W9-BVT-972

Caribbean Sea

75°W   60°W
15°N

ATLANTIC OCEAN

Maracaibo
Santa Marta   Barquisimeto
Barranquilla   Coro   Caracas   Barcelona
Cartagena   Cumaná
                              Maturín
CENTRAL AMERICA
          Mérida   Valencia   Maracay
          Cúcuta   Ciudad Guayana
          Bucaramanga   San Cristóbal   Ciudad Bolívar   Georgetown
          Medellín   Paramaribo
          Manizales   Tunja   VENEZUELA   GUYANA   FRENCH GUIANA (France)
          Pereira   Bogotá   SURINAME
          Cali   Villavicencio   Boa Vista
Galápagos Islands (Ecuador)   COLOMBIA   Macapá
          Neiva
Gulf of Panama   Pasto   Florencia   Negro R.
          ECUADOR   Quito   Ibarra   Amazon R.   Manaus   Santarém   Belém   São Luis
          0°   Portoviejo   Ambato   Iquitos   ATLANTIC
          Guayaquil   Riobamba   0°   Fortaleza
          Machala   Cuenca   Xingu R.   OCEAN   Teresina
          Loja   Iquitos   Tapajós R.   Natal
          Piura   Rio   Madeira R.   Tocantins R.   João Pessoa
          Chiclayo   Cajamarca   Branco   Porto Velho   BRAZIL   Recife
          Trujillo   Pucallpa   São Francisco R.   Maceió
          Chimbote   Huánuco   Aracaju
          PERU   Cerro de Pasco   Huancayo   Salvador
          Lima   Cusco
          Ayacucho   Trinidad
          Ica   Juliaca   BOLIVIA   Cuiabá   Brasília
          Arequipa   La Paz   Santa   Goiânia   Belo
PACIFIC   Cochabamba   Cruz   Paraguay R.   Horizonte
OCEAN   Tacna   Oruro   Sucre   Uberlândia   Vitória
          Arica   Potosí   Campo Grande   Belo Horizonte
          Iquique   Tarija   Pedro Juan   Campinas   Rio de Janeiro
                    San   Caballero   São Paulo   Niterói
          Antofagasta   Salvador   PARAGUAY   Ciudad   Santos
                    de Jujuy   Salta   Asunción   del Este   Curitiba
          Copiapó   San Miguel   Resistencia   Posadas   Florianópolis
          Catamarca   de Tucumán   Santiago   Encarnación
          CHILE   La Rioja   del Estero   Corrientes   Porto Alegre
          La Serena   Santa   Rivera
          30°S   Córdoba   Fe   Salto   30°S
          San Juan   Mendoza   Paysandú
          Valparaíso   San Luis   Rosario   URUGUAY
          Santiago   Rancagua   Buenos   Montevideo
          Talca   Aires   Río de la Plata   45°W
          Concepción   Chillán   ARGENTINA
          Temuco   Bahía   Mar del Plata   ATLANTIC
          Neuquén   Blanca   OCEAN
          Puerto Montt
          45°S   Comodoro   45°S
                    Rivadavia
          Falkland Islands
          (Islas Malvinas)
          (U.K.)
          Strait of Magellan
          Punta Arenas
          Ushuaia
          75°W   60°W

South America

Elevation in Feet   Major Cities
15,000   ✪ Capital city
10,000   ■ Over 5,000,000
5,000   ● 1,000,000–5,000,000
2,000   ■ 500,000–999,999
1,000   ● 250,000–499,999
0   ■ 100,000–249,999
Below sea level   ○ Less than 100,000

0   250   500 mi.
0   250   500 km

ENCYCLOPEDIA OF

LATIN AMERICAN HISTORY AND CULTURE

EDITORIAL BOARD

ENCYCLOPEDIA OF

LATIN AMERICAN HISTORY AND CULTURE

SECOND EDITION

Volume 2

C–D

Jay Kinsbruner

EDITOR IN CHIEF

Erick D. Langer

SENIOR EDITOR

CHARLES SCRIBNER'S SONS
A part of Gale, Cengage Learning

Detroit • New York • San Francisco • New Haven, Conn • Waterville, Maine • London

Encyclopedia of Latin American History and Culture

Jay Kinsbruner, Editor in Chief
Erick D. Langer, Senior Editor

For product information and technology assistance, contact us at
Gale Customer Support, 1-800-877-4253.
For permission to use material from this text or product, submit all requests online at **www.cengage.com/permissions.**
Further permissions questions can be emailed to
permissionrequest@cengage.com

While every effort has been made to ensure the reliability of the information presented in this publication, Gale, a part of Cengage Learning, does not guarantee the accuracy of the data contained herein. Gale accepts no payment for listing; and inclusion in the publication of any organization, agency, institution, publication, service, or individual does not imply endorsement of the editors or publisher. Errors brought to the attention of the publisher and verified to the satisfaction of the publisher will be corrected in future editions.

Library of Congress Cataloging-in-Publication Data

Encyclopedia of Latin American history and culture / Jay Kinsbruner, editor in chief; Erick D. Langer, senior editor. -- 2nd ed.
    p. cm. --
Includes bibliographical references and index.
    ISBN 978-0-684-31270-5 (set) -- ISBN 978-0-684-31441-9 (vol. 1) -- ISBN 978-0-684-31442-6 (vol. 2) -- ISBN 978-0-684-31443-3 (vol. 3) -- ISBN 978-0-684-31444-0 (vol. 4) -- ISBN 978-0-684-31445-7 (vol. 5) -- ISBN 978-0-684-31598-0 (vol. 6)
    1. Latin America--Encyclopedias. I. Kinsbruner, Jay.

F1406.E53 2008
980.003--dc22   2008003461

Gale
27500 Drake Rd.
Farmington Hills, MI, 48331-3535

978-0-684-31270-5 (set)   0-684-31270-0 (set)
978-0-684-31441-9 (vol. 1)   0-684-31441-X (vol. 1)
978-0-684-31442-6 (vol. 2)   0-684-31442-8 (vol. 2)
978-0-684-31443-3 (vol. 3)   0-684-31443-6 (vol. 3)
978-0-684-31444-0 (vol. 4)   0-684-31444-4 (vol. 4)
978-0-684-31445-7 (vol. 5)   0-684-31445-2 (vol. 5)
978-0-684-31598-0 (vol. 6)   0-684-31598-X (vol. 6)

This title is also available as an e-book.
ISBN-13: 978-0-684-31590-4 ISBN-10: 0-684-31590-4
Contact your Gale, a part of Cengage Learning, sales representative for ordering information.

Printed in the United States of America
1 2 3 4 5 6 7 12 11 10 09 08

CONTENTS

CAAGUAZÚ. Caaguazú department in east-central Paraguay with an area of 8,345 square miles and a 1990 population of 462,000. The capital city is Coronel Oviedo (population 21,782). The main physical feature of the department is the Cordillera de Caaguazú, a steplike massif at the southern edge of the Amambay plateau. The forests of the area are timbered, and Yerba Maté is grown. Some iron and copper veins add mining resources to the chiefly forest and agricultural bases of the economy.

See also **Paraguay, Geography.**

BIBLIOGRAPHY

Gerd Kohlhepp, "Problems of Dependent Regional Development in Eastern Paraguay," in *Applied Geography and Development* 22 (1983): 7–45.

Additional Bibliography

Paredes, Roberto. *Los sucesos de Caaguazú.* Paraguay: s.n., 2000.

CÉSAR N. CAVIEDES

CAAGUAZÚ, BATTLE OF. Battle of Caaguazú (28 November 1841), a major victory of Unitarist general José María Paz in the Argentine civil wars. It was fought on the bank of the Corrientes River in the province of the same name, which was maintaining a precarious independence vis-à-vis the dictatorship of Juan Manuel de Rosas. Corrientes had placed its forces under the command of Paz, who faced a large invading force led by Rosas's ally General Pascual Echagüe, governor of neighboring Entre Ríos. Having worn down the invaders by delay, Paz employed a masterful combination of battlefield tactics to virtually annihilate the enemy force. The victory gave Corrientes a breathing spell but did not break the power of Rosas, whose armies had meanwhile crushed Unitarist forces elsewhere in the country. Moreover, disunity among Paz, the governor of Corrientes, and their ally Uruguayan president Fructuoso Rivera precluded taking full advantage of the military success.

See also **Paz, José María; Rosas, Juan Manuel de; Unitario.**

BIBLIOGRAPHY

José María Paz, *Memorias,* vol. 4 (1968), chaps. 30–31.

Pablo Santos Muñoz, *Años de lucha (1841–1845): Urquiza y la política del litoral rioplatense* (1973), chaps. 1–2.

Additional Bibliography

Goldman, Noemí and Ricardo Donato Salvatore. *Caudillismos rioplatenses: Nuevas miradas a un viejo problema.* Buenos Aires: Eudeba, Facultad de Filosofía y Letras, Universdad de Buenos Aires, 1998.

Halperín Donghi, Tulio, and Jorge Raúl Lafforgue. *Historias de caudillos argentinos.* Buenos Aires: Extra Alfaguara, 1999.

Szuchman, Mark D., and Jonathan C. Brown, eds. *Revolution and Restoration: The Rearrangement of Power in Argentina, 1776-1860.* Lincoln: University of Nebraska Press, 1994.

DAVID BUSHNELL

CAAMAÑO DEÑÓ, FRANCISCO (1932–1973).

Francisco Caamaño Deñó (*b.* 11 June 1932; *d.* 16 February 1973), leader of the 1965 constitutionalist revolt in the Dominican Republic and president of the Dominican Republic (1965). Born in Santo Domingo, Caamaño began a career in the military in 1949, following in the footsteps of his father, Fausto Caamaño Medina, one of Rafael Leonidas Trujillo's most notorious generals. His father's influence enabled Caamaño to advance rapidly through the military ranks. When the April 1965 revolt split the military, Colonel Caamaño sided with the rebels in their efforts to reinstate the constitutional government of Juan Bosch (elected December 1962; overthrown September 1963). Caamaño became the leader of the revolutionary troops, and in an emergency session on 4 May 1965, the Dominican National Assembly elected him constitutional president, a position lasting until 31 August. The United States intervened, installing Héctor García-Godoy as interim president of the republic in September. In 1966, following the renewal of hostilities between the rebels and the conservatives, Caamaño was sent to London, effectively exiled, to assume a diplomatic post. A year later he abandoned the position and fled to Cuba, where he spent the next six years planning a campaign to overthrow the government of Joaquín Balaguer (elected 1966). On 3 February 1973, Caamaño landed with a guerrilla band on Dominican soil. Less than two weeks later, he was captured and executed.

See also **Dominican Revolt (1965).**

BIBLIOGRAPHY

Gregorio Ortega, *Santo Domingo, 1965* (1965).

Richard W. Mansbach, *Dominican Crisis, 1965* (1971).

Piero Gleijeses, *The Dominican Crisis: The 1965 Constitutionalist Revolt and American Intervention,* translated by Lawrence Lipson (1978).

Hamlet Hermann, *Francis Caamaño* (1983).

Tony Raful, *La revolución de abril de 1965* (1985).

Additional Bibliography

Matos Moquete, Manuel. *Caamaño: La última esperanza armada.* Santo Domingo, República Dominicana: Videocine Palau, 2000.

Rius, Hugo, and Ricardo Sáenz Padrón. *Caamaño.* República Dominicana: Ediciones Revolución, 2001.

SARA FLEMING

CAAMAÑO Y GÓMEZ CORNEJO, JOSÉ MARÍA PLÁCIDO (1838–1901).

José María Plácido Caamaño y Gómez Cornejo (*b.* 5 October 1838; *d.* 31 December 1901), president of Ecuador (1884–1888). Caamaño, a wealthy coastal cacao grower from Guayaquil, was selected to follow President Gabriel García Moreno (1861–1865, 1869–1875) in office in 1865. However, he refused. He also opposed the dictatorship of Ignacio de Veintimilla (1876–1883), which led to his arrest and exile in Peru. In 1883 he returned and helped organize the overthrow of Veintimilla. Caamaño joined the provisional government; the subsequent National Convention elected him president. The first of three Progresista (1883–1895) presidents, Caamaño sought to remain independent of both Liberals and Conservatives; his family ties in both the sierra and the coast afforded a further measure of neutrality.

Caamaño had hoped to implement a program of public works but instead spent his term fighting efforts to throw him out of office, employing particular brutality in quelling the revolts of coastal guerrillas (*montoneras*). After his presidency he served as governor of Guayas province (1888–1895). Critics saw Caamaño as leader of a corrupt clique, "the ring" (*la argolla*), thought to be a conspiracy of coastal financial interests who secretly controlled the nation. Caamaño was implicated in the Esmeraldas affair (1894–1895), a scandal that involved the use of the Ecuadorian flag to cover the sale of a Chilean warship to Japan. Accused of taking a bribe (a charge he denied), the former president fled Ecuador when angry citizens laid siege to his home. Caamaño traveled to Spain, where he spent the rest of his life in poverty. He died in Seville.

See also **García Moreno, Gabriel.**

BIBLIOGRAPHY

On nineteenth-century Ecuadorian politics, see Osvaldo Hurtado's interpretive *Political Power in Ecuador,* translated by Nick D. Mills, Jr. (1985); Frank MacDonald Spindler's descriptive *Nineteenth Century Ecuador: An Historical Introduction* (1987). For a brief analysis of Ecuadorian political economy in the nineteenth century, consult David. W. Schodt, *Ecuador: An Andean Enigma* (1987).

RONN F. PINEO

CAATINGA.

Caatinga denotes the spiny, stunted, predominantly xerophytic vegetation of the most arid zones of northeastern Brazil's Sertão, a region extending from the interior of Minas Gerais and Bahia to the interior of Piauí and Maranhão. *Caatinga*, literally "the white forest" in the Tupi language, it also refers to areas featuring such vegetation. Characteristic of the driest regions of the *Sertão catingueras* (a general term for the hardy plants of the *caatinga*) can withstand droughts lasting as long as three years.

The expansion of cattle ranching in the 1700s prompted European settlement of the inhospitable *caatinga*. During the 1800s cotton strains suited to the harsh climate were developed and cultivated. The population in the *caatinga* remained small, impoverished, and vulnerable to drought and disease.

See also **Brazil, Geography.**

BIBLIOGRAPHY

De La Rüe, Edgar Aubert. *Brésil Aride: La vie dans la Caatinga*. Paris: Gallimard, 1957.

Emperaire, Laure. *La Caatinga du sud-est du Piauí: Étude ethnobotanique*. Paris: Editions Recherche sur les civilizations, 1983.

Nemesio, Vitorino. *Caatinga e terra caída: Viagens no nordeste e no Amazonas*, 2nd edition. Lisbon: Imprensa. Nacional, Casa da Moeda, 1998.

Vitt, Laurie J. *The Ecology of Tropical Lizards in the Caatinga of Northeast Brazil*. Norman: University of Oklahoma Press, 1995.

CARA SHELLY

CABALLERÍA.

Caballería, a unit of land beyond the perimeter of a city (usually in Mexico) granted by the crown or its officials for the sole purpose of farming (as opposed to stock raising). Theoretically, the *caballería* was calculated to be large enough to provide subsistence for a *caballero*, a gentleman or cavalry man, and his family, in contrast to the *peonía*, a smaller grant of farmland deemed sufficient for a footman and his descendants. Although Viceroy Antonio de Mendoza established a standard size in 1536, in fact the *caballería* varied in expanse according to climate and soil quality. Some reports describe the *caballería* as about twice the size of the *peonía*. In central Mexico, an average-sized *caballería*, according to scholar Charles Gibson, measured 1,104 by 552 *varas de castilla*, or 0.024 square leagues (0.17 square miles or 105 acres).

See also **Mendoza, Antonio de.**

BIBLIOGRAPHY

Charles Gibson, *The Aztecs Under Spanish Rule. A History of the Indians of the Valley of Mexico, 1519–1810* (1964).

Victor Westphall, *Mercedes Reales: Hispanic Land Grants of the Upper Rio Grande Region* (1983).

Additional Bibliography

Horn, Rebecca. *Postconquest Coyoacan: Nahua-Spanish Relations in Central Mexico, 1519-1650*. Stanford, CA: Stanford University Press, 1997.

Pastrana Flores, Gabriel Miguel. *Historias de la Conquista: Aspectos de la historiografía de tradición náhuatl*. México, D.F.: Universidad Nacional Autónoma de México, 2004.

SUSAN E. RAMÍREZ

CABALLERO, BERNARDINO (1839–1912).

Bernardino Caballero (*b.* 20 May 1839; *d.* 26 February 1912), Paraguayan military leader and president (1880–1886). Born in the interior town of Ybycuí, Caballero spent his early career in the cavalry and by the beginning of the War of the Triple Alliance in 1864, had risen to the rank of sergeant. He participated in almost every engagement of the war, from the Mato Grosso campaign to those of Humaitá and the Cordilleras. His success in harassing the advancing Brazilians, as well as his exceptional loyalty, drew the attention of President Francisco Solano López. Advancements for Caballero came rapidly, until 1869, when he achieved the rank of general and with it command over what was left of López's army. Even after the fall of Asunción, he continued the fight, until, in March 1870, the Brazilians cornered and killed López at Cerro Corá. Caballero was taken prisoner shortly thereafter.

Caballero's star rose much higher in the postwar period. As one of the only Paraguayan generals to survive the war, he naturally caught the eye of various contending factions, who sought to use him as a figurehead. A Conservative movement led by

Cándido Bareiro secured his appointment as war minister in 1878, but he proved to be his own man.

Caballero assumed the presidency in 1880 after the death of Bareiro. His administration made only limited contributions to the public welfare. It disposed of thousands of hectares of state land by selling them to foreign buyers. Caballero also founded the National Bank and the National Law School. The most important innovation of his tenure, however, was in the political realm. In 1887, with the help of José Segundo Decoud, he founded one of the country's traditional parties, the Asociación Nacional Republicana, or Partido Colorado. He continued to direct this organization long after he left the presidency in the hands of his colleague Patricio Escobar. Caballero died in Asunción.

See also **War of the Triple Alliance.**

BIBLIOGRAPHY

Harris G. Warren, *Rebirth of the Paraguayan Republic: The First Colorado Era* (1985), esp. pp. 51–61.

Carlos Zubizarreta, *Cien vidas paraguayas,* 2d ed. (1985), pp. 184–188; *The Cambridge History of Latin America,* vol. 5 (1986), pp. 475–496.

Additional Bibliography

Bergonzi, Osvaldo. *Bernardino Caballero: El auténtico.* Asunción(?): O. Bergonzi, 2005.

Prieto Ruiz, Leandro José. *Breve historia de la línea nacional y popular: Mensaje a mis contemporaneous.* Asunción: Editorial Cuadernos Republicanos, 2002.

                                    THOMAS L. WHIGHAM

CABALLERO, PEDRO JUAN (1786–1821).

Pedro Juan Caballero (*b.* 1786; *d.* 13 July 1821), Paraguayan soldier and politician of the independence era. Born in Tobatí, Caballero spent his early youth in the Paraguayan countryside, where he learned to ride and, like many men of his class, to command small bands of troops in the colonial militia. He evidently participated in the Indian campaigns of the first years of the nineteenth century and by 1810 had attained the rank of captain.

The following year Caballero was catapulted into prominence. The revolutionary junta in Buenos Aires, seeking to gain Paraguay's adherence to the patriot struggle against Spain, had sent an expeditionary force to the province. Commanded by Manuel Belgrano, this small army anticipated little resistance. The Paraguayans, however, had no desire to be controlled from Buenos Aires, and their militia proceeded to defeat Belgrano in two separate engagements.

In the aftermath of these battles, some Paraguayan officers, Caballero included, actively fraternized with the defeated *porteños,* who convinced them that some form of independence was desirable. Together with colonels Fulgencio Yegros and Manuel Atanasio Cavañas, Caballero organized a conspiracy against the royal government in Asunción. When the plot was discovered in May 1811, Caballero acted in the absence of his associates, seizing the *cabildo* offices and arresting the governor at dawn on the fifteenth of the month.

The rebellion brought Paraguay independence but not political stability. Over the next three years a provisional junta composed of Caballero, Yegros, and three other notables ruled the country, though often in an erratic fashion. Their inability to govern effectively made possible the ascendancy of José Gaspar Rodríguez de Francia, the one outstanding political figure in Paraguay, and a man whom Caballero detested. In 1814, when Francia became dictator, Caballero wisely retired to Tobatí, but six years later he was implicated in a major plot against the dictator. Jailed by Francia's police, he committed suicide in his cell.

See also **Paraguay: The Colonial Period.**

BIBLIOGRAPHY

Louis G. Benítez, *Historia de la cultura en el Paraguay* (1976), p. 99.

John H. Williams, *The Rise and Fall of the Paraguayan Republic, 1800–1870* (1979), pp. 27–53.

Carlos Zubizarreta, *Cien vidas paraguayas,* 2d ed. (1985), pp. 93–98.

Additional Bibliography

Jara Goiris, Fabio Aníbal. *Descubriendo la frontera: Historia, sociedad y política en Pedro Juan Caballero.* Ponta Grossa, Brasil: Industria Pontagrossente de Artes Gráficas, 1999.

                                    THOMAS L. WHIGHAM

CABALLERO CALDERÓN, EDUARDO (1910–1993).

Eduardo Caballero Calderón (*b.* 6 March 1910; *d.* 3 April 1993), Colombian novelist and essayist. Author of more than two dozen books, Caballero Calderón is one of Colombia's major novelists of the twentieth century. He has also published numerous essays on literary, cultural, political, and historical topics. Caballero Calderón began writing in the 1940s and rose to prominence in the 1950s and 1960s. His major novel, *El buen salvaje* (The Good Savage) appeared in 1966, receiving international acclaim in Spain and throughout the Hispanic world. His ten novels, four volumes of short stories, and eleven books of essays have placed him at the forefront of Colombian writers.

Caballero Calderón's earliest publications were essays. The first, a volume titled *Tipacoque* (1941), is a set of nostalgic portraits of rural, provincial life in Colombia. In his book of essays, *Breviario del Quijote* (1947), the author demonstrates the importance of Spanish literary tradition for him and for Latin American writers in general: he writes about his admiration for the *Poema del Cid, Don Quijote,* writings of the Spanish Golden Age, and other classic Spanish texts. For the remainder of his career, he remained closely aligned to the culture of Spain.

Caballero Calderón's early novels dealt with the Colombian civil war commonly known as La Violencia, a conflict that took place primarily from 1948 to 1958. Many interests were represented in this conflict, but the primary antagonists were the traditional Conservative Party and the Liberal Party. In his novel *El Cristo de espaldas* (1952; Christ on His Back) a son in the Liberal Party is accused of killing his father of the Conservative Party, and the town priest becomes the sacrificial victim when he attempts to justify the son's act. The protagonist of *Siervo sin tierra* (1954) is also a victim of *La Violencia*. The basic thesis of the novel *Manuel Pacho* (1962) is that each person has one opportunity in life to be a hero. In *El buen salvaje,* Caballero Calderón rises above local stories of violence and constructs a self-conscious fiction about a young Latin American intellectual in Paris.

See also **Literature: Spanish America.**

BIBLIOGRAPHY

Leon Lyday and Luis Carlos Herrera et al., "Trayectoria de un novelista: Eduardo Caballero Calderón," in *Boletín Cultural y Bibliográfico* 12, no. 2 (1969): 13–103.

John S. Brushwood, *The Spanish American Novel: A Twentieth-Century Survey* (1975).

Seymour Menton, *La novela colombiana: Planetas y satélites* (1977).

Additional Bibliography

Boletín Cultural y Bibliográfico. Special Edition. 40: 62 (2003).

Roldán, Mary. *Blood and Fire: La Violencia in Antioquia, Colombia, 1946–1953.* Durham, NC: Duke University Press, 2002.

RAYMOND LESLIE WILLIAMS

CABALLEROS ORIENTALES. Caballeros Orientales, the name of a Masonic lodge that existed in Montevideo, Uruguay, in 1823. The territory was occupied by the Portuguese, who in 1820 had finalized their invasion with the rout of José Artigas. The 1822 Grito de Ypiranga declaring Brazilian independence from Portugal divided Portuguese and Brazilians and created an atmosphere of reaction in which residents of the Banda Oriental sought to return to the sanctuary of the United Provinces of the Río De La Plata—the principal objective of the Caballeros Orientales. Their attempts failed, however, because of lack of support from the rural *caudillos* and fear of Brazilian reprisals in the provinces that are now part of Argentina. Members of the group included Manuel and Ignacio Oribe, Santiago Vázquez, Antonio Díaz, and Juan Francisco Giró, all of whom became outstanding figures in the following years. The secret society produced various underground publications in Montevideo and practically dominated the town council in 1823. On withdrawal of the Portuguese and the beginning of Brazilian domination, the Caballeros Orientales ceased their activities, many of them going into exile in Buenos Aires.

See also **Brazil, Independence Movements; Masonic Orders; Orientales.**

BIBLIOGRAPHY

John Street, *Artigas and the Emancipation of Uruguay* (1959).

Alfredo Castellanos, *La Cisplatina: La independencia y la república caudillesca, 1820–1838* (1974).

Additional Bibliography

Golletti Wilkinson, Augusto. *Guerra contra el imperio del Brasil: A la luz de sus protagonistas.* Buenos Aires: Editorial Dunken, 2003.

Narancio, Edmundo M. *La independencia de Uruguay.* Madrid, Spain: Editorial MAPFRE, 1992.

JOSÉ DE TORRES WILSON

siglo XIX. Mexico: Comisión de Estudios de Historia de la Iglesia en América Latina: Fondo de Cultura Económica, 1990.

Rodríguez O., Jaime E. *The Origins of Mexican National Politics, 1808–1847.* Wilmington, DE: SR Books, 1997.

VIRGINIA GUEDEA

CABALLEROS RACIONALES, SOCIEDAD DE.

Sociedad de Caballeros Racionales, one of the first secret societies established in New Spain. (The other was Los Guadalupes.) The Caballeros Racionales, with Masonic affiliations, was originally founded in Cádiz in 1811 by American Spaniards interested in furthering home rule in their native countries. Several lodges were then established in London and various parts of Spanish America such as Caracas and Buenos Aires. The lodge in New Spain was founded in Jalapa at the beginning of 1812. Its aim was to promote the establishment of an American government in New Spain, and its members supported the insurgent movement against the colonial regime. Besides an organized directorate, the society developed initiation rites, in which the members swore to maintain secrecy, as well as signs by means of which associates recognized one another. The membership of the society exceeded seventy when the colonial authorities discovered its existence in May 1812. They imprisoned many of its members. Others managed to flee, and some, like Mariano Rincón, who later became one of the outstanding insurgent leaders in the Veracruz region, were members of the Governing Junta of Naolingo.

See also **Colonialism; Masonic Orders.**

BIBLIOGRAPHY

"Logia de los 'Caballeros Racionales' en Jalapa. Fragmentos del proceso del canónigo Cardeña," in *Boletín del Archivo general de la Nación* 3, no. 3 (1932): 390–407.

Virginia Guedea, "Las sociedades secretas durante el movimiento de independencia," in *The Independence of Mexico and the Creation of the New Nation,* edited by Jaime E. Rodríguez O. (1989), pp. 45–62.

Additional Bibliography

Bastian, Jean Pierre. *Protestantes, liberales y francmasones: Sociedades de ideas y modernidad en América Latina,*

CABALLERO Y GÓNGORA, ANTONIO

(1723–1796). Antonio Caballero y Góngora (*b.* May 1723; *d.* March 1796), viceroy of New Granada (1782–1789). A native of Córdoba Province, Spain, Caballero y Góngora became bishop of Yucatán in 1776 and archbishop of Santa Fe de Bogotá in 1779. He later entered the secular realm when, after defusing the Comunero Revolt of 1781, he became viceroy on 15 June 1782. The archbishop-viceroy championed enlightened education and science, and secured the creation of a mining reform mission. He also imposed centralized control on the colonial army and, to sustain royal authority, gained approval to establish in Santa Fe a veteran regiment reinforced by a disciplined militia.

During much of his administration, Caballero y Góngora resided at Turbaco, near Cartagena, directing ambitious military operations to pacify the aboriginals of Darién. He enhanced treasury receipts impressively but spent huge sums on the military and the bureaucracy. In the name of economy, his successors would dismantle much of his program. Replaced by Francisco Gil De Taboada y Lemos in January 1789, Caballero y Góngora returned to Córdoba, serving as archbishop until his death.

See also **Comunero Revolt (New Granada).**

BIBLIOGRAPHY

José Manuel Pérez Ayala, *Antonio Caballero y Góngora, virrey y arzobispo de Santa Fe, 1723–1796* (1951).

Allan J. Kuethe, *Military Reform and Society in New Granada, 1773–1808* (1978).

John Leddy Phelan, *The People and the King: The Comunero Revolution in Colombia, 1781* (1978).

Additional Bibliography

Tisnés Jiménes, Roberto María. "El arzobispo virrey, 1723–1796." *Boletín de Historia y Antigüedades* 83: 794 (July–September 1996): 729–756.

ALLAN J. KUETHE

CABALLERO Y RODRÍGUEZ, JOSÉ AUGUSTÍN

(1762–1835). José Augustín Caballero y Rodríguez (*b.* 28 August 1762; *d.* 7 April 1835), Cuban priest, philosopher, and educator. Along with Francisco Arango y Parreño, Caballero was a pioneer of reformism in Cuba. Born in Havana, he was ordained as a priest in 1785. He became professor of philosophy (1785) and later director at San Carlos Seminary, where he was able to influence the intellectual formation of Father Félix Varela y Morales, doubtless the most famous of his disciples. An eloquent orator and a gifted writer and critic, Caballero put his exceptional abilities at the disposal of Cuba's Patriotic Society, a respectable colonial institution where he pleaded constantly for a more flexible approach to human problems. Along with his newspaper articles and his speeches (some of which are magnificent rhetorical pieces), he left us a treatise on logic written in Latin, *Lecciones de filosofía electiva* (1796), the first text for the teaching of philosophy ever produced in Cuba by a Cuban.

Although he mentions in his work empiricist thinkers such as John Locke, Francis Bacon, and Étienne Bonnot de Condillac, Caballero was by no means a radical innovator. Basically he was a follower of the Spanish thinker Benito Jerónimo Feijóo, whose chief concern was to free philosophy from its submission to Aristotle and scholasticism, maintaining that all authorities were acceptable provided they taught the truth. Caballero's contribution to modernity, therefore, never went beyond trying to reconcile Cartesian rationalism with Aristotelianism. Faithful to the church, he never hesitated to place faith above reason, although he did favor the teaching of experimental physics and advocated greater freedom for university teachers and broader and deeper techniques of inquiry.

Caballero was also a believer in self-government, and in 1811 he put forward a proposal for the establishment of quasi-autonomist rule in Cuba. Never favoring the separation of Cuba from Spain, he was a moderate, politically and socially. Moreover, he thought that, given the prevailing conditions, slavery was an inevitable crime, although he wrote numerous articles urging slave owners to treat their slaves better. Despite his moderation, Caballero must be credited with laying the groundwork upon which later Cubans built their more radical thoughts.

See also **Cuba, Political Movements, Nineteenth Century; Slavery: Abolition.**

BIBLIOGRAPHY

There are few studies on Caballero's life and work; see Isabel Monal, "Tres filósofos del centenario," in *Universidad de La Habana* 192 (1968): 116–122; also, Emilio Roig De Leuchsenring, ed., *Homenaje al ilustre habanero pbro. Dr. José Agustín Caballero y Rodríguez en el centenario de su muerte, 1835–1935* (1935).

Additional Bibliography

Castellanos, Jorge. *Raíces de la ideología burguesa en Cuba.* Habana: Editorial Páginas, 1944.

Massip, Salvador. *Conferencias de geografía política, social y económica de Cuba (1939–40).* Habana: Editorial Páginas, 1944.

JOSÉ M. HERNÁNDEZ

CABALLO MUERTO.

Caballo Muerto, a complex of early sites located near the modern city of Trujillo in the Moche Valley on the north coast of Peru. The complex, probably the center of a larger multivalley polity, consists of eight U-shaped mound structures that are made of stone set in mud mortar and were sequentially constructed between 1700 BCE and 400 BCE.

The structure called Huaca de los Reyes (shrine of the kings) is the most elaborate architecturally. Built around 1500 BCE, this site contains several platform mounds, colonnades, stairways, and over fifty rooms, all precisely arranged along three sides of two large plazas and two small plazas. Access to the site is gained from the east, where one enters the largest plaza, which could hold several hundred people. Access to the three remaining smaller plazas could only be gained through very narrow, restricted passageways and staircases.

Niches and column faces within the various plazas are decorated with impressive mud sculptures that probably depicted various aspects of the builders' mythology. The largest plaza is lined with repetitive heads of creator deities as well as full-figure depictions of a main ancestral cultural hero. Just to the west, the smaller of the two main plazas contains more varied depictions of the ancestral cultural hero, possibly reflecting different myths involving this hero. Immediately north and south of this plaza are two small plazas, each containing a mound frontally decorated with paired profile jaguar sculptures. The restricted access to three of the plazas, their small size, and the special nature of their associated mud sculptures suggest these plazas were the scenes of special ceremonial activities by privileged groups within the society that built the structure.

BIBLIOGRAPHY

Thomas Pozorski, "The Early Horizon Site of Huaca de los Reyes: Societal Implications," in *American Antiquity* 45 (1980): 100–110, "Early Social Stratification and Subsistence Systems: The Caballo Muerto Complex," in *Chan Chan: Andean Desert City,* edited by Michael Moseley and Kent Day (1982), pp. 225–253, and "The Caballo Muerto Complex and Its Place in the Andean Chronological Sequence," in *Annals of Carnegie Museum of Natural History* 52 (1983): 1–40.

Additional Bibliography

Campana D., Cristóbal. *Tecnologías constructivas de tierra en la costa norte prehispánica.* Trujillo: Instituto Nacional de Cultura—La Libertad, 2000.

Moseley, Michael E. *The Incas and their Ancestors: The Archaeology of Peru.* New York: Thames and Hudson, 1992.

Pozorski, Thomas. "Huaca de los Reyes Revisited: Clarification of the Archaeological Evidence (in Reports)." *Latin American Antiquity,* Vol. 6, No. 4. (Dec., 1995): 335–339.

SHELIA POZORSKI
THOMAS POZORSKI

CABANAGEM. Cabanagem, a popular insurrection in the Brazilian Amazon (1835–1840). Decultured indigenous people known as *tapuios* and the rest of the formerly free population essentially constituted by people of color were subject to coercive labor arrangements, to army and navy recruitment, and to personal indignities.

In contrast with other parts of Brazil, whites constituted a very small minority in Pará. With the declaration of Brazilian independence, the metropolitan Portuguese sought to maintain the colonial status quo in the province. Although they were forced to concede in 1823, they managed to retain control of the region and to maintain the labor system. Popular uprisings in 1823, 1824, and 1831, supported by the nationalist portion of the elite, sought to end the

power of the Portuguese. They were put down with the help of the national army and navy. Massacres like that of 256 prisoners on the prison ship *Palhaço* (1823) contributed to the hostility of the lower classes (*cabanos*) against the white, Portuguese upper class.

In 1834 the authoritarian governor, Lobo de Souza, increased army and navy recruitment to strengthen authority in the province. Conflict within the elite was increased by the suppression of an anti-Masonic pastoral letter of the bishop. The governor, who was a Mason, took action against the popular bishop, Batista Campos, who had published the letter in the diocesan newspaper. The burning of the *fazenda* (ranch) of Campos's protector, Félix Antônio Clemente Malcher, in October 1834 and the subsequent death of the bishop made armed resistance appear to be the only solution for the *cabanos*.

The festival of São Tomé, during which people traveled to Belém, was a propitious time to prepare for the insurrection, which erupted on 6 January 1835. The rebels were led by Antônio Vinagre, a *fazendeiro* whose brother Manuel had been shot by government troops during the expedition against Bishop Campos. *Cabanos* soon took Belém, and most of the government troops joined them. The governor was executed, the Masonic temple was destroyed, and Malcher was freed from jail and proclaimed governor. The rebels sent a message to the imperial court in Rio de Janeiro, telling the government to send no more governors to Pará.

Malcher, a member of the dominant class, was not disposed to support fundamental changes and adopted a conciliatory attitude, seeking to stop acts of vengeance and appealing for a return to work. A month after his installation as governor, he was overthrown and the more popular Francisco Vinagre was proclaimed the new governor. Once in power, however, Vinagre also came into conflict with the *cabanos,* and in June finally agreed to hand power over to the designated governor, Manuel Jorge Rodrigues, a naturalized Portuguese. *Cabano* troops then left Belém but did not lay down their weapons. Persecution of *cabanos* by the new government led to new confrontations.

In the third and most crucial phase of the Cabanagem, Eduardo Angelim Nogueira, a tenant farmer on one of Malcher's properties, assumed leadership of the *cabanos.* Belém was again seized by *cabano* troops in August 1835. Black slaves joined the movement, which clearly envisaged the abolition of coerced labor and of slavery. Angelim Nogueira, seeking to establish government in the traditional way, opposed acts of vengeance and "excesses." Dissension within the *cabano* ranks, the outbreak of disease, and the arrival of government troops led the rebels to abandon Belém in May 1836.

The following years saw brutal repression of *cabanos,* many of whom were executed. The last groups surrendered in Amazonia in 1840. Some found shelter among indigenous groups, such as the Mura, who had supported the movement. About one-fifth of the population of Amazonia is said to have perished.

The Cabanagem is distinguished from most other insurrections of the regency by its popular character and leadership, especially in the last phase, and its power over an entire province.

See also **Slavery: Brazil.**

BIBLIOGRAPHY

Domingos Antônio Raiol, *Motins políticos ou história dos principais acontecimentos políticos de província do Pará desde o ano 1821 até 1835,* 2d ed., 3 vols. (1970).

Renato Guimarães, "Cabanagem: A revolução no Brasil," in *Cadernos do CEAS* 71 (January–February 1981).

Julio José Chiavenato, *Cabanagem: O povo no poder* (1984).

Carlos De Araújo Moreira Neto, *Indios de Amazônia, de maioria a minoria (1750–1850)* (1988).

Additional Bibliography

Di Paolo, Pasquale. *Cabanagem: A Revolucao Popular Da Amazonia.* Belem: Edicoes CEJUP, 1990.

Guimarães, Renato. *Dios estudos para a mão esquerda.* Rio de Janeiro: Revan, 2000.

Lima, Ana Renata Rosario de. *Cabanagem: Uma revolta camponesa no Acará-Pa.* Belém: s.n., 2004.

Oliveira, Roberto Monteiro de. *Utopia de uma região: Estudos regionais-Cabanagem.* Brasilia: SER, 2000.

Palheta, Aércio. *A revoluçao dos cabanos: Em perguntas e respostas.* Belem: Editora Amazonia, 2004.

Pinheiro, Luis Balkar Sá Peixoto. *Visões da Cabanagem: Uma revolta popular e suas representações na historiografia.* Manaus: Valer Editora, 2001.

Salles, Vicente. *Memorial da Cabanagem: Esboço da pensamento político-revolucionário no Grão-Pará.* Belém: Edições CEJUP, 1992.

MATTHIAS RÖHRIG ASSUNÇÃO

CABAÑAS, JOSÉ TRINIDAD (1805–1871).

José Trinidad Cabañas (*b.* 9 June 1805; *d.* 8 January 1871), military figure and president of Honduras (1852, 1853–1855). Born a creole, the son of José María Cabañas and Juana María Faillos, Cabañas was a Liberal politician whose role in Honduran history dates from his participation in the civil war of 1826–1829 as a follower of Francisco Morazán. In 1844 he defended León, Nicaragua, against Francisco Malespín's forces. In 1845 he led Salvadoran forces against the same Malespín. He served as constitutional president from 1 March 1852 to 28 October 1852 but was deposed by Conservatives in Guatemala (and within Honduras). When war resumed between Honduras and Guatemala, he led Honduran forces to triumph at Chiquimula and Zacapa, in southeast Guatemala, in July 1853 but was unable to hold these positions. Guatemala's capture of the castle of Omoa on 24 August 1853 removed Honduras from the conflict.

Cabañas returned to power as constitutional president from 31 December 1853 to 6 October 1855. Among the important accomplishments of his second presidency were the ratification of a railroad contract with Ephraim George Squier and the formation of the Ferrocarril Interoceánico de Honduras (Interoceanic Railway Company) on 28 April 1854. Interference in Guatemalan affairs led to his overthrow once again, and this time he fled to El Salvador.

A prominent general as well as a politician, Cabañas took to the battlefield again. He was defeated by Guatemalan forces under Rafael Carrera (1814–1865) at the Battle of Masagua on 6 October 1855. Although his successor, Santos Guardiola, was a Conservative, Cabañas remained active in Central American affairs and participated in a Salvadoran uprising in 1865. (In 1860 he had been connected with an abortive attempt by William Walker to return to Central America.) His presidencies faced not only Guatemalan opposition but other challenges, such as British efforts to colonize the Bay Islands and frustrated attempts to reunite the Central American federal government. A unionist movement failed when a constituent assembly dissolved shortly after his first presidential term on 10 November 1852.

See also **Honduras.**

BIBLIOGRAPHY

Medardo Mejía, *Trinidad Cabañas, soldado de la república federal* (1971).

Luis Mariñas Otero, *Honduras,* 2d ed. (1983).

José Reina Valenzuela, *José Trinidad Cabañas: Estudio biográfico* (1984).

Additional Bibliography

Cabañas, José Trinidad. *Pensamiento social y político: Edición conmemorativa del bicentenário de su nacimiento (1805–2005).* Tegucigalpa: Alcaldía Municipal del Distrito Central, 2005.

Montúfar, Lorenzo, and Raúl Aguilar Piedra. *Walker en Centroamérica.* Alajuela, Costa Rica: Museo Histórico Cultural Juan Santamaría, 2000.

JEFFREY D. SAMUELS

CABAÑAS, LUCIO (1936–1974).

The leader of a Mexican guerrilla group and promoter of the "revolution of the poor men," Lucio Cabañas Barrientos was born in El Porvenir, a municipality of Atoyac de Álvarez, one of the poorest regions of the state of Guerrero. He came from a family of coffee peasants, and as a child, he worked in the fields. A long family revolutionary tradition sparked his interest in politics. At the Rural Normal School in Ayotzinapa, Guerrero, he became a student leader. In 1960 he also became a local leader, in the movement headed by the teacher Genaro Vázquez Rojas and Guerrero's Civic Association to overthrow the state governor, Raúl Caballero Aburto. In 1962 Cabañas was elected general secretary of the Mexican Socialist Student Peasants Federation, and a year later, in Mezcaltepec, he fought against the forest companies that exploited the mountain range of Atoyac. In 1965, as an elementary school teacher in Atoyac, he helped remove the principal of the school for abusing the authority of her office and also became a member of the Mexican Communist Party. He participated in the Revolutionary Movement of Teachers and in the formation of the regional section of the Central Independent Peasant Organization. In 1967 he was an adviser in the movement against the principal of the "Juan Álvarez" elementary school. During a rally in Atoyac's civic plaza (18 May 1967) the judicial police tried to assassinate Cabañas, and in the melée that followed seven people died. Cabañas hid himself in the mountain range to prepare a guerrilla war to promote the "revolution of the poor against the rich." There he formed an armed group, the Peasant Brigade for Justice, and a secret support base, the Party of the Poor Men. His guerrilla war moved through three stages: (1) organizing the support bases (1967–1969); (2) financing their activities via bank robberies and kidnappings (1970–1971); and (3) attacking military objectives (1972–1974). The Mexican army conducted several campaigns that eventually wiped outthe armed group. In 1974 Cabañas's guerrillas had kidnapped the official candidate to govern Guerrero, Rubén Figueroa. In its rescue mission the army surrounded the guerrillas and secured the release of Figueroa, but Cabañas fell in a confrontation in Tecpan de Galeana, Guerrero. He later became a cult figure for the organizations of the radical Left.

See also **Guerrilla Movements; Mexico, Political Parties: Partido Comunista Mexicano.**

BIBLIOGRAPHY

Bartra Verges, Armando. *Guerrero Bronco. Campesinos, ciudadanos y guerrilleros en la Costa Grande.* México: Era, 2000.

Bellingeri, Marco. *Del agrarismo armado a la guerra de los pobres. Ensayos de guerrilla rural en el México contemporáneo: 1940–1974.* México: Casa Juan Pablos-Secretaría de Cultura del Distrito Federal, 2003.

Suárez, Luis. *Lucio Cabañas, el guerrillero sin esperanza.* México: Roca, 1976.

ADELA CEDILLO

CABEZA DE VACA, ALVAR NÚÑEZ

(c. 1490–1564). Alvar Núñez Cabeza de Vaca (*b.* ca. 1490; *d.* 1564), Spanish explorer, conquistador, and author. Cabeza de Vaca was most likely born in Jerez de la Frontera, Andalusia. He was treasurer and marshal of Pánfilo de Narváez's expedition to Florida (1527–1537) and was appointed governor of the Río de la Plata, in present-day Paraguay (1540–1545). For different reasons, both enterprises proved disastrous for Cabeza de Vaca, the first beginning in shipwreck, the latter ending in political failure.

After accidentally landing south of Tampa Bay in the spring of 1528, the ill-fated expedition of Narváez progressively deteriorated. It was not until eight years later that Cabeza de Vaca, Andrés Dorantes de

Carranza, Alonso del Castillo Maldonado, and an African slave named Estevanico, the only four survivors, encountered a party of Spaniards on the west coast of Mexico. Cabeza de Vaca's account, known in Spanish as the *Naufragios* (Shipwrecks), tells the story of his travails and coexistence with the Mariame, Avavare, and Opata peoples. He became a merchant and, with the three other survivors practiced shamanism with such success that hundreds of Indians formed a cult about them and traveled with them across the continent. The *Naufragios* is at once an account of an officer of the crown and the story of a European who penetrated and was penetrated by Native American cultures. On his return to Spain, he was given the governorship of Río de la Plata. The *Comentarios*, written by his amanuensis Pedro Hernández, tells of Cabeza de Vaca's journey from the island of Santa Catalina (Brazil) to Asunción (Paraguay), and the subsequent rebellion of Domingo Martínez de Irala that ended with Cabeza de Vaca's return to Spain in chains in 1545. He died in Seville.

Although a pirated edition of *Naufragios* appeared in 1542, while Cabeza de Vaca was in Paraguay, the authorized version was published with the *Comentarios* in 1555. The *Naufragios* is the more compelling of the two in its narration of a complete loss of material civilization and total dependence on the Indians. In this regard the *Naufragios* manifests the dubious nature of Western civilization's claims to superiority, since it is the Spaniards who are naked and unable to feed themselves or build boats, who fall into anomie and resort to cannibalism.

Cabeza de Vaca's story is the antithesis to *Robinson Crusoe* as it testifies that the Western individual does not embody the knowledge of European civilizations and must learn from Native Americans to survive. His account of cannibalism among the Spaniards includes a condemnation of the act by the Indians and a description of a highly ritualized consumption of the ashes of dead shamans. Thus, Europeans come to embody the savagery conventionally attributed to Indians.

See also **Cannibalism; Conquistadores.**

BIBLIOGRAPHY

The most complete edition of Cabeza de Vaca's writing is Alvar Núñez Cabeza De Vaca, *Relación de los naufragios y comentarios,* edited by Manuel Serrano y Sanz, *Colección de libros y documentos referentes a la historia de América,* vol. 5 (1906); volume 6 of this collection contains other documents by and on Cabeza de Vaca. For a more recent critical edition, see Alvar Núñez Cabeza De Vaca, *Relación,* edited by Enrique Pupo-Walker (1992). For an English version of the *Naufragios,* see Alvar Núñez Cabeza De Vaca, *Castaways,* edited by Enrique Pupo-Walker and translated by Frances M. López-Morillas (1993). The standard biography still is Morris Bishop, *The Odyssey of Cabeza de Vaca* (1933). More recent studies are Rolena Adorno, "The Negotiation of Fear in Cabeza de Vaca's *Naufragios,*" in *Representations,* no. 33 (1991): 163–199; Maureen Ahern, "The Cross and the Gourd: The Appropriation of Ritual Signs in the *Relaciones* of Alvar Núñez and Fray Marcos de Niza," in *Early Images of the Americas: Transfer and Invention,* edited by Jerry M. Williams and Robert E. Lewis (1993); and José Rabasa, "Allegory and Ethnography in Cabeza de Vaca's *Naufragios* and *Comentarios,*" in *Violence, Resistance, and Survival in the Americas: Native Americans and the Legacy of Conquest,* edited by William B. Taylor and Franklin Pease G.Y. (1994).

Additional Bibliography

Adorno, Rolena, Alvar Nuñez Cabeza de Vaca, and Patrick Charles Pautz. *Alvar Nuñez Cabeza de Vaca: His Account, His Life, and the Expedition of Pánfilo de Narváez.* 3 Vols. Lincoln: University of Nebraska Press, 1999.

Howard, David A. *Conquistador in Chains: Cabeza de Vaca and the Indians of the Americas.* Tuscaloosa: University of Alabama Press, 1997.

Montané Martí, Julio C. *El mito conquistado: Alvar Nuñez Cabeza de Vaca.* Hermosillo, Sonora, México: Universidad de Sonora, 1999.

                                                    JOSÉ RABASA

CABEZAS LACAYO, OMAR (1950–).

The Nicaraguan Omar Cabezas Lacayo is best known as the author of two testimonial works, *La montaña es algo más que una inmensa estepa verde* (1982; published in English as *Fire From the Mountain*, 1985) and *Canción de amor para los hombres* (Love for All Men, 1988) that narrate Cabezas's role in the popular uprising against the government of Anastasio Somoza and epitomize the fluid colloquial prose and oral communicative strategies characteristic of the testimonial genre.

The first work chronicles his own revolutionary coming of age as a university student, whereas the second describes his actions as a Sandinista *comandante* from 1974 to 1979 and reflects his growing awareness as first-person narrator and protagonist. Because of his themes and the accessibility of his texts to a wide reading public, Cabezas has frequently been read alongside the works of other Central American testimonials that also give voice to broader and traditionally marginalized populations.

Cabezas joined the Student Revolutionary Front (FER) in the late 1960s. After serving with the Sandinista National Liberation Front (FSLN) in the mountains of northern Nicaragua, Cabezas was named deputy interior minister for the FSLN government during the 1980s. After the Sandinista defeat at the polls in 1990, Cabezas became involved with human rights activities in Nicaragua and Central America, most recently as Nicaragua's autonomous Ombudsman for Human Rights (*Procurador para la Defensa de los Derechos Humanos*).

See also **Nicaragua, Political Parties: Sandinista National Liberation Front (FSLN); Sandino, Augusto César; Somoza Debayle, Anastasio.**

BIBLIOGRAPHY

Barbas Rhoden, Laura H. "El papel del testimonio después de la victoria: Omar Cabezas y el discurso revolucionario en Nicaragua." *Confluencia* 14: 2 (1999): 63–75.

Cabezas, Omar. *La montaña es algo más que una inmensa estepa verde.* Managua: Editorial Nueva Nicaragua, 1982.

Cabezas, Omar. *Fire from the Mountain: The Making of a Sandinista.* Translated by Kathleen Weaver. New York: Crown Publishers, 1985.

Cabezas, Omar. *Canción de amor para los hombres.* Managua: Editorial Nueva Nicaragua, 1988.

Cabezas Lacayo, Omar. "Testimonio de mis testimonios (sobre preguntas de Edward Walters Hood)." *Hispamérica* 22: 64–65 (1993): 111–120.

Delgado Aburto, Leonel. "Proceso cultural y fronteras del testimonio nicaragüense." *Istmo*, 12 March 2004. Available from http://www.denison.edu/collaborations/istmo/v01n02/articulos/proceso.html.

Hood, Edward Walters. "Form and Content in Cabezas Lacayós Works: Testimonio literario, literatura testimonial." *PCCLAS Proceedings* 15 (1991): 1–2; (1991–1992): 87–95.

Mantero, José María. "Omar Cabezas, Gioconda Belli y Sergio Ramírez: Autobiografías, sandinismo e identidad nicaragüense." *Salina* 18 (2004): 235–242.

Mantero, José María. "La mitificación de la revolución sandinista: El caso de Omar Cabezas y *La montaña es más que una inmensa estepa verde*." *Revista de Estudios Hispánicos* 30: 2 (2003): 47–57.

McCallister, Rick. "La cuestión de género en *La montaña es algo más que una inmensa estepa verde*." In *La literatura centroamericana: Visiones y revisiones*, edited by Jorge Román Lagunas. Lewiston, NY: Mellen, 1994.

Ross, Peter. "Between Fiction and History: Omar Cabezas's *La montaña es algo más que una inmensa estepa verde*." In *War and Revolution in Hispanic Literature*, edited by Roy Boland and Alun Kenwood. Melbourne, Australia: Voz Hispánica, 1990.

Ward, Thomas. "Omar Cabezas y el testimonio de aprendizaje." In *La resistencia cultural: La nación en el ensayo de las Américas*, edited by Thomas Ward. Lima: Editorial Universitaria, Universidad Ricardo Palma, 2004.

JOSÉ MARÍA MANTERO

CABILDO, CABILDO ABIERTO. *Cabildo* and *abierto cabildo*, town or city council and its "open" meeting. The *cabildo* or *ayuntamiento* was created at the founding of a municipality. Each *cabildo* had four or more aldermen (*regidores*) and one or two magistrates (*alcaldes ordinarios*). Other municipal officials, such as the standard-bearer (*alférez real*), chief constable (*alguacil mayor*), and inspector of weights and measures (*fiel ejecutor*), were subordinate to the council.

The cornerstone of Spanish rule and settlement, the *cabildo* distributed town lots and nearby garden plots, supervised the construction and maintenance of roads and public works, provided protection against fraud in the markets and against criminal activities in general, regulated holidays and processions, and performed a variety of other duties essential to a settled, civilized existence. For revenue, the *cabildos* relied on the rent or lease of town property, judicial fines, and other modest sources.

The authority and responsibility of the *cabildo* gave its members power, prestige, and (in some cases) income. As a result, particularly in the sixteenth century, there was substantial interest in securing *cabildo* positions. The crown responded by selling many of those posts of life and, in 1606, confirming that they could be bequeathed upon payment of specified taxes. The result was the solid entrenchment of local families in local offices for generations.

The substantial authority *cabildos* enjoyed in the sixteenth century declined in the seventeenth and eighteenth centuries. In the late eighteenth century, intendants reinvigorated many councils and increased their ability to meet their responsibilities. As representatives of local interests, the *cabildos* were well positioned to take the initiative in response to the abdications of Charles IV and Ferdinand VII in 1808, and many advocated greater local and regional autonomy.

In times of local crisis, eminent citizens were convoked to meet and deliberate with the *cabildo* in a *cabildo abierto*. In Buenos Aires, for example, a *cabildo abierto* convoked in 1810 set the course that ultimately led to independence.

See also **Colonialism; Spanish Empire.**

BIBLIOGRAPHY

Clarence H. Haring, *The Spanish Empire in America* (1947).

John Preston Moore, *The Cabildo in Peru Under the Hapsburgs* (1954), and *The Cabildo in Peru Under the Bourbons* (1966).

Peter Marzahl, *Town in the Empire: Government, Politics, and Society in Seventeenth-Century Popayán* (1978).

Additional Bibliography

Aguilar Gaxiola, Víctor Hugo. *Las familias poderosas del cabildo de Culiacán, 1872–1910.* Culiacán, Mexico: Universidad Autónoma de Sinaloa: H. Ayuntamiento de Culiacán, 2004.

Díaz-Cosuelo, José María. *El Cabildo de Buenos Aires y el otorgamiento de las cartas de ciudadanía.* Santiago: Ediciones Universidad del Desarrollo, 2005.

Din, Gilbert C., and Jon E. Harkins. *The New Orleans Cabildo: Colonial Louisiana's First City Government, 1769–1803.* Baton Rouge: Louisana State University Press, 1996.

MARK A. BURKHOLDER

CABOCLO. *Caboclo,* a Brazilian term originally applied to Amerindians. It was later expanded to refer to people of mixed Amerindian and European origin, and now commonly refers to the non-Indian people and culture of the Amazon region. The term is often used to distinguish the *caboclos* as "traditional" rural Amazonian inhabitants, as opposed to migrants and other newcomers—although the forebears of present-day Amazonian *caboclos* were also migrants,

many of whom came during the rubber booms of the late nineteenth and early twentieth centuries.

The *caboclo* way of life and adaptation to the Amazon forest are similar to those of the Amerindian population. Scientists now study *caboclo* communities to learn more about the complex ecology of the rain forest. The present-day rubber tappers, Brazilnut gatherers, and other riverine populations involved in newly established Amazonian extractive reserves can all be considered *caboclos.*

The term *caboclo* is often used pejoratively and, depending on the context, can means someone of a lower class, a person of indigenous heritage, a "hick" or a "bumpkin." Similar southern Brazilian terms include *jeca* and *caipira.* In Afro-Brazilian religions such as Candomblé and Umbanda, the *caboclo* is a deity in the pantheon, represented as an Indian.

See also **Race and Ethnicity.**

BIBLIOGRAPHY

Emilio F. Moran, "The Adaptative System of the Amazonian Caboclo," in *Man in the Amazon,* edited by Charles Wagley (1974).

Charles Wagley, *Amazon Town* (1976).

Eugene Philip Parker, ed., *The Amazon Caboclo: Historical and Contemporary Perspectives* (1985).

Additional Bibliography

Fraxe, Therezinha J. P. *Homens anfíbios: Etnografia de um campesinato das aguas.* São Paulo, SP, Brasil: Annablume, 2006.

Nugent, Stephen. *Amazonian Caboclo Society: An Essay on Invisibility and Peasant Economy.* Providence: Berg, 1993.

Pace, Richard. "The Amazon Cabolco: What's in a Name?" *Luso-Brazilian Review.* 34:2 (Winter 1997): 39-55.

Stephens, Thomas M. *Dictionary of Latin American Racial and Ethnic Terminology.* Gainesville: University of Florida Press, 1989.

JUDITH LISANSKY

CABOT, SEBASTIAN (c. 1474–1557). Sebastian Cabot (*b.* ca. 1474, *d.* 1557), Venetian or English navigator. Cabot was born in Bristol or Venice, the son of the explorer John Cabot. He served as cartographer to Henry VIII, accompanied an English force to Spain, and was appointed in

1518 by Holy Roman Emperor Charles V to the Spanish Council of the New Indies. He was named pilot major and in 1525 entrusted with an expedition to develop commercial ties with the Orient. Upon reaching South America and hearing tales from native inhabitants of enormous riches to be found upriver, Cabot chose to explore the Río de la Plata instead of continuing on to the Pacific. He also explored the Paraguay and Paraná rivers, but returned empty-handed to Spain in 1530. As punishment for the failure of his expedition, he was banished to Africa for two years, but he was then pardoned and regained his title of pilot major. In later life, he returned to England, where he organized an association of merchants to sponsor future expeditions. He died in London.

See also **Explorers and Exploration: Spanish America.**

BIBLIOGRAPHY

Henry Harrisse, *John Cabot, the Discoverer of North America and Sebastian His Son* (1896).

Juan Gil, *Mitos y utopías del descubrimiento*, vols. 2–3 (1989).

                                      HILARY BURGER

CABRA.   *See* **African Brazilians, Color Terminology.**

CABRAL, MANUEL DEL (1907–1999).

Manuel del Cabral (*b*. 7 March 1907, *d*. 14 May 1999), Dominican poet and writer. Cabral is considered the greatest poet of his country and one of the best of Latin America. He is admired for the variety of his themes, which range from the African roots of Dominican culture to eroticism. His writings include short stories, novels, essays, plays, poems, autobiographies, epistolary confessions, and parables. Cabral has received prizes and awards from many hispanic countries, including the Premio de la Fundación Argentina para la Poesía. His published works include *Trópico negro* (1941), *Manuel cuando no es tiempo, Compadre Mon* (1942), *Sangre mayor* (1945), *De este lado del mar* (1949), *Los huéspedes secretos* (1951), *La isla ofendida* (1965), *Los relámpagos lentos* (1966), *Los anti-tiempos* (1967), *Egloga de 2,000* (1970), and *Obra poética* (1987).

See also **Literature: Spanish America.**

BIBLIOGRAPHY

Additional Bibliography

Fernández Spencer, Antonio. *Nueva poesía dominicana.* Madrid: Ediciones Cultura Hispánica, 1953.

Ugarte, Manuel. *Cabral, un poeta de América: Su poesía, la tierra, el hombre, el drama.* Buenos Aires: Editorial Américalee, 1955.

                                   KAI P. SCHOENHALS

CABRAL, PEDRO ÁLVARES (1468– c. 1520).

Pedro Álvares Cabral (*b*. 1467 or 1468; *d*. ca. 1520), Portuguese explorer, leader of the follow-up fleet to Vasco da Gama's first voyage to India. His expedition made the first recorded sighting of Brazil by the Portuguese on 22 April 1500.

On 15 February 1500, King Manuel I of Portugal chose Cabral, a *fidalgo* of the royal household, to command a fleet of thirteen ships and 1,200–1,500 men to sail for India. The purpose of the voyage was to establish trade and diplomatic relations with the *samorim* of Calicut and other rulers in India.

Cabral left Lisbon on 9 March 1500. On 22 April, Monte Pascoal, a mountain in what is now Brazil, was sighted. Cabral thought he had discovered an island, which he called Ilha de Vera Cruz. Sailing northward, he reached a harbor that he called Porto Seguro (now known as Baía Cabrália). He remained there for eight days and was on friendly terms with the region's inhabitants. The first Catholic Mass in Portuguese America was officiated by Frei Henrique Soares de Coimbra, one of eight Franciscans accompanying Cabral. He also celebrated the second Mass, which was attended by fifty or sixty Amerindians.

On 2 May, Cabral continued on to India. To announce to King Manuel I the discovery of the new land, soon to be called Santa Cruz and then Brazil, he sent one of his supply ships carrying reports by Cabral and by his captains, pilots, and other members of the fleet. Only two of the documents survived: the reports of Pero Vaz de Caminha and Mestre João Faras. Both are addressed to King Manuel and dated 1 May 1500. These two documents are the original manuscripts and seem to have been unknown to all the great chroniclers of the sixteenth century.

After sailing around the Cape of Good Hope and then reaching Calicut on 13 September 1500, Cabral battled Muslim traders and bombed Calicut. However, he established friendly relations with the Hindu ruler of Cochin before beginning his return voyage to Portugal. The *Anunciada,* one of the ships in the Cabral expedition, arrived in Lisbon on 23 June 1501. Cabral himself did not arrive in Lisbon until the end of July.

Despite the importance of Cabral's visit to Brazil and India, relatively little is known about the man, the expedition, and the motives behind the sighting of Brazil and Cabral's brief stay there. In the past, there has been considerable debate over whether Cabral's visit to Brazil was intentional or accidental and whether the Portuguese were aware of its existence before 1500. Although the issue continues to be debated, most scholars now believe that Cabral was unaware of Brazil's existence until winds and currents brought him within sight of land.

See also **Explorers and Exploration: Brazil.**

BIBLIOGRAPHY

The only serious biography of Cabral in English is a short one by James Roxburgh McClymont, *Pedraluarez Cabral (Pedro Alluarez de Gouveia): His Progenitors, His Life, and His Voyage to America and India* (1914). The most important documents about Cabral's voyage (with an excellent introduction) have been compiled and translated by William Brooks Greenlee in *The Voyage of Pedro Álvares Cabral to Brazil and India, from Contemporary Documents and Narratives* (1938). Included are the letters of Pero Vaz de Caminha and Mestre João Faras. The major documents in Portuguese have been collected in Abel Fontoura Da Costa and António Baião, eds., *Os sete únicos documentos de 1500, conservados em Lisboa/Referentes à viagem de Pedro Álvares Cabral,* 2d ed. (1968). For the most recent analyses of Cabral's voyage, see Harold Johnson and Maria Beatriz Nizza Da Silva, *Nova História da Expansão Portuguesa.* Vol. VI, *O império luso-brasileiro, 1500–1620* (1992), and Francis A. Dutra, "The Discovery of Brazil and Its Immediate Aftermath," in *Portugal, the Pathfinder,* edited by George D. Winus (1994). Other useful discussions are found in Luis De Albuquerque, *Os descobrimentos portugueses* (1983).

Damião Peres, *História dos descobrimentos portugueses,* 3d ed. (1983).

Max Justo Guedes, "O descobrimento do Brasil," in *História Naval Brasileira,* vol. 1, pt. 1 (1975), pp. 139–174.

Additional Bibliography

Greenlee, William Brooks. *The Voyage of Pedro Alvares Cabral to Brazil and India.* Nendeln: Kraus Reprint, 1967.

Marcondes de Souza, Thomaz Oscar. *O descobrimento do Brasil.* Sao Paulo: Companhia Editora Nacional, 1946.

FRANCIS A. DUTRA

CABRAL DE MELO NETO, JOÃO.

See **Melo Neto, João Cabral de.**

CABRERA, ANGEL LEOPOLDO

(1969–). Angel Cabrera, an Argentine professional golfer born September 12, 1969, in Córdoba, surprisingly won the U.S. Open Tournament in June 2007. Before that, in a professional career that began in 1989, the cigarette-puffing Cabrera, nicknamed El Pato (The Duck), had played mainly in Europe and had never won in the United States, though he had earned $2,888,983 and tied for eighth at the 2006 Masters Tournament. His first professional victories were at the 1995 Paraguay and Colombian Opens. He qualified for the European tour in 1996 and has since ranked in the top fifteen six times, winning three events there and six others around South America. Cabrera is Argentina's best known golfer since Roberto De Vicenzo, who won 231 tournaments, including five PGA Tour events and the 1967 British Open.

See also **Sports.**

BIBLIOGRAPHY

Shipnuck, Alan. "Grand Opening." *Sports Illustrated,* June 25, 2007.

JOSEPH L. ARBENA

CABRERA, LYDIA (1900–1991). Lydia

Cabrera (*b.* 20 May 1900; *d.* 19 September 1991), Cuban writer and anthropologist. Daughter of a well-known lawyer and historian, she was tutored at home, where she also became entranced by the tales of the black servants. After her father's death, she studied painting and Oriental art at L'école du Louvre in Paris (1927–1930). Her stay in France coincided with European interest in primitive cultures, a trend that reawakened her childhood fascination with African Cuban culture. She began her new studies at the Sorbonne and did her research in Cuba in 1930. In Paris again, she wrote *Cuentos negros de Cuba* (1934), published in French (1936) to great acclaim. In 1938 she moved back to Cuba, intent on continuing her studies in African Cuban folklore and conducting interviews among the black population. A second collection of short stories (*¿Por qué?... Cuentos negros de Cuba*), written in the same direct and colorful style, appeared in 1948. In 1954 she published her first anthropological work, *El monte: Notas sobre las religiones, la magia, las supersticiones y el folklore de los negros criollos y del pueblo de Cuba,* considered by some to be her most important contribution to African Cuban culture. In the 1950s Cabrera became a consultant to the National Institute of Culture and published three major works: *Refranes de negros viejos* (1955), *Anagó: vocabulario Lucumí* (1957), and *La sociedad secreta Abakuá* (1958).

The Cuban Revolution burst upon her whirlwind of activity, and Cabrera moved to Miami, losing most of her research. Slowly, she reestablished her career and in 1970 published *Otán Iyebiyé: Las piedras preciosas* and the fictional tales of *Ayapá: Cuentos de Jicotea* (1971). After a stay in Spain to research some of her lost sources, Cabrera returned to Miami. She received two honorary degrees—from Denison (1977) and the University of Redlands (1981)—and continued her anthropological research: *La laguna sagrada de San Joaquín* (1973), *Yemayá y Ochún* (1974), *Anaforuana: ritual y símbolos de la iniciación en la sociedad secreta Abakuá* (1975), *La Regla Kimbisa del Santo Cristo del Buen Viaje* (1977), *Trinidad de Cuba* (1977), *Reglas de Congo, Palomonte Mayombe* (1979), *Los animales en el folklore y la magia de Cuba* (1988), *La lengua sagrada de los Ñáñigos* (1988), and *Supersticiones y buenos consejos* (1988). She also published two collections of short stories: *Francisco y Francisca: Chascarrillos de negros viejos* (1976) and *Cuentos para grandes, chicos y retrasados mentales* (1983).

See also **Africans in Hispanic America.**

BIBLIOGRAPHY

José Antonio Madrigal and Reynaldo Sánchez, eds. *Homenaje a Lydia Cabrera* (1978).

Nicolás Kanellos, ed., *Biographical Dictionary of Hispanic Literature in the United States: The Literature of Puerto Ricans, Cuban Americans, and other Hispanic Writers* (1989).

Julio A. Martínez, ed., *Dictionary of Twentieth-Century Cuban Literature* (1990).

Additional Bibliography

Castellanos, Jorge. *Pioneros de la etnografía afrocubana: Fernando Ortiz, Rómulo Lachatañeré, Lydia Cabrera.* Miami: Ediciones Universal, 2003.

Gutiérrez, Mariela. *Lydia Cabrera: Aproximaciones mítico-simbólicas a su cuentística.* Madrid: Editorial Verbum, 1997.

Rodríguez-Mangual, Edna M. *Lydia Cabrera and the Construction of an Afro-Cuban Cultural Identity.* Chapel Hill, NC: University of North Carolina Press, 2004.

MARÍA A. SALGADO

CABRERA, MIGUEL (1695–1768). Miguel Cabrera (*b.* 1695; *d.* 16 May 1768), Mexican painter. Although doubts exist about the authenticity of the document that gives his birth date and nothing is known about his training, Cabrera's will makes it clear that he was a native of Oaxaca. It is believed that by 1719 Cabrera was in Mexico City, where he became the most important painter of his day. With other artists he attempted to found an academy in Mexico City in 1753, and in 1756 he published *Maravilla americana,* an account of his examination of the original image of the Virgin of Guadalupe. Among his many works, those for the Jesuits are outstanding in number and quality; but he had numerous other important patrons, including the archbishop of Mexico City and the miner José de la Borda in Taxco. His paintings display a sense of ample space and often brilliant, light coloring. Sweetness of expression is a hallmark of his religious figures, whose repetitive portrayal was much appreciated in his time and in the nineteenth century, but has occasioned twentieth-century criticism. Cabrera's reputation has also suffered because of the disparate quality of many paintings signed by or attributed to him, a number of them executed in what must have been a large workshop. He is also known for his portraits and for an extraordinary series of *casta* paintings, depictions of the mixed races that peopled New Spain.

See also **Art: The Colonial Era.**

BIBLIOGRAPHY

Abelardo Carrillo y Gariel, *El pintor Miguel Cabrera* (1966).

María Concepción García Saiz, *La pintura colonial en el Museo de América*, vol. 1 (1980).

Additional Bibliography

Carrera, Magali Marie. *Imagining Identity in New Spain: Race, Lineage, and the Colonial Body in Portraiture and Casta Paintings*. Austin: University of Texas Press, 2003.

Katzew, Ilona. *Casta Painting: Images of Race in Eighteenth-Century Mexico*. New Haven, CT: Yale University Press, 2004.

Martí Cotarelo, Mónica, and Dolores Dahlhaus. *Miguel Cabrera: un pintor de su tiempo*. México, D.F.: Consejo Nacional para la Cultura y las Artes, Dirección General de Publicaciones, 2002.

Tovar de Teresa, Guillermo. *Miguel Cabrera: Pintor de cámara de la reina celestial*. México: InverMéxico Grupo Financiero, 1995.

CLARA BARGELLINI

CABRERA INFANTE, GUILLERMO

(1929–2005). Guillermo Cabrera Infante (*b.* 22 April 1929, *d.* 21 February 2005), Cuban novelist and essayist. Cabrera Infante was born in Gibara in Oriente Province. In 1947 he moved to Havana with his parents and began studying medicine at the University of Havana. After quickly deciding to take up writing, he abandoned medicine for journalism. In 1952 he was arrested and fined for publishing a short story that contained English profanities. In the late 1950s he began to earn prizes with his short stories.

Meanwhile, his passion for the cinema led him to film reviewing. Under the pseudonym G. Caín, he wrote film reviews and articles on the cinema for the weekly *Carteles,* becoming its editor in chief in 1957. He was the founder of Cinemateca de Cuba, the Cuban Film Society, over which he presided from 1951 to 1956. In 1959 he became director of the Cuban Film Institute and of the literary magazine *Lunes de revolución.* In 1962 he served the Cuban government as cultural attaché in Belgium. In 1964 he received the prestigious Biblioteca Breve Prize for his novel *Tres tristes tigres* (1971). In 1965 he decided to break with the Cuban government, leaving his diplomatic post and permanently settling in London.

By the mid-1990s, Cabrera Infante was the best-known living Cuban author. *Tres tristes tigres,* translated into English as *Three Trapped Tigers,* won him worldwide recognition. In this novel, as has been pointed out by such eminent critics as Emir Rodríguez Monegal, language itself is the main preoccupation. Here, too, as in all of Cabrera Infante's work, there is a great deal of humor, especially word games and puns. Because of this aspect of his work, he has been compared to Russian emigré writer Vladimir Nabokov. His mastery of the English language—one of his later novels, *Holy Smoke* (1985), was written in English—has also begged comparison with Joseph Conrad. Cabrera Infante, who became a British citizen, has said ironically that he is as English as muffins and is a happy subject of the queen. He died in London, and was survived by his second wife, actress Miriam Goméz, and two daughters from his first marriage.

Besides *Tres tristes tigres,* some of his best-known works are *La Habana para un infante difunto* (1984) and *Vista del amanecer en el trópico* (1974). His novels have been widely translated.

See also **Literature: Spanish America.**

BIBLIOGRAPHY

Rosa María Pereda, *Guillermo Cabrera Infante* (1979).

Stephanie Merrim, *Logos and the Word: The Novel of Language and Linguistic Motivation in* Grande sertao, veredas *and* Tres tristes tigres (1983).

Rosemary Geisdorfer Feal, *Novel Lives: The Fictional Autobiographies of Guillermo Cabrera Infante and Mario Vargas Llosa* (1986).

Dinorah Hernández Lima, *Versiones y re-versiones históricas en la obra de Cabrera Infante* (1990).

Additional Bibliography

Alvarez-Borland, Isabel. *Cuban-American Literature of Exile: From Person to Persona*. Charlottesville: University of Virginia Press, 1998.

Nelson, Ardis. *Guillermo Cabrera Infante: Assays, Essays and Other Arts*. New York: Twayne Publishers, 1999.

Souza, Raymond. *Guillermo Cabrera Infante: Two Islands, Many Worlds*. Austin: University of Texas Press, 1996.

ROBERTO VALERO

CABRERA LOBATO, LUIS (1876–1954). Luis Cabrera Lobato (*b.* 17 July 1876; *d.* 1954), leading Mexican intellectual remembered

for a brilliant speech before the Chamber of Deputies advocating an agrarian reform law in 1912, for hundreds of political essays written under the pen name of Blas Urrea, and for his complete intellectual independence from successive post-revolutionary governments.

Cabrera, the son of a humble baker, Gertrudis Lobato, attended the National Preparatory School (1889–1893). He went on to complete his law degree from the National School of Law in 1901, after which he practiced law and taught. A cofounder of the Anti-Reelectionist Party in 1909, he became dean of the National School of Law and a federal deputy in 1912, later serving as an agent of the Constitutionalists in the United States and as Venustiano Carranza's treasury secretary. He retired from politics in 1920, and though he was twice offered the presidential candidacy by opposition parties—in 1933 and 1946—he declined to run.

See also **Agrarian Reform.**

BIBLIOGRAPHY

Luis Cabrera, *Obras Completas,* 4 vols. (1972–1975).

Ramón Eduardo Ruiz, "Review of *Obras Completas,* vols. 1–4, by Luis Cabrera," in *Hispanic American Historical Review* (February 1978): 127–130.

Fernando Zertuche Muñoz, *Luis Cabrera: Una visión de México* (1988).

Additional Bibliography

Uhthoff López, Luz María. *Las Finanzas Públicas durante la Revolución: El Papel de Luis Cabrera y Rafael Nieto al Frente de la Secretaría de Hacienda.* México, D.F.: Universidad Autónoma Metropolitana, Unidad Iztapalapa, 1998.

RODERIC AI CAMP

CACAO INDUSTRY.

The cacao bean (*theobroma cacao*) comes from the large fleshy pod of a tropical bush or small tree. The plant is American, probably Amazonian in origin, and by the time of the European conquest had long ago diffused by unknown means to other parts of tropical America.

The bean yields chocolate, a nutritious fatty food or drink. In Mesoamerica cacao was domesticated many centuries before the Europeans arrived, and although tended groves grew on various parts of the Caribbean coast, such as the Gulf of Honduras and Tabasco, it was on the Pacific coastal plain, stretching all the way from Colima to the Gulf of Fonseca, that most production concentrated. Cacao beans were used for coinage, even into the Spanish colonial period, but it was as a drink that it found most favor, and the areas where it was cultivated were coveted by merchants and military states. Large quantities were collected as tribute and traded, and the drink enjoyed considerable prestige, so much so that in at least some areas only the aristocracy was permitted to drink it.

Whatever limits that were placed on its production and consumption disappeared after the European conquest, and cacao became a drink of mass consumption among the Mesoamerican native peoples, especially those of Central Mexico. Spaniards at first found the various chocolate concoctions, most of which contained maize gruel, chiles, and annatto for coloring, to be unpalatable, but they quickly seized the business opportunities involved, and merchants and *encomenderos* dominated cacao plantations and sales.

Soconusco, a satellite of the Aztec Empire, was the first area of extensive growth and export in the sixteenth century, but as it declined Izalcos, in present-day El Salvador, became the main producer. It, in its turn, was challenged and surpassed by the area around Guayaquil in Ecuador and then by the tropical valleys of Venezuela, and these two regions remained the main rivals for and suppliers of the Mexican market throughout the colonial centuries.

Europeans found that the addition of sugar and vanilla made chocolate tasty, and its consumption spread from Spain all over western Europe. Although eventually surpassed by coffee and tea, it remained entrenched in Catholic countries because although nutritious and filling, it was not prohibited during fasts.

As its use increased, the Dutch, who had captured the offshore island of Curaçao in 1634, began to trade illegally for Venezuelan cacao. Plantations then sprouted in Trinidad, Jamaica, Santo Domingo, and in the French colony of Saint-Domingue. In spite of these rivalries Guayaquil supplied most of Mexico's needs, and Venezuelan cacao dominated the European market throughout the eighteenth century.

Venezuelan production began to decline around 1800, and the destruction caused by the wars of independence further weakened the industry. Amazonian Brazil, long a producer of wild Marañón cacao, filled some of the gap, but Guayaquil, where production quadrupled in the second decade of the nineteenth century, was the main beneficiary.

In the 1820s, with Guayaquil still dominant, important changes in chocolate manufacturing and consumption pushed demand to new heights. In Holland, Conrad Van Houten developed a process for extracting cacao butter, and for manufacturing oil- and fat-free cocoa, a more digestible drink for children. About half a century later the Swiss pioneered the production of milk chocolate and, by the end of the century, hard chocolates, with cut flowers, had become the gifts associated with courtship.

Chocolate soon passed from being a luxury product for women and children to being an item of mass consumption. The emergence of giant firms such as Hershey in the United States; Fry, Cadbury, and Rowntree in Great Britain; Lindt and Tobler in Switzerland transformed marketing and consumption and created massive demand and new areas of production. The growth of the chocolate industry in the twentieth century has been spectacular. Concentrated in New York and London, the cacao market is now worldwide and highly competitive.

Ecuador, the leader in the 1820s, was the first producer for the world market, and the Guayaquil basin, supplied with labor from the depressed *sierra,* produced about 7,000 tons per year by the early 1840s. There it stagnated. Yellow fever and political turbulence hampered Ecuadorian growth until the 1870s, when a new spurt sent annual export to twenty thousand tons by 1900, a trade which supplied almost two-thirds of state revenues.

Venezuelan cacao, while it never regained the prosperity of 1800, remained in second place among Latin American producers until it was passed by Brazil and Trinidad around 1870. Coffee had become Venezuela's leading export.

Competition among Latin American states was not the main problem, however. From early intensive plantations on the islands of São Tomé and Principe, the leading suppliers of cacao in the world in the first decade of the twentieth century, intensive cultivation spread to the African mainland, where Cameroon, Nigeria, Ghana, and, more recently, the Ivory Coast became the world leaders.

Ecuador more or less kept its place until the end of World War I, although competition was affecting prices. Then the groves were hit by witch broom disease. Ecuador converted gradually to bananas, as Venezuela had to coffee, although Ecuador still exports large quantities of cacao. Brazil's cacao, most of which went to the United States, had ceased to be of the "wild" variety, and was now produced in southern Bahia. The Hershey company grew its own cacao in Cuba until its plantations were confiscated by the Cuban revolutionary government in the late 1950s. The Dominican Republic and Venezuela also export considerable quantities.

The great days of American cacao seem to have gone, however, and this American cultigen, which moved through so many Latin American tropical regions and which supplied Latin America with a major trade and export commodity for about four centuries, has now retreated to a minor role. In the early twenty-first century, the Ivory Coast supplies about 40 percent of the world's cacao. Ghana and Indonesia each have roughly 15 percent of the market. Latin American countries have begun to compete in the expanding premium chocolate market by producing organic crops, and farmers have started to produce cacao according to Fair Trade Standards, which stipulate living wages and good working conditions.

See also **Agriculture; Food and Cookery.**

BIBLIOGRAPHY

Alden, Dauril. *The Significance of Cacao Production in the Amazon Region During the Late Colonial Period: An Essay in Comparative Economic History* (1976).

Assomou, Jean. *L'économie du cacao* (1977).

Bergman, James F. "The Distribution of Cacao Cultivation in Pre-Columbian America," in *Annals of the Association of American Geographers* 59 (March 1969): 85–96.

Chiriboga, Manuel. *Jornaleros y gran propietarios en 135 años de exportación: Cacaotera, 1790–1925* (1980).

Harwich, Nikita. *Histoire du Chocolat* (1992).

León, Dora Borja and Adám Szászdi. "El comercio de cacao de Guayaquil," in *Revista de Historia de América* 57–58 (1964): 1–50.

McNeil, Cameron L. *Chocolate in Mesoamerica: A Cultural History of Cacao.* Gainesville: University Press of Florida, 2006.

Piñero, Eugenio. *Veracruz and the Caracas Cacao Trade* (1994).

Topik, Steven, Carlos Marichal, and Zephyr L. Frank. *From Silver to Cocaine: Latin American Commodity Chains and the Building of the World Economy, 1500–2000.* Durham, NC: Duke University Press, 2006.

Murdo J. MacLeod

CACAXTLA. One of many sites in highland Mexico that flourished between the seventh and tenth centuries CE, Cacaxtla is located approximately eighty miles east of Mexico City in the state of Tlaxcala. It contains some of the best-preserved pre-Columbian murals ever discovered in Mesoamerica. The main mound (*el gran basamento*), stretching over an area approximately twelve hundred feet long and rising more than eighty feet, was first excavated in 1975. In its heyday this great structure rose in giant horizontal terraces interrupted by massive vertical buttresses of masonry. Stairways and columned buildings had shaded portals facing outward from all sides and at all levels. The buildings show at least eight major stages of construction, each with its own pattern of stucco-covered adobe walls, indicating that the *gran basamento* was a combination palace and administrative center.

Cacaxtla means "the place of the merchant's backpack" in Nahuatl, and its murals show warrior-traders carrying weapons and standard consumer goods such as obsidian, textiles, and feathers as they traveled among other pre-Columbian groups. It is not definitively known which people built and inhabited this site, but scholars are leaning toward the Olmeca-Xicalanca, an obscure group with possible origins on the Gulf Coast of Mexico. Its location in the so-called Teotihuacán Corridor enabled its residents to dominate the traffic between the Gulf Coast and the cities of the Central Valley of Mexico.

The justly famous murals show in impressive detail a combat scene representing a military victory or staged postwar sacrificial ceremony in which jaguar warriors spear unarmed soldiers dressed as birds who writhe hideously at their feet, spreading blood everywhere. Dominating all the murals are Venus symbols, representing the dreaded "wasp star," which, some argue, celestially determined the occurrence of battles. In their totality, the murals depict a vision of the cycle of life.

Archaeologists date the last paintings at Cacaxtla at approximately 790 CE. The decline of Teotihuacán set off a chain reaction of collapse throughout Mesoamerica. This, together with increased military competition from other newly emerging and neighboring city-states, eventually caused residents to abandon the site.

See also **Art: Pre-Columbian Art of Mesoamerica.**

BIBLIOGRAPHY

Garcia Cook, Angel, and B. Leonor Merino Carrion. *Guia illustrada de Cacaxtla.* Tlaxcala: Instituto Nacional de Antropologia e Historia, Mexico, 1997.

Lombardo De Ruiz, Sonia, et al. *Cacaxtla: El lugar donde muere la lluvia en la tierra.* Mexico City: Secretaría de Educación Pública, 1986.

Stuart, George. "Cacaxtla." *National Geographic* 182 (September 1992): 120–136.

George Stuart
Kenneth Hirth

CÁCERES, ANDRÉS AVELINO (1833–1923). Andrés Avelino Cáceres (*b.* 1833; *d.* 1923), Peruvian military hero and president (1886–1890, 1894–1895), commander of the highland guerrilla resistance to the Chilean occupation of coastal Peru during the War of the Pacific (1879–1883). Like Francisco Bolognesi, Cáceres was drawn to military life in the 1850s in support of General Ramón Castilla against Generals José Rufino Echenique and Manuel Ignacio Vivanco. During Castilla's second term in office, Cáceres served as military attaché to the Peruvian legation in France. Upon his return to Peru he supported Colonel Mariano Ignacio Prado's 1865 revolution against General Juan Antonio Pezet's unpopular though legitimate government. When Manuel Pardo was elected as the first civilian president in 1872, Cáceres served as a faithful military officer. At this time he began to express political differences with his life-long foe Nicolás de Piérola, who conspired against Pardo.

Born in Ayacucho, Cáceres had extensive family and landowning interests in the south-central and central highlands of Peru, which provided him with the power base necessary to conduct his military campaigns against the Chilean army and to advance his own political ambitions. During the War of the Pacific, Cáceres fought in the battles of San Francisco and Tarapacá and in the 1881 defense of Lima in San Juan and Miraflores. Wounded in the latter battle, he hid in Lima and later went to the strategic central highland town of Jauja to initiate and lead his military and political resistance, the La Breña campaign. His guerrilla tactics earned him the name "Wizard of the Andes." The support his forces received from peasant communities fighting for their livelihood constituted the key factor of this protracted resistance.

However, Peruvian military and political leaders during the Chilean occupation were divided into several factions. Some, like Francisco García Calderón, had been imprisoned and exiled by the Chilean army. One such faction, led by General Miguel Iglesias, signed the Treaty of Ancón (1883), which allowed the Chilean army to withdraw from Lima. Cáceres opposed and fought Iglesias and assumed the presidency in 1886. During his term of office the Grace contract (1889), a costly settlement with foreign creditors, was signed to establish the bases for the economic recovery of Peru in the 1890s. In 1890, Cáceres handed power to General Remigio Morales Bermúdez, who died in office in 1894. Cáceres's subsequent attempts to regain power faced a popular insurrection led by Piérola, who succeeded in forcing Cáceres to resign and leave the country. After a long exile Cáceres returned to Peru and was awarded the honorific title of marshal in 1919. He died in Lima.

See also **Peru: Peru Since Independence.**

BIBLIOGRAPHY

Rory Miller, "The Making of the Grace Contract: British Bondholders and the Peruvian Government, 1885–1890," in *Journal of Latin American Studies* 8 (1978): 73–100.

Florencia E. Mallon, *The Defense of Community in Peru's Central Highlands: Peasant Struggle and Capitalist Transition, 1860–1940* (1983).

Additional Bibliography

Cáceras, Andrés Avelino. *Memorias del Mariscal Andrés A. Cáceras.* Lima: Editorial Milla Batres, 1986.

                                        ALFONSO W. QUIROZ

CÁCERES, ESTHER DE (1903–1971).

Esther de Cáceres (*b.* 1903; *d.* 1971), Uruguayan poet and educator. After earning a degree in medicine (1929), Cáceres taught humanities at the Teacher Training Institute and the Institute of Advanced Studies, both in Montevideo. She belonged to a cohort of leading women intellectuals and literary figures. Her first book of poetry was *Las ínsulas extrañas* (1929), followed in rapid succession by *Canción* (1931), *Libro de la soledad* (1935), *Los cielos* (1935), and many others. Especially noteworthy is "*Concierto de amor*" *y otros poemas,* with a prologue by Gabriela Mistral (1951). In Cáceres's early poetry, the mood alternates between melancholy and joy, as felt through mystical communion with God and other religious experiences. Later works—*Los cantos del destierro* (1963), *Tiempo y abismo* (1965), and *Canto desierto* (1969)—focus more on the subjective anguish caused by metaphysical displacement and the poet's immersion in the turbulent social and political circumstances of the time.

See also **Literature: Spanish America.**

BIBLIOGRAPHY

Sarah Bollo, *Literatura uruguaya, 1807–1965,* vol. 2 (1965).

Francisco Aguilera and Georgette Magassy Dorn, *The Archive of Hispanic Literature on Tape: A Descriptive Guide* (1974).

Additional Bibliography

Pickenhayn, Jorge Oscar. *Voces femeninas en la poesia de Uruguay.* Buenos Aires: Editorial Plus Ultra, 1999.

                                        WILLIAM H. KATRA

CÁCERES, RAMÓN (1866–1911).

Ramón Cáceres (*b.* 15 December 1866; *d.* 19 November 1911), president of the Dominican Republic (1906–1911). Born in Moca, in the north-central part of the country, to a distinguished and prosperous family, Cáceres, a landowner, was in the forefront of the opposition to president Ulises Heureaux (1882–1899). Cáceres earned national recognition when, on 26 July 1899, he assassinated the dictator during a public appearance in Moca. The ensuing political chaos resulted in several years of unstable regimes. Cáceres was forced into exile in 1903 but returned in 1904 to become vice president under Carlos Morales. When the latter abandoned his post in 1906, Cáceres assumed the office.

Cáceres's presidency was one of the most peaceful and prosperous periods in Dominican history. He expanded federal power without debilitating local government, reformed the constitution, began an ambitious public works program, and transferred many privately owned utilities to the public realm. The shifts in economic power engendered by his reform earned him powerful enemies, and there were several unsuccessful plots against his government. In 1905, a United States customs receivership was established. Cáceres welcomed the prosperity it brought but remained concerned about financial dependence on the United States. Then in 1911, as he took his evening ride, Cáceres was assassinated. His death was followed by a resurgence of political and economic disorder and, ultimately, by the U.S. occupation of the Dominican Republic in 1916.

See also **Dominican Republic.**

BIBLIOGRAPHY

Selden Rodman, *Quisqueya: A History of the Dominican Republic* (1964), pp. 102–127.

Pedro Troncoso Sánchez, *Ramón Cáceres* (1964).

SARA FLEMING

CACIQUE, CACIQUISMO. When the Columbian expeditions reached the Greater Antilles, they found most of the land dominated by chiefdoms. Hispaniola had probably reached a more consolidated level, with fewer, larger, and more powerful entities, some of them perhaps monarchies. The rulers called themselves, at least to the Spanish ear, "caciques," and those who did not immediately oppose the Spaniards found themselves in the tenuous position of brokers or administrators for the Spanish regime. Nearly all finally revolted and were killed in battle or executed.

Spaniards carried the word *caciques* to their conquests of the mainland and took to using the term to describe Indian leaders at the town or village level across the Americas. For example, Andean local leaders called *curacas* were inevitably still called *caciques*. Similar linguistic distortions of local power occurred in most areas that were conquered.

There is considerable academic debate as to the roles and fate of this indigenous lower aristocracy.

Some have emphasized their importance as brokers, tax collectors, and petty administrators for the local Spanish officials or the *encomenderos,* and discuss how caciques in many areas were squeezed between increasing demands from a growing Spanish population and a declining number of Indian subjects. Evidence for this position consists of data on the number of caciques killed or demoted, and of instances of usurpers placed in theoretically hereditary positions, often, after the early years, by Spanish manipulation of elections. These scholars also show that the imposition of Spanish systems of town government—*cabildos,* or town councils, headed by *alcaldes, regidores,* and sometimes *gobernadores*—was sometimes an attempt to shunt aside traditional cacique kinships.

Others have debated these conclusions, arguing that the native aristocracy survived in some areas for the entire colonial period. These caciques became true brokers and fended off some Spanish intrusions as well as provided for community needs. They became the repositories for native traditions and cultural resistance. This view also points to instances where *cabildos* were skillfully taken over by members of old ruling lineages, so that these caciques became the *alcaldes* and *regidores*. In a few areas there is also evidence that where the office of *gobernador* existed, it was sometimes reserved for a member of a hereditary ruling group. In other cases the position was clearly a direct Spanish imposition, and dominated the elected *cabildo*.

It would be safe to say only that the activities, cultural attitudes, and ultimate fates of the colonial cacique class varied widely over time and place between the extremes of rapid extinction and relatively prosperous independence and continuity.

The nineteenth-century history of the term *cacique,* and of its extension, *caciquismo,* is unclear, but they came to be used to describe various kinds of rural *patrones* (bosses, or strongmen) and their systems of wielding power, both in Spanish-speaking America and in Spain. (The Brazilian institution of Coronelismo has many similarities.)

Some have found the origins of caciquismo in the authoritarian regime of the colonial period, and in the regionalism and disarticulation of that era. Others consider the outbreak of independence, the disappearance of the colonial system, and the resultant legitimacy vacuum as the situation that led to the emergence of local bosses. Some reject explanations based on the colonial or independence periods and have emphasized such factors as: the weakness of the infant nation states which fostered anarchy or virtual autonomy on the peripheries; the lack of political institutions or parties which led people to pledge their allegiances to persons rather than movements; the necessity for a network of patron-client relationships in a hierarchically structured society with chronic insecurity and a tradition of paternalism and Latifundia; and, in some cases, the desire of undemocratic elites to retain power by using strongmen puppets to do their work of social control.

All of these propositions have been contradicted by yet other scholars. National rulers in the capital, for example, have used coalitions of regional caciques to maintain and even increase their power. Elites have been humbled by local populists, especially when these rural bosses make their bids for the presidency and national power.

The connection between the rural cacique and the national Caudillo has also caused debate. Some see them as different generically. Others argue that the caudillo was often an insurgent regional cacique who had seized power in the capital; that is, functionally and systemically the two institutions were linked.

Either the terms require further scrutiny or, perhaps, they have become so stretched by the diversity of explanations and processes packed into them that they have become somewhat empty generalizations.

See also **Encomienda; Patronage.**

BIBLIOGRAPHY

Díaz, Fernando Díaz. *Caudillos y caciques: Antonio López de Santa Anna y Juan Álvarez* (1972).

Guerra Manzo, Enrique. *Caciquismo y orden público en Michoacán, 1920–1940.* Múxico: El Colegio de Múxico, Centro de Estudios Sociológicos, 2002.

Haigh, Roger M. *Martín Güemes: Tyrant or Tool? A Study of the Sources of Power of an Argentine Caudillo* (1968).

Haskett, Robert S. *Indigenous Rulers: An Ethnohistory of Town Government in Colonial Cuernavaca* (1991).

Kern, Robert. *The Caciques, Oligarchical Politics, and the System of Caciquismo in the Luso-Hispanic World* (1973).

Knight, Alan, and W. G. Pansters. *Caciquismo in Twentieth-Century Mexico.* London: Institute for the Study of the Americas, 2005.

Lynch, John. *Caudillos in Spanish America, 1800–1850* (1992).

Maldonado Aranda, Salvador. *Grupos políticos y cacicazgos sindicales en el estado de Múxico.* Zamora, Múxico: El Colegio de Michoacán, 2002.

Pease García-Yrigoyen, Franklin. *Curacas, reciprocidad y riqueza.* Lima: Pontificia Universidad Católica del Perú Fondo Editorial, 1992.

Ramírez, Susan. "The 'Dueño de Indios': Thoughts on the Consequences of the Shifting Bases of Power of the 'Curaca de los Viejos Antiguos' Under the Spanish in Sixteenth-Century Peru," in *Hispanic American Historical Review* 67, no. 4 (1987): 575–610.

Roniger, Luis. "Caciquismo and Coronelismo: Contextual Dimensions of Patron Brokerage in Mexico and Brazil," in *Latin American Research Review* 22, no. 2 (1987): 71–99.

Varón Gabai, Rafael. *Curacas y encomenderos acomodamiento nativo en Huaraz, siglos XVI y XVII.* Lima: P. L. Villanueva, 1980.

Wilson, Samuel M. *Hispaniola: Caribbean Chiefdoms in the Age of Columbus* (1990).

MURDO J. MACLEOD

CAFÉ FILHO, JOÃO (1889–1970).

João Café Filho (*b.* 3 February 1889; *d.* 20 February 1970), president of Brazil (1954–1955). Lawyer, strike leader, and popular opposition figure in his native state of Rio Grande do Norte, Café Filho helped the 1930 revolution that brought Getúlio Vargas to the Brazilian presidency. Without completing the required course work for a degree, he passed an examination that admitted him to the bar. Elected to Congress in 1934, he opposed repression by Vargas. In 1937–1938 he spent six months in exile in Argentina to avoid arrest. He did not return to politics until 1945, near the end of the Vargas dictatorship, and, together with São Paulo's Ademar de Barros, founded what became the Partido Social Progressista (PRP), which returned him to Congress.

Following Barros's 1950 alliance with Vargas, Café Filho became Vargas's running mate and was narrowly elected vice president despite Catholic objections to his leftist past. When Vargas committed suicide on 24 August 1954, Café Filho assumed the presidency. Members of his cabinet, regarded as conservative and anti-Vargas, opposed the inauguration of Juscelino Kubitschek, elected in 1955, but war minister Henrique Lott favored the inauguration and carried out a coup on 11 November 1955, while Café Filho was hospitalized for a heart ailment. When Café Filho was released from the hospital later in November, Lott's troops prevented him from resuming the presidency. Congress, favoring Kubitschek's inauguration, declared Café Filho unable to govern, a judgment upheld by the Supreme Court. Before his death, Café Filho served (1961–1969) on the accounts tribunal responsible for ruling on the legality of financial steps taken by the Guanabara state government.

See also **Vargas, Getúlio Dornelles.**

BIBLIOGRAPHY

João Café Filho, *Do sindicato ao Catete* (1966).

John W. F. Dulles, *Unrest in Brazil: Political-Military Crises, 1955–1964* (1970).

Additional Bibliography

Silva, Hélio and Maria Cecília Ribas Carneiro. *Café Filho, A Crisis Institucional, 1954–1955.* São Paulo: Grupo de Comunicação Três, 1983.

JOHN W. F. DULLES

CAFÉ TACUBA. This musical band achieved popular acclaim through *roc en español*. In 1989 four students from the Mexico City industrial suburb of Naucalpan formed the band Alicia Ya No Vive Aquí, after the Martin Scorsese movie *Alice Doesn't Live Here Anymore*. They soon renamed the group for the restaurant in the capital's central historical zone. The band's eponymous first album (1992) was and remains compared to the Beatles' *White Album*. As of 2007, the band has released ten recordings, including *Cuatro Caminos* (2003), which won a Grammy Award in the United States. In 2004 the group issued *Un Viaje*, a three-disc compilation to celebrate the band's fifteen-year existence.

All four members play various instruments. Full name: Rubén Isaac Albarrán Ortega is known for his vocals and has also played in the instrumental band Villa Jardin. Emmanuel "Meme" del Real Díaz, who plays keyboards, has established a reputation in the electronica genre as "DJ Angustias" and as a producer for several popular music stars. Enrique "Quique" Rangel Arroyo plays bass. José Alfredo "Joselo" Rangel Arroyo plays electric guitar and has released two solo albums.

The band has been heard on the soundtracks for various movies, most notably *Amores Perros* and *Y Tu Mamá También*. It also played on two popular tribute albums to José José and Los Tigres del Norte.

See also **Music: Popular Music and Dance; Tigres del Norte, Los.**

BIBLIOGRAPHY

Café Tacuba Official Web Site, http://www.cafetacuba.com.mx/.

WILLIAM H. BEEZLEY

CAFUSO/CAFUS. *See* African Brazilians, Color Terminology.

CAILLET BOIS, RICARDO (1903–1977). Ricardo Caillet Bois was one of the best known figures of twentieth-century Argentine historiography. He studied history at the National Institute of Secondary Education and served as a professor in the School of Liberal Arts of the University of Buenos Aires, in the National Institute of Secondary Education, and in the Buenos Aires National College. He was one of the favorite disciples of Emilio Ravignani, whom he supported in many professional enterprises. He was also one of the central figures of the so-called New School of History. Like Ravignani, he was forced to leave the university environment during Juan Domingo Perón's first period.

After the fall of the Perón government in 1955, Bois was named director of the Institute of Historic Research of the Liberal Arts School, known from then on as the E. Ravignani Institute of Argentine and American History. He was a member of the National Academy of History and served as its president from 1970 to 1972, and he was also president of the National Council of Education. Among his most important works are "Ensayo sobre el Río de la Plata y la Revolución Francesa" (1959; Essay on the La Plata River region and the French Revolution) and "Las Islas Malvinas" (1953; The Malvinas Islands).

See also **Perón, Juan Domingo.**

BIBLIOGRAPHY

Barcala de Moyano, Graciela G. *Bibliografía del Doctor Ricardo R. Caillet-Bois*. Buenos Aires: Academia Nacional de la Historia, 1982.

PABLO BUCHBINDER

CAIRÚ, VISCONDE DE. *See* **Silva Lisboa, José da.**

CAJAMARCA. Cajamarca, a Quechua word meaning "place or town of cold" that is the name of an important city, province, and department (created in 1855) in northern Peru. Because the department encompasses semitropical valleys and Andean highlands, agricultural and mining production is varied and rich. Its most important commercial crops are sugar, tobacco, and rice. Dairy farming is also important. Miners extract copper, lead, silver, zinc, and iron, especially from the mines of Hualgayoc and Chilete. More than 1.3 million inhabitants live in the department and 119,615 in the capital (2004).

Cajamarca has long been important in the history of Peru. It was the indigenous population center where in 1532 Francisco Pizarro first made contact with the Inca Atahualpa, eventually imprisoning and executing him there, despite the payment of a large ransom. Soon thereafter, the native inhabitants of Cajamarca were given in *encomienda* to Melchor Verdugo, their first and perhaps most famous trustee. It was Verdugo who began Spanish silver mining at Chilete as early as 1540, using the Cajamarquinos as laborers.

For most of the colonial era, Cajamarca was known for its abundant crops of wheat, barley, and corn; its deer and smaller game; and its good pastures for cattle grazing. The systematic exploitation of Hualgayoc's silver deposits begun in the late eighteenth century brought a new round of prosperity to the region. The inhabitants had, by this time, also earned fame for their weaving skills.

In the nineteenth century, Cajamarca was the home base of Miguel Iglesias's efforts to influence Peruvian politics. During the War of the Pacific (1879–1883), the department was invaded by the Chileans. The city served as the site of a congress of delegates from Peru's northern provinces who elected Iglesias president. In late 1882, this meeting of congress resulted in negotiations leading to the Treaty of Ancón and the end of the war.

See also **Iglesias, Miguel; War of the Pacific.**

BIBLIOGRAPHY

Carlos Burga Larrea, *Diccionario geográfico e histórico de Cajamarca* (1983).

Fernando Silva Santisteban, Waldemar Espinoza Soriano, Rogger Ravines, et al., comps., *Historia de Cajamarca: Siglos XVI–XVIII,* vol. 3 (1986).

Additional Bibliography

Christiansen, Tanja K. *Disobedience, Slander, Seduction, and Assault: Women and Men in Cajamarca, Peru, 1862-1900.* Austin: University of Texas Press, 2004.

Dammert Bellido, José. *Cajamarca en el siglo XVI.* Lima: Pontificia Universidad Católica del Perú: Instituto Bartolomé de Las Casas: Centro de Estudios y Publicaciones, 1997.

Drinot, Paulo, and Leo Garofalo. *Más allá de la dominación y la resistencia: Estudios de historia peruana, siglos XVI-XX.* Lima: IEP, Instituto de Estudios Peruanos, 2005.

Frías Coronado, Carlos. *Pobreza campesina: Sólo un problema rural: Cajamarca: Economía, espacio, y tecnología.* Lima: ITDG, 1995.

Mujica Bermúdez, Luis. *Poncho y sombrero, alforja y bastón: La iglesia en Cajamarca, 1962-1992.* Lima, Perú: IBC, Instituto Bartolomé de las Casas: ISET JUAN XXIII: CEP, 2005.

SUSAN E. RAMÍREZ

CAJAMARCA, PRE-COLUMBIAN. Situated in a large intermontaine basin at 9,022 feet (2,750 meters), Cajamarca is the picturesque capital of Cajamarca Department, Peru. Its ancient occupation dates back to around 1500 BCE, but it is famous as the place for the historic meeting between Spanish conquistadors and the Inca Atahualpa in 1532.

Early inhabitants relied on the hunting-gathering of diverse resources, including wild plants and animals, especially deer. By 1200 BCE, at the Huacaloma excavation site, the first public buildings appeared for small-scale ritual practices, especially the burning of offerings in hearths and ceremonial maintenance. Later architecture at Huacaloma and the larger Layzón site featured terraced platform pyramids with stonemasonry, monumental staircases, drainage canals, and painted plaster murals, indicating greater populations and political centralization. The Cumbemayo Canal formed part of an elaborate religious system focused on water and fertility in economic production. Agriculture and the herding of camelids became predominant by around 500 BCE.

The Initial and Early Cajamarca periods (200 BCE–500 CE) witnessed an increase in fortified settlements, probably of competitive, ranked societies. By 700 CE, fine Middle Cajamarca "cursive" pottery was popular in many parts of the Andes for funerary and status displays. Trade for the pottery and other products was facilitated by Wari state expansion into a zone characterized by large fortified centers, such as Coyor. Ceremonial architecture focused on mortuary practices: cliff tombs, subterranean chambers, and aboveground *chullpa* mausolea. These represented key places to keep and venerate honored deceased, often in association with fine Cajamarca tradition ceramics and stone sculptures. Cajamarca's later prehistory saw the spread of the cult of Catequil (a major pre-Hispanic divinity and pilgrimage center), the now-extinct Culle language, and the resurgence of large, wealthy chiefdoms, said to have been integrated as part of the Cuismanco ethnic confederation, which the Incas conquered around 1460 CE.

In Cajamarca, the Incas established a key provincial capital to administer the client populations and economies of northern Peru, especially its prosperous metal and textile industries. Political structures and alliances changed with the Spanish Conquest. Despite a ransom payment filling a room with gold and silver (the modern Cuarto de Rescate), Francisco Pizarro and his men executed Atahualpa, which precipitated the conquest of the Inca Empire.

See also **Atahualpa; Incas, The; Pizarro, Francisco.**

BIBLIOGRAPHY

Silva Santisteban, Fernando, Waldemar Espinoza Soriano, and Rogger Ravines, eds. *Historia de Cajamarca*, 2nd edition. 2 vols. Cajamarca, Peru: Instituto Nacional de Cultura, 1995.

Terada, Kazuo, and Yoshio Onuki. *Excavations at Huacaloma in the Cajamarca Valley, Peru, 1979.* Tokyo: University of Tokyo Press, 1982.

GEORGE F. LAU

CAJEME (1837–1887). Cajeme (José María Leyva; *b.* 1837; *d.* 21 April 1887), Yaqui Indian leader. After leaving the Yaqui valley in southern Sonora in his youth, he became a dependable volunteer member of the state forces backing the liberal *caudillo* Governor Ignacio Pesqueira whenever there was a crisis, including campaigns against his own people in the late 1860s. Rewarding Cajeme with the post of district administrator of the Yaqui valley (1874), the Pesqueira government assumed he would help obtain the Yaquis's total and permanent submission. Instead, he mobilized them (and neighboring Mayos) to achieve the status of separate nations which the two tribes had long claimed was rightfully theirs. Cajeme restructured and disciplined Yaqui society toward greater economic security and military preparedness: instituting a tax system; controlling external trade; reviving the mission practice of community plots and institutionalizing the tribal tradition of popular assemblies as decision making bodies; amassing war material. But by the early 1880s, the advantage of political instability from Pesqueira's fall had given way to national and state governments united in their zeal to colonize the rich lands of the Yaqui and Mayo valleys, employing a large, unrelenting, military force to do so. Though Cajeme was defeated and captured by Ángel Martínez at San José de Guaymas, and executed, Yaqui guerrilla resistance continued through 1910.

See also **Yaqui Rebellion, 1885–1898.**

BIBLIOGRAPHY

Ramón Corral, "Biografía de José María Leyva Cajeme," *Obras históricas,* vol. 1 (1886), pp. 147–192.

Claudio Dabdoub, *Historia de El Valle del Yaqui* (1964), pp. 115–138.

Evelyn Hu-Dehart, *Yaqui Resistance and Survival: The Struggle for Land and Autonomy, 1821–1910* (1984), pp. 93–117.

Additional Bibliography

Zavala Castro, Palemón. *El Indio Cajame y su nación yaqui.* Hermosillo: Gobierno del Estado de Sonora, Secretaría de Fomento Educativo y Cultura, 1985.

STUART F. VOSS

CAKCHIQUELS. *See* **Kaqchikel.**

CALAKMUL. Calakmul is a large Maya ruin of the Classic period (514–990 CE), located in the central Petén in the state of Campeche, Mexico. Huge (over 1.2 miles in diameter), Calakmul has yet to be fully mapped. Most of its 113 stelae—a record for any Maya site—have been recovered. Seventy-nine of these stelae are sculptured and forty are plain. Most are large and flat—more or less in the Tikal style—but a few are unique in having a male figure on one side and a female on the other, as well as male and female figures facing each other on the same stelae—perhaps representing a royal marriage or a period of joint rule. Recently attempts have been made to decipher some of these stelae, and there are indications of long periods of rule by local dynasties. In fact, Calakmul may have been one of the four initial empires of the Maya lowlands starting as early as 731 CE, for the city has its own distinctive emblem glyph. Although its pyramids lack the elaborate roof combs of Tikal, the architecture, city planning, and other artistic features of Calakmul show that it fell within the Tikal sphere of influence. There are also indications of conflict with Tikal.

A distinctive feature of Calakmul, unlike other Maya sites, is a limestone ledge sculpture, 21 feet long and 17 feet wide, showing a line of captive figures with their hands tied behind their backs and connected to a huge captive figure standing 9 feet tall. Future explorations were anticipated to reveal other distinctive features, and full deciphering of Calakmul's many stelae and sculptures may well write another unique history for the Maya region.

See also **Architecture: Architecture to 1900; Maya, The.**

BIBLIOGRAPHY

Joyce Marcus, *The Inscriptions of Calakmul* (1987).

Additional Bibliography

Folan, William J. *Las ruinas de Calakmul, Campeche, México: Un lugar central y su paisaje cultural.* Campeche, Mexico: Universidad Autónoma de Campeche, Centro de Investigaciones Históricas y Sociales, 2001.

Martin, Simon and Nikolai Grube. *Chronicle of the Maya Kings and Queens: Deciphering the Dynasties of the Ancient Maya.* New York: Thames & Hudson, 2000.

RICHARD S. MACNEISH

CALCAÑO, JOSÉ ANTONIO (1900–1978). José Antonio Calcaño (*b.* 23 March 1900, *d.* 11 September 1978), Venezuelan composer. Calcaño was born and educated in Caracas. After studying for a year at the Academy of Music in Bern, Switzerland, he returned to Caracas, where he had an outstanding career as a music teacher, music historian, and choir director. His compositions contributed greatly to giving Venezuelan music its particular character. His best-known work is the ballet *Miranda en Rusia.* Also well-known is his cantata "Desolación y gloria," written in honor of Simón Bolívar. Calcaño's book *La ciudad y su música* (1958) presents an overview of the musical life of Caracas from colonial times to the 1950s.

See also **Music: Art Music.**

BIBLIOGRAPHY

Perli, Rebeca. *Vida coral de José Antonio Calcaño.* Caracas: Lagoven, 1990.

OSCAR G. PELÁEZ ALMENGOR

CALCHAQUÍ, JUAN (?–*d.* 1600?). Juan Calchaquí (*d.* ca. 1600), Indian chief. In the middle of the sixteenth century, Juan Calchaquí was the principal chief of the region of Tolombón, in the territory which today bears his name, the Calchaquí Valley. In the latter half of the sixteenth century he led the rebellion that spread across almost all of northwest Argentina and part of the southern high plateau of Bolivia. He gained control over the various indigenous groups in the area of the Calchaquí Valley as well as the Omaguaca of the Quebrada de

Humahuaca; the Casabindo, the Apatama, and Chicha of La Puna; and the Jurí of Santiago del Estero.

The founding of the Spanish settlements at Córdoba of Calchaquí, Londres in the Hualfín Valley, and Cañete in Tucumán pushed the Indians to the point of war. In 1561, with Juan Calchaquí in the lead, they attacked these new European centers, causing their evacuation. The prestige of Chief Juan Calchaquí was such that his authority extended across all of the northwest of Argentina as well as the eastern plains and the south of La Puna in Bolivia. His reputation gained an almost sacred air. In 1563 the Audiencia of Charcas reported to the king that "they honor him as if he were a burial mound."

See also **Indigenous Peoples.**

BIBLIOGRAPHY

Hernando De Torreblanca, *Relación histórica de Calchaquí* (1984).

Additional Bibliography

Cerda Rodríguez, Joselín. *Chelemín y su época.* Córdoba: Alción, 1995.

                                    JOSÉ ANTONIO PÉREZ GOLLÁN

CALDAS, FRANCISCO JOSÉ DE (1768–

1816). Francisco José de Caldas (*b*. 4 October 1768; *d*. October 1816), astronomer, cartographer, mathematician, and engineer in New Granada's pro-Independence army. Born in Popayán, Caldas was urged by his family to practice law. Instead he became one of the most prominent creole scientists of the early 1800s, participating in the Royal Botanical Expedition of José Celestino Mutis (1805) and later becoming director of the Royal Astronomy Observatory of Bogotá. His journal, *El Semanario del Nuevo Reino de Granada,* was one of the first scientific periodicals to be published in Latin America. As professor of mathematics at the progressive Colegio del Rosario in Bogotá, Caldas encouraged the dissemination of modern science, including Newtonian experimental physics and Copernican cosmography.

Although he benefited from his contacts with the influential German investigator Alexander von Humboldt, Caldas called on American scientists to end their dependence on Europeans. He discovered independently that the temperature of boiling water was proportional to atmospheric pressure and devised a formula to measure altitude with a thermometer. He also studied the properties and value of cinchona (quinine) bark and of cochineal.

Caldas personified the late colonial Latin American striving for scientific, economic, and, eventually, political independence. After 1810, he served the independence cause as coeditor of the official *Diario Político* and as captain of the newly created Corps of Engineers. Captured by the Spanish royalists in 1816, he was executed as a rebel. His death, and that of other creole insurgent scientists, dealt a near fatal blow to the continuity of scientific inquiry from the colony to the republic.

See also **Science.**

BIBLIOGRAPHY

The *Obras completas* (Bogotá, 1966) includes a biographical note by Alfredo D. Bateman. See also Thomas Glick, "Science and Independence in Latin America (with Special Reference to New Granada)," in *Hispanic American Historical Review* 71, no. 2 (1991): 307–334.

John Wilton Appel, *Francisco José de Caldas: A Scientist at Work in New Granada* (1994).

Additional Bibliography

González Pérez, Marcos. *Francisco José de Caldas y la ilustración en la Nueva Granada.* Bogotá: Ediciones Tercer Mundo, 1984.

                                    IRIS H. W. ENGSTRAND
                                    LOUISA S. HOBERMAN

CALDERA RODRÍGUEZ, RAFAEL

(1916–). Rafael Caldera Rodríguez (*b*. 24 January 1916), president of Venezuela (1969–1974; reelected 5 December 1993). In 1936, Caldera helped found the National Student Union (Unión Nacional Estudiantil), an anti-Marxist Catholic student organization. He served as attorney general of the republic in 1946, and between 1959 and 1961 as president of the Chamber of Deputies. In 1946, he organized the Independent Political Electoral Organization Committee (Comité de Organización Política Electoral Independiente, COPEI), which became the Social Christian Party (Partido Social Cristiano, COPEI). Elected president in 1968 on a "democratic

CALDERÓN, SILA MARÍA

progressive" platform, Caldera formed a government that addressed popular issues such as distribution of wealth, housing, and education. He also established an accord with leftist guerrillas that ended a decade of internal warfare. His foreign policy broke with his predecessors' anticommunism, accepted international social justice, and reflected a growing anxiety over the expansion of Brazil's power. Caldera also negotiated an agreement with Guayana in which both nations agreed not to claim each other's territory for twelve years.

See also **Venezuela, Political Parties: Social Christian COPEI Party.**

BIBLIOGRAPHY

Rafael Caldera, *Ideario: La democracia cristiana en América Latina* (1970).

Daniel H. Levine, *Conflict and Political Change in Venezuela* (1973).

David J. Myers, *Democratic Campaigning in Venezuela: Caldera's Victory* (1973).

John D. Martz and David J. Myers, *Venezuela: The Democratic Experience* (1977).

Jesús Araújo, *Política y realidad* (1979).

Donald L. Herman, *Christian Democracy in Venezuela* (1980).

José Antonio Gil Yepes, *The Challenge of Venezuelan Democracy,* translated by Evelyn Harrison, Lolo Gil de Yanes, and Danielle Salti (1981).

Additional Bibliography

Cartay Ramírez, Gehard. *Caldera y Betancourt: Constructores de la democracia.* Caracas: Ediciones Centauro, 1987.

Méndez, Ana Irene. *Democracia y discurso político: Caldera, Pérez y Chávez.* Caracas: Monte Avila Editores Latinoamericana, 2004.

Perry, William, and Norman Bailey. *Venezuela 1994: Challenges for the Caldera Administration.* Washington DC: Center for Strategic and International Studies, 1994.

WINTHROP R. WRIGHT

CALDERÓN, SILA MARÍA (1942–). Serving one term as the seventh governor of the Commonwealth of Puerto Rico (2000–2004), Sila María Calderón became the first woman to occupy the highest elective office in the history of this Caribbean nation. She was born into an affluent family in the capital city of San Juan, where she lived until attending college in the United States. After earning her degree in government from Manhattanville College in New York (1964), she returned to Puerto Rico to lead a successful career in corporate business, completed a master's degree in public administration from the University of Puerto Rico (1972), and started working in public service. As a member of the pro-commonwealth Popular Democratic Party, Calderón landed her first government appointments in the first administration of Governor Rafael Hernández Colón (1972–1976). She began as executive assistant to the labor secretary, and later became the governor's special assistant for economic development. Upon his reelection in 1984, Colón assigned Calderón even greater responsibilities, making her the first woman ever to hold the position of secretary of state.

In the early 1990s Calderón participated in grass-roots community redevelopment projects in San Juan. This experience provided the blueprint for the Special Communities Program, the urban community revitalization initiative that she spearheaded as mayor of San Juan (1996–2000), and that as governor she transformed into a far-reaching plan to fight poverty and marginalization across the country. The program trained local leaders from impoverished urban and rural areas in community organizing methods. Communities themselves identified their most pressing needs (such as infrastructure, housing, health care, and job training) and together decided on a course of action. These locally generated initiatives were financed from a trust fund run by the Office of Special Communities. Calderón also played a decisive role as governor in securing the total withdrawal of the U.S. Navy from Vieques. For decades, the U.S. Navy had used this inhabited island off eastern Puerto Rico as a live-fire training facility. Governor Calderón's steadfast position on this issue earned her widespread admiration, both nationally and internationally. Calderón did not seek reelection in 2004 and has retired from electoral politics. In the early 2000s she continued to pursue her interests in public policy and social justice through philanthropy, creating an endowment fund to support faculty research and graduate student training in public administration at Rutgers University–Camden.

See also **Puerto Rico, Political Parties: Overview; Puerto Rico, Political Parties: Popular Democratic Party (PPD); Vieques Protests.**

BIBLIOGRAPHY

"A New Governor Ushers in a New Era in Puerto Rico." *New York Times*, January 6, 2001, p. A8.

Fernández, Ronald, Serafín Méndez Méndez, and Gail Cueto. *Puerto Rico Past and Present: An Encyclopedia.* Westport, CT: Greenwood Press, 1998.

LUIS A. GONZÁLEZ

CALDERÓN DE LA BARCA, FANNY

(1804–1882). Fanny Calderón de la Barca (*b.* 23 December 1804; *d.* 6 February 1882), writer and educator. Born Frances Inglis in Edinburgh she, with her family, immigrated to the United States in 1831, after her father's bankruptcy and death. Her mother established schools in Boston and then Staten Island, where in 1838 Frances married Spain's minister to the United States, Ángel Calderón de la Barca. From 1839 to 1842, as wife of Spain's first ambassador to Mexico, she wrote journals and letters from which she gathered the two-volume *Life in Mexico* (1843), a richly detailed portrait of postindependence society. Particularly noteworthy are her observations on politics and daily life in the national capital and surrounding central valley, and in the neighboring regions of Michoacán, Morelos, and Puebla. Upon her husband's death in 1861, she became governess and companion to the Spanish royal family. In 1876, she was accorded the title of *marquesa*.

BIBLIOGRAPHY

Charles Dumas, *L'Europe et les Européens au Mexique vers 1840: Selon l'oeuvre de Mme. Calderón de la Barca* (1962).

Howard T. Fisher and Marion Hall Fisher, *Life in Mexico: The Letters of Fanny Calderón de la Barca* (1966).

Guadalupe Appendini, *La vida en México en 1840* (1974).

STUART F. VOSS

CALDERÓN FOURNIER, RAFAEL ÁNGEL

(1949–). Rafael Ángel Calderón Fournier (*b.* 14 March 1949), president of Costa Rica (1990–1994) and founder of the Social Christian Party. Rafael Ángel Calderón Fournier has spent virtually his whole life involved in Costa Rican partisan politics. He served as a leading member of the national legislature while still a law student at the University of Costa Rica—he received his law degree in 1977—and he has been deeply involved in public life ever since.

He shared with his father, Rafael Ángel Calderón Guardia (1940–1944), the distinction of being the youngest president in Costa Rican history. They were both only forty years old when elected. (After that, thirty-nine-year-old José María Figueres Olsen was elected in 1994.) From birth, Calderón Fournier was destined to be in politics, his life intertwined with that of his famous father. He was born in Managua, Nicaragua, while his father was in exile after the defeat of the progovernment forces in the 1948 civil conflict and later was reunited with his exiled father in Mexico, where he spent much of his early youth. When the family returned to Costa Rica, his father's many followers passed their loyalty to his son and namesake.

Following a term in the national legislature (1974–1978), he led the Calderónists into the Unidad coalition that elected Rodrigo Carazo Odio president in 1978. He then served as foreign minister from 1978 to 1982 and as a member of the board of the social security system.

After running unsuccessful presidential campaigns in 1982 and 1986, Calderón Fournier was elected for a four-year term in 1990 on a platform that emphasized privatization of the economy while maintaining intact the extensive national social welfare program, much of which his father initiated during his presidency. After leaving office, Calderón Fournier faced serious legal problems. In 2004, the government convicted Calderón Fournier of corruption charges and placed him in jail and later under house arrest, while waiting for his trial.

See also **Calderón Guardia, Rafael Ángel; Carazo Odio, Rodrigo; Corruption.**

BIBLIOGRAPHY

Rodrigo Carazo Odio, *Acción para la historia* (1982), covers his administration's foreign policy initiatives while Calderón served as foreign minister; see also Marc Edelman and Joanne Kenen, *The Costa Rica Reader* (1989).

Additional Bibliography

Rovira Mas, Jorge, ed. *La democracia de Costa Rica ante el siglo XXI* San José: Editorial de la Universidad de Costa Rica, 2001.

JOHN PATRICK BELL

CALDERÓN GUARDIA, RAFAEL ÁNGEL

CALDERÓN GUARDIA, RAFAEL ÁNGEL (1900–1970). Rafael Ángel Calderón Guardia (*b.* 10 March 1900; *d.* 9 June 1970), president of Costa Rica (1940–1944). Calderón Guardia was born in San José, Costa Rica, to a bourgeois, Catholic family. After completing secondary school, he went to Belgium to pursue his medical career. He studied at the Catholic University of Lovain, where he was influenced by Christian-socialist ideas. He then went to the Free University of Brussels, from which he graduated as a surgeon in 1927. In Belgium he married Ivonne Clays before returning to Costa Rica. He later married Rosario Fournier, with whom he had three children, including Rafael Ángel Calderón Fournier (president of Costa Rica, 1990–1994). In Costa Rica he practiced medicine, dedicating himself to the poor, an experience that influenced his populist ideas.

Calderón Guardia began his political career in 1930, when he was elected councilman and president of the municipality of San José. In 1934 he was elected to Congress, and in 1936 he became third alternate (vice president) of the Republic. In 1938 he was reelected to Congress and was chosen as its president due to his gift as a political leader. In 1939 he was the presidential candidate of the National Republican Party, and with little opposition he was elected. Even though Calderón Guardia had the support of the oligarchy and the liberal politicians of the time, once in power, he decided to implement a series of social reforms. He recognized the urgency of making changes in society in order to attend to the needs of the working class and avoid serious future conflicts.

His vision and success were shaped by his Christian-socialist ideals, his medical profession, and the Costa Rican economic crisis brought on by World War II and a dependent economy. Domestically, a series of conditions made the country ripe for reformism. The Catholic Church, led by Monsignor Víctor Manuel Sanabria and following papal encyclicals, supported laws in favor of the working class. The Communist Party under Manuel Mora was advocating state intervention on behalf of the proletariat and the peasants. The union movement had been growing since the beginning of the twentieth century. And several new reformist and revolutionary political parties were demanding reforms in the country. These factors allowed the government of Calderón Guardia to create the University of Costa Rica in 1941, establish a social-security system in 1942, and institutionalize a labor code in 1943. The reforms were made possible by an alliance between the government, the Catholic Church, and the Communist Party. For these reasons, Calderón Guardia is remembered as a statesman, a willful leader, and a social reformer. However, he also displayed a lack of fiscal planning and a tendency toward political favoritism, and he failed to confront Costa Rica's economic problems.

After his term as president, Calderón Guardia continued to exercise a strong influence in the administration of Teodoro Picado (1944–1948). In 1948 he was again a presidential candidate but lost to the opposition, led by the journalist Otilio Ulate. Not accepting the defeat, Calderón Guardia demanded that Congress nullify the election, which it did. With a strong political opposition and an armed movement under the leadership of José Figueres, the country was thrown into civil war in April 1948. After the military triumph of Figueres, Calderón Guardia, Picado, and other leaders went to Nicaragua. Backed by Anastasio Somoza, Calderón Guardia invaded Costa Rica in 1948, but the mission failed. In 1955, again backed by Somoza, he undertook another invasion and failed. He lived in Mexico until 1958, when he returned to Costa Rica upon being elected to Congress. In 1962 he ran again for the presidency, but lost. From 1966 to 1970 he served as ambassador to Mexico, then returned to Costa Rica. He died in San José. In 1973 the Congress declared him a national hero in honor of his political legacy and work as a social reformer.

See also **Costa Rica.**

BIBLIOGRAPHY

Carlos Araya Pochet, *Historia de los partidos políticos: Liberación nacional* (1968).

Ralph Lee Woodward, Jr., *Central America: A Nation Divided,* 2d ed. (1985).

Additional Bibliography

Salazar Mora, Jorge Mario. *Calderón Guardia.* San José: Editorial Universidad Estatal a Distancia, 1980.

JORGE MARIO SALAZAR

CALEDONIA. Caledonia, a Scottish colony at Darién (in present-day Panama), 1698–1700. Also known as Fort Saint Andrew, New Edinburgh, and New Saint Andrew. Under the leadership of William Paterson and with backing from London merchants, the Company of Scotland Trading to Africa and the Indies was established in June 1695. In hopes of developing lucrative trade with the Spanish Indies as well as expanding agricultural and mining operations on the isthmus, this company planted a colony of settlers on the Caribbean coast near the Gulf of Darién in 1698. They named the colony Caledonia and established a town called New Edinburgh. Fort Saint Andrew (sometimes called New Saint Andrew) was built on a platform overlooking the site. This first attempt at colonization failed, however, in the face of short supplies and Spanish raiding. Leaving more than four hundred graves at Caledonia, Paterson and all but a dozen of the remaining colonists abandoned the site on 18 June 1699 and left for Scotland via Jamaica and New York. A few weeks later, a Spanish force under Juan Delgado arrived and destroyed the fort, burned New Edinburgh, and captured one of the survivors.

A second expedition reestablished the colony and fort in November 1699, but internal dissension, disease, Spanish threats, and the inability of the company to sustain its own support led to its final abandonment. Fort Saint Andrew surrendered to the Spanish on 30 March 1700 with the understanding that the settlement would be vacated within two weeks. More than a thousand Scots had died in the venture before the remainder left Caledonia on 12 April 1700.

This disaster contributed to ill feeling between England and Scotland as well as between Britain and Spain. A flurry of publications immediately following the disaster reflected the intensity of feeling and interest in the matter.

See also **Panama.**

BIBLIOGRAPHY

Among the contemporary publications, see especially *A full and exact collection of all the considerable addresses, memorials, petitions ... relating to the Company of Scotland Trading to Africa and the Indies....* (1700).

Walter Harris, *A Short Vindication of Phil. Scot's Defence of the Scots abdicating Darién* (1700).

[George Ridpath], *An Enquiry into the causes of the miscarriage of the Scots Colony at Darién* (1700).

[Robert Ferguson], *A just and modest vindication of the Scots design....* (1699). Several rather full treatments of the Darién colonization effort were published early in the twentieth century, notably J. S. Barbour, *A History of William Paterson and the Darién Company* (1907).

Frank Cundall, *The Darién Venture* (1926).

George P. Insh, *The Company of Scotland Trading to Africa and the Indies* (1932).

Francis Russell Hart, *The Disaster of Darién: The Story of the Scots Settlement and the Causes of Its Failure, 1699–1701* (1929), the latter containing a large documentary appendix. The most complete account is John Prebble, *The Darién Disaster: A Scots Colony in the New World* (1968).

Additional Bibliography

Gallup-Diaz, Ignacio. *The Door of the Seas and Key to the Universe: Indian Politics and Imperial Rivalry in the Darién, 1640–1750.* New York: Columbia University Press, 2004.

Watt, Douglas. *The Price of Scotland: Darien, Union and the Wealth of the Nations.* Edinburgh: Luath Press, 2006.

SUE DAWN MCGRADY

CALENDARS, PRE-COLUMBIAN. Mesoamerican civilizations developed a very intricate and detailed system to identify days and years. This region was home to diverse languages and ethnicities, including the Maya and the Aztec, yet the method for determining the days and years was similar among the heterogeneous communities. These calendars varied in appearance among the different groups in that their sizes, names, and glyphs, among other features, were often different. Despite these variations, the calendars share their origin in addition to many essential features.

Calendars were based on astronomical observations over time and correlated with religion. The first basic feature of the calendar is the sacred day count, totaling 260 days. This sacred calendar correlated with rituals of the gods and has many names among the civilizations, including *tonalpohualli* in Nahuatl and *tzol kin* in Yucatec. The days are counted by twenty and by thirteen concurrently. The separate counts are referred to as the *veintena* and the *trecena*, respectively. The 260-day cycle is used along with the year cycle of 365 days, which is also called the secular calendar. This was used to determine agricultural patterns and seasons. Here the year is divided into eighteen months comprising twenty days each with a final month of five fateful days. The names of the years come from a combination of the two cycles. These names were not repeated for a cycle of fifty-two years. Because of the long lapse between year names, many Mesoamerican cultures believed that historical events would reoccur every fifty-two years. This system, comprising combinations of days, months, and years, serves as the basis for Mesoamerican calendars. These calendars include those of the Maya, Aztec, Zapotec, Quiche, Tikal, Mixe, and Tilantongo among many others, the most prominent one being that of the Aztec.

The Sun Stone, a widely known artifact with some of the features of the Aztec calendar, was recovered in Mexico in 1790. Antonio de León y Gama was the first person to attempt to uncover the true meaning behind its glyphs after its discovery. Some of his research has been contested and expanded upon by later researchers such as Alexander von Humboldt and Ezequiel Ordóñez, yet many of his findings are still accepted in the early twenty-first century. While many people consider the Sun Stone to be the Aztec calendar, it is important to note that this monolith was actually a commemorative stone; it represents the days and the stages of the sun but it is not the calendar. The real Aztec calendar does follow the basic pattern set forth by that of the other Mesoamerican calendars. The Sun Stone represents the glyphs of the twenty days and the four previous ages, or suns, and the current age. The twenty days surround the glyphs that represent the ages in the center of the artifact. The days should be read counterclockwise beginning with Cipactli, the crocodile. The other nineteen days are represented by Ehécatl (wind), Calli (house), Cuetzpallin (lizard), Cóatl (serpent), Miquiztli (skull), Mázatl (deer), Tochtli (rabbit), Atl (water), Itzcuintli (dog), Ozomatli (monkey), Malinalli (herb), Ácatl (cane), Océlotl (jaguar), Cuauhtli (eagle), Cozcacuauhtli (vulture), Ollin (movement), Técpatl (knife), Quiahuitl (rain), and Xóchitl (flower). This stone measures 141.73

inches in diameter and its proper positioning is horizontal, not vertical, as previously believed.

See also **Astronomy; Aztec Calendar Stone.**

BIBLIOGRAPHY

Edmonson, Munro S. *The Book of the Year: Middle American Calendrical Systems.* Salt Lake City: University of Utah Press, 1988.

Malsmström, Vincent H. *Cycles of the Sun, Mysteries of the Moon: The Calendar in Mesoamerican Civilization.* Austin: University of Texas Press, 1997.

Matos, Eduardo, and Solís, Felipe. *The Aztec Calendar and Other Solar Monuments.* Córdoba: Conaculta-Instituto Nacional de Antropología e Historia, 2004.

AMANDA LAIS GRAY

CALFUCURÁ (1770–1873).

Calfucurá (*b.* late 1770s; *d.* 1873), Araucanian leader. Calfucurá headed the rise of an important intertribal confederation in the Argentinian pampas that flourished in the last half of the nineteenth century until subjugation by the Argentine army in the 1880s.

In 1835 a group of Araucanians (also called Mapuches) headed by Calfucurá moved east from Chilean homelands near Llaima, in the southern cordillera (in the region of the Imperial River and Cautín), to establish a permanent encampment near a large salt deposit called the Salinas Grandes. Following a struggle for power over control of the Salinas Grandes with the Voroganos—a loosely organized group of Pampas and Araucanian followers of Mariano Rondeau—Calfucurá emerged victorious, and Rondeau's followers joined Calfucurá's Araucanian settlement.

Calfucurá's leadership was derived primarily from personal charisma as well as from military knowledge and status within the Araucanian world. Under his leadership, this Araucanian confederation in the pampas expanded to enjoy relative prosperity and autonomy and to become a large, well-organized threat to Argentine lives and property. Between 1834 and 1856, Calfucurá negotiated temporary alliances between neighboring Pampas, Tehuelches, Ranqueles, and other Araucanian bands or tribes, and also entered into a structured alliance with the government of Juan Manuel de Rosas in exchange for annuity payments in goods. Because of their control of the salt mines in the Salinas Grandes, Calfucurá's people escaped dependency on the payments and thrived on intra-tribal trade in salt—necessary for making *charqui* (salted meat)—and livestock (mostly cattle and horses).

When the annuity program ended after the fall of Rosas in the 1850s, the Araucanian followers of Calfucurá responded with raids called *malones* (also called *malocas*). In the next two decades in a series of highly organized raids against creole ranching interests in the southern Argentina frontier, Calfucurá's Voroganos acquired hundreds of thousands of head of cattle and horses and hundreds of *cautivos* (captives) to tend to these herds. When Calfucurá died of natural causes in 1873, he left a confederation of Araucanians that included over 224 tribes. This confederation, under the leadership of Manuel Namuncurá, Calfucurá's son, continued to resist Argentine subjugation until 1879.

See also **Araucanians.**

BIBLIOGRAPHY

Estanislao S. Zeballos, *Callvucurá y la dinastía de los Piedra* (1961).

Judith Ewell and William Beezeley, eds. *The Human Tradition in Latin America: The Twentieth Century* (1989), pp. 175–187.

Additional Bibliography

Poggi, Rinaldo Alberto. "Releyendo cartas de Calfucurá." *Investigaciones y Ensayos* 47 (February 1997): 469–493.

                                    KRISTINE L. JONES

CALI. Cali, the third-largest city in Colombia, located at the southwestern end of the Cauca Valley. The city was founded in 1536 by Sebastián de Belalcázar, a lieutenant of Pizarro. Despite its early foundation, its landlocked position long retarded its economic growth.

During colonial times, Cali was the economic center of slave-owning haciendas that provided supplies for the mining areas of Popayán, Antioquia, and Chocó. In the nineteenth century, the breakdown of mining and the lack of an adequate outlet to the Pacific Ocean kept the area isolated from world markets. One of the main battlegrounds during the slave-owners' rebellion of 1851 and the religious civil war of 1876, Cali remained a small town of 11,000 people, bypassed by the dynamic effects of the tobacco boom and even, at first, by the coffee economy.

The Panama Canal, which opened in 1914, provided an important stimulus to both Cali and the Pacific port of Buenaventura from the 1920s to the 1960s, ultimately establishing Cali as the main commercial center of the Cauca Valley. The importance of this outlet, as compared to the outlet of the Magdalena Valley, was greatly increased not only by the opening of the canal but also by the completion of the railroad (begun in 1878) connecting Cali with Buenaventura. In 1912 Cali had a population of 27,000; by 1918 it had grown to 45,000. By 2004 the city's population reached 2,369,696.

The transformation of the old haciendas into large-scale agribusinesses provided another stimulus to growth in the 1940s and 1950s. The influx of foreign capital into the manufacturing and the intermediate goods sectors made Cali one of the important industrial centers of the country. Industrialization in the region made Cali one of the fastest-growing urban centers in a very short time. Indeed, these economic prospects attracted rural-urban migrants. Rural violence and subsequent intensification of armed conflict also spurred significant migration and displacement to Cali.

Industry did not continue to expand after the 1960s, however. Whatever economic expansion there was came from commerce (including textiles, construction materials, tobacco products, and clothing) and public investment. By the 1990s, moreover, the city showed a prosperity that seemed to come from dubious sources, such as narcotics and related illicit ventures. Indeed, Cali was the base for one of two rival national groups involved in the cocaine and heroine trade. In the second half of the 1990s and first years of the twenty-first century, Colombia, including Cali, experienced a severe economic recession. Although difficult to prove, the jailing in 1995 of Cali's drug cartel leaders was a factor in the city's recession.

See also **Belalcázar, Sebastián de; Drugs and Drug Trade; Panama Canal; Slave Trade.**

BIBLIOGRAPHY

Arboleda, Gustavo. *Historia de Cali: Desde los orígenes de la ciudad hasta la expiración del período colonial,* 3 vols. (1956).

Barbary, Olivier, and Fernando Urrea Giraldo, eds. *Gente negra en Colombia: Dinámicas sociopolíticas en Cali y el Pacífico*. Cali, Colombia: Centro de Investigaciones y Documentación Socioeconómicas, Facultad de Ciencias Sociales y Económicas de la Universidad del Valle; Paris: Institut de recherche pour le développement; Colombia: COLCIENCIAS, 2004.

Colmenares, Germán. *Cali: Terratenientes, mineros, y comerciantes. Vol. I, Sociedad y economía en el Valle del Cauca* (1983).

Cuevas Arenas, Héctor Manuel. *La república de indios. Un acercamiento a las encomiendas, mitas, pueblos de indios y relaciones interestamentales en Cali, siglo XVII*. Cali, Colombia: Archivo Histórico de Cali, 2005.

Dávila, Julio D. *Urban Poverty Reduction Experiences in Cali, Columbia: Lessons from the Work of Local Nonprofit Organisations*. London: IIED, 2002.

Diego Romero, Mario. *Poblamiento y sociedad en el Pacífico colombiano, siglos XVI al XVIII*. Cali, Colombia: Universidad del Valle, Editorial Facultad de Humanidades, 1995.

Escorcia, José. *Desarrollo político, social y económico, 1800–1854. Vol. III, Sociedad y economía en el Valle del Cauca* (1983).

Luz Roldán, Clara. *Hacia la construcción de un modelo para el tratamiento integral e integrador del desplazamiento forzoso en Cali y el suroccidente colombiano*. San José, Costa Rica: Fundación Arias para la Paz y el Progreso Humano, 2000.

Ocampo, José Antonio. "El desarrollo económico de Cali en el Siglo XX," in *Santiago de Cali, 45 años de historia* (1981), pp. 127–148.

Ordóñez Burbano, Luis Aurelio. *Industrias y empresarios pioneros, Cali 1910–1945*. Cali, Colombia: Editorial Facultad de Humanidades, 1995.

Ulloa, Alejandro. *Globalización, ciudad y representaciones sociales: El caso de Cali*. Medellín, Colombia: Editorial Universidad Pontificia Bolivariana, 2000.

Vanegas Muñoz, Gildardo. *Cali tras el rostro oculto de las violencias: Estudios etnográficos sobre la cotidianidad, los conflictos y las violencias en las barriadas populares*. Cali, Colombia: Instituto CISALVA, Universidad del Valle, 1998.

Waxer, Lise A. *The City of Musical Memory: Salsa, Record Grooves, and Popular Culture in Cali, Colombia*. Middletown, CT: Wesleyan University Press, 2002.

JOSÉ ESCORCIA

CALIFORNIA. During the eighteenth century, California consisted of two mission frontiers— Baja California, developed after 1697 by the Jesuits, and Alta California, controlled by the Franciscans from 1769. Until 1804, both areas were included in the same administrative jurisdiction.

With the exception of a small region in the southern part of the peninsula where small-scale commercial farming and marginal silver mining developed after 1750, Baja California held little attraction for colonists. On this frontier the Jesuits did not establish the first missions until after 1697 and without government financial support. Between 1697 and 1840 twenty-seven missions were established, by the Jesuits (1697–1768), the Franciscans (1769–1773), and the Dominicans (1774–1840). The Indians who were resettled in the mission communities experienced high rates of mortality from disease and other factors and declined in total numbers from an estimated 50,000–60,000 in the 1690s to a mere 2,000 by the mid-1840s. Following the secularization of the missions in the 1830s, Baja California remained an isolated territory until a French mining company began to exploit its copper deposits in the 1870s.

In response to reports of Russian activities in Alaska and Captain James Cook's exploration of the Pacific islands, the Spanish began their occupation of Alta California, the modern state of California, in 1769 under the direction of Visitor-General José de Gálvez. The Spanish government encountered such considerable difficulty in populating the region with settlers that Alta California remained a mission frontier until the early years of the nineteenth century. Between 1769 and 1823 the Franciscans established twenty-one missions in the region, and the viceregal government founded four presidios (military garrisons) and three pueblos (civilian communities). The death rates among the Indians gathered into the missions were high, but until the 1820s the Franciscans, backed by the military, were able to resettle thousands of Indians in the missions. Between 1769 and 1832 the Franciscans baptized nearly 88,000 Indians in the missions, but during those years almost 64,000 of them died.

After about 1800 a vibrant but illegal trade in hides and tallow developed. Foreign merchants bartered manufactured goods for cattle hides and tallow from mission herds in a trade legalized by the newly independent Mexican government in 1823. The outbreak of the war for independence in central Mexico in 1810 placed increased pressure on the Franciscans to produce surplus goods to supply military garrisons cut off from their traditional sources of supplies there and intensified illegal trade with foreign merchants. Growing production levels in turn forced the Franciscans to recruit additional workers to replace the Indian converts, who died at alarming rates in the missions.

In 1833 a short-lived liberal congress in Mexico legislated the secularization of the Alta California missions. Theoretically, the missions were to be converted to formal autonomous Indian pueblos, with their land, livestock, and other communal goods distributed among the Indians. However, local politicians were able to establish de facto independence from Mexico City and to administer the secularized missions for their own benefit. Under the colonization laws passed by the Mexican government in the 1820s, different governors of California made more than 800 grants of large tracts of land in the province to prominent politicians and settlers. The recipients of such grants stocked their ranches with livestock from the mission herds and increased their exports of hides and tallow.

In the 1830s and 1840s a growing number of Anglo-Americans and Europeans settled in Alta California. A small minority married into local families and became Mexican citizens, but the majority remained hostile to Mexicans and the Mexican government. In 1846 in Sonoma they declared an independent California republic. Within a month of this so-called Bear Flag Revolt, U.S. forces began the conquest of the province. (As early as the 1820s, the U.S. government had tried to buy California from Mexico.) U.S. forces also occupied Baja California in 1846 and 1847, but they returned the province to Mexico under the terms of the 2 February 1848 Treaty of Guadalupe Hidalgo. It is the northernmost state of Mexico and became an official state therein in 1953. Due to its proximity to the U.S. border, there are large immigrant populations from both the United States and Central America. The majority of the population is mestizo (a mix of Amerindian and European heritages).

See also **Copper Industry; Missions: Spanish America; Slavery: Indian Slavery and Forced Labor.**

BIBLIOGRAPHY

Altamirano, Graziella, et al. *Vida social y cotidiana en la historia regional de México.* San Juan Mixoac, Mexico: Instituto Mora, 2001.

Amao, Jorge Luis. *Mineros, misioneros y rancheros de la antigua California.* México, D. F.: Plaza y Valdés, 1997.

Cook, Sherburne F. *The Conflict between the California Indians and White Civilization.* Berkeley: University of California Press, 1976.

Engelhardt, Zephyrin, O.F.M. *Missions and Missionaries of California,* 4 vols. San Francisco: J. H. Barry, 1929–1930.

González Montes, Soledad. *Mujeres, migración y maquila en la frontera norte.* México, D.F.: Colegio de México, Programa Interdisciplinario de Estudios de la Mujer, 1995.

Jackson, Robert H. "Demographic Change in Northwestern New Spain." *The Americas* 41, 4 (April 1985): 462–479.

Jackson, Robert H. "Population and the Economic Dimension of Colonization of Alta California: A Study of Four Mission Communities." *Journal of the Southwest* 33, no. 3 (1991): 387–439.

Meigs, Peveril. *The Dominican Mission Frontier of Lower California.* Berkeley: University of California Press, 1935.

Truett, Samuel, and Elliott Young. *Continental Crossroads: Remapping U.S.-Mexico Borderlands History.* Durham, NC: Duke University Press, 2004.

Weber, David J. *The Mexican Frontier 1821–1846: The American Southwest under Mexico.* Albuquerque: University of New Mexico Press, 1982.

ROBERT H. JACKSON

CALIFORNIOS.

Californios, technically, the Spanish-speaking residents of Alta California during the Spanish and Mexican era (1769–1848). More commonly the term referred to the property-holding elite, the 500 families who were given land grants during this period, including the most politically prominent families: the Bandinis, Carrillos, Picos, de la Guerras, Vallejos, Coronels, Castros, Alvarados, and others. Together they enjoyed economic and political dominance during the Mexican era (1821–1848). Among their numbers were a few Americans who had married into Californio families, such as Abel Stearns and John Warner.

Prominent Californios served as members of the State Constitutional Convention that met at Monterey in 1849. Others served as officials of town and county governments during the first few decades after the American takeover. After 1848, however, the economic and political fortunes of the Californios generally declined because of the immigration of more than 100,000 people to California during the gold rush. The newcomers' demand for land prompted squatter violence and the passage of several discriminatory laws that led to the loss of Californios' land. The Land Act, passed by Congress in 1851, established a lengthy process, lasting an average of twenty years, of legitimizing Californio land claims, leading to increased squatterism and speculation. In order to pay new, higher land taxes (Americans based land value on future productivity rather than actual usage) and lawyers' fees, the Californios mortgaged their grants; many ultimately lost them to banks, lawyers, and moneylenders. Some of the sons of the Californios became bandits, such as Nicolás Sepúl-veda, Chico Lugo, Pedro Vallejo, and Ramón Ama-dor; others continued to be active in politics; and many Californio families intermarried with Anglo immigrants.

See also **California.**

BIBLIOGRAPHY

Leonard Pitt, *The Decline of the Californios: A Social History of the Spanish-Speaking Californians, 1846–1890* (1966).

Richard Griswold Del Castillo, *The Los Angeles Barrio, 1850–1890: A Social History* (1979).

Douglas Monroy, *Thrown Among Strangers: The Making of Mexican Culture in Frontier California* (1990).

Additional Bibliography

Río, Ignacio del. *Crónicas jesuíticas de la antigua California.* México: Universidad Nacional Autónoma de México, Coordinación de Humanidades, Programa Editorial, 2000.

RICHARD GRISWOLD DEL CASTILLO

CALIMA. Calima, archaeological region located in the western highlands and the middle Cauca Valley, Colombia. Human occupation dates from the eighth millennium BCE to the sixteenth century. The first inhabitants were hunters and gatherers who made use of the abundant plants available in the region. Evidence of this early occupation has been found at several open sites, notably El Pital. Dates for these locations range from about 7500 to 2200 BCE. Pollen diagrams suggest maize was present in the region about 5000 to 3000 BCE, but it is not

clear yet if it played an important role in the economy of these early settlers.

Later periods include Ilama (*ca.* 1000 to 0 BCE), Yotoco (0 to 1200 CE) and Sonso (1200 to 1600 CE). The Ilama period marks the introduction of pottery richly decorated with incisions. There is evidence that Ilama people cultivated maize and developed metallurgy. Burials suggest there were some differences between the elite and the commoner in terms of access to exotic goods. Elite items generally copied designs from afar; gold objects sometimes imitated statuary from the Upper Magdalena region to the west.

Pottery was painted during the Yotoco period. Agriculture consisting of beans, maize, and gourds is associated with this development stage, as is the elaboration of some impressive large adornments of gold. Agricultural intensification is suggested by evidence of ridges and drainage systems in the valleys associated with the Yotoco period. Some Yotoco burials were extremely lavish, with gold objects and adornments elaborated in exotic raw materials such as seashells. Other burials, in contrast, contained only pottery vessels. This evidence suggests some degree of social inequality. Also, as Yotoco sites are more abundant than Ilama sites, it has been suggested that the Yotoco population was larger.

The Sonso period is described as one of dramatic change in social organization in the Calima region. Pottery was more simple, lacking the well-crafted designs of the Yotoco ceramics. Gold objects were not as impressive as those of the Yotoco period, generally consisting of small earrings. Agricultural practices also changed. Instead of in the valleys, the Sonso people cultivated on the slopes of the mountains.

Sonso is frequently described as a period of decadence. Nonetheless, evidence of social complexity continues to be found from this period, and some burials evidence an impressive number of pots. Also, the large number of Sonso sites reported suggests continuation of population growth. At the time of the Spanish Conquest, the native populations in the area were dominated by European colonizers and few traces of the pre-Columbian inheritance remained in the region.

See also **Archaeology.**

BIBLIOGRAPHY

The basic source for archaeological studies in the Calima region is *Pro Calima* (1980–1988), published in English in Basel, Switzerland. See also Leonor Herrera, Marianne Cardale, and Warwick Bray, "El Hombre y su medio ambiente en Calima," in *Revista Colombiana de Antropología* (1983), and "Costa del Pacífico y vertiente oeste de la Cordillera Occidental," in *Colombia Prehispánica-Regiones Arqueológicas* (1989). For a general discussion on social complexity in the area, see Carl Henrik Langebaek, "Estilos y culturas en Colombia prehispánica," in *Gran Enciclopedia de Colombia* (1991). A recent overview of Colombian archaeology is Carl Henrik Langebaek, *Noticias de Caciques muy Mayores: Orígen y desarrollo de sociedades complejas en el nororiente de Colombia y norte de Venezuela* (1992).

Additional Bibliography

Cardale de Schrimpff, Marianne, ed. *Calima and Malagana: Art and Archaeology in Southwestern Colombia.* Bogotá: Pro Calima Foundation, 2005.

Labbé, Armand J., and Warwick Bray. *Shamans, Gods, and Mythic Beasts: Colombian Gold and Ceramics in Antiquity.* New York: American Federation of Arts; Seattle: University of Washington Press, 1998.

Langebaek, Carl Henrik, and Alejandro Dever. *Arqueología en el Bajo Magdalena: Un estudio de los primeros agricultores del Caribe colombiano.* Bogotá: Departamento de Antropología, Universidad de los Andes, 2000.

Rodríguez, Carlos Armando. *El Valle del Cauca prehispánico: Procesos socioculturales antiguos en las regiones geohistóricas del Alto y Medio Cauca y la Costa Pacífica colombo-ecuatoriana.* Santiago de Cali: Universidad del Valle, Departamento de Historia, Facultad de Humanidades; Washington, DC: Fundación Taraxacum, 2002.

Rodríguez Cuenca, José Vicente, Sonia Blanco, and Alexander Clavijo. *Pueblos, rituales y condiciones de vida prehispánicas en el Valle del Cauca.* Bogotá, D.C.: Universidad Nacional de Colombia, 2005.

CARL HENRIK LANGEBAEK R.

CALLADO, ANTÔNIO (1917–1997).

Antônio Callado (*b.* 26 January 1917; *d.* 28 January 1997), Brazilian journalist, playwright, and novelist. Born in Niterói, Rio de Janeiro, Callado worked in London for the BBC from 1941 to 1947. Callado began writing fiction in the 1950s, primarily focusing on theater. His best-known play is *Pedro Mico*, which was later made into a film directed by Paulo Francis. However, he is best known for his novels that deal with religious and political themes. Perhaps his most famous work, *Quarup* (1967) describes the transformation of a missionary priest into a revolutionary who discovers his own sexuality in the process. This work also reflects Callado's own political activism and his opposition to the military regime, for which he was jailed twice. *Bar Don Juan* (1971) relates the points of view of six would-be revolutionaries who conspire to overthrow the military government. Callado has received literary prizes that include the Golfinho de Ouro, the Prêmio Brasília, and the Goethe Prize for fiction for *Sempreviva* (1981). He has also written nonfiction.

See also **Literature: Brazil.**

BIBLIOGRAPHY

Wilson Martins, "Le Roman politique d'Antônio Callado," in *Europe: Revue littéraire mensuelle* no. 640–641 (1982): 43–47.

Malcolm Silverman, "A ficção em prosa de Antônio Callado," in *Moderna ficção brasileira*, 2d ed. (1982), pp. 19–33.

Cristina Ferreira Pinto, *A viagem do herói no romance de Antônio Callado* (1985).

Naomi Hoki Moniz, "Antônio Callado," in *Dictionary of Brazilian Literature*, edited by Irwin Stern (1988), pp. 69–71.

Additional Bibliography

Ferreira-Pinto, Cristina. "Antonio Callado: A Identidade Latino-Americana da Nação Brasileira." *La Chispa* (1997): 135-143.

Leite, Ligia Chiappini Moraes. *Quando a patria viaja: Uma leitura dos romances de Antonio Callado.* La Habana: Casa de las Américas, 1983.

GARY M. VESSELS

CALLADO JUNIOR, JOAQUIM ANTÔNIO DA SILVA (1848–1880).

Joaquim Antônio da Silva Callado Junior (*b.* 11 July 1848; *d.* 20 March 1880), Brazilian flute virtuoso, teacher, prolific composer of popular instrumental dance pieces, and key figure in the history of Brazilian music. Son of a bandmaster in Rio de Janeiro, Callado received an appointment to teach flute at the Imperial Conservatory of Music in 1870, during which time he organized a popular musical ensemble called "Choro carioca." The first of many Choro ensembles in Rio, the traditional group included a solo flute or other woodwind instrument, with various guitar-type and occasional percussion instruments. Repertoire consisted of polkas, quadrilles, schottisches, waltzes, *lundus* (Afro-Brazilian dance), and polka-*lundus*. With the addition of a singer, the performance was called a *seresta*. Callado became famous as the composer of *Querida por todos,* a polka dedicated to a well-known woman composer, Chiquinha Gonzaga.

One of Callado's principal contributions was to establish the *choro* as a form of popular music and to develop an individualized style of popular composition that served as a model for later composers. The *choro* became the favored form of Heitor Villa-lobos to express musical elements that were distinctively Brazilian.

See also **Music: Popular Music and Dance.**

BIBLIOGRAPHY

Gérard Béhague, *Music in Latin America* (1979).

David P. Appleby, *The Music of Brazil* (1983).

Additional Bibliography

Diniz, André. *Joaquim Callado: O pai dos chorões*. Rio de Janeiro: Ourocard, 1970.

Livingston-Isenhour, Tamara Elena, and Thomas George Caracas Garcia. *Choro: A Social History of a Brazilian Popular Music*. Bloomington: Indiana University Press, 2005.

Siqueira, Baptista. *Três Vultos Históricos da Música Brasileira*. Rio de Janeiro, 1970.

DAVID P. APPLEBY

CALLAMPAS. Callampas (literally, mushrooms), a Chilean expression used to describe the shantytowns that have developed in urban centers. The dwellers in these centers often illegally occupy marginal land on which they erect homes consisting of wood and discarded materials. Without running water, gas, or power, unless they illegally tap into an electrical grid, these homes provide housing for those seeking work in the city. They became known as *callampas* because they appear so quickly and spread so rapidly. During the Allende years (1970–1973), *callampas* were often organized politically by members of the Movement of the Revolutionary Left (MIR), who converted them into centers of support for the Unidad Popular government. Through organization, residents of *callampas* in this era sometimes won legal status for the land they inhabited and thus city services such as potable water, paved roads,

and recreational spaces. In the early twenty-first century these long-standing and officially recognized *callampas* are considered permanent residential areas and are somewhat less marginal.

See also **Chile, Political Parties: Movement of the Revolutionary Left; Favela.**

BIBLIOGRAPHY

Arriagada, Alejandro González. *Surviving in the City: The Urban Poor of Santiago de Chile, 1930–1970*. Uppsala, Sweden: Upsaliensis Academiae, 2000.

Caviedes, César L. *The Politics of Chile: A Sociogeographical Assessment* (1979).

Garcés, Mario. *Tomando su sitio: El movimiento de pobladores de Santiago, 1957–1970*. Santiago: LOM, 2002.

Gómez Leyton, Juan Carlos. *Las poblaciones callampas: Una expresión de la lucha social de los pobres, Santiago, 1930–1960*. Santiago: FLACSO, 1994.

MacEoin, Gary. *No Peaceful Way: Chile's Struggle for Dignity* (1974).

Schneider, Cathy Lisa. *Shantytown Protest in Pinochet's Chile*. Philadelphia, PA: Temple University Press, 1995.

WILLIAM F. SATER

CALLAO. Callao, city of Peru (2006 population 839,271) and the port for the capital city of Lima, located about 10 miles from the heart of Lima. Although Callao was separated from the capital throughout most of its history, today the two cities merge into one megalopolis. But Callao has retained its uniqueness, and *chalacos,* as its citizens call themselves, still like to distinguish themselves from the residents of Lima.

Callao was founded in 1537 and served as a small way station along the Rímac River and a port of entry for Lima, which was founded by Francisco Pizarro in 1535. Its harbor, protected by San Lorenzo Island, is one of the best along Peru's generally open desert coastline, and by the end of the colonial period Callao had taken on a naval and commercial importance of its own.

It has witnessed many earthquakes, coups, and sieges, beginning as long ago as 1624, when Dutch raiders bombarded the port. A terrifying earthquake and tidal wave destroyed the entire city in 1746. The fortress of Real Felipe, which emerged in the rebuilt city of the late eighteenth century, played an important role in the independence of Peru, its control often being key to the control of the capital.

On 2 May 1866 Callao withstood a bombardment by a Spanish fleet bent on reducing the port to ashes, and that day is remembered as one of the grandest in the history of Peruvian arms. The action also persuaded the Spanish to give up their amorphous pretensions to reestablish their empire in that part of the world.

Facing the sea, Callao played an important role in the commercial history of Peru. In the nineteenth century a series of export-based booms focused attention on the port. Guano exports triggered the first modernization of the country from the 1840s through the 1870s, and Callao prospered from the hundreds of ships employed in that trade that visited annually to refit and revictual after loading guano at the Chincha Islands south of Callao. Later in the century the railroad boom in Peru spurred further economic growth of the city, and when the great copper and silver mines of the interior were once again tapped by modern technology and foreign capital in the early twentieth century, much of the prosperity flowed through Callao.

Callao emerged in the twentieth century as an industrial leader and the first fishing port of Peru. From cement factories to beer breweries, Callao grew as industry located there to take advantage of its proximity to the sea and to the capital. And when Peru became the world's leading fish-exporting nation in the 1950s, based on the rich catches in the waters of the Humboldt Current, Callao was the leading seaport for this booming industry, servicing the fleets and building the boats and ships in its shipyards.

Streetcars, modern sanitation, and constantly improving port facilities kept Callao as the nation's major port. When Lima relocated its principal airport to Callao with the opening of the modern Jorge Chávez International Airport in 1962, Callao also became the principal port of entry for air travelers to Peru.

See also Humboldt Current.

BIBLIOGRAPHY

Jorge Basadre's *Historia de la república del Perú* 7th ed. 11 vols. (1983) contains numerous references to the history of Callao.

Additional Bibliography

Catalán, Alfonso Cerda. *La Guerra entre España y las repúblicas del Pacífico, 1864-1866: El bombardeo de Valparaíso y el combate naval del Callao*. Providencia: Editorial Puerto de Palos, 2000.

Quiroz, Francisco. *Descripciones del Callao: Textos, planos grabados y fotografías (siglos XVI al XIX)* Callao: Centro de Investigaciones Históricas del Callao: Instituto Nacional de Cultura, 1990.

LAWRENCE A. CLAYTON

CALLEJA DEL REY, FÉLIX MARÍA, CONDE DE CALDERÓN (1757–1828).

Félix María, Conde de Calderón Calleja del Rey (b. 1757; d. 24 July 1828), commander of royalist forces in the War of Mexican Independence and viceroy of New Spain (1813–1816). Born in Medina del Campo, Castilla la Vieja, Spain, Calleja entered the infantry regiment of Savoy as a cadet in 1772. He saw wartime service in the abortive 1775 expedition to Algiers, served aboard the floating artillery platforms during the 1782 siege of Gibraltar, and was present at the siege of Menorca. Promoted to the rank of captain in 1789, Calleja accompanied his patron, Viceroy Conde de Revillagigedo, to Mexico. From 1790 to 1797 he held important commissions to inspect frontier districts, to raise militia units, and to conduct detailed geographical and resource studies. After promotion to colonel in 1798, he took command of the Tenth Militia Brigade, based at San Luis Potosí, in 1799. Calleja further strengthened his position in the Mexican north through marriage in 1807 to María Francisca de la Gándara, daughter of a wealthy landowner. He was promoted to brigadier in 1810 and to field marshal in 1811.

Although surprised by the Hidalgo revolt of September 1810, Calleja acted quickly to mobilize the militia brigade at San Luis Potosí, which formed the core of the effective royalist Army of the Center, and successfully dispersed the rebels at Aculco (7 November 1810), Guanajuato (25 November 1810), and Puente de Calderón (17 January 1811). In 1812, following the defeat of Hidalgo, Calleja led his army out of the Bajío provinces to raze the insurgent town of Zitácuaro and south to Cuautla, where his army besieged the defensive positions of José María Morelos. Both sides suffered terrible hardships during the seventy-two-day siege, and starvation forced the insurgents to flee Cuautla.

Calleja introduced a controversial counterinsurgency system designed to mobilize the urban and rural populations and to free army units to chase major insurgent forces. On 4 March 1813, he was named viceroy of New Spain. By 1815 his forces had eliminated Morelos and fragmented if not defeated the insurgency. By the time he transferred command to Viceroy Juan Ruíz De Apodaca on 19 September 1816, Calleja had come to believe his own propaganda that the royalists had won the war.

Calleja returned to Madrid, where he received the title of Conde de Calderón. In 1819, King Ferdinand VII named him captain-general of Andalusia, governor of Cádiz, and general in chief of the Spanish army that was being assembled to reconquer the Americas. In the military campaign of 1820 and the restoration of the constitution, Calleja was arrested and experienced political difficulties that continued until the return of absolutism in 1823. In 1825, he went to Valencia, where he remained until his death.

See also **Mexico, Wars and Revolutions: War of Independance.**

BIBLIOGRAPHY

Material on Calleja's campaigns during the War of Mexican Independence can be found in Lucas Alamán, *Historia de México desde los primeros movimientos que prepararon su independencia en el año de 1808 hasta la época presente*, 5 vols. (1849–1852; repr. 1942); Wilbert H. Timmons, *Morelos: Priest Soldier Statesman of Mexico* (1963); Hugh M. Hamill, *The Hidalgo Revolt: Prelude to Mexican Independence* (1966); Christon I. Archer, "La Causa Buena: The Counterinsurgency Army of New Spain and the Ten Years' War," in Jaime E. Rodríguez O., ed., *The Independence of Mexico and the Creation of the New Nation* (1989); Brian R. Hamnett, *Roots of Insurgency: Mexican Regions, 1750–1824* (1986). For biographical data, see José De Jesús Núñez y Domínguez, *La virreina mexicana: Doña María Francisca de la Gándara de Calleja* (1950); and Christon I. Archer, *The Army in Bourbon Mexico, 1760–1810* (1977).

Additional Bibliography

Orozco Linares, Fernando. *Fechas Históricas de México*. México City: Panorama Editorial, 1988.

CHRISTON I. ARCHER

CALLEJAS ROMERO, RAFAEL LEONARDO

(1943–). Rafael Leonardo Callejas Romero (*b.* 14 November 1943), president of Honduras (1990–1994) who promoted economic development along neoliberal lines. The son of a landowning family, Callejas earned B.S. (1965) and M.S. (1966) degrees in agricultural economics at Mississippi State University. Beginning in 1967 he was an economic planner in the Honduran government and a board member of several Honduran public and private corporations.

Callejas was an unsuccessful National Party presidential candidate in 1981 and 1985 before winning in 1989 as head of the MONARCA (Rafael Callejas National Renovation Movement) faction of the National Party. He favored development under U.S. president Ronald Reagan's Caribbean Basin Initiative and enjoyed strong U.S. support in his campaign. His popularity with conservative leaders in the industrial nations helped him gain favorable international financial agreements that contributed to economic gains early in his administration as he devalued the currency, privatized government enterprises, and pursued other structural adjustments favored by the U.S. Agency for International Development (AID). By 1993, however, Honduras was in serious financial difficulty and suffered severe shortages of foodstuffs, problems that contributed to a Liberal victory in the November 1993 presidential election. Although Callejas was the third elected civilian president to rule Honduras in succession since 1980, the armed forces, which remained autonomous under Callejas, continued to be a strong force in Honduran politics.

See also **Honduras, National Party (PNH).**

BIBLIOGRAPHY

For a more detailed biographical sketch of Callejas, see the entry by Ralph Lee Woodward, Jr., in the *Encyclopedia of World Biography*, vol. 18, edited by David Eggenberger (1994). For a detailed overview of recent Honduran political history, see Alison Acker, *Honduras: The Making of a Banana Republic* (1988); James Dunkerley, *Power in the Isthmus, a Political History of Modern Central America* (1988); and Tom Barry and Kent Norsworthy, *Honduras: A Country Guide* (1990). More detail on Callejas's presidential administration may be found in Howard H. Lenter, *State Formation in Central*

America: The Struggle for Autonomy, Development, and Democracy (1993).

Additional Bibliography

Flores Valeriano, Enrique. *Moralización de la administración pública*. Tegucigalpa: Editorial Guaymuras, 1995.

RALPH LEE WOODWARD JR.

CALLEJÓN DE HUAYLAS.

Callejón de Huaylas, a well-watered, mostly temperate, and healthy valley between the Cordillera Blanca and the Cordillera Negra in the Department of Ancash, Peru. The Callejón de Huaylas has attracted attention several times during its history. In the 1540s it was the site of an uprising by Alonso de Cabrera against Diego de Almagro and his son after Francisco Pizarro's murder. Toward the end of the sixteenth century, the Spanish discovered silver at Cerro Colqueporco (Quechua for "well of silver"). The ore proved low yielding and the site never prospered. Both the liberators José San Martín and Simón Bolívar used the valley as a base during the Wars of Independence because of its strategic value and its easy communications with the coast on the west, Trujillo on the north, and Huanuco to the southeast. In 1885, the valley was the staging ground for a serious uprising, led by Pedro Pablo Atusparia, against the abuses of peasant authorities, increased taxes, and the growing use of forced labor. The valley was and still is famous for its fertile soil and agricultural abundance.

In 1970 a strong earthquake known as the Callejón de Huaylas shook the Santa Valley. More than 50,000 people died, and 186,000 houses were damaged. Yungay was the city most damaged; it practically disappeared.

In July 1975 the Parque Nacional Huascarán, which is located in the Callejón de Huaylas, was designated a World Biosphere Reserve by UNESCO. It had been created to protect and preserve the Cordillera Blanca's flora, fauna, archaeological sites, and scenic beauty.

See also **Bolívar, Simón; Earthquakes.**

BIBLIOGRAPHY

Bode, Barbara. *No Bells to Toll: Destruction and Creation in the Andes*. New York: Scribner, 1989.

Díaz Bustos, Felipe. *Callejón de Huaylas y Cordillera Blanca*. Lima: Información Turística Kuntur, 1989.

Stein, William W. *El levantamiento de Atusparia* (1988).

Ugarte, Ruben Vargas. *Historia general del Perú*, 10 vols. (1971).

Varón Gabai, Rafael. "Estrategias políticas y relaciones conyugales: El comportamiento de incas y españoles en Huaylas en la primera mitad del siglo XVI." *Bulletin de l'IFEA* 22, no. 3 (1993): 721–737.

Werlich, David P. *Peru: A Short History* (1978).

SUSAN E. RAMÍREZ

CALLES, PLUTARCO ELÍAS (1877–1945).

Plutarco Elías Calles (*b.* 25 September 1877; *d.* 19 October 1945), president of Mexico (1924–1928). The poor relation of a notable family in the northwestern state of Sonora, Calles was an aspiring young professional and entrepreneur who had met with only limited success before the Mexican Revolution. Initially on the periphery of Francisco Madero's movement against the Porfirio Díaz regime, from a minor appointment in the new state government he rose steadily in the ranks of what became the constitutionalist army, becoming Alvaro Obregón's principal political associate. As president, and then as *jefe máximo* (supreme chief) in the wake of the assassination of president-elect Obregón (1928), Calles dominated the national government for more than a decade and initiated the institutionalization of the Revolution.

Until the Revolution, Calles's life had been punctuated with misfortune and disappointments. He was the illegitimate son of Plutarco Elías, scion of one of the most prominent families in northeast Sonora in the nineteenth century. Following the death of his mother when he was four, he was raised by his stepfather, Juan B. Calles, who owned a small cantina in Hermosillo (and from whom he took his second family name). After being educated in Hermosillo, Calles became a schoolteacher. The death of his first wife, Francisca Bernal, in 1899 prompted him to move to the port of Guaymas, where he began a decade-long search for economic success and social mobility. To do so, he relied on his connections with, and the support of, his father's family, the Elíases. First a school inspector and newspaper editor in the port, Calles next was

Plutarco Elías Calles, Teneria, Mexico, 1928. Ascending to the presidency of Mexico in 1924, Calles attempted to enact some of the promised reforms of the Mexican Revolution. Though Calles himself was sent into exile in 1936, his legacy endured with his creation of the National Revolutionary Party, an organization which ruled Mexico under different names for over seventy years. © BETTMANN/CORBIS

appointed municipal treasurer (he lost the post when funds were discovered missing), followed by a stint as manager of his half brother's hotel until it burned. He moved in 1906 to Fronteras, where he managed his father's modest hacienda, was bookkeeper for and shareholder in a small flour mill, and served as municipal secretary—at last achieving modest success and some local prominence. But he then became embroiled in the Elíases' conflict with the local cacique (boss) and in a dispute with farmers over water rights. As a result he returned to Guaymas in 1910 to manage a hotel and open a commission business in partnership.

Though not an active participant in the local Maderista movement, Calles lent it some support—his store as a meeting place. He used this connection to run unsuccessfully for the state legislature in 1911. Again he returned to northeast Sonora, opening a general store (in partnership) in the

border town of Agua Prieta, a most fortunate choice. The railroad running through the town connected Arizona with important mining districts in the interior of Sonora; and the new governor, José M. Maytorena, was looking for a loyal follower who, as the town's police chief, would secure customs revenues, quiet disgruntled former insurgents, and forestall a rumored invasion from Arizona by the radical Magonista revolutionaries. His choice of Calles proved to be the turning point of the latter's life. Calles proved to be a capable, diligent local official, against the Orozquista rebels (1912) and the Huerta coup a year later (being among the first to proclaim armed resistance in the state).

Calles soon developed a working relationship with Obregón, who was emerging as the leader of the revolutionary *jefes* in the northwest. While Obregón carried the constitutionalist movement beyond the state, Calles remained to manage the military and political affairs of Sonora. As governor of Sonora (1915–1916, 1917–1919) and working with Obregón's other principal Sonoran associate, Adolfo De La Huerta (governor, 1917, 1919–1920), Calles set forth a radical program to promote education on a broad scale; break up monopolies (including the cancellation of all prior government concessions which had tax exemptions) and support small entrepreneurs; extend secularization (including the legalization of divorce and the expulsion of all priests); establish an agrarian commission to distribute the expropriated land of those deemed enemies of the Revolution; foster government patronage of workers, assisting in their organization and legislating rights and benefits; and limit foreign influence (principally, severe economic and social restrictions on Chinese immigrants, and cancelling contracts with some large foreign investors). This radical program put Calle at loggerheads with President Venustiano Carranza. Obregón sought to moderate these concepts, but failed in his efforts to establish singular control over the state. He was forced to work with Calles and de la Huerta, forming a triumvirate.

When Obregón announced his presidential candidacy, Calles resigned as secretary of industry, commerce, and labor (1919–1920). Soon after, he led the military forces and proclaimed the Plan of Agua Prieta against Carranza's attempt to impose his successor, and then served as Obregón's interior secretary (1920–1923). When Obregón chose to support Calles over de la Huerta as his successor, and de la Huerta led a revolt, Calles commanded the troops in the northwest. As president, Calles pressed his radical anticlericalism in the face of the Catholic Church's challenge to the restrictions of the 1917 Constitution and then of the Cristero Rebellion (1926–1929). But his support of agrarian reform and the workers' movement ebbed as he moderated his policies and concentrated on the development of the nation's infrastructure (especially irrigation, roads, air and postal service, a telephone network, national banking and investment institutions) and on the promotion of enterprise, even to the point of supporting large-scale domestic and foreign investors.

To retain control over the national government in the wake of the assassination of president-elect Obregón, Calles and his followers pursued a limited and expedient institutionalization of the hierarchical, personalist system that had bound the ruling coalition of revolutionary *jefes* together: the National Revolutionary Party. However, the *Maximato* (the oligarchic rule of the Callista political machine) increasingly lost a popular base, as it turned away from the Revolution's promises of reform and as the Great Depression deepened. Reformers in the party used its structure to institute a radical program and mobilize popular support, coalescing around Lázaro Cárdenas. Again employing expediency, Calles responded by acceding to some of the reformist demands and settling on Cárdenas for the 1934 presidential elections, as the best option to contain growing party dissidence and rising popular alienation. This time, however, his expedient adjustments set in motion forces he could not control. Cárdenas mobilized popular support and employed the institutional prerogatives of the party and the presidency to the fullest. When Calles resisted, he was deported (April 1936). He remained in California until Cárdenas's successor, Manuel Ávila Camacho, permitted his return in 1941 and accorded him full honors at his funeral four years later.

See also **Mexico, Political Parties: National Revolutionary Party (PNR); Mexico: Since 1910.**

BIBLIOGRAPHY

Juan De Dios Bojórquez, *Calles* (1923).

Ramón Puente, *Calles* (1933).

Francisco R. Almada, *La Revolución en el Estado de Sonora* (1971).

Hector Aguilar Camín, *La frontera nómada: Sonora y la Revolución Mexicana* (1977).

Alejandra Lajous, *Los orígenes del partido único en México* (1981).

Luis Javier Garrido, *El partido de la Revolución institucionalizada (medio siglo de poder político en México)* (1982).

Additional Bibliography

Krauze, Enrique. *Plutarco E. Calles: Reformar desde el origen.* Mexico, D.F.: Fondo de Cultura Economica, 1987.

Silva, Carlos. *Plutarco Elias Calles.* Mexico, D.F.: Planeta, 2005.

STUART F. VOSS

CALÓGERAS, JOÃO PANDIÁ (1870–1934).

João Pandiá Calógeras (*b.* 19 June 1870; *d.* 21 April 1934), Brazilian statesman, minister, and author. Educated as an engineer, Calógeras served as a federal deputy (1897–1899 and 1903–1914). He sponsored a law giving the government control over subsoil resources, and was active in boundary and military questions. Close to reformist army officers, who backed his appointment as minister of agriculture, industry, and commerce in 1914, he rose to minister of economy (Fazenda) in 1915–1917. He reorganized government finances and foreign loans, thereby preventing foreign creditors from gaining control over customs receipts.

At the Versailles Conference, he served as delegation chief after Epitácio Pessoa was elected president. In 1919, Pessoa named him the first and only civilian to serve as the republic's minister of war (1919–1922). He oversaw the reorganization of the army, the establishment of army aviation and the French Military Mission, the creation of new training schools, a re-armament program, the massive building of new barracks, and the development of a national defense policy. Military professionalization contributed to the revolt of July 1922 that began the cycle of rebellion leading to the Revolution of 1930. Calógeras backed Getúlio Vargas in the 1930 election and was participating in the constituent assembly when he died in 1934. A convert to Catholicism, in 1932 he was president of the Liga Eleitoral Católica. His books and articles ranged from history and government to engineering and religion.

See also Brazil, Revolutions: Revolution of 1930.

BIBLIOGRAPHY

Egydio Moreira De Castro E Silva, Á margem do ministério Calógeras (1961).

Lawrence H. Hall, "João Pandiá Calógeras, Minister of War, 1919–1922: The Role of a Civilian in the Development of the Brazilian Army," Ph.D. diss., New York University (1983).

João Pandiá Calógeras, A History of Brazil, translated and edited by Percy A. Martin (1939).

FRANK D. McCANN JR.

CALPULLI. Calpulli (from calpolli, big house), a Nahuatl term for a subdivision of an Altepetl, sometimes used synonymously with or replaced by Tlaxilacalli. There have been several definitions

for calpulli, ranging from kin group to temple to the better-known territorial district (such differences arising from regional variation). There is greater agreement on the functional nature of the calpulli, often combined in groups of four, six, or eight within a single altepetl. The calpulli was the basic holder and distributor of usufruct on land to citizens, and the unit responsible for tribute collection and delivery. Each had its own leader and nobility, as well as a temple and market area. Calpulli were ranked in importance and proportionally represented in rotation at the level of altepetl administration. They were often divided into even smaller units, sometimes called calpulli or tlaxilacalli themselves. After the Spanish invasion, the calpulli persisted, retaining much of its pre-Hispanic organization.

See also Ayllu; Indigenous Peoples; Precontact History: Mesoamerica.

BIBLIOGRAPHY

Among the many scholars who have addressed the nature of the calpulli are Edward Calnek, "The Internal Structure of Tenochtitlán," in Ancient Mesoamerica, Selected Readings, edited by John Allen Graham (1981), pp. 337–338; Frances Berdan, The Aztecs of Central Mexico: An Imperial Society (1982), pp. 56–59; Rudolf Van Zantwijk, The Aztec Arrangement: The Social History of Pre-Spanish Mexico (1985); S. L. Cline, Colonial Culhuacán, 1580–1600: A Social History of an Aztec Town (1986); Susan Schroeder, Chimalpahin and the Kingdoms of Chalco (1991); James Lockhart, The Nahuas After the Conquest: A Social and Cultural History of the Indians of Central Mexico, Sixteenth through Eighteenth Centuries (1992), esp. pp. 16–19.

ROBERT HASKETT

CALUSA. Calusa, a native group in southwest Florida during the colonial period. The Calusa and their pre-Columbian ancestors inhabited the Gulf coast from Charlotte Harbor south to the Ten Thousand Islands (Florida Keys). They developed a powerful chiefdom based on the collection of marine foods rather than farming.

On his initial voyage to La Florida in 1513, Juan Ponce De León tried to introduce a settlement among the Calusa but was driven away. In 1566 Pedro Menéndez De Avilés established a Spanish garrison staffed with soldiers and Jesuit priests in the village of Calos; it was withdrawn in 1569. Spanish contact remained sporadic until 1697, when a Franciscan attempt to missionize the Calusa also failed. Diseases and raids by other native groups soon devastated the Calusa. Only remnants were still surviving in 1743, when Jesuits established the short-lived mission of Santa María de Loreto on the Miami River.

See also **Indigenous Peoples; Missions: Spanish America.**

BIBLIOGRAPHY

Goggin, John M., and William C. Sturtevant. "The Calusa: A Stratified Nonagricultural Society (with Notes on Sibling Marriage)," in *Explorations in Cultural Anthropology: Essays in Honor of George Peter Murdock,* edited by Ward H. Goodenough (1964).

Hann, John H., ed. and trans., *Missions to the Calusa* (1991).

Lewis, Clifford M. "The Calusa," in *Tacachale: Essays on the Indians of Florida and Southeast Georgia during the Historic Period,* edited by Jerald Milanich and Samuel Proctor (1978).

Randolph J. Widmer, *The Evolution of the Calusa: A Nonagricultural Chiefdom on the Southwest Florida Coast* (1988).

JERALD T. MILANICH

CALVO, CARLOS (1822–1906).

Carlos Calvo (*b.* 26 February 1822; *d.* 3 May 1906), Argentine diplomat and jurist. Born in Montevideo and educated in Buenos Aires, Calvo lived in the tumultuous early years after independence in the Río de la Plata region. In 1859, the president of Paraguay, Carlos Antonio López, appointed him Paraguay's representative to mediate a conflict between Great Britain and Paraguay. His mission was a success. Thereafter he retired from public life to write. In 1868, he published a book that gave him international recognition, *Derecho internacional teórico y práctico de Europa y América,* which contained the essence of what has come to be known as the Calvo Doctrine.

He argued that America as well as Europe consisted of free and independent nations and that their sovereignty not be ignored. He declared that sovereign states enjoyed the right to freedom from intervention by other states. Moreover, foreigners were not entitled to rights not accorded to nationals. Thus, the essence of Calvo's ideas were nonintervention and the absolute equality of foreigners with nationals. According to Calvo, European interventions in Latin America were a violation of the equality of sovereign nations, and no nation had the right to employ force against another for the enforcement of contracts or agreements between its citizens and those of the other. Many Latin American countries have incorporated this clause into contracts with international corporations.

Calvo enjoyed a long diplomatic career. In 1878, he served as a delegate to the International Congress of Geography that met in Paris. He was minister plenipotentiary to the postal congress of Paris (1878) and Vienna (1891). In 1883 he became special envoy and minister plenipotentiary to Berlin and to the Russian and Austrian emperors in 1889 and 1890, respectively. In 1899, Calvo was appointed minister to France and the Holy See. He died in Paris.

See also **Calvo Doctrine.**

BIBLIOGRAPHY

Percy Bordwell, "Calvo and the 'Calvo Doctrine,'" *Green Bag* 18 (July 1906): 377–382.

José Yves Limantour, *Memoria sobre la vida y obra de D. Carlos Calvo* (1909).

A. S. De Bustamante, "Carlos Calvo" in *Encyclopaedia of the Social Sciences,* vol. 3 (1930).

Additional Bibliography

Obregón, Liliana. "Completing Civilization: Nineteenth Century Criollo Interventions in International Law." Thesis, Harvard Law School, 2002.

Pérez Calvo, Eduardo Ricardo, and Lucio Ricardo Pérez Calvo. *Vida y trabajos de Carlos Calvo.* Buenos Aires: Ediciones Dunken, 1996.

JUAN MANUEL PÉREZ

CALVO DOCTRINE.

The Calvo Doctrine was a principle of international law developed by the Argentine diplomat and legal scholar Carlos Calvo (1822–1906). The doctrine states that the authority to settle international investment disputes resides in the government of the country in which that investment is located. The doctrine was based on two key principles: the equality of the rights of foreign and domestic investors and the sovereignty of the Latin American states. The doctrine was first articulated in Calvo's *Derecho internacional teórico y práctico de Europa y América* (International law: Theory and practice in Europe and America), published in Paris in 1868. Ironically, he developed the doctrine largely in response to France's imperialist adventure in México (1861–1867), which outraged Pan-Americanist intellectuals across the region.

With the establishment of Latin America's nationalist populist governments of the 1930s and 1940s Calvo's doctrine was incorporated into numerous political constitutions and civil codes. As a legal instrument, the Calvo Clause (as the applied doctrine became known) guided most Latin American states' attitudes toward international investment arbitration until the 1970s. But with the neoliberal turn of the 1980s Latin American governments abandoned the Calvo Clause in favor of multilateral conventions on international commercial arbitration. Given the region's current reversal of many neoliberal policies, however, it may be too soon to dismiss the relevance of the Calvo Doctrine to Latin America affairs.

See also **Argentina: The Nineteenth Century; Calvo, Carlos; Drago, Luis María; Neoliberalism; Pan-Americanism.**

BIBLIOGRAPHY

Bishop, R. Doak, and James E. Etri. "International Commercial Arbitration in South America." King & Spalding, LLP. Available from http://www.kslaw.com/library/pdf/bishop3.pdf.

Calvo, Carlos. *La doctrine de Monroe.* Paris: A. Eyméoud, 1903.

Calvo, Carlos. *La República del Paraguay y sus relaciones exteriors: Una página de derecho internacional,* 2nd ed. Asunción: Editorial Araverá, 1985.

Shea, Donald Richard. *The Calvo Clause: A Problem of Inter-American and International Law and Diplomacy.* Minneapolis: University of Minnesota Press, 1955.

JAMES A. WOOD

CALYPSO. Calypso, a Caribbean music and dance form with West African roots, was once criticized for its sharp social commentary and considered uncivilized. In the early twenty-first century it is sanctioned by Trinidad's government and is a popular and important feature of Trinidad's Carnival season. Sometimes sung in French creole, calypso is derived from earlier musical forms such as kaiso, calinda, and belair. Although Trinidad is regarded as calypso's home, the music is popular throughout the Caribbean.

Calypso's lyrics deal with themes of inequality, slavery, colonialism, and governmental fraud. Due to the subversive content and the elites' characterization of calypso as uncivilized, the music has been censored, particularly in the late nineteenth and early twentieth centuries. Nevertheless, the "calypso tent tradition" (calypso performances in tents) beginning in January and lasting into the Carnival season has been a mainstay since the 1920s. Artists such as Attila the Hun (1892–1962), Mighty Sparrow (b. 1935), Lord Executor Kitchener (d. 1952), and Growling Tiger (1915–1993) broke barriers, gaining fans in the Caribbean and abroad during calypso's golden age between 1930 and 1950. Harry Belafonte (b. 1927) brought a stylized calypso to mainstream U.S. audiences with the hit "Banana Boat (Day-O)."

Some critics have argued that the genre has been corrupted by the use of rhythms from popular U.S. songs rather than local bands, as well as by corporate sponsorships and the new predominance of "smut songs" (compositions with sexual content). At the same time, new variations of calypso such as "soca" (short for "soul calypso") and "Soca Chutney" (influenced by Trinidad's Indian population) point to continuing innovation and a widening fan base.

See also **Music: Popular Music and Dance.**

BIBLIOGRAPHY

Cowley, John. *Carnival, Canboulay and Calypso: Traditions in the Making.* Cambridge, U.K.: Cambridge University Press, 1996.

Dudley, Shannon. *Carnival Music in Trinidad: Experiencing Music, Expressing Culture.* New York: Oxford University Press, 2004.

Hill, Donald R. *Calypso Calaloo: Early Carnival Music in Trinidad.* Gainesville: University Press of Florida, 1993.

Liverpool, Hollis "Chalkdust." *From the Horse's Mouth: Stories of the History and Development of the Calypso from the 1920s to 1970s.* Trinidad: Juba Publications, 2003.

Regis, Louis. *The Political Calypso: True Opposition in Trinidad and Tobago, 1962–1987.* Gainesville: University Press of Florida, 1999.

MEREDITH GLUECK

CAMACHO ROLDÁN, SALVADOR

(1827–1900). Salvador Camacho Roldán (*b.* 1 January 1827; *d.* 19 June 1900), Colombian Liberal politician, publicist, and businessman. Born in Nunchía, Casanare, Camacho received his doctorate in law and became a judge in 1848. His prominence brought him increasingly higher appointments during the 1850s, including the governorship of Panama (1852–1853). Camacho was elected to the House of Representatives in 1854 and served both there and in the Senate for the next thirty years. A fiscal expert, he served successively as minister of finance and development (1870–1872) and of foreign affairs (1878). He had been president designate (1868–1869) and acting president (December 1869) but never became president, except for one day in July 1871. Camacho's decades of public service left him poor until 1887, when he established the Librería Colombiana and the dry goods firm of Camacho Roldán y Tamayo, in Bogotá. He edited numerous important newspapers from 1849 to 1881. Camacho advocated a technologically oriented educational system as the means to economic growth. His *Escritos varios* (3 vols., 1892–1895, repr. 1983) were culled from his extensive corpus of economic and political works. His travels are recorded in *Notas de viaje* (1898). Camacho is best known for his *Memorias* (2 vols., 1894, 1924, repr. 1946). He died at *El Ocaso*, his country house, at Zipacón, Cundinamarca, about thirty miles from Bogotá.

See also **Colombia: Since Independence.**

BIBLIOGRAPHY

Antonio José Iregui, *Ensayo biográfico: Salvador Camacho Roldán* (1919).

Additional Bibliography

Cacua Prada, Antonio. *Salvador Camacho Roldán.* Tunja: Publicaciones de la Academia Boyacense de Historia, 1990.

Vallejo Morillo, Jorge. *Cuatro economistas colombianos.* Bogotá: Norma, 2003.

J. León Helguera

CAMACHO SOLÍS, MANUEL (1946–).

Manuel Camacho is a Mexican politician, author, and *El Universal* columnist. Victor Manuel Camacho Solís was born in Mexico City on March 30, 1946. He received his degree in economics from the Universidad Nacional Autónoma de México and became a member of the Party of the Institutional Revolution (PRI) in 1965. Camacho's political career began in 1985, when he was elected deputy. In 1986 he was named minister of urban development. Under President Carlos Salinas de Gortari, Camacho was appointed head of government of the Federal District (Mexico City) in 1988 and minister of foreign affairs in 1993. That appointment was brief, however, as Salinas later summoned Camacho to be the chief negotiator for a resolution to the conflict with the Zapatistas in Chiapas in 1994.

After the announcement of Salinas's support for Luis Donaldo Colosio and later Ernesto Zedillo for the PRI presidential candidate, Camacho's differences with the PRI became more pronounced. In 1995 Camacho left the PRI, and in 2000 he campaigned for president from the short-lived Party of the Democratic Center (PCD). Camacho later joined the Party of the Democratic Revolution (PRD), and in 2003 he was elected deputy for the second time. Camacho participated actively in the 2006 presidential campaign of Andrés Manuel López Obrador. After decades of service in the Mexican government in various capacities, Manuel Camacho continues to be one of the most influential political insiders in Mexico.

See also **Salinas de Gortari, Carlos.**

BIBLIOGRAPHY

Camacho Solís, Manuel. *El desacuerdo nacional: Orígenes, consecuencias y propuestas de solución.* Mexico: Aguilar, 2006.

Osorno, Guillermo. "Manuel Camacho Solís: El solitario sin palacio." *Letras Libres* (June 2000).

Travis Scott High

CÂMARA, HÉLDER (1909–1999). Hélder

Câmara (Dom Hélder; *b.* 7 February 1909, *d.* 27 August 1999), Brazilian Catholic archbishop. Born in the poor northeastern state of Ceará, Câmara was ordained as a priest at age twenty-two. As a young cleric, he joined Ação Integralista Brasileira, a movement that sympathized with fascism. In 1936, he went to Rio de Janeiro to work with archbishop Sebastião Leme. In the 1940s, when he served as national assistant to Brazilian Catholic Action, Câmara moved toward liberal theological and political positions.

In 1952, Câmara was named auxiliary bishop of Rio. That same year, he helped create the National Conference of Brazilian Bishops (CNBB), which became the most important organization within the Brazilian Catholic Church. From 1952 until 1964, he served as secretary-general of the CNBB. In 1955, Câmara created the São Sebastião Crusade, a liberal organization whose objective was to improve the living conditions in Rio's *favelas* (slums).

On 12 March 1964, three weeks before the military coup, Câmara was named archbishop of Recife and Olinda. The new archbishop repeatedly denounced the military regime for human rights abuses, for neglecting the poor, and for imposing an economic model that concentrated wealth. His courageous statements in the face of constant intimidation made the diminutive cleric the most famous church leader in Brazil. At first relatively isolated in his criticisms of the military government, by the late 1960s Câmara had the support of a substantial part of the church hierarchy. He and many of his close associates in the archdiocese were frequently harassed by the military government; some were expelled from Brazil, tortured, and even killed. Câmara was a leading figure in the turn of the Brazilian church toward more progressive ecclesiastical and political positions in the 1960s and 1970s.

After retiring as archbishop in 1985, Câmara continued to work in Recife, mostly among the urban poor. His successor, José Cardoso Sobrinho, dismantled many of the programs Câmara had established and clashed with many who had worked with the retired archbishop. Up until his death Camara remained committed to the church though he also was a strong advocate of the poor and against world hunger.

See also **Brazil, Organizations: National Conference of Brazilian Bishops (CNBB); Catholic Church: The Modern Period.**

BIBLIOGRAPHY

José De Broucker, *Dom Hélder Câmara* (1970).

Additional Bibliography

Piletti, Nelson. *Dom Hélder Câmara: Entre o poder e a profecia*. São Paulo: Editora Atica, 1997.

Regan, David. *Why Are They Poor?: Helder Camara in Pastoral Perspective*. Münster: Lit, 2002.

Serbin, Kenneth. "Dom Helder Camara: The Father of the Church of the Poor." P. Beattie, ed. *The Human Tradition in Modern Brazil*. Wilmington, SR Books, 2004.

SCOTT MAINWARING

CÁMARA NACIONAL DE LA INDUSTRIA DE LA TRANSFORMACIÓN (CANACINTRA).

The Cámara Nacional de la Industria de la Transformación (National Chamber of the Manufacturing Industry) is a Mexican public organization grouping small and medium manufacturers. It is usually portrayed as having been the most pro-government employers' organization in Mexico during the rule of the Partido Revolucionario Institucional (PRI; Institutional Revolutionary Party), at least until the early 1980s. Although it is considered a public organization, its members formally control it under a one-firm-one-vote principle. CANACINTRA was created in 1941 on the initiative of ninety-three manufacturers interested in the modification of the 1936 Law of Chambers. It was also known as the CNIT.

Formally, CANACINTRA is one of the umbrella organizations of the Confederación de Cámaras Industriales (CONCAMIN; Industrial Chambers Confederation), the industrial chamber representing big manufacturers. However, CANACINTRA actually takes different positions on economic and political issues. CANACINTRA has represented the small manufacturers that appeared during the import-substitution industrialization process in Mexico between the late 1930s and the late 1960s. It was, therefore, a strong defender of protectionist policies. In 1985 CANACINTRA opposed the country's entrance to the General Agreement on Tariffs and Trade (the predecessor of the World Trade Organization). CANACINTRA's criticisms of the North American Free Trade Agreement (NAFTA) were moderated only after Canada's inclusion in the negotiations. During the 1990s CANACINTRA slowly shifted its protectionist position, emphasizing instead the establishment of conditions that small and medium manufacturers needed to compete in international markets: tax reforms, creation of infrastructure, and labor reforms.

See also **Mexico, Political Parties: Institutional Revolutionary Party (PRI); North American Free Trade Agreement.**

BIBLIOGRAPHY

Camp, Roderic Ai. *Entrepreneurs and Politics in Twentieth-Century Mexico.* New York: Oxford University Press, 1989.

"CANACINTRA Mexico." Available from http://www.canacintradigital.com.

SERGIO SILVA-CASTAÑEDA

CAMARENA, ENRIQUE (1947–1985).

Enrique Camarena (*b.* 26 July 1947; *d.* February 1985), a U.S. Drug Enforcement Administration (DEA) agent who was abducted on 7 February 1985, and then tortured and murdered, while on assignment in Mexico. Camarena's body was discovered one month later on a ranch in Guadalajara. Mexican officials placed blame for the murder on a Guadalajara drug kingpin, Rafael Caro Quintero. The DEA, however, conducted a lengthy and controversial investigation that linked high-ranking Mexican officials to the murder, including Rubén Zuno Arce, a prominent Mexican businessman and brother-in-law of former Mexican President Luis Echeverría. The controversy heightened when Mexican officials refused to allow DEA agents to participate in the investigation or view evidence as it was uncovered. Eventually, the U.S. government claimed that the Camarena case was intimately linked to members of Mexico's political elite, and the DEA charged that some Mexican officials were involved in a cover-up.

The Camarena case strained relations between the United States and Mexico. Frustrated by the slow pace of the case, in February 1985 the U.S. government brought pressure to bear on the Mexican government by ordering detailed inspections of all vehicles entering the United States from Mexico, virtually closing the border and threatening the economies of Mexican border cities and states. The difficulties intensified when DEA agents masterminded the April 1990 kidnapping and forcible extradition of a Guadalajara physician, Humberto Alvarez Machain, who was implicated in the torture of Camarena. The U.S. Supreme Court ruled, in 1993, that Alvarez Machain's forcible abduction

from a foreign country did not prohibit his trial in the United States. The court's decision, while hailed as a victory against terrorism and drug trafficking, was seen as a major threat to national sovereignty by Mexico and other Latin American countries.

At the end of numerous trials in the United States and Mexico, nineteen Mexican citizens, ranging from civilians to police officers and high-ranking persons, were indicted in the kidnapping, torture, and/or murder of DEA agent Camarena. The case produced great resentment in Mexico because of the overbearing attitude of the U.S. officials and violations of Mexican sovereignty; it reinforced images in the United States of corruption and noncooperative attitudes on the part of Mexican officials.

See also **Drugs and Drug Trade.**

BIBLIOGRAPHY

Andreas Lowenfeld, "Mexico and the United States, an Undiplomatic Murder," in *Economist*, 30 March 1985.

U.S. House of Representatives, Committee on the Judiciary, *Drug Enforcement Administration Reauthorization for Fiscal Year 1986: Hearing Before the Subcommittee on Crime. May 1, 1985* (1986).

Andreas Lowenfeld, "Kidnapping by Government Order: A Follow-Up," in *American Journal of International Law* 84 (July 1990): 712–716.

William Dirk Raat, *Mexico and the United States: Ambivalent Vistas* (1992).

Additional Bibliography

Lindau, Juan David. "Percepciones xexicanas de la política exterior de Estados Unidos: El caso Camarena Salazar." *Foro Internacional* 27 (April–June 1987): 562–575.

PAUL GANSTER

CAMARGO, SERGIO DE (1930–1990).

Sergio de Camargo (*b.* 8 April 1930, *d.* 1990), Brazilian sculptor. A native of Rio de Janeiro, Camargo left Brazil in the 1940s. In 1946 he entered the Academia d'Altimira art school in Buenos Aires, where he studied with the artist Emilio Pettoruti and one of the school's founders, the painter Lucio Fontana. He went to Europe for the first time in 1948, and studied philosophy at the Sorbonne in Paris. Influenced by Constantin Brancuçsi, Jean Arp, and Georges Vantongerloo, he began to sculpt. From 1948 to 1974, Camargo lived in Paris. In 1953, he traveled to Rio de Janeiro, where he exhibited several of his sculptural works in Rio's National Salon of Modern Art. He also made a brief trip to China.

Although figural sculpture predominated in his early years, Camargo experimented with wood reliefs, geometric abstractionism, and constructivism. Along with contemporaries Julio Le Parc and Carlos Cruz Diez, Camargo was also one of the pioneers of kinetic art. Using a cylinder or cube, he arranged forms and explored the "madness of order." He received the International Sculpture Prize at the 1963 Paris Biennale. In 1965, he began sculptural pieces for Oscar Niemeyer's Foreign Ministry Building in Brasília. In the same year, he was named best national sculptor in the São Paulo Bienal. He returned to Rio de Janeiro in 1974, and in 1977 he won the sculpture award given by the São Paulo Association of Art Critics. In the 1980s Camargo had solo exhibitions in both the Rio and São Paulo museums of modern art, and he participated in the 1982 Venice Biennale.

See also **Art: The Twentieth Century.**

BIBLIOGRAPHY

Arte no Brasil, vol. 2 (1979), esp. p. 933.

Dawn Ades, *Art in Latin America* (1989), esp. pp. 270–275.

Additional Bibliography

Brecheret, Vítor. *Brazilian sculpture from 1920 to 1990.* Washington, DC: Cultural Center, Inter-American Development Bank, 1997.

Brito, Ronaldo. *Sergio Camargo: Espacos da arte brasileira.* São Paulo: Cosac & Naify Edições, 2000.

CAREN A. MEGHREBLIAN

CAMARILLA.

Camarilla, popular term to describe a political network in Mexico. Throughout much of the nineteenth and twentieth centuries, Mexican political leaders have relied on personal networks or contacts to achieve successful careers in public life. These groups, which are frequently known as *camarillas,* have been described as the cement of Mexican politics. Since the 1940s, the most important locus of *camarilla* formation has been at the universities, especially the National University, and within the federal bureaucracy. Generally, politicians use their influence as professors and public officials to promote the careers of their disciples and to expand personal ties vertically and horizontally throughout the public arena.

See also **National Autonomous University of Mexico (UNAM).**

BIBLIOGRAPHY

Peter H. Smith, *Labyrinths of Power* (1979).

Roderic A. Camp, "Camarillas in Mexican Politics," in *Mexican Studies* 6 (1990): 85–107.

Additional Bibliography

Colosio Murrieta, Luis Donaldo, and Jaime González Graf. *Colosio: Un candidato en la transición: Frente al México nuevo.* México, D.F.: Grijalbo, 1994.

Muñoz Patraca, Víctor Manuel. *Del autoritarismo a la democracia: Dos decenios de cambio político en México.* México: Siglo Veintiuno, 2001.

RODERIC AI CAMP

CAMBACERES, EUGENIO (1843–1889).

Eugenio Cambaceres (*b.* 24 February 1843; *d.* 14 June 1889), Argentine novelist. Cambaceres was born in Buenos Aires into a wealthy landholding Argentine family of French heritage. Like other young Argentines of fortune, he frequently traveled to Europe, making his headquarters in Paris. There and in his native city he was known as a man-about-town, very fond of the ladies; he married an opera diva shortly before his death. During the 1870s, Cambaceres engaged unsuccessfully in politics, and only during middle age, in the 1880s, did he start writing novels. In six short years, he produced four volumes—*Sin rumbo* (1885) is his masterpiece. This promising literary career was cut short when he died of tuberculosis.

All of his novels—*Potpourri* (1882), *Música sentimental* (1884), *Sin rumbo,* and *En la sangre* (1887)—are cast in the naturalist mold, influenced by the French writer Émile Zola. Cambaceres bitterly attacks society, but unlike Zola fails to give moral guidance. In most of his work, we find a typical naturalistic stress on the sordid; the romantic love of earlier nineteenth-century Spanish American novels has given way to an obsession with sex. In its best moments, however, *Sin rumbo* transcends its naturalist theme and trappings and becomes a powerfully dramatic novel, written with intensity and great narrative art. It has become a classic, one of the most dynamic and significant works of nineteenth-century Spanish American literature.

See also **Literature: Spanish America.**

BIBLIOGRAPHY

Myron I. Lichtblau, "Naturalism in the Argentine Novel," in his *The Argentine Novel in the Nineteenth Century* (1959), pp. 163–184.

R. Anthony Castagnaro, *The Early Spanish American Novel* (1971), pp. 119–129.

María Luisa Bastos, introduction to *Sin rumbo* (1971), pp. 7–29.

Additional Bibliography

Laera, Alejandra. *El tiempo vacío de la ficción: Las novelas argentinas de Eduardo Gutiérrez y Eugenio Cambaceres.* Buenos Aires: Fondo de Cultura Económica de Argentina, 2004.

Tcachuk, Alexandra, "Eugenio Cambaceres: Vida y obra." Ph.D. diss., Northwestern University, 1976.

GEORGE SCHADE

CAMBIO 90-NUEVA MAYORÍA (C90-NM).

Alberto Fujimori founded Cambio 90 to support his candidacies for the Peruvian senate and presidency in 1990. Prominent among the party's initial members were technically oriented university professors, evangelical Protestants, and emerging, informal entrepreneurs of mostly indigenous and mestizo descent. After Fujimori unexpectedly became president, implemented neoliberal economic policies, and carried out a presidential coup, Nueva Mayoría was organized to channel support from more affluent Peruvians. With only skeletal organizations, both parties were little more than electoral vehicles for Fujimori. C90 and NM maintained independent registrations but constituted pro-Fujimori alliances in national elections held in 1992, 1995, 2000 (along with Vamos Vecino), 2001, and 2006.

See also **Peru: Political Parties: Overview; Fujimori, Alberto Keinya.**

BIBLIOGRAPHY

Levitsky, Steven, and Maxwell A. Cameron. "Democracy without Parties? Political Parties and Regime Change in Fujimori's Peru." *Latin American Politics and Society* 45, no. 3 (2003): 1–33.

Schmidt, Gregory D. "Fujimori's 1990 Upset Victory in Peru: Electoral Rules, Contingencies, and Adaptive Strategies." *Comparative Politics* 28, no. 3 (1996): 321–354.

Schmidt, Gregory D. *Peru: The Politics of Surprise.* New York: McGraw-Hill Primis, 2004.

GREGORY D. SCHMIDT

CAMILLE, ROUSSAN (1912–1961).

Roussan Camille (*b.* 27 August 1912; *d.* 7 December 1961), Haitian poet and journalist. Camille first wrote for *Le temps,* often publishing poems along with his regular columns. He was named editor in chief of *Haïti Journal* (1935) and director (1936), after the death of Charles Moravia. From 1947 to his death, he held several official positions: division head in the ministry of public instruction (during World War II), vice-consul of Haiti in New York City (1947–1948), secretary to President Dumarsais Estimé (1948–1950), and director of cultural affairs. Camille was imprisoned briefly after serving President Estimé. At the news of Camille's death, Franck Fouché published a poem to "celebrate the multiple presence of a great poet" (*Symphonie en noir majeur,* 1962).

Camille moved away from French poets toward the inspiration of Langston Hughes and Nicolás Guillén. He wrote with empathy for the victim—whether slave, prostitute, or child—and a sense of fraternity with his fellow poets. He was awarded the Dumarsais Estimé Prize for his collected poetry when he submitted the manuscript of *La multiple présence* in 1961. Among his other works are *Assaut à la nuit* (1940), and *La multiple présence, derniers poèmes* (1978).

See also **Literature: Spanish America.**

BIBLIOGRAPHY

Naomi M. Garret, *The Renaissance of Haitian Poetry* (1963), pp. 167–175.

F. Raphaël Berrou and Pradel Pompilus, *Histoire de la littérature haïtienne illustrée par les textes,* vol. 3 (1977), 237–252.

CARROL F. COATES

CAMNITZER, LUIS (1937–).

Luis Camnitzer (b. 1937), Uruguayan artist. German born, Camnitzer emigrated with his family to Uruguay in 1939. He studied sculpture and architecture at the Universidad de la República Oriental del Uruguay in Montevideo in the 1950s, and at the Akademie der Bildenden Künste in Munich (1957). He received a John Simon Guggenheim Memorial Fellowship in 1964 and moved to New York City, where he was also granted a Memorial Foundation for Jewish Culture Fellowship (1965–1966). He was a founding member of the New York Graphic Workshop (1967). During this period he used text without images to describe spaces and objects in installations. He has taught at the Pratt Institute, Fairleigh Dickinson University, and, since 1969, at the State University of New York College at Old Westbury.

In the 1980s he addressed themes related to human rights and environmental decay in Latin America. An outsider to the art market system, Camnitzer has devoted a great deal of his time to writing about art and organizing noncommercial exhibitions. In 1994, he published a book, *New Art of Cuba*. As of 2007, he lived in Great Neck, New York.

See also **Art: The Twentieth Century.**

BIBLIOGRAPHY

Angel Kalenberg, *Luis Camnitzer* (1987).

Luis Camnitzer, Gerardo Mosquera, and María Del Carmen Ramírez, *Luis Camnitzer: A Retrospective Exhibition 1966–1990* (1991).

Additional Bibliography

Farver, Jane. *Luis Camnitzer, Retrospective Exhibition, 1966–1990*. Bronx, NY: Lehman College Art Gallery, 1991.

MARTA GARSD

CAMÕES, LUÍS VAZ DE (1525–1580).

Luís vaz de Camões (b. 1525?; d. 10 June 1580), Portuguese poet. One of the most renowned figures of Portuguese letters, Luís de Camões authored a substantial corpus that includes the epic poem *Os Lusíadas* (*The Lusiads*, 1572), a cornerstone of his fame in world literature, lyric poetry (principal editions published in 1595 and 1598), plays, and familiar epistles. Little biographical information is known about Camões, although it is certain that he spent many of his adult years as a soldier in the Portuguese Empire. His poetry, written in both Portuguese and Spanish, was composed in the traditional style (the *medida velha*, as it was known in the poet's time) as well as in the *dolce stil nuovo*, introduced into Portugal by Francisco de Sá de Miranda. *Os Lusíadas* consists of 1,102 stanzas in ottava rima divided into ten cantos and reflects the epic imagination of the sixteenth-century Portuguese. The theme is nothing less than the history of Portugal—and it is the nation that emerges as the collective hero—articulated around the voyage of Vasco da Gama to India in 1497. *Os Lusíadas* was the model for Bento Teixeira's *Prosopopéia* (1601), an encomiastic poem about Jorge de Albuquerque Coelho, governor of Pernambuco.

See also **Portuguese Empire.**

BIBLIOGRAPHY

Jorge De Sena, *Trinta anos de Camões, 1948–1978: Estudos camonianos e correlatos* (1980).

Maria De Lourdes Belchior and Enrique Martínez-López, eds., *Camoniana Californiana: Commemorating the Quadricentennial of the Death of Luís Vaz de Camões; Proceedings of the Colloquium Held at the University of California, Santa Barbara, April 25 and 26, 1980* (1985).

David Quint, "Voices of Resistance: The Epic Curse and Camões's Adamastor," in *New World Encounters*, edited by Stephen Greenblatt (1993).

Additional Bibliography

Madeira, José. *Camões Contra a Expansão e o Império: Os Lusíadas como Antiepopeia*. Lisboa: Fenda, 2000.

JOSIAH BLACKMORE

CAMPA SALAZAR, VALENTÍN (1904–1999).

The Mexican labor union leader Valentín Campa Salazar was a controversial figure in the railroad workers' union and a longtime activist of the Mexican Communist Party. Born on February 14, 1904, in Monterrey, Nuevo León, Campa completed only his first year of secondary education before going to work in 1920 for La Corona, a subsidiary of the Royal Dutch Company. As a labor activist he cofounded the Sindicato Unitario Mexicano. Beginning in 1927 he was imprisoned thirteen times for his labor organizing; he spent ten years in Lecumberri prison after a 1958–1959 railroad strike. Campa ran unsuccessfully for president on the Mexican Communist Party (PCM) ticket in 1976 and served as a federal deputy from 1979 to 1982. He died on November 25, 1999.

See also **Labor Movements; Mexico, Political Parties: Partido Comunista Mexicano.**

BIBLIOGRAPHY

Valentin, Campa Salazar. *Mi testimonio: Experiencias de un comunista mexicano.* Mexico: Ediciones de Cultura Popular, 1978.

Valentin, Campa Salazar. *Una voz en la tribuna.* Mexico: Camara de Diputados, 1994.

RODERIC AI CAMP

CAMPBELL, FEDERICO (1941–). Born in Tijuana on July 1, 1941, Federico Campbell is considered one of the founding writers of border literature from northern Mexico. He became known as a journalist in 1972 with *Infame turba* (Infamous Mob). He is the author of "La hora del lobo" (The Hour of the Wolf), a weekly column in the news weekly *Milenio*. In 2000 he won the Colima Prize for Fiction with his novel *Transpeninsular*. He has also published *Pretexta* (1979), *Todo lo de las focas* (1982; All about Seals), *Tijuanenses* (1989; *Tijuana: Stories on the Border*, 1995), *La memoria de Sciascia* (1989; Sciascia's Memory), *La invención del poder* (1994; The Invention of Power), *Post scriptum triste* (1994), *Máscara negra* (1995; Black Mask), *La clave Morse* (2001; The Morse Code), and *El imperio del adiós* (2002; The Empire of Farewell). Other works include *Conversaciones con escritores* (1972; Conversations with Writers) and an anthology of critical essays on Juan Rulfo, *La ficción de la memoria* (2003; The Fiction of Memory). He has translated Harold Pinter, David Mamet, and Leonardo Sciascia into Spanish. In 1995 he was awarded the J. S. Guggenheim Fellowship.

See also **Journalism; Journalism in Mexico; Literature: Spanish America.**

BIBLIOGRAPHY

Additional Bibliography

Campbell, Federico. *Conversaciones con escritores.* México: Secretaría de Educación Pública, 1972.

Pino, Hernán Becerra, Javier Aranda Luna, et al., eds. *La máquina de escribir: Entrevistas con Federico Campbell.* Tijuana, D.F.: Centro Cultural Tijuana; Mexico: Consejo Nacional para la Cultura y las Artes, 1997.

ROSINA CONDE

CAMPERO, NARCISO (1813–1896). Narciso Campero (*b.* 29 October 1813; *d.* 12 August 1896), president of Bolivia (1880–1884). Campero was born in Tojo in the department of Tarija. Near the beginning of his military career, he fought in the battle of Ingavi in November 1841. He attended military school in Paris in 1845. From 1859 to 1879 Campero served in military, diplomatic, and administrative posts, usually under Liberal presidents. When the War of the Pacific began in 1879, he was appointed general of the Fifth Division. Because of their confidence in Campero, the Bolivian directors of the Huanchaca Silver Company sent provisions to the Fifth Division. When the inhabitants of La Paz overthrew President Hilarión Daza on 27 December 1879, they named Campero as their new leader. Following the advice of the silver barons, Campero gradually removed Bolivia from the war by 1884. Meanwhile, to legitimize his new government, Campero called a constituent assembly, which met in 1880. The delegates not only confirmed Campero as president but also approved a new constitution for Bolivia that remained in force until 1938. By cooperating with the mining oligarchy, Campero brought an end to unstable caudillo rule and, through the Constitution of 1880, allowed a small elite of mine owners to open Bolivia to the industrial world.

See also **Mining: Modern.**

BIBLIOGRAPHY

Julio Díaz Arguedas, *Los generales de Bolivia (rasgos biográficos) 1825–1925* (1929), pp. 247–261.

Herbert S. Klein, *Parties and Political Change in Bolivia, 1880–1952* (1969), pp. 14, 18.

ERWIN P. GRIESHABER

CAMPESINO. *Campesino,* the Spanish word for "peasant." In modern times the term has taken on a broader meaning in Spanish America. Now *campesino* is used to refer to all members of the Latin American rural working class. This includes agricultural wage laborers (*jornaleros*) and small landholders (*minifundistas*). The term also still refers to peasants (*mozos colonos*) who perform labor for the right to farm a small plot of land or in exchange for agricultural produce. *Campesino* is a very general term which encompasses all rural people of the lower economic strata, including men, women, and children. In some countries such as Peru, the term *campesino* sometimes refers to peoples of indigenous heritage when they are from the working class.

See also **Colono.**

BIBLIOGRAPHY

Additional Bibliography

Boyer, Christopher R. *Becoming Campesinos: Politics, Identity, and Agrarian Struggle in Postrevolutionary Michoacán, 1920-1935.* Stanford, CA: Stanford University Press, 2003.

Katz, Friedrich. *Riot, Rebellion, and Revolution: Rural Social Conflict in Mexico.* Princeton, NJ: Princeton University Press, 1988.

Salvatore, Ricardo Donato. *Wandering Paysanos: State Order and Subaltern Experience in Buenos Aires during the Rosas Era.* Durham, NC: Duke University Press, 2003.

Zamosc, León, Manuel Chiriboga Vega, and Estela Martínez. *Estructuras agrarias y movimientos campesinos en América Latina [1950-1990].* Madrid: Ministerio de Agricultura, Pesca y Alimentación, 1997.

RACHEL A. MAY

CAMPISTEGUY, JUAN (1859–1937).

Juan Campisteguy (*b.* 7 September 1859; *d.* 1937), president of Uruguay (1927–1931). Campisteguy, born in Montevideo, entered politics when he joined the revolutionary movement against the autocratic regime of Máximo Santos in 1886. His career within the ruling Colorado Party was closely linked to José Batlle y Ordóñez, of whose newspaper *El Día* he was one of the founding editors.

After two terms as member of the House of Representatives (1891–1897), Campisteguy was minister of finance (1897–1898) during Juan Lindolfo Cuestas's constitutional presidency as well as during his autocratic period following the 1898 coup. In 1903/1904, as minister of government under Batlle y Ordóñez, Campisteguy was one of the architects of the government victory over the Blanco rebellion led by Aparicio Saravia. He was subsequently a senator (1905–1911); a member of the Constituent Assembly for the Colorado Party's Riverista faction, which opposed Batlle's plans for the introduction of a *colegiado* system (1917); a deputy (1920–1923); and a member of the National Council of Administration (1921–1927).

Important achievements of Campisteguy's presidency were the creation of the state-owned Frigorífico Nacional (National Meat Packing Plant, 1928) and the Comité de Vigilancia Económica (Committee of Economic Vigilance, 1929).

See also **Batlle y Ordóñez, José; Uruguay, Political Parties: Colorado Party.**

BIBLIOGRAPHY

Taylor, Philip Bates, *Government and Politics of Uruguay* (1960).

Lindahl, Göran E., *Uruguay's New Path: A Study in Politics During the First Colegiado, 1919–33* (1962).

DIETER SCHONEBOHM

CAMPO, ESTANISLAO DEL (1834–1880).

Estanislao Del Campo (*b.* 7 February 1834; *d.* 6 November 1880), Argentine poet, legislator, journalist, civil servant, and officer of the Civic Guard. His admiration for Hilario Ascasubi and the Gauchesca literature prompted him to write poetry in this style. He even adopted the pseudonym of Anastasio el Pollo (Anastasio the Chicken) as a sign of respect for Ascasubi's *Aniceto el Gallo* (Aniceto the Rooster). In 1866 del Campo wrote the gauchesca poem *Fausto,* in which one gaucho, chatting with another, tells the plot of the Gounod opera that he happened to see in Buenos Aires's Teatro Colón. The novelty of this text is that del Campo injected an urban, highly cultured subject into gauchesca literature. He erased the disparity between the popular language and the cult subject of the Faustian legend by reducing it to the concrete reality and perceptions of the gaucho. In spite of the hilarity of the text, the gaucho-narrator and his friend are never ridiculed. On the contrary, their deep friendship is emphasized. The poem is also famous for its romantic descriptions, without parallel in gauchesca literature.

Committed to the party of General Bartolmé Mitre, del Campo fought at the battles of Cepeda (1859) and Pavón (1861) for a Buenos Aires state separate from the Argentine Confederation. In the late 1860s del Campo was elected to the House of Representatives of the province of Buenos Aires as a member of the Liberal Party. In 1874 he was made lieutenant colonel of the Civil Guard. Del Campo took part in the Mitre revolution against Nicolás Avellaneda. He retired from public life in April 1880 and died six months later in Buenos Aires.

See also **Gauchesca Literature.**

BIBLIOGRAPHY

Manuel Mújica Láinez, *Vidas del Gallo y el Pollo* (1966).

Enrique Anderson Imbert, *Análisis de "Fausto"* (1968).

Teresa Salas and Henry Richards, "La función del marco y la armonía simétrica en el *Fausto* de Estanislao del Campo," in *Kentucky Romance Quarterly* 17 (1970): 55–66.

Ollie Olympo Oviedo, "The Reception of the Faust Motif in Latin American Literature: Archetypal Transformations in Works by Estanislao del Campo, Alberto Gerchunoff, João Guimaraes Rosa, Carlos Fuentes, and Jaime Torres Bodet" (Ph.D. diss., New York University, 1978).

Additional Bibliography

Chiappini, Julio O. *Borges y Estanislao del campo.* Rosario: Zeus Editora, 1997.

ANGELA B. DELLEPIANE

Walker, sending Salvadoran troops to Nicaragua under Ramón Belloso and Gerardo Barrios. Upon returning from the war in Nicaragua, Barrios failed in an effort to overthrow Campo in June 1857. Barrios gained power in 1858, however, when Campo stepped down on 1 February of that year, after the serious cholera epidemic of 1857 had exhausted the country. Campo later served as foreign minister under Francisco Dueñas, and was president of the Constitutional Convention of 1871. A critic of the Liberal governments that followed, Campo was in exile in Nicaragua for most of the decade following, but in 1882 he returned to Sonsonate, his birthplace, where he worked for the establishment of the hospital there. He died in Acajutla.

See also **El Salvador.**

BIBLIOGRAPHY

Philip F. Flemion, *Historical Dictionary of El Salvador* (1972), pp. 29–30.

María Leistenschneider and Freddy Leistenschneider, *Gobernantes de El Salvador: Biografías* (1980), pp. 103–105.

Additional Bibliography

Rivera, Abraham. *Apuntes biográficos del Honorable ex-presidente de El Salvador Don Rafael Campo.* San Salvador: Editorial Delgado, 1985.

RALPH LEE WOODWARD JR.

CAMPO, RAFAEL (1813–1890). Rafael Campo (*b.* 24 October 1813; *d.* 1 March 1890), president of El Salvador (1856–1858). Educated at the University of San Carlos de Guatemala, Campo continued his father's successful agricultural and commercial enterprises in El Salvador and was among the first coffee planters in the country. He became politically active in the Conservative Party and was elected president on 30 January 1856, taking office on 12 February. He turned over power to his vice president, Francisco Dueñas, on 12 May of the same year, but resumed the presidency on 19 July. Regarded by many as a puppet of Guatemalan caudillo Rafael Carrera, the conservative Campo allowed greater political freedom than in other Central American states of the period.

In July 1856 Campo joined the other Central American states in the National War against William

CAMPOBELLO, NELLIE (1900–1986). María Francisca "Xica" Moya Luna (Nellie Campobello) was born in Villa Ocampo, Durango (Northern Mexico). She published fifteen poems entitled *¡Yo!* under her given name, Francisca, in 1929. She and her sister, Gloria, excelled in dance and became authorities on Mexican folk dance. Nellie was renowned as a dancer and teacher and became director of the National School of Dance, which was renamed in honor of the sisters in 1989. Their collaborative work preserves indigenous Mexican dance and culture, and Campobello's memoirs of the revolution in the North provide a unique firsthand perspective. Campobello's year of birth and the place and manner of her last illness and death remain controversial.

See also **Music: Popular Music and Dance.**

BIBLIOGRAPHY

Primary Works

Yo! versos [Francisca, pseud.]. México: Ediciones L.I.D.A.N., 1929.

Cartucho: Relatos de la lucha en el Norte de México. México: Ediciones integrales, 1931; Factoría, 1999; Era, 2001. English version, *Cartucho; and, My Mother's Hands.* Translated by Doris Meyer and Irene Matthews. Austin: University of Texas Press, 1988.

Apuntes sobre la vida militar de Francisco Villa. México: Iberoamericana de publicaciones, 1940. This work is also included in *Mis libros,* below.

Nellie and Gloria Campobello. *Ritmos indígenas de México.* México, n.p., 1940.

Mis libros "Prologo" Nellie Campobello. 1st ed. Mexico: Compañía General, 1960.

Las manos de mamá. Mexico: Juventudes, 1937; Grijalbo, 1991; Factoria, 1999.

Francisca Yo! El libro desconocido de Nellie Campobello. Edited by Jesús Vargas Valdés and Flor García Rufino. Chihuahua, México: Nueva Vizcaya Editores y la Universidad Autónoma de Ciudad Juarez, 2004.

Secondary Works

Dávila Valero, Patricia. *Nellie Campobello.* Durango, México: Poder Legislativo del Estado de Durango, 2000.

García, Clara Guadalupe. *Nellie: El caso Campobello.* México: Cal y Arena, 2000.

Matthews, Irene. *Nellie Campobello: La centaura del Norte.* México: Cal y Arena, 1997.

ELIZABETH WILLINGHAM

CAMPO GRANDE.

Campo Grande, frontier capital of Mato Grosso do Sul State in central-west Brazil. This city first obtained its economic importance in 1914 when Brazil's railroad pushed through southern Mato Grosso, making Campo Grande an economic hub of the region. The railroad drew immigrants from the five neighboring states as well as Bolivia and Paraguay. Prior to this, the majority of transportation through southern Mato Grosso was dependent upon water routes. Government plans to settle the frontier states, devised in the 1950s, resulted in waves of migrants by the 1960's for large-scale agricultural production and cattle raising. In 1979 Campo Grande became the capital upon the division of Mato Grosso into Mato Grosso and Mato Grosso do Sul. As of 2005 the estimated population of Campo Grande was 741,100. The principal agricultural products include rice, soybeans, and wheat. With its proximity to the Pantanal wetlands, tourism, along with education and commerce, are growing industries.

See also **Mato Grosso.**

BIBLIOGRAPHY

Arruda, Angelo Marcos Vieira de, Gogliardo Vieira Maragno, and Mário Sérgio Sobral Costa. *Arquitetura em Campo Grande.* Campo Grande, Brazil: UNIDERP, 1999.

Arruda, Gilmar. *Cidades e sertões: Entre a história e a memória.* Bauru, Brazil: EDUSC, 2000.

Corrêa, Valmir Batista. *Coronéis e bandidos em Mato Grosso, 1889–1943.* Campo Grande, Brazil: Editora UFMS, 1995.

CAROLYN E. VIEIRA

CAMPOMANES, PEDRO RODRÍGUEZ, CONDE DE

(1723–1802). Pedro Rodríguez, Conde De Campomanes (*b.* 1 July 1723; *d.* 3 February 1802), president of the Council of Castile (1783–1791). The son of a poor Asturian hidalgo, Campomanes, an attorney, became a *fiscal* (crown attorney) of the Council of Castile in 1762. Committed to royal absolutism yet open to Enlightenment ideas, Campomanes was essentially a utilitarian who believed that the interests of special groups like the *Mesta* (sheepowners' corporation), clergy, and guilds were detrimental to the welfare of the state. In his capacity as policymaker and royal adviser to Charles III, Campomanes embarked upon a program of agrarian reform that advocated free grain trade within Spain, limits on ecclesiastical entailment of land, crown incorporation or *señorios* (noble or aristocratic estates), and elimination of guild restrictions. He was instrumental in the movement to repopulate deserted regions of Spain (1767), founded the Royal Economic Society of Madrid (1775), and used his position as president of the *Mesta* (1779) to weaken that institution and its agricultural privileges. More importantly, he was a supporter of the expulsion of the Jesuits and helped compose a plan to support their removal from the nation. After the expulsion of the Jesuits, Charles III enhanced his support of the Franciscans and they soon replaced the Jesuits in their mission fields in California and elsewhere. In the end, Campomanes' policy toward Latin America included promoting colonial trade and limiting American manufacture.

See also **Franciscans; Jesuits.**

BIBLIOGRAPHY

Laura Rodríguez Díaz, *Reforma e ilustración en la España del siglo XVIII: Pedro Rodríguez de Campomanes* (1975).

Manuel Bustos Rodríguez, *El pensamiento socio-económico de Campomanes* (1982).

Additional Bibliography

Engstrand, Iris H.W. "The Enlightenment in Spain: Influences upon New World Policy" *The Americas* (April 1985): 436–444.

Llombart, Vicent. *Campomanes: Economista y político de Carlos III*. Madrid: Alianza, 1992.

SUZANNE HILES BURKHOLDER

CÁMPORA, HECTOR JOSÉ (1909–1980).

Hector José Cámpora, an Argentine politician and dentist, served as president of Argentina in 1973. Born in the province of Buenos Aires on March 26, 1909, he began his political activity as a member of the Conservative Party (*conservadurismo*). In 1945 he joined the Peronists, and in 1946 he was elected national deputy. He gave unconditional support to the government of Juan Domingo Perón and served as president of the chamber of deputies between 1948 and 1952. After the military coup in 1955, he was arrested along with other Peronist leaders but escaped to exile in Chile.

In 1971 he was named the personal delegate (principal representative in Argentina) of Perón, who trusted in his extreme loyalty. In 1973 Perón was disqualified as a candidate by the outgoing dictatorship and arranged for Cámpora to take his place for the Justicialista Liberation Front. After his victory, he attempted in vain to find a balance between the views of the young Peronists and the more conservative factions. He endorsed amnesty for political prisoners and restored diplomatic relations with Cuba. His closeness to the Peronists left led him to a confrontation with the extreme right wing

of the party. However, without Perón's support and under enormous political pressure as well as pressure from the labor unions, he resigned his post and opened the way for Perón to become president. He was then appointed ambassador to Mexico, and returned home in 1975. After the 1976 coup, he was forced to find refuge in the Mexican embassy. Years later, and very ill, he was allowed by the regime to gain asylum in Mexico, where he lived until his death on December 18, 1980.

See also **Argentina: The Twentieth Century; Argentina, Political Parties: Justicialist Party; Perón, Juan Domingo.**

BIBLIOGRAPHY

Acuña, Carlos Manuel. *Por amor Al Odio: Crónicas de guerra: De cámpora a la muerte de Perón*. Buenos Aires: Del Pórtico, 2003

De Riz, Liliana. *La política en suspenso: 1966–1976*. Buenos Aires: Paidós, 2000.

James, Daniel. *Resistencia e integración: El peronismo y la clase trabajadora Argentina, 1946–1976*. Buenos Aires: Sudamericana, 1990.

VICENTE PALERMO

CAMPOS, AUGUSTO DE (1931–).

Augusto de Campos has earned a place as one of Brazil's foremost poets and translators of poetry (from the French, English, and other languages) as well as literary and music critics. Born on February 14, 1931, in São Paulo, he, his brother Haroldo de Campos, and Decio Pignatari formulated the mid-century avant-garde movement of Concrete poetry in Brazil, and he is a key figure in the development of material poetry and other experimental forms. His critical writings of the late 1960s prompted recognition of the poetry and experimentation in *CAP-Música CAP-Popular Brasileira* (MPB), especially *tropicalismo*. He is also an important critic of nonconventional art music, such as that of the American composer John Cage and twelve-tone (dodecaphonic) composers.

Campos's 1984 poem "pós-tudo" ("post-everything") mocked postmodernism as fashion and sparked a discussion of vanguard aesthetics. In the mid-1990s he began performing, declaiming texts (both his own poems and translations) with musical accompaniment (notably electric guitars and synthesizers) as well as video-digital graphic projections. He has made many texts available both as Web art on the Internet and as items recorded on disc. In 2004 his volume of computer-generated poetry, *Não* (No), was named Brazil's National Library book of the year, and the national cultural-heritage institution organized an event and multimedia retrospective to honor his work.

See also **Campos, Haroldo de; Literature: Brazil; MPB: Música Popular Brasileira; Tropicalismo.**

BIBLIOGRAPHY

Aguilar, Gonzalo. *Poesía concreta brasileña: Las vanguardias en la encrucijada modernista.* Rosario, Argentina: B. Viterbo, 2003.

Perrone, Charles A. *Seven Faces: Brazilian Poetry since Modernism.* Durham, NC: Duke University Press, 1996.

Süssekind, Flora, and Júlio Castañón Guimarães, eds. *Sobre Augusto de Campos.* Rio de Janeiro: Fundação Casa de Rui Barbosa / 7Letras, 2004.

CHARLES A. PERRONE

CAMPOS, FRANCISCO LUIZ DA SILVA (1891–1968).

Francisco Luiz da Silva Campos (*b.* 18 November 1891; *d.* 1 November 1968), Brazilian presidential adviser. The son of Jacinto Alves da Silva Campos and Azejúlia de Souza e Silva, Campos was born in Dores de Indaiá, Minas Gerais. A lawyer, politician, and educator, he married Lavinia Ferreira da Silva, with whom he had two children. The couple eventually separated; later he lived with Margarita Leite.

As an educator, Campos was a professor at the Faculty of Law in his home state and a tenured professor at the Federal University of Rio de Janeiro. As a politician he held various posts, including state legislator, federal legislator, secretary of the interior for the state of Minas Gerais, and mayor of Belo Horizonte. He was also a leader in the Liberal Alliance, which supported the presidential candidacy of Getúlio Vargas, a movement that culminated in the Constitutionalist Revolution of 1930.

As the country's first minister of health and education (1930–1932), Campos reformed the training procedures for primary school teachers and established a federal university educational system. He wrote a number of works on education, including *Educação e cultura* (1940). As a jurist, Campos authored case studies and opinions that still appear in constitutional, administrative, and civil law texts.

In 1932, as Vargas's interim minister of justice, Campos had a great impact on the implantation of the *Estado Novo* (New State) program and authored the 1937 *Estado Novo* charter, in which many corporatist features were outlined. In addition, he was the main author of the Institutional Act No. 1, which juridically incorporated the revolution in the spring of 1964. He died in Belo Horizonte in 1968.

See also **Brazil, Political Parties: Liberal Alliance; Brazil, Revolutions: Revolution of 1930.**

BIBLIOGRAPHY

Michael L. Connif and Frank D. Mc Cann, eds., *Modern Brazil* (1989).

Alfred Stepan, ed., *Democratizing Brazil* (1989).

Additional Bibliography

Moraes, Maria Célia Marcondes de. "Educação e política nos anos '30: A presença de Francisco Campos." *Revista Brasileira de Estudos Pedagógicos* 73 (May–Aug. 1992): 291–321.

IÉDA SIQUEIRA WIARDA

CAMPOS HAROLDO DE (1929–2003).

Haroldo de Campos was an influential Brazilian intellectual and poet. Born on August 19, 1929, in São Paulo, the capital of Brazilian modernism, in 1952 he formed the group Noigandres with his brother Augusto de Campos and Décio Pignatari. This group, which initiated the concrete poetry movement, had a great impact on Brazilian and international literature, reciting its poetry in Germany, Japan, Italy, Spain, Switzerland, Argentina, and England. With a clearly cosmopolitan approach to literature, Campos translated ground-breaking modernist works from English (Ezra Pound and James Joyce), German (Eugen Gomringer, Helmut Heissenbüttel), and French (Stéphane Mallarmé, Francis Ponge), among other languages. He met Pound in Europe in the late 1950s and sustained a significant correspondence with him for years. He also connected with the Argentine avant-garde Grupo Sur (guided by Victoria Ocampo); poets and novelists such as the Chilean Pablo Neruda, the Mexican Octavio Paz, and the Peruvian Mario Vargas Llosa; and the Uruguayan literary critic Emir Rodriguez Monegal.

Campos was fundamental to the cultural and intellectual life of Brazil not only for his theoretical and creative work, but also for his efforts to revive interest in the oeuvres of traditional Brazilian writers such as Oswald de Andrade and Sousandrade. In the later 1960s and early 1970s he was linked to such diverse currents as *tropicalismo* and the Cinema Novo filmmakers. During the 1980s and 1990s he produced innovative studies on semiotics and literary criticism. His most important creative and critical works are *Auto do Possesso* (1950), *Re visão de Sousandrade* (1965), *Teoría da Poesia Concreta* (with Augusto de Campos and Décio Pignatari, 1965), *Morfologia do Macunaíma* (his doctoral thesis; 1972), and *Xadrez das Estrelas* (1976). He died in São Paulo on August 16, 2003.

See also **Campos, Augusto de; Literature: Brazil; Neruda, Pablo; Ocampo, Victoria; Paz, Octavio; Vargas Llosa, Mario.**

BIBLIOGRAPHY

Campos, Haroldo de. *Os melhores poemas de Haroldo de Campos*, 3rd edition. Rio de Janeiro: Global, 2005.

Jackson, K. David. *Haroldo de Campos: A Dialogue with the Brazilian Concrete Poet*. Oxford: Centre for Brazilian Studies, Oxford University, 2005.

PAULA HALPERIN

CAMPOS, JULIETA (1932–). Born in Havana, Cuba, on May 8, 1932, the novelist, essayist, and translator Julieta Campos has resided in Mexico since 1960 and is a Mexican citizen, active in Mexican cultural politics. Campos was writer-in-residence at the Centro Mexicano de Escritores (1966–1967) and on staff at the Instituto de Investigaciones Estéticas at the National University of Mexico (1970). She joined the editorial board of *Vuelta* in 1977 and directed the *Revista de la Universidad de México* from 1981 to 1984. Campos's novel *Tiene los cabellos rojizos y se llama Sabina* (1974) won the Xavier Villaurrutia Prize. Rejecting linear narrative, her writing demonstrates a self-reflexive, imaginative perspective on identity, nostalgia, love, time, and death. Critical works include assessments of literary authors and periods, discussions of the nature and function of literature,

and the study of Nahuatl stories within the problematics of oralism and literacy.

During the 1990s Campos addressed issues of poverty, writing and lecturing about indigenous populations. *Qué hacemos con los pobres* and *Tabasco, un jaguar despertado* are studies of poverty in Mexico. In 2001 she became the president of the Mexico City Tourism Authority, focusing on the cultural and historical patrimony of the city.

See also **Literature: Spanish America.**

BIBLIOGRAPHY

Primary Works

Muerte por agua. México, D. F.: Fondo de Cultura Económica, 1965.

Celina or the Cats [*Celina o los gatos*]. Translated by Leland H. Chambers and Kathleen Ross. Pittsburgh, PA: Latin American Literary Review Press, 1995. Original Spanish version, México: Siglo Veintiuno Editores, 1968.

Función de la novela. México, D. F.: J. Mortiz, 1973.

She Has Reddish Hair and Her Name Is Sabina [*Tiene los cabellos rojizos y se llama Sabina*]. Translated by Leland H. Chambers. Athens: University of Georgia Press, 1993. Original Spanish version, México, D. F.: J. Mortiz, 1974.

El miedo de perder a Eurídice. México, D. F.: J. Mortiz, 1979.

La herencia obstinada: Análisis de cuentos nahuas. México, D. F.: Fondo de Cultura Económica, 1982.

Qué hacemos con los pobres?: La reiterada querella por la Nación. México, D. F.: Aguilar, 1996.

Tabasco, un jaguar despertado: Alternativos a la pobreza. México, D. F.: Aguilar, 1996.

Ice Cream. In *Out of the Mirrored Garden: New Fiction by Latin American Women*, edited by Delai Poey. New York: Anchor Books, 1996.

Reunión de familia. México, D.F.: Fondo de Cultura Económica, 1997.

La forza del destino. México, D. F.: Alfaguara, 2004.

With Fabienne Bradu. *Razones y pasiones*. México, D. F. : Fondo de Cultura Económica, 2005.

Secondary Works

Barreto, Reina. "Blurred Boundaries: Theory and Practice in Julieta Campos's Writing." Ph.D. diss. Florida State University, 2002.

Bradu, Fabienne. "Julieta Campos: La cartografía del deseo y la muerte." In her *Señas particulares: Escritora*, 71–85. México, D.F.: Fondo de Cultura Económica, 1987.

Bruce-Novoa, Juan. "Julieta Campos' *Sabina:* In the Labyrinth of Intertextuality," *Third Woman* 2, no. 2 (1984): 43–63.

Garfield, Evelyn Picon. "Julieta Campos." In her *Women's Voices from Latin America*, 73–96. Detroit: Wayne State University Press, 1985.

Hansberg, Olbeth, and Julio Ortega, eds. *Crítica y literatura: América Latina sin fronteras.* México, D. F.: Coordinación de Humanidades, Universidad Nacional Autónoma de México, 2005.

Lagos-Pope, María Inés. "Cat/Logos: The Narrator's Confession in Julieta Campos' *Celina o los gatos.*" In *Splintering Darkness: Latin American Women Writers in Search of Themselves*, edited by Lucia Guerra-Cunningham, 31–42. Pittsburgh: Latin American Literary Review Press, 1990.

DEBORAH CAPLOW

CAMPOS, LUIS MARÍA (1838–1907).

Luis María Campos (*b.* 1838; *d.* 1907), Argentine military leader. Born in Buenos Aires, Campos entered the army in 1859 as a sublieutenant in the national guard regiment. He fought in the battles of Cepeda and Pavón, which ended the long struggle among the provinces, earning the rank of sergeant major. Campos served throughout the War of the Triple Alliance (1864–1870), perhaps the bloodiest in Latin American history. He fought at Paso de la Patría, Estero Bellaco, and Curupayty. Seriously wounded at San Ignacio, Campos was sent to the province of San Juan to recover. Returning to the war, he fought at most major engagements, including Lomas Valentinas and Angostura. Late in the war he was decorated by the commander in chief of Allied Forces, Conde D'eu, for his bravery.

Between 1870 and 1873 Campos fought against Ricardo López Jordán, the rebellious caudillo of Entre Ríos. In 1875 he was named inspector general of arms, and in 1892 he was appointed chief of staff of the army and then minister of war and navy until 1896. In March 1896 he mobilized the national guard for a possible international conflict, and in 1898 he again became minister of war. At this time the Army War College was established under his supervision. He was promoted to lieutenant general in 1899 and retired in January 1906.

BIBLIOGRAPHY

Ejército argentino: Cronología militar argentina, 1806–1980 (1982).

Felix Best, *Historia de las guerras argentinas,* 2 vols. (1983).

Additional Bibliography

Morales Gorleri, Claudio. *Luis María Campos: El General Petit.* Buenos Aires: Edivérn, 2005.

ROBERT SCHEINA

CAMPOS, MANUEL JORGE (1847–1908).

Manuel Jorge Campos (*b.* 22 April 1847; *d.* 15 December 1908), Argentine general who led troops in support of the Radical Party rebellion against President Miguel Juárez Celman in July 1890. Born in Buenos Aires, Campos was a career military officer who saw service in the War of the Triple Alliance, fought to support the national government against regional caudillos, and served with General Julio Roca in campaigns to conquer the Indians of Argentina's southern plains.

In 1890 the leader of the Radical Party, Leandro Alem, sought assistance from expresident Bartolomé Mitre and General Campos in a revolt against the Conservative president. Campos led his troops in a desultory fashion while Mitre negotiated the resignation of the president and the assumption of Vice President Carlos Pellegrini, a compromise that angered Alem. In 1892 Campos became the chief of police in the federal capital, and he later served as a senator, then a national deputy, in Congress.

See also **Argentina, Political Parties: Radical Party (UCR).**

BIBLIOGRAPHY

David Rock, *Argentina, 1516–1987: From Spanish Colonization to Alfonsín* (1987), provides a good description of the revolt of 1890 within the framework of the development of middle-class politics. For more on Campos's participation in the revolt, see Douglas W. Richmond, *Carlos Pellegrini and the Crisis of the Argentine Elites, 1880–1916* (1989), esp. pp. 42–44.

JAMES A. BAER

CAMPOS, ROBERTO (DE OLIVEIRA)

(1917–2001). Roberto (de Oliveira) Campos (*b.* 17 April 1917; *d.* 9 October 2001), Brazilian minister of planning and economic coordination (1964–1967). Diplomat, economist, professor, public official, and legislator, Campos has been a central participant in Brazilian economic affairs since joining the foreign service in 1939. He is known for his neoliberal (conservative) economic positions, including less state intervention and fewer restrictions on foreign capital investment. He attended many of the international economic conferences held in the 1940s, including the Bretton Woods Conference. As a government economic adviser in the 1950s, Campos helped found the National Economic Development Bank (Banco Nacional de Desenvolvimento Econômico—BNDE) to finance infrastructure and served as its director-superintendent (1955–1958) and president (1958–1959). He has held many posts in government, acting as ambassador to the United States (1961–1963) and to London (1975–1982), federal senator (1983–1991), and federal deputy (1991–2001).

As minister of planning and economic coordination (1964–1967), Campos was the principal architect of the Economic Action Plan of the Government (Plano de Ação Econômica do Governo—PAEG), which included budget-balancing and restrictions on money-supply growth to fight inflation and institutional reforms to provide the foundation for further economic expansion. Among the reforms enacted were indexed government bonds, called Readjustable Obligations of the National Treasury (Obrigações Reajustáveis do Tesouro Nacional—ORTN), and a general indexation system, termed *correção monetária* (monetary correction); a noninflationary and regressive wage policy; a weakening of job security; a housing finance system; limited, pro-production land reform; and a central bank. PAEG brought down inflation, but at the cost of an unpopular recession. The reforms established the basic institutional framework for subsequent Brazilian economic life and provided the foundations for the subsequent high-growth period called the Economic Miracle (1968–1974).

He also served as the senator for Mato Grosso (1983–1991) and federal deputy of Rio de Janeiro during two legislatures (1991–1999). In addition, in 1998 he ran for the Federal Senate losing by only a 5 percent margin. His autobiography *A lanterna na popa* (2001) recounts the economic history of Brazil as well as the various interactions and acquaintances which helped form Campos throughout his life.

See also **Delfim Neto, Antônio; Economic Development; Furtado, Celso; Simonsen, Mário Henrique.**

BIBLIOGRAPHY

Israel Beloch and Alzira Alves De Abreu, eds., *Dicionário histórico-biográfico brasileiro, 1930–1983*, vol. 1 (1984).

Leôncio Martins Rodrigues, *Quem é quem na constituinte: Uma análise sócio-política dos partidos e deputados* (1987).

Werner Baer, *The Brazilian Economy: Growth and Development*, 3d ed. (1989).

Additional Bibliography

Perez, Reginaldo Teixeira. *Pensamento político de Roberto Campos*. Editora FGV, 1999.

RUSSELL E. SMITH

CAMPOS CERVERA, HÉRIB

(1905–1953). Hérib Campos Cervera (*b.* 1905; *d.* 28 August 1953), Paraguayan poet. Widely considered to be Paraguay's finest poet of the post–Chaco War (post-1935) generation, Campos Cervera has left an indelible mark on the literature of his country. Descended from a well-known family of artists and writers, he began his life's work in poetry while teaching engineering at the Colegio Nacional and at the Escuela Normal de Profesores. Initially, his poems appeared only in student newspapers, but he soon gained a literary following in intellectual circles in Asunción.

Campos Cervera's earliest works were heavily influenced by the modernism of Rubén Darío and other turn-of-the-century writers. After a time, however, he became attracted to the *vanguardista* school and soon became its principal exponent in Paraguay. During the 1930s Campos Cervera was forced into exile because of his political associations. This stay outside of the country was actually helpful in developing his talent: in Buenos Aires, he discovered the writings of Federico García Lorca (who became his personal friend), and he helped found the literary group *Vy'araity*, which counted among its members his aunt Josefina Plá, the novelist Augusto Roa Bastos, and such figures as Hugo Rodríguez Alcalá and Oscar Ferreiro.

Campos Cervera's finest work can be found in his poetic compilation *Ceniza redimida*. He also was among the first to popularize poetry in the Guaraní language. He died in Buenos Aires.

See also **Literature: Spanish America.**

BIBLIOGRAPHY

Raúl Amaral, *Escritos paraguayos* (1984), pp. 217–227.

Carlos Zubizarreta, *Cien vidas paraguayas,* 2d ed. (1985), pp. 322–325.

MARTA FERNÁNDEZ WHIGHAM

CAMPOS-PARSI, HÉCTOR (1922–1998).

Héctor Campos-Parsi (*b.* 10 October 1922; *d.* 30 January 1998), Puerto Rican composer, music critic, teacher, and concert manager. Campos-Parsi completed his early education in Ponce and then went on to study biology and psychology at the University of Puerto Rico. In 1945 he entered the school of medicine at the National University of Mexico, but ill health forced him to abandon this pursuit. He received a fellowship to the New England Conservatory from 1947 to 1950 and, while in New England, also studied with Aaron Copland who arranged for him to work in Paris under Nadia Boulanger from 1950 to 1953. He was named director of the music division of the Institute of Puerto Rican Culture in 1958 and in 1970 to the Academy of Arts and Sciences. A prolific composer in various styles, he is best known for his *Sonatina para piano y violín* for which he won the Maurice Ravel Prize in 1953, *Tres fantasías para piano* (1950), and *Juan Bobo y las fiestas* (1957). Copland's influence is most evident in Campos-Parsi's folkloric works such as *Yerba bruja* (1962) and *Arawak* (1970). In addition, his work was featured on the album *Sonetos Sagrados* (1992) which commemorated the 500th anniversary of Columbus's voyage and features sonnets based on the music of Spain in the seventeenth and eighteenth centuries.

See also **Music: Art Music.**

BIBLIOGRAPHY

General overviews of his life and work can be found in Fernando Callejo y Ferrer, *Música y músicos puertorriqueños* (1971) and Fernando H. Caso, *Héctor Campos-Parsi en la historia de la música puertorriqueña del siglo XX* (1980).

Additional Bibliography

Montalvo, José A. *Héctor Campos Parsi His Life and Music: A Biographical Study with an Analysis of Four Selected Works.* New York: New York School of Education, Health, Nursing and Arts Professions, 1992.

JACQUELYN BRIGGS KENT

CAMPOS SALES, MANUEL FERRAZ DE (1841–1913).

Manuel Ferraz de Campos Sales (*b.* 13 February 1841; *d.* 28 June 1913), president of Brazil (1898–1902). Born in Campinas, São Paulo, Campos Sales studied and practiced law before being elected a provincial deputy by the Liberal Party in 1867. He became an organizing member of the Republican Party of São Paulo in 1871, and was elected to the provincial chamber in 1881 and the national legislature in 1885 as a Republican and doctrinaire federalist. He was voluble, principled, and politically astute.

With the establishment of the Republic, Campos Sales served as minister of justice in General Manoel Deodoro da Fonseca's governments and built the administrative and judicial basis of the new republic. Weathering the political conflicts of the 1890s, he was elected president in 1898. His administration is best known for the reconstruction of the nation's finances and the creation of the political process that characterized the Republic until 1930.

In the economic crisis characterized by rampant inflation and speculation, known as the *Encilhamento,* Campos Sales made financial reconstruction the priority of the administration. Bolstered by the "funding loan" he negotiated with the Rothschilds, the government carried out deflationary currency policies, cut spending, abandoned public works, increased taxes and tariffs, and emphasized agriculture over industry. Notwithstanding considerable unpopularity for his policies, by 1902 Campos Sales had rehabilitated the national finances and international credit.

Elected in an atmosphere of regional revolts and fractious party politics, Campos Sales proclaimed himself above partisan politics. He articulated the Política dos Governadores, in which incumbent state governments supplied loyal federal congressional delegations in exchange for nonintervention in state affairs. Relying heavily on the larger states' economic and demographic strengths, the political system revolved around São Paulo and Minas Gerais. This reciprocity created a hierarchy of interlocking interests and loyalties down to the *coroneis,* the local bosses who delivered the votes for patronage and financial favors.

Sales died in Santos, São Paulo.

See also **Coronel, Coronelismo.**

BIBLIOGRAPHY

Manuel Ferraz De Campos Sales, *Da propaganda a presidencia* (1908; repr. 1983).

Celio Debes, *Campos Sales: Perfil de um estadista,* 2 vols. (1978).

Additional Bibliography

Camargo de Villegas, María Zelia de. *El gobierno de Manuel Ferraz de Campos Salles, el restaurador de las finanzas, 1898-1902.* Caracas: Instituto de Altos Estudios de América Latina, 1993.

WALTER BREM

CANALES, NEMESIO ROSARIO
(1878–1923). Nemesio Rosario Canales (*b.* 18 December 1878; *d.* 14 September 1923), Puerto Rican writer and statesman. Nemesio R. Canales interrupted his studies of medicine in Saragossa, Spain, in 1898, when Puerto Rico came under United States sovereignty. He left the island two years later to study at the Baltimore School of Law. After graduating in 1903, he returned to Puerto Rico to practice law and began a career in politics. He wrote articles for the *Revista de las Antillas* and *La Semana,* and a column for the Ponce newspaper *El Día;* he also cofounded *Juan Bobo,* a weekly, and edited *Cuasimodo,* an inter-American journal on culture. Concerned with politics and the economy as well as social, labor, and cultural issues, he served in the Puerto Rican Congress and in the Department of Justice. His most famous work is a collection of humorously ironic articles entitled *Paliques* (Chit-chat, 1913). Canales also published a novel, *Mi voluntad se ha muerto* (My will has died), in 1921, and a drama, *El héroe galopante* (The galloping hero), in 1923, the year of his death in New York.

See also **Journalism.**

BIBLIOGRAPHY

José Gelpí, ed., *Nuevos Paliques y otras páginas de Nemesio R. Canales* (1965).

María Teresa Babín, *Genio y figura de Nemesio R. Canales* (1978).

ESTELLE IRIZARRY

CANANEA.
Cananea, a copper mining center in the northwestern state of Sonora that became for the Mexican Revolution a symbol of North American control over the economy, of the Porfirio Díaz regime's compliance in it, and of the rise of the labor movement to correct abuses and resist that alliance.

Though mines in the locality had been worked since the 1760s by a series of owners, they had remained small operations due to limited capital and Apache raiding (1820s–1860s). The North American adventurer-entrepreneur William Greene—through the application of large-scale corporate finance and organization beginning in 1896—transformed Cananea into one of the leading mining centers in Mexico. In addition to the mining of copper, Greene formed land, cattle, lumber, and railroad companies which, along with government concessions to supply basic services, enabled him to attain hegemony over the area's economy. Close ties with the political circle of Luis Torres that controlled the state government ensured cooperative local authorities.

Syndicalist ideas among workers from the United States and a cell of followers of the opposition Mexican Liberal Party helped foster unionist sentiment among the nearly 5,400 Mexican workers. The strike of 1–3 June 1906 involved a large proportion of the latter. Alarmed North American employees initiated the subsequent widespread violence, which brought in federal troops and "volunteers" from Arizona, whose presence sparked a formal national inquiry. Strike leaders Manuel M. Dieguez and Esteban Baca Calderón figured prominently in the Revolution.

See also **Torres, Luis Emeterio.**

BIBLIOGRAPHY

Esteban Baca Calderón, *Juicio sobre la guerra del Yaqui y génesis de la huelga de Cananea* (1956).

David M. Pletcher, *Rails, Mines, and Progress: Seven American Promoters in Mexico, 1867–1911* (1958).

Manuel J. Aguirre, *Cananea: Las garras del imperialismo en las entrañas de México* (1958).

Ramón Eduardo Ruiz, *The People of Sonora and Yankee Capitalists* (1988).

Additional Bibliography

Gonzalez, Michael J. "U.S. Copper Companies, the Mine Workers' Movement, and the Mexican Revolution, 1910–1920." *The Hispanic American Historical Review* 76, no. 3 (August 1996): 503–534.

STUART F. VOSS

BIBLIOGRAPHY

The standard reference on the Andean Indians is still Julian H. Steward, ed., *Handbook of South American Indians*, vol. 2, *The Andean Civilizations* (1946). Information can also be found in Garcilaso De La Vega, *Royal Commentaries of the Incas and General History of Peru*, translated by Harold V. Livermore (1966).

Burgos Guevara, Hugo. *La identidad del pueblo cañari: Deconstrucción de una nación étnica*. Quito: Abya-Yala, 2003.

RONN F. PINEO

CAÑARI.

Cañari (also Kanari), Indians of the southern Ecuadorian Andean provinces of Canar and Azuay. In the pre-Inca period the Cañari were one of the major groups of advanced sedentary peoples in Ecuador. The Cañari were especially noted for their fine gold working. During the mid-1400s Inca conquest, the Cañari organized a powerful resistance, but they were defeated by the 1470s. The Inca forceably relocated many Cañari to other parts of the empire. Some Cañari served in the elite Inca imperial guard. Inca emperor Tupac Yupanqui (r. c. 1471–1493) married a Cañari princess who bore him a child, Huayna Capac (r. c. 1493–1527). The Inca valued the region, creating a new imperial center at Tomebamba. Inca Quechua language replaced Cañari and closely related Puruha. The Cañari sided with Huascar (r. c. 1527–1532) in the war against his half-brother Atahualpa (r. c. 1532–1533). Victorious Atahualpa cruelly punished the Cañari. The Cañari assisted the conquering Spaniard Sebastián de Belalcázar, beginning in 1534.

As of 2003, the Consejo de Desarrollo de las Nacionalidades y Pueblos de Ecuador (CONDEPE) estimates a Cañari population of 150,000 residing in 387 communities. Most Cañari speak both Kichwa (Quechua) and Castilian, and dedicate themselves to subsistence farming and small-scale animal husbandry. A recent phenomenon is international migration, mostly to the United States and Spain. CONDEPE estimates that at least one person in each family has migrated and that 60 percent of Cañari families are dependent on money sent home from abroad.

See also **Art: Pre-Columbian Art of South America; Indigenous Peoples.**

CANARY ISLANDS.

The Canary Islands are a group of ten small islands (Tenerife, La Palma, Gomera, Hierro, Grand Canary, Fuerteventura, Lanzarote, Alegranza, Graciosa, and Isla de Lobos) lying 50 miles (80 kilometers) west of the coast of Morocco that comprise two provinces of Spain. Known to the ancient world as the Fortunate Islands, they received their later name from Pliny the Elder in reference to the large dogs (*canes*) found there by King Juba II of Mauretania when he explored the islands around 40 BCE. Along with the dogs, Juba found the islands inhabited by Guanches, a people of obscure origin, who successfully defended their domain against the king.

The details of first contact with Europe are contradictory. Europeans first visited the Canaries some time between 1330 and 1334, when a French or Iberian ship landed on the islands. This was followed fourteen years later by an expedition led by Luis de la Cerda, a grandson of Alfonso X of Castile, with the objective of converting the Guanches under a papal grant. This and similar attempts by the Spanish failed, both in their religious intent and in establishing a European colony there. Finally in 1402 two Frenchmen, Jean de Bethencourt and Gadifer de la Salle, successfully conquered most of the Canaries. Henry III of Castile gave Bethencourt money and the title of king of the islands in return for recognition of Castile's legal claim to possession. Spain began to consolidate its conquests when Alonso de Lugo signed a treaty with the local leader Tanasú in 1493. When some local residents resisted, de Lugo laid siege to the island, conquering it and freeing him up to invade Gran Canary that same year. By 1496 the islands were completely under the Spanish flag. The British often challenged the Spanish for possession of the Canaries. It was in the town of Santa Cruz on Tenerife during one of these forays that Lord Nelson lost his arm in 1797.

A sugar industry on the Canary Islands had long thrived until the seventeenth and eighteenth centuries when competition from the West Indies and Brazil proved overwhelming. The Canaries did, however, become a prime producer of cochineal dye, striking a blow at the dye industry of Central America. In turn the Canary dye industry was destroyed by the introduction of chemical dyes in the 1870s. Since the voyage of Columbus, the islands have served as a stopping point for ships to replenish their supplies before continuing on to the Americas. In the early twenty-first century, some Canarians identify more with Latin America than Spain, listening to Andean and Mariachi music.

See also **Cochineal; Colonialism; Sugar Industry.**

BIBLIOGRAPHY

Mercer, John. *Canary Islands: Fuerteventura.* Harrisburg, PA: Stackpole Books, 1973.

Fernández-Armesto, Felipe. *The Canary Islands after the Conquest: The Making of a Colonial Society in the Early Sixteenth Century.* New York: Oxford University Press, 1982.

White, Colin. *1797: Nelson's Year of Destiny: Cape St. Vincent and Santa Cruz de Tenerife.* Stroud, U.K.: Sutton Publishing, 1998.

SHEILA L. HOOKER

CAÑAS, JOSÉ MARÍA (1809–1860).

José María Cañas (*b.* 1809; *d.* 30 September 1860), commander of the Central American army in the National War against William Walker in Nicaragua. Born in El Salvador, Cañas was an officer in Francisco Morazán's army and later rose to prominence in Costa Rica as an ally of his brother-in-law, President Juan Rafael Mora Porrás. After General Cañas distinguished himself at the battle of Rivas (11 April 1856), Mora named him inspector general of the Central American allied army in January 1857 and later commander in chief of the Central American forces. When Mora was ousted from the presidency of Costa Rica in 1859, Gerardo Barrios put Cañas in command of the Salvadoran army. In 1860, after supporting Mora's unsuccessful attempt to return to power in Costa

Rica, Cañas and Mora were executed at Puntarenas. Cañas also represented Costa Rica in the intrigues relating to U.S. and British efforts to gain canal rights through Guanacaste in the border area between Nicaragua and Costa Rica during Mora's administration.

See also **National War.**

BIBLIOGRAPHY

Rafael Obregón, *Costa Rica y la guerra contra los filibusteros* (1991), has a detailed biographical sketch of Cañas on pages 291–293. Also useful are Alejandro Bolaños-geyer, *William Walker, the Gray-Eyed Man of Destiny*, vol. 4 (1990), and A. Paul Woodbridge, *Los contratos Webster-Mora y las implicaciones sobre Costa Rica y Nicaragua* (1967).

RALPH LEE WOODWARD JR.

CAÑAS, JOSÉ SIMEÓN (1767–1838).

José Simeón Cañas (*b.* 18 February 1767; *d.* 4 March 1838), Salvadoran intellectual and politician. Born in Santa Lucía Zacatecoluca, El Salvador, to a wealthy family, Cañas was educated as a priest in Guatemala, where he received his doctorate in theology. He became rector of the University of San Carlos in 1802. He joined with José Matías Delgado and Manuel José Arce in supporting Central American independence in 1821. As a member of the Central American Congress, on 31 December 1823 Cañas made the motion to abolish slavery in Central America, enacted the following year. He subsequently supported the cause of Central American unity. He died, and is buried, in San Vicente, El Salvador.

See also **Central America; Slavery: Abolition.**

BIBLIOGRAPHY

Miguel Ángel Espino, *La vida de José Simeón Cañas, padre de los esclavos* (1955), originally published in Adolfo Pérez Menéndez and José Luis Andreu, eds., *Colección patria grande. Época de la independencia. Biografías populares de los hombres símbolos de Centro América* (1938).

Ramón López Jiménez, *José Simeón Cañas: Su obra, su verdadera personalidad y su destino* (1970).

Manuel Vida, *Nociones de historia de Centro América (especial para El Salvador)*, 5th ed. (1957), pp. 143–147.

Ramón López Jiménez and Rafael Díaz, *Biografía de José Simeón Cañas* (1968).

Additional Bibliography

Alvarado, Hermógenes. *José Simeón Cañas: Y la abolición de la esclavitud en Centro América.* El Salvador: Delgado, 2000.

RALPH LEE WOODWARD JR.

CANCHA RAYADA, BATTLE OF.

Battle of Cancha Rayada, a clash between the patriot army and Royalist forces on 19 March 1818, during Chile's war for independence. The Argentine general José de San Martín had been pursuing the Spanish forces near Talca when he decided to stop for the night. Fearing an assault, San Martín was repositioning his troops when the Royalists suddenly attacked under cover of darkness. Surprised, some of the patriot units panicked. While San Martín's men were mauled, the Chileans had to absorb heavier losses, and their commander, Bernardo O'Higgins, who had his horse shot out from under him, suffered an arm wound. Given the high casualty rate, rumors spread that both O'Higgins and San Martín had perished. These tales proved false: the independence army, though badly battered, regrouped. Fortunately for the patriot cause, although O'Higgins's units had suffered heavy losses, the elements under the command of the other patriot officer, Juan Gregorio de Las Heras, emerged unscathed and hence able to actively pursue the war.

See also **O'Higgins, Bernardo; San Martín, José Francisco de.**

BIBLIOGRAPHY

Stephen Clissold, *Bernardo O'Higgins and the Independence of Chile* (1968), pp. 62, 159–169, 171.

Simon Collier, *Ideas and Politics of Chilean Independence, 1808–1833* (1968), p. 231.

Additional Bibliography

Archer, Christon I., ed. *The Wars of Independence in Spanish America.* Wilmington, DE: Scholarly Resources, 2000.

Jocelyn-Holt Letelier, Alfredo. *La independencia de Chile: Tradición, modernización y mito.* Santiago: Planeta/Ariel, 1992.

Ibáñez Vergara, Jorge. *O'Higgins, el Libertador.* Santiago: Instituto O'Higginiano de Chile, 2001.

WILLIAM F. SATER

CANCIÓN RANCHERA.

Canción Ranchera, a Mexican variation of the Spanish *canción* (song) brought to America during the sixteenth to nineteenth centuries and popularized in the 1940s and 1950s by such Mexican matinee idols as Jorge Negrete and Pedro Infante. It is commonly sung by mariachi groups, the *conjunto*, the *dueto*, the *trío*, and the country singer. It is a genre associated with the rural, agricultural worker—*ranchera* means "from the ranches," or "from the countryside." A rural working-class dialect of Spanish commonly characterizes the lyrics. Frequent themes include unrequited love, abandonment by a lover, and unfaithful women. The brokenhearted lover, mostly male but not always, narrates a tale of woe regarding a love affair gone awry and the subsequent drinking sprees the spurned lover undertakes to ease the pain. The genre has also become popular in the United States. Well-known *canción ranchera* composers include Tomás Méndez, José Alfredo Jiménez, and Cuco Sánchez.

See also **Bolero; Infante, Pedro; Music: Popular Music and Dance; Negrete, Jorge.**

BIBLIOGRAPHY

Vicente T. Mendoza, *La canción mexicana: Ensayo de clasificación y antropología* (1982).

María Herrera-Sobek, *Northward Bound: The Mexican Immigrant Experience in Ballad and Song* (1993).

Additional Bibliography

Broyles-González, Yolanda. *Lydia Mendoza's Life in Music: Norteño Tejano Legacies = La historia de Lydia Mendoza.* New York: Oxford University Press, 2001.

Peña, Manuel H. *Música Tejana: The Cultural Economy of Artistic Transformation.* College Station: Texas A & M University Press, 1999.

Pedelty, Mark. *Musical Ritual in Mexico City: From the Aztec to NAFTA.* Austin: University of Texas Press, 2004.

MARÍA HERRERA-SOBEK

CANDAMO, MANUEL (1842?–1904).

Manuel Candamo Iriate (ca. 1842–7 May 1904) was the son of one of the wealthiest merchants of mid-nineteenth-century Peru, whose fortune rested on shipping (especially the trade in indentured Asians), guano, and railroad construction. The family was typical of that group of merchants and entrepreneurs who replaced the aristocracy as the ruling elite of the country. Because political parties gave power to the masses, the aristocracy had banned them as tasteless and dangerous. But Candamo was active in the Civilista Party and in 1902 he gained public attention as an activist president of the Lima Chamber of Commerce. He became a candidate for president of Peru in 1903 as a moderate conciliator between two intransigent factions of the Democratic and Civilista parties.

Candamo's political views were established in his *Política peruana: Discurso-programa del nuevo presidente de Perú* (1903), an important document from the period. The Civilista Party disappeared briefly when leading members joined former Democrats in the Liberal Party. This action prompted another faction of Civilistas to form a surprise alliance with the Constitutionalist Party, the party of the military. Candamo remained the single Civilista trusted by and popular with all factions, although he was censured by Manuel González Prada. Inaugurated as president in November 1903 after he won the election, he fell ill and died the following May. Thereafter, mutual distrust sowed discord once again among party factions.

See also **Cáceres, Andrés Avelino; González Prada, Manuel; Peru, Political Parties: Civilista Party; Piérola, Nicolás de.**

BIBLIOGRAPHY

Basadre, Jorge. *Historia de la República del Perú, 1822–1933*, 7th edition. Lima: Editorial Universitaria, 1983.

Candamo, Manuel. *Política peruana: Discurso-programa del nuevo presidente de Perú.* Asunción: Talleres Nacionales de H. Kraus, 1903.

González Prada, Manuel. "Los partidos y la Unión Nacional." In *Horas de Lucha*, pp. 201–220. Caracas: Biblioteca Ayacucho 1976.

González Prada, Manuel. "Manuel Candamo." In *Textos inéditos de Manuel González Prada*, pp. 71–75. Lima: Biblioteca Nacional, 2001.

Kristal, Efraín. *The Andes Viewed from the City: Literary and Political Discourse on the Indian in Peru, 1848–1930.* New York: Peter Lang, 1987.

Mc Evoy, Carmen. *La utopía republicana: Ideales y realidades en la formación de la cultura política peruana, 1871–1919.* Lima: Pontificia Universidad Católica del Perú, Fondo Editorial, 1997.

Pike, Fredrick B. *The Modern History of Peru.* New York: Praeger, 1967. See especially pp. 190–191.

Werlich, David P. *Peru: A Short History.* Carbondale: Southern Illinois University Press, 1978. See pp. 131–132.

VINCENT PELOSO

CANDANEDO, CÉSAR (1906–1993).

César Candanedo (*b.* 12 May 1906; *d.* 29 March 1993), Panamanian writer. Candanedo was born in David, Panama. Self-taught, he was awarded a scholarship by the World Health Organization to pursue studies in the School of Public Health of the University of Chile. After completing his studies, he worked as a public health inspector for the Department of Public Health in Panama. This position gave him the opportunity to travel and to become familiar with the diverse regions of the country and, in particular, to become aware of the hopelessness that permeates every aspect of the daily existence of Panama's rural population.

In his first book, *Los clandestinos* (1957; The Clandestine Ones), he depicted the impact of the United Fruit Company and the Canal Zone on the living conditions of Panama's rural population. His later works, *La otra frontera* (1967; The Other Frontier), *El cerquero y otros relatos* (1967; The Encloser and Other Stories), *Memorias de un caminante* (1970; Memories of a Traveler), *Palo duro* (1973; Hard Truncheon), and *El perseguido* (1991; The Fugitive) reaffirmed his reputation as both a writer of vigorous works of social protest and a writer of regional literature. *El perseguido* received first prize in the 1986 Ricardo Mirõ competition.

See also **Literature: Spanish America.**

BIBLIOGRAPHY

Elsie Alvarado De Ricrod, "Reseña de *Los clandestinos* de César Candanedo," in *El Panamá América* (1958).

Carlos Guillermo Wilson, *Aspectos de la prosa narrativa panameña contemporánea* (Ph.D. thesis, 1987), pp. 108–110.

David Foster, comp., *Handbook of Latin American Literature*, 2d ed. (1992), pp. 463–464.

Additional Bibliography

Pilolli, Mariapia. *Sociología de la literature panameña.* Panamá: Universidad de Panamá Centro de Investigaciones, 1984.

ELBA D. BIRMINGHAM-POKORNY

CÂNDIDO DE MELLO E SOUZA, ANTÔNIO

(1918–). Antônio Cândido de Mello e Souza, an outstanding twentieth-century scholar of Brazilian literature, was born in Rio de Janeiro on July 24, 1918. He spent his childhood and early youth in Poços de Caldas in southern Minas Gerais, the homeland of his family. Son of a prestigious physician, he had access to an extensive home library from childhood. He originally planned to study at the traditional law school in São Paulo, but eventually gave up the idea and instead entered the new school of philosophy, sciences, and letters (Faculdade de Filosofia, Ciências, e Letras) at the University of São Paulo to study social sciences. In the 1940s during World War II, he, along with friends, founded the magazine *Clima*, which became an essential arts and literature reference for his generation. Professor Gilda de Mello e Souza (1919–2005), who was to become his wife, also collaborated on the magazine.

Antônio Cândido worked in the field of sociology up to 1958, when he joined the state faculty at the University of São Paulo at Assis as a Brazilian literature professor. In 1961 he joined the Faculdade de Filosofia, Ciências, e Letras as a professor on literary theory and comparative studies, where he remained until his retirement in 1978. After retirement he continued publishing books on literature and other major cultural fields. He was also active in left-wing politics, being one of the founders of the late Brazilian Socialist Party (dramatically dissolved during the military dictatorship in 1964) and of the present Worker's Party.

He wrote on a variety of subjects during the course of his career, but his major work was the huge *Formação da literatura brasileira: Momentos decisivos*, published in 1959. The two-volume book focused on the process of creating an autonomous Brazilian literature during the eighteenth century, through the pale but consistent Brazilian Enlightenment and the vigorous, although late (compared with Europe), Brazilian romantic movement, led by generations of writers who were strongly conscious of having a mission to fulfill for the new nation. In the *Formação* Cândido also established some fundamental concepts of Brazilian and later Latin American criticism, such as the idea of a *sistema literário* (literary system) based on the triangle of writers-books-public and this triad's continuity in time. His work formed the basis for a consistent tradition that helped to define a Brazilian national literature.

In the 1970s and early 1980s Cândido worked with Uruguayan professor Ángel Rama (1926–1983) in an effort to define a conceptual framework to encompass Latin American literature as a whole, including Brazil. As a scholar and a professor Cândido contributed to the development of at least three generations in the Brazilian academic world of literature.

Other major works by Antônio Cândido include *Ficção e confissão* (1956; on Graciliano Ramos); *Os parceiros do Rio Bonito* (1964; on the cultural life of São Paulo rural areas); *Tese e antítese* (1964 and 1971); *Literatura e sociedade* (1965); *Vários escritos* (1970); *Tese e antítese* (1971); *A educação pela noite e outros ensaios* (1987); and *O discurso e a cidade* (1993).

See also **Literature: Spanish America.**

BIBLIOGRAPHY

Aguiar, Flávio, ed. *Antonio Candido: Pensamento e militância*. São Paulo: Fundação Perseu Abramo/Humanitas, 1999.

D'Incao, Maria Angela, and Eloísa Faria Scarabôtolo, eds. *Dentro do texto, dentro da vida*. São Paulo: Companhia das letras, 1992.

Lafer, Celso, ed. *Esboço de Figura: Homenagem a Antonio Candido*. São Paulo: Duas Cidades, 1979.

FLAVIO AGUIAR

CANDIOTI, FRANCISCO ANTONIO

(1743–1815). Francisco Antonio Candioti (*b.* 1743; *d.* 25 August 1815), Argentine landowner and supporter of the independence movement. With large landholdings in the present-day provinces of Santa Fe and Entre Ríos, Candioti, "prince of the gauchos," generously provided arms and provisions for his friend Manuel Belgrano at the outbreak of the independence movement in 1810. Responding to widespread provincial sentiment against the centralist ambitions of *porteño* (Buenos Aires) leaders, he sought out the support of José Gervasio Artigas, whose federalist sympathies he largely shared. In 1815 Artigas loyalists led by José Eusebio Hereñú dislodged the *porteño* army under José Miguel Díaz Vélez, dissolved the provincial junta, and constituted the newly autonomous province of Santa Fe, with Candioti as its first governor. Aged and sickly, however, Candioti could contribute little to the province's defense against destructive Indian raids after the rapid departure of federalist forces. He died shortly after *porteño* troops reoccupied the city and put a temporary end to the newly won autonomy.

See also **Gaucho.**

BIBLIOGRAPHY

Jorge Newton, *El príncipe de los gauchos* (1941).

WILLIAM H. KATRA

CANDOMBLÉ. Candomblé, an Afro-Brazilian religion of Yoruba, Fon, and Bantu origin developed primarily in the Northeast by African slaves from Nigeria and their descendants. Candomblé may have been introduced as early as the eighteenth century, but it became firmly entrenched in Afro-Brazilian culture in the early nineteenth century, when enslaved members of the Oyo and Dahomey empires flowed into Brazil. The Candomblé community of Engenho Velho in Bahia, perhaps the oldest in Brazil, was founded around 1830. Oral tradition also dates the Casa das Minas of Maranhão to the mid-nineteenth century. "Candomblé" is the term specifically given to the religious traditions developed by Africans from the Gulf of Guinea, but it is often broadly applied to any Afro-Brazilian religion incorporating divination and possession ritual. In the Americas, it is most closely related to Santería, developed in Cuba by slaves from the same regions of West Africa.

Candomblé is based on the principles of harmony and balance between human beings and the forces of nature. All living beings and natural phenomena are considered creations of one supreme god, called Olodumare, and each is made of *axe*, divine energy. Different complexes of *axe* make up individual people, as well as phenomena such as rainbows, thunder, and wind. *Axe* may also take the specialized form of Orixás, deities who personify specific aspects of Olodumare.

In Brazil, *orixás* are the principal intermediaries between humans and God; ancestor worship was not equally cultivated, although it is an integral part of the religion's African tradition. Through divination and possession rituals, priests communicate with *orixás* to determine the causes of specific problems, and to find out the steps necessary to correct them. Devotees of Candomblé undergo extensive initiation, during which time they learn the various means of communicating with spiritual forces in order to maintain a harmonious balance of sacred energies.

In the Oyo and Dahomey empires each town worshipped a patron *orixá*. Some, like Xangô, the royal *orixá* of the Oyo kings, became popular throughout the entire empire. During the slave trade African towns such as Kêtu and Abeokuta lost large numbers of inhabitants to Brazil. These people brought with them the cults of their *orixá*, and eventually Afro-Brazilians incorporated the worship of all the major *orixás* in each community of devotees. Candomblé represents an adaptation of many traditions to the conditions of the New World. Because African slaves were forcibly baptized and converted to Catholicism, they were unable to practice Candomblé openly. They continued to secretly worship African deities by outwardly equating them with Catholic saints in a process of Syncretism.

In Brazil, Candomblé has an important social aspect. Each community is divided into houses (*iles*), which create new familial relationships among devotees. The senior initiate, traditionally a woman, is considered a spiritual mother (*mãe de santo*). As head of the household, she is responsible for the spiritual well-being of all the initiates, including the observance of obligations and annual celebrations for the *orixás,* as well as for the household's material needs. Seniority is based upon the number of years an individual has been initiated, regardless of chronological age. Respect for elders is rigidly observed, as are other values imparted through the social aspect of Candomblé. The distribution of responsibilities, hierarchies, and specific cultural and ritual traditions varies, based on the size and ethnic origins of the house. Many houses identify themselves with the names of African "nations," such as Kêtu, Gege, or Mina. These communities are also known as *terreiros* or *roças*, references to the land they occupy. In Brazil, portions of the *terreiro* are devoted to a specific *orixá*, where its sacred objects are kept.

Candomblé worship has been traditionally discouraged by supporters of the Catholic Church and other Christian sects. In the 1920s and 1930s police regularly raided *terreiros* in major cities such as Salvador and Recife, confiscating ritual objects and imprisoning worshippers. Candomblé began to gain broader acceptance in the 1930s, as international scholars convened in two Afro-Brazilian congresses. These academics pressed for the acceptance and appreciation of Candomblé as part of Brazil's African cultural heritage. Simultaneously, Candomblé principles were gaining wider acceptance through the related syncretic religions of Umbanda, and to a lesser extent, Macumba, Caboclo, and Quimbanda. In each of these religions, devotees consult deities or spirits for answers to their problems through divination or possession ritual. Some of these traditions, such as Candomblé Caboclo, originated during slavery through the intermingling of African and indigenous religious rituals.

Candomblé is now practiced openly, although it remains concentrated in its area of origin, the northeastern region. Although traditionalism is a hallmark of most *terreiros,* innovation can also be seen as Candomblé continues to evolve. Some Candomblé houses maintain ongoing relationships with their counterparts in West Africa and in other communities in the Caribbean and North America where Yoruba-based religion is practiced.

See also **African-Latin American Religions: Brazil.**

BIBLIOGRAPHY

Raymundo Nina Rodrigues, *O Animismo Fetichista dos Negros Bahianos* (1935).

Donald Pierson, *Negroes in Brazil: A Study of Race Contact at Bahia* (1942).

Edison Carneiro, *Candomblés da Bahia,* 3d ed. (1961).

Roger Bastide, *The African Religions of Brazil: Toward a Sociology of the Interpenetration of Civilizations,* translated by Helen Sebba (1978), and *O Candomblé da Bahia,* 2d ed. (1978).

Gary Edwards and John Mason, *Black Gods: Orisa Studies in the New World* (1985).

Manuel Querino, *Costumes africanos no Brasil,* 2d ed. (1988).

Additional Bibliography

Harding, Rachel E. *A Refuge in Thunder: Candomblé and Alternative Spaces of Blackness.* Bloomington: University of Indiana Press, 2000.

Johnson, Paul C. *Secrets, Gossip, and Gods: The Transformation of Brazilian Candomblé.* New York: Oxford University Press, 2002.

Landes, Ruth. *The City of Women.* Albuquerque, NM: University of New Mexico Press, 1994.

Matory, James Lorand. *Black Atlantic Religion: Tradition, Transnationalism, and Matriarchy in the Afro-Brazilian Candomblé.* Princeton, NJ: Princeton University Press, 2005.

Parés, Luis Nicolau. *A formação do candomblé: História e ritual da nação jeje na Bahia.* Campinas: Editora Unicamp, 2006.

KIM D. BUTLER

CANÉ, MIGUEL (1851–1905). The Argentine politician and writer Miguel Cané was born in Montevideo on 27 January 1851. His father, a relatively important writer and journalist, had been exiled to Uruguay because of his opposition to the Argentine dictator Juan Manuel de Rosas. When Rosas was defeated in the Battle of Caseros (1852) against the exiled sons of Argentina (a group that included Miguel Cané), the exiles were automatically recognized as Argentine citizens. Miguel settled in Buenos Aires, where he pursued studies that culminated in a law degree. Law was not his principal occupation, however; he divided his time between politics (including diplomacy) and literature. As a very young man, he joined the Autonomist Party and was elected provincial deputy and national deputy for the province of Buenos Aires. He devoted himself to diplomacy during the 1880s and part of the 1890s, and represented Argentina in Colombia, Venezuela, Germany, Austria, Spain, and France. After his return to Argentina he served briefly as mayor of Buenos Aires (1892–1893), minister of foreign relations, and finally as national senator. During his later years he was dean of the recently formed philosophy department (1901–1904) at the University of Buenos Aires, where he strongly promoted studies in the humanities.

As a member of the ruling party (National Autonomist Party) Cané maintained unorthodox opinions and always supported the leadership of his dear friend Carlos Pellegrini. As such, he was a liberal conservative concerned about the modernization of Argentina. His political and social ideas embodied the contradictions that were typical of his times. This was his opinion, for example, of the role he thought the Jockey Club should play: "The Jockey Club of Buenos Aires will not be, and cannot ever be, an imitation of its counterparts in Paris or Vienna, a closed and narrow circle, a caste-based clique, in which an accident of birth, and at times an accident of fortune, takes the place of the entire human condition." He added that it should be "a cross-section of society, vast and open, that includes and must include all educated and honorable men" (1897). His intention was clear: to create a republican elite, one that was open to social mobility but at the same time subject to a worldly routine of "aristocratic" roots.

Cané's most lasting contributions were in the field of literature. His output was huge and fragmentary; his best-known works include *En Viaje* (Traveling; 1882), *Prosa Ligera* (Light Prose; 1900), and a translation of Shakespeare's *Henry IV*. However, his highest achievement was undoubtedly the publication of *Juvenilia* (1884), a well-written and refreshing portrait of student life that remained a favorite of Argentine students.

See also **Argentina, Political Parties: National Autonomist Party (PAN); Jockey Club; Literature: Spanish America; Pellegrini, Carlos; Rosas, Juan Manuel de; Uruguay: Before 1900.**

BIBLIOGRAPHY

Hayes, Ricardo Saenz. *Miguel Cané y su Tiempo (1851–1905)*. Buenos Aires: G. Kraft, 1955.

Terán, Oscar. *Vida intelectual en el Buenos Aires fin-de-siglo (1880–1910)*. Buenos Aires: Fondo de Cultura Economica, 2000.

                                        EZEQUIEL GALLO

CANECA, FREI JOAQUÍM DO AMOR DIVINO (1779–1825).

Frei Joaquím do Amor Divino Caneca (*b.* 20 August 1779; *d.* 13 January 1825), Brazilian Carmelite friar, priest, journalist, and revolutionary. Born in Recife, Pernambuco, Caneca joined the Carmelite order in his native province and achieved prominence as a teacher of geometry and rhetoric. In 1817 he joined the Pernambucan republican revolt, for which he forfeited a nomination to be bishop of Maranhão and spent four years in prison in Salvador da Bahia. Freed after the 1821 liberal coup in Bahia, Frei Caneca returned to Pernambuco, where he became a member of the provincial junta. In 1822 he disavowed the regional republicanism of 1817 and advocated Pernambuco's adherence to the independent Brazilian monarchy proclaimed by Emperor Pedro I in Rio de Janeiro. He founded a newspaper, *Typhis Pernambucano,* to propagate his liberal-federalist-constitutionalist ideology.

Frei Caneca denounced the emperor's closing of the national Constitutional Convention of 1823 and led the fight in Pernambuco against the ratification of Pedro's centralist Constitution of 1824. After Pedro declared the constitution ratified, despite its rejection by the municipal councils of Recife and other northeastern cities, Frei Caneca declared it void in Pernambuco and called for the formation of an autonomous government for the Northeast. The result was the separatist Confederation of the Equator, which was crushed by imperial troops in 1824. Frei Caneca and fifteen other confederation leaders were condemned for insurrection; he died before a firing squad in Recife.

See also **Pernambuco.**

BIBLIOGRAPHY

Joaquím Do Amor Divino Caneca, *Ensaius políticos de Frei Caneca* (1976).

João Afredo De Souza Montenegro, *O liberalismo radical de Frei Caneca* (1978).

Additional Bibliography

Carvalho, Gilberto Vilar de. *Frei Caneca: Gesta da liberdade, 1779-1825* Rio de Janeiro: Mauad, 2004.

                                        NEILL MACAULAY

CAÑEDO, FRANCISCO (1839–1909).

Francisco Cañedo (*b.* 1839; *d.* 5 June 1909), governor of the state of Sinaloa. One of many migrants from neighboring Tepic, Cañedo began work as an errand boy and then clerk in large merchant houses, first in Mazatlán and then in Culiacán. Aided by marriage into the notable Batiz family, by the patronage of Culiacán's leading political family (the Vegas), and by his cultivation of close ties with Porfirio Díaz, Cañedo rose to preeminence in Sinaloan politics through the 1870s. Serving as governor (1877–1880, 1884–1888, 1892–1909), he assumed sole control of the state government thereafter until his death. He incorporated Mazatlán's notables into his political circle, ending the bitter and destructive rivalry between the state's two cities. Cañedo followed Porfirista policies faithfully. He consolidated control by eliminating all *municípios* (municipalities) but the district seats, which were firmly controlled by the prefects he appointed.

See also **Mexico: 1810–1910.**

BIBLIOGRAPHY

Eustaquio Buelna, *Apuntes para la historia de Sinaloa, 1821–1882* (1924; 2d ed., 1966).

Amado González Dávila, *Diccionario geográfico, histórico, y estadístico del Estado de Sinaloa* (1959), pp. 82–86.

Stuart F. Voss, "Towns and Enterprise in Northwestern Mexico: A History of Urban Elites in Sonora and Sinaloa, 1830–1910," (Ph.D. diss., Harvard University, 1972), pp. 126–154, 343–444.

Additional Bibliography

Figueroa Díaz, José María. *Los gobernadores de Sinaloa, 1831-1996.* Culiacán: Imp. Once Ríos Editores, 1996.

STUART F. VOSS

CAÑEDO, JUAN DE DIOS (1786–1850). Juan de Dios Cañedo (*b.* 18 January 1786; *d.* 28 March 1850), Mexican politician and diplomat. A scion of one of the great families of Jalisco, Cañedo studied law in Guadalajara. He was active in politics from 1811 until his death, distinguishing himself as a champion of legislative power and of federalism. Cañedo served in various elected positions: the *ayuntamiento* (city council) of Guadalajara (1811); the Cortes in Spain (1813; 1820–1821); the Mexican Constituent Congress (1823–1824); senator from Jalisco (1825–1828); deputy from Jalisco (1830–1831; 1849); and president of the *ayuntamiento* of Mexico City (1844). He also served as minister of foreign affairs from 1828 to 1829 and again from 1839 to 1840. He was Mexico's minister to South America (1831–1839); England (1846); and France (1847). A leader of the political opposition, Cañedo was brutally murdered in March 1850. Those responsible were never brought to justice.

See also **Jalisco.**

BIBLIOGRAPHY

Robert Joseph Ward Henry, "Juan de Dios Cañedo: Político y diplomático" (licentiate thesis, Universidad Iberoamericana, Mexico, 1968).

Jaime E. Rodríguez O., "Intellectuals and the Mexican Constitution of 1824," in *Los intelectuales y el poder en México,* edited by Roderic Ai Camp, Charles A. Hale, and Josefina Zoraida Vázquez (1991); "The Origins of the 1832 Revolt," in *Patterns of Contention in Mexican History,* edited by Jaime E. Rodríguez O. (1992); "The Constitution of 1824 and the Formation of the Mexican State," in *The Evolution of the Mexican Political System,* edited by Jaime E. Rodríguez O. (1993).

JAIME E. RODRÍGUEZ O.

CANEK, JACINTO (c. 1731–1761). Jacinto Canek (*b.* ca. 1731; *d.* 14 December 1761), a Maya who led an Indian uprising in Yucatán. Born Jacinto Uc de los Santos, this Indian from Campeche led a Maya cultural revitalization movement that ultimately challenged Spanish rule in colonial Yucatán. In 1761 in the village of Cisteíl he proclaimed himself to be King Canek (the legendary name of Maya kings), whose coming had been foretold in Maya prophecy. Thousands of Indians joined his movement, which combined traditional Maya and Christian elements and sought both cultural and political autonomy. The Spanish colonial authorities, using their military might, finally defeated Canek's forces in battle, thus crushing the movement. Canek was captured, tried, and executed by being torn limb-from-limb.

See also **Maya, The.**

BIBLIOGRAPHY

María Teresa Huerta and Patricia Palacios, eds., *Rebeliones indígenas de la época colonial* (1976).

Nancy M. Farriss, *Maya Society Under Colonial Rule: The Collective Enterprise of Survival* (1984).

Additional Bibliography

Farriss, Nancy M. *Maya Society Under Colonial Rule: The Collective Enterprise of Survival.* Princeton, NJ: Princeton University Press, 1992. Updated, corrected edition of 1984 work.

ROBERT W. PATCH

CANELONES. Canelones, second-largest department of Uruguay in terms of population (359,700 in 1985) and part of Greater Montevideo. Originally this department was the main supplier of vegetables and fruits for the capital city, but urban sprawl has engulfed most of the valuable agricultural land. Food-processing plants, factories for manufacturing durable goods, a paper mill, and granite/mica schist quarries are among the main supporters of the department's economy. Its major center is the town of Canelones (17,316 inhabitants in 1985), 27 miles north of Montevideo. Founded in 1774, it was for a short time the capital of Uruguay (in 1828). Canelones caters to the needs of the vegetable growers and small industries of the department.

See also **Uruguay, Geography.**

BIBLIOGRAPHY

Beatriz Torrendell, *Geografía histórica de Canelones* (Montevideo, 1986).

Additional Bibliography

Grupo Interdisciplinario de Economía de la Energía (Uruguay) and Universidad de la República (Uruguay). *Canelones: Economía del departamento: Análisis y perspectivas al año 2010.* Montevideo: Convenio UTE-Universidad de la República, 1996.

Gutiérrez Laplace, Juan Manuel. *Crónicas de la costa: Canelones: Historias, personajes y memorias del arroyo Carrasco al Solís Grande.* Montevideo, Uruguay: Ediciones de la Banda Oriental, 2000.

Villegas, Juan. *El Departamento de Canelones, Uruguay: Sus números hacia 1877–1878.* Montevideo, Uruguay: Centros de Estudios de Historia Americana, 2006.

CÉSAR N. CAVIEDES

CANGACEIRO.

CANGACEIRO. Cangaceiro, bandit of northeastern Brazil. *Cangaceiros* operated in the Sertão (backlands) during the nineteenth and early twentieth centuries. Feared and sometimes revered by rural tenants and small landholders, they represented a challenge to authorities and unscrupulous *coronéis* (local political bosses). Many began their careers by exercising private vengeance on family enemies, but most became bandits for personal gain and notoriety. *Cangaceiros* reflected the breakdown of traditional authority in the *sertão* and often operated with the protection of competing *coronéis.* Increased political centralization and more efficient policing led to their demise by the 1930s. *Cangaceiros* are a popular subject of regional literature, music, and art.

See also **Banditry; Coronel, Coronelismo; Jagunço; Lampião; Sertão, Sertanejo.**

BIBLIOGRAPHY

João Guimarães Rosa, *The Devil to Pay in the Backlands,* translated by James L. Taylor and Harriet De Onís (1963).

Billy Jaynes Chandler, *The Bandit King: Lampião of Brazil* (1978).

Linda Lewin, "The Oligarchical Limitations of Social Banditry in Brazil: The Case of the 'Good' Thief Antônio Silvino," and Billy Jaynes Chandler, "Brazilian *Cangaceiros* as Social Bandits: A Critical Appraisal," in *Bandidos: The Varieties of Latin American Banditry,* edited by Richard W. Slatta (1987), pp. 67–112.

Additional Bibliography

Barros, Luitgarde Oliveira Cavalcanti. *A derradeira gesta: Lampião e nazarenos guerreando no sertão.* Rio de Janeiro: Mauad: FAPERJ, 2000.

Grunspan-Jasmin, Elise. *Lampião, senhor do sertão: Vidas e mortes de um cangaceiro.* São Paulo: Editora da Universidade de São Paulo, 2006.

Lins, Daniel Soares. *Lampião: O homem que amava as mulheres: O imaginário do cangaço.* São Paulo: Annablume, 1997.

ROBERT WILCOX

CANNIBALISM.

CANNIBALISM. While anthropophagy, the eating of humans by other humans, has been a sign of difference between ethnic groups since earliest recorded history (for example, when the fifth-century BCE historian Herodotus employs the concept to distinguish between Greeks and barbarians), the term *cannibalism* was coined through the contact between Europe and the Americas. Upon landing in the Caribbean islands in 1492, Christopher Columbus wrote of friendly natives who claimed that their neighbors, the Caribs, consumed human flesh, and soon thereafter, the word *cannibal,* derived from the name of this people, became common usage. Over the course of the early colonial period, explorers and conquerors continued to hear rumors of cannibals. The 1516 disappearance of the Solís expedition is attributed to an anthropophagic River Plate tribe. The Aztecs of Mexico performed human sacrifices on prisoners of war and may have eaten parts of their victims. The Tupinambá and other tribes of Brazil engaged in ritual cannibalism consisting of assimilating their enemies into tribal life, then killing and eating them in order to symbolically absorb their strength. In the sixteenth century, the shipwrecked German sailor Hans Staden and the French Protestant missionary Jean de Léry lived among anthropophagic tribes of coastal Brazil and upon their return to Europe recorded their experiences. Both Léry and his countryman Michel de Montaigne arrived at the conclusion that European civilization was morally inferior to anthropophagic Amerindians.

The anthropologist William Arens inspired controversy by contending in his 1979 *The Man-Eating Myth* that there are virtually no verified eyewitness accounts of indigenous cannibalism. Instead of focusing on cannibalism as a gastronomic reality, Arens emphasizes the existence of a powerful cultural discourse marking the distinction between "civilized" Europeans and "savage" natives. As Arens observes, in the early years of the conquest, the Spanish monarch Queen Isabella sought to protect her new subjects who accepted Christianity by mandating that only cannibals, sodomites, and idolaters could be enslaved, and as a result these labels were liberally applied to peoples whom the Spaniards wished to conquer. Thus, throughout the colonial period cannibalism continued to be invoked by the conquerors in order to justify the imperial enterprise.

In the postcolonial period, the term *cannibal* has often been resignified by Latin American creative writers and cultural critics, who embrace it as a positive sign of their difference from colonial and neocolonial centers. In 1928, the Brazilian modernist Oswald de Andrade published his "Manifesto antropófago," which asserts that the former colonies must consume, digest, and transform metropolitan influences in order to generate cultural products that reflect their own hybrid national identity. In this way, Andrade employs an image formerly used to disparage colonized peoples and appropriates it as a symbol of empowerment. In the twentieth and twenty-first centuries various Latin American novelists and filmmakers have drawn upon the ambiguous image of anthropophagy in their artistic production. Some salient literary and cinematographic examples are Mário de Andrade's *Macunaíma* (Brazil, 1928), Nelson Pereira dos Santos's *Como Era Gostoso o Meu Francês* (*How Tasty Was My Little Frenchman*, Brazil, 1971), and Carlos Balmaceda's *Manual del caníbal* (Argentina, 2005).

These artistic endeavors have inspired a number of scholars to meditate on the significance of cannibalism both as a literal act and as a cultural metaphor for Latin American identity. In particular in the years surrounding the quincentenary of the European discovery of the Americas, there was a surge of creative and critical interest in interrogating the connection between cannibalism and colonialism, and its continued significance in postcolonial Latin America.

See also **Anthropology.**

BIBLIOGRAPHY

Arens, William. *The Man-Eating Myth: Anthropology and Anthropophagy.* New York: Oxford University Press, 1979.

Barker, Francis, Peter Hulme, and Margaret Iverson, eds. *Cannibalism and the Colonial World.* Cambridge, U.K.: Cambridge University Press, 1998.

Boucher, Philip P. *Cannibal Encounters.* Baltimore and London: Johns Hopkins University Press, 1992.

Brown, Paula, and Donald Tuzin, eds. *The Ethnography of Cannibalism.* Washington, D.C.: Society for Psychological Anthropology, 1983.

Hulme, Peter. *Colonial Encounters.* London and New York: Routledge, 1986.

Kilgour, Maggie. *From Communion to Cannibalism: An Anatomy of Metaphors of Incorporation.* Princeton, NJ: Princeton University Press, 1990.

Lestringant, Frank. *Cannibals.* Translated by Rosemary Morris. Berkeley and Los Angeles: University of California Press, 1997.

Madureira, Luís. *Cannibal Modernities: Postcoloniality and the Avant-Garde in Caribbean and Brazilian Literature.* Charlottesville: University of Virginia Press, 2005.

Root, Deborah. *Cannibal Culture.* Boulder, CO: Westview, 1998.

Sanday, Peggy Reeves. *Divine Hunger.* Cambridge, U.K.: Cambridge University Press, 1986.

KIMBERLE S. LÓPEZ

CANNING, GEORGE (1770–1827).

George Canning (*b.* 11 April 1770; *d.* 8 August 1827), British statesman. Despite a long career in public service, George Canning distinguished himself primarily during his term as Great Britain's foreign secretary between 1822 and 1827. He had, in fact, previously served as foreign secretary, from 1807 to 1809, before resigning amid controversy following British military losses to Spain.

In his second term as foreign secretary, Canning broke new ground in recognizing the legitimacy of several newly independent nations in Latin America. After separating Great Britain from the so-called Holy Alliance in 1823, Canning helped prevent other European nations from aiding Ferdinand VII of Spain in his bid to recapture his former colonies. Canning sent the first British consul to Buenos Aires and served as mediator in the Argentine-Brazilian territorial dispute which led to the establishment of the state of Uruguay.

Canning's diplomatic successes in Latin America and elsewhere led to his ascendancy to prime minister in 1827, an office he held for only a few months before his death.

See also **British–Latin American Relations; Holy Alliance.**

BIBLIOGRAPHY

Leslie Bethell, *George Canning and the Independence of Latin America* (1970).

Wendy Hinde, *George Canning* (1989).

Additional Bibliography

Manchester, Alan K. *British Preeminence in Brazil: Its Rise and Decline: A Study in European Expansion.* Chapel Hill: University of North Carolina Press, 1933.

JOHN DUDLEY

CANO, MARÍA DE LOS ÁNGELES

(1887–1967). María de los Ángeles Cano (*b.* 12 August 1887; *d.* 26 April 1967), Colombian labor leader and feminist. An icon of the Colombian Left, Cano was born into a prominent family in Medellín. Small in stature, she had great energy combined with a deeply felt social conscience. Reared in a liberal-minded home, she absorbed secular literature, encouraged by her educator father. She became a journalist in Medellín, thereby gaining access to international wire services, which from 1922 on, reported on the Soviet Union. Cano came to admire that nation greatly and also began to meet with artisans and workers, who as part of May Day festivities proclaimed her the "Flower

of Medellín Labor" in 1925. Over the next several months, Cano made seven nationwide tours in which she spoke out for socialism and workers' rights. Despite official persecution, workers' groups proclaimed her the "National Flower of Labor," in November 1926. She was among the founders of the Partido Social Revolucionario in September 1927. Although she was not a participant in the banana workers' strike against United Fruit Company (November–December 1928) at Santa Marta, her oratory on behalf of labor did help to create a climate favorable for such action. Cano was imprisoned and harassed, yet she continued her activities. After the mid-1930s, her health deteriorated, however, and her political activities ceased. Cano died in Medellín.

See also **Communism; Feminism and Feminist Organizations; Labor Movements.**

BIBLIOGRAPHY

Ignacio Torres Giraldo, *María Cano, mujer rebelde* (1972).

María Cano, *Escritos* (1985).

Gilberto Mejía V., *Memorias: El comunismo en Antioquia (María Cano)* (1986).

León Zuleta Ruiz, comp., *Flor del trabajo y semilla de esperanza: Memorias de su centenario* (1988).

Robert H. Davis, *Historical Dictionary of Colombia* (1993).

Additional Bibliography

Arango Jaramillo, Mario. *Maria Cano, Flor Eterna, Siempreviva.* Medellín: Cátedra María Cano, UMC, Fundación Universitaria María Cano, 2001.

J. LEÓN HELGUERA

CANTILO, JOSÉ LUIS (1871–1944).

José Luis Cantilo (*b.* 6 February 1871; *d.* 11 October 1944), Argentine politician and journalist. First elected a provincial deputy for Buenos Aires in 1896, Cantilo rose through the ranks of the Unión Cívica Radical, participating in the Radicals' last armed protest in 1905. Cantilo was a close associate of Hipólito Irigoyen and joined the national Congress in the wake of the reform of the suffrage law in 1912. President Irigoyen named him intervenor in the province of Buenos Aires in 1917, in an effort to defuse the opposition of conservatives. Soon afterward, Cantilo returned to the capital as intendant (1917–1922); there he dealt with the social upheaval of 1917 to 1921. He did not stand out as either a great conciliator or an effective administrator, but he was a loyal follower of the Radical faction led by Irigoyen. From 1922 to 1926, Cantilo served as governor of the province of Buenos Aires, where he was charged repeatedly by Conservatives and dissident Radicals with undiluted partisanship but nevertheless succeeded in displacing the Conservatives and consolidating a Radical hold. He was again intendant of the capital from 1926 to 1930. Had Irigoyen not stood for reelection in 1928, Cantilo would have been the logical Radical candidate. With the coup d'état in September 1930, Cantilo was forced to leave politics. A decade later, with signs that the country would return to unobstructed democratic rule, he was elected to Congress in 1940. He served very briefly as a foreign minister until March 1941, when he was replaced by a Conservative Hispanophile. From 1941 until his resignation in June 1943, he was president of the Cámara (lower House of Representatives). As the country polarized between archconservatives and rising trade unions, and faced military rumblings, the political room for a liberal like Cantilo quickly contracted.

See also **Argentina, Political Parties: Radical Party (UCR).**

BIBLIOGRAPHY

Richard J. Walter, *The Province of Buenos Aires and Argentine Politics, 1912–1943* (1985), esp. pp. 44–74, and *Politics and Urban Growth in Buenos Aires: 1910–1942* (1993).

Additional Bibliography

Blasi, Hebe Judith. *José Luis Cantilo: Interventor y gobernador*. La Plata: Asociación Amigos del Archivo Histórico de la Provincia de Buenos Aires, 2005.

Cabral, César Augusto. *Alem: Informe sobre la frustración argentina*. Buenos Aires: A. Peña Lillo, 1967.

Chiarenza, Daniel Alberto. *Historia general de la Provincia de Buenos Aires*. Buenos Aires: Ediciones Pre-Escolar, 1997.

JEREMY ADELMAN

CANTINFLAS (1911–1993). (Mario Moreno; *b.* 12 August 1911; *d.* 20 April 1993), Mexican comedian and film star. Cantinflas began studies in medicine at the National Autonomous University of Mexico (UNAM), but dropped out

for a career as a popular stage comedian in *carpas* (traveling stage shows). From the onset, Cantinflas created a unique comic persona, dressing in ragged clothes, his pants close to falling off, and using a rapid, nonsensical manner of speech. He debuted in cinema with a small part in *No te engañes corazón* (1936). The two films that followed, *Así es mi tierra* (1937) and *Águila o Sol* (1937), marked Cantinflas as a rising star. His role in *Ahí está el detalle* (1940) assured his popularity and success. Cantinflas went on to star in over forty features. Among his best-known and praised films are *El gendarme desconocido* (1941), *El 7 machos* (1951), *El bombero atómico* (1952), *Ni sangre ni arena* (1941), *El señor fotógrafo* (1952), and *Abajo el telón* (1954). He also starred in two Hollywood productions, *Around the World in 80 Days* (1956) and *Pepe* (1960). Cantinflas, whose career spanned over fifty years, is Mexico's best-known film celebrity, both nationally and internationally.

See also **Cinema: From the Silent Film to 1990.**

BIBLIOGRAPHY

Luis Reyes De La Maza, *El cine sonoro en México* (1973).

E. Bradford Burns, *Latin American Cinema: Film and History* (1975).

Carl J. Mora, *Mexican Cinema: Reflections of a Society: 1896–1980* (1982).

John King, *Magical Reels: A History of Cinema in Latin America* (1990).

Additional Bibliography

Gómez, Cristina. *Mario Moreno Cantinflas*. Madrid: Dastín, 2003.

Rutiaga, Luis. *Mario Moreno Cantinflas*. Mexico, D.F.: Grupo Ed. Tomo, 2004.

Stevens, LLan. *The Riddle of Cantinflas*. Albuquerque: University of New Mexico Press, 1998.

DAVID MACIEL

CANTÓN, WILBERTO (1925–1979). Wilberto Cantón (*b.* 15 July 1925; *d.* 5 March 1979), Mexican dramatist. Cantón was a prominent, popular playwright who wrote more than two dozen plays. He also was a director, translator, critic, and journalist, holding such posts as head of the theater department of Mexico's National

Institute of Fine Arts. He wrote two basic types of plays: those employing historical Mexican settings for dramatic action and those treating contemporary Mexican social problems. Outstanding works include *El nocturno a Rosario* (1956), *Malditos* (1958), and *Nosotros somos Dios* (1963). The theater at the General Society of Mexican Writers in Mexico City is named for him.

See also **Theater.**

BIBLIOGRAPHY

Samuel Trifilo, "The Theater of Wilberto Cantón," in *Hispania* 54, no. 4 (1971): 869–875.

Carl R. Shirley, "A *Curriculum Operum* of Mexico's Wilberto Cantón," in *Latin American Theatre Review* 13, no. 2 (1980): 47–56, and "The Metatheatrical World of Wilberto Cantón," in *Latin American Theatre Review* 23, no. 2 (1990): 43–53.

Additional Bibliography

Vélez, Joseph Francisco. "Entrevista con Wilberto Cantón." *Latin American Theatre Review* 13 (Fall 1979): 71–75.

CARL R. SHIRLEY

CANTORIA.

Cantoria, a tradition of improvised, sung popular poetry practiced in Northeastern Brazil. It consists of two poets, or *cantadores*, singing alternate strophes in a given style while accompanying themselves on musical instruments: *repentistas* on the guitarlike *viola*, *emboladores* on tambourines or shakers. Because of its improvised nature the poetry is referred to as the *repente*, from the Portuguese word for "sudden." Sometimes the singing takes on the character of a *desafio* (challenge) between contestants. The tunes are repetitive and melodically simple; the focus is on the content and beauty of the poetry and on adherence to a given metric pattern and rhyme scheme. These patterns derive from traditional European poetics, reflecting the historical roots of *cantoria* in the troubadour tradition of southern Europe. Historically *cantoria* belonged to the rural interior of the Northeast. Currently it is finding its way into urban centers.

See also **Baião; Banda de Pífanos; MPB: Música Popular Brasileira.**

BIBLIOGRAPHY

F. Coutinho Filho, *Violas e repentes* (1953).

Leonardo Mota, *Violeiros do Norte,* 4th ed. (1976), and *Cantadores,* 5th ed. (1978).

Luís Da Camara Cascudo, *Coleção reconquista do Brasil.* Vol. 81, *Vaqueiros e cantadores* (1984), pp. 126–226.

Additional Bibliography

Crook, Larry. *Brazilian Music: Northeastern Traditions and the Heartbeat of a Modern Nation.* Santa Barbara: ABC-CLIO, 2005.

Fox, Jennifer Colleen. "O vate canta: Experiencing the Cantoria Tradition of Northeastern Brasil." Ph.D. diss., University of Texas, at Austin, 1997.

Murphy, John P. *Music in Brazil: Experiencing Music, Expressing Culture.* New York: Oxford University Press, 2006.

JENNIFER FOX

CANTÚ, FEDERICO (1908–1989).

Federico Cantú (*b.* 3 March 1908; *d.* 1989), Mexican painter. Born in Cadereyta, Nuevo León, Cantú studied at the San Carlos Academy of Fine Arts in Mexico City and later lived and worked in France between the world wars. While in Europe, he was exposed to the works of Botticelli, El Greco, and the English Pre-Raphaelites. Back in Mexico, Cantú became one of a group of painters who rejected the politics of muralism and returned to easel painting with an intimate and classicizing sensibility. As a devout Christian, Cantú made the central theme of his art a contemporary representation of Christian subjects, such as annunciations and crucifixions. A virtuoso engraver, he produced prints depicting the Passion and other devotional themes. He also executed many frescoes in churches, among them a monumental crucifixion in the Santísima Trinidad in Mexico City. For many years, Cantú was an instructor of drawing and painting at the Esmeralda School of Fine Arts. He died in Mexico City.

See also **Art: The Twentieth Century.**

BIBLIOGRAPHY

McKinley Helm, *Modern Mexican Painters* (1948).

Augustín Arteaga, *Federico Cantú, una nueva visión* (1989).

Additional Bibliography

Abraham, Nuncio. *El espejo habitado: Federico Cantu y su obra.* Monterrey: Universidad Autonoma de Nuevo Leon, Facultad de Filosofía y Letras, Consejo para la Cultura de Nuevo Leon, 1999.

ALEJANDRO ANREUS

CANUDOS CAMPAIGN.

Canudos Campaign, military action of 1896–1897, aimed at dispersing the backlands, religiously based community of Canudos in Bahia, Brazil. Republican authorities mistakenly thought that the messianic community headed by Antônio Conselheiro was a base for monarchist restoration, and a series of misunderstandings made it the object of a bloody campaign. In November 1896 and January 1897, two successively larger units of federal and state troops marched on Canudos. Both units were routed decisively.

Oddly, senior commanders ignored the after-action reports of the defeated officers and so planned their responses based on rumor and conjecture. As Canudos took on the press image of a monarchist hotbed, frustrated Republican extremists, called *Florianistas* after deceased acting president Marshal Floriáno Vieira Peixoto (*d.* June 1895), hoped that victory in Bahia would bring them back to power.

Ardent Florianista colonel Antônio Moreira César, leading 1,300 soldiers and state police and exuding overconfidence, refused a briefing from his unfortunate predecessor and attacked the now reinforced and well-entrenched townspeople on 2 March 1897. Moreira César had a reputation for violence and a willingness to shoot civilians. His impulsiveness and the lack of an army supply service led him to march through a hot, arid region without adequate water supplies. He was mortally wounded in an ill-considered attack made without an attempt to parley. Although well armed and occupying the high ground, the troops fled in panic after the colonel's death, abandoning their equipment and wounded to the townspeople.

The defeat coincided with President Prudente José de Morais's return from sick leave, a subsequent shake-up in army administration, and suppression of a revolt at the Rio de Janeiro military school. The extreme turbulence of 1897 saw four ministers of war and five adjutants-general. Forced recruitment filled the battalions ordered to advance on Canudos in two columns from Salvador and Aracajú under Generals Arthur Oscar de Andrada Guimarães, João da Silva Barbosa, and Cláudio do Amaral Savaget. The planned pincer attack failed and, in late June 1897, the troops were trapped on Favela Hill before the town. Soldiers' wives did a lively business selling hoarded food to the hungry. Women played roles on both sides in this disaster. On 14 July, the encircled units broke out, taking about 1,700 casualties in the process, but finally able to send requests for reinforcements. Engaged in daily combat, the soldiers slit the throats of over 2,000 prisoners.

Minister of War Carlos Machado de Bittencourt took charge of the reinforcements, but General Arthur Oscar's mismanagement was so unnerving that officers excused themselves from joining the expedition. The only general who would command the new battalions was Carlos Eugênio de Andrada Guimarães, Arthur Oscar's brother. State police from São Paulo, Pará, and Amazonas eagerly joined the fray. By the end of September, siege lines surrounded the town, where hundreds of dead lay unburied, as fifteen cannons fired at point-blank range. An assault on 1 October left 587 army dead or wounded, with perhaps as many as 5,500 townsfolk either dead or missing. The next day the first parley between the combatants produced the surrender of several hundred, mostly women and children. On 4 October dynamite bombs and kerosene eliminated the last resistance.

The fighting cost the army heavily; of the 9,542 officers and men sent to Canudos, 4,193 were wounded between July and October 1897, while the townsfolk dead were estimated in the thousands. The campaign showed the army to be ill-organized, ill-equipped, ill-trained, and ill-led, with deficient recruitment and supply systems, and a willingness to fire on those defined as "bad Brazilians." The dreary experience would be used in coming decades to justify military reforms.

See also **Conselheiro, Antōnio; Peixoto, Floriano Vieira.**

BIBLIOGRAPHY

Henrique Duque-Estrada De Macedo Soares, *A Guerra de Canudos* (1902).

Euclydes Da Cunha, *Canudos (diario de uma expedição)* (1939), and *Rebellion in the Backlands,* translated by Samuel Putnam (1944).

Tristão De Alencar Araripe, *Expedições militares contra Canudos: Seu aspecto marcial*, 2d ed. (1985).

Marcos Evangelista Da Costa Villeja, Jr., *Canudos: Memórias de um combatente* (1988).

E. Bradford Burns, "The Destruction of a Folk Past: Euclides da Cunha and Cataclysmic Cultural Clash," in *Review of Latin American Studies* 3, no. 1 (1990): 17–36.

Robert M. Levine, *Vale of Tears: Revisiting the Canudos Massacre in Northeastern Brazil, 1893–1897* (1992).

Additional Bibliography

Martins, Paulo Emílio Matos. *A reinvenção do sertão: A estratégia organizacional de Canudos*. Rio de Janeiro: Editora FGV, 2001.

FRANK D. MCCANN JR.

CAPABLANCA, JOSÉ RAÚL (1888–1942).

José Raúl Capablanca (*b.* 19 November 1888; *d.* 8 March 1942), Cuba's foremost chess player and world champion. Ever since 1894, when a world chess championship began to be recognized by most nations, only three non-Europeans have held the title—two Americans, Paul Morphy and Bobby Fischer, and the Cuban Capablanca. Having learned to play when he was not quite five years old, he soon amazed his father and the members of the prestigious Chess Club in Havana. In 1906 he made a name for himself when he participated in a lightning (speed chess) tournament at the Manhattan Chess Club in New York. Three years later he defeated the United States champion, Frank J. Marshall, and from then onward he achieved a series of brilliant successes that culminated when he ended Emanuel Lasker's long reign over the world of chess in March 1921. Capablanca held most of the world's chess records during his lifetime, and has been regarded by some experts as the greatest chess player of all time. He lost his crown in 1927 to the Russian Alexander Alekhine, who later always found pretexts to avoid Capablanca's repeated challenges for a rematch.

See also **Sports.**

BIBLIOGRAPHY

See William Winter, *Kings of Chess: Chess Champions of the Twentieth Century* (1966); David Hooper and Dale Brandeth, *The Unknown Capablanca* (1975); Irving Chernev, *The Golden Dozen: The Twelve Greatest Chess*

Players of All Times (1976). A short biography of Capablanca may be found in José I. Lasaga, *Cuban Lives: Pages of Cuban History,* vol. 2, translated by Nelson Durán (1988), pp. 373–383.

Additional Bibliography

Bjelica, Dimitrije. *José Raúl Capablanca.* Madrid: Zugarto Ediciones, 1993.

JOSÉ M. HERNÁNDEZ

CAPELLANÍA.

Capellanía, an ecclesiastical endowment. The *capellanía,* or chantry, was one of several pious works commonly founded during the colonial period. The purpose of the chantry was to say masses in perpetuity for the spiritual benefit of the founder and his family. The chantry consisted of a capital endowment invested in real estate as a mortgage or lien at a standard rate of interest (7 percent until 1622, 5 percent thereafter). Other forms of endowment were also accepted, including real estate and voluntary encumbrances on previously unencumbered property.

In general the chantry served as a means of maintaining capital within one extended family, as a hedge against Spanish inheritance laws, which tended to fragment wealth. The founder of the chantry might indicate that one son would serve as the chaplain, another the patron or administrator, and a third, perhaps, the borrower of the capital endowment who would pay the interest. Although an ecclesiastical institution, the church intervened only in instances of legal disputes over the administration of the chantry. The chantry was one of several forms of permanent income recognized by the Catholic Church as sufficient for the purpose of ordination. Consequently the chantry was a means of providing family members with an income upon entering the clergy.

See also **Catholic Church: The Colonial Period.**

BIBLIOGRAPHY

Arnold J. Bauer, "The Church in the Economy of Spanish America: *Censos* and *Depósitos* in the Eighteenth and Nineteenth Centuries," in *Hispanic American Historical Review* 63 (1983): 707–733.

John F. Schwaller, *Origins of Church Wealth in Mexico: Ecclesiastical Revenues and Church Finances, 1523–1600* (1985), esp. pp. 111–127.

Additional Bibliography

Rodríguez Gonzalez, Ana Luz. *Cofradías, capellanías, epidemias y funerales: Una mirada al tejido social de la Independencia*. Bogotá: Banco de la República: El Ancora Editores, 1999.

Saguier, Eduardo R. "Las pautas hereditarias del Régimen Capellánico Ríoplatense." *The Americas* Vol. 51, No. 3 (Jan., 1995): 369-392.

Wobeser, Gisela von. *Vida eterna y preocupaciones terrenales: Las capellanías de misas en la Nueva España, 1700-1821*. México: Universidad Nacional Autónoma de México, 1999.

JOHN F. SCHWALLER

CAPELO, JOAQUÍN (1852–1928).

Joaquín Capelo, born in Lima, was a Peruvian intellectual involved in diverse pursuits, including politics and sociology. As an engineer, he headed Fomento, a development organization during the second presidency (1895–1899) of Nicolás de Piérola. He understood the need for a better trans-Andean transportation system and worked on the construction of a central highway from the central highlands to the coast. His study of the project was published as *La vía central del Perú* (1895–1896). Later he represented Junín in the senate. He was also interested in worker and indigenous rights, and as a professor at San Marcos University in Lima did important though somewhat forgotten work in the field of sociology. During the 1870s he co-founded the Amantes del Saber organization with the noted Puerto Rican essayist and sociologist Eugenio Maria de Hostos. He also became active in Pedro Zulen's Asociación Pro-Indígena.

Among his heterogeneous works, his *Sociología de Lima* (1895–1902) stands out, along with *Los menguados* (1912). Unlike latter-day sociologists, Capelo imparts a multidimensional framework to understanding Lima, discussing sociological, physical, historical, economic, institutional, and moral attributes. He dedicates a good deal of attention to associations and the role they play in the positive development of society. Capelo, like other early Latin American sociologists (as in the 1909 study *Pueblo enfermo* by the Bolivian Alcides Arguedas), approached the city as a diseased organism that could be cured with the proper treatment. Following the life path of many other Latin American intellectuals, Capelo ended up in Paris, where he died.

See also **Arguedas, Alcides; Hostos y Bonilla, Eugenio María de; Indigenismo; Piérola, Nicolás de; Zulen, Pedro S., [and] Dora Mayer de Zulen.**

BIBLIOGRAPHY

Joseph, Gilbert M., and Mark D. Szuchman, eds. *I Saw a City Invincible: Urban Portraits of Latin America*. Wilmington, DE: Scholarly Resources, 1996.

Kapsoli, Wilfredo, ed. *El pensamiento de la Asociación Pro-Indígena*. Cuzco, Peru: Centro de Las Casas, 1980.

Morse, Richard M. "The Lima of Joaquin Capelo: A Latin American Archetype." *Journal of Contemporary History* 4, no. 3, "Urbanism" (1969): 95–110.

THOMAS WARD

CAPE VERDE ISLANDS.

Cape Verde Islands, a group of volcanic islands with a population (2006 estimate) of 485,000 in the Atlantic Ocean, 400 miles west of Senegal. Uninhabited when they were first visited by Portuguese sailors in 1456, the Cape Verde Islands became the first Portuguese colony in Africa in 1462. Because of an arid climate, they had relatively little agricultural potential, although the Portuguese tried to make plantation crops viable. Some Europeans settled there, including exiles of various sorts and Flemish colonists, but the majority of the people were Africans, most brought as slaves from the mainland. They created a cotton-cloth industry whose unique products were much valued in the African trade. Some free Africans and political refugees of noble rank also came to the island, and the island's political elite and its major landowners were primarily of mixed race (mestizos).

Cape Verde's primary value was as a way station for Europeans trading in Africa and sailing to American and Asian locations, thanks to its prevailing winds and currents. Its location and arid climate made its inhabitants often turn to maritime pursuits, as crews on merchant ships and whalers, and to immigration, especially to Portugal, Brazil, and North America.

In the 1950s local inhabitants who resented the privileges given to metropolitan Portuguese in the government and economy developed an independence party linked to Portuguese Guinea. The Portuguese revolution of 1974 resulted in the freedom of all its African colonies. Cape Verde became an independent republic on 5 July 1975.

See also **Portuguese Empire.**

BIBLIOGRAPHY

Batalha, Luís. *The Cape Verdean Diaspora in Portugal: Colonial Subjects in a Postcolonial World.* Lanham, MD: Lexington Books, 2004.

Broecke, Pieter van den., and J.D La Fleur. *Pieter van den Broecke's Journal of Voyages to Cape Verde, Guinea and Angola, 1605-1612.* London: Hakluyt Society, 2000.

Langworthy, Mark, and Timothy J. Finan. *Waiting for Rain: Agriculture and Ecological Imbalance in Cape Verde.* Boulder, CO: Lynne Reinner Publishers, 1997.

Lobban, Richard. *Cape Verde: Crioulo Colony to Independent Nation.* Boulder, CO: Westview Press, 1995.

Santos, Maria Emília Madeira, and António Correia e Silva. *História geral de Cabo Verde.* v. 2-3. Lisboa: Centro de Estudos de História e Cartografia Antiga, Instituto de Investigação Científica Tropical; Praia: Instituto Nacional da Cultura de Cabo Verde, 1995.

JOHN THORNTON

CAPISTRANO DE ABREU, JOÃO

(1853–1927). João Capistrano de Abreu (*b.* 23 October 1853; *d.* 13 August 1927), Brazilian historian, scholar, and journalist. A landowner's son born in Maranguape, Ceará, Capistrano's formal education stopped at the *colégio* (secondary school). Widely read in French, English, and German, he was profoundly influenced by Auguste Comte and Herbert Spencer. In 1875, Capistrano moved to Rio de Janeiro, where he lived until his death, and worked as a schoolteacher, journalist, and bureaucrat. His historical writings drew on a formidable talent for archival research and displayed an original, penetrating mind. However, this work was largely restricted to short articles and reviews that did not sustain the promise of his first book, *O descobrimento do Brasil e seu desenvolvimento no século XVI* (1883). A distrust of worldly success, deep pessimism about life, the premature death of his wife, and time spent on scholarly translations and ethnographic research explain Capistrano's failure to write what contemporaries expected of him: a definitive study of colonial Brazil. *Capítulos de história colonial, 1500–1800* (1907), a commissioned work, is no more than suggestive of such a study. Nonetheless, his writings remain invaluable for their insights and analytical power, and Capistrano stands at the forefront of Brazilian historians.

See also **Positivism.**

BIBLIOGRAPHY

José Aurélio Saravia Câmara, *Capistrano de Abreu tentativa biobibliográfico* (Rio de Janeiro, 1965).

José Honório Rodrigues, *História e historiadores do Brasil* (São Paulo, 1965), pp. 34–53.

Additional Bibliography

Fringer, Katherine. "The Contribution of Capistrano de Abreu to Brazilian Historiography." *Journal of Inter-American Studies and World Affairs* 13 (April 1971): 258–278.

Holanda, Firmino. *Capistrano de Abreu.* Fortaleza: Edições Demócrito Rocha, 2002.

RODERICK J. BARMAN

CAPITANÍA. *See* **Captaincy System.**

CAPITÃO DO MATO. Capitão do Mato, literally, bush captain. During slavery in Brazil, bush captains were recruited from among the free population, usually mulattoes. Their job was similar to that of "patrollers" in the U.S. South: bush captains were contracted by plantation owners to hunt down and return escaped slaves. In the sugar areas of the North and Northeast they were used to locate *quilombos,* maroon communities of fugitives. Bush captains became infamous for their brutal tactics.

See also **Slavery: Brazil.**

BIBLIOGRAPHY

Mary C. Karasch, *Slave Life in Rio de Janeiro, 1808–1850* (1987).

Additional Bibliography

Gomes, Flávio dos Santos. *Histórias de quilombolas: Mocambos e comunidades de senzalas no Rio de Janeiro, século XIX.* Rio de Janeiro: Arquivo Nacional, 1995.

Nishida, Mieko. *Slavery and Identity: Ethnicity, Gender, and Race in Salvador, Brazil, 1808-1888.* Bloomington: Indiana University Press, 2003.

KIM D. BUTLER

CAPITÃO MOR.

CAPITÃO MOR. Capitão Mor, regimental colonel who was a military assistant to the governors of the captaincies. In Brazil's early colonial period, a *capitão mor* was a military commander of a front-line regiment. Each Donatário (lord proprietor) had a *capitão mor* of his territory. The early *capitão mor* was the person who governed new colonies for a period of three years. Since such a vast distance separated the colony from the kingdom, the *capitães mor* increased their power and became the political bosses of their districts. Often despotic in their application of local rule, they were in charge of enforcing royal laws, recruiting the militias, and serving as provincial governors. After 1764 they could impress men into the army, act as judges of final authority, and imprison deserters and vagrants. They could intervene in court trials or ecclesiastical affairs and even prevent couples from getting married. Usually they were local landowners of prominent families, who frequently abused their powers.

After their military power was curtailed, the *capitães mor* remained political bosses of their districts, exercising local autonomy in the sparsely populated rural areas where they were the real power. By the eighteenth century the title *capitão mor* was held by a governor of an unincorporated territory or by the commandant of a military company.

See also **Militias: Colonial Brazil.**

BIBLIOGRAPHY

Bailey W. Diffie, *Latin American Civilization: Colonial Period* (1945).

Additional Bibliography

Costa, Samuel Guimarães da. *O último capitão-mor, 1782-1857.* Curitiba: Scientia et Labor, 1988.

Monteiro, Rodrigo Bentes. *O rei no espelho: A monarquia portuguesa e a colonização da América, 1640-1720.* São Paulo: Editora Hucitec, 2002.

                                        PATRICIA MULVEY

CAPITULATIONS OF SANTA FE.

CAPITULATIONS OF SANTA FE. Capitulations of Santa Fe, the April 1492 agreements between the Catholic monarchs, Ferdinand II and Isabella I, and Christopher Columbus detailed the terms of royal support for Columbus's voyage to the New World. The capitulation is similar to a royal patent, in this case authorizing and regulating the relationship between the crown and an agent. By these agreements at the military encampment of Santa Fe on the edge of Granada, Isabella and Ferdinand bestowed on Columbus the offices of viceroy, admiral, and governor in any newly found lands. Further, Columbus received the right to one-tenth the value of the sale of "pearls, precious stones, gold, silver, spices," and other commodities. He was given the title of Don, and the capitulation was transferable to his heirs in perpetuity. In return, Columbus was to undertake the expedition, providing leadership and part of the funding. Many have questioned why the monarchs were so generous in their bestowal of privileges to the Italian; perhaps it was due to the recent fall of Granada, the prospect of converting pagan peoples, or the belief that if Columbus was successful, the crown could recover its investment.

See also **Columbus, Christopher.**

BIBLIOGRAPHY

Samuel Eliot Morison, *Journals and Other Documents on the Life and Voyages of Christopher Columbus* (1963).

William D. Phillips, Jr., and Carla Rahn Phillips, *The Worlds of Christopher Columbus* (1992).

Additional Bibliography

Nader, Helen, and Luciano Formisano, eds. *The Book of Privileges issued to Christopher Columbus by King Fernando and Queen Isabel, 1492–1502.* Eugene: Wipf & Stock, 2004.

Thomas, Hugh. *Rivers of Gold: The Rise of the Spanish Empire, from Columbus to Magellan.* New York: Random House, 2003.

                                        NOBLE DAVID COOK

CAPOEIRA.

CAPOEIRA. Capoeira is a stylized martial art of Afro-Brazilian origin, rhythmically performed to the music of drums and the *berimbau*, a bow-shaped instrument using a gourd as a resonating chamber to amplify the low tones produced by tapping its single string. With graceful and powerful movements resembling gymnastic floor exercise, the *capoeirista* strikes simulated blows primarily with the feet and head, which the partner/opponent parries, evades, and returns.

Capoeira practice, Rio de Janeiro, Brazil, 2003. With roots in Afro-Brazilian religious traditions, capoeira blends martial art techniques with the rhythmic thump of drums and the *berimbau*, an indigenous single-stringed instrument. © MIMI MOLLICA/ CORBIS

Historically, capoeira began to be recognized in the late eighteenth century and flourished through the nineteenth. Although the modern form is has become known and practiced to some degree in most parts of Brazil, the main historical centers were Rio de Janeiro and Salvador, Bahia. In the latter city capoeira is often associated with the Afro-Brazilian religious tradition known as *candomblé*. Often assisted by daggers, razors, stones, and clubs, it was practiced by individual slaves and free men of the urban lower class and by groups organized into gangs known as *maltas*. A concerted effort by police and judicial systems to eliminate the threat to urban public security that capoeira represented was generally successful by the early twentieth century. Beginning in the 1940s and 1950s it was revived as a martial art and dance/ fight with accompanying music, developed in organized clubs and training schools presided over by master teachers. By moving off the streets and into organized academies, capoeira has emerged as a legitimate and respected cultural form, Brazil's contribution to the variety of formalized martial arts, accompanied by strict training regimens and ranks achieved by performance tests. As such, it has enjoyed phenomenal growth in popularity among middle-class youths, both in Brazil and in other parts of the world.

Several hypotheses exist on the etymology of terms associated with capoeira. *Capoeira*, which in standard Brazilian Portuguese also refers to second-growth brushland, is derived from the Tupi linguistic elements *caá* (vegetation, forest) and *puêra* (that which has disappeared). Also called *capoeira* is a partridge-like bird native to Brazil. Typically inhabiting scrubland, the male of this species aggressively resists intrusions into its territory by attacking and clawing rivals. *Malta* may be related to old Lisbon slang for itinerant laborers and street rowdies who stereotypically were migrants from the island of Malta, or it may denote the clannishness of members who stuck together like the wax-and-tar sealing mixture of the same name. Whereas most studies of capoeira suggest it is a uniquely Brazilian phenomenon, some modern sources, particularly those focusing on the Afro-Brazilian culture of Salvador, Bahia, surmise it may have remote Angolan origins.

See also **Sports.**

BIBLIOGRAPHY

Almeida, Bira. *Capoeira: A Brazilian Art Form.* Richmond, CA: North Atlantic Books; Pao Alto, CA: Sun Wave, 1981.

Assunção, Matthias. *Capoeira: A History of an Afro-Brazilian Martial Art.* London and New York: Routledge, 2005.

Holloway, Thomas H. "'A Healthy Terror:' Police Repression of Capoeiras in Nineteenth-Century Rio de Janeiro." *Hispanic American Historical Review* 69, no 4 (1989): 637–676.

Lewis, John. *Ring of Liberation: Deceptive Discourse in Brazilian Capoeira.* Chicago: University of Chicago Press, 1992.

Pastinha, Vicente Ferreira. *Capoeira Angola.* Salvador, Brazil: Impresso na Escola Gráfica N.S. de Lorêto, Convente da Piedade, 1964.

Rego, Waldeloir. *Capoeira Angola; Ensaio sócio-etnográfico.* Il de Carybé, Rio de Janeiro: Gráf. Lux, 1968.

Rego, Waldeloir (text), and Fernando Goldgaber (photos). *Capoeira.* Salvador, Brazil: Secretaria da Educação e Cultura do Estado da Bahia, 1969.

THOMAS H. HOLLOWAY

CAPTAINCY SYSTEM.

CAPTAINCY SYSTEM. The captaincy system in Brazil had its roots in the late medieval Portuguese royal grant of *senhório* (seignory), which, in turn, had been slightly modified as the Portuguese began to settle the uninhabited Atlantic islands of the Azores, Madeiras, and Cape Verdes in the fifteenth century. In those cases certain individuals had been given the jurisdiction, rights, and revenues that had pertained to the king and were called *donatários* (donataries), because they had been given a *doação* (gift) by the crown—often as rewards for services. The *carta de doação* was accompanied by a *foral*, which in careful detail explained the rights and duties of the colonists in relation to both the *donatário* and the crown. The grants were perpetual and hereditary, but if the line died out, the grant reverted to the crown.

In response to increasing French threats to Brazil and to better settle the region, King João III (r. 1521–1557) instituted the captaincy system, which had worked well in the Atlantic Islands. Between 1534 and 1536 fifteen grants, each extending along the coast from ten to a hundred leagues (with three-fifths of them stretching fifty leagues or more), were made to twelve lord-proprietors or captains. Beginning with the Amazon River and extending southward to the present-day state of Santa Catarina, they were Pará (João de Barros and Aires da Cunha); Maranhão (Fernão Álvares de Andrade); Piaui and Ceará (António Cardoso de Barros); Rio Grande (João de Barros and Aires da Cunha); Itamaracá (Pero Lopes de Sousa); Pernambuco (Duarte Coelho Pereira); Bahia (Francisco Pereira Coutinho); Ilheus (Jorge Figueiredo Correia); Porto Seguro (Pero do Campo Tourinho); Espírito Santo (Vasco Fernandes Coutinho); São Tomé (Pero de Gois); Rio de Janeiro (Martim Afonso de Sousa); Santo Amaro (Pero Lopes de Sousa); São Vicente (Martim Afonso de Sousa); and Santa Ana (Pero Lopes de Sousa). Each *donatário* was granted extensive administrative, fiscal, and judicial powers by the Crown in exchange for settling and defending at their own cost the lands granted to them. They could make land grants (*sesmarias*) and found towns.

Only ten of the above-mentioned captaincies were settled in the sixteenth century. Two were left abandoned by their *donatários*, and several exchanged hands. Porto Seguro was sold to the first Duke of Aveiro and Ilheus to the wealthy merchant Lucas Giraldes. In addition, two small hereditary captaincies were established: Ilha de Itaparica (1556) in the Bay of All Saints and Paraguasu (1566) in the Recôncavo of Bahia. By the end of the sixteenth century, Rio Grande do Norte, Paraiba, Bahia, and Rio de Janeiro had become royal colonies. However, in the seventeenth century the Crown created a new set of hereditary captaincies in both the State of Brazil and in the State of Maranhão, the latter having been separated from the State of Brazil in 1621. Though five new proprietary captaincies were established in the State of Brazil, only two survived to be of some importance: Campos de Goitacases, given to Salvador Correia de Sá and his descendants, and Nossa Senhora da Conceição de Itanhaém. During the reign of João V (r. 1706–1750), five proprietary colonies in the State of Brazil were incorporated by the Crown. By 1759 the remaining ones were also absorbed. In the 1630s the captaincies of Cumá, Caete, Cametá, and Cabo do Norte were created in the State of Maranhão. In 1665 Ilha Grande de Joanes (the island of Marajó) was made a hereditary captaincy. In 1685 Xingu was created but never settled. But between 1752 and 1754 the six above-mentioned captaincies were incorporated into the State of Grão Pará and Maranhão.

Efforts by earlier writers on the subject to characterize the captaincies as either feudal or capitalistic have added little to the understanding of this important institution.

See also **Barros, João de; Coelho Pereira, Duarte; João III of Portugal; João V of Portugal.**

BIBLIOGRAPHY

Dutra. Francis A. "Duarte Coelho Pereira, First Lord-Proprietor of Pernambuco: The Beginning of a Dynasty." *The Americas* 29, no. 4 (1973): 415–441.

Johnson, H. B., Jr. "The Donatary Captaincy in Perspective: Portuguese Backgrounds to the Settlement of Brazil," *Hispanic American Historical Review* 52, no. 2 (1972): 203–214.

Saldanha, António Vasconcelos de. *As Capitanias do Brasil: Antecedentes, Desenvolvimento e Extinção de um Fenómeno Atlântico.* Lisbon: Comissão Nacional para as Comemorações dos Descobrimentos Portugueses, 2001.

Vianna, Hélio. *História do Brasil: Periodo Colonial*, 2nd rev. edition. São Paulo: Edições Melhoramentos, 1963.

FRANCIS A. DUTRA

CAPTAIN-GENERAL

This entry includes the following articles:

BRAZIL

SPANISH AMERICA

BRAZIL

The captain-general was a military man who acted as head of the captaincy. He was a provincial governor whose duties were primarily military and defensive in nature as the supreme commander of all the armed forces in his captaincy. He was also the chief administrative officer responsible for exercising absolute power and administering the king's justice in his domain. As a colonial governor, the captain-general embodied the king and royal authority. After 1720 the captain-general of Bahia was elevated to the office of viceroy, and after 1763 so, too, was the captain-general of Rio de Janeiro. Although the captain-general could be a dictator by local standards, his power was curtailed by royal authorities overseas and the local town councils. The geographic vastness of Brazil also limited the governor's power. The governors meddled in municipal affairs by controlling nominations to governmental office and extending the terms of office of local officials. The captains-general could also initiate public works. The earliest captains-general had to subjugate and pacify the Indians, Christianize them, build forts and towns, introduce agriculture and commerce, and make the new colonies self-sufficient. Soldiers of fortune and daring military men like Tomé de Sousa and Martim Afonso de Sousa made effective captains-general, because they were able administrators and courageous commanders.

See also **Militias: Colonial Brazil.**

BIBLIOGRAPHY

Bailey W. Diffie, *A History of Colonial Brazil, 1500–1792* (1987).

Additional Bibliography

Puntoni, Pedro. *A guerra dos bárbaros: Povos indígenas e a colonização do sertão nordeste do Brasil, 1650–1720*. São Paulo, SP, Brazil: FAPESP, 2000.

PATRICIA MULVEY

SPANISH AMERICA

A captain-general was the chief executive of an audiencia district whose location made it susceptible to internal or external military threats. The title was combined with that of viceroy for the chief executives of the viceroyalties, and commonly with those of president and governor in non-viceregal districts. A captain-general has less prestige and authority than a viceroy, but because of his assignment to oversee the *audiencia*'s defense, he had more responsibility than an executive who bore only the titles of president or president/governor of an *audiencia*. In his combined roles, the captain-general was a powerful official with administrative, judicial, military, and legislative responsibilities.

The Crown's decision to employ the title of captain-general was explicit recognition that some portions of the empire were militarily vulnerable. Since the vast viceroyalties of New Spain and Peru each had vulnerable areas, the viceroys were also titled captains-general and charged with overseeing their defense. By the late sixteenth century, however, the incursions of foreign interlopers in the Caribbean region and the continued conflict between Spanish settlers and the Araucanians in Chile led the Crown to start using the title in conjunction with those of president and governor for the chief executive of several *audiencias*. Specifically, it named captains-general for Chile in 1567, for Santo Domingo in 1577, for Tierra Firme in 1596, and for Guatemala in 1609. When an *audiencia* was created in Manila in 1583, its chief executive was also named a captain-general.

As part of their increased reliance upon military administrators, the Bourbon monarchs converted the presidencies of Guadalajara (1708) and Quito (1767) into captaincies-general, created the captaincy-general of Venezuela (1777), and reestablished captaincies-general in Chile (1778) and Manila (1783).

A captain-general was responsible for the defense of the captaincy-general and specifically charged with maintaining fortifications, arms, and equipment in good condition. As commander in chief, a captain-general was also responsible for military justice and served as the court of appeal for any cases that involved persons entitled to the military *fuero* or judicial privileges.

The Crown selected captains-general from among experienced army or navy officers and appointed them for a specific term, normally eight years. At the conclusion of their term, they were subject to a judicial review (*residencia*).

See also **Audiencia; Militias: Colonial Spanish America.**

BIBLIOGRAPHY

Clarence H. Haring, *The Spanish Empire in America* (1947).

Additional Bibliography

Andrien, Kenneth J. *The Kingdom of Quito, 1690–1830: The State and Regional Development.* Tuscaloosa: University of Alabama Press, 2004.

Hawkins, Timothy. *José De Bustamante and Central American Independence: Colonial Administration in an Age of Imperial Crisis.* Tuscaloosa: University of Alabama Press, 2004.

Sanciñena Asurmendi, Teresa. *La audiencia en México en el reinado de Carlos III.* México: Universidad Nacional Autónoma de México, 1999.

MARK A. BURKHOLDER

CAPUCHIN FRIARS.   Capuchin Friars, an autonomous branch of the Franciscan order of priests and brothers of the Roman Catholic Church. In early-sixteenth-century Italy a group of Franciscans sought to reform the order and return to a more pure observance of the rule established by Saint Francis. The result was the formation of the Capuchin branch, which became a separate order in 1528. The name "Capuchin" derives from the long, pointed hood of the order's habit, a distinctive mode of dress adopted when the order was founded. The friars became known as some of the most effective preachers and missionaries of the sixteenth and seventeenth centuries.

Beginning in 1578, the Capuchins established themselves in Spain, and from there joined other religious orders in sending missionaries to the New World. The first Capuchin community in the Americas was founded in Darién (on the Caribbean coast of Panama) in 1648, but was abandoned soon thereafter. In 1650, the Capuchins established a successful mission at Cumaná in Venezuela. Within a short period of time Capuchins staffed missions in Caracas, Trinidad, Guayana, Santa Marta, and Maracaibo. In the eighteenth century, in particular, they founded numerous settlements in northern South America. Based on a system of both common responsibility and private ownership, Indians at the missions were expected to work for the community a total of twelve hours per week. The Capuchins directed classes in catechism, reading, writing, and crafts.

As a result of the struggle for independence, the friars were imprisoned or forced out of New Granada beginning in 1812. The missions were restaffed in

1835, however, when friars fled the suppression of religious communities in Spain. In 1849, expelled from the missions once again, the Capuchins dispersed and founded communities in Guatemala, El Salvador, and Ecuador.

In Brazil, French Capuchins made advances into the Amazon region in the first decades of the seventeenth century, but they were almost immediately replaced by Portuguese. These friars, with varying degrees of success, established missions throughout the seventeenth and eighteenth centuries, as they had in northern South America. In the process they began valuable ethnographic and linguistic studies of the native peoples. In the nineteenth century the influence of freemasonry led the government to undertake the dissolution of the monasteries, and the Capuchins suffered loss of property and personnel. Direct persecution, however, ended with the establishment of laws separating church and state at the end of the nineteenth century.

Today the Capuchin friars work in nearly every country of Latin America. They are active in ministries, in such areas as preaching, hospital work, and education.

See also **Anticlericalism; Franciscans.**

BIBLIOGRAPHY

Antonio De Egaña, *Historia de la Iglesia en la América Española*, vol. 2 (1966).

Additional Bibliography

Adoáin, Esteban de., and Padre Lázaro de Aspurz, O.F.M. Cap. *Memorias: Cuarenta años de campañas misioneras en Venezuela, Cuba, Guatemala, El Salvador, Francia y España, 1842-1880.* Caracas: Universidad Católica Andrés Bello: Vicepostualación Esteban de Adoáin, 2000.

Langer, Erick, and Robert H. Jackson, eds. *The New Latin American Mission History.* Lincoln, NE: University of Nebraska Press, 1995.

Reynal, Vicente. *Los capuchinos valencianos en Hispanoamérica.* Vol. 1. Valencia: Gráficas Hurtado, 1994.

BRIAN C. BELANGER

CARABINEROS DE CHILE. The Chilean Constitution assigns the task of law enforcement to the *Carabineros de Chile* and the *Policía de Investigaciones.* The first institution was formed in 1927 with the definitive unification of the state and municipal police with the army's *Cuerpo de Carabineros* (Corps of Carbineers).

From this period on, both police forces were to report to the ministry of the interior, who was responsible for preserving the public order. Under the military regime of Augusto Pinochet (1973–1990), Carabineros underwent considerable transformations, as its general director became a member of the military junta. During this time, both the Carabineros and the investigative police were placed under the ministry of defense. Law Decree no. 444 established this change under the argument that ensuring the united action of Carabineros required that the police not be required to report to a secretary of state primarily concerned with politics, which would hamper the technical efficiency of the police. This institutional change ensured a high degree of operational autonomy of the police, because the ministry of defense was not involved in the preservation of public order.

The role of the Carabineros traditionally has been that of security police, including the preservation of the public order and the control and regulation of vehicular traffic. In recent years, this role has evolved and now the Carabineros also investigate crimes.

In the early twenty-first century, the Carabineros de Chile has 36,777 officers.

The Carabineros are organized along military lines, as evidenced in the institution's discipline and training. Like the army, the Carabineros have separate schools for commissioned and noncommissioned officers, and they fall under the jurisdiction of the military courts for violations of the law committed in the course of their service.

Following the transition to democracy, the first democratic governments maintained closer relations with the Policia de Investigaciones de Chile than with Carabineros, due to the perception that the officers of the later institution identified with the military regime. Nonetheless, the prestige Carabineros enjoyed throughout the region—due to its professional competence and disciplined structure—helped palliate this mistrust. Another factor was the increasing concern of the population with the growing rates of crime, which led them to seek the presence of carabineros in their neighborhoods.

With regard to this increase in citizen insecurity, in the late 1990s Carabineros undertook a restructuring process to increase operative personnel, which implied that the institution ceased to fulfill twenty-four of the sixty-seven tasks assigned by law. In 2007 the institution began the periodic evaluation of its operations using new performance indicators that were developed by its planning department. Carabineros began to incorporate the notion of community participation in the institution's discourse, in keeping with that of the government and the municipalities.

Thus, during 1999, in response to increasing insecurity due to the growing crime problem, the Carabineros put into action the *Plan Cuadrante* (Quadrant plan). One primary objective of this program was to increase the presence of police on the street. The area under supervision by each command was divided into small sectors or quadrants. Vehicles and human resources were assigned according to the specific needs of each quadrant. Responsibility for the management of each quadrant is assigned to police officers who bear the title of *delegado* or the lower-ranking *subdelegado*. These police are to attend to and resolve the problems brought to them by the citizens in their quadrant. The Carabineros have also adopted the practice of public accountability by sharing statistical information on police activities with community leaders and local public officials.

Public support for Carabineros and for Investigaciones is notoriously higher than that received by other components of the criminal justice system, such as the courts. Surveys on public perceptions of Carabineros demonstrate public confidence in the institution. The 2003 survey on the perception of Carabineros asks whether in the past twelve months the respondent has been the victim of or witness to a Carabinero using his or her post for personal gain. A negative response was given by 88 percent of the respondents. Only 6 percent had witnessed a Carabinero acting for personal gain, and 2 percent had been the victim of such abuse.

A victimization survey carried out in 2003 listed a series of statements regarding officers of Carabineros and asks respondents whether they agree. The statements that received more positive responses were Carabineros are responsive (78.9%); Carabineros are disciplined (73.9%); Carabineros are efficient (66.2%); and Carabineros treat people well (63.2%). In the response to the question as to whether Carabineros treat people well there are more positive opinions of respondents from the highest income bracket than from the lowest.

See also **Chile: The Twentieth Century; Chile, Constitutions; Criminal Justice.**

BIBLIOGRAPHY

Candina, Azun. "Carabineros de Chile: Una mirada histórica a la identidad institucional." In *Seguridad y Reforma Policial en las Américas,* edited by Lucía Dammert and John Bailey. Buenos Aires: Siglo XXI Editores.

Frühling, Hugo. "Carabineros y consolidación democrática en Chile." *Pena y Estado* 3, no. 3 (1998): 81–116.

Frühling, Hugo. "La Policía en Chile: Los nuevos desafíos de una coyuntura Compleja." *Perspectivas* 3 (1999): 63–90.

HUGO FRÜHLING

CARABOBO, BATTLE OF. Battle of Carabobo, the last major military engagement of the War of Independence in Venezuela, named after the savanna southwest of Valencia on which it took place. On the morning of 24 June 1821 the patriots, under the command of Simón Bolívar, faced royalist troops under the leadership of General Miguel de la Torre. The latter had taken command of the Spanish forces after the departure of General Pablo Morillo the previous year. Bolívar's forces consisted of the Colombian troops that had marched with him over the Andes. These troops were joined at Carabobo by the *llaneros* ("plainsmen") of José Antonio Páez. The patriot force of approximately six thousand outnumbered the royalists by perhaps a thousand. The battle lasted less than an hour, with light casualties on both sides. Losses were reportedly heaviest on the patriot side, with approximately two hundred killed and wounded, including nearly all of the British legion. Half of the royalist force was captured, the rest fleeing to the fort at Puerto Cabello. The patriots also gained important munitions, including artillery pieces and a large amount of ammunition.

The battle was important as a symbol of the strength of the patriot forces fighting on their territory, and their victory in effect freed Venezuela and New Granada from the Spanish. Bolívar entered Caracas less than a week later. In addition, with patriots now in charge of northern South America, Bolívar was able to focus his efforts on the south. In 1821 the Liberator organized a government at Cúcuta on the border of New Granada and Venezuela, marking the beginning of the construction of the Venezuelan nation.

See also **Cúcuta, Congress of.**

BIBLIOGRAPHY

Lino Duarte Level, *Cuadros de historia militar y civil de Venezuela* (1917).

Daniel Florencio O'Leary, *Bolívar and the War of Independence* (1970).

John V. Lombardi, *Venezuela: The Search for Order, the Dream of Progress* (1982).

Additional Bibliography

Bencomo Barrios, Héctor. *Los héroes de Carabobo.* Caracas: Ediciones de la Presidencia de la República, 2004.

Thibaud, Clément. *Repúblicas en armas: Los ejércitos bolivarianos en la guerra de Independencia en Colombia y Venezuela.* Lima: Instituto Francés de Estudios Andinos, 2003.

GARY MILLER

CARACAS. Caracas, the capital of Venezuela as well as that of the municipality of Libertador and the Federal District. The city lies in a narrow valley some 15 miles from east to west. Its northern boundary is a spur of the Coastal Range, whose most famous peak, El Ávila (7,100 feet), dominates the center of the metropolitan area, and whose tallest peak, Naiguaitá (9,000 feet), stands at the eastern end of the valley. The name Caracas honors one of the indigenous peoples of the area.

The Federal District, created in 1909, included the municipalities of Libertador (Caracas) and Vargas (La Guaira). About 12 miles by road from Caracas, La Guaira was until recently the major port of the country. The Metropolitian Area of Caracas was created in 1950 and includes five municipalities (Libertador, Sucre, Baruta, El Hatillo, and Chacao). The city, at an average altitude of 3,400 feet, has a balmy climate. The valley is subject to seismic activity, and Caracas has suffered a number of earthquakes, notably in 1641, 1812, and 1967.

FOUNDATION AND COLONIAL PERIOD

The forbidding coastline of central Venezuela and the resistance of local tribes, particularly under the leadership of Guaicaipuro, delayed the process of Spanish conquest and colonization of the valley. Diego de Losada founded Santiago de León de Caracas in mid-1567. The site, at the western end of the valley, consisted of a central plaza and twenty-four blocks. The first Cabildo (municipal council) to which there is written reference was held in 1568, and the lands and peoples of the valley were divided as booty among the Spaniards who accompanied Losada.

Caracas became the capital of the province of Venezuela in 1578, with a Spanish population of 60 *vecinos* (entitled residents), corresponding to some 300 persons, and some 7,000 Indians among the *encomiendas* of the valley. The town received a royal patent as a city in 1591.

By the early 1600s, the economy was based on the production of cacao, corn, and wheat as well as cattle and mules, all of which were traded through the port of La Guaira; the valley also produced sugar, beans, fruit, and other agricultural items for local consumption. In 1636 the bishopric was officially transferred from Coro to Caracas, where the bishops had been resident since 1613. The seventeenth century was one of slow growth, retarded severely by the earthquake of 1641. Estimated population by the end of the century was only some 350 *vecinos,* or about 1,750 people who could claim to be of Spanish origin.

In the eighteenth century there were important changes in the activities of the city. The Royal and Pontifical University of Caracas was founded in 1725, and in 1728 the Caracas Company (Compañía Guipuzcoana) began its monopoly of the commerce between Spain and Venezuela. In the last quarter of the century, Caracas became the seat for fiscal matters with the creation of the intendancy (1776); for military and political matters with the creation of the captaincy-general of Venezuela (1777), which included the provinces of Cumaná, Guayana, Maracaibo, Margarita, and Trinidad; for judicial and administrative matters with the creation of the audiencia Real (1786); and for commercial and agricultural affairs with the creation of the Consulado Real (1793). In 1804 an archbishopric was established in Caracas and the city became the official religious administrative center. In 1808 it received the first printing press in the colony.

By the end of the colonial period Caracas had an estimated population of 42,000 inhabitants and a very prosperous economic base and had become the administrative center of the colony, but the city itself did not reflect this importance. Its most distinguished public building was the recently constructed San Carlos military barracks. The Plaza Mayor was used as an open-air market. Water flowed down the center of the streets, and sidewalks were unknown, in part because there was no wheeled transport. Although foreigners praised the city for its climate and magnificent geographical setting, its clean streets and pleasant inhabitants, a fellow colonial from Mérida, Antonio Ignacio Rodríguez Picón, said of Caracas in 1803 that only the central streets, where the rich and aristocratic lived, were well paved and pleasing of aspect; that the city was full of blacks, mulattoes, and Canary Islanders; and that it had little more than cockfights as public entertainment. There was no public lighting, and the city retired for the night at nine.

THE NINETEENTH AND EARLY TWENTIETH CENTURIES

Independence was declared in Caracas on 5 July 1811, and between the long years of warfare and the devastating earthquake of 1812, the city suffered damages that were not fully repaired for more than fifty years. Between 1870 and 1888, however, Antonio Guzmán Blanco held effective power in Venezuela and made a concerted effort to beautify and dignify the capital city. The center of the city received particular attention: the Plaza Bolívar (Mayor) was redesigned, the Capitol was built, and El Calvario became an elegant park. Churches, theaters, aqueducts, boulevards, and the new cemetery General del Sur, which became a monument to mortuarial art, were all constructed. The streets were lighted by gas, a telephone system was installed, and the Caracas–La Guaira railroad was opened in 1883. Railroad connections were extended to Puerto Cabello and Valencia by 1895. This was the last face-lift Caracas would receive for sixty years.

CONTEMPORARY CARACAS

After 1936, improved public-health measures and the development of the petroleum industry combined to increase the population of Caracas at a rapid rate. As can be seen in the accompanying

Caracas: Population, 1881–1990		
Census year	Caracas	Metropolitan area
1881	55,638	77,911
1936	203,342	258,513
1950	495,064	693,896
1971	1,658,500	2,183,935
1990	1,824,892	2,784,042
2004	1,975,254	3,276,000

Table 1

table, the metropolitan area is growing faster than Caracas itself, but attempts to design an overall plan for urban growth have not had much success. The military government of the 1950s built, extended, and improved streets and highways, facilitating the city's expansion and improving connections with the port and airport on the coast. It also continued the urban renewal in the center of the city that was begun by the government of Isais Medina Angarita in the 1940s.

Caracas remains the administrative, commercial, and cultural center of Venezuela. The petroleum revenues that are distributed by the national government tend to stay close at hand, and many companies locate in Caracas because of the ease of communications. Caracas has a number of public and private universities, numerous publishers and newspapers, various theater and ballet groups (both public and private), and several orchestras and ensembles. Cultural life tends to coalesce in the environs of the Teresa Carreño Cultural Complex in the sector of Los Caobos. Nearby are the Ateneo, the National Gallery of Art, the Museum of Fine Arts, the Museum of Contemporary Art Sofia Imber, and the Children's Museum.

In the last few decades of the twentieth century new buildings sprung up to such an extent that the valley is completely urbanized; Caracas has passed from being an overgrown town characterized by one- and two-story buildings with red-tiled roofs to a city more defined by skyscrapers. Although the Sierra del Ávila was declared a park, most of the other hillsides have been built up, and the two extremes of the valley are characterized by *ranchos* (slum housing). The Caracas metropolitan area as of 2007 suffers greatly from inadequate public services, particularly with regard to water and sewage systems. The complex terrain, the rate of growth, and the complications of various local jurisdictions in the metropolitan area are having a devastating effect on the city.

Since the Bolivarian presidency of Hugo Chávez began in 1999, the city has become the site of demonstrations by the working classes in his support and by traditional elites, his detractors, who control most of the media outlets. Juan Barreto, elected mayor in 2004, has forged a sister-city project with London, England, has declared the expropriation of Caracas's most exclusive golf courses to build new housing for the city's underclass, and has declared the capital a "homophobia-free zone." The Caracas Metropolitan District is made of five subdivisions, each with its own mayor—some for and some against Chávez's presidency—so the direction Caracas will eventually take remained unclear.

See also **Caracas Company; Chávez, Hugo; Colonialism; Indigenous Peoples.**

BIBLIOGRAPHY

The most comprehensive study of Caracas is the multi-volume collection produced by the Universidad Central De Venezuela, *Estudio de Caracas*, 8 vols. in 15 pts. (1967–1973). One classic study of the city, also published in commemoration of its 400th anniversary, is José Antonio De Armas Chitty, *Caracas: Origen y trayectoria de una ciudad*, 2 vols. (1967).

Almandoz Marte, Arturo, ed. *Planning Latin America's Capital Cities, 1850–1950*. New York: Routledge, 2002.

De Sola Ricardo, Irma. *Contribución al estudio de los planos de Caracas: La ciudad y la provincia, 1567–1967* (1967). Among the hundreds of books describing the city and its customs, a frequently cited one is Arístides Rojas, *Crónicas de Caracas: Antología* (1962).

García Ponce, Antonio. *Los pobres de Caracas, 1873–1907: Un estudio de la pobreza urbana*. Caracas: Instituto Municipal de Publicaciones, Alcaldía de Caracas, 1995.

López Bohórquez, Alí Enrique. *La Real Audiencia de Caracas: Estudios*. Mérida, Venezuela: Ediciones del Rectorado de la Universidad de Los Andes, 1998.

Mago de Chópite, Lila, and José Jesús Hernández Palomo. *El Cabildo de Caracas (1750–1821)*. Caracas: Cabildo Metropolitano de Caracas: Universidad Pedagógica Experimental Libertador, 2002.

Márquez, Patricia C. *The Street Is My Home: Youth and Violence in Caracas*. Stanford, CA: Stanford University Press, 1999.

Martín Frechilla, Juan José. *Diálogos reconstruidos para una historia de la Caracas moderna*. Caracas: Universidad Central de Venezuela, Consejo de Desarrollo Científico y Humanístico, 2004.

Moreno, Antonio Arellano. *Caracas: Su evolución y su régimen legal*, 2d ed. (1972). A specialized book of interest is Marco Aurelio Vila, *Área Metropolitana de Caracas* (1965).

Myers, David J., and Henry A. Dietz, eds. *Capital City Politics in Latin America: Democratization and Empowerment*. Boulder, CO: Lynne Rienner, 2002.

Núñez, Enrique Bernardo. *La ciudad de los techos rojos: Calles y esquinas de Caracas*, 4th ed. (1973).

Paiva, Antonio. *Relevance of Metropolitan Government in Latin American Cities: Inter-institutional Coordination in Caracas, Venezuela and Monterrey, Mexico*. Delft, Netherlands: Eburon, 2003.

Sanoja, Mario, and Iraia Vargas Arenas. *El agua y el poder: Caracas y la formación del estado colonial caraqueño, 1567–1700*. Caracas: Banco Central de Venezuela, 2002.

SUSAN BERGLUND

CARACAS, AUDIENCIA OF.

Audiencia of Caracas, the juridical and administrative tribunal established by the Spanish crown in the province of Caracas. Created by a royal *cédula* of 31 July 1786 as part of the Bourbon dynasty's politics of centralization of control over its American dominions, it had jurisdiction over all the territory of the captaincy general of Venezuela.

From the beginning of the eighteenth century, there was a special commitment to reorganize the Spanish Empire in hopes of guaranteeing royal authority, centralizing colonial administration, and obtaining more wealth in order to maintain Spain's internal economy and recover its imperial status in Europe. During the first few decades of that century, the Compañía Guipuzcoana was established (1728); the posts of lieutenant governor and judge advocate were created; the power of the town magistrates was eliminated; and the viceroyalty of New Granada was formed.

In the latter part of the eighteenth century, during the reign of Charles III, the politics of centralization and control was pushed even further through the creation of the intendancy of the army and royal finances (1776), the captaincy general of Venezuela (1777), the Royal Council of Caracas (1793), and the Royal Audiencia of Caracas (1786). Altogether these reforms tended to consolidate Bourbon absolutism, enhance the economic prosperity of the colonial territories, and raise the efficiency of their administrations.

The object of the Spanish system of *audiencias* was to restore royal authority in the American dominions and to regulate the activities of colonial authorities and society in general. They were organs of enormous relevance not only from a judicial standpoint, but in terms of government and administration of the most diverse affairs. Before the creation of the Audiencia of Caracas, judicial affairs of the provinces belonging to the captaincy general of Venezuela were handled by the *audiencias* of Santo Domingo and Santa Fé de Bogotá. In 1673 the ministers of the tribunal of Santo Domingo solicited the king to establish a tribunal in Caracas. A similar solicitation was made in 1753 by the governor of the province of Venezuela, and another in 1769 by the Cabildo of Caracas. In this last petition, the officials stressed the high costs of administration of justice due to the great distances involved and the increase in the number of cases as a result of population increase. They also denounced the corruption and delays which plagued the system of *audiencias*. Nevertheless, the petition was denied in 1770. Not until the separation of the provinces of Maracaibo and Barinas from the Viceroyalty of New Granada and their incorporation into the captaincy general of Venezuela would the creation of the Audiencia of Caracas take place.

The creation of the Audiencia of Caracas meant the centralization of all the judicial, political, and administrative functions within the territory known today as Venezuela, which before had been handled by the *audiencias* of Santo Domingo and Santa Fé de Bogotá. Its first members were the commander in chief of Venezuela, Juan Guillelmi, who presided; the regent, Antonio López de Quintana; the judges, Francisco Ignacio Cortínes, Juan Nepomuceno de Pedrosa, and José Patricio de Ribera; and the civil and criminal prosecutor, Julián Díaz de Saravia. Administrative personnel included a chief warrant officer, a court clerk, a court reporter, a recording chancellor, an attorney for the poor, litigating attorneys, four solicitors, an appraiser, a distributor, two ordinary receivers, a receiver of court punishments, and assistants.

The *audiencia,* or tribunal, had various functions: It saw to the maintenance of royal authority, controlled the functionaries of the Crown, advised the governor, resolved ecclesiastical affairs, saw to the supervision of the royal finances, intervened in military statutes, ensured fair treatment of the Indians, and maintained constant communication with the king and the Council of the Indies to keep them up to date on provincial affairs.

The fact that the *audiencia* possessed the highest judicial authority also meant that its actions were determining factors regarding political control of the territories within its jurisdiction. This helped integrate judicial and political forces throughout the disjointed and dispersed provinces which made up the Venezuela of the day. This integration was a basic contributing factor toward the development of legal studies in Venezuela, aiding the founding of the Caracas Academy of Attorneys in 1788 and the creation of the Academy of Spanish and Public Law in 1790, both initiatives sponsored by the regent Antonio López de Quintana.

Nevertheless, the administration of justice was irregular and arbitrary, which resulted in the arrival of Joaquín Mosquera y Figueroa, who was sent to investigate accusations against the Audiencia of Caracas which had been brought before the Crown. Moreover, the predominance of Spanish ministers occupying high positions, the large amount of power with which the *audiencia* was invested, and its fierce reaction against any move to alter the colonial order resulted in numerous confrontations between the creole elite and the predominantly Spanish authorities of the *audiencia*. The Caracas city council made known its reservations regarding the authority of the tribunal. The prerogatives invested in the *audiencia* resulted in a loss of municipal autonomy and affected the political interests of the prominent citizens of Caracas. The Royal Council of Caracas, again under the control of the powerful creoles, also had reservations. As a result of this attitude, when the emancipation movement broke out, one of the first measures taken by the Junta Suprema of Caracas was the dismissal and expulsion of the ministers of the *audiencia*. It was reestablished in 1812, but because of the war it functioned irregularly. In 1813 it was dissolved, then reinstated for a short time in 1814, and dissolved once again in 1816 by order of Fernando VIII. With the final defeat of Spanish forces in 1821, the Royal Audiencia was permanently dissolved.

See also **Bourbon Reforms; Caracas; Charles III of Spain; Colonialism.**

BIBLIOGRAPHY

Hector Parra Márquez, *Historia del Colegio de Abogados de Caracas,* 2 vols. (1952–1971).

Alí Enrique López Bohorquez, *La Real Audiencia de Caracas: Su origen y organización 1786–1805* (1976).

Guillermo Morón, *Proceso de integración de Venezuela, 1776–1793* (1977).

Mario Briceño Iragorry, *El Regente Heredia, o la piedad heróica* (1980).

Teresa Albornoz De López, *Una visita a la Real Audiencia de Caracas entre 1804–1809* (1981).

Alí Enrique López Bohorquez, *Los ministros de la Real Audiencia de Caracas, 1786–1810* (1984).

José Francisco Heredia, *Memorias del Regente heredia,* 3d ed. (1986).

Additional Bibliography

López Bohórquez, Alí Enrique. *La Real Audiencia de Caracas: Estudios.* Mérida, Colombia: Ediciones del Rectorado de la Universidad de Los Andes, 1998.

Mago de Chópite, Lila, and José Jesús Hernández Palomo. *El Cabildo de Caracas (1750–1821).* Caracas: Cabildo Metropolitano de Caracas: Universidad Pedagógica Experimental Libertador, 2002.

Suárez, Santiago Gerardo. *Los fiscales indianos: Orígen y evolución del Ministerio Público.* Caracas: Academia Nacional de la Historia, 1995.

INÉS QUINTERO

CARACAS COMPANY. Caracas Company, a mercantile enterprise chartered to control trade between Venezuela and Spain from 1728 to 1784.

The Caracas Company, or Real Compañía Guipuzcoana de Caracas, was formed in Spain in 1728 by José de Patiño. The company was given the exclusive right to control the cacao trade between Venezuela and Spain. In return for this monopoly, the Caracas Company agreed to suppress the contraband trade, defend the Venezuelan coast, stimulate regional production of cacao, and provide slaves to the colony.

The Caracas Company was a mixed success. The first four decades of its existence were marked by expansion and profit. The production and legal exportation of cacao increased significantly, from 2.5 million pounds per year in the 1720s to over 6 million pounds annually in the early 1760s. This expansion, however, did little to enhance the overall condition of the colony. The planters elected to increase production in order to counteract the lower prices paid by the Caracas Company for cacao. This pushed the expansion of the plantation system—a classic case of growth without development. The efforts to halt contraband activities were not totally successful. Finally, the Caracas Company was unable to supply the colony with sufficient numbers of black slaves or European goods. These problems, the Bourbon Reforms, and the wars that disrupted trading patterns caused the company's fortunes to decline; the crown terminated the company's charter in 1784.

The Caracas Company's most enduring legacy was that it ensured the primacy of Caracas over the remainder of the captaincy-general. By expanding the economic sphere of the capital, in terms of both area and power, the activities of the Caracas Company preceded the political centralization of the colony later in the eighteenth century.

See also **Commercial Policy: Colonial Spanish America.**

BIBLIOGRAPHY

Roland Denis Hussey, *The Caracas Company, 1728–84: A Study in the History of Spanish Monopolistic Trade* (1934).

Francisco Morales Padrón, *Rebelión contra la Compañía de Caracas* (1955).

Robert J. Ferry, *The Colonial Elite of Early Caracas: Formation and Crisis, 1567–1767* (1989).

Additional Bibliography

Ferrigni, Yoston. *La crisis del régimen económico colonial en Venezuela, 1770-1830.* Caracas: Banco Central de Venezuela, 1999.

Vivas Pineda, Gerardo. *La aventura naval de la Compañía Guipuzcoana de Caracas.* Caracas: Fundación Polar, 1998.

GARY M. MILLER

CARACAS CONFERENCE (1954). *See* **Pan-American Conferences: Caracas Conference (1954).**

CARACOL. Caracol, the largest Maya archaeological site in the modern country of Belize. It is centrally located near the resource-rich Maya Mountains about 2.5 miles from the Guatemalan border. Caracol played a prominent role in Classic Maya history, and its archaeological remains document the existence of a sizable middle level of Classic Maya society.

Around 650 CE, Caracol occupied over 35 square miles and contained appoximately 36,000 structures and 150,000 people. The site maintained over 28 miles of internal roads that linked outlying architecture to epicentral groups; intervening areas contained households and terraced field systems, making Caracol a true "garden city." The earliest remains known from Caracol date to approximately 300 BCE; the latest are dated to just before 1100 CE. A hieroglyphic text records Caracol's defeat of Tikal, Guatemala, in 562 CE. Following this and other war events, the site prospered and controlled much of the southern Maya lowlands until 700 CE. The site also records a period of prosperity following 800 CE. At this time Caana, a massive building complex rising some 139 feet, was completely refurbished and new monuments erected. Even though Caracol carved no new monuments following 850 CE, archaeological remains indicate that the site was occupied for another 200 years.

Besides its extensive hieroglyphic record and size, Caracol is also noted for its burial practices and for evidence pertaining to the existence of a middle level of Classic Maya society. Of 176 burials investigated, 74 were in formal tombs; 8 tombs contained painted Maya dates. Together with caches and incense burners, the contents and distribution of these chambers throughout the site have aided in the identification of a sizable middle level of Classic Maya society, which arose following Caracol's successful warfare activities.

Despite Caracol's earlier size and prosperity, pottery and other remains left on building floors suggest that warfare may have led to an abrupt and nearly total abandonment of epicentral Caracol shortly before 900 CE. However, portions of the site continued to be occupied sporadically for another 200 years.

See also **Maya, The.**

BIBLIOGRAPHY

Diane Chase and Arlen Chase, *Investigations at the Classic Maya City of Caracol, Belize, 1985–1987* (1987), *Mesoamerican Elites: An Archaeological Assessment* (1992), pp. 30–49; *Studies in the Archaeology of Caracol, Belize* (1994).

Additional Bibliography

Aimers, James J. *Cultural Change on a Temporal and Spatial Frontier: Ceramics of the Terminal Classic to Postclassic Transition in the Upper Belize River Valley.* Oxford: Archaeopress, 2004.

Demarest, Arthur A., Prudence M. Rice, and Don Stephen Rice. *The Terminal Classic in the Maya Lowlands: Collapse, Transition, and Transformation.* Boulder: University Press of Colorado, 2004.

Garber, James, ed. *The Ancient Maya of the Belize Valley: Half a Century of Archaeological Research.* Gainesville: University Press of Florida, 2004.

Lucero, Lisa Joyce. *Social Integration in the Ancient Maya Hinterlands: Ceramic Variability in the Belize River Area.* Tempe: Arizona State University, 2001.

Martin, Simon, and Nikolai Grube. *Chronicle of the Maya Kings and Queens: Deciphering the Dynasties of the Ancient Maya.* New York: Thames & Hudson, 2000.

ARLEN F. CHASE
DIANE Z. CHASE

CARAL. The city of Cuzco is known as the capital of the Inca Empire and Machu Picchu as the base of one of the last Inca rulers. But very few people know that the Sacred City of Caral, in north-central Peru, was built by the first political state to be formed in America, 4,400 years before the rule of the Incas. The Caral civilization laid the foundations of social, political, and religious organization, of the cross-management of territory and its resources, of the production of knowledge and its technological application, and of other cultural expressions that were to last throughout the Andean cultural process.

The Caral civilization is one of the oldest civilizations on earth. Originating in a geographically diverse territory, it was based on a specialized but mixed economy of fishing and farming and within a complex sphere of interaction that integrated coastal, mountain, and high jungle populations.

The Caral-Supe social system took shape on the American continent in the same period as the other early civilizing centers of Mesopotamia, Egypt, India, and China. The people of Caral predated by at least 1,800 years those who inhabited Mesoamerica, where another of the world's six known centers of civilization has been identified. However, as opposed to other civilizations such as those in Mesopotamia, Egypt, and India, which exchanged goods, knowledge and experiences, the Caral civilization achieved an early development in complete isolation from its contemporaries in America.

THE SACRED CITY OF CARAL

This urban center is located at the start of the middle reaches of the Supe River valley, in the province of Barranca, department of Lima, near Km 184 on the North Pan-American Highway in north-central Peru. Of the urban settlements identified in this area as dating from the Late Archaic period (3000 to 2000 BCE), Caral is the most remarkable because of its ordering of space and architectural complexity. Each settlement contains public buildings and the characteristic sunken circular plaza, plus various groups of dwelling areas. Caral is not the largest urban center, but it is distinguished by its elaborate architectural design—notably its spacious areas for public gatherings—and the heavy investment of labor evident in its construction. It covers 66 hectares, in which one can distinguish a central area and an outlying area. In the central area, the buildings are arranged in two sections: the *upper section*, containing the more exceptional public and residential constructions organized in sectors and streets, a sunken circular plaza, three areas for public gatherings, the homes of officials, and an extensive residential grouping of dwellings for specialists and public servants; and the *lower section*, with smaller buildings including the amphitheater architectural complex and a group of residences covering an area of equally small dimension. The outlying area, located on the periphery, has numerous residences grouped and arranged in the shape of an archipelago over the alluvial plain adjoining the river valley.

The public and residential constructions did not have a single exclusive religious, political, or residential use but instead served multiple functions and also contained workspaces. The homes of the elite replicated, on a smaller scale, some of the dimensions of the public buildings to which they were related.

The buildings display a similar architectural design and some recurring components, although their differences are denoted by their location within the city, their alignment with astral bodies, their size, and the materials used in their construction. The public buildings have a central section and two lateral sections, one on each side. The elements they share include a central stairway as an ordered axis of the construction, stepped terraces, a ceremonial room on the top with a fire pit in the center, a back room with a platform and two side rooms in addition to other rooms off to the side, and a small altar with a fire pit fed by underground ventilation shafts. This altar, with a single exception, is circular in shape in the lower-section buildings and quadrangular in those of the upper section. Every building had adjacent workshops as well as rooms for the eating and drinking that accompanied the more private ceremonies and rites. As for the artisans' and laborers' quarters, although smaller in size, they also had an area for receiving work and patios where work was performed, in addition to enclosures and small storerooms.

The constructed space in the Sacred City of Caral reveals a long history of change covering almost one thousand years, ranging from construction of the early buildings, to their enlargement and formalization, and then to a period of lesser investment in labor and materials at the end of the occupation. Caral had been inhabited for several centuries before it began its profound architectural transformation into a city based on a design that had been previously prepared and was then executed by functionaries with the necessary authority to organize the labor and ensure that specifications were met.

The symbolic significance of the public buildings is worthy of note. Although they were periodically renovated, their builders took care each time to retain the link between the old and the new, between the past and the present. In these spaces that belonged to their forbears and to them, Caral authorities, representing the collective, spoke with their ancestors and the gods. Both ancestors and deities were shared by the members of the group through their authorities and the constructed space. This identification bound each individual to the social fabric while providing emotional security.

ECONOMIC CONDITIONS THAT SUPPORTED SUPE SOCIETY

The technological progress achieved in agriculture and fishing in the inter-Andean valleys and on the coast, and the organization of the inhabitants and trade in goods, all influenced the development of the productive forces among the various human groups inhabiting the north-central area and those of the Supe River basin in particular.

In Supe society, the cultivation of food and industrial plants (including the cotton used in making textiles, especially fishing nets) and the massive extraction of fish (especially anchovies) and mollusks fostered the local specialization of labor and economic complementarity through an ongoing trade in products between farming and fishing communities. This made it possible to accumulate a production surplus and to establish labor specialization, short- and long-distance trade, the social division of labor, and the rise of political authorities.

THE SOCIAL FABRIC AND FORMATION OF THE STATE

The surplus of society's production in agriculture and in fishing was distributed unequally to the benefit of the representatives of higher-status families and specialists in charge of the activities necessary to ensure reproduction of the system. In this way, farming and fishing communities formed in the north-central area, where they were called *pachaca* communities and were led by their political authorities. These authorities ordered the construction of public buildings for administrative and ceremonial purposes plus residential units and defined their territory of economic production.

The accumulation of a production surplus mainly benefited the populations settled in the middle reaches of the Supe River valley, in the best location for trade in goods. The added value in the manufacture of cotton fiber and the processing of anchovies and sardines for trade purposes enriched and enhanced the prestige of the political authorities in charge of local and interethnic trade. Chief among the political authorities was the *hunu*, or "lord of the lords" of the settlements in the valley and along the coast. This model of sociopolitical organization was to continue to reach far into pre-Hispanic Peru.

The pristine Caral-Supe state was able to mobilize enormous workforces and, through complex social networks, was able to attract for its own benefit the surplus produced over a wide territory consisting of the coastal valleys of Chancay, Huaura, Supe, Pativilca, and Fortaleza, the inter-Andean valleys of the Callejón de Huaylas and the area of Conchucos, and the upper Huallaga and Marañón river valleys in the high jungle. An extensive sphere of interaction was established in the area in which goods and knowledge circulated, thus linking populations on the Pacific coast to those in the Amazon Basin.

Although increased net-fishing activity and canal-irrigated agriculture generated production surpluses, and access to a variety of goods and experiences that supported scientific and technological development was made possible, there were no similar benefits in the social sphere. Hierarchical social strata formed, with a highly unequal distribution of social production.

This social division is evident in the residential architecture and in clothing and personal ornaments such as necklaces, the large earplugs of the male authorities, and the mantillas of the upper-society women. This distinction is also evident in the human remains, contrasting individuals with chronic anemia or with physical evidence of forced labor to children who received various treatments, all based on the social status of the particular individual's family.

THE IMPORTANCE OF KNOWLEDGE IN THE DEVELOPMENT OF A CIVILIZATION

These socioeconomic conditions supported the work of specialists. Various sciences, technologies, and arts developed. Astronomy, mathematics, biology, medicine, and other fields of knowledge were applied to predicting the weather, devising a calendar, building works of monumental architecture, managing soils and water by constructing irrigation and drainage canals and preparing fields for cultivation, genetically improving plants, treating disease, devising means of public administration, and manufacturing artifacts for ceremonial, business, and sumptuary purposes. The production of knowledge, fulfilled by specialists, also gave them power and enhanced living conditions for the populations of the north-central area during the emergence of civilization.

IDEOLOGY AND THE ROLE OF RELIGION

An elaborate system of beliefs, rituals, and ceremonies permeated the societies of the valleys on the coast between the Santa and Chillón rivers and in the neighboring regions of the Andes and surrounding jungle, linked by the dominant political state of Supe, or attracted by its prestige. Complex mythological universes were thus linked, sharing content and symbols and becoming identified as the Kotosh tradition.

In the absence of a military organization and armed forces, religion was used to achieve cohesion within the human group and to exercise control of society. The people lived their daily lives engaged in labor to produce for their own sustenance and for the service of their gods, authorities, and specialists, as well as to participate in construction, burial, and public remodeling works.

SIGNIFICANCE AND IMPORTANCE OF THE CARAL-SUPE CIVILIZATION

The first contribution that archaeological investigation in the Sacred City of Caral has made to present-day society is in the field of historical knowledge: This was a civilization of an antiquity comparable to that of Old World civilizations, providing evidence that allows scholars to question prior ideas regarding the formation of civilization, the state, and urban life and making it possible to evaluate the human condition on the planet.

In the specific case of Peru, this knowledge provides information on the great chronology and depth of the civilizing process and reveals the responses of the societies administering this territory and, as in other parts of the world, such knowledge serves to evaluate those experiences in order to recover each society's positive accomplishments and learn from its failures.

The Sacred City of Caral reveals the extraordinary creative capacity of the inhabitants of the varied north-central Andean territory, who, through effort and organization, were able to attain autonomously the state of civilization.

The relevance of Caral-Supe is based not only on its position as the oldest civilization in America, whose prestige lasted from 3,000 to 2,000 BCE, but also on its having been the mother culture that established a model of sociopolitical organization that was to spread to other societies in contemporary Peru and to survive into later historic periods. From the era of Caral come the *ayllu-* and *pachaca*-based social and political systems, symbolic architectural elements such as atria and double-jamb doorways and niches, agricultural terraces, the calendar, geoglyphs and mastery of astronomy to determine climate changes, record keeping on quipus, and more. Despite differences in lifestyles, cultures, and languages in pre-Hispanic Peru, there was a cultural process with a shared substratum.

From a cultural perspective, the Sacred City of Caral is sure to become one of the most important instruments to strengthen Peru's cultural identity and social cohesion, to develop into a prominent identifying symbol that enhances the nation's self-esteem. And in terms of economics, the importance being attached to the Sacred City of Caral, through the investigation, consolidation, and restoration of its stunning public and residential buildings, will make it a first-class archaeological tourist attraction nationally and internationally and a source of significant income for improving the living conditions of the local population and of the country as a whole.

See also **Archaeology; Indigenous Peoples.**

BIBLIOGRAPHY

Shady, R., et al. "Dating Caral, a Preceramic Site in the Supe Valley on the Central Coast of Peru." *Science* 292 (April 27, 2001): 723–726.

Shady, R., and C. Leyva, eds. *La Ciudad Sagrada de Caral-Supe.* Lima: Inst. Nat. de Cultura, 2003.

RUTH SHADY SOLÍS

CARAMURÚ (?–1557). Caramurú (Diogo Álvares Correia; *d.* 5 April 1557). Born in Viana do Castelo, northern Portugal, Caramurú arrived in Bahia de Todos os Santos, Brazil, sometime between 1509 and 1511 under uncertain circumstances: he may have been a *degredado* (criminal), a shipwrecked sailor, or a deserter. Because of his skills with firearms, he was befriended by the local Tupinambá Indians, one of whom he married.

With his knowledge of Tupi and of the lands and waters around All Saints Bay, Caramurú, the "Man of Fire," as the indigenous people dubbed him, proved extremely useful to a succession of Europeans who came to Bahia, among them ship captains; a lord proprietor, Francisco Pereira Coutinho; Brazil's first two governors-general, Tomé De Sousa and Duarte da Costa; and the first members of the Society of Jesus. He became an adviser to the proprietor, though it remains unknown whether he ignited or defused an indigenous uprising against him. He also aided Tomé de Sousa in the selection of a site for the city of Salvador, Brazil's first capital. He left part of his estate to the Jesuits and became the first civilian to be interred in their church in Salvador, where he died.

See also **Sousa, Tomé de; Tupinambá.**

BIBLIOGRAPHY

Joel Serrão, ed., *Dicionário de história de Portugal* (1971), vol. 1, pp. 479–480, which includes an extensive bibliography.

Additional Bibliography

Doria, Francisco Antonio. *Caramuru e Catarina.* São Paulo: Editora Senac, 1999.

Gruzinski, Serge, et al. *A passagem do século.* São Paulo: Companhia das Letras, 1999.

DAURIL ALDEN

CARAMURUS. Caramurus, a Brazilian political movement that called for the return of Brazil's first emperor after his abdication in 1831. The departure of Dom Pedro I, the first monarch of independent Brazil, ushered in a period of political confusion in the country. Moderate and radical liberals, many of whom had been instrumental in forcing Pedro I to give up his throne, struggled to enact a series of reforms, many of which promised to decentralize the young nation's political system. In reaction to this wave of liberalism and also to the anti-Portuguese sentiment the liberals often exhibited, a range of highly placed political and military figures, most of them born in Portugal, came together in a conservative political coalition. Centered on a simple restorationist program—a call for the return of Dom Pedro I either as monarch or as regent for his six-year-old son—the Caramurus managed to gain some popular support in both urban and rural areas and became a serious threat to the moderate liberal-controlled government of the early regency (1831–1840).

During the short life of their movement, the Caramurus acted as a provocative conservative opposition. They were active in the press; in fact, the movement took its name from the title of its leading newspaper, *O Caramuru.* They also organized their own association, the Sociedade Conservadora da Constituição Jurada do Império (Society for Con-

serving the Constitution as Sworn), which later became the Sociedade Militar (Military Society). The attacks that the Caramurus launched through these various organs came to a head in a conspiracy against the liberal government in 1832. Though suppressed easily, this plot demonstrated the seriousness of the conflict between these largely Portuguese conservatives and the state. The simplicity of the Caramuru program ultimately proved to be a fatal weakness. With the death of Pedro I in Portugal in 1834, the movement lost its definition and its members drifted into coalitions with other political factions.

See also **Pedro I of Brazil.**

BIBLIOGRAPHY

Thomas Flory, "Race and Social Control in Independent Brazil," in *Journal of Latin American Studies* 9, no. 2 (1977): 199–224.

Roderick J. Barman, *Brazil: The Forging of a Nation, 1798–1852* (1988).

Leslie Bethell and José Murilo De Carvalho, "1822–1850," in *Brazil: Empire and Republic, 1822–1930,* edited by Leslie Bethell (1989).

Additional Bibliography

Fagundes, Antonio Augusto. *Revoluçao farroupilha: Cronologia do "Decenio heróico, 1835–1845."* Porto Alegre: Martins Livreiro Editor, 2003.

Flores, Moacyr. *Negros na Revolução Farroupilha: Traição em Porongos e farsa em Ponche Verde.* Porto Alegre: EST, 2004.

Hasse, Geraldo, and Guilherme Kolling. *Lanceiros negros.* Porto Alegre: JA Editores, 2006.

Spalding, Walter. *Farroupilhas e caramurús, A brasildade dos farrapos; história, documentos, e bibliografia sobre o movimento reivindicador de 1835/45.* Porto Alegre: Imprensa oficial, 1944.

Telles, Jorge. *Farrapos: A guerra que perdemos.* Porto Alegre: Martins Livreiro Editor, 2004.

Ubim, Carlos. *Os farrapos.* Porto Alegre: Zero Hora, 2003.

ROGER A. KITTLESON

CARA SUCIA. Cara Sucia, a large Late Preclassic (400 BCE–250 CE) site located on the Pacific coastal plain, in the southwest corner of the Department of Ahuachapán in western El Salvador. Very little archaeological research has been done at Cara

Sucia, but a general chronology of historical and cultural development has been determined. The site is composed of low clusters of temple mounds, whose architecture and arrangement are characteristic of the Pacific coastal plain centers of the Late Preclassic period. This architectural organizational pattern contrasts with that of the nearby Salvadoran piedmont and highland basins. Piedmont sites typically have wide, artificial terraces that support potbelly monuments and jaguar heads, while highland sites have larger and more complex ceremonial centers.

In addition to its large size, Cara Sucia's impressive inventory of sculpture also emphasizes that this was an important ceremonial center. Cara Sucia is notable for its numerous Late Preclassic "jaguar head" sculptures. These jaguar heads are squarish, stylized stone faces. The dominant decorative motifs that form the face are rectangles and scrolls.

During the Middle Classic (400–700 CE), the massive Valley of Mexico center of Teotihuacán influenced much of the southern Pacific coastal plain. Cara Sucia is strongly linked by style of ceramics, architecture, and sculpture to the site of Bilbao, Guatemala in the Late Classic period (700–900 CE). Bilbao, in turn, appears to have strong connections to Teotihuacán. Thus, Cara Sucia was probably indirectly influenced by Teotihuacán.

Trade of cacao (*Theobroma cacao*) and obsidian (volcanic glass), both ritually important and utilitarian goods, appears to have been the basis of long distance interactions with Teotihuacán. Excavations have shown that cacao was present at Cara Sucia. A deposit of carbonized tree seeds included some tentatively identified as *Theobroma cacao*. A fragment of a life-sized cacao pod effigy found at Cara Sucia also indicates the ritual importance of cacao cultivation there. An U-shaped ball court, Balsam Coast–style sculpture, and ceramics indicate that the Postclassic-period (900–1500 CE) Cara Sucia settlement prospered, probably largely due to trading cacao.

See also **Archaeology.**

BIBLIOGRAPHY

Stanley H. Boggs, "Las esculturas espigadas y otros datos sobre las ruinas de Cara Sucia, Departamento de Ahuachapán," in *Anales del Museo Nacional "David J. Guzmán"* nos. 42–48 (1968–1975): 37–56.

Paul E. Amaroli, "Cara Sucia: Nueva luz sobre el pasado de la costa occidental de El Salvador," in *Universitas* 1 (1984): 15–19.

Arthur A. Demarest, *The Archaeology of Santa Leticia and the Rise of Maya Civilization,* in publication 52 of the Middle American Research Institute, Tulane University (1986); *Informe preliminar de las excavaciones arqueológicas en Cara Sucia, Departamento de Ahuachapán, El Salvador,* manuscript on file, Patrimonio Cultural, El Salvador, and the Department of Anthropology, Vanderbilt University (1987).

Additional Bibliography

Cobos, Rafael. *Síntesis de la arqueología de El Salvador (1850-1991).* San Salvador: Dirección General de Publicaciones e Impresos, Consejo Nacional para la Cultura y Arte, Dirección General del Patrimonio Cultural, 1994.

Dull, Robert A., John R. Southon, and Payson Sheets. "Volcanism, Ecology and Culture: A Reassessment of the Volcán Ilopango Tbj Eruption in the Southern Maya Realm." *Latin American Antiquity* Vol. 12, No. 1 (March 2001): 24-44.

Fowler, William R., and Federico Trujillo. *El Salvador: Antiguas civilizaciones.* San Salvador: Banco Agrícola Comercial de El Salvador, 1995.

McNeil, Cameron L. *Chocolate in Mesoamerica: A Cultural History of Cacao.* Gainesville: University Press of Florida, 2006.

KATHRYN SAMPECK

CARAZO ODIO, RODRIGO (1926–).

Rodrigo Carazo Odio (*b.* 27 December 1926), president of Costa Rica (1978–1982), founder of the University for Peace (1980). Born in Cartago, Rodrigo Carazo began his distinguished career in public service in the aftermath of the 1948 revolution, when he was named a city councilman in Puntarenas. Shortly after receiving his degree in economics and administration from the University of Costa Rica (1951), he served at the national level during the first elected presidency of José Figueres Ferrer (1953–1958).

Carazo began his political career as a follower of Figueres and held high positions in his administration and in that of Francisco Orlich Bolmarcich (1962–1966). He broke with the National Liberation Party (PLN) and formed the Democratic Renovation Party, a group that later joined with other parties to form the Unity Party, which supported his successful candidacy in 1978.

Although he came to the presidency on a ground swell of popular support for reform, his administration became embroiled in logistical support for the Sandinista revolution in Nicaragua. Because of charges of arms trafficking against members of his administration and oil crisis–induced inflation, his administration came to be popularly identified with high inflation and declining living standards after a generation of sustained economic growth. Despite many positive programs and high initial popularity, Carazo could not overcome the twin blows of rising oil prices and falling coffee prices.

Carazo later became a private businessman, although in 1983–1984 he did briefly attempt to create a new political party, Partido Radical Democrático (Radical Democratic Party).

See also **Costa Rica; Costa Rica, National Liberation Party.**

BIBLIOGRAPHY

Rodrigo Carazo Odio, *Acción para la historia* (1982).

Richard Biesanz, Karen Zubris Biesanz, and Mavis Hiltunen Biesanz, *The Costa Ricans* (1982; rev. ed. 1988).

Additional Bibliography

Abarca, Carlos A. *Rodrigo Carazo y la utopía de la dignidad: 1970–1983.* Heredia, Costa Rica: EUNA, 1995.

Mora A., Jorge A. *El valor de la independencia.* Heredia, Costa Rica: Universidad Nacional, 1996.

JOHN PATRICK BELL

CARBALLIDO, EMILIO (1925–). Emilio Carballido (*b.* 22 May 1925), Mexican playwright. Carballido, a native of Córdoba, Veracruz, has been at the center of the Mexican theater since the 1950s. A prolific playwright with nearly 100 plays published and performed, he has set the standard of quality and originality in the contemporary theater while championing a younger generation of writers. Imbued with boundless energy, enthusiasm, and a superb sense of humor, Carballido is identified primarily with the theater, although he also has written several stories, novels, and movie scripts. His creative spirit has led him to experiment with virtually all forms of theater, including farce, children's theater, allegory, opera, and monologue, as he plays constantly with elements of tragedy, comedy, folklore, classical myth, satire, and politics.

Beginning with his earliest play in 1948, Carballido has mixed realism and fantasy in innovative ways, building a pattern of experimentation in his search for ways to express a Mexican reality deeply rooted in tradition. His provincial plays, such as *Rosalba y los Llaveros* (1950) and *La danza que sueña la tortuga* (1955), were surpassed by daring experiments with magic and symbolic figures such as those in *La hebra de oro* (1956). His farces, such as *¡Silencio, pollos pelones, ya les van a echar su maíz!* (1963), are entertaining and provocative. In 1966 *Yo también hablo de la rosa*, a dramatization of the creative process built around the metaphor of the rose and the infinite ways of perceiving reality, became a classic of the Mexican theater. Carballido continued his experimentation with plays such as *Tiempo de ladrones: La historia de Chucho el Roto* (1984) which glorifies a Mexican-style Robin Hood in a complex play written for two settings (*dos tandas*). His *Rosa de dos aromas* (1987) has been particularly popular for its portrayal of two women "married" to the same man.

In addition to his numerous plays Carballido received the *Ariel de Oro* for his grand career in film, most notably *Nazarín* (2002) which was produced in collaboration with Luis Buñuel. In addition, Caraballido was awarded the *Premio Nacional de Literatura* (1996) in Mexico. Carballido has set the standards, then broken them, throughout his long and productive career.

See also **Theater.**

BIBLIOGRAPHY

Margaret S. Peden, *Emilio Carballido* (1980).

Jacqueline Eyring Bixler, "A Theatre of Contradictions: The Recent Works of Emilio Carballido," *Latin American Theatre Review* 18, no. 2 (1985): 57–65.

Judith Ishmael Bissett, "Visualizing Carballido's *Orinoco:* The Play in Two Imagined Performances," *Gestos* 5, no. 9 (April 1990): 65–74.

Diana Taylor, "Theatre and Transculturation: Emilio Carballido," in *Theatre of Crisis: Drama and Politics in Latin America* (1991).

Additional Bibliography

Bixler, Jacqueline Eyring. *Convention and Transgression in the Theater of Emilio Carballido.* Lewisberg: Bucknell University Press, 1997.

Coria-Sánchez, Carlos. *Visiones: Perspectivas literarias de la realidad social hispana.* New Haven, CT: Yale University Press, 2002.

Gordon, Samuel. *Teatro mexicano reciente: Aproximaciones críticas.* El Paso: University of Texas, 2005.

GEORGE WOODYARD

CARBALLO, AIDA (1916–1985).

Aida Carballo (*b.* 1916; *d.* 19 April 1985), Argentine printmaker, illustrator, and ceramist. Carballo studied in Buenos Aires at the Prilidiano Pueyrredón School of Fine Arts, at the Ceramics National School, and at the De la Cárcova School of Fine Arts. In 1959 the French government awarded her a grant to study in Paris. She also studied engraving and drawing in Madrid and Barcelona. Her engravings describe Buenos Aires life in its rich local color. Carballo's use of engraving, instead of the popular industrial materials of the period, made her work the center of critique by other Modernist artists. The majority of her works include autobiographical themes and self-portraiture though they also include portraits of suburban landscapes largely featuring female images and heterosexual erotica. She produced work of marked linear accent, which has a haunting, overwhelming effect, presenting a complex, ironic vision of the contemporary world.

See also **Art: The Twentieth Century.**

BIBLIOGRAPHY

Lily Sosa De Newton, *Diccionario biográfico de mujeres argentinas,* 3d ed. (1986).

Vicente Gesualdo, Aldo Biglione, and Rodolfo Santos, *Diccionario de artistas plásticos en la Argentina* (1988).

Additional Bibliography

García de la Mata, Helena. *El personaje de la colina.* Buenos Aires: El francotirador Ediciones, 1998.

Perrone, Alberto. *Aída Carballo: Arte y locura.* Buenos Aires: Emecé Editores, 1995.

AMALIA CORTINA ARAVENA

CARBO Y NOBOA, PEDRO JOSÉ

(1813–1895). Pedro José Carbo y Noboa (*b.* 19 March 1813; *d.* 24 December 1895), leading proponent of liberalism in nineteenth-century Ecuador. A persistent voice for coastal interests, Carbo, a native of Guayaquil, served in Congress and as a diplomat in the early decades of the republic. His fierce ideological battles against archconservative dictator Gabriel García Moreno (1861–1865, 1869–1875) proved to be the defining struggles of Carbo's career. He led the opposition to García Moreno's concordat with the Holy See of 1862. Named president of the Senate in 1867, Carbo used his position to battle the figurehead presidents named by García Moreno. In 1869 Liberals supported Carbo in his bid for the presidency, but he was defeated and exiled to Panama.

During the dictatorship of Ignacio de Veintimilla (1876–1883), Carbo accepted appointments as minister of the Treasury (1876) and supreme chief of Guayaquil province (1883). His anticlerical policies, including steps toward the secularization of education, greatly angered the Catholic hierarchy and led to armed revolts against the government. As Veintimilla grew increasingly corrupt and violent, Carbo left the government, ultimately joining the Liberal opposition. After Veintimilla's defeat in 1883, Carbo served as head of the provisional government. In the last years of his life Carbo wrote *Páginas de la historia del Ecuador* (1898), a work that brought together his liberal perspectives on nineteenth-century Ecuadorian politics.

See also **Ecuador: Since 1830.**

BIBLIOGRAPHY

On nineteenth-century Ecuadorian politics, see Osvaldo Hurtado's interpretive *Political Power in Ecuador,* translated by Nick D. Mills, Jr. (1985).

Frank MacDonald Spindler's descriptive *Nineteenth Century Ecuador: An Historical Introduction* (1987). For a brief analysis of Ecuadorian political economy in the nineteenth century, consult David W. Schodt, *Ecuador: An Andean Enigma* (1987).

Additional Bibliography

Cabo, Pedro. *Obras.* Guayaquil: Lit. e Impr. de la Universidad de Guayaquil, 1983.

RONN F. PINEO

CÁRCANO, MIGUEL ÁNGEL (1889–

1978). Miguel Ángel Cárcano was an Argentine lawyer, politician, and historian. In 1929 he was elected national deputy for the province of Córdoba. Following the coup d'état in 1930 that overthrew President Hipólito Irigoyen and dissolved the congress, Cárcano organized the Concordancia (Concordance), an alliance chiefly of anti-Irigoyen radicals, for the fraudulent elections of 1931; he was reelected as deputy.

In 1933 Cárcano was part of the Argentine delegation charged with signing the controversial Roca–Runciman Pact in London. The treaty awarded a broad range of benefits to British enterprises; in exchange, Argentina was allowed to continue exporting beef to the United Kingdom in the adverse international economic context set off by the world economic crisis of 1929. In 1936 he was named minister of agriculture by President Agustín P. Justo (1932–1938).

From 1942 to 1946 he held the post of ambassador to Great Britain. In 1945 he led the Argentine delegation that signed the United Nations Charter in San Francisco, in spite of opposition by the Soviet Union, who reproached Argentina for its neutral stance during the war. In 1961 Cárcano, a well-known spokesperson for the liberal wing of the Argentine conservative movement at the time, was named minister of foreign relations by the intransigent radical president, Arturo Frondizi (1958–1962). During Cárcano's brief period of service, Argentina abstained on the vote to expel Cuba from the Organization of American States in 1962, notwithstanding U.S. pressure, and lobbied for a stronger Alliance for Progress to keep communism from spreading on the continent. Having published *Evolución histórica del régimen de la tierra pública* (Historical evolution of the regime of public lands) in 1917, in which he described the process of land concentration in Argentina, he was strongly motivated by confidence in a promising "manifest destiny" for an Argentine nation founded on the value of its "genuinely European" citizenry.

See also **Alliance for Progress; Argentina: The Twentieth Century; Concordancia; Frondizi, Arturo; Irigoyen, Hipólito; Justo, José Agustín Pedro; Roca-Runciman Pact (1933).**

BIBLIOGRAPHY

Cárcano, Miguel Ángel. *La sexta república.* Buenos Aires: Araujo, 1958.

Cárcano, Miguel Ángel. *Evolución histórica del régimen de la tierra pública, 1810–1916,* 3rd edition. Buenos Aires: Eudeba, 1972.

Paradiso, José. *Debates y trayectoria de la política exterior argentina.* Buenos Aires: Grupo Editor Latinoamericano, 1993.

Tulchin, Joseph S. *Argentina and the United States: A Conflicted Relationship.* Boston: Twayne, 1990

VICENTE PALERMO

CÁRCANO, RAMÓN JOSÉ (1860–1946).

Ramón José Cárcano (*b.* 18 April 1860; *d.* 2 June 1946), Argentine politician and historian. Born and raised in, and long-time political chieftain of, the province of Córdoba, Cárcano was a remarkably successful conservative politician. Educated at the University of Córdoba, he affiliated with governors Antonio del Viso and Miguel Juárez Celman (the latter was elected president in 1886). Cárcano was elected to the national Congress in 1884 and two years later returned to Córdoba, where he occupied several key ministerial posts, including justice and education. Between 1890 and 1910 he devoted himself to teaching law and writing. Elected again to Congress in 1910, he returned to public life as one of the most respected politicians of the interior provinces. Cárcano was passed over repeatedly, though always in the running, as candidate for president. He was instrumental in the rise of President Roque Sáenz Peña, who promulgated the suffrage law of 1912. In 1913 he returned to Córdoba as governor and dominated the province for the next several decades. During his terms, he earned the reputation for sponsoring transportation and public works development. He also served as ambassador to Brazil (1933–1938). Cárcano wrote several classic accounts of mid-nineteenth-century Argentine politics and was twice president of the National Academy of History.

See also **Argentina: The Nineteenth Century; Argentina: The Twentieth Century.**

BIBLIOGRAPHY

Ramón José Cárcano, *Del sitio de Buenos Aires al campo de Cepeda (1852–1859)* (1921); *Guerra del Paraguay, acción y reacción de la Triple Allianza* (1941); and *Mis primeros ochenta años* (1945).

Natalio Botana, *El orden conservador: La política argentina entre 1880 y 1916* (1977).

JEREMY ADELMAN

CARDENAL, ERNESTO (1925–).

Ernesto Cardenal (*b.* 20 January 1925), Nicaraguan writer and minister of culture (1979–1988). Born into a wealthy family in Granada, Cardenal received his early education from the Christian Brothers and the Jesuits. A precocious writer, he allied himself with Carlos Martínez Rivas and others of the Generation of 1940. As a student of philosophy at the Universidad Nacional Autónoma de México (1942–1947), Cardenal joined other Nicaraguan exiles opposed to the dictatorship of Anastasio Somoza García. Reading T. S. Eliot and the Imagists (Ezra Pound and Amy Lowell, among others) during two subsequent years of study at Columbia University (1947–1949) shaped his emerging *exteriorista* poetics, which emphasized nonmetaphoric language and concrete (frequently historical) detail.

Cardenal's political, poetic, and critical abilities were evident in *La ciudad deshabitada* (1946), *Proclama del conquistador* (1947), and his introduction to *Nueva poesía nicaragüense* (1949; translated as *New Nicaraguan Poetry*). Following a year of study in Spain (1949–1950), he returned to Managua for seven years, where he operated a bookstore and formed a small publishing company (both called El Hilo Azul) with ex-*vanguardista* José Coronel Urtecho. He continued to write poetry on romantic and, increasingly, political themes.

Influenced by the Chilean poet Pablo Neruda and others, Cardenal explored Latin American indigenous culture and native resistance to domination, concerns that are prominent in *Con Walker en Nicaragua* (1952). His participation in the anti-Somoza April Rebellion of 1954 supplied themes for *La hora cero* or *Hora O* (1957–1959), especially that of the renewal of life through revolutionary activity. A religious conversion in 1956 led him to two years (1957–1959) of study with Thomas Merton at a Trappist monastery in Gethsemane, Kentucky, and two more years at a Benedictine monastery in Cuernavaca, Mexico; ultimately he went to Colombia to study for the priesthood (1961–1965). Cardenal's evolving political and religious views issued in the lyrical poems of *Gethsemani, Kentucky* (1960), *Epigramas* (1961), *Salmos* (1964; a recasting of the Psalms in terms of present-day political realities and language), and *Oración por Marilyn Monroe y otras poemas* (1965).

In 1966 Cardenal established on the island of Solentiname in Lake Nicaragua, an experimental Christian contemplative colony oriented to agricultural, social, political (anti-Somoza), and cultural work among the largely illiterate rural population. During the Solentiname years, Cardenal published the political poems of *El estrecho dudoso* (1966), *Homenaje a los indios americanos* (1969), and *Canto nacional* (1972) and the Christian-Marxist exegetical dialogues of *El evangelio en Solentiname* (1975). The Solentiname community was destroyed by Somoza's National Guard in 1977. Increasingly Marxist in orientation during the 1970s, Cardenal became a cultural ambassador for the anti-Somoza FSLN (Sandinista National Liberation Front) in 1976. Appointed minister of culture by the new Sandinista government in 1979, he projected a "revolutionary, popular, national, and anti-imperialist" cultural policy modeled substantially upon the earlier Solentiname experiments (especially the controversial *exteriorista* poetry workshops and primitivist painting). Ambitious plans for film production and a national system of centers for popular culture, libraries, museums, and theater and dance companies were frustrated by the post-1982 budget crisis, exacerbated by the Contra war financed by the United States. The Ministry of Culture ceased to exist as a separate entity in 1988.

At the end of the twentieth century Cardenal published his first two volumes of memoirs *Vida Perdida* (1998) and *Las ínsulas extrañas* (2002) and toured Germany, Italy, and Spain where his works had been translated. Upon his return he was invited to Cuba for *La Semana del Autor* (the Week of the Author) (2003) where he was honored with the José Martí Award. Subsequently he was awarded the Nicolás Guillén Literary Prize in Italy (2004). In May 2005, Cardenal was nominated—but did not receive—the Nobel Prize in Literature.

See also **Liberation Theology; Nicaragua, Sandinista National Liberation Front (FSLN).**

BIBLIOGRAPHY

The best single source on Cardenal is Paul W. Borgeson, Jr., *Hacia el hombre nuevo: Poesía y pensamiento de Ernesto Cardenal* (1984). On the Ministry of Culture see David E. Whisnant, "Sandinista Cultural Policy: Notes Toward an Analysis in Historical Context," in *Central America: Historical Perspectives on the Contemporary Crises,* edited by Ralph Lee Woodward, Jr. (1988), and *The Politics of Culture in Nicaragua* (1995). Cardenal's own major statements on culture, together with those of other members of the FSLN's national directorate, appear in Nicaragua, Ministry of Culture, *Hacia una política cultural de la Revolución Popular Sandinista* (1982), esp. pp. 162–273. An illuminating set of interviews (including one with Cardenal) is in Steven White, ed., *Culture and Politics in Nicaragua: Testimonies of Poets and Writers* (1986). Also useful is John Beverley and Marc Zimmerman, *Literature and Politics in the Central American Revolutions* (1990).

Additional Bibliography

Pastor Alonso, Ma Angeles. *La poesía cósmica de Ernesto Cardenal.* Huelva: Diputación Provincial, 1998.

Sheesley, Joel et al. *Sandino in the Streets.* Bloomington: Indiana University Press, 1991.

DAVID E. WHISNANT

CÁRDENAS, BERNARDINO DE (1579–1668).

Bernardino de Cárdenas (*b.* 1579; *d.* 20 October 1668), bishop of Paraguay (1642–1651) and opponent of the Jesuits. Born in La Paz, Upper Peru, Cárdenas joined the Franciscan order at the age of fifteen. After ordination, he preached for twenty years in native languages to the Quechua and Aymara peoples of Peru and Upper Peru, who reputedly revered him. His reputation caused King Philip IV in 1638 to nominate, and Pope Urban VIII in 1640 to appoint, Cárdenas bishop of Paraguay. Consecrated in Santiago del Estero in 1641, Cárdenas then left for Asunción, where the bulls of his investiture were read in 1642.

Cárdenas allied himself with labor-hungry Paraguayan settlers who coveted the Guaranís in Jesuit missions as workers. He also insisted on visiting all curacies and parishes of his bishopric, including the Jesuit missions, a policy that Jesuits opposed. These disputes intensified friction between colonial Franciscans and Jesuits. The Jesuits challenged the validity of the bishop's consecration, hoping to remove him from the province. Cárdenas also fought with Governor Gregorio de Hinestrosa, a Jesuit ally, who brought Guaraní forces from the Jesuit missions to Asunción to shield the Jesuits from the Paraguayans, an action that the Paraguayans resented.

Cárdenas criticized Jesuit economic practices and accused the fathers of teaching false doctrine. In 1644 the governor expelled Cárdenas from

Paraguay. Supported by Franciscans throughout South America, the exiled bishop spoke against his adversaries and persuaded the Audiencia of Charcas to order his reinstatement. He returned to Asunción in 1647 to face a new governor, Diego de Escobar Osorio, whose death in 1649 allowed the Paraguayans to name Cárdenas to the post. This right, they claimed, they had possessed since the Conquest. Applauded by the Asunción *cabildo*, the bishop-governor expelled the Jesuits from the capital, and a mob vandalized their property. Jesuit interests, however, finally prevailed; a mission army defeated the Paraguayan militia near San Lorenzo in 1650 and occupied and sacked Asunción. Although Cárdenas was then exiled from Paraguay, the king in 1660 ordered him reinstated as bishop. Old and feeble, he rejected further Paraguayan conflicts and instead accepted the bishopric of Santa Cruz de la Sierra, Upper Peru, where he served until his death. His legacy in Paraguay was an intensified anti-Jesuit feeling, and later rebellions in the 1720s and 1730s recalled his anti-Jesuit efforts.

See also **Franciscans; Jesuits.**

BIBLIOGRAPHY

Colección general de documentos tocantes á la persecución que los regulares de la Compañía suscitaron y siguieron tenazmente por medio de sus jueces conservadores desde 1644 hasta 1660 contra el Ilmo. Rmo. Sr. Fr. D. Bernardino de Cárdenas, Obispo del Paraguay, 2 vols. (1768).

Harris Gaylord Warren, *Paraguay: An Informal History* (1949).

Adalberto Lopez, *The Revolt of the Comuneros, 1721–1735* (1976).

Additional Bibliography

Priewasser, Wolfgang. *El Ilmo. Don Fray Bernardino de Cárdenas.* Asunción: FONDEC: Academia Paraguaya de la Historia, 1998.

JAMES SCHOFIELD SAEGER

CÁRDENAS, VICTOR HUGO (1951–).

Victor Hugo Cárdenas is a Bolivian politician and public intellectual. Born on July 4, 1951, in Sank'ay Jawira (River of Cactus Flowers) near Lake Titicaca, Cárdenas entered national politics in the mid-1970s as a partisan of *Katarismo*, a multifaceted movement favoring the indigenous majority. After serving in the chamber of delegates from 1985 to 1989, he became the leader of the Movimiento Revolucionario Tupaj Katari de Liberación (Revolutionary Liberation Movement of Tupaj Katari; MRTKL), a Katarist faction that supported alliances with other progressive political parties. In 1993 Cárdenas joined his party with Gonzalo Sánchez de Lozada's Nationalist Revolutionary Movement (MNR). This coalition carried the national elections, and Cárdenas became vice president, the first native American to occupy the post.

Cárdenas's political legacy is mixed. The MNR-MRTKL administration is best known for its now-discredited neoliberal agenda, which Cárdenas publicly supported. However, his concern for Bolivia's native people bore fruit through increased expenditures for rural education and a heightened awareness of native traditions as legitimate cultural expressions. Cárdenas lives in La Paz, researching and promoting rural education.

See also **Bolivia, Political Parties: Nationalist Revolutionary Movement (MNR); Katarismo.**

BIBLIOGRAPHY

Albó, Xavier. "And from Kataristas to MNRistas?" In *Indigenous Peoples and Democracy in Latin America*, edited by Donna Lee Van Cott, 55–79. New York: St. Martin's, 1994.

Van Cott, Donna Lee. "From Exclusion to Inclusion: Bolivia's 2002 Elections." *Journal of Latin American Studies* 35, no. 4 (2003): 751–775.

DAVID BLOCK

CÁRDENAS ARROYO, SANTIAGO

(1937–). Santiago Cárdenas Arroyo (*b.* 4 December 1937), Colombian painter. Born in Bogotá, Cárdenas studied painting at the Rhode Island School of Design (B.F.A. in 1960). After traveling in Europe, he returned to the United States and enrolled in the School of Fine Arts at Yale University, where he studied with Alex Katz, Jack Tworkov, and Neil Welliver, receiving his M.F.A. in 1964. Even before graduation, his work had appeared in his native Colombia at the Asociación de Arquitectos Javerianos, Bogotá (1963). He won first prize for painting at the Art Festival of New Haven, Connecticut (1964). In 1965 he returned to Bogotá

and began teaching painting and drawing at the National University, the University of the Andes, and the University of Bogotá. He continued exhibiting his work and won national first prize and regional first prize in painting, III Croydon Salon, Bogotá (1966). In 1967 he had solo exhibitions at the Museum La Tertulia, Cali, and the Belarca Gallery. In 1972 he won first prize at the III Biennale of Art Coltejer, Medellín, Colombia, and was named director of the School of Fine Arts of the National University of Colombia, Bogotá. The following year he had a solo show at the Center for Inter-American Relations, New York, followed by another at the Museum of Modern Art, Bogotá (1976), and the Art Museum, National University, and the Garcés Valásquez Gallery, Bogotá, in 1980.

His paintings have embodied many different styles. His earlier art includes landscapes and nude portraits which then transitioned to objects (clothespins, ironing boards). Cardenas has also experimented with modernist techniques such as cubism and expressionism as well as various mediums such as oil painting and lighting techniques.

See also **Art: The Twentieth Century.**

BIBLIOGRAPHY

Gloria Peña De Kahn, comp., *Panorama artístico colombiano* (1981).

Eduardo Serrano, *Cien años de arte colombiano, 1886–1986* (1986).

Additional Bibliography

Alloway, Lawrence. *Realism and Latin American Painting, The 70's.* New York: Center for Inter-American Relations, 1980.

Ardila, Jaime, and Camilo Lleras. *Verdades sobre arte, mentiras sobre papel.* Bogotá: 1994.

BÉLGICA RODRÍGUEZ

CÁRDENAS DEL RÍO, LÁZARO

(1895–1970). Lázaro Cárdenas del Río (*b.* 21 May 1895; *d.* 19 October 1970), president of Mexico, 1934–1940. Born in the small provincial town of Jiquilpán, in the western state of Michoacán, Mexico, Cárdenas was the oldest son of a shopkeeper. He left school after the fourth grade and worked as a clerk in the local tax office.

Following his father's death in 1911, Cárdenas, a quiet, serious, conscientious youth, became a surrogate parent for his many siblings; several of his brothers emulated him by pursuing careers in the military and politics. A fierce patriotism nurtured by the liberal school curriculum and a hungry though unfocused ambition lurked behind Cárdenas's stolid mien, and in 1913, three years after the Mexican Revolution broke out, the eighteen-year-old enlisted with rebels resisting the military regime of Victoriano Huerta. After initial setbacks (he was captured in 1923, escaped, and had to lie low in Guadalajara for some months), Cárdenas began a rapid rise through the ranks, helped by the friendship and patronage of his commanding general, Plutarco Elías Calles. After campaigns against the Yaquis in Sonora, the Villistas in Chihuahua, and the rebel-bandit forces of Chávez García in his home state, Cárdenas became interim governor of Michoacán (1920) and military commander on the isthmus (1921) and in the oil country of the Huasteca (1925–1928), where he condemned the corruption and arrogance of the foreign oil companies. During these years he developed close political alliances with President Elías Calles (1924–1928), with his fellow Michoacano, the radical Francisco Múgica, and with his own chief of staff, Manuel Ávila Camacho, member of a powerful revolutionary clan in the state of Puebla. As a military leader Cárdenas was bold to a fault, his impetuosity leading to defeats in 1918 and 1923, on which occasion he was severely wounded.

POLITICAL CAREEER

In 1928 Cárdenas was elected governor of his home state, where he undertook to accelerate agrarian reforms, develop education, and foster labor and peasant organizations, which he did through the radical anticlerical Confederación Revolucionaria Michoacana de Trabajo. His creation of a solid political base, however, was compromised by several leaves of absence, which he took in order to serve as president of the nascent National Revolutionary Party (PNR) (1930–1931), as minister of government (1932), and as minister of war (1933). Politically shrewd beneath a sphinx-like exterior, Cárdenas grasped—as some rival revolutionary caudillos, such as Adalberto Tejeda of Veracruz, failed to do—that the federal government, considerably strengthened and consolidated by the presidency

and *maximato* of Calles, was the surest ladder of political advancement. Loyalty paid off, and in 1933 Cárdenas was chosen—in effect by Calles—as the PNR presidential candidate. Calles, who had governed through the medium of three relatively pliant presidents, no doubt expected that he could control his old protégé, in which respect, political opinion concurred. However, the onset of the Depression had undermined the broadly export-oriented economic project of the 1920s, and those who favored both a more interventionist state and a greater commitment to social legislation saw Cárdenas, known as a reformist governor of Michoacán, as the best hope within the party.

Cárdenas's radicalism—a practical, populist desire for social betterment rather than any bookish Marxism—was further stimulated by his extensive presidential campaign of 1934, which set the style for a peripatetic presidency: a quarter of his six years in office were spent on the road, touring Mexico, reaching remote villages, listening to local complaints, distributing patronage and public works, often by executive fiat. The rapport Cárdenas thus achieved with popular groups, which endured long after his presidency, served him in good stead when, in 1935–1936, he challenged Calles's authority, marshaling trade unions and peasant groups, generals and politicos, in order to force the dismayed *jefe máximo* (highest chief) into exile. By mid-1936, Cárdenas was emphatically master in his own house; the authority of the presidency had been reinforced, an assertion of presidential power that had been unusually bloodless.

During the middle years of his *sexenio*, Cárdenas enacted a raft of reforms that changed the political face of Mexico. Most important, he confiscated some 45 million acres of private land and distributed it in the form of *ejidos*—peasant communities in which the land was individually worked or, as on the big Laguna cotton estates, collectively farmed. With the *ejidos* came a rapid expansion of rural schools, now commited to a form of socialist education which sought to instill nationalism, class consciousness, and anticlericalism. Welcomed by some, this ambitious program of social engineering offended many, especially devout Catholics. In the face of protests, parental boycotts, and a good deal of local violence, Cárdenas, who had never shared Calles's dogmatic anticlericalism, reined in revolutionary anticlericalism, declaring that material betterment was the greater priority. Meanwhile, the president encouraged the political organization of the peasantry under the aegis of a national confederation which, in 1938, formally incorporated itself into the offical party as the National Campesino Federation (CNC).

A similar process of mobilization and incorporation affected the considerably smaller working class. During the *maximato,* the hegemony of the once-dominant Regional Confederation of Mexican Workers (CROM) was splintered, and the ravages of the Depression, though less severe and prolonged in Mexico than in some other Latin American countries, encouraged a new working-class militancy, upon which Cárdenas could capitalize, especially as the economy revived after 1933. Major industrial unions were formed in the leading sectors of industry—oil, mining, railways—and they began to press, strenuously and effectively, for national collective contracts. Meanwhile, the Mexican Federation of Labor (CTM), led by the flamboyant Marxist Vicente Lombardo Toledano, arose from the ashes of the CROM; and, by virtue of a politically close alliance with the president, Lombardo and the CTM came to play a role in the 1930s similar to that of Luis N. Morones and the CROM in the 1920s. The CTM benefited from sympathetic official arbitration in strikes and, in return, it backed the government, as did the Mexican Communist Party (PCM), which, pledged to a collaborationist popular-front strategy, now enjoyed a brief heyday as a political, ideological, and cultural force. In 1938 the CTM joined the CNC as corporate pillars of the new official party, the Party of Mexican Revolution (PRM).

NATIONALIZATION OF INDUSTRIES

The radical thrust of the Cárdenas administration was evident in a series of nationalizations. Several mines and factories that threatened closure became workers' cooperatives. In 1937–1938 the railways were nationalized and placed under a workers' administration (conservative critics pointed to the inefficiency of the operation; radicals contended that the workers—seeking to run a decrepit system at low cost—made the best of a bad job). Most dramatic of all was the petroleum nationalization of March 1938, the first major seizure of oil assets by a developing

country. Confronted by a long-running labor dispute, intransigent managers, and a perceived threat to Mexico's economic well-being and national sovereignty, Cárdenas expropriated the Anglo-American companies and established a state oil company, Petróleos Mexicanos (PEMEX). Two consequences followed. Relations with the United States, which had been tolerably cordial since the late 1920s, cooled. But Cárdenas reassured the United States that oil was a special case, that further nationalizations were not contemplated, and that an adequate indemnity would be paid. And President Roosevelt, pilloried by big business at home and alarmed by the rise of fascism overseas, was reluctant either to champion the companies or to offend a friendly, anti-fascist Mexico. Indeed, with his condemnation of fascist aggression in Europe, Abyssinia (now Ethiopia), and China and his vigorous support of the Spanish Republic (a policy that elicited strong criticism from pro-Franco Mexicans), Cárdenas now appeared as a stalwart ally of the democratic powers. The United States therefore refrained from political or military reprisals and entered negotiations over the proposed oil indemnity, which was agreed to in 1942.

The oil crisis, followed by an oil company boycott of PEMEX, harmed the Mexican economy. Exports, the peso, and business confidence declined. Inflation quickened. Workers in the nationalized industries were required to tighten their belts and Cárdenas spent much of his final two years in office wrestling with the problems of the oil and railroad industries. Meanwhile, the presidential succession began to absorb political attention. International tensions—in particular, the global fascist–popular front confrontation—affected domestic politics. Right-wing groups, on the defensive since the Depression, staged a comeback. The National Sinarquista Union (UNS), a popular, Catholic, quasi-fascist movement founded in 1937, inveighed against Cardenista collectivism and "atheism." Conservative elements also mobilized behind dissident caudillos, on the right of the PRM, and in the pro-business, pro-Catholic National Action Party (PAN), founded in 1939. Some working-class Cardenistas broke ranks. Fearing destabilization, Cárdenas tacked to the center, reining in his radical policies and opting for a right-of-center successor, Ávila Camacho, rather than the radical Francisco Múgica. In the July 1940 presidential election Ávila Camacho easily defeated the challenge of the conservative caudillo Juan Andréu Almazán, but did so amid scenes of fraud and violence. The Cárdenas presidency, which had indelibly marked Mexican political life, thus ended in dissent and controversy.

After 1940, the rightward drift of official policy was accelerated. Agrarian reform slowed, socialist education ended, détente with the church and the United States advanced. The structures set in place by Cárdenas—PEMEX, the corporate party, the collective *ejido*—remained, but they now contributed to a national project dedicated to industrialization and capital accumulation, goals that Cárdenas had neither set nor endorsed. The ex-president, however, remained loyal to the system he had helped create. He served as minister of war in 1942–1945, reassuring nationalist sentiment as Mexico collaborated increasingly closely with the United States. During the 1950s and 1960s he headed two major regional development projects, working, as in the past, for the material betterment of the poorer regions of southern and southwestern Mexico, thereby reinforcing his popular and populist reputation (a factor that would prove significant with the rise of neo-Cardenismo, the leftist movement headed by Cárdenas's son, Cuauhtémoc Cárdenas, in the late 1980s). Loyalty to the system did not, however, prevent him from exercising significant influence: against the proposed reelection of President Miguel Alemán in 1951–1952; against the Vietnam War and U.S. policy toward Cuba in the 1960s; and in favor of political dissidents within Mexico. At the time of his death in 1970, Cárdenas was criticized by some as an authoritarian populist and a dangerous fellow-traveler, and revered by others, particularly in the Cardenista countryside, as the greatest constructive radical of the Mexican Revolution.

See also **Mexico, Organizations: National Peasant Federation (CNC); Mexico, Political Parties: National Revolutionary Party (PNR); Mexico, Political Parties: Party of the Mexican Revolution (PRM).**

BIBLIOGRAPHY

Luis González, *Historia de la Revolución Mexicana: Los días del presidente Cárdenas* (1979) is a deft, sensitive narrative of the Cárdenas presidency.

Nora Hamilton, *The Limits of State Autonomy: Post-revolutionary Mexico* (1982) gives a perceptive Marxist analysis of the post-revolutionary state, focusing on the 1930s.

Alan Knight, "The Rise and Fall of Cardenismo, c. 1930–c. 1946," *Mexico since Independence,* edited by Leslie

Bethell (1991), provides a recent general overview and contains a bibliography.

Enrique Krauze, *General misionero: Lázaro Cárdenas* (1987) is an intelligent popular biography, critical of Cárdenas and well illustrated. A hagiographic biography by a United States admirer of Cárdenas is William Cameron Townsend, *Lázaro Cárdenas: Mexican Democrat* (1952). For a succinct, sympathetic analysis of Cardenista politics and philosophy see Tzví Medín, *Ideología y praxis política de Lázaro Cárdenas* (1972).

Additional Bibliography

Becker, Marjorie. *Setting the Virgin on Fire: Lazaro Cardenas, Michoacan Peasants, and the Redemption of the Mexican Revolution.* Berkeley: University of California Press, 1995.

Fallaw, Ben. *Cárdenas Compromised: The Failure of Reform in Postrevolutionary Yucatán.* Durham, NC: Duke University Press, 2001.

ALAN KNIGHT

CÁRDENAS SOLORZANO, CUAUHTÉMOC

(1934–). Prominent Mexican politician Cuauhtémoc Cárdenas was born May 1, 1934, in Mexico City. Cárdenas's 1988 presidential candidacy, representing a coalition of opposition parties, provoked the strongest support against the Institutional Revolutionary Party (PRI) since 1952. Cárdenas's parties, which included the Partido Popular Socialista (PPS), the Partido Auténtico de la Revolución Mexicana (PARM), the Partido Mexicano Socialista (PMS), and the Partido del Frente Cardenista de Reconstrucción Nacional (PFCRN), won four senate seats in Michoacán and the Federal District and captured most of the congressional seats in the key states of México, the Federal District, Michoacán, and Morelos. Cárdenas himself received a reported 31 percent of the vote to Carlos Salinas de Gortari's reported 51 percent.

Most observers believe extensive fraud took place, and some analysts assert that Cárdenas actually defeated Salinas. In the 1991 congressional elections, however, support for Cárdenas's Party of the Democratic Revolution (PRD) declined to only 8 percent of the electorate. In 1994 Cárdenas once again ran for the presidency on his party's ticket. The PRI was successful in associating electoral violence with the PRD among many voters, and combined with Cárdenas's poor performance in the televised debates, he was unable to build on his strong showing six years earlier, coming in at a distant third place with 17 percent of the vote. Despite this poor showing, when the leadership of the Federal District was converted to an elective position in 1997, Cárdenas became the party's candidate, easily defeating both the PRI and National Action Party (PAN) nominees.

Using the Federal District's thirty congressional seats as a base, the PRD restored its strength in the four states where it performed strongly in 1988. Cárdenas became the party's standard bearer in 2000, and based on his and the party's resurgence in 1997, he imposed himself as the presidential candidate a third time, producing further splits in the party. Again, he ran a distant third in the presidential race, capturing 17 percent of the vote. His influence declined within the PRD after 2000, and when he did not run for the party's nomination in 2005, he opened the way for Andrés Manuel López Obrador, the head of the Federal District, to become the party's candidate. López Obrador restored the PRD's congressional influence and almost won the 2006 election, with 35 percent of the vote.

Cárdenas is the son of General Lázaro Cárdenas, without doubt Mexico's most popular president of the twentieth century. This fact accounts in part for his own political popularity, especially among the *campesinos*, who considered Lázaro Cárdenas an agrarian savior. The son studied at public and private schools, and at the Colegio de San Nicolás in Morelia. He graduated from the National School of Engineering on January 22, 1957. Cárdenas then studied abroad on a Bank of Mexico fellowship, interning in France and for Krupp in Germany (1957–1958)

Cárdenas received his first taste of electoral politics in 1951, when as a preparatory student he supported the candidacy of General Miguel Henríquez Guzmán, who—as Cárdenas would later do—left the government's fold to oppose the official party presidential candidate. Later he joined the Movimiento de Liberación Nacional (MLN), a loosely constituted leftist opposition movement supported by his father, serving on the national committee with Heberto Castillo, who would join him in the 1988 presidential campaign.

After engaging in a private engineering practice in the 1960s, Cárdenas began holding various public

positions. In 1970 he became subdirector of the Las Truchas steel complex, a decentralized federal agency, and in 1973 served as director of the public trust fund for the city of Lázaro Cárdenas. In 1976 he was elected senator from his home state, but he left his post that same year to serve as undersecretary of forest resources and fauna in the secretariat of agriculture and livestock. In 1980 he resigned this position to run for governor of Michoacán as the PRI candidate. Elected, he served until 1986, when he began his efforts to reform the official party. He and other reformers advocated democratizing the internal structure of the PRI and the electoral system in general. Their economic policies were populist, focused on debt renegotiation, deficit spending, and an increased state role in the economy. When the government leadership refused to accept their views, Cárdenas, Porfirio Muñoz Ledo (a former president of the PRI), and other leaders left the party in 1987. Not all the reformists followed their lead. Some, who called themselves the critical current, remained within the PRI.

Following the 1988 elections, Cárdenas's coalition reorganized itself as the Partido de la Revolución Democrática and offered intensive opposition in races for mayor and state legislative and gubernatorial posts. The strength of Cárdenas's opposition movement, and its persistence after the 1988 presidential elections, contributed significantly to the pressure for electoral reform and internal change within the government party. Many PRD members and candidates were persecuted before the 1994 election. Cárdenas used his personal stature within Mexico and abroad to appeal for honesty in the electoral process, thus contributing significantly to Mexico's democratic transformation.

See also **López Obrador, Manuel Andrés; Mexico, Political Parties: Democratic Revolutionary Party (PRD); Mexico: Since 1910; Salinas de Gortari, Carlos.**

BIBLIOGRAPHY

Ascencio, Esteban. *Cuauhtémoc Cárdenas: El hombre, el político, el líder.* México, D.F.: Editorial Rino, PRD, 2000.

Bruhn, Kathleen. *Taking on Goliath: The Emergence of a New Left Party and the Struggle for Democracy in Mexico.* University Park: Pennsylvania State University Press, 1997.

Cárdenas, Cuauhtémoc. *Cuauhtémoc Cárdenas: Política, familia, proyecto, y compromiso.* México, D.F.: Grijalbo, 2003.

Cornelius, Wayne A., Judith Gentleman, and Peter H. Smith, eds. *Mexico's Alternative Political Futures*. La Jolla, CA: Center for U.S.-Mexican Studies, University of California, San Diego, 1989.

RODERIC AI CAMP

CARDIM, FREI FERNÃO (1540–1625).

Frei Fernão Cardim (*b.* 1540; *d.* 27 January 1625), Portuguese Jesuit and writer. Cardim accompanied the visitador Cristóvão de Gouveia to Brazil. Arriving in Bahia on 9 May 1584, Cardim described their activities in a report on the Jesuits entitled *Narrativa epistolar, ou Informação da missão do padre Cristóvão de Gouveia às partes do Brasil*. The two had visited the captaincies of Bahia, Ilhéus, Porto Seguro, Pernambuco, Espírito Santo, Rio de Janeiro, and São Vicente. Cardim was nominated dean of the Jesuit *colégio* in the city of Salvador, where he served until 1593, and then as dean in Rio de Janeiro in 1596. Returning from a 1598 mission to Rome, he was captured by Flemish pirates and kept in England until 1601.

By 1604 Cardim was provincial of the Jesuits in Brazil, and in 1607 he was nominated for the second time as dean of the Bahian *colégio*, the position he occupied when the Dutch attacked Salvador in 1624. The Jesuits took refuge in the Indian village of Espírito Santo, where Cardim died in 1625. He summarized his Brazilian experiences in two treatises: *Do princípio e origem dos índios do Brasil e de seus costumes e cerimônias* and *Do clima e terra do Brasil e de algumas coisas notáveis que se acham assim na terra como no mar*, both published anonymously in Samuel Purchas's *Purchas his Pilgrimes* (London, 1625).

See also **Jesuits.**

BIBLIOGRAPHY

João Capistrano De Abreu, *Ensaios e estudos: Crítica e história* (1st and 2d ser., 1975, 1976).

José Honório Rodrigues, *História da história do Brasil*, vol. 1, *Historiografia colonial* (1979).

MARIA BEATRIZ NIZZA DA SILVA

CARDOSO, FELIPE SANTIAGO (1773–1818).

Felipe Santiago Cardoso (*b.* 1 May 1773; *d.* 17 September 1818), Uruguayan politician. Cardoso played an important role in the period of the revolution of the Provincia Oriental, known today as Uruguay. He was elected representative for Canelones to the Congress of April 1813, which produced the famous Instructions of 1813—the first expression of federalist thought of the eastern caudillo José Artigas. Cardoso acted as a confidential agent of Artigas in Buenos Aires, attempting to win the inclusion of representatives from the Provincia Oriental in the constituent assembly, which the government of Buenos Aires opposed. The representatives were finally rejected for technical reasons, the real reason being their federalist ideas, which ran contrary to the centralism of the capital. Cardoso was a member of the town council of Montevideo in 1815, a time during which Artigas, from his camp in Purificación on the Uruguay River, exercised a protectorate over the provinces of the Argentine littoral.

See also **Uruguay: Before 1900.**

BIBLIOGRAPHY

John Street, *Artigas and the Emancipation of Uruguay* (1959).

Washington Reyes Abadie and Andrés Vázquez Romero, *Crónica general del Uruguay*, vol. 2 (1984).

Additional Bibliography

García, Flavio A. *El ciudadano Felipe Cardoso*. Montevideo: Dirección General de Extensión Universitaria, División Publicaciones y Ediciones, 1980.

JOSÉ DE TORRES WILSON

CARDOSO, FERNANDO HENRIQUE (1931–).

Fernando Henrique Cardoso is a Brazilian statesman and sociologist who became well known as an academic exponent of dependency theory, which he later disavowed. He was president of Brazil from 1995 through 2002.

Cardoso studied sociology with Roger Bastide and Florestan Fernandes at the University of São Paulo, and taught there until the 1964 military coup, after which he left Brazil. While in exile in Santiago, Chile, Cardoso contributed signally to dependency analysis at a moment when import-substitution industrialization (ISI) seemed to have failed. The structuralist economist Celso Furtado had already asserted the connection between development and underdevelopment, and argued that economic phenomena had to be understood in a historical framework. In the mid- and latter 1960s Cardoso and his collaborator Enzo Faletto extended the analysis into social relations. Pessimistic about development led by national bourgeoisies as a result of his earlier research, Cardoso saw dependency as a historical situation not solely determined by a dynamic capitalist center, but one in which a complex internal dynamic of class conflict also existed in dependent countries of the less-industrialized periphery. He accepted the structuralists' argument that the center gains more from exchange than the periphery through the latter's deteriorating terms of trade. But he stressed mutual interests among social classes across the international system-in particular, those of the bourgeoisies of center and periphery. Cardoso and Faletto linked the failure of populism with the stagnation of ISI, viewing authoritarian regimes as necessary to secure political demobilization of the masses.

Yet unlike some other contributors to dependency theory (notably Andre Gunder Frank and Ruy Mauro Marini), Cardoso emphasized shifting alliances and a range of historical possibilities. For Latin American economies controlled by local bourgeoisies, he saw the option of associated dependent development. Like other dependency theorists he saw the international system, not the nation-state, as the proper unit of analysis; development and underdevelopment were locations in the international economic system, not stages. Cardoso also denied that dependency theory (for him, a variety of Marxism) could be made to yield a useful method of quantitative analysis, but saw it as a framework for historical analysis of a specific dialectical process.

Cardoso returned to Brazil in 1968, opposed the military dictatorship, and became head of Centro Brasileiro de Análise e Planejamento (CEBRAP), a social science research institute in São Paulo. He was elected to the Brazilian senate in 1983 on the ticket of the Partido do Movimento Democrático Brasileiro (PMDB). In 1988 he helped form the Partido da Social Democracia Brasileira (PSDB), a group that split away from the PMDB.

Following the impeachment of President Fernando Collor de Melo, Cardoso became foreign minister in the cabinet of Itamar Franco, Collor's successor, in October 1992. In May 1993, Cardoso was named finance minister, the most powerful cabinet post. In this capacity, he began the process that brought Brazil's rampant inflation under control by introducing a new unit of currency, the *real*, and its success made him the leading candidate for the presidency. In October 1994 Cardoso was elected by direct popular vote, having publicly disavowed many of his theses about dependency.

Cardoso broke inflation partly through budget cuts and higher taxes, but chiefly by borrowing abroad and later by selling state assets to cover revenue shortfalls. Inflation fell from 2,400 percent per annum in 1994 to 9 percent in 1999, and Cardoso ended indexation, his predecessors' device for raising prices and wages together to avoid relative distortions. Yet during the Cardoso years, overall GDP growth was unimpressive and erratic, buffeted by the Mexican, Asian, Russian, and Argentine financial crises of 1993 to 2001. Brazil could attract foreign capital only with high interest rates, which provided the prop for a high exchange rate for the real. As a consequence Brazilian goods were less competitive in the world market, and high domestic interest rates discouraged private investment. In the late 1990s the government took over a number of failed state banks and Brazil's international debt increased sharply.

Privatization of electricity and telecommunications also increased government revenues. Even the national oil monopoly, Petrobrás, privatized some ancillary operations. Through a combination of peasant mobilization by the Movimento dos Sem Terra and government legal action, some 600,000 families gained title to land in the Cardoso administration. Although the government instituted a number of other social reforms (e.g., the Bolsa Escola, to keep poor children in school) it was unable to reform the national pension plan, a costly fiscal burden at state and national levels. Government weakness arose from Cardoso's absorption in amending the constitution to permit his re-election in 1998, and from his fissiparous coalition in Congress, which remained unstable throughout his second term. He was succeeded by Luis Inácio Lula da Silva in 2003. Cardoso remained one of the leading figures in the PSDP, and the country's most prestigious elder statesman. As of 2007, he was also active in international circuits concerned with North-South relations, lecturing frequently in foreign universities.

See also **Brazil, Political Parties: Party of Brazilian Social Democracy (PSDB); Dependency Theory; Economic Development; Inflation.**

BIBLIOGRAPHY

Baer, Werner. *The Brazilian Economy: Growth and Development.* 5th ed. Westport, CT: Praeger, 2001.

Cardoso, Fernando Henrique, and Enzo Faletto. *Dependency and Development in Latin America.* Translated by Marjory Mattingly Urquidi. Berkeley: University of California Press, 1979.

Cardoso, Fernando Henrique, with Brian Winter. *The Accidental President of Brazil: A Memoir.* New York: Public Affairs, 2006.

Goertzel, Ted G. *Fernando Henrique Cardoso: Reinventing Democracy in Brazil.* Boulder, CO: Lynne Rienner, 1999.

Love, Joseph L. "The Origins of Dependency Analysis." *Journal of Latin American Studies* 22, no. 1 (February 1990): 143–168.

JOSEPH L. LOVE

CARDOZA Y ARAGÓN, LUIS (1904–1992).

Luis Cardoza y Aragón (*b.* 21 June 1904; *d.* 4 September 1992), Guatemalan poet, essayist, and art critic. Widely recognized for his book *Guatemala: Las líneas de su mano* (1955), Cardoza y Aragón was one of modern Guatemala's most important literary figures. Following the surrealist tradition of the 1920s, he used experiences in Europe to nourish his aesthetic and social preoccupations through poetic works such as *Luna Park* (1923) and *Maelstrom* (1926). With the French anthropologist Georges Raynaud he translated a pre-Columbian Maya-Quiché drama, *Rabinal Achí* (1928).

In 1931 Cardoza chose exile in Mexico over a return to Guatemala, which was entering one of the most brutal and repressive periods of its modern history under the dictatorship of Jorge Ubico y Castañeda (1931–1944). He continued to publish his poetry—*Soledad* (1936) and *El sonámbulo* (1937)—and began to write critical essays on contemporary Mexican art, including the controversial volume *La nube y el reloj* (1940).

Cardoza returned to Guatemala in October 1944, on the eve of the revolution. He was cofounder of *Revista de Guatemala* (1945) and continued his artistic and political commitment to the revolution until its defeat in 1954.

Cardoza returned to Mexico, where he completed and published *Guatemala: Las líneas de su mano* (1955), in which he underscores his personal experiences through a presentation of Guatemala's cultural and political heritage. His poetic account of Guatemala, and the hopes of the October Revolution, establish this work as essential reading for understanding Guatemala and its people as well as Cardoza y Aragón's life. He died in Mexico City.

See also **Literature: Spanish America.**

BIBLIOGRAPHY

A brief overview and a selected bibliography are in Francisco Albizúrez Palma and Catalina Barrios y Barrios, *Historia de la literatura guatemalteca*, vol. 2 (1986), pp. 205–213. A collection of critical essays, including articles by Arturo Arias, Augusto Monterroso, and José Emilio Pacheco, is in *Homenaje a Luis Cardoza y Aragón* (1987). Most of Cardoza's poetry, and some prose, with an excellent prologue by José Emilio Pacheco, is in *Poesías completas y algunas prosas* (1977). For further information on Cardoza's life, see his autobiography, *El río: Novelas de caballería* (1986).

Additional Bibliography

Díaz Castillo, Roberto. *Luis Cardoza y Aragón: Ciudadano de la vía láctea.* Guatemala, C.A.: Librerías Artemis Edinte, 2001.

Pinto Díaz, David and Rafael Gutiérrez. *Luis Cardoza y Aragón: Centenario, 1901-2001.* Guatemala, C.A.: Fondo de Cultura Económica de Guatemala, 2001.

SHELLY JARRETT BROMBERG

CARDOZO, EFRAÍM (1906–1973).

Efraím Cardozo (*b.* 16 October 1906; *d.* 10 April 1973), Paraguayan diplomat and historian. Born in Villarrica, Efraím Cardozo was the son of noted educator and journalist Ramón I. Cardozo and Juana Sosa. Given his parents' interest in the study of history, it is little wonder that Cardozo became a professional historian, one of Paraguay's best. He received a doctorate in law and social sciences at the National University of Asunción in 1932, and set off immediately on a diplomatic career, participating in the cease-fire negotiations that ended the Chaco War (1932–1935) and in the 1938 signing of the final peace treaty with Bolivia.

Cardozo was a Liberal, and on several occasions, officially (1970–1972) as well as unofficially, was president of the Liberal Radical Party. His political affiliations brought him considerable hardships during the Higinio Morínigo dictatorship (1940–1948), including exile to Argentina on eight occasions. He later served in the Chamber of Deputies and in the Senate, while simultaneously working as a professor at the National University and the Catholic University in Asunción.

Cardozo is best remembered for his many historical studies, which were scrupulously researched and which betrayed none of the partisan fanaticism so common in Paraguayan historiography. His thoroughly documented *El imperio del Brasil y el Río de la Plata: Antecedentes y estallido de la guerra del Paraguay* (1961) won the Alberdi-Sarmiento Prize for its incisive analysis of South American diplomacy prior to the War of the Triple Alliance (1864–1870). His other publications include *Paraguay independiente* (1949), *Vísperas de la guerra del Paraguay* (1954), *El Paraguay colonial: Las raíces de la nacionalidad* (1959), *Historiografía paraguaya* (1959), and *Hace cien años: Crónicas de la guerra 1864–1870* (13 vols., 1967–1976).

See also **Paraguay: The Twentieth Century.**

BIBLIOGRAPHY

Dennis Joseph Vodarsik, "Efraím Cardozo (1906–1973)," in *Hispanic American Historical Review* 54, no. 1 (1974): 116.

Jack Ray Thomas, *Biographical Dictionary of Latin American Historians and Historiography* (1984).

Efraím Cardozo, *Paraguay independiente* (Asunción, 1987).

MARTA FERNÁNDEZ WHIGHAM

CARDOZO, RAMÓN INDALECIO

(1876–1943). Born in Paraguay's interior department of Guairá in the period following the War of the Triple Alliance (1864–1870), Ramón Cardozo dedicated himself from an early age to public education, which, in his country, he saw as poorly administered and woefully grounded in the old-fashioned. For sixteen years he was the director of schools in the town of Villarrica, where he experimented with an approach that eschewed the "encyclopedic" methods of the past. He eventually moved on to Asunción, where the Eligio Ayala government asked him in 1924 to prepare a comprehensive plan for the reform of the nation's schools. Cardozo responded with a practical, more scientific, and vocational curriculum that he believed would better suit the needs of the rural population. He also brought many young people into Paraguay's teaching colleges and saw the number of primary schools expand exponentially during his career of more than thirty years of public service. Cardozo also contributed extensively in historical work and journalism, and in half a dozen studies made a name for himself as the chief scholar of his home district. In 1937 he was one of the founders of the Instituto Paraguayo de Investigaciones Históricas. He died in Buenos Aires.

See also **Ayala, Eligio; Education: Overview; War of the Triple Alliance.**

BIBLIOGRAPHY

Parker, William Belmont, ed. *Paraguayans of To-Day*. New York and London: Hispanic Society of America, 1921.

Zubizarreta, Carlos. *Cien vidas paraguayas*. Asunción: Araverá, 1985.

THOMAS L. WHIGHAM

CAREW, ROD

(1945–). Rodney Cline Carew was born on October 1, 1945, in the Panama Canal Zone, the son of a canal worker and a Panamanian mother. Carew moved to New York in 1962, signed a contract with the Minnesota Twins in 1964, and became American League Rookie of the Year in 1967. Playing second, then first base for the Twins (1967–1978) and California Angels (1979–1985), he won seven batting titles, played in eighteen All-Star games, had 3,053 career hits, and a .328 career average. He won the Roberto Clemente Award and election to the National Baseball Hall of Fame. After his retirement in 1985 he worked as a hitting coach and charity fundraiser. His popularity earned him Panama's Medal of Honor and the country's national stadium was renamed in his honor.

See also **Sports.**

BIBLIOGRAPHY

Carew, Rod, with Ira Berkow. *Carew*. New York: Simon and Schuster, 1979.

Carew, Rod, with Frank Pace and Armen Keteyian. *Art and Science of Hitting*. New York: Penguin Books, 1986.

JOSEPH L. ARBENA

CARÍAS ANDINO, TIBURCIO (1876–1969). Tiburcio Carías Andino (*b.* 15 March 1876; *d.* 23 December 1969), president of Honduras (1933–1948).

Carías was born in Tegucigalpa, the youngest son of General Calixto Carías and Sara Andino de Carías. An excellent student, he received his law degree from the Central University of Honduras in 1898; later he taught mathematics at the National Institute as well as night classes for poor children and workers. Standing six feet, two inches in height, unusually tall for a Central American, Carías developed natural leadership ability. As early as 1891 he was campaigning for the dominant Liberal Party, in which his father was active. Thereafter he became involved in the military conflicts related to Central American politics.

In 1903 Carías left the Liberals to support Manuel Bonilla in founding the National Party, a successor to the nineteenth-century Conservative Party. Although his part in a 1907 revolt earned him the rank of brigadier general, he was not primarily a military man but rather a skillful politician who used the military to build an effective political machine. As a congressman and governor of several departments, Carías became the National Party leader and in 1923 its presidential candidate. He won a plurality but lacked the required majority, and when the Congress failed to resolve the stalemate, his armed forces seized Tegucigalpa in 1924. Subsequent elections, assisted by United States mediation, elected Carías's running mate, Miguel Paz Baraona, as president. When, in 1928, Carías lost to the Liberals by twelve thousand votes, many of his supporters called for revolt, but Carías accepted the official results, a move that won him wide respect.

Honduran politics of the 1920s were closely related to the rise of the U.S. banana companies, which were responsible for much of the political turbulence of the era. Samuel Zemurray's Cuyamel Fruit Company supported the Liberals, while the United Fruit Company backed Carías's National Party. In 1932 Carías won a convincing victory over José Ángel Zúñiga Huete and took office in 1933 after putting down an opposition revolt. Revisions of the constitution in 1939 allowed Carías to remain in office, first to 1944 and later through 1949. When he finally stepped down on 31 December 1948, having ruled his country longer than any other president in Honduran history, he turned over power to his protégé and minister of war, Juan Manuel Gálvez Durón, following the first presidential election in the country since 1932.

Carías has been compared to contemporary dictators in the other Central American states: Jorge Ubico in Guatemala, Maximiliano Hernández Martínez in El Salvador, and Anastasio Somoza in Nicaragua. His regime had similar fascist tendencies, and he achieved order and a measure of economic growth at the cost of civil liberties and the general welfare. Ángel Zúñiga kept up a propaganda campaign against Carías from exile in Mexico and there was an occasional revolt attempted from within, but Carías's firm control of the military assured his continued rule. He also cooperated closely with American business and government interests, including support of the Allies in World War II. Although he promoted modernization and made his country the leader in the development of Central American commercial aviation, Honduras continued to be the least developed of the isthmian states.

Unlike his "Dictators' League" counterparts in one important respect, Carías abandoned the Liberal Party. Although he had come from a Liberal Party background, his National Party retained some of the nineteenth-century Conservative Party philosophy, which defended a curious alliance of the leading families of the elite with the masses and adopted a somewhat friendlier attitude toward the Roman Catholic Church than had the Liberals. While all of the Central American dictators were repressive and often brutal, Carías was somewhat more benign than the others, and he was the only one of them to step down gracefully. The overthrow of Hernández and Ubico by popular uprisings in 1944 probably contributed to Carías's decision to leave the presidency in 1948, for he, too, began to face student and labor unrest in 1944. In reality, his National Party, still a force in Honduras today, represented a union of nineteenth-century Liberal and Conservative elitist attitudes, allowing the Honduran Liberal Party of today to become more closely identified with middle-class interests. The major role of the military in modern Honduran politics was another legacy of Carías's dictatorship.

In the election of 1954, the seventy-nine-year-old Carías sought unsuccessfully to return to the presidency. A subsequent coup reduced his political influence even more, although he continued to live in Honduras until his death.

See also **Banana Industry; Honduras, Political Parties: National Party (PNH).**

BIBLIOGRAPHY

Mario Argueta, *Tiburcio Carías: Anatomía de una época, 1923–1948* (1989).

Filander Díaz Chávez, *Carías, el último caudillo frutero* (1982).

Gilberto González y Contreras, *El último caudillo* (*ensayo biográfico*) (1946).

James A. Morris, *Honduras: Caudillo Politics and Military Rulers* (1984), which reviews his regime in some detail. See also William S. Stokes, *Honduras: An Area Study in Government* (1950).

James D. Rudolf, ed., *Honduras: A Country Study* (1984).

Franklin Dallas Parker, *The Central American Republics* (1964).

Additional Bibliography

Contreras, Carlos A. *Hacia la dictadura cariísta: La campaña presidencial de 1932.* Tegucigalpa: Editorial Iberoamericana, 2000.

Dodd, Thomas J. *Tiburcio Carías: Portrait of a Honduran Political Leader.* Baton Rouge: Louisiana State University Press, 2005.

RALPH LEE WOODWARD JR.

CARIBBEAN ANTILLES. The Caribbean can be defined in several different ways. What is commonly referred to as the Caribbean Basin is a multicultural group of twenty-six states (thirteen insular and thirteen littoral) plus assorted territories. It can also be defined in terms of its cultural-linguistic subgroups, including Spanish-speaking Cuba, the Dominican Republic, and U.S.-controlled Puerto Rico; an expanding English-speaking bloc of ten insular and two littoral states plus five insular territories; a French-speaking bloc made up of Haiti, the French departments of Martinique, Guadeloupe, and French Guiana, plus half of the island of Saint Martin; a Dutch-speaking section comprising independent Suriname on the South American littoral, Aruba, and the Netherlands Antilles (including Bonaire, Curaçao, Saba, Saint Eustatius, and the remaining half of Saint Martin, known as Sint Maarten). The last definition, and the focus of this essay, is that of the multicultural insular Caribbean that includes the Greater and Lesser Antilles (along with other scattered islands and the French, Dutch, and British littoral territories that have been historically grouped with their island counterparts).

The Greater Antilles is composed of Cuba; Hispaniola, which is divided between the Dominican Republic and Haiti; the Commonwealth of Puerto Rico; and Jamaica. The Lesser Antilles arcs southward from the Bahamas toward Trinidad and includes the Leeward and Windward island groupings that together form a majority of the states and colonies of the Commonwealth Caribbean, the U.S. Virgin Islands, plus French and Dutch possessions. Most have common features. In addition to their European colonization and the general replacement of eradicated native Arawaks and Caribs by African slaves and a much lesser number of indentured workers from Asia and Europe, they share small size, restricted resources, and, in general, irregularly performing economies that remain highly dependent on metropolitan markets and goods. Except for Cuba, all adopted elected governments by 1995.

Haiti, although culturally rich, remains the most economically disadvantaged state in the Americas and one of the poorest globally. The Dominican Republic, which since the 1970s has been a democratic success story, frequently suffers strikes and food riots and faces additional controversy resulting from the sentencing of its president, Salvador Jorge Blanco (1982–1986) for corruption in office. Along with Haiti and most of the larger Commonwealth Caribbean states, the Dominican Republic has severe economic problems, including restructuring imposed by the International Monetary Fund (IMF). Cuba, which is not eligible for IMF or World Bank assistance—or its conditionalities—also faces severe economic dislocations in the face of major cutbacks in economic and political assistance from Russia and Eastern Europe as well as rising frustration

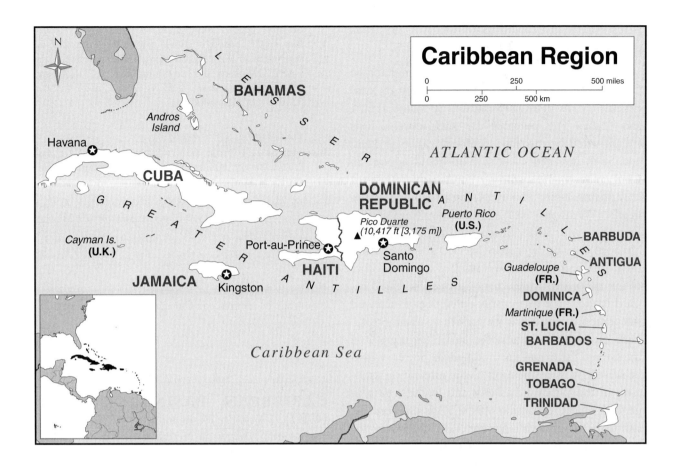

with the slowness of democratization in this Communist bastion. In the Commonwealth Caribbean, only Belize and a few of the smaller islands, especially the Commonwealth Dependencies most oriented to offshore banking (the Cayman Islands, the British Virgin Islands, and the Turks and Caicos Islands), have escaped the economic downturn of the 1990s. Cases of corruption and drug trafficking have followed the economic adversities in much of the region, requiring increased vigilance from all area governments.

Considerable regional change may accompany the Commonwealth Caribbean countries and Suriname, all of which are small and weak. Most have relatively open societies with memories of earlier good times promoting a sense of relative deprivation that is increased in intensity by the reality of popular demonstrations or coup attempts in several during the 1980s and 1990s. The authoritarian governments of Cuba and Haiti, the two exceptions to open societies in the insular Caribbean, are besieged with even greater anxieties as Cuba

faces a probable revolution-altering economic and political crisis, and Haiti must cope with post-1994 intervention changes that included the restoration of President Jean-Bertrand Aristide and another attempt at electoral democracy.

Greater emphasis on regionalism must be part of the answer in the post–cold war era, in view of the fact that both Russia and the United States appear preoccupied with internal domestic problems and higher-priority concerns in eastern Europe and Asia. Regional solutions in the Caribbean include a deepening and widening of the Caribbean Common Market (CARICOM); possible confederation of the Windward Islands (whose members in the early 2000s hold individual memberships in both the Organization of Eastern Caribbean States [OECS] and CARICOM); and expansion of the North American Free Trade Association (NAFTA) as outlined at the end of 1994 by President Bill Clinton; plus a possible enhancement of trade and economic assistance by regional intermediate powers such as Canada, Venezuela, Colombia, and Mexico, the

ENCYCLOPEDIA OF LATIN AMERICAN HISTORY & CULTURE 117

latter following resolution of its own domestic troubles.

CARICOM membership, now restricted to the Commonwealth Caribbean, has been sought by Venezuela, the Dominican Republic, Suriname, Haiti, and Cuba. The potential for such expansion is strengthened by increased democratization in Haiti and Suriname, and eventually, it would appear, in Cuba, a status that will enhance the desirability of their membership. The deepening of integrative ties in the Windward Islands (Grenada, Saint Lucia, Dominica and Saint Vincent and the Grenadines) has been impaired, ironically, by electoral democracy, since each time a plebiscite is planned one or another of the nations is facing a national election. The Leeward Islands have temporarily opted out of increased integration as the result of growth in their economies, especially in Antigua-Barbuda. The interests of the United States and the intermediate powers would be served by their attention to the integration processes in the Windward Islands and in the region in general. Finally, expansion of NAFTA is also possible, although fraught with perceived difficulties for local manufacturing and overall industrialization by Jamaica and other regional entities. Nevertheless, in 2005 the Dominican Republic joined Central American countries in signing a free trade pact with the United States.

See also **Caribbean Common Market (CARIFTA and CARICOM); Caribbean Sea, Commonwealth States; North American Free Trade Agreement.**

BIBLIOGRAPHY

Latin America and Caribbean Contemporary Record is an annual reference work (from 1983). *Caribbean Insight* is a current and accurate updated volume on the multicultural insular Caribbean. See also Charles Ameringer, *Political Parties of the Americas, 1980s to 1990s* (1992) and Robert J. Alexander, ed., *Biographical Dictionary of Latin American and Caribbean Political Leaders* (1988). Franklin Knight, *The Caribbean* (1978, rev. ed. 1990), is one of the best one-volume histories. Gordon K. Lewis, *The Growth of the Modern West Indies* (1968) and *Main Currents in Caribbean Thought* (1983), remain near classics. Carl Stone, *Power in the Caribbean Basin* (1986), is an excellent cross-cultural comparison of political economies. Howard Wiarda, *The Dominican Republic: Nation in Transition* (1969), and Wiarda and Michael J. Kryzanek, *The Dominican Republic: A Caribbean Crucible* (1992), are among the better works on that troubled country. Jorge I. Domínguez, *Cuba: Order and Revolution* (1978), though dated, remains a front-running assessment of this Marxist regime. Andres Serbin, "The CARICOM States and the Group of Three," in *Journal of Interamerican and World Affairs* 33, no. 2 (1991): 53–89, is of high value.

Additional Bibliography

Buscaglia-Salgado, José F. *Undoing Empire: Race and Nation in the Mulatto Caribbean.* Minneapolis: University of Minnesota Press, 2003.

Grafenstein, Johanna von, and Laura Muñoz Mata. *El Caribe región, frontera y relaciones internacionales.* México, D.F.: Instituto Mora, 2000.

Heuman, Gad J. *The Caribbean.* London: Hodder Arnold, 2006.

Rodríguez Juliá, Edgardo. *Caribeños.* San Juan, P.R.: Editorial del Instituto de Cultura Puertorriqueña, 2002.

W. MARVIN WILL

CARIBBEAN BASIN INITIATIVE (CBI).

Caribbean Basin Initiative (CBI), a twelve-year program that went into effect on 1 January 1984, under which designated Caribbean and Central American countries could ship a wide range of products duty-free to the United States. First proposed by President Ronald Reagan in February 1982, the program was not approved by Congress until July 1983. The primary motivation for this policy was to help strengthen the stability and economies of these countries in order to prevent leftist movements from growing as they had in Central America. Reagan's original proposal called for an emergency appropriation of $350 million for currency support; duty-free entry into the United States for exports, except textiles and apparel; and tax incentives for U.S. firms investing in manufacturing plants in the region. When approved by Congress, only the emergency appropriation remained unchanged. The duty-free list was altered to exclude footwear, handbags, luggage, flat goods (cloth materials), work gloves, leather apparel, canned tuna, petroleum and petroleum products, and certain watches and parts. Bowing to U.S. labor group pressure, Congress jettisoned the investment tax incentives. Communist-ruled countries—a clear reference to Cuba and Nicaragua—were denied any benefits under the plan.

From the outset the CBI was fraught with problems. More than half of the initial emergency allocation went to Costa Rica and El Salvador, the two countries most affected by Reagan's efforts to dislodge the Sandinistas from power in Nicaragua. The Bahamas and the Cayman Islands refused to participate in the CBI because the program required them to share tax information with the United States (an attempt to discourage offshore banking). Heads of Caribbean states immediately began to pressure Reagan to expand the duty-free list. The only concessions included the admission of garments manufactured with fabrics made in the United States and the implementation of a "twin plant" program by the Commonwealth of Puerto Rico, by which Puerto Rican–based industries could establish subsidiary operations in other Caribbean countries to produce products that would be sent back to Puerto Rico for final assembly. By 1990 the CBI had not generated broad-based economic growth, alleviated debt problems, generated lasting employment opportunities, or improved trade relations with the United States. Efforts by Reagan and his successor, George Bush, to expand and extend the program until 2007 failed to win congressional approval. However, in 2000, the Caribbean Basin Trade Partnership Act was passed. A planned economic agreement for Latin America, the Free Trade Area of the Americas (FTAA), would also include Caribbean countries.

See also **Economic Commission for Latin America and the Caribbean (ECLAC); Nicaragua, Sandinista National Liberation Front (FSLN); United States–Latin American Relations.**

BIBLIOGRAPHY

Bakan, Abigail B., David Cox, and Colin Leys, eds. *Imperial Power and Regional Trade: The Caribbean Basin Initiative.* Waterloo, ON: Wilfrid Laurier University Press, 1993.

"The Reagan Caribbean Basin Initiative," *Congressional Digest* 62 (1983): 69–96.

Tirado de Alonso, Irma, ed. *Caribbean Economies in the Twenty-First Century.* Gainesville: University Press of Florida, 2002.

U.S. Congress. House Committee On Ways and Means, Subcommittee on Oversight, *Review of the Impact and Effectiveness of the Caribbean Basin Initiative,* 99th Congress, 2d session, February 1986.

Whitney, Peter D. *Five Years of the Caribbean Basin Initiative* (1990).

THOMAS M. LEONARD

CARIBBEAN COMMON MARKET (CARIFTA AND CARICOM).

The search for Caribbean economic viability through some form of economic integration was initiated in 1965 by the political leaders of Guyana, Barbados, and Antigua. The proposal was modeled on the European custom union, the European Free Trade Association (EFTA). By May 1968 all the other English-speaking Caribbean nations had joined in the creation of the Caribbean Free Trade Association (CARIFTA). The ultimate goals of the union were, first and foremost, to encourage the kind of economic development that would provide the highest rates of employment, and second, to reduce the region's external economic dependence.

In October 1972 Jamaica, Trinidad and Tobago, Guyana, and Barbados (called the "more developed countries" within CARIFTA) agreed to deepen the integration process, forming the Caribbean Community and Common Market (CARICOM), which was formalized by the Treaty of Chaguaramas on July 4, 1973, with the following countries as members: Antigua and Barbuda, the Bahamas, Barbados, Belize, Dominica, Grenada, Guyana, Jamaica, Montserrat, Saint Lucia, St. Kitts and Nevis, St. Vincent and the Grenadines, Trinidad and Tobago. Haiti and Suriname were later admitted as full members. This agreement called for the establishment of a common external tariff, the harmonization of fiscal incentives for industry, double-taxation agreements, and the formation of a Caribbean Investment Corporation (CIC). The latter was geared toward helping the "less developed countries" (LDGs) of the area.

The English-speaking Caribbean nations had agreed to a very comprehensive institutional structure that went beyond economics. The highest decision-making body is the annual heads of Government Conference. Its decisions are given shape by the Common Market Council and implemented by the Caribbean Community Secretariat based in Georgetown, Guyana. Finances, specifically the Caribbean Development Bank and the Caribbean Investment Corporation, are under the purview of the ministers of finance and their administrative arm, the Council of Central Banks and Monetary Authorities. Whatever the potential of such a structure for future political integration, it was always felt that CARICOM would stand or fall on the basis of its economic performance. Using the best single measure of economic success—the rates of growth of intraregional trade as a share of total trade—the record appears to be mixed. Between 1967 and 2005 that rate has oscillated between 7 and 15 percent, with export from oil and gas-rich Trinidad counting for the lion's share.

Aware that the Caribbean is facing a changed global economy, including competition from Mexico and Asia and the disappearance of privileged protocols on sugar, bananas, rum, and a series of other traditional products, the CARICOM nations have amended the Treaty of Chaguaramas to launch the CARICOM Single Market and Economy (CSME). In 2007 it was still a work in progress, but its formal goals were to "allow CARICOM goods, services, people and capital to move throughout the Caribbean community without tariffs and without restrictions to achieve a single large economic space" (CARICOM Internet site). Achieving these goals will confront two challenges: (1) the perception in the smaller islands of the Organization of Eastern Caribbean States that they are at a terrible disadvantage and, consequently, need special allowances; and, increasingly more important, (2) the impatience of more developed countries (namely, Trinidad and Tobago, and Jamaica), which leads them to engage in bilateral national deals that contravene CSME arrangements and understandings.

See also **Economic Development; Economic Integration.**

BIBLIOGRAPHY

Bernal, Richard J. "CARICOM Single Market and Economy Charts Destiny: Progressing beyond a Common Market, Members in This Group of Caribbean Nations Are Implementing Economic Integration and Cooperative Development, Leading to a Greater Variety and Better Production of Goods and Services." *Americas* (English edition) 59, no. 3: 46–52.

Caribbean Community (CARICOM) Secretariat Internet site. Available from http://www.caricom.org/.

Caribbean Free Trade Association (CARIFA) Available from http://www.caricom.org/jsp/community/carifta.jsp?menu=community.

ANTHONY P. MAINGOT

CARIBBEAN LEGION. Caribbean Legion, a term applied to a conglomerate of exile groups that actively opposed the dictatorial regimes in the Caribbean during the period 1946 to 1950. Though the legion never existed as a specific military unit, certain personalities and matériel were common elements in a series of filibustering expeditions. Among the most prominent of these were Cayo Confites (1947), an ill-fated attempt to invade the Dominican Republic from Cuba; Costa Rica (1948), where Cayo Confites remnants based in Guatemala and augmented by Nicaraguan exiles aided José Figueres Ferrer (1906–1990) in his War of National Liberation; and Luperón (1949), wherein Dominican exiles, primarily using Guatemala as a base, carried out an unsuccessful raid on their homeland. Although each of these events was under distinct leadership and sponsorship, none boasted a coherent military force, such as the term "Caribbean Legion" would imply. Supported by the presidents of Cuba (Ramón Grau San Martín and Carlos Prío Socarrás, successively) and Guatemala (Juan José Arévalo Bermejo), these armed bands were comprised principally of Cubans and by Dominican, Honduran, Nicaraguan, and Salvadoran exiles at one time or another.

The core unit of these expeditions was the Liberation Army of America, founded in 1946 by General Juan Rodríguez García, as the military arm of a coalition of Dominican exiles opposing the dictator Rafael Trujillo Molina. The first use of the term "Caribbean Legion," however, occurred during the Costa Rican civil war, when it was used to designate a small force of exiles airlifted from Guatemala to seize Puerto Limón. The name caught on. Even Trujillo and Anastasio Somoza Debayle utilized it in the hope of depicting their adversaries as adventurers and mercenaries.

The phantom army ceased to exist altogether in 1950, after the Organization of American States imposed on Caribbean governments a series of "principles and standards" that severely restricted the activities of political exiles. The involvement of certain Central American exiles in Guatemalan affairs, particularly the implication of the Honduran Miguel Francisco Morazán in the 1949 assassination of Francisco Javier Arana, chief of the Guatemalan armed forces, also accounted for the eventual disappearance of the so-called Caribbean Legion.

See also **Filibustering.**

BIBLIOGRAPHY

Alberto Bayo, *Tempestad en el Caribe* (1950).

Enrique V. Corominas, *In the Caribbean Political Areas,* translated by L. Charles Foresti (1954).

Rosendo Argüello, Jr., *By Whom We Were Betrayed ... And How* (1955).

Horacio Ornes, *Desembarco en Luperón* (1956).

John Patrick Bell, *Crisis in Costa Rica: The 1948 Revolution* (1971).

Charles D. Ameringer, *The Democratic Left in Exile: The Antidictatorial Struggle in the Caribbean, 1945–1959* (1974) and *Don Pepe: A Political Biography of José Figueres of Costa Rica* (1978).

Additional Bibliography

Ameringer, Charles D. *The Caribbean Legion: Patriots, Politicians, Soldiers of Fortune, 1946-1950.* University Park: Pennsylvania State University Press, 1996.

CHARLES D. AMERINGER

CARIBBEAN SEA.

Defined geographically, the Caribbean Sea is the body of water surrounding the islands of the West Indies that also washes the mainland, Antilles-facing shores of Belize, Honduras, Nicaragua, Costa Rica, Panama, Colombia, and Venezuela. As a cultural designation, the word "Caribbean" may also be used to identify not only the diverse peoples who inhabit the territory outlined above but also the population of Guyana.

The term "Caribbean" has long suffered from lack of precision. Carl O. Sauer put the matter succinctly: "The whole of the Caribbean area came to be known in English as the Spanish Main, including the sea. Thus, sailing *to* the Spanish Main became called sailing *on* the Spanish Main." For two decades after Columbus made landfall, what the Spaniards called the Ocean Sea was thought to be a vast, unbroken expanse lying to the west between Europe and Asia. After Balboa traversed Darién, the Ocean Sea was divided in two, with the Pacific Ocean called the Mar del Sur (South Sea) and the Atlantic, with its Caribbean indentation, called the Mar del Norte (North Sea). In the English-language world, the designation dates to the eighteenth century and is attributed by Sauer to Thomas Jefferys, whose introduction to the *West-India Atlas* (1775) states that "it has been sometimes called the Caribbean-Sea, which name would be better to adopt, than to leave this space quite anonymous." "Caribbean" derives from Carib, the name given to a group of people

originally from mainland South America who later island-hopped their way across the Lesser Antilles, displacing other cultures as they went and raiding eastern Puerto Rico until Spanish intrusion halted their expansion.

See also **Belize; Costa Rica; Honduras; Nicaragua; Panama.**

BIBLIOGRAPHY

The best account of the tragedy that befell the native peoples of the Caribbean, a bitter experience of enslavement, exploitation, demographic collapse, and cultural extinction, is Carl O. Sauer's masterly reconstruction *The Early Spanish Main* (1966; 2d ed. 1992.) Also authoritative is Mary W. Helms's "The Indians of the Caribbean and Circum-Caribbean at the End of the Fifteenth Century," in *The Cambridge History of Latin America,* edited by Leslie Bethell, vol. 1 (1984), pp. 37–58. A more controversial depiction of the encounter between natives and newcomers is Kirkpatrick Sale, *The Conquest of Paradise: Christopher Columbus and the Columbian Legacy* (1990). An enduring classic is the textbook by Robert C. West and John P. Augelli, *Middle America: Its Lands and Peoples* (1966; 3d ed. 1989).

Additional Bibliography

Arciniegas, Germán. *Caribbean, Sea of the New World.* Princeton, NJ: Markus Wiener Publishers, 2003.

Britto García, Luis. *Señores del caribe: Indígenas, conquistadores y piratas en el mar colonial.* Caracas, Venezuela: Fundación Tradiciones Caraqueñas, 2001.

Duval, David Timothy. *Tourism in the Caribbean: Trends, Development, Prospects.* New York: Routledge, 2004.

Prevost, John F. *Caribbean Sea.* Minneapolis: Abdo Pub. Co., 2003.

Salazar–Vallejo, Sergio. "Huracanes y biodiversidad costera tropical." *Revista de biología tropical* 50, no. 2 (June 2002): 415–428.

Taylor, L.R., and Norbert Wu. *The Caribbean Sea.* Woodbridge, CT: Blackbirch Press, 1998.

W. GEORGE LOVELL

CARIBBEAN SEA, COMMONWEALTH STATES.

The Commonwealth Caribbean (generally known as the West Indies) encompasses twelve independent countries and six British dependent territories with a total population of approximately 6 million in the early twenty-first century. Spread throughout the insular and littoral Caribbean basin, this assemblage stretches from the Bahamas in the north to the South American country of Guyana (formerly British Guiana) in the south. The Commonwealth includes the countries of Jamaica and Belize (formerly British Honduras) on the Central American littoral and Trinidad and Tobago and insular Barbados on the Atlantic rim of the Caribbean. The remaining six independent countries and four of the six dependent territories are found in the Leeward and Windward Islands of the eastern Caribbean.

In the seventeenth and eighteenth centuries the Caribbean territories served primarily as pawns in European power struggles. Most were ruled consecutively by two, sometimes three, colonial masters. Saint Lucia, for instance, changed hands fourteen times (explaining why the official language is English but the lingua franca is French patois). Every island experienced alternating patterns of European attention and neglect. The phase of conquest ended with the defeat of France in the Napoleonic Wars. The Congress of Vienna (1815) established the basic geopolitical outlines of the Caribbean Commonwealth islands.

The next major watershed for the Commonwealth territories came with the abolition of the slave trade followed by emancipation (1834–1838). The impact and consequences of these two events were not everywhere the same. Islands with ample land outside the plantation system, such as Trinidad and British Guiana, were known as open economies because former slaves could leave plantations and settle the land as subsistence farmers. In closed economies, such as those on Barbados and Saint Christopher (Saint Kitts), there was no free land, so former slaves stayed on the plantations as wage labor.

Severe labor shortages developed in the open economies, a problem addressed by the adoption of a system already used in Mauritius in the Indian Ocean: importing indentured labor from India. The project lasted from 1854 to 1917 and led to a historical watershed in certain West Indian islands. By 1870 there were 28,500 Indians (mostly Hindus) in Trinidad, and by 1883 the number had risen to 48,000, about one-third of the island's population. In the same year there were 65,000 Indians in British Guiana out of a population of a quarter of a million. This steady supply of migrant labor enabled the sugar estates to expand production and put the

two colonies on the road to prosperity. It also allowed former slaves to migrate to the cities where they became the indispensable craftsmen of the building trades. At the same time, many free villages had been established, creating a landed peasantry.

By 1870, British colonial interests had shifted to India and slave-grown sugar was more cheaply imported from Brazil and Cuba. In the islands, community development through ownership and education began to falter and local leadership disappeared. Social and political inertia characterized the rest of the nineteenth century. The West Indies became the backwater of the British Empire.

The twentieth century began with the aggressive entry of a new imperial power: the United States. The rapid increase in the United States's influence in the region corresponded with the diminishing power of British colonization. At the same time the building of the Panama Canal had a dramatic impact on both the strategic importance and the economy of the Caribbean. A major part of that impact was through the recruitment of labor and the remittances sent home.

Once the employment opportunities generated by the canal project ended, population pressures combined with poor wages to create explosive conditions in the islands. The population of the British West Indies had increased from 1,719,000 in 1896 to 2,514,000 in 1936, and there were no outlets for emigrants. In 1941 the Panamanian constitution forbade the immigration of "the negro race, whose native language was not Spanish, the yellow race, and the native races of India, Asia Minor, and North Africa." In 1942 the United States promised to abide by the Panamanian restrictions when recruiting labor for the Canal Zone. Costa Rica, Cuba, and the United States all either closed the door completely to West Indian immigrants or left only a small space for a few to enter.

Discontent erupted first in 1935 in Saint Kitts when sugar workers struck for higher wages. Some months later the tension mounted in Saint Vincent. In Saint Lucia there were strikes among the coal workers, but no violence. Blood was shed in the Trinidad oilfields, and arms had to be used to quell the disturbance and to restore order. Soon after, rioting broke out in Barbados. In June 1938, there were serious disorders in Guiana and in Jamaica.

The first enduring labor and political organizations of the British West Indies emerged out of these disorders. After 1938 this growth was encouraged by the colonial government. Between 1939 and 1945 some sixty-five trade unions were formed and legislation was passed setting up departments of labor and providing machinery for regulating labor disputes. In every Commonwealth country, with the exception of Trinidad, trade union leaders became the political leaders who later led the decolonization movement.

The outbreak of World War II delayed the implementation of some reforms. The Caribbean, strategically located between the United States and Germany's South American sources of fuel and raw materials, became a shooting gallery for German U-boats. In 1940, Britain agreed to exchange fourteen bases on British West Indian islands for forty-four U.S. destroyers. The resulting U.S. influence on the islands would be profound.

The postwar decolonization process in the Commonwealth Caribbean proceeded with none of the conflict and violence evident in other parts of the British Empire. London hoped to create a single state out of all the islands, and the West Indies Federation was created in 1958. Powerful insular forces brought this experiment to an end in 1962. This unleashed independence movements in virtually all the islands. Despite periodic spurts of violence and ongoing racial conflict, the Commonwealth Caribbean islands have established themselves as stable two-party systems with entrenched social democratic values. Their efforts to organize a true common market have been torturous, but persistently pursued given the region-wide awareness of just how vulnerable small countries are in the global market place.

See also **Labor Movements; Panama Canal; Slavery: Spanish America; United States-Latin American Relations.**

BIBLIOGRAPHY

Knight, Franklin W. *The Modern Caribbean*. Chapel Hill: University of North Carolina Press, 1989.

Lewis, Gordon K. *The Growth of the Modern West Indies*. Kingston, Jamaica: Ian Randle Publishers, 2004.

ANTHONY P. MAINGOT

CARIBS. The term "Carib" was used by Europeans for political purposes rather than to identify ethnic groups in the Caribbean. Three groups of people have been called Caribs: Island Caribs, Main-land Caribs, and Black Caribs. The Caribbean contained many distinct ethnic groups, but after 1492 Europeans distinguished simply between the "peaceful Arawak" of the Greater Antilles and the "warlike Carib" of the Lesser Antilles, although the former resisted conquest and the latter spoke an Arawakan language, distinct from the Cariban languages spoken by people on the mainland of what is now Venezuela, Guyana, Surinam, and French Guiana. The Spanish called those who attacked them Caribs and extended the category conveniently in order to enslave people because Caribs were excluded from the Spanish law forbidding the enslavement of Indians. For example, they declared the people of Trinidad to be Carib in 1511, declassified them in 1518, and declared them Carib again in 1530, to meet Spanish labor requirements.

EUROPEAN IMPACT

The nature of the migration patterns, interactions, and relationships between the island and mainland Caribs remains controversial, but it is generally thought that Caribs originated on the mainland and migrated northward to the Guianas and the Lesser Antilles. At the time of conquest and colonization there were no firm ethnic boundaries between Amerindian people, and no clear Carib ethnic identity existed. Carib society was largely coastal and seafaring, based on its lowland, rain forest environment. Its economy was based on slash-and-burn agriculture, the chief crops being manioc, maize, beans, and squashes, supplemented by hunting and fishing. Caribs had a tradition of raiding, using clubs and poisoned arrows for economic as well as political reasons, and had an extensive trading system by river and sea, using dugout canoes. War leaders obtained influence over several related villages. Men moved into villages where their wives lived and each village contained four hundred or more persons. With considerable local variations, the colonization of the Caribs took about 300 years, partly because Europeans (Spanish, Dutch, French, and British) committed fewer resources to their region than others and partly because Carib resistance, which depended on a network of village alliances, was decentralized and hard to defeat decisively. When European merchants provided various groups with arms to fight or enslave members of other groups, some became known as Dutch and others as Spanish Caribs. Any potential Carib unity was shattered when rival leaders engaged in alliances with different Europeans, but the consolidation of a Carib identity emerged partly through their resistance to the European impact.

Prior to contact with Europeans there were more than one hundred thousand Caribs on the mainland, about twenty-five thousand in Trinidad, and several thousand on the other islands. The European impact on Carib societies was devastating. The combination of military campaigns, enslavement, and diseases from which Caribs lacked immunities reduced their mainland population by about 80 percent in the eighteenth century. The efforts of missionaries added to this impact. When peaceful persuasion failed to convert Caribs, violent means were used to capture, resettle, and "convert" them. In the early nineteenth century the Carib population was about ten thousand on the mainland; less than one thousand in Trinidad; and smaller numbers in Dominica, Martinique and St. Vincent.

REMNANTS OF THE CARIB SURVIVORS

Estimates of the present population vary greatly according to who is classified as Carib, as there has been a great deal of genetic and cultural mixing. Many Caribs of the mainland, who have still not recovered to their pre-conquest population levels, live in relatively remote areas. In the early twenty-first century, all the Amerindians of Venezuela and Guyana, not all of whom are Caribs, are only about 7 percent and 4 percent, respectively, of the populations. In the Caribbean islands, where few Amerindians survive, their culture persists in some place names and vocabulary (including the words hurricane, tobacco, hammock, and canoe) and in subsistence practices, diet, and technology, especially as associated with cassava production. However, Amerindian culture influenced the Africans who largely replaced them in the seventeenth and eighteenth centuries. On Dominica fewer than three thousand persons, constituting the largest Carib community of the islands, live in eight villages in a designated Carib Territory of less than 4,000 acres, which are communally owned. They live mostly by agriculture, especially through cultivating bananas as a cash crop, and by selling craft items to visitors. Their housing and recreational activities, however, differ little from those of other rural communities on Dominica. Although the assimilation process persists, there has been a cultural revival that includes a concern for the need to recognize their distinct history and an effort to develop a greater sense of identity.

THE GARIFUNA

In the sixteenth and seventeenth centuries, Caribs of the Lesser Antilles, more properly called Kalinago, raided European settlements and sometimes took enslaved Africans back home, where they became incorporated into Carib society. Other Africans were shipwrecked or escaped and joined Carib communities. Most of these Africans may have been men, and the children they had with Carib women were raised largely in their mothers' culture. By the seventeenth century these people were called "Black Caribs" to distinguish them from those that Europeans called "Red" or "Yellow." Physically and culturally distinct because of their mixed ancestral origins, they became a new ethnic group whose members prefer to be called Garifuna, the term for their own language. On St. Vincent, between 7,000 and 8,000 Garifuna, who outnumbered the surviving Caribs, engaged in protracted resistance against French and British colonizers. In 1795 a full-scale war broke out between the British and Garifuna, who were supported by some Carib, African, and French people. Britain almost lost control of the island, but in 1796 thousands of British troops destroyed Carib and Garifuna villages, canoes, and provision grounds, and many rebels surrendered. More than of half the captive Garifuna died. Of the survivors, 2,248 were separated from Caribs and former slaves and transported in 1797 to the island of Roatan in the Bay of Honduras. Many did not survive the journey, but the population of scarcely 2,000 grew after settling on the mainland. They flourished through a combination of subsistence farming, fishing, trade, and wage work and a strong historical consciousness of their unique origins and identity. In the early twenty-first century more than 200,000 Garifuna live in more than seventy communities along the Caribbean coast of Belize, Guatemala, Honduras, and Nicaragua, and many thousands live in the United States.

The Garifuna maintain distinctive cultural traditions and consider themselves an indigenous Caribbean people. Their language is essentially Arawakan, influenced by Carib and the European languages they have encountered. Central to their culture are music; oral literature; cuisine, in which cassava is prominent; and religious traditions, including an ancestral ritual called *dugu* in which their epic journey and resettlement is reenacted. Through these traditional rituals and activities they maintain their historical consciousness and identity by communicating with their ancestors and each other. In 1966 three St. Vincent Caribs visited the principal Garifuna community in Belize, at the invitation of Belizeans, to celebrate Garifuna Settlement Day and reestablish their ancestral connections. As the Garifuna continue to migrate, however, often living in poor and culturally heterogeneous urban conditions, their village-based traditions are hard to maintain, so their distinct culture and identity is increasingly threatened. Garifuna intellectuals have organized revivals of their traditions, and they undertook an initiative that resulted in UNESCO proclaiming Garifuna culture a Masterpiece of Oral and Intangible Heritage of Humanity in 2001.

See also **Belize; Dominica; Indigenous Peoples; Martinique and Guadeloupe; Saint Vincent; Suriname and the Dutch in the Caribbean; Trinidad and Tobago.**

BIBLIOGRAPHY

Basso, Ellen B., ed. *Carib-Speaking Indians: Culture, Society, and Language.* Tucson: University of Arizona Press, 1977.

Gonzalez, Nancie L. *Sojourners of the Caribbean: Ethnogenesis and Ethnohistory of the Garifuna.* Urbana: University of Illinois Press, 1988.

Palacio, Joseph O., ed. *The Garifuna: A Nation across Borders: Essays in Social Anthropology.* Benque Viejo del Carmen, Belize: Cubola Productions, 2005.

Whitehead, Neil L. *Lords of the Tiger Spirit: A History of the Caribs in Colonial Venezuela and Guyana, 1498–1820.* Providence, RI: Foris Publications, 1988.

Wilson, Samuel M., ed. *The Indigenous People of the Caribbean.* Gainesville: University Press of Florida, 1997.

O. NIGEL BOLLAND

CARIMBÓ. *Carimbó,* a type of *atabaque* (conical single-headed drum) and the African-derived dance performed with it in the north of Brazil. The instrument is made of a hollowed trunk with an animal-skin drumhead. The drummer sits on the trunk and strikes the skin with his hands. Historically,

the *carimbó* was used in the *batuque,* a dance brought from Africa by enslaved Africans. Also influenced by Portuguese and Native American cultures, the *carimbó* dance developed in Belém, a city located in the Pará region, during the colonial era. In the *carimbó,* men and women dance in a circle. Often dressed as a *Bahiana,* a woman then leaves the circle, dances into the center and, in a teasing manner, throws her flared skirt over the head of a male dancer. *Carimbó* can be found among the peasants and fishermen of the state of Pará. In the 1960s and 1970s, with the influence of electronic instruments, the rhythms of the *carimbó* helped produce the lambada.

See also **Lambada; MPB: Música Popular Brasileira; Musical Instruments.**

BIBLIOGRAPHY

David P. Appleby, *The Music of Brazil* (1983).

Luis Da Camara Cascudo, *Dicionário do folclore brasileiro,* 5th ed. (1984).

Additional Bibliography

Crook, Larry. *Brazilian Music: Northeastern Traditions and the Heartbeat of a Modern Nation.* Santa Barbara: ABC-CLIO, 2005.

Murphy, John P. *Music in Brazil: Experiencing Music, Expressing Culture.* New York: Oxford University Press, 2006.

BERNADETTE DICKERSON

CARIOCA. Carioca, anyone or anything from or pertaining to the city of Rio de Janeiro; thus, residents of Rio de Janeiro are called Cariocas, just as people from São Paulo are known as Paulistas. The name comes from the Carioca River, which originates in the valley between the Tijuca and Paineiras mountains, flows through the neighborhoods of Laranjeiras and Catete, and empties into Guanabara Bay at Flamengo and Glória beaches. Today almost entirely subterranean and extremely polluted, due to the emptying of raw sewage into it, the Carioca River was once famed for the purity and pleasant temperature of its water, which was believed to have medicinal qualities. The Tamoio, a Tupí community that lived on the margins of Guanabara Bay in the sixteenth century, believed the Carioca's waters sacred and inspirational for musicians and poets. Until the late nineteenth century, the river was the city's major source of potable water. A monumental aqueduct built in the early eighteenth century brought water from the Carioca to public fountains in the center of the city. Part of this Roman-style aqueduct, built in stone and mortar, which is today called the Arcos de Lapa, is one of Rio de Janeiro's most striking man-made landmarks.

See also **Rio de Janeiro (City).**

BIBLIOGRAPHY

Cunha, Maria Clementina Pereira. *Ecos da folia: Uma história social do carnaval carioca entre 1880 e 1920*. São Paulo: Companhia das Letras, 2001.

Lessa, Carlos. *O Rio de todos os Brasis: Uma reflexão em busca de auto-estima*. Rio de Janeiro: Editora Record, 2000.

Pechman, Robert M. *Cidades estreitamente vigiadas: O detetive e o urbanista*. Rio de Janeiro: Casa da Palavra, 2002.

SUEANN CAULFIELD

CARLÉS, MANUEL (1872–1946).

Manuel Carlés (*b.* 30 May 1872; *d.* 25 October 1946), Argentine politician, teacher, and president of the anti-leftist Argentine Patriotic League (1919–1946).

Carlés was born in Rosario, Santa Fe, to a prominent family. Although he never joined the Radical Civic Union (Unión Cívica Radical), he favored efforts to reform politics and participated in the Radical revolt of 1893. He served as national deputy from 1898 to 1912 and supported President Roque Sáenz Peña (1910–1914), who helped institute electoral democracy. After 1912 he devoted himself to the law and to his teaching at several schools, including the Colegio Militar de la Nación and Escuela Superior de Guerra, where he influenced many future military officers. He initially sympathized with the government of the Radical leader Hipólito Irigoyen (1916–1922, 1928–1930), who appointed him *interventor* (temporary administrator) in Salta in 1918. The next president, the Radical Marcelo T. de Alvear (1922–1928), appointed him *interventor* in San Juan in 1922.

Nevertheless, Carlés, like other middle- and upper-class Argentines, thought that the Irigoyen government was not doing enough to repress leftism. During the Semana Trágica (Tragic Week) disturbances between labor and the forces of order in Buenos Aires in 1919, military officers and civilians, including Carlés, formed militias to protect bourgeois neighborhoods and attack worker areas. Militias spread throughout the country. On 20 January 1919 these groups united to form the Argentine Patriotic League and on 5 April, Carlés was elected its president, a post he retained until his death. In the early postwar years, the League violently suppressed strikes and leftist groups. In 1923 an anarchist unsuccessfully attempted to kill Carlés. Fearing a leftist resurgence and disorder, Carlés influenced the League and the public to turn against Irigoyen in 1930 and thus helped inspire the coup of that year. General José F. Uriburu's (1930–1932) antidemocratic excesses, however, led Carlés to denounce this administration and return to his Radical roots. While he continued to criticize leftism, during the 1930s Carlés opposed electoral fraud and supported Marcelo Alvear's efforts to unite and strengthen Radical forces.

See also **Argentina, Organizations: Argentine Patriotic League (LPA).**

BIBLIOGRAPHY

Pedro P. Maglione Jaimes, "Una figura señera—Manuel Carlés," *La Nación*, 12 January 1969.

David Rock, *Politics in Argentina, 1890–1930: The Rise and Fall of Radicalism* (1975).

Sandra McGee Deutsch, *Counterrevolution in Argentina, 1900–1932: The Argentine Patriotic League* (1986).

Additional Bibliography

Caterina, Luis María. *La liga patriótica argentina: Un grupo de presióm frente a las convulsiones sociales de la década del veinte*. Buenos Aires: Corregidor, 1995.

SANDRA MCGEE DEUTSCH

CARLOS, ROBERTO (1943–).

Roberto Carlos (*b.* 1943), Brazilian pop singer and songwriter. Carlos has been one of Latin America's most popular recording artists throughout his career. He started out singing rock and roll, cowriting songs with Erasmo Carlos (no relation), and gained fame singing the 1963 hits "Calembeque" and "Splish

Splash" (a cover of the American hit). In 1965, he and Erasmo led the *jovem guarda* movement, a post–Bossa-Nova manifestation of domestic rock by several young Brazilian musicians. Roberto and Erasmo hosted the "Jovem Guarda" show on the TV Record network from 1965 to 1968, and cowrote hit songs like "Parei na contramão" (I Parked the Wrong Way), "É proibido fumar" (No Smoking), and "Garota do baile" (Dance Girl).

In the 1970s, Roberto transformed himself into a romantic interpreter of ballads and boleros, although he and Erasmo continued their songwriting partnership. During that decade, Roberto was the top-selling recording artist in Brazil, selling an annual average of one million records (quadruple-platinum) with each new album. With recordings frequently hitting the top ten in numerous Latin American and European countries, he also became an international star. In the 1980s, Carlos recorded hits in Portuguese, Spanish, French, and English, but was supplanted as Brazil's number-one recording artist in the late 1980s by the children's music singer Xuxa. After his wife's death in 1999, Carlos tried to keep on with his career, producing the album *Amor sem limite* but then broke his contract with Sony due to hardship. However, he went on to win the 2005 Latin Grammy for Best Romantic Album

See also **Music: Popular Music and Dance.**

BIBLIOGRAPHY

Rock, a música do século XX, edited by Pedro Paulo Popovic Consultores Editorias Ltda. (1983).

Rita Caúrio, ed., *Brasil Musical* (1988).

Chris McGowan and Ricardo Pessanha, *The Brazilian Sound: Samba, Bossa Nova, and the Popular Music of Brazil* (1991).

Additional Bibliography

Alves Júnior, Carlos. *Rock Brasil: O livro.* São Paulo: Editora Esfera, 2003.

Araújo, Paulo Cesar. *Roberto Carlos em detalhes.* São Paulo: Planeta, 2006.

CHRIS MCGOWAN

CARLOTA (1775–1830). Carlota (Carlota Joaquina de Borbón y Parma; *b.* 25 April 1775; *d.* 7 January 1830), Spanish princess, queen consort of Portugal, and royalist leader in South America. Daughter of King Carlos IV and Queen María Luisa of Spain, Princess Carlota Joaquina consummated her arranged marriage to Prince João, heir to the Portuguese throne, in 1790. The royal pair thoroughly disliked each other and were constantly at odds over political and personal matters; nevertheless, they produced nine children, including Pedro, who became emperor of Brazil, and Miguel, who usurped the Portuguese throne—although the paternity of the latter as well as that of two of his sisters is in doubt. Carlota reluctantly joined the emigration of the Portuguese court to Brazil in 1807, when Portugal was invaded by France in alliance with Spain.

In Rio de Janeiro, after the French had deposed her brother, King Fernando VII of Spain, Carlota in 1808 set out to establish herself as the regent of Spain's empire in the Americas in the name of her imprisoned brother. Carlota enlisted the aid of her good friend, British admiral Sir Sidney Smith, and initially had her husband's acquiescence in the regency project. But Prince João, regent of Portugal for the insane Queen Maria I, perceived a united Spanish America ruled by his wife as a threat to his own domains. His concern was shared by the British government, which, in 1809, recalled Admiral Smith and forestalled his scheme to sail with Carlota to Buenos Aires and install her there as Spanish regent.

A new opportunity for Carlota arose with the revolution in Buenos Aires in May 1810. From Rio she established contact with members of the Buenos Aires junta, offering herself as their leader. João was disconcerted by his wife's willingness to deal with revolutionaries to further her ambitions. In the end, however, Carlota's royal absolutism found few partisans in Spanish America and Fernando's return to the throne in Spain in 1814 obviated any need for a regency in his name.

In 1821 Carlota returned with her husband, now King João VI, to Portugal, where she continued to conspire against him. In 1824 she and her favorite son, Miguel, seized the government in Lisbon and forced João to seek refuge on a British warship. The British demanded and got João's restoration. After João's death in 1826, Carlota vigorously supported Miguel as king of Portugal, denying the claim of Maria II, Pedro's daughter.

With Miguel seemingly secure on the Portuguese throne, Carlota died in 1830.

See also **Joaõ I of Portugal.**

BIBLIOGRAPHY

Julián María Rubio, *La infanta Carlota Joaquina y la política de España en América, 1808–1812* (1920).

Marcus Cheke, *Carlota Joaquina, Queen of Portugal* (1947).

Additional Bibliography

Azevedo, Francisca L Nogueira de. *Carlota Joaquina na Corte do Brasil.* Rio de Janerio: Civilização Brasileira, 2003.

NEILL MACAULAY

CARMELITES (DISCALCED).

Carmelites (Discalced), a religious order of the Roman Catholic Church with separate branches for men and women. The order was founded in the Holy Land during the Crusades of the twelfth century when Albert, patriarch of Jerusalem, wrote a rule for the purpose of organizing the hermits living on the slopes of Mount Carmel into one community. Carmelites look to the Old Testament prophet Elijah as their spiritual father, for he is said to have inspired their lifestyle of silence, solitary prayer, and contemplation. With an invasion of the Holy Lands in 1238, the Carmelites dispersed, bringing the rule with them to Europe. From that time until the sixteenth century there was a general relaxation of the strict rule, but Saint Teresa of Ávila then succeeded in reversing the trend. This sixteenth-century Spanish mystic traveled throughout her country founding communities of Carmelites, for men and for women, based on a return to the strict rule. Those who chose to adopt this life of silence, contemplation, and abstinence from eating meat became known as Discalced (Barefoot) Carmelites. It is this branch of the order that first went to the Americas.

Carmelites had traveled to the New World as early as 1527, but not with the intention of founding monasteries. It was not until Quivira (a mythical town) and New Mexico became slated for colonization that there was an opportunity for the Carmelites to join in the missionary activities of the Spanish church. In 1585 the order petitioned the king's council for permission to establish a monastery for men in New Spain. The request was granted, and in September of that year eleven Carmelites arrived. This settlement led eventually to the founding of the province of San Alberto of New Spain by 1590. In the sixteenth century, there were Carmelite communities in Mexico City, Puebla, Atlixco, Morelia, Guadalajara, and Celaya, which were followed by other foundations throughout the colonial period.

A characteristic discipline of the order is the building of a "desert," a monastery of individual cells designed to accommodate a reclusive life. One such desert, El Desierto de los Leones, was founded in 1606 near Mexico City. At its peak in the middle of the eighteenth century, the order counted over 500 members. The Reform Laws of the nineteenth century all but extinguished the order, though in 1884 a novitiate opened and Carmelites began to be trained once again. The province of San Alberto, however, was not restored until 1960.

In the seventeenth century monasteries were erected elsewhere in Latin America, including Colombia (Bogotá, 1606), Argentina (Córdoba, 1628), Peru (Lima, 1643), Ecuador (Quito, 1653), Bolivia (Sucre, 1665), and Chile (Santiago, 1690). In Brazil there were six monasteries by the end of the sixteenth century, and three separate provinces by 1720. At present there are nearly one hundred Carmelite houses in fifteen countries of Latin America, with new foundations as recent as 1980.

The first community of Discalced Carmelite nuns in the Americas was established in Puebla in 1604, with four Spanish women under the direction of the Carmelite friars. In the colonial period and nineteenth century, eleven convents were founded in Mexico. Spanish women also founded communities in Argentina, Bolivia, Chile, Colombia, Ecuador, Peru, and Cuba; convents were established by Portuguese women in Brazil. These are cloistered, contemplative communities. Currently there are Carmelite convents in eight Latin American countries.

See also **Anticlericalism.**

BIBLIOGRAPHY

León Lopetegui and Felix Zubillaga, *Historia de la Iglesia en la América Española,* vol. 1 (1965).

Agustín De La Madre De Dios, *Tesoro escondido en el Santo Carmelo Mexicano* (1984).

Alfonso Martínez Rosales, *El gran teatro de un pequeño mundo: El Carmen de San Luis Potosí, 1732–1859* (1985).

Additional Bibliography

Dávila Munguía, Carmen Alicia. *Los Carmelitas Descalzos en Valladolid de Michoacán, siglo XVII*. Morelia: Instituto Michoacano de Cultura, 1999.

Fiori, Iride Rossi de., Rosanna Caramella de Gamarra, and Helena Fiori Rossi. *Primera escritura femenina en la República Argentina: Poemas del Carmelo de Córdoba (1804)*. Salta: Biblioteca de Textos Universitarios, 2002.

Gómez de la Parra, José. *Fundación y primero siglo: Crónica del primer convento de carmelitas descalzas en Puebla, 1604 1704*. México: Universidad Iberoamericana, Departamento de Historia: Comisión Puebla V Centenario, 1992.

Prat, André. *Notas historicas sobre as misões carmelitas no extremo norte do Brasil (seculo XVII-XVIII)*. Recife, 1941.

Ramos Medina, Manuel. *Místicas y descalzas: Fundaciones femeninas carmelitas en la Nueva España*. Chimalistac: Centro de Estudios de Historia de México Condumex, 1997.

BRIAN C. BELANGER

CARNEIRO DE CAMPOS, JOSÉ JOAQUÍM (1768–1836).

José Joaquím Carneiro de Campos (Caravelas, Marquês de; *b*. 4 March 1768; *d*. 8 September 1836), Brazilian statesman. Campos first pursued a religious career as a Benedictine monk, but then abandoned the ecclesiastic life to study law in Coimbra, Portugal. After receiving a doctor of jurisprudence degree, Campos began his political career in the kingdom of Portugal. He followed the royal family into exile in Brazil in 1807, shortly before the Napoleonic invasion. As aide to Prince Regent Dom João (later João VI), Campos rose quickly within the court. After independence in September 1822, Campos was elected to the constituent assembly, where he was one of the principal authors of the constitution of the monarchy. By 1823 Campos was already a cabinet member. In 1826 he was elected to the Senate from Bahia and ennobled by Emperor Pedro I. Subsequently, he served twice more in the cabinet during the First Empire (1822–1831).

José Campos and his brother Francisco, also a senator and cabinet officer, were as politically prominent as the Andrada Brothers of São Paulo and the Cavalcanti brothers from Pernambuco. In April 1831, when Pedro I abdicated and retreated to Portugal, Campos was one of the three provisional regents elected to govern Brazil in the name of the child emperor, Pedro II. In June 1831 Campos was elected one of the three permanent regents who ruled in Pedro's name until 1835.

See also **Brazil: The Empire (First); Brazil: The Regency.**

BIBLIOGRAPHY

Sacramento Augusto Victorino Alves Blake, *Diccionario bibliographico brasileiro*, 7 vols. (1897).

Eul-Soo Pang, *In Pursuit of Honor and Power: Noblemen of the Southern Cross in Nineteenth-Century Brazil* (1988).

EUL-SOO PANG

CARNEY, JAMES "GUADALUPE"

(1924–1983). James "Guadalupe" Carney (*b*. 28 October 1924; *d*. probably 16 September 1983), U.S. Catholic missionary in Honduras, revolutionary priest. Carney, a native of Chicago, entered the Jesuit seminary in 1948 and was ordained a priest in 1961. He was sent to Honduras, where he served as chaplain for the National Association of Honduran Peasants (ANACH), championed land reform, and helped establish Christian base communities in the department of Yoro. Expelled from the country in 1979, he was assigned to rural Nicaragua, where he was impressed by Sandinista social programs. After writing his autobiography and declaring himself a Christian Marxist, he resigned from the Jesuits and then crossed into Honduras in July 1983 with ninety-six Honduran guerrillas. Although U.S. and Honduran authorities claim he died in the jungle from starvation, subsequent investigations have led some scholars to conclude that he had been captured, tortured, and executed by the Honduran military. His body was never found.

See also **Christian Base Communities.**

BIBLIOGRAPHY

J. Guadalupe Carney, *To Be a Revolutionary* (1985).

Donna Whitson Brett and Edward T. Brett, *Murdered in Central America: The Stories of Eleven U.S. Missionaries* (1988), pp. 38–66.

Additional Bibliography

Carías, Marcos. *Vernon y James: Vidas paralelas.* Tegucigalpa: Acción Cultural Popular Hondureña: Centro de Estudios Históricos de Honduras, 1992.

EDWARD T. BRETT

CARNIVAL. Carnival ("farewell to flesh") is a pre-Lenten festival celebrated throughout much of Europe and Latin America. Origins of the festival are diverse, dating back to ancient Greek Bacchanal and Roman Saturnalia feasts, as well as other pre-Christian rites that coalesced in the cities of Europe during the medieval era. Taking place in the days just prior to Ash Wednesday, Carnival became a time of revelry and excess, marked by masquerades, processions, dances, and various public games and competitions.

In the eighteenth century, Spanish, Portuguese, and French versions of Carnival were exported to the Americas, where they absorbed local festival practices and soon created distinct regional and national traditions. Due to its placement in the calendar year, marking the seasonal change from winter to spring in the Northern Hemisphere and the height of the summer growing season in the South, many manifestations of Carnival, especially in rural areas, were tied to previously existing fertility rites and agricultural celebrations.

In the cities, a rigid distinction was maintained between the practices of social elites, whose masked balls were exclusive affairs, and the far more raucous world of the street, where the poor parodied the habits of the upper class in songs, dances, and skits in a quintessential "rite of reversal," and flagrantly broke other social taboos on cross dressing, public intoxication, and fighting. Street processions with music and dancing were and remain common, usually featuring competitions between rival Carnival *comparsas*, or troupes.

Race played an important and contentious role in the formation of Carnival in Latin America, with indigenous persons and African slaves (and free coloreds) often masquerading as whites or members of other ethnic groups. A number of extant Carnival practices of the early twenty-first century in Latin America, such as the French quadrilles danced by indigenous residents in Tlaxcala, Mexico, and the *caporales* ("slave drivers") dance of Oruro, Bolivia, can trace their roots to these activities.

In the twentieth century, the popularity of street processions largely eclipsed the practice of elite balls, and the former were promoted by civic authorities in various locales as expressions of local or national identity. Previously subversive practices were institutionalized as folkloric spectacles and promoted as tourist attractions to a growing international audience, particularly in Trinidad and Brazil. Social and political commentary remained a mainstay of many Carnival traditions, however, and old rituals of competition have been retained in the formal contests that are the centerpieces of present-day official celebrations.

SOUTH AMERICA

Though Carnival in Brazil is by far the most famous internationally, the festival is found with varying levels of participation throughout South America. One of the largest celebrations outside of Brazil takes place in Oruro, Bolivia, where *diablada* "devil dancers" and other masked and costumed groups depict figures drawn from local syncretic religious beliefs and other aspects of regional history. In more rural parts of the Andes, fertility rites honoring pre-Hispanic deities and ritual battles, known as *tinkuy*, exist alongside the processions and other practices introduced during the colonial era. In most other parts of South America, Spanish and African influences predominate, such as in the urban *murgas* (music and dance groups) of Uruguay and Argentina, or the Caribbean-style festivals held in the northern coastal cities of Colombia and Venezuela.

Carnival is Brazil's largest and most important popular festival, and is considered one of the major components of the country's national identity. The festival's origins lay in the urban atmosphere of the former capital, Rio de Janeiro, where two prototypical Carnival celebrations took place, one in the streets and the other in the salons. These old celebrations of Portuguese origin known as the *entrudo* were banned in 1853 when a visiting French architect, Grandjean de Montigny, died of pneumonia after being doused with water during Carnival. After the incident, the police and the state felt obligated to intervene and discipline perpetrators of public meetings that might "disturb the public peace."

With the abolition of slavery in 1888, settlements of former slaves formed in the hills around Rio. These Afro-Brazilians re-created their own cultural practices and went through an internal reorganization, one result of which was the resurrection of some of the Carnival celebrations banned since 1853. The bourgeois celebration of the festival, in contrast, attracted members of Rio's elite to carnivalesque encounters, first in hotels and later in exclusive clubs.

For many years the two forms of Carnival remained separate. They grew closer in the twentieth century, however, and reached a climax during the first administration of Getúlio Dornelles Vargas (1930–1945). In the 1930s Carnival in Rio became a street festival that attracted the well-to-do, and the example of the capital spread throughout Brazil. The festival was restructured around the samba

schools, and from the beginning received significant attention from the press.

When Brazil's period of modernization began in the 1960s, and especially during the military dictatorship (1964–1985), the government adopted Carnival as a tool for political propaganda. Foreign capital was being courted, and the televised parades in Rio usefully depicted a happy, organized, and orderly Brazilian people, especially after 1984, when the event was moved off of the street to the Sambódromo, a 100,000-seat, open-ended stadium built for the purpose. The popularity of the Rio Carnival led to a resurgence of other regional traditions with distinct musical styles, including in Salvador in Bahia, Olinda and Recife in Pernambuco, Ouro Prêto in Minas Gerais, and Florianópolis in Santa Catarina. All remain vibrant in the early twenty-first century.

CARIBBEAN
Carnival is ubiquitous in the Caribbean region, with major festivals celebrated (sometimes on alternate

Costumed dancers in Pinar del Rio, Cuba's carnival parade, July 23, 2006. Although Brazil's Carnival is the best known, carnival celebrations take place throughout Latin America and the Caribbean. AP IMAGES

dates) in Haiti, Cuba, Martinique, Guadeloupe, Antigua, and especially Trinidad and Tobago. Most feature resplendent floats, large groups of costumed dancers, and constantly evolving forms of popular music. Afro-Caribbean peoples have made the festival their own in all of these places, and as a result their cultural and musical influences predominate. In Haiti, for example, the carnivalesque celebration of *rara* that follows on Carnival, lasting throughout the Lenten season, is closely tied to the religious beliefs and ritual practices of voodoo. *Rara* is also typical of the Caribbean in its tradition of biting social and political commentary, which has made the festival a frequent target for government repression or attempts at cooptation, but also a popular site of resistance to those very regimes.

Trinidad hosts the largest Carnival festival in the Caribbean. Though the island was colonized by Spain in the late fifteenth century, the event did not take root until after 1783 with the arrival of French and Creole plantation owners, who hosted fancy-dress balls and made house calls on one another while costumed as black slaves. The emancipation of slaves in 1838 led to the first public processions, in which Afro-Trinidadians adopted the festival as a symbolic rite of their own liberation, engaging in a form of stick fighting called *kalenda* and a midnight torchlight parade known as *canboulay* (from the French *cannes brulées*, or "burning cane").

By the twentieth century, Afro-Trinidadians were joined during Carnival by other immigrants to the island, including Chinese and East Indian indentured laborers, in large *mas* (from *masquerade*) parades through the streets of Port of Spain. Calypso song competitions, held in large tents, also emerged at this time, providing a more focused listening environment for the elaborate wordplay that came to mark the genre. Efforts by the middle and upper classes to "clean up" Carnival eventually directed all activities toward formal competitions, and these dominate the event in the early twenty-first century. In addition to the official *mas* competitions for best group, best costumes, and best song, the contests for best children's group ("Kiddie Mas") and best steel band or "pan" ensemble (the "Panorama" championship) are tremendously popular.

DIASPORIC CELEBRATIONS

In recent decades, Carnival has spread to North American and European cities with a significant Latin American (especially Caribbean) diasporic population, where often it is held on a more seasonably appropriate date. The West Indian American Day Carnival held on Labor Day each year in Brooklyn, New York, Toronto's Caribana festival in July, and London's Notting Hill Carnival in August all feature street parades, music concerts, and masquerades that have become expressions of cultural pride for immigrant populations, as well as major tourist attractions that draw millions of spectators.

See also **Music: Popular Music and Dance; Race and Ethnicity; Slavery: Brazil.**

BIBLIOGRAPHY

Cowley, John. *Carnival, Canboulay, and Calypso: Traditions in the Making.* Cambridge, U.K.: Cambridge University Press, 1996.

Da Matta, Roberto. *Carnivals, Rogues, and Heroes: An Interpretation of the Brazilian Dilemma.* Translated by John Drury. Notre Dame, IN: University of Notre Dame Press, 1992.

Dudley, Shannon. *Carnival Music in Trinidad.* New York: Oxford University Press, 2004.

Harris, Max. *Carnival and Other Christian Festivals, Folk Theology, and Folk Performance.* Austin: University of Texas Press, 2003.

Mauldin, Barbara, ed. *¡Carnaval!* Santa Fe, NM: Museum of International Folk Art, 2004.

Meihy, José Carlos Sebe Bom. *Carnaval, Carnavais.* São Paulo, Brazil: Editora Atica, 1986.

Nunley, John, and Judith Bettelheim, eds. *Caribbean Festival Arts: Each and Every Bit of Difference.* Seattle: University of Washington Press, 1988.

Vásquez Rodriguez, Chalena, and Abilio Vergara Figueroa. *Chayraq! Carnaval Ayacuchano.* Ayacucho, Peru: Centro de Desarollo Agropecuario, 1988.

JOSÉ CARLOS SEBE BOM MEIHY
JONATHAN RITTER

CARO, JOSÉ EUSEBIO (1817–1853). José

Eusebio Caro (*b.* 5 March 1817; *d.* 28 January 1853), Colombian Conservative publicist and romantic poet. Caro was born in Ocaña, Norte de Santander. His mother's amorous relationships with Simón Bolívar, Francisco de Paula Santander, and José Ignacio de Márquez shadowed his impoverished youth. He received his doctorate in law in 1837 and became a government clerk (1838). A political libertarian, Caro wrote articles for the press and started composing verse. Among his best-loved poems are "El bautismo" and "Estar contigo." The violence of the War of the Supremes (1839–1842), in which he served sporadically but with distinction, caused Caro to move to more conservative political ground. He rose in the bureaucracy to chief of a section in the Secretariat of Interior and Foreign Relations (1843), and expounded his increasingly authoritarian ideas in *El Granadino*, which appeared sporadically between 1840 and 1845. A partisan, he deplored the bipartisanship (after 1846) of Tomás Cipriano de Mosquera's administration, though he did serve briefly as finance minister (1848). Caro's vehement opposition to the Liberal José Hilario López (1849–1853) caused his removal from government service (September 1849). With Mariano Ospina Rodríguez, he fashioned the first Conservative Party platform (1849) and was an editor of the newspaper *La Civilización* (1849–1850), whose editorials were a devastating indictment of López's presidency that resulted in Caro's exile (1850–1853) to New York. Upon returning to Colombia, Caro died of yellow fever in Santa Marta.

See also **Journalism; Literature: Spanish America.**

BIBLIOGRAPHY

Fernando Galvis Salazar, *José Eusebio Caro* (1956).

José Luis Martín, *La poesía de José Eusebio Caro ... Contribución estilística al estudio del romanticismo hispanoamericano* (1966).

Robert Henry Davis, "Acosta, Caro, and Lleras: Three Essayists and Their Views of New Granada's National Problems, 1832–1853" (Ph.D. diss., Vanderbilt University, 1969), pp. 243–299.

Lucio Pabón Núñez, ed., *Poesías completas. José Eusebio Caro* (1973).

Simón Aljure Chalela, comp., *Artículos y escritos histórico-políticos de José Eusebio Caro* (1981).

Additional Bibliography

Orjuela, Héctor H., ed. *Poesía Escogida*. Colombia: Editora Guadalupe, 2005.

J. LEÓN HELGUERA

CARO, MIGUEL ANTONIO (1843–1909).

Miguel Antonio Caro (*b.* 10 November 1843; *d.* 5 August 1909), Colombian president (1894–1898). Miguel Antonio Caro lived his entire life in the area of Bogotá, where he was born, and was a staunch defender of traditional Catholic and Hispanic values. A professor of Latin at the Universidad Nacional and expert in Spanish grammar and linguistics, Caro achieved distinction as a scholar (collaborating with Rufino José Cuervo) but is chiefly remembered as one of the architects of the regeneration that put an end to Liberal hegemony in Colombia. He was the principal author of the centralist, proclerical Constitution of 1886. As a "Nationalist" Conservative he became vice president under Rafael Núñez in 1892 but in reality was acting president, completing the term (1894–1898) after Núñez's death. His doctrinaire rigidity alienated both Liberals and the "Historical" faction of Conservatives, thus contributing to the outbreak of the War of the Thousand Days that began shortly after he left the presidency.

See also **Colombia, Constitutions: Overview; War of the Thousand Days.**

BIBLIOGRAPHY

Guillermo Torres García, *Miguel Antonio Caro, su personalidad política* (1956).

Jaime Jaramillo Uribe, *El pensamiento colombiano en el siglo XIX* (1964), chap. 19.

Charles W. Bergquist, *Coffee and Conflict in Colombia, 1886–1910* (1978), pp. 42–47 and passim.

Additional Bibliography

Sierra Mejía, Rubén. *Miguel Antonio Caro y la cultura de su época*. Bogotá: Universidad Nacional de Colombia, Sede Bogotá, 2002.

Valderrama Andrade, Carlos. *Miguel Antonio Caro y la regeneración: Apuntes y documentos para la comprensión de una época*. Santafé de Bogotá: Instituto Caro y Cuervo, 1997.

DAVID BUSHNELL

CARONDELET, FRANÇOIS-LOUIS HECTOR (1747–1807).

François-Louis Hector Carondelet, Baron de (*b.* 27 July 1747; *d.* 10 December 1807), governor of San Salvador and Louisiana; president of the Audiencia of Quito. A prototype of the bureaucratic *ilustrados* who staffed the late eighteenth-century Spanish colonies, Carondelet trod an ambiguous path between progress and reaction. Born at Cambray or Flanders, in what is the present-day French department of Nord, he entered the military service of Charles III of Spain at fifteen and saw brief action at the conclusion of the Seven Years' War. After serving at Algiers in 1775 and writing a book on infantry training and strategy, he was assigned to the Caribbean, where he fought with Bernardo de Gálvez against the British at Pensacola (1781).

In 1789 Carondelet became governor–intendant of San Salvador, an indigo-producing region on the Pacific coast of the Audiencia of Guatemala. He strove to rationalize dye production and marketing, and to establish settlements for those displaced by expanding commercial agriculture. Two years later, he was promoted to the governorship of Louisiana and West Florida.

The succeeding five years severely tested Carondelet's determination to keep the lower Mississippi watershed under permanent Spanish sovereignty. With paltry resources, he bluffed and badgered the local French Jacobins, the region's mercurial Indian groups, land-hungry American frontiersmen, free colored, a slave population equaling that of the free (including Europeans), and intriguers of many stripes. He deftly out-maneuvered a range of antimonarchical forces and challenged American use of the Mississippi and the right of deposit at New Orleans.

Carondelet was reassigned to the presidency of the remote Audiencia of Quito (where he was also governor-general) late in 1798. There he found a declining textile trade, widespread native unrest, and bickering among the clerical orders. Although at a loss to cope with internal issues of an unfamiliar society, Carondelet managed to complete a road to the north coast and to facilitate the expedition of Alexander von Humboldt. He died in Quito.

See also **Louisiana; San Salvador.**

BIBLIOGRAPHY

Arthur Preston Whitaker, *The Spanish-American Frontier, 1763–1795* (1927).

Thomas M. Fiehrer, "The Baron de Carondelet as Agent of Bourbon Reform" (Ph.D. diss., Tulane University, 1977).

Carlos Manuel Larrea, *El barón de Carondelet* (1978).

Eric Beerman, "Baron de Carondelet," in *The Louisiana Genealogical Register* 29, no. 1 (March 1982): 5–19.

THOMAS FIEHRER

CARPENTIER, ALEJO (1904–1980).

Alejo Carpentier (*b.* 26 December 1904; *d.* 24 April 1980), Cuban novelist and short-story writer. Carpentier was born in Havana and studied music with his mother, through whom he developed a love of music that became central to his life and work. In 1921 he studied architecture at the University of Havana and that same year began writing for local newspapers and magazines. Together with the noted Cuban composer Amadeo Roldán he organized concerts of new music, bringing to Cuba the works of Stravinsky, Poulenc, Satie, and Malipiero. He also wrote the librettos for two ballets with music by Roldán.

In 1928, with the help of Cuban poet and then-diplomatic official Mariano Brull, Carpentier moved to Paris, where he met André Breton, Paul Éluard, Ives Tanguy, Arthur Honegger, and Pablo Picasso, among others. With the 1933 publication of his first novel, *¡Ecue-Yamba-O!*, in Madrid, he traveled to Spain, where he met the celebrated Spanish poets Federico García Lorca, Rafael Alberti, Pedro Salinas, and José Bergamín. In 1937, along with fellow Cuban writers Juan Marinello, Nicolás Guillén, and Félix Pita Rodríguez, he represented Cuba at the Second Congress for the Defense of Culture, held in Madrid and Valencia.

In 1939 Carpentier returned to Cuba to work for the Ministry of Education and to teach the history of music at the National Conservatory, where he later conducted research that led to the rediscovery of neglected Cuban composers Esteban Salas and Manuel Saumell. In 1945 he moved to Venezuela to work in radio and advertising. While there, he traveled extensively in 1947–1948 through the Amazon region, an area vividly evoked in his novel *Los pasos perdidos* (1953; *The Lost Steps*, 1956). After the Cuban Revolution in 1959 Carpentier returned to Cuba, where he was appointed vice-president of the National Council on Culture. He was also a vice-president of the powerful Cuban Union of Writers and Artists (UNEAC) and from 1963 to 1968 the director of the Cuban National Publishing House. He traveled widely as a representative of the Cuban government on both cultural and political missions. In 1968 he was named Ministerial Counsel for Cultural Affairs at the Cuban embassy in Paris, a post he occupied until his death in 1980.

Carpentier's novels and short stories have been greatly acclaimed both in Cuba and abroad. He received many national honors as well as the international prizes Cino del Duca and Alfonso Reyes (1975). His work frequently evokes a particular historical period and is characterized by an ornate, meticulous, and rhythmical prose in which his love of music and architecture is evident. Among his other well-known works are *El reino de este mundo* (1949; *The Kingdom of This World*, 1957); *El siglo de las luces* (1962; *Explosion in a Cathedral*, 1963); and *El recurso del método* (1974; *Reasons of State*, 1976).

See also **Literature: Spanish America.**

BIBLIOGRAPHY

Roberto González Echevarría, *Alejo Carpentier: The Pilgrim at Home* (1977) and *Alejo Carpentier: Bibliographical Guide* (1983).

Araceli García-Carranza, *Bibliografía de Alejo Carpentier* (1984).

Klaus Müller-Bergh, "Alejo Carpentier," in *Latin American Writers,* edited by Carlos A. Solé and Maria Isabel Abreu (1989), pp. 1019–1031.

Simon Gikandi, *Writing in Limbo: Modernism and Caribbean Literature* (1992).

Barbara J. Webb, *Myth and History in Caribbean Fiction* (1992).

Additional Bibliography

González Echevarría, Roberto. *Alejo Carpentier, el peregrino en su patria.* Madrid: Biblioteca románica hispánica, 2004.

Padura, Leonardo. *Un camino de medio siglo: Alejo Carpentier y la narrativa de lo real maravilloso.* México, D.F.: Fondo de Cultura Económica, 2002.

ROBERTO VALERO

CARPINTERÍA, BATTLE OF.

On September 19, 1836, near the Carpintería Arroyo in the center of the Eastern State of Uruguay, the government's army, commanded by Ignacio Oribe (1795–1866) triumphed over the troops of former president of Uruguay José Fructuoso Rivera (1789?–1854). The opposition troops had risen up in July with the support of Argentine emigrés from the unitary (*unitario*) camp led by Juan Lavalle (1797–1841), who were opposed to the federal troops (*federales*) led by Juan Manuel de Rosas (1793–1877), the governor of Buenos Aires. Following their defeat, they were forced to seek asylum in Brazil.

The two sides were distinguished by colored sashes (*divisas*) that lent their names to two Uruguayan political parties that still exist in the early twenty-first century. The government loyalists wore white sashes with the words "Defender of the Law," whereas the troops that Rivera commanded bore red (*colorado*) sashes.

The territorial borders along the River Plate had not been fully established, and power struggles led to the formation of alliances among factions loyal to different states. Rivera took up arms again, and in 1838 the colorados and the unitarios, supported by France, forced the president of the Republic, Manuel Oribe (1792–1857), to resign and head for Buenos Aires.

See also **Uruguay, Political Parties: Blanco Party; Uruguay, Political Parties: Colorado Party.**

BIBLIOGRAPHY

Acevedo, Eduardo. *Anales Históricos del Uruguay.* Vol. I. Montevideo, Uruguay: Barreiro y Ramos, 1933.

Pivel Devoto, Juan E. *Historia de los partidos y de las ideas políticas en el Uruguay,* Vol. II: *La definición de los bandos, 1829–1838.* Montevideo, Uruguay: Medina, 1956.

ANA FREGA

CARRANZA, VENUSTIANO (1859–1920).

Venustiano Carranza (*b.* 29 December 1859; *d.* 21 May 1920), first chief of the Constitutionalist forces during the Mexican Revolution (1913–1917), president of Mexico (1917–1920). Carranza was born at Cuatro Ciénegas in the northeastern frontier state of Coahuila, son of a well-to-do landed proprietor who had supported Benito Juárez. After a conventional liberal education in Saltillo and Mexico City, Carranza returned to Coahuila, where, during the Porfiriato (1876–1911), he farmed and engaged in politics. After election as mayor of his hometown in 1887, Carranza was ousted by the autocratic state governor, José María Garza Galán, against whom he successfully rebelled (1893). Porfirio Díaz acquiesced in the installation of a state government congenial to the Carranza family and sympathetic to the great caudillo of the northeast, Bernardo Reyes of Nuevo León. Carranza, a loyal Reyista, served as mayor, state deputy, and federal senator, combining cautious political advancement with the acquisition of land and other property.

During the 1900s, political opposition to Díaz mounted and Reyes became a major contender for power. As the Reyista movement boomed (1908–1909), Carranza ran for the governorship of Coahuila. However, Díaz, resentful of overly powerful subjects, froze Reyes out of national politics and ensured Carranza's defeat. In retaliation, Carranza then forged an alliance of expedience with fellow Coahuilan Francisco Madero, who dared challenge Díaz for the presidency. Although he was linked to the Madero family by old political ties and shared Madero's liberal philosophy, Carranza lacked Madero's naïve optimism; he was, rather, a crafty and hardened practitioner of realpolitik. Thus, while Carranza supported the successful Madero revolution (1910–1911), he did so with typical caution, exercising his role as revolutionary commander of the northeast from the sanctuary of Texas. He also criticized Madero for being too generous to the defeated Porfiristas when he signed the Treaty of Ciudad Juárez (May 1911).

During Madero's presidency (November 1911–February 1913) Carranza served as governor of Coahuila, adhering to a moderate liberal program that stressed municipal democracy, educational and fiscal reform, and temperance. He also built an independent state military, which defended Coahuila against rebel incursions, afforded the state government a certain political autonomy, and gave rise to serious wrangles between himself and Madero. Indeed, there were rumors that Carranza and some like-minded northern governors—"hawks" who rejected Madero's dovish conciliation of conservative opponents—flirted with outright rebellion.

MEXICAN REVOLUTION
In February 1913, when military rebels ousted and killed Madero, installing General Victoriano Huerta in power, Carranza refused to recognize the coup. While his admirers depict this as an act of immediate outrage, the truth was more complex. For two weeks after the coup the telegraph wires

between Coahuila and the capital hummed. Carranza negotiated with Huerta, whose characteristic bullheadedness prevented a deal from being made. Instead, Carranza marshaled his forces and declared himself in revolt. His military fortunes soon faltered. A rebel attack on Saltillo was a costly failure; during the summer of 1913 he was forced to flee to the northwestern state of Sonora, where a similar rebellion had begun with greater success.

However, Carranza's stand was politically decisive. As the senior Maderista rebel, he became the figurehead—and to some extent the actual leader—of a broad anti-Huerta movement. On 26 March 1913, Carranza and his entourage drew up and promulgated the Plan of Guadalupe, in which they repudiated Huerta and promised the return of constitutional rule. (Hence Carranza became "First Chief of the Constitutionalist Army.") However—at Carranza's insistence and to the disgust of some young radicals—the Plan made no reference to broader socioeconomic reforms.

During 1913–1914, as the revolt against Huerta spread, Carranza established an alternative government in the north. He decreed, taxed, issued currency, dealt with foreign powers, and tried to control the heterogeneous Constitutionalist forces. He succeeded, to the extent that Huerta was forced from power; and he succeeded, too, in securing U.S. backing without ceding an iota of Mexican sovereignty. (Indeed, his prickly nationalism made him, in American eyes, a difficult ingrate.) But his relations with Emiliano Zapata, in the distant south, were tenuous and mutually suspicious. Francisco "Pancho" Villa, the charismatic caudillo of Chihuahua, who was victorious in the campaigns against Huerta in 1914, chafed under Carranza's persnickety authority. He resented Carranza's interference in Chihuahua and applauded the U.S. occupation of Veracruz—which tightened the noose around Huerta's neck—even as Carranza outspokenly condemned it. Differences were patched up until the fall of Huerta in July 1914.

Thereafter, the Constitutionalist revolution fragmented. The Zapatistas of Morelos had little time for Carranza, an elderly Porfirian politico whose commitment to agrarian reform was suspect. Villa, too, regarded Carranza with suspicion and personal dislike; when Villa and Zapata met in December 1914, they broke the ice by trading insults about Carranza.

More important, the grand revolutionary convention that met at Aguascalientes in October 1914 proved incapable of reconciling the major caudillos of the Revolution—Carranza spurned it, and Villa effectively hijacked it. Mexico's many lesser caudillos were forced to choose, and the forces that had been briefly united against Huerta now split apart and embarked on a bloody internecine conflict.

The civil war resolved itself into a struggle between Villa, loosely allied to Zapata, and Carranza, whose chief ally was the Sonoran general Álvaro Obregón. For some historians, this last great bout of revolutionary warfare was a clear-cut conflict between a popular and peasant coalition led by Villa and Zapata and the "bourgeois" forces of Carranza. However, this interpretation overlooks the sameness of the two sides' social makeup (nationwide, the Carrancistas included many peasants, just as the Villistas included landlords and bourgeoisie) and political programs (the rival programs differed little).

But the struggle was not irrelevant to Mexico's future. For while a victory of Villa and Zapata would probably have resulted in a weak, fragmented state, a collage of revolutionary fiefs of varied political hues presided over by a feeble central government, a victory by Carranza and his Sonoran allies would—and did—lay the foundations of a more ambitious, centralizing state dedicated to national integration and nationalist self-assertion. In this respect, Carranza, a product of Porfirian politics, helped lend a "neo-Porfirian" coloration to the revolutionary regime after 1915; he served, as Enrique Krauze observes, as the bridge between two centuries.

Carranza's triumph over Villa and Zapata, like his previous successes, owed more to political shrewdness than to military prowess. During 1914–1915 he overcame his ingrained political caution and promised agrarian and social reforms, legitimizing the efforts of his more radical supporters and undercutting the popular appeal of his enemies. He allowed Obregón to form an alliance with the workers of Mexico City and dispatched proconsuls to the states of southern Mexico, compelling those states to enter the revolutionary fold and—in Yucatán—skimming off valuable export revenues.

All this would have been in vain had not Obregón triumphed on the battlefield, repeatedly defeating Villa in a series of battles between April and June 1915, forcing him to relinquish claims to national power. Carranza was therefore recognized as de facto president by the United States in October 1915, establishing his administration in Mexico City, and, following elections, inaugurated as constitutional president in May 1917.

THE PRESIDENCY

Carranza's three years as president were difficult. Rebellion still simmered. Large areas of the country remained ungovernable. The economy was in disarray, the currency had collapsed, and 1917 became known, in popular memory, as the "year of hunger." Over two-thirds of government expenditures went to the military, on whose bayonets Carranza depended. Politics remained the preserve of the Carrancista faction (their enemies were proscribed) and elections, though boisterous, were rigged and unrepresentative. A constituent congress, summoned by Carranza, produced a new constitution (1917) embracing radical measures: labor and agrarian reform, anticlericalism, and economic nationalism. (Carranza probably wanted a more moderate document, but was content to go with the tide.) Implementation came slowly. Land reform remained minimal, while Carranza ordered the wholesale restitution of haciendas seized during the revolution. The brief alliance with the Mexico City workers ended and, in 1916, when he was de facto president, a general strike was ruthlessly crushed. When, in 1918, a new national labor confederation (the Confederación Regional Obrera Mexicana [CROM]; Mexican Regional Labor Confederation) was established, Obregón, rather than Carranza, was the chief political sponsor—and beneficiary.

As in the past, Carranza displayed more skill and consistency in the international arena. After Villa's defeat, the U.S. government grudgingly recognized the Carranza administration, without extracting any quid pro quo from the obstinate Mexican leader. When, in 1916–1917, U.S. troops entered Mexico in pursuit of Villa, Carranza demanded their unconditional withdrawal, ultimately successfully. He flirted with Germany, the better to keep the United States at bay; but he spurned the offer of an alliance, communicated in the notorious Zimmerman telegram. He also made a determined, if unsuccessful, attempt to enforce the provisions of the new constitution that claimed subsoil deposits (including petroleum) as the patrimony of the state. The booming oil companies were obliged to yield vital additional revenue to the penurious state, but they refused to acknowledge their new constitutional status. The impasse remained a source of serious contention into the 1920s.

Carranza thus stoutly defended the integrity of Mexico and the principles of the revolution in the face of foreign pressure. But domestically, Carranza soft-pedaled reform and displayed a poor grasp of the populist politics the Revolution had ushered in. After 1918 his authority waned. As the presidential election of 1920 neared, and Obregón launched a powerful campaign, Carranza attempted to impose a chosen successor, a little-known diplomat named Ignacio Bonillas. The military balked; the CROM backed Obregón; and the Sonoran leaders initiated a coup that swiftly drove Carranza from Mexico City into the Puebla sierra. There, in May 1920, he was killed at Tlaxcalantongo or, as Krauze hypothesizes, he committed suicide rather than give his enemies the satisfaction of killing him. This was to be the last successful rebellion of Mexico's revolutionary history. Obregón and the Sonorans, the architects of Carranza's rise and fall, shared his hardheaded opportunism, but they displayed a better grasp of the mechanisms of popular mobilization, allied to social reform, that would form the bases of a durable revolutionary regime after 1920. For this reason, Carranza has often been regarded as a conservative revolutionary who was overtaken by events and outflanked by younger, more "populist" revolutionaries. He did, however, forge a winning revolutionary coalition, defeating both Huerta and Villa and sponsoring the 1917 constitution. In addition, most critics concede, he was a strenuous and successful defender of Mexican sovereignty against the United States.

See also **Mexico, Constitutions: Constitution of 1917; Mexico, Wars and Revolutions: Mexican Revolution; Plan of Guadalupe.**

BIBLIOGRAPHY

Douglas W. Richmond, *Venustiano Carranza's Nationalist Struggle, 1893–1920* (1983), is the fullest recent biography; well researched, it is uncritically charitable toward its subject. Enrique Krauze, *Puente entre siglos: Venustiano Carranza* (1987), is brief, intelligent, and replete with illustrations. Of several older Mexican studies, Alfonso Junco, *Carranza y los orígenes de su rebelión* (1955), is a telling critique of Carranza's conduct toward Madero and Huerta. Detailed general histories of the revolution, which necessarily give much attention to Carranza and the Constitutionalists, are Charles C. Cumberland, *The Mexican Revolution: The Constitutionalist Years* (1972).

Alan Knight, *The Mexican Revolution* (1986), vol. 2, *Counterrevolution and Reconstruction;* and Ramón Eduardo Ruíz, *The Great Rebellion: Mexico 1905–1924* (1980), which sharply contrasts with Richmond's laudatory biography. Carranza's important international role has been analyzed in several good studies, including Mark T. Gilderhus, *Diplomacy and Revolution: U.S.-Mexican Relations Under Wilson and Carranza* (1977).

P. Edward Haley, *Revolution and Intervention: The Diplomacy of Taft and Wilson with Mexico 1910–17* (1970); and an outstanding piece of research, Friedrich Katz, *The Secret War in Mexico: Europe, the United States and the Mexican Revolution* (1981). Robert Freeman Smith, *The United States and Revolutionary Nationalism in Mexico, 1916–1932* (1972), offers a cogent analysis of economic nationalism during the Carranza years and after.

Additional Bibliography

Barron, Luis F. "Porfirian Politics in Revolutionary Mexico: Venustiano Carranza and the Mexican Revolution, 1859-1913." Ph.D. diss., University of Chicago, 2004.

Stout, Joseph Allen. *Border Conflict: Villistas, Carrancistas, and the Punitive Expedition, 1915-1920.* Fort Worth: Texas Christian University Press, 1999.

                                          ALAN KNIGHT

CARRANZA FERNÁNDEZ, EDUARDO (1913–1985).

Eduardo Carranza Fernández (*b.* 23 July 1913; *d.* 13 February 1985), Colombian poet, born in Apiay. Carranza started to achieve recognition in 1934 through the publication of his poetry and his collaboration on the journal *Revista de las Indias.* His first sonnets, written between 1937 and 1944 and collected in *Azul de ti* (1947), made him famous. Carranza was an important member of the Piedra y Cielo group, influenced by the poetry of Juan Ramón Jiménez and, to a lesser extent, Pablo Neruda. The works of Jiménez, Rafael Alberti, and Gerardo Diego were the models for Carranza's poetry, which is metaphorical, musical, and reminiscent of traditional Spanish styles. In the early 1940s his aesthetic confronted the modernist poet Guillermo Valencia, who was then the model of Colombian poets. While Valencia cultivates the perfection of the meter and shows preference for exotic landscapes, Carranza prefers intimate and vernacular landscapes. Carranza's work is also marked by a purity of language and faithfulness to love, Catholicism, and country, and is untouched by Colombia's political violence of the 1950s and 1960s. In the 1940s and 1950s, his poetry circulated widely in Spain and Chile, countries in which he traveled and resided because of his work in the Colombian diplomatic service. Other collections of his poetry are *Los pasos cantados* (1975), *Los días que ahora son sueños* (1973), and *Veinte poemas* (1980).

See also **Literature: Spanish America.**

BIBLIOGRAPHY

Gloria Serpa De De Francisco, *Gran reportaje a Eduardo Carranza* (1978).

Teresa Rozo De Moorhouse, *La evolución del hablante lírico en Eduardo Carranza* (1985).

Giovanni Quessep, *Eduardo Carranza* (1990).

Additional Bibliography

Carranza, Eduardo. *Antología poética*. Bogotá: Ediciones Brevedad, 2000.

JUAN CARLOS GALEANO

CARRASCO, BARBARA (1955–).

A key figure in the Chicano Arts Movement, Barbara Carrasco is a visual artist who works in a variety of mediums, including painting, lithography, silkscreen, and computer animation. Her pieces range from pen-and-ink sketches to large public murals. Carrasco was born in El Paso, Texas, but grew up in the Los Angeles area, for the most part in ethnically mixed housing projects. This experience fomented her social awareness and community involvement. From an early age she demonstrated an affinity for art, which her parents encouraged. Her father introduced her to the work of the Mexican muralists, and her mother was intensely interested in Japanese art. Carrasco earned a fine arts degree from UCLA in 1978 and a master of fine arts degree from California Institute of the Arts in 1991. Between 1976 and 1991 she worked closely with labor leaders César Chávez and Dolores Huerta of the United Farm Workers, creating various banners for UFW events. Carrasco is socially and politically engaged as an artist, and issues of gender and ethnicity have been a theme in much of her work. Her pieces have been

shown in exhibitions in the United States, Latin America, and Europe. Since 1993 she has been married to the Chicano artist, writer, and activist Harry Gamboa, Jr.

See also **Art: The Twentieth Century; Chaves, Julio César; Hispanics in the United States; United Farm Workers Union.**

BIBLIOGRAPHY

Artistas Chicanas: A Symposium on the Experience and Expression of Chicana Artists. Ten videotapes. Santa Barbara: University of California, 1991.

Carrasco, Barbara. Oral history interview by Jeffery J. Rangel, April 13–26, 1999. Archives of American Art, Smithsonian Institution. Available from http://www.aaa.si.edu/.

Venegas, Sybil. "Image & Identify: Recent Chicana Art from 'La Reina del Pueblo de Los Angeles de la Porcincula.'" *The Art of Greater Los Angeles in the 1990s* 2, no. 1 (1990). Laband Art Gallery series, Loyola Marymount University, Los Angeles.

CARYN C. CONNELLY

CARRASQUILLA, TOMÁS (1858–1940).

Tomás Carrasquilla (*b.* 1858; *d.* 1940), Colombian fiction writer. One of Colombia's greatest classic prose writers, Carrasquilla is best known for two novels, *Frutos de mi tierra* (1896) and *La Marquesa de Yolombó* (1926); between the publication of these two novels and afterward, he published several other novels, short novels, and numerous short stories with folkloric, psychological, fantastic, and symbolic perspectives. Carrasquilla believed that themes of rural, provincial life in Colombia were enough to make for good fiction; as such, his writings fall within the category of *costumbrista* (local color), which consists of providing vivid descriptions of popular customs and recreating the language of the popular classes. Nevertheless, Carrasquilla's fiction transcends the moralizing tone and didactic goal of *costumbrista*.

In one sense, his narrative success lies in his ability to draw upon such literary traditions of Spanish literature as the picaresque novel and stories portraying Spanish customs. While *Frutos de mi tierra* is a Cinderella story, it relies on local color, proverbs, legends, and the oral tradition to provide anecdotes that focus on hypocrisy in small, provincial towns. Carrasquilla does not just extol the good life in the provinces but also exposes moral issues centered on bigotry and cruelty. *La Marquesa de Yolombó* is Carrasquilla's most ambitious effort. The action takes place during the Spanish American colonial period of the late nineteenth century and criticizes the colonial government for inefficiency, corruption, and waste.

See also **Literature: Spanish America.**

BIBLIOGRAPHY

Kurt Levy, *Tomás Carrasquilla* (1980).

Additional Bibliography

Rodríguez-Arenas, Flor María. *Tomás Carrasquilla: Nuevas aproximaciones críticas*. Medellín: Editorial Universidad de Antioquia, 2000.

                                        DICK GERDES

CARREÑO, MARIO (1913–1999). Mario

Carreño (*b.* 24 June 1913; *d.* 20 December 1999), Cuban-born painter. Born in Havana, Carreño trained at the Academy of San Alejandro in Havana, the Academy of San Fernando in Madrid, and the École des Arts Appliqués in Paris. During the 1920s he worked as a political cartoonist for *Revista de Havana* and *Diario de la Marina*, both in Cuba. In the 1930s Carreño lived in Spain, where he designed revolutionary posters (1932–1935). After meeting the Mexican muralists in 1936, he returned to Paris, where he met the surrealist Oscar Domínguez and Pablo Picasso (1937). His paintings from the late 1930s combined traditional European painting techniques with the influence of the school of Paris and classical Picasso.

At the outbreak of World War II Carreño fled first to Italy, then to New York City, returning to Cuba in 1941. Influenced by David Alfaro Siqueiros, he experimented with industrial paint, a medium he had tried in the late 1930s (*Cane Cutters,* 1943). In 1946 he was appointed professor of painting at the New York School for Social Research and in the late 1940s turned to a late cubist vocabulary with distinctively Afro-Cuban themes (*Caribbean Enchantment,* 1949). He moved to Chile in 1957 at the urging of his friend, poet Pablo Neruda. For a brief period he worked on an abstract geometric style. In the late 1950s Carreño began to paint surrealist petrified and fragmented human figures in volcanic landscapes.

In the 1960s he collaborated with Chilean architects in the design of three-dimensional murals. The most distinguished examples are a freestanding, double-faced wall designed with glazed bricks for the Central Plaza of the University of Concepción (1962); an exterior wall for the Saint Ignatius Loyola School in Santiago (1960); and a freestanding wall and pool monument designed for the United Nations Regional Building, also in Santiago (1963–1964). Carreñ work ranks among the most sought-after from Latin America in the international art market. In 1982 he won the National Prize for Art in Chile and was recognized for his great contributions in the country. He died in Chile in 1999, leaving behind his wife from a second marriage and two daughters.

See also **Art: The Twentieth Century.**

BIBLIOGRAPHY

José Gómez Sicre, *Carreño* (1947).

Marta Traba et al., eds., *Museum of Modern Art of Latin America: Selections from the Permanent Collection* (1985), pp. 172–173.

Eva Cockroft, "The United States and Socially Concerned Latin American Art: 1920–1970," in Luis Cancel et al., *The Latin American Spirit: Art and Artists in the United States, 1920–1970* (1989), pp. 195–199.

Additional Bibliography

Ernesto, Saul. *Artes Visuales 20 años 1970-1990*. Santiago: Ministerio de Educación, 1991.

Pérez, Alberto. *La soledad en dos pintores chilenos*. Santiago: Editorial Fértil Provincia, 1992.

                                        MARTA GARSD

CARRERA, JOSÉ MIGUEL (1785–

1821). José Miguel Carrera (*b.* 15 October 1785; *d.* 4 September 1821), Chilean patriot and revolutionary. Carrera came from an old and distinguished family. A troublesome youth, he was sent in 1806 by his father to Spain, where he fought in at least thirteen actions in the Peninsular War. In July 1811 he returned to Chile and immediately immersed himself in the struggle for independence, using his sway over the military to seize power (15 November 1811). Handsome and personable, Carrera was a popular leader. During his dictatorship Chile's first newspaper, *La Aurora de Chile,* was published and the first national flag created. However, no declaration of independence was forthcoming.

With the arrival of a royalist expedition from Peru early in 1813, Carrera took command of the patriot forces in the south, leaving the government in the hands of a junta, over which his adversaries later assumed control. Given his limited military success, the junta transferred command to Bernardo O'Higgins (1778–1842), thereby opening up a serious rift between the two men. Soon afterward Carrera was captured by the royalists, but he escaped and returned to Santiago, where he staged a second coup d'état 23 July 1814. Civil war between the followers of O'Higgins and Carrera was averted only by the arrival of a new and powerful royalist expedition under the command of General Mariano Osorio (1777–1819). Carrera's failure to send relief to O'Higgins's valiant defense against Osorio at Rancagua (1–2 October 1814), resulted in a complete royalist triumph and the collapse of patriot Chile.

Carrera and two thousand others fled across the Andes to Mendoza, where the governor of Cuyo, José de San Martín, preferring the more reliable support of O'Higgins, ordered Carrera on to Buenos Aires. In November 1815 Carrera traveled to the United States, procured two warships, and then returned to Buenos Aires. Denied a part in the liberation of Chile now underway, he moved to Montevideo and launched a propaganda war against the new O'Higgins government.

Temperamentally incapable of remaining inactive for long, he next involved himself in the fighting then raging in the Argentine interior, lending support to various provincial caudillos. He was finally captured and executed at Mendoza, where his brothers Juan José (1782–1818) and Luis (1792–1818) had been shot three years earlier. These executions roused resentment against the O'Higgins regime in Chile. The remains of the three Carreras were repatriated in 1828. Following in his father's footsteps, Carrera's son, José Miguel Carrera Fontecilla (1820–1860), fought in the Chilean rebellions of 1851 and 1859.

See also **O'Higgins, Bernardo.**

BIBLIOGRAPHY

Julio Alemparte Robles, *Carrera y Freire, fundadores de la República* (1963).

Simon Collier, *Ideas and Politics of Chilean Independence* (1967), chap. 3.

Additional Bibliography

Barros Franco, José Miguel. "El archivo del General José Miguel Carrera y don Armando Moreno Martín." *Revista Chilena de Historia y Geografía.* 165 (1999–2000): 353–357.

Gutiérrez, Manuel Reyno. *Carrera: Su vida, sus sicisitudes, su época.* Santiago: Edit. Andujar, 2003.

SIMON COLLIER

CARRERA, JOSÉ RAFAEL (1814–1865). José Rafael Carrera (*b.* 24 October 1814; *d.* 14 April 1865), chief of state of Guatemala (1844–1848, 1851–1865). Born to poor parents in Guatemala City, Carrera joined the Central American federal army as a drummer at age twelve, and rose rapidly in the ranks during the civil war of 1826–1829. The army, dominated by the Guatemalan conservative elite, not only provided military training but also indoctrinated him in conservative ideology. After Francisco Morazán defeated this army in 1829, Carrera drifted for several years, eventually settling in Mataquescuintla, where he became a swineherd. Father Francisco Aqueche influenced him there and was instrumental in Carrera's marriage to Petrona García, the daughter of a local landowner.

Carrera emerged as a natural leader of the peasants and landowners of eastern Guatemala against the liberal reforms of the Guatemalan governor, Dr. Mariano Gálvez. The rural population, spurred on by the clergy, opposed his anticlericalism, taxes, judicial reforms, and land, labor, and immigration policies that appeared to favor foreigners over natives. With these grievances already strong, the Gálvez government's efforts to check the cholera epidemic that broke out in 1837 led to uprisings, especially in eastern Guatemala. Although Carrera did not instigate the 1837 revolt, and in fact had accepted assignment as commander of a government quarantine patrol, local residents soon persuaded him to join the revolt. At Santa Rosa, on 9 June 1837, he led a ragged band of insurgents to a stunning victory, sending government troops fleeing back to the capital.

Aided by serious divisions between Gálvez and José Francisco Barrundia, Carrera's peasant army took Guatemala City on 1 February 1838, bringing down the Gálvez government. This resulted temporarily in a more liberal government under Lieutenant Governor Pedro Valenzuela, who succeeded in persuading Carrera to leave the capital in return for promised reform and military command of the district of Mita. Resurgent strength of the conservative elite of the capital, however, and failure of the Valenzuela government to move fast enough with the reforms caused Carrera to resume the war in March 1838. President Morazán brought federal troops from El Salvador into the struggle, but on 13 April 1839 Carrera once more took the capital, this time installing a conservative government under Mariano Rivera Paz. In March 1840 Carrera decisively defeated Morazán at Guatemala City, effectively ending the Central American national government. From this point until his death, except briefly in 1848–1849, Carrera was the military master of Guatemala. He consolidated the power of his army during the early 1840s, especially by the Convenio of Guadalupe on 11 March 1844.

In December 1844 Carrera assumed the presidency of Guatemala. Although his policies were conservative, during this period he sometimes supported moderate liberal political leaders as a check against the pretensions of the conservative ecclesiastical and economic elite of the capital. On 21 March 1847 Carrera completed the process of Guatemalan secession from the defunct Central American union by establishing the Republic of Guatemala.

Liberal opposition, combined with continued rebel activity in eastern Guatemala, led to Carrera's resignation and exile in Mexico in August 1848. The new Liberal government, however, failed to achieve unity or solve the country's problems, and Carrera re-entered the country in March 1849 at the head of an "army of restoration" composed heavily of Indians. When Carrera took Quetzaltenango, several generals defected to him and an agreement was reached in June that made him a lieutenant general in the Guatemalan army, followed in August by his appointment once more as commanding general of the army. Thereafter he strengthened the army as he carried out campaigns against continuing rebellions within Guatemala and against the liberals' attempts to revive the Central American union in El Salvador,

Honduras, and Nicaragua. He dealt those forces a major blow with a stunning victory against the "national army" at San José la Arada on 2 February 1851. This victory assured the dominance of the conservatives in Guatemala for many years to come.

After 1850 Carrera allied himself closely with the conservative and ecclesiastical elite of Guatemala City. His government restored close relations with Spain and signed a concordat with the Vatican guaranteeing the clergy a major role in the regime. Although Carrera was often described as reactionary by his opponents, Guatemala enjoyed considerable economic growth during the next twenty years as coffee began to replace cochineal as its leading export. Carrera once more became president of Guatemala on 6 November 1851. He consolidated his strength and greatly increased his power when he became president for life, a virtual monarch, on 21 October 1854.

As the most powerful caudillo in mid-nineteenth-century Central America, Carrera affected the development of neighboring states as well, frequently intervening to assure conservative rule in El Salvador and Honduras. When the North American filibuster William Walker came to the aid of Nicaraguan liberals and subsequently became president of Nicaragua, Carrera provided substantial aid to the combined Central American force that routed Walker in 1857. Although he declined an invitation to command the Central American army, leaving that to Costa Rica's Juan Rafael Mora, Carrera sent more troops than any other state in the National Campaign.

In 1863 Carrera challenged the rise in El Salvador of Gerardo Barrios, who had begun to pursue liberal, anticlerical reforms. Although initially repulsed at Coatepeque in February, he returned to conquer San Salvador later in the year, removing Barrios from office.

When he died in 1865, probably from dysentery, Carrera had achieved considerable stability and economic growth for Guatemala, but had also established a stifling political dictatorship that had reserved many of the benefits of the regime for a small elite in Guatemala City. At the same time, Carrera deserves credit for protecting the rural Indian masses of the country from increased exploitation of their land and labor and for bringing Indians and mestizos into positions of political and military leadership. Perhaps the most lasting legacy of his long rule, however, was the establishment of the military as the dominant political institution in the country.

See also **Central America.**

BIBLIOGRAPHY

Luis Beltranena Sinibaldi, *Fudación de la República de Guatemala* (1971).

Keith L. Miceli, "Rafael Carrera: Defender and Promoter of Peasant Interest in Guatemala, 1837–1848," in *The Americas* 31, no. 1 (1974): 72–95.

Ralph Lee Woodward, Jr., *Rafael Carrera and the Emergence of the Republic of Guatemala, 1821–1871* (1993).

Additional Bibliography

Sullivan-González, Douglass. *Piety, Power and Politics: Religion and Nation Formation in Guatemala, 1821-1871.* Pittsburgh, PA: University of Pittsburgh Press, 1998.

RALPH LEE WOODWARD JR.

CARRERA ANDRADE, JORGE (1903–1978).

Jorge Carrera Andrade (*b.* 18 September 1903; *d.* 11 November 1978). Possibly Ecuador's greatest poet of the twentieth century, Carrera Andrade was also a diplomat and anthropologist who traveled extensively both inside and outside his native land. In constant evolution throughout Carrera Andrade's life, his literary works comprise more than two dozen books of poetry spanning fifty years, numerous prose works, translations, and several literary studies of Ecuadorian, French, and Japanese literature. In his poetry, the luscious, diverse land of Ecuador and its strong telluric magnetism symbolize, in the vein of the European romantics and French symbolists, the origins of cosmic man and woman. Carrera Andrade's verse is a vehicle that constantly takes him back to the center of his poetic world: Ecuador.

Early on, his poetry reads like a carefully crafted, melodious song dedicated to his native land and the American landscape, and it continues to impart a musical quality to the land through innovative visual imagery and metaphor. Through his poetry, Carrera Andrade rediscovers his identity in the beauty and order of nature, which gives rise to certain constants in his poetry: optimism, despite growing world problems throughout his long career; social concern for the less fortunate in the world; and a search for ways to deal with

solitude. *Hombre planetario* (1957–1963) is his best book of poetry, for in it he reconfirms his long-standing conviction concerning the need to understand our relationship with the land and with each other. Carrera Andrade also pioneered the adaptation of haiku to the Spanish language.

See also **Literature: Spanish America.**

BIBLIOGRAPHY

Enrique Ojeda Castillo, *Jorge Carrera Andrade: Introducción al estudio de su vida y de su obra* (1972).

Peter R. Beardsell, *Winds of Exile: The Poetry of Jorge Carrera Andrade* (1977).

Additional Bibliography

Gleason, Robert M. "The Reaffirmation of Analogy: An Introduction to Jorge Carrera Andrade's Metaphoric System." *Revista Iberoamericana* 68: 200 (July–September 2002): 567–582.

Lara, A. Darío. *Jorge Carrera Andrade: Memorias de un testigo.* Quito: Casa de la Cultura Ecuatoriana, 1998.

DICK GERDES

CARRERA DEL PARAGUAY.

For 400 years the only practical outlet of Paraguay to the rest of Spanish America, and then to the outside world, was by means of the Paraguay-Paraná River system. Colonial exports, mainly high-bulk, low-profit commodities as tobacco, timber, and yerba maté flowed south to Santa Fe for transshipment to the interior, or on to the estuary.

Paraguayan-built and -crewed river craft dominated the Carrera to the early 1800s, as did Paraguayan-produced products. In the Bay of Asunción flat-bottomed craft for the one-way trip south were constructed. Elsewhere along the Paraguay River or the multitude of tributaries, rafts and log-booms were gathered. Skilled pilots and helmsmen guided these boats through the treacherous mud shoals of the Paraná, bound for their destination at Sante Fe or Las Conchas, a delta settlement serving Buenos Aires. Salaried peons from the Paraguayan countryside supplied the necessary muscle for rowing and lightering. For the return trip, small sailing vessels loaded with passengers and finished goods made the four-month voyage north to Asunción from Las Conchas. By the viceregal era, a complex web of credit from Buenos Aires merchants held this commercial network together.

After a twenty-year hiatus during the tenure of José Gaspar de Francia, the Carrera again served Paraguay well during the era of Don Carlos Antonio López (1844–1862). However, after the destructive War of the Triple Alliance (1864–1870), Argentine entrepreneurs and their steamers captured control of commerce on the Carrera. It remained the primary external transport for Paraguay into the twentieth century.

See also **Paraguay River.**

BIBLIOGRAPHY

Jerry W. Cooney, *Economía y sociedad en la Intendencia del Paraguay* (1990).

Thomas Whigham, *The Politics of River Trade: Tradition and Development in the Upper Plata, 1780–1870* (1991).

Additional Bibliography

Irigoin, María Alejandra, Roberto Schmit, and Carlos Sempat Assadourian. *La desintegración de la economía colonial: Comercio y moneda en el interior del espacio colonial, 1800-1860.* Buenos Aires: Biblos, 2003.

JERRY W. COONEY

CARRILHO, ALTAMIRO (1924–).

Brazilian flutist Altamiro Carrilho, born in the state of Rio de Janeiro on December 21, 1924, is one of the most respected performers of choro, a Brazilian instrumental popular music genre. A precocious musician, he began his career at age twelve after winning an amateur talent competition. For many years he worked in a pharmacy during the day and played his instrument in the evenings. After forming his own ensemble, he had a television show in Rio de Janeiro in the 1950s. Altamiro's talent extended to popular and classical music, and beginning in the 1960s he was invited to give concerts throughout the world. In the 1980s he was an active participant in the revival of choro. Carrilho has composed approximately two hundred pieces for flute, has made an extensive number of recordings, and remained an active performer into the twenty-first century. He has been called a living legend.

See also **Choro, Chorinho.**

BIBLIOGRAPHY

Encyclopédia da música brasileira: Popular, erudite e folclórica. São Paulo: Art Editora, 1998.

Livingston-Isenhour, Tamara Elena, and Thomas George Caracas Garcia. *Choro: A Social History of a Brazilian Popular Music.* Bloomington: Indiana University Press, 2005.

THOMAS GEORGE CARACAS GARCIA

CARRILLO, JULIÁN [ANTONIO]

(1875–1965). Julián [Antonio] Carrillo (*b.* 28 January 1875; *d.* 9 September 1965), Mexican composer, theorist, conductor, violinist, and teacher. Born in Ahualulco, San Luis Potosí, Carrillo studied at the National Conservatory in Mexico City, where he took violin with Pedro Manzano, composition with Melesio Morales, and acoustics with Francisco Ortega y Fonseca. He went to Europe in 1899, remaining there until 1905 and studying at the Leipzig Conservatory with Salomon Jadassohn (composition), Carl Reinecke (theory), Jean Becker (violin), and Arthur Nikisch and Sitt (conducting). He also studied violin with Albert Zimmer at the Ghent Conservatory. In Leipzig he led the Gewandhaus Orchestra. During that epoch Carrillo started to develop his new musical theory about dividing a violin string in such a way as to create a ratio of 1:1–007246. Carrillo divided the octave into microtones (intervals smaller than the semitone), calling his system "Sonido 13"—the "thirteenth sound." He also developed a method of music notation for the microtonal system. Carrillo's Symphony no. 1 (1902) was premiered under his baton by the Leipzig Conservatory Orchestra. In it he used what he called "ideological unity and tonal variety." He continued to experiment and began using an excessively complex musical vocabulary, even though one third of his works are written without microtones.

Carrillo returned to Mexico and was appointed professor of composition at the National Conservatory (1906), inspector general of music for Mexico City (1908), and director of the National Conservatory (1913–1915, 1920–1924). Beginning in 1926 Carrillo's musical works and theoretical writings were very much praised abroad, by the New York League of Composers, the Philadelphia Orchestra, in Belgium, and in France. In 1961 the Lamoureux Orchestra of Paris recorded twenty of his microtonal and tonal works. A special piano for use with Carrillo's new system was built by the firm of Carl Sauter. Carrillo composed two operas as well as several symphonies, orchestral works, chamber music, and works for guitar, violin, and piano, and published numerous essays about his musical theory. He died in San Ángel.

See also **Music: Art Music.**

BIBLIOGRAPHY

Julian Carrillo, *Julian Carrillo: Su vida y su obra* (1945).

Gerald R. Benjamin, "Julian Carrillo and 'sonido 13,' " in *Yearbook, Inter-American Institute for Musical Research,* vol. 3 (1967), pp. 33–68.

Juan A. Orrego-Salas, ed., *Music from Latin America Available at Indiana University* (1971), p. 168; *New Grove Dictionary of Music and Musicians,* vol. 3 (1980).

Additional Bibliography

Carrillo, Julián. *Julián Carrillo: Testimonio de una vida.* San Luis Potosí: Comité Organizador "San Luis 400," 1992.

Contreras Soto, Eduardo. "Julián Carrillo y Ricardo Castro: Dos clásicos salvajes." *Nexos* 19: 226 (October 1996): 22–29.

SUSANA SALGADO

CARRILLO COLINA, BRAULIO (1800–1845).

Braulio Carrillo Colina (*b.* 20 March 1800; *d.* 15 May 1845), president and later dictator of Costa Rica (1835–1837; 1838–1842). Carrillo was an opponent of the Central American Federation as led by Francisco Morazán, in whose execution he was implicated. However, he followed essentially radical liberal policies in internal economic affairs. He was most strongly identified with the supremacy of coffee-growing interests and of the new national capital of San José. After studying law in León, Nicaragua, he returned to serve as deputy from his native city of Cartago (1827–1829), San José's principal rival as capital. He was chosen as a compromise chief of state in 1835 and then deposed his successor, Manuel Aguilar, to become virtual dictator in 1838. He was overthrown by Morazán's expeditionary force in 1842. Later, after engineering Morazán's capture and execution, he was forced into exile in El Salvador and assassinated near San Miguel.

During his first term Carrillo forcefully resolved the question of the site of the new capital by ending the system of "ambulatory," or rotating,

capitals in favor of San José. When challenged in revolt (Guerra de la Liga) in 1835, he defeated the anti–San José forces despite his forces being outnumbered nearly three to one. This was followed by an abortive invasion of exiles (led by Manuel Quijano) from Nicaragua to Guanacaste, in June 1836, with even less success.

During his dictatorship Carrillo abrogated the 1825 Constitution and replaced it with the Ley de Bases y Garantías in 1841, which named him ruler for life. Although that provision was short-lived, the larger document proved more significant, greatly influencing the Constitution of 1871 in further strengthening the central government and liquidating the power of local municipal authorities. He also convened a Constituent Assembly in 1838 which declared Costa Rica's independence from the collapsing Central American Federation. Severely tested by Morazán's occupation, this policy was reaffirmed in 1848.

Carrillo's policies were consistently in favor of coffee exports and the city of San José, despite his origins in the rival city of Cartago. He ordered municipalities to provide coffee seedlings to all who would plant them, as well as terms for purchase or rental of public lands for coffee cultivation. He also abolished the collection of the tithe on coffee production after 1835, a policy of great importance in both stimulating production and undermining the power of the church thereafter.

See also **Coffee Industry; Costa Rica; Morazán, Francisco.**

BIBLIOGRAPHY

Basic material on Carrillo can be found in Carlos Monge Alfaro, *Historia de Costa Rica,* 16th ed. (1980), pp. 193–199, 223–227. The most detailed examination of his policies is found in Rodolfo Cerdas Cruz, *Formación del estado de Costa Rica,* 2d ed. (1978). A more recent study with some new information is Clotilde Obregón, *Carrillo: Una época y un hombre, 1835–1842* (1989). See also Victor Hugo Acuño Ortega and Ivan Molina Jiménez, *El desarrollo económico y social de Costa Rica: De la colonia a la crisis de 1930* (1986); Jorge Sáenz Carbonell, *El despertar constitucional de Costa Rica* (1985); José Luis Vega Carballo, *Orden y progeso: La formación del estado nacional en Costa Rica* (1981); and Alberto Sáenz Maroto, *Braulio Carrillo, reformador agrícola de Costa Rica* (1987).

Additional Bibliography

Villalobos Rodríguez, José Hilario, and Luz Alba Chacón de Umaña. *Braulio Carrillo.* San José: Impr. Nacional, 1998.

LOWELL GUDMUNDSON

CARRILLO FLORES, ANTONIO
(1909–1986). Antonio Carrillo Flores (*b.* 23 June 1909; *d.* 20 March 1986), leading political figure in Mexican financial affairs since 1952. Born in Mexico City, he was the son of a famous musician Julián Carrillo. With Miguel Alemán, Carrillo Flores was a member of the 1929 law school graduating class at the National University. From 1946 to 1970 he held a succession of influential political posts, including secretary of the treasury (1952–1958), ambassador to the United States (1958–1964), and secretary of foreign relations (1964–1970). Through his public service and teaching careers he trained two generations of disciples who became mentors to Mexico's new political technocrats of the 1980s and 1990s. He was the brother of the distinguished scientist Nabor Carrillo Flores.

See also **Mexico: Since 1910.**

BIBLIOGRAPHY

Diccionario biográfico de México, vol. 1 (1968), pp. 121–122; and *Excélsior,* 1 March 1980, p. 4A.

RODERIC AI CAMP

CARRILLO FLORES, NABOR (1911–1967). Nabor Carrillo Flores (*b.* 23 February 1911; *d.* 19 February 1967), educator, scientist, and intellectual. Born in Mexico City, he was the younger brother of Antonio Carrillo Flores, and the son of the musician Julián Carrillo. He received a civil engineering degree from the National University in 1938 and a doctorate from Harvard in 1942. Internationally renowned for his work in subsoil mechanics, Carrillo Flores studied with Sotero Prieto before receiving a Guggenheim fellowship (1940). He directed various scientific research projects at the National University, and served as its rector from 1952 to 1961. He received the National Prize in Sciences in 1957 and pioneered the use of atomic energy in Mexico. He died in Mexico City.

See also **Science.**

BIBLIOGRAPHY

"Presente y futuro de la UNAM," in *Hispano Americano* 22 (27 February 1953): 35–37; and *Excélsior,* 21 August 1971, p. 7A.

RODERIC AI CAMP

CARRILLO PUERTO, FELIPE (1874–1924). Felipe Carrillo Puerto (*b.* 8 November 1874; *d.* 3 January 1924), one of the Mexican Revolution's most radical agrarian leaders. During his short-lived governorship of Yucatán (1922–1923), Carrillo Puerto presided over what was arguably the Americas' first attempted transition to socialism. Assassinated in January 1924 by insurgent federal troops allied with powerful members of Yucatán's henequen oligarchy, he has since become one of the most enduring martyrs of Mexico's twentieth-century revolution.

Carrillo Puerto was born in Motul—the heart of Yucatán's henequen zone—the second of fourteen children of a modest mestizo retail merchant. As a young man he was a *ranchero* (small landholder), mule driver, petty trader, and railroad conductor during Yucatán's henequen export boom, which descendants of the original Maya fieldworkers still recall as the *época de esclavitud* (age of slavery). Carrillo Puerto learned the Maya vernacular as part of his daily life, and developed close ties to Yucatán's rural underclass in the process. An autodidact who read a bit of Marx and other leftist European thinkers along with the more standard fare of mainstream Mexican liberalism, Carrillo Puerto was jailed several times for his political activities against the local oligarchical machine. Following the fall of the Porfiriato in 1911, his political aspirations within the state were frustrated by his backing of the wrong Maderista politician, and he left Yucatán for Morelos in late 1914 to volunteer his services to the celebrated agrarian movement of Emiliano Zapata. Six months later, however, he was back on his native soil, determined to work with the new populist governor, General Salvador Alvarado, to bring agrarian reform to Yucatán.

Carrillo Puerto proved both too popular and too radical for the authoritarian Alvarado, who kept him on a short leash prior to departing the peninsula in 1918. Once Carrillo Puerto assumed control of Alvarado's Socialist Party of the Southwest (Partido Socialista del Sureste—PSS) later that year, the Mexican Revolution moved steadily to the left in Yucatán. Whereas Alvarado had been reluctant to let the rural masses participate in the political process, Carrillo Puerto encouraged them to accept responsibility for their political destiny.

And while Alvarado had been prepared to initiate only a limited agrarian reform, under Carrillo Puerto's leadership, the pace of agrarian reform accelerated to the point that Yucatán distributed more land than any other state, save perhaps Zapata's Morelos. By the time of his death, Carrillo Puerto had made sure that virtually every one of the state's major pueblos had received at least a basic ejidal grant. His regime and life were snuffed out just as he seemed ready to initiate a more sweeping agrarian reform, one that would have expropriated the region's henequen plantations and turned them into collective farms owned and operated by the workers.

Under Carrillo Puerto the Mexican Revolution in Yucatán became a genuinely Yucatecan movement. He used locally trained cadres of agrarian agitators and activist schoolteachers, and allied with local caciques (power brokers). Moreover, Carrillo Puerto reinforced the regional character of his revolution in a variety of symbolic ways, most of which sought to wean the Maya campesino away from the institutions and passive attitudes of the old regime and to develop a sense of ethnic pride as a prelude to class consciousness. He encouraged the speaking of Maya and the teaching of Maya culture and art forms, began earnest restoration of the great archaeological sites of Chichén Itzá and Uxmal, and made every effort to recall the great revolutionary tradition of protest to which the campesinos were heir.

Ultimately, Carrillo Puerto's homegrown variant of "Yucatecan socialism" proved threatening, not only to the regional oligarchy, but also to the more moderate regime then consolidating its control over the republic under the leadership of Sonoran caudillos Alvaro Obregón Salido and Plutarco Calles. When, under cover of the De La Huerta rebellion, insurgent federal troops were contracted by the henequen kings to expunge bolshevism, Mexico City abandoned Carrillo Puerto. Yucatán's socialist experiment ended tragically when Felipe Carrillo Puerto and many of his closest supporters in Mérida were hunted down and summarily executed by a firing squad on 3 January 1924. Following the defeat of the de la Huerta rebellion, the remnants of the PSS were absorbed by the new corporatist structure in Mexico City. Only the outer trappings of the Americas' first attempted socialist transition—the red shirts, the radical slogans, the formal organization of the PSS—survived its leader's untimely death.

See also **Mexico, Wars and Revolutions: Mexican Revolution.**

BIBLIOGRAPHY

Francisco J. Paoli Bolio and Enrique Montalvo, *El socialismo olvidado de Yucatán* (1977).

Gilbert M. Joseph, *Revolution from Without: Yucatán, Mexico, and the United States, 1880–1924,* rev. ed. (1988).

Additional Bibliography

Berzunza Pinto, Ramón. *En el pórtico de la historia: Biografía de Felipe Carrillo Puerto.* Campeche: Gobierno del Estado de Campeche, Instituto de Cultura de Campeche, 2001.

GILBERT M. JOSEPH

CARRINGTON, LEONORA (1917–).

Leonora Carrington is a painter, writer, and sculptor born April 6, 1917, in Clayton Green, England. Against her family's wishes, she attended the academy of the French cubist Amédée Ozenfant (1886-1966), where in 1937 she met the German surrealist artist Max Ernst in 1937 and moved with him to Paris. In 1939 Ernst was arrested by the Gestapo but escaped to the United States with the help of the American art patron Peggy Guggenheim. Carrington fled to Spain, where she suffered a nervous breakdown and was institutionalized by her parents. When she was released to recover in the care of a nurse in Lisbon, she escaped and took refuge in the Mexican consulate. There she met the Mexican reporter and ambassador Renato Leduc; they married and went first to New York City, then to Mexico in 1942. Soon after, the couple divorced amicably, and Leonora became involved with a group of refugee artists, including the painter Remedios Varo (1908–1963). In 1946 Carrington married the Hungarian photographer Emerico Weisz, and they had two sons together.

Leonora's written works include *En Bas* (Down Below, 1945) and *Une Chemise de Nuit de Flanelle* (A Flannel Nightgown, 1951). Her graphic works were inspired by Celtic, Egyptian, Syrian, Mesopotamian, and Mexican mythology. She has exhibited her work in Mexico, New York, Paris, Tokyo, and many other cities. Further works include *Are You Really Syrius* (1953), *Habdalah Asejaledha* (1959), the mural *El mundo mágico de los mayas* (The Magical World of the Mayas, 1964), and *Tower of Nagas*

(1991). The sculpture *La fuente cocodrilo* (The Crocodile Fountain, 1998) was exhibited in Mexico, where she lived as of 2007.

See also **Art: The Twentieth Century.**

JORGE ALBERTO MANRIQUE

CARRIÓ DE LA VANDERA, ALONSO

(c. 1714–1783). Alonso Carrió de la Vandera was born in Guijón, Asturias, circa 1714–1716. In 1736 he arrived in Mexico City, where he lived for ten years. His business endeavors took him to different places in Mexico and to Guatemala, Hispaniola, and Puerto Rico. He moved to Lima, capital of the Viceroyalty of Peru, in 1746. He returned to Spain only once, when he volunteered to escort the 181 Jesuits expelled from Peru in 1767. He died in Lima in 1783.

Once in Lima, he devoted his life to public office. Among his most important public posts was that of inspector of the postal system between Buenos Aires and Lima. This particular post, which he held between 1771 and 1773, was crucial for the creation of his most influential work, *El lazarillo de ciegos caminantes* (Guide for Blind Travelers, c. 1775). His visit to this territory prompted his disagreement over how to better improve the postal system with the administrator of the postal system, José Antonio Pando, which eventually resulted in his dismissal from his post as second commissioner. To retaliate, Carrió published in Lima a pseudonymous manifesto between 1777 and 1778 attacking Pando's views on reforming the postal system. The colonial authorities considered the document dangerous, and had Carrió arrested and incarcerated. He was later released due to delicate health and old age.

El lazarillo de ciegos caminantes was published under very enigmatic circumstances: false authorship, false license, false publisher, and false place of publication. Carrió never received an official license to publish because there was no printing press in Guijón at the time. He hid his name under the pseudonym of Calixto Bustamente, alias Concolorcorvo, a mestizo Indian who accompanied Carrió during part of his trip between Buenos Aires and Lima. In a letter found in the Archive of the Indies dated 24 April 1776, Carrió confesses that he indeed used Concolocorvo's name to avoid

censorship. Many critics in the nineteenth and early twentieth centuries granted authorship to Concolorcovo to ascribe *El lazarillo* Latin American authorship.

El lazarillo is a hybrid text, sharing characteristics of discursive genres such as travel literature, diary, chronicle, *relación* (forensic account), and popular romance. It is characterized by its descriptive, didactic, and critical nature. It is a valuable source of information about social, political, cultural, and religious practices in what encompasses a great part of present-day South America. The book provides a complex picture of how knowledge of distant territories and peoples by the Spanish crown was often characterized by ambiguities, contradictions, and an incomplete view of the diverse realities of colonial societies at the time.

See also **Carrió de la Bandera, Alonso (Concolorcorvo).**

BIBLIOGRAPHY

Carrió de la Vandera, Alonso. *El lazarillo de ciegos caminantes.* Edited by Antonio Lorente Medina. Caracas: Ayacucho, 1985.

Hill, Ruth. *Hierarchy, Commerce, and Fraud in Bourbon Spanish America: A Postal Inspector's Exposé.* Nashville, TN: Vanderbilt University Press, 2005.

Meléndez, Mariselle. *Raza, género e hibridez en El Lazarillo de ciegos caminantes.* Chapel Hill: University of North Carolina Press, 1999.

Stolley, Karen. *El lazarillo de ciegos caminantes: Un itinerario crítico.* Hanover, NH: Ediciones del Norte, 1993.

MARISELLE MELÉNDEZ

CARRIÓN, ALEJANDRO (1915–1991).

Alejandro Carrión (*b.* 11 March 1915; *d.* 1991), Ecuadorian writer. Born in Loja, Alejandro Carrión is known in Ecuador principally as a political journalist. Many of his writings were signed with the pseudonym "Juan sin Cielo." Carrión also wrote poetry and narrative fiction. Among his most cited works are *La manzana dañada* (1948), a collection of short stories that depicts the sordid aspects of a school system controlled by the Catholic Church in southern Ecuador, and *La espina* (1959), a novel of solitude in which the protagonist tries to reconstruct the image of his mother, who had died during his birth. Because of his political views, which ran the gamut from socialism in his early life to conservatism in his later years, Carrión was a controversial figure in Ecuador. During the government of León Febres Cordero (1984–1988), many accused Carrión of being the president's principal apologist; in his journalism, Carrión defended the government's neoliberal economic policies and its conservative political agenda. In 1985, President Febres awarded Carrión the Eugenio Espejo Prize for Literature.

See also **Literature: Spanish America.**

MICHAEL HANDELSMAN

CARRIÓN, JERÓNIMO (1801–1873).

Jerónimo Carrión (*b.* 6 July 1801; *d.* 5 May 1873), president of Ecuador (1865–1867). Carrión served as governor of Azuay province (1845–1847), deputy (1845, 1852) and senator (1847–1849) from Loja province, and vice president of Ecuador in 1859 during the administration of Francisco Robles (1856–1859). In 1865 he accepted the invitation of archconservative dictator Gabriel García Moreno (1861–1865, 1869–1875) to succeed him. The retiring president arranged a landslide electoral victory for Carrión, who, to García Moreno's dismay, proved unwilling to be a puppet ruler. He chose his own cabinet, naming several liberals, and dispatched García Moreno on a diplomatic mission to Chile.

Yet on policy matters Carrión did not diverge significantly from the García Moreno agenda, save for his unwillingness to savage political opponents with violent repression. Under Carrión freedom of expression returned, bringing the reemergence of a lively—if often reckless and irresponsible—opposition press. In 1867 his leading minister, Manuel Bustamante, angered powerful Liberal elements then ascendant in Congress. In the ensuing political showdown with Senate president Pedro Carbo y Noboa, Congress censured Carrión. He was overthrown and replaced by Pedro José Arteta in 1867. Lacking support, Carrión agreed. Contemporaries generally regarded him as honest if not especially bright or energetic.

See also **Espinosa y Espinosa, (Juan) Javier.**

BIBLIOGRAPHY

On nineteenth-century Ecuadorian politics, see Osvaldo Hurtado's interpretive *Political Power in Ecuador,* translated by Nick D. Mills, Jr. (1985); Frank MacDonald Spindler's descriptive *Nineteenth Century Ecuador: An Historical*

Introduction (1987). For a brief analysis of Ecuadorian political economy in the nineteenth century, consult David W. Schodt, *Ecuador: An Andean Enigma* (1987).

Additional Bibliography

Hurtado, Osvaldo. *El poder político en el Ecuador.* Quito: Planeta, 2003.

RONN F. PINEO

CARRIÓN, MANUEL BENJAMÍN (1897–1979).

Manuel Benjamín Carrión (*b.* 20 April 1897; *d.* 8 March 1979), Ecuadorian essayist. Originally from Loja, Benjamín Carrión spent his life writing about the major social, political, and cultural problems of both his native Ecuador and the rest of Latin America. During his youth, he was one of the early founders of Ecuador's Socialist Party (1925). His contributions to the continent's many democratic causes were formally recognized when the Mexican government awarded him in 1968 the prestigious Benito Juárez Prize. In 1944, Carrión founded Ecuador's Casa de la Cultura Ecuatoriana (House of Ecuadorian Culture), which through the years has become one of the country's principal institutions charged with developing among all Ecuadorians the many forms of cultural and intellectual expression. In Ecuador, Carrión is revered for his efforts to stimulate and guide others in their creative endeavors. His most celebrated works are *Atahuallpa* (1934) and *Cartas al Ecuador* (1943). In 1975 he received the Eugenio Espejo Prize, Ecuador's highest literary and cultural honor.

See also **Journalism.**

BIBLIOGRAPHY

Handelsman, Michael H. *El ideario de Benjamín Carrión: Selección y Análisis Crítico.* Quito: Planeta, 1992.

Orero de Julián, José, and Liliana del Castillo Rojas. *El pensamiento vivo de Benjamín Carrión.* Guayaquil: Casa de la Cultura Ecuatoriana, Núcleo del Guayas, 1998.

MICHAEL HANDELSMAN

CARTAGENA.

Cartagena, the northern province of the New Kingdom of Granada, whose capital, Cartagena de Indias, was the principal Spanish port and defense center on the northern Caribbean littoral.

Located on the Caribbean coast of modern-day Colombia in the Bolívar Department between the Magdalena and Sinú rivers and extending southward to the town of Mompós, Cartagena was an eminent colonial jurisdiction dominated by activity in the port of Cartagena de Indias. When the Spanish explorers Juan de la Cosa and Rodrigo de Bastidas first reconnoitered the area in 1502, they recognized the potential afforded by a large bay reminiscent of the bay at Cartagena, Spain. Cosa and others, however, did not return to the site until 1509.

As in 1502, they confronted Caramari, Turbaco, and other Indians who resisted the Spanish incursion. In a February 1510 battle, for example, Turbaco warriors killed Cosa and seventy others, dealing Spanish troops their worst defeat yet in the Caribbean conquest. Cosa's compatriot, Alonso de Ojeda, and recently arrived reinforcements commanded by Diego de Nicuesa successfully counterattacked, but they abandoned the field for territories farther south and west. Modern scholarship continues to examine the origins and cultural affinities of these Indians, but sixteenth-century Spaniards knew them to be stout fighters, skillful archers, and active merchants, trading salt, fish, and cotton hammocks for gold and clothing.

Not until 1533 did Spanish colonists, led by Pedro de Heredia, establish a permanent settlement at Cartagena. Because of continuing Indian hostility at Turbaco and the island of Tierra Bomba, upon their arrival, Heredia selected a deserted Caramari village site for his new town. Heredia's efforts paid off in great dividends for imperial Spain. Within the decade, Cartagena de Indias developed into a major imperial entrepôt for the shipment of American bullion to Spain as well as for slaves and manufactures intended for northern South American markets. In turn, this commerce energized economic life within the city itself.

Foreigners, too, recognized the significance of Cartagena de Indias and so sought to appropriate its wealth and deal Spain a military and political blow. French pirates sacked the city in 1544 and 1559. A decade later (1568), John Hawkins took the port, as did Francis Drake in 1586. French troops captured Cartagena in 1697. British forces twice besieged the port, in 1727 and 1741, the second time with a force of twenty thousand men and nearly two hundred ships under the command of Admiral Edward Vernon.

Because of the commercial and strategic prominence of the port, Spanish authorities ordered substantial fortifications for the city, raising there some of the best and most impressive colonial military architecture. Highlighted by walls eight feet thick and the looming fortress of San Felipe de Barajas, these defenses—constructed between 1560 and 1780—demonstrated royal resolve, declared imperial pretensions and power, and marked the colonial greatness of the port. The battlements remain even today a constant reminder of one of the most celebrated historical events in Colombian historiography: the defeat of Vernon's 1741 assault on the city. Aided by tropical disease, which devasted the English forces, and guided by Viceroy Sebastián de Eslava (1740–1749) and naval commander Blas de Lezo (1689–1741), the defenders withstood the British attacks and thus earned the port the appellation "heroic."

Cartagena de Indias was also an ecclesiastical and political hub, rivaled only in New Granada by Santa Fe de Bogotá. It was an episcopal see and possessed one of three American offices of the Inquisition (established in 1610), charged with responsibility for northern South America, Panama, and the Spanish Caribbean. It contained four monasteries, two convents, and the San Juan de Dios hospital. Moreover, one of the most famous Jesuit missionaries of the colonial period, Saint Pedro Claver, labored there among Africans between 1610 and 1654, when the city was a major slave distribution center for the Caribbean. Governors and treasury officials also served in Cartagena, and, in the eighteenth century, viceroys occasionally ruled from there.

The fame of Cartagena de Indias notwithstanding, more people lived in the provincial hinterlands than in the city, especially in times of foreign hostilities. Whereas in the eighteenth century, for example, the population of the port generally fluctuated between ten and sixteen thousand, as many as nine times that many people lived in the rest of the province. The commercial milieu that dominated port life also characterized activity in and around Mompós (founded 1537) and Tolú, two towns known for their contraband fairs and centrality in regional trade networks.

In the twenty-first century Cartagena, home to more than 800,000 residents (2002), remains the country's most important harbor. Despite bombings and violence in the early years of the decade related to country's civil war, Cartagena's beaches, cultural heritage sites, and colonial architecture draw increasing numbers of Colombian and international tourists each year.

See also **Indigenous Peoples; Slavery: Spanish America.**

BIBLIOGRAPHY

For a representative sampling of works available in English, see James Nelson Goodsell, "Cartagena de Indias: Entrepôt for a New World (1533–1597)" (Ph.D. diss., Harvard University, 1966); Linda L. Greenow, *Family, Household, and Home: A Microgeographic Analysis of Cartagena (New Granada) in 1777* (1976); and Lance R. Grahn, "Cartagena and Its Hinterland in the Eighteenth Century," in *Atlantic Port Cities: Economy, Culture, and Society in the Atlantic World, 1650–1850,* edited by Franklin W. Knight and Peggy K. Liss (1991), pp. 168–195. Essential, however, are these books in Spanish: Enrique Marco Dorta, *Cartagena de Indias: Puerto y plaza fuerte* (1960), which is exceptional in its survey of the military architecture of the port; Eduardo Lemaitre Román, *Cartagena colonial* (1973), a fine general history; Donaldo Bossa Herrazo's guide to the geography and place names of the city and province, *Nomenclatur cartagenero* (1981); and Orlando Fals-Borda's multivolume study of the provincial hinterlands of Cartagena, *Historia doble de la costa,* 4 vols. (1979–1986).

Ceballos Gómez, Diana Luz. *Hechicería, brujería, e Inquisición en el Nuevo Reino de Granada: Un duelo de imaginarios.* Bogotá: Editorial Universidad Nacional, 1994.

Conde Calderón, Jorge. *Espacio, sociedad y conflictos en la provincia de Cartagena, 1740–1815.* Barranquilla, Colombia: Fondo de Publicaciones de la Universidad del Atlántico, 1999.

Cunin, Elisabeth. *Identidades a flor de piel: Lo "negro" entre apariencias y pertenencias: Categorías raciales y mestizaje en Cartagena (Colombia).* Bogotá: Instituto Colombiano de Antropología e Historia, 2003.

Helg, Aline. *Liberty and Equality in Caribbean Colombia, 1770–1835.* Chapel Hill: University of North Carolina Press, 2004.

Navarrete, María Cristina. *Prácticas religiosas de los negros en la colonia: Cartagena, siglo XVII.* Santiago de Cali, Colombia: Universidad del Valle, Editorial Facultad de Humanidades, 1995.

Olsen, Margaret M. *Slavery and Salvation in Colonial Cartagena de Indias.* Gainesville: University Press of Florida, 2004.

Redondo Gómez, Maruja. *Cartagena de Indias: Cinco siglos de evolución urbanística.* Bogotá: Fundación Universidad de Bogotá Jorge Tadeo Lozano, Facultad de Arquitectura, 2004.

Rodríguez-Bobb, Arturo. *Exclusión e integración del sujeto negro en Cartagena de Indias en perspectiva histórica.* Madrid: Iberoamericana, 2002.

Saldarriaga Roa, Alberto, et al. *Restoring Architecture: The Work of Alvaro Barrera.* Bogotá: Villegas Editores, 2003.

Solano Alonso, Jairo. *Salud, cultura y sociedad: Cartagena de Índias, siglos XVI y XVII.* Barranquilla, Colombia: Universidad del Atlántico, 1998.

LANCE R. GRAHN

CARTAGENA MANIFESTO. The first major political statement of Simón Bolívar, at the time a relatively obscure fugitive from the collapse of Venezuela's First Republic, was the manifesto that he published at Cartagena in neighboring New Granada (1812). In the form of a pamphlet titled *Memoria dirigida a los ciudadanos de la Nueva Granada por un caraqueño,* it contained Bolívar's analysis of the reasons for the recent failure of the Venezuelan patriots and anticipated many of the themes of his later writings. He placed particular emphasis on the errors of doctrinaire theorists whose infatuation with foreign ideas and with federalist forms of organization—which Bolívar considered unsuited to Spanish American conditions—had caused them to ignore the need for a strong central executive. He urged New Granadans both to avoid repetition of the same mistakes and to support a new campaign to liberate Venezuela.

See also **Bolívar, Simón.**

BIBLIOGRAPHY

Selected Writings of Bolívar, compiled by Vicente Lecuna, edited by Harold A. Bierck, Jr., translated by Lewis Bertrand (1951), vol. 1, pp. 18–26.

Gerhard Masur, *Simón Bolívar* (1948; rev. ed. 1969), chap. 9.

Additional Bibliography

Lynch, John. *Simón Bolívar: A Life.* New Haven, CT: Yale University Press, 2006.

Mendizábal, Francisco Javier de. *Guerra de la América del Sur, 1809–1824.* Buenos Aires: Academia Nacional de la Historia, 1997.

DAVID BUSHNELL

CARTAGO. Cartago, capital of the province of Cartago, the second most densely populated Costa Rican province after San José. Cartago competes with Heredia and Alajuela for the distinction of being the second city of the *meseta central,* the Costa Rican heartland. As the site of the basilica of the Black Virgin (Nuestra Señora de los Angeles), it retains an unrivaled place in the religious sentiments of the people and is the destination of an impressive annual pilgrimage. Cartago and its residents played pivotal roles in the watershed 1948 revolution. Costa Ricans always remember Cartago for the devastating earthquake it suffered in 1910 and its sporadic episodes with the nearby Irazu volcano.

Cartago's greatest glory came in the colonial period. From the time of its foundation in 1564, it was the capital and most important city in one of Spain's most isolated and neglected colonies. By the independence era (c. 1821) the city had a scant seven thousand residents. In 1823 Cartago was defeated by the more dynamic and republican San José in the struggle to be the new nation's capital city.

See also **Costa Rica.**

BIBLIOGRAPHY

For the independence period, see Ricardo Fernández Guardia, *La independencia: historia de Costa Rica* (1971); for the role of Cartago in the crisis of the 1940s, see John Patrick Bell, *Crisis in Costa Rica* (1971); for the impact of coffee production and its aftermath, see Carolyn Hall, *Costa Rica: A Geographical Interpretation in Historical Perspective* (1985); and for its place in Costa Rican society over the years, see Richard Biesanz, Karen Zubris Biesanz, and Mavis Hiltunen Biesanz, *The Costa Ricans* (1982; rev. ed. 1988).

Additional Bibliography

Moya Gutiérrez, Arnaldo. *Comerciantes y damas principales de Cartago: Vida cotidiana, 1750–1820.* Cartago, Costa Rica: Editorial Cultural Cartaginesa, 1998.

JOHN PATRICK BELL

CARTAVIO. Cartavio, a sugar-producing landed estate in northern Peru dating from Spanish colonial times. In 1882 this 1,447-acre hacienda was surrendered by its Peruvian owner, Guillermo Alzamora, to the U.S. commercial firm W. R. Grace and Company in payment of its accumulated debt. In the 1890s the Grace firm formed the Cartavio Sugar Company as a subsidiary corporation. A pioneering U.S. direct investment of 200,000 pounds sterling was used to modernize the estate and build a sugar mill. In this way the Grace interests contributed to a process of land consolidation by giant estates (Cartavio, Casa Grande, and Laredo) which displaced smaller landowners in the northern Chicama valley of Peru. In the 1970s, during the implementation of the agrarian reform sponsored by the military regime, the Cartavio estate's ownership and administration were transferred to an agrarian cooperative.

See also **Sugar Industry.**

BIBLIOGRAPHY

Peter Klarén, *Modernization, Dislocation, and Aprismo* (1973).

Michael González, *Plantation Agriculture and Social Control in Northern Peru, 1875–1933* (1985).

Additional Bibliography

Piel, Jean, and Francis Eherran. *Capitalismo agrario en el Perú.* Lima: IFEA; Buenos Aires: U. Nacional de Salta, 1995.

ALFONSO W. QUIROZ

CARTER, JIMMY (1924–). Jimmy Carter (James Earl Carter, Jr.) was thirty-ninth president of the United States (1977–1981). His presidency was known for his human rights policy, the Panama Canal treaties returning the Canal to Panamanian control, and the Camp David peace accords between Israel and Egypt. After he lost his reelection bid to Ronald Reagan, Carter and his wife returned to Georgia and founded the Carter Center, a non-profit center to resolve conflict, promote democracy, protect human rights, and prevent disease and other afflictions in developing countries.

Carter was born 1 October 1924, in the small farming town of Plains, Georgia. He was educated in the public school of Plains, attended Georgia Southwestern College and the Georgia Institute of Technology, and received a B.S. degree from the United States Naval Academy in 1946. In the Navy he served on submarines and was promoted to the rank of lieutenant.

In 1946, he married Rosalynn Smith of Plains. When his father died in 1953, Carter resigned his commission in the Navy and went back to Georgia to operate the Carter farms. In 1962 he was elected to the Georgia Senate. Losing the race for governor in 1966, he won the election in 1970. In 1972 he was the Democratic National Committee's campaign chairman for the congressional and gubernatorial elections of 1974. He announced his candidacy for president of the United States with the Democratic Party in 1974 and was elected president on 2 November 1976.

Carter served as president from 1977 to 1981. His major foreign policy achievements included the Camp David Accords leading to the peace treaty between Egypt and Israel, the SALT II treaty with the Soviet Union, and the establishment of U.S. diplomatic relations with the People's Republic of China. He supported human rights worldwide and particularly in Latin America, where he advanced the transition from military to civilian governments in many countries. He negotiated the Panama Canal treaties, which led to a return of the Canal Zone to Panama. It won ratification in the U.S. Senate by just one vote and was politically costly for Carter.

Domestically, the Carter administration's accomplishments included a comprehensive energy program conducted by a newly created Department of Energy. Other achievements on the domestic front included deregulation in energy, transportation, communications, and finance; major educational programs under a new Department of Education; and major environmental protection legislation, including the Alaska National Interest Lands Conservation Act.

Carter is the author of numerous books, including *Palestine: Peace Not Apartheid* (2006). In 1982 he became University Distinguished Professor at Emory University in Atlanta, Georgia, and founded the Carter Center. Under his leadership the Carter Center has sent sixty-three international election-monitoring delegations to elections in the Americas, Africa, and Asia. The Latin American nations include Panama (1989), Nicaragua (1990), Guyana (1992), Venezuela (1998), and Mexico (2000). In 2002, Carter made an historic trip to Cuba, the first sitting or former U.S. president to visit since the 1959 Cuban Revolution.

In 2002 Carter was awarded the Nobel Peace Prize "for his decades of untiring effort to find peaceful solutions to international conflicts, to advance democracy and human rights, and to promote economic and social development" ("The Nobel Peace Prize of 2002," http://nobelpeaceprize.org).

See also **Carter Center; Panama Canal; Panama Canal Treaties of 1977.**

BIBLIOGRAPHY

Gherman, Beverly. *Jimmy Carter.* Minneapolis, MN: Lerner Publications Co., 2004.

Horowith, Daniel. *Jimmy Carter and the Energy Crisis of the 1970s: A Brief History with Documents.* New York: Bedford/St. Martins, 2004.

Joseph, Paul. *Jimmy Carter.* Edina, MN: ABDO Publishing Co., 2002.

Waxman, Laura Hamilton. *Jimmy Carter.* Minneapolis, MN: Lerner, 2006.

JENNIFER McCOY

CARTER CENTER.

Founded in 1982 by Jimmy Carter, the Carter Center is a nonprofit, public policy institute that is associated with Emory University in Atlanta, Georgia. Its programs aim to contribute to resolving conflicts, eradicating disease, and promoting human rights and democracy all over the world. Of these, the Latin American and Caribbean Program was established in September 1985. It sponsored a conference in April 1986 to propose strategies for solving the Latin American debt crisis. The program officially opened the Carter Center's new facilities, dedicated in October 1986, with a major conference the following month called Reinforcing Democracy in the Americas. Co-chaired by Carter and former president Gerald Ford, the gathering included fourteen current and former presidents and prime ministers. These leaders formed a Council of Freely Elected Heads of Government, which expanded to thirty-five members. The Council has promoted democracy and advanced free trade and development in the Americas and beyond.

Beginning in 1987 with a visit to try to shore up the electoral process in Haiti, the council became deeply engaged in monitoring and helping to mediate democratic transitions. They sent a team under Carter and Ford to observe elections in Panama in May 1989. When General Manuel

Noriega tried to manipulate the results, Carter denounced him and encouraged the Organization of American States to take action to restore democracy. In August 1989 the Carter Center was invited by Nicaragua's leaders to observe the country's elections in February 1990. During the next six months, Carter and council members developed election mediation as a new technique of conflict resolution whereby the council would mediate the terms of a free and fair election among the leaders of the country. That model was then applied to more than sixty countries in the Americas and the world. The program was renamed the Americas Program in 1990 and has continued to work to deepen the democratic process in the Americas.

See also **Carter, Jimmy; Democracy; Human Rights; United States-Latin American Relations.**

BIBLIOGRAPHY

Brinkley, Douglas. *The Unfinished Presidency: Jimmy Carter's Quest for Global Peace.* New York: Penguin, 1999.

Robert A. *Exiting the Whirlpool: U.S. Foreign Policy toward Latin America and the Caribbean.* Boulder, CO: Westview Press, 2001.

ROBERT A. PASTOR

CARTOGRAPHY

This entry includes the following articles:
OVERVIEW
THE SPANISH BORDERLANDS

OVERVIEW

A map does more than represent physical space. It situates space in time and in a particular social, political, cultural, and scientific context. Geographic maps make select elements of natural spaces into cultural places whose physical features have meaning for humans who use them, among other purposes, to navigate voyages and claim land or govern peoples. Mapping in the Americas existed before the arrival of Europeans in 1492, but, as Argentine urban historian Jorge Hardoy noted in 1983, there is no history of Latin American cartography, perhaps because of distinct national and imperial histories and multiple mapmaking traditions derived from and sometimes combining Amerindian and European practices.

PRE-COLUMBIAN MAPPING
Pre-Columbian mapping to represent space was most developed among the Nahua and Aztecs (Mexica), a people without a word for map because their pictorial representation on paper, cloth, and hides of landholdings, territories, routes, war plans, and rivers did not differ significantly from their image-based writing. Although the Maya are reported to have created similar maps, only pre-Columbian cosmographical maps representing sacred space survive. Scholars identify Andean peoples as representing secular and religious space using abstract images on ceramics and textiles, but only Mexica scribes are known to have made maps to facilitate conquistadors' travels, confirming not only their expertise but their ability to make representations legible to heirs of a different symbolic tradition.

MAPPING IN THE AGE OF DISCOVERY
From initial sketches to methodically constructed and lavishly illustrated maps, European cartography from Columbus's earliest expeditions not only depicted geographical space but claimed literal and figurative control over land and inhabitants and reflected Europe's changing understanding of the globe. Europeans were the first to map the Americas as a unit comprising the Caribbean and North, Central and South America, setting the stage for justifications for controlling this unit. The Portuguese, under Prince Henry the Navigator, were perhaps the most advanced cartographers in Europe, but the Spanish-sponsored Columbus expeditions were the first to map American lands. Initial maps identifying Central America's coast as part of Asia were soon replaced with more accurate renderings of continents that undermined the medieval understanding that only water separated Western Europe from Asia to the west. They also highlighted claims by European states to control specific territories by naming or renaming places, using saints' names (San Salvador), names of metropolitan centers (New Spain), or geographic features (Buenos Aires), applying hybrid names (San Luís Potosí) to existing villages. In this way they largely inscribed European territorial control across American places.

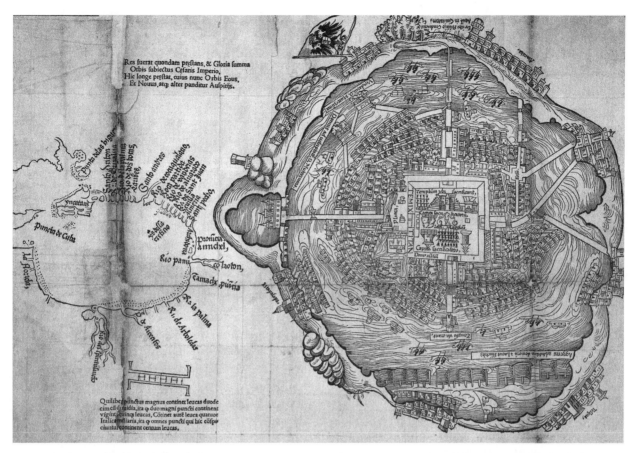

Map of Mexico, 1524. Few early Spanish or Portuguese maps of the New World were available to the public, as rulers feared information about their access to highly profitable trade routes would land in enemy hands. Instead, cartographers would attempt to sketch maps of the Americas based on reports received from explorers, often adding their own Eurocentric biases to the drawing. HIP/ART RESOURCE, NY

Iberian Manuscript Maps. Few detailed Spanish or Portuguese maps, particularly city plans or maps of shores, harbors, and sea routes, were published in the sixteenth century, for fear of use by rival European powers, particularly France and England, whose pirates, privateers, and naval vessels sought to hijack bullion and develop contraband trade. Instead, pilots' reports and maps were likely to be held in manuscript form in government archives. Such maps might include navigational innovations, such as scales of latitude and longitude that put locating grids on rhumb lines or formerly empty space, transforming medieval-style maritime charts, such as the 1500 portolan world map by Spanish cartographer Juan de la Cosa, into precursors of modern maps. Or they might include navigational charts, such as Lisbon cartographer João Teixeira's 1630 manuscript atlas of secret maps of Portugal's empire that, among other things, pushed the line separating Spanish

from Portuguese possessions to the west. So foreigners such as Britain's Sir Walter Ralegh were particularly delighted to collect "a secret mappe of those partes made in Mexico. . . . for the King of Spaine" (Harley 1988, p. 64).

Published World Maps and Atlases. Outside Iberia, New World discoveries prompted multiple innovations in cartography, as mapmakers who had never visited the New World developed and published maps for European consumption, based on explorers' reports. In 1507, cosmographer Martin Waldseemüller published the first map to label the continents as the Americas, probably due to Amerigo Vespucci's identification of this "unknown land" as a continent unheard of by Ptolemy and the classical world, and to show the Pacific Ocean as a separate body of water. The Eurocentric world map, with north on top, would remain a standard (and seemingly objective) representation until twentieth century cartographers not only flipped the world upside down, but also made Afrocentric or Asia-centric maps, revealing how this seemingly neutral map actually symbolized and naturalized Western European power.

Abraham Ortelius published the first full world atlas, *Theatrum Orbis Terrarum* (1570, Antwerp), a map in book form made for transport, not walls; Cornelius Wytfliet's first atlas of the Americas, *Descriptionis Ptolemaicae augmentum* (1597, Louvain), followed, along with Gerardus Mercator's cylindrical projection, which is still used for navigation charts and world maps. By 1601, with information widely available, the chronicler of Spain's Council of the Indies, Antonio de Herrera y Tordesillas, published Spain's first official atlas of fourteen folding maps of its American territories as part of his four-volume *Historia General de los hechos de los castellanos en las islas i tierra firme del mar océano* (1601, Madrid).

Despite extensive exploration and mapping, lacunae remained in early imperial cartography; California was occasionally represented as an island, and the fabled city of Cíbola and the Northwest Passage sometimes appeared as real places. In addition, shores, bays, and rivers connecting coastal settlements were more accurately depicted than the interiors, which Europeans had neither settled nor fully controlled. Early European maps of the New World thus showed a progression in understanding basic geography and topography, and the limits of control over territorial interiors (which served as refuges for many indigenous peoples as well as maroon, or runaway slave, communities).

COLONIAL MAPPING

As colonization followed exploration, early Latin American cartography developed a syncretism in which both American and European world views mixed in maps by both groups, maps meant to make policy as well as represent territory.

Syncretic Cartography.

One European hybrid map is the 1524 woodcut of Tenochtitlán, the Aztec capital on whose ruins Hernán Cortés founded Mexico City. The art historian Barbara Mundy believes the woodcut's sources is one of two maps, now lost, that Cortés sent to Charles V to promote his conquest: a detailed city map of Tenochtitlán of unknown authorship and "a cloth with all the coast painted on

it, and . . . a river which ran to the sea" (Mundy 1998, p. 25). Mundy makes a convincing case that the European representation "translated" Mexica towns into Renaissance villages, showing both how "civilized" and "well-ordered" this society was and its "barbaric" practice of human sacrifice, seen in the city's temple precinct and skull rack, which justified Spain's conquest. A public domain image of this map can be found on the Web site of the History Project at the University of California, Davis; a black-and-white image is also available from the Library of Congress.

In Mexico, caciques (chieftains) and other holders of pre-Columbian documents converted manuscripts of primarily historical or genealogical content into "written maps" by adding text to indicate boundaries, probably for use as evidence in Spanish courts, and continued to use footprints for roads and bell shapes for communities on postconquest maps. Native authors also integrated their own symbols into maps commissioned by Europeans. The most well-known examples of hybrid cartography are the surviving 160 maps (of 191) produced (*relaciones geográficas*) in the 1570s in response to Spain's demands for information from all parts of the Americas, a process dubbed "mapping by questionnaire" (Edwards 1969). The Crown asked for details on demographics, political jurisdictions, languages, physical terrain, and native vegetation, as well as city plans, to provide data for metropolitan scholars including Juan López de Velasco author of the 1571–1574 manuscript *Geografía y descripción universal de las Indias*. Relación geográfica plans of Mexican towns such as Cholula and Culhuacán depict a Spanish grid pattern but add Tlaxcalan glyphs and mountains next to Spanish churches or footprints to indicate pathways, hinting that indigenous informants and authors were as prevalent in this project as in previous and subsequent inquiries into geographic, ethnographic, and natural history.

European Mapping.

As Europeans' control and knowledge of the Americas increased, their methods and techniques came to dominate maps produced for and by colonial and later national governments whose elites shared Western values and education. Spanish, Portuguese, Dutch, British, and French officials in the Americas mapped the towns and land of colonial districts; individuals and town councils commissioned cadastral surveys of private land claims and property; governors asked for maps of proposed new roads; mariners took soundings and charted bays and shores; priests and missionaries issued statistical and geographical information from their parish and bishopric *visitas*; engineers drafted plans of cities and fortresses, and architectural renderings of new buildings accompanied reports to colonial and metropolitan military, commercial, and administrative authorities. Neither the Spanish nor their competitors seem to have expended much energy mapping mining centers, which may have been a strategic decision. European audiences without access to such official maps might turn to books published by the occasional traveler to Spanish or Portuguese America. The Briton Thomas Gage lived as a Dominican friar in Mexico and Central America before returning to England, where he published a critique of Spanish colonialism with maps based on first-hand observations.

Eighteenth-Century Mapping. Eighteenth-century mapmaking continued as part of a larger project of collecting and disseminating encyclopedic information about a region, and as well as extending power over territory by placing particular regions, landmarks, and borders, on an imperial power's map. Military engineers and civilians with training in mathematics, astronomy, and geometry mapped to answer scientific questions. If Latin America did not develop novel cartographic science, it once again proved important to its advancement. Famous maps emerged from surveys done by scientists such as Charles de la Condamine and his associates who traveled to the Audiencia of Quito in 1736 to determine the length of a degree of latitude, and so settle the question of the shape of the earth. Spanish experts on the expedition, Jorge Juan and Antonio de Ulloa, contributed not only scientific measurements but commentary on problems with colonial society. The most famous cartographer of late colonial Spanish America was, however, the Prussian naturalist Alexander von Humboldt, who explored South America, Cuba, and Mexico with French naturalist and illustrator Aimé Bonpland from 1799 to 1804. Like sixteenth-century chroniclers, Humboldt carried not just scientific instruments but "sacks of verbiage" with which to inscribe peoples and places on maps, in copious illustrations, tables, and charts, and in his multivolume travel narratives describing political, social, economic, and cultural as well as geographic,

climatological, and biological elements (Burnett 2000, p. 94). Among his other contributions to geographic knowledge, Humboldt was the first to suggest that the Americas and Africa might once have been joined, and his four-month, 1725-mile trip down the Orinoco led to confirmation of the communication of the Orinoco and Amazon River water systems. In a way, Humboldt's work extended the cartographic syncretism of the early colonial cartogra-phers, as he relied on local knowledge as well as his own scientific investigation; however, he drew not from Aztec lords but Creole elites.

Spanish naval officers, including Alejandro Malaspina and José de Bustamante, continued to map for political purposes as part of imperial cartography's emphasis on defending claims to poorly explored areas, such as the Pacific Northwest and South America's interior, which had dense forests, difficult mountains, and challenging climates, and lacked easily exploitable natural resources and labor pools. As Europeans moved inland, notional boundaries, such as the 1494 division of Spanish and Portuguese South America under the Treaty of Tordesillas, came to need real markers. As a result, after 1750 and 1770 treaty attempts proved fruitless; the Portuguese and Spanish mounted joint expeditions starting in 1778 to determine the boundaries between their South American colonies.

THE NATIONAL PERIOD

By the early nineteenth century, as most Spanish and Portuguese territories became independent of their European metropolises, the new national governments harnessed cartography (much as did other governments of the time) to fill in blanks, set boundaries, catalogue natural and human resources, and project an image of the legitimacy and authority of their states for both internal and external audiences.

Defining Countries. Who mapped in this period? National governments worked assiduously to create maps that would define their territorial boundaries in what historian Raymond Craib has called "state fixations": attempts to control "fugitive landscapes" in which competing forces—individual landowners, village elders, military officials, tax agents—fought over boundaries, water or drilling rights, and other issues. Such mapping projects continued the colonial tradition of seeking to improve knowledge and accuracy of representation of topographic features, and resulted in locally authored atlases, such as Miguel Rivera Maestre's 1832 atlas of Guatemala's seven departments and a national map and Antonio García Cubas's 1858 General Map of Mexico. Maps were compiled using information from expeditions and surveys, colonial records, and even vignettes from nineteenth-century travel accounts, to provide not just a topography but a more complex physical and political geography that incorporated distant and sometimes autonomous populations into the new states, fixing them on the map and, symbolically, under the control of national elites, while providing a catalogue of local customs, costumes, products, flora, and fauna. Agustín Codazzi, an Italian-born military officer and engineer, was hired in the 1830s by Venezuela with a mandate that shows just how closely the new republics correlated having an accurate map with good governance. Codazzi was to "facilitate military operations, further the knowledge of provincial limits, determine what the exact tributary contributions should be, aid in the development of agriculture, facilitate the opening and construction of roadways, help in the drainage of lakes and swamps and facilitate the navigation of rivers" (Del Castillo 2004, n. 5).

International Borders. Marking national and international boundaries motivated a significant part of nineteenth-century Latin American cartography, because the outer limits of the colonial administrative districts forming most present-day Latin American states were often unclear. For example, Rivera Maestre's 1832 Guatemala atlas left its border with Mexico undefined while claiming parts of Honduras far beyond colonial boundaries. Codazzi later directed Colombia's Chorographic Commission (1849–1859); his recommendations for where to set the country's borders in the Caquetá region with Ecuador and Brazil largely hold. In general, as in the case that settled the Honduran-Nicaraguan border in 1906 using (among other sources) nineteen German, Dutch, and British maps dated from 1597 to 1777, historical maps of varying accuracy were called on to support both sides. Such disputes also prompted new surveys. The British government sent Robert Schomburgk to Guyana in the 1830s to explore the colony's backlands, as Venezuela, Brazil, and British colonial authorities disputed its national boundary (much as independent Guyana and Venezuela still do, despite U.S. arbitration in 1899).

Schomburgk, like Codazzi, used the traverse survey that Humboldt favored, which allowed a small group to chart altitude and latitude and longitude positions, transcribe their route and sight lines, and later create a map that provided detail on the colony's rivers, mountains, and territory. The trigonometric survey technique, while more accurate, required unfeasibly larger and more expensive teams of surveyors.

Nineteenth-century conflicts created additional cartographic demands, from the War of the Pacific to the Mexican-American War. After the latter, a Mexico Boundary Commission demarcated the border after it had been described and agreed upon in the 1848 Treaty of Guadalupe Hidalgo. Changing riverbeds and water rights disputes led to the creation of a permanent body, the International Boundary Commission (1889; as of 1944, the International Boundary and Water Commission), to address disagreements and preserve the boundary at the Rio Grande and Colorado River. As the post-independence civil wars largely drew to a close by the late nineteenth century, governments institutionalized national cartography by creating geographical and statistical institutes charged with mapping political boundaries, populations, mineral resources, and road and river systems; they also established military institutes that mapped for military purposes, with cartographers trained in U.S. and European techniques and schools. Mexico's Geographic Exploration Commission, created by Porfirio Díaz, was one such institution. Business, academic, and leisure travelers, too, grew in numbers and supplemented official maps with cartography about themes that interested them: plans of Maya ruins, geological surveys of valleys with mining potential, charts locating ethnic groups or volcano chains.

TWENTIETH-CENTURY MAPPING

Twentieth- and twenty-first century Latin-American cartography has been affected by changing technologies and international organizations. After World War II, aerial photography enabled cartographers to combine ground observations and remote sensing to increase the accuracy of maps, and in the 1970s and 1980s computers allowed databases of information to be stored in geographic information systems (GIS) in which there are multiple ways to store, analyze, and display georeferenced information. These techniques have resulted in more complete and accurate maps produced by government agencies and private companies. By the 1940s many states had established national geographic institutes, eventually combining cartographic offices with other statistics-gathering agencies to create institutions such as Brazil's Institution Brasileiro de Geografia e Estatística (IBGE, 1937) and Mexico's INEGI (Instituto Nacional de Estadística, Geografía, e Informática, 1980), which produce not only maps but demographic and other important population and economic statistics. Equally important, America's nations created regional organizations which promoted multinational and regional geographical and cartographic advances. The twenty-two-member Instituto Panamericano de Geografía e Historia (1928) based in Mexico City became a specialized agency of the Organization of American States (1948) in 1949, and has spent eighty years funding, promoting, and coordinating cartographic, geographic, geophysical, and historical studies.

Maps and Travel. The twentieth century also produced two relatively novel kinds of mapping projects. First, starting in the early part of the century, there was a boom in mapping for business travelers and tourists who could choose road, rail, or air travel to visit modern cities, ancient ruins, sunny beaches, or folkloric villages. National touring clubs promoted the travel business and developed specialized maps and guidebooks for a new group of map consumers, travelers who scheduled their own flights and hired their own cars to visit formerly difficult-to-access places on newly paved roads. In Mexico, the result was the *Guia Roja* series, and in Brazil, the *Guía Rodivaria* of the Río de Janeiro branch of the national auto club. In the United States, Rand McNally and General Drafting, among other companies, provided maps for foreigners planning driving tours on parts of the Pan-American Highway. Such maps, in addition to including practical information such as distances and driving times, might include icons of sombreros or happy tourists throwing beach balls in water, emphasizing the tourists' interest in Latin America as a place for pleasure and entertainment, and one in which natural wonders—whether agricultural export items or caves and rivers to explore—abounded. In the early twenty-first century it is not unusual for a tourist center such as Antigua, Guatemala, to distribute maps of its colonial center ringed with advertisements for the hotels, restaurants, and boutiques that underpin the local economy.

Indigenous Knowledge and Cartography. Until the late twentieth century, state and private mapping followed late colonial and early national precedent, often ignoring indigenous knowledges and methods of representing or marking space. More recently, the political success (with international support) of indigenous movements has resulted in the second mapmaking novelty, indigenous participation in cartographic projects from Belize to Panama and from Venezuela to Guyana and Brazil to secure land titles, sometimes in coordination with conservationists. Quechua- and Aymara-speakers living near Lake Titicaca use maps that blend both Western and Andean representational precepts in negotiations with Peruvian officials, and there are foreign-funded GIS labs in both Bolivia and Perú. In the early 1990s, Colombia launched a *mapas parlantes* (speaking maps) project, intended to recover and promote history as recalled and spoken by indigenous peoples. Activist geographers have fostered such projects. Peter Herlihy and Bjorn Sletto, among others, have returned to a syncretic cartographic tradition and work with native groups using new technologies, including GIS, to allow these groups to create their own representations of the territory they occupy. In the Honduran *La Mosquitia* region (the Mosquito Coast), Herlihy developed a form of "participative cartography" that invited Garifuna, Miskito, Pech, and other indigenous populations to give interviews to help "ascertain their popular geographical conceptions" in the 1990s. In 2001, sponsored by the Honduran and German governments, the same team worked on "participatory research mapping" to develop a zoning and management plan for Central America's oldest biosphere reserve, "transforming cognitive knowledge of local peoples into standard maps and data, seeking to catalyze partnerships for conservation" (Herlihy 2001).

ART AND CARTOGRAPHY

Cartographers, official and unofficial, were not the only authors of influential maps of Latin America. Artists have used maps across the centuries to create and display knowledge and challenge power. In the colonial period, portraits of viceroys and explorers might locate the subject standing next to or seated at a table on which a map of newly conquered or visited territory symbolized control. In 1943 Uruguayan artist Joaquín Torres-García inverted a map of South America by flipping the continent so that Patagonia and the "South Pole" were at the top, drawing in white on a black background to emphasize the oppositional politics of his message. Nestling the map in between a sun and moon that appear to be derived from Inca iconography, the "upside-down" continent seems to propose a world in which North America and Mexico are not even on the map. Why? Some argue that the image promoted a Latin American art with indigenous as well as European roots, one intended to displace Northern artistic production with Southern creativity. Such a map, combining scientific and artistic aspects, is a reminder that cartography of and from this region is part of a long tradition of using representations of physical space to claim and contest power.

See also **America; Bonpland, Aimé Jacques; Codazzi, Agustín; Colonialism; Columbus, Christopher; Cortés, Hernán; Díaz, Porfirio; Explorers and Exploration: Brazil; Explorers and Exploration: Spanish America; Gage, Thomas; Guadalupe Hidalgo, Treaty of (1848); Herrera y Tordesillas, Antonio de; Humboldt, Alexander von; Malaspina, Alejandro; Mexico, Wars and Revolutions: Mexican-American War; Rivera Maestre, Miguel; Torres García, Joaquín; Ulloa, Antonio de; Vespucci, Amerigo; War of the Pacific.**

BIBLIOGRAPHY

Burnett, D. Graham. *Masters of All They Surveyed: Exploration, Geography, and a British El Dorado.* Chicago: University of Chicago Press, 2000.

Butzer, Karl W. "From Columbus to Acosta: Science, Geography and the New World." *Annals of the Association of American Geographers* 82, no. 3 (1992): 543–565.

Chapin, Mac, Zachary Lamb, and Bill Threlkeld. "Mapping Indigenous Lands." *Annual Review of Anthropology* 34 (2005): 619–638.

Craib, Raymond B. *Cartographic Mexico: A History of State Fixations and Fugitive Landscapes.* Durham, NC: Duke University Press, 2004.

Del Castillo, Lina. "The Science of Nation-Building: Agustín Codazzi's Scientific Expeditions and the Construction of Political Power in Venezuela and Colombia, 1830–1861." Panel, "Reading Technology, Re-reading History" at the Latin American Studies Association, October 2004, Las Vegas, NV.

Edwards, Clinton R. "Mapping by Questionnaire: An Early Spanish Attempt to Determine New World Geographical Positions" *Imago Mundi* 23 (1969): 17–28.

Gartner, William Gustav. "Mapmaking in the Central Andes." In *Cartography in the Traditional African, American, Arctic, Australian Societies,* edited by David Woodward and G. Malcolm Lewis (Vol. 2, Book 3 of *The History of Cartography,* edited by David Woodward and J. B. Harley). Chicago: University of Chicago Press, 1998.

Hardoy, Jorge E. "Urban Cartography in Latin America during the Colonial Period." *Latin American Research Review* 18, no. 3 (1983): 127–134.

Harley, J. Brian. "Silences and Secrecy: The Hidden Agenda of Cartography in Early Modern Europe." *Imago Mundi* 40 (1988): 57–76.

Harley, J. Brian. *Maps and the Columbian Encounter.* Milwaukee: Golda Meir Library, University of Wisconsin–Milwaukee, 1990.

Herlihy, Peter H. "Indigenous and Ladino Peoples of the Río Plátano Biosphere Reserve, Honduras." In *Endangered Peoples of Latin America: Struggles to Survive and Thrive,* edited by Susan C. Stonich, 100–120. Westport, CT: Greenwood Press, 2001.

Instituto Brasileiro de Geografia e Estatística. Online at http://www.ibge.gov.br/.

Instituto Nacional de Estadística, Geografía e Informática (Mexico) Available from http://www.inegi.mx.

Instituto Panamericano de Geografía e Historia. Available from http://www.ipgh.org/.

Lewis, G. Malcolm, ed. *Cartographic Encounters: Perspectives on Native American Mapmaking and Map Use.* Chicago: University of Chicago Press, 1998.

Library of Congress, Hispanic Division. "The Portuguese Role in Exploring and Mapping the New World." Available from http://www.loc.gov/rr/hispanic/portam/role.html.

Library of Congress, Kislak Collection. Online exhibition. Available from http://www.loc.gov/exhibits/kislak/kislak-exhibit.html.

Mundy, Barbara E. "Mesoamerican Cartography." In *Cartography in the Traditional African, American, Arctic, Australian Societies,* edited by David Woodward and G. Malcolm Lewis (Vol. 2, Book 3 of *The History of Cartography,* edited by David Woodward and J. B. Harley). Chicago: University of Chicago Press, 1998.

Mundy, Barbara E. *The Mapping of New Spain: Indigenous Cartography and the Maps of the Relaciones Geográficas.* Chicago: University of Chicago Press, 1996, 2000.

Mundy, Barbara E. "Mapping the Aztec Capital: The 1524 Nuremberg Map of Tenochtitlan, Its Sources and Meanings." *Imago Mundi* 50 (1998): 11–33.

Padrón, Ricardo. "Mapping Plus Ultra: Cartography, Space and Hispanic Modernity." *Representations* 79 (2002), 28–60.

Planos de ciudades iberoamericanas y Filipinas existentes en el Archivo de Indias. 2 Vols. Madrid: Instituto de Estudios de Administración Local, 1951.

Rebert, Paula. *La Gran Linea: Mapping the United States-Mexico Boundary, 1849–1857.* Austin: University of Texas Press, 2001.

Reinhartz, Dennis, and Gerald D. Saxon, eds. *Mapping and Empire: Soldier-Engineers on the Southwestern Frontier.* Austin: University of Texas Press, 2005.

Sletto, Bjorn. "Mapping the Gran Sabana." *Américas* (Nov.–Dec. 2005): 6–13.

Stocks, Anthony. "Too Much for Too Few: Problems of Indigenous Land Rights in Latin America." *Annual Review of Anthropology* 34 (2005): 85–104.

University of California, Davis. The History Project. "U.S. History Images." Available from http://historyproject.ucdavis.edu/khapp.php.

University of Texas at Austin, Benson Library. *Relaciones Geográficas* Collection. Online at http://www.lib.utexas.edu/benson/rg/.

Whitehead, Neil L. "Indigenous Cartography in Lowland South America and the Caribbean." In *Cartography in the Traditional African, American, Arctic, Australian Societies,* edited by David Woodward and G. Malcolm Lewis (Vol. 2, Book 3 of *The History of Cartography* edited by David Woodward and J. B. Harley). Chicago: University of Chicago Press, 1998.

Woodward, David, and G. Malcolm Lewis. *Cartography in the Traditional African, American, Arctic, Australian Societies.* Vol. 2, Book 3 of *The History of Cartography,* edited by David Woodward and J. B. Harley. Chicago: University of Chicago Press, 1998.

JORDANA DYM

THE SPANISH BORDERLANDS

Many precontact cultures in Latin America had concepts of space and methods for representing that space visually. The Europeans who came to the region brought with them new techniques.

Spanning the 300-year colonial era, European mapping of the Spanish Borderlands began with efforts to understand the discovery of the New World, advanced with attempts to define competing claims, and culminated in surveys to determine international boundaries.

The first cartographic efforts, accomplished with early technology, sometimes militated against accuracy. Latitude determination, with astrolabe or cross-staff, was imprecise; there was no dependable means of computing longitude. However crude, the work

was significant and influential. As data accrued from the early discoveries, King Ferdinand designated the Casa De Contratación in Seville as the repository for geographical data. Cosmographers there kept a master chart, called the *padrón real.* As reports came in, cartographers drafted the data into finished maps. Crown policy kept this knowledge from other nations, and each copy of the *padrón real* was destroyed when superseded. Hence, mapmakers of other nations, using whatever Spanish data were at their disposal, shaped Europeans' concepts of the Spanish discoveries.

Following Juan Ponce De León's discovery of Florida in 1513, Spanish North America was mapped in three chronological stages: (1) the Gulf coast, (2) the Atlantic coast from Florida northward, and (3) the Pacific coast.

From a 1519 voyage dispatched by Francisco de Garay, governor of Jamaica, came the first crude map sketch of the Gulf of Mexico. This expedition, commanded by Alonso Álvarez De Pineda, explored the coast from Ponce's Florida landing to Hernán Cortés's new settlement of Villa Rica on the Veracruz coast. It discovered the mouth of the Mississippi River (named Río del Espíritu Santo) and proved there was no strait linking the Gulf with the Pacific. The "Pineda sketch," preserved in the Archivo General de Indias in Seville, was a cartographic cornerstone. It was the first European map to portray the Gulf based on actual exploration. Its Gulf configuration, with data from Atlantic coast explorations north of Florida by Lucas Vázquez De Ayllón's pilots in 1520–1521 and by Estevão Gomes in 1525, enabled cosmographers to present a portion of the continent in recognizable outline. It aided especially the 1529 world maps by Diogo Ribeiro, chief cosmographer in the Casa de Contratación, which became prototypes.

Not until the coastlines were roughly established did maps begin to show significant interior detail. The so-called De Soto map, found among the papers of the cosmographer Alonso de Santa Cruz about 1572, was the first to supply information on rivers and native towns. Although most of the information was derived from Hernando de Soto's expedition (1539–1543), the map also drew from other explorers: Ponce de León and Vasquez de Ayllón in the East and Alvar Núñez Cabeza De Vaca and Francisco Vázquez de Coronado in the

Southwest. It influenced Borderlands cartography for half a century.

Influenced by Coronado's march onto the Great Plains, voyages around 1540, including those of Francisco de Ulloa, Hernando de Alarcón, and Juan Rodríguez Cabrillo, focused on the Pacific Coast. Domingo del Castillo, a pilot with both Ulloa and Alarcón, drew a map showing the results of these two voyages, which traced 2,000 miles of coastline, proved California was not an island, and discovered the Colorado River. By 1570 Abraham Ortelius, with his landmark *Americae sive novi orbis nova descriptio,* was able to portray North America to its far limits, using the Mercator projection introduced the previous year.

Maps of the seventeenth century reflected little new knowledge of the Borderlands. Spanish secrecy continued to deny the most accurate data to cartographic centers in other European countries. The French explorer René-Robert La Salle, in descending the Mississippi River from Illinois to the Gulf of Mexico in 1682, had no reliable map to guide him. The lack of geographical data and faulty cartography have been blamed for his subsequent landing in Texas while seeking the mouth of the Mississippi from the Gulf.

The Spaniards' three-year search for La Salle's Gulf Coast colony constituted a rebirth of exploration. The pilot Juan Enríquez Barroto, on a 1686–1687 search voyage that circumnavigated the Gulf, mapped the shoreline and named its features. Although his maps have been lost, his diary survives, revealing the source of many place names appearing on a host of non-Spanish maps, including those of the French geographer Guillaume Delisle.

Delisle and his father, Claude, brought to the mapping of America a level of scholarship not previously attained, as is evident in the 1703 *carte du Mexique et de la Floride.* This joint effort utilized sources from Pánfilo de Narváez and Cabeza de Vaca to Louisiana founder Pierre Le Moyne d'Iberville. Delisle's 1718 *Carte de la Louisiane et du cours du Mississippi* utilized information from explorers such as Louis Juchereau de Saint-Denis and small-area maps like those of François Le Maire.

In the Far West, Jesuit Father Eusebio Kino settled, with his 1702 map, confusion that since Ulloa's time had made California an island. Later in the eighteenth century, military inspections of New Spain's interior provinces brought a new dimension to Borderlands cartography, notably the series of six maps by Francisco Álvarez Barreiro, engineer with Pedro de Rivera's inspection team (1724–1727), and the 1771 map by Nicolás de Lafora, engineer with the Marqués de Rubí's visit of 1766–1768. Both these examples extended from the Gulf of California to Louisiana.

With the end of the Seven Years' War in 1763, both England and Spain faced the need to explore and map their new territories. Thus came into play the work of cartographers in English service such as George Gauld, Philip Pittman, and Bernard Romans along the Gulf coast and the Mississippi.

A lack of accurate coastal mapping was recognized by Bernardo de Gálvez, campaigning against the British on the Gulf Coast during the American Revolution. Having reclaimed the Floridas, Gálvez sent José de Evía to explore and map the Gulf coast from Florida to Tampico, in 1785–1786. Evía's work served as the basis for subsequent maps by the Spanish Hydrographic Service and contributed to José Antonio Pichardo's 1811 map of New Mexico and adjacent regions, meant to be used in the settlement of the Louisiana-Texas boundary dispute. The Hydrographic Office charts, in turn, provided the Gulf of Mexico configuration for Alexander von Humboldt's map of New Spain (1811). Zebulon M. Pike's *A Map of the Internal Provinces of New Spain,* based in part on his own military reconnaissance, and Aaron Arrowsmith's *A New Map of Mexico,* both showing the western Borderlands, drew on Humboldt's data.

Philadelphia publisher John Melish facilitated the eventual division of lands between the United States and Mexico under the 1819 Adams-Onís Treaty with his 1816 *Map of the United States.* In its six sheets this map epitomized the state of cartographic knowledge as Florida passed to the United States, and Spain, in 1821, yielded the rest of the Borderlands to independent Mexico.

Anglo-American colonization of Mexican Texas brought forth maps by Stephen F. Austin (1830) and David H. Burr (1833), showing Texas and adjacent Mexican states, north to the Arkansas River. Pertinent to the question of annexation of Texas to the United States, after it gained independence from Mexico, was William H. Emory's 1844

Map of Texas and the Countries Adjacent, which embraced the territory west to the Pacific Ocean.

Texas was annexed in 1845, and the Treaty of Guadalupe Hidalgo, ending the Mexican-American War, also gave the United States title to the present states of Arizona, California, Nevada, New Mexico, and Utah. The map used in the treaty negotiations was John Disturnell's *Mapa de los Estados Unidos de Méjico* (1847). Following the treaty, jointly appointed commissions from Mexico and U.S. conducted surveys that yielded new maps and corrected Disturnell's errors. Together, the commissions significantly expanded geographic knowledge of the borderlands region and influenced future cooperation on bilateral boundary issues, from the Gadsen Treaty of 1853 into the twenty-first century.

See also **America; Cartography: Overview; Garay, Francisco de; Mayan Epigraphy; Ponce de León, Juan.**

BIBLIOGRAPHY

Buisseret, David. *Monarchs, Ministers, and Maps: The Emergence of Cartography as a Tool of Government in Early Modern Europe.* Chicago: University of Chicago Press, 1992.

Cumming, William Pratt, R. A. Skelton, and D. B. Quinn, *The Discovery of North America* (1972).

Delanglez, Jean. *El Río del Espíritu Santo: An Essay on the Cartography of the Gulf Coast and the Adjacent Territory During the Sixteenth and Seventeenth Centuries* (1945).

Evia, José de, and Jack David Lazarus Holmes. *José de Evia y sus reconocimientos del Golfo de México, 1783–1796 (diarios, cartas, explicaciones, descripciones, planos y mapas).* Madrid: Ediciones J. Porrúa Turanzas, 1968.

Martin, James C., and Robert Sidney Martin, *Maps of Texas and the Southwest, 1513–1900* (1984).

Mignolo, Walter G. *The Darker Side of the Renaissance: Literacy, Territoriality, and Colonization.* 2nd edition. Ann Arbor: University of Michigan Press, 2003.

Mundy, Barbara E. *The Mapping of New Spain: Indigenous Cartography and the Maps of the Relaciones Geográficas.* Chicago: University of Chicago Press, 1996.

Rebert, Paula. *La Gran Línea: Mapping the United States–Mexico Boundary, 1849–1857.* Austin: University of Texas Press, 2001.

Reinhartz, Dennis, and Gerald D. Saxon. *The Mapping of the Entradas into the Greater Southwest.* Norman: University of Oklahoma Press, 1998.

Roa-de-la Carrera, Cristián Andrés. *Histories of Infamy: Francisco López de Gómara and the Ethics of Spanish Imperialism.* Boulder: University Press of Colorado, 2005.

Ross, Kurt, ed. *Codex Mendoza: Aztec Manuscript.* Fribourg, Switzerland: Productions Liber SA, 1978, 1983.

Schwartz, Seymour J., and Ralph E. Ehrenbert, *The Mapping of America* (1980).

Taliaferro, Henry G., Jane A. Kenamore, and Uli Haller, *Cartographic Sources in the Rosenberg Library* (1988), esp. pp. 3–36.

Weddle, Robert S. *Spanish Sea: The Gulf of Mexico in North American Discovery, 1500–1685* (1985), pp. 103–104, 232–233.

Weddle, Robert S. *The French Thorn: Rival Explorers in the Spanish Sea, 1682–1762* (1991).

ROBERT S. WEDDLE

CARTOLA

CARTOLA (1908–1980). The Brazilian composer, guitarist, and singer Cartola—real name Angenor de Oliveira—is considered one of the greatest samba composers of the twentieth century. Born in Rio de Janeiro on October 11, 1908, he helped found the Mangueira samba school in 1928 and for many years was its principal composer. He experienced success as a songwriter in the 1930s, writing hits for Francisco Alves and Carmen Miranda, among others. During the 1940s Cartola disappeared from the musical scene, leading to speculation that he was dead until he was rediscovered in 1956 washing cars in Ipanema. During the 1960s he and his wife Zica ran Zicartola, a restaurant in downtown Rio that served as an important meeting place for both older samba singers and young bossa nova artists. Cartola recorded his first LP at the age of sixty-six in 1974 and made three more before his death on November 30, 1980. His many compositions include "As Rosas Não Falam," "O Sol Nascerá," "Acontece," "O Mundo é um Moinho," and "Alvorada."

See also **Alves, Francisco; Bossa Nova; Miranda, Carmen; Music: Popular Music and Dance; Samba; Samba Schools.**

BIBLIOGRAPHY

Autran, Margarida. "Samba, artigo de consumo nacional." In *Anos 70: Ainda sob a tempestade,* ed. Adauto Novaes. Rio de Janeiro: Aeroplano, Editora Senac Rio, 2005.

Barboza da Silva, Marília T., and Arthur L. de Oliveira Filho. *Cartola: Os Tempos Idos.* Rio de Janeiro: FUNARTE/ Instituto Nacional de Música, Divisão de Música Popular, 1983.

Marcondes, Marcos Antônio, ed. *Enciclopédia da Música Brasileira: Popular, Erudita e Folclórica,* 2nd edition. São Paulo: Art Editora, Publifolha, 1998.

ANDREW M. CONNELL

CARTOONS IN LATIN AMERICA.

The history of Latin American cartoons offers a blend of immense popularity, mystery, and intense drama; state oppressiveness; economic perseverance; imitation; and, of course, the usual characteristics of comic art, such as high levels of commercialization and corporatism.

In Mexico comic books were once so popular that a few titles were published daily in the 1940s (one of them, *Pepín,* eight times per week). Though cartoonists worldwide have suffered at the hands of the authorities, in parts of Latin America the perils of drawing comics and cartoons have been grave. Take the 1977 "disappearance," engineered by Argentine government officials, of comics publisher/writer Héctor Oesterheld and his four daughters, two of whom were pregnant; or the plight of Rius (Eduardo del Río), the famous Mexican artist of social documentary comics, who lost the rights, by order of the president, to his popular *Los supermachos* comic book, and in 1969 was taken to the mountains by police to be executed (he was spared). Other examples of government interference in cartooning in Latin America are abundant, though perhaps not as mystery- or drama-laden.

Perseverance also has marked Latin American cartooning, the most exemplary case being that of Cuba, where cartoonists "reinvented" the genre long before that tendency became fashionable in the computer age. Because of the hardships caused by the U.S.-orchestrated economic embargo and later the "special period" at the dawn of the 1990s, Cubans generally, and cartoonists in particular, have become masters at coping. Severe shortages of paper, inks, and printing equipment forced cartoonists to rethink cartooning. One cartoonist made inks out of plant roots and juices, others converted to ceramics, paper cutouts, and other mediums, and the humor

magazine *Palante,* for a while, stopped printing and instead appeared as a television program. In Chile during Salvador Allende's short presidency (1970–1973), the comic book *La firme* persisted in providing an alternative perspective to the capitalistic and unsympathetic viewpoints of the Disney comics very popular in Latin America. Though *La firme* survived the harsh criticism of Chile's right-wing press and the United States' overthrow of Allende, its effectiveness gradually diminished.

EARLY FORMS OF CARTOONING

Precursors of cartoons include the codices and the drawings on plates and vessels of Late Classic Mayan culture (600–900), the latter showing that the Maya were capable of cartoon-style depictions of direction, perspective, gesturing, framing, motion, sound, and smell. Contemporary Latin American cartoon history has several sources. Illustrations on Mexican cigar and cigarette boxes and premiums in the 1880s told stories in sequential comic-strip fashion, and handbills appearing in Mexico, Cuba, and Colombia during the first half of the nineteenth century satirized political figures.

Satirical periodicals carrying cartoons were also prevalent. Early examples include *El toro* (1826–1832), *La orquestra* (1861–1874) and *El ahuizote* of Mexico; *La caricature* (1896) of Venezuela; *El zancudo* (1890s), *El gráfico* (1910–1941), *Cromos* (1916), and *Bogotá cómico* (later *La semana cómico,* 1917–1925) of Colombia; *El esquife* (1813–1814) and *El moro muza* (1859–1875) of Cuba; *El negro Timoteo* (1890–1898) of Uruguay; and Argentina's *Caras y caretas,* distributed throughout Latin America by 1912. Most were critical of government, except for *El ahuizote,* which successfully promoted Porfirio Díaz's campaign for the Mexican presidency.

COMIC STRIPS AND COMIC BOOKS

Comic strips are largely a twentieth-century phenomenon in most of the world, but in Brazil, Angelo Agostini drew *As aventuras de Nhô Quim ou impressões de uma viagem à Corte* beginning in 1869, making it one of the world's first comic strips. U.S. newspaper comic strips had a huge influence in Latin America after 1900, as some newspapers used *dominicales* (translations of U.S. strips) or created their own characters adapted from or imitative of those of North America. But the region also had its own very popular strips, including *Patoruzu*, created in 1928 by Dante Quinterno in Argentina; Mexico's *Don Lupito* (1903); and Cuba's *El bobo*. As elsewhere, many strips featured children, animals, families, bums, fools, and politicians. Magazines too were home to Latin American strips; prominent among them were *O Tico-Tico* (1905) in Brazil and *El tony* (1928) and *Rico tipo* (1944) in Argentina.

Latin America was one of the world's first developers of comic books. In Brazil, *Suplemento juvenil* reprinted North American comic strips as a tabloid, first weekly in 1934, and then thrice weekly. An indigenous comic industry started soon after when the publishing houses Editora-Brasil America Ltda (EBAL, 1945) and Editora Abril (1950) were established exclusively to produce comic books. Mexican comic books evolved from the *dominicales*, and in the beginning all were published or otherwise allied with large daily newspapers. At the peak of comics' popularity in 1943, one-half million comics were purchased daily. Publishers and comics creators outdid one another in employing promotional gimmicks to attract readers.

From the 1950s through 1970s cartooning and comics thrived in the region, producing world-renowned cartoonists such as Argentina's Alberto Breccia, Roberto Fontanarrosa, Quino (Joaquín Salvador Lavado), Landrú (Juan Carlos Colombres), and Guillermo Mordillo; Brazil's Mauricio de Sousa, Ziraldo Alves, Pinto, and Henfil (Henrique de Souza Filho); Cuba's Manuel, Santiago "Chago" Armada, René de la Nuez, Carlucho, and Orestes Suárez; Honduras' Hermes Bertrand; Nicaragua's Róger Sánchez Flores; and Mexico's Rius, Gabriel Vargas, Antonio Gutiérrez, Yolanda Vargas Dulché, and Abel Quezada. Equally famous globally were many Latin American comic-book and comic-strip titles and characters. A few among the many that stand out are those featuring female characters, such as *Mafalda*, Quino's precocious little girl who represents Argentina's bourgeoisie lifestyle; Mauricio de Sousa's *Mônica*, which describes the antics of an irascible girl that its creator fashioned into a publishing and merchandising empire; Vladimir ("Vladdo") Flórez's *Aleida*, a frivolous, petty woman popular in Venezuela; Argentina's *Flopi Bach*, a strip by Argentineans Ernesto García Seijas and Carlos Trillo that

deals with raw sexuality, and *Maitena*, the work of Maitena Burundarena, also of Argentina, focusing on women in their twenties through middle age.

CONTEMPORARY SITUATION

All types of cartooning have remained popular throughout Latin America. Even though comic books have had their heyday, they continue to be a main form of reading material in the region. Mexico is considered one of the world's only comics cultures (along with Japan), with large numbers of comic books and huge audiences. At one time in the 1980s, 60 percent of all paper used in Mexico went to publishing 159 comics titles. Political cartoons continue to be hard-hitting in much of Latin America, despite abrupt changes in power, totalitarian regimes, fascist ideologies of state and church, and augmented corporate takeovers of mass media that have made cartooning difficult and even hazardous. Political cartoonists and their periodicals often have had to contend with government oppression, the results of which have been closure of media, censorship, arrest of cartoonists, or, as in the cases of Oesterheld and Rius, worse penalties. Control of cartooning is also exercised through oligopolistic ownership of the media, especially in Brazil and Mexico, and corporate and state economic and other tie-ins. Despite formidable obstacles, cartooning survives as an important component of Latin American popular culture.

See also **Journalism; Journalism in Mexico.**

BIBLIOGRAPHY

Hinds, Harold E. Jr., and Charles M. Tatum. *Not Just for Children: The Mexican Comic Book in the Late 1960s and 1970s.* Westport, CT: Greenwood Press, 1992.

Lent, John A., ed. "Latin American Comic Art: A Symposium." *International Journal of Comic Art* 3 (Fall 2001): 1–137.

Lent, John A., ed. *Cartooning in Latin America.* Cresskill, NJ: Hampton Press, 2005.

Rubenstein, Anne. *Bad Language, Naked Ladies, and Other Threats to the Nation: A Political History of Comic Books in Mexico.* Durham, NC: Duke University Press, 1998.

Tamayo, Évora, Juan Blas Rodríguez, and Oscar Hurtado. *Más de cien años de humor político*, tom 01. Santíago de Cuba: Editorial Oriente, 1984.

JOHN A. LENT

CARVAJAL, LUIS DE (1566–1596).
Luis de Carvajal (*b.* 1566; *d.* 8 December 1596), prominent crypto-Jew (secret Jew) in Mexico. Carvajal was born in Benavente, Castile, and studied at the Jesuit school in Medina del Campo. In 1580 he and his family immigrated to Mexico at the invitation of Luis's uncle, Luis de Carvajal y de la Cueva, conquistador and governor of Nuevo León, who was unaware that his relatives secretly practiced Judaism. Carvajal tried his hand at a variety of trades, raising sheep, and working as an itinerant merchant. The Carvajals established extensive contacts with other crypto-Jews and became the cynosure of the Inquisition's first major campaign against Judaizers. On 9 May 1589 agents of the Inquisition arrested Carvajal and his mother. While in prison, Carvajal had several dreams that convinced him that God had chosen him to sustain the Jewish community in Mexico. He therefore feigned repentance, formally abjured his heresy, and was reconciled to the Catholic Church. But he continued to practice Judaism in secret and persuaded other members of his family to do the same.

While serving in the Colegio de Santiago de Tlatelolco as part of his penance, he used the library to further his knowledge of the Old Testament and correct Jewish practice. In early 1595 Carvajal wrote his *Memoirs,* a mystical autobiography in which he referred to himself as Joseph Lumbroso ("the Enlightened"). Shortly after, he was again arrested by the Inquisition and condemned as a relapsed heretic. He and several other family members were burned at the stake in the century's largest auto-da-fé. According to some reports, Carvajal made a last-minute conversion to Christianity and was garroted before being burned.

See also **Inquisition: Spanish America; Jews.**

BIBLIOGRAPHY

Luis De Carvajal, *The Enlightened: The Writings of Luis de Carvajal, el Mozo,* edited and translated by Seymour B. Liebman (1967).

Additional Bibliography

Cohen, Martin A. *The Martyr: The Story of a Secret Jew and the Mexican Inquisition in the Sixteenth Century.* Albuquerque: University of New Mexico Press, 2001.

Costigan, Lúcia Helena Santiago. "Manifestaciones del judaísmo y 'colonización de lo imaginario' en Iberoamérica durante la primera fase moderna del imperio español." *Revista Iberoamericana* 66: 191 (April-June 2000): 299–308.

R. DOUGLAS COPE

CARVALHO, ANTÔNIO DE ALBUQUERQUE COELHO DE (1655–1725).
Antônio de Albuquerque Coelho de Carvalho (*b.* 1655; *d.* 25 April 1725), Portuguese colonial administrator. Born in Lisbon and baptized on 14 September 1655, Carvalho was the son of the governor of Maranhão (1667–1671) of the same name; the nephew of Feliciano Coelho de Carvalho, the first lord-proprietor of the captaincy of Camutá (also known as Cametá); the grandson of Francisco Coelho de Carvalho, first governor-general (1626–1636) of the newly established state of Maranhão and Grão-Pará; and the great-grandson of Feliciano Coelho de Carvalho, Indian fighter and governor of Paraíba in the 1590s. He accompanied his father to America, leaving Portugal in 1666 and returning in 1671. In 1678 young Carvalho returned to Maranhão to serve as *capitão-mor* of his family's captaincy of Camutá until 1682. That same year, he fathered by Angela de Bairros, whose parents were said to be *pardos* from Pernambuco, the bastard Antônio de Albuquerque Coelho (1682–1746), who later gained fame as the one-armed governor and captain-general of Macau. From 1685 to 1690 Carvalho served as governor and *capitão-mor* of Grão-Pará. On 17 May 1690, he became governor and captain-general of the state of Maranhão, Grão-Pará, and Rio Negro, administering that vast territory until 1701.

After returning to Portugal, Carvalho served in the War of Spanish Succession. For his services in Portuguese America, Carvalho, already a knight in the Order of Christ, was awarded a commandery worth 300 milreis and the post of *alcaide-mor.* Since there was no single commandery available with annual receipts for that amount, he was given the commandery of Santo Ildefonso de Val de Telhas in the Order of Christ, two other commanderies in Setúbal, and the post of *alcaide-mor* of Sines—the latter three in the Order of Santiago.

In March 1709, Carvalho was named governor of Rio de Janeiro. He arrived in June 1709, departed for Minas Gerais in July, and spent the next few months pacifying the area in the wake of the War of the Emboabas, the civil conflict between the Paulistas who had discovered the area's mineral wealth and the newcomers from Portugal and coastal Brazil. In the late fall he returned to Rio de Janeiro, where he remained until his appointment as governor of the newly created captaincy of São Paulo and Minas do Ouro. Installed in São Paulo in June 1710, he remained in the captaincy, erecting new townships and strengthening crown authority, until late September 1711. Upon hearing that an armada of eighteen ships under the French corsair René Duguay-Trouin had arrived at Rio de Janeiro, he quickly mobilized six thousand men from the mining areas and marched to the city's rescue. But it was too late: Rio had already been occupied and plundered by the French, and most of the ransom they had demanded had been paid. After the French departed on 13 November 1711, Carvalho helped restore order and rebuild Rio de Janeiro, holding the post of governor (October 1711–June 1713) while he continued to hold his governorship of São Paulo and Minas do Ouro.

Late in 1713 he set sail for Portugal. Enroute he spent eighteen days in Recife's harbor in the aftermath of Pernambuco's War of the Mascates and, upon his return to Portugal, he lobbied for the planter faction.

Carvalho married Dona Luisa Antônia de Mendonça, daughter of Dom Francisco de Melo and Dona Joana de Abreu e Melo. From this marriage, a son, Francisco de Albuquerque Coelho de Carvalho, was born. On 22 March 1722, Carvalho took office as governor of Angola, where he died.

See also **Portuguese Empire.**

BIBLIOGRAPHY

The best treatment to date of Antônio de Albuquerque Coelho de Carvalho's Brazilian experience is found in C. R. Boxer, *The Golden Age of Brazil, 1695–1750* (1962). Also useful is the same author's *Fidalgos in the Far East, 1550–1770* (repr. 1968). There is a short biography in Portuguese by Aureliano Leite, *Antônio de Albuquerque Coelho de Carvalho: Capitão-General de São Paulo de Minas do Ouro, no Brasil* (1944). For Carvalho's services in Angola, see the late-eighteenth-century account of his governorship by Elias Alexandre Silva Correia, *História de Angola*, vol. 1 (1937), pp. 353–357.

FRANCIS A. DUTRA

CARVALHO E MELLO, SEBASTIÃO JOSÉ DE.

See **Pombal, Marquês de (Sebastião José de Carvalho e Melo).**

CASA DA INDIA.

See **Portuguese Overseas Administration.**

CASA DA SUPLICAÇÃO.

Casa da Suplicação, a Portuguese High Court of Appeal that served as a model for the Brazilian High Court. It was originally joined with the Casa do Cível, from which it was separated at the end of the fourteenth century. The main body of the Casa da Suplicação consisted of *desembargadores* (high court magistrates), including *desembargadores extravagantes* (unassigned judges) and *desembargadores dos agravos* (appellate judges). The *desembargadores* were divided into two chambers, or *mesas*, one for civil cases and one for criminal cases. Each was directed by a *desembargador dos agravos*, who bore the title of *corregedor*. A plenary session, called a *mesa grande*, could be convened for matters of great importance. A chancellor served as a kind of chief justice and assigned judges to hear litigation, issued sentences, and reviewed decisions to avoid conflict with existing statutes.

The Casa da Suplicação heard appeals in criminal cases, in civil cases involving sums of money above the amount established for the Casa de Cível, and in appeals of judicial decisions made in the colonies. Because it was the highest court of appeal, the Casa da Suplicação made some of the most important decisions affecting life in colonial Brazil.

See also **Judiciary in Latin America, The.**

BIBLIOGRAPHY

Stuart B. Schwartz, *Sovereignty and Society of Colonial Brazil* (1973).

Additional Bibliography

Barrios, Feliciano, ed. *El gobierno de un mundo: Virreinatos y audiencias en la América hispánica*. Cuenca, Ecuador: Ediciones de la Universidad de Castilla-La Mancha: Fundación Rafael del Pino, 2004.

Burkholder, Mark A., ed. *Administrators of Empire.* Brookfield, VT: Ashgate, 1998.

Ross Wilkinson

CASA DA TORRE.

Casa Da Torre, a dynasty of northeastern Brazilian cattle barons founded in 1549 by Garcia d'Avila, a protégé of Governor Tomé de Sousa. The name "Casa da Torre" came from the family seat at Tatuapara, Bahia, a fortified tower citadel. Garcia d'Avila and his grandson, Colonel Francisco Dias d'Avila, expanded into the backlands of Pernambuco, Piauí, and Sergipe, winning a series of land grants from the crown in the seventeenth century for their efforts in organizing mining expeditions, defending Bahia against the Dutch, and "pacifying" (massacring) Amerindians. By 1700 the Casa possessed nearly the entire interior of Pernambuco. In 1711 João Antônio Andreoni recorded that it controlled 260 leagues (league = 6,600 meters) along the Rio São Francisco and another 70 leagues between the São Francisco and the Parnaíba.

See also **Indigenous Peoples; Livestock.**

BIBLIOGRAPHY

João Capistrano De Abrue, *Capítulos de história colonial, 1500–1800,* 4th ed. (1954), p. 215.

Pedro Calmon, *História da Casa da Tôrre, uma dinastia de pioneiros,* 2d ed. (1958); *Nôvo dicionário de história do Brasil* (1971).

John Hemming, *Red Gold: The Conquest of the Brazilian Indians, 1500–1760* (1978), pp. 346–354.

Additional Bibliography

Baldessarini, Sonia Ricon. *A arquitectura da Casa da Torre Garcia D'Avila: Introdução a Teoria 'Arche" e sua manifestação em estruturas monumentais.* Salvador, Brazil: Secretaria da Cultura e Turismo, Fundação Cultural do Estado: Empresa Gráfica da Bahia, 2001.

Bandeira, Moniz. *O feudo: A Casa da Torre de Garcia d'Avila: Da conquista dos sertões á independencia do Brasil.* Rio de Janeiro: Civilizaçao Brasileira, 2000.

Holanda, Gastao de, and Adenor Gondim. *A Casa de Torre de Garcia d'Avila.* Rio de Janeiro: Arte & Cultura, 2002.

Judy Bieber Freitas

CASA DE CONTRATACIÓN.

The "House of Trade," was established by the crown in Seville in 1503, initially with the limited but vital brief of overseeing the purchase, transport, warehousing, and sale of merchandise exported to and imported from Spain's newly discovered American territories. As discovery and conquest spread during the next two decades from Hispaniola to Cuba and Jamaica, Venezuela, Central America, and Mexico, the Casa's commercial and financial responsibilities multiplied. Moreover, as the only crown agency competent in this period to deal with American affairs as a whole, it also regulated the flow of passengers and assumed a wide range of additional responsibilities, including the training of pilots, the preparation and provision of maps and charts, the exercise of probate in respect of the estates of Spaniards who died in America, and the resolution of legal disputes concerning commerce.

The broader administrative responsibilities of the Casa were curtailed by the creation of the Council of the Indies in 1524. Thereafter, the Casa functioned primarily as a Board of Trade. It was headed by three key officials: a factor, responsible for the provisioning and inspection of shipping and the purchase on behalf of the crown of strategic commodities required in America, including arms, munitions, and mercury; a treasurer, entrusted with the registration and safe custody of all bullion and jewels landed in Seville; and an accountant-secretary, responsible for maintaining accounts relating to the Casa's internal and external activities. These functions were exercised from the body's splendid headquarters in the Alcázar of Seville, a prestigious base that emphasized the importance to the monarchy of the regulation of imperial commerce, not only in terms of the provision of revenue—the Casa oversaw the collection of the Almojarifazgo, or tax on maritime trade, the Avería, or defense tax, and other taxes—but also as a means of preserving America as a uniquely Spanish, Catholic environment.

In this and related matters, including the control of contraband, the Casa, like other Hapsburg organs of government, tended by the seventeenth century to become obsessed with bureaucratic detail, losing sight of the broader need to adjust commercial policies and practices to take account of the changing economic conditions in America. Its registers of shipping, passengers, and cargoes were meticulously maintained, for example (and constitute a source of fundamental importance for historians of imperial trade), but little consistent effort was made to curb widespread fraud and contraband even within Seville, let alone in American ports.

The history of the Casa is closely related to the role of Seville as the only Spanish port licensed to trade with America for the greater part of the Hapsburg period. By the end of the seventeenth century this monopoly had been transferred, in effect, to Cádiz, which enjoyed easier access to the sea (and, thus, to the foreign manufactures required for re-export to America), although administrative inertia delayed the transfer of the Casa to Cádiz until 1717. It functioned there with diminishing efficiency until 1790, when it was abolished in the wake of the radical restructuring of imperial trade undertaken in 1778–1789.

See also **Commercial Policy: Colonial Spanish America.**

BIBLIOGRAPHY

Eduardo Trueba, *Sevilla marítima (siglo XVI)* (1986).

Antonia Heredia Herrera, *Sevilla y los hombres del comercio (1700–1800)* (1989).

José Miguel Delgado Barrado, "Las relaciones comerciales entre España e Indias durante el siglo XVI: Estado de la cuestión," in *Revista de Indias* 50, no. 188 (1990): 139–150.

Additional Bibliography

Romano, Ruggiero. *Mecanismo y elementos del sistema económico colonial americano, siglos XVI-XVIII*. México: El Colegio de México, Fideicomiso Historia de las Américas: Fondo de Cultura Económica, 2004.

Topik, Steven, Carlos Marichal, and Zephyr L. Frank. *From Silver to Cocaine: Latin American Commodity Chains and the Building of the World Economy, 1500-2000*. Durham, NC: Duke University Press, 2006.

JOHN R. FISHER

CASA DE LAS AMÉRICAS.

Founded in Havana, Cuba, in 1960, it is one of the major institutions for the publication and dissemination of scholarly, cultural, and political studies in the Caribbean. Since Castro's rise to power it has become a powerful center for promoting national culture, Marxism, and the reinterpretation of history. Casa de las Américas publishes books by authors from throughout the Western Hemisphere as well as a bimonthly review guide. It also is a principal forum for Latin Americans' intellectual exploration of Third World issues. The most prestigious Cuban literary award is given annually by this organization to promising Latin American novelists, playwrights, and poets. Despite Cuba's severe economic problems, its "special period" that came after the fall of the Soviet Union in 1989, La Casa de las Americas continues to be a potent cultural force, in Cuba and in Latin America as a whole.

See also **Soviet-Latin American Relations.**

BIBLIOGRAPHY

Lie, Nadia. *Transición y transacción: La revista cubana Casa de las Américas, 1960–1976*. Leuven, Belgium: Leuven University Press; Gaithersburg, MD: Hispamérica, 1996.

Maclean, Betsy, ed. *Haydée Santamaría*. Melbourne, Australia and New York: Ocean Press, 2003.

Quintero-Herencia, Juan Carlos. *Fulguración del espacio: Letras e imaginario institucional de la Revolución Cubana, 1960–1971*. Rosario, Argentina: B. Viterbo, 2002.

Weiss, Judith A. *Casa de las Américas: An Intellectual Review in the Cuban Revolution* (1977).

DARIÉN DAVIS

CASA DEL OBRERO MUNDIAL.

Casa del Obrero Mundial, an anarcho-syndicalist organization advocating working-class control of the means of production that led the way in mobilizing Mexican labor between 1911 and 1916. While violence grew in the countryside, Mexican workers joined unions on an unprecedented scale. Enabled by revolutionary zeal, unrest, and the weakness of the new state, they confronted employers and the new government of Francisco Madero with strikes, boycotts, sit-ins, and violence. The Casa grew out of small groups of anarchist intellectuals and artisans, such as the Mexican Typographic Confederation, and anarcho-syndicalist industrial workers to mobilize the working class. Formed in Mexico City in 1912 as the Casa del Obrero, by 1914 it could claim national standing and had adopted its formal name, becoming one of the most important entities of the revolutionary era.

The formation by 5,000 or more Casa members of the Red Battalions, which joined with the under-manned Constitutionalist Army during the Revolution, proved instrumental in the critically important victory over the forces of Francisco Villa in the battle of El Ebano, fought in late 1914 for control of Mexico's oil fields along the Gulf Coast. Fifteen hundred women members of the Casa, many of them textile workers, adopted the name Acratas (those opposed to all authority) and formed military nursing units offering essential support to the male combat units. By agreement with the Constitutionalist government, the Casa was to have an independent command staff and the exclusive right to organize workers in the areas that came under government control.

While never becoming part of the independent officer corps, the Casa did grow rapidly and comprised 150,000 members by early 1916. Following the Constitutionalist victory over the Villistas in 1915, the Casa and the new government quickly came into conflict. Military demobilization of the Casa in 1915 presaged general strikes in the spring and summer of 1916, before the Constitutionalist government of Venustiano Carranza used the regular army to crush and disband the Casa.

See also **Anarchism and Anarchosyndicalism.**

BIBLIOGRAPHY

John M. Hart, *Anarchism and the Mexican Working Class, 1860–1931* (1978), and *Revolutionary Mexico: The Coming and Process of the Mexican Revolution* (1987).

Additional Bibliography

Lear, John. *Workers, Neighbors, and Citizens: The Revolution in Mexico City.* Lincoln: University of Nebraska Press, 2001.

Robles Gómez, Jorge Alfredo, and Angel Luís Gómez. *De la autonomía al corporativismo: Memoria cronológica del movimiento obrero en México, 1900-1980.* Mexico, D.F.: El Atajo Ediciones, 1995.

JOHN MASON HART

CASADO, CARLOS (1833–1899). Carlos Casado (*b.* 16 March 1833; *d.* 29 June 1899). Born in Valencia, Spain, Casado immigrated to Argentina in 1857 and opened a business in the city of Rosario in Santa Fe Province. He also established a private bank that became one of the foundations for the offices of the Bank of London and the Río de la Plata that opened in Rosario in 1868. In 1870 he set up the Candelaria agricultural colony, promoting the immigration of European agricultural workers and realizing the first major export shipment of wheat to Europe. Casado organized a company of wheat mills, promoted the construction of docks in the Rosario port, and was a founder and president of the Banco de Santa Fe, a leading commercial bank. He was also elected counselor of the city government of Rosario.

See also **Rosario.**

BIBLIOGRAPHY

William Perkins, *Las colonias de Santa Fe: Su orígen, progreso y actual situación* (1864).

Michael Mulhall, *Handbook of the River Plate* (1885).

Ezequiel Gallo, *La pampa gringa: La colonización agrícola en Santa Fe* (1984).

Additional Bibliography

Marco, Miguel Angel de. *Carlos Casado del Alisal y el progreso argentino.* Buenos Aires: Grupo Editor Latinoamericano, 1994.

CARLOS MARICHAL

CASA GRANDE. Casa Grande, the main house or family residence on a plantation during Brazil's colonial era and the Empire. Architectural style varied by region, era, and degree of wealth of the planter. The more elaborate homes were grand, two-story dwellings with separate sitting, dining, and ball rooms; numerous bedrooms; a kitchen and a pantry, and sometimes even a chapel. Family living quarters occupied the upper floor; the ground floor was divided into locked areas for storage of supplies, tools, and the products of the plantation. Rather than being set apart in a spacious garden, the *casa grande* typically formed one of a cluster of buildings—workshops, mill or waterwheel, storage sheds, and slave quarters—that made up the living and administrative core of a plantation. Sociologist Gilberto Freyre used the term *casa grande* in his famous study of slavery and race relations, *Casa grande e senzala,* published in 1933 and subsequently translated into English as *The Masters and the Slaves* (1946), to connote the constellation of cultural assumptions that characterized the patriarchal family and relations between masters and slaves, describing both the institutionalized brutality of slavery and the contributions of Afro-Brazilians to the larger patterns of Brazilian culture.

See also **Fazenda, Fazendeiro; Senzala.**

BIBLIOGRAPHY

Barickman, Bert Jude. "Revisiting the 'Casa-Grande': Plantation and Cane-Farming Households in Early Nineteenth-Century Bahia." *Hispanic American Historical Review.* 84:4 (November 2004): 619-659.

SANDRA LAUDERDALE GRAHAM

CASAL, JULIÁN DEL (1863–1893).

Julián del Casal (*b.* 7 November 1863; *d.* 21 October 1893), Cuban poet who used the pseudonyms the Count of Camors, Hernani, and Alceste at times during his literary career. Casal was born in Havana and showed a great talent for poetry from an early age. His first poems were published in *El Estudio,* an underground publication that he founded with a group of friends. He began studies for a career in law in 1881 at the University of Havana but never finished them. Instead, he became finance minister while writing articles and working in diverse capacities for newspapers and literary publications, among them *La Discusión, El Fígaro,* and *La Habana Literaria.* Casal published a series of articles on Cuban society in the magazine *La Habana Elegante.* The first, a derogatory piece about the Spanish captain-general Sabas Marín, cost him his government post. In his short life Casal earned a place as one of the great poets in Cuban history. Along with three other poets, fellow Cuban José Martí, Colombian José Asunción Silva, and Mexican Manuel Gutiérrez Nájera, he was an initiator of modernism, the first literary movement to originate in Spanish-speaking America.

See also **Journalism.**

BIBLIOGRAPHY

Some of the most notable of Casal's contemporaries, including Martí, José Lezama Lima, Ramón Mesa, Enrique Varona, and Cintio Vitier, have written about Casal and his poetry. See Emilio De Armas, *Casal* (1981). An excellent study in English is Robert J. Glickman, *The Poetry of Julián del Casal,* 3 vols. (1976–1978).

Additional Bibliography

Figueroa, Esperanza. *Poesías completas y pequeños poemas en prosa (en orden cronológico).* Miami: Ediciones Universal, 1993.

ROBERTO VALERO

CASALDÁLIGA, PEDRO (1928–). Pedro

Casaldáliga (*b.* 1928), bishop of São Félix do Araguaia, Brazil. Casaldáliga was born in Barcelona and raised on his family's cattle ranch in Catalonia. In 1952 he was ordained into the Claretian order, and sixteen years later he arrived in Brazil. By 1971 he had attracted the attention of Brazilian authorities by writing a critical report titled "Feudalism and Slavery in Northern Mato Grosso." In the following year Casaldáliga was consecrated as the first bishop of São Félix do Araguaia, a large but remote region in the states of Goiás and Mato Grosso.

In subsequent years, however, the prolific writer and poet found himself in direct conflict with the landowners of Goiás and Mato Grosso, the Brazilian government, and the Catholic hierarchy because of his emphasis on developing community leadership among the peasants within his diocese, providing health care and education, and resisting the continued expansion of ranches at the expense of peasants' rights. In 1973, the same year that the Missionary Council to Indigenous Peoples was founded in Brazil, Francisco Jentel, a priest under Casaldáliga's authority, was tried under Brazil's National Security Law for inciting class warfare as the government sought resolutions to continuing conflicts at Santa Terezinha. In October 1976 Casaldáliga was present when Brazilian authorities shot and killed a Jesuit missionary, João Bosco Penido Burnier, for interfering with the interrogation and torture of two women. After 1973 public criticism began to surface from Archbishop Sigaud and Cardinal Joseph Ratzinger about Casaldáliga's pastoral work as well as his theological convictions.

In 1985 Casaldáliga began traveling extensively throughout Central America, including Nicaragua, El Salvador, and Cuba, in "a ministry of borders and consolation." As a result of criticism for these trips, as well as for his writings supportive of liberation theologians and his characterization of Archbishop Oscar Romero as a martyr, in 1988 the Vatican issued an order that Casaldáliga not speak publicly, publish any further writings, or leave his diocese without explicit permission. After his seventy-fifth birthday he was ordered to retire and he decided to remain in the same spartan residence where he had lived for more than thirty-five years. Though diagnosed with Parkinson's disease, he chose to remain in Brazil to continue to fight for rights for the poor. In both 1989 and 1992 he was nominated for the Nobel Peace Prize.

See also **Catholic Church: The Modern Period; Liberation Theology.**

BIBLIOGRAPHY

Teófilo Cabestrero, *Mystic of Liberation: A Portrait of Pedro Casaldáliga* (1981).

Penny Lernoux, *Cry of the People*, rev. ed. (1982).

Scott Mainwaring, *The Catholic Church and Politics in Brazil, 1916–1985* (1986).

Kevin Neuhouser, "The Radicalization of the Brazilian Catholic Church in Comparative Perspective," in *American Sociological Review* 54, no. 2 (1989): 233–244.

Pedro Casaldáliga, *In Pursuit of the Kingdom*, translated by Philip Berryman (1990).

Additional Bibliography

Beozzo, José Oscar. *Brazil: People and Church(es)*. London: SCM Press, 2002.

Escribano, Francesc. *Descalzo sobre la tierra roja*. Barcelona: Ediciones Península, 2002.

CAROLYN E. VIEIRA

CASALS, FELIPE (1937–). Felipe Casals (*b.* 28 July 1937), Mexican film director, born in France but raised in Zapopán, Jalisco, and Mexico City. Casals studied film in Paris. He is one of the leading directors of the generation of 1968, which contributed greatly to a brief flowering of Mexican cinema in the 1970s. Among the most celebrated of his films are *Canoa* (1974), *El apando* (1975), *Las poquianchis* (1976), *El año de la peste* (1978), *Bajo la metralla* (1982), *Los motivos de Luz* (1985), and *El tres de copas* (1986). In 2006 he won the Mexican Silver Ariel award for his film *Vueltas del citrillo*. Casals's films are characterized by hard-hitting, violent portrayals of Mexican national issues, particularly social strife and the underclass. Most of his films have been produced by the state. He received the Ariel from the Mexican Film Academy for best director for *El año de la peste* and *Bajo la metralla*. He has filmed other minor features for the video market, such as *Las abandonadas* and a musical biography of the popular singer Rigo Tovar, entitled *Rigo es amor*.

See also **Cinema: From the Silent Film to 1900.**

BIBLIOGRAPHY

Luis Reyes De La Maza, *El cine sonoro en México* (1973).

E. Bradford Burns, *Latin American Cinema: Film and History* (1975).

Carl J. Mora, *Mexican Cinema: Reflections of a Society: 1896–1980* (1982).

John King, *Magical Reels: A History of Cinema in Latin America* (1990).

Additional Bibliography

García Tsao, Leonardo. *Felipe Cazals habla de su cine*. Guadalajara: Universidad de Guadalajara, 1994.

DAVID MACIEL

CASA MATA, PLAN OF. *See* **Plan of Casa Mata.**

CASANARE. Casanare, an intendancy of Colombia located in the eastern plains (Llanos Orientales) and occupying an area of 17,169 square miles, it is bounded on the west by the Cordillera Oriental, on the north by the Casanare River, and on the south and east by the Meta River. Mostly low-lying grassland, it has a tropical climate with alternating wet and dry seasons.

In the sixteenth century Spanish and German conquistadores explored Casanare in a futile search for El Dorado. Later, *encomenderos* and missionaries competed for control of the Indians. Before their expulsion in 1767, the Jesuits established eleven missions and eight haciendas in Casanare, an empire second in size only to their reductions in Paraguay. By this time, cattle raising—the principal economic activity—had produced a mestizo subculture of *llaneros* (cowboys).

Casanare was a major theater in the War of Independence. After royalists reconquered the new Granada highlands, Simón Bolívar sent Francisco de Paula Santander to the plains to forge the fiercely patriotic *llaneros* into a new army. In June 1819, Bolívar led this force in an epic march over the Andes to defeat the Spanish in the battle of Boyacá (7 August 1819).

The ravages of war and systematic neglect precipitated Casanare's decline in the nineteenth century from a modestly self-sufficient region to an isolated, forgotten province. Until recently, subsistence agriculture and ranching predominated, but since 1983 large-scale extraction of petroleum near the capital of Yopal promises a more prosperous future.

See also **Colombia: From the Conquest through Independence; El Dorado.**

BIBLIOGRAPHY

James J. Parsons, "Europeanization of the Savanna Lands of Northern South America," in *Human Ecology in Savanna Environments,* edited by David R. Harris (1980), pp. 267–289.

Jane M. Rausch, *A Tropical Plains Frontier: The Llanos of Colombia, 1531–1831* (1984).

Héctor Publio Pérez Ángel, *La participación de Casanare en la guerra de independencia, 1809–1819* (1987).

Additional Bibliography

Lamus Gélvez, Julio César. *Territorios de Arauca y Casanare: La provincia de Casanare en la Nueva Granada, 1832–1857.* Bucaramanga, Colombia: Editorial, 2003.

Pearce, Jenny. *Más allá de la malla perimetral: El petróleo y el conflicto armado en Casanare, Colombia.* Bogotá, D.C.: Cinep, 2005.

JANE M. RAUSCH

CASANOVA Y ESTRADA, RICARDO

(1844–1913). Ricardo Casanova y Estrada (*b.* 10 November 1844; *d.* 14 April 1913), archbishop of Guatemala (1886–1913). Casanova was born in Guatemala City and studied law at the University of San Carlos. He served in governmental positions until 1874, when he angered President Justo Barrios by deciding a case in favor of an abolished religious community. Being forced by Barrios to parade through the city in a cassock convinced the lawyer to become a priest. Ordained in 1875 and consecrated archbishop in 1886, he issued several pastoral letters defending the church against the Liberals. He was exiled by President Manuel Barillas in 1887 and returned to Guatemala in 1897, spending the rest of his life guiding the church during the dictatorship of Manuel Estrada Cabrera. Casanova was also a poet, writing under the pseudonym of Andrés Vigil.

See also **Anticlericalism.**

BIBLIOGRAPHY

José M. Ramírez Colóm, *Reseña biográfica del ilustrísimo y reverendísimo señor arzobispo de Santiago de Guatemala don Ricardo Casanova y Estrada* (1896).

Agustín Estrada Monroy, *Datos para la historia de la iglesia en Guatemala,* vol. 3 (1979), pp. 199–308.

EDWARD T. BRETT

CASA ROSADA. Casa Rosada (the Pink House), the presidential palace and seat of the executive branch in Argentina. Located in the Plaza de Mayo near the Río de la Plata, the palace began to be built during the presidency of Domingo Sarmiento (1868–1874) and was completed in 1882, during the presidency of Julio A. Roca (1880–1886; 1898–1904). Its name, which intentionally evokes its North American antecedent, came as a result of Sarmiento's decision to paint it with a blend of the Federalists' red and the Unitarians' white—the colors of the two major political factions that competed for power in Argentina after its break from Spain in 1810.

In the twentieth century the Casa Rosada has been the site of many of the most important demonstrations and rallies in Argentine history. During the presidency of Juan Domingo Perón, Perón's wife Eva spoke to large groups of workers from the balcony of the Casa Rosada. In 1955 a dissident group within the military bombed the Casa Rosada in an attempted coup against Perón; this attack killed more than 300 people. In the 1980s the Madres de Plaza de Mayo walked around the plaza where the Casa Rosada is located to protest against the military government that "disappeared" their children.

See also Buenos Aires; Perón, Juan Domingo; Perón, María Eva Duarte de.

BIBLIOGRAPHY

Gálvez, Lucía. *Casa Rosada: Su Historia Y Su Plaza*. Buenos Aires: Manrique Zago Ediciones, 1997.

Scobie, James R. *Argentina: A City and a Nation*, 2d ed. (1971), pp. 163, 165.

DANIEL LEWIS

CASAS GRANDES. Casas Grandes, an archaeological site in north-central Chihuahua state in Mexico. Although it has a number of Mesoamerican features, it is separated from the northernmost Mesoamerican sites in Zacatecas by many miles and really belongs in the southernmost part of the Southwestern culture area.

The earliest occupation at Casas Grandes is called the Medio period (1060–1340), although for half a millennium earlier a Mogollon-like population occupied the area, lived in pit houses, and made red pottery. During the earliest part of the Medio period, the Buena Fé phase (1060–1205), a large town was built, featuring twenty or so house clusters around plazas enclosed by a fortification wall. The houses were made of mud concrete poured walls, had T-shaped doorways, and were usually one story. The people made polychrome pottery and kept breeding boxes for macaws imported from Mesoamerica. Charles Di Peso interpreted this entire construction as built by the *pochteca* traders from central Mexico who invaded and ruled Casas Grandes.

During the next phase, the Paquimé (1205–1261), the town blossomed. Four- or five-story adobe apartment complexes were built, as well as effigy mounds and pyramids. A complex irritation system and a road system were constructed, features attributable to Mesoamerican influences. The amount of Mexican imports—copper bells, armlets, rings, pendants, shells, and perhaps obsidian—also increased.

Almost as fast as the Paquimé rise was the decline in the Diablo phase (1261–1340). The multistoried apartments fell into disrepair and the ceremonial structures ceased to be used, although fine polychrome pottery continued to be made and the population may have increased. By the 1350s, however, the site was abandoned, and the Casas Grandes culture ceased to exist.

See also Archaeology.

BIBLIOGRAPHY

Charles C. Di Peso, *Casas Grandes: A Fallen Trading Center of the Gran Chichimeca*, 7 vols. (1974), and *Casas Grandes and the Gran Chichimeca* (n.d.).

Additional Bibliography

Lekson, Stephen H. *The Chaco Meridian: Centers of Political Power in the Ancient Southwest*. Walnut Creek: AltaMira Press, 1999.

Nárez, Jesús, Araceli Rivera, and José Luis Rojas Martínez. *Casas Grandes*. México, D.F.: Instituto Nacional de Antropología e Historia: Consejo Nacional para la Cultura y las Artes, 1991.

Schaafsma, Curtis F., and Carroll L. Riley. *The Casas Grandes World*. Salt Lake City: University of Utah Press, 1999.

Townsend, Richard F., Ken Kokrda, and Barbara L. Moulard. *Casas Grandes and the Ceramic Art of the Ancient Southwest*. Chicago: Art Institute of Chicago; New Haven, CT: Yale University Press, 2005.

VanPool, Christine S., and Todd L. *Signs of the Casas Grandes Shamans*. Salt Lake City: University of Utah Press, 2007.

Whalen, Michael E., and Paul E. Minnis. *Casas Grandes and Its Hinterland: Prehistoric Regional Organization in Northwest Mexico*. Tucson: University of Arizona Press, 2001.

RICHARD S. MACNEISH

CASASOLA, AGUSTÍN (1874–1928). Agustín Casasola (*b.* 1874; *d.* 1928), Mexican photographer. Born in Mexico City, Agustín Casasola worked as a reporter for numerous periodicals, including the Porfirian daily *El Imparcial*. There he began to collect illustrations, documents, books, and photographs which would eventually become the Casasola Archives, containing nearly one million photographs, the richest pictorial documents of twentieth-century Mexican history. The most prolific Mexican photographer of his day, Casasola captured the last years of the Porfiriato, the revolutionary struggle, and its aftermath. Like Matthew Brady, distinguished photographer of the American Civil War, he witnessed and recorded history; his photographs include figures such as Pancho Villa and Emiliano Zapata, rebels hanged from trees or executed by firing squads, and *soldaderas* riding atop boxcars and shouldering rifles. A collection of his photography, including some of what he collected from others, was published by his son Gustavo in *Historia gráfica de la Revolución Mexicana: 1900–1940,* edited by Luis González Obregón and Nicolás Rangel.

See also **Photography: The Twentieth Century.**

BIBLIOGRAPHY

Diccionario Porrúa de historia, biografía y geografía de México, 5th ed. (1986).

Victor Sorell, "Mexposición 2: Images of the Revolución, Casasola" (1976).

Jacobo Wiebe, "Hazañas fotográficas de Casasola," in *Contenido* 152 (January 1976): 82–87.

Additional Bibliography

Ortiz Monasterio. *Mexico, the Revolution and Beyond: Photographs by Augustín Victor Casasola, 1900-1940.* New York: Aperture; Mexico City, 2003.

MARY KAY VAUGHAN

CASÁUS Y TORRES, RAMÓN (1765–1845).

Ramón Casáus y Torres (*b.* 1765; *d.* 10 November 1845), archbishop of Guatemala (1811–1845). Born in Jaca, Huesca, Spain, Casáus entered the Dominican order in Saragossa and later earned his doctorate in Mexico City. He was bishop of Oaxaca when appointed archbishop of Guatemala in 1811. As archbishop, he worked to improve educational facilities and donated his library to the University of San Carlos. He was especially interested in Indian languages and arranged for teaching Quiché and Cakchiquel at the university and the seminary. He opposed independence from Spain and Mexico and became closely associated with conservative political interests in the civil wars following independence. He strongly resisted establishment of a separate diocese for El Salvador.

Liberal victory in 1829 resulted in Casáus's exile from Central America by Francisco Morazán. He spent the remainder of his life in Havana. The state of Guatemala declared him a traitor on 13 June 1830. After Rafael Carrera came to power, in 1839, the Guatemalan government invited him to return, but the continuing turmoil on the isthmus deterred the archbishop from returning to his

see before his death. His remains were brought to Guatemala for burial in 1846.

See also **Guatemala.**

BIBLIOGRAPHY

Francisco Fernández Hall, "Historiadores de Guatemala posteriores a la independencia nacional: El Doctor don Francisco de Paula García Peláez," in *Anales de la Sociedad de Geografía e Historia* 15, no. 3 (1939): 261–278.

Mary P. Holleran, *Church and State in Guatemala* (1949).

Carlos C. Haeussler Yela, *Diccionario general de Guatemala,* vol. 1 (1983), p. 323.

RALPH LEE WOODWARD JR.

CASEROS, BATTLE OF.

The Battle of Caseros took place on February 3, 1852, to the west of the city of Buenos Aires. The troops of the governor of that province, Juan Manuel de Rosas (1793–1877), were pitted against an alliance led by the governor of Entre Ríos, Justo José de Urquiza (1801–1870). The alliance included the province of Corrientes, the Empire of Brazil, and Rosas's enemies in Uruguay. The Buenos Aires forces were defeated, and Rosas fled to England.

Between 1831 and 1852, the provinces of the River Plate formed the loose Argentine Confederation based on the Federal Pact of 1831. This treaty preempted the eventual organization of a Constitutional Congress. Rosas, who had been given authority over foreign relations and had considerable influence over the other provinces, managed to delay the nationalization of the country. In an attempt to allow Buenos Aires to monopolize customs revenue, he also opposed direct commerce between the riverine provinces—the only ones with access to navigation—and foreign ships. In 1851 Entre Ríos relieved Rosas of his involvement in the province's foreign relations and sought allies against him, and at the same time pressed for the organization of a nation-state. Brazil, already at loggerheads with Rosas, supported Urquiza because of Brazilian interests in river navigation and opposition to the concentration of power in Buenos Aires. The Uruguayan political faction that controlled Montevideo also joined the alliance, together with its allies who had emigrated from Buenos Aires.

With Rosas defeated, Urquiza led a process of nationwide organization that culminated in the Constitution of 1853. However, Buenos Aires abstained from this process until 1860.

See also **Argentina, Constitutions; Argentina, Federalist Pacts (1831, 1852); Rosas, Juan Manuel de; Urquiza, Justo José de.**

BIBLIOGRAPHY

Sarobe, José María. "Campaña de Caseros: Antecedentes con referencia a la política interna y externa." In *Academia Nacional de la Historia: Historia de la Nación Argentina*, 3rd edition, Ricardo Levene. Buenos Aires: El Ateneo, 1962.

Scobie, James. *La lucha por la consolidación de la nacionalidad argentina, 1852–1862.* Buenos Aires, Librería Hachette, 1964.

EDUARDO MIGUEZ

CASHEW INDUSTRY.

Before the arrival of the Portuguese, the Tupi Indians used the ripened fruit of the cashew (*acajou*) to mark the passage of time. Portuguese explorers soon discovered this fruit, which they called *cajú,* and by the 1550s, they were exporting its nuts to other parts of their empire. Ranging in color from off-white to red, the fruit is shaped like an upside-down, shiny-skinned pear with a nut growing from its top. Brazilians now value the *cajú* more for its fruit than the cashew nut, which they export. Although cashew trees can be found throughout Brazil, they are most prevalent in the Amazonian rain forest.

Cajús ripen in November, when the Brazilians use the fruit to make pies and jellies and its juice for alcoholic liqueurs, or *suco de cajú.* The nut can only be eaten after roasting it to eliminate the poisonous oil found between the nut's inner and outer shells. Starting in World War II, the oil from the shell, which contains insulating and protective properties, was essential in arms production. Since that time, the cashew industry uses 600,000 tons of nuts annually in wood preservation, waterproofing paper, plastics, varnishes, paints, printing ink, and candy. Realizing the growth potential of the cashew market, the Brazilian government encouraged settlers participating in the Polonoroeste development plan of the 1970s to plant cashew trees, and has continued to press for mass production of

cajú products since that time. As of 2004, Brazil was among the largest exporters of cashews in the world and small producers were responsible for 80 percent of Brazil's production.

See also **Forests.**

BIBLIOGRAPHY

Clara Inés Olaya, "Cajú/Maranón/Merey/Acaiu/Cashew Nut," in *Americas* 42, no. 3 (1990): 52–53.

Additional Bibliography

Moreira, Agio Augusto. *O cajueiro: Vida, uso e estórias.* Fortaleza, Ceará, Brazil: A. A. Moreira, 2002.

CAROLYN JOSTOCK

CASIQUIARE CANAL.

Casiquiare Canal, a remarkable stream in southern Venezuela that provides a permanent, natural link between the Orinoco River and the Río Negro (a major tributary of the Amazon River). Originating at the bifurcation of the Orinoco into separate rivers, the Casiquiare is about 222 miles long. It flows across a relatively smooth plain, picking up velocity as its volume increases. Most of this water is supplied by three large tributaries, rather than by the Orinoco itself.

By the mid-seventeenth century some Europeans, probably Spaniards traveling the upper Orinoco, knew of the Casiquiare's existence and must have been surprised to encounter Portuguese-speaking people who had come entirely by water from the Brazilian Amazon in search of slaves. Native Americans had long been using this route. By the 1740s information on the Casiquiare had reached Europe, arousing the interest of scholars there. Among Alexander von Humboldt's goals when he came to America in 1799 were to see and measure the Casiquiare. Even though Humboldt mapped it correctly nearly two centuries ago, some cartographers still cannot bring themselves to draw the Casiquiare as a natural, navigable link between the Orinoco and the Amazon rivers. That is because at a fork in a stream, cartographers assume one is joining the other, not leaving it. So some depict the Casiquiare as disconnected from either the Orinoco or the Río Negro.

The Casiquiare is generally believed to represent an example of stream capture, in which the Amazon Basin is growing at the expense of the

Orinoco Basin. Because the capture has been so slow, the Casiquiare is an important route for the dispersal of numerous types of plants and animals, including freshwater dolphins.

See also **Indigenous Peoples; Orinoco River.**

BIBLIOGRAPHY

U.S. Army Corps of Engineers, *Report on Orinoco-Casiquiare-Negro Waterway Venezuela-Colombia-Brazil* (1943).

Douglas Botting, *Humboldt and the Cosmos* (1973).

Additional Bibliography

Tellería, Ma. Teresa. *La comisión naturalista de Löfling en la expedición de Límites al Orinoco.* Madrid, Spain: Real Jardín Botánico, Consejo Superior de Investigaciones Científicas, Caja Madrid, 1998.

Whitehead, Neil L. *Histories and Historicities in Amazonia.* Lincoln: University of Nebraska Press, 2003.

WILLIAM J. SMOLE

CASO Y ANDRADE, ALFONSO

(1896–1970). Alfonso Caso y Andrade (*b.* 1 February 1896; *d.* 30 November 1970), Mexican archaeologist, intellectual, and public figure who wrote numerous works on Middle American indigenous populations. From 1931 to 1943 he directed the explorations of Monte Albán, one of Mexico's major archaeological sites.

The son of the engineer Antonio Caso y Morali and Maria Andrade, brother of the distinguished intellectual Antonio Caso y Andrade, and the brother-in-law of a leading intellectual and labor leader, Vicente Lombardo Toledano, Caso was part of a significant generation of Mexican intellectuals. A longtime professor at the National University, he directed the National Preparatory School and, in 1944, after directing the National Institute of Anthropology and History, became rector of the National University. Caso briefly served (1946–1948) in Miguel Alemán's cabinet as the first secretary of government properties and in 1949 he founded and became director of the National Indigenous Institute, a position he held until his death. A member of the National College, an honorary society of distinguished Mexicans, Caso was awarded the National Prize in Arts and Sciences for his intellectual contributions.

See also **Archaeology; National Institute of Anthropology and History.**

BIBLIOGRAPHY

Alfonso Caso, "Discursos," in *Memoria* (1953).

Luis Calderón Vega, *Los 7 sabios de México* (1961).

Alfonso Caso, *A un joven arqueólogo mexicano* (1968).

Additional Bibliography

Salas Ortega, Antonio. *La política en el pensamiento de Alfonso Caso: Testimonio.* México, D.F.: Editormex Mexicana, 1990.

RODERIC AI CAMP

CASO Y ANDRADE, ANTONIO

(1883–1946). Antonio Caso y Andrade (*b.* 19 December 1883; *d.* 6 March 1946), a leading Mexican philosopher who wrote numerous books on values and sociology but is more important for his contribution to the cultural emancipation of the Mexican and the destruction of positivism. He is also remembered for his notable debates on academic freedom in 1933 and for his impact on dozens of major intellectual and political figures who passed through the National University from 1910 through the 1920s.

The son of engineer Antonio Caso y Morali and Maria Andrade, and brother of Alfonso Caso y Andrade, he became first secretary of the National Treasury in 1910 and was a founding member of the first graduate school in 1913. He was among the members of the distinguished intellectual generation of the Ateneo de la Juventud. Caso directed the National Preparatory School, the School of Philosophy and Letters, and, in 1921–1923, the National University. He served briefly as an ambassador in South America and was an original member of the prestigious National College, an honorary society of distinguished Mexicans.

See also **Philosophy: Overview; Positivism.**

BIBLIOGRAPHY

Antonio Caso, *El concepto de la historia universal y la filosofía de los valores* (1933).

Luís Garrido, *Antonio Caso: Una vida profunda* (1961).

John H. Haddox, *Antonio Caso: Philosopher of Mexico* (1971).

María Caso, *20 lecciones de español* (1972).

Additional Bibliography

Chávez González, Mónica. "Antonio Caso y los paradigmas de la nación mexicana." *Cuicuilco* 11: 30 (January-April 2004): 217–236.

Hernandez Prado, Jose. *La filosofía de la cultura de Antonio Caso: La concepcion casiana del conocimiento de la historia, la sociedad y la cultura.* Mexico, D.F.: Universidad Autonoma Metropolitana, 1994.

RODERIC AI CAMP

CASS, LEWIS

CASS, LEWIS (1782–1866). Lewis Cass (*b.* 9 October 1782; *d.* 17 June 1866), U.S. general, secretary of state, diplomat, Democratic presidential candidate in 1848. Characterized as hawkish and anglophobic, Cass was one of the nineteenth century's leading exponents of Manifest Destiny in the United States. Cass backed the annexation of Texas and argued in 1847 that the Mexican War offered the United States a great opportunity for westward expansion. He called upon the Senate to approve the military expenditure necessary to force Mexico to surrender all its land north of the Sierra Madre. Cass urged the annexation of the Yucatán Peninsula in 1848, and he was an advocate of U.S. political and economic interests in Central America in the 1850s.

See also **Mexico, Wars and Revolutions: Mexican-American War; United States-Latin American Relations.**

BIBLIOGRAPHY

Albert K. Weinberg, *Manifest Destiny: A Study of Nationalist Expansion in American History* (1935).

Thomas D. Clark, *Frontier America: The Story of the Westward Movement* (1959).

Thomas R. Hietala, *Manifest Design: Anxious Aggrandizement in Late Jacksonian America* (1985).

Additional Bibliography

Klunder, Willard Card. *Lewis Cass and the Politics of Moderation.* Kent, OH: Kent State University Press, 1996.

HEATHER K. THIESSEN

CASTAÑEDA, FRANCISCO DE PAULA

CASTAÑEDA, FRANCISCO DE PAULA (1776–1832). Francisco de Paula Castañeda (*b.* 1776; *d.* 12 March 1832), Argentine educator and journalist. Born in Buenos Aires, Castañeda studied at the College of San Carlos, became a Franciscan friar, and was ordained a priest in 1800. He taught moral theology for three years and staunchly supported the May Revolution of 1810. He was a firm advocate of public education and in 1815 founded a school of design and drawing. In the same year he became the superior of the Franciscans.

Castañeda opposed Bernardino Rivadavia's anticlerical measures (e.g. abolishing tithes, prohibiting persons under twenty-five from entering monastic life, and limiting the number of monks that could reside in monasteries), for which he was banished from Buenos Aires (1821–1823). He wrote prolifically and energetically against Rivadavia's reforms, characterizing his rule as "insane, heretical, immoral, and despotic." Among his publications are *La verdad desnuda* (1822), *Derecho del hombre,* and *Buenos Aires cautiva.* He founded schools for Indians of Paraná and San José de Feliciano. Castañeda died in Paraná.

See also **Franciscans; Rivadavia, Bernardino.**

BIBLIOGRAPHY

Ricardo Levene, *A History of Argentina* (1963).

Additional Bibliography

Fúrlong Cárdiff, Guillermo. *Vida y obra de Fray Francisco de Paula Castañeda: Un testigo de la naciente patria argentina, 1810-1830.* San Antonio de Padua: Ediciones Castañeda, 1994.

NICHOLAS P. CUSHNER

CASTAÑEDA CASTRO, SALVADOR

CASTAÑEDA CASTRO, SALVADOR (1888–1965). Salvador Castañeda Castro (*b.* 6 August 1888; *d.* 5 March 1965), general and president of El Salvador (1945–1948). Born in Chalchuapa to a well-connected family, Salvador Castañeda Castro received his education under the Chilean mission to El Salvador and had attained the position of lieutenant by age eighteen. He rose quickly through the ranks and served in a variety of political positions after 1931, the most important being director of the military school, minister of the interior under General Maximiliano Hernández Martínez, and governor of various departments. Following the overthrow of Hernández Martínez in 1944, General Castañeda Castro ran unopposed in a presidential election marred by violence and intimidation. His victory represented the supremacy of the army's old guard and a return to *martinista*-style politics without Martínez. In December 1945 a group led by the aged liberal Miguel Tomás Molina invaded El Salvador from Guatemala, but the expected military rebellion against Castañeda Castro never materialized. Less than a year later, popular discontent manifested itself in the general strike of October 1946, which was effectively repressed.

Among the major events of Castañeda's presidency were visits by Chilean and French missions in 1945, the creation of a national tourism commission, and the dedication of both a major thoroughfare in San Salvador and the Pan-American Highway to Franklin Delano Roosevelt. During his administration, Castañeda brought the control of notaries under the direction of the Supreme Court and passed a so-called law of social majority designed to tighten the government's control over the population. His most significant undertaking, however, was the passage in 1945 of a new, regressive constitution that alienated even the younger cadres within the military. The latter, led by Colonel Oscar Osorio, overthrew Castañeda in 1948 when it became clear he would seek to extend his rule through a second term. Castañeda continued to reside in San Salvador until his death.

See also **El Salvador; Military Dictatorships: 1821–1945.**

BIBLIOGRAPHY

Jorge Larde y Larín, *Guía histórica de El Salvador* (1958).

Maria Leistenschneider and Freddy Leistenschneider, *Gobernantes de El Salvador* (1980).

James Dunkerley, *The Long War* (1982).

Tommie Sue Montgomery, *Revolution in El Salvador* (1982).

Additional Bibliography

Soto Gómez, Arturo. *Todos los presidentes, 1821-2004: Elecciones presidenciales en El Salvador.* San Salvador: Insta Prints, 2005.

KAREN RACINE

CASTE AND CLASS STRUCTURE IN COLONIAL SPANISH AMERICA.

During most of the colonial era, Spanish American society had a pyramidal structure with a small number of Spaniards at the top, a group of mixed-race people beneath them, and at the bottom a large indigenous population and small number of slaves, usually of African origin. Although the size of these groups varied between regions and fluctuated over the course of three centuries, they comprised the hierarchy of power and social status during most of the colonial period.

SPANIARDS

The upper echelons of colonial society were dominated by Spaniards, who held all of the positions of economic privilege and political power. However, a sharp split existed between those born in Europe, "peninsulars," and those born in the Americas, creoles. Although the relationship between these two groups was sometimes friendly, as when peninsular men married into creole families, it could also be antagonistic. Peninsulars sometimes perceived creoles as lazy, mentally deficient, and physically degenerate, whereas creoles often saw peninsulars as avaricious. In the sixteenth century rivalries between European-born and American-born friars for control of the religious orders led to violence that resulted in a formal policy of alternating terms of leadership between creoles and peninsulars. The Spanish crown's preference for European-born Spaniards in government and church posts in the eighteenth century provoked deep resentment among elite creole men, who had come to expect positions of influence. Their resentment helped fuel anti-Iberian sentiment in the colonies before the wars for independence.

Creoles attributed greed to peninsulars because it was far more possible to make a fortune in the Americas than in Europe. Opportunities were present in retail and transatlantic commerce, in gold and silver mining, and in bureaucratic posts that offered opportunities to trade in native goods and exchange influence for favors. In the sixteenth century many peninsulars made their New World fortunes in order to retire in comfort in Spain, but by the eighteenth century, peninsulars were apt to enmesh themselves in the communities of the Americas.

The numerous opportunities for enrichment made the Crown tremendously reluctant to grant titles of nobility to creoles who became wealthy in the Americas. Thus, although there were many extraordinarily wealthy creole families, there were comparatively few creole noble titles. This lack of titles created one of the distinctive characteristics of Spanish society in the New World: In Spain a title of nobility clearly indicated an elevated social rank, but in the Americas there were too few titles to identify all the individuals with wealth and power. Nor were all the families that were ennobled by the Crown able to retain their economic positions, and this made noble titles uncertain guides to social status. Power and status depended far more upon the recognition of one's peers than upon the external and readily identifiable labels of nobility, and the absence of noble titles contributed to a sense of shared status among all Spaniards. Although there were clear, though usually unstated, limits to ideas of equality between elite and nonelite Spaniards, the absence of noble titles and the small size of the European population relative to the indigenous population contributed to sentiments of equality.

Despite the common prejudice against laboring with one's hands, many Spaniards did so, though unskilled labor was performed by Indians. Spanish craftsmen were employed for their skills, even when they were hired out on a daily basis. In rural settings Spaniards were likely to be the managers and foremen over Indians, who did the hard physical labor of planting, weeding, and harvesting crops.

Introduced to the Americas by the Spaniards, horses became symbols of European superiority; they represented wealth (for horses were not cheap), a superior physical vantage point, greater mobility and speed, and the superiority of European society. The horse and iron-based arms were the keys to many military successes during the Spanish Conquest, and were broadly considered to be indicators of the superior social status shared by Spaniards, from which all conquered native peoples and slaves were excluded. By Spanish statute, Indians and slaves were forbidden to bear arms, for military reasons. The enforcement of this prohibition was greatly assisted by the popularity of the belief that bearing arms, like riding a horse, was a prerogative of social rank and being Spanish.

CASTAS (RACIALLY MIXED GROUPS)

Members of the intermediate racial groups were called "castes" or, in Spanish, *castas*. They included the offspring of black and white parents, called mulattoes; of white and Indian parents, called *mestizo*; and of black and Indian parents, to whom no single term was ever applied. The *mestizos*, mulattoes, and black Indians also intermingled and produced descendants of even greater racial mixture—part Indian, part Spanish, part black. No distinctive name was ever applied to these offspring; they were usually called simply *castas*.

For the first 150 years of Spanish colonial rule the number of *castas* was relatively small, and racially mixed offspring were usually absorbed into the Spanish, Indian, or black groups. During this time only a handful were categorized as *castas*, and these were usually divided into either *mestizos* or mulattoes. About the middle of the seventeenth century, these groups began to develop an identity of their own. Instead of merely being people who lacked either the tribal affiliation of native peoples or the social prerogatives of Spaniards, they came increasingly to constitute groups in their own right. Women of these intermediate groups were more often employed than their Spanish counterparts, whereas the men were apt to be artisans, but journeymen rather than masters.

Racially mixed people were officially banned from positions of influence in colonial society. They could not sit on town councils, serve as notaries, or become members of the more exclusive artisan guilds such as the goldsmiths. They were barred from the priesthood and from the universities. Those designated as *mestizos* were exempt from the tribute payment owed by their Indian relatives, but no such exemption was granted mulattoes; even when freed, they were subject to the traditional payments of conquered peoples to their rulers.

The dramatic growth of the *castas* in the eighteenth century was an increase in sheer numbers of *castas* as well as a proliferation in the number of racial categories. From the simple divisions of *mestizo* and mulatto emerged categories such as the *castizo*, an intermediate position between Spaniard and *mestizo*, and *morisco*, the equivalent between mulatto and Spaniard. And the steady rise of intermarriages among the racially mixed population itself produced an enormous range of physical types, in turn generating a number of novel, often fanciful names for the sheer physical variety apparent for the first time in large numbers during the eighteenth century.

INDIANS

The Indians were a conquered people, and many of the earliest social distinctions regarding them, such as

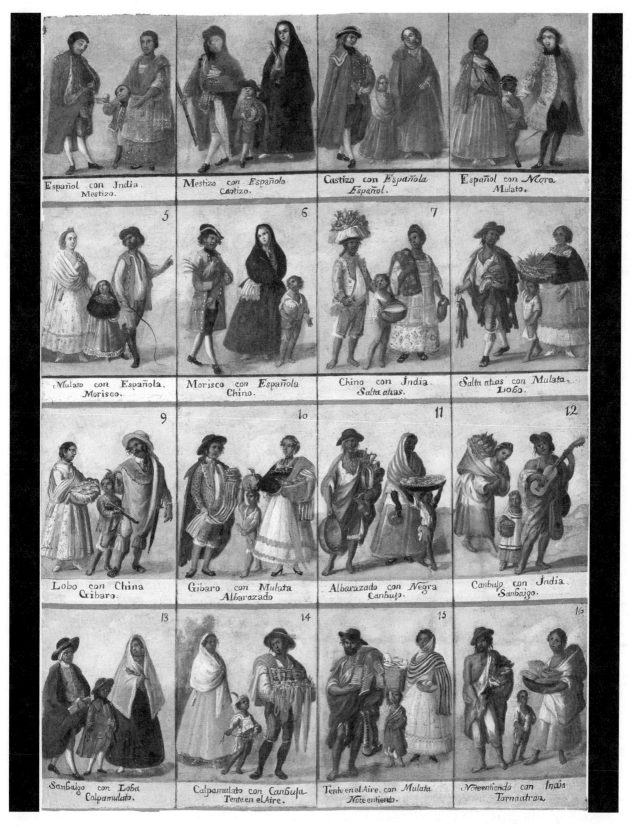

Castes, anonymous, 18th century. This Mexican painting catalogs the various different racial combinations possible in the racially diverse society of eighteenth-century Mexico. PHOTO BY BOB SCHALKWIJK

the payment of tribute, stemmed from their initial relationship to the Crown as conquered subjects. Spanish rulers exempted indigenous elites from payment of tribute and granted them the honorific "Don," characteristic of the Spanish lesser nobility. But whereas such titles and exemptions from tribute were hereditary among Spaniards, these titles were held only by Indians who were incumbents. Because the offices they held were rarely hereditary—instead they were passed among members of the community, often by elections—the exemptions from tribute were rarely permanent.

Indigenous communities in the New World were overwhelmingly agricultural. Indians farmed land, either their own or that of Spaniards. Some resided in communities near Spanish settlements, others were forcibly removed and "congregated" near such settlements. In some regions Indians engaged in fishing or hunting. In the urban areas of the Americas, Indians were more apt to be construction workers (e.g., bricklayers, stonemasons), day laborers, or vendors of agricultural products.

In the mining regions of Central and South America, Spaniards used Indians to mine the gold and especially the silver found in regions located away from major population centers. Spaniards uprooted Indians, temporarily or permanently, and relocated them in communities near the mines. Slaves were rarely employed in the mines, and never in large numbers. Mining was the labor of Indians.

SLAVES

In the early years of the Spanish Conquest a great number of Indians were captured and enslaved on the Caribbean islands and nearby landfalls. Slavery was blamed by many for the devastation of indigenous communities, and the practice was outlawed by the New Laws of 1542, though natives who fought the Spaniards in frontier regions were often enslaved as late as the seventeenth century.

Following the devastation of native peoples in the Caribbean, blacks were introduced as slave labor. The largest number of black slaves arrived in the Spanish colonies between 1550 and 1650, corresponding with growth in the cultivation of sugar in Spanish America. But with the surpassing success of sugar production in seventeenth-century Brazil, the Spanish American industry shrank substantially,

along with the number of imported slaves. In the nineteenth century, both the number of imported slaves of African origin and the sugar industry were revived in the Spanish Caribbean. But on the mainland, the numbers of imported slaves fell off sharply after 1650. In addition to the slaves in sugar-growing regions, there were a small number of slaves in the entourages of the wealthy and powerful in Spanish American capitals. These slaves were often pages, working in the urban homes of the well-to-do.

Between the middle of the seventeenth century and the end of the next century, the slaves of African origin disappeared as a readily identifiable social group in Spanish America. In some cities the African presence persisted into the nineteenth century. In the last years of Spanish rule, approximately one-third of the population of Buenos Aires was considered black, but by the end of the nineteenth century the percentage of Afro-Argentines had dropped to 2 percent. Nevertheless, their integration into the racially mixed population was central to the transformation of Spanish New World society in the eighteenth and nineteenth centuries.

HISTORICAL CHANGES

The longest running debates over eighteenth-century society in Latin America have concerned the nature of its economic and social transformation. Historians have long noted an increase in economic opportunities during the era. Increased silver production, growing domestic markets for agricultural products and textiles, and increased trade, both licit and illicit, produced unprecedented population and economic growth. This growth allowed many outside the traditional economic and social elites to acquire fortunes. There was a marked increase in the number of prosperous elites, accompanied by an unusual rise in the wealth of traditionally lower-status groups, including those of mixed racial ancestry. Historians have disagreed over whether Spanish society barred entrance to those with new wealth, particularly those of racially mixed origin.

Some historians have argued that there was a rigid social structure known as a society of castes (*sociedad de castas*), and they support their view with reference to the continuing legal and economic disabilities of natives and descendants of African-born people. Furthermore, they point to well-known paintings commissioned in the eighteenth century by wealthy Spaniards showing a proliferation of racial categories. These paintings depict the dress, food, and activity of various racial types in their homes. The paintings are arranged in a series of miniportraits that follow the order of a written or printed page, beginning at the upper left side of the page and depicting a family group sitting down to a meal in a well-appointed home. The label at the top of this miniportrait describes them in genealogical terms: "From Spaniard and Indian comes mestizo." The next portrait portrays in equally favorable terms the intermarriage of mestizo and Spaniard, producing "castizo." The third or fourth portrait begins the sequence all over again portraying a Spanish man and a black woman. But after two or three portraits of Spanish-black unions, reading from left to right, one gradually encounters a profusion of intermediate scenes, depicting various mixtures of Indian and black, often with highly fanciful names, such as "there you are," or derogatory ones, such as "wolf." The final portrait is often one of a poor hut, badly furnished, and depicting a woman with a frying pan chasing her husband. Not only is the lowest caste poor, but the paternalism of the Spanish family is inverted, and the woman dominates the man, thus indicating how far they are from the Spanish norm in the upper left. These portraits reveal the prejudice that accompanied the legal liabilities of various categories, and often have been cited as evidence of the difficulties of social mobility in the eighteenth century. However, newer interpretations have detected more creole pride and identity in these painting: Some scholars have suggested that some of the paintings subtly defend Spanish-American culture against European stereotypes and prejudices.

Other historians have focused on the ways in which rigid legal categories and physical distinctions appear to have been overcome. In some cases racial categories were altered on christening records, and a humble origin could be overcome by reputation and wealth. The regional differences of Latin America appear to have had a bearing on such nobility. Some studies suggest that by the time Mexico achieved independence, several members of the titled nobility were *mestizos*; in Peru fewer such examples can be found.

The differences between the terms *caste* and *class* have been drawn more commonly by U.S. historians than by Latin American scholars. Their use as labels to differentiate open and closed societies was first

Peasants in Mexico City, 1860s (engraving) by French School (19th century). PRIVATE COLLECTION / KEN WELSH / THE BRIDGEMAN ART LIBRARY

suggested in the 1930s by the U.S. sociologist William Lloyd Warner (1898–1970). On the basis of his work and U.S. sociology of the 1950s and 1960s, the ways of distinguishing between a caste and a class society have focused on interracial marriage as the key to integration and the definition of an open society. As a result, much of the controversy generated by the dispute has centered on questions such as whether the Spaniards were intermarrying with members of the castes, which racial groups (castes) were marrying members of other groups, and what were the marriage patterns of the black community, which became integrated during the eighteenth century.

Among Latin American historians, class has been addressed in terms of the emergence of a bourgeoisie, or middle class. The question for many Latin American historians has been whether the individuals who profited from or led the economic revival of the eighteenth century should be considered members of an emerging bourgeoisie, and questions of a class society tend to revolve around the economic attitudes and behavior of the emerging economic elites. Latin American historians, and some U.S. historians of Marxist orientation, have been more apt to use the term *feudal* rather than *caste* to designate a closed society.

The final transformation of caste and class structure in colonial Spanish America came with independence. Peninsular Spaniards were officially expelled by many resentful creole communities. Tribute payments by native communities were suspended throughout Spanish America, either at independence or shortly thereafter. Slavery was usually abolished by the new republics within the first two decades of independence, except in the remaining Spanish possessions in the Caribbean, where it endured well into the nineteenth century. Men of mixed racial origin had access to arms and became skilled in using those arms against Spanish troops during the wars for independence. Arms and the horse remained symbols of power, but were no longer identified with Spanish rule and the caste system.

Throughout most of Spanish America, the close of the colonial era removed the rigid racial hierarchy that had lasted for three centuries. The legal distinctions of tribute payers and slaves disappeared, and in many regions, the superiority automatically conferred upon Spaniards gradually disappeared. In its place emerged a society also stratified by wealth and power, but one where those distinctions were no longer automatically registered by differences of race.

See also **Castizo; Class Structure in Modern Latin America; Creole; Marriage and Divorce; Mestizo; New Laws of 1542; Peninsular; Race and Ethnicity; Slavery: Spanish America; Slavery: Indian Slavery and Forced Labor; Sociology.**

BIBLIOGRAPHY

Anderson, Rodney. "Race and Social Stratification: A Comparison of Working Class Spaniards, Indians, and Castas in Guadalajara, Mexico, in 1821." *Hispanic American Historical Review* 68, no. 2 (1988): 209–243.

Bennett, Herman L. *Africans in Colonial Mexico: Absolutism, Christianity, and Afro-Creole Consciousness, 1570–1640.* Bloomington: Indiana University Press, 2003.

Chance, John K. *Race and Class in Colonial Oaxaca.* Stanford, CA: Stanford University Press, 1978.

Cope, R. Douglas. *The Limits of Racial Domination: Plebeian Society in Colonial Mexico, 1660–1720.* Madison: University of Wisconsin Press, 1994.

Katzew, Ilona. *Casta Painting: Images of Race in Eighteenth-century Mexico.* New Haven, CT: Yale University Press, 2004.

Lavallé, Bernard. *Las promesas ambiguas: Ensayos sobre el criollismo colonial en los Andes.* Lima: Pontificia Universidad Católica del Perú, Instituto Riva-Agüero, 1993.

Lutz, Christopher. *Santiago de Guatemala, 1541–1773: City, Caste, and the Colonial Experience.* Norman: University of Oklahoma Press, 1994.

Marín Bosch, Miguel. "Puebla neocolonial, 1777–1831 casta, ocupación y matrimonio en la segunda ciudad de Nueva España." Ph.d. diss., Columbia University, 2004.

McAlister, Lyle. "Social Structure and Social Change in New Spain." *Hispanic American Historical Review* 43 (1963): 349–370.

Mörner, Magnus. *Race Mixture in the History of Latin America.* Boston: Little, Brown, 1967.

Seed, Patricia. "Social Dimensions of Race: Mexico City, 1753." *Hispanic American Historical Review* 62, no. 4 (1982): 569–606.

Seed, Patricia, and Philip Rust. "Estate and Class in Colonial Oaxaca Revisited." *Comparative Studies in Society and History* 25 (1983): 703–709, 721–724.

Twinam, Ann. *Public Lives, Private Secrets: Gender, Honor, Sexuality, and Illegitimacy in Colonial Spanish America.* Stanford, CA: Stanford University Press, 1999.

PATRICIA SEED
BYRON CRITES

CASTELLANOS, AARÓN GONZÁLEZ

(1800–1880). Aarón González Castellanos (*b.* 8 August 1800; *d.* 1 April 1880), commonly regarded as the greatest promoter of agricultural colonization of nineteenth-century Argentina. Born in the city of Salta, as a young man he joined the cavalry forces led by a regional caudillo named Martin Güemes, who fought against the Spanish. After the conclusion of the wars of independence, he went to Peru, where he engaged in trade in the mining center of Cerro de Pasco. Subsequently he became involved in an ambitious colonization scheme on the Río Bermejo but was persecuted by Paraguayan dictator José Francia, who held him prisoner from 1825 to 1830. Later Castellanos established himself in Buenos Aires Province, where he raised cattle. In the late 1830s he sold his properties and went to Paris, where he became known for writing several descriptive publications on Argentina. Castellanos returned to Argentina in 1853 and convinced the provincial government of Santa Fe to support his colonization scheme in the Chaco region. He helped finance the emigration of 200 families of agricultural workers from Dunkirk and Antwerp, then founded the agricultural colony of Esperanza in Santa Fe, which is still a prosperous grain-producing town. Castellanos also promoted the construction of docks in the port of Rosario and served in the municipal government of that city.

See also **Argentina: The Nineteenth Century.**

BIBLIOGRAPHY

Martin Mulhall, *Handbook of the River Plate* (1885).

Additional Bibliography

Caro Figueroa, Gregorio A. "Aarón Castellanos y las colonias en la Argentina." *Todo es Historia* 32:371 (June 1998): 38–40.

CARLOS MARICHAL

CASTELLANOS, GONZALO (1926–).

Gonzalo Castellanos (*b.* 1926) Venezuelan composer and conductor. Born in Caracas to a musical family, Castellanos studied piano and organ with his father before apprenticing with the great Vicente Emilio Sojo at the National Modern School. This institution and its graduates initiated a new movement in Venezuelan music that was based on a postimpressionist aesthetic. Castellanos traveled to Paris, where he was active in the Schola Cantorum, and later received training from the European pianist Sergiu Celibidache. Upon his return to Venezuela, Castellanos conducted the Venezuela Symphony Orchestra and served at the collegium of the Museum of Caracas. Among his most famous pieces are *Suite caraqueña, Symphonic Fantasy,* and *Andelación e imitación fugaz.*

See also **Music: Art Music.**

BIBLIOGRAPHY

Helen Delpar, ed., *Encyclopedia of Latin America* (1974).

José Antonio Calcano, *La ciudad y su música: Crónica músical de Caracas* (1985).

Luís Felipe Ramón y Rivera, *50 Años de música en Caracas, 1930–1980* (1988).

Additional Bibliography

Astor, Miguel. *Aproximación fenomenológica a la obra musical de Gonzalo Castellanos Yumar.* Caracas: Comisión de Estudios de Postgrado, 2002.

KAREN RACINE

CASTELLANOS, JUAN DE (1522–1607).

Juan de Castellanos (*b.* 9 March 1522; *d.* 27 November 1607), Spanish poet-chronicler, soldier, and priest. Born to farmers in Alanís (Seville province), Spain, as a teenager with some command of Latin, Castellanos went to Puerto Rico, where he continued his studies. In 1540, he traveled to Cubagua, an island off the Venezuelan coast, to work as a pearl fisherman, then joined the army and traveled to New Granada and Venezuela (1541–1545). From 1545 to 1554 he campaigned in the Bogotá and Pamplona regions, before being ordained a Roman Catholic priest in Cartagena (ca. 1554). Castellanos was curate and diocesan treasurer of Cartagena from 1557 to 1558, when he became curate of Riohacha, a position he served in until 1560. He moved to Tunja, in the highlands, as an assistant curate sometime after 1561; in 1568 he became curate. In Tunja, Castellanos devoted much of his time to writing. His *Elegías y elogios de varones ilustres de Indias* was composed between 1570 and 1590. Its nearly 114,000 verses narrate the discovery, conquest, and settlement of Spanish America, especially New Granada and Venezuela.

See also **New Granada, Viceroyalty of; Venezuela: The Colonial Era.**

BIBLIOGRAPHY

Ulíses Rojas, *Juan de Castellanos: Biografía* (1958).

Mario Germán Romero, *Juan de Castellanos* (1964).

Additional Bibliography

Pardo, Isaac. *Juan de Castellanos: Estudio de las elegías de varones ilustres de Indias.* Caracas: Academia Nacional de la Historia, 1991.

Restrepo, Luis Fernando, ed. *Antología crítica de Juan de Castellanos: Elegías de varones ilustres de Indias.* Bogotá: Editorial Pontificia Universidad Javeriana, 2004.

J. LEÓN HELGUERA

CASTELLANOS, ROSARIO (1925–1974).

Rosario Castellanos (*b.* 25 May 1925; *d.* 7 August 1974), Mexican author and diplomat. Born in Mexico City, Castellanos spent her youth in the state of Chiapas, a region with a high concentration of Indians and a history of conflict between the Tzotzil Indians and the wealthy landowners. In two prize-winning novels, *Balún-Canan* (1957; *The Nine Guardians,* 1960) and *Oficio de Tinieblas* (1962), and in the short stories of *Ciudad Real* (1960), Castellanos depicted the psychology and cosmology of the Chiapas Indians without romanticizing or stereotyping her characters, a marked departure from earlier "indigenist" writers.

Castellanos, educated at the National Autonomous University and in Madrid, also pioneered new territory in her exploration of gender relations. Her published master's thesis, *Sobre cultura femenina* (1950), provided the intellectual underpinnings for the contemporary women's movement in Mexico. Her essays, published regularly in Mexican periodicals and compiled in collections such as *Juicios sumarios* (1966) and *Mujer que sabe latín* (1973), as well as her dramatic works, particularly *El eterno femenino* (1975), and some thirteen volumes of poetry, often probed issues relating to the place of women in Mexican culture and history.

Castellanos was also a teacher and diplomat. She taught Latin American literature in Mexico, the United States, and Israel. From 1971 until her accidental death in 1974, she was Mexico's ambassador to Israel.

See also **Feminism and Feminist Organizations; Literature: Spanish America.**

BIBLIOGRAPHY

Maureen Ahern and Mary Seale Vázquez, eds., *Homenaje a Rosario Castellanos* (1980), contains several excellent critical studies in English of Castellanos's work, as well as a useful bibliography. For an insightful analysis of the relationship between Castellanos's life and works, see Oscar Bonifaz Caballeros, *Remembering Rosario,* translated and edited by Myralyn F. Allgood (1990). For understanding the intellectual development of Castellanos as a writer, see the interview in Enrique Carballo, *Diecinueve protagonistas de la literatura mexicana del siglo XX* (1965).

Additional Bibliography

Ahern, Maureen, ed. *A Rosario Castellanos Reader: An Anthology of Her Poetry, Short Fiction, Essays, and Drama.* Austin: University of Texas Press, 1988.

Galindo Ulloa, Javier. *La farsa y la mujer mexicana en el eterno femenino de Rosario Castellanos.* México, D.F.: Consejo Nacional para la Cultura y las Artes, 2004.

VIRGINIA M. BOUVIER

CASTELLI, JUAN JOSÉ (1764–1812).

Juan José Castelli (*b.* 19 July 1764; *d.* 12 October 1812), Argentine independence leader. The son of an Italian father and Spanish mother, Castelli was born in Buenos Aires and studied law at the University of Chuquisaca in Upper Peru (modern Bolivia). He practiced in Buenos Aires, where, along with his cousin Manuel Belgrano and other creoles who had absorbed Enlightenment ideas, he worked to promote liberal reforms.

In 1810 Castelli took an active part in the May Revolution and was one of the secretaries of the revolutionary junta. That same year the junta sent him to accompany an expeditionary force to Upper Peru, where he proposed the elimination of monastic houses and other radical religious innovations, while also seeking to enlist the Indian population in the struggle. When Upper Peru was lost in mid-1811, Castelli's rivals sought to make him a scapegoat; he stood trial in Buenos Aires, but before a verdict could be handed down he died of cancer.

See also **Argentina: The Colonial Period.**

BIBLIOGRAPHY

Julio César Chaves, *Castelli, el adalid de mayo,* 2d ed. (1957).

John Lynch, *The Spanish-American Revolutions, 1808–1826* (1973).

Additional Bibliography

Delgado, Josefina. "Andrés Rivera y el sueño eterno de Castelli." *Todo Es Historia* 27:315 (October 1993): 56–59.

Lesser, Rocardo. *La infancia de los próceres: Belgrano, Rivadavia, Moreno, Castelli, Azcuénaga.* Buenos Aires: Editorial Biblos, 2004.

DAVID BUSHNELL

CASTELLO BRANCO, HUMBERTO DE ALENCAR

(1900–1967). Humberto de Alencar Castello Branco (*b.* 20 September 1900; *d.* 18 July 1967), president of Brazil (1964–1967). A *nordestino* (northeasterner) from Fortaleza, Castello Branco was born of a long line of military officers. After studying at the Military Preparatory School of Rio Prado in Rio Grande do Sul from 1912 to 1917, he enrolled as a cadet in the Realengo Military Academy in Rio de Janeiro. Commissioned into the army in 1921, he married Argentina Vianna the next year. Devout Catholics, the couple formed a close union until her death in 1963.

EARLY CAREER

As a young lieutenant devoted to professionalism and the rule of law, Castello Branco declined to participate in the various military uprisings of the 1920s. Instead he fought against the Luís Carlos Prestes Column in Mato Grosso and Bahia and remained loyal to the government during the Revolution of 1930.

Castello Branco was promoted to captain in 1932, and then named assistant director at Realengo, where he had previously served as an instructor. He was also attached to the French military mission. Subsequently he was sent to Paris to attend the Superior War College, which enhanced his academic reputation.

In 1940 Castello Branco, now a major, was posted to assist the minister of war, Eurico G. Dutra, who later became president (1946–1951). In preparation for dispatching the Brazilian Expeditionary Force (FEB), Castello Branco was enrolled in the U.S. Army Command and General Staff College at Fort Leavenworth, Kansas, in 1943. As a lieutenant colonel he embarked the next year for Italy, where he was chief of operations (G-3) of the Brazilian Expeditionary Force. After advancing to colonel in 1945 for his effectiveness during that campaign, he returned to Brazil, where he alternated between general staff and field assignments. In 1952 he was named brigadier general and assumed command of the Tenth Military Region (Ceará). In 1954 he signed the General's Manifesto of 23 August calling for the resignation of President Getúlio Vargas.

After commanding the army's general staff college in 1954–1955, Castello Branco moved on to the Escola Superior da Guerra (ESG), Brazil's Superior War College, as assistant commandant and director of the armed forces and command course in 1956–1958. As general of division he was transferred in 1958–1960 to head the Amazonia and Eighth Military Region headquartered in Belém, Pará, and went on to assume the directorship of army instruction, which allowed him to remain in close contact with the war college.

The ascension to the presidency of reformist Jânio da Silva Quadros in 1961 and his subsequent resignation and replacement by populist João Goulart provoked a crisis in the officer corps that polarized into legalist and hard-line factions. In spite of Goulart's pro-Castro stance, nonaligned foreign policy, counterproductive economic policies, and support for a radical syndicalist republic, Castello Branco remained a legalist until early 1964.

Named a four-star general and posted to command the Fourth Army at Recife in 1962, Castello Branco found the Northeast unsettled by Peasant League–provoked turmoil, fomented, he believed, by Pernambuco governor Miguel Arraes and President Goulart's brother-in-law, Leonel Brizola, leader of one of the socialist parties. Once elevated to army chief of staff in mid-1963, Castello Branco sought to persuade President Goulart to abandon certain of his allegedly unconstitutional actions. Failing to do so, he agreed, in the name of legality, to head a long-prepared military-civilian conspiracy to oust the chief executive.

THE PRESIDENCY

A well-planned coup led by the army, state governors, and opposition congressmen came off easily, with little loss of life on 31 March 1964. Discussions among the various governors, congressmen, business leaders, politicians, and high-ranking military men resulted in Castello Branco's selection as president. On 11 April 1964, by a wide margin the congress confirmed him as president to complete the remaining two years of Goulart's term. While pledging to respect the Constitution of 1946, Castello Branco appointed coconspirator General Artur da Costa e Silva as war minister.

The new chief executive hoped to turn this joint military-civilian coup into a revolution dedicated to controlling inflation, containing Communism, fomenting economic development, and promoting political, social, and educational reform. A team player, Castello Branco selected Roberto Campos as minister of finance and Octavio Bulhões as minister of planning. Together they instituted an indexation system to neutralize economic distortions caused by a high rate of inflation, as well as a tax-reform structure that forced firms and individuals to adopt realistic accounting methods.

A long-term economic policy that endured for some fifteen years was launched under Castello Branco, who sought to promote capital formation, expand the market for durable consumer goods, reduce wages, foster industrial exports, and stimulate foreign capital investment. This growth strategy, however, was designed to perpetuate the country's basic economic and social structure, thereby permitting the traditional agricultural elite to support the regime while the industrial sector expanded. Hence, the nation's potential was developed while its agricultural and industrial sectors retained control. Because foreign as well as domestic stability was deemed essential to development, Brazil avoided being drawn into conflict with the United States, the dominant power in the hemisphere, and sought to associate itself with the United States in global affairs. The latter in turn reciprocated with generous financial aid and investment.

The Castello Branco regime further insured internal order by a series of measures known as Institutional Acts. The first, promoted by the hard-liners and enacted on 9 April 1964, actually prior to Castello Branco's inauguration, sought to purify the government. Three former presidents—Jânio da Silva Quadros, João Goulart, and Juscelino Kubitschek De Oliveira—as well as seventy others were stripped of their political rights. In addition, the granting of tenure to civil servants was suspended for six months and military police courts, called IPMs, were established to investigate subversion.

The Second Institutional Act, effective 27 October 1965, was provoked by the reaction of hard-liners to state elections that went against the regime. Under this act all political parties were dissolved, indirect election of the president by congress was mandated, the government's right to dismiss civil servants was reinstated, citizens' political rights were canceled, and the Supreme Court was packed. The next month Brazil's political parties were re-formed. A government party, the National Renovating

Alliance (Arena), and an opposition party, the Brazilian Democratic Movement (MDB), were established in congress.

Early in 1966, Castello Branco's presidential term was extended, against his wishes, for another year, to 15 March 1967. Protests against these measures then erupted, led by the National University Students Union and by certain socially sensitive Catholic clergy, notably Hélder Cámara, archbishop of Olinda and Recife.

Tensions increased as presidential candidates proliferated. Castello Branco favored a civilian successor. União Democrática Nacional leader Olavo Bilac Pinto, Senator Daniel Krieger of Rio Grande do Sul, and Foreign Minister Juracy Magalhães were his top choices. Nevertheless, the hard-liners prevailed. War Minister Costa e Silva, who was nominated and inaugurated on 15 March 1967, served as president until 1969.

In retirement, Castello Branco continued to exert a moderating influence on national affairs until his untimely death in an airplane accident.

See also **Brazil, Political Parties: Brazilian Democratic Movement (MDB); Brazil, Political Parties: National Renovating Alliance (ARENA); Institutional Acts.**

BIBLIOGRAPHY

Richard Bourne, *Political Leaders of Latin America* (1970).

Rollie E. Poppino, *Brazil: The Land and People* (1973).

John W. F. Dulles, *Castello Branco: The Making of a Brazilian President* (1978) and *President Castello Branco, Brazilian Reformer* (1980).

Hélio Vianna, "O pensamento militar de Castello Branco," in *Revista do Instituto Histórico e Geográfico Brasileiro* 321 (1978): 242–249.

Vernon A. Walters, *Silent Missions* (1978).

Eurico De Lima Figueiredo, *Os Militares e a democracia: Análise estrutural da ideologia do Pres. Castello Branco* (1980).

Additional Bibliography

Neto, Lira. *Castello: A marcha para a ditadura*. São Paulo: Editora Contexto, 2004.

Silva, André Luiz Reis da. *A diplomacia brasileira entre a segurança e o desenvolvimento: A política externa do governo Castelo Branco, 1964–1967*. São Paulo: Editora Contexto, 2004.

LEWIS A. TAMBS

CASTE WAR OF YUCATÁN.

Regarded by many as the most militarily successful Indian rebellion in Latin American history, the Guerra de Castas (Caste War) remains the central historical event in the regional popular mind. In fact, many Yucatecans often assume that when one speaks of "the Revolution," one is referring to the great peasant rebellion unleashed in 1847, not the more recent national upheaval that began in 1910.

The rash of agrarian revolts and caste wars that erupted in several key Mexican regions in the aftermath of independence points up both the disintegration of the imperial central state and the political and economic disenfranchisement of Indian minorities during the early national period. In Yucatán, hostilities broke out on the state's southeastern frontier of commercial sugar expansion. Here the Maya peasantry bitterly resented increased taxation, the loss of their *milpa* (maize lands), and debt peonage and physical abuse on the sugar plantations. Also, the Church caused widespread resentment among the Maya. Although priests lost power after independence, according to some scholars they remained owners of large properties and used their position to repress Native American communities. But unlike their more domesticated counterparts in the older northwestern zone of corn-and-cattle haciendas, the frontier Maya still had the cultural capacity and the mobility to resist white domination. When a series of petty disputes between elite political factions expediently put guns into Indian hands, the frontier Maya turned these guns on the white leaders.

Recent ethnohistorical research, particularly in Maya language sources, has helped to clarify the racial or caste nature of the war. A dominant theme in the communications of Indian leaders is that the laws should apply equally to all peoples, whatever their ethnic background. In this sense, the free Maya made a social revolution to erase caste distinctions. These demands began with the dismantling of the colonial order. During the independence movement, indigenous communities cited the liberal Spanish constitution of 1812 to argue for equality and lower taxes. On the other hand, the fearful and skittish white elites bore most of the responsibility for redefining a social conflict into a brutal race war. During the earliest days of the rebellion they decided not to honor the distinction that then existed between rich Indian Caciques (or *hidalgos,* as they were then called) and the majority of poor, landless Indians. Many of these educated, politically powerful Maya had connections in, and identified closely with, white society. By persecuting and actually lynching members of this privileged class, the whites forced such caciques as Jacinto Pat and Cecilio Chi to identify as Indians and contribute their leadership abilities to the rebel movement. Interestingly, while the war was generally fought along racial lines, many Maya peons tied to the haciendas of northwestern Yucatán remained loyal to their white *patrones.* Indeed, their support may have been crucial in preventing their masters from being killed or driven from the peninsula during the darkest days of the war in 1848. It is the participation of these Maya auxiliaries—as well as the defection of some mestizo and white troops to the rebel Maya side—that has led some historians to argue that the War of the Castes is badly named.

Other nineteenth-century indigenous peasant rebellions would last longer than the Caste War of Yucatán (for example, the Yaqui rebellion in Sonora), encompass a greater geographical area (the Sierra Gorda revolt in central Mexico), or range more freely in their depredations against the dominant white society (the Cora rebellion of Manuel Lozada). Yet none had as many advantages as the rebel Maya: a homogeneous ethnic base still animated by a vigorous pre-Hispanic cultural tradition; the absence of serious natural obstacles (mountains, rivers, and so forth), which reinforced this ethnic identity and strategically facilitated mobility across the frontier of white settlement; the proximity of British arms and supplies from Belize; and the weak economic, political, and logistical ties between Yucatán and central Mexico, which permitted the revolt to proceed for some time without federal intervention.

It is not surprising, therefore, that the Yucatecan rebellion was the most violent of this turbulent age, nor that its regional consequences were likely the most profound. Estimates of human loss and economic dislocation are staggering: the peninsula's population declined at least 30–40 percent. The southeastern sugar industry was destroyed; Yucatán's economic and demographic center of gravity would shift from the southeast to the northwest, the site of the future Henequen boom.

But Henequen's development would begin only after the northwest had been cleared of rebel Maya. At the point of their furthest advance, in June and July 1848, these indios bravos controlled three-fourths of the Yucatán peninsula—and were on the verge of capturing the last two important white strongholds, Mérida and Campeche, before their campaign was interrupted by the economic and cultural imperative to return home for the planting season. In the meantime, the whites were able to regroup—receiving food and ammunition from Havana, Veracruz, and New Orleans, and reinforcements from the federal government. By 1853, the Maya had been driven across the southeastern frontier of settlement into remote portions of Yucatán and what are today the states of Campeche and Quintana Roo. That year a substantial number of the rebels—known henceforth as the *pacíficos del sur*—signed a truce that permitted them a relatively autonomous existence in the Chenes region of Campeche. Meanwhile, however, to the northeast, in the chicle forests of Quintana Roo, a diehard faction of rebel Maya, the Cruzob, would have no truck with the hated whites. Remarkably, they would maintain an independent Maya state centered on a millenarian cult of the Talking Cross until they were finally overrun by a large, combined force of Yucatecan and federal troops in 1901.

See also **Messianic Movements: Spanish America; Race and Ethnicity.**

BIBLIOGRAPHY

Bricker, Victoria R. *The Indian Christ, the Indian King* (1981).

Campos García, Melchor. *Guerra de Castas en Yucatán: Su origen sus consecuencias y su estado actual, 1866.* Mérida, Yucatán, México: Universidad Autónoma de Yucatán, 1997.

Joseph, Gilbert M. *Rediscovering the Past at Mexico's Periphery: Essays on the History of Modern Yucatán* (1986).

Reed, Nelson. *The Caste War of Yucatan* (1964).

Rugeley, Terry. *Yucatán's Maya Peasantry and the Origins of the Caste War.* Austin: University of Texas Press, 1996.

Sullivan, Paul. *Unfinished Conversations: Mayas and Foreigners Between Two Wars* (1991).

GILBERT M. JOSEPH

CASTILE. Castile, sovereign territory of the kings of Spain, was united with Aragon by the marriage in 1469 of Ferdinand II of Aragon and Isabella I of Castile. The kingdom of Castile was carved out by the Reconquest of Spain, which shaped its enduring political, social, and economic structures, and by the regional division of the Castilian *meseta* (tableland) into a northern area of small land proprietors and villages called Old Castile and a southern area dominated by larger landowners and towns known as New Castile. Superficially united under the crown of Aragon during the reign of Ferdinand and Isabella, its growing economic strength allowed it to become an imperial power colonizing the New World. The Catholic monarchs contracted with Columbus to explore "the Indies." Their successor, Charles I, expanded Columbus's conquests to include large swaths of Mesoamerica and the Andes. Madrid became the empire's capital in 1561, when Philip II took the court there and the concept of Spain began to take precedence over Castile. Its culture and legal system were used to bring its transatlantic colonies into the fold. In the early twenty-first century the language of Castile is the official language of most Hispanic American republics.

See also **Columbus, Christopher; Explorers and Exploration: Spanish America; Ferdinand II of Aragon; Isabella I of Castile.**

BIBLIOGRAPHY

Elliott, John H. *Imperial Spain, 1469–1716.* 1963. Reprint, New York: New American Library, 1977; see in particular pp. 24–43.

Carr, Raymond. *Spain, 1808–1975,* 2nd edition. Oxford: Clarendon Press, 1982. See in particular pp. 1–37.

Kamen, Henry. *Spain, 1469–1714: A Society of Conflict.* London; New York: Longman, 1983. See in particular pp. 9–15.

Moraña, Mabel, ed. *Ideologies of Hispanism.* Nashville, TN: Vanderbilt University Press, 2005.

Pagden, Anthony. *Lords of All the World: Ideologies of Empire in Spain, Britain and France c. 1500–c. 1800.* New Haven, CT: Yale University Press, 1995.

SUZANNE HILES BURKHOLDER
THOMAS WARD

CASTILHOS, JÚLIO DE (1860–1903).

Júlio Prates de Castilhos (b. 29 June 1860; d. 24 October 1903) was a Brazilian statesman and founder of the positivist dictatorship of Rio Grande do Sul. A graduate of the São Paulo law school, Castilhos agitated for a federal republican regime as the editor of Rio Grande's republican newspaper. He led the state delegation at the federal constituent assembly following the collapse of the Empire of Brazil in 1889. Returning to Porto Alegre, he imposed an authoritarian state constitution. Castilhos was elected governor in 1891, but was deposed for supporting Manoel Deodoro da Fonseca's failed coup. Castilhos's countercoup and second election in 1893 provoked a major but unsuccessful rebellion (1893–1895) by the Liberals (later called the Federalists). The governor left office in 1898, but continued to rule through his highly disciplined Republican Party until his early death from cancer in 1903.

Castilhos's state constitution, in effect till 1930, gave the governor decree power on all issues except setting the budget, and allowed him to serve indefinitely. The document was inspired by Auguste Comte (1798–1857), who had believed scientific laws would soon explain all social behavior, and that a "monocrat" should preside over the transition to the "positive" stage of history. Despite his authoritarianism, Castilhos's policies were progressive concerning rural land taxation and public education, and on these matters Rio Grande led the nation.

Castilhos's triumph over the Liberals also resulted in an economic power shift, diminishing the political influence of ranchers and raising that of farmers and industrialists. Even labor, by 1917, would receive some redress for low wages from the paternalistic government of Antônio Augusto Borges de Medeiros, Castilhos's successor. Borges used Castilhos's regime to rule the state from Castilhos's death until 1930, and most of that time served as governor.

See also Borges de Medeiros, Antônio Augusto; Brazil, The Empire (Second); Fonseca, Manoel Deodoro da.

BIBLIOGRAPHY

Axt, Gunter, et al., eds. *Júlio de Castilhos e o paradoxo republicano.* Porto Alegre, Brazil: Nova Prova, 2005.

Franco, Sérgio da Costa. *Júlio de Castilhos e sua época.* Porto Alegre, Brazil: Editora Globo, 1967.

Love, Joseph L. *Rio Grande do Sul and Brazilian Regionalism, 1882–1930.* Stanford, CA: Stanford University Press, 1971. See chapters 2–4.

JOSEPH L. LOVE

CASTILLA, RAMÓN (1797–1867).

Ramón Castilla (*b.* 27 August 1797; *d.* 25 May 1867), military officer and twice president of Peru (1845–1851, 1855–1862), he contributed to the formation of the Peruvian republican state during the nineteenth-century struggle by military strongmen (caudillos) after independence from Spain. His efforts were aided considerably by the dawn of the Guano Age, which brought considerable income from export activities to the Peruvian state.

Castilla was born in Tarapacá. During his early military career he was trained by the Spanish colonial army and fought against the forces of independence led by the Argentine General José de San Martín in Chacabuco, Chile (1817). Taken prisoner, he escaped to Brazil and then in 1818 to Peru. Castilla switched allegiances only in 1822, when he offered his military services to General San Martín in southern Peru. He fought in the army of Simón Bolívar against the Spanish army in the decisive battle of Ayacucho (1824), which guaranteed Peruvian independence.

After independence in 1825, Castilla was named subprefect of his native province of Tarapacá. He started his career as a rather conservative and creole-patriotic military caudillo by opposing Bolívar's constitutional designs. In 1829, Castilla rejected General Andrés de Santa Cruz's liberal leanings, instead supporting the protectionist and conservative General Agustín Gamarra. In 1833, Castilla fell from grace with Gamarra and transferred his support to generals Luis José de Orbegoso and Felipe Santiago Salaverry. When Santa Cruz seized power in 1836 for the second time, Castilla traveled to Chile and once again joined Gamarra in a successful Chilean military expedition against Santa Cruz's Peru-Bolivia Confederation. During Gamarra's second administration (1839–1841) Castilla was appointed minister of the treasury and in that capacity arranged the first guano export contracts with native businessman

Francisco Quirós. In 1841, Castilla was taken prisoner at Ingaví, Gamarra's failed last adventure against Bolivian forces. Soon, however, Castilla was politically active again in Cuzco.

By 1845, Castilla had surfaced as supreme chief from the complex caudillo struggles that pitted Generals Juan Crisóstomo Torrico, Francisco Vidal, and Manuel Ignacio Vivanco against each other. During Castilla's first administration his most important measure was the introduction of the first national budget. New contracts for guano marketing abroad were signed with local and foreign merchants. Eventually the British firm Antony Gibbs y Cía assumed the distribution of guano to Great Britain and the French firm Montané the distribution to France. Consequently, transportation began to improve (steamship lines, the first railway between Lima and Callao in 1851), and state finances, military facilities, and payroll became organized. Most important, Castilla regularized the service of the internal and external debts, introducing in 1850 the Law of Consolidation (amortization and repayment) of the floating national debt.

Castilla saw in General José Rufino Echenique a deserving successor and peacefully handed power to him in 1851. However, Echenique's supporters manipulated the consolidation of the internal debt to their own advantage through corrupt means. Politically, the archconservative Echenique began to drift away from Castilla's watchful eye. Sensing growing popular opposition, Castilla decided to lead a motley group of liberals and radicals who fought Echenique in a civil war (1854–1855). To obtain support, Castilla followed the advice of liberals Pedro Gálvez and Manuel Toribio Ureta and abolished slavery and the Indian tribute in 1854. Castilla regained power in 1855 after the battle of La Palma, in which Echenique was finally defeated.

During his second term of office, Castilla initially complied with the liberal faction that had supported him, pressing for the liberal constitution of 1856. However, after the defeat of the conservative reaction led by Vivanco in 1858, Castilla turned against his liberal supporters and promoted instead an executive-biased constitution that was enacted in 1860. His preoccupation with such constitutional matters earned him the name of "Soldier of the Law." A successful short war over boundaries with Ecuador in 1859 enhanced Castilla's conservative constitutionalist and nationalist stand.

At the end of his second term in 1862, Castilla once again peacefully handed power to elected General Miguel de San Román. However, San Román died in office and was succeeded by Vice President Juan Antonio Pezet, who, like Echenique before him, disregarded the influential Castilla. The unpopular Pezet was deposed as a result of the nationalist movement led by Colonel Mariano Ignacio Prado against the Spanish aggression of 1864–1866. Prado, however, was opposed by Castilla, who went into exile in Chile to organize yet another revolution. Castilla died in Tivilichi.

See also **Peru: Peru Since Independence; Peru-Bolivia Confederation.**

BIBLIOGRAPHY

Jorge Basadre, *Historia de la República del Perú*, vols. 2–3 (1963).

Alberto Regal, *Castilla constructor: Las obras de ingeniería de Castilla* (1967).

Celia Wu, *Generals and Diplomats: Great Britain and Peru, 1820–40* (1991).

Additional Bibliography

Cayo Córdoba, Percy. *Ramón Castilla*. Lima: Editorial Brasa, 1994.

Garibaldi, Rosa. *La política exterior del Perú en la era de Ramón Castilla: Defensa hemisférica y defensa de la jurisdicción nacional*. Perú: Fondo Editorial Fundación Academia Diplomática del Perú, 2003.

ALFONSO W. QUIROZ

CASTILLA DEL ORO. Castilla del Oro, the name given by a royal decree of 27 July 1513 to Pedro Arias ("Pedrarias") de Ávila as governor and captain-general, to "land which until now has been called Tierra Firme, [which] we now order be called Castilla del Oro." The name applies to a long stretch of mainland running west from the Peninsula of Paría in Venezuela past the Colombian port cities of Santa Marta and Cartagena into the Gulf of Darién and beyond to that part of Panama known in the early sixteenth century as Veragua.

Even by the rapacious standards of the day, the utter ruin wrought by Pedrarias was remarkable for its swiftness and brutality. The conqueror enlisted under his command such an assortment of wrongdoers that King Ferdinand II wrote to Pedrarias expressing concern, correctly but in vain, about "the quality of the men who have gone with you, soldiers who have been in Italy, [ones] accustomed to very great vices, so that you will have some difficulties." Pedrarias and his men looted and enslaved, torched people as well as property, threw native rulers who could not furnish quantities of gold quickly enough to killer dogs, and generally behaved with such demonic abandon that one official informed the Crown that "the land has become so aroused and alarmed by the grave indignities, killings, brutal robbery, and the burning of settlements that all the Castilians maintain themselves only like birds of prey and all the land is lost and desolate." The excesses committed by Pedrarias were never forgotten, even by chroniclers writing decades after his death.

See also **Ávila, Pedro Arias de; Ferdinand II of Aragon; Las Casas, Bartolomé de.**

BIBLIOGRAPHY

Carl O. Sauer, *The Early Spanish Main* (1966; 2d ed. 1992), tells the sorry tale of Castilla del Oro in all its squalor and sadness. The region's demise also figures in the sixteenth-century account of Bartolomé De Las Casas, *History of the Indies* (1971), translated and edited by Andrée M. Collard.

Additional Bibliography

Mena García, María del Carmen. *Sevilla y las flotas de Indias: La gran armada de Castilla del Oro (1513–1514)*. Sevilla, Spain: Universidad de Sevilla, Secretariado de Publicaciones, 1998.

W. GEORGE LOVELL

CASTILLO, ANA

CASTILLO, ANA (1953–). Ana Castillo is an acclaimed Chicana/Latina poet, novelist, and essayist as well as editor and translator. Born in Chicago on 15 June 1953, she received a B.A. degree from Northern Illinois University in 1975, an M.A. from the University of Chicago in 1979, and a PhD from the University of Bremen, Germany, in 1991. A self-proclaimed Xicanista, or Chicana, feminist, Castillo is innovative and provocative in her writing. She is known for her poetry collections, novels such as *The Mixquiahuala Letters* (1986), *So Far from God* (1993), and *Peel My Love Like an Onion* (1999), and nonfiction such as *Massacre of the Dreamers: Essays on Xicanisma* (1994). Castillo's honors include two NEA fellowships (1990, 1995), the Before Columbus Foundation American Book Award (1987) and the Carl Sandburg Literary Award in Fiction (1993). The Ana Castillo Archives are housed at the University of California, Santa Barbara.

See also **Hispanics in the United States; Literature: Spanish America.**

BIBLIOGRAPHY

Poetry by Castillo

Women Are Not Roses. Houston, TX: Arte Público Press, 1984.

My Father Was a Toltec: Poems. Albuquerque, NM: West End Press, 1988.

My Father Was a Toltec and Selected Poems, 1973–1988. New York: Norton, 1995.

I Ask the Impossible. New York: Doubleday, 2001.

Novels and Short Stories by Castillo

The Mixquiahuala Letters. Binghamton, NY: Bilingual Press, 1986. Reprinted, 1992.

Sapogonia: An Anti-Romance in 3/8 Meter. Tempe, AZ: Bilingual Press, 1990.

So Far from God. New York: Norton, 1993.

Las cartas de Mixquiahuala. Translated by Mónica Mansour. Mexico City: Grijalbo/Conaculta, 1994.

Loverboys: Short Stories. New York: Norton, 1996.

Peel My Love Like an Onion. New York: Doubleday/Random House, 1999.

Desnuda mi corazón como una cebolla. Mexico City: Alfaguara, 2001.

Watercolor Women, Opaque Men (Novel in Verse). Willimantic, CT: Curbstone Press, 2005.

Other Works by Castillo

PSST . . . I Have Something to Tell You, Mi Amor (play). San Antonio, TX: Wings Press, 2005.

My Daughter, My Son, the Eagle, the Dove: An Aztec Chant (children's book). New York: Dutton, 2000.

Editions and Translation by Castillo

Esta puente, mi espalda: Voces de mujeres tercermundistas en los Estados Unidos, ed. Cherríe Moraga and Ana

Castillo; trans. Ana Castillo and Norma Alarcón. San Francisco: ISM Press, 1988.

Massacre of the Dreamers: Essays on Xicanisma. Edited by Ana Castillo. Albuquerque: University of New Mexico Press, 1994.

Secondary Works

Delgadillo, Theresa. "Forms of Chicana Feminist Resistance: Hybrid Spirituality in Ana Castillo's *So Far from God.*" *Modern Fiction Studies* 44, no. 4 (1998): 888–916.

Quintana, Alvina E. "Ana Castillo's *The Mixquiahuala Letters*: The Novelist as Ethnographer." In *Criticism in the Borderlands: Studies in Chicano Literature, Culture, and Ideology,* ed. Héctor Calderón and José David Saldívar. Durham, NC: Duke University Press, 1991.

CLAIRE JOYSMITH

CASTILLO, JESÚS (1877–1946). Jesús Castillo (*b.* 9 September 1877; *d.* 23 April 1946), Guatemalan composer and student of native Indian music. Castillo was born in San Juan Ostuncalco, near Quezaltenango in the western highlands of Guatemala. As a young man he became interested in traditional Indian music. He composed his "First Indian Overture" based on the Dance of the Little Bulls, a traditional dance at fiestas. Traveling from village to village in the highlands, he collected data about the music of the different Indian groups. Castillo used themes and melodies in a classical tradition to compose his symphonic poems, suites, operas, and ballets. He became a leading authority on Indian music and instruments. His writings include *La música Maya-Quiché* (1941) and *Legado folklórico a la juventud guatemalteca* (1944). He died in Quezaltenango.

See also **Music: Popular Music and Dance.**

BIBLIOGRAPHY

Donald Thompson, "Castillo, Jesús," in *New Grove Dictionary of Music and Musicians,* vol. 3 (1980).

Additional Bibliography

Tánchez, J. Eduardo. *La música en Guatemala: Algunos músicos y compositores.* Guatemala: Editorial Impresos Industriales, 1987.

DAVID L. JICKLING

CASTILLO, OTTO RENÉ (1937–1967). Otto René Castillo (*b.* 1937; *d.* 19 March 1967), Guatemalan poet. He is the best known of Guatemalan contemporary poets because of his revolutionary militancy and his heroic death. Castillo is one of the "guerrilla poets" who flourished throughout the continent during the 1960s, and is the author of Guatemala's best-known contemporary poem, "Vámonos patria a caminar" ("Let's start walking").

Castillo was born in Quezaltenango, Guatemala's second city. He was a student organizer and led the Association of High School Students. As a result, when the country was invaded in 1954, he was exiled to El Salvador. In 1955 he shared the Premio Centroamericano de Poesía with the Salvadoran poet Roque Dalton. He returned to Guatemala in 1957 and enrolled at the University of San Carlos. In 1959 he left for East Germany, where he studied literature at the University of Leipzig. In the early 1960s he trained as a filmmaker with the well-known Dutch documentary directory Joris Ivens. Castillo returned to Guatemala in 1966 and joined the ranks of the Rebel Armed Forces (FAR). In March 1967, after eating nothing but roots for fifteen days, his guerrilla group was ambushed and captured. Four days of torture ensued, after which Castillo was burned to death. His books are *Vámonos patria a caminar* (1965), *Informe de una injusticia* (1975), and *Sabor de luto* (1976).

See also **Guerrilla Movements.**

BIBLIOGRAPHY

Otto René Castillo et al., *Clamor de América: Antología de poesía latinoamericana* (1970).

Otto René Castillo, *Tomorrow Triumphant: Selected Poems,* edited by Magdaly Fernández and David Volpendesta and translated by Roque Dalton (1984).

Additional Bibliography

Iffland, James. *Ensayos sobre la poesía revolucionaria de Centroamérica.* San José: EDUCA, 1994.

ARTURO ARIAS

CASTILLO, RAMÓN (1873–1944). Ramón Castillo (November 20, 1873–October 12, 1944), a conservative born in the northern province of Catamarca, became vice president of Argentina in the fraudulent presidential elections of 1937. As appointed governor of Tucumán during the Uriburu dictatorship and former minister of education under President José Agustín Pedro Justo, Castillo's candidacy won support from nationalist and religious sectors. His rise to power was facilitated by the illness of President Roberto Ortiz, who handed over his office in 1940.

The historical context in which Castillo governed was marked by three principal issues: the nature and form of state intervention in the economy; the problem of the legitimacy of political authority, given the contradiction between democratic principles and their enactment in practice; and the conflict during World War II between supporters of the Allies and those who promoted neutrality in international affairs. On the first issue, there was clearly a policy of state intervention closely linked to the promotion of industries with ties to the military. On the second issue, the institutional framework under Castillo showed a clear break with the more pro-democratic programs of his predecessor. In contrast with Ortiz, Castillo agreed to electoral fraud and legitimated it, first in the provinces of Mendoza and Santa Fe and then in the province of Buenos Aires itself. He governed under a state of siege and outlawed hundreds of public events.

At the Conference of Rio de Janeiro in January 1942, the Argentine government, in contrast to Mexico, refused to support a break in relations with Germany and Italy. Clearly illustrating the regime's sympathies with Germany was a ban on exhibiting the Charlie Chaplin film *The Great Dictator* (1940) in Argentina. Although Castillo lacked his own base of support—a circumstance that explains a certain degree of ambivalence in his political discourse—his administration had the backing of nationalist segments of the army and the Catholic Church. He was overthrown in a military coup in June 1943 that opened the way for the political ascendance of Colonel Perón, and died on October 12 of that year.

See also **Argentina: The Twentieth Century; Justo, José Agustín Pedro; Ortiz, Roberto Marcelino; Uriburu, José Félix.**

BIBLIOGRAPHY

Bisso, Andrés. *Acción Argentina: Un antifascismo nacional en tiempos de guerra mundial.* Buenos Aires: Prometeo Libros, 2005.

Buchrucker, Cristián. *Nacionalismo y Peronismo: La Argentina en la crisis ideológica mundial (1927–1955).* Buenos Aires: Editorial Sudamericana, 1987.

Ciria, Alberto. *Parties and Power in Modern Argentina (1930–1946).* Translated by Carlos A. Astiz with Mary F. McCarthy. Albany: State University of New York Press, 1974.

Halperin Donghi, Tulio. *La República imposible.* Buenos Aires: Ariel, 2004.

Ibarguren, Carlos. *La historia que he vivido.* Buenos Aires: Editorial Sudamericana, 1999.

Klich, Ignacio, ed. *Sobre nazis y nazismo en la cultura argentina.* College Park, MD: Hispamerica, 2002.

Potash, Robert. *El ejército y la política en la Argentina, 1928–1945: De Yrigoyen a Perón.* Buenos Aires: Editorial Hispamerica, 1985.

Sabsay, Fernando. *Los presidentes argentinos: Desde Rivadavia hasta Kirchner.* Buenos Aires: Editorial El Ateneo, 2005.

Zanatta, Loris. *Del estado liberal a la nación católica: Iglesia y ejército en los orígenes del peronismo, 1930–1943.* Buenos Aires: Universidad Nacional de Quilmes, 1996.

CÉSAR TCACH

CASTILLO ARMAS, CARLOS (1914–1957).

Carlos Castillo Armas (*b.* 4 November 1914; *d.* 26 July 1957), president of Guatemala (1954–1957). Born into a provincial Ladino family in the department of Escuintla, Castillo Armas pursued a military career, rising to the rank of colonel and director of the national military academy in 1947.

Obsessed by the July 1949 assassination of army chief and presidential candidate Colonel Francisco Javier Arana (an act he attributed to Arana's political rival, Lieutenant Colonel Jacobo Arbenz, who was elected president in November 1950), Castillo Armas launched a five-year rebellion against the Arbenz regime. In November 1949 he led an abortive attack on a Guatemala City military base. He was shot, but he revived while being taken to the cemetery. Sentenced to death, he tunneled out of the Central Penitentiary in June 1951 and took refuge in the Colombian embassy, which granted him political asylum. From Colombia he moved to Honduras, where, with a number of other Guatemalan political dissidents, he launched the National Liberation Movement. Supported by the Central Intelligence Agency (CIA), this offensive succeeded in overthrowing Arbenz on 2 July 1954 and established Castillo Armas as leader of a five-man governing junta set up in San Salvador under the auspices of U.S. Ambassador John Peurifoy. On 10 October 1954 Castillo Armas was elected president in an unopposed plebescite.

The presidency of Carlos Castillo Armas followed three broad interrelated policies: the dismantling of most of the governmental programs and institutions established by the Cerezo Arévalo and Arbenz regimes during the so-called revolutionary decade (1944–1954); a socioeconomic strategy that can be termed "conservative modernization"; and close cooperation with the United States. The "liberationist" regime banned all existing political parties, labor federations, and peasant organizations; disenfranchised three-quarters of the electorate by excluding illiterates; annulled the Arbenz agrarian reform law; and restored the right of the Roman Catholic Church to own property and conduct religious instruction in the public schools.

Seeking to become a "showcase of capitalist development," the regime encouraged foreign investment by granting tax concessions and by repealing laws restricting foreign oil exploration and investments in public utilities. It secured substantial loans and credits from the United States for road building and beef and cotton production. It also sought to stimulate internal investment by maintaining low taxes and wage rates.

The July 1957 assassination of President Castillo Armas by one of his personal bodyguards in the National Palace has been attributed to a power struggle in his political party, the National Democratic Movement.

See also **Guatemala.**

BIBLIOGRAPHY

Richard N. Adams, *Crucifixion by Power: Essays on Guatemalan National Social Structure, 1944–1966* (1970).

Thomas Melville and Marjorie Melville, *Guatemala—Another Vietnam?* (1971).

Stephen Schlesinger and Stephen Kinzer, *Bitter Fruit: The Untold Story of the American Coup in Guatemala* (1982; repr. 1983).

James Dunkerley, *Power in the Isthmus: A Political History of Modern Central America* (1988).

Additional Bibliography

Streeter, Stephen M. *Managing the Counterrevolution: The United States and Guatemala, 1954-1961.* Athens: Ohio University Center for International Studies, 2001.

ROLAND H. EBEL

CASTILLO LEDÓN, AMALIA (1902–1986).

Amalia Castillo Ledón (*b.* 18 August 1902; *d.* 3 June 1986), prominent early feminist in Mexico. A native of San Jerónimo, Tamaulipas, and daughter of a schoolteacher, Castillo Ledón completed graduate studies in the humanities at the National University. After her marriage to the prominent historian Luis Castillo Ledón, she established herself as an early feminist in United Nations and Mexican organizations. She served as president of the Inter-American Commission of Women in 1949, and in 1953 she addressed the Mexican Senate on women's suffrage, the first woman to do so. The first female Mexican diplomat, she was minister plenipotentiary to Sweden (1953), Finland (1956), and Switzerland (1959). She was the first woman to serve as undersecretary of education (1958–1964).

See also **Feminism and Feminist Organizations.**

BIBLIOGRAPHY

Aurora M. O'Campo and Ernesto Prado Velázquez, *Diccionario de escritores mexicanos* (1967), pp. 143–144; and *Hispano Americano* 39 (17 June 1986): 41.

RODERIC AI CAMP

CASTILLO Y GUEVARA, FRANCISCA JOSEFA DE LA CONCEPCIÓN DE (1671–1742).

Francisca Josefa de la Concepción de Castillo y Guevara (*b.* 6 October 1671; *d.* 1742), Colombian nun and author. The daughter of a Spanish official, Francisca Josefa was born in Tunja and entered the convent of Saint Clare in 1689. She remained there until her death, holding various offices in the community, including that of abbess.

Madre Francisca is remembered for two literary works, which she undertook upon the advice of her confessor. The first of these is her autobiography, known as the *Vida,* which was published in 1817. In this work she recounts her physical and spiritual travails, including her conflicts with fellow nuns and her visions of Jesus Christ, the Virgin Mary, and others. The second is the *Afectos espirituales,* also known as *Sentimientos espirituales,* which was published in 1843. The *Afectos* consists of 195 meditations on religious themes that express her longing for union with God. Because of their clear, forceful style and their spirituality, Madre Francisca's writings are often compared to those of other mystics, notably Saint Teresa of Avila.

See also **Literature: Spanish America.**

BIBLIOGRAPHY

Obras completas, 2 vols., edited by Darío Achury Valenzuela (1968). See also María Teresa Morales Barrero, *La madre Castillo: Su espiritualidad y su estilo* (1968).

Julie G. Johnson, *Women in Colonial Spanish American Literature* (1985).

Additional Bibliography

Mújica, Elisa. "250 Anos de la Muerte de la Madre Castillo" *Revista credencial historia* (June 1992).

HELEN DELPAR

CASTIZO. *Castizo,* a term used for a person of mostly Spanish and some indigeneous ancestry. In the eighteenth century, Spaniards officially described a *castizo* as a person with one-quarter Indian and three-quarters Spanish ancestry, but genealogical investigations were rare, and most assessments of *castizo* status were based on such criteria as physical appearance, occupation, residence, dress, and income. A person of mixed Hispanic and indigenous ancestry who appeared darker or was lower in the social or economic order was called a *mestizo.* The term *castizo* was used most frequently in Spanish records during the eighteenth century and appears to have disappeared following independence.

See also **Race and Ethnicity.**

BIBLIOGRAPHY

Nicholás León, *Las castas del México colonial* (1924).

Lyle McAlister, "Social Structure and Social Change in New Spain," in *Hispanic American Historical Review* 43, no. 3 (1963): 349–370.

Magnus Mörner, *Race Mixture in the History of Latin America* (1967).

John K. Chance, *Race and Class in Colonial Oaxaca* (1978).

Patricia Seed, "Social Dimensions of Race: Mexico City, 1753," in *Hispanic American Historical Review* 62, no. 4 (1982): 569–606.

Patricia Seed and Philip Rust, "Estate and Class in Colonial Oaxaca Revisited," in *Comparative Studies in Society and History* 25 (1983): 703–709, 721–724.

Rodney Anderson, "Race and Social Stratification: A Comparison of Working Class Spaniards, Indians, and Castas in Guadalajara, Mexico, in 1821," in *Hispanic American Historical Review* 68, no. 2 (1988): 209–243.

Douglas Cope, *The Limits of Racial Domination* (1994).

Additional Bibliography

Carrera, Magali M. *Imagining Identity in New Spain: Race, Lineage, and the Colonial Body in Portraiture and Casta Paintings.* Austin: University of Texas, 2003.

Katzew, Ilona. *Casta Painting: Images of Race in Eighteenth-Century Mexico.* New Haven, CT: Yale University Press, 2004.

Katzew, Ilona, ed. *New World Orders: Casta Painting and Colonial Latin America.* New York: Americas Society, 1996.

Stephens, Thomas M. *Dictionary of Latin American Racial and Ethnic Terminology.* Gainesville: University of Florida Press, 1989.

PATRICIA SEED

CASTRO, CIPRIANO (1858–1924). Cipriano Castro (*b.* 12 October 1858; *d.* 4 December 1924), president of Venezuela (1899–1908). Born and raised in Capucho, Táchira, Castro attended schools in Colombia. During the 1880s and 1890s he brought Colombian liberalism to his native Venezuela when he participated in Tachiran politics.

In 1899, Castro launched his Revolution of Liberal Restoration against the government of President Ignacio Andrade, whom he defeated in a campaign that lasted from 23 May to 22 October. He established a coalition government that even included some of the Caracas liberals whom he had overthrown. Basically, Castro attempted to continue the process of centralization begun by Antonio Guzmán Blanco, but financial problems and a series of major conflicts with foreign powers restricted his government. His personal behavior further inhibited his effectiveness as a national leader.

During his reign, Castro adopted a highly nationalistic policy. In 1902, his belligerence led to a blockade of Venezuela by European powers. The intervention of the United States eventually ended the blockade, but Castro remained hostile to foreign governments, including that of the United States. In retaliation for the blockade, Castro closed most Venezuelan ports to trade from the Antilles and imposed a 30-percent surcharge on all goods shipped from the British West Indies.

As a dictator, Castro faced a number of revolts, most notably those led by Manuel Antonio Matos (1902–1903), José Manuel "El Mocho" Hernández (1900), and Antonio Paredes (1907). Over 12,000 died in the fighting. These struggles, and the nation's fiscal difficulties, meant that Castro accomplished very little in the way of reform. He enriched friends and allies through monopoly concessions but did little to improve the nation's transportation, sanitation, or education facilities.

In December 1908, Castro left Venezuela to seek medical treatment in Europe for a urinary tract infection caused by his heavy drinking, use of aphrodisiacs, and venereal disease. Upon his departure, Juan Vicente Gómez seized power. Castro died in exile in Puerto Rico.

See also **Venezuela since 1830.**

BIBLIOGRAPHY

William M. Sullivan, "The Rise of Despotism in Venezuela: Cipriano Castro, 1899–1908" (Ph.D. diss., University of New Mexico, 1974).

José Rafael Pocaterra, *Memorias de un venezolano de la decadencia* (1979).

Cipriano Castro, *El pensamiento político de la Restauración Liberal*, 2 vols. (1983); *La oposición a la dictadura de Cipriano Castro* (1983).

Carlos Siso, *Castro y Gómez: Importancia de la hegemonia andina* (1985).

Mariano Picón-Salas, *Los días de Cipriano Castro* (1986).

For more general treatment, see Edwin Lieuwen, *Venezuela* (1961); Guillermo Morón, *A History of Venezuela*, edited and translated by John Street (1964); Judith Ewell, *Venezuela: A Century of Change* (1984).

Additional Bibliography

McBeth, B.S. *Gunboats, Corruption, and Claims: Foreign Intervention in Venezuela, 1899-1908.* Westport, CT: Greenwood Press, 2001.

Torres Iriarte, Alexander. "Anarquía, traición y locura en 1899: Breves consideraciones histórico-historiográficas acerca de la Revolución Liberal Restauradora." *Boletín de la Academia Nacional de la Historia (Venezuela)* 68:200 (July-September 2004): 145–162.

WINTHROP R. WRIGHT

CASTRO, JOSÉ GIL DE (c. 1785–c. 1841). José Gil de Castro (*b.* ca. 1785; *d.* ca. 1841), Peruvian artist and cartographer. Known as "El Mulato Gil," he was first to paint portraits of the heroes of the South American Wars of Independence. Born in Lima under Spanish viceroyal rule, he probably apprenticed with a master of the old colonial school. His *Portrait of Fernando VII* (1812) was influenced by Francisco de Goya. He accompanied Bernardo O'Higgins in his military campaign for Chilean independence. In Santiago he executed several portraits, including those of General José de San Martín, O'Higgins, and their military collaborators. O'Higgins appointed him captain of the engineering corps of the revolutionary army for his expertise in engineering and cartography.

Gil de Castro returned to Peru via Argentina with San Martín's troops and in 1822 was named chamber painter of the Peruvian state. He became the Peruvian aristocracy's favorite portrait painter. In his several portraits of Simón Bolívar, Gil de Castro displayed his fascination with military regalia. His portrayal of sitters in frontal and full-length images recalls votive paintings. Craftsmanship, absence of perspective, and the incorporation of inscriptions into framed plaques in his paintings relate Gil de Castro to colonial painting traditions. A provincial neoclassicist, he was the first representative in Latin America of an independent and naive pictorial school.

See also **Act: The Nineteenth Century.**

BIBLIOGRAPHY

Jaime Eyzaguirre, *José Gil de Castro: Pintor de la independencia americana* (1950).

Dawn Ades, *Art in Latin America: The Modern Era, 1820–1980* (1989), pp. 17–21.

Additional Bibliography

Mariátegui Oliva, Ricardo. *José Gil de Castro.* Lima: 1981.

MARTA GARSD

CASTRO, JUAN JOSÉ (1895–1968).

Juan José Castro (*b.* 7 March 1895; *d.* 5 September 1968), Argentine composer and conductor. Born in Avellaneda, Buenos Aires Province, Castro began his musical education in Buenos Aires, studying piano and violin under Manuel Posadas, harmony under Constantino Gaito, and fugue and composition under Eduardo Fornarini. As a winner of the Europa Grand Prize, he went to Paris to study composition with Vincent D'Indy at the Schola Cantorum, attending Edouard Risler's piano classes. Returning to Buenos Aires, he founded the Sociedad del Cuarteto in 1926 and performed there as first violin; two years later he started a conducting career with Orquesta Renacimiento. Castro was appointed conductor of the ballet season at the Teatro Colón in 1930 and traveled abroad conducting that ensemble. In 1933 he was named director of the Colón.

Parallel with extensive tours as principal conductor of several Latin American orchestras, Castro began a productive career in composition as a founder-member of the Grupo Renovación; nevertheless, his music was individualistic and he remained independent of group theories. His works exhibit three influences: nationalism, Spanish subject matter, and a free cosmopolitan style, the latter a product of his Parisian years. The last quality applies to the color and sonority of his orchestral works, in which he achieved a sort of American impressionism. He became internationally known when Ernest Ansermet conducted the award-winning *Allegro Lento e Vivace* (1930) at the International Society of Contemporary Music (ISCM) Festival. Among Castro's five stage works there are two operas after Federico García Lorca: *La zapatera prodigiosa* (1943), first performed in Montevideo in 1949, and *Bodas de sangre* (1953), which premiered at the Teatro Colón in 1956. *Proserpina y el extranjero,* a three-act opera, first performed at Milan's La Scala, was the recipient of the first International Verdi Prize in 1951. Among his orchestral pieces is *Corales criollos* No. 3, a first prize winner at the Caracas Interamerican Music Festival (1954). As a teacher, Castro was appointed by Pablo Casals as dean of studies and professor at the National Conservatory in San Juan, Puerto Rico, from 1959 to 1964.

See also **Music: Art Music.**

BIBLIOGRAPHY

Composers of the Americas, vol. 4 (1958).

V. Gesualdo, *Historia de la Música en la Argentina* (1961).

R. Arizaga, *Juan José Castro* (1963) and *Enciclopedia de la Música Argentina* (1971).

John Vinton, ed., *Dictionary of Contemporary Music* (1974).

Gerard Béhague, *Music in Latin America* (1979).

Stanley Sadie, ed., *The New Grove Dictionary of Music and Musicians,* vol. 3 (1980), and *The New Grove Dictionary of Opera,* vol. 1 (1992).

SUSANA SALGADO

CASTRO, JULIÁN (1815–1875).

Julián Castro (*b.* 1815; *d.* 1875), provisional president of Venezuela from March 1858 to August 1859, during which time the Constitutional Convention of Valencia created the Constitution of 1858. Castro began his career as an officer in the republican army of Venezuela. As a captain he participated in the Revolution of the Reforms in 1835–1836. He joined the Liberal Party at its inception in 1840. Before being chosen as provisional president of the nation, he was governor of the province of Carabobo.

Castro assumed office on 18 March 1858 as the titular head of a coalition of Conservatives and dissident Liberals who conspired to overthrow President José Tadeo Monagas. His "gobierno de fusión" was doomed from the start. The only goal the Conservatives and Liberals shared was their desire to remove Monagas from office. Both groups jockeyed for Castro's approval. The Conservatives quickly alienated the Liberals by pushing through Congress a bill making government employees responsible for past embezzlements. The Castro government's refusal to free Monagas and other prominent Liberals who had sought refuge in the French embassy resulted in a blockade of Venezuela's two major ports by the French and British in 1858. Castro's attempts to placate rebellious Liberals through concessions, along with the fact that his government was weak and unpopular, led to the Federal War, a civil war that lasted from 1859 to 1864.

On 1 August 1859, Castro was overthrown by a Conservative-led coup known as the Federalist Revolution. He was imprisoned by government troops, then tried and convicted for treason but later absolved. He completed his career as a general in the Liberal armies of Antonio Guzmán Blanco.

See also **Venezuela: Venezuela since 1830.**

BIBLIOGRAPHY

Garrido Mezgiita y Compania, ed., *Diccionario biográfico de Venezuela* (1953).

William D. Marsland and Amy L. Marsland, *Venezuela Through Its History* (1954).

Guillermo Morón, *A History of Venezuela* (1964).

Rafael Páez, *Los hombres que han hecho Venezuela* (1983).

DAVID CAREY JR.

CASTRO, RICARDO (1864–1907).

Ricardo Castro (*b.* 7 February 1864; *d.* 20 November 1907), Mexican pianist and composer. Castro was the leading piano virtuoso in Mexico when that tradition was in full flower at the end of the nineteenth century. After study and a debut in Europe, where his music and his pianistic prowess gained immediate success, he returned to Mexico, propagating a European style marked by his own formidable technique and clarity of expression. His orchestral works (two symphonies and two concertos) and operatic music (*La Légende de Rudel*, 1906) were favorably accepted in his own epoch but have not had the enduring appeal of his works for solo piano.

See also **Music: Art Music.**

BIBLIOGRAPHY

Robert Stevenson, *Music in Mexico: A Historical Survey* (1952).

Additional Bibliography

Aguirre Aguilera, José Ramón. *Ricardo Castro: Semblanza de la obra musical.* Durango: Secretaría de Educación, Cultura y Deporte, 1994.

ROBERT L. PARKER

CASTRO ALVES, ANTÔNIO DE (1847–1871).

Antônio de Castro Alves (*b.* 14 March 1847; *d.* 6 July 1871), Brazilian poet. Castro Alves was the last and the greatest Brazilian romantic poet. He is also remembered as a playwright and an orator. Born on a large plantation in Bahia into a family of slave owners, he developed a passionate opposition to slavery; he is called "the poet of the slaves." Castro Alves is also known as the leader of the *condoreiros* (condor poets), who used the condor, strong and high flying, as their symbol. Their poetry is marked by ardent sentiment and grandiloquence, abounding in daring figures of speech.

Castro Alves led a tragic life. When very young, he fell in love with an actress, Eugênia Câmara. They had an amorous liaison, but after two years Eugênia left him. His mother's early death, the insanity and suicide of his brother, and the amputation of his foot after an accident deeply affected the poet. At sixteen he contracted tuberculosis, which killed him at the age of twenty-four. He loved life and did not want to die: "To die ... when this world is a paradise," he wrote in "Mocidade e morte" (Youth and Death), which appeared in the collection *Espumas flutuantes* (Floating Foam, 1870). "Mocidade e morte" was written during a critical point in his illness, and it marks the beginning of his great art. Grief awoke in him the supreme accents that he later would extend to the sufferings of humanity.

Castro Alves became known through poems appearing in periodicals and recited at meetings. During his lifetime only one volume of his poetry was published, *Espumas flutuantes,* a collection of erotic, patriotic, and plaintive lyric verses. His antislavery poems appeared posthumously in *A cachoeira de Paulo Afonso* (The Waterfalls of Paulo Afonso, 1876) and *Os escravos* (The Slaves, 1883). The latter contains some of his most celebrated poems, such as "Vozes d'áfrica" (Voices of Africa), an oration from Africa imploring God's justice, and "O navio negreiro" (The Slave Ship), a dramatic composition picturing all the horrors of an African slaver. Additional works include *Obra completa* (1960) and *Gonzaga ou a revolução de Minas* (Gonzaga or the Revolution in Minas, 1875).

See also **Literature: Brazil.**

BIBLIOGRAPHY

Jorge Amado, *ABC de Castro Alves* (1941).

Samuel Putnam, *Marvelous Journey* (1948).

Raymond S. Sayers *The Negro in Brazilian Literature* (1956), pp. 112–117.

Jon M. Tolman, "Castro Alves, poeta amorosa," in *Luso-Brazilian Review* 12 (1975): 241–262.

Ivan Cavalcanti Proença, *Castro Alves Falou* (1979).

Thomas Braga, "Castro Alves and the New England Abolitionist Poets," in *Hispania* 67 (1984): 585–593.

David T. Haberly, "Antônio de Castro Alves," in *Latin American Writers*, edited by C. Solé and M. I. Abreu, vol. 1 (1989), pp. 289–297.

Additional Bibliography

Matos, Edilene. *Castro Alves: Imagens fragmentadas de um mito*. São Paulo: EDUC, 2001.

MARIA ISABEL ABREU

CASTRO JIJÓN, RAMÓN (1915–1984).

Ramón Castro Jijón (*b.* 1915, *d.* 1984), representative of the navy in the military junta that ruled Ecuador from 11 July 1963 until 1966. Born in Esmeraldas, Castro Jijón received advanced military training in Chile and the United States. He served as a naval attaché in Western Europe. When the military overthrew the government of Carlos Julio Arosemena Monroy, Commander Castro was the only member of the junta from the coast. The movement that overthrew Arosemena's government was the first institutional intrusion of the military into politics since the coup of 23 October 1937.

The junta, which had wide public support during its first year, announced that the armed forces had the responsibility to promote new socioeconomic structures that would provide a foundation for true democracy. After suppressing leftist critics and purging the government of Arosemena supporters, the junta began to implement a program of structural reforms, including agrarian and tax reforms, which quickly alienated important civilian groups. The junta created a personal income tax; rationalized taxation by suppressing hundreds of levies that directly financed public agencies and autonomous institutions; and transferred revenue collection from autonomous agencies to the Central Bank. The latter measure prompted widespread public criticism, against which the junta retaliated by imposing martial law. The Agrarian Reform Law of 11 July 1964, which abolished the *huasipungo* labor system, and the establishment of maximum limits for the size of landholdings, sought to redress one of the most unequal distributions of land in South America. Although the law was relatively weak and threatened only the most inefficient producers, its passage galvanized sierra elite opposition to the junta.

When the economy began to falter in 1964, government deficits burgeoned. The junta sought to stabilize public finances by increasing import duties, but was forced to back down in the face of widespread public criticism, which culminated in a general strike in Guayaquil. When the junta again sought to increase import duties in early 1966, a second general strike spread throughout the nation and resulted in the resignation of the junta on 29 March 1966.

See also **Arosemena Monroy, Carlos Julio.**

BIBLIOGRAPHY

República Del Ecuador, *Plan político de la Junta Militar de Gobierno* (1963) and *La junta militar de gobierno y la opinión pública* (1964).

Martin Needler, *Anatomy of a Coup d'état: Ecuador 1963* (1964).

John Samuel Fitch, *The Military Coup d'état as a Political Process: Ecuador, 1948–1966* (1977), esp. pp. 55–73.

Additional Bibliography

Pyne, Peter. *Ecuador's Junta Militar, 1963-1966: A Case Study of Military Reformism*. New York: New York University of Ulster, 1990.

LINDA ALEXANDER RODRÍGUEZ

CASTRO MADRIZ, JOSÉ MARÍA

(1818–1871). José María Castro Madriz (*b.* 1818; *d.* 1871), president of Costa Rica (1847–1849, 1866–1868). Born in San José, Costa Rica, Castro Madriz studied law in León, Nicaragua. In 1848 he severed Costa Rica's ties with the United Provinces of Central America and declared the country's independence. As a result of strong political pressure, he was obliged to leave the presidency in 1849. When reelected in 1866, he supported improvements in the public education system, opened the bay of Limón to trade, and inaugurated Costa Rica's first telegraph. Overthrown in a military coup in 1868, Castro Madriz served as minister in subsequent governments. He was given the title Benemérito de la Patria

(National Hero) and is called the founder of the republic.

See also **Costa Rica.**

BIBLIOGRAPHY

Cleto González Víquez, *Dos proceres* (1918).

Rafael Obregón Loría, *Dr. José María Castro Madriz, paladín de la libertad y de la cultura* (1949).

Cleotilde María Obregón, *Costa Rica: Relaciones exteriores de una república en formación, 1847–1849* (1984).

Additional Bibliography

Díaz Arias, David. *Construcción de un estado moderno: Política, estado e identidad nacional en Costa Rica, 1821-1914.* San José: Editorial de la Universidad de Costa Rica, 2005.

Yashar, Deborah J. *Demanding Democracy: Reform and Reaction in Costa Rica and Guatemala, 1870s–1950s.* Stanford, CA: Stanford University Press, 1997.

OSCAR PELÁEZ ALMENGOR

CASTRO POZO, HILDEBRANDO

(1890–1945). Hildebrando Castro Pozo (*b.* 1890; *d.* 1 September 1945), Peruvian intellectual and writer from the northern border state of Piura. Castro Pozo first entered the national arena after he had already written strong essays on the misery and extreme poverty of sharecroppers on the coastal plantations. In 1920, President Augusto Leguía named him to head the section on Indian affairs in the national Ministry of Development, a post he held until 1923. He then became one of the most articulate and forthright defenders of the rights of Indians in the country. Quickly parting with Leguía, he understood *indigenismo* through the spectacles of socialism; stressing that the exploitative, capitalist plantation agriculture of the coastal valleys of Peru could be ended only by the imposition of socialism. He felt further that the Indians, who had been communal village farmers since Incan times, would be the group in society most likely to carry out such a transformation. With landowners opposing him, he was sent into exile in 1923; he returned in 1924. His *Nuestra comunidad indígena* (1924) is a long essay on the naturally socialist character of indigenous village traditions. This and other writings influenced José Carlos Mariátegui, his contemporary among Peruvian *indigenistas* and the founder of the Socialist

Party. A pragmatic leader, Castro Pozo encouraged party members to take positions in the government to help indigenous villagers. The Socialists hoped the government would introduce technological improvements into the villages, thereby better equipping them to compete with the big landowners. Two years after he died, the government passed a new, comprehensive sharecropping law.

See also **Indigenous Peoples; Journalism.**

BIBLIOGRAPHY

Henry F. Dobyns and Paul L. Doughty, *Peru: A Cultural History* (1976), p. 230.

Jesús Chavarría, *José Carlos Mariátegui and the Rise of Modern Peru, 1890–1930* (1979), pp. 108, 115.

Additional Bibliography

Franco, Carlos. *Castro Pozo: Nación, modernización, endógena y socialismo.* Lima: Centro de Estudios para el Desarrollo y la Participación, 1989.

VINCENT PELOSO

CASTRO RUZ, FIDEL

(1926–). After leading a revolutionary force that overthrew the Cuban dictator Fulgencio Batista in 1959, Fidel Castro became Cuba's undisputed leader and one of the best-known political figures in the world, holding the positions of prime minister and commander in chief (1959–2008), first secretary of the Communist Party of Cuba (1965), and president of the Council of State and Council of Ministers (1976–2008).

Castro's life can be divided into two periods: his early years as a revolutionary, and later as a politician and leader of Cuba for more than forty years. As of 2008 this second phase is not over: Although Castro underwent surgery in 2006 and handed over temporary presidential authority to his brother, Raúl Castro, Fidel remained in power, and longtime observers were reluctant to make predictions about a leader who, since 1959, has shown a remarkable ability to challenge the might of the United States, his ally the former Soviet Union, and the world community, without losing his grip on political and economic control. In 2008 Fidel resigned as president and Raúl was officially elected to the post.

Fidel Castro and his compatriots in the Cuban jungle, June 1957. This small group of revolutionary forces, including Raul Castro (kneeling in the foreground) and Che Guevara (second from left), would eventually bring down Batista's government. © BETTMANN/CORBIS

EARLY LIFE

Castro was born on 13 August 1926, near the town of Mayarí in Oriente Province (present-day Holguín province) in eastern Cuba to an affluent landowning family. His father, Angel Castro y Argiz, was a native of Galicia, Spain, while his mother, Lina Ruz González, was born in Cuba. Castro attended Catholic boarding schools and graduated in 1945 from Belen College in Havana, also a Catholic school. He entered law school at the University of Havana in 1945 and began practicing law in 1950. At the university Castro became involved in campus politics and even shot a political opponent. In 1947 he took part in a plan, never carried out, to invade the Dominican Republic and overthrow the dictator Rafael Trujillo. The following year, 1948, Castro attended an anti-imperialist conference in Bogotá, Colombia, during which the Colombian populist leader Jorge Gaitán was assassinated and riots broke out. While there, he was

arrested for trying to incite mutiny in a police barracks and was released and returned to Cuba only upon the intervention of the Cuban ambassador to Colombia.

It was nationalism, not socialism, that served as the driving force of Castro's early political activism. Castro's hero was José Martí, not Lenin or Marx. As a student, Castro could have joined the Cuban Communist Party (as his brother Raúl had done), but Fidel steered away from Cuba's communist movement in favor of the nationalism that influenced so many of Castro's generation. Because Cuba was subjected to the imperialism of both Spain and the United States, Castro hoped to establish a nation free of the colonialism and neocolonialism of past years. To this end Castro joined the reform-minded Orthodox Party in 1947 and ran for Congress in 1952. In the midst of the campaign, however, Fulgencio Batista spearheaded a coup that suspended elections and left Batista dictator of the island. This coup convinced Castro of the futility of trying to transform Cuba's government through legal means and so was converted to a revolutionary strategy.

CASTRO AS REVOLUTIONARY

Committed to a revolutionary course, Castro led at first a failed attempt to overthrow the U.S.-backed Batista regime before leading his victorious forces into the capital city of Havana in 1959. Castro responded to Batista's coup of 1952 by organizing a guerrilla organization to launch attacks against the Batista government. On 26 July 1953, Castro led an assault on the Moncada Barracks in Santiago. Whereas this attack was sheer folly and easily defeated, Castro nonetheless became a nationally known figure for his prominent role in the attack. Castro was captured and put on trial, which he skillfully used to spread his anti-Batista message. In court testimony defending the attack, Castro gave his famous "History Will Absolve Me" speech in which he listed, with unique flair, the corruption and shortcomings of the Batista regime as well as his own solutions to the problems besetting Cuba. His speech embraced liberal nationalism, not socialism, and called for a democratic government, better education and health care, economic diversification, and an end to the overbearing influence of the United States in Cuba's politics and economy. Not only were nationalists and socialists drawn into Castro's camp but also members of the Cuban middle class resentful of Batista's alliance with U.S. businesses and Cuba's elite as well as the uneven development of the Cuban economy.

After the trial Castro was jailed for his role in the attack on the Moncada Barracks and released as part of a general amnesty two years later. Castro went to Mexico to plot his next move, and it was there that he joined forces with Ernesto "Che" Guevara, an Argentine Marxist and medical doctor. Guevara's anti–United States position grew out of his firsthand experience of the U.S.-backed coup in Guatemala in 1954. Along with Guevara and Raúl Castro, Fidel and seventy-nine others landed in Oriente Province, Cuba, on 2 December 1956, in the boat *Granma*. Most of the Castros' forces were captured or killed, but Fidel, Raúl, and Guevara survived. It was this small, poorly equipped army that would rally broad popular support among the Cuban people and overthrow Batista.

Batista's army failed to capture him, and Castro's image among the Cuban people grew. Starting from his base in the mountains of eastern Cuba, Castro's 26th of July Movement (named for the day the attack was launched on the Moncada Barracks) quickly made contact with other groups disillusioned with Batista's rule. While most observers, including most of the leaders of the Cuban Communist Party (Partido Socialista Popular), were startled at Castro's success, Castro never doubted the eventual outcome of his struggle. On 1 January 1959, Castro's forces marched triumphantly into Havana just hours after Batista had fled Cuba.

CASTRO CONSOLIDATES POWER

Castro at first took the position of commander in chief of the armed forces and was also sworn in as prime minister when José Miró Cardona abruptly resigned. Once in power, Castro gained world attention for his defiant stand against the United States. As head of the Cuban government, Castro was committed to nationalizing Cuba's largest industries and landholdings, especially the sugar industry. On a visit to the United States, Castro was refused an audience with President Eisenhower. Refusing to bow to U.S. economic and political pressures, Castro then met for the first time with Soviet premier Nikita Khrushchev. These positions led to a cooling of U.S.-Cuban relations, while at the same time the Castro government turned increasingly toward the Soviet Union to counter U.S. pressure.

On 17 April 1961, U.S.-backed Cuban exiles launched an invasion at the Bay of Pigs on the southern coast of the island, an offensive both ill conceived and poorly planned. First developed during the Eisenhower administration, the invasion was carried out under the newly elected administration of John F. Kennedy and was a conclusive failure. Cuba's local police force and militia defeated the counterrevolutionaries, and Castro was hailed both at home and abroad as one of the few leaders capable of standing up to the North American giant. It was after the failed invasion, on 2 December 1961, that Castro publicly declared himself a Marxist, a conversion whose sincerity has since been the subject of much debate. The timing of his conversion does suggest, however, that Castro's move was more pragmatic than heartfelt. Whatever his motives, Castro was left with few alternatives: The U.S. government was patently hostile to his rule and would be satisfied only with the continuation of a Batista-style government sans Batista. Thus, Castro embraced communism and drew ever closer to the Soviet Union.

CUBAN MISSILE CRISIS

In October 1962, U.S. intelligence detected Soviet nuclear missiles on the island, and a tense period known as the Cuban Missile Crisis followed. U.S. president Kennedy demanded that the Soviet Union remove its missiles from Cuba, and Soviet premier Khrushchev countered by demanding that the United States remove its nuclear missiles from Turkey. For days it appeared that the United States and the Soviet Union were headed toward war. According to documents released years later, Castro was willing to call Washington's bluff, whereas the Soviets were more reluctant to start a nuclear war. While the world anxiously waited, Premier Nikita Khrushchev gave an eleventh-hour order to turn back a Soviet ship allegedly carrying nuclear missiles and to recall the Soviet nuclear missiles from Cuba. Castro was privately furious at Khrushchev's decision, but the crisis sealed Cuba's fate: The United States would work to undermine Cuba at every turn, as well as try to assassinate Castro himself. From the early 1960s to the early 2000s, Castro led the country, with varied success, on the path of Soviet-style socialism. By the late 1960s the Cuban government had nationalized all economic endeavors, no matter how small, in an effort to centralize the economy and the distribution of resources. Fearful of another U.S.-backed coup, all political activities, the press, and education were closely monitored by the state.

MASTER POLITICIAN

Starting in 1956, before the ouster of Batista, until 1965, when Castro formally became the head of the Cuban Communist Party, Castro adeptly maneuvered around the various factions vying for power in revolutionary Cuba. In his march to power Castro manipulated varied political groupings within Cuba to help achieve his revolutionary goal without relinquishing any real power. For example, in April 1958 Castro at first supported a general strike planned by the urban wing of the underground 26th of July Movement. This strike was opposed by the PSP and backed by the liberal wing of Castro's own movement. But when the strike proved unsuccessful, Castro reversed course and opposed the strike. From that time forward, Castro was the undisputed leader

of the movement to oust Batista. Not only did the failed strike discredit the liberals of the movement, but it also allowed Castro to absorb many PSP members into his 26th of July Movement. Although Castro mistrusted the leadership of the PSP, he nonetheless recognized that their commitment to rank-and-file organization and their well-organized party structure could be useful to his own aims.

With Batista gone, Castro first designated Manuel Urrutia Lleó president of Cuba, a post Castro would take over himself once he had consolidated the necessary power. To do this, he turned again to the well-disciplined PSP, whose members he placed in key positions within the government. Resignations of liberals and moderates quickly followed, accompanied by predictable claims that Cuba's government was turning too far to the left. But the wave of resignations and dismissals by liberals and moderates, and the arrest of the popular anti-Communist guerrilla commander Major Hubert Matos, only allowed Castro to consolidate further his political and economic power.

As supreme leader, Castro similarly balanced competing forces in order to maintain his uncontested rule. With the dismissal and exile of the liberals and moderates of the anti-Batista movement, Castro turned increasingly to his brother Raúl and the charismatic Che Guevara for support. Guevara in particular played a crucial role in government economic planning in the mid-1960s. But while Guevara's lasting contribution as a revolutionary is undeniable, his role as economic planner was largely a failure.

Seeking to shift Cuba's economy away from its traditional reliance on sugar production, Guevara embarked on a disastrous plan of diversification. When it became clear that sugar was still the only Cuban product of significant value on the world market, Guevara "recruited" armies of workers to get out the sugar harvest. Despite his calls for Cubans to sacrifice for the good of the revolution (presumably by working sixteen-hour days with no days of rest), the sugar harvest continued to falter because of poor economic planning. Yet Castro took little direct blame for the serious economic decline of the middle and late 1960s. Instead, Castro succeeded in directing the blame variously toward Guevara, the unyielding government bureaucracy, or the United States. While events leading up to Guevara's

Castro with Venezuelan president Hugo Chávez, on Castro's 75th birthday, 2001. The close ties between Cuba and oil-rich Venezuela that emerged after the election of leftist president Hugo Chávez in 1998 have provided a sorely needed boost to the Cuban economy. CARLOS SOLORZANO/AFP/GETTY IMAGES

departure are poorly documented, it is clear that Castro and Guevara had a parting of the ways. Guevara left Cuba for the final time in 1965 and was killed while fighting in Bolivia in 1967.

CASTRO IN POWER

Over the years Castro has relied on a core of individuals to carry out his rule. Second in power to Castro is his brother Raúl, longtime first vice president of the Council of State and the Council of Ministers and second secretary of the Communist Party, who on 31 July 2006, was appointed by his ailing brother as the acting president of Cuba as well as the commander in chief of the armed forces. Another power of longstanding in Castro's ruling circle, Osmani Cienfuegos, whose brother Camilo Cienfuegos was a comrade of Castro's during the guerrilla war, has served as a vice president of the Council of Ministers and member of the Central Committee of the Communist Party. Other Castro loyalists include Ricardo Alarcón,

president of the Cuban National Assembly and former Cuban ambassador to the United Nations, and Ramiro Valdés, minister of information science and communication, who fought with Castro at the Moncada Barracks attack in 1953. Valdés has served many posts under Castro, including minister of the interior and member of the Politburo. One of the few leaders besides Fidel to wear the olive-green uniform of the revolution, Valdés is one of only three veterans to carry the title Comandante de la Revolución, a position not even Raúl Castro enjoys. Castro also relied on Carlos Rafael Rodríguez both before and after the revolution to rally crucial support for the regime. Rodríguez was head of the PSP before the revolution, and while he gave his support to Castro only just prior to Batista's ouster, he became a close friend and ally of Castro's after the revolution. Rodríguez served as a vice president of both the Council of State and the Council of Ministers and was a member of the Politburo before his death in 1997

While Castro's political genius has allowed him to enjoy unchallenged power in Cuba, the U.S. government has tried every method conceivable to oust him. After the failure of the Bay of Pigs operation, the Kennedy administration initiated Operation Mongoose, with the purpose of assassinating the Cuban leader. One plan was to contaminate Castro's clothing with thallium salts that would make his beard fall out. Another idea was to spray the broadcasting booth with hallucinogens before a televised speech. There were also plans to poison Castro's cigars or to place explosive shells at his favorite diving spots.

Because he has squelched most opposition within Cuba, Castro has relied on a charismatic rule that places personality ahead of practical programs. Castro is forever the advocate, and up until age and illness limited his movements, he was known to travel up, down, and across the island to meet with as many Cubans as possible. A brilliant speaker, he is capable of convincing huge crowds to endorse programs they may have been opposed to minutes earlier. His speeches are legend, both for their length (he has been known to speak for up to nine hours straight) and their ability to persuade. Castro places great importance on his ability to move massive crowds (and Cuba's television audience) to endorse with their shouts and cheers whatever programs or policy he might be pushing for at the time.

Despite U.S. efforts to undermine Castro's regime, the Cuban economy grew throughout the 1970s and 1980s. Despite criticism at home and abroad, Castro could justifiably claim that the standard of living for Cubans was better than for other Caribbean peoples. In some categories, such as life span or low infant mortality, Cuba led all Latin American nations. Literacy rates in Cuba rivaled that of the United States and the western European nations. And though scarcities were common, Cuba did not have the army of homeless beggars that populated the streets of other Latin American nations.

Critics argued that Cuba's relative affluence was the result of financial support from the Soviet Union, not of what many considered the failed polices of Castro's socialist government. While true, it is also true that the United States has funneled large sums of economic and military support to Latin American nations such as Guatemala, El Salvador, Honduras, and Haiti, where economic misery and political strife were constant. Thus, Castro could argue that while Soviet aid helped build a nourished and housed population with an exceptional health care system, U.S. aid to many Latin American nations only exacerbated the cycle of poverty and violence so prevalent in the region.

MARIEL BOATLIFT

Because Cuba's economy relied on Soviet support and subsidies, when the Soviet economy began to falter in the late 1970s so too did Cuba's. With food and housing shortages spreading throughout the island, in April 1980 a group of Cubans ran the gates of the Peruvian embassy in Havana and requested asylum. As news spread throughout Cuba, an estimated ten thousand Cubans flocked to the Peruvian embassy hoping to leave the island. This was a genuine crisis for Castro's government, because it suggested a high level of discontent among Cubans living in Cuba. Castro, the master politician, however, successfully diverted attention from the failings of his government and caused a public embarrassment for the U.S. government and its president, Jimmy Carter.

In response to the crisis, Carter publicly expressed solidarity for all Cubans wanting to leave Cuba. Castro responded by declaring that any Cuban who wanted to leave the island could now do so. Overnight, thousands of ships from Florida crossed the Florida Straits to collect Cubans wanting to leave Cuba. This caused an immediate problem for the United States, especially state officials in Florida, who had neither the money nor the facilities to handle such a large exodus. When Carter denounced Castro for keeping political prisoners, Castro freed many Cubans in prison or state hospitals. The result was an unmanageable crisis for the United States, and Carter was forced to request that Castro once again enforce Cuba's border and prevent Cubans from leaving the island without legal permission.

COLLAPSE OF THE SOVIET UNION

With the collapse of the Soviet Union in 1991 the Cuban economy declined dramatically, and anti-Castro forces in the United States waited for the collapse of Cuba's socialist system. Rationing was expanded, malnourishment appeared in some areas, and a fuel shortage forced more and more Cubans to walk or ride bicycles. But by the late 1990s Cuba's economy had recovered slightly, and the election of Hugo Chávez as president of Venezuela gave a boost to the Cuban economy. With Chávez in power, oil-rich Venezuela could now provide Cuba with the oil it had lacked since the collapse of the Soviet Union. In 2006 the Cuban economy was in full rebound and reported a 12 percent growth. Though this estimate is considered high, independent analysts figured Cuba's growth to be a still robust 9 percent in 2006.

PERSONAL LIFE

For all his visibility as a public figure, little is known about Castro's private life. In 1948 he married Mirta Díaz-Balart, with whom he had one son before divorcing in 1955. Castro later married Dalia Soto del Valle and had five sons with her. Most of Castro's old comrades have died off, and he lacks close personal friendships with all but a few. He is still in touch with his ex-wife, Mirta, and also keeps in contact with his eldest son, Fidelito, who is married and has two children. Trained as a physicist, Fidelito served as head of the Cuban Nuclear Commission until Castro had him removed from the post. Castro's daughter Alina Fernández-Revuelta (whose mother Naty Revuelta had an affair with Castro while he was still married to Mirta Díaz-Balart) left Cuba in 1993 and has been a strong critic of her father's rule.

Castro maintains varying degrees of cordiality with his siblings. He is closest to his brother Raúl, a relationship born of their unique shared experiences starting with the attack on the Moncada Barracks. One sister, Juana, is actively hostile toward him, however, and attacks him often from her self-imposed exile in Miami. The Castro family landholdings were gradually turned over to government control starting in 1959. Castro's former nephew by marriage, Lincoln Diaz-Balart, is a Republican Congressman from Florida.

If Castro has a lover, her identity is unknown, and since the death of Celia Sánchez Manduley in 1980, Castro has shown no interest in elevating another woman to this position. Despite never marrying Fidel, Celia Sánchez played the role of first lady of Cuba. In addition to her role as companion, she exercised considerable political power as secretary of the Council of State and member of the party's Central Committee. After her death, numerous monuments and parks were erected in her honor.

Castro was a habitual smoker throughout much of his career, but he quit smoking in 1986 in order to set an example to other Cubans. Although the cigar industry brings in hundreds of millions of dollars in revenue every year, Castro has embarked on a campaign to get Cubans to quit smoking.

Castro's health has been the subject of rumors since he first emerged as a international figure in the 1950s. Despite numerous claims of ill health (or death), Castro was an active, visible leader of Cuba from the 1950s until 2006, when he temporarily gave all governing power to his brother Raúl while he underwent surgery for "acute intestinal crisis with sustained bleeding." For months Castro was not seen in public, but video footage of him a year later suggested that his health was improved. In February 2008 Castro announced his resignation as leader of Cuba.

ASSESSMENT

When the Soviet bloc collapsed, Castro faced still another challenge to his rule and the Cuban state he built. In his eighties, Castro cannot rule for very much longer, and some argue that after his death Cuba will revert to the control of the Cuban exile community based in Miami. Yet the political pundits have never given Castro his due, and there is no reason to think that Castro's brand of socialism will collapse once he dies. It was considered folly to attack the Moncada Barracks in 1953 and even more foolhardy to launch a sea invasion of Cuba in 1956. Yet Castro silenced his critics with his record

of success. Since the establishment of his socialist regime in Cuba, many have counted by the day or week, not year, the time it would supposedly take for Castro to be ousted, yet he has clung to power for nearly fifty years.

It is also common to regard Castro as nothing more than a caudillo, and in fact he displays many of the traits associated with other Latin American strongmen. Yet if his only goal had been to replace Batista, certainly a man of Castro's considerable abilities and class background could have reached the pinnacle of power in Cuba through the accepted military and social channels. While Castro's early days in the mountains of eastern Cuba nearly cost him his life, they also established that he was fighting for more than just personal aggrandizement and perpetuation of the old order. From his earliest days as a student, Castro has been an ardent nationalist fighting to rid Cuba of foreign control and the humiliation of poverty and illiteracy. Although foreign influences remain after his much-publicized break with the United States, certainly Cuba enjoyed greater leeway with the Soviet Union than it did in its relations with its North American neighbor. And while poverty and illiteracy there have not been eliminated, Cuba far surpasses the rest of Latin America in education and the fulfillment of basic needs. Although he cannot claim sole responsibility for this, Fidel Castro can take at least partial credit for overseeing the transformation of Cuba into a modern, secular, healthy, and well-educated society.

See also **Cuba: Cuba Since 1959; Cuban Intervention in Africa; Cuban Missile Crisis; Cuba, Revolutions: Cuban Revolution; Cuba, Twenty-Sixth of July Movement.**

BIBLIOGRAPHY

Primary Work

Castro, Fidel, and Ignacio Ramonet. *Fidel Castro: My Life; A Spoken Autobiography.* New York: Simon & Schuster, 2008.

Secondary Works

Bourne, Peter G. *Fidel: A Biography of Fidel Castro.* New York: Dodd, Mead, 1986.

De la Cova, Antonio Rafael. *The Moncada Attack: Birth of the Cuban Revolution.* Columbia: University of South Carolina Press, 2007.

Franqui, Carlos. *Diary of the Cuban Revolution.* New York: Viking, 1980.

Latell, Brian. *After Fidel: The Inside Story of Castro's Regime and Cuba's Next Leader.* New York: Palgrave Macmillan, 2005.

Lievesley, Geraldine. *The Cuban Revolution: Past, Present, and Future.* New York: Palgrave Macmillan, 2004.

Lockwood, Lee. *Castro's Cuba, Cuba's Fidel.* New York: Vintage, 1969.

Shierka, Volker. *Fidel Castro: A Biography,* trans. Patrick Camillar. Cambridge, U.K., and Malden, MA: Polity, 2004.

Szulc, Tad. *Fidel, a Critical Portrait.* New York: Morrow, 1986.

MICHAEL POWELSON

CASTRO RUZ, RAÚL

CASTRO RUZ, RAÚL (1931–). Raúl Castro, Cuban revolutionary and military leader, is the younger brother of Cuban leader Fidel Castro and one of the original members of the 26th of July Movement that organized the successful overthrow of the Cuban dictator Fulgencio Batista in 1959. Raúl Castro was born on 3 June 1931, in Oriente Province (now Holguín province) to an affluent landowning family. His father, Angel, was a native of Galicia, Spain; his mother, Lina Ruz González, was Cuban. As a youth he attended Catholic schools in Oriente Province and went on to study at the University of Havana. Unlike his brother Fidel, Raúl was early attracted to Marxism, and while a student at the university he joined the Socialist Youth Branch of the Partido Socialista Popular (PSP).

Raúl and Fidel Castro found common ground, however, in their hatred of the regime of Fulgencio Batista and the pervasive role the United States played in all aspects of Cuban life. Raúl fought alongside his brother during the struggle to overthrow the Batista regime. In 1953 Raúl was imprisoned along with Fidel for the attack on the Moncada Barracks and joined his brother in exile in Mexico after Batista declared a general amnesty in 1955. Raúl helped Fidel plan the 1956 landing of a small band of revolutionaries from the boat *Granma* in southeastern Cuba. This invasion culminated in the ouster of Batista in 1959, and when the new revolutionary government took power, Raúl was named minister of Cuba's Revolutionary Armed Forces.

As hostilities with the United States grew after the revolution, both Raúl Castro and Che Guevara were instrumental in influencing Fidel Castro to turn to the Soviet Union for economic and military aid. Whereas Fidel initially denied he was a communist, Raúl openly courted the Soviets while attacking the United States. With the Bay of Pigs invasion in 1961 and the Cuban Missile Crisis the following year, Raúl played an integral role in moving Cuba from the U.S. to the Soviet sphere of influence.

As a trusted adviser to Fidel, Raúl has increased his power considerably over the years. Many have charged the Castro brothers of running the Cuban government as a family-owned business. While Fidel holds the title of president of the Council of Ministers and president of the Council of State, Raúl holds the offices of vice president of both the Council of Ministers and the Council of State. In addition, Raúl is second in command of the armed forces behind his brother Fidel. Raúl is also a member of the Politburo and second secretary of the Cuban Communist Party. He has been president of the Agrarian Reform Institute since 1965 and is responsible for the Council of Ministers, the Ministry of the Interior, the Secretariat of the President, the Ministry of Public Health, and the Children's Institute. In 2006 Fidel name Raúl temporary head of state while Fidel underwent surgery for gastrointestinal bleeding. He was officially elected president in February 2008, upon Fidel's resignation.

Raúl Castro and his supporters built a modern army capable of protecting Cuba against U.S. aggression and of launching military forays abroad. With the collapse of the Soviet Union and economic crises at home, the Cuban military, led by Raúl, is increasingly prominent in Cuban industries such as manufacturing and tourism. Once regarded as an ideologue by comparison with his pragmatic brother Fidel, Raúl Castro has since shown greater flexibility, especially in guiding the direction of Cuba's economy. Raúl has endorsed limited capitalist foreign investment, as well as market incentives for Cuban producers, as a remedy for the nation's economic ills. Although Raúl possesses considerable power, he lacks Fidel's charisma, and most Cuba-watchers doubt that he would be able to fill his brother's shoes if Fidel were to die.

Raúl Castro's wife, Vilma Espín Guillois, also played a prominent role both during the revolution, when she fought with the Castro brothers against Batista, and after the revolution, when she founded the Federation of Cuban Women. Because Fidel lacked an official "wife," Vilma played the role of official first lady. Vilma Espin and Raúl Castro had four children; she died in 2007.

While there has been much criticism of Raúl, he and his brother Fidel did lead a successful revolt against both a despised dictator and the overbearing economic and political hegemony of the United States. Although it was widely accepted that Cuba could not survive without massive Soviet military and economic support, since the collapse of the Eastern bloc, Cuba shows few signs of internal turmoil, and since the late 1990s the Cuban economy has been growing. Raúl Castro can take part of the credit for that.

See also **Cuban Intervention in Africa; Cuba, Revolutions: Cuban Revolution; Cuba, Twenty-Sixth of July Movement.**

BIBLIOGRAPHY

Primary Work

Castro, Raúl, and Fidel Castro. *Selección de discursos acerca del partido.* Havana: Editorial de Ciencias Sociales, Instituto Cubano del Libro, 1975.

Secondary Works

Fitzgerald, Frank T. *Managing Socialism: From Old Cadres to New Professionals in Revolutionary Cuba.* New York: Praeger, 1990.

Latell, Brian. *After Fidel: Raúl Castro and the Future of Cuba's Revolution.* New York: Palgrave Macmillan, 2007.

McManus, Jane, ed. *From the Palm Tree: Voices of the Cuban Revolution.* Secaucus, NJ: L. Stuart, 1983.

Suárez, Luis, ed. *Entre el fusil y la palabra.* Mexico: Universidad Nacional Autónoma de México, 1980.

MICHAEL POWELSON

CATALONIAN VOLUNTEERS. The

Free Company of Catalonian Volunteers was formed in Barcelona in 1767 as part of the Bourbon reorganization of the Spanish military in the Americas. The company participated in the Sonora expedition of 1767–1771, the establishment of California in 1769, the Colorado River Campaign of 1781–1782, the voyage of the *expedición de los limites* to the Pacific Northwest and Alaska during 1790–1793, as well as the royalist effort to quell the movement for Mexican independence. From 1767 to 1815, the Compañía Franca de Voluntarios de Cataluña assisted in Spain's last great push to secure the northwestern portion of its empire in the Western Hemisphere.

See also **Mexico, Wars and Revolutions: War of Independence.**

BIBLIOGRAPHY

Joseph P. Sánchez, *Spanish Bluecoats: The Catalonian Volunteers in Northwestern New Spain, 1767–1810* (1990).

Additional Bibliography

Soler Vidal, Joseph, and Martín Olmedo. *California: La aventura catalana del noroeste.* Tlalpan, D.F.: Colegio de Jalisco, 2001.

JOSEPH P. SÁNCHEZ

CATAMARCA. Catamarca, capital city of the

province of the same name in northwestern Argentina, with 141,000 inhabitants (2001 census). It was founded in 1558 with the unusual name of London, to commemorate the marriage of Philip II of Spain to Mary Tudor of England, and was destroyed by Diaguita Indians in 1563, 1607, and 1683. Its location today in a well-sheltered valley between Sierra de Ancasti and Sierra de Ambato was chosen by Fernando Mendoza, who was attracted, as were other settlers from Santiago del Estero, by the good soils and by the numerous Indian farming communities that flourished in the valley. On the basis of the region's famed Indian textiles in colonial times, cotton fields and textile mills were established around Catamarca during republican times. However, fruit orchards in the well-irrigated valley dominated the agrarian economy until the late twentieth century.

The hinterland of Catamarca was formerly part of the Diaguita cultural realm extending from Argentina across the Andes into the Norte Chico region of Chile and famous for its fine ceramics. East of the Sierra de Famatina, the interior valley of the Colorado River is still the seat of the traditional Indian-Mestizo agrarian populations, Fiambalá and Tinogasta counting among their centers.

See also **Argentina, Geography.**

BIBLIOGRAPHY

Carlos Villafuerte, *Catamarca: Camino y tiempo* (Buenos Aires, 1968).

CÉSAR N. CAVIEDES

CATAVI MASSACRE. Catavi Massacre, slay-

ing of Bolivian workers during a miners' strike in 1942. In September 1942, the miners' union in the

Catavi tin ore concentration plant presented the Patiño Company with demands for wage increases ranging from 20 percent to 70 percent. The company refused even to negotiate with the union, and union negotiators failed to obtain the support of the government of General Enrique Peñaranda. When the union announced a strike for 14 December, the government declared a state of siege in the tin-mining departments, and troops moved into Catavi. When union leaders were arrested on 13 December, the workers mobilized to demand their release, and the police fired on the crowd, killing and wounding several.

The strike continued. On 21 December, workers demonstrating in front of company offices in Catavi were fired on by soldiers, who killed or wounded 35 people. The workers then mobilized some 8,000 people, who descended on the company headquarters in Catavi. Soldiers shot into the crowd and for the next two days roamed through workers' living quarters, beating up and killing miners and members of their families. The government admitted that 19 people were killed—including 3 women—but other sources claimed the deaths were as high as 400.

This incident shocked the country. The Catavi union's secretary general got to La Paz and informed Víctor Paz Estenssoro, leader of the Nationalist Revolutionary Movement (MNR) of what had occurred. MNR deputies then intensively interrogated government ministers, establishing a bond between the MNR and the miners that lasted several decades.

The Catavi massacre provoked wide international protest. The U.S. State Department and the Pan-American Union expressed concern, and the AFL and the CIO sent to Bolivia a joint delegation, roundly denouncing the Peñaranda government.

The Catavi massacre was undoubtedly a major factor undermining the Peñaranda regime, which was overthrown a year later by a coalition of young military men and the MNR.

See also **Mining: Modern.**

BIBLIOGRAPHY

Augusto Céspedes, *El presidente colgado* (1966).

Guillermo Lora, *A History of the Bolivian Labour Movement* (1977).

Additional Bibliography

Ibáñez Rojo, Enrique. *La política desde el socavón: El movimiento obrero en la historia de Bolivia, 1940-1970*. Serie Con-textos de ciencias sociales, 5. Madrid: Entinema, 1999.

ROBERT J. ALEXANDER

CATEAU-CAMBRÉSIS, TREATY OF (1559).

Treaty of Cateau-Cambrésis (1559), agreement between France and Spain ending the Hapsburg-Valois wars. The treaty ended four decades (1521–1559) of armed conflict over Navarre, Aragon's borders, Flanders, Artois, Burgundy, and Milan. According to its terms, France kept imperial cities in northern Europe but was almost totally excluded from the Italian peninsula, underscoring the existing balance of power in continental Europe. The reigning monarchs when the treaty was signed on 3 April 1559, Philip II of Spain and Henry II of France, were forced by bankruptcy and heresy to make peace. The treaty also marked the end of an Anglo-Spanish alliance that had been crucial in foreign policy during the end of Charles I's reign and left Philip II with the problem of defending the Low Countries without an English alliance. The New World was ignored in the treaty by mutual consent and peace was thus limited to the European domain.

See also **Charles I of Spain; Philip II of Spain.**

BIBLIOGRAPHY

William S. Maltby, *Alba: A Biography of Fernando Álvarez de Toledo, Third Duke of Alba, 1507–1582* (1983), esp. pp. 110–116.

John Lynch, *Spain 1516–1598* (1991), pp. 101–137, 251–253.

SUZANNE HILES BURKHOLDER

CATHERWOOD, FREDERICK (1799–1854).

Frederick Catherwood (February 27, 1799–September 27, 1854) was an English architect, artist, explorer, and illustrator who worked with American diplomat and journalist John Lloyd Stephens to carry out the first formal surveys of several Maya archaeological sites in present-day Mexico, Guatemala, Belize, and Honduras between 1839 and 1842. Catherwood produced more than two hundred detailed drawings of Maya architecture, sculpture, monuments, and other material culture, as well as plan maps that were turned into steel lithograph engravings. These were published in two double-volume travelogues authored by Stephens, entitled *Incidents of Travel in Central America, Chiapas, and Yucatan* (1841) and *Incidents of Travel in Yucatan* (1843). He later published on his own a two-volume folio set of hand colored plates entitled *Views of Ancient Monuments in Central America, Chiapas, and Yucatan* (1844).

Catherwood used a camera lucida technique to project outlines of his subjects directly onto graph paper. This was the first time this technique was used outside of Europe. In the history of Mesoamerican studies, Stephens and Catherwood's publications are revolutionary contributions in several ways. Catherwood did not depict Maya architecture and monuments through an Old World lens or filter, but rather focused on detailed representations of the styles and relief of the sculpture itself, thereby emphasizing the elements that were unique to Maya art and architecture, including hieroglyphic inscriptions that clearly depicted a language unknown anywhere else in the world.

Stephens and Catherwood championed the idea of indigenous development of complex society in the Americas rather than a migration of civilized peoples from the Near East, Mediterranean, or Classical Greek or Roman world sometime in the remote past. Their ideas were based on comparing the details of Maya monuments and architecture with Old World forms, in which Catherwood's illustrations provided key visual evidence. Stephens and Catherwood argued that Maya cities were probably built between the fifth and thirteenth centuries CE, dates much later than most scholars of the time thought and within the range supported by modern archaeological investigations. They also suggested that the ancient Maya civilization was ancestral to the contemporary indigenous population living in southern Mexico and Central America.

Frederick Catherwood died in 1854 when the steamship *S.S. Arctic*, upon which he was a passenger returning to New York from Liverpool, England, was rammed by another ship and sank in the North Atlantic.

See also **Archaeology; Maya, The.**

BIBLIOGRAPHY

Bartlett, William Henry. *Walks about the City and Environs of Jerusalem*. London: G. Virtue, 1884.

Bourbon, Fabio. *The Lost Cities of the Mayas: The Life, Art, and Discoveries of Frederick Catherwood*. New York: Abbeville, 2000.

Briggs, Peter. *The Maya Image in the Western World: A Catalogue to an Exhibition at the University of New Mexico*. Albuquerque: University of New Mexico Press, 1986.

Catherwood, Frederick. *Explanation of the Large Map of Jerusalem: From Actual Survey in the Year 1835*. New York: Israel Sacket, 1838.

Catherwood, Frederick. *Views of Ancient Monuments in Central America, Chiapas, and Yucatan*. New York: Bartlett & Welford, 1844.

Evans, R. Tripp. *Romancing the Maya: Mexican Antiquity in the American Imagination, 1820–1915*. Austin: University of Texas Press, 2004.

DYLAN J. CLARK

CATHOLIC ACTION. Catholic Action was the generic name for Catholic lay associations that were founded throughout the world in response to Pope Pius XI's call for Catholics to participate more actively in support of the church and to defend Catholicism against the dangers of liberalism, Communism, positivism, and Protestantism. Most Catholic Action national associations in Latin America were founded in the 1930s: Argentina and Chile in 1931, Colombia in 1933, Peru in 1935, and Bolivia in 1938. Based on the Italian model, Catholic Action had branches for men, women, and youth. There were also specialized groups for workers, students, businessmen, secretaries, and rural workers. Many Catholic Action groups had strong ties with the schools run by religious orders, especially the Jesuits. Catholic Action drew its inspiration from the papal social encyclicals and European intellectuals such as Jacques Maritain, Gilbert Keith Chesterton, and Hilaire Belloc. Drawing its leadership mainly from the urban upper and middle classes, Catholic Action received a strong impulse from the bishops and papal nuncios. In some cases, leading Catholic laymen took the initiative. In Brazil, Jackson de Figueiredo founded the Centro Dom Vital (Dom Vital Center) in 1922, and his successor, Alceu Amoroso Lima, became the most important spokesmen for Brazilian Catholic Action.

In many cases the specialized groups had a greater long-term influence than the general association. The most important Catholic Action group among workers was the Juventud Obrera Católica (JOC; Young Catholic Workers). Modeled on the original movement founded in 1925 by a Belgian priest, Joseph Cardijn, JOC aimed to counteract the influence of Communist or Socialist-run unions. In Chile, Clotario Blest, a Catholic Action leader, was also an important figure in the national union movement. In Cuba the Catholic university student movement, Agrupación Católica Universitaria (ACU), founded in 1931 by the Jesuits, was the most important Catholic Action group on the island. In Brazil, the Juventude Universitária Católica (JUC; Catholic University Youth) numbered many thousands in the 1960s.

Although Catholic Action was officially forbidden to participate in partisan politics, in fact it served as a school of political leadership for an entire generation of Catholics. Most of the founders of the Christian Democratic parties began as youth leaders in Catholic Action. Many of the leaders of the Cristero movement in Mexico, notably René Capistrán, had their beginnings in the Centro de Estudiantes Católicos (Catholic Student Center), founded by the Jesuits in Mexico City in 1913. Rigoberta Menchú in Guatemala, the winner of the Nobel Peace Prize in 1992, was somewhat an exception to the rule, because Catholic Action groups normally did not extend to the countryside. The daughter of a catechist who was killed in a massacre, she acquired many skills as a catechist and as a member of Catholic Action in her village that served her later when she became a union organizer. Her simple indigenous Catholicism was a source of strength in the face of much personal adversity. It also led her to take a sympathetic attitude toward liberation theology and to be highly critical of conservative groups in the church.

Although all members were united in their determination to defend Catholicism, not all shared the same views on politics. Some, such as Jackson de Figueiredo, thought along integralist lines and espoused the creation of a Catholic corporatist state. Most Catholic Action leaders, however, were swayed by Jacques Maritain's concept of a "Christian democracy." By the 1960s some of the university groups had become quite radicalized. The JUC in Brazil took such a leftist and independent course that it was eventually marginalized by the bishops.

By the late 1950s Catholic Action had begun to decline, to be replaced by other, newer movements. Its most important contribution to Latin American Catholicism was the fostering of a new social awareness among Catholics. It represented the transition from an older, elitist Catholicism to the more modern and pluralistic Catholicism of Vatican II.

See also **Catholic Church: The Modern Period; Figueiredo, Jackson de; Liberation Theology; Lima, Alceu Amoroso.**

BIBLIOGRAPHY

Bailey, David C. *¡Viva Cristo Rey! The Cristero Rebellion and the Church-State Conflict in Mexico.* Austin: University of Texas Press, 1974.

Bidegain, Ana María. *Iglesia, pueblo, y política: Un estudio de conflictos de intereses, Colombia, 1930–1955.* Bogotá, Colombia: Pontificia Universidad Javeriana, Facultad de Teología, 1985.

Cleary, Edward L. *Crisis and Change: The Church in Latin America Today.* Maryknoll, NY: Orbis Books, 1985.

Dussel, Enrique, ed. *The Church in Latin America, 1492–1992.* Maryknoll, NY: Orbis Books, 1992.

Klaiber, Jeffrey. *The Church, Dictatorships, and Democracy in Latin America.* Maryknoll, NY: Orbis Books, 1998.

Landsberger, Henry A., ed. *The Church and Social Change in Latin America.* Notre Dame, IN: University of Notre Dame Press, 1970.

Mainwaring, Scott. *The Catholic Church and Politics in Brazil, 1916–1985.* Stanford, CA: Stanford University Press, 1986.

Menchú, Rigoberto, and Elizabeth Burgos Debray. *Me llamo Rigoberta Menchú.* Havana: Casa de las Américas, 1983.

JEFFREY KLAIBER

CATHOLIC CHURCH

This entry includes the following articles:
THE COLONIAL PERIOD
THE MODERN PERIOD

THE COLONIAL PERIOD

The Catholic Church in colonial Latin America is often seen as a monolithic institution. In actual fact there were significant divisions within it. The church was divided internally into two basic parts: the secular clergy and the regular clergy. The regular clergy consisted of all priests, friars, and monks who were members of religious orders. Since membership in a religious order called upon the individual to pursue a special rule of life, *regula* in Latin, these clerics were called regulars. The secular clergy was made up of the clerics and priests involved in the day-to-day affairs of parish life. They lived out "in the world," *saeculum* in Latin, from which the term *secular* derives.

The secular clergy in the New World fell under the administrative control of the Iberian monarchs, under the Patronato Real (in Portuguese *Padrado Real*) as developed during and immediately following the discovery and conquest. Each order of the regular clergy, on the other hand, had its own internal organization and leadership, directly under the pope.

Both seculars and regulars existed in Iberian and indigenous societies, and both relied on the gifts, alms, and taxes of the Iberians to help subsidize their work among the Indians.

EARLY SETTLEMENT

In the first phase of the Spanish and Portuguese settlement of the New World, the regulars played a very important role. In each of the major conquering armies one member of a religious order served as the spiritual director of the expedition; in addition, there were also secular clerics involved in the expeditions. Pope Adrian VI empowered the religious orders to engage in missionary activities with his bull *Exponi nobis feciste*, known as *Omnimoda* (1522), which authorized the Franciscans, in particular, to do anything necessary for the conversion of the Indians whenever they were out of the immediate jurisdiction of a bishop (defined as a two-days' ride). Other religious orders eventually received the same or similar powers.

The major effort of conversion fell rather naturally to the religious orders. Structurally they were better suited to the work because they carried with them a sense of institutional direction and oversight, usually arriving in organized groups, normally of twelve, in imitation of the Apostles.

The Iberian powers engaged in an extensive moral debate over the treatment of the natives of the New World. Bartolomé de Las Casas, a Dominican friar, and other outspoken critics, decried the harsh treatment which the conquerors had meted out on the natives. In 1537 Pope Paul III, in his bull *Sublimis deus,* declared that the natives were fully human and thus were not to be deprived of their freedom or mastery of their possessions. Another camp, manifest in the work of Juan Ginés de Sepúlveda, argued that the natives were naturally inferior to the Europeans, and thus force could be used against them. Legal provisions were adopted to protect the natives, although in actual application most of these failed.

In confronting the huge indigenous population, which spoke dozens of different and mutually unintelligible languages, the missionaries had to adopt certain operational rules, as there were too many converts and too few clergy. For instance, in administering the sacrament of baptism, the clergy could not engage in a long and complex catechumenate before admitting the Indians to Christianity. It was far more practical to baptize the masses and concentrate later on their spiritual preparation. Clearly it was not practical to teach all of the Indians Spanish or Portuguese in order to then instruct them in Christianity. Consequently the clergy learned the native languages and preached and indoctrinated in them; as a consequence there are scores of books, mostly catechisms and other doctrinal works, printed in native American languages. Many missionaries concentrated on amassing as much knowledge about the native cultures as possible and in the process produced such works as the *Florentine Codex,* a twelve-volume encyclopedia of Aztec life, written in the Aztec language, Nahuatl, by a Franciscan, Friar Bernardino de Sahagún. In Peru one finds the legends of Huarochirí collected by the secular priest Francisco de Ávila. Although modern scholars are thrilled to have this wealth of detail about native culture at the time of contact, one must keep in mind the purpose for which it was compiled: to extirpate all vestiges of the pre-Columbian civilization. The need to learn the native languages also produced scores of other books, grammars, and dictionaries of the New World languages, from Floridian Timucua to Chilean Araucanian, from Aymara of Bolivia to Zapotec of Mexico and Tupi of Brazil.

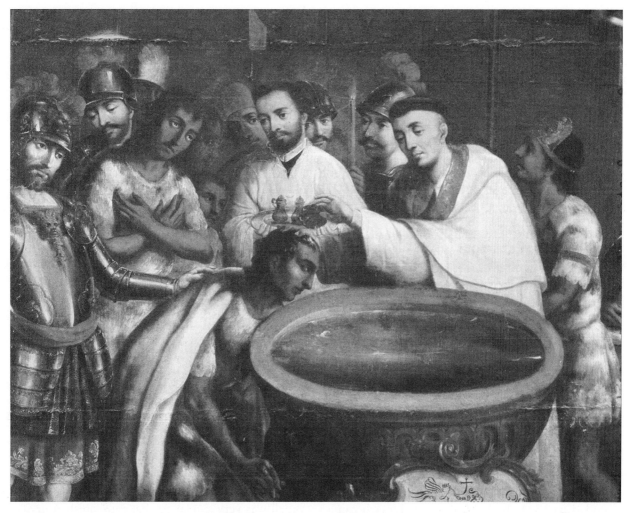

First Baptism of the Indians by the Dominicans (oil on canvas) by Mexican School (18th century). MUSEO NACIONAL DE HISTORIA, MEXICO CITY, MEXICO/ GIRAUDON/ THE BRIDGEMAN ART LIBRARY

The religious orders were the most active in the early phases of European settlement. The first organized missionary expedition to Mexico, a group of twelve Franciscans, arrived in 1524, led by Friar Martín de Valencia. It was followed in 1526 by twelve Dominicans led by Friar Tomás Ortiz and in 1533 by seven Augustinians under the guidance of Friar Francisco de la Cruz. By 1559 the missionary corps of New Spain had swelled to some 802 religious in some 160 monasteries.

The first missionary efforts in Brazil were conducted principally by Franciscans who accompanied the early voyages of discovery. The first organized missionary effort to Brazil was an expedition of six Jesuits under the leadership of Manuel da Nóbrega in 1544. By the end of the century there were 128 Jesuits active in Brazil. The secular clergy were active in Brazil from a very early date. The first parishes were erected in 1532, and in 1551 the diocese of Brazil was created. The first convent for nuns was not established until 1665, the second in 1735.

In Peru a similar pattern emerged. The Franciscans were among the first missionaries to arrive, along with Dominicans and Mercedarians, shortly following the Conquest. The Franciscan mission was initially led by Fray Marcos de Niza, who came down from Mexico with a small expedition but apparently returned home upon reaching what is southern Panama. In 1534–1535 the Franciscans established monasteries in Quito and in Los Reyes (modern-day Lima). In 1540 twelve Dominicans, the second expedition organized by the order, arrived under the leadership of Friar Francisco Toscano. The first Mercedarians appeared in Lima in 1535, and by 1540 they had established four monasteries, in Lima, San Miguel de Piura, Cuzco, and Guamanga.

Although active in Mexico, the Augustinians did not participate in the early missions in Peru. The Mercedarians arrived in Mexico in the late sixteenth century. In 1593 they established a college and a novitiate under the direction of the Guatemalan province. It was not until 1619 that the Mercedarians established an independent Mexican province. In the mid-sixteenth century the Jesuits became active throughout Hispanic America.

THE SECULAR CLERGY

The first dioceses were erected in the Caribbean in 1511, including Santo Domingo, Cuba, Concepción, and Puerto Rico. On the mainland the first diocese, called Carola, was founded in 1519 and inspired by the ongoing conquest of the Aztecs. Following the confusion of the Conquest, the diocese was resurrected as Tlaxcala in 1526. The seat of the diocese later moved to the Spanish city of Puebla de los Ángeles, and thus the diocese is known variously as Tlaxcala, Puebla, or Tlaxcala-Puebla. The diocese of Mexico was erected in 1530 with Friar Juan de Zumárraga as first bishop. In South America, the diocese of Cuzco was the first to be erected, in 1537, with Vicente de Valverde, a Dominican and chaplain to Pizarro, as first bishop. Lima was founded in 1541. Both Mexico and Lima became archbishoprics in 1546, along with Santo Domingo.

The church in the Hispanic Americas was divided into three provinces, under the three archdioceses. Each of the three archdioceses had a number of suffragan, or subject, dioceses. The Province of Santo Domingo included all the dioceses erected in the Caribbean. The Province of Mexico included all the dioceses of Mexico, Central America, and the Philippines, until 1595, when Manila was elevated to an archdiocese. Later, in 1743 Guatemala became an archdiocese. The Province of Peru included all of South America. In 1564 Santa Fe de Bogotá became an archdiocese, controlling the northern part of the continent and Panama. In 1609, La Plata (modern-day Sucre, Bolivia) was elevated to an archdiocese.

The Portuguese placed all of their overseas possessions into one ecclesiastical province, centered in Funchal, on the island of Madeira. In 1551 the various territories within Brazil were placed under the administrative control of the newly created bishopric of Salvador da Bahia. In 1676 Bahia was made an archdiocese and Rio de Janeiro and Pernambuco were made suffragan dioceses. The African dioceses of São Tomé and Angola were also placed under the administrative control of the archbishop of Bahia. The following year Maranhão became a diocese, followed in 1719 by Pará, and in 1745 São Paulo and Mariana (Minas Gerais).

The secular clergy was organized under the authority of the local bishop; clerics were assigned to the cathedral, to provide it with ecclesiastical staff and to assist the bishop in his administration of the diocese. These clerics were collectively known as the cathedral chapter, or *cabildo eclesiástico,* which had a maximum of twenty-seven clerics, including five dignitaries, ten canons, six *racioneros,* and six *medio-racioneros.* The dignitaries, dean, archdeacon, *chantre* (precentor), *maestrescuelas* (schoolmaster), and treasurer, all received the honorific title *don,* and theoretically oversaw specific areas of the church's life. The canons and *racioneros* both participated in the daily round of religious observations. All these functionaries received stipends from the ecclesiastical tax, the tithe. The terms *racionero* and *medio-racionero* signify that these clerics received either a full or half ration from the tithe.

The organization of the cathedral chapters in Brazil was very similar to that in Spanish America. Yet in addition to the structure seen in the Hispanic world, the Brazilian church was also divided into prelacies. There were territories within established dioceses, which functioned as proto-dioceses. For example, in 1575 the Prelacy of Rio de Janeiro was created by Pope Gregory XIII. The territory was fully subject to the bishop of Bahia, but had its own local prelate. The prelate, often called a vicar, exercised most of the functions of the bishop for the southern territories of Brazil. At the same time a prelacy was created for the far north, in Pernambuco. Both would become independent dioceses in 1676.

The parish priest might fulfill several obligations. His principal responsibility was the spiritual cure of souls. If he enjoyed an income guaranteed by the crown or by some other patron, he would be the beneficiary of that stipend, or *beneficiado,* signifying that he held his office for life. If he served as an ecclesiastical judge, whose power emanated from the bishop, the ordinary ecclesiastical judge of the diocese, he would be known as a *vicario*.

THE REGULAR CLERGY

Just as the secular clergy was divided into dioceses and grouped into provinces, so, too, was the regular clergy divided into provinces. In Mexico, the Franciscans had two. The Province of the Santo Evangelio de México encompassed the central region of the colony, mostly the dioceses of Puebla and Mexico; the Discalced Franciscans administered the Province of San Pedro y San Pablo in the western area, in the dioceses of Michoacán and Guadalajara. The Augustinians likewise had two provinces: in the west was the Province of San Nicolás Tolentino, and in the central zone was the Province of the Santísimo Nombre de Jesús. The Dominicans had a province in the central area, the Province of Santiago. In the south, in the dioceses of Oaxaca and Chiapas, there was another Dominican province, that of San Hipólito. Thus, in each instance the orders established one province in the central area and another in a more distant region. As the church developed, additional provinces were added, especially in Central America.

Likewise in South America the orders divided into provinces. The Dominicans had the Province of San Juan Bautista, serving Peru; the Province of Santa Catalina Mártir for Quito and Popayan; and the Province of San Lorenzo Mártir for Upper Peru and Río de la Plata. The Franciscans had the Province of the Twelve Apostles for Peru, the Province of San Francisco for Quito, the Province of La Santísima Trinidad for Chile, the Province of San Antonio for Upper Peru, and the Province of Santa Fe for Bogotá. Similarly the Mercedarians and Augustinians divided the region into their own provinces.

Several of the religious orders were active in Brazil. The Jesuits and the Franciscans had the longest history in the region, dating from the first decades of Portuguese occupation. Each order had one province to administer their activities in Brazil. In the seventeenth century the Benedictines, Carmelites, and Trinitarians established missions, convents, and monasteries. Other orders had a smaller presence, including the Capuchins, the Discalced Carmelites, and the Oratorians. The Mercedarians and Augustinians arrived only in the eighteenth century.

NONRELIGIOUS ACTIVITIES

In addition to providing for the spiritual needs of the faithful, the church took an active role in education. While the Dominicans had established some grammar schools, as had the Franciscans, education in Ibero-America came to be dominated by the Jesuits. Three universities were founded in the mid-sixteenth century in Santo Domingo, Mexico, Peru. Most dioceses established seminaries for the secular clergy in the seventeenth century, although these relied heavily on the Jesuits.

In Brazil the Jesuits were also at the forefront of higher education. The Jesuit colleges in Bahia and Rio de Janeiro were the first authorized to grant degrees and prepare students for further study at the University of Coimbra, in Portugal. Later in the colonial period other schools were founded by the Jesuits, Oratorians, and local bishops, yet none was ever granted the title of university.

The church also acted as a bank. In general, colonial Hispanic and Portuguese America was cash poor. Many transactions relied on credit. The principal source of institutional credit was the church. Through the institution of pious works, and specifically chantries, Capellanías, the church acquired significant amounts of cash which had to be loaned at interest to generate more income. The church only loaned money when real estate was used as collateral. The loan took the form of a mortgage or lien. The important difference was that the church did not want, or expect, the loan to be paid off or the mortgage amortized. The church needed the constant income to pay for her various ministries and projects. Thus the impositions became nearly perpetual. If an individual lacked cash but still wished to found a *capellanía,* he could do one of two things: he could give real estate to the church, which would then rent or sell the property to generate the needed income; or he could give part of a piece of property or voluntarily impose a lien on a free and clear property and begin to pay the interest, thereby donating money which he did not actually possess. This latter method provided the colonial economy with a means of capital formation.

The secular clergy and religious orders acquired large tracts of land. By far the leader in this regard was the Society of Jesus (Jesuits). The religious orders depended on the rents and revenues generated by rural and urban property for their long-term sustenance. The only order to eschew this practice was the Franciscans. The Franciscans found that the possession of property was antithetical to their ideal of apostolic poverty. Nevertheless, when taken as a whole, the lands held by the church constituted a significant portion, some estimates have even placed it as high as a third, of the arable agricultural land of the Ibero-American colonies.

INTERNAL STRUCTURE

As the religious orders accepted sons of the local elite, a significant change occurred in their social composition. By the beginning of the seventeenth century, membership in the religious orders was evenly divided among those born in Europe (peninsulars) and those born in the New World (Creoles). As the orders were largely self-governing on the local level, the social division between peninsulars and creoles led to factionalism whenever elections were held. In order to ameliorate the effects of this division, a system in which control would alternate between the two factions was developed. This system, the *alternativa*, eventually was adopted throughout most of the religious orders and also came to include the European-born Spaniards who had entered the orders in the New World.

In the seventeenth century there were many conflicts between the secular and regular clergy. In 1574 Phillip II of Spain had decreed that all parishes would eventually be subject to the control of the seculars, but the indigenous population was so large and the clerical population still so small, that it was necessary to keep the regulars in the parishes. The process through which parishes passed from the regular to the secular clergy was usually a bitter one and did not end until the 1740s.

The second area of conflict between the seculars and regulars concerned the payment of the tithe. The regular clergy claimed to be exempt from payment, since the church should not rightly tax itself. On the other hand the local bishops felt that as long as the religious orders did not recognize the bishop's supervisory power over their actions in the parishes, the orders were not truly subject to the bishop. Therefore, they had to pay the tithe. This conflict came to a head in the diocese of Puebla, in New Spain, during the episcopacy of don Juan de Palafox y Mendoza (*d.* 1659), when the Jesuits refused to tithe. Eventually the religious orders accepted both the duty to tithe and to subjugate themselves to the local bishop.

THE CROWN VERSUS THE CLERGY

What had been a series of conflicts between the seculars and the regulars in the seventeenth century turned into an assault by the monarch on ecclesiastical privilege in the eighteenth century. The monarch favored the seculars, since under the *patronato real* he controlled the seculars far more completely. Consequently the monarch attempted to limit the independent action of the regulars or to place them firmly under the control of local bishops. There were several decrees of the early eighteenth century which placed limits on the construction of new monasteries, moratoria on entrance into the religious orders, and limits on bequests to the orders. This pattern came to a dramatic conclusion in 1767, when the crown expelled the Jesuits from the New World. (They had been expelled from Brazil in 1759–1760.) While the expulsion of the Jesuits responded to many concerns emanating from Europe, it can clearly be seen as part of a general royal attempt to bring the orders under royal authority.

The fourth provincial council of Mexico (1771) and the sixth provincial council of Peru (1772) clearly recognized the monarch's rights and privileges as patron of the church and accorded him all deference and honor, in essence making him the pope for the New World. The Mexican decrees were so excessively favorable to the monarch that they were somewhat of an embarrassment in Madrid and received neither royal nor papal approval.

The pattern of increasing royal control over the church culminated in the early nineteenth century. In 1804 the monarch called in all of the loans, liens, and mortgages extended by the church. In a desire for more capital the crown demanded the amortization of the loans and promised to pay the church the annual interest based on royal bonds, or *juros*. In 1812, in the wake of the French invasion of Spain and the flush of liberal power, the ecclesiastical *fuero*, the right of clerics to have their legal cases heard in church courts, was abolished—an act that clearly defined the clergy as just another royal bureaucracy.

See also **Anticlericalism; Augustinians; Capellanía: Dominicans; Franciscans; Mercedarians.**

BIBLIOGRAPHY

Mariano Cuevas, *Historia de la iglesia en México,* 5 vols. (1921–1928).

Lewis Hanke, *The Spanish Struggle for Justice in the Conquest of America* (1949).

Antonine Tibesar, *Franciscan Beginnings in Colonial Peru* (1953).

Rubén Vargas Ugarte, *Historia de la iglesia en el Perú*, vols. 1 and 2 (1953–1959).

Leon Lopetegui and Antonio De Egaña, *Historia de la iglesia en la América española*, 2 vols. (1965–1966).

Robert Ricard, *The Spiritual Conquest of Mexico* (1966).

Michael P. Costeloe, *Church Wealth in Mexico, 1800–1856* (1967).

Nancy M. Farriss, *Crown and Clergy in Colonial Mexico, 1759–1821* (1968).

Eduardo Hoornaert et al., *História da igreja no Brasil* (1977).

John F. Schwaller, *Origins of Church Wealth in Mexico* (1985) and *Church and Clergy in Sixteenth-Century Mexico* (1987).

Arlindo Rubert, *Historia de la iglesia en Brasil* (1992).

Additional Bibliography

Brading, D. A. *Church and State in Bourbon Mexico: The Diocese of Michoacán, 1749-1810.* New York: Cambridge University Press, 1994.

Brading, D. A. *First America: The Spanish Monarchy, Creole Patriots, and the Liberal State, 1492-1867.* New York: Cambridge University Press, 1991.

Burns, Kathryn. *Colonial Habits: Convents and the Spiritual Economy of Cuzco, Peru.* Durham, NC: Duke University Press, 1999.

Dean, Carolyn. *Inka Bodies and the Body of Christ: Corpus Christi in Colonial Cuzco, Peru.* Durham, NC: Duke University Press, 1999.

Díaz, María Elena. *The Virgin, the King, and the Royal Slaves of El Cobre: Negotiating Freedom in Colonial Cuba, 1670–1780.* Stanford, CA: Stanford University Press, 2000.

Mills, Kenneth. *Idolatry and Its Enemies: Colonial Andean Religion and Extirpation, 1640-1750.* Princeton, NJ: Princeton University Press, 1997.

Peñafort, Luisa Zahino. *Iglesia y sociedad en México, 1765-1800: Tradición, reforma y reacciones.* México: Universidad Nacional Autónoma de México, 1996.

Schwaller, John F. *The Church in Colonial Latin America.* Wilmington, DE: Scholarly Resources Books, 2000.

Souza, Laura de Mello e. *The Devil and the Land of the Holy Cross: Witchcraft, Slavery, and Popular Religion in Colonial Brazil.* Trans. Diane Grosklaus Whitty. Austin: University of Texas Press, Teresa Lozano Long Institute of Latin American Studies, 2003.

Taylor, William B. *Magistrates of the Sacred: Priests and Parishioners in Eighteenth-Century Mexico.* Stanford, CA: Stanford University Press, 1996.

Vainfas, Ronaldo. *A heresia dos índios: Catolicismo e rebeldia no Brasil colonial.* São Paulo: Companhia das Letras, 1995.

JEFFREY KLAIBER

THE MODERN PERIOD

The Catholic Church was the most important colonial institution to survive the Wars of Independence. Throughout the nineteenth and twentieth centuries, the church was the principal symbol of tradition and stability in the midst of political and social change. It touched the lives of everyone, but its influence was felt most deeply among the lower classes and the rural peasantry. Religion not only offered consolation, but Sunday morning Mass or the patron saint's feast day were natural occasions to socialize or sell wares in the village plaza. But this most traditional of all institutions, after undergoing a series of prolonged crises in the post-Independence period, experienced a profound transformation in the 1960s. Since that time the church has emerged as an advocate of human rights, democracy, and social change.

INDEPENDENCE

The Wars of Independence produced internal cleavages within the ranks of the clergy. The upper clergy (which consisted of six archbishops, thirty-one bishops, and other dignitaries), most of whom were Spanish, remained loyal to the king, whereas large sectors of the lower clergy, most of whom were creoles, supported the insurgent movement. When independence was finally achieved, most of the bishops and many priests and religious were obliged to return to Spain. The church also contributed much of its wealth, sometimes unwillingly, to both sides.

In spite of these difficulties, the church as a whole came out of the wars relatively intact. In Mexico, Miguel Hidalgo, José María Morelos, and other priests who fought and died for the independence of their country were considered patriots and heroes. Liberal clergymen such as Francisco Javier de Luna Pizarro in Peru and Deán Gregorio Funes in Argentina helped to write the constitutions of their respective nations and played important roles in politics.

Most of these liberal priests belonged to the secular clergy.

The religious clergy, which unlike the secular clergy included many Spanish missionaries in colonial times, fared less well. The liberals associated the religious orders with the old regime, and in many countries they confiscated monasteries and enacted laws severely limiting membership in the orders. Impoverished national governments saw the extensive lands and possessions of the church as a potential source of funds with which to support their governments. For liberals especially, diminishing the power of the orders fulfilled both a political and an economic goal. As a result, the religious way of life for both men and women underwent an institutional crisis from which it did not recover until the end of the nineteenth century, when more cooperative regimes took office.

RESTORATION AND ROMANIZATION IN HISPANIC AMERICA

The major post-Independence crisis, however, concerned the episcopal vacancies. The new republican governments attempted to assume control over the church by creating a national patronage in place of the old Patronato Real, or royal patronage. But the Holy See refused to recognize these claims of the new governments. As a result, most dioceses of Spanish America remained vacant for lengthy periods. Finally, the different governments and the Holy See entered into formal agreements (concordats) or arrived at informal arrangements by which the state could name bishops, who in turn would have to be approved by Rome. By the middle of the 1830s, the episcopacy had been restored in most countries of Spanish America.

In the process, however, the Latin American church also became "romanized." If before the church was principally a Spanish church, now it became a Roman church, reorganized and centralized under the pope. Although all the new bishops were Latin Americans, Rome preferred men who were obedient to the papacy, and that implied not being sympathetic to liberalism. But overdependence on Rome also limited the church's ability to deal creatively with Latin American realities.

The bishops reopened the seminaries and standardized them according to criteria laid down in Rome. In 1858 a seminary (known as the South American College) for Latin Americans was founded in Rome. The majority of Latin America's bishops have been drawn from priests who have studied there. At the same time, liberal clergymen were marginalized in the church. Rome's ties to Latin America were further strengthened when the Latin American bishops participated in the First Vatican Council (1869–1870) and again, in 1899, when the bishops attended a special plenary council for Latin America, convoked by Pope Leo XIII.

Brazil and Cuba. For different reasons Brazil and Cuba escaped the general pattern for the church that emerged elsewhere in Latin America. When Brazil achieved its independence in 1822, the monarchy assumed control of national patronage of the church. As a result, the Brazilian church did not fall under Rome's direct jurisdiction until the end of the monarchy in 1889. Also, liberal clergymen such as Diogo Antônio Feijó, who served as regent of the empire (1835–1837), enjoyed greater freedom from Rome than their counterparts in Spanish America. The otherwise harmonious relations between Pedro II and the church were interrupted by the "religious question" between the years of 1872 and 1875. The emperor imprisoned two bishops when they followed papal orders that forbade Catholics from participating in Masonic activities. The provisional republican government separated the church from the state in 1890. For its part, Cuba remained under the church in Spain until its independence in 1898. After that, as in Brazil, it came under Roman jurisdiction.

THE CHURCH'S STRUGGLE WITH LIBERALISM

After 1850 the liberals enacted more laws to curb the church's influence in society and to transfer its wealth and lands to the state or to private hands. The church reacted by organizing the laity into associations such as the Catholic Union and by publishing periodicals defending its positions. The church also sought out the protection of conservative caudillos and parties, a factor that further alienated it from the progressive middle classes. The persecution against the church was especially severe in Mexico as a result of the Reform Laws and the liberal struggle for power in the Reform Wars (1857–1860) and in Ecuador under the Eloy Alfaro Delgado regime at the turn of the century.

In the midst of the struggle with liberalism, the church suffered another, more serious crisis.

Beginning in the middle of the nineteenth century, the number of vocations to the priesthood declined considerably, especially in countries with a small middle class or with a large indigenous population. The reasons for the decline are varied. The liberal governments cut off economic support to the church, and the conservative image the church projected did not attract vocations from progressive sectors of society. Also, the church required that candidates for the seminaries be able to read and write, a factor that disqualified the Indians and most peasants. In Central America in particular, the number of clergy declined precipitously in the late nineteenth century as a result. In Peru, Bolivia, and Nicaragua, among other countries, close to 60 percent of the clergy remains foreign born.

In the second half of the nineteenth century the church, concerned over its waning influence in society, brought over many different religious orders and congregations from Europe. The Daughters of Charity, the Good Shepherd Sisters, and similar congregations established many hospitals and charitable institutions for the poor. The Jesuits, the Sacred Heart nuns, the Ursulines, the Salesians, the Marists, and other teaching orders and congregations founded numerous schools, usually for the middle and upper classes, throughout all of Latin America.

Popular Piety. Liberalism made many inroads among the middle classes, but it did not touch the lower classes. The church continued to exercise considerable influence among the Indians, peasants, blacks, and mestizos who made up the lower classes, especially through the many local devotions that nourished popular religiosity. Some of the more famous popular devotions are Our Lady of Guadalupe in Mexico, the Lord of Miracles in Lima, the Virgin of Luján in Argentina, Our Lady of Copacabana in Bolivia, and the Dolorosa of Ecuador. As a result of the spread of liberalism, many middle- and upper-class men ceased to practice their religion. The women, who did continue to practice, virtually became the mainstay of Catholicism in that social milieu.

Catholic Action. At the behest of Pope Pius XI, nearly every local church created a national branch of Catholic Action in the 1920s and 1930s. Catholic Action was an association of laypeople committed to the task of bringing new life to the church, defending

Crowds gather to greet Pope Benedict XVI on his first official visit to Brazil, 2007. © MARCELO SAYAO/EPA/ CORBIS

it against its critics, and spreading the church's doctrine of social justice. In Brazil, Archbishop Sebastião Leme of Rio de Janeiro became the leading promoter of Brazilian Catholic Action. In Chile, Eduardo Frei Montalva in 1938 helped found the National Falange (National Phalanx), which drew together many young Christian intellectuals who were dissatisfied with the traditional church. Although not an official church organization, Frei's party (which became the Christian Democratic Party) contributed to the social awareness of Chilean Catholics. Mexico represented a unique case of Catholic Action in response to official government persecution. In reaction to the harsh anticlericalism of the Plutarco Elías Calles regime (1924–1928), many peasants led by middle-class Catholics, known as Cristeros (from their cry, "Long live Christ the King!"), took up arms against the central government in the Cristero Rebellion. But the church disavowed the movement and the Cristeros were forced into submission.

Most members of Catholic Action came from the urban middle classes. Some, such as Jackson de Figueiredo in Brazil and José de la Riva-Agüero in Peru, harbored integralist and authoritarian solutions to the problems of political unrest and the spread of socialism. But others, such as Frei in Chile and Victor Andrés Belaúnde in Peru, looked to the Western democracies as models for Latin America. Many of the leaders of Catholic Action became founders of the Christian Democratic parties.

MODERNIZATION

Although the Latin American church in general continued to be very conservative in the post–World War II period, frequently legitimizing anti-Communist dictatorships, it was nonetheless influenced by the same tendencies and intellectual currents that had begun to affect the church in the developed world. In response to the priest shortage, Pope Pius XII and his successor, John XXIII, called for missionaries from Europe and the United States to work in Latin America. Hundreds of priests, nuns, brothers, and lay volunteers from the Western democracies flocked to Latin America in the late 1950s and early 1960s, bringing with them progressive attitudes and plans for development projects. The Maryknoll Fathers and Sisters, the best-known American missionary society, had already arrived in Latin America in 1942.

Certain churchmen were especially influential in awakening other Catholics to the need for change. José María Cardinal Caro, the archbishop of Santiago (1939–1958), fostered many social works for the poor. Juan Landázuri Ricketts, the cardinal-archbishop of Lima (1955–1989), built parishes and medical posts to aid the dwellers in the growing shantytowns. The massive migrations of the rural or mountain peasants to the big cities spurred church planners to be more innovative and creative. Other socially progressive churchmen were Dom Hélder Câmara of Recife, who won fame for his work among the poor; Bishop Leonidas Proaño of Riobamba, Ecuador, who was noted for his support of the peasants; and Bishop Manuel Larraín of Talca, Chile, who played a key role in preparing the way for the Medellín conference. In 1955 the bishops founded the Episcopal Latino Consemerricano Conselho Episcopal Latino Americano (CELAM), the permanent Conference of Latin American Bishops, for the purpose of coordinating the church's pastoral activities.

The Second Vatican Council (1962–1965) was also instrumental in changing the mentality of many Latin American Catholics. The nearly six hundred bishops of Latin America who attended the council, though they contributed little to the theological discussions, acquired a deeper sense of identity as Latin Americans.

In the wake of the Cuban Revolution of 1959, the church felt the urgency of finding social solutions to Latin America's poverty, preferably by democratic means. In 1966 Camilo Torres Restrepo, a Colombian priest, joined a guerrilla movement and was killed shortly afterwards. His action dramatically underlined the fact that practicing Catholics were being subjected to the same dilemmas over the use of peaceful versus violent means that were causing divisions among Latin Americans in general in those years.

Medellín and Liberation Theology. In 1968 in Medellín, Colombia, 130 bishops attended the second general assembly of the Latin American episcopate. The bishops gave the church a mandate to foster social justice and to work in solidarity with the poor. The Medellín conference constituted a dramatic change for the traditionally conservative Latin American church. The bishops were especially influenced by liberation theology, which called for the church to help the poor in their struggle to free themselves from unjust social structures. Some of the principal liberation theologians included Gustavo Gutiérrez, Leonardo Boff, Juan Luis Segundo, and Jon Sobrino. Also, the ideas of Brazilian educator Paulo Freire on education as a tool of liberation influenced many church groups. The basic nucleus in which liberation theology was put into practice was the base ecclesial community. A pastoral innovation created by the Brazilian bishops, a base ecclesial community consists of a small group of people who apply the lessons of the Bible to their everyday lives and to society in general. In the wake of Medellín, base ecclesial communities sprang up throughout Latin America. By 1991 Brazil alone had more than 150,000 of these communities.

Both Vatican Council II and the Medellín conference encouraged greater lay participation in the church. Besides forming base ecclesial communities, the laity also exercised leadership by becoming adult catechists, or delegates of the word. Other lay movements that flourished after Vatican II were the Cursillos de Cristiandad (Christian short courses: weekend retreats geared originally for men), the charismatic movement, and Encuentro Matrimonial (Marriage encounter). Religious women also changed their lifestyle and diversified their pastoral activities. Before Medellín, most religious women taught in schools or worked in hospitals. After Medellín they expanded their activities to include work in the shantytowns, the Andes, or the Amazon jungle as catechists, community organizers, and chaplains in prisons as well as health and social advisers. The church also diversified its educational presence. While it continued to administer many colleges and a few universities, it also opened up numerous schools for the poor and sponsored specialized short courses for working adults. The Fe y Alegría (Faith and Joy) schools founded by the Jesuits in many Latin American countries are among the more notable of these popular educational centers.

These radical changes led to conflict between the church, on the one hand, and on the other, dictators, the political right, and most of the military regimes that came to power in the 1960s and 1970s. In sharp contrast to the past, when it supported the military and conservative groups, the church, with few exceptions, took a leading role in denouncing violations of human rights and in encouraging democratic popular participation. Relations between the military, its right-wing sympathizers, and the church were very tense, and many bishops, priests, nuns, and laypeople were executed, tortured, or imprisoned in retaliation for their critical stance. Peru and Argentina were exceptions to this rule, for different reasons. In Peru, the military under General Juan Velasco Alvarado, was reformist and thus was supported by the church. In Argentina, where a right-wing military government (1976–1983) suppressed basic liberties and tortured and killed dissidents, the church hierarchy either sympathized with the military or maintained neutrality.

But the situation in Brazil manifested the general pattern more exactly. During the period of military rule (1964–1985), the national bishops' conference fully supported the movement to return to civilian government. Hélder Câmara, Cardinals Pablo Arns of São Paulo and Aloisio Lorscheider of Fortaleza,

and Pedro Casaldáliga, a bishop in the Amazon, stood out especially for their denunciations of police and paramilitary brutality. In Chile, under the Augusto Pinochet regime (1973–1990), Raúl Cardinal Silva Henríquez of Santiago created the Vicariate of Solidarity, an organization intended to protect victims of political persecution and to search for missing persons. He and his successor, Juan Francisco Cardinal Fresno Larrain, were instrumental in organizing civilian opposition to the government. The church played a similar role in Bolivia, especially during the Hugo Bánzer Suárez and Luis García Mesa governments, and in Paraguay under Alfredo Stroessner.

In Central America and in the Caribbean, Catholics also stood out for their progressive positions. Nicaragua provided the most dramatic example of Catholic participation in a revolution. Early on, a moderate sector led by Archbishop Miguel Obando y Bravo of Managua took a critical stance regarding the Anastasia Somoza regime, and more radical Catholics from the base ecclesial communities, including many priests, actively fought with the Sandinistas to overthrow the dictator. After the revolution, however, the church was sharply divided. A few priests, notably Ernesto Cardenal, Miguel D'Escoto, and Fernando Cardenal, held important posts in the Sandinista government, much to the displeasure of the pope and Miguel Cardinal Obando. In 1980 unknown assassins shot and killed Bishop Oscar Romero of El Salvador. Romero, a leading critic of the military's excesses, became the most celebrated martyr bishop in Latin America. In Haiti, Jean-Bertrand Aristide, a priest influenced by liberation theology, was elected president of the country in 1990. After the Cuban Revolution, the church vehemently opposed the Castro regime, and many priests went into exile. The government in turn marginalized the church's role in public affairs. After Medellín, however, the church sought to end its isolation by becoming a part of mainstream life on the island. By the middle of the 1980s, the state and the church had arrived at a mutually acceptable modus vivendi.

During the third general meeting of the bishops in Puebla, Mexico, in 1979, tensions surfaced between progressives and conservatives. Pope John Paul II, elected in 1978, inaugurated the Puebla conference, and during the next decade he visited nearly every Latin American country. Everywhere he was received by enthusiastic crowds. He lent support to the bishops who were critical of liberation theology and other changes in the church. As a result, progressive-conservative tensions have loomed over church discussions since the Puebla conference. Over the last decades of the twentieth century, the church in Latin America became less clearly aligned with reformist politics and more focused on purely ecclesiastical issues and conservative social issues in keeping with papal teachings.

GENERAL STATISTICS

The percentage of Catholics in Latin America averages between 80 percent and 90 percent. In most countries, however, only about 10 percent of Catholics regularly attend church services. In 2004 there were 792 Catholic dioceses in Latin America, with 40,277 diocesan priests, 124,685 female religious, and 42,293 male religious (of whom 23,885 were priests). The average number of Catholics per priest is approximately 7,750. At one extreme is Panama (1 to every 4,542), at the other Honduras (1 to every 13,884).

See also **Alfaro Delgado, José Eloy; Aristide, Jean-Bertrand; Belaúnde, Víctor Andrés; Boff, Leonardo; Calles, Plutarco Elías; Câmara, Hélder; Cardenal, Ernesto; Catholic Action; Chile, Political Parties: National Phalanx; Conference of Latin American Bishops (CELAM); D'Escoto Brockmann, Miguel; Feijó, Diogo Antônio; Figueiredo, Jackson de; Frei Montalva, Eduardo; Freire, Paulo; Fresno Larraín, Juan Francisco; Funes, Gregorio; Guadalupe, Virgin of; Gutiérrez, Gustavo; Hidalgo y Costilla, Miguel; John Paul II, Pope; Landázuri Ricketts, Juan; Leo XIII, Pope; Liberation Theology; Morelos y Pavón, José María; Obando y Bravo, Miguel; Patronato Real; Pedro II of Brazil; Pius IX, Pope; Proaño Villalba, Leonidas Eduardo (Bishop); Riva Agüero y Osma, José de la; Romero, Oscar Arnulfo; Silva Henríquez, Raúl; Wars of Independence, South America.**

BIBLIOGRAPHY

Berryman, Phillip. *The Religious Roots of Rebellion: Christians in Central American Revolutions.* Maryknoll, NY: Orbis Books, 1984.

Burdick, John, and W. E. Hewitt. *The Church at the Grassroots in Latin America: Perspectives on Thirty Years of Activism.* Westport, CT: Praeger, 2000.

Cleary, Edward L. *Crisis and Change: The Church in Latin America Today.* Maryknoll, NY: Orbis Books, 1985.

Dussel, Enrique. *A History of the Church in Latin America: Colonialism to Liberation (1492–1979).* Translated and revised by Alan Neely. Grand Rapids, MI: Eerdmans, 1981.

Kirk, John M. *Between God and the Party: Religion and Politics in Revolutionary Cuba.* Tampa: University of South Florida Press, 1989.

Klaiber, Jeffrey L. *The Church in Peru, 1821–1985: A Social History.* Washington, DC: Catholic University of America Press, 1992.

Lernoux, Penny. *Cry of the People: U.S. Involvement in the Rise of Fascism, Torture, and Murder and the Persecution of the Catholic Church in Latin America.* Garden City, NY: Doubleday, 1980.

Levine, Daniel H., ed. *Religion and Political Conflict in Latin America.* Chapel Hill: University of North Carolina Press, 1986.

Mainwaring, Scott. *The Catholic Church and Politics in Brazil, 1916–1985.* Stanford, CA: Stanford University Press, 1986.

Mainwaring, Scott, and Alexander Wilde, eds. *The Progressive Church in Latin America.* Notre Dame, IN: University of Notre Dame Press, 1989.

Mecham, J. Lloyd. *Church and State in Latin America: A History of Politico-Ecclesiastical Relations.* Rev. edition. Chapel Hill: University of North Carolina Press, 1966.

Quirk, Robert E. *The Mexican Revolution and the Catholic Church, 1910–1929.* Bloomington: Indiana University Press, 1973.

Smith, Brian H. *The Church and Politics in Chile: Challenges to Modern Catholicism.* Princeton, NJ: Princeton University Press, 1982.

Tombs, David. *Latin American Liberation Theology.* Boston: Brill Academic Publishers, 2002.

JEFFREY KLAIBER
JOHN F. SCHWALLER

CATURLA, ALEJANDRO GARCÍA.

See García Caturla, Alejandro.

CAUCA RIVER.

Cauca River, Colombia's second longest river. The Cauca flows northward some 838 miles from its origin south of Popayán to its entrance into the Magdalena River at Pinillos, in the department of Bolívar. The waterway is comprised by three zones. The first, which defines the rich agricultural area of the Cauca Valley, is readily navigable. From here, the river then descends into the largely impassable "Cauca Canyon" (a source of gold in the colonial period) through the departments of Caldas, Risaralda, and Antioquia until reaching the town of Valdivia. Its fertile second valley merges into a vast swamp before joining the Magdalena basin, the third zone, a desolated region until the development of a coffee-based economy in the early twentieth century.

During the colonial period, the upper valley's cattle haciendas and tobacco production supplemented the gold-mining activities of the region's economy, products augmented by sugar and coffee production in the late nineteenth century. The region around Cali contains one of Colombia's most diversified and dynamic economic centers.

See also **Magdalena River.**

BIBLIOGRAPHY

David Bushnell, *The Making of Modern Colombia: A Nation in Spite of Itself* (1993).

Additional Bibliography

Cubillos, Julio César. *Arqueología del Valle del Río Cauca: Asentamientos prehispánicos en la suela plana del río Cauca.* Bogotá: Banco de la República, 1984.

Galindo Díaz, Jorge Alberto. *Arquitectura, industria y ciudad en el Valle del Cauca: Tipos y técnicas (1917-1945).* Cali: Universidad del Valle, 2002.

Galindo Díaz, Jorge Alberto. *Cruzando el Cauca: Pasos y puentes sobre el río Cauca en el departamento del Valle hasta la primera mitad del siglo XX.* Cali: J.A. Galindo Díaz, 2003.

Navarrete, María Cristina. *Inmigrantes de la India en el Valle del Río Cauca.* Colombia: Gobernación del Valle del Cauca, 1996.

DAVID SOWELL

CAUCA VALLEY.

Cauca Valley, an inland valley of southwestern Colombia between the western and central chains of the Andes. It is the site of one of Colombia's most developed networks of urban centers, with Cartago at the northern end and Cali, the main urban center of the valley, at the southern end. No other area of Colombia can boast such a significant network of middle-sized urban centers.

Considered one of the most fertile plains in Latin America, the region was stagnant economically for centuries and absent from participation in the world market. The opening of the Panama Canal, however, provided the impetus for economic transformation. Growth was further stimulated by the phenomenal sugar cane boom of 1930–1980, which transformed the inefficient haciendas into the large-scale sugar agribusinesses of today—a process that, unfortunately, provoked a certain amount of violence in the 1940s and 1950s. In the 1950s the entrepreneurial elite of Cali provided another economic boost by promoting the creation of a regional development corporation modeled after the Tennessee Valley Authority—the Corporación autónoma regional del Valle del Cauca (CVC)—which has been instrumental in promoting electrification, dam construction, and land reclamation.

The valley was immortalized in local resident Jorge Isaacs's canonical nineteenth-century novel *María*, read by most Latin American high school students, even today.

See also **Isaacs, Jorge.**

BIBLIOGRAPHY

Raymond E. Crist, *The Cauca Valley, Colombia: Land Tenure and Land Use* (1952).

Richard P. Hyland, *El crédito y la economía, 1851–1880. Vol. IV, Sociedad y economía en el Valle del Cauca* (1983).

José María Rojas, *Empresarios y Tecnología en la Formación del Sector Azucarero en Colombia, 1860–1980. Vol. V, Sociedad y economía en el Valle del Cauca* (1983).

Additional Bibliography

Cardale de Schrimpff, Marianne. *Caminos prehispánicos en Calima: El estudio de caminos precolombinos de la cuenca del alto río Calima, Cordillera Occidental, Valle del Cauca.* Santafé de Bogotá: Fundación de Investigaciones Arqueológicas Nacionales, Banco de la República, 1996.

Ramírez Santos, Alberto. *Maravillosa Colombia: El Folklore, El Valle del Río Cauca, Los Andes del Sur.* Madrid: Printer Latinoamericana Editorial, 2003.

Saavedra Rivera, Libardo. *Gorrones, salseros y montaneros: Una mirada antropológica al Valle del Cauca.* Bogotá: Fundayudas, 1995.

Salgado López, Héctor. *Asentamientos prehispánicos en el noroccidente del departamento del Valle del Cauca.* Bogotá: Fundación de Investigaciones Arqueológicas Nacionales, Banco de la República, 1986.

Trimborn, Hermann. *Señorío y Barbarie en el Valle del Cauca: Estudio sobre la Antigua civilización Quimbaya y Grupos afines del Oeste de Colombia.* Colombia: Editorial Universidad del Cauca, 2005.

JOSÉ ESORCIA

CAUDILLISMO, CAUDILLO.

Caudillo, caudillismo, an authoritarian form of leadership common throughout the history of the Hispanic world. Among the Spanish words for leader is *caudillo*, which derives from the Latin *capitellum*, the diminutive of *caput* (head). Although it is common to think of caudillos in the context of Spanish America, the prototypes are deep in the Iberian past.

Caudillismo is often narrowly interpreted to apply mainly to those leaders who emerged in the newly independent republics. There are, however, so many who deserve the name "caudillo"—from Pelayo (the eighth-century Asturian chieftain) to Augusto Pinochet—that it is too limiting to direct attention only to an early-nineteenth-century "Age of Caudillos." It is, nevertheless, important to employ qualifiers when dealing with individuals. Although caudillos are often military men, there are civilians like Gabriel García Moreno of Ecuador, who might be called "theocratic," and Rafael Núñez of Colombia, who was a lawyer, career politician, and poet. Many caudillos acquired sobriquets that set them apart. José Gaspar Francia of Paraguay was "El Supremo," Plutarco Elías Calles of Mexico was called "El Jefe Máximo" (the Ultimate Chief), Juan Vic-ente Gómez of Venezuela carried the nickname "El Bagre" (the Catfish), and Alfredo Stroessner was known to his foes in Paraguay as "El Tiranosauro."

The variety of caudillos is practically endless, but certain common qualities help distinguish them from other leaders: a personalist rapport with followers, the ability to create reciprocal advantages between leaders and the led, a combination of charisma and machismo, and access to political and economic power are fundamental characteristics. In a controversial book Glen Dealy argues that "public men" in Catholic societies—particularly in Latin America—surround themselves first with their family and *compadrazgo* (godparent) relations and then concentrically with aggregates of friends, who are more important to them than wealth. The Dominican Republic's Rafael Trujillo, "The Benefactor," arranged to be the *compadre* (godfather) at the baptism of thousands of babies to enhance his power.

Some caudillos were actually manipulated by elites, and only seemed to be dominant. Martín Güemes of Salta, in what later became Argentina, was a regional caudillo during the Independence wars (1810–1821) who prospered as long as he served the interests of his extended family, and was destroyed when he deviated.

Many caudillos have understood the value of ceremony and the need to look the part of a dominant personality, often in uniform, whether on horseback, in the back of an open limousine, or on a balcony. Part of this theatrical display and attendant propaganda is designed to fill the vacuum of moral authority lost in Spanish America with the end of the empire. From the days of Hernán Cortés to the present, caudillos have sought legitimacy. Peter Smith (whose essay is included in this author's edited work, *Caudillos*) examines Max Weber's criteria for legitimacy—"traditional," "legal," and "charismatic"—and then adds two of his own: "dominance" and "achievement-expertise," or the technical ability to solve a nation's problems. Chile's Augusto Pinochet skillfully manipulated the military's hierarchy and the traditions of the country's presidency to ensconce himself in power for fifteen years (1973–1988) before the democratic process reasserted itself. Many caudillos cleverly utilized rigged elections, plebiscites, and constitutional amendments to extend themselves in power in a process called Continuismo. Anastasio "Tacho" Somoza and his two sons were particularly adept at this in Nicaragua, and managed for a time to overcome the problem of political succession that has plagued most caudillos. That such undemocratic maneuvers often succeeded suggests that caudillismo does not necessarily always carry a pejorative connotation within the culture. On the contrary, José de Palafox, a hero of Spanish resistance against the French in 1808, was called "El Caudillo Palafox," and Francisco Franco, the victor in the Spanish Civil War (1936–1939) and autocrat of Spain until his death in 1975, proudly dubbed himself "El Caudillo."

Military dependency has been widespread among caudillos, but it is not universal. Antonio López de Santa Anna of Mexico, Francisco Solano López in Paraguay, and Marcos Pérez Jiménez of Venezuela banked heavily on their armies. But adroit politicians like Porfirio Díaz in Mexico recognized that a strong army might threaten their power and thus played generals against each other and against civilian factions and corporations. Díaz, for example, expanded a paramilitary force called the Rurales to parry the army's pretensions. Juan Perón sought to broaden his support beyond the military in Argentina by cultivating labor.

Caudillos have often been characterized by their violence, intimidation of their enemies, and the use of torture. Resort to such practices is a function of the problem of succession. Caudillos most often have come to power through coups d'état, and are conscious of the fact that the "out" factions are waiting—usually in exile—for an opportunity to repeat the process. Vigilance, oppression, and wealth from Venezuelan oil wells helped the notorious Juan Vicente Gómez to remain in power from 1908 to 1935. He died of old age. One of the most vicious of caudillos was Manuel Estrada Cabrera of Guatemala (1898–1920), who became the model for the novel *El señor presidente* by the Nobel laureate Miguel Ángel Asturias.

In historical perspective caudillismo—already well developed in the reconquest of the Iberian Peninsula—arrived in the Americas with the explorers and conquistadores. Bands were almost always centered about leaders like Cortés and Francisco Pizarro. The mutual reliance of followers and their chiefs was always dependent upon *caudillaje*, the essence of close personal ties. These relationships, however, were often tenuous—witness the difficulties that Cortés had with the followers of Governor Diego Velázquez in Cuba and the factional divisions that beset Pizarro. Once the goals of conquest were achieved, the sometime soldiers quickly dispersed and settled down or returned to Spain as civilians to enjoy the fruits of their victories.

As the colonial era developed, it was local political bosses or caciques who tended to characterize leadership. They could be bureaucrats, *hacendados*, miners, merchants, militia officers, or priests as well as bandits and peasant leaders. These frequently formed personal networks to which they turned after Napoleon's invasion of Spain in 1808 broke down the royal mechanisms to resolve disputes among colonial factions. These caciques moved into the political vacuums everywhere evident in the Independence wars, and some rose to national caudillo status.

New constitutional forms in the early republics lacked the moral authority once associated with the crown. The ambitious caudillos who emerged had their own agendas or *pronunciamientos* in which ideology was less important than the degree of stability and economic control a given leader might guarantee his supporters. Some used liberalism as an excuse to exploit the communal property of indigenous peoples, while others, like José Rafael Carrera of Guatemala, became what E. Bradford Burns calls "folk caudillos" bent upon preserving traditional patterns of property and institutions.

Weak states and powerful regions so characterized mid-nineteenth-century Spanish America that later caudillos like Rafael Núñez abandoned federalism in favor of recentralizing authority.

Caudillismo since 1900 has been an uneven but persistent phenomenon. Countries such as Costa Rica and Venezuela (after Pérez Jiménez left in 1958) have had little recent experience with caudillos. Mexico has developed the dominant party to replace the dominant individual. But Cuba (with Fulgencio Batista and Fidel Castro), Panama (with Omar Torrijos and Manuel Noriega), the Dominican Republic (with Trujillo and Joaquín Balaguer), Paraguay (chiefly with Stroessner), and Argentina (with Perón and a succession of military strongmen), as well as Chile, have had their histories punctuated by caudillos during the middle and later decades of the twentieth century.

See also **Militias: Colonial Spanish America.**

BIBLIOGRAPHY

For a comprehensive guide to the interpretive and illustrative literature on caudillismo, see Hugh M. Hamill, ed., *Caudillos: Dictators in Spanish America* (1992), and John Lynch, *Caudillos in Spanish America, 1800–1850* (1992). Efforts to explain caudillismo include Peter H. Smith, "Political Legitimacy in Spanish America," in *New Approaches to Latin American History*, edited by Richard Graham and Peter Smith (1974); Glenn Caudill Dealy, *The Public Man: An Interpretation of Latin American and Other Catholic Countries* (1977); Torcuato S. Ditella, *Latin American Politics: A Theoretical Framework* (1990). Robert L. Gilmore makes a useful distinction in his *Caudillism and Militarism in Venezuela, 1810–1910* (1964). A Chilean woman's view of caudillismo is in Isabelle Allende's novel *The House of the Spirits,* translated by Magda Bogin (1985). John Hoyt Williams treats Francia, Carlos Antonio López, and his son, Francisco Solano López, in *The Rise and Fall of the Paraguayan Republic, 1800–1870* (1979). A sample of the massive literature on individual caudillos includes Roger M. Haigh, *Martín Güemes: Tyrant or Tool? A Study of the Sources of Power of an Argentine Caudillo* (1968); Howard J. Wiarda, *Dictatorship and Development: The Methods of Control in Trujillo's Dominican Republic* (1968); John

Lynch, *Argentine Dictator: Juan Manuel de Rosas, 1829–1852* (1981); Joseph A. Page, *Perón: A Biography* (1983); James William Park, *Rafael Núñez and the Politics of Colombian Regionalism, 1863–1886* (1985); Genaro Arriagada, *Pinochet: The Politics of Power,* translated by Nancy A. Morris, Vincent Ercolano, and Kristen A. Whitney (1988); Sebastian Balfour, *Castro* (1990); Carlos R. Miranda, *The Stroessner Era: Authoritarian Rule in Paraguay* (1990); Ralph Lee Woodward, Jr., *Rafael Carrera and the Emergence of the Republic of Guatemala, 1821–1871* (1993).

Additional Bibliography

Buchenau, Jürgen. *Plutarco Elías Calles and the Mexican Revolution.* Lanham, MD: Rowman & Littlefield, 2007.

Castro, Pedro. *A la sombra de un caudillo: Vida y muerte del general Francisco R. Serrano.* México, D.F.: Plaza & Janés, 2005.

De la Fuente, Ariel. *Children of Facundo: Caudillo and Gaucho Insurgency During the Argentine State-Formation Process (La Rioja, 1853–1870).* Durham, NC: Duke University Press, 2000.

HUGH M. HAMILL

CAUPOLICÁN

CAUPOLICÁN (?–1558). Caupolicán (*d.* 1558), Araucanian warrior and hero. The cacique of Palmaiquén, he was active in the Araucanian resistance to the Spanish conquistadores from early on. He rose to prominence among his people after the death of Lautaro (April 1557), when he was chosen as *toqui* (chief). He was a principal adversary of the newly arrived Spanish governor García Hurtado De Mendoza (1535–1609). Caupolicán's attacks on the new governor's hastily constructed fort near Concepción were repulsed. The Spaniards, now reinforced, defeated the Araucanians at the battles of Lagunillas (or Bío-Bío) and Millarapue in November 1557. Caupolicán rejected all Hurtado de Mendoza's offers of peace. In mid-1558 a Spanish captain, Alonso de Reinoso, organized a surprise raid on the *toqui*'s encampment at Palmaiquén and succeeded in capturing him. A woman, presumably his wife, revealed his identity to the Spaniards by reproaching him for being taken alive and dashing her infant son to the ground. (The name traditionally given to her, Fresia, is probably an invention of the poet Alonso de Ercilla y Zúñiga.) Reinoso took Caupolicán back to the newly founded settlement at Cañete, where he was executed by impalement. He is remembered as second only to Lautaro among the Araucanian heroes of the sixteenth century.

See also **Araucana, La.**

BIBLIOGRAPHY

Márquez, Antonio. *Historia de Chile ilustrada.* Santiago: Ercilla, 2000.

SIMON COLLIER

CAVALCANTI, NEWTON

CAVALCANTI, NEWTON (1930–2006). Newton Cavalcanti (*b.* 20 June 1930; *d.* 12 August 2006), Brazilian engraver and illustrator. Although born in Pernambuco and trained in Europe, Cavalcanti moved in 1952 to Rio de Janeiro, where he met the Brazilian metal engraver Raimudo Cela. In 1954 he studied wood engraving at the National School of Fine Arts in Rio de Janeiro under Oswaldo Goeldi. Along with fellow Pernambucan Gilvan Samico, Cavalcanti dedicated himself to xylography, the art of wood-block printing. Cavalcanti's woodcuts and wood engravings focused mainly upon themes from the legends, myths, and stories of Brazil's Northeast. Lyrical, grotesque, and fantastic animals and saints drift in and out of his nearly monochromatic green and black compositions. Examples of this style include *The System of the Doctor* and *The Counselor.* In 1960 he accepted a position teaching printmaking at the Educational Center in Niterói. Although best known for his graphic art, Cavalcanti has also produced illustrated books and has worked on film projects. In addition, he has been the subject of two film documentaries, *Newton Cavalcanti-Um artista brasileiro* (1973) and *Newton Cavalcanti Quadro a Quadro* (1983).

See also **Art: The Twentieth Century.**

BIBLIOGRAPHY

Dawn Ades, *Art in Latin America* (1989), p. 342.

Additional Bibliography

Centro Brasileiro de Cultura. *4 Grabadores del Brasil.* Santiago: Ed. Universitaria, 1966.

CAREN A. MEGHREBLIAN

CAVALLÓN, JUAN DE (1524–1565).

Juan de Cavallón (*b.* 1524; *d.* 1565), first conqueror of Costa Rica during the early 1560s. Although largely unsuccessful on his own, his invasion from Nicaragua in 1561 both set in motion the process and established the mechanisms by which subordinates such as Juan Vázquez de Coronado would conquer the province. Cavallón held a licenciate in law and came from Castillo de Garcimuñoz, Cuenca, New Castile. He married Leonor de Barahona, the daughter of one of Cortés's associates in the conquest of Mexico. He was named *alcalde mayor* of Nicoya in the 1550s. From this base he led 80 to 90 men, recruited in Guatemala in 1560, as an expeditionary force to claim the province of Costa Rica.

In January 1561 the force left its base and landed on the coast near the modern port of Puntarenas. They attempted to establish two settlements, Landecho as a port and Castillo de Garcimuñoz further inland, but both soon failed. Relations with the Indians deteriorated quickly as their leader, Garabito, organized resistance to Cavallón's requisitioning of corn supplies. Cavallón financed this expedition in association with the Franciscan priest Juan de Estrada Rávago, a native of Guadalajara, New Castile, long resident in the Salvadoran Indian parishes of the cacao-rich Izalco district. Cavallón claimed to have lost nine thousand pesos of his own funds in the enterprise, and Estrada may have invested six or seven thousand. Estrada also undertook an expedition along the Atlantic coast, in coordination with Cavallón's march from the Pacific side, but with even more dismal results.

Cavallón was named *fiscal* of the *audiencia* in Guatemala in 1562 and left Estrada in charge of a rapidly declining force. Estrada also left Costa Rica, returning eventually to Spain, but several members of the conquering band remained to claim positions and *encomiendas* after the more lasting conquest expedition of Vázquez de Coronado in 1563.

See also **Costa Rica.**

BIBLIOGRAPHY

The best sources of Cavallón's exploits in Costa Rica are those of Carlos Meléndez Chaverri: *Conquistadores y pobladores: Orígines histórico-sociales de los costarricenses* (1982), and *Juan Vázquez de Coronado, conquistador y fundador de Costa Rica,* 2d ed. (1972).

LOWELL GUDMUNDSON

CAVOUR, ERNESTO (1940–).

The Bolivian folkloric musician Ernesto Cavour is renowned worldwide as a *charango* (Andean stringed instrument) soloist. Born April 9, 1940, in La Paz, he received his first major distinction in 1965, as "best instrumentalist" at the Latin American Folklore Festival in Salta, Argentina. The next year he founded Los Jairas—arguably Bolivia's most influential folkloric ensemble—with fellow La Paz residents Julio Godoy and Edgar "Yayo" Joffré along with the Swiss musician Gilbert Favre. Cavour also formed the Trio Domínguez-Favre-Cavour, known for its innovative instrumental repertoire. In 1969 both ensembles became the first Bolivian folkloric groups to tour Europe. Cavour returned to La Paz in 1971, devoting his attention to running the folkloric music venue Peña Naira (closed in 1996) and the Museum of Bolivian Musical Instruments (still in operation as of 2007). Cavour has authored widely read method books for various instruments and texts about local musical traditions. He serves as president of the Bolivian Charango Society, which he helped establish in 1973.

See also **Music: Popular Music and Dance.**

BIBLIOGRAPHY

Primary Works

Instrumentos musicales de Bolivia. La Paz: Producciones CIMA, 1994.

El charango: Su vida, costumbres y desventuras. 2nd edition. La Paz: Producciones CIMA, 2001.

Secondary Works

Rios, Fernando. "Music in Urban La Paz, Bolivian Nationalism, and the Early History of Cosmopolitan Andean Music: 1936–1970." Ph.D. diss., University of Illinois at Urbana-Champaign, 2005.

FERNANDO RIOS

CAXIAS, DUQUE DE. *See* **Lima e Silva, Luís Alves de.**

CAYENNE, BRAZILIAN INVASION OF.

On 22 March 1808, Portuguese forces, aided by the British, invaded the French colony of Cayenne in retaliation for the French invasion of Portugal in 1807. The original purpose of the mission under the count of Linhares was to completely destroy the colony. In May 1809 Dom João (later João VI) made the decision to keep the colony and to build it up for trade and military purposes. With Manuel Marques serving as intendent and Maciel da Costa as civilian administrator, Portuguese rule was relatively enlightened and accepted by the French colonists. However, European powers at the Congress of Vienna forced the return of Cayenne to the French on 8 November 1817.

See also **João VI of Portugal; Portuguese Empire.**

BIBLIOGRAPHY

Pedro Calmon, *A história do Brasil,* vol. 4 (1963), pp. 1419–1420.

Sérgio Buarque De Hollanda, ed., *História geral da civilização brasileira,* vol. 1, no. 2 (1963), pp. 283–299; *South American Handbook,* 67th ed. (1991), p. 1125.

Additional Bibliography

Schultz, Kirsten. *Tropical Versailles: Empire, Monarchy, and the Portuguese Royal Court in Rio De Janeiro, 1808–1821.* New York: Routledge, 2001.

Soublin, Jean. *Cayenne 1809: La conquête de la Guyane par les Portugais du Brésil.* Paris: Karthala, 2003.

ROBERT A. HAYES

CAYMAN ISLANDS.

Cayman Islands, a British dependency in the Caribbean located south of Cuba and northwest of Jamaica. Consisting of the islands of Grand Cayman, Cayman Brac, and Little Cayman, the territory covers an area of about 100 square miles. Sighted by Christopher Columbus in 1503, the island group was named Las Tortugas on account of its native sea turtles. By 1530 the name "Caimanas," or "Caymans," derived from a word meaning crocodile in the language of the Caribs, early island visitors, came into acceptance. Permanent settlers arrived after the Treaty of Madrid (1670), by which Spain recognized English claims to these islands in exchange for restraint of pirates whose haunts included the Caymans. From 1863 to 1959, the Cayman Islands were officially a dependency of Jamaica. Upon Jamaican independence in 1962, they chose to remain a British Crown Colony. Since the Constitution of 1972 was implemented, the Caymans have been internally autonomous under an appointed governor.

Aided by government promotion, tourism has become the most important industry, even despite setbacks with terrorist attacks on the United States in 2001 and the landing of Hurricane Ivan in 2004. Cruise ship stopovers to the island are major explanations for the industry's strength.

Offshore finance, another industry of recent prominence, developed in response to banking confidentiality legislation and the absence of direct taxation, making the Caymans an international financial center. As of year-end 2005, there were 305 banks. More significantly, since the mid-1990s, mutual funds have become widely prevalent. At year-end 2005, there were 7,107 registered mutual funds.

In 1996, stricter legislation against money-laundering was passed. In 2002, a tax information exchange agreement with the United States was passed, with which the United States can access information on criminal tax evasion and administrative matters related to U.S. federal income tax. It went into full effect in 2006.

See also **Madrid, Treaty of (1670); Tourism.**

BIBLIOGRAPHY

George S. S. Hirst, *Notes on the History of the Cayman Islands* (1910; repr. 1967).

H. B. L. Hughes, "Notes on the Cayman Islands," in *Jamaican Historical Review* 1, no. 2 (1946): 154–158.

Neville Williams, *A History of the Cayman Islands* (1970).

Brian Uzzell, ed., *The Cayman Islands Yearbook and Business Directory* (annual).

PAULA S. GIBBS

CAYMMI, DORIVAL

(1914–). Dorival Caymmi (*b.* 1914), Brazilian songwriter. Beginning in the 1930s, Salvador-born Caymmi composed a wide variety of highly successful tunes that explored Bahian and Afro-Brazilian culture and were popularized by singers such as Carmen Miranda, Anjos do Inferno, Ângela Maria, João Gilberto, Elis Regina, Gal Costa, Gilberto Gil, and Caetano Veloso, as well as by foreign interpreters such as Andy Williams and Paul Winter. Caymmi worked in many different musical styles, including *sambas, marchas, toadas, modinhas, canções praieiras* (fishermen's songs), *cocos, sambas de roda,* and *pontos de candomblé* (*candomblé* invocations). Like novelist Jorge Amado, with whom he composed "é doce morrer no mar" (It's Sweet to Die in the Sea), he is closely identified with Bahian culture. Due to his unique style of singing and song-writing and the venerating themes of his music Caymmi is largely responsible for national image. His songs include folkloric influences from the streets of Bahia as well as guitar techniques unique to his music.

Caymmi gained fame with "O que é que a baiana tem?" (What Is It That the Baiana's Got?), sung by Carmen Miranda in the films *Banana da terra* (1938) and *Greenwich Village* (1944); Caymmi recorded a duet with the actress in 1939. Other Caymmi standards include: "Samba da minha terra" (Samba of My Land), "Marina," "Nem eu" (Me Neither), "Saudade de Itapoã," "Oração de mae menininha" (a tribute to a famed *mae-de-santo* in Salvador), "Rosa morena," "Saudade da Bahia," "João Valentão," "Requebre que eu dou um doce," "Doralice," "Das rosas," and "Promessa de pescador" (Promise of a Fisherman). His three children (singer Nana, singer-songwriter Dori, and flutist-composer Danilo) are also musicians.

See also **Music: Popular Music and Dance.**

BIBLIOGRAPHY

Dorival Caymmi, *Cancioneiro da Bahia* (1978).

Rita Caúrio, ed., *Brasil Musical* (1988).

Chris Mc Gowan and Ricardo Pessanha, *The Brazilian Sound: Samba, Bossa Nova, and the Popular Music of Brazil* (1991).

Additional Bibliography

Caymmi, Stella. *Dorival Caymmi: O mar e o tempo.* São Paulo: Editora 34, 2001.

Risério, Antonio. *Caymmi: Uma utopis de lugar.* São Paulo: Editora Perspectiva, 1993.

CHRIS MCGOWAN

CAZNEAU, WILLIAM LESLIE (1807–1876). William Leslie Cazneau (*b.* 5 October 1807; *d.* 7 January 1876), a wealthy Texan and supporter of William Walker's filibustering scheme in Nicaragua. As an expansionist in the 1840s, Cazneau encouraged the annexation of Cuba and Mexico's northern states to the United States. Subsequently, he fought in the Mexican-American War (1846–1848), for which he received the rank of general. In 1853 Secretary of State William L. Marcy appointed Cazneau special minister to Santo Domingo to negotiate a commercial treaty and to obtain Samaná Bay as a coaling station. The mission failed, and Cazneau returned to the United States in 1855. In 1856, he contracted with Walker to send one thousand colonists to Nicaragua within a year to be established in settlements of not fewer than fifty families, each settler to be given title to eighty acres of land. In return, Cazneau was to receive a considerable land grant. The effort failed with Walker's ouster from Nicaragua in May 1857.

See also **Filibustering; Walker, William.**

BIBLIOGRAPHY

Sumner Welles, *Naboth's Vineyard: The Dominican Republic, 1844–1924,* 2 vols. (1928).

Charles C. Tansill, *The United States and Santo Domingo, 1798–1873* (1938).

Robert E. May, "Lobbyists for Commercial Empire: Jane Cazneau, William Cazneau, and U.S. Caribbean Policy, 1846–1878," *Pacific Historical Review* 48 (1979): 383–412.

Additional Bibliography

Hudson, Linda. *Mistress of Manifest Destiny: A Biography of Jane McManus Storm Cazneau, 1807–1878.* Austin: Texas State Historical Association, 2001.

THOMAS M. LEONARD

CEARÁ. Ceará, a state in northeastern Brazil, covers 58,150 square miles and in 2000 had an estimated population of 6.5 million. Its capital is Fortaleza. Located partly on the sandy coastal plain and partly on semiarid uplands, Ceará suffers periodic droughts. The state is economically reliant upon cotton, sugar, tobacco, carnauba wax, and other agricultural products. Forty percent of the population lives in the countryside, and rural poverty has been widespread throughout its history.

The French presence among Indian populations inhibited early Portuguese settlement of the area, but ranchers pressed into the interior during the 1600s. Occupied by the Dutch from 1637 until 1654, the region was part of Maranhão until 1680, when it became a dependency of Pernambuco. Ceará became an independent captaincy in 1799, a province of the empire in 1822, and a state of the republic in 1889.

In the 1700s the economy centered on cattle ranching and sugar. In the 1800s the long-staple cotton crop rose to prominence, particularly during the American Civil War. Ceará's unprecedented prosperity, resulting from a surge in cotton exports, ended with a severe drought in 1877–1879. The drought overwhelmed attempts to provide relief, and an estimated 200,000 to 500,000 people died of starvation and disease. Roughly 30 to 50 percent of Ceará's population emigrated or perished.

By 1880 property had been devastated throughout the northeast, and slaves were virtually the only negotiable commodity. Many slaves were shipped south in exchange for food and in order to conserve local food supplies. Since the 1860s and perhaps earlier, free workers had performed most of Ceará's agricultural labor, but access to southern markets bolstered slave prices. In the early 1880s, laws restricting interprovincial slave trading undercut slaves' value in Ceará. Abolitionism gained momentum, and the province abolished slavery in 1884, four years before the national emancipation law. Ceará's action served a symbolic function for abolitionism elsewhere in Brazil.

Between 1877 and 1915 four major droughts struck the state, prompting massive migrations of *sertanejos* (inhabitants of the interior). Some fled to cities within Ceará, while others were attracted to coffee production in the south and work in the rubber tree forests of Amazonas and Pará. Although Ceará's government collected a head tax on emigrants, the loss of manpower resulted in a chronic labor shortage lasting into the 1920s. Economic hardships during this period also abetted the coalescence of *sertanejos* around Padre Cícero Romão Batista of Joaseiro (now Juazeiro do Norte). The priest held sway over much of the state from the mid 1910s until his death in 1934.

Despite Ceará's chronic and intractable problems, which are similar to those in the rest of the northeast, the state became known nationally and internationally in the 1990s for a series of pragmatic and effective governments led by Tasso Jereissati and Ciro Gomes. Their public works programs provided employment in an expeditious fashion to many during the 1987 drought, and evidently operated in something other than the traditional patron–client fashion. Health care improved, and infant mortality declined significantly. Ceará became the first Latin American government to receive UNICEF's Maurice Pate Award for its children's programs. Agriculturally, there have been some setbacks, especially in terms of the damage that the boll weevil has done to cotton production.

See also **Messianic Movements: Brazil; Slavery: Brazil; Slave Trade.**

BIBLIOGRAPHY

Conrad, Robert. *The Destruction of Brazilian Slavery, 1850–1888.* Berkeley: University of California Press, 1972.

Della Cava, Ralph. *Miracle at Joaseiro.* New York: Columbia University Press, 1970.

Tendler, Judith. *Good Government in the Tropics.* Baltimore, MD: Johns Hopkins University Press, 1997.

ANDREW J. KIRKENDALL

CEDEÑO, JUAN MANUEL (1914–1997).

Juan Manuel Cedeño (*b.* 28 December 1914, *d.* 11 August 1997), Panamanian painter. Cedeño studied under Humberto Ivaldi and Roberto Lewis at the Escuela Nacional de Pintura in Panama and at the Chicago Art Institute (B.F.A., 1948). In addition he was invited to study at the Polytechnical Institute of Mexico where he worked with artists Sigueiros and Diego Rivera. His role as an educator is one of his greatest contributions to Panama. He was director of his alma mater, in 1952 renamed the Escuela Nacional de Artes Plásticas (1948–1967) and professor at the University of Panama (1967–1978). His prolific paintings earned him the title of "Graphic Chronicler of the Panamanian Nationality," although he preferred to be called the "painter from Los Santos."

In his work with local folklore themes, Cedeño was one of the first Panamanian artists to experiment with the geometrization of forms derived from cubism and futurism, as in *Domingo de Ramos* (1955). Although he also paints landscapes and still lifes, he is best known for his many commissioned portraits, for example, *Octavio Méndez Pereira* (1950) and in 1995 he was contracted to complete series depicting significant events of Panama's history for the Foreign Minister, Gabriel Lewis Galindo.

See also **Art: The Twentieth Century.**

BIBLIOGRAPHY

Mónica Kupfer, ed., *Exposición Retrospectiva de la obra de Juan Manuel Cedeño* (1983).

P. Padros, *Exposición Maestros-Maestros* (1987).

Additional Bibliography

Cedeño, Juan Manuel, and Monica Kupfer. *Exposición retrospectiva de la obra de Juan Manuel Cedeno*. Panamá: Museo de Arte Contemporaneo, 1983.

MONICA E. KUPFER

CEDILLO MARTÍNEZ, SATURNINO

(1890–1939). Saturnino Cedillo Martínez (*b.* 29 November 1890; *d.* 11 January 1939), Mexican politician and rebel leader. An important revolutionary general and the regional boss of the state of San Luis Potosí, Cedillo led the last military rebellion against the government in the post-Revolutionary period and was killed in battle.

Born at Rancho de Palomas, Ciudad del Maíz, San Luis Potosí, the son of landowning peasants, he obtained a primary school education. He joined the Maderistas, but later, with his brothers Magdaleno and Cleofas, he sided with Emiliano Zapata and fought against Madero on the side of Pascual Orozco in 1912. He was captured and imprisoned. He later joined the Constitutionalists, but abandoned Venustiano Carranza to support the Plan of Agua Prieta in 1920. He remained in the army, holding top military commands, and supported the government against rebel causes in 1923 and 1929. After serving as governor of his home state, he provided decisive peasant support for Lázaro Cárdenas's presidential candidacy in 1934, for which he was rewarded with the post of secretary of agriculture (1935). He broke with the president in 1937, leaving the cabinet. He then organized his supporters into a small army and opposed the Cárdenas government.

See also **Mexico: Since 1910.**

BIBLIOGRAPHY

Nathaniel Weyl and Sylvia Weyl, *The Reconquest of Mexico: The Years of Lázaro Cárdenas* (1939).

Additional Bibliography

Ankerson, Dudley. *El Caudillo Agrarista: Saturnino Cedillo y la Revolución Mexicana en San Luis Potosí*. México, D.F.: Instituto Nacional de Estudios Históricos de la Revolución Mexicana, 1994.

RODERIC AI CAMP

CÉDULA. Cédula, legislation signed, at least in theory, by the ruling monarch of Castile. A *cédula* or *real cédula* was a form of legislation issued by the sovereign to dispense an appointment or favor, resolve a question, or require some action. When solicited from America it was a *cédula de parte*. When initiated by the Council of the Indies, it was a *cédula de oficio*. A *cédula* began with the heading *El Rey* or *La Reina* and was signed by the monarch or in his or her name. As a direct communication from the monarch, a *cédula* took precedence over royal decrees or orders issued by the Council of the Indies or royal ministers.

See also **Castile.**

BIBLIOGRAPHY

Diccionario de la lengua española, 18th ed. (1956).

Additional Bibliography

Twinam, Ann. *Public Lives, Private Secrets: Gender, Honor, Sexuality, and Illegitimacy in Colonial Spanish America*. Stanford, CA: Stanford University Press, 1999.

MARK A. BURKHOLDER

CEIBO. The ceibo (seíbo), or *Erythrina cristagalli,* is a tree common in well-watered areas of central and northern Argentina. The cockspur coral tree or cockspur coral bean tree is bushy and thorny, with wide, lustrous, dark green leaves about four inches (ten centimeters) long and three inches wide. It sprouts bright red blooms and beanlike pods. It generally grows to twenty or thirty feet in height but can reach eighty feet. Residents of the Río de la Plata developed many medicinal uses for the tree, including bathing wounds, gargling, and treating hemorrhoids.

See also Medicinal Plants.

BIBLIOGRAPHY

Coluccio, Félix. *Diccionario folklórico argentino*, vol. 1. Buenos Aires: Lasserre, 1964.

Oitaven, Alberto V. *El ceibo: Flor nacional Argentina*. La Plata, Argentina: Estrella, 1943.

RICHARD W. SLATTA

CELAM. *See* **Conference of Latin American Bishops (CELAM).**

CELAYA, BATTLES OF. Battles of Celaya, the critical encounters in central Mexico between Venustiano Carranza's Constitutionalist forces and Francisco Villa's Division of the North. The two battles of Celaya turned the course of the revolution in favor of the Carrancistas.

The Constitutionalists, commanded by Álvaro Obregón, met the Division of the North at Celaya, Guanajuato, on 6 April 1915. Villa used his predictable but effective tactic of relentless cavalry assaults against Obregón's fortified positions. After Villa's forces exhausted themselves, Obregón attacked Villa's flanks and repulsed the Division of the North, which suffered heavy casualties and captives. Villa attempted a second assault on Celaya on 13 April. Using the same tactics, he again met defeat with many casualties. As in the first encounter, Obregón's casualties were remarkably light.

Obregón's victories of Celaya are attributed to Villa's poor planning, faulty supply lines, ammunition shortages, and inaccurate and inefficient use of artillery; rain and mud, which slowed Villa's assaults; the professionalism of the Constitutionalist forces and the soundness of Obregón's tactics; and division and dissension among Villa's officers.

After defeating Villa at Celaya, Obregón pushed further north. In May 1915 he defeated Villa's rejuvenated and resupplied army at León. A month later, Obregón routed the Division of the North at Aguascalientes. By July 1915 the once invincible Villistas were reduced to small guerrilla bands in northern Mexico. In contrast, Obregón's popularity and power increased within the Constitutionalist movement.

See also **Mexico, Wars and Revolutions: Mexican Revolution.**

BIBLIOGRAPHY

Charles C. Cumberland, *Mexican Revolution: The Constitutionalist Years* (1972), pp. 200–201.

Alan Knight, *The Mexican Revolution*. Vol. 2, *Counter-Revolution and Reconstruction* (1986), pp. 322–325.

John Mason Hart, *Revolutionary Mexico: The Coming and Process of the Mexican Revolution* (1987), p. 311.

Additional Bibliography

Barrón, Luis. *Historias de la Revolución Mexicana*. México, D.F.: Centro de Investigación y Docencia Económicas: Fondo de Cultura Económica, 2004.

Katz, Friedrich. *The Life and Times of Pancho Villa*. Stanford, CA: Stanford University Press, 1998.

AARON PAINE MAHR

CEMENTOS MEXICANOS. Founded in Monterrey, Mexico, in 1906, Cementos Mexicanos (CEMEX), over the course of the twentieth century, became the third-largest cement supplier in the world, as well as one of the largest building materials suppliers. Originally called Cementos Hidalgo, the company began to dominate the local market in 1931, when it merged with Portland Monterrey and officially changed its name to Cementos Mexicanos. CEMEX slowly expanded in the mid-twentieth century by purchasing local companies. When Lorenzo Zambrano, grandson of the founder, became the chief executive officer in 1985, CEMEX had become the second-largest producer in Mexico. Zambrano initiated an aggressive international expansion. First, the company began buying companies in Spanish-speaking countries like Spain and Panama. In 1994 the company purchased its first U.S. company and later in the decade moved into Asia and Africa. As of 2003, CEMEX relied on Mexico for only a third of its sales. The United States followed with 15 percent. Business case studies have examined how CEMEX management aggressively utilized computers and satellite tracking technology to increase efficiency. For instance, when CEMEX took over the Rugby plant in England, the new management improved the production from 70 percent to 93 percent capacity. With this productivity and vigorous expansion, analysts predicted that CEMEX would continue to be among the most competitive cement producers in the world.

See also **Industrialization.**

BIBLIOGRAPHY

Agtmael, Antoine W. van. *The Emerging Markets Century: How a New Breed of World-Class Companies Is Overtaking the World.* New York: Free Press, 2007.

Barragán, Juan. *Juan F. Brittingham y la industria en México, 1859–1940.* Monterrey, Nuevo León: Urbis Internacional, 1993.

BYRON CRITES

CEMPOALA. Cempoala (Zempoala), one of several Totonac states located near Veracruz Vieja, where Cortés's expedition disembarked to penetrate central Mexico. It contained a large population (20,000–30,000 tributaries) clustered around a ceremonial center. The name which translates to "place of twenty waters" derives from numerous rivers in the area. The Totonacs, who had a culture similar to the Maya, populated the area approximately 1500 years before the Spanish encounter. Cempoala had just recently been conquered by the Aztecs, and the people rankled at the empire's tribute demands. Cortés therefore found them willing allies. The Spanish had to protect Cempoala from Aztec retribution. In 1520 Cempoala was swept by a smallpox epidemic that left virtually no survivors. The remaining population was congregated in a neighboring town in 1569.

See also **Totonacs.**

BIBLIOGRAPHY

Peter Gerhard, *A Guide to the Historical Geography of New Spain* (1972).

Additional Bibliography

Brüggemann, Jürgen K. *Zempoala: El estudio de una ciudad prehispánica.* México, D.F.: Instituto Nacional de Antropología e Historia, 1991.

Platas Domínguez, Julio. *Cempoala: El amor al terruño.* Xalapa, Veracruz: J. Platas Domínguez, 1994.

JOHN E. KICZA

CENSORSHIP. To sketch a historical context for understanding censorship in Latin America, we must begin by defining the term. By providing competing conceptions of censorship, crucial issues involved in debates concerning freedom of the press emerges. Two points of view predominate. The liberal-pluralist stance understands censorship in a relatively narrow manner and focuses on whether there are any formal impediments to the exercise of free expression by the media. The other view implies a more nuanced conception of mass communication: regardless of whether the media are privately owned or government-controlled, the notion of censorship is related to the degree of access available to the population, either as individual citizens or as members of interest groups, and to their potential capacity to define public issues. Thus, in addition to legal and formal obstacles to free expression, informal means of restricting access to the public sphere may also be considered forms of censorship.

Both formal and informal censorship practices have existed since early colonial times in what today is Latin America. In precolonial civilizations, such as the Maya and the Inca, the definition of the social order was the exclusive privilege of the ruling elites. The Spanish and Portuguese authorities banned books, usually on religious and moral grounds, throughout the colonial empire, thus marking the start of censoring practices in the New World. However, only with the appearance and subsequent prohibition of patriotic *pasquines* (political pamphlets) during the independence period did the curtailment of press freedom occur that people later associated with censorship.

Once the new nations had gained independence, daily newspapers proliferated. This was a partisan press, which openly espoused the political views of its publishers. Throughout the nineteenth century, these partisan newspapers ebbed and flowed according to the fortunes of their sponsors. It was customary for the party in power to harass and outlaw the partisan press sponsored by its political opponents, in the understanding that, when power shifted, as it often did, that party's own newspapers would be banned from circulation. Such "censorship" was an integral part of the political modus operandi of the times.

The situation was not the same for all Latin American countries. In Chile, for example, a country where caudillo politics of the nineteenth century were less entrenched and eventually gave way to a remarkably stable democratic system in the twentieth century, the first nonsectarian newspaper was founded as early as 1855. In contrast, Venezuela, where *caudillismo* remained strong well into the twentieth century, did not enjoy a free press until recently.

The structure of media ownership, particularly television, is the key factor in determining the subtler forms of censorship that were outlined above in terms of limited access and ability to define issues. Electronic media in Latin America grew on a commercial basis, and the vast majority of television stations are privately owned. Thus, messages tend to favor the worldview of the urban privileged, fostering consumerism and political conservatism.

A movement aimed at alleviating this situation took hold in several countries during the 1960s and early 1970s, eventually resulting in a 1976 meeting sponsored by UNESCO, where representatives of twenty Latin American nations discussed communication policies. The recommendations of this conference, which sought to increase popular participation and access to media, were seldom implemented. By the time they were formulated, the political climate that favored government intervention to promote greater media democratization had passed, and a wave of dictatorial regimes was sweeping the region, particularly the Southern Cone. Censorship increased greatly during the 1960s through the 1980s under these military regimes. Many newspapers were shut down and their reporters and editors assassinated, "disappeared," or hounded from the country. A famous example is Jacobo Timerman, the editor of *La Opinón*, who was imprisoned, tortured and deported from Argentina in the 1970s. In Nicaragua, Pedro Joaquín Chamorro, owner of *La Prensa*, in Managua, Nicaragua, was assassinated in 1978.

After redemocratization in the 1980s, censorship diminished throughout the region. The power of the private broadcasters themselves became formidable and few governments could afford to antagonize them. In Brazil, for instance, the Globo television network had far more influence and power than any current political force. A separate case was that of Mexico. After the loss of the Institutional Revolutionary Party (PRI) in the presidential elections of 2000, newspapers and other media took a more independent stance, not as bound to the ad revenue that the Mexican government provided to media outlets.

Censorship has begun to emerge in Latin America again under the aegis of populist-leftist regimes. Most important in this respect was Venezuela, where in 2004 the National Assembly controlled by President Hugo Chávez promulgated a law that restricted the type of programming in radio and television. In 2005, it became a crime to insult public officials, but this law has been used mainly to keep journalists quiet rather than to punish them for transgressions. These actions were followed in May 2007 by Venezuelan government's decision not to renew the broadcasting license of Radio Caracas Televisión (RCTV). The government, which has argued that most private media outlets are against it, asserted that RCTV had helped the plotters in the 2002 coup and that it was within its rights to close the station. This decision brought about massive protests throughout the country, but the government did not back down. In communist Cuba, censorship of all media remains the rule. In Colombia, death threats against reporters by paramilitary and drug dealers promote self-censorship. Likewise, in Mexico the murder of nine journalists in 2007 highlights the problems of censorship, especially of media outlets along the U.S. border, where drug traffickers threaten to harm those reporting on their activities.

Overall, systematic censorship by governments in Latin America is relatively rare except in Cuba and Venezuela. In Cuba even the Internet is strictly controlled. The most important barriers are self-censorship because of threats from criminal elements. Thus, censorship is becoming less an issue since the rise of the Internet has made control of information very difficult.

See also **Journalism.**

BIBLIOGRAPHY

Two major contributions that, from different perspectives, deal with issues of censorship in Latin American twentieth-century media are Marvin Alisky, *Latin American Media: Guidance and Censorship* (1981), and Elizabeth Fox, ed., *Media and Politics in Latin America: The Struggle for Democracy* (1988). On censorship during colonial times, see Pablo González Casanova, *La Literatura perseguida en la crisis de la colonia* (1986). For a discussion of press harassment in the twentieth century, see María Teresa Camarillo Carbajal, *La represión a la prensa en América Latina: Hemerografía, 1978–1982* (1985) and Richard R.Cole, ed. *Communication in Latin America: Journalism, Mass Media, and Society.* Four interesting national studies respectively, are Andrés Avellaneda, *Censura, autoritarismo y cultura: Argentina, 1960–1983* (1986); Silvana Goulart Guimaraes, *Sob a verdade oficial: Ideologia, propaganda e censura* (1990); and Hernán Millas, *Los señores censores* (1985).

Additional Bibliography

Smith, Anne-Marie. *A Forced Agreement: Press Acquiescence to Censorship in Brazil.* Pittsburgh, PA: University of Pittsburgh Press, 1997.

The best up-to-date resource for censorship issues is Reporters Without Borders, whose website is http://www.rsf.org.

OMAR HERNÁNDEZ
ERICK D. LANGER

CENTER FOR ADVANCED MILITARY STUDIES (CAEM).

Center for Advanced Military Studies (CAEM), a Peruvian institution for specialized higher military education created in 1950 under the rule of the de facto president General Manuel Odría. Its original objectives were to define national war doctrines, train Peruvian colonels aspiring to higher military posts, and relate the issues of national defense to national problems. It was similar in scope to contemporary military centers in France, the United States (Inter-American Defense College), Argentina, and Brazil.

Peruvian military training and education had been modeled since 1896 on the French military school (in part as a reaction to the German model used by the Chilean army at the time). The French model perceived the role of the military in a wider social and administrative dimension. With this perspective the Peruvian general Oscar Torres, President José Luis Bustamante y Rivero's minister of war, called as early as 1945 for the establishment of a specialized military training institution.

The CAEM's graduates and teaching staff began a gradual transformation in the military mentality toward a "new professionalism." They favored institutional military intervention in matters of national development, Indian "integration," and diminished foreign dependency. The CAEM played an important role in the military suppression of the peasant uprisings in Cuzco in the early 1960s through "civic action." In Cuzco the military introduced the first land reform ever executed in Peru in order to avoid further insurrections.

It has been assumed that the CAEM had a decisive influence among those who supported the 1968 military coup led by General Juan Velasco Alvarado against constitutional President Fernando Belaúnde. While some supporters of Velasco were CAEM graduates (such as General Jorge Fernández Maldonado), recent studies point to the much more important bearing of concepts of strategic internal and external defense (rather than the CAEM's developmental doctrines) expounded by the newly expanded military intelligence.

See also **Armed Forces.**

BIBLIOGRAPHY

Alfred Stepan, *The State and Society: Peru in Comparative Perspective* (1978).

Daniel Masterson, *Militarism and Politics in Latin America: Peru from Sánchez Cerro to Sendero Luminoso* (1991).

Additional Bibliography

Masterson, Daniel M. *Fuerza armada y sociedad en el Perú moderno: Un estudio sobre relaciones civiles militares, 1930–2000.* Lima: Instituto de Estudios Políticos y Estratégicos, 2001.

ALFONSO W. QUIROZ

CENTRAL AMERICA.

The term "Central America" is often used to designate the region stretching southeastward from the isthmus of Tehuantepec, in Mexico, to the boundary between Panama and Colombia. Historically, however, it has more often been used with reference to the five states that once made up the Central American federation—Guatemala, El Salvador, Honduras, Nicaragua, and Costa Rica—but also including Belize, which has long been claimed by Guatemala. The Spanish colonial Kingdom of Guatemala also

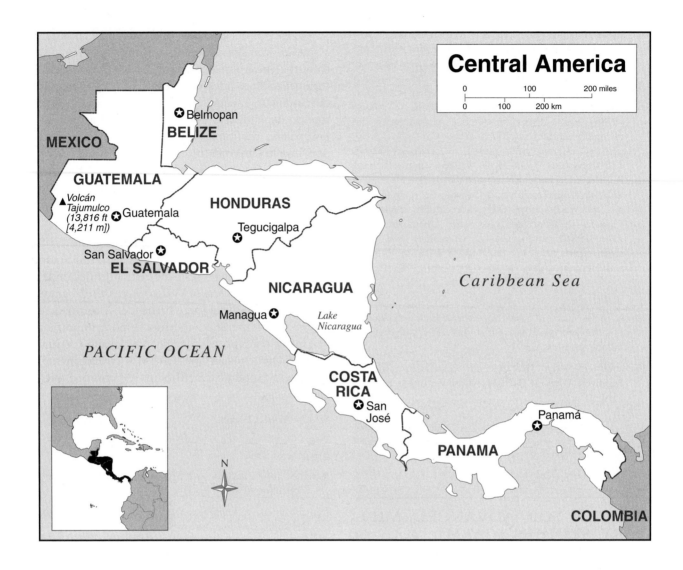

Central America

0   100   200 miles

0   100   200 km

MEXICO

BELIZE
⊕ Belmopan

GUATEMALA
▲ Volcán Tajumulco (13,816 ft [4,211 m])
⊕ Guatemala

HONDURAS
⊕ Tegucigalpa

San Salvador ⊕
EL SALVADOR

NICARAGUA

Managua ⊕   Lake Nicaragua

PACIFIC OCEAN

Caribbean Sea

COSTA RICA
⊕ San José

Panamá ⊕
PANAMA

N

COLOMBIA

included the area occupied by the present-day Mexican state of Chiapas; that state is sometimes included in considerations of Central America. And since its independence from Colombia in 1903, Panama has increasingly been thought of politically as well as geographically as a part of Central America.

Before the arrival of the Europeans, Central America, an archaeological bridge between North and South America, was home to a variety of nomadic and sedentary peoples. Mayan civilization occupied much of the isthmus, from Chiapas and Yucatán through Guatemala, Honduras, Belize, El Salvador, and into Nicaragua. Various tribes of Nahuatl origin had moved along the Pacific watershed from central Mexico as far as Nicaragua. Chibcha and other South American Indians occupied lower Central America into Nicaragua. Although the

Maya were the most advanced pre-Columbian civilization, they were neither unified nor cohesive. Unlike the Aztecs or Incas, their autonomous city-states remained independent, presaging the political fragmentation that would characterize modern Central America. What unity existed was cultural rather than political.

These Indian peoples suffered greatly under the Spanish military conquest. Efforts to enslave the natives decimated their numbers, but far more destructive were the biological consequences of the conquest. Epidemics of smallpox, plague, syphilis, and other diseases killed millions, perhaps 80 to 90 percent of the population. The population continued to decline until about 1750, then began to grow slightly through the nineteenth century and to rise at a surprising pace in the twentieth century.

Much of the contemporary writing on Central America focuses on individual states, offering rather myopic analyses with little sense of the larger regional issues. Even most of the growing number of works concentrating on the contemporary crises in Central America for the most part deal with the region on a state-by-state basis. This is not, of course, altogether unjustified or unwelcome, for there has been a need for more careful studies of individual states and most of these works contribute to understanding the dynamics of Central American development. At the same time, there is a Central American regional cohesiveness across a broad spectrum of activity. The concept of Central American nationality is deeply ingrained in isthmian history, and although the period since the 1870s has fostered the nationalism of the separate city-states, Central American reunification remains a possibility many Central Americans desire.

THE COLONIAL PERIOD

Central American history reveals a strong thread of unity. Although political union was not a feature of pre-Columbian Central America, there was considerable cultural similarity among the peoples occupying the present-day states of Central America, with extensive commercial relations among them and some sense of common enemies from without. In the early sixteenth century, however, the Spanish imposed political, economic, social, and cultural unity. As the Kingdom of Guatemala, for three centuries the region evolved as a single political unit, governed from Santiago de Guatemala (present-day Antigua). Moved occasionally because of natural disasters, that city became the home of a patrician creole elite and the peninsular bureaucrats who ruled these provinces. Their progeny extended into the provinces and formed the nucleus of the local aristocracy in each provincial capital.

While varying degrees of allegiance and amounts of colonial tribute were paid to the viceregal capital at Mexico City and to Spain, the immediate and real center of the Central American universe was Santiago de Guatemala. Until the very last years of Spanish rule, it contained the only university in the kingdom (the University of San Carlos, founded in 1681), and was the headquarters for every religious order on the isthmus, the center for overseas trade and finance, and, of course, the administrative

capital of the kingdom. The cream of the local creole stock came from the provinces to be educated, to enter commerce, to join the bureaucracy, and to establish closer ties with the families at the center of the kingdom.

To be sure, there were centrifugal forces as well. Inadequate transportation facilities caused much of the region to be remote from the capital and its advantages. The kingdom often represented an intrusion on local subsistence, a burden in the form of taxes and service to crown or cross. There was the conflict between the two great socioeconomic systems that have characterized Central America since 1524: feudalism and capitalism. The conquistadores established a kingdom with feudal concepts, institutions, and customs. The vestiges of that kingdom can still be seen in institutions and attitudes in modern Central America, but there also was a Renaissance capitalism carried to Central America that emphasized mineral exploitation, agro-export production, development of infrastructure, and greater unity among the provinces of the kingdom. This capitalist trend slowed during the seventeenth century and, if anything, feudal institutions became stronger then. But as Spain declined economically, her rivals gained strength and the industrial revolution caused them to probe the isthmus for trade and plunder, which contributed ultimately to greater overseas trade. The eighteenth-century Bourbons especially promoted increased agricultural export production in the backwater regions of the Spanish Empire that had been predominantly subsistence-oriented.

In Central America this produced some very substantial changes. Provinces formerly subservient to Guatemala began to gain importance in their own right. Honduras exploited silver mines and, as in Nicaragua, a flourishing ranching community emerged that drove large herds to markets in El Salvador and Guatemala. Costa Rica exported cacao and tobacco. And, most of all, El Salvador's indigo became the major export of the isthmus. This greater economic importance of the provinces contributed to their resentment against the persistent economic and political dominance of Guatemala City, but it also caused some severe economic dislocations. During the final half-century of Hispanic rule, strong divisions began to emerge among the colonial elite regarding economic development, the role of the

Roman Catholic Church, provincial representation, and, ultimately, the question of independence from Spain.

INDEPENDENCE TO 1850

All the various issues crystallized the educated creole class into two factions that emerged after independence as the conservative and liberal parties. The liberals advocated a continuation of Bourbon policies that promoted liberal capitalism, while the conservatives looked back to the perceived harmony of Hapsburg times, with strong feudal overtones. This would have major consequences for the future of Central American nationalism.

Conservatives looked toward maintenance of the two-class society that had so long characterized Spain and Central America. They favored policies that would preserve the landholding elites in their traditional, dominant roles but also, in noblesse oblige fashion, they assured the peasants of some protection against exploitation by the liberal modernizers. Overcoming initial liberal gains at the outset of independence, these conservatives and their caudillos controlled most of Central America in the mid-nineteenth century. They preserved traditional Hispanic values and institutions, especially the Roman Catholic Church, and they rewarded loyal Indian and mestizo peasants with paternalism and respect for their communal lands. They made real, if limited, demands on the peasants, for most of whom subsistence agriculture continued to be the principal activity. In feudal style, they relied on the clergy and local caudillos and landowners for social control, peace, and security. They thus defended states' rights against national unity and were xenophobic toward foreigners who threatened their traditional society with Protestantism, democracy, and modernization.

While the conservatives welcomed expansion of agroexports, they were sensitive to the danger of upsetting native labor and land tenure patterns, and they were forcefully opposed to granting the nation's land and resources to foreigners who generally did not share their religion, language, or social and cultural values, and who might threaten the preeminent place that the conservatives held in the social structure of the provinces. Peasant insurgency against liberal innovators in the 1830s, sometimes instigated by small landlords, was instrumental in the conservative accession to power.

Liberals, by contrast, represented the segment of the Creole elite and an incipient bourgeoisie that wished to modernize Central America by imitating the economic and political success of western Europe and the United States. These "modernizers" rejected traditional Hispanic values and institutions, especially the church. They espoused classical economic liberalism, opposing monopolies while encouraging private foreign trade, immigration, and investment. They emphasized exports and treated the rural masses and their land as the principal resources to be exploited in this effort. Although republican and democratic in political theory, they became much influenced first by utilitarianism and later by positivist materialism, and were contemptuous of, even embarrassed by, the indigenous heritage of their countries. Once in power they often resorted to dictatorship to accomplish their economic goals and to defend their gains.

Thus the professionalization of the military, which became their power base, was an important trend in the late nineteenth and early twentieth centuries. The absence of stronger middle sectors in the traditional two-class Central American society and the persistence of elitist attitudes toward the masses meant, however, that in practice the liberals proceeded very differently than did the industrialized nations. Instead, there emerged elite oligarchies of planters and capitalists who cynically, and without the noblesse oblige of their conservative predecessors, continued to live off the labor of an oppressed rural population that shared little if any of the benefits of the expanded export production. On the contrary, they found their subsistence threatened by encroachment on their lands for production of export commodities.

Few Central Americans at the beginning of the nineteenth century envisioned or favored independence for the separate city-states of the Kingdom of Guatemala. But the peculiar circumstances, which Mario Rodríguez has described brilliantly in his *Cádiz Experiment* (1978), brought together both provincial resentment toward Guatemala City and greater local autonomy through the reforms of the Cádiz government in 1810 to 1814. Independence from Spain came through endorsement of Agustín Iturbide's "Plan of Iguala" on 15 September 1821, by a council of notables in Guatemala City. Following the brief continuation of the Kingdom of Guatemala within Iturbide's Mexican Empire (1822–1823), an elected assembly dominated by liberals met in Guatemala City and on 1 July 1823 declared independence from Mexico and organized the United Provinces of the Center of America (Provincias Unidas del Centro de América). In 1824 it adopted a republican constitution providing for a loose federation of Guatemala, El Salvador, Honduras, Nicaragua, and Costa Rica. Chiapas had elected to stay with Mexico in 1823, and Panama had become part of Gran Colombia in 1821.

From the outset, the failure of federal leaders to enforce the constitutional provisions led to fragmentation of the union. Provincial jealousies and ideological differences that had emerged in the late colonial period had already sown the seeds of disunion. In the first presidential election (1825) Manuel José Arce, a liberal Salvadoran army officer, won a disputed election over a moderate Honduran attorney and prominent intellectual, José Cecilio del Valle. The intrigue connected with the electoral process alienated not only conservatives supporting Valle but also extreme liberals, who accused Arce of selling out to conservatives in the congress. Arce did, in fact, ally himself with conservative interests in Guatemala City, and when the liberal Guatemalan state government became hostile toward him, he deposed Governor Juan Barrundia and replaced him with the staunchly conservative Mariano Aycinena. This act prompted the Salvadoran state government to rebel, touching off a civil war in 1826 that produced animosities throughout the federation that would last beyond the brief life of the United Provinces.

Liberal victory in 1829, under the leadership of Honduran general Francisco Morazán, resulted in a sweeping reform program that included strong anticlericalism, promotion of infrastructure and agroexports, integration of the Indian population, and approval of new judicial and penal codes, notably including trial by jury and, in Guatemala, the ill-advised adoption of the Livingston Codes. Under Morazán's presidency (1831–1839), the liberals exiled prominent conservatives, including the archbishop and other clergy. Morazán also moved the federal capital from Guatemala City to San Salvador in 1834.

This disintegration of the old kingdom is of crucial importance to Central America's subsequent history. Struggles emerged between conservative and liberal creole elites in every province, as well as between provinces. Fighting was especially bitter between Guatemala City and San Salvador and between the Nicaraguan cities of Granada and León. But nearly as serious were conflicts between Comayagua and Tegucigalpa in Honduras and among the four towns of the Costa Rican central valley, where liberal San José ultimately emerged victorious over traditional Cartago. Quetzaltenango and other towns of western Guatemala also harbored separatist sentiments that surfaced in unsuccessful secession movements in 1839 and in 1848.

Resistance to the liberal reforms arose among the rural masses in El Salvador in the rebellion of the Indian leader Anastasio Aquino, beginning in 1833, but Morazán suppressed this insurrection. Disenchantment with the liberal reforms was also evident in the presidential election at the end of 1833, when opposition candidate José Cecilio del Valle defeated Morazán, but died before taking office. Morazán, as the runner-up, remained constitutionally in office, confirmed by a new election in February 1835. In Guatemala, opposition to the liberal policies of Governor Mariano Gálvez—including anticlericalism, land grants to foreigners, judicial reform, and imposition of a general head tax—combined with panic caused by a serious cholera epidemic ignited a peasant revolt beginning in 1837. Encouraged by the rural clergy and led by the charismatic Rafael Carrera, the peasants toppled Gálvez and sharply divided the liberals in Guatemala, allowing the conservatives to gain control.

Meanwhile, western Guatemala, under liberal leadership, seceded and formed a sixth state, called Los Altos. Carrera quickly reconquered these departments in January 1840, however, and when Morazán brought federal troops into the conflict, Carrera defeated him decisively at Guatemala City in March 1840. The federation was already in disarray, as Nicaragua, Honduras, and Costa Rica had seceded in 1838. Morazán fled to Chiriquí in Colombian Panama. He returned two years later and briefly took over the government of Costa Rica, but in this action he not only failed to reunite the states but also inspired a Costa Rican reaction that ended in his own execution before a firing squad on 15 September 1842.

Even at that, conservatives as well as liberals were reluctant to abandon national union. The states formed a conservative alliance in 1842, which served to prevent the liberals from regaining control. Despite their declared preference for reunion, however, the conservative caudillos of the mid-nineteenth century laid the foundations for the modern city-state republics of Central America. Guatemala in 1847 and Costa Rica in 1848, in their fervor to prevent a return of the Morazanistas, declared their states to be republics, and the other states followed their lead within a decade.

1850 TO 1945

Even in the symbolic declarations of independence from the defunct federation, the countries reiterated their hopes for reunion at "a more propitious time." Carrera's stunning defeat of a liberal National Army at Arada, Guatemala, in February 1851 destroyed whatever chances a reunification effort organized by José Francisco Barrundia and other liberals might have had, and a conservative "National Campaign" under the leadership of Costa Rica's Juan Rafael Mora defeated William Walker's unionist aspirations in 1857. Walker had come to the aid of Nicaraguan liberals and then established himself as president of that state. A strong Costa Rican–Guatemalan axis throughout the mid-nineteenth century, both before and after the Walker episode, prevented the middle states from returning to liberalism.

That "more propitious time" has come and gone frequently, with more than a hundred attempts at reunification between 1824 and 1965. The liberal resurgence that recovered control of all the states before 1900 appeared propitious to some, especially to liberal caudillos Justo Rufino Barrios (1873–1885) of Guatemala and José Santos Zelaya of Nicaragua (1893–1909), who sought to reunite the isthmus under their respective military leadership.

In reality, the liberal caudillos brought a different kind of unity to the isthmus in their common policies of welcoming foreign, especially United States, capital to the region. In a very real sense, the United States provided the kind of external unity over the region in the twentieth century that Spain had lost at the beginning of the nineteenth century and that Great Britain had only partially achieved in the mid-nineteenth century.

Estimates of Central American population (1500–2025)	
Year	Population
1500	2,500,000
1778	805,339
1810	1,000,000
1824	1,287,491
1855	2,000,000
1915	4,915,133
1930	6,018,880
1945	8,141,493
1955	9,155,000
1965	12,515,000
1975	17,670,000
1985	24,218,000
1995	28,910,000
2000	32,201,000
2005	35,544,000
2015	42,590,000
2025	49,288,000

SOURCE: R.L. Woodward, Jr., *Central America, a Nation Divided*, 2nd ed. (1985); U.S. Census Bureau, Population Division, International Database (IDB), http://www.census.gov/ipc/www/idb/. Panama is not included in these figures.

Table 1

In the early twentieth century, Nicaraguan writer Salvador Mendieta spearheaded another unionist movement that, although it failed, helped to generate interstate cooperative agencies and laid a foundation for the later integration movement. A Mendieta-inspired Unionist Party won the Guatemalan presidency briefly in 1920, but traditional liberals displaced it a year later.

Central Americans have often charged that foreign nations—Britain in the nineteenth century, the United States in the twentieth—have sabotaged unity, following a divide-and-conquer policy. Certainly there is some truth to the charge with regard to the activities of nationals and diplomats of both English-speaking countries. It was, for example, easier for the giant fruit companies to deal with small, weak states than with a larger, united republic. Yet had there not been substantial internal causes of disunity for foreigners to exploit, Central Americans might still have achieved union.

After World War II foreign aid programs, particularly from the United States but also from international organizations, focused on the need for Central American unity and engendered a spirit of cooperation. Working with the United States Agency for International Development (formerly

International Cooperation Administration) and United Nations organizations, the Central American states launched multilateral programs that promoted a spirit of unity at least among the technocrats and politicians associated with them. Cultural and ideological unity came more gradually with programs to eliminate unnecessary duplication in Central American universities and vocational schools.

These foreign assistance programs imposed a kind of unity over the region. Studies made by private corporations and foundations, by national and international governmental agencies, and by academicians in several disciplines encouraged the five states to collaborate in facing common problems. Movement toward economic integration and its accompanying interstate organizations promoted cooperation and unity on the isthmus, as did a rise in interstate investment and the advent of better transportation and communication among the states. Symbolically, the printing of "Centro-América" on the automobile license tags in all five states reflected the new spirit of unity.

Unfortunately, aide programs were often ill conceived and not applicable to the particular problems of Central America. The failure of the United States to support the socioeconomic reforms of Juan José Arévalo, the Sandinistas, and other progressive forces attached an aura of reaction to United States programs that made them suspect to many Central Americans. At the same time, the military grew and often became the principal beneficiary of aid programs. The refusal of most U.S. aid programs to recognize the need for basic restructuring of the society and economy of the region was at the heart of the failure of the programs to achieve greater change. Many Central Americans saw the programs simply as devices to maintain the region in economic dependence on the capitalists.

FROM 1945 TO 1994
With more progressive governments in Guatemala, Costa Rica, and El Salvador following World War II—and even some spirit of the benefits of cooperation evidence in Honduras and Nicaragua—the movement for unity picked up. Guatemalan and Salvadoran initiatives led to a general meeting of Central American foreign ministers in October 1951, from which came plans for the formation of the Organization of Central American States

(ODECA), formally founded in 1955. In 1952 economic ministers of the five states met in Tegucigalpa with the United Nations Economic Commission for Latin America, leading eventually to a 1958 treaty for Central American economic integration that included the Central American Common Market (CACM), a series of trade agreements, and planned industries, which expanded through the 1960s. Costa Rica, the most prosperous state, was reluctant to cooperate fully, fearing competition from countries with cheap labor and especially distrustful of Nicaragua. Thus, a full common market was never achieved, but substantial advances were made, particularly in Guatemala, El Salvador, and Honduras, where new industrial establishments blossomed. Panama also was a limited member of the CACM. Other results of the cooperation included an acceleration in road building and completion of the Pan-American Highway to Panama in 1964. These improvements promoted interstate trade, industry, and tourism, although political instability limited these advances.

The two-week Football War between El Salvador and Honduras in the summer of 1969 brought a halt to the growth of the CACM and emphasized that without stronger political cooperation, economic union was precarious. The Central American states had settled most disputes amicably since World War II, but the outbreak of this war brought back memories of the frequent civil wars and the meddling in each other's affairs so common earlier. It abruptly interrupted a decade of growth and economic diversification. Although interstate trade soon reached pre-1969 levels and there was modest commercial growth throughout most of the 1970s, in the aftermath of that clash careful analysis revealed not only that economic union could go only so far without closer political confederation but also that the CACM had not been uniformly beneficial for all five states. The Permanent Secretariat for Economic Integration of Central America (SIECA) concluded that if it was truly to benefit the entire region, there would have to be provision for redistribution of the generated wealth that flowed from one region to another as a result of trade patterns.

The worsening economic and social conditions stimulated by rampant inflation and the worldwide oil crisis led to the formation of the High-Level Committee, which drafted a treaty in 1976 that, if adopted, would have extended the integration movement to total trade liberalization, standardization of foreign investment rules, tax harmonization, free movement of labor and capital, a common agricultural policy, a coordinated system of basic industries, and a unified social policy that promoted health, nutrition, housing, support of labor unions, and harmonization of social security and minimum wages. This progressive proposal, however, was rejected by all five states, and the integration movement lost its earlier momentum. The failure of the Central American elites to seize this opportunity was far more damaging than the Football War, reflecting selfish concerns to protect privileged positions within their respective city-states.

The economic problems and political turmoil of the late 1970s fragmented the isthmus and made integration seem remote. The rise of the Sandinistas in Nicaragua and the guerrilla warfare in El Salvador and Guatemala curtailed traffic on the Pan-American Highway, meanwhile the real value of exports fell for all of the states. Yet hope did not die, and the violence and economic decline of the 1980s once again emphasized the desirability of unity. Encouraged especially by Presidents Vinicio Cerezo of Guatemala, Oscar Arias Sánchez of Costa Rica, and Daniel Ortega of Nicaragua, this new interest in unity resulted by 1990 in renewed plans for integration and a Central American parliament modeled on that of the European community. Although Costa Rica's legislature kept that state aloof from this initiative, the other four states proceeded to hold elections and organize the Central American Parliament with guarded optimism.

By 1980 political and economic crisis in Central America had made it the focus of an East-West confrontation that brought new manifestations of U.S. hegemony over the region. The pattern of military dictatorship in all of the states except Costa Rica had intensified in reaction to the rise of Fidel Castro after 1959. A military phase of the Central American integration movement was the formation, beginning in 1963, by Guatemala, Honduras, El Salvador, and Nicaragua of the Central American Defense Council (CONDECA) with strong U.S. support. The 1969 war weakened this organization when Honduras pulled out, and in the 1970s it faded into near obscurity, with greater emphasis being placed on economic and social development. After the 1968 Medellín Episcopal Conference, the Roman Catholic church began to promote, with some success, greater attention to the plight of the poor and oppressed, contributing to a new international awareness of the problem of human rights violations and social injustice in Central America. International organizations began to focus on Guatemala, Nicaragua, and El Salvador, and they often scored the United States for its support of repressive regimes in those countries. When Secretary of State Henry Kissinger visited Costa Rica and Guatemala in February 1976, he was greeted with riots and outcries against U.S. support of reactionary regimes in Latin America.

President Jimmy Carter (1977–1981) sought to establish a more humanitarian United States policy, but his pro-human rights policy brought stiff opposition from elites in Guatemala and El Salvador, especially after the 1979 overthrow of Anastasio Somoza in Nicaragua. Carter also pushed through treaties under which the United States agreed to turn over the Panama Canal to Panama by the year 2000, ending severely strained relations between the United States and Panama, and helping the government of strongman Omar Torrijos to reverse the unfavorable economic trends in his country. Although the Carter government opposed the Sandinistas in Nicaragua, it accepted their victory gracefully, and in late September 1979 the U.S. Congress approved a Nicaraguan aid package.

The election of Ronald Reagan in 1980, however, brought a sharp reversal of these policies. Reagan had opposed transfer of the Canal Zone, and his administration obstructed implementation of the 1977 treaties, risking deteriorating relations with Panama in a period when that state was undergoing political adjustments following the 1981 death of Torrijos in a plane crash. Reagan cultivated better relations with the Central American armies, however. Soon after taking office he resumed sales of military items to Guatemala, sent military advisers to El Salvador, and suspended aid to Nicaragua. By November 1981 Reagan had begun support of covert operations against the Nicaraguan government, and soon afterward the Nicaraguan Contras emerged to launch a civil war aimed at overthrowing the Sandinistas. He also increased U.S. support against guerrilla opposition forces in El Salvador.

From the outset of his administration, it was clear that Reagan intended to roll back the revolutionary tide in Central America and to make the isthmus a theater in the escalating confrontation with Soviet power. The U.S. presence was most obvious in Honduras, where a massive U.S. military and naval buildup supported the militarization of Honduras and aid to the Nicaraguan contras in an effort to intimidate both the Sandinistas and the Salvadoran guerrillas. In 1983, with the strong backing of the Reagan administration, Honduras, Guatemala, El Salvador, and Panama resurrected CONDECA, with Nicaragua excluded and Costa Rica, emphasizing its neutrality, declining participation. But the Reagan administration played on traditional Costa Rican fear of Nicaragua to encourage a military buildup in that country as well.

As debate over U.S. policy heightened, Reagan named Henry Kissinger in 1983 to head a bipartisan commission to study Central America. The committee's report, although providing considerable evidence that the basic problems on the isthmus were socioeconomic, concluded with an endorsement of the military policies of the Reagan government. It also called, however, for a massive economic and social aid program, which the Reagan government began to implement. A rapidly deteriorating economic crisis in Nicaragua accompanied continued United States support of the contras after 1985. After much negotiation a peace initiative by Costa Rican president Oscar Arias Sánchez finally succeeded in 1989. The United States agreed to disband the contras and the Sandinistas agreed to hold free elections, which in 1990 brought to power an anti-Sandinista coalition strongly linked to the old Conservative Party and United States interests under the presidency of Violeta Barrios De Chamorro, widow of the slain *La Prensa* editor who had opposed the Somoza dynasty.

Reagan's successor, George Bush (1989–1993), continued the military approach to Central American problems, however. In Panama, General Manuel Noriega challenged American interests there after having collaborated with the CIA for years. President Bush cited Noriega's role in drug trafficking as justification for a U.S. invasion of Panama in December 1989 but was obviously concerned about Noriega's ties to Cuba. Noriega was captured and brought to the United States, where he was convicted of violating U.S. drug laws. A successor government under Guillermo Endara,

widely regarded as a U.S. puppet government, however, appeared to allow continuation of the drug trafficking at an even higher level than under Noriega. Meanwhile, the collapse of the Eastern bloc, beginning in 1989, ended the perceived Soviet threat in Central America, and U.S. direct interest in the region dropped sharply.

As the twentieth century closed, the middle and working classes were continuing to challenge the power of creole oligarchies that had inherited power at independence. Yet while the Reagan-Bush Central American policy had verbalized a great deal about its support of the democratization of Central America, much of the progress was superficial and limited to the supervision of free elections. A 1991 poll of Latin American academic specialists in the United States (the 1991 Fitzgibbon-Johnson Image-Index on Latin American Democracy, conducted by Phil Kelly of Emporia State University) rated Costa Rica as the most democratic of the twenty Latin American republics; Nicaragua placed tenth, and Honduras (seventeenth), Guatemala (eighteenth), and El Salvador (nineteenth) ranked above only Haiti in the poll. While some of the more visible manifestations of military rule in those states have been camouflaged, the serious social and economic obstacles to democracy remain strong.

Chances of Central American reunion as of 2007 seem more unlikely than at any time since 1839, but the appeal of union remains irresistible. If governments representing a broader segment of the population gain power and can check the self-serving policies of the elites, then the hopes of Francisco Morazán and Salvador Mendieta for a single Central American republic may yet come to fruition. Steve Ropp has written an article entitled "Central America in Search of a Cavour," which notes striking similarities between nineteenth-century Italy and contemporary Central America. Once initiated, a progress toward a rejuvenated Central American republic could come rapidly, and the new Central American Parliament may well be a step in that direction. But for the early twenty-first century, while cooperation at many levels will probably resume, it is just as likely that Central America will remain divided into five sovereign states with strong nationalistic elements that emphasize their unique differences rather than their common problems.

See also **Central America, Independence of; Indigenous Peoples; Organization of Central American States (ODECA); United States-Latin American Relations.**

BIBLIOGRAPHY

There are useful bibliographical volumes on each Central American country in Clio Press's World Bibliographical Series. Ralph Lee Woodward, Jr., *Central America, a Nation Divided*, 3d ed. (1993), is a general history of Central America in English; for the post-Independence period James Dunkerley, *Power in the Isthmus: A Political History of Modern Central America* (1988), is much more detailed. Héctor Pérez Brignoli, *A Brief History of Central America*, translated by Ricardo B. Sawrey and Susana Stettri de Sawrey, 2d ed. (1989), and Rodolfo Pastor, *Historia de Centroamérica* (1988), offer Central American interpretations. Leslie Bethell, ed., *Central America Since Independence* (1991), conveniently provides the pertinent chapters from *The Cambridge History of Latin America*, 10 vols. (1984–1994). Although over a century old, Hubert Howe Bancroft, *History of Central America*, 3 vols. (1883–1887), still has much utility, especially in its presentation of the liberal interpretation. Mary W. Helms, *Middle America: A Culture History of Heartlands and Frontiers* (1975), surveys isthmian history from an anthropological perspective from pre-Columbian to modern times. For the colonial period, see Murdo J. Macleod, *Spanish Central America: A Socioeconomic History, 1520–1720* (1973), and Miles Wortman, *Government and Society in Central America, 1680–1840* (1982). Severo Martínez Peláez, *La patria del criollo* (1971), is an extended interpretive essay by a leading Guatemalan historian that offers a detailed description of the colonial social structure and the formation of the creole mentality. Mario Rodríguez, *The Cádiz Experiment in Central America, 1808 to 1826* (1978), is a superb study on the independence period and the influence of the Spanish Constitution of 1812 in Central America; Thomas L. Karnes, *The Failure of Union: Central America, 1824–1975*, rev. ed. (1976), describes the failure of the Central American federation and surveys attempts to revive it throughout the nineteenth and twentieth centuries. Ralph Lee Woodward, Jr., *Rafael Carrera and the Emergence of the Republic of Guatemala, 1821–1871* (1993), deals with the first half-century of independence, with particular attention to Guatemala.

Lowell Gudmundson, *Costa Rica Before Coffee: Society and Economy on the Eve of the Export Boom* (1986), provides an excellent reevaluation of the early development of Costa Rica, including considerable discussion of the myths of Costa Rican history and its historiography. David Browning, *El Salvador, Landscape and Society* (1971), is an excellent description of land use and tenure in El Salvador, with relevance for understanding the relation between land and history throughout the region. E. Bradford Burns, *The Poverty of Progress: Latin America in the Nineteenth Century* (1980), pays considerable attention to Central America and calls attention to the damage done to folk culture by the liberal economic policies of the nineteenth century. E. Bradford Burns, *Patriarch and Folk: The Emergence of Nicaragua, 1798–1858* (1991), interprets nineteenth-century Nicaragua within that framework. The early-twentieth-century problems of Central America are described in excruciating detail in Salvador Mendieta, *Alrededor del problema unionista de Centro-América*, 2 vols. (1934), and *La enfermedad de Centro-América*, 3 vols. (1910–1934).

Victor Bulmer-Thomas, *The Political Economy of Central America Since 1920* (1987), stresses the difficulties created by Central American emphasis on export-led economic development. Robert G. Williams, *Export Agriculture and the Crisis in Central America* (1986), focuses on the cotton and beef industries since World War II, explaining their impact on the social and political crises of the 1980s. William Durham, *Scarcity and Survival in Central America: Ecological Origins of the Soccer War* (1979), is a superb study that pursues the underlying causes of the 1969 war between El Salvador and Honduras and exposes many of the socioeconomic problems of Central America and their long-term historical consequences. A number of anthologies focus on the crises of the 1980s, but from a historical perspective the most useful include Steve C. Ropp and James A. Morris, eds., *Central America: Crisis and Adaptation* (1984), and Ralph Lee Woodward, Jr., ed., *Central America: Historical Perspectives on the Contemporary Crises* (1988). See also Steve C. Ropp, "Waiting for Cavour: The Current Central America Crisis and Unification," in *Proceedings of the Pacific Coast Council on Latin American Studies* 12 (1985–1986): 109–118.

Additional Bibliography

Dym, Irene, and Christophe Belaubre, eds. *Politics, Economy, and Society in Bourbon Central America, 1759–1821.* Boulder: University Press of Colorado, 2007.

Gambone, Michael D. *Capturing the Revolution: The United States, Central America, and Nicaragua, 1961–1972.* Westport, CT: Praeger, 2001.

Leiva Vivas, Rafael. *La unión centroamericana: Utopía, lirismo y desafío.* Tegucigalpa, Honduras: ENAG, Empresa Nacional Artes Gráficas, 2004.

RALPH LEE WOODWARD JR.

CENTRAL AMERICA, INDEPENDENCE OF.

At the end of the eighteenth century the captaincy general of Guatemala, also known as the Kingdom of Guatemala, encompassed the five modern-day Central American republics as well as the state of Chiapas y Soconusco, today part of Mexico. At the time, the area had a population of about 1 million. Its urban centers did not boast large populations. Among the most important were Guatemala City, with approximately 20,000 inhabitants, and San Salvador, with fewer than 15,000. Communications among the provinces was difficult. Compared to New Spain and Peru, the captaincy general of Guatemala was of peripheral importance. The chief sources of wealth for its colonizers were land and Indians. Natural dyes were its chief exports.

The turn of the nineteenth century marked the beginning of events that would determine the destiny of the entire captaincy general of Guatemala. First, the Bourbon reforms gave political power to several cities, San Salvador among them, through the creation of Intendancies. Second, Napoleon's invasion of Spain in 1808 broke the economic connections necessary for the commercialization of Central America's prime source of revenue: indigo. Third, there was political upheaval, which brought about the revolt led by Miguel Hidalgo y Costilla and José Morelos y Pavón in Mexico.

During this period, rash attempts to secure independence occurred in Nicaragua, El Salvador, and Honduras from 1811 to 1813. In 1814 a conspiracy against Spanish power arose in Guatemala City, but the authorities managed to quell it at its beginning. An important figure in these events was Field Marshal José Bustamante y Guerra, who from 1811 to 1818 fought any separatist attempts with a firm hand.

The political atmosphere in Guatemala City began to change in 1820, with the restoration of the liberal Constitution of 1812. On one side, radical professionals, educated at the University of San Carlos and led by Pedro Molina, attacked the old colonial system. On the other, a more conservative group, led by José Cecilio del Valle, kept hope alive for the continuation of Spanish power. Members of the Guatemalan elite sought to break the Spanish commercial monopoly that had brought them serious economic problems.

In 1821 events in Mexico changed the panorama. The Mexican *criollos*, under the leadership of Agustín de Iturbide, managed to move without major violence from an absolute to a constitutional monarchy. News of Mexican independence and the Plan of Iguala spread rapidly throughout Central America. Chiapas joined the movement in September of that

year. Field Marshal Gabino Gaínza yielded to demands for a meeting of the different institutions on 15 September. That day, after a stormy session, Guatemalan political independence was declared. Although control of the government remained in the hands of the Spanish bureaucracy under Gaínza, through a maneuver by conservatives, Guatemala was annexed to the Mexican Empire of Iturbide on 5 January 1822. In July of that same year, Iturbide sent Vicente Filísola to take possession of the captaincy general.

Rejection of the annexation by several Central American cities resulted in war, particularly against San Salvador. With the destruction of the Mexican Empire, Filísola convoked a constituent assembly that began 24 June 1823. On 1 July 1823 the assembly declared Central America free and independent, adopting the name United Provinces of Central America. This put an end to Spanish domination and the annexation to Mexico, and was the definitive beginning of independent life for the region.

See also **Central America; El Salvador; Guatemala; Guatemala City; Honduras; Iturbide, Agustín de; Molina, Pedro; Morelos y Pavón, José María; Nicaragua.**

BIBLIOGRAPHY

Mario Rodríguez, *The Cádiz Experiment in Central America* (1978).

Julio César Pinto Soria, *Centroamérica: De la independencia al estado nacional (1800–1840)* (1989).

Carlos Meléndez, *La independencia de Centroamérica* (1993).

Ralph Lee Woodward, Jr., *Rafael Carrera and the Emergence of the Republic of Guatemala, 1821–1871* (1993).

Additional Bibliography

Dym, Irene, and Christophe Belaubre, eds. *Politics, Economy, and Society in Bourbon Central America, 1759–1821.* Boulder: University Press of Colorado, 2007.

Hawkins, Timothy. *José De Bustamante and Central American Independence: Colonial Administration in an Age of Imperial Crisis.* Tuscaloosa: University of Alabama, 2004.

OSCAR G. PELÁEZ ALMENGOR

CENTRAL AMERICA, UNITED PROVINCES OF. United Provinces of Central America, a loose confederation of former Spanish colonies that had comprised most of the captaincy general of

Guatemala from the middle of the sixteenth century until their independence from Spain in 1821. This captaincy or "kingdom," as it was popularly known, included present-day Guatemala, El Salvador, Honduras, Nicaragua, and Costa Rica, as well as other jurisdictions, such as Chiapas, no longer considered part of Central America. As the United Provinces, they clung together with varying degrees of unity until their complete separation and the disintegration of any semblance of a central government in 1838.

Three centuries of colonial experience provided scant evidence that these provinces might ever become a single nation-state. The Central American region had been conquered by expeditions launched from Panama, Santo Domingo, and Mexico, creating a variety of interests, loyalties, and responsibilities. Poor communications meant that these feelings extended most strongly to the village or town around which settlers tended to cluster. The larger communities, generally greater distances apart, were usually governed by a council or *ayuntamiento* in something of the manner of a city-state. While higher-ranking colonial officials almost always were Spanish-born and Spanish-oriented, the members of the *ayuntamientos* tended to be creoles, American-born persons of Spanish ancestry. With the passage of time, council members in the larger towns often formed a small, tight aristocracy, not democratic but strongly representing local interests of the elite against Spain and forming the nucleus of a growing Americanism.

Such developments were, of course, not Spain's intent. The Hapsburgs created an elaborate centralism for America, and their Bourbon successors in the eighteenth century attempted to tighten the system even more. Central Americans fell under the jurisdiction of the vast viceroyalty of New Spain with its capital in faraway Mexico City; one division of the viceroyalty was the audiencia of Guatemala, whose presiding officer was generally a captain-general. Time, distance, and travel conditions meant that in most administrative matters Mexico City was bypassed by the Central Americans.

By the eighteenth century the capital at Guatemala had become a city of some stature, as effective as a viceroyalty; its aristocratic families carried out their roles in commensurate fashion. But even this kingdom could not reach authoritatively to most of Central America; the provincials ran their own affairs as much as possible, and viewed Guatemala as something of an expensive nuisance. Worse, the large city of San Salvador yearned to run more of its own political and religious affairs.

Lacking the mineral wealth of Peru or Mexico, the kingdom of Guatemala never equaled their importance in the Spanish scheme of things. Most of the folk in the kingdom were peasants or small farmers living out their lives in obscure labor; a few others were into the export business and made good profits by working with Europeans. So the decades passed slowly, sometimes peacefully, sometimes in turbulence, but gradually strengthening local feelings.

Although in the backwash of Spanish intellectualism, the Central Americans were not ignorant of the ideas of freedom the Enlightenment brought to Europe. Napoleon I's invasion of Spain and his overthrow of the monarchy disconnected the metropolitan power from its colonies and forced some rethinking by colonial *ayuntamientos* about their future status. Dreams of a brighter place in the empire's sun died with the return of King Ferdinand VII and his reactionary regime.

Barring a few minor skirmishes, no Central American war of independence took place. But the issue of freedom was argued in every *ayuntamiento,* some colonials favoring a return to the empire and others seeking improved status within the Mexican orbit. Still others demanded "independence from Spain, Mexico, and every other power." In the end, the last group won out, and following a brief annexation to the Mexican Empire of Agustín de Iturbide (1822–1823), Central American provinces—and towns—made individual decisions about their sovereignty. The majority agreed upon a consolidated government for Central America, free from Spain *and* Mexico.

The United Provinces of Central America drew up a constitution in 1824, the same five states of Guatemala, El Salvador, Honduras, Nicaragua, and Costa Rica now calling themselves the Federal Republic of Central America. Partially copying several constitutions, including that of the United States and that of Spain (1812), the framers called for a federal type of government with certain powers retained by the states and others granted to the national government. Given time, a nation might have evolved. But there was no time. The rulers of the old kingdom wanted a strong governmental presence in Guatemala; the provinces wanted greater rights for the states; the old tax structure had been destroyed and poorly replaced; San Salvador wanted its own bishop; there was electoral fraud, village rivalries, and suspicions—these matters and many others surfaced on the withdrawal of Spain's restraining hands.

A Salvadoran Liberal, Manuel José Arce, was elected president in 1825, governing from the temporary capital in Guatemala City. Needing support against the demands—and accusations—of Liberals outside the capital, Arce linked himself with the elite families, frightening his original backers. Salvadorans brought up the bishop question. In each state personalist and ideological issues surfaced. Most states faced local civil war; Costa Rica tried to ignore all the others. A series of battles between 1826 and 1829 resulted in victory for the Liberals, now led by Francisco Morazán, a Honduran who forced the Arce government into exile and assumed the presidency of the federation.

Morazán, reelected in 1835, has since been recognized by most Central Americans as the soul of the federation movement. But his liberal reforms were too broad and too sudden for many of his people, and they caused fear. Secession movements, a cholera epidemic, and a revolt of peasants led by an able caudillo, José Rafael Carrera, led to Morazán's overthrow. Government reverted to localism, and the federation came to an end. The five states went their own ways.

On twenty-five or more occasions since 1838, groups of Central American states have attempted to reunite in some fashion. Failure followed every effort, even when all five states participated in the attempt. In spite of all the obvious advantages that a greater Central America might bring, the five states still cling tenaciously to their sovereignty.

See also Arce, Manuel José; Central America; Central America, Independence of; Costa Rica; El Salvador; Ferdinand VII of Spain; Guatemala; Guatemala City; Honduras; Napoleon I; Nicaragua.

BIBLIOGRAPHY

Hubert H. Bancroft, *History of Central America*, vol. 3 (1887).

Salvador Mendieta, *Alrededor del problema unionista de Centro-América* (1926).

Rodrigo Facio, *Trayectorio y crisis de la Federación Centroamericana* (1949).

Robert S. Chamberlain, *Francisco Morazán: Champion of Central American Federation* (1950).

Pedro Joaquín Chamorro Cardenal, *Historia de la Federación de la América Central* (1951).

Alberto Herrarte, *La unión de Centro América* (1955).

Andrés Townsend Ezcurra, *Las provincias unidas de Centroamérica* (1958).

Thomas L. Karnes, *The Failure of Union: Central America, 1824–1975*, rev. ed. (1976).

Ralph Lee Woodward, Jr., *Central America: A Nation Divided* (1976).

Additional Bibliography

Gudmundson, Lowell, and Héctor Lindo-Fuentes. *Central America, 1821–1871: Liberalism Before Liberal Reform.* Tuscaloosa: University of Alabama Press, 1995.

Leiva Vivas, Rafael. *La unión centroamericana: Utopía, lirismo y desafío.* Tegucigalpa, Honduras: ENAG, Empresa Nacional Artes Gráficas, 2004.

THOMAS L. KARNES

CENTRAL AMERICA, UNITED PROVINCES OF, CONSTITUTION OF 1824.

The Constitution of 1824, the first constitution of the United Provinces of the Center of America, was put into effect in November 1824 by the National Constituent Assembly but was not ratified by the first elected congress until August 1825.

The constitution was based heavily on the Spanish Constitution of 1812, with some influence from the U.S. Constitution of 1789. José Cecilio del Valle played a leading role in its formulation as a compromise between liberal and conservative principals. It came to be regarded as the prototype of liberal constitutions in the subsequent Central American republics of Guatemala, El Salvador, Honduras, Nicaragua, and Costa Rica throughout the nineteenth century. It established Roman Catholicism as the state religion, excluding any other public worship, but limited the clergy's participation in government. It outlawed slavery and guaranteed individual liberties and provided for a unicameral congress with a relatively weak executive, except for his command of the armed forces. The constitution also provided for a senate (with two senators from each state) that had to approve all legislation and could veto acts of the congress, which could override senate votes with a two-thirds majority. The senate could not initiate legislation and was actually more of an executive council than part of the legislature. Supreme Court justices were elected for two-year, staggered terms. In providing the framework for a federation of the five autonomous states, a major weakness of the document was the lack of sufficient power at the national level.

See also **Central America, United Provinces of; Valle, José Cecilio del.**

BIBLIOGRAPHY

The Constitution of 1824 may be found in Luis Mariñas Otero, *Las constituciones de Guatemala* (1958), as well as in other compilations of the constitutions of the Central American states. Jorge Mario García Laguardia has written extensively on the development of this constitution, most notably in *La génesis del constitucionalismo guatemalteco* (1971); Mario Rodríguez has described the importance of the Constitution of 1812 to its formulation in *The Cádiz Experiment in Central America, 1810 to 1826* (1978). For briefer discussions of its relevance to Central American history, see Thomas Karnes, *Failure of Union* (1965); and Ralph Lee Woodward, Jr., "The Aftermath of Independence, 1821–c. 1870," in *Central America Since Independence*, edited by Leslie Bethell (1991), pp. 10–12.

Additional Bibliography

Gudmundson, Lowell, and Héctor Lindo-Fuentes. *Central America, 1821–1871: Liberalism Before Liberal Reform.* Tuscaloosa: University of Alabama Press, 1995.

Leiva Vivas, Rafael. *La unión centroamericana: Utopía, lirismo y desafío.* Tegucigalpa, Honduras: ENAG, Empresa Nacional Artes Gráficas, 2004.

RALPH LEE WOODWARD JR.

CENTRAL AMERICAN COMMON MARKET (CACM).

The Central American Common Market (CACM) is an economic agreement among the five Central American countries (Costa Rica, El Salvador, Guatemala, Honduras, and Nicaragua). This movement toward regional economic integration commenced in 1951 with adoption of a resolution by the United Nations Economic Commission for Latin America (ECLA). Years of study and negotiation followed.

In 1958, the five countries, under the tutelage of ECLA, concluded two agreements: the Multilateral Treaty on Central American Free Trade and Economic Integration and the Convention on the Regime of Central American Integration Industries. The former, entered into force on 2 June 1959, provided for limited intraregional free trade, with additional items to be made subject to free trade over a ten-year period. The latter agreement provided for protected regional "integration industries" (those requiring free access, without competition, to the entire Central American market in order to be economically viable). The industries were to be allocated among the five countries. Costa Rica signed, but did not ratify, the agreements. Its failure to do so rendered the convention inoperational.

In 1960, a three-country (El Salvador, Guatemala, and Honduras) agreement backed by the United States—the Treaty of Economic Association—was signed. It created an expanded and accelerated movement toward integration. Only fifty-five items were exempted from regional free trade. The treaty created a development assistance fund and a set of regional institutions—neither were provided for in the earlier protocols. The free-trade area would become a common market after five years, provided that the signatories had equalized external tariffs. The treaty did not incorporate integration industries.

The Treaty of Economic Association created crisis in the regionwide movement toward economic integration and prompted all five Central American countries to conclude yet another agreement, the General Treaty of Central American Economic Integration, this time under ECLA tutelage, in December 1960. This treaty provided for immediate regional free trade for all except a very small number of products. It stipulated that virtually all exempted products would be freely traded in five years. It also provided for a uniform external tariff and a common market in five years. Integration industries were incorporated. Additionally, the treaty established a set of institutions and provided for the establishment of the Central American Bank for Economic Integration. The treaty was signed and ratified by all but Costa Rica, which offered economic reasons for its refusal but in reality acted out of a sense of distinctiveness from the rest of Central America. In 1963 it reversed its position.

Under the free-trade provisions, intra–Central American trade grew dramatically—from $8.3 million in 1950 to $32.7 million in 1960 to $213.6 million in 1967. Central America experienced considerable economic growth in the 1960s and into the 1970s, averaging 5.8 percent per year. Most of the growth took place in the urban industrial sector under the stimulus of the common market. The common market, by creating a regional market free of most trade barriers, made feasible a greater degree of industrial development than would have been possible in five separate markets.

The common market's impact was not entirely positive. It did nothing to promote development of the agrarian sector. And because the common market adhered to free-market forces, the bulk of the industrial development that followed its creation was concentrated in El Salvador and Guatemala, already the most developed Central American countries. Much of the industrialization was capital-intensive rather than labor-intensive. The opportunities created by the common market were mainly exploited by foreign investors.

Operation of the common market was disrupted by the 1969 war between El Salvador and Honduras and its aftermath. It was even more seriously disrupted by the economic-political crises of the 1970s and 1980s. In 2004, the Central American countries, along with the Dominican Republic, negotiated a new economic agreement with the United States, called the Central American Free Trade Agreement (CAFTA). Despite the opposition of numerous civil society organizations in the United States and Central America, the treaty was ratified.

See also **Central America; Costa Rica; El Salvador; Guatemala; Honduras; Nicaragua; United Nations.**

BIBLIOGRAPHY

Bulmer-Thomas, Victor. *Integración regional en Centroamérica.* San José, Costa Rica: FLACSO; New York: Social Science Research Council, 1998.

Cline, William R., and Enrique Delgado, eds., *Economic Integration in Central America* (1978).

Cochrane, James D. *The Politics of Regional Integration: The Central American Case* (1969).

Harding, Alan S., and Jan Hoffman. *Trade between Caribbean Community (CARICOM) and Central American Common Market (CACM) Countries: The Role to Play for Ports and Shipping Services.* Santiago, Chile: United Nations CEPAL Natural Resources and Infrastructure Division Transport Unit, 2003.

Nye, Joseph S., Jr. "Central American Regional Integration," in *International Conciliation* 562 (March 1967).

Orantes, Isaac Cohen. *Regional Economic Integration in Central America* (1972).

Rodlauer, Markus, and Alfred Schipke. *Central America: Global Integration and Regional Cooperation.* Washington, DC: International Monetary Fund, 2005.

Wardlaw, Andrew B. *The Operations of the Central American Common Market* (1966), and *Achievement and Problems of the Central American Common Market* (1969).

JAMES D. COCHRANE

CENTRAL AMERICAN COURT OF JUSTICE.

Central American Court of Justice, a body created at the Central American Conference held in Washington, D.C., in November and December 1907. Escalating isthmian political turmoil and the threat of international conflict prompted the United States and Mexico—nations with specific interests in Central America—to host the meeting. Once the conference began, however, the host powers played a passive role in the proceedings, thus allowing the Central Americans to resolve their outstanding differences without any significant outside interference. Luis Anderson Morúa of Costa Rica, elected president of the conference, advocated the adoption by the Central American nations of the principle of obligatory arbitration of international disputes. With the support of the Salvadoran delegation, Anderson was able to convince the other delegates of the need to establish a Central American Court of Justice.

The court was the first international tribunal requiring mandatory adjudication of international disputes among the contracting parties, and thus represented a precedent-breaking step in international jurisprudence. The promise of the court, however, was never really fulfilled as political partisanship, more often than not, tended to influence the decisions of the judges who represented the various isthmian nations. The court ceased to function in 1918 following Nicaragua's denunciation, in the previous year, of the 1907 Washington Treaties. The Nicaraguan action came as the result of the Central American Court's ruling on the Bryan-Chamorro Treaty. The court decreed that Nicaragua, by signing the treaty with the United States, had violated preexisting treaty rights held by Costa Rica and El Salvador. Rather than accept the court's interpretation of the Bryan-Chamorro Treaty, the Nicaraguan authorities chose in effect to destroy the 1907 treaty system, and with it the Central American Court of Justice.

Though the Organization of Central American States created a regional court system in 1962, it was the Protocol of Tegucigalpa in December 1991 whereby Costa Rica, El Salvador, Guatemala, Honduras, and Nicaragua officially reestablished the Central American Court of Justice. At this time, Panama joined as a new member and Belize obtained observer status. The Protocol of Tegucigalpa established the Central American Integration System (SICA), which promoted the economic, political, and social integration of the region. As an intra-governmental decision-making body, the court contributes to this goal. Headquartered in Managua, Nicaragua, the court's principal mandate is to resolve conflicts between member nations, member and nonmember countries, and states and individuals. It also hears disputes between constitutional organs of member states. The formation of the court spurred the development of consistent norms, procedures, and jurisdictions throughout the isthmus. Headed by a secretary general, the court is run by a president and vice president from different countries.

See also **Bryan-Chamorro Treaty (1914); Central America; Organization of Central American States (ODECA); United States-Latin American Relations.**

BIBLIOGRAPHY

Dana G. Munro, *Intervention and Dollar Diplomacy in the Caribbean, 1900–1921* (1964), esp. pp. 152–153, 402–403.

Carlos José Gutiérrez Gutiérrez, *La corte de justicia centroamericana* (1978).

Additional Bibliography

Archivo Nacional (Costa Rica); Corte de Justicia Centroamericana. *Guía del fondo documental Corte de Justicia Centroamericana: 1908–1918.* Madrid: Fundación Histórica Tavera, 2000.

Chamorro Mora, Rafael. *La Corte de Justicia de la Comunidad Centroamericana.* Managua: R. Chamorro M., 2000.

Corte de Justicia Centroamericana; Universidad Nacional Autónoma de Honduras. *El tribunal centroamericano: La Corte Centroamericana de Justicia.* Tegucigalpa, Honduras: Editorial Universitaria, 1995.

Corte Centroamericana de Justica. *La Competencia de la Corte Centroamericana de Justicia.* Managua: La Corte, 1996.

Giammattei Avilés, Jorge Antonio. *Conciencia centroamericana.* 2 vols. Managua: Editorial Somarriba, 1996–2000.

Metcalf, Katrin Nyman, and Ioannis Papageorgiou. *Regional Integration and Courts of Justice.* Antwerp, Belgium: Intersentia; Holmes Beach, FL: Gaunt Inc., 2005.

RICHARD V. SALISBURY

CENTRAL AMERICAN DEFENSE COUNCIL (CONDECA).

The Central American Defense Council (Condeca) is a special regional defense organization established in 1965. Its founding member states were Guatemala, Honduras, El Salvador, and Nicaragua. Costa Rica and Panama were offered observer status. Panama accepted observer status but opposed U.S. pressure to upgrade its status to full membership; Costa Rica refused membership at any level. CONDECA was closely linked to the U.S. Southern Command (SOUTHCOM) in Panama and thus enjoyed substantial U.S. backing. Its establishment was considered the military phase of a growing movement toward Central American integration.

CONDECA emphasized development of coordinated military action against guerrilla activity to counter any perceived Soviet penetration of Central America and to foster cooperation between the national armies of the region. CONDECA proved ineffective, and its military coordination was hampered by the withdrawal of Panama in 1968, Honduras in 1973, and Nicaragua in 1979. In 1983, however, CONDECA was revived at the insistence of the Reagan administration that Nicaragua was destabilizing the region. El Salvador, Honduras, and Guatemala, with U.S. backing, reestablished CONDECA. The revival was criticized for being under the influence of Washington and for undermining the Contadora peace initiative. Despite the original intention to coordinate regional strategy, CONDECA's revival only served to strengthen the relationship between the Pentagon and the military governments of the region. With the end of the cold war and increased political stability in Central America, CONDECA ceased to exist.

See also **Central America; Costa Rica; El Salvador; Guatemala; Honduras; Nicaragua; Panama; Soviet-Latin American Relations; United States-Latin American Relations.**

BIBLIOGRAPHY

Calvert, Peter, ed. *The Central American Security System: North-South or East-West?* (1988).

Gambone, Michael D. *Capturing the Revolution: The United States, Central America, and Nicaragua, 1961–1972*. Westport, CT: Praeger, 2001.

Leiken, Robert S., ed. *Central America: Anatomy of Conflict* (1984).

LeoGrande, William M. *Our Own Backyard: The United States in Central America, 1977–1992*. Chapel Hill: University of North Carolina Press, 1998.

Rouquié, Alain. *Guerras y paz en América Central*. Mexico: Fondo de Cultura Económica, 1994.

Schooley, Helen. *Conflict in Central America* (1987).

HEATHER K. THIESSEN

CENTRAL AMERICAN MISSION (CAM).

The Central American Mission (CAM) is a nondenominational Protestant faith mission based in Dallas, Texas, for the evangelization and proselytization of Central Americans. CAM was founded in 1890 by Cyrus I. Scofield, a businessman and biblical scholar who is best remembered for his authorship of a reference Bible which still bears his name. Scofield, an adherent of dispensationalist theology, believed that the conversion of all humanity was a precondition of Christ's second coming, and he founded the CAM with the belief that the conversion of Central America to Protestantism would hasten the fulfillment of biblical prophecy. The CAM organization, while not a true denomination, continued to adhere to dispensationalist theology.

The first CAM missionaries went to Costa Rica in 1891. Three years later, a missionary couple named Dillon was sent to establish missions in northern Central America; both succumbed to fever outside the Salvadoran port of Acajutla and were buried at sea on the way there. Missions were eventually established in El Salvador and Honduras in 1896. CAM began mission work in Guatemala in 1899, and in Nicaragua in 1900.

Although CAM has always considered its primary purpose to be evangelization, it is involved in many secular projects. Until the 1960s, CAM never attracted many local converts in Central America; however, CAM-run schools and linguistic projects have long given the mission an influence disproportionate to its size. Most CAM projects in Central America are based in Guatemala, where CAM has historically enjoyed the greatest number of native converts, although prior to the 1960s, even there converts numbered less than a few thousand.

CAM first became involved in linguistic work in 1919, when a CAM missionary, Cameron Townsend, developed a grammar and dictionary in the Maya language Cakchiquel in order to translate the New Testament. Townsend eventually left CAM to found the Wycliffe Bible Translators/Summer Institute of Linguistics, a nondenominational organization devoted to translating religious literature into the languages of the indigenous peoples of the Americas. Despite Townsend's departure, linguistic work has remained central to CAM's work to the present day.

CAM also established a number of elementary and secondary schools in the early twentieth century, the largest of which, the Jardín de las Rosas, was founded in Guatemala City in 1914. In the early 2000s, CAM runs the Theological Seminary of Central America (formerly the Central American Biblical Institute) in Guatemala City, which is the largest and most influential fundamentalist seminary on the isthmus.

Officially named CAM International, the organization's mission has changed slightly. Whereas Guatemala and Honduras remain important areas of work, CAM International also has programs in Mexico and among Spanish-speaking communities in the United States, Canada, and Albania.

See also **Missions: Spanish America; Protestantism.**

BIBLIOGRAPHY

Carpenter, Joel A., and Wilbert R. Shenk. *Earthen Vessels: American Evangelicals and Foreign Missions, 1880–1980*. Grand Rapids, MI: W. B. Eerdmans, 1990.

Dow, James, and Alan R. Sandstrom, eds. *Holy Saints and Fiery Preachers: The Anthropology of Protestantism in Mexico and Central America*. Westport, CT: Praeger, 2001.

Garrard-Burnett, Virginia. *Protestantism in Guatemala: Living in the New Jerusalem*. Austin: University of Texas Press, 1998.

Nelson, Wilton M. *El protestantismo en Centro América* (1982).

Nelson, Wilton M. *Historia del protestantismo en Costa Rica* (1983).

Steigenga, Timothy J. *The Politics of the Spirit: The Political Implications of Pentecostalized Religion in Costa Rica and Guatamala*. Lanham, MD: Lexington Books, 2001.

Stoll, David. *Fishers of Men or Founders of Empire? The Wycliffe Bible Translators in Latin America* (1982).

Winn, Wilkins Bowdre. "A History of the Central American Mission as Seen in the Work of Albert Edward Bishop, 1896–1922" (Ph.D. diss., University of Alabama, 1964).

VIRGINIA GARRARD-BURNETT

CENTRAL AMERICAN PARLIAMENT.

The Central American Parliament was a Guatemalan proposal approved in 1986 by the Central American presidents during a summit at Esquipulas, Guatemala, which was held to negotiate peace in Central America. The articles were approved in 1987 by mandatories (leaders) from Guatemala, El Salvador, Honduras, Nicaragua, and Costa Rica. As of 2007, the Congress of Costa Rica had not yet ratified it.

As envisioned in the Declaration of Esquipulas, the parliament would seat twenty representatives from each country, and would develop "strategies, analyses and recommendations" on Central America's political and economic problems. Its headquarters, as designated by the declaration, is Esquipulas. Former presidents and vice presidents are, ex officio, representatives of the parliament. Among its powers would be advising the *buena vecindad* and the Central American Common Market, the entities of Central American integration. The European Community supported the initiative, offering financial support for its realization.

As of 2008, Guatemala, El Salvador, Honduras, Nicaragua, Panama, and the Dominican Republic had all elected representatives to the parliament.

See also **Central America; Central American Common Market (CACM); Costa Rica; El Salvador; Guatemala; Honduras; Nicaragua.**

BIBLIOGRAPHY

Tratado constitutivo del parlamento centroamericano y otras instancias políticas (1988).

M. S. Gloria Abraham, *El parlamento centroamericano: Su incidencia en el desarollo futuro del istmo* (1989).

Additional Bibliography

Tangermann, Klaus-D. *Ilusiones y dilemas: La democracia en Centroamérica.* San José, Costa Rica: FLACSO, Programa Costa Rica, 1995.

Walker, Thomas W., and Ariel C. Armony. *Repression, Resistance, and Democratic Transition in Central America.* Wilmington, DE: Scholarly Resources, 2000.

FERNANDO GONZÁLEZ DAVISON

CENTRAL INTELLIGENCE AGENCY (CIA).

The history of the Central Intelligence Agency is inseparable from that of cold war relations between the United States and Latin America. Established by the 1947 National Security Act only to collect, coordinate, and evaluate intelligence, the new agency got off to an inauspicious start. Rioting at the 1948 Inter-American Conference held in Bogotá, Colombia, elicited charges that the CIA had failed to forewarn the State Department. Although the first director (DCI), Rear Admiral Roscoe H. Hillenkoetter, successfully fended off Capitol Hill critics, he failed to convince bureaucratic rivals, especially J. Edgar Hoover and the Federal Bureau of Investigation (FBI), that they should cede their responsibilities in Latin America to the fledgling CIA.

The CIA's reputation improved, and it overcame its competitors' opposition when, empowered by a series of secret National Security Council (NSC) directives, it became progressively more involved in covert activities. It scored some immediate successes, and the selection of the respected General Walter Bedell Smith as DCI in 1950 solidified the Agency's standing. Three years later the CIA's golden era began. Bringing to the White House an enthusiasm for clandestine operations and psychological warfare developed during his World War II military command, President Dwight D. Eisenhower increased the CIA's authority and resources. To succeed Smith as DCI, he appointed Allen W. Dulles, Office of Strategic Services (OSS) veteran, principal author of the 1949 report that granted the CIA exclusive aegis over covert projects, and Smith's deputy director for plans. Eisenhower named Smith chief deputy to Secretary of State John Foster Dulles, Allen's brother.

Within Eisenhower's first year in office, the CIA rewarded the president by orchestrating the ouster of Iran's prime minister, Muhammad Mussadegh, and the shah's return to the Peacock Throne. It was in Guatemala the next year, however, that the Agency achieved legendary status. Since Guatemala's

1944 revolution, the United States had become increasingly concerned with the perceived leftward drift of presidents Juan José Arévalo Bermejo and Jacobo Arbenz Guzmán. These concerns escalated when the Arbenz government enacted agrarian reform legislation in 1952 that appropriated some 400,000 acres held by Guatemala's largest landowner, the United Fruit Company. CIA analysts ascribed this behavior to the influence on Arbenz of Guatemalan Communists. Unless checked, these presumed agents of the Kremlin would, it was argued, promote Soviet penetration of the Western Hemisphere, thereby confronting the United States with a strategic nightmare.

Later scholars have rejected the CIA's estimate of the threat. Eisenhower never questioned it; he instructed the Agency to develop plans to rid the hemisphere of the menace. After the CIA failed to prevent the arrival in Guatemala of Czech-manufactured arms, Eisenhower approved Operation Success. On 18 June 1954, under the leadership of Carlos Castillo Armas, the U.S.-sponsored Army of Liberation invaded Guatemala from Honduras. Its progress, however, was less a determinant of the outcome than was the CIA's intensive program of psychological warfare that all but paralyzed Arbenz and his military. On 27 June, Arbenz resigned and left the country. Guatemala's next president was Castillo Armas. Subsequently many North and South American commentators have judged the United States culpable for Guatemala's internal strife and dismal record of human rights abuses. Although not diminishing the role of the United States, other scholars have focused on how the actions of the Guatemalan government were an attempt to control and reduce the country's large Mayan population.

The Eisenhower administration basked in the glory of the Guatemalan success. Predictably, therefore, notwithstanding CIA failures during the ensuing years, when Fidel Castro embraced the Soviet Union after overthrowing Cuba's longtime caudillo Fulgencio Batista, Eisenhower again asked the Agency to eradicate what was seen as a hemispheric cancer. Dulles delegated primary responsibility for planning to Richard M. Bissell, Jr., who had joined the CIA just in time to play an important role in Operation Success, and by masterminding the U-2 overflights program had become Dulles's heir apparent. Bissell modeled the plan to depose Castro after the Guatemalan venture and assigned many of the

same personnel to it. By the time Operation Zapata took its final form, it had grown in size and degree of risk. Moreover, John F. Kennedy had become U.S. president.

Kennedy was never comfortable with Bissell's scheme, and many of his advisers were hostile to it. But Bissell gave assurances that when confronted with a brigade of Cuban exiles spread across three beachheads along the Bay of Pigs, Castro would suffer the same loss of nerve as Arbenz and his military had. In the worst-case scenario a stalemate would result that the Organization of American States (OAS) would resolve in favor of the United States. On 17 April 1961, Kennedy sanctioned the operation's implementation, but he curtailed the concomitant air strikes to reduce U.S. exposure. Castro's fighter planes retained air superiority, and his forces either killed or captured the defenseless invaders stranded on the beach. The Bay of Pigs fiasco strengthened Castro in Cuba and ended Dulles's and Bissell's careers in the CIA.

Its early warning of Soviet missile emplacements in Cuba in 1962 and the 1967 assassination of Castro's lieutenant Ernesto "Che" Guevara in Bolivia helped restore some of the CIA's lost luster. But after Operation Mongoose failed to eliminate Castro, and as it became increasingly preoccupied in Southeast Asia, the Agency in the 1960s and 1970s confined most of its Latin American enterprises to assisting the counterinsurgency efforts of U.S. clients. The major exception came in Chile, where the CIA expended great energy and resources to prevent the socialist Salvador Allende from securing the presidency. In 1970 he did so nonetheless. Debate continues over the extent of the CIA's direct involvement in the military coup three years later that ended in Allende's death. What is unambiguous is that between 1970 and 1973 the CIA distributed millions of dollars among Allende's opponents, and that it knew about and encouraged the successful plot against him.

Ronald Reagan's election in 1980 and his appointment of OSS veteran William Casey as DCI brought a revival of CIA activism, in Central America above all. The fundamental objectives were to bring about the collapse of Nicaragua's leftist Sandinista regime and to bolster the government of El Salvador in its battle against the guerrilla forces associated with the Farabundo Martí National Liberation Front (FMLN). Assuming that the FMLN depended on the Sandinistas, the administration concentrated on the Nicaraguan front. Reagan proclaimed the indigenous opposition to the Sandinistas to be "freedom fighters," and Casey, aided by White House staffers and private citizens who had participated in the CIA's secret war in Laos, funneled human, financial, and material support to Contra units operating inside Nicaragua and across neighboring borders. Often this assistance required circumventing congressional prohibitions, the most notorious case of which led to the Iran-Contra scandal. The combination of Casey's sudden death, grants of immunity to key witnesses, the Sandinistas' electoral defeat, and the negotiated end to the Salvadoran insurrection has left many details of the CIA's operations in Central America unclear. The greater openness that accompanied the end of the cold war seemed to promise that additional information would be forthcoming. Although many documents still remain classified, the government has released important new information, such as CIA training manuals used in Latin America during the 1980s that discuss how to coerce captured enemies. Furthermore, the Kerry Committee in the U.S. Senate in 1998 found that the CIA often knew about the close ties between the Nicaraguan contras and drug traffickers.

See also **Allende Gossens, Salvador; Arbenz Guzmán, Jacobo; Arévalo Bermejo, Juan José; Bay of Pigs Invasion; Castillo Armas, Carlos; Castro Ruz, Fidel; Cuba: Cuba Since 1959; Cuban Missile Crisis; Guatemala; Guevara, Ernesto "Che"; Honduras; Nicaragua; Nicaragua, Sandinista National Liberation Front (FSLN); United States-Latin American Relations.**

BIBLIOGRAPHY

General histories of the CIA include John Ranelagh, *The Agency: The Rise and Decline of the CIA* (1986); Loch Johnson, *America's Secret Power: The CIA in a Democratic Society* (1989); Rhodri Jeffreys-Jones, *The CIA and American Democracy* (1989). Equally insightful are biographies of the two most influential DCIs: Thomas Powers, *The Man Who Kept the Secrets: Richard Helms and the CIA* (1979); Peter Grose, *Gentleman Spy: The Life of Allen Dulles* (1994). The most comprehensive survey of the CIA's covert operations is John Prados, *Presidents' Secret Wars: CIA and Pentagon Covert Operations Since World War II* (1986). For the project in Guatemala, see Richard Immerman, *The CIA in Guatemala: The Foreign Policy of Intervention* (1982); Stephen

Schlesinger and Stephen Kinzer, *Bitter Fruit: The Untold Story of the American Coup in Guatemala* (1982); and Piero Gleijeses, *Shattered Hope: The Guatemalan Revolution and the United States, 1944–1954* (1991).

The best studies of the Bay of Pigs are Peter Wyden, *Bay of Pigs: The Untold Story* (1979); and Trumbull Higgins, *The Perfect Failure: Kennedy, Eisenhower, and the CIA at the Bay of Pigs* (1987).

Gregory Treverton, *Covert Action: The Limits of Intervention in the Postwar World* (1987), is excellent on the CIA and Allende. Starting points for examining CIA activity in Central America in the 1980s are Bob Woodward, *Veil: The Secret Wars of the CIA, 1981–1987* (1987); Robert A. Pastor, *Condemned to Repetition: The United States and Nicaragua* (1987); and Walter La Feber, *Inevitable Revolutions: The United States in Central America* (1993).

Blum, William. *Killing Hope: U.S. Military and CIA Interventions since World War II.* Monroe, ME: Common Courage Press, 2004.

Cullather, Nick. *Secret History: The CIA's Classified Account of Its Operations in Guatemala, 1952–1954,* 2nd edition. Stanford, CA: Stanford University Press, 2006.

Gambone, Michael D. *Capturing the Revolution: The United States, Central America, and Nicaragua, 1961–1972.* Westport, CT: Praeger, 2001.

Kornbluh, Peter. *The Pinochet File: A Declassified Dossier on Atrocity and Accountability.* New York: New Press, 2003.

LeoGrande, William M. *Our Own Backyard: The United States in Central America, 1977–1992.* Chapel Hill: University of North Carolina Press, 1998.

Rouquié, Alain. *Guerras y paz en América Central.* Mexico: Fondo de Cultura Económica, 1994.

Webb, Gary. *Dark Alliance: The CIA, the Contras, and the Crack Cocaine Explosion.* New York: Seven Stories Press, 1998.

RICHARD H. IMMERMAN

CENTRO DE ALTOS ESTUDIOS MILITARES. *See* **Center for Advanced Military Studies (CAEM).**

CENTROMÍN. Centromín, state-owned Peruvian mining company. After prolonged and sometimes acrimonious negotiations from 1971 to 1973 between the Cerro De Pasco Corporation and the Peruvian State for the purchase of the company, the government of Juan Velasco Alvarado finally nationalized it, as well as its huge copper mining complex in the central high-lands. Cerro was one of the oldest foreign companies operating in Peru and long a nationalist target; its takeover set off a country-wide celebration in December 1973. The nationalized company became Centro-mín-Perú, a branch of Minero-Perú, which comprised all state mining operations.

See also **Cerro de Pasco Corporation; Mining: Modern; Velasco Alvarado, Juan.**

BIBLIOGRAPHY

Additional Bibliography

Abeyta, Loring. *Resistance at Cerro De Pasco Indigenous Moral Economy and the Structure of Social Movements in Peru.* Ph.d. diss., University of Denver, 2005.

Alarcón Aliaga, Carlos. *Catástrofe ecológica en la Sierra Central del Perú: Incidencia de la actividad minero-metal-úrgica en el medio ambiente.* Lima: IPEMIN, 1994.

PETER F. KLARÉN

CENTURIÓN, CARLOS R. (1902–1969).

Carlos R. Centurión (*b.* 1902; *d.* 1969), Paraguayan historian. Born into an old and established family, Centurión chose to enter the legal profession but also spent many years in academic pursuits. His first literary undertaking, a two-volume account of the Gran Chaco dispute, *El conflicto del Chaco: Gestiones diplomáticas,* published in 1937, was well received, and a year later, he produced a detailed examination of Paraguay's first constitutional convention, *Los hombres de la convención del 70* (1938).

These two early works gave Centurión excellent preparation for his magnum opus, *Historia de las letras paraguayas.* This study, which appeared in three volumes between 1947 and 1951, has long been regarded as the most complete and best-researched intellectual history of Paraguay. Perhaps its only rival is Efraím Cardozo's *Historiografía paraguaya,* which addresses only the colonial period. Centurión's work received considerable acclaim when it first appeared. Subsequent critics have nonetheless charged that it avoids in-depth analysis of Paraguayan writers in favor of a superficial thoroughness. Even these critics, however, have failed to duplicate Centurión's efforts.

See also **Literature: Spanish America.**

BIBLIOGRAPHY

Carlos Centurión, *Historia de la cultura paraguaya,* 2 vols. (1961).

Charles J. Kolinski, *Historical Dictionary of Paraguay* (1975).

THOMAS L. WHIGHAM

CENTURIÓN, JUAN CRISÓSTOMO (1840–1903).

Juan Crisóstomo Centurión (*b.* 1840; *d.* 12 March 1903), Paraguayan diplomat, journalist, and author. Born in Itauguá in 1840, Centurión received his early education in Asunción, where he studied literature with European tutors. In the late 1850s, the government selected him as one of several young Paraguayans sent abroad for further education at state expense. He went to Britain, where he learned English and French and studied international law. He returned to Paraguay in 1863 and immediately became a key adviser to President Francisco Solano López. Two years later, when his country became deeply involved in a war with Argentina and Brazil, Centurión contributed his part, acting as a military officer, magistrate, and state propagandist. Faithful to López to the end, he fought at Itá-Ybaté and, in 1870, was with his commander at Cerro Corá, where he suffered a painful face wound. His Brazilian captors took him to Rio de Janeiro after the war.

Released a few months later, Centurión made his way to London, where he married a Cuban acquaintance. He and his wife then moved to Cuba, where he practiced law. In 1877 he published a short memoir in New York. In 1878 he returned to Asunción, where he edited a key newspaper, *La Reforma,* served as attorney general under President Bernardino Caballero, and began writing another set of memoirs. Centurión joined General Caballero in organizing the Partido Colorado in 1887 and served as foreign minister under Patricio Escobar. In 1895, Centurión was elected senator, a post he held until his death in Asunción. His three-volume *Memorias o reminiscencias históricas sobre la guerra del Paraguay* (Buenos Aires,

1894–1897) is still regarded as the best war memoir from the Paraguayan side.

See also **Journalism.**

BIBLIOGRAPHY

Charles Kolinski, *Historical Dictionary of Paraguay* (1973), p. 49.

Harris G. Warren, *Rebirth of the Paraguayan Republic: The First Colorado Era, 1878–1904* (1985), p. 292.

Additional Bibliography

Guerra, Sergio. *Paraguay: De la independencia a la dominación imperialista, 1811–1870.* Paraguay: C. Schauman, 1991.

Lewis, Paul H. *Political Parties and Generations in Paraguay's Liberal Era, 1869–1940.* Chapel Hill: University of North Carolina Press, 1993.

THOMAS L. WHIGHAM

CENTURIÓN, ROQUE MIRANDA

(1900–1960). Roque Miranda Centurión (*b.* 1900; *d.* 1960), Paraguayan dramatist. Born in Carapeguá, Centurión completed his secondary education at the National College in Asunción and began his theatrical career in the capital city in 1926 as an actor in Félix Fernández's *Mborayjhú pajhú.* That same year, his first play, *Cupido sudando,* was performed. From 1926 to 1928, he lived in France and Spain. In 1932, he collaborated with Josefina Plá in the Spanish-Guarani play *Episodios chaqueños.* In 1933, his play *Tuyú,* in Guarani, was performed, and in 1942 and 1943, he again collaborated with Plá in *Desheredado* and *Sobre en blanco.*

Centurión was the founder of the Escuela Municipal de Declamación y Arte Escénico, which he directed until 1960. He was one of the founders of the Academia de la Lengua y Cultura Guaraní. A radio pioneer, in 1936, Centurión promoted "La Peña," a broadcast created to provide the airways with cultural programs. In 1939, with Plá, he initiated the radio series "Proal," and he created the program "La Voz Cultural de la Nación."

See also **Radio and Television; Theater.**

BIBLIOGRAPHY

Carlos R. Centurión, *Historia de la cultura paraguaya,* vol. 2 (1961).

Additional Bibliography

Rodríguez-Alcalá, Hugo, and Dirma Pardo de Carugati, eds. *Historia de la literatura paraguaya.* Asunción: Editorial El Lector, 1999.

THOMAS E. CASE

CEPEDA, BATTLES OF.

Battles of Cepeda, two conflicts at the *cañada* (ravine) of Cepeda in Buenos Aires Province in 1820 and 1859. The first of the two battles, over the issue of centralism versus federalism, took place on 1 February 1820. It was fought by the Federalist army under General Francisco Ramírez of Entre Ríos, and the Buenos Aires army, headed by General José Rondeau. Rondeau failed to secure assistance from José de San Martín and Manuel Belgrano—as they were busy elsewhere—and the *porteño* (Buenos Aires) army was dispersed at the first cavalry attack.

Porteño officers convinced the Buenos Aires *cabildo* to disband the directorate, Congress dissolved itself, and on 19 February 1820, the *cabildo* was replaced by a junta. On 23 February, Manuel de Sarratea, head of the Buenos Aires junta, met with Estanislao López and Ramírez at the Capilla del Pilar, Buenos Aires Province, to sign a peace treaty, which the junta approved the following day. The public portion of the treaty provided for the security of the provinces of Buenos Aires, Entre Ríos, and Santa Fe and, anticipating the federal pact of 1831, accepted the principle of federation as the basis for national organization. Sixty days after the ratification, freely elected provincial representatives were to meet in San Lorenzo to form a constitutional convention. Entre Ríos and Santa Fe were to withdraw their forces from Buenos Aires, and free trade on the rivers bordering those provinces would resume. The national Congress would settle all boundary disputes. The treaty's secret portion stipulated that Ramírez would ask José Artigas to ratify the treaty for the Banda Oriental, to join them, and to suspend military operations against Brazil. Ramírez entered Buenos Aires on 15 February and left it on 12 April, when he learned that Artigas, who disapproved of the Pilar treaty, had invaded Entre Ríos. The arrangements made at Pilar broke down when López and Juan Manuel de

Rosas signed a treaty at Benegas on 24 November 1820, in order to isolate Ramírez.

The second battle of Cepeda was fought 23 October 1859 over the tariff war between Buenos Aires and the Argentine Confederation, the refusal of Buenos Aires Province to join the union, and the national Congress's decision to authorize President-General Justo José de Urquiza to bring a recalcitrant Buenos Aires into the union. Urquiza commanded the confederation's army, and Governor Bartolomé Mitre, the army of Buenos Aires. Fighting alongside the *porteños* was a Uruguayan division under General Venancio Flores. The Buenos Aires forces were dispersed, and Mitre withdrew. Urquiza then negotiated an armistice at San Nicolás, mediated by Francisco Solano López of Paraguay.

Cepeda ended a war that the international community had tried to avoid. The Pact of the Union was signed on 11 November 1859, and Buenos Aires became a member of the Argentine Confederation. In accordance with the treaty, Buenos Aires proposed amendments to the national constitution that were accepted in 1860. The defeat did not end the influence of Buenos Aires. In 1862, Bartolomé Mitre was elected president of Argentina for a six-year term. During his presidency, Mitre founded many of the federal government's essential institutions.

See also **Argentine Confederation; López, Estanislao; Ramírez, Francisco.**

BIBLIOGRAPHY

Cárcano, Ramón J. *Del sitio de Buenos Aires al campo de Cepeda*, 2d ed. (1921).

Bethell, Leslie, ed. *Spanish America After Independence, c. 1820–c. 1870* (1987), pp. 331, 352.

Bosch, Beatriz. *Urquiza y su tiempo*, 2d ed., rev. (1980). In English, see José Luis Romero, *A History of Argentine Political Thought*, translated by Thomas F. McGann (1963), pp. 88, 89, 108.

Halperín Donghi, Tulio. *Historias de caudillos argentinos.* Edited by Jorge Raúl Lafforgue. Buenos Aires: Extra Alfaguara, 1999.

Lynch, John. *The Spanish-American Revolutions, 1808–1826* (1973), pp. 69, 100, and *Argentine Dictator: Juan Manuel de Rosas* (1981), p. 26.

Molinari, Diego Luis. *"¡Viva Ramírez!" El despotismo en las provincias de la Unión del Sur (1816–1820)* (1938).

Pasquali, Patricia. *La instauración liberal: Mitre, Urquiza y un estadista olvidado, Nicasio Oroño.* Buenos Aires: Planeta, 2003.

Szuchman, Mark D., and Jonathan C. Brown, eds. *Revolution and Restoration: The Rearrangement of Power in Argentina, 1776–1860.* Lincoln: University of Nebraska Press, 1994.

JOSEPH T. CRISCENTI

CEPEDA, ORLANDO (1937–). Orlando Cepeda was born September 17, 1937, in Ponce, Puerto Rico. A baseball player with slugging power who starred with the San Francisco Giants and St. Louis Cardinals, he was one of the most visible Latinos in the game.

Baseball was a part of Cepeda's life from childhood. His father, Pedro, known simply as Perucho and The Bull, had built a legendary career as one of the island's all-time leading sluggers. Young Cepeda, tabbed Peruchin and Baby Bull by the local media, acquired the mantle and carried on his father's reputation. While he was in his teens Cepeda's baseball prowess on the high-school circuit caught the attention of major-league scouts. In 1956 he signed with the then New York Giants who, by the time of his 1958 arrival at the big leagues, had moved to San Francisco. He had a banner season that year, which included a .312 batting average, 25 home runs, and 96 runs batted in (RBIs). He earned the National League Rookie of the Year award, and the hearts of San Francisco baseball fans.

As his career developed, so too did his reputation as one of the league's most ferocious sluggers. In his seventeen major-league seasons, the Baby Bull compiled a .297 batting average, with 379 home runs and 1,365 RBIs. He earned the 1967 Most Valuable Player award after leading the St. Louis Cardinals to that year's world championship.

One year after his 1974 retirement, federal agents arrested Cepeda when they found marijuana in his luggage at the San Juan airport. He spent ten months in prison and, upon his release, vowed to reconstruct his damaged image. Though he spent countless hours working with humanitarian organizations and youth baseball programs, by 1996, after several attempts, he failed to win enough votes for induction into the National Baseball Hall of Fame. In 1999, however, the Veterans Committee elected to induct the Baby Bull into Cooperstown, where his plaque sits near that of Roberto Clemente, the only other Puerto Rican to be honored in the Hall of Fame.

See also **Clemente Walker, Roberto; Sports.**

BIBLIOGRAPHY

Cepeda, Orlando. *Baby Bull: From Hardball to Hard Time and Back.* Dallas, TX: Taylor Publishing, 1998.

Markusen, Bruce. *The Orlando Cepeda Story.* Houston, TX: Pinata Books, 2001.

SAMUEL O. REGALADO

CERDO GORDO, BATTLE OF. Battle of Cerdo Gordo, an engagement on 18 April 1847 in which the Mexican Army was decisively defeated by the United States Army at a mountain pass between Veracruz and Mexico City. Following the indecisive engagement at Buena Vista, Antonio López de Santa Anna rushed south to deal with political problems in Mexico City and to confront the U.S. Army led by General Winfield Scott. Santa Anna chose to meet Scott at a narrow pass named Cerdo Gordo just east of Jalapa. He blocked the road with 25 pieces of artillery and 4,000 of his best troops and fortified the nearby heights of El Telégrafo and La Atalaya, holding 8,000 troops in reserve.

On 12 April, General David Twiggs, commanding some 2,500 men, ordered a precipitous attack on the Mexican position but escaped disaster by the overeagerness of the Mexican gunners. Scott arrived the following day with 6,000 men and ordered a reconnaissance of the formidable Mexican position. Engineer officers Captain Robert E. Lee and Lieutenant George Derby discovered a path around the Mexican position, which was unknown to Santa Anna.

Early on the morning of 18 April, Scott opened his assault with an artillery barrage. While part of the U.S. Army engaged the Mexicans along their front, Twiggs advanced along the path in order to cut off the Mexican line of retreat. Before reaching the Mexican rear as ordered, Twiggs prematurely attacked El Telégrafo and La Atalaya. After three hours of fighting, the Mexican Army broke and fled in disarray; Santa Anna barely escaped capture.

The Mexicans lost approximately 3,000 men, and a like number were captured along with a large quantity of munitions. The United States suffered 64 dead and 353 wounded.

The victory at Cerdo Gordo allowed the U.S. Army to escape the unhealthy lowlands at the beginning of the yellow fever season. Also, the Mexicans lost most of their remaining better-trained units. Although the Mexican-American War continued for another year, the Mexican Army was no longer capable of executing offensive maneuvers.

See also **Mexico, Wars and Revolutions, Mexican-American Wars.**

BIBLIOGRAPHY

Hubert Howe Bancroft, *History of Mexico* (1883).

José Fernando Ramírez, *Mexico During the War with the United States,* edited by Walter V. Scholes and translated by Elliott B. Scherr (1950).

Additional Bibliography

Heidler, David Stephen, and Jeanne T. Heidler. *The Mexican War.* Westport, CT: Greenwood Press, 2006.

Vázquez, Josefina Zoraida. *México al tiempo de su guerra con Estados Unidos, 1846–1848.* México: Secretaría de Exteriores: El Colegio de México: Fondo de Cultura Económica, 1997.

ROBERT SCHEINA

CERÉN. Cerén, a small Late Classic (650–900 CE) residential site that was buried during the eruption of the Laguna Caldera volcano in the sixth or seventh century. Located in the Zapotitán Valley in central El Salvador, Cerén consists of two houses, outbuildings, activity areas, and a *milpa* (cornfield). The descending cloud of volcanic ash and gases burned palm-thatch roofs and wooden supports in walls, and blanketed the surfaces of all structures. The thirteen-foot-thick blanket of ash insulated site remains from erosion and decay, and the high temperatures of ash and gas at deposition fired the architectural features to nearly indestructible hardness.

Cerén appears to represent part of a dispersed settlement pattern of farmers living near their fields. Besides two houses, excavations have revealed storehouses containing storage pots for chiles, corn, and beans; a sweathouse; a kitchen; and workshop areas.

The house most fully excavated had *bajareque* (mud-and-pole) walls and floors made of a thick layer of clay. Thatch-roof construction resembled that in modern Maya houses.

Evidence of domestic activities that occurred in sections of the house were preserved. Behind a dividing wall on the raised floor were four large pots and a maul, much like modern kitchens in traditional areas of El Salvador. In the central portion of the house were a spindle whorl, for spinning cotton thread, and a miniature ceramic vessel, perhaps made by a child learning the craft. The southeastern end of the house had the vestiges of a grass floor mat, probably used for sleeping.

The *milpa* at Cerén had parallel cultivation ridges with intervening furrows, a method very different from that used by modern traditional Maya agriculturalists. The plant casts indicate that the Cerén site was buried by ash shortly after the onset of the growing season, in May or early June.

See also **Archaeology.**

BIBLIOGRAPHY

Payson D. Sheets, "Maya Recovery from Volcanic Disasters: Ilopango and Cerén," in *Archaeology* 32 (1979): 32–42.

Payson D. Sheets, ed., *Archaeology and Volcanism in Central America: The Zapotitán Valley of El Salvador* (1983).

Payson D. Sheets et al., "Household Archaeology at Cerén, El Salvador," in *Ancient Mesoamerica* 1 (1990): 81–90.

Payson D. Sheets, *The Cerén Site: A Prehistoric Village Buried by Volcanic Ash in Central America* (1992).

Additional Bibliography

Allison, Penelope M., ed. *The Archaeology of Household Activities.* New York: Routledge, 2002.

Ardren, Traci, ed. *Ancient Maya Women.* Walnut Creek: AltaMira Press, 2002.

Dietler, Michael, and Brian Hayden, eds, *Feasts: Archaeological and Ethnographic Perspectives on Food, Politics, and Power.* Washington, DC: Smithsonian Institution Press, 2001.

Lentz, David L., Marilyn P. Beaudry-Corbett, Maria Luisa Reyna de Aguilar, and Lawrence Kaplan. "Foodstuffs, Forests, Fields, and Shelter: A Paleoethnobotanical Analysis of Vessel Contents from the Ceren Site, El Salvador (in Reports)." *Latin American Antiquity* 7, no. 3. (Sept. 1996): 247–262.

Plunket, Patricia Scarborough. *Domestic Ritual in Ancient Mesoamerica.* Los Angeles: Cotsen Institute of Archaeology, University of California, 2002.

Sheets, Payson D. *Before the Volcano Erupted: The Ancient Cerèn Village in Central America.* Austin: University of Texas Press, 2002.

KATHRYN SAMPECK

CEREZO ARÉVALO, MARCO VINICIO

(1942–). Marco Vinicio Cerezo Arévalo (*b.* 26 December 1942), president of Guatemala (1986–1991). Vinicio Cerezo was born in Guatemala City into a politically prominent family. His grandfather was murdered for opposing Jorge Ubico (1931–1944) and his father served on the Guatemalan Supreme Court. In 1954 Cerezo's political inclinations were awakened by the U.S.-sponsored overthrow of Jacobo Arbenz (1951–1954). He joined the Christian Democratic Party (DCG) while a law student at the University of San Carlos. After completing his degree in 1968, he studied at Loyola University in New Orleans, Louisiana, and in Chile, Venezuela, West Germany, and Italy. He was elected to the congress in 1974. During the repressive regime of General Lucas García (1978–1982), he survived at least three attempts on his life.

In 1986 Vinicio Cerezo became the first elected civilian president since 1970 and only the second since Juan José Arévalo (1945–1951). Cerezo faced a difficult situation in 1986: a troublesome insurgency on the left, an intransigent military on the right, an increasingly mobilized peasantry, and an economy in a state of crisis (declining GNP, escalating inflation, 40 percent unemployment, and scarce foreign exchange). To address these problems Cerezo launched a neoliberal program of export diversification, currency devaluation, removal of price controls, and increased taxes. The results were generally favorable for the national economy, but living standards for most people were reduced. This led to a series of massive strikes in 1987, 1988, and 1989.

Although supported by the military high command, Cerezo was opposed by field commanders who thought that domestic concerns were taking precedence over the government's counterinsurgency efforts. Coup attempts by disgruntled officers were launched in May 1988 and again in 1989.

In January 1987 Cerezo renewed the diplomatic relations with Britain that had been ruptured in 1981 by the granting of independence to Belize.

In 1986 and 1987, he hosted the Central American peace talks in Esquipulas which led to the successful implementation of the Arias peace plan, whose goal was the settlement of the insurgency wars in Central America.

Although elected on a platform to bring peace to Guatemala, Cerezo made little progress in ending the leftist insurgency or improving the country's human rights record. The coalition of four major guerrilla groups, the Guatemalan National Revolutionary Union (URNG), expanded its operations, and the number of assassinations by alleged right-wing death squads increased in Guatemala City. The problem was exacerbated by the massacre of fourteen men and boys in the Indian village of Santiago Atitlan in December 1990, which resulted in the cutoff of U.S. military aid.

Plagued by charges of corruption and drug trafficking, Cerezo was unable to secure the election of his handpicked successor, but he did preside over the first successive democratic presidential election in 151 years. Jorge Serrano Elías (*b.* 1945) was inaugurated in January 1991. In 1999 Cerezo won one of the two National Congress seats and was then reelected in the 2004–2008 term.

See also **Arévalo Bermejo, Juan José; Guatemala; Guatemala, Political Parties: National Guatemalan Revolutionary Unity (URNG).**

BIBLIOGRAPHY

Stephen Kinzer, "Walking the Tightrope in Guatemala," in *New York Times Magazine,* 9 November 1986.

Inforpress Centroamericana, *Guatemala—1986, The Year of Promises* (1987).

James Painter, *Guatemala: False Hope, False Freedom: The Rich, the Poor, and the Christian Democrats* (1987).

Stephen Kinzer, "What Has Democracy Wrought," in *New York Times Magazine,* 26 March 1989.

Roland H. Ebel, "Guatemala: The Politics of Unstable Stability," in *Latin American Politics and Development,* edited by Howard J. Wiarda and Harvey F. Kline (1990).

Additional Bibliography

Amaro, Nelson. *Guatemala, historia despierta.* Guatemala: IDESAC, 1992.

ROLAND H. EBEL

CERNA, VICENTE (c. 1810–1885). Vicente Cerna (*b.* ca. 1810; *d.* 27 June 1885), field marshal and president of Guatemala (1865–1871). A military officer who became by 1847 a close associate of the dictator Rafael Carrera (1840–1865), Cerna played an important role at the battle of Arada (1851). This battle established Carrera as the dominant military figure in Central America and as president for life (formally so in 1854). Outside Carrera's family no military man was closer to the dictator than Cerna, who was politically and militarily dependable and a devout Catholic, as was Carrera. Cerna later received the rank of field marshal for his performance in the difficult 1863 campaign against El Salvador's Liberal president Gerardo Barrios. Shortly before his death in April 1865, Carrera named Cerna to succeed him. In the close presidential election that followed in May this endorsement gave Cerna his margin of victory.

Carrera's regime had been in large measure reactionary but provided peace and encouraged development of coffee culture. Cerna continued most of Carrera's policies, seeking sufficient modernization for economic development under traditional institutions such as monopoly franchises (*estancos*) and the Consulado de Comercio, which favored a restricted circle of landowners, entrepreneurs, and merchants. Under Cerna Guatemala became more closely connected with the world trading system, which favored free trade. Cerna's regime improved the infrastructure of transportation and communication: the Pacific port of San José was built up; some roads and highways were improved; railroads were commissioned, though not built; and the telegraph was introduced, although it would not become effective until after 1871. In 1870–1871 an ambitious currency reform was introduced, a reform of land tenure sought, and a modern public market, which would stand for a century, was completed.

Despite some successes, pressures on the regime grew. A series of insurrections began in 1867 and Cerna's church-dominated government had poor relations with Benito Juárez's victorious Liberal regime in Mexico. Both foreign and Guatemalan entrepreneurs associated with the expanding coffee culture became impatient with Cerna's policy. His reelection in 1869 involved manipulation, and in 1870 political repression ended parliamentary debate. Miguel García Granados, leader of the opposition, was forced into exile, from whence both Guatemalan and Mexican allies aided his organization of the Liberal revolution of 1871. Joined by those impatient for modernization in Guatemala, García Granados and Justo Rufino Barrios defeated Cerna's army on 29 June 1871 and took control of the government the next day.

See also **Guatemala; Military Dictatorships: 1821–1945.**

BIBLIOGRAPHY

Jorge Skinner Klee, *Revolución y derecho: Una investigación sobre el problema de la revolución en el derecho guatemalteco* (1971), esp. pp. 65–74.

Wayne M. Clegern, "Transition from Conservatism to Liberalism in Guatemala, 1865–1871," in *Hispanic-American Essays in Honor of Max Leon Moorhead,* edited by William S. Coker (1979), pp. 98–110.

Ralph Lee Woodward, Jr., *Central America: A Nation Divided,* 2d ed. (1985), and *Rafael Carrera and the Emergence of the Republic of Guatemala, 1821–1871* (1993).

Carol A. Smith, ed., *Guatemalan Indians and the State, 1540–1988* (1990), esp. pp. 52–136.

Wayne M. Clegern, *Origins of Liberal Dictatorship in Central America* (1994).

Additional Bibliography

Taracena Arriola, Arturo. *Invención criolla, sueño ladino, pesadilla indígena: Los Altos de Guatemala: De región a estado, 1740–1871.* Antigua: Centro de Investigaciones Regionales de Mesoamérica, 1999.

WAYNE M. CLEGERN

CERRADO. *Cerrado* is host to over 10,000 species of plants, 45 percent of which are unique to the Cerrado, making it one of the world's most biologically abundant tropical savannas. Located in the Brazilian central plateau covering more than 700,000 square miles, or 22 percent of Brazil, the Cerrado is rolling terrain with deep sandy soils of low fertility. Rainfall is heavy in the summer (November to March), while there is little precipitation the rest of the year. Vegetation consists of grasses, low bushes, and scattered trees. Cerrado has supported a cattle industry since the seventeenth century and is now the most important ranching region of Brazil. It also hosts vast soybean agribusinesses. However, ranching and farming have taken their toll on the Cerrado, contributing to the environmental degradation of this largely unprotected area. In 2001, two protected areas of the Cerrado,

Chapada dos Veadeiros and Emas National Parks, were added to the UNESCO World Heritage List.

Cerrado was probably formed and maintained by the action of fire. Since the arrival of humans, it has been exposed to seasonal burning first by the original inhabitants and later by ranchers. Fire combined with overgrazing has caused severe erosion in some areas and the replacement of native grasses by tough invader species that first entered Brazil in explorer and slave ships. Several species of plants and animals in this region are on the endangered list due to habitat pressure.

Cerrado native peoples have also suffered significant population loss over the last century due to the expansion of permanent settlement originating in more populated regions of Brazil. The national capital city of Brasília is located in the middle of Cerrado. The government and the region are often referred to by the term *planalto* (plateau).

See also **Brazil, Geography; Indigenous Peoples.**

BIBLIOGRAPHY

G. Eiten, "Brazilian 'Savannas,'" and L. M. Coutinho, "Ecological Effect of Fire in Brazilian Cerrado," in *Ecology of Tropical Savannas,* edited by B. J. Huntley and B. H. Walker (1982), pp. 25–47, 273–291.

Kurt Hueck, "A primitividade dos 'campos cerrados' brasileiros e novas observações em seu limite meridional," in *Boletim Geográfico* (*Rio de Janeiro*) 31, no. 230 (1972): 215–225.

Lindalvo Bezerra Dos Santos, "Campo cerrado," in *Tipos e aspectos do Brasil,* 10th ed. (1975), pp. 469–470.

G. Sarmiento, "The Savannas of Tropical America," in *Tropical Savannas,* edited by François Bourlière (1983), pp. 245–288.

Additional Bibliography

Oliveira, Paulo S., and Robert J. Marquis. *The Cerrados of Brazil: Ecology and Natural History of a Neotropical Savanna* (2002).

ROBERT WILCOX

CERRO CORÁ, BATTLE OF. Battle of Cerro Corá, the final engagement of the War of the Triple Alliance on 1 March 1870. The remnants of the Paraguayan army under Field Marshal Francisco Solano López had been in flight for nearly a year when Brazilian cavalry units closed in on them at a spot along the Aquidaban-Nigui creek in northeastern Paraguay. In the battle, really more of a skirmish, the Brazilians quickly overwhelmed the defenders. The Paraguayan vice president, several ministers, and high military officers were all killed. So was Field Marshal López, who, when called upon to surrender, purportedly refused in the most florid terms, crying, "Muero con mi patria!" (I die with my country!). Extremist writers and hagiographers later converted that expression into a virtual national slogan for Paraguay. In reality, López's demise at Cerro Corá ended a bloody war that had taken the lives of at least 100,000 people.

See also **War of the Triple Alliance.**

BIBLIOGRAPHY

Charles A. Washburn, *The History of Paraguay, with Notes and Personal Observations* (1871), vol. 2, *passim;* Charles J. Kolinski, "The Death of Francisco Solano López," *The Historian* 26, no. 1 (1963): 75–91, and *Independence or Death! The Story of the Paraguayan War* (1965).

Additional Bibliography

Bethell, Leslie. *The Paraguayan War (1864–1870).* London: Institute of Latin American Studies, 1996.

Leuchars, Chris. *To the Bitter End: Paraguay and the War of the Triple Alliance.* Westport, CT: Greenwood Press, 2002.

Marco, Miguel Angel de. *La Guerra del Paraguay.* Buenos Aires: Planeta, 1995.

Whigham, Thomas. *The Paraguayan War.* Lincoln: University of Nebraska Press, 2002.

THOMAS L. WHIGHAM

CERRO CORPORACIÓN. *See* **Gran Minería.**

CERRO DEL CUBILETE.

The monument to Christ the King on the Cerro del Cubilete (Cubilete Hill) is considered to be the geographical center and heart of the Republic of Mexico. It is an important symbol of Catholicism in the twentieth century, built to defy the secularizing policies of the Mexican state. Its aim was to unite the nation's Catholics, and it served as a balm for the wounds inflicted by the Cristero War (Guerra Cristera, 1926–1929), which ended with the expulsion of the combatants. The monument's construction (1919–1960) survived several conflicts as the Catholic Church struggled to preserve its diminishing hegemony; today it stands as a material embodiment of the country's history of religious belief in the power of Christ, if only symbolic, over and above earthly powers. The shrine is visited by hundreds of pilgrims every year.

See also **Cristero Rebellion; Mexico: Since 1910; Religion in Mexico, Catholic Church and Beyond.**

BIBLIOGRAPHY

Torres Septién, Valentina. "De cerro a montaña santa: La construcción del monumento a Cristo Rey (1919–1960)." *Historia y Grafía* 22 (2004): 113–154.

VALENTINA TORRES SEPTIÉN

CERRO DE PASCO CORPORATION.

Cerro de Pasco Corporation, foreign-owned Peruvian mining company. Cerro was founded in 1902 by an American syndicate composed, among others, of J. P. Morgan, Henry Clay Frick, and Darius Ogden Mills. It shortly came to control the majority of mines in Cerro de Pasco and Morococha, spearheading a general trend toward the denationalization of the Peruvian mining industry during the first three decades of the twentieth century. The labor force at Cerro was recruited from the surrounding peasantry and, at its peak prior to the depression, amounted to some 13,000 workers, or about 30 percent of the total mining proletariat in the country. Between 1916 and 1937 Cerro's gross earnings amounted to some $375 million, of which $207 million or (55 percent) was returned to the local economy and $169 million (45 percent) went abroad to pay for imports and as profits. As one of the largest multinational corporations operating in Peru during the twentieth century, Cerro not only had a huge impact on the national and local economy but also intervened directly and indirectly in both internal and external affairs, leading it to become a source of deep resentment to the Peruvian people prior to its nationalization in 1973 as Centromín.

See also **Mining: Modern.**

BIBLIOGRAPHY

Dirk Kruijt and Menno Vellinga, *Labor Relations and Multinational Corporations: The Cerro de Pasco Corporation in Peru (1902–1974)* (1979).

Additional Bibliography

Jochamowitz, Luis. *Hombres, minas y pozos: 1896–1996: Un siglo de minería y petróleo en el Perú.* Lima: Sociedad Nacional de Minería y Petróle, 1996.

PETER F. KLARÉN

CERRO NARRÍO. Cerro Narrío, an important archaeological site in the south-central highlands of Ecuador. Stratigraphic excavations conducted at the site in the 1940s produced some of the earliest known pottery in the highlands and yielded a lengthy ceramic sequence that has been used as a baseline for interpreting the regional archaeology. The site is also significant for the evidence it has produced of early connections between the sierra, coastal Ecuador, and the Amazonian lowlands.

The site of Cerro Narrío is situated on a hilltop across the river from the modern town of Cañar, at an elevation of 10,230 feet. The surface of this barren hilltop is literally paved with ceramic potsherds. In the early 1920s, a find of several gold objects at Cerro Narrío induced indiscriminate looting of the site on a massive scale. For all the activity, very little gold was actually recovered and the site of Cerro Narrío was all but destroyed.

Twenty years later, two North American scholars, recognizing the archaeological significance of the site, undertook limited excavations in the remaining undisturbed areas. Their excavations produced enormous quantities of sherds, the principal variety being that which the excavators classified as Narrío Red-on-Buff. This pottery type, most often a jar form decorated with painted red bands, is found in all occupation levels at the site. Almost as common numerically, though confined to the lower levels, is the spectacularly thin-walled pottery identified as Narrío Red-on-Buff Fine. This was the index ware (the pottery type that marks or indicates a specific chronological period) for the archaeological culture or phase known as Chaullabamba. In addition to the local pottery, exotic styles and influences identified at Cerro Narrío include Valdivia and Chorrera elements from coastal Ecuador, the "Group X" components possibly deriving from the eastern Andean slopes or lowlands, Puruhá and Tuncahuán wares from further north, Kotosh styles from the Peruvian Montaña, and Chimú pieces from Peru's north coast.

Based on the relative changes in the percentages of these wares found in different stratigraphic levels, the occupational history of the site was divided into an earlier and a later phase. Though work at the site was conducted prior to the advent of radiocarbon dating, subsequent assays of charcoal collected from the lower levels of the site gave a date of 1978 BCE. This and other carbon 14 dates from sites in the Cañar Valley having an Early Cerro Narrío component associate this phase with the Early Formative period of Ecuadorian prehistory. Cross-referencing of exotic styles found primarily in the upper levels of the site associate the Late Cerro Narrío phase with the Late Formative period (about 1500–500 BCE).

In addition to pottery, occupational debris found at the site includes stone beads, bone awls and whistles, shell beads and figurines, copper objects, and cylindrical pottery "drums." Charred remnants provide direct evidence of maize cultivation, while numerous deer and rabbit bones indicate that hunting continued to be an important subsistence activity. Postholes encountered in some excavation units indicate that the dwellings constructed by the site's inhabitants were both circular and rectangular in form, with the latter type perhaps postdating the former. The burials encountered were simple and generally lacking in funerary offerings.

The ceramic sequence at Cerro Narrío and the cross-correlation of exotic styles found at the site with other regions have been taken as evidence of early contact between the southern Ecuadorian highlands, coast, and eastern lowlands; of trade with the north coast of Peru; of indirect links with the civilizations of Central America; and of possible influences from the Middle Horizon cultures of southern Peru. Cerro Narrío is thus considered a key site in the reconstruction of Ecuadorian prehistory.

See also **Archaeology; Precontact History: Latin America in the Precontact Period.**

BIBLIOGRAPHY

Donald Collier, and John V. Murra, *Survey and Excavations in Southern Ecuador,* Field Museum of Natural History, Anthropological Series, Publication 523, vol. 35 (1943).

Betty J. Meggers, *Ecuador* (1966), especially pp. 53–55, 108–111.

Robert Braun, "The Formative as Seen from the Southern Ecuadorian Highlands," in *Primer simpósio de corelaciones antropológicas Andino-Mesoamericano,* edited by Jorge Marcos and Presley Norton (1982), pp. 41–53.

Additional Bibliography

Garzón Espinoza, Mario. *Evolución cultural del Cañar prehistórico.* Azogues: Casa de la Cultura Ecuatoriana "Benjamín Carrión" Nucleo del Cañar, 2005.

Molina, Manuel J. *Arqueología ecuatoriana: Los canaris.* Roma: LAS; Quito: Ediciones Abya-Yala, 1992.

Stahl, Peter W. "Pre-Columbian Andean Animal Domesticates at the Edge of Empire." *World Archaeology* 34, no. 3, *Luxury Foods* (Feb. 2003): 470–83.

TAMARA L. BRAY

CERROS. Cerros, a Late Preclassic (300 BCE–250 CE) Maya site located in Belize on a narrow spit of swampy land where the New River empties into Chetumal Bay. Cerros underwent a dramatic transformation from an egalitarian fishing and trading community to a cosmopolitan political capital during the Late Preclassic period.

Inhabitants fished in fresh and salt water and also worked wood extensively, probably making dugout canoes. Raised agricultural fields were located both at the site center and near the river's mouth. A large, low platform bordering the nucleated village's shoreline appears to have been a dock. Imported ceramics and foreign stylistic affinities indicate that Cerros was a trading community.

The initial phase of settlement (300–200 BCE) was a nucleated village. Slightly later, an elaborately decorated pyramid was built. The south side and lower terraces flanking the stairway of the pyramid were decorated with polychrome painted panels and modeled stucco masks. The use of this pyramid and the nucleated settlement ended in an elaborate ritual, evinced by ceramics and jade that were smashed and left in place. Elite residences and ceremonial structures were subsequently erected over this same area.

From 200 to 50 BCE, residential settlement gradually became more dispersed. The transition from nucleated to dispersed settlement and additions to ceremonial architecture at the center were completed by 150 CE. An elaborate system of artificial drainage was used during this period, probably to help compensate for the seasonal availability of fresh water. A massive artificial canal bordered the dispersed settlement zone and drained the central precinct. This hydraulic system rapidly deteriorated following the Late Preclassic collapse of Cerros as a political capital. Settlement at Cerros persisted after 250 CE, but the site never regained the political, economic, or religious importance it had during the Late Preclassic.

See also **Maya, The.**

BIBLIOGRAPHY

David A. Freidel, "Maritime Adaptation and the Rise of Maya Civilization: The View from Cerros, Belize," in *Prehistoric Coastal Adaptations,* edited by Barbara L. Stark and Barbara Voorhies (1978), pp. 239–265.

Robin A. Robertson, *Archaeology at Cerros, Belize, Central America,* vol. 1, *An Interim Report* (1986).

David A. Freidel and Linda Schele, *A Forest of Kings: The Untold Story of the Ancient Maya* (1990), esp. pp. 96–129.

Additional Bibliography

Freidel, David A., and Robin A. Robertson, eds. *Archaeology at Cerros, Belize, Central America.* v. 1–3. Dallas: Southern Methodist Univeristy Press, 1986.

Lewenstein, Suzanne M. *Stone Tool Use at Cerros: The Ethnoarchaeological and Use-Wear Evidence.* Austin: University of Texas Press, 1987.

Mock, Shirley Boteler, ed. *The Sowing and the Dawning: Termination, Dedication, and Transformation in the Archaeological and Ethnographic Record of Mesoamerica.* Albuquerque: University of New Mexico Press, 1998.

KATHRYN SAMPECK

CERRUTO, ÓSCAR (1912–1981). Óscar Cerruto (*b.* 13 June 1912; *d.* 10 April 1981), Bolivian poet, novelist, and storyteller. One of the most important figures of contemporary Bolivian literature, Cerruto wrote his first group of poems, *Cifra de las rosas* (1957), within the aesthetics of modernism. This poetical composition is followed by *Patria de sal cautiva* (1958), *Estrella segregada* (1973), and *Reverso de la transparencia* (1975), wherein Cerruto explores the possibilities of avant-gardism. His imagery is harsh and in harmony with the high plateau landscapes of Andean Bolivia. Of great intensity and linguistic precision, Cerruto's works denounce the excesses of power and examine the topics of hate, solitude, fear, and death. His poetry, embedded in the Judeo-Christian notion of guilt, dissociates itself from his early revolutionary ideals of social transformation, admirably set forth in his novel *Aluvión de fuego* (1935). The absence of social redemption can be perceived in his later narrative, particularly in *Cerco de penumbras* (1958), a volume of short stories.

See also **Literature: Spanish America.**

BIBLIOGRAPHY

A brief but excellent study of Cerruto's poetry may be found in Eduardo Mitre, *El árbol y la piedra: Poetas contemporáneos de Bolivia* (1988). Two major contributions on Cerruto are Luis H. Antezana, "Sobre 'Estrella segregada' de Óscar Cerruto," in his *Ensayos y lecturas* (1986); and Óscar Rivera-Rodas, "La poesía de Óscar Cerruto," in *Cuadernos Hispanoamericanos* 417 (1985): 146–154.

Additional Bibliography

Arduz Ruiz, Heberto. "La soledad en la obra poética de Oscar Cerruto." *Signo* 50 (January–December 1997): 41–44.

Bourne, Luis. "Un Boliviano declara su amargura: La soledad plural de Oscar Cerruto." *Signo* 57 (January–April 2001): 191–198.

JAVIER SANJINÉS C.

CERUTI, ROQUE (c. 1683–1760).

Roque Ceruti (*b.* ca. 1683; *d.* 6 December 1760), Italian composer active in Peru. Born in Milan, then under Spanish rule, Ceruti studied the violin there until 1706. When the Marquis Castell dos Ríus, viceroy of Peru, appointed him director of music, Ceruti settled in Lima, where he conducted the premiere of his opera *El mejor escudo de Perseo* at the viceroyal palace on 17 September 1708. In 1720 he moved to Trujillo and was named *maestro de capilla* of the cathedral there (1721–1728). In 1728 Ceruti succeeded Tomás de Torrejón y Velasco as *maestro de capilla* of the Lima cathedral, remaining in that position until his death. During Ceruti's tenure the cathedral continued to be an active music center. Ceruti composed and published numerous works: mythological operas and pastorals, secular and religious music, some in Spanish, others on Latin texts. His manuscripts are kept in the Lima Archives,

in the San Antonio Abad Seminary in Cuzco, in Sucre cathedral, in Santa Clara Conventín Cochabamba, in private collections, and at the archive of the church of San Francisco de Asís in Montevideo. He died in Lima.

See also **Music: Art Music.**

BIBLIOGRAPHY

Robert M. Stevenson, *The Music of Peru* (1960) and *Renaissance and Baroque Musical Sources in the Americas* (1970); *New Grove Dictionary of Music and Musicians,* vol. 4 (1980).

Additional Bibliography

Estenssoro, Juan Carlos. *Música y sociedad coloniales: Lima, 1680–1830.* Lima: Editorial Colmillo Blanco, 1989.

SUSANA SALGADO

CERVANTES, VICENTE (1755–1829).

Vicente Cervantes (*b.* 1755; *d.* 26 July 1829), distinguished botanist of Bourbon Mexico. Born in Zafra, Badajoz, Spain, Cervantes began his career as an apprentice to an apothecary, studying pharmacy part-time. After passing the pharmacist's examination, he served as chief pharmacist at the general hospital in Madrid until Charles III chose him as a member of the royal botanical expedition to New Spain. The expedition arrived in New Spain in 1787; Cervantes, appointed professor of botany at the University of Mexico, began teaching the following year. His popular courses, which emphasized Linnaean principles, introduced a generation of Mexican creoles to the modern study of botany.

Cervantes also was a founder of the Royal Botanical Gardens, located in the viceregal palace, and its head from 1802. There, he and his assistants cultivated some 1,400 species of plants; the New World flora came mostly from central Mexico, though some species were imported from as far away as Havana. Cervantes, who remained in Mexico when the rest of the expedition departed, faced difficulties after 1810. The hard-pressed viceregal government progressively slashed the Royal Botanical Gardens' budget, and Cervantes was unable to prevent the institution's gradual deterioration. He died in Mexico City.

See also **Medicine: Colonial Spanish America.**

BIBLIOGRAPHY

The most complete study of Cervantes and the Royal Botanical Gardens is Harold William Rickett, *The Royal Botanical Expedition to New Spain, 1788–1820* (1947). For a more general treatment of botanical studies under the Bourbons, see Arthur R. Steele, *Flowers for the King: The Expedition of Ruíz and Pavón and the Flora of Peru* (1964), esp. pp. 3–49.

Additional Bibliography

Aceves Pastrana, Patricia. *Química, botánica, y farmacia en la Nueva España a finales del siglo XVIII*. México, D.F.: Universidad Autónoma Metropolitana, Unidad Xochilmico, 1993.

Lozoya, Xavier. *Plantas y luces en México: La real expedición científica a Nueva España (1787–1803)*. Barcelona: Ediciones del Serbal, 1984.

R. DOUGLAS COPE

CERVANTES KAWANAGH, IGNACIO (1847–1905).

Ignacio Cervantes Kawanagh (*b.* 31 July 1847; *d.* 29 April 1905), pioneer of Cuban musical nationalism. Cervantes, a native of Havana, was not the first Cuban nationalist musician, but it was in his *contradanzas* that this musical genre found its fullest expression. He benefited from the friendship of the American composer Louis M. Gottschalk, who in 1865 advised Cervantes's parents to send him to study in Paris, where he won numerous awards. Like José White, another Cuban musician, he was forced by the Spaniards to leave Cuba (to which he had returned in 1870) during the Ten Years' War (1868–1878). He later became a friend of José Martí, whom he assisted in his revolutionary activities. As a composer his magnum opus was his series of Cuban dances (some forty of which are extant). Because of their richness and complexity, they became concert music. They have been described as "the soul of Cuba in full bloom." He died in Havana.

See also **Music: Popular Music and Dance.**

BIBLIOGRAPHY

José I. Lasaga, *Cuban Lives: Pages from Cuban History* (1984), vol. 1, pp. 223–231. See also Alejo Carpentier, *La música en Cuba* (1946).

Additional Bibliography

Mikowsky, Solomon Gadles. *Ignacio Cervantes y la danza en Cuba*. La Habana: Editorial Letras Cubanas, 1988.

JOSÉ M. HERNÁNDEZ

CERVETTI, SERGIO (1940–).

Sergio Cervetti (*b.* 9 November 1940), Uruguayan composer. Born in Dolores, Cervetti studied piano in Montevideo with Hugo Balzo and counterpoint and harmony with Carlos Estrada and Guido Santórsola. He then studied composition at the Peabody Conservatory in Baltimore under the direction of Ernst Krenek and Stefan Grové. Later he worked in electronic music under the guidance of Mario Davidovsky, Vladimir Ussachevsky, and Alcides Lanza. He received the composition prize at the Caracas Festival in 1966. In 1968 he was artist-in-residence with the DAAD (German exchange program) for the city of Berlin and received important commissions from Baden-Baden and the Art Academy in Berlin. His music for ballet includes *Transatlantic Light* (1987) for the Dance Company of Nina Wiener and *40 Second/42 Variations* (1979) for the Holland Festival.

Until 1971 Cervetti's work was characterized by dodecaphonic tendencies with some incursions into aleatoric languages. Following his move to New York City, he became part of the minimalist movement. Even if his aesthetics separated him completely from other Latin American musical schools modeled after the European, particularly Polish, composers, Cervetti created his own version of minimalism, producing works with strong lyrical lines, thick counterpoint, and a hypnotic atmosphere. He later transformed this style to include pop and nationalist styles. In 1979, he became a U.S. citizen.

Other important works by Cervetti include Five Episodes for chamber ensemble (1965); *Divertimento* for woodwinds (1964); *Plexus* for orchestra (1970), commissioned by the Fifth Inter-American Music Festival, Washington, D.C.; *Zinctum* for string quartet (1967); *The Bottom of the Iceberg* for solo guitar (1975); *Transatlantic Light* for electronic keyboard (1987); *Lucet in Tenebris* for choir (1970); *Bits and Pieces and Moving Parts* for chamber ensemble and tape (1970); Trumpet Concerto (1977); *4 Fragments of Isadora* for soprano and piano (1979); *Wind Devil* for electronic tape (1983); *Llanto, muerte y danza* for harpsichord (1984); *3 Estudios australes* for piano (1989); Concerto for harpsichord and eleven instruments (1990); *Leyenda* for soprano and orchestra (1991); and *Las indias olvidadas,* a concerto for harpsichord and chamber group (1992), commissioned by the Festival of Alicante, Spain. Until 1997, he taught at Tisch School of Arts at New York University.

See also **Music: Art Music.**

BIBLIOGRAPHY

John Vinton, ed. *Dictionary of Contemporary Music* (1974), p. 134.

Gérard Béhague, *Music in Latin America: An Introduction* (1979), pp. 341–342; *Octavo festival internacional de música contemporánea* (1992), pp. 46–47, 110–111.

Additional Bibliography

Alcaraz, José Antonio. *Hablar de música.* Iztapalapa: Unidad Iztapalapa, 1982.

ALCIDES LANZA

CÉSAIRE, AIMÉ (1913–).

Aimé Césaire (*b.* 25 June 1913), West Indian writer. Born in Martinique, Césaire graduated from the well-known Lycée Victor Schoelcher in Fort-de-France in 1931. He later studied in Paris at the Lycée Louis-le-Grand, where he met Léopold Sédar Senghor from Senegal and many other young black students from African and Caribbean countries. In 1934 Césaire invented the neologism négritude as an expression of pride in the African cultural heritage. Césaire helped found the black magazine *L'étudiant Noir* (1934–1936). In 1939, the same year that his now classic epic poem *Cahier d'un retour au pays natal* (1939; Notebook of a Return to the Native Land) came out in Paris, Césaire returned to Martinique.

During World War II, Césaire worked as a teacher and founded the magazine *Tropiques* (1941–1945) in order to maintain contact with French-language literature. In spring 1941, the famous surrealist poet André Breton payed Césaire a visit. This historic encounter not only confirmed the strong identification Césaire felt with the antirationalism of the surrealist movement but also inspired Bretón to write a preface to a new edition of the *Notebook* (1947), in which he described Césaire as the "Great Black Poet."

In the meantime, Césaire, who had written about the Haitian hero of independence Toussaint Louverture in his *Notebook,* undertook a trip to Haiti, where he remained from May to December of 1944.

Although Césaire's poetry is highly regarded, he is better known for his polemical essays and plays. In 1945 he was elected mayor of Fort-de-France and, after denouncing the French Communist Party in 1956, he founded his own independent socialist party, the Martinican Progressive Party, or PPM, two years later. His political ideas are reflected in his essay against colonialism, *Discours sur le colonialisme* (1950); the letters against communism, *Lettres à Maurice Thorez* (1956); and a historical interpretation of *Toussaint L'Ouverture* (1960). In his plays—such as *La Tragédie du roi Christophe, Une saison au Congo* (1967), and *Une tempête* (1969)—he concentrates on the problems of newly independent African countries against the background of Caribbean history. He retired from politics in 1993, at the age of 80. In 2002, he received the honor of *Commander of the Order of Merit of Cote d'Ivoire.*

BIBLIOGRAPHY

An extensive biographical and critical overview is provided by two African scholars: Mbawil A Mpaang Ngal, *Aimé Césaire: Un homme à la recherche d'une patrie* (1975), and Aliko Songolo, *Aimé Césaire, un poétique de la découverte* (1985). Jean-Claude Bajeux, *Antilia retrouvée* (1983), compares Césaire's work with the poetry of Claude McKay and Luis Palés Matos from Puerto Rico. Josaphat B. Kubayanda in *The Poet's Africa: Africanness in the Poetry of Nicolás Guillén and Aimé Césaire* (1990), links Césaire's poetry to the work of the Cuban poet Nicolás Guillén. Also in English is Janis Pallister, *Aimé Césaire* (1992).

Additional Bibliography

Davis, Gregson, *Aimé Cesaire.* Cambridge, U.K.: Cambridge University Press, 1997.

Suk, Jeannie. *Postcolonial Paradoxes in French Caribbean Writing: Césaire, Glissant, Condé.* Oxford: Clarendon, 2001.

Wright, Michelle. *Becoming Black.* Durham, NC: Duke University Press, 2004.

INEKE PHAF

CÉSPEDES, CARLOS MANUEL DE (THE ELDER) (1819–c. 1874).

Carlos Manuel de Céspedes (The Elder) (*b.* 18 April 1819; *d.* c. 22 March 1874), nineteenth-century Cuban revolutionary. Son of a sugar planter in Cuba's Oriente Province, Céspedes received his baccalaureate degree in Havana in 1840. He then went to study law in Spain where he was exposed to the ideas of Freemasonry, participated in revolutionary activities for which he was exiled to France, and committed himself to opposing colonial repression. When he returned to Cuba, Céspedes joined with other like-minded eastern planters and cattle ranchers, including Ignacio Agramonte, Salvador Cisneros Betancourt, Bartolomé Masó, Pedro Figueredo, and Francisco Vicente Aguilera, who were convinced that Cuba would only win its freedom through the military defeat of Spain. Hence, in the isolated and less-developed corners of the Oriente, Céspedes and the other conspirators used Masonic lodges to organize and coordinate their activities.

On 10 October 1868, without consulting the other leaders, Céspedes held a public meeting at his plantation, La Demajagua, at which he freed his slaves. He then encouraged his listeners to follow the path of such Latin American freedom fighters as Simón Bolívar and José de San Martín. Finally, he issued the Grito De Yara, in which he proclaimed Cuban independence from Spain.

But despite their commitment to independence, Céspedes and his co-conspirators envisioned independence as a transitional step in the process of union with the United States. Only weeks after the independence proclamation, Céspedes led a delegation of Cuban revolutionaries to Washington, D.C., to petition the American secretary of state to consider Cuba's admission to the Union. A year later the revolutionary Constituent Assembly of Guáimaro explicitly proclaimed annexation as the ultimate purpose of the Cuban rebellion.

Despite an initial setback, by 1869 Céspedes was the acknowledged leader of the insurrection and on 10 April he was chosen to be president of the republic declared by the Constituent Assembly. However, divided by petty regionalism, class origins, and conflicts over military strategy, the revolutionaries lacked the unity and discipline essential for victory. Céspedes's authoritarian disposition only intensified the centrifugal forces of the revolutionary movement. In 1873 Céspedes was deposed in absentia as president, and on 22 March of the following year he was killed in a skirmish with Spanish forces.

See also **Bolívar, Simón; Cuba, War of Independence; Masonic Orders.**

BIBLIOGRAPHY

Charles E. Chapman, *History of the Cuban Republic* (1927).

Teresita Martínez Vergne, "Politics and Society in the Spanish Caribbean during the Nineteenth Century" (1989).

Louis A. Pérez, Jr., *Cuba: Between Reform and Revolution* (1989), and *Cuba and the United States* (1990).

Leslie Bethell, *Cuba: A Short History* (1993).

WADE A. KIT

CÉSPEDES Y QUESADA, CARLOS MANUEL DE (1871–1939).

Carlos Manuel de Céspedes y Quesada (*b.* 1871; *d.* 1939), Cuban diplomat and writer. Céspedes y Quesada was the son of Carlos Manuel de Céspedes, the Elder, the Cuban revolutionary who was elected president in 1869 and who was killed in battle during the Ten Years' War. As a child he studied in the United States, France, and Germany, and in 1901 he received a degree in public and civil law from the University of Havana.

Like his father, Céspedes y Quesada played an active role in the movement for Cuban independence. He was among the leading participants of the 1895 Cuban Revolution. Prior to American involvement in the war, he served as governor of Oriente Province, representative of the Second Army Corps, secretary of the Assembly of La Yaya, colonel of the General Staff of the Inspector General, and secretary of the *junta consultiva.*

During the two American interventions (1899–1902, 1906–1909), Céspedes y Quesada withdrew entirely from political life. But upon the creation of the republic, he initiated a long and fruitful diplomatic and political career that lasted for more than thirty years. Among the most important posts he occupied were congressional representative from Oriente; president of the Commission on Tariffs and Codes; ambassador successively to Italy (1909–1912), to Argentina (1912–1913), and to the United States (1913–1922); secretary of state (1922–1926); and ambassador to France (1930–1933). While minister in Washington he negotiated the sale of the Cuban sugar crops of 1917 and 1918 to the United States and the Allies. Upon the overthrow of Cuban dictator Gerardo Machado y Morales in 1933, Céspedes y Quesada, by virtue of his brief tenure as secretary of state, became president of the republic, a position he held from 12 August until 5 September.

Besides being a member of numerous learned societies and the recipient of countless Cuban and foreign honors, he also was a renowned writer. Among the many works he authored, the most noteworthy are *Cuba y el derecho de la fuerza, El problema de la haciendas comuneras, La oración fúnebre del Mayor General Bartolomé Masó,* and *Carlos Manuel de Céspedes y Loynaz.*

See also **Cuba: The Republic (1898–1959).**

BIBLIOGRAPHY

Louis A. Pérez, *Cuba Under the Platt Amendment, 1902–1934* (1986), and *Cuba: Between Reform and Revolution* (1989).

Leslie Bethell, *Cuba: A Short History* (1993).

Additional Bibliography

Hernández, José M. *Política y militarismo en la independencia de Cuba, 1868–1933.* [S.l.]: Editorial Colibrí, 2000.

WADE A. KIT

CEVALLOS, PEDRO ANTONIO DE

(1715–1778). Pedro Antonio de Cevallos (*b.* 29 June 1715; *d.* 24 December 1778), governor of Buenos Aires (1756–1766); viceroy of Río de la Plata (1777–1778). Born in Cádiz, the son of the general superintendent of customs of that city, Cevallos studied for a military career at the Seminario de Nobles in Madrid. Promoted to field marshal by 1747, Cevallos arrived in the Río de la Plata in 1756 as governor and chief of a sizable military expedition charged with containing the Portuguese. During his tenure as governor, Cevallos traveled extensively in the Misiones area. He returned to Spain in 1767, but in 1776 was again called upon to confront the Portuguese. Proving himself to be a fine strategist, he successfully ousted the Portuguese from Colonia in 1777, proceeding to Buenos Aires as first viceroy of the Río de la Plata. During his brief term of office, Cevallos promulgated free-trade ordinances. Shortly after taking office, he fell ill on a trip to Córdoba and died. A lifelong

bachelor, Cevallos left at least one illegitimate son in Buenos Aires, born shortly after his father's death.

See also **Argentina: The Colonial Period.**

BIBLIOGRAPHY

Enrique Udaondo, *Diccionario biográfico colonial argentino* (1945), pp. 249–252.

Hialmar Edmundo Gammalsson, *El virrey Cevallos* (1976).

Enrique M. Barba, *Don Pedro de Cevallos,* 2d ed. (1978).

Additional Bibliography

Lesser, Richard. *La última llamarada: Cevallos, primer virrey del Río de la Plata.* Buenos Aires: Editorial Biblos, 2005.

SUSAN M. SOCOLOW

CEVALLOS, PEDRO FERMÍN (1812–

1893). Pedro Fermín Cevallos was a Supreme Court judge, congressman, biographer, and the father of modern historiography in Ecuador. With a doctoral degree in jurisprudence from the Colegio de San Luís in Quito, he began his political career in 1844 as a deputy in the national Congress. A supporter of liberal political ideas, he helped to establish the first Liberal Party in Ecuador and served as secretary of the 1852 Constitutional Congress that brought General Francisco Urvina to power.

Cevallos was appointed minister of state during the *urvinista* administration (1851–1859); he authorized important decrees implementing such elements of the liberal agenda as the abolition of slavery and the expulsion of the Jesuits. He was elected to Congress in 1867 and in 1875 was appointed minister of the Supreme Court in Quito. Despite his important political contributions, Cevallos is remembered primarily for his six-volume history of Ecuador, *Resumen de la historia del Ecuador* (A summary of the history of Ecuador, 1870). This work, based on his earlier writings in his column *Cuadro sinóptico de la República del Ecuador* (A synoptic picture of the republic) in the liberal newspaper *Democracia,* represents the first systematic study of Ecuadoran history. Continuing the work of the Jesuit historian Juan de Velasco (1727–1792), Cevallos offers a general history of Ecuador starting with the reign of Huayna-Cápac, the last great Inca; and concluding with the *marcista* (march) Revolution of 1845. Although it has been criticized for not offering an in-depth analysis of the historical events, *Resumen* represents an important contribution to Ecuadoran historiography.

See also **Ecuador: Since 1830; Huayna Capac; Liberalism; Mera, Juan León; Urvina Jado, Francisco.**

BIBLIOGRAPHY

Arias, Augusto. "Vida de Pedro Fermín Cevallos." *Augusto Arias: Obras selectas.* Quito: Casa de la Cultura Ecuatoriana, 1962.

Barrera, Isaac J. "Pedro Fermín Cevallos." *Historiografía del Ecuador.* México, D. F.: Instituto Panamericano de Geografía e Historia, 1956.

Thomas, Jack Ray. *Biographical Dictionary of Latin American Historians and Historiography.* Westport, CT: Greenwood Press, 1984.

KENNETH ATWOOD

CHACABUCO, BATTLE OF.

Battle of Chacabuco (12 February 1817), a clash between the Spanish Royalists and the pro-independence Army of the Andes. Chacabuco was an important military encounter in Chile's struggle to win independence from Spain. The rebel force, raised in Mendoza by the Argentine general José de San Martín and Chilean patriot Bernardo O'Higgins, crossed the Andes at Uspallata and Los Patos, surprising and defeating the troops of Francisco Casimiro Marcó del Pont before he could mass his soldiers. Although some Spanish troops remained in Chile, requiring additional mopping up, the insurgent victory at Chacabuco constituted the first successful step in the struggle which culminated in Chile's independence.

See also **O'Higgins, Bernardo.**

BIBLIOGRAPHY

Luis Galdames, *A History of Chile* (1941), pp. 195, 209.

Stephen Clissold, *Bernardo O'Higgins and the Independence of Chile* (1968), pp. 144–146, 148.

Additional Bibliography

Archer, Christon I., ed. *The Wars of Independence in Spanish America.* Wilmington, DE: Scholarly Resources, 2000.

Jocelyn-Holt Letelier, Alfredo. *La independencia de Chile: Tradición, modernización y mito.* Santiago: Planeta/ Ariel, 1992.

Ibáñez Vergara, Jorge. *O'Higgins, el Libertador.* Santiago: Instituto O'Higginiano de Chile, 2001.

WILLIAM F. SATER

CHACARA. *See* **Land Tenure, Brazil.**

CHACMOOLS.

A *chacmool* (literally, "red" or "great jaguar paw") is a Mesoamerican human figural sculpture in a distinctive semireclining position, with legs flexed, chest raised at an incline, head looking toward the viewer, and holding a receptacle on its stomach. Twelve *chacmools* have been discovered at Chichén Itzá, eight are known from Tula, Hidalgo, and many others have been found at Tenochtitlán and sites in Veracruz, Tlaxcala, Michoacán, Querétaro, and Central America. They date from the Terminal Classic to Early Postclassic periods (c. 800–1521).

The *chacmool* generally has been considered a Toltec sculptural form, introduced at Chichén Itzá from Tula between about 900 and 1000. Some scholars question this view, however, since no pre-Toltec central Mexican prototype exists, and since a greater number come from Chichén Itzá. Mary Ellen Miller (1985) proposed that the *chacmool* derives from recumbent captives depicted in Classic Maya art.

The functions and cult associations of the *chacmool* may have varied over time. Late versions have been associated with fertility deities such as Tezcatzoncatl, a México pulque god, or the rain god Tlaloc. Earlier *chacmools* from Tula and Chichén Itzá lack distinctive deity associations but hold platelike receptacles for sacrificial offerings, suggesting they served as divine messengers.

See also **Tula.**

BIBLIOGRAPHY

Enrique Juan Palacios, "El simbolismo del chac-Mool: Su interpretación," in *Revista Mexicana de Estudios Antropólógicos* 4, nos. 1–2 (1940): 43–56.

César Lizardi Ramos, "El Chacmool mexicano," in *Cuadernos Americanos* 14 (March–April 1944): 137–148.

J. Corona Núñez, "Cual es el verdadero significado del Chac Mool?" in *Tlatoani* 1, nos. 5–6 (1952): 57–62.

Alfredo Cuellar, *Tezcatzoncatl escultórico: El "Chac Mool"* (*el dios mesoamericano del vino*) (1981).

Mary Ellen Miller, "A Re-Examination of the Mesoamerican Chacmool," in *Art Bulletin* 67, no. 1 (1985): 7–17.

Additional Bibliography

Jiménez García, Elizabeth. *Iconografía de Tula: El caso de la escultura*. México, D.F.: Instituto Nacional de Antropología e Historia, 1998.

Macazaga Ordoño, César. *Chac Mool: El señor de nuestro sustento*. México, D.F.: Editorial Innovación, 1985.

Miller, Mary Ellen. *Maya Art and Architecture*. New York: Thames & Hudson, 1999.

JEFF KARL KOWALSKI

CHACÓN, LÁZARO (1873–1931).

Lázaro Chacón (*b.* 27 June 1873; *d.* 1931), president of Guatemala (1926–1930). Lázaro Chacón was born in Teculután, Zacapa. His grandfather was a military officer and his father was a cattle rancher. A career army officer, General Chacón assumed the presidency of Guatemala on 27 September 1926, the day following the fatal heart attack of General José María Orellana, his boyhood friend. Chacón's critics charged that the new president "was a man of very little intelligence, less education and no experience in government affairs."

Upon assuming the presidency, Chacón committed his government to the continuation of the policies of his predecessor. Also, with the country in the midst of a remarkable economic boom, Chacón announced his intention to prevent all forms of social and political unrest. Supported by a large majority of Guatemalan liberals, Chacón easily won the December 1926 presidential election. From most reports, the outcome of the election was never in doubt. Most of Guatemala's traditionally powerful landed elite had little reason to oppose Chacón's promises of prosperity and stability. While the opposition Progressive Party candidate, future president Jorge Ubico y Castañeda, ran a campaign that was vaguely reformist, Chacón capitalized on his links to the Guatemalan military and on the economic prosperity enjoyed by the nation's coffee elite to secure an easy victory.

When the Guatemalan economy was crippled by the effects of a worldwide depression in the late 1920s, Chacón's government was already unpopular with the Guatemalan upper and middle classes. Accused of mismanagement, corruption, and inept administration, the Chacón government appeared to be on the verge of anarchy. In December 1930, Chacón suffered a massive stroke. With Chacón incapacitated, the government wallowed in a sea of indecision until Jorge Ubico was elected president in early February 1931.

See also **Guatemala.**

BIBLIOGRAPHY

Joseph A. Pitti, "Jorge Ubico and Guatemalan Politics in the 1920's" (Ph.D. diss., University of New Mexico, 1975).

Wade Kit, "Precursor of Change: Failed Reform and the Guatemalan Coffee Elite, 1918–1926" (Master's thesis, University of Saskatchewan, 1989).

Additional Bibliography

Gaitán, Héctor. *Los presidentes de Guatemala: Historia y anécdotas*. Guatemala de la Asunción: Artemis-Edinter, 2004.

WADE A. KIT

CHACO REGION.

Chaco Region (El Gran Chaco) is a vast alluvial plain in the interior of South America which is shaped like a cone. The Chaco region occupies more than 100,000 square miles of western Paraguay, eastern Bolivia, and northern Argentina. It is extremely flat, rising only gently from the Paraná–Paraguay river system in the east to western Argentina and the lowlands of eastern Bolivia. It is divided by rivers into three sections: the Chaco Austral between the Salado and Bermejo rivers, the Chaco Central between the Bermejo and Pilcomayo rivers, and the Chaco Boreal from the Pilcomayo to just north of the Paraguay–Bolivia border.

During the summer, many areas are drenched with rain, leaving lagoons, swamps, and rivulets overflowing in every direction. In winter these same areas are arid wastelands cut irregularly by thorn forests. The region is home to a vast array of fauna, including jaguars, tapirs, parrots, and a species of peccary long thought to be extinct. Usually cited as one of the continent's last great wildernesses, much of it remains sparsely settled and infrequently visited, although it produces timber, livestock, and cotton.

In pre-Columbian times the Chaco region was synonymous with the unknown. The pre-Hispanic inhabitants of the Altiplano simply called it *chacu*, a Quechua word meaning "great hunting ground." The Guarani from Paraguay and Brazil crossed it to trade with Andean peoples. Sixteenth-century Spanish explorers followed the Guaranis across the Chaco to Peru; but after the Chaco peoples, including the Mocobís, Abipones, and Tobas, acquired horses and resisted Spanish incursions, the Spaniards forgot the route and rarely ventured into the region.

In the eighteenth century Spanish ranchers and timber merchants penetrated the Chaco. Late in the century, government expeditions probed the interior, and minor missions were sent to the Abipones and Mocobís. During the late nineteenth century, venture capitalists from Argentina and Europe sought to open the Chaco to commercial exploitation. They focused primarily on the region's hardwoods—lapacho, curupay, petereby, and especially quebracho (a source of tannin for curing leather). Their efforts were hampered by the climate, terrain, and native resistance. The local communities of the Argentine Chaco were finally subdued in the 1880s, those of the Bolivian Chaco in the 1890s. Only Mennonite farmers, who came from Eastern Europe to the Paraguayan Chaco in the beginning of the twentieth century seemed to make the land thrive. They raised cattle and grew cotton.

Border disputes—and a lingering rumor that the region possessed sizable reserves of petroleum—led to the Chaco War (1932–1935), in which Paraguay bested Bolivia, gaining most of the Chaco Boreal, at the cost of tens of thousands of lives.

After the war, colonization increased, especially in the eastern part of the Chaco. Ranches and farms gradually replaced military posts. The Chaco indigenous groups—Chiriguanos, Makas, Nivaklés, Lenguas, Ayoreos, and others—hired out as wranglers or day-laborers chiefly on Mennonite lands. National and foreign companies exploited the Argentine Chaco. Oil companies explored the Chaco without success. By the late 1980s, stockraising, dairy farming, and cotton growing had transformed the Argentine Chaco and the eastern Paraguayan Chaco. The traditional isolation and natural purity of these areas were becoming things of the past. Daily commuters from Asunción now crossed a new bridge over the Paraguay River to Chaco communities, and Chaco products traveled to Asunción. Nevertheless, vast stretches of the Chaco, especially in the center and west, were still nearly empty of human population.

In September of 1995, the Bolivian government established the Kaa–Iya National Park (Parque Nacional y área natural de manejo integrado Kaa–Iya del Gran Chaco), home to Latin America's most diverse population of mammals. Developed in partnership with the Guaraní peoples known as Isoceño, and the Wildlife Conservation Society, the 3.44 million hectare Kaa–Iya National Park is managed solely by the indigenous people themselves through the Capitanía de Alto y Bajo Isoso (CABI).

See also **Argentina, Geography; Chaco War; Paraguay, Geography.**

BIBLIOGRAPHY

Martin Dobrizhoffer, *An Account of the Abipones: An Equestrian People of Paraguay*, 3 vols., translated by Sara Coleridge (1822; repr. in 1 vol., 1970).

Pedro Lozano, *Descripción corográfica del Gran Chaco Gualambra* (1941).

Alfred Métraux, "Ethnography of the Chaco," in *Handbook of South American Indians*, vol. 1, edited by Julian H. Steward (1946).

Juan Belaieff, "The Present–Day Indians of the Gran Chaco," in *Handbook of South American Indians*, vol. 1, edited by Julian H. Steward (1946), pp. 197–370, 371–380.

David H. Zook, *The Conduct of the Chaco War* (1960).

Harry Robinson, *Latin America: A Geographic Survey* (rev. ed., 1967), pp. 432–435, 464–466.

Luis Jorge Fontana, *El Gran Chaco: Estudio preliminar de Ernesto J. A. Maeder* (1977).

Andrew Nickson, *Historical Dictionary of Paraguay* (rev. ed., 1993), pp. 111–123.

Additional Bibliography

Andrew Taber, Gonzalo Navarro, Miguel Angel Arribas. "A New Park in the Bolivian Gran Chaco—An Advance in Tropical Dry Forest Conservation and Community-based Management." *Oryx* 31, no. 3 (July 1997): 189–198.

JAMES SCHOFIELD SAEGER
THOMAS L. WHIGHAM

CHACO WAR. The Chaco War was a conflict that began in June 1932 when Bolivian and Paraguayan outposts clashed at a brackish lake in the northern Chaco Boreal, a territory over which the two nations disputed sovereignty. This spark began a bloody war that lasted until 1935.

The Chaco Boreal was a vast, inhospitable, and sparsely populated area bordering the two countries. In the summer (November–February) the sun parched the hot, dry earth, and in the rainy season (March–October) heavy rains created huge marshes that bred disease-carrying insects. Both Bolivia and Paraguay looked upon the Chaco as a potential site of development and wealth. Some Bolivians believed that they could regain their access to the sea, which they had lost in the War of the Pacific (1879–1883), by developing a port on the Paraguay River at the northeastern corner of the disputed territory. Much of Paraguay's foreign exchange was earned by exports of quebracho bark and cattle hides from the Chaco. In order to improve their claims to the territory, both countries had accelerated exploration and the establishment of outposts.

Although both sides had been preparing for this war for decades, neither really appreciated the logistical obstacles that they would face. As a result, prewar operational plans were useless and soon abandoned. Bolivia's situation was made significantly more difficult by the differences in strategy and priorities between President Daniel Salamanca and the country's military leaders, whose antagonism grew as the war progressed. In contrast, General José Estigarribia emerged as the de facto commander of the Paraguayan Army and won the unconditional support of recently elected President Eusebio Ayala.

Following the fighting at Lake Pitiantuta, the Bolivian army conducted a limited offensive in the east-central Chaco, capturing a number of *fortines* (small forts), the most important being Boquerón. Salamanca then ordered the army to suspend operations, fearing that Argentina might intervene on the side of Paraguay. Estigarribia immediately attacked Boquerón, and after a stout defense by the Bolivians, the Paraguayans captured it on 29 September. Each side sustained some 3,000 casualties.

The Bolivian public was shocked at this defeat and demanded the recall of General Hans Kundt from exile. Kundt had headed a German military mission to Bolivia prior to World War I, and following the war he returned, became a Bolivian citizen, and resumed command of the army. During the late 1920s he had been exiled for political activity.

Many Bolivians believed that, as the creator of the modern army, he could win the day. In December 1932 Kundt launched a series of offensives against Paraguayan *fortines*, focusing on Nanawa in the east-central Chaco. Time and time again, Kundt unsuccessfully threw masses of infantry against well-prepared defensive positions. Nanawa earned the nickname the Verdun of South America. After a year of unimaginative, costly tactics, Kundt was relieved by General Enrique Peñaranda.

In October 1932 Estigarribia began his offensive, driving the Bolivians from *fortín* to *fortín* across the central Chaco. He was finally halted before Fortín Ballivián on the bank of the Pilcomayo River in the southwest corner of the Chaco. Although the *fortín* had no special military significance, it had become the symbol of Bolivia's presence in the Chaco. Nonetheless, General Peñaranda ordered General David Toro to abandon the *fortín* in order to shorten Bolivia's overstretched defenses. Toro refused to obey and Peñaranda acquiesced.

By July 1934 a large Paraguayan force commanded by Colonel Rafael Franco had driven across the central Chaco north of Ballivián and into undisputed Bolivian territory. Estigarribia realized that Franco had outdistanced his supply system and ordered him to fall back slowly. Toro, on his own initiative, decided to attempt to cut off Franco's retreating force, so he marched north with a significant part of Fortín Ballivián's garrison. Estigarribia perceived the Bolivian move and ordered Franco to fight a delaying action against Toro's superior numbers. Toro attempted to circle Franco's force but failed. Slowly, Toro was enticed farther and farther into the Chaco by the retreating Franco. Finally, in December 1934, Estigarribia rushed significant reinforcements to Franco's aid. The Paraguayans captured the wells supplying water to the Bolivians. A significant part of Toro's force was surrounded and captured. Of approximately 11,000 Bolivians, perhaps only half escaped the Paraguayan trap. In the meantime, the Paraguayans captured the now weakly defended Fortín Ballivián.

By early 1935 the Paraguayans had won almost all of the disputed Chaco and were besieging the Bolivian town of Villa Montes. But the balance of power had begun to shift in favor of the Bolivians as the Paraguayans overextended their supply lines. Also, Bolivia finally declared a general mobilization, thus taking advantage of its significantly larger population. Both sides were exhausted and nearly bankrupt. On 12 June 1935 they agreed to a cease-fire, which took effect on the 14th, and the war was formally ended in 1938.

Paraguay won most of the entire Chaco during the war and was awarded most of it during the peace negotiations. Bolivia sustained about 57,000 dead and Paraguay some 36,000. The war destroyed the fragile democratic governments in both countries: Salamanca was overthrown on 27 November 1934 and Ayala on 17 February 1936.

See also **Chaco Region; War of the Pacific.**

BIBLIOGRAPHY

Angel Rodríguez, *Autopsia de una guerra* (1940).

Pablo Max Ynsfrán, ed., *The Epic of the Chaco: Marshal Estigarribia's Memoirs of the Chaco War, 1932–1935* (1950).

David H. Zook, *The Conduct of the Chaco War* (1960).

Ramón César Bejarano, *Síntesis de la guerra del Chaco* (1982).

Additional Bibliography

Farcau, Bruce W. *The Chaco War: Bolivia and Paraguay, 1932–1935*. Westport, CT: Praeger, 1996.

Lorini, Irma. *El nacionalismo en Bolivia de la pre y posguerra del Chaco, 1910–1945*. La Paz: Plural Editores, 2006.

ROBERT SCHEINA

CHACRA. *Chacra*, meaning "land for sowing" in the Quechua language, is a word widely used in the Andes and surrounding cities and towns (even on the coast). It is used today to refer generally to a small plot of land for market gardening. The specific meaning of *chacra* varies by locale and time. Generally it denotes modest plots of land devoted in part to the production of agricultural goods for household consumption, and in part to small surpluses for sale in local markets. As such, *chacras* are important sources of household income, usually tended by women and children while men work on nearby estates or in cities for wages. They flourish particularly in agrarian zones around cities, for which they are important sources of foodstuffs. In some regions and times, the *chacra* may produce for market more than for subsistence and provide full employment for all household members.

See also **Agriculture; Quechua.**

BIBLIOGRAPHY

Apffel-Marglin, Frédérique. *The Spirit of Regeneration: Andean Culture Confronting Western Notions of Development*. New York: Zed Books, 1998.

Mayer, Enrique. *The Articulated Peasant: Household Economies in the Andes*. Boulder, CO: Westview Press, 2002.

JEREMY ADELMAN

CHACRINHA (1918–1989). Chacrinha (José Abelardo de Barbosa Medeiros; *b.* 1918; *d.* 1989), Brazilian television variety show host. Born in Pernambuco, he was one of the longest-running stars of radio, starting in 1943, then of television, with a leading show on TV Rio by 1958. He was considered very innovative in developing one of the two major Brazilian television entertainment forms, the live variety show (*show de auditório*). (The other major form is the *telenovela*.) His programs were characterized by his dressing in a flamboyant clown costume, an outrageous style of comedy, and close interaction with his audience. His shows relied on amateur performances, comedy, music, guests, dancers, and games. His two best-known shows were *Buzina de Chacrinha* (Chacrinha's Horn) and *Discoteca de Chacrinha*. In the 1960s and 1970s, Chacrinha was identified with the movement known as *tropicalismo* to revive authentic Brazilian popular culture, particularly in music. He was mentioned in Gilberto Gil's salute to Brazilian tropical culture, the song "*Alegria, Alegria*" (Joy, Joy). While Chacrinha was considered in dubious taste by some, including TV Globo's management, which fired him in 1972, many popular culture experts, both Brazilian and foreign, considered his shows the best forum for authentic Brazilian popular culture. He was called one of Brazil's best communicators for his rapport with his audience. His programs, along with other live programs, were banned by the military governments from 1972 to 1979 because they were too difficult to control. In the 1980s, Chacrinha appeared on several competing Brazilian networks.

See also **Radio and Television.**

BIBLIOGRAPHY

Joseph Straubhaar, "Brazilian Television Variety Shows," in *Studies in Latin American Popular Culture* 2 (1983): 71–78.

Additional Bibliography

Barbosa, Florinda, and Lucia Rito. *Quem não se comunica se trumbica*. São Paulo: Editora Globo, 1996.

JOSEPH STRAUBHAAR

CHADBOURNE PLAN.

During the Great Depression, New York lawyer Thomas L. Chadbourne supervised two agreements to alleviate the problem of stockpiled Cuban sugar. The 1930 Cuban Stabilization Law imposed production controls on the sugar industry. The following year, the Chadbourne Plan established international guidelines for sugar production and marketing.

The continuing depression and concomitant autarky, however, ended the plan's hope that world consumption would climb as sugar tariffs ended. By imposing the largest production reduction on Cuba, the plan benefited only U.S. banks holding stockpiled sugar, while hurting Cuban sharecroppers and cane cutters. Therefore, it only added anticapitalist fuel to Cuban nationalism, already inflamed by the Platt Amendment.

See also **Platt Amendment.**

BIBLIOGRAPHY

Harry F. Guggenheim, *The U.S. and Cuba: A Study in International Relations* (1934).

Boris Swerling, *International Control of Sugar, 1910–1941* (1949).

Jules Benjamin, *The United States and Cuba: Hegemony and Dependent Development, 1880–1934* (1977).

Additional Bibliography

Ayala, César J. *American Sugar Kingdom: The Plantation Economy of the Spanish Caribbean, 1898–1934.* Chapel Hill: University of North Carolina Press, 1999.

Santamaría García, Antonio, and Carlos Malamud. *Sin azucar no hay país: La industria azucarera y la economía cubana (1919–1939).* Sevilla: Secretariado de Publicaciones de la Universidad de Sevilla: Diputación de Sevilla, Servicio de Archivo y Publicaciones, 2001.

Zanetti Lecuona, Oscar and Alejandro García Alvarez. *Sugar & Railroads: A Cuban History, 1837–1959.* Chapel Hill: University of North Carolina Press, 1998.

Zanetti Lecuona, Oscar. *Las manos en el dulce: Estado e intereses en la regulación de la industria azucarera cubana, 1926–1937.* La Habana: Editorial de Ciencias Sociales, 2004.

EDMOND KONRAD

CHAGAS, CARLOS RIBEIRO JUSTINIANO

(1879–1934). Carlos Ribeiro Justiniano Chagas (*b.* 9 July 1879; *d.* 8 November 1934), Brazilian medical scientist. Chagas is remembered for discovering a new human disease, *Trypanosomiasis americana,* commonly known as Chagas' disease, which to this day afflicts millions of people in South America.

Chagas was born in Minas Gerais and trained in medicine in Rio de Janeiro, where he obtained his medical degree in 1902. In 1907 he joined the staff of the Oswaldo Cruz Institute, which later sent him to Lassance, 300 miles from Rio, to organize an anti-malaria campaign. It was while he was in Lassance that Chagas took up the study of a biting insect commonly known as the *barbeiro* (a *triatoma*), which lived in the walls and thatched roofs of the local dwellings. Finding a trypanosome in the gut of the insect, he suspected that it might produce disease and that humans might be its natural host. Therefore, Chagas proceeded to test its pathogenic effects in animals. He went on to discover trypanosome in the heart and brain tissues of patients whose diverse clinical symptoms had escaped understanding until that time.

The announcement of a new human disease in 1909 initiated years of research into its insect vectors; the life cycle of the causative agent, the *Trypanosoma cruzi* (named after Oswaldo Cruz, Chagas's friend and director of the Oswaldo Cruz Institute); and its clinical symptoms. The disease has acute and chronic forms and causes cardiac, gastrointestinal, and neurological symptoms.

In 1917, Chagas took over the direction of the Oswaldo Cruz Institute; in 1919 he also became director of the federal public health program, where he oversaw the extension of public health campaigns into the rural areas of Brazil. Nevertheless, Chagas was primarily known as a medical scientist. His work on *Trypanosomiasis americana* gave him an international reputation in medicine; he received the Schaudinn Prize for protozoology in 1913 and several honorary degrees.

See also **Diseases; Medicine: The Modern Era.**

BIBLIOGRAPHY

The *Annals of the International Congress of Chagas' Disease,* 5 vols. (1960), contains a complete bibliography of Chagas's writings; his career is described in Nancy Stepan, *Beginnings of Brazilian Science: Oswaldo Cruz, Medical Research, and Policy, 1890–1920* (1976).

Additional Bibliography

Scliar, Moacyr. *Oswaldo Cruz e Carlos Chagas: O nascimento de ciência no Brasil.* São Paulo: Odysseus, 2002.

NANCY LEYS STEPAN

CHALCATZINGO. Chalcatzingo, an archaeological site located in the modern state of Morelos, Mexico, approximately 60 miles southeast of Mexico City. It was one of the earliest and largest ceremonial centers and one of the first complex chiefdom societies to develop in central Mexico.

Chalcatzingo is located at the base of a large mountain known as Cerro Chalcatzingo. Between 1000 and 100 BCE, terraces were constructed across the hillside where household gardens were planted adjacent to individual residences. A large upper terrace immediately adjacent to Cerro Chalcatzingo was the focus of the site's elite and ritual activity. A large platform (77 feet long by 33 feet wide by 3 feet high), a large public plaza, and an elite residential area were the center of the community's ritual life. After 700 BCE the ceremonial zone expanded and ritual architecture was constructed on adjacent terraces, which included rectangular stone-faced platforms with one or more carved stelae (stone monuments) and an enclosed patio with a tabletop altar.

Chalcatzingo is famous for its Olmec-style rock carvings, many of which are located on the talus above the site's ceremonial core. These carvings reflect Chalcatzingo's role as a major ritual center and its participation in long-distance trade networks throughout Mesoamerica. Chalcatzingo grew to its greatest size between 700 and 500 BCE, when it covered slightly more than 88 acres and had a population of between four hundred and one thousand people. During this period Chalcatzingo brought the Amatzinac region under its direct political control and developed perhaps central Mexico's first chiefdom-level society based on social ranking, the inheritance of status, and differential access to wealth.

See also **Precontact History: Mesoamerica.**

BIBLIOGRAPHY

David Grove, et al., "Settlement and Cultural Development at Chalcatzingo," in *Science* 192 (1976): 1203–1210; *Chalcatzingo, Excavations on the Olmec Frontier* (1984); *Ancient Chalcatzingo* (1987).

Kenneth Hirth, "Interregional Trade and the Formation of Prehistoric Gateway Communities," in *American Antiquity* 43 (1978): 35–45.

Additional Bibliography

Diehl, Richard A. *The Olmecs: America's First Civilization.* New York: Thames & Hudson, 2004.

Grove, David C. "Faces of the Earth at Chalcatzingo, Mexico: Serpents, Caves, and Mountains in Middle Formative Period." *Iconography in Olmec Art and Archaeology in Mesoamerica,* edited by John E. Clark and Mary E. Pye. Washington, DC: National Gallery of Art; New Haven, CT: Distributed by Yale University Press, 2000.

Grove, David C., and Rosemary A. Joyce, eds. *Social Patterns in Pre-Classic Mesoamerica.* Washington, DC: Dumbarton Oaks Research Library and Collection, 1999.

KENNETH HIRTH

CHALCHUAPA, BATTLE OF. Battle of Chalchuapa. On 28 February 1885, the president of Guatemala, Justo Rufino Barrios, issued a declaration calling for the establishment of a Central American Union. As the self-proclaimed supreme military commander of Central America, Barrios asked each of the Central American states (Costa Rica, Honduras, El Salvador, Nicaragua, and Guatemala) to recognize the union and to send delegates to Guatemala City to create the institutions of the new government.

The governments of Costa Rica, Nicaragua, and El Salvador opposed the union immediately. As a result, on 31 March 1885, Barrios initiated a military campaign against El Salvador to crush the resistance of Salvadoran president Rafael Zaldívar. Two days later, on 2 April 1885, Barrios was killed in battle and the Guatemalan army was soundly defeated at Chalchuapa, El Salvador. Following the defeat, the

Guatemalan forces dispersed and the war with El Salvador came to a rapid conclusion. In subsequent weeks, Barrios's proclamation recognizing the creation of the Central American Union was revoked and his dream of unity thwarted.

See also **Barrios, Justo Rufino.**

BIBLIOGRAPHY

Thomas L. Karnes, *The Failure of Union, Central America, 1824–1960* (1961), pp. 152–162.

Additional Bibliography

Leiva Vivas, Rafael. *La unión centroamericana: Utopía, lirismo y desafío.* Tegucigalpa: ENAG, Empresa Nacional Artes Gráficas, 2004.

Yashar, Deborah J. *Demanding Democracy: Reform and Reaction in Costa Rica and Guatemala, 1870s–1950s.* Stanford, CA: Stanford University Press, 1997.

WADE A. KIT

CHALCO AGRARIAN REBELLION OF 1868.

The Chalco peasant rebellion of 1868, originating in the Chalco region of south-central Mexico, had its ideological origins in the currents of radical utopian socialism and anarchism espoused by the school of Plotino Rhodakanaty. Texcoco native Julio López Chávez led the uprising, and at its zenith it mobilized a poorly armed force of more than fifteen hundred peasants. The quickly growing militia attacked towns and confiscated haciendas between Puebla and Chalco, in the area to the immediate southeast of Mexico City. A contingent of the national army commanded by General Rafael Cuéllar succeeded in capturing López Chávez in August 1869, after a brutal campaign that included the forced relocation of entire villages. The Juárez government executed López Chávez in September 1869, effectively ending the insurrection.

The Chalco rebellion was the first of the nineteenth century to advance a coherent ideological critique of the Mexican state based on the principles of agrarian socialism. The imported European concept of class struggle gave form to the long-festering grievances of the Mexican peasantry, many of whom had come to see the *hacendados* as allied with the state and the church to deprive them of their communal land rights. López Chávez, in a manifesto

released preceding the major phase of the rebellion, enshrined the ideal of *municipios libres*, or communally organized and politically autonomous villages. In the decades to come, the *municipio libre* would become a central demand of the agrarian movement.

See also **Agrarian Reform; López Chavez, Julio.**

BIBLIOGRAPHY

Hart, John M. *Anarchism & the Mexican Working Class, 1860–1931.* Austin: University of Texas Press, 1978.

Valadés, José C. *El socialismo libertario mexicano (siglo XIX).* Mexico: Universidad Autónoma de Sinaloa, 1984.

JAMES ELLIOT MCBRIDE

CHALMA.

Chalma (or Chalmita), a renowned pilgrimage site in Mexico and symbol of folk Catholicism, combining elements of indigenous and European faiths. According to legend, in 1539, Augustinian friars found an idol (possibly representing Tezcatlipoca) and evidence of sacrifices to it in a cave at Chalma. Later, when they went to replace the idol with a cross, they reputedly found the image broken in pieces and a crucifix already in its place. The idol had been the object of pilgrimages in pre-Hispanic times; subsequent treks were made from great distances to worship the miraculous new god and the nearby town's new patron, St. Michael, who also came to occupy a place at the sacred shrine. Which deity Oztoteotl (the "cave god"), as the idol came to be called, truly represented, and whether his attributes were transferred to Christ and/or St. Michael in the hearts of the indigenous people, are unresolved questions. Modern pilgrimages are lively events marked by floral displays, song, dance, and fireworks.

See also **Augustinians.**

BIBLIOGRAPHY

Erna Fergusson, *Fiesta in Mexico* (1934), pp. 47–67, and Alejandra González Leyva, *Chalma: Una devoción agustina* (Toluca, 1991), provide an example of the folklore surrounding the shrine at Chalma. Gilberto Giménez offers details of a modern pilgrimage to Chalma in his *Cultura popular y religión en el Anáhuac* (1978).

Additional Bibliography

Rodríguez-Shadow, María, and Robert Dennis Shadow. *El pueblo del Señor: Las fiestas y peregrinaciones de*

Chalma. Toluca: Universidad Autónoma del Estado de México, 2000.

STEPHANIE WOOD

CHAMBI, MARTÍN (1891–1973). Martín
Chambi (*b.* 5 November 1891; *d.* 1973), Peruvian photographer. Although all biographical facts about Chambi are currently under scrutiny, it is safe to say that he was born into a modest peasant family of Indian stock in the village of Coaza, near Lake Titicaca, in the southern highlands of Peru. His first experience with photography occurred when his father was working for the British Santo Domingo Mining Company, near Carabaya. The curious boy eagerly sought to help the company photographer, who was taking survey views of the area. Around 1908, Chambi moved to Arequipa, where he allegedly pursued a high school education and until 1917 was an apprentice at the studio of the then famous photographer Max T. Vargas. That same year he married Manuela López Viza; they had six children.

In 1917, seeking to establish his own business, Chambi moved to the thriving town of Sicuani. Some three years later he moved on to Cuzco, where he sought out Juan Manuel Figueroa Aznar, a former pupil of Vargas. For a while Chambi and Figueroa shared a studio in Cuzco. At the time, that ancient capital of the Incas was undergoing a cultural renaissance and the beginning of an economic recession. Indigenismo became a major intellectual and political force in Cuzco. Chambi befriended such leading *indigenista* intellectuals as José Uriel García, Luis Valcárcel, Gamaliel Churata, Roberto Latorre, and Luis Valesco Aragón. Chambi's work was published in illustrated magazines like *Variedades*. Politically, he sympathized with the early APRA party and contributed to the radical avant-garde magazine *Kosko* by taking ads for his studio in it.

During the 1920s Chambi's prestige as a photographer peaked, and his clientele included wealthy families such as the Lomellinis and the Montes. Some of his most memorable images are commissioned portraits to which he added a social commentary. Yet, his ethnographic work and documentation of Cuzco's colonial and Inca architecture is probably his most systematic. Many of the images for which he is famous today were never shown in the exhibitions curated by Chambi himself. The American photographer Edward Ranney, largely responsible for Chambi's rediscovery in 1977, has played an important role in the appreciation and perception of his work.

See also **Photography: The Twentieth Century.**

BIBLIOGRAPHY

Roderic Ai Camp, "Martín Chambi: Photographer of the Andes," in *Latin American Research Review* 13, no. 2 (1978): 223–228, and "Martín Chambi: Pioneer Photographer of Peru," in *Américas* 30, no. 3 (March 1978): 5–10.

Edward Ranney, "Martín Chambi: Poet of Light," in *Earthwatch News* 1 (Spring–Summer 1979): 3–6.

Fernando Castro, *Martín Chambi: De Coaza al MoMA* (1989).

José Carlos Huayhuaca, *Martín Chambi, fotógrafo* (1991); *Martín Chambi: Photographs, 1920–1950,* translated by Margaret Sayers Peden (1993).

Additional Bibliography

Hopkinson, Amanda. *Martín Chambi*. New York: Phaidon, 2001.

FERNANDO CASTRO

CHAMIZAL CONFLICT. From 1864 to
1963, the United States and Mexico claimed sovereignty over the El Chamizal tract ("the thicket"), located between El Paso, Texas, and what is now Ciudad Juárez, Chihuahua. Changes in the course of the Rio Grande caused this land, formerly on the Mexican side of the river, to shift to the U.S. side, thereby altering the international boundary. Both nations claimed the Chamizal. The dispute was submitted to international arbitration in 1911. The United States rejected the arbitral tribunal's award, which divided the area between the claimants.

Settlement of problems between the United States and Mexico was impeded by the continued Chamizal conflict. For instance, the petroleum expropriation controversy of the 1930s could not immediately be resolved because Mexico distrusted the intentions of the United States and refused to submit the matter to arbitration.

In 1963 President John F. Kennedy agreed to settle the dispute on the basis of the 1911 arbitration award. This action eliminated a source of propaganda directed against United States imperialism and allayed Mexican fears about further U.S. expansion into its territory.

See also **United States-Mexico Border.**

BIBLIOGRAPHY

Sheldon B. Liss, *A Century of Disagreement: The Chamizal Conflict, 1864–1964* (1965).

Alan C. Lamborn and Stephen P. Mumme, *Statecraft, Domestic Politics, and Foreign Policy Making: The El Chamizal Dispute* (1988).

Additional Bibliography

Gómez Robledo, Antonio. *México y el arbitraje internacional: El Fondo Piadoso de las Californias, la Isla de la Pasión, el Chamizal*. México: Porrúa, 1994.

Utley, Robert Marshall. *Changing Course: The International Boundary, United States and Mexico, 1848–1963*. Tucson, AZ: Southwest Parks and Monuments Association, 1996.

SHELDON B. LISS

CHAMORRO, FRUTO (1804–1855).
Fruto Chamorro (*b*. 20 October 1804; *d*. 12 March 1855), first director of state and first president of Nicaragua (1853–1855). Chamorro is considered one of the most influential and significant figures in the political life of Nicaragua. He restored order to the republic after the chaos of the incessant post-independence wars caused by friction between Conservatives and Liberals.

Born in Guatemala to a Nicaraguan father, Pedro José Chamorro, Fruto Chamorro left his homeland for Nicaragua in early 1827. Soon realizing that Nicaragua suffered from anarchy, factionalism, and militarism, he focused his energy on the fight for liberty and order. In 1836 Chamorro was elected deputy to the Granada state legislature, a position he used to establish public education in that state. He considered education basic to social progress and saw it as a way to mend the fatal localism afflicting the country. Chamorro also was instrumental in the establishment of elections to create a Constituent Assembly that would reform the constitution of 1838. From 1839 to 1842 he was a senator.

By the end of 1842 Chamorro was managing the first newspaper in Granada, *Mentor Nicaragüense,* an organ of the Universidad de Oriente in whose pages he revealed his moral personality. He was an intensely faithful Christian, a staunch supporter of public education, an enemy of ignorance, a concerned political activist, and a dedicated public servant who devoted himself to the preservation of order in Nicaragua. The maintenance of order was Chamorro's major objective upon his assumption of the office of supreme director on 1 April 1853. The new constitution, promulgated on 4 March 1854, provided that the State of Nicaragua be renamed the Republic of Nicaragua and that the title supreme director be changed to president of the republic; thus, Chamorro served as the first and only supreme director and the first president of Nicaragua.

On 1 June 1855, U.S. adventurer William Walker landed fifty-seven men at Realjo in order to take over Nicaragua. After initial military setbacks, Walker captured Granada in October 1855 and was appointed armed forces chief. Patricio Rivas served as a figurehead president. Although Walker himself was elected president in June 1856, Honduras, El Salvador, and Guatemala allied against him. Nicaraguan forces ousted Walker in May 1857, and he spent the next three years trying to incite other revolutions. British marines eventually captured Walker in Honduras. He was executed in Trujillo on 12 September 1860. Nicaragua returned to peace, which the Conservative presidents who followed Chamorro maintained until 1893.

Chamorro's legacy, then, rests on the fact that his administration provided the foundation for the orderly succession of mainly civilian Conservative presidents. In addition, Chamorro was responsible for the formation of political clubs that evolved into the Conservative Party. His family has been an active and integral element in the Conservative Party ranks for generations. The Conservatives posthumously honored Chamorro as the founder of their party in 1859.

See also **National War; Nicaragua.**

BIBLIOGRAPHY

Sara Luisa Barquero, *Gobernantes de Nicaragua, 1825–1947* (1945), esp. pp. 81–85.

Pedro Joaquín Chamorro Zelaya, *Fruto Chamorro* (1960).

Francisco Ortega Arancibia, *Cuarenta años (1838–1878) de historia de Nicaragua* (1975).

Ricardo Paíz Castillo, *Breve historia del Partido Conservador de Nicaragua y estampas conservadoras* (1984), esp. pp. 29–31, 109–119.

Additional Bibliography

Díaz Lacayo, Aldo. *Gobernantes de Nicaragua (1821–1979): Guía para el estudio de sus biografías políticas.* Managua: Aldilà Editor, 2002.

Kinloch Tijerino, Frances. *Nicaragua: Identidad y cultura política (1821–1858).* Managua: Banco Central de Nicaragua, 1999.

SHANNON BELLAMY

CHAMORRO, VIOLETA. *See* Barrios de Chamorro, Violeta.

CHAMORRO CARDENAL, PEDRO JOAQUÍN (1924–1978).

Pedro Joaquín Chamorro Cardenal (*b.* 23 September 1924; *d.* 10 January 1978), Nicaraguan political activist. Chamorro came from a prominent Nicaraguan family with a long history of participation in partisan politics (four of his ancestors held the Nicaraguan presidency). Chamorro's father, Pedro Joaquín Chamorro Zelaya, had founded the daily newspaper *La Prensa* in 1926; upon his father's death in 1952, Chamorro became editor in chief and owner of the paper, which became a vehicle for his opposition to the dictatorship of the Somoza family. Chamorro also condemned the government in a number of books he wrote. In 1948 he cofounded the short-lived National Union of Popular Action and Justice (UNAP). In 1954 he was a member of the Internal Front, which attempted to overthrow Somoza García. He participated in an invasion of Nicaragua from Costa Rica in 1959, the first air invasion in Latin American history and another failed attempt to overthrow the Somoza dictatorship. In 1974 he brought together much of the middle-class opposition to Somoza in the Democratic Union of Liberation (UDEL).

Chamorro paid a high price for his activism. He suffered repeated imprisonment, torture, house arrest, and exile before his assassination in 1978. The public response to his death was a series of general strikes leading to mass insurrection. His death closed off the option of a negotiated end to the Somoza dictatorship. Instead, guerrillas of the Sandinista Liberation Front (Frente Sandinista de la Liberación Nacional—FSLN) overthrew the dictatorship in July 1979.

Chamorro's legacy is still debated. His widow, Violeta Barrios De Chamorro (who was elected president of Nicaragua in 1990), and two of his children, Pedro Joaquín and Cristiana, all favor a conservative interpretation of that legacy. They argue that Chamorro was a nationalist devoid of Communist leanings, and that he was a staunch and traditional Catholic. They believe he would have struggled against the Sandinistas, just as they have done.

But his brother Xavier and two other of Pedro Joaquín's children, Carlos Fernando and Claudia, claim that his legacy was far more radical. They note that his nationalism led him to oppose the imperialist aggression of the United States and that his Catholicism led him to work for social justice through what he called "Christian revolution." They claim he would have been a Sandinista revolutionary as they are.

See also Nicaragua.

BIBLIOGRAPHY

Pedro Joaquín Chamorro, *Estirpe Sangrienta: Los Somoza* (1980), and *Diario de un Preso* (1981).

Patricia Taylor Edmisten, *Nicaragua Divided: La Prensa and the Chamorro Legacy* (1990).

Additional Bibliography

Everingham, Mark. *Revolution and the Multiclass Coalition in Nicaragua.* Pittsburgh: University of Pittsburgh Press, 2002.

KAREN KAMPWIRTH

CHAMORRO VARGAS, EMILIANO (1871–1966).

Emiliano Chamorro Vargas (*b.* 11 May 1871; *d.* 26 February 1966), president of Nicaragua (1917–1921; 1926). The Nicaraguan who led more revolutions than any other began his military career in 1903, when he commanded an uprising against the Liberal dictator José Santos Zelaya. Although unsuccessful, this armed rebellion catapulted the Conservative Emiliano Chamorro into the forefront of Nicaraguan politics. Chamorro's animosity toward Zelaya seemingly stemmed not only from party politics and personal ambition but also from Zelaya's mistreatment of Chamorro's father. Chamorro became Zelaya's primary military rival when he joined forces with Juan José Estrada and José María Moncada to overthrow the dictator. By 1909, Zelaya had resigned under pressure from Conservative and anti-Zelaya Liberal forces. Chamorro not only proved himself through this success but also solidified his position as leader of the Conservative Party, a position he maintained until his death.

After Zelaya's ouster, Chamorro served as head of the Constituent Assembly. He returned to the battlefield in 1912, when Minister of War Luis Mena revolted against President Adolfo Díaz. After Chamorro defeated Mena, he expressed his own presidential ambitions. The United States, however, supported Díaz and offered Chamorro the position of envoy to the U.S., thereby eliminating any potential challenge to its old friend Díaz.

As envoy, Chamorro negotiated and signed the controversial Bryan–Chamorro Treaty, which gave the U.S. the option on a canal through Nicaragua. After the completion of the Panama Canal, the U.S. wanted to ensure that no other country would build a canal in Nicaragua. Besides the canal option, the U.S. received a ninety-nine-year lease on the Corn Islands in the Caribbean and on a naval base in the Gulf of Fonseca that would be under U.S. jurisdiction. In turn, the U.S. agreed to pay $3 million in gold to Nicaragua upon ratification. William Jennings Bryan, the U.S. secretary of state under President Woodrow Wilson, and Chamorro signed the treaty in 1914, and the U.S. Senate ratified it in 1916.

The treaty met with strong opposition, particularly from Costa Rica, El Salvador, and Colombia. Costa Rica argued that Nicaragua had violated an arbitral award by U.S. President Grover Cleveland (1888) that bound Nicaragua not to make a canal grant without consulting Costa Rica, because of their common San Juan River boundary. El Salvador expressed outrage at the casual treatment of its territorial rights in the Gulf of Fonseca. Colombia protested Nicaragua's usurpation of the Corn Islands because Colombia claimed sovereignty over them. Chamorro maintained that the treaty provided the best means of solving Nicaragua's economic woes.

Not until 1938 did he recognize his mistake in supporting and signing the treaty, for it jeopardized the sovereignty not only of other Latin American countries but also of Nicaragua itself.

Chamorro resigned his position as envoy in 1916 and returned to Nicaragua in order to seek the presidency. The U.S. had previously expressed doubts about Chamorro's military background—it preferred civilian leaders—but after his service as envoy, the U.S. supported Chamorro during the 1916 election, which he won. Upon assuming the presidency, he faced an empty treasury, a national debt, and a foreign debt outstanding since the days of Zelaya. He therefore focused his efforts on obtaining payment of the $3 million in gold promised to Nicaragua upon ratification of the Bryan–Chamorro Treaty. The U.S., however, tied its payment to the settlement of Nicaragua's foreign debt; consequently, Chamorro spent most of his term embroiled in lengthy negotiations.

Chamorro was elected president a second time in 1926, after he overthrew the Conservative government of Carlos Solórzano. Ostensibly, the coup was intended to neutralize the Liberal influence of Vice President Juan Bautista Sacasa, but Chamorro's own desire for the presidency was widely known. Once again, Conservatives and Liberals waged war against one another. Although Chamorro's forces performed well at first, he had fallen out of favor with the U.S. He therefore resigned on 30 October 1926.

During the dictatorship of Anastasio Somoza García, Chamorro continued his political machinations in the form of abortive uprisings and assassination attempts against the Liberal dictator. Nonetheless, in 1950 Chamorro and Somoza signed the Pact of the Generals, which guaranteed Conservatives one-third of the seats in Congress and one seat on the Supreme Court. Thus, the Conservatives obtained positions within the government while Chamorro's action, as leader of the Conservative Party, gave a boost to the regime's image. These benefits, however, were reaped at great cost, for the Conservative Party ultimately became a mere appendage of the Somoza dictatorship. The consequences were monumental: younger Conservatives who were disenchanted with their party and its leadership sought new avenues for political expression. Their quest led to the creation of the Frente Sandinista de Liberación Nacional, which overthrew the Somoza dynasty on 19 July 1979.

Chamorro, as head of the Conservative Party during this period, failed to provide true leadership, for in reality he represented only his personal ambitions and the interests of a small, elite class. The perennial revolutionary was merely an opportunist.

See also **Bryan-Chamorro Treaty (1914); Nicaragua; Panama Canal.**

BIBLIOGRAPHY

Calvin B. Carter, "The Kentucky Feud in Nicaragua: Why Civil War Has Become Her National Sport," in *The World's Work* 54 (July 1927): 312–321.

Sara Luisa Barquero, *Gobernantes de Nicaragua, 1825–1947* (1945).

William Kamman, *A Search for Stability: United States Diplomacy Toward Nicaragua, 1925–1933* (1968).

Emiliano Chamorro, *El último caudillo: Autobiografía* (1983).

Lester D. Langley, *The Banana Wars: United States Intervention in the Caribbean, 1898–1934* (1983).

Additional Bibliography

Guido, Clemente. *Emiliano Chamorro: Estadista y guerrero.* Managua: Fondo Editorial CIRA, 2002.

SHANNON BELLAMY

CHANCAY. Chancay, culture of ancient Peru that developed in the central coast valleys of Chancay and Chillón at the southern end of Chimú territory. This culture, which appears to have originated after the Huari collapse (c. 900 CE), was incorporated by the Chimú Empire and ultimately was conquered by the Incas around 1470.

Chancay culture is defined archaeologically by a distinctive and homogeneous ceramic style. These ceramics are known from extensive cemeteries in the Chancay region, where they were included in burials as grave goods. They are generally mold-made of a peculiarly gritty clay that leaves an unpolished matte surface, sometimes as rough as sandpaper. Over this is painted a white slip, decorated with black or dark brown designs, in a style known as Chancay Black on White. Vessel forms included both single- and double-chambered bottles, face-neck jars, ring-based plates, and open bowls. Clay figurines representing humans and animals also were produced. These often had yarn hair attached to a row of holes along the top of the head and were clothed in miniature textiles. One theory is that the llamas and human figurines were sacrificial surrogates for living animals and people, and as such were interred to accompany the dead.

The major artistic achievement for which the Chancay are known is their mastery of textiles. They produced plain weave, brocade, and openwork textiles in which open spaces were deliberately woven into the cloth as part of the decorative design. Plain woven cloth was also decorated with painted designs. Chancay weavers specialized particularly in delicate gauze work. Cloth was produced for clothing and decoration, and no doubt served the typical pre-Columbian function as a medium of value and prestige. Curious small dolls or human figurines made of cloth were included in burials. These figurines were sometimes arranged in scenes of activities perhaps suggesting the daily life of the deceased.

Beyond their art, little is known of the Chancay people; they seem to have left no cities nor great architectural monuments. Like all peoples of the dry desert coast, however, they must have been irrigation farmers and must have derived part of their living from the sea as well. They probably exploited the same food crops as other coastal peoples, growing cotton and importing wool for textiles.

See also **Archaeology; Art: Pre-Columbian Art of South America.**

BIBLIOGRAPHY

Sources on the Chancay are few. See Edward P. Lanning, *Peru Before the Incas* (1967); and Luis G. Lumbreras, *The Peoples and Cultures of Ancient Peru,* translated by Betty J. Meggars (1974).

Additional Bibliography

Fernando Márquez, Miranda, Grete Stern, and Horacio Coppola. *Huacos, cultura chancay* (1943).

GORDON F. McEWAN

CHAN CHAN. Chan Chan, the capital of the Chimú Empire. Located in the Moche valley of Peru's north coast, the city of Chan Chan was founded between 850 and 900 CE. As the imperial capital of the Chimú, it eventually grew to be one of the largest pre-Columbian cities in South America.

The city, constructed of adobe bricks, covered nearly ten square miles. Ten huge palace-like structures, called *ciudadelas,* which are believed to correspond to the ten rulers of the Chimú dynasty, dominate the city. Surrounded by walls thirty feet or more in height, these structures contained rooms and corridors in a complex labyrinthine arrangement. Architecturally, they were a radical break with the earlier Moche tradition of ceremonial centers dominated by pyramids. Whereas Moche monumental architecture was principally religious, the most complex Chimú structures seem to have been rulers' residences, which suggests that the rulers had become divine. The form of the *ciudadela* probably derived from earlier Huari architecture, which was widely distributed throughout ancient Peru and would have provided a model for prestigious imperial buildings.

These *ciudadelas* have been interpreted as the residence and treasure vault of the reigning emperor and, after his death, his mortuary monument, for they include kitchens, wells, shrines, living quarters, numerous storerooms, and burial platforms. The many storerooms are thought to have housed the accumulated valuables of the ruler, such as fine cloth, gold and silver objects, *spondylus* shells, and other high-status goods.

Between the large *ciudadelas,* lesser compounds housed the nobles and lower-ranking elite. These were simpler versions of the great compounds and housed many of the same functions on a reduced scale. The city also contained residential districts for artisans and their workshops; these buildings were much smaller and lacked the elaboration of the elite buildings.

See also **Chimú; Moche.**

BIBLIOGRAPHY

The principal sources on the city of Chan Chan are Rogger Ravines, *Chan Chan metrópoli Chimú* (1980); Michael Moseley and Kent C. Day, eds., *Chan Chan: Andean Desert City* (1982). See also John H. Rowe, "The Kingdom of Chimor," *Acta Americana* 6 (1948): 26–59; and Michael Moseley and Alana Cordy-Collins, *The Northern Dynasties: Kingship and Statecraft in Chimor* (1990). For a discussion of the architectural origins of Chan Chan, see Gordon F. Mc Ewan, "Some Formal Correspondences Between the Imperial Architecture of the Wari and Chimú Cultures of Ancient Peru," *Latin American Antiquity* 1, no. 2 (1990): 97–116.

Additional Bibliography

Sakai, Masato. *Reyes, estrellas y cerros en Chimor: El proceso de cambio de la organización espacial y temporal en Chan Chan.* Lima: Editorial Horizonte, 1998.

Stone, Rebecca. *Art of the Andes from Chavín to Inca.* New York: Thames and Hudson, 1996.

Valle Alvarez, Luis. *Aportes para la historia de Chan Chan.* Trujillo: Ediciones SIAN, 2004.

                                    GORDON F. MCEWAN

CHANGADOR.

In the River Plate region in the eighteenth century, the role of the *changador* was to slaughter livestock and to collect skins and tallow for illicit sale to the Spaniards, Portuguese, or anyone who wanted them. The word *changador* was associated with the term *gaucho.* Although there is still no agreement on the origin of the word, its derivation may have to do with the fact that the contraband skins and tallow sold to Portuguese territories were transported in canoes or light boats known as *jangadas* in Portuguese; the boats' owners were called *jangadoiros* or *jangadeiros.*

Around the middle of the nineteenth century the word was applied to day laborers hired for seasonal agricultural work (*changa*). On the docks, it was used for porters.

See also **Gaucho; Gaúcho; Livestock.**

BIBLIOGRAPHY

Assunçao, Fernando. "El Gaucho." *Revista del Instituto Histórico y Geográfico del Uruguay* 24 (1958–1959): 369–918.

Bouton, Roberto J. "La vida rural en el Uruguay." *Revista Histórica* 29, no. 85–87 (July 1959): 1–200.

                                    ANA FREGA

CHAPALA, LAKE.

Lake Chapala, Mexico's largest lake. It lies in a long depression 5,000 feet above sea level in the state of Jalisco. The lake is part of the Lerma-Chapala-Santiago system in which the Lerma River empties into, and the Santiago River flows out from, Chapala. The lake has experienced numerous oscillations in its shoreline. By 1954 a combination of drought and water diversion caused

Chapala to recede 2.5 miles, a deficit from which the lake has never fully recovered.

Farmers exploit the exposed lake-bed soils, and small, informal restaurants dot the shores. Increased demands by Mexico City on the Lerma and diversions from Chapala to supply Guadalajara with water are again threatening the viability of the lake. Still, Chapala's beautiful setting and recreational attractions draw many Mexican visitors, and it is a favorite retirement site for a growing colony of North Americans.

See also **Jalisco.**

BIBLIOGRAPHY

David Barkin and Timothy King, *Regional Economic Development: The River Basin Approach in Mexico* (1970), esp. pp. 113–115.

José Rogelio Alvarez, ed., *Encyclopedia de México,* 3d ed., vol. 5 (1978), pp. 265–268.

Robert C. West and John P. Augelli, *Middle America: Its Lands and Peoples,* 3d ed. (1989).

Additional Bibliography

De Anda, José, and Ulrich Maniak. "Modificaciones en el régimen hidrológico y sus efectos en el fosforo y fosfatos en el lago Chapala, Mexico." *Interciencia* 32, no. 2 (2007): 100–108.

Durán Juarez, Juan Manuel, and Alicia Torres Rodríguez. "Crisis ambiental en el lago de Chapala y abastecimiento de agua para Guadalajara." *Carta Económica Nacional* 14, no. 78 (October 2001): 10–11.

Hansen, Anne M., and Manfred Van Afferden, eds. *The Lerma–Chapala Watershed: Evaluation and Management.* New York: Springer, 2001.

Hargraves, Michael. *Lake Chapala: A Literary Survey: Plus an Historical Overview with Some Personal Observations and Reflections of this Lakeside Area of Jalisco, Mexico.* London: Hargraves, 1992.

MARIE D. PRICE

CHAPARE. Chapare is a river and region in east central Bolivia, notorious as the center of nontraditional coca cultivation in the country. The river and its fertile valley lie to the east of Cochabamba and have long attracted immigration from the highlands. In the mid-twentieth century road construction and agricultural investments sponsored by the U.S. Agency for International Development opened the region to intensive colonization. Ironically, this infrastructure later channeled a large migrant stream, displaced by the collapse of tin mining and a series of droughts, who began large-scale coca cultivation. These growers, *cocaleros,* carried on a twenty-year struggle against a variety of coca eradication programs. From this resistance, the Chapare formed the base for the Movimiento al Socialismo (Movement toward Socialism; MAS) political party and for Evo Morales's rise to power.

See also **Morales, Evo; Venezuela, Political Parties: Movement to Socialism (MAS).**

BIBLIOGRAPHY

Kohl, Benjamin H., and Linda C. Farthing. *Impasse in Bolivia: Neoliberal Hegemony and Popular Resistance.* London and New York: Zed Books, 2006.

Montes de Oca, Ismael. *Geografía y recursos naturales de Bolivia,* 3rd edition. La Paz: EDOBOL, 1997.

DAVID BLOCK

CHAPULTEPEC, ACT OF. *See* Pan-American Conferences: Mexico City Conference (1945).

CHAPULTEPEC, BATTLE OF. The last major engagement of the U.S.-Mexican War and the fourth of General Winfield Scott's invasion of central Mexico, the Battle of Chapultepec took place in the morning of September 13, 1847, on the hill and forest of that name, just outside Mexico City. It consisted in the assault of a Mexican position on Chapultepec hill, manned by some 900 troops under General Nicolás Bravo (most of them regular soldiers, plus the San Blas Battalion of the National Guard and a handful of cadets from the military academy) by two divisions of the U.S. Army (five regular regiments and volunteer units from New York, Pennsylvania, and South Carolina), under Generals John A. Quitman and Gideon J. Pillow. As in almost all of the war's encounters, the U.S. Army emerged victorious, partially because of its organizational superiority but also because the Mexican command, until the last minute, considered the attack a diverting maneuver and kept preparing for a direct offensive on the city. The battle lasted about two hours; around 9:30 a.m., General

Bravo surrendered to a New York volunteer. Less than twenty-four hours later—after a combat at the city gates—General Scott's troops were taking possession of Mexico's National Palace.

Unremarkable as a feat of arms, and somewhat irrelevant from a political point of view (inasmuch as the conflict was not decided on that day), the battle would nevertheless become the war's most significant episode in Mexican imagination. Its transformation to national myth comprised three moments. Up to the mid-1850s, it was mostly linked to the San Blas Battalion's annihilation and thus was part of a larger campaign intended to contrast the national guard's sacrifice to the professional army's incompetence and cowardice. During the civil wars of the 1850s, two cadets who had been present at Chapultepec (Leandro Valle and Miguel Miramón) rose to positions of power, and the battle became yet another instance of the liberal-conservative conflict. The most enduring phase began in the late nineteenth century, around the battle's fiftieth anniversary, as the Porfirian army found in the cadets the best emblem of its (presumed) apolitical professionalism. Six of them were identified as the true martyrs and enshrined as the *niños héroes* (young heroes) of that day: Juan de la Barrera, Juan Escutia, Francisco Márquez, Agustín Melgar, Fernando Montes de Oca, and Vicente Suárez. In an implausible stroke of luck, their bodies were discovered in 1947. That allowed for the construction of a mausoleum on the slopes of Chapultepec hill—the "motherland's altar"—and, in an ironic twist, the homage paid by U.S. president Harry Truman during the war's hundredth anniversary as well.

See also **Mexico, Wars and Revolutions: Mexican-American War; Scott, Winfield.**

BIBLIOGRAPHY

Plascencia de la Parra, Enrique. "Conmemoración de la hazaña épica de los Niños Héroes: Su origen, desarrollo y simbolismos." *Historia Mexicana* 45, no. 2 (October 1995): 241–280.

                                        LUIS FERNANDO GRANADOS

CHAPULTEPEC, BOSQUE DE.   Bosque de Chapultepec, a centrally located park in Mexico City and the oldest recreational space in the Americas. The park takes its name from the hill

called *Chapulín* on which Chapultepec Castle was constructed in the 1780s. In the park are found the presidential residence (Los Pinos), the National Museum of Anthropology, the Tamayo Museum, the Museum of Modern Art, the National Auditorium, a renovated zoo, athletic fields, recreational areas, and several lakes. It was once a forest of giant cypress (*ahuehuete*), but these have almost disappeared due to the loss of lands that surrounded their marshy habitat.

In about 1250 a roving tribe of Aztecs settled in Chapultepec. Upon gaining power in the Valley of Mexico and consolidating Tenochtitlán as the capital of their confederacy with Texcoco and Tlacopán, they made it a sacred place and alternative residence of their emperors. Nezahualcóyotl, king of Texcoco, designed it as a park in about 1450 and constructed an aqueduct that supplied drinking water first to Tenochtitlán and later to the colonial city. It is believed that the hill was the burying place of the Aztec emperors, some of whose effigies are preserved as rock carvings.

During the siege of 1521, Chapultepec was heroically defended by the Aztecs. Hernán Cortés added it to his possessions. Carlos V took it from Cortés's estate and gave it back to Mexico City. The viceroy Bernardo de Gálvez began construction of the castle as a summer residence in 1786 and had finished a great part of it the following year when he died. It was finished in 1842, when the Military Academy occupied it. During the battle for the capital in 1847, 200 cadets defended it to the death against the forces of Winfield Scott. Maximilian and Carlota made the castle their imperial palace from 1864–1867. Porfirio Díaz divided it for use as the presidential residence, often called El Alcázar, and the Military Academy. Almost every postrevolutionary president resided in it until Lázaro Cárdenas moved to Los Pinos in 1936. In 1944 the castle was opened as the National Museum of History.

Between 1898 and 1910 the ancient forest was converted to a French park in the style of the Bois de Boulogne in Paris. From that time until the completion of the subway in 1969 it was the preferred promenade of the middle class. Today it is overwhelmed by the public for recreation. Visits are free, and each week more than 1.5 million people pass through it. The construction of freeways and public buildings around its perimeter has caused the park to suffer devastating consequences. Lying in the middle of a city of 20 million inhabitants, with an excessive number of factories and automobiles, it shows evidence of damage from pollution. As an attempt to alleviate this problem, the central part has been closed to vehicular traffic. The zoo is one of the only one in the world where pandas and sea lions have reproduced in captivity.

See also **Mexico City.**

BIBLIOGRAPHY

Most books about Mexico City discuss Chapultepec as well. See, for example, Jonathan Kandell, *La Capital* (1988).

Additional Bibliography

Aguilar, Miguel Angel, Amparo Sevilla, and Abilio Vergara Figueroa, eds. *La ciudad desde sus lugares: Trece ventanas etnográficas para una metropolis.* México: Miguel Angel Porrua: CONACULTA, Culturas Populares e Indígenas: Universidad Autónoma Metropolitana, Unidad Iztapalapa, 2001.

Cueva, Hermilo de la. *Chapultepec, biografía de un bosque.* México, D.F.: Libro Mex, 1957.

Fernández, Miguel Angel. *Documentos para la historia de Chapultepec.* México, D.F.: Instituto Nacional de Antropología e Historia, 2001.

Novo, Salvador. *Los paseos de la Ciudad de México.* México: Fondo de Cultura Economica, 1974.

J. E. PACHECO

CHARCAS, AUDIENCIA OF. Audiencia of Charcas, the high court of Charcas, which had its seat in the city of La Plata (now Sucre), in the eastern Andes in what is now Bolivia. It was often known as the Audiencia of La Plata and sometimes as that of Chuquisaca, another name for the same town. Proposals for its foundation date back to 1551, inspired in part by the great silver strike in 1545 at Potosí, 50 miles to the southwest. The resultant rise of local population called for a firmer royal presence. Final arrangements were made in 1558–1559, and the first set of four *oidores* (judges) took office in 1561.

After 1570 the northern limit of the audiencia's district was set 120 miles south of Cuzco and ran down on the Pacific coast to the Copiapó River valley in Chile. Inland the district extended east to a vague line in the interior, but a projection southward covered Tucumán, Paraguay, and the settlements along the Río de la Plata. Buenos Aires, after its refounding in 1580, became the district's southeastern extremity. This was the largest audiencia jurisdiction in South America, and it remained little changed until 1783, when an *audiencia* was permanently set up in Buenos Aires to take cases from Tucumán, Paraguay, and Buenos Aires Province.

The Audiencia of Charcas, like others in colonial Spanish America, combined judicial and administrative functions. Constant dispute over the exercise of *gobierno* (adminstration) took place, however, between the audiencia and the viceroy in Lima, in whose broad adminstrative domain it resided (until 1776, when it passed to the new Viceroyalty of the Río de la Plata). The Audiencia's district, in its reduced post-1783 form, was the direct ancestor of the territory of modern Bolivia.

See also **Audiencia; Bolivia: The Colonial Period.**

BIBLIOGRAPHY

Ernesto Schäfer, *El Consejo Real y Supremo de las Indias; Su historia, organización y labor adminstrativa hasta la terminación de la casa de Austria* (1947).

Inge Wolff, *Regierung und Verwaltung der Kolonialspanischen Städte in Hochperu, 1538–1650* (1970).

Herbert S. Klein, *Bolivia: The Evolution of a Multi-Ethnic Society* (1982).

Additional Bibliography

Escobari de Querejazu, Laura. *Caciques, yanaconas y extravagantes: La sociedad colonial en Charcas s. XVI–XVIII.* La Paz, Bolivia: Embajada de España en Bolivia, 2001.

Presta, Ana María. *Encomienda, familia, y negocios en Charcas colonial (Bolivia): Los encomenderos de La Plata, 1550–1600.* Lima, Peru: IEP, Instituto de Estudios Peruanos, 2000.

PETER BAKEWELL

CHARLES, EUGENIA (1919–2005). Eugenia Charles (later Dame Charles) was known to the world as the Iron Lady of the Caribbean, but in Dominica as Mamo. Born Mary Eugenia on 15

May 1919, in the fishing village of Pointe Michel, she died on 6 September 2005, at age 86. Her father had parlayed his small farm into a substantial import-export business and established the first colored-owned bank in Dominica, catering to small farmers. Eugenia took after her father and worked and cared for him until his death at age 107. Devoutly religious (Roman Catholic), she was always independent-minded and outspoken. She never abandoned her no-nonsense style even as her detractors taunted her for her lifelong unmarried and childless state. She earned degrees from the University of Toronto and the London School of Economics and returned to Dominica in 1949 as the island's only female barrister. In 1968 she helped form the Dominica Freedom Party (DFP) to counter the authoritarian and corrupt tendencies evident in the Patrick John regime, which had governed since 1974. As a member of the party, she served in the Dominican parliament.

Charles was elected prime minister of Dominica in 1980, making her the first female prime minister in the Caribbean, and served three terms (21 July 1980–14 June 1995) which were characterized by probity, constant lobbying for the endangered banana industry, and efforts in favor of Caribbean integration. These were hardly tranquil years however. She survived two coup attempts organized by ousted prime minister Patrick John and backed by the U.S. Mafia and the Ku Klux Klan. In 1983 Charles backed U.S. president Ronald Reagan's decision to intervene in Grenada. Facing strong criticism from leftist intellectuals for her stance, she was characteristically direct: "The Grenadians wanted it and that's all that counts. I don't care what the rest of the world thinks," she told the Associated Press in a 1995 interview recounted in her *New York Times* obituary. Her conservative and profoundly honest philosophy of leadership was perhaps best summed up when she was asked what makes a good leader. "Leaders," she said, "must look after the things that need looking after without looking after themselves" (Chouthi 1997).

See also **Dominica; Grenada.**

BIBLIOGRAPHY

Chouthi, Sandra. "Dame Eugenia Today: As Blunt as Ever." *Express*, November 24, 1997, sec. 2, p. 1.

"Eugenia Charles, 86, Is Dead; Ex-Premier of Dominica, Called 'Iron Lady.'" *New York Times*, September 9, 2005.

ANTHONY P. MAINGOT

CHARLES I OF SPAIN (1500–1558).
Charles I of Spain, born on February 24, 1500, was king of Spain from 1516 to 1556 and Holy Roman emperor, as Charles V, from 1519 to 1558. The grandson of Ferdinand II and Isabella I as well as the emperor Maximilian I, Charles inherited an empire that stretched from Germany to the Americas. Throughout his reign he struggled to keep his inheritance intact in the face of Protestant threats in Germany, French threats in Italy, and Turkish threats on the Mediterranean coast. Despite tremendous military expenditures, Charles was unable to check all three forces simultaneously. The war against France kept him, for instance, from giving the necessary attention to the spread of Lutheran doctrine in Germany. Charles's solution there was to delegate authority to his brother, Ferdinand (king of Bohemia and Hungary), who ultimately negotiated a religious settlement in the Peace of Augsburg (1555). Toward the end of his reign Charles began a division of the Hapsburg inheritance by giving to his son Philip II the territories of Naples, Milan, the Netherlands, and Spain (1554–1556) and relinquishing his imperial title (1556–1558) to his brother, who reigned as Emperor Ferdinand I.

Because of his Burgundian origins, Charles I was initially not well received in Spain. He faced his first political crisis in 1519 with the revolt of the *comuneros* (Castilian rebels) who demanded that he exclude foreigners from high positions at court and give the Cortes a greater role in government. When Charles granted the participating cities a general pardon, he inaugurated a more favorable relationship with his Spanish subjects.

Charles respected the autonomy of his widespread domains and ruled through a system of viceroys or regents (often family members) to preserve his personal rule. The viceroys acted as liaisons with his various councils. The central governing institution and highest administrative body was the Council of Castile, staffed largely by non–aristocratic jurists. Grandees served on an advisory council of state. To these bodies were added councils of finance (1523) and the Indies (1524). Charles's main sources of royal revenue were Castile, Aragon, the Church, and America, although he also drew upon resources in the Netherlands and Italy.

One of Charles's most important partnerships was with Hernán Cortés (1485–1547), who would become conquistador of the Aztec empire of Montezuma. All of Cortés's actions in New Spain were in the name of his monarch, Charles V. For his part, Cortés suggested that Charles add the designation of Emperor of the Indies to his lengthy list of titles, but he declined. Charles maintained a eurocentric attitude toward his New World possessions and for most of his reign European mines produced greater quantities of silver than those in the colonies. However, he capitalized on the influx of American silver to secure monetary loans from European financiers.

See also **Cortés, Hernán; Ferdinand II of Aragon; Isabella I of Castile; Spanish Empire; Viceroyalty, Viceroy.**

BIBLIOGRAPHY

Blockmans, Wim. *Emperor Charles V: 1500–1558.* Translated by Isola van den Hoven-Vardon. London: Arnold, 2002.

Brandi, Karl. *The Emperor Charles V* (1939; repr. 1980).

Elliott, J. H. *Imperial Spain: 1469–1716.* London and New York: Penguin Books, 1963, 1990.

Elliott, J. H. *Empires of the Atlantic World: Britain and Spain in America, 1492–1830.* New Haven, CT: Yale University Press, 2006.

Fernández Álvarez, Manuel. *Charles V* (1975).

Kamen, Henry. *Empire: How Spain Became a World Power, 1492–1763.* New York: Harper Collins, 2003.

Kleinschmidt, Harald. *Charles V: The World Emperor.* Stroud, U.K.: Sutton, 2004.

Maltby, William S. *The Reign of Charles V.* Houndmills U.K., and New York: Palgrave, 2002.

Thobar, Ramón Carande. *Carlos V y sus banqueros,* 3 vols. (1943–1967).

SUZANNE HILES BURKHOLDER

CHARLES II OF SPAIN (1661–1700).

Charles II of Spain (*b.* November 1661; *d.* 1 November 1700), king of Spain, Naples, and Sicily (1665–1700). Chronically ill throughout his life, Charles II

ruled early on through his mother, as regent, and a five-member government junta, which was an aristocratic faction headed by his illegitimate brother, Don John of Austria. Toward the end of his reign, he ruled through titled prime ministers. Charles's reign was marked by increasing governmental decentralization accompanied by a resurgence of aristocratic influence in government and a revival of provincial liberties.

During Charles's tenuous rule, Spain fought the French to retain the Spanish Netherlands but lost strategic territory at considerable cost to the ailing economy. In addition to this costly war, Castile suffered a number of natural disasters—harvest failures caused by a drought-and-deluge cycle, locusts, an earthquake, and epidemics—all of which exacerbated the effects of monetary depression. Yet Castile's very weakness forced its ministers to recognize the need for administrative and economic reforms and to act upon it, a policy that characterized the reigns of Charles's Bourbon successors. One of the bright spots of his reign was the 1680 publication of a vast compendium of the local laws of America, known as the *Recopilación de las leyes de Indias.* The crown intended to use this information to keep the legal codes of Spain and the Americas as close in nature as possible. The local precedent often trumped the laws encoded in the *Recopilación*; however, such as in 1685 when the Viceroyalty of Peru printed its own *Recopilación provincial*, a compendium of laws created by Peruvian viceroys.

See also **Spanish Empire.**

BIBLIOGRAPHY

John Lynch, *Spain Under the Habsburgs*, vol. 2, *Spain and America 1598–1700* (1964–1969), esp. pp. 229–280.

Henry Kamen, *Spain in the Later Seventeenth Century, 1665–1700* (1980).

Additional Bibliography

Elliott, John. *Empires of the Atlantic World: Britain and Spain in America, 1492–1830.* New Haven, CT: Yale University Press, 2006.

Elliott, John. *Imperial Spain: 1469–1716.* New York: Penguin Books, c. 1963, 1990.

Kamen, Henry. *Empire: How Spain Became a World Power, 1492–1763.* New York: Harper Collins, 2003.

Kamen, Henry. *Spain, 1469–1714. A Society of Conflict.* London: Longman, 1991.

Lynch, John. *The Hispanic World in Crisis and Change, 1598–1700*. London: Blackwell Publishers, 1994.

SUZANNE HILES BURKHOLDER

CHARLES III OF SPAIN   (1716–1788).

Charles III of Spain (*b.* 20 January 1716; *d.* 14 December 1788), king of Spain (1759–1788) and Naples and Sicily (1734–1759). Often termed an "enlightened despot," Charles III is chiefly known for the administrative and economic reforms during his reign and for the expulsion of the Jesuits (1767). He brought to the Spanish throne twenty-five years of experience as the king of Naples. Charles was a proponent of royal absolutism whose main concern was the welfare of the state, which he intended to strengthen through domestic reforms, imperial defense, and stringent colonial control. He attempted neutrality in the Seven Years' War but was drawn into the losing side of the conflict by a desire to fortify Spanish land and sea power with a French alliance. In 1779, Charles entered into the war between America and Britain to regain control over the Gulf coast and the Mississippi and destroy British colonial power in Central America. His rewards for this effort were Florida and Minorca.

Charles's domestic and foreign policies were influenced by a succession of enlightened ministers who pressed for varying degrees of reform within a framework of absolute monarchy. His first administration was dominated by such Italians as Leopoldo de Gregorio Squillace and Grimaldi, who supported the reforms of Campomanes, which infringed on the privileges of the clergy and aristocracy. Initial reforms sparked riots in Madrid and other cities (1766) and led to the dismissal of Squillace, the minister of finance. The count of Aranda dominated the second administration as president of the Council of Castile (1766–1773). Aranda's political rival, the count of Floridablanca, later served as secretary of state (1776–1792) and essentially ran the government during the latter years of Charles's reign.

In centralizing control over colonial affairs, Charles III created new administrative units, reduced the political power of the creoles, expelled the Jesuits, and expanded the army with American-born recruits. However, his increased taxation and new colonial inspections (*visitas*) were met with rebellions in the early 1780s. These uprisings in turn led to tighter control under the secretary of the Indies, José de Galvéz (1776–1787), who favored the introduction of the intendant system of royal administrators as a link between the districts and the central authorities. In 1765 the crown began to reduce the restrictions on colonial trade so as to expand commerce within the empire, while at the same time reinforcing the Spanish monopoly. By 1789 this system of free trade within the empire encompassed all of Spain's New World colonies.

Despite much talk about increasing state revenues through tax reforms, the reincorporation of noble estates (*señorios*), and confiscation of church property, there was little opportunity for structural change during the reign of Charles III. In addition to resistance from privileged groups, the king and his ministers had limited resources and often deferred domestic investment to meet the costs of war.

See also **Gálvez, José de; Intendancy System; Spanish Empire.**

BIBLIOGRAPHY

Vicente Rodríguez Casado, *La política y los políticos en el reinado de Carlos III* (1962).

Anthony H. Hull, *Charles III and the Revival of Spain* (1980).

Javier Guillamón Álvarez, *Las reformas de la administración local durante el reinado de Carlos III* (1980).

John Lynch, *Bourbon Spain, 1700–1808* (1989), esp. pp. 247–374.

Additional Bibliography

Elliott, John. *Empires of the Atlantic World: Britain and Spain in America, 1492–1830*. New Haven, CT: Yale University Press, 2006.

Ferández Díaz, Roberto. *Carlos III*. Madrid: Arlanza Editores, 2001.

Kamen, Henry. *Empire: How Spain Became a World Power, 1492–1763*. New York: HarperCollins, 2003.

Sánchez Blanco, Francisco. *El Absolutismo y las luces en el reinado de Carlos III*. Madrid: Marical Pons, 2002.

Stein, Stanley J. *Apogee of Empire: Spain and New Spain in the Age of Charles III, 1759–1789*. Baltimore, MD: Johns Hopkins University Press, 2003.

Weber, David J. *Bárbaros: Spaniards and Their Savages in the Age of Enlightenment*. New Haven, CT: Yale University Press, 2005.

SUZANNE HILES BURKHOLDER

CHARLES IV OF SPAIN (1748–1819).

Charles IV of Spain (*b.* 12 November 1748; *d.* 19 January 1819), king of Spain (1788–1808). Charles IV had neither experience nor interest in government when he came to the throne. Although he began his rule with ministers inherited from his father, he soon handed the reins of government to Manuel de Godoy, whose rapid rise to power earned him widespread unpopularity in both Spain and the colonies. Distracted by revolutionary events in France, Charles and Godoy presided over the demise of the old regime while doing little to acknowledge or avert it.

War and the threat of state bankruptcy determined Charles's foreign and domestic policy. The Spanish monarch's decision to intercede on behalf of his cousin, the king of France, led to war (1793–1795), a subsequent alliance with France (1796), and costly conflicts with England (1796–1802 and 1804–1808). In the Indies, what was left of the Spanish monopoly eroded during the reign of Charles IV with the legalization of neutral trade.

Quests for further sources of state revenue dominated domestic policy during the reign of Charles IV. The few reforms generated by the crown's fiscal needs were lost amid the demands of wartime conditions and did little to improve Godoy's popularity. Opposition to him as the court favorite ultimately manifested itself in aristocratic support for the king's heir, Ferdinand VII, and in a revolt at Aranjuez (1808) demanding that Charles abdicate in favor of his son. Shortly thereafter, Napoleon I lured Charles and Ferdinand to France, where he forced them to abdicate in favor of his brother, Joseph Bonaparte.

See also **Ferdinand VII of Spain; Spanish Empire.**

BIBLIOGRAPHY

Carlos Corona, *Revolución y reacción en el reinado de Carlos IV* (1957).

John Lynch, *Bourbon Spain, 1700–1808* (1989).

Additional Bibliography

Elliott, John. *Empires of the Atlantic World: Britain and Spain in America, 1492–1830.* New Haven, CT: Yale University Press, 2006.

La Parra López, Emilio. *Manuel Godoy: La aventura del poder.* Barcelons: Tusquets, 2002.

Portillo Valdés, José M.*Crísis Atlántica: Autonomía e independencia en la crisis de la monarquía Hispana.* Madrid: Marcial Pons, 2006.

Rodríguez, Jaime E. O. *The Independence of Spanish America.* Cambridge, U.K.: Cambridge University Press, 1998.

Weber, David J. *Bárbaros: Spaniards and their Savages in the Age of Enlightenment.* New Haven, CT: Yale University Press, 2005.

SUZANNE HILES BURKHOLDER

CHARLOT, JEAN (1898–1979).

A French-Mexican illustrator, muralist, writer, and archaeologist, Jean Charlot was born in France on February 8, 1898, and attended the École des Beaux-Arts National School of Fine Arts in Paris. In 1921 Charlot and his widowed mother immigrated to Mexico. Charlot played a major role in the postrevolutionary florescence of Mexican art, becoming friends with many leading muralists. Charlot's mural *The Massacre in the [Aztec] Main Temple* is usually considered the Mexican mural movement's first true fresco.

Charlot expended a good deal of artistic energy producing prints, and early on he recognized the importance of the satirical prerevolutionary printmaker José Guadalupe Posada. Throughout Charlot's career he stressed his commitment to creating popular, reproducible, and even useful art for the people. While in Mexico he also wrote many articles, collaborated closely with the writer Anita Brenner, and became a lifelong friend of the photographer Edward Weston. Despite his circle of radical friends, he remained a devout Catholic and incorporated religious themes and images in his art.

His art style strongly reflects the pre-Columbian sculptural traditions of Mexico, with their ties to the earth and stress on geometric forms and volume. From 1926 through 1928 Charlot was the expedition artist for the Carnegie Institution of Washington's excavations at Chichén Itzá. As a coauthor of the *Temple of the Warriors* report, he gained fame as "the painter turned archaeologist."

In fall 1928 Charlot moved to New York City to seek new opportunities; however, Mexico remained the prime inspiration for the subject and style of his art. In 1945 he received a Guggenheim Fellowship to return to Mexico to write his masterwork, *The Mexican Mural Renaissance: 1920–1925.* In 1949 he was invited to join the faculty of the University of Hawaii, where his Mexican experience, now transformed into Polynesian settings, reverberated in his murals, paintings, and prints. He remained at the university until his death on March 20, 1979.

See also **Archaeology; Art: The Twentieth Century; Chichén Itzá.**

BIBLIOGRAPHY

Primary Works

The Mexican Mural Renaissance, 1920–1925. New Haven, CT: Yale University Press, 1963.

An Artist on Art: Collected Essays of Jean Charlot. Honolulu: University Press of Hawaii, 1972.

Secondary Works

Klobe, Thomas, ed. Jean Charlot: A Retrospective. Honolulu: University of Hawaii Art Gallery, 1990.

Koprivitza, Milena, and Blanca Garduño Pulido, eds. México in la obra de Jean Charlot. México: Consejo Nacional para la Cultura y las Artes, 1994.

Morse, Peter. Jean Charlot's Prints: A Catalogue Raisonné. Honolulu: University Press of Hawaii and Jean Charlot Foundation, 1976.

DONALD McVICKER

CHARQUI. Charqui, term for sun-dried salted meat used in Chile and other Andean regions. Throughout the colonial period and well into the twentieth century, *charqui*, beef, llama, or horse meat cut into strips, salted and dried, was a food staple for rural peasants in Chile as well as for the Mapuches. *Charqui* was prepared for consumption by pounding or grinding the dried meat into a coarse meal to be served in stews, accompanied by toasted wheat. *Charqui* became increasingly important in the native Chilean economy in the early nineteenth century, when it was exported north for use in the mines. A major export product, *charque* played an important economic role in nineteenth century Rio Grande do Sul, Brazil.

See also **Food and Cookery.**

BIBLIOGRAPHY

Rodolfo Lenz, *Diccionario etimológico* (1910).

Additional Bibliography

Bell, Stephen. Campanha gaúcha: A Brazilian Ranching System, 1850–1920. Stanford, CA: Stanford University Press, 1998.

Briones, Claudia, and José Luis Lanata. Archaeological and Anthropological Perspectives on the Native Peoples of Pampa, Patagonia, and Tierra del Fuego to the Nineteenth Century. Westport, CT: Bergin & Garvey, 2002.

Gorla, Carlos María. Las carnes patagónicas y fueguinas en el marco de la economía nacional y en relación al contexto de la economía mundial (1930–1957). Buenos Aires: Ediciones Dunken, 1998.

Norman, G.A., and O. O. Corte. Dried Salted Meats: Charque and Carne-de-sol. Rome: Food and Agriculture Organization of the United Nations, 1985.

KRISTINE L. JONES

CHARREADA. Charreada, Mexican roping and riding contest. The precursor of the American rodeo, a *charreada* is a contest consisting of the *suertes* (events) of *charrería*, the national sport of Mexico. Such *suertes* as *coleadero* (downing a bull by twisting its tail) and *jaripeo* (bull riding) originated in sixteenth-century *corridas*. Others developed from cattle ranching: *jineteo* (riding wild mares and young bulls), *paso de la muerte* (death pass: jumping from a tame horse to the back of a wild horse), *piales* (roping the hind legs of a running mare), *manganas* (roping the forelegs of a running mare), and *terna en el ruedo* (team roping: one charro ropes the bull's head and the other, the hind legs). *Charreadas* reached their greatest popularity as part of nineteenth-century hacienda fiestas during roundups and branding. This popularity was enhanced by Ponciano Díaz, an exceptionally skilled *charro* and bullfighter who organized the first professional shows and made several international tours.

The Mexican Revolution and the breakup of the haciendas ended the heyday of the *charro*. To preserve the cultural heritage, a group of former *charros* in 1921 wrote standard rules, making *charreadas* team contests among members of amateur *charro* clubs. Held in special arenas known as *lienzos*, contemporary *charreadas* include the events of the past four centuries, as well as the *cala de caballo*, a form of dressage, and *escaramuza charra*, precision sidesaddle riding by women's teams. As in the nineteenth century, *charreadas* end with the *jarabe tapitío* (Mexican hat dance). Since 1933 *charrería* has been regulated by the Federacíon Nacional de Charros. In 1991 fifty U.S. clubs broke away and formed the rival

Federacíon de Charros, U.S., Inc. Mexican-Americans have long held *charreadas* and are important to the Mexican-American community in the United States.

See also **Sports.**

BIBLIOGRAPHY

Higinio Vázquez Santa Ana, *La charrería mexicana* (1950).

Enrique Guarner, *Historia del toreo en México* (1979).

Mary Lou Le Compte, "The Hispanic Influence on the History of Rodeo, 1823–1922," in *Journal of Sport History* 23 (1983): 21–38.

José Alvarez Del Villar, *La charrería mexicana* (1987).

Kathleen Sands, *Charrería Mexicana: An Equestrian Folk Tradition* (1993).

Additional Bibliography

Arbena, Joseph, and David G. LaFrance. *Sport in Latin America and the Caribbean.* Wilmington, DE: Scholarly Resources, 2002.

Rendon, Al, et al. *Charreada: Mexican Rodeo in Texas.* Denton: University of North Texas Press, 2002.

Vélez-Ibañez, Carlos G., Anna Sampaio, and Manolo González-Estay. *Transnational Latina/o communities: Politics, Processes, and Cultures.* Lanham, MD: Rowman & Littlefield, 2002.

MARY LOU LECOMPTE

which are somewhat like American rodeos except that competition is by team rather than individual, with rules and events more like those of earlier centuries.

See also **Gaucho; Sports.**

BIBLIOGRAPHY

Carlos Rincón Gallardo, *El charro mexicano* (1939).

Alfonso Rincón Gallardo, "Contemporary Charrería," in *Artes de México* 14, no. 99 (1967): 41–42 (entire issue is devoted to *charrería*).

James Norman Schmidt, *Charro: Mexican Horseman* (1969).

José Alvarez Del Villar, *Men and Horses of Mexico: History and Practice of "Charrería,"* translated by Margaret Fischer de Nicolin (1979).

Kathleen M. Sands, "*Charreada:* Performance and Interpretation of an Equestrian Folk Tradition in Mexico and the United States," in *Studies in Latin American Popular Culture* 13 (1994): 77–100.

Additional Bibliography

Carreño King, Tania. *El charro: La construcción de un estereotipo nacional, 1920–1940.* México: Instituto Nacional de Estudios Históricos de la Revolución Mexicana, 2000.

MARY LOU LECOMPTE

CHARRO. Charro, Mexican horseman skilled in roping and riding. The first *charros* were elite Spaniards who perpetuated *jineta* (Moorish-style riding) on their New World *encomiendas.* The group subsequently included mestizos, many of whom were landowners or hacienda overseers. Over time they combined *jineta* with events derived from cattle ranching and developed the whole into a sport called *charrería,* which became the national sport of Mexico. Always known for their distinctive riding style and flamboyant costumes, *charros* gained fame in the Mexican Revolution because they formed a great part of the insurgent groups. Both Pancho Villa and Emiliano Zapata were *charros.* Since 1921, most *charros* have been members of one of over 800 amateur *charro* clubs in Mexico and the United States. Unlike their rural predecessors, contemporary *charros* usually live in cities, and many follow professions like law or medicine. Clubs regularly compete against one another in Charreadas,

CHARRY LARA, FERNANDO (1920–2004). Fernando Charry Lara (*b.* 1920), Colombian poet, born in Bogotá. His love poetry is erotic and characterized by a sense of mystery inspired by the night. Charry Lara's importance lies in his occupying a transitional position between the poets of the Piedra y Cielo group and those of the Mito group, which is known for its universalist poetry. The members of Piedra y Cielo, following the style of Spanish poetry, concentrated on purity of forms, whereas the members of Mito, influenced by existentialism, worried less about form and meditated on reality, love, and poetry itself. Charry Lara became famous with the publication of his first poems in 1944 in the poetry magazine *Cántico.* In the 1950s he was a part of the Mito group, whose magazine is notable for its criticism of the Colombian literary and social situation. Charry Lara's poetry collections are *Nocturnos y otros sueños* (1949), *Los adioses* (1963), *Pensamientos del amante* (1981) and *Llama de amor viva* (1986,) which is considered by many to be his master work. Of the Mito group members, Charry Lara contributed the most to the criticism of Colombian poetry with his essay collection *Lector de poesía* (1975). His poetry was influenced by such Spanish poets as Vicente Aleixandre, by Pablo Neruda and Jorge Luis Borges, and by the German Romantic poets. In 2000, he won the José Ausunción Silva National Poetry Prize in Colombia, and in 2003 the National University of Antioquía awarded him the National Poetry Prize for his life's work. He died in the United States in 2004.

See also **Literature: Spanish America.**

BIBLIOGRAPHY

Francisco Aguilera and Georgette Magassy Dorn, *The Archive of Hispanic Literature on Tape* (1974).

Rafael Gutiérrez Girardot, "Poesía y crítica literaria en Fernando Charry Lara," in *Revista Iberoamericana* 50 (1984): 839–852.

Armando Romero, "Fernando Charry Lara o la obsesión de la noche," in his *Las palabras están en situación* (1985), pp. 86–96.

Juan Gustavo Cobo Borda, *Poesía colombiana 1880–1980* (1987), pp. 172–178.

Jaime García Maffla, *Fernando Charry Lara* (1989).

Additional Bibliography

Bonnett, Piedad. *Imaginación y oficio: Conversaciones con séis poetas colombianos.* Medellín, Colombia: Editorial Universidad de Antioquía, 2003.

García Maffla, Jaime. *Fernando Charry Lara.* Bogotá: Procultura, 1989.

Serrano Serrano, Samuel. "Entrevista a Fernando Charry Lara." *Cuadernos hispanoamericanos* (Sep–Oct 2004): 651–652.

JUAN CARLOS GALEANO

CHARTERED COMPANIES. *See* **Companies, Chartered.**

CHATEAUBRIAND BANDEIRA DE MELO, FRANCISCO DE ASSIS (1892–1968).

Francisco de Assis Chateaubriand Bandeira de Melo was one of the most important figures in the evolution of the mass media in twentieth-century Brazil. Born October 4, 1892, in Umbuzeiro, Paraíba, he stuttered as a child and did not learn to read and write until he was around age twelve. He began to work as a reporter while still a teenager in Recife. He gained national attention when, as a recent law school graduate in 1915, he competed for a teaching position at his alma mater; he went to Rio de Janeiro to argue his case and made valuable allies while demonstrating polemical and political skills in the process. Never to spend a day in the classroom again, he relocated to Rio. A practicing lawyer as well as a journalist, he aspired to become a newspaper publisher. After working as a foreign correspondent and a managing editor of the *Jornal do Brasil*, he got his chance in 1924 when he became publisher of *O Jornal* and quickly doubled advertising revenues. Over the next several decades he created the largest empire of newspapers, magazines, radio stations, television stations, and advertising agencies in Latin America, Diários e Emissoras Associados. He regularly acq-uired the latest technology to improve the look and style of his newspapers and magazines. In 1935 he founded his first radio station; in 1950 he launched the first television station in South America. His national preeminence in his field led him to be elected senator (representing his home state, as well as Maranhão) and ambassador to the United Kingdom in the 1950s, but he paid scant attention to his duties in either position. One of his lasting achievements was the creation of the Museu de Arte de São Paulo. Paralyzed for much of the last decade of his life, he continued to play an active role in the management of his many businesses. He died April 4, 1968.

See also **Radio and Television; Journalism; Journalism in Mexico.**

BIBLIOGRAPHY

Morais, Fernando. *Chatô: O rei do Brasi.* São Paulo, Brazil: Companhia das Letras, 1994.

ANDREW J. KIRKENDALL

CHATFIELD, FREDERICK (1801–1872).

Frederick Chatfield (*b.* 6 February 1801; *d.* 30 September 1872), key British agent in Central America (1833–1840, 1842–1852).

A native of London, Chatfield had already outlined British policy in Central America before his arrival as minister plenipotentiary. But the territorial question of Belize (British Honduras) stirred up nationalistic reactions that frustrated England's political and economic objectives. The 1839 takeover of Roatán (one of the Bay Islands) and the promotion of protectorate status for the Miskito Shore further complicated relationships.

Although Chatfield had pursued a constructive line with the Unionist Party, assisting the Central American Federation in making financial and customs reforms, the Roatán takeover forced him into a negative stance. Having become the leader of the States' Righters, he devised favorable "doctrines" and employed financial claims to bring on blockades for political objectives. Aiming at establishing a British protectorate in Central America before North Americans took control of a transisthmian interoceanic route, he seized Tigre Island (Honduras) on 16 October 1849. War with "Brother Jonathan" (North Americans) seemed inevitable. Lord Palmerston's parliamentary enemies defeated the aggression by signing the Clayton–Bulwer Treaty (1850). Palmerston's dismissal in 1851 and Chatfield's recall in 1852 underscored the reversal in British policy.

See also **British–Latin American Relations.**

BIBLIOGRAPHY

Mary Wilhelmine Williams, *Anglo-American Isthmian Diplomacy, 1815–1915* (1916).

Richard W. Van Alstyne, "The Central American Policy of Lord Palmerston, 1846–1848," in *Hispanic American Historical Review* 16, no. 3 (1936): 339, 359, and "British Diplomacy and the Clayton–Bulwer Treaty, 1850–60," in *Journal of Modern History* 11, no. 2 (1939): 149–183.

Thomas Karnes, *Failure of Union: Central America, 1824–1860* (1961).

Mario Rodríguez, *A Palmerstonian Diplomat in Central America: Frederick Chatfield, Esq.* (1964).

Additional Bibliography

Quesada Monge, Rodrigo. *Recuerdos del imperio: Los ingleses en América Central, 1821–1915.* Heredia: EUNA, 1998.

MARIO RODRÍGUEZ

CHAUVET, MARIE VIEUX (1916–1973).

Marie Vieux Chauvet (*b.* 16 September 1916, *d.* 19 June 1973), Haitian novelist and playwright. Chauvet is the most widely known Haitian woman novelist, and yet her audience has remained restricted. She received early recognition for her first novel, *Fille d'Haïti* (1954), which received the prize of the Alliance Française. In *Danse sur le volcan* (1957), she brought a feminist perspective to bear on the Haitian Revolution, at a moment when women's movements were virtually nonexistent in Haiti. *Fonds des Nègres* (1960) depicts a young city woman who regains the taste for traditional culture when she is caught in a small town. *Amour, colère et folie* (1968) has received high critical acclaim for the combination of a lucid style and unadorned insights into the fearful grip of François Duvalier and his Tonton Macoutes on the Haitian bourgeoisie and intellectuals. It was banned in Haiti, however, and the Chauvet family bought back all rights. *Les rapaces* (1986) was published posthumously after the fall of Jean-Claude Duvalier.

Although the Haitian political situation and a faltering literary establishment have kept Chauvet from gaining wide readership, she is increasingly recognized as a powerful writer and an early Haitian advocate of women's rights.

See also **Feminism and Feminist Organizations.**

BIBLIOGRAPHY

Works by Marie Vieux Chauvet include: *La légende des fleurs* (play, 1947); *La danse sur le volcan* (novel, 1957), translated by Salvator Attanasio as *Dance on the Volcano* (1959); and *Fonds des Nègres* (novel, 1960).

Maryse Condé, *La parole des femmes: Essais sur les romancières des Antilles de langue française* (1979), pp. 98–110; Joan Dayan, "Reading Women in the Caribbean: Chauvet's *Love, Anger, and Madness,*" in *The Politics of Tradition,* edited by Joan De Jean and Nancy Miller (1990).

Additional Bibliography

Dominique, Max. *Esquisses critiques,* Port-au-Prince: Editions Mémoire, 1999.

Shelton, Marie-Denise. "Hatian Women's Fiction." *Callaloo* 15, no. 3 (Summer 1992): 770–777.

CARROL F. COATES

CHAVES, FEDERICO (1882–1978).

Federico Chaves (*b.* 1882; *d.* 24 April 1978), Paraguayan political leader and president (1949–1954). The son of Portuguese immigrants, Federico Chaves spent his early life as a lawyer and judge in Asunción and other locales. His affiliation with the Asociación Nacional Republicana (or Partido Colorado) in the 1930s and 1940s brought him some national prominence, and by 1946, he was vice president of the party. In that year, the dictator Higínio Morínigo brought Chaves into the government as a concession to the Colorados. This coalition regime did not last, however, and in the 1947 civil war that followed, Chaves clarified his position as chief of the "democratic" wing of the party. By so doing, he had placed himself in opposition to the violent Guión Rojo faction, led by Juan Natalicio González. In 1948 a coup d'état gave Chaves the chance to ally himself with the new president, Felipe Molas López, with whom he purged the government of González followers.

This housecleaning paved the way for Chaves's own accession to the presidency in 1949. During his administration the Paraguayan economy was plagued by inflation, which Chaves sought to relieve through a close economic union with Perón's Argentina. At home, his policies were repressive, but his arbitrary use of police power failed to curb the opposition of former Guionistas and army officers, one of whom, General Alfredo Stroessner, launched a revolt in May 1954. After some fierce fighting, Chaves stepped down. A year later, Stroessner rewarded his predecessor's noninterference in the new government by making him ambassador to Paris. He died in Asunción.

See also **Paraguay, Political Parties: Colorado Party; Paraguay: The Twentieth Century.**

BIBLIOGRAPHY

Leo B. Lott, *Venezuela and Paraguay: Political Modernity and Tradition in Conflict* (1972).

Paul H. Lewis, *Paraguay Under Stroessner* (1980), esp. pp. 28–60.

Alfredo M. Seiferheld, comp., *La caída de Federico Chaves: Una visión documental norteamericana* (1987).

Riorden Roett and Richard S. Sacks, *Paraguay: The Personalist Legacy* (1991), esp. pp. 51–54.

Additional Bibliography

Amaral, Raúl. *Los presidentes del Paraguay (1844–1954): crónica política.* Asunción: Centro Paraguayo de Estudios Sociológicos, 1994.

López Benítez, Adriano Abab. *Historia política del Paraguay: 1940 a 2005.* Asunción: Paraguay, 2005.

THOMAS L. WHIGHAM

CHAVES, FRANCISCO C. (1875–1961).

Francisco C. Chaves (*b.* 7 June 1875; *d.* 1961), Paraguayan educator and statesman. Chaves was born in the city of Asunción in the period in which Paraguay was recovering from the disastrous War of the Triple Alliance. His well-connected family was involved in the country's reconstruction at many levels and contributed several sons and grandsons to serve in high office. Chaves was educated at the Colegio Nacional, graduating with a bachelor's degree in 1895, and at the National University, from which he received a doctorate in law in 1901. He spent the rest of his career teaching law to young students.

After receiving his doctorate, the government named him a justice of the Superior Court and a professor of civil law at the university. Over the next ten years, he held numerous offices, including minister of justice, national deputy, minister to Brazil, and rector of the university.

Chaves taught a generation of lawyers in Paraguay and added a great deal to the professionalization of that field within the country. In later life, he became special envoy to a dozen international conferences while simultaneously serving as a national senator and president of the central bank. He capped his legal career by being named president of the Supreme Court.

See also **Paraguay: The Twentieth Century.**

BIBLIOGRAPHY

William Belmont Parker, *Paraguayans of To-Day* (1921), pp. 189–190.

Charles J. Kolinski, *Historical Dictionary of Paraguay* (1975), p. 54.

THOMAS L. WHIGHAM

CHAVES, JULIO CÉSAR (1907–1988).

Julio César Chaves (*b.* 1907; *d.* 20 February 1988), Paraguayan historian and diplomat. Born into an old and distinguished Asunción family, Chaves spent his early years in the Paraguayan capital, where he later studied international law. After receiving his law degree from the National University in 1929, he went on to hold various educational and diplomatic posts. Chaves was ambassador to Bolivia after the conclusion of the Chaco War (1932–1935), and in 1940 he became President José Félix Estigarribia's ambassador to Peru. Two years later, political conditions at home forced him to leave the diplomatic service, and he relocated to Buenos Aires, where he remained for eleven years.

In Argentina, Chaves began to pursue his interest in historical topics. He eschewed the blind nationalism of many of his contemporaries and made every effort to give his investigations a measure of empirical depth. To this end, he conducted extensive research in South American and European archives and incorporated his findings in many publications. These included *Historia de las relaciones entre Buenos Aires y el Paraguay* (1938), *Castelli: El Adalid de Mayo*, 2d cd. (1957), *San Martín y Bolívar en Guayaquil* (1950), *El presidente López: Vida y gobierno de Don Carlos* (1955), *La conferencia de Yataity-Corá* (1958), and *Descubrimiento y conquista del Río de la Plata y el Paraguay* (1968). By common consent, however, Chaves's greatest work was *El supremo dictador* (1942), the first modern biographical treatment of the nineteenth-century Paraguayan dictator Dr. José Gaspar Rodriguez de Francia.

After his return to Asunción in the mid-1950s, Chaves resumed his teaching career. His good relations with the Stroessner government (his brother was longtime president of the Colorado Party) assured him freedom of action in the country as well as considerable prestige. He became an unofficial spokesman for his country's intellectuals, traveling to scores of international scholarly conferences and acting as head of the Paraguayan PEN Club and of the Academia Paraguaya de la Historia.

See also **Paraguay: The Twentieth Century.**

BIBLIOGRAPHY

Julio César Chaves, *El Supremo Dictador,* 3d ed. (1958).

Luis G. Benítez, *Historia de la cultura en el Paraguay* (1976), pp. 239–240.

Additional Bibliography

Valleau de Talavera, Andrés Avelino. "Biografía de historiadores paraguayos y sus obras." Ph.D. diss.,Universidad Nacional de Asunción, 1982, 1986.

                                            THOMAS L. WHIGHAM

CHÁVEZ, CARLOS (1899–1978).

Carlos Chávez (*b.* 13 June 1899; *d.* 2 August 1978), Mexican composer, conductor, educator, and administrator. Chávez began piano studies with his brother and continued with Manuel Ponce and Luis Ogazón. His penchant for improvisation led him to begin composing at an early age. He wrote his first symphony at age sixteen, but most of his early works were miniatures derivative of European styles or drawn from the Mexican song tradition. A concert of his works in 1921 brought public awareness of a new creative voice in Mexico. Travels in 1922 left him discouraged over the conservative state of music in Europe. Back in Mexico he produced new music concerts, but impatient for a better response, he moved to New York City (1926–1928) and received professional encouragement from the new music establishment, notably Aaron Copland, Roger Sessions, and Edgard Varèse. Chávez returned to Mexico in 1928 and was appointed director of the Symphony Orchestra of Mexico (remaining twenty-one years). Quick success led to directorships of the National Conservatory and fine arts department in the Ministry of Education. His conducting reputation grew rapidly through engagements with the New York Philharmonic and NBC Orchestras (1937–1938). In 1947 President Miguel Alemán named him founding director of the National Institute of Fine Arts with sweeping authority over all of the arts.

Chávez was an active and productive writer, lecturer, conductor, teacher, and statesman, but claimed these activities were no more than a means for him to compose. His most widely accepted composition was the nationalistic work employing Mexican Indian themes, *Sinfonía india* (1935). His more abstract and cerebral style in later years signaled a move away from nationalism.

See also **Music: Art Music.**

BIBLIOGRAPHY

Robert L. Parker, *Carlos Chávez: Mexico's Modern-Day Orpheus* (1984).

Additional Bibliography

Alcaraz, José Antonio. *Carlos Chávez, un constante renacer.* México, D.F.: Instituto Nacional de Bellas Artes, Centro Nacional de Investigación, Documentación e Información Musical, 1996.

Cuesy, Silvia L. *Carlos Chávez.* México: Planeta DeAgostini, 2002.

ROBERT L. PARKER

CHÁVEZ, HUGO (1954–). In the years following his election as president of Venezuela in 1998, Hugo Chávez became a controversial and influential political figure in Latin American and worldwide. His close friendship with, and frequent praise of, Fidel Castro created fears that he intended to copy the Communist model at the same time that he was replacing the aging Cuban leader as Latin America's leading leftist icon. Castro, however, publicly advised Chávez that he did not need to follow the Cuban path in order to achieve his ambitious goals.

Chávez was born on July 28, 1954, into a lower-middle-class family in Sabeneta, a town in the rural state of Barinas. He entered the army after graduating from Venezuela's military academy in 1975, and in December 1982 he founded a clandestine group of middle-level officers that became the Movimiento Bolivariano Revolucionario—200 (MBR-200). As an affirmation of its democratic commitment, the group called for a "civilian-military alliance" and held six clandestine congresses that were attended by disenchanted civilian leaders. The ranks of the MBR-200 swelled as a result of discontent among officers due to the harsh repression unleashed during the week of widespread disturbances and looting known as the "Caracazo," beginning on February 27, 1989. On February 4, 1992, the MBR-200 led an abortive coup against President Carlos Andrés Pérez involving middle-level army officers, but the insurgents failed to receive backing from higher-ranking officers or other branches of the armed forces. In March 1994 the recently elected president, Rafael Caldera, granted Chávez and the other coup participants amnesty. Chávez's MBR was virtually alone in the 1990s in calling for electoral abstention, but in April

1997, when it changed its name to the Movimiento Quinta República (MVR), it launched the candidacy of Chávez for the 1998 presidential elections. During the nearly two-year campaign, Chávez moderated his positions on economic issues such as payment of Venezuela's foreign debt obligations and concentrated on his main campaign slogan, which was the calling of a constituent assembly. He was elected with 56 percent of the vote.

REVERSING NEOLIBERALISM

The first two years of the Chávez presidency saw the drafting of a new constitution and its ratification in a national referendum in December 1999, followed by general elections in July 2000, in which Chávez increased his vote from 56 percent to 59 percent. The Constitution embodied the concept of participatory democracy, which promoted direct popular input into decision making and was designed as a corrective to domination by political party elites, which was sometimes referred to as representative democracy. In spite of his moderation during this first stage, Chávez halted the plans for privatization undertaken by the previous government of Caldera. Thus, he rejected the position of his right-hand man Luis Miquilena, who favored the transfer of the social security system to the private sector in accordance with legislation passed in 1997. Furthermore, the new constitution prohibited the sale of stocks by the state oil company, PDVSA.

The government's enactment in 2001 of a package of forty-nine special laws that definitively reversed the neoliberal trends of the 1990s signaled the beginning of a second, more leftist stage. Most important, the Organic Hydrocarbons Law established majority government ownership of all mixed companies in charge of oil operations. The Lands Law subjected idle land to expropriation, while a special tax was devised for the owners of underutilized land. A broad coalition of employers, FEDECAMARAS, the labor confederation Confederación de Trabajadores de Venezuela (CTV; Confederation of Venezuelan Workers), and opposition parties united to oppose the legislation and organize general strikes that culminated in a violent confrontation in downtown Caracas on April 11, 2002, which set off a military coup. Two days later, tens of thousands of pro-Chavista poor people surrounded the presidential palace as well as military bases calling on officers to rebel against the provisional government. The concept of a civilian-military alliance developed by Chávez in the

1980s played itself out as he returned to power on April 13. In December 2002 an insurgent movement led by FEDECAMARAS and the CTV engineered a two-month general strike in another abortive attempt to oust Chávez by peaceful means. On August 15, 2004, the opposition attempted to force Chávez out of office for the third time, in this instance by a recall election in which the president emerged triumphant with 59 percent of the vote.

FURTHER RADICALIZATION

With his government firmly in control and the opposition thoroughly demoralized, Chávez promoted further radicalization at the same time that a new economic model began to emerge. Chávez declared his government "anti-imperialist," and, in 2005, he called for the construction of a novel brand of "socialism for the twenty-first century." He also announced a policy of respect for private property rights under normal circumstances while demanding that property holders fulfill social obligations. The government began to apply the Lands Law of 2001 to the private sector and also expropriated several companies that had closed down. In addition, it established free programs in barrios. Known as "missions," these programs were mainly in the areas of health and education. The educational missions ranged from literacy classes to university education and included modest stipends for enrollees. Twenty thousand Cuban doctors, along with a much smaller number of Venezuelan physicians, lived and set up offices in barrios, dispensing free medicine and working with community groups in order to promote preventive medicine. In sharp contrast with the past, business interests went unrepresented in the key government ministries in charge of economic decision making. In another action that undermined those interests, the federal tax agency, SENIAT, made use of new legislation to enforce the income tax system, which until then had been largely unenforced.

In December 2006 Chávez won the presidential elections with 63 percent of the vote, the highest in the modern democratic period beginning in 1958. A few days later he announced additional steps toward radicalization. In the first half of 2007, the state took control of the telephone company, CANTV; the Electricidad de Caracas; and the companies that exploited the heavy, unconventional oil of the Orinoco region. In short, throughout his first eight and a half years in power, Chávez has taken advantage of his position of strength following each political victory—such as the ratification of the constitution in 1999, the defeat of the coup in April 2002, the defeat of the general strike of 2002–2003, his triumph in the recall election of 2004, and his reelection in 2006—to introduce increasingly radical changes and consolidate his control.

See also **Caldera Rodríguez, Rafael; Castro Ruz, Fidel; Pérez, Carlos Andrés; Venezuela: Venezuela since 1830.**

BIBLIOGRAPHY

Ellner, Steve. "Revolutionary and Non-Revolutionary Paths of Radical Populism: Directions of the *Chavista* Movement in Venezuela." *Science and Society* 69, no. 2 (April 2005): 160–190.

Ellner, Steve, and Daniel Hellinger, eds. *Venezuelan Politics in the Chávez Era: Class, Polarization and Conflict.* Boulder, CO: Lynne Rienner, 2003.

Ellner, Steve, and Miguel Tinker Salas, eds. *Venezuela: Hugo Chávez and the Decline of an "Exceptional" Democracy.* Lanham, MD: Rowman & Littlefield, 2007.

Garrido, Alberto. *Chávez, plan andino y guerra asimétrica.* Caracas: Los Libros El Naciona, 2006.

Gott, Richard. *Hugo Chavez and the Bolivarian Revolution in Venezuela.* London: Verso, 2005.

Guevara Guevara, Aleida, interviewer. *Chávez: Venezuela and the New Latin America.* Melbourne, Ocean Press, 2005.

Harnecker, Marta, interviewer. *Understanding the Venezuelan Revolution: Hugo Chávez Talks to Marta Harnecker.* New York: Monthly Review Press, 2005.

Jones, Bart. *Hugo! The Hugo Chávez Story: From Mud Hut to Perpetual Revolution.* Hanover, NH: Steerforth Press, 2007.

Kozloff, Nicolás. *Hugo Chávez: Oil, Politics, and the Challenge to the U.S.* New York: St. Martin's Press, 2006.

López Maya, Margarita. *Del viernes negro al referendo revocatorio.* Caracas: Alfadil, 2004.

McCaughan, Michael. *The Battle of Venezuela.* London: Latin American Bureau, 2004.

McCoy, Jennifer, and David J. Myers, eds. *The Unraveling of Venezuelan Democracy in Venezuela.* Baltimore: Johns Hopkins University Press, 2004.

STEVE ELLNER

CHÁVEZ, MARIANO (1808–c. 1845).

Mariano Chávez (*b.* 1808; *d.* c. 1845), president of the New Mexico Assembly and interim governor (1844). Like many of the political actors of the

Mexican period, Chávez became wealthy through his participation in the trade between Santa Fe and Missouri during the 1830s. His wealth and elevated social status brought Chávez the opportunity to demonstrate his leadership during the popular revolt of northern New Mexicans in 1837 against the centralist governor, Albino Pérez. Chávez exhorted those who chose to show their allegiance to Santa Anna and his centralist government to follow the leadership of General Manuel Armijo. The Plan de Tomé denounced the rebel governor, José González, and named Armijo as the New Mexican leader and Chávez as his lieutenant. Together Armijo and Chávez defeated the rebels, reoccupied Santa Fe, and apprehended and executed González.

Chávez's status as a *rico* and his family connections to Manuel Armijo aided his election in 1844 as president of the New Mexican Assembly and explains his appointment as interim governor shortly afterward by Armijo, who became ill. As Assembly president, Chávez swore loyalty to Santa Anna and his recently promulgated *bases orgánicas* while protesting the neglect of New Mexico by the central government.

During his brief tenure as governor, Chávez distinguished himself by becoming involved in a feud between Father Antonio José Martínez of Taos and Charles Bent and his business associates. In 1844, in response to a petition by Martínez, Chávez revoked the enormous Beaubien-Miranda grant made by Armijo, thereby adding to its already complicated history. The year before, the governor's brother, Antonio José Chávez, had been robbed and murdered by American bandits. Agreeing with Martínez that increasing foreign influence and interest in New Mexico threatened Mexican sovereignty, Chávez sought to enforce a ban on foreigners holding an interest in Mexican land grants, apparently believing that Charles Bent held a share of the Beaubien-Miranda grant. On 15 May 1844, Chávez was replaced by a Santa Anna appointee, General Mariano Martínez.

Known as a wealthy and educated political operator during his short career, Chávez used his moment in power to diminish the growing political and economic power that American expatriates were gaining in New Mexico. Just before sending his son José Francisco to school in Saint Louis in 1841, Chávez apparently said to him: "The heretics are going to overrun all this country. Go and learn their language and come back prepared to defend your people."

See also **New Mexico; Pérez, Albino.**

BIBLIOGRAPHY

Angelico Chávez, *Origins of New Mexico Families* (1954).

Howard Roberts Lamar, *The Far Southwest, 1846–1912: A Territorial History* (1966).

Marc Simmons, *The Little Lion of the Southwest: A Life of Manuel Antonio Chaves* (1973).

David J. Weber, *The Mexican Frontier, 1821–1846: The American Southwest under Mexico* (1982).

Victor Westphall, *Mercedes Reales: Hispanic Land Grants of the Upper Rio Grande Region* (1983).

Additional Bibliography

Alba, Victor. *Mexicanos para la historia: Doce figuras contemporáneas.* México: Libro-Mex Editores, 1995.

Etulain, Richard W. *Western Lives: A Biographical History of the American West.* Albuquerque: University of New Mexico Press, 2004.

Laezman, Rick. *100 Hispanic-Americans Who Shaped History.* San Mateo, CA: Bluewood Books, 2002.

Machamer, Gene. *Hispanic American Profiles.* New York: One World, 1996.

ROSS H. FRANK

CHÁVEZ MORADO, JOSÉ (1909–2002).

José Chávez Morado was a Mexican painter and educator. Born in Siloa, Guanajuato, Mexico, on 4 January 1909, Chávez Morado belongs to the second generation of Mexican mural painters. He studied engraving and lithography at San Carlos Academy in Mexico City. In 1937, together with Feliciano Peña, Francisco Gutiérrez, and Olga Costa, he painted the murals of the Escuela Normal. In one year alone (1948) he painted over fifteen public buildings, using various techniques. Later he painted frescoes at the Alhóndiga de Granaditas and the Exhacienda Minera (now called Pastita) in Guanajuato. He served as vice president of the Latin American section of the Worldwide Artists' Council of UNESCO. In 1974 he won the National Prize of Sciences and Arts in Mexico. In 1985 the Academy of Arts of Mexico appointed him a member, and the Universidad Nacional Autónoma de México (UNAM) awarded him an honorary doctorate.

He exhibited his easel paintings in important galleries and museums throughout Latin America, Europe, Asia, and the United States. He died in Guanajuato on 2 December 2002.

See also **Art: The Twentieth Century.**

BIBLIOGRAPHY

Martínez, Jesús. "José Chávez Morado, creador de espacios para el arte." *Plural* 23 (November 1994): 40–47.

Santiago, José de. *José Chávez Morado: Vida, obra, y circunstancias.* Mexico: Ediciones La Rana, 2001.

Tibol, Raquel. *José Chávez Morado: Imágenes de identidad mexicana.* Mexico: Coordinación de Humanidades, Universidad Nacional Autónoma de México, 1980.

BÉLGICA RODRÍGUEZ

CHAVÉZ SÁNCHEZ, IGNACIO (1897–1979).

The Mexican educator and cardiologist Ignacio Chávez Sánchez was a member of a distinguished generation of intellectuals and politicians from the Colegio Nacional de San Nicolás, Morelia, Michoacán. Born on January 31, 1897, Chávez became one of the youngest figures ever to direct a major Mexican university, the Colegio Nacional de San Nicolás, in 1920. He obtained both medical (1920) and Ph.D. (1934) degrees from the National Autonomous University of Mexico (UNAM), and he also studied in Europe (1926–1927). He taught in the National Medical School for five decades, serving as dean in 1933–1934. In 1944 he founded the National Institute of Cardiology, which he directed for many years. He was rector of the UNAM from 1961 to 1966, a period of student unrest. Personal physician to many presidents beginning with Plutarco Elias Calles (1924–1928), Chávez left an important legacy of institutionalizing Mexican heart research. He was awarded Mexico's National Prize of Arts and Sciences in 1961.

See also **Education; Medicine: The Modern Era.**

BIBLIOGRAPHY

Arreola Cortés, Raúl. *Infancia y juventud de Ignacio Chávez.* Morelia, Mexico: Universidad Michoacana, 1997.

Romo Medrano, Lilia. *Un relato biográfico: Ignacio Chávez, rector de la UNAM.* Mexico: Colegio Nacional, 1997.

RODERIC AI CAMP

CHAVÍN.

Chavín, the first of the widespread, great art styles of the Andes. Chavín is named for the archaeological site of Chavín De Huántar in the northern Peruvian highlands, a temple complex that exhibits the greatest formal expression of this style. Its widespread distribution corresponds generally to the Early Horizon of the Andean chronological sequence (c. 1400–400 BCE).

Around 1400 BCE a religious movement began to spread across northern Peru that archaeologists term the cult of Chavín. It incorporated elements from older prehistoric Andean coastal religions represented by temples with sunken circular courts and later U-shaped temples, and combined them with elements from the tropical forests of the Amazon basin. Many of the images most commonly represented in Chavín art are wild animals found in the tropical jungle of the Amazonian lowlands. Prominent are the cayman, the jaguar, the serpent, and raptorial birds such as hawks or harpy eagles. Features of these animals, especially fangs and claws, are used even on nonanimal and human representations in Chavín art, probably as a sign of divinity. These features occur in a great variety of contexts even on a single image. Hair is represented as snakes, limbs end in feet with large raptorial bird claws or jaguar claws, junctions of the limbs with the trunk of the body are often shown as snarling, fanged feline or cayman mouths, as is the waist, or even the knees. Feathers may end in eyes, snakes' heads, or feline mouths. It has been suggested that the constant use of these features represents a system of visual metaphors. These are thought to be analogous to kenning, or comparison by substitution. The audience for Chavín art would have understood the references, so that, for example, as a result of an artist's consistently substituting snakes for hair in an image, snakes would eventually come to symbolize hair or represent the qualities of hair. It would also be possible to make kennings of well-known kennings and thus add more complexity to the images.

Chavín art conformed to a specific set of canons. In addition to the use of kennings, the principles of Chavín art include bilateral symmetry, reversible images, and double-profile heads. Bilateral symmetry was extensively used but was rarely perfect, for compositions often have at least one unsymmetrical element, typically a face looking to one side in the center. Many Chavín compositions also contain reversible imagery, whereby a work rotated side to side and/or inverted will still present a right-side-up image. This is usually achieved by clever and careful use of mouth and eye images in kennings on the major intersections of body parts, typically at the junction of the legs, arms, and head with the trunk of the figure. Double-profile heads are achieved through careful placement of two profile heads. Facing each other, the elements of the two heads can be visually combined and read as a single face.

By 1300–1200 BCE temples and artworks associated with this cult had been built in the north highlands of Peru and on the Peruvian north coast. In the highlands, the temples were built of stone and decorated with low-relief carvings of Chavín deities and icons. The coastal temples were built of adobe and embellished with sculpted mud friezes that were painted in bright colors. By 1000 BCE Chavín influence had appeared as far south as the area near the modern city of Lima. The cult continued to expand, and by 500 BCE, Chavín influence extended from the modern cities of Cajamarca in the north to Ayacucho in the south. Enduring for centuries, the Chavín cult was enormously successful, but by about 400 BCE it seems to have disappeared, as a number of new regional traditions asserted themselves.

See also **Archaeology; Art: Pre-Columbian Art of South America; Incas, The; Moche; Paracas.**

BIBLIOGRAPHY

An excellent synthesis of archaeological research on Chavín can be found in Richard L. Burger, "Unity and Heterogeneity within the Chavín Horizon," in *Peruvian Prehistory*, edited by Richard W. Keatinge (1988), pp. 99–144. See also Richard L. Burger, *The Prehistoric Occupation of Chavín de Huantar, Peru* (1984). For a discussion of kenning in Chavín art, see John H. Rowe, "Form and Meaning in Chavín Art," in *Peruvian Archaeology: Selected Readings,* edited by John H. Rowe and Dorothy Menzel (1967), pp. 72–103. See also Peter G. Roe, *A*

Further Exploration of the Rowe Chavín Seriation and Its Implication for North Central Coast Chronology (1974); and Richard L. Burger, *Chavín and the Origins of Andean Civilization* (1992).

Additional Bibliography

Julio C. Tello, *Chavín, cultura matriz de la civilización andina* (1960).

Musée du Petit Palais (Paris, France). *Peru: Art from the Chavín to the Incas.* Milano: Skira, 2006.

GORDON F. MCEWAN

CHAVÍN DE HUÁNTAR.

Chavín de Huántar, an archaeological site in the Mosna Valley in Peru's northern highlands. From 900 BCE until 200 BCE Chavín de Huántar was an important religious and economic center. At its height, it played a key role within a sphere of interaction that included cultures distributed nearly to the current Ecuadorian border on the north and to the highlands of Ayacucho and the coast of Ica in southern Peru.

In 1919 the pioneering Peruvian archaeologist Julio C. Tello initiated investigations at Chavín de Huántar. Over the next three decades he argued that the developments there had provided the cultural matrix out of which later Andean civilization developed. More recent investigations have demonstrated that many of the distinguishing features of the site's art and monumental architecture had been based on earlier cultural traditions from the coast and highlands. Nevertheless, the distinctive blend of these older styles constitutes a major artistic accomplishment, and the Chavín style is considered by many to have been among the greatest artistic achievements of indigenous South America.

The public constructions consist of a series of pyramid-platforms arranged in a U-shaped ground plan. Their exteriors were faced in cut and polished masonry, and decorated with stone carvings of tropical forest animals like the jaguar, caiman, harpy eagle, and anaconda. The largest of these structures reached a height of 52.5 feet. They were catacombed with subterranean passageways and chambers, some of which were used for religious rituals. The principal cult object, a large granite sculpture of a fanged anthropomorphic figure (known as the Lanzón), can still be found in situ in the center of the oldest temple structures. While many of the religious rites were held on building summits and in the subterranean chambers, most of the ceremonial activities probably took place in the open-air, semisubterranean, rectangular and circular courts built at the foot of the platforms.

At the outset, a small residential population was associated with Chavín's ceremonial complex, but after 400 BCE this settlement grew to a considerable size (104 acres, including the public architecture), and the population may have reached two thousand or more. Located at the intersection of two natural routes of communication, the center at Chavín de Huántar became an important focus of interregional trade and religious pilgrimage. While the local subsistence economy was based on a mixed agropastoral system of high-altitude crops (such as potatoes), maize, and llama herding, substantial amounts of exotic utilitarian items and ritual goods were acquired from distant sources. There is evidence of socioeconomic stratification at Chavín de Huántar by 300 BCE, and it is likely that the center of Chavín de Huántar served as the focus of one of the first complex societies to develop in the Central Andes.

See also **Cupisnique Culture; Kotosh; Tello, Julio César.**

BIBLIOGRAPHY

A synthesis on the archaeology of Chavín de Huántar and its significance for Andean prehistory may be found in Richard L. Burger, *Chavín and the Origins of Andean Civilization* (1992). More detailed descriptions of excavations in the temple sector are provided in Julio C. Tello, *Chavín: Cultura Matriz de la Civilización Andina* (1960), and Luis Lumbreras, *Chavín de Huántar en el Nacimiento de la Civilización Andina* (1989). The best-known studies of the Chavín art style are John H. Rowe, *Chavín Art: An Inquiry into Its Form and Meaning* (1962), and Peter Roe, *A Further Exploration of the Rowe Chavín Seriation and Its Implications for North Central Coast Chronology* (1974).

Additional Bibliography

Burger, Richard L. *Excavaciones en Chavín de Huántar.* Peru: Pontificia Universidad Católica del Perú, Fondo Editorial, 1998.

Campana D., Cristóbal. *El arte chavín: Análisis estructural de formas e imagines.* Lima: Universidad Nacional Federico Villarreal, 1995.

Druc, Isabelle C. *Ceramic Production and Distribution in the Chavín Sphere of Influence (North-central Andes).* Oxford: J. and E. Hedges: Distributed by Hadrian Books, 1998.

Vaughn, Kevin, Dennis E. Ogburn, and Christina A, Conlee. *Foundations of Power in the Prehispanic Andes.* Arlington: American Anthropological Association, 2005.

RICHARD L. BURGER

CHAYANTA, REVOLT OF (1777-1781).

Revolt of (1777–1781) Chayanta, an indigenous insurrection in Chayanta Province of Upper Peru (modern Bolivia). It began earlier than the more famous 1780–1781 revolt of Túpac Amaru, with which it became associated.

In 1777 the Aymaras in Macha began protesting the colonial government's failure to protect traditional land practices and rights to *cacicazgo* (chieftainship). A *corregidor* (provincial governor), Nicolás Usarinqui, appointed as a *cacique* (chief) of Macha a mestizo, who had no legitimate claim to leadership within the *ayllu* (kinship unit). Among other duties the *cacique* allocated *ayllu* lands, but this one did so to his own rather than to the community's advantage. By so doing he harmed the villagers, who depended on their agricultural production to pay tributes and provide food and other things for their ill-paid *mitayos* drafted for the mines of Potosí. To protect his people, Tomás Catari, the rightful *cacique*, protested this corruption and abuse to royal treasury officials in Potosí, who decreed the false *cacique's* removal. Nonetheless, the new *corregidor*, Joaquín Alós, disregarded the ruling.

Between early 1778 and January 1781, Catari appealed four times to the Potosí officials and four times to the royal Audiencia of Charcas. Seeking redress, he also traveled by foot to Buenos Aires, where he met with the viceroy. The colonial bureaucracy repeatedly approved his petitions but did not force local officials to comply. For his troubles, Catari suffered beatings, five arrests, and ten months in jail. Threats and riots by his followers secured his release. Violence mounted, and disturbances spread to neighboring provinces. The *audiencia* and Alós conspired to eliminate Catari, who was murdered during the night of 15 January 1781.

The insurrection in Chayanta intensified following Catari's death, with his brothers Dámaso and Nicolás helping lead the movement. Chayanta was crucial in spreading rebellion throughout Upper Peru, where dissatisfaction with *repartos* (forced distribution of merchandise to Indians), the Mita (forced labor), and the colonial system generally was explosive. Although the Spanish suspected that the revolts of Tomás Catari and Túpac Amaru were linked, and in fact there was correspondence between the two, the causes of the Chayanta revolt were peculiar to its Aymara peasantry.

See also **Aymara; Bolivia: The Colonial Period.**

BIBLIOGRAPHY

An excellent analysis of the revolt's causes is Sergio Serulnikov, *Reivindicaciones indígenas y legalidad colonial: La rebelión de Chayanta (1777–1781)* (1989). Also see Lillian Estelle Fisher, *The Last Inca Revolt, 1780–1783* (1966), esp. pp. 53–94; and María Cecilia Cangiano, *Curas, caciques, y comunidades: Chayanta a fines del siglo XVIII* (1988).

Additional Bibliography

Hylton, Forrest, ed. *Ya es otro tiempo el presente: Cuatro momentos de insurgéncia indígena.* La Paz: Muela del Diablo Editores, 2003.

Jacobsen, Nils, and Cristóbal Aljovín de Losada. *Political Cultures in the Andes, 1750–1950.* Durham, NC: Duke University Press, 2005.

Serulnikov, Sergio. *Subverting Colonial Authority: Challenges to Spanish Rule in Eighteenth-Century Southern Andes.* Durham, NC: Duke University Press, 2003.

Stavig, Ward. *The World of Túpac Amaru: Conflict, Community, and Identity in Colonial Peru.* Lincoln: University of Nebraska Press, 1999.

Stern, Steve J. *Resistance, Rebellion, and Consciousness in the Andean Peasant World, 18th to 20th Centuries.* Madison: University of Wisconsin Press, 1987.

Walker, Charles C. *Smoldering Ashes: Cuzco and the Creation of Republican Peru, 1780–1840.* Durham, NC: Duke University Press, 1999.

KENDALL W. BROWN

CHAYANTA, REVOLT OF (1927).

Revolt of (1927) Chayanta, one of the largest peasant rebellions in twentieth-century Bolivian history, in which up to 10,000 indigenous rebels attacked haciendas and towns throughout the central highlands between Potosí, Sucre, and Oruro. The uprising lasted about a month, and although it was violently suppressed by the army, the revolt effectively ended the period of hacienda expansion at the expense of highland traditional communities. During the early 1920s community Indians of south-central Bolivia, who had previously fought the alienation of their lands primarily through nonviolent means, became radicalized as legal methods and passive resistance failed. Organized around new leaders, including Manuel Michel, a monolingual Quechua-speaking mestizo, the movement attempted to incorporate not only community Indians but also hacienda peons and urban intellectuals (including the Bolivian Socialist Party). The leaders' principal goals were to fight for the establishment of schools in the communities and for a redistribution of hacienda lands to Indians, whether peons or community members. Shortly after the revolt broke out on 25 July 1927, the rebels took control of a number of haciendas in the Chayanta area (northern Potosí). They killed a landowner but caused few other fatalities. Indigeneous communities elsewhere attempted to rise up but were quickly suppressed. The government mobilized the army and by mid-August had brought the rebellion under control after killing hundreds of Indians. Hundreds more were jailed and the leaders exiled. Armed conflict continued in the countryside at much lower levels of violence for some years thereafter.

See also **Indigenous Peoples: Quechua.**

BIBLIOGRAPHY

The most thorough general description of the revolt is contained in René Arze Aguirre, *Guerra y conflictos sociales: El caso rural boliviano durante la campaña del Chaco* (1987), pp 11–25. See also Olivia Harris and Xavier Albo, *Monteras y guardatojos: Campesinos y mineros en el norte de Potosí,* rev. ed. (1984), pp. 59–71; and Erick D. Langer, "Andean Rituals of Revolt: The Chayanta Rebellion of 1927," in *Ethnohistory* 37, no. 3 (1990): 227–253.

Additional Bibliography

Barnadas, Josep M., and Guillermo Calvo. *Diccionario histórico de Bolivia.* Sucre: Grupo de Estudios Históricos, 2002.

Grindle, Merilee Serrill, and Pilar Domingo. *Proclaiming Revolution: Bolivia in Comparative Perspective.* Cambridge, MA: David Rockefeller Center for Latin American Studies, Harvard University, 2003.

Grunberg, Angela. *The Chayanta Rebellion of 1927, Potosí, Bolivia.* Oxford: Oxford University Press, 1996.

Klein, Herbert S. *A Concise History of Bolivia.* Cambridge: Cambridge University Press, 2003.

Schultze M., Juan Carlos, and Roberto Casanovas Sainz. *Tierra y campesinada en Potosí y Chuquisaca.* La Paz: Centro de Estudios para el Desarrollo Laboral y Agrario, 1988.

Stern, Steve J. *Resistance, Rebellion, and Consciousness in the Andean Peasant World, 18th to 20th Centuries.* Madison: University of Wisconsin Press, 1987.

ERICK D. LANGER

CHE GUEVARA. *See* Guevara, Ernesto "Che".

CHESS. *See* Sports.

CHIAPA DE CORZO.

Chiapa de Corzo, an important Mesoamerican site because of its occupation from 1400 BCE to the present. It is located on the Grijalva River, in the central section of the Isthmus of Tehuantépec near the modern town of Tuxtla Gutiérrez, Chiapas, Mexico. This location has a tropical lowland environment but the surrounding hills are arid and lack similar pre-Columbian occupations. The site is important for its long ceramic sequence and its location, which facilitates comparisons with regions to the east and west.

The earliest evidence of occupation in the Cotorra phase consists of adobe plaster from a construction and pottery jars and bowls. This pottery was decorated with a variety of surface techniques: punctation, stamping, and appliqué. By 550 BCE there were pyramids and civic buildings, and by 150 BCE there was social differentiation, indicated by palaces of cut stone and polished stucco. Tomb 1 of this period held an important personage. Built of unfired brick, it contained a burial with an obsidian-bladed lance, unusual pottery vessels, and jade jewelry. Bones and sculptures were carved in the Izapan style. Mound 5 of the same period was notable for large quantities of pottery in great variety.

See also Mesoamerica.

BIBLIOGRAPHY

Gareth W. Lowe, *Research in Chiapas, Mexico,* New World Archaeological Report no. 2 (1959).

New World Archaeological Foundation, *Excavations at Chiapa de Corzo, Mexico,* papers 8–11 (1960); *Mound 5 and Minor Excavations, Chiapa de Corzo, Chiapas, Mexico,* 12 (1962); and "Archaeological Chronology of Eastern Mesoamerica," in *New World Chronologies,* edited by Royal Ervin Taylor and Clement Woodward Meighan (1973).

Additional Bibliography

González Cruz, Arnoldo, and Martha Cuevas García. *Canto versus canto: Manufactura de artefactos líticos en Chiapa de Corzo, Chiapas.* México, D.F.: Instituto Nacional de Antropología e Historia; San Cristóbal de las Casas, Chiapas: Centro de Investigaciones Humanísticas de Mesoamérica y el Estado de Chiapas, 1998.

Lee, Thomas A., and Susanna Ekholm-Miller. *The Artifacts of Chiapa de Corzo, Chiapas, Mexico.* Provo: New World Archaeological Foundation, Brigham Young University, 1969.

Powls, Terry G., et al. "Sprouted Vessels and Cacao Use among the Preclassic Maya." *Latin American Antiquity* 13, no. 1 (March 2002): 85–106.

EUGENIA J. ROBINSON

CHIAPAS.

Mexico's southernmost state is bounded on the southwest by the Pacific Ocean, on the east by Guatemala, on the north by the state of Tabasco, and on the west by the states of Veracruz and Oaxaca. The state's population in 2005 was 4,293,459, mostly mestizos with about one-quarter indigenous people of Maya descent. The capital is Tuxtla Gutiérrez. Owing to its varied and often spectacular topography, Chiapas has several clearly defined regions, each with its distinct history, demographic base, climate, and means of production. The lowlands are hot and humid; the Valle Central is relatively dry and hot. The Meseta Central is a plateau ranging from 5,000 to 8,000 feet, with a temperate climate and a good deal of forest. North of the Meseta are valleys that drop into Tabasco; east of the Meseta lies the Lacandón rain forest. By most estimates, the forest is home to up to one-fourth of Mexico's biodiversity, but human activity since 1950 (primarily farming, logging, and ranching) has reduced its size by more than two-thirds.

Chiapas was on the western boundary of the great Maya civilization and is home to important archaeological sites of the Late Classic period (600–900 CE) such as Bonampak, Palenque, Yaxchilán, and Toniná. At their first contact, the Spaniards found a variety of ethnic states that occupied distinct territories. Among the most important were the Zoques, the Chiapanecos, the Tzotzils, and the Tzeltals. To the east were the Ch'ols, the Tojolobals, and the reclusive Lacandons. Native society in Chiapas was stratified, with a nobility, commoners, and slaves.

COLONIAL PERIOD

The definitive conquest of the province took place in 1528, when Captain Diego de Mazariegos suppressed an indigenous revolt and founded the first Spanish township, Villa Real (today known as San Cristóbal de Las Casas). Mazariegos distributed the first encomiendas (grants of land and indigenous labor) in the province.

The Conquest triggered a demographic disaster among the native population of Chiapas, chiefly through disease, slavery, and onerous tribute demands. Within fifty years, an estimated two-thirds of the indigenous population had perished; along the Pacific Coast, the natives were wiped out. The depredations of the encomenderos drew the attention of Chiapas' first bishop, Bartolomé de Las Casas. During his brief tenure (1545–1547), this Dominican friar tried unsuccessfully to enforce the 1542 decree abolishing Indian slavery. Las Casas then took his case to the royal court; in time, the local clergy (including the Dominicans) joined the encomenderos and their descendants in extracting labor and tribute from the surviving indigenous population.

MODERN PERIOD

When the wars of independence broke out in New Spain in 1810, Chiapas was a marginalized, impoverished intendancy of the capitanía of Guatemala. Economic stagnation and neglect fed a spirit of separatism among the province's oligarchy. After Spain recognized the independence and sovereignty of the Mexican empire in August 1821, Chiapas' provincial assembly declared independence from both Spain and Guatemala and solicited annexation with its northern neighbor. Chiapas became a Mexican state in 1824, and the boundaries with Guatemala were finally settled in 1882.

After independence, factions of Chiapas' ladino (non-Indian) elite fought to control access to Indian land and labor. By 1850 the lands that the Spanish crown had preserved as a buffer around Indian communities—the terrenos baldíos—were claimed by

ladinos, and the original occupants were reduced to a serf-like status known as baldiaje. After 1890 modernizing governors invited foreign surveying companies to sell remaining vacant lands and indigenous communal lands. Mexican and foreign capitalists invested in lucrative cash crops such as sugar, bananas, rubber, and, most notably, coffee. The development of plantation agriculture in the lowlands created a demand for seasonal labor that was increasingly met by highland Indians who entered into debt peonage arrangements. Although the press in Mexico City denounced slavery in Chiapas, local landowners and merchants argued that the benefits of coerced labor far outweighed the costs.

The Mexican revolution ran an idiosyncratic course in Chiapas. It was imposed from without, and when it finally arrived in late 1914 it engendered no significant grassroots mobilization. Indians were considered not potential allies, but part of the spoils. When troops loyal to First Chief Venustiano Carranza entered the state, they announced a series of land, labor, and anticlerical reforms. A loose coalition of ranchers and planters called the Mapaches (raccoons) resisted the Carrancistas and eventually won a war of attrition in 1920. The Mapaches' leader, Tiburcio Fernández Ruiz, became Chiapas' first postrevolutionary governor. He and his immediate successors resisted or undermined most of the federal reforms associated with the Revolution. President Lázaro Cárdenas (1934–1940) and his allies introduced land and labor reform and indigenismo (official Indian policy) to the state, but these and other reforms were neutralized or undermined in subsequent years by local ranchers, coffee planters, alcohol merchants, and their allies in the state government.

SINCE THE LATE TWENTIETH CENTURY

Chiapas is one of Mexico's leading producers of corn, coffee, timber, sugar, beans, and cattle. In the 1970s the Mexican government completed two major dam projects in the state, and Chiapas now produces half of Mexico's hydroelectric power. The state also has important oil reserves. However, increased economic productivity has tended to exacerbate preexisting social inequities in Chiapas, as most of the benefits have accrued to non-Indian landowners and entrepreneurs. As the hunger for land grew, so too did frustration with the agrarian reform process. In the 1980s the political system grew increasingly corrupt and the state apparatus more repressive. Caciquismo (bossism) in the indigenous highlands flourished, nurtured and protected by the state and federal governments. Highland indigenous communities loyal to the ruling Institutional Revolutionary Party (PRI) expelled residents on a variety of economic, political, and religious grounds. Many expelled Maya settled in eastern Chiapas, where they governed themselves democratically and joined independent peasant unions.

Matters reached a breaking point when the Mexican government accelerated the country's integration into the globalized market through neoliberal economic policies. In 1992 Mexican president Carlos Salinas de Gortari suspended land reform as a precondition for entering the North American Free Trade Agreement (NAFTA). Many indigenous communities in eastern Chiapas voted for war.

On January 1, 1994, Mexico officially entered NAFTA, and Chiapas exploded in violence. The indigenous rebels, most hailing from eastern Chiapas, called themselves Zapatistas, after Emiliano Zapata, who led the fight for agrarian reform during the Mexican Revolution. Their list of denunciations was long—political corruption, caciquismo, the recent decision to end land reform, inadequate medical care, and a useless and culturally insensitive education system, among others. Their spokesperson, a pipe-smoking mestizo who called himself Subcomandante Marcos, called NAFTA "a "death certificate for the Indian peoples of Mexico." After seizing several towns and suffering heavy losses, the Zapatistas retreated to the eastern forest. Better prepared for guerrilla theater than guerrilla warfare, they entered into negotiations with the federal government, exposed the illegitimacy of Mexico's one-party state, and forced Mexican society to contemplate a multiethnic nation.

Although negotiations between the Zapatistas and the federal government failed to produce meaningful accords on indigenous rights and culture, some observers have argued that the Zapatista conflict played a role in ending the PRI's seventy-one-year hold on federal power. In August 2000, several weeks after Vicente Fox's unprecedented defeat of the PRI's candidate in the presidential election, an opposition coalition orchestrated an equally unprecedented defeat of the PRI's candidate for governor of Chiapas. The opposition's victory shook the political landscape. Many indigenous communities in Chiapas had been among the PRI's most loyal supporters, and the PRI's defeat broke the bonds of patronage that had cemented their loyalty. In the 2006 presidential elections, many indigenous communities voted for Andrés Manuel López Obrador, the candidate of the left-leaning Party of the Democratic Revolution (PRD).

Meanwhile, the Zapatista conflict remained unresolved. Denied a legal avenue to autonomy, in 2003 Zapatistas in eastern Chiapas created five Juntas de Buen Gobierno (Good Government Boards) and put their notion of regional autonomy into practice. The state and federal governments did nothing to block this development, perhaps hoping that, after ten years, the Zapatista movement would fade into irrelevancy.

In the first decade of the twenty-first century, an estimated 76 percent of the population of Chiapas earned less than $8 a day. Approximately 300,000 residents of Chiapas have found work in the United States. Remittances sent to Chiapas from the United States have increased so much that Chiapas as of 2007 ranks among more traditional "sending" states like Michoacán and Zacatecas. Unless measures are taken to restore the viability of small-scale agriculture in Chiapas, this trend is expected to continue.

See also **Agrarian Reform; Encomienda; Indigenismo; Indigenous Peoples; Las Casas, Bartolomé de; Mexico: The Colonial Period; Mexico, Political Parties: Institutional Revolutionary Party (PRI); North American Free Trade Agreement (NAFTA); Slavery: Indian Slavery and Forced Labor; Zapata, Emiliano.**

BIBLIOGRAPHY

Benjamin, Thomas. *A Rich Land, A Poor People: Politics and Society in Modern Chiapas*, rev. ed. Albuquerque: University of New Mexico Press, 1996.

Harvey, Neil. *The Chiapas Rebellion: The Struggle for Land and Democracy.* Durham, NC: Duke University Press, 1998.

Lewis, Stephen E. *The Ambivalent Revolution: Forging State and Nation in Chiapas, 1910–1945.* Albuquerque: University of New Mexico Press, 2005.

Rus, Jan. "The 'Comunidad Revolucionaria Institucional': The Subversion of Native Government in Highland Chiapas, 1936–1968." *In Everyday Forms of State Formation: Revolution and the Negotiation of Rule in Modern Mexico*, edited by Gilbert M. Joseph and Daniel Nugent, pp. 265–300. Durham, NC: Duke University Press, 1994.

Rus, Jan, Rosalva Aída Hernández Castillo, and Shannon L. Mattiace, eds. *Mayan Lives, Mayan Utopias: The Indigenous Peoples of Chiapas and the Zapatista Rebellion.* Lanham, MD: Rowman and Littlefield, 2003.

Ruz, Mario Humberto. *Savia india, floración ladina: Apuntes para una historia de las fincas comitacas (siglos XVIII y XIX).* Mexico: Consejo Nacional para la Cultura y las Artes, 1992.

Viqueira, Juan Pedro. *Encrucijadas chiapanecas: Historia, economía, religion e identidades.* Mexico: El Colegio de México/Tusquets, 2002.

Vos, Jan de. *La paz de Dios y del rey: La conquista de la selva lacandona, 1525–1821.* Mexico: Secretaría de Educación y Cultura de Chiapas y Fondo de Cultura Económica, 1988.

STEPHEN E. LEWIS

CHIARI, RODOLFO E. (1870–1937). Rodolfo E. Chiari (*b.* 15 November 1870; *d.* 16 August 1937), Panamanian politician, president (1924–1928), and businessman. Born in Aguadulce, he held many government posts before and after the country's separation from Colombia. He was a deputy to the National Convention in 1904, treasurer of Panama City (1905–1906), deputy secretary of the treasury in the national government (1908), and manager of the national bank (1909–1914). In 1910 he was elected third designate to the presidency, and in 1912 he briefly took charge of the executive office. In 1914 he became the secretary of government and justice, and in 1922 he was appointed director general of the telegraph service. Chiari was a prominent member of the Liberal Party, perhaps second only to Belisario Porras. Following his election in 1924, Chiari substituted Porras's populist style with a more business-oriented administration, which led to a quarrel and ultimately to a split in the party.

In 1925 Chiari faced two serious crises. The first was a rebellion by the Cuna Indians on the San Blas Islands, which he quelled successfully. Then, the Tenants Revolt (*movimiento inquilinario*) paralyzed the city for two days. The strike was defeated only after Chiari requested the help of U.S. troops stationed in the Canal Zone.

Chiari negotiated a new treaty with the United States in 1926, but it was never ratified by the National Assembly because of concern over one article that made Panama an instant ally of the United States whenever the latter became involved in an armed conflict.

See also **Panama.**

BIBLIOGRAPHY

Manuel María Alba, *Cronología de los gobernantes de Panamá, 1510–1967* (1967).

Manuel Octavio Sisnet, *Belisario Porras o la vocación de la nacionalidad* (1972).

Walter La Feber, *The Panama Canal: The Crisis in Historical Perspective* (1978).

Jorge Conte Porras, *Diccionario biográfico ilustrado de Panamá,* 2d ed. (1986).

Additional Bibliography

Córdoba Araba, Abel Abraham. *100 años de gobierno: Panama 1903–2003: Compendio cronológico de nuestros gobernantes.* Panama: Imprenta Caribean, 2004.

JUAN MANUEL PÉREZ

CHIARI REMÓN, ROBERTO FRANCISCO (1905–1981). Roberto Francisco Chiari Remón (*b.* 2 March 1905; *d.* 1981), Panamanian president (1949, 1960–1964). A liberal and popular politician, he was the son of Rodolfo E. Chiari, who had been president of Panama from 1924 to 1928. Before becoming president he was deputy to the National Assembly (1940–1945) and minister of health and public works (1945). In 1948 he was elected second vice president, and in the following year he was president for five days (20–24 November 1949) after the overthrow of Daniel Chanis. Chiari resigned after the Supreme Court declared him ineligible for the presidency. In 1952 he was the presidential candidate of a popular coalition called the Civilista Alliance, whose victory was not recognized because of the opposition's imposition of Colonel José Antonio ("Chichi") Remón Cantera.

Chiari was elected president in 1960 as the candidate of a four-party coalition, the first opposition candidate to win an election in Panama. He entered office with a reformist attitude and was intent on breaking the oligarchy's grip on power. However, most of his reform measures were blocked by the National Assembly. Seeking better relations with the United States, Chiari traveled to

Washington, D.C., and won some concessions from the Kennedy administration, including the right to fly the Panamanian flag at certain sites in the Canal Zone. However, as a result of the 1964 flag riots, Chiari broke diplomatic relations with the United States and demanded the abrogation of the 1903 treaty. He was succeeded in 1964 by Marcos Aurelio Robles.

See also **Panama Canal: Flag Riots.**

BIBLIOGRAPHY

Walter La Feber, *The Panama Canal: The Crisis in Historical Perspective* (1978); *Panama: A Country Study* (1989).

Additional Bibliography

Major, John. *Prize Possession: The United States Government and the Panama Canal, 1903–1979.* Cambridge, MA: Cambridge University Press, 2002.

Soler, Ricaurte. *Panamá, nación y oligarquía: 1925–1975.* Panamá: Ediciones de la Revista Tareas Panamá, 1989.

JUAN MANUEL PÉREZ

CHIBÁS, EDUARDO (1907–1951). Eduardo Chibás (*b.* 26 August 1907; *d.* 5 August 1951), founder of the Cuban Orthodox Party. Born in Oriente, Chibás was one of the founders of the Directorio Estudiantil at the University of Havana in the mid-1920s. He studied law and then lived in exile in Miami, Florida (1927–1933), because of his sharp criticism of Gerardo Machado's government (1925–1933). Following Machado's downfall, Chibás returned to Cuba to support the candidacy of Ramón Grau San Martín, who became president on 10 September 1933. On 14 January 1934, Fulgencio Batista orchestrated Grau's removal from power. Chibás became strongly critical of the series of governments headed by puppet presidents, and particularly of Batista. In 1938, he joined the Authentic Party and in 1940 again backed Grau for the presidency. After Grau was elected president in 1944, Chibás became disillusioned with his nepotism and governmental corruption.

In 1947, Chibás broke away from the Authentic Party and founded the Orthodox Party. He was a candidate for the presidency in 1948, finishing third in the race. During Carlos Prío Socarrás's tenure (1948–1952), Chibás used weekly radio broadcasts to attack government policies and corruption.

Chibás committed suicide by shooting himself during an emotional radio broadcast on 5 August 1951. His death created a political vacuum and rift in the Orthodox Party, facilitating Batista's coup on 10 March 1952.

See also **Cuba, Political Parties: Cuban People's Party (Ortodoxos).**

BIBLIOGRAPHY

Hugh Thomas, *Cuba: The Pursuit of Happiness* (1971).

Jaime Suchlicki, *Historical Dictionary of Cuba* (1988) and *Cuba: From Columbus to Castro*, 3d ed. (1990).

Additional Bibliography

Argote-Freyre, Frank. "The Political Afterlife of Eduardo Chibás: Evolution of a Symbol, 1951–1991." *Cuban Studies/Estudios Cubanos* 32 (2001): 74–79.

Alavez Martín, Elena. *La ortodoxia en el ideario americano.* La Habana: Editorial de Ciencias Sociales, 2002.

Rodríguez Salgado, Ramón. *La ortodoxia chibasista: Nacimiento, liderazgo y acción política de un movimiento.* Cuba: Editora Historia, 1998.

JAIME SUCHLICKI

CHIBATA, REVOLT OF THE. Revolt of the Chibata, Brazilian sailors' mutiny (1910). Brazil began an ambitious naval expansion program in 1907, purchasing two dreadnoughts, the *Minas Gerais* and the *São Paulo,* in 1908–1909, then the world's largest battleships. Soon Brazil had the world's fifth largest navy in tons displaced. An enormous gulf separated officers from seamen. Serving fifteen-year tours, seamen were mostly black and often forcibly recruited. Officers were white and aristocratic. Despite abolition (1888) and the naval prohibition of flogging with the *chibata* on the second day of the Republic in 1889, the practice continued.

A week after Marshal Hermes da Fonseca was inaugurated as president in November 1910, the squadron in the waters of Rio de Janeiro, the capital, revolted. Four officers were killed as the crews of the two dreadnoughts and lesser ships mutinied. The immediate cause was a brutal whipping of a sailor aboard the *Minas Gerais.* The command of the squadron and 2,400 rebel sailors passed to a thirty-year-old black, semiliterate seaman.

João Candido Felisberto, the son of a slave, directed the ships, coordinating their movements and loading coal, ammunition, and provisions. He demanded the abolition of corporal punishment and an amnesty for all mutineers. When Congress tarried, he fired on the capital. The president and naval authorities wanted to punish the rebels, but feared destruction of the city and loss of the costly warships. Congress capitulated to the demands.

In December a revolt of marines broke out, but João Candido and his dreadnought crew remained loyal to the government, even after officers had abandoned his ship. The revolt was quelled, and some participants in the second uprising were shot, while others were sent to Amazonian rubber plantations. The previously amnestied rebels of the first rebellion were put into prison, where sixteen suffocated. João Candido, who nearly suffocated, was tried for participation in the second revolt, but was acquitted. The first rebellion was the world's only mutiny in which a common sailor led a squadron, and one containing the most powerful war machines of its time. The *chibata* became a symbol of black and lower-class resistance.

See also **Fonseca, Hermes Rodrigues da.**

BIBLIOGRAPHY

Edmar Morel, *A Revolta da Chibata,* 2d ed. (1963).

Robert L. Scheina, *Latin America: A Naval History, 1810–1987* (1987), pp. 80–86, 105–107.

Hélio Leôncio Martins, *A revolta dos marinheiros: 1910* (1988).

Additional Bibliography

Granato, Fernando. *O Negro da chibata.* Rio de Janeiro: Objetiva, 2000.

Lopes, Moacir C. *O almirante negro: Revolta da chibata: A vigança.* São Paulo: Casa Amarela, 2003.

Maestri, Mário. *Cisnes negros uma história da revolta da Chibata.* São Paulo: Moderna, 2000.

Roland, Maria Ines. *A revolta da Chibata: Rio de Janeiro, 1910.* São Paulo: Saraiva, 2000.

Silva, Marcos A. da. *Contra a chibata: Marinheiros brasileiros em 1910.* São Paulo: Brasiliense, 1982.

Vieira, César. *João Candido do Brasil: A revolta da chibata.* São Paulo: Casa Amarela, 2003.

JOSEPH L. LOVE

CHIBCHAS. *See* **Muisca.**

CHICAGO BOYS. Known by the name Chicago Boys, this influential international network of economists advocates limited governments and unhindered markets. In the mid-1950s, the U.S. government and private foundations funded the first cohorts of Latin American economics students at the University of Chicago to counter the prevailing developmentist thinking in the region that favored state interventionism and economic nationalism. Some Chicago professors, most prominently Arnold Harberger, advised transforming economics education along neoclassical principles to offset the influence of Marxist and other heterodox currents of economic thought. Twenty years later, under Pinochet's military dictatorship, Chilean government ministers Sergio de Castro, Pablo Baraona, Miguel Kast, and Rolf Lüders and a large group of other Chicago-trained economists implemented radical market reforms. Results were mixed, but conservatives everywhere, including University of Chicago Nobel laureates Milton Friedman and Friedrich August von Hayek, extolled the virtues of Chile's neoliberal revolution. Since then, neoliberalism has been the blueprint for marketization around the world.

See also **Neoliberalism.**

BIBLIOGRAPHY

Harberger, Arnold C. "Good Economics Comes to Latin America, 1955–95." In *The Post-1945 Internationalization of Economics,* edited by Alfred W. Coats, pp. 301–311. Durham, NC, and London: Duke University Press, 1996. Annual supplement to *History of Political Economy,* vol. 28.

Valdés, Juan Gabriel. *Pinochet's Economists: The Chicago School in Chile.* Cambridge, U.K., and New York: Cambridge University Press, 1995 [*La Escuela de Chicago: Operación Chile.* Buenos Aires: Grupo Editorial Zeta S.A., 1989].

VERONICA MONTECINOS

CHICHÉN ITZÁ. Chichén Itzá is a legendary place that exists in spiritual discourses, cultural imaginaries, scientific visions, and political projects that reach beyond the four square miles that it occupies in the state of Yucatán, Mexico. Chichén, especially represented by iconic images of the main Pyramid of Kukulcan (a.k.a. El Castillo) and unique statuary, is a pervasive symbol of identity for Yucatec society, the Mexican nation, contemporary Maya peoples, Maya civilization, New Age spiritualisms, and even competing newspapers.

As a pre-Columbian Maya city that rose to power in the Late Classic (c. 800–1250 CE), Chichén was the capital of a province that held hegemony over a constellation of sixteen or eighteen other Maya lineage state-kingdoms in northern Yucatán Peninsula. They formed a geopolitical-cultural unity known as Mayab or U Kal Peten (Yukalpeten). These names became widely recognized in the twentieth century as the authentic and true indigenous names of the Maya world that was labeled Yucatán by the Spaniards in an over-interpreted and highly debated origin. *Chichén Itzá* translates as "The Mouth of the Well of the Magicians of Water"—*chi* (mouth, edge), *ch'en* (well), *itz* (magic, witchery), and *há'* (water). According to interpretations of the Books of the Chilam Balams, Uuc Habnal (Seven Year Flintstone) or Uuc Yabnal (Seven Much Corn) is either a mythic personage associated with the Itzá founding of Chichén or is the previous name of Chichén prior to the Itzá takeover.

Chichén and the Itzá are privileged protagonists in the Books of the Chilam Balams and play a special role in the history of Spanish colonization of Yucatán. Archaeological research in Yucatán has primarily sought to substantiate understandings of the pre-Columbian Maya provided by the Chilam Balams and Spanish colonial documents. Key debates center on the ethnic identity of the Itzá as Maya, Toltecs, or Mexicanized Gulf Coast peoples. The predominant interpretation asserts that the Itzá were Toltecs (ancient Mexicans) who conquered Chichén and thereby brought war, moral decadence, and human sacrifice-as well as new gods (Quetzalcoatl), art, and architecture-to the otherwise peaceful Maya who worshipped the rain god Chac. Contrary arguments observe that the Toltec elements of Chichén are historically earlier at Chichén than at Tula (Toltec capital), or that the two cultural periods are, instead, either totally or partially contemporaneous styles. Historical periodization for Chichén and other Yucatec cities is notoriously difficult given the lack of inscriptions in Yucatán of dates written in the Long Count calendar system typical of the southern Classic Maya cities (e.g., Palenque).

Archaeological study of Chichén began in the nineteenth century by foreign travelers such as John Lloyd Stephens, Désiré Charnay, Augustus Le Plongeon, and Edward H. Thompson. Reconstruction (1923–1941) by U.S. and Mexican archaeologists sponsored by the Carnegie Institution of Washington and the federal Monumentos Prehispanicos had the explicit goal of creating a tourist attraction. Today, Chichén is the third most important (visited) tourism site in Mexico behind only Tulum and Teotihuacan. Ethical and political controversies surround the U.S. archaeologists E. H. Thompson, who looted or illegally exported valuable artifacts from Chichén, and Sylvanus G. Morley, who used archaeology as a "cloak" under which he conducted U.S. Naval intelligence in Mexico during World War I. The 1920s to 1930s archaeological reconstruction of Chichén generated a brief neo-Mayan revivalism in architecture, inspired innovations in art deco building facades, and fueled the development of a Yucatec movement of regionalist modernism in art, literature, and architecture, as occurred throughout Latin America.

Chichén, the best-known pre-Columbian Maya city, was placed on Mexico's list of UNESCO-sanctioned World Heritage sites in 1988 and was designated fifth among the New Seven Wonders of the World by the N7W Foundation on July 7, 2007. Although archaeological materials are legally defined as national patrimony owned by the nation (under stewardship of the National Institute of Anthropology and History), the land in which the material artifacts and monuments of Chichén exist are actually owned as private property by an established oligarchic family of Yucatán, the Barbachanos. While the Barbachano family has sought to privatize Chichén and monopolize its tourism market, Maya communities (e.g., Pisté) have contested the legality of Barbachano privatization, asserted rights of cultural ownership of Chichén as Maya heritage, and demanded the expropriation of the archaeological ruins. Further, Neo-Aztecs, U.S.-based New Age spiritualists, and Gnostics claim Chichén to be a religious-spiritual site of initiation into cosmic growth, healing, and transformation. These groups appropriate Chichén to perform hybrid rituals during the spring equinox descent of Kukulcan; they invented additional ceremonies on other dates that are derived from ad hoc New Age interpretations of Maya calendars fundamentally at odds with both archaeological orthodoxy and commonsense knowledge. Maya from nearby communities, such as Pisté, have also re-appropriated Chichén as intangible heritage by having created a new and aesthetically innovative form of art, a wood sculpture called *arte pisteño*, that is inspired by the statuary, iconography, paintings, and murals of Chichén Itzá and other Classic Maya cities.

See also **Archaeology; Chilam Balam; Maya, The; Privatization; Toltecs; Tourism; Yucatán.**

BIBLIOGRAPHY

Argüelles, José. *The Mayan Factor: Path beyond Technology.* Santa Fe, NM: Bear, 1987.

Arochi, Luis E. *La pirámide de Kukulcán: Su simbolismo solar.* Mexico: Panorama Editorial, 1974.

Castañeda, Quetzil E. *In the Museum of Maya Culture: Touring Chichén Itzá.* Minneapolis: University of Minnesota Press, 1995.

Harris, Charles H., III, and Louis R. Sadler. *The Archaeologist Was a Spy: Sylvanus G. Morley and the Office of Naval Intelligence.* Albuquerque: University of New Mexico Press, 2003.

Himpele, Jeffrey, and Quetzil E. Castañeda, filmmakers. *Incidents of Travel in Chichén Itzá* (film). Watertown, MA: Documentary Educational Resources, 1997.

Jones, Lindsay. *Twin City Tales: A Hermeneutical Reassessment of Tula and Chichén Itzá.* Boulder: University Press of Colorado, 1995.

Morley, Sylvanus G. "Chichén Itzá: An Ancient American Mecca." *National Geographic* 47 (1925): 63–95.

Ramírez Aznar, Luis. *El Saqueo del Cenote Sagrado de Chichén Itza.* Mérida, Yucatán: Dante, 1990.

Schele, Linda, and David Freidel. *A Forest of Kings: The Untold Story of the Ancient Maya.* New York: Morrow, 1990l.

Sullivan, Paul. *Unfinished Conversations: Mayas and Foreigners between Two Wars.* Berkeley: University of California Press, 1991.

Tozzer, Alfred M. *Chichén Itzá and Its Cenote of Sacrifice.* Memoirs of the Peabody Museum of Archaeology and Ethnology. Cambridge, MA: Harvard University Press, 1941.

QUETZIL E. CASTAÑEDA

CHICHIMECS. Chichimecs, a term for various groups of nomadic, warlike peoples to the north of Mexico City. From the Nahuatl *chichi* (dog) and *mecatl* (lineage), the term may have been pejorative, or it may have had totemic significance. The chronicler Fernando de Alva Ixtlilxóchitl rejects these possible meanings, suggesting a relationship with eagles. Long before the Spanish Conquest, the term was applied to succeeding waves of invading bands of Anahuac peoples. In the sixteenth century it encompassed the Guachachiles, Guamares, Pames, and Zacatecos, all of whom lived to the north of Mexico City. With the great silver discoveries of mid-century, the Chichimecs resisted the Spanish advance to the north. Because of the Chichimecs' ferocity and successful resistance, the colonists consistently called for a total war of extermination or enslavement. The proposed war was roundly condemned by the bishops of the Third Mexican Council (1585). Eventually, the Chichimecs were pacified by a combination of Presidio and missions that were directed by the Jesuits.

The Chichimecs descended from the north and fused culturally with the Toltec or Toltec successor peoples. This is essentially the story as narrated by the Chichimec historian Fernando de Alva Ixtlilxóchitl.

See also **Aztecs; Indigenous Peoples; Nahuas; Precontact History: Mesoamerica.**

BIBLIOGRAPHY

Alva Ixtlilxóchitl, Fernando de. *Obras Históricas.* 3rd Edition. 2 vols. Edited by Edmundo O'Gorman. Mexico City: Universidad Nacional Autónoma de México, Instituto de Investigaciones Históricas, 1975–1977.

Alva Ixtlilxóchitl, Fernando de. *Historia de la nación chichimeca.* Edited by Germán Vázquez. Madrid: Historia 16, 1985.

Anders, Ferdinand, Maarten Jansen, and Luis Reyes Garcia. *Códex Ixtlilxoxhitl.* Vol. 2. Graz, Austria: Akademische Druck und Verlagsanstalt; Mexico City: Fondo de Cultura Económica, 1996.

Poole, Stafford, C.M. "War by Fire and Blood: The Church and the Chichimecas in 1585," in *The Americas* 55 (1965): 115–137.

Powell, Philip Wayne. *Soldiers, Indians, and Silver: North America's First Frontier War* (1952, repr. 1975).

Ward, Thomas. "From the 'People' to the 'Nation': An Emerging Notion in Sahagún, Ixtlilxóchitl and Muñoz Camargo." *Estudios de Cultura Náhuatl* 32 (2001): 223–234.

STAFFORD POOLE C. M.

CHICLE INDUSTRY.

Chicle Industry, the extraction of resin from chicle trees for use as a base in the manufacture of chewing gum. The chicle tree (*Achras sapota* or *Manikara sapota*) is a broad-leaf evergreen found in the tropical lowlands of several Latin American countries. In some regions chicle is also known as *níspero* or *tuna*. The primary sources of chicle are Mexico, Belize (formerly British Honduras), and the Petén region of northern Guatemala. Although the export of chicle never assumed great national importance, the industry was and remains significant to these local economies.

John Curtis of the United States is credited with the first commercial production of chewing gum in 1848. Curtis used spruce resin as a base, but by the 1870s manufacturers had come to prefer chicle resin. Commercial interests from the United States began their chicle operations in Mexico in 1869. A dramatic increase in chewing gum consumption took place during World War I. Advertising campaigns by the Wrigley Company promoted chewing gum for soldiers and civilians to relieve tension and satiate thirst. The growth of chewing gum sales led to the expansion of the chicle industry. By 1930 the United States imported 15 million pounds of chicle resin a year, a boom that lasted until the 1940s, when synthetic substitutes came on the market. Chicle production continues, but the industry is threatened. Competition from synthetics and deforestation are major problems. Attempts to cultivate chicle trees on commercial plantations have failed. Indeed, as of 2007 natural chewing gum only represented 3.5 percent of the chewing gum market. However, there is a growing niche market for products based on sustainable development. Thus, Mexican producers have tried to promote natural chicle as helping low-wage workers attain decent wages, while also preserving the environment.

The backbone of the industry is the individual *chiclero* (chicle gatherer). Although they operate out of a common base camp for several months, *chicleros* work alone in the jungle to locate chicle trees, tap them, and collect the sap. A *chiclero* might locate and tap ten trees on an average day. A single tree can yield from 1 to 5 pounds of resin, depending on its age and the number of times it has been tapped. The same tree cannot be tapped successfully for another four to eight years. Tap-ping requires that the *chiclero* climb the tree and cut a vertical line of V-shaped notches along the trunk. At the base of this line a bucket is placed to catch the resin. The accumulated resin will be returned to camp, where it is boiled down to reduce its water content and then poured into molds. A contractor pays the *chiclero* according to the weight and water content of the resin molds.

BIBLIOGRAPHY

Robert Hendrickson, *The Great American Chewing Gum Book* (1976).

Herman W. Konrad, "Una población chiclera: Contexto histórico-Económico y un perfil demográfico," in *Boletín de la Escuela de Ciencias Antropológicas de la Universidad de Yucatán* 8 (December 1981): 2–39.

Norman B. Schwartz, *Forest Society: A Social History of Petén, Guatemala* (1990).

Additional Bibliography

Forero, Oscar A., and Michael R. Redclift. "The Role of the Mexican State in the Development of 'Chicle' Extraction in Yucatán, and the Continuing Importance of 'Coyotaje.'" *Journal of Latin American Studies* 38, no. 1 (February 2006): 65–93.

Vadillo López, Claudio. *Los chicleros en la región de la Laguna de Términos, Campeche, 1890–1947.* Ciudad del Carmen, México: Universidad Autónoma del Carmen, 2001.

STEVEN S. GILLICK

CHICO ANÍSIO

(1932–). Chico Anísio (Francisco Anísio de Oliveira Paulo Filho) is a Brazilian television personality and fiction writer. Chico Anísio created a variety of memorable television characters, including Santelmo, Coronel Limoeiro, and the Mayor of Chico City. His style of humor has been equally successful in his fiction. Chico Anísio aims for the jugular through satire and social critique presented in a direct, oral, and truly popular language and style. A predominant theme in his work is the desperation of society's marginalized population. The stories in *Feijoada no Copa* (1976) censure the upper classes for their insensitivity toward the reality surrounding them. The collection of stories *Teje preso* (1975) focuses on his own northeastern roots and the region's traditions. He produced various television programs, including *Lingüinha x Mr. Yes*, a children's show that ran from 1971 to 1972; *Chico City* (1973–1980); *Chico Total* (1981); and *Chico Anísio Show* (1982–1990). Between 1990 and 2001, his show *A Escolinha do Professor Raimundo* ran on Brazil's TV Globo network. He played the protagonist's father in the Brazilian movie *Tieta do Agreste* (1996). He is also the author of *Como segurar seu casamento* (2005).

See also **Cinema: Since 1990.**

BIBLIOGRAPHY

Khoury, Simon. *Bastidores.* Entrevistas a Simon Khoury de Tônia Carrero et al. 6 vols. Rio de Janeiro: Leviatã, 1994–1997.

Silverman, Malcolm. *A moderna sátira Brasileira.* Rio de Janeiro: Nova Fronteira, 1987.

Stern, Irwin. "Anísio, Chico," in *Dictionary of Brazilian Literature* (1988).

IRWIN STERN

CHIHUAHUA.

CHIHUAHUA. Chihuahua, the largest state in Mexico, with an area of 95,400 square miles and a population of 3.31 million (2005). The state lost territory as a result of the Treaty of Guadalupe Hidalgo (1848) and increased in size slightly with the Chamizal Agreement of 1963. Bounded on the north by Texas and New Mexico and on the west, south, and east by Sonora, Sinaloa, Durango, and Coahuila, the region has long been a sparsely populated frontier zone characterized by mining and large landed estates dedicated to livestock raising. Chihuahua is divided into three basic geographical zones: the Sierra Madre Occidental, cut by deep canyons, in the west; the eastern slopes of the mountains with their basins, ranges, and valleys; and the huge desert depression in the east known as the Bolsón de Mapimí. These geographical features, an arid climate, the absence of water, isolation from the rest of Mexico, and a history of endemic violence have led historians to describe Chihuahua as a harsh and violent land.

The region has a long record of human habitation. Twenty-five to thirty thousand years ago, hunters entered the area. New arrivals from the north about 900 CE, linked to the Mogollon culture in southern Arizona and New Mexico and influenced by the Anasazi, built and inhabited the site of Casas Grandes (Paquimé) in northwestern Chihuahua between 1060 and 1340. This cultural and trading center also displayed probable Toltec influences, including L-shaped ball courts. By the sixteenth century, the region of Chihuahua was inhabited principally by Tarahumares, or Raramuri, estimated to number twenty thousand at the time of contact with the Spaniards, as well as Conchos, Tobosos, Sumas, Mansos, Jumanos, Warihios, and various Apache bands in the far north. Spanish settlement and demands for mine labor, combined with mission activity, led to rebellions and the eventual disappearance of Amerindian peoples, except the Raramuri and Apache. Endemic violence and the lack of a large, sedentary Indian population limited race mixture, weakened the hold of the Catholic Church, encouraged the development of labor forms characterized by mobility and wage relationships, and fostered the creation of Presidios and ranches for defensive purposes.

The Spaniards first settled the mining district of Santa Bárbara, founded in 1567. The discovery of silver ore at Parral in 1631 and nearby Nuevas Minas (now Villa Escobedo) in 1634 prompted governors to run the province of Nueva Vizcaya from Parral for the next hundred years. Later, a similar find converted Santa Eulalia (1708) and the newly founded San Felipe el Real de Chihuahua into mining, commercial, and administrative centers and the headquarters of the newly organized Commandancy General of the Internal Provinces after 1776.

Although political factionalism, war with the United States, Indian raids, drought, and epidemic laid waste to much of newly independent Chihuahua, with economic activity reaching a low point in the mid-nineteenth century, after 1880 foreign investment in railroads, mining, forestry, and land made for rapid economic expansion. After the defeat of the Apache in 1880 and the construction of the Mexican Central Railroad in 1884, U.S. companies took over the state's mining industry and foreigners controlled the largest commercial firms. At the same time, a local oligarchy, the Terrazas-Creel family, monopolized economic power, becoming one of the largest landowners in the country, and centralized political power. This pattern of economic development, resentment of the Terrazas-Creel oligarchy, and the loss of village lands prompted mountain communities, political "outs," the middle class, and displaced artisans to revolt in 1910, leading, subsequently, to the identification of Chihuahua as "the cradle of the Revolution."

Despite the changes ushered in by the Mexican Revolution, including the demise of the great estate, restriction in the power of the church, land reform, and labor legislation, subsequent developments in Chihuahua have continued previous patterns. Beginning with the creation of a free-trade zone in 1885 (eliminated in 1905) and Mexican migration to the United States in the late nineteenth century, the border, not regulated until 1929, has drawn people and investment. The Bracero Program (1942–1964) and an accompanying undocumented movement of an even larger magnitude, along with the Border Industrialization Program, established by the Mexican government in 1965, and the import of many commodities duty-free (*artículos ganchos*) since 1971 have contributed to phenomenal population growth in Ciudad Juárez (population of over 1,400,000 in 2005), as well as to the establishment of assembly plants known as Maquiladoras. Such plants, allowing the tariff-free importation of parts and equipment and return of finished goods to the United States with tariffs charged only on the value added, numbered more than 300 in 2002 and employed 250,000 workers, mostly young women. Despite the relocation of some plants to China in the 1990s, the *maquiladoras* have stimulated migration and consequent overcrowding and have increased the region's dependence on inputs from the United States.

Since the early 1990s, international attention has focused on Chihuahua, and especially Ciudad Juárez, because of the unsolved murders of more than 70 women, many of them young, poor maquiladora workers.

The economic and cultural influence of the United States combined with a long history of resistance to the centralizing Mexican state (the area was a bastion of federalism, liberalism, and anticlericalism in the nineteenth century) have made Chihuahua a center of organized political opposition and popular antipathy to the central government. An opposition party, National Action Party (PAN), made significant gains in municipal elections in 1983, gubernatorial elections in 1986, the water-

shed national election that made Vicente Fox Quesada (b. 1942) president in 2000, and the 2006 presidential election of Felipe de Jesús Calderón Hinojosa (b. 1962).

See also **Maquiladoras; North American Free Trade Agreement; United States-Latin American Relations.**

BIBLIOGRAPHY

Almada, Francisco R. *Resumen de la historia del estado de Chihuahua* (1955).

Aziz Nassif, Alberto. *Los ciclos de la democracia: Gobierno y elecciones en Chihuahua.* México: M.A. Porrúa Grupo Editorial, 2000.

Bernstein, Marvin D. *The Mexican Mining Industry, 1890–1950: A Study of the Interaction of Politics, Economics, and Technology* (1964).

Deeds, Susan M. *Defiance and Deference in Mexico's Colonial North: Indians under Spanish Rule in Nueva Vizcaya.* Austin: University of Texas Press, 2003.

French, William E. *A Peaceful and Working People: Manners, Morals, and Class Formation in Northern Mexico.* Albuquerque: University of New Mexico Press, 1996.

Jones, Oakah L., Jr. Nueva Vizcaya: *Heartland of the Spanish Frontier* (1988).

Katz, Friedrich. *The Life and Times of Pancho Villa.* Stanford, CA: Stanford University Press, 1998.

Lister, Florence C., and Robert H. Lister, *Chihuahua: Storehouse of Storms* (1966).

Martin, Cheryl. *Governance and Society in Colonial Mexico: Chihuahua in the Eighteenth Century.* Stanford, CA: Stanford University Press, 1996.

Middlebrook, Kevin J., ed. *Party Politics and the Struggle for Democracy in Mexico: National and State-Level Analyses of the Partido Acción Nacional.* San Diego: Center for U.S.-Mexican Studies, University of California, 2001.

Preston, Julia, and Sam Dillon. *Opening Mexico: The Making of a Democracy.* New York: Farrar, Straus, and Giroux, 2004.

Salzinger, Leslie. *Genders in Production: Making Workers in Mexico's Global Factories.* Berkeley: University of California Press, 2003.

Santiago Quijada, Guadalupe. *Propiedad de la tierra en Ciudad Juárez, 1888 a 1935.* Tijuana, México: Colegio de la Frontera Norte: New Mexico State University: Ediciones y Gráficos, 2002.

Vanderwood, Paul J. *The Power of God against the Guns of Government: Religious Upheaval in Mexico at the Turn of the Nineteenth Century.* Stanford, CA: Stanford University Press, 1998.

Wassserman, Mark. *Capitalists, Caciques, and Revolution: The Native Elite and Foreign Enterprise in Chihuahua, Mexico, 1854–1911* (1984).

WILLIAM FRENCH

CHILAM BALAM.

Chilam Balam, a Maya priestly class whose members' predictions form the basis for local historiography. Literally translated from Classical Yucatecan Maya, *Chilam Balam* means "spokesmen of the jaguar." The *Books of Chilam Balam* are a set of Yucatecan Maya documents that were compiled during the seventeenth to nineteenth centuries covering events of the seventh to nineteenth centuries. Several types of documents have been titled *Chilam Balam*. The most widely recognized are fourteen manuscripts (twelve survive) that are named after the community of the Yucatán Peninsula of southern Mexico where they were found.

Although the term *Chilam Balam* implies priests who could foretell the future, only five of the books (those from Chan Kan, Chumayel, Kaua, Mani, and Tizimin) include prophetic texts. They are histories of the past and at the same time predictions of the future. These books are grounded in the belief that events occurring during certain periods of time will recur in particular future periods. Specifically, *katuns*, or cycles of 20 tuns (the 360-day Maya civil year), that end on days with the same name and coefficient will contain analogous events. In the books containing the prophetic texts, close attention is given to historical and calendrical accuracy; a reliable picture of what the future held was at stake.

Topics covered in the nonprophetic books include astrology, calendrics, and medicine. *The Book of Chilam Balam of Nah* contains the greatest amount of medical information, including descriptions of ailments, etiology, and various means of treatment.

The Chilam Balam of Chumayel, because of multiple translations, is the most widely known. The book reveals many details of everyday life including cuisine. It also offers a glimpse of the indigenous view of the Spanish: certain passages suggest that the Maya understood the arrival of Christianity as the fulfillment of calendrical predictions.

The *Books of Chilam Balam* have been and will continue to be important documents for understanding the present and future Maya of Yucatán.

See also **Annals of the Cakchiquels; Maya, The; Mayan Epigraphy; Popol Vuh.**

BIBLIOGRAPHY

Ralph L. Roys, trans. *The Book of Chilam Balam of Chumayel* (1913).

Eugene R. Craine and Reginald C. Reindorp, *The Codex Pérez and the Book of Chilam Balam of Mani* (1979).

Munro S. Edmonson, trans. *The Ancient Future of the Itza: The Book of Chilam Balam of Tizimin* (1982).

Additional Bibliography

Alfredo Vásquez Barrera, Silvia Rendón, trans. *El libro de los libros de Chilam Balam* (1948).

Bolles, David. "Colonial Mayan Literature Sheds Light on the Mayan Calendar, the Solar-Agricultural Year, and Correlation Questions." *Latin American Indian Literatures Journal* 14, no. 1 (Spring 1998): 26–53.

González Ortega, Nelson. *Relatos mágicos en cuestión: La cuestión de la palabra indígena, la escritura imperial y las narrativas totalizadoras y disidentes de Hispanoamérica.* Madrid/Frankfurt: Iberoamericana/Vervuert; 2006.

Mercedes Garza, Miguel León Portilla. *Literatura maya* (1980).

MATT KRYSTAL

CHILDREN.

Children in Latin America have been deeply influenced by the impact of race, economic and social status, and a shift in ideas regarding the roles of family and government in the education and socialization of children. From the time of the Conquest, families, especially fathers, were invested with extensive powers over and responsibilities for their children. Gradually governmental authorities, as well as mothers, began to share the responsibility. Severe economic, political, and racial differences, however, have resulted in the inability or unwillingness to care for children. The result has been periodic surges in the numbers of abandoned or homeless children.

The basic unit of Latin American society is the legally and religiously sanctioned biological family. The offspring of these unions historically have transmitted familial economic, social, political, and religious status. During the colonial era, legitimate children perpetuated the patriarchal name as well as the material fortunes of both parents. In the case of upper-class families, this meant that the child inherited their social status, and efforts were made to prepare that child to perpetuate or enhance the family's reputation. Often selected children were promised to the Catholic Church as an indication of family piety. If the child were female, upon marriage she would assume the status of her husband's family.

Most Latin American children, however, were born to poor families who rarely were sanctioned by either the state or the Catholic Church. Furthermore, racial miscegenation (*mestizaje*) and poverty usually prevented offspring from improving family status by marriage or by service to the church. Instead of property and social status, children born to African or Afro-Latin American slave women inherited the stigma of slavery, regardless of the status of the father.

Indian mothers faced other realities. If the father was Indian, the children inherited the burdens of the family's tribute payments in the form of labor, produce, or money. The children, particularly the young women who learned how to weave and embroider, also helped celebrate indigenous identity through custom and clothing. If the father was not Indian, the mestizo offspring of Indian women lost both their Indian identity and their obligation to pay tribute.

From the Independence era onward, Latin American governments began to revise the significance of both children's legal birthrights and (thus) their political, social, and economic value. From the nineteenth century on, governments began to insist on greater involvement in education, public health, and the development of the economy. Consequently, many patriarchal privileges, such as the right to select an occupation and provide an education for offspring, were limited. There was also a weakening of economic responsibility for children through the decline of the dowry for young brides, and child abandonment. The inability of an unmarried mother to force the father to recognize his paternity, along with development of religious and secular institutions designed to care for unwanted children, exacerbated these conditions. By the twentieth century a father's

patriarchal privileges over his children (*patria potestad*) were further restricted by laws regarding parents accused of abandonment, maltreatment, or moral turpitude. In practice, however, governments rarely enforce the laws and have been unwilling to pay the financial costs of rearing most of the children involved.

Thus, from the Conquest to the present, the social and emotional value that society has placed on children has been highly contradictory. At the same time that childbirth was often a welcome event, illegal abortions were common, and high infant mortality and popular Catholicism led to the belief that the death of young, baptized children transformed them into angels. There are patterns of ritualized celebration of infant death through portraiture and, by the nineteenth century, of photographs of the child. Examples of the *angelito* (*anjinho* in Portuguese) phenomenon are still common in Mexico and Brazil. The children, regardless of economic status, are adorned with a crown of flowers and often dressed in white.

During the same time periods, parents who could not afford the social stigma or the economic burden of illegitimate children gave them to better-off families or abandoned them on a *turno* (*roda* in Portuguese; foundling wheel), usually at a convent, or left them at the doorsteps of churches or town council halls, or in the doorways of families they believed would take pity on the child. These traditions dated from European medieval times and allowed children to be taken into new homes without the stigma of their birth. Despite this Catholic tradition, the strength of blood ties was so strong that fostered children could never share equal inheritance with legitimate offspring unless their identities were falsified. The practice of legal adoption reached many Latin American countries only in the twentieth century. Reforms of the Civil Codes authorizing adoption occurred in Brazil in 1917; Peru in 1936; Chile in 1934; Uruguay in 1868, 1934, and 1945; and Argentina in 1948. The enactment of these laws took place in the midst of debates regarding the right of parents to have legal heirs as well as the right of orphaned or abandoned children to have parents. Adoption laws have been reexamined after military antiterrorist campaigns in the 1970s and 1980s in Central and South America left significant numbers of orphans who were illegally adopted after their parents were executed.

Street children sleeping on a sidewalk, Rio de Janeiro, Brazil, 1993. In Brazil, widespread poverty and the lack of governmental intervention has forced many poor children to fend for themselves. H. JOHN MAIER JR./TIME LIFE PICTURES/ GETTY IMAGES

The formation in the late nineteenth and early twentieth centuries of a cadre of physicians specializing in public health took up the challenge of infant mortality by providing new technologies of childbirth, inoculations against childhood diseases, and improved water and sewage services, and by advocating programs for infant nutrition. Initially breast-feeding was the recommended strategy to save children of poor mothers, and campaigns against the sale of breast milk by wet nurses were launched. Until 1888 and the end of slavery, Brazilian doctors diverged from their counterparts elsewhere due to their belief in the superior qualities of black women's breast milk. By the early twentieth century, the availability of reliable sources of pasteurized milk in urban areas, along with the development of powdered milk and prepared baby formulas, created new opportunities for physicians to teach mothers how to feed their

children. Some of these campaigns were influenced by principles of eugenics.

Elite women also had a significant role to play in the campaign against infant mortality. The Sociedad de Beneficiencia, for example, in 1823 was authorized by the Argentine government to care for sick women and children. By the 1880s it fed and provided shelter for hundreds of orphaned or abandoned children in Buenos Aires. Eventually, through government subsidies and private donations, it built children's homes throughout the province of Buenos Aires. Similar organizations were founded in Chile, Uruguay (1857), Costa Rica (1887), Cuba, and Mexico. Feminist women, often of upper- and middle-class origins, as well as socialist women in many Latin American countries encouraged *puericultura* (the scientific study of child rearing) and persuaded their male counterparts to enact legislation to help both women and their children. In addition to these organizations, municipal Defensores de Menores and the Patronato de la Infancia in Argentina (1892), the Mexican Asociación Nacional de Protección a la Infancia (1925), Gotas de Leche (Chile, Cuba, Argentina), the Asociación Uruguaya de Protección a la Infancia (1925), the Comisión Nacional de Protección de la Maternidad e Infancia (Cuba), and the Patronato de la Infancia (Costa Rica, 1930) worked to aid orphans or abused and neglected children.

Latin American child specialists began to meet in scientific and politically sponsored congresses. The Pan-American Union, predecessor of the Organization of American States, sponsored children's congresses from 1916 to 1984. In addition, Argentina hosted one in 1913, as well as a congress on abandoned and delinquent children in 1933. Mexico held one in 1923 and then another in 1925. Costa Rica's congress took place in 1931, and Venezuela held its first Congreso Nacional del Niño in 1936. Among the topics discussed were the need for special legislation to establish appropriate forms of re-education for delinquent children and juvenile courts, and ways to enable government authorities to intervene in what had previously been considered family matters.

These meetings resulted in the enactment of significant legislation in several Latin American nations. In 1919 Argentine legislators enacted the Ley Agote. For the first time judges had clear guidelines as to when the courts could remove the right of *patria potestad* from parents who were considered immoral or irresponsible, or who had abandoned their children. It identified the degree of responsibility for a child's crime by age and authorized expansion of reform schools for delinquent children so that they would not have to be jailed with adult prisoners, but provided no funds to accomplish this. (A newer, more comprehensive, version of this legislation, called Códigos del Niño, was promulgated in Uruguay in 1933.) It also created juvenile courts. Colombia already had the beginning of a juvenile court system in 1946, when the Estatuto Orgánico del Niño was promulgated. In 1934 Venezuela established its Código del Niño, which was superseded by the Estatuto de Menores in 1950.

Despite the early efforts to promote a scientific yet caring governmental policy dealing with children, recent economic and political events have made it difficult for Latin American nations to live up to both the spirit and the letter of the law. Extreme poverty, militarism, and the burdens of governmental debt have led to the abandonment of strong state intervention in the needs and care of children, and have relegated much of the social assistance to children to nongovernmental organizations. Impoverished children in the twenty-first century face the challenge of survival on the streets, often because of the actions of government elements. For example, in Brazil, in recent years, death squads of the military police have been murdering *meninos da rua* (street children).

See also **Education: Overview; Family.**

BIBLIOGRAPHY

Memorias del VII Congreso panamericano del niño reunido en la Ciudad de México del 12 al 19 de octubre de 1935, 2 vols. (1937); *Actos y trabajos del Primer Congreso nacional de puericultura, 7–11 de octubre de 1940,* 2 vols. (1941), for Argentina.

Carlos Bueno-Guzman, "The Child in the Civil Law of the Latin American States," in *The Child and the Law* (1975).

Silvia M. Arrom, "Changes in Mexican Family Law in the Nineteenth Century: The Civil Codes of 1870 and 1884," in *Journal of Family History* 10, no. 3 (1985): 305–317.

Donna J. Guy, "Lower-Class Families, Women and the Law in Nineteenth-Century Argentina," in *Journal of Family History* 10, no. 3 (1985): 318–331.

Patricia Seed, *To Love, Honor, and Obey in Colonial Mexico: Conflicts over Marriage Choice, 1574–1821* (1988).

John Boswell, *The Kindness of Strangers: The Abandonment of Children in Western Europe from Late Antiquity to the Renaissance* (1990).

Emilio García Méndez, and Elías Carranza, eds., *Infancia, adolescencia y control social en América Latina: Argentina, Colombia, Costa Rica, Uruguay, Venezuela* (1990).

Mary Del Priore, ed., *Historia da criança no Brasil* (1991).

Joseph M. Hawes, and N. Ray Hiner, eds., *Children in Historical and Comparative Perspective: An International Handbook and Research Guide* (1991).

Elizabeth Anne Kuznesof, "Sexual Politics, Race, and Bastard-Bearing in Nineteenth-Century Brazil: A Question of Culture or Power?" in *Journal of Family History* 16, no. 3 (1991): 241–260.

Nancy Stepan, *"The Hour of Eugenics": Race, Gender, and Nation in Latin America* (1991).

Additional Bibliography

Alcubierre, Beatriz, and Tania Carreño King. *Los niños villistas: Una mirada a la historia de la infancia en México, 1900–1920*. México: Instituto Nacional de Estudios Históricos de la Revolución Mexicana, 1996.

Ardren, Traci, and Scott Hutson. *The Social Experience of Childhood in Ancient Mesoamerica*. Boulder: University Press of Colorado, 2006.

Bolin, Inge. *Growing up in a Culture of Respect: Child Rearing in Highland Peru*. Austin: University of Texas Press, 2006.

Ciafardo, Eduardo O. *Los niños en la ciudad de Buenos Aires (1890–1910)*. Buenos Aires: Centro Editor de América Latina, 1992.

González Uribe, Guillermo. *Los niños de la guerra*. Bogotá: Planeta, 2002.

Hecht, Tobias. *Minor Omissions: Children in Latin American History and Society*. Madison: University of Wisconsin Press, 2002.

Klich, Kent, and Elena Poniatowska. *El Niño: Niños de la calle, Ciudad de México*. Syracuse: Syracuse University Press, 1999.

Kramer, Karen. *Maya Children: Helpers at the Farm*. Cambridge, MA: Harvard University Press, 2005.

Marten, James Alan. *Children in Colonial America*. New York: New York University Press, 2007.

Mickelson, Roslyn Arlin. *Children on the Streets of the Americas: Homelessness, Education, and Globalization in the United States, Brazil and Cuba*. New York: Routledge, 2000.

Post, David. *Children's Work, Schooling, and Welfare in Latin America*. Boulder: Westview Press, 2002.

Potthast-Jutkeit, Barbara, and Sandra Carreras. *Entre la familia, la sociedad y el Estado: Niños y jóvenes en América Latina (siglos XIX–XX)*. Madrid: Iberoamericana, 2005.

Premo, Bianca. *Children of the Father King: Youth, Authority, & Legal Minority in Colonial Peru*. Chapel Hill: University of North Carolina Press, 2005.

Reimers, Fernando. *Unequal Schools, Unequal Chances: The Challenges to Equal Opportunity in the Americas*. Cambridge, MA: Harvard University, David Rockefeller Center for Latin American Studies: Distributed by Harvard University Press, 2000.

DONNA J. GUY

CHILE

This entry includes the following articles:
FOUNDATIONS THROUGH INDEPENDENCE
THE NINETEENTH CENTURY
THE TWENTIETH CENTURY

FOUNDATIONS THROUGH INDEPENDENCE

Perched on one of the remotest edges of the Spanish American empire, the captaincy-general of Chile was never counted among the richest or most developed territories of the Spanish crown. Isolation was a keynote of Chilean history from the outset. Until the advent of the steamship, the territory was rarely less than four months by sea from Europe. Yet from the first, Spaniards arriving in Chile were attracted by its fertile soil and its usually moderate climate: "This land is such that for living in and perpetuating ourselves in there is none better in the world," wrote Pedro de Valdivia (c. 1498–1553) to Emperor Charles V (1500–1558) on 4 September 1545. Valdivia was the first conquistador to establish permanent settlements in Chile; his first "city" was Santiago (founded 12 February 1541), the hegemonic focus of Chilean life from that day forward.

Encounter between Native Americans and European explorers at Cape Horn, 1616. Conflict and warfare characterized relations between Spanish colonizers and the Mapuche people who defended their land in southern Chile into the nineteenth century. © CORBIS

The first decades of the new colony's existence were dominated by warfare. Resistance to the invading Spaniards was fiercest in the south, in the lands beyond the Bío-Bío River, where the Mapuche, who had successfully fought off the Inca army, again proved more than able to hold their own. The Spaniards came to refer to the native Chileans as Araucanians. The indigenous people the Spanish encountered, estimated to number between 800,000 and 1,200,000, shared a language but were in fact of varying tribes; their military prowess was generously eulogized by Alonso de Ercilla y Zúñiga (1533–1594), the soldier-poet whose epic *La Araucana* narrated the early phases of the prolonged struggle of the Spaniards and Mapuche.

After extending the colony to the south of the Bío-Bío, Valdivia himself was killed by the Mapuche in December 1553. His successors as governor were obliged to give most of their attention to warfare. By the end of the sixteenth century, it was clear that the colony was impossibly overextended: its Spanish-creole population at that point was less than eight thousand. In 1599 the point was proved by a major Araucanian offensive that drove the invaders from their settlements south of the Bío-Bío—Valdivia's "seven cities"—and confined them to the northern half of the Central Valley.

For the rest of the colonial period and well beyond, the Bío-Bío became a frontier zone. From the early seventeenth century a small standing army (financed by the Viceroyalty of Peru) was based in the south to protect the frontier, but Chile was not important enough to the empire to warrant a full-scale military assault on Araucania. The Mapuche preserved their political independence until the mid-nineteenth century. Their culture and society, however, undoubtedly were altered as a result of contact with Spanish Chile, an observation supported by developments in both agriculture and cross-frontier trade. Warfare continued at regular intervals throughout the seventeenth century. In 1723, however, an Araucanian offensive was curtailed because of the disruption it was causing to trade, and there was only one further serious flurry of warfare (1766) in colonial times. Missionaries tried more peaceful methods of winning over the Mapuche, but with no conspicuous success.

As a result of the Araucanians' success in defending their trans-Bío-Bío homeland, the dimensions of

colonial Chile were fairly compact, the main nuclei of population concentrated in the northern section of the Central Valley and in the adjacent Aconcagua Valley (or Vale of Chile). A few small clusters of population existed further north, toward the desert, and by the second half of the eighteenth century, the mining town of Copiapó marked the rough northern limit of Spanish settlement. South of "indomitable Araucania" there were diminutive outposts at Valdivia and on the island of Chiloé, remote appendages of the captaincy-general that counted for very little in colonial times. Colonial Chilean life thus developed in a relatively limited area. Geographical isolation contributed to the formation of a distinctive and increasingly homogeneous culture.

The evolving social structure of the colony resembled that of other parts of the Spanish Empire, but was also marked by certain local differences. The basic shapes and forms of Chilean life were developed during the sixteenth and (especially) seventeenth centuries, and consolidated in the eighteenth. During this period the population became increasingly less diversified: mestizos were already a conspicuous group by 1600, and continued miscegenation meant that 200 years later they were the numerically dominant component in the Chilean population of 700,000 or so. Native Chilean numbers north of the Bío-Bío declined rather sharply as European pathogens took their toll. (How many natives made their way to the free redoubt of Araucania is impossible to say, although some did.) The Spanish-creole elite was not rich enough to constitute a market for African slaves: in 1800 there were approximately five thousand of these.

The Chile that developed in colonial times essentially consisted of a largely mestizo majority and a small upper class of Spaniards and creoles. Upper-class culture was basically Spanish. Mestizo culture reflected both Spanish and native influences, observable in such things as games, diet, vocabulary, and popular superstitions. By the end of colonial times, however, mestizos tended where possible to pass themselves off as Spaniards. Their names, language, and religion were all Spanish.

Societies built on brutal conquest are often sharply stratified. In the Chilean case, economic imperatives reinforced stratification. The main aim of the conquistadors themselves was to mobilize native labor through the encomienda for washing gold from the rivers and for ranching and agriculture. In theory the *encomienda* was not a grant of land but an allocation of natives. In practice many natives were assigned a place in the large seigneurial landholdings that grew up after the Conquest. With the decline of the native population, the *encomienda* lost its importance, though surviving in outlying areas like Chiloé and the north until the 1780s. Alternative sources of labor (the enslavement of Mapuche captured in war, or the transfer of natives from Cuyo across the Andes) proved unsatisfactory. A more stable rural labor system was needed and one gradually evolved.

The seventeenth century is often described as Chile's "tallow century." Tallow, *charqui* (jerked beef), and cattle hides were exported to Lima and Potosí, while Chilean mules were sent to the great annual fair at Salta. Ranching helped to consolidate the great estate, a process that was enhanced at the end of the century by the growth of a demand for wheat both domestically (as mestizos developed European dietary preferences) and in the Peruvian market. Haciendas, as Chilean estates were now usually called, began to adopt cereal cultivation. The mestizos and poor Spaniards who had been enticed onto the earlier ranches as renters (given a small plot in exchange for help with the livestock) were gradually transformed into a permanent class of tied peasants, known in Chile as *inquilinos*. (Use of this term became customary in the second half of the eighteenth century, by which time the classic Chilean hacienda was more or less fully formed.) The stable hacienda population of *inquilinos* was complemented, in the countryside, by a large mass of casual and frequently itinerant peons, whose lack of opportunities often forced them into vagabondage and petty banditry—a phenomenon that was especially noticeable in the area between the Maule and Bío-Bío rivers.

Though overwhelmingly dominant in the Chilean countryside, haciendas were never universal. In the vicinity of the townships, fruit and vegetables were often grown on small farms called *chacras*

Silver and copper works in the Andes, illustration from *Travels into Chile* by Peter Schmidtmeyer, 1824 (litho) by English School (19th century). In the late eighteenth century, hundreds of small, labor-intensive copper, silver, and gold mines sprang up in Chile's *Norte Chico* region, supplying the high-grade ore for the country's flourishing export economy. PRIVATE COLLECTION/ THE BRIDGEMAN ART LIBRARY (often owned by hacendados), while numerous subsistence plots were worked by peons wherever they were able to squat. The position of the great estate, however, was enhanced over the years. Ownership of a hacienda was one of the clearest marks of upper-class status. Agriculture was the principal motor of the eighteenth-century colonial economy, with wheat usually accounting for 50 percent of Chile's exports to Peru. At the end of the colonial period, the mining of gold, silver, and copper in the thinly populated north (the area Chileans now refer to as the Norte Chico) assumed a new importance, prefiguring its spectacular nineteenth-century profile. There were hundreds of mines in the semi-desert north, mostly very shallow, worked with primitive technology, and rich in high-grade ores. The new salience of mining was acknowledged in 1787 by the creation of a mines administration on the model of Mexico's.

EIGHTEENTH-CENTURY GROWTH

By the end of colonial times, metals were becoming increasingly important in the colony's trading pattern. In the seventeenth century, the captaincy-general was no more than an economic appendage of Peru and, because of the highly regulated imperial system, at the end of a long commercial chain that extended through Lima and Panama to Spain. This made European merchandise impossibly expensive. The eighteenth-century Bourbon reforms had a notably stimulating effect on Chilean trade. From 1740 ships were permitted to sail directly from Spain to Chile, and trade with the Río De La Plata provinces was finally legalized. Thus the colony could now trade directly with Spain, with the Río de la Plata (whence came the Yerba Maté so popular in Chile), and with Peru. The powerful Consulado (merchant guild) of Lima tried to resist such developments, but in vain. Chile shook free from its irksome dependence on the Viceroyalty: after 1750 the colony could mint its own coins, and in 1796 a separate consulado was set up in Santiago. The only real advantage now enjoyed by Peru was control of the shipping that carried Chilean wheat to Lima. This enabled Peruvian merchants to fix the wheat price—a long-running Chilean grievance.

While it is important not to exaggerate the scale of Chile's eighteenth-century commercial expansion, it is undeniable that new opportunities attracted a flow of Spanish immigrants into the colony—some twenty-four thousand Spaniards between 1700 and 1810. Roughly half of these were Basque or Navarrese. The most enterprising immigrants accumulated sufficient capital (usually in trade) to insert themselves into the creole upper class by marriage and by the purchase of haciendas. Some of these newcomers founded impressive family networks. The so-called Basque-Castilian aristocracy thus formed played a dominant part in Chilean affairs until the twentieth century. Taking *mayorazgos* (strict entails) and titles of nobility as a fairly reliable indicator, this Chilean creole elite looks much less impressive than its counterparts in the viceroyalties. In 1800 there were only seventeen *mayorazgos* and twelve titles (seven *marqueses* and five *condes*) held by Chilean families. Very few creoles were really well-to-do; not until the trade booms of the nineteenth century did agriculture and mining yield large fortunes.

Nevertheless the creoles, old and new, were clearly the leaders of colonial society by the second half of the eighteenth century. High political office was generally denied them, a practice which in due course became a grievance. Chile's political status was that of a captaincy-general, formally subordinate to the Viceroyalty of Peru (until 1798), but for all practical purposes ruled separately by a governor and an audiencia (operating temporarily in 1567–1575 and permanently after 1609). As part of the Bourbon overhaul of imperial administration, the colony was divided in 1786–1787 into two Intendancies, Santiago and Concepción, under a governor acting as the senior intendant. These changes do not seem to have impinged as negatively on creoles as may have been the case elsewhere in the empire. In any case, the Chilean elite was adept at exerting informal pressure on colonial officials.

It is difficult to find evidence of serious disaffection from the imperial political system. This perhaps became more likely with the rising educational level of creoles: the University of San Felipe opened in 1758, and by 1813 nearly two thousand students had passed through it. In the same period the university conferred 299 doctorates: 128 in law, 106 in theology.

THE BREAK WITH COLONIAL RULE

However isolated and remote, the colony could not remain entirely cut off from the new trends of thought then emanating from the outside world. A number of educated creoles assimilated the ideas of the Enlightenment. Those few who traveled to Europe were especially exposed to its influence. Some of them developed a strong interest in economic reform. Manuel de Salas (1754–1841), a conspicuous member of this group, wrote a classic account of the colony's economy and society (1796), in which he contrasted the material backwardness of the territory with its abundant physical potential. Such feelings fueled a growing sense of creole patriotism. Salas and similar figures were neomercantilists, impressed by movements for enlightened reform in Spain itself, and they placed a good deal of faith in the imperial state. However, it is also clear that they deeply desired improvements, and this stance doubtless inclined them to favor creole run national governments when the time came.

A much smaller group of creoles, probably no more than a handful, was enthused by the Enlightenment, by the anticolonial struggle in British North America, and (less straightforwardly) by the French Revolution, and aspired to complete independence and the creation of a Chilean republic. Representative of this group was Bernardo O'Higgins (1778–1842), a frontier landowner who had been educated in England, where he had met Francisco de Miranda (1750–1816) and had been converted to Miranda's separatist vision. All that radicals like O'Higgins could do was bide their time and wait for an opportunity that might never come. It came sooner than they could have imagined possible.

Napoleon's invasion of Spain in 1808 caused consternation in Chile, as everywhere else. Creole leadership had already been perturbed by the attempted British conquest of the Río de la Plata in 1806–1807. The initial feelings of loyalty to Spain expressed by the *cabildo* (municipal government) of Santiago lasted several months, but soon lost ground to the notion of establishing an autonomous (and creole-directed) government, if only to preserve the colony for the dethroned King Ferdinand VII (1784–1833). The governor, Francisco Antonio García Carrasco (1742–1813), a military man with little political subtlety, interpreted creole aspirations as subversive, an attitude also taken by the Audiencia. In what it saw as a preemptive move against the creole-dominated Cabildo, the Audiencia prevailed on García Carrasco to resign in favor of a rich and well-respected

creole, Mateo de Toro Zambrano (1727–1811). Emboldened by the news of the May Revolution in Buenos Aires, the *cabildo* responded by invoking colonial precedent and calling for a *cabildo abierto,* an open meeting of leading citizens. Toro Zambrano eventually agreed, and the assembly was convened on 18 September 1810 with about four hundred people in attendance. A national junta of seven members was chosen, and the governor himself installed as president. The stated aim of the junta was to preserve Chile for the "unfortunate" monarch Ferdinand VII. But the promise to convene a national congress (which met, to no great effect, in July 1811) owed nothing to colonial precedent and was a revolutionary step toward dismantling colonial rule.

It may be doubted whether more than a small minority of creoles yet favored outright independence. In fact none of the "patriot" governments of the next four years—the period Chileans call the Patria Vieja (old homeland)—made a formal declaration of independence. And in any case, divisions within the patriot leadership soon emerged. These were not merely the predictable divisions between moderates and radicals, but a serious rivalry between the powerful (and highly extended) Larraín family and its adversaries, whose self-appointed leader was an ambitious army officer returning from Spain—José Miguel Carrera (1785–1821). In November 1811 Carrera used his sway over the military to seize power, dissolving the first national congress and, over the next few months, neutralizing his opponents, who had entrenched themselves in the south. With the Carrera dictatorship, the impetus for reform gained momentum. Chile's first newspaper, *La Aurora de Chile,* did much to spread new revolutionary doctrines. Yet Carrera made no real move toward a final break with Spain.

This ambiguous stance did not deter the Viceroy of Peru, José Fernando de Abascal y Sousa (1743–1821) from sending three successive task forces to Chile to form the nucleus of royalist armies (1813–1814). So began Chile's War of Independence. Carrera's lack of success against the royalists weakened his position. Power in Santiago passed into the hands of a series of juntas. Carrera's successor as commander-in-chief, Bernardo O'Higgins, was neutralized by the second major royalist offensive, and a short-lived peace treaty ensued (May 1814).

On 23 July 1814 Carrera once again seized power in Santiago, and civil war between O'Higginistas and Carreriños seemed unavoidable, but a third royalist army, commanded by General Mariano Osorio, swept up the Central Valley from the south and overwhelmed the patriot forces at Rancagua (1–2 October 1814). O'Higgins, Carrera, and many other patriots fled to Argentina, and Chile reverted to colonial rule. This "Spanish reconquest" lasted two years and four months, and was an unhappy time of persecutions and occasional atrocities. This in itself weaned most creoles from the idea of colonial rule.

INDEPENDENCE AND THE NEW STATE

It fell to the great Argentine general José Francisco de San Martín (1778–1850) to effect the final liberation of Chile. He saw this as an essential step in his plan for a seaborne invasion of the Viceroyalty of Peru. At the start of 1817, San Martín's Army of the Andes (more than four thousand men) crossed the high passes of the Cordillera and won a decisive victory over the royalists at Chacabuco (12 February 1817). O'Higgins, by this stage a close associate of San Martín, was selected as supreme director of the new Chilean state. A massive royalist counterattack, led once again by Osorio, was finally checked at the very bloody battle of Maipú on 5 April 1818, by which time O'Higgins had formally proclaimed the independence of Chile (February 1818).

The patriots then created a small Chilean navy, which was placed in the command of the redoubtable Scottish admiral-adventurer Lord Thomas Cochrane (1775–1860), whose audacious forays cleared the seas of Spanish shipping and enabled San Martín's Chilean-financed (and largely Chilean-manned) expedition to set off for Peru in August 1820. The rest of the South American war of independence was waged far from Chile, whose part had been both decisive and heroic. In Benjamín Vicuña Mackenna's great phrase, "free, she freed others."

Independence enabled the creoles of the Basque-Castilian aristocracy to assume their place as the governing class of the new state. It was more than a decade, however, before they found an adequate form of government. Meanwhile the apparatus of separate nationality was adopted with enthusiasm, and reforms were enacted: O'Higgins abolished titles of nobility and the display of coats of arms (1817), and reestablished institutions such as the Instituto Nacional (National Institute of Higher Education) and the National Library, abolished under the Spanish reconquest. Slavery was abolished in 1823.

Commercial reforms—four ports were thrown open to international trade in 1811—stimulated mild economic expansion: the value of Chile's external trade nearly tripled between 1810 and 1840 (from 5 million pesos to 14 million pesos). Agriculture, it is true, was seriously disrupted by the wars of independence, especially in the south, where recovery did not come much before the 1840s. But the mining zone, unaffected by fighting, benefited immediately from the increase in commercial traffic. Silver production may have doubled between 1810 and 1830, while the export of copper showed a threefold rise between the 1810s and the 1830s. Imports also flooded into the country, though the limited market was quickly saturated. Overall, Chile's economic capacity was appreciably heightened by independence, even if it took several decades for genuine commercial booms to set in, as they did in the later 1840s and again in the 1860s.

Politically, the search for an appropriate framework was by no means easy. O'Higgin's regime was essentially a war dictatorship until 1820 and, as such, brilliantly successful. With the tide of war receding, however, he was less able to handle domestic political pressures. His abdication on 28 January 1823 was followed by several years of makeshift constitutional experiment, with the main role assumed by Liberal politicians. A strangely idiosyncratic constitution devised by Juan Egaña in 1823 was soon jettisoned. A brief flirtation with federalist ideas in the mid-1820s proved similarly fruitless. In 1828, under President Francisco Antonio Pinto (1775–1858), the Liberals succeeded in enacting yet another constitution, and for a while the prospects for stable Liberal government seemed promising. Unfortunately, certain Liberal actions and a mild tendency toward anticlericalism provoked hostility from the Conservative opposition. A clear-cut differentiation of Liberals and Conservatives, however, is difficult: the Conservative Party probably included the best-established section of the elite, whereas the Liberals had a greater share of professional men, intellectuals, and so forth. In the Chile of the 1820s the influence of the Conservatives was always potentially stronger.

The Conservative rebellion of 1829–1830, captained by the remarkable and resolute Diego Portales (1793–1837), ended the Liberal phase and inaugurated a long period of political stability with the new Constitution of 1833 as its legal framework. The new regime was at times repressive: It depended on strong presidential power and the systematic manipulation of elections, a practice that did not cease until after 1891. With all its blemishes, however, the Conservative Republic gave Chile internal tranquillity and provided the basis for commercial expansion, and it was flexible enough to allow an eventual transition to Liberal-dominated politics in the 1860s and 1870s.

In political terms, the aftermath of Chile's struggle for independence was the most unusual story in nineteenth-century Spanish America. It was due in part to the strength of the colonial legacy: Isolation, separate cultural development, and relative homogeneity were all factors that influenced the Chile that emerged from the colonial chrysalis into the light of freedom.

See also **Carrera, José Miguel; Colonialism; Indigenous Peoples; O'Higgins, Bernardo; Salas, Manuel de; Spanish Empire; Viceroyalty, Viceroy; Wars of Independence, South America.**

BIBLIOGRAPHY

Archer, Christon I., ed. *The Wars of Independence in Spanish America*. Wilmington, DE: Scholarly Resources, 2000.

Barbier, Jacques A. *Reform and Politics in Bourbon Chile, 1755–1796* (1980).

Bauer, Arnold J. *Chilean Rural Society from the Spanish Conquest to 1930* (1975), chap. 1.

Carmagnani, Marcello. *Los mecanismos de la vida económica en una sociedad colonial: Chile 1680–1830*. Santiago: Ediciones de la Dirección de Bibliotecas, Archivos y Museos, Centro de Investigaciones Diego Barros Arana, 2001.

Collier, Simon. *Ideas and Politics of Chilean Independence, 1808–1833* (1967).

Collier, Simon, and William F. Sater. *A History of Chile, 1808–2002*, 2d ed. Cambridge and New York: Cambridge University Press, 2004.

Cóngora, Mario. *Orígen de los 'inquilinos' de Chile central,* 2d ed. (1974).

De Armond, Louis. "Frontier Warfare in Colonial Chile." *Pacific Historical Review* 23 (1954): 125–143.

De Ramón, Armando, and José Manuel Larraín, *Orígenes de la vida económica chilena, 1659–1808* (1982).

Felstiner, Mary Lowenthal. "Kinship Politics in the Chilean Independence Movement." *Hispanic American Historical Review* 56 (1976): 58–80.

Foerster, Rolf. *Jesuitas y mapuches, 1593–1767.* Santiago: Editorial Universitaria, 1996.

Loveman, Brian. *Chile: The Legacy of Hispanic Capitalism,* 2d ed. (1988), chaps. 2–3.

Pocock, H. R. S. *The Conquest of Chile* (1967).

Retamal Avila, Julio, ed. *Testamentos de indios en Chile colonial, 1564–1801.* Chile: Universidad Andrés Bello, Departamento de Derechos Intelectuales de Chile, RIL Editores, 2000.

Solano, Francisco de. *Relaciones económicas del reino de Chile (1780).* Madrid: Consejo Superior de Investigaciones Científicas, Centro de Estudios Históricos, Departamento de Historia de América, 1994.

Uribe-Uran, Victor, ed. *State and Society in Spanish America during the Age of Revolution.* Wilmington, DE: SR Books, 2001.

SIMON COLLIER

THE NINETEENTH CENTURY

The defeat of the Spanish at Chacabuco on 12 February 1817 marked a milestone on, but not the end of, Chile's quest for liberty. Since Chileans fought for both the Royalists and the *independistas,* their struggle to end Madrid's rule was both a civil war and a rebellion. The defeat of the Spanish army did not end conflict; it simply permitted the latent tensions which had riven Chilean society to surface. Thus, the end to the struggle against Spain set the stage for a more prolonged civil war.

AFTER CHACABUCO

Following Chacabuco, three groups vied for power: the followers of José Miguel Carrera, who sought radical economic and social change; Bernardo O'Higgins's supporters, who hoped to introduce mild reforms; and the traditionalists, who wished to limit change by substituting the Chilean elite for the old colonial bureaucracy. O'Higgins enjoyed certain advantages: he had led the triumphant army and hence had won some personal popularity. Unlike his rivals, moreover, he already wielded power. However, the traditional elements disliked O'Higgins because he revoked their titles of nobility, thereby diminishing their social status, and because he

José de San Martín and Bernardo O'Higgins with their army in the Andes during the Spanish-American wars for independence. After a painting by Agosto Ballerini. Accompanied by O'Higgins of Chile, San Martín led his army through the treacherous Upsalata Pass to defeat the Spanish at Chacabuco in 1817. The people of Santiago proclaimed San Martín the liberator of Chile. © BETTMANN/CORBIS

abolished the entailed estate, thus threatening their economic base. But as much as they loathed O'Higgins, the traditionalists dared not move against him, fearful that the more radical Carrera might take over.

The execution of Carrera and his brothers in 1821 and the expulsion of the Spanish from the south emboldened O'Higgins's foes. Consequently, the opposition forced the Supreme Director to enact a constitution. Presumably undertaken to ensure popular sovereignty, this document in fact sought to limit O'Higgins's power. Although O'Higgins's social, political, and economic policies were somewhat restrained by the new constitutional strictures, they continued to alienate, especially the most powerful. Even nature seemed to turn on him: poor harvests, which produced a famine, and a terrible earthquake ravaged O'Higgins's Chile. The combination proved too much;

discontent finally blossomed into unrest. Rather than fight a fratricidal civil war, O'Higgins resigned on 28 January 1823 and fled to Peru.

O'Higgins's premature departure from office initiated a period of political turmoil that lasted until 1830. For approximately seven years, Chileans embraced, then rejected, different leaders, constitutions, and political systems, and even established a federal republic. Chile's presidential palace, the Moneda, became a way station. First Ramón Freire ruled, as both president and dictator, until 1826. Next, Manuel Blanco Encalada and his associate Agustín Eyzaguirre lasted until 1827, when Freire briefly returned to power. Then he gave way first to Francisco Antonio Pinto and then to Francisco Ramón Vicuña.

While turbulent, this period was not without accomplishments. The new republic won U.S. and

British diplomatic recognition; it abolished slavery in 1823; and three years later it finally drove out the last Spanish garrison, although Madrid waited until 1844 before belatedly acknowledging the existence of its former colony. Yet, despite these achievements, the economic elite and the landholding aristocracy had tired of the unrest. In 1829, after seeing their candidate unfairly denied victory, these elements rebelled as southern aristocrats, who resented Santiago's rule, raised an army under General Joaquín Prieto, who marched on the capital. At the Lircay River, on 17 April 1830, Prieto's troops defeated the government's forces under the leadership of general and former president Ramón Freire.

THE 1830S: NEW STABILITY

The victory brought to power the conservatives, men who wanted to restore to Chile many of the colonial system's institutions. Under the guiding genius of Diego Portales, a new state emerged, authoritarian by nature, albeit republican in name. The Constitution of 1833 created a political system that restricted the vote and the right to hold public office to less than 10 percent of the nation. While clearly undemocratic, the constitution recognized the reality of Chile: The wealthy were in control, and unless they could dominate the political system, unrest would roil the nation. But in return for receiving control of the state, the oligarchy had to submit to its authority.

This social contract worked. From 1831 to 1871, only four men—Joaquín Prieto (1831–1841), Manuel Bulnes (1841–1851), Manuel Montt (1851–1861), and José Joaquín Pérez (1861–1871)—governed Chile. In contrast to nearby nations, which seemed to change presidents with each new season, Chile's political life seemed staid, if not stodgy. Thus, while Santiago's potentially richer neighbors wallowed in seemingly perpetual political turmoil, Chile could devote its energies to developing its economy, instead of squandering its treasure and blood maintaining internal order.

The passage of the Constitution of 1833 alone did not guarantee order. Diego Portales made sure that it worked, by purging the military and the bureaucracy of anyone whom he suspected of harboring treasonous thoughts. His policies were brutal but efficient: by the late 1830s, Chile had become strong enough to fight a war to destroy

the Peru-Bolivian Confederation. True, the president did have to rule by extraordinary decree—which meant that he could suspend the precious few civil liberties remaining—but he managed to quell domestic as well as foreign foes. Indeed, it was a tribute to the strength of the state that it could survive the loss of its progenitor when Portales died in an abortive coup (1837). Hence, Chile emerged from the decade of the 1830s stronger domestically and, after forcing the dissolution of the confederation, more powerful internationally.

Economic prosperity seemed to follow in the wake of Chile's political stability. During the 1830s, and particularly in the 1840s, Chilean farmers thrived by exporting their foodstuffs first to hemispheric customers and later to England. Chile's real wealth, however, lay not in the agrarian central valley but in the arid Norte Chico. The discovery of silver—as well as copper—first in La Serena and then in Chañarcillo, provided the state with a generous source of income in the form of export taxes. Trade also buttressed Chile's prosperity. By constructing an enormous complex of warehouses and wharf facilities that allowed foreigners to store their cargoes for minimal fees and by providing repair facilities and victualing for vessels arriving from Europe or the United States, Portales's minister of economics, Manuel Rengifo Cárdenas, made Valparaiso into the hemisphere's most important Pacific entrepôt.

THE 1840S: DISCOVERY AND DEVELOPMENT

The 1840s proved a decade of development for Chile. Its new president and hero of the war against the defunct Peru-Bolivian Confederation, General Manuel Bulnes, ruled in a relatively benign fashion, attempting to reconcile the nation politically. Economically, Chile hummed. The discovery of gold in California proved a boon to the nation's farmers, who grew rich feeding the Forty-Niners, as did the merchants of Valparaíso, who revictualed the California-bound ships. The discovery of additional silver deposits in the north, in conjunction with the development of domestic coal pits in Lota, increased the vitality of the mining sector. Chile's first railroad, connecting the port of Caldera with the northern center of Copiapó, began to function.

The state invested many of its new revenues in developing the nation's infrastructure, creating the

Students in different levels of education, Chile, 1880–1900

Year	Primary	Secondary	Higher	Total
1880	65,288	2,082	780	68,150
1900	157,330	12,624	1,228	171,182

Note: In 1880 the total population of Chile was calculated at 2,271,040; in 1900 it was 2,973,992. Data provided by author.

Table 1

University of Chile and a normal school as well as various other cultural and technical institutions. To protect the country's trade routes to Europe, Chile occupied the Strait of Magellan and founded the city of Magallanes (later Punta Arenas). It also encouraged German immigrants to settle in the country's virgin forests in the south.

The influence of foreign political refugees—Argentines like Domingo Faustino Sarmiento and the Venezuelan Andrés Bello—as well as European ideas, particularly those associated with the revolutions of 1848, became more pronounced. Chilean thinkers like José Victorino Lastarria, Francisco Bilbao, Santiago Arcos, and Eusebio Lillo spread these ideas, along with many of their own, throughout the nation.

MID-CENTURY: GROWING POLITICAL MATURITY

The growing social and intellectual diversity in Chile's elites eventually undermined the nation's monolithic political system. A squabble between two former ministers of the interior, Manuel Montt and Camilo Vial, erupted into a schism in the Conservative Party. Political dissidents, whom Portales had driven underground, surfaced, joining the supporters of Vial to form the Liberal Party. The new organization demanded a more open political environment: abolition of the Senate, an end to presidential succession, an extension of suffrage, local autonomy (including the right to select local officials), and greater personal freedom. The demise of the old consensus might, many feared, signal a return to political unrest.

The pessimists proved right: revolution did follow liberalization. In 1851, Chileans rebelled for the first time, opposing Bulnes's attempt to select Manuel Montt as his successor. The son of impoverished gentry, Montt rose to occupy several important governmental positions. But although he was an extremely competent and hard-working man, the prospect of Montt's presidency managed to fuse traditionally disparate groups into a solid phalanx of hate. Rebellions erupted throughout the country when it became clear that Montt would indeed become president. Violence spread from the mining north even as far south as Magallanes. The government was unable to restore order until early 1852.

Initially, Montt reacted vindictively, sentencing many of the rebels to death. Although he subsequently commuted these sentences, he still held tight to the reins of power: For almost half of his ten-year regime, Montt governed either under a state of siege or under the rubric of his extraordinary presidential powers.

Even this formidable authority could not assure Montt a tranquil administration. He became involved in a series of fruitless struggles with the Roman Catholic Church when its hierarchy under Archbishop Rafael Valentín Valdivieso y Zañartu challenged his authority to regulate the clergy. The president became so infuriated with the church that he broke with the ultramontane Conservatives to found a new political bloc, the National Party, or the Montt-Varistas, which would rule Chile for the next several decades. Except for its repudiation of ultramontane ideals, the Nationals shared many of the old Conservative ideologies. Montt's decision to create his own political party drove the Liberal and Conservative opposition elements to form an alliance to oppose him.

Despite a turbulent beginning, Montt ruled well. He modernized the economy by abolishing the entailed estates, or Mayorazgos, in 1852. He initiated the construction of a rail line between Santiago and Valparaíso, as well as another connecting the capital with the agrarian south. Montt established telegraph service connecting Santiago with Valparaíso and Talca. Of equal importance, his government published a new commercial code, organized a mail service, founded a credit bank, and authorized the creation of private lending institutions and public corporations.

A downturn in the economy turned Montt's second term sour. The agricultural boom generated by gold rushes in the United States (1849) and Australia (1853) evaporated when these areas became self-sufficient in food production. The loss of the Californian and Australian markets caused economic dislocation in Chile, whose farmers and millers suffered even more when exports of U.S. farm surplus began to drive down prices for Chile's agricultural commodities. Mineral production also fell when the mines of Chañarcillo began to peter out. The downturn in the fields and mines reduced the flow first of exports, then of imports, and finally of the states' revenues, impoverishing both the commercial sector and the government.

Montt, like his predecessors, tried to handpick the man who would replace him as president. His choice was his alter ego, Antonio Varas, whose career and ideals seemed a mirror image of his mentor's. The political parties, however, would no longer tolerate the old ways. In 1859 rebellions erupted in the north as well as the south. Although the government's troops crushed the uprisings, the rebels made their point: the political system would have to become more open. Rather than perpetuate the existing venomous feelings by accepting Montt's support for the presidency, Varas bowed out of the race for president. In his stead Montt selected José Joaquín Pérez, a jovial, benign politician whose presence neither antagonized nor frightened anyone. Pérez immediately amnestied all those involved in the 1851 and 1859 rebellions. He ruled Chile during a ruinous war with Spain. Santiago joined the hemispheric outrage when Madrid, in 1862, seized the Chincha Islands, off the coast of Peru. The Spanish fleet eventually retreated, but before leaving Chilean waters it cannonaded Valparaíso, devastating the port and the nation's economy.

Happily, Chile's domestic political scene seemed more placid. Helped by the affable Pérez, who included members of the Liberal-Conservative Fusion in his government, Chile's political system continued to evolve. In the early 1860s, a group of dissident Liberals created the Radical Party. Its ferocious name notwithstanding, this new group sought not to change the political system drastically but to secularize society by stripping the Roman Catholic Church of its special privileges. Eventually, four political parties proclaimed that they would not tolerate operating under the old strictures.

In 1865, with the election of an antigovernment majority, the Congress enacted laws that guaranteed increased religious freedom, particularly for Protestants. Five years later the legislature revised the election laws, including mechanisms intended to prevent vote fraud. The culmination of the reform movement was an 1870 constitutional amendment limiting the president to a single five-year term.

The first man elected under this new law was Federico Errázuriz, who, like many of his contemporaries, had been jailed for opposing the Montt regime. The standard bearer of the Liberal Party, Errázuriz was also a friend of Archbishop Rafael Valdivieso, whose support he cultivated in order to win the 1870 presidential election, defeating a candidate of the National and Radical Parties. Errázuriz, however, would turn against his Conservative allies.

Perhaps this political split was inevitable, for what united the Liberals and Conservatives was not a shared ideology but a hatred of the National Party. Once Errázuriz came to power, he had to deal with the Conservative agenda. The new president increasingly disliked the fact that various Roman Catholic institutions seemed to enjoy certain extralegal prerogatives such as controlling the rite of marriage and the use of cemeteries. In 1872 the Catholic minister of education, Abdón Cifuentes, ordered the University of Chile to admit students who had passed entrance exams administered not by the university but by church schools. Cifuentes's edict unleashed a political firestorm. Subjected to fierce parliamentary questioning, Cifuentes and his Conservative colleagues resigned their cabinet posts.

With the Conservatives gone, Errázuriz moved to the left, thus accelerating the pace of reform and the secularization of society. In 1873 and 1874, for example, the Congress liberalized the constitutional requirements for legislative quorums and for naturalization, extended the right of free association, required that senators be elected directly from specific districts—previously they had been selected at large—and created a joint congressional committee that could, under certain conditions, request the president to convoke an extraordinary legislative session.

The impetus to convert Chile's government into a quasi-parliamentary system accelerated: it became easier for the legislature to challenge ministers, and harder for the president to declare a state of siege. Changes were also made in the electoral process. Henceforth, the local communities' most affluent people would maintain the voting rolls,

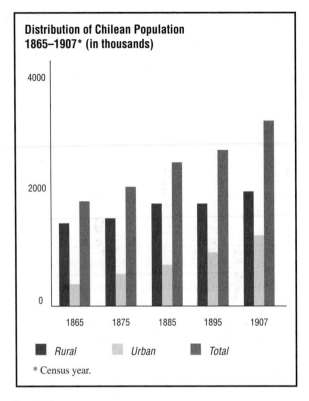

Distribution of Chilean Population
1865–1907* (in thousands)

4000

2000

0

1865   1875   1885   1895   1907

■ Rural   ■ Urban   ■ Total

* Census year.

Figure 1

and the state eliminated the provision that individuals must possess property in order to vote. The Congress also passed a law enhancing the ability of minority parties to win office.

Theoretically, these measures prevented the government from manipulating the political process. In fact, they made it only slightly more difficult while permitting local oligarchies, particularly rural landowners, a free hand in influencing elections. Other significant reforms included the promulgation of a new criminal code, which among its provisions restricted the powers of the clergy, and a mining code.

THE 1870S: GROWTH AND DECLINE

Chile had changed dramatically by the mid-1870s. The population numbered 2 million and the number of urban centers had increased, as had the population of Santiago and Valparaíso. The nation's economy, based on a mix of mining, commerce, and agriculture, became increasingly diversified. But a more significant shift took place.

Although the nation had flirted with free trade beginning in the 1870s, the legislature began, on a piecemeal basis, to pass laws protecting national

industries as they began producing consumer goods like textiles or shoes. The manufacture of agricultural tools as well as heavy machinery began. Chileans constructed mineral refineries in the south where, using local coal, they smelted imported and domestic ores into ingots of pure silver and copper. Linked by an ever-expanding rail system and a merchant marine, and backed up by telegraph and mail service, Chile's economy became integrated into that of the world. Cereals were exported not merely to Latin America but to England, and metals were sold everywhere.

Blessed with increasing revenues, particularly from the development of the Caracoles silver mines in Bolivia, the government constructed various public-works projects and even purchased two iron-clad warships for its navy. Then the good times came to a halt. Beginning in 1873, a series of unrelated events short-circuited Chile's economy. First, various European nations adopted the gold standard, depreciating the value of silver, by then Chile's most lucrative export. And roughly at the same time that the silver mines in Chile and Bolivia became less productive, copper output also declined. In the interim, a depression enveloped both the United States and Europe. Hence, Chile simultaneously lost both its markets and its principal source of income.

Errázuriz's term of office expired in 1876. His handpicked successor, Aníbal Pinto, however, needed massive intervention by Errázuriz to force the Liberal Party to nominate him. After his election, Pinto almost did not take office. Elements within the army considered launching a coup and imposing Pinto's rival, Benjamín Vicuña Mackenna, on the nation. The government, however, managed to crush the potential putsch, exiling the conspirators.

During the ensuing years, Pinto might have wished that Vicuña Mackenna had triumphed. The year Pinto took office, floods destroyed the crops in Chile's south while drought devastated them in the north. The enormous drop in agricultural output not only reduced exports but drove up domestic food prices. The following year brought no respite. Famine became widespread, forcing people into the cities in a futile search for food. Desperate people turned to crime or fled the nation in search of work.

Pinto initially attempted to deal with the crisis by reducing government expenditures. When that

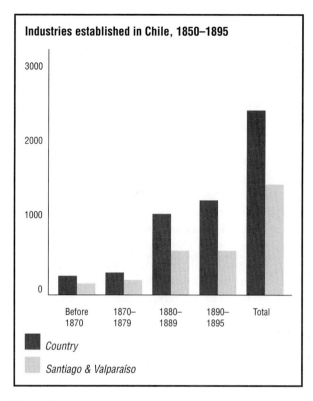

Industries established in Chile, 1850–1895

■ Country
▨ Santiago & Valparaíso

Figure 2

measure failed to balance the budget, he and the Congress passed a tax on income and inheritances as well as gifts. While not substantial, these imposts nevertheless represented a milestone in Chile's economic history. This was the first time the government had imposed direct taxes on its citizens and the first time the levies were designed to fall mainly upon the affluent.

The combination of the declines in mining and agriculture continued to devastate Chile. By 1878 it became clear that virtually all but one of the nation's financial institutions were bankrupt. Fearing a panic, the government decreed that the public could no longer convert the banks' paper money into specie. Not just the financial institutions suffered. The Moneda, literally without gold or silver, had to print paper money.

As Pinto attempted to confront this economic Armageddon, his nation became embroiled in a bitter border dispute with Argentina over the ownership of Patagonia and control of the Strait of Magellan, which threatened to plunge Chile into war. No sooner had Pinto temporarily resolved this

problem, when Bolivia initiated a series of steps that would push not only Chile but also Peru into war.

In late 1878, Bolivia's president, Hilarión Daza, increased taxes on nitrates, or *salitre*, mined by a Chilean corporation operating in Bolivia's Atacama Desert. This tax increase violated an earlier treaty under which Chile had ceded to Bolivia control of the desert in return for its promise not to raise taxes on any Chilean corporation operating in that area.

Pinto did not wish a confrontation with La Paz. His decision to negotiate with Argentina, however, infuriated his domestic enemies. Fearing that his political opponents might use the dispute with Bolivia to their advantage, Pinto recognized that he had to defend strenuously Chile's interests in Bolivia. Thus, in February 1879 Pinto acted, ordering his troops to occupy the territory that Santiago had earlier ceded to La Paz in return for its concessions to the Chilean mining interests. Daza responded by declaring war.

Six years earlier, Peru and Bolivia had signed a secret military alliance binding both nations to support each other in case either one became involved in a war with Chile. Chile knew of the treaty's existence but had never reacted. Pinto de-manded to know officially whether Peru had signed an alliance with Bolivia and, if so, whether Lima would join in the war against Chile. Faced with an ultimatum, Peru's envoy admitted that it would honor its military commitment to Bolivia. Hence, in April 1879 Chile declared war on both Peru and Bolivia.

THE WAR OF THE PACIFIC
The ensuing struggle, known as the War of the Pacific, lasted for four years. Although Chile eventually triumphed, its victory was neither easy nor guaranteed. Indeed, outnumbered and geographically smaller than its enemies, Chile seemed to be at great risk. Santiago, however, managed to win control of the sea lanes, allowing it to launch an attack. By late 1879, Chile had driven the combined Peruvian and Bolivian armies from the nitrate-rich province of Tarapacá. The next year Pinto's army tortuously invaded Tacna and Arica, eventually capturing the area. In January 1881 the victorious army seized Lima.

The fall of Lima did not end the war, however, since Peru's leader, Nicholás de Piérola, refused to cede territory to Chile in return for a peace treaty. Instead he and other zealots organized centers of resistance in Peru's interior. Faced with this resistance, Santiago tried to form a rump government that would sign a peace treaty. It required two years of diplomatic badgering and bloody fighting before Peru capitulated, granting Chile Tarapacá as well as the right to occupy Tacna and Arica for a period of ten years. Bolivia quickly followed suit, agreeing to an armistice allowing Chile to occupy the Atacama.

AFTERMATH OF THE WAR OF THE PACIFIC

The War of the Pacific severely taxed Chile's economic, military, and political resources. Not until the conquest of Tarapacá, which permitted the Chilean government to export nitrates, did the Moneda receive a more constant source of income. The Chilean public had quickly tired of war. Faced with a lack of volunteers, the army began impressing society's less fortunate—drunks and vagrants—and eventually peasants and urban workers. Pinto also had problems with his professional military. Too many officers proved incapable of directing the war, causing the president to send civilians to help prod the army into action and to take charge of plotting strategy as well as provisioning the army.

Finally, the war threatened Chile's political system. The capture of a transport ship, the *Rimac,* in the winter of 1879 unleashed a series of riots in Santiago which threatened Pinto's regime and required force to quash. Had the war not shifted in Santiago's favor, the Chileans might have turned their president out of office. Pinto enjoyed only slightly less support within the Congress. The president's enemies used every opportunity to harass Pinto, unsuccessfully trying to use the war to force him to form a cabinet of national unity.

Having surmounted the earlier crisis, Pinto managed to finish his term of office. His successor, Domingo Santa María (1881–1886), was, like Pinto, handpicked. Given his lack of broad support, Santa María encountered even more political problems than had Pinto. The intense partisan bickering that would characterize the Parliamentary Regime had begun in the latter days of the Pinto government and came into full flower during Santa María's administration. The Conservative opposition, for example, delayed the passage of a budget—even

though the nation was at war—in hopes of forcing the government to invite them to join the cabinet. Santa María refused. Instead of capitulating, he solved this problem by shamelessly manipulating the 1882 congressional elections so that none of the opposition Conservatives won.

With a relatively tame legislature, Santa María achieved one of his most cherished goals: secularizing Chilean society. In the mid-1880s the president prodded the legislature into passing measures that made marriage a civil, not a religious, contract and gave the state control over the civil registry and cemeteries. (The latter measure had particularly ghoulish results as the pious, rather than allowing their deceased loved ones to lie beside possible nonbelievers or, even worse, Protestants, clandestinely disinterred them to rebury them in consecrated ground.) The ultramontanes and the Catholic Church accused Santa María of launching a *Kulturkampf* against them, but to no avail; short of complete separation, the Moneda had effectively curtailed the Church's power.

Santa María's greatest achievement was Chile's victory over Peru and Bolivia. In 1883, Lima signed the Treaty of Ancón, which ceded Tarapacá to Chile. A year later, Bolivia reluctantly permitted Santiago to take Antofagasta. Regrettably, the status of two additional provinces, Tacna and Arica, as well as a final resolution of the War of the Pacific, remained to vex the belligerents for decades.

Now one-third larger, Chile had incorporated the nitrate-rich northern provinces into the nation, thereby creating a market for locally produced consumer goods as well as giving the state control over the world's nitrate supply. Rather than operate these mines itself, the government sold the mines (called *salitreras*) to private interests. Many subsequently lamented that the Chilean state did not retain ownership of the *salitreras*. However, had Santiago opted to operate the mines, it would have had to liquidate an enormous debt before it could own them outright. Thus, rather than indenturing itself and assuming the responsibility for running the mines—a task for which it was unsuited—the state preferred to levy a heavy tax on the export of nitrates.

Nitrates, which at first blush appeared to be a boon to the Chilean economy, eventually poisoned the country. The easy money from nitrates encouraged congress to abandon the earlier taxes on land, income, and estates—levies which obviously fell upon the wealthy—and instead place the economic burden on the foreign consumer. Chileans preferred to invest their capital in nitrate shares, which guaranteed them a high rate of return, rather than in national industries. Hence, the country's revenues and its economy, which earlier had been so diversified, increasingly depended upon the good fortune of the *salitreras*.

These problems did not surface immediately. On the contrary, Chile seemed to have entered the promised land. The newly rich government launched numerous public-works projects, erected palatial *belle époque* public buildings, expanded the bureaucracy, and extended the railroads deeper into the south. The Moneda dedicated substantial sums to modernizing the army, which had finally vanquished the Araucanian Indians, as well as to the navy, which possessed some of the world's finest warships.

The man destined to follow in Santa María's footsteps was his former minister of the interior, José Manuel Balmaceda. The new president, who like so many of his predecessors achieved office through chicanery if not brute force, took his oath of office in September 1886.

When Balmaceda became president, he controlled a vast source of revenue, which he hoped to use to fund numerous public-works projects. Unfortunately, many members of the president's own party, as well as the opposition, vied with him for control of the purse strings. Balmaceda resented their intrusions, preferring to retain power so that he alone could dispense patronage. He also objected to the fact that congress had become obstreperous. Like his predecessor, Balmaceda manipulated the congressional elections to pack the legislature with his supporters. Balmaceda's intervention incensed not only those who lost but also some Liberals, who increasingly disliked this policy. They also disliked the fact that Balmaceda often acted without winning their prior approval.

As his opposition grew and coalesced, Balmaceda's own followers became divided over the issue of presidential succession. Balmaceda wished to select his successor, but his Liberal colleagues opposed his choice. It became clear that Balmaceda would have to act in consort with the legislature, in effect making Chile a de facto parliamentary republic, if he wished to govern effectively. The strong-willed Balmaceda, who before he became president

The battle of Valparaiso, 1891. Nitrate fortunes from the Tarapacá, won by Chile in the War of Pacific (1879–1883), created new political struggles. A brief civil war with Congress triumphing over President José Manuel Balmaceda (1881–1886) converted the country to a parliamentary republic, privileging the oligarchy. © ARCHIVO ICONOGRAFICO, SA/ CORBIS

had spearheaded a drive to weaken the president's power, refused to accept this possibility.

In late 1890 the Congress refused to approve Balmaceda's budget unless he agreed to form a cabinet which enjoyed the legislature's approval. The president refused, declaring that he would use the 1890 budget for 1891 as well. Outraged at this violation of the 1833 Constitution, the congressional forces rebelled.

Backed by the Chilean navy, Balmaceda's opposition, the congressionalists, fled to Iquique, where they established their headquarters. Better equipped, and apparently better led, the rebels defeated the loyalist army at the battles of Placilla and Concón, then seized the capital. Although Santiago was declared an open city, the victorious congressional forces looted the homes of Balmaceda's supporters and murdered some of his officials. Balmaceda wisely took refuge in the Argentine embassy, where he remained until his term of office expired. The following day, he committed suicide.

THE PARLIAMENTARY REGIME

The death of Balmaceda ushered in the Parliamentary Regime, which would rule, but not govern, Chile until 1924. The passage of new legislation transferred the supervision of elections from the central to the local governments. Presumably designed to prevent fraud, the new law merely changed the malefactors. Henceforth, corrupt provincial officials, under the thumb of the landed aristocracy or urban political bosses, rather than the president's minions, perverted the electoral process. Thus, instead of having to appeal to the electorate, candidates needed only to satisfy the aspirations of the power elite.

Chile's rampant corruption perpetuated a political order that remained insensitive, if not deaf, to the nation's pressing social and economic ills. In fairness, it should be noted that new political parties appeared. The Democratic Party, in 1887, became Chile's first avowedly working-class political party, and the Balmacedistas, after futilely attempting to overthrow the Parliamentary Regime, eventually joined it in the 1890s by creating the Liberal Democratic Party. Eventually, both the Democrats and the Balmacedistas compromised their principles, moving from opposing the regime to joining it.

The parliamentary regime marked the beginning of Chile's decline. The existence of so many parties—six, competing for the votes of 150,000 people, or less than 10 percent of the nation's total population—virtually guaranteed political instability and hence administrative paralysis. An indication of potential problems was the fact that during the government of Federico Errázuriz Echaurren (1896–1901) alone, there were more cabinet changes than had occurred between 1830 and 1851. Unfortunately, since the president could not fill the political vacuum precipitated by so much parliamentary shuffling, the nation seemed inert.

At the same time, Chile was no longer the Southern Cone's principal political force. Argentina, which had finally put its house in order, was larger, wealthier, and more populated. Using the revenues generated by its pastoral and cereal economy, Buenos Aires purchased a navy that successfully challenged Santiago's hegemony on the seas.

OVERVIEW

At the end of the nineteenth century, Chile's future seemed to have taken a turn for the worse. When the century began, Chile had indeed been an oligarchic republic. Still, as it matured it had become more open, permitting the dissemination of new ideas and the creation of new political parties. This openness created a climate that, while maintaining order, permitted the economy to grow. Indeed, the economy seemed to represent as many different economic interests as the nation's political parties did ideologies. The nation, which owed its success to the development of a diversified economy, became addicted to nitrates. Then the Revolution of 1891 unleashed latent forces that had existed for years, if not decades, mortally wounding the domestic political process at precisely the time when it would have to confront foreign enemies and internal social problems.

See also **Arcos, Santiago; Bello, Andrés; Bilbao Barquín, Francisco; Blanco Encalada, Manuel; Bulnes Prieto, Manuel; Carrera, José Miguel; Chile, Parliamentary Regime; Freire Serrano, Ramón; Lastarria, José Victorino; Mining: Modern; Moneda Palace; Montt Torres, Manuel; Nitrate Industry; O'Higgins, Bernardo; Peru-Bolivia Confederation; Piérola, Nicolás de; Pinto Díaz, Francisco Antonio; Pinto Garmendia, Aníbal; Prieto Vial, Joaquín; Santa María González, Domingo; Sarmiento, Domingo Faustino; Vicuña Mackenna, Benjamin; War of the Pacific.**

BIBLIOGRAPHY

The references have been selected because they are in English and for the most part readily available. A good place to begin a study of this era is two important essays in the *Cambridge History of Latin America:* Simon Collier, "Chile from Independence to the War of the Pacific," vol. 3 (1985), pp. 583–613, and Harold Blakemore, "Chile from the War of the Pacific to the World Depression, 1880–1930," vol. 5 (1986), pp. 449–551.

Diplomatic studies include Fredrick B. Pike, *Chile and the United States, 1880–1962* (1963); Robert N. Burr, *By Reason or Force* (1965); and William F. Sater, *Chile and the United States: Empires in Conflict* (1990).

Economic topics are discussed in Stefan de Vylder, *From Colonialism to Dependence: An Introduction to Chile's Economic History* (1974); Markos Mamalakis, *The Growth and Structure of the Chilean Economy: From Independence to Allende* (1976); C. Carriola and O. Sunkel, "Chile," in Roberto Cortés Conde and Stanley J. Stein, eds., *Latin America: A Guide to Economic History, 1830–1930* (1977); Luis Ortega, "Economic Policy and Growth in Chile from Independence to the War of the Pacific," in Christopher Abel and Colin Lewis, *Latin America, Economic Imperialism, and the State* (1985); Cristóbal Kay, "The Development of the Chilean Hacienda System," in Kenneth Duncan et al., *Land and Labour in Latin America* (1977), pp. 103–

139; John Mayo, *British Merchants and Chilean Develop-ment, 1851–1886* (1987); William F. Sater, "Economic Nationalism and Tax Reform in Nineteenth-Century Chile," in *The Americas* 22 (1976): 311–335.

For different aspects of mining, see Leland R. Pederson, *The Mining Industry of the Norte Chico, Chile* (1966); Luis Ortega, "The First Four Decades of the Chilean Coal-mining Industry, 1840–1879," in *Journal of Latin American Studies* 14, no. 1 (1982): 1–32; William Culver and Cornel Reinhart, "The Decline of a Mining Region and Mining Policy: Chilean Copper in the Nineteenth Century," in *Miners and Mining in the Americas,* edited by Thomas Greaves and William Culver (1985), 68–81. Specifically on nitrates, see Thomas O'Brien, *The Nitrate Industry and Chile's Crucial Transition, 1870–1891* (1982).

On railroad development, see Robert Oppenheimer, "Chile's Central Valley Railroads and Economic Development in the Nineteenth Century," in *Proceedings of the Pacific Coast Council on Latin American Studies* 6 (1977–1979): 73–86.

Intellectual, political, and social history includes Fredrick B. Pike, "Aspects of Class Relations in Chile, 1850–1960," in *Hispanic American Historical Review* 43, no. 1 (1963): 14–33; Simon Collier, *Ideas and Politics of Chilean Independence, 1808–1833* (1967); Solomon Lipp, *Three Chilean Thinkers* (1975); Allen Woll, *A Functional Past: The Uses of History in Nineteenth-Century Chile* (1982). The War of the Pacific is covered in William F. Sater, *Chile and the War of the Pacific* (1986). For the postwar period, see Harold Blakemore, *British Nitrates and Chilean Politics, 1886–1896: Balmaceda and North* (1974); Karen L. Remmer, "The Timing, Pace, and Sequence of Political Change in Chile, 1891–1925," in *Hispanic American Historical Review* 57, no. 2 (1977): 205–230.

Additional Bibliography

Bethell, Leslie, ed. *Chile since Independence.* Cambridge, U.K.; New York: Cambridge University Press, 1993.

Clissold, Stephen. *Bernardo O'Higgins and the Independence of Chile.* New York: Praeger, 1969.

Collier, Simon. *Chile: The Making of a Republic, 1830–1865: Politics and Ideas.* New York: Cambridge University Press, 2003.

Collier, Simon. *History of Chile: 1808–2002.* Cambridge, U.K.; New York: Cambridge University Press, 2004.

García de la Huerta I., Marcos. *Chile 1891, la gran crisis y su historiografía: Los lugares comunes de nuestra conciencia histórica.* Santiago: Centro de Estudios Humanísticos, Universidad de Chile, 1981.

Hervey, Maurice H. *Dark Days in Chile: An Account of the Revolution of 1891.* Philadelphia: Institute for the Study of Human Issues, 1979.

Scully, Timothy. *Rethinking the Center: Party Politics in Nineteenth- and Twentieth-century Chile.* Stanford, CA: Stanford University Press, 1992.

WILLIAM F. SATER

THE TWENTIETH CENTURY

As the 1910 centennial approached, marking the beginning of the revolution and the war that had made Chile an independent republic (1810–1818), Chilean society still retained quite a few of the characteristics it had inherited from the colonial era (1541–1810). Above all, it remained sharply stratified along socioeconomic lines and still constituted a "pigmentocracy," as the Creole oligarchy played a dominant role in all realms.

What had changed during the nineteenth century were the economic, cultural, and ideological tendencies of the ruling class, which throughout the century had enjoyed the modernizing influences of Europe and North America. Likewise, the Creole elite had diversified its economic activities, augmenting its traditional agricultural and livestock production with the active promotion of mining as well as domestic and foreign trade. With the advent of these new branches of production, some representatives of the middle class, along with better-off immigrants of European origin, had joined the ranks of the oligarchy. The cities had grown in importance as they were transformed into loci of modernization for the elites and centers for the development of the middle classes and urban workers.

The political hegemony of this expanded oligarchy had consolidated following the 1891 civil war. The oligarchy was organized into several conservative and liberal factions that had paved the way for a parliamentary republic in which these factions shared power and took turns at ruling.

Moreover, during the second half of the nineteenth century, the Republic of Chile had attained the geographic size and shape that it has today. The chief milestones in this process had included the delimitation of its border with Argentina in the southern region, the occupation of the Mapuche territories in the south, and the annexation of the northern regions known today as Tarapacá and Antofagasta following the war against Peru and Bolivia (1879–1884).

Since that time, the history of Chile has played out over its 292,258 square miles of territory, which runs 2,610 miles from north to south, with an average width of just 87 miles from the Andes mountain range and the Pacific Ocean. Chile's regions include the desert-like Great North (Tarapacá and Antofagasta), the semiarid Small North (Atacama and Coquimbo), the Mediterranean climate of the Central Region (Valparaíso, Santiago, O'Higgins, Maule), the rainy South (Bío Bío, Araucanía, Los Lagos), and the cold Far South (Aysén and Magallanes). Within these borders there were just over 3.2 million inhabitants, according to the 1907 census, of which some 60 percent were illiterate and 43 percent lived in cities.

CHALLENGES OF MODERNIZATION AND DEMOCRACY (1900–1973)

The addition of the new regions to the north facilitated an enormous increase in the resources available to Chile through the development of saltpeter mining. Chile had a monopoly on the world production of this resource in an age of huge growth in the demand for fertilizers to supply the expansion of agricultural development around the world. Although the mining was principally carried out by British and German companies, the Chilean government received a share of their hefty profits by imposing a tax on their activities. The development of the saltpeter economy laid the groundwork for a series of trends that transformed Chilean society at the turn of the century into one that was more complex, modern, and diversified.

Although the manufacturing sector was showing some signs of expansion at the beginning of the twentieth century—as were agriculture, transportation, trade, communications, financial activities, and copper mining—it was undeniably saltpeter that sustained the Chilean economy, accounting for the largest share of exports and tax revenues. During the last two decades of the nineteenth century and the two first decades of the twentieth, the state significantly expanded its reach thanks to saltpeter revenues, vastly increasing its promotion of public works and education, and at the same time modernizing the armed forces and increasing public-sector employment for the middle class.

Several factors came together to bring about change in Chile's social structure, as well as in the rules and key actors of the political process. On the one hand, middle-class sectors, particularly

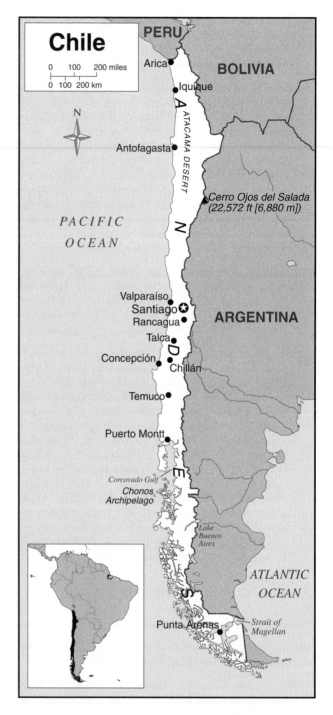

professionals, teachers, and the military, were gaining in social and cultural strength. On the other hand, a broad and organized working class began to appear in both the mines and ports of the saltpeter region, as well as in the central and southern cities, which had begun to grow rapidly. However, halfway through the second decade of the century, the interruptions in transportation brought about by World War I, and particularly the appearance of synthetic saltpeter in Europe, revealed that Chile's extreme dependence on salt-peter revenues was also a structural weakness of its economy. In the midst of the economic upheavals of the 1920s and 1930s, movements led by the middle class and workers challenged the oligarchic nature of the prevailing political and social order. These movements were democratic, nationalist, social Christian, and socialist, based on the ideologies that were motivating political and social debates around the world at the time.

During the first two decades of the century the workers' movement had organized trade unions and political organizations grounded in socialism and anarchism, and had managed to play a limited role in the representative institutions of the political system. They faced state harassment and even violence as their demands and mobilizations surpassed the threshold of tolerance of both the ruling elite and bourgeois public opinion, causing these two factions to close ranks around the defense of public order. The violence, which at times reached true repression, cost the lives of dozens and even hundreds of workers in incidents that included a massacre at the Santa María de Iquique School on December 21, 1907. In that context, Luis Emilio Recabarren Serrano, a typesetter by trade, founded the Socialist Workers' Party (Partido Obrero Socialista, or POS) in 1912; in 1922 it became the Communist Party (Partido Comunista, or PC).

The movements of the middle classes spanned a broad range of ideologies, and they established ties with both oligarchic and working-class sectors. In this way, their upward and downward social boundaries were not at all clear. The middle-class and anticlerical Radical Party (Partido Radical, or PR) of the nineteenth century managed to make the transition to social liberalism, and even to social reformism, at the start of the twentieth century. The PR forged an alliance with the reformist sector of liberalism, enabling the presidency of Arturo Alessandri (1920–1925). That alliance lasted until the mid-1930s, when Alessandri and the liberals joined forces with the Right during his second term in office (1932–1938).

Divisions between the liberal and conservative wings of the traditional elite began to diminish once they achieved agreement on the separation between the Catholic Church and the Chilean state, a measure that was reiterated in the 1925 Constitution. At the same time, the emergence of new political and social movements prompted them to jointly defend the economic order based on the fundamental nature of property and the market, the social order based on historically established hierarchies, and the political order that was republican and only somewhat democratic.

From 1924 to 1932 the officer corps of the armed forces was the standard-bearer and front line of middle-class ambitions and concerns, in terms of resisting both pressure from above and the revolutionary threat from below. It was a time of militaristic and social nationalism, which in 1924 and 1925 was in harmony with the social and civic liberalism of the first Alessandri government. The result was a rewritten constitution that established a democracy strongly dominated by the executive branch, as well as the introduction of labor and social reforms that both acknowledged and regulated the formation of trade unions, collective bargaining, and strikes. The Alessandri presidency also laid the early groundwork for a state-sponsored social safety net.

The break between Alessandri and the military led to the presidency of Carlos Ibáñez del Campo (1927–1931), a military leader who attempted to institute modernization by authoritarian means. Although hampered by the devastating local effects of the 1929 world economic crisis, he built the foundation of a modern state with the ability to intervene in the economy and society. Ibáñez was overthrown in 1931, and following a period of instability that included attempts to set up a socialist republic in 1932, the other chief leader of the military youth movement of the 1920s, Marmaduke Grove, co-founded the Socialist Party (Partido Socialista, or PS) in 1933. The PS brought together populists, democratic socialists, and anti-Stalinist Marxists from the middle and working classes. Its goal was the revolutionary transformation of the economic and social order, based on "Marxism enhanced by constant social evolution."

During the 1930s, the most promising young members of the Chilean conservative movement, together with academics and professionals belonging to the traditional elite and emerging middle classes, split off from the socially traditional and economically liberal Conservative Party in 1938 to form the National Falangist Movement (Falange

Chile

Population:	16,284,741 (2007 est.)
Area:	292,258 sq mi
Official language:	Spanish
Languages:	Spanish, indigenous languages, German
National currency:	Chilean peso (CLP)
Principal religions:	Roman Catholic 70%, Evangelical 15.1%, Jehovah's Witness 1.1%, other Christian 1%, other 4.6%, none 8.3% (2002)
Ethnicity:	white and white-Amerindian 95%, Amerindian 3%, other 2%
Capital:	Santiago
Other urban centers:	Antofagasta, Concepción, Temuco, Valparaíso, Viña del Mar
Annual rainfall:	Ranges from none in the northern desert to 30 inches in central Chile and up to 160 inches in the south.
Principal geographical features:	*Mountains:* The Andes Mts. run along the entire eastern border and feature many tall peaks such as Ojos del Salado (22,579 ft) and Tupungato (22,310 ft). Lower ranges run along the coast. *Rivers:* Bío-Bío, Loa *Lakes:* Llanquihue, General Carrera (Buenos Aires), many others in the lake district. *Islands:* Easter Island, Juan Fernandez Islands, Sala y Gómez, San Ambrosio, and San Felix in the open Pacific Shares Tierra del Fuego with Argentina, thousands of smaller islands along the southern coast.
Economy:	*GDP per capita:* $12,600 (2006 est.)
Principal products and exports:	*Agricultural:* fish, fruits, meat, wool *Manufacturing:* food processing, metal refining, textiles, transport machinery, wood products *Mining:* copper, lithium, iron, nitrates
Government:	Chile declared independence from Spain in 1810. It is governed as a republic, with the president as both chief of state and head of government. The legislature is a bicameral National Congress, with a 38-seat Senate and a 120-seat Chamber of Deputies, all popularly elected.
Armed forces:	*Army:* 47,700 *Navy:* 19,398 *Air force:* 11,000 *Paramilitary:* 38,000 *Reserves:* 50,000
Transportation:	*Rail:* 4,092 mi *Ports:* Antofagasta, Arica, Huasco, Iquique, Lirquen, San Antonio, San Vicente, Valparaiso *Roads:* 9,992 mi paved; 39,473 mi unpaved *National airline:* National Airlines of Chile (LAN-Chile) *Airports:* 79 paved runways, 279 unpaved
Media:	Over 30 major newspapers, including: *La Tercera, La Cuarta, Las Últimas Noticias, El Mercurio; Caras* and *Qué Pasa?* are popular magazines. 80 AM and 64 FM radio stations; 63 television stations.
Literacy and education:	*Total literacy rate:* 95.7% Children ages 6 to 18 are required to attend school. Public education is free. Major universities include the University of Chile and the University of Santiago de Chile.

Nacional), a political movement rooted in social Catholicism. That same year saw the climax of confrontations between the second Alessandri governmnet (1932–1938), supported by the Liberal and Conservative Parties, and the Ibáñez and Naci movement (which used the letter "c" to distinguish itself from the German Nazis, although it identified with the latter in several aspects). The Nacis had authoritarian and populist nationalist leanings, and fought equally hard against the Left and the Right. The massacre of dozens of Nacis just weeks before the presidential elections, during the suppression of a putsch against Alessandri, led Ibáñez to withdraw as his party's candidate. Therefore the electorate had to choose between a liberal-conservative right-wing candidate and the candidate of the Popular Front, which brought together the Radical, Socialist, and Communist parties along with several lesser groups.

The victory in 1938 by the Radical Pedro Aguirre Cerda launched a cycle of ten governments made up of center-right coalitions and Radical presidents. After the death of Cerda in 1941, Juan Antonio Ríos was elected president, and he also died during his term in office. The next president elected, Gabriel González Videla (1946–1952), put an abrupt end to the alliance between Radicals and the Left in response to the outbreak of the cold war. He expelled the Communists from the government in 1947 and outlawed them in 1948, establishing a Chilean version of McCarthyism that kept

Chuquicamata Copper Mine, Atacama Desert, Chile, 1996. As part of a plan to increase the state's role in the economy, the socialist-democratic coalition government of Salvador Allende (1908–1973) expanded agrarian reform and nationalized copper mines, such as the one seen here. © CHARLES O'REAR/CORBIS

communism on the sidelines of Chile's political system until 1958.

The world economic crisis of 1929 had forced Chile to seek a new direction for its development strategy. Although there is still debate about when the Chilean economy actually recovered from the crisis and when exactly it began to industrialize based on a strategy of import substitution, the fact is that at the close of the 1930s, Chile's gross domestic produce (GDP) was still 7 percent lower than in 1929. It was not until the government of Aguirre Cerda (1938–1941) that Chile definitively abandoned its previous economic model and began a new phase that would last around three decades. Industrialization was promoted nationwide, with a focus on the energy sector and import substitutions. The state played a central role in this effort as a direct participant in the production of electricity, petroleum, transportation, iron and steel, banking, and communications. The government also set steep tariffs to protect national

products, and at the same time played a regulatory role in labor relations.

A network of government institutions was set up during that period to provide health care, social welfare, credit, and housing, chiefly for the benefit of salaried workers in the public and private sectors. Thus, state spending on social services as a percentage of the GDP grew from 2.1 percent in 1925 to 17.9 percent in 1955 and to 25.8 percent by 1972. In the area of education, enrollment at all levels continued to increase, and institutions were created to provide meals and school supplies to low-income students. The national literacy rate grew from 58.3 percent in 1940 to 82.4 percent in 1960 and to 89.8 percent by 1970. Industry grew and diversified from the 1940s to the 1960s, attaining an annual growth rate of 5.2 percent between 1940 and 1970, but the GDP grew at a rate of only 3.8 percent per year. All in all, the effort to industrialize Chile met with only partial success, and the nation continued to depend heavily on copper; the resource had replaced saltpeter as its principal source of wealth and was controlled by U.S. companies. The result was inflation and repeated crises in the government's budget and balance of payments.

From the 1940s through the 1960s the rate of urbanization, which had risen gradually throughout the previous century, began to accelerate rapidly, reaching 60 percent of the population in 1950 and more than 70 percent during the 1960s. In those urban spaces a rich and complex social fabric developed that was tightly interwoven with political activity. Between 1932 and 1970 the number of unionized workers increased tenfold, from 54,800 to 551,000, and the number of trade unions grew from 421 to 4,001 during the same period. Business associations continued to have great influence, as did professional associations that represented the educated middle class.

The emergence of new social actors onto the national stage, and profound changes among those who had already been participating, transformed the way Chileans thought about and imagined their nation, and the way that historically marginalized actors were portrayed. Intellectuals and artists played a decisive role in this transformation. These men and women of middle-class and working-class origins, urban and rural, would become the most dynamic segment of the cultural elite.

During that same period, the modernization and democratization of society in the cities and the mining regions stood in increasingly stark contrast to the traditional forms of production and social relations that continued in the rural areas, where trade-union organizations among rural workers were legally banned until the mid-1960s.

Rapidly accelerating migration from the countryside to the cities, where the majority of the nation's population became increasingly concentrated, led to a worsening of problems in urban marginalized communities. Neither the economy nor public policy was capable of assimilating an expanding population that lived on the outskirts of the large cities in precarious conditions with regard to work, housing, nutrition, and healthcare. The inability of the import-substitution model of industrialization and of the state-run social safety net to meet the needs of the new urban workers, compounded by the effects of inflation on the salaried working and middle classes, and a constant

struggle between the various productive sectors seeking benefits through state regulation, all amounted to a broad wave of social discontent at the end of the 1940s that finally forced the Radical Party out of office.

Thus, in 1952, the former dictator Carlos Ibáñez won the presidential elections with the support of a motley coalition of populist and nationalist groups, joined by a faction of socialists. But the nation's economic and social problems remained unresolved under the Ibáñez government, which this time upheld the 1925 Constitution. This led to the breakup of the coalition that had brought him to power and an increase in popular discontent. In April 1957 dissatisfaction with the government turned into an explosion of social violence that was harshly repressed by the police and military troops, leaving dozens of people dead.

In that context, the 1958 elections saw a narrow victory by the right-wing candidate, the independent engineer Jorge Alessandri Rodríguez, son of the former president (Arturo Alessandri Palma), who had the support of both the Conservative and Liberal Parties and won with 32 percent of the vote. Alessandri was closely followed by the left-wing candidate, the socialist physician Salvador Allende, who received 29 percent of the vote and was supported by the Socialist Party, the Communist Party, and other smaller groups that made up the Popular Action Front (Frente de Acción Popular, or FRAP) created in 1956. Third place went to an attorney and leader of the Falangists since the 1930s, Eduardo Frei Montalva, who had the support of the Christian Democratic Party (Partido Demócrata Cristiano, or PDC), which was founded in 1957 when the Falangists merged with the Social Christian wing of the Conservatives and with smaller groups created after the breakup of Ibáñez-style populism. The formerly dominant Radical Party was left in fourth place, with 15 percent of the vote.

The government of Jorge Alessandri was unable to pursue his goal of modernizing the economy along capitalist lines due to resistance from the nation's business sectors. These groups had consolidated under the aegis of the protectionist, regulatory, and interventionist state created by the Radicals and followers of Ibáñez. They were joined by an alliance that was founded on Radical ideology, and this enabled them to achieve a parliamentary majority.

Downtown Santiago, c. late 20th century. Flanked by the Andes, Santiago, the financial, cultural, and political capital of Chile, experienced high population increase and growth throughout the twentieth century. PHOTOGRAPH BY SUSAN D. ROCK. REPRODUCED BY PERMISSION

In addition, the Right was placed on the defensive by a wave of social mobilization led by the United Federation of Workers (Central Única de Trabajadores, or CUT), created in 1953, and by steadfast political opposition from FRAP and the PDC.

Chilean women had won the right to vote in all elections in 1949, and the electoral system was reformed in 1958, the same year that the 1948 restrictions on political pluralism were abolished. Thus, starting in the 1960s, the universal suffrage that had been decreed almost a century earlier was finally put into practice. This expansion of the rights of citizens regardless of ideology, social class, or gender extended the true promise of political participation in the nation's institutions to all social sectors in Chile.

In the 1960s two alternative programs for effecting qualitative changes in Chilean society emerged with strong popular support. The first,

the Revolución en Libertad (Revolution in Liberty), came to power in 1964 and was headed by the Christian Democratic president Eduardo Frei Montalva; the second was the Vía Chilena al Socialismo (Chilean Road to Socialism), an effort begun in 1970 by the Socialist president Salvador Allende. The two programs agreed in their analysis of the main issues preventing national progress: foreign control over the huge copper-mining industry, and lack of development in the agricultural sector, which they attributed to the structure of rural landholding and to the kinds of social relations that prevailed in the countryside. Likewise, both programs agreed to work to ensure that social groups that were still marginalized (rural workers and poor urban dwellers) would become integrated into political life. They found relatively little agreement, however, on the right strategies to resolve the problems they had identified, and particularly on the ideological orientation underlying the profound changes they were determined to make.

In the 1964 presidential elections, the Christian Democratic candidate Eduardo Frei received 56 percent of the vote, defeating the FRAP candidate, Salvador Allende, who received 39 percent. The Radical candidate won only 5 percent of the vote after losing the backing of the Right, whose supporters gave their votes to Frei not because they supported his platform but rather to prevent the Left from winning. The elections were characterized by a widespread terror campaign against Allende financed by the United States, whose goal was to establish a link in the public mind between the Chilean Left and the Communist dictatorships of the Soviet Union and Cuba. This campaign created a split between the Christian Democrats and the Left and fostered deep antagonism between the Socialist Party and the PDC.

The Frei Montalva government (1964–1970) implemented a program of agrarian reform that changed the structure of rural landholding, and the state became involved in ownership of the great copper mines, the benefits of which were meant to be used to promote economic modernization with the participation of the state and national business interests. Likewise, the government pressed for the organization of rural workers, women, and the urban poor, who until then had played no significant role in the nation's political or social life. Rural trade unions were established by law and promoted by the government, growing from about 1,000 members in 1964 to more than 100,000 in 1970. The policy of grassroots organizing, meant to transform the "marginalized masses" into "an organized people," resulted in the creation of local organizations in which more than one million people were involved. These groups also reaped the benefits of state-run popular education programs. At the same time, the government enacted reforms in the nation's educational system to substantially broaden coverage of primary and secondary education. It also carried out an ambitious program to build low-income housing.

The agrarian reform that brought about such a profound transformation of Chile's rural life was made possible by a constitutional amendment passed by the Congress in 1967, thanks to votes from the PDC and the Left, that subordinated property rights to the social cause. That amendment also laid the groundwork for the potential future socialization of other sectors of the economy, as long as there was a parliamentary majority willing to pass such legislation.

The agrarian reform, and the constitutional amendment that enabled it, transformed the Right, which in 1966 regrouped to form the National Party. Together with the business associations, they became unyielding opponents of the reformist government, which they perceived as unleashing a wholesale assault on private property rights. At the other extreme, the Left was busy denouncing the weaknesses and inadequacies of the government's reforms in terms of truly benefiting the majority of the population, as Frei was unwilling to go beyond the limits of a social market economy.

For the 1970 presidential elections, the Left once again chose as its candidate Salvador Allende, the leader of a new coalition called Popular Unity (Unidad Popular) that brought together Socialists, Communists, Radicals, a group that had split off from the PDC in 1969, and other smaller organizations. In the coalition's view, solutions to the nation's economic and social problems could be found only by going beyond "dependent capitalism" to build socialism. Between 1967 and 1970, the Left had managed to position itself as the voice of those who desired true change. It spoke for many of the new social movements that had arisen during the Frei government but whose expectations had only been partially fulfilled by existing government policies.

The presidential election of 1970 was a contest of candidates representing three different ideologies: the Right, the Christian Democratic center, and the Left. The Left won with 36 percent of the vote, followed closely by the Right with 35 percent, and the PDC was relegated to third place with 28 percent. Because none of the candidates had won an absolute majority of the popular vote, the National Congress was called upon to decide between the two frontrunners. Allende's simple majority gave him the presidency after he won support from the PDC in the National Congress.

In order to win that support, Allende and his Popular Unity coalition were forced to draft a constitutional amendment in which they promised to carry out their governing program with full respect for democratic practices, political pluralism, and citizens' rights and freedoms. This constitutional amendment transformed Chile's political and legal institutional framework into one of the most democratically advanced in the world. However, what one part of the Left did not understand was that under the new pact, respect for the Constitution and the rule of law had become essential prerequisites for the success of their revolutionary program. Nor did that sector of the Left, which included the majority of the Socialist Party and the Movement of the Revolutionary Left (Movimiento de Izquierda Revolucionaria, or MIR), understand that the pact required some type of shared understanding with the Christian Democrats with regard to the radical changes that the government hoped to effect in the economy and in society.

Allende worked hard with his closest advisers, with the Communist Party, and with a minority wing of his own party to achieve socialist changes within a constitutional and legal framework. Nevertheless, they were unable to reach agreements with the PDC to pass legislation that would socialize key sectors of the Chilean economy. This was due not only to stubborn opposition from one segment of the governing coalition itself, but also to the weight of the conservative wing of the Christian Democrats, led by Frei, who espoused a deeply anticommunist ideology and were opposed to state control over the economy.

With support that varied from just over one-third to almost one-half of the nation's citizens, Allende's government tried to bring about radical, socialist changes in the Chilean economy. Allende nationalized the large copper mines, broadened the agrarian reform, and nationalized the banking system along with the majority of Chile's principal industries. Thus, he reinforced the role of the state as the most important player in the nation's economy, cutting back the role of the private sector and subordinating it to that of the state.

The nationalization of the copper mines was the only measure that met with unanimous support in Congress, including from the PDC and even the right wing. By the same token, the agrarian reform was extended and stepped up within the framework of the rules set by the Frei government. However, when Allende attempted to subordinate the industrial economy and the distribution of goods to social causes, he was forced to resort to administrative

Chile's presidential palace, La Moneda, in Santiago, under siege, September 11, 1973. Domestic unrest and division, economic problems, and international pressure resulted in a coup d'état by the military and national police, ushering in authoritarian dictatorship until 1988. © BETTMANN/ CORBIS

measures that the opposition viewed as "legal loopholes" that allowed Allende to forcibly implement a revolutionary program that lacked majority support.

These public policies enacted by the government drew intense opposition from those whose interests were being undermined and those who opposed the ideas they embodied. All the nation's institutions were politically polarized, and this cut through the entire fabric of society. Chile was in a state of permanent mobilization, and antagonism between supporters and opponents of the government grew, reaching critical levels by the end of 1972. The situation was worsened by the critical state of the economy as a consequence of the enormous problems created by the transition from capitalism to socialism, by disagreements on that issue within the ruling coalition, and by resistance to the process from the private sector, both in Chile and abroad.

The polarization of Chilean society during those years was whipped into a frenzy by the ideological confrontations between the major world powers of that time. Locally, the confrontation was between the dominant power in the western hemisphere-the United States-and the leftist movements that had gathered force in Latin America since the Cuban Revolution in 1959. The U.S. government's backing of Chilean opposition to Allende ranged from support for an attempt to prevent his rise to power, which resulted in the October 1970 assassination of the commander-in-chief of the army, René Schneider (1913–1970), to covert support for opposition political parties, mass media, and social movements, with the aim of making the nation ungovernable from late 1972.

In that context, with the support or acquiescence of the majority of Allende's opponents, and despite the 43.5 percent of Chileans who supported the government in the parliamentary elections of March 1973, and following several weeks of an insurrectionary strike led by business associations with the support of the entire opposition, a military conspiracy culminated in a coup d'état on 11 September 1973. Participating in this overthrow was the entire ensemble of military forces, with General Augusto Pinochet at its head. The result was the establishment of a dictatorship in Chile that lasted for more than sixteen years. With an iron fist, the dictatorship transformed the Chilean economy and society, turning it in a direction diametrically opposed to the prevailing model of the previous decades.

NATIONAL GLOBALISM AND SOCIAL RECONSTRUCTION (1973–1990)

The advent of the military regime brought the expulsion of citizen representatives from government institutions, prohibitions on political party activities, controls over the mass media, and the loss of autonomy for civil society organizations. At the same time, the regime placed strict limits on individual rights and freedoms. State power was concentrated exclusively in the hands of the military junta, which assumed the functions of the executive, legislative, and constituent branches, and at the same time subordinated the judicial branch to a "permanent state of emergency." The power of the junta was subsequently placed in the hands of Pinochet.

The most tragic aspect of the breakdown of the rule of law and of the concentration of power was the violation of the rights of supporters of the deposed government—their physical safety and even their lives were endangered—and this applied equally to those who attempted to organize any new opposition to the regime. To this end, the regime created a secret police force with unlimited powers to watch and punish any real or potential opponent, both inside and outside the country.

The vast scale of repression under the Pinochet regime left 3,500 to 4,000 persons dead or "disappeared," as well as about 150,000 detainees and political prisoners, many of whom were tortured. In addition, around 200,000 fled a nation whose population in 1973 had totaled 10 million. A systematic, state-sponsored program used terror to destroy an entire democratic political and social way of life that had been deeply rooted in Chilean history over the previous decades. In its place, the government built an authoritarian and highly selective regime on a foundation of fear and division. The use of terror was rooted in an ideology of "national security" that was radically anticommunist as well as contrary to liberal political democracy. This ideology was increasingly combined with an extremist "neoliberal" vision for the Chilean economy and its role in the world economy.

Pinochet's national globalist dictatorship brought about qualitative changes in the structure and functioning of the economy and society. It was guided by a view that placed market forces at the center of not only how resources were allocated, but also how society itself was shaped. Thus, private capital became the fundamental driving force of the economy. The businesses that had been taken over by the state during the Allende government were returned to their previous owners; subsequently, the large state-run public enterprises that had always been part of the government were also privatized. Domestic price controls were abolished, and tariff barriers that protected domestic production from foreign competition were progressively reduced. The capital market was liberalized, and incentives were provided to encourage foreign investment. Similar measures were taken in the fields of urban planning, transportation, and the environment. The government focused its social policies on the poorest of the poor, and transferred the administration of workers' benefits to profit-making

Public rally in Santiago, Chile, 1984. Following years of severe military repression, large-scale demonstrations for and against the dictatorship of General Augusto Pinochet (1973–1988) resumed in the early 1980s, emboldened in the face of economic crisis. © CARLOS CARRION/SYGMA/CORBIS

enterprises. Private-sector involvement in health and education was also increased.

The ruling bloc, which was made up of military officers under the command of the dictator, the nation's economic elites, and professionals and technocrats allied with the government, planned to institutionalize the dictatorial regime headed by General Pinochet so that it would last through the end of the twentieth century. Its long-term outlook was to build a permanent regime of restricted democracy with military oversight. This new institutional framework represented a break with Chile's historical political culture. Its goals were to protect the economic model that had been imposed and to ensure the lasting dominance of the economic elites and technobureaucrats who rose to prominence under the dictatorship.

To that end, the authoritarian regime led by Pinochet drafted and implemented a new constitution in 1980 that extended his term in office until 1988. His expectation was that the plebiscite

scheduled for that year would renew his mandate for an additional eight years. However, an economic crisis befell the nation in the first half of the 1980s, and its social effects were devastating. As a result, in 1983 the opposition began to ignore the strict limits imposed on expressions of dissent, setting off a prolonged period of political and social confrontation.

May 1983 saw the first massive social protest against the dictatorship, and in September 1986 a combat unit of the Manuel Rodríguez Patriotic Front (Frente Patriótico Manuel Rodríguez), a political-military organization created by the Communist Party in late 1983, tried unsuccessfully to assassinate Pinochet. Between May and September, Chile had seen sharp clashes between broad sectors of society—those who were fighting to bring down the regime using the widest possible variety of social protest, and those fighting to uphold the regime using all the coercive powers available to the state, including a suffocating degree of control

Pinochet supporter with portrait at public rally in 1999. International courts attempted to bring General Augusto Pinochet to trial, sparking debate on past human rights violations in Latin America. © REUTERS/CORBIS

over the mass media. Chilean society again was as politically divided as it had been from 1970 to 1973, or even more so. Meanwhile, activists overran the narrow limits imposed on political activity despite the government's use of repressive violence and injury (both massive and selective, legal and clandestine) to quash its opponents.

The opposition forces agreed on the need to mobilize against the dictatorship, but differed in their views on the best strategies to forge a path toward democracy. The PDC favored a combination of peaceful mobilization and negotiations with the ruling clique. One faction of the socialists joined with other left-wing organizations in their belief that continuous social mobilization could push the regime into crisis. Another socialist sector agreed with the MIR and the Communist Party that mobilization needed to be complemented by armed actions in order to provoke such a crisis. The ruling bloc, meanwhile, had set up a series of organizations

that took the form of government-sponsored political parties to run against the opposition.

In the end, the solution to the catastrophic stalemate between opponents and supporters of the regime was the "no" vote in the October 1988 plebiscite that rejected another term for Pinochet as head of state. This was followed the next year by an agreement between the government and the leading opposition party to ratify a partial amendment to the 1980 Constitution in order to make it more democratic.

TRANSITION TO DEMOCRACY, AND GLOBALIZATION (1990–2000)

Democratic governance was restored in Chile in 1990, but the partial constitutional amendment ratified in 1989 left intact a set of rules and institutions from the previous regime, known as "authoritarian enclaves." General Pinochet himself remained as commander-in-chief of the army until 1998.

Broad political blocs became consolidated during the 1990s. Most of the center-Left forces were in the Concertation (Concertación), a coalition that included the Christian Democratic, Socialist, Pro-Democracy, and Radical parties; the coalition supported the candidacies of presidents Patricio Aylwin (1990–1994), Eduardo Frei Ruiz Tagle (1994–2000), Ricardo Lagos (2000–2006), and Michelle Bachelet (2006–2010). The opposition Right coalition was made up of the National Renovation (Renovación Nacional) and Independent Democratic Union (Unión Demócrata Independiente) parties. The political process unfolded in an extraordinarily peaceful fashion, despite the sharp conflicts and painful experiences of the military regime, with which society has yet to come to terms.

In October 1998, just a few months after retiring from the army, Pinochet was arrested in London at the request of a Spanish judge to be tried for crimes against humanity. He was returned to Chile in March 2000, where he faced several judicial prosecutions for those crimes, as well as for corruption, until his death in December 2006.

The Concertation governments elected beginning in 1990 retained the existing framework of free and open markets, stressing investment in infrastructure and greater participation in the world economy. Most of the changes made were in the areas of social equity and poverty reduction, through public policies financed by moderate tax increases. The nation's GDP grew at an average annual rate of 7.7 percent from 1986 to 1997, inflation gradually declined to below 5 percent, and exports managed to make up approximately 35 percent of the GDP. Chile's country risk-index figure has become the lowest in all of Latin America.

Chile's population has grown fivefold since the turn of the twentieth century, totaling 15,116,435 inhabitants in 2002. The cities, which held 43.3 percent of Chileans in 1907, now are home to approximately 85 percent of the nation's inhabitants. Chile's illiteracy rate was as high as 60 percent at the start of the century and less than 5 percent at century's end. Infant mortality, which was measured at 267 per 1,000 in 1910, had dropped to 10 per 1,000 in 1997. Average life expectancy had increased from thirty to seventy-five years. At the same time, society has progressed in its recognition and appreciation of its diversity. In the 1992 census, some 10 percent of the population identified themselves as belonging to one of the indigenous groups. That said, Chile still must overcome deep divisions and economic and social inequalities. This challenge can be summed up by the fact that at the end of the twentieth century, the richest 10 percent of the population accounted for approximately 50 percent of the GDP, whereas the poorest 10 percent represented scarcely 2.5 percent.

Issues that Chilean society faces in the twenty-first century include narrowing this economic and social gap, producing better-quality goods and services that contain more added value, protecting the environment, fully establishing a shared democratic political order that is capable of integrating the new generations, and renewing its national identity in this era characterized by multiculturalism and globalization.

See also **Agrarian Reform; Class Structure in Modern Latin America; Creole; Globalization; Junta: Spanish America; Labor Movements; Mining: Modern; Pinochet Ugarte, Augusto; Privatization; Salt Trade: Andean Region.**

BIBLIOGRAPHY

Angell, Alan. *Politics and the Labour Movement in Chile.* New York: Oxford University Press, 1972.

Arellano, José Pablo. *Políticas sociales y desarrollo. Chile 1924–1984.* Santiago: Corporacion de Estudios para Latinoamérica, 1985.

Barr-Melej, Patrick. *Reforming Chile: Cultural Politics, Nationalism, and the Rise of the Middle Class.* Chapel Hill: University of North Carolina Press, 2001.

Bengoa, José, ed. *La Memoria Olvidada, Historia de los Pueblos Indígenas de Chile.* Santiago: Cuadernos Bicentenario, 2004.

Bethell, Leslie, ed. *Chile since Independence.* Cambridge, U.K.: Cambridge University Press, 1993.

Borzutzky, Silvia. *Vital Connections: Politics, Social Security, and Inequality in Chile.* South Bend, IN: University of Notre Dame Press, 2002.

Collier, Simon, and William F. Sater. *A History of Chile: 1808–1994.* Cambridge, U.K.: Cambridge University Press, 1996.

Correa, Sofía, Consuelo Figueroa, Alfredo Jocelyn-Holt, et al. *Historia del siglo XX chileno.* Santiago: Editorial Sudamericana, 2001.

Cristi, Renato, and Pablo Ruiz-Tagle. *La república en Chile. Teoría y práctica del constitucionalismo republicano.* Santiago: LOM Ediciones, 2006.

Drake, Paul, and Ivan Jaksic, eds. *The Struggle for Democracy in Chile*. Lincoln: University of Nebraska Press, 1995.

Drake, Paul, and Ivan Jaksic, eds. *El modelo chileno: Democracia y desarrollo en los noventa*. Santiago: LOM Ediciones, 1999.

Fermandois, Joaquín. *Mundo y fin de mundo: Chile en la Política Mundial 1900–2004*. Santiago: Ediciones Universidad Católica de Chile, 2005.

Garretón, Manuel Antonio. *La faz sumergida del iceberg. Estudios sobre la transformación cultural*. Santiago: Centro de Estudios Sociales and LOM Ediciones, 1994.

Haslam, Jonathan. *The Nixon Administration and the Death of Allende's Chile: A Case of Assisted Suicide*. London: Verso, 2005.

Huneeus, Carlos. *El régimen de Pinochet*. Santiago: Editorial Sudamericana, 2002.

Hutchison, Elizabeth. *Labors Appropriate to Their Sex: Gender, Labor, and Politics in Urban Chile, 1900–1930*. Durham, NC: Duke University Press, 2001.

Instituto Nacional de Estadísticas. *Estadísticas de Chile en el siglo XX*. Santiago: Author, 1999.

Loveman, Brian. *Chile, the Legacy of Hispanic Capitalism*. 3rd ed. New York: Oxford University Press, 2001.

Meller, Patricio. *Un Siglo de Economía Política Chilena (1890–1990)*. Santiago: Editorial Andrés Bello, 1996.

Moulian, Tomás. *Fracturas: Desde Pedro Aguirre Cerda hasta Salvador Allende (1938–1973)*. Santiago: LOM Ediciones, 2006.

Pinto, Julio, ed. *Cuando Hicimos Historia. La experiencia de la Unidad Popular*. Santiago: LOM Ediciones, 2005.

Portales, Felipe. *Los mitos de la democracia chilena*. Santiago:Catalonia, 2004.

Puryear, Jeffrey. *Thinking Politics: Intellectuals and Democracy in Chile, 1973–1988*. Baltimore, MD: Johns Hopkins University Press, 1994.

Ramón, Armando de. *Historia de Chile. Desde la invasión incaica hasta nuestros días (1500–2000)*. Santiago: Catalonia, 2003.

Rolle, Claudio. *1973: La vida cotidiana en un año crucial*. Santiago: Planeta, 1973.

Salazar, Gabriel. *Violencia Política Popular en las Grandes Alamedas*. Santiago: Ediciones Sur, 1990.

Stabili, María Rosaria. *El sentimiento aristocrático. Elites chilenas frente al espejo (1860–1960)*. Santiago: Editorial Andrés Bello-Centro de Investigaciones Diego Barros Arana, 2003.

Stern, Steve. *Remembering Pinochet's Chile: On the Eve of London, 1998*. Durham, NC: Duke University Press, 2004.

Subercaseaux, Bernardo. *Historia de las ideas y de la cultura en Chile, El Centenario y las vanguardias*. Santiago: Editorial Universitaria, 2004.

Valenzuela, Arturoand Pamela Constable. *A Nation of Enemies. Chile under Pinochet*. New York: W. W. Norton, 1991.

Varas, Augusto, Felipe Agüero, and Fernando Bustamante. *Chile, Democracia, Fuerzas Armadas*. Santiago: Facultad Latinoamericana de Ciencias Sociales, 1980.

ALFREDO RIQUELME SEGOVIA

CHILE, CONSTITUTIONS.

Two seminal constitutions provided the legal framework for ruling Chile from 1833 until 1973.

CONSTITUTION OF 1833

Chile's 1833 Constitution, while not the nation's first, was the most durable, lasting until 1925. By initially insisting that only men at least twenty-one years old, literate, and affluent could vote, it sought to empower only the most conservative. Predictably, the requirements for becoming legislators were substantially more demanding than those for mere voters: the indirectly elected senators, who served for nine years, had to be at least thirty-five years old and own more property than the popularly elected deputies, who served for three years and had to be at least thirty years old. The president, who had to be older and wealthier than any of the legislators, enjoyed enormous powers. He appointed men to the judiciary, provincial office, and the cabinet; he could veto laws and could, if needed, declare a state of siege, thereby suspending an already limited number of political freedoms. Initially, the legislature could do little to restrain the president. Every eighteen months it could deny him the right to collect taxes, refuse to pass his budget, and limit the size of the armed forces.

The 1833 Constitution successfully restored order to Chile. As the nation's political system became less monolithic, demands for change became more vocal. As early as 1846, the legislature won the right to interpolate ministers; eleven years later the congress threatened to withhold funds unless

President Manuel Montt changed the composition of his cabinet. The proliferation of parties, all of which wanted a chance to participate in the political system, increased the pace of change. In the 1860s the legislature passed laws granting increased religious freedom to non-Catholics and preventing the president from succeeding himself in office. Within a few years Congress altered the requirements on legislative quorums, liberalized the naturalization process, granted the right of free association, increased the number of deputies, established electoral districts for senators—who previously had been elected at large—limited the president's right to rule by decree or to invoke his extraordinary powers, created a panel to protect civil liberties, and increased the legislature's right to question ministers. Subsequent measures extended suffrage by reducing the voting age and eliminating property requirements. During the 1880s the constitution was altered to end the church's control over cemeteries and the civil registry while making marriage a civil contract.

The 1891 revolution that forced President José Manuel Balmaceda Fernández from power decisively altered the 1833 Constitution. After 1891 a hybrid parliamentary system ruled Chile. As in other parliamentary democracies, the ministry remained in power only as long as it enjoyed the confidence of the legislature. Unfortunately, it became increasingly difficult for anyone to govern. From 1891 to 1924, 121 separate cabinets attempted to rule, and there were more than five hundred ministerial changes. This instability resulted from the fact that widespread bribery, intimidation, and simple fraud permitted candidates to win office without having to appeal to the electorate. The combination of proportional representation and vote fraud led to a proliferation of political parties, which virtually required the formation of coalition governments. Insulated from the electorate's legitimate wrath, congress ignored the country's pressing social problems and the widening economic gap separating the oligarchy from the rest of the country. Finally, the post–World War I collapse of the nitrate markets forced Chile to confront the political debacle. In 1925, following two rebellions and the resignation of Arturo Alessandri Palma, Chileans abandoned the 1833 Constitution in favor of a new charter.

CONSTITUTION OF 1925

Politically, the 1925 Constitution restored the presidential form of government, allowing the people to elect the chief executive directly for a single term of six years. Following the legislature's approval, the cabinet would serve at the president's pleasure, although the Chamber of Deputies could impeach a minister for cause.

Chile remained a highly centralized nation. The president appointed virtually all the members of the judiciary as well as provincial officials (except for city councilmen), initiated the budget, and still retained the power to declare a state of siege. The president also enjoyed the right to authorize certain laws and expenditures by decree.

The 1925 Constitution retained a bicameral legislature in which the term for senators fell from nine to eight years and that for congressmen rose from three to four. Reflecting the experience of the Parliamentary Regime, the legislature's ability to influence the budgetary process was diminished from that enjoyed under the 1833 Constitution. Under the 1925 Constitution, the president could put the budget into effect if Congress failed to act within four months.

While guaranteeing civil liberties and the right of private property, the 1925 Constitution empowered the state to guarantee its citizens' right to work and to provide them with certain minimum benefits for themselves and their families. In addition, the constitution called for the government to stimulate agriculture, mining, and industrialization. To accomplish these and other goals, the central government enjoyed the right to subordinate private property to the public good.

Despite its dual commitment to the preservation of political freedoms as well as the promotion of social and economic change, the 1925 Constitution suffered from certain defects. For one thing, it adopted the complicated d'Hondt system of proportional representation, which effectively denied minority parties their fair share of legislative representation while seating individuals who often had not won a majority of the votes. The new constitution also perpetuated the political parties that had long outlived their rationale. Thus, presidents still had to build fragile coalitions, which resulted in some of the same political instability that characterized the Parliamentary Regime. The constitution, moreover, enfranchised neither women, who finally received the right to vote in 1949, nor illiterates. Because it did not call for reapportioning legislative districts, rural precincts enjoyed more political power than industrial urban centers. Political corruption remained quite common. Landowners often either cajoled or forced their workers to vote for their candidates, and in the cities the parties resorted to buying votes or stuffing the ballot boxes. It was not until the passage of reform laws in 1958 and 1962 that many of these abuses ended.

Still, the 1925 Constitution served Chile well, advancing efforts to protect its citizens' political rights and promoting the cause of social justice. Under its aegis, Chileans implemented sweeping economic changes like agrarian reform while enjoying ample political freedom. Unfortunately, the constitution could not settle the intensely partisan conflicts that arose during the Allende years, nor prevent the 1973 coup. In 1980 the Pinochet government submitted a substitute for the 1925 Constitution to the Chilean public which, following a referendum of questionable value, approved the new document.

See also **Alessandri Palma, Arturo; Balmaceda Fernández, José Manuel; Chile: The Nineteenth Century; Chile: The Twentieth Century.**

BIBLIOGRAPHY

Paul V. Shaw, *The Early Constitutions of Chile, 1810–1833* (1930).

Luis Galdámes, *A History of Chile* (1941).

Julio Heise González, *La Constitución de 1925 y las nuevas tendencias político-sociales* (1951).

Fernando Campos Harriet, *Historia constitucional de Chile* (1956).

Julio Heise González, *150 años de evolución institucional* (1960).

Fredrick B. Pike, *Chile and the United States, 1880–1962* (1963), pp. 182–185.

Federico G. Gil, *The Political System of Chile* (1966).

Karen L. Remmer, *Party Competition in Argentina and Chile* (1984).

WILLIAM F. SATER

CHILE, GEOGRAPHY. With 16,284,741 inhabitants (2007 estimate), Chile stretches from tropical (17 degrees south) to subantarctic (56 degrees south) latitudes. Between the high summits of the Andes and the shores of the Pacific Ocean, Chile occupies a narrow fringe of land with a minimum width of 7 miles and a maximum width of 220 miles. Despite the fact that most of the country's northern segment lies within the tropical belt, the influence of the cold Humboldt Current (Peruvian Current) lowers temperatures considerably, so that most of the country has a temperate climate. Rainfall, however, varies from almost none in the extremely arid and always sunny climate of the north to quite a bit in the humid areas of the south. Toward the central part of the country the humidity is moderate, caused mostly by winter rains. As one progresses southward, the rainy season grows longer and includes a good part of autumn, all of winter, and most of spring. Finally, in the high latitudes, it rains all year long as the humid air masses are carried to the continent by the constantly blowing westerly winds.

The great variability in rainfall means that there is a corresponding variability in vegetation. In the northern segment of the country, desert conditions dominate. Along the coast, the desert climate is mitigated by fogs, but they never render any real precipitation. The desert extends into the interior, with the exception of some piedmont oases that are fed by ground water generating from the snowmelt of numerous volcanoes. Advancing south, shrubs and cacti dominate the landscape as humidity increases. In central Chile, the Mediterranean region of the country, the winter rains and constant snowmelt from the Andes contribute to maintain a vegetation consisting of hardwoods, shrubs, and winter grass. Farther south, with more rainfall, the hardwoods give way to the evergreen and deciduous trees of the temperate rain forests. In the southern extreme of the country, cooler temperatures and perennial rains favor the growth of large coniferous trees that are interspersed with dense rain forest.

Given the extensive desert regions, the high mountains, and the boggy land under the southern rain forests, only 27 percent of the territory is considered habitable. In this area, which stretches between latitudes 27 and 42 degrees south, 90 percent of the national population is concentrated. Even within this ecumene there are considerable variations: Metropolitan Santiago is home to nearly 39 percent of the Chilean population; another 13 percent live in the neighboring region of Valparaíso and Viña del Mar. Eighty-four percent of all

Chileans live in urban centers. This increasing urbanization of the population is probably responsible for the modern demographic character of the country. The population growth rate is .916 percent, fertility is 1.97 children per woman, life expectancy is 77 years, and infant mortality is 8.4 per thousand—the lowest in Latin America.

The national economy depends on three major activities: industry, services, and agriculture; these provide 49 percent, 45 percent, and 6 percent of the gross domestic product, respectively. The highest percentage of employment, at 63 percent, is in the service sector, followed by 23.4 percent in industry, and nearly 14 percent in agriculture. Mining comprises much of the industrial sector and hinges on the production of copper (Chuquicamata, Salvador, Río Blanco, and El Teniente), iron ore (Romeral), and nitrate (mines in the provinces of Tarapacá and Antofagasta). The agricultural activities are concentrated in the temperate Central Valley, where grapes, apples, and wine are major export commodities. With its planted pine and natural forests, Chile has been a leading exporter of timber and paper pulp in Latin America since the 1980s. Fishing is a dominant activity in the north, yielding sardines, anchovies, and jack mackerel, most of which goes into the production of fish meal and fish oil for export; farmed species are also important. These are indicators of the strong export economy that was initiated by General Augusto Pinochet during his rule (1973–1990) and that has continued since.

Traditionally Chile has been divided into six regions: (1) the Norte Grande (Great North), the region of deserts, mining settlements, and coastal towns dedicated mostly to fishing and the shipping of minerals; (2) the Norte Chico (Little North), a transitional region in which greater precipitation allows the growing of fruit but where mining is still a strong supporter of the economy; (3) the Central Region, which encompasses most of mediterranean Chile (the core of the temperate zone), the capital city, and the large conurbations of Valparaíso–Viña del Mar and Concepción–Talcahuano, where most of the industrial establishments are concentrated; (4) La Frontera (the Frontier), a region of predominantly Mapuche ethnic composition, which was incorporated and colonized only after 1881; (5) Los Lagos (the Lakes Region), a territory mostly colonized by Europeans, where dairy products,

sugar beets, and grains are the main commodities and tourism is one of the major assets; and (6) the Great South, which comprises the islands, fjords, channels, and rain forests of the Strait of Magellan, Chilean Patagonia, and Tierra del Fuego, formerly inhabited by Alakaluf and Fuegino Indians. Citizens of Punta Arenas must contend with UVB radiation caused by the Antarctic ozone hole.

The central valley of Chile is the name given to a central depression extending between the Andes and the Coastal Range (Cordillera de la Costa), latitudes 33 to 41.5 degrees south. This tectonic trench has been filled by volcanic, fluvial, and glacial materials carried from the Andes by numerous torrential rivers, among them, the Mapocho, Maipo, Cachapoal, Maule, Ñuble, Bío-bío, and Toltén. Owing to its good soils and adequate irrigation facilities, the Central Valley is the core of the agricultural region, which specializes in grapes, wine, dry fruits, wheat, cattle, and vegetables. In colonial times a string of agricultural settlements—Rancagua, Curicó, Talca, Linares, Los Angeles, Temuco, and Osorno—was established and in 1921 was connected by a railway line that runs between Santiago and Puerto Montt, at the southern extreme of the Central Valley. Originally the region was occupied by large haciendas and was considered the cradle of the landowning aristocracy. In the 1960s large landed estates were expropriated, and most of the land was given to the workers by the agrarian reform implemented by presidents Eduardo Frei and Salvador Allende. The best wines are produced in the Maipo, Cachapoal, and Teno river valleys. In the Bío-bío segment, sandy volcanic soils are excellent for growing pine trees, which support the paper pulp and lumber industries. The southern portion of the Central Valley is predominantly dedicated to dairy farming.

Historically, Chile was the name given by Peruvians to the country between the Aconcagua and Maule rivers settled by friendly Indians. To the south lies Araucania, the territory of the belligerent Mapuches. Just after the conquest of the country, colonization efforts by Spaniards incorporated Cuyo, on the east side of the Andes. The Governancy of Chile also claimed jurisdiction over the Strait of Magellan and Terra Australis (the name given to Tierra del Fuego and the lands thought to expand to the south). After the War of the Pacific

(1879–1884) against Bolivia and Peru, Chile occupied the Bolivian segment of the Pacific coast and the southern Peruvian department of Tarapacá. In the South Pacific, Easter Island became a dependency in 1889, after three decades of French missionary presence on the remote island.

See also **Indigenous Peoples; Volcanoes.**

BIBLIOGRAPHY

Caviedes, César N. *The Politics of Chile: A Sociogeographical Assessment* (1979).

Collier, Simon, and William F. Sater. *A History of Chile, 1808–2002*, 2nd Edition. Cambridge, U.K., and New York: Cambridge University Press, 2004.

Cunill, Pedro. *Geografía de Chile* (1986).

Ffrench–Davis, Ricardo. *Economic Reforms in Chile: From Dictatorship to Democracy.* Ann Arbor: University of Michigan Press, 2002.

Fuentes, Jordi, et al. *Diccionario histórico de Chile,* 8th ed. (1984).

Loveman, Brian. *Chile: The Legacy of Hispanic Capitalism* (1988).

Quezada Vergara, Abraham. *Diccionario de conceptos históricos y geográficos de Chile.* Santiago: RIL Editores, 2004.

Rector, John Lawrence. *The History of Chile.* Westport, CT: Greenwood Press, 2003.

Romero, Hugo. "Fundamentos geográficos del territorio nacional," in Instituto Geográfico Militar, *Geografía de Chile* (1984).

Scarpaci, Joseph L. *Primary Medical Care in Chile* (1988). On the Central Valley, see Eugene E. Martin, *La división de la tierra en Chile Central* (Santiago, 1960).

Tinsman, Heidi. *Partners in Conflict: The Politics of Gender, Sexuality, and Labor in the Chilean Agrarian Reform, 1950–1973.* Durham, NC: Duke University Press, 2002.

Vío, Dionisio. "Geografía de la actividad agropecuaria," in *Geografía de Chile,* vol. 17 (Santiago, 1987).

CÉSAR N. CAVIEDES

CHILE, ORGANIZATIONS

This entry includes the following articles:
CHILEAN NITRATE COMPANY (COSACH)
CORPORATION OF AGRARIAN REFORM (CORA)
DEVELOPMENT CORPORATION (CORFO)

FEDERATION OF CHILEAN STUDENTS (FECH)
FEDERATION OF CHILEAN WORKERS (FOCH)
GRUPO CRUZAT-LARRAÍN
MOVIMIENTO PRO-EMANCIPACIÓN DE LA MUJER CHILENA
SOCIEDAD NACIONAL DE AGRICULTURA (SNA)
SOCIETY OF EQUALITY
VICARIATE OF SOLIDARITY

CHILEAN NITRATE COMPANY (COSACH)

Owned by the government of Chile and private interests, the Chilean Nitrate Company (Compañía de Salitre de Chile, or COSACH) was founded to produce nitrate. In the 1920s, the Guggenheim family interests introduced a new technique to refine nitrate. Although more economical, the natural nitrates, or *salitre,* had difficulty competing with synthetics, particularly those produced by German chemical firms using the Haber-Bayer process. In hopes of lowering production costs and thus the price, the Guggenheims requested that the government of Carlos Ibáñez rescind the export tax on nitrates, but the government needed money and could not grant the concession. As a compromise, the Guggenheims and Ibáñez created COSACH in 1931. Since the new corporation virtually controlled the mining and marketing of natural nitrates, the U.S. and Chilean interests hoped that COSACH could maintain prices. In return for the abolition of the export tax, the Guggenheims gave the Chilean government $80 million over a four-year period. From then on, the Chilean government and the corporation agreed to share equally in COSACH's profits or losses. Consistent with Ibáñez's policy of economic nationalism, Chileans would have to constitute at least 80 percent of COSACH's workforce.

COSACH never fulfilled the expectations of either the government or the Guggenheims. Although the new technology did increase production, it also dramatically cut—by more than 85 percent—the number of people working in the nitrate mines. What was worse, the onset of the Great Depression reduced world demand so that the price of nitrates fell and even the more efficient COSACH could not make a profit. Arturo Alessandri abolished COSACH in 1933, heavily in debt and denounced by nationalists who claimed that Ibáñez had sold out to the Guggenheims. It was replaced in 1934 by COVENSA (Corporation for the Sale of Nitrate and Iodine), a solely government-owned company that produced and marketed nitrates. As of the mid-1990s Chilean nitrates constituted 69 percent of the world's annual production.

See also **Alessandri Palma, Arturo; Ibáñez del Campo, Carlos; Mining: Modern.**

BIBLIOGRAPHY

Frederick M. Nunn, *Chilean Politics: The Honorable Mission of the Armed Forces 1920–1931* (1970), pp. 157–158, 169, 171–172.

Thomas O'Brien, "Rich beyond the Dreams of Avarice: The Guggenheims in Chile," in *Business History Review* 63 (1989):122–159.

Additional Bibliography

Conti, Viviana E. and Marcelo Lagos, eds.. *Una tierra y tres naciones: El litoral salitrero entre 1830 y 1930.* San Salvador de Jujuy, Argentina: Unidad de Investigación en Historia Regional, Facultad de Humanidades y Ciencias Sociales, Universidad Nacional de Jujuy, 2002.

Robles-Ortiz, Claudio. "Agrarian Capitalism in an Export Economy: Chilean Agriculture in the Nitrate Era, 1880–1930." Ph.D. diss., University of California, Davis, 2002.

WILLIAM F. SATER

CORPORATION OF AGRARIAN REFORM (CORA)

Created during the government of Jorge Alessandri (1958–1964), the Corporation of Agrarian Reform (Corporación de la Reforma Agraria—CORA) oversaw the agrarian reform process by buying land and dividing it into parcels for individual or cooperative development, as well as by providing these new agricultural units with technical assistance and funding. CORA, representing a commitment by the state to provide assistance to the rural poor, initially concentrated on converting largely government-owned property into individual plots. The enabling legislation granted CORA the right to pay for expropriated property in a combination of cash and long-term government bonds, which represented a radical departure from earlier laws, as well as the power to take land that was abandoned or inefficiently operated. The government charged CORA with ensuring that landlords respected the rights of agrarian workers. The agrarian reform program also included education programs and family centers. While the educational content emphasized male

dominance, rural women were able to increase their involvement in the public sphere through these projects.

Although CORA was accused of being paternalistic and failing to provide needed technical assistance, during the administration of Eduardo Frei (1964–1970) it still expropriated 18 percent of Chile's irrigated land and 12 percent of its nonirrigated property, converting this property either into individual holdings, cooperatives, or temporary communal farms called *asentamientos*. Despite its failures, which included creating a largely unneeded bureaucracy, CORA did achieve certain reforms until its demise in 1978. More significantly, it constituted the first agency to deal in a realistic fashion with the problem of agrarian reform in Chile.

See also **Agrarian Reform; Agriculture; Alessandri Rodríguez, Jorge.**

BIBLIOGRAPHY

Robert B. Kaufman, *The Politics of Land Reform in Chile, 1950–1970: Public Policy, Political Institutions and Social Change* (1972).

Brian Loveman, *Struggle in the Countryside: Politics and Rural Labor in Chile, 1919–1973* (1976), pp. 233–240, 268–272.

Additional Bibliography

Fontaine Aldunate, Arturo. *La tierra y el poder: Reforma agraria en Chile (1964–1973).* Santiago, Chile: Zig-Zag, 2001.

Tinsman, Heidi. *Partners in Conflict: The Politics of Gender, Sexuality, and Labor in the Chilean Agrarian Reform, 1950–1973.* Durham, NC: Duke University Press, 2002.

WILLIAM F. SATER

DEVELOPMENT CORPORATION (CORFO)

This Chilean development agency was begun as a government entity to supervise the reconstruction of Chile's south following a disastrous 1939 earthquake that inflicted enormous damage and took approximately 30,000 lives. The Pedro Aguirre Cerda regime (1938–1941) subsequently gave Corporación de Fomento (CORFO) the task of developing the Chilean economy, particularly by increasing the country's power supplies and creating basic industries. Funded initially by special taxes, particularly on largely U.S.-owned copper mines, and by foreign loans, this government agency grew. CORFO has also financed private ventures, as well as state enterprises, if they seemed to lead to import substitution and to produce products that might improve the nation's standard of living.

As one of its many achievements, CORFO succeeded in developing hydroelectric projects as well as a state-owned steel mill, and in discovering petroleum in Magallanes. CORFO often acted as a minority stockholder in privately owned corporations. During the Salvador Allende regime (1970–1973), CORFO received additional funds which it used to purchase shares of public corporations, in effect transferring them from the private to the public sector. Then, consistent with its economic philosophy, the Augusto Pinochet administration (1973–1990) sold many of CORFO's assets to private individuals. In the twenty–first century, CORFO has given new attention to market changes, diversification, and expansion of Chi-lean businesses in all regions of the country. It plays an important role in offering credit and resources to small and medium-size enterprises (*pequeñas y medianas empresas.* CORFO not only has provided significant assistance to Chile's industrial sector but also has demonstrated the role of the state in fostering economic development.

See also **Aguirre Cerda, Pedro; Pinochet Ugarte, Augusto.**

BIBLIOGRAPHY

Casaburi, Gabriel G. *Dynamic Agroindustrial Clusters: The Political Economy of Competitive Sectors in Argentina and Chile.* Basingstoke, U.K.: Macmillan, 1999.

Collier, Simon, and William F. Sater. *A History of Chile, 1808–2002.* 2d ed. New York: Cambridge University Press, 2004.

Ellsworth, P. T. *Chile: An Economy in Transition* (1954).

Finer, Herman. *The Chilean Development Corporation* (1947).

Mamalakis, Markos. "An Analysis of the Financial and Investment Activities of the Chilean Development Corporation: 1939–1964." *Journal of Development Studies* 5 (Jan. 1969): 118–137.

Ortega M., Luis, et al., *Corporación de Fomento de la Producción, 50 años de realizaciones, 1939–1989* (1989).

Tiffin, Scott, ed. *Entrepreneurship in Latin America: Perspectives on Education and Innovation.* Westport, CT: Praeger, 2004.

WILLIAM F. SATER

FEDERATION OF CHILEAN STUDENTS (FECH)

Founded in 1906 as the official student organization of the University of Chile, the Federation of Chilean Students (Federación de Estudiantes de Chile—FECH) was the first, largest, and politically most powerful student federation in Chile until 1973. Because the university was the largest institution of higher education in the country and the source of much of Chile's political and professional elite, FECH exercised strong influence on national affairs. Since its inception, FECH has contributed significantly to political change through alliances with unions and political parties, or through massive mobilizations that have affected policy at the national or university levels. In 1931, for example, it contributed to the demise of General Carlos Ibáñez Del Campo. In 1957 FECH again challenged Ibáñez during his second administration. During the 1960s and early 1970s, it became part and parcel of political struggles at the national level and mobilized the student population to an unprecedented degree. During this period, FECH secured a 25 percent representation in rectorship elections, thus achieving the university reform ideal of *cogobierno* (co-government). In 1973, FECH was banned and its leaders driven underground. In conjunction with the resurrection of other democratic forces in the mid-1980s, FECH once again entered the political fray, but this time in a weakened and less ideological position, reflecting the overall decline of the university. In 1993 it closed down, but was restarted by Rodrigo Roco in 1995. In March 2006 FECH once again engaged in activism by supporting the protests of high school students, who demanded education reforms. This new student movement, the largest in thirty years, peaked on 30 March with 790,000 students participating in a strike. In June the government announced policies that largely met student demands.

See also **Universities: The Modern Era.**

BIBLIOGRAPHY

Bonilla, Frank, and Myron Glazer. *Student Politics in Chile* (1970).

Bravo Lira, Bernardino. *La universidad en la historia de Chile, 1622–1992.* Santiago: Pehuén, Universidad Santo Tomás, 1992.

Cifuentes Seves, Luis, ed. *La reforma universitaria en Chile (1967–1973)*. Santiago: Editorial Universidad de Santiago, 1997.

Huneeus Madge, Carlos. *La reforma en la Universidad de Chile* (1973).

Jaksić, Iván, and Sonia Nazario, "Chile," in *Student Political Activism: An International Reference Handbook*, edited by Philip G. Altbach (1989).

Levy, Daniel C. *Higher Education and the State in Latin America: Private Challenges to Public Dominance* (1986).

IVÁN JAKSIĆ

FEDERATION OF CHILEAN WORKERS (FOCH)

A Chilean labor union created in 1909, the Federation of Chilean Workers (Federación Obrera de Chile—FOCH) was originally a mutual-aid organization of railroad workers who contributed small sums monthly to provide members with medical assistance. Named FOCH in 1917, it was reorganized in 1919 into a confederation of skilled and unskilled workers who called for unions to operate the factories and who opposed capitalism. FOCH initially included socialists, anarchists, nonpolitical Social Democrats, and even bourgeois Radicals as well as Communists. Eventually the Communist members purged the non-Communists from positions of leadership within the federation. By the mid-1920s, FOCH was identifying itself as part of the Communist Party and tending to recruit its members from among the nitrate and coal miners, with whom the Communists had made the most inroads. At its height, FOCH's membership may have numbered as many as 150,000. The federation eventually collapsed during the late 1920s as the result of government oppression, particularly during the Ibáñez period (1927–1931), and declining economic conditions in FOCH's most important constituencies, the nitrate mines.

See also **Labor Movements.**

BIBLIOGRAPHY

Alan Angell, *Politics and the Labour Movement in Chile* (1972), pp. 32–38.

Peter De Shazo, *Urban Workers and Labor Unions in Chile, 1902–1927* (1983).

Additional Bibliography

Garcés, Mario, and Pedro Milos. *FOCH, CTCH, CUT: Las centrales unitarias en la historia del sindicalismo* *chileno*. Santiago: Educación y Comunicaciones Ltda., 1988.

Rojas Flores, Jorge. *La Dictadura de Ibáñez y los sindicatos (1927–1931)*. Santiago: Dirección de Bibliotecas, Archivos y Museos, Centro de Investigaciones Diego Barros Arana, 1993.

WILLIAM F. SATER

GRUPO CRUZAT-LARRAÍN

The Grupo Cruzat-Larraín was one of the largest of the *grupos económicos* (economic conglomerates) that came to dominate the Chilean financial system under the neoliberal economic policies implemented in the mid-1970s. Led by financiers Manuel Cruzat Infante and Fernando Larraín Peña, the group purchased controlling interests in virtually every sector of the Chilean economy during the privatization of public enterprises in the early years of the Pinochet regime. Liberalization of the domestic financial markets, an absence of government regulation, and easy access to international credit allowed for their spectacular growth. Their growth was also facilitated by close relations with key economic policymakers, some of whom periodically took positions with the groups. At its peak the Grupo Cruzat-Larraín had a virtual monopoly in petroleum distribution and owned at least 109 companies. The free-market policies of the Chicago Boys seemed to encourage this extreme economic concentration, further exacerbating the uneven distribution of wealth. The economic crisis of 1981–1982 resulted in the bankruptcy and liquidation of both the Grupo Cruzat-Larraín and the Grupo Vial, and led to a reform of the banking system. Popular discontent and street protests stemming from this economic crisis challenged the survival of the Pinochet regime.

See also **Pinochet Ugarte, Augusto.**

BIBLIOGRAPHY

Fernando Dahse, *El mapa de la extrema riqueza* (1979).

Lois Hecht Oppenheim, *Politics in Chile: Democracy, Authoritarianism, and the Search for Development* (1993).

David E. Hojman, *Chile: The Political Economy of Development and Democracy in the 1990s* (1993).

Additional Bibliography

Fuentes E., Luis Arturo. *Grandes grupos económicos en Chile y los modelos de propiedad en otros países*. Santiago: Dolmen Ediciones, 1997.

Mönckeberg, María Olivia. *El saqueo de los grupos económicos al Estado chileno*. Santiago de Chile: Ediciones B Grupo Zeta, 2001.

J. DAVID DRESSING

MOVIMIENTO PRO-EMANCIPACIÓN DE LA MUJER CHILENA

Founded in 1935 by members of the Asociación de Mujeres Universitarias under the leadership of the lawyer Elena Caffarena, MEMCH advocated full legal rights and equal work and pay opportunities for women and pursued a broad-based agenda of social concerns as it attacked poverty, prostitution, and the high rate of infant mortality. The association published the magazine *La Mujer Nueva*. MEMCH's involvement in women's health issues led it to support the use of contraceptives and, within limits, access to abortion. Particularly during the years of the Popular Front, MEMCH organized women in many provinces into local committees and laid the groundwork for the Federación Chilena de Instituciones Femeninas (FECHIF). MEMCH's organizational tactics, strategies, and membership base later served as the sustaining force of FECHIF. MEMCH's ten-year drive to circulate petitions and stage street demonstrations was instrumental in finally gaining the right for women to vote in 1949. In addition to pursuing women's rights, MEMCH supported the families of strikers and victims of political oppression. Though nonpartisan, MEMCH had a leftist orientation that, along with internal tensions, led to its marginalization in the cold war climate of the late 1940s and its dissolution in 1953.

Named for the original MEMCH, MEMCH83 was founded in 1983 as an umbrella group to coordinate the activities of Chilean feminist and nonfeminist women's groups working to restore democracy to the nation. Though at first women's issues were not addressed, MEMCH83's first large-scale demonstration, on November 28, 1983, not only opposed the Pinochet government but called for peace and women's rights. In 1985 MEMCH reestablished itself as a nongovernmental organization. Beginning in 1987 partisan splits, sectarian conflict, and shifting political alliances resulted in changes in the groups claiming or disclaiming affiliation with MEMCH83. Since the transition to democracy in Chile in 1988 to the present day, MEMCH has joined a broad coalition of NGOs in Chile that continue to advocate for women's equality, sexual and reproductive rights, and sustainable development.

See also **Feminism and Feminist Organizations.**

BIBLIOGRAPHY

Antezana-Pernet, Corinne. "Peace in the World and Democracy at Home: The Chilean Women's Movement in the 1940s," in *Latin America in the 1940s,* edited by David Rock (1994).

Baldez, Lisa. *Why Women Protest: Women's Movements in Chile*. Cambridge, U.K., and New York: Cambridge University Press, 2002.

Churchryk, Patricia M. "Feminist Anti-Authoritarian Politics: The Role of Women's Organizations in the Chilean Transition to Democracy," in *The Women's Movement in Latin America,* edited by Jane S. Jaquette (1989).

Gaviola, Edda, Eliana Largo, and Sandra Palestro. *Una historia necesaria: Mujeres en Chile, 1973–1990*. Chile: Akí and Aora, 1994.

Godoy, Lorena, et al., eds. *Disciplina y desacato: Construcción de identidad en Chile, siglos XIX y XX*. Santiago: SUR, CEDEM, 1995.

Poblete, Olga. *Una Mujer, Elena Caffarena*. Santiago: Ediciones la Morada/Editorial Cuarto Propio, 1993.

Rock, David, ed. *Latin America in the 1940's: War and Postwar Transitions*. Berkeley: University of California Press, 1994.

Rosemblatt, Karin Alejandra. *Gendered Compromises: Political Cultures and the State in Chile, 1920–1950*. Chapel Hill: University of North Carolina Press, 2000.

CORINNE ANTEZANA-PERNET
FRANCESCA MILLER

SOCIEDAD NACIONAL DE AGRICULTURA (SNA)

The Sociedad Nacional de Agricultura (SNA), founded in 1869, is a voluntary association of landowners in Chile. Successor to the Sociedad Chilena de Agricultura, established in 1838, the SNA has been dominated by the large landowners of the Central Valley, many of them also members of the national social and political elites. During the nineteenth century its primary mission was to promote the modernization of agricultural practices. By 1900 the organization had become more explicitly political in response to the creation of competing economic interests. With the rise of working-class organizations and militancy following World War I, the SNA became increasingly identified with the defense of landowners on social issues, including food price controls, unionization of agricultural workers, and, by the 1930s, land reform. To meet these challenges, the SNA reached beyond its elite core by recruiting smaller landowners and founding the Confederación de la Producción y del Comercio (CPC), a multi-sectoral business pressure group, in 1934.

With the intensification of political challenges in the 1960s, the SNA became the most visible symbol of elite resistance to reform, but its efforts could not forestall the agrarian reform legislation that began dismantling the traditional rural estate in 1967. Defeated in the legislative arena, the SNA was instrumental in forging the *gremio* (guild) movement that began in the late 1960s and mushroomed after the 1970 election of Salvador Allende. A broad-based, militant coalition of large entrepreneurial associations with their smaller counterparts, the *gremio* movement used "bosses' strikes" and street demonstrations to weaken the Allende government in preparation for its overthrow.

During the Pinochet dictatorship (1973–1990) large landowners recovered most of the land they had lost to agrarian reform and, backed by the military regime, regained their traditional control over the rural population. Despite internal dissension over the Chicago Boys' neoliberal economic project, which cut some agricultural subsidies, the SNA regained prestige and influence. Since the return of elected government in 1990, large landowners have benefited from over-representation in congress, and the dynamic, socially retrograde, export-oriented agricultural economy that emerged during the dictatorship has continued to flourish. After nearly 140 years, the SNA remains one of Chile's most powerful economic interest associations.

See also **Agrarian Reform; Chicago Boys.**

BIBLIOGRAPHY

Carrière, Jean. *Landowners and Politics in Chile: A Study of the Sociedad Nacional de Agricultura, 1932–1970.* Amsterdam: Centrum voor Studie en Documentatie van Latijns-Amerika, 1981.

Izquierdo Fernández, Gonzalo. *Un estudio de las ideologías chilenas: La Sociedad de Agricultura en el siglo XIX.* Santiago: Universidad de Chile, 1968.

Wright, Thomas C. *Landowners and Reform in Chile: The Sociedad Nacional de Agricultura, 1919–1940.* Urbana: University of Illinois Press, 1982.

THOMAS C. WRIGHT

SOCIETY OF EQUALITY

The Society of Equality was a radical political organization formed in Chile on 14 April 1850 by Santiago Arcos (1818–1874), Francisco Bilbao (1823–1865), and others. Originally intended as an organization for educating artisans (and for making them aware of their political rights), the Sociedad quickly became associated with the growing opposition to the presidential candidacy of Manuel Montt (1809–1880). It had a membership of several hundred, including many artisans, though it cannot be regarded as a genuinely spontaneous artisan movement. Its meetings sometimes attracted more than a thousand participants. Enrolling members were asked to accept the three principles of "popular sovereignty," "the sovereignty of reason," and "love and universal fraternity." *Escuelas populares* (people's schools) organized by the Sociedad held classes in Spanish, English, music, mathematics, history, and drafting.

Highly unusual in the quiet Santiago of the period, the marches and processions of the *igualitarios* dismayed the authorities. On 19 August 1850 the Sociedad's premises were assaulted by a group probably hired by the police. In November 1850 the imposition of a state of siege brought the dissolution of the Sociedad, without popular protest. Politically, the effect of the Sociedad's agitation caused the ruling Conservative Party to accept the controversial candidacy of Montt, the consequence of which was two civil wars (1851, 1859). Many of the ideas of the Society of Equality continued in the Radical Party, which formed in 1863. The Radical Party remained active through the twentieth century, but gradually lost popularity. In 1994 it merged with another party to form the Social Democrat Radical Party.

See also **Arcos, Santiago; Bilbao Barquín, Francisco.**

BIBLIOGRAPHY

Collier, Simon. *Chile: The Making of a Republic, 1830–1865: Politics and Ideas.* New York: Cambridge University Press, 2003.

Gazmuri, Cristián. *El "48" Chileno: Igualitarios, reformistas, radicales, masones y bomberos* (1992).

SIMON COLLIER

VICARIATE OF SOLIDARITY

The Vicariate of Solidarity (Vicaría de la Solidaridad) was the principal human rights organization in Chile during the military government of General Augusto Pinochet (1973–1990). Established by the Catholic Church in January 1976, the vicariate took over the activities of the ecumenical Committee of Cooperation for Peace, which had been formed after the 11 September 1973 coup that overturned the Socialist government of Salvador Allende. The brutality of the new regime had caused Catholic, Protestant, and Jewish leaders to establish this humanitarian relief agency for the victims and their families. When the committee was closed in 1975, due in part to government pressure, Cardinal Raúl Silva Henríquez established the Vicariate of Solidarity as part of the archdiocese of Santiago.

The vicariate focused on providing legal, medical, and humanitarian assistance to Chileans throughout the country. Its legal department became renowned for its creativity in using existing national and international law to defend political prisoners, secure the release of those illegally detained, and investigate assassinations, torture, and disappearances. It also provided technical assistance to human rights organizations in other countries.

In addition to its legal work, the vicariate established medical services, communal kitchens, consumer and producer cooperatives, and basic educational and job training programs, and provided technical assistance and credit, particularly to poor communities. In one year, its facilities provided 5 million meals for children. By the 1980s, public opinion surveys indicated that the vicariate was the most trusted institution in Chile. Also, the pluralism of the organization helped create new relationships between the Left and Christian Democrats, who have worked together since the democratic transition.

With the return of elected civilian government in March 1990, the vicariate began scaling down its human rights activities on the grounds that civic and other organizations could assume such tasks. The vicariate provided the majority of the documents used by the Commission of Truth and Reconciliation in the latter's final report in 1991. The Vicariate of Solidarity closed in December 1992.

See also **Allende Gossens, Salvador; Chile, Truth Commissions; Human Rights; Pinochet Ugarte, Augusto; Silva Henríquez, Raúl.**

BIBLIOGRAPHY

Juan Ignacio Gutiérrez Fuente, *Chile: La Vicaría de la Solidaridad* (Madrid, 1986).

Hannah W. Stewart-Gambino, *The Church and Politics in the Chilean Countryside* (1992).

Additional Bibliography

Aranda, Gilberto C. *Vicaría de la Solidaridad: Una experiencia sin fronteras.* Santiago, Chile: CESOC, 2004.

Lowden, Pamela. *Moral Opposition to Authoritarian Rule in Chile, 1973–90.* New York: St. Martin's Press, 1996.

                                    MARGARET E. CRAHAN

CHILE, PARLIAMENTARY REGIME.

Chile's Parliamentary Regime, the political system under which Chile was ruled from 1891 to 1925. The 1891 Revolution effectively destroyed the presidential form of government that had been in effect in Chile since 1833. Henceforth, the chief executive acted as a figurehead while the Congress, under the leadership of the minister of the interior, the Chilean equivalent of a prime minister, dictated national policy.

While not intrinsically defective, Chile's parliamentary system suffered significant flaws. In order to ensure honest elections, the Law of Municipalities (1891) shifted control of the electoral system from the central government to the provinces. This transfer of power, however, merely permitted urban bosses and rural landowners to control the political process. Consequently, these individuals selected their own candidates, ensuring their electoral triumph through bribery, intimidation, or fraud. Since the candidates no longer had to court voters but merely the power brokers, they could safely ignore the needs of the nation. Dishonest elections also preserved parties that possessed no distinctive ideologies or rationales for existing, other than the egos of their own members.

Chile's extremely limited electorate divided their votes between an increasing number of parties. One of the results of the dishonest electoral system was that no one party could achieve a parliamentary majority. Hence, coalition politics became the standard. Regrettably, the creation of parliamentary majorities became increasingly complicated: politicians demanded high prices in terms of patronage for their cooperation, and even members of the same party would sometimes not cooperate with each other. The number of complete cabinet changes accelerated from eight during the government of Jorge Montt (1891–1896) to seventeen under Juan Luis Sanfuentes (1915–1920). During the period of 1891–1920, more than eighty cabinets attempted to rule the nation. Since few ministries retained power long enough to formulate and implement a coherent program, the nation foundered.

Meanwhile, Chile's problems in this period desperately needed attention. The process of urbanization was crowding the nation's poor into filthy and unhealthy housing, where they perished at a higher rate than in India. Working conditions were equally perilous: men and women were injured or even died laboring in the nation's ill-ventilated factories and *salitreras*. The fortunes of Chile's domestic economy ebbed and flowed according to the price of nitrates. When revenues were high, the government prospered, but when they declined the nation retrenched. In bad times, the state made up its deficits by borrowing or selling off nitrate lands to private interests.

For decades, Chile's working class endured poor pay, wretched living and working conditions, and an inflation that eroded their purchasing power. Eventually, when they demanded change, the political elites, depending upon their beliefs, either could or would not respond. The post–Word War I collapse of the nitrate economy so distorted Chile's economy in conjunction with this inept political system that it forced radical change. In 1925 the nation ratified a new constitution which restored a presidential system to Chile and guaranteed the need of the state to intervene in order to address the nation's social and economic needs.

See also **Chile: The Nineteenth Century; Montt Álvarez, Jorge; Sanfuentes Andonaegui, Juan Luis.**

BIBLIOGRAPHY

Karen L. Remmer, "The Timing, Pace and Sequence of Political Change in Chile, 1891–1925," in *Hispanic American Historical Review* 57, 2 (1977): 205–230, and *Party Competition in Argentina and Chile* (1984), pp. 23–24, 85–86.

Additional Bibliography

Stuven, Ana María. *La seducción de un orden: Las elites y la construcción de Chile en las polémicas culturales y políticas del siglo XIX*. Santiago, Chile: Ediciones Universidad Católica de Chile, 2000.

Villablanca Z., Hernán. *Estructuración sociopolítica y desarrollo capitalista en Chile, 1820–1900*. Santiago, Chile: Bravo y Allende Editores, 1999.

WILLIAM F. SATER

CHILE, POLITICAL PARTIES

This entry includes the following articles:

CHRISTIAN DEMOCRATIC PARTY (PDC)
CHRISTIAN LEFT
COMMUNIST PARTY
CONCENTRACIÓN NACIONAL
CONSERVATIVE PARTY
DEMOCRATIC PARTY
FEMININE PARTY
LIBERAL-CONSERVATIVE FUSION (LIBERAL-CONSERVADORA)
LIBERAL PARTY
MOVEMENT OF NATIONAL UNITY (MUN)
MOVEMENT OF THE REVOLUTIONARY LEFT (MIR)
NATIONAL PARTY
NATIONAL PHALANX
POPULAR ACTION FRONT
POPULAR ACTION UNITARY MOVEMENT (MAPU)
POPULAR FRONT
POPULAR UNITY
RADICAL PARTY
SOCIALIST PARTY

CHRISTIAN DEMOCRATIC PARTY (PDC)

The Chilean Christian Democratic Party (Partido Demócrata Cristiano; PDC) traces its roots to a movement led by Catholic youth groups associated with the Conservative Party who had become increasingly alienated by what they perceived as their party's lack of social consciousness. Basing their ideas on the principles outlined in the papal encyclicals *Rerum Novarum* (1891) and *Quadragesimo Anno* (1931), which set down the foundations for Christian humanism, these students formed the Falange Nacional (National Falangist Party) and formally broke from the Conservative Party in 1938. The Falangists merged with the Social Christian Conservative Party to formally found the Christian Democratic Party on 28 July 1957. The PDC's ideology advocates a so-called third way between unbridled capitalism and socialism. It professes a conservative, Catholic-based doctrine on social issues such as divorce, abortion, and homosexuality, yet supports limited state intervention in the economy and progressive policies on poverty and income distribution.

The PDC has been one of the dominant political parties in Chile since the mid-1950s. Its meteoric rise to power culminated in the election of the first PDC president, Eduardo Frei Montalva, in 1964. Frei initiated a program of agrarian reform, public works, and social reform. Frei's personal popularity failed to translate into support for PDC candidate Radomiro Tomic in the 1970 elections, when Socialist Salvador Allende won the presidency with a plurality of the vote, though lacking a majority in congress. The polarization, instability, and deadlock that followed prompted military intervention, inaugurating the brutal seventeen-year military regime of Augusto Pinochet, who seized power in a military coup on 11 September 1973. Though initially attempting to work out a peaceful solution to the conflicts of the 1970s, ultimately the PDC's leadership backed military intervention, never expecting the military to stay in power so long, or to engage in such extensive human rights abuses.

Despite its initial support for military intervention, the PDC rather quickly began to oppose military rule. The party was legally proscribed in 1977, but remained active in opposition, playing a crucial role in the democratic transition. In the period leading up to the return to democracy in 1990, the PDC reemerged as one of Chile's most important parties, playing a key role in building the Concertación de Partidos por el No (Coalition of Parties for the No) to campaign against Pinochet's bid to remain in power in a 1988 plebiscite. After victory in the plebiscite, the Concertación evolved into the Coalition of Parties for Democracy (Concertación de Partidos por la Democracia), an alliance of parties that also included the Socialist Party, the Party for Democracy, and a few smaller parties that has ruled Chile since the return of democratic rule. Two Christian Democrats served consecutive terms as presidents in the immediate post-authoritarian period (Patricio Aylwin from 1990 to 1994, and Frei Montalva's son, Eduardo Frei Ruiz-Tagle, from 1994 to 2000). Though Socialists have ruled Chile since 2000 (Ricardo Lagos from 2000 to 2006 and Michele Bachelet, who assumed power in 2006), the Christian Democrats have retained important

leadership roles in the coalition, serving as ministers in the Concertación's multiparty cabinets.

The party is as of 2007 led by Soledad Alvear, who was defeated by Michele Bachelet in the internal Concertación primary to choose the alliance's candidate for the 2005 presidential elections. In legislative terms, at the return to democracy in 1990 the PDC had the largest contingent in the Chamber of Deputies (38 of 120 members). Though still one of Chile's most important parties, its fortunes waned in the early twenty-first century and for the 2006–2010 legislature it held only 21 of 120 seats.

See also **Frei Montalva, Eduardo; Frei Ruiz-Tagle, Eduardo; Tomic, Radomiro.**

BIBLIOGRAPHY

Angell, Alan. "Party Change in Comparative Perspective." *Revista de Ciencia Política* 23, no. 2 (2003): 88–108.

Castillo Infante, Fernando. *La Flecha Roja.* Santiago: Editorial Francisco de Aguirre, 1997.

Fleet, Michael. *The Rise and Fall of Chilean Christian Democracy.* Princeton, NJ: Princeton University Press, 1985.

Mainwaring, Scott, and Timothy R. Scully, eds. *Christian Democracy in Latin America: Electoral Competition and Regime Conflicts.* Stanford, CA: Stanford University Press, 2003.

Petras, James F. *Chilean Christian Democracy: Politics and Social Forces.* Berkeley: Institute of International Studies, University of California, Berkeley, 1967.

Scully, Timothy. *Rethinking the Center: Party Politics in Nineteenth- and Twentieth-Century Chile.* Stanford, CA: Stanford University Press, 1992.

Walker, Ignacio. *El futuro de la democracia cristiana.* Santiago, Chile: Ediciones B., 1999.

PETER M. SIAVELIS

CHRISTIAN LEFT

A breakaway faction of Chile's Christian Democratic Party (PDC), the Christian Left was active during the regime of Salvador Allende (1970–1973). Comprised of the more leftist members of the PDC and under the leadership of Senator Renán Fuentealba, these elements demanded that Eduardo Frei and his followers support Allende's economic policies. Hoping to remain politically potent, many of the PDC initially supported many of the Christian Left's positions. In a 1971 Christian Democratic Party meeting, the leaders of what became the Christian Left submitted a proposal suggesting that the PDC cease cooperating with the conservative National Party (PN). When their motion failed, those who believed it not inconsistent for Christians to support Allende's struggle to bring socialism to Chile broke with the PDC, forming the Christian Left. While the new party, which included six former PDC deputies, attracted some of the members of the United Movement of Popular Action, or MAPU (another PDC splinter group), it failed to bolster the Allende coalition. As just one of many leftist parties, the Izquierda Cristiana won only 1.1 percent of the vote in the 1973 congressional elections, indicating its lack of popular support. Banned by the Pinochet government, it continued to operate clandestinely, joining the Movimiento Democrático Popular to try to restore democracy in Chile.

See also **Chile, Political Parties: Christian Democratic Party (PDC).**

BIBLIOGRAPHY

Paul E. Sigmund, *The Overthrow of Allende and the Politics of Chile, 1964–1976* (1977), p. 135.

Carmelo Furci, *The Chilean Communist Party and the Road to Socialism* (1984).

Additional Bibliography

Corvalán, Luis. *El gobierno de Salvador Allende.* Santiago: LOM Ediciones, 2003.

Lomnitz, Larissa Adler de and Ana Melnick. *Chile's Political Culture and Parties: An Anthropological Explanation.* Notre Dame, IN: University of Notre Dame Press, 2000.

WILLIAM F. SATER

COMMUNIST PARTY

The Communist Party of Chile (Partido Comunista) traces its origins to the left wing of the Democratic Party and its successor, the Partido Obrero Socialista (POS). In 1922, after six years of its independent existence, Luis Emilio Recabarren led the POS into the Communist International. Persecuted by the Carlos Ibáñez government, it also suffered from internal schisms. Politically isolated even after Ibáñez's 1931 overthrow, it agreed to cooperate with other parties, largely by order of the Communist International, which commanded its members to work with progressive elements to stop the spread of fascism. Although the Communist Party proved instrumental in the creation and triumph of the Popular Front (Frente Popular), it would not accept any ministerial posts in that government, apparently not wishing to suffer a possible loss of prestige if the Front should fail.

The Soviet Union's 1939 nonaggression pact with Germany and struggle for control of the unions led the Communists to quit the Front until the Nazi invasion of Russia forced a reconciliation between the Communists and their old allies. The Communists' support of the Radical candidate Gabriel González Videla led to their participation in his government. Apparently fearing that the Communists were becoming too powerful, and encouraged by the British and Americans, González Videla expelled the party from his cabinet. When the Communists retaliated by launching a series of deadly strikes, González Videla banned the party and struck its members from the voting rolls. As political repression slowly eased, the party reappeared under the new name of the Democratic Party, and much of its literature became available. Although it still remained clandestine, the Communist Party announced in 1956 at its tenth congress that it would use peaceful means to achieve its goals of ending U.S. imperialism; promoting state ownership of all industries, land, and credit institutions; and empowering the working class. Following the Ibáñez government's 1958 rescinding of the Law for the Defense of Democracy, which had outlawed them, the Communists returned to political life.

The Communists helped create Popular Action Front (FRAP), which supported Salvador Allende's presidential aspirations in 1958 and 1964. The party also played a significant role in the 1970 Popular Unity (Unidad Popular) government, a coalition of the Communist, Socialist, and Radical Parties that again nominated Allende. Unlike the Socialists, the Communists were willing to cooperate with bourgeois political parties or individuals regardless of their class. These differences between parties became more pronounced during Allende's regime, when the Communists urged the government to consolidate its gains rather than press for more drastic change. With the adoption of this position, the party appeared less hostile to the interests of small property owners and the middle class. Conversely, the Socialists urged Allende to become more radical.

Well-disciplined, cohesive, and possessed of a history of operating successfully underground, the Communists survived the 1973 Pinochet coup. Within a relatively short period, the party was meeting clandestinely and publishing its journals. In 1980, after studying Chile's political situation, the party announced that it would use force to overthrow the Pinochet government. Although it denied any involvement, the Communists organized the Frente Patriótico Manuel Rodríguez (FPMR), described as the armed vanguard of the resistance movement. This group's most audacious act was an attempted assassination of General Pinochet. While initially refusing to cooperate with other antigovernment forces, the Communists subsequently did go along with the measures that ultimately led to the 1989 plebiscite which brought Patricio Aylwin to power. Although the Communists failed to elect anyone to the Congress, the party remains viable, and the FPMR continues to use violent means to remind people of its existence. In the twenty-first century the Communist Party has supported the election of two Socialist presidents, Richard Lagos (2000-2006) and Michelle Bachelet, elected in 2006.

See also **Allende Gossens, Salvador; Bachelet, Michelle; Gonzálcz Videla, Gabriel; Lagos, Ricardo; Pinochet Ugarte, Augusto.**

BIBLIOGRAPHY

Ernest Halperin, *Nationalism and Communism in Chile* (1965).

Hernán Ramírez Necochea, *Origen y formación del Partido Comunista de Chile* (1965).

Federico G. Gil, *The Political System of Chile* (1966), pp. 277–283.

Carmelo Furci, *The Chilean Communist Party and the Road to Socialism* (1984).

Julio Faúndez, *Marxism and Democracy in Chile* (1988), pp. 94–95, 168–169, 174–175, 195–196, 201–202.

Additional Bibliography

Ibáñez Santa María, Adolfo. *Abrazado por la revolución: Ideología y totalitarismo en Chile 1960–1973*. Santiago: Editorial Biblioteca Americana, 2004.

Scully, Timothy. *Rethinking the Center: Party Politics in Nineteenth- and Twentieth-century Chile*. Stanford, CA: Stanford University Press, 1992.

WILLIAM F. SATER

CONCENTRACIÓN NACIONAL

The Concentración Nacional was a post–World War II Chilean political alliance. Following his 1946 election, Gabriel González Videla initially created a government that included members of the Communist Party. In 1947, however, he reshuffled his cabinet, this time excluding the Communists, who he felt had become too popular. Infuriated, the Communists launched a series of strikes, some of which became violent. Claiming that the Communists were threatening Chile's political stability, González Videla created a new cabinet, the Concentración Nacional, which consisted of the Radical, Conservative, Democratic, and Liberal parties. In 1948 this coalition cabinet passed a measure called the Law for the Permanent Defense of Democracy, which outlawed the Communist Party. The Concentración Nacional lasted until 1950, when a split over labor and prices led to the cabinet's resignation.

See also **González Videla, Gabriel.**

BIBLIOGRAPHY

César Caviedes L., *The Politics of Chile: A Sociogeographical Assessment* (1979), pp. 184–185.

Julio Faúndez, *Marxism and Democracy in Chile* (1988), p. 75.

Additional Bibliography

Moulian, Tomás. *Fracturas de Pedro Aguirre Cerda a Salvador Allende (1938–1973)*. Santiago: LOM Ediciones, 2006.

Scully, Timothy. *Rethinking the Center: Party Politics in Nineteenth- and Twentieth-century Chile*. Stanford, CA: Stanford University Press, 1992.

WILLIAM F. SATER

CONSERVATIVE PARTY

Other than possessing a commitment to maintaining social order and preserving property rights, the original Conservative Party (Partido Conservador) did not hold its first convention until 1878. Lacking an ideology for their first forty years of existence did not seem to trouble the Conservatives. Emerging victorious from the Battle of Lircay (1830), the Conservatives happily turned power over to Diego Portales, who created a strong centralized government wielding enough power to keep order. Once the Conservatives lost control of the Moneda (government house), they tried to reduce the power of the central government and enhance political liberties. Paradoxically, they still insisted that the state support the Catholic Church's desire to deny Protestants religious freedom. Even after losing the presidency, the Conservatives continued to hold ministerial posts. In the 1870s, however, the Conservatives broke with the other parties over the issue of the role of the Roman Catholic Church and did not participate in government until after the 1891 revolution.

Although numerically small, the Conservative Party remained highly disciplined. It managed to preserve its share of the seats in the legislature largely because most of its members were large landowners who cynically forced their *inquilinos* (tenant farmers) to vote for Conservative candidates. The so-called reforms produced by the 1891 revolution enhanced the Conservatives' power base by permitting local governments, not the Moneda, to supervise the electoral process. This power, plus the fact that rural communities were overrepresented in the legislature, breathed new life into the Conservative cause.

At its 1901 party convention some Conservatives, under the influence of Pope Leo XIII's 1891 encyclical *Rerum Novarum*, began to advocate social and economic reforms: the construction of housing for the poor, improvement of working conditions, and increased educational opportunities. Social and economic reform continued to be one of the party's concerns.

The party managed to survive, but when it turned to the right, in the early 1930s, it lost several of its brightest members, some of whom bolted to form what became the Christian Democratic Party (PDC). After 1945, those who remained within the Conservative Party split into two groups: the Social Christian wing and the traditionalists. Later the Social Christians would join the PDC. The party managed to retain wide support, often outpolling the Left. Changes in the election process and a refusal of the *inquilinos* to accept passively their patrons' control led to a collapse of the Conservative Party's base of support. In 1965, for example, the Conservatives won only 5 percent of the vote in the congressional elections, losing all its places in the Senate and retaining only three places in the lower house. In order to unify the right wing and not dissipate their power, the Conservatives, in league with the Liberals, formed the National Party in 1966.

The Conservative Party retains its faith in the teachings of the Roman Catholic Church. While it does not question democracy, it wishes to reduce the power of the central government. Economically, it favors the free-enterprise system, but admits that private property rights can be subordinated to the needs of society. It remains an elitist, upper-class party, whose members are large provincial property owners. Needless to say, these elements resisted attempts at agrarian reform, which they often denounced as a U.S. plot.

The National Party continued its opposition to the Allende administration, working in league with the Christian Democrats in crucial by-elections and in supporting various antigovernment labor actions. The Nationals fielded candidates in the 1989 congressional elections but elected none.

See also **Agrarian Reform; Allende Gossens, Salvador; Leo XIII, Pope; Portales Palazuelos, Diego José Pedro Víctor.**

BIBLIOGRAPHY

Fredrick B. Pike, *Chile and the United States, 1880–1962* (1963), pp. 250–256.

Federico G. Gil, *The Political System of Chile* (1966), pp. 245–252.

Germán Urzúa Valenzuela, *Los partidos políticos chilenos* (1968), pp. 102–134.

Ben Burnett, *Political Groups in Chile: The Dialogue Between Order and Change* (1970), pp. 161–170, 178–181.

Karen L. Remmer, *Party Competition in Argentina and Chile* (1984), pp. 12–15, 72–74, 76–80, 117–120.

Additional Bibliography

Pereira L., Teresa. *El Partido Conservador, 1930–1965: Ideas, figuras y actitudes.* Fundación Mario Góngora, 1994.

Scully, Timothy. *Rethinking the Center: Party Politics in Nineteenth- and Twentieth-century Chile.* Stanford, CA: Stanford University Press, 1992.

WILLIAM F. SATER

DEMOCRATIC PARTY

The Democratic Party (Partido Demócrata) was the first Chilean political party dedicated to advancing the cause of the workers. Created in 1887 by an offshoot of the Radical Party, the Democrats held their first convention two years later. This party was the first in Chile seeking to protect the economic and political interests of the lower classes, calling for honest elections, laws to provide decent housing and improved working conditions, a return to the gold standard, and economic nationalism.

Unlike other political organizations, the Democratic Party's directors included professionals and intellectuals like lawyer Malaquías Concha and physician Alejandro Bustamante, but more significantly, it also included workers, such as printer Luis Emilio Recabarren. Not surprisingly, this party, which seriously challenged Chile's status quo, encountered difficulties. Its support of José Manuel Balmaceda during the 1891 revolution led to the persecution of its leaders at the hands of the congressionalist victors. Perhaps because it included various political extremists such as anarchists, the party initially refused to participate in any of the parliamentary political coalitions. It also provided leadership in organizing various strikes and demonstrations, such as the 1905 Santiago Meat Riots.

Eventually, anxious to participate in government, and perhaps in patronage as well, the Democrats abandoned their principles of noncooperation, often supporting extremely reactionary candidates such as those of the Conservative Party, in return for ministerial portfolios. This willingness to cooperate with bourgeois parties, which gained the Democrats a ministerial post, precipitated various schisms. The conflict between the traditionalists and those advocating socialism ultimately led, in 1912, to the creation of the Socialist Workers Party (Partido Obrero Socialista—POS).

Electing its first deputy to the national Congress in 1894, the Democratic Party continued to win additional victories. In 1904 six Democratic congressmen and, for the first time, a senator, won legislative seats. Triumph at the polls, however, did not always translate into political power, as the Congress sometimes refused to seat Democratic legislators. The party nevertheless enjoyed increasing popularity, particularly in the nitrate pampas and among urban workers. The Democrats seemed to reach their political zenith in 1932, when the party elected thirteen deputies. Too conservative for the Left and too radical for the Right, the party began to lose support, particularly when some of its more progressive members, like Recabarren, left the party. Even

those who remained seemed without direction: in the 1958 presidential election the members of the Democratic Party supported each of the three candidates. By this time the party had won but 5 percent of the vote, and by 1965 it had ceased to be of any real importance.

Although it eventually went out of existence, the Democratic Party nonetheless fulfilled an important function. It was one of the first of Chile's parties to articulate such ideas as creating a labor section and providing social security, worker compensation, and accident insurance to protect the nation's working class.

See also **Balmaceda Fernández, José Manuel; Democracy; Labor Movements; Recabarren Serrano, Luis Emilio.**

BIBLIOGRAPHY

Hector De Petris Giesen, *Historia del partido democrático* (1942).

Germán Urzúa Valenzuela, *Los partidos políticos chilenos* (1968), pp. 53–55.

Ben G. Burnett, *Political Groups in Chile* (1970), pp. 161–170, 178–181.

Peter De Shazo, *Urban Workers and Labor Unions in Chile, 1902–1927* (1983), pp. 90–92, 109–113, 119–122, 126, 139–140, 175, 177.

Karen L. Remmer, *Party Competition in Argentina and Chile: Political Recruitment and Public Policy, 1890–1930* (1984), pp. 67–70, 85–86, 118–120.

Additional Bibliography

Hutchison, Elizabeth Q. *Labors Appropriate to Their Sex Gender, Labor, and Politics in Urban Chile, 1900–1930*. Durham, NC: Duke University Press, 2001.

WILLIAM F. SATER

FEMININE PARTY

Founded in 1946 by María de la Cruz, this party joined the umbrella group FECHIF (Federación Chilena de Instituciones Femeninas) the same year. De la Cruz was influenced by Juan and Eva Perón, and the Feminine Party platform stressed "justice and social harmony." The party reflected de la Cruz's beliefs about women's moral superiority, defended traditional gender roles and femininity, and argued that female "emotionality" was a necessary counterweight to male "rationality." Journalist Georgina Durand and lawyer Felícitas Klimpel were on the Feminine Party board of directors. In 1951 the party split over de la Cruz's personalist leadership, but both factions supported the successful independent presidential candidacy of Carlos Ibáñez in 1952. Running as the Feminine Party candidate, de la Cruz was the first woman to be elected to the Chilean Senate in 1952; the party disintegrated following her expulsion from the Senate in 1953.

See also **Feminism and Feminist Organizations.**

BIBLIOGRAPHY

Felícitas Klimpel, *La mujer chilena (el aporte femenino al progreso de Chile) 1910–1960* (1962).

Corinne Antezana-Pernet, "Peace in the World and Democracy at Home: The Chilean Women's Movement in the 1940s," in *Latin America in the 1940s,* edited by David Rock (1994).

Additional Bibliography

Rosemblatt, Karin Alejandra. *Gendered Compromises: Political Cultures and the State in Chile, 1920–1950.* Chapel Hill: University of North Carolina Press, 2000.

CORINNE ANTEZANA-PERNET

LIBERAL–CONSERVATIVE FUSION (LIBERAL-CONSERVADORA)

The Fusion grew out of a Chilean political alliance formed in January 1858 to fight against President Manuel Montt (1851–1861) and his National Party (founded December 1857) in the congressional elections of that year. It consisted of the Liberals, who had been in opposition since 1830, and those Conservatives (probably a majority) then defecting from Montt, partly provoked by his handling of the Question of the Sacristan. This alliance of old enemies was more resilient than its opponents suspected it would be: It lasted fifteen years. In 1859 the Fusion mounted unsuccessful armed rebellions against Montt. His tolerant successor, José Joaquín Pérez (1861–1871), invited the alliance into the cabinet in July 1862. Though opposed by the now-displaced Nationals and also by the "unreconstructed" Liberals known as Radicals, the Fusion retained its power, and in 1871 elected its own president, Federico Errázuriz Zañartu (1871–1876). It finally broke up in 1873 over a contentious dispute about private education, when the Conservatives went into opposition.

See also **Chile, Political Parties: National Party; Montt Torres, Manuel.**

BIBLIOGRAPHY

Collier, Simon. *Chile: The Making of a Republic, 1830–1865: Politics and Ideas.* New York: Cambridge University Press, 2003.

Stuven, Ana María. *La seducción de un orden: Las elites y la construcción de Chile en las polémicas culturales y políticas del siglo XIX.* Santiago: Ediciones Universidad Católica de Chile, 2000.

SIMON COLLIER

LIBERAL PARTY

The first Liberal Party of Chile (Partido Liberal) consisted of a group of men who shared vague ideals rather than a cohesive ideology. Crushed by the Conservatives at the battle of Lircay in 1830, the party dissolved, and its supporters went to ground. The Manuel Bulnes administration (1841–1851) proved more benign than its predecessor, permitting a more open political atmosphere. A split in Conservative ranks provided the impetus and the leadership for the creation of the Liberal Party. The dissident Conservatives attracted the support of pre-1830 Liberals as well as a new generation of political mavericks, such as Francisco Bilbao and José Victorino Lastarria, who were strongly influenced by events in Europe, particularly the various revolutions of 1848. Together they founded the Liberal Party in 1849.

The newly created Liberals did not fare well. Twice, in 1851 and 1859, they participated in rebellions intended to bring political change to Chile. Displeased by the Manuel Montt administration (1851–1861), the Liberals began to side with Conservatives to form an antigovernment opposition. The conclusion of the Montt regime, however, brought the Liberals into increasing prominence and even into the José Joaquín Pérez administration's cabinet. Under their aegis the legislature gave rights to non-Catholics, reduced the powers of the president to suspend the Constitution, and limited his tenure to one term.

From 1871 to 1891, Liberal presidents ruled Chile, initiating legislation that amplified civil rights, reduced the power of the government, enfranchised more people, and secularized many institutions. The party, however, suffered on various occasions from numerous splits, which limited its effectiveness, often forcing it to forge coalitions in order to rule.

Like the Conservative Party, the Liberal Party did not hold its first convention until late: in September 1892, when it announced its support for the parliamentary system and free elections. Because of its propensity for internal disputes and lack of organization, the party lost much of its effectiveness during the first half of the parliamentary period. The Liberal Party rarely lived up to its name: other than calling for separation of church and state, it tended to concentrate on political change rather than demand substantive socioeconomic reforms. Even the Conservatives were more liberal.

The Liberals continued to splinter after 1925, with each faction often supporting different candidates. Periodically, Liberals participated in various cabinets, even working with Communists on one occasion, thereby indicating that political consistency was not their strong suit. Despite its problems, the Liberal Party still elected candidates largely from rural areas where it could control the peasant vote. For the same reasons the Conservatives lost congressional power—changes in the electoral law and an end to election fraud—the Liberals lost as well. By 1965 they had attracted but 7.3 percent of the congressional vote, electing only six deputies and five senators. Increasingly, the Liberal Party functioned as part of a coalition. Its last experience, working with Conservatives and Radicals to elect a congressional candidate, failed dismally. Recognizing the problems confronting it, in 1966 the Liberals joined the Conservatives, once their mortal foes, to create the National Party which lasted until the early 1990s.

See also **Bilbao Barquín, Francisco; Bulnes Prieto, Manuel; Lastarria, José Victorino; Liberalism.**

BIBLIOGRAPHY

Sergio Guilisasti, *Partidos políticos chilenos* (1964), pp. 71–128.

Federico G. Gil, *The Political System of Chile* (1966), pp. 231–243, 252–256, 308–309.

James O. Morris, *Elites, Intellectuals, and Consensus: A Study of the Social Question and the Industrial Relations System in Chile* (1966), pp. 9, 101, 144–171, 180–184, 187, 217, 233–234.

Ben G. Burnett, *Political Groups in Chile* (1970), pp. 161–170, 178–181.

Karen L. Remmer, *Party Competition in Argentina and Chile: Political Recruitment and Public Policy, 1890–1930* (1984), pp. 12–19, 23, 74–76, 80, 82, 85, 117–120.

Additional Bibliography

Collier, Simon. *Chile: The Making of a Republic, 1830–1865: Politics and Ideas.* New York: Cambridge University Press, 2003.

Scully, Timothy. *Rethinking the Center: Party Politics in Nineteenth- and Twentieth-century Chile.* Stanford, CA: Stanford University Press, 1992.

Stuven, Ana María. *La seducción de un orden: Las elites y la construcción de Chile en las polémicas culturales y políticas del siglo XIX.* Santiago: Ediciones Universidad Católica de Chile, 2000.

WILLIAM F. SATER

MOVEMENT OF NATIONAL UNITY (MUN)

In late 1983 the Movement of National Unity (Movimiento de Unión Nacional—MUN) was formed by traditional and younger-generation rightists who were critical of the military government's economic policies and of restrictions on political activity. Projecting itself as a civilian alternative capable of consolidating General Augusto Pinochet's work, it signed the 1985 National Accord that called for a more rapid return to democratic rule. In 1987 the group joined with other right-wing movements to form the National Renovation Party (RN), which supported Pinochet in the 1988 plebiscite and campaigned on a pro-regime platform in the 1989 election. Although the MUN supported some early initiatives of the government of Patricio Aylwin Azócar, it subsequently opposed him and worked closely with the more stridently rightist Independent Democratic Movement (UDI).

See also **Pinochet Ugarte, Augusto.**

BIBLIOGRAPHY

Cavallo, A., et al. *La historia oculta del regimen militar* (Santiago, 1989).

Drake, P. W., and I. Jaksic, eds. *The Struggle for Democracy in Chile, 1882–1990* (1991).

Mireya, Dávila A., and Claudio Fuentes. *Promesas de cambio: Izquierda y derecha en el Chile contemporáneo.* Santiago: FLACSO-Chile: Editorial Universitaria, 2003.

Pollack, Marcelo. *The New Right in Chile, 1973–1997.* New York: St. Martin's Press, 1999.

MICHAEL FLEET

MOVEMENT OF THE REVOLUTIONARY LEFT (MIR)

The Movement of the Revolutionary Left (Movimiento de la Izquierda Revolucionaria—MIR) is an extremist Marxist political organization founded in the 1960s largely by young, middle-class students who accused both the Socialist and the Communist parties of lacking sufficient revolutionary zeal. Influenced by Régis Debray and the Cuban experience, the MIR believed that the working class should eschew cooperation with the bourgeoisie and take power immediately. In 1969, just prior to the presidential elections, the MIR went underground and began a series of assaults and bank robberies to finance their activities. While refusing to participate in the political process, the MIR nonetheless supported Salvador Allende's 1970 candidacy for the presidency. Upon his election, members of the MIR organized illegal seizures of farmland called *tomas*, as well as organized urban centers of political support called *cordones industriales* (industrial zones), which they ran. Apparently, the organization also helped plan the abortive 1973 naval mutiny that immediately preceded the fall of Allende's government.

Although most of the MIR's leadership escaped the repression following the September 1973 coup, taking refuge in foreign embassies and ultimately leaving Chile under safe-conduct passes, some clandestinely reentered Chile to launch a series of urban assaults, assassinations, and attempts to create a guerrilla base in Chile's south. Operating from abroad, the MIR maintained close relations with various terrorist organizations, publishing a newsletter and in a few cases joining other groups such as the Argentine People's Revolutionary Army (ERP).

The Pinochet government that followed Allende's seemed to enjoy some success running to ground leaders of the MIR. Eventually, the group seemed to lose its enthusiasm for continuing the revolutionary struggle and was replaced in large part by the Communist-backed (Frente Patriótico) Manuel Rodríguez. Since the late 1980s, the MIR has faded from the public eye.

See also **Allende Gossens, Salvador; Debray, [Jules] Régis; Pinochet Ugarte, Augusto.**

BIBLIOGRAPHY

Carmelo Furci, *The Chilean Communist Party and the Road to Socialism* (1984), pp. 98–100, 120, 124, 137–139, 150–152, 155, 157–162, 164, 166–167.

William F. Sater, *The Revolutionary Left and Terrorist Violence in Chile* (1986).

Additional Bibliography

Ibáñez Santa María, Adolfo. *Abrazado por la revolución: Ideología y totalitarismo en Chile 1960–1973.* Santiago: Editorial Biblioteca Americana, 2004.

Scully, Timothy. *Rethinking the Center: Party Politics in Nineteenth- and Twentieth-century Chile.* Stanford, CA: Stanford University Press, 1992.

WILLIAM F. SATER

NATIONAL PARTY

The National Party, a Chilean political organization which functioned between 1857 and 1932, was the creation and the vehicle of President Manuel Montt and his protégé Antonio Varas. Initially conservative, it was distinguished from other contemporary parties by its predilection for authoritarian methods—not all that unusual at the time—and an intense hostility toward the Roman Catholic Church. In truth, the party owed its existence as much to a fight between Montt and his political opponents on both the Right and the Left as to a clash between the hierarchy and the Moneda, or administration, over the right of the civil government to assert jurisdiction over clerics. Still, the new organization became known as the National Party presumably because it sought to protect national interests from Chilean ultramontanes who wished to subordinate Santiago to the will of Rome.

Once in power, the Nationals, whose motto was "liberty within order," enjoyed only a brief place in the political sun. When it became clear that Montt could not impose Varas as his successor, the party began to lose its power. The Montt-Varistas lost their parliamentary majority in 1864, and a coalition including the Nationals proved unable to elect its candidate in the 1871 election. After President José Joaquín Pérez, the Nationals would not win the Moneda, although numerous Montt–Varistas held ministerial portfolios and the party supported the election of Aníbal Pinto and Domingo Santa María González. The Nationals were among the last to abandon José Manuel Balmaceda. Perhaps because of this fact, they suffered heavy losses in the 1894 parliamentary elections. The party, however, did enjoy a resurgence during the parliamentary period of the 1890s and saw its founder's son, Pedro Montt, become president in 1906. It also elected a total of sixteen deputies in 1909. After that date, however, the Nationals again began to lose ground slowly, though often backing winning candidates in ensuing presidential elections. In return for their support, the Nationals occupied, however briefly, various cabinet posts.

Fundamentally the brainchild of Manuel Montt, the Nationals initially lacked any clear ideology beyond a willingness to adhere to their founder's wishes. Once it lost control of the Moneda, the party, like many of those which no longer dominated the government, advocated reducing the powers of the chief executive, expanding individual liberties, and restricting the power of the church. While it was perhaps not politically unique, the National Party did provide a vehicle for the emerging Chilean middle class, particularly those involved in the civil service and later commerce as well as finance.

Insulted by the Chilean political system, the party continued to function even after its political rationale had ceased to exist. Moreover, the party began to fracture, thus accelerating its decline. After 1925 the National Party lost its appeal. Although it participated in selecting the Thermal Congress (1930–1932), the National Party ceased to exist. In 1932 it joined with various Liberals and some long-time supporters of Balmaceda to form the United Liberal Party.

See also **Montt Torres, Manuel; Varas de la Barra, Antonio.**

BIBLIOGRAPHY

Collier, Simon. *Chile: The Making of a Republic, 1830–1865: Politics and Ideas.* New York: Cambridge University Press, 2003.

Galdames, Luis. *A History of Chile* (1941), pp. 294–298.

Scully, Timothy. *Rethinking the Center: Party Politics in Nineteenth– and Twentieth-century Chile.* Stanford, CA: Stanford University Press, 1992.

Stuven, Ana María. *La seducción de un orden: Las elites y la construcción de Chile en las polémicas culturales y políticas del siglo XIX.* Santiago: Ediciones Universidad Católica de Chile, 2000.

Urzúa Valenzuela, Germán. *Diccionario político institucional de Chile* (1979), pp. 103–104.

WILLIAM F. SATER

NATIONAL PHALANX

The National Phalanx (Falange Nacional), a Chilean political party, was the precursor of the Christian Democratic Party. Influenced by Christian Socialism, the Falange broke from the Conservative Party in 1938. It advocated domestic social and economic reforms, espousing a neutralist foreign policy which included supporting the refusal of Juan Antonio Ríos to declare war on the Axis powers and opposing Chile's alignment with the United States during the cold war. The Falange continued to function during the 1940s, reaching its political high point in 1957, when it elected fourteen deputies and a senator. Consistent with its centrist tendencies, its members served as ministers in the government of Juan Antonio Ríos, Alfredo Duhalde, and Gabriel González Videla. In 1957 the Falange merged with the Social Christian Conservative Party to form the Christian Democratic Party.

See also **González Videla, Gabriel; Ríos Morales, Juan Antonio.**

BIBLIOGRAPHY

Federico G. Gil, *The Political System of Chile* (1966), pp. 67, 71, 266.

César Caviedes L., *The Politics of Chile: A Sociogeographical Assessment* (1979), pp. 57–59.

Additional Bibliography

Díaz Nieva, José. *Chile: De la Falange Nacional a la Democracia Cristiana.* Madrid: Universidad Nacional de Educación a Distancia, 2000.

WILLIAM F. SATER

POPULAR ACTION FRONT

A left-wing political alliance, the Popular Action Front was formed in 1956. The coalition was composed of Socialists, Popular Socialists, the Laborites, the People's Democratic and Democratic parties, as well as the outlawed Communists. The FRAP represented the first time that the Socialists and Communists, who were permitted to return to public life in 1958, formed a cohesive unit. FRAP's 1958 presidential candidate, Salvador Allende Gossens, called for the empowerment of workers, nationalization of the country's basic industries and financial institutions, agrarian reform, and the adoption of a neutralist, if not overtly anti-American, foreign policy.

Though Allende lost to Jorge Alessandri Rodríguez, the Conservative candidate, the FRAP's popularity increased. Because of changes in the electoral law, the coalition did well in predominantly agricultural districts. Thus the FRAP won 31 percent of the popular vote in the 1961 congressional contest, virtually doubling its seats in the Chamber of Deputies while increasing, by 50 percent, its power in the Senate; three years later FRAP won almost 40 percent of the vote.

In 1964, the FRAP again nominated Allende, who advocated extending suffrage, increasing social benefits, and calling for the state to take a more active role in developing the economy. Eduardo Frei Montalvo, the Christian Democratic candidate, easily defeated Allende, who lost the heavily populated cities of Santiago and Valparaíso as well as the rural areas. Although the FRAP was dissolved in 1969, it constituted the first movement that successfully welded Chile's Marxist parties into a formidable political bloc.

See also **Allende Gossens, Salvador.**

BIBLIOGRAPHY

Gil, Federico G. *The Political System of Chile* (1966), pp. 204–205, 229–243, 276–277, 299–307.

Ibáñez Santa María, Adolfo. *Abrazado por la revolución: Ideología y totalitarismo en Chile 1960–1973.* Santiago: Editorial Biblioteca Americana, 2004.

Petras, James. *Politics and Social Forces in Chilean Development* (1969), pp. 174–196, 209, 245–246, 262, 266–269, 276–283.

Scully, Timothy. *Rethinking the Center: Party Politics in Nineteenth- and Twentieth-century Chile.* Stanford, CA: Stanford University Press, 1992.

WILLIAM F. SATER

POPULAR ACTION UNITARY MOVEMENT (MAPU)

The Popular Action Unitary Movement (Movimiento de Acción Popular Unitaria—MAPU) was formed in 1969 by radical Christian Democrats unhappy with the slow pace of reform under the government of Eduardo Frei Montalva (1964–1970) and with their party's unwillingness to work with Marxists and other leftists in the construction of a socialist society. MAPU joined the Popular Unity coalition that backed Salvador Allende for president in 1970, and several of its members served in his cabinet. Some *mapucistas* wanted to create a distinctively Christian socialist party, and in 1971 they formed the Christian Left (IC) movement with other dissident Christian Democrats. Those who remained moved farther left, embracing orthodox, and increasingly secular, Marxist-Leninist positions and either abandoning or setting aside their Christian faith.

During the next year, two wings emerged in MAPU: the more moderate wing, led by Jaime Guzmuri, aligned with the Chilean Communist Party and committed to the development of a national political force; and the more radical wing, led by Oscar Garretón, which favored the Socialist Party (PS) and stressed the development of social movements at the local level. A formal split occurred early in 1973, with the moderates forming MAPU Obrero-Campesino (MAPU—OC, or MOC) and the radicals continuing to function as MAPU.

During the years of military rule, most *mapucistas* abandoned their radical Leninist positions. Those associated with the MOC, such as Manuel Antonio Garretón and José Antonio Viera-Gallo, were particularly influential in critical discussions, in Chile and among exiles in Italy and Holland, of the Popular Unity experience and the future of Chilean socialism. They were active in promoting the *renovación* (moderate renewal) and reunification of the Socialist Party, with whose moderate Nuñez wing most were identified, and to which many of their erstwhile MAPU comrades were later attracted. A smaller number of *mapucistas*, most of whom were younger Christian community activists, were active in the paramilitary MAPU-Lautaro, which carried out sporadic armed attacks against the military government.

Former *mapucistas* who have held influential position in postmilitary governments include Viera-Gallo (PS), who was president of the chamber of deputies and later a senator; Enrique Correa (PS), who was general secretary of the government under Patricio Aylwin Azócar; and José Miguel Insulza (PS), who was minister of foreign relations under Eduardo Frei Ruiz-Tagle, minister of interior under Ricardo Lagos, and later secretary general of the Organization of American States.

See also **Allende Gossens, Salvador; Aylwin Azócar, Patricio; Frei Montalva, Eduardo; Frei Ruiz-Tagle, Eduardo; Lagos, Ricardo.**

BIBLIOGRAPHY

Edwards, Carlos Bascuñán. *La izquierda sin Allende*. Santiago, Chile: Planeta, 1990.

Israel Zipper, Ricardo. *Politics and Ideology in Allende's Chile*. Tempe: Center for Latin American Studies, Arizona State University, 1989.

"La Ruta de un CamaleLón." *Punto Final* no. 5172 (July 2004); "Rebeldes con Vocación de Poder." *Punto Final* no. 5173 (August 2004).

MICHAEL FLEET

POPULAR FRONT

The Popular Front (Frente Popular) was a political coalition of the Communist, Socialist, Democratic, Radical-Socialist, and Radical parties, as well as the Chilean Confederation of Workers, that ruled Chile from 1938 until 1941. Fearing the rise of fascism and Nazism in Europe, the Communist International ordered its members to cooperate with democratic elements in order to achieve progressive programs. The Chilean Communist Party complied, forming an alliance, the Popular Front, with the Socialist Party and the more powerful Radicals. The front sought to strengthen democratic government as well as civil rights; institute reforms to redistribute the wealth, stimulate the economy, and foment national industries; and regulate working and living conditions as well as encourage education.

The Popular Front's slate of congressional candidates did so well that it agreed to run a candidate, Pedro Aguirre Cerda, a member of the Radical Party, for the presidency in 1938. A surprise victor, Aguirre Cerda won the presidency by a scant nine thousand votes, and the Popular Front ruled Chile until infighting between the Communists and Socialists, in part precipitated by Stalin's signing of a nonaggression pact with Hitler, destroyed the fragile coalition.

During its brief tenure, the Popular Front passed legislation favoring unionization, increased social benefits for the nation's needy, and called for increased government intervention in Chile's economic development.

See also **Aguirre Cerda, Pedro; World War II.**

BIBLIOGRAPHY

John R. Stevenson, *The Chilean Popular Front* (1942).

Richard Super, "The Chilean Popular Front Presidency of Pedro Aguirre Cerda, 1938–1941," (Ph.D. diss., Arizona State University, 1975).

Additional Bibliography

Bravo Lira, Bernardino. *Régimen de gobierno y partidos políticos en Chile, 1924–1973*. Santiago de Chile: Editorial Jurídica de Chile, 1978.

Moulian, Tomás. *Fracturas: De Pedro Aguirre Cerda a Salvador Allende (1938–1973)*. Santiago: LOM Ediciones, 2006.

WILLIAM F. SATER

POPULAR UNITY

The Popular Unity (Unidad Popular—UP) Chilean political coalition ruled Chile from 1970 to 1973. The successor to Popular Action Front (FRAP), the Unidad Popular was founded in 1969. Initially it consisted of Marxist and progressive parties—the Socialists, the Communists, the Social Democrats, the Movimiento de Acción Popular Unida (MAPU), Acción Popular Independiente (AP), and the Radicals—but later it added the Izquierda Cristiana, while losing some elements of the Radical Party. The Popular Unity party provided ministerial portfolios to its members, but the Socialists and Communists dominated the coalition.

Calling for radical economic change—nationalization of the mines, a neutralist foreign policy, an accelerated program of agrarian reform, state control of the banks and insurance companies and major means of production—the party nominated Salvador Allende as its candidate in the 1970 presidential election. Given its eclectic composition, the UP suffered from internal schisms, with the Communists favoring consolidation of its gains and the Socialists demanding yet more radical change. The extreme Left often refused to cooperate with the government and adopted various policies, such as sponsoring illegal seizures of land and factories, assassinating Edmundo Pérez Zujovic, pushing for an ideological education program, and attempting to politicize the military, that alienated elements who might have been willing to support the Allende government. Moreover, establishing a quota system that accorded each UP faction a share of the government's appointments based upon a party's importance within the coalition handicapped the Unidad Popular's performance. Riven by internal disputes and under increasing pressure, the Unidad Popular government succumbed to a coup in 1973.

See also **Allende Gossens, Salvador.**

BIBLIOGRAPHY

Arturo Valenzuela, *The Breakdown of Democratic Regimes, Chile* (1978), pp. 64–68, 83, 89, 109, 123.

Julio Faúndez, *Marxism and Democracy in Chile* (1988), pp. 154, 159, 170–171, 174, 176, 191–194, 199–200, 203–204, 221–223.

Additional Bibliography

Ibáñez Santa María, Adolfo. *Abrazado por la revolución: Ideología y totalitarismo en Chile 1960–1973.* Santiago: Editorial Biblioteca Americana, 2004.

Rodrigo Baño, and Hugo Fazio. *La Unidad Popular treinta años después.* Santiago, Chile: Departamento de Sociología, Facultad de Ciencias Sociales, Universidad de Chile, 2003.

Scully, Timothy. *Rethinking the Center: Party Politics in Nineteenth- and Twentieth-century Chile.* Stanford, CA: Stanford University Press, 1992.

WILLIAM F. SATER

RADICAL PARTY

The Radical Party (Partido Radical) began in the early 1850s, influenced by European ideas as well as those of the radical Francisco Bilbao, when various members of the Liberal Party objected to cooperating with the Conservative Party. In 1857 these men, many of whom were identified with the newly emerging mining elites, split from the Liberals to form the Radical Party. Their commitment to a secular state and, more significantly, their opposition to an authoritarian central government attracted the attention of the Manuel Montt government, which exiled many of the new party's leaders. Within ten years, the Radicals had elected members to the Congress. After 1875 they served in the cabinets of Federico Errázuriz Zañartu, Aníbal Pinto, and Domingo Santa María González. The Radicals joined the anti-Balmaceda forces during the 1891 Revolution.

The party did not hold its first convention until 1888, when it called for municipal autonomy; the separation of church and state; an expansion of individual liberties; state support for a free, obligatory secular education; and improved conditions for workers and women. In 1906, at its third convention, the Radical Party confronted the issue of growing social and economic inequality. Valentín Letelier Madariaga advocated that the party adopt a program calling for state-sponsored social reforms to end the nation's endemic poverty. His main opposition came from Enrique MacIver Rodríguez, who argued that a lack of moral fiber, not economic deprivation, was what was causing Chile's social problems. Letelier carried the day, and, henceforth, the Radical Party sponsored various pieces of social legislation.

From 1912 to 1921 the Radicals doubled their number of seats in the legislative branch, but electoral fraud prevented them from winning the presidency. Over the years, the party's composition changed as the urban middle class, professionals, and the bureaucracy joined its ranks. Rhetorically, it seemed to become more left wing as it competed with the Democratic Party for votes. In fact, this political change was more cosmetic than real.

In 1931, either in response to the economic dislocations of the Great Depression or to undercut the increasing popularity of the leftist parties, the Radical Party denounced capitalism, advocating instead a collectivization of the means of production. Despite this switch, the Radicals did not get a chance to direct the nation until the Popular Front's 1938 triumph brought Pedro Aguirre Cerda to power. Aguirre Cerda did institute certain social programs and create basic industries, but, fearing political retaliation, he refused to deal with the more vexing issue of agrarian reform. His Radical successors, Juan Antonio Ríos Morales and Gabriel González Videla, seemed incapable of successfully instituting political and economic reforms or ending a crippling inflation. By 1958, when it had become clear that the Radicals were more interested in preserving their political position than in instituting significant change, the public became disenchanted with the party, and by 1963 the Christian Democrats were outpolling them. Anxious to retain some share of power, the Radicals became the handmaiden of the Unidad Popular (UP). This opportunistic policy proved disastrous. The party began to suffer defections, with many people bolting to join the anti-UP forces. By 1971, many of the party's most senior leaders had quit to form a new party, the Radical Left Party. In the 1973 congressional elections the Radicals won a paltry 3.7 percent of the popular vote. The Radical Party had become a shadow of its once-powerful self.

See also **Aguirre Cerda, Pedro; Bilbao Barquín, Francisco; Errázuriz Zañartu, Federico; Letelier Madariaga, Valentín; Mac-Iver Rodríguez, Enrique; Pinto Garmendia, Aníbal; Santa María González, Domingo.**

BIBLIOGRAPHY

Peter G. Snow, *The Radical Parties of Chile and Argentina* (1963).

Sergio Guilisasti, *Partidos políticos chilenos* (1964), pp. 129–197.

Federico G. Gil, *The Political System of Chile* (1966), pp. 42–43, 67–69, 231–243, 257–266, 308–309.

Luis Palma, *Historia del Partido Radical* (1967).

Karen L. Remmer, *Party Competition in Argentina and Chile: Political Recruitment and Public Policy, 1890–1930* (1984), pp. 14–17, 63–67, 85–86, 118–120.

Additional Bibliography

Moulian, Tomás. *Fracturas: De Pedro Aguirre Cerda a Salvador Allende (1938–1973).* Santiago: LOM Ediciones, 2006.

Sepúlveda Rondanelli, Julio. *Los radicales ante la historia.* Santiago de Chile: Editorial Andrés Bello, 1993.

WILLIAM F. SATER

SOCIALIST PARTY

A conglomeration of various Marxist groups—the Nueva Acción Pública, the Acción Revolucionaria Socialista, the Partido Socialista Marxista, the Orden Socialista, and the Partido Socialista Unificado—became the Socialist Party on 19 April 1933. Created to fill a political vacuum caused by the collapse of the Carlos Ibáñez government and the failure of the Socialist Republic of 100 Days, the party endured repression at the hands of the Arturo Alessandri Palma government, which exiled many of its leaders, including Marmaduke Grove Vallejo. The Socialists created a special niche for themselves: they favored the class struggle and the dictatorship of the proletariat, and opposed capitalism and imperialism, particularly that of the United States. But while ideologically akin to the Communists, they refused to accept the domination of Moscow.

Initially acting alone, the Socialists urged an alliance with other left-wing parties to form the Bloque de Izquierda in 1935. Two years later, the Communists joined the Socialists and other elements, including the Radical Party, to establish the Popular Front. Although they held various ministerial portfolios in the Aguirre Cerda government, some dissidents accused the party's leaders of betraying Socialist principles by supporting the reformist, but hardly revolutionary, Aguirre Cerda government.

This dispute, which led to the creation of the Socialist Workers Party (Partido Socialista de Trabajadores), constituted the first of many splits which shattered the party's cohesion. Grove later led another splinter group out of the Socialist fold and into the Partido Socialista Auténtico when radicals criticized his support of the Ríos regime. Given the party's eclectic composition, it is not surprising that schisms appeared. By 1946 the Socialists had formed three parties, and not surprisingly, their collective fortunes declined in the elections. Two years later, the party coalesced into just two factions: the Partido Socialista de Chile and the Partido Socialista Popular.

The Partido Socialista Popular unexpectedly supported the candidacy of Carlos Ibáñez, a former dictator associated with conservative policies. Although the party attempted to rationalize this policy, its decision represented an attempt to jump on the Ibáñez bandwagon in order to win back some of its former supporters. This opportunistic policy bore fruit when the party won certain ministerial posts and increased its congressional representation. But when Ibáñez's policies began to misfire, the Socialist faction withdrew its support. In 1957 the Socialists managed to reconcile their two factions. Earlier, in 1956, the Socialists had joined the Communists to create the Popular Action Front (FRAP), which would nominate Salvador Allende as its presidential candidate in 1958 and 1964. They also participated in the 1970 Popular Unity government.

The largely working-class Socialists sought to establish a broad-based authoritarian government to reorder drastically the nation's economic, social, and political priorities. Unlike the Communists, the Socialists believed that Chile's own experience should shape the revolutionary process. The Socialists became more vociferous during the Allende period, advocating armed revolution, seeking the abolition of the bourgeois state, and refusing to compromise with the Christian Democrats. Many believe that Socialist intransigence prevented Allende from compromising on certain essential issues, thus hastening the collapse of his government.

Since 1973, the party has split into various factions, including one led by Ricardo Lagos, which appeared willing to compromise with non-Marxists, and another under the control of the more radical Clodomiro Almeyda Medina, which was not. Despite these differences, the Socialists cooperated with the anti-Pinochet forces, helping to elect Patricio Aylwin in 1989 and electing representatives to both houses of Congress. Continuing their partnership with other leftist parties, the Socialists won the presidency in 1999 with candidate Ricardo Lagos. Again, in 2006, the socialist candidate Michelle Bachelet won the presidential contest and also became Chile's first female chief executive.

See also **Alessandri Palma, Arturo; Allende Gossens, Salvador; Aylwin Azócar, Patricio; Bachelet, Michelle; Chile, Socialist Republic of 100 Days; Grove Vallejo, Marmaduke; Ibáñez del Campo, Carlos; Lagos, Ricardo.**

BIBLIOGRAPHY

Julio César Jobet Burquez, *El socialismo chileno a través de sus congresos* (1965) and *El partido socialista de Chile*, 2 vols. (1971).

Miriam R. Hochwald, "Imagery in Politics: A Study of the Ideology of the Chilean Socialist Party" (Ph.D. diss., UCLA, 1971).

Paul W. Drake, *Socialism and Populism in Chile, 1932–52* (1978).

Benny Pollack and Hernán Rosenkranz, *Revolutionary Social Democracy—The Chilean Socialist Party* (1986).

Additional Bibliography

Baño, Rodrigo, ed. *La Unidad Popular treinta años después.* Santiago: Departamento de Sociología, Facultad de Ciencias Sociales, Universidad de Chile, 2003.

Ponce Durán, Pedro. *Oscar Schnake Vergara: Comienzos del socialismo chileno, 1933–1942.* Santiago: Ediciones Documentas, 1994.

WILLIAM F. SATER

CHILE, REVOLUTIONS

This entry includes the following articles:
REVOLUTIONS OF 1851 AND 1859
REVOLUTION OF 1891

REVOLUTIONS OF 1851 AND 1859

Two political upheavals during the Manuel Montt regime both cost Chile dearly in treasure and blood. Each had its roots in deep-seated economic causes and, in some cases, conflicting ideologies. Fundamentally, a loathing of Montt and the system he represented drove two politically and geographically disparate elements into rebellion.

THE REVOLUTION OF 1851

Manuel Montt, best described as the law personified, came to power in 1851, threatening to perpetuate a highly centralized government that would limit the opposition parties' access to the political system. As a result, even before Montt took office a rebellion erupted in two areas: La Serena, in the nation's north, and Concepción, Chile's third most important city.

The northern rebellion was spearheaded by mainly middle-class liberal intellectuals, many of whom were members of the Society of Equality (a reform group influenced by European liberalism), but it was supported by various lower-class elements as well. The 1851 insurgency, which began on 7 September, was organized by José Miguel Carrera's son, José Miguel Carrera Fontecilla, who became the provincial intendant. Carrera organized a militia, which eventually numbered about 1,000 men to defend the fledgling revolution.

While successfully occupying various cities, the northerners committed a crucial mistake in seizing a British ship, the *Fire Fly,* which was anchored in Coquimbo. The administration in the Moneda requested and received naval assistance from the British, who blockaded the port. Meanwhile, Montt ordered his troops to attack the insurgents, who were advancing toward the Central Valley and Santiago, where they hoped to link up with southern rebels. These elements, however, proved unequal to the regular troops, who destroyed the insurgent army of approximately 2,000 men at the battle of Petorca in October 1851.

Suffering heavy casualties, the rebels withdrew to La Serena, where, reinforced by the arrival of numerous miners, they prepared for a siege. The government troops first had to quash an abortive uprising in Coquimbo, but having wiped out this pocket of insurgents, they joined the units that had vanquished the rebels at Petorca to attack La Serena.

Surprisingly, the inexperienced rebels repelled three infantry assaults. When it became clear that the insurgents could not survive, their leaders offered to capitulate, but the popular elements refused. Unfortunately, discipline among the rebels collapsed, leading to widespread looting and allowing the regular army to capture the city. The last rebel units, led by Bernardino Barahona, a miner from Huasco, held out until routed by the troops of Victorino Garrido at the battle of Linderos on 8 January 1852.

The southern rebels, who began their uprising on 13 September, seemed the ideological opposites of their northern brethren. This insurgency was fundamentally rooted in a colonial-era rivalry between Concepción and Santiago. The old landholding elites rallied to the cause of General José María de la Cruz, a dissatisfied officer who had been relieved of both his command and the post of intendant of Concepción. After raising an army of 4,000, de la Cruz planned to attack the loyalist army under General Manuel Bulnes. Unfortunately for him, however, various units which had promised to support the rebellion either could not join his troops or changed their minds about siding with the insurgents.

Bulnes created a 3,000-man army composed of militia and regular units. Outnumbered and running low on ammunition, he had to retreat. On 8 December 1851, he decided to make his stand near the banks of the Loncomilla River. De la Cruz, who early in the battle had foolishly lost his cavalry, could not repel Bulnes's infantry, which, after outflanking the rebel commander, attacked his rear. Under deadly fire, de la Cruz had to withdraw while Bulnes kindly ceased fire in order to spare the lives of his opponents. De la Cruz managed to escape but was cornered by Bulnes on the banks of the Purapel River, where, on 14 December 1851, he capitulated.

While the extreme north and the south constituted the main thrusts of the 1851 rebellion, an uprising also occurred in Valparaíso. The fall of this city could have proven fatal for the central government, since it would have prevented the Bulnes administration from reinforcing its garrisons. Fortunately for President Montt, the local intendant, Admiral Manuel Blanco Encalada, drove the rebels from their positions.

Inspired by the activities in the central part of Chile, some officers under the leadership of José Miguel Cambiazo rebelled on 21 November, supporting de la Cruz's candidacy for the presidency. Cambiazo evacuated the city and set sail for Europe, using a captured merchant vessel. The crew managed to seize the rebel ship, turning the leaders over to the authorities, who tried and executed them.

THE REVOLUTION OF 1859

The agreements ending the 1851 Revolution should be seen as more an armistice than a definitive solution. Many of the forces that precipitated the earlier upheaval caused the second: a political system that purported to represent if not the will of the people then at least that of the oligarchy, but which existed merely so that Manuel Montt could continue to rule. Thus, many of the same Liberals who had rebelled in 1851 did so again eight years later. Curiously, the Conservatives also joined the anti-Montt forces. Since they no longer controlled the government, they refused to allow the secular National Party to enjoy the same unlimited power it had once wielded. The Conservative Senate tried to hamstring Montt by refusing to ratify his budget unless he would shuffle his cabinet. Although he agreed to do so, thus opening the door to an incipient parliamentary system, the Liberals demanded more. These elements published a journal called *La asamblea constituyente*, which sought to revamp the 1833 Constitution. When the supporters of this drive met, government forces arrested them and later exiled them, declaring a state of siege. Aware that the opposition could not legally obtain power, the anti-Montt forces rebelled.

As before, the focus of the revolt was the mining north, Copiapó. Pedro León Gallo, who had become rich mining silver in Chañarcillo, organized a coup and seized the city on 5 January 1859. The rebel chieftain formed a 1,500-man army with which he hoped to capture Santiago.

The rebels had planned for uprisings to follow in Valparaíso, Concepción, Talca, and San Felipe. Unfortunately for their cause, those outbreaks that did erupt lacked the intensity of those of the northern insurgents. Most of the rebel groups consisted of small bands, some under the protection of local landed barons who disliked the Montt government for a variety of reasons. These units sought to harass the central government and to cut its lines of communication with the Concepción region. Rebel bands also captured the towns of Talca and San Felipe, while their compatriots organized guerrilla bands in the south.

In the 1859 Revolution the army, unlike that of 1851, remained loyal to the central government. De la Cruz, who had been asked to lead the rebellion, refused. First blood went to the rebels, who, on 14 March 1859, defeated the regular troops at Los Loros. An outraged Montt then raised another army under Juan Vidaurre, the same general who had put down the 1851 rebellion.

Vidaurre, at the head of a substantial expeditionary force, sailed north from Valparaíso, landed at Tongoy, and marched overland, with the cavalry in tow, to Cerro Grande, where Gallo's forces had taken up positions defending La Serena. Vidaurre's troops, enjoying naval support from the *Esmeralda,* attacked Gallo's men, half of whom had no weapons. On 29 April the regular troops easily vanquished the rebels, who took flight, occupying La Serena the next day.

While Vidaurre was mounting his northern campaign, the rest of the regular army was eradicating pockets of rebel resistance, including Valparaíso, in the Central Valley. Most of these cities surrendered, although it took twenty-two days before Talca capitulated. Various rebel leaders, including José Miguel Carrera, organized guerrilla bands in the south. One of these units, composed in part of Araucanians and numbering more than 2,000 men, attacked Chillán. Although Montt's army vanquished the rebels, peace was not restored to the south until mid-April. The rebels' final stand occurred on 18 September 1859, when an armed band attacked Valparaíso. Vidaurre, who had been appointed intendant of the province, successfully organized a bayonet charge, which ended the rebellion. Ironically, Vidaurre died in this skirmish, shot during this afterthought of the 1859 Revolution.

See also **Bulnes Prieto, Manuel; Chile, Political Parties: National Party; Montt Torres, Manuel.**

BIBLIOGRAPHY

Benjamín Vicuña Mackenna, *Historia de la jornada del 20 de abril de 1851* (1878).

Pedro Pablo Figueroa, *Historia de la Revolución Constituyente* (1889).

Luis Galdames, *A History of Chile* (1941), pp. 288, 298–299.

Daniel Riquelme, *La revolución de 20 de abril de 1851* (1966).

Luis Vitale, *Interpretación marxista de la historia de Chile* (1969), pp. 223–287, and *Las guerras civiles de 1851 y 1859 en Chile* (1971); *Historia del ejército de Chile* (1981), vol. 4, pp. 67–158.

Maurice Zeitlin, *The Civil Wars in Chile* (1984).

Additional Bibliography

Collier, Simon and William F. Sater. *A History of Chile, 1808–1994.* Cambridge, U.K.: Cambridge University Press, 1996.

Hudson, Rex A. *Chile: A Country Study.* Washington, DC: Federal Research Division, 1994.

Scully, Timothy. *Rethinking the Center: Party Politics in Nineteenth- and Twentieth-Century Chile.* Stanford, CA: Stanford University Press, 1992.

Valenzuela, J. Samuel. *Building Aspects of Democracy before Democracy: Electoral Practices in Nineteenth-century Chile.* Notre Dame, IN: University of Notre Dame, 1996.

WILLIAM F. SATER

REVOLUTION OF 1891

In 1891 a seminal civil war dramatically altered the nature of Chilean political life. José Manuel Balmaceda, who became chief executive in 1886, tried to rule in an authoritarian manner. Times had changed, however. The legislature now demanded to participate in the decision-making process, particularly to dispense political patronage, and it resented Balmaceda's attempt to select his successor. After months of bickering, the two sides collided when the Congress refused to approve Balmaceda's budget for 1891 until he reshuffled his cabinet. The president responded by unilaterally declaring that he would simply use the authorization for the 1890 budget for 1891. At this, a faction of the legislature, the congressionalists rebelled. Having won the support of the navy, they sailed for the north and eventually established their seat of government in the nitrate port of Iquique.

The capture of Iquique provided the insurgents with crucial economic support with which to finance the rebellion. Their control of the fleet ensured that the army, most of which had remained loyal to Balmaceda, could not attack the rebel stronghold. His lack of a fleet—Balmaceda's forces consisted of but two torpedo boats and a converted transport—

gave the congressionalists the time to raise and equip an army.

In addition to the navy, Balmaceda's foes enjoyed certain other key advantages: they possessed unlimited funds to purchase arms and, thanks to the defections of various high-ranking army officers, including that of a German-born military adviser, Emil Körner, excellent leaders. Finally, the Balmaceda government's clumsy crushing of a nitrate strike so alienated the miners that they flocked to join the congressionalist army at the outbreak of the revolution.

In mid-August, the rebel forces under Körner's direction, landed north of Valparaíso and moved inland toward the vital port. Better equipped—the insurgents had the more rapid-firing Mannlicher rifles—and better led, the congressionalist forces defeated Balmaceda's army first at the battle of Concón on 21 August 1891, then at Placilla a week later. The loyalist army suffered enormous casualties, including the loss of their generals, whose bodies were mutilated after they were brutally murdered. Valparaíso, though not a battle site, nonetheless suffered substantial property damage and loss of life when the congressionalist victory turned into an opportunity for looting and vengeance.

Fearful that the capital would suffer a similar fate, the Balmaceda government declared Santiago an open city and turned its administration over to the hero of the War of the Pacific, General Manuel Baquedano. Despite his sometimes desultory efforts to preserve order, the homes of various Balmaceda supporters were looted. Balmaceda himself took refuge in the Argentine embassy, where he remained until 19 September 1891, the day after his term of office had legally ended. Then the former president committed suicide.

The 1891 Revolution marked the culmination of a movement begun decades before to limit the power of the presidency. Until 1924 it would be the Congress, not the chief executive, that ruled Chile.

See also **Balmaceda Fernández, José Manuel; Baquedano, Manuel.**

BIBLIOGRAPHY

Maurice Hervey, *Dark Days in Chile* (1891).

James H. Sears and B. W. Wells, Jr., *The Chilean Revolution of 1891* (1893).

Julio Bañados E., *Balmaceda, su gobierno y la revolución de 1891,* 2 vols. (1894).

Harold Blakemore, "The Chilean Revolution of 1891 and Its Historiography," in *Hispanic American Historical Review* 44, 3 (1965): 393–421; and *British Nitrates and Chilean Politics, 1886–1896: Balmaceda and North* (1974).

Additional Bibliography

Bañados Espinoso, Julio. *La revolución de 1891.* Santiago: Editorial Andujar, 2001.

Bañados Espinoso, Julio, and Alejandro San Francisco. *Balmaceda: su gobierno y la revolucón de 1891.* Santiago: Ediciones Centro de Estudios Bicentario, 2005.

Nuñéz P., Jorge. *1891, crónica de la guerra civil.* Santiago: LOM Ediciones, 2003.

Rector, John Lawrence. *The History of Chile.* Westport, CT: Greenwood Press, 2003.

San Francisco, Alejandro. *La guerra civil de 1891.* Santiago: Ediciones Centro de Estudios Bicentario, 2007.

Zeitlin, Maurice. *The Civil Wars in Chile, or, the Bourgeois Revolutions that Never Were.* Princeton, NJ: Princeton University Press, 1994.

WILLIAM F. SATER

CHILES. Chiles (in English, chilies) are hot peppers that are indigenous to the New World and are one of the significant food contributions to the world following the Columbian period. Members of the *Capsicum* genus number over two hundred, with over one hundred Mexican species. Chiles vary in shape, size (from the huge *chile de agua* to the half-inch-long *pequín*), and color (common green and red to unusual black, yellow, and white). They are used fresh, dried, pickled, and smoked in various cuisines, especially in Mexican cooking.

Known for their spicy character, each variety has a distinctive taste and piquancy, from mild to hot. Chile aficionados rely on Scoville units, devised by Wilbur L. Scoville, to measure the hotness of the capsaicin (an enzyme) contained in the peppers.

Besides their use as a spice, chiles have also been an essential ingredient in numerous folk remedies of the Americas. Medical science today acknowledges that chiles are higher in vitamin A than carrots and higher in vitamin C than most citrus fruits. Chiles are used as a decongestant and expectorant, and as an aid in weight loss and pain relief. Promising experiments are under way by arthritis and rheumatism researchers using capsaicin in lotions that reduce pain and inflammation in joints. One 2006 study suggested that capsaicin may stop the spread of prostate cancer. Other capsaicin creams have been successfully used to treat severe itching that affects many patients who undergo kidney dialysis.

The most widespread use of chiles is in the production of *salsa*, or hot sauce, which has become so popular in the United States that it has surpassed the rather bland catsup in consumer purchases. In the early twenty-first century, even more exotic varieties of chiles, such as the chipotle (a smoked ripe jalapeño), have become popular in U.S. cuisine.

See also **Food and Cookery: Medicinal Plants; Nutrition.**

BIBLIOGRAPHY

Diana Kennedy, *The Cuisines of Mexico* (1972).

Janet Long-Solís, *Capsicum y cultura: La historia del chilli* (1986); *Dallas Morning News*, 7 December 1992, sec. C, pp. 3–4, and 9 June 1993, sec. F, pp. 2, 4.

Additional Bibliography

Alvarez, Robert R., Jr. *Mangos, Chiles, and Truckers: The Business of Transnationalism.* Minneapolis: University of Minnesota Press, 2005.

Long Solís, Janet, Manuel Álvarez, and Aranzazú Camarena. *El placer del chile.* Mexico City: Clío, 1998.

WILLIAM H. BEEZLEY

CHILE, SOCIALIST REPUBLIC OF 100 DAYS.

The Socialist Republic of 100 Days, a radical political regime which ruled Chile from 4 June 1932 to 13 September of that year. Juan Esteban Montero, elected president in late 1931, could not revive Chile's Depression-devastated economy. In June 1932, the Chilean Air Force, under the command of Marmaduke Grove, rebelled, forced Montero from power, and established the Socialist Republic. In truth, this republic was a series of juntas which had seized power illegally and hence ruled without the consent of the nation.

The first junta consisted of General Arturo Puga, Socialist politician Eugenio Matte, and former ambassador to the United States Carlos Dávila. This junta dissolved the Congress Carlos Ibáñez had appointed, declared a moratorium on the collection of all debts, and returned all goods held in pawn at the government-owned Banco de Crédito Popular. On 16 June, Dávila forced Matte from power, exiling him with Grove to Easter Island.

The second junta, firmly under Dávila's control, while less socialist than its predecessor, nonetheless passed various laws giving the state more power to intervene in the economic process, including the right to establish prices and to seize and operate any private business. Eventually, in July, Dávila seized power for himself, only to be deposed in September by General Bartolomé Blanche, who, although tempted to remain in power, held elections which restored democracy to Chile and put Arturo Alessandri back into the presidency.

The Socialist Republic did accomplish some things. For one, it led to the creation of the Socialist Party, which would emerge as one of the nation's most powerful political blocs. It also enacted some laws which, while not sanctioned by a popularly elected congress, allowed the Allende administration (1970–1973) to attempt to seize control of Chile's industrial sector.

See also **Allende Gossens, Salvador; Chile, Political Parties: Socialist Party.**

BIBLIOGRAPHY

Paul W. Drake, *Socialism and Populism in Chile: The Origins of the Leftward Movement of the Chilean Electorate, 1932–52* (1971), pp. 71–83, 91, 94, 96, 149–152.

Manuel Dinamarca, *La république socialista chilena: Orígenes legítimos del partido socialista* (1987), pp. 159–218.

Additional Bibliography

Faúndez, Julio. *Izquierdas y democracia en Chile, 1932-1973.* Santiago de Chile: Ediciones Bat, 1992.

Ponce Durán, Pedro. *Oscar Schnake Vergara: Comienzos del socialismo chileno, 1933–1942.* Santiago, Chile: Ediciones Documentas, 1994.

WILLIAM F. SATER

CHILE, TRUTH COMMISSIONS.

The National Commission for Truth and Reconciliation (TRC) was established in April 1990, with a nine-month mandate to produce a report on the human rights violations (HRV) under military rule (1973–1990) that resulted in death or disappearance of civilian and to recommend reparations and reforms to guarantee respect for HR. The TRC was a vehicle for political and moral—not criminal—justice, and lacked powers of subpoena.

The nonpartisan TRC was composed of eight members of varying political persuasions. It received more than four thousand testimonies and made about two thousand official requests for information from state institutions, receiving responses in about 80 percent of cases. The bulk of information came from the archives of human rights organizations (HROs) and of the Vicariate of Solidarity. The TRC Report was released in February 1991 by the president in a nationally televised ceremony and became available in the form of serialized supplements. It established that the armed forces had been institutionally responsible for 2,115 deaths and that 641 people had died as a result of terrorist actions.

The public reception of the report was very positive, with the strongest support coming from HROs and the church. Victims' organizations were somewhat critical because the report did not include all violations, and the names of violators were not published. The political right, unable to deny the facts, was obliged to resort to criticism of the historical interpretation of events leading to HRV. None of the branches of the armed forces apologized, all confirmed the existence of the "state of war" dismissed by the report, and all reaffirmed their commitment to the military coup and regime. No sector made an attempt to disprove the facts contained in the report.

See also **Chile: The Twentieth Century; Chile, Organizations: Vicariate of Solidarity; Truth Commissions.**

BIBLIOGRAPHY

Barahona de Brito, Alexandra. *Human Rights and Democratization in Latin America: Uruguay and Chile.* Oxford and New York: Oxford University Press, 1997.

Brett, Sebastian. *Chile, a Time of Reckoning: Human Rights and the Judiciary.* Geneva: International Committee of Jurists, 1992.

Brown, Cynthia G. *Human Rights and the "Politics of Agreement": Chile during President Aylwin's First Year.* New York: Americas Watch, 1991.

Comisión Nacional de la Verdad y la Reconciliación. *Informe de la Comisión Nacional de la Verdad y la Reconciliación.* Santiago: Ornitorrinco, 1991.

Correa Sutil, Jorge. "Dealing with Past Human Rights Violations: The Chilean Case after Dictatorship." *Notre Dame Law Review* 67, no. 5 (1992): 1455–1485.

Garretón, Manuel Antonio. "Human Rights and Processes of Democratization." *Journal of Latin American Studies* 26, no. 1 (1994): 221–234.

Human Rights Watch. *Chile: The Struggle for Truth and Justice for Past Human Rights Violations.* New York: Human Rights Watch, 1992.

Human Rights Watch. *Chile: Unsettled Business: Human Rights at the Start of the Frei Presidency.* New York: Human Rights Watch, 1994.

Report of the Chilean National Commission on Truth and Reconciliation. U.S. Institute for Peace. Truth Commissions Digital Collection. Available from http://www.usip.org/library/tc/doc/reports/chile/chile_1993_toc.html.

Zalaquett, José. *The Ethics of Responsibility: Human Rights: Truth and Reconciliation in Chile.* Issues on Human Rights Paper 2. Washington DC: Washington Office on Latin America, 1991.

ALEXANDRA BARAHONA DE BRITO

CHILE, WAR WITH SPAIN.

The War with Spain was a late-nineteenth-century conflict between Chile and Peru and Spain. In the early 1860s, Spain seized Peru's Chincha Islands, which, by virtue of their enormous deposits of guano, constituted the mainstay of Lima's economy. When Peru called upon its hemispheric neighbors for support, Chile responded by forbidding Chileans from selling the Spanish fleet fuel or supplies and by joining an inter-American conference to stop Spanish aggression. Madrid turned on Chile for permitting its citizens to make what it considered scurrilous remarks about the Spanish queen and for placing an embargo on Spanish ships. As compensation for the insults, on Chile's independence day Spain demanded that Chile pay a large indemnity as well as fire a twenty-one-gun salute to the Spanish flag. When the Chileans refused, Spanish admiral Juan Manuel Pareja instituted a naval blockade. This decision actually went against the orders of the newly elected Spanish prime minister, Leopoldo O'Donnell. The government in Santiago responded by declaring war on September 24, 1865.

During the conflict, which was essentially a naval contest, the larger Spanish flotilla quickly asserted control of Chile's coast, blockading Valparaíso. After suffering some minor losses, the Spanish fleet warned the Chileans that unless they paid damages and fired a twenty-one-gun salute, its fleet would fire on the port. Although nearby U.S. and British fleets could have protected Valparaíso from the Spanish, they elected not to do so.

On March 31, 1866, the Spanish ships opened fire on a virtually defenseless Valparaíso, inflicting substantial damage. The Spanish fleet remained in the area until mid-April, when it sailed for Callao, where it subsequently suffered a major defeat at the hands of Peruvian coastal batteries. This battle effectively ended the war. However, an official resolution was not reached with Spain until 1879. Chile's naval defeat prompted the Chilean government to rebuild and improve the navy. Chile was then able to defeat Bolivia and Peru in the War of the Pacific (1879–1884).

Because the United States chose not to invoke its Monroe Doctrine to protect Chile from a European aggressor, relations between Santiago and Washington suffered. The war with Spain also demonstrated to the Chileans their need both to fortify its principal ports and to acquire a fleet to defend its frontiers.

See also **Chile: The Nineteenth Century.**

BIBLIOGRAPHY

Cerda Catalán, Alfonso. *La Guerra entre España y las repúblicas del Pacífico, 1864–1866: El bombardeo de Valparaíso y el combate naval del Callao.* Providencia, Chile: Editorial Puerto de Palos, 2000.

Davis, W. C. *The Last Conquistadores: The Spanish Intervention in Peru and Chile, 1863–1866* (1950).

Galdames, Luis. *A History of Chile* (1941), pp. 306–310.

Heredia, Edmundo A. *El imperio del guano: América Latina ante la guerra de España en el Pacífico.* Córdoba, Argentina: Alción, 1998.

WILLIAM F. SATER

CHILOÉ. Chiloé, island archipelago province with nearly 155,000 inhabitants (2002) in southern Chile. The earliest known inhabitants of the islands were the nomadic people called the *Chonos* and also the Huilliche, with links to the Mapuche. On the Isla Grande de Chiloé, the largest island, the Spaniards established several fortified settlements (Castro, Ancud, Curaco de Vélez) to protect the southern flank of the Viceroyalty of Peru from English and Dutch corsairs sailing into the Pacific after crossing the Strait of Magellan or Cape Horn. With strong attachments to Spain, Chiloé was Chile's loyalist stronghold during the Wars of Independence. Since the nineteenth century residents of the islands, called *Chilotans*, have migrated to Argentine Patagonia or the Chilean province of Magallanes for work. Tourism and aquaculture are important to the economy. The island's unique wooden architecture has received international attention. The particular style, evident in small wooden churches, developed with the arrival of Jesuit missionaries in the seventeenth century; the churches combine native and Christian belief systems. Set at the water's edge, the buildings have wooden shingles carved from the Alerce tree known as *tejuelas*, and besides creating a striking geometric design, can keep out rain.

See also **Chile, Geography; Tourism.**

BIBLIOGRAPHY

Renato Cárdenas, *Apuntes para un diccionario de Chiloé* (Castro, 1978).

Philippe Grenier, *Chiloé et les chilotes* (Aix-en-Provence, 1984).

Additional Bibliography

Berg Costa, Lorenzo. *Iglesias de Chiloé: Conservando lo infinito, proyecto y obras 1988–2002..* Santiago de Chile: Universidad de Chile, 2005.

Guarda, Gabriel. *Los encomenderos de Chiloé.* Santiago: Ediciones Universidad Católica de Chile, 2002.

Urbina B., Rodolfo. *La vida en Chiloé en los tiempos del Fogón, 1900–1940.* Valparaíso: Universidad de Playa Ancha Editorial, Editorial Puntángeles, 2002.

CÉSAR N. CAVIEDES

CHILPANCINGO, CONGRESS OF. Congress of Chilpancingo, Mexico's first political assembly. The need for military and political organization prompted the principal leaders of the insurgents, particularly Ignacio Rayón (1773–1832) and José María Morelos y Pavón (1765–1815), to form a governing junta. Their first effort, the *Junta de Zitácuaro*, proved unsuccessful. The divisions among its members convinced Morelos to accept Carlos María de Bustamante's (1774–1848) proposal to convene a Congress, the Supremo Congreso Nacional Americano, with representatives from the provinces, at Chilpancingo in September 1813. Because elections could not be completed in all provinces, only two deputies, José Manuel de Herrera (c. 1776–1831) and José María Murguía y Galardi, were elected. Morelos named three other proprietary deputies, López Rayón, José María Liceaga (c. 1780–1818), and José Sixto Verduzco, and three substitutes, Bustamante, José María Cos y Pérez (d. 1819) and Andrés Quintana Roo (1787–1851). The *Reglamento* (the regulations) for its organization was issued on 11 September, and Morelos's views on government, the *Sentimientos de la Nación*, were read at its inauguration on 14 September. Once installed, Congress selected Morelos for the executive and determined how the judiciary should be established. On 6 November the Congress issued its *Acta solemne de la declaración de independencia*, the declaration of national independence.

The establishment of the Congress, however, did not resolve the divisions among the insurgents, and the conflicts between the military leaders and the lawyers resulted in a decline of the movement. Pursued by the royalists, Congress wandered in search of safety. It increased its number of deputies early in 1814, but functioned in an irregular manner. In October 1814 it issued the Apatzingán constitution, the *Decreto constitucional para la libertad de la América mexicana*. After Morelos was captured by the royalists (November 1815), Manuel Mier y Terán (1789–1832) dissolved Congress in Tehuacán on 15 December 1815.

See also **Mexico: 1810–1910.**

BIBLIOGRAPHY

Archer, Christon I. *The Birth of Modern Mexico, 1780–1824.* Wilmington, DE: Scholarly Resources Inc., 2003.

Guedea, Virginia. "Los procesos electorales insurgentes," *Estudios de Historia Novohispana* 11 (1991): 201–249.

Lemoine, Ernesto. "Zitácuaro, Chilpancingo y Apatzingán. Tres grandes momentos de la insurgencia mexicana,"

in *Boletín del Archivo General de la Nación,* 2d series, vol. 4, no. 3 (1963).

Lemoine, Ernesto, ed. *Manuscrito Cárdenas, Documentos del Congreso de Chilpancingo hallados entre los papeles del caudillo José María Morelos, sorprendido por los realistas en la acción de Tlacotepec el 24 de febrero de 1814* (1980).

VIRGINIA GUEDEA

CHIMALPAHIN

CHIMALPAHIN (1579–1660). Chimalpahin (*b.* 26 May 1579; *d.* 1660), premier writer of Nahuatl prose. Don Domingo Francisco de San Antón Muñón Chimalpahin Quauhtlehuanitzin, who was born in Amecameca, Mexico, and was most active in the first two decades of the seventeenth century, produced a mass of historical writings on indigenous Mexico. Although he never lost his close identification with his homeland, his career unfolded in Mexico City. Chimalpahin wrote copiously about both Chalco and Mexico Tenochtitlán, covering both pre-conquest and post-conquest periods. His annals represent a large range of Nahuatl thought and expression.

See also **Nahuatl.**

BIBLIOGRAPHY

Susan Schroeder, *Chimalpahin and the Kingdoms of Chalco* (1991).

Additional Bibliography

Benoist, Valérie. "La construcción de una comunidad nahua/española en las relaciones de Chimalpahin." *Estudios de Cultura Náhuatl* 34 (2003): 205–208.

Namala, Doris Mathilde. "Chimalpahin in His Time: An Analysis of the Writings of a Nahua Annalist of Seventeenth-Century Mexico Concerning His Own Lifetime." Ph.D. diss., University of California, Los Angeles, 2002.

JAMES LOCKHART

CHIMÚ

CHIMÚ. Chimú, Between 900 and 1460 CE the north coast of Peru was dominated by an empire controlled by an ethnic group called the Chimú. This empire, called by the Spanish "the Kingdom of Chimor," controlled at its maximum extent more than 620 miles of the Peruvian coast. The Chimú Empire is the only pre-Columbian Peruvian state other than the Incas for which there exists ethnohistoric information. The Incas had conquered the Chimú between 1460 and 1470, only sixty to seventy years before the European invasion. As a result, Spanish chroniclers were able to record a limited amount of information about the Chimú culture as it existed before the Inca conquest. Unfortunately, only a few fragments of this information from the chronicles have survived. These bits of information, together with Spanish legal documents of the early colonial period and recent archaeological studies, have shed some light on the Chimú culture.

Chimú origin stories collected as oral histories by the Spaniards name Taycanamu as the legendary founder of the first Chimú dynasty. He is said to have arrived in the Moche valley after having traveled by sea on a balsa raft. Saying he was sent by a great lord across the sea to govern this land, he established a settlement in the lower valley. The son and the grandson of Taycanamu, whose names were Guacricaur and Ñançenpinco, established control over the entire valley. Archaeological and ethnohistoric data suggest that the Chimú then began a two-phase expansion.

Ñançenpinco, having completed the conquest of the Moche valley, began the first phase of imperial expansion around 1350. His conquests extended to the Jequetepeque valley in the north and the Santa valley in the south. Following a series of unnamed successors, the seventh or eighth king, Minchancaman, continued a second phase of imperial expansion. Completed by about 1450, the second expansion brought the empire to its maximum extent, from the Chillón valley in the south to Tumbes in the north. Shortly thereafter, the Chimú fell to the invading Inca armies. By 1470 the Inca had conquered Chimor and carried off Minchancaman (whom the Incas called Chimú Capac) to Cuzco as a royal hostage.

The economy of the Chimú Empire was based primarily on agriculture, but fishing and shellfish gathering were also important. Highly complex irrigation systems were used to bring water to the vast number of fields in the Chimú domain. These enormous networks of canals were the largest ever created in ancient Peru. The construction and maintenance of the canals and the proper distribution of water required an extensive administrative bureaucracy. Archaeological studies have identified a hierarchy of provincial administrative centers throughout the empire that provided state control over production. These centers carried out the will of the emperor, who governed from the imperial capital at Chan Chan. State construction projects such as canals, roads, and cities, and staffing of the imperial army, were accomplished by the citizens of the empire paying their taxes in labor.

Chimú society was a rigid hierarchy of social classes. The most powerful class, the hereditary nobility, exercised complete control over the production, storage, and redistribution of the wealth of the state. Luxury goods seem to have been concentrated in the hands of the elite. Class distinction was so absolute that kings were held to be divine. Kings and nobles were believed to have had a separate origin from that of commoners. Beyond the distinction between nobles and commoners, people were ranked by their occupation. In a society with an economy based on complex hydraulic works, people having technical knowledge were especially valued. Artisans, working for the elite, had special status and special privileges: they could wear ear spools and live next to the nobility.

Ethnohistoric accounts give some insight into the Chimú legal system. Society was regulated by strict laws with severe punishments for offenders. Chimú society seems to have been especially concerned about theft, which may have been regarded as an offense against the gods as well as against humans. Although artistic expression was standardized in terms of the motifs used, the Chimú were superb artisans and craftsmen. They particularly excelled in the arts of weaving and metalwork. Chimú goldsmiths were carried off to work for the Incas, and much of the golden treasure captured from the Inca by the Spanish was of Chimú origin.

See also **Archaeology; Art: Pre-Columbian Art of South America; Chavín; Incas, The; Moche.**

BIBLIOGRAPHY

The classic source of the Chimú is John H. Rowe, "The Kingdom of Chimor," *Acta Americana* 6 (1948): 26–59. See also Michael Moseley and Kent C. Day, eds., *Chan Chan: Andean Desert City* (1982); and Michael Moseley and Alana Cordy-Collins, *The Northern Dynasties: Kingship and Statecraft in Chimor* (1990).

Additional Bibliography

Leicht, Hermann. *Arte y cultura preincaicos: Un milenio de imperio chimú* (1963).

Ravines, Rogger, and Anthony P. Andrews *Chanchán: Metrópoli chimú* (1980).

GORDON F. MCEWAN

CHINAMPAS.

CHINAMPAS. *Chinampas,* a term from the Nahuatl *chinámitl* that refers to an indigenous method of agriculture used to promote the high yields required to support a dense population. By extending strips of land (*chinampas*) into the shallow lakes and wetlands of Mesoamerica, the farmers have the benefit of year-round irrigation. Best known in the Basin of Mexico and dating there from as early as 1100, *chinampas* are still extant in, for example, Xochimilco. Some sources employ the Spanish term *camellones* as a synonym for *chinampas*. Recent archaeological and historical research may be broadening the temporal and spatial framework for this type of agriculture, pointing to the importance of "raised fields" as a means of sustaining state formation in the Maya sphere.

For centuries foreign observers have mistaken chinampas for "floating gardens," possibly because *chinampas* often have woven reed structures fortifying their banks. Alternatively, the confusion may be owing to some movable nurseries that were towed about Lake Chalco-Xochimilco.

BIBLIOGRAPHY

S. L. Cline, *Colonial Culhuacán, 1580–1600: A Social History of an Aztec Town* (1986), pp. 132–135, provides data derived from indigenous sources on *chinampas*. See also Jeffrey R. Parsons, "The Role of Chinampa Agriculture in the Food Supply of Aztec Tenochtitlán," in *Cultural Change and Continuity: Essays in Honor of James Bennett Griffin,* edited by Charles E. Cleland (1976), pp. 233–257, and Pedro Armillas, "Gardens on Swamps," in *Science* 174 (1971), pp. 653–661, for a discussion of the importance of this type of farming for the support of a large population.

Additional Bibliography

Rojas Rabiela, Teresa. *Presente, pasado y futuro de las chinampas.* México, D.F.: CIESAS, 1995.

STEPHANIE WOOD

CHINANDEGA.

CHINANDEGA. Chinandega, an important agricultural center in western Nicaragua. In 1842 Chinandega served as the site of unsuccessful Central American unification talks among Honduras, El Salvador, and Nicaragua, and it subsequently was often mentioned as a possible capital of a new Central American Union. In 1855 it served as one of the bases for William Walker's invasion of Nicaragua. In February 1927 an aerial bombardment of Chinandega was carried out by two U.S. pilots as part of the effort to control Liberal insurrectionists who were located there. Several hundred women and children were killed, and widespread destruction resulted from what was considered to be the first tactical use of air power in warfare. In 1978–1979 heavy fighting took place around Chinandega between the Sandinistas and government troops. Today it is a prosperous commercial and agricultural processing center. Traditionally, the region was famous for corn, coffee, and oranges. Cotton production was expanded in the 1950s, but there have been difficulties in controlling pests. Sugarcane continues to be grown. The largest sugar refinery in the country is near Chinandega. The city is estimated to have a population of 100,000 people (2005).

See also **Nicaragua.**

BIBLIOGRAPHY

Jeffrey L. Gould, *To Lead as Equals: Rural Protest and Political Consciousness in Chinandega, Nicaragua, 1912–1979* (1990).

Additional Bibliography

Gobat, Michel. *Confronting the American Dream: Nicaragua under U.S. Imperial Rule.* Durham, NC: Duke University Press, 2005.

Ortega Hegg, Manuel, and Marcelina Castillo Venerio. *La gestión de los gobiernos locales desde la perspectiva de los ciudadanos: Así piensan los residentes de Chinandega.* Managua: Centro de Análisis Socio-Cultural, 2001.

Romero, Jilma, and Teresa Cabrera. *Tierra ardiente: El occidente de Nicaragua a través de su historia.* Managua: Departamento de Historia de la Universidad Nacional Autónoma de Nicaragua (UNAN-Nicaragua), 2005.

DAVID L. JICKLING

CHINA POBLANA.
China Poblana, a style of dress worn by Mexican women in Puebla from the sixteenth through the late nineteenth century. The word *china* has little to do with China. *China poblana* was originally the name given to domestic servants but also was used to refer to a pulque seller, a woman who wrapped cigars, a laundress, or a prostitute. A *china poblana* was distinguished by her ornate style of dress, which was distinct from indigenous and European upper-class modes. Her skirt of colorful, sturdy wool was dotted with sequins of gold and silver. Cinched at the waist and very wide at the bottom, it covered billowing petticoats and was complemented by ribbons, silk stockings, and satin slippers. Her finely embroidered blouse was immaculately white. She wrapped a rebozo around her arms and coiffed her abundant hair in thick braids, interwoven with colored ribbons and gathered on the top of her head by a fine comb. She completed her costume with long gold earrings and fine bracelets. She did not merely walk. She sauntered with elegance and arrogance along the streets.

The popular image and inspiration for the *China poblana* dress style derives from the life and legend of Catarina de San Juan (c. 1607–1688). Although she was born into an aristocratic family in India, Catarina was baptized and sold into the slave trade before arriving in New Spain. Considered a visionary, Catarina not only achieved sainthood, but also became an important symbol of mestizo womanhood and the city of Puebla, where a monument of *La China Poblana* stands.

During the Wars of the Reform, the *china poblana* became a national symbol, accompanying her husband into battles and adorning her costume with tricolor ribbons. Although her dress fell into disuse in Puebla in the 1880s, it has preoccupied writers and poets as material for legend and folkloric color since the colonial period. Stylizations of the dress are still used in festivals, especially in central Mexico. The tricolor skirt with an eagle embroidered in sequins is one of the best-known versions.

See also **Mexico, Wars and Revolutions: The Reform.**

BIBLIOGRAPHY

Artes de México. *La china poblana.* México, D.F.: Artes de México, 2003.

Cordero y Torres, Enrique. *Historia compendiada del estado de Puebla,* vol. 2 (1965).

Lavín, Lydia, and Gisela Balassa. *Museo del traje mexicano.* México, D.F.: Editorial Clío, 2001.

Myers, Kathleen Ann. *Neither Saints Nor Sinners: Writing the Lives of Women in Spanish America.* New York: Oxford University Press, 2003.

Puente, R. Carrasco. *Bibliografía de Catarina de San Juan y de la china poblana* (1950).

Santamaría, Francisco J. *Diccionario de Mejicanismos* (1959).

Vigil, Angel. *The Eagle on the Cactus: Traditional Stories from Mexico/ El águila encima del nopal: Cuentos tradicionales de Mexico.* Westport, CT: Libraries Unlimited, 2000.

MARY KAY VAUGHAN

CHINCHA.
Chincha is the name of both a province and a city in Peru. The province, located 124 miles south of Lima in the Peruvian department of Ica, has a population of 168,578 and a city population of 52,661 (2000 census). *Chincha*—a Quechua word for "north," indicating its location relative to Cuzco, the center of the Inca empire—also refers to the pre-Hispanic people who lived in this area. Conquistador Diego de Almagro founded the city Villa de Almagro in Chincha in 1537. Grand estates, holding the largest slave population in Peru, produced wine, sugar, and cotton developed in the rich soil. During the nineteenth century, guano exports from the Chincha Islands led to an economic boom for Peru, which provoked a massive importation of workers from Canton, China. In the early twenty-first century, Chincha is a major agricultural center and the heart of Peru's black culture. An earthquake of 8.0 on the Richter scale shook the region in 2007 causing major destruction.

See also **Archaeology; Art: Pre-Columbian Art of South America; Indigenous Peoples.**

BIBLIOGRAPHY

Feldman, Heidi Carolyn. *Black Rhythms of Peru: Reviving African Musical Heritage in the Black Pacific.* Middletown, CT: Wesleyan University Press, 2006.

Cushner, Nicholas P. *Lords of the Land: Sugar, Wine and Jesuit Estates of Coastal Peru, 1600–1767.* Albany: State University of New York Press, 1980.

Rodríguez Pastor, Humberto. *Hijos del Celeste Imperio en el Peru (1850–1900): Migración, agricultura, mentalidad y explotación.* Lima: Sur Casa de Estudios del Socialismo, 2001.

Uhle, Max. *Explorations in Chincha*, ed. A. L. Kroeber. Berkeley: University of California Press, 1924.

MÓNICA RICKETTS

CHINCHA ISLANDS.

Chincha Islands, the best-known group of some thirty major islands and scores of islets and rock outcrops located off the coast of Peru. Under the administration of Ramón Castilla in the 1850s, the guano-rich islands assumed increased importance in the economic history of Peru. Guano, the excrement from the guanay (Peruvian cormorant) and other seabirds, was in increased demand as a fertilizer for agriculture around the world. This led to increased foreign investment and immigration, much of it forced Chinese labor, and to the systematic exploitation of the islands. Production was erratic in the twentieth century, but the islands remained commercially important producers of guano.

See also **Guano Industry.**

BIBLIOGRAPHY

Robert Cushman Murphy, *Bird Islands of Peru* (1925).

Emilio Romero, *Perú: Una nueva geografía*, 2 vols. (1973).

Additional Bibliography

Campbell, Michael T. *Guano and Manpower: the Case of Mona Island, Navassa Island and the Chincha Islands.* Barbados: Paper Presented at the 28th Annual Conference of the Association of Caribbean Historians, 1996.

Hollett, D. *More Precious than Gold: The Story of the Peruvian Guano Trade.* Madison: Fairleigh Dickinson University Press, 2007.

JOHN C. SUPER

CHINCHA ISLANDS WAR.

This unexpected conflict (1864–1866) between Spain and a coalition of several Latin American countries represented a belated attempt by Spain to reassert control over its former colonies. Taking advantage of the United States' involvement in its own civil war, which undermined its ability to strenuously enforce the Monroe Doctrine (a policy that prohibited European nations from meddling in Latin America), Spain occupied the territory of the present-day Dominican Republic and then sent a naval expedition to Peru. Ostensibly on a scientific mission, the squadron's commander, Admiral Luis Hernández Pinzon, carried secret orders to support Spanish citizens if they complained that their host nations maltreated them. The Spanish soon found reason to intervene.

In 1863 group of Spanish workers charged that a Peruvian *hacendado* abused them. When the local courts upheld the landowner, Spain sent an envoy to protect its nationals. The Peruvian government, however, refused to meet with him until Spain recognized the existence of the Peruvian republic.

Insulted by Peru's actions, and arguing that a state of war still existed between the two nations—they had never signed a peace treaty—Spain seized Peru's Chincha Islands, some guano-covered spits of land. The Spanish act infuriated Peru because exports of this nitrate-rich fertilizer funded its economy. It also distressed Peru's neighbors, particularly Chile, which organized an international congress to protest Madrid's aggression. The Spanish remained unmoved, demanding that Peru pay 3 million pesos if it wished to regain possession of the islands. Without the revenues from guano sales, which constituted Peru's main source of income, Lima had no choice but to capitulate. Thus in January 1865 Peru paid the extortion.

The matter still did not end: Madrid, distressed by Chilean insults, ordered its fleet south. When Chile refused to apologize for insulting the Madrid government or to fire a salute to the Spanish flag, Pareja blockaded Valparaiso. Chile responded not merely by declaring war on Spain but, by February 1866, it also convinced Bolivia, Ecuador, and Peru to join an anti-Spanish coalition. In the maritime war that followed, Chile captured a Spanish corvette, the *Covadonga*, which so depressed Pareja that he committed suicide.

His replacement, Admiral Casto Méndez, failed to defeat the allied fleet. Finally he demanded that Chile either fire a twenty-one gun salute to Spain or he would bombard Valparaiso. When Chile refused, on 31 March 1866, Méndez's ships bombarded the defenseless port, reducing it to ruins. The Spaniards then sailed north to attack Peru's principal port Callao. But on 2 May 1866, the Peruvian coastal batteries repulsed Méndez. Isolated, without supplies and facing mutinious crews, Méndez returned to Spain. The expedition had been a fiasco, gaining Spain little but the emnity of Latin America, the United States, which looked foolish for not strenuously enforcing the Monroe Doctrine, and Europe.

See also **Chincha Islands.**

BIBLIOGRAPHY

Cortada, James W. *Spain and the American Civil War: Relations at Mid-Century, 1855–1868.* Philadelphia: American Philosophical Society, 1980.

Davis, William C. *The Last Conquistadores: The Spanish Intervention in Peru and Chile, 1833–1866.* Athens: University of Georgia Press, 1950.

WILLIAM F. SATER

CHINCHA KINGDOM.

Chincha, one of the most important pre-Inca kingdoms in Peru. It ruled the Chincha valley, about 130 miles south of Lima, but the exact dates of the kingdom are unknown. It probably controlled the valley by 1300 CE and was incorporated into the Inca Empire about 1450. Relations between Chincha and the Inca were cordial. The lord of Chincha was traveling with the Inca Atahualpa at the time the Inca was captured by the Spanish at Cajamarca in 1532. The archaeological site known as La Centinela, near modern Chincha Baja, apparently served as the Chincha capital.

The Chincha valley, shallow but very wide at its mouth, is probably the richest Peruvian coastal valley south of Lima. María Rostworowski's studies of early colonial documents have provided evidence of a population divided into specialized economic groups of farmers, fishermen, and long-distance traders. These traders were the most intriguing feature of Chincha social and economic organization. It is believed that they sailed hundreds of boats on the ocean and had a virtual monopoly on trade with the area that is modern Ecuador. While there is no certainty of the nature of this trade, it is believed that it mainly involved an exchange of metals from inland regions to the south and east for the highly valued spondylus shell from the warm waters off the Ecuadorian coast. The Pacific coast of Peru is influenced by the cold Humboldt current, which fosters one of the richest regions of marine plant and animal life in the

world. However, this region does not include the spondylus, or spiny oyster, which appeared in the south only during the periods of El Niño events, when cold currents were displaced by a southward movement of warmer water. The rare appearances of spondylus corresponded with rains on the Peruvian desert coast. The association between rains and spondylus apparently resulted in the belief that the spondylus brought rain. The red shells became sacred and extremely valuable. It is believed that Chincha dominated the trade that brought the shells from the north by boat, supplying large areas of the Andean highlands.

Archaeological studies have not yet located installations used by the traders. Evidence of the fisherfolk referred to in the written sources has been identified at a seaside site called Lo Demas. Numerous sites of various sizes in the inland heart of the well-irrigated valley were probably related to agricultural activities. These sites include Huacarones and Las Huacas. While the most dense occupation of the Chincha valley dates to the period between 1300 and 1532, its occupation and use began in the early periods of Andean prehistory. Archaeological sites dating to the time of the Paracas and Nazca cultures are prominent in the valley, demonstrating that the great wealth and large populations documented by both the archaeological and written sources for the immediately pre-Columbian periods extended back for more than a millennium.

See also **Precontact History: Andean Region.**

BIBLIOGRAPHY

Dorothy Menzel and John Rowe, "The Role of Chincha in Late Pre-Spanish Peru," in *Ñawpa Pacha* 4 (1966): 63–79.

María Rostworowski De Díez Canseco, "Mercaderes del valle de Chincha en la Época prehispánica: Un documento y unos comentarios," in *Revista Española de Anthropologia Americana* 5 (1970): 135–177.

Craig Morris, "Más allá de las fronteras de Chincha," in *La frontera del estado Inca,* edited by Tom D. Dillehay and Patricia Netherly (1988), pp. 131–140.

Daniel H. Sandweiss, *The Archaeology of Chincha Fishermen: Specialization and Status in Inka Peru* (1992).

CRAIG MORRIS

CHINCHULÍN, PACT OF.

The Pact of Chinchulín (Pork-Barrel Pact) was an October 1931 power-sharing agreement between two of the principal party factions in Uruguay. Under the 1919 Constitution, executive authority was divided between the president and a nine-member National Council of Administration. Reflecting votes cast in the 1928 elections for the council, the Colorado Party had five seats (of which three went to the Batllist faction) and the Blancos, four. The Batllists sought support for their proposal to create a new public corporation Ancap (National Administration of Fuel, Alcohol, and Cement). The urban-oriented, elitist *principista* faction of the Blancos agreed to enter the pact with the Batllists on the condition that the directorates of all public corporations reflect the party composition of the National Council of Administration. The Blancos thus secured an enhanced share of patronage in the public sector. The pact was opposed by the Herrerist Blancos, who supported the overthrow of the constitution by Gabriel Terra in 1933.

See also **Terra, Gabriel; Uruguay: The Twentieth Century; Uruguay, Constitutions; Uruguay, Political Parties: Blanco Party; Uruguay, Political Parties: Colorado Party.**

BIBLIOGRAPHY

Göran G. Lindahl, *Uruguay's New Path: A Study in Politics During the First Colegiado, 1919–1933* (1962).

Gerardo Caetano and Raúl Jacob, *El nacimiento del terrismo, 1930–1933* (1989).

HENRY FINCH

CHINESE LABOR (PERU).

Imports of Chinese labor into Peru began when social and diplomatic pressure to end black slavery by 1854 forced coastal export planters to seek substitute cheap labor. They began contracting peasant labor from Macao. Between 1849 and 1874, nearly 100,000 men were kidnapped or lured from wharfside taverns, shackled on ships, and traded at Peruvian ports for about 300 pesos apiece in groups of fifty or more. The purchasers legally had contracted the labor of each man for eight years, after which he would return to China. The men worked in the guano fields, on the railroads, and in the sugar and cotton fields. On the plantations, housed in former slave barracks, they received meager food rations—a pound of rice and some vegetables once or twice a day. Ill-clothed and housed, the men lacked good medical care. Uric acid in the guano dust undoubtedly infected the lungs of many. Overwork also plagued the indentured men. Workdays were fourteen to sixteen hours long, and holidays were few and far between. Public officials rarely intervened between contract owners and contractees. Disease, poor nutrition, neglect, and overwork took their toll. One estimate places the death rate before 1865 in all venues at about 50 percent.

After 1860 the previously sluggish demand for indentured Chinese resumed when the market for cotton grew with the havoc wrought by the Civil War in the United States. Without legal recourse and not understanding Spanish, many men resisted indenture by fighting—often with one another in the barracks at night—attacking their overseers, fleeing, and in some cases committing suicide. Owners sought to dull resistance by distributing opium and cheap liquor in the barracks, to little avail. The guano mines, rail construction sites, and plantation fields were dangerous and volatile areas subjected to high security. Nevertheless, some men fled successfully, hiding in forests and no doubt aided on occasion by sympathetic local peasants despite offers of rewards. Those who were caught were returned to the work sites, where they underwent severe public whippings, time in the stocks, and other humiliations. They also were isolated from their fellow workers. Suicide occurred rarely enough among the contractees that there is reason to believe that their worldview was largely informed by Confucius, who celebrated the sanctity of all life, and perhaps they became fatalistic. They also may have realized that landlords in Peru were not much different from landlords in China. There is some speculation that suicides were prompted by the conviction that death would mean transportation of the soul back to China. But few of those who outlived indenture ever returned to their homeland.

By 1874 the reorganized Chinese government demanded the abolition of indenture in Peru. Peruvian leaders acceded to the demand with the proviso that the contracts for labor be resolved locally. This method allowed the contract owners to demand a resolution of debts incurred over the life of the contracts. Many men had incurred debts that plantation owners could document for days of work missed due to illness and flight, breakage of tools, personal loans at interest, unpaid purchases of clothing and "luxuries" (firecrackers and candles to celebrate religious holidays), and the like. In these cases contract owners could claim labor for years into the future. Indenture thus was prolonged in some cases into the 1890s, but the importation of new Chinese labor ended in 1874.

As indenture waned and agricultural labor remained scarce, itinerant Chinese plantation labor gangs bargained for wages along with other workers. Competition between ethnic work gangs became common, and by the end of the century indigenous Andean highlanders joined in. Fear of the Chinese may have stirred jealousies within the Afro-Peruvian and indigenous populations. Ethnically divided conflict occurred periodically on the coastal plantations until the War of the Pacific (1879–1883), when conflict between Asians and Peruvians reached new heights with massive attacks on Chinese peasants. After the war Chinese workers once more joined the ethnically mixed plantation labor force. By the early twentieth century a new wave of Chinese and Japanese immigrated voluntarily to Peru. Many were petty merchants and shopkeepers. A Chinese community arose in Lima, and gradually Chinese foods and cooking styles joined the indigenous and European influences in making up a diverse Peruvian cuisine.

See also **Asians in Latin America; Plantations.**

BIBLIOGRAPHY

Peter Blanchard, *The Origins of the Peruvian Labor Movement, 1883–1919* (1982), esp. pp. 123–125.

Michael Gonzáles, *Plantation Agriculture and Social Control in Northern Peru, 1875–1933* (1985).

Humberto Rodríguez Pastor, *Hijos del celeste imperio en el Perú (1850–1900): Migración, agricultura, mentalidad y explotación* (1989).

Additional Bibliography

Derpich, Wilma. *El otro lado azul: 150 años de inmigración China al Perú.* Lima: Fondo Editorial del Congreso del Perú, 1999.

McKeown, Adam. *Chinese Migrant Networks and Cultural Change: Peru, Chicago, Hawaii, 1900–1936.* Chicago: University of Chicago Press, 2001.

Rodríguez Pastor, Humberto. *Herederos del dragón: Historia de la comunidad China en el Perú.* Lima: Fondo Editorial del Congreso del Perú, 2000.

Trazegnies Granda, Fernando de. *En el país de las colinas de arena: Reflexiones sobre la inmigración china en el Perú del S. XIX desde la perspectiva del derecho.* Lima: Pontificia Universidad Católica del Perú, Fondo Editorial, 1994.

VINCENT PELOSO

CHINESE–LATIN AMERICAN RELATIONS. Traces of the first Chinese in Mexico can be found as far back as 1585. The Manila Galleons (1571–1814) that crossed the Pacific, bringing to Mexico and other Spanish colonies in the Western Hemisphere silk, brocades, linen, tea, and spices from China and other Asian lands, also brought many Chinese sailors and merchants, some of whom stayed in the New World. In 1810, the Portuguese contracted with several hundred Chinese workers to plant tea in the capital of Brazil. (*Chá*, the Portuguese word for tea, is a transliteration of the Chinese word for tea.) To remedy the labor shortage in Peru, Mexico, and the Caribbean toward the end of the nineteenth century, more than 300,000 Chinese "coolies" were imported. Since the early twentieth century, there have been few new Chinese arrivals in Latin America due to restrictive immigration laws. Today, Chinese are found in all Latin American countries, assimilated into their societies. Apart from the Manila galleon trade, early contact between China and Latin America arose from emigration.

With the founding of the People's Republic of China (PRC) in 1949, relations between China and Latin America were strained by complex ideological and political factors. During the pre-Cuban Revolution period, Beijing (Peking) had neither the opportunity nor the incentive for involvement in Latin America. The Cuban Revolution in 1959 gave the PRC an opportunity to break the American policy of "containing China," and to establish relations with Latin American countries. However, except for Cuba, China made no diplomatic breakthroughs in the Western Hemisphere in the 1960s. By the 1970s, most of the trade and cultural exchanges between China and Latin America were concentrated on Cuba.

After the PRC's joining the United Nations and the U.S.–China rapprochement, Chinese diplomatic representation in Latin America increased, and by 1978 China had embassies in twelve Latin American countries. This paralleled the growth of Chinese economic activities in Latin America. Nonetheless, the political and economic ties between the two regions were very limited before China adopted an "open-door" policy in 1978.

Since the late 1970s, however, Chinese–Latin American relations have undergone a radical change. Economic interactions have intensified; financial, commercial, investment, and technical ties have been formed where, in general, few existed before. By the end of 1993, China had established diplomatic relations with most of the countries in the region. Taiwan maintains diplomatic and close economic ties with several Central American and the Caribbean countries.

China's 1992 trade volume with Latin American countries reached nearly $3 billion, an all-time high, compared with only $2 million in 1950. Chinese import volume accounted for nearly $1.9 billion, a 21.5 percent increase over the previous year. Export volume climbed to $1.1 billion, a rise of 35.3 percent over 1991. In 1991, Cuba was the only country in the region to which China's exports exceeded $100 million. In 1992, imports of Mexico, Panama, Chile, and Argentina from China also exceeded this figure. Enormous changes have also taken place in the composition of Chinese exports to Latin America. Prior to the 1990s, China's exports to the region were confined to textiles and some raw materials. In recent years, alongside sustained increases in exports of textiles, those of machinery, motor vehicles, airplanes, ships, electrical appliances, and farm machinery rose rapidly. Under the Chinese policy of modernization, imports from Latin America, such as copper, lumber, lead, and zinc are of prime importance. Latin American agricultural exports of wheat, fish meal, and maize have been long-term staples for Chinese consumption.

From 1993 to 2003, trade between Latin America and China expanded 600 percent. China has begun to ship large amounts of manufactured goods to Latin America, creating stiff competition for *maquiladoras*, Mexican factories on the U.S.–Mexican border. Yet China's economic rise has greatly helped the agricultural exports of Latin American countries, especially Brazil and Argentina. Venezuela has also sought and received Chinese investment in its oil industry. Some analysts believe that Venezuela hopes to use China so as to counterbalance its dependence on the United States.

See also **Asians in Latin America.**

BIBLIOGRAPHY

Appelbaum, Nancy P., Anne S. Macpherson, and Karin Alejandra Rosemblatt, eds. *Race and Nation in Modern Latin America.* Chapel Hill: University of North Carolina Press, 2003.

Bradley, Anita. *Trans-Pacific Relations of Latin America* (1942).

Connelly, Marisela, and Romer Cornejo Bustamente, *China–América Latina* (1992).

Cornejo Bustamente, Romer. "El comercio exterior de China con América Latina," in *Comercio Exterior* 35, no. 7 (July 1985): 714–720.

Ding, Sha, et al. *Zhongguo he ladinmeizhou guanxi jianshi* (1987).

Gómez Izquierdo, José Jorge. *El movimiento antichino en México (1871–1934): Problemas del racismo y del nacionalismo durante la Revolución Mexicana.* Colección Divulgación. Mexico: Instituto Nacional de Antropología e Historia, 1992.

Herrera Jerez, Miriam, and Mario Castillo Santana. *De la memoria a la vida pública: Identidades, espacios y jerarquías de los chinos en La Habana republicana (1902–1968).* Havana: Centro de Investigación y Desarrollo de la Cultura Cubana Juan Marinello, 2003.

Johnson, Cecil Earle. *Communist China and Latin America, 1959–1967* (1970).

Leite, José Roberto Teixeira. *A China no Brasil: Influências, marcas, ecos e sobrevivências chinesas na sociedade e na arte brasileiras.* Coleção Viagens da voz. Campinas, Brazil: Editora da Unicamp, 1999.

Li, He. *Sino–Latin American Economic Relations* (1991).

McKeown, Adam. *Chinese Migrant Networks and Cultural Change: Peru, Chicago, Hawaii, 1900–1936.* Chicago: University of Chicago Press, 2001.

Rodríguez Pastor, Humberto. *Hijos del Celeste Imperio en el Perú (1850–1900): Migración, agricultura, mentalidad y explotación* (1989).

Ruilova, Leonardo. *China Popular en América Latina* (1978).

Trazegnies Granda, Fernando de. *En el país de las colinas de arena: Reflexiones sobre la inmigración china en el Perú del S. XIX desde la perspectiva del derecho.* Lima:

Pontificia Universidad Católica del Perú, Fondo Editorial, 1994.

HE LI

CHIQUINHA. *See* Gonzaga, Francisca Hedwiges.

CHIQUINQUIRÁ.
Chiquinquirá, a city of about 60,000 in Colombia's Boyacá Department, is the seat of the shrine of the Virgin of the Rosary of Chiquinquirá. The painting of the Chiquinquirá Virgin, showing her between Saint Anthony of Padua and Saint Andrew, has been dated at about 1550. After being neglected for some years, it was restored to its pristine state, according to witnesses, on 26 December 1586. Custody of the miracle-working image was given to the Dominicans, and an increasingly larger shrine was constructed over the centuries by the order. Until recently the Chiquinquirá region specifically and Boyacá in general were the major source of novices for the Dominicans in Colombia. Since 1919, the Virgin of Chiquinquirá has been the patroness of Colombia. She has devotees in Venezuela as well.

See also **Dominicans.**

BIBLIOGRAPHY

Andrés Mesanza, O.P., *Nuestra Señora de Chiquinquirá: Y monografía histórica de esta villa* (1913).

Pedro De Tobar y Buendía, O.P., *Verdadera histórica relación del origen, manifestación y prodigiosa renovación por sí misma y milagros de la imagen de la Sacratíssima Virgen María ... de Chiquinquirá,* 2d ed. (1986).

Additional Bibliography

Rojas Peña, Víctor Raúl. *La coronación de la Virgen de Chiquinquirá: Mentalidad religiosa e imaginario mariano, 1891-1919: (Historia de Boyacá).* Tunja: Consejo Editorial de Autores Boyacenses: Instituto de Cultura de Boyacá, 2001.

J. LEÓN HELGUERA

CHIRIBOGA, LUZ ARGENTINA
(1940–). Luz Argentina Chiriboga is perhaps the most accomplished contemporary Afro-Latina writer in Ecuador. Born in Esmeraldas on 1 April 1940, she has emerged as an integral voice in Ecuador's search for a pluralistic national identity. The widow of Nelson Estupiñán Bass (author of the first major Afro-Ecuadorean novel, *Cuando los guayacanes florecían*), Chiriboga has established her own reputation with a series of important novels. The first, *Bajo la piel de los tambores* (1991), was translated into English in 1996 with the title *Drums under My Skin.* She contributed to the growing phenomenon of the neo-slave narrative in her critically acclaimed novel *Jonatás y Manuela* (1994). In the novel, Chiriboga rescues the memory of Manuela Sáenz's (Simón Bolívar's companion) slave woman. This important novel rearticulates Afro-Ecuadorean identity in terms of the country's earliest national traditions. In addition to her novels and short stories, Chiriboga has worked to document and preserve Afro-Ecuadorean identity and culture. In *Diáspora por los caminos de Esmeraldas: Décimas, cuentos, adivinanzas, leyendas, coplas, refranes, dichos, rompecabezas, trabalenguas, chigualo, arrullos, recetas de cocina* (1997) she mines African diaspora discourse to preserve the jokes, riddles, legends, sayings, tongue-twisters, and recipes that help define coastal Ecuadorian identity.

See also **Literature: Spanish America.**

BIBLIOGRAPHY

DeCosta-Willis, Miriam. "The Poetics and Politics of Desire: Eroticism in Luz Argentina Chiriboga's *Bajo la piel de los tambores.*" *Afro-Hispanic Review* 14, no. 1 (1995): 18–25.

Feal, Rosemary Geisdorfer. "Entrevista con Luz Argentina Chiriboga (Followed by Poems from Her *La contraportada del deseo,* Translated by Rosemary Geisdorfer Feal)." *Afro-Hispanic Review* 12, no. 2 (1993): 12–16.

O'Donnell, William E. "*Bajo la piel de los tambores: Post-Colonial Bildungsroman.*" In *The Image of the Outsider in Literature, Media, and Society,* edited by Will Wright and Steven Kaplan, pp. 131–136. Pueblo, CO: Society for the Interdisciplinary Study of Social Imagery, University of Southern Colorado, 2002.

Zielina, María Carmen. "*Jonatás y Manuela*: La historia de una amistad transnacional y étnica." *Revista Iberoamericana* 65 (1999): 681–695.

V. DANIEL ROGERS

CHIRIGUANOS. The Chiriguanos, the descendants of the Tupi-Guaraní migrated in the fifteenth century from what is now Brazil to the foothills of the southeastern Bolivian Andes, where they conquered and intermingled with the resident Chané Indians. Superb warriors, the Chiriguanos presented a threat to the Incas, who constructed numerous fortresses to defend themselves, not always successfully. When the Spanish conquered the Andean peoples, the Chiriguanos raided deep into the highlands, almost reaching the silver-mining center of Potosí. Viceroy Francisco Toledo mounted a large expedition against the Chiriguanos, but was forced to retreat. He then adopted the Inca strategy of creating a number of fortress-towns to contain the Indians. Chiriguano demographic growth in the seventeenth century and a society organized for war made it possible to resist Spanish encroachment.

By the end of the century, the Chiriguano population may have approached 250,000. A highly decentralized system of government, based on consensual politics under village-level chiefs who accepted the loose leadership of regional chiefs, remained a distinguishing feature of Chiriguano politics. Jesuit attempts at missionizing the Chiriguanos in the eighteenth century failed, but between 1780 and 1810 the Franciscans were able to establish a string of missions in the region. The Wars of Independence led to the destruction of the mission system, and participation on the patriots' side by Chiriguano groups under the leadership of Cumbay helped them to reconquer much of the territory lost earlier.

In the second half of the nineteenth century Creoles were able to regain the initiative when the Bolivian mining economy improved and cattle ranching, the main creole economic activity, became lucrative. Creole settlers drove their cattle onto the Indians' cornfields and, with better weapons, were able to subjugate the Chiriguanos. A sharp demographic decline set in; whereas the Chiriguanos numbered around 100,000 at the beginning of the nineteenth century, by the early twentieth those remaining in Bolivia numbered only 26,000. By this time, many Indians had migrated to Argentina. At the same time a new Franciscan mission system, in which Chiriguano groups sought refuge from the exactions of the settlers, helped in the conquest of the region. In an effort to avoid the onerous living conditions on haciendas or the restricted environment of the missions, many Chiriguanos left their homes and, through labor contracts mediated by their chiefs, became migrant laborers on the sugar plantations of Jujuy in northern Argentina. Valued very highly for their hard work, the Chiriguanos were the most important workers on the plantations from the late nineteenth century to the 1930s.

The Chaco War (1932–1935) brought about the destruction of the Franciscan missions and the dispersal of the Chiriguanos into Paraguay and especially Argentina. Because they spoke Guaraní like many Paraguayans, the Bolivian military saw the Chiriguanos as traitors and often refused to permit them to return to their homeland. As a result, Chiriguano groups are dispersed throughout southeastern Bolivia, the Salta province of Argentina, and the Paraguayan Chaco, living as hacienda peons or in independent villages.

See also **Indigenous Peoples; Tupi-Guarani.**

BIBLIOGRAPHY

The most inclusive histories of the Chiriguanos are Francisco Pifarré, *Los Chiriguano-Guaraní: Historia de un pueblo* (1989); and Giuseppe Calzavarini, *Nación chiriguana: Grandeza y ocaso* (1980). A collection of brilliant essays spanning much of Chiriguano history is Thierry Saignes, *Ava y karai: Ensayos sobre la frontera chiriguana: Siglos XVI–XXX* (1990). Hernando Sanabria Fernández, *Apiaguaiqui Tumpa* (1972), and Erick D. Langer, *Economic Change and Rural Resistance in Southern Bolivia: 1880–1930* (1989), treat the nineteenth and twentieth centuries.

ERICK D. LANGER

CHIRINO, JOSÉ LEONARDO (?–1796). José Leonardo Chirino (*d.* 10 December 1796), leader of the 1795 slave uprising in Coro, Venezuela. Chirino was a *zambo*, the freeborn son of a male slave and an Indian woman. He worked for a rich Coro trader named José Tellería, whom Chirino had accompanied on one of his commercial ventures to Haiti. While there, Chirino became aware of the early black and mulatto insurrectionary movements. In 1795, he and fellow conspirator José Caridad González, an African slave who had fled Curaçao for Coro, instigated an uprising of blacks in which they favored the establishment of a republic based on French law and proclaiming social equality and the abolition of privileges. Chirino was pursued, imprisoned, and condemned to death by hanging. He was executed in the central plaza of Caracas. His head was hung in a cage at the door of the city, and his severed hands were displayed in two towns in the area of Falcón.

See also **Slave Revolts: Spanish America.**

BIBLIOGRAPHY

Pedro Manuel Arcaya, *Insurrección de los negros de la serranía de Coro* (1949).

Additional Bibliography

Ramos Guédez, José Marcial. *Bibliografía y hemerografía sobre la insurrección de José Leonardo Chirino en la serranía de Coro, 1795–1995*. Caracas: Universidad Central de Venezuela, 1996.

Rodríguez, Luis Cipriano. *José Leonardo Chirino y la insurrección de la Serranía de Coro de 1795: Insurrección de libertad o rebelión de independencia: Memoria del simposio realizado en Mérida los días 16 y 17 de noviembre de 1995*. Mérida: Universidad de Los Andes: Universidad Central de Venezuela, 1996.

Wright, Winthrop R. *Café con leche: Race, Class, and National Image in Venezuela*. Austin: University of Texas Press, 1990.

INÉS QUINTERO

CHIRIPÁ. Gauchos of the Río de la Plata adopted many elements of pre-Columbian culture, including clothing. The original peoples of South America developed the *chiripá* (a word of probable Quechua origin), a rectangular cloth worn like a diaper. After passing the cloth between his legs, a man secured it around his waist with a stout belt (*tirador*). The seamless garment provided great comfort while riding. Underneath the *chiripá*, gauchos sometimes wore white, lace-fringed leggings called *calzoncillos blancos*. During the late nineteenth century, the traditional *chiripá* gave way to imported *bombachas*, bloused (usually black) pants taken in at the ankle.

See also **Gaucho.**

BIBLIOGRAPHY

Madaline Wallis Nichols, *The Gaucho* (1968), p. 13.

Richard W. Slatta, *Gauchos and the Vanishing Frontier* (1983), p. 73.

Additional Bibliography

Assunção, Fernando O. *Historia del gaucho: El gaucho, ser y quehacer*. Buenos Aires: Editorial Claridad, 1999.

Gari, Abel. *Del chiripá al pantalón y algo más—*. Ayacucho: Museo Histórico Regional Ayacucho, 1999.

Slatta, Richard W. *Comparing Cowboys and Frontiers*. Norman: University of Oklahoma Press, 1997.

Stedile Zattera, Véra. *Pilchas do gaúcho: Vestuário tradicional, arreios e avios de mate*. Porto Alegre: Pallotti, 1998.

RICHARD W. SLATTA

CHISPAS. *See* **Violencia, La.**

CHOCANO, JOSÉ SANTOS (1875–1934). José Santos Chocano (*b*. 14 May 1875; *d*. 13 December 1934), Peruvian poet. Acclaimed as Poet of America, Chocano was born in Lima to a father whose origin can be traced to Don Gonzalo Fernández de Córdoba, a famous Spanish soldier known as the "Great Captain"; his mother was a wealthy miner's daughter. Nevertheless, Chocano was not a happy child; he made the motto of his family coat of arms his own: Either I find a way, or I make one. On entering the University of San Marcos, at age 16, he began three careers: student, poet, and politician. In politics he learned that in Peru, family name means more than personal skills. His success as a poet was outstanding: he began writing before the age of ten and published his first book at twenty. His *Poesías completas* was published in Spain in 1902. King Alfonso XIII received from Chocano's hand the book *Alma América* (1906); Spanish American countries demanded his presence and applauded his recitals; and, in 1922, the Peruvian nation crowned him National Poet.

Chocano did not achieve political power because his creed accepted the so-called organizational dictatorships. But as a diplomat, he scored resounding victories arbitrating disputes between Guatemala and El Salvador, Colombia and Peru, and Peru and Ecuador. Twice Chocano escaped the firing squad. Once he eluded an angry mob in Guatemala, and on another occasion, after receiving a slap in the face, he fatally shot his adversary. One biographer characterized Chocano's adventurous and colorful life as a "mixture of vigor, audacity, and the picaresque." Disheartened, he moved with his young wife, Margarita, and their son to Chile. The Chileans welcomed Chocano, who continued writing, reciting, and trying his hand at business ventures. He died when an assassin fatally stabbed him on a streetcar. One of his verses inadvertently became a prophecy: "He who took a life by assault/could only die by a sword thrust."

See also **Literature: Spanish America.**

BIBLIOGRAPHY

Augusto Tamayo y Vargas, "J.S.C.," in *Latin American Writers*, edited by Carlos A. Solé and Maria Isabel Abreu, vol. 2 (1989), pp. 543–549.

Additional Bibliography

Rodríguez-Peralta, Phyllis W. *José Santos Chocano.* New York: Twayne Publishers, 1970.

Rodríguez-Peralta, Phyllis W. *Tres poetas cumbres en la poesía peruana: Chocano, Eguren, y Vallejo.* Madrid: Playor, 1983.

Salgado, María Antonia. *Modern Spanish American Poets. Second Series.* Detroit: Gale, 2004.

Sánchez, Luis Alberto. *Aladino: O, vida y obra de José Santos Chocano.* México: Libro Mex, 1960.

BALBINA SAMANIEGO

CHOCÓ. Chocó, a department in northwestern Colombia, comprising approximately 18,000 square miles. One of the most isolated and least developed regions of Colombia, the Chocó is covered by dense tropical vegetation and is cut off from the interior of the country by the Western Cordillera. It is one of the rainiest places on earth, with an average annual rainfall of 420 inches. In 1985 the department had a population of 234,000, 90 percent of whom were blacks and mulattoes, concentrated along the San Juan and Atrato rivers. The capital, Quibdó, which is located on the Atrato, had a population of more than 74,000 in 1985.

In the sixteenth century the region was inhabited by the Chocó and Cuna Indians, who resisted Spanish occupation. Spaniards were eager to exploit the rich gold deposits of the Chocó, but it was not until the late seventeenth century that the Indians were subdued and mining could begin on a large scale. Blacks were used increasingly as laborers and by 1778 accounted for 60 percent of the population.

The Chocó was part of the state (later department) of Cauca in the nineteenth century but became a separate department in 1947. The mining of gold and platinum remained the basis of the economy, but individual miners rarely prospered because of the primitive methods used and the large share of the profits taken by intermediaries. As a result, the Chocó remained one of Colombia's poorest departments; a 1980s government study found that 83 percent of the population lacked the basic necessities of life.

See also **Cauca Valley.**

BIBLIOGRAPHY

Robert C. West, *The Pacific Lowlands of Colombia: A Negroid Area of the American Tropics* (1957).

William Frederick Sharp, *Slavery on the Spanish Frontier: The Colombian Chocó, 1680–1810* (1976).

Peter Wade, *Blackness and Race Mixture: The Dynamics of Racial Identity in Colombia* (1993), esp. pp. 94–148.

Additional Bibliography

Jimeno, Myriam; Sotomayor, María Lucía, and Valderrama, Luz María. *Chocó: Diversidad cultural y medio ambiente.* Bogotá: Fondo FEN Colombia, 1995.

Losonczy, Anne–Marie. *Les saints et la forêt: Rituel, société et figures de l'échange avec les indiens Emberá chez les Négro-Colombiens du Chocó.* Paris, France: L'Harmattan, 1997.

Tayler, Donald. *Embarkations: Ethnography and Shamanism of the Chocó Indians of Colombia.* Oxford: University of Oxford, 1996.

Uribe Hermosillo, Julio César. *El Chocó: Una historia permanente de conquista, colonización y resistencia.* Chocó, Colombia: s.n., 1992.

Urrutia, María Ezequiela, Antún Castro Urrutia, and Arminda Castro Urrutia. *Apuntes sobre geografía e historia del Chocó.* Colombia: Promotora Editorial de Autores Chocoanos, 1992.

Williams, Caroline. *Between Resistance and Adaptation: Indigenous Peoples and the Colonization of the Chocó, 1510–1753.* Liverpool: Liverpool University Press, 2005.

HELEN DELPAR

CHOCRÓN, ISAAC (1932–).

Isaac Chocrón is a Venezuelan playwright, director, actor, critic, and novelist. Born in Maracay on 25 September 1932, he was trained in the United States and England as an economist. One of the moving forces in the contemporary Venezuelan theater, along with José Ignacio Cabrujas and Román Chalbaud, Chocrón, a native of Maracay, founded the Nuevo Grupo in 1967 and pioneered a vanguard, independent theater in Caracas that set the standards of quality for a new generation. The Nuevo Grupo offered an international repertoire as well as original plays by Venezuelan authors.

Chocrón's theater is varied and polemical. His first play, *Mónica y el florentino* (1959), focused on problems of alienation and communication within an international guest house. In 1963 he won the Premio del Teatro de Ateneo in Caracas. His popular *Asia y el lejano oriente* (1966), about the selling of a nation, was revived in 1984 for the grand opening of the Venezuelan National Theater Company, which Chocrón was invited to head. Chocrón dealt with consumerism in *O.K.* (1969) and with homosexuality in *La revolución* (1972). Other plays include *El acompañante* (1978) and *Mesopotamia* (1979). *Simón* (1983) presents Simón Bolívar and his mentor Simón Rodríguez in a challenging encounter between the would-be hero and his wiser master, who obliges him to face up his potential and to the promise of his leadership. Chocrón is also the author of a major book on American playwrights of the twentieth century, and the plays *Escrito y Sellado* (1993), *Tap Dance* (1999), and *Los Navegaos* (2006).

See also **Art: The Twentieth Century; Bolívar, Simón.**

BIBLIOGRAPHY

Durbin, Joyce Lee. *La dramaturgia de Isaac Chocrón.* Dissertation Abstracts International 50, no. 6 (Dec. 1989), 1673A.

Friedman, Edward H. "The Beast Within: The Rhetoric of Signification in Isaac Chocrón's *Animales feroces,*" *Essays on Foreign Languages and Literatures* 17 (1987): 167–183.

Márquez Montes, Carmen. *La dramaturgia de Isaac Chocrón: Experiencia del individualismo crítico.* Caracas: Comisión de Estudios de Postgrado, Facultad de Humanidades y Educación, Universidad Central de Venezuela, 2000.

Mujica, Barbara. "Isaac Chocrón: Tap Dancing Until the End." *Américas* 52 (January–February 2002): 63.

Nigro, Kirsten F. "A Triple Insurgence: Isaac Chocrón's *La revolución,*" *Bulletin of the Rocky Mountain MLA* 35, no. 1 (1981): 47–53.

Roldán, Julia Z. *Isaac Chocrón: Una lectura de sus textos teatrales.* Caracas: Fondo Editorial de la Universidad Pedagógica Experimental, 1996.

Rotker, Susana. *Isaac Chocrón y Elisa Lerner: Los transgresores de la literatura venezolana: Reflexiones sobre la identidad judía.* Caracas: FUNDARTE, Alcaldía del Municipio Libertador, 1991.

GEORGE WOODYARD

CHOLERA. *See* Diseases.

CHOLO.

Cholo, term used in Ecuador, Peru, small parts of northern Argentina, and especially Bolivia as a synonym for Mestizo, specifically a person of mixed Andean and European heritage, usually a white father and an Aymara or Quechua mother. The term can be derogatory, but also can express ethnic pride, or a term of endearment.

What mainly identifies *cholos* is their lifestyle as well as their occupational and educational status. They are fluent in Spanish and the Indian languages (Quechua, Aymara). Most are engaged in petty trade, small farming, and herding. *Cholas* dress colorfully in rich material, with several full petticoats, embroidered blouses, and hats that vary by locality (such as a stylish derby). A change in lifestyle, a university education, Western dress, and speaking Spanish nearly always move them into the Europeanized middle class. Sometimes the middle class uses the term *cholo* to characterize undignified behavior. Since the 1950s, when the social revolution gained power in Bolivia, and increasingly in the 1980s and 1990s, many *cholos* were elected to political office, including the vice presidency in 1993 and the presidency in 2006. Therefore the derogatory use of the term has become improper, and the ethnic pride of many *cholos* is noticeable. This change in attitude is also occurring in Ecuador and Peru, but to a lesser extent.

See also **Race and Ethnicity.**

BIBLIOGRAPHY

Daniel Pérez Velasco, *La mentalidad chola en Bolivia* (1928).

José Varallanos, *El cholo y el Perú* (1962).

Anthony Vetrano, *The Ecuadorian Indian and Cholo in the Novels of Jorge Icaza: Their Lot and Languages* (1974).

Paulovich [Alfonso Prudencio Claure], *Diccionario del cholo ilustrado* (1978).

Hernán Barra, *Indios y cholos* (1992).

Additional Bibliography

Cadena, Marisol de la. *Indigenous Mestizos: The Politics of Race and Culture in Cuzco, Peru, 1919–1991.* Durham, NC: Duke University Press, 2000.

Peredo, Elizabeth. *Recoveras de los Andes: Una aproximación a la identidad de la chola del mercado.* La Paz: Fundación Solón, 2001.

Rivera Cusicanqui, Silvia, and Denise Y. Arnold. *Ser mujer indígena, chola o birlocha en la Bolivia postcolonial de los años 90.* La Paz: Ministerio de Desarrollo Humano, Secretaría Nacional de Asuntos Étnicos, de Género y Generacionales: Subsecretaría de Asuntos de Género, 1996.

Stephens, Thomas M. *Dictionary of Latin American Racial and Ethnic Terminology.* Gainesville: University of Florida Press, 1989.

CHARLES W. ARNADE

CHOLULA. Cholula (Cholula de Rívadabia), city in the state of Puebla, Mexico. A city of 82,964 inhabitants (2005 census) situated at an altitude of 7,095 feet, Cholula is 72 miles southeast of Mexico City and 8 miles west of the state capital, Puebla. Founded on 27 October 1537, Cholula is primarily an agricultural and commercial center, a tourist site, and increasingly a bedroom community of the nearby state capital; however, it is best known for its pre-Columbian history, its role in the Spanish conquest of Mexico, and its many colonial-era churches.

Cholula ("place from which one jumps or flees" in Nahuatl) was one of the principal centers of pre-Columbian civilization. Its origins are obscure, but probably it was occupied by migrating Nahuatl-Olmec peoples. In the seventh century, Toltecs conquered the area, turned Cholula into an important religious site, and built what would become the largest pyramid in the Americas. It was here that the high priest Quetzalcoatl stayed after fleeing from Tula and before the fall of the Toltec civilization in 1116. The Spanish conquerer Hernán Cortés stopped in Cholula on his march from Veracruz to Tenochtitlán (Mexico City) in October 1519. Fearing an ambush, Cortés ordered a preemptive attack that resulted in the deaths of perhaps as many as ten thousand Indians.

See also **Puebla (State).**

BIBLIOGRAPHY

Luz María Josefina Walles Morales, *Cholula* (1971).

Guillermo Bonfil Batalla, *Cholula: La Ciudad sagrada en la era industrial* (1973).

Michael C. Meyer and William L. Sherman, *The Course of Mexican History,* 4th ed. (1991), esp. pp. 24, 36, 39, 108–110.

Additional Bibliography

Ashwell, Anamaría. *Creo para poder entender: La vida religiosa en los barrios de Cholula.* Puebla: Benemérita Universidad Autónoma de Puebla: Gobierno del Estado de Puebla, 2002.

Binford, Leigh, ed. *La economía política de la migración internacional en Puebla y Veracruz: Siete estudios de caso.* Puebla: Benemérita Universidad Autónoma de Puebla, 2004.

Castillo Palma, Norma Angélica. *Cholula, sociedad mestiza en ciudad india: Un análisis de las consecuencias demográficas, económicas y sociales del mestizaje en una ciudad novohispana (1649–1796).* México, D.F.: Plaza y Valdés Editores: Universidad Autónoma Metropolitana, Unidad Iztapalapa, División de Ciencias Sociales y Humanidades, 2001.

DAVID LAFRANCE

CHOLULA (PRE-COLUMBIAN). Cholula is located in the municipality of San Andrés Cholula and San Pedro Cholula, in the state of Puebla, Mexico. Some two hundred years before the modern era it was an agricultural village with a ceremonial center. Cholula had several different names in pre-Hispanic times, all related to the concept of the hill as a sacred place. It shows evidence of being populated for a long time, from the preclassical period (1500 BCE–100 CE) until the arrival of the Spaniards (in the sixteenth century). Originally an agricultural village, from the onset of the modern era it became a ceremonial center with an urban layout, divided into four neighborhoods. The town flourished during the classical period (300–900) with the development of a structured city, which had territorial divisions like those of Teotihuacan and included the largest pyramid in the whole of Mesoamerica. This building consisted of a pattern of geometric structures that were gradually added to over the years. Mural paintings can be seen in some of the buildings, of which the most famous is the one known as *The Drinkers*, a naturalistic representation of a ceremony in which individuals are drinking *pulque* (a fermented drink from a cactus plant named maguey). A type of polychrome ceramic, known as *cholulteco*, was produced in this location, and from here its production spread to other regions. The local population declined significantly after the classical period.

Cholula was visited and written about by chroniclers such as Hernán Cortés, Antonio de Torquemada, and Bernal Díaz del Castillo, who described the main covered pyramid he saw upon his arrival as "like a great hill." Toward the end of the sixteenth century the colonial magistrate (*corregidor*), Gabriel Rojas, carried out an excavation at the top of the Great Pyramid and unearthed snail conchs that served as ritual trumpets. During the colonial period, the Church of Our Lady of Good Remedy (*Nuestra Señora de los Remedios*) was built on the town's pre-Hispanic foundation.

In 1931 the Monuments Department, under the leadership of the architect Emilio Cuevas, Ignacio Herrera, and Mariano Gómez, began the first series of studies of the area, in which they constructed tunnels in order to explore the covered buildings. In the 1960s Ignacio Marquina had six kilometers of tunnels dug to explore the substructures and analyze the building system that had been used. The archeological site is currently under the protection of the INAH (National Institute of Anthropology and History), and the area has sufficient infrastructure to allow for tourism.

See also **Mesoamerica; Puebla (State); Teotihuacán.**

BIBLIOGRAPHY

Marquina, Ignacio, coordinator. *Proyecto Cholula*. México: INAH, 1970.

SARA LADRÓN DE GUEVARA

CHONCHOL, JACQUES (c. 1926–). Jacques Chonchol is a Chilean political leader and agrarian reform expert. A member of the Christian Democratic Party (PDC), Chonchol advocated the creation of a communitarian society as the way to solve Chile's economic problems and to avoid the excesses of socialism and capitalism. A member of the PDC's left wing, he served as a functionary of Eduardo Frei's agrarian reform program. In 1968, distressed by what he considered Frei's conservative policies, he broke with the PDC, creating the United Movement of Popular Action (MAPU). Chonchol later served as Salvador Allende's minister of agriculture, accelerating the pace of agrarian reform. He subsequently bolted from MAPU, which he claimed had become too Marxist, to form the Christian Left. Later he resigned from Allende's cabinet over political differences. After the coup of 1973, he was exiled. He took up a post at the Instituto de los Altos Estudios de América Latina at the University of Paris. In 1994 he returned to Chile, where he continued to serve as an outspoken critic of the neoliberal economic-political system of the early twenty-first century. In 2005 he participated in "The Lessons from Chile," the first conference of the Transnational Institute, a fellowship of global scholars and activists, held in Amsterdam.

See also **Chile, Political Parties: Christian Democratic Party (PDC); Chile, Political Parties: Popular Action Unitary Movement (MAPU).**

BIBLIOGRAPHY

Collier, Simon, and William F. Slater. *A History of Chile, 1808–2002*, 2nd edition. Cambridge, U.K., and New York: Cambridge University Press, 2004.

Loveman, Brian. *Struggle in the Countryside* (1976), pp. 280, 285–286, 291–292, 296–300.

Oppenheim, Lois Hecht. *Politics in Chile: Socialism, Authoritarianism, and Market Democracy*, 3rd edition. Boulder, CO: Westview Press, 2007.

Rector, John L. *The History of Chile*. Westport, CT: Greenwood Press, 2003.

Sigmund, Paul. *The Overthrow of Allende and the Politics of Chile, 1964–1976* (1977), pp. 52–53, 62–63, 72, 79, 84, 89, 91, 130, 139, 151–152.

WILLIAM F. SATER

CHONG NETO, MANUEL (1927–).

Manuel Chong Neto is a Panamanian artist. Chong Neto studied painting at the San Carlos Academy in Mexico (1963–1965). He began his professional career as a high school art teacher and, after 1970, he also taught at the Casa de la Escultura, the Escuela Nacional de Artes Plásticas, and the National University.

A figurative artist, Chong Neto creates compositions characterized by formal balance and the contrast of darks and lights. His early renderings of human characters and urban landscapes show the influence of Mexican social realism. He is best known for the large, sensuous, and enigmatic woman who appears in most of his paintings. She is often accompanied by men, voyeurs, and symbolic birds or owls, as in his dramatic drawings series *Poemas Eróticos* (1976). In 1972 he won the first prize in the Concurso Xerox in Panama. He participated in several biennial exhibitions, including the Bienal de Arte Latinoamericano at the University of Eastern Tennessee (1970,) the Bienal Coltejar in Medellín, Colombia (1973), and the Bienal de São Paulo (1982). From 1970 to 1975 he was an art professor at the Escuela Naciónal de Artes Plásticas de Panamá, and from 1975 to 1985 he taught art at the University of Panama. He was a special invited guest for the 1991 Bienal de Cuenca, in Ecuador. In 1986 he retired from university life to paint in his studio in Panama City.

See also **Art: The Twentieth Century.**

BIBLIOGRAPHY

Artistas Panameños. Bogota: Biblioteca Luís-Ángel Arango del Banco de la República, 1973.

Oviero, R. "Chong Neto y el tema como pretexto estético," in *La Prensa* (Panama) (June 1982).

Kupfer, Mónica, ed. *Manuel Chong Neto: Visión Retrospectiva, 1955–1985* (1986).

MONICA E. KUPFER

CHORO, CHORINHO.

Chorinho Choro, a small Brazilian urban band or the kind of music performed by such a band; a word literally meaning "to cry." A *choro* ensemble typically includes flute, clarinet, trombone, trumpet, large and small guitars, *cavaquinhos* (Brazilian ukulelelike instruments), and a few percussion instruments.

Appearing as a musical genre in the late 1880s, *choro* was at first strictly an instrumental style, and was marked by its improvisational character and the virtuosity of its solos. Thus it has often been compared with ragtime and early-twentieth-century New Orleans–style jazz. Formally, its structure is in three parts in the pattern A-B-A-C-A. Vocal forms of *choro* in which the voice substitutes for a solo wind instrument began to appear in the 1920s and 1930s. Among notable examples of the genre are "Urubu," by Pixinguinha, and "Sai faísca." This music style had lost a great deal of popularity by the 1960s. However, two national *chorinho choro* festivals broadcast in 1977 and 1978 helped revive the genre. Consequently, the *choro* remains an important and vibrant part of the Brazilian music scene.

See also **Lundu; Maxixe; MPB: Música Popular Brasileira; Samba.**

BIBLIOGRAPHY

Oneyda Alvarenga, *Música popular brasileira* (1982).

Mário De Andrade, *Dictionário musical brasileiro*, coordinated by Oneyda Alvarenga and Flávia Camargo Toni (1982–1989).

Charles A. Perrone, *Masters of Contemporary Brazilian Song* (1989).

Additional Bibliography

Diniz, André. *Almanaque do choro: A história do chorinho, o que ouvir, o que ler, onde curtir*. Rio de Janeiro: Jorge Zahar Editor Ltda., 2003.

Murphy, John P. *Music in Brazil: Experiencing Music, Expressing Culture*. New York: Oxford University Press, 2006.

ROBERT MYERS

CHORRERA.

Chorrera, a pre-Columbian culture located in western Ecuador, also called Engoroy by some archaeologists. Scarcely investigated, Chorrera's existence has been dated variously from 1500 to 500 BCE to as recently as 800 to 100 BCE. These temporal differences may in fact date occupations in different geographical areas. Chorrera is known principally for technically innovative and aesthetically pleasing ceramics, often depicting the local fauna and the wild and cultivated plants of the Pacific coast, savanna, and tropical forests of western Ecuador.

Chorrera existed during the Late Formative period of Ecuadorian prehistory. Archaeologists describe Formative period cultures as initiating many of the developments that later became the foundations of "high" civilization in the Central Andes, culminating in the Inca empire-state. These novel developments included settled life in permanent villages, highly productive agricultural systems, the invention and elaboration of pottery, social-status differences reinforced by differential access to exotic goods, and the beginnings of monumental constructions undertaken through corporate labor projects.

Two contrasting views have been proposed to explain the origins of Chorrera culture. One view argues for strong links between Chorrera and Formative cultures in Mesoamerica, with the latter region as the proposed place of origin. The presence of ceramic traits such as iridescent painting and napkin-ring ear spools in both areas suggests to some that long-distance contacts existed. Mesoamerica is seen as the more precocious region, and therefore as the donor of many cultural traits to the Andean region. According to the opposing view, many purported Mesoamerican traits in Chorrera ceramics occurred earliest in Ecuador, and therefore its origins were elsewhere, either in the forested eastern Andes or southern highlands of Ecuador. The representations of plants and animals in Chorrera pottery are seen as indications of a well-established tropical-forest cultural pattern, similar to ethnographically known groups from present-day Amazonia.

Much of the information archaeologists use to reconstruct Chorrera culture comes from the carefully crafted naturalistic depictions on Chorrera pottery. Chorrera bottles, jars, and bowls often incorporate a variety of forest mammals and reptiles, as well as numerous species of birds. The depiction of marine animals suggests the exploitation of maritime resources. Chorrera pottery also offers information about agricultural practices. Various types of squashes and tropical fruits appear on bottles. Botanical analyses from archaeological excavations indicate that maize and root crops were cultivated. In addition, many wild plants from the forests appear to have played an important role in subsistence.

Ceramic human figurines were also made by Chorrera potters. The fronts of figurines appear to have been fashioned using molds, while the backs were modeled by hand. Although neither the archaeological context nor the use of these figurines is known, they do provide clues as to possible clothing and hair styles, and may reflect the practice of tattooing or body painting.

Archaeologists have recovered little information regarding Chorrera mortuary practices. Excavations at a cemetery site in southwestern Ecuador uncovered several burials. Individuals were sometimes accompanied by grave goods, including stone beads, ceramic bowls, and effigy bottles. Other perishable items may have been included in burials, but were not preserved over time. Also recovered were secondary collective burials documenting the practice of reburying the disarticulated bones of several individuals together in circular pits.

See also **Archaeology; Art: Pre-Columbian Art of Mesoamerica.**

BIBLIOGRAPHY

Clifford Evans and Betty J. Meggers, "Formative Period Cultures in the Guayas Basin, Coastal Ecuador," in *American Antiquity* 22 (1957): 235–247.

Emilio Estrada, *Las culturas pre-clásicas: Formativas o arcaicas del Ecuador* (1958).

Carlos Zevallos Menéndez, "Informe preliminar sobre el Cementerio Chorrera, Bahía de Santa Elena, Ecuador," in *Revista del Museo Nacional* 34 (1965–1966): 20–27.

Betty J. Meggers, *Ecuador* (1966).

Donald W. Lathrap, *Ancient Ecuador: Culture, Clay, and Creativity, 3000–300 B.C.* (1975).

Henning Bischof, "La fase Engoroy—períodos, cronología y relaciones," in *Primer Simposio de Correlaciones Antropológicas Andino-Mesoamericano* (1982), pp. 135–176.

EVAN C. ENGWALL

CHOTUNA. Chotuna, a major archaeological site located in the lower part of the Lambayeque Valley of northern Peru. It is thought to have been associated with a legendary dynasty, founded by Naymlap, that came to this valley centuries before European contact in the early sixteenth century. According to the legend, Naymlap came by sea on a fleet of balsa rafts, bringing with him many concubines, a chief wife named Ceterni, and many people who followed him as their captain and leader. Among the latter were forty officials who served in his royal court.

Naymlap and his followers are said to have beached their boats at the mouth of a river, and then followed that river approximately one-half mile inland. Naymlap built a palace for his principal wife, and nearby, at a place called Chot, he built a palace for himself where he lived for many years. When he was about to die, he had his trusted servants bury him in a room and spread the word among his people that he had grown wings and flown away. Chotuna is thought to be Chot of the Naymlap legend, and Chornancap, another archaeological site approximately one-half mile west of Chotuna, is thought to be where Naymlap built the palace for Ceterni.

Today, the site of Chotuna consists of a series of pyramids, palaces, and walled enclosures scattered over an area of approximately 50 acres. In 1941 grave robbers at Chotuna uncovered walls with elaborate low-relief friezes. Their designs were so similar to friezes at Dragon, an archaeological site in the Moche Valley, approximately 110 miles to the south, that it was thought that the two sites were somehow related. Major excavation at Chotuna between 1980 and 1982 revealed that the site was first inhabited approximately 700 CE, and continued to be occupied until 1100, when a major period of flooding destroyed much of the ancient architecture. After 1100 the site was reoccupied by people with different ceramics who lived there until the early part of the Colonial Period, around 1650. If Naymlap was a real person, his story probably relates to the founding of the site, and the period prior to the flooding. The friezes date to the period after the flooding, probably between 1100 and 1250.

See also Archaeology.

BIBLIOGRAPHY

Alfred L. Kroeber, *Peruvian Archaeology in 1942* (1944).

Christopher B. Donnan, "An Assessment of the Validity of the Naymlap Dynasty" and "The Chotuna Friezes and the Chotuna-Dragon Connection," in *The Northern Dynasties: Kingship and Statecraft in Chimor,* edited by Michael E. Moseley and Alana Cordy-Collins (1990).

Additional Bibliography

Cavallaro, Raffael and Izumi Shimada. "Some Thoughts on Sican Marked Adobes and Labor Organization." *American Antiquity* 53, no. 1 (Jan. 1988): 75–101.

Davies, Nigel. *The Ancient Kingdoms of Peru.* New York: Penguin Books, 1997, pp. 88–90.

CHRISTOPHER B. DONNAN

CHRISTIAN BASE COMMUNITIES.

Christian Base Communities (Comunidades Eclesiales de Base—CEB) are small groups within a parish who meet regularly for Bible study, led by a priest, nun, or lay member; who elect their own leaders; and who decide democratically with what other activities the community should be concerned. At their inception, CEBs were seen as a mechanism by which the liberal Catholic doctrine developed during the Second Vatican Council (1962–1965) and the Bishops' Conference held at Medellín, Colombia (1968), could be implemented. The goal was to bring the laity into the life of the church, to bring the church into dialogue with the world, and to teach that the church is a community of equals before God in which everyone has obligations to each other and responsibilities to share. CEBs reflect a rupture with the past, when the church was allied with wealth and power, and demonstrate a new commitment to a "preferential option for the poor." It is not surprising, therefore, that CEBs have flourished in poor parishes across Latin America but are virtually unknown in middle- and upper-class parishes.

Lay leaders are known as catechists and delegates of the Word. They are chosen by the community for their leadership qualities, moral rectitude, Christian commitment, and willingness to serve. Catechists prepare parishioners for baptism, first communion, and marriage. Delegates lead the community in worship services; in many countries they are also authorized to give communion, to perform marriages, and to conduct burial services. Both catechists and delegates receive training from clergy and nuns and/or attend short courses at lay training centers.

The content of Bible study courses rejects the church's traditional message, preached from the Con-quest onward, that one should accept one's lot on earth and wait patiently for one's reward in heaven. Through the CEBs (in line with Medellín documents), the people receive a different message: that God, who is a God of justice, has acted throughout human history on behalf of the poor and oppressed; that it is not God's will that they be poor; that, before God, they are equal to the rich; that they have a basic human right to organize and take control of their own lives; and that the church has responsibility to "accompany" them in that journey.

The impact of this process is profound. More than one peasant has commented that when the priest or nun came to organize CEBs, it was the first time anyone had asked what she or he thought about anything. Nuns report observing their parishioners' traditional fatalism change over a few months to a new sociopolitical awareness: "It's 'God's will' when a child dies becomes 'The system caused this.'" Religious workers also report that CEB members change physically: "They walk upright, their heads high, with self-confidence," rather than shuffling along with heads bowed.

CEBs can continue for years and develop in different ways. All, however, share four characteristics. First, the CEBs provide an organization, a means by which the people can meet together on a regular basis. Since the poor have been unorganized in most societies, this is usually the first experience of its kind for CEB members. Furthermore, the form and function of each CEB are determined by the members of the community, not by the priest or nun, whose role is that of facilitator, resource, and occasionally advocate. It is the people who decide what they want and who organize themselves to get it, whether "it" be literacy classes, an agricultural cooperative, or paramedical training for a member of the community.

Second, the CEBs produce grass-roots leadership by selecting their own catechists and delegates. Among people who have been treated as objects for almost five centuries, the opportunity to develop local leadership has meant that for the first time since the Conquest, the poor have their own spokespeople who are willing and able to advocate on behalf of their communities.

Third, CEBs are working models of participatory democracy. The lay leaders never have the right to impose their will on the community; if they try to do so, they will be removed by the people. The same applies to priests. Traditionally it is unheard of for parishioners, especially peasants, to talk back to a priest. But two CEBs stopped a priest cold in one Central American country when he tried to discredit the nun who had been working with them for years, accusing her of "political work." The people told him he was wrong and refused to entertain the priest's charges.

Fourth, together with the Mass, CEBs provide the means by which the people reflect on God's word in the Bible, which contributes to *concientización* (or *consentização,* a word coined by Brazilian educator Paulo Freire), the process by which the people become aware (conscious) of the interconnectedness of God's Word, their lives, and their world.

The growth of CEBs has been explosive in some countries and virtually nonexistent in others. In still other countries there are great variations among dioceses. The data suggest two critical variables. First, there appears to be a correlation between the extent of poverty in a country and the number of CEBs. CEBs are few and far between in Argentina, Uruguay, Chile, and Costa Rica, countries that have enjoyed a relatively higher standard of living than the rest of Latin America. Second, there is a clear and even stronger correlation between the support a bishop gives the development of CEBs in his diocese and the number of CEBs that are organized. Brazil, with well over a hundred thousand CEBs, best illustrates both variables: widespread poverty and the most progressive bishops of any national church in the world. At the other end of the theological spectrum, Colombia, with equally widespread poverty and one of the most conservative hierarchies in Latin America, has relatively few CEBs. El Salvador, Guatemala, and Mexico also qualify on both points, but the development of CEBs in each of these countries has been highly erratic: in dioceses with progressive bishops large numbers of CEBs flourish, while dioceses headed by conservatives have few.

It should not be surprising that conservative episcopal reaction echoes in the larger society. CEBs have come to be regarded as subversive by elites bent on maintaining the economic and political status quo. Dozens of priests and nuns involved with CEBs have been harrassed, exiled, tortured, or murdered. Hundreds of catechists and delegates and even some bishops have met the same fate.

Scholars have begun to assess the impact of over two decades of CEB activity, amid the explosion of evangelical Protestantism and Catholic Charismatic Renewal (CCR), whose practitioners were initially known as Pentecostal Catholics. Evidence shows a decrease in CEBs, with the poor in Latin America offering only limited support for liberation theology. Nevertheless, the Conference of Latin American Bishops (CELAM) has called for greater CEB growth, and in some regions, such as the Amazon, CEBs remain vibrant and significant. Representing a significant development in the history of the Catholic Church, CEBs endure in the twenty-first century's competitive religious marketplace.

See also **Catholic Church: The Modern Period; Conference of Latin American Bishops (CELAM); Liberation Theology.**

BIBLIOGRAPHY

Adriance, Madeleine. *Promised Land: Base Christian Communities and the Struggle for the Amazon*. Albany: State University of New York Press, 1995.

Berryman, Philip. *The Religious Roots of Rebellion: Christians in Central American Revolutions* (1984).

Burdick, John, and W. E. Hewitt, eds. *The Church at the Grassroots in Latin America: Perspectives on Thirty Years of Activism*. Westport, CT: Praeger, 2000.

Cardenal, Ernesto. *The Gospel in Solentiname*, 4 vols. (1979).

Cook, Guillermo. *The Expectation of the Poor: Latin American Base Ecclesial Communities in Protestant Perspective* (1985).

Dawson, Andrew. *The Birth and Impact of the Base Ecclesial Community and Liberative Theological Discourse in Brazil*. Lanham, MD: International Scholars Publications, 1998.

Drogus, Carol Ann. *Women, Religion, and Social Change in Brazil's Popular Church*. Notre Dame, IN: University of Notre Dame Press, 1997.

Galdámez, Pablo. *Faith of a People: The Life of a Basic Christian Community in El Salvador*, translated by Robert R. Barr (1986).

Hewitt, W. E. *Base Christian Communities and Social Change in Brazil* (1991).

Lernoux, Penny. *Cry of the People* (1980).

Loreto Mariz, Cecilia. *Coping with Poverty: Pentacostals and Christian Base Communities in Brazil* (1994).

Mainwaring, Scott, and Alexander Wilde, eds. *The Progressive Church in Latin America* (1988).

Tombs, David. *Latin American Liberation Theology*. Boston: Brill Academic Publishers, 2002.

TOMMIE SUE MONTGOMERY

CHRISTIE AFFAIR. Christie Affair, a series of reprisals taken by the British Navy against Brazilian merchantmen from December 1862 to 5 January 1863. Named for William Christie, the British ambassador to Brazil at the time, it brought to a head thirty-five years of growing animosity between the two governments concerning slavery in Brazil. In 1861, the British ship *Prince of Wales* sank off the coast of Brazil. The British suspected foul play because the Brazilian government would not, or could not, produce the bodies of any of the last crewmen or any of the ship's cargo, which had been stolen by local inhabitants. A year later, three out-of-uniform British sailors were arrested in Brazil for drunkenness and disorderly conduct. The British government viewed these arrests as deliberate provocation and demanded an apology for the arrests and immediate restitution for the *Prince of Wales*. It authorized Christie to use reprisals if these demands were not met. Christie subsequently ordered British naval vessels to blockade Rio de Janeiro harbor; during a six-day blockade the British seized five Brazilian ships. Thereupon, the Brazilian government agreed to pay for the *Prince of Wales* and put the matter of the sailors' arrests to an arbitrator.

The arbitrator decided in favor of Brazil, ruling that no insult to Great Britain had been intended. Brazil then demanded restitution for its five ships. The British refused, and the Brazilians severed diplomatic relations with Great Britain. Although the British never paid for the seized Brazilian ships, Brazil restored diplomatic relations five years later for economic reasons.

Since William Christie and the British government were keenly interested in the abolition of slavery in Brazil, this affair was seen in Brazil as a warning that Britain was willing to use force, if needed, to push Brazil toward the abolition of slavery.

See also **British–Latin American Relations.**

BIBLIOGRAPHY

Richard Graham, "Causes for the Abolition of Negro Slavery in Brazil: An Interpetive Essay," *HAHR* 46, no. 2 (1966): 123–137, and *Britain and the Onset of Modernization in Brazil, 1850–1914* (1968), pp. 169–183.

Bradford E. Burns, *Nationalism in Brazil: A Historical Survey* (1968).

Additional Bibliography

Bethell, Leslie. *The Abolition of the Brazilian Slave Trade; Britain, Brazil and the Slave Trade Question, 1807–1869.* Cambridge, U.K.: Cambridge University Press, 1970.

Florentino, Manolo. *Tráfico, cativeiro e liberdade: Rio de Janeiro, séculos XVII–XIX.* Rio de Janeiro: Civilização Brasileira, 2005.

Rivière, Peter. *Absent-Minded Imperialism: Britain and the Expansion of Empire in Nineteenth-Century Brazil.* London: Tauris Academic Studies, 1995.

MICHAEL J. BROYLES

CHRISTMAS, LEE

CHRISTMAS, LEE (1863–1924). Lee Christmas (*b.* 22 February 1863; *d.* 24 January 1924), North American soldier of fortune in Honduras. Christmas was probably the most famous of a generation of North American adventurers and filibusters who migrated to Central America from the 1890s until World War I. He left New Orleans in 1894 and got a job railroading on the north Honduran coast. From then until his return to the United States after World War I, he was involved in the political turmoil of Honduras and Guatemala. He served as national police chief of Honduras, fought in the Honduran-Nicaraguan war of 1907, and plotted with former Honduran president Manuel Bonilla and Guy "Machine-Gun" Molony to restore Bonilla to power, a plan that culminated in the attack on La Ceiba in January 1911. Christmas was rewarded with a sinecure at Puerto Cortés, and Sam "The Banana Man" Zemurray gained valuable concessions for his Cuyamel Fruit Company on the north Honduran coast. In 1915 Christmas lost favor with the Honduran regime and joined Manuel Estrada Cabrera's secret service in Guatemala. He returned virtually penniless to the United States in March 1922 and died of tropical sprue.

See also **Filibustering; Honduras.**

BIBLIOGRAPHY

Hermann Deutsch, *The Incredible Yanqui: The Career of Lee Christmas* (1931).

Additional Bibliography

Acker, Allison. *Honduras: The Making of a Banana Republic.* Boston: South End Press, 1988.

Cáceres Lara, Víctor. *El golpe de estado de 1904.* Tegucigalpa: Universidad Nacional Autónoma de Honduras, Editorial Universitaria, 1985.

Garcia Buchard, Ethel. *Poder político, interés bananero e identidad nacional en Centro América: Un estudio comparativo: Costa Rica (1884-1938) y Honduras (1902-1958).* Tegucigalpa: Editorial Universitaria, 1997.

LESTER D. LANGLEY

CHRIST OF THE ANDES

CHRIST OF THE ANDES. Christ of the Andes, monument, also known as Cristo Redentor (Christ the Redeemer), standing on Uspallata Pass (13,860 feet) on the old dirt road from Mendoza (Argentina) to Los Andes (Chile). It was erected in 1904 to commemorate the peaceful solution of long and bitter boundary disputes by the treaty signed in 1902 after British arbitration. Made from the bronze of melted-down cannons, the 25-foot-high statue is of Christ standing on a globe, holding a cross in his right hand and raising his left arm in the sign of peace. The inscription at the base reads "Let these mighty mountains turn to dust before two sister nations wage war against each other."

See also **Uspallata Pass.**

BIBLIOGRAPHY

Salvatore Bizzarro, *Historical Dictionary of Chile* (1987).

Additional Bibliography

León Gallardo, René E. *Breve historia del Cristo de Los Andes.* Chile: Ediciones de Santa Rosa de Los Andes, 2004.

Sevilla, Fabián, Ariel Sevilla, and María Sáenz Quesada. *El Centinela de la Paz: Historia del monumento Cristo Redentor de Los Andes.* Mendoza: Ediciones Culturales de Mendoza, 2004.

CÉSAR N. CAVIEDES

CHRISTOPHE, HENRI

CHRISTOPHE, HENRI (1767–1820). Henri Christophe (*b.* 6 October 1767; *d.* 8 October 1820), president of the State of Haiti (1806–1811) and king (1811–1820). In the inky darkness of a mountain night, an exhausted entourage of royalty and servants led by Queen Marie-Louise reached the outer gates of the fortress of Citadelle la Ferrière. Once inside the compound, two royal aides hurriedly looked for shovels and a place to dispose of their cargo, an unshrouded body in a hammock. Finally, unable to inter the cadaver in suitable fashion, they simply dumped their cargo into a pile of quick lime and left. Later Haiti would entomb the remains on this site with the occupant's own prepared epitaph: "I shall be reborn from my ashes."

Always the showman, Henri Christophe left Haitians with the fear that he just might return. He had cleverly built a personal mythology to buttress his tyrannical rule of the northern State of Haiti. Historian James Leyburn called Christophe Haiti's best nineteenth-century ruler, which he was. And Simon Bolívar might have been thinking of Christophe when he stated in his Jamaica Letter (1815) that Latin America needed strong, paternalistic rulers who would govern for life and who would educate and guide their people to assume democratic responsibilities.

Born a slave on Grenada, Christophe became the property of a ship captain and then the chattel of Saint-Domingue sugar planter Master Badechi, who soon put him to work at Couronne, a hostelry in Le Cap François. In 1778 Christophe served as a slave orderly for the French at Savannah, Georgia, where he suffered injury. In 1790 in northern Saint-Domingue he rode with a dragoon unit that suppressed the rebellion of Vincent Ogé (1755?–1791). It is probable that by this time Christophe had become a free black. He cherished his British origins, always gave the English spelling, "Henry," and chose George III for hero worship.

When Toussaint L'ouverture joined the French in 1794, Christophe's military career had been languishing, as he had attained only the rank of captain of the infantry at the garrison of Le Cap François. But Toussaint recognized in the young officer the qualities of good leadership. Christophe served his commander well in the La Petite-Anse district, where he and Colonel Vincent introduced the *fermage* (system of forced labor and government management) to maintain the plantation system. Under this profit-sharing plan, laborers had to surrender a great deal of personal freedom and submit to corporal punishment. Toussaint was impressed and used the scheme widely across Saint-Domingue. In 1799 Christophe, by then a colonel, commanded the garrison at Le Cap François and would later join Toussaint in crushing the Moyse Rebellion (October 1801).

When the expedition of General Charles Leclerc reached Haiti from France, Christophe at first fought well by torching Le Cap François and moving to the interior. But then came an unexpected event, Christophe's surrender to the French on 26 April 1802, and his agreement to command a French unit under General Jean Hardy. Ralph Korngold has argued that Christophe betrayed Toussaint, but his belief is not shared by biographer Hubert Cole. Christophe himself defended his action by saying that he was tired of living like a savage. In October 1802, he deserted the French and joined the rising tide of black rebels opposed to the restoration of slavery.

In February 1807, Christophe was angered when the mulatto-dominated assembly at Port-au-Prince handed him a weakened presidency. There followed a civil conflict in which Christophe ruled the State of Haiti in the north and Alexandre Pétion and a mulatto clique governed the Republic of Haiti in the south.

From the beginning of his rule, Christophe pursued an effective social policy. He hired English teachers to establish a system of national schools. He demanded that his subjects have church marriages. On this issue he often wandered about the countryside looking for wayward lovers. If they suffered his apprehension, their fate was an altar and a priest. He even tried to impose desirable personal habits upon his people. The Royal Dahomets, his special African police force, inspected Haitians for neatness and honesty. They tested this second quality by dropping a wallet and other valuables in a public place, hiding, and then arresting any culprit who found the items without making a police report. Public awe of Christophe grew as his subjects often sighted him attended by an aide with a telescope. Popular rumor maintained that Christophe saw all and punished all.

Economically, Christophe followed Toussaint's maintenance of the plantation system without slavery. But Christophe did break up some of the large estates late in his rule and sold the parcels to small farmers, a point Hubert Cole believes other historians may have missed. To further his economic plans, Christophe became King Henry I on 28 March 1811. Surrounding his crown was a new Haitian nobility. To them he gave generous land grants and pompous titles. To him they gave loyalty and maintained prosperous plantations.

On 8 October 1820 a dying Christophe committed suicide at his plush palace, Sans Souci. Faithful followers carried his body to Citadelle La Ferrière, the great monument to black work skills, which Christophe had constructed during his rule. Their monument was fittingly his last resting place.

See also **Haiti.**

BIBLIOGRAPHY

W. W. Harvey, *Sketches of Haiti* (1827).

C. L. R. James, *The Black Jacobins* (1938).

James Leyburn, *The Haitian People* (1941).

Ralph Korngold, *Citizen Toussaint* (1944).

Hubert Cole, *Christophe: King of Haiti* (1967).

Thomas O. Ott, *The Haitian Revolution, 1789–1804* (1973).

David Nicholls, *From Dessalines to Duvalier: Race, Colour, and National Independence in Haiti* (1979).

Additional Bibliography

Dubois, Laurent. *Avengers of the New World: The Story of the Haitian Revolution.* Cambridge, MA: Belknap Press of Harvard University Press, 2004.

Fick, Carolyn. *The Making of Haiti: The Saint Domingue Revolution from Below.* Knoxville: University of Tennessee Press, 1990.

Geggus, David Patrick, ed. *The Impact of the Haitian Revolution in the Atlantic World.* Columbia: University of South Carolina Press, 2001.

Geggus, David Patrick, ed. *Haitian Revolutionary Studies.* Bloomington: Indiana University Press, 2002.

THOMAS O. OTT

CHRIST THE REDEEMER. *See* Corcovado.

CHUBUT.
Chubut is a southern province of Argentina located in the Patagonia region and bordered on the west by Chile. It has 400,000 inhabitants (2001 national census) and its capital is Rawson. Following the Conquest of the Desert in 1884, in which the national government took control of western Patagonia, the National Territory of Chubut was created; it became a province in 1955. Other important cities in the province are Puerto Madryn, Trelew, and Comodoro Rivadavia. There is a small Welsh community in Chubut. More than one in ten families in the province is indigenous (Mapuches or Tehuelches).

The Patagonian plateau region is arid and cold, with precipitation levels decreasing toward the east. The economy depends on petroleum extraction, aluminum mining, sheep rearing, fishing, and tourism. The Valdés Peninsula along the Atlantic coast is the province's main tourist attraction. From the peninsula one can observe the mating rituals of the southern right whale, sea lions, elephant seals, and penguins. There is a popular ski resort in the city of Esquel, in the Andean region of Chubut, near the Los Alerces National Park. This region has a great variety of flora and fauna as well as dense conifer forests, lakes, and meltwater rivers. Fishing and hunting of certain exotic species such as elk and fallow deer are allowed in the national park.

See also **Argentina: The Nineteenth Century; Argentina: The Twentieth Century; Argentina, Geography; Conquest of the Desert; Petroleum Industry.**

BIBLIOGRAPHY

Dumrauf, Clement I. *Historia de Chubut.* Buenos Aires, Plus Ultra, 1992.

VICENTE PALERMO

CHUCUITO.
Chucuito, a province in the department of Puno, Peru. Juli is its capital. Bordered by Lake Titicaca to the east and Bolivia to the south, the province's elevations range from 12,500 to 13,200 feet. The region was an important center of pre-Hispanic cultures. The published official inquiry (*visita*) by Garci Diez de San Miguel in 1567 describes in great detail the Lupaca people of the region, thus constituting a crucial source on the precolonial and early Conquest periods. Commerce with Bolivia and livestock raising are the province's major economic activities today.

See also **Indigenous Peoples.**

BIBLIOGRAPHY

Cortázar, Pedro Felipe. *Department del Puno,* vol. 21 of *Documental del Perú,* 2d ed. (1972).

Diez De San Miguel, Garci. *Visita hecha a la provincia de Chucuito por Garci Diez de San Miguel en al año 1567,* edited by Waldemar Espinoza Soriano (1964).

Premo, Bianca. "From the Pockets of Women: The Gendering of the Mita, Migration, and Tribute in Colonial Chucuito, Peru." *The Americas* 57, no. 1 (July 2000): 63–93.

CHARLES F. WALKER

CHUMACERO, ALÍ (1918–).

Alí Chumacero, born on 9 July 1918, is a Mexican poet, editor, and essayist. Early in his career Chumacero was associated with the literary journals *Tierra Nueva* (1940–1942) and *El Hijo Pródigo* (1943–1946) and subsequently with *México en la Cultura* and *La Cultura en México,* among others. He has held important positions with the publisher Fondo de Cultura Económica, has edited works of nineteenth-century Mexican Romantic poets and of Alfonso Reyes and Xavier Villaurrutia, and has collaborated with Octavio Paz, José Emilio Pacheco, and Homero Aridjis in the preparation of the influential anthology *Poesía en movimiento* (1966). Since 1964 he has been a member of the Academia Mexicana de la Lengua. His essays range across the fields of poetics, literary history and criticism, and contemporary Mexican art. Chumacero's poetry, almost all of it written before 1956, is a very carefully crafted, subtle exploration of existential desolation, solitude, and the inadequate consolations of love. The earlier poems (*Páramo de sueños* [1944] and *Imágenes desterradas* [1948]) are quite hermetic, bearing traces of his predecessors, the Contemporáneos (most notably José Gorostiza and Villaurrutía). The later poems (*Palabras en reposo* [1956]) are more accessible, though no less complex. He has won many prizes for his poetry, including the Premio Javier Villaurrutia (1984), the Premio Internacional Alfonso Reyes (1986), the Premio Nacional de Ciencias y Artes (for Language and Literature, in 1987), the Premio Estatal de Literatura Amado Nervo (2003), and the Medalla Belisario Domínguez del Senado de la República in 1996.

See also **Reyes Ochoa, Alfonso; Villaurrutia, Xavier.**

BIBLIOGRAPHY

Marco Antonio Campos has edited the *Poesía completa* (1980). Miguel Angel Flores presents a fine selection of Chumacero's essays in *Los momentos críticos* (1987). For an extended discussion of the poetry and additional bibliography, see Frank Dauster, *The Double Strand* (1987).

Gordon, Samuel, ed. *Poéticas mexicanas del siglo XX.* Mexico: Ediciones y Gráficos Eón, Universidad Iberoamericana, 2004.

Pacheco, Cristina, and Mauricio Sanders. *Al pie de la letra.* Mexico: Fondo de Cultura Económica, 2001.

Paz, Octavio, et al. *Poesía en movimiento.* Mexico: Siglo Veintiuno Editores, 1980.

Villarino, Roberto. *Catorce perfiles.* Mexico: Coordinación de Difusión Cultural, Dirección de Literatura/ UNAM, 1997.

MICHAEL J. DOUDOROFF

CHUMASH INDIANS.

The Chumash Indians are an Indian group that inhabited an extensive south-central California territory that stretched from the southern Salinas Valley in the north to the Santa Monica Mountains in the south. The Chumash territory also included the Santa Barbara Channel Islands. They numbered an estimated 18,500 when the Spaniards came to Alta California in 1769.

The Chumash had a sophisticated matrilineal tribal government and were, at the time of Spanish arrival, in the process of a social evolution that was leading to social differentiation. They practiced food-resource management and utilized a variety of food sources from the diverse ecologies found within their territory. They used burning to maximize seed production and selectively promoted the growth of certain grasses that produced more seeds. Fish, marine mammals, and shellfish were also exploited. The Chumash are renowned for the sophisticated construction of seaworthy plank canoes, called *tomols,* as well as cave paintings and money made of shells.

The Franciscan missionaries established five missions in Chumash territory: San Luis Obispo (1772), San Buenaventura (1782), Santa Barbara (1786), La Purísima (1787), and Santa Ynez (1804). During the course of some fifty years, the Franciscans resettled the bulk of the Chumash in these five missions, where life proved unhealthy for them because of disease, the stress of cultural change, and crowded living conditions. The rate of population decline reached about 85 percent from contact population levels, so that by 1832, there were only 2,259 Chumash converts living in the five missions. Infant mortality was particularly high—about two-thirds of all children died before reaching age five, and only one-fourth reached puberty. A small number of Chumash survive today in the Santa Barbara–San Luis Obispo county areas and preserve much of their culture.

At the turn of the twenty-first century, only one of the existing fourteen bands of Chumash in California is a federally recognized tribe, the *Samala* or Santa Ynez Chumash. In 2002 Californians voted to give exclusive rights of a Las Vegas–style casino operation to Native Americans. Feuding within the Chumash tribe over blood quantum (one must be able to document one-quarter tribal blood to be an enrolled member) has increased since the opening of the Chumash Casino Resort because enrolled members (approximately 200) generally receive $30,000 per month from casino profits.

See also **California; Indigenous Peoples; Missions: Spanish America.**

BIBLIOGRAPHY

Arnold, Jeanne E., ed. *The Origins of a Pacific Coast Chiefdom: The Chumash of the Channel Islands.* Salt Lake City: University of Utah Press, 2001.

Johnson, John R. "The Chumash and the Missions" in David H. Thomas, ed., *Columbian Consequences,* vol. 1, *Archaeological and Historical Perspectives on the Spanish Borderlands West* (1989), pp. 365–375.

Kroeber, Alfred L. *Handbook of California Indians* (1925, repr. 1976).

ROBERT H. JACKSON

CHUQUICAMATA MINE.

Chuquicamata Mine, world's largest open-pit copper mine, located in the northern Atacama Desert in Chile, approximately 150 miles northeast of the port city of Antofagasta. At 9,500 feet above sea level, it measures 2 miles in length, 1.5 miles in width, and almost half a mile in depth. With estimated reserves of 600 million to 1 billion tons of 1.6 percent copper content, the mine produced 667,000 metric tons in 1991, almost half of Chile's copper output and 13 percent of its foreign revenues. Operated by the state-owned Chile Copper Corporation, it employed 10,000 workers in 1992. Originally

purchased by the Guggenheim interests, the mine be-gan operation in 1915. It was sold to the Chile Exploration Company, a subsidiary of U.S.-based Anaconda, in 1923. In the 1920s bitter strikes, led by the leftist Federation of Chilean Workers, and harsh retaliation by the mine's management led to demonstrations of Chilean nationalistic sentiment and to congressional inquiries. In spite of persistent disturbances, Chuquicamata yielded consistently higher profits than Anaconda's domestic operations. The Christian Democratic government of Eduardo Frei Montalvo (1964–1970) "Chileanized" the mine, putting 51 percent of its stock under state control with compensation paid to Anaconda over a twelve-year period. During the Popular Unity government of Salvador Allende Gossens (1970–1973), Congress unanimously approved full nationalization. Charging Anaconda with excess profits in the past, the Allende government denied compensation, further provoking the United States opposition to his regime. In 1974 the Augusto Pinochet Ugarte government promised compensation of $253 million; the claim was settled in 1975. The Chuquicamata Mine is still operated by the state company, Codelco, and it currently produces about a third of Chile's exports.

See also **Copper Industry.**

BIBLIOGRAPHY

Marcial Figueroa, *Chuquicamata: La tumba del chileno* (1928).

Fredrick B. Pike, *Chile and the United States, 1880–1962* (1963), esp. pp. 161, 234, and 409 for the early period.

Theodore H. Moran, *Multinational Corporations and the Politics of Dependence: Copper in Chile* (1975) for the post-1945 era.

Paul W. Drake, *Socialism and Populism in Chile 1932–1952* (1978), esp. pp. 19, 44, 200, 287, 319, 355.

Additional Bibliography

Finn, Janet L. *Tracing the Veins: Of Copper, Culture, and Community from Butte to Chuquicamata.* Berkeley: University of California Press, 1998.

CHRISTEL K. CONVERSE

CHUQUITANTA. *See* El Paraíso.

CHURCH-STATE CONFLICTS. *See* Anticlericalism.

CHURRASCO.

Churrasco is chunks of beef or mutton roasted over a wood or charcoal fire with a combination of salt and spices. Gauchos and other rural inhabitants of the Río de la Plata region relished fresh beef cooked in this way. In some cases, the cook wrapped the meat in a hide and laid it on a bed of hot coals. This technique better retained the meat's flavor and juices. Gauchos could seemingly subsist on a diet consisting largely of *churrasco* and their favorite beverage, Mate. A gaucho used only his long knife (Facón) to slice and eat the meat. Traditionalists in the Río de la Plata region continue to prepare *churrasco, carne asado,* and other beef delicacies. This style of cooking has been exported to other countries such as Chile, Peru, and Spain, where fine restaurants in Santiago, Lima, and Madrid offer choice cuts of beef roasted in the *churrasco style.* Brazilian steakhouses known as *churrascarias* where roasted meats are served *rodizio* style have become popular in the United States. In many cases the beef is eaten with a traditional *chimichurri* sauce made from olive oil, lemon juice, garlic, and basil.

See also **Asado; Food and Cookery; Gaucho.**

BIBLIOGRAPHY

Bell, Stephen. *Campanha Gaúcha: A Brazilian Ranching System, 1850–1920.* Stanford, CA: Stanford University Press, 1998.

Cascudo, Luís da Câmara. *História da alimentação no Brasil.* São Paulo: Editora da Universidade de São Paulo, 1983.

Coluccio, Félix. *Diccionario folklórico argentino,* vol. 1 (1964), p. 121.

Slatta, Richard W. *Comparing Cowboys and Frontiers.* Norman: University of Oklahoma Press, 1997.

RICHARD W. SLATTA

CHURRIGUERESQUE.

Churrigueresque, a style of architectural decoration of eighteenth-century Latin America. Named after José Benito Churriguera (1665–1725) of Madrid, its origin and character in Mexico are actually based on the work of Jerónimo de Balbás, whose Retablo de los Reyes (1718–1737) in the cathedral of Mexico City is the first Churrigueresque work in New Spain. In Peru, the pulpit in the Iglesia San Blas in Cuzco is an outstanding example of this style as is the Basílica Menor de Nuestra Señora de la Merced in Lima. Academic neoclassicism put an end to Churrigueresque by around 1790. Its identifying feature is the *estípite* (a pillar whose lower section is an elongated and inverted truncated pyramid), but just as significant are the changes in proportions and, consequently, in compositional principles. Freestanding figure sculpture and a more naturalistic style of ornament with rococo elements also accompany the *estípite*. The historical inaccuracy of the word "Churrigueresque" has led many scholars to reject or limit its use. Alternatives are "ultrabaroque," "balbasiano," or, simply and most commonly now, "*estípite* baroque."

See also **Architecture: Architecture to 1900.**

BIBLIOGRAPHY

Justino Fernández, *El Retablo de los Reyes* (1972), pp. 279–282.

Additional Bibliography

Early, James. *The Colonial Architecture of Mexico.* Dallas: Southern Methodist University Press, 2001.

Mullen, Robert Jame. *Architecture and Its Sculpture in Viceregal Mexico.* Austin: University of Texas Press, 1997.

Peraza Guzmán, Marco Tulio, and Pablo A Chico Ponce de León. *Arquitectura y urbanismo virreinal.* Mexico City: Consejo Nacional de Ciencia y Tecnología, 2000.

CLARA BARGELLINI

CHURUBUSCO, BATTLE OF.
See **Mexico, Wars and Revolutions: Mexican-American War.**

CÍCERO, PADRE.
See **Batista, Cícero Romão.**

CIELITO.

Cielito, a traditional folk dance of the rural Río de la Plata region and Chile, also called *cielo*. The slow, stately dance, dating from colonial days, is performed by couples who dance around one another. Partners do not touch each other. Over time, the rural lower classes enlivened the dance with variations, such as snapping their fingers. *Cielito* shared some similarities with the nineteenth-century *pericón,* which came to be considered the most patriotic and typical dance of Argentina.

See also **Music: Popular Music and Dance.**

BIBLIOGRAPHY

Carlos Vega, *Las danzas populares argentinas* (1952).

Félix Coluccio, *Diccionario folklórico argentino,* vol. 1 (1964), p. 77.

Additional Bibliography

Barrera, Rosita. *Abrazo de identidad: Danzas paralelas de Argentina y Chile.* Santiago de Chile: [s.n.], 1996.

Veniard, Juan María. "El minué. Supervivencia de una danza aristocrática en el salón romántico rioplatense." *Latin American Music Review/Revista de Música Latinoamericana* 13 (Autumn 1992): 195–212.

RICHARD W. SLATTA

CIENFUEGOS, CAMILO (1931–1959).

Camilo Cienfuegos (*b.* 1931; *d.* October 1959), Cuban revolutionary and chief of staff of the rebel army. Born to a poor family in the Layanó district of Havana, Camilo Cienfuegos nevertheless had a happy childhood. He managed to secure an eighth-grade education while selling shoes to support his family, and he displayed his social conscience at an early age, collecting money in 1937 to aid the orphans of the Spanish Civil War. Cienfuegos's father resisted formal education for his children, preferring instead that Camilo and his older brother Osmany receive private lessons from an old Communist acquaintance. Nevertheless, Camilo was drawn to more social forms of activity and joined the anti-Fascist student paper *Lídice* in 1945. He was a handsome, popular, and athletic young man with red hair and a quick laugh. In 1947 Cienfuegos won the national *pelota* championships and was the pride of his family.

After ending his formal education for good, Cienfuegos worked at odd jobs in Havana and took up sculpting. The on-air suicide of political activist and radio personality Eddy Chibás in 1951 prompted Cienfuegos to leave Cuba for the United States, where he hoped to make his fortune. In 1955 he was back in Cuba and participating in demonstrations against Batista and the police on behalf of Fidel Castro's Twenty-Sixth of July

Movement. With his forceful personality, Camilo Cienfuegos quickly caught Castro's eye, and he joined the exile group in Mexico that was preparing for an invasion of Cuba. He was one of the eighty-one men who set out with Fidel Castro in November 1956 on the *Granma* to start a revolution.

After the initial landing, Cienfuegos became one of the *comandantes* of the rebel forces. He appears to have been an avowed Marxist at a time when the revolutionaries had not yet declared an official ideology; in his districts Cienfuegos set up schools that taught literacy and socialist doctrine.

After the rebels' victory on 1 January 1959, Cienfuegos was appointed chief of staff of the armed forces and became the second most popular figure of the revolution after Castro himself. He disappeared mysteriously on a solo flight from Camagüey to Havana in October 1959; no trace of the wreckage was ever found, and the disappearance remains controversial.

See also **Cuba, Revolutions: Cuban Revolution.**

BIBLIOGRAPHY

Ernesto "Che" Guevara, *José Martí, Antonio Guiteras, Antonio Maceo, Camilo Cienfuegos* (1977).

William Gálvez, *Camilo, señor de la vanguardia* (1979); Carlos Franquí, *Diary of the Cuban Revolution,* translated by Georgette Felix et al. (1980).

Tad Szulc, *Fidel: A Critical Portrait* (1986).

Additional Bibliography

Batista Moreno, René. *Camilo en Las Villas.* Barcelona: Seix Barral, 2001.

Franqui, Carlos. *Camilo Cienfuegos.* La Habana: Editorial Gente Nueva, 2004.

Gálvez, William. *Camilo Cienfuegos.* La Habana: Editora Política, 1998.

KAREN RACINE

CIENTÍFICOS.

Científicos, Mexican political faction in the Porfiriato. Supporters of the dictatorship of Porfirio Díaz (1876–1910), the *científicos* were a group of young lawyers and journalists who, in the periodical *La Libertad,* articulated a theory of "scientific" politics based upon the positivism of Auguste Comte and Herbert Spencer as an alternative to "doctrinaire" and "metaphysical" liberalism. They advocated strong government marked by technocratic management and were concerned less with rights and liberties than they were with issues of order, peace, and economic growth. The original group included Justo Sierra, Telesforo García, Francisco Cosmes, Francisco Bulnes, Pablo Macedo, and José Yves Limantour.

In 1892, these powerful tenured public servants in the Díaz government formed the Liberal Union to advocate a third term for Díaz. With a developmentalist platform, they called for a money-saving reorganization of the ministry of war, rationalization of the tax system, and a commercial and fiscal policy to accelerate foreign investment. They also sought constitutional amendments that would create institutional safeguards against persistent dictatorial rule. To strengthen the separation of powers, they advocated a vice presidency independent of the supreme court and the irremovability of judges. In the debate over these reforms, the group was dubbed "Científicos."

Only partially successful in their constitutional reform proposals, the *científicos* were more effective with their developmentalist agenda. As minister of finance, José Yves Limantour created a budget surplus after repaying the foreign debt; reorganized finances and credit; suppressed the *alcabala*, or internal sales tax; lowered tariffs on imports; negotiated foreign loans; put Mexico on the gold standard; and succeeded in enacting new mining and land legislation to encourage unfettered growth through foreign investment.

In 1903 the *científicos* once again organized the reelection of Díaz through a second Liberal Union convention and at the same time sought constitutional safeguards for institutionalizing the transfer of power. As Díaz's Mexico City–centered power group, the *científicos* were clearly one of the two major contending political factions. Opposed to their European-oriented development policy to offset U.S. penetration were the *reyistas*, supporters of the Nuevo León governor Bernardo Reyes, who were more closely allied with the military and with peripheral, regional bases of power. The political contention between these two factions gave rise to the crisis of succession and the Revolution of 1910.

After the Revolution of 1910, *científico* became a derogatory term applied to those most closely associated with the dictatorship who had accumulated capital, wealth, and power at the expense of the Mexican people and their development.

Interpretations of the *científicos* vary among historians. François Javier Guerra and Charles Hale see them as constitutionalists. Guerra, however, believes that they clearly distinguished themselves from liberalism after 1893. Hale sees their liberal derivation as always fundamental. Friedrich Katz sees them as a key political faction motivating the crisis of succession in 1910. Leopoldo Zea and Arnaldo Córdova see them as ideologues and administrators of the Mexican bourgeoisie and managers of dictatorship for capitalist development.

See also **Díaz, Porfirio.**

BIBLIOGRAPHY

Córdova, Arnaldo. *La ideología de la revolución mexicana: La formación del nuevo régimen* (1974).

Cosío Villegas, Daniel. *Historia moderna de México*, vol. 9 (1955–1972); Jesús Reyes Heroles, *El liberalismo mexicano*, 3 vols. (1957–1961).

Guerra, François Javier. *Mexico, del antiguo régimen a la revolución*, 2 vols. (1988).

Hale, Charles. *The Transformation of Liberalism in Late Nineteenth Century Mexico* (1989).

Katz, Friedrich. *The Secret War in Mexico* (1982).

Tenorio-Trillo, Mauricio. *Mexico at the World's Fairs: Crafting a Modern Nation.* Berkeley: University of California Press, 1996.

Villegas Revueltas, Silvestre. *El liberalismo moderado en México, 1852–1864.* México, D.F.: Universidad Nacional Autónoma de México, 1997.

Weiner, Richard. *Race, Nation, and Market: Economic Culture in Porfirian Mexico.* Tucson: University of Arizona Press, 2004.

Zea, Leopoldo. *El positivismo en México* (1968).

MARY KAY VAUGHAN

CIEZA DE LEÓN, PEDRO DE (c. 1520–1554).

Pedro de Cieza de León (*b.* c. 1520; *d.* 2 July 1554), "prince of the Peruvian chroniclers." Born in Llerena, Spain, the son of Lope de León and Leonor de Cazalla, Pedro had at least three sisters and one brother. Little is known of his early years. On 3 June 1535 he set sail for the Indies, heading for Santo Domingo. He first entered South America via Cartagena on the north coast of present-day Colombia and participated in minor expeditions in search of riches, some of which were little more than grave-robbing episodes. In 1536 he joined the Entrada of Juan de Vadillo to explore the Gulf of Urabá; the next year he followed the same leader in the discovery of the province of Abibe—both were financial disasters. In 1539 he set out to explore the Cauca and Atrato basin with a new force under Jorge Robledo that later founded Ancerma and Cartago (1540) in the rich Quimbaya region. It was in Cartago in 1541 that Cieza first began to keep copious notes on what he saw and experienced. The following year he was representing Jorge Robledo in the Audiencia of Panamá, where he probably met for the first time those escaping the conflict in Peru. The same year he helped found the city of Arma and received an Encomienda for his efforts.

With the rising of Gonzalo Pizarro in Peru, Cieza traveled to serve the royalists under Pedro de la Gasca, president of the Audiencia of Lima. In September 1547 he crossed the Pacasmayo Valley with the king's forces, continued into highland Jauja, and marched southward toward Cuzco. He fought at the battle of Jaquijahuana (9 April 1548) and witnessed the execution of the rebels Gonzalo Pizarro and Francisco de Carvajal. Gasca must have been impressed by young Cieza's scholarly capabilities, for he seems to have appointed Cieza official chronicler of events in Peru. During 1549 the young chronicler traveled into southern Charcas (modern Bolivia) under the president's orders. For a few months in 1550 he resided in Cuzco, where he took oral testimony about the Inca past from several Indians, including Cayu Tupac, descendant of the ruler Huayna Capac. Cieza completed the first part of his multivolume history in Lima on 8 September 1550.

In 1551 Cieza voyaged back to Spain and was in Toledo by mid-1552 to present Philip II with a copy of the manuscript. Following his return to Spain, Cieza married Isabel López de Abreu, daughter of Maria de Abreu and the prosperous merchant Juan de Llerena. Cieza died before he could complete his massive narrative and was buried in Seville in the Church of San Vicente alongside his wife, who died at age thirty-four only two months earlier.

Cieza de León intended to publish a four-part history of Peru. Part one, the only section printed during the author's lifetime, was a geographical and ethnological account of South America's Andean region; part two, the "Señorío de los Incas," was a history of the Incas; part three was the account of the Spanish discovery and conquest of the realm; and part four, made up of five book-length manuscripts, examined the civil wars: Las Salinas, Chupas, Quito, Huarina, and Jaquijahuana. Cieza became a sixteenth-century "best-seller" with the 1553 Seville edition of part one, which was quickly followed by three Spanish editions in Amberes in 1554 and seven Italian translations between 1555 and 1576.

See also **Peru: From the Conquest Through Independence.**

BIBLIOGRAPHY

Pedro De Cieza De León, *The Incas of Pedro de Cieza de León* (1959).

Francesca Cantu, ed., *Pedro de Cieza de León e il "Descubrimiento y Conquista del Perú"* (1979).

Additional Bibliography

Estrada Ycaza, Julio. *Andanzas de Cieza por tierras americanas.* Guayaquil, Ecuador: Banco Central del Ecuador: Archivo Histórico del Guayas, 1987.

Figueroa, Luis Millones. *Pedro de Cieza de León y su Crónica de Indias: La entrada de los incas en la historia universal.* Lima: Pontificia Universidad Católica del Perú Fondo Editorial, 2001.

NOBLE DAVID COOK

CIHUATÁN.

CIHUATÁN. Cihuatán, a large Early Postclassic (900–1250 CE) settlement located atop a hill with a commanding view of the Acelhuate River floodplain in the Paraíso Basin of central El Salvador. This site has yielded unequivocal evidence of the intrusion and dominance of Mexican (Pipil) or Mexicanized populations in central El Salvador during the Early Postclassic period.

Strong contrasts in settlement pattern and material culture distinguish the preceding Late Classic (550–900 CE) Fogón phase from the Early Postclassic Guazapa phase. Fogón settlements near Cihuatán are tightly nucleated clusters arranged in *plazuela* groups and located on river terraces. Guazapa settlements at the site are in a dispersed pattern, surrounding a central zone of monumental public buildings and elite residences. Guazapa settlements occur on the floodplain, on relict terraces, and atop hills. Mexican architectural traits, such as the *talud-tablero* form, I-shaped ball courts, and T-shaped temple platforms, characterize the public buildings at Cihuatán.

Unlike Maya-looking Fogón ceramics, the Guazapa ceramic complex emphasizes forms and decorative techniques from central Mexico and the southern Gulf Coast area. Large spiked censers are very similar to those from Tula. Life-sized modeled effigies of Mexican deities such as Tlaloc and Xipe Totec are very much like those from central Mexico and central and southern Veracruz. Mold-made, wheeled figurines are almost identical to those from Tula and the Veracruz Gulf Coast. These new traits that emerged during the Early Postclassic had antecedents not in any nearby region but in central and southern Mexico, indicating that Cihuatán was occupied by a foreign population during the Early Postclassic.

The fall of Cihuatán may be linked to struggles among recently arrived and established populations in El Salvador and Guatemala. It was destroyed by fire around 1250 CE.

See also **Precontact History: Latin America in the Precontact Period.**

BIBLIOGRAPHY

William R. Fowler, Jr., "The Pipil-Nicarao of Central America" (Ph.D. diss., University of Calgary, 1981).

William R. Fowler, Jr., and Howard H. Earnest, Jr., "Settlement Patterns and Prehistory of the Paraíso Basin of El Salvador," in *Journal of Field Archaeology* 12 (1985): 19–32.

William R. Fowler, Jr., *The Cultural Evolution of Ancient Nahua Civilizations: The Pipil-Nicarao of Central America* (1989).

Additional Bibliography

Fowler, William R., and Federico Trujillo. *El Salvador: Antiguas civilizaciones.* San Salvador: Banco Agrícola Comercial de El Salvador, 1995.

Kelley, Jane Holden, Marsha P. Hanen, and William R. Fowler. *Cihuatán, El Salvador: A Study in Intrasite Variability.* Nashville: Vanderbilt University, 1988.

Lubensky, Earl H. *The Excavation of Structures P-12 and P-20 at Cihuatán, El Salvador = Excavación de las estructuras P-12 y P-20 de Cihuatán, El Salvador.* San Francisco: San Francisco State University, 2005.

KATHRYN SAMPECK

CIMARRÓNES. *See* **Maroons (Cimarrones).**

■

CINCHONA. Cinchona, a genus of thirty-eight species of trees and shrubs, is found on the western slopes of the Andes, from Colombia to Peru. Although some of these plants are known for their fever-reducing properties, there is no evidence that the Incas were aware of their medicinal value. The earliest recorded use of cinchona was in 1630, when Jesuits treated the viceroy of Peru for fever with the bark of the plant. This bark, in pulverized form called "Jesuit powder," proved to be extremely popular as a preventive and cure for malaria for Europeans in the tropics. Linnaeus named the plants in 1742 after the Countess of Chinchón, who was said to have recovered from malaria after being treated with the powdered bark. Although the story was without factual basis, the name stuck.

The active ingredients in the bark of the cinchona are any one of four alkaloids—cinchonine, cinchonidine, quinidine, and quinine—this last being the most important of the four. As the amount of quinine in each species varies greatly, efforts were made to separate the drug from the bark. In 1820 French chemists Pierre Pelletier and Joseph Caventou successfully produced crystallized quinine from cinchona.

After 1821 the Jesuit practice of planting five trees for every one cut was discontinued by the governments of the newly liberated countries, a decision that led to the destruction of most of the cinchona in Peru and Colombia. From 1844 to 1851, Bolivia passed laws regulating the export of cinchona bark and forbidding the export of cinchona seeds. These policies resulted in an insufficient European supply, which spurred efforts to smuggle the seeds out of South America. Clements R. Markham, an Englishman, safely brought plant seeds of the *succirubra* and *oficialis* varieties of cinchona to Europe in 1858, and seven years later

Charles Ledger arrived in Europe with seeds of *C. ledgeriana*, a superior variety. Ledger learned about the different kinds of cinchona plants and their properties from a Bolivian Aymara guide, Manuel Incra Mamani, who pointed out the red-bark cinchona as having the greatest curative powers. It is this variety that bears Ledger's name.

The Dutch were the most successful in establishing cinchona plantations. Their East Indies properties yielded enough quinine for European needs until World War II interrupted production. Synthetic quinine, such as atebrin, which was developed by I. G. Farbenindustrie in 1930, then became an important substitute for the natural product. Synthetics remain the major source of quinine, whereas cinchona is used mostly for flavoring tonics such as quinine water.

See also **Medicinal Plants; Medicine: Colonial Spanish America; Medicine: The Modern Era.**

BIBLIOGRAPHY

Jaramillo-Arango, Jaime. *The Conquest of Malaria*. London: Heinemann, 1950.

Gramiccia, Gabriele. *The Life of Charles Ledger (1818–1905): Alpacas and Quinine*. London: Macmillan, 1988.

SHEILA L. HOOKER

CINCO DE MAYO. Cinco de Mayo, a Mexican national holiday commemorating the triumph of the Mexican army over the French on 5 May 1862, the battle of Puebla. General Ignacio Zaragoza led the Mexican army, consisting of about 2,000 conscript soldiers, to victory over a French force of some 6,000 well-equipped professional soldiers commanded by General Charles Latrille, Count of Lorencez. The battle was part of a campaign by the French to place the Austrian Archduke Maximilian on the Mexican throne and to establish an American empire. Although the French were ultimately successful in defeating the Mexicans and imposing Maximilian, the Mexican victory at Puebla, in the face of inadequate manpower and weaponry, inspired the Mexican nation to fight with new determination. Mexico, in honor of the victory, made Cinco de Mayo a holiday and an important national symbol. Cinco de Mayo has been celebrated for many years

in the United States, especially in the Southwest and other areas with substantial communities of Mexican origin. It is often confused with Mexican Independence Day (16 September).

See also **Puebla, Battle and Siege of.**

BIBLIOGRAPHY

Jack Autrey Dabbs, *The French Army in Mexico, 1861–1867: A Study in Military Government* (1963).

Lilia Díaz López, *Versión francesa de México: Informes diplomáticos (1853–1858)* (1963).

Ernesto De La Torre Villar, *La intervención francesa y el triunfo de la república* (1968).

Francisco P. Troncoso, *Diario de las operaciones del sitio de Puebla en 1863* (1972).

David G. Lafrance, "A Battle for Nationhood," *Vista* 5 (6 May 1990): 8–10, and "Dashed Ambition," *Vista* 6 (5 May 1991): 12–13, 18.

Additional Bibliography

Cunningham, Michele. *Mexico and the Foreign Policy of Napoleon III*. Houndmills, New York: Palgrave, 2001.

García Cantú, Gastón. *La intervención francesa en México*. México: Clío, 1998.

Meyer, Jean A. *Yo, el francés: La intervención en primera persona: Biografías y crónicas*. México: Tusquets Editores, 2002.

PAUL GANSTER

CINEMA

This entry includes the following articles:
FROM THE SILENT FILM TO 1990
SINCE 1990

FROM THE SILENT FILM TO 1990

Cinema has played a vigorous role in shaping Latin American popular culture and in portraying Latin America to the world. Its economic history has been influenced by the role of the state, positively and negatively, through nationalization, subsidies, government development corporations, exhibition quotas, and censorship. In the last years of the nineteenth century, from the capitals of Mexico and Argentina to the highlands of Bolivia, entrepreneurs trucked film equipment and novelty shorts. In clubs, cafés, and theaters, audiences watched comedy routines, advertisements, images of great rural estates, and scenes of military and political pomp.

SILENT FILM

Silent films became entertainment staples in urban Latin America, accompanying immigration and industrialization. Production remained, however, artisanal, complementing the burgeoning products of European and U.S. studios, which occupied 90 to 95 percent of screen time. World War I, which limited European film production, benefited U.S. producers. U.S. distributors offered U.S. films, which had recouped costs at home, at rates far lower than those Latin American producers could afford to charge for their films. Latin American productions often mimicked competing products from Europe or the United States. In Brazil, for example, directors making "Westerns" even took Anglo-Saxon pseudonyms. Nonetheless, an indigenous film culture was born. In Mexico, silent-film actresses became national icons; in Brazil, the "golden age" (1898–1912) was marked by romantic, even idyllic versions of the countryside and portraits of fashionable society.

Documentary subjects predominated, with some filmed theater and occasional fiction, such as the wildly successful Mexican *María* (1922), drawn from the romantic novel by Colombian Jorge Isaacs. Censorship honored the power of the documentary as early as 1913; newsreels in many places, already flickering reflections of the powerful, came to have something of an officialist character. Sometimes fiction subjects were drawn from headlines, such as the murder tale *El pequeño heroe del arroyo de oro* (The Little Hero of the Arroyo de Oro [Uruguay, 1929]) or the Mexican crime story *La banda de automóvil gris* (The Gray Car Gang [1919]). Religious and historical subjects were also popular.

Working-class culture gradually became a theme of popular silent film. The Argentine José Agustín ("El Negro") Ferreyra made films about the life of the *arrabales* (working-class suburbs) such as *La muchacha de Arrabal* (Neighborhood Girl [1922]), which incorporated a tango played by an orchestra. The Brazilian Humberto Mauro explored the relationship between country and city in several films, including *Braza dormida* (Dying Embers [1928]). Rarely was film a medium for the fine arts, with the notable exception of Mario Peixoto's *Limite* (Limit [1929]).

SOUND FILM

When sound film was introduced in 1929, U.S. studios produced simultaneous remakes in Spanish and later dubbed (in hilariously heterogenous Spanish) versions in response to audiences' clamor to see the original stars. The U.S. Good Neighbor Policy in the 1930s vigorously fostered free-trade agreements backed strongly by U.S. industry groups, establishing a diplomatic tradition of U.S. cultural export. Latin American sound-film production thus was low throughout the 1930s.

National industries in Mexico and Argentina were fostered by corporatist states in the 1930s. There, as in lesser production centers such as Brazil, Peru, and Cuba, radio provided an important source of stars, plots (especially from soap operas and series), themes, styles, and soundtracks. The studio model was borrowed from the United States, often with integrated exhibition. One indication of U.S. dominance was Brazil's first sound film, *Broadway Melody* (1929; original title in English), which was about Brazilians backstage in New York.

In Argentina, sound films started early. The tango generated a popular musical genre that developed within a decade from vigorously populist to cloying cliché as the cinema sought a middle-class audience. The star Carlos Gardel made several tango movies before continuing his career in Europe. Some productions went beyond populist celebration, for instance, Mario Soffici's 1939 *Prisioneros de la tierra* (Prisoners of the Land), about the exploitation of maté workers, and the psychological dramas of Leopoldo Torres Ríos, such as *La vuelta al nido* (Return to the Nest [1938]), about a family in crisis. Import-substitution policies, urbanization, and cutbacks in Spanish-language competition because of the Spanish Civil War fueled the business. However, Argentina's neutrality in World War II caused the United States to suspend shipments of raw stock, further intensifying national filmmakers' demands for state protection. After 1946, Juan Domingo Perón introduced quotas, government loans, and an admissions tax; production was boosted, but *churros* ("quota quickies," low-quality films made simply to fill mandatory screen time) were also common.

In Mexico, the Lázaro Cárdenas government established a tradition of heavy state involvement, bankrolling studios, and establishing loan policies as well as quotas from 1935 on. U.S. support during World War II, quotas, and state financing— including the purchase of some distribution companies in 1947—garnered 15 percent of the home market for Mexican production. A studio system flourished, complete with major stars such as María Félix, Pedro Armendáriz, and Dolores Del Rio, and the 1940s became the "golden age" of Mexican commercial cinema. Genre films arose, such as the *cabaretera* (brothel) films, *comedias rancheras* (cowboy films), historical films of the Revolution, and redolent melodramas playing on the virgin/whore female image. Among the best-known directors of the period was Emilio ("El Indio") Fernández, who produced a trilogy on the Mexican Revolution and has been compared to John Ford for his creation of a national iconography. Cantinflas, the comedian whose character and films have had enduring popularity throughout the region, rose to celebrity in the late 1930s. As the system consolidated, state support for studios also entrenched a group of veteran filmmakers and, along with the international market, encouraged filmic clichés. Centralized distribution after 1953 fostered the production of *churros.*

The uncompleted epic work of Soviet filmmaker Sergei Eisenstein in Mexico in 1930–1931 acquainted several Mexican filmmakers, including the renowned cinematographer Gabriel Figueroa, with his vision and style. (By contrast, the Spanish exile Luis Buñuel's postwar stay in Mexico, while resulting in some remarkable films, had little stylistic impact except on the work of his associate Luis Alcoriza.)

In Brazil, whose major trading partner was the United States, and whose options to control film production were correspondingly reduced, mild quotas from 1930 on encouraged entrepreneurs. They produced films that sentimentally celebrated the lives of the poor and disenfranchisesd, such as Humberto Mauro's *Ganga bruta* (Thugs [1933]) and *Favela dos meus amores* (Slum of My Desires [1935]), and also films that transformed radio musical tradition into the *chanchada* musical. A clutch of production companies, including Cinédia—started by the self-styled nationalist entrepreneur Adhémar Gonzaga—were formed, featuring carnivalesque films that were precursors to *chanchadas.* The Rio production company Atlántida, later to become a foremost producer of *chanchadas,* was founded in 1941 to produce films involving themes of daily life; *Moleque Tião* (Kid Tião [1943]) featured the great black comedian and actor Grande Otelo. Vera Cruz was started by a São Paulo industrialist in 1949 to upgrade Brazilian cinema and

appeal to an international audience. It produced the internationally acclaimed *O cangaceiro* (The Bandit, [1953]), a film about backlands bandits that showed the influence of the U.S. Western genre, but also treated a national subject that would be well worked in Cinema Novo. However, the U.S. studio Columbia Pictures owned international distribution rights to Vera Cruz, and it calculatedly failed to find the international audience. The company went bankrupt in 1954, a year after *O cangaceiro* won a prize at the Cannes film festival.

In the late 1930s and 1940s, Mexican cinema became preeminent throughout Latin America, and Mexicans both produced and influenced production in other countries, such as Guatemala, Colombia, Venezuela, and Cuba. Argentine cinema—both its capital and talent—spread to Chile and Uruguay. The forms pioneered by both cinemas became models, even to the extent that Brazilian movie music sometimes had a Caribbean flavor. Censorship affected the choice of subject and tone. For instance, *Manuel García* (Cuba [1941]) was censored in Cuba for its Robin Hood–like theme. Mexican censorship forced a happy ending in the first of Fernando de Fuentes's films about the Revolution, *El prisionero trece* (Prisoner Number Thirteen [1933]).

NUEVO CINE
In the 1950s, studio production declined and an energetic wave of film production developed on completely different terms, for a variety of reasons. It came to be called Nuevo Cine Latino Americano after a film festival in Viña del Mar, Chile, in 1967. U.S. wartime support for national production did not continue, and the trade association Motion Picture Export Association zealously guarded distribution networks for U.S. films. Film audiences declined and film studios collapsed for other reasons as well. Latin American government production policies all too often produced low-quality films, and admission prices set by the state limited capital. Television proved a fierce rival for cinema.

At the same time, political forces—the rise of postcolonial nations in Africa and Asia, the Cuban Revolution international lending policies for development, and U.S. diplomacy—fostered nationalist and populist rhetoric. Culturally, Italian neorealists and the French New Wave variously demonstrated the creative power of the socially engaged or dissident artist.

In Latin America, middle-class, mostly male youths typical of the international youth and student culture of the 1950s—both political and individualistic, in opposition to and yet part of the nation's cultural elite—established film clubs, film magazines, and cinematheques. In Argentina in 1956, Fernando Birri, who like several other Latin American filmmakers had studied with the Italian neorealists, founded a production center at the National University of the Littoral in Santa Fe, soon known as the Documentary Film School of Santa Fe and inspiring among others a center called Cine Experimental at the University of Chile.

Some strove to be missionaries of "cultured cinema" and to produce personal artistic statements within the dramatic conventions of international feature film. Argentine Leopoldo Torre Nilsson's Bergmanesque elaborations on middle- and upper-class alienation; Argentine Fernand Ayala's *Paula la cautiva* (The Captive Paula [1963]), portraying a decadent artistocracy; the Brazilian Anselmo Duarte's *O pagador de promessas* (The Given Word [1962]), a tale of a backlands simpleton who comes to the city to fulfill a promise to an Afro-Brazilian saint; and several Mexican adaptations of Gabriel García Márquez stories, including Arturo Ripstein's *Tiempo de morir* (A Time to Die [1965]), each demonstrate a simultaneous search for indigenous themes, a personal style, and a conformity to existing conventions of feature cinema.

Many strove to both reflect and to affect social reality, while also reaching mass audiences. This goal took many expressive forms. Films such as Venezuelan Margot Benacerraf's *Araya* (1958); the early films of the Argentine Santa Fe film school, such as the documentary *Tire dié* (Throw Me a Dime [1956–1958]) and the fiction feature *Los inundados* (The Flooded Ones [1961]); the early films of Brazilian *cinema novo* leader Nelso Pereira dos Santos, including *Vidas secas* (Barren Lives [1963]); Argentine Leonardo Favio's *Crónica de un niño solo* (Tale of an Orphan [1964]); Chilean Aldo Francia's *Valparaíso mi amor* (Valparaiso My Love [1968]); and Chilean Miguel Littin's *El chacal de Nahueltoro* (The Jackal of Nahueltoro [1969]), refracting the mandate of Italian neorealism, plunged with documentary or documentary-like realism into long-hidden social realities. In some cases film served as exposé and testament, as in the Mexican Central University of Film Studies *El Grito* (1968), the chronicle of the Mexican student movement whose clash with authorities resulted in the Tlatelolco massacre of 1968.

"Militant cinema" called for a divorce both from studio and art cinema and from traditional lowest-common-denominator goals of entertainment, aiming instead to provoke heightened political awareness. Aesthetic polemics ensued over what was variously called "the cinema of hunger" (the Brazilian Glauber Rocha), "imperfect cinema" (the Cuban Julio García Espinosa), "revolutionary cinema" (the Bolivian Jorge Sanjinés), and "third cinema" (the Argentines Fernando Solanas and Octavio Getino). Stylistically innovative films, whose formal challenge was motivated by a desire to break through social clichés and stereotypes, included Jorge Sanjinés and Oscar Soria's *Revolución* (1964); Glauber Rocha's astonishingly rich opus *Deus e o diabo na terra do sol* (Black God/White Devil [1964]); Fernando Solanas and Octavio Getino's *La hora de los hornos* (Hour of the Furnaces [1968]); Argentine Raymundo Gleyzer's *México: La revolución congelada* (Mexico, the Frozen Revolution [1970]); Cuban Manuel Octavio Gómez's *La primera carga al machete* (First Charge of the Machete [1969]); Cuban Tomás Gutiérrez Alea's abundant and brilliant opus, including his early *Memorias de subdesarrollo* (Memories of Underdevelopment [1968]); and the early work of Chilean Raúl (later Raoul) Ruíz.

This spectacular flourishing of cinematic creativity was heralded in film festivals and international retrospectives worldwide. This recognition also made possible some international coproductions, such as those between Italian national television and Jorge Sanjinés in the production of *El Coraje del Pueblo* (The Courage of the People [1971]). The Latin American audience, however, was always sparse for such films, partly because they were often formally challenging and partly because of political suppression, especially in the Southern Cone. Governments increasingly censored, exiled, and even "disappeared" filmmakers. Works of distinction were produced in exile, including the remarkable three-part documentary of the Allende regime *Batalla de Chile* (Battle of Chile [1975, 1976, 1979]). In a few cases institutions endured, such as the Cinemateca

Uruguaya, which resisted censorship and kept open doors throughout military rule.

FILM INSTITUTIONS

Even governments that found the Nuevo Cine Latinoamericano profoundly threatening sought to promote quality cinema. In Argentina, the National Institute of Cinema, offering loans to filmmakers from box-office taxes, was responsible for a rise in cinematic production in the mid-1970s, including Héctor Olivera's internationally acclaimed *La Patagonia rebelde* (Rebellion in Patagonia [1974]). In Brazil, Embrafilme was launched in the early 1970s, the result of filmmakers' lobbying, and thereafter perpetually reorganized until its abolition in 1990. In the mid-1970s it controlled some distribution, produced up to half the Brazilian films made, and exercised a screen quota. Brazilian commercial production tended to be raucous and rowdy, with the *pornochanchada,* a debased form of the earlier musical genre, flourishing along with slapstick comedy.

In Mexico, the state continued to play a powerful, controversial, and erratic role. In the early 1960s a corrupt and financially stagnant industry produced low-quality films with a virtual government guarantee of profitability. Independent filmmakers of the Nuevo Cine generation agitated and developed projects. Beginning in 1970, the Luis Echeverría Alvarez government founded new film institutions and supported many independent filmmakers, including Arturo Ripstein, Jaime Hermosillo, Felipe Cazals, Luis Alcoriza, and Paul Leduc, but his successor, José López Portillo, quickly reversed much of this policy. The presidency of Miguel de la Madrid Hurtado reinstated the goal of producing quality cinema by creating the Mexican Institute of Cinema (IMCINE), which coordinated state roles in production, distribution, and exhibition. Occasional works of quality have emerged, although most Mexican movies have been low-quality features aimed at a Mexican and U.S.-Hispanic audience.

Other governments throughout Latin America supported cinema as a tool of cultural self-discovery, with mixed results. In 1952 a nationalist military government in Bolivia established the Bolivian Film Institute, which lasted for more than a decade and involved Bolivia's major film producers, Antonio Eguino, Oscar Sonia, and Jorge Sanjinés, who headed it briefly. After a tempestuous history, the institute was shut down by a military government in 1967. In 1968 Peru's nationalist military government stimulated film production, mostly in shorts, by invoking quotas and lifting import fees on equipment. Francisco Lombardi's 1977 *Muerte al amanecer* (Death at Dawn) was a rare box-office success; he later enjoyed several others. In Colombia, entertainment taxes were targeted from 1971 to support cinema, in combination with mandated screen time, and in 1978 a development company, Focine, was established. Several interesting Colombian films resulted, including Carlos Mayolo's *Carne de tu carne* (Flesh of Your Flesh [1983]) and Luis Ospina's *Pura sangre* (Pure Blood [1982]), both obliquely referencing Colombian politics through vampire metaphors. In Venezuela, where oil profits were fueling cultural policy, state film financing and required exhibition of national films promoted cinema from 1975 on. Additional support came from the Venezuelan development company Focine, a mixed public-private corporation founded in 1981 that was responsible for an uneven record of commercial production. In Panama, the left-leaning Torrijos government established in 1972 the Grupo Experimental de Cine Universitário, which produced several shorts and maintained a magazine and film exhibition center. The Chilean national film institute did not survive the 1973 coup.

The Cuban government's Institute of Cinematic Art and Industry (ICAIC), established months after the revolution, was a uniqe institution, with profound effects for Nuevo Cine. Growing from an aggressively experimental documentary and newsreel base—one that drew heavily on the montage tradition of early Russian formalists—the small industry soon began producing fiction features on themes of revolutionary life. After a censorship controversy in 1961, Fidel Castro described the industry's role with the dictum, "Within the Revolution, everything; against the Revolution, nothing"—a phrase that did not inhibit a vigorous internal history of conflict over aesthetics and politics at ICAIC.

ICAIC became an important coproduction and postproduction site for Latin American left filmmakers under pressure at home by the late 1960s. By 1979, Cuba was ready to offer an international showcase for Latin American film in its annual Festival of New Latin American Cinema. For a decade, before Cuba began suffering from the collapse of its socialist allies, it flourished as the premier Latin American film festival and became a major marketplace as well (although the Latin American marketplace for Latin cinema continued to be poor). In 1986 an international school of cinema and television, headed by Nuevo Cine veteran and visionary Fernando Birri, was founded in Cuba to foster a new generation of socially conscious filmmakers. By 1990, it had weathered several crises, some caused by the clash of expectations between teachers and highly diverse students, but had an uncertain future. At the same time the Foundation for Latin American Cinema, an international organization headed by Gabriel García Márquez and also based in Cuba, experimented with international coproduction with mild success. On the model of ICAIC, the Nicaraguan Sandinista government established in 1979 a national film institute, INCINE, which produced some provocative documentaries and newsreels with ample help from ICAIC and international media makers, but was crippled by lack of resources and the gradual collapse of the Sandinista government.

AFTER THE MILITARY

As civilian rule was restored in the Southern Cone in the 1980s and film clubs revived, Nuevo Cine veterans began making films with a social edge and high production values, such as Brazilian Ruy Guerra's *Eréndira* (1982) and Argentine Fernando Solanas's *Tangos: El exilio de Gardel* (Tangos [1985]). Others who had trained in advertising also made films that offered social criticism along with entertainment, including Marcos Zurinaga's *La gran fiesta* (The Grand Ball, Puerto Rico [1986]) and Argentine Luis Puenzo's *La historia oficial* (The Official Story [1985]). Women met internationally, formed production units, and produced documentary and fiction work. Among the leading female directors were Brazilian Suzana Amaral (*A hora da estrela* [Hour of the Star, 1985]), Argentine María Luisa Bemberg (*Camila* ;ob1984]), and Mexican María Novaro (*Danzón* [1991]).

Although European television programmers created funding possibilities for filmmakers, satellite signal piracy also fostered the growth of low-cost television services throughout Latin America. Movie attendance shrank dramatically with hard times, unrenovated theaters, and the threat of street crime at night. The collapse of the socialist bloc, long a dependable if not lucrative venue, especially for

documentaries, also affected the market. International coproductions often lacked a distinctive style. Thro-ughout Latin America, national film boards and institutes were battered by economic crises in the late 1980s. Argentina's INC was repeatedly threatened with abolition under sweeping and draconian economic measures; Brazil's Embrafilme was abolished in 1990, and with it much of Brazil's production.

Some of the producer/distributor cooperatives begun in the 1970s, including the Colombian Cine Mujer, the Mexican Zafra, and the Peruvian Grupo Chaski, seized on the grassroots potential of video. Left-wing media makers increasingly turned to video as a mode of communication. The Brazilian Workers' Center, part of a large metallurgical union, launched ambitious grassroots video production, and grassroots video burgeoned in Colombia, Ecuador, and elsewhere. In some areas, particularly lowlands Brazil, indigenous groups experimented with video. In El Salvador, video became a propaganda weapon.

For some filmmakers, the advent of portable video and digital editing, combined with economic recession and the high cost of film, suggested the end of filmmaking as they had known it. But some of the old guard of Nuevo Cine held out hope that video makers of tomorrow would continue the social inquiry of new Latin American film. As Paul Leduc said to his colleagues at the Havana film festival in 1987, "Cinema, the cinema we always knew, is a dinosaur becoming extinct; but the lizards and salamanders that survived the catastrophe are beginning to appear.... Dinosaur cinema is extinct! Long live the salamander cinema!"

See also **Alcoriza, Luis; Armendáriz, Pedro; Bemberg, María Luisa; Buñuel, Luis; Cantinflas; Cinema Novo; Del Rio, Dolores; Félix, María; Fernández, Emilio "El Indio"; Figueroa, Gabriel; García Márquez, Gabriel; Gardel, Carlos; Grande Otelo; Guerra, Ruy; Gutiérrez Alea, Tomás; Hermosillo, Jaime-Humberto; Leduc, Paul; López Portillo, José; Mauro, Humberto; Ripstein, Arturo; Rocha, Glauber Pedro de Andrade; Santos, Nelson Pereira dos; Solanas, Fernando E; Torre Nilsson, Leopoldo.**

BIBLIOGRAPHY

Jorge A. Schnitman, *Film Industries in Latin America: Dependency and Development* (1984).

Paulo Paranagua, *Cinema na América Latina: Longe de Deus e perto de Hollywood* (1985).

Tim Barnard, ed., *Argentine Cinema* (1986).

Julianne Burton, ed., *Cinema and Social Change in Latin America: Conversations with Filmmakers* (1986).

Randal Johnson, *The Film Industry in Brazil: Culture and the State* (1987).

Peter. B. Schumann, *Historia del cine latinoamericano* (1987).

Patricia Aufderheide, ed., *Latin American Visions* (1989).

Carl. J. Mora, *Mexican Cinema: Reflections of a Society*, rev. ed. (1989).

Jorge Sanjines and the Ukamau Group, *Theory and Practice of a Cinema with the People* (1989).

Julianne Burton, ed., *The Social Documentary in Latin America* (1990).

John King, *Magical Reels: A History of Cinema in Latin America* (1990).

PATRICIA AUFDERHEIDE

SINCE 1990

The 1990s was a period of boom and bust in Latin American film industries. In Argentina, President Carlos Menem's neoliberal economic program encouraged multimedia television conglomerates to apply for state subsidies to invest in national cinema. These companies created commercial hits based on television shows such as *Comodines* (*Cops*, 1997) and *La furia* (*The Fury*, 1997). Two animated films for children, *Dibu: La película* (Dibu: The Movie, 1998) and *Manuelita* (1999), were national chart toppers. In Brazil Fernando Collor de Mello's government dismantled Embrafilme, the nation's film institute. In Mexico the Carlos Salinas government gutted what little state funding was available via the Instituto Mexicano de Cinematografía (IMCINE), the Mexican film institute.

GLOBAL AND LOCAL
In the first decade of the twenty-first century, a series of global hits emerged from Latin America, made possible by the availability of co-production funding and private investment. These films displayed a hip, youth-oriented style well-suited to the global aesthetic of the international film festival market, while at the same time maintaining a commitment to local storytelling. Examples of films with well-honed scripts and high production values that translated well in international venues include the British–Latin American co-production *Diarios de motocicleta* (*The Motorcycle Diaries*, 2004),

directed by Walter Salles; Alejandro González Iñárritu's *Amores perros; Nueve reinas* (*Nine Queens*, 2000), directed by the Argentine Fabian Bielinsky; and *Secuestro Express* (2005), a Venezuelan hit that was shot digitally and directed by Jonathan Jakobowicz.

Concurrently, younger, first-time filmmakers made low-budget independent films, some shot in black and white, and some using new technologies such as digital video. In Argentina the prevalence of many private and a few state-run film schools have helped to train new directors interested in making small, intimate films rather than big-budget, commercial ones. Since the end of the Cold War, and the decades of trauma inflicted by military dictatorships, civil wars, and other forms of national strife, Latin American filmmakers have moved toward the telling of micro-histories rather than grand, sweeping narratives. Rather than make bold ideological films, they are making films that address social issues, but in a less polemical form than their 1970s predecessors. With the support of European film festival funds, such as the Rotterdam festival's Hubert Bals Fund, the Toulouse festival's Cine en Construccion, and the French foundation Fonds Sud, new filmmakers have attained the money and exhibition platform they need to screen their completed films. Uruguayan directors Juan Pablo Rebella and Pablo Stoll were supported by the Hubert Bals Fund in producing the gritty *25 Watts* (2001); later, Ibermedia helped them complete a more aesthetically polished *Whisky* (2004), which won a jury prize at the Cannes Film Festival. After making the critically acclaimed black-and-white film *Mundo grúa* (*Crane World*, 1999) Pablo Trapero made three more features, each premiered at Rotterdam. Mexican first-time director Fernando Eimbcke's *Temporada de patos* (*Duck Season*, 2004), shot in black and white, concerned young people facing alienation in the modern city.

MEXICO
Unlike other Latin American film industries, especially those of Brazil and Argentina, Mexico's has not been able to push the government to create a strong funding mechanism to work as an incentive for production. Since 1997 production figures have been low. Although state support exists under the auspices of IMCINE, private film companies have increasingly produced both critically acclaimed films and

box office hits without government funding. From 1997 to 2004 between one-half and one-third of all films produced in a given year were financed entirely with private monies. It is these film companies, mostly funded by wealthy entrepreneurs, who are waking up the close-to-moribund film industry. For example, the Mexican conglomerate CIE (Interamerican Entertainment Corporation) partnered with the venture-capital arm of the Grupo Financiero Inbursa (owned by billionaire Carlos Slim Helú) to create Alta Vista Films. Another company, Anhelo, is funded by CEO Carlos Vergara, who made his fortune through Omnilife, an herbal supplement company. These production companies worked with such film directors as Alfonso Cuarón and Guillermo del Toro, who made films in Mexico, then became successful in Hollywood, and later returned to make more films at home in Mexico. Iñárritu achieved success by making a hit film in Mexico and then directing in Hollywood. Cuarón's *Y tu mamá también* (2001) and del Toro's *El espinazo del Diablo* (*The Devil's Backbone*, 2001), both produced by Anhelo, and Iñárritu's *Amores perros* (*Love's a Bitch*, 2000), produced by Altavista, gained critical acclaim in art-house circles abroad but were equally successful at the domestic box office. The three directors are friends and have remarked in interviews that they feel ostracized by the traditional Mexican film community because of their work in Hollywood. They do not lament the loss of state funding for films. In 2007 each one had a film nominated for an Academy Award, causing critics to herald a "Mexican film renaissance." Only del Toro's film, *El laberinto del fauno* (*Pan's Labyrinth*, 2006) had partial financing from Mexico.

BRAZIL

In 1998 Walter Salles's *Central do Brasil* (*Central Station*), achieved worldwide recognition with a Golden Bear at the Berlin Film Festival and two Academy Award nominations. But it was not until after 2000 that Brazil made a comeback in terms of critically acclaimed, box-office hits. The film *Carandiru* (2000) brought in 4.5 million viewers, *Cidade de Deus* (2002) 3.3 million, and *Deus e Brasileiro* (God Is Brazilian) 1.6 million. All of these films benefited from provisions of the Lei do Audiovisual (Audiovisual law), legislation passed in the mid-1990s that gave incentives to corporations for investing in national cinema. These incentives also spurred investment by Hollywood studios that distributed and co-

produced star vehicle films such as children's superstar actress and singer Xuxa, as well as for the comedian Renato Aragão. These stars, as well as television actors made famous on the Globo television stations, boosted the box office for commercial movies in partnership with TV Globo.

PERU, COLOMBIA, BOLIVIA, ECUADOR

The Andean region of Latin America has had some success in cultivating young directors in directorial debuts. Since 1999 a spate of high-quality films have been produced in Peru. *Paloma de papel* (*Paper Dove*, 2003), directed by Fabrizio Aguilar, addresses the issue of the recruitment of children by the Shining Path guerrilla movement; in Josue Mendez's *Días de Santiago* (*Days of Santiago*, 2004), a young man experiences psychological trauma after serving as a soldier in the Peru-Ecuadorian border war; and *El destino no tiene favoritos* (*Destiny Has No Favorites*, 2003), by first-time director Alvaro Velarde, offers a send-up of telenovela culture starring Angie Cepeda, a well-known Colombian actress. New film journals have also sprung up in Peru, such as *La gran illusion*, *Butaca sanmarquino*, and *Tren de Sombras*, published by young film critics with university support.

The Colombian government passed legislation in 2003 earmarking 10 percent of box-office receipts for reinvestment in film production. This gave a boost to the fledgling industry and led to national hits such as Emilio Maillé's *Rosario Tijeras* (2005), based on a novel about a *sicaria* (hitwoman) in the underworld of narcotic trafficking, and Rodrigo Triana's *Soñar no cuesta nada* (Dreaming Costs Nothing, 2006; released in the U.S. as *A Ton of Luck*), a comedy based on a true story of military men who stumble across forty million dollars. The film's release coincided with the soldiers' trial and sentencing.

A surge in production has also occurred in the Bolivian film industry. Rodrigo Bellott's *Dependencia sexual* (*Sexual Dependency*, 2003), shot digitally, was lauded at film festivals for its stylistic and narrative innovation. Fernando Vargas's *Di buen día a papá* (Say Good Morning to Dad, 2005), a Bolivian-Argentine-Cuban co-production, examines Che Guevara's death in Bolivia and explores his last days; the film resonates with the countries' decision to capitalize on the tourism potential of Guevara's death in the countryside. Juan Carlos Valdivia's *American Visa* (2005), a co-production with Mexico, deals with the frustrations of U.S. immigration.

The first film by Ecuador's up-and-coming director, Sebastián Cordero, *Ratas, Ratones, Rateros* (*Rodents*, 1999), which was shot digitally, is the highest-grossing Ecuadorian film of all time. Cordero then raised co-production funds to make a higher-budget film with an international cast called *Crónicas* (Chronicles, 2004), starring the Colombian-born American actor John Leguizamo. It grapples with the ethical dimensions of crime reporting and international tabloid journalism.

CENTRAL AMERICA, THE CARIBBEAN, CUBA

In the Central American and Caribbean regions, film production is still emerging. Some forms of funding have been made available through the film fund Cinergia, created in 2004 with funds from a private Costa Rican film school called Veritas, the Dutch foundation Hivos, and the Foundation for New Latin American Cinema (founded by the Colombian novelist and Nobel laureate Gabriel García Márquez). Cinergia has been called a Central American version of Ibermedia. Member countries include Belize, Costa Rica, El Salvador, Guatemala, Honduras, Nicaragua, Panama, and Cuba. Cinergia has helped Central American filmmakers financially, but another of its main goals is to help train young screenwriters and film technicians via workshops led by Latin American and European professionals. This fund encourages the creation of a regional pan-American source of collaboration. Films such as Juan Carlos Cremata Malberti's *Viva Cuba* (2005) won twenty-seven prizes, including one at Cannes; Panamanian director Pituka Ortega directed *Los puños de una nación* (The Fists of a Nation, 2005), a documentary about the life of a boxing champion. *Entre los muertos* (Between the Dead, 2006), by El Salvadorian director Jorge Dalton, explores the cultural meanings of death in El Salvador. The film was screened at festivals in Malaga, Spain, Biarritz, France, and Viña del Mar, Chile.

After the disintegration of the Soviet Union, the Cuban film industry, formerly dependent on Soviet funding, struggled to survive. During what is known as the "special period," film production was diminished to two or three films per year, depending on whether directors could obtain co-production grants. Some Cuban films achieved international recognition: *Fresa y chocolate* (*Strawberry and Chocolate*, 1994), co-directed by Tomás Gutiérrez Alea, one of Cuba's finest directors, confronted Cuba's legacy of discrimination against homosexuality. Fernando Pérez directed *Madagascar* (1994), *La vida es silbar* (*Life Is to Whistle*, 1998), and *Suite Habana* (Havana Suite, 2003), all of which were lyrical films that also showed the everyday lives of Cubans. Other Cuban filmmakers have managed to cut costs by using digital video. Humberto Solás made the first digital Cuban feature film in 1999 with *Miel para Oshún* (Honey for Oshún, 2001). A lower-budget film, *Mañana* (Tomorrow, 2007), by Alejandro Moya Iskánder, was shot digitally but featured veteran actors Mario Balmaceda and Enrique Colina. Some independent films have been made independently of ICAIC, the state-run film institute. Directors Gloria Rolando, Esteban García Insausti, and Arturo Infante are among those who have raised funds on their own, typically working in video.

FUNDING

In 1997 the Ibero-American co-production fund Programa Ibermedia was founded as a film finance pool headed by and housed in Spain, to which each member country contributes a minimum of $100,000; director-producers can enter annual competitions to win co-production funding from this pool. Filmmakers in Peru, Uruguay, and other countries have depended in large part on these funds, often lobbying their governments to ensure payment of dues. In 2002 and 2005 respectively, Puerto Rico and Panama joined this co-production fund to spur filmmaking activity.

A novel co-production treaty was announced in January 2005 between the Argentine Film Institute (INCAA) and cultural entities in Galicia and Catalonia, two autonomous regions of Spain. The Fondo Raices de Cine (Roots of Cinema Fund), to which each partner contributes equally, totals $600,000. Two notable films have benefited from this fund: *No sos vos, soy yo* (*It's Not You, It's Me*, released in Argentina 2004, in Spain 2005), an Argentine-Catalan co-production directed by Juan Taratuto, and *Cama adentro* (*Live-in Maid*, released in Spain 2004, in Argentina 2005), directed by Jorge Gaggaro. Both films performed well at the box office, but *No sos vos* defied expectations by playing to packed houses in

Madrid for two months, thus earning the status, in terms of audience figures, of one of the top ten films in Spain in 2005.

THE RELATIONSHIP WITH TELEVISION

In many European as well as Latin American countries, particularly Mexico, Argentina, and Brazil, there has been a symbiotic relationship between the film industry and television. Many television channels have chosen to produce or co-produce films to gain prestige, to advertise their product at minimal cost, and finally, to provide content for their stations. Television channel investment and distribution have been an important addition to smaller film industries, such as in Uruguay, where such participation began in the 1990s. Channel Ten of Uruguay agreed to donate technicians, goods, and services to a few low-budget films. Cable television companies in Uruguay were also asked to support local film production by contributing a "tax" toward production in Montevideo. The result is a small fund called FONA that has supported low-budget films shot on video. This television-film partnership has paved the way for stronger integration between television, a wealthy and resourceful enterprise, and the film industry, which is usually in need of financial support.

EXHIBITION OUTLETS

Newer film exhibition outlets include the Buenos Aires International Independent Film Festival, founded in 1999. This festival, founded by Eduardo "Quintin" Antin, creator of the independent film magazine *El Amante*, obtained funding from the city of Buenos Aires to bring independent filmmakers from all over the world to show their work and showcase those of Argentine and Latin American directors. Only first- and second-time directors may show their work. Veteran Cuban director Humberto Solás founded an independent film festival, Festival Internacional de Cine Pobre, in the city of Gibara, Cuba, in 2003. The festival is an attempt to give filmmakers on the margins a chance to exhibit their films; most are shot digitally with budgets under $50,000.

Spaces for Latin American film exhibition expanded in the mid-1990s with the surge in transnational investment in new multiplex cinemas.

Multinational companies principally from Australia and the United States built lavish movie theaters with stadium-style seating and American-style concessions, all within the confines of upscale shopping malls that have been built in suburban areas and wealthy neighborhoods of Lima, Mexico City, Buenos Aires, São Paulo, and Rio de Janeiro, among other major cities. Filmmakers hoped that the presence of more screens might translate into additional spaces to screen national works, but this did not materialize.

Historically, Hollywood movies have supplanted national ones in theaters because of exhibitor preference. The Latin American film market continues to be dominated by Hollywood films. In 2004, to counter Hollywood's long-standing domination, the Argentine congress passed legislation to strengthen national exhibition: This new screen quota measure was meant to legally ensure that national films gain a fair share of screening space. Mexico also passed a screen quota (Article 9 of the 1999 law modified from 1992) dedicating 10 percent of theater space to national cinema, but the practice is rarely, if ever, enforced. Both Brazil and Colombia also have the screen quota on their books, but it is unclear how much enforcement exists.

Another trend has emerged in Argentina, Mexico, and Brazil, perhaps in response to the screen quota: The Hollywood majors have invested in co-production and distribution deals with Latin American film producers in these nations. Rather than relying solely on state funding or co-production funding from Europe (usually Spain), more collaboration is taking place between the Hollywood studios represented by the Motion Picture Association (MPA; the overseas arm of the Motion Picture Association of America) and Latin American producers. Latin American co-producers stand to gain from Hollywood involvement. In addition to money invested, they also gain greater exposure with the wider distribution that the Hollywood studios command.

In the case of Mexico, the MPA, via studios such as Disney, Warner Bros., Fox Universal, and Columbia TriStar, has produced, co-produced, and distributed film and television programs. The films co-produced with Hollywood studio money generally have very low budgets by Hollywood standards (typically between US$1–2 million). The majority of Mexican films that receive co-production funding from Hollywood studios are relatively more expensive by Latin American standards, but they tend not to be "quality" productions, but rather popular movies that appeal to younger, upwardly mobile, upper-middle-class audiences who enjoy comedies and trendy urban youth culture. These films make money at the box office but are not exported to film festivals for world recognition. Buena Vista International/Disney has actively co-produced and distributed films that have commercial potential, such as Marcelo Piñeyro's *Kamchatka* (2002) and Daniel Barone's comedy *Cohen vs. Rosi* (1998), both films from Argentina. In Brazil, films starring the pop star Xuxa were produced with investment by Warner Bros., and the art-house film *Casa de Areia* (*House of Sand*, 2005), by Andrucha Waddington, was co-produced by Sony Pictures Classics in addition to Brazilian corporate financing given under the auspices of the Audiovisual Law.

Latin American cinema in the twenty-first century is gaining recognition both in domestic venues and on the world stage. Latin American nations are teaming up with private and state sources of funds, as well as international partners from Spain and the United States. This has helped elevate the production values of the films and has provided some access to wider distribution outlets. The larger industries remain Argentina, Brazil, and Mexico, but emerging industries are blossoming slowly in countries such as Peru, Colombia, Bolivia, and a few nations in Central America. Some countries with smaller home markets, such as Cuba and Uruguay, cannot sustain a viable industry without the support of co-production funding from wealthier nations.

See also **Cuaron, Alfonso; García Márquez, Gabriel; González Iniarritu, Alejandro; Gutiérrez Alea, Tomás; Radio and Television; Salles, Walter; Solas, Humberto.**

BIBLIOGRAPHY

Chanan, Michael. *Cuban Cinema.* Minneapolis: University of Minnesota Press, 2003.

Cortes, Maria Lourdes. *La pantalla rota: Cien años de cine en Centroamérica.* Mexico: Taurus, 2005.

Elena, Alberto, and Marina Díaz López, eds. *The Cinema of Latin America.* London: Wallflower Press, 2003.

Falicov, Tamara L. *The Cinematic Tango: Contemporary Argentine Film.* London: Wallflower Press, 2007.

Getino, Octavio. *Cine argentino: Entre lo posible y lo deseable,* 2nd edition Buenos Aires: Fundación CICCUS, 2005.

King, John. *Magical Reels: The History of Cinema in Latin America,* new edition. London: Verso, 2000.

Martin, Michael T., ed. *The New Latin American Cinema,* 2 vols. Detroit, MI: Wayne State University Press, 1997.

Mora, Sergio de la. *Cinemachismo: Masculinities and Sexuality in Mexican Film.* Austin: University of Texas Press, 2006.

Nagib, Lúcia, ed. *The New Brazilian Cinema.* London and New York: I. B. Taurus, 2003.

Noble, Andrea. *Mexican National Cinema.* London and New York: Routledge, 2005.

Shaw, Deborah, ed. *Contemporary Latin American Cinema: Breaking into the Global Market.* Lanham, MD: Rowman and Littlefield, 2007.

Shaw, Lisa, and Stephanie Dennison, eds. *Latin American Cinema: Essays on Modernity, Gender, and National Identity.* Jefferson, NC: McFarland, 2005.

TAMARA L. FALICOV

CINEMA NOVO.

Cinema Novo, a movement that marks the beginning of modern cinema in Brazil. Although Cinema Novo ceased to exist as a unified movement by the early 1970s, virtually every significant Brazilian film made since the late 1950s has been directly or indirectly influenced by the movement and its critical vision of Brazilian society.

Cinema Novo arose in the late 1950s and early 1960s as part of a broad, heterogeneous movement of cultural transformation that involved theater, popular music, and literature as well as the cinema. It evolved through a number of discernible phases, each corresponding to a specific sociopolitical conjuncture. Between 1960 and 1964, the year of the military coup d'état that overthrew the government of João Goulart, questions such as agrarian reform and social transformation were debated at almost every level of society. The films of this period attempted to contribute to the debate with films about the country's lower classes.

Initially, Cinema Novo sought to reveal the truth about the country's underdevelopment, in the hope that the Brazilian people would gain a critical consciousness and then participate in the struggle for national liberation. As Glauber Rocha wrote in his 1965 manifesto, "An Aesthetic of

Hunger," "Cinema Novo is ... an evolving complex of films that will ultimately make the public aware of its own misery."

In their attempt to raise the Brazilian people's level of consciousness, filmmakers initially set their stories in areas of Brazil where social contradictions were most apparent: poor fishing villages, urban slums, and the country's impoverished Northeast. Glauber Rocha's *Barravento* (1962; The Turning Wind) denounces Afro-Brazilian religion as a form of alienation while at the same time affirming its value as a means of preserving cultural identity and as a potential site of collective resistance. Nelson Pereira dos Santos's *Vidas secas* (1963; Barren Lives), based on the Graciliano Ramos novel, outlines the plight of a peasant family during a period of drought, including its conflict with an absentee landowner. Ruy Guerra's *Os fuzis* (1964; The Guns) concerns soldiers who guard a landowner's food warehouse to keep its contents from starving peasants. Rocha's *Deus e o diablo na terra do sol* (1964; Black God, White Devil) indirectly discusses the feudal structures that impede a more just distribution of land in the Northeast.

From 1964 until 1968, the year of the military government's Fifth Institutional Act, which inaugurated a period of extremely repressive military rule, political liberties were restricted and censorship increased, but there was still a degree of space for discussion and debate. During this period, the focus of Cinema Novo shifted from rural to urban Brazil as filmmakers turned their cameras on the urban middle class, and more specifically on intellectuals like themselves, in an attempt to understand the failure of the Left in 1964.

Paulo César Saraceni's *O desafio* (1966; The Challenge) deals with a young, anguished, and socially impotent journalist in the period immediately following the coup. Glauber Rocha's *Terra em transe* (1967; Land in Anguish) dissects the populist arrangements that have long dominated Brazilian politics by tracing the trajectory of a poet as he moves between Left and Right and his final, suicidal option for individual armed struggle. Gustavo Dahl's *O bravo guerreiro* (1968; The Brave Warrior) focuses on the futile struggle of an idealistic young congressman, and ends with a scene in which he looks into a mirror and points a gun into his mouth. In Nelson Pereira dos Santos's *Fome de*

amor (1968; Hunger for Love), the revolutionary leader is deaf, dumb, and blind. These films express the pessimism, disillusion, and despair of many intellectuals after 1964.

The final phase of Cinema Novo ran from 1968 until around 1972. During this period of extremely harsh military rule, it was difficult for filmmakers to express opinions directly, so allegory became the preferred mode of cinematic discourse of what is known as *tropicalismo* in Brazilian cinema. Glauber Rocha's *O dragão da maldade contra o santo guerreiro* (also called *Antônio das Mortes*, 1968) uses a highly allegorical, quasi-operatic style to portray a metaphysical struggle between good and evil that shifts, at the end of the film, to a struggle against imperialism. Joaquim Pedro de Andrade's adaptation of Mário de Andrade's modernist novel *Macunaíma* (1969) develops cannibalism as a metaphor for exploitative social relationships. Nelson Pereira dos Santos's *Como era gostoso o meu francês* (1972; How Tasty Was My Little Frenchman) uses the same metaphor for the often conflictive relationship between Brazilian and European cultures and the development of a national cultural identity in Brazil.

The period since 1972 has been characterized by stylistic and thematic diversity, and Cinema Novo's legacy has continued to be one of its major driving forces. Its practitioners have remained in the forefront of Brazilian cinema with films such as Joaquim Pedro de Andrade's *O homem do pau-brasil* (1982; The Brazilwood Man), Carlos Diegues's *Bye bye Brasil* (1980), Ruy Guerra's *A queda* (1978; The Fall), Leon Hirszman's *Eles não usam black-tie* (1981; They Don't Wear Black-Tie), Arnaldo Jabor's *Tudo bem* (1978; All's Well), Glauber Rocha's *A idade da terra* (1980; Age of the Earth), and Nelson Pereira dos Santos's *Memórias do cárcere* (1984; Prison Memoirs).

Following Cinema Novo's lead, the best of Brazilian cinema has continued to express certain historical moments as few other art forms have been able to do. The influence of the movement's critical vision of Brazilian society is evident in films such as Hector Babenco's courageous *Lúcio Flávio* (1977), the first film to depict police torture, and the same director's *Pixote* (1980), a brutal portrait of street kids. It is also clear in Roberto Farias's *Pra frente Brasil* (1982; Onward Brazil), which deals with the torture and murder of an innocent man by the military police on a day when the nation's attention was turned toward the 1970 World Soccer championship in Mexico, and in Tizuka Yamasaki's *Patriamada* (1984; Beloved Country), which is set during the 1984 campaign for direct elections. *Patriamada* combines fiction and documentary sequences with highly original effects. With its highly creative films and its continuing rich legacy, Cinema Novo is virtually synonymous with modern Brazilian cinema.

See also **Cinema: From the Silent Film to 1990.**

BIBLIOGRAPHY

Jean-Claude Bernardet, *Brasil em tempo de cinema*, 2d ed. (1977), and *Cinema brasileiro: Propostas para uma história* (1979).

Ismail Xavier, *Sertão mar: Glauber Rocha e a estética da fome* (1983).

Randal Johnson, *Cinema Novo x 5: Masters of Contemporary Brazilian Film* (1984) and *The Film Industry in Brazil: Culture and the State* (1987).

Randal Johnson and Robert Stam, eds., *Brazilian Cinema* (1988).

Additional Bibliography

Dennison, Stephanie, and Lisa Shaw. *Popular Cinema in Brazil, 1930–2001.* Manchester: Manchester University Press, 2004.

Oricchio, Luiz Zanin. *Cinema de novo: Um balanço crítico da retomada.* São Paulo: Estação Liberdade, 2003.

Stam, Robert. *Tropical Multiculturalism: A Comparative History of Race in Brazilian Cinema and Culture.* Durham, NC: Duke University Press, 1997.

Tal, Tzvi. *Pantallas y revolución: Una visión comparativa del cine de liberación y el cinema novo.* Tel Aviv: Universidad de Tel Aviv, Instituto de Historia y Cultura de América Latina, 2005.

Viany, Alex, and José Carlos Avellar. *O processo do cinema novo.* Rio de Janeiro, RJ: Aeroplano Editora, 1999.

Xavier, Ismail. *Allegories of Underdevelopment: Aesthetics and Politics in Modern Brazilian Cinema.* Minneapolis: University of Minnesota Press, 1997.

                                                    RANDAL JOHNSON

CIPRIANI, ARTHUR ANDREW (1878–1945).

Arthur Andrew Cipriani was born in 1878 to Corsican immigrants in the British colony of Trinidad. Upon completing his secondary education he entered the family's successful cocoa business. His interests, however, were mainly political and reformist. His political career can be said to have begun in World War I when he led a one-man campaign for the creation of a regiment of nonwhite West Indian soldiers. The regiment was formed in 1916 as the British West Indian Regiment, and Cipriani rose to the rank of captain and commander. He was thereafter known as Captain Cipriani, Champion of the Barefoot Man. In 1919 he became president of the Trinidad Workingmen's Association (TWA) which led to the formation of the Trinidad Labour Party (TLP), allied with the Fabian socialist British Labour Party. He fought for the eight-hour work day, minimum wage, workers' compensation, old-age pensions, representative government, legalization of trade unions, universal suffrage, and equal rights for women. He was elected mayor of Port-of-Spain on eight separate occasions and between 1925 and 1945 and repeatedly elected to the Legislative Council. Trinidadian author C. L. R. James called him the most important preindependence figure in the struggle for social justice and political rights in Trinidad and in much of the eastern Caribbean.

See also **Trinidad and Tobago.**

BIBLIOGRAPHY

James, C. L. R. *The Life of Captain Cipriani: An Account of British Government in the West Indies.* Nelson, U.K.: Coulton, 1932.

                                                    ANTHONY P. MAINGOT

CIRANDA. Ciranda, a round dance of Portuguese origin found throughout Brazil in both children's and adult versions. The children's *ciranda* is a round game with sung verses. The adult version is a group dance performed in a circle around a small ensemble of musicians and a singer. In one common form, dancers hold hands facing the center as they collectively take several steps to the right and one back to the left so that the circle slowly moves counterclockwise. The ensemble usually includes a trumpet or saxophone, a snare drum, a *bombo* (tenor drum), and a *mineiro* (metal shaker). The songs are performed in call-and-response form between the *mestre* (lead singer) and the dancers.

See also **Music: Popular Music and Dance.**

BIBLIOGRAPHY

Evandro Rabello, *Ciranda: Dança de roda, dança da moda* (1979).

Oneyda Alvarenga, *Música popular brasileira*, 2d ed. (1982), esp. pp. 195–197.

Additional Bibliography

Crook, Larry. *Brazilian Music: Northeastern Traditions and the Heartbeat of a Modern Nation.* Santa Barbara: ABC-CLIO, 2005.

Murphy, John P. *Music in Brazil: Experiencing Music, Expressing Culture.* New York: Oxford University Press, 2006.

Schreiner, Claus. *Música brasileira: A History of Popular Music and the People of Brazil.* New York: Marion Boyars, 1993.

LARRY N. CROOK

CÍRCULO MILITAR. The Círculo Militar began as a social club for officers in the Argentine army in the wake of the War of the Triple Alliance (1864–1870). Founded in 1881, it expanded and became a center for the promotion of corporate interests and political activity within the military.

After 1900, members of the Círculo Militar used organizational meetings as a forum for the discussion of the place of the armed forces in Argentine politics and society. The rise of the Radical Party to political dominance in 1916 sparked a transformation of the club. When President Hipólito Irigoyen promoted loyalist officers to positions of authority within the armed forces, conservatives used the club to organize an opposition movement. In 1920 members of a secret organization, the Logia General San Martín, took control of the club. The club quickly developed as a center of conservative political opposition.

The club and its leaders actively supported the armed forces' intervention in politics after 1930. It published books and pamphlets by nationalists, including Leopoldo Lugones. Generals Agustín P. Justo and Arturo Rawson, both having served as presidents of the Círculo Militar, helped lead coups against civilian regimes in 1930 and 1943. As the military became more deeply involved in politics, in particular during the Proceso de Reorganización Nacional (1976–1983), the club in its publications and its public forums continued to apologize for military interventions and dictatorships that occurred in Argentina between 1955 and 1983.

See also **Irigoyen, Hipólito; Justo, José Agustín Pedro; War of the Triple Alliance.**

BIBLIOGRAPHY

García Enciso, Isaías. *Los 100 años del Círculo Militar.* Buenos Aires: Círculo Militar, 1982.

Potash, Robert A. *The Army and Politics in Argentina, 1928–1945.* Stanford, CA: Stanford University Press, 1969.

DANIEL K. LEWIS

CISNEROS, BALTASAR HIDALGO DE (1755–1829). Baltasar Hidalgo de Cisneros (*b.* 12 June 1755; *d.* 9 June 1829), viceroy of Río de la Plata (1809–1810). A military man and the last viceroy of the Río de la Plata, Cisneros was born in Cartagena, Spain, the son of a high-ranking naval officer. Following in his father's footsteps, Cisneros entered the navy, progressing through the ranks and serving in the Pacific, in Algeria, and in the Spanish campaigns against the revolutionary government of France. He arrived in Buenos Aires in June 1809, sent by the Seville junta that was ruling Spain in the name of the deposed king. His nine months in office were marked by a disintegration of the political scene and a worsening of economic conditions. He also was unable to bring the local militia, emboldened by their victories in repelling two British invasions (1804, 1806–1807), under his control. By May 1810, forced into an emergency created by the fall of Seville to the French, Cisneros decided to call an open town council meeting (*cabildo abierto*). Although the viceroy believed that he would be called upon to form a new government, the *cabildo abierto* voted to depose Cisneros; however, he was allowed to return to Spain.

Able to absolve himself of any blame for the loss of Buenos Aires, Cisneros was successively named commandant general of Cádiz, minister of the navy, and director general of the fleet. Appointed captain-general of Cartagena by the Constitutionist government during the 1820 uprising, he held this post until his death.

See also **Río de la Plata, Viceroyalty of.**

BIBLIOGRAPHY

Enrique Udaondo, *Diccionario biográfico colonial argentino* (1945), pp. 442–443.

Additional Bibliography

Martínez Urrutia, Luis. *El virrey Cisneros en la Revolución Argentina de 1810.* Buenos Aires: Editorial Dunken, 2003.

Szuchman, Mark D., and Jonathan C. Brown, eds. *Revolution and Restoration: The Rearrangement of Power in Argentina, 1776–1860.* Lincoln: University of Nebraska Press, 1994.

SUSAN M. SOCOLOW

CISNEROS, FRANCISCO JAVIER

(1836–1898). Francisco Javier Cisneros (*b.* 28 December 1836; *d.* 7 July 1898), transportation developer in Colombia. Cisneros was educated in his hometown of Santiago de Cuba and in Havana, where he received his civil engineering degree (1857). He studied at Rensselaer Polytechnic Institute in Troy, New York, then engaged in railway construction in Cuba from 1857 to 1868. His pro-independence activities (1868–1871) forced him into exile in New York City. Cisneros attempted to work in Peru but in 1873 left for Colombia. There, the Antioquia Railroad (upon which he labored intermittently until 1885), the Cauca Railroad (1878–1883), the Barranquilla Railroad (1885–1895), plus dock construction at Puerto Colombia and the placement of steamboats on the Magdalena River (1877–1885; 1889–1898) all testify to Cisneros's developmental vision. Colombia's unsettled politics and weak economy were structural liabilities that Cisneros found insurmountable. He died in New York City.

See also **Railroads.**

BIBLIOGRAPHY

Alfredo D. Bateman, *Francisco Javier Cisneros* (1970).

Hernán Horna, *Transport Modernization and Entrepreneurship in Nineteenth Century Colombia* (1992).

Additional Bibliography

Bateman, Alfredo D., and Alfonso Orduz Duarte, eds. *Historia de los ferrocarriles de Colombia.* Bogotá: Página Maestra, 2005.

Mayor Mora, Alberto. *Francisco Javier Cisneros y el inicio de las comunicaciones modernas en Colombia.* Bogotá: Banco de la República: El Ancora Editores, 1999.

J. LEÓN HELGUERA

CISNEROS, SANDRA

(1954–). Cisneros is a critically acclaimed Chicana-Latina novelist, poet, short story writer, and essayist. Born on 20 December 1954, in Chicago to a Mexican father and Mexican American mother, Cisneros received a BA degree from Loyola University in Chicago in 1976 MFA from the University of Iowa in 1978. Her first novel was *The House on Mango Street* (1983), a series of vignettes told from the perspective of a young girl growing up in Chicago; it has been translated into Spanish by the Mexican writer Elena Poniatowska and into more than a dozen other languages. In the early twenty-first century it is required reading in secondary schools throughout the United States as well as a staple of many college and university courses and has sold well over two million copies. Both *Woman Hollering Creek and Other Stories* (1991) and *Caramelo; or, Puro Cuento* (2002) were designated as notable books of the year by the *New York Times* and have been translated into Spanish and many other languages. Cisneros is the recipient of numerous honors, including National Endowment for the Arts fellowships for poetry (1982) and fiction (1988) and the prestigious MacArthur Foundation Fellowship (1995). She founded the Macondo Writing Workshop in 1995 and Los Macarturos, a collective of Latino/a MacArthur Fellows, in 1997.

See also **Hispanics in the United States; Literature: Spanish America.**

BIBLIOGRAPHY

Poetry by Cisneros

Bad Boys. San Jose, CA: Mango Press, 1980.

My Wicked, Wicked Ways. Bloomington, IN: Third Woman Press, 1987.

The Loose Woman. New York: Alfred A. Knopf, 1994

Novels, Stories, and Collections by Cisneros

Hairs/Pelitos. New York: Knopf, 1994. Bilingual children's book translated from the English by Liliana Valenzuela.

Vintage Cisneros. New York: Vintage, 2004.

Secondary Sources

Elliott, Gayle. "An Interview with Sandra Cisneros." *Missouri Review*, 25, no. 1 (2002): 93–109.

Joysmith, Claire. "Desplazamiento y reconstrucción: "Eyes of Zapata de Sandra Cisneros." In *Las formas de nuestras voces: Chicana and Mexicana Writers in Mexico*, pp. 167–183. Mexico and Berkeley: CISAN, UNAM and Third Woman Press, 1995.

Mullen, Harryette "'A Silence between Us like a Language': The Untranslatability of Experience in Sandra Cisneros's *Woman Hollering Creek*." *MELUS* 21, no. 2 (Summer 1996): 3–20.

Poniatowska, Elena. "Sandra Cisneros en Tepoztlán." *La Jornada*, January 24, 2006; "Sandra Cisneros parte II," January 25, 2006.

Rebolledo, Tey Diana. "La Chicana Bandera: Sandra Cisneros in the Public Press—Constructing a Cultural Icon (1996–1999)." In her *The Chronicles of Panchita Villa and Other Guerrilleras. Essays on Chicana/Latina Literature and Criticism*, pp. 124–128. Austin: University of Texas Press, 2005.

Saldivar-Hull, Sonia. "Feminism on the Border: From Gender Politics to Geopolitics." In *Criticism in the Borderlands: Studies in Chicano Literature, Culture, and Ideology*, ed. Héctor Calderón and José David Saldívar. Durham, NC: Duke University Press, 1991.

Valenzuela, Liliana. In *Caramelo o Puro Cuento*. New York: Alfred A. Knopf, 2002.

CLAIRE JOYSMITH

CISNEROS BETANCOURT, SALVADOR (1828–1914).

Salvador Cisneros Betancourt (*b.* 10 October 1828; *d.* 28 February 1914), Cuban independence leader and legislator. Cisneros Betancourt was born in Camagüey, central Cuba, to a wealthy and noble family. After independence, people affectionately continued to call him by his title, Marqués of Santa Lucía. As a young man, he was imprisoned in Spain for his conspiratorial activities. Cisneros Betancourt was involved in Cuba's two wars of independence and was president of the insurgent provisional government in both. He also participated in the framing of the insurgent constitutions and was a delegate to the constituent assembly that approved Cuba's first constitution as an independent nation (1900–1901). Cisneros Betancourt strongly urged the rejection of the Platt Amendment, accusing the

United States of exercising "the power of the strong over the weak." He was a member of the Cuban Senate from 1902 until his death. Cisneros Betancourt died in Havana.

See also **Cuba, Constitutions.**

BIBLIOGRAPHY

For Cisneros Betancourt's role in the wars of independence, see José M. Hernández, *Cuba and the United States: Intervention and Militarism, 1868–1933* (1993); for his opposition to the Platt Amendment, see Philip S. Foner, *The Spanish-Cuban-American War and the Birth of American Imperialism* (1972), vol. 2, pp. 534–632.

Additional Bibliography

Bernal, Andrés Avelino. *Salvador Cisneros Betancourt: Marqués de Santa Lucía y presidente de la República de Cuba,* Madrid: Editorial Verbum, 1993.

JOSÉ M. HERNÁNDEZ

CISPLATINE CONGRESS.

Cisplatine Congress, a meeting convened by the Portuguese in Montevideo, Uruguay (15 July–8 August 1821), after having defeated the resistance led by José Artigas. At this congress, the Provincia Oriental was incorporated into the United Realm of Portugal, Brazil, and Algarve as the State of Cisplatine. King João VI of Portugal had returned to Lisbon after residing in Río de Janeiro since 1808. Liberal ideas predominated in Portugal. One leader who espoused them was Chancellor Silvestre Pinheiro Ferreira, who believed that the people of the Provincia Oriental themselves should decide their fate. Nevertheless, Carlos Federico Lecór, baron of Laguna and commander of the invading army, had a decisive influence on the outcome of the congress.

See also **Artigas, José Gervasio.**

BIBLIOGRAPHY

Pivel Devoto, Juan E. "El Congreso Cisplatino (1821)," in *Revista del Instituto Histórico y Geográfico del Uruguay* 3 (1936): 111–409.

Street, John. *Artigas and the Emancipation of Uruguay* (1959).

Castellanos, Alfredo. *La Cisplatina: La independencia y la república caudillesca, 1820–1838* (1974).

Barrios Pintos, Aníbal. *Historia de los pueblos orientales: sus orígenes, procesos fundacionales, y sus primeros años.* Montevideo, Uruguay: Academia Nacional de Letras, 2000.

JOSÉ DE TORRES WILSON

CISPLATINE PROVINCE.

Cisplatine Province, the buffer territory of the eastern bank of the Uruguay River. In 1821 a weak and subservient Uruguayan congress formally annexed the Banda Oriental to Portuguese Brazil as the Cisplatine Province. Between 1825 and 1828 the region was a battleground between Argentina and Brazil. Argentina regarded the area as its east bank; Brazil considered it the Cisplatine Province, or Estado Cisplatino. Great Britain, anxious to enlarge its trade in the Plata region, persuaded Brazil to end the conflict. The Cisplatine Province was recognized as the independent state of Uruguay in 1828.

See also **Boundary Disputes; British–Latin American Relations.**

BIBLIOGRAPHY

Alisky, Marvin. *Uruguay: A Contemporary Survey* (1969), pp. 19–20.

Archer, Christon. *The Wars of Independence in Spanish America.* Wilmington, DE: Scholarly Resources, 2000.

Barman, Roderick J. *Brazil: The Forging of a Nation* (1988).

Ocampo, Emilio. *Alvear en la guerra con el imperio del Brasil.* Buenos Aires: Claridad, 2003.

Vale, Brian. *A War Betwixt Englishmen: Brazil against Argentina on the River Plate, 1825–1830.* London: I. B. Tauris, 2000.

Willis, Jean L. *Historical Dictionary of Uruguay* (1974), pp. 101–102.

ORLANDO R. ARAGONA

CISPLATINE WAR.

Cisplatine War, struggle between Uruguayan patriots and the Brazilian army of occupation between 1825 and 1828. In April 1825, thirty-three Uruguayan patriots, led by Juan Antonio Lavalleja, crossed the river from Buenos Aires at night to rally their countrymen against the Brazilian army. In an effort to enlarge their efforts, the band of thirty-three leaders gathered around them groups of fighting gauchos. For three years, a few thousand Uruguayans successfully harassed the Brazilian regiments in Uruguay. In 1828 British mediation brought Brazilian recognition of independent Uruguay and an end to the war.

See also **Cisplatine Province.**

BIBLIOGRAPHY

Roderick J. Barman, *Brazil: The Forging of a Nation* (1988).

Additional Bibliography

Ocampo, Emilio. *Alvear en la guerra con el imperio del Brasil.* Buenos Aires: Claridad, 2003.

Vale, Brian. *A War Betwixt Englishmen: Brazil against Argentina on the River Plate, 1825–1830.* London: I.B. Tauris, 2000.

ORLANDO R. ARAGONA

CITADELLE LA FERRIÈRE.

Citadelle la Ferrière, a Haitian fortress situated atop Pic La Ferrière at 3,100 feet. The structure was begun by Jean Jacques Dessalines in 1804 and completed by Henri Christophe (King Henry I) in 1817. Access to this huge granite fortress in northern Haiti is by a precipitous road from the king's plush palace of Sans Souci at the foot of the mountain. The fortress itself has walls up to 140 feet high and 13 feet thick. In area it is 10,750 square yards and could house 15,000 soldiers. Protecting the citadel's outer walls were three galleries of 365 cannons. Two huge roof cisterns provided an internal water supply.

Dessalines began the fortress as a final place of retreat should France reinvade Haiti, and Christophe shared this purpose in completing it. But Christophe had additional motives. He wanted to show the world that blacks were capable of a grand construction—even with severe human loss. Further, it made him more mysterious and powerful in the eyes of the masses. For enraging the king, an errant duke or baron or even the monarch's own son might find himself sentenced there to hard labor among the granite. Fittingly, Christophe is buried inside the fortress with an epitaph boasting that he would rise to life from his ashes.

See also **Haiti.**

BIBLIOGRAPHY

W. W. Harvey, *Sketches of Haiti* (1827).

James Leyburn, *The Haitian People* (1941).

Hubert Cole, *Christophe, King of Haiti* (1967).

Additional Bibliography

Sheller, Mimi. *Democracy After Slavery: Black Publics and Peasant Radicalism in Haiti and Jamaica.* Gainesville: University Press of Florida, 2000.

THOMAS O. OTT

CITIES AND URBANIZATION.

Cities occupy a central place in history, and have played a particularly important role in the Latin American experience. The cities of ancient Latin America, from Teotihuacán in Mexico to Cuzco in Perú, offered unique expressions of urban life. The conquering Spanish were quintessentially urban people, and the cities they built served as focal points for colonial exploitation. In the early twenty-first century Latin America has become the most urbanized of the less-developed regions of the world.

Defining what "urban" means has always been problematic. Certainly urban areas are places of more people and higher population density. Cities were the places where labor specialization developed and distinct social classes emerged. Cities are centers of commerce, crafts, and industry. Cities serve as administrative, ecclesiastical, intellectual, and cultural centers, and as seats of government. Some urbanization experts have insisted that a numerical threshold must be reached for a place to qualify as a city: the U.S. Bureau of the Census in 1920 defined "urban" as a location with a population of 2,500 or more. But urbanism is probably better defined not just by population size or density but by function as well. Most scholars hold that places should be regarded as cities if administrative, social, religious, trade, or economic activities are carried on in them that do not and cannot take place in rural zones. This more generous conception of what constitutes a city encompasses the variety of urban habitats in Latin America.

ANCIENT URBANIZATION

The emergence of the first cities in what is present-day Latin America depended upon the establishment of sedentary agriculture, a development that occurred in the New World around 4000 BCE or perhaps earlier. The earliest urban settlements of Latin America, in the Norte Chico region of central coastal Perú, may date from as far back as 3500 BCE. However, it was not until after about 1800 BCE that steadily increasing clusters of villages emerged in which sedentary farming was a full-time occupation, especially in Mesoamerica and the Andean region of South America. The farming settlements of these regions—in Mexico, northern Central America, Perú, and Bolivia—provided the critical mass for the subsequent development of civilizations and cities. These were probably the only places in Latin America where cities emerged in the pre-Columbian period, although some have argued for urban developments in the ancient Amazon.

Urban complexes appeared in each of the major and many of the minor civilizations of ancient Latin America. Three cities stand out as most significant. One was Teotihuacán, located in central Mexico, the largest urban complex of Latin America in the pre-Columbian period. Teotihuacán reached its greatest efflorescence between 450 and 650 CE, sustaining a population of at least 200,000 people. The city served as an artisan production center (especially of obsidian), a religious center and place of pilgrimages, and a focal point for commerce. So important were the trade ties that Teotihuacán fostered that the decline and ultimate abandonment of the city after 650 may have contributed to the decline and abandonment of several leading cities of the Maya and other Mesoamerican civilizations.

Tenochtitlán, founded in 1325, was the leading city of the Aztec of Mexico. At its peak, during the reign of Moctezuma II (1502–1520), Tenochtitlán reached a population of at least 160,000. When the Spanish first arrived in the city in 1519 they marveled at Tenochtitlán's appearance: They had never seen a city so large, clean, orderly, and well-governed. In two years, however, the city lay in ruins, destroyed in the combat of the Spanish conquest. Hernán Cortés and the conquering Spanish built their capital, Mexico City, on the ruins of Tenochtitlán.

Cuzco, in southern highland Peru, grew in significance as the Inca empire expanded in the mid- to late-fifteenth century. At its peak Cuzco may have supported a population of 50,000. The

Teotihuacán's Avenue of the Dead. Teotihuacán, in central Mexico, was one of the most important religious, commercial, and cultural centers of pre-Columbian Latin America. © ANGELO HORNAK/CORBIS

city served as the Inca capital and focal point for tribute collection. Every year local lords (*kurakas*) from across the Inca empire were required to travel to Cuzco and deliver gold, silver, cloth, corn, coca, and young female virgins into the hands of the Inca hierarchy. The Inca built temples and sacred gardens in Cuzco decorated with the vast quantities of silver and gold taken in tribute. In 1533 the Spanish arrived and looted these treasures, establishing colonial control over the city and the empire.

THE COLONIAL PERIOD

Cites were central to the establishment of Spanish colonialism in the Americas. When Hernán Cortés arrived in Mexico in 1519 one of his first acts was the founding of a city, Villa Rica de la Veracruz (modern day Veracruz), which gave him the legal legitimacy he needed to proceed with the conquest of Mexico. As Spanish conquistadores became settlers, they seldom chose to live in rural districts; they directed the colonial exploitation of Latin America from the cities they constructed. By

1580 nearly all the great Spanish American cities had been founded, the most notable exceptions being Medellín, Colombia (founded in 1616) and Montevideo, Uruguay (1726). The conquistador Francisco Pizarro himself founded twenty-two cities, including Lima, Perú, in 1535.

While it has often been asserted that the plaza-and-grid design of most colonial Spanish American cities grew out of a rigid set of royal orders pertaining to city construction, this is probably not the case. Town planning was seldom practiced in Spain in the late fifteenth century, even if it was in other parts of Europe. True, rules for the building of Spanish colonial cities were set down in the 1523 Laws of the Indies, and King Phillip II drew together the existing laws in one long decree in 1573, *The Ordinances for the Discovery, New Settlement, and Pacification of the Indies*. But as urban historian Jorge Hardoy noted in 1975, "legislation only formalized a situation already perfectly defined in practice" (p. 30).

City fathers in colonial Spanish America usually followed the successful example of Santo Domingo, in the modern-day Dominican Republic, an urban model that most Spanish were familiar with. Santo Domingo was settled in 1496 and formally founded in 1498, but the city was moved in 1502 to a better location on the other side of the Ozama River. The relocated Santo Domingo was laid it out in a grid, although not in conformity with any preexisting Spanish design. Santo Domingo was the leading Spanish American city until the completion of the conquest of Mexico in 1521, and until that date functioned as the center of trade, exploration, and conquest. Santo Domingo was therefore the place where Spanish American urban forms and political arrangements were pioneered; most cities subsequently erected by the conquering Spanish followed its model, whether founded by the conquistadores or by the clergy for purposes of conversion of the native peoples.

Still, some cities founded by the Spanish did not follow any plan. In these cases, as in for example in Asunción, Paraguay, the imposition of an orderly urban design often came long after the initial founding and a period of chaotic growth. Brazilian cities typically did not follow the grid design or any other plan, instead growing naturally without externally imposed order.

Latin American colonial cities were initially alien European enclaves focused on the consumption of the economic surplus created by the labor of indigenous or African slave workers. But in time these cities developed into more than the white exploiters' headquarters, becoming home to a growing population of *mestizos* (people of mixed race). Cities that began as military staging areas gradually became transformed into administrative centers, ecclesiastical seats, and, more gradually, commercial entrepôts. The Spanish and Portuguese naturally located their

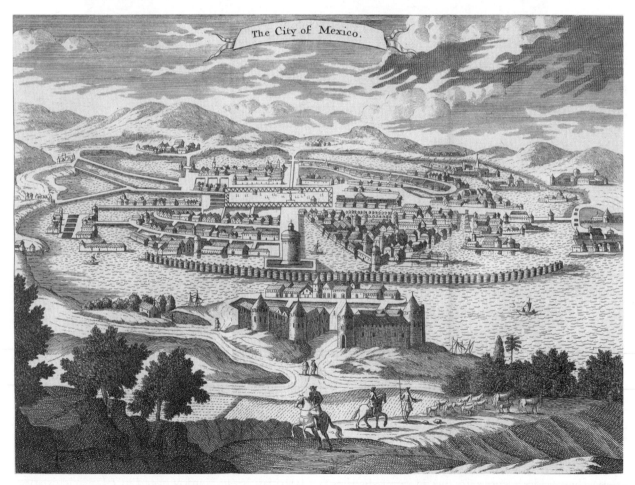

***The City of Mexico,* 1723.** (engraving) by John Clark (fl. 1710–1723). STAPLETON COLLECTION, UK/ THE BRIDGEMAN ART LIBRARY

cities so to facilitate trade, and most were on the coast, although some were situated in the interior along navigable rivers, near exploitable indigenous populations, or by silver mines. Despite the catastrophic population loss in the Americas in the wake of the conquest (90 percent in 110 years), cities grew steadily, and Latin America became more urban.

The largest city in colonial Latin America was Potosí, in modern-day Bolivia, which by the sixteenth century had a population of more than 140,000. However, as production from the silver mines around Potosí declined during the seventeenth century, so too did the population of the city, which fell to about 30,000. Other large colonial-era cities included Mexico City, which by 1700 had a population of more than 100,000. Six others had populations of 50,000 or greater: Rio de Janeiro and Salvador (formerly called Bahia), Brazil; Puebla and Guanajuato, Mexico; Havana; and Lima. By the end of the colonial period other sizeable cites appeared, including Buenos Aires (42,000 in 1810), Santiago (40,000 in 1790), and Querétaro, Mexico (30,000 in 1790). Overall, late colonial Spanish America was more urban than the young United States. Mexico City was the largest city in the hemisphere, with a population in 1800 of 120,000, compared to 80,000 in New York City.

THE NINETEENTH AND EARLY TWENTIETH CENTURIES

The post-independence period was a time of economic depression and political instability for much of Latin America. As a consequence, the early nineteenth century was the historical low point for the political and economic importance of Latin American cities. Political power tended to shift toward rural-based *caudillos* and away from the capitals. Economically the cities were in retreat as well. As exports languished, cities' population growth stagnated or in some cases even declined. Even by 1870 fewer Latin Americans lived in cities than had in 1800.

However, changes in the world economy by the late nineteenth century, especially the spread of industrialization in Western Europe and the United States, generated more demand for raw materials and food products from Latin America. The rise of the Latin American export economies of the late nineteenth century triggered a resurgence in urban growth. Urbanization progressed most rapidly in

southern Brazil, Uruguay, and Argentina, places that attracted waves of immigration from Portugal, Spain, and Italy. Starting in the 1870s and ending with the Great Depression of the 1930s, the net influx of immigration to southern Brazil, Uruguay, and Argentina reached some seven million. These zones, temperate regions of recent settlement—prime farmlands without large pre-existing labor forces—drew workers for the expanding export trade: the coffee industry in Brazil, sheep in Uruguay, and wheat and beef in the Argentine pampa. While many immigrants found work in these enterprises, many more took jobs in ancillary occupations in the booming cities of Santos, São Paulo, Montevideo, and Buenos Aires. Elsewhere in Latin America urban growth was directly associated with economic growth: Those nations with the strongest ties to the world economy grew the most rapidly, and those that remained more economically isolated grew the least.

In 1850 there were only four Latin American cities with populations of 100,000 or more: Rio de Janeiro, Salvador (Bahia), Mexico City, and Havana. By 1900 there were ten, led by Buenos Aires, 870,000; Rio de Janeiro, 690,000; Mexico City, 540,000; Montevideo, 309,000; Santiago, 287,000; and São Paulo, 239,000. By 1930 there were twenty-eight such cities. The growth of some cities in this period was especially rapid: Buenos Aires from 90,000 in the 1850s to more than 3 million by 1930; Rio de Janeiro from 186,000 in the 1850s to more than 1.5 million by 1930; Mexico City from 200,000 in the 1850s to 1.3 million by 1930; and São Paulo, from 26,000 in the 1850s to 1 million by 1930.

As cities grew the need for services—potable water, sewers, transportation, street paving, electricity, street lights, hospitals, schools, jails—became more urgent. It fell to the state to supply these necessities, and the role of government expanded accordingly. As export economies blossomed and urban areas grew, political power shifted back to the cities.

Latin American cities in the late nineteenth and early twentieth centuries showed considerable variability in the achievement of urban social reform. This wide range was reflected in urban death rates in this period. While not every city has been studied, some comparative numbers are available. Guayaquil was arguably the most unhealthy city in Latin America in

View of Rio de Janeiro from the church of St. Bento. Black and white photo of an engraving by French School (19th century) after an 1838 drawing by Fleury and engraving by Aubert. PRIVATE COLLECTION/ THE BRIDGEMAN ART LIBRARY

this period: in 1879 and 1880 the death rate exceeded 100 per thousand in population, although it fell to 38 per thousand in the early 1920s. Other Latin America cities showed lower death rates. For example, Santiago had a death rate averaging 35 in the years 1920–1924; Valparaíso had death rates ranging from 33 to 26 in the early 1920s; and the average death rate in Río de Janeiro in the years from 1901 to 1920 was 23. Nevertheless, these numbers compare unfavorably to cities of the developed world in the period 1905 to 1908: New York City 17, Paris 17, Berlin 17, London 16, and Chicago 14.

Several factors explain the variability in Latin America urban death rates from 1870 to 1930. Certainly geography played a key role. Cities in tropical settings experienced continuing problems with malaria and yellow fever, although these diseases were of course not unknown in many temperate cities. However, highland cities, such as Mexico City, Bogotá, Quito, or La Paz, never suffered

malaria or yellow fever epidemics: mosquitoes cannot live at the elevation of these cities.

More important than geography, however, were financial resources. The cities that had the best-performing export economies could best afford the cost of urban reform. Such cities were also more likely to develop the political circumstances that could lead to reform, for the achievement of urban social reform was principally a political matter. Clearly, being able to pay the costs of providing potable water and constructing modern sewers did not automatically assure that these developments would occur. Powerful groups or classes had to force government to take these actions. Historically, the broad array of urban reforms of the late nineteenth and early twentieth centuries, including public health care reforms, went furthest in those places where labor was effectively organized and the middle class was the strongest. Whereas these conditions applied chiefly in the premier cities of the developed world, in Latin America they could be found, albeit to a somewhat lesser

Avenida de Mayo, Buenos Aires, 1941. Buenos Aires's wide avenues were part of the urban reforms some of the more prosperous Latin American cities implemented in the late nineteenth and early to mid-twentieth centuries. © BETTMANN/CORBIS

extent, in Buenos Aires and Montevideo. To the extent that other Latin American cities lagged behind in the achievement of urban social reform, the principal reason was that the formation of these key political actors was weaker.

THE MID-TWENTIETH CENTURY AND AFTER

The years from 1950 to 1980 were Latin America's period of most rapid urbanization to date. Many of Latin America's cities grew by more than 4 percent per year in these decades. Some grew even faster: Lima, Mexico City, and São Paulo grew at more than 5 percent, Caracas at greater than 6 percent, and Bogotá grew at the astonishing rate of more than 7 percent per year in this period. Urbanization, if defined as the percentage of population living in towns or cities of 20,000 or more, rose with each decade: in 1930, 17 percent of Latin Americans lived in urban areas; in 1940, 33 percent; in 1960, 44 percent; in 1970, 64 percent; and in 1990, 72 percent of Latin Americans lived in cities. At the beginning of the twentieth century

Latin America had three cities with half a million or more; by 1950 there were six. By 1990 there were thirty-nine cities with a million and eleven with three million or more. And whereas the population of Latin America rose 33 percent from 1960 to 1970, the urban population rose 54 percent. Latin America became by the closing decades of the twentieth century the most urbanized region in the developing world. From the late nineteenth century to the closing decades of the twentieth, leading Latin American cities grew at roughly double the rate of most U.S. cities.

The main reason for the explosive growth of Latin America's cities in these decades was a basic demographic change. From the postwar period to the 1980s, births greatly exceeded deaths. Until the mid-1930s the Latin American death rate was about 20 per thousand while the birth rate was 30 per thousand, but by the 1970s the death rate had dropped below 10 and the birth rate had climbed to more than 40. Moreover, Latin American life expectancy, which had averaged 31 years in 1920, had risen to 56 by 1960. Infant mortality rates (the annual number of deaths, age 0–1, per 1,000 live births) fell too, dropping in Chile, for example, from 250 for the years 1920 to 1924 to 92 by 1967, and in Mexico from 178 in 1920–1924 to 63 in 1967. Latin America's population grew at 1.9 percent per year in the 1930s, but rose by 2.3 percent annually in the 1940s, 2.7 percent in the 1950s, and 2.8 percent in the 1960s, a rate at which the population would double every twenty-five years.

Part of this may be explained by the fact that more women were living into their childbearing years, and more were surviving through multiple pregnancies. Likewise, more pregnancies resulted in live births. Yet beyond these gains, the larger question remains of why the death rates fell so markedly. There are several probable causes. One certainly was the mass introduction of antibiotics, sharply reducing deaths from pneumonia, tuberculosis, and various bacterial enteric disorders. Another factor was the widespread, if controversial, application of the insecticide DDT, which killed anopheles mosquitoes, the malaria vector. The anti-malaria campaigns of the 1950s, led by the Pan American Sanitary Bureau (later called the Pan American Health Organization) were highly successful in this regard. DDT spraying, by the Pan American Sanitary Bureau, by Latin American governments, or just by individuals who purchased gallon jugs of the insecticide at hardware stores, killed many other disease-bearing insects, including flies that contributed to the spread of microbes that spread digestive illnesses.

Perhaps even more important in explaining the surge in Latin American population growth in the 1950s to the 1980s were the notable improvements in urban sanitation, the provisioning of potable water, and the digging of sewers. Nevertheless, the factor that was probably most responsible for the dramatic lowering of death rates was improvement in diet. The best defense against disease is not medicine or even public sanitation but one's own immune system, and the strength of this system depends on proper nutrition. Admittedly, it is all but impossible to prove that diets improved for ordinary Latin Americas in these years—it is always hard to know for certain what and how much people ate. But because the other factors alone or together

cannot account for the dramatic drop in the Latin America death rates of the postwar years, improvement in diet must be the most likely explanation.

Rural-to-urban migration also underlies the expansion of urbanization in the postwar period and after. Indeed, two-thirds of Latin America's urban growth from 1940 to 1970 came from migration from the countryside. Peasants left the countryside for a variety of reasons, but foremost was increasing land scarcity due to rural population growth. Moreover, as agriculture became more mechanized fewer could find steady work. Young men migrated to cities looking to find jobs in the many new factories or in construction. Young women, who outnumbered male migrants, often found work as domestic servants. However, not all migrants to the cities found good jobs or improvement in their lives. The shantytowns of urban Latin America were a creation of the post-World War II population boom. By the 1960s a quarter to a third of urban Latin Americans lived in newly created slum areas.

Latin America's economic policies from the late 1940s through the 1970s also contributed strongly to rising urbanization. State-led import substitution industrialization (ISI) policies fostered economic growth and development across much of Latin America, especially in Brazil, the Southern Cone, and Mexico. Protected behind high tariffs, many new industries appeared in Latin America's leading cities. Although ISI policies had their critics, by one key measure, economic growth rates, they proved a remarkable success. For Latin America as a whole, the economy grew at an annual rate of 5.3 percent from 1950 to 1981, a rate even faster than that of the developed world. Many of the migrants to Latin American cities in this period could realistically hope to find jobs in industry and enjoy an improvement in their standard of living. Because ISI policies expanded the role of the state, there was also a significant increase in the number of white-collar employees working for government bureaucracies. These concentrated, like industry, in the primate cities (cities that had a quarter or more of the national population and which also served in most cases as the capital, leading port, and intellectual center). As industries multiplied and construction boomed, Latin American cities took on a more modern appearance. Some built subway systems.

Poor neighborhood on a hillside in Caracas, Venezuela, 1996. The period from the 1950s to the 1980s was one of rapid urbanization in Latin America, resulting in the proliferation of slums and shantytowns. © PABLO CORRAL V/CORBIS

That of Buenos Aires had opened in 1913, but most were built later: Mexico City's opened in 1969, São Paulo's in 1974, Rio de Janeiro's in 1979, and Caracas's in 1983.

THE 1980S AND THE END TO RAPID URBANIZATION

Populations everywhere have usually taken two or three generations to adjust their birth rates downward to match lower death rates, and Latin America has been no different. After 1960 birth rates began to fall, dropping from 42 births per thousand in the early 1960s to 27 by the early 1990s. This was due in part to the urbanization process itself, for urban women tend to have fewer children than do rural women, in Latin America typically two to three fewer per woman in a lifetime. Latin American population growth fell from an annual average of 2.8 percent in the years 1950 to 1980, to 1.8 percent per year from 1980 to 1995. As Latin American population growth slowed, urbanization slowed too.

The decrease in rural population growth put less pressure on landless poor to move to cities in search of work. Moreover, by the 1980s there were fewer employment opportunities in the cities. The 1980s were a "lost decade" for Latin America, its worst period economically ever. After the Mexican debt crises of 1982, foreign investors withdrew, domestic capital fled abroad, industries shut down, businesses closed, and new foreign loans, even to service existing debts, became all but unavailable. Although Latin American economic growth had been strong during the entire ISI period, in the 1980s the per capita GDP of Latin America fell by more than 8 percent. Everywhere factories closed down and governments laid off employees. The newly created middle class was dumped into the working class, and the number of urban poor doubled during the decade of the 1980s.

The economic free fall of the 1980s halted urbanization growth. Mexico City, for example,

Medellín, Colombia, 2004. A metro train runs past the Gothic-inspired Palacio de la Cultura Rafael Uribe Uribe in Colombia's second-largest city. © FERNANDO BENGOECHEA/BEATEWORKS/CORBIS

had had an annual population growth rate of 5 percent in the 1950s, 5.6 percent in the 1960s, and 4.2 percent in the 1970s, but the rate fell to just 0.9 percent per year in the 1980s, before climbing to 1.6 percent in the 1990s. While Mexico City had grown faster than Mexico as a whole in the 1950s and 1960s, it grew more slowly in the 1970s, and much more slowly in the 1980s. In Mexico and across Latin America cities were no longer homes to rural-to-urban migrants; they had become places where the children of these migrants lived.

URBANIZATION IN THE AGE OF NEOLIBERALISM

With the end of ISI by the 1980s, Latin America shifted from inward-directed to externally directed economic development. The widespread adoption of "neoliberal" or "free–market" economic policies meant the abandonment of state-run industrialization and government programs designed to stimulate industrialization. Instead came policies designed to open Latin America's economies and encourage the development of raw material and industrial exports that could compete in global markets. The face of urban Latin America changed. Factories shut down and whole urban districts came to be abandoned, boarded over, and quiet.

With industrialization in retreat in many of the older primate cities, the pool of un- and under-employed workers rose markedly. Many former factory workers fell into the informal sector, that of the marginalized poor who seek to make a living any way they can, from buying a sewing machine and taking in piecework at home, to itinerant retail sales, garbage picking, prostitution, or petty crime. The size of the informal economy is countercyclical, declining as hiring rises during economic good times, expanding to take in newly unemployed during each economic downturn. In most Latin American countries at least 40 percent of the economically active urban population labors in the informal sector. In some nations, Perú and Ecuador for example, the informal sector encompasses the majority.

This large and growing informal sector raises some troubling urban issues. Informal sector workers are overwhelmingly poor. They earn far less than formal sector workers, have no benefits, no health plans, and are not covered by social security programs. Moreover, meager informal sector earnings are clearly on the decline. While during the 1990s real wages in the public sector fell 30 percent in Latin America, informal sector wages fell as much as 42 percent. The very presence of such a massive urban labor surplus serves to drive down wages for all.

Most Latin American cities have suffered under neoliberalism. The neoliberal agenda includes anti-union policies, undermining workers' collective bargaining strength. Neoliberal policies have brought sharp cuts in government social spending, hitting the urban poor hardest. Privatization of urban potable water and electricity services have brought steep rate hikes and popular protests, most spectacularly in Cochabamba, Bolivia, in 2000. Overall, under neoliberalism poverty in urban Latin America has grown at twice the rate of rural poverty. At least a third of the urban population of Latin America live in poverty. More than half of the urban dwellers in Latin America live in homes or shelters that they constructed themselves. In a historic shift, Latin American poverty is no longer concentrated in rural areas, and by the 1990s nearly two thirds of the poor people in Latin America lived in urban areas. Latin America's poor have become an urban population.

The impact of neoliberalism is not the same in all places, and in Latin America it has contributed to the growth of some nonprimate cities as production centers linked to the global economy. By the 1990s the fastest growing Latin American cities were Medellín and Tijuana, both of which were increasing in population at faster than 9 percent per year. Whereas secondary cities are increasing at a faster rate than the older primate cities, in Latin America as a whole urbanization continues to advance, in old cities and new, in small cities and large. Overall, about half of the Latin American population lives in one of the forty-one cities in Latin America with at least one million people.

While the growth of nonprimate cities has been noteworthy, the largest cities of Latin America remain the older urban centers. Indeed, of the fifteen largest cities in the world, four are older Latin American cities: Mexico City, São Paulo, Rio de Janeiro, and Buenos Aires. The emergence of these massive megacities of ten million or more raises new health concerns. As E. Fuller Torrey and Robert H. Yolken warn in their book *Beasts of the Earth*, "Such population concentrations are likely to create novel patterns of infectious disease transmission and also lead to the emergence of new microbes that require huge populations for their natural reservoirs" (p. 131).

See also Tenochtitlán; Santo Domingo; Aztecs; Migration and Migrations; Buenos Aires; Cuzco; Economic Development; Incas, The; Industrialization; Maya, The; Mexico City; Neoliberalism; Rio de Janeiro: The City; São Paulo (City); Teotihuacán.

BIBLIOGRAPHY

Cross, Malcolm. *Urbanization and Urban Growth in the Caribbean: An Essay on Social Change in Dependent Societies.* Cambridge, U.K. and New York: Cambridge University Press, 1979.

Gilbert, Alan. *The Latin American City.* London: Latin America Bureau, 1998. Gilbert is one of the leading scholars of Latin American urbanization. This work remains a very valuable reference.

Greenfield, Gerald M., ed. *Latin American Urbanization: Historical Profiles of Major Cities.* Westport, CT: Greenwood Press, 1994.

Gwynne, Robert N., and Cristóbal Kay, eds. *Latin America Transformed: Globalization and Modernity.* London: Arnold, 2004.

Hardoy, Jorge E. "Two Thousand Years of Latin American Urbanization." In *Urbanization in Latin America: Approaches and Issues*, edited by Jorge E. Hardoy. Garden City, NY: Anchor Press, 1975.

Harris, Walter D., Jr., with Humberto L. Rodriguez-Camilloni. *The Growth of Latin American Cities.* Athens: Ohio University Press, 1971.

Kinsbruner, Jay. *The Colonial Spanish-American City: Urban Life in the Age of Atlantic Capitalism*. Austin: University of Texas Press, 2005.

Merrick, Thomas W. "The Population of Latin America, 1930–1990." In *The Cambridge History of Latin America*, Vol. VI: *1930 to the Present*, Part 1: *Economy and Society*, edited by Leslie Bethell. Cambridge, U.K., and New York: Cambridge University Press, 19945.

Morse, Richard M. "Trends and Patterns of Latin American Urbanization, 1750–1920." *Comparative Studies in Society and History* 16, no. 4 (September 1974): 416–447. Morse was one of the pioneers in the field of Latin American urban history.

Oliveira, Orlandina de, and Bryan Roberts. "Urban Growth and Urban Social Structure in Latin America, 1930–1990." In *The Cambridge History of Latin America*, Vol. VI: *1930 to the Present*, Part 1: *Economy and Society*, edited by Leslie Bethell. Cambridge, U.K., and New York: Cambridge University Press, 1995.

Pattnayak, Satya R., ed. *Globalization, Urbanization, and the State: Selected Studies on Contemporary Latin America*. Lanham, MD: University Press of America, 1996.

Pineo, Ronn F. *Social and Economic Reform in Ecuador: Life and Work in Guayaquil, 1870–1925*. Gainesville: University Press of Florida, 1996.

Pineo, Ronn, and James A. Baer, eds. *Cities of Hope: People, Protests, and Progress in Urbanizing Latin America, 1870–1930*. Boulder, CO: Westview Press, 1998.

Portes, Alejandro. "Latin American Urbanization During the Years of the Crisis." *Latin American Research Review* 24, no. 3 (1989): 7–44.

Portes, Alejandro, and John Walton. *Urban Latin America: The Political Condition from Above and Below*. Austin: University of Texas Press, 1976.

Roberts, Bryan R. *Cities of Peasants: The Political Economy of Urbanization in the Third World*. London: Arnold, 1978; Beverly Hills, CA: Sage Publications, 1979.

Roberts, Bryan R. *The Making of Citizens: Cities of Peasants Revisited*. London: Arnold; New York: Halsted Press, 1995.

Roberts, Bryan R. "Globalization and Latin American Cities." *International Journal of Urban and Regional Research* 29, no. 1 (March 2005): 110–123.

Sánchez-Albornoz, Nicolás. *The Population of Latin America: A History*. Translated by W. A. R. Richardson. Berkeley: University of California Press, 1974.

Schaedel, Richard P., Jorge E. Hardoy, and Nora Scott Kinzer, eds. *Urbanization in the Americas from Its Beginnings to the Present*. The Hague: Mouton, 1978.

Scobie, James R. "The Growth of Latin America Cities, 1870–1930." In *The Cambridge History of Latin America*, Vol. IV: *c. 1870–1930*. Cambridge, U.K., and New York: Cambridge University Press, 1986. Written by a leading founder of modern Latin American urban history.

Torrey, E. Fuller, and Robert H. Yolken. *Beasts of the Earth: Animals, Humans, and Disease*. New Brunswick, NJ: Rutgers University Press, 2005.

RONN PINEO

CIUDAD BOLÍVAR.

CIUDAD BOLÍVAR. Ciudad Bolívar, Venezuelan city situated on the Orinoco River some 250 miles from its mouth and the capital of the state of Bolívar. Founded in 1764 as Santo Tomé de la Nueva Guayana, it took on the name of Angostura in 1768 because of its location at a narrows. In 1849, it was renamed Ciudad Bolívar in honor of Venezuela's liberator.

During the Wars of Independence, Simón Bolívar established his headquarters at Angostura and on 15 March 1819 convened the Congress of Angostura, the ruling body of his loyalist government. Ciudad Bolívar suffered from the war in the region and never fully recovered its prewar prosperity because of local struggles for power that followed the independence movement.

Ciudad Bolívar always provided an important link in Venezuela's waterway system. Its principal exports included gold, cattle, cacao, horses, mules, tobacco, rubber, bitters, hides, timber, and other forest products. The city inaugurated the first bridge crossing the Orinoco River, the *puente* Angostura, in 1967, linking the region to the rest of the country. In 2005 the population was estimated at 292,833 inhabitants.

See also **Angostura, Congress of; Bolívar, Simón.**

BIBLIOGRAPHY

Briceño, Tarcila. *Comercio por los ríos Orinoco y Apure durante la segunda mitad del siglo XIX*. Caracas: Gobernación del Estado Bolívar, Dirección de Educación, Comisión de Historia Regional, Fondo Editorial Tropykos, 1993.

Ewell, Judith. *Venezuela: A Century of Change* (1984).

Lombardi, John V. *People and Places in Colonial Venezuela* (1976), and *Venezuela: The Search for Order, the Dream of Progress* (1982).

Rodríguez, Manuel Alfredo. *La ciudad de la Guayana del Rey*. Caracas: Ediciones Centauro, 1990.

WINTHROP R. WRIGHT

CIUDAD DEL ESTE. Ciudad del Este, a city of 223,350 inhabitants (2002), is the capital of the department of Alto Paraná in Paraguay. Located in a corner of the country bordering on Paraguay, the Argentine province of Misiones, and the Brazilian state of Paraná, the city, originally Puerto Aguirre, turned into an important hub during the construction of the Itaipú Dam (1970–1984) and its hydroelectric complexes. Named Puerto Stroessner in those years, after the Paraguayan dictator General Alberto Stroessner, it became the second-largest urban center of Paraguay, after Asunción, by incorporating neighboring towns such as Hernandarias (64,074) and Puerto Presidente Franco (54,400).

The location of Ciudad del Este on the international route that connects southeastern Bolivia with Curitiba and Porto Alegre has contributed to turning this city into a smuggling post between Paraguay and Brazil and of cocaine between southern Bolivia and the large cities of São Paulo, Curitiba, Porto Alegre, and Florianapolis. Because of this negative reputation, many Argentine and Brazilian tourists visiting Lake Itaipú and the Iguazú Falls, both on the Paraná River, avoid Ciudad del Este.

See also **Paraguay: The Twentieth Century; Paraguay, Geography; Paraná River; Stroessner, Alfredo.**

BIBLIOGRAPHY

Lewis, Daniel K. *A South American Frontier: The Tri-Border Region.* New York: Chelsea House, 2006.

Ynstrand, Edgard L. *Un giro geopolítico: El milagro de una ciudad.* Asunción: Instituto Paraguayo de Estudios Geopolíticos e Internacionales, 1990.

CÉSAR N. CAVIEDES

CIUDADELA, LA. *See* **La Ciudadela.**

CIUDAD REAL. *See* **San Cristóbal de las Casas.**

CIUDAD TRUJILLO. Ciudad Trujillo, official name given to the city of Santo Domingo, Dominican Republic, on 8 January 1936, in honor of President Rafael Leónidas Trujillo Molina. On 21 November 1961, almost six months after Trujillo's assassination, the city was renamed Santo Domingo, as it had been called since its founding in 1496. During Trujillo's domination (1930–1961) the city grew from a population of less than 100,000 to nearly 400,000 and experienced considerable modernization. The metropolitan area in 2005 had more than 2,000,000 inhabitants.

See also **Trujillo Molina, Rafael Leónidas.**

BIBLIOGRAPHY

Germán E. Ornes, *Trujillo: Little Caesar of the Caribbean* (1958).

Robert D. Crassweller, *Trujillo: The Life and Times of a Caribbean Dictator* (1966).

Howard Wiarda, *Dictatorship, Development, and Disintegration: Politics and Social Change in the Dominican Republic* (1975).

Jacinto Gimbernard, *Historia de Santo Domingo,* 7th ed. (1978).

Additional Bibliography

Alvarez López, Luis. *Estado y sociedad durante la dictadura de Trujillo.* Santo Domingo, República Dominicana: Editora Cole, 2001.

Diederich, Bernard. *Trujillo: The Death of a Dictator.* Princeton, NJ: Markus Wiener, 2000.

López-Calvo, Ignacio. *God and Trujillo: Literary and Cultural Representations of the Dominican Dictator.* Gainesville: University Press of Florida, 2005.

Roorda, Eric. *The Dictator Next Door: The Good Neighbor Policy and the Trujillo Regime in the Dominican Republic, 1930–1945.* Durham, NC: Duke University Press, 1998.

RALPH LEE WOODWARD JR.

CLAIR, JANETE (1925–1983). Janete Clair (*b.* 1925; *d.* 1983), Brazilian *telenovela* author, was born in Minas Gerais. She was the most prominent scriptwriter of *telenovelas* (prime-time serial dramas) for TV Globo from the late 1960s to 1983. She started as a radio actress in 1943 for Rádio Tupi in São Paulo, and turned to writing after she married playwright Dias Gomes, who also became a prominent scriptwriter for TV Globo. Clair's first major success came in 1956 with the *radionovela Perdão, meu filho* for Radio Nacional. She wrote a few *telenovelas,* such as *Paixão proibida*

(Prohibited Passion), for TV Tupi in the mid-1960s, then moved to TV Globo in 1967, at the time it began to invest heavily in *telenovela* production, including hiring all the best talent available. After 1968, TV Globo began to dominate the market for *telenovelas,* in part due to Clair's writing. She was the most popular author for the most watched *telenovela* time slot, 8 P.M. Her personal popularity contributed to an unusual phenomenon in popular television: some of the major scriptwriters for Brazilian *telenovelas* became major public figures, as popular and well known as the most prominent actors and actresses. Clair wrote nineteen *telenovelas* for TV Globo from 1967 to 1983. Her first was *Anastácia, a mulher sem destino* (Anastasia, the Woman Without a Destiny, 1967). Two of her more popular *telenovelas* were for *Selva de pedra* (Jungle of Stone, 1972) and *Pecado capital* (Mortal Sin, 1975–1976). After her death in 1983, her writing style and popular touch remained standards by which *telenovelas* were judged by critics and public. The TV Globo Center for Production (Casa da Criação) was named for her.

See also **Radio and Television; Telenovelas.**

BIBLIOGRAPHY

Joseph Straubhaar, "The Rise of the *Telenovela* as the Preeminent Form of Popular Culture in Brazil," in *Studies in Latin American Popular Culture* 1 (1982): 138–150.

Niko Vink, *The Telenovela and Emancipation* (1990).

Additional Bibliography

Ferreira, Mauro, and Cleodon Coelho. *Nossa Senhora das Oito: Janete Clair e a evolução da telenovela no Brasil.* Rio de Janeiro: MAUAD Editora, 2003.

Xexéo, Artur. *Janete Clair: A usineira de sonhos.* Rio de Janeiro: Relume Dumará, 1996.

JOSEPH STRAUBHAAR

CLARK, LYGIA (1920–1988). Lygia Clark (*b.* 1920; *d.* 1988), Brazilian painter and sculptor. Clark began her artistic training in the late 1940s at the School of Fine Arts in Belo Horizonte, where she was born. Her first teachers were the painter Alberto da Veiga Guignard and the landscape architect Roberto Burle Marx. Upon graduating, she traveled to Europe and studied in Paris for two years with Ferdinand Léger. In 1952 she returned to Rio de Janeiro, where she began to experiment with the geometric abstract language common to constructivist and concrete art. In 1954, with the concrete movement in full swing, Clark joined Lygia Pape, Hélio Oiticica, Decio Vieira, and other concrete artists as members of Grupo Frente. Eschewing representation, these artists opposed the imitation of nature as well as lyrical nonfigurative art.

By 1959, with the fragmentation of the concrete movement, Clark, Ferreira Gullar, Lygia Pape, Hélio Oiticica, and others formed the neoconcrete group. In their manifesto they declared that the neoconcrete movement had "emerged out of the need to express the complex realities of modern man with a new plastic language." They rejected the scientific and positivist attitudes permeating the concrete movement and called for the incorporation of "new verbal dimensions" in art. Through painting and sculpture, Clark sought to create "real," kinetic space. Toward this end, she extended her canvases beyond the confines of the frame, searching for an organic dimension within geometry so that the spectator could enter the painting and participate, such as in *Animals,* a sculpture formed of metal surfaces, which the spectator can manipulate.

In the 1960s Clark experimented with other tactile artistic projects such as short films and body art. By the 1970s her interests ventured away from art into the psychological implications of spectator participation and in 1976 led her to declare herself a "nonartist."

See also **Art: The Twentieth Century.**

BIBLIOGRAPHY

Lygia Clark, "O homem como suporte vivo de una arquitetura biológica imanente," in *Arte Brasileira Hoje,* edited by Ferreira Gullar (1973), pp. 159–160.

Dawn Ades, *Art in Latin America* (1989), esp. pp. 264–265.

Additional Bibliography

Cabo, Paula Terra. "Resignifying Modernity: Clark, Oiticica and Categories of the Modern in Brazil." Ph.D. diss., University of Essex, 1997.

Carneiro, Beatriz Scigliano. *Relâmpagos com claror Lygia Clark e Hélio Oiticica, vida com arte.* São Paulo: Imaginário, 2004.

ART AND ARCHITECTURE

Interior view of the dome of the Catedral Metropolitana, Brasília. The cathedral, also known as Our Lady of Aparecida, was built in the 1960s for the new capital of Brazil. © Peter M. Wilson/Corbis

LEFT: Mask of Lord Pacal, 7th century. This mosaic jade death mask covered the face of Lord Pacal, the great ruler of Mayan Palenque, in his tomb in the funerary pyramid known as the Temple of Inscriptions. THE ART ARCHIVE/DAGLI ORTI/THE PICTURE DESK, INC.

RIGHT: The Three Fridas. A museum curator, wearing a shawl with Frida Kahlo's image on it, stands in front of Kahlo's *The Two Fridas*. Kahlo has become a pop icon since the late twentieth century, her image appearing on such diverse items as dinner plates, coffee mugs, and T-shirts. JOHN D. McHUGH/AFP/GETTY IMAGES

BELOW: Trove of stolen art, Lima, Peru, May 2003. Peruvian police captured these art works, dating from the seventeenth through nineteenth centuries, from smugglers intending to sell them in illegal art markets in the United States. AP IMAGES

Christ the Redeemer. The great-granddaughter of Heitor da Silva Costa, designer of Rio de Janeiro's famous monument, *Christ the Redeemer*, poses in front of representations of the statue on exhibit to celebrate its seventy-fifth anniversary. The 100-foot-tall statue, which stands at the peak of Corcovado mountain overlooking the city, has become a symbol of Rio de Janeiro. Antonio Scorza/AFP/Getty Images

LEFT: **A man examines art for sale at an open-air market, Santa Clara, Cuba.** Paintings of iconic Cuban images such as Che Guevara, 1950s-era automobiles, and the *campo* (countryside) are displayed for sale to tourists. JORGE REY/GETTY IMAGES

BELOW: **Quechua women weaving, Cuzco, Peru.** These weavers, indigenous Quechua people of the southern Andes, practice an art handed down by generations of ancestors. There is concern that traditional forms and patterns are giving way to meet the preferences of the tourist market. © DANNY LEHMAN/CORBIS

RIGHT: Faces painted on organ pipes at San Agustin Church, Oaxaca, Mexico. The custom of painting faces on the pipes of church organs, while not unique to Oaxaca, was practiced widely there. Painted faces such as these can be found on the pipes of church organs throughout the state. © MACDUFF EVERTON/CORBIS

BELOW: Hillside rowhouses in Valparaíso, Chile. The historic quarter of the port of Valparaíso has been declared a UNESCO World Heritage Site because of its colonial and nineteenth-century architecture. MARCO SIMONI/RISER/GETTY IMAGES

ABOVE: **La Iglesia de los Remedios with the twin peaks of the volcanoes Popocatepetl and Iztaccihuatl in the background, Cholula, Mexico.** The Church of Our Lady of Remedies was built by the Spanish on top of the Great Pyramid of Tepanapa. Many of Cholula's churches sit on the ruins of pre-Columbian pyramids and monuments. Hernán Cortés was said to have declared that he would have a church built for every pyramid destroyed in Cholula. SISSE BRIMBERG/ COTTON COULSON/KEENPRESS/GETTY IMAGES

LEFT: **Exterior of the Templo da Boa Vontade (Temple of the Legion of Goodwill), Brasília, Brazil.** The modernist design of the Templo da Boa Vontade, an ecumenical temple and national headquarters of the Legion of Goodwill, is at home in Brasília, a city designed by urban planners to become the capital of Brazil. Construction began on Brasília in 1956. © DIEGO LEZAMA OREZZOLI/CORBIS

Stencil graffiti in Recoleta, Buenos Aires, Argentina. This graffiti, created by stencils, first showed up in the areas around the University of Buenos Aires in 2001 and now can be seen throughout the city. The graffiti ranges from satiric political images to the simply artistic. Despite the omnipresence of these images, graffiti remains illegal in Argentina. Krzysztof Dydynski/Lonely Planet Images/Getty Images

Milliet, Maria Alice. *Lygia Clark: Obra-trajeto.* São Paulo: Edusp, 1992.

CAREN A. MEGHREBLIAN

CLARK MEMORANDUM.

Clark Memorandum (1930), a statement written by Undersecretary of State Joshua Reuben Clark during the administration of Herbert Hoover. The Clark Memorandum was a restatement of the Monroe Doctrine made necessary by rising Latin American criticism of U.S. interventionist policy, especially in Nicaragua, in the 1920s. Theodore Roosevelt had expanded the scope of the Monroe Doctrine in the Roosevelt Corollary (1904), justifying U.S. intervention in Latin America in order to protect the region from European interference. Latin American governments had condemned this interpretation as self-serving. The Clark Memorandum did not repudiate intervention but declared that the United States had the right to safeguard its national security under international law, and thus did not require the Roosevelt Corollary. Nonetheless, scholars contend that the memorandum helped to lay the groundwork for the noninterventionist declaration of Franklin D. Roosevelt.

See also **Big Stick Policy; Good Neighbor Policy; United States-Latin American Relations.**

BIBLIOGRAPHY

Alexander De Conde, *Herbert Hoover's Latin American Policy* (1951).

Dexter Perkins, *A History of the Monroe Doctrine,* rev. ed. (1963).

Additional Bibliography

Gilderhus, Mark T. *The Second Century: U.S.—Latin American Relations Since 1889.* Wilmington, DE: Scholarly Resources, 2000.

Schmitz, David F. *Thank God They're on Our Side: The United States and Right-Wing Dictatorships, 1921–1965.* Chapel Hill: University of North Carolina Press, 1999.

LESTER D. LANGLEY

CLASS STRUCTURE, COLONIAL.
See **Caste and Class Structure in Colonial Spanish America.**

CLASS STRUCTURE IN MODERN LATIN AMERICA.

The class structures of Latin America are determined by the social relationships of basic economic activities. These relationships include property ownership, labor arrangements, forms and sources of income, and patterns of supervision and subordination, among others. In addition, some groups of people may be confined to certain jobs or discriminated against on the basis of gender, race, ethnicity, and so on. All of these factors contribute to the formation and characteristics of contemporary social classes. Given the great diversity among Latin American countries, the following discussion should be considered mainly as a portrayal of general regional patterns.

CLASS STRUCTURE IN HISTORICAL PERSPECTIVE

To understand modern-day class structures, it is imperative to review the historical forces that have shaped them since the mid-nineteenth century. Between roughly 1850 and 1930, national governments pursued an "outward-looking" development model based on the export of primary agricultural and mineral commodities and the import of manufactured goods from Europe (and later the United States). The creation of large-scale export economies entailed profound transformations of class relations.

In the countryside, landholding patterns were altered, legally and/or forcibly, to facilitate the creation of large enterprises devoted to export crops, such as coffee in Central America, northern South America, and Brazil, and wheat in the Southern Cone. Estate labor needs were met by transforming rural migrants into full-time or part-time laborers. Where labor was scarce, as in Argentina and southern Brazil, European immigrants were contracted. In the Caribbean, meanwhile, growth was driven by the creation of a banana export economy and the revival of sugar, mainly on foreign-owned plantations. Labor forces were largely recruited from among ex-slaves and their descendants.

In highland regions the rise or resurgence of mining export economies reflected new demands for industrial minerals. Copper and tin mining altered the course of development in Chile, Bolivia, and Peru, while oil discoveries transformed Venezuela and

Mexico. The organization of mining economies followed that of plantation agriculture in their dependence on foreign capital and permanent wage labor forces.

These developments had several important effects on social structures. Landowning classes were greatly empowered, politically as well as economically. The industrial-style organization of plantation and mining economies facilitated the emergence of the first large labor unions in the region. In the cities, the largest urban merchants linked to export-import trade began to emerge among national elites. Manufacturing remained relatively small and largely artisanal in nature. Middle classes were weak, although by the turn of the century they were expanding in the larger countries with the growth of public sector employment.

The export-import national development model was highly vulnerable to the shifting fortunes of the international economy, and the narrow distribution of benefits impeded the creation of dynamic domestic markets. Consequently the Great Depression of the 1930s and the drastic downturn in international trade, which persisted until after World War II, created a general sense of crisis throughout the hemisphere.

One response to this crisis was populism, such as the movements led by Juan Perón in Argentina, Víctor Raúl Haya de la Torre in Peru, Getúlio Vargas in Brazil, and Lázaro Cárdenas in Mexico. Populist governments shared such features as anti-imperialism and hostility to foreign capital, mass-based appeals to play off against traditional elites, support for labor unions, and a new emphasis on state intervention in the economy. Elsewhere in the region, authoritarian regimes clamped down on popular unrest in response to the crisis. These governments, however, also felt compelled to take a more active role in economic management. Thus one far-reaching outcome of the crisis of the old model was a dramatic expansion of Latin American states.

The new economic model of the period was import-substituting industrialization (ISI), defined by the replacement of manufacturing imports with the output of domestic industries. Where local private investment was inadequate to sustain this process, the state was assigned a leading role in building an industrial base. After 1945, protectionist policies were adopted to shield the new industries from European and North American competition. In the larger countries of the region (and later in the smaller ones, following the implementation of regional integration schemes), the protected domestic markets proved attractive to new foreign investment, chiefly by U.S.-based firms.

The growth of industry and expansion of the state ignited a rapid process of urbanization. With both working-class and middle-class employment growing, the major Latin American cities proved irresistible magnets for migrants from smaller towns and the countryside. Rural–urban migration was also spurred by the transformation of agrarian economies. New postwar export opportunities, as well as the growing urban demand for food, generated a renewed expansion of large-scale agriculture. This development generally was unfavorable to rural smallholders and laborers because new employment opportunities were offset by reduced access to good farmland and the effects of labor-saving technologies. Combined with high rates of population growth, these changes swelled the cityward exodus.

Class structures were profoundly altered by these developments. Dominant class interests were diversified to incorporate domestic and transnational manufacturing sectors alongside the traditional export and mercantile groups. A growing middle class was nurtured by the rapid growth of state bureaucracies as well as opportunities among larger private firms. Industrial working classes were expanding as well. By 1960 the majority of Latin America's economically active population was employed in nonagricultural work, and the proportion in manufacturing had reached as high as 34 percent in Argentina, 30 percent in Chile, and around 20 percent in Mexico, Peru, and Brazil.

Nonetheless, this expansion was outpaced by high population growth and migration. Consequently Latin American cities witnessed the proliferation of the informal sectors. Growing numbers of residents were forced to improvise their livelihoods as street vendors, providers of personal services, and part-time or temporary wage laborers. Characterized by myriad subsistence strategies, the informal sectors were largely unregulated by the state and bereft of benefits or security for workers. Their most visible manifestation was the

A woman and child stand in the doorway of their home on the side of the freeway in São Paulo, Brazil, 2001.
Migrants from Brazil's poorest regions come to São Paulo in search of work, leading to overcrowding and the expansion of urban slums. AP IMAGES

sprawling shantytowns and squatter settlements that spread across Latin American cities during the 1950s and 1960s.

In the countryside, as small farms became more difficult to sustain, rural workers and smallholders were increasingly forced to depend on seasonal wage labor and nonagricultural employment. Remittances from family members in the cities came to play an important role in many rural communities. Most Latin American governments attempted to shore up rural agriculture and employment with agrarian reform programs during the 1960s, but in general these programs were hampered by dominant class opposition and government inability to provide support (such as credit, technical assistance, and market access) for reform projects.

Agrarian reform did serve to mobilize the rural population politically, however, and the 1960s saw rising working-class protests linked to both populist and socialist political movements. Growing elite

resistance to reforms fueled an increasing willingness on the left to embrace revolutionary alternatives. The resulting confrontational spiral was brought to a violent halt by the authoritarian, military-led regimes that swept across the region beginning with Brazil in 1964.

The advent of repressive military regimes in the 1960s and 1970s did not greatly alter the state-centered, ISI-based development model. During the 1970s military governments presided over major state initiatives drawing on cheap, easily obtained credit from international banks. In the early 1980s, however, debt repayment and interest obligations began to mount just as a global recession reduced new capital inflows and depressed Latin America's trade balances. Most governments were compelled to rely on the assistance (and policy prescriptions) of the International Monetary Fund (IMF) and other global financial institutions. Facing rising popular opposition, decreasing support from dominant groups, and economic crisis, military leaders were forced to restore executive office to civilian hands.

The new civilian leaders faced the daunting challenge of strengthening democracy while pursuing the reactivation of their economies within the context of IMF restrictions. Thus, since the mid-1980s, diverse governments have pursued similar economic strategies. They have opened up their economies by removing protectionist tariffs and other trade barriers, promoting foreign investment, privatizing state enterprises, and reducing subsidies for public services. This neoliberal approach has generated substantial popular resistance but remains the predominant development model in the early twenty-first century and an important determinant of class structures.

RURAL CLASS STRUCTURES
SINCE THE 1990S

The traditional relationships of landlord and peasant that helped to define Latin American societies all but disappeared in the 1990s. Large estates are no longer so large, in many cases having been curtailed by agrarian reform in the 1960s, and farms devoted to exports are more likely to be run according to strictly capitalistic criteria. Moreover, rural society in general is much more closely linked to the major urban centers and national economic and political forces. The incidence of poverty, however, remains 60 percent of the rural population for Latin America as a whole.

Agrarian elites are less easily characterized as oligarchies. Large farms are likely to be run by managers, while owners may be impersonal corporations or city dwellers with diversified economic interests. A typical example is the transformation between the mid-1980s and the mid-1990s of the Salvadoran coffee oligarchy into a modernized elite based on banking and industrial and commercial assets. Rural elite interests tend to be promoted through professional associations and political parties rather than through the direct exercise of coercive power. This evolution has fundamentally altered rural class relations; small landholders and rural workers now deal with entrepreneurs, commercial intermediaries, and state agencies rather than traditional large landowners.

The rural population has both gained and suffered as a result of these changes. On the one hand, rural people are freer to organize themselves, pursue political alliances, and negotiate with state agencies. The disappearance of military regimes has also contributed to the rise of organized rural activism in countries such as Bolivia, Brazil, and Peru. Rural educational levels and access to basic services have risen as well. On the other hand, the advancing modernization of agriculture has reduced employment opportunities. In the context of continuing population growth, the migratory outflow from the countryside has continued.

A further challenge to the rural economy since 1980 has been the elimination of the agrarian reform policies that had sought to shore up smallholders' agriculture. Even where such policies had not been suspended earlier by military dictatorships, the prescriptions of economic liberalization have been to curtail state efforts to redistribute land and organize production, relying instead on market forces to drive rural development.

The net effect of these changes has been to accelerate both the differentiation of Latin American peasantries and their integration into larger social structures. Viable small farms persist in some regions, especially where proximity to urban centers guarantees a stable demand for food crops. The largest farm enterprises still provide permanent wage employment for a significant group of workers. The majority of rural families, however, are pursuing diversified subsistence strategies that may combine cultivation of tiny plots, occasional wage labor on larger farms, and off-farm sources of income. Among the most important sources of the latter are nonagricultural employment (for instance, in rural food-processing or manufacturing assembly plants) and remittances from family members who have moved to the city or even out of the country. Many rural communities in Mexico, El Salvador, and the Dominican Republic, for example, increasingly were sustained by family remittances from the United States by the early 1990s. In the early twenty-first century the remittance stream coming in from the United States and some countries of the European Union (especially Spain) is a vital lifeline for the rural and the urban poor population. Data from the UN Economic Commission for Latin America and the Caribbean (ECLAC) indicate that the outgoing remittance stream from the United States to Latin America alone was $45 billion in 2004, a quantity larger than the volume of the direct

Vineyard workers, Vina Caliterra, Chile, 1996. As technological improvements decreased the demand for farm workers and land costs became prohibitively expensive in Latin America, large numbers of rural citizens looked to support themselves by combining seasonal farm work with other sources of income. © CHARLES O'REAR/CORBIS

foreign investment and the amount of foreign aid together. Of this total, 55 percent went to Mexico and Central America. An annual remittance stream of $8 billion keeps the economies of El Salvador, Honduras, Guatemala, and Nicaragua afloat.

URBAN CLASS STRUCTURES
SINCE THE 1990S

The dominant classes are a very small proportion of the economically active population in modern Latin American societies. Their ranks are characterized by diverse interests, however, including the traditional export and mercantile sectors, transnational and domestic manufacturing, services (banking in particular), and even large state-owned enterprises. The crisis of the 1980s and the ascendance of neoliberalism have altered the dominant class profile. Privatization policies are gradually doing away with state enterprises; transnational firms have acquired many of them. Among private firms, those best able

to cope with prevailing economic conditions have been those least reliant on the domestic market and more geared toward nontraditional exports, as well as those with the capacity to spread their resources across borders and foreign currencies. Increasingly, transnational capital refers not just to U.S.-, European-, or Asian-based firms operating in Latin America but also to Latin American firms and investors who have looked abroad for greater security or greater returns.

The middle classes include professionals, mid-level managerial and technical personnel, and career-oriented government employees. While these groups remain considerably better off than the working classes, the economic downturn of the 1980s represented a blow, as the expectations of upward mobility and increased consumer buying power that earlier had accompanied economic growth were suddenly dashed. Emigration has become a more attractive option among these groups, as has that of abandoning work in large firms to start small businesses.

Public sector employees have been especially affected. By the 1980s the public sector accounted for between 15 and 30 percent of total urban employment in most Latin American countries. The curtailment of government spending resulting from the debt crisis and readjustment policies has signified a major decrease in real wages and living standards for public sector employees, although the number of jobs has generally remained stable. The incidence of poverty has risen to encompass around one-fourth of all civil servants in Brazil, Mexico, and Venezuela.

The formal working class has been perhaps the hardest hit of all classes by economic trends since the 1980s. During that decade employment in manufacturing throughout the region declined sharply relative to services, and in several cases declined in absolute terms as well. The number of workers in manufacturing in Argentina declined by 29 percent from 1980 to 1990; Peru and Brazil experienced drops of 19 percent and 13 percent respectively. Open unemployment rates soared in most major cities. For those who kept their jobs, incomes headed downward. Over the same decade, real wages in the manufacturing sector fell by 45 percent in Venezuela, 24 percent in Argentina, 18 percent in Brazil, and 8 percent in Mexico.

Workers have found it difficult to defend their interests. Labor unions, weakened during the years of repression and military rule, have been further affected by declining employment in some of the industries where they were once strongest, notably mining. A related factor of the "lost decade" of the 1980s was the shrinking electoral fortunes of Socialist and Communist political parties in the 1990s, once devoted to the cause of organized labor but now forced to seek compromise in electoral coalitions. Both on the right and on the left, an important political shift has occurred, as traditional class-based strategies have been replaced by coalition-building and cross-class appeals.

One noteworthy exception to the pattern of declining industrial employment has been the phenomenal growth of maquiladoras, best known in Mexico but also expanding in Central America and in some Andean countries. These are export processing plants established under special concessionary regulations; textiles and clothing, food processing, and electronics are the typical industries. In Mexico, employment in this sector more than quadrupled during the 1980s. Perhaps the most significant contribution of the maquiladora industries to the changing class structure of Latin America has been their heavy reliance on female labor.

The evolution of the informal sectors since 1980 has been complex. On the one hand, many informal workers have experienced deteriorating living standards. Contributing factors include the swelling of the informal labor force by those displaced from formal employment, the further overcrowding of housing in the shantytowns and poor neighborhoods, the decline in part-time or casual wage labor (in such fields as construction), and the reduction in state services, subsidies, and other programs aimed at the poor. On the other hand, the same downturn produced new economic opportunities. Depressed earnings of middle- and working-class consumers have translated into greater demand for goods produced cheaply by informal businesses and street vendors. Other informal entrepreneurs are producing inputs needed by large formal sector firms through piece-rate work and home work—arrangements replacing inputs previously produced by formal sector firms.

Thus increasing urban poverty levels have masked some informal success stories. In Otavalo, Ecuador, Indian entrepreneurs have established small weaving operations in which workers turn out jeans and shirts for the national market and luxury woolen items for export. In another case, Uruguayan women working in cooperatives have also developed a thriving garment industry using an umbrella organization that operates wholesale outlets in the capital city of Montevideo, supplying both domestic and export markets.

Perhaps the most remarkable example is Gamarra, a former slum conglomerate near the very center of Peru's capital city, Lima, where a kind of informal middle class of textile entrepreneurs emerged from the formerly self-employed and informal workers. The most audacious entrepreneurs diversified their assets afterward to other economic sectors. The first unregistered micro-enterprises

Selling cold water to bus passengers, Managua, Nicaragua, 1993. The depressed economies of Latin America have increased demand by consumers for inexpensive goods produced by street vendors, such as the bagged water sold by these Nicaraguan girls. © KEITH DANNEMILLER/CORBIS

started in the early 1970s as house-and-work *talleres* of the new provincial migrants around Lima's popular food and groceries market of those days in the La Victoria district. Houses were transformed in *talleres*, thirty or forty per block, generally 50 percent of the existing quarters. Specialized financial institutes discovered a potential clientele: entrepreneurs, with their extended and symbolic family as backbone and *confianza* (personal trust) as the basic relation between the entrepreneur and the work force and between the members of the entrepreneurial circuit. By 2007 more than sixty thousand artisans and micro-entrepreneurs with their workers were associated in industrial-commercial cooperatives that administered the Gamarra industrial and commercial infrastructure. Other clusters of interdependent *talleres* and small service enterprises specializing in a certain sector (textiles, shoes, metallurgy, plastics) are the typical advance industries in all slum cities around Lima.

These examples demonstrate the increasing class differentiation within the informal economy and society. It is, however, also a fact of life that most of those who find employment in the informal economy are surviving under very precarious conditions.

SIGNIFICANCE OF OTHER SOCIAL CLEAVAGES

It is important to recognize that other social divisions cut across class structure and help to determine the specific characteristics and identities associated with social classes. The most important of these distinctions are gender and ethnicity.

Between 1950 and 1980 Latin America witnessed a slow but steady expansion of women's participation in the labor force. This was largely the consequence of broader patterns of social change, including urbanization, higher educational achievement, evolving labor markets, and associated changes in cultural values. Women's employment was highly segmented, however, with jobs concentrated in the areas of personal (including domestic) services, office services, and sales.

As with the informal sector as a whole, women experienced contradictory developments during the crisis of the 1980s. Unemployment rates for women generally increased faster than those for men, reflecting a relative decline in formal employment opportunities. At the same time, however, younger women were entering the labor force at an accelerated rate because families needed additional workers to offset the declining incomes of those already working. Much of this additional labor was absorbed in small-scale informal sector activities.

New opportunities arose with the appearance of nontraditional export industries. In the countryside, large firms producing commodities such as cut flowers in Colombia or fresh fruit in Chile hired women to do the processing or packing. This gender-based preference was mirrored in the maquiladora industries. Women were also hired preferentially for "home work": jobs in which parts of production processes (such as for shoes and clothing) are subcontracted to individual workers to carry out in their homes. These opportunities have carried a cost, however: women workers have been consistently subject to discriminatory wage rates (relative to men), extreme job insecurity, and difficult work environments. The persistence of discriminatory practices, along with other gender-based issues, has helped spark the rapid growth of women's organizations. These movements represent an increasingly active presence in the Latin American political arena.

Ethnic divisions represent a defining aspect of Latin American and Caribbean class structures. The colonial reliance on native Americans and African slaves as a labor force for European conquerors has been an enduring legacy. Despite the vast changes that have since occurred, it remains true that throughout the hemisphere, to be identifiably Indian or black is to rank lower in economic, political, and social status than those who are nonindigenous or non-black. There is great variation across countries and regions in how these inequalities are expressed, but a few major trends are worth noting.

Latin America's original indigenous peoples have been largely assimilated or confined to remote areas in many countries of the region but remain a substantial component of the population in Mesoamerica (especially Guatemala and Mexico) and the Andean countries. Long concentrated in rural communities that provided the basis for maintaining separate ethnic identities, these groups by the mid-twentieth century had joined migration streams toward the cities. Indigenous ethnicity has proven remarkably resilient. In many cases urban migrants have maintained community-based identities through the social networks that led them to settle in the same neighborhoods as their family and friends.

The relationship between class and ethnicity has been no less complex. In the Caribbean the demise of the plantation system, with its sharply defined racial hierarchy, has produced varied outcomes. On the smaller islands, where white elites never constituted more than a tiny minority, blacks and mulattoes have acquired greater political and economic status. In the larger countries, such as Cuba or the Dominican Republic, where the white population was considerably more substantial, racial stratification has been more persistent. In general the evolution of social and political movements based on racial awareness has been marked more by selective strategies than by polarization on the U.S. model. Movements centered on black self-awareness, for instance, have focused at various times on achieving national independence, resisting U.S. interventions, or opposing transnational corporations, but rarely on opposition to whites in general. In other instances, once-racial distinctions have come to be expressed more in ethnic terms, as with black and mulatto populations in Haiti or black and Asian Indian groups in Trinidad and Guyana.

Brazil offers yet another pattern. There the discriminatory heritage of slave plantations was reinforced until the mid-twentieth century by the spatial concentration of blacks in the economically depressed Northeast, whereas the white population (enlarged by European migration) inhabited the more prosperous South. Despite increasing black migration from the Northeast to the South, however, racial inequality has not lessened. During the "economic miracle" of the 1970s, despite general gains for Brazilian workers, the black and mulatto populations remained concentrated in the most disadvantaged educational categories and occupations. One result has been, since the late 1980s, the rise of social movements and organizations articulating a distinct Afro-Brazilian identity.

CONSOLIDATION OF HETEROGENEITY IN CLASS STRUCTURES

The Latin American class structure of the early twenty-first century is more heterogeneous than that of the 1950s–1980s period. Data from ECLAC, the International Labour Organization (ILO), and the United Nations Development Program (UNDP) demonstrate certain trends. In the first place, poverty, informality, and social exclusion have become a massive urban phenomenon. Data from 1990 to the early 2000s show a consistent proportion of urban income poor in Latin America of more than one-third of the total urban population, with a tendency to increase after 2000. With the urban population still growing (and at a significantly faster rate than the rural population) during the 1990s, the absolute number of urban poor increased. In 2002 roughly 144 million (or 65 percent) out of the total 221 million of income poor in Latin America lived in cities and towns. Fifty million people lived in extreme poverty (*indigencia*). Of the total Latin American population 75 percent lived in cities and a significant segment of them in megacities and metropolitan conglomerates. This development is reflected in high persistent inequality in the distribution of urban income and wealth, in the expansion of slums, and the deterioration of popular neighborhoods since the 1980s.

A second characteristic of the class structure is the implicit duality of the formal and informal economy and society. Originally interpreted as a short-term under- and unemployment phenomenon, employment in the informal economy appears in the early twenty-first century to be consolidated, and the informal economy thus shapes a kind of informal society, partially inserted in the formal order and partially forming a parallel social structure with its internal social hierarchies. Ethnicity is a stratifying factor within the informal economy and society. Mechanisms for survival predominate: ties of ethnicity, religion, real or symbolic family relationships, closeness to the place of birth, local neighborhood relations. In the Andean countries, Central America, and Mexico, features of Quechua or Maya culture mix with elements of informal society. In Table 1 one can observe the over-time consolidation of the formal-cum-informal order.

This heterogeneous class structure reflects the growing pattern of segregation, restriction, poverty, and de facto second-class citizenship in the second half of the twentieth century. It reflects the precarious implantation of (urban) second-class citizenship as the long-term result of the mainstream model of economic crisis and reforms in the 1980s and 1990s. The resulting class structure is related to an intergenerational process of informalization and social exclusion in the urban—more precisely the metropolitan—environments, nourished by a continuous migration stream from the rural hinterland of the countries of Latin America and the larger island states of the Caribbean. Latin America has thus become the continent where, in most of its countries, a significant segment of the population is at once poor, informal, and excluded.

There are some marked changes within the Latin American urban class structures. The chronically poor are now joined by the "new poor," descending from the former strata of the middle and industrial working classes. Old and new poor converge as informal micro-entrepreneurs and self-employed in search of survival and livelihood strategies. The decomposition of the formerly substantive working classes has not only led to the formation of a new edifice of social stratification but also to changes in the size and composition of poor households' family structures. The traditional role of men as heads of families is ebbing away with the enlarged number of female-headed households in the popular neighborhoods and slum cities.

Structure of urban employment in Latin America, 1990–2003 (percentages)

	1990	2003
Public sector	14	14
Private sector	43	40
Self-employed	22	24
Workers in microenterprises	15	16
Household servants	6	7

SOURCE: Elaboration of data from ILO, *Panorama laboral 2004*, pp. 97–101.

Table 1

Furthermore, the informal economy and society even generates hidden migration cycles, demographic breakdowns, and cleavages within the family structure.

Central America, with its poverty-stricken and war-torn societies, may provide the best example of disruption at the family level. The displacement process of war refugees fleeing violence followed by even more substantial migration in peacetime to the United States and Mexico is in fact a population exodus migration to Mexico and the United States. Their remittances create other patterns of consequences such as a structurally reduced employment market, high unemployment rates for women and younger people, broken families and the despair of the family at home after the "temporary" migration of the male members, and the bitter choice between self-employment and emigration.

This overflow of poverty and exclusion bursting its banks and generating the new basin of informality and second-class citizenship has been portrayed as the *desborde popular*. It has the potential to trigger the decline of the institutional pillars of traditional formal society, overwhelmed by the growth of Latin America's slums and its consequences in terms of the emergence of a qualitatively new (urban) society. It prompted the birth of a diversity of organizations representing the informal entrepreneurs and self-employed, such as local and regional chambers of craftsmen and community-run food canteens in the slum cities. What all of these have in common is an ambivalent relationship of dependency on the professional development organizations that finance them, such as religious and ecclesiastical foundations, NGOs, donor agencies, private banks "with a social face," and municipal and central government organizations.

This process also started the collapse of the traditional support institutions of the democratic order: the decline of political parties, the erosion of the status of the legislature and the judiciary, the dwindling stature of the magistrates as the legitimate authorities in the sphere of law and order, the collapse of the once-powerful trade union confederations, and the weakening of other conventional entities of civil society, such as the chambers of industry and commerce and the professional organizations of doctors, lawyers, and

engineers. The parallel institutions, parallel hierarchies, and parallel sectors that have emerged along the lines of poverty, informality, and social exclusion may well have formed a more durable—albeit heterogeneous—economic, social, political, and cultural order.

The newly emerging class structure also has consequences with respect to the political order. It is interesting to notice that between 1997 and 2007 all Latin America's nonelectoral government changes were instigated not by military coup but by social movements of the poor—the slum dwellers, the urban *informales*, the ethnic movement in the urban informal society—that have mainly taken the form of ad hoc popular protest movements, mass meetings, regional protest alliances, sit-down meetings, and hunger marches. Several substitutions of presidential regimes—in Argentina (four in 2001), Bolivia (two in two years: 2003 and 2005), Ecuador (eight between 1997 and 2007) and in Peru with the fall of Alberto Fujimori (2000)—were the result of this new *democracia de la calle*. Latin America's complex class structure is producing substantive changes in the region's social and political landscape.

See also **Migration and Migrations; African Brazilians: Color Terminology; Brazil: Economic Miracle (1968–1974); Economic Development; Maquiladoras; Slavery: Brazil; Slavery: Spanish America.**

BIBLIOGRAPHY

Bodemer, Klaus, and Eduardo Gamarra, eds. *Centroamérica 2020: Un nuevo modelo de desarrollo regional*. Caracas, Editorial Nueva Sociedad, 2002.

Cardoso, Fernando Henrique, and Enzo Faletto. *Dependency and Development in Latin America*. Translated by Marjory Mattingly. Berkeley: University of California Press, 1979.

CEPAL. *Panorama social de América Latina 2005*. Santiago de Chile: Comisión Económica para América Latina LC/G.2288-P, 2006.

Fernandes, Florestan. *Capitalismo dependente e clases sociais na América Latina*. Rio de Janeiro: Zahar, 1973.

ILO. *Panorama laboral 2004*. Lima, Organización Internacional de Trabajo–Oficina Regional para América Latina y el Caribe, 2004.

Kruijt, Dirk, Carlos Sojo, and Rebeca Grynspan. *Informal Citizens: Poverty, Informality, and Social Exclusion in Latin America*. Amsterdam: Rozenberg, 2002.

Matos Mar, José. *Desborde popular y crisis del estado: Veinte años después.* Lima: Fondo Editorial del Congreso del Perú, 2004.

Perez Saínz, Juan Pablo. *The New Faces of Informality in Central America.* Boulder, CO: Lynne Rienner, 1996.

Portes, Alejandro. "Latin American Class Structures: Their Composition and Change during the Last Decades." *Latin American Research Review* 20, no. 3 (1985): 7–40.

Portes, Alejandro, and Kelly Hoffman. "Latin American Class Structures: Their Composition and Change during the Neoliberal Era." *Latin American Research Review* 38, no. 1 (2003): 41–82.

Tardanico, Richard, and Rafael Menjívar. *Global Restructuring, Employment, and Social Inequality in Urban Latin America.* Miami: North-South Center Press, 1997.

UNDP. *La democracia en América Latina: Hacia una democracia de ciudadanas y ciudadanos: Argentina, Bolivia, Brasil, Chile, Colombia, Costa Rica, Ecuador, El Salvador, Guatemala, Honduras, México, Nicaragua, Panamá, Paraguay, Perú, República Dominicana, Uruguay.* New York: United Nations Development Programme, 2004. Available from http://www.democracia.UNDP.org.

DIRK KRUIJT

CLAVÉ, PELEGRÍN (1811–1880).

Pelegrín Clavé (*b.* 17 June 1811; *d.* 13 September 1880), painter. Trained in his native Barcelona and in Rome, Clavé was in Mexico between 1846 and 1867 as director of the reestablished Academia de San Carlos. In Rome he studied with Tommaso Minardi and, like the sculptor Manuel Vilar, he was sympathetic to the Nazarenes (a group of German artists who sought to revitalize Christian art). While in Mexico he executed many portraits reminiscent of those of Jean Auguste Dominique Ingres, with which he must have become familiar in Rome; these are considered his most significant work. With his pupils Clavé decorated the interior of the dome of the church of the Profesa (1860–1867; destroyed by fire in 1914). He was instrumental in the formation of the collection of colonial paintings in the galleries of the Academia de San Carlos. Political difficulties led Clavé to return to Barcelona in 1868. There he lectured and wrote about Mexican painting, and worked on plans to decorate the dome of the church of the Merced.

See also **Art: The Nineteenth Century.**

BIBLIOGRAPHY

Salvador Moreno, *El pintor Pelegrín Clavé* (1966).

Additional Bibliography

Camacho Becerra, Arturo. *Pelegrín Clave.* Zapopan: Colegio de Jalisco [Barcelona]: Generalitat de Catalunya, 1998.

Hernandez-Duran, Raymond. "Reframing Viceregal Painting in Nineteenth-century Mexico: Politics, the Academy of San Carlos, and Colonial Art History." Ph.D. diss., 2005.

CLARA BARGELLINI

CLAVER, PEDRO (1580–1654).

Pedro Claver (*b.* 26? June 1580; *d.* 8 September 1654), Catalan Jesuit missionary in Colombia who became a saint. Born in Verdú, Spain, Claver joined the Jesuits in 1602. He arrived in Cartagena in 1610, then quickly went on to Bogotá and Tunja, where he studied until 1615. Ordained in Cartagena in 1616, Claver worked among the black slaves as a protégé of Father Alonso Sandoval. In 1622 he signed his final vows as "Pedro Claver, slave of the negroes forever." For the next three decades he met the slave ships coming to Cartagena, the main slave emporium in Spanish America, and ministered to the needs of their human cargo. Claver had black translators fluent in African languages who questioned, instructed, and aided the slaves in religious and health matters. He also sought out the destitute in hospitals and jails and provided them with medicine, food, and clothes. When asked how many he had baptized, he answered, "more than three hundred thousand." Claver died in Cartagena. He was beatified by Pius IX in 1851 and canonized by Leo XIII in 1888.

See also **Slavery: Spanish America.**

BIBLIOGRAPHY

A good survey is Angel Valtierra, S.J., *Pedro Claver: El santo redentor de los negros,* 2 vols. (1980); the earlier edition (1954) is available in English as *Peter Claver: Saint of the Slaves,* translated by Janet H. Perry and L. J. Woodward (1960). A succinct account can be found in Juan Manuel Pacheco, S.J., *Historia extensa de Colombia,* vol. 13; *Historia eclesiástica,* Tomo 2, *La consolidación de la iglesia, siglo xvii* (1975), esp. pp. 633–637.

Additional Bibliography

Abston, Emanuel Jordan. "Catholicism and African-Americans: A Study of Claverism, 1909–1959." Ph.D. disseration, Florida State University, 1998.

Rey Parrado, Maria Lucía. *Historia de la Congregación Hermanas de los pobres de San Pedro Claver, 1874–1984.* Bogotá: Editorial Kelly, 1984.

Splendiani, Anna Marí, and Tulio Aristizábal Giraldo. *Proceso de beatificación y canonización de San Pedro Claver.* Bogotá: Pontificia Universidad Javeriana: Universidad Católica del Táchira, 2002.

MAURICE P. BRUNGARDT

Charles E. Ronan, S.J. *Francisco Javier Clavigero (1731–1787)* (1977).

Additional Bibliography

Ronan, Charles E. *Francisco Javier Clavigero, S.J. (1731–1787): Figura de la ilustración mexicana, su vida y obras.* Guadalajara: Instituto Technologico y de Estudios Superiores de Occidente, Universidad de Guadalajara, 1993.

Villegas, Juan. *El P. Francisco Javier Clavijero S.J.: Americano y novohispano ilustrado.* Montevideo: Centro de Estudios de Historia Americana, 2004.

CHARLES E. RONAN S.J.

CLAVIGERO, FRANCISCO JAVIER

(1731–1787). Francisco Javier Clavigero (Clavijero; *b.* 9 September 1731; *d.* 2 April 1787), historian and promoter of the Mexican Enlightenment. Clavigero, a native of Veracruz, is noted for his role in introducing modern philosophy into Mexico (a modified Aristotelian cosmology influenced by eighteenth-century sciences with an emphasis on empirically based critical analysis). He taught in the Jesuit *colegios* in Valladolid (modern-day Morelia) and in Guadalajara, where he was residing when the Jesuits were expelled from the Spanish Empire in 1767. Exiled to Bologna in the Papal States, Clavigero turned to history to consolidate the record of pre-Hispanic Mexico and also to refute the so-called theory of American degeneracy that some European writers, like Corneille de Pauw, were propagating to the effect that America and her native inhabitants were far inferior to Europe because of America's wretched climate and other factors. The outcome was his *Storia antica del Messico* (1780–1781) that not only accomplished his purpose but also fostered a spirit of regionalism and neo-Aztecism among certain Mexican patriots which they used to justify their revolt against Spain. Noteworthy also is his posthumously published *Storia della California* (1789), written to counteract charges against the Jesuits and their California missions and to acquaint Europe with that peninsula and its inhabitants. He died in Bologna.

See also **Philosophy: Overview.**

BIBLIOGRAPHY

Antonello Gerbi, *The Dispute of the New World: The History of a Polemic, 1750–1900,* rev. and enl. ed., translated by Jeremy Moyle (1973), pp. 196–211.

CLAY, HENRY

(1777–1852). Henry Clay (*b.* 12 April 1777; *d.* 29 June 1852), U.S. statesman who served as secretary of state (1825–1829). Clay was one of the country's great political leaders before the Civil War. A native of Virginia, Clay achieved success as a lawyer and state legislator in Kentucky before entering the Senate in 1806. He was an unsuccessful presidential candidate in 1832 and 1844. Although Clay identified the movements for Latin American independence with the U.S. colonial struggle against the British, he wanted the United States to remain neutral during the conflict because he thought it would hinder the U.S. effort to acquire the Floridas from Spain. Anticipating commercial opportunities and wanting to secure the Caribbean region from European interlopers, by 1818, Clay urged the granting of recognition to the independent South American nations. Clay's advocacy of an American system of independent states to counterbalance the European Holy Alliance led to his support of the Monroe Doctrine, which proclaimed the western hemisphere off limits to foreign intruders, and his hope that the Panama Congress (1826) would declare its support for the doctrine. Subsequently, Clay lost his fraternalistic spirit with the South American nations as more information about their corruption surfaced following their independence. To secure the U.S. position in Latin America, Clay encouraged the signing of favorable treaties of amity and commerce, illustrated by the treaty signed in 1825 with the Federation of Central America. Late in his career, Clay opposed the annexation of Texas over the slavery issue, but he supported the Mexican-American War once it had begun (1846).

See also **Monroe Doctrine.**

BIBLIOGRAPHY

H. L. Hoskins, "The Hispanic American Policy of Henry Clay, 1816–1828," *Hispanic American Historical Review* 7, no. 4 (1927): 460–478.

Glyndon G. Van Deusen, *The Life of Henry Clay* (1937).

Clement Eaton, *Henry Clay and the Art of American Politics* (1957).

Additional Bibliography

Clay, Henry. *Las instrucciones de Henry Clay.* México: Secretaría de Relaciones Exteriores, 1985.

Serna Herrera, Juan Manuel de la. "Del tiempo y el poder en la historia de América Latina." *Revista de Historia de las Ideas* 10 (1990): 271–275.

THOMAS M. LEONARD

CLAYTON-BULWER TREATY (1850).

Clayton-Bulwer Treaty (1850), an agreement between Britain and the United States codifying Anglo-American relations with regard to Central America. The treaty was signed 19 April 1850 by U.S. Secretary of State John M. Clayton and Sir Henry L. Bulwer, British minister to the United States. Seeking to end a dangerous rivalry, the treaty prohibited colonization, fortification, or the exercise of exclusive influence in Central America by either side and provided joint Anglo-American protection for any interoceanic canal built on the isthmus. It remained in effect until superseded by the Hay-Pauncefote Treaties of 1901, which granted the United States exclusive rights to build and operate an isthmian canal.

The treaty was the diplomatic meeting ground of British informal colonialism in mid-nineteenth-century Central America and the Caribbean phase of U.S. Manifest Destiny. Historians have variously claimed the treaty as a victory for both sides, but it appears to have been a compromise in which the interests of both benefited, although no canal was realized. As Mary W. Williams pointed out early in this century, however, the treaty was arrived at by avoiding certain basic questions, namely, what to do with existing British holdings in the region: Belize, the Bay Islands, and the Mosquito Protectorate. Belize was excluded from the treaty's provisions by

a subsequent exchange of diplomatic notes. The Bay Islands question, however, was muddled by the British Colonial Office's proclamation of the Bay Islands Colony in 1852 without consulting the British Foreign Office. British efforts to relinquish the Mosquito Protectorate were frustrated first by Nicaragua's defiance and then by its collapse amidst civil war and filibuster invasion. British absorption in the Crimean War (1853–1856) and the bellicose posturing of the Pierce administration (1853–1857) postponed an Anglo-American rapprochement over Central America and threatened to undermine the treaty itself.

The treaty (and the mutually self-denying compromise it represented) was finally preserved by a series of British treaties signed in 1859 and 1860 with Guatemala, Honduras, and Nicaragua, relinquishing or otherwise clarifying British holdings in the region to the satisfaction of the United States, and by the Buchanan administration's (1857–1861) formal repudiation of filibustering. Ultimately, the U.S. Civil War slowed the momentum of Caribbean Manifest Destiny, thereby removing the most serious challenge to the 1850 treaty until the end of the nineteenth century.

See also **British–Latin American Relations; Hay-Pauncefote Treaties (1901).**

BIBLIOGRAPHY

Lester D. Langley, *Struggle for the American Mediterranean: United States–European Rivalry in the Gulf-Caribbean, 1776–1904* (1976), pp. 81–106, provides an excellent introduction to the Anglo-American rivalry in Central America. Wilbur D. Jones, *The American Problem in British Diplomacy, 1841–1861* (1974) gives an excellent account of the British side, while Mary W. Williams, *Anglo-American Isthmian Rivalry, 1815–1915* (1916) remains extremely useful. A later view of the "Clayton-Bulwer process" is provided in Richmond F. Brown, "Charles Lennox Wyke and the Clayton-Bulwer Formula in Central America, 1852–1860," in *The Americas* 47 (April 1991): 411–445.

RICHMOND F. BROWN

CLEMENTE WALKER, ROBERTO

(1934–1972). Roberto Clemente Walker was born August 18, 1934, in Carolina, Puerto Rico, near San Juan. Clemente signed with the Los Angeles Dodgers (1954) out of high school, but played his entire major league career (1955–1972) with the Pittsburgh Pirates. In his 2,433 Pirate games, he had 3,000 hits and a .317 batting average. He won four batting titles and twelve Gold Glove Awards, was named his league's Most Valuable Player (MVP) in 1966 and World Series MVP in 1971, and appeared in twelve Major League All-Star Games. Until 1971 he repaid his native country by playing in the Puerto Rican winter league. To achieve all this and earn deserved praise in the United States he had to overcome racism and prejudice against blacks and Hispanics and persistent physical ailments that hampered him and brought cruel accusations that he was a hypochondriac and malingerer.

He died in a plane crash on December 31, 1972, while trying to deliver relief aid that he had collected for earthquake victims in Nicaragua. In 1973 a special election made him the first Latino to enter baseball's Hall of Fame. In life, as on the field, Clemente displayed a capacity for toughness and tenderness, aggressiveness and compassion. In Puerto Rico his widow Vera and others operate the youth sports center named in his honor. Major League Baseball's annual award to the player who best exemplifies community service is named for him, and his career and humanitarianism were again recognized at the 2006 All-Star Game in Pittsburgh's new PNC Park.

See also **Hispanics in the United States; Sports.**

BIBLIOGRAPHY

Bjarkman, Peter C. *Baseball with a Latin Beat: A History of the Latin American Game.* Jefferson, NC: McFarland, 1994.

Maraniss, David. *Clemente: The Passion and Grace of Baseball's Last Hero.* New York: Simon & Schuster, 2006.

Musick, Phil. *Who Was Roberto? A Biography of Roberto Clemente.* Garden City, NY: Doubleday, 1974.

O'Brien, Jim. *Remember Roberto: Clemente Recalled by Teammates, Family, Friends, and Fans.* Pittsburgh: James P. O'Brien Publishing, 1994.

Wagenheim, Kal. *Clemente!* New York: Praeger, 1973.

JOSEPH L. ARBENA

CLEMENTINA. *See* **de Jesus, Clementina.**

CLIMATE. *See* **Environment and Climate.**

CLINE, HOWARD F. (1915–1971). Howard F. Cline (June 12, 1915–June 1, 1971) was a leading specialist in Mexican history and a key figure in the development of Latin American area studies. He received his undergraduate degree from Harvard; before returning to Harvard for graduate study, Cline traveled in Mexico and worked briefly in the Department of Indian Affairs during the administration of President Lázaro Cárdenas. From the latter experience he acquired a lifelong interest in ethnohistory. His best-known work, *The United States and Mexico* (1953) deals chiefly with Mexico and offers a wide range of detailed information and analysis on twentieth-century Mexican developments. Cline taught Latin American history at Harvard, Yale, and ultimately Northwestern, but left full-time teaching in 1952 to become director of the Hispanic Foundation of the Library of Congress. In that capacity he supervised one of the world's great collections of materials dealing with Spain, Portugal, and Latin America. Increasingly, he also took a leading role in the professional activities of Latin American specialists, particularly when, after the Cuban Revolution, there was a sharp rise of interest in and support for Latin American studies. He was one of the organizers of the Latin American Studies Association, founded in 1966, and served as its first executive secretary.

See also **Latin American Studies Association.**

BIBLIOGRAPHY

Finan, John J. "Howard F. Cline (1915–1971): Obituary." *Hispanic American Historical Review* 51, no. 4 (November 1971): 646–653.

DAVID BUSHNELL

CLIPPERTON ISLAND. An uninhabited island in the Pacific Ocean, 1,300 miles (2,090 kilometers) southwest of Mexico, Clipperton Island is a coral atoll (2 square miles [5 square kilometers]). Discovered by Ferdinand Magellan in 1521, it was named after the English pirate John Clipperton in

1705. In 1858 the French explorer Victor le Coat de Kervéguen annexed the island to France, though he could not land on it. In 1897 the Mexican ruler Porfirio Díaz sent a military expedition to occupy the island. There was a Mexican garrison on it between 1897 and 1917. After a long legal dispute between Mexico and France, King Victor Emmanuel III of Italy in 1931 arbitrated the conflicting claims in favor of France. In 1979 France assumed direct administration of the dependency.

See also **Díaz, Porfirio; Magellan, Ferdinand.**

BIBLIOGRAPHY

González Avelar, Miguel. *Clipperton, isla mexicana*. Mexico City: Fondo de Cultura Económica, 1992.

Granados Barba, A. "El atolón de Clipperton: Aspectos históricos y ecológicos." *Ciencia y desarrollo* 25, no. 149 (November–December 1999): 16–23.

Juet, Hubert. *Clipperton, l'île passion*. Paris: Editions Thélès, 2004.

Labarraque-Reyssac, Claude. *Les oubliés de Clipperton*. Paris: André Bonne, 1970.

Niaussat, Pierre-Marie. *Le Lagon et l'atoll de Clipperton*. Paris: Académie des sciences d'outre-mer, 1978.

Ongay Méndez, Alfredo Fernando. "El arbitraje de la isla Clipperton. Modos de adquirir y enajenar en derecho internacional público." PhD diss., Universidad Nacional Autónoma de México (UNAM), 1945.

Orozco, Ricardo. *La pasión es México!: La terrible tragedia de la Isla de Clipperton*. Mexico, D.F.: Centro de Estudios Históricos del Porfiriato, 1998.

Sachet, Marie Hélène. "Monographie physique et biologique de l'île Clipperton." *Annales de l'Institut Océanographique* 40, no. 1 (1962): 1–108.

Skaggs, Jimmy M. *Clipperton: A History of the Island the World Forgot*. New York: Walker, 1989.

REYNALDO YUNUEN ORTEGA ORTIZ

CLOSED CORPORATE PEASANT COMMUNITY (CCPC).

Closed Corporate Peasant Community (CCPC) is an organizational framework for analysis of peasant communities developed by anthropologist Eric Wolf in the 1950s. Wolf applied his typology of peasant organization to communities in Central Java and Mesoamerica, specifically Mexico and Guatemala. The CCPC, according to

Wolf, is a "relatively autonomous economic, social, linguistic, and politico-religious system." The community is corporate because it maintains a body of rights and membership, and closed because it limits its benefits to members and discourages participation with the larger society. Wolf believes the development of the closed corporate peasant community was a result of the serious social and cultural crises of indigenous communities brought on by the Spanish Conquest of Latin America. Peasant communities closed into themselves in response to the economic and social changes wrought by colonization. Thus the CCPC can be understood as a protective device of peasant and indigenous communities to ensure their self-preservation in light of such radical change. Social science scholarship varies in the degree of adherence to the theory that outside factors are the main determinants of local community behavior. Instead, many scholars argue that the interpretations of Wolf's theory lose sight of other specificities in local communities that may affect the development (or dissolution) of a CCPC, such as personal agency, ecological changes, historical autonomy, religious movements, and political organizing.

See also **Indigenous Peoples; Mesoamerica.**

BIBLIOGRAPHY

Wolf, Eric. "The Closed Corporate Peasant Communities in Mesoamerica and Central Java." *Southwestern Journal of Anthropology* 13, no. 1 (1957): 1–18.

Wolf, Eric. "The Vicissitudes of the Closed Corporate Peasant Community." *American Ethnologist* 13 (May 1986): 325–329.

HEATHER K. THIESSEN

CLOUTHIER DEL RINCÓN, MANUEL J. (1934–1989).

A leading Mexican opposition politician and 1988 presidential candidate, Clouthier was a native of Culiacán, Sinaloa. Born on June 13, 1934, he attended high school in the United States at the Brown Military Academy in San Diego and graduated in 1957 from the Institute of Technology and Higher Education in Monterrey, Mexico, with a degree in agricultural engineering. Clouthier was a successful local businessman; he became active in a variety of regional business interest groups, including the United Fresh Fruit and Vegetable Association and the Businessman's Coordinating Council. He presided over the national Businessman's Coordinating Council, one of Mexico's most influential private-sector organizations from 1981 to 1983. Known for his hard-line defense of powerful agricultural interests, Clouthier became politically involved in the National Action Party (PAN), joining the party only in 1985. After losing as a PAN candidate for Congress and governor, he ran against Carlos Salinas in the 1988 presidential election, running an aggressive and charismatic campaign and endearing himself to many voters. He lost the election but helped many congressional candidates from his party to win, including Vicente Fox, his political disciple and future president of Mexico. Clouthier was killed in an auto accident in Sinaloa on October 1, 1989, under suspicious circumstances.

See also **Mexico, Political Parties: National Action Party (PAN).**

BIBLIOGRAPHY

Bañuelos Rentería, Javier. *Maquío: La fuerza de un ideal, biografía política*. Mexico: PAN, 2002.

Nanti Fernández, Enrique. *El Maquío Clouthier: La biografía, 1934–1989*. Mexico City: Planeta, 1998.

RODERIC AI CAMP

CLUZEAU-MORTET, LUIS [RICARDO] (1889–1957).

Luis [Ricardo] Cluzeau-Mortet (*b.* 16 November 1889; *d.* 28 September 1957), Uruguayan composer, violist, and pianist. Born in Montevideo, Cluzeau-Mortet studied piano, harmony, and composition with his maternal grandfather, Paul Faget, a winner of the Grand Prix of the Paris Conservatory. Later he studied violin and viola with María Visca. In 1914 he joined the Asociación Uruguaya de Música de Cámara, for whom he played viola until 1931, when he accepted the position as first viola in the Uruguayan state orchestra (OSSODRE), where he remained until his retirement in 1946. Cluzeau-Mortet received an invitation from the British Council to visit London in 1938, to which he responded by giving concerts of his vocal and piano works there and in Paris.

Cluzeau-Mortet's musical output comprises nearly two hundred works. His career can be divided into three periods: a brief romantic-impressionist phase that produced songs based on French poetry; a nationalist period; and a universalist phase. It is for his nationalist works that he is best known; indeed, Cluzeau-Mortet, with Alfonso Broqua and Eduardo Fabini, is considered a progenitor of Uruguayan nationalism. About half of his output, which includes several orchestral pieces, is made up of chamber music works. Among them the vocal and piano compositions are the masterpieces of his career. *Pericón* for piano (1918), premiered by Artur Rubinstein, and *Canto de chingolo* for voice and piano (1924), recorded by RCA Victor in 1930, are the most well-known and representative works from his nationalist period. Other important works are: *Llanuras* (1932); *Soledad campestre* (1936); *Rancherío* (1940), premiered by Jasha Horenstein in 1947 and winner of a SODRE composition competition; and *Sinfonía Artigas* (1951), all for orchestra. He died in Montevideo.

See also **Music: Art Music.**

BIBLIOGRAPHY

Composers of the Americas, vol. 14 (1968), pp. 47–64; *New Grove Dictionary of Music and Musicians*, vol. 4 (1980).

Susana Salgado, *Breve historia de la música culta en el Uruguay*, 2d ed. (1980), and *Cluzeau-Mortet* (1983).

Additional Bibliography

Ficher, Miguel, Martha Furman Schleifer, and John M Furman. *Latin American Classical Composers: A Biographical Dictionary*. Lanham, MD: Scarecrow Press, 1996.

SUSANA SALGADO

COAHUILA.

Coahuila, third largest state in Mexico. With a population of 2,495,200 (2005) and an area of 58,522 square miles, Coahuila lies south of Texas along the big bend of the Rio Grande known to Mexicans as the Río Bravo. The Spanish settlement of Coahuila, known as Nueva Extremadura, began in the late sixteenth century, and in 1577 the present-day capital of Saltillo was founded. Due to its scarcity of water, fertile land,

and valuable minerals, and because of the presence of nomadic and often hostile native groups, Coahuila remained a sparsely occupied ranching, farming, and mining frontier during the colonial era. As part of Spain's administrative reorganization of the northern frontier during the eighteenth century, Coahuila was incorporated into the Interior Provinces, and in 1785 it became part of the Commandancy of the East, along with Texas, Nuevo León, and Tamaulipas. In 1824, after Mexico had gained its independence, Coahuila and Texas (and for a brief time, Nuevo León) were established as one state. The union of Coahuila and Texas was challenged in 1836 by the Texas declaration of independence, and again in 1845 with the annexation of Texas by the United States. As a result of the Mexican-American War, Coahuila lost all of its territory north of the Río Bravo, and U.S. soldiers occupied Saltillo and other areas of the state.

During the Reform period of the mid-nineteenth century, Coahuila was annexed to the neighboring state of Nuevo León (1856–1864). It regained independent status by order of President Benito Juárez, who briefly sojourned in Saltillo during the French intervention in Mexico (1862–1867). The era of Porfirio Díaz (1877–1911) and the relatively peaceful conditions of the late nineteenth century encouraged the growth of Coahuila's agriculture, ranching, and mining sectors. The construction of railroads added to the state's prosperity and promoted the development of a manufacturing sector. During the Mexican Revolution, Coahuila played a prominent role, producing several leaders and serving as an important strategic base. Francisco Madero's revolt against Porfirio Díaz began in Coahuila, and the later Constitutionalist revolution was led by another native son, Venustiano Carranza. The state suffered severe destruction during the revolution, as competing armies struggled for control of this important northern area. Coahuila emerged from the revolution with a depressed economy, and during the 1920s and 1930s it continued to experience periodic unrest, including two minor manifestations of the Cristero Rebellion. During the 1940s, Coahuila began a slow economic recovery, visible in the growth of industry and an increase in population.

Generally speaking, economic development has been very important, and Coahuila has remained a center of foreign, especially American, investment.

The Saltillo-Ramos Arizpe industrial "corridor" is home to two large auto plants operated by Chrysler and General Motors, and Coahuila is the site of Mexico's largest steel plant, Altos Hornos de Mexico.

Throughout the twentieth century as well, Coahuila has remained a center of the Mexican workers' movement. In 1918, Saltillo hosted the conference that gave rise to the Confederación Regional de Obreros Mexicanos (CROM), and the governor at that time, Gustavo Espinosa Mireles, played a key part in its organization. Workers in Coahuila's coalmining region have always been especially active, and in the 1950s they struck against the American Smelting and Refining Company, which operated mines in the areas of Nueva Rosita and Cloete. Miners' demands for better working conditions were met with repression by the government and the mining company, which tried to starve workers into submission (blocking supplies of food sent by union sympathizers in the Laguna region), thereby precipitating the Caravan of Hunger—a protest march of some 5,000 workers from Coahuila to Mexico City, where workers were repressed, and many thrown in jail.

See also **Juárez, Benito.**

BIBLIOGRAPHY

Calderón, Roberto. *Mexican Coal Mining Labor in Texas and Coahuila.* College Station: Texas A&M University Press, 2000.

Cuéllar Valdés, Pablo. *Historia de la ciudad de Saltillo* (1975), and *Historia del estado de Coahuila* (1979).

Favret Tondato, Rita. *Tenencia de la tierra en el estado de Coahuila (1880–1987)* (1992).

Jones, Richard. *Ambivalent Journey.* Tucson: University of Arizona Press, 1995.

Pasztor, Suzanne. *The Spirit of Hidalgo: The Mexican Revolution in Coahuila.* Calgary, Canada: University of Calgary Press, 2002.

Robles, Vito Alessio. *Coahuila y Texas, desde la consumación de la independencia hasta el tratado de paz de Guadalupe Hidalgo,* 2 vols. (1945–1946).

Terrazas, Eduardo Enríquez, and José Luis García Valero. *Coahuila: Una historia compartida* (1989).

Terrazas Eduardo Enríquez, and Martha Rodríguez García, comps. *Coahuila: Textos de su historia* (1989).

Villarello Vélez, Ildefonso. *Historia de la revolución mexicana en Coahuila* (1970).

SUZANNE B. PASZTOR

COATEPEQUE, BATTLE OF.

Battle of Coatepeque (22–24 February 1863, near Santa Ana, El Salvador). At Coatepeque, Salvadoran forces under Gerardo Barrios and Liberal Nicaraguans under Máximo Jérez stopped the Guatemalan army of Rafael Carrera. Carrera invaded El Salvador in an effort to crush the Liberal government of Barrios. He occupied Santa Ana with little resistance on 21 February. Hoping to end the war quickly, the next day he marched his troops to Coatepeque without sufficient provision for food and water. Well-entrenched Salvadorans engaged the Guatemalans in a twelve-hour artillery duel on 23 February. On the following day Barrios's forces repulsed the hungry and thirsty Guatemalans. Heavy losses, however, prevented the Liberals from pursuing Carrera, who retreated into Guatemala with only moderate losses. Instead, joined by Honduran forces who entered the war as a consequence of the Liberal victory at Coatepeque, Barrios and Jérez marched into Nicaragua in an unsuccessful effort to take León.

Carrera launched a new, more cautious offensive in June 1863, leading to his capture of San Salvador in October, ending the war. Barrios escaped to La Unión and sailed to Costa Rica.

See also **Barrios, Gerardo.**

BIBLIOGRAPHY

Federico Hernández De León, *El libro de las efemérides*, vol. 5 (1963), pp. 307–312.

Pedro Zamora Castellanos, *Vida militar de Centro América*, 2d. ed. (1967), vol. 2, pp. 193–206.

Additional Bibliography

Gudmundson, Lowell, and Héctor Lindo-Fuentes. *Central America, 1821–1871: Liberalism before Liberal Reform.* Tuscaloosa: University of Alabama Press, 1995.

Leiva Vivas, Rafael. *La unión centroamericana: Utopía, lirismo y desafío.* Tegucigalpa: ENAG, Empresa Nacional Artes Gráficas, 2004.

Woodward, Ralph Lee. *Rafael Carrera and the Emergence of the Republic of Guatemala, 1821–1871.* Athens: University of Georgia Press, 1993.

Yashar, Deborah J. *Demanding Democracy: Reform and Reaction in Costa Rica and Guatemala, 1870s–1950s.* Stanford, CA: Stanford University Press, 1997.

RALPH LEE WOODWARD JR.

COATLICUE.

Coatlicue, Aztec deity, mother of the Mexica patron and war god Huitzilopochtli. Coatlicue is one of a complex of Aztec female supernaturals associated with the earth, reproduction, and sacrificial death. According to myth, Coatlicue (Serpent-skirt) was magically impregnated by a ball of down while sweeping the temple atop the mythical mountain of Coatepec (Serpent Mountain). Her 400 sons and her daughter, Coyolxauhqui, shocked that their mother had become pregnant while engaged in temple service, plotted to murder her and the unborn child. One of the sons revealed the plot to the unborn Huitzilopochtli. After Coatlicue was beheaded by her daughter, Huitzilopochtli burst from the womb armed with the Fire Serpent and vanquished his sister and brothers.

The southern portion of the Great Temple in Tenochtitlán was intended to replicate Coatepec. The colossal stone sculpture of Coatlicue, discovered in 1790, probably originally stood in that temple. A masterpiece of Aztec art, the statue presides over the Mexica Hall of Mexico's National Museum of Anthropology. It depicts the deity dressed in a skirt of intertwined serpents and a necklace of human hearts and hands. Blood flows from her severed neck in the form of two serpents, whose adjoined profiles create a monstrous face.

See also **Aztecs; Mesoamerica.**

BIBLIOGRAPHY

Esther Pasztory, *Aztec Art* (1983).

Bernardino De Sahagún, *Florentine Codex: General History of the Things of New Spain*, bk. 3, translated by Arthur J. O. Anderson and Charles E. Dibble (1978).

Johanna Broda, Davíd Carrasco, and Eduardo Matos Moctezuma, *The Great Temple of Tenochtitlán* (1987).

Inga Clendinnen, *Aztecs: An Interpretation* (1991).

Additional Bibliography

León Portilla, Miguel, and Antonio Valeriano. *Tonantzin Guadalupe: Pensamiento náhuatl y mensaje cristiano en el "Nican mopohua."* México: Colegio Nacional: Fondo de Cultura Económica, 2000.

Read, Kay Almere and Jason J. González. *Mesoamerican Mythology.* New York: Oxford University Press, 2002.

Vera, Luis Roberto. *Coatlicue en Paz: La imagen sitiada: La diosa madre azteca como imagen mundial y el concepto binario de analogía: Ironía en el acto de ver: Un estudio de los textos de Octavio Paz sobre el arte*. Puebla: Benemérita Universidad Autónoma de Puebla, Dirección General de Fomento Editorial, Facultad de Filosofía y Letras, Maestría en Literatura Mexicana, 2003.

LOUISE M. BURKHART

COATZACOALCOS RIVER. Coatzacoalcos River, a relatively small river that drains a basin of 8,448 square miles. It forms on the north slope of the Sierra Atravesada, flows northward across the Isthmus of Tehuantepec, and empties into the Gulf of Mexico near its namesake city. A major tributary, the Jaltepec, rises on the northern side of the Sierra de Oaxaca.

Despite its size, the river always has been important because of its association with transisthmian communications. In 1521 Hernán Cortés sent Gonzalo de Sandoval to explore it as a potential route to the Pacific. During the colonial period, goods were carried by boat to an upriver landing on the Coatzacoalcos and thence overland to Tehuantepec on the Pacific side of the isthmus.

In 1774, the viceroy of New Spain, Antonio María de Bucareli ordered a survey of the isthmus for construction of a canal through the mountains to connect the upper reaches of the Coatzacoalcos with the Pacific. Almost a century later, in 1870, as interest in a U.S. canal developed after the Civil War, Admiral Robert W. Shufeldt surveyed the Coatzacoalcos and recommended that it be built there. Proposals for a railway that would carry fully laden ships across the isthmus were advanced in 1880 (by James B. Eads) and again in the 1940s (by the Mexican engineer Modesto Rolland), but neither of these remarkably ambitious projects got beyond the planning stage.

The earliest petroleum finds on the Gulf side of the isthmus were in 1907, but it was not until additional discoveries were made in the 1970s that the region became an important center of petroleum production. The Coatzacoalcos River is navigable for more than 100 miles and is the port for the city of Coatzacoalcos. Mexico's busiest port, Pajaritos, which serves a massive Pemex complex, is adjacent to the river.

One of the biggest petroleum spills in the Coatzacoalcos River occurred on 22 December 2004; it spread as far as Nanchital, Veracruz. The spill could have been contained, but because of the negligence of the Mexican Petroleum (PEMEX) personnel, the pumping of crude was not suspended even though there was a fire and an explosion at the pumping station at Mazumiapan, 120 kilometers from the spill. The spill of five thousand barrels of crude petroleum contaminated the stream of Tepeyac, the Coatzacoalcos River, and the beaches of Coatzacoalcos and Congregation of Beyond.

See also **Bucareli y Ursúa, Antonio María; Petróleos Mexicanos (Pemex).**

BIBLIOGRAPHY

Coe, Michael D., and Richard A. Diehl. *In the Land of the Olmec*. Austin: University of Texas Press, 1980.

Glick, Edward B. *Straddling the Isthmus of Tehuantepec*, School of Inter-American Studies, Latin American Monograph Series no. 6 (1959).

Tamayo, Jorge L. *Geografía general de Mexico*, 2d ed., vol. 2 (1962), pp. 326–328.

Vergara, Rosalía. "Desastre por imprevisión: Derrame petrolero en río Coatzacoalcos." *Proceso* (January 2005): 28–30.

West, Robert Cooper, ed. *Handbook of Middle American Indians*, vol. 1 (1964), pp. 87–88, 92–93.

JOHN J. WINBERRY

COBÁ. Cobá, an ancient Maya metropolis in central Quintana Roo, Mexico, less than 12 miles from the eastern coast of the Yucatán peninsula. During the eighth century an estimated forty thousand people lived at the site, making it one of the largest urban centers anywhere in Mesoamerica at that time. Cobá, an important trade link between the coast and inland cities, also figures prominently in the traditional Maya histories of the late pre-Hispanic period, with legendary ties to many of the city-states and royal lineages that dominated Yucatán at the time of contact with the Spanish. At the height of its power, this lowland city probably dominated much of the northeastern Yucatán peninsula and competed with other regional centers at Tizimín, Izamal, Uxmal, and Edzna.

Cobá is probably best known for its radiating *sacbeob*, wide causeways that connected the city's monumental core to residential neighborhoods, nearby towns, and more-distant centers up to 60 miles away. At the core of the city were four major pyramid and palace complexes linked by *sacbeob* and dispersed around four large, shallow lakes. Minor temples, the residences of lesser nobility, and countless walled commoners' compounds packed the surrounding urban sprawl, which covered an additional 28 square miles around the core.

Researchers believe that from 600 to 800 CE, Cobá was a diversified city of residential wards and craft guilds at the center of a powerful regional state. By the time the great center of Chichén Itzá (1000–1200 CE) had risen a little more than 60 miles to the east, Cobá had declined to a less important shrine center where the magnificent stelae (with more than thirty carved stone markers depicting male and female rulers holding ceremonial bars) and temples of an earlier age were probably revered and maintained as powerful symbols of the postclassic nobility's links to a more glorious past.

See also **Maya, The.**

BIBLIOGRAPHY

William J. Folan, Ellen R. Kintz, and Laraine A. Fletcher, *Cobá: A Classic Maya Metropolis* (1983).

Linda Manzanilla, *Cobá, Quintana Roo: Análisis de dos unidades habitacionales mayas* (1987).

Additional Bibliography

Evans, Susan Toby. *Ancient Mexico & Central America: Archaeology and Culture History.* London: Thames & Hudson, 2004.

Kintz, Ellen R. *Life under the Tropical Canopy: Tradition and Change among the Yucatec Maya.* Fort Worth, TX: Holt, Rinehart and Winston, 1990.

Paxton, Merideth. *The Cosmos of the Yucatec Maya: Cycles and Steps from the Madrid Codex.* Albuquerque: University of New Mexico Press, 2001.

Robles C., Fernando. *La secuencia cerámica de la región de Cobá, Quintana Roo.* México, D.F.: Instituto Nacional de Antropología e Historia, 1990.

THOMAS W. KILLION

COBO, BERNABÉ (1580–1657). Bernabé Cobo (*b.* 1580; *d.* 1657), Spanish Jesuit scholar of the New World. Father Bernabé Cobo arrived in Lima from Spain in 1599. He spent the rest of his life in different locations in Peru and Mexico, working as a missionary, teacher, and writer. Of the original forty-three books making up his *Historia del nuevo mundo* (History of the New World, finished 1653, published 1890), seventeen are extant. The first fourteen comprise a study of New World natural history and the history of the Incas; the last three treat the foundation of Lima.

Cobo, like other historians of his era, based his writing on personal observations, interviews with native informants, and the chronicles of other Spanish historians. His views on Inca beliefs and practices are highly judgmental, condemning native religion as diabolical. He provides excellent information on many Inca monuments as they were in the early seventeenth century. The *Historia* also contributes to our knowledge of the customs of everyday life in Peru before and after the Conquest. The prose is straightforward and clear, tending toward observation and description rather than interpretation.

See also **Peru: From the Conquest Through Independence.**

BIBLIOGRAPHY

There are two volumes of Cobo's *Historia* in English translation; each one includes two books of the original Spanish manuscript. They also offer short, useful introductions to the author and his work. See Bernabé Cobo, *History of the Inca Empire* (1979) and *Inca Religions and Customs* (1990), both translated and edited by Roland Hamilton.

Additional Bibliography

Millones-Figueroa, Luis. "La historia natural del padre Bernabé Cobo: Algunas claves para su lectura." *Colonial Latin American Research* 12:1 (June 2003): 85–87.

Olmo Pintado, Margarita del. "La historia natural en la Historia del Nuevo Mundo del p. Cobo." *Revista de Indias* 52 (May–December 1992): 795–823.

KATHLEEN ROSS

COBOS, FRANCISCO DE LOS (c. 1477–1547). Francisco de Los Cobos (*b.* ca. 1477; *d.* 10 May 1547), official under King Charles I. The son of an impoverished noble family of Ubeda, Francisco de los Cobos devoted his career to government service. Aided by Lope Conchillos, who in 1507 was given substantial authority over New World affairs,

Cobos's fortunes rose and he ultimately became secretary, and thus a leading adviser, to King Charles I (Emperor Charles V). In the 1520s Cobos served as secretary of a number of councils, including the new Council of the Indies. He remained influential until his death.

Cobos used his position to advance relatives and clients and to build a fortune. He amassed numerous royal favors, including grants from Indies' revenues, and gifts from persons, including the conquistador Hernán Cortés, who sought royal favor. Cobos invested in commerce in the Indies, participating with conquistador Pedro de Alvarado in sending black slaves to Guatemala. To guarantee the perpetuation of his fortune, Cobos established an entailed estate (*mayorazgo*). His career vividly illustrates the rewards available to a trusted servant of the monarch.

See also **Council of the Indies.**

BIBLIOGRAPHY

Hayward Keniston, *Francisco de los Cobos: Secretary of the Emperor Charles V* (1959).

Additional Bibliography

Moreno Mendoza, Arsenio. *Francisco de los Cobos y su época.* Madrid: Electa, 1997.

                                    MARK A. BURKHOLDER

COCAINE. *See* **Drugs and Drug Trade.**

COCHABAMBA. Cochabamba, city and department in Bolivia.

THE CITY
Cochabamba City is the capital of its department and the third largest city in Bolivia. The estimated 2003 population of the city was 559,872, and with its immediate environs, over 800,000. Although its population has more than quadrupled since 1963, it has lost its position as the second largest city of Bolivia to the even faster growing Santa Cruz, in the eastern lowlands.

Cochabamba was founded in 1574 by Sebastián Barba de Padilla, who named it Villa de Oropeza

(Oropesa). In 1783 the name was changed to the Quechua *Kocha-pampa* (eventually *Cochabamba*), meaning "a plain with small ponds." The creator and first president of Bolivia, Simon Bolívar, wanted Cochabamba to be the new nation's capital, but he failed to convince the colonial elite.

The city is located in a fertile valley, about 15 miles long and 6 miles wide at an altitude of 8,400 feet, facing the Tunari range, which in the winter is covered with snow. The valley has a moderate climate, with an average temperature of 66 degrees Fahrenheit. Considered the granary of Bolivia, it produces a variety of fruits, and has considerable herding. Cochabamba has some small industries and an oil refinery. It is an active trade center with a large and colorful weekly market (La Cancha). The University of San Simón has a fine medical school.

Although modernization has destroyed some of the colonial residences, Cochabamba still has a number of architectural treasures, such as the cathedral, the municipal palace, churches, and a cloistered convent with paintings by Goya. There are also notable nineteenth-century buildings, including the mansion of the late tin magnate Simón Patiño, which is now a museum and conference center.

THE DEPARTMENT
One of the nine departments of Bolivia, Cochabamba has sixteen provinces. Under the nation's unitary form of government, the head of the department (*prefecto*) is appointed by the president. Cochabamba is the most centrally located department in Bolivia; it covers 23,300 square miles. In 2003 its population was estimated at 1.6 million, slightly more than triple the number in 1973.

The department has a varied topography. The famous eighteenth-century German naturalist Thaddeus Haenke, author of a classic account of Cochabamba, described the region as a continuous descent from the high peaks of the Andes in the west to the tropical plains in the east, from over 16,000 feet to 500 feet. The western and central parts, the most populated, have large, fertile valleys with a year-round temperate climate. The capital of the department, the city of Cochabamba, is located in the largest valley. In the north is the continuation of the Yungas, subtropical forested valleys that are accessible from La Paz. East of the Cochabamba Valley is the subtropical Chaparé region, which is well suited for the cultivation of coca. Although it is a traditional crop, the increased production of coca since the 1960s, much of it for illegal export, has become a focus of intense controversy and international attention.

The population is heavily Mestizo and Quechua with a Europeanized urban sector. In the rural areas Que- chua is the predominant language. There is a modern airport in the city of Cochabamba. The only railroad link is with the city of Oruro, where it connects with railroads to La Paz (the de facto capital of Bolivia), Argentina, and Chile. An all-weather highway goes to Santa Cruz. All the rivers of the department join the vast eastern Bolivian fluvial system, which connects with the Amazon system.

The main production is agricultural, especially cereals and fruits in the fertile valleys. There is also considerable herding and some small industry, mostly in the city of Cochabamba and its surroundings.

Water is a controversial issue in Cochabamba. The influx of migrants from poor rural communities has taxed municipal resources. More than 40 percent of Cochabamba's population lacks running water. In January 2000 protestors from the city mobilized over the privatization of sanitation services and the municipal water supply, which had doubled or tripled their water bills. The protests later spread to the agricultural sector because the same water company also had concession rights for irrigation water. Ultimately, popular pressure forced the Bolivian government to rescind the contract, but the problems of access to and supply of water continues.

See also **Bolívar, Simón; Bolivia, Agrarian Reform; Drugs and Drug Trade.**

BIBLIOGRAPHY

For both city and department, see Augusto Guzmán, *Cochabamba: Panorama geográfico, proceso histórico* (1972), and *Geografía de Cochabamba* (1978); S. R. L. Viajes Tejada, *Cochabamba: Su belleza y sus riquezas* (1974).

For the city, see José Benito Guzmán, *Crónica de la villa de Oropesa* (1884); José Macedonio Urquidi, *El orígen de "la noble villa de Oropesa,"* Cochabamba (1950); Ricardo Anaya, *La ciudad de Cochabamba* (1959); Fernando Calderón G., *La Cancha: Un gran feria campesina en la ciudad de Cochabamba* (1984).

For the department, see Guillermo Urquidi, *Monografía del departamento de Cochabamba* (1954); Thaddeus Haen- ke, *Taddeo Haenke, su obra en los Andes y la selva boliviana* (1974); Centro De Investigación y Desarrollo Regional, *Monografía del trópico del departamento de Cochabamba* (1990); Humberto Solares Serrano, *Historia, espacio y sociedad de Cochabamba, 1550–1950* (1990).

Fernando, Calderón G., and Alicia M. Szmukler. *La política en las calles: Política, urbanización y desarrollo.* La Paz: Plural Editores 2000.

Goldstein, Daniel M. *The Spectacular City: Violence and Performance in Urban Bolivia.* Durham, NC: Duke University Press, 2004.

Jackson, Robert H. *Regional Markets and Agrarian Transformation in Bolivia: Cochabamba, 1539–1960.* Albuquerque: University of New Mexico Press, 1994.

Larson, Brooke. *Cochabamba, 1550–1900: Colonialism and Agrarian Transformation in Bolivia.* Durham, NC: Duke University Press, 1998.

Ledo García, Carmen. *Urbanisation and Poverty in the Cities of the National Economic Corridor in Bolivia: Case Study, Cochabamba.* Delft, Netherlands: Delft University Press Science, 2002.

Urquidi Zambrana, Jorge E. *La evolución urbana de la ciudad de Cochabamba: A través de ordenanzas y reglamentos municipales 1786–1982: Comentarios.* Cochabamba, Bolivia: Colegio Arquitectos de Cochabamba, 1995.

Vargas, Humberto, Jaqueline Garrido Cortés, and Víctor Calisaya Hinojosa. *Las travesías de la participación ciudadana: Casos de Sucre y Cochabamba.* Cochabamba, Bolivia: FORHUM, 1994.

CHARLES W. ARNADE

COCHASQUÍ. Cochasquí, an important archaeological site in Ecuador located approximately 30 miles north of the capital city of Quito in Pichincha province. Excavated in the mid-1960s by a team of German archaeologists, Cochasquí remains the best studied of a class of sites found in the equatorial Andes comprising earthen mounds, or *tolas* as they are locally known. The distribution of these mound sites is coterminous with the territory of the ethnic group known as the Caranqui, who occupied the northern Ecuadorian highlands at the time of the Spanish invasion. Mound sites in this region date to the late prehistoric period, approximately 1000 to 1500 CE, and represent pre-Columbian centers of political power. Ethnohistoric accounts of the Inca invasion of the Caranqui region suggest that Cochasquí was an important center of local resistance.

The number of *tolas* per site varies greatly, ranging from a few to well over one hundred. At Cochasquí, there may have originally been forty-five mounds, though less than two-thirds of that number still remain. Two basic types of mounds are found at Cochasquí and elsewhere in the region: the round, hemispherically shaped variety and the truncated pyramidal forms, which may or may not have associated ramps. The former range from 20 to 132 feet in diameter and represent both mortuary features and house sites. The largest of the truncated pyramidal mounds at Cochasquí is 264 by 297 feet at the base and 66 feet tall. These quadrilateral mounds are generally thought to have served as house platforms for elite residences and are also often assigned a ceremonial function. The hemispherical habitation mounds tend to predate the quadrilateral mounds, with the construction of the latter thought to signal fundamental changes in the level of sociopolitical organization.

See also **Andes; Archaeology.**

BIBLIOGRAPHY

The primary reference works are those of the German archaeologists who directed excavations: Udo Oberem, *Cochasquí: Estudios arqueológicos* (1981), and Udo Oberem and Wolfgang Wurster, *Excavaciones en Cochasquí, Ecuador, 1964–1965* (1989). Luis Lumbreras, *Cronología arqueológica de Cochasquí* (1990), offers a critical evaluation of the work conducted at Cochasquí and considers the site in its regional context. For a more general study of mound sites in the northern highlands, see J. Stephen Athens, "Ethnicity and Adaptation: The Late Period-Cara Occupation in Northern Highland Equador," in *Resources, Power, and Interregional Interaction,* edited by Edward Schortman and Patricia Urban (1992), pp. 193–219.

Additional Bibliography

Bray, Tamara L. "The Panzaleo Puzzle: Non-Local Pottery in Northern Highland Ecuador." *Journal of Field Archaeology* 22, no. 2 (Summer 1995): 137–156.

Lippi, Ronald D. *Una exploración arqueológica del Pichincha Occidental, Ecuador.* Quito: Pontificia Universidad Católica del Ecuador: Museo Jacinto Jijón y Caamaño, 1998.

Pullas De la Cruz, Virgilio. *Historia hecha en Cangahua: Guia del centro monumental arqueologico y vida socio-cultural de Cochasqui.* Quito: Ediciones Abya-Yala, 1997.

TAMARA L. BRAY

COCHINEAL. Cochineal (*grana cochinilla*), a bright red dye made from the bodies of small insects found on the nopal cactus. The production of cochineal dates to pre-Hispanic times. The Indians of southern Mexico and Guatemala traded cochineal extensively and used it as a dye for textiles. The process of extracting cochineal was extremely tedious and required great skill. It took approximately 25,000 live insects to make one pound of dye, and 70,000 dried ones to make the same amount.

Although indigenous peoples harvested the cochineal insect from wild plants, the Spaniards raised and produced cochineal on commercial estates or *nopalerías*. In pre-Hispanic times, cochineal grew in great quantities in the Mixteca region, in Oaxaca, and around Puebla in Mexico, and these areas continued to be important centers of production after the Conquest. By 1600, Spaniards shipped between 250,000 and 300,000 pounds of Mexican cochineal annually from Veracruz to Spain, where it was usually sold to textile makers in the Netherlands. During the colonial period, cochineal was worked almost exclusively by Indian labor.

The successes of the Mexican cochineal trade encouraged Spaniards in Central America to cultivate the dye, particularly after the profitable cacao market collapsed in the early seventeenth century. In 1611, the arrival of an ambitious governor, the Conde de la Gómera, signaled the beginning of a brief boom in the cochineal industry in Central America. With his encouragement, *nopalerías* appeared in the western highlands of Guatemala, in Totonicapán, Suchitepequez, Guazacapán, and south of Lake Atitlán, as well as throughout northern Nicaragua. The boom lasted until 1621 and then ended abruptly, possibly due to plagues of locusts which ravaged the crop in 1616 and 1618.

After 1621, the production of cochineal was centered almost completely in Mexico, which had always remained the primary producer of the crop. Although a lack of skilled Indian labor hampered the industry's expansion during the seventeenth century, the rich red dye was in such demand by Flemish, Dutch, and English textile weavers that it remained a vital commodity for Mexico throughout the entire colonial period. While the work was dangerous, labor scarcity gave indigenous workers some power in the colonial order, according to recent research. Indeed, the *repartimiento* (distribution or assessment) system, traditionally explained as a way of forcing indigenous communities to buy unwanted goods, actually provided an incentive to keep the laborers producing. This interpretation suggests that the repartimiento was a form of forced credit to keep the labor force motivated. By the early eighteenth century, the growing textile industry in Europe and expanded economic policies under the Bourbon rulers of Spain greatly enhanced cochineal's popularity as an export commodity. In the 1760s, the Portuguese attempted to cultivate cochineal with limited success in Rio Grande de São Pedro and the island of Santa Catarina, but New Spain remained Europe's main supplier of the dye. By the mid-eighteenth century, cochineal had become Mexico's second most valuable export, after silver. It was grown mainly in Oaxaca, where as many as thirty thousand Indians were employed in the industry. Cochineal remained a vital export for Mexico into the nineteenth century, until the international textile industry converted to the use of cheaper synthetic red dyes. Cochineal is now produced in Mexico primarily for use by local artists and craftsmen.

See also **Indigo.**

BIBLIOGRAPHY

William B. Taylor, *Landlord and Peasant in Colonial Oaxaca* (1972).

Murdo J. Mac Leod, *Spanish Central America: A Socioeconomic History 1520–1720* (1973).

Miles L. Wortman, *Government and Society in Central America 1680–1840* (1982).

Michael Meyers and William Sherman, *The Course of Mexican History* (3d ed., 1987).

Richard J. Salvucci, *Textiles and Capitalism in Mexico: An Economic History of the Obrajes* (1987).

Additional Bibliography

Baskes, Jeremy. *Indians, Merchants, and Markets: A Reinterpretation of the Repartimiento and Spanish-Indian Economic Relations in Colonial Oaxaca, 1750–1821.* Stanford, CA: Stanford University Press, 2000.

Cervantes, Mayán. *La grana cochinilla del nopal: Patrimonio cultural y propuesta económica.* Mexico City: Escuela Nacional de Antropología e Historia, 2004.

VIRGINIA GARRARD-BURNETT

COCHRANE, LORD THOMAS ALEXANDER (1775–1860).

Lord Thomas Alexander Cochrane (*b.* 14 December 1775; *d.* 30 October 1860), naval commander in wars for Latin American independence. A member of the Scottish nobility with a distinguished record in the Royal Navy during the Napoleonic Wars, Cochrane came to South America in 1818, at the invitation of the independent Chilean government, which gave him command of its fledgling navy. Consisting of odds and ends of warships and heavily dependent on foreign adventurers for skilled seamen, this force under Cochrane's leadership harassed Spanish-held ports along the Pacific coast and was instrumental in the capture of the key fortress of Valdivia in southern Chile (1820). In 1820 Cochrane convoyed the army of José de San Martín on its way to invade Peru. But he soon quarreled with San Martín over questions of strategy as well as over what he considered inadequate support of his naval forces.

Cochrane's pursuit of Spanish shipping in the Pacific took him as far north as Mexico before he finally returned in 1822 to Chile, where he had an estate. He did not stay there long, for in 1823 he accepted an invitation from the new Brazilian monarchy to head its naval forces in the struggle for independence from Portugal. Once again he had a heterogeneous collection of ships and a large number of foreign sailors, including British seamen whom he induced to desert their own ships. However, when Cochrane sailed against Bahia in mid-1823, the fear inspired by his reputation, quite as much as the forces he commanded, led the Portuguese military entrenched there to depart without a struggle—and Cochrane harassed their fleet all the way to the coast of Portugal. He next helped evict the Portuguese from ports they still held on the north coast of Brazil. In 1825, however, he had a falling out with the Brazilian government and returned to Europe. There he volunteered his services to help in the Greek struggle for independence from Turkey in 1827, and was reinstated in the Royal Navy in 1832.

See also **British–Latin American Relations.**

BIBLIOGRAPHY

Basic sources on Cochrane are his own *Narrative of Services in the Liberation of Chili, Peru, and Brazil from Spanish and Portuguese Domination*, 2 vols. (1859), and his *Autobiography of a Seaman*, 2 vols. (1869). For his Chilean and Peruvian service, see Donald E. Worcester, *Sea Power and Chilean Independence* (1962). His contribution to Brazilian independence is covered in Neill Macaulay, *Dom Pedro: The Struggle for Liberty in Brazil and Portugal, 1798–1834* (1986), chap. 5.

Additional Bibliography

Harvey, Robert. *Thomas Cochrane, 1775–1860: Libertador de Chile, Brasil y Grecia*. Barcelona: Edhasa, 2001.

López Urrutia, Carlos. *Más allá de la audacia: Vida de Thomas Cochrane, Décimo Conde de Dundonald*. Barcelona: Editorial Andrés Bello, 2002.

DAVID BUSHNELL

COCKFIGHTING. *See* Sports.

CÔCO. Côco, a popular northeastern Brazilian form of song and dance of African and Amerindian origin, found especially in Alagoas. *Côco* songs consist of choruses and refrains that are both traditional and improvised. As the name suggests, the earliest *côcos* were work songs of the Afro-Brazilians of Palmares, who would harvest and break coconuts to a rhythmic beat. The form now goes by a variety of names, such as *côco de ganzá, côco de zambê, côco de usina,* and *côco da praia*. It was also danced in the salons of Alagoas and Paraiba under the names *samba, pagode, zambê,* and *bambelô*.

In a common form of the dance, men and women form a circle with a soloist in the center who sings and performs a ritual dance, inviting the next soloist into the center with an *umbigada* (belly bounce) or courteous bow. Most of the instruments driving this lively exchange are percussion, namely *ingonos, cuícas, pandeiros, ganzás,* or wooden boxes.

See also Musical Instruments.

BIBLIOGRAPHY

David P. Appleby, *The Music of Brazil* (1983).

Luis Da Camara Cascudo, *Dicionário do folclore brasileiro,* 5th ed. (1984).

Chris Mc Gowan and Ricardo Pessanha, *The Brazilian Sound: Samba, Bossa Nova, and the Popular Music of Brazil* (1991).

Additional Bibliography

Ayala, Maria Ignez Novais and Marcos Ayala. *Cocos: Alegria e devoção*. Natal: Editora da UFRN, 2000.

Crook, Larry. *Brazilian Music: Northeastern Traditions and the Heartbeat of a Modern Nation*. Santa Barbara, CA: ABC-CLIO, 2005.

Murphy, John P. *Music in Brazil: Experiencing Music, Expressing Culture*. New York: Oxford University Press, 2006.

BERNADETTE DICKERSON

CODAZZI, AGUSTÍN (c. 1793–1859).

Agustín Codazzi (*b.* ca. 12 July 1793; *d.* 7 February 1859), military officer and cartographer. Born in Lugo, on the northeastern coast of Italy near Ravenna, Codazzi was a veteran of the Napoleonic armies and one of the European volunteers who joined Simón Bolívar's troops in the War of Independence. However, his main contribution to both Venezuela and New Granada was as a geographer, by charting the maps of both countries and by actually visiting many unknown territories of both nations. After the war he remained in the Venezuelan Army as a geographer and cartographer for almost three decades.

In 1848, Codazzi became involved in one of the many civil wars between Páez and Monagas. Ending up on the losing side, he was exiled to New Granada, where he was put in charge of the Comisión Corográfica, a group that studied in detail most of the Colombian provinces and territories known and unknown, producing maps and descriptions of the local economies and advising how to build needed roads. Codazzi died in Colombia in a town on the Caribbean coast. The town and the National Geographic Institute of Colombia now bear his name.

See also Cartography: Overview.

BIBLIOGRAPHY

José Manuel Restrepo, *Historia de la Nueva Granada,* Vols. 1, 2 (1952–1963).

Mario Longhena, *Memorias de Agustín Codazzi* (1973).

Additional Bibliography

Antei, Giorgio. *Los héroes errantes: historia de Agustín Codazzi, 1793-1822.* Santafé de Bogotá: Planeta Colombiana Editorial, 1993.

Lovera, José Rafael. "Geografía y política en la naciente Venezuela: Codazzi y la Comisión Corográfica, 1830-1841." *Boletín de la Academia Nacional de la Historia (Venezuela)* 82:326 (April–June 1999): 331–353.

Sánchez, Efraín. *Gobierno y geografía: Agustín Codazzi y la Comisión Corográfica de la Nueva Granada.* Santa fé de Bogotá: Banco de la República, 1999.

JOSÉ ESCORCIA

CODESIDO, JULIA (1883–1979). Julia Codesido was a Peruvian artist. Codesido, known as one of the *indigenistas sabogalinos* (close followers of painter José Sabogal) was born on 5 August 1883, in Lima. As a young girl, she and her family traveled to Europe with her diplomat father. Over the next eighteen years, she was introduced to the great museums and master works of Europe. In 1918 she returned to Peru, and in 1919 she enrolled in the Escuela Nacional de Bellas Artes del Perú, where she studied with Daniel Hernández and later José Sabogal. In 1924 she had her first individual exhibition in the Palacio de Bellas Artes.

Like other *indigenistas*, she aimed at creating a Peruvian school of painting based on the exploration of native themes and the depiction of Andean local scenes and customs. She studied at the National School of Fine Arts, in Lima, where she later taught. In 1935, she visited Mexico to study the muralist movement. After this visit, the influence of Siqueiros became evident in her work.

Codesido abstracted some pictorial elements in her paintings—trees, architecture—although she always stayed within the boundaries of realism.

In 1936, Codesido participated in the First Congress of American Artists, held in New York City. She exhibited in Mexico City and New York (1935 and 1936). When in 1943 Sabogal was relieved of his position as director of the National School of Fine Arts over artistic differences, Codesido resigned in solidarity with him. Subsequently, she dedicated herself to forming, with other members of the *indigenista* movement, a collection of popular art and artisanal work for the National Museum of Peruvian Culture. In 1946 she was named a member of the Instituto de Arte Peruano. She died on 8 May 1979.

See also **Art: The Twentieth Century.**

BIBLIOGRAPHY

Acha, Juan. *Art in Latin America Today: Perú* (1961)

Chase, Gilbert. *Contemporary Art in Latin America* (1970), p. 101.

Codesido, Julia. *Julia Codesido (1938–1979): Muestra antológica.* Lima: Centro Cultural, Pontificia Universidad Católica del Perú, 2004.

Moll, Eduardo. *Julia Codesido, 1883–1979.* Lima: Editorial Navarette, 1990.

MARTA GARSD

CODICES. Codices, a term that is applied to diverse native-style documents produced in the pre-Hispanic and early colonial period by the indigenous peoples of central Mexico, the Mixtecs of southern Mexico, and the Maya of Yucatán. Earlier examples have been discovered, but were too fragile to survive excavation. Most postclassic native books were destroyed by the Spanish, and the extant corpus probably represents a small fraction of the total number produced in the New World.

These documents are mistakenly called codices, although none of the pre-Hispanic books is actually a volume bound on one side of the page. Instead, they are screenfold manuscripts (*amoxtli* in Náhuatl, *tutu* in Mixtec, and *vuh* in Maya) that were painted on strips of animal hide in the highlands and on native paper among the Maya. The strips were cut to the same width, sewn or glued together, and folded in accordion pleats into pages. Pigments were derived from mineral and vegetable sources. Some examples are painted on only one side. When both sides are painted, one side is designated as the obverse and the other as the reverse. Several have protective covers.

The manuscripts have no consistent starting point. Some are read from right to left, some from left to right, and some from the bottom to the top of the page. Genealogical manuscripts are usually read one page at a time, while divinatory information frequently stretches across two or more pages.

A detail of the *Codex Cospi*, one of a small number of surviving pre-Columbian pictorial documents. The *Codex Cospi* is likely of Mixteca-Puebla origin. © WERNER FORMAN/CORBIS

Red or black guidelines divide sections and subjects or establish a meandering reading pattern.

Information is conveyed through conventionalized pictures that illustrate actions, gestures, and rituals; figures of speech; and complex linguistic puns in the indigenous language of a manuscript's patron. Pictographic, ideographic, and phonetic signs may be used in a single document. In Mexican examples, pictorial forms indicate basic outlines of a story or ritual, and the pre-Hispanic reader drew from his or her store of knowledge for details. The Mayan manuscripts also employ extensive hieroglyphic inscriptions. Europeans sometimes added glosses to identify ceremonies or the name of an owner, but frequently these glosses have no relationship to the pre-Hispanic pictorial information.

The codices are an elite art describing dynastic histories of rulers and records of ritual, calendrical, and divinatory matters. Genealogical manuscripts may have been recited to affirm or assert claims of dynasties to territories, while ritual and divinatory manuscripts may have been consulted on less public occasions for their guidance. In the decades

soon after contact, the manuscripts were sent to Europe, presumably as curios to inform various sacred and secular authorities about native books. Their exact New World provenances are generally unknown, and they are named for the collections and libraries in which they have been deposited, or for the family or individuals who owned or made them known to the public.

Written in Náhuatl, Spanish, and Latin, well-known Aztec codices include the *Codex Borbonicus*, treating pre-Conquest and Conquest era calendars, rituals and ceremonies; the *Codex Mendoza* (1541), with dynastic histories, tributes, and records of quotidian Aztec life; the *Florentine Codex*, supervised by the Franciscan Bernardino de Sahagún during the later years of the sixteenth century, consisting of twelve books, with Book Twelve chronicling first contact with the Spanish; and the *Aubin Codex*, narrating the mythical Aztec migration from Aztlán, the arrival in the Valley of Mexico, and subsequent history to the early Conquest period. The *Boturini Codex, Codex Cozcatzin,*

Codex Ixtlixochitl, *Codex Magliabechiano*, and *Codex Osuna* are also of interest to scholars of Aztec culture.

The Borgia Group manuscripts, named for one member of the group, Codex Borgia, also include Codices Vaticanus 3773, Laud, Fejéváry-Mayer, and Cospi. All are concerned with ritual and divinatory matters, including the 260-day ritual calendar, the dispensations of repeating cycles of twenty- and thirteen-day periods, prognostications for auspicious and inauspicious days for traveling, auguries for marriage, and predictions about years with good and lean harvests. They may be deciphered to some extent through information in central Mexican chronicles. Nevertheless, they are not a unified group in style or emphasis. Various provenances have been suggested, but a Mixteca-Puebla origin may be correct for some of them.

The Mixtec manuscripts include Codices *Selden* 3135 (A.2), *Bodley* 2858, *Colombino-Becker* I (two fragments of a single document), *Becker* II, *Sánchez-Solís*, and *Vindobonensis Mexicanus* I. These six are concerned primarily with dynastic histories that describe the marriages, offspring, wars, and occasionally the deaths, of rulers of small city–states in southern Mexico. *Codex Vindobonensis* is a ritual manuscript that describes the beginning of the world, the first performances of rituals, and the establishment of Mixtec territories.

Only four Mayan manuscripts survived the Conquest: the Codices Dresden, Madrid, Paris, and Grolier (the last of which came to light only in 1971). Mayan manuscripts are concerned with ritual and astronomical matters, including tables of the movements of the planet Venus, eclipses, the 260-day count, rituals concerned with rain, agriculture, and prophecies for individual years and larger cycles of time.

See also **Maya, The; Mayan Alphabet and Orthography; Nahuatl.**

BIBLIOGRAPHY

Most of the manuscripts have been published in photographic facsimiles with accompanying commentaries by the Akademische Druck- und Verlagsanstalt of Graz, Austria. See also Karl Anton Nowotny, *Tlacuilolli* (1961); Mary Elizabeth Smith, *Picture Writing from Ancient Southern Mexico* (1973); John Glass, "A Survey of Native Middle American Pictorial Documents," in *Handbook of Middle American Indians* 14 (1975): 3–80; John Glass in collaboration with Donald Robertson, "A Census of Native Middle American Pictorical Manuscripts," in *Handbook of Middle American Indians* 14 (1975): 81–252; Thomas A. Lee, Jr., *Los Códices Mayas* (1985).

Boone, Elizabeth Hill. *Stories in Red and Black: Pictorial Histories of the Aztecs and the Mixtecs*. Austin: University of Texas Press, 2000.

Lockhart, James, ed. *We People Here: Náhuatl Accounts of the Conquest of Mexico*. Berkeley: University of California Press, 1993.

Mignolo, Walter. *The Darker Side of the Renaissance: Literacy, Territoriality, and Colonization*. 2d ed. Ann Arbor: University of Michigan Press, 2003.

JILL LESLIE MCKEEVER-FURST

CODOVILLA, VITTORIO (1894–1970).

The Italian-born Vittorio (also Victorio and Víctor) Codovilla was the principal figure of the Argentine Communist Party (PCA) from the mid-1920s until his death in 1970. Known less as a strong theorist than as a strict enforcer of the Moscow political line, Codovilla has remained a controversial figure for the non-Communist left.

Commonly credited as one of the PCA's principal founders, Codovilla first joined the party's Central Committee in 1921 and, together with Rodolfo Ghioldi, quickly came to dominate the party. Before the end of the decade, Codovilla had become head of the Latin America Bureau of the Communist International, a position from which he intervened in disputes surrounding Peruvian Marxist José Carlos Mariátegui and the Mexican Communist Party's reactions to the presence of the exiled Leon Trotsky in that country. Codovilla traveled to Spain in 1932 as agent Medina of the Comintern, charged with the task of unifying the ranks of the Spanish Communist Party (PCE). With the outbreak of the Spanish Civil War Codovilla played an even greater role in the PCE, working to enforce the demobilization of anarchist and Trotskyist militias in Barcelona and other areas of the Spanish Republic.

Upon his return to Buenos Aires in 1941, Codovilla once again took up the reins of the PCA, making the party a driving force in assembling the Unión Democrática coalition of parties that unsuccessfully challenged Juan Domingo

Perón in the 1946 presidential elections. Though Codovilla tempered the party's stance toward Peronism for the rest of the decade, the PCA supported the 1955 military coup that deposed Perón. In the course of the 1960s, Codovilla embraced the early success of the Cuban Revolution while also working to marginalize Guevarist, New Left, and Maoist currents within the PCA and in the Latin American left more generally. Vittorio Codovilla died in Moscow 15 April 1970.

See also **Communism; Ghioldi, Rodolfo; Mariátegui, José Carlos; Perón, Juan Domingo.**

BIBLIOGRAPHY

Caballero, Manuel. *Latin America and the Comintern, 1919–1943.* Cambridge, U.K., and New York: Cambridge University Press, 1996.

Codovilla, Victorio. *Vigencia y proyección: Breve selección de trabajos.* Buenos Aires: Editorial Fundamentos, 1980.

Dominguez, Pablo. *Victorio Codovilla: La ortodoxia comunista.* Buenos Aires: Capital Intelectual, 2006.

Radosh, Ronald, Mary Habeck, and Grigory Sevostianov, eds. *Spain Betrayed: The Soviet Union in the Spanish Civil War.* New Haven, CT: Yale University Press, 2001.

Ramos, Jorge Abelardo. *El partido comunista en la política argentina: Su historia y su crítica.* Buenos Aires: Editorial Coyoacán, 1962.

JAMES CANE

COE, MICHAEL (1929–). American archaeologist and anthropologist Michael Coe's career spanned more than five decades and produced pathbreaking research in pre-Columbian Mesoamerican studies. Coe was born on March 14, 1929, and after a comfortable Long Island childhood, he attended Harvard University and made his first trip to the Yucatan Peninsula, sparking an interest in Mayan archaeology. Following a post as a CIA operative in the Far East during the Korean War, Coe returned to Harvard for graduate school, engaging in study of the Maya, the Olmecs, and many other early American civilizations. Upon receiving his Ph.D. in anthropology, Coe worked as an assistant professor at the University of Tennessee from 1958 to 1960. Much of his career, however, was spent at Yale University, where he

was a professor and served as the curator of the Peabody Museum of Natural History's anthropology collection from 1968 until his retirement in 1994. Over his career, Coe's work overturned many previously held beliefs about Mesoamerican culture, perhaps most notably the one that Mayan hieroglyphics were actually a writing system. While establishing a reputation as one of the foremost Mayanist scholars of the twentieth century, Coe also did research at archaeological sites across North America, South America, and Southeast Asia. Coe's extensive body of writing on archaeological, anthropological, and ethnohistorical topics also includes a number of popular works for nonspecialist audiences. In addition to his many travels and research passions, Coe and his wife, the late Sofie Dobzhansky, raised five children. As of 2007, Coe was the Charles J. MacCurdy Professor of Anthropology, Emeritus, at Yale University and Curator Emeritus of the Peabody Museum.

See also **Anthropology; Archaeology; Mayan Ethnohistory.**

BIBLIOGRAPHY

Coe, Michael D. *The Maya.* New York: Praeger Press, 1966.

Coe, Michael D. *Final Report: An Archaeologist Excavates His Past.* London: Thames & Hudson Press, 2006.

ALISON FIELDS

COELHO, JORGE DE ALBUQUERQUE (1539–1601/2). Jorge de Albuquerque Coelho (April 23, 1539–1601/2) was the third lord-proprietor of Pernambuco (1582–1601). Albuquerque was born in Olinda in the captaincy of Pernambuco, a younger son of Duarte Coelho Pereira, Pernambuco's first lord-proprietor. He and his older brother, Duarte Coelho de Albuquerque, were sent for their education to Portugal, where Jorge soon gained a reputation for his military skills. In 1560 he accompanied his brother, second lord-proprietor of Pernambuco, to Brazil to deal with Native American threats to the family's captaincy. Albuquerque was placed in charge of the Portuguese offensive. After almost five years of fierce warfare, he managed to remove hostile indigenous peoples from the coastal region south to the Rio São Francisco as well as from much of the fertile interior.

His task completed, he left Recife for Portugal in mid-1565 on the 200-ton *Santo Antônio*, never to return to the land of his birth. This four-and-a-half-month voyage, described by the sixteenth-century historian Frei Vicente do Salvador in his *História do Brasil* as "one of the worst and most dangerous seafarers had seen," was the subject of a famous Portuguese shipwreck narrative. By 1601 an account written by Afonso Luís had gone through at least two printings of a thousand copies each.

After recovering from the effects of the voyage, Albuquerque served at the court of young King Sebastian I. In 1574 he was a participant in the first of that monarch's two expeditions to North Africa. Wounded badly and captured, he and his brother were among the eighty nobles ransomed at great expense. He was back in Portugal by 1579. His brother, however, died in 1581 in Morocco on the journey home. Permanently crippled, Albuquerque officially succeeded him as lord-proprietor of Pernambuco in 1582.

By the mid-1580s, because of revenues from his captaincy, Albuquerque was considered one of the wealthiest of those men who gained their riches from Portuguese America. His captaincy of Pernambuco continued to prosper, especially from sugar. In 1591 a crown official reported that there were sixty-three sugar mills in that captaincy and tithes of 28,500 cruzados. Albuquerque encouraged the religious life of the captaincy and was generous to the Franciscans, the Benedictines, and the Carmelites. He was, however, an absentee lord-proprietor, and in his absence there were charges of corruption. From 1593 to 1595 a visitor from the Inquisition was stationed in Olinda, taking testimony from the inhabitants. In 1595 the English pirate James Lancaster seized Recife, sacking the port for several months before sailing on. As a result, Albuquerque suffered great financial losses as well as the loss of confidence of Pernambuco's inhabitants in the security of their port city.

After the death of his first wife, Albuquerque married the daughter of Dom Alvaro Coutinho, commander of Almourol in Portugal. From this union there were two sons. The first, born in 1591, was Duarte de Albuquerque Coelho, who became fourth lord-proprietor of Pernambuco and author of *Memorias diarias de la guerra del Brasil* (1654), the

eyewitness account of the early years (1630–1638) of the struggle against the Dutch in Pernambuco. The second, Matias de Albuquerque, born in 1595, later became *capitão-mor* of Pernambuco and governor-general of Brazil. Jorge de Albuquerque Coelho died in Lisbon and was buried in the Church of São Nicolau.

See also **Coelho Pereira, Duarte.**

BIBLIOGRAPHY

Boxer, Charles R. "Jorge d' Albuquerque Coelho: A Luso-Brazilian Hero of the Sea, 1539–1602." *Luso-Brazilian Review* 6, no. 1 (Summer 1969): 3–17.

Boxer. Charles R., ed. and trans. *Further Selections from the Tragic History of the Sea, 1559–1565.* Cambridge, U.K.: Published for the Hakluyt Society at the University Press, 1968. See Boxer's translation of "Shipwreck Suffered by Jorge d'Albuquerque Coelho, Captain and Governor of Pernambuco" (pp. 108–157) and his useful introduction to the subject (pp. 12–21).

Dutra, Francis A. "Notas sobre a vida e morte de Jorge de Albuquerque Coelho e a tutela de seus filhos." *Studia* 37 (December 1973): 261–286. Contains new information on the lord-proprietor's life and death.

Vicente, do Salvador Frei. *História do Brasil, 1500–1627,* 5th ed. São Paulo: Edições Melhoramentos, 1965.

FRANCIS A. DUTRA

COELHO, PAULO (1947–). Born into a middle-class Rio de Janeiro family, the Brazilian author Paulo Coelho has become a worldwide cultural and marketing phenomenon. Before selling 65 million copies of his books—translated into fifty-eight languages in more than 150 countries—in less than two decades, Coelho led a turbulent and adventurous young life. He was three times a patient at a mental institution, a heavy drug addict, a practitioner of black magic, an anarchist community leader, and a political prisoner. He also became, in his twenties, a shrewd and successful pop music lyricist in partnership with the iconoclastic Raul Seixas, Brazil's legendary rock star. At the age of thirty and relatively wealthy, Coelho had studied various religions and converted to Catholicism while traveling around the world. He soon started his bestselling, award-winning literary career. Whether his books (from *The Pilgrimage*, 1987, to

Eleven Minutes, 2003) belong in the categories of self-help and esoterica, as many critics say (some of them with explicit disdain), or of literature and philosophy, as scores of award referees and the author himself claim, all of them speak of mysticism, mystery, magic, self-reliance, and personal redemption through spiritual faith.

See also **Literature: Brazil.**

BIBLIOGRAPHY

Arias, Juan. *Paulo Coelho: Confessions of a Pilgrim.* New York: HarperCollins, 2001.

Maestri, Mário. *Por que Paulo Coelho teve sucesso.* Porto Alegre, Brazil: Age, 1999.

Pons, Pedro. *Paulo Coelho: su obra, pensamiento, filosofía y enseñanza.* Geroma, Spain: Tikal, 1999.

DÁRIO BORIM

COELHO NETO, HENRIQUE (1864–1934).

Henrique Coelho Neto (*b.* 21 February 1864; *d.* 28 November 1934), Brazilian writer. Born in Caxias, in the state of Maranhão, he was a prolific novelist as well as a journalist, essayist, short-story writer, and playwright. Some of his chief novels are *Miragem* and *O rei fantasma*, both published in 1895, *Inverno em flor* (1897) and *A capital federal* (1893). His principal work, *Turbilhão*, was published in 1906. He is best known for his narratives, in which he employed many innovative literary techniques for which Brazilian letters would become known following the introduction of its modernist movement to the world during Modern Art Week, held in São Paulo in 1922. His work, however, is classified as premodernist, for it exhibits many Parnassian and symbolist characteristics. He also proposed a return to Brazilian nationalistic themes and sentiments. In fact, according to critics, Coelho Neto spoke vehemently against the modernist direction Brazilian letters was taking during the last years of his life. Coelho Neto also had an active political career. He was a public lecturer, and in 1909 he was elected as a federal deputy. He was subsequently reelected to two more legislatures. In addition, he occupied several diplomatic and other government posts. In 1926, he was elected president of the Brazilian Academy of Letters.

See also **Literature: Brazil.**

BIBLIOGRAPHY

Claude Hulet, *Brazilian Literature*, vol. 2 (1974).

Assis Brasil, *O livro de ouro da literatura brasileira* (1980).

Lemuel A. Johnson, "The *Romance Bárbaro* as an Agent of Disappearance: Henrique Coelho Neto's *Rei Negro* and Its Conventions," in *Voices from Under: Black Narrative in Latin America and the Caribbean,* edited by William Luis (1984).

Additional Bibliography

Daniel, Mary L. "Coelho Neto revisitado." *Luso-Brazilian Review* 30:1 (Summer 1993): 175–180.

ROSÂNGELA MARIA VIEIRA

COELHO PEREIRA, DUARTE (late fifteenth century–1553 or 1554).

Duarte Coelho Pereira was the first lord-proprietor of Pernambuco (1534–1553 or 1554). Coelho was one of the most important figures in sixteenth-century Brazil; he established a strong Portuguese foothold there. The circumstances surrounding Coehlo's birth and early career are shrouded in mystery. It is known, however, that he was the illegitimate son of a certain Gonçalo Coelho and that a brother, João de Azevedo, was a priest and chaplain. In 1509 Coelho joined an armada going to India under the leadership of Dom Fernando Coutinho. During the next twenty years, Coelho's actions in the Far East earned him praise and mention in almost all the chronicles of the period. He also amassed an immense fortune that later served him well in his efforts to colonize Brazil. In 1521 he was made a *hidalgo* in the king's household. Sometime around 1529 he arrived back in Portugal. After a diplomatic mission to France in 1530, Coelho returned to Portugal by late April or early May of 1531 and shortly thereafter was named *capitão-mor* of the annual armada sent to the African fortress of São Jorge da Mina. On the return voyage he rendezvoused in the Azores with ships arriving from India. Later in the year 1532 he was again in charge of an armada, this one on coast guard duty along the Malagueta coast. On this voyage Coelho captured a French galleon. Toward the end of January 1533 he and his armada were ordered to the Azores to await that year's armada from India. He was back in Portugal by the end of July or early August 1533.

By 1534 Coelho was married to Dona Brites de Albuquerque, niece of Jorge de Albuquerque, twice captain of Malacca and a former comrade-in-arms. In that year he was one of twelve men awarded captaincies in Brazil. Because of his exploits in Asia and as one of King João III's most trusted and dependable military men, Coelho received on 10 March 1534 the choicest grant of land in Brazil: a sixty-league territory with fertile soil, a good port, previous settlement, and proximity to Portugal. Roughly the area from the Rio São Francisco northward to the southern banks of the Rio Igaraçu (including all of present-day Alagoas and most of Pernambuco), the grant came with a vast number of powers and privileges. On 24 September 1534 the king issued Coelho's *foral* (charter), a statement of the obligations of the donatário (lord-proprietor) and his settlers. Like the other lords-proprietor, Coelho was granted extensive administrative, fiscal, and judicial powers by the crown in exchange for settling and defending at his own cost the land granted him.

Early in 1535, with his wife and her brother, Jerôanimo de Albuquerque, plus a good-sized armada of personnel and supplies, Coelho left Lisbon for Pernambuco. The lord-proprietor took firm hold of his captaincy and brought it order and prosperity by leading the fight against the hostile local population as well as French interlopers and by providing the blueprint for a stable agrarian colony.

Even though brazilwood had been the region's most important product before the era of the captaincies and continued to play a major role during the first lord-proprietor's lifetime, it was soon supplanted by sugar as the chief money crop. Exactly when the first sugarcane was planted in Coelho's colony is not known, but by April 1542 the lord-proprietor was reporting to the king that much cane had been planted and that a large sugar mill was almost ready for operation. At the same time, Coelho requested permission to import black slaves from Guiné (Guinea). Eight years later, in 1550, there were five *engenhos* (sugar mills) in use and many others under construction. Thus, in less than twenty years, Coelho had set his captaincy on a path of agro-industrial development that it would follow for the remainder of the Portuguese colonial era and well into the national period of Brazilian history.

Coelho, who had been granted his own coat of arms in 1545, reacted strongly to the crown's program in 1548 to cut back on donatarial prerogatives and establish a system of royal and centralized government in Brazil. As he informed King João III in 1550: "All the people of this Nova Lusitania were and are very much upset with these changes" (Dutra 1973, p. 438). In mid-1553 or 1554 Coelho returned a second time to Portugal to plead his case personally but died shortly after his arrival. He was buried in the tomb of Manuel de Moura in Lisbon's church of São João da Praça. He left as his heirs two teenage sons, Duarte Coelho de Albuquerque and Jorge de Albuquerque Coelho, who succeeded him as second and third lords-proprietor of Pernambuco.

See also **Albuquerque, Matias de; Brazil: The Colonial Era, 1500–1808; Brazilwood; Coelho, Jorge de Albuquerque; João III of Portugal; Sugar Industry.**

BIBLIOGRAPHY

Dutra, Francis A. "Duarte Coelho Pereira, First Lord-Proprietor of Pernambuco: The Beginning of a Dynasty." *The Americas* 29, no. 4 (1973): 415–441. Uses new archival material.

Mello, José Antônio Gonsalves de, and Cleonir Xavier De Albuquerque, eds. *Cartas de Duarte Coelho a el rei.* Recife, Brazil: Imprensa Universitária, 1967. The best edition of Duarte Coelho Pereira's correspondence.

Mota, A. Teixeira da. *Duarte Coelho, capitão-mor de Armadas no Atlântico (1531–1535).* Lisbon: Junta de Investigacões do Ultramar, 1972.

Porto, José da Costa. *Duarte Coelho.* Rio de Janeiro: Ministério da Educação e Cultura, Serviço de Documentação, 1961.

Saldanha, Antônio Vasconcelos. *As capitanias o regime senhorial na expansão ultramarina portuguesa.* Funchal, Brazil: Secretaria Regional do Turismo, Cultura e Emigração: Centro de Estudos de História do Atlântico, 1992. An important newer work on the *donatarios* (lords-proprietors) of Portuguese America (as well as other parts of the Portuguese Empire).

FRANCIS A. DUTRA

COFFEE, VALORIZATION OF (BRAZIL).

Valorization of (Brazil) Coffee, the government's efforts to prop up (valorize) the price of coffee by reducing the world supply. The first valorization

(1906–1914) was occasioned by an unusually large crop that threatened to decimate coffee prices. The governors of São Paulo, Minas Gerais, and Rio de Janeiro agreed to reduce production and remove coffee stocks from the market. The valorization did not raise coffee prices, but it successfully prevented prices from falling further, since Brazil controlled 80 percent of world coffee production.

The success of the first program convinced the federal government to finance another valorization program in 1917, when coffee prices again slumped. Undertaken only with Brazilian funds, it enjoyed great success because a severe frost in 1918 reduced production and ended the threat of glut. The last stocks were sold off two years later. In 1921 the federal government along with São Paulo intervened again to prevent low prices. European and U.S. lenders and exporters provided the funds to sustain prices until 1924.

In the 1920s São Paulo, Rio de Janeiro, and Minas Gerais established state institutes to finance and regulate coffee's flow to market. In 1931 the new government of President Getúlio Vargas created the National Coffee Council (changed to the National Department of Coffee in 1933) to control coffee marketing and financing. This arrangement was effective as long as Brazil produced most of the world's coffee, but after the late 1920s its share declined. In 1946 the Brazilian government signed the Inter-American Coffee Agreement to stabilize prices within the Americas through a quota system. This program was expanded to producers in the rest of the world in 1962 with the signing of the International Coffee Agreement, which made coffee one of the most closely state-controlled commodities in the world. The agreement remained in effect until 1989, when Brazil abandoned it in a dispute over quotas and at the same time, abolished the National Department of Coffee. The next year Brazil lost its place as the world's leading coffee producer to Colombia, though it subsequently regained its preeminence.

See also **Coffee Industry.**

BIBLIOGRAPHY

Carlos Manuel Pelaez, "Análise econômica do programa brasileiro de sustentação do café, 1906–1945," in *Revista Brasileira de Economia* 25, no. 4 (1971): 5–211.

Thomas Holloway, *The Brazilian Coffee Valorization of 1906: Regional Politics and Economic Dependence* (1975).

Antônio Delfim Netto, *O problema do café no Brasil*, 2d ed. (1979).

Steven Topik, *The Political Economy of the Brazilian State, 1889–1930* (1987).

Additional Bibliography

Teixeira de Oliveira, José. *História do café no Brasil e no mundo*. Rio de Janeiro: Barléu Edições, 2004.

Perissinotto, Renato M. "Estado, capital cafeeiro e crise política na decada de 1920 em Sao Paulo, Brasil." *The Hispanic American Historical Review* 80, no. 2 (May 2000): 299–332.

STEVEN TOPIK

COFFEE INDUSTRY. The coffee industry is a major economic activity of several Latin American countries, with consequent influence on patterns of land use, population distribution, and social relations. Native to northeast Africa, coffee was introduced into the Caribbean and the Guianas in the eighteenth century, but it became a major commercial crop only in the nineteenth century, as demand grew in Europe and North America and transportation technology connected remote producing areas to seaports. Coffee requires a frost-free, temperate climate with well-distributed rainfall and fairly rich soils—conditions met by the interior uplands of southeast Brazil as well as the highland areas of Colombia, Central America, southern Mexico, and the larger Caribbean islands. While it is a perennial shrub with a normal life span of twenty to forty years, yields can vary markedly from one year to the next. Aggregate world demand changes only slowly, but abrupt fluctuations in supply, and consequently prices, make coffee a risky business. Nations heavily dependent on coffee for foreign exchange earnings and government revenue have gone through cycles of boom and bust, mitigated somewhat since World War II by a series of international coffee agreements intended to regulate production levels and even out price swings.

In Brazil coffee replaced sugar as the most important export by 1830, holding that position until superseded by soybeans in about 1980. When leaf-rust disease decimated coffee groves in Ceylon

Harvesting coffee beans. A worker separates green and ripe coffee beans, Comasagua, El Salvador, 2004. Although coffee production fell from 50 percent of El Salvador's gross domestic product in 1988 to only 3.5 percent in 2002, the rise of speciality coffees such as these has allowed Salvadorean coffee farmers some measure of recovery. ROBERTO ESCOBAR/AFP/GETTY IMAGES

and Java in the 1870s, Brazil became the world's primary producer. Coffee spread south and west from Rio de Janeiro, with African slaves providing the labor force on large plantations. That pattern extended into western São Paulo with the construction of railroads connecting the port of Santos to the interior. In the late 1880s, during a decade of high prices and rapid growth, European immigrants replaced slaves as the mainstay of the labor force in São Paulo, just before the final abolition of slavery in 1888. In the first two decades of the twentieth century, Brazil produced three-quarters of the world's coffee, with the state of São Paulo accounting for fully half the world's supply. A bumper crop in 1906 of 20 million 132-pound bags, the highest recorded in Brazil for many years, prompted a government program of price supports and market controls that became a recurring feature of Brazilian coffee policy. During the 1930s

such policies included the purchase and destruction of large quantities in the face of depressed world prices. The coffee trade brought mass immigration from Europe, high government revenues, and complementary economic activity—all fundamental in the eventual emergence of São Paulo as South America's largest industrial center.

Colombia first exported small quantities of coffee in 1835, and by the early twentieth century was exporting about 500,000 bags per year (at a time when Brazilian exports averaged some 12 million bags annually). The formation of the National Federation of Coffee Growers in 1927 institutionalized a system whereby the coffee of many medium and small farms was marketed through what became a powerful political and financial organization controlling the country's principal export. By specializing in higher-quality varieties and astute marketing, Colombia's production expanded steadily after

World War II, so that by the 1980s the aggregate value of its coffee exports rivaled that of Brazil (whose large internal market absorbs about half of its total production).

Cultivation began in the highland areas of Central America also in the nineteenth century, as newly consolidating national elites encroached on indigenous village lands through privatization laws and usurpation, and many formerly autonomous peasants were forced or drawn into the labor force of the new export sector. German planters and trading firms were important from the 1870s to World War I in some areas of Guatemala and Chiapas, Mexico. Costa Rica's coffee sector, like that of Colombia, has had a greater proportion of small and medium-sized producing units than was the case in Guatemala and El Salvador, where larger plantations have been the norm. Although coffee became dominant in the profile of exports in several countries, none rivaled Brazil in total production, and the vagaries of Brazil's annual crop continued to influence world price levels. Since World War II, production in central Africa also expanded, led by Ivory Coast, Uganda, and Kenya, so that by the 1980s Latin America accounted for 55 to 60 percent of world exports, down from nearly 90 percent in the early 1900s.

Since the 1980s, increased competition from African and Asian producers has brought down the prices paid to growers. One of the ways coffee estates have combated low prices is through specialization and quality. The fair trade movement, an effort to guarantee workers a fair wage and producers a fair price, has brought a higher premium and better quality. Increasingly, coffee marketers are creating brands based on the unique qualities of coffees grown in particular regions.

See also **Coffee, Valorization of (Brazil); Colombia, Organizations: National Federation of Coffee Growers.**

BIBLIOGRAPHY

Bergad, Laird. *Coffee and the Growth of Agrarian Capitalism in Nineteenth-Century Puerto Rico* (1983).

Bergquist, Charles. *Coffee and Conflict in Colombia* (1986).

Fisher, Bart S. *The International Coffee Agreement: A Study in Coffee Diplomacy* (1972).

Holloway, Thomas H. *Immigrants on the Land: Coffee and Society in São Paulo, 1886–1934* (1980).

Palacios, Marco. *Coffee in Colombia, 1850–1970* (1980).

Roseberry, William. *Coffee and Capitalism in the Venezuelan Andes* (1983).

Stein, Stanley. *Vassouras, a Brazilian Coffee County, 1850–1900* (1957).

Wickizer, Vernon D. *The World Coffee Economy, with Special Reference to Control Schemes* (1943).

Winson, Anthony. *Coffee and Democracy in Modern Costa Rica* (1989).

Thomas H. Holloway

COFRADÍA.

COFRADÍA. Cofradía, a religious sodality, also known as a confraternity. The *cofradía* was an ecclesiastical institution of the laity based on the veneration of a specific image or religious attribution, such as the Blessed Sacrament (*Santísimo Sacramento*), Saint Peter, or the Virgin Mary. The *cofradía* was popular among all racial and caste groups, although the individual sodalities were not ethnically integrated. The institution provided spiritual security and collective identity through common acts of piety, such as sponsoring processions, celebrations, and masses. At the very minimum it was a burial society in which members paid dues to offset the costs of burial. The very largest and wealthiest *cofradías* owned large tracts of land and controlled vast amounts of capital. Among native communities the *cofradía* came to form part of a civil-religious hierarchy in which males in the community would advance by assuming a series of increasingly important offices in the *cofradía* and municipal government during the course of their life. In Spanish and mixed communities the *cofradía* often came to serve as an extension of the guild, or Gremio, fostering social cohesion and reinforcing common values.

See also **Brotherhoods; Catholic Church: The Colonial Period.**

BIBLIOGRAPHY

Asunción Lavrín, "La Congregación de San Pedro: Una cofradía urbana del México colonial, 1640–1730," in *Historia Mexicana* 29 (1980): 562–601.

Richard Greenleaf, "The Inquisition Brotherhood: *Cofradía de San Pedro Mártir* of Colonial Mexico," in *The Americas* 40 (1983): 171–208.

Additional Bibliography

Guerra, Manuel Patricio. *La Cofradía de la Virgen del Pilar de Zaragoza de Quito*. Quito: Ediciones Abya-Yala, 2000.

Hernández Soto, Carlos. *Kalunga eh!: Los Congos de Villa Mella*. Santo Domingo: Editorial Letra Gráfica, 2004.

Luque Alcaide, Elisa. *La Cofradía de Aránzazu de México, 1681-1799*. Pamplona: Ediciones Eunate, 1995.

Martínez de Sánchez, Ana María. *La Cofradía del Carmen en la Iglesia de Santa Teresa de Córdoba*. Córdoba: Prosopis Editora, 2000.

Meyers, Albert and Diane Elizabeth Hopkins, eds. *Manipulating the Saints: Religious Brotherhoods and Social Integration in Postconquest Latin America*. Hamburg: Wayasbah, 1988.

Molina, Alonso de., Barry D. Sell, Larissa Taylor, and Asunción Lavrin. *Nahua Confraternities in Early Colonial Mexico: The 1552 Nahuatl Ordinances of Fray Alonso de Molina, OFM*. Berkeley: Academy of American Franciscan History, 2002.

Rodríguez Gonzalez, Ana Luz. *Cofradías, capellanías, epidemias y funerales: Una mirada al tejido social de la Independencia*. Bogotá: Banco de la República: El Ancora Editores, 1999.

JOHN F. SCHWALLER

COHEN PLAN. Cohen Plan, an Integralist Party forgery that alleged plans for a Communist overthrow of the Brazilian government. The Cohen Plan was used to justify the imposition of the Estado Novo. The plan, "discovered" in September 1937, was actually authored by a Brazilian Army captain, Olympio Mourão Filho, head of the Integralist propaganda section.

The fictitious plan was passed to army chief of staff and Getúlio Vargas confidant General Góes Monteiro. It became public on September 29 when War Minister Eurico Dutra, while speaking on a national radio program, urged a renewal of previous national emergency decrees. This request was overwhelmingly approved by Congress. The Cohen Plan was widely accepted by the press and the public as legitimate, and its publication was followed by an executive decree that suspended many of the personal rights granted by the Constitution of 1934.

The "Cohen" part of the plan's title was deliberately chosen to create a linkage between Judaism and communism, a false linkage, but one held to be true by many associated with the Vargas regime. According to Mourão Filho, he originally signed the document with the name of the Hungarian Communist Bela Kun as a joke. Later, he recalled, "I remembered that one of our leaders always referred to Kun as Cohen [so I] crossed out the surname Kun and wrote Cohen." The forgery, when released, appeared to be authorized by the nonexistent Cohen, presumably a Jew and a Communist.

See also **Vargas, Getúlio Dornelles.**

BIBLIOGRAPHY

Levine, Robert. *The Vargas Regime: The Critical Years, 1934–1938* (1970), esp. pp. 138–158.

Trindade, Helgio. *Integralismo: O fascismo brasileiro na década de 30* (1979).

Silva, Hélio, Maria Cecília Ribas Carneiro, and José Augusto Drummond, *A ameaça vermelha: O Plano Cohen* (1980).

Rose, R. S. *One of the Forgotten Things: Getúlio Vargas and Brazilian Social Control, 1930–1954*. Westport, CT: Greenwood Press, 2000.

Williams, Daryle. *Culture Wars in Brazil: The First Vargas Regime, 1930–1945*. Durham, NC: Duke University Press, 2001.

JEFFREY LESSER

COICOU, MASSILLON (1867–1908). Massillon Coicou (*b.* 9 October 1867; *d.* 15 March 1908), Haitian writer. Coicou became secretary of the cabinet of President Tirésias Sam in 1897. He later served as secretary and chargé d'affaires of the Haitian legation in Paris from 1900 to 1903. Several of his plays were produced in Paris, and he became known in literary circles. Several volumes of his poetry were also published in Paris. After returning to Port-au-Prince, Coicou founded the journal *L'oeuvre*. He taught philosophy at the Lycée Pétion from 1904 on and founded the Théâtre Haïtien during this period. After becoming involved in clandestine opposition to President Nord Alexis, Coicou was arrested and summarily executed with his two brothers and eight other persons.

Coicou was the author of numerous plays—tragedies, comedies, and one-act plays—most of them unpublished. The historical drama *Liberté* (produced in Haiti, 1894; in Paris, 1904), on the Haitian revolution, was highly praised by Parisian reviewers. While his surviving dramas have been criticized for weak structuring, Coicou was a master of French versification, and his poem "L'alarme" was memorized by most Haitian secondary students.

See also **Theater.**

BIBLIOGRAPHY

Poésies nationales (1892); *Impressions* (1903); *Passions* (1903); *Poésies nationales* (1904); *La noire* (novel, published in the newspaper *Le soir*, 1905); *L'empereur Dessalines* (drama, 1906); and *Le génie français et l'âme haïtienne* (essay, 1904).

See also Naomi M. Garret, *The Renaissance of Haitian Poetry* (1963), pp. 35–37; Robert Cornevin, *Le théâtre haïtien des origines à nos jours* (1973), pp. 110–115; F. Raphaël Berrou and Pradel Pompilus, *Histoire de la littérature haïtienne illustrée par les textes*, vol. 1 (1975), pp. 423–492.

Additional Bibliography

Gaillard, Roger. *Le grand fauve (1902-1908)*. Port-au-Prince, Haïti: R. Gaillard, 1995.

CARROL F. COATES

COIMBRA, UNIVERSITY OF.

The University of Coimbra is the oldest university in the Iberian world. It dates from 1288, when the church established a school known as the Studium Generale in Lisbon. It received its charter of incorporation from King Diniz and Pope Nicholas IV in 1290. Frequent quarrels between the students and the townspeople over the high costs of lodging and food led the king to move the university to the quieter surroundings of Coimbra. By 1308, when King Diniz issued the charter at Coimbra, the university offered degrees in canon and civil law, medicine, and grammar. In the Middle Ages the university moved back and forth between Coimbra and Lisbon until it was established permanently in Coimbra by the end of the fifteenth century.

At the end of the thirteenth century the Studium Generale was a simple school little more advanced than the previous episcopal and monastic schools. Its first curriculum included the study of arts, grammar, and logic. Later, chairs of medicine, physics, philosophy, and theology were added. Faculties of law included the study of both civil and canon law and Roman law. In the Middle Ages the university was small, with never more than two dozen professors. Elite males of all ages attended; a large percentage of them were clergymen.

The university conferred degrees through the archbishop or vicar. In addition to the bachelor's degree (which required three years of study), there were also licentiate and doctorate degrees. To acquire a licentiate, the student had to follow a course of study for seven to nine years, undergo examinations, and pay expensive fees. The title "doctor" required public examinations and a costly ceremony only the wealthy could afford. Clerical students usually were subsidized by the church.

In the Middle Ages Portuguese students had preferred to travel to Paris for their university educations, but due to religious disputes with the French the Portuguese court revived learning at home. In 1537 the university was reestablished at Coimbra, where it undertook the teaching of law, rhetoric, mathematics, theology, medicine, grammar, and Greek. Ten years later a college of arts was established to teach Latin and philosophy. It was headed by Andre de Gouveia who brought teachers from Paris and Bordeaux. In 1548 the school's enrollment rose to 1,200, and by 1550 it was 1,500. In 1555 King João III turned the school over to the Jesuits.

The Enlightenment brought a backlash against Jesuit teaching methods that favored scholasticism over the natural sciences, and when the Marques of Pombal became prime minister he expelled the Jesuits in 1759. He reorganized the curriculum of study by adding faculties of mathematics and natural science, tore down an old castle and added new buildings, including laboratories, a natural history museum, a botanical garden, and an observatory. He proposed new courses in legal history, church history, and biblical exegesis. New professors were brought in from Italy. By the end of the eighteenth century metallurgy and hydraulics were taught at the university.

Because there was no university in Brazil until the twentieth century, many colonial Brazilians were educated at the University of Coimbra. In the sixteenth century, the missionaries José de

Anchieta (1534–1597) and Manuel da Nóbrega (1517–1570) did their training at Coimbra for civilizing the native peoples of Brazil. In the eighteenth century the revolutionary changes sweeping Europe influenced the Coimbra's Brazilian students, instilling a nationalistic spirit.

After the expulsion of the Jesuits, Coimbra was the only university in Portugal until 1911. Coimbra is one of the oldest university cities in Europe. For many centuries it was the intellectual and spiritual center of Portugal.

See also **Anchieta, José de; Education: Overview; Jesuits; João III of Portugal; Nóbrega, Manuel da; Pombal, Marquês de (Sebastião José de Carvalho e Melo).**

BIBLIOGRAPHY

Boxer, Charles R. *The Portuguese Seaborne Empire*. New York: Knopf, 1969.

Brandão, Mário, and Manuel Lopes d'Almeida. *A Universidade de Coimbra—esboço da sua história*. Coimbra, Portugal: Por Ordem da Universidade, 1937.

Diffie, Bailey. *Latin American Civilization*. Harrisburg, PA: Stackpole, 1945.

Livermore, Harold Victor. *A New History of Portugal*. Cambridge, U.K.: Cambridge University Press, 1966.

Marques, A. H. de Oliveira. *Daily Life in Portugal in the Middle Ages*. Madison: University of Wisconsin Press, 1971.

Payne, Stanley G. *A History of Spain and Portugal*, 2 vols. Madison: University of Wisconsin Press, 1973.

PATRICIA A. MULVEY

COINAGE (COLONIAL SPANISH AMERICA).

With gold and silver dominating the export economy of the Spanish Indies, not surprisingly, the minting of gold and silver coins became a significant colonial enterprise. Apparently, the first coins appeared in Española in 1497—crude gold specie fashioned in Santo Domingo as a convenience for the growing population and trade on the island. As the Spanish presence expanded in the Caribbean and elswhere, so too did the stamping of gold coins in Santo Domingo. In fact, by 1520 over 14,000 kilograms of gold in bars and specie reached Seville from the Indies. Moreover, until about 1535, the standard monetary unit in the Indies was the *peso de oro*, also called a *castellaño* or *peso de minas*, with a value of 450 *maravedís*, a weight of 4.6 grams, and a fineness of 22.5 carats, or one-fiftieth of a mark (*marco*) of gold.

In 1535, with the successful conquest of Mexico, Peru, and New Granada, Charles I ordered the founding of mints (*casas de moneda*) in Mexico City, Lima, and Santa Fe de Bogotá. Set up ten years later at Potosí was a Temporary mint, which functioned until a permanent structure was erected in 1572. In Mexico the first coins issued by the Casa de Moneda in 1536 were gold *pesos de tupuzque*, valued at 272 maravedís. Appearing in 1537, the first silver peso (also called the *peso fuerte*, *patacón*, *duro*, or piece of eight by the English), became a standard monetary unit in the Indies for the next three centuries. Royal edicts also called for the minting of silver coins of a quarter, half, one, two, three, four (*tostones*), and eight reales, in addition to the peso. The two-real coin was the most commonly used.

Pesos of eight reales oscillated in size between 33 and 40 millimeters. Although they varied somewhat in their inscriptions, during the sixteenth and seventeenth centuries most coins were circular, with one side depicting castles and lions, separated into four parts by a cross, and carrying an inscription of the value of the coin. On the reverse side were two columns representing the pillars of Hercules with the inscription *plus ultra* in the middle; on the edge were the name of the monarch in Latin and a name or letter designating the site of the mint—*M* for Mexico, *L* for Lima, *P* for Potosí, and so forth.

Until the seventeenth century coins were fashioned crudely by stamping pieces of silver bars (*trozos*) with a round-mold hammer, but the coins were seldom perfect circles or of the proper weight or fineness. By 1600, however, better technology, more precise assay methods, and more stringent oversight of mint empresarios by royal officials established the Spanish American piece of eight as one of the most reliable monetary units in the world. In fact at the end of the sixteenth century, merchant contracts in faraway Turkey often specified payment in pesos of Potosí.

Despite the spate of gold discovered or seized during the early years of the Conquest, silver quickly replaced gold as the only metal being minted in

Mexico, Lima, and Potosí. In the late sixteenth and seventeenth centuries, only the gold coins of Spain circulated in these placs, at least until 1675, when Charles II once again authorized mintage of gold. In New Granada, however, where gold output vastly overshadowed silver production, crude gold coins stamped in Bogotá or Cartagena and gold dust circulated as a means of exchange in the sixteenth century. By 1627 Turillo de Yebra, a royal treasurer in Bogotá, had begun minting both gold and silver coins, an enterprise which continued in New Granada through the Wars of Independence.

The wide variety of specie circulating in Spain and the Indies during the sixteenth and seventeenth centuries led to the establishment of imaginary monetary units of account to ensure reduction of the myriad currencies to a single common denominator. For this purpose the crown used the maravedí with a real valued at 34 maravedís, a peso of eight reales at 272 maravedís, and a *peso de oro* at 450 maravedís. In Peru and Upper Peru the *peso ensayado* of 450 maravedís was another common, imaginary unit of account which existed until about 1735. This imaginary *peso ensayado* reflected the traffic in silver bars valued at 2,250 maravedís from which 5 pesos of 450 maravedís could be coined. Still another imaginary monetary unit used primarily in the sixteenth century, the *ducado,* or ducat, valued at 375 maravedís, provided another conversion unit more convenient than the tiny maravedí. Unlike Spain, where copper coins called *moneda de vellón* circulated widely in various denominations of maravedís, no copper money or maravedís were coined in America, preserving the integrity of the *peso de ocho* and reales both in the Indies and worldwide.

Despite the continual debasement or devaluation of the currency in Spain, the Hapsburgs did not pursue a similar policy in the Indies. From 1535 to 1728 the piece of eight was valued at 272 maravedís, had a silver content of 25.561 grams, and weighed 27.468 grams. In 1728, however, Philip V lowered the silver content to 24.809 grams. Then later in 1772, Charles III decreased it still further to 24.433 grams, and finally in 1786 to 24.245 grams. Thus, the fine silver content of a peso decreased by about 5 percent over the course of the eighteenth century, or expressed another way, the amount of fine silver contained in one *peso de ocho* was 0.9306 from 1535 to 1728, 0.9167 from 1728 to 1772, 0.9028 from 1772 to 1786, and 0.8958 from 1786 to 1825.

At the same time the Bourbon regime began reducing the silver content of American coins, it transformed the mintage system in the Indies. Bourbon monarchs set up new mints in Santiago de Chile, Guatemala, Guanajuato, Guadalajara, and Popayán. Later, during the Wars of Independence, *casas de moneda* emerged in Mexico at Durango and Zacatecas and at Cuzco in Peru. Moreover, throughout the Indies, private mint operators, formerly supervised by royal assayers and treasury officials, gave way to royal control and management of all mint activity.

In another reform, the Crown also ordered mintage of new coins with ridged edges and with the bust of the king inscribed on the specie. Although silver specie was issued in the same denominations as before, the Bourbon bureaucracy hoped that the new silver coins with the ridged edges would stop the practice of shaving or clipping. In Bogotá and Popayán, mint officials began stamping gold *escudos* of eight, four, two (*doblón*), or one *escudo* (*escudo sencillo*). At the same time, mints at Potosí, Lima, and Mexico City increased their output of gold coins. In still another move to tighten metropolitan control of colonial coinage in the late eighteenth century, mint officials in the Indies were required to send samples of their coins to Spain every six months for inspection and assay.

During the Wars of Independence (1808–1825) royal *casas de moneda* continued to operate, at least until they fell to rebel forces, but mint activity declined sharply. In 1812 the mint in Lima, for example, coined 3,876,000 pesos (456,000 marks) of silver and 575,000 pesos (4,228 marks) of gold; in 1821 the same Casa de Moneda minted approximately 476,000 pesos (56,000 marks) of silver and 272,000 pesos (2,000 marks) of gold. In Mexico in 1808 various mints stamped almost 25 million pesos in silver coins and a bit over 1 million pesos in gold; in 1821, however, mint output amounted to only 5,600,000 pesos in silver and 300,000 pesos in gold, evidence of the devastation wrought by the struggle for independence.

See also **Charles I of Spain; Mining: Colonial Spanish America.**

BIBLIOGRAPHY

Humberto Burzio, "El 'peso de oro' hispanoamericano," in *Historia* 1, no. 4 (1956): 9–24, and "El 'peso de plata' hispanoamericano," in *Historia* 3, no. 12 (1958): 21–52.

A. M. Barriga Villalba, *Historia de la Casa Moneda*, 2 vols. (1969).

Julio Benavides M., *Historia de la moneda en Bolivia* (1972).

Manuel Moreyra Paz Soldán, *La moneda colonial en el Perú* (1980).

Additional Bibliography

Beltrán Martínez, Antonio. *Introducción al estudio de la moneda hispanoamericana*. Zaragoza: Gobieno de Aragón, Departamento de Educación y Cultura, 1997.

Gilboy, Frank F. *The Milled Columnarios of Central and South America: Spanish American Pillar Coinage, 1732 to 1772*. Regina: Prairie Wind Pub., 1999.

Menzel, Sewall H. *Cobs, Pieces of Eight and Treasure Coins: The Early Spanish-American Mints and their Coinages, 1536–1773*. New York: American Numismatic Society, 2004.

Proctor, Jorge A. *The Forgotten Mint of Colonial Panama: A Look into the Production of Coins in America during the 16th Century and Panama's Spanish Royal House for Minting Coins*. Laguna Hills: Jorge A. Proctor, 2005.

JOHN JAY TEPASKE

COLEGIO DE MÉXICO. The Colegio de México is a prestigious institution of higher education in Mexico City. Its origins go back to the Casa de España en México, created by a presidential decree of Lázaro Cárdenas in 1938 to receive Spanish Republican artists, scientists, and intellectuals in the face of imminent Republican defeat in the Civil War. The first members of the Casa were three Spaniards who were already in Mexico: Luis Recaséns Siches, León Felipe, and José Moreno Villa. The first to arrive from abroad were José Gaos, Enrique Díez-Canedo, Juan de la Encina, Gonzalo Lafora, Jesús Bal y Gay, Adolfo Salazar, Isaac Costero, and Agustín Millares Carlo. Membership implied a salary, a requirement to give talks and courses, and a possibility of publishing. In 1940 the Casa de España was transformed into the Colegio de México to guarantee its continuity. The first president, Alfonso Reyes, who was familiar to the cultural elite in Spain ever since his decade in Madrid (1914–1924), continued in office. Reyes guided the early

growth of the institution and continued to lead it until his death in 1959. His principal collaborator was Daniel Cosío Villegas, named initially as secretary and, after Reyes's death, president until 1963. Conceived initially as a space for research, the Colegio de México gradually became a center for both research and teaching in the humanities and the social sciences. Since 1976 the institution has been housed in a striking modern building in the south of the capital. In the 1950s Reyes had the shrewd idea of offering grants to young writers (among them, Luis Cernuda, Octavio Paz, Juan Rulfo, Juan José Arreola, and Tomás Segovia). The Colegio always had a close relationship with the state publishing house, the Fondo de Cultura Económica, founded by Cosío Villegas in 1934. The first centers dedicated to research and teaching were the Centro de Estudios Históricos, created in 1941; Estudios Sociales, in 1943; and Estudios Filológicos (now the Centro de Estudios Lingüísticos y Literarios), in 1948. The first and third of the preceding centers coexist in the early twenty-first century with five others: Estudios Internacionales, Estudios Económicos; Estudios Sociológicos; Estudios de Asia y Áfricap; and Estudios Demográficos, Urbanos y Ambientales. The prestige of the Colegio de México can be measured by the quality of its staff and graduates, by its contributions to problems of knowledge, and by some of the great publishing ventures that established new paradigms, including the ten volumes of the *Historia moderna de México* (1955–1972) or the five volumes of the *Cancionero folklórico de México* (1975–1985). The institution received international attention through its journals, the first of which were the *Nueva revista de filología hispánica* (from 1947), *Historia mexicana* (from 1951), and *Foro internacional* (from 1960). Since the late twentieth century, it has undergone moderate growth and a deep process of internationalization.

See also **Reyes Ochoa, Alfonso.**

BIBLIOGRAPHY

Lida, Clara E. *La Casa de España en México*. Mexico City: Colegio de México, 1988.

Lida, Clara E., and José A. Matesanz. *El Colegio de México: Una hazaña cultural, 1940–1962*. Mexico City: Colegio de México, Centro de Estudios Históricos, 1990.

Zoraida Vázquez, Josefina. *El Colegio de México: Años de expansión e institucionalización, 1961–1990.* Mexico City: Colegio de México, Centro de Estudios Históricos, 1990.

ANTHONY STANTON

COLEGIO MILITAR (ARGENTINA).

The Colegio Militar (Military Academy) trains the future officers of the Argentine army. Brief attempts to consolidate its foundations had been made since 1810, but difficulties surrounding the process of national organization prevented this from happening. Once the disputes between Buenos Aires and the interior provinces had been resolved in 1862, the national state began to take shape, thus allowing for the creation of the National Military Academy in 1869 as part of the "modernization" program promoted by President Domingo F. Sarmiento (1811–1888). The first director of the academy was Colonel Juan F. Czetz (1822–1904), an Argentine of Hungarian background.

Officer training was increasingly inspired by the German model. Nationalism based on territorial identity and conservative values rooted in Catholicism were also decisive influences. The ideological orientation of the Colegio Militar was not far removed from the view that the armed forces was the ultimate guardian of the nation, over and above even the nation's constitution.

Key changes in the organization and orientation of the Colegio Militar took place after the Falkland Islands (Islas Malvinas) War in 1982. The collapse of the military dictatorship of 1976 in 1982 forced the armed forces to democratize its ranks. In the early twenty-first century, the Colegio Militar allows women to enroll on equal terms with men, and it also serves as a university-level institute.

See also **Sarmiento, Domingo Faustino.**

BIBLIOGRAPHY

García Enciso, Isaías José. *Historia del Colegio Militar de la Nación.* Buenos Aires, Círculo Militar, 1970.

Potash, Robert. *El Ejército y la política en la Argentina.* Buenos Aires, Sudamericana, 1994.

Sarni, Miguel Angel. *Educar para este siglo.* Buenos Aires, Dunken, 2005.

VICENTE PALERMO

COLEGIO NACIONAL DE BUENOS AIRES.

Colegio Nacional de Buenos Aires, a secondary school established on 14 March 1863 as part of president Bartolomé Mitre's policy for improving public instruction. Its five-year program of studies was developed under the minister of justice and public instruction, Eduardo Costa. The curriculum consisted of humanities and letters (languages and literature), moral sciences (philosophy and history), and natural sciences (mathematics and science). The school occupied the site of the early Jesuit headquarters in Argentina. Its prestigious location, only a few blocks from the central Plaza de Mayo and bounded by Alsina, Bolívar, Moreno, and Peru streets, was the site of several previous schools, including Colegio Máximo de San Ignacio (1767), the Colegio Convictorio y Universidad Máxima de San Carlos (1768), Real Colegio de San Carlos (1783), and Real Colegio de la Unión del Sur (1817). In 1821 the new Universidad de Buenos Aires had opened on this site.

The Colegio's first rector in 1863 was Eusebio Agüero. Later that year he was replaced by Amadeo Jacques, who served until his death in 1865. In 1911 Argentine president Roque Sáenz Peña placed the Colegio under the administration of the Universidad de Buenos Aires as the Colegio Nacional Central. From 1919 to 1945 it was called Colegio Nacional San Carlos. In 1945 it returned to the name Colegio Nacional de Buenos Aires. During the military dictatorship of 1976–1983, the Colegio suffered severe political repression. The government fired professors and "disappeared" 105 students.

The Colegio remains one of the most prestigious secondary schools in Argentina. It has produced many prestigious alumni, including two Nobel laureates, presidents of the republic, and world-renowned musicians.

See also **Education: Overview.**

BIBLIOGRAPHY

Diego Abad De Santillán, ed., *Gran enciclopedia Argentina,* vol. 2 (1951), pp. 330–331. For additional facts on the early history of the school, see Ione S. Wright and Lisa M. Nekhom, *Historical Dictionary of Argentina* (1978).

Garaño, Santiago, and Werner Pertot. *La otra juvenilia: Militancia y represión en el Colegio Nacional de Buenos Aires, 1971–1986.* Buenos Aires: Editorial Biblos, 2002.

Zago, Manrique, and Fernando Alonso, eds. *El Colegio Nacional de Buenos Aires.* Buenos Aires: Manrique Zago Ediciones, 1995.

JAMES A. BAER

COLÉGIOS (BRAZIL).

COLÉGIOS (BRAZIL). Colégios (Brazil), literally "schools," a term that refers to a range of secondary educational institutions in Brazil, from the earliest times to the present. During the first two centuries of colonization, the Jesuits, who held almost a monopoly over education, established eleven *colégios,* stretching from Pará to São Paulo. The teaching comprised classes on the humanities (but with the native Indian language in place of Greek), philosophy, mathematics, and, in Salvador and Rio de Janeiro, theology. In the eighteenth century, the Oratorians also held classes in Bahia and Pernambuco, but the episcopal seminaries in Rio de Janeiro (1739) and Minas Gerais (1750) were the only new institutions that could properly be called *colégios.* All the Jesuits' activities, however, collapsed in 1759, when the Marquês de Pombal expelled the order from the realm and began a far-reaching educational reform. The buildings of the *colégios* were neglected, and they were replaced by a small number of *aulas régias* (royal classes) throughout the territory. Ecclesiastics retained a strong influence on education, however, and in 1800 a new episcopal seminary was founded at Olinda. Conceived after the reform of Coimbra University by Pombal, it was intended to train a skilled colonial elite to share in the administration of the overseas dominions. *Aulas avulsas* (loose classes, each conducted by a different teacher at a different address) and private tuition continued to flourish. But the Olinda Seminary represented a return to a systematic educational policy and became an important model for the *colégios* of the first half of the nineteenth century. In 1821 Lazarist priests created the Colégio do Caraça in Minas Gerais. A few years later Pernambuco became the first province to have its public *colégio,* the Liceu Pernambucano (1826).

With the Additional Act (1834), the provinces were granted authority over local educational matters, but it was an enterprise from the central government that looms largest in this period. The imperial Colégio Pedro II (1837) was designed to be the exemplar for Brazilian secondary education and to provide the nation with bureaucrats.

Moreover, it proclaimed to the local elites the primacy of Rio de Janeiro as the intellectual capital of an empire beset by regional strife. The intent of secondary education, however, remained above all to prepare students for matriculation in the law, medical, and engineering schools that had been created since 1827. In this objective, private institutions, which enjoyed their golden age between 1860 and 1890, were much more successful than the public, provincial *colégios* and normal schools. Among the former, some established prominent reputations, such as the Colégio do Dr. Kopke, Colégio Briggs, Colégio Abilio, and the Externato (half-day school) Aquino, all in the Rio de Janeiro area. Besides the Colégio do Caraça, which was then in full bloom, the Benedictines founded a *colégio* in Rio de Janeiro (1858), and the Jesuits regained a role in the educational field, although they were not as prominent as before. Even a few Methodist and Presbyterian *colégios* were created.

Colégios for women were rare, and only in the last quarter of the century did coeducational institutions emerge. With the republic (1889), a large-scale educational reform was undertaken, but it was unable to change the narrow scope of secondary education in Brazil.

See also **Education: Overview; Jesuits.**

BIBLIOGRAPHY

Fernando De Azevedo, *A cultura brasileira,* 4th ed. (1964).

Laerte Ramos De Carvalho, "A educação e seus métodos," and Maria José Garcia Werebe, "A educação," in *História geral da civilização brasileira,* edited by Sérgio Buarque de Holanda and Pedro Moacyr Campos, vol. 2, 3d ed. (1973), pp. 78–87, and vol. 6, 2d ed. (1974), pp. 366–383.

Manoel Da Silveira Cardozo, "The Modernization of Portugal and the Independence of Brazil," in *From Colony to Nation* (1975), by A. J. R. Russell-Wood, pp. 185–210.

José Ricardo Pires De Almeida, *História da instrução pública no Brasil, 1500–1889,* translated by Antonio Chizzotti (1989).

Additional Bibliography

Lopes, Eliane Marta Santos Teixeira, Luciano Mendes de Faria Filho and Cynthia Greive Veiga. *500 anos de educação no Brasil.* Belo Horizonte: Autêntica, 2000.

Niskier, Arnaldo. *Educação brasileira: 500 anos de história.* São Paulo: FUNARTE: Ministerio de Culutra, 2001.

LÚCIA M. BASTOS P. NEVES
GUILHERME PEREIRA DAS NEVES

COLLOR, LINDOLFO (1890–1942).

Lindolfo Collor (*b.* 4 February 1890; *d.* 21 September 1942), Brazilian statesman. Born in Rio Grande do Sul of German descent, Collor received a pharmacy degree in 1909, but his first professional endeavors involved journalism and literature. His career in politics began when Antônio Augusto Borges De Medeiros, virtual dictator of Rio Grande, asked him to direct the state Republican Party newspaper in 1919. Thereafter, Collor rose rapidly in Riograndense politics and entered congress in 1925. After fellow Riograndense Getúlio Vargas was defeated for the presidency in 1930, Collor participated in the October revolution of that year, a movement which overthrew the Constitution of 1891. One of the first acts of Vargas's provisional government was to create a labor ministry, headed by Collor.

Collor legalized those unions approved by the labor ministry, which could also intervene in their internal operation. In addition, he introduced the so-called two-thirds law, which required that two-thirds of the work force of all industrial enterprises be Brazilian nationals. He also set up conciliation boards to settle labor disputes, regulated working conditions of women, and established a minimum wage.

Collor's labor system has expanded and survived all the regimes since 1930. Fundamentally corporative, it was also eclectic, inspired by Catholic social doctrine (though Collor was Protestant), the welfarism of Uruguayan José Batlle y Ordoñez, the Comtian paternalism of Julio de Castilhos, and Vargas's new commodity syndicates in Rio Grande.

Collor resigned his ministry in 1932, protesting Vargas's continuing dictatorship, and remained an opponent of his former colleague. A grandson, Fernando Collor De Mello, became president of Brazil in 1990 but resigned at the end of 1992 following impeachment.

See also **Brazil: Since 1889.**

BIBLIOGRAPHY

John W. F. Dulles, *Vargas of Brazil* (1967), pp. 1–116.

Joseph L. Love, *Rio Grande do Sul and Brazilian Regionalism, 1882–1930* (1971), chaps. 10–11.

Edgard Carone, *A república nova (1930–1937)* (1974), pp. 98–151.

Rosa Maria Barboza De Araujo, *O batismo do trabalho: A experiencia de Lindolfo Collor* (1981): Israel Beloch and Alzira Alves De Abreu, eds., *Dicionário histórico-biográfico brasileiro, 1930–1983* (1984), pp. 2142–2151.

Additional Bibliography

Costa, Licurgo. *Ensaio sobre a vida de Lindolfo Collor.* Florianópolis, Santa Catarina: Editora Lunardelli, 1990.

Weinstein, Barbara. *For Social Peace in Brazil: Industrialists and the Remaking of the Working Class in São Paulo, 1920-1964.* Chapel Hill: University of North Carolina Press, 1996.

JOSEPH L. LOVE

COLLOR DE MELLO, FERNANDO AFFONSO (1949–).

Fernando Affonso Collor de Mello, president of Brazil from 1990 to 1992, was born on 12 August 1949, in Rio de Janeiro. His father, Arnon de Mello, was a journalist, senator, and governor of Alagoas. His mother, Leda Collor de Mello, was the daughter of Lindolfo Collor, who served as minister of labor in the first administration of Getúlio Vargas. After attending the Padre Antônio Vieira, São Vicente de Paulo, and São José schools in Rio de Janeiro, in 1966 he transferred to the Centro Integrado de Ensino Médio (CIEM) in Brasília. He studied economics at the University of Brasília, then attended the Federal University of Alagoas, and returned to Brasília to obtain a degree in social communication. In his youth, Collor was an avid athlete and attained a black belt in karate. In 1975, Collor married Celi Elizabeth Monteiro de Carvalho, with whom he had two sons. They divorced in 1981, and the following year he married Rosane Malta, a member of a prominent family from Alagoas and manager of Rosane Enterprises.

In 1979, the National Renovating Alliance (ARENA), a government party, named Collor mayor of Maceió, where he served until 1982, when he was elected federal deputy by the Social Democratic Party (PDS). After changing his party affiliation to the Brazilian Democratic Movement Party (PMDB), he was elected governor of Alagoas (1987–1989). As governor and an outspoken critic of then president José

Sarney, he attracted national attention for his anti-corruption measures aimed at public servants who received exorbitant salaries, often without working full time. Collor fought against powerful sugar-mill owners who refused to pay their debts to the state bank, Produban, which was eventually closed by the federal government.

Rejected by the PMDB, Collor launched his presidential campaign almost single-handedly, preaching the need for a crackdown on political corruption and promising a clean, efficient government. For months he remained third in the national polls, but eventually began to take the lead. In November 1989, among twenty-one candidates, he received the highest number of votes during the first round of elections, and he went on to the second round in a two-way contest against Luís Inácio (Lula) da Silva. On 17 December 1989, Collor was elected president with 43 percent of the vote to Lula's 38 percent. At age forty, he became the youngest president in Brazilian history.

During his inauguration speech, Collor declared that the federal government could no longer continue to subsidize a bloated bureaucracy. Breaking with Sarney's Cruzado Plan II, the newly elected president announced economic policies of austerity and cutbacks. In May 1991 he revamped his economic team and formulated new economic policies signaling a greater flexibility in negotiations with international banks. In the spring of 1992, Collor again made major ministerial changes. During that year, Brazil hosted the United Nations Conference on Environment and Development (Earth Summit), which won praise from the international community. By that time, however, the president had become the target of corruption charges. Following Collor's impeachment by the Chamber of Deputies, Vice President Itamar Franco was named acting president on 2 October 1992. Collor was officially removed from office by the Senate on 29 December and was charged with corruption in June 1993.

He was eventually acquitted of any wrongdoing due to lack of evidence. His only punishment was an eight-year ban on holding public office in Brazil. This did not dissuade Collor from maintaining his involvement in Brazilian politics, however, and in 1998 he sought to run in the presidential election. A federal court upheld the ruling suspending his political rights. In 2000 he tried to run for mayor of São Paulo, but the courts again declared his candidacy invalid. That same year his wife Rosane was convicted of corruption and sentenced to eleven years in prison on charges of embezzling money from a charity in her care during her husband's time in office. In 2002 Collor was able to reenter politics and ran unsuccessfully for governor of Alagoas. In 2006 he was elected to the senate, representing Alagoas.

See also **Alagoas; Brazil, Political Parties: National Renovating Alliance (ARENA); Corruption.**

BIBLIOGRAPHY

Conti, Mario Sergio. *Notícias do Planalto: A imprensa e Fernando Collor*. São Paulo: Companhia das Letras, 1999.

Isto é Senhor, 27 December 1989.

Mendes, Candido. *Collor: Anos-luz, ano zero*. Rio de Janeiro: Editora Nova Fronteira, 1993.

Rosenn, Keith S., and Richard Downes, eds. *Corruption and Political Reform in Brazil: The Impact of Collor's Impeachment*. Coral Gables, FL: North-South Center Press, 1999.

Schneider, Ronald M. *Order and Progress: A Political History of Brazil* (1991).

Zaverucha, Jorge. *Frágil democracia: Collor, Itamar, e os militares, 1990–1998*. Rio de Janeiro: Civilização Brasileira, 2000.

IÊDA SIQUEIRA WIARDA

COLL Y TOSTE, CAYETANO (1850–1930).

Cayetano Coll y Toste (*b.* 30 November 1850; *d.* 19 November 1930), Puerto Rican physician, politician, historian. Born in Arecibo, Puerto Rico, Coll y Toste was educated in both Puerto Rico and Barcelona, Spain. Although he practiced medicine and wrote articles in that field, Coll y Toste is best known for his historiographical contributions. After retiring from the practice of medicine, he wrote numerous biographies of distinguished Puerto Ricans, compiled legends, and published the *Boletín histórico de Puerto Rico*, a multivolume collection of documents on the island's history. In 1913 he was given the title of official historian of Puerto Rico. Coll y Toste died in Madrid, Spain.

See also **Puerto Rico.**

BIBLIOGRAPHY

Biographical sketches of Coll y Toste appear in Adolfo De Hostos, *Diccionario histórico bibliográfico comentado de Puerto Rico* (1976), pp. 275–277; Isabel Cuchí Coll, Introduction to *Puertorriqueños ilustres* (1978); Donald E. Herdeck, ed., *Caribbean Writers: A Bio-Bibliographical-Critical Encyclopedia* (1979).

OLGA JIMÉNEZ DE WAGENHEIM

COLMÁN, NARCISO (1876–1954).

Narciso Colmán (*b.* 1876; *d.* 1954), Paraguayan poet and anthologist. Born in poor circumstances in the interior town of Ybytymí, Colmán relocated to Asunción in the late 1880s to study at the Escuela Normal. In search of better opportunities, he went to Buenos Aires, where for several years he worked as a telegraphist for the Argentine National Railways. He finally returned to Paraguay in 1901 to assume the post of chief telegrapher with the postal administration, and spent a good part of the rest of his life in that position and in various juridical posts.

Colmán's true interest, however, lay in developing a public interest in Guaraní, the native Indian language of Paraguay. He collected folklore in the *campo* (countryside) and popularized it for the generation of the 1920s and 1930s. Writing under the pen name Rosicran, he published his own poetry in Guaraní, including *Ocara Poty* (Wild Flowers), in two volumes, and, more important, *Ñande Ypy Cuera* (Our Forefathers), an evocation of Guaraní myths. In many ways, Colmán could take credit for rescuing Guaraní from the ignominy to which it had been relegated by Paraguayan writers who worked exclusively in Spanish and who, disdaining the Indian tongue, produced simple imitations of European styles.

See also **Guaraní (language).**

BIBLIOGRAPHY

William Belmont Parker, *Paraguayans of To-Day* (1921), pp. 212–214.

Rafael Eladio Valázquez, *Breve historia de la cultura en el Paraguay* (1980), pp. 259–260.

Additional Bibliography

Micó, Tomás L. *Leyendas del Paraguay: Mitología guaraní.* Asunción, Paraguay, 1998.

Romero, Roberto A. *Narciso R. Colmán. El poeta de los guaraníes.* Asunción, Paraguay: Editorial Ñandereko, Misión de Amistad, 1991.

THOMAS L. WHIGHAM

COLOMBIA

This entry includes the following articles:
FROM THE CONQUEST THROUGH INDEPENDENCE
SINCE INDEPENDENCE

FROM THE CONQUEST THROUGH INDEPENDENCE

Spanish discovery of Colombian territory began in 1499, when Alonso de Ojeda, accompanied by Juan de la Cosa and possibly Amerigo Vespucci, sailed the northern shores of South America from Guyana to the Guajira Peninsula. In 1500 Rodrigo de Bastidas mounted another voyage to that area, known as Tierra Firme. With Juan de la Cosa he sailed from Cabo de la Vela to the Gulf of Urabá, thus traversing virtually the entire length of Colombia's Caribbean shoreline. They left Urabá with a cargo of treasure looted from the local indigenous population, and the prospect of taking gold and slaves lured further expeditions to the region in the years that followed. Juan de la Cosa returned in 1505, capturing indigenous peoples for slaves at Cartagena, raiding native settlements on the Sinú coast, and seizing towns at Urabá and Darién before sailing back to Hispaniola.

In 1508 Ojeda and Cosa joined in another expedition, this time with a view to establishing a settlement at Cartagena. Repelled by a native attack that killed Cosa and many others, Ojeda moved west to the Gulf of Urabá, where he established Spain's first permanent settlements in Colombian territory. The first was at San Sebastián de Urabá, founded in 1510. It was quickly superseded by Santa María de la Antigua, based on the Amerindian town of Darién on the western side of the Gulf of Urabá, which the Spaniards took over. For a time Santa María was the main base for exploration in Tierra Firme; when it was abandoned in 1524, Spanish settlement had spread to other points on the coast, all of which were to act as springboards for conquest and colonization in the interior. One was on the Isthmus of Panama, in the land known to Spaniards as Castilla del Oro (Golden Castile); another was at Santa Marta, founded by Bastidas in 1526; a third was Cartagena de Indias, established by Pedro de Heredia in 1533. Settlements in Panama were to be stepping stones to the Pacific and thus to western Colombia and Peru; those at Santa Marta and Cartagena became bases for exploring and conquering the Colombian interior.

Spanish exploration of the interior began in earnest after Francisco Pizarro's conquests of Peru in 1533. Excited by the possibility of finding new riches in the lands between the Caribbean coast and Peru, bands of adventurers entered Colombia's interior from several directions. Penetration from the south was spearheaded by Sebastián de Belalcázar, the conqueror of Quito. In 1535, his agents, Pedro de Añasco and Juan de Ampudia, entered the Pasto region and passed into the Cauca Valley; they were shortly followed by Belalcázar, who founded Cali in 1536 and Popayán in 1537.

After briefly returning to Quito, Belalcázar reentered Colombian territory in 1538 and from Popayán headed northward along the Magdalena River toward the Eastern Cordillera. There, in 1539, Belalcázar converged with other Spaniards who had entered the interior from the north and had discovered the rich and populous lands of the Chibchas. These expeditions came from two bases on the northern coasts. The first, led by Gonzalo Jiménez de Quesada, started out from Santa Marta in October 1536 and found the rich Chibcha civilization in the mountains of Colombia's Eastern Cordillera. In April 1537 Quesada entered the main Chibcha town of Bogotá, extracted a large booty in gold and emeralds from the inhabitants, and claimed the surrounding territory for Spain, calling it the Nuevo Reino de Granada (Kingdom of New Granada) after his native city. The other expedition that entered Chibcha lands from the north came from Coro in Venezuela and was led by the German Nicholas Federmann. Federmann's arrival coincided with Belalcázar's, and in March 1539 the two leaders joined with Jiménez de Quesada to found Santa Fe de Bogotá; they also pooled their forces to strengthen the Spanish presence in the area and agreed to have the crown adjudicate their conflicting claims to rights of conquest.

Meanwhile, Spaniards at Cartagena and Urabá were active in exploring central and western Colombia. From 1534, Pedro de Heredia ranged over the Sinú and Ayapel regions, ransacking indigenous peoples' tombs for gold; in 1535, he mounted an expedition southward on the river Atrato, an initiative that was soon followed by others in search of gold in the Central and Western Cordilleras. The most important of these was organized by Juan de Vadillo, who left Urabá in 1538, crossed the Central Cordillera and followed the river Cauca south to Cali, where he met with Spaniards commanded by Lorenzo de Aldana. While Vadillo returned to Cartagena via Quito and Santo Domingo, Aldana sent Jorge de Robledo northward, initiating the conquest and colonization of Antioquia.

COLONIZATION

By the mid-sixteenth century Spaniards had carved out the major spaces within which colonial society was to develop in Colombia and had established rudimentary forms of communication between them. On the Caribbean coast stood Santa Marta and Cartagena; of these Cartagena soon became the more important, emerging as the principal point of entry into the interior and the major port for trade with Spain. In the center of the country, Jiménez de Quesada's Kingdom of New Granada became another key area for colonization, attracting Spaniards who fanned out from Bogotá in search of gold and tribute from indigenous communities. By midcentury Spanish settlement had extended from Bogotá throughout Colombia's Eastern Cordillera and beyond.

To the north, settlement reached through Vélez, Tunja, and Málaga to Pamplona; westward, Spaniards crossed the river Magdalena, founding towns at Ibagué, Mariquita, and Honda; eastward, they moved down the slopes of the Andes to the fringes of the Llanos, establishing strongholds at Medina de las Torres, Santiago de las Atalayas, and San Juan de los Llanos. To the south, the towns founded at Neiva, Timaná, and La Plata facilitated contact with Belalcázar's sphere of influence in Popayán, first by the Guanacas trail, which led to Popayán by way of Neiva and Timaná, and then, from 1550, through the Quindío Pass across the Central Cordillera into the Cauca Valley. There lay the heart of Belalcázar's great province of Popayán, which extended over a vast area of southern and western Colombia. For some years, it seemed that Popayán would become a separate dominion, independent of both Peru to the south and New Granada to the north; this possibility finally disappeared in 1563, when Antioquia was removed from its jurisdiction and brought under the Audiencia of Santa Fe de Bogotá.

Conquest Colombia was, then, a fragmented entity. Spanish settlements were widely dispersed, and their tendency toward autonomy was accentuated by difficulties of communication over long distances and rugged terrain. The development of the colonial population is difficult to ascertain, but it was still small in the mid-sixteenth century. Contemporary estimates suggest that by 1560 there were probably between 6,000 and 8,000 colonists scattered over the country, with small clusters of Spaniards living in rudimentary towns that usually held no more than about 100 Spanish *vecinos* (householders) and their families. The largest urban center was Santa Fe de Bogotá, with a core of about 600 vecinos, whereas Cartagena and Tunja had about 200 and 250 respectively. There was also a growing population of blacks and people of mixed race, between 5,000 and 7,000 in 1560, and a surviving indigenous population of around 1.26 million. Of course, the indigenous population was greatly diminished, as within a few decades of the Europeans' arrival almost all indigenous peoples were adversely affected by the consequences of war, epidemic disease, and exploitation.

INDIGENOUS CULTURES

Many different indigenous peoples inhabited Colombia at the time of the Spanish invasions. At one extreme were the simple hunting and gathering bands that lived in the tropical rain forests of the Pacific coast and in the great plains crossed by the tributaries of the Orinoco and Amazon rivers. At the other extreme stood two great cultural complexes: the Taironas of the Sierra Nevada de Santa Marta and the Chibchas of the Eastern Cordillera. Both were at a relatively advanced stage of social and political organization, uniting densely populated federations of villages under leaders who combined political and religious roles. Between these extremes, most indigenous peoples were organized in the groups the Spaniards called *cacicazgos* (chiefdoms). In the Central Cordillera, these were frequently at war with each other, and according to Spanish commentators, they routinely practiced ritual cannibalism. On the Caribbean coast such warfare was less common, and the cacicazgos seem to have organized more for religious than military purposes. Whatever their differences, Colombia's indigenous peoples shared a common fate after the Conquest; within half a century, their population had been severely depleted, beginning a decline that was never fully reversed.

It is difficult to gauge the full extent of indigenous demographic decline after the Conquest, because the size of the native population before the arrival of Europeans cannot be fixed with any certainty. Some historians believe that Colombia's pre-Conquest native population was about 850,000; others estimate that it was at least three million and possibly more than four million. Indeed, one calculation suggests that more than a million people lived in the Eastern Cordillera region, another million in the Cauca Valley, at least half a million on the Caribbean coast, and between 300,000 and 400,000 in the upper and middle Magdalena Valley and its central slopes and in the southern Altiplano region around Pasto. If the size of the pre-Conquest population is still in dispute, there is no doubt that in the decades after the arrival of the Spaniards, most indigenous communities experienced catastrophic reductions and some were completely obliterated.

ECONOMY

Decimation of indigenous societies, sudden and violent in some areas, more gradual in others, was paralleled by the formation of new types of social and economic organizations designed to meet Spanish needs and aspirations. Two basic patterns emerged. One was a rural economy in which arable farming was combined with extensive cattle raising. The other was a mining economy that extracted gold, essential for trade with Europe. These economies were established in the same general pattern that Spaniards employed throughout the Americas. They founded towns from which to dominate and exploit the local population and used the institution of *encomienda* (a grant of the right to take tribute from a group of indigenous people as a reward for service to the crown) to obtain the goods and labor needed to support nascent settler communities, while also seeking sources of precious metals in order to pay for imports from Europe.

A Prospect of the Town and Harbour of Carthagena, by English School (18th century). Cartagena was the region's chief port for international trade throughout the colonial period. PRIVATE COLLECTION/ THE BRIDGEMAN ART LIBRARY

The discovery of gold and the development of gold mining played a central role in shaping Colombia's colonial economy. In the early years of settlement, Spaniards acquired gold by looting indigenous communities of their ornaments and mortuary regalia; then, as permanent Spanish towns were founded in the interior, plunder gave way to mining the underground veins and gold alluvions found through Colombian territory. Some gold was found in the Eastern Cordillera, at Pamplona, and on the western banks of the Magdalena River; however, the richest and most enduring sources were in the south and west of the country, in the provinces of Popayán, Antioquia, and later, the Chocó. The most important mining districts of the sixteenth century were developed along the course and slopes of the river Cauca, at Cáceres and Santa Fe de Antioquia in the north, around Arma, Anserma, and Cartago to the south, and in the headwaters of the Cauca near Popayán. To

these gold fields, others were added during the second half of the sixteenth century when Spaniards pushed into the Pacific lowlands and found the gold-rich rivers of the lower Chocó.

The first great cycle of Colombian gold mining was roughly between 1550 and 1640. It started with the exploitation of gold deposits in Pamplona and the western slopes of the Magdalena, mostly mined by Spaniards from Bogotá. Gold production in the south and west was also underway in these years but was less stable and less valuable, partly because of the scarcity of indigenous labor. Around 1580 mining suffered a temporary crisis as the indigenous workforce declined dramatically in the districts controlled from Bogotá. However, gold production recuperated as new mines opened in western Colombia after 1580, mainly in Cáceres and Zaragoza. There, deposits were so rich that miners could afford to buy black slaves to work them, and so production soared, reaching its highest point in 1595–1599 with an average production equivalent to about 1.8 million pesos per year. The boom then tailed off as miners reached the limits of their technical capacity until, between 1640 and 1644, gold output fell to a fraction of late-sixteenth-century levels.

The second major cycle of gold production began at the close of the seventeenth century and lasted until the end of the colonial period. It was based on fresh discoveries of gold, found chiefly in the alluvions of the Pacific lowlands (in Chocó province and in Raposo, Iscuandé, and Barbacoas) and the Central Cordillera (in the province of Antioquia). Unlike the first mining boom, this late colonial phase of mining expansion used very little indigenous labor. The gold frontier of the Pacific lowlands relied heavily on imported African slaves, while growing gold output in Antioquia depended mainly on the activities of individual prospectors and miners with small slave gangs. The value of gold production during the eighteenth century is, again, impossible to measure accurately from official records. Contemporary statistics do nonetheless suggest a powerful upward trend: in 1700 gold to the value of just over 250,000 silver pesos was minted at Bogotá; by 1800, the mints of Bogotá and Popayán were producing 2 million pesos.

Gold mining was vital to colonial society because it both supplied the means to buy European imports and stimulated the development of internal trade and production. Colonial Colombia was nonetheless an overwhelmingly agrarian society that provided for its own basic needs from agricultural holdings of many different types. In the early years of colonization, Spaniards relied for subsistence on products and services supplied by natives as tribute, channeled through the encomienda system. *Encomenderos* and other settlers also appropriated Amerindian land, and in the core regions of colonization they created large estates on which to raise cattle and cultivate commercial crops such as wheat, barley, and sugar. Before the end of the sixteenth century, landholdings of this kind were replacing the encomienda as a major source of wealth, as the latter was undermined by the falling indigenous population. However, early in the seventeenth century, the prosperity of agriculture diminished when mining declined, stunting the growth of domestic markets. As poor whites and

mestizos (people of mixed indigenous and European ancestry) found it increasingly difficult to live in the dwindling economy of the encomenderos and mine-owners, they spread into the countryside and created farming settlements that later became Spanish parishes. Such, for example, were the origins of the villages and towns of the San Gil and Socorro regions north of Tunja, and the Medellín area of Antioquia, all of which subsequently became important centers of population.

As gold mining contracted during the seventeenth century, the Spanish provinces in the Colombian region showed a tendency toward ruralization and greater domestic self-sufficiency. This was not necessarily a sign of generalized retreat into economic decline. Depleted though it undoubtedly was, the output of gold continued to fuel the regional interchange of foodstuffs and basic manufactures. Indeed, interregional trade was fostered after 1620 by the establishment of a mint in Santa Fe de Bogotá and by the introduction of a silver coinage that facilitated trade within the domestic economy. Information on internal trade during the seventeenth century is scarce, but competition over the farming of river port revenues around midcentury suggests that internal commerce in domestic products was reasonably buoyant. There were also signs that the colony was developing rudimentary manufactures.

In the final decade of the sixteenth century, the president of the Audiencia of Santa Fe de Bogotá called upon the *corregidores* (district magistrates) of his jurisdiction to organize indigenous labor in *obrajes* (workshops) for producing woolen cloth, coarse woolen skirts, blankets, and hats. By 1610 there were eight such obrajes in the city of Tunja, and during the seventeenth century the city became the hub of a flourishing trade conducted with other regions in Colombia and with neighboring Venezuela. The growth of interregional trade was further reinforced during the late seventeenth century by the development of farming communities in the San Gil and Socorro regions, producing crude cotton textiles both for domestic use and sale in regional markets. Thus, the colonial economy went through a long phase of change and consolidation, during which it became self-sufficient in basic foodstuffs and crude textiles and less dependent on gold mining and imports from Spain.

Throughout the colonial period, Cartagena de Indias was the region's chief port for overseas trade, providing colonial Colombia with a direct connection to the Spanish commercial system through the Tierra Firme fleet which supplied Spanish South America. Fueled by gold, this trade declined when the mining sector contracted in the mid-seventeenth century and revived when growth in gold output resumed during the eighteenth century. Bourbon monarchs introduced a succession of measures to guarantee Spain's monopoly of such trade, beginning with the 1720 *Proyecto para Flotas y Galeones* (Project for fleets and galleons), which sought to rebuild the system of annual fleets between Spain and America, proceeding to the abolition of the galleons in 1739, and culminating in *comercio libre*, or imperial free trade, which was decreed in 1778. The deregulation allowed by comercio libre stimulated a short phase of vigorous growth during the 1780s, but per capita exports remained relatively small compared to other areas in Spanish America and, despite official efforts to encourage diversification, continued to consist largely of gold remittances. At the turn of the nineteenth century, Spanish commerce with the region declined dramatically. Disrupted by the Anglo-Spanish wars of 1796–1802 and 1804–1808, it was finally ended by the break with Spain in 1810.

SOCIETY

Colombian colonial society was built on three ethnic groups. At first, European invasion created a dual society of conquering Spaniards and conquered indigenous peoples. Later, the growing importation of African slaves added an additional ethnic component, and miscegenation produced intermediate groups of people of mixed race, known to Spaniards as the *castas* (mixed groups of people). Over the colonial period as a whole, two major demographic trends stand out: a steep fall in the indigenous population, and a gradual increase in the numbers of whites, blacks, and people of mixed race. According to one estimate, there were roughly 50,000 whites, 60,000 blacks, 20,000 mestizos, and 600,000 Amerindians in the region in 1650, giving a total population of about 730,000. By the late eighteenth century, this population had increased to at least 850,000 people, and the castas had become the single largest group. The first countrywide census, taken in 1778–

1780, shows that people of mixed race made up 46 percent of the population, whites about 26 percent, Amerindians 20 percent, and black slaves 8 percent. The preponderance of mestizos is striking, as is the decline of indigenous peoples. At the end of the eighteenth century, the only areas where Amerindians were still a local majority were in the province of Pasto, in the Llanos of Casanare, and in frontier areas along the Pacific and Caribbean coasts where indigenous peoples had successfully resisted or evaded white encroachments. Elsewhere, they had become a minority in their own land, outnumbered by whites and mestizos in a demographic structure that contrasted sharply with those of the Andean lands to the south in Ecuador, Peru, and Bolivia.

Colombia's conversion into an essentially mestizo society had important implications for its development. The dual society of indigenous and Spanish republics envisaged by early Spanish law had been almost completely undermined by *mestizaje* (miscegenation between whites and indigenous peoples), and compared to the Andean territories to the south, indigenous communities made only a small contribution to the Hispanic state and economy, whether in labor, markets, or taxes. There were, of course, regional variations within Colombia, but generally the absence of large indigenous populations based in the corporate ownership of land and standing in a special relationship to the Spanish state, had produced a social order different from those regions of the empire where indigenous peoples were in the majority. Racial divisions reinforced by economic inequalities stratified society as they did in other parts of Spanish America, but colonial Colombia was in many ways a less rigid society than those where indigenous cultures had remained strong, as in the highlands of Quito, the southern Andean regions of Peru and Upper Peru, or southern Mexico.

GOVERNMENT AND POLITICS

The earliest forms of Spanish political authority in Colombia were the leaders of conquering expeditions. Having contracted with the crown to bring new territories under Castilian sovereignty in return for political and economic privileges, the captains of conquest were usually the first royal governors. Thus, Bastidas was first governor of Santa Marta, while Heredia held the same post in Cartagena, Belalcázar in Popayán, and Jiménez de Quesada in New Granada. By establishing towns, these men also implanted a second pillar of Spanish political authority, the *cabildo*, or municipal council. Its members were originally chosen by the governor from amongst the powerful encomenderos; members then chose new officers from among their peers, setting a pattern in which cabildos tended to become self-perpetuating oligarchies, dominated first by encomenderos and later by leading landowners, miners, and merchants.

Royal authority was strengthened in the later sixteenth century by the creation of the Audiencia of Santa Fe. Installed at Bogotá in 1550, the audiencia was established after the abortive efforts of Juan Díaz de Armendáriz to impose the New Laws of Charles I (1542). With the audiencia in place, the crown commissioned a series of *visitas* (official inspections) with a view to improving government, imposing a regulated system of tribute on the indigenous peoples, and providing the indigenous peoples with protection from unrestrained exploitation by settlers. In practice, relatively little was achieved in any of these spheres. For whereas the presence of royal judges signaled the Crown's determination to centralize authority, the audiencia failed to exert close control over Spanish settlers and their creole descendants, even when it was led by strong and active presidents such as Andrés Venero de Leiva (1563–1574) or Antonio González (1590–1597).

At the start of the seventeenth century, the Crown sought to enhance the audiencia's authority in two ways. First, it endowed the audiencia president with military powers and duties, appointing Juan de Borja as the first presidente de Capa y Espada in 1605. Borja proved to be an unusually energetic and effective official, and in the twenty-two years that he held the office (1605–1628), he strengthened the royal government in several ways. Borja brought new areas under its jurisdiction, oversaw the establishment of a Tribunal de Cuentas (a supreme court of audit for the royal treasury), and put the royal mint into operation at Bogotá. In his war against the Pijaos and in other anti-indigenous campaigns, Borja crushed important redoubts of indigenous resistance to Spanish rule and thereby extended the frontier for colonial settlement.

The appointment of his successor, Sancho Girón, marquis of Sofraga (1630–1637), saw a second innovation designed to enhance the authority of New Granada's audiencia: the appointment to the presidency of members of the Spanish nobility. This did not guarantee good or effective government, however. At the end of the seventeenth century the visita conducted by Carlos Alcedo y Sotomayor (1695–1698) revealed that royal authority, while acknowledged in principle, was flouted in practice. Administered by corrupt officials acting in collusion with local elites, colonial government was undermined by widespread tax evasion, fraud, and graft.

Defenses against foreign attack and territorial encroachment also weakened in the later seventeenth century. In 1697 Cartagena de Indias fell to a French naval attack led by Baron de Pointis, and in 1698 a Scottish colony was established at Darién, threatening Spanish sovereignty in a strategic frontier area. Thus, when Hapsburg rule finally ended with the death of Charles II in 1700, Spanish control over the provinces subject to the Audiencia of Santa Fe had become highly attenuated. Provincial governments run by venal governors frequently ignored orders from Bogotá; the audiencia judges were themselves invariably concerned more with private than public business; royal finances were a shambles; and colonial resources, particularly gold, were being diverted by contrabandists into the hands of foreigners.

The Bourbon succession to the Spanish throne, guaranteed by the Treaty of Utrecht in 1713, prepared the way for changes in these conditions. In 1717 the Crown sent Antonio de la Pedrosa y Guerrero to New Granada with orders to investigate and overhaul the region's administration, finances, and defenses, and to prepare the territory for government by a viceregency based in Santa Fe de Bogotá. The Viceroyalty of New Granada (also known as the Viceroyalty of Santa Fe, after its capital) was duly created but did not survive long. The first viceroy, Jorge de Villalonga (1719–1723), was an inept politician and poor administrator, and when he proved unable to protect Spanish fleets against fierce competition from foreign contrabandists on Colombia's Caribbean shores, he was sacked and the experiment with viceregal government ended. A quarter century later the viceroyalty was revived when the Crown again decided that such a structure was essential if it was to tighten control of

New Granada's government and finances and harden defenses against foreign attack.

Reestablishment of the Viceroyalty of New Granada in 1739 inaugurated a distinctive period in Colombia's colonial history. The viceroys exercised jurisdiction over a huge area (equivalent to the modern republics of Colombia, Ecuador, Panama, Venezuela, and the Guayanas), but in practice they focused their authority mainly on the provinces of New Granada and Popayán (an area roughly coterminous with modern Colombia). In so doing, successive viceroys improved government finances, brought previously autonomous provincial governments under closer supervision, and strengthened Bogotá's role as a center for a more integrated system of government.

On these foundations, Charles III (1759–1788) intensified reform of the region's government and commerce during the 1770s and 1780s. As part of its wider program for revitalizing the empire, the crown opened the region's ports to imperial free trade in 1778 and, at the same time, sent a visitor-general to Bogotá with orders to increase tax yields and to make government more responsive to central command. These plans met with strong opposition. When Visitor-General Juan Gutiérrez de Piñeres took steps to restructure administration and taxation, he alienated sectors of both patrician and plebeian society and triggered the Comunero Revolt of 1781. This great regional uprising mobilized a force of 20,000 people at its height, and under the slogan "Long live the king and down with bad government," merged the discontents, ideas, and aspirations of more than one social group. Some historians have portrayed the rebellion as a protonationalist movement and precursor of Colombian independence; some have regarded it as an aborted social revolution that revealed underlying conflicts between rich and poor; others have seen it as an essentially "constitutionalist" movement defending customary procedures and practices in government and creole rights to consultation in important matters of policy.

Whatever the causes of the Comunero revolt, its consequences were clear. The authorities were forced temporarily to retract tax increases and permanently to abandon plans to introduce the system of regional government by intendants favored by Minister of the Indies José de Gálvez and widely implemented elsewhere in the empire. Charles III's program of colonial reform was, therefore, less fully and effectively implemented in Colombia than in other parts of Spanish America.

After the Comunero revolt, other signs of opposition to colonial government appeared within the ranks of the creole elite. In 1794 the authorities arrested a number of creoles in Bogotá on charges of sedition, alleging that, inspired by North American and French republican ideas, they had plotted to overthrow Spanish rule. Among those arrested was Antonio Nariño, who admitted translating and printing the French Assembly's Declaration of the Rights of Man and who, after escaping from Spanish custody, began a career as a revolutionary that was eventually to lead him to a prominent role in the struggle for independence. At the time, however, Nariño and the tiny group of dissidents arrested in 1794 (mostly young men drawn together by a common interest in modern science, philosophy, and political ideas) were not a significant threat to the established order, because they were poorly organized and politically isolated. Their dislike of colonial government did nonetheless reflect an emerging creole consciousness, in which enthusiasm for the ideas of the Enlightenment blended with resentment toward Spain for its discrimination against creoles. So long as Spanish authority remained intact, creole criticism of the parent power was contained within the colonial political system; when the monarchy faltered, such criticism was used as justification for breaking with the system.

INDEPENDENCE

The movement toward Colombian independence was initially triggered by crisis in Spain, caused by Napoleon's capture of the Spanish throne in 1808 and the subsequent war of national liberation against France. Without a legitimate monarch at the center of the empire, the colonies were left in a political vacuum; while Spanish government was weak and discredited, creole dissidents seized the opportunity for self-government. The first revolt in the Viceroyalty of New Granada occurred in Quito in August 1809 and was suppressed by force. The second came in Caracas in April 1810 and established a junta that soon sought independence from Spain. In Colombia the first effective move to overthrow Spanish colonial authority took place in Cartagena de Indias, which replaced its royal governor with a junta of local notables on 14 June 1810. Similar moves were made in the first half of July at

Cali, Pamplona, and Socorro. Most important, Bogotá followed on 20 July 1810. There the overthrow of the viceregal government was achieved by a small group of creole conspirators who, by manipulating urban crowds and neutralizing the local garrison, succeeded in replacing Viceroy Antonio Amar y Borbón with a Supreme Junta that claimed to hold authority in the name of King Ferdinand VII.

Overthrowing the viceroy proved easier than creating an alternative government. In December 1810 the junta convoked a congress of representatives from all provinces in the viceroyalty, but only six representatives attended. Even this small group failed to agree, and in February 1811 the congress dissolved itself, having achieved nothing. Thus, the first attempt to create a central government failed, as the country split into competing provinces, each dominated by urban elites determined to pursue their local interests. In March 1811 centralists in Bogotá created the state of Cundinamarca, which recognized the authority of Ferdinand VII; through it they hoped to impose their authority over the rest of the country. It was led first by Jorge Tadeo Lozano, then by Antonio Nariño. Other provinces joined in the rival Federation of New Granadan Provinces, with Tunja as its capital and Camilo Torres as its first president, while Cartagena declared itself an independent and sovereign state. When the state of Cundinamarca itself became an independent republic in 1813, there were three rival patriot governments in Colombia. Tension between them eventually led to war, and in December 1814 Cundinamarca was defeated by the Federation and Nariño's government was overthrown.

While the autonomous provinces fought amongst themselves, royalist forces in Popayán, Pasto, and Santa Marta were regrouping and regaining territory. In 1813 and 1814 they came to dominate a large area of the Caribbean coast and gained ground in both the south, at Pasto, and in the Magdalena Valley. This prepared the way for the reestablishment of Spanish rule. In July 1815 a military expedition from Spain led by Pablo Morillo landed at Santa Marta and from there began the successful reconquest of New Granada.

Reimposition of Spanish rule by military force did not bring a permanent reconstruction of the colonial order. Weariness with civil conflict and

Bogotà, Colombia, c. 1880. Artist rendering of Bogotá, Colombia, at the end of the nineteenth century. Once the main city of the pre-Columbian Chibcha people, Bogotá became a leading city during Spanish colonial rule and eventually a capital city after Colombia became independent in 1819. © NORTH WIND/NORTH WIND PICTURE ARCHIVES — ALL RIGHTS RESERVED

regional disunion facilitated Spanish reconquest in 1815–1816, but the savage repression that followed rekindled opposition to the colonial regime. In some regions, rebels mounted an anti-Spanish insurgency that, if it could not create a nation, did harass the royalists and keep alive the idea of independence. In 1818, when Morillo withdrew some of his troops for deployment against rebels in Venezuela, Simón Bolívar sent the New Granadan Francisco de Paula Santander into the Casanare plains where he rallied resistance to Spain. Then, in mid-1819, Bolívar led his own forces out of the Venezuelan plains and across the Andes to defeat Spanish forces near Bogotá at the battle of Boyacá on 7 August 1819. With this decisive victory, Bolívar retook central new Granada and laid the foundations of the Republic of Colombia. In December 1819 the Congress of Angostura formally established the republic, which was to be based on the erstwhile Viceroyalty of Santa Fe. Known to historians as Gran Colombia, this state was essentially the brainchild of Bolívar who became and remained its first president while continuing the war of liberation against Spain throughout South America.

The constitution of the new state, drawn up at the Congress of Cúcuta in 1821, was centralist and conservative. It united the colonial territories of New Granada, Panama, Venezuela, and Quito under a single government in Bogotá, endowed the president with greater power than the legislature, and limited the franchise to propertied and literate members of society. But Bogotá's domination of such a huge area could not endure. Even before Bolívar had completed the task of liberating South America from Spain, underlying regional and ideological divisions fractured Gran Colombian unity. In Bogotá, liberals resented Bolívar's authoritarianism and federalists disliked his centralism; in Venezuela, separatists led by the *caudillo* José Antonio Páez wanted their own government and in 1826 broke away from Bogotá; and finally, in 1830, Ecuador also seceded from the remains of Gran Colombia, leaving Bogotá to govern the old Audiencia of Santa Fe and the adjoining province of Popayán. Reconstituted in 1832 as the Republic of New Granada, this territory formed the basis of the modern Republic of Colombia.

See also **Agriculture; Bogotá, Santa Fe de: The Audiencia; Bolívar, Simón; Cabildo, Cabildo Abierto; Caste and Class Structure in Colonial Spanish America; Castilla del Oro; Caudillismo, Caudillo; Charles I of Spain; Charles II of Spain; Charles III of Spain; Commercial Policy: Colonial Spanish America; Comunero Revolt (New Granada); Conquistadores; Corregidor; Ferdinand VII of Spain; Gálvez, José de; Gran Colombia; Independent Republics (Colombia); Mestizo; Mining: Colonial Spanish America; Nariño, Antonio; New Granada, United Provinces; New Granada, Viceroyalty of; Obraje; Ojeda, Alonso de; Páez, José Antonio; Santa Marta; Vespucci, Amerigo; Villalonga, Jorge; Wars of Independence, South America.**

BIBLIOGRAPHY

Avellaneda Navas, José Ignacio. *The Conquerors of the New Kingdom of Granada.* Albuquerque: University of New Mexico Press, 1995.

Blossom, Thomas. *Nariño, Hero of Colombian Independence.* Tucson: University of Arizona Press, 1967.

Bushnell, David. *The Santander Regime in Gran Colombia.* Newark: University of Delaware Press, 1954.

Colmenares, Germán. *Historia económica y social de Colombia.* Vol. 1: *1537–1719.* Cali, Colombia: Universidad del Valle, División de Humanidades, 1973; Vol. 2: *Popayán: Una sociedad esclavista, 1680–1800.* Bogotá: La Carreta, 1979.

Earle, Rebecca A. *Spain and the Independence of Colombia, 1810–1825.* Exeter, U.K.: University of Exeter Press, 2000.

Fisher, John R., Allen J. Kuethe, and Anthony McFarlane, eds. *Reform and Insurrection in Bourbon New Granada and Peru.* Baton Rouge: Louisiana State University Press, 1990.

Gómez, Thomas. *L'envers de l'Eldorado: Économie coloniale et travail indigène dans la Colombie du XVIème siècle.* Toulouse: Association des publications de l'Université Toulouse-Mirail, 1984.

Helg, Aline. *Liberty and Equality in Caribbean Colombia, 1770–1835.* Chapel Hill: University of North Carolina Press, 2004.

Jaramillo Uribe, Jaime. *Ensayos sobre la historia social colombiana.* Bogotá: Universidad Nacional de Colombia Dirección de Divulgación Cultural, 1968.

König, Hans-Joachim. *En el camino hacia la nación: Nacionalismo en el proceso de formación del Estado y de la Nación de la Nueva Granada, 1750–1856.* Bogotá: Banco de la República, 1994.

Marzahl, Peter. *Town in the Empire: Government, Politics, and Society in Seventeenth-Century Popayán.* Austin: Institute of Latin American Studies, University of Texas at Austin, 1978.

McFarlane, Anthony. *Colombia before Independence: Economy, Society, and Politics under Bourbon Rule.* Cambridge, U.K., and New York: Cambridge University Press, 1993.

Melo, Jorge Orlando. *Historia de Colombia,* Vol. 1: *El Establecimiento de la dominación española.* Medellín, Colombia: La Carreta, 1977.

Ortíz, Sergio Elías. *Génesis de la revolución de 20 de julio de 1810.* Bogotá: Kelly, 1960.

Phelan, John Leddy. *The People and the King: The Comunero Revolution in Colombia, 1781.* Madison: University of Wisconsin Press, 1978.

Rausch, Jane M. *A Tropical Plains Frontier: The Llanos of Colombia, 1531–1831.* Albuquerque: University of New Mexico Press, 1984.

Ruíz Rivera, Julián B. *Encomienda y mita en Nueva Granada en el siglo XVII.* Sevilla, Spain: Escuela de Estudios Hispano-Americanos, 1975.

Saether, Steinar. *Identidades e independencia en Santa Marta y Riohacha, 1750–1830.* Bogotá: Instituto Colombiano de Antropología e Historia (ICANH), 2005.

Sauer, Carl Ortwin. *The Early Spanish Main.* Berkeley: University of California Press, 1966.

Sharp, William F. *Slavery on the Spanish Frontier: The Colombian Chocó, 1680–1810.* Norman: University of Oklahoma Press, 1976.

Silva, Renán. *Los Ilustrados de Nueva Granada, 1760–1808: Genealogía de una comunidad de interpretación.* Medellín, Colombia: Banco de la República: Fondo Editorial Universidad EAFIT, 2002.

Thibaud, Clément. *Repúblicas en armas: Los ejércitos bolivarianos en la guerra de independencia en Colombia y Venezuela.* Lima: Instituto Francés de Estudios Andinos; Bogotá: Planeta, 2003.

Twinam, Ann. *Miners, Merchants, and Farmers in Colonial Colombia.* Austin: University of Texas Press, 1982.

West, Robert C. *Colonial Placer Mining in Colombia.* Baton Rouge: Louisiana State University Press, 1952.

Williams, Caroline. *Between Resistance and Adaptation: Indigenous Peoples and the Colonisation of the Chocó, 1510–1753.* Liverpool, U.K.: Liverpool University Press, 2004.

ANTHONY MCFARLANE

SINCE INDEPENDENCE

Leading citizens of Cartagena, Pamplona, Socorro, Bogotá, and other provincial towns initiated the movement toward Colombian independence in 1810. The power struggle of the Patria Boba (Foolish Fatherland) period (1810–1816) foreshadowed the nineteenth-century disputes surrounding the issue of regional autonomy (federalism) versus centralized rule. Miguel Pombo and Camilo Torres Restrepo drew upon Enlightenment thought and the example of the United States in their defense of federalism within the United Provinces of New Granada—a governmental model well suited to the starkly divided Colombian topography, but not, perhaps, to Colombian political dispositions. The precursor, Antonio Nariño, however, insisted on a centralized structure for reasons of military expediency and political authority. The conflict between these factions facilitated the 1816 Spanish reconquest by General Pablo Morillo, whose pacification techniques included the execution of Torres and some three hundred other patriots. After Morillo's 1816 capture of Bogotá, patriot forces retreated to the plains of Casanare, where they joined the *llanero* (plainsman) chief José Antonio Páez. Francisco de Paula Santander, a Cúcuta-born lawyer, helped Simón Bolívar march over the Andes and defeat the Spaniards at the Battle of Boyacá on August 7, 1819. Shortly thereafter, the Congress of Angostura created the Republic of [Gran] Colombia, comprised of contemporary Colombia, Venezuela, Panama, and Ecuador.

The Congress of Cúcuta in 1821 established a constitutional framework that shaped the subsequent Colombian constitutions of 1832 and 1843. These centralized regimes allowed for the division of authority among the executive, legislative, and judicial branches, with a clause providing the executive with emergency authority. Bolívar was selected as president, but it was vice president Santander who gave the new government administrative shape and direction while the Liberator led the independence struggle further to the south. The regime instituted the standard reforms, including the elimination of the Inquisition, Indian tribute, and the *alcabala* (sales tax); the opening of ports; the assertion of patronage over the church; and the gradual emancipation of slaves. A moderately protective tariff was retained for fiscal purposes, as were monopolies on tobacco and aguardiente (sugarcane alcohol).

Regional tensions doomed the Gran Colombian experiment. The 1826 federalist revolt by José Antonio Páez forced Bolívar to dampen the uprising and impose a dictatorship upon the country, an assumption of extraordinary powers that many Colombian presidents later used in the interest of public order. Bolívar survived an assassination attempt in September; the failure earned Santander several years of exile in Europe and his co-conspirators death. Gran Colombia collapsed two years later as both Venezuela and Ecuador charted their own national destinies. Santander returned from exile to assume the presidency of the Republic of New Granada in 1832.

REGIONALISM, ECONOMIC PATTERNS, AND SOCIAL STRUCTURES

Regionalism, determined by geography, patterns of economic and social development, and political jurisdiction, has profoundly influenced Colombian history. Leading cities dominated each region: Popayán was the center of the Cauca; Medellín, Antioquia; Cartagena, la costa; Bogotá, the central highlands; and the multiple nodes of Vélez, Socorro, and Pamplona were associated with the northeast; only the *llanos* to the east of the Andes lacked a major city. These regions continue to define the country, though Cali has long eclipsed Popayán as the leader of the Cauca. Further, late-nineteenth-century migration created the coffee regions of Caldas and Quindío.

Independence changed colonial economic patterns very little. Agriculture remained the most

Colombia

important activity in a regionally dispersed economy, with larger estates (often dedicated to raising cattle) more prevalent in the Cauca, coastal, and central highland regions, and smaller peasant production dominant elsewhere, especially in areas around Socorro–San Gil, Pasto, and Medellín. Sugar estates to the north of Popayán, which had relied upon slave labor, suffered a significant decline as wartime emancipation and the flight of enslaved peoples stimulated the emergence of widespread subsistence activities (as well as social strife). As the most important export earner until well into the century, gold from the Pacific lowlands of the Chocó and the Antioquia slopes sustained substantial mercantile activity. Manufacturing remained in the hands of multitalented rural and urban artisans, especially in the production of domestic textiles in the

Socorro–San Gil region. Efforts by the New Granadan government to stimulate the manufacturing industry through a system of privileges in the 1830s proved largely unsuccessful, although they did sustain a fledgling iron industry in the central highlands.

The early national social structure is poorly understood, but several characteristics are apparent. An elite bound by kinship ties dominated regional social hierarchies, drawing their strength from large landholdings and positions in the civil bureaucracy, church, and mercantile communities. Most members of rural societies, especially those of the central highlands and Cauca regions, were highly deferential, bound by tradition and dependence upon landholders. Native inhabitants of the *resguardos* (common lands) maintained more independent lives and defended themselves against efforts to abolish their corporate privileges. Small farmers and artisans of the northeast and central highlands had considerable social, economic, and political autonomy. Antioqueño society was dominated by large landholders, the Church, and the mining elite, but also included numerous independent small farmers.

Colombia

Population:	44,379,598 (2007 est.)
Area:	439,736 sq mi
Official language:	Spanish
National currency:	Colombian peso (COP)
Principal religions:	Roman Catholic, 90%
Ethnicity:	mestizo 58%, white 20%, mulatto 14%, black 4%, mixed black-Amerindian 3%, Amerindian 1%
Capital:	Bogotá
Other urban centers:	Barranquilla, Cali, Medellín, Cartagena
Annual rainfall:	42 in
Principal geographical features:	*Mountains:* Andes Mts., including the Cordillera Occidental, Cordillera Central, Cordillera Oriental, Sierra de los Andes, and Sierra de Perijá; Sierra Nevada de Santa Maria includes the highest peaks in the country, Cristóbal Colón and Simon Bolivar (both 18, 947 ft); Serranía de Baudó *Rivers:* Cauca, Magdalena; the Amazon and Orinoco form portions of the southern and eastern borders *Islands:* San Andrés and Providencia archipelagos, Gorgona, Gorgonilla, and Malpelo islands (ownership is disputed by Nicaragua)
Economy:	*GDP per capita:* $8,600 (2006 est.)
Principal products and exports:	*Agricultural:* bananas, coffee, flowers, rice, shrimp, sugar *Manufacturing:* chemicals, food processing, textiles *Mining:* coal, emeralds, gold, petroleum *Other:* Production of illicit drugs such as cocaine is an important part of the Colombian economy in areas outside the effective control of the government.
Government:	Formed as an independent nation after the breakup of Gran Colombia in 1830, Colombia is governed as a republic, but the president holds particularly broad powers and is both chief of state and head of government. The legislature is popularly elected, with some seats reserved for certain minority groups, and consists of a 102-seat Senate and a 166-seat House of Representatives. Rebel and drug trafficking organizations limit the effectiveness of the government in some regions.
Armed forces:	As of 2007, armed conflict between government forces and rebel and narcotics organizations within Colombia had been underway for decades. *Army:* 178,000 *Navy:* 22,000 *Air force:* 7,000 *Paramilitary:* roughly 8,000 rural militia and 121,000 national police *Reserves:* 60,700
Transportation:	*Rail:* 2,053 mi *Ports:* Barranquilla, Buenaventura, Cartagena, Muelles El Bosque, Puerto Bolivar, Santa Marta, Turbo *Roads:* 10,110 mi paved; 60,098 mi unpaved *National airline:* Avianca *Airports:* 103 paved and 831 unpaved runway airports, with 6 major airports; 2 heliports
Media:	Numerous newspapers, including *El Colombiano, El Espacio, El Heraldo, El Nuevo Siglo, El País,* and *El Tiempo.* 463 AM and 35 FM radio stations, 60 television stations.
Literacy and education:	*Total literacy rate:* 92.8% Nine years of primary education are compulsory. Public education is free. The Roman Catholic Church exerts great influence over public schools; private schools are also available. Secondary schools are generally only present in urban centers. Universities include the National University in Bogotá, Universidad Javierana, Universidad de los Andes, and Universidad Libre.

The degree of autonomy enjoyed by these social sectors shaped patterns of political affiliation social strife. More rigid patron-client relations produced long-term partisan loyalties and more stable social hierarchies, which was evident, for example, in the Boyacá region around Tunja. By contrast, Socorreño craftsmen, Antioqueño freeholders, and the newly liberated slaves of the Cauca valley resisted the reimposition of elite control. Migrants to the frontier zones of the coffee regions carved out enclaves of relative political autonomy. Urban artisans, especially those of Bogotá, exercised considerable social and political independence throughout the nineteenth century.

Regionalism manifested itself in the initial bipartisan alignment of the Conservative and Liberal Parties. Men with ready access to centers of authority, education, religion, and political position during the late colonial and early national periods tended to align themselves into the Conservative Party by the late 1840s. By contrast, the elite and middling sectors of secondary provincial centers such as Vélez or Socorro formed the Liberal Party at the same time. Other issues affected party alignment, such as the Bolívar-Santander division of the 1820s and alliances during the War of the Supremes (1839–1842), but social location seems to have been a key variable in the development of factions. After the 1830s, members of the Conservative and Liberal Parties dominated the system of formal politics until well into the twentieth century, engaging in numerous civil wars shaped more by party loyalty than by any other factor.

EARLY NATIONAL POLITICS

The presidential election of 1837 and the War of the Supremes opened the door to partisan rivalries and conflicts. Santander had wanted General José María Obando to succeed him as president, but Obando's military background, ambiguous social station in the aristocratic Popayán region, and alleged involvement in the assassination of Antonio José de Sucre embittered other groups, who supported José Ignacio Márquez, the eventual winner. In the aftermath of the election, both sides mobilized urban middle sectors, especially artisans, in the attempt to expand their bases of popular support, a critical step in the development of the party

system. In 1839 the National Congress ordered the closing of several minor convents in the highly religious community of Pasto, a move that sparked the War of the Supremes, in which Obando played an important role as the alleged protector of religion and federalism. Several other pro-Santander leaders declared themselves in revolt, which the government did not suppress until 1842.

By the mid-1840s the nation seemed to be making little progress, leaving leaders ready for significant reforms. The liberal reforms that began with the presidency of the nominal Conservative Tomás Cipriano de Mosquera (1845–1849) included the reduction of tariff rates and the abolition of the tobacco monopoly, antecedents to the widespread reforms undertaken by the Liberal José Hilario López (1849–1853). López's government abolished slavery, expelled the Jesuits, decentralized the nation's fiscal structure, declared absolute freedom of the press, and began political decentralization. The Constitution of 1853 established the separation of church and state, allowed for civil marriage and divorce, extended suffrage to all male citizens over the age of twenty-one, instituted the popular election of governors and many other officials, and weakened executive powers. Several years later, in the wake of the civil war of 1859 to 1861, a final set of reforms privatized corporate properties for public sale and outlawed convents and monasteries.

Despite basic agreements on economic issues between the Conservative and Liberal Parties, serious conflicts erupted over several reforms, especially those concerning social order and public morality. Conservatives tended to view the church as the proper foundation, whereas Liberals placed their faith in an educated and self-reliant citizenry. The abolition of slavery threatened vested interests in both the Cauca and Antioquia regions; this was a primary factor in the unsuccessful Conservative revolt of 1851. Reduction of tariff rates inspired Bogotá's craftsmen to mobilize politically into the Democratic Society of Artisans, and eventually to align themselves with moderate (Draconiano) Liberals who, like Obando, opposed the reduction of executive powers and the threats to the military contained within the Constitution of 1853. This alignment of forces, generally drawn from the middle sectors of rural and urban society, produced General José María Melo's 1854 coup d'état, a movement whose defeat by a Conservative-Liberal elite alliance paved the way for the election of the Conservative Mariano Ospina Rodríguez as president in 1857.

The Constitution of 1863 established a federalist system of quasi-independent state governments within the United States of Colombia. States were allowed their own armies, and all nine had to agree upon constitutional revisions. A president served for two years without opportunity for reelection, a system that ensured near-continual campaigning and political strife throughout the thirty-some years of Liberal hegemony.

ECONOMIC, SOCIAL, AND POLITICAL TRANSFORMATIONS

Economic liberalization offered Colombia limited success in the 1800s, but it oriented the economy toward the world market over the long term. Initially, Colombian commodities enjoyed only sporadic success. Exports earned an estimated $1.88 per capita in the 1830s and $4.77 in 1880, figures that suggest a general increase in value but actually ranked Colombia's export economy among the least important in nineteenth-century Latin America. Furthermore, the fate of exports caused serious political and social instability. Tobacco boomed in the lowland Ambalema region after demonopolization in the 1840s, but declined in the 1870s due to inconsistent quality and Javanese competition. Cotton, cinchona bark (a source of quinine), Panama hats, indigo, and coffee experienced similar booms (and busts), with only coffee surviving in the export mix, along with gold.

Coffee spurred the great southward migration of Antioqueños to the frontiers of south-central Colombia. This was the country's most important nineteenth-century social and economic phenomenon. The movement gained force in the 1830s and 1840s, fueled by a rate of demographic increase substantially above that of the rest of the country. Pioneer farmers (colonos) sought freehold for subsistence crops on the forested slopes of what were largely unclaimed public lands, or lands whose claims were disputed by inheritors of earlier grants, who more often than not were men of considerable economic and social prestige. The colonization of the frontier spurred a tremendous amount of litigation, most of it involving access to land and control of labor for the production of coffee; this pattern of conflict persisted well into the 1930s. Through decades of struggles, thousands of colonos established small, family farms that sustained the twentieth-century coffee industry.

Migrants also came from the Cauca, though not in the same numbers as those from Antioquia. A significant demographic pool of mulattoes, blacks, and mestizos existed in the central Cauca as wage laborers, but these groups preferred subsistence farming and relative autonomy on abandoned lowlands and slopes and the establishment of medium-sized farms. These "dangerous" social sectors were at the center of several social conflicts, as when Obando mobilized them in support of his cause during the War of the Supremes, and in the protests against large landholders near Cali in the early 1850s. Conflicts over access to land and the social order played roles in the 1851 Conservative rebellion, the Melo coup of 1854, and regional insurrections in the 1870s.

The Conservative intellectual and Cauca political leader Sergio Arboleda (1822–1888) decried this lack of order in the early 1870s, suggesting that a combination of Catholic social restraint and capitalist development could save the region from social and political disorder. The failure of Conservatives and Catholic leaders to achieve public order led to the civil war of 1876 to 1877, perhaps the only armed conflict in Colombia with a genuine religious core. Importantly, that conflict divided the Liberal Party into Radicals and Independents, the latter which would align itself with Conservative in the 1880s.

THE REGENERATION AND BIPARTISAN RULE

Economic, political, and social tensions forced a fundamental realignment of the Colombian polity in the 1880s. The failure of export commodities undermined the fiscal resources of the state and engendered social unrest. Rafael Núñez's 1880 and 1884 Independent Liberal presidential victories propelled Radical Liberals to rebellion in 1885. Conservatives joined with Independents to repress the Radicals, thereby allowing Núñez to undertake the Regeneración (Regeneration) of the country. With the crucial assistance of Conservative philosopher and politician Miguel Antonio Caro, Núñez engineered passage of the Constitution of 1886, which swept aside the tenets of mid-century liberalism and established a centralized state with departments instead of sovereign states. Núñez accepted a six-year presidency with increased executive authority, including the power to direct fiscal policy through a national bank. Núñez increased tariffs and signaled state support for industrial development. Taking advantage of the government's ability to print paper money, Núñez ordered several large issues, with disputed economic effect. Caro's concern for a "proper" social hierarchy restored Roman Catholicism as the state religion, reestablished its strong role in public education, and helped produce a concordat with the Vatican in 1887.

Independents and Conservatives cooperated in the establishment of the National Party, whose purpose was to end partisan contention in support of the new regime. Núñez's preference for his native city of Cartagena to the highland capital made this mission impossible. (Núñez's absence from the capital meant that executive power rested in the hands of vice president Caro.) Both the dogmaticism and heavy-handedness of Caro alienated many Regeneration leaders, especially "historical" Conservatives led by Antioqueño Marceliano Vélez Barreneche (1832–1923) who were less willing to cooperate with Independents. The 1892 presidential election formalized this split, as Caro and Barreneche contended for the vice presidential position (Caro succeeded). The Liberal Party attempted to regain its political voice in 1893, but its members faced arrest and overt repression.

Partisan political strife escalated through the 1890s, culminating in the War of the Thousand Days (1899–1902). Inflationary pressures from the release of paper money and the erratic performance of coffee called into question the fiscal leadership of Caro's government. The more aggressive "war liberals," who had failed in an 1895 insurrection, redoubled their efforts after the inefficacious presidential election of 1897 placed the feeble, eighty-three-year-old Manuel A. Sanclemente (1814–1902) at the head of the government. Economic and political crises merged into war in October 1899. The "gentlemen's war" soon gave way to bitter conflict between Liberal guerrillas and government forces assisted by their own guerrillas. Although the zones of coffee agriculture in Huila, Cundinamarca, the Cauca, and Santander were the primary zones of conflict, few regions of the country were spared before the

struggle came to a merciful conclusion in 1902. The estimated 100,000 deaths fail to resolve the bitter social animosities engendered by the conflict, many of which persisted as social vendettas for decades. Nor does the human loss reflect the traumatic national impact, which created the conditions for the successful separation of the department of Panama from Colombia with the assistance of the United States.

The Conservative General Rafael Reyes (1849–1921) emerged victorious in the suspiciously corrupt 1904 presidential election. The well-born Reyes favored cooperative politics, and named several Liberals to his cabinet. Reyes practiced the interventionist style of the Mexican dictator Porfirio Díaz, instituting reforms intended to restore stability to the fiscal system, improve the country's rail infrastructure, boost industrial activity through protective tariffs, and increase the production of coffee. Reyes also mirrored Díaz's penchant for personal rule, dismissing the Congress in 1905 in favor of a handpicked "national assembly," which immediately extended the length of the president's term. Reyes sought to restore the friendly relations with the United States that had been disturbed by the U.S. role in the independence of Panama. The proposed treaty to resolve outstanding issues required the approval of the national assembly, which, when called back into session, rejected Reyes's proposal in March 1909, in keeping with public opinion. The president resigned his position and left the country several months later.

Most presidents in the 1910s shared Reyes's tendency toward bipartisan rule, though not his predilection toward strong-handedness. The constitutional reform of 1910 mandated minority representation and reduced the presidential term to four years. Carlos E. Restrepo, a Conservative who headed the bipartisan Republican Union Party, assumed the presidency in 1910. The increased social polarization that marked his rule and that of his successors represented the diverging interests of conservative church reformers, organized labor, peasants, and an emerging middle class. The Liberal Rafael Uribe Uribe symbolized some of these sentiments, abandoning his party's commitment to dogmatic theory in his call for state socialism. The assassination of Uribe Uribe in 1914 blunted this tendency within his party until the emergence of Jorge Eliécer Gaitán in the 1930s. More traditional

Banana vendor at market in Armenia, Colombia, late 20th century. New and traditional exports comprise an important part of Colombia's economy. ENZO AND PAOLO RAGAZZINI/CORBIS

Conservatives came to dominate the party and most national offices until 1930.

COFFEE, INDUSTRY, AND URBANIZATION

Coffee is central to an understanding of twentieth-century Colombia. For most of the century, it dominated the export economy and helped to redefine several regions of the country. Production boomed after the War of the Thousand Days as Antioqueño colonization pushed the coffee frontier southward. One million 60-kilogram (132-pound) bags were exported in 1913: 32.8 percent from Santander, 20.0 percent from Cundinamarca, and 16.1 percent from Antioquia. By the early 1930s, exports surpassed 3 million bags and constituted almost 70 percent of the country's exports, with the new zones of production in the departments of Caldas, Risaralda, Quindío, Tolima, and Valle del Cauca accounting for well over half of the exports. National exports topped 5 million bags in 1943 and 6 million bags ten years later—a level of production maintained through the 1990s. By the 1990s the price of coffee had fallen dramatically, as

had its importance in the export economy, when it accounted for less than 10 percent of the value of exports.

Family-owned-and-operated farms accounted for three-fourths of the 150,000 to 200,000 coffee farms in the 1930s to 1950s. These small farmers tended toward economic and social conservativism in defense of their relative social autonomy; they generally resisted efforts to mobilize their collective energies in labor struggles, and they aligned themselves with either local Conservative or Liberal patrons. Although they produced the vast majority of the country's coffee, the product has been marketed since 1927 by the National Federation of Coffee Growers (Fedecafe), which itself is dominated by large producers. Large producers supplanted the output of small producers in the 1950s through the planting of a type of coffee tree more conducive to large-scale labor and harvesting, and came to dominate the industry through their control of marketing, credit, and distribution systems.

Coffee produced large quantities of capital that helped stimulate rapid changes in the Colombian economy and polity. Annual export earnings increased from an average of $26 million during the Reyes period to an average $200 million in the late 1920s. Industrial entrepreneurs, especially in the Medellín region, created an industrial base, most significantly in textiles. A $25 million indemnification from the United States for its role in the separation of Panama (stipulated by the 1922 Urrutia-Thomson Treaty) opened the way for $260 million in foreign loans, much of which was invested in infrastructural and municipal development. Foreign loans accompanied foreign investment, which included the establishment of a United Fruit Company banana enclave near Santa Marta, oil extraction and refining by the Tropical Oil (Jersey Standard, now Exxon) Company near Barrancabermeja, and the Barco concession to Gulf and Socony (now Mobil) south of Lake Maracaibo. Railways, highways, maritime traffic, and other infrastructural improvements knitted much of central-western Colombia into a single economic unit.

Urbanization and population growth transformed Colombia into a "nation of cities" over the course of the twentieth century. Only 5 percent of the nation's 3.89 million people in 1900 lived in cities, but thereafter both population and urbanization figures increased dramatically. The national population reached 17.5 million (54 percent urban) in 1964, 33 million (70 percent urban) in 1990, and approximately 43 million (77 per cent urban) in 2006. Bogotá led the urban increase, from about 150,000 in 1918 to 355,000 in 1938; 1,697,311 in 1964; just under 3 million in 1973; 4.2 million in 1985; and perhaps 6.8 million in 2006. Estimates from 2006 show that Cali (2.3 million), Medellín (2 million), Barranquilla (1.3 million), and Cartagena (900,000) experienced similar rates of urbanization, as have smaller provincial cities such as Manizales, Cucutá, Ibagué, and Bucaramanga.

Coffee and urbanization helped to transform the nation's labor force. Slightly over one-half of the 8.7 million people counted in the 1938 census were considered "economically active," with 75 percent of them involved in the production of primary materials, including coffee. Barely 10 percent of the population labored in industrial activities, three-quarters of which were cottage industries of fewer than five people that produced just over one-third of all manufacturing output. Although numbering only 3 percent of the total

laboring population, larger industrial shops doubled the output of the smaller establishments. The larger shops received significant import-substitution support during the Great Depression. Oil workers, transportation workers, and industrial laborers were numerically few but of critical economic importance. Urbanization, increased commercial activity, and industrialization created service and professional occupations that provided the foundation for the middle class, which became increasingly important after World War II.

Changing social and economic realities affected the character of Colombian politics. Protests by transportation and dock workers on the coast shook the nation in 1918. The initial government response to labor militancy was to institute a right-to-work law, force mediation, and ban strikes in strategic sectors, including transportation. Strikes in the oil zone of Barrancabermeja (1924 and 1927) and in the banana enclave of Santa Marta (1928) resulted in mass arrests and violent repression. Fledgling leftwing groups such as the Socialist Revolutionary Party (PSR) attempted to mobilize these social forces under the leadership of dynamic orators such as María de los Ángeles Cano, the "Revolutionary Red Flower." However, most workers tended to channel their political energies into the Conservative or Liberal Parties. The young Liberal Jorge Eliécer Gaitán emerged as a prominent national figure in leading the investigation of the 1928 "banana massacre," which revealed the intimate relationship between Conservative politicians and foreign investors. Foreign loans began to dry up in 1927 and government revenues declined, undermining the Conservative presidency of Miguel Abadía Méndez. The economic foundation of the Colombian state suffered a serious blow with the 1929 collapse of the world economy. The resulting conditions enabled the Liberal Enrique Olaya Herrera to win the 1930 presidential election as Conservatives split their votes between two of their own candidates.

THE REVOLUCIÓN EN MARCHA AND LA VIOLENCIA

The administration of Olaya Herrera proved to be the calm before the partisan political storm. The Liberal president appointed Conservatives to both national and regional offices, resuming a pattern of bipartisan representation and dialogue. Nevertheless, armed strife broke out between local Liberals and Conservatives over the spoils of office. Gaitán used the short-lived Unión Izquierdista Revolucionaria (UNIR) Party to rail against the *país político* in favor of the *país nacional*—populist rhetoric that disturbed many in the upper class. UNIR and Communist organizers attempted to mobilize disgruntled coffee farmers in favor of assertive land and labor reforms.

The presidency of Alfonso López Pumarejo (1934–1938) moderated the tensions surrounding land, labor, and foreign investment by asserting the role of the state in social management in the Revolution on the March. The constitutional reform of 1936 stipulated that property had a social function and that ineffective use of property could lead to its expropriation by the state. Law 200 of the same year applied this principle to land, favoring squatters and others who had occupied land as opposed to landlords with dubious and unverifiable titles. The López regime tended not to use the power of the state in support of capital in disputes and favored labor in the establishment of the Federation of Colombian Workers (CTC), the first such nationwide organization. The state expanded its support for education, removing its control from local officials and lessening the influence of the church. Finally, taxes were increased somewhat and collection improved, especially taxes on foreign firms.

The effects of these reforms were generally more symbolic than revolutionary, but they called Conservative opponents to action, even as they drew new workers and the urban middle class into the Liberal ranks. Even Liberal leaders such as President Eduardo Santos (1938–1942) found the resulting tenor to be unsettling, and assumed a more moderate stance. A decidedly less reformist López returned to office in 1942, reversing some of the land and labor policies initiated in his first administration.

The Conservative Laureano Gómez Castro served as the intellectual and political counterweight to these Liberal leaders. Gómez seized control of the party in the early 1930s, using it as forum to analyze the failures of Liberalism in favor of traditional, principled Conservativism. Gómez criticized the reduction of Catholic authority in the 1936 constitutional reform and the role of Communists in the first López government. Gaitán, too, criticized López, but in the name of the small capitalist and members of the middle class

who lacked political authority. The weakened López resigned in favor of Alberto Lleras Camargo in 1945.

The presidential election of 1946 spurred a wave of partisan bloodshed that initiated La Violencia (The Violence). Gaitán and the moderate Liberal Gabriel Turbay split the Liberal vote, enabling the moderate Conservative Mariano Ospina Pérez, an Antioqueño industrialist and former head of Fedecafe, to emerge victorious. The first stage of the violence began in rural areas with the transfer of power, just as it had in 1930, even though the president named Liberals to his regime. Ospina Pérez shifted government support of organized labor to the newly founded and more conservative Union of Colombian Workers (UTC). When Gaitán gradually convinced moderate Liberals of the futility of their cooperation with Ospina Pérez, they withdrew from the government in March 1948.

Gaitán's assassination on 9 April 1948, led to a massive riot that ravaged Bogotá, leaving hundreds of people dead and much physical damage, and initiated the second stage of La Violencia. Liberals throughout the country joined in the outrage against Conservatives, so frightening the party leadership that they rejoined the Ospina Pérez regime to calm partisan tensions. Indeed, violence soon ebbed, but it did not disappear. Gómez won the uncontested presidential election in late 1949, sparking a sharp increase in violence, to which his regime reacted with brutal repression. Partisan civil war soon ravaged the countryside. Gómez responded in 1952 with an unsuccessful attempt to create a corporatist constitution to impose his ideology upon the Colombian polity. By 1953, with an estimated 160,000 people killed in the violence since 1946, the Colombian political framework was in shambles.

General Gustavo Rojas Pinilla came to power in a coup sponsored by moderate Conservatives in June 1953. Partisan violence had scarred most of rural Colombia, especially the coffee zones and *llanos*, sparing only the coast and the department of Nariño. An amnesty reduced the level of violence temporarily, but it had resumed by 1954 in widespread political banditry with greater social and class undertones. An additional 17,000 people died during the Rojas regime (1953–1957) and

Colombian troops take position in Bogotá during a state of siege, November 1949.
Political feuding and violent attacks between the Liberal and Conservative political parties characterize the era known as "La Violencia," which lasted from 1946 to 1964. More than 200,000 people lost their lives. BETTMANN/CORBIS

some 16,000 more before 1966, the unofficial end of La Violencia.

THE FRENTE NACIONAL

As Rojas Pinilla became more popular and less reliant on the traditional parties, Conservative and Liberal leaders set aside their differences to form the Frente Nacional (National Front), a bipartisan effort to dominate the political landscape. In mid-1956 Lleras Camargo and Laureano Gómez initiated a power-sharing formula that eventually stipulated that the presidency would alternate between the Conservative and Liberal Parties for sixteen years, during which time appointed and elective positions would be shared on an equal basis. A national plebiscite approved these terms by an overwhelming majority. Lleras Camargo once again assumed the presidency in August 1958.

The National Front put an end to partisan violence and facilitated modernization of the nation's economy; it did not, however, end violence or expand democratic politics. The Conservative Guillermo León Valencia (1962–1966) and Liberal Carlos Lleras Restrepo (1966–1970) both took office according to the National Front formula without incident. In 1970 the Conservative Party split its votes for the last guaranteed Conservative presidency of the National Front among several candidates in an election that was complicated by the presidential candidacy of Rojas Pinella. Drawing strength from his Conservative roots and dissident Liberal supporters, Rojas Pinella had helped the Popular National Alliance Party (ANAPO) to win one-fifth of the congressional seats in 1966. The extremely close election on April 19, 1970, generated charges of vote fraud by the government, which allowed the Conservative Misael Pastrana Borrero (1970–1974) to emerge victorious. The urban guerrilla Movement of 19 April (M-19) emerged to challenge the oligarchic control of the government in 1973, a year before Alfonso López Michelsen, the former head of the dissident Movement of Revolutionary Liberals, became the first non–National Front president in sixteen years (1974–1978).

A truck carrying ballots burns in the Cundinamarca Mountains. The truck was intercepted by FARC rebels during the 2002 presidential elections. Guerrilla groups continue to hold sway in Colombia, particularly in remote regions such as Cundinamarca. © REUTERS/CORBIS

The National Front governments brought various producers' associations into the government to coordinate national economic development. The National Association of Industrialists (Andi), Fedecafe, the Colombian Bankers Association (Asobancaria), and other producers' groups, all bipartisan in nature and elite in leadership, supported the new regimes. So, too, did international bodies such as the World Bank, the Agency for International Development (AID), and the Rockefeller Foundation, which served the anti-Communist agenda of the Alliance for Progress.

Despite some differences, most domestic and international groups supported development and political reform initiatives. These included the implementation of an agreement with Renault to develop a national automobile industry, the establishment of the Andean Common Market, and further import-substitution industrialization. The Colombian Agricultural

Society (SAC), by contrast, opposed the 1961 land-reform program of Lleras Camargo, leaving Lleras Restrepo the task of putting some power (however small) into land reform. Restrepo, however, did help organize the National Association of Peasants (ANUC), which asserted itself quite forcefully in the 1970s. He also oversaw reforms that strengthened the executive's hand in economic development and allowed for the gradual dismantling of shared offices in the National Front, which eventually ended in 1978. President Misael Pastrana Borrero helped launch Operation Colombia, which stimulated housing construction, promoted nontraditional exports, increased agricultural productivity, and supported effective taxation. But Pastrana Borrero capitulated to land-owning groups by undercutting the strength of earlier land-reform measures.

The National Front, though effective at ending partisan violence, did not sponsor political democratization. Numerous guerrilla groups rose to challenge the oligarchic control of politics during this period, including the Colombian Revolutionary Armed Forces (FARC), the Fidel Castro–inspired National Liberation Army (ELN), the Maoist Popular Liberation Army (ELP), and the M-19. Though the guerrillas were contained by an increasingly professionalized military, persistent social inequality, popular support, and inhospitable terrain have prevented their elimination. Guerrilla groups attracted considerable national attention as a possible alternative to bipartisan rule, but none gained sufficient power to challenge the Colombian state effectively.

CONTEMPORARY COLOMBIA

After the end of the National Front in 1978, Colombia departed significantly from its historic roots. In the early 2000s coffee is now the sixth most important export product. The country has entered a strategic alliance with U. S. foreign policy. Some things have not changed: Colombia still lacks a political culture that responds to the popular sector. Drug lords, guerrillas, and paramilitary forces have added to the violence that still plagues the country. Still, regular elections take place, even while there is much to suggest that the bipartisan heritage might be eroding. Colombia's internal and external economies continue to "muddle through," while recent high commodity prices, especially for oil and coal, offer a promise for the future.

Colombia's export economy is historically one of the more balanced and profitable in Latin America. While most Latin American economies stagnated in the 1980s, Colombia's export-led economy grew at an annual rate of 3.5 percent. In the period 1995 to 2004, Colombian exports increased by 5 percent annually, a significant factor in the nation's 17-percent GDP increase in the same period. Colombia is Latin America's largest producer of coal and its third-largest producer of petroleum, with newly discovered fields of more than two billion barrels yet to be put into production. The World Trade Organization reported that in 2004, petroleum and mining products constituted some 40 percent of Colombia's exports, manufactured products just over 38 percent, and agricultural products just over 20 percent. Coffee, which dominated the nation's exports for most of the twentieth century, has seen a dramatic decline

in importance, from 80 percent in the 1920s to 50 percent in the 1970s, and about 6 percent in 2003. The production of cut flowers, a semi-industrialized agricultural product from the high plains around Bogotá, employs about 140,000 people, mostly women. African palms, cacao, sorghum, and bananas are increasingly important exports. The United States continues to absorb the largest percentage of Colombian exports (42%), but its exports to Colombia have declined to barely 28 percent, down from 45 percent in 1990.

Political and drug-related violence ravaged the country in the 1980s. The Conservative Belisario Betancur Cuartas (1982–1986) offered FARC, M-19, and ELN guerrillas the opportunity to lay down their arms and enter into the political arena. In a positive response, FARC created the Patriotic Union Party (UP) as its political front in 1985, placing candidates in local and departmental elections. Right-wing paramilitary organizations, many of them linked to the military, declared de facto war upon the UP. Hundreds of UP candidates were assassinated in a bloodbath that drove the FARC back into overt warfare against the state. In November 1985 members of the M-19 seized the Supreme Court's Palace of Justice; the assault by the Colombian military left the building in flames and eleven of the twelve justices dead. Faced with the public outcry, the M-19 stopped its military activity and entered the political process.

Violence and the fragmentation of the political process created the environment in which Colombians reconsidered their constitutional structure. Highlighting the violence were the assassinations in 1989 and 1990 of three presidential candidates, "New Liberal" Luis Carlos Galán (1943–1989), UP Bernardo Jaramillo Ossa (1956–1990), and M-19 Carlos Pizarro Leongómez (1951–1990). The mainstream Liberal César Agusto Gaviria Trujillo (1990–1994) eventually won the election. An overwhelming popular vote in December 1990 led to a constituent congress that produced a new constitution in 1991. Under the new constitution the executive lost considerable power to the legislature, which itself was democratized and less beholden to regional party bosses. The judicial system was overhauled and extradition to foreign states banned. Elections to the first congress revealed a fundamental schism in the venerable Conservative Party, and saw the decline of the Liberal Party to a mere plurality. The short-term emergence of Democratic Alliance M-19 as the country's second-largest political association suggested the destabilization of the historic bipartisan political culture.

The tremendous demand for marijuana and cocaine from drug-consuming societies (chiefly the United States and Europe) has had profound and mostly negative impacts upon Colombia. High-quality marijuana, grown mostly on small farms on the northern coast in the early 1970s, stimulated regional economic activity and increased the standard of living before U.S. pressure on the Julio César Turbay Ayala regime (1978–1982) led to extensive spraying of defoliants that the United States had banned in its own country. The processing of cocaine by a limited number of producer cartels resulted in widespread social and political violence as well as an influx of U.S. dollars to the Medellín and Cali regions. The administration of U.S. president Ronald Reagan (1981–1989) demanded the extradition of drug barons for trial in the United States, prompting drug lords such as Pablo Escobar (1949–1993) to develop social programs and forge political ties to forestall extradition. When New Liberal politicians Luis Carlos Galán and Rodrigo Lara Bonilla (among others) assumed a decidedly antitrafficking stance, there was a wave of assassinations, including the minister of justice, Lara Bonilla, in 1984. President Belisario Betancur Cuartas then enforced the extradition treaty, setting off all-out war between Escobar and the government. Complicating the situation was the movement into the drug trade by FARC and ELN guerrillas. Scores of bombings, assassinations, and finally the murder of the favored presidential candidate, Luis Carlos Galán, in 1989, led the government to attack the Medellín cartel, by first killing the drug lord Gonzalo Rodríguez Gacha in late 1989. By the time the government finally killed Escobar in 1993, the violence of the drug trade had further destabilized the political process.

The economic importance of cocaine and the violence associated with its production increased during the 1990s. The Liberal president Ernesto Samper (1994–1998), despite having been wounded in a drug attack in 1989, was widely thought to have received money from the Cali cartel in support of his campaign. Samper proved unable—or unwilling—to curb production or distribution networks. In addition, coca

production moved from Bolivia and Peru to Colombia during the 1990s, so that by 2000 70 percent of the world's coca was being grown in the country by some 300,000 farmers. Guerrilla and paramilitary organizations became actively involved in both production and protection rackets, bringing violence to new areas of the country. Between 1985 and 2000 an estimated two million people were displaced by violence, leading to the rapid growth of many regional urban centers and an increase in urban poverty.

The Conservative Andrés Pastrana Arango (b. 1954) came to the presidency in 1998 with promises to attack the basic problems of political instability and the misdistribution of economic resources. Returning to the policies of Betancur, Pastrana opened negotiations with the FARC and ELN, offering the former a 40,000-square-kilometer demilitarized zone as an inducement to serious dialogue. The next year, his government proposed a Plan Colombia to achieve political peace and economic development. The United States significantly revised Plan Colombia to emphasize security concerns, enhancing the power of the military and potent antidrug initiatives, including the widespread use of defoliants on coca fields. After four years of frustrating and unsuccessful talks, Pastrana ordered the army to retake the zone.

The dissident Liberal Álvaro Uribe Vélez rode public sentiment in favor of a stronger position against guerrillas to victory in the 2002 presidential election. Though critics blasted his alleged relations with paramilitary organizations, Uribe fits well within the pattern of Colombian presidents assuming extraordinary powers with little regard to the niceties of civil power. Uribe has forged close relations with the government of U.S. president George W. Bush (2001–2009), which offered Colombia almost $4 billion in aid under Plan Colombia to combat "terrorism" and *narcotraficantes*. Considerable progress has been made in limiting drug trafficking, with Colombian cocaine production falling almost 40 percent from an estimated annual peak of 700 metric tons in 2001, the year Plan Colombia was initiated, to 430 metric tons in 2004. The amount of land dedicated to coca production, however, has not declined, despite energetic efforts on the part of the government. Although fighting between guerrilla, paramilitary, and state forces continues to ravage areas of the countryside, urban Colombia has been spared the violence it experienced in the 1980s. After the Congress changed the constitution allowing Uribe to run for a second term, 62 percent of the voting population preferred Uribe in the May 2006 presidential contest. In the electoral process, traditional Conservative and Liberal candidates fared very poorly, another indication of the changing political landscape

See also **Banana Industry; Coffee Industry; Drugs and Drug Trade.**

BIBLIOGRAPHY

Appelbaum, Nancy P. *Muddied Waters: Race, Region, and Local History in Colombia, 1846–1948.* Durham, NC: Duke University Press, 2003.

Bergquist, Charles. *Coffee and Conflict in Colombia, 1886–1910.* Durham, NC: Duke University Press, 1978.

Bergquist, Charles. *Labor in Latin America: Comparative Essays on Chile, Argentina, Venezuela, and Colombia.* Stanford, CA: Stanford University Press, 1986.

Braun, Herbert. *The Assassination of Gaitán: Public Life and Urban Violence in Colombia.* Madison: University of Wisconsin Press, 1985.

Bushnell, David. *The Santander Regime in Gran Colombia.* Westport, CT: Greenwood Press, 1970.

Bushnell, David. *The Making of Modern Colombia: A Nation in Spite of Itself.* Berkeley: University of California Press, 1993.

Delpar, Helen. *Red Against Blue: The Liberal Party in Colombian Politics, 1863–1899.* Tuscaloosa: University of Alabama Press, 1981.

Fluharty, Vernon Lee. *Dance of the Millions: Military Rule and the Social Revolution in Colombia, 1930–1956.* Pittsburgh, PA: University of Pittsburgh Press, 1971.

Green, W. John. *Gaitanismo, Left Liberalism, and Popular Mobilization in Colombia.* Gainesville: University Press of Florida, 2003.

Gutiérrez de Pineda, Virginia. *Familia y cultura en Colombia: Tipologías, funciones y dinámica de la familia.* Bogotá: Instituto Colombiano de Cultura, 1975.

Hartlyn, Jonathan. *The Politics of Coalition Rule in Colombia.* New York: Cambridge University Press, 1988.

Helg, Aline. *Liberty and Equality in Caribbean Colombia, 1770–1835.* Chapel Hill: University of North Carolina Press, 2004.

Henderson, James. *Conservative Thought in Twentieth-Century Latin America: The Ideas of Laureano Gómez.* Athens: Ohio University Press, 1988.

Journal of Inter-American Studies and World Affairs 30, nos. 2–3 (1988).

Legrand, Catherine. *Frontier Expansion and Peasant Protest in Colombia, 1830–1936.* Albuquerque: University of New Mexico Press, 1986.

Levine, Daniel H. *Religion and Politics in Latin America: The Catholic Church in Venezuela and Colombia.* Princeton, NJ: Princeton University Press, 1981.

Lynch, John. *The Spanish American Revolutions, 1808–1826.* 2nd ed. New York: W. W. Norton, 1986.

McFarlane, Anthony. "The Transition from Colonialism in Colombia, 1819–1975." In *Latin America, Economic Imperialism, and the State,* edited by Christopher Abel and Colin Lewis. London: Athlone Press, 1985.

McGreevey, William Paul. *An Economic History of Colombia, 1845–1930.* New York: Cambridge University Press, 1971.

Ocampo, José Antonio. *Colombia y la economía mundial, 1830–1910.* Bogotá: Fedesarrollo y Siglo Veintiuno Editores, 1984.

Ospina Vásquez, Luis. *Industria y protección en Colombia, 1810–1930.* Medellín, Colombia: Oveja Negra, 1974.

Oquist, Paul. *Violence, Conflict, and Politics in Colombia.* New York: Academic Press, 1980.

Palacios, Marco. *Coffee in Colombia, 1850–1970: An Economic, Social, and Political History.* New York: Cambridge University Press, 1980.

Palacios, Marco. *Between Legitimacy and Violence: A History of Colombia, 1875–2002,* translated by Richard Stoller. Durham, NC: Duke University Press, 2006.

Park, James W. *Rafael Núñez and the Politics of Colombian Regionalism, 1863–1886.* Baton Rouge: Louisiana State University Press, 1985.

Reinhardt, Nola. *Our Daily Bread: The Peasant Question and Family Farming in the Colombian Andes.* Berkeley: University of California Press, 1988.

Safford, Frank, and Marco Palacios. *Colombia: Fragmented Land, Divided Society.* New York: Oxford University Press, 2002.

Sanders, James E. *Contentious Republicans: Popular Politics, Race, and Class in Nineteenth-Century Colombia.* Durham, NC: Duke University Press, 2004.

Urrutia, Miguel. *The Development of the Colombian Labor Movement.* New Haven, CT: Yale University Press, 1969.

Wade, Peter. *Blackness and Race Mixture: The Dynamics of Racial Identity in Colombia.* Baltimore, MD: Johns Hopkins University Press, 1993.

Zamosc, Leon. *The Agrarian Question and the Peasant Movement in Colombia: Struggles of the National Peasant Association, 1967–1981.* Cambridge, U.K.: Cambridge University Press, 1986.

DAVID SOWELL

COLOMBIA, CONSTITUTIONS

This entry includes the following articles:
OVERVIEW
CONSTITUTION OF 1863

OVERVIEW

On 4 July 1991, Colombia officially adopted a new constitution, which replaced the Constitution of 1886, one of the world's oldest. Through its independent history the nation functioned under a number of charters, but after the early years there developed patterns more stable than in neighboring countries. An Act of Federation signed on 27 November 1811, created a federation known as the United Provinces of New Granada, but meaningful independence came only after the victory by patriot forces at the battle of Boyacá in August 1819, which established the state of Gran Colombia under the Constitution of Cúcuta (1821). Providing for a strong executive, a bicameral legislature, an appointed judiciary, and indirect elections, it also recognized departments, provinces, cantons, and parishes.

Criticized as being too centralized, it was replaced by a new document following the 1830 breakup of Gran Colombia, when Venezuela and Ecuador went their own ways. The 1832 charter recognized the Republic of New Granada as a decentralized entity, and the conflict between centralism and federalism remained at the center of politics throughout the nineteenth century. The centralist impulse was enshrined in the Constitution of 1843, which represented in part a reaction to the 1832 document. A strong president was granted unlimited power of appointment plus the authority to initiate legislative debates, while provincial assemblies were subordinated to the national government. Within a few years, however, the trends were in the direction of decentralization, leading to the constitutions of 1853, 1858, and 1863.

The first of these documents was notable for a wide range of liberal reforms, including the abolition of slavery, separation of church and state, recognition of press freedom, trial by jury, and a strengthening of provincial legislatures. Five years later the Constitution of 1858 renamed the nation the Granadine Confederation. Eight sovereign states were recognized, each with residual powers. The national government's authority was restricted largely to foreign affairs and defense.

It was the Constitution of 1863, adopted on 8 May by a convention of delegates assembled in Rionegro, that carried the federalist approach to its extreme. Nine states established the United States of Colombia, the central government of which was prohibited from interference in state affairs. Each of the federated states enjoyed sovereignty and was permitted to have its own army. Individual liberties were virtually unlimited, and capital punishment was abolished. The presidential term was shortened from four to two years, with immediate reelection prohibited. The Rionegro constitution was among the most extreme federalist documents ever known. In practice, its decentralization of authority was such that more than fifty uprisings broke out in the next quarter century, accompanied by a cavalcade of state constitutions.

An eventual alliance between Conservatives and so-called Independent Liberals in 1885 supported Rafael Núñez as president and moved for a change of the system. The Constitution of 1886 created the Republic of Colombia along unitary lines. Strong centralism was restored, while the authority of the provinces was subordinated to Bogotá. Governors were to be appointed, rather than elected, to serve four-year terms. Reelection was permitted after one term out of office. A bicameral legislature was to be elected for four-year terms. This charter proved to be Colombia's most durable and was amended in 1936, 1945, 1957, and 1968.

The most far-reaching of these amendments came in 1957, legitimizing a sixteen-year period of controlled rule by the Conservative-Liberal hegemony known as the National Front. Parity of representation, along with alternation in executive power, constituted the cornerstone of the arrangement, as further modified by reforms in 1968. This arrangement served to stabilize the system, while also assuring unchallenged control by traditional party elites.

By the 1980s, rising political pressures called for major reforms, as was manifested by a popular vote in 1990 approving the convening of a constitutional assembly, the body that subsequently wrote the Constitution of 1991. Popular participation was encouraged, congressional privilege was restricted, electoral procedures were democratized, the judicial system was reorganized, and party clientelism was reduced. Individual rights—socioeconomic as well as political—were spelled out in detail. The presidential term remained four years, but reelection was ruled out, while the office of vice president was created for the first time. The management and organization of fiscal and economic policy were also restructured.

The new constitution was lengthy, and many reforms were outlined in considerable detail. The intention of opening up the constitutional and political system had carried the constitutional assembly further than had been expected. The impact on the Colombian political system can be judged only with the passing of time. However, the constitutional changes from 1886 to 1991 were unquestionably extensive and destined to have a powerful impact on Colombia. Despite the ongoing civil war, the constitution has remained in place with only one major change. In 2004, President Álvaro Uribe lobbied Congress to allow for the reelection of the president. When the Congress passed this proposal, Uribe ran and won a second term in office.

See also **Cúcuta, Congress of; Federalism.**

BIBLIOGRAPHY

Jesús María Henao and Gerardo Arrubla, *History of Colombia*, translated by J. Fred Rippy (1938).

Helen Delpar, *Red Against Blue: The Liberal Party in Colombian Politics, 1863–1899* (1981).

Harvey F. Kline, *Colombia: Portrait of Unity and Diversity* (1983).

Robert H. Dix, *The Politics of Colombia* (1987).

Jorge Pablo Osterling, *Democracy in Colombia: Clientelist Politics and Guerrilla Warfare* (1989).

Additional Bibliography

Cárdenas Rivera, Miguel E., ed. *La reforma política del estado en Colombia: Una salida integral a la crisis.* Bogotá: Friedrich Ebert Stiftung en Colombia (Fescol), 2005.

Gómez Ortiz, Armando, Orlando Pardo Martínez, and Amado Antonio Guerrero Rincón, eds. *Las constituciones políticas del Gran Santander, 1853–1885.* Bucaramanga, Colombia: Escuela de Historia, Universidad Industrial de Santander, 2004.

JOHN D. MARTZ

CONSTITUTION OF 1863

In effect from 1863 to 1885, the constitution, produced by an all-Liberal assembly at Rionegro, Antioquia, was the maximum expression of Colombian federalism, outstripping its already federalist predecessor of 1858. Colombia's nine sovereign states were permitted to raise armies, set electoral laws, and do most anything else of consequence; the federal president was limited to a nonrenewable two-year term, and he was indirectly elected by the states. The document's libertarian bent, providing for absolute freedom of the press (including libel) and unrestricted traffic in arms, led the French novelist Victor Hugo to deem it a constitution for a "nation of angels." Conservatives, and many Liberals, blamed the document for Colombia's persistent instability and underdevelopment. In January 1886 President Rafael Núñez, after crushing a Liberal revolt, declared that the 1863 constitution had "ceased to exist"; its successor, in force until 1991, reverted to a centralist and quasi-authoritarian model.

See also **Federalism; Mosquera, Tomás Cipriano de.**

BIBLIOGRAPHY

Salvador Camacho Roldán, "La convención de Rionegro," in his *Memorias* (1923).

William M. Gibson, *The Constitutions of Colombia* (1948).

James William Park, *Rafael Núñez and the Politics of Colombian Regionalism, 1863–1886* (1985).

Additional Bibliography

Gómez Ortiz, Armando, Orlando Pardo Martínez, and Amado Antonio Guerrero Rincón, eds. *Las constituciones políticas del Gran Santander, 1853–1885.* Bucaramanga, Colombia: Escuela de Historia, Universidad Industrial de Santander, 2004.

RICHARD J. STOLLER

COLOMBIA, GREAT BANANA STRIKE.

Colombia's Great Banana Strike, a violent labor dispute in 1928. The target of the strikers was the United Fruit Company, which controlled banana production and marketing in the coastal department of Magdalena. In mid-November 1928 about twenty thousand workers went on strike against United Fruit and Colombian growers. The strikers' main demand was that they be recognized as company employees so that they might receive benefits guaranteed by law. To avoid providing these benefits, the company used labor contractors in hiring and firing. The strikers also sought wage increases and collective contracts. Intransigence on both sides prolonged the strike, and as tension mounted, the government declared martial law on 5 December. Early the next morning General Carlos Cortés Vargas ordered a crowd of 1,500 strikers and family members camped in the plaza of Ciénaga to disperse. When the order was ignored, his soldiers fired, killing thirteen. Strikers then attacked and burned company buildings in Sevilla, where soldiers killed twenty-nine. A wave of repression that followed produced additional deaths. The total number of victims is not known, but a historian has estimated the total between sixty and seventy-five. Many strike leaders were also jailed.

The Conservative government's handling of the strike, and especially the use of the army in defense of a foreign enterprise, provoked outrage and contributed to the Liberal victory in 1930. Jorge E. Gaitán, then a Liberal member of Congress, excoriated the government in an inflammatory debate that solidified his reputation as a friend of labor. The strike occupies an important place in Colombian national consciousness. It is the focal point of Álvaro Cepeda Samudio's novel *La casa grande* (1962) and the subject of a key episode in Gabriel García Márquez's *Cien años de soledad* (1967).

See also **Banana Industry.**

BIBLIOGRAPHY

Miguel Urrutia, *The Development of the Colombian Labor Movement* (1969), esp. pp. 99–109.

Judith White, *Historia de una ignominia* (1978).

Roberto Herrera Soto and Rafael Romero Castañeda, *La zona bananera del Magdalena* (1979).

Carlos Arango Z., *Sobrevivientes de las bananeras* (1981).

Additional Bibliography

Bucheli, Marcelo. *Bananas and Business: The United Fruit Company in Colombia, 1899–2000.* New York: New York University Press, 2005.

Green, W. John. *Gaitanismo, Left Liberalism, and Popular Mobilization in Colombia.* Gainesville: University Press of Florida, 2003.

HELEN DELPAR

COLOMBIA, ORGANIZATIONS

This entry includes the following articles:
COLOMBIAN INDIGENIST INSTITUTE
COLOMBIAN INSTITUTE FOR AGRARIAN REFORM (INCORA)
CONFEDERATION OF COLOMBIAN WORKERS (CTC)
DEMOCRATIC SOCIETY OF ARTISANS
NATIONAL ASSOCIATION OF INDUSTRIALISTS
NATIONAL FEDERATION OF COFFEE GROWERS
NATIONAL SCHOOL OF MINES OF MEDELLÍN
UNIFIED CENTRAL OF WORKERS (CUT)
UNION OF COLOMBIAN WORKERS (UTC)
UNION SOCIETY OF ARTISANS

COLOMBIAN INDIGENIST INSTITUTE

This organization was established in 1942 to promote the founding of indigenist groups to advise governments on official Indian policy. Formed in response to the call of the First Inter-American Indigenist Congress (at Pátzcuaro, Mexico), the institute was a private entity founded by leading Colombian intellectuals, including Gregorio Hernández de Alba, Antonio García, Juan Friede, Gerardo Reichel Dolmatoff, and Alfredo Vásquez Carrizosa. Its objectives included the publication of cultural, historical, and socioeconomic studies of Colombian Indians as well as the promotion of applied anthropology projects aimed at the rational integration of Indians into the national life of Colombia. The Colombian Indigenist Institute was active in confronting official policies, and it was critical of the liquidation of indigenous communities and government support of Catholic missions among indigenous people. The institute was incorporated into the National University of Colombia in 1947, but was dissolved during the Violencia of the following decade.

See also **Labor Movements.**

BIBLIOGRAPHY

Roberto Pineda Camacho, "La reivindicación del indio en el pensamiento social colombiano (1850–1950)," in *Un siglo de investigación social: Antropología en Colombia,* edited by Jaime Arocha and Nina S. de Friedemann (1984).

Additional Bibliography

Gros, Christian. *Políticas de la etnicidad: Identidad, estado y modernidad.* Bogotá: Instituto Colombiano de Antropología e Historia, 2000.

Postero, Nancy Grey, and León Zamosc, eds. *The Struggle for Indigenous Rights in Latin America*. Portland, OR: Sussex Academic Press, 2004.

Rappaport, Joanne. *Intercultural Utopias: Public Intellectuals, Cultural Experimentation, and Ethnic Pluralism in Colombia*. Durham, NC: Duke University Press, 2005.

JOANNE RAPPAPORT

COLOMBIAN INSTITUTE FOR AGRARIAN REFORM (INCORA)

Law 135 of 1961 created the Colombian Institute for Agrarian Reform (INCORA) to address the inequities of rural Colombia amid the challenges of the Cuban Revolution and the social upheaval of *La Violencia*. Carlos Lleras Restrepo, the leader of the Liberal Party, served as the intellectual author of the project, sought to distribute public lands, expand zones of colonization, offer credits for agricultural development, and improve rural infrastructure through road and irrigation projects. He did not, however, envision the purchase or nationalization of private property. Even with its limited scope, INCORA distributed a very small percentage of lands it intended to make available, largely because of elite political influence from the Society of Agriculturalists (SAC) and the Federación Nacional de cafeteros de Colombia (Federation of Colombian Coffee Growers, FEDECAFE). Perhaps as a result of this shortcoming, Lleras Restrepo, during his presidency (1966–1970), helped to found the Asociación Nacional de Usarios Campesinos (ANUC, 1968), a national peasants' organization that also proved ineffective in addressing problems of rural poverty or landlessness.

See also **Lleras Restrepo, Carlos; Violencia, La.**

BIBLIOGRAPHY

Tobón, Alonso. *La tierra y la reforma agraria en Colombia*. Bogotá: La Oveja Negra, 1972.

Zamosc, León. *The Agrarian Question and the Peasant Movement in Colombia: Struggles of the National Peasant Association, 1967–1981*. New York: Cambridge University Press, 1986.

DAVID SOWELL

CONFEDERATION OF COLOMBIAN WORKERS (CTC)

The Confederation of Colombian Workers (Confederación de Trabajadores de Colombia—CTC) was the first national labor confederation in Colombia. The return of the Liberal Party to power in 1930 was followed by extensive unionization, culminating in the establishment of the CTC in 1935 to represent all unionized workers. Transportation workers were the backbone of the CTC, which was weakened by bitter rivalry between Communist and Liberal factions. In exchange for supporting Liberal candidates the CTC received government funds, yet it could not shed its image as a radical organization of the extreme left.

The Liberal government crushed a major strike by river dockworkers in 1945 because it felt that the CTC had become too powerful. In 1947 the CTC had 109,000 members, who belonged to 427 affiliated unions. When the Conservative Party returned to power in 1946, it supported, at the urging of the Catholic Church, a rival confederation, the Union of Colombian Workers (UTC). By 1950, the UTC had replaced the CTC as the largest labor organization. Defections from the CTC to the UTC and the growing ranks of unaffiliated unions further weakened the CTC, which by 1959 represented only 27 unions.

Following the Cuban Revolution the U.S. government, through the CIA, convinced the CTC to expel remaining Communist members. In return, the CTC received funds and backing to revive itself as an attractive alternative for those workers not comfortable with the Catholic and Conservative ideas of the UTC. The expelled Communists set up the Syndical Confederation of Colombian Workers (CSTC) in 1964, while the CTC, with support from the Colombian and U.S. governments, was able to push its membership figures back above 100,000. In 1979 the CTC claimed to have more than 400,000 members, almost the same number as the rival UTC. By then the CTC was a hollow organization whose corrupt leaders had lost contact with the rank and file. Many unions defected to the new Unified Central of Workers (CUT). By the early 1990s the CTC represented less than 13 percent of unionized workers in Colombia; its membership had dropped below 80,000. Although still weak, the CTC managed to survive into the early twenty-first century.

See also **Labor Movements.**

BIBLIOGRAPHY

Cabrera Mejía, María Alicia. *El sindicalismo en Colombia: Una historia para resurgir*. Bogotá, Colombia: M. A. Cabrera Mejía, 2005.

Caicedo, Edgar. *Historia de las luchas sindicales en Colombia.* Bogota: Ediciones Suramerica, 1982.

De La Pedraja, René. "Colombia." In *Latin American Labor Organizations,* ed. Gerald Greenfield and Sheldon L. Maram, pp. 179–212. New York: Greenwood, 1987.

López-Alves, Fernando. "Explaining Confederation: Colombian Unions in the 1980s." *Latin American Research Review* 25 (1990): 115–133.

RENÉ DE LA PEDRAJA

DEMOCRATIC SOCIETY OF ARTISANS

Members of the Democratic Society of Artisans (Sociedad Democrática de Artesanos) articulated a critical assessment of the liberal reform process and of elite-dominated politics in mid-nineteenth century Colombia. In Bogotá, where the Democratic Society emerged in 1849 from the Society of Artisans, members initially focused upon increasing tariffs and other popular policies, despite the influence of Liberal politicians who sought to manipulate the organization. In Cali, the Democratic Society sought racial equality and the return of *ejido* lands (common lands—some were indigenous, some not), reflecting the distinct social characteristics of the region. Artisans and disgruntled Draconiano (followers of President José María Obando) regained control of the capital's chapter in 1851, after which it became closely aligned with the presidential administration of General Obando (1853–1854). Its earlier myopic focus on higher tariff rates evolved into a potent criticism of elite-dominated liberalism, leading chapters in Bogotá, Cali, and San Gil to support the unsuccessful 1854 *golpe de estado* (coup d'état) of José María Melo.

See also **Colombia, Political Parties: Liberal Party; Ejidos; Golpe de estado (coup d'état); Melo, José María; Obando, José María.**

BIBLIOGRAPHY

Sanders, James E. *Contentious Republicans: Popular Politics, Race, and Class in Nineteenth-Century Colombia.* Durham, NC: Duke University Press, 2004.

Sowell, David. "'*La teoría i la realidad*': The Democratic Society of Artisans of Bogotá, 1847–1854." *Hispanic American Historical Review* 67, no. 4 (November 1987): 611–630.

DAVID SOWELL

NATIONAL ASSOCIATION OF INDUSTRIALISTS

Founded 18 November 1944 in Medellín at a meeting of several of the country's largest manufacturers, the National Association of Industrialists (Asociación Nacional de Industriales—ANDI) is one of the best-organized and most powerful producer groups (*gremios*) in Colombia. Its emergence reflected not only the rapid growth of Colombian industry at the time but also the desire of industrialists, led by the Echavarría clan and other wealthy capitalists from Medellín, to promote their interests by urging the government to pursue protectionist economic policies. Speaking for major sectors of Colombian business, the group has had an impact through its outspoken support of the free-enterprise system, as well as the work of its economists and the advice of its consultants.

BIBLIOGRAPHY

Harvey Kline, *Colombia: Portrait of Unity and Diversity* (1983), pp. 79–80.

Eduardo Sáenz Rovner, "The Industrialists and Politics in Colombia, 1945–1950" (Ph.D. diss., Brandeis University, 1989).

Additional Bibliography

Dávila L de Guevara, Carlos. *Empresas y empresarios en la historia de Colombia: Siglos XIX–XX: Una colección de estudios recientes.* Bogotá: Norma: CEPAL: Uniandes, 2003.

Sáenz Rovner, Eduardo. *Colombia años 50: Industriales, política y diplomacia.* Bogotá: Universidad Nacional de Colombia, Sede Bogotá, 2002.

PAMELA MURRAY

NATIONAL FEDERATION OF COFFEE GROWERS

The National Federation of Coffee Growers (Federación Nacional de Cafeteros—Fedecafé) is an organization that seeks to represent domestic producers and sellers of coffee, Colombia's primary export commodity. It was founded in 1927 by prominent landowners and politicians who have played a vital role in the development of the Colombian coffee industry. Supported by a government tax on coffee exports, Fedecafé has stimulated coffee productivity by disseminating information on modern farming methods, improving marketing, and promoting trade policies to make Colombia's crop competitive worldwide. Despite its claim to speak for both small and big growers, the federation has mainly represented Colombia's largest coffee interests, including some of the oldest and wealthiest landowning families in the country. Its leadership has included members of the political elite, such as Mariano Ospina Pérez, who served as the federation's first president (1927–1934) before becoming president of Colombia. This connection explains the federation's quasi-governmental influence not only on the coffee industry but on national economic policies as well.

See also **Ospina Pérez, Mariano.**

BIBLIOGRAPHY

Bennett E. Koffman, "The National Federation of Coffee Growers of Colombia" (Ph.D. diss., University of Virginia, 1969).

Marco Palacios, *Coffee in Colombia, 1850–1970: An Economic, Social, and Political History* (1980).

Additional Bibliography

Gómez Jaramillo, Arturo, Otto Morales Benítez, and Diego Pizano Salazar. *Arturo Gómez Jaramillo, zar del café.* Bogotá: Fondo Cultural Cafetero, 2003.

Ramírez Bacca, Renzo. *Formación y transformación de la cultura laboral cafetera en el siglo XX.* Medellín: Carreta Editores, 2004.

PAMELA MURRAY

NATIONAL SCHOOL OF MINES OF MEDELLÍN

Founded in 1887, the National School of Mines is Colombia's second oldest engineering school. Although originally designed to train mining engineers, by the mid-1940s it trained mainly civil engineers known for their practical bent and versatility. More important, it became a seedbed of entrepreneurs and industrialists who, in the first half of the twentieth century, helped make Medellín the undisputed cradle of modern Colombian manufacturing industry. The School also forged a technocratic elite. Through the 1960s its graduates played key roles in departmental and national government, routinely serving as superintendents of the Antioquia Railway and Empresas Publicas de Medellín; as cabinet ministers; and as directors of powerful producer organizations such as the National Federation of Coffee Growers and the National Association of Industrialists. To supply the country with its own professionals for the energy (especially oil) industry, moreover, the School developed the nation's first program in geological and petroleum engineering. It has continued to develop specialties to meet the country's increasingly complex technical and administrative challenges, in the late 1970s, for example, founding a Coal Research Center. Now part of Colombia's National University, it maintains a reputation for excellence.

See also **Mining: Modern; Petroleum Industry.**

BIBLIOGRAPHY

Mayor Mora, Alberto. *Etica, Trabajo, y Productividad en Antioquia: Una interpretación sociológica sobre la influencia de la Escuela Nacional de Minas en la vida, costumbres e industrialización regionales.* Bogotá: Ediciones Tercer Mundo, 1984.

Murray, Pamela S. *Dreams of Development: Colombia's National School of Mines and its Engineers, 1887–1970.* Tuscaloosa: University of Alabama Press, 1997.

PAMELA MURRAY

UNIFIED CENTRAL OF WORKERS (CUT)

The largest labor confederation in Colombia since 1986, the Unified Central of Workers (Central Unitaria de Trabajadores—CUT) has at various times represented from 50 to possibly 80 percent of unionized workers. The creation of the CUT reflected the growing disenchantment of the rank and file with the corrupt and ineffective leadership of the two traditional labor confederations, the Union of Colombian Workers (UTC) and the Confederation of Colombian Workers (CTC). When, starting in 1980, employers launched an antiunion campaign to drastically slash wages, the workers became militant and began to sympathize with the Communist organization, the Syndical Confederation of Colombian Workers (CSTC), itself reeling from a combined government–employer offensive.

To preempt the Communists, in 1985 President Belisario Betancur appointed a union leader, Jorge Carrillo Rojas, as minister of labor. Carillo Rojas decided to merge the four existing labor confederations into a new one, the CUT. This unwieldy coalition survived while he remained as minister but disintegrated as soon as he resigned to become the head of the CUT in 1986. Most unions stayed in the CUT, however, so that it continued to represent at least half of the unionized workers. Likewise, many unaffiliated unions joined the CUT. When the CSTC merged with the CUT, the CTC and UTC leaders charged that the new confederation was under Communist control. Against the advice of Carrillo Rojas, militants voted to participate in two general strikes, in 1987 and 1988, both of which ended in failure.

Employers and the government had wanted the CUT to end Communist influence but not to become an independent force. In an attempt to undermine support for the CUT, the government funded and supported the nearly moribund CTC and UTC. Since 1988 the CUT has concentrated on backing workers in specific struggles, such as those on banana plantations and in government agencies threatened with privatization.

See also **Labor Movements.**

BIBLIOGRAPHY

René De La Pedraja, "Colombia," in *Latin American Labor Organizations,* edited by Gerald Greenfield and Sheldon L. Maram (1987), pp. 179–212.

Fernando López-Alves, "Explaining Confederation: Colombian Unions in the 1980s," in *Latin American Research Review* 25 (1990): 115–133.

Additional Bibliography

Cabrera Mejía, María Alicia. *El sindicalismo en Colombia: Una historia para resurgir.* Bogotá, Colombia: M.A. Cabrera Mejía, Editorial Nomos, 2005.

Delgado, Alvaro. *El sindicalismo bogotano del nuevo siglo.* Bogotá: Alcaldía Mayor de Bogotá, Instituto Distrital de Cultura y Turismo (Observatorio de Cultura Urbana), 2003.

Silva Romero, Marcel. *Flujos y Reflujos: Reseña histórica sobre la autonomía del sindicalismo colombiano.* Bogotá: Universidad Nacional de Colombia, Facultad de Derecho, Ciencias Políticas y Sociales, 1998.

RENÉ DE LA PEDRAJA

UNION OF COLOMBIAN WORKERS (UTC)

The Union of Colombian Workers (Unión de Trabajadores de Colombia—UTC) was the most important labor confederation in Colombia from 1950 to 1980. It was created in 1946 at the urging of the Catholic Church to counter the leftist Confederation of Colombian Workers (CTC). The strong religious tendency within the early UTC (Jesuit advisers remained active until the 1960s) made the confederation acceptable to female workers and traditional factory owners. During the wave of industrialization in Colombia after 1945, the UTC organized the new industrial workers, and by 1950 it had replaced the CTC as the largest confederation.

During its early years, the UTC had tried to avoid partisan issues, but in 1963 a new UTC president, Tulio Cuevas, linked the UTC with the Conservative Party. Backing and funds from the Colombian and U.S. governments fueled the expansion of the UTC, whose membership reached half a million workers in 1971. The rank and file became disenchanted with the corrupt and autocratic leadership, and in 1980 the 100,000 members from Cundinamarca bolted from the UTC. Other unions followed, many of which later joined the new Unified Central of Workers (CUT). By 1986, the UTC's membership had dropped to 80,000, representing barely 13 percent of unionized workers in Colombia. The UTC has continued to decline, and its future survival is seriously in doubt, as is that of the CTC. The obsession of leaders with preserving their plush posts, however, has blocked attempts to merge the former rivals, which have been eclipsed by the CUT.

See also **Labor Movements.**

BIBLIOGRAPHY

Hernando Gómez B. et al., *Sindicalismo y política económica* (1986).

René De La Pedraja, "Colombia," in *Latin American Labor Organizations,* edited by Gerald Greenfield and Sheldon L. Maram (1987), pp. 179–212.

Fernando López-Alves, "Explaining Confederation: Colombian Unions in the 1980s," in *Latin American Research Review* 25 (1990): 115–133.

Additional Bibliography

Farnsworth-Alvear, Ann. *Dulcinea in the Factory: Myths, Morals, Men, and Women in Colombia's Industrial Experiment, 1905–1960.* Durham, NC: Duke University Press, 2000.

Silva Romero, Marcel. *Flujos y reflujos: Reseña histórica sobre la autonomía del sindicalismo colombiano.* Santafé de Bogotá: Universidad Nacional de Colombia, Facultad de Derecho, Ciencias Políticas y Sociales, 1998.

RENÉ DE LA PEDRAJA

UNION SOCIETY OF ARTISANS

The Union Society of Artisans (Sociedad Unión de Artesanos), a labor organization, culminated twenty years of political activities by Bogotá's artisans during the liberal reform era. Founded in 1866 in the aftermath of the 1859–1862 civil war, amidst a serious economic recession, it attempted to forge a nonpartisan alliance of artisans. Membership in the society ranged from perhaps 300 to 500 artisans during its first year, before partisan upheaval caused by Tomás Cipriano de Mosquera's abortive coup divided the organization. The society finally dissolved after the November 1868 overthrow of the Cundinamarcan state government. The society's newspaper, *La Alianza* (The Alliance), articulated an ideology of artisan republicanism, based in part on a labor theory of value. It advocated the return to centralized government, a restitution of clerical temporal authority, a biparty government, and protection of native industries. José Leocadio Camacho, Antonio Cárdenas, Saturnino González, and Felipe Roa Ramírez were the most visible leaders of the society.

See also **Labor Movements.**

BIBLIOGRAPHY

David Sowell, *The Early Colombian Labor Movement: Artisans and Politics in Bogota, 1832–1919* (1992).

Additional Bibliography

Gaviria Liévano, Enrique. *El liberalismo y la insurrección de los artesanos contra el librecambio: Primeras manifestaciones socialistas en Colombia.* Bogotá: Universidad de Bogotá Jorge Tadeo Lozano, 2002.

Mayor Mora, Alberto. *Cabezas duras y dedos inteligentes: Estilo de vida y cultura técnica de los artesanos colombianos del siglo XIX.* Colombia: Instituto Colombiano de Cultura, 1997.

DAVID SOWELL

COLOMBIA, PACIFIC COAST. Colombia's Pacific Coast, a geographic unit between the Pacific shore and the western highlands of Colombia. In terms of archaeology, knowledge remains so scant that processes of social development in the area can only be described in the most general terms. Even in the early 2000s major interpretations still claim migrations and diffusion as the most important variables shaping the societies that the Spaniards described in the region upon their arrival early in the sixteenth century.

Colombia was probably occupied by human societies coming from lower Central America about 10,000 to 12,000 BCE. Thus, early preceramic occupation along the Pacific coast is important for the understanding of the very early human societies that settled South America. Early human presence in the region is inferred from tools that have been found in surface collections without pottery. Two projectile points found in the Golfo de Urabá, not far from the border with Panama, suggest hunting activities around 8000 BCE. Very little is known in terms of other economic activities, settlement patterns, and cultural features.

Knowledge improves somewhat for much later periods, when pottery and goldwork were introduced in the area. Early radiocarbon dates have been obtained for sites in the Tumaco area, close to the Colombia-Ecuador border. About 325 BCE human societies in this region elaborated fine pottery and used gold adornments. Other sites this old have been found farther north, in the Lower Calima and near the Munguidó River. Pottery from Tumaco shows similarities with pottery excavated along the Pacific coast of Ecuador (Chorrera) and sites in the Calima region near Cali (the Ilama period). In Tumaco one of the main features in pottery manufacture is the elaboration of fine figurines. This period is also known for the construction of mounds locally known as *tolas*. Economic activities included fishing and the exploitation of mangroves, hunting, and agriculture. It seems that intensive cultivation of maize was present in some areas from about 200 to 100 BCE, although earlier dates in the neighboring Calima region to the east would suggest maize was known long before its consumption became important. Other plants seem to have been at least as relevant as maize during early times.

Later periods in Tumaco are described as a sequence of changes in pottery styles, including the progressive modification of figurines that become more and more rudimentary. Construction of *tolas* disappears about 1000 CE. Nonetheless, social changes in the region do not suggest a decadence in social organization or economic activities. Between 800 and 1500 CE there is evidence of agricultural progress, including labor-intensive practices of fertilization. Also, the elaboration of metal adornments continued to the time of the Spanish Conquest. Trade activities along the Pacific coast were described during the sixteenth century and there is some speculation that long-distance trade networks linked the Pacific coast with Ecuador and Panama. Archaeological evidence of this trade, however, remains scant.

See also **Calima; Indigenous Peoples.**

BIBLIOGRAPHY

A summary of archaeological research in the area is provided by Leonor Herrera, "Costa del Pacífico y vertiente oeste de la cordillera occidental," in *Colombia Prehispánica-Regiones Arqueológicas* (1989). Excavations in Tumaco are reported by Francois Bouchard, "Excavaciones arqueológicas en la Región de Tumaco, Nariño, Colombia," in *Revista Colombiana de Antropología* (1985). Also see Diógenes Patiño, *Asentamientos Prehispánicos en la Costa Pacífica Caucana*. A description in English of archaeological research in the area is Warwick Bray, "Across the Darien Gap: A Colombian View of Isthmian Archaeology," in *The Archaeology of Lower Central America*, edited by Frederick W. Lange and Doris Z. Stone (1984). For a general overview of Colombian archaeology, see Carl Henrik Langebaek, *Noticias de Caciques muy Mayores: Orígen y desarrollo de sociedades complejas en el nororiente de Colombia y norte de Venezuela* (1992).

Additional Bibliography

Corsetti, Giancarlo. *Cambios tecnológicos, organización social y actividades productivas en la Costa Pacífica colombiana*. Bogotá: Ecoe, 1990.

Pardo, Mauricio. *Acción colectiva, estado y etnicidad en el pacífico colombiano*. Bogotá: Instituto Colombiano de Antropología e Historia, Conciencias, 2001.

Seeliger, U., and Kjerfve, B., eds. *Coastal Marine Ecosystems of Latin America*. New York: Springer, 2000.

Velásquez, R. *Fragmentos de historia, etnografía y narraciones del Pacífico colombiano negro*, Bogotá: Instituto Colombiano de Antropología e Historia, 2000.

CARL HENRIK LANGEBAEK R.

COLOMBIA, POLITICAL PARTIES

This entry includes the following articles:
OVERVIEW
CONSERVATIVE PARTY
LIBERAL PARTY
NATIONAL FRONT
NATIONAL POPULAR ALLIANCE (ANAPO)
RADICAL OLYMPUS

OVERVIEW

Colombia's party system is the oldest in Latin America. Its two traditional parties, the Liberals and Conservatives, date back to the late 1840s and have controlled national politics until the 1990s, when their electoral dominance subsided notably. In the early twenty-first century, the Colombian party system is in a period of flux; the traditional Liberal and Conservative Parties continue to exist, but they have been challenged by a vibrant democratic left, as well as by more personalist parties supportive of the highly popular president Alvaro Uribe Vélez (2002–).

Historically, the Liberal and Conservative parties were divided over significant policy issues. In the nineteenth and early twentieth centuries, Conservatives favored a strong centralized state in contrast to the Liberals' preference for a federal association of individually powerful states. Conservatives advocated close ties between church and state; the Liberals did not. And Conservatives wanted government involvement in economic policymaking, whereas Liberals championed a nineteenth-century laissez-faire view of the economy. These differences, along with regional rivalries and personal ambitions, characterized party conflict for a century.

While the parties were organizations of notables rather than forces for mass political participation, the leadership built strong support and loyalties that were strengthened by patron-client relationships. Liberal and Conservative leaders generated substantial backing for the succession of civil wars and uprisings that took place in the nineteenth century. The struggle for power was often violent and was only stabilized in the 1880s, when Rafael Núñez Moledo moved toward establishing a strong central government. This arrangement was legitimated by the Constitution of 1886, which drastically reduced the authority of individual states while also recognizing Catholicism as Colombia's official religion. By the time of Núñez's death in 1894, structures had been erected that would strengthen Conservative domination.

Civil strife was by no means ended: There was a brief insurgency in 1895 and then the War of the Thousand Days (1899–1902). Yet Conservative rule continued until 1930, when the Liberals returned to power. Four years later, when the Liberal Alfonso López Pumarejo won the presidency and instituted a number of reforms, the level of partisan debate rose. López and his followers sought an expansion of the state, greater activity in labor and welfare policy, and a redefined relationship with the Catholic Church. He met with fierce opposition from within his own party as well as from the Conservatives. These differences eventually led to a Liberal division in 1946, enabling the Conservatives to regain power under Mariano Ospina Pérez. The next few years saw a progressive deterioration of the party system, fueled by growing violence between Liberals and Conservatives in the countryside. This period of extremely bloody partisan conflict (known in the twenty-first century simply as La Violencia) brought a collapse of the civilian regime and the reluctant intervention by the armed forces in 1953.

Following the collapse of the military regime in 1957, Liberal and Conservative party leaders negotiated a power-sharing arrangement intended to bring an end to partisan violence. The resultant National Front (1958–1974) assured sixteen years during which congressional, ministerial, and other major positions would be divided equally between the Liberal and Conservative parties, while the presidency would alternate between them. These measures guaranteed that third parties were relegated to a minor position in the system, while traditional Conservative and Liberal elites could retain control of public policy.

With the return of competitive elections in 1974, the Liberals proved to be the majority party. From 1974 to 1998, they lost the presidency only once—in 1982 when two Liberal candidates divided the vote—and they consistently maintained control of both houses of Congress. At the same time, amendments to the original National Front provisions adopted in 1968 called for continuing participation in government by both parties, thus ensuring access to bureaucratic posts for the minority Conservative Party.

Meanwhile, the two party organizations had weakened internally, with national leaders increasingly relying upon local and regional bosses for votes and services. Customary elitist control over the traditional parties diminished. National Front rules also discouraged participation in elections, and abstention rates were high. Levels of public cynicism rose, increasing pressure for reforms and political modernization. In 1990, Liberal president César Gaviria Trujillo (1990–1994) backed a movement that eventually led to the new constitution of 1991. The 1991 Constitution weakened traditional party domination, with new electoral regulations sharply limiting the old control mechanisms of local leaders.

Poor governance further undermined two-party dominance after the 1991 Constitution. The Liberal Party suffered a significant blow to its image during the presidency of Ernesto Samper Pizano (1994–1998), who was accused of having accepted several million dollars from the Cali drug cartel to finance his campaign. Although Samper survived two impeachment processes in Congress, the Liberal Party was badly shaken and lost the 1998 presidential election to Conservative Andrés Pastrana Arango (1998–2002). Pastrana, in turn, proved to be highly unpopular when his efforts to achieve peace with the leftist FARC and ELN guerrillas failed utterly. In the 2002 presidential election, the Conservatives declined to run a candidate and the official candidate of the Liberal Party was soundly defeated by the dissident Liberal Alvaro Uribe Vélez. Having broken with the Liberal Party, Uribe governed as an independent; his immense popularity led to his re-election with 62.3 percent of the vote in 2006.

The two-party system was further weakened by a package of constitutional amendments approved in 2003 intended to establish more cohesive and responsible parties. In the 2006 congressional elections, the Liberal and Conservative parties together garnered only 35.3 percent of the seats in the Senate (down from 83.3 percent as recently as 1998) and 38.6 percent of the seats in the Chamber of Representatives (down from 81.4 percent in 1998). A democratic leftist party, the Polo Democrático Alternativo (Alternative democratic pole), won 9.8 percent of the seats in the Senate and 4.8 percent in the Chamber, and its presidential candidate came in second with 22.0 percent of the vote, nearly twice the votes of the official Liberal Party candidate. The other two major parties in Congress, Cambio Radical (Radical change) and the Partido Social de Unidad Nacional (National unity social party, known as el Partido de la U), were composed largely of former Liberals and Conservatives who had broken away to support President Uribe. It is unclear whether these parties will continue to exist after Uribe's presidency and, if not, whether their adherents will return to the folds of the Liberal and Conservative parties. The Colombian party system is unstable in the early twenty-first century, but the days of the exclusive two-party system appear to be definitively over.

See also **Colombia, Revolutionary Movements: Revolutionary Armed Forces of Colombia (FARC); Colombia, Revolutionary Movements: Army of National Liberation (ELN); Drugs and Drug Trade; Gaviria Trujillo, César Augusto; López Pumarejo, Alfonso; Núñez Moledo, Rafael; Ospina Pérez, Mariano; Violencia, La; War of the Thousand Days.**

BIBLIOGRAPHY

Archer, Ronald P. "Party Strength and Weakness in Colombia's Besieged Democracy." In *Building Democratic Institutions: Party Systems in Latin America*, edited by Scott Mainwaring and Timothy R. Scully. Stanford, CA: Stanford University Press, 1995.

Dix, Robert H. *The Politics of Colombia*. New York: Praeger, 1987.

Hartlyn, Jonathan. *The Politics of Coalition Rule in Colombia*. Cambridge, U.K., and New York: Cambridge University Press, 1988.

Pizarro Leongómez, Eduardo. "La crisis de los partidos y los partidos en la crisis." In *Tras las Huellas de la Crisis Política*, edited by Francisco Leal Buitrago. Bogotá: Tercer Mundo: FESCOL: Instituto de Estudios Políticos y Relaciones Internacionales (IEPRI), Universidad Nacional, 1996.

Roll, David. *Rojo Difuso y Azul Pálido: Los partidos tradicionales en Colombia: Entre el debilitamiento y la persistencia*. Bogotá: Universidad Nacional de Colombia, Facultad de Derecho, Ciencias Políticas y Sociales, 2002.

JOHN D. MARTZ
JOHN C. DUGAS

CONSERVATIVE PARTY

Colombia's Conservative Party was founded in 1849, making it one of the oldest functioning political parties in Latin America. For more than 150 years it has struggled for power in Colombia against its traditional adversary, the Liberal Party. During much of the nineteenth and early twentieth centuries it was characterized by its support for a strong central government, economic protectionism, and close ties with the Catholic Church. The Conservative Party in the early twenty-first century is a mainstream center-right party with multiclass support, but remains characterized in many regions by patron-client relations between party leaders and followers. Since the return of fully competitive elections in 1974, it has also clearly been the minority party. Nonetheless, it has won the presidency twice under Belisario Betancur Cuartas (1982–1986) and Andres Pastrana Arango (1998–2002). In the 2002 and 2006 elections, it chose not to run a presidential candidate, but rather to support Alvaro Uribe Vélez, a Liberal Party dissident running as an independent (and the winner both times), because of his strong conservative positions.

See also **Betancur Cuartas, Belisario.**

BIBLIOGRAPHY

Dugas, John C. "The Conservative Party and the Crisis of Political Legitimacy in Colombia." In *Conservative Parties, the Right, and Democracy in Latin America*, edited by Kevin J. Middlebrook. Baltimore, MD: Johns Hopkins University Press, 2000.

Pachón, Mónica. "Partido Conservador y sus dinámicas políticas." In *Degradación o cambio: Evolución del sistema político colombiano*, edited by Francisco Gutiérrez Sanín. Bogotá: Grupo Editorial Norma, 2002.

JOHN C. DUGAS

LIBERAL PARTY

Colombia's Liberal Party was founded in the late 1840s and is one of Latin America's oldest functioning political parties. In the nineteenth and early twentieth centuries, the Liberal Party was characterized by its positions in favor of decentralized political authority, free trade, and a clear separation between church and state. During the twentieth century, the party began to address the concerns of peasants and the working class, although it continued to be dominated by social and economic elites. In the early twenty-first century the party is a mainstream, center-left political party that is still characterized by patron-client ties in many regions. Since the return to freely contested elections in 1974, the Liberal Party has, for the most part, dominated the political arena. However, it has had difficulty recovering from the widely publicized drug corruption scandal of Liberal President Ernesto Samper (1994–1998), and has lost its longstanding control of both houses of Congress as well as the presidential elections of 1998 (to a Conservative, Andres Pastrana) and 2002 and 2006 (to a dissident Liberal, Alvaro Uribe, running as an independent with Conservative Party support).

See also **Colombia, Political Parties: Radical Olympus.**

BIBLIOGRAPHY

Archer, Ronald P. "Party Strength and Weakness in Colombia's Besieged Democracy." In *Building Democratic Institutions: Party Systems in Latin America*, edited by Scott Mainwaring and Timothy R. Scully. Stanford, CA: Stanford University Press, 1995.

Gutiérrez Sanín, Francisco. "Historias de democratización anómala: El Partido Liberal en el sistema politico colombiano desde el Frente Nacional hasta hoy." In *Degradación o cambio: Evolución del sistema politico colombiano*, edited by Francisco Gutiérrez Sanín. Bogotá: Grupo Editorial Norma, 2002.

JOHN C. DUGAS

NATIONAL FRONT

The National Front was a coalition between Colombia's two main political parties, in force between 1958 and 1974. In 1956 Liberal leader Alberto Lleras Camargo and exiled Conservative leader Laureano Gómez started discussions on a long-term accord to end the partisan Violencia that had claimed 200,000 lives since the 1940s, and to replace the military regime in power since 1953. The final accord, ratified in the plebiscite of December 1957, provided for alternation of the presidency between the two parties; parity in the cabinet, the judiciary, and in all elected bodies; and the requirement for a two-thirds majority to pass important legislation. (This last provision was amended in 1968.) The Frente regimes were successful in controlling the *Violencia* and in redefining its remnants as apolitical or subversive. The Frente's social and economic record was generally mediocre; politically, the Frente's provisions increased the level of intraparty conflict and eventually encouraged abstentionism. The Frente lapsed in 1974, its mission completed; a residual provision for "equitable participation" by the opposition party in the cabinet was abolished in the 1991 constitution.

See also **Lleras Camargo, Alberto.**

BIBLIOGRAPHY

Berry, R. Albert, Ronald G. Hellman, and Mauricio Solaun, eds. *Politics of Compromise: Coalition Government in Colombia* (1980).

Hartlyn, Jonathan. *The Politics of Coalition Rule in Colombia* (1988).

Leal Buitrago, Francisco. *La seguridad nacional a la deriva: Del Frente Nacional a la posguerra fría*. Bogotá, Colombia: Universidad de los Andes, CESO, 2002.

Martz, John D. *The Politics of Clientelism: Democracy & the State in Colombia*. New Brunswick, NJ: Transaction Publishers, 1996.

RICHARD J. STOLLER

NATIONAL POPULAR ALLIANCE (ANAPO)

The National Popular Alliance (Alianza Nacional Popular—ANAPO) was founded in 1961 by former President Gustavo Rojas Pinilla of Colombia to help him stage a political comeback. It was initially a movement sponsoring candidates under Conservative and Liberal factional labels, which were the only ones permitted under the National Front (1958–1974). In 1970, Rojas Pinilla ran for the presidency as a Conservative and was narrowly defeated. Many claimed that he was fraudulently deprived of victory by political elites alarmed by his antiestablishment, populist rhetoric. In 1974, a newly formed guerrilla group, the 19th of April Movement (M-19), derived its name from the date of 1970 presidential election. ANAPO refused to endorse the guerrillas but M-19 went on to become the largest guerrilla movement in Colombia in the 1980s.

In 1974, ANAPO, by now constituted as a party, chose Rojas's daughter, María Eugenia Rojas de Moreno, as its presidential candidate, but she ran a poor third behind the Liberal and Conservative contenders. Thereafter the party declined, partly because of internal divisions and the death of the elder Rojas in 1975. In 1982, ANAPO endorsed the victorious Conservative candidate, Belisario Betancur, who appointed María Eugenia Rojas director of an important housing agency.

See also **Rojas Pinilla, Gustavo.**

BIBLIOGRAPHY

R. Albert Berry et al., eds., *Politics of Compromise: Coalition Government in Colombia* (1980), pp. 31–179.

Additional Bibliography

Ayala Diago, César Augusto. *Resistencia y oposición al establecimiento del Frente Nacional: Los orígenes de la Alianza Nacional Popular, ANAPO: Colombia, 1953–*

1964. Bogotá: Universidad Nacional de Colombia, Facultad de Ciencias Humanas, Departamento de Historia, 1996.

Serpa Erazo, Jorge. *Rojas Pinilla: Una historia del siglo XX.* Bogotá: Planeta, 1999.

HELEN DELPAR

RADICAL OLYMPUS

Radical Olympus was a name applied to leaders of the Radical wing of Colombia's Liberal Party in the late nineteenth century. Among the principal members of the group were three presidents of the period: Manuel Murillo Toro (1864–1866, 1872–1874), Santiago Pérez (1874–1876), and Aquileo Parra (1876–1878). Admirers used the name as a tribute to the integrity and devotion to principle they found characteristic of the gods of Mount Olympus. Critics referred instead to a Radical oligarchy which held the national government in an iron grip. Most members of the Olympus came from eastern Colombia. They were generally identified with the federalist constitution of 1863, a belief in limited government, and anticlericalism, but in reality they held a wide range of positions on these issues. After 1878 the Radicals lost control of the national government but remained active in opposition.

See also **Murillo Toro, Manuel.**

BIBLIOGRAPHY

Rodríguez Piñeres, Eduardo. *El Olimpo Radical: Ensayos conocidos e inéditos sobre su época, 1864–1884* (1950).

Delpar, Helen. *Red Against Blue: The Liberal Party in Colombian Politics, 1863–1899* (1981).

Rivadeneira Vargas, Antonio José. *Aquileo Parra y la ideología radical.* Bogotá, Colombia: Editorial Planeta Colombiana, 2001.

HELEN DELPAR

COLOMBIA, REVOLUTIONARY MOVEMENTS

This entry includes the following articles:

ARMY OF NATIONAL LIBERATION (ELN)

One of Colombia's leftist guerrilla groups, the Army of National Liberation (Ejército de Liberación Nacional—ELN) was founded in 1964 by a group of mostly college-educated activists, some with Communist or dissident Liberal antecedents. The ELN was (and remained in the 1990s and early 2000s) strongly Castroite both in its goal of socialist revolution and in its strategy of establishing zones of dominance (*focos*). The ELN's first action was the seizure of Simacota, Santander, on 7 January 1965, but it first came to public attention when Father Camilo Torres Restrepo, organizer of the United People's Front movement in Bogotá, died in combat in February 1966, shortly after joining the ELN. The movement was weakened by a brutal purge in 1966–1967; an army assault in August 1973 nearly finished it off. In the 1980s the ELN returned to prominence under the defrocked Spanish priest Manuel Pérez, first as the lone holdout during the peace initiative of President Belisario Betancur (1984), and, since 1986, for its attacks on eastern Colombia's oil production and pipeline network. In the 1990s the ELN also became a leader in kidnappings. However, the ELN and the Colombian government began peace talks in the early twenty-first century.

BIBLIOGRAPHY

Arenas, Jaime. *La guerrilla por dentro: Análisis del E.L.N. colombiano.* Bogota: Tercer Mundo, 1971.

Hernández, Milton. *Rojo y negro: Historia del ELN.* Tafalla, Spain: Txalaparta, 2006.

Osterling, Jorge P. *Democracy in Colombia.* New Brunswick, NJ: Transaction Publisher, 1989. See pp. 307–313.

RICHARD J. STOLLER

ARMY OF POPULAR LIBERATION (EPL)

A guerrilla group active from 1967 to 1991, the Army of Popular Liberation (Ejército Popular de Liberación—EPL) had its origins in the Partido Comunista Colombiano Marxista-Leninista (PCC-ML), a pro-Chinese party founded in 1964. It was most active in the northwestern department of Córdoba, a zone of conflict between peasant settlers and expanding cattle interests. The EPL, which numbered perhaps 600 fighters at its peak, made little progress in the face of army pressure. Attempts to organize an urban front in Cali in the mid-1970s also failed. In 1984 it signed a cease-fire accord with the Belisario Betancur regime; but after the assassination of Oscar William Calvo Ocampo, EPL negotiator and one of the group's founders, the group returned to armed struggle in November 1985. The EPL's Córdoba base was seriously threatened by the army's new aggressiveness in 1990. A new round of negotiations led to the group's demobilization in March 1991 and a political alliance with the Alianza Democrática M-19. It then changed its official name to Esperanza, Paz y Libertad (Hope, Peace, and Liberty). A hardline faction of the EPL has rejected the demobilization and now operates in league with the Army of National Liberation (ELN). Its main leader, Francisco Caraballo, was arrested in 1993, but the faction continues to operate. Today its activities are mainly in Caldas, Antioquia, northern Santander, and La Guajira. It is overseen by commandant Juan Montes.

See also **Colombia, Revolutionary Movements: M-19.**

BIBLIOGRAPHY

Bejarano, Jesús Antonio. *El proceso de paz en Colombia y la política exterior de los Estados Unidos.* Washington, DC: Latin American Program, Woodrow Wilson International Center for Scholars, 2000.

Braun, Herbert. *Our Guerilla, Our Sidewalks: A Journey into the Violence in Colombia.* Lanham, MD: Rowman and Littlefield, 2003.

Calvo Ocampo, Fabiola. *EPL: Diez hombres, un ejército, una historia* (1985).

Kline, Harvey F. *State Building and Conflict Resolution in Colombia, 1986–1994.* Tuscaloosa: University of Alabama Press, 1999.

Lucas, Kintto. *Plan Colombia: La paz armada.* Ecuador: Editorial Planeta, 2000.

Osterling, Jorge P. *Democracy in Colombia* (1989), 314–317.

Peñaranda, Ricardo, and Javier Guerrero Barón. *De las armas a la política.* Bogotá: TM Editores, 1999.

Rabasa, Angel, and Peter Chalk. *Colombian Labyrinth: The Synergy of Drugs and Insurgency and Its Implications for Regional Stability.* Santa Monica, CA: Rand, 2001.

Ruiz, Bert. *The Colombian Civil War.* Jefferson, NC: McFarland, 2001.

Villaraga, Álvaro, and Nelson Plazas. *Para reconstruir los sueños: Una historia del EPL.* Bogotá: Fundación Cultura Democrática, 1994.

RICHARD J. STOLLER

M-19

Active from 1974 to 1990, the M-19 guerrilla group was an offshoot of the National Popular Alliance (ANAPO) of former dictator Gustavo Rojas Pinilla; its name comes from the date in 1970 when electoral fraud allegedly deprived him of the presidency. Unlike Rojas himself, M-19 was decidedly leftist (though not Marxist) in its populism and "anti-imperialism." Its early actions, under Jaime Bateman Cayón (*d.* 1983), were highly theatrical, such as the theft of Simón Bolívar's sword in January 1974; the 1979 arms theft from the main army depot; and the 1980 seizure of the Dominican Republic Embassy were high points of the group's visibility and prestige. A truce with the government in 1984 collapsed after several attacks on M-19 leaders and continued extortion by the guerrillas. In late 1985, M-19 suffered critical defeats at the Palace of Justice in Bogotá and in Cali's Siloé neighborhood; many of the group's remaining leaders were killed. After renewed negotiations, M-19 demobilized in early 1990. This portion of the Alianza Democrática M-19 has garnered significant electoral support under the leadership of Antonio Navarro Wolff, one of the few surviving leaders of the armed movement. The group operated successfully as a political party for ten years, participating in notable events such as the writing of the 1991 Colombian constitution. At the same time, other former leaders, including Ever Bustamante, Rosemberg Pabón (b. 1950) and Luis Alberto Gil have joined the mainstream government of President Alvaro Uribe. By 2003 the AD-M-19 had been absorbed into the Independent Democratic Pole coalition, and it ceased to exist in its former incarnation.

See also **Rojas Pinilla, Gustavo.**

BIBLIOGRAPHY

Ardila Galvis, Constanza. *The Heart of the War in Colombia.* London: Latin American Bureau, 2000.

Behar, Olga. *Noches de humo* (1988).

Bejarano, Jesús Antonio. *El proceso de paz en Colombia y la política exterior de los Estados Unidos.* Washington, DC: Latin American Program, Woodrow Wilson International Center for Scholars, 2000.

Kline, Harvey F. *State Building and Conflict Resolution in Colombia, 1986–1994.* Tuscaloosa: University of Alabama Press, 1999.

Lara, Patricia. *Siembra vientos y recogerás tempestades* (1982).

Osterling, Jorge P. *Democracy in Colombia* (1989), pp. 300–307.

Peñaranda, Ricardo, and Javier Guerrero Barón. *De las armas a la política.* Bogotá: TM Editores, 1999.

Villamizar Herrera, Darío. *Jaime Bateman: Biografía de un revolucionario.* Bogotá: Editorial Planeta Colombiana, 2002.

RICHARD J. STOLLER

REVOLUTIONARY ARMED FORCES OF COLOMBIA (FARC)

The Revolutionary Armed Forces of Colombia (Fuerzas Armadas Revolucionarias de Colombia—FARC) is the largest ongoing insurgency in Latin America. The FARC originated in 1966 as the armed branch of the Communist Party from among survivors of La Violencia, the period of nationwide violence that began in 1948. It was led by Manuel Marulanda Veléz (*nom de guerre* for Pedro Antonio Marín), later known as Tirofijo (sureshot). Marulanda survives into his late seventies as the titular head of the FARC. The FARC undertook guerrilla warfare against the Colombian state and was almost wiped out by the military through a campaign of counterinsurgency. Originally motivated by the principles of reform and social justice, these goals became corrupted by money from cocaine, which provided much of the organization's budget for operations.

By the late 1990s the FARC had grown to become a formidable military threat, inflicting defeats on the Colombian army. The FARC operates in the vast, uncontrolled rural areas of Colombia, fielding a force estimated at from twelve thousand to sixteen thousand fighters, including forcibly recruited children and women. Benefiting from economic and military assistance from the United States under Plan Colombia and with more capable leadership, the administrations of presidents Andrés Pastrana and Alvaro Uribe crafted an effective military strategy and an expansion of the armed forces and the police. Accordingly, the FARC were placed on the defensive and experienced desertions and repudiation. But they were by no means defeated. The activities of the FARC helped spawn the self-defense paramilitary groups, Autodefensas Unidas de Colombia

(UAC), which contested FARC over territory, the support of the population, and the cocaine economy.

See also **Drugs and Drug Trade.**

BIBLIOGRAPHY

Alape, Arturo. *Las vidas de Pedro Antonio Marín, Manuel Marulanda Vélez.* Bogota: Planeta, 2004.

Pizarro Leongómez, Eduardo. *Insurgencia sin revolución: La guerrilla en Colombia en una perspectiva comparada.* Bogota: Tercer Mundo, 1996.

Rochlin, James F. *Vanguard Revolutionaries in Latin America: Peru, Colombia, Mexico.* Boulder, CO: Lynne Rienner Publishers, 2003.

GABRIEL MARCELLA

UNITED SELF-DEFENSE FORCES OF COLOMBIA (AUC)

The United Self-Defense Forces of Colombia (Autodefensas Unidas de Colombia—AUC) is an organization created in April 1997 to consolidate scattered counterguerrilla paramilitary units that had emerged in several areas of the country since the 1980s. These private armed groups were organized by landowners, local elites, drug traffickers, and victimized communities, to retaliate against aggressions by the Fuerzas Armadas Revolucionarias de Colombia (Armed Revolutionary Forces of Colombia, FARC) and Ejército de Liberación Nacional (National Liberation Army, ELN) guerrilla groups. Their declared objective was to protect supporters from kidnapping, killing, and extortion by these insurgent groups. The AUC did not oppose the Colombian state, but their actions were based on claims that the national army had failed to protect them from rebel groups. Their main areas of operation were rural zones of northern Colombia, but they had a presence all over the country, and were also affiliated with urban units operating in the poorer sectors of major Colombian cities, particularly Medellín. The AUC was financed mostly by illegal drug trafficking, but also by voluntary or imposed contributions from land and business owners in the areas they operated. They were added to the U.S. and European Union lists of terrorist organizations in 2001. In 2003 the AUC signed an agreement with the Colombian government, as a result of which around 30,000 combatants disarmed by 2006, and their top commanders stepped down to face sentences of five to ten years, some of which could be served out of prison. The law that allowed this demobilization created controversy within the country and abroad, as well as objections among human rights organizations, which considered it too lenient.

Members of the AUC were known for their brutal methods of aggression, involving massacres and severe victimization of targeted populations. Their attacks were often directed toward individuals or communities suspected of being guerrilla sympathizers, and they also engaged regularly in direct combat with the guerrillas. Several human rights organizations claimed that the Colombian army tolerated AUC operations, and there were frequent allegations of close links between the AUC, the army, and some members of the Colombian government. Some of these claims have been confirmed through official investigations by judiciary entities in Colombia. The centralized structure of the AUC was dismantled after the demobilization, but a number of AUC units have refused to disarm and continue operating in several areas of the country.

See also **Colombia: Since Independence; Colombia, Revolutionary Movements: Revolutionary Armed Forces of Colombia (FARC); Colombia, Revolutionary Movements: Army of National Liberation (ELN).**

BIBLIOGRAPHY

Arnson, Cynthia J., ed. *The Peace Process in Colombia with the Autodefensas Unidas de Colombia-AUC.* Washington, DC: Woodrow Wilson International Center for Scholars, 2005.

Rangel, Alfredo, ed. *El poder paramilitar.* Bogotá: Planeta y Fundación Seguridad y Democracia, 2005.

Romero, Mauricio. *Paramilitares y autodefensas, 1982–2003.* Bogotá: Planeta y IEPRI, 2003.

MARIA HELENA RUEDA

COLOMBRES, JOSÉ EUSEBIO (1778–

1859). José Eusebio Colombres (*b.* 16 December 1778; *d.* 11 February 1859), ecclesiastic and signer of the Argentine Declaration of Independence. Colombres was born in Tucumán, received his doctorate from the University of Córdoba in 1803, and was ordained a priest the same year. He served as a parish priest in Catamarca and supported the May Revolution of 1810. Colombres was elected to the Congress of Tucumán (24 March 1816) and was a signer of the Declaration of Independence of the United Provinces of La Plata on 9 July 1816, by which the political bonds with Spain were broken. While the leaders of the United Provinces were busy establishing their independence, Spain had reasserted its rule in the surrounding areas and overthrown the newly established regime.

Colombres played an active political role in Tucumán, but he is also known for reintroducing sugarcane cultivation there. Sugarcane had been introduced in the 1550s and fostered by the Jesuits on their estates, but at their expulsion in 1767 the industry collapsed. Colombres planted extensive fields and built ox-driven mills to crush the cane. In 1831, however, Juan Facundo Quiroga's forces burned the fields, and Colombres was imprisoned.

Colombres became a government minister under Governor Bernabé Aráoz. He supported the formation of the Coalition of the North, but when the unitarist forces were defeated, he went into exile in Bolivia. After the fall of Juan Manuel de Rosas (1852), Colombres returned and held ecclesiastical positions in Salta. He died in Tucumán.

See also **Rosas, Juan Manuel de.**

BIBLIOGRAPHY

Tulio Halperín-Donghi, *Politics, Economics, and Society in Argentina in the Revolutionary Period,* translated by Richard Southern (1975).

Additional Bibliography

Acevedo, Edberto Oscar. *La revolución y las intendencias.* Buenos Aires: Ciudad Argentina, 2001.

Adelman, Jeremy. *Republic of Capital: Buenos Aires and the Legal Transformation of the Atlantic World.* Stanford, CA: Stanford University Press, 1999.

Harari, Fabián. *La contra: Los enemigos de la revolución de Mayo, ayer y hoy.* Buenos Aires: Ediciones RyR, 2006.

Szuchman, Mark D and Jonathan Brown, eds. *Revolution and restoration: The Rearrangement of Power in Argentina, 1776–1860.* Lincoln: University of Nebraska Press, 1994.

NICHOLAS P. CUSHNER

COLONIA. Colonia, department of Uruguay with 112,800 inhabitants and city of 21,714 (2004) inhabitants west of Montevideo, on the shores of the Río De La Plata. This historical emplacement was founded in 1680 by the governor of Río de Janeiro, Manuel de Lobo, according to instructions from the Portuguese crown to occupy for Brazil the northern shore of the estuary to counteract the influence of Buenos Aires on the southern shore. Because there had been no significant Spanish presence on the northern shore since Captain Juan Romero's colonization attempt had been foiled by the Charrúa Indians in 1552, the Portuguese established a colony and fortified a small town overlooking the estuary. The threat of a Portuguese enclave in the middle of the Spanish Río de la Plata, aggravated by the active smuggling of French and English merchandise, called for immediate action from Buenos Aires. Since repeated attempts to forcefully dislodge the invaders failed, Colonia del Sacramento was put under siege by Pedro Antonio de Cevallos in 1762. It was not until the signing of the Treaty of San Ildefonso (1777) that the Spanish regained control of the settlement and Portugal withdrew its claims on the Río de la Plata.

In the early 2000s, Colonia is a picturesque and pleasant town, an active station on the route between Montevideo and Buenos Aires via a hydrofoil that crosses the 25-mile-wide estuary, and a vacation spot for residents of Montevideo. Vineyards, fruit groves, and vegetable gardens dot the route connecting Colonia with Montevideo, 95 miles away.

See also **Uruguay, Geography.**

BIBLIOGRAPHY

Assunção, Fernando. *Etopeya y tragedia de Manuel Lobo: Biografía del fundador de Colonia del Sacramento.* Montevideo, Uruguay: Linardi y Risso, 2003.

Blixen, Diego. *De prostituta a señora: La historia reciente de Colonia del Sacramento.* Montevideo, Uruguay: Ediciones del Caballo Perdido, 2005.

Moreira, Omar. *Colonia del Sacramento* (Montevideo, 1984).

CÉSAR N. CAVIEDES

COLÔNIA DO SACRAMENTO. *See* Sacramento, Colônia del.

COLONIALISM.

The colonial period (1492–1820) has traditionally been studied from the perspective of the colonizer and colonialism understood as the conquest and control of other people's land and goods. Colonialism is also, however, a fundamentally unequal encounter between peoples and cultures, unsought by the colonized, in which the colonizer is incomparably more powerful. As such, it constitutes a complex multilayered network of social and cultural actions and interactions. It was just such a relationship that began to develop when Christopher Columbus set foot in the Americas in 1492.

The Iberian colonization of the Americas entailed—aside from military conquest, direct economic exploitation, and political domination—centuries of trade and intercultural exchange with indigenous peoples, who were far from a homogenous population. In the New World, Europeans encountered, among others, Nahuatl-speaking peoples in central Mexico, Quechuas in the Andean Incan empire, and Mayas in southern Mexico and Central America, as well as Arawaks and Caribs in the Caribbean, Otomí, Zapotec, Mixtec, and Tarascan peoples in Mexico, Cunas in Central America, and Mapuches, Aymaras, and Guarani in South America. The cultural richness, political, economic, and social structures, and religious expression of these conquered peoples entered into dialogue with and became part of the Christian norms and practices that the Iberians attempted to impose.

Following the lead of Edward Said's analysis of Eurocentric prejudice toward the East in *Orientalism* (1978) and the work of the Subaltern Studies Group on the Third World, studies of Latin American colonialism have shifted from a focus on colonial "letters" toward the study of colonial "discourse." Thus, studies that traditionally focused on the writings of the conquerors and the "tyranny of the alphabet" (Mignolo) have been opened to many previously ignored voices and ways of thinking. In addition to the writings of the conquerors, colonizers, and missionaries (including Columbus, Bartolomé de las Casas, Hernán Cortés, Bernal Díaz del Castillo, Bernardino de Sahagún, and others), the notion of colonial discourse includes pre-Hispanic oral traditions and written records (the *Nahuatl huehuetlahtolli* or *Word of the Ancients*, the fewer than twenty extant pre-Hispanic picto-ideographic codices, the *Popol Vuh*, the *Chilam Balam*, and the *Quechua Quipus*) as well as indigenous and mestizo expressions of the colonial period (the writings of Inca Garcilaso de la Vega, Felipe Guaman Poma de Ayala, and Fernando de Alva Cortés Ixtlilxóchitl; Diego de Castro Titu Cussi Yupanqui's Ynstrucción del Ynga). In the colonization of Latin America, Europeans systematically imposed their ways of thinking and being, suppressing and marginalizing indigenous ways and forms of knowledge (Restrepo 53). As Europe wrote colonial history it sought to control knowledge—a process central to colonialism (Mignolo 2000). As contemporary scholars have investigated the cultures that resulted from the colonial encounters of the New World, they have begun to hear the multilingual voices of the Americas' past expressed in a numerous forms: architecture, painting, theater, sculpture, pottery, textiles—the Paradise Garden Murals of Malinalco, Mexico, where indigenous tlacuilo or painters wove native flora and fauna into the Christian message of paradise in the sixteenth century; the baroque synthesis of indigenous symbolism and Christian theology in the Church of Santa María Tonantzintla in Cholula; the transformation of Spain's Apostle Santiago in the New World. Conceiving colonialism in Latin America as a series of cross-cultural encounters, not between the "self" and the "other" but between many "selves" and many "others," that take multiple and diverse forms—juxtaposition, acculturation, syncretism, transculturation, empowerment, mestizaje, hybridity, resistance—engenders better understanding of Latin American cultures of today.

See also **Argentina: The Colonial Period; Bolivia: The Colonial Period; Brazil: The Colonial Era, 1500–1808; Caste and Class Structure in Colonial Spanish America; Catholic Church: The Colonial Period; Colombia: From the Conquest through Independence; Cuba: The Colonial Era (1492–1898); Ecuador: Conquest Through Independence; Indigenous Peoples; Mestizo; Mexico: The Colonial Period; Paraguay: The Colonial Period; Peru: From the Conquest Through Independence; Race and Ethnicity; Slavery: Brazil; Slavery: Spanish America; Slavery: Indian Slavery and Forced Labor; Venezuela: The Colonial Era.**

BIBLIOGRAPHY

Campos, Araceli and Louis Cardaillac. *Indios y Cristianos: Cómo en México el Santiago Español se hizo indio*. Mexico City: El Colegio de Jalisco, Universidad Nacional Autónoma de México, Editorial Itaca, 2007.

Mallon, Florencia. "The Promise and Dilemma of Subaltern Studies: Perspectives from Latin American History." *American Historical Review* 99:5 (December 1994), 1491–1515.

Mignolo, Walter D. *Local Histories/Global Designs: Coloniality, Subaltern Knowledges, and Border Thinking*. Princeton, NJ: Princeton University Press, 2000.

Restrepo, Luis Fernando. "The Cultures of Colonialism." *The Companion to Latin American Studies*, edited by Philip Swanson. London: Arnold, 2003.

Said, Edward. *Orientalism*. New York: Pantheon, 1978.

COLLEEN EBACHER

COLONO.

Colono, a term that in Spanish and Portuguese refers to a class of rural workers tied to the land, often with a status similar to that of sharecroppers in U.S. history. As a general rule, *colonos* provide their labor in exchange for either access to land or for a portion of the harvest on large Latifundia. In Argentina the term *colono* simply implies a member of a colony of agricultural immigrants. In Peru, it can refer to a day laborer on a hacienda.

The actual practice of *colonage* varies widely by region, but generally it is associated with the rise of debt peonage and dependent labor that accompanied the consolidation of the large landed estates in Latin America. This solution to labor shortages offered the laborer a minimum of basic needs in exchange for the landowners' guarantee of work during harvests and other peak labor demand periods.

In Brazil, *colono* generally refers to a small (tenant) farmer. In the nineteenth century it was associated with foreign immigrants whom planters introduced to work their estates as an alternative to slave labor. Private and public sources financed the transatlantic transportation and settlement of tenant farmers under contract arrangements that stipulated the number of coffee trees to cultivate, process, and harvest. The *colono* received half of the profits from the sale of the coffee he harvested after processing, transport, and other expenses were deducted. Payment might be made at the termination of the harvest or on an annual basis.

Initial experiments with colonization plans involving immigrant *colonos* proved a costly and, in the long run, unfeasible labor alternative. They faced large debts and tropical illnesses, lacked clergymen and legal counsel, and were subject to the disciplinary measures of local planters and police authorities. A second wave of European immigration to Brazil introduced contract farm laborers into the expanding coffee areas of São Paulo in the 1880s and 1890s. In Rio de Janeiro, Minas

Gerais, and Espírito Santo, where postemancipation labor needs were met mostly with Brazilian labor, *colonos* referred to foreigners and Brazilians who were contracted individually or in family units as sharecroppers, tenants, and in some cases part-time salaried laborers on rural estates.

See also **Campesino.**

BIBLIOGRAPHY

Warren Dean, *Rio Claro* (1976).

Emília Viotti Da Costa, *Da senzala a colónia*, 2d ed. (1982).

Additional Bibliography

Cortés López, José Luis. *Esclavo y colono: Introducción y sociología de los negroafricanos en la América española del siglo XVI*. Spain: Ediciones Universidad de Salamanca, 2004.

Juarez-Dappe, Patricia Isabel. "Cañeros" and "Colonos": Cane Planters in Tucumán, 1876–1895." *Journal of Latin American Studies* 38:1 (February 2006): 123–147.

TODD LITTLE-SIEBOLD
NANCY PRISCILLA SMITH NARO

COLORADO RIVER. The Colorado River is in the south of Argentina, marking the border between the provinces of Mendoza and Neuquén, La Pampa, and Río Negro. With a length of 684 miles, the river is commonly considered the northern border of the Patagonian region of Argentina. The Colorado River begins in the Andes mountain range in the province of Mendoza, at the confluence of the Barrancas River and the Grande River (its principal tributary). It flows into the Argentine Sea (Mar Argentino) in the Atlantic Ocean, to the south of the province of Buenos Aires. Its average volume of flow is more than 4,900 cubic feet per second.

The river basin can be divided into two sectors: the upper, made up of the Grande and Barrancas rivers all the way to Buta Ranquil, and the middle and lower, from Buta Ranquil to the Atlantic Ocean. The river runs in an east-southeasterly direction through a sparsely populated region. Its waters are used for irrigation, although the river could also be transformed in the future into a key waterway for shallow draft vessels.

See also **Argentina, Geography; Mendoza; Neuquén; Patagonia.**

BIBLIOGRAPHY

Schard, Wernher. *Los ríos mas australes de la tierra*. Buenos Aires: Marymar Ediciones, 1983.

RICHARD REED

COLOSIO MURRIETA, LUIS DONALDO (1950–1994). The Mexican political leader Luis Donaldo Colosio Murrieta was assassinated after becoming a presidential candidate. Born February 10, 1950, in Magdaleno de Kino, Sonora, the son of a meat packer and self-educated accountant, he graduated from the Institute of Technology and Higher Studies in Monterrey in economics. He received an M.A. in economics from the University of Pennsylvania and spent a year in Vienna before taking a position at the Secretariat of Programming and Budgeting in 1979 as a member of Carlos Salinas's political network. In 1985 Colosio was elected to Congress from Sonora, and during Salinas's presidential campaign three years later, he served as *official mayor* of the Institutional Revolutionary Party (PRI). After a brief stint as senator in 1988, Colosio became party president from 1988 to 1992 and presided over the crucial 1991 congressional elections and internal party reforms. In 1992 President Salinas appointed him as the first secretary of the newly reconstituted Social Development Secretariat, where Colosio directed the politically influential Solidarity program before his designation by President Salinas in 1993 as the PRI's candidate for president. It was expected that he would win the August 1994 presidential election, but he was assassinated in Tijuana in mid-campaign. Colosio's murder produced numerous consequences for the political system, and coming so soon after the indigenous uprising in Chiapas, contributed to political instability. President Salinas was forced to select a replacement candidate, Colosio's campaign manager Ernesto Zedillo, who did not generate as much support within the party. Although the Salinas administration claimed Colosio was killed by a single, deranged gunman, President Zedillo later reopened the investigation, which alleged a wider plot. However, no charges ensued from that investigation to support such assertions. Colosio's death on March 23, 1994, contributed to further splits within the PRI leadership, as many of his former disciples and supporters left the party, thus furthering democratic pluralization.

See also **Mexico, Political Parties: Institutional Revolutionary Party (PRI).**

BIBLIOGRAPHY

Eguía, Colilá. *A quemarropa.* Mexicali, Mexico: BusCa Libros, 1994.

González Graf, Jaime. *Colosio, un candidato en la transición: Frente al México nuevo.* Mexico City: Grijalbo, 1994.

RODERIC AI CAMP

COLTEJER. The Compañía Colombiana de Tejidos, one of the oldest and largest textile firms in Colombia, was founded in 1907 in Medellín by the wealthy Echavarrías family of merchants. Developed initially as an extension of Alejandro Echavarría's cloth import and retail business, Coltejer grew to become the country's single largest industrial enterprise within the next half century. Most of the company's growth occurred in the 1930s and 1940s, when the worldwide economic depression and World War II disrupted the supply of foreign-made goods and gave Colombian manufacturers a chance to fill the breach. Besides expanding plant size and acquiring modern equipment, such as the two hundred automated looms imported from England in 1932, Coltejer also took the lead in technological innovations. With the help of machines imported from Czechoslovakia in the early 1930s, it became the first manufacturer of printed cloth in Colombia, setting the pace for other Colombian textile companies.

By 1940 Coltejer was able to compete with foreign producers in the production of fine fabrics, and its merger with the Rosellón company in 1942 marked the peak of its expansion in this period. Acquisition of Rosellón, third or fourth largest producer in the country at the time, doubled Coltejer's plant size and capital reserves. By 1943 the company had 1,900 looms and close to 4,000 workers. Its labor force had also changed, from all female in the early years to virtually all male after 1945. Coltejer has prided itself on its paternalistic policies toward workers, which, in the late 1940s and 1950s, began to include provisions for social security, annual paid vacations, overtime compensation, low-interest home loans, and various other services that preceded national legislation on these matters.

See also **Textile Industry: Modern Textiles.**

BIBLIOGRAPHY

Enrique Echavarría, *Historia de los textiles en Antioquia* (1943).

Fernando Gómez and Arturo Puerta, *Biografía económica de las industrias de Antioquia* (1945).

Fernando Botero Herrera, *La industrialización en Antioquia: Génesis y consolidación, 1900–1930* (1984).

Alberto Mayor Mora, "Historia de la industria colombiana 1930–1968," in *Nueva historia de Colombia,* vol. 7, edited by Jesús Antonio Bejarano (1989).

Additional Bibliography

Farnsworth-Alvear, Ann. *Dulcinea in the Factory: Myths, Morals, Men, and Women in Colombia's Industrial Experiment, 1905–1960.* Durham, NC: Duke University Press, 2000.

PAMELA MURRAY

COLUMBUS, BARTHOLOMEW (c. 1454–1514). Bartholomew Columbus (Bartolomé Colón: *b.* ca. 1454; *d.* 1514). A wool carder in his youth in Genoa, Bartholomew played a key role in the achievements of his more famous brother, Christopher. A skilled chartmaker and a superb navigator, he preceded Christopher to Lisbon, where he endured poverty while making charts and planning the "great enterprise." Sharing his brother's hardships and suffering the same indignities, Bartholomew remained steadfast and resolute during the many years of frustration. Sent by Christopher in 1488 to seek the aid of Henry VII of England, he was unsuccessful; and though he fared no better at the court of Charles VIII of France in 1490, he was at least consoled by the king's sister Anne de Beaujeu, at Fontainebleau. Meanwhile, unknown to Bartholomew, Christopher had reached the Indies. By the time he learned of the feat and made his way to Spain (1493), Christopher had already sailed on his second voyage. Bartholomew was sent with three ships to Hispaniola, where he served as captain-general from 1494 to 1496 and founded the city of

Santo Domingo. In the absence of Christopher from the island, he acted as governor until 1498, then as captain-general again until 1500, after which he returned to Castile. In recognition of Bartholomew's services, Christopher conferred on him the prestigious rank of Adelantado of the Indies.

A brave and bold leader, in 1497 Bartholomew faced a violent rebellion led by Francisco Roldán because he enforced strict and unrealistic rules on the colonists and meted out severe punishment. When Indians defiled sacred Christian religious images, the *adelantado* burned some of the natives at the stake. Continuing disorder in the colony resulted in the sending in 1500 of a royal agent, Francisco de Bobadilla, who arrested the Columbus brothers and shipped them in chains to Spain. Later Bartholomew was sorely tested when he accompanied Christopher on the disastrous fourth voyage (1502–1503) to Central America. With Christopher ill much of the time, Bartholomew explored Veragua, finding some gold and bravely fighting off Indians and mutineers, suffering two wounds in the process. Bartholomew returned to Spain but sailed again to Hispaniola with his nephew Diego in 1509. He continued to serve the crown until his death in Santo Domingo.

See also **Columbus, Christopher; Explorers and Exploration: Spanish America; Hispaniola; Santo Domingo.**

BIBLIOGRAPHY

The most important work in English on the Columbus family is Samuel Eliot Morison, *Admiral of the Ocean Sea: A Life of Christopher Columbus*, 2 vols. (1942). See also Fernando Colón, *The Life of the Admiral Christopher Columbus by His Son Ferdinand*, edited and translated by Benjamin Keen (1959), and Troy Floyd, *The Columbus Dynasty in the Caribbean, 1492–1526* (1973).

Additional Bibliography

Alponte, Juan María. *Colón: El hombre, el navegante, la leyenda*. México, D.F.: Aguilar, 1992.

Davidson, Miles H. *Columbus Then and Now: A Life Reexamined*. Norman: University of Oklahoma Press, 1997.

Heers, Jacques. *Cristóbal Colón*. México: Fondo de Cultura Económica, 1992.

Yewell, John, Chris Dodge, and Jan DeSirey. *Confronting Columbus: An Anthology*. Jefferson, NC: McFarland & Co., 1992.

WILLIAM L. SHERMAN

COLUMBUS, CHRISTOPHER (c. 1451–1506).

Christopher Columbus (*b.* ca. 1451; *d.* 1506), Genoese explorer.

EARLY LIFE IN GENOA AND PORTUGAL

Christopher Columbus was born in the republic of Genoa. His father, Domenico Colombo, was a wool weaver, wool merchant, tavern keeper, and political appointee. Columbus's early education was limited, although he read widely after reaching adulthood. He went to sea at an early age and sailed the Mediterranean on merchant vessels, traveling as far east as the island of Chios. In the mid-1470s, he settled in Portugal, joining other Italian merchants in Lisbon. Columbus sailed north to England and Ireland, and possibly as far as Iceland. He also visited the Madeira and Canary Islands and the African coast as far south as the Portuguese trading post at São Jorge da Mina (in modern Ghana).

In 1478 or 1479, Columbus married Felipa Moniz, member of a prominent Italian-Portuguese family. Her father and brother were hereditary captains of the island of Porto Santo, and her mother came from a noble family. In 1480 Felipa bore Columbus a son named Diogo (Diego in Spanish), who would later have a bureaucratic career in the lands his father claimed for Spain. Columbus's marriage provided connections to the Portuguese court, important ties to Madeira and Porto Santo, and at least some wealth.

THE ENTERPRISE OF THE INDIES

Columbus based his ideas about the size of the world and the possibility of a westward voyage to the fabled riches of Asia on rumors of unknown Atlantic islands, unusual objects drifting ashore from the west, and wide reading of academic geography in printed books. He was also influenced by the Italian humanist-geographer Paulo del Pozzo Toscanelli, who described the feasibility of a westward route to Asia. Although Columbus knew that the world was spherical, he underestimated its circumference and believed that Asia stretched some 30 degrees farther east than it really does, and that Japan lay 1,500 miles east of the Asian mainland. Columbus estimated that the Canary Islands lay only 2,400 nautical miles from Japan, instead of the actual distance of 10,600 nautical miles. Neither Columbus nor anyone else in Europe suspected that two vast continents lay in the way of a westward passage to Asia.

Probably in 1485, on the basis of his miscalculations, Columbus tried to interest Dom João II of Portugal in his scheme for a westward passage to Asia, his "enterprise of the Indies." After assembling a learned committee to examine Columbus's ideas, the king turned him down, for unrecorded reasons, although he licensed other westward probes.

SPAIN BACKS COLUMBUS

Columbus left Portugal for Spain in 1485. After meeting Columbus early in 1486 at Alcalá de Henares, Isabella I of Castile and her husband, Ferdinand II of Aragon, appointed a commission to investigate the details of Columbus's plan. The spherical shape of the world was never in question. Although the commission disputed Columbus's flawed geography, the monarchs suggested that they might support him once they conquered Muslim Granada, and they even provided him with periodic subsidies.

During his years of waiting, Columbus established a liaison with a young woman in Córdoba, Beatriz Enríquez de Arana. In 1488, they had a son named Hernando, whom Columbus later legitimized. Hernando accompanied Columbus on his fourth transatlantic voyage and ultimately wrote a biography of his father.

In January 1492, during the final siege of Granada, Queen Isabella summoned Columbus to court. In the Capitulations of Santa Fe, signed in April, the monarchs contracted to sponsor a voyage and to grant Columbus noble status and the titles of admiral, viceroy, and governor-general for any islands or mainlands he might discover.

THE FIRST VOYAGE, 1492–1493

Columbus secured the use of two caravels, the *Pinta* and the *Niña*, and a larger *nao*, the *Santa María*. With the help of Martín Alonso Pinzón, a prominent local mariner and captain of the *Pinta*, Columbus gathered a crew of around ninety men, including three from the local jail. The three ships sailed from Palos on 3 August 1492. After repairs

Map of Hispaniola, frontispiece of *Letter to Santangel* (1494). Columbus's letter to his patron Luis Santangel, later published in book form, described his journey and the things he encountered in the New World. CORBIS

and reprovisioning in the Canaries on 6 September 1492, the fleet headed west into the open ocean, propelled by the northeast trade winds. The voyage went smoothly, with fair winds and remarkably little grumbling among the crew. On 12 October, at 2 A.M., the lookout on the *Pinta* saw a light; shortly after dawn the fleet dropped anchor at an island in what are now the Bahamas that local people called Guanahaní and that Columbus renamed San Salvador. Believing they were in Asia, the Europeans called the islanders "Indians."

The fleet sailed through the Bahamas and visited Cuba, seeking the vast commerce and rich ports of Asia. From Cuba, Martín Alonso Pinzón, without permission, sailed off in the *Pinta* to explore on his own. The two ships remaining with Columbus sailed to the island they named

Christopher Columbus reaching the New World, by D. K. Bonatti (fl. 1720–1780). © HISTORICAL PICTURE ARCHIVE/ CORBIS

Hispaniola and explored its northern coast. On Christmas Eve 1492, the *Santa María* ran aground and broke up. Columbus founded a settlement, Villa de la Navidad, for the thirty-nine men he had to leave behind. Afterward Pinzón rejoined Columbus, and on 16 January the *Niña* and *Pinta* set sail for home with six captured Indians.

Columbus first tried a course directly east, but contrary winds forced him northward until he found winds blowing from the west. After a stormy passage, during which the caravels were separated, and a stopover in the Azores, the *Niña* reached Lisbon on 4 March. Columbus paid a courtesy call to Dom João II and departed for Spain on 13 March 1493, arriving in Palos two days later. Pinzón brought the *Pinta* into port later that same day, having first landed at Bayona, on the northwest coast of Spain.

Isabella and Ferdinand received Columbus warmly in Barcelona in mid-April. They confirmed all his privileges and gave him permission for a second voyage. Columbus asserted that the Asian mainland lay close to the islands he had found.

THE SECOND VOYAGE, 1493–1496

The Spanish monarchs facilitated Columbus's colonizing effort, and the queen ordered that the native islanders be treated well and converted to Christianity. Columbus found 1,200 men to accompany him as settlers. On 3 November 1493, the fleet of seventeen vessels reached an island in the Caribbean that Columbus named Dominica, then sailed through the Lesser Antilles and the Virgin Islands, past Puerto Rico, to Hispaniola.

They found that the men left in La Navidad the previous January were all dead, most of them killed by the islanders. Columbus founded a new settlement, named Isabella for the queen, on a poor site without fresh water. He then began to enslave some of the islanders. According to Spanish law, if the local people peacefully accepted takeover by the Europeans, they were protected against enslavement as subjects of the Castilian crown, but if they made war, they could be seized as slaves. Some islanders were certainly at war against the Europeans, and Columbus used their resistance as a justification for outright conquest. He and his men marched through the island with horses, war dogs, and harquebuses, seeking gold through barter but conquering and taking captives when they met opposition.

In April 1494, leaving Hispaniola under the control of his brother Diego, Columbus took an expedition to explore the southern shore of Cuba, which he believed was part of the Asian mainland. He even made his crewmembers sign a document to that effect. Columbus's brother Bartholomew had arrived on Hispaniola during Columbus's absence and found the colony in chaos. Disappointed colonists returned to Spain on a fleet dispatched by Columbus in 1494 and spread stories about the Columbus brothers' misdeeds and ineptitude as administrators. The Spanish rulers sent out an investigator named Juan Aguado, who observed many deaths among the Amerindians, and disease and desertions among the Europeans. To defend his administration in person, Columbus departed for Spain on 10 March 1496, leaving Bartholomew in charge on Hispaniola. He reached Cádiz on 11 June.

THE THIRD VOYAGE, 1498-1500

Despite reports about Columbus's failings as an administrator, the monarchs confirmed his previous grants and gave him permission for a third voyage, with a *nao* and two caravels for exploration and three more caravels to carry provisions to Hispaniola, plus 300 men and 30 women as additional colonists, including 10 pardoned criminals.

Departing from Spain on 30 May 1498, Columbus took his three ships south to the Cape Verde Islands before heading west, reaching the island of Trinidad on 31 July. He then sailed to the mainland of South America, realizing from the vast flow of water from the Orinoco River that he had encountered an enormous landmass, which he believed to be in Asia and near the Garden of Eden described in the Bible. After briefly exploring the coast of Venezuela, Columbus sailed on to Hispaniola.

Although Bartholomew had moved the main settlement from Isabella to Santo Domingo, the situation was in crisis. Some of the colonists had mutinied, the Indians were increasingly hostile, and neither Bartholomew nor Diego Columbus had been able to maintain order. Columbus himself had little better luck. Ferdinand and Isabella sent out Francisco de Bobadilla to investigate and restore authority. He arrested the three Columbus brothers, seized their money, and sent them home in chains in December 1500. Columbus was summoned to court in Granada, but the monarchs delayed granting his request for reinstatement to his official posts.

Eventually Ferdinand and Isabella allowed Columbus to keep some of his titles and all of his property, but the titles were thereafter empty of authority. They also delayed granting him permission for another voyage. Instead, they began to establish a bureaucratic structure outside Columbus's control, appointing Nicolás de Ovando governor of Hispaniola and dispatching a large colonization fleet. In March 1502 Ferdinand and Isabella finally granted Columbus permission for a fourth voyage.

THE FOURTH VOYAGE, 1502–1504

With Columbus and his son Hernando sailing on the flagship, a fleet of four rickety caravels with second-rate crews left Spain on 11 May 1502. Departing the Canaries on 25 May, they arrived at Hispaniola on 29 June, even though Columbus was specifically forbidden to land there. Columbus knew that Governor Ovando was about to send a fleet home and saw that a hurricane was brewing. He warned Ovando of the approaching storm and asked to anchor in the harbor. Ovando refused and ordered the fleet to depart, just before the hurricane struck. Twenty-five of the fleet's ships were sunk.

Thereafter, Columbus and his men spent much of the voyage sailing along the coast of Central America. Bad weather and adverse currents and winds kept the crews from learning much about the lands and peoples, and the hostility of local Indians forced them to abandon plans for a settlement in Panama. Unable to reach Hispaniola, Columbus landed in northern Jamaica and awaited rescue for a year. He sailed back to Spain, broken in health, and reached Seville on 7 November 1504, never again to return to the Indies.

LAST YEARS

Columbus struggled to have all his grants and titles restored. He remained a wealthy man, but he felt betrayed and slighted by his royal patrons. For their part, the Spanish sovereigns justified their withdrawal of support on the basis of Columbus's mismanagement. Colonial settlement had grown too complex for any one person to manage.

Surrounded by family and friends, Columbus died in Valladolid in 1506, rich but dissatisfied. With the perspective of five centuries, we can recognize the extraordinary changes that resulted from his voyages. Instead of finding a new route to Asia, Columbus made the lands and peoples of the Western Hemisphere known to Europeans and set in motion a chain of events that altered human history on a global scale. The origin of many characteristics of the modern world, including the interdependent system of world trade, can be traced directly to his voyages.

COLUMBUS IN HISTORY AND MYTH

The myths surrounding Columbus make it difficult to put his accomplishments into their proper context. Often he is depicted as a perfect hero in advance of his time who conceived the idea of a spherical earth and had to fight traditional religious beliefs and prejudice before succeeding, and who died poor and alone. None of this is true. A product of his times, Columbus was strongly influenced by the powerful religious and economic currents of his day. In pursuit of profits, he established a slave trade in Caribbean natives, arguing that such slavery would allow them to be converted and reformed. Far from being oppressed by Christian beliefs, he hoped that some of the profits from his ventures would be used to recapture Jerusalem from the Muslims, in fulfillment of Christian

prophecy. Neither the simple hero portrayed by generations of textbook writers nor the unredeemable villain depicted by some recent writers, Columbus was a complex human being who exemplified the virtues and the flaws of his time and place in history.

See also **Columbus, Diego (d. 1515); Explorers and Exploration: Spanish America; Ferdinand II of Aragon; Isabella I of Castile; Hispaniola; Pinzón, Martín Alonso.**

BIBLIOGRAPHY

The most important primary sources dealing with Columbus are Bartolomé De Las Casas, *Historia de las Indias,* edited by Agustín Millares Carlo, 3 vols. (1951); Ferdinand Columbus, *The Life of the Admiral Christopher Columbus by His Son Ferdinand,* translated by Benjamin Keen (1959); Cristóbal Colón, *Textos y documentos completos,* edited by Consuelo Varela, 2d ed. (1984); and Oliver C. Dunn and James E. Kelley, Jr., eds. and trans., *The Diario of Christopher Columbus's First Voyage to America, 1492–1493, Abstracted by Fray Bartolomé de las Casas* (1989). For a half century, the standard English-language biography, stressing the maritime facets of Columbus's career, was Samuel Eliot Morison, *Admiral of the Ocean Sea: A Life of Christopher Columbus,* 2 vols. (1942). A Spanish-language biography of the same period deserves to be better known: Antonio Ballesteros Beretta, *Cristóbal Colón y el descubrimiento de América,* 2 vols. (1945). Since the 1940s, numerous scholars have added important new interpretations. A detailed biography on Columbus's life up to 1492 is provided by the Genoese historian and Italian senator Paolo Emilio Taviani, *Christopher Columbus: The Grand Design,* translated by William Weaver (1985).

Antonio Rumeu De Armas has written many studies clarifying particular aspects of the Columbus story, including *Nueva luz sobre las Capitulaciones de Santa Fe de 1492* (1985). Juan Manzano Manzano provides a detailed but not totally convincing study of Columbus in Spain before the first voyage, *Cristóbal Colón: Siete años decisivos de su vida, 1485–1492,* 2d ed. (1989); and, with Ana María Manzano Fernández-Heredia, a lengthy study of Columbus's Spanish collaborators: *Los Pinzones y el descubrimiento de América,* 3 vols. (1988). Marvin Lunenfeld, ed., *1492: Discovery, Invasion, Encounter: Sources and Interpretations* (1991), serves as an excellent introduction to the heated controversies surrounding the quincentenary. Based on the documents and recent scholarship, William D. Phillips, Jr., and Carla Rahn Phillips place the actions of Columbus and the consequences of his voyages in the broad context of world history in *The Worlds of Christopher Columbus* (1992). *The Christopher Columbus Encyclopedia,* edited by Silvio A. Bedini, 2 vols.

(1992), offers an array of articles on Columbus and his times.

Additional Bibliography

Alponte, Juan María. *Colón: El hombre, el navegante, la leyenda.* México, D.F.: Aguilar, 1992.

Davidson, Miles H. *Columbus Then and Now: A Life Reexamined.* Norman: University of Oklahoma Press, 1997.

Heers, Jacques. *Cristóbal Colón.* México: Fondo de Cultura Económica, 1992.

Yewell, John, Chris Dodge and Jan DeSirey. *Confronting Columbus: An Anthology.* Jefferson, NC: McFarland & Co., 1992.

WILLIAM D. PHILLIPS JR.

COLUMBUS, DIEGO (1468–1515).

Columbus, Diego (Giacomo Colombo; *b.* c. 1468; *d.* before 20 February 1515), youngest brother of Christopher Columbus. He left Genoa to join Christopher in Spain and sailed with him on the second voyage to America. Described as amiable, virtuous, and peaceful, Diego had no instincts for seamanship, warfare, or administration. Nevertheless, Christopher's devotion to his brother led to Diego's appointment as president of a ruling council for Hispaniola during Christopher's absence on another voyage, a heavy responsibility for the young man. Francisco Roldán, the alcalde mayor, offended at Diego's superior position, led the island's malcontents in rebellion. Christopher returned to find the colony in anarchy. He sought to bring about order by removing the hapless Diego, who was sent to Spain in February 1495 to defend Christopher against their enemies at court. Months later Diego returned to Hispaniola, endeavoring as best he could to assist his beleagured brothers against rebellious colonists. In 1500 the concerned sovereigns sent Francisco de Bobadilla as chief justice to pacify the island. Diego, by then governing in the port city of Santo Domingo, with uncharacteristic backbone defied Bobadilla, who clapped Diego in irons, along with his brothers, and shipped him to Spain. The same year Diego finally found his true vocation when he took holy orders. Although Christopher sought to obtain a bishopric for Diego from the Queen, the request was denied on grounds of his foreign birth. In 1509 Diego made a brief visit to Santo Domingo, then returned to Seville, where he died.

BIBLIOGRAPHY

Fernando Colón, *The Life of the Admiral Christopher Columbus by His Son Ferdinand*, edited and translated by Benjamin Keen (1959); Troy Floyd, *The Columbus Dynasty in the Caribbean, 1492–1526* (1973).

WILLIAM L. SHERMAN

COLUMBUS, DIEGO (c. 1480–1526).

Diego Columbus (Diego Colón; *b.* ca. 1480; *d.* 1526), eldest son of Christopher Columbus. Following the death in 1485 of his mother, Felipa Perestrello, a Portuguese noblewoman, Diego was left by his father at the Franciscan friary of La Rábida (Spain) for education. In 1494, he began court life, attached to the infante Don Juan, at whose death he became a page to Queen Isabella II, and later a member of her bodyguard. When Isabella died in 1504, Diego continued in crown favor, owing in part to his marriage to María de Toledo, a cousin of the king. At his father's urging, Diego endeavored for years to secure titles and financial rewards for the family, but with little success. In 1505, he sought appointment as governor and viceroy of Hispaniola, but having spent his years as a privileged courtier, and being still a young man who had not seen military action, he was judged too inexperienced to govern the ruffians in the Indies. On his father's death in 1506, Diego inherited the title Admiral of the Indies, and in 1509 the sovereign conferred on him the governorship he sought. In 1511, he was appointed viceroy of the islands as well, but not "of the Indies," as he had hoped. For fifteen years, Diego served as a capable governor of the turbulent islands. Though he continued to press for further honors and compensation for the Columbus family, he died with his hopes unfulfilled.

See also **Columbus, Christopher; Hispaniola; Spain; Spanish Empire.**

BIBLIOGRAPHY

Troy Floyd, *The Columbus Dynasty in the Caribbean, 1492–1526* (1973), contains many references to Diego. See also Samuel Eliot Morison, *Admiral of the Ocean Sea: A Life of Christopher Columbus*, 2 vols. (1942).

Additional Bibliography

Alponte, Juan María. *Colón: El hombre, el navegante, la leyenda*. México, D.F.: Aguilar, 1992.

Davidson, Miles H. *Columbus Then and Now: A Life Reexamined*. Norman: University of Oklahoma Press, 1997.

Heers, Jacques. *Cristóbal Colón*. México: Fondo de Cultura Económica, 1992.

Yewell, John, Chris Dodge and Jan DeSirey. *Confronting Columbus: An Anthology*. Jefferson, NC: McFarland & Co., 1992.

WILLIAM L. SHERMAN

COLUNJE, GIL (1831–1898). Gil Colunje (*b*. 1831; *d*. 1898), Panamanian jurist who spent most of his life in Colombia, where he became a senator. In his writings he often speaks against government corruption and injustice, which gained the admiration and respect of the people. He was repeatedly harassed by the government because of his ideas. Colunje held many government posts throughout his life. He served as minister of foreign relations, member of the Supreme Court, president of the Bank of Bogotá, and rector of the Colegio Mayor del Rosario. In 1865 he occupied briefly the presidency of the Sovereign State of Panama.

See also **Colombia: Since Independence; Panama.**

BIBLIOGRAPHY

Ernesto De Jesús Castillero Reyes, *Historia de Panamá*, 7th ed. (1962).

Jorge Conte Porras, *Diccionario biográfico ilustrado de Panamá*, 2d ed. (1986)

Additional Bibliography

Araúz, Celestino Andrés, and Patricia Pizzurno Gelós. *El Panamá colombiano (1821-1903)*. Panamá: Primer Banco de Ahorros y Diario La Prensa de Panamá, 1993.

Bonilla, Heraclio, and Gustavo Montañez. *Colombia y Panamá: La metamorfosis de la nación en el siglo XX*. Bogotá: Universidad Nacional de Colombia, 2004.

JUAN MANUEL PÉREZ

COMALCALCO. Comalcalco is a Mayan settlement located in Tabasco, in the southeastern part of Mexico, on a flood plain surrounded by tropical rain forest. This setting gave the inhabitants access to plentiful and diverse resources, although the swampy environment brought them an array of physical ailments and other problems. The original name of the settlement was Joy Chan (knotted sky) and its civilization reached its apex between the sixth and ninth centuries CE.

Located on the right bank of the Mezcalapa-Mazapa River (known today as the Río Seco, or dry river), the site measures 2.3 square miles. It is made up of three aligned groups of monumental architecture surrounded by over three hundred scattered mounds, where common people built their houses with perishable materials. Nearby were fields for growing corn and cacao, which has been the primary trade product in the region from pre-Hispanic times to the present day.

The earliest monumental architecture consisted of building earthen platforms with thick coat of lime plaster. The invention and widespread use of bricks allowed the old constructions to be resurfaced, and enabled the construction of new masonry buildings with high vaulted ceilings and wide bays and passageways.

The spaces that were created were used as plazas, courtyards, residences, sanctuaries, a *popol nah* (council house), temples, and administrative areas. A unique characteristic of these bricks is that some were decorated on one side with paint, incisions, or impressions representing anthropomorphic features such as animals, plants, or geometric designs, which were hidden inside the masonry. With clay widely available, villagers modeled it into large funeral urns, spindles, weights for fishing nets, personal ornaments, figurines, and vessels for domestic use and trade.

The first descriptions and illustrations of Comalcalco were made in 1880 by the French explorer Desire Charnay. Since that date, several archaeologists have researched the site, the most notable among them being Ponciano Salazar, who explored six buildings from 1972–1982, and the Ricardo Armijo project which began in 1993. The latter has excavated eleven structures in the monument area and made substantial research progress, including the ability to read text inscriptions that reveal a portion of the dynastic history of the site, a record of a possible eclipse, the celebration of regular rituals, and particularly the history of the priest Aj Pakal Than, who held prestigious posts and titles in local society. The ceramic and stone materials used show that the people of Comalcalco maintained trade and political relations with settlements and regions as far away as Xcambó, Yucatan, southern Campeche, Los Tuxtlas, Veracruz, and northern Chiapas, traveling on rivers as well as by sea around the Yucatán peninsula. History relates that Palenque conquered Comalcalco in the year 649 CE. Before that, Comalcalco was an important settlement, with its own glyphic emblem. Its geographic location and the productivity of its soil to cultivate cacao must have upheld its status within the pre-Hispanic Mayan world.

See also **Maya, The.**

BIBLIOGRAPHY

Alvarez, Luis Fernando, María Guadalupe Landa, and José Luis Romero. *Los ladrillos de Comalcalco*. Villahermosa, Mexico: Instituto de Cultura de Tabasco, 1990.

Andrews, George F. *Comalcalco, Tabasco, Mexico: Maya Art and Architecture*, 2nd edition. Culver City, CA: Labyrinthos, 1989.

Armijo, Ricardo, Marc U. Zender, and Miriam Judith Gallegos. "La urna funeraria de Aj Pakal Than, un sacerdote del siglo VIII en Comalcalco, Tabasco, México." *Temas Antropológicos* 22, no. 2 (2001): 242–253.

Armijo, Ricardo. "Comalcalco la ciudad maya de ladrillos." *Arqueología Mexicana* 61 (2003): 30–37.

Gallegos Gómora, Miriam Judith, and Ricardo Armijo. "La corte real de Joy'Chan a través de las mujeres, hombres y dioses de barro. Estudio preliminar de género." *Los Investigadores de la Cultura Maya* 12, no. 2 (2004): 304–318.

Centro Studi Americanistici and Universidad Veracruzana, Perugia, Italia "Sistemas constructivos y materiales en la arquitectura de Comalcalco, Tabasco." *Quaderni di Thule. Rivista italiana di studi americanistici, Atti del XXV Convengo Internazionale di Americanistica*, III-2 (2005): 391–398.

MIRIAM JUDITH GALLEGOS GÓMORA

COMANCHES.

Comanches, a Shoshonean tribe in the Uto-Aztecan language family, migrated southward to the plains of Texas and New Mexico in the late seventeenth century. They represented the epitome of Plains Indian culture: They were master warriors and hunters on horseback. Comanche raids against northern Mexican settlements, missions, and the pueblos of New Mexico began in the mid-1700s; by the 1820s the Comanches were attacking towns and ranches as far south as Zacatecas. Migrating to the Apachería at the turn of the eighteenth century, Comanches brought additional difficulties for the Apaches, who struggled to protect their territories from Spanish, Anglo-American, and other indigenous powers. In an effort to subdue Apache aggression toward Spanish settlers, the Spaniards brokered a loose and unsuccessful alliance with the Apaches to combat the Comanches. However, by 1786 a peace was negotiated between the Spanish and the Comanches that lasted into the late colonial era and in some cases through Independence. The fragmented nature of Comanche social organization, however, prevented the general observance of any peace treaty, and different bands continued to raid in northern Mexico.

The Comanches became valuable allies to the New Mexicans and some Texan settlements in the wars (c. 1750s) against certain Apache groups, and the Comanches often allied with the Kiowas in their wars against the Apaches. Men known as *comancheros* traded between the New Mexicans and the Comanches and developed a lively commerce in guns, ammunition, supplies, stolen horses, and captives on the plains. However, as Anglo-Americans pushed into Texas in the 1860s, the Comanches raided deeper into Mexico. Ultimately, the increased number of westward-migrating Anglo settlers and ranchers prompted renewed Comanche warfare on the southern plains. As a result of the Red River War of 1874 between the U.S. Army and the Comanches and their Kiowa allies, the Comanches were forced to settle on small reservations in Oklahoma. As of 2007, the Comanche Nation of Oklahoma numbers approximately 13,000 enrolled tribal members, many of whom live in or near Lawton, Oklahoma.

See also **Indigenous Peoples.**

BIBLIOGRAPHY

Griffen, William B. *Utmost Good Faith: Patterns of Apache-Mexican Hostilities in Northern Chihuahua Border Warfare, 1821–1848* (1988), chap. 9.

John, Elizabeth A. H. "Nurturing the Peace: Spanish and Comanche Cooperation in the Early Nineteenth Century," in *New Mexico Historical Review* 59, no. 4 (1984): 345–369.

Kenner, Charles L. *A History of New Mexico-Plains Indians Relations* (1969).

Rodriguez-García, Martha. *Historias de resistencia y exterminio: Los indios de Coahuila durante el siglo XIX.* Tlalpan, Mexico: CIESAS, 1995.

Vizcaya Canales, Isidro. *Tierra de guerra viva: Incursiones de indios y otros conflictos en el noreste de México durante el siglo XIX, 1821–1885.* Monterrey, Mexico: Academia de Investigaciones, 2001.

AARON PAINE MAHR

COMANDANTE RAMONA (1959?–2006).

Comandante (Commander) Ramona was the leader of the Zapatista Army of National Liberation (EZLN), an indigenous rights movement begun in southern Mexico. The Zapatistas gained international attention on 1 January 1994, when they launched their rebellion and under Ramona's leadership seized control of San Cristóbal de las Casas, the capital of Chiapas state. Until her untimely death on 6 January 2006, of kidney cancer, this diminutive Mayan Tzotzil woman, born near San Andrés de Larrainzer, was a spokesperson and symbol for indigenous people and women's rights.

In addition to being a key military figure, Ramona participated in the peace dialogue known as the San Andrés accords between the Zapatistas and the Mexican government. As a vocal advocate for indigenous community autonomy, Ramona convened the National Indigenous Congress (Congreso Nacional Indigena), a meeting of indigenous peoples from across Mexico, and flew to Mexico City in the fall of 1996 to participate. While there she received a kidney transplant from her brother, with funds for the operation coming from the Zapatistas' civilian supporters.

Until forced by ill health out of a more public role, Ramona spoke on behalf of women in general but also more specifically on behalf of poor women and indigenous women within their communities. She demanded that indigenous women have a say in community decision making and the freedom to choose a romantic partner and to determine the number of children they would bear. She spoke out against physical abuse of women, and for poor women everywhere she stressed the need for access to education and health care.

See also **Chiapas; Mexico, Organizations: Zapatista Army of National Liberation.**

BIBLIOGRAPHY

Cay y Mayor, Aracely Burguete, ed. *Indigenous Autonomy in Mexico.* Copenhagen: IWGIA, 2000.

Hernández Castillo, Rosalva Aída. *La otra palabra: Mujeres y violencia en Chiapas, antes y después de Acteal.* Mexico: CIESAS: Grupo de Mujeres de San Cristóbal: Centro de Investigación y Acción para la Mujer, 1998.

Ross, John. *Rebellion from the Roots: Indian Uprising in Chiapas.* Monroe, ME: Common Courage Press, 1995.

Speed, Shannon, Rosalva Aída Hernández Castillo, and Lynn Stephen, eds. *Dissident Women: Gender and Cultural Politics in Chiapas.* Austin: University of Texas Press, 2006.

MEREDITH GLUECK

COMANDANTE ZERO. *See* **Pastora Gómez, Edén.**

COMARCA.

Comarca, a judicial district. A territorial subdivision within the Brazilian captaincies, the *comarca* was a judicial district composed of two or more counties. Ordinarily the *comarca* incorporated a district larger than a municipality. Usually there were two *comarcas* per captaincy. In the colonial period and the early empire, they were often sizeable. The *comarca* of São Francisco represented more than half of the territory of Pernambuco before it was ceded to Bahia. In 1720 Brazil was divided into three *comarcas,* with centers in Paraíba, Bahia, and Rio de Janeiro, each of which was headed by a *corregidor.* Pernambuco and all of Brazil north of it was under the jurisdiction of Paraíba, which served as a court of appeals for all the cases before the judges and *ouvidores* of Pernambuco, with further appeals and matters outside of Paraíban jurisdiction going to the Relação (High Court) in Lisbon. After the discovery of gold and diamonds in the interior, new *comarcas* were set up in Minas Gerais, Goiás, and Mato Grosso to see that the king's justice moved westward. Sudden shifts of population as a result of new mining discoveries made a visible judicial presence desirable. By the nineteenth century *juizes de direito*—district judges—were under central control. As instruments of royal justice and control, the *comarcas* brought law and order to frontier areas and contributed to the administrative incorporation of Brazil.

See also **Pernambuco.**

BIBLIOGRAPHY

Dutra, Francis A. "Centralization *vs.* Donatorial Privilege: Pernambuco, 1602–1639," in *Colonial Roots of Modern Brazil,* edited by Dauril Alden (1973).

Fragoso, João Luís Ribeiro, Maria Fernanda Bicalho, and Maria de Fátima Gouvêa. *O Antigo Regime nos trópicos: A dinâmica imperial portuguesa, séculos XVI–XVIII.* Rio de Janeiro: Civilização Brasileira, 2001.

Levine, Robert M. *Historical Dictionary of Brazil,* translated by Suzette Macedo (1979), p. 59; *The Cambridge History of Latin America,* edited by Leslie Bethell, vol. 2 (1984).

Prado, Caio, Jr. *The Colonial Background of Modern Brazil* (1967).

PATRICIA MULVEY

COMAYAGUA. Comayagua, the former capital of Honduras (2005 population of 58,784), located on a plain bearing the same name in a central valley. An agricultural center for cattle, sugarcane, and food staples as well as an economic link for the western portion of the country, Comayagua is also the name of the department, one of the first seven departments established in 1825. It boasts a broad agricultural valley as well as extensive pre-Columbian ruins.

Founded in 1537 as Valladolid de Santa María de Comayagua, the city participated in a celebrated rivalry with Tegucigalpa after silver deposits led to an expansion of the latter after 1578. Political and economic rivalry continued between the two cities throughout the colonial period, independence, annexation to Mexico, membership in the Central American federation, and the national period until the triumph of more Liberal Tegucigalpa over more Conservative Comayagua during the presidency of Marco Aurelio Soto (1876–1881). Soto moved the capital to Tegucigalpa in 1880, after it had alternated several times between the two cities. The older Camino Real was replaced in 1970 by a highway linking the cities of San Pedro Sula, Comayagua, and Tegucigalpa and providing needed transportation infrastructure to an economy

historically plagued by regional isolation. In later decades, the city's colonial architecture attracted tourists, and this industry came to play a growing role in the economy.

See also **Honduras.**

BIBLIOGRAPHY

José Reina Valenzuela, *Comayagua antanona, 1537–1821* (1968).

Steven J. Reif, *Comayagua: A City in Central Honduras* (1980).

Luis Mariñas Otero, *Honduras* (1983).

Additional Bibliography

Euraque, Darío A. *Reinterpreting the Banana Republic: Region and State in Honduras, 1870–1972.* Chapel Hill: University of North Carolina Press, 1996.

Fernández Hernández, Bernabé. *El gobierno del Intendente Anguiano en Honduras, 1796–1812.* Sevilla: Universidad de Sevilla, Secretariado de Publicaciones, 1997.

Turcios Vijil, Julio César. *Monumentos, costumbres y tradiciones de Comayagua.* Tegucigalpa, D.C., Honduras: Universidad Nacional de Honduras, Editorial Universitaria, 2000.

Zelaya, Gustavo. *El legado de la Reforma Liberal.* Tegucigalpa: Editorial Guaymuras, 1996.

JEFFREY D. SAMUELS

COMECHINGONES. Comechingones, an ethnic group that, until the middle of the sixteenth century, occupied the mountainous region in what are now the central Argentine provinces of Córdoba and San Luis. The economy of the Comechingones was based on agriculture using irrigation. Their chief crops were corn, squash, beans, and chili peppers. The Algarrobo (genus *Prosopis*), whose fruit they collected, served as another important resource. They also tended *auchenidos* (llama, alpaca, vicuña, and guamoco). The two most common linguistic variants of the Comechingones were Camiare and Henia, although different dialects existed. They lived in settlements consisting of as many as forty pit-dwellings, the bottom half of which were constructed underground. As protection, the settlement was surrounded by an enclosure made of thorny plants. The group's rich pictorial legacy continues to intrigue scholars; a thousand Comechingón cave-paintings are scattered throughout present-day Argentina. Each settlement was home to a kinship group (probably similar to the Andean *ayllu*) and under the authority of a chief (*curaca*). There is almost no information available on the religious life of the Comechingones, except that during ceremonies they consumed cebil (genus *Anadenanthera*). Ceremonial dances took place inside branch enclosures that contained animal figures carved in wood. Documents testify that by the end of the sixteenth century the population, spread among some six hundred settlements, was perhaps 30,000. One hundred years later, due either to demographic shift, cultural homogenization, or interbreeding, Comechingón culture was thought to be nonexistent. However, in 1998 the first annual "Encuentro de Descendientes de Indígenas Comechingones" was held, demonstrating a renewal of ethnic pride that hints at a recovery and revitalization of Comechingón culture in the twenty-first century.

See also **Indigenous Peoples; Precontact History: Southern Cone.**

BIBLIOGRAPHY

Michieli, Catalina Teresa. *Los Comechingones según la crónica de Gerónimo de Bibar y su conformación con otras fuentes* (1985).

Signorile, Analía, and Griselda Benso. *Comechingones y los primeros españoles en Calamuchita*. Córdoba, Argentina: Ediciones del Boulevard, 2005.

JOSÉ ANTONIO PÉREZ GOLLÁN

COMIBOL. Comibol, the Mining Corporation of Bolivia (Corporación Minera de Bolivia). On 2 October 1952 the government of Víctor Paz Estenssoro established Comibol as an autonomous public corporation. The government's objective was to centralize control over approximately 163 mines and mineral properties nationalized by the April 1952 revolution. These different mines produced zinc, silver, gold and tin. In a short span, Comibol became the single most important source of foreign exchange for Bolivia. However, while Comibol subsidized nearly every other bureaucracy and allowed for spending in education and other areas, the government did not reinvest in the enterprise, thus allowing it to suffer a severe process of decapitalization.

Under the Nationalist Revolutionary Movement (MNR), the mine workers federation (Federación Sindical de Trabajadores Mineros de Bolivia—FSTMB) enjoyed worker comanagement in Comibol, a fact that accounted for slight improvements in working conditions but also both politicized the institution and eroded its finances. Efforts to end worker comanagement often led to violent confrontations between workers and the state. In 1964 the military coup that ended the MNR's twelve-year revolutionary experiment also terminated worker comanagement through outright repression. Over the course of the next eighteen years, several military governments attempted to downsize Comibol through the use of force, periodically stationing troops in mining districts to prevent worker unrest.

Military repression failed to bring Comibol workers under control. Paradoxically, in 1985 Paz Estenssoro, the very person who had established Comibol, accomplished what years of coercion had not. In launching his New Economic Policy (NPE) he downsized Comibol considerably, firing 23,000 mineworkers and closing nonproductive mines. The NPE also called for the privatization and decentralization of Comibol.

See also **Mining: Modern.**

BIBLIOGRAPHY

Melvin Burke, *The Corporación Minera de Bolivia (Comibol) and the Triangular Plan: A Case Study in Dependency* (1987).

Additional Bibliography

Bedregal, Guillermo. *COMIBOL, una historia épica*. La Paz: Fondo Editorial de los Diputados, 1998.

EDUARDO A. GAMARRA

COMINTERN. *See* **Communism.**

COMISIÓN NACIONAL DE DERECHOS LOS HUMANOS. Mexico's National Human Rights Commission (CNDH) was established in 1990 by the Mexican Interior Ministry for the promotion, study, and protection of the human rights of persons in Mexican territory. From 1847 to 1989 there were no fewer than nine efforts to legally enshrine and institutionalize respect for human rights in Mexico, without significant success. Although the commission was designed to be an independent entity, it was not until 1999 that the CNDH enjoyed juridical, organizational, and functional autonomy from the federal government.

A ten-member panel, headed by a president who since 1999 has been appointed by the Senate, governs the commission. As of 2007, its most salient work involves spurring investigations into people's disappearances, issuing human rights reports, addressing sexual abuse and inequality, and advocating for greater transparency. Since its founding, the human rights record of the Mexican federal government has improved, an achievement noted by NGOs such as Human Rights Watch. However, human rights concerns persist with regard to state and municipal governments in Mexico, especially in the most impoverished regions of the country, where lawlessness and drug trafficking thrive.

See also **Human Rights; Truth Commissions.**

BIBLIOGRAPHY

Comisión Nacional de Derechos los Humanos. Available from http://www.cndh.org.mx.

SEAN H. GOFORTH

COMMERCIAL POLICY

This entry includes the following articles:
COLONIAL BRAZIL
COLONIAL SPANISH AMERICA

COLONIAL BRAZIL

From the beginning of its expansion down the coast of Africa in 1420, the Portuguese crown always drew a clear distinction between the free access it granted to foreign ships coming to the metropolis and adjacent islands (Madeira, Azores) via seas that had "long been open to all," and its prohibition on their entry into seas and adjacent coasts that it had recently discovered; unlicensed ships found there were subject to seizure. The coast of Brazil fell into the latter category; thus its commerce was, from the beginning, a monopoly reserved for the Crown and its subjects.

Shortly after the discovery of Brazil in 1500, the Portuguese crown decided to lease out its monopoly rights there to a group of merchants led by Fernão de Loronha, a naturalized Portuguese of Italian ancestry. This original lease lasted for three years, with the crown taking, in the final year, 25 percent of the proceeds. In 1506 the lease was renewed for another ten years upon payment of a lump sum, after which Brazilian trade was "royalized" and conducted by the crown for its own account via salaried *comisários* (agents).

With the definite decision in 1532 to settle Brazil, royal trade policy changed. Portuguese settlers, as well as metropolitan and foreign merchants, were allowed to trade freely with Brazil on condition of paying a 10 percent duty and securing royal licenses for the cargoes. Nonetheless, foreigners were compelled to channel their trade through the Portuguese inhabitants, who were the only persons authorized to deal directly with the Indians. Control was further tightened circa 1550 with the creation of *alfândegas* (customs houses) in most of the captaincies to collect crown duties.

Trade was conducted through a variety of ports both in Portugal (such a Lisbon, Oporto, Viana do Castelo, and Aveiro) as well as in Brazil (such as Recife, Bahia, Porto Seguro, Vitória, Rio de Janeiro, and São Vicente), although some commodities, such as brazilwood, had to go through the *Casa da Índia* (India House) in Lisbon, which acted as the crown agency for its monopoly trades. Varying duties, too complex to describe in detail, were levied on both exports and imports at points along the way: this was the primary benefit derived by the crown from the trade. Additional duties were added (and sometimes subtracted) from time to time. For example, in 1592, all import and export trade with Brazil carried a 3 percent ad valorem duty (the Consulado) to defray the expense of an armada to protect shipping to and from Brazil.

Portugal's primary problem during the sixteenth century and the first half of the seventeenth was the growth of illegal (unlicensed) trading in its empire by other European nations: primarily the French in the sixteenth century; the Dutch in the period 1590–1600; and the English intermittently throughout. After 1580, when Philip II of Spain became king of Portugal, the latter found itself swept up into the world conflicts of the House of

Hapsburg. At war with the Dutch and the English, Philip closed all the ports of the Iberian Peninsula to their merchants (laws of 1591 and 1605). This drove the Dutch, in particular, to increase their direct trade with Brazil in order to secure the sugar that they had previously been able to acquire in Lisbon. After a short truce (1609–1621) the Dutch renewed their attack on Brazil with the occupation of Bahia in 1624–1625 and the conquest of Pernambuco in 1630–1654, which they gradually extended to all the other northern captaincies. Coupled with these losses, the Dutch also seized Portuguese slave stations in Africa. Piracy at sea also increased after 1625, leading to severe losses until Portugal finally severed its connection with Spain in 1640 and signed a truce with the Dutch in 1641, leading to peace in 1661.

In 1649 the Portuguese crown chartered, on the Dutch model, a joint-stock company that was to control trade and protect commerce via a system of fleets between Portugal and its colony. About the same time, a series of commercial treaties was negotiated with the nations that had been the main interlopers in Portugal's imperial trade monopoly—with the English in 1642, the Dutch in 1661, and the French in 1667. Due to the ambiguous language used, these treaties permitted those nations extensive, though ill-defined, rights to trade within the Portuguese Empire.

During the next century, Portugal attempted to control and profit from its Brazilian commerce more via the establishment of monopoly companies than through the earlier policy of a blanket prohibition on unlicensed foreign shipping. In 1755 a company was created to monopolize the trade with the northern area of Brazil (Grão-Pará and Maranhão), and in 1759 a similar company was established to revitalize the sugar trade with Pernambuco and Paraíba.

Throughout the colonial era Portugal used the products of its empire to balance its trade with the exterior. It achieved this in the period up to 1570 with pepper from India and, from circa 1570 to 1670, with sugar exports from Brazil. The decline in the latter near the end of the seventeenth century, at least partly due to the establishment of competing plantations by the English, French, and Dutch in the Caribbean, forced the crown to initiate a policy of industrialization to lessen Portugal's dependence on foreign imports. The discovery, however, of gold in Brazil circa 1690 again permitted Portugal to balance its trade with a colonial commodity, and the industrial policy was scrapped only a couple of decades after it was begun. When gold gave out at the end of the 1750s, Portugal once again turned to an industrial policy to lessen its dependence upon imports. In the sixteenth and seventeenth centuries, Portugal had not made any attempt to stifle the development of industry in Brazil; in fact, it had encouraged sugar refining there by prohibiting it in the homeland (1559), fearful that the process might consume so much wood that it would deforest the kingdom. At the end of the eighteenth century, however, Brazilian industry was seen as a threat to the exports of a newly industrialized Portugal, and was generally prohibited. Nonetheless, Brazil after 1770 found a new prosperity in a revived and diversified agriculture, much of which benefited Portugal itself, and the colonial period closed on a note of a general prosperity both in Brazil and in Portugal.

See also **Captaincy System; Trade, Colonial Brazil.**

BIBLIOGRAPHY

Joel Serrão, ed., *Dicionário de História de Portugal* (1963). V. M. Godinho, *Ensaíos II: Sobre a história de Portugal* (1978), pp. 295–315.

Jose Gonçalves Salvador, *Os Cristãos-Novos e o comércio no Atlântico meridional* (1978), pp. 195 *passim*; Leslie Bethell, ed., *The Cambridge History of Latin America* (1984).

Frédéric Mauro, *Portugal, o Brasil e o Atlântico*, vol. 2 (1989), pp. 183–248.

Additional Bibliography

McCusker, John J., and Kenneth Morgan. *The Early Modern Atlantic Economy.* Cambridge: Cambridge University Press, 2000.

Nardi, Jean-Baptiste. *O fumo brasileiro no período colonial: Lavoura, comércio e administração.* São Paulo: Editora Brasiliense, 1996.

HAROLD B. JOHNSON

COLONIAL SPANISH AMERICA

The essential characteristic of Spanish commercial policy toward Spanish America throughout the colonial period was the firm belief that the benefits of commercial intercourse between metropolitan Spain and its empire should be reserved for Spaniards alone. The definition of "Spaniards" included American as well as peninsular Spaniards, but the needs and interests of the former were considered to be secondary to those of the Spanish monarchy and peninsular producers and exporters. This general policy was articulated in different ways, and with variable success, throughout the three centuries of Spanish rule in America. In the Hapsburg period it was built around the formal restriction of transatlantic trade to a single peninsular port (first Seville, subsequently Cádiz), and to a limited number of American ports in the Caribbean basin. (Moreover, intercolonial trade which might compete with that from Spain was restricted and sometimes prohibited.) In the eighteenth century the gradual introduction of free trade in the period 1765–1789 eventually permitted the major ports of Spain and Spanish America to trade directly with each other. Even in the late eighteenth century, however, the formal policy of excluding foreign ships from direct participation in the commercial exchange between the metropolis and its American dependencies was breached (by the grudging grant of permission for neutral ships to enter Spanish American ports) for only limited periods during the long French revolutionary wars, when Spanish ships were kept in port by British naval blockades. This monopoly, although undermined in practice by both contraband and the inefficiency of peninsular industry, was consistent with the commercial policies also implemented by Portugal, France, England, and Holland in their overseas empires, and thus reflected the general mercantilistic view that the ideal economic relationship between a European imperial power and its overseas territories was one in which the dependencies provided fiscal surpluses and raw materials for processing in the factories of the metropolis (and for re-export to third parties), and protected markets for its manufactured goods. In reality, for most of the colonial period the actual commercial relationships between Spain and Spanish America deviated considerably from this notional norm, partly because of the preponderance of bullion in exports from America (even in the late eighteenth century, when Spain first sought to exploit systematically America's

agricultural potential, precious metals constituted almost 60 percent of the value of exports), and partly because of the related problem that the majority of the manufactured goods exported from Spain to America were produced not in the peninsula but in other European countries.

THE HAPSBURG COMMERCIAL SYSTEM

Spanish Mercantile Communities. During the first five decades of Spanish discovery and exploration in America, the nature and the value of trade was determined in large measure by the rhythm of conquest, the seizure of the accumulated treasure stocks of native civilizations, and the steady export from Seville of the basic commodities (primarily flour, oil, and wine) that the settlers required for their subsistence, together with tools, weapons, animals, and building materials. Short-term fluctuations in the value of this trade were caused primarily by the availability of gold as a return cargo and by the state of Spain's relations with France. By the 1540s, the bonanza of native gold was over, and the more farsighted colonists were turning from looting and barter to the development of silver mining, which was well-established at both Potosí (in modern Bolivia) and Zacatecas (Mexico) by 1550.

The decade of the 1550s was one of depression in the Indies trade, primarily as a consequence of Franco-Spanish hostilities. At the onset in the early 1560s there was a prolonged period of growth that gathered pace in the 1580s and 1590s and soared to its apex in the first decade of the seventeenth century before entering a period of gradual but inexorable decline that continued until the end of the seventeenth century. During the half-century of expansion up to about 1610—in 1608, the record year for westbound sailings, over two hundred ships left for America, and the two years that followed also saw very large fleets dispatched from Seville—despite occasional interruptions caused by, for example, the diversion of merchant ships to carry the ill-fated Spanish invasion force to England in 1588 and Francis Drake's attack on Cádiz in 1596, imports of American bullion reached record levels, averaging almost 7 million pesos a year in the 1590s, and, although tailing off slightly in the first quarter of the sevententh century, remained above 5 million pesos a year until 1630. Thereafter, for both external and internal reasons, including a clear tendency for a greater proportion of the output of the American mines to be retained in the empire to meet the soaring costs of defense, remittances fell sharply to an estimated average of 3.3 million pesos in the 1630s, 2.6 million pesos in the 1640s, and 1.7 million in the 1650s, before plunging to truly insignificant levels in the last two decades of the seventeenth century.

The Spanish Crown. In the short term the Spanish crown was somewhat better protected from commercial decline in the seventeenth century than were the mercantile communities of Spain and America, for it was in the advantageous position of being able to increase taxation. In the long term, of course, resort to this device merely intensified the crisis by encouraging both fiscal fraud at the Spanish end of the system and outright contraband in the Americas. It is important to stress, however, that throughout the sixteenth century and for a substantial part of the seventeenth, the crown could rely upon the receipt of a secure, significant income from America, and succeeded in protecting both the sources of that wealth, its American possessions, and the commercial system that conveyed it to Spain from the hostile attentions of emerging imperial rivals and their agents, both official and unofficial.

Throughout this period Seville served as the only port for trade to and from America. Although strongly criticized by eighteenth-century reformers, its monopoly (which was definitively transferred in 1717 to Cádiz, primarily as a consequence of the silting-up of the Guadalquivir River) reflected not an artificial privilege but a natural concentration of both administrative and commercial authority in the principal city of southwestern Spain, whose natural advantages included a secure port, a rich agricultural hinterland, and a sophisticated commercial-financial-artisan infrastructure capable of satisfying the needs of the rapidly developing American enterprise.

Casa de Contratación. The defense of Spain's monopoly of American trade, and in the process the control of emigration, was based initially upon the administrative control over trade provided by the creation in Seville in 1503 of the Casa De Contratación, or House of Trade. This powerful body combined a variety of commercial, political, scientific, and judicial functions, the majority of which it

retained even after the formal establishment of the Council of the Indies in 1524. The Casa registered every ship sailing to and from the Indies, organized convoys, trained pilots, made maps and charts, functioned as a post office and a receptory for royal treasure, and fulfilled important legal functions. From 1543 it worked closely with the Consulado, or incorporated merchant guild, of Seville, whose members—drawn from the city's leading commercial families—received from the crown a grant of a formal monopoly of the Indies trade in the form of an obligation to organize the financing and defense of periodic fleets.

Convoy System. The organization of shipping into convoys protected by warships was a further key feature of the Hapsburg imperial commercial system that those instrumental in the Bourbon Reforms were wont to criticize as a hindrance to commercial freedom and flexibility. The system again represented, at least in its origins, an institutionalization from 1564 of two natural devices for the protection of Indies shipping from both privateers and the naval forces of other European powers rather than the imposition from above of an artificial structure. From this date the *Carrera de las Indias,* or Indies trade, assumed the configuration that it was to retain until the War of the Spanish Succession, without any significant structural modification other than an increasing practical inability to dispatch fleets on time, particularly in the second half of the seventeenth century, when there were frequently gaps of several years between them.

In principle two fleets a year sailed from Seville: the *flota,* which left in April for Veracruz, and the Galeones, intended primarily to trade indirectly with the viceroyalty of Peru, which departed in August for Nombre de Dios—(superseded in 1598, after Sir Francis Drake and John Hawkins sacked it, by Portobelo) on the isthmus of Panama. The principal armed escort, the Armanda de la Guardia de la Carrera de las Indias, usually consisting of at least two and more commonly up to eight large, well-armed vessels, was never able to prevent attacks upon isolated ships or those involved in local Caribbean trade. The returning *galeones* were never plundered in their entirety, however, and the treasure of the New Spain *flota* was lost only once, when the Dutch privateer, Piet Heyn, captured it at

Matanzas, on the north coast of Cuba, in 1628. The Armada de Barlovento, a separate squadron based in Puerto Rico, paid for by an increase in the rate of Alcabala (sales tax) levied in New Spain and consisting of ships built in Havana, was established in principle in 1636. It succeeded in preventing another Matanzas but was incapable of curbing both the settlement of uninhabited islands and widespread contraband by Dutch, English, and French intruders. Similarly, the Armada De La Mar Del Sur, although established too late to prevent Drake from seizing bullion worth 450,000 pesos off the coast of Peru during his 1577–1580 circumnavigation, succeeded thereafter in ensuring the security of silver fleets in the Pacific.

If on the whole the fleet system functioned effectively in its prime task of protecting transatlantic shipping and the subsidiary Pacific convoys that carried silver from Arica (Peru) to Callao (Peru) and on to Panama, it also had the negative effects of constricting trade, both geographically and structurally, and failing to provide the commercial flexibility necessary to respond to the changing needs of American consumers and producers, particularly in the late seventeenth and early eighteenth centuries. In part, this inflexibility resulted from the restriction of transatlantic trade at the American end of the system to Veracruz, the isthmus of Panama, and to a lesser extent Santo Domingo.

Contraband Trade. Although both historical and geographical considerations made Panama, for example, the natural supply route for Peru and the return of its silver to Spain in the sixteenth century, the consequent failure of the crown and merchants alike to respond in the later Hapsburg period to the growth of contraband trade in the Río De La Plata by legalizing trade with Buenos Aires starkly demonstrated the inflexibility of vested commercial interests. To a large extent this rigidity derived from not only legal restrictions but also the monopoly of trade within the American system enjoyed by the *consulados* of Mexico and Lima, incorporated in 1592 and 1593, respectively, along similar lines to that of Seville, with whose members the Mexican and Peruvian merchants enjoyed extremely close ties of business, friendship, and often family. For these merchants, whose capital and influence controlled the dispatch of fleets from Seville, the conduct of the trade fairs of Veracruz and Portobelo, and the subsequent transfer of merchandise to the warehouses of Mexico and Callao for distribution throughout New Spain and Peru, shortages of goods did not necessarily constitute a problem, for scarcity guaranteed high prices and easy profits. In fact, the fundamental economic problem of the Hapsburg commercial system was that the merchandise required by American consumers increasingly could not be supplied in adequate quantities and at acceptable prices, not only because of the restrictionist attitudes of the monopolists but also because by the end of the Hapsburg period Spain possessed neither the productive capacity nor the initiative to satisfy even the basic needs of the American market.

Throughout America the perennial shortage of goods supplied through official channels, and the exorbitant prices charged for those which did arrive, induced American producers and consumers, particularly in areas remote from the viceregal capitals, to indulge in contraband with foreign ships, which sailed into the many unguarded harbors open to them along the Atlantic and Caribbean coasts, and local officials to turn a blind eye to and even participate in their illegal practices. Not surprisingly, Spain's clear inability to preserve the commercial integrity of its American possessions encouraged its imperial rivals to go beyond mere contraband to engage in selective territorial expansion, acquiring in the course of the seventeenth century Caribbean bases such as Jamaica and Saint Domingue, which built their prosperity upon both the smuggling and the production of sugar and tobacco for the European market.

THE BOURBON ERA

The advent of the Bourbon dynasty in 1700 brought the question of the reform of the American commercial system to the forefront of discussions about national regeneration from late-Hapsburg decline and the ravages of the War of the Spanish Succession (1702–1713). During the war only one trade fair was held at Portobelo (in 1708)—like that of 1713 it was a commercial flop, largely because licensed French merchantmen and contrabandists had saturated the market—although the five *flotas* dispatched in the same period to Veracruz enjoyed more success. In the short term the prospects for postwar commercial recovery were not strong, partly because of the grant in 1713 to the English South Sea Company by the *asiento* (contract) to supply slaves to Spanish American ports, and the supplementary right to send a merchant ship to each of the trade fairs attended by the *galeones* and *flotas*. Before their abolition in 1750, these privileges provided a smokescreen for widespread contraband activity. In the meantime, despite the clamor of influential writers such as José del Campillo y Cossío (1693–1744), minister of finance under Philip V, for a more liberal commercial structure, the crown—under pressure from the *consulados* of Cádiz, Mexico City, and Lima—limited structural change to the formal abolition in 1740 of the Portobelo fairs (the last of which was held in 1731) in favor of the use of individual register ships, an increasing number of which sailed to Pacific ports.

During the first half of the eighteenth century, registered Spanish trade with America grew modestly, primarily as a consequence of economic growth in America: the index of tonnage increased from a base figure of 100 at the beginning of the century to 160 in the period 1710–1747, and to 300 in the period 1748–1778. Despite this encouraging trend many commentators argued that the need for the abolition of the fleet system and the Cádiz monopoly remained urgent if contraband were to be curbed and major commercial growth secured. The crown considered further radical reform in 1754, but, under pressure from conservative forces, confirmed that biennial fleets would continue to be dispatched from Cádiz to New Spain: in fact, only six fleets sailed in the 1757–1776 period, and the majority found it very difficult to sell their cargoes in a market saturated by contraband goods. In the meantime, a new king, Charles III (1759–1788), and his advisers moved gradually in the wake of Spain's humiliating defeat in the final stages of the Seven Years' War (1756–1763) toward genuine structural reform, which culminated in the famous "Decree of Free Trade" of 1778.

Free Trade. The principal features of the new Bourbon commercial policy were the decision in 1765 to open the Spanish islands in the Caribbean to direct trade with nine peninsular ports; the 1778 Free Trade Act, which increased the peninsular ports licensed to trade to thirteen, and extended the new system to all of Spanish America except Venezuela and New Spain; and, finally, in 1789, the definitive admission of all Spanish America to the free trade system. Although these changes were radical, the slowness of their introduction reflects the durability of the Hapsburg system and the timidity of the Bourbon reformers. However, there is no doubt that the new system (which allowed Spanish and Spanish American ports to trade freely with each other but not with foreigners) ushered in a fourfold increase in the value of Spanish exports to America in the period 1782–1796, and an elevenfold increase in the value of the return trade. It was less successful in breaking the practical monopoly of Cádiz—which controlled 80 percent of this trade—and in promoting significant industrial growth in the peninsula: although there was some expansion in textile production in Catalonia, the principal beneficiaries of free trade in Spain were the agricultural and viticultural sectors.

In America, the results were more spectacular: although bullion continued to dominate exports to Spain (in the late eighteenth century its share fell from 76 percent of the value to 56 percent), the agricultural and pastoral economies of formerly neglected regions such as Venezuela, the Río de la Plata, and Cuba grew rapidly, as did that of New Spain.

This economic and commercial growth ground to an abrupt halt in 1797, following Spain's 1796 entry into what turned out to be a prolonged war against Britain. The crown's reluctant decision in November 1797 to allow trade to be conducted in the ships of neutral nations encouraged some vessels to test the British blockade of Cádiz, but the principal beneficiaries were North American merchants who brought foreign manufactures and foodstuffs to Spanish American ports, and returned directly to their home ports with silver, sugar, and other products rather than taking them to Spain. Aware of this abuse, the crown revoked the general grant of neutral trade in 1799, although it was subsequently forced to endorse its partial restoration, as local officials simply flouted the prohibition, citing wartime necessity as their excuse. Official Spanish trade made a brief recovery in 1802–1804, with the suspension of hostilities in Europe, and again picked up marginally in 1809–1810 and 1815–1816.

During the period 1797–1820 as a whole, however, the average value of exports from Spain to America was only 9 percent higher than in 1778. Throughout the last two decades of imperialism, Charles IV and Ferdinand VII refused consistently to introduce genuine free trade. The result was that the quest for the right to trade freely with the world at large was a major factor in persuading many Spanish Americans by 1810 that real commercial freedom could not be secured without political emancipation from Spain.

See also **Armada del Mar del Sur; Charles III of Spain; Colonialism; Fleet System; Colonial Spanish America; Seven Years' War.**

BIBLIOGRAPHY

Huguette Chaunu and Pierre Chaunu, *Séville et l'Atlantique,* 8 vols. (1955–1956).

Valentín Vázquez De Prada, "Las rutas comerciales entre España y América en el siglo XVIII," in *Anuario de Estudios Americanos* 25 (1968): 197–237.

Antonio García-Baquero González, *Cádiz y el Atlántico (1717–1778),* 2 vols. (1976).

Geoffrey J. Walker, *Spanish Politics and Imperial Trade, 1700–1789* (1979).

Lutgardo García Fuentes, *El comercio español con América, 1650–1700* (1980).

Enriqueta Vila Vilar, "Las ferias de Portobelo: Apariencia y realidad del comercio con Indias," in *Anuario de Estudios Americanos* 39 (1982): 275–340.

John R. Fisher, *Commercial Relations Between Spain and Spanish America in the Era of Free Trade, 1778–1796* (1985).

Josep Fontana and Antonio Miguel Bernal, eds., *El "comercio libre" entre España y América (1765–1824)* (1987).

Peter T. Bradley, *The Lure of Peru: Maritime Intrusion into the South Sea, 1598–1701* (1989).

Hector R. Feliciano Ramos, *El contrabando inglés en el Caribe y el Golfo de México (1748–1778)* (1990).

Additional Bibliography

Arazola Corvera, Ma Jesús. *Hombres, barcos y comercio de la ruta Cádiz-Buenos Aires, 1737–1757.* Sevilla: Diputación de Sevilla, 1998.

Bustos Rodríguez, Manuel. *Los comerciantes de la carrera de Indias en el Cadiz del siglo XVIII (1713–1775).* Cádiz: Servico de Publicaciones, Universidad de Cádiz, 1995.

Hill, Ruth. *Hierarchy, Commerce and Fraud in Bourbon Spanish America: A Postal Inspector's Exposé.* Nashville, TN: Vanderbilt University Press, 2005.

JOHN R. FISHER

COMMISSIONS REGARDING 1968 MASSACRES IN TLALTELOLCO.

On November 27, 2001, President Vicente Fox Quesada created this Special Prosecutor's Office, under the Office of the Government Attorney, to investigate the massacres, torture, disappearances, and genocide of dissidents and opponents of the authoritarian regime of the Institutional Revolutionary Party (Partido Revolucionario Institucional, or PRI). The PRI had just lost the elections of 2000, after having been in power for more than seventy years, to a great extent through repressive measures that reached the extreme of crimes against humanity. The main cases that this office was to investigate and punish were the massacre of hundreds of students by the army and paramilitary groups in 1968 and 1971; and the "dirty war" that led to the murder, torture, and "disappearance" of mainly leftist militants in the 1970s.

Some relatives of the victims—who would have preferred a truth commission in the form of those of South Africa, El Salvador, and Guatemala—were suspicious of the newly created Special Prosecutor's Office, believing that the powerful criminals of the old regime would be able to pressure for impunity, as in other legal instances. Some members of Fox's cabinet supported the idea of a truth commission because, given Mexico's weak judicial system, it would be the only way to have an effective instrument of transitional justice. Nevertheless, the more conservative elements in the cabinet won the debate, arguing that a commission would not have the legal power to put the offenders in prison, and that the Special Prosecutor's Office would help to channel the demands for justice through qualified institutional avenues.

The Special Prosecutor's Office was a failure and closed on March 27, 2007, less than four months after Felipe Calderón assumed the presidency. In shutting it down, the government argued that it lacked jurisdiction and produced poor results. Special Prosecutor Ignacio Carrillo Prieto was not only suspected of embezzlement of at least part of the budget of 300 million Mexican pesos but had also made grave juridical errors in the trials (raising suspicion of concealment) and did not manage to win a single conviction. Nevertheless, Carrillo claimed that the office was closed down through an agreement between the

Fox and Calderón administrations and the PRI and high army commanders. Relatives of the victims assert that the administrations in power during the transition to democracy have granted a de facto amnesty to the criminals of the old regime, perpetuating their impunity.

See also **Mexico, Political Parties: Institutional Revolutionary Party (PRI).**

BIBLIOGRAPHY

Aguayo Quezada, Sergio, and Javier Treviño. "Neither Truth Not Justice: Mexico's De Facto Amnesty." *Latin American Perspectives* 33 (March 2006): 56–68.

Castellanos, Laura. *México Armada. 1943–1981.* Mexico City: Era, 2007. See chapter 7.

FROYLÁN ENCISO

COMMUNISM. Between the years immediately after the founding of the Soviet Union in 1917 until its collapse in 1991, the Latin American Communist movement was closely tied to Moscow. The long-term strategy of Communist parties as well as positions on specific issues generally coincided with Moscow's thinking, sometimes referred to as "orthodox Communism." Nevertheless, during this extended period, Latin American Communists occasionally assumed positions and engaged in actions that to varying degrees were temporarily at odds with the official Moscow line.

The basic Moscow-approved Communist strategy during these seven decades (with the exception of the World War II years) was the prioritization of the struggle against imperialism, specifically U.S. domination. The anti-imperialism of the Communist movement was tied to the concept of a dual revolutionary process, which supposedly corresponded to the sequence of the Soviet revolutions of February and October in 1917. According to this scheme, the first revolution was supported by a "national progressive bourgeoisie" and consisted of the establishment of a democratic government that promoted agrarian reform and national industrial development. The achievement of the objectives of the first stage was seen as a prerequisite for advancing to the second stage, which was socialist. While some sectors of the non-Communist left also defended this thesis,

others questioned the existence of a "progressive bourgeoisie" in Latin America and argued that this entire class was inextricably tied to the imperialist system.

EARLY YEARS AND POPULAR FRONTISM
Communist parties were formed throughout Latin America during the decade and a half following the Soviet revolution. Some, as in the case of Argentina, were split-offs of existing socialist parties, whereas others, such as the Communist Party of Mexico, consisted of many former anarchists. In the case of Chile, the Socialist Workers Party, founded in 1912, changed its name to the Communist Party under the influence of its main leader, ex-typographical worker Luis Emilio Recabarren. The Communist Party of Venezuela, as that of several other countries, was founded in 1931 by nonveterans with little previous organizational ties. The early Communists were students, intellectuals, and other members of the middle sectors; few of them belonged to the working class (the Chilean Communist Party being an exception).

The Communist parties joined the Communist International (the Comintern), which was created shortly after the Soviet revolution and saw itself as one worldwide party. Various international Communist organizers aided in the founding of Communist parties throughout Latin America. The most prominent was M. N. Roy, from India, who unsuccessfully attempted to win over delegates at the Second Comintern Congress in 1920 to the thesis that the political struggles of underdeveloped countries was central to the world revolutionary process.

During its early years, the Latin American Communist movement was more independent than at any other time. The most heterodox thinker was José Carlos Mariátegui, founder of the Peruvian Socialist Party in 1928, which refrained from calling itself "Communist" although it affiliated with the Comintern. Mariátegui glorified the collective spirit that the Peruvian peasants inherited from their Incan past, which he saw as the seeds of a socialist society. In an action that was largely independent of the Comintern, the Salvadorian Communist Agustín Farabundo Martí led an armed insurrection in 1932 that the army brutally crushed. Another icon of the Communist movement, former military officer Luís

Carlos Prestes, led an uprising with heavy participation by Brazilian Communists against the government of Getúlio Vargas in November 1935, an insurrection that was contrary to the Comintern's prodemocratic line at the time.

At its Seventh Congress in July 1935, the Comintern initiated its strategy of broad alliances known as "popular fronts," with parties to the right of the Communist parties in opposition to the threat of fascism. At first popular frontism was designed to achieve far-reaching economic and political reforms, but after the German invasion of the Soviet Union in 1941 it consisted of Communist support of governments opposed to Germany. The one popular front that came to power was the coalition of the Communist, Socialist, and Radical Parties in Chile, whose candidate Pedro Aguirre Cerda won the presidential elections in 1938. Several Communist parties supported presidents during World War II. Two leading Communists, Juan Marinello and Carlos Rafael Rodríguez, entered the cabinet of the first government of Fulgencio Batista (1940–1944) in Cuba; the party of Venezuelan President Isaías Medina Angarita formed an alliance with Communists for the 1944 municipal elections.

COLD WAR YEARS
In the latter years of World War II, splinter groups emerged in the Communist parties of Venezuela, Mexico, Colombia, and Peru that were opposed to conciliatory stands, including the "no-strike" policy promoted by Earl Browder, the secretary-general of the U.S. Communist Party. With the beginning of the Cold War in 1946, Latin American Communists hardened their positions and denounced "Browderism." The political polarization set off by the Cold War turned former allies against the Communists. Thus the Radical government of Gabriel González Videla in Chile, elected in 1946 with Communist endorsement as a continuation of popular frontism, passed the Law for the Permanent Defense of Democracy in 1948, which outlawed the Communist Party. While the Chilean Communist Party went underground, its counterparts in countries run by military dictatorships in the 1950s, such as that of Batista in Cuba and Marcos Pérez Jiménez in Venezuela, faced ever harsher repression. Polarization also split the continental labor movement the Confederation of Workers of Latin America (CTAL), which was under the direction of the Mexican trade unionist Vicente Lombardo Toledano and under strong Communist influence. Motivated by Cold War considerations, Serafino Romualdi of the American Federation of Labor (AFL) played an active role in pushing for the CTAL's schism in 1948.

The pro-Soviet Communist movement in Latin America was generally reluctant to support armed movements; not surprisingly, the Cuban Communist Party, known as the Partido Socialista Popular (PSP), at first criticized Fidel Castro's clandestine Movimiento 26 de Julio for being *putschist* (supporting a military seizure of power). But Castro's advent to power on January 1, 1959, was a milestone event for Latin American Communists and resulted in the merging of the PSP and the Movimiento 26 de Julio into a new Communist Party of Cuba. Most, but not all, Latin American Communist parties opposed Castro's call to arms in the 1960s. Ironically, in Venezuela, which was one of the continent's more solid democracies, the Communist Party initiated the guerrilla struggle in 1962, although it gradually extricated itself from the movement after 1965. Communists in several other nations also engaged in armed warfare. After considerable hesitation, the Communist Party in El Salvador joined the guerrilla front Farabundo Martí National Liberation Front (FMLN) in 1979. The party's secretary general, Jorge Handal, became a guerrilla commander and, in 2004, the FMLN's presidential candidate. In the 1960s the Revolutionary Armed Forces of Colombia (FARC), which represented the armed wing of the Communist Party, reactivated the previous decade's armed struggle, known as "La Violencia," between Liberals and Conservatives, and has maintained itself as the nation's largest guerrilla organization since then. Finally, the Communist Party of Chile joined the far-leftist Movement of the Revolutionary Left (MIR) in forming the Manuel Rodríguez Patriotic Front (FPMR) in 1983; it carried out sabotage, kidnappings of military personnel, and, in 1986, an attempt on the life of dictator Augusto Pinochet.

EUROCOMMUNISM AND THE COLLAPSE OF THE SOVIET UNION
Beginning in the 1970s, in a phenomenon known as Eurocommunism, European Communist parties

rejected long-standing Marxist dogma. This development, together with the liberalization policies known as *perestroika*, initiated in 1986 by Soviet leader Mikhail Gorbachev, inspired some Latin American Communists to follow a flexible line. Eurocommunism influenced Venezuelan Communist Party dissidents to break off from the main party to form the Movement toward Socialism (MAS) in 1971, which advocated a democratic "Venezuelan road to socialism" and soon became the nation's largest leftist party. Ten years later, the Communist Party of Mexico coalesced, with four smaller parties, into the Socialist Unified Party of Mexico (PSUM), which in turn dissolved itself to enter the Party of the Mexican Revolution (PRD), led by Cuauhtémoc Cárdenas. By uniting organically with leftists who defended diverse ideological currents, the Mexican Communists abandoned dogmatic notions long associated with the international Communist movement.

The developments culminating in the collapse of the Soviet Union in 1991 weakened the Communist movement in Latin America. Thus the Chilean Communist Party (PCC), historically the largest in Latin America dating back to Recabarren, saw its electoral intake severely diminished to 3 percent for its secretary general and candidate Gladys Marín in the 1999 presidential elections. Furthermore, beginning in the late 1980s the Communists' long-standing ally the Chilean Socialist Party maintained an ongoing electoral alliance with the Christian Democratic Party, which excluded the PCC. Those few who stayed in Communist parties hardened their stand after 1991. With the election of Hugo Chávez as president of Venezuela in 1998 signaling leftist electoral inroads, Latin American Communists sided with the radical brand of leftism over the moderate one. Thus the Communist Party of Venezuela avidly supported President Chávez; the Communist Party of Bolivia ran candidates on the slate of Evo Morales's Movement toward Socialism (MAS) and supported his candidacy in 2005 when he was elected president; and the Communist Party of Peru endorsed the candidacy of Ollanta Humala in the 2006 presidential elections. In contrast, the Communist Party of Argentina maintained a more critical attitude toward President Néstor Kirchner, elected in 2003.

THE BALANCE SHEET OF SOVIET INFLUENCE

Although Latin American Communist parties generally hewed to the Moscow-endorsed line, they occasionally assumed relatively independent positions. Examples include the thinking and actions of first-generation Communist leaders such as Mariátegui, the emergence of anti-Browder Communist factions at a time when the U.S. Communist leader enjoyed considerable prestige, and the influence of the Cuban Communist Party on some Latin American parties at a time when Fidel Castro was considered a maverick within the international Communist movement.

The balance sheet of pro-Soviet Communist influence in Latin America was mixed. On the one hand, the local Communist Party failed to play a major role in the two successful leftist Latin American revolutions, namely that of Cuba in 1959 and Nicaragua in 1979. On the other hand, after defying the Soviets during the first decade of the Cuban revolution, Castro's qualified support for the Soviet invasion of Czechoslovakia in 1968 signaled a convergence of Cuban-Soviet positions lasting until 1991. In addition, the Communists maintained major influence over a period of time in a number of labor movements. Examples include the General Confederation of Workers of Peru (CGTP), which was founded by Mariátegui in 1929 and since the late 1960s has been the nation's largest labor confederation; the Chilean Workers' Central (CUT), founded in 1953, as well as its two major precursor organizations; and the Communist-controlled Unionist Confederation of Colombian Workers, founded in 1964. Finally, the colorful careers of various important Communists added prestige to the movement. These figures included, in addition to Mariátegui and Prestes, Julio Antonio Mella, the founder of the Cuban Communist Party who was assassinated in 1929; Gustavo Machado, a long-time Communist head from an aristocratic family; and Pablo Neruda, the Chilean poet who died days after the Pinochet-led coup in 1973.

See also **Pérez Jiménez, Marcos; Labor Movements; Aguirre Cerda, Pedro; Batista y Zaldívar, Fulgencio; Cárdenas Solorzano, Cuauhtémoc; Castro Ruz, Fidel; González Videla, Gabriel; Lombardo Toledano, Vicente; Mariátegui, José Carlos; Marinello, Juan; Martí, Agustín Farabundo; Medina Angarita, Isaías; Prestes, Luís Carlos; Rodríguez, Carlos Rafael; Vargas, Getúlio Dornelles.**

BIBLIOGRAPHY

Alexander, Robert J. *Communism in Latin America*. New Brunswick, NJ: Rutgers University Press, 1957.

Alexander, Robert J. *The Communist Party of Venezuela*. Stanford, CA: Hoover Institution Press, 1969.

Caballero, Manuel. *Latin America and the Comintern, 1919–1943*. Cambridge, U.K., and New York: Cambridge University Press, 1986.

Carr, Barry. "Marxism and Anarchism in the Formation of the Mexican Communist Party, 1910–19." *Hispanic American Historical Review* 63, no. 2 (1983): 277–305.

Carr, Barry. "Mexican Communism 1968–1981: Eurocommunism in the Americas?" *Journal of Latin American Studies* 17, no. 1 (1985): 201–228.

Carr, Barry. "Crisis in Mexican Communism: The Extraordinary Congress of the Mexican Communist Party (Part 2)." *Science and Society* 51, no. 1 (1987): 43–67.

Carr, Barry, and Steve Ellner, eds. *The Latin American Left: From the Fall of Allende to Perestroika*. Boulder, CO: Westview Press, 1993.

Chilcote, Ronald, H. *The Brazilian Communist Party: Conflict and Integration, 1922–1972*. New York: Oxford University Press, 1974.

Ellner, Steve. "Factionalism in the Venezuelan Communist Movement, 1936–1948." *Science and Society* 45, no. 1 (1981): 52–70.

Fuenmayor, Juan Bautista. *1928–1948: Veinte Años De Política*. Caracas, Miguel Angel García e Hijo, 1969.

Furci, Carmelo. *The Chilean Communist Party and the Road to Socialism*. London: Zed Books, 1984.

Halperin, Ernst. *Nationalism and Communism in Chile*. Cambridge, MA: MIT Press, 1965.

Poppino, Rollie E. *International Communism in Latin America: A History of the Movement, 1917–1963*. New York: Free Press, 1964.

Ramírez Necochea, Hernán. *Origen y formación del Partido Comunista de Chile: Ensayo de historia del partido*. Santiago, Chile: Editora Austral, 1965.

Ravines, Eudocio. *The Yenan Way*. New York: Scribner, 1951. Repr., Westport, CT: Greenwood, 1972.

STEVE ELLNER

COMMUNITY ACTION. *See* **Panama, Community Action.**

COMODORO RIVADAVIA. Comodoro Rivadavia, a city of 137,000 inhabitants (2001), is the largest urban center of the Province of Chubut in Argentine Patagonia. The first site of the settlement was an anchorage at the southern edge of the Golfo San Jorge known as Puerto Tilly, in remembrance of the Spanish captain Tilly y Peredes, who in 1794–1795 repelled repeated attacks by Portuguese raiders on the Río de la Plata estuary. In 1889 the private entrepreneur Francisco Pietrobelli used this port to serve the *estancias* located along the Chubut River, on which Welch colonists had been settling since 1885. The name Comodoro Rivadavia was given to the set of shacks in 1901 to honor the navy officer Martin Rivadavia, who had surveyed the coast of Patagonia between 1890 and 1892. The discovery of petroleum deposits in 1907 spurred development of the humble settlement and gave rise to the Argentine oil industry, which peaked in 1922 with the founding of Yacimientos Petrolíferos Fiscales (YPF), which is one of the country's largest corporations in the early twenty-first century. Comodoro Rivadavia is an important base for the Argentine army and air force, and in 1974 it was chosen as the site for the Universidad Nacional de la Patagonia San Juan Bosco. In 2007 there were 10,000 students on this campus, and more on secondary campuses in Trelew, Puerto Madryn, Puerto Gallegos, and Ushuaia. An inflow of Chilean immigrants has contributed to the rapid growth of Comodoro Rivadavia, the 2006 population of which reached an estimated 148,000.

See also **Argentina, Geography; Patagonia.**

BIBLIOGRAPHY

Thomas, John M., et al. *Una frontera lejana: La colonización galesa del Chubut, 1865–1935*. Buenos Aires: Fundación Antorchas, 2003.

CÉSAR N. CAVIEDES

COMONFORT, IGNACIO (1812–1863). Ignacio Comonfort (*b.* 1812; *d.* 13 November 1863), president of Mexico (1855–1858). Born in the state of Puebla, he pursued a military career from the period of the 1830s onward. After the war against the United States (1846–1848), he became the chief customs official in Acapulco and a close associate of Juan Álvarez, the *caudillo* of Guerrero. Comonfort was one of

the authors of the Plan of Ayutla (1 March 1854), which began the military movement to oust Antonio López de Santa Anna from the presidency and put in place a Liberal government. He then traveled to the United States to raise funds for the war effort.

Returning to Mexico, Comonfort became the general in charge of operations in Jalisco and Michoacán. His mentor, Juan Álvarez, led the Ayutla Revolution to victory, became president in late 1855, and appointed his protégé his minister of war. Álvarez governed only briefly; Comonfort replaced him on 11 December 1855. A moderate Liberal, Comonfort tried to harmonize the demands of the radicals for rapid implementation of a reform program with the more gradual approach advocated by the moderates. He signed and promulgated the famous Ley Lerdo (25 June 1856) calling for the alienation of church and municipal properties, written by his treasury minister Miguel Lerdo De Tejada. He vigorously crushed a Conservative revolt in Puebla in early 1856 and he also promulgated the Constitution of 1857. By late 1857, however, he was concerned that the radicals were too influential and were leading Mexico into a civil war. He then conspired with Conservatives to bring them to power, an act that started the war he had hoped to avoid, the War of the Reform (1858–1860).

Comonfort left the presidency in early 1858, remained in exile in the United States until 1861, and then returned to Mexico. He was rehabilitated by the Liberals, given a commission, served in President Benito Juárez's cabinet, and took an active role in confronting the French Intervention. He was killed in a skirmish.

See also **Mexico: 1810–1910.**

BIBLIOGRAPHY

The following works are all by Ray F. Broussard: "Ignacio Comonfort: His Contributions to the Mexican Reform, 1855–1857" (Ph.D. diss., University of Texas at Austin, 1959); "Comonfort y la revolucíon de Ayutla," in *Humanitas* 8 (1967): 511–528; "El regreso de Comonfort del exilio," in *Historia Mexicana* 16, no. 4 (1967): 516–530; and "Viduarri, Juárez, and Comonfort's Return from Exile," in *Hispanic American Historical Review* 49 (1969): 268–280. In addition, see Rosaura Hernández Rodríguez, *Ignacio Comonfort: Trayectoría política, documentos* (1967).

Additional Bibliography

Hamnett, Brian. "The Comonfort Presidency, 1855–1857." *Bulletin of Latin American Research* 15:1 (July–December 2001): 53–81.

Villegas Revueltas, Silvestre. *Ignacio Comonfort.* México, D.F.: Planeta DeAgostini, 2003.

CHARLES R. BERRY

COMPADRAZGO. Compadrazgo, a special bond between two social equals. Rooted in personal trust, *compadrazgo* is a relationship between individuals who rely upon one another for mutual support in times of need. Practiced throughout the Americas, *compadrazgo* is not defined by social hierarchy (as in patron-client relations) or even necessarily blood or affinal relationship (birth or marriage); rather it is a "ritual" kinship.

Originally the term referred to the relationship between the sponsor and the candidate at the Catholic sacraments of baptism and confirmation. Medieval Catholic doctrine treated this ritually instituted kinship as identical to blood kinship and labeled marriages between participants "incestuous." In the early 2000s only the sense of an intimate bond remains, not necessarily one created by a ritual or joint participation in a rite of passage. Sometimes used for in-laws, this bond is secondary to the primary pact of mutual help and trust.

See also **Catholic Church: The Colonial Period.**

BIBLIOGRAPHY

Sidney W. Mintz and Eric R. Wolf, "An Analysis of Ritual Co-Parenthood (Compadrazgo)," in *Southwestern Journal of Anthropology* 6, no. 4 (1950): 341–368.

Julian Pitt-Rivers, *The People of the Sierra* (1954).

Additional Bibliography

Cerón Velásquez, María Enriqueta. *Redes sociales y compadrazgo: Indicadores de vitalidad etnolingüística en una comunidad indígena de Puebla.* México, D.F.: Instituto Nacional de Antropología e Historia, 1995.

McAnany, Patricia Ann. *Living with the Ancestors: Kinship and Kingship in Ancient Maya Society.* Austin: University of Texas Press, 1995.

Schweizer, Thomas, and Douglas R. White, eds. *Kinship, Networks, and Exchange.* New York: Cambridge University Press, 1998.

PATRICIA SEED

COMPADRESCO. Compadresco, a godparent relationship. *Compadresco* is a form of religious kinship in Luso-Brazilian Catholic society whereby a person acquires one or two godparents at baptism, confirmation, and marriage. By acting as a spiritual sponsor at baptism, the godparents (*padrinho* and *madrinha*) become coparents, assuming the responsibility of watching over the child's spiritual life and material well-being. In Brazil, as in other Catholic countries, the godparent relationship is taken very seriously and involves lifelong obligations, including adopting godchildren in case of the death of their parents and awarding dowries. The *compadrio* ties allow families to strengthen and enlarge kinship links with wealthy individuals of higher social class. The *parentela* (kinship network) thus created is a vital institution in Brazilian society and politics. Since family counts for everything, a lone individual could be included in family groups by a favorable marriage alliance and godparent relationships. In colonial times the *compadrio* relationships helped ambitious families to secure favorable political positions and alliances with wealthy landowning and merchant families, thereby strengthening and reinforcing the existing *parentelas*. Social linkages were vital in colonial times, when the cycles of boom and bust could reduce even the wealthiest families to poverty. Slaves commonly sought godparents for their children from the free population and among their owners to aid in freeing their children.

See also **Compadrazgo.**

BIBLIOGRAPHY

Sidney W. Mintz and Eric R. Wolf, "An Analysis of Ritual Co-Parenthood (Compadrazgo)," in *Southwestern Journal of Anthropology* 6, no. 4 (1950): 341–368.

A. J. R. Russell-Wood, *Fidalgos and Philanthropists: The Santa Casa da Misericordia of Bahia, 1550–1755* (1968).

Stephen Gudeman, "The *Compadrazgo* as a Reflection of the Natural and Spiritual Person," in *Proceedings of the Royal Anthropological Institute* (1971), pp. 45–71.

Stephen Gudeman and Stuart B. Schwartz, "Baptismal Godparents in Slavery: Cleansing Original Sin in Eighteenth-Century Bahia," in *Kinship, Ideology, and Practice in Latin America*, edited by Raymond T. Smith (1984), pp. 35–58.

Additional Bibliography

Graham, Sandra Lauderdale. *Caetana Says No: Women's Stories from a Brazilian Slave Society*. New York: Cambridge University Press, 2002.

Higgens, Kathleen J. *"Licentious Liberty" in a Brazilian Gold-Mining Region: Slavery, Gender, and Social Control in Eighteenth-Century Sabaráa, Minas Gerais*. University Park: Pennsylvania State University Press, 1999.

PATRICIA MULVEY

COMPADRITO. Compadrito, one of the most colorful figures in Argentine literature and music of the early twentieth century, the flashy urban dandy mentioned in tango lyrics. Usually of lower-class origin, the *compadrito* was familiar with the language and habits of the denizens of *la mala vida,* the easy—and often criminal—life of Buenos Aires. He rarely had a job, often bragged about exploits in which he had never participated, and tried to dress as if he were affluent.

Many Argentine intellectuals identify the *compadrito* as emblematic of the deleterious consequences of the urban transformation that made Buenos Aires unique. There, men no longer dressed as gauchos (cowboys) but instead put brilliantine on their hair, dangled cigarettes from their lips, wore hats that obscured their eyes, donned flashy scarves, and wore shoes with thick heels. This uniform separated these urban men from their rural counterparts and indicated their integration into a Europeanized modern city. The *compadrito's* female counterpart was the dance-hall girl, often a prostitute. To middle- and upper-class critics of lower-class culture both social types were considered immoral. In fact, what the *compadrito* and the music-hall girl represented was the most marginal, yet visible, group of lower-class inhabitants: those who responded to the poverty and lack of well-paid work in Buenos Aires by turning to more remunerative, but less socially acceptable, activities. The different types of tango styles also revealed diverse and changing images of the compadrito and gender relations. In the ruffianesque, an aggressive style tango, the *compadrito* typically deceived and successfully seduced women. Yet, the romantic style tango portrays the *compadrito* encountering more independent women who are able to choose their companion.

See also **Music: Popular Music and Dance; Tango.**

BIBLIOGRAPHY

Andrés M. Carretero, *El compadrito y el tango* (1964).

Jorge Luís Borges and Silvina Bullrich, *El compadrito: Su destino, sus barrios, su música* (1968).

Fernando Guibert, *The Argentine Compadrito,* translated by Eric Gibson (1968).

Additional Bibliography

Collier, Simon, Artemis Cooper, Maria Susana Azzi, and Richard Martin. *Tango! The Dance, the Song, the Story.* New York: Thames and Hudson, 1995.

Lamas, Hugo and Enrique Binda. *El tango en la sociedad porteña, 1880–1920.* New York: Thames and Hudson, 1998.

Savigliano, Marta E. *Tango and the Political Economy of Passion.* Boulder: Westview Press, 1994.

DONNA J. GUY

COMPANHIA GERAL. *See* **Trade, Colonial Brazil.**

COMPANHIA VALE DO RIO DOCE (CVRD). The world's largest iron-mining company, Companhia Vale do Rio Doce (CVRD), also known as Vale, was created in 1942 as Brazil began to industrialize its economy. Originally confined to the exploration and production of iron ore in the southeastern region of the country, the company has become a diversified international firm operating in fourteen Brazilian states and sixteen countries on five continents. In 1997 a consortium of companies acquired 45 percent of the government-owned shares of Vale and turned the company into a giant mineral conglomerate.

Vale produces iron ore and pellets, pig iron, copper, bauxite, alumina, nickel, coal, kaolin, potassium, manganese, and ferro alloys. Between 2004 and 2006 the company's revenue went from $8.5 billion to $28.7 billion. Accordingly, its net earnings soared from $2.6 billion to $8 billion. For the first quarter of 2007, revenue reached US$7,680 million—33.4 percent from the Americas, 43.4 percent from Asia, and 20.1 percent from Europe. China has become Vale's most important market (16.1% of worldwide sales), followed by Brazil (14.8%), Japan (11.5%), and the United States (9.9%). This means 85 percent of Vale's business is outside the country.

Employing 33,000 people, the company participates in the federal campaign against hunger (Zero Fome) program by providing transportation of food and other sustenance necessities as well as direct donation of goods and cash to communities where it operates. It has become an important engine of development for the country.

See also **Iron and Steel Industry; Mining: Modern.**

BIBLIOGRAPHY

Companhia Vale do Rio Doce. Available from www.cvrd.com.br.

Companhia Vale do Rio Doce. *CVRD–2006 Production Report.* Rio: CVDR, 2007.

Companhia Vale do Rio Doce. *Reaping the Rewards of Diversification: CVRD Performance in the First Quarter of 2007.* Rio de Janeiro: CVRD Department of Investor Relations, 2007.

EUL-SOO PANG

COMPAÑÍA GUIPUZCOANA. Compañía Guipuzcoana, a company established for the monopoly control of commerce between Spain and the province of Venezuela (1728–1785). From the beginning of the Spanish presence in America, commercial activity with the overseas provinces was controlled by the House of Contracts in Seville. After two centuries this system had not yielded successful results. Bureaucratic red tape, smuggling, conflicts of interest, supply problems, and diverse restrictions all led many subjects to propose the creation of private companies to deal with trade. It was not until the beginning of the eighteenth century and the ascendancy of the Bourbon dynasty to the Spanish throne that the lessons of the French concerning the benefits of a commercial monopoly began to be applied. The idea of creating a company responsible for commerce with the province of Venezuela grew in favor when Pedro José de Olavarriaga visited it from 1720 to 1721 and made a report on the conditions of commerce there, including the boom in Venezuelan cocoa and the obvious deterioration of trade between the province and Spain.

The Compañía Guipuzcoana was created with broad powers by the royal decree of 25 September

1728. In 1730 its first ships sailed, and its business was rapidly established. Three years later it declared a dividend, and its volume of trade was steadily rising. The *compañía* extended its area of activity to include Maracaibo in 1752. It achieved a substantial reduction in the price of cocoa, increased production, extended areas of cultivation, and increased the crown's revenues.

The formation of the *compañía* and its success caused great uneasiness in the province, however. Andresote's uprising in Yaracuy occurred between 1730 and 1733, and later the displeasure of the creole elite would be felt with greater force, since the *compañía*'s activities destabilized the business that the local merchants and harvesters had with other Spanish colonies.

In 1749 Juan Francisco de León, backed by a great number of notables and important cocoa growers, led a revolt against the *compañía*. Added to the discontent were accusations that the directors were benefiting illicitly by making private deals, by not paying dividends to shareholders, and by rendering inadequate accounts to the crown. All of this resulted in the convocation of a general junta to investigate the *compañía* and the imposition of severe restrictions upon it. A price-regulating junta was formed; the *compañía* was obliged to reserve up to one-sixth of its ships' capacity for use by the shippers of Caracas; and it was required to take on shareholders from Caracas and Maracaibo. When the intendancy was created in 1776, the *compañía*'s activities were subject to the control of the intendant, José de Abalos. And in 1779, when war with England broke out, its business declined. By 1780 the *compañía* had lost its privileges, and in 1785 it was finally dissolved by the royal decree of 10 March.

See also **Colonialism; Commercial Policy: Colonial Spanish America.**

BIBLIOGRAPHY

Roland Dennis Hussey, *The Caracas Company, 1728–84* (1934).

Eduardo Arcila Farías, *Economía colonial de Venezuela* (1946).

Ramón De Basterra, *Una empresa del siglo XVIII, los navios de la ilustración: Real Compañía Guipuzcoana de Caracas y su influencia en los destinos de América* (1954).

Vincente De Amezaga Aresti, *Hombres de la Compañía Guipuzcoana* (1963).

Mercedes Margarita Álvarez Freites, *Comercio y comerciantes, y sus proyecciones en la independencia venezolana,* 2d ed. (1964).

Additional Bibliography

Aizpurua, Ramón. *Curazao y la costa de Caracas: Introducción al estudio del contrabando de la provincia de Venezuela en tiempos de la Compañía Guipuzcoana, 1730–1780.* Caracas: Academia Nacional de Historia, 1993.

Cohen, Jeremy David. "Informal Commercial Networks, Social Control, and Political Power in the Province of Venezuela, 1700–1757." Ph.D. diss., University of Florida 2003.

INÉS QUINTERO

COMPANIES, CHARTERED.

Chartered Companies. Corporations formed through a grant by a sovereign power for the purposes of foreign trade. These companies had Italian origins and became popular among European countries such as Great Britain in the sixteenth and seventeenth century. After a long economic depression in the sixteenth century, proposals for the formation of trading companies within the Spanish empire abounded during the eighteenth century, and companies reached their heyday at mid-century. Principally directed at expanding trade between Spain and its American kingdoms, companies were established with varying degrees of success for trade with Honduras (1714); Caracas (1728); the Philippines (1733); Cuba (1740); Portugal (1746); Buenos Aires, Cartagena, Veracruz, and Panama (1747); and the islands of Santo Domingo, Puerto Rico, and Marguerita (1755). After negotiation between merchants and the crown, the king would typically issue a charter (*cedula real*) directing formation of a company for either exclusive or privileged trade with specific American ports. The charter would establish a starting capital and sometimes designate the number of years for which the contract was valid. Shares would then be sold and when the company had attained sufficient funds, business would begin.

The establishment of trading companies was influenced by Colbertian mercantilism, the philosophy and practice of state sponsorship of factories and monopolies to stimulate production, with two primary intentions in the Americas: to support a growing state apparatus and to keep out imperial rivals. Moreover, Spanish authorities hoped to end the widespread illegal trade conducted through English, Dutch and French trading partners. The companies were an alternative to the fleet system, by which once a year, each of two treasure ship convoys left Spain at different times, one to Veracruz and the other to Terra Firme. By the early eighteenth century the fleet system was generally acknowledged to be seriously outmoded to the needs of empire. It was slow, costly, and because of its predictability, highly susceptible to piracy. Compounding these ills, the fleet system prevented Spain from maximizing the profits of empire, kept the colonies undersupplied, restrained the development of industry in Spain, encouraged contraband, and created powerful interest groups antithetical to the Bourbon, absolutist ideal.

Company formation was intended to increase trade in areas peripheral to traditional Spanish interests where contraband had flourished. These regions typically did not produce precious metals, but rather cash crops such as indigo, tobacco, and cacao. At the same time, companies theoretically would reduce the influence of merchant monopolies in Cádiz, Mexico, and Lima by expanding the number of ports open to trade. Companies further provoked opposition in the Americas by obliging colonists to sell produce for less and to buy imported goods for more than they had been accustomed to. While the goal of the chartered companies was to increase trade, the monopolistic nature of the companies consequently went against free trade capitalist philosophy.

Despite opposition on several fronts, the monarchy was encouraged by the early success of the Compañía Guipuzcoana, or Caracas Company, which drove out foreign trade and eliminated the need for an annual subsidy from New Spain. Trade between Spain and the Americas did increase under chartered companies, but the success of the Caracas Company, which was created in 1728 and endured until 1784, was not repeated. Several companies never began trade after receiving charters. Even those that achieved early success fell apart by the century's final quarter, because of internal dissension, corruption, and the beginnings of intercolonial free trade introduced in 1765.

See also **Caracas Company; Commercial Policy: Colonial Spanish America.**

BIBLIOGRAPHY

Roland D. Hussey, *The Caracas Company, 1728–1784* (1934).

Jorge Pinto Rodríguez, "Los Cinco Gremios Mayores de Madrid y el comercio colonial en el siglo XVII," in *Revista de Indias* 51 (May–August 1991).

Carmelo Saenz De Santamaría, "La Compañía de Comercio de Honduras, 1714–1717" in *Revista de Indias* 40 (January–December 1980).

Additional Bibliography

Arazola Corvera, Ma Jesús. *Hombres, barcos y comercio de la ruta Cádiz–Buenos Aires, 1737–1757.* Sevilla: Diputación de Sevilla, 1998.

Cavieres Figueroa, Eduardo. *Servir al soberano sin detrimento del vasallo: El comercio hispano colonial y el sector mercantil de Santiago de Chile en el siglo XVIII.* Valparaíso: Ediciones Universitarias de Valparaíso de la Universidad Católica de Valparaíso, 2003.

Fisher, John Robert. *The Economic Aspects of Spanish Imperialism in America, 1492–1810.* Liverpool, U.K.: Liverpool University Press, 1997.

Martínez Shaw, Carlos and José María Oliva Melgar. *Sistema atlántico español: Siglos XVII–XIX.* Madrid: Marcial Pons Historia, 2005.

Romano, Ruggiero. *Mecanismo y elementos del sistema económico colonial americano, siglos XVI–XVIII.* México: El Colegio de México, Fideicomiso Historia de las Américas: Fondo de Cultura Económica, 2003.

Vila Vilar, Enriqueta and Allan J. Kuethe. *Relaciones de poder y comercio colonial: Nuevas perspectivas.* Sevilla: Escuela de Estudios Hispano–Americanos: Texas Tech University, 1999.

PHILIPPE L. SEILER

COMPAY SEGUNDO (1907–2003). Compay Segundo was one of the most prominent musicians in recent Cuban history. Born Francisco Repilado and raised in Santiago de Cuba, he started his music career in the 1930s playing the clarinet in the municipal band. In his early years he became familiar with the origins of Son Cubano—a mix of African beats and Spanish guitar and songs. In 1934 Repilado moved to Havana, where he played both the clarinet and the armónico—his own seven-string variation of the tres guitar—and formed a number of bands with famous Cuban musicians, beginning with Ñico Saquito. Repilado and Lorenzo Hier-rezuelo, another musician from Santiago, formed Los Compadres in 1942, when Repilado adopted his professional name, "Compay Segundo." Los Compadres became successful in Cuba, playing mainly sones and boleros, but broke up in 1955. Segundo went solo until the 1970s, when he gave up music and worked in a cigar factory. In 1996 he returned to professional music, featuring on the *Buena Vista Social Club* recording. Within two years of the release of the recording, Repilado became an international star, winning a Grammy, playing in famous halls worldwide, and making several more records.

See also **Music: Popular Music and Dance.**

BIBLIOGRAPHY

Orovio, Helio. *Cuban Music from A to Z.* Durham, NC: Duke University Press, 2004.

Sweeney, Philip. *Cuban Music: The History; the Artists; the Best CDs.* London: Rough Guides, 2001.

SMITH DOUGLAS MONSON

COMPOSICIÓN. Composición, a proce-dure used in the Spanish Indies to settle legal dis-putes by payment of fees to the royal treasury. Initially, *composición* was used to legitimize or revoke titles to guardianships (encomiendas) over the Indians in cases where the original title could not be produced by the holder (*composición de encomiendas*). Later it was used to validate land-ownership in cases of land seized, often illegally, from Indian communities by Spaniards or land occupied by colonizers as squatters for farming or cattle raising. Usually, after residing on the land for an appropriate time, the claimant asked authorities for a *composición* to validate his land title in return for a payment of a fee (*composición de tierras*).

The procedure was useful to Spaniards wish-ing to acquire native lands, particularly as indigen-ous communities were decimated by disease or were moved to other areas away from their villages to be Christianized and thus unable to challenge the *composición*. Moreover, it provided the Real Hacienda (royal treasury) with revenues, and it also allowed foreigners to remain in Spanish

America despite strong prohibitions against their presence there. In return for payment of a yearly assessment, approved aliens were permitted to remain in the Indies (*composición de extranjeros*). Foreign women and foreign priests were exempt from this levy.

See also **Colonialism; Real Hacienda.**

BIBLIOGRAPHY

Arranz Lara, Nuria. *Instituciones de derecho indiano en la Nueva España.* Chetumal, Quintana Roo, México: Editora Norte Sur, 2000.

Knight, Alan. *Mexico: The Colonial Era.* Cambridge, UK: Cambridge University Press, 2002.

Recopilación de leyes de los reynos de las Indias, 4 vols. (1681; repr. 1973), libro IV, título XII; leyes XV–XXI; libro IX, título XXVII: leyes XI–XXXI.

JOHN JAY TEPASKE

COMPUTER INDUSTRY. During the 1960s governmental agencies, banks, and large busi-nesses became the first in Latin America to use U.S.-produced mainframe computers for internal control applications. By the early 1980s more than a dozen computer firms had established plants in Mexico by means of different business arrangements: Mexican majority ownership (e.g., Apple, Burroughs, Hewlett Packard, Honeywell), agreements with local manufac-turers (NCR, Sperry), or retention of complete con-trol, as IBM had in exchange for exporting 90 percent of production and distributing software in Spanish.

Brazil attempted to develop its own computer hardware industry in the early 1970s when poten-tial computer manufacturers, including major banks and "frustrated nationalist technicians," lob-bied the Brazilian military government to foster a national industry. They founded the Comissão Coordenodora dos Atividados de Processamento Electronico (CAPRE) in April 1972 and in July 1974 the first national company, Computadores e Sistemas Brasileiros, S.A. (COBRA), was formed to manufacture minicomputers. Beginning in 1977 the government prohibited imports of mini- and microcomputers, terminals, printers, other periph-erals, and software, and severely limited foreign investment in these areas. In 1979 a new regulatory body, the Special Informatics Secretariat (SEI) replaced CAPRE and in 1984 the Informatics Law formalized the strict prohibitions already in effect. Beginning with the election of Fernando Collor in 1989, however, the government removed import prohibitions and lowered tariffs on foreign computers, peripherals, and software. In 1992 Brazil permitted the entry of foreign technology and capital, easier formation of joint ventures, and the establishment of wholly owned subsidiaries of foreign manufacturers, allowing the construction of American, European, and Asian plants.

The Brazilian experiment failed for the very reasons most Latin American nations have not tried to develop their own industries outside of implementing equipment import conditions and setting research and training standards to encourage local development. Domestic technology generation could not keep pace with global changes in the industry; neither national entrepreneurs nor the government could provide adequate resources for local technology and software development; computer users and manufacturers needed access to up-to-date technology at lower cost; and foreign manufacturers and governments, particularly the United States, exerted pressure to end piracy and copyright violation. However, foreign computer companies have set up offices and factories in Latin America. In 2001 Dell Computers, for instance, opened an assembly plant in Brazil.

The advent of the microcomputer in the 1980s made computing affordable to smaller businesses and educational institutions in Latin America and created a market for locally produced software, as well as for the cheaper Asian personal computer (PC) clones. Latin American computer users, especially those in rural areas, still contend with unreliable power supplies, the lack of trained support personnel, systems and documentation available only in English, difficulties in getting supplies and spare parts, and expensive imported equipment. However, these problems have not prevented the adoption of computers; the few studies and reliable statistics show that in 1993 there were approximately 13 computers per 1,000 Mexicans, 6 per 1,000 Brazilians, and 2 per 1,000 Guatemalans, whereas the United States counted 265 computers per 1,000 citizens.

In 1990 the small Latin American market represented only 3.2 percent of the international revenues for U.S. software producers that dominate the PC-based systems software and programming markets worldwide. As of 2007, Internet penetration stood at 13 percent of the region's population. Brazil and Mexico are the two most important sources of software demand, followed by Argentina, Venezuela, and Chile. Because unauthorized copying of software by users and computer dealers is rampant, U.S. software producers have brought successful cases against dealers in Argentina and Mexico. Meanwhile, on the applications side, there are hundreds of small software development companies that serve the needs of local clients according to demand in each country's marketplace.

Latin American telecommunications services are intimately related to regional computer software and hardware industries. Creating links to worldwide computer networks has been a slow process, mainly because of difficulties in obtaining reliable and cost-effective communications links from government-owned telephone companies. By the late 1980s most of the traffic was email, based on personal computers and carried mainly on direct dial-up connections. The APC (Association for Progressive Communications), for example, established nodes in Brazil (Alternex), Ecuador, Nicaragua, and Uruguay. By the early 1990s a growing number of countries (including Brazil, Argentina, Peru, Mexico, Costa Rica, and Chile) were linking up to the Internet and developing networks within their borders. In 1991 the Organization of American States launched its Hemisphere Wide Inter-University Scientific and Technological Information Network to foster the interconnection of academic computer systems throughout Latin America and the Caribbean, supporting efforts in the Caribbean (CUNet), Jamaica (JAMNet), Central America (RedCACyT), Argentina, Chile, and the Andean countries.

The information revolution is ending Latin American isolation, and has already affected revolutions of a different sort there. In 1995 it was widely reported that Sub-Comandante Marcos, leader of the Zapatista revolt in Chiapas, Mexico, plugs his laptop computer into cigarette lighter outlets in Jeeps to send messages worldwide. Cries for help, complete with President Ernesto Zedillo's FAX number, were spread through the Internet during an army crackdown, resulting in a deluge of communications at the Presidential Palace and perhaps a suspension in hostilities. Latin Americans participate in the latest Internet trends in the early twenty-first century. Citizens from all over the Americas have started blogs using

MySpace and Facebook accounts. Snippets from Latin American *telenovelas* and news programs can be found on the popular video site YouTube. Despite these important cultural changes, a sizable digital divide exists in Latin America.

BIBLIOGRAPHY

Adler, Emanual. *The Power of Ideology: The Quest for Technological Autonomy in Argentina and Brazil.* Berkeley: University of California Press, 1987.

Caetano, Gerardo and Rubén M. Perina, eds. *Informática: Internet & política.* Montevideo: Centro Latinoamericano de Economía Humana: Washington, DC: Organización de los Estados Americanos, 2003.

Chahin, Ali, et al. *E-gov.br: A próxima revolução brasileira: Eficiência, qualidade e democracia: O governo eletrônico no Brasil e no mundo.* São Paulo: Pearson Prentice Hall, 2004.

Castelazo-Morales, Luis. *The Microcomputer Industry in the U.S. and Opportunities in Mexico Professional Report.* Austin: University of Texas at Austin, Graduate School of Business, 1985.

Evans, Peter B. "State, Capital, and the Transformation of Dependence: The Brazilian Computer Case." *World Development* 14, no. 7 (1986): 791–808.

Rada, Juan F. *The Impact of Microelectronics and Information Technology: Case Studies in Latin America.* Paris: UNESCO, 1982.

Ronfeldt, David F. *The Zapatista Social Netwar in Mexico.* Santa Monica, CA: Rand Arroyo Center, 1998.

Tigre, Paulo B. *Computadores brasileiros.* Rio de Janeiro: Campus, 1984.

GRETE PASCH
JOSEPH STRAUBHAAR

COMUNERO REVOLT (NEW GRANADA).

Comunero Revolt (New Granada), large-scale rebellion (March–October 1781) against colonial authority in what is now northeastern Colombia. On 16 March 1781, a crowd in Socorro, led by Manuela Beltrán, tore down an edict on new sales tax (*alcabala*) rates, one of a package of fiscal measures promulgated by the royal visitador, Juan Francisco Gutiérrez De Piñeres. Similar disturbances occurred in other towns in the region, and on 16 April leading figures of the Socorro elite endorsed the movement. One of them, Juan Francisco Berbeo, was named leader (*capitán*). The rebellious towns quickly organized a force of between 10,000 and 20,000 men to march on Santa Fe de Bogotá, and in late May they arrived at Zipaquirá, just north of the viceregal capital. Viceroy Manuel Antonio Flores was in Cartagena, and Gutiérrez fled the capital, leaving a junta under Archbishop Antonio Caballero y Góngora in charge.

Caballero traveled to Zipaquirá to parley with the rebels (and to exploit the substantial differences among them), and on 5 June Caballero and Berbeo agreed to a set of thirty-four articles—the Capitulations of Zipaquirá. These articles dealt with the full range of the northeasterners' complaints against the fiscal and administrative aspects of Bourbon reformism, including sales tax and head tax increases, restrictions on tobacco cultivation (the region's only viable cash crop), abuses of the liquor monopoly, the one-way flow of public monies to Bogotá, and others. Several of the articles called for improvements in the lot of Indians and free blacks, two groups whose numbers were insignificant in the movement's mestizo heartland—although Indians were more numerous in the neighboring provinces of Pamplona to the north and Tunja to the south, which were nominally part of the rebellion. (The Comunero revolt, it should be noted, was unrelated to the far more threatening and violent Túpac Amaru insurrection in Peru in 1780.)

After Berbeo and most of the *comuneros* returned home, Caballero and Flores promptly denounced the *capitulaciones* as null and void. After granting amnesty to the vast majority of the *comuneros*, including Berbeo and other elite leaders, Caballero then spent six months in the northeast, preaching obedience to royal authority and restoring many (though not all) of Gutiérrez's fiscal measures. Berbeo and other patricians were happy to avoid punishment for their involvement; plebeians, however dissatisfied, had to return to their precarious livelihoods. Only a small core of *comuneros*, led by José Antonio Galán, a small farmer from Charalá, continued the armed struggle. They were captured in October 1781, and Galán was executed along with three of his lieutenants in February 1782. The visible long-term consequences of the rebellion were slight, though subsequent viceroys took care to draw up defensive plans lest Bogotá again find itself threatened by *socorranos*.

For many decades the Comunero episode was practically unknown outside the Socorro region; only in 1880 did Manuel Briceño publish his study *Los comuneros* and a version of the *capitulaciones*. Like many Colombian historians after him, Briceño saw the movement as a precursor to independence, not just chronologically but programmatically as well. This idea has been effectively refuted by recent studies, which note that elites and plebeians gladly invoked the figure of the king against the abuses of his officials, a typical colonial gambit. However, authors differ as to the overall import of the demands codified in the *capitulaciones*.

John L. Phelan, in *The People and the King* (1978), argues that the rebellion reflected societal rejection of centralizing Bourbonist infringements upon local autonomy, whereas Mario Aguilera Peña, in *Los comuneros: guerra social y lucha anticolonial* (1983), emphasizes the importance of agrarian and other socioeconomic conflicts in Socorro. Given the dominant characteristics of Socorro society circa 1781—the relative autonomy of the region's smallholder/artisan majority, their increasingly tenuous economic situation, and the role of the fiscal system in ensuring the elite's viability—the power of a literalist view that takes the *capitulaciones* at face value should not be underestimated.

See also **Bourbon Reforms.**

BIBLIOGRAPHY

Besides the works cited above, see Anthony Mc Farlane, *Colombia Before Independence* (1993).

Additional Bibliography

Aguilera Peña, Mario. *La rebelión de los Comuneros.* Bogotá: Panamericana Editorial, 1998.

Arciniegas, Germán. *Los comuneros.* Caracas: Biblioteca Ayacucho, 1992.

Caballero, Enrique and Alfredo Iriarte. *Incensio y pólvora: Comuneros y precursores.* Bogotá: Amazonas Editores, 1993.

Silva, Renán. *La ilustración en el virreinato de Nueva Granada: Estudios de historia cultural.* Medellín: La Carreta Editores, 2005.

Silva, Renán. *Saber, cultura, y sociedad en el Nuevo Reino de Granada, siglos XVII y XVIII.* Medellín: La Carreta Editores, 2004.

RICHARD STOLLER

COMUNERO REVOLT (PARAGUAY, 1730–1735).

The revolt originated in the long-standing hostility of Paraguayans to the Society of Jesus. Paraguayans coveted Jesuit lands, commercial privileges, and the monopoly on Guarani labor in Jesuit missions. This hostility first appeared in the violence of the 1640s, when Bishop Bernardino de Cárdenas articulated Paraguayan grievances; it surfaced again during the incendiary governorship of José de Antequera y Castro. Under Antequera, in 1724, Paraguayans routed a Guarani army from the missions, expelled Jesuits from their Asunción *colegio*, and remained largely unchastised when Antequera fled in 1725.

Although Paraguayans were relatively quiescent during the governorship of Martín de Barúa, resentment smoldered. Paraguayans disliked but accepted the return of the Jesuits to Asunción. In 1730 the appointment as governor of Ignacio de Soroeta, a client of Viceroy José de Armendáriz, marqués de Castelfuerte, the jailer of Antequera and the restorer of the Jesuits to their properties in Asunción, roused Paraguayans to renew their resistance. Soroeta's pro-Jesuit associations goaded Paraguayans past the boundaries of good sense and overcame the counsels of local moderates and Jesuit partisans.

Bishop José de Palos, a Franciscan who supported the Jesuit position, was unable to soothe tempers. A shadowy figure named Fernando Mompox De Zayas, a fugitive from Lima, encouraged rebellion. An acquaintance of Antequera's and a fellow prisoner in the viceregal jail in Lima, Mompox was a person to whom Jesuit writers and other critics of the rebellious Paraguayans ascribed inordinate influence. Modern Paraguayan patriots have suggested that he was a premature antimonarchist. The theory of natural rights that Mompox supposedly revealed to Paraguayans held that political authority was vested in the people, or *común* (thus *comuneros*), and they delegated it to the monarch. This view of the limited powers of kingship was reactionary, not revolutionary. It was an approach to monarchy predating eighteenth-century absolutism, and it flourished in provincial Asunción, where men treasured the exploits of the heroes of the sixteenth century.

Paraguayans in 1731 expelled Soroeta from the province, incidentally condemning to death Antequera in Lima. Some Paraguayans, whose leadership centered on the Asunción *cabildo,* created the *junta gobernativa,* a committee that hoped to direct the province. Although offensive to royal authority, this body was not a truly revolutionary creation. Its aim was to rival the city council. Direction of the insurrection came from the Asunción elite. For a time, the *alcalde ordinario* José Luis Barreiro, who expelled Mompox from the province, directed local affairs. Leadership then fell to Miguel de Garay and the former Antequera partisan Antonio Ruíz de Arellano. In 1732, Paraguayans again expelled the Jesuits from Asunción, showing the continuity between earlier uprisings and the 1730s. In July 1733, Governor-designate Manuel Agustín de Ruiloba y Calderón, another Castelfuerte appointee, arrived in Paraguay. Paraguayans shot him. The elderly bishop of Buenos Aires, Juan de Arregui, who was visiting the province, then served briefly as governor. Unable to command respect, he departed. Cristóbal Domínguez de Obelar, a Paraguayan *encomendero* and local magistrate, took charge of the government until 1735, when pacification of the province again fell to Buenos Aires governor Bruno Mauricio de Závala, who was more repressive than when he had suppressed the earlier insurrection in 1725. He sentenced to death four leaders of the uprising, ordered thirteen exiles, removed municipal officials from their posts, and prohibited public meetings.

Later interpreters have followed the argument of Father Pedro Lozano, the Jesuit chronicler of the revolt, who wished to discredit Paraguayans by picturing them as radicals. Many twentieth-century authors have also seen the rebellion as a precursor to modern revolutions, which it was not. Its leaders never pursued revolutionary goals. They saw themselves as patriots loyal to the Spanish monarchy. Nevertheless, present-day Paraguayans cherish the memory of the *comuneros* and consider them patriots and precursors of independence.

See also **Jesuits; Mompox de Zayas, Fernando.**

BIBLIOGRAPHY

Antonio Zinny, *Historia de los gobernantes del Paraguay* (1887).

Pedro Lozano, *Historia de las revoluciones de la provincia del Paraguay,* 2 vols. (1905).

Carlos Zubizarreta, *Historia de mi cuidad: Etopeya de la Asunción colonial* (1964).

James Schofield Saeger, "Origins of the Rebellion of Paraguay," in *Hispanic American Historical Review* 52, no. 2 (1972): 215–229.

Adalberto López, *The Revolt of the Comuneros, 1721–1735: A Study in the Colonial History of Paraguay* (1976).

Additional Bibliography

Castillo, David R. *Reason and Its Others: Italy, Spain, and the New World.* Nashville, TN: Vanderbilt University Press, 2006.

Franzen, Beatriz Vasconcelos. *Jesuítas, portugeses y espanhóis no sul do Brasil e Paraguai coloniais: novos estudos.* São Leopoldo, Brazil: Editora UNISINOS, 2003.

Ganson, Barbara Anne. *The Guaraní under Spanish Rule in the Río de la Plata.* Stanford, CA: Stanford University Press, 2003.

Millones Figueroa, Luis and Domingo Ledezma. *El saber de los Jesuitas, historias naturales, y el nuevo mundo.* Madrid: Iberoamericana, 2005.

Techo, Nicolás del, Manuel Serrano y Sanz, and Bartomeu Melía. *Historia de la provincia del Paraguay de la compañia de Jesús.* Asunción: Centro de Estudios Paraguayos Guasch, 2005.

JAMES SCHOFIELD SAEGER

CONCEPCIÓN, CHILE.

Concepción, capital of the central Chilean province of the same name and of the Bío-Bío region. The city, which has a population of 391,733 (2003) inhabitants, along with the sister port city Talcahuano (2003 pop. 288,666), is now the second-largest urban center of the country after Greater Santiago, with close to 700,000 people in the metropolitan areas combined, followed by Valparaíso–Viña del Mar. Concepción was founded by Pedro de Valdivia in 1550 as a stronghold against the Mapuche Indians of the Bío-Bío region. After being repeatedly destroyed by earthquakes, tidal waves, and Indian attacks, the city was established in its present location on the northern margin of the Bío-Bío River in the eighteenth century. During colonial times it developed into a strong, independent power that used its strategic location and proximity to the sea to challenge

Santiago for its position as capital city. Between 1858 (when coal was discovered in Lota) and 1940, Concepción and its surroundings became a bustling industrial center (textiles, steel mill, glass factories). It is also the location of several universities, including the University of Concepción. During the 1960s and 1970s the active militancy of students and workers converted Concepción into the most powerful political stronghold of the Left.

Concepción remains one of the most important industrial and harbor sites in Chile. The growing economic importance of the lumber, pulp, paper, and chemical industries, as well as fisheries, has attracted migrants in recent years, yet unemployment and social segregation within the city are salient problems. The contamination of soil, water, and air due to the proximity of industrial zones to residential areas has raised questions about Concepción's zoning laws.

See also **Chile, Geography.**

BIBLIOGRAPHY

Glaeser, Edward L., and John Robert Meyer. *Chile: Political Economy of Urban Development.* Cambridge, MA: Harvard University Press, 2002.

Instituto Geográfico Militar, "La región del BioBio," in *Geografía de Chile,* vol. 30 (Santiago, 1986).

Mazzei de Grazia, Leonardo. *La red familiar de los Urrejola de Concepción en el siglo XIX.* Santiago: Universidad de Concepción Centro de Investigaciones Diego Barros Arana, 2004.

Nimia, Jaque Peña. *El arbol que florecía hijos: Golpe militar de 1973, relatos de mujeres de Concepción.* Santiago: Julio Araya Editorial, 2003.

Rojas Miño, Claudio. *El desarrollo después de la crisis del estado de bienestar: Sus posibilidades en el caso de Concepción, Chile.* Santiago: Instituto Latinoamericano y del Caribe de Planificación Económica y Social–ILPES, Universidad del Bío–Bío, 1995.

Silveira, Vera L., Ximena Valdés, Ana María Arteaga, and Catalina Arteaga. *Mujeres, relaciones de género y agricultura.* Santiago: Centro de Estudios para el Desarrollo de la Mujer, 1995.

CÉSAR N. CAVIEDES

CONCEPCION, DAVE (1948–). David Ismael (Benitez) Concepcion was born 17 June 1948, in Maracay, Aragua State, Venezuela. He played major-league baseball for the Cincinnati Reds and stood out as one of the game's finest shortstops.

Concepcion signed with the Cincinnati Reds as a free agent in 1967, and in April 1970 made his playing debut. Concepcion's stellar play was such that the Reds' players named him team captain in 1973. Contributing to four Cincinnati World Series appearances, Concepcion earned five Rawlings Gold Glove Awards, was named to nine All-Star teams, and, in 1977, was named the Roberto Clemente Award winner. In 1982, he was named Most Valuable Player in that year's All-Star game. The Venezuelan played his entire nineteen-year career with the Reds until his 1988 retirement and fell only forty-four games short of Larry Bowa's National League record for games played at shortstop. Following a distinguished line of Venezuelan shortstops such as Chico Carrasquel and Luis Aparicio, he inspired players like Omar Vizquel to maintain the legacy of great shortstops from his country.

See also **Sports.**

BIBLIOGRAPHY

Bjarkman, Peter C. *Baseball with a Latin Beat.* Jefferson, NC: McFarland, 1994.

Oleksak, Michael M., and Mary Adams Oleksak. *Béisbol: Latin Americans and the Grand Old Game.* Grand Rapids, MI: Masters Press, 1991.

Wendel, Tim. *The New Face of Baseball: The One-Hundred Year Rise and Triumph of Latinos in America's Favorite Sport.* New York: Rayo, 2003.

SAMUEL O. REGALADO

CONCEPCIÓN, PARAGUAY. Concepción, city founded 31 May 1773 by Spanish colonel Agustín Fernando de Pinedo y Valdivieso on the east bank of the Paraguay River, 193 miles north of Asunción, to dominate the Mbayá Indians, to contain the Portuguese, and to explore the *yerbales* (agricultural prospects) between the rivers Jejúi and Apa. It remained a small town, with the population increasing from 44 families and three military companies in the 1780s to 2,768 in 1846; 14,640 in 1950; 18,232 in 1962; 22,866 in 1982; and 25,607 in 2001.

Although Concepción was laid out in the Spanish rectangular pattern, its commerce was concentrated around the port. The town was a center of the yerba trade in the eighteenth century, and by 1864 it boasted lime and brick factories, several general stores, and half a dozen *pulperías* (grocery stores). It exported Yerba Maté, Quebracho, lumber, and cattle, and it protected the northern frontier with Brazil. From 1826 to 1831 the town served as a place of exile for Europeans, Corrientinos, and Paraguayans who questioned the authority of dictator José Gaspar de Francia. Although the region lost population during the War of the Triple Alliance (1864–1870), its northern position protected it from destruction, though not from declining prosperity after the war. Because Concepción opposed General Higínio Morínigo in the 1947 civil war, it suffered neglect from both General Alfredo Stroessner and the Colorado Party.

Although river trade has declined, Concepción is a strategic location for road transport leading to Asunción, the country's capital, and to the Gran Chaco region. It is also free port for trade with Brazil. In the early 2000s the municipality has begun to promote tourism.

See also **Paraguay, Geography.**

BIBLIOGRAPHY

Natalico Olmedo, *Album gráfico de Concepción* (1927), deals with both the province and the city between 1870 and 1925. Guillermo A. Cabral Giménez, *Semblanzas de Concepción* (1970), while including historical material from the colonial period to 1970, is inclined to concentrate on political issues post-1870. See also John Hoyt Williams, *The Rise and Fall of the Paraguayan Republic, 1800–1870* (1979), esp. pp. 12, 56, 60, 67, 77, and 217–218, the best available nineteenth-century history.

Ashwell, Washington. *Concepción, 1947: Cincuenta años después.* Asunción: W. Ashwell, 1998.

Martínez, Ofelia, and Mary Monte. *Dios proteja destino patria: Las concepcioneras de 1901.* Asunción: Centro de Documentación y Estudios, 1999.

Pereira, Humberto Osnaghi. *La libertad viene del norte: Revolución de Concepción, 1947.* Asunción: Arandurã Editorial, 2004.

VERA BLINN REBER

CONCHA, ANDRÉS DE LA (c. 1554–1612).

Andrés de la Concha (*b.* ca. 1554; *d.* after 1612), painter and architect. Born in Seville and trained there in the mannerist style, possibly under Peter Kempeneer, Concha went to New Spain in 1567, with a contract to execute the main retablo at Yanhuitlán. Among the many works by Concha referred to in documents, numerous paintings and altarpieces were for the Dominican order in Oaxaca and Mexico City. A good number survive, such as the panels at Yanhuitlán, Coixtlahuaca, and Tamazulapán. In addition, the paintings that were formerly attributed to the Master of Santa Cecilia are now credited to Concha. Concha was named *maestro mayor* of the cathedral of Mexico City in 1601, and most of his activity after that year was architectural. This lends weight to a recent hypothesis that there were two artists of the same name, one a painter and the other an architect.

See also **Retablos and Ex-Votos.**

BIBLIOGRAPHY

José Guadalupe Victoria, "Sobre las nuevas consideraciones en torno a Andrés de la Concha," in *Anales del Instituto de investigaciones estéticas* 50, no. 1 (1982): 77–86.

Additional Bibliography

Fernández, Martha. "Andrés de Concha: Nuevas noticias, nuevas reflexiones." *Anales del Instituto de Investigaciones Estéticas* 15:59 (1998): 51–68.

Vences Vidal, Magdalena. "Incidencias en el proceso artístico, mixteca alta, Oaxaca." *Latino América* 30 (1997): 29–49.

CLARA BARGELLINI

CONCHA, JOSÉ VICENTE (1867–1929).

José Vicente Concha (*b.* 21 April 1867; *d.* 8 December 1929), president of Colombia (1914–1918). A member of the Conservative Party's traditionalist, or "Historical" wing, Concha, a native of Bogotá, became a critic of the Nationalist regime of Miguel Antonio Caro (1892–1898). In 1900 he conspired with fellow Historicals and with members of the Liberal Party to overthrow Nationalist President Manuel Antonio Sanclemente. The plotters replaced Sanclemente with José Manuel Marroquín, who headed the government until 1904. Concha served as Marroquín's minister of war, and in 1902 was sent to Washington, D.C., to conclude negotiations on the Hay–Herran Treaty.

Concha was a leader in the struggle against the authoritarian regime of President Rafael Reyes, whose five-year term (1904–1909) is known in Colombian history as El Quinquenio. Concha's term as president coincided with World War I, during which Colombia remained neutral in the face of U.S. pressure to declare war on Germany. Philosophically committed to administrative decentralization, to laissez-faire economics, and to a nonpartisan political style, Concha was frequently praised by leaders of the opposition Liberal Party.

Following his presidency, Concha served in the Colombian Senate, taught university courses, wrote literary essays, and authored legal treatises, especially in the areas of penology and constitutional law. He served as Colombia's minister to the Vatican under President Miguel Abadía Méndez (1926–1930). He died in Rome.

See also **Colombia, Political Parties: Conservative Party.**

BIBLIOGRAPHY

See the essay by Juan Lozano y Lozano on José Vicente Concha in Lozano's *Ensayos críticos* (1934). For additional information see David Bushnell, *The Making of Modern Colombia, a Nation in Spite of Itself* (1993).

Additional Bibliography

Arizmendi Posada, Ignacio. *Manual de historia presidencial: Colombia, 1819-2004*. Bogotá, D.C.: Planeta, 2004.

Posada-Carbo, Eduardo. "Limits of Power: Elections Under the Conservative Hegemony in Colombia, 1886–1930." *The Hispanic American Historical Review* 77:2 (May 1997): 245–279.

JAMES D. HENDERSON

CONCILIAÇÃO.

Conciliação, the program of conciliation and unity adopted by the ministry of the Marquês de Paraná (1853–1856). Two developments motivated the conciliação program. First, party politics established in Brazil during the 1840s generated a factionalism that polarized and corrupted public life while stultifying the administrative system. Second, industrialization and the growth of infrastructure in Europe and the United States had created a sense of backwardness among educated Brazilians. Abolition of the slave trade with Africa and a burgeoning coffee economy generated a sense of optimism and a willingness to experiment. As interpreted by the Paraná ministry, *conciliação* meant a government willing to employ all men of talent, regardless of previous party allegiance. The associated term *melhoramentos* (improvements) referred to the construction of a modern infrastructure both physical (e.g., railroads) and social (e.g., mass education). This twofold program proved difficult to implement. The political goals were too vague to generate broad and solid support, while the creation of a national infrastructure required a mobilization of resources and a reordering of society more sweeping than the ministry could accept. The personal prestige and authority of the Marquês de Paraná alone kept the cabinet and its policies functioning, so that his death in September 1856 effectively ended this experiment in conservative reformism.

See also **Coffee Industry.**

BIBLIOGRAPHY

Costa, Emília Viotti da. *The Brazilian Empire: Myths and Histories*. Chapel Hill: University of North Carolina Press, 2000.

Mattos, Ilmar Rohloff de. *O tempo saquarema*. São Paulo: Editora Hucitec, com o apoio técnico e financeiro do MinC/Pró-Memória e Instituto Nacional do Livro, 1987.

RODERICK J. BARMAN

CONCORDANCIA.

Concordancia (1931–1943). Formed in the wake of the Revolution of 1930, the Concordancia was a coalition of three political factions that shared power during Argentina's Infamous Decade: the National Democratic Party, the Independent Socialist Party, and the Anti-Personalist wing of the Radical Civic Union. The most important of the three was the Anti-Personalists, who had two of their members—José Agustín Justo (1932–1938) and Roberto Ortiz (1938–1940)—elected president. During the Concordancia, opposition groups faced electoral fraud, censorship, and repression. With opponents effectively blocked from national politics, coalition members pursued policies that protected the conservative interests of the Argentine elite. Through the Great Depression and into World War II, its governments used a blend of economic orthodoxy and pragmatism, including reduced spending, exchange controls, and trade promotions, to protect agriculture and preserve Argentina's foreign markets. When political divisions and economic challenges crested during World War II, the military removed the coalition from power in June 1943.

See also **Argentina, Political Parties: Antipersonalist Radical Civil Union; Argentina, Political Parties: Independent Socialist Party.**

BIBLIOGRAPHY

Béjar, María Dolores. *Uriburu y Justo: El auge conservador, 1930–1935* (1983).

Falcoff, Mark, and Ronald H. Dolkart, eds. *Prologue to Perón: Argentina in Depression and War, 1930–1943* (1975).

Persello, Ana Virginia. *El partido radical: Gobierno y oposición, 1916–1943*. Buenos Aires: Siglo Veintiuno Editores Argentina, 2004.

DANIEL LEWIS

CONCORDAT OF 1887.

The Concordat of 1887 was a treaty (December 31, 1887) between the Colombian government and the Vatican that regulated church-state relations in that country for more than five decades. It gave the Roman Catholic Church a privileged position in the religious and educational life of Colombia.

The negotiation of a concordat was authorized by the Constitution of 1886, which established a regime dominated by Conservatives eager to undo the anticlerical policies of their Liberal predecessors. Ratified by the Colombian Congress in 1888, the concordat declared Catholicism the religion of the nation. While public authorities were to protect the Catholic Church and ensure that it be respected, the church was to enjoy complete freedom and independence from the state, including the right to own property. The president of Colombia was given a major voice in the nomination of archbishops and bishops, however. The concordat also stipulated that religious instruction was to be compulsory in all educational institutions and that marriage in accordance with the Catholic rite was to be valid for civil

purposes. Subsequent conventions (1892, 1902) regulated the power of the church in other areas, such as the control of cemeteries and mission fields.

After 1930 the slow but perceptible waning of Catholic influence in Colombia led to limitations on the powers of the church through constitutional reform (1936) and the signing of new concordats (1942, 1973). The Constitution of 1991 guaranteed religious freedom and forbade compulsory religious instruction in public schools. Although Catholicism lost its status as Colombia's official religion, many argue that it still maintains a privileged position.

See also **Catholic Church: The Colonial Period; Catholic Church: The Modern Period.**

BIBLIOGRAPHY

Castillo Cárdenas, Gonzalo. *The Colombian Concordat in the Light of Recent Trends in Catholic Thought Concerning Church–State Relations and Religious Liberty.* Cuernavaca, Mexico: Centro Intercultural de Documentación, 1968.

González, Fernán E. *Poderes enfrentados: Iglesia y estado en Colombia.* Bogotá, Colombia: Cinep, 1997.

Mecham, J. Lloyd. *Church and State in Latin America*, rev. ed. (1966), esp. pp. 115–138.

HELEN DELPAR

CONCRETISM.

Concretism, a term incorporating a broad panoply of Brazilian neovanguardist movements in the plastic arts and in literature launched in the 1950s and active through the 1970s. The term "concrete," drawing on "concrete music" of the early European musical vanguards, refers in Brazilian poetics to a rigidly simplified and exteriorized structure of composition based on the mathematical, graphic, and spatial awareness of artistic language as object. It also came to refer to a syncretic tradition of literary innovation in the art of representation, exemplified by certain modernist writers such as Stéphane Mallarmé and Ezra Pound. Brazilian concretism is largely circumscribed and defined by the Poesia Concreta (Concrete Poetry) movement of São Paulo, with its international and universalizing dimensions, that has proved to be highly influential on subsequent literary theory and production.

The constructivist, rationalist, and mathematical structures in the geometrical abstractionism of Max Bill and Eugen Gomringer at the I Bienal De São Paulo in 1951 influenced the formative phase of Brazilian neovanguard groups in the plastic arts. Abstract Brazilian art was exhibited by the Grupo Ruptura at the São Paulo Museum of Modern Art in 1952, followed by the I Exposição Nacional de Arte Abstrata (Petrópolis, 1953), the Grupo Frente de Artistas Plásticos (Instituto Brasil-Estados Unidos/Rio de Janeiro, 1954), and the first Exposição Nacional de Arte Concreta at the Museum of Modern Art (São Paulo, 1956). The definitive launching of the concrete aesthetic as a polemical, experimental movement occurred at the Exposição Nacional de Arte Concreta at the Ministry of Education in Rio de Janeiro (4–11 February 1957). Later concretist groups include the short-lived neoconcretism of Rio de Janeiro, Mário Chamie's "poema praxis," and Waldimir Dias Pino's "poema processo."

The concrete poems of São Paulo provided concretism with an extensive theoretical apparatus and many literary works published in their magazines *Invenção* and *Noigandres* in the 1950s and later codified in *Teoria de poesia concreta* (1965; Theory of Concrete Poetry). Viewing their work as a continuation of experimentalism and aesthetic modernization, of which João Cabral De Melo Neto's *O engenheiro* (1945; The Engineer) is a credible predecessor, the Paulista concrete poets—Décio Pignatari, Haroldo de Campos, and Augusto de Campos, with the participation at different times of Ronaldo de Azeredo, Edgar Braga, José Lino Grünewald, José Paulo Paes, Dias Pino, Ferreira Gullar, and others—defined concrete works as the "tension of word-objects in space-time" and sought to relate concrete poetry to international graphic and representational trends. Supporting theory includes a synthetic chronology of texts by such diverse figures as Mallarmé, Pound, James Joyce, Paul Klee, e. e. cummings, William Carlos Williams, Anton von Webern, and Karlheinz Stockhausen.

At the same time, through its rejection of discursive writing and its radical revision of artistic form through semiotics, concrete poetry took a position in the open debate of the early 1960s on national literary values, particularly the role of experimental art in underdevelopment. Poetry was to embody the constructive rationality and the aesthetic sensibilities of the concrete city. After 1968, concrete poetry sought association with the Tropicália counterculture movement in popular music and with the anthropophagic critical metaphors of modernist writer Oswald de Andrade. Critical dimensions are present in many of the most widely read and cited poems: Pignatari's "Beba Coca Cola" (Drink Coca Cola set to music by composer Gilberto Mendes); Augusto de Campos's "Luxo lixo" (Luxury garbage); and Haroldo de Campos's "Servidão de passagem" (Passageway).

Recovery of a Brazilian literary tradition of innovation and translation of world poetry are two complementary areas of concretist production. The poetry of Oswald de Andrade, Sousândrade, and Pedro Kilkerry was republished with critical studies, while selected works of Joyce, Pound, cummings, William Blake, and troubadour poets, Dante, and others were translated into Portuguese.

See also **Art: The Twentieth Century; Literature: Brazil; Modernism, Brazil.**

BIBLIOGRAPHY

Brazilian concrete works can be found in such English anthologies as Mary Ellen Solt, ed., *Concrete Poetry: A World View* (1968), and Emmet Williams, ed., *An Anthology of Concrete Poetry* (1967). For scholarly views, see Douglas Thompson, "Pound and Brazilian Concretism," *Paideuma* (Winter 1977): 279–294; Claus Clüver, "Languages of the Concrete Poem," in *Transformations of Literary Language in Latin American Literature,* edited by K. David Jackson (1987), pp. 32–43. The theoretical texts are reunited in Augusto De Campos, Décio Pignatari, and Haroldo De Campos, *Teoria da poesia concreta,* 2d ed. (1975). Summaries of concretist movements can be found in the concretism issue of *Revista de cultura: Vozes,* no. 1 (1977), and in Iumna Maria Simon and Vinicius Dantas, *Poesia concreta* (1982).

Additional Bibliography

Bois, Yve Alain. *Geometric Abstraction: Latin American Art from the Patricia Phelps De Cisneros Collection. Abstracción Geométrica Arte Latinoamericano En La Colección Patricia Phelps De Cisneros.* Cambridge, MA: Harvard University Art Museums, 2001.

Cintrão, Rejane, and Ana Paula Nascimento. *Grupo Ruptura: Arte concreta paulista.* São Paulo, SP: Cosac & Naify, 2002.

Bandeira, João. *Arte concreta paulista: Documentos.* São Paulo: Cosac & Naify, 2002.

K. DAVID JACKSON

CONDÉ, MARYSE

CONDÉ, MARYSE (1937–). Maryse Condé is a Guadeloupean writer and teacher. She was born on 11 February 1937. After studying in Guadeloupe and Paris, Condé taught in Guinea, Ghana, and Senegal for twelve years. Returning to Paris in 1972, she began a doctoral thesis and helped produce her first play, "Le morne de Massabielle." Condé complained that her early novels were badly received in the Caribbean and Africa, but she enjoyed wide success with the first volume of her trilogy, *Ségou*, distributed by a French book club in 1984. *Moi, Tituba sorcière . . .* received the Grand Prix Littéraire de la Femme in 1987.

Condé writes of the search for Caribbean identity. She is an influential commentator on questions of the triple colonization of Caribbean women in sexist, racist, and colonialist cultures. She also writes novels for young people. Since 1986 she has lived both in the United States and in Guadeloupe. She has taught at various universities, including the Sorbonne, Harvard University, the University of Virginia, the University of Maryland, and the University of California at Berkeley. Her works include *La colonie du nouveau monde* (1993), *La Migration des coeurs* (1995), *Desirada* (1997), and *Who Slashed Celanire's Throat? A Fantastical Tale* (2004). In 2004 she retired from her post in the French department at Columbia University and became a professor emeritus. As of 2007, she lives in New York with her husband Richard Philcox, who has translated many of her works into English.

See also **Martinique and Guadeloupe.**

BIBLIOGRAPHY

The Hills of Massabielle (theater, 1972), translated by Richard Philcox (1991); *La mort d'Oluwémi d'Ajumako* (theater, 1972); *Hérémakhonon* (novel, 1976), translated by Richard Philcox (1982); *La civilisation du bossale* (essay, 1978); *La parole des femmes: Essai sur des romancières des Antilles de langue française* (essay, 1979); *Ségou*, vol. 1, *Les murailles de terre* (1984), translated by Barbara Bray as *Segu* (1987); *Ségou*, vol. 2, *La terre en miettes* (novel, 1985), translated by Linda Coverdale as *The Children of Segu* (1989); *Moi, Tituba sorcière . . .* (novel, 1986), translated by Richard Philcox as *I, Tituba, Black Witch of Salem*, 1992; *La vie scélérate* (novel, 1987), translated by Victoria Reiter as *Tree of Life* (1992); *Pension des Alizés* (theater, 1988); *Traversée de la mangrove* (novel, 1989); *Les derniers rois mages* (novel, 1992).

See also Vèvè Clark, "I Have Made Peace with My Island: An Interview with Maryse Condé," in *Callaloo* 12:1 (1989), 85–133; Ann Armstrong Scarboro, *I, Tituba, Black Witch of Salem*, pp. 187–227; *Callaloo* 15:1 (1992), special issue on the literature of Guadeloupe and Martinique, edited by Condé.

Hewitt, Leah D. *Autobiographical Tightropes: Simone de Beauvoir, Nathalie Sarraute, Marguerite Duras, Monique Wittig, and Maryse Condé*. Lincoln: University of Nebraska Press, 1990.

CARROL F. COATES

CONDE D'EU.

CONDE D'EU. *See* **Gastão d'Orléans.**

CONDOR

CONDOR. The condor is a large vulture that feeds mainly on carrion. *Gymnogyps californianus*, the California condor, is found in the mountains of southern California. It is extremely endangered, with 140 birds surviving as of 2007. Its body is about 50 inches long, and it has a bald yellow head. The bare, reddish neck is circled by a black feathered ruff. There are white feathers on the underside of the wings.

Vultur gryphus, the Andean condor, found in the Andes from Venezuela to the Strait of Magellan, is also threatened with extinction. The body length varies from 52 to 63 inches, and the wingspan can be up to ten feet. A bald, reddish, crest-crowned head tops a bare, reddish neck circled by a white feathered ruff. There are white feathers on the wings. Both species have long, powerful, hooked beaks. Their bodies and wings are covered by dark gray feathers. All species of condor are strictly protected.

When the Incas ruled the central Andes the condor was considered an *apu* or spirit. When a dead condor fell from the sky into the central patio of the capital Cuzco's *Acllawasi*, or House of the Virgins, it was interpreted as a bad omen. Shortly thereafter Pizarro arrived at Cajamarca. After the Conquest by the Spanish, a new cultural tradition developed called *Yawar Fiesta* or *Blood Celebration* where the Spanish bull and the Andean condor struggle to the death. This is topic of José María Argueda's novel of the same name and in the early twenty-first century exists in popular culture being depicted in *retablos*, usually one of three scenes, the other two being the harvest and the birth of Christ representing the hybrid culture of the Andes. In this tripartite cultural and political construction, the indigenous harvest coexists alongside the Birth of Christ, but Spanish and Andean cultures continue in conflict as represented by the bloody struggle between bull and the condor.

When the first Spaniards arrived in South America in the 1530s, the condor was flourishing along the Andes from northern Venezuela down to the Tierra del Fuego. Regrettably, loss of habitat, hunting by humans, and pesticides have taken their toll. One of the few places were the *Vultur gryphus* thrives is the Colca Cañon in Peru, a favorite stop for ecotourists. The Andean condor is today the national symbol of Argentina, Bolivia, Chile, Ecuador, and Peru and is the subject of the popular song "El condor pasa" ("The condor Passes By") arranged by the Peruvian folklorist Daniel Alomía Robles in 1913.

See also **Environment and Climate.**

BIBLIOGRAPHY

Arguedas, José María. *Yawar Fiesta*. Austin: University of Texas Press, 1985.

Andrews, Michael Alford. *The Flight of the Condor: A Wildlife Exploration of the Andes*. Boston: Little, Brown, 1982.

Baschieri Salvadori, Francesco B. *Rare Animals of the World*. New York: Mallard Press, 1990.

Bierhorst, John. "The Condor Seeks a Wife." In his *Black Rainbow: Legends of the Incas and Myths of Ancient Peru*. New York: Farrar, Straus and Giroux, 1976.

Cohn, Jeffrey P. "The Return of the California Condor." In *Endangered Species*, edited by Shasta Gaughen. Detroit: Greenhaven Press, 2006.

Dorr, Kirstie A. "Mapping 'El Condor Pasa': Sonic Translocations in the Global Era." *Journal of Latin American Cultural Studies* 16, no. 1 (March 2007): 11–25.

Jara, Víctor. "El condor pasa." Performed by Conjunto Kollahuara, Víctor Jara solist. On *Music of the Andes*. Compact disc. [S.l.]: Hemisphere, 1994.

Luthin, Herbert W. "Condor Steals Falcon's Wife" (Yowlumni Yokuts, 1930). In *Surviving through the Days: Translations of Native California Stories and Songs: A California Indian Reader*. Berkeley: University of California Press, 2002.

Patzelt, Erwin. *Fauna del Ecuador*. Quito: Banco Central del Ecuador, 1989.

Wilcove, David Samuel. *The Condor's Shadow: The Loss and Recovery of Wildlife in America*. New York: W.H. Freeman and Co, 1999.

THOMAS WARD

CONFEDERACIÓN DE CÁMARAS NACIONALES DE COMERCIO (CONCANACO).

The Confederation of National Chambers of Commerce is a Mexican organization that groups together local chambers of commerce to represent commercial-sector interests at a national level. Although it is considered a public organization, its members formally control it under a one-firm-one-vote principle. It was created on 3 November 1917, during the National Congress of Commerce by forty-two local chambers in the presence of President Venustiano Carranza. Its legal existence was recognized in the Law of Chambers of Commerce and Industry in 1936. In 1941 this law was modified to denominate the chambers and confederations as autonomous public institutions. The law was modified once more in 1997 and again in 2005. The main change was that affiliation to any chamber was no longer mandatory.

Although the role of Mexican government in the creation and development of CONCANACO is clear, it has always conducted an independent discourse about public policy; the economic independence of its membership seems to be the reason for this. CONCANACO criticized protectionism in particular and was always resentful of government participation in the national economy. However, CONCANACO's position and strategy was usually more moderate than the position of more independent organizations such as the Confederation of Employers of the Mexican Republic (COPARMEX). In the late 1980s CONCANACO supported Mexican economic liber-alization.

See also **Carranza, Venustiano.**

BIBLIOGRAPHY

Camp, Roderic Ai. *Entrepreneurs and Politics in Twentieth-Century Mexico*. New York: Oxford University Press, 1989.

"Confederación de Cámaras Nacionales de Comercio: Servicios y Turismo." Available from http://www.concanacored.com.

RODERIC AI CAMP

CONFEDERACIÓN DE NACION-ALIDADES INDÍGENAS DEL ECUA-DOR (CONAIE).

Building on the initiatives of earlier indigenous organizations, in November 1986 five hundred delegates formed the Confederación de Nacionalidades Indígenas del Ecuador (Confederation of Indigenous Nationalities of Ecuador; CONAIE) at the Nueva Vida (New Life) camp outside Quito. Their goal was to combine all indigenous peoples into one large pan-Indian movement to defend indigenous concerns and to agitate for social, political, and educational reforms. In June 1990 CONAIE emerged at the forefront of a powerful indigenous uprising that paralyzed the country for a week. Since then, the organization has led repeated popular protests for land, economic development, education, and recognition of indigenous nationalities.

See also **Indigenismo; Indigenous Organizations.**

BIBLIOGRAPHY

Confederación de Nacionalidades Indígenas del Ecuador (CONAIE). *Las nacionalidades indígenas en el Ecuador: Nuestro proceso organizativo*, 2nd ed. Quito: Ediciones Tincui-Abya-Yala, 1989.

MARC BECKER

CONFEDERACIÓN DE TRABAJADO-RES DE AMÉRICA LATINA (CTAL).

The Confederación de Trabajadores de América Latina (CTAL), a regional labor organization, was formed by union delegates from twelve Latin American nations in Mexico City in September 1938. Vicente Lombardo Toledano, the intellectual and Marxist leader of the Confederación de Trabajadores de México (CTM), served as president throughout the life of the organization. In the context of World War II, Mexico played an important ideological role in the effort to create an international labor confederation. The CTAL sought to end exploitation of the working class, promote democracy, obtain political and economic autonomy for Latin America, and join the popular front movement against international fascism. The CTAL brought together national labor organizations of diverse political orientations, including Communists, socialists, Auténticos, and Apristas. To focus on this international effort, in 1941 Lombardo reduced his involvement with the CTM. By 1944 more than 3.3 million people in sixteen countries were CTAL members.

The CTAL's influence and hemispheric labor unity deteriorated in the postwar and incipient cold war period. Argentina's Confederación General de Trabajadores (CGT) withdrew in 1944 to create a rival, Peronist regional labor organization Agrupación de Trabajadores Latinoamericanos Sindicalistas (ATLAS). The CGT's withdrawal and the heightened influence of Communists in several national labor confederations led to Marxist domination by the time of the CTAL's December 1944 Congress. The CTAL joined the leftist World Federation of Trade Unions (WFTU) in 1945. Noncommunist labor groups abandoned the CTAL to join the Confederación Inter-Americana de Trabajadores (CIT), established in 1948 with support from the American Federation of Labor. More concerned with domestic issues, Mexico's CTM left the CTAL and expelled Toledano from the CTM in 1948. CTAL influence waned throughout the 1950s, and the confederation officially dissolved in 1962.

See also **Labor Movements.**

BIBLIOGRAPHY

Alba, Victor. *Politics and the Labor Movement in Latin America* (1968).

Alexander, Robert J. *Organized Labor in Latin America* (1965), esp. pp. 246–248.

Bernal Tavares, Luis. *Vicente Lombardo Toledano y Miguel Alemán: Una bifurcación en la revolución mexicana.* Mexico: Facultad de Filosofía y Letras, UNAM, Centro de Estudios e Investigación para el Desarrollo Social, 1994.

Bethell, Leslie, and Ian Roxborough, eds. *Latin America between the Second World War and the Cold War.* Cambridge, U.K., and New York: Cambridge University Press, 1993.

Lombardo Toledano, Vicente. *Vicente Lombardo Toledano: Acción y pensamiento.* Edited by Martín Tavira Urióstegui. Mexico: Fondo de Cultura Económica, 1999.

López Portillo, Felicitas, ed. *Movimiento obrero en América Latina.* Mexico: Universidad Nacional Autónoma de México, 1995.

Poblete Troncoso, Moisés, and Ben G. Burnett. *The Rise of the Latin American Labor Movement* (1960), pp. 134–139.

Spalding, Hobart A., Jr. *Organized Labor in Latin America* (1977), pp. 255–256.

STEVEN S. GILLICK

CONFEDERACIÓN NACIONAL DE INSTITUCIONES EMPRESARIALES PRIVADAS (CONFIEP).

The Confederación Nacional de Instituciones Empresariales Privadas (CONFIEP, the National Confederation of Private Enterprise Institutions) was founded in 1984 by seven associations with the principal objective of "reinforcing the private enterprise system" in Peru. CONFIEP became a force to be reckoned with in 1987 when it prevented the nationalization of the financial system and increased the number of its member associations to twenty. As the chief spokesperson for the Peruvian private sector, CONFIEP holds regular talks with governments, political parties, trade unions, and other civic organizations. Its influence has diminished somewhat since three of its founding member associations withdrew in 1998. Moreover, as the Peruvian economy has become more involved in the global economy, the government has tended to discuss issues more frequently and closely with foreign companies.

BIBLIOGRAPHY

Confederación Nacional de Instituciones Empresariales Privadas. "Primer Congreso Nacional de la Empresa Privada: Conclusiones y propuestas integrales." Working paper, 1986.

Confederación Nacional de Instituciones Empresariales Privadas. *La empresa privada y el orden constitucional.* Lima: Author, 1988.

Durand, Francisco. *Los empresarios y la concertación.* Lima: Fundación Friedrich Ebert, 1987.

Durand, Francisco. "Collective Action and the Empowerment of Peruvian Business." In *Organized Business, Economic Change, and Democracy in Latin America,* ed. Francisco Durand and Eduardo Silva. Miami, FL: North-South Center, 1998.

Levaggi, Virgilio. "The Role of Formal Business Organizations in Latin America." Workshop on Market Reforms and Democracy in Latin America and the Caribbean. Center for International Private Enterprise, Washington, DC, 1993.

Levaggi, Virgilio. *Organizaciones empresariales en América Latina.* Lima: Confederación Nacional de Instituciones Empresariales Privadas, 1994.

FRANCISCO DURAND

CONFEDERACIÓN PATRONAL DE LA REPÚBLICA MEXICANA (COPARMEX).

The Confederación Patronal de la República Mexicana (COPARMEX, or Employers' Confederation of the Mexican Republic) is a Mexican employers' organization created in 1929 to oppose government intervention in the economy. The main difference between COPARMEX and other entrepreneurs' organizations is its independence from the Mexican government in institutional and political terms. This independence enabled COPARMEX to be more straightforward in its criticisms of policy making in Mexico, but it also reduced COPARMEX's capacity to gain government favors for its members. Unlike other employers' organizations that were led by businessmen from Mexico City (such as CONCANACO or CANACINTRA), COPARMEX's leadership originated in the northern city of Monterrey.

During the first thirty years of its existence, COPARMEX was unattractive to many entrepreneurs because other employers' organizations—those organizationally and financially dependent on the state—were in a better position to influence policy making. However, during the 1960s and 1970s, as government favoritism declined, COPARMEX's confrontational stance became more appealing. Although COPARMEX never advocated the creation of a political party (what the scholar Roderic Ai Camp has called the "last logical step" of COPARMEX's strategy), the organization has a close relationship with the Partido Acción Nacional (PAN), and many of COPARMEX members have run for political office under the PAN banner, including the 1988 presidential candidate Manuel J. Clouthier (1934–1989).

See also **Cámara Nacional de la Industria de la Transformación (CANACINTRA); Clouthier del Rincón, Manuel J; Confederación de Cámaras de Comercio, CONCANACO; Mexico, Political Parties: National Action Party (PAN).**

BIBLIOGRAPHY

Camp, Roderic Ai. *Entrepreneurs and Politics in Twentieth-Century Mexico.* New York: Oxford University Press, 1989.

COPARMEX Internet site. Available from http://www.coparmex.org.mx.

SERGIO SILVA-CASTAÑEDA

CONFEDERATES IN BRAZIL AND MEXICO.

After the American Civil War, thousands of former rebels fled the South, seeking new homes in Latin America. Because of proximity and a welcome from Emperor Maximilian, Mexico attracted many settlers, among them a number of well-known ex-Confederates, including oceanographer Matthew Fontaine Maury; generals Joseph Shelby, Sterling Price, J. B. Magruder, and Thomas C. Hindman; and former governors Isham G. Harris of Tennessee and Henry W. Allen of Louisiana. Confederate émigrés scattered across Mexico, but Córdova and the Tuxpan region were the two most important areas of settlement. For most emigrants, settlement in Mexico was of brief duration because of the political turmoil attendant upon Maximilian's overthrow in 1867, the hardships of pioneering, and the lack of capital. British Honduras (now Belize) and Venezuela also attracted ex-Confederates, but the country which received the most Confederate emigrants, a conservatively estimated 2,500 to 4,000, was Brazil.

Former rebels who settled in Brazil feared the onset of a harsh Reconstruction in the United States and dreamed of rebuilding their plantation way of life. Prior to the war, Matthew Fontaine Maury had propagandized for the settlement of fertile lands in Brazil. In 1865 and 1866 emigrant agents toured Brazil, made arrangements to purchase land and bring settlers, and wrote enthusiastic books and letters on the prospects of settlement. Former leaders of the Confederacy and the Southern press were hostile, however, viewing emigration as abandonment of the South.

The peak years of emigration were 1867 and 1868. Since most confederados lacked adequate means for settlement, Brazil's attraction was a liberal immigration policy with good land offered at prices as low as twenty-two cents an acre and mortgages payable in five equal installments. Equally important was the presence of slavery and cheap labor in general. There were four distinct areas of rural settlement: 200 pioneers located at Santarém on the Amazon River 500 miles from the coast; 50 or more families settled at Lake Juparana (the Rio Doce settlement) 30 miles from the coast and 300 miles north of Rio de Janeiro; 150 families formed a community on the Juquiá River near Iguape, some 100 miles south of São Paulo; and some 75 families located in a cluster of communities (Retiro, Campo, and Villa Americana) in the Santa Barbara area, 80 to 100 miles northwest of São Paulo. After clearing land and planting, most settlers soon failed because of their remoteness from markets and lack of transportation and capital. Disillusioned, they moved on to São Paulo and Rio, or returned to the United States. By the mid-1870s most had abandoned rural life, and Brazil's two largest cities had the greatest numbers of remaining confederados, the most successful of whom were doctors, dentists, and engineers.

The only successful rural settlement was Americana. Located 30 miles from a rail line to São Paulo, Estação or Villa Americana, as it was first called, was initially a cotton-growing settlement; settlers later switched to other crops, among them the Georgia rattlesnake watermelon, which they introduced to Brazil. The confederados of Americana tried to maintain a "Southern way of life," but by the third generation they had become Brazilianized. Today Americana is a city of 160,000 where descendants of the first settlers still celebrate the Fourth of July and the Fraternidade Descendência Americana meets quarterly at the American Cemetery to remember the past.

See also **Brazil: 1808–1889; Maximilian; United States-Latin American Relations.**

BIBLIOGRAPHY

Peter A. Brannon, ed., "Southern Emigration to Brazil: Embodying the Diary of Jennie R. Keyes, Montgomery, Alabama," in *Alabama Historical Quarterly*, 1 (Summer 1930): 74–75 (Fall 1930): 280–305 (Winter 1930): 467–488.

Lawrence F. Hill, "The Confederate Exodus to Latin America," in *Southwestern Historical Quarterly*, 39, no. 2 (October 1935): 100–134, no. 3 (January 1936):161–199, no. 4 (April 1936): 309–326.

Blanche Henry Clark Weaver, "Confederate Emigration to Brazil," in *Journal of Southern History*, 27, no. 1 (February 1961): 33–53.

Andrew R. Folle, *The Lost Cause: The Confederate Exodus to Mexico* (1965).

Bell J. Wiley, "Confederate Exiles in Brazil," in *Civil War Times Illustrated*, 15 (January 1977):22–32.

Eugene C. Harter, *The Lost Colony of the Confederacy* (1985).

William Clark Griggs, *The Elusive Eden: Frank McMullan's Confederate Colony in Brazil* (1987).

Additional Bibliography

Dawsey, Cyrus B., and James M. Dawsey. *The Confederados: Old South Immigrants in Brazil.* Tuscaloosa: University of Alabama Press, 1995.

Gussi, Alcides Fernando. *Os norte-americanos (confederados) do Brasil: Identidades no contexto transnacional.* Americana: Prefeitura Municipal de Americana, SP, 1997.

Horne, Gerald. *The Deepest South: The United States, Brazil, and the African Slave Trade.* New York: New York University Press, 2007.

Oliveira, Ana Maria Costa de. *O destino (não) manifesto: Os imigrantes norte-americanos no Brasil.* São Paulo: União Cultural Brasil-Estados Unidos, 1995.

CARL OSTHAUS

CONFEDERATION OF THE EQUATOR.

Confederation of the Equator, a separatist movement in Northeast Brazil in 1824. Reaction by provinces in Brazil's Northeast to the dissolution of the 1823 Constituent Assembly by Dom Pedro I is usually cited as the main cause for the rebellion, although others point to the political ambitions of rebel leaders, especially Manuel de Carvalho Pais de Andrade. Andrade, a member of the governing junta in 1824, issued a series of proclamations renouncing Dom Pedro's control and establishing a republic called the Confederation of the Equator. Royal troops commanded by Brigadier Francisco de Lima e Silva, supported by a five-ship armada under Lord Thomas Cochrane, attacked the port city of Recife, Pernambuco. The revolt, however, spread to the provinces of Paraíba, Rio Grande do Norte, and Ceará, provoking further fighting in those areas. Several principal leaders, including the famous Frei Joaquim do Amor Divino Rabelo e Caneca, editor of the newspaper, *O Tífis Pernambucano,* were captured, tried, and executed. Others, including Pais de Andrade, who took refuge aboard a British naval vessel, escaped to the exterior. Order was reestablished in the area by Francisco de Lima e Silva by 1 December 1824. Andrade later (7 March 1825) was permitted to swear allegiance to the Imperial Constitution and reenter public life with an appointment as senator from Pernambuco.

See also **Brazil: 1808–1889.**

BIBLIOGRAPHY

Sérgio Buarque De Holanda, ed., *Historia geral da civilzação brasileira,* vol. 1, pt. 1 (1962), pp. 227–237; *Dicionário de história do Brasil* (1973), pp. 474–475.

E. Bradford Burns, *A History of Brazil,* 2d ed. (1980), pp. 168–169.

Additional Bibliography

Barman, Roderick. *Brazil: The Forging of a Nation, 1798–1852.* Stanford, CA: Stanford University Press, 1988.

Barman, Roderick. *Citizen Emperor: Pedro II and the Making of Brazil, 1825–91.* Stanford, CA: Stanford University Press, 1999.

Graham, Richard. *Patronage and Politics in Nineteenth-century Brazil.* Stanford, CA: Stanford University Press, 1990.

Janscó, István. *Independencia: Historia e historiografia.* São Paulo: Editora Hucitec, 2005.

Mosher, Jeffrey. "Challenging Authority: Political Violence and the Regency in Pernambuco, Brazil, 1831–1835." *Luso-Brazilian Review* 37 (Winter 2000): 33–57.

Rohrig, Matthias Assuncao. "Elite Politics and Popular Rebellion in the Construction of Post-colonial Order. The Case of Maranhao, Brazil (1820–41.)" *Journal of Latin American Studies* 31 (February 1999): 1–38.

ROBERT A. HAYES

CONFERENCE OF LATIN AMERICAN BISHOPS (CELAM).

Conference of Latin American Bishops (CELAM) emerged in 1955 as an initial step toward modernizing the structures of Latin American Catholicism. The major function of its various departments has been to promote communication across national lines by means of conferences, training institutes, and publications. The General Conferences of CELAM held at Medellín, Colombia (1968), and Puebla, Mexico (1979), are important milestones in the recent history of the Latin American church.

The Medellín conference, the agenda of which was heavily influenced by a small group of progressive Latin American clergy and by the modernizing tendencies of the Second Vatican Council (1962–1965), began an effort to apply the principles of Vatican II to Latin America. Medellín established the importance of the church's addressing contemporary socioeconomic realities, endorsed new pastoral practices, and marked the emergence of the new, distinctly Latin American "theology of liberation." These changing perspectives had a great impact on the religious and political life of Latin America. First, they reoriented a significant part of the Catholic clergy and hierarchy away from its former preoccupation with the needs of the elite and the preservation of the status quo. Second, they promoted the power and participation of the lay Catholic masses in both religious and political affairs.

The 1979 Puebla conference reflected the influence of more conservative forces, which had assumed control of CELAM in 1972. While there was some slowing of the process of change associated with Medellín, the bishops nevertheless reaffirmed their earlier positions and stressed their commitment to a "preferential option for the poor."

The fifth General Conference, held in 2007 at the Basilica of Aparecida in São Paulo, Brazil, generally reaffirmed the positions taken at Medellín, Puebla, and Santo Domingo. The bishops emphasized the "preferential option for the poor" and reaffirmed support for Base Christian Communities (CEBs). In addition to addressing the continuing expansion of fundamentalist Protestantism in Latin America, they also focused on new concerns, including human rights violations, migrant issues, and globalization. The clergy also upheld the institution of marriage and condemned abortion.

See also **Catholic Church: The Modern Period; Liberation Theology.**

BIBLIOGRAPHY

No single book is devoted to CELAM. Edward L. Cleary, *Crisis and Change: The Church in Latin America Today* (1985), and Phillip Berryman, *Liberation Theology* (1987), both do an excellent job of presenting CELAM and its work.

CELAM. *Globalización y nueva evangelización en América Latina y el Caribe: Reflexiones del CELAM, 1999–2003*. Bogota: Publicaciones CELAM, 2003.

Hennelly, Alfred T., ed. *Santo Domingo and Beyond: Documents and Commentaries from the Fourth General Conference of Latin American Bishops*. Maryknoll, NY: Orbis Books, 1993.

BRUCE CALDER

CONGADA. Congada (also called congado or congo), a Brazilian folk dance and music form of African, Portuguese, and Spanish origin. First observed among African slaves during the late seventeenth century, the congada is a processional dance, fusing elements of Iberian popular drama and Catholicism with African indigenous ceremonies. Dressed as members of the royal court, the participants of the congada enact such themes as military victory and the crowning of Queen Nginga Nbandi of Angola.

While the congada is indigenous to central and southern Brazil, the congo is found in the northern sections of the country. Because women were historically excluded from participating in the congo, the coronation theme has centered around King Henrique. In the congo procession dancers sing to the sounds of drums, *chocalhos, pandeiros,* and violas.

Congadas are observed during the Christmas season and are often enacted throughout the year depending upon region and symbolic significance. Although the congada originated among African slaves, it has been known to include Indian participants who have incorporated their own native dances. According to scholars the congada, despite its distinctly African thematic and stylistic influences, is a uniquely Brazilian art form; no performances of the congada have been found on the African continent.

See also **Music: Popular Music and Dance.**

BIBLIOGRAPHY

Gilbert Chase, *The Music of Spain*, 2d rev. ed. (1959).

David P. Appleby, *The Music of Brazil* (1983).

Chris Mc Gowan and Ricardo Pessanha, *The Brazilian Sound: Samba, Bossa Nova, and the Popular Music of Brazil* (1991).

Additional Bibliography

Kinn, Marli Graniel. "Negros congadeiros e a cidade costumes e tradicões nos lugares e nas redes da congada de Uberlandia-MG." M.A. Diss. São Paulo, 2006.

Souza, Marina de Mello e. *Reis negros no Brasil escravista: História da festa de coroacão de rei congo*. Belo Horizonte: Editora UFMG, 2002.

JOHN COHASSEY

CONGREGACIÓN. From the decade of the 1570s throughout the rest of the colonial period, the Spanish authorities regularly instituted *congregación*, or forced resettlement programs, also known as *reducciónes*. As a result of the pestilence and population mobility unleashed by the Spanish conquest of the Americas, many previously densely populated regions were depopulated. As the system of colonial administration developed in the sixteenth century, the Spanish recognized the need to consolidate widely scattered native populations in nucleated villages for ease of control.

Three resettlement programs have received considerable scholarly attention. The earliest of these was the program initiated by Don Francisco de Toledo, viceroy of Peru, in the 1570s. Later, from 1599 to 1604, there was an extensive program in New Spain. The last was initiated in the eighteenth century by Jesuit and Franciscan missionaries in the region of present-day Paraguay and the Californias.

The *congregaciones* aided Spanish missionaries and crown officials. Yet the policy had serious disadvantages for the Indians, including loss of land, disruption of traditional political and social ties, and an increased susceptibility to disease. On the positive side, some have argued that the Jesuit settlements protected the natives of Paraguay from mistreatment at the hands of colonists and slave raids of the Portuguese.

See also **Aldeias; Missions: Jesuit Missions (Reducciones).**

BIBLIOGRAPHY

Cardiff, Guillermo Furlong. *Misiones y sus pueblos de Guaraníes.* Buenos Aires: Ediciones Theoría, 1962.

Cline, Howard F. "Civil Congregations of the Indians of New Spain, 1598–1606." In *Hispanic American Historical Review* 29 (1949): 349–369.

Solano, Francisco. "Política de concentración de la población indígena: Objetivos, proceso, problemas, resultados." *Revista de Indias* 36, nos. 145–146 (1976): 7–29.

JOHN F. SCHWALLER

CONGRESS OF APRIL 1813.

Congress of April 1813, an important meeting convened in the headquarters of José Artigas on 5, 6, 13, and 20 April 1813, during the second siege of Montevideo, at which for the first time Artigas fully expressed his federalist ideas. Artigas had returned from his "Exodus," that is, the emigration that resulted from the Montevideo and Buenos Aires peace accord. The Constituent Assembly that was meeting in Buenos Aires to determine the fate of the provinces that had belonged to the Viceroyalty of Río de la Plata solicited Artigas to send delegates. As requested, he convened the Congress of April, also known as the Congress of Three Crosses, for the place near Montevideo where it was held (near the present-day Hospital Británico).

Artigas maintained that the Constituent Assembly must be recognized "by agreement" and not "out of obedience." The conditional clauses for recognizing the provinces in question were drawn up, along with a set of instructions the six delegates were to take to the Assembly. The delegates were rejected by the Assembly on technicalities, the real reason perhaps being the federalist character of their proposals, which ran contrary to the "unitarism" or "centralism" of Buenos Aires. Despite Artigas's efforts to appeal, the delegates were again rejected. The opposition of unitarism and federalism remained a clearly defined cause of the revolution in Río de la Plata. Artigas attempted to reach an agreement with General José Rondeau, commander of the forces of Buenos Aires in the second siege of Montevideo, but the confrontation between the two factions was by then inevitable.

See also **Artigas, José Gervasio.**

BIBLIOGRAPHY

John Street, *Artigas and the Emancipation of Uruguay* (1959).

Washington Reyes Abadie, *Artigas y el federalismo rioplatense* (1974).

Washington Reyes Abadie and Andrés Vázquez Romero, *Crónica general del Uruguay,* vol. 2 (1984).

Additional Bibliography

Barrios Pintos, Aníbal. *Historia de los pueblos orientales: Sus orígenes, procesos fundacionales, sus primeros años.* Montevideo: Academia Nacional de Letras, 2000.

Goldmen, Noemí, and Ricardo Donato Salvatore. *Caudillismos rioplatenses: Nuevas miradas a un viejo dilema.* Buenos Aires: Eudenba, Universidad de Buenos Aires, 2005.

Maggi, Carlos. *La nueva historia de Artigas.* Montevideo: Ediciones de la Plaza, 2005.

Narancio, Edmundo M. *La independencia de Uruguay.* Montevideo: Editorial Ayer, 2001.

Ribeiro, Ana. *Los tiempos de Artigas.* Montevideo: El País, 1999.

JOSÉ DE TORRES WILSON

CONI, EMILIO R.

CONI, EMILIO R. (1854–1928). Emilio R. Coni was one of Argentina's pioneer public-health physicians. Born in Corrientes in 1854, he attended medical school at the University of Buenos Aires during the 1870s and became well known in the medical community for his many statistical articles about diseases and mortality rates. Coni also published numerous books, including his autobiography, *Memorias de un medico higienista* (1918), and a study of Buenos Aires's public and private social assistance agencies, *Asistencia y previsión social. Buenos Aires caritativo y previsor* (1918). His wife and partner, the Socialist journalist Gabriela Laperrière (1866–1907), took part in the promotion of his antituberculosis campaigns and health crusades in Buenos Aires.

Coni is remembered as one of the fathers of Argentine demography studies, which he considered to be a main tool in improving public-health policies. In 1891 he became the first president of the Sociedad Médica Argentina (the Argentine Medical Society) and in 1892 he was named director of the Sanitary Administration and Public Assistance of Buenos Aires. Internationally recognized for his work in public health, he became a member of the Brazilian Medical Academy in 1878, and he participated in international health conferences in many cities including Amsterdam, London, and Washington, D.C. Coni was particularly interested in the control of venereal disease through medically supervised prostitution, the establishment of tuberculosis treatment centers, the regulation of wet nurses and milk supplies of all types, the treatment of alcoholics, and the creation of municipal medical facilities to shelter the indigent. He was also involved in efforts to improve sanitation in Buenos Aires. Many of these programs were implemented as a result of Coni's determination that the medical facilities of Buenos Aires should rival those in Europe.

See also **Diseases; Medicine: The Modern Era.**

BIBLIOGRAPHY
Primary Works

Asistencia y prevision social Buenos Aires caritativo y previsor. Buenos Aires: Imprenta Emilio Spinelli, 1918.

Memorias de un medico higienista. Buenos Aires: Biblioteca Méedica Argentina, 1918.

Secondary Works

Guy, Donna J. "Emilio and Gabriela Coni: Reformers, Public Health, and Working Women." In *The Human Tradition in Latin America: The Nineteenth Century*, ed. Judith Ewell and William H. Beezley. Wilmington, DE: SR Books, 1989.

Loudet, Osvaldo. *Figuras próximas y lejanas, al margen de la historia.* Buenos Aires: Academia Argentina de Letras, 1970.

DONNA J. GUY
VICENTE PALERMO

CONI, GABRIELA LAPERRIÈRE DE

CONI, GABRIELA LAPERRIÈRE DE (1866–1907). Gabriela Laperrière de Coni (*b.* 1866; *d.* January 1907), Argentine feminist and health-care activist. The public career of Gabriela Laperrière de Coni was intense but brief. Little is known about her early life except that she was born in Bordeaux, France, in 1866 and published a novel about a woman's efforts to help sick children. In her career, fiction mirrored reality. Once Laperrière became active in Argentina, she campaigned as a feminist socialist for improved working and health conditions for poor families. Her marriage in 1899 to Dr. Emilio R. Coni, a noted public-health physician, reinforced her commitment to health issues. One manifestation of this concern was the extensive lectures she gave about the dangers of tuberculosis.

Laperrière's Argentine career began in 1900, when she served as the press secretary for the Argentine National Council of Women. Two years later she was appointed Buenos Aires's first factory inspector by the city's mayor, Adolfo Bullrich. Her research led in April 1902 to recommend that legislation to protect workers be enacted. Such a law was enacted by the Argentine Congress in 1907.

A popular speaker on public-health issues, Laperrière also helped found the Centro Socialista Femenino (Socialist Women's Feminist Center). In one of her last public appearances she helped mediate a dispute between factory owners and working women in a shoe factory. Her death in January 1907 terminated her brief career, but her concerns about health and working conditions were implemented by others.

See also **Feminism and Feminist Organizations.**

BIBLIOGRAPHY

Enrique Dickmann, *Recuerdos de un militante socialista* (1949).

Donna J. Guy, "Emilio and Gabriela Coni: Reformers, Public Health, and Working Women," in *The Human Tradition in Latin America: The Nineteenth Century,* edited by Judith Ewell and William H. Beezley (1989), pp. 233–248.

Additional Bibliography

Armus, Diego. *The Years of Tuberculosis: Buenos Aires 1870–1950.* Ph.D. diss., University of California, Berkeley, 1996.

Guy, Donna J. *White Slavery and Mothers Alive and Dead: The Troubled Meeting of Sex, Gender, Public Health, and Progress in Latin America.* Lincoln: University of Nebraska Press, 2000.

DONNA J. GUY

CONQUEST OF THE DESERT.

The so-called Conquest of the Desert (*Conquista del desierto*) was carried out in 1879 in Argentina under the military command of Julio Argentino Roca (1843–1914), who was minister of war at the time. He organized a military offensive to put an end to the problem posed by the native peoples who were preventing him seizing full control of the territories to the south of the Colorado River (*Río Colorado*). The objective of the military campaign was, in Roca's words, to expel, subjugate, or wipe out the Indians. In doing this he hoped to complete the task of not only occupying those territories but also placing them under the control of the national government, a task begun in earlier times by ranchers, merchants, and Indian chiefs.

The occupation of this territory was seen as important for a number of reasons. These included the need to limit indigenous control of economic exchanges in the region, limit the role of their chiefs as political intermediaries, and secure the borders of the Patagonian territories.

To carry out the military campaign, the National Congress passed a law that provided the necessary resources. In 1878 troops had already attacked tribal chief Manuel Namuncurá's forces in their tents, Juan José Catriel's troops surrendered as prisoners, and tribal chief known as Pincén was ambushed and captured with his best men. In 1879 troops under the command of General Roca, which also included some indigenous soldiers, occupied Choele-Choel. Other divisions took and held La Pampa and the confluence of the Lima and Neuquén rivers. The advance of all these divisions was uncontainable, and in a short time they were able to occupy the region and decimate the indigenous communities. They took over 225,000 square miles of land that could be used for livestock and agriculture, and built villages and colonies along the banks of the Colorado, Negro, Neuquén, and Santa Cruz rivers. They also extended and improved communications in the inland provinces of the country, and gradually expanded the military telegraph network, which was then turned over to the civil authorities. Indigenous settlements were created to house some survivors, and others were dispersed throughout rural villages; women and children were assigned to wealthy families in Buenos Aires under the notion that work would help them adapt to "civilization."

See also **Argentina: The Nineteenth Century; Namuncurá, Manuel; Roca, Julio Argentino.**

BIBLIOGRAPHY

Argeri, Maria E. *De guerreros a delincuentes. La desarticulación de las jefaturas indígenas y el poder judicial. Norpatagonia, 1880–1930.* Madrid: Consejo Superior de Investigaciones Científicas, 2005.

Delrío, Walter Mario. *Memorias de expropiación: Sometimiento e incorporación indígena en la Patagonia (1872–1943).* Bernal: Universidad Nacional de Quilmas, 2005.

Mases, Enrique. *Estado y cuestión indígena. El destino final de los indios sometidos en el sur del territorio (1878–1919).* Buenos Aires: Prometeo/Entrepasados, 2002.

Quijada, Mónica. "La ciudadanización del 'indio bárbaro'. Políticas oficiales y oficiosas hacia la población indígena de La Pampa y La Patagonia, 1870–1920." *Revista de Indias,* 44, no. 217 (1999): 675–704.

Quijada, Mónica. "Indígenas: violencia, tierra y ciudadanía" In *Homogeneidad y nación. Con un estudio de caso: Argentina, siglos XIX y XX,* eds. Mónica Quijada, Carmen Bernand, and Arnd Schneider. Madrid, Consejo Superior de Investigaciones Científicas, 2000.

Vezub, Julio: "El Gobernador Indígena de las Manzanas. Don Valentín Sayhueque." In *Vivir entre dos mundos. Las fronteras del sur de la Argentina, siglos XVIII y XIX,* ed. Raúl Mandrini. Buenos Aires: Taurus/Alfaguara, 2006.

MIRTA ZAIDA LOBATO

CONQUISTADORES. Conquistadores,
the conquerors of a New World empire for Spain in
the sixteenth century. The conquistadores were men
who participated in the conquest of Mexico, Peru,
and other regions of what became the Spanish
Empire from the early sixteenth century to approximately 1570. They went to the New World seeking
a better life for themselves and their families, and
often endured incredible hardships in their pursuit
of this dream. While the vast majority were laymen,
a number of dedicated clerics also participated in the
conquests, adding a spiritual dimension to the military ventures.

The conquistadores represented every segment
of Spanish society except the high nobility. The early
conquistadores and their most celebrated leaders—
Hernán Cortés, Francisco Pizarro, Francisco de
Montejo, Hernando de Soto, and others—were
born in Spain, frequently in Estremadura, and
arrived in the New World as young men. Typically
they led privately financed expeditions and shared
any booty with their men. Most initially saw their
exploits as a means to provide wealth which would
enable them to return to Spain and live a life of
leisure. Except for some participants in the capture
and ransom of the Inca Atahualpa, however, few
realized their dream, for the rewards of conquest
were typically *encomiendas*, land, and offices, commodities not transferable to Spain. Most conquistadores remained in the New World, some moving
every few years in pursuit of "another Peru."

As a group, the conquistadores shared the desire
to own a big house and a horse; marry a Spanish wife;
be able to entertain family, retainers, and friends
lavishly; and live off the labor of natives held in
encomienda. Those who were successful diversified
their investments and engaged in stock raising, farming, mining, commerce, and officeholding. They and
their heirs were a central part of the early colonial
aristocracy.

See also **Cortés, Hernán; Encomienda; Pizarro, Francisco; Soto, Hernando de.**

BIBLIOGRAPHY

Bernal Díaz Del Castillo, *The True History of the Conquest of
New Spain, 1517–1521,* 5 vols. in 4, translated by
Alfred P. Maudslay (repr. 1967).

James Lockhart, *The Men of Cajamarca: A Social and Biographical Study of the First Conquerors of Peru* (1972).

Additional Bibliography

Elizondo, Carlos. *El escorpión de oro: Luces y sombras en la
extraordinaria vida de Hernán Cortés.* México, D.F.:
EDAMEX, 1996.

Grunberg, Bernard. "The Origins of the Conquistadores of
Mexico City." *Hispanic American Historical Review*
74, no. 2 (May 1994): 259–283.

López de Gómara, Francisco and Silvia L. Cuesy. *Historia
de la conquista de México.* México, D.F.: Editorial
Océano de México, 2003.

Thomas, Hugh. *Conquest: Montezuma, Cortés, and the Fall
of Old Mexico.* New York: Simon & Schuster, 1993.

                                    MARK A. BURKHOLDER

CONSELHEIRO, ANTÔNIO (1830–
1897). Antônio Conselheiro (*b.* 13 March 1830;
d. October 1897), a late-nineteenth-century Brazilian Catholic mystic and lay missionary. His career is
immortalized in Euclides da Cunha's *Os sertões*
(1902; *Rebellion in the Backlands*).

António Vicente Mendes Maciel was born in
Santo Antônio de Quixeramobim, deep in the
Ceará backlands. His grandparents were *vaqueiros*
(cowboys). His father, Vicente's, first marriage
ended disastrously; he deserted his wife after cudg-
eling her so savagely that she nearly died. Vicente's
common-law second wife, Maria Maciel, was the
boy's stepmother during his formative years.
Known in the village as Maria Chana, she compen-
sated by imposing strict religious discipline within
her household and meting out frequent punishments to her children and slaves. Gradually, Vicente's fortunes as a merchant and property owner
began to slip away. He grew morose and sullen,
and was frequently inebriated.

As a child, Antônio was unobtrusive and stu-
dious. The boy's complexion was tawny (*moreno*),
later attributed to partial Calabaça Indian ancestry.
His birth certificate listed him as *pardo* (dark), but
chroniclers who saw him generally referred to him
as white. His first formal instruction came from his
father, who wanted him to become a priest. He was
then enrolled in a school taught by Professor Manuel Antônio Ferreira Nobre, where he studied
arithmetic, geography, Portuguese, French, and

Latin. Some of his schoolmates later took their places in the regional elite as police chiefs, newspapermen, and lawyers.

The Mendes Maciel clan was a "good family" in the eyes of local inhabitants and, in the language of the day, part of the "conservative classes" although not particularly wealthy. At the age of twenty-five Antônio found himself responsible for four unmarried younger girls (two of them half sisters). He took over his father's business and filed papers to back the outstanding loans with a mortgage. In 1857, when he was twenty-seven, he married his fifteen-year-old cousin, Brasilina Laurentina de Lima, the daughter of Francisca Maciel, his father's sister. When she ran away with a soldier, Maciel sold his house and struck off to wander the backlands. He dressed austerely, fasted, and spent weeks and even months in small backlands towns, rebuilding dilapidated churches and cemetery walls. By the 1880s he began to acquire a reputation as a *conselheiro,* or religious counselor.

His wanderings took him through the backlands of Ceará, Pernambuco, Sergipe, and Bahia, in the heart of Brazil's Northeastern drought region. In 1887 he reached the seacoast, at Vila do Conde; he then turned back toward the semiarid interior. He wore a blue tunic tied with a sash, a turned-down hat to protect him from the sun, and sandals. He carried a leather bag with pen and ink, paper, and two prayer books.

Antônio lived on alms and slept in the back rooms of houses and in barns, always on the floor. His nightly orations from makeshift podiums in public squares entranced listeners, although he was not a particularly forceful speaker. The sophisticated called him a buffoon, laughing at his mixture of dogmatic counsels, vulgarized precepts from Christian morality, Latinate phrases, and prophecies. But he exerted a charismatic hold on the humble, many of whom began to follow him as he walked from place to place. In 1893, after a skirmish between his disciples and troops sent from the coast to arrest him, he set out for a remote abandoned cattle ranch on the banks of the Vasa-Barris River in the state of Bahia, a hamlet of 500 or so mud-thatched wooden shanties. Here, protected by a ring of mountains surrounding the valley (and by friendly landowners in the region as well as some local priests), he established a religious community called Canudos, or Belo Monte. As many as 25,000 pilgrims of all racial and economic groups (most of them impoverished backlands *caboclos* of mixed origin) took up residence there, making it Bahia's second most populous urban center by 1895.

Conselheiro's theological vision inverted the harsh and austere reality of the impoverished backlands: the weak, strengthened by their faith, would inherit the earth. Nature would be transformed: rains would come to the arid *sertão,* bringing forth the earth's bounty. Canudos would be a "New Jerusalem." As community leader, he retained his personal asceticism and humility. He dissuaded others from calling him a saint, and he never assumed the powers of the clergy. Although he borrowed from a Catholic apocalyptic missal used widely during the late nineteenth century (*A missão abreviada*), his teachings never strayed from traditional church doctrine. Conselheiro admonished his disciples to live austerely, to renounce luxury, and to await the imminent coming of the Day of Judgment at the millennium. He was a misogynist, and avoided eye contact with women. But he was no religious fanatic. His preachments fell squarely within the tradition of backlands popular Catholicism, which, cut off from church influence by the paucity of available clergy, always had emphasized the presence of sin, the need for penitence, and the personal role of saints and other intermediaries.

Politically, he opposed the (1889) Republic because he revered the exiled Emperor Pedro II and because Brazil's Constitution of 1891, influenced by positivist ideas, ceded jurisdiction over the registry of births, marriages, and deaths to the state. His enemies accused him of sedition and of advocating the violent restoration of the monarchy, presumably with aid from monarchists elsewhere in Brazil as well as from monarchies in Europe. Opposition to Conselheiro and his community was led by backlands landowners threatened by the loss of their traditionally docile labor force as thousands abandoned their residences and streamed to Canudos.

Conselheiro's community at Canudos was destroyed by a massive and bloody assault by the Brazilian army in October 1897, following four attacks over the space of more than a year. He had died, probably of dysentery, some days before, and had been buried by pious villagers. His body was disinterred, the head severed and mounted on a pike, and displayed at the head of military parades in Salvador and in other cities on the coast.

See also **Canudos Campaign.**

BIBLIOGRAPHY

Ronald H. Chilcote, *Power and the Ruling Classes in Northeast Brazil* (1990); *Luso-Brazilian Review,* special issue on messianism and millenarianism (Summer 1991).

Robert M. Levine, *Vale of Tears: Revisiting the Canudos Massacre in Northeastern Brazil* (1992).

Additional Bibliography

Conselheiro, Antônio, Walnice Nogueira Galvão, and Fernando da Rocha Peres. *Breviário de Antonio Conselheiro.* Salvador: Universidade Federal da Bahia, Centro de Estudos Baianos: EDUFBA, 2002.

Galvão, Walnice Nogueira. *O império do Belo Monte: Vida e morte de Canudos.* São Paulo: Editora Fundação Perseu Abramo, 2001.

ROBERT M. LEVINE

CONSELHO DA FAZENDA. Conselho da Fazenda (Treasury Council), founded in 1591 after Spain's annexation of Portugal as part of Philip II's attempt to centralize the state bureaucracy. The Conselho da Fazenda exercised jurisdiction over all matters pertaining to the crown's royal revenues. During the Portuguese Restoration, the Conselho assumed the appearance it would maintain throughout the early modern era. After 1642 it consisted of three *vedores* (inspectors), who were noblemen; four *conselheiros* (counselors), all of whom were university-trained lawyers (Letrados) and who by 1700 were judges (Desembargadores); and four scribes. Several subordinate tribunals worked under the Conselho, including customs (*alfândega*), mint, *Casa da India,* and *Casa dos Contos* (exchequer).

In addition to the collection and management of royal revenues, the Conselho dealt with wide-ranging problems affecting commerce at home and in the colonies. Apart from the daily management of the royal revenues, it is difficult to judge how much power the Conselho da Fazenda, or most of the other councils, actually wielded. Portuguese kings had no obligation to heed its decisions. Because noblemen frequently sat on several councils at the same time, the crown increasingly came to rely on a small group of advisers for important decisions. In 1761 the marquês de Pombal stripped most of the Conselho's authority by turning it into a voluntary claims tribunal and severely narrowing its jurisdiction. In 1790 the Conselho was consolidated with the royal exchequer and effectively dissolved.

See also **Philip II of Spain.**

BIBLIOGRAPHY

Padre Antônio Carvalho Da Costa, *Corografia portuguesa, e descripção topográfica do famoso reyno de Portugal,* 3 vols. (1706–1712).

Joel Serrão, ed., *Dicionário de história de Portugal,* 6 vols. (1979).

Additional Bibliography

Anderson, James Maxwell. *The History of Portugal.* Westport, CT: Greenwood Press, 2000.

WILLIAM DONOVAN

CONSELHO DA INDIA. *See* **Portuguese Overseas Administration.**

CONSELHO ULTRAMARINO. *See* **Overseas Council (Portugal).**

CONSERVATIVE PARTIES. Latin American conservative parties have been important political forces throughout the region since their formation during the 1830s and 1840s. Organized in response to the exigencies of republicanism, and in opposition to social, economic, and political reform, they struggled for power against rival liberal parties during the middle decades of the nineteenth century. Toward the end of the century, conservative and liberal elites achieved a modus vivendi in most parts of Latin America, first because their frequently bloody struggles had clearly harmed national interests, and second because leaders of both parties believed civil order would lead to progress.

Conservatives described the era of consensus as one of "national" or "progressive" conservatism. Liberals termed it a time of "conservative liberalism." In both instances all but the most doctrinaire found they could compromise ideological differences on a platform accentuating economic progress and social order.

Elite accommodation prevailed in Latin America until the early twentieth century, when a traditionally quiescent citizenry began to demand both a meaningful voice in political affairs and substantive social reform. The awakening of a constituency that historically had been passive, respectful of authority, and accepting of elite governance, destroyed conservative-liberal consensus and brought with it political ferment and partisan realignment. Conservatives were especially hard-pressed to recast their political message so as to maintain their constituencies.

The modernization of traditional party platforms came too late in Mexico, Brazil, and Argentina, where revolutionary change either destroyed the old parties or rendered them powerless. Elsewhere conservative parties either passed out of existence or shrank to insignificance. Only Colombia's and Nicaragua's Conservative parties retained their traditional platforms and remained important forces in national politics. In several countries, notably Chile and Venezuela, young conservatives formed new parties founded on conservative principles but aggressively promoting social reform. In so doing they heeded the call of Pope Pius XI, who in his 1931 encyclical *Quadragesimo Anno* gave motive force to what would become the Christian Democratic movement. Over the following decades, Christian Democratic parties appeared in most Latin American nations, and where they did not—in Colombia and Nicaragua, for example—existing conservative parties eventually adopted Christian Democratic–like platforms.

Twentieth-century social change thus produced an inexorable shift in the orientation of Latin America's conservative parties. In that they came to embrace reform programs, they stood poles apart from the hidebound organizations of earlier times. But in that their platforms and ideologies were rooted in Roman Catholic social and philosophic teachings, they proclaimed their descent from Latin America's original conservative parties.

CONSERVATIVE PARTY EVOLUTION

The motive force for conservative party formation in Latin America came from liberals who, following European and North American models, proposed ambitious programs of economic and social reform in decades following the wars of independence (1810–1824). Liberals sought to free their respective countries from traditional social constraints of every sort. In economics they pursued free-trade policies; in politics they endorsed a broadening of democracy; and in the social sphere they struck at limitations to individual freedom. Rational, utilitarian-minded liberals were especially intent on lessening the power of the Roman Catholic Church, which they perceived as the chief obstacle to national progress. The church enjoyed special legal privileges, or fueros, inherited from colonial times, and owned considerable property, which liberals believed should be placed at the disposal of individual citizens.

These policies and beliefs did violence to conservative interests and values at every point, driving adherents to organize politically. By 1850, conservative parties had been constituted in virtually all Latin American nations. Party leaders were united in both interest and ideology. Many of them were descended from landowning families favored by economic policies derived from Spanish mercantilism. At the same time, they viewed economic liberalism as a self-serving device promoting the interests of an upwardly mobile creole commercial elite. They saw liberal egalitarianism and democratic premises as both politically motivated and potentially disruptive of social tranquility. And conservatives were scandalized by liberal attacks on the church, which they viewed as both the repository of divinely inspired moral values and a vital social institution in its own right. Confessional Catholics almost to a man, Latin America's first conservatives could not but see liberal reforms as perverse—even atheistic—disruptions of national social hierarchies, and hence productive of social dissolution. Proponents of strong, even monarchical state leadership, they likewise viewed the extreme federalism endorsed by liberals as wrongheaded and antinational.

Conservative attempts to preserve the closed, inegalitarian system of earlier times, and liberal efforts to open it by striking at traditional institutions and beliefs, formed a common theme in civil wars fought throughout Spanish America during the middle decades of the nineteenth century. Notable figures emerged to orient and lead the traditionalists. Some, such as Rafael Carrera in Central America, José

Antonio Páez in Venezuela, and Juan Manuel de Rosas in Argentina, were military leaders. Others, among them Lucas Alamán in Mexico, Mariano Ospina Rodríguez in Colombia, Gabriel García Moreno in Ecuador, and Diego Portales Palazuelos in Chile, left the fighting to others, concentrating instead on providing their partisans with political, intellectual, and moral leadership. Only Brazil, which existed under a constitutional monarchy until 1889, managed to avoid bloodshed produced by conservative-liberal struggles.

As elites fought over issues of principle and self-interest, Latin America fell farther behind Europe and the United States in economic development. By the latter nineteenth century, the backwardness of the region had become galling to national leaders. Sensitivity to their backwardness, coupled with the appearance of new commercial elites, drove conservatives and liberals to reconcile their differences. For their part, conservatives became convinced that the masses would remain tractable. Having diversified their economic interests, they were no longer threatened by the freeing of national markets to international trade. Meanwhile, the liberals had softened their anticlericalism and had embraced the notion that social order demanded strong, even authoritarian rule. As Spanish America entered the twentieth century, peace springing from elite accommodation reigned everywhere in the region. The bourgeois calm prevailed in Brazil, too, where coffee-based prosperity and the positivist slogan "order and progress" united the new republic's political arbiters.

Latin America's social tranquility did not last past the first decade of the twentieth century. Economic progress had frequently been achieved at the expense of the rank and file, who continued to be, in overwhelming numbers, uneducated peasants having little or no voice in political affairs. Beginning in Mexico in 1910, where rural-based revolution destroyed the political establishment, Latin America woke abruptly from its premodern slumber. Economic change produced increased industrialization and urbanization, which gave rise to new social groups whose members demanded political representation. Their calls produced a plethora of new political parties, most of which employed radical, frequently revolutionary, messages to win constituents.

Conservative party leaders reacted to social and political change in several ways. Some, such as Colombia's Laureano Gómez Castro and Chile's Alberto Edwards Vives, resisted it; they based their political messages on a defense of elitist rule and attacks on liberalism and socialism alike. Elsewhere, in Ecuador, Peru, and Argentina, conservatives joined coalition movements or entered dominant political movements, such as Peru's APRA and Argentina's Peronist Party, coming to constitute right-wing factions in them.

In Nicaragua the Conservatives steadily lost ground to the Liberals over the course of the 1920s, prior to establishment of the Somoza dynasty (1933–1979). Throughout Somoza's regime the Conservative Party remained the leading official opposition in the country, although it splintered into several factions. In the upheavals of the late 1970s Conservatives, led by the editor of *La Prensa,* Pedro Joaquín Chamorro Cardenal, eventually joined with the Sandinistas to end the Somoza regime. The assassination of Chamorro on 10 January 1978 was a major catalyst in the popular uprising that brought an end to the dynasty.

Most Conservatives broke with the Marxist Sandinistas after 1979. Whereas some joined the CIA-backed Contras, most formed the nucleus of the opposition coalition within Nicaragua that eventually triumphed against the Sandinistas in the 1990 election, when Pedro Chamorro's widow, Violeta Barrios De Chamorro, was elected president.

The most significant conservative response to social change during the twentieth century lay in the formation of Christian Democratic parties. Young conservatives such as Eduardo Frei Montalva in Chile and Rafael Caldera Rodríguez in Venezuela rejected the authoritarianism of the extreme right, the threat to private property posed by the extreme left, and the secularism of doctrinaire liberals. They sought and found theoretical and practical inspiration for an alternative path to social change in the encyclical *Rerum Novarum,* issued by Pope Leo XIII in 1891 and commemorated by Pius XI forty years later in *Quadragesimo Anno.* For Frei and the others, *Rerum Novarum* showed Latin Americans a way of addressing social problems while remaining faithful to their oldest cultural value and moral precepts. In that regard the Christian Democrats remained squarely in the tradition of early-day conservatives such as Lucas

Alamán, Mariano Ospina Rodríguez, and Gabriel García Moreno.

Through Christian Democracy, Latin American conservatives found they could embrace nontraditional, progressive solutions of social problems, all the while remaining steadfast in their fundamental political principles.

MODERN PARTY PLATFORMS
At the end of the twentieth century, Latin American conservative parties frequently won presidential elections on political platforms with populist, liberal, and even socialist overtones. Yet on close analysis, those platforms bore clear signs of their conservative character. Party platforms called for social reform within a nonrevolutionary context, whether articulated by Colombia's Social Conservative Party; Ecuador's National Front conservative coalition, which bore Belisario Betancur and León Febres-cordero to victory during the 1980s; Nicaragua's anti-Somoza and later anti-Sandinista Conservative coalition; Costa Rica's Social Christian Unity Party; or Chile's Christian Democratic Party, whose leaders Rafael Calderón Guardia and Patricio Aylwin Azócar won national elections during the early 1990s. Those platforms stressed harmonious change on behalf of the "common good," a phrase, rooted in Roman Catholic social organicism conveying the belief that societies governed in accord with divine law are harmonious ones in which human beings enjoy justice of a distributive character. Modern conservative party platforms endorsed the notion that the social function of property takes precedence over its private function—a reversal of earlier conservatives' intransigent defense of the individual's right to private property.

A final, notable plank in modern conservative party platforms permitted them to support social order while opposing authoritarian or quasi-authoritarian forms of government. That opposition was justified through the principle of subsidiarity, which is rooted in corporatist theory and which holds that individuals and groups have a natural right to autonomy within the state. Mexico's Partido de Acción Nacional (PAN) bases its opposition to the hegemonic Partido Revolucionario Institucional (PRI) on the principle of subsidiarity.

Late-twentieth-century conservative party politicians employed the idiom of religion, morality, and virtue, coupled with explicit or implicit condemnation of relativism, moral laxness, and the loss of ethical standards. In so doing they presented to their respective electorates a modern version of the historic conservative condemnation of secularism, which they blamed for the decline of public and private virtue. Whereas the left has had major presidential victories in Venezuela, Argentina, and Bolivia in the early twenty-first century, center-right parties continue to win important elections. In 2006 Felipe Calderón of the PAN won a very close race in Mexico, promising to maintain economic stability. Another conservative, Álvaro Uribe, who won Colombia's presidential race in 2002 and 2006, gained popularity by taking a strong stance against rebels.

BIBLIOGRAPHY
Harold E. Davis touches on Conservative Party development in his *Latin American Thought: A Historical Introduction* (1972), as does James D. Henderson in *Conservative Thought in Twentieth Century Latin America* (1988). A useful anthology of writings by Latin American conservatives is *Pensamiento conservador, 1815–1898* (1978), edited by José Luis Romero. Romero's *El pensamiento político de la derecha latinoamericana* (1970) stands as of 2007 as the only attempt to survey nineteenth-century Latin American conservatism. Harold E. Davis, *Latin American Social Thought: The History of Its Development Since Independence, with Selected Readings* (1963), contains samples of nineteenth- and twentieth-century conservative writing in English translation. The process of late-nineteenth-century conservative-liberal accommodation is treated in Charles A. Hale, "Political and Social Ideas, 1870–1930," in *The Cambridge History of Latin America*, vol. 4 (1986), edited by Leslie Bethel. Hale also deals extensively with conservative-liberal reconciliation in *The Transformation of Liberalism in Late Nineteenth-Century Mexico* (1989). Eduardo Frei Montalva, *Aún es tiempo* (1942), is an early statement of progressive conservativism. Venezuelan Christian Democratic leader Rafael Caldera suggests the progressive thrust of most modern conservative thought in his *Ideario: La democracia cristiana en América Latina* (1970). Heinrich A. Rommen, *The State in Catholic Thought: A Treatise in Political Philosophy* (1969), is an excellent starting point for those wishing to understand the ideological foundations of Latin American political conservatism, while Noël O'Sullivan, *Conservatism* (1976), treats the subject within the context of post-Enlightenment Western politics.

Additional Bibliography
Deutsch, Sandra McGee. *Las Derechas: The Extreme Right in Argentina, Brazil, and Chile, 1890–1939*. Stanford, CA: Stanford University Press, 1999.

Fowler, William, and Humberto Morales Moreno, eds. *El conservadurismo mexicano en el siglo XIX*. Puebla, Mexico: Benemérita Universidad Autónoma de Puebla, 1999.

Middlebrook, Kevin J., ed. *Conservative Parties, the Right, and Democracy in Latin America*. Baltimore, MD: Johns Hopkins University Press, 2000.

Pereira, Teresa. *El Partido Conservador, 1930–1965: Ideas, figuras y actitudes*. Santiago: Fundación Mario Góngora, 1994.

JAMES D. HENDERSON

CONSOLIDACIÓN, LAW OF.

Law of Consolidación. The Spanish crown decreed the law of *consolidación* on 26 December 1804. The law, or more exactly collection of laws and implementing decrees, required that officials of the church's Juzgado de Capellanías recall all funds that had been invested by the court. The principal of the loans was to be handed over to royal officials, and the crown would pay the court 3 percent annual interest on the principal. Over the course of the Spanish colonial period, very large sums of money had been given to the church for the establishment of pious works. Those funds were normally invested in mortgages on real estate, both urban and rural. Many authors writing at the time believed that more than half of the available capital of the colonies was tied up in these loans. Many borrowers had held these loans for several generations and were hard put to come up with the cash necessary to pay them off, in accordance with the royal decree, and their recall posed an immediate and dire threat to the economic stability of the colonies. In the archdiocese of Mexico, within four years a total of over 2.5 million pesos was collected.

See also **Catholic Church: The Colonial Period.**

BIBLIOGRAPHY

Booker, Jackie. *Veracruz Merchants, 1770–1829: A Mercantile Elite in Late Bourbon and Early Independent Mexico*. Boulder, CO: Westview Press, 1993.

Costeloe, Michael P. *Church Wealth in Mexico: A Study of the "Juzgado de Capellanías" in the Archbishopric of Mexico 1800–1856* (1967).

Jáuregui, Luís. *La real hacienda de Nueva España: Su administración en la época de los intendentes, 1786–*

1821. México: Universidad Nacional Autónoma de México, Facultad de Economía, 1999.

JOHN F. SCHWALLER

CONSPIRACY OF THE TAILORS.
See **Inconfidência dos Alfaiates.**

CONSTANT BOTELHO DE MAGALHÃES, BENJAMIN (1836–1891).

Benjamin Constant Botelho de Magalhães (*b.* 18 October 1836; *d.* 22 January 1891), one of the founders of the Brazilian Republic. The son of a schoolteacher and a seamstress, Constant was instrumental in Brazil's transition from monarchy to republic. The army gave him the opportunity to rise above his humble birth. Trained as an engineer at Rio de Janeiro's Military Academy, Constant later taught mathematics at his alma mater. In 1866 he participated briefly in the War of the Triple Alliance, but illness forced his return to Rio de Janeiro.

A more successful teacher than soldier, Constant nonetheless was part of the new military that emerged from the Paraguayan war committed to more active participation in political affairs of the empire. He became a convert to positivist doctrines and was influential in spreading them among his students at the Military Academy and later at the War College. By the late 1880s Constant demonstrated vocal support for republicanism and conspired to bring down the empire in 1889. His prestige among students brought many cadets to support the republican cause. In November 1889, as vice president of the Military Club, he urged its president, General Manuel Deodoro da Fonseca, to lead the military against the Emperor Pedro II and proclaim the republic.

Under the Republican administration, Constant served first as minister of war, then as minister of public instruction and postmaster in 1890. The positivist slogan, "Order and Progress," emblazoned on the Brazilian flag is attributed to him.

See also **Positivism.**

BIBLIOGRAPHY

João Cruz Costa, *A History of Ideas in Brazil*, translated by Suzette Machado (1964), esp. pp. 143–148.

Heitor Lyra, *História da queda do império*, 2 vols. (1964).

Ronald Schneider, *"Order and Progress": A Political History of Brazil* (1991), esp. pp. 56–57.

Additional Bibliography

Castro, Celso. *Os militares e a república: Um estudo sobre cultura e ação política*. Rio de Janeiro: J. Zahar Editor, 1995.

Lemos, Renato. *Benjamin Constant: Vida e história*. Rio de Janeiro: Topbooks, 1999.

JOAN MEZNAR

CONSTITUTIONAL CHANGES TO MEXICAN CONSTITUTION. *See* Mexico, Constitutions: Constitution of 1917.

CONSTITUTIONS. *See* under individual countries.

CONSULADO.

The Spanish-American *consulados* (merchant guilds) had their roots in medieval Mediterranean institutions formed to protect merchant interests after the breakdown of the Roman Empire. Their central feature was a tribunal to hear commercial litigation. Although rooted in Greco-Roman legal precedents, the Spanish merchant guilds derived more directly from Italian sea consulates, which were highly organized by the end of the twelfth century at Genoa, Pisa, Siena, Bologna, and elsewhere. From Italy the institution spread northwestward through Provence and Languedoc to several towns along the Aragon coast from Perpignan to Valencia as well as to Majorca. The most important of these came to be Barcelona's Council of One Hundred (Concell de Cent), which James I authorized in 1249. In the foreign ports with which Barcelona traded, it appointed consuls who could govern, judge, and punish all the subjects of the Crown of Aragon who resided in those ports. The fourteenth-century *Libre del Consolat de mar* of the Barcelona guild thus became one of the earliest codes of maritime and commercial law. This Barcelona sea consulate (consolat de mar), although not officially chartered until 1347, became the model for those which followed in the Spanish world. By that date it had a commercial court elected by the merchants that heard commercial cases.

By 1450 eight towns in the Kingdom of Aragon had similar commercial courts. These courts eliminated the expense of lawsuits and strife in mercantile litigation because they circumvented the legalism and obstruction encountered in the ordinary courts. In addition, the merchants usually elected a junta to represent them in negotiations with other organizations and at trade fairs, to administer the finances of the guild, and to enforce trade regulations within the area of the *consulado*'s jurisdiction. The early *consulados* were closely allied to the municipal administration of their respective cities and played important roles in the economic and political structure of eastern Spain by 1450.

After the union of Aragon and Castile in 1479, Catalonian commercial customs influenced those of Castile as the Spanish Empire began to take shape. There had been merchant guilds in Burgos, Bilbao, and other northern Castilian towns for half a century before the union with Aragon, but it was not until after unification that the judicial court privileges were granted in Castile. Burgos (1494) and Bilbao (1511) were the first Castilian towns to receive royal sanction for *consulados*. In 1543 the Crown authorized a *consulado* to the merchants of Seville (Universidad de los Cargadores de las Indias), where it held a monopoly on the trade with America. To supervise the colonial trade, the Crown had established the Casa De Contratación (Board of Trade) in Seville in 1503, after the pattern of the Board of Trade established in Barcelona to supervise Mediterranean commerce in the fourteenth century. The Casa de Contratación controlled every detail of trade, and the *consulado* established in Seville in 1543 worked closely with it to protect the merchants of the city, strenuously resisting any curtailment of the monopoly they held on the trade with the Indies. The *consulado* of Seville supervised the fleet system that channeled legal trade with the Indies through the annual fairs at Portobelo for Peru and Veracruz (or Xalapa) for New Spain.

Establishment of *consulados* in Mexico and Lima extended the control of the Seville merchant guild.

Patterned after those in the Spanish towns, they were composed of the chief importers, mostly representatives of Seville merchants. These first Latin American *consulados* thus served to strengthen the Seville merchant monopoly over trade with the Indies. Agitation for a Mexican *consulado* began as early as 1580; it was authorized on 15 June 1592 and was formally established in Mexico City in 1604. The Crown authorized the Peruvian *consulado* on 29 December 1593, but its organization was not completed until February 1613. In the seventeenth century these two *consulados* enjoyed great power as the institution of the European residents, serving as a sympathetic tribunal to hear disputes over contracts, bankruptcy, shipping, insurance, and other commercial matters. They established consular deputations in towns throughout their respective viceroyalties and developed large funds that came to be an important source for development of public works and loans to the viceregal governments.

The merchants in the viceregal capitals jealously guarded their privileged monopolies and successfully opposed any new *consulados* in America for two centuries, despite petitions for such institutions from other cities from the mid-seventeenth century forward. With the exception of a *consulado* in Bogotá, which functioned between 1694 and 1712, outside of Lima and Mexico City the only mercantile organization permitted in Spanish America consisted of some commercial deputies who exercised limited functions as commercial judges and tax collectors in an ill-defined system that frequently led to confusion, delay, and sizable backlogs of cases.

Under Charles III and Charles IV, late in the eighteenth century, the efforts to liberalize commercial activity and to reduce the Seville-Cádiz monopoly finally led to formation of several new *consulados*. Manila gained a *consulado* in 1769, with jurisdiction over the Philippines. Then, between 1793 and 1795, the Crown erected new *consulados* in Caracas, Guatemala, Buenos Aires, Havana, Veracruz, Santiago de Chile, Guadalajara, and Cartagena. Several of these had already been operating limited commercial courts as consular deputations of the *consulados* of Mexico or Lima. Although apparently never formally chartered by the Crown, consular deputations in Montevideo and San Juan also evolved into institutions operating as

consulados in the early nineteenth century. All these new *consulados* had as their "principal duty" the protection and advancement of commerce. In addition to their judicial functions, these newer *consulados* came to have an important role in the development of the economic infrastructure of the colonies. There were also new *consulados* formed during the struggle for independence, including one at Puebla in Mexico and at Guayaquil, Cuenca, and Angostura in South America, all of them short-lived. At least one *consulado*, in Valparaíso, Chile, was established after independence.

Because of their close association with Spanish peninsular interests, most of the *consulados* were abolished during or soon after independence. The Spanish government abolished the institution in 1829, although Valencia revived its *consulado* in 1934. In Latin America, however, a few *consulados* survived well into the nineteenth century, notably in Chile until 1875, in Guatemala until 1871, and in Argentina until 1862. Representing the principle of commercial monopoly, however, all of them eventually fell before the dominance of classical liberal economic philosophy in the nineteenth century.

See also **Commercial Policy: Colonial Spanish America.**

BIBLIOGRAPHY

Robert Sidney Smith, *The Spanish Guild Merchant: A History of the Consulado, 1250–1700* (1940; repr. 1972), provides the best overview of the institution of the *consulado* in the Spanish world; Robert Sidney Smith, "Research Report on Consulado History," in *Homenaje a don José María de la Peña y Cámara* (1969), pp. 121–140, provides a useful survey of much of the literature on the topic. On the origins of the institution, Stanley S. Jados, *Consulate of the Sea and Related Documents* (1975), is useful; and on the Seville merchant society, Ruth Pike, *Aristocrats and Traders: Sevillean Society in the Sixteenth Century* (1972), is an excellent introduction.

Several of the Latin American *consulados* have received treatment. C. Norman Guice, "The Consulado of New Spain, 1594–1795" (Ph.D. diss., University of California, 1952) surveys the Mexican *consulado*. See also Louisa Schell Hoberman, *Mexico's Merchant Elite, 1590–1660: Silver, State, and Society* (1991); David A. Brading, *Miners and Merchants in Bourbon Mexico, 1763–1810* (1971); and Javier Ortiz De La Tabla Ducasse, *Memorias políticas y económicas del consulado de Veracruz, 1796–1822* (1985). On the Peruvian *consulado*, see Lawrence A. Clayton, "Sources in Lima for the Study of the Colonial Consulado of Peru," in *The Americas* 33 (1977): 457–469; and John Melzer, *Bastion of Commerce in the City of Kings: The Consulado de Comercio of Lima, 1593–1887* (1991). On Caracas, see Manuel Nunes Dias, *El real consulado de Caracas (1793–1810)* (1971), and Humberto Tandrón, *El real consulado de Caracas y el comercio exterior de Venezuela* (1976); on Guatemala, see Ralph Lee Woodward, Jr., *Class Privilege and Economic Development: The Consulado de Comercio of Guatemala, 1793–1871* (1966); on Buenos Aires, see Germán O. Tjarks, *El consulado de Buenos Aires y sus proyecciones en la historia del Río de la Plata* (1962). See also Susan Migden Socolow, *The Merchants of Buenos Aires, 1778–1810* (1978). On the brief history of the *consulado* in Bogotá, see Robert S. Smith, "The Consulado de Santa Fe de Bogotá," in *Hispanic American Historical Review* 45, no. 3 (1965): 442–451.

Additional Bibliography

Arazola Corvera, Ma Jesús. *Hombres, barcos y comercio de la ruta Cádiz-Buenos Aires, 1737–1757.* Sevilla: Diputación de Sevilla, 1998.

Bustos Rodríguez, Manuel. *Los comerciantes de la carrera de Indias en el Cadiz del siglo XVIII (1713–1775).* Cádiz: Servico de Publicaciones, Universidad de Cádiz, 1995.

Fisher, John Robert. *The Economic Aspects of Spanish Imperialism in America, 1492–1810.* Liverpool: Liverpool University Press, 1997.

Hausberger, Bernd, and Antonio Ibarra. *Comercio y poder en América colonial: Los consulados de comerciantes, siglos XVII–XIX.* Madrid: Iberoamericana, 2003.

Hill, Ruth. *Hierarchy, Commerce and Fraud in Bourbon Spanish America: A Postal Inspector's Exposé.* Nashville: Vanderbilt University Press, 2005.

Stein, Stanley J. and Barbara H. Stein. *Silver, Trade, and War: Spain and America in the Making of Early Modern Europe.* Baltimore, MD: Johns Hopkins University Press, 2000.

RALPH LEE WOODWARD JR.

CONTADORA. Contadora, an effort to achieve a peace treaty between the Central American nations of Guatemala, El Salvador, Honduras, Nicaragua, and Costa Rica in the late 1980s. The sponsoring countries were Mexico, Panama, Colombia, and Venezuela, with a support group consisting of Argentina, Brazil, Peru, and Uruguay. Contadora was so named for an island off the western coast of Panama where the first meeting took place in 1983. The principal objectives were to stop the war between the Sandinista government in Nicaragua and the U.S.-backed counterrevolutionary force based in Honduras, and to remove foreign military influence from Central America.

Daniel Ortega, representing Nicaragua, signed the first draft of Contadora in September 1984, but the other Central American executives balked. New language was inserted to pressure Nicaragua to adopt more democratic institutions. In June 1986, Ortega and Guatemalan president Vinicio Cerezo were ready to sign, but the United States achieved the abstention of Costa Rica, Honduras, and El Salvador. In February 1987, Costa Rican president Oscar Arias presented a new plan based on the original Contadora provisions. On 7 August 1987, all five countries signed the Arias Peace Plan (for which Arias received the 1987 Nobel Peace Prize).

The Contadora sponsors and support group have provided teams for the International Corps of Inspectors and the Verification Commission which have monitored various phases of the Arias Plan. In 1993 the functions of Contadora were absorbed by the United Nations and the Organization of American States.

See also **Arias Sánchez, Oscar; Cerezo Arévalo, Marco Vinicio; Esquipulas II; Organization of American States (OAS); Ortega Saavedra, Daniel.**

BIBLIOGRAPHY

Morris Blachman et al., eds. *Confronting Revolution: Security Through Diplomacy in Central America* (1986).

Center for International Policy, "Contadora Primer," in *International Policy Report* (November 1986).

Jim Morrell, "The Nine Lives of the Central American Peace Process," in *International Policy Report* (February 1989), pp. 1–7.

Additional Bibliography

Bagley, Bruce Michael. *Contadora and the Diplomacy of Peace in Central America.* Boulder, CO: Westview Press, 1987.

Zamora R., Augusto. *La paz burlada: Los procesos de paz de Contadora y Esquipulas.* Madrid: SEPHA, 2006.

MARK EVERINGHAM

CONTADURÍA. Contaduría, a general term referring to accounting procedures in Spain and the Indies. Throughout Spanish America royal accountants (*contadores*) kept records for the royal treasury (*caja*) in their district. In Lima and Mexico City similar officials labored over the ledgers of the viceregal matrix treasuries along with a host of other accountants who were responsible for keeping track of one specific tax category (*ramo*) such as tribute, indulgences, mercury, stamped legal paper, and sales taxes. In 1605, to strengthen the colonial accounting system, Philip III established in Bogotá, Mexico City, and Lima auditing bureaus (Tribunales de Cuentas) whose task was to audit the myriad of ledgers generated by regional and viceregal accountants. After the audits, the *tribunals* forwarded the accounts to the contaduría of the Council of the Indies in Spain. Here, more accountants subjected these books to still another vigilant review, before sending them to the archives—after 1783 to the General Archive of the Indies in Seville.

See also **Viceroyalty, Viceroy.**

BIBLIOGRAPHY

De Escalona y Agüero, Gaspar. *Gazofilacio Real del Perú*, 4th ed. (1941).

Jáuregui, Luís. *La real hacienda de Nueva España: Su administración en la época de los intendentes, 1786–1821.* México: Universidad Nacional Autónoma de México, Facultad de Economía, 1999.

Klein, Herbert S. *The American Finances of the Spanish Empire: Royal Income and Expenditures in Colonial Mexico, Peru, and Bolivia, 1680–1809.* Albuquerque: University of New Mexico Press, 1998.

Recopiliación de leyes de los reynos de las Indias, 4 vols. (1681; repr. 1973), libro II, título XI; libro VIII, título II; libro IX, título VIII.

JOHN JAY TePASKE

CONTEMPORÁNEOS, LOS.

Los Contemporáneos, a group of Mexican artists and writers in the 1920s who opposed the dogmatic character of the Escuela Mexicana (Mexican School) and disseminated the ideas of the European avant garde. Among its most important members were the writers Xavier Villaurrutía, Salvador Novo, Jaime Torres Bodet, and the artist and critic Agustín Lazo. Originally gathered around Antonieta Rivas Mercado and the first experimental theater in Mexico, Teatro Ulises, these writers and artists went on to form the group called Los Contemporáneos in 1927. They founded an important journal devoted to art and literature titled *Contemporáneos* (1928–1931). Often attacked by the members of the Escuela Mexicana for being overly concerned with European modernism, Los Contemporáneos nevertheless were important promoters of a number of lesser-known Mexican artists, including Abraham Angel, Manuel Rodríguez Lozano, Carlos Mérida, and Julio Castellanos. In 1935 they organized an exhibition of the work of Rufino Tamayo at the Galería de Arte Mexicano. Although Los Contemporáneos were condemned for not being fervent nationalists, they wrote extensively about Mexican art and literature.

See also **Literature: Spanish America.**

BIBLIOGRAPHY

Olivier Debroise, *Figuras en el trópico, plástica mexicana 1920–1940* (1984), esp. p. 141.

Jorge Alberto Manrique, "Rompimiento y rompimientos en el arte mexicano," in Museo de Arte Alvar y Carmen T. de Carrillo Gil, *Ruptura 1952–1965* (1988), pp. 25–42, and "Otras caras del arte mexicano," in Museo Nacional de Arte de Mexico, *Modernidad y modernización en el arte mexicano 1920–1960* (1991), pp. 131–143.

Additional Bibliography

Oropesa, Salvador A. *The Contemporáneos Group: Rewriting Mexico in the Thirties and Forties.* Austin: University of Texas Press, 2003.

Vento, Arnold C. *La generación Hijo pródigo: Renovación y modernidad.* Lanham, MD: University Press of America, 1996.

ILONA KATZEW

CONTESTADO REBELLION.

Contestado Rebellion, which pitted some 25,000 millenarian rebels against two-thirds of the Brazilian army (7,000 men) between 1912 and March 1916, was the last of three great millenarian movements (along with rebellions at Canudos and Juazeiro) that shook Brazil at the turn of this century. The rebellion was fought in the contested border region between the Brazilian states of Paraná and Santa Catarina ("the Contestado"). Rebels who followed the teachings of the "prophet" José Maria created "holy cities" for believers, attacked skeptics, and called for the return of the Brazilian monarchy (overthrown in 1889). An army scorched-earth campaign eventually starved the rebels into submission.

Rapid socioeconomic change at the beginning of the twentieth century prompted the rebellion. Before that time small-scale cattle ranching dominated the Contestado economy. Landowners secured their large, undefined holdings via usufruct land grants to Agregados (combination ranch hands and sharecroppers). An unequal, yet reciprocal, relationship developed between landowners and *agregados,* one maintained not only by material exchanges but also by the establishment of ritual kinship ties between the landowner, the *agregado,* and the latter's family.

But turn-of-the-century colonization projects and railroad construction transformed life in the Contestado. Between 1890 and 1912 thousands of new European immigrants colonized lands donated by state governments. In 1906 the American-owned Brazil Railway Company began construction of the first railroad through the region, at the same time promoting the colonization of thousands of hectares of Contestado land it had received as part of a federal government concession. Local landowners subsequently sold large portions of their holdings because of the booming real estate market, thereby dispossessing their *agregados* and their families.

The actions of "faceless" North American capitalists and local landowners threatened peasant subsistence in the Contestado. What emerged was not only a material crisis but also a spiritual crisis of values, for the profit-hungry landowners, the godfathers of *agregados* and their families, had broken their religiously sanctioned subsistence guarantees. By calling for landowners and peasants to live together in holy cities the millenarian movement led by José Maria promised to heal both the internal crisis of values and the material threat of peasant subsistence. It was this powerful dual message that fueled and inspired one of the largest popular rebellions in the history of Brazil.

See also **Batista, Cícero Romão; Conselheiro, Antônio.**

BIBLIOGRAPHY

Duglas Teixeria Monteiro, *Os errantes do novo século* (1974).

Maria Isaura Pereira De Queiroz, *O messianismo no Brasil e no mundo,* 2d ed. (1976).

Bernard J. Siegel, "The Contestado Rebellion, 1912–1916: A Case Study in Brazilian Messianism and Regional Dynamics," in *The Anthropology of Power,* edited by Raymond D. Fogelson and Richard N. Adams (1977), pp. 325–336.

Maurício Vinhas De Queiroz, *Messianismo e conflito social,* 3d ed. (1981).

Patricia Pessar, "Unmasking the Politics of Religion," in *Journal of Latin American Lore* 7, no. 2 (1981): 255–278.

Todd A. Diacon, *Millenarian Vision, Capitalist Reality: Brazil's Contestado Rebellion, 1912–1916* (1991).

TODD A. DIACON

CONTINUISMO. Continuismo, the practice of maintaining a president in office beyond his legal term. Because most Latin American constitutions contain one-term limitations for the president, a variety of devices have been used by resourceful chief executives to continue in office. Among the more common have been: (1) constitutional revision (Juan Domingo Perón [Argentina] in 1951 and Alfredo Stroessner [Paraguay] in 1954), (2) legislative enactment (Jorge Ubico [Guatemala] in 1941), (3) plebescite (Carlos Castillo Armas [Guatemala] in 1954 and Marcos Pérez Jiménez [Venezuela] in 1958), (4) internal coup (Getúlio Dornelles Vargas [Brazil] in 1938), (5) imposition of a weak candidate to serve as a figurehead while the outgoing president rules behind the scenes (Plutarco Calles's [Mexico] choice of Emilio Portes Gil to succeed him in 1928 and Luis Somoza's [Nicaragua] decision to install René Schick Gutiérrez in the presidency in 1963), (6) conferral of the title President for Life to François Duvalier in 1964 by the Haitian legislature, and (7) maintenance of a leader's power by a political movement or hegemonic political party (Fidel Castro [Cuba]).

Based on these practices, a number of types of *continuista* regimes can be identified. First is classical *continuismo,* which is the manipulation of the constitutional or legal system by a personal dictator to perpetuate himself in power. The "depression dictatorships" of Central America and the Caribbean, such as that of Maximiliano Hernández Martínez of El Salvador, are of this type. Second, dynastic *continuismo* is the passing of power from father to son (for example, the Duvaliers [Haiti] and the Somozas [Nicaragua]), from husband to wife (Juan Perón to Isabel Perón [Argentina] through the vice presidency in 1974), and, potentially, between brothers (Raúl Castro is generally considered to be Fidel Castro's heir apparent). A third type, institutional *continuismo,* is the perpetuation of a ruler in office or the naming of his successor by a hegemonic party (Mexico and Cuba). Finally, there is a type of military *continuismo,* which is the circulation of power among a succession of military rulers by the general staff, a practice evident in the bureaucratic-authoritarian regimes in Brazil, Argentina, and Uruguay.

See also **Military Dictatorships: Since 1945.**

BIBLIOGRAPHY

Mainwaring, Scott, and Matthew Soberg Shugart. *Presidentialism and Democracy in Latin America.* Cambridge, U.K.: Cambridge University Press, 1997.

Nohlen, Dieter, and Mario Fernández Baeza. *El presidencialismo renovado: Instituciones y cambio político en América Latina.* Caracas: Nueva Sociedad, 1998.

Rossi, Ernest E., and Jack C. Plano. "Continuismo," in *Latin American Political Dictionary* (1980).

ROLAND H. EBEL

CONTRABAND (COLONIAL SPANISH AMERICA).

Contraband (Colonial Spanish America), external trade and trade goods that flowed outside the bounds of formal Spanish taxation, regulation, and national monopoly.

Contraband and its economic cousins—smuggling, fraud, illicit commerce, and illegal trade—were integral elements in the economies of colonial Spanish America. Technically, each term referred to a specific element of the multifaceted phenomenon. Fraud, for example, consisted of trade that, although legal per se, occurred at levels disallowed by license or law. Trade of Spanish or Spanish American origin expressly forbidden by law was considered contraband. The illegal direct trade of foreigners with Spanish America was categorized as illicit commerce. But as Pedro González de Salcedo generalized in his *Tratado jurídico-político del contra-bando* (1654, 1729), and as the king of Spain, Charles III, reaffirmed in 1770, contraband was understood also to include all trade prohibited by law or ruled by the monarch to damage the public good. Generally, this economic interplay between restrictions and law-breaking called contraband applied to descriptions of external commerce. However, illegal trade and tax fraud also marked internal commerce and created

economic problems and opportunities in the interior similar to those afforded by smuggling in coastal regions of Spanish America.

Coastal contraband occurred throughout the empire, but it was especially prevalent in northern South America from Portobelo, in present-day Panama, to Cumaná, in present-day northern Venezuela, and in the Río de la Plata delta. Its practice, well-established by the 1590s, surged in the seventeenth century with the Dutch seizure of Curaçao in 1634, the British capture of Jamaica in 1655 and the subsequent suppression of piracy in the 1680s, and the Portuguese establishment of Colonia del Sacramento in 1680. The Treaty of Utrecht (1713) and the international wars of the eighteenth century furthered illegal trafficking through Spanish American ports. These developments reflect the general regionalism of Spanish American contraband. While England had merchants throughout the Americas, the Dutch primarily worked the southern Caribbean, the Portuguese the Río de la Plata basin, and the French the Pacific coasts.

There were two distinctly divergent points of view regarding contraband within the Spanish Empire. On one hand, peninsulars blamed illicit commerce on inordinate American consumer demands and insufficient American regard for law and custom. Americans, on the other, focused on the failure of the metropolis to appreciate sufficiently American needs and to service properly its American dominions. But, in either case, Spaniards—and foreigners, too—recognized the illegality of smuggling.

Contrary, then, to official will and purpose and to the principles of mercantilist theory, contraband trafficking in Spanish American colonies represented to policy-making elites and peninsular monopolists a serious threat to imperial well-being. They commonly called contraband a "cancer" that ate away at legitimate royal revenues, sapped the economic vitality of the empire, and eroded the moral fiber of Spanish vassals. Consequently, the Spanish crown sought to curb, if not eliminate, contraband. At times, it merely took a necessary public position. Smuggling could not go unchallenged without undermining the power and influence of Spanish law, royal authority, and the assertion of hegemonic economic dominance in Spanish America. At other times, however, the metropolis addressed the problem of contraband with significant and creative measures, including the creation of the viceroyalties of New Granada (1717 and 1739) and Río de la Plata (1776), the formation of the monopolistic Caracas Company in 1728, and the formulation of free trade policies in the late eighteenth century. More often than not, however, all of these efforts fell short of their goal, because imperial realities constrained them. Unwieldy Spanish bureaucracies, metropolitan commercial weaknesses, American consumer demands, the difficulties of law enforcement, official corruption, international war, unpacified indigeneous groups, the commercial interest of European rivals in Spanish American wealth, the smugglers' ingenious and practical methods of hiding their activities, and the long coastlines of the colonies all limited, if not undid, the effectiveness of these initiatives.

Given the inconstancies of legal Spanish commerce, smuggling also represented logical economic behavior and so complemented formal trade. In the absence of licensed Spanish shipping, only illicit commerce kept ports (including important entrepôts like Portobelo in present-day Panama) active and their respective markets supplied. Contraband provided American consumers with a wide variety of goods—new and used clothing; textiles of all sorts; common items such as scissors, toys, and candles; foodstuffs, including wheat flour and spices; and slaves—at prices that undercut those of licit goods. In return, Spanish Americans supplied silver, gold, gems, tobacco, cacao, livestock, hides, yerba, and dyewoods, according to local availability. Even local treasuries occasionally relied on the capture, sale, and taxation of contraband goods for major funding during the year.

Because contraband trade was illegal and therefore largely unrecorded, it is difficult to measure its volume, value, and movement and so to know fully its actual role in Spanish colonial economies. Both contemporary observers and modern scholars agree, however, on its importance. The openness with which smugglers sold their wares in the marketplaces of Cartagena and Buenos Aires testifies to the commercial prominence of contraband. So does the number of smuggling vessels that called on Spanish American ports. In 1706, for example, sixty Dutch ships called on Portobelo customers, and when the galleons arrived in 1708, twenty British merchantmen were in the harbor. Contemporary estimates of the value of contraband point as well to its vigor. In 1800, José Ignacio de Pombo, one of the most astute merchants and economic thinkers of viceregal New Granada, set the annual value of illegal Jamaican imports alone to Cartagena at 1 million pesos.

Contraband, furthermore, cut across social lines, employing high government officials and slaves; priests, soldiers, merchants, and indigenous peoples (especially Guajiros, Cunas, and Osage); males and females; outlaws and law-enforcement agents; and Spaniards and foreigners alike. So, albeit illegal, contraband played a significant role in the economic life of colonial Spanish America.

See also **Trade, Colonial Brazil.**

BIBLIOGRAPHY

Significant monographic studies of Spanish American contraband include Sergio Villalobos R., *Comercio y contrabando en el Río de la Plata y Chile, 1700–1811* (1965); Celestino Andrés Araúz, *El contrabando holandés en el Caribe durante la primera mitad del siglo XVIII* (1984); Cornelis Ch. Goslinga, *The Dutch in the Caribbean and in the Guianas, 1680–1791* (1985); Michel Morineau, *Incroyables gazettes et fabuleux métaux: Les retours des trésors américains d'après les gazettes hollandaises (XVIe–XVIIIe siècles)* (1985); Zacarías Moutoukias, *Contrabando y control colonial en el siglo XVII: Buenos Aires, el Atlántico, y el espacio peruano* (1988); and Héctor R. Feliciano Ramos, *El contrabando inglés en el Caribe y el Golfo de Mexico, 1748–1778* (1990).

Three pioneering articles in English are Vera Lee Brown, "Contraband Trade: A Factor in the Decline of Spain's American Empire," in *Hispanic American Historial Review* 8, no. 2 (1928): 178–189; Allan Christelow, "Contraband Trade Between Jamaica and the Spanish Main, and the Free Port Act of 1766," in *Hispanic American Historical Review* 22, no. 2 (1942): 309–343; and George H. Nelson, "Contraband Trade Under the Asiento," in *American Historical Review* 51, no. 1 (1945): 55–67.

Additional Bibliography

Garner, Richard L., and Spiro E Stefanou. *Economic Growth and Change in Bourbon Mexico*. Gainesville: University Press of Florida, 1993.

Grahn, Lance Raymond. *The Political Economy of Smuggling: Regional Informal Economies in Early Bourbon New Granada*. Boulder, CO: Westview Press, 1997.

Lozano Armendares, Teresa. *El chinguirito vindicado: el contrabando de aguardiente de caña y la política colonial*. México: Universidad Nacional Autónoma de México, 1995.

LANCE R. GRAHN

CONTRAS.

CONTRAS. Contras, an anti-Sandinista military force funded by the administration of President Ronald Reagan during the 1980s. Conceived in 1981 as an armed force to interdict arms supplies shipped from Nicaragua to anti-government guerrillas in El Salvador, the contras grew from a five-hundred-man force to an estimated twelve thousand men with the objective of ousting the Sandinistas from political power. The contras eventually represented Nicaragua's diverse political factions: ex-Somocistas, Miskito Indians and disgruntled Sandinistas, and members of Nicaragua's upper, middle, and lower social sectors. U.S. congressional discontent with the contras' attacks upon civilian targets and their continued human rights violations led in 1984 to the Boland Amendment, which cut military aid to them. The Reagan administration then turned to the National Security Council, where Lieutenant Colonel Oliver North solicited money from leaders of oil-rich nations and generated funds from missile sales to Iran. Operating from base camps in Honduras, the contras conducted forays into Nicaragua but never controlled any territory inside the country, nor did they ever gain popular support. As Reagan's Central American policy came under increasing criticism at home, Central American peace initiatives took hold. In 1989, first at Tesoro Beach, El Salvador, in February and then at Tela, Honduras, in August, the Central American presidents forged an agreement that provided for free elections in Nicaragua and the disbanding of the contras. Under these conditions, the U.S. Congress appropriated $49.7 million in humanitarian aid for the contras pending the results of the February 1990 elections. When Violeta Barrios de Chamorro defeated Daniel Ortega Saavedra for the Nicaraguan presidency, the justification for the existence of the contras disappeared. Under the supervision of a United Nations peacekeeping force, the contras were disbanded by June 1990, but not all returned to Nicaragua. Some remained scattered throughout Central America, while the wealthier supporters resided in the United States.

See also **Nicaragua, Sandinista National Liberation Front (FSLN); United States-Latin American Relations.**

BIBLIOGRAPHY

Robert A. Pastor, *Condemned to Repetition: The United States and Nicaragua* (1987).

Bob Woodward, *Veil: The Secret Wars of the CIA, 1981–1987* (1987).

U.S. Congress. House Of Representatives Select Committee to Investigate Covert Arms Transactions with Iran and Senate Select Committee on Secret Military Assistance to Iran and the Nicaraguan Opposition, *Iran-Contra Affair.* 100th Congress, 1st session, House Report No. 100–433, Senate Report No. 100–216 (1987).

Roy Gutman, *Banana Diplomacy: The Making of American Policy in Nicaragua, 1981–1987* (1988).

Additional Bibliography

Brown, Timothy C. *The Real Contra War: Highlander Peasant Resistance in Nicaragua.* Norman: University of Oklahoma Press, 2001.

Cameron, Bruce P. *My Life in the Time of the Contras.* Albuquerque: University of New Mexico Press, 2007.

Sobel, Richard. *Public Opinion in U.S. Foreign Policy: The Controversy over Contra Aid.* Lanham, MD: Rowman & Littlefield, 1993.

Webb, Gary. *Dark Alliance: The CIA, The Contras, and the Crack Cocaine Explosion.* New York: Seven Stories Press, 1999.

Zamora R., Augusto. *El conflicto Estados Unidos-Nicaragua, 1979–1990.* Managua: Fondo Editorial CIRA, 1996.

THOMAS M. LEONARD

CONTRERAS, GLORIA

CONTRERAS, GLORIA (1934–). Mexican choreographer Gloria Contreras (María del Carmen Gloria Contreras y Roeniger), has created more than 180 original works since beginning her dancing career at the School of American Ballet in New York City. In 1970 she founded a choreography workshop, Taller Coreográfico de la Universidad Nacional Autónoma de México, in Mexico City and served as the artistic director from its inception. Each year the workshop offers dance instruction to more than twelve hundred students.

Contreras studied with noted dancers and choreographers, including George Balanchine, Pierre Vladimiroff, Felia Doubrovska, Anatole Oboukhoff, and Muriel Stuart. Her ballets have been performed by the Royal Winnipeg Ballet, Oakland Ballet, and the Joffrey Ballet, as well as by companies in Russia, Mexico, and several other Latin American countries. In 1995 she won the Premio Universidad Nacional in the area of Artistic Creation, and was also given the Guillermina Bravo Award by the International Festival of Contemporary Dance. In addition to her career in dance, she has appeared in Chilean director Alejandro Jodorowski's 1989 film *Santa Sangre* (*Holy Blood*) and has edited nineteen books on ballet and Latin American culture.

See also **Jodorowski, Alejandro; Music: Popular Music and Dance.**

BIBLIOGRAPHY

Contreras, Gloria. *Latin American Culture Studies: Information and Materials for Teaching about Latin America.* Austin: Institute of Latin American Studies, University of Texas at Austin, 1987.

Contreras, Gloria. *Diario de una bailarina.* Mexico: Universidad Nacional Autónoma de México, 1997.

Horosko, Marian. "Balanchine's Guide to a Young Choreographer: Excerpts from Diary of Choreographer Gloria Contreras about Conversations with Choreographer George Balanchine." *Dance Magazine* (December 1996): 86–87.

Manzanos, Rosario, and Armando Ponce. "Gloria Contreras y la UNAM: De poder a poder." *Proceso* (September 2000): 70.

STACY LUTSCH

CONTRERAS BROTHERS.

Contreras Brothers (Hernando [*b.* c. 1529; *d.* 1550] and Pedro [*b.* c. 1531; *d.* 1550]), sons of Rodrigo de Contreras, governor of Nicaragua (1534–1544), and grandsons of Pedro Arias de Ávila; in 1550 they led one of the most serious revolts against Spanish royal authority during the colonial period. Their father, from a prominent Segovian family, was accused, among other abuses, of misappropriating to himself, his family, and his friends the best *encomiendas* in Nicaragua. When he was relieved of office, his sons and supporters faced the reduction or loss of their pueblos, along with diminished social and political influence. Emboldened by sulking *encomenderos* and malcontents from Peru, the brothers rebelled with some three hundred followers, a majority of the residents in Nicaragua.

In León, Hernando and others murdered Bishop Antonio de Valdivieso, a persistent critic of Rodrigo, after which other rebels proceeded to destroy livestock and crops, as well as surplus sailing vessels. They aimed to capture the silver fleet from Peru, commanded by the formidable Pedro de la Gasca, and take control of the city of Panama. Thereafter they planned to establish rule in Peru under Hernando Contreras, the "prince of liberty," spuriously claiming that kingdom because initial Spanish expeditions to the general region had sailed under the aegis of Ávila and that, accordingly, certain proprietary rights accrued to his grandsons.

Because of overconfidence, poor planning, and inept leadership, the uprising failed. Reared in luxury and enjoying the favor of the colonists, the leaders were inexperienced; Hernando, though a licentiate, was only twenty-one, and Pedro nineteen. They understood strategy very poorly, making the mistake of dividing their forces into small groups. After a clumsy attack on Panama City, the residents there fought back with unexpected skill and resolution. In disarray, the hapless rebels fled for their lives. Pedro was lost at sea, and Hernando drowned in a river. His head was displayed as a warning to would-be traitors.

See also **Ávila, Pedro Arias de.**

BIBLIOGRAPHY

The most complete study of the Contreras family is Marqués De Lozoya (Juan De Contreras), *Vida del segoviano Rodrigo de Contreras, gobernador de Nicaragua (1534–1544)* (1920), although the author, a descendant of Rodrigo, is biased in his presentation. In English, see Hubert Howe Bancroft, *History of Central America,* vol. 2 (1883). See also Antonio De Remesal, *Historia general de las Indias Occidentales y particular de la gobernación de Chiapa y Guatemala,* 2 vols. (1966), first published in 1619. Another publication of interest is Teodoro Hampe-martínez, *Don Pedro de la Gasca (1493–1567): Su obra política en España y América* (1990).

Additional Bibliography

Chamorro, Pedro Joaquín. *Limites de Nicaragua: Su formación histórico geográfica durante la conquista y el período colonial, 1502–1821.* Managua, Nicaragua: Fondo Editorial, CIRA, 2000.

Coronel Urtecho, José. *Reflexiones sobre la historia de Nicaragua: De la colonia a la independencia.* Managua, Nicaragua: Fundación Vida, 2001.

Mena García, María de Carmen. *Temas de historia panameña.* Panamá: Editorial Universitaria, 1996.

Montiell Argüello, Alejandro. *Nicaragua colonial.* Managua, Nicaragua: Banco Central de Nicaragua, 2000.

WILLIAM L. SHERMAN

CONVENTILLO. *Conventillo* refers to an urban tenement in Argentina established during the nineteenth century as thousands began to emigrate from Europe—particularly Spain and Italy. Home to sometimes as many as three to four hundred people during the peak years of immigration to Argentina, these residential structures derived either from subdivided elite family homes or were quickly constructed rental properties located on vacant, side, or back lots.

Conventillos generally had few windows and only a single street entrance that opened onto a patio interior that accessed several small rooms (usually 12 by 12 feet with ceilings somewhere between 9 to 14 feet high). Landlords provided only the most rudimentary access to electricity, heat, furniture, and waste removal. Residents found space for cooking, bathing, and toilet facilities significantly limited. Many single male renters slept in shifts over a twenty-four-hour period while women often worked from home as they did laundry, sewing, cigar rolling, and other piecework while also fulfilling child-care duties.

Around the turn of the twentieth century, the environment of the *conventillos* gave rise to an especially intimate working-class social culture. Residents constantly had to negotiate with neighbors. Familiarity also fostered cooperation and political solidarity as residents, on occasion, organized for better living conditions and reduced rents. Evidence of this can be seen in 1907 when residents in approximately 2,000 *conventillos* (out of a total of nearly 120,000) took part in a citywide rent strike. Similarly, the rough-and-tumble working-class culture of Buenos Aires, including early tango music, can be closely associated with the *conventillos*.

See also **Cities and Urbanization.**

BIBLIOGRAPHY

Moya, José C. *Strangers and Cousins: Spanish Immigrants in Buenos Aires, 1850–1930*. Berkeley and Los Angeles: University of California Press, 1998.

Scobie, James. *Argentina: A City and a Nation*. Oxford: Oxford University Press, 1971.

Scobie, James. *Buenos Aires: Plaza to Suburb, 1870–1910*. Oxford: Oxford University Press, 1974.

ANDREW G. WOOD

COOKE, JOHN WILLIAM (1920–1968). John William Cooke (*b.* 14 November 1920; *d.* 19 September 1968), principal Argentine theoretician of revolutionary Peronism, or *justicialismo*. Cooke was elected to Argentina's Congress in 1946 as a member of the Radical Party. He quickly gravitated to the charismatic Juan Domingo Perón, whom he supported in the pages of *De Frente,* a publication that to many Peronists became the political and moral conscience of the movement. With Perón's ouster in September 1955, Cooke developed a plan of resistance that had as its focus guerrilla warfare followed by general insurrection. Arrested in October 1955, he clandestinely directed from prison the Peronist resistance against both military and civilian governments. A dramatic escape in 1957 was followed in 1959 by exile in Cuba, where he arranged for the training of Argentine guerrillas.

By 1962 Cooke, still in Cuba, and Perón, in exile in Spain, had moved to different political positions and adopted different strategies. Cooke remained on the violent extreme left of the Peronist movement and felt that Perón had become little more than a symbolic memory. Perón considered Cooke "too Cuban" and unrepresentative of *justicialismo,* Perón's political and social philosophy. Cooke returned to Argentina in the mid-1960s, where he died of cancer.

See also **Argentina: The Twentieth Century; Argentina, Political Parties: Justicialist Party; Argentina, Political Parties: Radical Party (UCR); Frondizi, Arturo.**

BIBLIOGRAPHY

Daniel James, "The Peronist Left, 1955–1975," in *Journal of Latin American Studies* 8, no. 2 (1976):273–296.

Richard Gillespie, *John William Cooke: El peronismo alternativo* (1989).

Donald C. Hodges, *Argentina's "Dirty War": An Intellectual Biography* (1991), pp. 73–4, 78–9.

Additional Bibliography

Duhalde, Eduardo L., compiler. *John William Cooke: Obras completas.* Buenos Aires: Colihue, 2007.

Goldar, Ernesto, ed. *John William Cooke y el peronismo revolucionario.* Buenos Aires: Centro Editor de América Latina, 1985.

PAUL GOODWIN

COPACABANA FORT, REVOLT OF.

Revolt of Copacabana Fort (1922). Cannon fire shook Brazil's capital during the early morning of 5 July 1922, initiating a rebellion that became the epicenter of a series of military insurrections known as the *tenente* (lieutenant) revolts. Mutinies orchestrated by army coconspirators quickly ensued in other Carioca (Rio de Janeiro) garrisons, but legalist officers were forewarned and easily crushed these subsequent uprisings. Organized primarily by junior officers, the revolt included common soldiers, noncommissioned officers, cadets, and a handful of civilians. Incensed by the civilian government's corruption and the arrest of former president and army spokesman Marshal Hermes Da Fonseca, the junior officers acted to depose President Epitácio Pessoa.

The rebels of Copacabana Fort learned of the revolt's failure outside their battlements but refused to surrender, despite heavy bombardment. On 6 July the acting commander, Lieutenant Antônio de Siqueira Campos, allowed all soldiers not prepared to fight to the death to leave the fort. The eighteen troops and officers who remained sallied forth with shreds of the fort's Brazilian flag in their breast pockets. Eleven of them confronted loyalist forces in a suicidal gun battle on the beachfront Avenida Atlântica. This audacious act captured popular attention, providing martyrs and inspiration for succeeding *tenente* revolts.

See also **Tenentismo.**

BIBLIOGRAPHY

For a narrative account of the revolt, consult Glauco Carneiro, *História das revoluções brasileiras*, 2d ed. (1989). Another analysis of this insurrection can be found in José Augusto Drummond, *O movimento tenentista* (1986). Sources in English deal with this initial *tenente* revolt only in passing. A standard reference that focuses on the subsequent uprisings is Neill Macaulay, *The Prestes Column: A Revolution in Brazil* (1980).

Additional Bibliography

Borges, Vavy Pachecho. "Tenentes, tenetismo: tenetismo versus oligarquia: reflexões para uma revisão historiográfica." *Anais do museo Paulista* 34 (1985): 105–143.

Fausto, Boris. *A Concise History of Brazil.* Cambridge, U.K.: Cambridge University Press, 1999.

Levine, Robert M. *The History of Brazil.* New York: Palgrave Macmillan, 2003.

Sena, Davis Ribeiro de. *As revoltas tenentistas que abalaram o Brasil: 1922, 1924, 1925/7.* Brasília: s.n., 2004.

PETER M. BEATTIE

COPÁN.

Copán, a major pre-Hispanic Maya center on the western border of Honduras near Guatemala. It marks the eastern boundary of Maya territory and undoubtedly controlled trade between the Maya area and Central America during its time of major activity, the Late Classic Period. The earliest and latest dated monuments show 9.1.0.0.0 (455 CE) on stela 20 and 9.18.10.0.0 (790 CE) on altar 61. The site has been known since reported by Don Diego García de Palacios in 1576.

The site center consists of a large open plaza to the north, bounded by modest structures, in which stand numerous ornately carved stone stelae of the rulers of Copán. Many have burial caches beneath. In the southeast corner of the plaza are an elegant ball court and a hieroglyphic stairway with the longest known carved Maya inscription (1,500–2,000 glyphs), with details of Copán's long dynastic history. The southern half of the site center consists of a large elevated (120-foot) platform, the Acropolis, with multiple construction phases and numerous elite ceremonial buildings. The Copán River eroded a portion of the east side of the Acropolis, exposing an archaeological cross-section noted for its size (900 feet long by 120 feet high). (The river was rechanneled to protect the site.) From the northeast, a *sacbe* (causeway) leads to an area of elite residences with richly carved, full-figure hieroglyphic inscriptions. Recent studies show that wide areas of the Copán valley surrounding the site center were occupied. The site has several astronomical alignments and carved evidence of a new Maya method for finding the length of a lunar month.

The carved dynastic monuments, in concert with the stelae of nearby Quirigua, record the capture of Copán's ruler, 18 Rabbit, in 737 CE. Though two additional rulers are recorded, Copán's peak had passed and major activity ended abruptly after 800 CE. The site shows its own emblem glyph on monuments, and also mentions Tikal, Palenque, and Calakmul.

See also **Maya, The.**

BIBLIOGRAPHY

See Sylvanus G. Morley and George W. Brainerd, *The Ancient Maya*, 4th ed. (1983), pp. 320–328; Proyecto Arqueológico Copán (Instituto Hondureño de Antropología e Historia), *Introducción a la arqueología de Copán, Honduras,* 3 vols. and detailed maps (1983).

Additional Bibliography

Agurcia Fasquelle, Ricardo. *Secretos de dos ciudades mayas: Copán y Tikal.* San José: La Nación, 1994.

Andrews, E. Wyllys, and William Leonard Fash, eds. *Copán: The History of an Ancient Maya Kingdom.* Santa Fe: School of American Research: Oxford: James Currey, 2005.

Baudez, Claude F. *Maya Sculpture of Copán: The Iconography.* Norman: University of Oklahoma Press, 1994.

Becerra, Longino. *Copán, tierra de hombres, mujeres y dioses.* Nueva versión.Tegucigalpa: Baktun Editorial, 2001.

Bell, Ellen E., Marcello A. Canuto, and Robert J. Sharer. *Understanding Early Classic Copan.* Philadelphia: University of Pennsylvania Museum of Archaeology And Anthropology, 2004.

Martin, Simon, and Nikolai Grube. *Chronicle of the Maya Kings and Queens: Deciphering the Dynasties of the Ancient Maya.* New York: Thames and Hudson, 2000.

Newsome, Elizabeth A. *Trees of Paradise and Pillars of the World: The Serial Sela Cycle of "18-Rabbit-God K," King of Copan.* Austin: University of Texas Press, 2001.

Newsome, Elizabeth A., and Heather S. Orr. *The "Bundle" Altars of Copán: A New Perspective on their Meaning and Archaeological Contexts.* Bernardsville, Washington, DC: Center for Ancient American Studies, 2003.

Webster, David L. *The Fall of the Ancient Maya: Solving the Mystery of the Maya Collapse.* New York: Thames & Hudson, 2002.

Willey, Gordon R. *Ceramics and Artifacts from Excavations in the Copan Residential Zone.* Cambridge, MA: Peabody Museum of Archaeology and Ethnology, Harvard University, 1994.

WALTER R. T. WITSCHEY

COPARTICIPACIÓN.

Coparticipación (Coparticipation), the doctrine under which the government administration in Uruguay was shared by the two traditional political parties, the Blancos and the Colorados. During the nineteenth century and until 1904, this system took the form of a territorial division, with departments under the control of one party or the other. Later, under the 1919 Constitution, Coparticipation was redefined as the share of the national government by the two parties, with the president sharing his power with a national bipartisan council. Between 1952–1966 the two parties formed the National Council of Government and with democratization (at the end of the 1980s) the two parties formed several coalitional governments. Notwithstanding, with the emergence of the left movement Frente Amplio (Broad Front) in 1971 the whole system began slowly to crack. In 2004 the Frente Amplio won the national elections for the first time.

See also **Uruguay, Political Parties: Blanco Party; Uruguay, Political Parties: Broad Front; Uruguay, Political Parties: Colorado Party.**

BIBLIOGRAPHY

Göran G. Lindahl, *Uruguay's New Path: A Study in Politics During the First Colegiado, 1919–1933* (1962).

Additional Bibliography

Caetano, Gerardo. *Marco histórico y cambio político en dos décadas de democracia: De la transición democrática al gobierno de la izquierda (1985–2005) en 20 años de democracia: Uruguay 1985–2005.* Montevideo, Uruguay: Santillana, 2005.

HENRY FINCH
VICENTE PALERMO

COPPER INDUSTRY.

Early Andean copper mining was prompted by the need to develop symbolic objects that served political power, the display of social status, and communication of religious belief. Gold-plated and alloyed copper objects were common in the pre-Inca Chavín culture of about 1000 BCE. Electrochemical replacement and depletion silvering and gilding on copper surfaces were devised in pre-Columbian times to give a precious-metal appearance. The first known Andean example of copper-silver alloy is a Peruvian bead from the Lurin valley site of Malposo. Tumbaga, a gold-copper alloy, was first produced in the central Andes, but later became common to many parts of pre-Columbian South America and as far north as Mexico. In 1494, Columbus reportedly initiated gold mining with a copper by-product in the Dominican Republic. The Spanish conquistadores valued copper for use in armaments.

The first European copper mine in Latin America opened in 1522 at Taxco, Mexico. Mexico produced a total of 8,000 tons of copper by 1890, averaged about 65,000 tons annually by 1905, and more than 200,000 tons per year by the early 1970s. The most important Mexican deposits are located at Cananea and Nacozari (La Caridad) in Sonora and, formerly, at El Boleo in Baja California.

The nineteenth century was a time of political turmoil in Chile, and copper mining became increasingly important. The War of the Pacific, involving Chile, Bolivia, and Peru (1879–1883) resulted in the incorporation of the copper-rich Regions I and II into northern Chile. Copper mining expanded in Chile following the introduction of the first reverberatory furnace in 1842, which permitted smelting of copper sulfide minerals. Chile was the foremost world producer until 1882, when the United States took the lead. A new era for Chilean copper evolved in the early 1900s through U.S. investment and mining technology. Using the U.S.-developed froth flotation for concentration of copper ores and large-scale open-pit mining methods, low-grade Chilean copper porphyries could be exploited.

The Chilean Cordillera possesses several major copper porphyry deposits at Chuquicamata, El Salvador, Potrerillos, Rio Blanco, El Teniente, and La Escondida and La Candelaria. Chile's largest, the Chuquicamata Mine (600,000 tons per year), began large-scale production in 1912. La Escondida Mine (300,000 tons per year) started production in late 1990. The mostly U.S.-owned large Chilean copper mines were nationalized on July 16, 1971. The government-owned copper company, Corporación Nacional del Cobre de Chile (CODELCO-Chile), is the largest copper mining and refining company in the world. In the early twenty-first century, Chile is the world's largest copper producer, having regained that position in 1982, when it surpassed the United States. Chile's annual copper production was more than 1.6 million tons of copper. In 2004 Chile's copper production increased to more than 4 million tons per year.

Peruvian production is about 400,000 tons of copper per year, but Peru's copper industry did not grow significantly until after the War of the Pacific, aided by the completion of the central railway, and between 1940 and 1960, by the significant exploration and mining development efforts of U.S.-owned companies. Though significant reserves are known in the Carajas District of Brazil, mines of the Rio Grande do Sul area have been the most important and currently produce about 46,000 tons of copper per year. Copper also has been mined in Argentina, Bolivia, Colombia, Cuba, Ecuador, Guatemala, Haiti, Honduras, Nicaragua, Panama, and Venezuela, but although some countries have undeveloped resources, the amount mined has been small. Between 1800 and 1926, the copper mines in the Bolivian province of Pacajes near the Chilean border had an annual production of about 20,000 tons of copper per year. Argentina, Bolivia, Honduras, and Ecuador currently produce less than 600 tons per year of copper each. Cuba has produced copper from the Pinar del Río Province near Matahambre since the end of the nineteenth century. Copper has been mined near Caracas, Venezuela, and from deposits near the port of Cabello in the state of Yaracuy since the early sixteenth century. Copper mining in Haiti began in 1728, and with development of the Meme copper deposit in the late 1950s, continued through 1971.

In 2004 the countries of Latin America contributed 44 percent of the world copper mine production. Chile produced approximately 35 percent of world copper production, Peru 6 percent, and Mexico 3 percent, according to the U.S. Geological Survey. These countries also had a substantial percentage of the world copper ore reserve base. Chile had approximately 38 percent, Peru 6 percent, and Mexico 4 percent. Like many other commodities, prices have gone up considerably for copper because of the industrialization of China and overall growth in the world economy. Chile in particular has benefited from this high demand.

See also **Mining: Colonial Spanish America; Mining: Modern.**

BIBLIOGRAPHY

Benavides, Alberto Q. "Exploration and Mining Ventures in Peru." *Economic Geology* 7 (November 1990): 1296–1302.

Brundenius, Claes. *Technological Change and the Environmental Imperative: Challenges to the Copper Industry.* Cheltenham, U.K.; Northampton, MA: Edward Elgar, 2003.

Finn, Janet L. *Tracing the Veins: Of Copper, Culture, and Community from Butte to Chuquicamata.* Berkeley: University of California Press, 1998.

Klubock, Thomas Miller. *Contested Communities: Class, Gender, and Politics in Chile's El Teniente Copper Mine, 1904–1951.* Durham, NC: Duke University Press, 1998.

Lechtman, Heather. "Pre-Columbian Surface Metallurgy." *Scientific American* 250, no. 6 (June 1984): 56–63.

Méndez Beltrán, Luz María. *La exportación minera en Chile, 1800–1840: Un estudio de historia económica y social en la transición de la Colonia a la República.* Santiago de Chile: Editorial Universitaria, 2004.

Parsons, A. B. *The Porphyry Coppers.* New York: AIME, 1933. See pp. 320–354

Reyna, Jenaro González. *Riqueza minera y yacimientos minerales de México.* Mexico D. F., 1947. See pp. 173–183.

U.S. Bureau of Mines. "Copper." In *Minerals Yearbook,* vol. I, 1900–1989 issues.

JANICE L. W. JOLLY

CORCOVADO.

Part of the Gavea-Tijuca Massif, Corcovado (the "Hunchback") stands near the entrance to Guanabara Bay in Rio De Janeiro (see illustration). During the nineteenth century, Corcovado was the site of early coffee plantations and a refuge for runaway slaves, who lived in *quilombos* (huts) on its slopes. A cog railway, built in 1884 by engineer Pereira Passos, afforded easy access to the peak, which had long been a tourist attraction. Guglielmo Marconi designed an electrical system to light the mountain, which began operating in 1912, further enhancing the area's appeal.

The mountain is best known for the 98-foot concrete and soapstone statue of Christ the Redeemer, which stands at its peak. The statue, planned and directed by Brazilian engineer H. Silva Costa, was completed in 1931. It was designed by French sculptor Paul Landowski and funded by contributions from the people of Rio.

See also **Slavery: Brazil.**

BIBLIOGRAPHY

Bruce Weber "On High," in *New York Times Magazine,* 22 July 1990, p. 46.

Additional Bibliography

Delfino, Jean-Paul. *Corcovado.* Paris: Métailié, 2005.

de Semenovich, Jorge Scévola. *Corcovado, a conquista da montanha de Deus: A história da Estrada de Ferro e do Monumento ao Cristo Redentor.* Rio de Janeiro, Brazil: Editora Lutécia, 1997.

Winter, Agnés P., de Souza Hue, Jorge, and Horta, Luís Paulo. *Cor quo vado.* Rio de Janeiro, Brazil: Casa da Palabra, 2003.

SHEILA L. HOOKER

CORDEL, LITERATURE OF THE.

Literature of the Cordel. Originally presented in oral form in the tradition of epic and other popular literature in the world, these ballads, primarily of northeastern Brazil, were eventually printed as *folhetos* (pamphlets or little books) and sold dangling from a *cordel* (string). The cover, usually in pastel colors, has a photograph or print not always related to the text. The reader, often illiterate, may recognize a familiar tale and be persuaded to buy according to its cover design. A picture of the author and some information are often found on the back cover. Contemporary storytellers, frequently well-known writers, continue to develop the tradition. Read now rather than recited, and without musical accompaniment (both hands are needed to turn pages), the ballads usually consist of high dramatic dialogue as befits the customary content.

The traditional *cordel* is a collection of folktales in verse (usually *sextilhas,* six lines of seven syllables each, rhymed *a b c b d b*) on a wide variety of subjects that express the strict morality of the extended community of the Northeast. To name but a few, there are *cordel* versions of news events; the lives and exploits of famous bandits, cowboys, saints, and other historical personages; as well as of Romeo and Juliet, Sleeping Beauty, and numerous other European, Asian, and African figures. Fabled animals, such as mysterious bulls, are part of the vast body of *cordel* material.

A carefully balanced trial between good and evil, in which the former always clearly wins, is a constant theme in the *cordel.* Most of the personages are either saints or sinners. The protagonist generally undergoes a test of character which he or she may fail, but usually passes. In narratives of actual or would-be incest, for example, the besieged daughter ascends into heaven at the end, while the father who has assailed or tempted his child descends into hell. In a formula usually resembling a court trial comprising an opposition between honor and dishonor, an initial pact is tested, after which there is a response and a counter-response, followed by a judgment and a final confirmation of the pact.

The stories are offered to the people as models of how daily life should be lived ideally. The traditional pattern is both a literary convention and a means of reasserting a code of ethics. Their authors do not merely protest or chide the dominant class from the point of view and in the language of the proletariat, however, but express politicized and ideological struggles in terms that may not always be literary.

See also **Literature: Brazil.**

BIBLIOGRAPHY

Candace Slater, *Stories on a String: Brazilian Literatura de Cordel* (1982).

Additional Bibliography

Abreu, Márcia. *Histórias de cordéis e folhetos.* Campinas, SP, Brasil: Mercado de Letras, 1999.

Curran, Mark J. *História do Brasil em cordel.* São Paulo, SP, Brasil: Edusp, 1998.

RICHARD A. MAZZARA

CORDERO, JUAN (1822–1884).

Juan Cordero (*b*. 10 June 1822; *d*. 28 May 1884), Mexican painter. After having attended the Academia de San Carlos during what was probably its most difficult period, Cordero went in 1844 to Rome, where he came into contact with the Nazarenes (a group of German artists who sought to revitalize Christian art) and executed religious and historical canvases as well as portraits. On his return to Mexico in 1853, Cordero was disappointed at not being named director of painting at the Academia de San Carlos, a post then occupied by Pelegrín Clavé. Nevertheless, he produced numerous fine portraits and received important commissions. Contrasts in lighting characterize a good number of his works, and a realistic bent informs even his most idealized portraits. Cordero painted the vaults and dome of the Church of Santa Teresa and the dome of the Church of San Fernando. An allegorical mural for the Escuela Nacional Preparatoria, known only through a copy, has been considered an antecedent of twentieth-century muralism by nationalist historians.

See also **Art: The Nineteenth Century.**

BIBLIOGRAPHY

Elisa García Barragán, *El pintor Juan Cordero* (1984).

CLARA BARGELLINI

CORDERO, ROQUE (1917–).

Roque Cordero (*b*. 16 August 1917), Panamanian composer and pedagogue. Born in Panama City, Cordero studied composition at Hamline University in St. Paul, Minnesota, and orchestral conducting at Tanglewood. Among his teachers were Ernst Krenek, Leon Barzin, and Dimitri Mitropoulos. He was the director of the National Institute of Music in Panama from 1953 until 1964 and artistic director and conductor of the National Orchestra of Panama from 1964 to 1966. He then became professor of composition at the Latin American Music Center at Indiana University. Cordero's compositional style evolved from a guarded nationalistic approach near the beginning of his career to an atonal language with twelve-tone procedures. His own version of a serially organized atonal language became his most prevalent compositional technique from 1950 on. It is applied to pitch classes and intervals but also determines the evolution of his complex rhythmic structures and the overall form of the piece. In 1976 he received the First Inter-American Composition Prize in Costa Rica. Cordero has been music adviser to Peer International Corporation in New York City and has been invited to judge many international composition competitions. He has been a professor of music at Illinois State University since 1972. As of 2007, he was a distinguished professor emeritus.

His more nationalistic works include *Capricho interiorano* (1939), *Sonatina rítmica* (1943), *Obertura Panameña* (1944), and *Rapsodia campesina* (1953). Those early works show Cordero expressing himself through elaborations of typical Panamanian dance rhythms, such as the *mejorana* and the *tamborillo*. His first twelve-tone composition is his 1946 Sonatina for violin and piano. Other important works are the Symphony no. 2 (1956); String Quartet no. 1 (1960); *Mensaja fúnebre* for clarinet and string orchestra (1961), written in memory of

Dimitri Mitropoulos; Violin Concerto (1962), written in a virtuoso style and full of intricate rhythms; Soliloquies for alto sax; Sonata for cello and piano (1963); Symphony no. 3 (1965), a work with one theme and five variations, commissioned by the Third Music Festival in Caracas, Venezuela; *Sonata breve* for piano (1966); *Circumvolutions and Mobiles* for fifty-seven instruments (1967); String Quartets no. 2 and no. 3 (1968, 1973); Cantata (1974); *Permutaciones* (1974); *Variations and Theme for Five* (1975); and *Paz, Paix, Peace* for chamber ensemble (1970).

See also **Music: Art Music.**

BIBLIOGRAPHY

Béhague, Gérard. *Music in Latin America: An Introduction* (1979); *New Grove Dictionary of Music and Musicians* (1980).

Béhague, Gérard. *Octavo festival internacional de música contemporánea* (1992), pp. 47–48, 122.

Congdon, Kristin G., and Kara Kelley Hallmark. *Artists from Latin American Cultures: A Biographical Dictionary.* Westport, CT: Greenwood Press, 2002.

Filós Goch, Priscilla. *El piano en las obras de Roque Cordero.* Panamá: Compañía de Seguros Chagres, 1985.

Vinton, John, ed. *Dictionary of Contemporary Music* (1974).

ALCIDES LANZA

CORDERO CRESPO, LUIS (1833–1912).

Luis Cordero Crespo (*b.* 6 April 1833; *d.* 30 January 1912), president of Ecuador (1892–1895). Born into a prominent family of Azuay, Luis Cordero Crespo studied law at the University of Quito but chose to devote himself to letters and politics rather than jurisprudence. As a man of letters he was most noted for his *Poesías serias* (1895), *Poesías jocosas* (1895), and a Spanish-Quechua dictionary. He founded several newspapers, was a professor of literature at the National College in Cuenca, and helped to inaugurate the universities of Guayaquil and Cuenca. He served as rector of the University of Cuenca from 1911 to 1912.

In 1883, Cordero helped found the Republican Party. After serving in Congress as a deputy and then as a senator, he was elected president in 1892. He attempted unsuccessfully to conciliate warring Liberals and Conservatives. His declaration that church interests were superior to those of the state turned Liberals against him. Revelation of his government's secret involvement in the sale of a Chilean warship to Japan aroused public indignation and forced Cordero to resign. The fall of the government brought the Liberal general Eloy Alfaro to power, thus ending twelve years of civilian rule.

See also **Ecuador: Since 1830.**

BIBLIOGRAPHY

Remigio Crespo Toral, *Luis Cordero* (1917).

Luis Robalino Dávila, *Diez años de civilismo* (1968), pp. 437–701.

Frank Macdonald Spindler, *Nineteenth-Century Ecuador: An Historical Introduction* (1987), pp. 137–147.

Additional Bibliography

Ayala Mora, Enrique. *Historia de la revolución liberal ecuatoriana.* Quito: Corporación Editora Nacional, 1994.

MARK J. VAN AKEN

CÓRDOBA.

THE PROVINCE

The central province of Argentina, Córdoba encompasses 65,161 square miles and has a population of 3,066,801 (2001). Located between the Río Dulce in the north and the Río Quinto in the south, the province of Córdoba stretches across three physiographic units: the eastern pampa, the Sierra de Córdoba, and the interior pampa. Its center is occupied by the Sierra de Córdoba, a crystalline-metamorphic massif rising to a maximum height of 9,817 feet in the Cerro Champaquí. Among the minerals extracted from this sierra and adjacent ranges are manganese, beryl, bismuth, and wolfram. Air purity and cooler temperatures have converted many mountain villages (especially in the Punilla Valley) into spa resorts, frequented by Córdobans and residents of the pampa during the hot summers. In the humid pampa plains east of the sierra, the dominant activity is raising cattle for either meat or dairy production. However, owing to the relatively ample water supply from the Sierra de Córdoba, large areas along the eastern slope and the pampa have specialized in the production of wheat (the main agricultural commodity of the province), rye, maize, flax, peanuts, millet, and alfalfa. Recently, the land dedicated to soybean production has increased to the same degree that the land producing wheat has decreased. Of lesser agricultural significance is the segment of the pampa between the western slope of the sierra and the foothills of the Andes. Excessive aridity and lack of water have created a semidesert landscape; the salt flats of Salinas Grandes and Pampa de Salinas are the most significant examples.

THE CITY

The city of Córdoba (2001 population 1,272,334) was founded on 6 July 1573 by Jerónimo Luis de Cabrera, governor of Tucumán, in order to facilitate the transit between Alto Perú and Santa María del Buen Aire (now Buenos Aires) on the Río De La Plata estuary. The city lies on the banks of the Río Primero, at the eastern slopes of the Sierra de Córdoba. By 1584 forty landholders with trusted Indians settled in the peaceful town to practice agriculture and cattle ranching, and in 1599 the Jesuits opened a mission there. In 1623 Bishop Fernando de Trejo y Sanabria founded the University of Córdoba on the site of what had been a Jesuit academy (1613), and several administrative services were established in the growing town as agricultural activities developed and wealth accumulated. Soon Córdoba competed with Tucumán as a major trading center in the Río de la Plata hinterland: In 1622 an inland custom was instituted to stop the smuggling of European merchandise from the estuary into the interior.

When it was declared the seat of the Intendancy of Córdoba in 1783, with jurisdiction over the provinces of Córdoba, La Rioja, Mendoza, San Juan, and San Luis, the city of Córdoba gained in prestige as one of the most prosperous, cultured, aristocratic, and Spain-oriented settlements in the Río de la Plata region. In the seventeenth and eighteenth centuries, religious orders flocked to the city. The numerous churches, such as the cathedral and the Church of the Compañía de Jesús, are testimony to their presence and influence. At the time independence was declared by the Buenos Aires junta on 25 May 1810, the authorities of Córdoba voted to remain faithful to the king of Spain. A split from and rivalry with Buenos Aires ensued, and Córdoba became one of the most stubborn supporters of the autonomy of the Platine provinces. Rulers of Buenos Aires, such as Bernardino Rivadavia, Juan Manuel de Rosas, Manuel Dorrego, Juan Galo Lavalle, Juan Quiroga, and Manuel López, tried to subdue the rebellious interior province, which in the process was torn apart by internal strife. It was not until 1868 that Governor Félix de la Peña was able to establish order and harmony in the province.

In 1870 a railway line was opened between Córdoba and the capital city of Buenos Aires, accelerating the integration of the region into the national mainstream and promoting active colonization of the interior Pampa. Yet occasional outbursts of dissension continued to perpetuate the traditional enmity between Córdoba and Buenos Aires: in 1880 conservative and Catholic sectors of Córdoba strongly opposed the laicist laws discussed in the congress of Buenos Aires, and throughout republican times the city's elites were at odds with the political leaders of Buenos Aires over accepting foreigners without a patriarchal family background. In the 1950s Juan Perón was resisted not only because of his attacks against the Catholic hierarchy but also because of his plebeian origin, and in 1955 the army uprising that overthrew Perón was started by General Eduardo Leonardi in the artillery barracks of Córdoba. Similarly, Cristina Fernández de Kirchner, a member of the Peronist Party and Argentina's first woman president, did not win in this city.

Nonconformism and rebelliousness have not been the hallmark exclusively of the conservative circles of Córdobans. In 1969 workers and students from that city initiated the Cordobazo, a massive rebellion that brought an end to the rule of General Juan C. Onganía. During subsequent military governments, *montonero* guerrillas effectively attacked military and government targets in the city of Córdoba, keeping military rulers at bay.

The metropolitan perimeter of Córdoba stretches over a gentle slope between 1,320 and 1,650 feet. Originally the settlement spread out from the left bank of the Río Primero. Later, it expanded along the river into the General Paz and San Vicente boroughs. Early in the twentieth century the city grew toward the western slope, where today most military garrisons are established. After World War II the most accelerated development took place along the highway leading to Buenos Aires and Rosario. Along this artery are located most of the industrial establishments of the city: automobile factories, chemical and fertilizer plants, factories of electromechanical equipment, and food-processing plants.

Since colonial times, Córdoba has benefited from good communications with neighboring and distant regions. Railway lines of the General Belgrano and Bartolomé Mitre systems connect the city with Rosario and Buenos Aires to the southeast; with Tucumán, La Rioja, and San Juan to the north and west across the Sierra de Córdoba; and with Mendoza to the southwest, after connecting with the General San Martín railway at Mercedes. Airport Coronel Olmedo secures communications with the nation's capital and with major cities in western Argentina.

The main cultural center is the University of Córdoba, supported by the Catholic University of Córdoba, and the National Technological University. The city and province are centers for Argentine space research. An observatory was established at the University of Córdoba in 1869, and researchers there produced the first star atlas of the Southern Hemisphere, in the early 1900s. Teofilo Tabanera Space Center, devoted to space investigation, is located in the province. In addition to being an important educational and economic center, Córdoba is the birthplace of a popular musical genre known as the *cuarteto*.

See also **Argentina, Geography; Córdoba, University of; Jesuits; Onganía, Juan Carlos; Perón, Juan Domingo.**

BIBLIOGRAPHY

Alfredo Terzaga, *Geografía de Córdoba* (Córdoba, 1963).

Efraín Bischoff, *Historia de la provincia de Córdoba* (Buenos Aires, 1968).

Raúl J. Arias, *Córdoba: Cuatro siglos* (Buenos Aires, 1973).

María C. Vera, *Córdoba: Una historia para los argentinos* (Buenos Aires, 1989.)

Additional Bibliography

Arcondo, Aníbal B. *En el reino de Ceres: La expansión agraria en Córdoba, 1870–1914.* Córdoba, Argentina: Universidad Nacional de Córdoba, 1996.

Boixadós, María Cristina. *Las tramas de una ciudad, Córdoba entre 1870 y 1895: Elite urbanizadora, infraestructura, poblamiento.* Córdoba, Argentina: Ferreyra Editor, 2000.

Bravo, Fernán. *Los viajes de don Jerónimo Luis de Cabrera: La fundación de Córdoba y la formación del talante ciudadano.* Córdoba, Argentina: Editorial Espartaco Córdoba, 2006.

Brennan, James P. *The Labor Wars in Córdoba, 1955–1976: Ideology, Work, and Labor Politics in an Argentine Industrial City.* Cambridge, MA: Harvard University Press, 1994.

Cena, Juan Carlos. *El cordobazo: Una rebelión popular.* Buenos Aires: La Rosa Blindada, 2000.

Florine, Jane L. *Cuarteto Music and Dancing from Argentina: In Search of the Tunga-Tunga in Córdoba.* Gainesville: University Press of Florida, 2001.

Mayo, Carlos A., and O. Alborés. *La Historia agraria del interior: Haciendas jesuíticas de Córdoba y el Noroeste.* Buenos Aires: Centro Editor de América Latina, 1994.

Parra Garzón, Gabriela. *El Cabildo de Córdoba del Tucumán a través de sus documentos (1573–1600): Estudio diplomático.* Córdoba, Argentina: Centro de Estudios Historicos Prof. Carlos S. A. Segreti, 2005.

Segreti, Carlos S. A. *Córdoba, ciudad y provincia, siglos XVI–XX: Según relatos de viajeros y otros testimonios.* 2nd ed. Córdoba, Argentina: Centro de Estudios Históricos, 1998.

CÉSAR N. CAVIEDES

CÓRDOBA, FERNÁNDEZ/HERNÁNDEZ DE. *See* **Fernández (Hernández) de Córdoba, Francisco.**

CÓRDOBA, JOSÉ MARÍA (1799–1829).

José María Córdoba (also Córdova; *b.* 8 September 1799; *d.* 17 October 1829), Colombian military hero. Born in La Concepción, Antioquia, the son of the alcalde, Córdoba joined the patriots in 1814. His valor brought him a captaincy in 1817; he was named lieutenant colonel in 1819 and, after the battle of Boyacá (7 August 1819), commandant of Antioquia (1819–1820). He proceeded to eliminate royalist remnants from Chocó and the northern Cauca and Magdalena basins (1820–1821), and was promoted to colonel. He joined General Antonio José de Sucre Alcalá in Ecuador, distinguished himself at Pichincha (24 May 1822), and became a general (3 January 1823). In Peru, Córdoba went on to win further laurels. He led the Colombian infantry's decisive charge at Ayacucho (9 December 1824), the apex of his career.

Although Córdoba had killed one of his sergeants at Popayán on 28 December 1823, and had threatened the lives of two other subordinates in 1824, he was acquitted by a court-martial for murder and threats to murder (1827). Then he became engaged to Fanny Henderson, daughter of James Henderson, the British consul general in Bogotá. Although Córdoba was Bolívar's minister of war (1828), the two men became estranged over Bolívar's flirtation with monarchy. Falsely accused of disloyalty by Tomás Cipriano de Mosquera, he rebelled against the government and attempted to raise Antioquia. Wounded and a prisoner, with his little force routed, he was cut down at El Santuario by Colonel Rupert Hand.

See also **Wars of Independence: South America.**

BIBLIOGRAPHY

Pilar Moreno De Ángel, *José María Córdova* (1977); and "Córdoba, José María," in *Historical Dictionary of the Spanish Empire, 1492–1975,* edited by James S. Olson.

Additional Bibliography

Earle, Rebecca. *Spain and the Independence of Colombia 1810–1825.* Exeter: University of Exeter Press, 2000.

J. León Helguera

CÓRDOBA, TREATY OF (1821).

Treaty of Córdoba (1821), an agreement that recognized Mexico's independent sovereignty and arranged for the withdrawal of remaining Spanish forces. Arriving at Veracruz in 1821 after most of Mexico had fallen to Agustín de Iturbide's Army of the Three Guarantees, Captain-General Juan O'Donojú, a liberal and Mason who had served as Spanish minister of war under the Constitution of 1812, entered negotiations with Iturbide at Córdoba rather than unnecessarily prolong the revolutionary war. Recognizing that the Plan of Iguala sought to maintain the Bourbon dynasty and strong links between Spain and Mexico, O'Donojú signed the Treaty of Córdoba on 24 August 1821. The sixteen articles of the treaty followed the spirit of the Plan of Iguala. For most Mexicans, the fact that the Spanish government later repudiated the treaty was irrelevant. After assisting with the

transition of power, O'Donojú died in Mexico City of a disease contracted during his stay at Veracruz.

See also **Iturbide, Agustín de; O'Donojú, Juan; Plan of Iguala; Three Guarantees, Army of the.**

BIBLIOGRAPHY

Jaime Delgado, *España y México en el siglo XIX,* 3 vols. (1950).

William Spence Robertson, *Iturbide of Mexico* (1968).

Timothy E. Anna, *The Mexican Empire of Iturbide* (1990).

Christon I. Archer

CÓRDOBA, UNIVERSITY OF.

University of Córdoba, Argentina's oldest university, established in 1613 by the Jesuits, and the center of the city's civic and cultural life from colonial times to well into the twentieth century. The university remained under the control of the Jesuits until their expulsion from the Spanish colonies in 1767, at which point it came under the direction of the Franciscans. In 1858, the national government of Justo José Urquiza officially assumed control of its administration. But almost two and a half centuries of church control of education, as well as isolation from the secularizing influences to be found in Buenos Aires, imbued the city with a strong Catholic ethos, and the church retained a preponderant influence in the university, with the clergy continuing to hold the majority of faculty and administrative positions well into the twentieth century.

From early in its history, the city's aristocratic families developed a close relationship to the university and the title of "doctor" was considered the highest social distinction. Throughout the nineteenth and early twentieth centuries, the university was a bastion of traditionalism, with a curriculum heavily weighted in favor of a scholastic education in law and theology. Because of its hidebound conservatism and social influence, it became the target of an important reform movement in 1918. In the wake of the Radical Party's 1916 electoral victory, middle-class students organized boycotts and an eventual occupation of the university, demanding a series of reforms, most notably university autonomy, student participation in the election and administration of university councils, modernization of the curriculum, and the competitive selection and periodic review of all professors. To coordinate the reform campaign, students established the Federación Universitaria de Córdoba (FUC), an organization that would dominate student university politics for the next half century.

International influences such as the Mexican and Russian revolutions fired the young minds of the student reformers and radicalized the movement, bringing support from both the Socialist Party and the labor movement and leading to demands for free university education and the establishment of university extension courses for the working class. University issues again found common cause with social unrest in the 1969 uprising known as the Cordobazo. International influences included the Cuban Revolution and the events in Paris of May 1968. The alliance of the university with the trade unions led to an even more explosive social protest, highlighting once again that the university was a central part of public life in Córdoba.

During the dictatorship of 1976 to 1983, the military government slashed funding for the university. It also censored social science classes and scholarship on subjects such as historical materialism and psychoanalysis. To silence critics, the government also "disappeared" many professors and students. In reaction numerous faculty members left the country. When the military government fell in 1983 and an elected government returned, the UC once again followed the democratic principles of 1918 reform. Tension and activism still exist. Students and teaching staff went on strike in 2005 to protest low wages and reached limited agreements with the government to improve compensation.

See also **Argentina, University Reform; Universities: The Modern Era.**

BIBLIOGRAPHY

Bischoff, Efrain U. *Historia de Córdoba* (1979).

Buchbinder, Pablo. *Historia de las universidades argentinas.* Buenos Aires: Sudamericana, 2005.

Ferrero, Roberto A. *Historia crítica del movimiento estudiantil de Córdoba.* Córdoba, Argentina: Alción Editora, 1999, 2005.

Flachs, Vera de, María Cristina, and Remedios Ferrero Micó. *Finanzas y poder político en las universidades hispanoamericanas: El caso de Córdoba 1613–1854.* Córdoba, Argentina: Ediciones del Copista, 1996.

Walter, Richard J. *Student Politics in Argentina: The University Reform and Its Effects, 1918–1964* (1968).

JAMES P. BRENNAN

CORDOBAZO, EL. El Cordobazo, a social protest in the Argentine industrial city of Córdoba that took place 29–30 May 1969. The city's militant trade union movement found common cause with student protesters and the general citizenry in an uprising directed against the dictatorship of Juan Carlos Onganía and the provincial government. The independent structures and combative practices of the Peronist unions, together with a radicalized local political culture, permitted a broad alliance in the uprising and an exceptionally violent protest in which symbols of both the government and imperialism were attacked. Fourteen persons were killed. The Cordobazo was the seminal political event of the 1960s, fatally weakening the Onganía dictatorship and serving as a powerful symbol for the Peronist and Marxist left in the following years.

See also **Aramburu, Pedro Eugenio; Argentina: The Twentieth Century; Córdoba; Krieger Vasena, Adalberto; Onganía, Juan Carlos.**

BIBLIOGRAPHY

James P. Brennan, *The Labor Wars in Córdoba, 1955–1976: Ideology, Work, and Labor Politics in an Argentine Industrial City* (1994).

James P. Brennan and Mónica B. Gordillo, "Working Class Protest, Popular Revolt, and Urban Insurrection in Argentina: The 1969 Cordobazo," in *Journal of Social History* 27, no. 3 (Spring 1994): 477–498.

JAMES P. BRENNAN

CÓRDOVA, ARTURO DE (1908–1973). Arturo de Córdova (b. 8 May 1908; d. 1973), Mexican film actor. Born Arturo García Rodriguez in Mérida, Yucatán, Córdova studied in Argentina. Upon his return to Mexico in 1930, he worked in radio. He made his cinematic debut in Hollywood with a small part in the film *For*

Whom the Bell Tolls. In Mexico, his first acting part was in *Celos* (1936). By the 1940s, he had become one of the most sought-out and popular leading men of the golden age of the Mexican cinema. He starred in over 300 films in Mexico, Hollywood, Brazil, Spain, and Venezuela, and received three Ariels from the Mexican film academy for best performance by an actor for the films *En la palma de tu mano* (1950), *Las tres perfectas casadas* (1952), and *Feliz año amor mío* (1955).

See also **Cinema: From the Silent Film to 1990.**

BIBLIOGRAPHY

Luis Reyes De La Maza, *El cine sonoro en México* (1973).

E. Bradford Burns, *Latin American Cinema: Film and History* (1975).

Carl J. Mora, *Mexican Cinema: Reflections of a Society: 1896–1980* (1982).

John King, *Magical Reels: A History of Cinema in Latin America* (1990).

Additional Bibliography

Sánchez, Francisco. *Luz en la oscuridad: Crónica del cine mexicano, 1896–2002.* México: CONACULTA: Cineteca Nacional, 2002.

DAVID MACIEL

CÓRDOVA, JORGE (1822–1861).

Jorge Córdova (*b.* 1822; *d.* 23 October 1861), president of Bolivia (1855–1857). Córdova's parents remain unknown. He joined the army of Andrés de Santa Cruz as an ordinary soldier and rose rapidly in rank. Córdova's marriage to the daughter of President Manuel Isidoro Belzú facilitated his entrance into politics.

Córdova succeeded his father-in-law as president. The transferal of power from Belzú to Córdova was the first peaceful one in Bolivia's history. Although Córdova was elected, he was overthrown by a military revolt and escaped to Peru. He returned to Bolivia several years later as a private citizen and died violently in the Massacre de Yáñez, which marred the presidency of José María Achá.

Córdova had a reputation as a man of pleasure. As president he was fair and unpretentious and desperately tried to foster internal peace, tolerance, and cooperation among the political factions. These activities consumed so much of his time that little of substance was accomplished during his tenure.

See also **Bolivia: Since 1825.**

BIBLIOGRAPHY

Moisés Ascarrunz, *De siglo a siglo: Hombres célebres de Bolivia* (1920).

Alcides Arguedas, *La plebe en acción,* in *Obras Completas,* vol. 2 (1959).

Additional Bibliography

Peralta Ruiz, Victory, and Marta Irurozqui. *Por la concordia, la fusión y el unitarismo: Estado y caudillismo en Bolivia, 1825–1880.* Madrid: Consejo Superior de Investigaciones Científicas, 2000.

CHARLES W. ARNADE

CÓRDOVA RIVERA, GONZALO S. (1863–1928).

Gonzalo S. Córdova Rivera (*b.* 15 July 1863; *d.* 13 April 1928), president of Ecuador. Born in Cuenca, Córdova Rivera completed a law degree at the Universidad de Cuenca. He served as deputy from Cañar Province from 1892 to 1897 and as governor of that province from 1898 to 1902. He was minister of the interior from 1903 to 1906. In 1912 he served as senator from Carchi Province and as vice president of the senate. He was Ecuador's minister to Chile, Argentina, and the United States in the period 1911–1913, and minister to Venezuela in 1922. He was popularly elected to the presidency in 1924. On July 9, 1925, a group of young lieutenants overthrew the Córdova government.

See also **Ecuador, Revolutions: Revolution of 1925.**

BIBLIOGRAPHY

Linda Alexander Rodríguez, *The Search for Public Policy: Regional Politics and Government Finances in Ecuador, 1830–1940* (1985), esp. pp. 51–52, 123–129.

Additional Bibliography

Muñoz Borrero, Eduardo. *En el palacio de Cardondelet: Del presidente Flores al presidente Noboa Bejarano 1830-2002.* Quito: Francisco Andrade Ortiz, F.S.C., 2002.

LINDA ALEXANDER RODRÍGUEZ

CORNEJO, MARIANO H. (1873–1942).

Mariano H. Cornejo (*b.* 1873; *d.* 25 March 1942), one of a group of positivist social scientists in late-nineteenth-century Peru. In 1896 he was appointed to the first chair of sociology at the National University of San Marcos. Cornejo relied upon precepts and convictions learned from European thinkers and adapted them to the society around him. He expressed optimism that an open-ended Peruvian aristocracy that admitted "new blood," together with the nation's scientists, could discover the sociological laws necessary to carry out the task of national progress. He scorned revolutionary change, favoring universal education and gradualism as the keys to national improvement. He denied that either race or class antagonisms governed history and foresaw utilitarian cooperation as a more useful framework of analysis.

See also **Positivism.**

BIBLIOGRAPHY

Fredrick B. Pike, *The Modern History of Peru* (1967), pp. 162–164.

Thomas M. Davies, Jr., *Indian Integration in Peru, 1900–1948* (1974).

Additional Bibliography

Mc Evoy, Carmen. *La utopía republicana: Ideales y realidades en la formación de la cultura política peruana, 1871–1919.* Lima, Perú: Pontificia Universidad Católica del Perú, Fondo Editorial, 1997.

VINCENT PELOSO

CORN ISLANDS.

Corn Islands, two small islands about 40 miles off of the east coast of Nicaragua, near the coastal town of Bluefields. Little Corn and Great Corn islands became increasingly important tourist destinations in the late twentieth century. Their historical significance, however, derives from their location rather than their beaches. As part of its attempts to construct a canal linking the Atlantic and Pacific oceans, the United States sought and gained the right to fortify these islands to protect the approach to a potential canal across Nicaragua. The concession was part of a much broader struggle between Britain and the United States for control of potential canal routes as well as political and economic dominance throughout the Caribbean Basin in the late nineteenth and early twentieth centuries. The islands also were considered as a possible resort by the dictator of Nicaragua, Anastasio Somoza, who invited U.S. millionaire Howard Hughes to Nicaragua to discuss plans for the islands in 1972.

See also **Bluefields; Somoza Debayle, Anastasio.**

BIBLIOGRAPHY

Additional Bibliography

Riverstone, Gerald. *Living in the Land of Our Ancestors: Rama Indian and Creole Territory in Caribbean Nicaragua.* Managua, Nicaragua: ASDI, 2004.

Romero Vargas, Germán. *Las sociedades del Atlántico de Nicaragua en los siglos XVII y XVIII.* Managua: Fondo de Promoción Cultural-Banic, 1995.

TODD LITTLE-SIEBOLD

CORONA, RAMÓN (1837–1889).

Ramón Corona (*b.* 1837; *d.* 11 November 1889), Liberal military commander and governor of Jalisco. Born to a family of modest social position in the southern Jaliscan village of Tuxcueca, Corona was the administrator of some mining operations near the Sinaloa–Tepic border when the Reform war began in 1858. Over the next decade, he emerged as the leader of the migrants driven from Tepic who sought to restore white and mestizo dominance over that territory and its Indians, whom Manuel Lozada had united and allied with the imperialist cause. Rising to command the Tepic Brigade, and then the Army of the West during the Intervention (1862–1867), Corona became the dominant military and political figure in west-central Mexico in the postwar years. His career culminated in his defeat of Lozada in 1873. After serving as ambassador to Spain and Portugal for twelve years, Corona returned as the elected governor of Jalisco in March 1887. An activist who promoted infrastructure and education, he acquired a growing national reputation and became a leading presidential candidate. Corona was assassinated in Guadalajara.

See also **Mexico: 1810–1910.**

BIBLIOGRAPHY

Daniel Cosío Villegas, *Historia moderna de México: La República restaurada—la vida política* (1955) and

Historia moderna de México: El Porfiriato—la vida política interior, 2 vols. (1970).

Stuart F. Voss, *On the Periphery of Nineteenth Century Mexico: Sonora and Sinaloa, 1810–1877* (1982).

Additional Bibliography

García, Clara Guadalupe. *El general Corona*. Zapopan, Jalisco: Colegio de Jalisco, 1998.

Peregrina, Angélica. *Ramón Corona y la educación pública*. Guadalajara: Programa de Estudios Jaliscienses, Secretaría de Educación y Cultura, 1990.

STUART VOSS

CORONADO, JUAN VÁZQUEZ DE

(1523–1565). Juan Vázquez de Coronado (*b.* 1523; *d.* October 1565), conquistador and governor of Costa Rica (1562–1565). Founder of the Costa Rican city of Cartago (1564), Coronado headed a series of expeditions that brought most of Costa Rica under Spanish control by 1565.

Born in Salamanca, Spain, of noble parents, Coronado left Spain in 1540 to seek his fortune. He traveled to Mexico, joining his uncle, conquistador Francisco Vázquez de Coronado. In 1548, Juan Vázquez de Coronado departed for Guatemala with a *cedula real* (royal letters patent) recommending him to the *audiencia*. Upon his arrival he was named *alcalde mayor* (royal governor) of El Salvador and Honduras. In subsequent years Coronado distinguished himself as a capable administrator and an adept conquistador. He was made *alcalde mayor* of Nicaragua in 1561. One of his first acts in this post was to subvert a rebellion of Spanish soldiers led by Lope de Aguirre.

In 1562, King Philip II designated him *alcalde mayor* of the provinces of Nueva Cartago and Costa Rica. Coronado began an extended campaign, tending to administrative problems in the cities of León, Nicoya, and Garcimuñoz, and pursuing the rebel cacique (local ruler) Garabito. In interactions with caciques, he proved to be a skillful negotiator and was far more moderate in his treatment of the Indians than were many of his contemporaries.

Coronado journeyed to Quepo and through the Guarco Valley in 1563, encountering strong Indian resistance in the town of Cuoto. A prolonged and bloody battle there ended in a Spanish victory. Coronado remained in the valley briefly, negotiating a peace with neighboring caciques and founding the city of Cartago, which became the capital of Costa Rica. After overseeing the provisioning and settlement of the city, he headed north, taking possession of the valley of Guaymi and the provinces of Texbi and Duy. He discovered gold in the Estrella River and in 1564 organized a registry of mines to facilitate the exploitation of the river's wealth.

In 1565, Coronado traveled to Spain to give Philip II a personal account of his progress. The Spanish monarch named him *adelantado* (governor) in perpetuity of the province of Costa Rica. In addition, Coronado received an annual salary, royal recognition of Cartago, and a three-year appointment as governor of Nicaragua. He was never to enjoy these privileges, however; on the return voyage, his ship, the *San Josepe*, was wrecked in a storm, leaving no survivors.

See also **Conquistadores; Costa Rica.**

BIBLIOGRAPHY

Academia De Geografía E Historia De Costa Rica, *Juan Vázquez de Coronado: Cartas de relación sobre la conquista de Costa Rica* (1964).

Carlos Meléndez Chaverri, *Juan Vázquez de Coronado: Conquistador y fundador de Costa Rica* (1966).

Victoria Urbano, *Juan Vázquez de Coronado y su ética en la conquista de Costa Rica* (1968); *Revista del Archivo Nacional de Costa Rica* 33, nos. 1–12 (January–December 1969): 13–17, 45–64.

Ricardo Fernández Guardia, *El descubrimiento y la Conquista* (1975), pp. 107–127.

Additional Bibliography

Bray, Warwick. *The Meeting of Two Worlds: Europe and the Americas, 1492–1650*. Oxford: Published for the British Academy by Oxford University Press, 1993.

Molina Montes de Oca, Carlos. *Garcimuñoz: La ciudad que nunca murió: Los primeros cien días de Costa Rica*. San José: Editorial Universidad Estatal a Distancia, 1993.

SARA FLEMING

CORONEL, CORONELISMO.

Coronel is a rural political boss during the predominantly agrarian phase of Brazilian history (c. 1870–1940);

coronelismo is the phenomenon of local and regional political rule by one or more *coronéis*.

A coronel was a member of the local economic and social elite, generally a landowner, merchant, lawyer, or even a priest, who rose to political prominence in his region because of his status in society. The title of coronel, or colonel, a military rank, was frequently associated with Brazil's National Guard (1834–1917). Prominent citizens took part in guard activities and held military rank. The use of military titles became pervasive in rural Brazil, where the elite seldom had formal higher education. Many influential political coronels never held official rank in the guard, however.

By using his economic and social resources, the coronel controlled a large dependent population, whose well-being was his concern. In return, the common folk obeyed their coronel. The First Republic (1889–1930) observed the rituals of the electoral process, however fraudulent and manipulated, and coronéis came to play the role of vote producers for state and national politicians, exchanging votes for favors.

By the 1910s, intricate alliances of coronéis and state and national politicians emerged. Influential coronéis were able to bring in public works—frequently roads, dams, and even railroads—which opened up backward agricultural enclaves to urban and export centers. Attentive national and state politicians made sure that key coronéis got what they wanted. The coronéis in turn appointed all local and state officials in their towns and exacted absolute loyalty from them. Many important coronéis never held public office.

This system of personal parallel governance especially thrived in the north, northeast, and far west, the country's agrarian bastion and backwaters. In the center-south, coronéis were often loyal members of regional parties. After 1930 *coronelismo* as an informal form of government for rural Brazil began to wane as the country experienced intensive urbanization, industrialization, and political centralization.

See also **Caudillismo, Caudillo; Patronage.**

BIBLIOGRAPHY

Corrêa, Valmir Batista. *Coronéis e bandidos em Mato Grosso, 1889–1943.* Campo Grande, Brazil: Editora UFMS, 1995.

Leal Nunes, Victor. *Coronelismo: The Municipality and Representative Government in Brazil,* translated by June Henfrey (1977).

Pang, Eul-Soo. *Bahia in the First Brazilian Republic: Coronelismo and Oligarchies, 1889–1934* (1979).

Pereira De Queiroz, Maria Isaura. *O mandonismo local na vida política brasileira e outros ensaios* (1976).

Walker, Thomas W., and Agnaldo de Sousa Barbosa. *Dos coronéis à metrópole: Fios e tramas da sociedade e da política em Ribeirão Preto no século XX.* Ribeirão Preto, Sao Paulo, Brazil: Palavra Mágica, 2000.

EUL-SOO PANG

CORONEL, PEDRO (1923–1985).

Pedro Coronel (*b.* 25 May 1923; *d.* 23 May 1985), Mexican painter and sculptor. Born in Jerez, Zacatecas, Coronel left in 1940 for Mexico City, where he studied at the National School of Painting and Sculpture (La Esmeralda) until 1945. He taught sculpture there in 1945–1946. In 1946, Coronel traveled to Europe. While living in Paris he studied painting in the studio of Victor Brauner and sculpture with Constantin Brancusi. In later years he was a friend of Sonia Delaunay, the Ukrainian-born painter and designer who was married to Robert Delaunay. Throughout his life Coronel traveled extensively in Mexico, Europe, Africa, and Asia, assembling collections of artifacts from these countries. Coronel returned to Mexico in 1952 and in 1954 had his first important exhibition in the Proteo Gallery, Mexico City, which was very well received and reviewed. From that point on he exhibited regularly in Mexico, the United States, and Europe, most notably in Mexico City at the Gallery of Mexican Art.

Coronel's mature work draws heavily upon the tenets of abstraction while incorporating figural imagery derived from ancient artifacts of Mexico, Europe, Africa, and Asia. His works on canvas are heavily textured and aggressively colored. Sculptures are executed in marble, onyx, and bronze. In 1959, Coronel received the National Prize of Painting; in 1984, he was awarded the National Prize of Plastic Arts.

See also **Art: The Twentieth Century.**

BIBLIOGRAPHY

Justino Fernández, *Pedro Coronel: Pintor y escultor* (1971), and *Exhibition of Paintings by Pedro Coronel: Lunar Poetics* (1972).

Sergio Pitol et al., *El universo del Pedro Coronel* (1981).

Erika Billeter, ed., *Images of Mexico* (1988).

Additional Bibliography

Torres Arroyo, Ana María. *Pedro Coronel: Variación en el color y la forma.* Mexico: Círculo de Arte, 2003.

CLAYTON KIRKING

CORONEL, RAFAEL (1931–). Rafael Coronel is a Mexican painter and collector of masks, puppets and other artwork, much of which is on display at the Rafael Coronel Museum in his native city of Zacatecas. The son-in-law of renowned Mexican muralist Diego Rivera, Coronel has shown at the Museum of Modern Art in New York, the Royal Museum of Art and History in Brussels, and the Museum of Modern Art in Mexico City. He is known for portraits with subtle colors and somewhat foggy appearances. Coronel's older brother Pedro (1923–1985) was also an accomplished artist. A museum in Pedro Coronel's name, also in Zacatecas, boasts a fine collection of pre-Columbian art as well as paintings by Picasso, Dalí, and others.

See also **Coronel, Pedro; Rivera, Diego.**

BIBLIOGRAPHY

Coronel. Rafael, *Rafael Coronel: Cincuenta años de pintura, 1949–1999.* Mexico City: Instituto de Seguridad y Servicios Sociales de los Trabajadores del Estado, 1999.

PATRICK BARR-MELEJ

CORONEL URTECHO, JOSÉ (1906–1994). José Coronel Urtecho (*b.* 28 February 1906; *d.* March 1994), except for Rubén Darío considered to be Nicaragua's most important writer. Born in Granada and educated at the Colegio Centroamérica, Coronel Urtecho studied for several years in the United States before returning to Nicaragua in 1925, bringing back a passionate interest in the "new American poetry" of Ezra Pound and others. With Luís Alberto Cabrales in 1931 he founded the *vanguardia* movement, which included Pablo Antonio Cuadra, Luís Downing, Joaquín Pasos, and others, most of them disaffected from their conservative upper-class Granada families. Taking as a motto "Beside our ancestors we go against our fathers," the iconoclastic *vanguardistas* reacted against Darío's imitators, bourgeois culture, the academy, and U.S. intervention in Nicaraguan political affairs. They proclaimed support for the patriotism of Augusto César Sandino and fomented a rediscovery of *"lo nicaragüense"* (that which is Nicaraguan). The best work of the *vanguardistas* revitalized interest in the indigenous roots of national culture, introduced vigorous new North American and European literature (much of which they translated into Spanish) into Nicaragua, and produced an influential body of innovative writing in a variety of genres. Unfortunately, their paradoxical fascination with the elitist and antidemocratic ideals of emerging European fascism led them into a naive attempt to put their ideas into practice by supporting and taking part in the embryonic Somoza dictatorship.

Coronel Urtecho's own writing has embraced many genres: short stories and short novels, poetry, essays, translations, literary criticism, political commentary, and history. Loath to write books, he left the task of collecting his widely dispersed writings mostly to others. Major collections are *Rápido tránsito (al ritmo de norteamérica)* (1953), an account of his North American sojourn; *Pól-la d'anánta katánta paránta: Imitaciones y traducciones* (1970), a collection of his poetry edited by Nicaraguan poet Ernesto Gutiérrez; *Prosa* (1972), edited by Carlos Martínez Rivas; and *Prosa reunida* (1985), which includes portions of his influential *Panorama y antología de la poesía norteamericana* (1949). A major historical work is *Reflexiones sobre la historia de Nicaragua* (3 vols., 1962–1967). Both Coronel Urtecho's writings and his politics have evolved continuously. In *Mea máxima culpa* (1975), he publicly regretted having served in the Somoza regime, as subsecretary of external relations, from the 1930s into the 1950s. In the 1970s, he moved into sympathy with the emerging Sandinista movement, writing *exteriorista* poetry in the manner of Ernesto Cardenal. His *Conversación con Carlos* (1986) praises FSLN (Sandinista National Liberation Front) founder Carlos Fonseca Amador. In 2001, his book on Nicaraguan history, *Reflexiones sobre la historia de Nicaragua: De la*

Colonia a la Independencia, was republished. He died in March 1994 on his farm in southern Nicaragua.

See also **Nicaragua.**

BIBLIOGRAPHY

An excellent biographical source is Manlio Tirado, *Conversando con José Coronel Urtecho* (1983).

Additional Bibliography

Salgado, Maria A., ed. *Modern Spanish American Poets.* Second Series. Detroit, MI: Gale, 2004.

Tünnermann Bernheim, Carlos. *Valores de la cultura nicaraguense.* 2nd ed. San José: Educa, 1998.

DAVID E. WHISNANT

Delmar Leon Beene, *Sonora in the Age of Ramón Corral, 1875–1900* (1972).

Stuart F. Voss, *On the Periphery of Nineteenth-Century Mexico: Sonora and Sinaloa, 1810–1877* (1982).

Manuel R. Uruchurtu, *Apuntes biográficos de don Ramón Corral 1854–1900* (1984).

Additional Bibliography

Hernández Silva, Héctor Cuauhtémoc. *Insurgencia y autonomía: Historia de los pueblos yaquis, 1821–1910.* México, D.F.: CIESAS: Instituto Nacional Indigenista, 1996.

Tinker Salas, Miguel. *In the Shadow of the Eagles: Sonora and the Transformation of the Border during the Porfiriato.* Berkeley: University of California Press, 1997.

RODERIC AI CAMP

CORRAL VERDUGO, RAMÓN (1854–1912).

Ramón Corral Verdugo (*b.* 10 January 1854; *d.* 10 November 1912), Mexican politician and vice president (1904–1911). Influential figure in Sonoran state politics and a fixture of the Porfirio Díaz administration from 1900 to 1911, he was a prototypical political-financial leader of the Porfiriato.

Corral was born in the mining town of Álamos, Sonora, on the Hacienda de Las Mendes, where his father operated a small store in the Palmarejo mines and later became mayor of Chinipas. Sharing his father's interest in politics, Corral wrote for opposition newspapers in an attempt to oust a succession of governors. In 1876 he joined the political faction of Luis E. Torres, serving as vice-governor, then governor (1895–1899) of Sonora. Although Corral was responsible for many public works in Sonora, thousands of Yaqui Indians were killed or deported to Yucatán during his administration. In 1900 he served in cabinet-level posts, beginning with governor of the Federal District (1900–1903), and in the key agency of secretary of government (1903–1911) while simultaneously holding office as vice president. Corral had many financial investments in Sonora. He died in exile in Paris.

See also **Porfiriato.**

BIBLIOGRAPHY

Jesús Luna, *The Public Career of Don Ramón Corral* (1979).

CORREA, JUAN (c. 1645–1716).

Juan Correa (*b.* ca. 1645; *d.* 3 November 1716), Mexican painter. An almost exact contemporary of Cristóbal de Villalpando, Correa is more sober and conservative but equally productive and uneven. His works are found throughout Mexico and even in Europe. His first known painting is *Saint Rose of Lima* (1671). Notable are the two great canvases for the sacristy of the cathedral of Mexico City (1689–1691) and many devotional images. The catalog of his work lists nearly 400 paintings. A mulatto, Correa had a large and successful workshop and numerous followers, many of them relatives. The extensive and detailed knowledge of this workshop gained through recent studies sheds much light on the practice of painting in colonial Mexico.

See also **Art: The Colonial Era.**

BIBLIOGRAPHY

Elisa Vargas Lugo et al., *Juan Correa, su vida y su obra* (1985).

Additional Bibliography

Velázquez Gutiérrez, María Elisa. *Juan Correa: Mulato libre, maestro de pintor.* México, D.F.: Círculo de Arte, 1998.

CLARA BARGELLINI

CORREA, JULIO MYZKOWSKY (1890–1953).

Julio Myzkowsky Correa (*b.* 1890; *d.* 14 July 1953), Paraguayan dramatist, poet, and short-story writer. Son of a Brazilian who fought against Paraguay in the War of the Triple Alliance and grandson of a Polish immigrant who fought for Paraguay in the same war, Correa was raised in the Guaraní-speaking countryside. He became known as the creator of the Guaraní theater as it is known today. At the time of the Chaco War, he began to write down his plays, and to perform them with the help of his actress wife. He also did the staging, costuming, and training of the actors. Although Correa did not have a formal education in the theater and his works are crude and lacking in technique, his powerful characterizations of national types and his ability to dramatize the political feelings of his countrymen in Guaraní guaranteed his success. A prevalent theme in his works is the injustice of the *latifundia* and the deprivation of land and opportunity for the Paraguayan peasant. His bold and poignant satire landed him in jail more than once. He also defended the poor Guaraní-speaking peasant in his poetry and short stories.

See also **Guaraní (language).**

BIBLIOGRAPHY

Julio Correa, *ñame mba' era' ín. sainete en tres actos* (1964), and *Sombrero Ka'a y cuentos* (1969).

Hugo Rodríguez-Alcalá, *Historia de la literatura paraguaya* (1971), pp. 113–116.

Additional Bibliography

Delgado, Susy. *25 nombres capitales de la literatura paraguaya*. Asunción: Servilibro, 2005.

CATALINA SEGOVIA- CASE

CORRÊA DE AZEVEDO, LUIZ HEITOR (1905–1992).

Born in Rio de Janeiro in 1905, Luiz Heitor Corrêa de Azevedo began his career as a pianist and composer, but ultimately became one of Brazil's most distinguished musicologists and ethnologists. His research begin in the 1920s, the era of Brazilian modernism: artists began to turn away from Europe, to focus instead on their own nation's richness, vitality, and history, and to search for and define the "authentically Brazilian." Azevedo's interests—which encompassed both folklore and music by classical composers such as Carlos Gomes—was in harmony with this important cultural movement. Using equipment borrowed from the U.S. Library of Congress, he recorded for posterity a trove of endangered songs from the states of Minas Gerais and Ceará and established an archive of rapidly disappearing work.

Azevedo helped to found numerous institutions, including the Associacô Brasileira de Música, the Centro de Pesquisas Folclóricas, and the groundbreaking journal *Revista Brasileira de Música*; he was named the very first professor of folklore at the Instituto Nacional. Azevedo worked briefly in Washington, D.C., as a consultant for the Organization of American States. In 1947 he departed for Paris, where he played a major role in the United Nations Educational, Scientific and Cultural Organization (UNESCO) as a music programmer and taught at the Institut des Hautes Etudes de L'Amérique Latine at the University of Paris. He died in Paris on November 10, 1992.

See also **Andrade, Mário de; Gomes, Antônio Carlos.**

BIBLIOGRAPHY

Béhague, Gerard. "Azevedo, Luiz Heitor Corrêa de." In *The New Grove Dictionary of Music and Musicians*, 2nd ed., vol. 2, edited by Stanley Sadie. London: Grove/Macmillan Publishers, 2001.

Horta, Luiz Paulo. "Lembrando Luiz Heitor." In *Revista Brasiliana* 13 (Janeiro 2003). Available from http://www.abmusica.org.br/brasili13.htm#31.

Magalhaes, Carolina. "Luiz Heitor Correa de Azevedo et les Relations Musicales entre la France et le Bresil" In *Cahiers du Bresil Contemporain* 12 (1990). Available from http://www.revues.msh-paris.fr/vernumpub/12-%20C-%20MAGALHAES.pdf.

Mariz, Vasco. *Três musicólogos brasileiros: Mário de Andrade, Renato Almeida, Luiz Heitor Correa de Azevedo*. Rio de Janeiro: Civilização Brasileira, 1983.

Travassos, Elizabeth. "Brazil's Indigenous Universe (to ca. 1990): The Xavate, Kamayra, and Suya." In *Music in Latin America and the Caribbean: An Encyclopedic History*. Vol. 1, edited by Malena Kuss. Austin: University of Texas Press, 2004.

Works by Azevedo

Dois pequenos estudos de folclore musical [Two short studies of musical folklore], 1938.

Escala, ritmo e melodia na musica dos indios brasileiros [Scale, rhythm and melody in the music of Brazilian Indians], Rio de Janeiro, 1938.

ABCD

"Mario de Andrade e o folklore" [Mario de Andrade and folklore] in *Revista brasileira de musica* IX (1943): 11–14.

A musica brasileira e seus fundamentos [Brazilian music and its foundations]. Washington, DC: Pan American Union, Department of Cultural Affairs, 1948.

Musica e musicos do Brasil [Music and musicians of Brazil]. Rio de Janeiro: Libraria-Editôra da Casa do Estudante do Brasil, 1950.

With Cleofe Person de Matos and Mercedes de Moura Reis. *Bibliografia musical brasileira (1820–1950)* [Brazilian musical bibliography, 1820–1950]. Rio de Janeiro, Ministério da Educação e Saúde—Instituto Nacional do Livro.

"The Present State and Potential of Music Research in Latin America." In *Perspectives in Musicology: The Inaugural Lectures of the Ph.D. Program in Musicology at the City University of New York*, edited by Barry S. Brook, Edward O. D. Downes, and Sherman Van Solkema. New York: Norton, 1972.

Music of Ceara and Minas Gerais. Compact disc (CD) produced by Mickey Hart and Alan Jabbour. Washington, DC: Library of Congress Endangered Music Project, 1997.

KAREN S. BACKSTEIN

CORREGIDOR.

Corregidor, administrator of a territorial unit known as a *corregimiento* in Peru and some other parts of the Spanish Empire. His judicial, administrative, military, and legislative responsibilities were indistinguishable from those of Alcaldes Mayores in New Spain. There were eighty-eight corregidores in Peru in 1633.

The post of corregidor was introduced in the sixteenth century both to provide sustenance for Spaniards and to expand royal authority from the urban centers into the countryside and over the indigenous population. Most corregidores served a single term of five years or less. The crown preferred men with military, or at least militia, backgrounds.

From the stabilization of the position until 1677, most corregidores were named by viceroys or other regional chief executives. The Crown's decision to sell corregidor appointments in 1677 reduced the viceroys' patronage. In addition, the sales, which continued until at least 1750, forced corregidores to increase their pressure on the native populations of their districts in order to recoup their investment and make a profit.

Working closely with wholesale merchants, corregidores routinely required the natives to purchase animals and merchandise from them (*repartimiento de mercancías* or *bienes*) at inflated prices, and in some cases they forced the natives to sell their produce to them at below market prices. These abuses led to repeated local rebellions in the Andes and, in some cases, to the death of the corregidor. The Túpac Amaru II Revolt in Peru (1780–1783) was provoked in part by the exactions of corregidores and one of its objectives was to end the hated *repartimiento de mercancías*.

To correct the abuses of the corregidores and their lieutenants, the Crown replaced them with intendants in most of the empire during the late eighteenth century.

See also **Intendancy System.**

BIBLIOGRAPHY

Fisher, John Robert. *Government and Society in Colonial Peru: The Intendant System, 1784–1814* (1970).

Haring, Clarence H. *The Spanish Empire in America* (1947).

Lohmann Villena, Guillermo. *El Corregidor de indios en el Perú bajo los Austrias.* Lima: Pontificia Universidad Católica del Perú, Fondo Editorial, 2001.

Robins, Nicholas A. *Priest-Indian Conflict in Upper Peru: The Generation of Rebellion, 1750–1780.* Syracuse, NY: Syracuse University Press, 2007.

MARK A. BURKHOLDER

CORREIA, DIOGO ÁLVARES. *See* Caramurú.

CORREOSO, BUENAVENTURA (1831–1911).

A Panamanian military man, educator, and journalist, Correoso was one of the standard bearers of nineteenth-century Panamanian liberalism. From an early age he showed great interest in books and was encouraged to read by his family. He entered the Colombian Army Academy, where he soon demonstrated leadership abilities and gained the favor of such prominent military men as Generals Tomás Herrera, Tomás Cipriano de Mosquera, and Juan José Nieto. In

1856 he headed the investigation of the Watermelon Riot in Panama City, where a dispute between a white American and an Afro-Panamanian watermelon vendor led to a conflict between Americans and Panamanians in which seventeen people died.

Correoso was a populist leader, greatly admired by the lower classes. In 1868, with the support of the lower-class neighborhoods in the capital, he led a successful uprising against the government. He brought many reforms to the Federal State of Panama and enacted what was the first fiscal code in Panama. He was president three times (August 29, 1868, to April 1, 1872; acting from August 29 to October 1, 1868; January 1, 1878, to December 29, 1878). As president Correoso founded numerous schools and the first public library in the country. Correoso's public life also included serving as president of the Colombian Congress, consul general of Colombia in Peru, minister plenipotentiary to the Central American Republics, judge, and deputy to the National Congress.

According to the Panamanian historian Jorge Conte Porras, Correoso was a great orator who was able to attract the lower classes to his side. He knew how and when to interject humor into his speeches and engage his audience. It was owing to him that the Plaza de Santa Ana became the focal point of mass political concentrations well into the mid-twentieth century.

See also **Liberalism; Watermelon Riot (Panama Riot).**

BIBLIOGRAPHY

Castillero Reyes, Ernesto de Jesús. *Historia de Panamá*, 9th ed. Panamá: Editora Renovación, 1986.

Conte Porras, Jorge. *Diccionario biográfico ilustrado de Panamá.* 2nd ed. Panamá: Editorial Diego de Almagro, 1986.

Conte Porras, Jorge. *Panameños ilustres.* Panamá: Instituto Nacional de Cultura, 2004.

JUAN MANUEL PÉREZ

CORRIDO. Corrido, a type of song presented by a traveling storyteller, narrating a lengthy tale of heroic or tragic deeds, noteworthy events, and interesting (often satirical) anecdotes. Although the *corrido* has Spanish antecedents and developed in various Latin American nations, it is most closely associated with northern Mexico and its frontier, where it may have appeared as early as the seventeenth century. During the 1800s it was commonly used as a vehicle for the lampoon of public figures and for the description of technological progress. The revolution against Porfirio Díaz caused an outpouring of *corridos* that recounted battles, endurance of hardship, feats of bravery, and deeds of treachery. Several leaders had personal *corrido* singers, such as Pancho Villa's Samuel Lozano, who continued composing after the war.

The standard song was in 2/4 or 3/4 time, with verses of four lines and four beats to the line over which a musical statement of verse length was repeated. The song's content was stated at the beginning, and a finale somewhat formally bade the listener "good-bye." The record industry required that *corridos* be shortened to fit the length of a 78-rpm disc. Radio and singing stars widely popularized the form, and new songs, such as Victor Cordero's "Juan Charrasqueado" became popular. The widely known "Adelita" is actually a popular song. During the Tlatelolco uprising in 1968, student protests appeared in *corrido* form, and national competitions in the 1970s helped stimulate its revival. *Corridos* such as "Gregorio Cortez" are a vital part of Mexican-American culture. Within the past few decades, however, the *narcocorrido* has become a popular subgenre, often portraying drug traffickers as social bandits.

See also **Music: Popular Music and Dance.**

BIBLIOGRAPHY

See listing under "Mexico" in *New Grove Dictionary of Music* (1980), and record series, "Corrido," released by Arhoolie, with extensive notes.

Additional Bibliography

Valenzuela Arce, José Manuel. *Jefe de Jefes: Corridos y narcocultura en México.* Barcelona: Plaza & Janés Editores, 2002.

Wald, Elijah. *Narcocorrido: A Journey into the Music of Drugs, Guns, and Guerrillas.* New York: Rayo, 2001.

GUY BENSUSAN

CORRIENTES. Corrientes, capital city of the province of the same name in Argentina. With 339,067 inhabitants (2005), it is located on the eastern bank of the Paraná River south of the confluence with the Paraguay River. The settlement was founded by Spanish scouts from Asunción, Juan Torres de Vera y Aragón and Alonso de Vera y Aragón, on 3 April 1588 and was given the name San Juan de Vera de las Siete Corrientes, indicating the number of streams that converge into the Paraná River. The purpose of this outpost was to secure the southern edge of the Paraguayan governance from Indian attacks and facilitate communications between Asunción and Santa María del Buen Aire (now Buenos Aires). The development of the settlement was not easy: not only did the city have to fight off the fierce Guaraní Indians, but it was also a favorite raiding post of Brazilian slave hunters (*bandeirantes*), not to speak of its frictions with the authorities of both Asunción and Buenos Aires. In 1782 Corrientes became an integral part of the Intendancy of Buenos Aires, but during the struggle for independence it was a bone of contention among independents from Uruguay, federalists from Buenos Aires, and annexists from Paraguay. Not until 1852 did Corrientes become a full-fledged Argentine province.

The city of Corrientes is mainly a service hub for the agricultural hinterland, which focuses on the production of beef and the cultivation of cotton, tobacco, rice, and yerba maté. Until recent times Corrientes exported timber products, among them *quebracho* wood, which was shipped on ocean vessels expressly equipped to reach the fluvial port of Corrientes. The city is the center of a cultural region known as *El Litoral* (The Riverfront), famed for its indigenous musical folklore (the *chamamé*), and its inhabitants proudly call themselves *correntinos*. Decay of the traditional agrarian activities in the province led to massive migration downriver to the industrial cities of Rosario and Buenos Aires.

See also **Argentina, Geography.**

BIBLIOGRAPHY

Cristina M. Sonsogni, *La población de la ciudad de Corrientes a mediados del siglo XIX* (Corrientes, 1980).

James R. Scobie, *Secondary Cities of Argentina: The Social History of Corrientes, Salta, and Mendoza, 1850–1910* (1988).

Additional Bibliography

Bolsi, Alfredo S. C.; Foschiatti de dell'Orto, Ana María H. *La población de la ciudad de Corrientes entre 1588 y 1980.* Publication: Buenos Aires: Academia Nacional de Geografía, 1995.

Covalova, Adriana and Adriano Nalda. *La alta burguesía urbana de Corrientes en las primeras décadas del siglo XX: Un exponente, Adriano Nalda.* La Plata: Ediciones Al Margen, 2003.

Salinas, María Laura *Los indios de encomienda en Corrientes y Santa Fe: La visita del oidor Garabito de León (1650-1653).* Resistencia: Instituto de Investigaciones Geohistóricas, Conicet, 1999.

Whigham, Thomas. *The Politics of River Trade: Tradition and Development in the Upper Plata, 1780–1870.* Albuquerque: University of New Mexico Press, 1991.

César N. Caviedes

CORRUPTION. Corruption in the broadest sense involves immoral or illegal activity, but the term frequently refers to political corruption, or the abuse of public office for private gain. Political corruption takes many forms, including the acceptance of bribes in exchange for favors that violate government procedures, the refusal to perform one's governmental duties without an extralegal payment, and the misappropriation of public funds. Corrupt exchanges range from small bribes to larger kickback schemes, in which government officials responsible for assigning public works contracts receive a percentage of the value of the contract from the firm receiving that contract and, at times, to even larger embezzlement efforts.

Political corruption has a long history in Latin America and beyond. When Spanish and Portuguese colonizers established mercantilist restrictions on commerce, some businesspeople bribed colonial officials to avoid punishment for using internal trade routes not authorized by the crown and for trading outside the colonial empire. Both before and after Latin American countries gained independence, propertied citizens sometimes offered bribes in pursuit of favorable government decisions to acquire title to land or to avoid paying taxes. The emergence of electoral politics after independence paved the way for vote-buying as an additional form of corruption; many Latin American political parties gained a reputation for buying votes with public funds.

As public revenues and government activity expanded over the course of the twentieth century, the potential for larger corrupt exchanges also grew.

In Cuba and elsewhere, government officials allegedly used the lottery to funnel public money to themselves, their relatives, and their supporters. Higher levels of taxation on income, sales, and property tempted more citizens to pay bribes if and when they were caught evading taxes. The expansion of public works projects increased the opportunities for kickback schemes involving contracts for public buildings and transportation links; to cite two examples from the 1950s, the elected government of Juscelino Kubitschek in Brazil and the dictatorship of Marcos Pérez Jiménez in Venezuela faced widespread allegations of corruption in the awarding of public contracts. Throughout Latin America, many people spoke of an embedded culture of corruption and of a circle of impunity in which the executive, legislative, and judicial branches often protected one another from prosecution.

Whereas corruption occurs in both authoritarian and democratic settings, democratization from the 1980s through the early twenty-first century began to change the dynamics of political corruption in Latin America. Corruption scandals contributed to the premature end of several chief executives' mandates between 1992 and 2001, including Fernando Collor de Mello in Brazil, Carlos Andrés Pérez in Venezuela, Jamil Mahuad in Ecuador, Alberto Fujimori in Peru, and Fernando de la Rúa in Argentina. Past presidents faced formal corruption investigations during the years 1993 into 2007 in Argentina, Bolivia, Chile, Costa Rica, Ecuador, Guatemala, Haiti, Nicaragua, Panama, Paraguay, Peru, and Venezuela. Contemporary anticorruption efforts include the creation of new government auditing agencies, the expansion of legislative oversight, the growth of investigative journalism, and the rise of nongovernmental watchdog groups such as Citizen Power (Poder Ciudadano) in Argentina, the Civic Alliance (Alianza Cívica) in Mexico, and a regional network of Transparency International chapters. These developments raise the question: Will the twenty-first century witness a decrease in corruption in Latin America?

See also **Narcotráfrico.**

BIBLIOGRAPHY

Johnston, Michael. *Syndromes of Corruption: Wealth, Power, and Democracy.* Cambridge, U.K.; New York: Cambridge University Press, 2005.

Peruzzotti, Enrique, and Catalina Smulovitz, eds. *Controlando la política: Ciudadanos y medios en las nuevas democracias latinoamericanas.* Buenos Aires: Temas, 2002.

Tulchin, Joseph S., and Ralph H. Espach, eds. *Combating Corruption in Latin America.* Washington, DC: Woodrow Wilson Center Press, 2000.

CHARLES H. BLAKE

CORTÁZAR, JULIO (1914–1984). Argentine writer Julio Cortázar, a major figure in twentieth-century Latin American literature, is best known for his masterful short stories and his novel *Rayuela* (1963; *Hopscotch*, 1966).

Cortázar was born to Argentine parents in Belgium on August 26, 1914. In 1918 the family returned to Argentina, and Cortázar's father abandoned them soon thereafter. Cortázar cut short his university studies to support his mother and sister, working as a teacher in the provinces and later as a translator in Buenos Aires. Motivated in part by his disaffection with Peronist politics, in 1951 he left Argentina for France, where he would reside until his death. Cortázar was married twice, to Aurora Bernárdez in 1953 and to Carol Dunlop in 1980.

Politics and polemics were central to Cortázar's later life. The target of frequent criticism from fellow Argentines who accused him of abandoning his homeland, he contended that, paradoxically, his move to Paris helped him recover his Latin American identity. Cortázar's involvement in politics and human rights included his support of the Cuban and Nicaraguan revolutions and his denunciation of the military dictatorship in Argentina. He died in Paris on February 12, 1984.

Cortázar's literary career was launched in 1951 with the publication of *Bestiario* (*Bestiary: Selected Stories*, 1998), his first collection of short stories. Typical of Cortázar's use of the fantastic to express psychological states, the beasts in these stories are manifestations of a repressed realm of censored desire. One of Cortázar's influences was Poe, whose complete prose works he translated. Subsequent story collections include *Las armas secretas* (Secret weapons, 1959) and *Final del juego* (1956; *End of the Game and Other Stories*, 1967). Frequent themes are the double, the writing process, obsession with the mother, frustrated love relationships, and the world of childhood and games. Reflecting Cortázar's personal circumstances, the opposition between Buenos Aires and Paris is often present, along with interstitial spaces such as bridges and passageways. Later stories employ the fantastic to explore political issues. Another side to Cortázar is his sense of whimsy and playfulness, as evidenced in the short pieces of *Historias de cronopios y famas* (1962; *Cronopios and Famas*, 1969).

Rayuela follows the wanderings of Horacio Oliviera, an Argentine intellectual living in Paris. An experimental novel that incorporates linguistic innovation and offers an alternative reading by changing the order of the chapters, *Rayuela* has been considered the quintessential novel of the "Boom" in Latin American literature. Recent criticism, however, points out that "the text is profoundly derisive of its own experimentality" and that Cortázar's "shifting and questioning of the ground on which . . . identity rests align him more closely with . . . post-Boom literary production" (Alonso, 11, 13–14). A creative and imaginative writer who challenged the conventional idea of genre, Cortázar published other innovative novels as well as several volumes of miscellany, poetry, and theater.

See also **Borges, Jorge Luis; Cabrera Infante, Guillermo; Donoso, José; Fuentes, Carlos; García Márquez, Gabriel; Literature: Spanish America; Vargas Llosa, Mario.**

BIBLIOGRAPHY

Alazraki, Jaime. *Hacia Cortázar: Aproximaciones a su obra.* Barcelona: Anthropos, 1994.

Alonso, Carlos J., ed. *Julio Cortázar: New Readings.* New York: Cambridge University Press, 1998.

Boldy, Steven. *The Novels of Julio Cortázar.* New York: Cambridge University Press, 1980.

González Bermejo, Ernesto. *Conversaciones con Cortázar.* México, D. F.: Hermes, 1978.

Schmidt-Cruz, Cynthia. *Mothers, Lovers, and Others: The Short Stories of Julio Cortázar* Albany: State University of New York Press, 2006.

Standish, Peter. *Understanding Julio Cortázar.* Columbia: University of South Carolina Press, 2001.

Yovanovich, Gordana. *Julio Cortázar's Character Mosaic: Reading the Longer Fiction.* Toronto: University of Toronto Press, 1991.

Yurkievich, Saúl. *Julio Cortázar: Mundos y modos.* Madrid: Anaya y Mario Muchnik, 1994.

Works by Cortázar

Bestiario. Buenos Aires: Editorial Sudamericana, 1951. Translated by Alberto Manguel, Paul Blackburn, Gregory and Clementine Rabassa, and Suzanne Jill Levine as *Bestiary: Selected Stories.* London: Harvill Press 1998.

Final del juego. Buenos Aires, Editorial Sudamericana 1956. Translated by Paul Blackburn as *End of the Game and Other Stories.* New York, Pantheon Books, 1967.

Las Armas Secretas [Secret Weapons]. Buenos Aires: Editorial Sudamericana, 1959.

Historias de cronopios y famas. Madrid: Ediciones Alfaguara, 1962. Translated by Paul Blackburn as *Cronopios and Famas.* New York: Pantheon Books, 1969.

Rayuela. Buenos Aires: Editorial Sudamericana, 1963. Translated by Gregory Rabassa as *Hopscotch.* New York: Pantheon Books, 1966.

62: Modelo para armar. Buenos Aires: Editorial Sudamericana, 1968. Translated by Gregory Rabassa as *62: A Model Kit.* New York: Pantheon Books, 1972.

Blow-Up and Other Stories. New York: Collier Books, 1968.

Cuentos completos [Complete Stories]. 2 vols. Madrid: Alfaguara, 1994.

La autopista del sur y otros cuentos [The Southern Highway and Other Stories]. New York: Penguin Books, 1996.

Obras Completas [Complete works]. Barcelona: Galaxia Gutenberg: Círculo de Lectores, 2004–. Titles published to date are *Teatro Novelas I*, 2004; *Novelas II*, 2006; *Cuentos* 2006; *Poesia y Poetica*, 2006; and *Obra Critica* 2007.

CYNTHIA SCHMIDT-CRUZ

CORTÉS, HERNÁN (c. 1484–1547).

Hernán Cortés (Fernando, Hernando; *b.* ca. 1484; *d.* 2 December 1547), conqueror of Mexico. Hernán Cortés was born in Medellín, Spain, in the province of Extremadura. Best known for his conquest of the Aztecs (Mexica) of central Mexico, he is also renowned for his famous *Cartas de relación.* Cortés was often depicted as a psychological and tactical master, but his greatest achievement was neither military nor literary; instead, it lay in his understanding that successful conquest was dependent upon successful colonization.

Cortés studied law at the University of Salamanca. While he probably did not become a *bachiller*, his activities and writings betray legal knowledge, especially of the *siete partidas*, which aided him in the process of conquest.

Seeking wealth and power, Cortés sailed for Hispaniola in 1504. After briefly serving as a notary in Hispaniola, he joined Diego Velázquez in the conquest of Cuba, where he assumed the position of *alcalde* and in about 1515 married Catalina Suárez Marcaida. By 1517, he had acquired both an *encomienda* and several gold mines. Having shown little interest in the early exploratory voyages of Hernández de Córdoba and Juan de Grijalva, he was nevertheless chosen to lead an expedition to find Grijalva in late 1518. By the time Cortés was ready, Grijalva had returned. Cortés, nevertheless, set forth on what became a mission of trade and exploration to the Yucatán in November 1519.

With an army of 508 soldiers, Cortés set out on an expedition that was primarily intended for trade, but he also was instructed to evangelize the Indians and to take possession of any new lands discovered, two tasks he undertook with zeal. He was not instructed to colonize, however. In April 1519 Cortés reached what is now Veracruz, where he learned of a rich and powerful ruler, Motecuhzoma II, who was located inland but who held domain over a vast area extending to the coastal region. The subsequent events of Cortés's conquest of the Aztec king's domain were defined by Cortés's unshakable desire to deliver that empire to the kingdom of Castile.

Cortés also learned that Motecuhzoma and his army had many enemies who might be turned against the Mexica. But to carry out such a project, both to find Motecuhzoma and to make alliances with native groups, would take time and material resources. Expanding upon the orders of Pánfilo de Narváez, an ally of Velázquez, Cortés established a town with a *cabildo* (Villa Rica de la Vera Cruz) and placed the town directly under the king's authority.

Now in open rebellion against Velázquez, Cortés and his army destroyed their own ships to cut their means of connection to Cuba. Meanwhile, envoys carrying gold and examples of elaborate Mexica featherwork had been dispatched to Spain, seeking royal sanction of Cortés's actions. Velázquez sent a representative to Spain to brand Cortés a traitor and organized an army to move against him. By August 1519, Cortés and most of his army had set forth, moving west to find Motecuhzoma and the capital of his empire, the island city Tenochtitlán. By September, Cortés had reached Tlaxcala. He may have heard that the Tlaxcalans were longtime enemies of the Mexica and thus been motivated to find and make allies of them. It took fierce fighting to subdue the Tlaxcalans, but by late September, Cortés had formed a critical alliance with Tlaxcala. After next pacifying Cholula, Cortés was ready to march into the heart of the Valley of Mexico. Having negotiated with emissaries of Motecuhzoma several times during the march west, Cortés could not be persuaded against entering the heart of Mexica territory, and Cortés and Motecuhzoma met in early November.

While we can never know precisely what occurred during the first meetings of the representatives of these two very different societies, the ultimate outcome was the imprisonment of Motecuhzoma by the Spaniards. Cortés decisively beat back the forces of Pánfilo de Narváez sent by Velázquez and thereby gained needed reinforcements. The entire conquest project, however, was almost ruined by the slaughter at the Great Temple by Pedro de Alvarado, Cortés's lieutenant, and his forces. Cortés, meanwhile, released Motecuhzoma's brother, Cuitlahuac, who immediately rallied the Mexica in violent opposition to the Spanish.

The situation deteriorated so badly that Cortés decided that retreat was necessary. On the so-called Noche Triste many Spanish soldiers lost their lives. Revealingly, Cortés's accounts also lament the gold that was lost that night. Retreating to Tlaxcala in July 1520, Cortés prepared for a final siege of Tenochtitlán. He ordered the building of thirteen brigantines to blockade the island capital, and set forth for Texcoco on 28 December. Over the next months, the Spanish soldiers conducted a series of assaults on Indian towns surrounding Tenochtitlán to pacify the area and to increase the size of their allied Indian forces. Once the ships were ready, Cortés undertook the final assault, which was achieved by blockade, massive force, and great destruction of life and property. Tenochtitlán fell in August 1521.

Salvador de Madariaga, one of Cortés's biographers, says that he was conquered by his own conquest; the events of the sixteen years after it bear this out. While he was consolidating his leadership of New Spain, he received official recognition as its legitimate conqueror and governor. But many of his soldiers nursed grievances, other Spaniards were jealous and resentful, and his wife died under mysterious circumstances.

Cortés embarked on further territorial expansion, sending Pedro de Alvarado to conquer Guatemala and Cristóbal de Olid to conquer Honduras. Alvarado succeeded but with little gain; Olid, with Velázquez's encouragement, rebelled against Cortés's authority. Olid's betrayal prompted Cortés to set off on an ill-fated expedition to Honduras. Royal authorities became disturbed by his willingness to take the law into his own hands, and his absence from Mexico City provided an opening for his enemies to move against his followers, thus strengthening the royal conviction to bring New Spain under its own firm control.

In 1529, after personal entreaties from Cortés, who had traveled to Spain, Charles V granted him the title marqués del Valle de Oaxaca, twenty-two *encomienda* towns, and the right to entail his estate. While he returned again to Mexico in the mid-1530s, he never again held the governorship. Thus to others fell the task of solidifying the territorial gains and administrative structures Cortés had put in place. Dogged by lawsuits and investigations, the marqués spent much of his latter years defending himself. Brilliant, active, and cruel, Cortés was the conqueror of the largest single community pacified in the New World. He died in Spain still seeking the status and riches he believed he had been denied.

See also **Encomienda; Explorers and Exploration: Spanish America; Motecuhzoma II; Spanish Empire.**

BIBLIOGRAPHY

Salvador De Madariaga, *Hernan Cortés, Conqueror of Mexico* (1942).

Henry R. Wagner, *The Rise of Fernando Cortés* (1944).

Eulalia Guzmán, *Relaciones de Hernán Cortés a Carlos V sobre la invasión de Anáhuac* (1958).

Bernal Díaz Del Castillo, *The Conquest of New Spain*, translated by J. M. Cohen (1963).

Francisco López De Gómara, *Cortés: The Life of the Conqueror by His Secretary*, translated and edited by Lesley B. Simpson (1966).

Hernan Cortés, *Letters from Mexico*, translated and edited by Anthony Pagden (1971), pp. xiff.

Additional Bibliography

López de Gómara, Francisco. *Historia de la conquista de México*. México, D.F.: Editorial Océano de México, 2003.

Restall, Matthew. *Seven Myths of the Spanish Conquest*. Boston: Bedford/St. Martin's, 2003.

Schwartz, Hugh. *Victors and Vanquished: Spanish and Nahua Views of the Conquest of Mexico*. Boston: Bedford/St. Martin's, 2000.

Thomas, Hugh. *Conquest: Montezuma, Cortés, and the Fall of Old Mexico*. New York: Oxford University Press, 1993.

SUSAN KELLOGG

CORTÉS, MARTÍN (1533–1589).

Martín Cortés (*b.* 1532/1533; *d.* 13 August 1589), legitimate son of the conquistador Hernán Cortés and Juana de Zúñiga, born in Cuernavaca. Not to be confused with his stepbrother, also named Martín (son of Cortés and Malinche), this Martín was the second Marqués del Valle de Oaxaca. In 1540, he went to Spain, where he joined Charles V's royal service and later became a favorite in the entourage of Philip II. His return to Mexico in 1562 to claim his father's titles and property coincided with the Spanish crown's attempt to revoke the extension of the *encomienda* to the sons and grandsons of conquistadores. Indignant at the crown's assertiveness and eager to protect their inheritance, the criollos naturally looked to Martín Cortés for leadership. Don Martín, however, had an arrogant disposition and had an ostentatious lifestyle that offended many; more important, he seemed to lack the natural leadership abilities of his father. Though he tacitly agreed to their plan to make him king of Mexico, he never fully pledged his support for criollo plans to assassinate royal officials and overthrow the government. The plot failed, and the leaders were severely punished. Cortés was apprehended and sent to Spain to face trial in 1567; he was fined and sentenced to military duty. Though pardoned by the crown in 1574, Cortés never returned to Mexico. This failed uprising represented the last serious challenge to the crown's authority in Mexico by the early conquistadores and their families. Cortés died in Madrid.

See also **Conquistadores; Cortés, Hernán.**

BIBLIOGRAPHY

Irving Alber Leonard, *Baroque Times in Old Mexico* (1966).

Michael C. Meyer and William L. Sherman, *The Course of Mexican History* (1991).

Additional Bibliography

González Obregón, Luis. *Semblanza de Martín Cortés.* México, D.F.: Fondo de Cultura Económica, 2006.

Suárez de Peralta, Juan. *La conjuración de Martín Cortés y otros temas.* México: Universidad Nacional Autónoma, 1994.

J. DAVID DRESSING

CORTES, PORTUGUESE.

Portuguese Cortes, politico-administrative bodies that, according to some historians, had their roots in national councils of the Visigoth monarchy. The word *cortes* is derived from the Latin *cohors,* meaning assembly or party. From the thirteenth to the nineteenth century, the *cortes* had a significant influence on Portuguese politics. They were composed of members of the clergy, nobles, and lawyers of the towns and cities. They represented the country and legitimized the king's power. Convened by the sovereigns, they discussed economic and financial matters and heard protests brought before the crown by the religious orders. Besides being a primarily consultive body, they acted as mediators, serving to mete out royal power along classic absolutist lines. With the revolution of Pôrto in 1820, however, the *cortes* were convened by the Provisional Junta of the Supreme Government of the Realm rather than by the king. Although the liberals affirmed they were seeking the reestablishment of the former fundamental laws of the monarchy, the General and Special Cortes had quite a different character. They rejected the old representation by orders and established equitable representation for all citizens. Therefore they became the sole supreme constitutional authority expressing the will of the nation.

See also **Portuguese Empire.**

BIBLIOGRAPHY

Barman, Roderick J. *Brazil: The Forging of a Nation, 1798–1852* (1988), pp. 64–96.

Lyra, Maria de Lourdes Viana. *A utopia do poderoso império: Portugal e Brasil: bastidores da política, 1798–1822.* Rio de Janeiro: Sette Letras, 1994.

Martins De Carvalho, Alberto. "Cortes," in *Dicionário de história de Portugal,* vol. 1 (1963), pp. 711–715.

Maxwell, Kenneth. *Conflicts & Conspiracies: Brazil and Portugal, 1750–1808.* New York: Routledge, 2004.

Piteira Santos, Fernando. *Geografia e economia da revolução de 1820,* 3d ed. (1980).

LÚCIA M. BASTOS P. NEVES

CORTÉS CASTRO, LEÓN (1882–1946).

León Cortés Castro (*b.* 8 December 1882; *d.* 2 March 1946), president of Costa Rica (1936–1940). After receiving a law degree from the School of Law in San José, León Cortés Castro held many elected and appointed positions beginning with his appointment by the military dictator President Federico Tinoco Granados (1917–1919), to the post of commander of the Alajuela Garrison (Comandante de Plaza de Alajuela). Cortés served as president of the National Assembly (1925–1926), as minister of education (1929–1930), and as minister of public works (1930; 1932–1936). His tour as minister of public works under president Ricardo Jiménez Oreamuno consolidated Cortés's reputation as a no-nonsense and frugal administrator, which prompted the leaders of the National Republican Party to choose him as their standard-bearer in 1936.

During his administration Cortés was a proponent of fiscal responsibility, extending the nation's highway network and embarking on an ambitious construction program. His brick, mortar, and asphalt approach provided employment that helped ameliorate setbacks due to the Great Depression. He founded the National Bank of Costa Rica in 1936.

Although generally accredited even by his detractors with being an effective administrator, Cortés frequently was charged with arbitrary actions. While president he intervened in the 1938 and 1940 elections preventing opposition candidates from being elected; he also meddled in the presidential candidacy of three-time president Ricardo Jiménez.

Shortly after Rafael Angel Calderón Guardia's inauguration in 1940, Cortés, as the most prominent leader of the opposition forces, openly broke with Calderón and formed a rival party. When Cortés lost the 1944 election to Teodoro Picado Michalski (1944–1948), there were widespread charges that

Calderón had used his executive power to perpetrate electoral fraud on a grand scale.

Cortés remained the leader of the opposition until his sudden death following a heart attack in 1946.

See also **Costa Rica.**

BIBLIOGRAPHY

William Krehm, *Democracies and Tyrannies of the Caribbean* (1984), discusses Cortés as president and presidential candidate.

John Patrick Bell, *Crisis in Costa Rica* (1971), discusses Cortés's role in the turbulent events leading to the 1948 revolution.

Franklin D. Parker, *The Central American Republics* (1964), provides a succinct general history.

Carlos Calvo Gamboa, *León Cortés, y su tiempo* (1969), deals with Cortés and the politics of the period.

Additional Bibliography

Molina Jiménez, Iván, and Fabrice Edouard Lehoucq. *Urnas de lo inesperado: Fraude electoral y lucha política en Costa Rica (1901–1948)*. San José: Editorial de la Universidad de Costa Rica, 1999.

Salazar Mora, Jorge Mario. *Crisis liberal y estado reformista: Análisis político-electoral (1914–1949)*. San José: Editorial de la Universidad de Costa Rica, 1995.

JOHN PATRICK BELL

CORTÉS DE MADARIAGA, JOSÉ

(1766–1826). José Cortés de Madariaga (*b.* 8 July 1766; *d.* March 1826), priest and political activist in the Venezuelan independence movement. A native of Chile, Cortés de Madariaga was ordained in 1788. He arrived in Venezuela by chance in 1802 and obtained a canonry in the Cathedral of Caracas. He played an active role in the events of 19 April 1810 in Caracas and was a member of the Junta Suprema of Caracas. Cortés de Madariaga traveled to New Granada in 1811 and signed the first treaty of alliance and federation between Cundinamarca and Venezuela. At the fall of the republic in 1812, he was sent to the military prison at Ceuta, in Africa, from which he escaped two years later. When Venezuela regained its independence in 1817, he returned and promoted the founding of a representative, federal government. This plan was disclaimed and condemned by Simón Bolívar. Cortés de Madariaga later traveled to Jamaica, where he again worked for independence. In 1823 the Congress of Colombia granted him a pension for his services in the cause of independence.

See also **Venezuela: The Colonial Era.**

BIBLIOGRAPHY

Daniel Arias Argaez, *El canónigo don José Cortés y Madariaga* (1938).

Nicolás Perazzo, *José Cortés de Madariaga* (1972).

Additional Bibliography

Armas Chitty, José Antonio de. *La independencia de Venezuela*. Madrid: Editorial MAPFRE, 1992.

Ríos, Alicia. *La idea de nación y cultura nacional en la independencia Venezolana: 1810-1830*. Ph.D. diss., University of Maryland at College Park, 1992.

INÉS QUINTERO

CORTES OF CÁDIZ.

The placement of Joseph Bonaparte on the throne of Spain in 1808 by his brother Napoleon resulted in widespread resistance to the French organized by provincial juntas of Spanish patriots. With French troops occupying nearly all of the country by January 1810, the Central Junta of resistance at Seville turned authority over to a five-member regency to rule in the name of the captive Spanish Bourbon, Ferdinand VII. This regency, however, lacked the legitimacy of the popular resistance juntas, and thus it called for election of deputies to a General and Extraordinary Cortes that convened in Cádiz beginning on 24 September 1810. While British forces attacked the French in Spain through Portugal, the Cortes (Congress) of Cádiz directed loyalist guerrilla resistance to the French and sought to maintain the loyalty of Spain's American dominions.

The Cortes of Cádiz claimed legitimacy as the sole representative of Spanish sovereignty, assuming administration of the American dominions and granting them representation in the Cortes. In fact, colonial deputies to the Cortes played an important role in its deliberations, even though many did not reach Cádiz for some time. The Cortes supervised elections in the Cádiz region (the only area of Spain not held by the French) and throughout Spanish America for municipal offices and for the Cortes of 1812. These elections established an influential precedent for the subsequent political history of Spanish America. Many of the Cortes's actions reflected compromise between conservative and liberal deputies, but the Cortes had a discernible liberal tone, and its Constitution of 1812 became the fundamental charter of nineteenth-century liberalism in Spain and Spanish America. Colonial representation in the Cortes and the attack on aristocratic privilege and monopolies were especially important liberal advances. Although the Cortes retained the Roman Catholic Church as the established church, it suppressed the Holy Office of the Inquisition and limited the regular orders. The American representatives pressured their peninsular counterparts on free trade, on ending restrictions on agriculture and manufacturing in the colonies, and on granting them a guaranteed percentage of bureaucratic appointments.

With the defeat of Napoleon in 1814, Ferdinand VII replaced Joseph Bonaparte as king of Spain. He immediately dissolved the Cortes and nullified all of its acts with a single decree on 4 May 1814. He refused to recognize the constitution or the Cortes, beginning a period of strong repression that lasted until the Riego Revolt of 1820, which forced Ferdinand to accept restoration of the constitution.

See also **Bonaparte, Joseph.**

BIBLIOGRAPHY

The primary sources for research on the Cortes are *Actas de las Cortes de Cádiz,* 2 vols. (1964) and *El Perú en las Cortes de Cádiz,* 2 vols. (1974). Among secondary works, Mario Rodríguez, *The Cádiz Experiment in Central America, 1808 to 1826* (1978), is especially perceptive.

See also Cesareo De Armellada, *La causa indígena americana en las Cortes de Cádiz* (1959); Daniel A. Moreno, *Las Cortes de Cádiz y la Constitución de 1812* (1964); Nettie Lee Benson, ed., *Mexico and the Spanish Cortes, 1810–1822* (1966); Dardo Pérez Guilhou, *La opinión pública española y las Cortes de Cádiz frente a la emancipación hispanoamericana, 1808–1814;* (1981); Raymond Carr, *Spain 1808–1975,* 2d ed. (1982); María Teresa Berruezo, *La participación americana en las Cortes de Cádiz, 1810–1814* (1986); Jorge Mario García La Guardia, *La Constitución de Cádiz y su influencia en América (175 años 1812–1987)* (1987).

Blanco Valdés, Roberto Luis. *El "problema americano" en las primeras cortes liberales españolas, 1810–1814.* México: Universidad Nacional Autónoma de México, 1995.

Chust Calero, Manuel. *La cuestión nacional americana en las Cortes de Cádiz (1810–1814).* Valencia, Spain: Fundación Instituto Historia Social, 1999.

HEATHER THIESSEN

CORVALÁN LEPE, LUIS (1916–).

Luis Corvalán Lepe is a politician and the secretary general of Unidad Popular, the Chilean Communist Party. A professor by education, Corvalán worked his way up in the party to serve as a senator representing the south. Then, selected by his predecessor, he became head of the party in 1957. Always a supporter of Moscow, he was nevertheless willing to cooperate with progressive elements. Corvalán rationalized the Unidad Popular's policies, arguing that it was possible to achieve socialism in Chile without revolution. Captured in the 1973 coup that overthrew Allende, Corvalán suffered torture at the hands of the Pinochet government. He was then imprisoned, and during his incarceration he was awarded the Lenin Peace Prize for 1973–1974. In 1976 he was exchanged for the Soviet political prisoner Vladimir Bukovsky. He received asylum in the USSR and relocated there. From exile, he continued to head the Communist Party of Chile. He returned to Chile in October 1989, just before the plebiscite to decide whether Pinochet would continue his rule. He immediately began campaigning for Patricio Aylwin, Pinochet's opponent, who won the election.

See also **Chile, Political Parties: Communist Party.**

BIBLIOGRAPHY

Bascuñán Edwards, Carlos. *La izquierda sin Allende.* Santiago: Planeta, 1990.

Faúndez, Julio B. *Marxism and Democracy in Chile* (1988), p. 172.

Furci, Carmelo. *The Chilean Communist Party and the Road to Socialism* (1984), pp. 19, 37, 56, 85–88, 153, 167.

Loyola T., Manuel, and Jorge Rojas F., eds. *Por un rojo amanecer: Hacia una historia de los comunistas chilenos.* Santiago: Instituto de Ciencias Alejandro Lipschutz (ICAL), 2000.

Piñera Echenique, José. *Una casa dividida: Como la violencia política destruyó la democracia en Chile.* Chile: Proyecto Chile, 2005.

Shragin, Victor. *Chile, Corvalán, Struggle*. Translated by Yuri Sviridov. Moscow: Progress Publishers, 1980.

WILLIAM F. SATER

CORZO, EL. *See* Ruiz, Antonio.

COS, MARTÍN PERFECTO DE (1800–1854).

Martín Perfecto De Cos (*b.* 1800; *d.* 1854), Mexican general. A native of Veracruz, Cos joined the Veracruz regiment in 1820. He became a lieutenant under Augustín de Iturbide during 1821, but supported the formation of a Mexican republic by 1823. After Cos became a general in 1833, President Antonio Lopéz de Santa Anna sent him to control unrest in the North. In December 1835 he lost San Antonio to the Texans. Cos fought at the Alamo (1836) before being captured at San Jacinto in early 1836. Federalists defeated him in battle at Tampico in 1838 and at Tuxpan in 1839. During 1847 he fought against the U.S. Army at Tuxpan. Cos acted as government leader for Tehuantepec before his death.

See also **Mexico: 1810–1910.**

BIBLIOGRAPHY

Walter Lord, *A Time to Stand* (1961).

Joseph Milton Nance, *After San Jacinto: The Texas-Mexican Frontier, 1836–1841* (1963); "Cos, Martín Perfecto de," in *Diccionario Porrúa de historia, biografía y geografía de México* (1986).

Alwyn Barr, *Texans in Revolt: The Battle for San Antonio, 1835* (1990).

Additional Bibliography

Vázquez, Josefina Zoraida. *México al tiempo de su guerra con Estados Unidos, 1846-1848*. México: Secretaría de Exteriores: El Colegio de México: Fondo de Cultura Económica, 1997.

ALWYN BARR

COSIATA, LA (1826).

La (1826) Cosiata, a politico-military movement for the secession of Venezuela from Gran Colombia. When Gran Colombia was formed in 1821, conflicts arose in the territory of Venezuela over political and administrative difficulties resulting from the location of the center of power in Bogotá. Rejection of the conscription system imposed by the government of Bogotá was widespread. Also, there were outright confrontations between entities of civil and military power, stemming both from their insufficiently defined powers and the lack of institutionalized authority.

Several factors contributed to the restless climate leading up to Venezuela's eventual decision to ignore Bogotá's authority and to the Municipality of Caracas's appointment of José Antonio Páez as chief of the department of Venezuela in 1826. One was the imprecision as to the authority and jurisdiction of the various local, departmental, and national entities of power. A second was the great distances between the various political and administrative bodies. A third was the newness of the Gran Colombia experiment, and a fourth involved tensions between political factions and problems brought about by the war.

The series of events that comprise La Cosiata began in the city of Valencia on 27 April 1826, when the municipal council expressed its regret over the suspension of Páez as military commander in chief of the department of Venezuela earlier in the year. Discontent spread rapidly throughout most of the territory formerly known as the captaincy general of Venezuela. An assembly of Venezuelan municipalities called for a convention and the adoption of a federal system. General Francisco de Paula Santander declared Páez a rebel and deployed troops. In December, Simón Bolívar entered Venezuela, declared an amnesty, and named Páez chief civil and military leader of Venezuela. The integrity of the Colombian Republic was thus provisionally maintained.

See also **Bolívar, Simón.**

BIBLIOGRAPHY

José Antonio Páez, *Autobiografía de José Antonio Páez*, vol. 1 (1973).

Graciela Soriano De García-Pelayo, *Venezuela, 1810–1830: Aspectos desatendidos de dos décadas* (1990).

Additional Bibliography

Felice Cardot, Carlos. *Mérida y la Revolución de 1826, o "La Cosiata."* Meridá: Universidad de los Andes, 1963.

González, Eloy Guillermo. *Dentro de la Cosiata*. Caracas: Imprenta Nacional, 1907.

León de Labarca, Alba Ivonne, and Juan Carlos Morales Manzur. *Venezuela y el ideario de la unidad continental*. Maracaibo: FAMUSC, 2004.

Tarver Denova, Hollis Micheal, and Julia C. Frederick. *The History of Venezuela*. Westport, CT: Greenwood Press, 2005.

INÉS QUINTERO

COSÍO MEDINA, JOSÉ GABRIEL

(1887–1960). Juan Gabriel Cosío Medina was born in the town of Accha, Cuzco, Peru, on March 18, 1887, to Timoteo Cosío and Juana Medina. In 1903 he began advanced studies at San Antonio de Abad University in the Faculty of Letters and Law. After receiving his doctorate in 1908, he held professorships in the history of ancient and modern civilization, the history of America, and sociology, the three fields in which he excelled. He also served as an assistant to the rector (president) of the university, Alberto Giesecke. He is best known for his exploratory work with Hiram Bingham to discover Machu Picchu in 1911.

Later on Cosío Medina served as director of the San Carlos de Puno High School (1927–1931), of the San Juan de Trujillo High School (1935–1944), and at one point served as interim rector of San Antonio de Abad University. Due to his fervent intellectual activity, he was named "académico de número" at the prestigious Instituto Histórico del Perú. He also was well known to readers of *El Sol*, an important newspaper published in Cuzco, the ancient Incan capital. He wrote a prologue for the 1917 edition of Clorinda Matto's *Tradiciones cuzqueñas* as well as a number of well-received books, including *Americanismo literario* (1909), *Cuzco prehispánico y colonial* (1918), and *El Cuzco histórico y monumental* (1924).

In addition to being an educator and a journalist, Cosío Medina was also a politician, serving as Cuzco's mayor on more than one occasion. He died in Lima on November 23, 1960.

See also **Archaeology; Bingham, Hiram; Machu Picchu; Matto de Turner, Clorinda.**

BIBLIOGRAPHY

Bingham, Hiram. *The Lost City of the Incas: The Story of Macchu Picchu and Its Builders*. New York: Duell, Sloan and Pierce, 1948.

WILFREDO KAPSOLI

COSÍO VILLEGAS, DANIEL (1898–

1976). Daniel Cosío Villegas (*b*. 23 July 1898; *d*. 10 March 1976), Mexican intellectual figure and cultural entrepreneur. A graduate of the National Preparatory School and the National School of Law, he became a prominent student leader and began teaching before graduating with degrees in law and literature. He was a disciple of Pedro Henríquez Ureña and a political collaborator of José Vasconcelos. He became one of the first members of his generation to study economics abroad. In 1938 he founded *El Trimestre Económico* and the leading publishing house Fondo de Cultura Económica, directing both until 1948. Known for his collaborative historical projects on the Porfiriato, he directed *Historia Mexicana* (1951–1961) and cofounded and directed the Colegio de Mexico, where he produced many distinguished disciples. He was awarded the National Prize in Letters in 1971, and was a member of the National College from 1951 until his death.

See also **Literature: Spanish America.**

BIBLIOGRAPHY

Daniel Cosío Villegas, *Ensayos y notas*, 2 vols. (1966) and *Memorias* (1976).

Charles A. Hale, "Review of *Memorias* by Daniel Cosío Villegas" in *Hispanic American Historical Review* vol. 58 (1978): 132–133.

Enrique Krauze, *Daniel Cosío Villegas: Una biografía intelectual* (1980).

Gabriel Zaid, comp., *Daniel Cosío Villegas, imprenta y vida público* (1985).

Additional Bibliography

Hale, Charles Adam. "Edmundo O'Gorman, Mexican National History, and the 'Great American Dichotomy'." *Journal of Latin American Studies* 36:1 (October–December 2004): 131–145.

Márquez, Graciela. *Daniel Cosío Villegas, sus años como economista*. México: Centro de Estudios Económicos, El Colegio de México, 2001.

Vizcaíno, Fernando. *Cien años de Daniel Cosío Villegas*. México: Clío, 1998.

RODERIC AI CAMP

COSTA, CLÁUDIO MANUEL DA

(1729–1789). Cláudio Manuel da Costa (also Manoel; *b*. 5 June 1729; *d*. 4 July 1789), considered the father of Brazilian literature and its major neoclassic poet. He was born in Mariana, Minas Gerais, to a well-to-do family. After studying with the Jesuits in Brazil, he obtained a law degree in Coimbra, Portugal, in 1753. Returning to Brazil, he set up residence in Ouro Prêto, where he pursued a career as a lawyer and public servant. Through investments in gold mining and money lending, he became one of the wealthiest men in the province. His collected poems were published as *Orbas* [*sic*] (1768), and he also wrote an epic poem on the history of his home town (published as *Vila Rica* in 1839). In 1789 he was arrested under the accusation of participating in a plot to declare Minas Gerais independent of the Portuguese crown (Inconfidência Mineira). After a month in jail, he compromised himself and several of his named co-conspirators. Broken and remorseful, he committed suicide. Without presenting serious documentation, some historians have tried to contest the official version of his death, accusing his jailer of murder.

See also **Literature: Brazil.**

BIBLIOGRAPHY

Samuel Putnam, *Marvelous Journey* (1948), pp. 81–95.

Kenneth R. Maxwell, *Conflicts and Conspiracies: Brazil and Portugal, 1750–1808* (1973).

Additional Bibliography

Alcides, Sérgio. *Estes penhascos: Cláudio Manuel da Costa e a paisagem das Minas Gerais 1753-1773*. São Paulo: Hucitec, 2003.

Brandão, Roberto de Oliveira. *Poética e poesia no Brasil (Colônia)*. São Paulo: Editora UNESP, 2001.

Lopes, Edward. *Metamorfoses: A poesia de Cláudio Manuel da Costa*. São Paulo: Editora UNESP, Fundação, 1997.

HEITOR MARTINS

COSTA (ECUADOR).

Costa (Ecuador), the coastal lowland region of Ecuador, comprising approximately one-quarter of the nation (roughly 27,000 square miles) in a strip ranging from 12 to 100 miles wide along the Pacific Ocean. The provinces of the *costa*—Esmeraldas, Manabí, Los Ríos, Guayas, and El Oro—contain about half of the nation's population. The port city of Guayaquil in Guayas is the nation's commercial center and largest city. Historically, the rivalry between the commercially oriented and politically liberal coast and the isolated and conservative sierra (site of the national capital of Quito) has shaped national politics. The costa developed close ties with international markets, and at various times was the world's leading producer of cacao and bananas. It is culturally distinct—less Andean, traditional, Catholic, and provincial than the rest of Ecuador.

See also **Ecuador, Geography; Quito.**

BIBLIOGRAPHY

Linda Alexander Rodríguez, *The Search for Public Policy: Regional Politics and Government Finances in Ecuador, 1830–1940* (1985).

Osvaldo Hurtado *Political Power in Ecuador*, translated by Nick D. Mills, Jr. (1985).

Preston James, *Latin America* (1986).

David W. Schodt, *Ecuador: An Andean Enigma* (1987).

Theodor Wolf, *Geography and Geology of Ecuador*, translated by James Flanagan (1933).

RONN F. PINEO

COSTA, HIPÓLITO JOSÉ DA (1774–1823).

Hipólito José da Costa (*b*. 25 March 1774; *d*. 11 September 1823), journalist. Born in the colony of Sacramento, Brazil, where his father served in the royal troops, da Costa graduated with a degree in philosophy (1796) and law (1798) from the University of Coimbra. He began his public career under the protection of minister of the colonies Rodrigo de Souza Coutinho, who placed him in charge of a visit to the United States and Mexico in 1798, and appointed him director of the royal press.

Da Costa undertook a voyage to England in 1802 with the aim of acquiring books, machinery, and other typographical equipment. When he returned, he was seized by the Inquisition and accused of being a mason. He escaped to London (1805), where, in 1808, he founded the liberal newspaper *Correio Braziliense,* a publication that had a decisive influence at the time of Brazil's independence, even though it did not advocate separation from Portugal until February 1822. As a result of new freedoms of the press and the proliferation of numerous periodicals, da Costa believed that Brazil no longer needed news emanating from abroad. Publication of *Correio Braziliense* ceased in 1822. After independence, da Costa was appointed the Brazilian representative in London, but he died soon after his nomination.

See also **Journalism.**

BIBLIOGRAPHY

Mecenas Dourado, *Hipólito da Costa e o Correio Braziliense* (1957).

Carlos Rizzini, *Hipólito da Costa e o Correio Braziliense* (1957).

Additional Bibliography

Costa, Hipólito José da, and Sergio Goes de Paula. *Hipólito José da Costa.* São Paulo: Editora 34, 2001.

Quevedo, Raul. *Em nome da liberdade: A saga de Hipólito José da Costa.* Pelotas: UFPEL, Editora Universitária, 1997.

LÚCIA M. BASTOS P. NEVES

COSTA, LÚCIO (1902–1998).

Lúcio Costa (*b.* 27 February 1902; *d.* 13 June 1998), Brazilian urban planner, best known for designing the city plan of Brasília. Born in Toulon, France, Costa was part of an extraordinary flowering of creative genius in Rio de Janeiro in the 1950s that included, among others, the architect Oscar Niemeyer, the landscape architect Roberto Burle Marx (Costa's neighbor), and the creators of Bossa Nova, such as Antônio Carlos Jobim and Luís Bonfa. Twenty-six plans, some with elaborate models labored over for months by entire architectural firms, were submitted in the 1955 design competition for the new capital. Costa produced his plan in sixty-four hours. His only expenditures were for paper, pencils, and an eraser. Disillusioned by Brasília's failure to catalyze social change, as he and Niemeyer had hoped, Costa said, "You don't solve the social problems of a country by simply moving its capital, and in Brazil the main problem is the huge base of poor in the country." He died in Rio de Janeiro in June 1998.

See also **Architecture: Modern Architecture.**

BIBLIOGRAPHY

Alex Shoumatoff, *The Capital of Hope* (1980).

Additional Bibliography

Buchmann, A. *Lúcio Costa: O inventador da cidade de Brasília, centenário de nascimento.* Brasília: Thesaurus Editora, 2002.

El-Dadah, Farés. *CASE: Lucio Costa, Brasilia's superquadra.* Cambridge, MA: Harvard University, Graduate School of Design, 2005.

Miranda, Wander Melo. *Anos JK: Margens da modernidade.* São Paulo: Imprensa Oficial, 2002.

Nobre, Ana Luiza. *Um modo de ser moderno: Lúcio Costa e a crítica contemporanea.* São Paulo: Cosac & Naify Ediçoes, 2004.

Wisnik, Guilherme, and Lúcio Costa. *Lúcio Costa.* São Paulo: Cosac & Naify Ediçoes, 2001.

ALEX SHOUMATOFF

COSTA (PERU).

Costa (Peru), one of the three principal geographic regions of Peru, with the *selva* and *sierra.* The *costa* is between the Pacific and the Andean mountains; it constitutes only 12 percent of the national territory but contains around 53 percent of the population—largely as a result of the massive migration from the less developed rural Andean interior during the second half of the twentieth century. Most of the coast is a desert where rainfall is scant due to the peculiarities of the Humboldt Current, but where numerous, fertile valley oases are watered by the fifty-two rivers that flow out of the Andes east to west, emptying into the Pacific. Historically, the coast, by virtue of its orientation toward Europe and the West, has tended to be more modernized and developed than the highland interior as well as more racially and ethnically mixed.

See also **Andes.**

BIBLIOGRAPHY

Instituto Nacional de Estadística e Informática, Migraciones Internas en el Perú. http://www.inei.gob.pe/biblioi neipub/bancopub /Est/Lib0018/cap31002.htm.

James Higgins, *Lima: A Cultural History* (2005).

PETER K. KLARÉN

COSTA E SILVA, ARTUR DA (1902–1969).

Artur da Costa e Silva (*b.* 3 October 1902; *d.* 17 December 1969), president of Brazil (1967–1969). Born in Taquarí, Rio Grande do Sul, Costa e Silva attended the Realengo Military Academy and graduated at the head of his class. As a young second lieutenant in 1922, he took part in the Copacabana Fort Revolt in Rio de Janeiro, for which he was imprisoned for six months. For supporting Getúlio Vargas in the Revolution of 1930, Costa e Silva was named to a federal government post. During World War II, he served as an officer in the Brazilian Expeditionary Force (FEB) in Italy, after which he joined a group of officers who removed Vargas from office in 1945. Costa e Silva became a brigadier general in 1952; six years later he was named a major general and commander of the second infantry division and of the armored vehicle division based in São Paulo.

He turned down President João Goulart's offer to become army chief of staff in 1961, but the following year he accepted command of the Fourth Army, based in northeastern Brazil. Costa e Silva played a key role in the March 1964 coup against Goulart, seizing the War Ministry Building in Rio, the armed forces' communication and bureaucratic center. The Supreme Revolutionary Command, which engineered the coup, named him head of the 200,000-man army. Two years later the Army High Command elected him to succeed fellow officer (and academy classmate) Humberto Castello Branco as president.

Costa e Silva's presidency was marked by the imposition of authoritarian rule. In December 1968, he recessed the National Congress when it refused to waive immunity for a member perceived to have criticized the military. Costa e Silva then issued a series of Institutional Acts that expanded executive and military powers, limited media freedom, and suspended federal, state, and municipal elections. He justified his regime with an improving economy. The government cut taxes on Brazilian businesses, attracted foreign investment, and provided incentives to ranchers. The gross domestic product rose 11 percent in 1968 and the World Bank approved a $1 billion development loan, marking the beginning of the Brazilian Economic Miracle.

In August 1969, while campaigning for a national referendum on revisions to the Constitution of 1967, Costa e Silva suffered an incapacitating stroke. A military junta composed of the three armed forces ministers assumed power, bypassed the constitutionally designated successor, Vice President Pedro Aleixo, and with the Army High Command named General Emílio Garrastazú Médici in October 1969 to succeed immediately to the presidency. Costa e Silva died in Rio de Janeiro.

See also **Brazil, Revolutions: Revolution of 1964.**

BIBLIOGRAPHY

Thomas E. Skidmore, *The Politics of Military Rule in Brazil, 1964–85* (1988).

Additional Bibliography

Gaspari, Elio. *A ditadura envergonhada.* São Paulo: Companhia das Letras, 2002.

Martins Filho, João Roberto. *O palácio e a caserna: A dinâmica militar das crises políticas na ditadura, 1964–1969.* São Carlos: Editora da Universidade Federal de São Carlos, 1995.

Reis Filho, Daniel Aarão, and Marcelo Ridenti. *O golpe e a ditadura militar: Quarenta anos depois (1964–2004).* Bauru: Editora da Universidade do Sagrado Coração, 2004.

ROSS WILKINSON

COSTA RICA.

Costa Rica has grown and prospered in a manner so distinct from that of other Latin American nations that its history warrants more extensive study than its small size and population would suggest. From an isolated and generally ignored colony of some sixty thousand inhabitants at the time of independence, it has developed into one of the most prosperous, educated, healthy, and democratic nations in Latin America. Its progress has been sustained and profound, without any great economic windfalls occasioned by the discovery and exploitation of such resources as petroleum or precious metals or precious stones. Its progress has come from the creativity, imagination, and common sense of its people, who have worked with a limited resource base and from a scant colonial material legacy of such items as infrastructure, wealth, roads, port facilities, and homes.

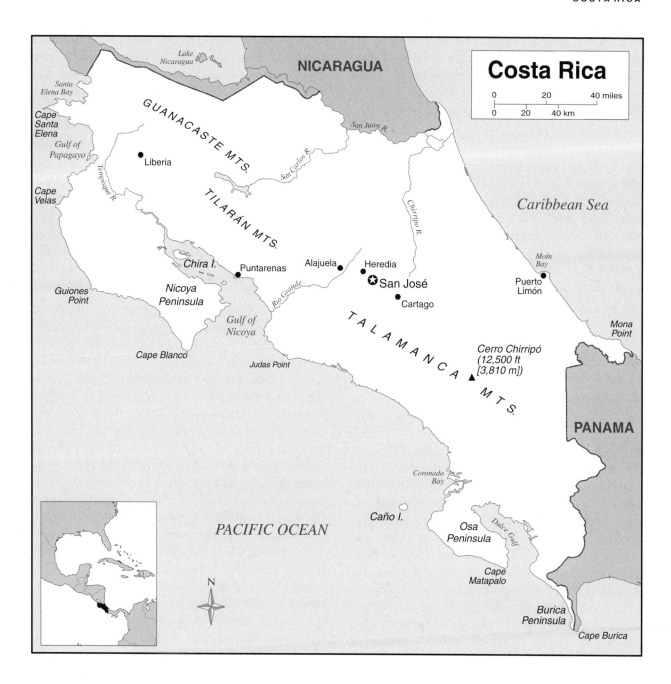

Costa Rica

0   20   40 miles
0   20   40 km

GEOGRAPHY

Costa Rica is the third smallest of the Central American republics (El Salvador and Belize have less land area) and is located wholly within the tropics (between 8 and 11 latitude). Despite its limited area of 19,575 square miles, Costa Rica contains a great variety of hot to moderate climatic zones because of its enormous variety of topography, coastlines on the Pacific Ocean and the Caribbean Sea, and variations in seasonal and annual precipitation.

The prevailing winds from the northeast that pass over the warm Caribbean waters account for the high annual rainfall along the Caribbean coast and the eastern slopes of the mountainous interior. Although there is a distinct rainy season in the humid tropical zone on the Caribbean side, it might be better designated the rainier season because there is substantial precipitation throughout the year. Much of the lowland area is tropical rain forest; at higher elevations dense vegetation and swift-flowing mountain streams are the norm. Along the Pacific coast and the western slopes of the mountains, there are pronounced rainy and dry seasons. The amount of precipitation increases as one moves from the northwestern region to the southwest. Guanacaste Province is a region of tropical dry forest and semiarid areas, whereas in the area around Golfito there is sufficient rainfall to sustain economically viable banana plantations.

Historically the country's most significant geographic feature has been the mountain ranges that run from the border with Nicaragua in the north to the southern border with Panama. The volcanoes not only add a dramatic element to the landscape but, when active, have had devastating effects on the surrounding areas. They also have benefited agricultural development by depositing rich volcanic soil at unpredictable intervals. The highest peaks are in the Talamanca Range in the southwestern part of the country.

The mountain valleys constitute the third major climate zone, which enjoys a moderate climate (*clima templada*). These valleys occur between 2,000 to 7,000 feet above sea level.

The heartland of Costa Rica is the great Central Valley and the Central Plateau (*meseta central*) within that valley. The principal cities of the early independence period, San José, Cartago, Heredia, and Alajuela, were all on the *meseta central,* and the vast majority of the colonial population lived in these cities and their environs. The national culture, character, and values emanate from this central region. The Costa Ricans, then, are a mountain people who, in over a century and a half of independence, have gradually moved out from the heartland to occupy and develop the other regions of the nation. As they have adjusted to different climates and embraced other environments, their national culture has remained essentially that of the *meseta*. The national values of democracy, individual liberty, egalitarianism, peace, and universal education were fostered and inculcated in the *meseta* and then spread throughout the nation.

NATIONAL ORGANIZATION

With the triumph of San José over Cartago in 1823, Costa Rica turned its back on Mexico and Agustín Iturbide's imperial model for independence and embraced republicanism and the Central American Federation. It was still too early to clearly discern the emergence of a distinct Costa Rican nation, but the victory at Ochomogo by the combined forces of San José and Alajuela over those of Cartago and its ally, Heredia, marked an important milestone along the path to nationhood. Future development became more predictable with San José's victory in the War of the League (1835) over the other three cities of the *meseta*. San José became the undisputed capital of an emerging nation soon to break with the Central American Federation.

Costa Rica's relative stability was the reason that the province of Guanacaste aligned itself with Costa Rica rather than Nicaragua in 1824. The Federation approved the annexation. Juan Mora Fernández's long tenure as head of state (1824–1833) also reflected a growing cohesiveness in contrast to conditions elsewhere in Central America.

Braulio Carrillo Colina provided effective if somewhat arbitrary leadership for the consolidation of Costa Rican nationhood during his two periods as head of state (1835–1837 and 1838–1842). Carrillo took the lead in establishing San José as the permanent capital and in separating Costa Rica from the Federation (1838). He also fostered the cultivation of coffee, which became the principal national export and the mainstay of the national economy. It is difficult to overestimate the importance of coffee in Costa Rica's economic development and modernization. The manner in which Carrillo promoted the new crop also served to reinforce the existing positive land-tenure pattern in the *meseta*. He distributed coffee saplings to the peasant farmers as a means of providing them with a cash crop and the nation with its most significant export as of 2007. This success confirmed in practice one of the major tenets of early liberal and republican dogma, that is, that more open trade and foreign capital—British capital was involved in the commercialization and shipping of coffee and in supplying trees—would contribute significantly to economic development and should be encouraged.

The liberal-conservative conflict that raged throughout the rest of Central America afflicted Costa Rica in a very attenuated form. National leadership placed Costa Rican interests above party or ideological interests so that the country did not suffer from the same deep divisions as other Central American countries, and remained on the sidelines in inter–Central American conflicts.

The ultimate fate of the great liberal leader from Honduras, Francisco Morazán, was determined by

Costa Rica

Population:	4,300,000
Area:	19,575 sq. mi
Official language:	Spanish
Languages:	Spanish, English
National currency:	Costa Rican colon (CRC)
Principal religions:	Roman Catholic 76.3%, Evangelical 13.7%, Jehovah's Witnesses 1.3%, other Protestant 0.7%, other 4.8%, none 3.2%
Ethnicity:	white (including mestizo) 94%, black 3%, Amerindian 1%, Chinese 1%, other 1%
Capital:	San José
Other urban centers:	Alajuela, Cartago, Heredia, Limón, Puntarenas
Annual rainfall:	Over 100 in
Principal geographical features:	*Mountains:* Cordillera de Guanacaste, including the Meseta Central. Chirripó Grande (12,500 ft) is the tallest peak. Irazú (11,260 ft) is an active volcano. *Rivers:* San Juan
Economy:	*GDP per capita:* $12,500 (2006 est.)
Principal products and exports:	*Agricultural:* bananas, cocoa, coffee, meat, sugar *Manufacturing:* fertilizers, food processing, microprocessors, plastics, textiles
Government:	Costa Rica has been a sovereign nation since 1838 and is governed as a democratic republic. The president is both chief of state and head of government. The legislature is popularly elected and consists of a 57-seat Legislative Assembly.
Armed forces:	Costa Rica's constitution forbids the formation of a military. Paramilitary forces consists of a 4,400-member Civil Guard, 2,000-member Border Security Police, and 2,000-member Rural Guards.
Transportation:	*Ports:* Caldera, Límon *Roads:* 5,357 mi paved; 16,596 mi unpaved *National airline:* Líneas Aéreas Costarricenses, S.A. (LACSA) *Airports:* 36 paved and 115 unpaved runway airports
Media:	Several daily newspapers in San José, including *Diario Extra, La Nación,* and *La República;* 65 AM and 51 FM radio stations; 20 television stations
Literacy and education:	*Total literacy rate:* 96% (2003 est.) Primary and secondary education is free; 6 years of primary education are compulsory. There are 39 universities, including the University of Costa Rica, and the Open University, which has campuses throughout the country and accepts all who apply.

Costa Rican reluctance to be party to these inter–Central American disputes. After the disintegration of the Federation, Morazán attempted to use Costa Rica as his base for military operations to reclaim his presidency and restore the Federation. Morazán's ascendancy in Costa Rica lasted less than six months and ended with his execution there in September 1842.

Throughout the Carrillo period and the 1840s, coffee production expanded at a prodigious rate, and the road building that he initiated continued apace. The most important advances were related to the exportation of this new crop, particularly the improvement of the cart road to the major Pacific port, Puntarenas.

The expansion of coffee production in Costa Rica can be attributed to the initiative of those involved in the trade but also to the propitiousness of the setting. The moderate temperatures of the Central Valley together with rich volcanic soil and tropical sun without excess heat made for nearly ideal growing conditions. The predictability of the dry season provided a natural means of drying the husked beans in *beneficios* (processing plants) and made the trails to Puntarenas passable at the time that the dried beans were ready for market.

As coffee production expanded to meet the increasing external demand, there emerged a new coffee elite, which also manifested distinct Costa Rican traits. It was not a mere carryover from a colonial landholding oligarchy that introduced coffee production to its large estates, which was the case in several other Latin American nations. The coffee elite in Costa Rica was more commercial in origin and developed from early investment in processing, transporting, and marketing the bean. Some of its members were descendents of the colonial elite; others were foreign nationals who became involved in the trade and later invested in land and production (hence such surnames as Dent and Rohrmoser). Some were Costa Ricans of relatively humble background who prospered with the coffee boom in ancillary enterprises and then invested in land for coffee production.

Members of the coffee elite extended their land holdings and created relatively large estates. However, they did not do so to the exclusion of the peasant producers. The general scarcity of workers made the bargaining position of agricultural labor stronger than elsewhere in Central America. The larger-scale producers were dependent on the independent peasant farmers who would work for wages at harvest time. The patron-peon relationship did not involve the extreme exploitation common in so many other areas of nineteenth-century Latin America. Nonetheless, the new elite based on coffee became the dominant socioeconomic group and, as such, played a major role in the social, cultural, political, and economic development of the nation.

The political situation after the execution of Morazán was fluid until the presidency of Juan Rafael Mora Porrás (1849–1859), who reestablished republican forms despite being something of a caudillo. As chief executive, Mora emphasized order and had the support of much of the emerging coffee elite.

THE NATIONAL WAR AND THE SENSE OF NATIONHOOD

The most dramatic events of Mora's presidency revolved around the military campaigns to repulse William Walker's (1824–1860) invading forces. For Costa Ricans, this war against the filibusters contributed to their sense of nationhood in much the same way as the struggle for independence did in many other countries. In a sense, the National War filled the void created by the absence of a war for independence and engendered the great national heroes, particularly the figure of Juan Santamaría (1831–1856).

Walker's ascendancy in Nicaragua (1855–1857) and his subsequent advance into the Guanacaste region of Costa Rica led President Mora to issue a call to arms to repel the invading forces. The Costa Rican forces that were organized on the *meseta* joined troops in Guanacaste and defeated the invading forces at Santa Rosa. The filibusters retreated to Nicaragua and were again defeated at Rivas (11 April 1856).

It was at Rivas that a simple soldier, Juan Santamaría, lost his life in a heroic and successful one-man attack that resulted in the fiery destruction of the filibusters' stronghold. Santamaría's sacrifice, coupled with his humble origin, made him a fitting hero for a nation that sought democratization and a greater spirit of equality among its people.

After the battle for Rivas, a cholera outbreak struck the Costa Rican forces, which then sought refuge in the Central Valley. The epidemic resulted in an estimated ten thousand deaths in a nation of approximately one hundred thousand inhabitants. This tragedy added to the indelible impression the National War left on Costa Rica and its people.

THE NEW LIBERALISM AND THE OPENING TO THE CARIBBEAN

After a decade of military-political instability, then colonel and later general Tomás Guardia Gutiérrez (1831–1882) seized power (1870). He remained the dominant figure in government until his death in 1882. Guardia, like several other Latin American presidents of the period, rationalized his departure from liberal principles by embracing positivist concepts. These authoritarian presidents maintained, and in the case of Guardia, even enhanced the mechanisms of republicanism, but they ruled by force of arms and personality. They placed great emphasis on economic development through modernization, particularly transportation infrastructure and trade expansion. Guardia's presidencies are somewhat ambivalently honored in Costa Rica because he contributed to political and economic development even though he relied on military power to govern.

He introduced the Constitution of 1871, which remained the fundamental law for over three-quarters of a century and in a sense beyond. When the Constituent Assembly met to write a new constitution following the 1948 revolution, it decided to discard the draft constitution presented by the revolutionary junta. The assembly chose to simply modify the 1871 Constitution. As a result, the 1949 Constitution bears a close resemblance to that formulated under Guardia.

The outstanding material achievement of Guardia's initiatives proved to be railroad construction. The project inspired and initiated but not completed by Guardia had immense implications for the future of the country. The major goal in contracting with the Keith brothers and Henry Meiggs to build a railroad from the Central Valley to the Caribbean or Atlantic coast was to have a more direct, quicker, and less costly means of exporting coffee to European and North American markets. With the death of his brother, Minor Cooper Keith emerged as the driving force for the project. The railroad, which finally became operational around 1890 after great expense and loss of life, brought several profound changes to Costa Rica. The most obvious difference was the connection between the heartland and the Atlantic coast, which facilitated new development along the whole course of the railway. In the space of just a few years, Puerto Limon on the Caribbean became the principal port.

The prevalence of endemic diseases, particularly yellow fever, malaria, and dysentery, in the hot, humid tropical lowlands created problems for the railroad builders that were as difficult to overcome as the mountainous and heavily forested terrain. The Costa Ricans living in the Central Valley and along the Pacific side of the mountains were reluctant to live and work along the notoriously unhealthy railroad route.

Minor Cooper Keith experimented with importing workers from Italy and China before finally finding the desired labor supply in the British West Indies, principally Jamaica. The Chinese and Italians became small but significant ethnic groups that contributed disproportionately to subsequent national development. The West Indian population became the principal population component of the Caribbean coastal area. This importation of workers gave the whole region a distinct character that has only been modified since 1945 with greater internal migration by the Afro–Costa Ricans to other regions and by people from other regions into Limon and the coastal area.

THE BANANA TRADE

The projected railroad from San José to Limon met many obstacles, not the least of which was the increasing financial burden. Keith came up with an idea that had long-term consequences of political, social, and economic importance: He began to cultivate bananas for export to the U.S. market.

The banana trade provided a means for exploiting the land grants conferred on Keith's railroad construction enterprise in order to subsidize the project. Banana production also provided a cargo for the ships that brought supplies for the railroad construction crews. In this way it partially resolved one of the problems inherent in building a railroad to connect the Central Valley to the Atlantic coast: construction had to proceed primarily from the coast inward because essential materials had to be imported. The principal potential export, coffee, could not reach the coast until the railway reached the Central Valley.

Keith's solution consisted of planting bananas along the right of way and then exporting them to an expanding U.S. market. The banana, which had elicited a favorable popular response from U.S. consumers at the 1876 Centennial Exposition, needed only refrigerated ships and regular sailings to reach a U.S. port from which the fruit could enter the already technologically advanced U.S. transportation system. By 1880 Costa Rica was developing a second major export that proved to be a consistent and significant source of revenue and foreign exchange from the late nineteenth century to the present.

The opening of the Atlantic coast area to banana cultivation intensified immigration from Jamaica. U.S. private investment and management coupled with a Jamaican labor force created an English-speaking enclave in the banana zone. Because the whole zone had previously been unexploited, the banana and railroad companies ultimately built the infrastructure, from hospitals and schools to wharfage and water-treatment facilities. This led to an impressive upsurge in Costa Rican contact with the outside world as these companies served as the catalysts for more rapid and predictable transportation to the coast and from Limon to Europe and North America. They introduced new technologies in communications as well.

Although the nation welcomed the material progress, the increased access to the outside world, and the new sources of revenues and foreign exchange, the fact that banana production led to an outwardly oriented, English-speaking enclave became a major political issue in the twentieth century. First, such reformers as Jorge Volio Jiménez (1882–1955) protested the enclave, and then mainstream political leaders such as Ricardo Jiménez Oreamuno (1859–1945) and José Figueres Ferrer (b. 1906) eventually enacted measures to integrate the enclaves into national life.

DEMOCRATIZATION AND EDUCATIONAL REFORM

When Costa Rica celebrated one hundred years of democratic government in 1989, it commemorated the watershed election in which President Bernardo Soto Alfaro (1885–1889) and his hand-picked successor, Ascensión Esquivel Ibarra, accepted electoral defeat. The victor, José Joaquín Rodríguez Zeledón (1890–1894), and subsequent governments sometimes deviated from the democratic norm, but the all-important transfer of power based on a free election had taken place.

Soto, through his revered education minister, Mauro Fernández Acuña (1843–1905), made one of the most important advances for the consolidation of the democratic tendencies that had been present in Costa Rica since its beginnings. They established a system of free, compulsory public education in practice, not just in theory. The commitment to universal literacy has endured from the time of Fernández and contributed to sustained cultural, political, and economic progress in the twentieth century. Fernández's democratic proclivities manifested themselves when on the grounds that it was an unjustifiable expense for the benefit of the elite he closed the university until the state first had provided an elementary education for all.

THE AGE OF DON CLETO AND DON RICARDO

The period from 1906 to 1936 was dominated by two civilian presidents of unusual dedication and ability: Cleto González Víquez (1906–1910 and 1928–1932) and Ricardo Jiménez Oreamuno (1910–1914, 1924–1928, and 1932–1936). Although personalism and ephemeral party organizations characterized political activity, it remained civilian, peaceful, and civil throughout the period except for the Federico Tinoco Granados (1870–1931) dictatorship (1917–1919).

González Víquez and Jiménez Oreamuno consolidated the civilian tradition. Both governed within the Constitution and presided over progressive, fiscally responsible administrations that continued to support popular education, civil rights, and economic expansion. During this period Costa Rica served as the site for the Central American Court of Justice and gained international recognition for its progressive and orderly ways.

Under the surface, however, there were growing problems of increased class distinction, rural poverty, and the concentration of economic power in the hands of the coffee elite and foreign enterprise. The United Fruit Company, which administered a virtual state within a state along the Caribbean coast, interfered less in Costa Rica than in several other Central American nations. However, the presence of an English-speaking enclave dominated by a foreign corporation met with increasing ambivalence despite its recognized contributions to national progress and well-being.

Alfredo González Flores's presidency (1914–1917) and the organization of Jorge Volio Jiménez's (1882–1955) Reformist Party in the 1920s served as precursors of the social reform movements that would transform the national agenda for two decades beginning in 1940. Both recognized that the emerging middle sectors, the urban laborers, and peasants suffered from social injustice and lack of economic opportunity.

Congress chose González Flores as president after the 1914 election failed to produce a clear victor. Despite assuming power without a substantial political base, he attempted a fundamental reform by successfully sponsoring an income tax that placed a heavier burden on those of greater wealth. His position was further weakened by an attempt to control the off-year elections in order to secure greater congressional support for his economic reform program. When economic crisis struck as a result of market disruptions occasioned by World War I in Europe, González Flores was overthrown by his war minister, Federico Tinoco Granados.

Tinoco's repressive ways and the nonrecognition of his government by U.S. president Woodrow Wilson (1913–1921) led to ever more vociferous protest and armed rebellion. He resigned and went into exile in 1919.

Jorge Volio Jiménez became a "general" in the armed struggle against the Tinoco dictatorship after having been a reform-minded priest who identified with the plight of small, independent, but poor farmers. After his fall Tinoco turned his talents to politics and organized the Reform Party, which championed popular causes. His ideas strongly influenced future generations. In exchange for the inclusion of some of his program in the platform of the National Republican Party (PRN), he supported the victorious candidacy of Ricardo Jiménez Oreamuno in 1924.

The more educated and better informed electorate searched for government programs that would improve their standard of living. Jiménez, with the support of Volio, advocated reforms in 1924, but his second term, like his first, was characterized by profound respect for democratic traditions and a concern for public works, but without major advances in social reform. He did, however, create a National Insurance Bank. In his third term Jiménez successfully sponsored the nation's first minimum wage and carried out a very modest program of land distribution in the Caribbean lowlands.

The Great Depression and the void left by the disappearance of the Reform Party presented an opportunity for the development of a new political movement that had profound impacts on the nation for decades to come. In 1931 a young law student, Manuel Mora Valverde organized a communist party, the Farmers and Workers Bloc (Bloque de Obreros y Campesinos). Mora and like-minded leaders such as the novelist Carlos Luis Fallas Sibaja and Jaime Cerdas Mora capitalized on the growing discontent and occupied a significant political space as an influential minority party. The communists' program emphasized realizable reforms, many of which were already commonplace in contemporaneous Europe and North America. By the mid-1930s they had demonstrated sufficient strength to have led a successful strike in the banana zone (1934) and to have two representatives in Congress. By 1930 the population had reached one-half million and the personalistic politics of the period no longer commanded the allegiance of all the voters. The more organized and ideologically defined Bloque had demonstrated its growing appeal.

The National Republicans met the challenge presented by the communists by electing a no-nonsense anticommunist, León Cortés Castro, in 1936. Cortés won high marks as an administrator and for extending public works. However, his record on civil rights was widely questioned as were his allegedly pro-German sympathies. The protest against his high-handed dissolution of the Electoral Tribunal to deny the communists a seat in Congress extended far beyond the aggrieved party and included much of the political and intellectual leadership.

In 1940, the National Republican Party's candidate was Rafael Angel Calderón Guardia (1940–1944). The opposition experienced difficulties in organizing behind a viable candidate when Ricardo Jiménez, elder statesman and three-time president, withdrew his candidacy charging President Cortés with obstructing the electoral process. The opposition finally supported Mora Valverde's unsuccessful candidacy.

SOCIAL REFORM AND POLITICAL REACTION

With the opposition in disarray and without a viable candidate, Calderón won an overwhelming victory that seemed to confirm the continuance of Cortés's policies. Calderón, however, broke sharply with the past and initiated a sweeping program of change and social progress and set in motion the conflicts that culminated in the 1948 civil war.

Calderón's inauguration marked the beginning of a tumultuous and decisive decade in Costa Rica. The events of the 1940s resulted in a new Costa Rica in which the democratic and egalitarian tendencies of the past reached a new level of definition and effectiveness; in which sustained economic development through diversification and modernization reached ever higher levels; and in which a national conscience formed in support of social justice. The decade of the 1940s served to break with the past and yet build on the very positive achievements of that past. The reform program elicited strong reactions that shook the nation to its very foundations.

There were many factors involved in shaping the Calderón administration. The president leaned on his friend and advisor, Víctor Manuel Sanabria Martínez, who ascended to the post of archbishop of San José in 1940. The two shared the conviction that the best answer to the communists' promise of a more just society was to be found in the social encyclicals of the Roman Catholic Church. The Franklin D. Roosevelt administration in the United States (the hegemonic power in Central America) favored welfare capitalism and assiduously courted the Latin American nations with the expectation of establishing Western Hemisphere solidarity for the Second World War. In response to the elite reaction against his reform program, Calderón took advantage of the wartime alliance between the United States and the Soviet Union to enlist the support of a renamed and supposedly democratic communist party (Popular Vanguard Party—PVP), which ostensibly accepted his social Christian approach to reform.

In this atmosphere of change, and with the disruptions and initiatives of wartime (price controls, intervention of enemy properties, financial and trade agreements with the Allies, a military training unit and intelligence operations from the United States), Calderón secured passage in Congress of his extensive reform program. Congress amended the Constitution to include social guarantees. The social security system included national health insurance as well as provisions for retirement and disability pensions. The labor code provided for the creation of a ministry of labor and a series of guarantees for workers, including the right to organize and strike, a minimum wage, protection against arbitrary dismissal, and obligatory collective bargaining.

Calderón, with support in Congress from his own majority National Republicans and the Popular Vanguard, passed extensive social legislation. The University of Costa Rica, the nation's first university in the twentieth century, was founded. Another bill provided for the distribution of uncultivated land to those who brought it under cultivation and for compensation if the land was privately held. Another program distributed shoes to school children.

This set of social programs, along with graft and mismanagement, elicited a strong response from much of the national elite, many of whom considered Calderón a traitor to his class. It also served to activate increasingly politicized members of the middle class who opposed Calderón because he was an oligarch and because his administration was fiscally irresponsible. They also opposed the communists because they were inherently undemocratic. These middle-class dissidents formed the Center for the Study of National Problems (1940) and Democratic Action (1944), which later coalesced to form the Social Democratic Party (1945).

In the 1944 election, the governing party selected Teodoro Picado Michalski (1944–1948) to confront the Democratic Party, newly reorganized to advance the candidacy of former president León Cortés. The campaign was vigorous, vehement, and sometimes violent. Picado won amid widespread charges of fraud and intimidation. Although he was on the defensive from the very beginning, Picado passed a progressive income tax. He hoped that electoral reform would diminish the growing discontent. It did seem to have a beneficial effect on the off-year election in 1946, but that proved to be little more than the calm before the storm.

During the next two years, Costa Rica suffered from acrimonious political confrontations that ran the gamut from street protests and gang clashes through press excesses and terrorism to attempts at and preparations for armed uprisings. On the electoral front, the opposition united behind the figure of the prominent liberal journalist Otilio Ulate Blanco, leader of the National Union Party (PUN).

Among the dissidents who doubted the efficacy of the electoral reforms was José Figueres Ferrer, who became more prominent and sought support nationally and internationally for arms to overthrow the Calderónist-communist regime. Upon entering into an alliance to overthrow dictatorship in the region by signing the Pact of the Caribbean, Figueres received assurance from the Guatemalan president Juan José Arévalo Bermejo (1944–1948) that arms and men would be made available to him in the future.

When the election held on 8 February 1948 resulted in a provisional count showing Ulate victorious over Calderón, the governing coalition maintained its unity in Congress and voted to annul the presidential election. Both sides charged fraud; the flawed electoral apparatus had failed.

CIVIL WAR AND REVOLUTIONARY JUNTA

Although Archbishop Sanabria, along with business and political leaders, continued to seek a compromise to avoid armed conflict, events moved quickly to a bloody confrontation. Government forces repressed opposition leaders. Figueres, from his estate in the south, called on the opposition to mobilize for revolution. As Figueres's forces mustered at his estate, La Lucha, he called on Arévalo to send arms and men from Guatemala. On 10

March 1948, Figueres's Army of National Liberation seized several strategic objectives in the south. Picado, unaware of Figueres's international connections and therefore of his potential strength, reacted reluctantly and somewhat ambivalently to the uprising. He did not maintain decisive control over the small army under his command so that the initiative remained with the insurgents. As a consequence, the major force that confronted the rebels was made up of PVP volunteers.

After several bloody battles, the rebels were poised to move on San José. At this crucial juncture the pro-government forces, now split by mutual suspicions and distrust, welcomed the intervention of the diplomatic corps to bring about a negotiated peace. At this point Mora, who controlled the most numerous and reliable progovernment forces, met in secret with Figueres at the Alto de Ochomogo, just outside Cartago. With assurances from Figueres that the National Liberation would respect the social legislation and that there would be no reprisals against the progovernment supporters, Mora agreed to abide by the peace treaty negotiated by Picado with Figueres's representative Father Benjamin Núñez Vargas.

Since the pretext for the rebellion had been Congress's annulment of the 1948 election, it was incumbent on the triumphant forces to recognize Ulate as president-elect. On 1 May, Ulate reached an agreement with Figueres under which he accepted that title. Figueres, who took the title of president of the Founding Committee of the Second Republic (Junta), organized the junta along the lines of a presidential cabinet, which then governed the nation for the next eighteen months. The victors recognized only the results of the 1948 presidential election; all other results remained annulled.

To the surprise of many within the former opposition, the junta consolidated rather than overturned the reforms of the previous eight years. It persecuted the PVP and Calderónist leadership, but enhanced their programs. However, Figueres gave them a social democratic orientation.

The most profound changes instituted by the junta were contained in the 1949 Constitution. The armed forces were abolished in favor of a national police force. The banking system was nationalized. The creation of an electoral tribunal as a fourth power within the government allowed Costa Rica to develop one of the world's fairest and most transparent systems for guaranteeing the validity of the exercise of suffrage. The junta also gave new impetus to the creation of cooperatives, the modernization of education, the extension of higher education, and the creation of autonomous institutions, such as the Costa Rican Insurance Institute (INS), which were created by the state but governed by an independent board of directors.

The social democratic orientation of the junta met with a strong negative response from Ulate's followers, the numerically dominant PUN members of the victorious coalition that had opposed Calderón. This political dissent even led to an abortive armed uprising headed by Figueres's defense minister, Edgar Cardona Quiros. PUN elected a clear majority in the Constituent Assembly, which then declined to ratify the draft document prepared for the junta, but instead updated the liberal constitution that had served the nation since 1871. The reformed constitution fell far short of the reforms that the junta espoused.

POLITICAL DEMOCRACY AND SUSTAINED GROWTH

After Ulate served his term, a new party committed to the ideals of the revolution, the National Liberation Party (PLN), successfully supported Figueres's candidacy. As the first president (1953–1958) elected under the new constitution, Figueres interpreted the great margin of victory that carried him to office as a popular mandate to implement the new party's social democratic program. From this election forward, the PLN has been the dominant political force in the nation and its principles have profoundly affected many aspects of national life. Its greatest strength has been a burgeoning, self-conscious middle class that transformed Costa Rica over the next generation into an unusually well-developed country, given its small population and limited resource base.

During the postwar period, Costa Rica sustained a remarkable rate of cultural and economic growth. Education on all levels reached all areas of the country; the arts flourished. Economic growth was fueled by increased productivity in traditional crops and by diversification into new crops and light industry. The expanding delivery system of medical care is rivaled in Latin America only by that of post-revolution Cuba. In the twenty-first century, telecommunications, manufacturing, services, and tourism rival primary exports. The rate of increase in living standards brought the nation nearly to the level of the industrialized nations in many areas, such as literacy and life expectancy. However, despite strong social indicators, geographic disparities persist.

The nation's remarkable growth was accomplished in the face of rapid population increase. By 1960 Costa Rica had one of the highest rates of population increase in the world (estimated to be nearly 4 percent). It declined to somewhere between 2 and 2.5 percent by 1970 and has remained within that range since then. From an estimated population of 1 million in 1956, it soared to 1,871,780 by the census of 1973, reached just over 3 million in 1990, and increased to an estimated 4.3 million in 2007. Some 500,000 to 1 million immigrants from Nicaragua, many undocumented, add to the population.

The PLN provided the nation with vital and viable alternatives for social, economic, and political development that were neither communistic nor dominated by an oligarchy. It provided the country with a stable political environment that permitted it to survive the cold war with its political democracy intact as well as to sustain a high rate of economic development and diversification.

The permanent, highly organized, and idcological nature of the PLN also marked a turning point in political development. In the face of the PLN challenge, the ephemeral, personalistic groupings of the past could no longer compete. For the generation following Figueres's election, political contests pitted the PLN against anti-PLN coalitions supported by the hugely successful daily newspaper *La Nación* (founded in 1946). The Liberationists controlled the legislature for the most part, but the presidency alternated between them and the opposition. After Figueres's term, a PUN leader, Mario Echandi Jiménez (1958–1962), was elected with support from the still potent National Republicans. He was followed in office by Francisco Orlich Bolmarcich (1962–1966), one of the leaders in the 1948 uprising and a contemporary and close friend of Figueres. Continuing this alternation in power, José Joaquín Trejos Fernández (1966–1970), a National Republican and longtime supporter of Calderón, was elected to the presidency in 1966 as the wounds from the

confrontations of the 1940s began to heal. The PLN recovered the presidency in 1970, when Figueres won his second term. (The Constitution had been amended to prohibit second terms, but the prohibition did not apply to Figueres or Echandi.) When Daniel Oduber Quirós was elected (1974–1978) to succeed him, Costa Rican pundits began to speculate about the possible creation of a one-party state similar to Mexico.

However, in the 1978 campaign the PLN candidate, Luis Alberto Monge Álvarez, met a revived coalition which demonstrated greater internal coherence than the previous challenges to its continued dominance. Calling itself simply Unidad, the anti-Liberation coalition nominated Rodrigo Carazo Odio (1978–1982), a former PLN leader, and won the election.

The Carazo presidency, however, did not live up to its promise. Concerns about the Sandinista revolution in Nicaragua, low coffee prices, and high petroleum costs plagued the administration. Cararzo failed to react quickly enough to the crisis, and the resultant inflation and excessive national debt broke the pattern of rapid and sustained development that had characterized Costa Rica for a generation. The Unidad coalition, however, laid the foundation for a second major party based on social Christian principles and less state intervention in the economy.

The PLN's Monge (1982–1986) defeated the discredited Unidad in the 1982 election but faced daunting tasks. Heavy debt coupled with American pressure to play a more active role in the U.S.-directed effort to bring down the Sandinista government in Nicaragua seriously crippled Monge's efforts to revive the economy and maintain political democracy and peace. Although avowing neutrality, the Monge adminstration was only partially able to avert U.S. and internal pressures to aid the contras. The continual influx of Central American refugees, particularly from Nicaragua, placed an added economic and social burden on the Monge administration and those of his successors.

After leading a generational revolt within the PLN that culminated in his nomination, Oscar Arias Sánchez (1986–1990) defeated the leader of the unified party that had emerged from the Unidad coalition, Rafael Angel Calderón Fournier. As president, Arias brought renewed vigor and vision to his party and nation. He went beyond Monge's neutrality to become the most prominent and successful leader seeking peace in Central America. He decreased the national debt through a series of initiatives. He asserted national interests despite American pressure and largely eliminated Costa Rica as a base for anti-Sandinista activities. His growing international stature, a result of being awarded the Nobel Prize for peace, helped Arias maintain an independent, pro-negotiations stance that greatly contributed to increased stability in Central America.

The election of Calderón Fournier in 1990 marked a new milestone in national political development. Calderón Fournier and Arias represented the rise of a new generation of political leaders who were not involved in the 1948 civil war. They are the beneficiaries of the reforms that transformed the nation between 1940 and 1970, but they do not carry the scars and rancor of many of their predecessors. Calderón Fournier brought a more internally coherent major party to power, the Christian Social Unity Party (PUSC), which was based on the social Christian principles that had inspired the reforms of the early 1940s. The earlier insistence by the Center for the Study of National Problems on the need for permanent, ideologically based political parties led to the formation of the PLN. The PLN's success had created the necessity for a similarly coherent rival. As of the election of 1990, that necessity seemed a reality.

In the twenty-first century, the PUSC and PLN continue to dominate, though new and viable political parties have emerged. In 2002 the Partido Acción Ciudadana (PAC; Citizens Action Party) captured 26 percent of the vote in the presidential elections, thereby forcing the country to hold its first-ever runoff. Again in 2006, the PAC proved strong. The party's presidential candidate, Ottón Solis Fallas, won enough votes against former President Oscar Arias Sanchez to require an unexpected manual recount. Arias, by a very slim margin, emerged the victor.

See also **Costa Rica, Constitutions; Costa Rica, National Liberation Party; Costa Rica, Second Republic.**

BIBLIOGRAPHY

Ameringer, Charles D. *Don Pepe* (1978).

Araya Pochet, Carlos. *Historia de los partidos políticos: Liberación nacional* (1968).

Bell, John Patrick. *Crisis in Costa Rica* (1971).

Biesanz, Richard, Karen Zubris Biesanz, and Mavis Hiltunen Biesanz, *The Costa Ricans* (1982; rev. ed. 1988).

Edelman, Marc, and Joanne Kenen, eds., *The Costa Rica Reader* (1989).

English, Burt H. *Liberación Nacional in Costa Rica* (1971).

Gudmundson, Lowell. *Costa Rica Before Coffee* (1986).

Hall, Carolyn. *Costa Rica: A Geographical Interpretation in Historical Perspective* (1985).

Harpelle, Ronald N. *The West Indians of Costa Rica: Race, Class, and the Integration of an Ethnic Minority.* Montreal: McGill–Queen's University Press, 2001.

Hayes, Anne M. *Female Prostitution in Costa Rica: Historical Perspectives, 1880–1930.* New York: Routledge, 2006.

Lehoucq, Fabrice Edouard, and Iván Molina Jiménez. *Stuffing the Ballot Box: Fraud, Electoral Reform, and Democratization in Costa Rica.* New York: Cambridge University Press, 2002.

Malavassi Aguilar, Ana Paulina. *Entre la marginalidad social y los orígenes de la salud pública: Leprosos, curanderos y facultativos en el Valle Central de Costa Rica (1784–1845).* San José: Editorial de la Universidad de Costa Rica, 2003.

Meléndez, Carlos. *Juan Santamaría* (1982).

Murillo Jiménez, Hugo. *Tinoco y los Estados Unidos* (1981).

Obregón, Clotilde María. *El proceso electoral y el poder ejecutivo en Costa Rica: 1808–1998.* San José: Editorial de la Universidad de Costa Rica, 2000.

Palmer, Steven Paul, and Iván Molina Jiménez, eds. *The Costa Rica Reader: History, Culture, Politics.* Durham, NC: Duke University Press, 2004.

Putnam, Lara. *The Company They Kept: Migrants and the Politics of Gender in Caribbean Costa Rica, 1870–1960.* Chapel Hill: University of North Carolina Press, 2004.

Quesada Camacho, Juan Rafael. *Historia de la historiografía costarricense, 1821–1940.* San José: Editorial de la Universidad de Costa Rica, 2001.

Sandoval-García, Carlos. *Threatening Others: Nicaraguans and the Formation of National Identities in Costa Rica.* Athens: Ohio University Press, 2004.

Sawchuk, Dana. *The Costa Rican Catholic Church, Social Justice, and the Rights of Workers, 1979–1996.* Waterloo, Canada: Wilfrid Laurier University Press, 2004.

Stewart, Watt. *Keith and Costa Rica* (1964).

Stone, Samuel F. *La dinastia de los conquistadores* (1975).

JOHN PATRICK BELL

COSTA RICA, CONSTITUTIONS.

The basic constitutional framework of Costa Rica has been established by documents of 1825, 1844 (as amended in 1847 and 1848), 1871, and 1949. However, constitutions of one sort or another were also written or rewritten in 1823, 1824, 1841, 1847, 1848, 1859, 1869, and 1917. Moreover, the existence of a Central American Federation Constitution of 1824 (amended in 1835) makes Costa Rican constitutional authority problematic until the 1840s at the very least. Finally, the earliest constitutional precedents date from both the Cortes of Cádiz experiment of 1812 and the Independence-era pacts and statutes of 1821–1823; major codifications of Costa Rican civil law were undertaken in 1841 and 1886.

Political participation as voter, elector, or office-holder was severely limited by property, literacy, and gender qualifications in all constitutions prior to 1949. However, major electoral changes were made somewhat earlier, with direct elections after 1913, the secret ballot in 1928, an increasingly nonpartisan electoral machinery after the 1930s, a much more inclusive literacy and property qualification in practice after the 1890s, and the vote for women, finally, in 1949. While pre-1870 experiments with dual-chamber assemblies were undertaken, the Chamber of Deputies, or Assembly, legislated while a Senate was a more advisory, quasi-judicial body. However, the single-assembly model has long dominated. In this, as in the fairly rigid nineteenth-century stance on indirect elections with stiff requirements for a limited electorate, the influence of the Spanish constitutionalism of Cádiz would appear to be more directly relevant than the North American model of the time.

According to the Costa Rican authority Hernán G. Peralta, the constitutional tradition draws most heavily upon the 1821 "Pacto de Concordia," the 1825 Ley Fundamental, and the 1871 and the 1949 constitutions. The sequential relationship of Costa Rican constitutions can be summarized as follows:

1. The independence-related Pacto de Concordia (also Pacto Social Interino; 1 December 1821), reformed by political statutes of 17 March and 16 May 1823

2. The Central American Federation Constitution of 1824 (amended in 1835, largely irrelevant after 1838)

3. As a consequence of the 1824 document, the Ley Fundamental of 25 January 1825, formally abrogated by the Ley de Bases y Garantías of 1841

4. The Constitution of 9 April 1844, which reinstated much of the 1825 law, amended in various ways by new constitutions of 10 February 1847, 30 November 1848, 26 December 1859, and 15 April 1869

5. The Constitution of 7 December 1871, amended by its promulgator, General Tomás Guardia, in 1882, and suspended by the Tinoco dictatorship of 1917–1919

6. The Constitution of 7 November 1949, which continues in force.

The constitutional tradition in Costa Rica has, in general, opposed Central American union tendencies regardless of the local attitudes toward centralization or decentralization of government. Until the 1871 Constitution, the legislative branch held most power with various schemes to restrain the executive, particularly after dictatorships led by Braulio Carrillo (1838–1842) and Juan Rafael Mora (1859).

Early in independent national life the supremacy of the legislative branch was extreme and a thin disguise for the power of municipal, localist authorities who doubled as deputies in early national assemblies. Carrillo defeated the most extreme of such tendencies—the rotation of the site of the capital—with the 1841 Ley de Bases y Garantías, which abrogated the 1825 Constitution. When Mora amassed great power in the late 1850s, in part as a consequence of his immense popularity as the victor over William Walker in Nicaragua, constitutional changes were again instituted to annul his reelection (1859) and restrain like-minded future executives. With the revolt led by Guardia Gutiérrez in 1870, the pendulum swung sharply back toward presidentialism and against the rule of family-based cliques in the Assembly. Although Guardia briefly abrogated the 1871 Constitution as dictator (1877–1882), he reinstated the document, along with the total elimination of the death penalty, shortly before his death in 1882.

The framework of the 1871 Constitution survived until the civil war of 1948 and the new Constitution of 1949, although some major changes were made in the interim. The preeminence of the executive was clear throughout the early

COSTA RICA, NATIONAL LIBERATION PARTY

twentieth century, in regimes led by such figures as three-time president Ricardo Jiménez, by Cleto González, and by León Cortés, as well as in the controversial actions of president Rafael Angel Calderón Guardia leading up to the conflict of 1948.

Only once was the Constitution of 1871 challenged directly prior to 1948: by the military coup and dictatorship of the Tinoco brothers, Federico and José Joaquín, in 1917. Their own constitution was short-lived, being abrogated in favor of the 1871 document with their downfall in 1919.

The document drawn up by the victors of 1948 remains in force today. While it was still largely presidentialist, efforts were made to avoid the worst of the earlier excesses. While no truly radical strengthening of the Assembly or the municipalities was attempted, each was recognized as an important seat of power. As a counterbalance to the perceived ills of presidentialism, the 1949 Constitution established the new category of "autonomous" or "decentralized" institutions in the public sector. The social security health system, the electrical and telecommunications services, and the national insurance institute, among others, were to be administered nonpartisanly, independent of executive branch control. While such control has been realized only partially, these agencies have become the largest employers and interest groups in the nation and, arguably, have provided an element of restraint on partisanship from the executive branch.

The 1949 Constitution also established a number of new departures. The social function of property and the need for state intervention in the economy were changes from earlier Liberal orthodoxy. As part of this thrust the banks were nationalized and a special one-time 10 percent tax on capital was levied to provide for reconstruction. The abolition of a standing army has often been credited to the authors of the 1949 Constitution, although professional military forces were few in number and had exerted little influence as a separate interest group for a long time. Most military figures leading revolts in the past—against Mora in 1859, by Guardia in 1871, or by the Tinoco brothers in 1917—did so at the behest of civilian forces against unpopular regimes. They acted as barracks commanders within an elite political contest with few troops and little in the way of institutional interests to defend.

Most important of the constitutional changes brought about in 1949 are the enfranchisement of women and the elimination of illiteracy and property qualifications for the vote. Likewise, the power of the independent Supreme Electoral Tribunal was strengthened significantly, as a consequence of the alleged fraud of 1948. The very visible success of this agency since then has been built upon similar, incremental reforms made since the 1920s, in reaction to the evident manipulation of votes by executives under the 1871 Constitution. Presidential reelection was also prohibited, putting to rest another of the means by which the executive controlled votes. This has led to a basically two-party or two-coalition alternation in power since 1948. Modern constitutional conflicts have been infrequent, although on the negative side, the political rights of those who lost in 1948 were denied them for some time thereafter. Nevertheless, perhaps the most serious and recurrent weakness of Costa Rican constitutionalism prior to 1948—the manipulation of electoral machinery and vote counting—appears to have been resolved by the 1949 Constitution.

See also **Central America, Constitution of 1824.**

BIBLIOGRAPHY

On Costa Rican constitutionalism the authority is Hernán G. Peralta, *Las constituciones de Costa Rica* (1962). Also useful is Jorge Sáenz Carbonell, *El despertar constitucional de Costa Rica* (1985). On the 1949 Constitution, see Oscar Aguillar Bulgarelli, *La constitucion de 1949: Antecedentes y proyecciones* (1973). On the disruptions of constitutional rule, see Rafael Orbregón Loría, *Conflictos militares y políticos de Costa Rica* (1951); and on the legislature, his *El poder legislativo en Costa Rica* (1966). On the question of suffrage, see Samuel Z. Stone, *La dinastía de los conquistadores* (1975), and Cleto González Víquez, *El sufragio en Costa Rica ante la historia y la legislación*, 2d ed. (1978).

Additional Bibliography

Trejos, Gerardo, and Hubert May. *Constitución y democracia costarricense.* San José, Costa Rica: Editorial Juricentro, 2001.

Yashar, Deborah J. *Demanding Democracy: Reform and Reaction in Costa Rica and Guatemala, 1870s–1950s.* Stanford, CA: Stanford University Press, 1997.

LOWELL GUDMUNDSON

COSTA RICA, NATIONAL LIBERATION PARTY.

The National Liberation Party became the dominant political party in Costa

Rica with the election of José Figueres Ferrer as president in 1953. Since that time a majority of the nation's chief executives have been PLN members, and the party generally has enjoyed a majority in the national legislature. Not only did the PLN achieve a dominant position in Costa Rican politics, but its organization and success induced a new politics. No longer could informal, transitory groups form around a charismatic candidate to contest an upcoming election. To meet the challenge of the highly organized, ideologically coherent PLN, its opponents had to become more organized and present the electorate with specific programs and a greater degree of continuity.

The PLN was founded in October 1951 by a group of insiders of the National Liberation movement, which had supported the successful 1948 armed uprising and the resultant de facto government under Figueres Ferrer's presidency (1948–1949). They met at Francisco Orlich Bolmarcich's *finca*, La Paz. They wanted to convert the movement into a permanent, highly structured political party by capitalizing on the immense popularity of Figueres. Although many of the participants had been active in the Social Democratic Party, they recognized that its poor showing in the December 1948 election indicated the need to form a more broadly based party and to take advantage of the National Liberation label and its association with military victory, social justice, political renewal, and a greater political role for the middle class.

The PLN traces its origins to the formation of the Center for the Study of National Problems (1940), with its strong affinity for social democratic ideas. The Center merged with the Democratic Action group to form the Social Democratic Party (1945), which unsuccessfully presented Figueres as its candidate to lead the united opposition in the 1948 election. It was a party born of national crisis. The successful revolt of 1948 vaulted the founders of the movement into prominent positions in government. Figueres's decisive victory in the 1953 election assured a bright future for the PLN.

See also **Ferrer, José; La Paz.**

BIBLIOGRAPHY

Ameringer, Charles D. *Don Pepe* (1978).

Araya Pochet, Carlos. *Historia de los partidos políticos: Liberación Nacional* (1968).

Bell, John Patrick. *Crisis in Costa Rica* (1971).

English, Burt H. *Liberación Nacional in Costa Rica* (1971).

Longley, Kyle. *The Sparrow and the Hawk: Costa Rica and the United States during the Rise of José Figueres.* Tuscaloosa: University of Alabama Press, 1997.

Obregón Valverde, Enrique. *Socialismo democrático y el Partido Liberación Nacional.* San José, Costa Rica: Editorial Universidad Estatal a Distancia, 2003.

JOHN PATRICK BELL

COSTA RICA, SECOND REPUBLIC.

The Second Republic is the name given to the government that resulted from the reorganization following Costa Rica's 1948 civil war. On 1 March 1948, outgoing Costa Rican president Teodoro Picado Michalski used his control over the Legislative Assembly (national congress) to annul the presidential election held in February, replacing the apparent winner, Otilio Ulate, with the defeated candidate, Rafael Ángel Calderón Guardia. Reacting to this violation of the constitutional order, José Figueres Ferrer (1906–1990), a little-known political activist, led a six-week War of National Liberation to restore legitimate government and enforce Ulate's claim to the presidency.

Raising a volunteer force and using arms supplied by antidictatorial exile elements in Guatemala, Figueres defeated the would-be usurpers and presided over the Founding Junta of the Second Republic for eighteen months (April 1948–November 1949). During its exercise of power, the Founding Junta abolished the national army and held elections for a constituent assembly for the purpose of drafting a new constitution. With the adoption of the Constitution of 1949, Figueres Ferrer and the Junta turned over the executive power to Ulate, beginning Costa Rica's Second Republic, a new political era characterized by free elections, stable government, diminished presidential authority, and a tilt toward socialism in economic and social affairs.

See also **Picado Michalski, Teodoro; Ulate Blanco, Otilio.**

BIBLIOGRAPHY

John Patrick Bell, *Crisis in Costa Rica: The 1948 Revolution* (1971).

Bert H. English, *Liberación Nacional in Costa Rica: The Development of a Political Party in a Transitional Society* (1971).

Charles D. Ameringer, *Don Pepe: A Political Biography of José Figueres of Costa Rica* (1978), and *Democracy in Costa Rica* (1982).

Additional Bibliography

Longley, Kyle. *The Sparrow and the Hawk: Costa Rica and the United States during the Rise of José Figueres.* Tuscaloosa: University of Alabama Press, 1997.

Rovira Mas, Jorge. *Estado y política económica en Costa Rica, 1948–1970.* San José: Editorial de la Universidad de Costa Rica, 2000.

CHARLES D. AMERINGER

COS Y PÉREZ, JOSÉ MARÍA (?–1819).

José María Cos y Pérez (*d.* November 1819), Mexican insurgent ideologue. Born in Zacatecas, he studied in Guadalajara, where he entered the Seminario Tridentino. A doctor of theology, he opposed the insurrection in 1810. When suspected of sedition, he joined Ignacio López Rayón (1773–1832) and became a writer and ideologue for the insurgency. In 1812 he wrote the *Plan de paz y plan de guerra,* and published the insurgent papers *Ilustrador Nacional* and *Ilustrador Americano.* He served as vicar general of the army and deputy for Zacatecas in the insurgent Congress. A signer of the Constitution of Apatzingán (1814), he became a member of the executive branch. When Congress reprimanded him for directing troops while serving in the executive, he disavowed that body in 1815. Although first condemned to death and later to life imprisonment, he was released by Rayón and later received amnesty from the colonial regime in 1817. He died in Pátzcuaro.

See also **Chilpancingo, Congress of.**

BIBLIOGRAPHY

Alejandro Villaseñor y Villaseñor, *Biografías de los héroes y caudillos de la Independencia,* vol. 2 (1910), pp. 1–12.

José María Miquel I Vergés, *La Independencia mexicana y la prensa insurgente* (1941) and *Diccionario de insurgentes* (1969), pp. 151–154.

Additional Bibliography

Jiménez Gassós, Teresita del Carmen. *José María Cos, ideólogo de la insurgencia mexicana.* Xalapa: Universidad Veracruzana, 1999.

VIRGINIA GUEDEA

COTAPOS BAEZA, ACARIO (1889–1969).

Acario Cotapos Baeza (*b.* 30 April 1889: *d.* 22 November 1969), Chilean composer. Born in Valdivia, Chile, Cotapos was one of the group of authors, poets, composers, architects, and visual artists known as Los Diez, the first group to comprise the Chilean cultural avant-garde. Initially self-taught, at the age of twenty-seven Cotapos moved to New York to study. For the ten years following, he counted among his associates Edgard Varèse, Aaron Copland, Henry Cowell, Ernest Bloch, and Darius Milhaud. In 1927, with Varèse and others, Cotapos founded the International Composers Guild, one of the first organizations with a mandate to perform new music. In 1927, Cotapos left New York for Paris and Madrid, where he composed a number of important works. Returning to his homeland in 1940, he served as secretary of the National Conservatory from 1940 to 1946. He was supervisor of the Instituto de Extensión Musical of the University of Chile from 1949 until his death in Santiago. His musical output includes works for voice, piano, orchestra, and chamber ensembles. Much of his music, characterized by a free and independent spirit, tends toward the dramatic and monumental.

See also **Music: Art Music.**

BIBLIOGRAPHY

Revista musical chilena (April 1961).

John Vinton, ed., *Dictionary of Contemporary Music* (1971).

Samuel Claro Valdés and Jorge Urrutia, *Historia de la música en Chile* (1973).

Gerard Béhague, *Music in Latin America: An Introduction* (1979).

Samuel Claro Valdés, *Oyendo a Chile* (1979).

Samuel Claro Valdés et al., *Iconografía musical chilena,* vols. 1 and 2 (1989).

Additional Bibliography

Aharonián, Coriún. "Un extraño señor llamado Acario Cotapos." *Revista Musical Chilena* 44 (January–June 1990): 114–117.

Merino Montero, Luis. "Jorge Urrutia Blondel y Acario Catapos: Reflexiones sobre dos facetas de la música chilena." *Boletín de la Academia Chilena de Bellas Artes* 2 (1989): 129–162.

Merino Montero, Luis. "Nuevas luces sobre Acario Cotapos." *Revista Musical Chilena* 37 (January–June 1983): 3–49.

SERGIO BARROSO

Eul-Soo Pang, *In Pursuit of Honor and Power: Noblemen of the Southern Cross in Nineteenth-Century Brazil* (1988).

EUL-SOO PANG

COTEGIPE, BARÃO DE (1815–1889).

Barão de Cotegipe (João Mauricio Wanderley; *b.* 23 October 1815; *d.* 13 February 1889), Brazilian politician. Cotegipe was identified with Bahian politics and slavocratic sugar interests throughout his life. After graduating from the Olinda Law Faculty in Pernambuco in 1837, Cotegipe set out on the path that eventually made him the archetypal imperial mandarin. He moved up steadily through the political ranks, holding a county judgeship and a variety of provincial elected offices before becoming a national deputy in the early 1840s. By 1856 he was a senator from Bahia, and a member of the cabinet. An important chieftain of the pro-slavery national Conservative Party, Cotegipe was himself a slave owner and a holder of several sugar plantations, all inherited by his wife, a daughter of the Conde de Passé, perhaps the richest planter in Bahia Province. In 1875 Cotegipe, then serving as minister of finance, authored the landmark legislation (Decree no. 2687 of 6 November 1875) that created the agricultural credit guaranteeing 7 percent interest on all investments to create the modern sugar mill complex, or *engenho central*. In 1885 Cotegipe became prime minister. His Conservative government, finally facing up to the reality that slavery in Brazil could not continue forever, introduced the Saraiva–Cotegipe Law of 1885 that freed all slaves over sixty-five years old, thereby immediately manumitting 120,000 older slaves. Typical of many imperial mandarins, Cotegipe was a poor businessman when it came to looking after his own interests and died poor, months before the monarchy was overthrown by a discontented army.

See also **Brazil: The Empire (Second); Slavery: Brazil.**

BIBLIOGRAPHY

Sacramento Augusto Victorino Alves Blake, *Diccionario bibliographico brasileiro*, 7 vols. (1897).

José Wanderley Pinho, *Cotegipe e seu tempo: Primeiro phase, 1815–1867* (1937), and *História de um engenho do Recôncavo, 1552–1944* (1946).

COTOCOLLAO.

Cotocollao, a large prehistoric village located in the northern highlands of Ecuador, is the regional type-site for the archaeological period known as the Formative. Prior to the discovery of this site in the 1970s, little was known about cultural life in the northern sierra during this period. The site takes its name from the modern barrio of Cotocollao, which is situated at the north end of the capital city of Quito. The site is strategically located near a pass that connects the Quito basin with the tropical forests of the western Andean foothills. Cotocollao was occupied from approximately 1800 to 500 BCE, a period corresponding to the Middle and Late Formative in Ecuadorian prehistory. The occupation levels at Cotocollao are capped by a thick layer of volcanic ash and lapilli associated with the eruption of Mount Pululahua, which is located about seventeen miles to the north. The eruption of this volcano, dated to approximately 467 BCE, is thought to have caused the abandonment of the site.

The Formative Period in Andean prehistory is defined by the appearance of pottery and incipient agriculture. These developments occurred at different times in different places. The earliest evidence of pottery in Ecuador is found on the coast, where Valdivia ceramics have been dated to circa 3200 BCE. This tradition was eventually replaced by Machalilla Phase pottery, around 2000 BCE. The Cotocollao ceramic assemblage exhibits decorative and morphological similarities with both Valdivia and Machalilla pottery, suggesting that connections existed between the highlands and the coast around the time of transition between these two coastal phases. The Cotocollao assemblage also evidences some stylistic affinities with ceramics from the southern highlands and the eastern slopes of the Andes.

Distinctive vessel forms in the ceramic assemblage from Cotocollao include straight-walled, flat-bottomed bowls; stirrup-spout bottles; and strap-handled bottles. The latter form is typical of the Chorrera pottery horizon, which follows Machalilla and is found throughout much of Ecuador during the Late Formative Period. The most important diagnostic element of the Cotocollao assemblage is the decorated, ground stone bowl. A ceremonial function is postulated for these objects on the basis of the technical expertise involved in their manufacture and the lack of apparent wear from use. The stone bowls from Cotocollao are the earliest known in the northern sierra, and the Quito region has been suggested as a possible locus of manufacture for these objects.

The pattern of spatial organization identified at the site of Cotocollao involves the arrangement of household clusters around a village cemetery. The cemetery apparently served as the ritual focal point of the community. This is in contrast to the pattern described for Formative Period sites on the coast, where dwellings are typically arranged around a central public-ceremonial space. The cemetery at Cotocollao has produced one of the largest samples of prehistoric skeletal remains from the northern sierra. Analysis of the approximately 200 sets of remains from the site has provided important information on diet, disease, and demography for the Late Formative Period population. In addition to the osteological evidence, finds of carbonized beans and maize in the earliest levels at Cotocollao, together with the quantity of *manos* (pestles), *metates* (mortars), and hoes recovered at the site, indicate that agriculture was the primary means of subsistence for the inhabitants of this site. Given the marshy environment of the northern Quito basin during the pre-Columbian era, waterfowl also figured significantly in the local diet.

See also **Archaeology; Chorrera; Valdivia Culture.**

BIBLIOGRAPHY

Fine-Dare, Kathleen. *Cotocollao: Ideología, Historia, y Acción en un barrio de Quito.* Quito: Abya-Yala Press, 1991.

Porras, Pedro. *Arqueología de Quito 1: Fase Cotocollao.* Quito: Centro de Investigaciones Arqueológicas, Pontífica Universidad Católica del Ecuador, 1982.

Raymond, J. Scott, and Richard Burger, eds. *The Archaeology of Formative Ecuador.* Washington, DC: Dumbarton Oaks Research Library and Collection, 2003.

Ubelaker, Douglas H. "Prehistoric Human Remains from the Cotocollao Site, Pichincha Province, Ecuador." *Journal of the Washington Academy of Science* 70, no. 2 (1980): 59–74.

Villalba, Marcelo. *Cotocollao: Una aldea formativa del Valle de Quito.* Quito: Serie Monográfica 2, Miscelánea Antropológica Ecuatoriana. Museos del Banco Central del Ecuador, 1988.

TAMARA L. BRAY

COTO WAR. Coto War (1921), an armed conflict between Panama and Costa Rica over the Coto, a region in Panama's Chiriquí Province along the Panamanian–Costa Rican border. The controversy began soon after independence from Spain. In 1911 the chief justice of the U.S. Supreme Court, Edward D. White, was asked to arbitrate. He rendered his decision in 1914, but Panama did not accept it, alleging that it favored Costa Rica. Hostilities broke out in 1921, when Costa Rica invaded the area. Panama recaptured the area easily. The conflict spread, however, when Costa Rica moved into the province of Bocas del Toro. Fearing that its interests might be threatened, the United States forced Panama to accept the White decision.

See also **Costa Rica; United States-Latin American Relations.**

BIBLIOGRAPHY

Manuel Octavio Sisnet, *Belisario Porras o la vocación de la nacionalidad* (1972).

Additional Bibliography

Cuestas G., Carlos H. *Panamá y Costa Rica, entre la diplomacia y la guerra.* Panamá: Litho Editorial Chen, 1999.

JUAN MANUEL PÉREZ

COTTON. Cotton, a plant native to most of the warmer regions on earth, including the tropical and semitropical regions of the Americas. It was cultivated and woven into cloth by all three of the great pre-Columbian civilizations: the Mayas, the Aztecs, and the Incas. Long before European contact with the Americas, cotton had been introduced into Europe from the Middle East, and consequently was not particularly impressive to the newly arrived Spanish conquerors. Nevertheless, cultivation of cotton continued after contact, and contributed to a cottage textile industry in Spanish and Portuguese America during the colonial period.

The mechanization of the spinning and weaving processes during the Industrial Revolution of the eighteenth century increased production of cotton textiles enormously. In the mid-1700s both the Portuguese colony of Brazil and the British Caribbean islands exported large amounts of cotton fiber for the rapidly growing British textile industy. By 1800, however, the United States had replaced the Caribbean islands as the major transatlantic source of cotton, thanks to Eli Whitney's cotton gin.

After independence, during the middle and late nineteenth century (the liberal/positivist period), many Latin American countries, particularly Mexico, Brazil, and Colombia, attempted to develop their own textile industries, and in conjunction with this effort they expanded cotton production. In addition, cotton became a very profitable export commodity for Latin American countries after the U.S. cotton industry was destroyed by the Civil War. By the end of World War I, textile manufacturing had been initiated in most Latin American countries, and most countries were producing cotton for domestic use, for export, or for both. Because cotton was intimately connected to industrialization and nascent capitalism, it produced a semiproletarian agricultural work force in many places. Accordingly, wage-earning cotton workers were often among the first agricultural laborers to organize unions.

Cotton again became important in the 1960s, when the United States and its Alliance for Progress encouraged the stimulation of nontraditional agricultural exports in Latin America. Cotton was a natural choice for Central Americans because improved pesticide technology made their Pacific coastal plain ideal for the crop. In Central America, access to credit and other incentives were available for those who would produce and export raw cotton. Consequently, Central American cotton production increased by 500 percent between 1961 and 1973. By 1977, Central America was the third largest producer of cotton for the world market, behind the United States and Egypt.

Vastly increased cotton production in Central America had disastrous economic effects for the poorest agricultural workers. Land that had previously been dedicated to subsistence farming of corn was turned over to cotton. This displacement

contributed to the proletarianization process that was taking place among agricultural workers in much of Latin America during the 1960s and 1970s. Unfortunately for the peasants who had previously inhabited this cropland, cotton did not provide stable employment for wage laborers. Because of the mechanized nature of modern cotton production, labor demands are relatively low for much of the growing season. Consequently, most of these newly proletarianized agricultural workers were forced to migrate.

Cotton, both as an export commodity and as an input for domestic textile production, continues to be an important Latin American industry. Cotton has also been a source of trade tension between the United States and Latin American countries. In 2007, the World Trade Organization (WTO) ruled that U.S. subsidies constituted an unfair trade practice. Consequently, the WTO allowed Brazil to raise tariffs on select U.S. products in retaliation.

See also **Textile Industry: Modern Textiles; Textile Industry: The Colonial Era.**

BIBLIOGRAPHY

José Romero Loza, *Algodón en Bolivia,* 2d ed. (1978).

Bertha Dodge, *Cotton: The Plant That Would Be King* (1984).

Forrest D. Colburn and Silvio De Franco, "Privilege, Production, and Revolution: The Case of Nicaragua," *Comparative Politics* 17, no. 3 (1985): 277–290.

Robert G. Williams, *Export Agriculture and the Crisis in Central America* (1986).

Barry Carr, "The Mexican Communist Party and Agrarian Mobilization in the Laguna, 1920–1940: A Worker-Peasant Alliance," *Hispanic American Historical Review* 67, no. 3 (1987): 371–404.

Dawn Keremitsis, *The Cotton Textile Industry in Porfiriato Mexico* (1987).

Michael J. Gonzales, "The Rise of Cotton Tenant Farming in Peru, 1890–1920: The Condor Valley," *Agricultural History* 65, no. 1 (1991): 51–71.

Additional Bibliography

Cueto, Marcos, and Jorge Lossio. *Innovación en la agricultura: Fermín Tangüis y el algodón en el Perú.* Lima: Universidad del Pacifico, Centro de Investigación, 1999.

Gómez-Galvarriato, Aurora, ed. *La industria textil en México.* Mexico City: Instituto Mora, Colegio de Michoacán: Colegio de México: Instituto de Investigaciones Históricas-UNAM, 1999.

RACHEL A. MAY

COUNCIL OF THE INDIES.

Council of the Indies, central administrative and judicial institution for the Spanish Empire. In 1524 Charles I created the Council of the Indies as a judicial, legislative, and executive body responsible for the administration of Spain's New World empire. Located in Spain, and ultimately based in Madrid, it had jurisdiction over the Spanish colonies analogous to that of the Council of Castile over much of Spain. Thus the Council of the Indies initially had jurisdiction in legislative, financial, judicial, military, ecclesiastical, and commercial matters in the New World.

The council prepared all legislation related to administration, taxation, and, initially, defense of the New World; no major project could be undertaken without its approval. It corresponded directly with both civil and ecclesiastical officials in the New World and exercised patronage, except during the existence of the Cámara of the Indies, over both lay and clerical positions.

The Council of the Indies also had judicial responsibilities and sat as the final court of appeals for civil cases tried by the colonial audiencias and for civil and criminal cases tried by the House of Trade. In addition, it held first-instance jurisdiction in cases concerning encomiendas and those initiated in Spain which dealt with matters in the Indies. The council also arranged judicial reviews (*residencias*) of high-ranking colonial officials and special inspections (*visitas*) of colonial officials and districts. Finally, the council exercised censorship over all books dealing with the Indies and had to approve any papal decree prior to its transmission to the New World.

During the sixteenth century, the Council of the Indies was at the peak of its power. In the seventeenth century, however, favoritism and corruption led to a reduction of its authority in favor of both other tribunals and royal favorites. From 1600 to 1609 and 1644 to 1701, a subcommittee of the council known as the Cámara of the Indies handled its patronage responsibilities. In 1717 and from 1721 to 1808, the *cámara* again was charged with fulfilling the council's patronage responsibilities.

In its early years, the council had a president, four or five councillors, a crown attorney (*fiscal*), and various subalterns. Initially, the councillors were men trained in law (*ministros togados*). However, in 1626, Philip IV began naming some councillors without any training in law. These were called *ministros de capa y espada* to distinguish them from the *ministros togados*. The rights and responsibilities of the two groups were identical, with the important exception that *ministros de capa y espada* could not vote on judicial matters. By the end of the seventeenth century, the quality of the *ministros de capa y espada* had eroded significantly as the Crown sold appointments and even named a nine-year-old boy as a reward for the services of his father. The dubious quality of the minister and the acknowledged inefficiency of the Council of the Indies at the close of the seventeenth century stimulated its reform and reduction of authority by Philip V in 1717.

When Philip V, the first Bourbon monarch in Spain, organized his government, he named a minister of the Indies (secretary of state for the Indies) with responsibility for American affairs in administration, war, finance, and commerce. A clarification in September 1717 left judicial matters, patronage (including making recommendations for high-ranking judicial and ecclesiastical appointments), and matters related to municipal government to the council. Although overshadowed by the minister, the council slowly increased its influence in the latter eighteenth century as its size increased in response to the growing population, wealth, and importance of the empire and as its ranks were increasingly filled with men who had personal experience in the New World. Declared equal in rank and prerogatives to the Council of Castile in 1773, the Council of the Indies enjoyed a renaissance of prestige and authority. From the 1773 decree to 1808, thirty-one of thirty-nine new *ministros togados* had American experience. When responsibility for both peninsular and American affairs was united in five ministerial portfolios organized by function rather than by territory in 1790, and the House of Trade was abolished in the same year, the Council of the Indies remained the only body in Spain devoted solely to American affairs.

The Cortes of Cádiz suppressed the council in 1812, but Ferdinand VII reestablished it in 1814, naming an unprecedented number of American-born ministers to its ranks in a modest effort to win favor in the New World. Belatedly, after the loss of Spain's colonies in the American mainlands, the council was finally abolished in 1834.

See also **Charles I of Spain; Spanish Empire.**

BIBLIOGRAPHY

Barrios, Feliciano. *El gobierno de un mundo: Virreinatos y audiencias en la América hispánica.* Cuenca, Ecuador: Ediciones de la Universidad de Castilla-La Mancha: Fundación Rafael del Pino, 2004.

Burkholder, Mark A. *Biographical Dictionary of Councilors of the Indies, 1717–1808* (1986).

Domínguez Ortiz, Antoni. *La sociedad americana y la corona española en el siglo XVII.* Spain: M. Pons, 1996.

Haring, Clarence H. *The Spanish Empire in America* (1947), pp. 102–118.

Schäfer, Ernesto. *El consejo real y supremo de las Indias,* vol. 1 (1935).

MARK A. BURKHOLDER

COUNTERINSURGENCY.

Since achieving independence, many Latin American governments have fought to stave off challenges to their legitimacy from armed segments of their own population. When, in the decades following the Bolshevik Revolution of 1917, many of these uprisings acquired an ideological dimension, the United States became increasingly concerned about what it had heretofore regarded as an internal problem of the countries involved. This concern peaked in the late 1950s and early 1960s after Fidel Castro's victory in Cuba and Soviet premier Nikita Khrushchev's declared support for wars of national liberation. Convinced that "the sweep of nationalism" presented "the most potent factor in foreign affairs today" and that insurgency had become the Communists' preferred method of expansion, U.S. president John F. Kennedy in 1961 made counterinsurgency the cornerstone of his strategic doctrine of Flexible Response for containing communism during the cold war.

In concept, counterinsurgency was a twist on traditional U.S. policies that posited a middle path between reactionary dictatorship on the Right and communist totalitarianism on the Left. With the focal point of the cold war having shifted to the less developed countries, the United States promoted a variety of programs designed to allow third world nationalists

to realize their aspirations for social, economic, and political change through peaceful reform instead of violent revolution. Extensive economic assistance from international sources, both public and private, together with structural reforms and better management of resources within recipient countries, presumably would pave the way for economic development, social mobility, and, where it did not already exist, political democracy. To protect this liberal reform program from Communist subversion, the United States would encourage a government's military forces to engage in civic action projects that would improve local conditions while winning the allegiance of the people. Indigenous police and military forces would also take military action against hard-core insurgents whose ideological commitment prevented them from accepting peaceful reform as a legitimate approach to progress and stability.

President Kennedy, according to an official memorandum, observed that "the most critical spot on the globe nowadays is Latin America, which seems made-to-order for the Communists." Consequently, during his administration, the preponderance of U.S. counterinsurgency efforts took place within the Western Hemisphere, with special attention given to Guatemala, Venezuela, Colombia, Peru, and Bolivia. The Alliance for Progress (1961) offered a plan for long-term economic development and political stability, while civic action and counterguerrilla activities offered short-term responses to the Communist threat. Latin American military forces seeking instruction in this comprehensive approach could attend courses at the U.S. Army School of the Americas in the Canal Zone and receive training from U.S. military advisory groups and from small, highly skilled teams of Special Forces (Green Berets). Weapons and equipment for counterinsurgency could be procured through a military assistance program that Kennedy reoriented from hemispheric defense to internal security.

The success of Latin American governments against leftist insurgencies in the 1960s seemed to prove the efficacy of the U.S. strategy. In reality, the failure of those insurgencies can be attributed not so much to U.S. assistance as to the inability to duplicate Cuba's *foco* model (the employment of a small armed band operating from a rural base to create the conditions for revolution) in other countries. Other factors were factionalism within guerrilla movements and the reformist or repressive responses of threatened governments.

After a brief hiatus, concern about Latin American insurgencies again mounted in Washington in the late 1970s, following the reemergence of leftist guerrillas in Guatemala and other countries and the success of the Sandinistas in Nicaragua. Compared with the insurgents of the 1960s, the new or rejuvenated movements placed greater emphasis on organization, received generous support from external sources, such as Cuba, and mastered the art of public relations directed at foreign agencies and public opinion, especially in the United States. The United States again assisted friendly governments seeking to suppress revolutionary movements, although the remembrance of Vietnam, a divided public, and an emphasis on human-rights issues placed constraints on U.S. counterinsurgency efforts, for example, in El Salvador, a major recipient of Washington's largess.

Entering the 1990s, most leftist insurgencies in Latin America again seemed under control, Guatemalan National Revolutionary Unity (URNG) and, in Peru, Shining Path (Sendero Luminoso) being two exceptions. But the conditions that gave rise to insurgent movements have not been removed in most countries, and trafficking in narcotics has added another dimension to the problem. Conversely, the demise of the Eastern bloc and the initiatives of several Latin American countries, including peace negotiations in El Salvador, have given rise to hopes that diplomacy might become an effective counterinsurgency tool.. In the late 1990s government documents in the United States were declassified that demonstrated the involvement of the United States in *Operation Condor*, the counterinsurgency campaign of dictatorships in the Southern Cone (Chile, Argentina, and Uruguay) during the 1970s and 1980s. Since 1999 *Plan Colombia*, the term used to describe American backed counterinsurgency and drug trafficking in Colombia, has been in effect. This *Plan* has received criticism due to the technique of aerial fumigation of coca crops, which damages legitimate agriculture and may lead to health problems. Scholars have argued that many of the counterinsurgency techniques developed in Latin America by the United States during the cold war have been reemployed elsewhere. In particular, some policy makers who helped establish the counterinsurgency in Latin America during the 1980s have put similar policies in practice against the large insurgency in the second Iraq war, which began in 2003.

See also **Communism; Guerrilla Movements; United States-Latin American Relations.**

BIBLIOGRAPHY

Armony, Ariel C. *Argentina, the United States, and the Anti-Communist Crusade in Central America, 1977–1984.* Athens: Ohio University Center for International Studies, 1997.

Blum, William. *Killing Hope: U.S. Military and CIA Interventions since World War II.* Monroe, ME: Common Courage Press, 2004.

Che Guevara, Ernesto. *Guerrilla Warfare* (1985).

Child, John. *Unequal Alliance: The Inter-American Military System, 1938–1978* (1980).

Fauriol, Georges, ed. *Latin American Insurgencies* (1985).

Gambone, Michael D. *Capturing the Revolution: The United States, Central America, and Nicaragua, 1961–1972.* Westport, CT: Praeger, 2001.

Grandin, Greg. *Empire's Workshop: Latin America, the United States, and the Rise of the New Imperialism.* New York: Metropolitan Books, 2006.

Gutman, Roy. *Banana Diplomacy: The Making of American Policy in Nicaragua, 1981–1987* (1988).

LeoGrande, William M. *Our Own Backyard: The United States in Central America, 1977–1992.* Chapel Hill: University of North Carolina Press, 1998.

Rouquié, Alain. *Guerras y paz en América Central.* Mexico: Fondo de Cultura Económica, 1994.

Schwarz, Benjamin C. *American Counterinsurgency Doctrine and El Salvador* (1991).

Wickham-Crowley, Thomas P. *Guerrillas and Revolution in Latin America* (1992).

LAWRENCE A. YATES

COUP D'ÉTAT. *See* **Golpe de estado (coup d'état).**

COURTS. *See* **Judicial Systems: Brazil; Judicial Systems: Spanish America; Judiciary in Latin America, The.**

COUTINHO, JOSÉ JOAQUIM DA CUNHA DE AZEREDO (1742–1821).

José Joaquim da Cunha de Azeredo Coutinho (*b.* 8 September 1742; *d.* 12 September 1821), bishop of Olinda (1794–1806) and author. A child of the late Portuguese Enlightenment, Coutinho was born into a landowning family from the Rio de Janeiro captaincy. He graduated with a degree in canon law from Coimbra University in 1780. Twelve years later he was elected to the Royal Academy of Sciences. In 1798, he left Lisbon for Olinda, Pernambuco, where he founded a renowned seminary, whose "Estatutos" (Ordinances) he wrote. Also serving as provisional head of Pernambuco's government, he took harsh measures against what he considered, given his enlightened outlook, abusive practices such as tax evasion, and private appropriation of funds from the royal treasury. By so doing, he offended powerful vested interests. In 1802, Coutinho was called back to Portugal, where he was nominated bishop of Elvas in 1806. He retired from his see in 1817, and was appointed the last general inquisitor of the realm the following year.

As an author, Coutinho was chiefly concerned with the economic policy of the crown. His *A Political Essay on the Commerce of Portugal and Her Colonies* was published in 1794, and was translated into English in 1801. Later, he wrote a number of important works in a polemic vein on religious and administrative matters. His physiocratic beliefs, shrouded in a conservative outlook, revealed his sympathies with the reform-minded officials of the times, but some extreme attitudes, such as the defense of the slave trade, kept him somewhat apart from the leading intellectuals of the period.

See also **Portuguese Empire.**

BIBLIOGRAPHY

E. Bradford Burns, "The Role of Azeredo Coutinho in the Enlightenment of Brazil," in *Hispanic American Historical Review*, no. 2 (1964): 145–160.

Sérgio Buarque De Holanda, "Apresentação," in *Obras econômicas de J. J. da Cunha de Azeredo Coutinho (1794–1804)*, edited by Sérgio Buarque de Holanda (1966).

Manoel Cardozo, "Azeredo Coutinho and the Intellectual Ferment of His Times," in *Conflict and Continuity in Brazilian Society,* edited by Henry H. Keith and S. F. Edwards (1969).

Severino Leite Nogueira, *O Seminário de Olinda e seu fundador o bispo Azeredo Coutinho* (1985).

Additional Bibliography

Alves, Gilberto Luiz. *O pensamento burguês no Seminário de Olinda, 1800–1836*. Ibitinga: Humanidades and Mato Grosso do Sul: U.F.M.S., 1993.

Férrer, Francisco Adegildo. "Proposta pedagógica do bispo Azeredo Coutinho para a educacão de rapazes e raparigas no Brasil colonial, 1798-1802." *Revista do Instituto do Ceará* 109 (1995): 365–387.

GUILHERME PEREIRA DAS NEVES

COUTINHO, RODRIGO DOMINGOS ANTONIO DE SOUSA (1755–1812).

Rodrigo Domingos Antonio de Sousa Coutinho (*b.* 3 August 1755; *d.* 26 January 1812), first count of Linhares (1808) and a Portuguese diplomat. From a noble family of important court and state functionaries, Coutinho was the son of Francisco Inocêncio de Sousa Coutinho, a governor and captain-general of Angola (1764–1772) and ambassador to Madrid (1774–1780).

After studying at the Nobles' College in Lisbon and at Coimbra University, Coutinho visited France and subsequently served at Turin as minister plenipotentiary from 1779 to 1796. In 1790 he published a discussion of the effects of the mining of precious metals on industry that implied the need for technological innovation in Brazil's Minas Gerais mining industry. Recalled to Lisbon in 1796 to succeed the deceased Martinho de Melo E Castro as state secretary for the navy and colonies, Coutinho developed the concept of a joint Luso-Brazilian imperial economic and political unit, declaring in 1798 that Portugal's vast overseas domains, especially those in the Americas, were the basis of the crown's power and that without them continental Portugal would be reduced to a province of Spain.

After a term as president of the treasury (1801–1803), Coutinho left Lisbon in October 1807 with the regent João and the court and government when the capital was transferred to Rio de Janeiro to escape French armies invading Portugal. In Brazil he served as secretary of state for foreign affairs and war (1808–1812) and advised the regent on the negotiations leading to the three Anglo-

Portuguese treaties of February 1810, which opened Brazilian ports to international trade and committed the Portuguese never to establish a tribunal of the Inquisition in the New World.

See also **Inquisition: Brazil.**

BIBLIOGRAPHY

Marquez Do Funchal, *O conde de Linhares: Dom Rodrigo Domingos António de Sousa Coutinho* (1908).

Maria Beatriz Nizza Da Silva, "O império Luso-Brasileiro, 1750–1820," in *Nova história da expansão portuguesa*, edited by Joel Serrão and Antônio Henrique de Oliveira Marques, vol. 8 (1986).

José Luís Cardoso, *O pensamento econômico em Portugal nos finais do século XVIII, 1780–1808* (1989).

Additional Bibliography

Raposo, Luciano. "Das arcas coloniais ao Palácio de Queluz: Dilemas luso-brasileiros no governo da fazenda real nas memórias do Códice 807." *Revista do Instituto Histórico e Geográfico Brasileiro* 163 (July–September 2002): 67–127.

Silva, Andrée Mansuy Diniz. *Portrait d'un homme d'état, D Rodrigo de Souza Coutinho, comte de Linhares, 1755–1812: Les anées de formation, 1755–1796.* Lisbon: Fundação Calouste Gulbenkian; Paris: Centre culturel Calouste Gulbenkian; Paris: Commission nationale pour les commémorations des découvertes portugaises, 2003.

Silva, Andrée Mansuy Diniz. *Portrait d'un homme d'état, D Rodrigo de Souza Coutinho, comte de Linhares, 1755–1812: L'homme d'état, 1796–1812.* Lisbon: Fundação Calouste Gulbenkian; Paris: Centre culturel Calouste Gulbenkian; Paris: Commission nationale pour les commémorations des découvertes portugaises, 2006.

DAVID HIGGS

COUTO, JOSÉ BERNARDO (1803–1862).

José Bernardo Couto (*b.* 1803; *d.* 1862), Mexican jurist, politician, and writer. Couto studied jurisprudence and humanities at San Ildefonso, Mexico City. In 1827 he became a lawyer, and in 1828 served in the Veracruz legislature. He was counselor of state in 1842 and minister of justice in 1845. Couto was one of the Mexican commissioners during the peace negotiations with the United States in 1847–1848. A distinguished jurist, he was known for his radical anticlerical views in his youth, particularly because of his *Disertación sobre la naturaleza y límites de la autoridad eclesiástica* (1825). Decades later he retracted his anticlerical position in *Discurso sobre la constitución de la iglesia* (1857).

Couto was a supporter of the arts, particularly painting and sculpture, and served as president of the governing committee of the Academy of San Carlos. In addition, he was a writer of note, translating Horace, publishing various novels and volumes of verse, and contributing to the *Diccionario universal de historia y geografía.*

See also **Mexico: 1810–1910.**

BIBLIOGRAPHY

José Rojas Garciadueñas, *Don José Bernardo Couto* (1964).

María Del Refugio González, "Ilustrados, regalistas, y liberales," in *The Independence of Mexico and the Creation of the New Nation,* edited by Jaime E. Rodríguez O. (1989).

JAIME E. RODRÍGUEZ O.

COVARRUBIAS, MIGUEL (1904–1957).

Miguel Covarrubias (*b.* 22 November 1904; *d.* 4 February 1957), Mexican artist. Miguel Covarrubias was extremely multifaceted, particularly in artistic and cultural endeavors. A native of Mexico City, he was a caricaturist, set designer, book illustrator, cartographer, painter, writer, art historian, ethnologist, and anthropologist. His work on the Olmec civilization made a major archaeological contribution, and his innovative museum installations forever changed the way exhibitions are designed. Toward the end of his life, as director of dance at the Instituto de Bellas Artes, he created a nationalist dance movement that initiated what has been termed the golden age of modern Mexican dance.

In everything that Covarrubias accomplished he remained an artist. He possessed a rare intuitive ability to capture and synthesize at a glance the essentials of character or situation, as demonstrated by his famous caricatures for *Vanity Fair* and his illustrations for his first books, *The Prince of Wales and Other Famous Americans* (1925) and *Negro Drawings* (1927).

Covarrubias married Rosemonde Cowan, a dancer and choreographer, in 1930. She became his collaborator as researcher and photographer for his next two books, *The Island of Bali* (1938) and *Mexico South* (1946). In the early 1940s, they returned to live permanently in Mexico, where they entertained many of the major intellectual and show-business figures of the time.

As he matured, Covarrubias immersed himself in studies of early historical happenings, peoples, folklore, and civilizations, principally on the American continent and in Polynesia. He wrote and illustrated *The Eagle, the Jaguar, and the Serpent* (1954) and *Indian Art of Mexico and Central America* (1957).

Terence Grieder has said, "In some ways, Covarrubias was a man out of his age. The typical thought of his day took mathematical or statistical form rather than the pictorial form, which was his, and incidentally the Renaissance way of expressing thought. But he typified the best of twentieth-century humanism: its fascination with the visual arts, its openness to other cultures, and its desperate and doomed struggle to preserve the humane virtues of the traditional societies against technocratic commercialism."

Miguel Covarrubias was the encyclopedic artist of Mexico's rebirth. When he died in Mexico City, he had won a lasting place as a distinguished artist, scholar, teacher, and advocate of Mexican cultural studies. His final gesture to the Mexican people was the gift of his extraordinary pre-Columbian collection to the National Museum.

See also **Art: The Twentieth Century.**

BIBLIOGRAPHY

Terence Grieder, "The Divided World of Miguel Covarrubias," in *Americas,* 23 (May 1971): 19–24.

Adriana Williams, *Covarrubias* (1994).

Additional Bibliography

Poniatowska, Elena. *Miguel Covarrubias: Vida y mundos.* Mexico City: Ediciones Era, 2004.

ADRIANA WILLIAMS

CRABB, HENRY A. (1827–1857). Henry A. Crabb (*b.* 1827; *d.* 7 April 1857), filibuster. A schoolmate of William Walker, a fellow filibuster, in Nashville, Tennessee, Crabb journeyed to California during the Gold Rush. After settling in Stockton in 1849, he led a brief expedition of adventurers to Nicaragua in 1855. Crabb returned to California the next year and married Filomena Ainsa, who came from a prominent Sonora, Mexico, family. Then, in 1857, he organized the American and Arizona Mining and Emigration Company in a bold attempt to colonize part of Sonora. Crabb outfitted a group of men and marched into Mexico. Ambushed on 1 April 1857 by Mexican troops and besieged for six days, Crabb and fifty-nine of his men were captured and brutally executed to serve as a warning to Americans that Mexico was not open to further colonizing ventures.

See also **Filibustering.**

BIBLIOGRAPHY

Rufus Kay Wyllys, "Henry A. Crabb—A Tragedy of the Sonora Frontier," *Pacific Historical Review* 9, no. 2 (June 1940): 183–194.

Joe A. Stout, "Henry A. Crabb—Filibuster or Colonizer?" *The American West* 8, no. 3 (May 1971): 4–9.

Diana Lindsay, "Henry A. Crabb, Filibuster, and the *San Diego Herald,*" *Journal of San Diego History* 19 (Winter 1973): 34–42.

Additional Bibliography

May, Robert E. *Manifest Destiny's Underworld: Filibustering in Antebellum America.* Chapel Hill: University of North Carolina Press, 2003.

Ruibal Corella, Juan Antonio. !*Y Caborca se cubrió de gloria …!": La expedición filibustera de Henry Alexander Crabb a Sonora.* Mexico City: Editorial Porrúa, 1976.

IRIS H. W. ENGSTRAND

CRAIGE, JOHN HOUSTON (c. 1890–?). U.S. Marine Corps captain John Houston Craige is best known for two books about his service in the Gendarmerie d'Haiti during the Marine occupation (1915–1934): *Black Baghdad* (1933) and *Cannibal Cousins* (1934). Writing for a popular audience, he stressed what he considered to be the exotic aspects of Haitian society and culture. His books offer a first-hand account of the occupation, and insight into the experience of U.S. soldiers engaged in Caribbean "banana wars."

By his own account, Craige first visited Haiti in 1912. After joining the Marines during World War I and serving in France, Craige returned to Haiti in 1925 to join the gendarmerie, the Haitian police force staffed with U.S. officers. He served in the mountain village of Hinche and ran a broadcasting station in Port-au-Prince. Craige learned about Haiti by reading works by the French historian Moreau de Saint-Méry (1750–1890), the Hatian historian Thomas Madiou (1814–1884), and the Haitian writer Louis-Joseph Janvier (1855–1911), among others. In his books, Craige describes the interactions between Marines and Haitians and includes many anecdotes about Haitian culture and traditions, providing perceptive if often exaggerated accounts. Generally, Craige supported U.S. efforts to "civilize" Haiti, though he also noted some of their shortcomings.

After returning from Haiti, Craige served as director of public relations for the Marines. He wrote several more books, including *What the Citizen Should Know about the Marines* (1941), *Guide to the United States Armed Forces* (1942), and *The Practical Book of American Guns* (1950).

See also **Haiti.**

BIBLIOGRAPHY

Primary Sources

Black Baghdad. New York: Minton, Balch, 1933.

Cannibal Cousins. New York: Minton, Balch, 1934.

Secondary Sources

Renda, Mary A. *Taking Haiti: Military Occupation and the Culture of U.S. Imperialism, 1915–1940.* Chapel Hill and London: University of North Carolina Press, 2001.

JOSEPH W. HORAN

CREEL, ENRIQUE CLAY (1854–1931).

Enrique Clay Creel (*b.* 30 August 1854; *d.* 17 August 1931), Mexican banker, governor of Chihuahua (1904–1911). Born in Chihuahua, Creel was the son of the U.S. consul there. He married the daughter of General Luis Terrazas and subsequently headed the financial and industrial enterprises of the Terrazas family. He was the leading Mexican banker of the pre-Revolutionary era and was a founder and manager of the Banco Minero de Chihuahua and several other banks. He also had widespread interests in food processing, mining, textiles, and manufacturing. He served as the most prominent Mexican officer or board member of several foreign corporations. Creel also entered politics, serving in Chihuahua's state legislature in

1882–1885 and 1897–1900. He was an alternate federal deputy from Chihuahua in 1892–1894 and a full deputy from Durango in 1900–1902 and from Chihuahua in 1902–1906.

In 1904 the governor of Chihuahua resigned in Creel's favor. Creel was elected on his own in 1907 and served to 1911. Creel was a member of the Científicos, a positivist group led by José Y. Limantour, the secretary of the treasury (1892–1911) under dictator Porfirio Díaz. As governor he tried to implement positivist principles by streamlining and modernizing state government, which caused protests from fiercely independent municipalities. While serving as governor, he was also Mexican ambassador to the United States (1907–1908) and secretary for foreign relations (1910–1911).

During the Mexican Revolution, when he fled for his life, Creel suffered heavy financial losses. He returned to Mexico from exile in the early 1920s and served as a financial adviser to President Álvaro Obregón Salido.

See also **Mexico, Wars and Revolutions: Mexican Revolution.**

BIBLIOGRAPHY

Francisco R. Almada, *Gobernadores del Estado de Chihuahua* (1980), furnishes basic biographical information. Mark Wasserman, "Enrique C. Creel: Business and Politics in Mexico, 1880–1930," in *Business History Review* 59 (Winter 1985): 645–662, examines Creel's public and business career.

Additional Bibliography

Wasserman, Mark. "Strategies for Survival of the Porfirian Elite in Revolutionary Mexico: Chihuahua during the 1920s." *Hispanic American Historical Review* 67 (February 1987): 87–107.

MARK WASSERMAN

CREELMAN INTERVIEW.

Creelman Interview, an interview given by Mexican president Porfirio Díaz (1876–1880, 1884–1911) to the U.S. journalist James Creelman of *Pearson's Magazine* and published on 17 February 1908. It subsequently appeared in Spanish in the Mexico City newspaper *El Imparcial* on 3 March 1908. In it

Díaz revealed his plans to retire from the presidency following the June 1910 election, when he would be eighty years old. He also called for the formation of opposition political parties, which effectively had been banned during his thirty-year dictatorship.

The purpose of Díaz's statement most likely was to calm both external and internal criticism of his rule. Others claim that Díaz expected his offer to resign to be met with demands from his supporters that he remain in power. Finally, it may have been designed to bring into the open those who opposed him. Whatever the motive, Díaz made a mistake, as the interview stimulated long-dormant political activity in the country resulting in his overthrow in May 1911.

See also **Díaz, Porfirio.**

BIBLIOGRAPHY

Barrón, Luis. *Historias de la Revolución mexicana.* México, D.F.: Centro de Investigación y Docencia Económicas, 2004.

Cumberland, Charles C. *Mexican Revolution: Genesis Under Madero* (1952).

Gonzales, Michael J. *The Mexican Revolution, 1910–1940.* Albuquerque: University of New Mexico Press, 2002.

Ross, Stanley R. *Francisco I. Madero: Apostle of Mexican Democracy* (1955), esp. pp. 46–48.

DAVID LAFRANCE

CREOLE. In Spanish America, the term "creole" (*criollo*) refers to people of European descent, especially Spaniards who were born in the New World—in contrast to *peninsulares,* born in Europe. Because few Spanish women came to the colonies, creoles often were not exclusively of European descent. Nevertheless, they represented a privileged group that held much of the land and economic power in the colonies, although they often felt discrimination from Spanish-born *peninsulares* in political and economic privileges. Creoles occupied many of the positions in the bureaucracy and were legally equal to *peninsulares,* although a tendency under the Bourbons to appoint *peninsulares* to office heightened the rivalry between these two groups in the eighteenth century and contributed to independence sentiment. Creoles led the independence movements in the early nineteenth century and were the group that inherited political power in Hispanic America. They imposed a strong conservative legacy in their domination of the higher clergy, military officer corps, and the landowning and merchant elites, often in collaboration with foreign investors.

The term *criollo* or *créole* also was used in Portuguese and French colonies to indicate those of European descent, while in Brazil *criolo* defines a black person of African descent. In modern Latin America the term often refers to characteristics that are especially native or traditional to the country, for example, "creole cuisine."

In English-speaking areas, especially those once ruled by France or Spain, the term has been corrupted to mean not only those of French or Spanish descent but also those of mixed, often African, descent, as in the British Caribbean, Haiti, or Louisiana; indeed, in modern times, it has come to be applied to virtually all the native inhabitants. In much of the Caribbean, it also often refers to the mixed European-African language spoken by natives of the former colonies.

Since the term is used in different ways in different regions, the context of its use is important for understanding its precise meaning.

See also **Peninsular; Race and Ethnicity.**

BIBLIOGRAPHY

Severo Martínez Peláez, *La patria del criollo: Ensayo de interpretación de la realidad colonial guatemalteca* (1970).

Mark A. Burkholder and D. S. Chandler, *From Impotence to Authority: The Spanish Crown and the American Audiencias, 1687–1808* (1977).

Barbara Lalla and Jean D'costa, *Language in Exile: Three Hundred Years of Jamaica Creole* (1990).

Additional Bibliography

Brading, D. A. *The First America: The Spanish Monarchy, Creole Patriots, and the Liberal State, 1492–1867.* Cambridge, U.K.: Cambridge University Press, 1991.

Cañizares-Esguerra, Jorge. *Nature, Empire, and Nation: Explorations of the History of Science in the Iberian World.* Stanford, CA: Stanford University Press, 2006.

Díz Caballero, Jesús. "El incaísmo como primera ficción orientadora en la formación de la nación criolla en las provincias unidas del Río de la Plata." *A Contracorriente* 3.1 (Fall 2005 | Otoño 2005): 67-113. http://www.ncsu.edu/project/acontracorriente/fall_05/Diaz-Caballero.pdf.

Mazzotti, José Antonio, ed. *Agencias criollas: La ambigüedad "colonial" en las letras hispanoamericanas.* Pittsburgh, PA: Instituto Internacional de Literatura Iberoamericana, Universidad de Pittsburgh, 2000.

Poupeney-Hart, Catherine, and Albino Chacón Gutiérrez. *El discurso colonial: Construcción de una diferencia americana.* Heredia: Editorial Universidad Nacional, 2002.

Stephens, Thomas M. *Dictionary of Latin American Racial and Ethnic Terminology.* Gainesville: University of Florida Press, 1989.

RALPH LEE WOODWARD JR.

CRESPO, JOAQUÍN (1845–1898).

Joaquín Crespo (*b.* 1845; *d.* 1898), Venezuelan president (1884–1886, 1892–1898). Crespo, a tough young *llanero,* joined the Liberal side in the Federal War (1859–1863) and, as a loyal supporter of Antonio Guzmán Blanco, became his minister of war (1877–1878). In 1879, as a reward for his loyalty to the dictator, Crespo was given the title "Hero of Duty Done." From 1884 to 1886 Crespo served as figurehead president for Guzmán Blanco, and in 1888 he ran unsuccessfully for president. From 1892 to 1894 he served as interim president after seizing power in a caudillo rebellion. His constitutional presidency (1894–1898) corresponded with an economic slump and with clashes with Great Britain over the border with British Guiana. Crespo is credited with initiatives to professionalize the national army. After his presidential term was completed, he led the forces of the new regime of General Ignacio Andrade against a rebellion headed by José Manuel ("El Mocho") Hernández. In one of its first engagements Crespo was killed in battle.

See also **Venezuela: Venezuela since 1830.**

BIBLIOGRAPHY

Robert L. Gilmore, *Caudillism and Militarism in Venezuela, 1810–1910* (1964).

Ramón J. Velásquez, *La caída del liberalismo amarillo* (1972).

Judith Ewell, *Venezuela: A Century of Change* (1984).

Additional Bibliography

Velásquez, Ramón J. *Joaquín Crespo (1841–1898): El último caudillo liberal.* Caracas, Venezuela: Editora El Nacional, 2005.

WINFIELD J. BURGGRAAFF

CREYDT, OSCAR (1906–1987).

Oscar Creydt was a Paraguayan Communist leader. Born in San Miguel, in southern Paraguay, Creydt was the scion of a wealthy family, and although trained as a lawyer, he dedicated his life and fortune instead to organizing the Paraguayan Communist Party.

During the early 1920s, Creydt was a leading figure in the University Students Federation, and in the Consejo Mixto de Obreros y Estudiantes. This latter group (not more than fifty individuals) formed the basis for the Paraguayan Communist Party (PCP), founded in 1928 and brought into the Comintern four years later.

At this time, the PCP could count on little meaningful support in Paraguay, even within the labor unions. After the Chaco War (1932–1935), the Communists found many of their social programs "hijacked" by the nationalist Febrerista Party, and, at the same time, the PCP itself was forced underground. Creydt, however, proved to be a talented clandestine organizer. Through discipline and hard work, he drove out the Trotskyists within the party and managed to weather the persecutions of the Morínigo dictatorship (1940–1948).

In 1947, Creydt got his only opportunity for a measure of national power. A civil war had erupted, and the Communists forged an alliance with disaffected soldiers, Febreristas, and Liberals, which came critically close to defeating the rival Colorados. The strength of the PCP at this juncture surprised many observers, but Creydt, who felt that the political work was finally paying off, was not surprised. Nonetheless, the victory of the Colorados and the subsequent terror sent him and most party members into exile.

Creydt retained his hold on the secretary-general's post for many years. In the 1960s, younger Paraguayan Communists accused him of mimicking Stalin in fostering a cult of personality. The PCP split over this issue in 1968, with a substantial minority shifting to Creydt's old associate, Obdulio Barthe, who now adopted a pro-Beijing line. In 1963 he published a book entitled *Formación histórica de la nación paraguaya*. In an attempt to heal the breach, Creydt negotiated with the Maoists, but in the end this gesture resulted only in a split of his own pro-Moscow wing. Creydt himself was supplanted as party chief by the much younger Miguel Angel Soler, whose arrest (and probable murder) by General Alfredo Stroessner's police in 1975 brought another round of factionalization from which the Communists did not recover. Until his death in 1987, Creydt remained active in Communist politics, leading a small faction of supporters in a party that was largely divided and ostracized.

See also **Paraguay, Political Parties: Colorado Party; Paraguay, Political Parties: Febrerista Party; Paraguay, Political Parties: Liberal Party.**

BIBLIOGRAPHY

Bonzi, Antonio. *Procéso histórico del Partido Comunista Paraguayo: Un itinerario de luces y sombras.* Asuncíon: Arandurá, 2001.

Creydt, Oscar. *Formación histórica de la nación paraguaya* (1963), pp. 48–55.

Lambert, Peter, and Ricardo Medina. "Contested Discourse, Contested Power: Nationalism and the Left in Paraguay." *Bulletin of Latin American Research* 26 (July 2007): 339–355.

Lewis, Paul H. *Paraguay Under Stroessner* (1980), pp. 32, 220–221.

Rosales, Humberto. *Historia del Partido Comunista Paraguayo (1928–1991)* (1991), *passim.*

THOMAS L. WHIGHAM

CRIMINAL JUSTICE.

Crime and violence were part and parcel of the conquest and settlement of the New World and persisted throughout the colonial era. Contemporary accounts are replete with references to crimes against property, crimes perpetrated by one individual on another, and, far less frequently, crimes against the state. Cases of robbery, assault, and homicide regularly reached colonial officials and provoked efforts to find and punish the perpetrators. Officials paid far less attention, however, to illegal physical and financial abuse of Indians and slaves. In urban centers, authorities devoted considerable effort to controlling crime and punishing criminals. In many rural areas, in contrast, much crime went unreported to royal bureaucrats in the audiencia's capital, and local officials meted out punishment. Indeed, the only types of crime that officials in rural communities had to report were homicides, aggravated assault, and sedition.

The most effective large-scale crackdown on crime took place in New Spain in the eighteenth century with the creation in 1710 of a new body, the Acordada, which actively pursued and punished criminals throughout the viceroyalty. An indication of the frequency of crime in late colonial New Spain can be found in the nearly forty-three thousand cases heard by a single judge of the *acordada* from 1782 to 1808.

Several types of officials shared responsibility for dealing with crime. Municipalities had *alguaciles,* sheriffs or constables who apprehended criminals and received as income a portion of the fines levied. In addition, the audiencias had Alguaciles Mayores who engaged in the same activities. Local magistrates (*alcaldes ordinarios*), provincial administrators (Alcaldes Mayores and Corregidores), and the regional high courts (*audiencias*) heard cases and pronounced sentences. Provincial administrators heard appeals from local magistrates; the *audiencias* heard appeals from both as well as from corporate bodies that enjoyed special judicial privileges (fueros). Viceroys and captains-general heard military cases, and ecclesiastical courts handled cases involving clerics. Appeals in criminal cases ended at the *audiencias.* In civil cases involving substantial sums of money, however, plaintiffs could appeal to the Council of the Indies.

Colonial judges invoked criminal statutes codified in the *Recopilación de leyes de los reynos de las Indias* (1681) and in Spanish legal compilations. These included the *Nueva recopilación de Castilla* (1659), the Laws of Toro (1505), and other legislation extending back to the Siete Partidas (1265). In addition, judges consulted local ordinances, viceregal decrees, and other legislation.

Interpersonal crime was commonplace and usually involved people who knew each other. The offenders, particularly those who used a deadly weapon such as a butcher or household knife, were usually young males, as were the victims. Most reported crimes against women, which included beating, stabbing, homicide, and sexual offenses, took place in the home.

Homicide was one of the few offenses that virtually all members of colonial society considered criminal. Consequently, records of homicides, although fragmentary, are more complete than those for any other crime. A review of these records for central Mexico reveals that rural homicide rates rose beginning in the late seventeenth century. Rural homicides usually took place after work and on Sundays.

The colonial authorities' toleration of crime and violence varied considerably over time. Behavior condoned during and immediately following the conquest of a region was often subsequently condemned and punished. The illegal branding and exportation of Indian slaves in Central America in the 1530s, for example, continued both because officials participated in the trade and because violators, on the occasions when they were punished, usually received light sentences. The race, class, and sex of the perpetrator and victim also affected the extent to which officials tolerated criminal activities and the vigor with which they pursued the perpetrators.

Spanish officials considered persons of mixed racial background to be of "vicious origins and nature," expected them to engage in crime and violence, and consequently were willing to tolerate a high level of criminality. When they finally took action against mestizos, mulattoes, and other *castas,* however, the punishment was apt to be severe and exemplary.

Legislation made Indians legal minors. From this paternalistic perspective, criminal behavior was expected as a result of their alleged lack of reason, and was not considered as serious as that of Spaniards. As a result, punishment was usually lenient.

A substantial body of royal and municipal legislation defined measures for controlling the behavior of black slaves. For example, blacks in Lima were subject to a curfew, forbidden to leave the city without official permission, and prohibited from carrying weapons. Punishments for violations were theoretically severe and included whipping of up to three hundred lashes, castration, exile, and hanging. In many cases, however, well-connected slave owners simply bribed the *alguaciles* to overlook the offense. The most common offense slaves committed was running away, but they also committed theft, assault, and murder with some

frequency. The victims of slave theft were usually Spaniards or Indians, while victims of assault or murder were apt to be persons of color. Blacks were often victims of assault and murder committed by Spaniards.

As the colonial period progressed, the number of Spaniards in the lower and lower-middle classes increased. Many Spanish criminals came from these groups. A review of the cases of 958 prisoners sentenced to service in a presidio or garrison of New Spain or elsewhere in the empire in 1799 and 1800 revealed that 28 percent of the men were Spaniards, most of them from the lower or lower-middle class.

Much justice, particularly in rural areas, was handled informally. The *hacendado* or plantation owner often took it upon himself to discipline workers and to punish petty theft and assault. Urban residents, on the other hand, especially Spaniards and *castas,* were much more apt to be punished following formal proceedings.

While every group in colonial society was victimized by criminals, women were particularly ill served by the judicial system. Physical abuse, wife beating, rape, and kidnapping were the most common crimes against women; most occurred in the home and were committed by a member of the family or another person known by the victim. Frequently the husband was the perpetrator, lashing out at his spouse in anger over her conduct, especially her sexual conduct. Many, perhaps most, wives were reluctant to file charges, for fear of provoking even harsher abuse.

When a woman sought legal redress, she found that a male judge questioned her closely, in search of any sign of blemished reputation. A woman had to document her pure behavior, and if any stain was found, her husband's conduct was condoned. Not surprisingly, accused husbands routinely countercharged that their wives had engaged in misconduct.

Assailants were seldom punished for the rape or kidnapping of a single woman. Only when a married woman had been raped did colonial judges consider the offense a serious crime—not for its heinous nature but because it damaged the honor of the victim's husband. If convicted, the assailant often was temporarily exiled.

In cases of adultery, the cuckolded husband could legally murder his wife and her lover, but this form of retribution happened only among the lower classes. For an elite male to take this step would stain his honor by publicly proclaiming his wife's infidelity. If a wife murdered an adulterous husband, she could expect no mercy.

Colonial authorities employed various punishments, depending on the specific crime committed; the class, race, age, health, and sex of the perpetrator; the length of time spent in prison prior to sentencing; and prior criminal record. The one crime certain to result in a death sentence was sodomy. Otherwise, capital punishment was rarely employed, even for homicide, and *audiencia* judges examined the cases carefully for evidence of premeditation, treachery, or assassination. For the most part judges reserved death sentences for highwaymen who had robbed and killed their victims and rape-murderers.

Labor service in the presidios of Havana or Veracruz from one to a maximum of ten years was the usual punishment for homicide in Mexico during the eighteenth century. Animal rustling and robbery also merited presidio sentences; vagrancy was frequently punished by two to four years of labor on a royal ship. Indians were not sentenced to military service, and only rarely to ship duty.

Terms of service as convict labor for private employers were common in Mexico, and many male criminals found themselves working in *obrajes* (textile workshops). Whippings were common, administered for many crimes committed by Indians, black slaves, and *castas*. Spaniards alone were exempt from the lash. Although women were punished less rigorously than men, they were sentenced to labor in artisans' workshops or in private households.

Most criminal offenses were misdemeanors and punished accordingly. Temporary confinement prior to sentencing or minor punishment—for example, a small fine—accounted for the vast majority of the sentences handed down by the judge of the *acordada* in Mexico in the closing decades of colonial rule.

One feature of criminal justice in colonial Spanish America that deserves special notice is the use of pardons. From time to time, the Crown declared general pardons in celebration of a coronation, a royal marriage, or the birth of a prince of princess. These resulted in numerous prisoners being released, although some crimes, such as robbery and fraud, were not covered by a pardon. A general pardon also reduced the number of unsolved crimes, for under the terms of the pardon, criminals who turned themselves in were absolved. In addition, viceroys could grant clemency and commute sentences.

See also **Judicial Systems: Brazil; Judiciary in Latin America, The.**

BIBLIOGRAPHY

Alderete, Roger, and Rosaura Andazabal. *Perú, estadística criminal, 1700–1821.* Lima: Seminario de Historia Rural Andina, Universidad Nacional Mayor de San Marcos, 2003.

Barreneche, Osvaldo. *Crime and the Administration of Justice in Buenos Aires, 1785–1853.* Lincoln: University of Nebraska Press, 2006.

Garcés, Carlos Alberto. *El cuerpo como texto: La problemática del castigo corporal en el siglo XVIII.* San Salvador de Jujuy, Argentina: Editorial Universidad de Jujuy, 1999.

Haslip-Viera, Gabriel. "Criminal Justice and the Poor in Late Colonial Mexico City," in *Five Centuries of Law and Politics in Central Mexico*, edited by Ronald Spores and Ross Hassig (1984).

Haslip-Viera, Gabriel. *Crime and Punishment in Late Colonial Mexico City, 1692–1810.* Albuquerque: University of New Mexico Press, 1999.

Johnson, Lyman L., ed. *The Problem of Order in Changing Societies: Essays on Crime and Policing in Argentina and Uruguay, 1750–1940* (1990).

MacLachlan, Colin M. *Criminal Justice in Eighteenth-Century Mexico: A Study of the Tribunal of the Acordada* (1974).

Premo, Bianca. *Children of the Father King: Youth, Authority, & Legal Minority in Colonial Lima.* Chapel Hill: University of North Carolina Press, 2005.

Salvatore, Ricardo Donato, Carlos Aguirre and G. M. Joseph. *Crime and Punishment in Latin America: Law and Society Since Late Colonial Times.* Durham, NC: Duke University Press, 2001.

Sosa Abella, Guillermo. *Labradores, tejedores y ladrones: Hurtos y homicidios en la provincia de Tunja, 1745–1810.* Santafé de Bogotá: Instituto Colombiano de Cultura Hispánica, 1993.

Taylor, William B. *Drinking, Homicide, and Rebellion in Colonial Mexican Villages* (1979).

Uribe Uran, Victor. *Honorable Lives: Lawyers, Family, and Politics in Colombia, 1780–1850.* Pittsburgh, PA: University of Pittsburgh Press, 2000.

MARK A. BURKHOLDER

CRIOULOS. *See* **African Brazilians, Color Terminology.**

CRISTÃOS NOVOS. *See* **Inquisition: Brazil.**

CRISTERO REBELLION. Cristero Rebellion, a peasant uprising from 1926 to 1929, pushed Mexico to the brink of political chaos. The Cristeros generally saw the conflict as a religious war against the anticlericalism of the Mexican government.

This anticlericalism originated in northern Mexico, where North American–style entrepreneurs, Protestant converts, and ambitious politicians built a movement to transform their traditionally Catholic nation into a center of secular economic expansion. The movement's leading proponent, Plutarco Elías Calles (president of Mexico, 1924–1928), placed rigid regulations on the church, including required registration of priests and the closing of church schools. The church responded with a strike—the cessation of religious services—which caused a panic among the faithful. In Jalisco and the surrounding states of central Mexico, this panic sparked a peasant rebellion.

Government claims that the rebels were superstitious tools of scheming priests were largely propaganda. Only about 45 of the 3,600 priests in Mexico supported the rebellion. The Cristeros were indigenous and mestizo peasants whose motives for rebellion were mixed. Most acted to defend their faith against an expansive secular state, while others seized the opportunity to demand more extensive land reform.

The Mexican army's early victories obscured the depth of popular support for the rebels. By July 1927 approximately 20,000 rebels operated in small, uncoordinated guerrilla bands that lost several skirmishes but grew in numbers. The Cristeros moved to a new level of military action under the leadership of Enrique Gorostieta, a professional military officer who developed disciplined units to confront the army with conventional battlefield tactics. His attack on Manzanillo in May 1928 forced the federal army to bring in several regiments to avoid a major defeat.

The federal army mounted an offensive in Jalisco in December 1928, but the Cristeros simply left the area to escape the army's superiority in numbers and firepower. The frustrated soldiers attacked and looted the local villages, whose outraged inhabitants actually strengthened the Cristero base of support. Gorostieta's largest offensive climaxed at the Battle of Tepatitlán on 19 April 1929, when José Reyes Vega (one of the few Catholic priests active in the fighting) commanded a 900-man force that defeated a federal contingent more than three times its size.

By 1929 the fighting was stalemated. The Mexican government saw that a complete victory in the field was unlikely because of massive popular support for the rebels in their home districts. However, in spite of their 50,000 recruits, the Cristeros did not have the resources to overthrow the central government, which had the support of the United States.

The end of the revolt came from the outside. A reluctant but shaken Mexican government heeded the pleas of U.S. ambassador Dwight Morrow and reached an agreement with representatives of the Catholic Church in Mexico and Rome. The government relaxed its clerical regulations, and on 21 June 1929 the Catholic clergy resumed public worship. By September of that year the Cristeros had disbanded.

See also **Anticlericalism.**

BIBLIOGRAPHY

Jean Meyer, *La Cristiada,* 3 vols. (1973–1974), is fundamental. An abridged translation by Richard Southern is available under the title *The Cristero Rebellion: The Mexican People Between Church and State, 1926–1929* (1976). See also David Bailey, ¡*Viva Cristo Rey! The Cristero Rebellion and the Church-State Conflict in Mexico* (1974).

Jim Tuck, *The Holy War in Los Altos: A Regional Analysis of Mexico's Cristero Rebellion* (1982).

Robert Quirk, *The Mexican Revolution and the Catholic Church, 1910–1929* (1973), pp. 145–247.

Ramón Jrade, "Inquiries into the Cristero Insurrection Against the Mexican Revolution," in *Latin American Research Review* 20, no. 2 (1985): 53–69.

Additional Bibliography

Arrias Urrutia, Angel. *Entre la cruz y la sospecha: Los cristeros de Revueltas, Yáñez, y Rulfo.* Madrid: Iberoamericana, 2005.

Butler, Matthew. *Popular Piety and Political Identity in Mexico's Cristero Rebellion: Michoacán, 1927–29.* Oxford; New York: Published for the British Academy by Oxford University Press, 2004.

Llano Ibañez, Ramón del. *Lucha por el cielo: Religión y política en el estado de Querétaro, 1910–1929.* Mexico, DF: Miguel Angel Porrua, 2006.

Mendoza Delgado, Enrique. *La guerra de los cristeros.* Mexico, DF: Instituto Mexicana de Doctrina Social Cristiana, 2005.

Purnell, Jennie. *Popular Movements and State Formation in Revolutionary Mexico: The Agraristas and Cristeros of Michoacán.* Durham, NC: Duke University Press, 1999.

JOHN A. BRITTON

CRISTIANI, ALFREDO

CRISTIANI, ALFREDO (1947–). Alfredo Cristiani was president of El Salvador from 1989 to 1994. Born on November 22, 1947, the scion of a family of coffee planters, he graduated from Georgetown University and was elected president during El Salvador's civil war (1979–1992). Before his nomination as candidate for the presidency, he was a businessman with little political experience. Although his party, the National Republican Alliance (ARENA), was founded by Roberto d'Abuisson, a cashiered army officer with alleged links to death squads, and represented the most conservative elements in Salvadoran society, Cristiani conveyed a moderate image. With his election ARENA won the presidency for the first time.

In November 1989 Cristiani had to face the first major crisis of his presidency, a guerrilla offensive that reached San Salvador. During the struggle for the capital, six well-known Jesuit priests were brutally murdered. The prosecution of the crime was seen as a test of the commitment of his administration to control the excess of the army. Two army officers were eventually convicted of the crime, but disagreements remained as to whether the investigation had uncovered the full extent of army involvement. Although the case was officially closed in 1993, in 2000 the university where the priests had worked pressed charges against Cristiani for his involvement in the incident.

The main priority of the Cristiani administration was to bring the civil war to a negotiated end. The negotiations between the government and the guerrillas, sponsored by the United Nations, culminated with a cease-fire agreement signed 16 January 1992 by Cristiani and the leaders of the guerrilla forces in Mexico City. His administration advocated free-market economic policies. Despite criticisms of the way in which his administration implemented the peace accords, when Cristiani's term ended in 1994, opinion polls ranked him as the most popular politician in El Salvador, thanks in part to the pacification of the country and a healthy rate of economic growth. After withdrawing from political life, he opened a brokerage firm. In 1996 a rebel group known as the Popular Revolutionary Life made an unsuccessful assassination attempt by planting a bomb outside his office.

See also **El Salvador, Political Parties: National Republican Alliance (ARENA).**

BIBLIOGRAPHY

As of 2007 there is no full biography. A profile was published in the *New York Times,* 21 March 1989. An excellent source for this period of Salvadoran history is the documents section of the journal *Estudios Centroamericanos.*

Didion, Joan. *Salvador.* London: Granta Books, 2006.

From Duarte to Cristiani: Where Is El Salvador Headed? Hearing before the Subcommittee on Western Hemisphere Affairs of the Committee on Foreign Affairs, U.S. House of Representatives, 101st Congress, First Session, Thursday, July 13, 1989. Washington, DC: United States Government Printing Office, 1989.

González, Luis Armando. "Perspectivas del nuevo gobierno: El legado de Cristiani y Calderón Sol." *Estudios Centroamericanos* 54 (May–June 1999): 607–608.

HÉCTOR LINDO-FUENTES

CROIX, MARQUÉS DE

CROIX, MARQUÉS DE (1699–1786). Marqués de Croix (*b.* 1699; *d.* 1786), viceroy of New Spain (1766–1771). Born in Lille, France, Carlos Francisco de Croix rose to the rank of general within the Spanish army. He was serving as captain-general of Galicia when he was designated viceroy of New Spain in 1766. His term overlapped the Visita of José de Gálvez (1765–1771), who had been sent by Charles III to inspect and reform the colony. Croix presided over the efficient expulsion of the Jesuits in 1767. He supported Gálvez's suppression of the resulting riots in Guanajuato and San Luis Potosí the following year. A staunch regalist in ecclesiastical matters, the viceroy successfully defied the Mexican Inquisition when he was summoned before it. Croix undertook the colonization of Alta California in 1769 to defend the northern boundary of the empire. By the end of his term, four settlements had been founded. Croix urged the creation of the Interior Provinces jurisdiction in the north, which was accomplished five years after his departure. He sought improvement of the militias being formed in Mexico and encouraged the addition of regular Spanish army units to bolster the defense of the colony. He departed Mexico in 1771 to become captain-general of Valencia, where he died.

See also **New Spain, Viceroyalty of.**

BIBLIOGRAPHY

Luis Navarro García, "El virrey Marqués de Croix," in *Los virreyes de Nueva España en el reinado de Carlos III*, edited by José Antonio Calderón Quijano, vol. 1 (1967), pp. 161–381.

JOHN E. KICZA

CROIX, TEODORO DE (1730–1791).

Teodoro de Croix (*b.* 30 June 1730; *d.* 8 April 1791), viceroy of Peru (1784–1790). Born in Lille, Flanders, into a military family, Croix went to America with his uncle, Carlos Francisco, who served as viceroy of New Spain (1765–1771) and, following his recall to Spain, as captain-general of Valencia. Not surprisingly, this powerful patronage brought Teodoro rapid promotion in the Mexican military hierarchy. He succeeded Jáuregui as viceroy of Lima as Peru began its slow economic and political recovery from the Túpac Amaru I rebellion, the administrative confusion associated with the *visita general* (general inspection), and the indebtedness of the exchequer in the early 1780s.

Although overanxious to protect the dignity of his office against the authority of the first generation of intendants (installed in 1784), Croix

succeeded in overseeing a period of stable government and economic and fiscal growth. He succeeded in 1787 in persuading the crown to restore the superintendency of exchequer affairs to the viceroy, thereby undermining a key feature of the intendant system.

See also **New Spain, Viceroyalty of.**

BIBLIOGRAPHY

Lillian Estelle Fisher, "Teodoro de Croix," in *Hispanic American Historical Review*, 9 (1929): 488–504.

Rubén Vargas Ugarte, *Historia del Perú: Virreinato (Siglo XVIII) 1700–1790* (1956), esp. pp. 435–467.

John R. Fisher, *Government and Society in Colonial Peru* (1970), esp. pp. 54–70.

Additional Bibliography

Jansen, André. *Charles et Théodore de Croix: Deux gardes wallons vice-roise de l'Amérique espagnole au XVIIIe siécle.* Gembloux: J. Duculot, 1977.

JOHN R. FISHER

CROWDER, ENOCH HERBERT

(1859–1932). Enoch Herbert Crowder (*b.* 11 April 1859; *d.* 7 May 1932), U.S. military officer and diplomat. After graduating from West Point in 1881, Crowder received a law degree in 1886. In 1891 he joined the staff of the advocate general of the U.S. Army and went to the Philippines as judge advocate general during the Spanish-American War. During the U.S. provisional government of Cuba in 1906, Crowder served as president of the Advisory Law Commission that wrote legislation for Cuban elections, civil service, the courts, and local and provincial government. He chaired the committee that oversaw the Cuban elections in 1908 and established new electoral laws there in 1919. In 1921 he returned as the personal representative of President Warren Harding to help out following the crash of the economy after the Dance of the Millions. He strongly impressed on President Alfredo Zayas the need for honest government, and was successful in eliminating some corrupt practices. In 1922 he helped secure a $50 million loan for Cuba. From 1923 until his retirement in 1927, Crowder served as ambassador to Cuba.

See also **Cuba: The Republic (1898–1959).**

BIBLIOGRAPHY

David Healy, *The United States in Cuba, 1898–1902: Generals, Politicians, and the Search for Policy* (1963).

Allan R. Millet, *The Politics of Intervention: The Military Occupation of Cuba, 1906–1909* (1968).

Louis A. Pérez, *Cuba Under the Platt Amendment, 1902–1934* (1986), and *Cuba: Between Reform and Revolution* (1989).

Leslie Bethell, *Cuba: A Short History* (1993).

Additional Bibliography

"Enoch Herbert Crowder." *American National Biography* vol. 5. New York: Oxford University Press, 1999.

WADE A. KIT

CRUZ, ARTURO (1923–).

Arturo Cruz is a banker, former Nicaraguan ambassador to the United States (1981), and former Contra leader. Born on 18 December 1923, in Jinotepe, Cruz attended Georgetown University and earned degrees in economics from the School of Foreign Service (B.S., 1947; M.S., 1971). Cruz joined the Conservative Party at an early age and helped form the National Union of Popular Action in 1948. In 1954, he participated in an unsuccessful effort by young Conservatives to overthrow Anastasio Somoza García, for which he was jailed for eleven months.

Cruz joined the Inter-American Development Bank as a finance officer in 1959. He was one of the architects of the Central American Common Market in the early 1960s. In 1977, the Sandinistas convinced him to join a prestigious group of Nicaraguans, known as "The Twelve," which supported the revolutionary movement. Cruz was president of the Central Bank of Nicaragua from July 1979 to May 1980, when he became a member of the Governing Junta of National Reconstruction. In March 1981, the Sandinista government named him ambassador to the United States; he resigned at the end of that year. Cruz started to run for president against Daniel Ortega in 1984, but never registered as a candidate. In 1985, he helped found the Nicaraguan Opposition Union, the political arm of the counterrevolutionary force. He resigned his post in February 1987 and from 1990 to 1994 served as the alternate executive director of the Inter-American Development Bank's section for Central America. In 1999 he sought information from the United States and Honduran governments regarding the death of his nephew, David Arturo Baez Cruz. A naturalized American citizen, Baez had served in the elite Green Beret division of the U.S. armed forces and then returned to Nicaragua to serve in Sandinista military intelligence. He died while acting as a military adviser in Honduras. Cruz's son, Arturo José Cruz Sequeira, was as of 2007 Nicaragua's ambassador to the United States.

See also **Nicaragua.**

BIBLIOGRAPHY

Díaz Araujo, Enrique. *El sandinismo nicaragüense.* Mendoza, Argentina: Ediciones la Rosa Blanca, 2004.

Fonseca Terán, Carlos. *El poder, la propiedad, nosotros: La Revolución Sandinista y el problema del poder en la transformación revolucionaria de la sociedad Nicaragüense.* Managua, Nicaragua: Editorial Hispamer, 2005.

Grove, Lloyd. "Arturo Cruz," in *Washington Post,* 19 February 1987, sec. B, pp. 1, 4; *The IDB Report* 17, no. 9–10 (1990): 6.

Latin American Studies Association, *The Electoral Process in Nicaragua* (1984).

Matamoros Hüeck, Bosco. *La contra: Movimiento nicaragüense, 1979–1990.* Madrid: Imaginediciones, 2005.

Smith, Calvin L. *Revolution, Revival, and Religious Conflict in Sandinista Nicaragua.* Leiden, Netherlands, and Boston: Brill, 2007.

MARK EVERINGHAM

CRUZ, CELIA (1925–2003).

Born in Havana, Cuba, Celia Cruz (October 21, 1925–July 16, 2003) began her career singing for a tourist, earning a pair of shoes for her effort at the age of six. She participated in amateur radio contests, landing her first radio job as a backup singer. Hired as lead singer, Celia debuted with the band La Sonora Matancera on August 3, 1950. She left Cuba in July 1960, fleeing Fidel Castro's revolution, bound for Mexico with the band.

In 1973 Cruz performed as La Gracia Divina in *Hommy*, Larry Harlow's salsa opera at Carnegie Hall. Afterward, she relocated to New York City. She recorded "Celia y Johnny," with Fania Records co-founder Johnny Pacheco in 1974. It was a hit, and Celia signed with the Fania label.

The Fania All Stars included Rubén Blades, Hector Lavoe, and Ray Barretto. Cruz also performed with bandleader Tito Puente hundreds of times.

In the male-dominated salsa world, Celia's powerful voice, improvisational abilities, and personality made her a superstar. To Cruz, the difference between the music she was singing in Cuba and salsa was imperceptible, but it was in the world of salsa where she achieved immortality. She recorded more than seventy albums. Cruz continued performing and recording until her death in Fort Lee, New Jersey, at age seventy-eight.

See also **Music: Popular Music and Dance.**

BIBLIOGRAPHY

Kent, Mary. *Salsa Talks! A Musical Heritage Uncovered.* Orlando, FL: Digital Domain, 2005.

Rondón, Cesar Miguel. *El libro de la salsa: Crónica de la músic del Caribe urbano.* Caracas, Venezuela, Editorial Arte, 1980.

MARY KENT

CRUZ, OSWALDO GONÇALVES

(1872–1917). Oswaldo Gonçalves Cruz (*b.* 5 August 1872; *d.* 11 February 1917), Brazilian pioneer in medicine and public health. Cruz's careers in medicine and public health were closely intertwined. As director of public health for the federal government between 1903 and 1909, he led the campaign to eliminate yellow fever, smallpox, and the plague from the federal capital of Rio de Janeiro. As director of the Oswaldo Cruz Institute, he created the first important center in the country for microbiological research and tropical medicine.

The son of a doctor, Cruz obtained his medical degree at the Rio Medical School in 1892 and pursued further training in bacteriology in Paris between 1896 and 1899. On his return to Brazil in 1899 he joined the staff of the Serum Therapy Institute at Manguinhos, outside Rio, rising quickly to the position of director. In 1902, Cruz came to the attention of the newly elected president of Brazil, Francisco Rodrigues Alves, who asked him to lead an ambitious campaign against

yellow fever, smallpox, and the plague, all of which were epidemic in the federal capital.

The campaign was based on the newest techniques of the sanitation sciences, notably the destruction of mosquitoes and their breeding sites, fumigation of houses, and isolation of sick individuals. Despite considerable opposition from doctors, sections of the military, and the poor, who were the main targets of the campaign and who objected to its intrusive nature, Cruz and his teams of "mosquito killers" were successful in controlling the plague and yellow fever. However, resistance to compulsory smallpox vaccination meant that many people were not vaccinated; as a result, the city experienced a severe epidemic in 1908, with more than 9,000 deaths.

In 1909 Cruz resigned his position in public health in order to devote his attention to the Serum Therapy Institute, which was renamed the Oswaldo Cruz Institute in his honor. There he established the first modern school of experimental medicine in Brazil. In early 1916 Cruz retired to Petrópolis, where he died at the age of forty-three.

See also **Diseases; Medicine: The Modern Era.**

BIBLIOGRAPHY

Donald B. Cooper, "Oswaldo Cruz and the Impact of Yellow Fever in Brazilian History," in *Bulletin of the Tulane Medical Faculty* 26 (1967): 49–52.

Clementino Fraga, *Vida e obra de Osvaldo Cruz* (1972).

Nancy Stepan, *Beginnings of Brazilian Science: Oswaldo Cruz, Medical Research, and Policy, 1890–1920* (1976).

Additional Bibliography

Scliar, Moacyr. *Oswaldo Cruz: Entre micróbios e barricadas.* Rio de Janeiro: Relume Dumará, Rio Arte, 1996.

NANCY LEYS STEPAN

CRUZ, SERAPIO

(?–1870). Serapio Cruz (*d.* 23 January 1870), Guatemalan military officer and revolutionary leader. Known by the nickname of "Tata Lapo," Cruz served under the command of José Rafael Carrera in the Guatemalan revolt of 1837. Cruz broke with Carrera in 1848. Though a leader in the revolution of 1848, he refused to collaborate with the new liberal government and continued to resist until he reached an agreement with President Mariano Paredes on 2 February 1849. Upon Carrera's return to power in August 1849, Cruz reestablished his relationship with Carrera. He was an important military leader at the Battle of Arada in 1851 and in the campaign against El Salvador in 1863. Carrera suspected Cruz of a plot against him in 1863 but retained Cruz's loyalty by promising to leave him the presidency. Infuriated by Carrera's deathbed designation of Vicente Cerna as his successor, Cruz launched a revolt in 1867 against Cerna's government. In a daring attack at Palencia, near the capital, early in 1870, he died, thus becoming one of the principal martyrs of the Liberal Reforma of 1871.

See also **Arada, Battle of; Carrera, José Rafael.**

BIBLIOGRAPHY

Rodolfo González Centeno, *El mariscal de campo Don Serapio Cruz: Sus notables campañas militares,* 2d ed. (1985).

Ralph L. Woodward, Jr., *Rafael Carrera and the Emergence of the Republic of Guatemala, 1821–1871* (1993).

Wayne M. Clegern, *Origins of Liberal Dictatorship in Central America: Guatemala, 1865–1873* (1994).

RALPH LEE WOODWARD JR.

CRUZ, VICENTE

CRUZ, VICENTE (?–1849). Vicente Cruz (*d.* 20 March 1849), one of the leading officers in José Rafael Carrera's 1837 revolt in Guatemala. Once in control of Guatemala, Carrera appointed Cruz Corregidor of the departments of Mita and of Guatemala. Cruz was Carrera's vice president in 1844–1848, and he exercised the office of president when Carrera stepped down briefly from 11 September to 31 October 1845 and again from 25 January to 4 February 1848. When Carrera resigned in August 1848, Cruz expected to succeed him. But because the legislature opposed Cruz, he resigned on 28 November 1848 and took up arms against the government. He accepted, however, the Convenio de Zacapa (2 February 1849) arranged by President Mariano Paredes and returned to the government's army. Little more than a month later, he died fighting rebels led by Agustín Pérez.

See also **Carrera, José Rafael.**

BIBLIOGRAPHY

For details on his career, see Ralph Lee Woodward, Jr., *Rafael Carrera and the Emergence of the Republic of Guatemala, 1821–1871* (1993). On the death of Cruz, see Federico Hernández De León, *El libro de las efemérides,* vol. 5 (1963), pp. 455–459.

RALPH LEE WOODWARD JR.

CRUZ DIEZ, CARLOS

CRUZ DIEZ, CARLOS (1923–). Carlos Cruz Diez is a Venezuelan artist. Born on August 17, 1923, in Caracas, Cruz Diez studied at the Cristóbal Rojas School of Fine and Applied Arts. He began his career as a graphic designer, working as an art director at several advertising agencies. While his paintings display a taste for social realism with portrayals of daily life and common people, his graphic work reflects a fascination with color. During a visit to Barcelona and Paris in 1955, he began experimenting with the kinetic possibilities of color in his series *Physichromies.* He returned to Caracas in 1957 and opened a studio of art and industrial design. Later he designed publications for the Venezuelan Ministry of Education and taught art history and design at the School of Fine Arts and Central University in Caracas.

Shortly after his solo show at the Museum of Fine Art in Caracas, he moved to Paris with his family (1960). Three years later he joined the Nouvelle Tendence group in Paris and his work began to appear in international group exhibitions: The Responsive Eye (New York, 1965) and Soundings Two (London, 1966). He won the grand prize at the Córdoba Bienal (Argentina, 1966), and the international prize of painting at the São Paulo Bienal (1967). His large chromatic works are in the Caracas international airport and the Guri Dam powerhouse. From 1986 to 1993, he was a professor at the International Institute for Advanced Studies in Caracas. In 2005 his work was shown at the Sicardi Gallery in Houston and the Galerie Denise René in Paris. In 2006 he received an honorary doctorate from the Universidad Simón Bolívar. That same year Oscar Lucién directed and produced a biographical film exploring his career and influence, *Carlos Cruz Diez, la vida en color.*

See also **Art: The Twentieth Century.**

BIBLIOGRAPHY

Boulton, Alfredo. *Cruz Diez* (1975).

Rodríguez, Bélgica. "Carlos Cruz Diez and the Transformable Work of Art" (Master's thesis, Courtauld Institute of Art, University of London, 1976), and *La pintura abstracta en Venezuela, 1945–1965* (1980).

Rubiano Caballero, Germán. "Three Masters of Abstract Art and Their International Impact." *Art Nexus* 16 (May 1995): 80–82.

Schara, Julio César. *Carlos Cruz Diez y el arte cinético.* Mexico: Consejo Nacional para la Cultura y las Artes, 2001.

BÉLGICA RODRÍGUEZ

CRUZ E SOUSA, JOÃO DA (1861–1898).

João da Cruz e Sousa (*b.* 24 November 1861; *d.* 19 March 1898), Brazilian poet. Born in Santa Catarina to freed slaves, Cruz e Sousa became one of the most notable men of letters of his time. His protector, the former master of his parents, sent him through high school (1874) and tutorials. After brief experiences in teaching and journalism, Cruz e Sousa joined a touring dramatic troupe in 1881. His travels around Brazil revealed to him the abject conditions of his fellow blacks. From 1882 to 1889, he collaborated on a pro-republican, abolitionist periodical that he published. In 1884 he was appointed to a government post in a provincial city but was barred from assuming his duties because of his race. At that time he issued his first books of verse, which reflect the dominant realist rhetoric of the period. In 1890, he moved to Rio to work in journalism and later in the archives of the railroad company. He soon launched symbolism in Brazilian letters, becoming the leader of the new aesthetic movement.

Cruz e Sousa suffered several tragedies: two of his four children succumbed to tuberculosis while the two that remained died of other causes, his wife went mad, and he himself became consumptive. The poet retired to a country home in Minas Gerais but soon passed away. While personal misfortune is reflected in his verse, Cruz e Sousa's awareness of the condition of blacks is historically more significant. His leadership role in symbolism is outstanding and important in terms of black participation in elite cultural production.

See also **Literature: Brazil.**

BIBLIOGRAPHY

Raymond Sayers, "The Black Poet in Brazil: The Case of João da Cruz e Sousa," in *Luso-Brazilian Review* 15 (suppl.) (1978): 75–100.

David Brookshaw, *Race and Color in Brazilian Literature* (1986).

Additional Bibliography

Almeida, Sandra Regina Goulart. "'Beyond the Frontiers of the Word': Cruz e Sousa and the Concept of Symbolist Poetry." Durham, NC: Duke University, Duke University of North Carolina Program in Latin American Studies, 1992.

Firmino, Carmen Lúcia Zambon. "A imagística sensoral de Pessanha e Cruz e Sousa." *Revista de Letras* 33 (1993): 129–140.

Montenegro, Abelardo Fernando. *Cruz e Sousa e o movimento simbolista no Brasil.* Florianópolis: FCC Edições, 1988.

CHARLES A. PERRONE

CRUZ UCLES, RAMÓN ERNESTO

(1903–1985). Ramón Ernesto Cruz Ucles (*b.* 3 January 1903; *d.* 1985), lawyer, president of Honduras (1971–1972). After a thirty-year career in law, much of it as a district judge and legal expert in Honduras's border disputes with Nicaragua, Cruz was nominated by the National Party as a compromise candidate in 1962. The elections were scuttled in 1963 by the coup of Oswaldo López Arellano. Cruz was again nominated for president of Honduras by the National Party when General López stepped aside to permit elections in 1971. Cruz won a bare plurality (49.3 %) and took office on 7 June 1971. During his brief eighteen months in office, he concentrated on foreign affairs, traveling widely and winning the return of the Islas de Cisne (Swan Islands) from the United States. This diplomatic master stroke, however, could not offset his rapid and total isolation from his own party. In the face of virtual economic collapse and the escalation of agrarian strife, cresting with the massacre of Olancho peasants at La Talanquera by angry cattle ranchers, President Cruz lost control. General López quietly removed him from office on 4 December 1972.

See also **Honduras, National Party (PNH).**

BIBLIOGRAPHY

James A. Morris, *Honduras: Caudillo Politics and Military Rulers* (1984).

KENNETH V. FINNEY

CUADRA, PABLO ANTONIO (1912–2002).

Pablo Antonio Cuadra (4 November 1912–2 January 2002), Nicaraguan poet, journalist, and director of the Nicaraguan Academy of Letters. Cuadra studied with the Jesuits and attended law school. At nineteen he co-founded the Vanguardia group and began his journalistic work. He edited and co-edited several publications, beginning with the *Vanguardia* (1931–1933) and ending with *La Prensa*, which he edited after the newspaper's founder and editor Pedro Joaquín Chamorro was assassinated by supporters of the Somoza regime in 1978.

Cuadra's poetry and political ideology grew together. He was a Sandinista who published his first book at twenty-two: *Poemas nicaragüenses* (1934), followed by *Cuaderno del Sur* (1934–1935), *Hacia la cruz del sur* (1936), and *Canto temporal* (1943). In the 1940s, away from Nicaragua, he wrote three essays: *Breviario imperial* (1940), *Promisión de México* (1945), and *Entre la cruz y la espada* (1946).

Back at home, *La tierra prometida* (1952) and *Libro de horas* (1954) appeared. Cuadra recorded his persecution after Somoza's assassination in *América o el purgatorio* (1955); he won important prizes in 1959 and 1964, and published *Cantos de Cifar y del Mar Dulce* (1971), *Tierra que habla* (1974), *Esos rostros que asoman en la multitud* (1976), *Siete árboles contra el atardecer* (1980), and *Poesía selecta* (1991).

The Sandinista government continued Cuadra's marginalization, closing *La Prensa* in 1986. Cuadra's international status grew, however. He lectured abroad, won Fulbright (1987) and Guggenheim (1989) fellowships, and published his *Obra poética completa* (1983–1989).

See also **Chamorro Cardenal, Pedro Joaquín; Literature: Spanish America; Nicaragua.**

BIBLIOGRAPHY

Arellano, Jorge, ed. *Pablo Antonio Cuadra: Valoración múltiple*. Managua: Ediciones JEA, 1994.

MARÍA A. SALGADO

CUARÓN, ALFONSO (1961–).

The young Mexican director Alfonso Cuarón, like Luis Puenzo, Héctor Babenco, and Guillermo del Toro, became one of Hollywood's most celebrated filmmakers in the 1990s. Born on 28 November 1961, he studied at Centro Universitario de Estudios Cinematográficos in Mexico City, but eventually he was expelled from this university. After serving as assistant director for such films as *Gaby Brimmer, una historia verdadera* (*Gaby: A True Story*, 1987), *Romero* (1989), and *Diplomatic Immunity* (1991), he directed his first feature film, the hugely successful *Sólo con tu pareja* (*Love in the Time of Hysteria*, 1991), for which he also cowrote the screenplay with his brother Carlos. Subsequent films in which Cuarón was both director and screenwriter include *Y tu mamá también* (2001), a segment of *Paris, je t'aime* (2006), and *Children of Men* (2006). As director his credits include such films as *A Little Princess* (1995), *Great Expectations* (1998), and *The Possibility of Hope* (2007). The biggest box-office success of his career as of 2007 came when Warner Brothers invited him to direct the third Harry Potter film, *Harry Potter and the Prisoner of Azkaban* (2004). Cuarón has also been a producer or executive producer for films including *Crónicas* (2004), *The Assassination of Richard Nixon* (2004), *Black Sun* (2005), and *El laberinto del fauno* (*Pan's Labyrinth*, 2006). Cuarón has received three Oscar nominations in addition to twenty-two wins and eighteen nominations for other prestigious awards.

BIBLIOGRAPHY

Ciuk, Perla. *Diccionario de directores del cine mexicano*. Mexico: Consejo Nacional para la Cultura y las Artes (CONACULTA) and Cineteca Nacional, 2000.

Cuarón, Carlos, and Alfonso Cuarón. *Y tu mamá también*. Mexico: Trilce Ediciones, 2001.

JUAN CARLOS GRIJALVA

CUARTELAZO.

Cuartelazo, a barracks revolt. *Cuartelazos* have been one of the means frequently used by disaffected factions within Latin American society to change the government. The term is derived from the Spanish *cuartel* ("quarter" or "barracks"), so it refers very specifically to the use of a key garrison to begin a generalized military move against the government. The leaders often issue a *plan* or Pronunciamiento outlining their goals. Mexican history in the nineteenth century is a particularly good example of the importance of the military revolt in dictating the rhythm and direction of political change. That country saw the issuing of over one hundred *planes* and many more attempted *cuartelazos*.

See also **Pronunciamiento.**

BIBLIOGRAPHY

Additional Bibliography

Betancourt, Rómulo, Alberto Carnevali, Rómulo Gallegos, Andrés Eloy Blanco, and Marco Tulio Bruni Celli. *El Cuartelazo del 24 de noviembre 1948.* Caracas: Acción Democrática, Departamento de Estudios, Doctrina y Capacitación, 1980.

Calvert, Peter. "The 'Typical Latin-American Revolution'" *International Affairs (Royal Institute of International Affairs 1944–)* 43, no. 1 (January 1967): 85–95.

González Prada, Manuel. "Nuestras revoluciones," "La Buena revolución," pp. 131–146; 147–156, in *Bajo el oprobio.* Paris: Louis Bellenard et Fis, 1933.

López González, Valentín. "El cuartelazo Morelos, 1913." *Cuadernos Morelenses.* Cuernavaca, Mexico: Ediciones Gobierno del Estado Libre y Soberano de Morelos, 1981.

Stokes, William S. "Violence as a Power Factor in Latin-American Politics" *Western Political Quarterly* 5, no. 3 (Sept. 1952): 445–468.

Tamariz L., Domingo. *La ronda del general testimonios inéditos del Cuartelazo de 1948.* Lima, Perú: J. Campodonico Editor, 1998.

TODD LITTLE-SIEBOLD

CUAUHTEMOC (c. 1494–1525).

Cuauhtemoc (*b.* ca. 1494; *d.* 1525), last ruler of Tenochtitlán-Tlatelolco and leader of the final defense against the Spanish invaders. Nephew of Emperor Moctezuma II, Cuauhtemoc was elected to the post of *tlatoani* after Cuitlahuac, Moctezuma's immediate successor, died of smallpox. Around twenty-five years old when he took power, Cuauhtemoc married a daughter of Moctezuma who was a widow of Cuitlahuac. Later baptized as Isabel Moctezuma, she wed three Spaniards in succession.

Though the Mexica under Cuauhtemoc put up a spirited resistance to Spanish attacks, lack of water and food, and mounting deaths from disease and combat took their toll. Abandoned by most of his allies, Cuauhtemoc finally embarked on 13 August 1521 with a large canoe-borne force (or, according to some indigenous accounts, in one canoe with a small number of companions), either to flee or to mount one last offensive. The *tlatoani*'s canoe was captured by the captain of one of the Spanish brigantines used in the siege, and though Cuauhtemoc is reported to have pleaded for death, he was instead brought as a prisoner before a jubilant Hernán Cortés.

Early in his captivity, Cuauhtemoc was pressed to reveal the location of the "lost" Mexica treasure by having his feet burned with hot oil. This torture led to nothing, and Cuauhtemoc remained a prisoner until October 1524, when Cortés took him and a number of other indigenous rulers on an expedition to Honduras to subdue Cristóbal de Olid, who had declared against the conqueror. Cortés and others seem to have feared that the Indian leaders might rebel if left behind, but the Spaniards soon came to suspect that Cuauhtemoc was somehow plotting an uprising. Accordingly, during Lent of 1525 Cuauhtemoc and two other rulers were convicted of treason and hanged from a *cieba* tree beside the trail to Honduras. As in the later Peruvian case of the captured Inca Atahualpa, who was executed on a similar charge, the conquerors became convinced that Cuauhtemoc had outlived his usefulness.

Though defeated in life, Cuauhtemoc, and not Cortés, ultimately triumphed as an important symbol of Mexican nationalism. Evidence of his heroic stature includes such work as the later-nineteenth-century libretto of the heroic opera *Guatimotzín* (ca. 1872), by Mexican composer Aniceto Ortega Del Villar. By the twentieth century Cuauhtemoc's valor was celebrated in everything from post-Revolutionary murals to a statue gracing a *glorieta* (traffic circle) on Mexico City's Paseo de la Reforma, and even in the name of Cuauhtémoc Cárdenas, opposition presidential candidate in the election of 1988.

See also **Tenochtitlán.**

BIBLIOGRAPHY

Many colonial chronicles, both indigenous and Spanish, contain information about Cuauhtemoc, including Bernal Díaz Del Castillo, *The Discovery and Conquest of Mexico,* translated by A. P. Maudslay (1956); Diego Durán, *The Aztecs: The History of the Indies of New Spain,* translated by Doris Heyden and Fernando Horcasitas (1964); Francisco López De Gómara, *Cortés: The Life of the Conqueror by His Secretary,* translated and edited by Lesley B. Simpson (1964); Bernardino De Sahagún, *Florentine Codex: General History of the Things of New Spain,* vol. 12, *The Conquest of Mexico,* translated and edited by Arthur J. O. Anderson and Charles E. Dibble (1971); Fernando De Alva Ixtlilxochitl, *Obras históricas,* 4th ed. (1985); and Hernando Cortés, *Letters from Mexico,* edited by Anthony Pagden (1986). Accessible syntheses can be found in Miguel León-portilla, ed., *The Broken Spears: The Aztec Account of the Conquest of Mexico* (1992); Patricia De Fuentes, ed. and trans., *The Conquistadors: First-person Accounts of the Conquest of Mexico* (1993); and Ross Hassig, *Mexico and the Spanish Conquest* (1993).

Additional Bibliography

Aguilar Moreno, Manuel. *Handbook to Life in the Aztec World.* New York: Facts on File, 2006.

Berdan, Frances. *The Aztecs of Central Mexico: An Imperial Society.* Belmont, CA: Thomas Wadsworth, 2005.

Hernández Chávez, Alicia. *Mexico: A Brief History.* Berkeley: University of California Press, 2006.

Townsend, Camila. *Malintzin's Choices: An Indian Woman in the Conquest of Mexico.* Albuquerque: University of New Mexico Press, 2006.

ROBERT HASKETT

CUAUTLA, SIEGE OF. Siege of Cuautla, the most famous engagement by the royalist armies against insurgents during the War of Mexican Independence. In early 1812, with 4,000 to 4,500 men, José María Morelos fortified the town of Cuautla, south of Mexico City. Morelos had threatened Puebla and Toluca before Viceroy Francisco Javier Venegas ordered Félix Calleja and the Army of the Center to march out of the Bajío provinces north of the capital and into the new center of insurgent activity. After destroying the rebel stronghold of Zitácuaro, Calleja arrived near Cuautla on 17 February 1812. As Morelos anticipated, the royalists lacked effective logistics and were short of munitions and provisions. Despite these difficulties, Calleja launched three frontal attacks that were repulsed by the insurgents. After this failure, Calleja called for reinforcements and commenced a formal siege, cutting off all communications, provisions, and water. After seventy-two days, during which the insurgents suffered starvation and disease, on 2 May 1812, Morelos and some of his troops broke through the royalist lines and escaped. Although victory went to the royalists, the fame and glory went to Morelos.

See also **Calleja del Rey, Félix María; Morelos y Pavón, José María.**

BIBLIOGRAPHY

Lucas Alamán, *Historia de México desde los primeros movimientos que prepararon su independencia en al año de 1808 hasta la época presente,* 5 vols. (1849–1852; repr. 1942).

Wilbert H. Timmons, *Morelos: Priest Soldier Statesman of Mexico* (1963).

Ernesto Lemoine Villicaña, *Morelos: Su vida revolucionaria a través de sus escritos y de otros testimonios de la época* (1965).

Brian R. Hamnett, *Roots of Insurgency: Mexican Regions, 1750–1824* (1986).

Additional Bibliography

Archer, Christon. *The Birth of Modern Mexico, 1780–1824.* Wilmington, DE: Scholarly Resources Inc., 2003.

Rodríguez O, Jaime E. *The Origins of Mexican National Politics, 1808–1847.* Wilmington, DE: SR Books, 1997.

CHRISTON I. ARCHER

CUBA

This entry includes the following articles:
THE COLONIAL ERA (1492-1898)
THE REPUBLIC (1898-1959)
SINCE 1959

THE COLONIAL ERA (1492–1898)

CONQUEST AND COLONIZATION

Christopher Columbus reached Cuba on 27 October 1492 and disembarked the next day in the port of Bariay, which he named San Salvador. Although impressed with its beauty, he lost interest in this land. He returned during his second voyage and sailed along the southern coast. He believed it to be part of the Asian continent, and not an island,

and registered it as such on 12 June 1494. The conquest of America began in Hispaniola, and Cuba was of secondary importance. In 1504 King Ferdinand II asked Nicolás de Ovando to verify that it truly possessed the riches attributed to it. Sebastián de Ocampo was charged in 1508 with measuring its perimeter, an undertaking concluded in July 1509, when Diego Columbus became governor of Hispaniola. Diego Columbus arranged for the conquest of the island in order to satisfy royal desires and to secure the territories discovered by his father, assigning the task to Diego Velázquez, whom he appointed as his Adelantado. The conquistador set out from Salvatierra de la Sabana, Spain, in 1510, accompanied by some 300 men. He disembarked on the southeastern coast between Guantánamo and Maisí, where he encountered a group of people led by Hatuey, a chief who had escaped from the abuses of the colonists in Hispaniola. The rebels resisted for some three months, but they were forced to flee to the mountains. Hatuey was captured and condemned to be burned at the stake.

Velázquez established his residence and organized the Cabildo in the indigenous region of Baracoa, which he named Our Lady of the Assumption. Then began excursions toward the west with the aim of subduing the inhabitants peacefully and avoiding the horrible consequences of the mistreatment in Hispaniola. Nevertheless, Francisco Morales dealt cruelly with the inhabitants of Maniabón and was dismissed. Pánfilo de Narváez proceeded with greater brutality but went unpunished, leading the massacre of Arawakan people in the area of the Zaza River. From 1512 to 1515, seven settlements were established: Baracoa, Bayano, Trinidad, Sancti Spíritus, La Habana (Havana), Puerto Príncipe, and Santiago de Cuba. In 1515 the island was named Fernandina, but the customary name of Cuba was the one that later prevailed.

When Velázquez was appointed as Indian distributor in 1513, the period of mining encomiendas began, opening the way for permanent settlement. The *encomiendas* became the most cruel form of slavery. Native Cubans were forced into intense labor, which was contrary to their social organization and traditions of production, and were annihilated. Through this exploitation of the indigenous, there ensued a period of rapid growth, based on gold

An Indian Cacique of the island of Cuba addressing Columbus (1451–1500) concerning a future state, frontispiece to *The History, Civil and Commercial of the British Colonies in the West Indies* (1794) by Bryan Edwards, engraved by Francesco Bartolozzi, after Benjamin West (1738–1820). PRIVATE COLLECTION/ THE BRIDGEMAN ART LIBRARY

mining and agriculture on Estancias, allowing the first colonists to amass great wealth.

Velázquez did not content himself with Cuba. He knew of the existence of Motecuhzoma's empire and attained royal authorization to begin expeditions in Mexico. He sent the expedition that conquered Mexico under the command of Hernán Cortés. Cortés betrayed Velázquez and routed Pánfilo de Narváez, who was sent to subjugate him. When Velázquez died in 1524, the island of Cuba had entered a period of decline owing to the exhaustion of its gold and the depopulation begun with the conquest of Mexico. Once news of Mexico's riches spread, the exodus from Cuba increased, leading to more and more native uprisings. As towns became increasingly endangered, it became necessary to prohibit people from abandoning the island.

As a consequence of gold depletion, uprising, and the work of Fray Bartolomé de Las Casas, the New Laws of 1542, declaring the indigenous to be free and subjects of the crown, were introduced.

The colonists opposed the New Laws and managed to delay their implementation until 1553.

THE INTRODUCTION OF SLAVERY

The second half of the sixteenth century brought significant changes. The establishment of a system of annual fleets (1561), the introduction of African slaves, and the distribution of land by the *cabildos* (town councils) all contributed to the long-term settlement of the towns and to the creation of bases for systematic exploitation. Economic activities included the raising of livestock, the cultivation of tobacco, and, primarily in Havana, service industries, and military construction. Toward the end of the century another slave-based undertaking arose, sugar production.

For a long time, the principal business of Havana was to house the crews and passengers of the fleets and to repair and supply galleons for the ocean crossings. In 1553 the residence of the governor was moved from Santiago de Cuba to Havana, which was reorganized and transformed into a stronghold, with fortifications paid for by revenues from New Spain, assuring its supremacy. Slavery of blacks, who were known as "black earners," became the norm in the town. Slaves were used in all types of labor, including military construction and agriculture. The great majority of their earnings went to their owners.

The occupation of the western territories assumed the form of Mercedes (land grants) or circular haciendas, overseen by the *cabildo* in Havana. The *mercedes* were of two types: *corrales,* dedicated to the raising of swine; and *hatos,* for livestock such as cows, oxen, horses, or mules. There were also *estancias* where minor crops were raised as well as gardens and cultivated plots surrounding the town. With some differences, the other *cabildos* functioned in the same manner. The so-called "ransom" (*rescate*) trade was practiced in the interior regions. This practice evaded the monopoly of the House of Trade in Seville by means of bartering goods, mainly leather and tobacco, for which ships from other European nations were brought in.

Despite the risk of attack to Cuba owing to continuing wars between Spain and other powers, as well as repeated menaces from corsairs and pirates, criollo society established itself during the seventeenth century. Cuba's strategic location made it a vital center of communication between Europe and America. While the fleet system continued, an economy existed in western Cuba that Manuel Moreno Fraginals has classified as service-production, split between shipbuilding and finished wood products. The need to supply the fleets and armadas stimulated both large- and small-scale operations, which coexisted with, and eventually displaced, extensive livestock raising.

The first half of the eighteenth century saw the establishment of the forms of land use that would come to characterize the Cuban agrarian structure. The bases for the development of slave plantations also took shape. Landowners amassed wealth through the extensive exploitation of enormous livestock farms and the destruction or subdivision of the primitive haciendas. This made possible investments in sugar production, the most important of which was slave acquisition. The sparse population made it possible for small-scale white farmers, mostly from the Canary Islands, to settle on small plots. Some blacks also had access to land, due to the existence of legal means by which slaves could obtain their freedom. The population of free blacks grew, and they began to hold positions in the cities. The presence of these middle sectors prevented Cuba from following the same route as most colonies in the Caribbean. Although there were the so-called "black earners" and domestic slaves, slavery in Cuba on the whole was a rural phenomenon. Nevertheless, the average sugar mill in the Havana area relied on twenty to thirty slaves.

Spain's continual wars had numerous effects on Cuba. The War of the Spanish Succession brought French squadrons accompanied by merchants and slaves. With the 1713–1714 Utrecht treaties' territorial concessions to the English, slaves began to arrive in greater numbers and under better conditions, and it became easier to thwart the Spanish commercial monopoly. The crown became more interested in exploiting Cuba's riches. With Cuban tobacco famous in Europe, a state monopoly company was established, which would sell all Cuban tobacco at a fixed price. This led to the 1717 uprising of Cuban tobacco growers, which forced a temporary suspension of the monopoly. An attempt to reimpose the monopoly led to a second uprising in 1720, after which it was agreed that the growers could sell surplus tobacco to Spain and its colonies after satisfying its quota for the Factoría (Royal Agency). A third uprising in 1723 was met with severe military force, resulting in some deaths, but free trade in tobacco was authorized.

Interest in land was growing, along with the hope of making a profit by selling it. A 1729 royal decree prohibited the municipalities from granting further *mercedes.* However, it was not ratified until ten years later. After that, land acquisition was accomplished through the so-called *"composición,"* wherein lands were sold at auction to benefit the royal treasury.

By 1740 the sugar industry had entered a crisis. In that year, a commercial monopoly was authorized under the control of the Royal Commerce Company of Havana. The monopoly adversely affected tobacco growers, imported goods became harder to find, and the cost of living went up. But the monopoly contributed to the growing predominance of the sugar industry and the slave plantation. Several thousand slaves were introduced, and the new oligarchy of criollos began to receive noble titles. There was a corresponding growth of cultural institutions, such as the Seminary of San Basilio el Magno, founded in Santiago de Cuba in 1722, and the University of Havana (1728). New urban centers arose, stimulating new civil and ecclesiastical construction. The first historians—such as Ambrosio Zayas Bazán, Pedro Agustín Morell de Santa Cruz, José Martín Félix de Arrate, and Ignacio José de Urrutia—appeared during this era.

The first direct offensive against Cuba by the English was the occupation of part of Guantánamo Bay in 1741. After failing to take Santiago de Cuba, they retreated after five months. In June 1762 an English squadron of more than 10,000 men arrived in Havana. Although fortified, the city had a weak point. The English took control of Las Cabañas, which allowed them to take the fort called El Morro. Despite strong resistance, the city was surrounded. It surrendered on 12 August. The substantial booty seized by the occupiers demonstrated the economic progress that Cuba had achieved. Although English domination technically extended throughout the territory under the jurisdiction of Havana, which comprised the western portion of the island, in practice it was limited to the area around the city itself.

Historians and ideologists from among the landowners, Francisco de Arango y Parreño foremost among them, have maintained that the English occupation provided a fundamental impulse to the Cuban economy. The historian Ramiro Guerra points out, however, that Havana was not a miserable outpost, but rather had already become a vital mercantile and cultural center, considered an emporium of wealth and one of the most important cities in the New World, with more inhabitants than Boston, New York, or Philadelphia. Later investigations have corroborated Guerra's assertion. Spain reclaimed Havana in 1763 in exchange for Florida, which was not productive and practically uninhabited.

After the occupation of the city, the new fortifications of La Cabaña, Atarés, and El Príncipe were built, as was a new arsenal. The economy revived and trade with other Spanish ports grew. Havana became one of the most important fortified cities in the world. The Royal Agency was reestablished and Cuban revenues began to increase. The Intendancy of Finance and Customs was organized. The 1778 regulation for free trade between Spain and the Indies raised the number of Spanish ports with which business could be conducted, authorized traffic between the colonies, reduced tariffs, and eliminated duties for ten years on some products, including Cuban sugar. During the U.S. War of Independence, France declared war on England. Spain supported France, and Cuba became a base of operations toward the reclaiming of Florida. In 1779 free trade with North America was authorized. It lasted four years and brought benefits to Cuba.

THE PLANTATION SYSTEM

The destruction of plantations and decline in the sugar trade during the Haitian Revolution were felt immediately in Cuba. Arango y Parreño saw the opportunity for Cuba to surpass the wealthy French colony in international trade. He received authorization for the free introduction of slaves and exemptions from start-up taxes for the new sugar mills. Institutions such as the Patriotic Society (1793) and the Royal Consulate of Agriculture, Industry, and Trade (1795) influenced economic transformation and cultural growth. With the decisive transformation of the sugar industry, the slave plantation began to flourish. The number and size of sugar mills increased. Cuba's participation in the international sugar trade increased dramatically. The open slave trade allowed for larger workforces and the regular replacement of slaves who had been

Old Colonial Architecture in Havana, Cuba, 1841 by J. M. de Andueza (fl. 1841). BRITISH LIBRARY, LONDON, UK/
© BRITISH LIBRARY BOARD. ALL RIGHTS RESERVED/ THE BRIDGEMAN ART LIBRARY

worn out by the hard labor. Traders in black slaves amassed huge fortunes, which they reinvested in sugar. The population, particularly that of the slaves, grew rapidly.

In a relatively short time, Cuba surpassed Haiti as a supplier of sugar and significantly increased its production of coffee for export. In 1792 Cuba had 84,496 blacks in slavery—30 percent of its population. The slaves did not submit passively, and as their exploitation intensified, so did their struggle against it. Chained and fugitive slaves were a common sight. The free blacks did not show open resistance until 1795, when Nicolás Morales led a conspiracy in Bayamo demanding equal rights. He was discovered and executed.

High-ranking criollos did not make a stand for independence, but a group of well-to-do youths did try to achieve it. Joaquín Infante, Román de la Luz, and Luis Francisco Basave were tried for inciting rebellion in 1810. They were deported to Spain, but Infante escaped to South America, where he published the first plan for an independent Cuban

constitution. José Antonio Aponte, a free black, organized a vast movement that spread to other regions and called for the abolition of slavery and the overthrow of the colonial regime. He and his principal collaborators were denounced and executed in 1812. The year 1820 saw the beginnning of a conspiracy inspired by movements on the Latin American continent. It was known as the Suns and Rays of Bolívar. The poet José María Heredia was involved before escaping to the United States. Francisco Agüero and Manuel Andrés Sánchez disembarked from an expedition originating in Jamaica and were captured and executed in Puerto Príncipe. The Black Eagle Conspiracy (1828), which had support in Mexico, was also uncovered.

From his professional chair at the Seminary of San Carlos, Félix Varela y Morales influenced the thinking of many young people. He was elected representative to the Spanish Cortes in 1822, and he proposed a constitution of autonomy for Spain's overseas provinces. He was not able to set forth his plan for the abolition of slavery because he was forced to flee when Ferdinand VII was restored to the throne in 1823. From Philadelphia he published the periodical *El Habanero*, in which he openly promoted his ideas favoring independence. Brilliant intellectuals among his followers and supporters included José Antonio Saco, Domingo del Monte, and José de la Luz y Caballero, all of whom powerfully influenced Cuban thought.

Several measures were stimulating economic development: the state monopoly on tobacco was eliminated, land granted by the *cabildos* (*mercedes*) was recognized, and an open market was decreed. In 1817 Spain was obliged to sign a treaty with England by which slave trading was outlawed. Although this treaty went into effect in 1820, it ended only legal slave trading; traffic in slaves continued and increased. White immigration to Cuba was encouraged, and new colonies were established in coastal areas. The prosperous economy and the racial imbalance created by the excessive increase in the slave population pitted the landowners against any pro-independence activity. Slave uprisings were repeatedly quelled. By 1827 the slave population had reached 286,946, some 40.7 percent of the total. Slaves and free blacks together accounted for 55 percent.

During the 1830s, use of the steam engine became common, large warehouses were constructed, and the first railroad was built (1837). But the colonial government was changing. In 1825 all-embracing powers had been granted to the captaincies general, and in 1837 it was agreed that the colonies would be ruled by special laws and would no longer have representatives in the Spanish Cortes.

With their exploitation intensifying, the slaves responded with uprisings in sugar mills and on coffee plantations. Whites lived in a state of terror. English abolitionists mounted an intense propaganda campaign. Outstanding among these were the consuls David Turnbull and Richard Madden. A vast conspiracy involving slaves and free blacks, which came to be called the Conspiracy of the Ladder (La Escalera), was uncovered in 1843, and a cruel and violent reaction against all blacks ensued. Among those implicated in the conspiracy was the mulatto poet Gabriel de la Concepción Valdés (Plácido). White intellectuals were also accused, including Domingo del Monte and José de la Luz y Caballero. The landowners began to grow alarmed at the increase in the black population and sought

the cessation of the slave trade. Their most brilliant voice was José Antonio Saco, who denounced the regime in power and was exiled.

THE SYSTEM IN CRISIS

Although the plantation-based economy continued to grow and factories relied on workforces of slaves, the decline of slavery in general began to be apparent. The rate of growth in the slave population decreased abruptly. Owing to the difficulty of replacing worked-out slaves, intense research began into labor-saving techniques that would allow reductions in the size of the work force. Asian coolies were introduced and contracted laborers were recruited from Spain and the Canary Islands.

From early on, U.S. politicians had shown interest in Cuba. The 1823 Monroe Doctrine affirmed a U.S. right to annex Cuba, but European opposition inhibited attempts to do so. The first annexation attempt from within Cuba was markedly proslavery. With the prospect of abolition looming, the support of the southern U.S. states was sought. Between 1846 and 1848, the annexationists came together as the Havana Club, comprised of prominent landowners and intellectuals. In Puerto Príncipe a group led by Gaspar Betancour Cisneros (El Lugareño) also put out annexationist propaganda. Both of these groups created the Cuban Counsel in New York City in 1848. During that period, U.S. president Polk made attempts to purchase Cuba for $100 million.

Backed by the southern U.S. states and with important participation by North Americans, Narciso López led an expedition which managed to take the city of Cárdenas and fly the Cuban flag for the first time in 1850. He met with a lack of support and retreated. His next attempt, at Pinar del Río, also failed. The group was captured and condemned to death. The movements of Joaquín de Agüero in Puerto Príncipe (1851) and Isidro Armenteros in Trinidad met with similar fates. The executions of Ramón Pintó and Francisco Estrampes in 1855 put an end to armed attempts at annexation.

The landowners returned to reformism. In 1865 José Ricardo O'Farrill and Miguel Aldama organized the Reformist Party, whose mouthpiece was the periodical *El Siglo*. They proposed tariff reform, the cessation of the slave trade, representation in the Spanish Cortes, and the gradual abolition of slavery with

The Mill of Cana, **1874** (oil on canvas) by Victor Patricio Landaluce (1828–1889). Landaluce's painting depicts a period in the early nineteenth century when sugar mills flourished in Cuba and with them, the institution of slavery. MUSEO NACIONAL PALACIO DE B. ARTES, HAVANA, CUBA/ INDEX/ THE BRIDGEMAN ART LIBRARY

compensation. The sugar mills had grown without restraint, and the introduction of new technologies reduced the need for slaves. Change and competition demanded new forms of organization.

In 1866–1867 the Board of Information on Reforms in Cuba and Puerto Rico, convened by Spain, met with Cuban reformers who sought gradual abolition with compensation, cessation of the slave trade, an immigration plan, free commerical exchange, and assimilation giving Cuba the character of a Spanish province. Spain responded with the application of a direct tax of 10 percent on revenue without eliminating tariffs, and it acceded to none of the other suggestions of the Board. This failure and the new tax led to a separatist rebellion (the Grito De Yara) on 10 October 1868. Led by Carlos Manuel de Céspedes, the uprising started the Ten Years' War, at the end of which the situation in the country became critical. Many criollos lost their capital to the skyrocketing war taxes, which rose to 30 percent of the

net yield. Areas that had seen combat were devastated.

The 1880 law calling for the establishment of a *patronato* (trusteeship) began a process of economic change that led to the social division of labor in the sugar industry, marking the transition from slave manufacture to capitalist industry. *Patronatos,* which offered monthly stipends and conditions for gaining freedom, replaced traditional slavery. The war contributed to the elimination of inefficient mills in the east and hastened the development of business districts. These economic changes made the atmosphere ripe for the effective abolition of slavery in 1886. With the abrogation that year of the *patronato* came a massive immigration of laborers from Spain for the sugar crops.

One consequence of the Pact of Zanjón, which put an end to the Ten Years' War, was a change in metropolitan policies that made possible the formation of political parties. Freedom of the press, assembly, association, and worship were also granted. Two parties developed: the Autonomist Party, which sought self-governance, and the Constitutional Union Party, which proposed some reforms but opposed independence. They represented the opposing interests of Cubans and Spaniards. The Autonomists, with Rafael Montoro, Eliseo Giberga, and Enrique José Varona among them, demanded civil and economic rights for Cubans equal to those that existed for Spaniards. Their few representatives to the Cortes repeatedly protested Cuba's wrongs and defended her interests. Among their ranks figured outstanding intellectuals and brilliant orators.

On the economic scene, the differential right of flags—a scale of tariffs, based on the national flag under which a ship sailed, that charged less from ships flying the Spanish flag—was suspended and the fiscal system was streamlined. Negotiations began toward the forging of treaties with the United States. Until 1890, relations with the United States were defined by policies that favored exports to that important market. The implementation of the McKinley Tariff Act (1890) placed this trade with the United States in danger. This act provided tax-free sugar imports to the United States in exchange for a reciprocal trade agreement. Financial corporations and political parties organized themselves into the Economic Movement. A treaty between Spain and the United States that favored raw sugar but not finished tobacco products was signed in 1891. The Wilson-Gorman Tariff Act in 1894 abrogated reciprocity, worsening the situation created by the crisis of 1893.

The Autonomists had not given up hope. A group of combatants from the Ten Years' War began to conspire. Upon being discovered in 1879, Guillermo Moncada, José Maceo, and Quintín Banderas led quick uprisings in the east, and another group rebelled in Las Villas. When Calixto García arrived in 1880, the movement known as the Little War had already failed. Among its conspirators was José Martí, who knew that the time was not ripe to renew the fight. There were, however, other isolated attempts. Between 1884 and 1886, Máximo Gómez and Antonio Maceo conspired in a movement known as the Gómez-Maceo Plan. Maceo traveled to Cuba in 1890 and affirmed that the ideal of independence was still alive.

Among the émigrés in the United States led by José Martí, the Cuban Revolutionary Party was already forming. The party was officially announced on 10 April 1892, and Martí was named its representative. From the start, the group dedicated itself to raising funds and unifying Cubans to prepare for war. With the critical economic situation, the drop in the price of sugar, and the failure of the reform plan proposed by Overseas Minister Antonio Maura, armed struggle appeared to be the only option. A plan for simultaneous uprisings suffered a setback when arms in Fernandina were confiscated. Nevertheless, the plan went ahead with a limited uprising on 24 February 1895. When Maceo, Martí, and Gómez arrived, the War of Independence took shape. Martí's death in Dos Ríos did not deter the revolution. The invasion headed toward the west and developed into generalized war that cost Cuba large-scale destruction, numerous lives, and the impoverishment of the great majority of its inhabitants. When autonomy was finally declared in 1897, the course of events could not be altered. The U.S. Congress approved a joint resolution clearing the way for U.S. intervention in the war. Proposals and ultimatums were sent to Madrid, but rejected. In May 1898 U.S. troops were sent to Santiago de Cuba. With the aid of Cuban troops, the city was surrounded and taken. It surrendered on 16 July.

Negotiations between Spain and the United States began. The main concern was Cuba's debt of $500 million, which weighed heavily on its treasury. To this were added the costs of both wars of independence, expeditions, and diplomatic activities with Spain. With the signing of the Treaty of Paris, the island was freed of this heavy burden. Cuban independence began on 20 May 1902, three years after General John R. Brooke took charge of the government of Cuba.

See also Columbus, Christopher; Cuba, Political Parties: Autonomist Party; Fleet System: Colonial Spanish America; New Laws of 1542; Slavery: Spanish America; Sugar Industry; Ten Years' War; Tobacco Industry.

BIBLIOGRAPHY

Additional Bibliography

Casanovas, Joan. *Bread or Bullets! Urban Labor and Spanish Colonialism in Cuba, 1850–1898.* Pittsburgh, PA: University of Pittsburgh Press, 1998.

Díaz, María Elena. *The Virgin, the King, and the Royal Slaves of El Cobre: Negotiating Freedom in Colonial Cuba,*

1670–1780. Stanford, CA: Stanford University Press, 2000.

Guimerá Ravina, Agustín, and Fernando Monge. *La Habana, Puerto Colonial (siglos XVIII–XIX).* Madrid: Fundación Portuaria, 2000.

Johnson, Sherry. *The Social Transformation of Eighteenth-Century Cuba.* Gainesville: University Press of Florida, 2001.

La Rosa Corzo, Gabino. *Runaway Slave Settlements in Cuba: Resistance and Repression.* Chapel Hill: University of North Carolina Press, 2003.

Pérez, Louis A. *Cuba between Empires, 1878–1902.* Pittsburgh, PA: University of Pittsburgh Press, 1983.

Pruna, P. M. *Ciencia y científicos en Cuba colonial: La Real Academia de Ciencias de la Habana, 1861–1898.* La Habana: Sociedad Económica de Amigos del País: Editorial Academia, 2001.

Tornero Tinajero, Pablo. *Crecimiento económico y transformaciones sociales: Esclavos, hacendados y comerciantes en la Cuba colonial (1760–1840).* Madrid: Ministerio de Trabajo y Seguridad Social, 1996.

FE IGLESIAS GARCÍA

THE REPUBLIC (1898–1959)

THE EARLY YEARS

Cuba ceased being a Spanish colony, only to become a protectorate of the United States. After the devastating War of Independence, the country was left in a lamentable condition. The war destroyed the economic base and casualties claimed a large part of the population, owing especially to epidemics and famine brought about by the decrees of General Valeriano to relocate the rural population.

One of the first measures of the new military government was to proceed with the country's reconstruction. A public administration was organized and an educational system established. Measures were taken to strengthen the economic base of the island, and tariffs on U.S. goods were unilaterally reduced. Despite the approval of the Foraker Amendment in 1899, which prohibited concessions to U.S. firms for the exploitation of Cuban natural resources, U.S. investments were on the rise.

The general disarmament of the Cuban populace in January 1899 gave way to the dissolution of the Liberation Army. Tomás Estrada Palma already had dissolved the Cuban Revolutionary Party in 1898. Even so, during the government of John R. Brooke, anti-annexationist sentiment was evident in Cuba. Brooke, who became known as a moderate,

was replaced in less than a year by Leonard Wood, who had annexationist ideas. But economic and political forces in the United States remained opposed to annexation.

A Constituent Assembly was convened in July 1900, and the Constitution of the Republic of Cuba was signed 21 February 1901. A commission was formed within the Assembly to deal with relations between Cuba and the United States. Criteria to define these relations was sought as an appendix to the constitution, but the U.S. government pushed instead for a congressional accord, proposed by Senator Orville Platt, creating the basis for them. Known as the Platt Amendment, its third article established the principle of U.S. intervention in the internal affairs of Cuba. One condition of its approval was the removal of occupying military forces. Despite strong opposition, a small majority of the commission approved the Platt Amendment on 12 June 1901.

Landowners and financial corporations advocated commercial reciprocity, which was of vital importance to reconstruction. A treaty to this effect was signed in December 1902 and approved by the U.S. Congress in December 1903. Cuban commodities received a tariff 20 percent lower than that of their counterparts from other countries, while the tariff on U.S. commodities was between 25 percent and 40 percent lower. This raised the value of U.S. exports to Cuba by 45 percent. The first elections were held on 31 December 1901. Tomás Estrada Palma was the sole candidate after Bartolomé Maso's withdrawal. On 20 May 1902 the Cuban flag was raised in El Morro and Leonard wood handed over the government to Estrada Palma, the new president, who returned from the United States upon his election.

The first years of the Republic were characterized by power struggles between liberals and conservatives. Despite the fact that almost all of the political leaders had been part of the struggle for independence, fraud, shady business deals, and dishonesty were rife among them. Estrada Palma, however, was one exception. Attempts to remain in power provoked political battles and power struggles that made consolidation difficult. Racial and labor disputes aggravated the unstable situation. From an economic viewpoint, the country was experiencing an accelerated process of reconstruction and population growth. Thousands of immigrants,

Santa Cecilia sugar mills, Guantanamo, Cuba, 1920. From 1920–1921, the value of sugar on the world market plummeted after years of speculation and artificially inflated prices. Cubans lost jobs, savings, and businesses in the crash, further convincing many that the country needed to lessen its dependence on the sugar industry. © BETTMANN/CORBIS

primarily Spanish, who were attracted by employment possibilities, contributed to the latter. Agriculture relied more and more exclusively on sugar, due to the dependence on the U.S. market.

By 1905 U.S. companies owned twenty-nine sugar mills, which were responsible for 21 percent of Cuba's total production. The process of land acquisition by U.S. interests had begun with the first intervention, and by 1905 an estimated 13,000 U.S. colonists lived in Cuba, primarily on the Isle of Pines (now called the Isle of Youth), whose status had not yet been determined. There were also U.S. investments in mining, tobacco, and the railroad. After World War I, control of the economy remained in the hands of U.S. monopolies, in alliance with the domestic bourgeoisie. The 1920–1921 crisis strengthened the financial domination of U.S. banks and further increased U.S. land holdings. Estrada Palma's reelection in 1906

produced an armed movement of liberals, led by José Miguel Gómez. Unable to control the situation, the president requested U.S. intervention, and Charles E. Magoon headed a provisional government from 1906 to 1909. To the already critical situation of a country in reconstruction were added the effects of the international economic crisis of 1907. There were numerous strikes centered on demands for better pay and an eight-hour workday.

José Miguel Gómez took power as elected president in 1909. Although he did not especially favor U.S. business, he ignored the hopes of Cubans and continued with the administrative corruption that had begun with Magoon. In 1912 there developed a racial movement opposed to the prohibition of organizations based on race, known as the Independents of Color. The movement's leaders, Pedro Ivonet and Evaristo Esternoz, perished in the struggle. U.S. troops landed, but the Cuban government opposed this intervention. That same year the lease turning over Guantánamo Bay to the United States for an indefinite period was signed.

The new president, Mario García Menocal (1913–1921), capitalized on the economic upswing that drove up sugar prices during World War I. Investments in sugar by U.S. monopolies, courted by the administration, continued to increase. Menocal was reelected through fraud, and the liberals returned to armed struggle in the 1917 movement known as La Chambelona. Again U.S. troops landed, and Enoch Crowder was sent as a mediator. The U.S. government announced that it would not recognize a government that had taken power through violence, and the movement failed.

A HISTORICAL TURN

Following the war, Cuba experienced the "dance of the millions." An abrupt rise in sugar prices caused euphoria and speculation. But the subsequent rapid drop in the price by over 70 percent from 1920 to 1921 resulted in a grave crisis in which vast amounts of capital were lost and the domestic banking industry was broken. Small businesses went under, savings were lost, and thousands were left unemployed. The years 1920 to 1925 can be considered a period of consolidation of civil society and the national conscience, marking a historical turn. The crisis had demonstrated the consequences of such an extreme dependence on sugar and on the U.S. market. The loss of domestic capital in favor of that from the United States reinforced anti-imperialist sentiment throughout society. Likewise, General Crowder's intervention in internal affairs during the administration of Alfredo Zayas (1921–1925) accentuated an attitude of rejection of U.S. policies toward Cuba and deepened nationalist sentiment.

In 1923 movements with a new orientation appeared on the political scene, in which intellectuals, youth, and students seeking solutions for national problems took an active role. These movements distinguished themselves from the traditional political parties, which until then had been involved in a struggle for power and privilege. Among them was the Cuban Junta for National Renovation, led by the outstanding intellectual Fernando Ortiz. Its manifesto highlighted national woes. Arising out of the so-called Protest of the Thirteen—a group of young

intellectuals, led by Rubén Martínez Villena, who challenged the fraudulent business practices of the Zayas administration—was the Minorista Group (*Grupo Minorista*), which united the vanguard of the Cuban intelligentsia. The Veterans' and Patriots' Movement was organized, and the First National Congress of Women, proposing equality of civil and political rights and the protection of children, was celebrated. Merchants, industrialists, and financial corporations also organized in defense of their interests.

Students became an important force in political life. Their struggles for university reform began in 1922. Out of them arose the University of Havana Student Federation (FEU), of which Julio Antonio Mella was an outstanding figure. The movement's strength earned it a participating role in the University Assembly, whose agenda was reform. With an anti-imperialist agenda, the First National Revolutionary Congress of Students was held in 1923. The Anti-Imperialist League, with Rubén Martínez Villena and Julio Antonio Mella at its forefront, was founded in 1925. That same year, the United States ratified the Hay-Quesada Treaty, which recognized Cuban sovereignty over the Isle of Pines. This treaty had been signed in 1904, and its ratification had been demanded by Cuban organizations ever since.

The labor movement was unified at the Third National Workers' Congress in 1925. The National Confederation of Cuban Workers (CNOC) also was formed, and a small group, including Carlos Baliño and Julio Antonio Mella, founded the country's first Communist Party in 1925. Outstanding social scientists such as Enrique José Varona, Fernando Ortiz, Emilio Roig De Leuchsenring, and Ramiro Guerra pointed out the evils of large landed estates, monoculture, foreign interests, and extreme dependence on the United States. Progressive intellectuals played an important role in public life; they also cofounded and taught at the José Martí Popular University.

The sugar industry had begun a modest recovery when the United States adopted a protectionist policy and raised the tariff on sugar. From 1926 to 1929 the price of sugar and volume of exports declined, resulting in a decrease in the value of the harvests. Beginning in 1929, the

Inauguration parade of General Gerardo Machado, Havana, Cuba, May 27, 1929. Taking power in 1924, General Machado encouraged foreign investment in Cuba, earning great wealth for himself and his fellow public officials. By 1930, resistance to his dictatorship and corruption became widespread, leading to crippling national strikes. He fled the country on August 12, 1933. © BETTMANN/CORBIS

Great Depression caused an increase in U.S. protectionism, and Cuba was forced to reduce production. Exports in 1932 were only 18 percent of what they had been in 1922–1923. Cuban sugar's share in the U.S. market dropped from 52.2 percent in 1922–1926 to only 25 percent in 1933. A policy restricting sugarcane harvests was put into effect. The 1932–1933 harvest was half of what it had been in 1922. Sugar revenues dropped about 80 percent.

THE REVOLUTION OF 1930

The dictatorship of Gerardo Machado began with his triumph at the polls in 1924. His government promoted a demagogic program and practiced political assassination and repressed civil-rights movements. Two labor leaders, Enrique José Varona and Alfredo López, were slain and various communists

jailed, Mella among them. He engaged in a hunger strike for nineteen days and, once freed, went to Mexico, where he was later assassinated.

Machado implemented his promised public-works plan, which turned into a very profitable business for him and his collaborators. With financing by Chase National Bank of New York and the Warren Brothers Company, both fronts for public officials, the cost of the central highway reached ten times its true value. U.S. investments in Cuba had increased from about $200 million in 1911 to $1.5 billion in 1927. Actual cash investments are thought to have been around $500 million. The rest were government subsidies, especially for the railroad, and reinvested dividends. Introduced in 1927 was a timid protectionist tariff reform which had no effect on U.S. interests but did aid the development of certain areas of production for the domestic market.

In order to remain in power, Machado applied what was known as cooperativism, with the backing of a group of politicians. Opposition parties were prohibited. The 1901 Constitution was reformed in 1928, and the presidential term of office extended to six years. The only candidate in the 1928 elections, Machado served a second term from 1929 to 1935. Public reaction was immediate. The Great Depression further exacerbated political contradictions. Thus began the convulsive period known as the Revolution of 1930. Resistance against the dictatorship involved diverse organizations and various social strata and assumed various forms, including strikes, public demonstrations, and armed insurrections.

Martínez Villena organized a general strike in March 1930. In a student demonstration on 30 September, Pablo de la Torriente Brau was wounded and Rafael Trejo killed. In reaction to the repression, the student movement was radicalized. The Student Directorate was formed to fight the dictatorship. From this the Student Left Wing split off in 1931. The government intensified its repression, using regular police and military forces as well as paramilitary groups. The opposition parties set up underground organizations. One such group, the Revolutionary Union, was formed by Antonio Guiteras in 1932. It was anti-imperialist and oriented toward armed struggle.

At the height of the revolutionary movement in 1933, Sumner Welles was appointed U.S. ambassador. His mission was to mediate between the dictator and the opposition. Negotiations were interrupted by the strikes in August, which began in the Havana bus system and developed into a general strike. The result was the overthrow of the dictatorship, and Machado fled to the Bahamas on 12 August 1933. The new president, Carlos Manuel de Céspedes (Junior), was deposed in a 4 September military coup, dominated by then Sergeant Fulgencio Batista. An administration called the Pentarchy was formed, and on 10 September Ramón Grau San Martín assumed the presidency.

The so-called government of a hundred days had as its secretary of the interior Antonio Guiteras, who promoted various measures beneficial to the rank and file, including an eight-hour workday, a minimum wage, legalization of unions, restitution of the university's autonomy, and nationalization of labor—a work guarantee for Cubans that challenged the control of jobs by Spanish employers.

But as chief of the army, Batista repressed the popular movements. Lack of unity among the forces that had overthrown the dictatorship made the situation very difficult for the government. Batista took advantage of these circumstances and led another military coup, deposing the new administration and installing Carlos Mendieta as president. In order to strengthen his position, Batista obtained the abrogation of the Platt Amendment, and a new treaty of relations between Cuba and the United States was signed in 1934. A plan for sugar quotas was approved, and a new treaty of trade reciprocity reducing the tariff on sugar was signed. The number of favored U.S. products increased, and tariffs on several other Cuban products were reduced. This affected industries that had sprung up in the period of tariff reform. Labor and peasant struggles continued, and Antonio Guiteras formed Young Cuba, which advocated further armed conflict. A strike in March 1935 was put down violently, and on 8 May Guiteras was assassinated. These events brought to a close the Revolution of 1930.

CONSOLIDATION OF THE REPUBLIC

A series of ephemeral governments followed. A 1940 Constituent Assembly provided Cuba with one of the most progressive constitutions in Latin America, a sign of the maturity the republic had achieved. Elected president in 1940, Fulgencio Batista abandoned his populist policies. His party lost to Ramón Grau San Martín in 1944, thus beginning a period of governments of the Authentic Cuban (or Revolutionary) Party, which abandoned its nationalist program and became characterized by corruption, scandalous fraud, and the repression of workers and students.

Standing out during this period is the figure of Eduardo Chibás. One of the original rank and file who had founded the Cuban People's Party, he launched an active campaign against the rampant political corruption. His suicide in 1951 brought increased popularity to the party, which had been favored to win in the election of 1952. Batista aspired to the presidency with the United Action Party. Knowing that he would lose in the election, he led a 10 March 1952 military coup that deposed President Carlos Prío Socarrás.

During World War II, the economic situation had improved. Harvests were brought in at profitable prices. But the 1950s saw a decline in sugar's share of the national product. Cuba began to nationalize the sugar industry and U.S. capital investment declined by $713 million. Sugar no longer yielded the tremendous profits it had in the early years, leading U.S. companies to sell their sugar holdings to Cuban interests. Although the overall economic pattern did not radically change, a process of diversification had begun. Between 1947 and 1958 national revenues increased by 31 percent, the gross national product by 32.6 percent, and per-capita income by 27.2 percent, to one of the highest in Latin America. Production other than sugar increased 20 percent over the 1953 level, and the value of sugar harvests increased 27 percent from 1955 to 1958. Nevertheless, sugar's share in national revenues dropped to 28 percent and agricultural revenues in general dropped to 27.9 percent, indicating growth in other areas. These economic indicators can be misleading, however. Although attributed to economic factors, the 1959 Revolution in fact stemmed from the political crisis reflected in the hardships of the poorest Cubans.

The adoption of constitutional statutes in April 1952 unleashed a struggle for the implementation of the Constitution of 1940, which was joined by all levels of society. A group of young people from the Orthodox Party, led by Fidel Castro, attacked the Moncada military quarters in Santiago de Cuba on 26 July 1953. This offensive was a military failure: Several of the insurgents were killed and a period of repression bringing about a national movement against the dictatorship followed. An underground struggle was organized in the cities, and in 1955 the popular movement obtained amnesty for Fidel Castro and his cohorts, who emigrated to Mexico. The student movement produced the Revolutionary Directorate, led by José Antonio Echevarría. The underground organization, especially in Santiago de Cuba, organized by Frank País, aided the return from Mexico of Castro and others on the small yacht Granma on 2 December 1956. The guerrilla front dug in in the mountains of the Sierra Maestra. Camilo Cienfuegos and Ernesto ("Che") Guevara were the leaders of the invasion that moved through Camagüey and Las Villas. In 1957 a coalition comprised of the Twenty-sixth of July Movement, the Revolutionary Directorate, and the People's

Socialist Party was born. Despite failures in the strike of 9 April and the attack on the presidential palace on 13 March, the conflict intensified. The war entered its final stage in November 1958, when strategic military points and important cities were occupied. December brought the decisive Battle of Santa Clara, and Batista fled at dawn on 1 January 1959. Attempts were made at establishing a government of compromise, but a general strike enabled the Rebel Army to take power.

See also **Cuba, Revolutions: Revolution of 1933; Cuba, Twenty-Sixth of July Movement; Estrada Palma, Tomás; Fleet System: Colonial Spanish America; Guantánamo Bay; Platt Amendment; Slavery: Spanish America; Sugar Industry; Tobacco Industry.**

BIBLIOGRAPHY

Ramiro Guerra, *Historia de Cuba*, 2d ed. (1922–1925), *Manual de historia de Cuba* (1938), and *Azúcar y población de las Antillas* (1976).

Leland H. Jenks, *Our Cuban Colony* (1928).

Ramiro Guerra et al., eds., *Historia de la nación cubana*, 10 vols. (1952); Havana, Oficina del Historiador de la Ciudad, *Revalorización de la historia de Cuba por los congresos nacionales de historia* (1959).

Oscar Pino-Santos, *Historia de Cuba: Aspectos fundamentales,* 2d ed. (1964).

Julio Le Riverand, *Economic History of Cuba* (1967), and *La república: Dependencia y revolución*, 3d ed. (1973).

Fernando Portuondo Del Prado, *Estudios de historia de Cuba* (1973).

José Luciano Franco, *Ensayos históricos* (1974); *La república neocolonial* (Yearbook of Cuban Studies), 2 vols. (1975–1979).

Lionel Soto, *La revolución del 33,* 3 vols. (1977).

Louis A. Pérez, *Cuba: Between Reform and Revolution* (1988).

Additional Bibliography

Bronfman, Alejandra. *Measures of Equality: Social Science, Citizenship, and Race in Cuba, 1902–1940.* Chapel Hill: University of North Carolina Press, 2004.

Dye, Alan. *Cuban Sugar in the Age of Mass Production: Technology and the Economics of the Sugar Central, 1899–1929.* Stanford, CA: Stanford University Press, 1998.

Fuente, Alejandro de la. *A Nation for All: Race, Inequality, and Politics in Twentieth-Century Cuba.* Chapel Hill: University of North Carolina Press, 2001.

García González, Armando, Raquel Alvarez Pelaez, and Consuelo Naranjo Orovio. *En busca de la raza perfecta:*

eugenesia e higiene en Cuba (1898–1958). Madrid: Consejo Superior de Investigaciones Científicas, 1999.

Guerra, Lillian. *The Myth of José Martí: Conflicting Nationalisms in Early Twentieth-Century Cuba*. Chapel Hill: University of North Carolina Press, 2005.

Helg, Aline. *Our Rightful Share: the Afro-Cuban Struggle for Equality, 1886–1912*. Chapel Hill: University of North Carolina Press, 1995.

Ibarra, Jorge. *Prologue to Revolution: Cuba, 1898–1958*. trans. Marjorie Moore. Boulder, CO: Lynne Rienner Publishers, 1998.

Montejo Arrechea, Carmen Victoria. *Sociedades negras en Cuba, 1878–1960*. La Habana: Editorial de Ciencias Sociales: Centro de Investigación y Desarrollo de la Cultura Cubana Juan Marinello, 2004.

Moore, Robin. *Nationalizing Blackness: Afrocubanismo and Artistic Revolution in Havana, 1920–1940*. Pittsburgh, PA: University of Pittsburgh Press, 1997.

Shaffer, Kirwin R. *Anarchism and Countercultural Politics in Early Twentieth-Century Cuba*. Gainesville: University Press of Florida, 2005.

Whitney, Robert. *State and Revolution in Cuba: Mass Mobilization and Political Change, 1920–1940*. Chapel Hill: University of North Carolina Press, 2001.

FE IGLESIAS GARCÍA

SINCE 1959

The Cuban Revolution has passed through three phases since it triumphed on 1 January 1959. In phase one, from 1959 to 1965, Fidel Castro consolidated political power with the collaboration of the popular classes; the second era, from 1965 to 1991, featured the institutionalization of communist rule with predominant economic and international alliances with Soviet Bloc and Third World countries; and the final phase, the Special Period, began with the fall of the Union of Soviet Socialist Republics (USSR). Although circumstances and external relationships differed from one phase to the next, several tendencies of the Cuban Revolution have endured. The revolutionary leadership maintained Cuba on a definite anti-U.S., anti-imperialist course. As a second consistent feature, the revolution has steadfastly upheld the power and authority of Castro, whose leadership has enforced redistributive social policies providing free educational, medical, and employment opportunities to all loyal citizens. Finally, the economy of Cuba has been so thoroughly subordinated to the previous three concerns that it has lost dynamism and became ever more dependent on outside factors, whether Soviet largess or currently a tightly controlled opening to non-U.S. capital and tourism. Of the three phases, the first was the most important in establishing these lasting features of the revolution.

REVOLUTION AND CONSOLIDATION OF POWER

New Year's Day of 1959 filled Cubans with possibilities and hope. The first crisis of the revolution consisted of dealing with an interim government set up by generals of the army of the dictator Fulgencio Batista. The dominant rebel armed force, the Movimiento 26 de Julio (M26) of Fidel Castro, quickly moved to eliminate this threat. Castro sent two guerrilla columns into Havana and called for a general strike that neutralized Batista's former supporters. The old army quickly collapsed, laying the groundwork for the hasty arrival of the government-in-exile, made up of M26 collaborators and distinguished political opponents of the dictatorship. By prior agreement, the government of President Manuel Urrutia with José Miró Cardona as its prime minister prepared to revive the Constitution of 1940 and to set up elections. Comandante (major) Castro served as chief of the revolutionary armed forces, which consisted of *batistiano* soldiers not involved in atrocities, officers previously imprisoned by Batista for insubordination, secondary rebel forces such as the Directorio Revolucionario (DR), and the more numerous guerrillas of M26. Officers from Castro's own revolutionary movement took over the highest commands of the new army.

In the first months of 1959, the principal question concerned the intentions of Castro. His entry into Santiago de Cuba on New Year's Day had been triumphal, as were his slow journey westward and his reception eight days later in Havana, the nation's capital. The people who filled the streets and stood in the blazing sun for his several-hours long orations attributed to Castro all of the credit for overthrowing the dictatorship. His pronouncements as a rebel against Batista had proclaimed elections as well as social reforms, but two of his closest associates in M26, his brother Raúl Castro (b. 1931) and the Argentine Ernesto "Che" Guevara (1928–1967), had espoused more radical ideas. One thing had already become evident:

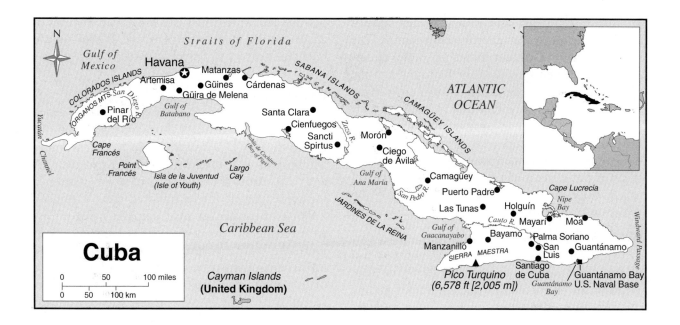

Castro's anti-Americanism. When foreign officials and news media criticized the revolutionary trials and executions of hundreds of *batistianos* for war crimes, Castro asked why the U.S. government had refrained from criticizing the Batista dictatorship for its torture and murder of the "heroic" youth of the revolution. He also demanded that American officials extradite to Cuba those "war criminals" who had fled to the United States with wealth plundered from the Cuban people. The American government did not respond. In the first six weeks of the revolution, the Cuban public seemed to respond more strongly to Castro's leadership than to that of the interim government. Therefore, when Prime Minister Miró Cardona resigned in mid-February, the cabinet quickly replaced him with the only logical choice—Fidel.

Castro moved speedily to institute several policies at once. He designed a land reform decree that divided up the largest sugar and tobacco plantations into smaller farms; established the National Institute of Agrarian Reform to administer the decree; and, without any publicity whatever, brought in members of the old communist party to take up positions in military and agrarian affairs. As American landowners complained about the lack of prompt compensation for their properties, Castro branded them agents of imperialism. As Catholic laypersons, the independent press, and even some members of M26 complained of the communist presence in the government,

Castro equated these whistleblowers with traitors and counterrevolutionaries. In the meantime, the prime minister attended labor meetings and urged the unions to rid their leadership of the former collaborators of the dictatorship. His armed forces, now commanded by Raúl Castro, began to raise militia units from among the unions and the universities. Their purpose was to defend the revolution against its enemies—foreign as well as domestic. Former M26 guerrilla comandantes like Huber Matos resigned, an act of betrayal that earned him a twenty-two-year jail sentence; another popular comandante, Camilo Cienfuegos, died mysteriously in a plane crash. In the universities, the government purged the faculties of counterrevolutionaries and replaced them with leftists. When students protested these changes, they faced dismissal by disciplinary committees. By the end of 1960, the last of the independent newspapers and radio stations reverted to state ownership.

The exodus of the Cuban middle class was also reaching alarming proportions. A few politicians and rebel army officers began leaving for exile, but the land reforms followed by seizure of rental properties under the urban reform laws shook the propertied and professional classes. Well-to-do families sent their children abroad and joined them after attempting to settle their affairs in Cuba. At that moment, armed opponents of the revolutionary regimes went into the Escambray and other mountains to begin guerrilla uprisings against Fidel, himself a former guerrilla commander. The involvement of Catholic priests in these underground movements exposed the hierarchy and the educational institutions of the church to government repression. Revolutionary leaders quickly raised peasant militias in areas infested with counterrevolutionary groups and ruthlessly hunted down hundreds of anticommunist rebels. So effective was the government campaign against the so-called *bandidos* (bandits) that armed opposition groups moved offshore to Central America, Puerto Rico, and increasingly Miami.

U.S. opposition to the Cuban Revolution had been tardy in forming. Throughout 1959, the State Department attempted to work with the dwindling numbers of moderates in the Revolutionary Government, even though Castro relentlessly attacked U.S. policymakers for supporting his enemies inside and outside the country. When an explosion in Havana Harbor sank a ship delivering weapons to the government in March 1960, Castro accused the Central Intelligence Agency of sabotage. This was the moment at which Castro introduced his motto, *patria or O muerte, veneceremos* ("fatherland or death, we will conquer"), and the photographer Alberto Korda took the iconic photograph of Che Guevara. Indeed, the Central Intelligence Agency was already actively aiding Cuban dissidents and exiles. Plans were afoot to launch an exile invasion of the island. Between 1960 and 1961, President Dwight D. Eisenhower reduced trade with Cuba by stages—and Castro responded by gradually confiscating all U.S. businesses there. Thus it was that a social revolution in an island nation of just 6.5 million inhabitants dragged Latin America into the cold war.

Fidel Castro had anticipated, even worked for, the United States retreat from Cuba. He nurtured relations with a reluctant Soviet Union, sending Che Guevara to conclude trade deals with the Eastern Bloc countries and Raúl Castro to sign defense pacts. Castro's collaboration with Cuban communists facilitated these overtures. Although the communists had refrained from the struggle against Batista, Castro offered them participation in the consolidation of the Revolution. He knew that communist infiltration into government would flush out moderate competitors for power, and the communists proved useful in carrying out revolutionary reforms and confiscations. His use of old-line party personnel had the added benefits of alienating the United States as well as winning the reluctant support of Soviet leaders.

BAY OF PIGS

In January 1961 the United States broke diplomatic relations with Cuba and prepared to bequeath the CIA's invasion plans to the incoming administration of President John F. Kennedy. CIA and U.S. Army training proceeded in Guatemala for approximately fifteen hundred men of Brigade 2506, as the exiles' combat unit was named. Castro's intelligence agents as well as Latin American journalists were reporting on these efforts, and the men and equipment moved to the Caribbean coast of Nicaragua for launching. President Kennedy agreed to the CIA invasion plans, which promised to rid him of this "communist beachhead" in the Americas. But Kennedy ordered that no U.S. military units engage in or support the émigrés in this invasion. The amphibious landing of exiles depended on several expectations: (1) that the "majority" of Cubans would rise up against the regime, (2) that the peasant militias would run away at the first sight of the invasion forces, and (3) that the invaders' bombers would destroy Castro's small force of fighter planes. As one CIA trainer told the Cubans of Brigade 2506, after you secure the beachhead, "turn left and go straight into Havana." However, when the Bay of Pigs invasion (named for the location of the landing) took place, not one of these three conditions materialized, and the invaders surrendered on the beach after three days of fighting. Castro himself arrived to command the Cuban defense forces. Pictures showed Castro directing the battle from the turret of a Soviet T-34 tank.

Although Castro eventually negotiated a U.S. "indemnity" for the return of the Bay of Pigs prisoners, he still predicted an invasion of American military units. Eastern Bloc weapons and Soviet military advisers arrived to help the Revolutionary Army and militias, some 150,000 in number, prepare for the defense of the Revolution. In the meanwhile, the popular classes of Cuba responded to Castro's militarization of the island. They joined various revolutionary organizations, such as the Committees for the Defense of the Revolution (CDRs), neighborhood watch groups that carried out surveillance against counterrevolutionary

Cuba

Population:	11,394,043 (2007 est.)
Area:	42,803 sq mi
Official language:	Spanish
National currency:	Cuban peso (CUP)
Principal religions:	Cuba was officially atheist until 1994. Roman Catholicism is believed to be the most widely practiced religion, with Protestantism, Santería, and Judaism are also practiced.
Ethnicity:	mulatto 51%, white 37%, black 11%, Chinese 1%
Capital:	Havana
Other urban centers:	Camagüey, Guantánamo, Holguín, Santa Clara, Santiago de Cuba
Annual rainfall:	45 inches in lowland areas, 70 inches in mountains
Principal geographical features:	*Mountains:* Sierra de los Órganos; Sierra Maestra, with Cuba's highest point: Pico Real del Turquino (6,578 ft); Trinidad (Escambray) Mts. *Rivers:* Cauto *Islands:* Isla de la Juventud, numerous small coastal islands
Economy:	*GDP per capita:* $4,100 (2006 est.)
Principal products and exports:	*Agricultural:* coffee, fruit, sugar, tobacco *Manufacturing:* agricultural machinery, sugar processing, pharmaceuticals *Mining:* nickel
Government:	Cuba gained complete independence in 1902. It has a Communist-led single-party government. The president is chief of state, head of government, and in practice has control over the government. A 609-seat legislature called the National Assembly of People's Power is popularly elected from a list of approved candidates, and it selects the president.
Armed forces:	Men and women are subject to 2 years of mandatory military service. *Army:* 38,000 *Navy:* 3,000 *Air force:* 8,000 *Paramilitary:* Over 1.1 million, mostly in the Territorial Militia *Reserves:* 39,000
Transportation:	*Rail:* 2,626 mi *Ports:* Cienfuegos, Havana, Matanzas *Roads:* 18,529 mi paved; 19,286 mi unpaved *National airline:* Cubana Airlines *Airports:* 75 paved runway, 95 unpaved runway airports
Media:	All print and broadcast media is under government control. Major newspapers include *Granma* and *Juventude Rebelde*. There are 150 AM and 5 FM radio stations, and 58 television stations.
Literacy and education:	*Total literacy rate:* 99.8% (2002) Public education is free, and children ages 6 to 11 are required to attend school. Cuba has five universities, including the University of Havana and Oriente University.

elements within Cuba. However, popular backing was not enough. Cuban authorities either requested or agreed to Soviet suggestions that medium-range missiles be activated for Cuba's defense. U.S. spy planes photographed the missile sites, and President Kennedy ordered a naval blockade of the island to prevent the Soviet ships from delivering the rockets. The resulting standoff in October 1962, known as the Cuban Missile Crisis, produced an agreement between Kennedy and Soviet Premier Nikita Khrushchev (1894–1971). The United States pledged that it would not invade Cuba and that it would remove U.S. missiles that were aimed at Moscow from Turkey. The Soviets promised to remove its own missiles from Cuba and permit Americans to inspect the disassembled installations. Castro and other Cuban leaders erupted in anger (and a long list of expletives) that they had not been consulted. Indeed, the U.S.-USSR agreement offered no assurances to the Cubans that the United States would halt attacks by mercenaries and exiled counterrevolutionaries or that it would terminate spy flights over the island. Castro adamantly refused to permit American inspectors to visit military installations on the island.

INSTITUTIONALIZATION OF COMMUNIST RULE

The Sovietization of Cuba began in the second half of the 1960s, as the alliance between the Cuban revolutionaries and the Eastern Bloc countries grew tighter. This process did not evolve without disagreements. The evidence indicates that Cuba did not serve as the Caribbean puppet of the Soviet state—far from it. In these developments, the resignation and disappearance of Che Guevara marked a turning point. During his administration of the revolutionary economy, he had instituted a policy of socialization of the markets and production, rapid industrialization, and rigid central controls. Sugar exports declined drastically and rationing became a revolutionary fact of life. Che pretended to be the strict Marxist-Leninist and charged the Russians with revisionism. His policies drew opposition from older communists, who favored the contemporary Soviet economic model featuring decentralization and emphasizing profitability in state industries. After Che left Cuba in 1965, Castro settled on an economic policy that split the difference. He kept the tight state controls while returning to sugar exports, mainly to the Eastern Bloc countries. The Soviets paid higher-than-market prices for Cuban cane sugar and charged its Caribbean partner below-world prices for its petroleum. Therefore, trade with the socialist countries of Eastern Europe amounted to a subsidy for the island nation. In addition, Soviet technical and military aid flowed into Cuba in a way that entrenched inefficiencies in Cuban productivity. Russian, East German, and Czech families inhabited the largest high-rise apartment complex in the Vedado district of Havana. Jokes circulated among the Cuban hosts about the Russian predilection for strong drink and aversion to regular bathing. Nonetheless, socialization meant that, with Eastern Bloc assistance, all Cubans had access to jobs, medical care, and free education.

Cuba was by no means subservient to Soviet direction; it was not a puppet regime. Castro dominated the Communist Party that he established in 1965, and occasionally purged communists who too zealously spoke in favor of policies with which he disagreed. In 1962 and again in 1968, he broke up a "microfaction of divisionists" led by long-time communist Aníbal Escalante. Castro also maintained an aggressive revolutionary policy abroad that clashed with Soviet ideology; Soviet leaders maintained that conditions in the Third World were not propitious for armed revolution and that the existing socialist countries would defeat the capitalist countries by out-producing them. If conditions

for revolution did mature, the old-line pro-Moscow communist parties would lead the workers in armed struggle. Therefore, trade and detente with the West—not armed insurrections—remained the order of the day in Soviet communism.

Cuban officials resisted this model because their experience in the Sierra Maestra mountains had taught a different lesson. As Che had written in 1960 in his primer *Guerrilla Warfare*, the Cuban struggle proved that the rural guerrillas could create the conditions for social revolution and that, with peasant backing, they could defeat the armies of dictators. During the Cuban insurrection, Castro added, the communists were hiding "under the bed." These ideas became the heart of the theory of the *rural foco* (guerrilla insurrections in rural areas). For these reasons, Che Guevara served as one of the architects of the export of revolution, and all those Latin American leftists who came to Cuba for military training returned to their countries with the idea of leading rebellions in the countryside. The Sino-Soviet rift between the communists of Chairman Mao Tse-Tung and those of the Kremlin complicated the relationship in Cuba. To the Soviets the *rural foco* looked too much like the Chinese Revolution of 1949. Essentially, the Cubans sponsored and assisted armed insurrections in Panama, the Dominican Republic, Haiti, Nicaragua, Guatemala, Argentina, Peru, Colombia, and Venezuela. Although none of these succeeded, the United States responded by engineering a break in relations between most member countries of the Organization of American States (OAS) and Cuba. Cuba became isolated in the Americas except for Mexico and Canada.

When he disappeared from view in 1965, Che Guevara led a Cuban expedition into Africa to train revolutionary guerrillas in Eastern Congo. He failed in this task and escaped back to Cuba, whence he launched a guerrilla incursion into Bolivia in 1966. Che had been operating there for several months before two members of his band captured by the Bolivian army revealed that he was still alive. Because no one had seen Che for two years, CIA analysts had speculated that Castro had had the Argentinean-born revolutionary executed over a policy disagreement. The United States immediately responded to a Bolivian request for military assistance, which partly contributed to Che's capture and execution in October 1967.

Despite the setback of Che's death, the Cuban revolutionaries continued diplomatic and military assistance to leftist governments and national liberation movements both in Africa and Latin America. Cuban troops supported the Angolan leftist government in 1988 and helped defeat mercenary forces supported by the CIA and South Africa's apartheid government. These aggressive policies forced the Soviet Union reluctantly to support Cuban international initiatives even though Soviet Premier Leonid Brezhnev (1906–1982) found them "adventurous." Leaders in Moscow deemed preserving the Cuban Revolution as a symbol of defiance against U.S. "capitalist imperialism" important enough to tolerate Castro's impulsiveness. Besides, Castro and the Soviets realized that the Caribbean island was located too far away for the Soviets to enforce its influence with tanks as they had in Hungary in 1956 and Czechoslovakia in 1968. The most that Moscow could expect was Castro's verbal backing of the Soviet tanks in the streets of Prague to preserve socialism in Eastern Europe. Something less might have jeopardized Soviet subsidies and military support. On other occasions, the Cubans were brutally frank with their Russian benefactors. Mikhail Gorbachev (b. 1931), the only Soviet premier to make a state visit to Cuba, stoically endured Castro's denunciation of his policies of *glasnost* (openness) and *perestroika* (restructuring) for their dangerous deviations from Marxism-Leninism.

The Mariel Boatlift. As for the American government, the only serious rapprochement developed during the presidency of Jimmy Carter (served 1977–1981). Diplomatic negotiations resulted in the easing of trade and travel restrictions, and a renewal of diplomatic relations between the two governments appeared possible. Then Castro turned an incident to his advantage to further tighten his grip on power: on 1 April 1980, a group of five dissidents crashed a bus through the fence around the Peruvian embassy seeking asylum, which the embassy granted. Over the next few days tensions mounted between Castro and the

Peruvian government. On Easter Sunday, ten thousand Cubans jammed onto the Peruvian embassy grounds. Castro led a parade of fervent supporters in wishing good riddance to these *gusanos* (worms) and any others who wished to abandon the fatherland. This open invitation caught President Carter and U.S. authorities by surprise. Overnight, hundreds of Cuban Americans piloted pleasure boats from Florida to the port of Mariel near Havana to pick up the thousands who gathered there to leave the country. Cuban authorities emptied the jails and mental health facilities, and these inmates also joined the exodus. The influx of so many refugees (and criminals) taxed U.S. infrastructure and prisons for years to come. The exodus of 1980 contrasted sharply with that of the 1960s: few of these newer refugees came from the professional class, and many were poorly prepared to take advantage of opportunities in the United States. American politicians thereafter recoiled at the idea of courting Castro and worried about future massive arrivals of refugees. The Cuban community in Florida mostly favored continued restrictions against the Castro regime as it built up a new generation of citizens and political power in South Florida.

THE SPECIAL PERIOD: THE POST-SOVIET ERA

In 1991 Cuba's number-one trade and military partner, the Soviet Union, along with the communist governments of Eastern Europe, collapsed. The Russians in Cuba returned home, and Soviet foreign aid dried up. The island's economy, never strongly self-supporting, declined precipitously. During this time, known as the Special Period in Time of Peace (*Período especial en tiempo de paz*), electrical production and transportation shut down for lack of affordable Russian oil supplies, unemployment spread, and the medical and educational infrastructure grew impoverished. The Cuban government had to ease some of its central controls to open up the economy to other than U.S. investors, especially in tourism. The influx of hard currency promoted a return of class divisions, as those workers with access to tourist dollars had higher incomes than those stuck earning wages paid in Cuban pesos. Sugar exports plunged, as Cuba could no longer compete on foreign markets for want of customers willing to pay high Soviet-era prices. The government defrayed maintenance of apartment buildings and roadways, and as a result Cuban cities grew shabby. Elements of prerevolutionary maladies, such as prostitution and corruption, resurfaced. Many Cubans grew nostalgic for the halcyon days of Soviet largess.

Finally, Cuba's plight since the fall of the Soviet Union has drawn the sympathy of the world community outside of the United States. Between 1972 and 2000, most Latin American nations abandoned the boycott and renewed diplomatic and trade relations with Cuba. Developments in the late twentieth and early twenty-first centuries have had a significant impact on Cuba: The rising giant of the Far East, the People's Republic of China, began seeking economic opportunities and widening trade with Cuba. Panama began widening its interoceanic canal to facilitate Asian-Caribbean trade. Socialist and left-of-center governments in Argentina, Bolivia, Brazil, and Venezuela have lent support to Cuba's recovery efforts. Hugo Chávez, a great admirer of Che Guevara and Castro who was elected president of Venezuela in 1998, began selling petroleum to Cuba at deeply discounted Soviet-style prices. At the United Nations, nearly all member nations supported nonbinding resolutions condemning the U.S. boycott on Cuban trade. During the Special Period church services resumed on the island, and in 1998 Pope John Paul visited Cuba and conducted Mass. In 2002 former President Carter also traveled to the island, denouncing American restrictions while also criticizing Castro's human rights record. Cuba also ended its program of fomenting armed revolutions abroad. Despite these changes, there remains no certainty that diplomatic relations between Cuba and the United States will normalize anytime soon.

Cubans have responded to the economic crisis with their characteristic resourcefulness and ingenuity. To provide political stability, the army under Raúl Castro has become partner with foreign investors in car rental agencies, resort hotels, and manufacturing plants. In towns and provincial cities, small-time entrepreneurs harness horses to wagons for public transportation and convert bicycles into service as affordable taxis. For Cuban drivers, lovingly maintained, Russian-made Ladas from the 1970s complement the American cars of the 1950s. The government has purchased late-model Japanese cars for the tourist trade. To stimulate food production, the government imports breeding stock for dairy and beef production and permits direct sales of vegetables and fruits in farmers' markets. The egalitarian revolution earns hard currency by exporting medical and education workers to Africa and Latin America. By the first decade of the twenty-first century, the Cuban economy had regained its balance if not its dynamism. As of this writing, Cuban leaders were pushing forward with recovery, helped by trade and tourism open to every country of the world save the United States, whose government maintains policies that prevent travel and trade between these natural economic partners. In 2008 Fidel Castro, who underwent surgery in 2006 and handed over temporary power to his brother Raúl, officially resigned. Raúl Castro was elected president on February 24, 2008.

See also **Batista y Zaldívar, Fulgencio; Bay of Pigs Invasion; Castro Ruz, Fidel; Castro Ruz, Raúl; Cuba, Political Parties: Communist Party; Guevara, Ernesto "Che"; Russian-Latin American Relations; United States-Latin American Relations.**

BIBLIOGRAPHY

Anderson, Jon Lee. *Che Guevara: A Revolutionary Life.* New York: Grove Press, 1997.

Balfour, Sebastian. *Castro.* 2nd ed. London: Longman, 1995.

Blight, James G., and Philip G. Brenner. *Sad and Luminous Days: Cuba's Secret Struggle with the Superpowers after the Missile Crisis.* Lanham, MD: Rowman & Littlefield, 2002.

Castro, Fidel. *Fidel Castro Speaks.* New York. Eds. Martin Kenner and James Petras. New York: Penguin Books, 1969.

Cordova, Efrén. *Castro and the Cuban Labor Movement: Statecraft and Society in a Revolutionary Period.* Lanham, MD: Rowman & Littlefield, 1987.

Dominguez, Jorge I. *Cuba: Order and Revolution.* Cambridge, MA: Belknap Press of Harvard University Press, 1978.

Fagan, Richard R. *The Transformation of Political Culture in Cuba.* Stanford, CA: Stanford University Press, 1969.

Franqui, Carlos. *Family Portrait with Fidel: A Memoir.* Translated by Alfred MacAdam. New York: Random House, 1984.

Guevara, Ernesto "Che." *Guerrilla Warfare.* Introduction by Marc Becker. Lincoln: University of Nebraska Press, 1998.

Johnson, Haynes, with Manuel Artime (and others). *The Bay of Pigs: The Leaders' Story of Brigade 2506.* New York: Dell, 1964.

Karol, K. S. *Guerrillas in Power: The Course of the Cuban Revolution.* Translated by Arnold Pomerans. New York: Hill & Wang, 1970.

Kornbluh, Peter. Editor. *Bay of Pigs Declassified: The Secret CIA Report on the Invasion of Cuba.* New York: The New Press, 1998.

Matthews, Herbert L. *Revolution in Cuba: An Essay in Understanding.* New York: Scribner, 1975.

Mesa-Lago, Carmelo. *The Economy of Socialist Cuba: A Two Decade Appraisal.* Albuquerque: University of New Mexico Press, 1981.

Paterson, Thomas G. *Contesting Castro: The United States and the Triumph of the Cuban Revolution.* New York: Oxford University Press, 1994.

Thomas, Hugh. *Cuba or the Pursuit of Freedom.* Updated ed. New York: Da Capo Press, 1998.

Zeitlin, Maurice. *Revolutionary Politics and the Cuban Working Class.* New York: Harper & Row, 1970.

JONATHAN C. BROWN

CUBA, CONSTITUTIONS.

Since its independence from Spain, Cuba has had three constitutions. The first was drafted in 1901, immediately following the Spanish-American War, and reflected the new hegemonic role the United States played in Cuban affairs. The second, the Constitution of 1940, represented a thorough reworking of the Constitution of 1901 and reflected the strong sense of nationalism and liberalism that had begun to emerge in Cuban society in the 1930s. And while one of the goals of the revolution of 1959 was the enactment of a new constitution, the third constitution was not approved until 1976, seventeen years after Fidel Castro's forces entered Havana and established a new regime.

Enacted under the shadow of a just-terminated U.S. military occupation and the passage of the imperialistic Platt Amendment by the U.S. Congress, the Constitution of 1901 failed to fulfill the Cuban dream of a truly independent nation. While Cuba had successfully thrown off the yoke of Spanish imperialism, the United States more than filled that void; through the Platt Amendment, it

delivered to Cuba conditions that limited independent action. The amendment limited Cuban authority to negotiate international treaties and to borrow money from abroad. The United States also claimed a coaling station on Cuban soil, and one clause of the amendment stated that "Cuba consents that the United States may exercise the right to intervene for the preservation of Cuban independence, the maintenance of a government adequate for the protection of life, property, and individual liberty. . . ." While nominally independent, Cuba was expected to incorporate the Platt Amendment into the drafting of the Cuban Constitution. Even efforts to modify the amendment were vetoed by the United States, and in the end Cuba was forced to incorporate the original U.S. version.

Not surprisingly, the Constitution of 1901 bitterly divided Cuban society, and while the Platt Amendment was abrogated by the United States in 1934, the fact that the first Cuban constitution had obediently followed the dictates of the U.S. government was not lost on future generations of Cuban nationalists. Support for the Constitution of 1901 was generally drawn along class lines, with the European upper class arguing that given U.S. support for Cuban independence against Spain, its northern neighbor had a legitimate role to play in Cuban affairs. The Cuban middle class, on the other hand, accepted the constitution as a distasteful inevitability, while working-class and poor Cubans, in general, believed that the Constitution of 1901 was a humiliating concession to the imperialist United States.

The effects of the Constitution of 1901 were immediately felt in Cuba, and a series of governments with little real power passed in and out of office under the watchful eye of the United States. Under the authority of the Cuban constitution, the United States intervened militarily from 1906 to 1909, sent troops to quell an uprising in 1912, and again deployed troops from 1917 to 1922. It was not until the collapse of the pro-U.S. dictator Gerardo Machado y Morales in 1933 that steps would be taken to draft a new constitution.

Cuba's second constitution would take years to draft, and both the amendments of 1934 and the Constitution of 1940 were an outgrowth of the political and economic crisis that swept the island in 1933. While Machado openly ruled as a dictator (he forced the Cuban Congress to extend his term of office), the island was crippled in the early 1930s by falling sugar prices. Growing unrest led Machado increasingly to employ brute force to maintain his rule. From Cuban students, influenced by the Russian and Mexican revolutions, came demands to reject U.S. political and economic control and to nationalize Cuban industry. From labor, both rural and urban, also came demands for nationalization as well as for higher wages and better social programs. Finally, even the army revolted, and hounded by the popular slogan "Cuba for the Cubans," the pro-U.S. Machado was forced to resign in 1933. During the 120-day reign of Ramón Grau San Martín, who replaced Machado and enjoyed widespread support, a number of revolutionary decrees were issued, some of which were included in the "provisional" Constitution of 1934. Many of the demands of the revolution of 1933, however, were not fulfilled, most prominent of which were demands to nationalize some of Cuba's largest industries. Even the mild reforms enacted by the amendments of 1934 were negated when the regime of Carlos Mendieta y Montefur suspended constitutional guarantees.

Advocates of more far-reaching reforms found an unexpected ally in Fulgencio Batista y Zaldívar, the Cuban army officer who supported the U.S.-backed Mendieta as president in the wake of the revolution of 1933. Ever the pragmatist, Batista recognized the need for some type of reform, and the Constitution of 1940 was, on paper, a radical departure from Cuba's 1901 Constitution. Article 24, for example, acknowledged the right of the government to expropriate property "for reason of public utility or social interest," while Article 66 authorized the government to use all of its powers to "provide jobs for everyone." Articles also banned *latifundia*, allowed for state control of the sugar industry, and placed restrictions on foreign ownership of land. Labor was a particular beneficiary of the Constitution of 1940, whose pro-labor articles reflected the growing numbers and collective strength of the Cuban working class. Pro-labor provisions included the right to a job, the eight-hour workday, minimum wages, mandatory union membership, vacation pay, collective bargaining, and old-age pensions. The fact that these provisions were spelled out in the new constitution, however, did not mean that they were ever enacted; a much more militant political and economic movement would have to emerge to forge the hopes of the 1940 Constitution into reality. The

Constitution of 1940 was nonetheless significant in two ways: it reflected in concrete form the aspirations of the revolutionary generation of 1933 and served as a rallying point of disappointed aspirations skillfully exploited by Fidel Castro in the 1950s.

While the Constitution of 1940 spelled out important reforms that were never carried out, the Cuban Revolution of 1959 enacted many of those reforms without embodying them in a new constitution. The constitution governing postrevolutionary Cuba was not to be enacted until 1976. With the victory of the Twenty-sixth of July Movement in 1959, the revolutionary government enacted the Fundamental Law, a provisional body of laws intended to guide the country until a permanent constitution could be drafted. Ignoring the Constitution of 1940, the Cuban government instead chose to govern by amending the Fundamental Law. Between 1959 and 1963 over one hundred new statutes were enacted, reflecting the rapid shift to the left that the Cuban government was then undergoing. These and other changes guided Cuba until the enactment of the Constitution of 1976.

The Constitution of 1976 reflected the Cuban government's commitment to a political and economic system modeled after the Soviet Union. To that end the constitution replaced previous civil law with "socialist" law. Marxism-Leninism was recognized as the state ideology and the Communist Party was made the only legal political party in the country (which in fact had already been the case for many years). While the Constitution defined state and political power as resting in the "dictatorship of the proletariat," power was actually concentrated in the bureaucratic class—not in the workers and peasants. The Council of Ministers was the "highest ranking executive and administrative organ" of the regime and was headed by a president (Fidel Castro) and vice president (Fidel's brother, Raúl Castro). The Council of Ministers was in theory accountable to the National Assembly. But given that the National Assembly met only a few days each year, real political power rested with Fidel Castro, much as it had with Batista before the 1959 revolution. A small step toward greater democracy was taken in 1993, when the first popular elections were held for the National Assembly. While no opposition was allowed to run candidates, voters were given the option to abstain from voting or to reject the

Communist Party candidate on the ballot. While the vote was, not surprisingly, an overwhelming victory for Castro's government, neutral observers acknowledged that the 1993 election proved once again that Fidel Castro and his government still enjoyed widespread support among Cubans.

See also **Batista y Zaldívar, Fulgencio; Castro Ruz, Fidel; Castro Ruz, Raúl; Platt Amendment; United States-Latin American Relations.**

BIBLIOGRAPHY

Ramón Eduardo Ruiz, *Cuba: The Making of a Revolution* (1970).

Samuel Farber, *Revolution and Reaction in Cuba, 1933–1960* (1976).

Max Azicri, *Cuba: Politics, Economics, and Society* (1988).

Louis A. Pérez, Jr., *Cuba: Between Reform and Revolution* (1988).

Sandor Halesky and John Kirk, eds., *Cuba in Transition: Crisis and Transformation* (1992).

Additional Bibliography

Bernal, Beatriz. *Cuba y sus leyes: Estudios histórico-jurídicos.* México: Universidad Nacional Autónoma de México, 2002.

Bronfman, Alejandra. *Measures of Equality: Social Science, Citizenship, and Race in Cuba, 1902–1940.* Chapel Hill: University of North Carolina Press, 2004.

Domínguez, Jorge I. *A Constitution for Cuba's Political Transition: The Utility of Retaining (and Amending) the 1992 Constitution.* Miami, FL: Institute for Cuban and Cuban-American Studies, University of Miami, 2003.

Whitney, Robert. *State and Revolution in Cuba: Mass Mobilization and Political Change, 1920–1940.* Chapel Hill: University of North Carolina Press, 2001.

MICHAEL POWELSON

CUBA, GEOGRAPHY.

In 2007 Cuba had an estimated population of 11.4 million. With its land mass of 44,218 square miles, this creates a population density of more than 250 people per square mile. It is the largest archipelago in the Antilles and is situated between the Straits of Florida on the north, the Caribbean Sea on the south, the Windward Passage on the east, and the Yucatán Channel on the West.

Cuba rests on a sea shelf that was formed by deep and calm seas and provides one of the richest ecological water habitats in the world. There are plentiful bays, estuaries, beaches, cliffs, and island keys. The terrain is mostly flat, with some hills. The highest point is Turquino Peak (6,560 feet), located in the Sierra Maestra in the eastern part of the island. The Sierra de Trinidad is located on the southern shore of the central section of the island.

Mineral deposits in Cuba include kaolin, nickel reserves in the northeast, copper, chromium, iron, manganese, and oil. The climate is tropical, with rain and intense heat from May to October. The annual mean temperature is about 72 degrees Fahrenheit, but can exceed 100 degrees in the summer. Annual rainfall averages 54 inches. June through November marks the cyclone season, and the island's location makes it prone to frequent hurricane strikes. From November to April the climate is fresh and dry. Only 22 percent of the annual rainfall occurs during the winter months, and it comes from cold air masses to the north. The eastern part of the island is most affected by the decline in temperature, with measurements as low as 34 degrees Fahrenheit.

Rivers that cut across Cuba are short due to the long and narrow formation of the island. The Cauto is the longest river, at 155 miles. Vegetation is highly *antropizada* mainly in the plains, the Zapata March, and the Guanahacabibes Peninsula. Many native species of flora and fauna are found in the mountain zones and the keys. Pine trees grow throughout the island, and the royal palm tree (*Roystonea regia*) is considered native to Cuba. Animals that are native to Cuba include the Santa María snake (*Epicrates angulifer*), the bat species *Philonycteris poeyi,* and the hummingbird species *Kellisuga relenae.* There are no large, dangerous animals native to Cuba.

The Cuba economy is based on agricultural production. Seventy-five percent of arable land is under cultivation: 30 percent is pasture, 23.5 percent is forest, 18 percent is devoted to sugarcane, 2 percent is in citrus groves, 1.7 percent is devoted to coffee and cacao, 1.5 percent to rice cultivation, and 1 percent to tobacco. In livestock, Cuba has 40 million poultry, 5 million head of cattle, and 100,000 head of oxen. The principal agricultural income producers are sugar and sugar derivatives, rum, tobacco, textiles, and construction materials. Biotechnical products have recently joined Cuba's traditional exports as commercial products, and the tourism sector has increased significantly since the 1990s. Cuba's main exports are sugar and its derivatives, minerals, fish and shellfish, citrus fruits, beverages, and tobacco. Cuba imports fuel, food, raw materials for industry, fertilizers, machinery, and equipment.

The Cuban population is multiethnic. Indigenous people initially mixed with the Spanish following the Conquest. But disease and mistreatment all but eliminated the Indian population. An imported laboring class consisted of African slaves and smaller groups of Chinese immigrants and indentured servants who arrived from the late eighteenth through early twentieth centuries. According to Cuban census data available in 2007, the Cuban population is 37 percent white, 51 percent mulatto, 11 percent black, and 1 percent Chinese. The major migratory flows in the twentieth century occurred immediately after independence, when many Spanish sought jobs in the former colony, and after the 1959 revolution, when many Cubans emigrated for political, economic, and family reasons. The current rate of population growth is 2.6 percent annually.

The employment rate is around 42.3 percent of the total population. The annual death rate is 7 per 1,000 people, and the mortality rate for newborns is 6.3 deaths per 1,000, also one of the lowest in the world. The average life expectancy is 77 years. There is one doctor for every 165 inhabitants of the island, and nearly everyone over five years of age is educated.

The country is divided into fourteen provinces and the municipality of the Isla de la Juventud (Isle of Youth). The capital, Havana, has a population of 2.2 million (2005). Other major cities are Santiago de Cuba (494,913), Camagüey (326,774), Holguín (329,995), and Guantánamo (244,180). Seventy-six percent of the population is urban.

See also **Africans in Hispanic America; Explorers and Exploration: Spanish America; Indigenous Peoples.**

BIBLIOGRAPHY

Gutiérrez Domech, Roberto, and Manuel Rivero Glean. *Regiones naturales de la isla de Cuba.* Havana: Editorial Científico-Técnica, 1999.

Hudson, Rex A., ed. *Cuba: A Country Study.* 4th Edition. Washington, DC: Federal Research Division, Library of Congress, 2002.

McCook, Stuart George. *States of Nature: Science, Agriculture, and Environment in the Spanish Caribbean, 1760–1940.* Austin: University of Texas Press, 2002.

Pérez, Louis A. *Winds of Change: Hurricanes and the Transformation of Nineteenth-Century Cuba.* Chapel Hill: University of North Carolina Press, 2001.

Pérez-López, Jorge F., and Jose Alvarez, eds. *Reinventing the Cuban Sugar Agroindustry.* Lanham, MD: Lexington Books, 2005.

Scarpaci, Joseph L., Roberto Segre, and Mario Coyula. *Havana: Two Faces of the Antillean Metropolis.* Chapel Hill: University of North Carolina Press, 2002.

RAÚL BENAVIDES

CUBAGUA.

Cubagua, the smallest (10 sq. mi.) of the three Venezuelan islands that comprise the state of Nueva Esparta (New Sparta). Though deserted today, Cubagua enjoyed a brief, prosperous heyday in the early sixteenth century due to the pearl-rich oyster beds near its shores. The island group was discovered by Columbus during his third voyage and later visited by Alonso de Ojeda, who gathered numerous pearls near the islands of Margarita and Cubagua. In 1500 Ojeda founded a small colony on the island, the first Spanish settlement in Venezuelan territory. The oyster beds were not systematically exploited until 1519, when the Audiencia de Santo Domingo decided to use Indian slaves to dive for pearls. Cubagua grew rapidly. In 1526 it was incorporated as the Villa of Santiago and in 1528 became known as the city of Nueva Cádiz, which had a population of 1,000. Intensive exploitation quickly exhausted the oyster beds and, by the late 1830s, new and richer beds were being discovered elsewhere. By 1539, the island was abandoned and in 1541 it was destroyed by either a hurricane or a tidal wave.

See also **Columbus, Christopher.**

BIBLIOGRAPHY

Cervigón, Fernando. *Cubagua, 500 años.* Caracas: Fundación Museo del Mar, 1997.

Gabaldón Márquez, Joaquín, ed. *Descubrimiento y conquista de Venezuela: Textos históricos y documentos fundamentales* (1962).

Gómez, Iván. *Cubagua: Un llamado a la conciencia nacional.* Carúpano, Venezuela: Abre Brecha, 1991.

López Bohórquez, Alí Enrique. *Margarita y Cubagua en el paraíso de Colón.* Mérida, Colombia: Rectorado de la Universidad de los Andes, 1997.

Otte, Enrique. *Las perlas del Caribe: Nueva Cádiz de Cubagua* (1977).

INÉS QUINTERO

CUBAN AMERICAN SUGAR COMPANY.

Following the United States war with Spain, which ended in 1898, Cuban property owners reeled from debt. American businessmen, interested in investment possibilities, flocked to the island. American occupation enhanced business opportunities, and in 1899, R. B. Hawley organized the Cuban American Sugar Company and acquired both extensive tracts of land (77,000 acres) and important sugar mills in the Matanzas, Pinar del Río, and Puerto Padre regions.

Along with other American-owned companies, the Cuban American Sugar Company not only generated tremendous wealth for its investors but promoted the development of American enclaves, usually in towns surrounding the sugar mills. These areas grew into privileged neighborhoods inhabited by American technicians, chemists, agronomists, administrators, and their families. The area surrounding the company's mill in Puerto Padre consisted of six hundred homes, racially differentiated social clubs, and schools. The infrastructure was also well established. While creating exclusive neighborhoods for Americans living in the region, the company's enclaves also came to dominate the local political and economic life.

See also **Spanish-American War.**

BIBLIOGRAPHY

Louis A. Pérez, Jr., *Cuba and the United States: Ties of Singular Intimacy* (1990).

Additional Bibliography

Ayala, César J. *American Sugar Kingdom: The Plantation Economy of the Spanish Caribbean, 1898–1934.* Sevilla: Secretariado de Publicaciones de la Universidad de Sevilla, 2001.

Santamaría García, Antonio, and Carlos Malamud. *Sin azucar no hay país: La industria azucarera y la economía cubana (1919–1939).* Chapel Hill: University of North Carolina Press, 1999.

ALLAN S. R. SUMNALL

CUBAN INTERVENTION IN AFRICA.

As part of its efforts to play a major role in third world affairs, the Cuban government of Fidel Castro directly involved itself with military and diplomatic efforts on behalf of several African socialist movements. Cuba's ties to Africa, however, also heightened opposition to those movements and increased cold war tension between the United States and the Soviet Union.

Cuban interest in African anticolonial movements began soon after Fidel Castro came to power. Cuba sent military and medical supplies to the Algerian National Liberation Front and upon achievement of Algerian independence in 1962, Castro established a Cuban military mission in Algeria. He had sent a similar military mission to Ghana in 1961.

More substantial involvement in African affairs began in 1964, when Ernesto "Che" Guevara visited with leaders of progressive movements in the Portuguese colonies. A year later, Cuba began sending them military missions. The main recipient of Cuban military assistance was Angola's Popular Movement of Liberation (MPLA). Although there were several revolutionary movements in Angola, the MPLA received Cuban support because its socialist ideology most closely reflected that of the Cuban Revolution, whereas others emphasized tribalism and racism, or were pro-Western. Cuban support of African socialist movements in the early 1960s began to replace declining Soviet aid to these movements, and Cuba was openly critical of the USSR for its failure to offer more assistance. This point of contention even hindered Cuban-Soviet relations for a number of years.

The support of other governments for different Angolan movements prompted Cuba and the USSR to reconcile their differences and unite in their support of the MPLA. The United States, China, and South Africa supported the National Union for the Total Independence of Angola (UNITA) and the Liberation Front of Angola (FNLA). Although the United States charged that the Soviets were dictating Cuba's actions in Angola, scholarly research on the subject suggests that Cuba was largely acting on its own behalf in initiating aid to the MPLA.

Cuban leader Fidel Castro and President Julius Nyerere (center) of Tanzania, Africa, 1977. While Cuba's involvement in African socialist movements has significantly declined in the early twenty-first century, it continues to maintain diplomatic relations throughout the continent, in cooperative education and sports programs and medical assistance. © BETTMANN/CORBIS

Cuban involvement intensified after the breakdown of peace negotiations in Portugal in 1975. As fighting escalated, Cuba sent 230 military instructors to the MPLA. South Africa, meanwhile, began to train FNLA and UNITA troops in Namibia. When these troops failed to make consequential gains against the MPLA, South African forces intervened directly. South Africa sought to maintain instability in the region, which it hoped would guarantee the continued economic dependence of southern African nations on South Africa. South Africa was also encouraged by the United States. With strong anti-Communist rhetoric, South Africa cited the presence of Cuban troops as grounds both for delaying Namibian independence and for continuing its policy of apartheid.

Direct South African intervention in Angola changed the scope of the struggle there. It prompted the Organization of African Unity (OAU) immediately to condemn South Africa while simultaneously avoiding any judgment against Cuba or the Soviet Union. Nigeria's strong protest against South Africa, combined with praise of the Soviet and Cuban action in Angola, demonstrated that the struggle embodied more than an East-West competition at the international level. Nigeria had been one of the West's strongest allies in the sub-Sahara region, but here sided with anticolonialism and against racist South Africa.

Cuban military aid was crucial to an MPLA victory. By March 1976 some 24,000 Cuban troops were in Angola, a number that grew to nearly 40,000 by 1984. With this assistance the MPLA drove the South Africans out of Angola. Negotiations over Namibian independence had complicated the issue. Namibia (Southwest Africa before 1968) had been mandated to South Africa following

Germany's defeat in World War I. After World War II, South Africa, having expanded its apartheid policies into the territory, refused to allow the United Nations to monitor its administration of the area. Although the United Nations nullified South African jurisdiction in 1966, resolution of the dispute came slowly. In the negotiations, South Africa linked Namibian independence to Cuban withdrawal from Angola. The Cubans, however, were unwilling to give South Africa the strategic geographic advantage that a removal of Cuban troops would cause. Moreover, as G. R. Berridge has pointed out, Cuba insisted that withdrawal had to be conducted in a way that emphasized a positive legacy of Cuban influence in African history. In 1988 a number of accords involving Cuba, Angola, Namibia, and South Africa were signed, with Cuba and Angola agreeing to remove Cuban troops by July 1991.

Cuba's presence in Mozambique was more subdued, involving by the mid-1980s seven hundred Cuban military and seventy civilian personnel. While Cuba's presence in Angola was vital in shifting the balance of power in southwest Africa, its presence in Mozambique was relatively insignificant.

In Ethiopia the Cubans also played a role, closely in concert with Soviet policy. Before 1974, both the USSR and Cuba had supported Ethiopia's adversary, Somalia. But in that year Ethiopia, suffering from much internal turmoil, began to move toward the Left. After Emperor Haile Selassie's overthrow in 1974, a bitter military struggle led to the victory of the socialist faction in 1977. Meanwhile, Cuba's former ally, Somalia, sponsored a revolutionary group in Ogaden, which had historically been a part of Ethiopia. As Ethiopia reshuffled its international alliances, Somalia found itself on the outside. Only two months after supplying aid to Somalia, in 1977, Cuba, in collaboration with Soviet policy, began sending arms and advisers to Ethiopia. After unproductive negotiations, Somalia broke relations with Cuba and sent its own troops into Ogaden. Cuba responded by sending 17,000 troops into war-torn Ethiopia, which by 1987 had established a Marxist-Leninist state and was suffering massive economic and social devastation, exacerbated by famine and drought. The end of the cold war resulted in foreign withdrawal from the area, leaving Ethiopia and Somalia to struggle with internal strife and continued economic and physical hardships.

Although Cuba's presence in Africa was beneficial to Angola, Ethiopia, and several other nations, there was a high cost in lives and material. Cuba had both gains and losses from its intervention in Africa. It greatly strengthened its ties to the Soviet Union, while further alienating it from the United States at a time when a willingness to normalize U.S.-Cuban relations had begun. In effect, it furthered Cuba's break with the West, solidifying its membership in the Soviet economic and political bloc.

Cuba's relations with Africa changed after the disintegration of the Soviet Union in 1991. Without Soviet support, Cuba entered an extended economic crisis in the 1990s and early twenty-first century, and consequently dramatically lessened its involvement in Africa. Despite its difficulties, Cuba did continue to send its doctors on medical missions. In 2002 Cuba had more than two thousand physicians working on numerous projects throughout the continent.

See also **Castro Ruz, Fidel.**

BIBLIOGRAPHY

Benemelis, Juan F. *Castro, subversión y terrorismo en Africa.* Madrid: Editorial San Martin, 1988.

Berridge, G. R. "Diplomacy and the Angolan/Namibia Accords." *International Affairs* 65, no. 3 (1989): 463–479.

Boahen, Albert Adu, ed. *Africa under Colonial Domination: 1880–1935.* Paris: UNESCO; Berkeley: University of California Press, 1990.

Brenner, Philip, et al., eds. *The Cuban Reader: The Making of a Revolutionary Society.* New York: Grove Press, 1989.

Davidson, Basil. *The People's Cause: A History of Guerrillas in Africa.* Essex, U.K.: Longman, 1981.

Gleijeses, Piero. *Conflicting Missions: Havana, Washington, and Africa, 1959–1976.* Chapel Hill: University of North Carolina Press, 2002.

Kahn, Owen Ellison. "Cuba's Impact in Southern Africa." *Journal of Inter-American Studies and World Affairs* 29 (Fall 1987): 33–54.

Liebenow, J. Gus. *African Politics: Crises and Challenges.* Bloomington: Indiana University Press, 1986.

Mesa-Lago, Carmen, and June S. Belkin, eds. *Cuba in Africa.* Pittsburgh, PA: Center for Latin American Studies, University of Pittsburgh, 1982.

Montgomery, Robin Navarro. *Cuban Shadow over the Southern Cones.* Austin: TX: Tyler Publishing, 1977.

Ohaegbulam, Festus Ugboaja. *Towards an Understanding of the African Experience from Historical and Contemporary Perspectives.* Lanham, MD: University Press of America, 1990.

Pérez, Louis A., Jr. *Cuba: Between Reform and Revolution* New York: Oxford University Press, 1988.

Ros, Enrique. *La aventura africana de Fidel Castro.* Miami, FL: Ediciones Universal, 1999.

ALLAN S. R. SUMNALL

CUBAN MISSILE CRISIS. On May 29, 1962, a high-ranking Soviet delegation, posing as an agricultural mission, but including the head of the Soviet Union's Raketnye voyska strategicheskogo naznacheniya (Strategic Rocket Forces) and two nuclear ballistic missile specialists, arrived in Havana to propose the installation of nuclear ballistic missiles on the island. Cuba agreed. Raul Castro and Che Guevara traveled to Moscow in early July to formalize the agreement. Nuclear missiles began arriving in Cuba secretly during the first half of September under a Moscow project code-named Operation Anadyr.

Several post-crisis accounts cite fears in both Moscow and Havana of a United States invasion of Cuba. They were provoked in part by U.S. activities surrounding Operation Mongoose, a post–Bay of Pigs covert effort by Washington aimed at removing Cuba's Fidel Castro, which was coupled with a Soviet desire to redress what was then a 17-to-1 nuclear missile imbalance in favor of the United States.

Rumors swirled for weeks of Soviet missiles in Cuba, but confirmation did not come until an American U2 surveillance flight over the island on October 14, 1962. By then, there were also 40,000 Soviet troops on the island. In a seventeen-minute, nationally televised October 22 speech, President John F. Kennedy cited "unmistakable evidence" of Soviet intermediate and long-range nuclear missiles and nuclear-capable bombers in Cuba. He also announced the imposition of a "strict quarantine on all offensive military equipment" headed for the island, warning the Soviet government that the United States will "regard any nuclear missile launched from Cuba against any nation in the Western Hemisphere as an attack by the Soviet Union on the United States, requiring a full retaliatory response upon the Soviet Union."

Soviet premier Nikita Khrushchev responded on October 27 in a message broadcast by Radio Moscow, in which he called for the dismantling of U.S. missile bases in Turkey in exchange for withdrawal of Soviet missiles in Cuba. Almost simultaneously, a Khrushchev letter to Kennedy arrived at the U.S. Embassy in Moscow with essentially the same message.

The basic agreement resolving the crisis called for removal of the Soviet missiles in Cuba under United Nations supervision while promising removal of the naval quarantine and a pledge by the Kennedy administration not to invade Cuba. While withdrawing the Jupiter missiles from Turkey was not a quid pro quo for withdrawing the Soviet missiles from Cuba, it was part of the discussions for settlement of the missile crisis. The settlement made no mention of withdrawal of U.S. missiles from Turkey, but that obviously was an unspoken part of the agreement, and the missiles were withdrawn within six months.

A new message from Khrushchev, broadcast over Radio Moscow on October 28, effectively terminated the crisis. In it, he said "the Soviet government, in addition to previously issued instructions on the cessation of further work at the building sites for the weapons, has issued a new order on the dismantling of the weapons which you describe as 'offensive,' and their crating and return to the Soviet Union."

An angry and recalcitrant Castro refused to allow on-site inspections of the missile removal from Cuba, which, as a result, was limited to aerial surveillance.

Although never formalized with a written agreement—and kept secret for many years—Kennedy's no-invasion pledge and its post-missile crisis implications continue to be apparent in the early twenty-first century, both in U.S. policy towards the island and the fact that Cuba remains under Castro's control nearly a half-century later.

There are those who argued that the no-invasion agreement was rendered invalid by Castro's refusal to allow on-site inspections to assure removal of the missiles. While the validity of that argument has never been tested, President Nixon reaffirmed the no-invasion pledge the early 1970s, when it appeared the Soviets might be building a submarine base at Cienfuegos, on Cuba's south coast.

See also **Castro Ruz, Fidel; Castro Ruz, Raúl; Communism; Guevara, Ernesto "Che"; Soviet-Latin American Relations.**

BIBLIOGRAPHY

Bohling, Don. *The Castro Obsession: U.S. Covert Operations against Cuba 1959–1965.* Washington, DC: Potomac Books, 2005.

Blight, James G., Bruce J. Allyn, and David A. Welch. *Cuba on the Brink: Castro, the Missile Crisis, and the Soviet Collapse.* New York: Pantheon Books, 1993.

Brugioni, Dino A. *Eyeball to Eyeball: The Inside Story of the Cuban Missile Crisis,* ed. Robert F. McCort. New York: Random House, 1991.

Chang, Laurence, and Peter Kornbluh, eds. *The Cuban Missile Crisis, 1962: A National Security Archive Documents Reader.* New York: New Press, 1992.

Frankel, Max. *High Noon in the Cold War: Kennedy, Khrushchev, and the Cuban Missile Crisis.* New York: Ballantine Books, 2004.

Fursenko, Aleksandr, and Timothy Nafatli. *One Hell of a Gamble: Khrushchev, Castro, and Kennedy, 1958–1964.* New York: Norton, 1997.

Gribkov, Anatoli I., and William Y. Smith. *Operation Anadyr: U.S. and Soviet Generals Recount the Cuban Missile Crisis,* ed. Alfred Friendly Jr. Chicago: Edition Q, 1994.

Jarman, Robert L., and Jane Priestland. *British Archives on the Cuban Missile Crisis 1962.* London: Archival Publications International, 2001.

Lechuga, Carlos. *Cuba and the Missile Crisis,* trans. Mary Todd. Melbourne, Australia, and New York: Ocean Press, 2001.

May, Ernest R., and Philip D. Zelikow, eds. *The Kennedy Tapes: Inside the White House during the Cuban Missile Crisis.* Cambridge, MA: Belknap Press of Harvard University Press, 1997.

U.S. Central Intelligence Agency. *CIA Documents on the Cuban Missile Crisis 1962,* ed. Mary S. McAuliffe. Washington, DC: History Staff, Central Intelligence Agency, 1992.

U.S. Department of State. Office of the Historian. *Foreign Relations of the United States, 1961–1963,* vol. 11: *Cuban Missile Crisis and Aftermath.* Washington, DC: U.S. Government Printing Office, 1996.

MICHAEL A. PALUSHIN
DON BOHNING

CUBA, ORGANIZATIONS

This entry includes the following articles:
CLUB FEMENINO
COMMITTEES FOR THE DEFENSE OF THE REVOLUTION (CDR)
DEMOCRATIC SOCIALIST COALITION
FEDERATION OF CUBAN WOMEN (FMC)
FEDERATION OF CUBAN WORKERS (CTC)

CLUB FEMENINO

The Club Femenino was formed in 1917 by a group of middle- and upper-class women to improve social conditions on the island and obtain suffrage for women. Members advocated the elimination of prostitution, establishment of women's prisons and juvenile courts, improvement of educational opportunities for women, and improved job conditions for working-class women.

The Club Femenino joined with five other women's rights groups in 1923 to form the umbrella organization *Federación Nacional de Asociaciones Femeninas.* The First Annual Women's Congress, headed by Club Femenino member Pilar Morlon y Menéndez, invited all women's organizations throughout the country. The congress addressed issues as varied as female participation in government to the beautification of Havana. Many of its leaders joined with the Veterans and Patriots Organization in calling for "regeneration" of the government.

By 1925, the Second Congress promised success because President Gerardo Machado pledged support for women's suffrage. When he reneged on his promises and began massive repression of opposition groups, Club Femenino members, led by Hortensia Lamar, formed another coalition, the Women in Opposition to Machado, and participated with students and labor unionists in street protests. Lamar met with U.S. ambassador Sumner Welles to call for Machado's removal from office. President Ramón Grau San Martín granted suffrage during his brief tenure, but the issue remained uncertain until it became a part of the formal Constitution of 1940.

After gaining suffrage, the club continued pressing for education and social reform, joining other women's organizations in running night schools and free classes for working-class women. In 1934 it successfully pressured the government to implement a 1913 law offering free breakfasts to school children.

The success of Club Femenino came from working within a male-dominated system in a manner that did not threaten the political structure of the island.

See also **Feminism and Feminist Organizations.**

BIBLIOGRAPHY

An excellent book on the members and activities of the women's movement in this period is K. Lynn Stoner, *From the House to the Streets: The Cuban Woman's Movement for Legal Reform, 1898–1940* (1991). Little else is available in English, but good sources for beginning a study are K. Lynn Stoner, *Latinas of the Americas: A Source Book* (1989), and Nelson Valdés, *Cuban Women in the Twentieth Century: A Bibliography* (1978).

Additional Bibliography

González Pagés, Julio César. *En busca de un espacio—historia de mujeres en Cuba.* La Habana: Ediciones de Ciencias Sociales, 2003.

Prins, Melissa Marisol, and K. Lynn Stoner. *A Guide to The Women's Movement in Cuba, 1898–1958: The Stoner Collection on Cuban Feminism.* Wilmington, DE: Scholarly Resources, Inc., 1990–1997?.

Sabas Alomá, Mariblanca. *Feminismo: Cuestiones sociales y crítica literaria.* Santiago de Cuba: Editorial Oriente, 2003.

JACQUELYN BRIGGS KENT

COMMITTEES FOR THE DEFENSE OF THE REVOLUTION (CDR)

Organization formed in Cuba on 28 September 1960 to combat counterrevolutionary activity through collective vigilance of the populace. One of many Cuban mass organizations, CDRs arose as a response to perceived internal and external threats to the Cuban Revolution. Early goals of the CDR included mobilization and unification of the people, and advancement of revolutionary ideals. Organized by neighborhood blocks, factories, labor unions, and state farms, their primary responsibilities involved community patrols and watchfulness against subversive activities.

With a membership of more than one-half million people by 1961, the function and scope of the CDRs gradually expanded to address other societal issues, such as public health, education, food distribution, conservation, the need for voluntary work, and community improvement. Throughout the 1960s, the CDRs acquired both legitimacy and permanent institutional status vis-à-vis the Cuban government and became an integral part of Cuban society. The organization was structured on three levels, with the block level being the most basic unit, followed by the district and national levels. Political autonomy, particularly on the local level, has been extremely limited, with policy and decision making instituted from the top echelons of the government and the Communist Party of Cuba. Leadership in the upper ranks of the CDR traditionally has been the domain of persons with strong party affiliations.

Membership in the CDR has fluctuated considerably, with the percentage of the adult population in its ranks rising from around 38 percent in 1963 to near 80 percent by the early 1970s. An easing of restrictions on membership led to the sharp increase in numbers, as did general changes in the association. While vigilance remained a priority, by the early 1970s the focus had shifted from counterrevolutionary to more common criminal activities. Criticized by its enemies as a totalitarian spy organization, the CDR nevertheless contributed to societal improvement in Cuba through participation in public-health programs, literacy campaigns, agricultural works, and construction.

See also **Cuba: Cuba Since 1959; Labor Movements.**

BIBLIOGRAPHY

Buch, Luis. *Gobierno revolucionario cubano: Génesis y primeros pasos.* Havana: Editorial de Ciencias Sociales, 1999.

Domínguez, Jorge I. *Cuba: Order and Revolution* (1978), pp. 208–209, 261–267.

Eckstein, Susan. *Back from the Future: Cuba under Castro.* New York: Routledge, 2003.

Harnecker, Marta, ed. *Cuba: Dictatorship or Democracy?* translated by Patrick Greanville (1979), pp. 56–70.

Rabkin, Rhonda Pearl. "The Cuban Political Structure," in *Cuba: Twenty-Five Years of Revolution, 1959–1984,* edited by Sandor Halebsky and John M. Kirk (1985), pp. 261–264.

D. M. SPEARS

DEMOCRATIC SOCIALIST COALITION

The Democratic Socialist Coalition was a broad alliance organized and controlled by Cuban dictator Fulgencio Batista y Zaldívar in the 1940s. The coalition consisted of Batista supporters, liberals, labor leaders, and the Cuban Communist Party. Formed in 1940, the coalition sought broad-based support for the election of Batista. In exchange for membership in the coalition, leftists received many favors from the Batista regime, including the appointment in 1942 of Communist Party member Juan Marinello as minister without portfolio in the Batista government. Marinello was the first member of a Communist organization in any Latin American country to become a government minister.

The coalition was used again in the elections of 1944, and again a Batista supporter ran for the presidency. But the opposition, led by Ramón Grau San Martín and his Auténtico Party, defeated the Batista candidate. Grau San Martín then turned on the leftists of the coalition who dominated organized labor, ousting its members from government positions. Those who participated in the Batista-controlled coalition were largely discredited among Cubans seeking sweeping reforms.

While leftist leaders in the coalition cynically lined up behind Batista, a revolutionary force, Fidel Castro's Twenty-sixth of July Movement, was formed with neither the knowledge nor the support of the Democratic Socialist Coalition, thus ensuring the coalition's isolation after the Cuban Revolution of 1959. The coalition members' lack of public credibility allowed Castro to dominate Cuba's labor unions, the Cuban Communist Party, and other organizations that comprised the Democratic Socialist Coalition.

See also **Batista y Zaldívar, Fulgencio.**

BIBLIOGRAPHY

Aguiar Rodríguez, Raúl. *El bonchismo y el gangsterismo en Cuba.* Havana: Editorial de Ciencias Sociales, 2001.

Argote-Freyre, Frank. *Fulgencio Batista: From Revolutionary to Strongman.* New Brunswick, NJ: Rutgers University Press, 2006.

Farber, Samuel. *Revolution and Reaction in Cuba, 1933–1960* (1976).

Pérez-Stable, Marifeli. *The Cuban Revolution: Origins, Course, and Legacy* (1993).

Ruiz, Ramón Eduardo. *Cuba: The Making of a Revolution* (1970).

Woodward, Ralph Lee, Jr. "Urban Labor and Communism: Cuba," in *Caribbean Studies* 3, no. 3 (1963): 17–50.

MICHAEL POWELSON

FEDERATION OF CUBAN WOMEN (FMC)

The Federation of Cuban Women (Federación de Mujeres Cubanas—FMC) is the official governmental body overseeing women's issues. Founded in 1960 by Fidel Castro and directed by Vilma Espín, the FMC sought to mobilize women following the 1959 Cuban Revolution. Called the "revolution within the revolution," the Cuban women's movement sent women into new regions of the country to teach the illiterate and nurse the ill. Women received professional training in traditional and nontraditional fields, and they were encouraged to participate in militia forces to respond to possible international threats. The FMC has pursued the objective of liberating women through revolutionary political activism, not through gender-based activism. It publishes *Mujeres* and *Muchachas.*

The FMC is not an autonomous organization; rather it is one of the popular-based institutions designed to convey government views to the populace and reflect women's needs to the government. This two-way communication was most evident at the FMC national congresses in 1962, 1974, 1980, 1985, and 1995. The FMC directly influenced the 1974 Maternity Law, the 1975 Family Code, the Protection and Hygiene Law, and the Social Security Law. By 1986 the FMC had established 838 child-care centers that supported 96,000 mothers.

Open to all women between the ages of fifteen and sixty-five, the FMC relies on modest membership dues for its financial sources. The group has various organizational levels (national, provincial, municipal, block, delegation, and individual), and its duties and responsibilities entail production, finance and transport, education, social work, ideological orientation, day care, and foreign relations.

The FMC has increased women's presence in the workforce, including managerial positions, and has raised the level of women's education. In 1986 women comprised 35 percent of the workforce and were concentrated in services, education, health, and technology. In 1981 the FMC formed the Commission for Coordinating Women's Employment to oversee what had been an unfavorable implementation of work laws regulating when and where women worked, maternity and hiring practices, and pay scales.

Over 50 percent of university students in Cuba are women. Eighty-five percent of all women have a ninth-grade education. Political ideology is provided at the Fe del Valle Cadre School for selected students, who are expected in turn to propagandize in their communities and work places.

The FMC has formed health brigades to conduct programs such as mother and infant care, environmental hygiene, uterine cancer diagnosis, and health education. It has sponsored a vigorous sex education campaign and promoted birth control.

The FMC has encouraged women to stand for national elections in the municipal, provincial, and national assemblies, and it has gained governmental approval for candidates. Nevertheless, in 1985 women accounted for only 22.6 percent of administrative leaders, including the National Assembly (22.6 percent), provincial (21.4 percent) and municipal (11.5 percent) assemblies, Communist Party members (21.9 percent), and trade union leaders (40.3 percent).

Criticism of the FMC surfaced in the 1990 *llamamiento* (mass evaluation) of the Revolution. The major complaint concerned the excessive amount of time spent in meetings, work, and voluntary activities, which was made worse by the generalized complications in obtaining food and managing transportation. Also, scarcity of goods has forced many young women into prostitution, which the government has tacitly supported. The FMC's effort to convert women into productive and moral revolutionaries is being undermined by a declining economy.

See also **Espín de Castro, Vilma; Feminism and Feminist Organizations.**

BIBLIOGRAPHY

Additional Bibliography

González Pagés, Julio César. *En busca de un espacio—historia de mujeres en Cuba.* La Habana: Ediciones de Ciencias Sociales, 2003.

Molyneux, Maxine. *State, Gender and Institutional Change in Cuba's 'Special Period': The Federación de Mujeres Cubanas.* London: Institute of Latin American Studies, 1996.

Randall, Margaret and Judy Janda. *Women in Cuba: Twenty Years Later.* New York: Smyrna Press, 1981.

Safa, Helen Icken. *The Myth of the Male Breadwinner: Women and Industrialization in the Caribbean.* Boulder, CO: Westview Press, 1995.

Pérez-Stable, Marifeli. *The Cuban Revolution: Origins, Course, and Legacy.* New York: Oxford University Press, 1993.

Séjourné, Laurette, and Tatiana Coll. *La mujer cubana en el quehacer de la historia.* México, D.F.: Siglo Veintiuno, 1980.

Shayne, Julie D. *The Revolution Question: Feminisms in El Salvador, Chile, and Cuba.* New Brunswick, NJ: Rutgers University Press, 2004.

Smith, Lois M. and Alfred Padula. *Sex and Revolution: Women in Socialist Cuba.* New York: Oxford University Press, 1996.

K. LYNN STONER

FEDERATION OF CUBAN WORKERS (CTC)

Cuba's primary labor confederation from its foundation in 1939 to the present has been the Federation of Cuban Workers (Confederación de Trabajadores Cubanos—CTC). Communists under Lázaro Peña controlled this organization until 1946. The CTC claimed over 400,000 members by the early 1940s. Eusebio Mujal, an Auténtico (nationalist-revolutionary), became secretary general of the CTC in 1947. Under Mujal the CTC suppressed strikes, organized pro-government rallies, and repressed labor dissidents in exchange for government support. Union corruption became a serious problem. Despite shortcomings, the CTC continued to grow and by 1959 represented over 1 million Cuban workers.

Cuban labor history changed dramatically with the onset of the Cuban Revolution in 1959. Mujal fled the country and the CTC went into decline. It remained largely inactive during the first decade of the revolution. After 1970, however, the government revitalized the CTC in an effort to counter declining worker productivity and high absenteeism. The CTC undertook initiatives in worker education, grievance committees became more active, and workers on the factory level began to take part in production decisions. The election of union officers became more open and democratic. New unions formed, and CTC membership rose to include 94 percent of Cuba's workforce.

See also **Peña, Lázaro.**

BIBLIOGRAPHY

Maurice Zeitlin, *Revolutionary Politics and the Cuban Working Class* (1967).

Rodolfo Riesgo, *Cuba: El movimiento obrero en su entorno socio-político, 1865–1983* (1985).

Efrén córdova, *Castro and the Cuban Labor Movement: Statecraft and Society in a Revolutionary Period (1959–1961)* (1987).

Linda Fuller, "The State and the Unions in Cuba Since 1959," in *Labor, Autonomy, and the State in Latin America,* edited by Edward C. Epstein (1989), pp. 133–171.

Additional Bibliography

Alexander, Robert Jackson. *A History of Organized Labor in Cuba*. Westport, CT: Praeger, 2002.

Córdova, Efrén. *Clase trabajadora y movimiento sindical en Cuba*. Miami, FL: Ediciones Universal, 1995–1996.

STEVEN S. GILLICK

CUBA, POLITICAL MOVEMENTS, NINETEENTH CENTURY.

Nineteenth Century Cuba: Political Movements. Cuban political attitudes in the nineteenth century were conditioned by a number of factors, particularly the hardening of Spanish colonial rule after the loss of the South American mainland colonies in 1825 and the development on the island of a prosperous sugar industry (1790–1830) that depended on the importation of an increasing number of African slaves. As a result, during the first half of the century the majority of Cuba's population was black or mulatto. In those days, slaves represented a great asset but also a menace. In 1791 there had been a slave revolt in Haiti that had lain waste the island, wiping out its white planter class. Haiti's specter never ceased to haunt Cuban slave owners.

A land like Cuba, therefore, was not receptive to political extremism. When the sense of national identity matured among Cubans, a process that roughly coincided with the sugar revolution, some small groups, encouraged by events in continental Spanish America, began to consider seriously the prospect of independence. But the planter class and the leading intellectuals refused to support the movement. Although they, too, were disgruntled with the existing order, they favored evolution over revolution; and whenever they became too impatient with Spanish despotism, they sought to preserve their wealth by making Cuba one of the slave states of the United States. These two attitudes gave rise to the two major political movements of the first two-thirds of the century: reformism and annexationism.

Generally speaking, reformists opposed abolition of slavery, proposing instead that the slave trade be suppressed and white colonization promoted. Some, like José Antonio Saco, dreaded Cuba's absorption by the United States, and others at times could live with it, but all of them dreamed about "building a fatherland," as José de la Luz y Caballero put it, and believed that Cuba was sufficiently rich and powerful to force Spain to make concessions.

Annexationism was basically supported by slave owners who feared that England would compel Spain to free the slaves in Cuba, although there were some who joined the movement for other reasons. Its influence pervaded the Cuban political milieu, either overtly or implicitly, until the eve of independence, but it reached its peak with the two futile attempts made in 1850 and 1851 by a former officer of the Spanish army, Narciso López, to carry the "annexationist revolution" into Cuba. In both cases López had U.S. backing.

Annexationism was little more than a dream after the U.S. Civil War, and the same fate befell reformism after the failure in April 1867 of the Junta de Información convened by the Madrid government to discuss the reforms that were necessary in Cuba. After this new setback, Cubans, who were then feeling the impact of an international economic crisis, began to think again that armed rebellion was the only way out of their predicament. And so it was that a group of planters and patriots rose up on 10 October 1868, the start of the Ten Years' War. The war was unsuccessful, but its consequences were lasting. It began the process of integration of all the various elements that made up Cuban society and solidified the nationalistic spirit that ultimately ignited the 1895–1898 war of independence. As far as Cuba is concerned, the history of the last third of the nineteenth century is the history of the rise and culmination of *independentismo,* the third great political movement of the period.

See also **Slavery: Spanish America; Slave Trade.**

BIBLIOGRAPHY

For a discussion of the subject in English, see Hugh Thomas, *Cuba: The Pursuit of Freedom* (1971). Further details are found in José Ignacio Rodríguez, *Estudio histórico sobre el origen, desenvolvimiento y manifestaciones prácticas de la idea de la anexión de la isla de Cuba* (1900); Francisco Figueras, *Cuba y su evolución colonial* (1959); Ramiro Guerra, *Guerra de los diez años, 1868–1878*, 2 vols. (1972); Sergio Aguirre, "Seis actitudes de la burguesía cubana en el siglo XIX," in his *Eco de caminos* (1974); Ramiro Guerra, *Manual de historia de Cuba* (1975); and Pedro Roig, *La guerra de Martí* (1984).

Balboa Navarro, Imilcy. *La protesta rural en Cuba: Resistencia cotidiana, bandolerismo y revolución 1878–1902*. Madrid, Spain: Consejo Superior de Investigaciones Científicas, 2003.

Childs, Matt D. *The 1812 Aponte Rebellion in Cuba and the Struggle against Atlantic Slavery*. Chapel Hill: University of North Carolina Press, 2006.

Ferrer, Ada. *Insurgent Cuba: Race, Nation, and Revolution, 1868–1898*. Chapel Hill: University of North Carolina Press, 1999.

JOSÉ M. HERNÁNDEZ

CUBA, POLITICAL PARTIES

This entry includes the following articles:
ABC PARTY
AUTHENTIC PARTY (PA)
AUTONOMIST PARTY
COMMUNIST PARTY
CUBAN PEOPLE'S PARTY (ORTODOXOS)

ABC PARTY

The ABC Party was a prominent clandestine organization opposing the Gerardo Machado regime (1925–1933) in the early 1930s. Composed of intellectuals, students, and members of the middle class, the ABC used the cellular concept for an underground organization. Each cell contained seven members who had no knowledge of the other cells. The directing cell was known as A, the second tier of cells was B, then C, and so on. In December 1932, the ABC issued its program manifesto, which opposed not only the Machado regime but also the circumstances that brought it into existence. ABC advocated the breakup of large landholdings, nationalization of public services,

limitations on landownership by U.S. interests, and political liberty and social justice.

In late 1932, the ABC conceived a two-phased plan to eliminate Machado. Phase 1 succeeded when Senate president Clemente Vásquez Bello was assassinated in Havana. Phase 2, which contemplated blowing up all top government leaders during Vásquez Bello's funeral in a Havana cemetery, failed when the Vásquez Bello family requested that he be buried in the family plot in a Santa Clara cemetery. Machado's police then launched a manhunt for members of the organization, driving most of the ABC leadership into exile. In 1933, the ABC supported the mediation efforts of U.S. ambassador Sumner Welles to ease Machado out of the presidency and bring an end to the violence. Following Machado's resignation on 12 August, the group participated in the short-lived regime of Carlos Manuel de Céspedes and later opposed the more radical regime of Ramón Grau San Martín (1933–1934). The ABC ceased to operate after those turbulent years, but many of its leaders came to occupy prominent positions in later administrations and exerted considerable influence until the 1950s.

See also **Cuba, War of Independence.**

BIBLIOGRAPHY

López Civeira, Francisca. *El proceso revolucionario de los años 30*. Havana: Editorial Félix Varela, 2000.

Suchlicki, Jaime. *Historical Dictionary of Cuba* (1988) and *Cuba: From Columbus to Castro*, 3d ed. (1990).

Thomas, Hugh. *Cuba: The Pursuit of Freedom* (1971).

Whitney, Robert. *State and Revolution in Cuba: Mass Mobilization and Political Change, 1920–1940*. Chapel Hill: University of North Carolina Press, 2001.

JAIME SUCHLICKI

AUTHENTIC PARTY (PA)

After Fulgencio Batista had engineered the downfall of Ramón Grau San Martín and the thwarting of the 1933 revolution, the students who had supported Grau were angry and disillusioned. Many who desired to continue fighting formed the Authentic Party (Auténtico Party—PA) in 1934. Their model was the party of Jose Martí (the Partido Revolucionario Cubano of 1892). Leaders of the Directorio Estudiantil Universitario joined the new party and Grau San Martín was appointed president. The Auténtico program called for economic and political nationalism, social justice, and civil liberties.

Through the mid-1940s the Auténticos consistently opposed Batista and his puppet presidents. In 1944, Grau and the Auténticos were elected, during a period in which organized use of violence to achieve political power increased. To many Cubans in the late 1940s, the Auténticos and Grau had failed to fulfill the aspirations of the anti-Machado revolution, especially with regard to administrative honesty. Eduardo Chibás and others split from the party in 1947, forming the Partido del Pueblo Cubano (Ortodoxo). The failure of the Auténticos to bring profound structural, economic, and political changes to Cuba was perhaps the most important factor contributing to Batista's 1952 coup.

See also **Batista y Zaldívar, Fulgencio; Chibás, Eduardo; Grau San Martín, Ramón; Martí y Pérez, José Julián.**

BIBLIOGRAPHY

Hugh Thomas, *Cuba: The Pursuit of Freedom* (1971).

Jaime Suchlicki, *Historical Dictionary of Cuba* (1988) and *Cuba: From Columbus to Castro*, 3d ed. (1990).

Additional Bibliography

Vignier, E., and Guillermo Alonso. *La corrupción política administrativa en Cuba, 1944–1952.* Habana: Editorial de Ciencias Sociales, Instituto Cubano del Libro, 1973.

Whitney, Robert. *State and Revolution in Cuba: Mass Mobilization and Political Change, 1920–1940.* Chapel Hill: University of North Carolina Press, 2001.

JAIME SUCHLICKI

AUTONOMIST PARTY

After the end of the Ten Years' War (1878), Spain dismantled Cuba's colonial regime, took steps to reduce its insular army, and allowed Cubans to elect deputies to the Spanish Cortes. These reforms led to the formation of the Liberal or Autonomist Party, made up of reformist Cubans and some Spaniards, most of middle-class origin. Its platform differed little from traditional Cuban reformism.

Essentially what it demanded was "the liberty of Cuba legally within Spanish nationality."

The Autonomist Party was the most critical movement in Cuba in the decade that followed the war, but it failed to make genuine headway. It was distrusted by conservative Spaniards, who thought that autonomy was merely the anteroom of independence. Spain, by contrast, breaking the promises it had made when the war ended, never fully granted Cubans the same political rights that Spaniards enjoyed. There was no real freedom of the press and assembly on the island, and the property qualification was so high that black and poor Cubans could not vote. Furthermore, elections were manipulated whenever necessary. By 1892 the Autonomists were thoroughly disillusioned. They issued a manifesto to the nation warning that Spain's obduracy would force Cubans to make "radical decisions." Their more distinguished men began openly to back the course of revolution.

On the eve of the Spanish-American War, Spain finally established in Cuba a home-rule government led by Autonomists. But by then the 1895 war of independence had been raging in the countryside for three years, and the Autonomist government was caught in the middle of the conflict staged by Spain, the United States, the diehard Spaniards in Cuba, and the Cuban insurgents. A few days before the U.S. declaration of war (25 April 1898), it sent a message to President William McKinley protesting U.S. intervention in Cuba and claiming that Cubans had the right to govern themselves. Apparently, McKinley did not reply.

See also **Cuba, War of Independence.**

BIBLIOGRAPHY

For an interesting non-Cuban view of the Autonomists, see J. C. M. Ogelsby, "The Cuban Autonomist Movement's Perception of Canada, 1865–1898: Its Implications," *The Americas* 48 (April 1992): 445–461; see also Antonio Martínez Bello, *Origen y meta del autonomismo, exégesis de Montoro* (1952).

Bizcarrondo, Marta, and Antonio Elorza. *Cuba-España: El dilema autonomista, 1878–1898.* Madrid, Spain: Editorial Colibrí, 2001.

Ferrer, Ada. *Insurgent Cuba: Race, Nation, and Revolution, 1868–1898.* Chapel Hill: University of North Carolina Press, 1999.

Piqueras Arenas, José A. *Cuba, Emporio y colonia: La disputa de un mercado interferido (1878–1895)*. Madrid, Spain: Fondo de Cultura Económica de España, 2003.

JOSÉ M. HERNÁNDEZ

COMMUNIST PARTY

Founded in 1925, the Cuban Communist Party underwent many changes in perspective and political program, from operating as an openly revolutionary party in the 1920s and 1930s to its tactical alignment with the Batista regime in the 1930s, through its demise in the late 1940s and 1950s, and its revival in the 1960s and 1970s. While the party played a significant role in twentieth-century Cuba, and while it worked hard to organize Cuba's working class, the party's leaders failed to recognize the growing revolutionary movement within Cuba in the 1950s, which culminated in the overthrow of Fulgencio Batista y Zaldívar on 1 January 1959. In fact the Cuban Revolution, led by Fidel Castro, was carried out largely without the support of the Cuban Communist Party, and Castro and his followers maintained a distrust of most of the party's leaders throughout this revolutionary period. Only with the defeat of Batista and with Castro firmly in power did the remnants of the Twenty-sixth of July Movement seek to reorganize the Cuban Communist Party—on terms dictated by Castro and his close associates. One cannot ignore the influence of Moscow on the party throughout its history, which helps at least in part to explain why it increasingly took positions contrary to the principles of revolutionary socialism. The revolutionary movement in the Soviet Union peaked in the 1920s and declined in the 1930s—a pattern repeated in the early history of the Cuban Communist Party. And just as the Soviet Union in the 1940s and 1950s abandoned all pretense to international revolution in favor of cooperation and coalitions with bourgeois democracies and dictatorships, this can also be said for the Cuban Communist Party.

Inspired by the Bolshevik Revolution, Julio Antonio Mella founded the Partido Comunista de Cuba in 1925, and from its inception it was successful at organizing Cuban workers, especially those in Cuba's sugar and railroad industries. The party published a weekly newspaper, *El Comunista,* and by the late 1920s its organizing and propaganda efforts bore fruit when one of its members, César Vilar, was elected secretary-general of the Confederación Nacional Obrera Cubana (CNOC), the central labor federation of Cuba. In the early 1930s, the party instigated and led many successful strikes, including walkouts by textile, cigar, transportation, and sugar workers.

The sugar workers' strike of 1933 led to the overthrow of the dictatorship of Gerardo Machado. But the party opposed the strike, claiming it would prompt U.S. intervention. International politics may have also played a role in the party's rejection of the strike, since 1933 was also a time when the Stalin-dominated Communist International had concluded a truce with the United States culminating in the recognition of the Soviet Union by Cuba's powerful northern neighbor. The party continued to grow throughout the 1930s, despite the Batista dictatorship. Even a crackdown on the party and the CNOC by Batista in 1935 hardly deterred the growth of the Communist-led labor movement, and by 1938 the party had even agreed to support the Cuban dictator. In exchange Batista granted legal recognition to the party, now named Partido Unión Revolucionaria (PUR), and allowed the publication of the party's organ, *Hoy,* edited by Aníbal Escalante.

This tactical alliance with the Batista dictatorship brought real benefits for the party; Batista's Ministry of Labor was dominated by party members; party candidates ran in, and won, elections; and its secretary-general, Blas Roca played a prominent role in drawing up the section dealing with labor in the Constitution of 1940. Party membership increased from 90,000 in 1940 to 150,000 in 1946. In 1944 the name of the party was changed to the Partido Socialista Popular (PSP), once again reflecting Moscow's influence.

The postwar period saw the decline of the party, as divisions within the PSP were exploited by the government. The new Cuban minister of labor was a vocal anti-Communist, and in 1947 he removed PSP members from the Workers' Palace then under construction in Havana. That same year the government arrested hundreds of PSP members, shut down their radio stations, and censored their newspaper.

Despite Castro's later espousal of communism, neither he nor his Twenty-sixth of July Movement worked with the PSP in the years leading up to the ouster of Batista. In fact, the official position of the PSP was *not* to back Castro's growing revolutionary movement, although many individual PSP members worked in support of it. After the revolution the PSP merged with Castro's Twenty-sixth of July Movement and the Revolutionary Student Directorate in 1961 to form the Integrated Revolutionary Organizations (ORI), to be renamed the Communist Party of Cuba in 1965. Further evidence of Castro's mistrust of the old guard of the Communist Party is evidenced by the fact that the reconstituted party's first congress, promised for 1967, was not held until December 1975. It is ironic that while the PSP claimed to be a revolutionary party of the working class, it played no official, and only a weak unofficial, role in the most important revolutionary movement within Cuba during the twentieth century.

Castro's government lost a great deal of funding when the Soviet Union collapsed in the early 1990s. However, the Communist Party remained the official party in Cuba. As the economy worsened in the 1990s, the Cuban state implemented limited economic reforms to allow for the expansion of the tourism industry. Still, the economy generally followed communist policies.

See also **Castro Ruz, Fidel; Cuba, Revolutions: Cuban Revolution; Cuba, Twenty-Sixth of July Movement.**

BIBLIOGRAPHY

Ralph Lee Woodward, Jr., "Urban Labor and Communism: Cuba," in *Caribbean Studies* 3, no. 3 (1963): 17–50.

Ramón Eduardo Ruiz, *Cuba: The Making of a Revolution* (1970).

Nelson P. Valdes, *Ideological Roots of the Cuban Revolutionary Movement* (1975).

Samuel Farber, *Revolution and Reaction in Cuba, 1933–1960* (1976).

Lionel Martin, *The Early Fidel: Roots of Castro's Communism* (1978).

Irving Louis Horowitz, ed., *Cuban Communism*, 4th ed. (1981).

Barry B. Levine, ed., *The New Cuban Presence in the Caribbean* (1983).

Additional Bibliography

Azicri, Max, and Elsie Deal. *Cuban Socialism in a New Century: Adversity, Survival, and Renewal.* Gainesville: University Press of Florida, 2004.

Eckstein, Susan Eva. *Back from the Future: Cuba under Castro.* 2nd ed. New York: Routledge, 2003.

Farber, Samuel. *The Origins of the Cuban Revolution Reconsidered.* Chapel Hill: University of North Carolina Press, 2006.

Rojas Blaquier, Angelina. *El primer Partido Comunista de Cuba.* Vol. 1: *Sus tácticas y estrategias, 1925–1935.* Santiago de Cuba: Editorial Oriente, 2005.

MICHAEL POWELSON

CUBAN PEOPLE'S PARTY (ORTODOXOS)

The Cuban People's (Ortodoxo) Party was created in 1947 by a faction that broke with the ruling Auténtico Party over the issues of the 1948 presidential nomination and the corruption of the Ramón Grau San Martín administration (1944–1948). Its leader was the mercurial senator Eduardo Chibás, a former student activist who had built a strong national following through his weekly radio broadcasts. He launched a national crusade against governmental corruption, promising to rescue the Cuban revolutionary tradition and to clean up Cuba's politics. Appropriately, he chose a broom as the party emblem. Under the slogan "vergüenza contra dinero" (honesty versus money), he entered the 1948 presidential race, and although he lost to the Auténtico candidate, Carlos Prío Socarrás, he was able to attract nearly 20 percent of the vote.

Since Auténtico scandals continued, Chibás pressed onward with his often immoderate campaign, increasing his political strength and contributing powerfully to the final discrediting of the Prío administration. When he again ran for president in 1951, it appeared that this time he had a good chance of winning. A few months before the election, however, he shot himself at the end of one of his broadcasts. His suicide was apparently an ill-conceived attempt to regain popularity that he had momentarily lost as a result of a campaign miscalculation. It dealt a severe blow to the hopes of the party, for although his candidacy was eventually filled, the new candidate, Roberto Agramonte, was a colorless university professor who lacked Chibás's dynamism and oratorical skill. It also paved the way for Fulgencio Batista, who, three months before the election, staged his 10 March 1952 coup d'état, thereby putting an end to the political aspirations of all parties. Thus forced into the opposition, many Ortodoxos, especially the younger elements who made up the party's more radical left wing, chose revolution as the way to overthrow Batista's dictatorship. One of them was a young lawyer who was running for Congress—Fidel Castro.

See also **Chibás, Eduardo; Grau San Martín, Ramón.**

BIBLIOGRAPHY

In English see Hugh Thomas, *Cuba: The Pursuit of Freedom* (1971); Samuel Farber, *Revolution and Reaction in Cuba, 1933–1960* (1976); Ruby Hart Phillips, *Cuba: Island of Paradox* (1959). On the corruption of the Auténtico administrations, see Enrique Vignier and Guillermo Alonso, *La corrupción política y administrativa en Cuba, 1944–1952* (1973); Chibás's life and work are studied by Luis Conte Aguero, *Eduardo Chibás, el adalid de Cuba* (1955), probably the most extensive treatment of the subject as of 2007.

Alavez Martín, Elena. *La ortodoxia en el ideario americano.* Havana: Editorial de Ciencias Sociales, 2002.

Argote-Freyre, Frank. *Fulgencio Batista: From Revolutionary to Strongman.* New Brunswick, NJ: Rutgers University Press, 2006.

José M. Hernández

CUBA, REVOLUTIONS

This entry includes the following articles:
CUBAN REVOLUTION
REVOLUTION OF 1933

CUBAN REVOLUTION

On 1 January 1959, the guerrilla forces of the Twenty-sixth of July Movement, led by Fidel Castro, entered Havana, the capital of Cuba, signaling the collapse of the dictatorship of Fulgencio Batista. From a small group of radical students and professionals, Castro had organized in less than three years a successful revolutionary force that not only toppled the Batista regime but also challenged Cuba's powerful northern neighbor, the United States.

The roots of the Cuban Revolution can be traced to the Ten Years' War (1868–1878), in which Cuban nationalists unsuccessfully battled to end Spanish control of the island. Despite defeat, the war fueled the determination of many Cubans to end foreign domination of their homeland. With the renewal of the struggle for independence at the turn

of the century, two significant events had a profound influence on later Cuban history. First, José Martí emerged as the ideological and symbolic leader of an independent Cuba. Cuba's greatest poet and thinker, Martí exhibited a genius that served the independence movement well. Second, the United States intervened in the struggle in 1898, and rather than full independence, gave Cuba protectorate status. Although the United States certainly hastened the departure of Spain's army from Cuba, the newly independent nation had a new, and far mightier, imperialist power to contend with.

The Platt Amendment, passed by the U.S. Congress in 1901, granted the United States access to Cuban ports and the right to intervene both to preserve Cuban independence and to "protect life, property, and individual liberty." Although most wealthy Cubans accepted U.S. suzerainty, many labor leaders and intellectuals refused to believe that Cuba would enjoy full independence. In the aftermath of the Spanish-American War and the Platt Amendment, there emerged a nationalist revival with Martí as its symbolic leader. In 1933, with Cuba suffering under the brutal dictatorship of Gerardo Machado, a general strike called by the Communists (known as the Popular Socialist Party—PSP) revived nationalist sentiment and led to the overthrow of Machado.

After a period of political instability, Ramón Grau San Martín emerged as the head of the new revolutionary government. Under his direction, Interior Minister Antonio Guiteras Holmes introduced a series of long overdue reforms, including the eight-hour workday, a cut in utility rates, the rights of peasants to occupy lands, and limits on foreign ownership of Cuban property. However, political infighting, U.S. opposition, and plots within the military led to Grau's resignation in January 1934. The failed revolution of 1933 proved to be a focus for Cuba's future generations, and the revolution of 1959 was clearly rooted in it.

Between 1934 and 1959, Fulgencio Batista was the de facto head of the Cuban government. Although he is most remembered as the dictator overthrown by Castro's forces, in the 1930s he was regarded as a reformer. Batista enacted many of the demands put forward in the revolution of 1933, including limits on women's work hours, a pension for veterans, expanded education, and guarantee of

Aftermath of the Moncada barracks attack, Santiago de Cuba, July 26, 1953. Insurgents lie dead at the site of Fidel Castro's first attack against the Batista government. Few of the surviving guerrillas managed to escape capture; most were imprisoned or killed. AP IMAGES

permanent land tenure to Cuba's medium-sized farmers. In 1939 Batista was confident enough of his power base to allow free elections, which he won, and in 1940 drafted a new constitution that guaranteed universal suffrage, freedom of political organization, mandatory public education, and a limit to foreign holdings. In addition, the death penalty was outlawed.

Between 1940 and 1952, Cuba had a series of constitutional governments, and each year brought greater prosperity for the working and middle classes. During this period, Cuban politics was dominated by the Authentic (Auténtico) Party, two of whose members, Grau (1944–1948) and Carlos Prío Sacorrás (1948–1952), became president. In 1944 Batista retired to the United States.

Conditions in the rural areas remained static or declined, however. And because Cuba's principal source of income was agriculture, and the majority of its population continued to reside in the country-side, social, economic, and political tensions

continued to brew outside the principal cities. Furthermore, the period leading up to the coup of 1952 was characterized by political cronyism, corruption, and incompetence. In 1946, charges of corruption led to a split in the Authentic Party ranks and the formation of the Orthodox (Ortodoxo) Party, which consisted of disgruntled professionals, intellectuals, and Cuba's growing middle class, all of whom considered themselves heirs to the 1933 revolution. Their slogan, "Honor Before Money," underscored their commitment to end corruption and cronyism in the government. Although not socialists, the Orthodox Party members resented the control exerted by U.S. business interests on the Cuban economy; many of its members advocated the nationalization of foreign-owned sugar plantations.

Elections were scheduled in 1952, and Fidel Castro ran for a seat in Congress as an Orthodox Party candidate. Although Batista, who had returned from exile, could not count on broad popular support, he knew he could amass the necessary cabal of cronies, army officers, and members of the national police to take control of the government. The coup of 1952 also had the implicit support of the Communists, who welcomed a return to political stability. The United States quickly recognized the new government, and despite scattered protests, there was little real resistance. However, although he had support from key power blocs, Batista was never able to legitimize his rule among the Cuban masses. Fidel Castro, deprived of his chance to serve in an elected position, recognized this, and immediately began the work of undermining the Batista regime.

Castro's earliest attack on the Batista government occurred on 26 July 1953, when Fidel, his brother Raúl, Ramiro Valdés, and others attacked the Moncada barracks in Santiago de Cuba. Although virtually all of the guerrillas were killed or captured, including the Castro brothers, the attack made Fidel a national figure. It was not the first time that a military defeat resulted in a political and propaganda victory for Castro. As a recent candidate of the Orthodox Party, he viewed the attack as the fulfillment "of what Martí wanted to do." At his trial, Fidel utilized his impressive oratorical skills to attack Batista's government and to call for the implementation of a constitutional government, agrarian reform, profit-sharing in key industries, and the confiscation of money gotten by corrupt politicians for political favors. Although he was certainly a reformist, Castro's program had little to do with Marxism-Leninism. Castro was jailed in 1953 and freed in a general amnesty in 1955. Fearing Batista's police, Fidel and his brother Raúl fled to Mexico City, where they formed the Twenty-sixth of July Movement with the intention of plotting the overthrow of the Batista regime. It was in Mexico that Castro joined forces with the Argentine revolutionary and Marxist Ernesto "Che" Guevara.

Castro's guerrillas were not the only organized force opposing the Batista dictatorship. The Revolutionary Directorate (DR), an offshoot of the University Students Federation (FEU), was an anti-communist urban-based guerrilla organization whose single goal was the ouster of Batista. Its leader, José Antonio Echeverría, was killed, along with other DR leaders, during an attack on the presidential palace in March 1957. This greatly weakened both the DR and the noncommunist guerrilla opposition to Batista.

There were also efforts throughout the 1950s to bring a peaceful end to the Batista dictatorship. Among these groups, the Society of Friends of the Republic (SAR), which included representatives of the Authentic Party, students, and members of the opposition, attempted to engage Batista in a "civic dialogue." Not surprisingly, their efforts got nowhere, since SAR had no clear political agenda, and its members were willing to do no more than engage in dialogue with the dictator, in the naive hope of convincing him of the necessity for reform.

While opposition to Batista grew, relative economic prosperity and cordial foreign relations undermined the dictator's efforts to step up repression by claims of threats to national security. On 2 December 1956, Castro landed eighty-two guerrillas on the southeast coast of the island, making good on his promise to return to Cuba. Although Castro's forces were initially routed, he was able to regroup and, with his brother Raúl and Che Guevara, launch attacks on Batista's forces. The Twenty-sixth of July Movement issued a manifesto, *Nuestro razón* (Our Purpose), which spelled out its political program. The manifesto attacked four aspects of Cuban political and economic life that needed thorough revision: the colonial mentality, foreign economic domination, corruption, and the military. The manifesto called for constitutional reforms, political pluralism, a "constructive friendship" with the United States, and an independent economy.

Castro's Twenty-sixth of July Movement also had an urban wing, which in 1958 called for a general strike. Although the liberals of the movement supported the strike, and Castro at first agreed, the Communists, including Guevara, considered the strike poorly planned and ill timed. After the strike proved to be a failure, Castro withdrew his support for it, thus undermining the influence of the noncommunists in the Twenty-sixth of July Movement. Officially, the PSP objected to Castro's tactics and believed them doomed to fail. Yet Castro appreciated their commitment to organization and their ability to follow commands. Once it was clear that Batista was doomed, PSP members increasingly backed Castro's Twenty-sixth of July Movement, and Castro in turn relied increasingly on Communists because of their loyalty and reliability.

The final blow to the Batista regime was a U.S.-imposed arms embargo in March 1958. The

U.S. State Department, which distrusted Castro, saw no option but to halt arms shipments until government repression lessened. Underestimating Castro's strength, State Department officials hoped that a decrease in repression would quiet the Cuban middle class, which had long protested the excesses of the Batista regime. Further, Castro had the foresight to use respected, educated liberals of the Twenty-sixth of July Movement to speak to the world press and diplomatic community, thus giving the impression that his forces were fighting solely to end the Batista dictatorship, not to restructure Cuban economic and social life.

By the end of 1958, even some of Batista's officers were ambivalent about the dictator's future or, worse, openly supported the guerrillas. With declining support within the army, political and material isolation from the United States, and no popular base of support, Batista fled the country on 1 January 1959. Although Manuel Urrutia Lleó was named the new president, Castro was clearly the true head of state. Once victorious, the revolutionaries worked to fulfill the promises of the revolution, including the nationalization of foreign-owned properties and a massive program of land redistribution. The United States officially objected to the programs of the new government, and privately plotted to overthrow the revolutionary regime. As with all revolutions, factions united against a common enemy before victory end up fighting each other for the right to control the new government. Castro and his Communist allies proved more than equal to the task, and within two years of the revolution, most of the noncommunists in the Twenty-sixth of July Movement had been removed from power, executed, or exiled. With the decline of the anticommunist faction in the new government and the increased hostility of the United States, Castro's programs grew increasingly radical: first nationalizing large landholdings, then medium-sized ones, and finally virtually all of the farms on the island.

U.S. hostility to the revolution peaked in April 1961 with the Bay of Pigs Invasion. The invasion, a military and propaganda disaster for the United States, solidified Castro's grip on the Cuban government. In December 1961, eight months after the invasion, Castro declared himself a Communist.

Although Castro's commitment to socialism has been the subject of intense debate, it is clear that Castro believed that only by endorsing communism and establishing a close relationship with the Soviet Union could Cuba hope to achieve the goals of nationalization and economic independence from the United States that had been the dream of so many Cubans since the Ten Years' War almost a century earlier.

See also **Castro Ruz, Fidel; Cuba, Constitutions.**

BIBLIOGRAPHY

Del Agulia, Juan M. *Cuba: Dilemmas of a Revolution,* rev. ed. (1988).

Farber, Samuel. *Revolution and Reaction in Cuba, 1933–1960* (1976).

Farber, Samuel. *The Origins of the Cuban Revolution Reconsidered.* Chapel Hill: University of North Carolina Press, 2006.

García Luis, Julio. *Cuban Revolution Reader: A Documentary History of 40 Key Moments of the Cuban Revolution.* Melbourne, Australia: Ocean Press, 2001.

Gilly, Adolfo. *Inside the Cuban Revolution,* translated by Felix Gutiérrez (1964).

Gott, Richard. *Cuba: A New History.* New Haven, CT: Yale University Press, 2004.

Matos, Huber. *Cómo llegó la noche.* Barcelona, Spain: Tusquets Editores, 2002.

Paterson, Thomas G. *Contesting Castro: The United States and the Triumph of the Cuban Revolution.* New York: Oxford University Press, 1994.

Ruiz, Ramón Eduardo. *Cuba: The Making of a Revolution* (1970).

Sweig, Julia. *Inside the Cuban Revolution: Fidel Castro and the Urban Underground.* Cambridge, MA: Harvard University Press, 2002.

Thomas, Hugh. *The Cuban Revolution* (1977).

MICHAEL POWELSON

REVOLUTION OF 1933

The revolution of 1933 resulted from the violent opposition of the Cuban people to President Gerardo Machado's attempt to perpetuate himself in power in 1928. Political dissent was further inflamed by the widespread misery caused by the economic collapse of 1929, and by the fact that the 1920s were for Cuba, as for the rest of Latin America, a period of unrest and transformation. A new and more radical type of nationalism appeared on the island; students and rising labor unions undertook to promote the creation of a new and different type of society; and new leftist political organizations arose to defend the rights of the masses. It was the concurrent action of these forces that metamorphosed the anti-Machado protest into a revolutionary upheaval.

From 1930 to 1933 Cuba was caught between the violent tactics of the opposition, spearheaded by the Student Revolutionary Directorate and a secret organization known as ABC, and the brutal repression of the government, supported by the army. The struggle seemed to have reached a stalemate when President Franklin D. Roosevelt, who needed political stability in Cuba in order to implement his New Deal Cuban policy, sent his trusted aide Sumner Welles to Havana to seek a peaceful solution to the unrest. At first Welles acted as a mediator, but subsequently he pushed Machado toward making concessions, encouraged the opposition, and undermined the army's loyalty to the president. Machado was desperately trying to stand up to Welles's pressure when, in August 1933, a general strike paralyzed the nation. Fearing a U.S. intervention, the army moved against Machado, who fled the island.

Following the coup, the first in Cuban history, Welles moved to fill the resulting political vacuum with a hastily organized provisional government supported by the ABC and the majority of the opposition. But the new government proved unable to cope with the situation. In September the Student Directorate (which had rejected Welles's good offices) and other elements turned a mutiny of army sergeants led by Fulgencio Batista into a triumphant revolutionary takeover. The officers were removed from the army and replaced with sergeants, and the provisional government was unceremoniously supplanted with a new leadership headed by Ramón Grau San Martín, a physician and professor at the University of Havana.

For four months the revolutionaries struggled to push forward a radical and ambitious program of social and profoundly nationalistic reforms. But Welles thought that theirs was a "frankly communistic" government, and consequently Washington confronted it with a stern nonrecognition policy. This was far more than Grau San Martín and his colleagues could withstand, especially after Batista, who was less radical and more pro-American than

the students, astutely withdrew his support from the government. On 15 January 1934, Grau San Martín resigned as president, thus ending the radical phase of the revolution.

Although the more advanced elements did not remain in power for long, the revolution of 1933 marked a turning point in the evolution of twentieth-century Cuba. It put new life into Cuban nationalism, helped to restrain U.S. influence on Cuban affairs, and opened the way for the enactment of new and progressive social legislation. Most of the trends that it initiated proved irreversible, and many of them were reflected and sanctioned in the Cuban Constitution of 1940. In many ways the type of society that existed in Cuba in 1958 grew out of the revolution.

See also **Cuba, Political Parties: ABC Party.**

BIBLIOGRAPHY

The most comprehensive account in English of the revolution is Luis E. Aguilar, *Cuba 1933: Prologue to Revolution* (1972). See also Jules R. Benjamin, "The 'Machado' and Cuban Nationalism, 1928–1932," *Hispanic American Historical Review* 55 (February 1975): 66–91; Harry Swan, "The Nineteen Twenties: A Decade of Intellectual Change in Cuba," *Revista/Review Interamericana* 8 (Summer 1978): 275–288; and Justo Carrillo, *Cuba 1933: Students, Yankees, and Soldiers,* translated by Mario Llerena (1994). On the role of the students, see Jaime Suchlicki, *University Students and Revolution in Cuba, 1920–1968* (1969). In Spanish the reader may wish to consult Ricardo Adam y Silva, *La gran mentira, 4 de septiembre de 1933* (1947); Lionel Soto, *La revolución del 33,* 3 vols. (1977).

Ibarra Guitart, Jorge Renato. *La mediación del 33: Ocaso del machadato.* Havana: Editora Política, 1999.

Osa, Enrique de la. *Crónica del año 1933.* Havana: Editorial de Ciencias Sociales, 1989.

Ros, Enrique. *La revolución de 1933 en Cuba.* Miami: Ediciones Universal, 2005.

Soto, Lionel. *Historia de Cuba: La revolución de 1933.* Havana: Editorial SI-MAR, 2003.

JOSÉ M. HERNÁNDEZ

CUBA, TWENTY-SIXTH OF JULY MOVEMENT.

The Twenty-Sixth of July Movement was the name given to the guerrilla campaign led by Fidel Castro, which overthrew the

Batista government of Cuba on January 1, 1959. The name originates from a coup plot that involved attacking the Moncada Barracks in Santiago de Cuba on July 26, 1953. The attack failed, but had the effect of catapulting the young Fidel into the leadership role of the anti-Batista movement. During his trial he gave an impassioned speech in which he proclaimed, "History will absolve me!" After being released from jail Fidel, his brother Raul, and others, including Ernesto "Che" Guevara and Camilo Cienfuegos, met in Mexico and renewed efforts to depose Batista. On December 2, 1956, Castro's 82 man army arrived in Cuba, a week after leaving Tuxpan, Veracruz on the yacht *Granma*. The invasion was botched; the forces landed during the day allowing the Cuban Air Force to have a devastating effect, and most of the force's supplies were left on the beach. Many men scrambled into the jungle only to be caught by the Cuban Army. By the time the army congregated in the Sierra Maestra mountains days later scarcely a dozen members remained. Still, the Twenty-Sixth of July Movement gained support, capitalizing on discontent among peasants and the increasingly brutal nature of Batista's repression. With armies under the command of Cienfuegos and Guevara the Twenty-Sixth of July revolutionaries waged a successful guerrilla war, first securing the Sierra Maestras, then over the next two years enjoying spectacular successes in Yaguajay and Santa Clara en route to Havana. In 1958, the guerrillas expanded their operations to include economic warfare, burning sugar cane fields, attacking tobacco factories, oil refineries, and railroads. Panicked and finding himself in an increasingly hostile city, Batista fled Havana for the Dominican Republic on New Year's Eve 1958. The Twenty-Sixth of July Movement overtook the capital on January 1, 1959.

Once in power, the Twenty-Sixth of July Movement transformed, assimilating several political parties, including the Cuban Communist Party and the Partido Socialista Popular. They officially merged to form the Communist Party of Cuba in 1965. It became clear that Castro envisioned the Twenty-Sixth of July as a revolutionary process, with the goal of realizing communist ideals, and not just a guerrilla movement. To this extent, the Twenty-Sixth of July Movement continues to symbolize the Cuban Revolution and remains a rallying cry for loyal communists on the island.

See also **Castro Ruz, Fidel; Castro Ruz, Raúl; Cienfuegos, Camilo; Cuba, Political Parties: Communist Party; Guevara, Ernesto "Che."**

BIBLIOGRAPHY

Benjamin, Jules R. *The United States and the Origins of the Cuban Revolution.* Princeton, NJ: Princeton University Press, 1990.

Perez, Louis A. *Cuba: Between Reform and Revolution.* New York: Oxford University Press, 1995.

SEAN H. GOFORTH

CUBA, WAR OF INDEPENDENCE.

Cuba: War of Independence (1895–1898), the culmination of the Cubans' struggle to gain their freedom from Spanish colonial rule. The armed separatists were committed to more than just independence. The Creole bourgeoisie was just as much the enemy of Cuba Libre as were the Spanish officeholders, and the revolutionaries recognized that inequity was not caused by Spanish political rule as much as by the Cuban social system. They believed that a transformation of Cuban society was the only remedy. Originally the war was primarily between the colony and the metropolis, but after 1896 the conflict expanded to become a struggle between the creole bourgeoisie and a populist coalition over competing claims of hegemony within the colony. The rebellion offered oppressed groups—poor blacks and whites, peasants and workers, the destitute and dispossessed—the promise of social justice and economic freedom.

Jose Martí, the father of Cuban independence, Máximo Gómez y Báez, Antonio Maceo, and other veterans of the Ten Years' War coordinated the war effortsin Cuba. On 24 February 1895, the insurrection began with the Grito De Baire (Declaration of Baire). On 24 March Martí presented the Manifesto de Montecristi, which outlined the insurgents' war policies: The war was to be waged by blacks and whites alike (participation of all blacks was deemed crucial for victory); Spaniards who did not object to the war effort were to be spared; private rural properties were not to be destroyed; and the revolution was to bring new economic life to Cuba. Martí said, "Cubans ask no more of the world than the recognition of and respect for their sacrifices."

Martí's death in 1895 did not stop the independence movement. In September representatives of the five branches of the Army of Liberation proclaimed the Republic in Arms. In July 1895 Gómez and Maceo sent orders to end all economic activity on the island that might be advantageous to the royalists. Defeat of the Spanish required destruction of the bourgeoisie's social and economic power, and so the insurrection became an economic war. The insurgents burned fields to stop sugar production. The population continued to support the rebellion despite its economic consequences, and the war did in fact destroy the Spanish bourgeoisie as a social class as well as end colonial rule.

Spanish authorities were stunned by the insurrection. They enlarged their army to 200,000 men and appointed General Valeriano Weyler y Nicolau to bolster the war effort. He instituted the reconcentration policy under which the rural population was ordered to evacuate the countryside and relocate in specially designated fortified towns. Subsistence agriculture was banned and villages, fields, homes, food reserves, and livestock were all destroyed. Over 300,000 Cubans were relocated into these concentration camps. Mass deaths resulted because the municipal authorities were not prepared to assume the responsibility of caring for the internal refugees. The policy proved to be counterproductive. As a result of the camps, more Cubans supported the insurrection; also, in the United States and even Spain there was a strong public reaction against the Spanish policy.

The Spanish controlled the cities and attacked the peasants, while the Cubans controlled the countryside and attacked the planters. By the end of 1897, Cuban victory was inevitable. Weyler was incapable of expelling the insurgents from the western area of the island, and the Cuban elites were appealing to the United States to intervene and restore order. The explosion on 15 February 1898 of the *U.S.S. Maine*, which had been sent to the Havana harbor to protect U.S. citizens, killed 260 enlisted men and officers. This tragedy provided the United States with an excuse to enter the war. On 25 April 1898, the U.S. Congress declared war against Spain, but the Teller Amendment stated that the United States would make no attempt to establish permanent control over the island. In June 1898 some 17,000 U.S. troops landed east of Santiago, Cuba. On 3 July the Spanish fleet was destroyed,

and a few subsequent land victories prompted Spanish surrender on 12 August.

Although the Cuban forces were instrumental in the outcome of the war, they were excluded from the peace negotiations that resulted in the Treaty of Paris. The terms of the treaty, which permitted the United States to dominate Cuba, reflected the view that the quick victory over Spain was attributable solely to the United States. That view did not acknowledge that the Cuban struggle for independence had been depleting the crown's resources for several decades, especially in the preceding three years. On 1 January 1899, the Spanish administration retired from Cuba, and General John R. Brooke installed a military government, establishing the U.S. occupation of the island, which ended in 1902.

See also **Spanish-American War.**

BIBLIOGRAPHY

Freidel, Frank. *The Splendid Little War* (1958).

Guerra, Sergio. *América Latina y la independencia de Cuba.* Caracas: Ediciones Ko'Eyú, 1999.

Helg, Aline. *Our Rightful Share: The Afro-Cuban Struggle for Equality, 1886–1912.* Chapel Hill: University of North Carolina Press, 1995.

Pérez, Louis A., Jr. *Cuba: Between Reform and Revolution* (1988).

Portell Vilá, Herminio. *Historia de Cuba en sus relaciones con los Estados Unidos y España* (1938).

Portell Vilá, Herminio. *Historia de la guerra de Cuba y los Estados Unidos contra España* (1949).

Pratt, Julius W. *Expansionists of 1898: The Acquisition of Hawaii and the Spanish Islands* (1936).

Roig De Leuchsenring, Emilio. *1895 y 1898: Dos guerras cubanas, ensayos de revaloración* (1945).

Roig De Leuchsenring, Emilio. *La guerra libertadora cubana de los treinta años, 1868–1898* (1952)

Roig De Leuchsenring, Emilio. *La Guerra Hispano-cubanoamericano fué ganada por el lugarteniente general de Ejército Libertador Calixto García Iñiguez* (1955).

Rudolph, James D. *Cuba: A Country Study* (1985).

Thomas, Hugh. *Cuba, or the Pursuit of Freedom* (1971).

Tone, John Lawrence. *War and Genocide in Cuba, 1895-1898.* Chapel Hill: University of North Carolina Press, 2006.

Torre, Mildred de la. *El autonomismo en Cuba, 1878-1898.* Havana: Editorial de Ciencias Sociales, 1997.

Varona Guerrero, Miguel. *La Guerra de la Independencia de Cuba, 1895–1898,* 3 vols. (1946).

DAVID CAREY

CUCHUMATANES.

CUCHUMATANES. The Sierra de los Cuchamatanes of Guatemala is the most massive and spectacular nonvolcanic region in all Central America. It lies at elevations ranging from 1,500 feet to more than 12,000 feet in the northwestern Guatemalan departments of Huehuetenango and El Quiché. The region's isolation and limited economic potential meant that Maya peoples there survived the Spanish Conquest and its destructive aftermath more resiliently than did native communities elsewhere in Latin America. The disruptions of the colonial period have had their modern-day equivalent in the form of violent civil war, the Cuchumatanes being the part of Guatemala hit hardest by counterinsurgency sweeps in the early 1980s. With the Guatemalan Peace Accords signed in 1996, one of Latin America's longest (36 years) and bloodiest civil wars came to an end. Remarkably, however, in light of the extreme poverty, and lack of basic infrastructure, education, and medical facilities, the Cuchumatán Maya endure, and culturally and demographically still constitute a visible, conspicuous element in the human landscape. The resolution of the bloody conflict has remarkably improved the capacity and success of both international nongovernmental organizations in Guatemala, and the relationship between the government of Guatemala and the local government. This has allowed large, integrated social services to grow.

See also **Guatemala.**

BIBLIOGRAPHY

W. George Lovell, "From Conquest to Counter-Insurgency" in *Cultural Survival Quarterly* 9:2 (1985): 46–49.

W. George Lovell, "Surviving Conquest" in *Latin American Research Review* 23, no. 2 (1988): 25–57.

W. George Lovell, *Conquista y cambio cultural* (1990).

W. George Lovell, *Conquest and Survival in Colonial Guatemala: A Historical Geography of the Cuchumatán Highlands* (1985, rev. ed. 1992).

Additional Bibliography

Blum, Leonor. "International NGOs and the Guatemalan Peace Accords." *Voluntas: International Journal of Voluntary and Nonprofit Organizations.* 12, no. 4 (2001): 327–353.

Perera, Victor, *Unfinished Conquest: The Guatemalan Tragedy* (1993).

Grandin, Greg. *The Blood of Guatemala: A History of Race and Nation.* Durham, NC: Duke University Press, 2000.

W. GEORGE LOVELL

CÚCUTA, CONGRESS OF.

CÚCUTA, CONGRESS OF. The constituent congress of Gran Colombia met at Cúcuta, on the border between Venezuela and New Granada, from May to October 1821. Though comprised only of representatives from Venezuela and New Granada, and not the present-day Ecuador, it confirmed the union of all sections of the former Viceroyalty of New Granada in a single independent republic. It adopted the first constitution, which was centralist in structure but typically liberal in providing for the separation of powers and a list of individual rights that did not, however, include freedom of religious worship. By separate enactments, the same congress adopted a first round of legal and institutional reforms that included abolition of the Inquisition and of various colonial taxes, and a free-birth law for the gradual elimination of slavery. To save time, it also elected the first president and vice president of the new nation: Simón Bolívar and Francisco de Paula Santander.

See also **Inquisition: Spanish America.**

BIBLIOGRAPHY

David Bushnell, *The Santander Regime in Gran Colombia* (1954; repr. 1970), chap. 2; *Congreso de Cúcuta de 1821: Constitución y leyes* (1971).

Additional Bibliography

Lynch, John. *Simón Bolívar: A Life.* New Haven, CT: Yale University Press, 2006.

Riaño Cano, Germán. *El gran calumniado: Réplica a la leyenda negra de Santander.* Bogotá, Colombia: Planeta, 2001.

DAVID BUSHNELL

CUECA.

CUECA. The cueca is a Chilean dance with its own music and words. It appeared during the first half of the nineteenth century, though there is some controversy surrounding its origin. Some say it came to Chile from Peru, bringing with it African and Caribbean influences. Other researchers argue that its origins are Arab-Andalusian. The dance was recreated in Chile and taken up in salons by the upper classes, and in bars and cafeterias by the common folk, reaching its height of popularity in the late nineteenth and early twentieth centuries as it spread through rural and urban areas. The dance is performed by a couple, accompanied by singing and guitar playing, in a style that evokes a rooster courting a hen. The movements are performed in a semicircle, with the man attempting to win over the woman while she responds with modesty, both of them flourishing handkerchiefs. The cueca has become less popular over the past several decades, but it is still performed during Chilean national celebrations, folk-dancing performances, and radio and television programs. The cueca was declared the national dance of Chile by military decree in 1979.

See also **Music: Popular Music and Dance.**

BIBLIOGRAPHY

Claro Valdés, Samuel, and Carmen Peña Fuenzalida. *Chilena o cueca tradicional.* Santiago: Ediciones Universidad Católica de Chile, 1994.

Garrido, Pablo. *Historial de la cueca.* Valparaíso: Ediciones Universitarias de Valparaíso, 1979.

León Echaiz, René. *Interpretación histórica del huaso chileno.* Buenos Aires and Santiago: Editorial Francisco de Aguirre, 1971.

HORACIO GUTIÉRREZ

CUE CÁNOVAS, AGUSTÍN (1913–1971).

Mexican historian and academic Agustín Cue Cánovas (August 28, 1913–April 23, 1971) was born in Villahermosa, Tabasco. He graduated with a law degree but never practiced law. He began teaching at the Higher Normal School and the National Teachers School in Mexico City, and later at the National School of Economics and National School of Political Science at the National Autonomous University of Mexico (UNAM). He became director of the Cultural Institutes of Mexico-Cuba and Mexico-Rumania. Politically active on the left, he ran as a candidate for congress on the Popular Socialist Party (PPS) ticket. Given his political interests, he also wrote for many newspapers, including *El Día*, *El Popular*, and *El Universal*. He has been described as belonging to a new wave of historians, and became a close friend of Ernesto de la Torre Villar, a leading figure of his generation. De la Torre Villar describes Cánovas's historical contributions as focused on revisionist interpretations which can be linked to universal developments.

See also **Mexico: Since 1910.**

BIBLIOGRAPHY

Torre Villar, Ernesto de la. *Estudios de Historia Moderna y Contemporánea de México*, Vol. 4. Mexico City: UNAM, 1972. See pages 195–201.

RODERIC AI CAMP

CUENCA.

Cuenca, the third largest city in Ecuador (2005 est. pop. 276,964) and capital of Azuay Province. Cuenca is located in the southern sierra of Ecuador, 8,500 feet above sea level, on the banks of the Tomebamba River. Pre-Incaic civilizations flourished in the region and attained their most highly developed cultural phase with the Cañari, known for their beautiful goldwork. The Cañari had no centralized authority and were not able to defend themselves effectively against the invading Incas, who came from Peru between 1463 and 1471. The Incas established a reputedly breathtaking city known as Tomebamba (Tumipampa) on the site of modern Cuenca. The nearby ruins of Ingapirca, on the great Incan highway, are the only Incan architectural monuments left in Ecuador today. The indigenous city was razed in 1557, when the Spanish conquerors arrived in the region after defeating the Incas. On the orders of Viceroy Gil Ramírez Dávlos, Fray Vicente Solano founded the city anew as a Spanish town, naming it Cuenca after a city in Spain.

During the colonial period, the Spanish built a picturesque tiled city, of which much architecture remains in the early 2000s. Cuenca became known for the devoutly religious and conservative character of its residents. The economy depended on agriculture and on the textile production of the indigenous peoples of the region. The population was not at first in favor of the independence movement; indeed, after independence the local economy suffered due to the sudden rise in imports of British textiles. During the nineteenth century, the misnamed "Panama hat," woven of straw and formerly made on the Ecuadorian coast, made its way to the highlands and became the basis for the dominant cottage industry among local native people. These hats and other artisan productions are exported in great numbers in the early 2000s. The economy also depends on agriculture, cattle ranching, and leather processing.

Another important component of the economies in Cuenca, Azuay province, and Ecuador is the funds its migrants send home. Since 1980, 10 to 15 percent of Ecuador's population has emigrated overseas, and in the first of two migration waves, Cuenca and Azuay province sent the most emigrants. Most of them were poor men from communities where women traditionally wove Panama hats, and they often sought work in the New York metropolitan area. In 2004 migrants sent $2 billion in remittances back to Ecuador, an amount equal to 6.7 percent of the country's GDP and second only to oil exports, according to the Inter-American Development Bank.

In 1999 the United Nations Educational, Scientific, and Cultural Organization (UNESCO) declared Cuenca's historic center of colonial Spanish architecture a World Heritage Site, boosting a growing tourist industry.

See also **Textile Industry: The Colonial Era; Textile Industry: Modern Textiles.**

BIBLIOGRAPHY

For an excellent summary of what is known about the ancient history of Cuenca, see Betty Jane Meggers, *Ecuador* (1966). For the transition from the colonial period to the modern, see Silvia Palomeque, *Cuenca en el siglo XIX: La articulación de una región* (1990).

Arteaga, Diego. *El artesano en la Cuenca colonial (1557–1670)*. Cuenca, Ecuador: Centro Americano de Artesanías: C.C.E. Nucleo del Azuay, 2000.

Chacón Z., Juan Pedro Soto, and Diego Mora. *Historia de la gobernación de Cuenca, 1777–1820: Estudio económico-social*. Cuenca, Ecuador: Universidad de Cuenca, Instituto de Investigaciones Sociales, 1994.

Idrovo Urigüen, Jaime. *Tomebamba, arqueología e historia de una ciudad imperial*. Quito: Banco Central del Ecuador, Dirección Cultural Regional Cuenca, 2000.

Jamieson, Ross W. *Domestic Architecture and Power: The Historical Archaeology of Colonial Ecuador*. New York: Kluwer Academic/Plenum Publishers, 2000.

Kyle, David. *Transnational Peasants: Migrations, Networks, and Ethnicity in Andean Ecuador*. Baltimore, MD: Johns Hopkins University Press, 2000.

Moldstad, Gro Mathilde. *"Guardiana de la fe": Oposición religiosa y negociación de identidad: Los nobles de Cuenca*. Quito: Ediciones Abya-Yala, 1996.

Paniagua Pérez, Jesús, and Deborah L. Truhan. *Oficios y actividad paragremial en la Real Audiencia de Quito (1557–1730): El corregimiento de Cuenca*. León, Ecuador: Universidad de León, Secretariado de Publicaciones y Medios Audiovisuales, 2003.

CAMILLA TOWNSEND

CUERNAVACA. Cuernavaca, Mexican municipality and capital of the state of Morelos. With 349,102 residents in the city in 2005, and a metropolitan population of 804,140 in 2003, it is located about 36 miles south of Mexico City at an elevation of 5,059 feet above sea level. Known as Cuauhnahuac (near the trees) in pre-Spanish times, it became the residence of the conqueror Hernán Cortés. Franciscan missionaries arrived in 1529.

In colonial times Cuernavaca was an important center of local indigenous government and the seat of a Spanish magistrate appointed by the administrators of Cortés's estate. The town's growing non-Indian population became enfranchised with the creation of a municipal government shortly before Mexican independence.

Cuernavaca was often involved in nineteenth-century politics; a junta held there in 1855 named Juan Álvarez as interim president of Mexico, and Emperor Maximilian von Hapsburg frequently vacationed there. In 1869 it became the capital of the new state of Morelos, and in 1891 its first bishop was consecrated. Railroads arrived in 1897, and Cuernavaca played a pivotal role in the Revolution of 1910.

During the 1920s a new highway to Mexico City enabled President Plutarco Elías Calles and many of his associates to commute easily to their vacation homes in Cuernavaca. In the last decades of the twentieth century the city has continued to be a favored weekend retreat of Mexico City residents. Such popularity does not come without problems:

traffic jams, congestion, and pollution have grown in recent years, detracting from the city's attractiveness.

See also **Morelos.**

BIBLIOGRAPHY

A scholarly treatment of the colonial period can be found in Robert S. Haskett, *Indigenous Rulers: An Ethnohistory of Town Government in Colonial Cuernavaca* (1991). For a highly personal account of events in Cuernavaca during the Revolution of 1910, see Rosa E. King, *Tempest over Mexico: A Personal Chronicle* (1970).

Chávez Galindo, Ana María. *La nueva dinámica de la migración interna en México 1970–1990.* Cuernavaca, Mexico: Universidad Nacional Autónoma de Mexico, 1999.

Haskett, Robert S. *Visions of Paradise: Primordial Titles and Mesoamerican History in Cuernavaca.* Norman: University of Oklahoma Press, 2005.

Mentz, Brígida von, and R. Marcela Pérez López. *Manantiales, ríos, pueblos y haciendas: Dos documentos sobre conflictos por aguas en Oaxtepec y en el valle de Cuernavaca (1795–1807).* Jiutepec, México: Instituto Mexicano de Tecnología del Agua, 1998.

Rueda Hurtado, Rocío. *Sistema urbano de Cuernavaca.* México, D.F.: Editorial Praxis, 2001.

Sánchez Santiró, Ernest. *Azúcar y poder: Estructura socioeconómica de las alcaldías mayores de Cuernavaca y Cuautla de Amilpas, 1730–1821.* México, D.F.: Editorial Praxis, 2001.

Wiesheu, Walburga. *Religión y política en la transformación urbana: Análisis de un proceso sociodemográfico.* México: Instituto Nacional de Antropología e Historia, 2002.

CHERYL ENGLISH MARTIN

CUERPO DE CARABINEROS. *See* **Carabineros de Chile.**

CUERVO, RUFINO JOSÉ (1844–1911).

Rufino José Cuervo (b. 19 September 1844; d. 17 July 1911), Colombian philologist. Rufino José Cuervo, born in Bogotá, was largely self-taught in his various specialties, which spanned ancient and modern languages and literature, including Native American tongues and American Spanish dialects. Among his earlier works are *Apuntaciones críticas sobre el lenguaje bogotano* (1867–1872) and *Gramática de la lengua latina* (1876), a Latin grammar he wrote with Miguel Antonio Caro. Cuervo traveled extensively in Europe, and after 1882 settled permanently in Paris, where he taught at the Sorbonne and contributed to European specialized journals. He also produced, in collaboration with his brother Ángel, a historically important life of their father, *Vida de Rufino Cuervo y noticias de su época* (1946). Cuervo also undertook a massive *Diccionario de construcción y régimen de la lengua castellana* (1886–1893), which he completed only to the letter D.

See also **Indigenous Languages.**

BIBLIOGRAPHY

Luis López De Mesa, *Miguel Antonio Caro y Rufino José Cuervo* (1944).

Fernando Antonio Martínez, *Rufino José Cuervo* (1954).

Additional Bibliography

Rufino José Cuervo: El reencuentro con la palabra. Bogotá: Instituto Caro y Cuervo, 1999.

Porto Dapena, J. Alvaro. *Elementos de lexicografía: El diccionario de construcción y régimen de R.J. Cuervo.* Bogotá: Instituto Caro y Cuervo, 1980.

Valle, José del. "Historical Linguistics and Cultural History: The Polemic Between Rufino José Cuervo and Juan Valera." In *The Battle Over Spanish Between 1800 and 2000: Language Ideologies and Hispanic Intellectuals,* edited by José del Valle and Luis Gabriel-Stheeman. London and New York: Routledge, 2002.

Valle, José del. "Lingüística histórica e historia cultural: Notas sobre la polémica entre Rufino José Cuervo y Juan Valera." In *La batalla del idioma: La intelectualidad hispánica ante la lengua,* edited by José del Valle and Luis Gabriel-Stheeman. Madrid: Iberoamericana, and Frankfurt am Main: Vervuert, 2004.

DAVID BUSHNELL

CUESTAS, JUAN LINDOLFO (1837–1905).

Juan Lindolfo Cuestas (b. 6 January 1837; d. 21 June 1905), president of Uruguay (1899–1903). A veteran politician, Cuestas was president of the Senate between 1895 and 1898 and provisional president between 1898 and 1899. In his early career he subscribed to the collectivist Colorado group led by Herrera y Obes, which had overseen the transition from militarism to civilian government. As president of the Senate exercising executive power after the death of the constitutional president, he modified his politics in order to broaden his base of support within both the Colorado and the Blanco (National) parties. The preceding president, Juan Idiarte Borda, assassinated in 1897, had left a legacy of revolution in the Blanco Party, led by Aparicio Saravia. Cuestas made a pact with Saravia, accepting what amounted to a formula for cogovernment. In 1898, unable to assure his own election by the Parliament, he dissolved the assembly by decree and assumed dictatorial powers. During his provisional presidency, military and presumably collectivist factions attempted a coup d'état and an invasion, which ultimately failed. Cuestas's constitutional presidency deserves credit for bringing the peace and order so longed for. José Batlle y Ordóñez succeeded him as president, beginning a new era in Uruguayan politics and suppressing the cogovernment of Cuestas and Saravia.

See also **Uruguay, Political Parties: Blanco Party; Uruguay, Political Parties: Colorado Party.**

BIBLIOGRAPHY

Eduardo Acevedo, *Manual de historia uruguaya: Desde el coloniaje hasta 1930* (1935), esp. pp. 241–298.

Enrique Méndez Vives, *El Uruguay de la modernización* (1977), esp. pp. 87–95, 117–122.

Additional Bibliography

Rock, David. "State-Building and Political Systems in Nineteenth-Century Argentina and Uruguay." *Past and Present* 167 (May 2000): 176–202.

FERNANDO FILGUEIRA

CUEVA, FRANCISCO DE LA (c. 1501–1576).

Francisco de la Cueva (*b.* ca. 1501; *d.* 1576), Spanish governor of Guatemala. Cueva accompanied the expedition of Pedro de Alvarado y Mesía to Guatemala (ca. 1524). Later, he married Alvarado's daughter Leonor, child of Alvarado's union with the Tlaxcalan princess Luisa Xicoténcatl.

Alvarado named Cueva acting governor and captain-general of Guatemala on two occasions. He was acting governor when news of Alvarado's death reached Guatemala in 1541. He was replaced by his cousin Beatriz de la Cueva De Alvarado, who was Alvarado's second wife. After her death (10 September 1541), Cueva and Bishop Francisco Marroquín were co-

governors until a replacement, Alonso de Maldonado, was sent from Mexico, 17 May 1542.

See also **Guatemala.**

MURDO J. MACLEOD

CUEVA DE ALVARADO, BEATRIZ DE LA (?–1541).

Beatriz de la Cueva de Alvarado (*d.* 10 September 1541), second wife of Pedro de Alvarado y Mesía and the only female governor during the Spanish-American colonial period. Niece of the duke of Albuquerque, she married Pedro de Alvarado, her deceased sister's husband, in Spain in 1538, after receiving a papal dispensation, and accompanied him to Guatemala when he returned there as governor the following year.

When news of Alvarado's death arrived in Guatemala in June 1541, she demanded the governorship. Her cousin, the acting governor, Francisco de la Cueva, gave it to her. The conquistador elite, already shocked by what it considered to be her excessive and sacrilegious mourning for her husband, resented her assumption of the governorship. She was killed on 10 September 1541 by the flood and mudslide that destroyed the city following rainstorms and earthquakes. Years later she was buried beside Alvarado in the cathedral of Antigua, Guatemala.

See also **Alvarado y Mesía, Pedro de; Cueva, Francisco de la.**

BIBLIOGRAPHY

Adams, Jerome R. *Notable Latin American Women: Twenty-Nine Leaders, Rebels, Poets, Battlers, and Spies, 1500–1900.* Jefferson, NC: McFarland & Co., 1995.

Dillon, Susana. *Mujeres que hicieron América: Biografías transgresoras.* Buenos Aires: Editorial Catari, 1992.

MURDO J. MACLEOD

CUEVA ENRÍQUEZ Y SAAVEDRA, BALTÁSAR DE LA (c. 17th century).

Baltásar de la Cueva Enríquez y Saavedra (count of Castellar), viceroy of Peru (1674–1678). An experienced administrator, Castellar attempted to reform colonial administration and increase crown revenues by streamlining accounting procedures and investigating tax collectors and regional treasuries throughout the viceroyalty. Through his efforts, hundreds of thousands of pesos in back taxes and other revenues owed to the crown were collected, many from the *consulado* (merchant guild). His anticorruption campaign resulted in the public execution of two treasury officials and sanctions against many others, one of whom attempted to assassinate Castellar in 1675. Disgruntled treasury officials and members of the powerful *consulado* of Lima complained so strenuously to the crown that Castellar was removed from office in 1678.

See also **Viceroyalty, Viceroy.**

BIBLIOGRAPHY

See the excellent account of colonial administration in Kenneth J. Andrien, *Crisis and Decline: The Viceroyalty of Peru in the Seventeenth Century* (1985), esp. pp. 184–189, which give details of Castellar's career. A more general discussion of colonial administration can be found in Mark A. Burkholder and Lyman L. Johnson, *Colonial Latin America* (1990).

Additional Bibliography

Hunefeldt, Christine. *A Brief History of Peru.* New York: Facts on File, 2004.

Mannarelli, María Emma. *Private Passions and Public Sins: Men and Women in Seventeenth-Century Lima.* Albuquerque: University of New Mexico Press, 2007.

San Cristóbal Sebastián, Antonio. *Obras civiles en Lima durante el siglo XVII.* Lima: Universidad Nacional de Ingeniería, 2005.

Torres Arancivia, Eduardo. *Corte de virreyes: El entorno del poder en el Perú en el siglo XVII.* Lima: Pontífica Universidad Católica del Perú, 2006.

ANN M. WIGHTMAN

CUEVAS, JOSÉ LUIS (1933–).

José Luis Cuevas is a Mexican artist. Born on 26 February 1933, Cuevas's talent became apparent in 1953, a crucial time in Mexican art when the hegemony of the Mexican School was in question. His pen and ink drawings of mad people, cadavers, freaks, and prostitutes brought him acclaim in 1954 at the Pan American Union under the tutelage of its director, José Gómez Sicre. Cuevas promoted himself with a publicity campaign that culminated in 1956 with his article "La cortina de nopal" (The Cactus Curtain) in the newspaper *Novedades,* in which he fulminated against the Mexican School. He initiated an expressive figurative and intimist drawing style based on monsters and the grotesque. His later work drew extensively from literary sources (Kafka, Dostoevsky, Quevedo) and from such artists as Van Eyck, Rembrandt, Goya, Dürer, Picasso, and Orozco. He did several thematic series, which include *The Worlds of Kafka and Cuevas* (1957), *Funerals of a Dictator* (1958), *The Spain of Franco* (1960), and *The Conquest of Mexico* (1961), as well as innumerable self-portraits. Cuevas has had a strong influence on neofigurative Latin American artists. In 1992 the Museo José Luis Cuevas opened in Mexico City. In 1997 he received the Tomas Francisco Pietro Award in engraving. Francisco Bolaños directed a biographical documentary about his life and work, *José Luis Cuevas … Ilustrador de su tiempo* (2006). He writes a weekly column in the Mexico City newspaper *Excelsior.*

See also **Art: The Twentieth Century.**

BIBLIOGRAPHY

Arnaldo Alcubilla, Francisco Javier. "José Luis Cuevas, armado con su firma." *Cuadernos Hispanoamericanos* 575 (May 1998): 15–18.

Arnaldo Alcubilla, Francisco Javier. "Una conversación con José Luis Cuevas en Madrid." *Cuadernos Hispanoamericanos* 575 (May 1998): 19–30.

Dimmick, Ralph, et al., trans., *Cuevas by Cuevas: Autobiographical Notes* (1965).

Fuentes, Carlos. *El mundo de José Luis Cuevas,* translated by Consuelo de Aerenlund (1969).

Gallo, Rubén. *Mexican Modernity: The Avant-Garde and the Technological Revolution.* Cambridge, MA: MIT Press, 2005.

Goldman, Shifra M. *Contemporary Mexican Painting in a Time of Change* (1981).

Peden, Margaret Sayers. *Out of the Volcano: Portraits of Contemporary Mexican Artists.* Washington, DC: Smithsonian Institution Press, 1991.

SHIFRA M. GOLDMAN

CUEVAS, MARIANO (1879–1949).

Mariano Cuevas (*b.* 1879; *d.* 1949), Mexican historian. Born in Mexico City, Cuevas studied there until joining the Society of Jesus in Loyola, Spain, in 1893. From 1902 to 1906, Cuevas taught literature and history in Saltillo and Puebla, Mexico. He went on to study theology in St. Louis,

Missouri (1906–1910). Cuevas was ordained a priest but continued to study archaeology, paleography, diplomacy, and historical methods. He spent most of the rest of his life researching and writing historical works. He published collections of documents as well as the results of his own investigations. His principal works include *Documentos inéditos del siglo XVI* (1914), *Cartas y otros documentos de Hernán Cortés* (1915), *Historia de la iglesia en México*, 5 vols. (1921–1928), and *La historia de la nación mexicana* (1940).

See also **Jesuits.**

BIBLIOGRAPHY

Carlos González Peña, *History of Mexican Literature*, translated by Gusta Barfield Nance and Florence Johnson Dunstan, 3d ed. (1968); *Diccionario Porrúa de historia, biografía y geografía de México*, 5th ed. (1986).

Additional Bibliography

Palmer, Dennis R. "The American Protestant Conspiracy Theory of Mexican History: A Case Study in the Literature of Mexican Militant Catholicism." Ph.D. diss., Graduate Theological Union, 1979.

D. F. STEVENS

CUGAT, XAVIER (1900–1990).

Xavier Cugat (*b.* 1 January 1900; *d.* 27 October 1990), Spanish musician and bandleader. Born near Barcelona, Spain, Cugat immigrated to Cuba with his family in 1904. At age six, he appeared as a guest violinist with the Havana Symphony and became a full-time member of that orchestra in 1912. Later that same year, he moved to the United States. Unable to find work as a classical musician, he drew caricatures of movie stars for the *Los Angeles Times* until Rudolph Valentino asked him to organize a band to accompany him in a film requiring tango music. He and his band, the Gigolos, appeared in several films of the 1940s and 1950s, making his name a household word. He introduced the rumba to American audiences in his movies and through his appearances at clubs like the Coconut Grove, the Hotel Chase, and Al Capone's Chez Paris in Chicago, and a ten-year run at the Waldorf Astoria. His full-time career as a big band leader spanned from the 1940s to the 1960s. In 1986, he formed his last band and began touring Spain. He was married and divorced five times and had no children.

See also **Arnaz, Desi; Music: Popular Music and Dance.**

BIBLIOGRAPHY

Cugat wrote two books that best define his life, *I, Cugat* (1981) and *My Wives*. His work with his band is discussed in George T. Simon, *The Big Bands*, 4th ed. (1981). The introduction and effects of Latin American music in the United States is the subject of John S. Roberts, *The Latin Tinge: The Impact of Latin American Music on the United States* (1979).

Additional Bibliography

Cushman, Gregory T. "¿De qué color es el oro? Race, Environment, and the History of Cuban National Music, 1898–1958." *Latin American Music Review* 26 (Fall/Winter 2005): 164–194.

Gasca, Luis. *Cugat*. Madrid: Ediciones del Imán, 1995.

JACQUELYN BRIGGS KENT

CUIABÁ.

Cuiabá, the capital of Mato Grosso State in central-west Brazil, lies in the geographical center of South America on the Cuiabá River, a tributary of the Paraguay River, and has a population of roughly 480,000 (2000). The city was founded in 1718 when the gold boom hit Mato Grosso, but its gold fields proved to be shallow, with most deposits lying within two feet of the surface. Cuiabá persisted as a permanent settlement, unlike most boom towns, becoming the provincial capital in 1820. At times it has taken center stage in the land struggles between the soybean agro-industry and Amerindians of Brazil. It is home to the first federally protected indigenous territory, the Xingu National Park, created in 1961.

Cuiabá is an important commercial and industrial center for much of Mato Grosso's economy, including rubber manufacturing, cattle raising, agriculture, tourism, and mining. It is responsible for roughly 20 percent of the state's gross domestic product (2003) and 23 percent of the electric energy generated in the state (2005). Its thermal power station runs on natural gas, most of which is imported from Bolivia. In August 2007 the station suspended its activities because of unsuccessful price negotiations between Brazil and Bolivia.

See also **Mato Grosso.**

BIBLIOGRAPHY

Foweraker, Joe. *The Struggle for Land: A Political Economy of the Pioneer Frontier in Brazil*. Cambridge, U.K., and New York: Cambridge University Press, 2002.

Poppino, Rollie E. *Brazil: The Land and People*, 2nd edition. New York: Oxford University Press, 1973.

Swarts, Frederick A., ed. *The Pantanal: Understanding and Preserving the World's Largest Wetland*. St. Paul, MN: Paragon House, 2000.

CAROLYN E. VIEIRA
ANA JANAINA NELSON

BIBLIOGRAPHY

Marquina, Ignacio. *Arquitectura prehispanica*. Mexico City: Instituto Nacional de Antropología e Historia, Secretaria de Educación Pública, 1964.

Parsons, Jeffrey, and Michael E. Whalen. *Prehispanic Settlement Patterns in the Southern Valley of Mexico: The Chalco-Xochimilco Region*. Ann Arbor: Museum of Anthropology, University of Michigan, 1982.

Saunders, William, Jeffrey R. Parsons, and Robert S. Santley. *The Basin of Mexico: Ecological Processes in the Evolution of a Civilization*. New York: Academic Press, 1979.

Schávelzon, Daniel. *La pirámide de Cuicuilco*. Mexico City: Fondo de Cultura Económica, 1983.

KENNETH HIRTH

CUICUILCO. Cuicuilco is an archaeological site located at the southern end of the Valley of Mexico on the outskirts of Mexico City. Between 300 and 1 BCE it was one of the largest and most influential communities in central Mexico. It is believed that the site grew to cover 1.4 square miles (3.6 square kilometers) and had a resident population of around 20,000 people. A large circular temple platform 405 feet (123 meters) in diameter at the base and 60 feet (18 meters) high was constructed as the center of ritual activity at the site. This was the first monumental temple platform to be constructed in the Valley of Mexico, predating similar constructions at Teotihuacán by several hundred years.

The Valley of Mexico appears to have been divided into several large chiefdom societies between 300 and 1 BCE. Cuicuilco was one of the biggest of these, and a large portion of the southwestern Valley of Mexico was under its sociopolitical control. Teotihuacán, in the northeast corner of the Valley of Mexico, was Cuicuilco's primary political competitor during this period.

The site of Cuicuilco was dramatically destroyed around 50 BCE by a volcanic eruption from Mount Xitle. The entire residential area was covered by a massive lava flow that encased the archaeological site in a thick layer of basalt up to 33 feet (10 meters) deep. The destruction of Cuicuilco had immediate and dramatic repercussions throughout the Valley of Mexico. Teotihuacán emerged as the region's undisputed political leader and underwent accelerated growth as populations throughout the Valley of Mexico were resettled within its limits.

See also **Teotihuacán.**

CUISINES. The cuisines of Latin America reflect the complexity and diversity of the history and culture of the region. Centuries of adaptations to the land have produced cuisines that are unique modifications of the food habits of Indians, Europeans, and Africans. Many of the staples upon which these cuisines are based have their origins in the early history of agriculture in Latin America. Maize, cassava, or manioc, and potatoes, the three most important of these staples, remain essential in Latin American cooking today. They have also become central to the cuisines of many other regions of the world.

Maize was the most widely cultivated of the New World staples. Considered a miraculous food because of its yield and a sacred food because of its ceremonial significance, it became the main component of a dietary complex that included varieties of beans, squash, chiles, tomatoes, and fruits. Traditionally, maize was prepared by shucking the kernels, either by hand or by using the cob as a tool. In much of Mexico, so dependent on maize, it was then soaked or boiled in water and lime, which prepared the kernels for milling, often done with stone *metates*. More water was then added to the mixture, known as *nixtamel*, to give it the texture and consistency necessary for cooking. The result was *masa*, commonly used to make tortillas, a versatile food that has long been the basis of Mexican cuisine. Tortillas came in all shapes and sizes, determined by history and custom, and were common accompaniments to meals. Served as a bread, tortillas help to accent the classic dishes of Mexican cuisine, such as fish, meat, and poultry carefully prepared with *mole* or *adobo* sauce. When wrapped around meat, poultry, beans, or cheese, tortillas became the tacos, enchiladas, quesadillas, and burritos so commonly associated with Mexican cuisine today. Tamales, made from maize flour with salt and fat added, were more labor intensive and generally reserved for special occasions.

Mexican maize was almost as versatile when served as a liquid. *Atole* was a thin drink prepared from maize water. *Pozole* was a heartier beverage, at times served with chunks of meat or vegetables. *Pinole* was made from lightly toasted maize that was ground into a flour and then mixed with water. Maize also achieved a culinary complexity in other areas of Latin America. In the Andes, people ate *macha,* roasted maize flour; *cancu,* special loaves of maize bread; *humitas,* similar to Mexican tamales; and *mote,* a maize gruel. In Colombia and Venezuela, *arepas,* a type of roasted maize bread served plain or stuffed, were favored over tortillas. In Brazil, maize was also prepared in many different ways, from *angu,* a cornmeal gruel, to *biscoitos de milho,* maize biscuits with sugar, eggs, fat, and a pinch of salt. Variations of these dishes were common through most of Latin America.

Maize, an Indian food associated with Indian agricultural and cultural practices, was often maligned by the Europeans for its bland taste and indigestibility, yet it was widely used. In the late sixteenth century, the popular writer Garcilaso De La Vega noted that "with maize flour the Spaniards make little biscuits, fritters, and other dainties for invalids and the healthy. As a remedy in all sorts of treatment, experienced doctors have rejected wheat flour in favor of maize flour."

Cassava, called *yuca* in much of the Caribbean and *mandioca* (manioc) in Brazil, was a staple for many lowland peoples. It was similar to maize in that it required processing before eating. The most popular cassava contained hydrocyanic acid, removed by peeling and grating the root, then pressing out the poisonous juices. Gratings were then toasted and used for gruels and bread. *Pan de casabe* was described by some Europeans as "very

white and savourie," but most Spaniards thought it tasteless and difficult to digest. In Brazil, *mandioca* achieved a special importance in the sixteenth-century diet as planters and explorers relied on it to provide cheap sustenance to Portuguese colonists, African slaves, and Indians. Bureaucrats encouraged its production, recognizing its centrality to Portuguese control over Brazil. However, manioc was a staple food in Africa and many slaves brought their cultivation of this root with them. In its most common form, it was a dried and toasted flour, known as *farinha* or *farofa,* eaten by rich and poor, though occasionally it emerged as *beijús,* tasty fritters for special occasions. Different types of *farinha,* used as thickeners, eaten as side dishes, or elaborately prepared with many different ingredients, are widely consumed in Brazil today.

Potatoes were the most localized of the three great staples. Found in the highlands of the central Andes, potatoes were a basic food source for the growing population of the Andean region. Variant soils, climatic conditions, and human experimentation had created a multitude of shapes, sizes, and colors of potatoes. Usually eaten boiled or in soups, potatoes were also frozen and dried to make *chuños.* Reverence for the potato is still seen in *papas a la huacaina,* a sturdy dish of potatoes (preferably those with yellow flesh), cheese, cream, peppers, and eggs.

Dozens of foods complemented the basic staples, some of them so widely consumed that during different times and places they almost achieved the status of staples. Grains, tubers, fruits, and vegetables such as quinoa, Amaranth, chia, oca, ulluco, jicama, sweet potatoes, beans (kidney, tepary, lima, black, navy, wax, and others) pumpkins, chayotes, squash, peppers, tomatoes, avocados, pineapples, papayas, sapotes, soursops, guavas, and much more came in such abundance that early writers frequently talked about the profusion of food.

Beans deserve special mention, since they, along with grains and tubers, figured prominently in the cuisine, offering a solid basis for many dishes. Their importance in the diet continues today, and several of the traditional dishes of Latin America are based on beans. Frijoles, served in innumerable ways in Mexico but commonly mashed and mixed with fat, salt, and chilies, accompany many dishes. The Brazilian *feijão* can be cooked with coconut milk and vegetables, or served as the classic *feijoada completa*, a combination of beans and meats.

Meat was not absent from the diet of pre-Columbian peoples. The llama served the multiple purposes of transportation, wool, leather, fuel, and food. Llama meat was often eaten as charqui, a type of jerky. In this sense, the llama was as important to highland Andean peoples as the camel was to nomads of the Arabian desert. The alpaca, better known for its fine wool, was also a source of meat. The *cui*, or small cavy, also known as *muca-muca* and *chucha*, was kept as a source of meat by households. Mesoamerican peoples did not have domesticated animals similar to the llama and *cui*, but they did keep ducks, turkeys, and dogs for the table. They were also hunters, and the iguana, peccary, tapir, coati, armadillo, rabbit, and deer, along with birds, fowl, and fish supplemented the diet. As Europeans were quick to point out, Indians also ate snakes, rats, lizards, insects, larvae, and lake scum—in other words, they effectively used their environment to enrich their diets and add diversity to their cuisines.

Foods introduced after 1492 altered the cuisines of the New World. The key European staples of wheat and rice challenged, and in some cases replaced, staples indigenous to the region. Introduced very early, wheat was the preferred food of Spaniards and Portuguese, who planted the crop wherever possible and relied on imported flour and hardtack when wheat could not be grown. Soon, the bakeries of cities produced several types of bread, some carefully refined and white, others dark and coarse with much of the bran remaining.

Rice also became important in local diets, often as a result of temporary shortages of more traditional foodstuffs. In the nineteenth and twentieth centuries, as larger populations sought new staples and as techniques for rice growing improved, Latin Americans ate more of it. Immigration affected the importance and method of consumption of rice. The arrival of large numbers of East Indian, Indonesian, Chinese, and Japanese immigrants led to increased consumption. While rice was prepared in many ways, a method common to many regions was to sauté the grains, often with a little onion, then cover with water and simmer. Examples of specialized techniques include *morisqueta* in Mexico, where rice is ground into a powder before

cooking. Rice flour is also the basis for specialty drinks with sugar, honey, cinnamon, and other ingredients added.

The cultural and regional interplay of food staples in Latin America has not yet been sufficiently studied. There is a disagreement among scholars about the ease with which European settlers adapted to a manioc-based cuisine in Brazil, thus reducing their reliance on imported foods. There are differing estimations of the importance of barley and wheat in the diet in regions with large Indian populations. In Cuba, at least according to Alexander von Humboldt, Old World grains had "become articles of absolute necessity" for some by about 1800, displacing the traditional staples of maize, cassava, and bananas. Whereas some traditional foods fell out of favor, others increased in importance. Bananas (and plantains), introduced only in the sixteenth century, spread quickly through tropical and subtropical Latin America; eaten raw, boiled, fried, or dried, they were versatile, nutritious, and economical additions to the cuisine.

Meat was so abundant in the sixteenth century that it became a staple for many. Meat was usually prepared in one of the four ways common in fifteenth-century Spain: *asado* (roasted), *cozida* (stewed), *frita* (fried), and *empanada* (baked, at times breaded). Today, the classic meat dishes in the cuisine are roasted, often over an open fire. Examples range from the almost dainty Peruvian *anticuchos*, succulent beef hearts marinated and then grilled, to the spectacular Argentine *asado* and Brazilian *churrasco*, different cuts of meat cooked slowly over open fires. This type of cooking is far more popular than the old methods of *barbacoa* in Mexico or *pachamanca* in Peru, where food is placed over heated rock, then sealed with earth for slow baking, similar to the New England clambake. A fifth method of preparation was dehydrating and salting, already in use before 1492. With the abundance of meat and the development of long-distance trade in meat, preservation techniques became more elaborate. The cattle regions of plains and pampas produced charqui, *cecina, tasajo, carne seca, carne-do-sol* and other types of dried, salted, and smoked meat.

In the cattle regions, beef was the mainstay of the cuisine, eaten three times a day. When meat was not available, animal fats generally were. Foods

Grilling meats on a ranch in Argentina. Asado, a selection of meats grilled over a charcoal fire, is popular throughout Argentina; beef in particular is a mainstay of the Argentine diet. © OWEN FRANKEN/CORBIS

previously only boiled or roasted could now be fried, and indulgence in fried, fatty foods became commonplace by the eighteenth century. The abundance of animal fat quickly reduced the dependence on olive oil, reducing it to a secondary role in cooking by the end of the sixteenth century.

The emerging cuisines of Latin America depended on a combination of flavors, some pronounced, others subtle. Chilies assumed prominence in the colonial cuisines of Mexico, Peru, and Brazil, much more so than vanilla or any other indigenous flavoring. In addition, black pepper, citrus, ginger, anise, cinnamon, nutmeg, and more regionally specialized flavorings such as *azeite de dende,* characteristic of Bahian cooking, and cilantro (Chinese parsley), so widely used in Mexican food, became characteristic of Latin American cuisine. In this way, American, African, European, and later Asian foods and cooking techniques mixed to form the Creole cuisines of Latin America.

Sugar, though lacking in nutritional value, was essential as a sweetener for chocolate, coffee, and tea, and as the principal ingredient of many diverse and creative foods. Sugar combined with all types of fruits and nuts yielded spectacular results. Cookbooks list innumerable recipes for *dulces* in Spanish America and *doces* in Brazil. Milk and eggs, other new ingredients in the cuisine, also became popular for desserts, especially flan, the caramelized custard common to Latin America. Chocolate, Latin America's gift to the desserts of much of the world, was consumed primarily as a beverage during its early history. In the nineteenth century its popularity increased as it took the form of modern milk chocolate. While still important as a beverage and dessert in Latin America, chocolate consumption there pales in comparison with that of many other regions of the world.

The encounter between different cultures established the basis for the cuisines of Latin America. Foods and methods of preparation that would endure into the twentieth century had already taken root by the end of the sixteenth century. Later external influences, especially those of France in the nineteenth century, affected cuisines but did not alter the basic foods and cooking techniques. The post–World War II global trends of commercialization, mass production, and food substitutes may ultimately change the cuisines of Latin America more profoundly than any other influences since the encounter.

See also **Alcoholic Beverages; Asado; Churrasco; Fruit Industry; Meat Industry; Nutrition; Sugar Industry.**

BIBLIOGRAPHY

Eugenio Pereira Salas, *Apuntes para la historia de la cocina chilena* (1977).

Amando Farga, *Historia de la comida en México* (1980).

Luís De Câmara Cascudo, *História da alimentaçao no Brasil,* 2 vols. (1983), offers good introductions to the history of food in individual countries. For specific foods, see Nelson Foster and Linda S. Cordell, *Chilies to Chocolate: Food the Americas Gave the World* (1992). Two good examples of the historical interpretation of individual foods are Gilberto Freyre, *Açúcar: Em tôrno da etnografia, da história, e da sociologia do doce no Nordeste canaviero do Brasil* (1969), and Alfredo Castillero Calvo, *El café en Panamá: Una historia social y económica* (1985). Early cookbooks, such as Simón Blanquel, *Novísimo arte de cocina* (1831), and Mariano Rivera Galván, *El cocinero mejicano,* 3 vols. (1831), are particularly valuable sources. For cookbooks in English, see Jonathan Norton Leonard, *Latin American Cooking* (1968), Elisabeth Lambert Ortiz, *The Complete Book of Mexican Cooking* (1967), and Mary Urrutia Randelman and Joan Schwartz, *Memories of a Cuban Kitchen* (1992), which offer interesting cultural and historical insights.

Additional Bibliography

Belasco, Warren James and Philip Scranton. *Food Nations: Selling Taste in Consumer Societies.* New York: Routledge, 2002.

Cascudo, Luís da Câmara. *A cozinha africana no Brasil.* Luanda: Publicações do Museu de Angola, 1964.

Houston, Lynn Marie. *Food Culture in the Caribbean.* Westport, CT: Greenwood Press, 2005.

Lima, Claudia. *Tachos e panelas: Historiografia da alimentação brasileira.* 2nd edition. Recife: Editora Comunicarte, 1999.

Lody, Raul Giovanni da Motta. *Santo também come.* Rio de Janeiro: Pallas, 1998.

Mintz, Sidney W. *Tasting Food, Tasting Freedom: Excursions into Eating, Culture, and the Past.* Boston: Beacon Press, 1996.

Morales, Edmundo. *The Guinea Pig: Healing, Food, and Ritual in the Andes.* Tucson: University of Arizona Press, 1995.

Pilcher, Jeffrey. *¡Que Vivan Los Tamales! Mexican Cuisine and National Identity.* Albuquerque: University of New Mexico Press, 1998.

Querino, Manuel. *A arte culinaria na Bahia.* Salvador: Progresso, 1951.

Schávelzon, Daniel. *Historias del comer y del beber en Buenos Aires: Arqueología histórica de la vajilla de mesa.* Buenos Aires: Aguilar Argentina, 2000.

Weismantel, Mary. J. *Food, Gender, and Poverty in the Ecuadorian Andes.* Philadelphia: University of Pennsylvania Press, 1989.

Wilk, Richard R. *Home Cooking in the Global Village: Caribbean Food from Buccaneers to Ecotourists.* New York: Berg, 2006.

JOHN C. SUPER

CUITLAHUAC   (1467–1520). Cuitlahuac (*b.* before 1467; *d.* 1520), Aztec ruler, son of Axayacatl and older brother of Motecuhzoma II. Cuitlahuac governed the disintegrating Aztec Empire for a brief period during the Spanish invasion. Ruler of the town of Iztapalapa and one of his brother's chief advisers, Cuitlahuac was already a seasoned warrior and statesman when the Spaniards entered Mexico. According to native histories, he advised Motecuhzoma against allowing Hernán Cortés and his army to enter Tenochtitlán, the Aztec capital. When Cortés occupied the city, he imprisoned Cuitlahuac along with Motecuhzoma. After the Aztecs turned against the invaders and laid siege to their headquarters, Cuitlahuac gained release on the pretense that he would reopen the market to allow food to reach the invaders.

Following Motecuhzoma's death and the flight of the Spaniards and their allies from the city on the night of 30 June—1 July 1520, Cuitlahuac was elected to succeed his brother (according to some accounts he assumed this role even before Motecuhzoma's demise). His leadership of the resistance to the ensuing Spanish-led siege was short-lived. Within a few months of his accession, he died. His death is frequently attributed to smallpox, the first of many Old World infectious diseases to strike

Mexico's native population, but the early sources do not state this explicitly. He was succeeded by his young nephew Cuauhtemoc.

See also **Mesoamerica; Motecuhzoma II.**

BIBLIOGRAPHY

Burr Cartwright Brundage, *A Rain of Darts: The Mexica Aztecs* (1972).

Fernando De Alva Ixtlilxochitl, *Obras históricas,* 3d ed. (1975).

Miguel León-Portilla, *The Broken Spears* (1992).

Additional Bibliography

Aguilar Moreno, Manuel. *Handbook to Life in the Aztec World.* New York: Facts on File, 2006.

Berdan, Frances. *The Aztecs of Central Mexico: An Imperial Society.* Belmont, CA: Thomas Wadsworth, 2005.

Hernández Chávez, Alicia. *Mexico: A Brief History.* Berkeley: University of California Press, 2006.

Townsend, Camila. *Malintzin's Choices: An Indian Woman in the Conquest of Mexico.* Albuquerque: University of New Mexico Press, 2006.

LOUISE M. BURKHART

CUMANÁ. Cumaná, the first permanent European-built settlement in Latin America. It was founded on the site of a Franciscan monastery on the northeastern Venezuelan coast in 1520. The pearl beds of Margarita and Cubagua for a short period in the early sixteenth century sustained the small colony and Spanish commercial interests. The German banking house of Welser obtained a grant from the Spanish crown to explore the region and used Cumaná as one of its bases of operation. The only other commercial interest in the region during this period was slave raiding, which predictably resulted in a high level of Indian hostility from the early sixteenth century into the seventeenth century.

The region was characterized by a high level of strife, not just between Spaniards and Indians, but between Spaniards themselves. Jurisdictional disputes arose frequently between rival conquistadores as royal territorial authorizations often overlapped. By the end of the 1500s, Spanish control of the region had been established. Religious missions were created by the

Franciscans in the early seventeenth century and the Capuchins in 1650. Cumaná was an important port that was economically associated with the Caribbean colonies. It also was one of the major links in the Caribbean defense network. The colony was governed by a captain-general from 1650 to 1830. Although economically focused on the Caribbean, it was Lima's central treasury that provided annual subsidies for the settlement. In the 1700s the Cumaná area supported a hide and cattle industry. Due to its coastal location and the nature of Spanish expansion, Cumaná's economic, political, and religious activities were directed toward the Caribbean rather than Caracas.

Today, Cumaná is the capital of the province of Sucre and functions as a minor seaport. Its economic and strategic importance declined, and its major commercial activities now center around resort hotels and sport fishing on the coast. The estimated population in 2003 was 257,783 inhabitants.

See also **Colonialism; Indigenous Peoples.**

BIBLIOGRAPHY

Raymond E. Crist and Edward P. Leahy, *Venezuela: Search for a Middle Ground* (1969).

John V. Lombardi, *Venezuela: The Search for Order, the Dream of Progress* (1982).

Additional Bibliography

Castillo Hidalgo, Ricardo Ignacio. *Asentamiento español y articulación interétnica en Cumaná (1560–1620).* Caracas: Academia Nacional de la Historia, 2005.

Hollis, Micheal, Denova Tarver, and Julia C. Frederick. *The History of Venezuela.* Westport, CT: Greenwood Press, 2005.

Laserna Gaitán, Antonio Ignacio. *Tierra, gobierno local, y actividad misionera en la comunidad indigena del Oriente venezolano: La visita a la provincia de Cumana de don Luis de Chavez y Mendoza (1783–1784).* Caracas: Academia Nacional de la Historia, 1993.

HEATHER K. THIESSEN

CUMBIA. Cumbia, a form of Latin American popular music originating on the Caribbean coast of Colombia. The name was originally applied to a traditional dance of the region as well as to the music of the dance and the musicians who play it.

Perhaps derived from the Spanish fandango, the dance is performed by couples who form a circle around the seated musicians. Carrying lighted candles in their right hands, the women dance with shuffling steps while the men perform zigzagging steps around them. The partners pass each other back to back but rarely touch. A similar folk dance is performed in Panama.

Music for the *cumbia* was once purely instrumental, but lyrics were later introduced. The music is played by either of two ensembles. In one, the *caña de millo,* an open pipe with a single reed, is the melodic instrument; in the other, the *gaita hembra,* a vertical-duct flute, provides the melody. All other members of the ensembles play percussion instruments. Starting in the 1930s, the *cumbia* began to gain popularity in the interior of Colombia, and by the 1960s commercialized versions had spread to Peru, Mexico, and other Latin American countries.

See also **Music: Popular Music and Dance.**

BIBLIOGRAPHY

George List, *Music and Poetry in a Colombian Village: A Tri-Cultural Heritage* (1983).

Thomas Turino, "Somos el Perú: 'Cumbia Andina' and the Children of Andean Migrants in Lima," *Studies in Latin American Popular Culture* 9 (1990): 15–37.

Additional Bibliography

Pombo Hernández, Gerardo. *Kumbia, legado cultural de los indígenas del Caribe colombiano.* Barranquilla, Colombia: Editorial Antillas, 1995.

Wade, Peter. *Music, Race & Nation: Música Tropical in Colombia.* Chicago: University of Chicago Press, 2000.

HELEN DELPAR

CUMPLIDO, IGNACIO (1811–1887). Ignacio Cumplido (*b.* 20 May 1811; *d.* 30 November 1887), Mexican publisher. Born in Guadalajara, Cumplido, the son of a doctor and medical school professor, grew up in Mexico City. While an employee at the National Museum, he began publishing newspapers. In 1829 he became the manager of the shop that printed *El Correo de la Federación,* soon followed by *El Fénix de la Libertad.* In 1838 he went to the United States to buy the equipment necessary for a first-class printing establishment, but he lost everything when the French blockaded the port of Veracruz. Nevertheless, he continued to publish the most celebrated authors of the day in *El Museo Mexicano, La Ilustración Mexicana,* and other periodicals. Although associated with liberal politics, Cumplido was imprisoned in 1840 for printing José María Gutiérrez Estrada's pamphlet advocating monarchy. Soon after he was named superintendent of prisons.

Cumplido is best known for founding *El Siglo XIX* on 8 October 1841; it became the foremost daily newspaper of nineteenth-century Mexico City and was published almost continuously through 1896. The list of its editors forms a who's who of Mexican intellectual life of the time and includes Guillermo Prieto, Manuel Payno, Ignacio Ramírez, Francisco Zarco, Francisco Sosa, and Francisco Bulnes. In 1842 he was elected to Congress first as deputy and then as senator, always giving his salary to charity. He founded a lithography school for orphans in his home. In 1847, during the war with the United States, Cumplido volunteered as head of a battalion of national guard and was subsequently promoted to captain.

In 1848 Cumplido went to Europe and purchased steam-powered presses. Following the French Intervention, Cumplido became a member of the 1873 Ayuntamiento of Mexico City in charge of boulevards. It was his idea to plant trees on both sides of the Paseo de la Reforma in emulation of the Champs-Élysées.

See also **Journalism in Mexico.**

BIBLIOGRAPHY

Ramiro Villaseñor y Villaseñor, *Ignacio Cumplido: Impresor y editor jalisciense del federalismo en México* (1974).

Additional Bibliography

Lombardo García, Irma. *El siglo de Cumplido: La emergencia del periodismo mexicano de opinión, 1832–1857.* Mexico City: Universidad Nacional Autónoma de México, 2002.

Villaseñor y Villaseñor, Ramiro. *Ignacio Cumplido, impresor tapatío.* Guadalajara: Gobierno de Jalisco, Secretaría General, Unidad Editorial, 1987.

BARBARA A. TENENBAUM

CUNA. *See* **Kuna (Cuna).**

CUNDINAMARCA.

Cundinamarca, a department in central Colombia, comprises an area of 9,300 square miles. While Bogotá serves as both the departmental and national capital, the Constitution of 1991 reorganized Bogotá and its metropolitan area into the politically autonomous Distrito Capital. Excluding Bogotá, Cundinamarca has 1.7 million inhabitants. Approximately 7 million reside within the capital.

Located between the Magdalena River valley and the eastern plains region, Cundinamarca varies in climate and terrain. The population is concentrated in high intermontane basins, the most important of which is the *sabana* (savanna) of Bogotá. Cundinamarca was a major center of Chibcha civilization, and Lake Guatavita, the site of the Chibcha ceremony believed to have inspired the El Dorado legend, is located here.

Cundinamarca's varied topography has encouraged agricultural diversification. During the mid-nineteenth century, tobacco and indigo grown in lowland areas near the Magdalena were important commercial crops. Cundinamarca also became a major coffee producer after 1870. In the coffee-growing areas of western Cundinamarca, such as Sumapaz, there was much agrarian unrest during the 1920s and 1930s and later much communist and guerrilla activity. In the early twenty-first century, Cundinamarca is one of the world's largest producers of cut flowers.

See also **El Dorado.**

BIBLIOGRAPHY

Bogotá: Portal Oficial del Distrito Capital. Available from http://www.bogota.gov.co.

DANE: Departamento Administrativo Nacional de Estadística. Available from http://www.dane.gov.co.

Gobernación de Cundinamarca. Available from http://www.cundinamarca.gov.co.

Jiménez, Michael F. "Traveling Far in Grandfather's Car: The Life Cycle of Central Colombian Coffee Estates. The Case of Viotá, Cundinamarca (1900–30)." *Hispanic American Historical Review* 69 (1989):185–219.

HELEN DELPAR
DOUGLAS SOFER

CÚNEO PERINETTI, JOSÉ (1887–1977).

José Cúneo Perinetti (b. 11 September 1887; d. 19 July 1977), Uruguayan artist. Cúneo Perinetti studied at the Circle of Fine Arts in his native Montevideo; in Turin, Italy, with Leonardo Bistolfi and Anton Mucchi (1907–1909); and in Paris at the Académie Vity with the Spanish painter Hermenegildo Anglada Camarasa (1911). Early in his career, he painted naturalist gardens under the belated influence of the Italian Macchiaioli and the contemporary Spanish painter Santiago Rusiñol. Back in Uruguay, he painted landscapes in Treinta Tres Orientales. In 1917 he returned to Paris to study with Kees van Dongen. Upon his return to Uruguay, he began painting geometrical landscapes, including Uruguayan rural huts (*ranchos*) and Spanish colonial sites in the town of Maldonado, and portraits involving pure, extended areas of color. In the 1930s he started the series of his so-called moon landscapes, for which he is best known (*The Moon Over the Ranch*, 1934).

Cúneo Perinetti's work from this period is characterized by a low palette, thick pigment, and compositions based on diagonals and dynamic lines. Swirling strokes give the impression of dragging everything—trees, dwellings, earth—into a vortex. These turbulent paintings reveal the influence of Vincent van Gogh and Chaim Soutine. Oversized moons give his expressionistic landscapes a cosmic quality. He won gold medals at the National Salon in Uruguay in 1941, 1942, and 1949. In the late 1940s he turned once more to naturalist landscapes. Despite his long career he had little influence on subsequent Uruguayan artists.

See also **Art: The Twentieth Century.**

BIBLIOGRAPHY

José Pedro Argul, *El pintor José Cúneo: Paisajista del Uruguay* (1949).

Raquel Pereda, *José Cúneo: Retrato de un artista* (1988).

Additional Bibliography

Cardis-Toulouse, Regine. "Jose Cuneo Perinetti 1887-1977, un peintre uruguayen monographie et catalogue de l'oeuvre." Ph.D. diss., Univeristé de Toulouse-Le Mirail, 1998.

MARTA GARSD

CUNHA, EUCLIDES DA (1866–1909).

Euclides da Cunha (b. 20 January 1866; d. 15 August 1909), Brazilian writer. Cunha began his career in 1888 as a journalist for the prestigious *A Província de São Paulo* after interrupting his studies at the Military Academy of Rio de Janeiro and resuming his military education at the Escola Superior de Guerra (Superior School of War) from which he would graduate in 1892 with an engineering degree. His fame as a writer began with the publication of his first articles, both titled "A nossa Vendéia" (Our Vendée), suggesting a comparison between the French Revolution of 1793–1796 and its Brazilian counterpart, the messianic movement of 1874–1897 headed by Antônio Conselheiro (Anthony the Counselor) in the northeastern backlands (*canudos*). Positive responses from readers and his own fascination with the subject prompted his newspaper to assign Cunha to cover the battles between the republican army and Antônio Conselheiro's followers. By the time he arrived at the war zone, the latter had crushed three military expeditions sent by local and federal governments. Thousands of republican soldiers had died and, baffled by the turn of events, government officials began to seek a plausible explanation for the series of defeats that had led the young and already fragile Brazilian republic into chaos and confusion.

During some thirty days spent in the battlefield, Cunha experienced scenes so tragic and horrifying that he was compelled to reevaluate his own view of the conflict. For Cunha, a confessed republican who had also been an ardent militant, it did not take long to realize that Canudos was not simply a clash involving primitive peasants and "civilized" men, but a brutal civil war.

Once home from the battlefield, Cunha began to write his most acclaimed book, *Os sertões* (*Rebellion in the Backlands*), a powerful account of the war at Canudos. In it he strives to show that a misunderstanding and a breakdown in communications were responsible for the war between the two groups. The republicans thought of Antônio Conselheiro's movement as a means to restore the monarchy with the help of the British crown. The poverty-stricken members of his flock believed, on the other hand, that they were fighting the forces of evil, Freemasonry, and heresy.

It may well be that no other Brazilian journalist before or since Cunha has acquired such a deep understanding of Brazil's tremendous social problems. His ambition in writing *Rebellion* was not only to analyze the war but also to provide an account of the formation of the national identity of Brazil. Thus, the book delves into geology, geography, sociology, anthropology, military and social history, literature, and philosophy. Cunha's language is precise, metaphorical, and, above all, oxymoronic. He takes liberties with the use of technical terminology to render clear, precise descriptions of the complex geography of Canudos.

Despite the reliable voice of the narrator at the beginning of *Rebellion*, when Cunha presents himself as an unbiased historian, the book is not a completely objective historical account of the war. A divergence between its literary achievements and its scientific accuracy is noticeable. In his quest for truth Cunha did some intriguing speculating and arguing, especially since he knew little of geology and botany and had never seen Canudos before the last thirty-five days of the war. While many are inclined to ascribe the difficulties in Cunha's book to his peculiar language, undoubtedly some of his theories, for example, on what he called "physical determinism" (the influence of the backlands upon the individual) and on genetic anthropology (degeneration of the white race through miscegenation), today sound arcane and obsolete, though expressed with vigor and intelligence. On the other hand, his sociological theory of cultural isolation is still viable.

Soon after its publication in 1902, *Rebellion* was enthusiastically received by critics and became a best-seller in Brazil. The success of the book guaranteed Cunha membership in the Brazilian Academy of Letters, which he joined in 1903. Following literary fame came opportunities to work with the Brazilian government. In 1906, after returning from an official trip to the Amazon, where he chaired a committee to survey the borders of northwestern Brazil, Cunha began to write a report that became his next most important book, *Contrastes e confrontos* (Contrasts and Comparisons), issued in 1907. Cunha spent the last two years of his life working on his third book, *À margem da história* (On the Margin of History), posthumously published in 1909. In this collection of essays he demonstrates his maturity as a writer and thinker, and replicates the artistic qualities of his masterpiece.

See also **Journalism; Literature: Brazil.**

BIBLIOGRAPHY

Samuel Putnam, " 'Brazil's Greatest Book': A Translator Introduction," in *Rebellion in the Backlands* (1945).

Olímpio De Souza Andrade, *História e interpretação de "Os sertões"* (1960).

Frederick C. H. Garcia, "Duas apresentaçoes de Euclides da Cunha," in *Luso-Brazilian Review* 7, no. 1 (1970): 23–34.

Walnice Nogueira Galvão, ed., "Euclides, elite modernizadora e enquadramento," in *Euclides da Cunha* (1984).

Luiz Costa Lima, "Nos sertões da oculta mimesis," in his *O controle do imaginário* (1984).

Leopoldo M. Bernucci, *História de un malentendido* (1989), esp. pp. 189–218.

Additional Bibliography

Brandão, Adelino. *Euclides da Cunha e a questão racial no Brasil: A antropologia de "Os sertões."* Rio de Janeiro: Presença, 1990.

Gomes, Gínia Maria. *Euclides da Cunha: Literatura e história.* Porto Alegre: Editora da UFRGS, 2005.

Levine, Robert M. *Vale of Tears: Revisiting the Canudos Massacre in Northeastern Brazil, 1893–1897.* Berkeley: University of California Press, 1992.

Lima, Luiz Costa. *Terra ignota: A construção de Os sertões.* Rio de Janeiro: Civilização Brasileira, 1997.

Ventura, Roberto, Mario Cesar Carvalho and José Carlos Barreto de Santana. *Retrato interrompido da vida de Euclides da Cunha.* São Paulo: Companhia das Letras, 2003.

LEOPOLDO M. BERNUCCI

CUNHA DOTTI, JUAN (1910–1985). Juan Cunha Dotti (*b.* 1910; *d.* 1985), Uruguayan poet. Born in Sauce de Illescas, Cunha left for Montevideo when he reached eighteen; his first book of poetry was published a year later. That volume, *El pájaro que vino de la noche* (1929), established his enduring fame through hermetic yet colloquial images that communicated well the nostalgia of the time for a less complicated and anguished existence. Other collections of poems—Cunha published twenty-six during his lifetime—demonstrated his agile versification skills in sonnets as well as free verse, in popular songs as well as difficult, esoteric verses. His poetry always registered subtle mutations of taste and concern with urgent social issues. During the 1940s he published little. Cunha's mature expression after 1951, in works such as *A eso de la tarde* (1961) and *Pastor perdido* (1966), communicates the poet's resentful solitude amid the silent streets and locked front doors of Uruguay's capital city. Additional works by Cunha include *Sueño y retorno de un campesino* (1951); *Hombre entre luz y sombra* (1955); and *Carpeta de mi gestión terrestre* (1960).

See also **Literature: Spanish America.**

BIBLIOGRAPHY

Franscico Aguilera and Georgette Magassy Dorn, *The Archive of Hispanic Literature on Tape: A Descriptive Guide* (1974).

Additional Bibliography

Bianchi, Matilde. "Juan Cunha." *Foro Literario* 8 (July–December 1985): 66-67.

WILLIAM H. KATRA

CUPISNIQUE CULTURE. In 1926 the Peruvian archaeologist Rafael Larco identified a distinctive cultural pattern that characterized the north coast of Peru during much of the second and first millennia BCE. While the Cupisnique culture was once considered to be simply a coastal variant of the Chavín culture, it was later recognized as an independent cultural tradition that provided one of the sources of inspiration for the slightly later Chavín culture. Although the Cupisnique culture was originally defined on the basis of fine pottery from burials in the Cupisnique drainage and adjacent Chicama valley, late-twentieth-century research favored a broader definition. As currently understood, the Cupisnique culture extended along the Peruvian coast from the Virú valley up to the Lambayeque drainage, and it maintained close relations with adjacent highland cultures and the occupants of the coastal valleys immediately to the north and south.

The center of Cupisnique culture was the rich but arid lands of the lower coastal valleys, and its economy was based mainly on irrigation agriculture and fishing. Besides numerous shoreline fishing villages and agricultural hamlets, there were larger centers where monumental architecture was built for civil ceremonial activities. The largest known Cupisnique sites, Purulén in the Zaña drainage and

Caballo Muerto in the Moche valley, have numerous mounds suggesting a pattern of organization very different from that found on the central coast. Public constructions were built of stone or conical adobes and usually featured combinations of low tiered platforms, elaborate colonnades, massive central inset stairways, and sunken rectangular courtyards. In many cases the public architecture was decorated with painted or sculpted religious iconography featuring feline, ophidian, and avian imagery.

Much of the information on the Cupisnique culture derives from cemeteries excavated by Larco and others. People of the Cupisnique culture buried their dead in irregular oval pits dug into subsoil. The carved bone rings, shell ornaments, necklaces of semiprecious stones (including lapis lazuli from northern Chile) and shell, and high-quality anthracite mirrors that often accompanied the deceased suggest a special interest in personal adornment. Among the other items left in the tombs were pottery vessels, especially modeled or incised stirrup-spouted bottles, and, more rarely, carved bone tablets or spatulas believed to have been used to ingest hallucinogenic snuff during rituals. Among the most distinctive Cupisnique artifacts are elaborate stone mace heads, perhaps used as symbols of authority, and ceramic stamps or seals, which may have been used for skin painting or decorating cloth.

Sometime after 500 BCE the north coast became integrated into the Chavín sphere of interaction, and Cupisnique culture, while still distinctive, came to share features with cultures in central and southern Peru. When the Chavín sphere of interaction collapsed at approximately 200 BCE the Cupisnique culture was replaced by a cultural pattern known as Salinar.

See also Archaeology; Art: Pre-Columbian Art of South America; Chavín de Huántar.

BIBLIOGRAPHY

A more detailed discussion is in Richard L. Burger, *Chavín and the Origins of Andean Civilization* (1992). A summary of Rafael Larco's pioneering research is available in his essay, "A Culture Sequence for the North Coast of Peru," in *The Handbook of South American Indians,* vol. 2, edited by Julian Steward (1946). For a widely available article on the excavations at Caballo Muerto, see Thomas Pozorski, "The Early Horizon Site of Huaca de los Reyes: Societal Implications," in *American Antiquity* 45 (1980): 100–110. The Huaca Lucia investigations are described in Izumi Shimada, "The Batan Grande–La Leche Archaeological Project—The First Two Seasons," in *Journal of Field Archaeology* 8, no. 4 (1981): 405–446. One of the few detailed discussions of Cupisnique symbolism is Lucy Salazar-burger and Richard L. Burger, "La araña en la iconografía del horizonte temprano en la costa norte del Perú," in *Beiträge zur Allgemeinen und Vergleichenden Archäologie* 4 (1983): 213–253.

RICHARD L. BURGER

CURAÇAO. The Netherlands Antilles, consisting of three Leeward (Aruba, Curaçao, and Bonaire) and three Windward islands (Saint Maarten, Statia, and Saba), were before 1954 officially known as "Curaçao and its dependencies." After they acquired autonomy within the Kingdom of the Netherlands in that year, Curaçao remained the administrative center, with 50 percent of its total population. The official language is Dutch; however, most of the people speak Papiamento, a Portuguese-based Creole language familiar to the Criolo of Cabo Verde. The people on the Windward Islands speak English; the population of those islands is largely Protestant, whereas those in the Leeward Islands are predominantly Catholic with a (mostly white) Protestant minority.

Curaçao was a trade post in colonial times, slaves, sugar and salt being its principal commodities. Slavery was common to all islands, with the exception of Aruba. Curaçao had a large slave population; in 1780 there were 13,000 slaves, 70 percent of the island's population. When slavery was abolished in 1863, a third of the population of the Netherlands Antilles was officially registered as having that status. For all the Antillean islands, but especially for Curaçao, the basis of the subsequent "segmented society," with its fascination and fixation on color and race relations, was laid out. The most obvious characteristic of the Curaçaoan social structure up to the 1970s (and perhaps into the early twenty-first century) was the powerful dividing line between "white" and "colored."

After the discovery of huge oil reserves in Venezuela, Shell built a refinery on Curaçao in 1916; Standard Oil was established on Aruba. In 1958 the per capita income of the Antilleans was almost one and one-half times as much as in the motherland. But when Venezuela built its own refineries, the Antillean ones were forced to cut back and rationalize. In 1966 between 15 and 20 percent of Curaçao's workforce was unemployed. The result was a transgenerational poverty underclass of from 20 to 25 percent of the population, concentrated in from ten to fifteen squatter neighborhoods.

Curaçao sought the solution to its economic woes in offshore banking, maintaining a certain standard of prosperity until the mid-1980s, when the U.S. government restricted access to Caribbean banks and tax havens. In the 1990s the island government tried, in a lukewarm way, to promote external tourism, an endeavor that had only a limited success. The island, together with the other remaining Antillean islands, became gradually more dependent on development aid from the Netherlands, thereby accumulating huge internal debts.

The political structure of the Netherlands Antilles—with six, and later five, islands—was established in 1954 with the perspective of incorporating Indonesia with the Antilles into a kind of commonwealth, with dual levels of "national (i.e., Antillean)" and "island" governments with overlapping powers and conflicting loyalties. In 1986 Aruba left the political structure of the Netherlands Antilles, considering Curaçao as a kind of colonizer. Aruba received a *status aparte* as the third "country" within the Netherlands, the Netherlands Antilles, and Aruba]. Political splits between the island governments and between the islands and the central Antillean government in Curaçao produced and produces ill-feeling towards what was called the "colonization by Curaçao." After several efforts at restructuring the complicated political relation between the European and the Caribbean parts of the kingdom, the Dutch in 2006 succeeded in convincing the government of the Antilles to dissolve the political structure of Antillean "country." The Dutch offered in return a privileged status of municipality in the case of Bonaire, Saba, and Statia and a *status aparte* like Aruba's for Curaçao and Saint Maarten. If the island populations would agree, the Dutch would exonerate the Antillean internal debt of around € 3 billion (US\$ 4.2 billion) in exchange for remission of the internal debt. The island government of Curaçao initially refused to agree and announced a renegotiation of the internal debt. After elections in mid-2007, however, Curaçao's island government also agreed with the new *status aparte*.

See also **Aruba; Leeward Islands; Suriname and the Dutch in the Caribbean; Windward Islands.**

BIBLIOGRAPHY

Oostindie, Gert. *Paradise Overseas; the Dutch Caribbean: Colonialism and Its Transatlantic Legacies.* Oxford: Macmillan, 2005.

Jong, Lammert de, and Dirk Kruijt, eds. *Extended Statehood in the Caribbean: Paradoxes of Quasicolonialism, Local Autonomy and Extended Statehood in the USA, French, Dutch and British Caribbean.* Amsterdam: Rozenberg Publishers, 2006.

DIRK KRUIJT

CURANDERO/CURANDEIRO.

A *Curandero/Curandeiro* is a folk healer. Terms such as *botánico, curioso,* or *empírico* are local variations. Folk healing is found in practically all Latin American cultures and can be traced back to the Iberian peninsula. Although its practice varies widely, the two major styles are American Indian and urban. The typical American Indian *curandero* is a shaman, often a respected community member, who bases his or her work on native beliefs, such as the idea that the soul can wander and be captured or that magical objects can be shot into the body. In addition to shamans, there are native specialists who prescribe herbal medicines, or set broken bones, or massage the body. Generally speaking, both styles offer healing for physical as well as spiritual ailments. The typical Indian *curandero,* whose work may seem exotic to non-Indians, follows a cultural pattern that is more orthodox than the eclectic, personal styles of most urban *curanderos.*

In the cities and towns of Latin America, religious ideas from all over the world have mingled to create a wide variety of urban folk-healing practices. The typical urban *curandero* is a healer who claims religious power and who uses techniques derived from different sources. Almost any religion or healing theory can be the basis for the urban *curandero*'s practice. Naturopathy, spiritism, spiritualism, Catholicism, Buddhism, African-American religions, homeopathy, and indigenous traditions all have had roles in Latin American urban *curanderismo.* The synthesis of practices and beliefs is the rule rather than the exception. In spite of the variety, a specific region may be known for a particular type of *curanderismo*. For example, some cities in Brazil (Belém, São Paulo, Rio de Janeiro, Pôrto Alegre) abound in *Umbandista* curing; Salvador da Bahia is known for *Candomblé* remedies; *Iquitos*, on the Peruvian Amazon, is known for healers who give their patients a hallucinogenic drug made from the *Banisteriopsis* vine; and healers on the north Peruvian coast conduct ceremonies in which the participants drink a potion derived from the San Pedro cactus.

The old Native American Indian traditions of folk healing were effective both psychologically and physiologically and have continued into the present. The high civilizations of the Andes and Mexico developed healing arts based on magic and medicinal knowledge. The Aztecs of central Mexico had both shamans and herbalists. Aztec herbal medicines were effective in correcting what was believed to be the cause of a disease. For example, if the healers felt that excess urine caused an illness, they prescribed an effective herbal diuretic. They used bleedings, baths, purges, dressings, plasters, and the extracts of plants, as well as magic. Aztec medicinal knowledge compared well with that of then-contemporary Europe. In Peru, Inca folk medicine men were low-level priests who divined the causes of illness and then provided cures. The ancient Peruvians developed extensive pharmacological knowledge. Skeletal remains and pottery drawings reveal that the ancient Peruvians also were excellent surgeons. The people from the Paracas region of Peru performed a prodigious number of successful skull trepanations probably to relieve pressure on the brain due to war club injuries.

Yet despite the long-standing popularity of folk remedies among Spanish and non-Spanish alike in both the cities and countrysides of Latin America, *curanderos* faced great scrutiny and even prohibition. *Curanderas* in Mexico City during the colonial era were denounced as witches in Inquisition trials. In Andean Peru, Catholic Church authorities led campaigns to rid the populace of ritual objects and materials used in healing. Still, the acceptance of some fluidity between magic, medicine, religion, witchcraft, and spirituality continued to be potent into the early twenty-first century.

In the early twenty-first century, Indian shamans are ritual specialists who claim to know about unseen, supernatural worlds. Male shamans are more numerous in Indian communities, but the office is open to women as well. Shamans may speak of a supernatural experience that has brought them the power to cure. They learn their profession from other shamans, and they may undergo a period of formal training, such as that given by the Ixil Maya shamans of Guatemala. In the regions where ancient civilizations once flourished, the profession of shaman may include such nonhealing services as priestly officiating. There is a tendency for shamans to deal more and more with the psychological components of illnesses as modern medicine becomes more successful in dealing with physical infections. Modern shamans often divide illness into a sorcery-caused type, which they will treat, and a natural type, which modern medicine and doctors treat.

Shamanic healing rituals have significant psychological effects. A belief in the shaman's magical power over animistic life forces supports the psychological component of shamanic work. Such a belief can be extended to include the power to harm or kill. Shamans often struggle on mythical battle lines between the good use of their power, curing, and the bad use of it, sorcery. In their rituals they combat the sorcery caused by the enemies of the patient. Sometimes they become involved in counter-sorcery aggressions themselves. However, many shamans prefer to be called *curanderos* (healers) to highlight the positive, healing function of their work. They prefer not to be called *brujos* (sorcerers).

In many parts of Latin America, Indian shamans take hallucinogenic drugs to induce visions. Various plants, such as *Banisteriopsis*, *Virola theiodora*, *Nicotiana tabacum* (tobacco), and *Datura*, aid the shaman in seeing into the supernatural world. The drugs are seldom given to patients; they are used primarily by shamans to arrive at the correct diagnosis of a disease or the solution of a personal problem.

The early European medical traditions introduced into Latin America also were effective models of disease and healing. Humoral theories introduced by the Moors influenced Iberian medical concepts of the sixteenth century. These concepts entered Latin America with the missionaries, who founded hospitals and ministered to the Indians. Once the accepted knowledge of educated people, these traditions became the lore of the people of Latin America. Popular *recetarios* (home-care manuals) published in the sixteenth and seventeenth centuries contained medical information for home use and explained illness in humorial terms. The humorial qualities of wet and dry became less significant, and the qualities of hot and cold came to dominate Latin American folk medicine. Many of today's folk-healing systems seek to maintain a balance between hot and cold essences in the body, particularly in reference to what is eaten. In Guatemala, for example, peaches, chocolate, and honey are thought to be "hot," while tomatoes, squash, and carrots are "cold." People are careful not to eat too much of one or the other type of food.

The modern urban *curandero* goes well beyond the common beliefs in hot-cold imbalances. He or she may perform psychic surgery, purification rituals, or other types of healings. He or she may treat magical illnesses, such as sorcery, *susto* (debilitating fright), or soul-loss, and "natural" illnesses, such as cancer, tuberculosis, and obesity. Each urban *curandero* seems to have a personal twist to what he or she does; idiosyncratic styles are prevalent. Urban *curanderos* diagnose illnesses by talking with the patient; by examining the patient's urine, iris, skin, hair, or personal object; or by using such instruments as stethoscopes and magnifying glasses. Urban *curanderos* are less socially involved with their patients than are shamans, and they seldom include the entire family in a treatment. Urban *curanderos* usually charge modest fees or accept only donations. Some religious groups in Latin America practice healing in larger group ceremonies. For example, the public attends Umbanda rituals in Brazil to obtain healing and spiritual benefits from possessed cult members.

See also **Diseases; Indigenous Peoples, Medicine.**

BIBLIOGRAPHY

Adams, Richard N., and Arthur J. Rubel, "Sickness and Social Relations." In *Handbook of Middle American Indians,* vol. 6, ed. Robert Wauchope. Austin: University of Texas Press, 1967.

Aguirre Beltrán, Gonzalo. *El negro esclavo en Nueva España: La formación colonial, la medicina popular y otros ensayos.* México: Fondo de Cultura Económica, 1994.

Armus, Diego, ed. *Entre médicos y curanderos: Cultura, historia y enfermedad en la América Latina moderna.* Buenos Aires: Grupo Editorial Norma, 2002.

Brown, Michael F. *Tsewa's Gift: Magic and Meaning in an Amazonian Society.* Washington, DC: Smithsonian Institution Press, 1986.

Ceballos Gómez, Diana Luz. *Hechicería, brujería, e Inquisición en el Nuevo Reino de Granada: Un duelo de imaginarios.* Bogota: Editorial Universidad Nacional, 1994.

Chalhoub, Sidney, et al. *Artes e ofícios de curar no Brasil: Capítulos de história social.* Campinas, Brazil: Editora UNICAMP, 2003.

Dobkin De Rios, Marlene. *Visionary Vine: Hallucinogenic Healing in the Peruvian Amazon.* New York: Oxford University Press, 1972.

Dow, James. *The Shaman's Touch: Otomí Indian Symbolic Healing.* Salt Lake City: University of Utah Press, 1986.

Farberman, Judith. *Las salamancas de Lorenza: Magia, hechicería y curanderismo en el Tucumán colonial.* Buenos Aires: Siglo Veintiuno Editores Argentina, 2005.

Finkler, Kaja. *Spiritualist Healers in Mexico: Successes and Failures of Alternative Therapeutics.* New York: Bergen and Garvey, 1985.

Foster, George F. "On the Origin of Humoral Medicine in Latin America." *Medical Anthropology Quarterly* 1, no. 4 (1987): 355–393.

Huber, Brad R., and Alan R. Sandstrom, eds. *Mesoamerican Healers.* Austin: University of Texas Press, 2001.

Irwin Press. "The Urban Curandero," *American Anthropologist* 73, no. 3 (1971): 741–756.

Joralemon, Donald, and Douglas Sharon. *Sorcery and Shamanism: Curanderos and Clients in Northern Peru.* Salt Lake City: University of Utah Press, 1993.

Kunow, Marianna Appel. *Maya Medicine: Traditional Healing in Yucatan.* Albuquerque: University of New Mexico Press, 2003.

Langdon, E. Jean Matteson. *Xamanismo no Brasil: Novas perspectives.* Florianópolis, Brazil: Editora da UFSC, 1996.

Lewis, Laura A. *Hall of Mirrors: Power, Witchcraft, and Caste in Colonial Mexico.* Durham, NC: Duke University Press, 2003.

Sharon, Douglas. *Wizard of the Four Winds: A Shaman's Story.* New York: Free Press, 1978.

Souza, Laura de Mello e. *The Devil and the Land of the Holy Cross: Witchcraft, Slavery, and Popular Religion in Colonial Brazil.* Translated by Diane Grosklaus Whitty. Austin: University of Texas Press, Teresa Lozano Long Institute of Latin American Studies, 2003.

Sowell, David. *The Tale of Healer Miguel Perdomo Neira: Medicine, Ideologies, and Power in the Nineteenth-century Andes.* Wilmington, DE: SR Books, 2001.

Torres, Eliseo. *Curandero: A Life in Mexican Folk Healing.* With Timothy L. Sawyer Jr. Albuquerque: University of New Mexico Press, 2005.

Voeks, Robert A. *Sacred Leaves of Candomblé: African Magic, Medicine, and Religion in Brazil.* Austin: University of Texas Press, 1997.

JAMES DOW

CURITIBA. Curitiba, capital of the state of Paraná, Brazil. In 2005, Curitiba had an area of 171 square miles and a population of 1.78 million and 3.15 million in the metropolitan area. Gold prospectors founded the settlement of Nossa Senhora da Luz dos Pinhais, which became the village of Curitiba in 1693. Until the end of the eighteenth century, the inhabitants lived on subsistence agriculture and marginal old gold sites. Progress came with cattle drives south to São Paulo's cattle market in Sorocaba and, in 1820, with the export of Yerba Maté through Paranaguá harbor. The village of Curitiba, the center of a community of large rural estates, was declared a city in 1842. After the territory of Paraná was separated from the province of São Paulo in 1853, Curitiba became the capital of the newly formed province. Together with the Indian and white populations, black and mulatto slaves constituted a significant work force, about 40 percent of the total population of Curitiba in the first half of the nineteenth century. In the second half of that century, European immigrants—primarily Germans, Italians, Ukrainians, and Poles—settled on the outskirts of the city, contributing their cultures to its development. At the beginning of the twentieth century, the city had acquired the features of a modern capital and had 30,000 inhabitants. In 1940 a Frenchman named Agache devised a plan to regulate the disorganized growth of the city. At the same time there was an expansion of coffee production, which resulted in increased wealth for the capital. In the twenty-first century, Curitiba boasts more green space per inhabitant than any other city, and is celebrated for its urban planning.

See also **Brazil, Geography.**

BIBLIOGRAPHY

Ermelino De Leão, *Dicionário histórico e geográfico do Paraná* (1929).

Altiva P. Balhana, Brasil Pinheiro Machado, and Cecília Maria Westphalen, *História do Paraná* (1969).

Louis Henry and Altiva Pilatti Balhana, "La population du Paraná depuis le XVIII siècle," in *Population, revue bimestrielle de l'Institut national d'études démographiques* (Nov. 1975).

José Francisco Da Rocha Pombo, *O Paraná no centenario: 1500–1900,* 2d ed. (1980).

Márcia Elisa De Campos Graf, "Economia e escravidão no Paraná" in *Boletim do Instituto histórico, geográfico e etnográfico do Paraná* 45 (1987); *Anúario estatístico do Brasil* (1990); *Sinopse preliminar do censo demográfico—1991* (1992).

Additional Bibliography

Irazábal, Clara. *City Making and Urban Governance in the Americas: Curitiba and Portland.* Burlington, VT: Ashgate, 2005.

Karvat, Erivan Cassiano. *A sociedade do Trabalho: Discursos e práticas de controle sobre a mendicidade e a vadiagem em Curitiba, 1890–1933.* Curitiba: Aos Quatro Ventos, 1998.

Martins, Romário. *Historia do Paraná.* 2d. ed. S. Paulo: Editora Rumo limitada, 1939.

Oliveira, Dennison de. *Curitiba e o mito da cidade modelo.* Curitiba: Editora UFPR, 2000.

Roderjan, Roselys Vellozo. *Os curitibanos e a formação de comunidades campeiras no Brasil meridional: Séculos XVI a XIX.* Curitiba: Instituto Histórico, Geográfico e Etnográfico Paranaense, 1992.

Sallas, Ana Luisa Fayet, and Rafael Duarte Villa. *Os jovens de Curitiba–esperanças e desencantos: Juventude, violência e cidadania.* Brasília, DF: Ediçoes UNESCO Brasil, 1999.

MÁRCIA ELISA DE CAMPOS GRAF

CURRENCY. Since the mid-nineteenth century, monetary instability has proven a major hindrance to Latin America's economic and political development. Internal political and social disruptions have frequently interfered with the ability of Latin American nations to implement and adhere to the sound economic policies that underlie stable currencies. At the same time, the capacity of many Latin American nations to promote monetary stability was hindered by their economic over-reliance upon the export of raw natural resources and the intake of foreign direct investment, making the region highly vulnerable to external shocks caused by factors such as investment cycles and global recessions.

Economic theory postulates that strong currencies tend to benefit domestic industry and consumers by improving access to international credit and lowering the real cost of imported consumer and industrial goods, whereas weak currencies encourage export activities by reducing the international prices of export goods. Governments maintain some control over currency valuations through their ability to adjust key interest rates, monetary supply, investment and trade restrictions and incentives, and foreign reserve deposits. To a large extent, however, currency valuation is determined by trade balances and public confidence in the governing authority that issues and guarantees the currency.

HISTORY

Following the Spanish wars of independence in the early to mid nineteenth century, the newly minted currencies of the young Latin American nations fluctuated wildly in response to the sporadic fighting among local elites, heavy debts incurred from years of military expenses and treasury-plundering caudillos, widespread infrastructure destruction, and vulnerability to the boom and bust cycles of the rapidly industrializing markets of Europe and the United States. Although Brazil's separation from Portugal proved less destructive, its currency also suffered tumultuous swings in response to a series of regional revolts and sustained dependency on exports.

As the situation stabilized during the latter half of the nineteenth century, foreign direct investment flows increased, the banking sectors expanded, and some countries—notably Mexico, Argentina, Brazil, and Chile—raised tariffs and implemented devaluation policies (raising interest rates and paying down debt when feasible) to encourage industrial growth and modernization. While heavier investment led to modernized transportation and communication systems, it also produced escalating national debts, engrained bureaucratic corruption, periodic bouts of inflation, and bank crises. Frequent and intense monetary policy shifts between alternating political administrations backed by industrial proponents and the traditional agricultural landowning class further undermined public confidence. Revolutions and populism, periods of military dictatorships, and persistent vulnerability to international commodity markets resulted in unsustainable public debt, bouts of

hyperinflation, the repeated introduction of new national currencies, bank runs, and public confidence crises in Latin America through much of the twentieth century.

TWENTIETH-CENTURY REFORMS

Since the 1990s, however, many nations have introduced innovative and effective reforms to restore confidence. Between 1991 and 1994, Mexico, Peru, Argentina, and Brazil all introduced new currencies to break the inflationary crises provoked by the poor economic administration of their predecessors, and augmented the purchase of dollars for their foreign reserves to support the value of these currencies. These policies were supported by the greater independence granted to federal bank ministers. Two of Latin America's most poorly administered economies, Ecuador and El Salvador, took the unprecedented step of adopting the U.S. dollar as their national currency.

Higher industrial growth and foreign direct investment followed, but these policies also left the nations more vulnerable to global monetary shocks. The downward spiral began with Mexico's failed attempt to manage a currency devaluation, which sparked the 1994 peso crisis. The "tequila effect" that followed and the subsequent financial collapse of Asian and Russian markets led international investors to yank so-called hot money investments from emerging markets. Brazil and Argentina responded by raising interest rates as high as 40 percent to defend their currencies, resulting in higher debt levels and sharp spikes in unemployment. Brazil and Argentina eventually conceded to floating their currencies in 1999 and 2001, which initially led to sharp devaluation and some inflation. Subsequently, however, strong fiscal administration and high commodity demands driven by emerging market growth inspired international investor confidence and enabled leaders to control inflation while lowering key interest rates, boost social and infrastructure spending, and pay down large amounts of foreign debt. Unfortunately, relatively tepid gross domestic product (GDP) growth and continued wealth imbalances increased political discontent with incumbent leaders. The question remains as to whether Latin America is entering a new era of industrial-led growth and monetary stability, or if a new wave of populism and the inevitable decline of international commodity prices will once again upset the balance.

See also **Economic Development; Foreign Investment.**

BIBLIOGRAPHY

Elson, Anthony. "What Happened? Why East Asia Surged Ahead of Latin America and Some Lessons for Economic Policy." *Finance and Development* 43, no. 2 (June 2006): 37–40.

Topik, Steven. *The Political Economy of the Brazilian State, 1889–1930.* Austin: University of Texas Press, 1987.

Zarazaga, Carlos E. "Argentina, Mexico, and Currency Boards: Another Case of Rules Versus Discretion." *Economic and Financial Policy Review, Federal Reserve Bank of Dallas* (fourth quarter 1995): 14–24.

CHRISTOPHER L. MURCHISON

CURRENCY (BRAZIL).

Brazil has had a complex monetary history, notable for a variety of mediums of exchange, chronic currency shortages, and in recent times, periods of hyperinflation. Until 1942 the basic unit of account was the *real* (plural *réis*), or *milreis* (1,000 *réis,* written as 1$000). Its origin was in silver and billon (silver and copper alloy) coins first struck in Portugal in the 1300s, and the name was derived from a similar Castilian piece. In time, the value of all gold, silver, billon, and copper coinage, of which there were many types and denominations, was expressed as so many *réis,* but identified also by specific name and as multiples of smaller coins or divisions of more valuable ones. Copper coins as small in value as a single or one and one-half *réis* were coined until the 1680s. Silver coins included the *vintém* (20 *réis*), *tostão* (100 *réis*), and *meio-tostão* (50 *réis*). The gold coins of the time were the *cruzado* (400 *réis*), *quarto de cruzado* (100 *réis*), and the *Portuguez* of 10 *cruzados,* or 4,000 *réis* (4$000). For large sums, such as the financial transactions of merchants and the state, the term *conto* (equal to 1,000 *milréis*) was employed (expressed as 1:000$000).

Early on, however, specie was used mainly in colonial ports. Cowrie shells (*zimbos*) and commodities (brazilwood, sugar, tobacco, cattle, cotton, cotton cloth or thread, even slaves) were customarily bartered for trade goods. Where coins were used, Spanish silver *pesos* were common. In the 1640s, during the era of West India Company occupation of the northeast coast, the Dutch were the first to mint money (florins) for local use. Currency debasement was the rule in Portugal in the late seventeenth century, but following the establishment of colonial mints after gold was discovered in the interior of Brazil (1697 onward), a policy of "strong money" for the mother country was adopted. Gold and silver products of mints at Bahia and Rio de Janeiro were valued differently for Brazilian and Portuguese usage in order to limit the outflow of money from the colony. Gold *dobras, peças,* and *escudos;* silver *patacas* and *tostões;* and silver and copper *vintems* and *réis* were produced by these mints. Gold, in the form of bars or ingots and gold dust, was allowed to circulate as legal tender, but only in the region of the mines. Locally restricted currency issues were common in other provinces as well.

Following independence from Portugal (1822), currency shortages spawned widespread counterfeit copper coins. Paper money, in very limited use in the late eighteenth century in Portugal, was promoted by the establishment of the Bank of Brazil (1808–1829; 1853 onward) and by the founding of provincial banks throughout the nineteenth century. A national monetary system was established in 1833, but old coins continued to circulate along with new mintings; foreign coins, such as British sovereigns and U.S. dollars, were also permitted. After 1922 the national bank became the sole issuer of paper notes, and gold coins ceased to be struck.

In 1942 the *cruzeiro* (equal to 1$000 and divided into 100 *centavos,* with its symbol Cr$) succeeded the venerable *milreis.* Subsequent currency reform in 1965 created the *cruzeiro novo.* Since then monetary policies designed to reverse inflation have introduced frequent currency shifts, including the *cruzado* (1986), *cruzado novo* (1989), the return of the *cruzeiro* (1990), and the *cruzeiro real* (1993). Currency reform in 1994, known as the Plano Real, restored the *real* (plural *réais*), first as a basic unit of account or Unit of Real Value (URV) pegged to the U.S. dollar (initially 647 *cruzeiros réais* = 1 URV). In mid-1994 the currency was renamed the *real* (R$), a name it has retained into the twenty-first century, although it has not held a fixed exchange rate since the late 1990s.

See also **Banking: Overview.**

BIBLIOGRAPHY

Cavalcanti, Amaro. *O meio circulante nacional,* vol. 1 (1983).

Dos Santos Trigueiros, F. *Dinheiro no Brasil,* 2d ed. (1987).

Franco, Gustavo Henrique Barroso. *The Real Plan and the Exchange Rate.* Princeton, NJ: International Finance Section, Department of Economics, Princeton University, 2000.

Frieden, Jeffry A., and Ernesto Stein. *The Currency Game: Exchange Rate Politics in Latin America.* Washington, DC: Distributed by the Johns Hopkins University Press for the Inter-American Development Bank, 2001.

Lopes Fernandes, M. B. *Memória das moedas correntes em Portugal,* 2 vols. (1856–1857).

Pandia Calogeras, João. *A política monetária do Brasil* (1960).

Prado, Maria Clara R. M., ed. *A real história do real.* Rio de Janeiro: Record, 2005.

Sombra, S. *História monetaria do Brasil colónial* (1938).

CATHERINE LUGAR

CURUPAYTY, BATTLE OF. Battle of
Curupayty, a major Paraguayan victory on 22 September 1866 during the War of the Triple Alliance. The Brazilian and Argentine expeditionary forces had been making steady, if very bloody, progress against the Paraguayans throughout 1866 and, by September, were approaching the fortress of Humaitá from the southwest. Hoping for real negotiations, or at least to buy time, Paraguayan President Francisco Solano López met with the Allied commander, General Bartolomé Mitre, at Yataity Corá.

Though this foray into diplomacy failed, it permitted López's British engineers time enough to construct a 2,000-yard line of deep trenches at Curupayty and to reinforce them with forty-nine cannon and Congreve rocket stands. Five thousand troops under the command of General José Eduvigis Díaz guarded this position, which the Allies assaulted in force on 22 September. Unknown to the advancing troops, their naval bombardment, which had begun in the morning, had been totally ineffectual, and when the 11,000 Brazilians and 7,000 Argentines came within range, Díaz poured concentrated blasts of grape and canister into

them. The carnage was so dreadful that Mitre gave early orders for a general retirement.

The Allied dead numbered about 9,000, including the son of Mitre's successor, Domingo Faustino Sarmiento. The Paraguayans lost only 50 men. As a result of this debacle, the Allies were unable to resume their advance into Paraguay for fourteen months.

See also **López, Francisco Solano; Mitre, Bartolomé; War of the Triple Alliance.**

BIBLIOGRAPHY

Charles J. Kolinski, *Independence or Death! The Story of the Paraguayan War* (1965); *The Cambridge History of Latin America,* vol. 3 (1985), pp. 787, 790.

Additional Bibliography

Bethell, Leslie. *The Paraguayan War (1864–1870).* London: Institute of Latin American Studies, 1996.

Leuchars, Chris. *To the Bitter End: Paraguay and the War of the Triple Alliance.* Westport, CT: Greenwood Press, 2002.

Marco, Miguel Angel de. *La Guerra del Paraguay.* Buenos Aires: Planeta, 1995.

Whigham, Thomas. *The Paraguayan War.* Lincoln: University of Nebraska Press, 2002.

THOMAS L. WHIGHAM

CUYAMEL FRUIT COMPANY. Cuyamel Fruit Company, a large banana-producing enterprise in Honduras founded by Samuel Zemurray. After arriving in Puerto Cortés, Honduras, in 1905, Zemurray purchased the properties and concessionaire's rights of William F. Streich. In 1911, with plans of expanding beyond the Honduran northern coast, Zemurray incorporated Cuyamel, only to discover that Honduran president Miguel Dávila had negotiated a customs receivership agreement with the United States. The agreement provided Dávila with a loan from New York bankers, secured by a U.S. customs receiver, who would have restricted Cuyamel's duty-free imports. To protect his interests, Zemurray supported Manuel Bonilla Chirinos in a coup that ousted Dávila in 1911. In return, the new president granted Zemurray generous concessions. Zemurray turned to large-scale irrigation, flooding of inferior lowlands, and selective pruning that enabled Cuyamel to compete successfully against the United Fruit Company (UFCO). In

1915, Zemurray expanded Cuyamel's holdings into the Motagua Valley along the disputed border between Honduras and Guatemala. In 1929, UFCO bought out Cuyamel for $31.5 million. The agreement also required Zemurray to retire from the banana industry. He returned to New Orleans as UFCO's largest shareholder, a position he subsequently used to take over the operations of that company.

See also **Banana Industry.**

BIBLIOGRAPHY

Charles D. Kepner and Jay H. Soothill, *The Banana Empire* (1935).

Charles M. Wilson, *Empire in Green and Gold: The Story of the American Banana Trade* (1947).

Stacy May and Galo Plaza, *The United Fruit Company in Latin America* (1958).

Thomas P. Mc Cann, *An American Company: The Tragedy of United Fruit* (1976).

Additional Bibliography

Argueta, Mario. *Bananos y política: Samuel Zemurray y la Cuyamel Fruit Company en Honduras.* Tegucigalpa: Editorial Universitaria, 1989.

García Buchard, Ethel. *Poder político, interés bananero e identidad nacional en Centro América: Un estudio comparativo: Costa Rica (1884–1938) y Honduras (1902–1958).* Tegucigalpa: Editorial Universitaria, 1997.

THOMAS M. LEONARD

CUYO. Cuyo was an old administrative region of the Spanish colonies in South America, founded during sixteenth century. At that time the region was inhabited by indigenous pampas (or *huarpes*). When the Spanish Crown created the viceroyalty of the River Plate in 1776, Cuyo was no longer under the administrative control of Santiago de Chile, and became part of this new political-administrative entity whose capital was Buenos Aires. During the war of independence, this region was the base of operations of the Army of the Andes. In the early twenty-first century, Cuyo is a geographic region of western Argentina that covers part of the Andes mountain range. Its main feature is the Andes mountain range—the mountains and their foothills—and

it straddles the provinces of Mendoza, San Juan, La Rioja, part of San Luis, and part of Neuquén. Excellent fine wines are among the chief products of this region. Other important products are olives, fruits, and vegetables. Tourism is a key activity. There are still small indigenous communities in the region.

See also **Argentina, Geography.**

BIBLIOGRAPHY

Borgononi, Mario. *Geografía Argentina.* Buenos Aires: Editorial Stella, 2002.

VICENTE PALERMO

CUZCO. Cuzco, also spelled Cusco, a city and department in southeastern Peru. The estimated population of the city in 2007 was 312,140. Geographic diversity characterizes the region as high mountains descend into river valleys that flow to eastern, tropical lowlands. The range of elevations and temperatures creates many distinct ecological zones that influence the economic and social life of the region.

Most likely the city's remote origins lie with pre-Inca groups residing there who were from or associated with the Huari (or Wari) culture. Later, the city of Cuzco became the religious and political center of the Quechua-speaking Inca Empire, or Tahuantinsuyu. Legend dates the founding of the city from the reign of Manco Capac, who may have entered the area around 1200. Under the Inca royal family the city and the empire expanded, especially toward the end of the fifteenth century, when the influence of Cuzco extended north to Ecuador and south to Chile. Tribute was essential to the city's growth. From the lowland valleys came tobacco, coca, cotton, chiles, and yucca; from the highlands, grains, wool, and tubers. Long river valleys, most notably that of the Urubamba, were major population and agricultural centers. Cuzco's location as a crossroad between north and south and highlands and lowlands helped it to emerge as an important economic and political center.

The city of Cuzco became more imposing as the wealth and power of the Incas expanded. In addition to some 4,000 residential structures, granaries, and storage sheds, the city boasted magnificent

Cuzco, Peru, 1880s, an engraving by French School (20th century). PRIVATE COLLECTION/ KEN WELSH/ THE BRIDGEMAN ART LIBRARY

religious and imperial structures, built of carefully shaped stones. Central to life in the city were the palaces of the former emperors and Coricancha (the Palace of the Sun). Many of the most important buildings were around the central square of Aucaypata. Just outside the city was Sacsahuamán, a massive fortress or ceremonial structure of crafted walls made from rocks that weighed up to 300 tons each.

Inca dominance of Cuzco was challenged with the arrival of a small group of Spaniards on the coast of Peru in 1532. Led by Francisco Pizarro, Spaniards entered Cuzco in November 1533, and declared it La Muy Noble y Gran Ciudad del Cuzco in 1543. Fighting among Spaniards and resistance from the Quechua-speaking peoples was intense but did not prevent Spanish control of Cuzco. New buildings rose

on the ruins of the old, at times made from the same stones and foundations of Inca structures. The center of the Inca city became the Spanish Plaza de Armas, the site of the seventeenth-century Cathedral and Jesuit Church of the Compañía, built on the Place of the Serpents. Any observer will notice that many of the central Spanish buildings were built on Incan foundations, creating a striking architectural contrast.

Spanish owners of landed estates, mines, and textile factories, along with merchants, bureaucrats, and clerics, relied on indigenous labor to generate the wealth of the city and region. Quechuan resistance continued to challenge Spanish control. Revolts in Cuzco in the eighteenth century, especially the revolt of (José) Tupac Amaru II in 1780, had an influence beyond the region. By the time of this revolt, Cuzco had become a city of complex social and ethnic relationships, a distinctive culture that was the result of centuries of contact between Europeans and Indians. The culture of the old and the new, the Andean and the European, is more evident in Cuzco than in many other Latin American cities. Carleton Beals perhaps captured it best in his *Fire on the Andes* (1934) when he described Cuzco as "two cities, locked in deadly embrace of love and hate."

Cuzco's cultural history includes significant intellectual and artistic achievements. The University of San Ignacio (1622) gave way to the University of San Antonio Abad (1692), which continued as the intellectual center of the city into the twentieth century. In the eighteenth century, an outpouring of art distinguished the city. Cuzco also had writers who achieved fame, beginning with El Inca Garcilaso De La Vega, best known for his *Comentarios reales* (1609). In the nineteenth century, Clorinda Matto De Turner captured the memories of Cuzco in her *Tradiciones cuzqueñas* and won international recognition for her *Aves sin nido* (1889), a portrayal of Quechuan struggles against the Creole elite in an imaginary town outside Cuzco. The old Incan capital became the Andean center of Indigenismo, a complex intellectual and social movement that sought to understand, protect, and further the interests of the indigenous peoples of the region.

Independence brought economic change to the city. The textile industry, so important during the colonial period, suffered as foreign cloth and garments entered the Peruvian market. But Cuzco still sat astride the old Lima-Potosí trade route and benefited temporarily from the Peru-Bolivia Confederation. With the confederation's collapse and the rise of the guano industry, the coast emerged as the dominant economic region of the country. Population data demonstrate the extent of the collapse. The population of the city dropped from 40,000 in 1834 to 18,370 in 1876. Recovery came slowly, and by 1912 the city still claimed only 19,825 residents. Impetus for growth came from railroad links with the outside and new highway construction. Sicuani was the railroad terminal for Cuzco until the arrival of a railhead in Cuzco. The corvée known as the *Conscripción vial,* which required men aged eighteen to twenty and fifty to sixty to work on the roads, was reminiscent of colonial labor drafts in the Andes. Cuzco continued to ship out agricultural products and textiles along these routes as it had done in the past. A new direction for growth in the late nineteenth and early twentieth centuries was the *montaña,* the lower elevations around Ollantaytambo and Machu Picchu. By the 1920s the tourism potential of these and other sites was recognized. This potential was realized beginning in the 1960s, as Cuzco and its many magnificent archaeological sites emerged as leading tourist attractions in the Andes.

The recent history of the city dates from the earthquake of 1950. The rebuilding that took place after the earthquake brought growth and expansion. Accelerated migration from rural areas added to the growth of the city. With the population increase came the *barriadas,* or *pueblos jóvenes,* the new communities common to the peripheries of all the major cities of Peru. While Cuzco still retains much of the past, evident in the carefully preserved monuments and architecture, and in the people, language, and culture of the city, it also has become a cosmopolitan hub as tourists from Asia, Europe, the United States, and other Latin American countries pass through en route to Machu Picchu, the Sacred Valley, the Inca Trail, or other ecotourism destinations. There is a thriving dining, café, and nightclub scene. A new cultural phenomenon, *cazadoras de gringos,* inverts and gives new meaning to the old Don Juan trope. The *cazadoras de gringos,* also called *bricheras,* are women from Cuzco who hunt gringos (foreign men), whom they seduce with the objective of an intercultural marriage.

See also **Garcilaso de la Vega, El Inca; Machu Picchu; Manco Capac; Matto de Turner, Clorinda; Sacsahuaman; Tahuantinsuyu.**

BIBLIOGRAPHY

Much good writing has been done on the history of Cuzco. John H. Rowe describes the architecture and pottery of the city in *An Introduction to the Archaeology of Cuzco* (1944). For Cuzco as the seat of the empire, see Burr Cartwright Brundage, *Lords of Cuzco* (1967); and John Hemming, *The Conquest of the Incas* (1970). Víctor Angles Vargas, *Historia del Cusco incaico,* 3 vols. (1988), narrates the early history of Cuzco in detail. Paulo O. D. De Azevedo, *Cuzco, ciudad histórica: Continuidad y cambio* (1982), provides a brief historical overview with specialized attention to architecture and recent problems. José Tamayo Herrera analyzes major changes in the city since independence in *Historia social del Cuzco republicano* (1978). He is also the author of *Historia del indigenismo cuzqueño* (1980), a social and intellectual history of

Indianist movements in Cuzco. Pierre L. Van Den Berghe and George P. Primov analyze the social, economic, and political structure of Cuzco in *Inequality in the Peruvian Andes: Class and Ethnicity in Cuzco* (1977).

Additional Bibliography

Bauer, Brian S.*Ancient Cuzco: Heartland of the Inca*. Austin: University of Texas Press, 2004.

Burns, Kathryn. *Colonial Habits: Convents and the Spiritual Economy of Cuzco, Peru*. Durham, NC: Duke University Press, 1999.

Cadena, Marisol de la. *Indigenous Mestizos: The Politics of Race and Culture in Cuzco, Peru, 1919–1991*. Durham, NC: Duke University Press, 2000.

Covey, R. Alan. *How the Incas Built Their Heartland: State Formation and the Innovation of Imperial Strategies in the Sacred Valley, Peru*. Ann Arbor: University of Michigan Press, 2006.

Dean, Carolyn. *Inka Bodies and the Body of Christ: Corpus Christi in Colonial Cuzco, Peru*. Durham, NC: Duke University Press, 1999.

Escandell-Tur, Neus.*Producción y comercio de tejidos coloniales: Los obrajes y chorrillos del Cusco, 1570–1820*. Cusco, Peru: Centro de Estudios Regionales Andinos, Bartolomé de Las Casas, 1997.

Matto de Turner, Clorinda. *Tradiciones cuzqueñas completas*. Lima: PEISA, 1976.

Seligmann, Linda J. *Peruvian Street Lives: Culture, Power, and Economy among Market Women of Cuzco*. Urbana: University of Illinois Press, 2004.

Tardieu, Jean-Pierre. *El negro en el Cuzco: Los caminos de la alienación en la segunda mitad del siglo XVII*. Lima: Pontificia Universidad Católica del Perú : Banco Central de Reserva del Perú, 1998.

Viñuales, Graciela María. *El espacio urbano en el Cusco colonial: Uso y organización de las estructuras simbólicas*. Lima: Epígrafe Editores, S.A., 2004.

Walker, Charles F. *Smoldering Ashes: Cuzco and the Creation of Republican Peru, 1780–1840*. Durham, NC: Duke University Press, 1999.

JOHN C. SUPER

CUZCO SCHOOL OF PAINTING.

Cuzco School of Painting, the most distinctive major school of painting in Spain's American colonies, which evolved during the seventeenth and eighteenth centuries in the old Inca capital of Cuzco. Indian and Mestizo artists transformed formal and iconographical types from European art to create a uniquely American style of religious painting, characterized by brilliant color, flattened space, and a strongly decorative aesthetic. Favorite subjects include anecdotal biblical narratives, hieratic figures of the Virgin and saints, and gaily dressed archangels, as well as brightly colored tropical birds and idealized imaginary landscapes without reference to local geography.

The origins of the school can be found in the many Flemish engravings and European paintings that were taken to Peru from Spain, as well as in works by European artists such as the Italian mannerist painter and Jesuit Bernardo Bitti, who was active in Peru and Bolivia between 1575 and 1610. The key figure in establishing the new style was the Indian painter Diego Quispe Tito (1611–after 1681), from a village outside Cuzco, whose uniquely American sensibility exerted a powerful effect on *cuzqueño* painting for over a century.

The popular style of painting that evolved in the eighteenth century from the work of Quispe and his immediate followers is frequently labeled "mestizo," a racial term that suggests a mixture of foreign and indigenous elements. From busy workshops in the prosperous city, painters such as Marco Zapata (active 1748–1764) produced sophisticated baroque compositions for major patrons and religious institutions while other, mostly anonymous painters worked in a more simplified, decorative style to service a vast market that stretched from Ecuador to Chile.

See also **Art: The Colonial Era.**

BIBLIOGRAPHY

The principal study of viceregal painting in Cuzco is José De Mesa and Teresa Gisbert, *Historia de la pintura cuzqueña*, 2d ed., 2 vols. (1982), which incorporates many earlier studies by this prolific Bolivian couple. Gisbert focuses on the distinct iconography of Andean painting in *Iconografía y mitos indigenas en el arte* (1980). Two of the most characteristic subjects of Cuzco painting are studied in the exhibition catalogue, *Gloria in Excelsis: The Virgin and Angels in Viceregal Painting of Peru and Bolivia* (1986). Earlier, more general catalogues in English are Leopoldo Castedo, *The Cuzco Circle* (1976); and Pal Keleman, *Peruvian Colonial Painting* (1971).

Additional Bibliography

Benavente Velarde, Teófilo, and Alejandro Martínez Frisancho. *Pintores cusqueños de la colonia*. Lima: Municipalidad del Qosqo, 1995.

Pastor de la Torre, Celso, and Luis Enrique Tord. *Perú: Fe y arte en el Virreynato*. Córdoba: Publicaciones Obra Social y Cultural CajaSur, 1999.

SAMUEL K. HEATH

D

DAINZÚ. Dainzú, an archaeological site located 12 miles east of Oaxaca City, near the village of Macuilxóchitl, in Oaxaca, Mexico. Located on the eastern side and at the base of a large, loaf-shaped mountain spur rising from the floor of the Valley of Oaxaca, Dainzú was excavated by Ignacio Bernal in the 1960s. Although the excavated remains are referred to as Dainzú and date from around the time of Jesus Christ, they actually are part of the site of Macuilxóchitl, which has both earlier and later occupations. The most spectacular of the excavated remains are some fifty carved stone slabs that form the vertical walls of a probable temple, called Building A, and are placed on both sides of the temple's stairway. Thought to represent ball players, many of the individuals portrayed on the slabs are attired in helmets and protective gear. They are shown in action and in dynamic positions with spherical objects (perhaps balls) in their hands. Most of the players are facing right, toward an important individual who faces them and stands on what is probably the top of a hill. Among the slabs depicting ball players are slabs carved with persons who may be priests, judging from their attire. Some scholars suggest that the carved stones form a ritual scene of calendrical significance associated with the ballgame. Others suggest that a battle scene is represented and that the individuals portrayed are soldiers. Down the slope from Building A are residences of the elite, one of which contains an elaborate tomb with a carved jaguar on its facade. A ball court, similar to those of Yagul and Monte Albán, lies some distance away. It dates to the Postclassic period (*ca.* CE 900–1521), however, and therefore was built about 1,000 years after the stones were carved. Dainzú is important because the carved stones represent a unique style in the Valley of Oaxaca.

See also **Archaeology; Ball Game, Pre-Columbian.**

BIBLIOGRAPHY

Ignacio Bernal and Andy Seuffert, *The Ballplayers of Dainzú,* translated by Carolyn B. Czitrom (1979).

George Kubler, *Art and Architecture of Ancient America,* 3d ed. (1984), pp. 160–161.

Marcus Winter, *Oaxaca: The Archaeological Record* (1989), pp. 55–56, 103–104.

Additional Bibliography

Bernal, Ignacio, and Arturo Oliveros. *Exploraciones arqueológicas en Dainzú, Oaxaca.* México, D.F.: Instituto Nacional de Antropología e Historia, 1988.

Marcus, Joyce, and Kent V. Flannery. *Zapotec Civilization: How Urban Society Evolved in Mexico's Oaxaca Valley.* New York: Thames and Hudson, 1996.

Newsome, Elizabeth A., and Heather S. Orr. *The "Bundle" Altars of Copán: A New Perspective on Their Meaning and Archaeological Contexts.* Washington, DC: Center for Ancient American Studies, 2003.

MICHAEL D. LIND

DALTON GARCÍA, ROQUE (1935–1975). Roque Dalton García (*b.* 14 May 1935; *d.* 10 May 1975), Salvadoran Marxist writer and activist. Born and educated in San Salvador, Dalton went to Chile to study law and there began his career as a poet, essayist, novelist, and biographer. Returning to El Salvador with strong leftist political leanings, he became part of the literary group known as the Committed Generation. His leftist views forced him into exile in 1961. After several years in Cuba, Dalton traveled extensively in Europe and became closely associated with the ideas of Che Guevara and Régis Debray in defense of the Cuban Revolution. After returning clandestinely to El Salvador, where he was the effective founder of the leftist Armed Forces of National Resistance (Fuerzas Armadas de Resistencia Nacional), he was executed by members of the rival Revolutionary Army of the People (Ejército Revolucionario del Pueblo), from which his FARN had broken away, in San Salvador. In addition to his many poems and novels, Dalton wrote a biography, *Miguel Mármol: Los sucesos de 1932 en El Salvador* (1972).

See also **El Salvador.**

BIBLIOGRAPHY

Roque Dalton, *El Salvador* (1963).

James Dunkerley, *The Long War: Dictatorship and Revolution in El Salvador* (1982).

Luis Gallegos Valdés, *Panorama de la literatura salvadoreña del período precolombino a 1980* (1987), esp. pp. 342–355, and 429–431.

John Beverley and Marc Zimmerman, *Literature and Politics in the Central American Revolutions* (1990), esp. pp. 115–141.

Additional Bibliography

Alvarenga, Luis. *El ciervo perseguido: vida y obra de Roque Dalton.* San Salvador: Dirección de Publicaciones e Impresos, 2002.

Iffland, James. *Ensayos sobre la poesía revolucionaria de Centroamérica.* San Jose: EDUCA, 1994.

Lara Martínez, Rafael. *La tormenta entre las manos: ensayos polémicos sobre literatura salvadoreña.* San Salvador: Dirección de Publicaciones e Impresos, 2000.

Lara Martínez, Rafael, and Dennis L. Seager, editors. *Otros Roques: la poetica multiple de Roque Dalton.* New Orleans: University Press of the South, 1999.

RALPH LEE WOODWARD JR.

DAMAS, LÉON-GONTRAN (1912–1978).

The Guyanese author, politician, and public intellectual Léon-Gontran Damas (March 28, 1912–January 22, 1978) was one of the leading figures of the twentieth-century French Négritude movement. He was born at Cayenne in the French colony of Guyana to a middle-class family of mixed African, European, and indigenous ancestry. He excelled in school, which took him to the French colony of Martinique and later to France, where he took classes and later collaborated with Aimé Césaire. His writings focused on his own mixed racial heritage as emblematic of the Caribbean experience, the importance of African origins, folklore as a key to Guyanese history, and the problems of colonial relations with France. He served in the French Chambre des Députés from 1948 to 1951, representing the overseas department of French Guyana, where his campaign stressed developmental and educational issues. After failing to win reelection, he returned to intellectual life by writing, teaching, publishing, and working for the United Nations Educational, Scientific, and Cultural Organization. In 1970 Damas moved to Washington, D.C, where he taught at Georgetown University and served as Distinguished Professor of African Literature at Howard University until his death in 1978.

See also **Césaire, Aimé; Guyana; Négritude.**

BIBLIOGRAPHY

Racine, Daniel L. *Léon-Gontran Damas: L'homme et l'œuvre.* Paris: Présence africaine, 1983.

Warner, Keith Q., ed. *Critical Perspectives on Léon-Gontran Damas.* Washington, DC: Three Continents Press, 1988.

MATTHEW CHILDS

DA MATTA, ROBERTO (1936–).

Roberto Augusto da Matta (b. Niterói, Rio de Janeiro, 1936) is one of Brazil's foremost cultural anthropologists, specializing in social and cultural anthropology, anthropological theory, rituals and symbols, film, literature, modernization and national identity. Da Matta received his Ph.D. from Harvard University.

Among his many books are *Carnivals, Rogues, and Heroes: An Interpretation of the Brazilian Dilemma* (1991), *A Divided World: Apinayé Social Structure* (1982), *The Brazilian Puzzle* (with David Hess, 1995), and, with Elena Soárez, *Aguias, Burros e Borboletas: Um Estudo Antropologico do Jogo do Bicho* (*Eagles, Donkeys, and Butterflies,* 1999). Da Matta writes about how to define Brazilian sociability. Of particular note is his theory about the difference between the individual and the person as he explores the fragility of social institutions, including governments, in Brazil. Da Matta has been a professor at the National Museum at the Federal University of Rio de Janeiro and is an emeritus professor from the University of Notre Dame. He began to write *crónicas* in 1995 and a weekly column in the newspaper *Estado de São Paulo,* in which he chronicles daily events of ordinary Brazilians and how the role of music and literature play foundational roles in their lives. With this column he weaves an optimistic view of society.

BIBLIOGRAPHY

Primary Works

A Divided World: Apinayé Social Structure. Cambridge, MA: Harvard University Press, 1982.

Carnivals, Rogues, and Heroes: An Interpretation of the Brazilian Dilemma. South Bend, IN, and London: University of Notre Dame Press, 1991.

"Estado e Sociedade e a Casa e a Rua." In *Revisão do Paraíso: Os Brasileiros e o Estado em 500 anos de História,* edited by Mary Del Priori. Rio de Janeiro: Campus, 2000.

"Back to Tristes Tropiques: Notes on Levi-Strauss and Brazil." *Brazil 2001: A Revisionary History of Brazilian Literature and Culture.* Dartmouth, MA: Center for Portuguese Language and Culture, 2001.

SUSAN CANTY QUINLAN

DANCE. *See* **Music: Popular Music and Dance.**

DANCE OF THE MILLIONS.

Dance of the Millions is the phrase used to describe the boom-and-bust prosperity associated with the rapid rise and collapse of sugar prices in Cuba at the conclusion of World War I. The war stimulated an unprecedented demand for Cuban sugar and great business growth in Cuba from 1914 through the conflict's end. The U.S. price of sugar was fixed at 5.5 cents per pound during the war, which allowed for substantial profits and encouraged rapid expansion of sugar cultivation and speculation in Cuban land and other businesses. Although the entire economy expanded rapidly, speculators and investors also incurred heavy debts in their rush to join the rising prosperity. When price controls ended after the war, prices soared, driven upward by widespread speculation. Sugar reached a peak of 22.5 cents per pound in the United States by May 1920. By this time, however, European beet sugar had resumed production and the shortage of sugar that had stimulated the initial rise in prices no longer existed. Once it became apparent that there was a surplus of sugar, prices plummeted to less than 4 cents per pound by December 1920. The collapse of sugar prices caused widespread financial and business failure.

A similar surge in foreign investment and speculation in Colombia in the 1920s has also been called the Dance of the Millions by some writers.

See also **Sugar Industry.**

BIBLIOGRAPHY

Hugh Thomas, *Cuba: The Pursuit of Freedom* (1971), pp. 525–563, provides a detailed description of the Cuban sugar boom of 1912–1920, and Robert F. Smith, *The United States and Cuba: Business and Diplomacy, 1917–1960* (1960), describes its relation to the U.S. economy. See also Leland Hamilton Jenks, *Our Cuban Colony: A Study in Sugar* (1928). Vernon Lee Fluharty, *Dance of the Millions: Military Rule and the Social Revolution in Colombia, 1930–1956* (1957), pp. 30–35, describes the Colombian Dance of the Millions.

Additional Bibliography

Ayala, César J. *American Sugar Kingdom: The Plantation Economy of the Spanish Caribbean, 1898-1934.* Chapel Hill: University of North Carolina Press, 1999.

Dye, Alan. *Cuban Sugar in the Age of Mass Production: Technology and the Economics of the Sugar Central, 1899–1929.* Stanford, CA: Stanford University Press, 1998.

Santamaría García, Antonio. *Sin azucar no hay país: La industria azucarera y la economía cubana (1919–1939).* Sevilla: Secretariado de Publicaciones de la Universidad de Sevilla: Diputación de Sevilla, Servicio de Archivo y Publicaciones; Madrid: Consejo Superior de

Investigaciones Científicas, Escuela de Estudios Hispano-Americanos, 2001.

RALPH LEE WOODWARD JR.

DANISH WEST INDIES.

DANISH WEST INDIES. Danish West Indies, also known as the Danish Virgin Islands, an island group that includes the islands of Saint Croix, Saint Thomas, and Saint John. Denmark's first settlement on Saint Thomas in 1665 failed. In 1670 King Christian V established the Danish West India Company to resettle Saint Thomas. Settlers arrived in 1672, among them bondmen and convicts. The company claimed Saint John in 1684 but did not occupy it until 1717. Denmark purchased Saint Croix from France in 1733.

A profitable plantation economy developed despite hardships. Generous land grants from the Danish West India Company attracted immigrants. Oddly, most settlers were not Danes but French, German, English, Dutch, and other foreigners. Plantations produced cotton, indigo, tobacco, and especially sugar. Saint Thomas thrived as a trade center. Crown rule came in 1755 and brought increased prosperity. Once free of the Danish West India Company's monopoly, planters could sell their commodities at higher free-market prices.

Bondmen and convicts proved insufficient as plantation laborers, a situation that the colonists resolved by importing African slaves. The first slave ship brought 103 Africans in 1673. The slave population rose steadily and peaked in 1803 at 35,727. Africans soon vastly outnumbered Europeans. Reliance on slave labor, however, had its problems. A slave rebellion, provoked by the harsh slave code of 1733, rocked Saint John in November 1733. The abolition of the slave trade in 1803 restricted the slave supply even though illegal imports continued. Meanwhile, sentiment in Denmark led the government to plan for gradual emancipation. In 1847 authorities passed a law of free birth and decreed the emancipation of all slaves in twelve years. Impatient slaves revolted in early July 1848, took over most of Saint Croix, and demanded immediate freedom. Governor-General Peter von Scholten complied, issuing an emancipation proclamation on 3 July 1848. The crown confirmed the action in September. Modest compensation to slave owners did not come until 1853.

Emancipation did not end labor unrest. To replace slave labor, authorities implemented the Labor Act of 1849, establishing a system of yearly contract labor. Opposition to the contract system led to violence in 1878. Protesters burned homes and shops in Frederiksted, and unrest spread into the countryside. Mary Thomas, dubbed "Queen Mary" by her followers, was one of the leaders of the uprising. The violence, which lasted several days, included the destruction of fifty-three plantations and cane fields. Three Europeans and seventy-four Africans died. Authorities later executed twelve protesters. On 1 October 1879 authorities abolished the Labor Act.

The United States had a long-standing interest in the Danish Virgin Islands. Efforts to purchase the islands failed in 1867 and 1902. Fearful that Germany would gain control over the islands during World War I, the United States forwarded a new proposal that was accepted in 1916. The United States paid $25 million for the islands, the most expensive land acquisition in its history. Formal transfer took place on 31 March 1917.

See also **Labor Movements; Plantations; Slave Revolts: Spanish America; Slavery: Spanish America; Slavery: Abolition.**

BIBLIOGRAPHY

Charles C. Tansill, *The Purchase of the Danish West Indies* (1932).

Darwin D. Creque, *The U.S. Virgins and the Eastern Caribbean* (1968).

Pearl Varlack, *The Virgins: A Descriptive and Historical Profile* (1977).

William W. Boyer, *America's Virgin Islands: A History of Human Rights and Wrongs* (1983).

Karen Fog Olwig, *Cultural Adaptation and Resistance on St. John: Three Centuries of Afro-Caribbean Life* (1985).

Additional Bibliography

Donoghue, Eddie. *Black Women/White Men: The Sexual Exploitation of Female Slaves in the Danish West Indies.* Bloomington: AuthorHouse, 2006.

Tyson, George. *Bondmen and Freedmen in the Danish West Indies.* St. Thomas: Virgin Islands Humanities Council, 1996.

STEVEN S. GILLICK

DANTAS, MANUEL PINTO DE SOUZA (1831–1894).

Manuel Pinto de Souza Dantas (*b.* 21 February 1831; *d.* 29 January 1894), prime minister of Brazil (1884–1885). One of the leading Liberal politicians of the last decades of the Brazilian Empire, Dantas began his career soon after finishing law school in 1851. He held a number of local and provincial political posts, including provincial president of Alagoas and of his native Bahia. At the same time he was a member of various sessions of the national Chamber of Deputies from 1852 to 1868 and was named minister of agriculture, commerce, and public works in the Zacarias de Góes cabinet in 1866. When that administration fell in 1868, Dantas retired temporarily from electoral politics.

Dantas gained his greatest recognition when he returned to politics as a senator in the 1880s. In a period when the abolition of slavery was increasingly seen as the nation's most pressing problem—it was abolished in 1888—the emperor asked Dantas in 1884 to form a new cabinet that would take steps toward emancipation. Moderate in his views, Dantas described the goals of his cabinet as "neither retreat, nor halt, nor undue haste." Nevertheless, the bill he presented, the central provision of which would free slaves over sixty years of age, set off a storm of opposition in Congress. After attacking the principle of liberating any slave without compensating the former master, his enemies finally forced Dantas's cabinet out of power in 1885. The Conservative ministry that followed then passed a watered-down version of Dantas's Sexagenarian Law that same year.

With the end of the Brazilian Empire in 1889, Dantas became director of the Bank of Brazil and then the Bank of the Republic, until his death.

See also **Slavery: Abolition.**

BIBLIOGRAPHY

Robert E. Conrad, *The Destruction of Brazilian Slavery, 1850–1888* (1972).

Robert Brent Toplin, *The Abolition of Slavery in Brazil* (1972).

Emília Viotti Da Costa, "Masters and Slaves," chap. 6 in her *The Brazilian Empire: Myths and Histories* (1985).

ROGER A. KITTLESON

DANTICAT, EDWIDGE (1969–).

Edwidge Danticat, a Haitian writer, was born in Port-au-Prince, Haiti, on January 19, 1969. Danticat's fiction interrogates Haiti's troubled past and the problems faced by the Haitian diaspora in the United States. In 1981, at age twelve, Danticat left Haiti for the United States, and she remains haunted by her ambivalent status as a Haitian exile. Her debut novel, *Breath, Eyes, Memory* (1994), begun in high school, heralded a potent new voice for the Haitian American diaspora. Subsequently it was a selection for Oprah Winfrey's Book Club. *Krik?Krak!* (1995), a collection of short stories, was followed by two exceptionally powerful novels, *The Farming of Bones* (1998) and *The Dew Breaker* (2004). The first chronicled the mass murder of Haitian cane cutters in the Dominican Republic during the Trujillo dictatorship; the second followed the lives of Haitians as they struggled to survive in the West Indian enclaves of New York. Even as the novels articulated unspeakable grief and trauma, they were distinguished by the gentle, redemptive voice that has become recognizably Danticat's. *Behind the Mountains* (2002) and *Anacaona, Golden Flower* (2005) are novels for young adults. The latter tells the story of a pre-Columbine queen of Haiti, Anacaona, who resisted the Spanish. *After the Dance* (2002) is a memoir and travelogue about the Haitian carnival.

See also **Carnival; Literature: Spanish America.**

BIBLIOGRAPHY

Scarboro, Ann Armstrong. *Edwidge Danticat Visits Her Haitian Roots, June, 2003.* Boulder, CO: Mosaic Media Arts. VHS tape. Danticat discusses life in Haiti, her family, immigration to the United States, and her work to promote young authors. Ends with a reading in French from *The Dew Breaker.*

Thomson, Ian. *Bonjour Blanc: A Journey through Haiti.* London: Penguin, 1992.

IAN THOMSON

DARIÉ, SANDU (1908–1991).

Sandu Darié (*b.* 1908, *d.* 1991), Cuban artist and art critic. Born in Romania, Darié studied law at the University of Paris. While there he continued to write art criticism for Romanian newspapers and contributed humorous sketches to the French press. Darié immigrated to Cuba in 1941 and embraced Cuban life and culture; he subsequently became a full citizen. In 1949 he had his first solo exhibit, at the Lyceum in Havana, and another showing in New York. He exhibited at shows in Brazil, Mexico, Italy, Argentina, and Japan, and has pieces in the permanent collection of the Museum of Modern Art in New York. Darié's work is uniquely interactive: through his transformable constructions, such as *Estructura espacial transformable* (1960), the viewer is able to participate in the creative process.

See also **Art: The Twentieth Century.**

BIBLIOGRAPHY

Government of Cuba, *Pintores Cubanos* (1962) and *Pintores Cubanos* (1974).

Adelaida De Juan, *Pintura cubana: Temas y variaciones* (1978).

Additional Bibliography

Merino Acosta, Luz, and Elsa Vega Dopico. *La razón de la poesía: arte concreto, exposición en el Museo Nacional de Bellas Artes, Colección Arte Cubano, La Habana: 6 de diciembre de 2002–9 de febrero de 2003.* La Habana: Museo Nacional de Bellas Artes, 2002.

KAREN RACINE

DARIÉN. Darién, the first Spanish settlement on the North American mainland, was established in 1510 when Martín Fernández de Enciso captured a village on the hot, swampy Caribbean coast of Panama, which he christened Santa María La Antigua de Darién.

Enciso was not an able leader, and one of his lieutenants, Vasco Núñez de Balboa, soon took over control of Darién. Balboa established an agricultural economic base for Darién, worked by native labor, and the settlement thrived. In 1513, Darién served as the base for Balboa's expedition to find the "Southern sea," during which Balboa became the first European to set eyes on the Pacific Ocean.

Although the crown rewarded Balboa with the title of "*adelantado* of the Southern sea," his own father-in-law, Pedrarias Dávila, contested his control over the settlement. In 1517 Pedrarias beheaded Balboa and assumed control of Darién.

Darién suffered under Pedrarias's administration. In 1519, Pedrarias moved the Spanish population from the swamplands of Darién to the more healthful climate of Panama City. In 1524, Darién was formally abandoned. Darién was also the site of Scotland's failed attempt to establish a colony at the Isthmus of Panama; the colony was abandoned in 1699 after less than a year.

See also **Balboa, Vasco Núñez de; Enciso, Martín Fernández de.**

BIBLIOGRAPHY

Murdo J. MacLeod, *Spanish Central America: A Socioeconomic History, 1520–1720* (1973).

Ralph Lee Woodward, Jr, *Central America: A Nation Divided* (2d ed., 1985).

VIRGINIA GARRARD BURNETT

DARIEN GAP. The Darien Gap is the "saddle," or ridge, in the Serranía del Darién over which, in September 1513, the expedition led by Vasco Núñez de Balboa crossed the Isthmus of Panama en route to the discovery of the Pacific Ocean. In 1510, Balboa had set out from Santa María la Antigua del Darién, the strategic base founded on the mainland of Central America, so that he would "pass to the other sea on the side of the south" which native informants told him "is very good to navigate in canoes, being always pacific, and does not turn wild as it does on this [Atlantic] coast" (letter to the king, January 1513). Like all conquistadors, Balboa was driven (and deluded) by the prospect not only of discovering new lands and peoples but of finding gold and, in this case, pearls as well. Indian leaders, with whom Balboa is said to have enjoyed less hostile relations than his counterparts elsewhere, assured him that gold was present in quantity in all the rivers of the other coast sufficient motivation to endure extreme hardship and privation, lack of food and unhealthy conditions above all. Balboa understood the necessity of native collaboration for the goals of Spanish conquest better than most of his more short-sighted contemporaries, especially his father-in-law, Pedro Arias (Pedrarias) de Ávila, who beheaded

Balboa in 1519 to assert his authority as "Captain and Governor of Tierra Firme." The treatment that Pedrarias meted out to his son-in-law was replicated time and again in his dealings with native inhabitants, so much so that Darién soon was lost and desolate, causing the Spanish base in the region to be relocated, in 1524, to Panama City.

An intrepid explorer who processed information relayed to him assiduously, Balboa took pains to document his deeds, even if others failed to record them properly. His sighting, "silent, upon a peak in Darien," of the Pacific Ocean was attributed by the English poet John Keats, famously but erroneously, to "stout Cortez." Balboa choreographed his trek into history to ensure that, following native counsel, he alone walked to the vantage point where he became the first European to contemplate the Pacific on either September 25 or 27, 1513. Two days later Balboa was among the first Christians wading in the South Sea, all trying the water with their hands and proving that it was salt. A ceremony of possession was performed. Balboa's party, after a four-month reconnaissance, returned to Santa María del Darién in early 1514.

Though native communities were able to furnish their Spanish masters with impressive amounts of gold and pearls, geographical setting was the chief reward for all those who sought to profit from establishing a presence in Darién. Realizing the wealth that could accrue by controlling transoceanic trade across the isthmus, an ill-fated colonization scheme in the late seventeenth century saw Scottish investors ruined, and naive countrymen of theirs fall sick and perish, in the Darién tropics. Scotland's disastrous endeavor is enshrined in Panamanian place names such as Cerro Caledonia and Punta Escocés. It would take the building of the Panama Canal in the early twentieth century, at considerable expense of money and men, for the vision of William Paterson, the Scottish merchant who attempted to transport cargoes overland at this site, to materialize. The environs of Darién may still be "door of the seas, and the key of the universe," but taking advantage of the location for entrepreneurial gain has always come at a price.

See also **Balboa, Vasco Núñez de; Panama; Panama Canal.**

BIBLIOGRAPHY

Mena García, Carmen. "La frontera del hambre: Construyendo el espacio histórico del Darién." *Mesoamérica* 45 (2003): 35–65.

Parsons, James J. "Santa María la Antigua del Darién." *Geographical Review* 50, no. 2 (April 1960): 274–276.

Prebble, John. *The Darien Disaster*. London: Secker & Warburg, 1968.

Romoli, Kathleen. *Balboa of Darien: Discoverer of the Pacific Ocean*. Garden City, NY: Doubleday, 1953.

Sauer, Carl O. *The Early Spanish Main*. Berkeley: University of California Press, 1966.

W. GEORGE LOVELL

DARÍO, RUBÉN (1867–1916). Rubén Darío (*b.* 18 January 1867; *d.* 6 February 1916), born Félix Rubén García Sarmiento in Nicaragua, was the leading poet writing in Spanish between 1888 and 1916.

Life and Works. Darío was born in Metapa (now Cuidad Darío). After his parents separated, he was reared by his great-aunt Bernarda Sarmiento Ramírez and her husband. He studied with the Jesuits and at the National Institute, reading the classics and publishing poetry from age twelve. By age fourteen he had joined the editorial staff of the local newspaper. In 1883 he traveled to El Salvador, where President Rafael Zaldívar enrolled him in school. Upon his return to Nicaragua (1884), he worked as a journalist and read voraciously at the National Library. In 1886 he moved to Chile. Through his friendship with the president's son, Pedro Balmaseda, he became immersed in French poetry, especially the Parnassians, which is the most salient influence in his *Azul,* a collection of short stories and verse, published in Valparaíso (1888).

In 1889, Darío returned to Central America and worked feverishly on his poetry and newspaper articles. The following year he married Rafaela Contreras. They moved to Costa Rica in 1891. In 1892 he was named secretary of Nicaragua's delegation to Spain's celebration of the fourth centennial of Columbus's voyage of discovery. Upon his return, he learned of his wife's death and was named Colombia's consul to Buenos Aires. He married Rosario Murillo in 1893, but left alone for Argentina via

Statue of Nicaraguan national poet Rubén Darío (1867–1916) in Managua, c. 20th century. A highly innovative and influential poet, Darío was the leader of the modernismo movement in the Spanish-speaking world. © NIK WHEELER/CORBIS

New York and Paris. In Paris he met Jean Moreas, Théodore de Banville, and Paul Verlaine, and in New York, José Martí. In Argentina, Darío discharged his consular duties, wrote for *La Nación* and other newspapers, and became the leader of a group of young and brilliant writers. With one of them, the Bolivian Ricardo Jaimes Freyre, he founded the literary journal *Revista de América*.

In 1896 Darío took over the leadership of the *modernismo* group. That same year, he published *Los raros*—a collection of essays on American and European writers—and *Prosas profanas*—a book influenced by French symbolism, although rooted in the Spanish classics. *Prosas,* a deliberate break with romanticism, became Darío's most imitated work for its innovative form, musicality, beauty,

and exoticism. In 1898, *La Nación* sent him to Spain to report on the aftereffects of the Spanish-American War. The results of this endeavor were later collected in *España contemporánea* (1901). While in Madrid he reaffirmed his leadership of modernism and met the younger poets, among them Antonio and Manuel Machado and Juan Ramón Jiménez. He also met Francisca Sánchez, the woman who became his lifetime companion and the mother of his son. In 1900 he moved permanently to Paris.

In 1905, Darío published *Cantos de vida y esperanza.* Its first poem, "Yo soy aquél...," rejected his previous "blue verse and profane songs," while continuing his revolutionary treatment of meter, rhythms, and poetic techniques. *Cantos* is perhaps Darío's most accomplished book. In it he also introduced a note absent from his earlier poetry: sociopolitical concerns for the future of Latin America and Hispanic culture. The Spanish defeat in 1898 and Theodore Roosevelt's policies in Central America had awakened Latin Americans to the fact that the United States could no longer be regarded as a trusted neighbor. Instead, it appeared as a menace capable of swallowing the southern half of the continent. *Cantos* manifests this new awareness and the new sense of allegiance to Spain as the mother country.

During the following years Darío maintained his residence in Paris, while visiting Spain and Latin America and publishing a number of important books: *El canto errante* (1907), *El viaje a Nicaragua* (1909), and *Poema del otoño* (1910). In 1911 he joined *Mundial* magazine in Paris. Its publishers took Darío on an advertising trip to the New World the following year. While in Buenos Aires, he wrote *Autobiografía,* a work serialized in *Caras y caretas.* He returned to Paris in 1913. When World War I erupted, Darío was ill and in serious economic straits, but he accepted another lecture tour throughout the Americas. He spoke at Columbia University in New York, where he contracted pneumonia. Taken to Nicaragua, he died in the city of León.

Significance. By the time Darío published his first book, *Epistolas y poemas* (1885), at age eighteen, he was the leading Central American poet. Three years later, with the publication of *Azul,* he became the leading poet of the Hispanic world. It has even been said that Darío's poetry divides Hispanic literary history into "before" and "after." His renovation of poetic expression was so thorough that he is still a leading force. In his quest for poetry, he broke away from traditional conventions and maintained no allegiance to any one set of aesthetic norms. He learned from the primitives and the standard-bearers of Golden Age poetics—Góngora, San Juan de la Cruz, Saint Teresa d'Ávila, Cervantes, Quevedo—as well as from Gustavo Adolfo Bécquer and the Romantics. To their invaluable lessons he added what he learned from the French Parnassians and Symbolists. He acknowledged his debt and achieved a style unequaled by any other Spanish poet of his day. His range of expression, his inventiveness, and his flawless rendering of music into words are still refreshingly new.

See also **Literature: Spanish America.**

BIBLIOGRAPHY

Charles D. Watland, ed. *Poet-Errant: Selected Poems of Rubén Darío,* translated by Lysander Kemp, prologue by Octavio Paz (1965, 1988).

Enrique Anderson Imbert, *La originalidad de Rubén Darío* (1967).

Ángel Rama, *Rubén Darío y el modernismo: Circunstancia socio-económica de un arte americano* (1970).

George D. Schade and Miguel González-Gerth, eds., *Rubén Darío: Centennial Studies* (1970).

Raymond Skyrme, *Rubén Darío and the Pythagorean Tradition* (1975).

Cathy Login Jrade, *Rubén Darío and the Romantic Search for Unity: The Modernist Recourse to Esoteric Tradition* (1983).

Enrique Anderson Imbert, "Rubén Darío," in *Latin American Writers,* edited by Carlos A. Solé and Maria Isabel Abreu (1989), vol. 1, pp. 397–412.

Additional Bibliography

Acereda, Alberto, and Rigoberto Guevara. *Modernism, Rubén Darío, and the Poetics of Despair.* Dallas: University Press of America, 2004.

Martínez Domingo, José María. *Rubén Darío, addenda.* Palencia: Cálamo, 2000.

Ortega, Julio. *Rubén Darío.* Barcelona: Ediciones Omega, 2003.

Urbina, Nicasio. *Miradas críticas sobre Rubén Darío.* Managua: Fundación International Rubén Darío, 2005.

Zanetti, Susana. *Rubén Darío en La Nación de Buenos Aires, 1892-1916.* Buenos Aires: EUDEBA, 2004.

MARÍA A. SALGADO

DARTIGUENAVE, PHILIPPE-SUDRÉ

(1863–1926). Philippe-Sudré Dartiguenave (*b.* 1863, *d.* 1926), president of Haiti (1915–1922). Installed as president by the U.S. Marines, he was the first Haitian president since 1879 to be from the south of Haiti and the first mulatto. Dartiguenave supported the U.S. occupation and customs receivership, and relied on the U.S. authorities for financial advice. Contrary to popular opinion, however, he did not surrender absolute control of the island to U.S. interests. In 1922 the vote of the mulatto elite in the south prevented his reelection.

See also **Haiti.**

BIBLIOGRAPHY

Cyril L. R. James, *The Black Jacobins,* 2d ed. (1963), is a classic study on Haitian history. A more recent analysis is Michel-Rolph Trouillot, *Haiti: State Against Nation* (1990).

Additional Bibliography

Renda, Mary A. *Taking Haiti: Military Occupation and the Culture of U.S. Imperialism, 1915–1940.* Chapel Hill, NC: University of North Carolina Press, 2001.

Shannon, Magdaline W. *Jean Price-Mars, the Haitian Elite and the American Occupation, 1915–1935.* New York: St. Martin's Press, 1996.

DARIÉN DAVIS

D'AUBUISSON, ROBERTO (1943–1992). Roberto d'Aubuisson (*b.* 23 August 1943; *d.* 20 February 1992), Salvadoran army officer and political leader. Roberto d'Aubuisson was a career intelligence officer who left the service when a new reformist government seized power in El Salvador on 15 October 1979. An outspoken anti-Communist who opposed social reforms and called for a hard line against leftist rebels in the country's civil war, d'Aubuisson was widely believed to be responsible for human rights violations. His name was frequently associated with the activities of death squads, most notably the assassination on 24 March 1980 of San Salvador's archbishop Oscar Arnulfo Romero, as well as with coup conspiracies against the reformist junta.

Youthful and charismatic, d'Aubuisson sought a political following. He founded the right-wing

Nationalist Republican Alliance (Alianza Republicana Nacionalista—ARENA) in 1981 and served briefly as president of the Constituent Assembly (1982–1984), but his higher ambitions were discouraged by the armed forces and by the administration of U.S. president Ronald Reagan, which feared that his reputation would jeopardize congressional support for military aid to El Salvador. Following his defeat by José Napoleón Duarte in the 1984 presidential election, d'Aubuisson yielded his party leadership post to Alfredo Cristiani, a less controversial politician. D'Aubuisson's political influence endured. When Cristiani was elected president in 1989, many observers believed that the charismatic former party leader would wield the real power, but d'Aubuisson's death from cancer three years later at age forty-eight brought a premature end to his career.

See also **El Salvador, Political Parties: National Republican Alliance (ARENA).**

BIBLIOGRAPHY

There is no biography of d'Aubuisson. A number of press and magazine accounts are useful, among them the obituary in the *New York Times,* 21 February 1992, and Christopher Dickey, "Behind the Death Squads," in the *New Republic* (26 December 1983): 16–21. General works on the Salvadoran crisis are Tommie Sue Montgomery, *Revolution in El Salvador: Origins and Evolution* (1982); Enrique A. Baloyra, *El Salvador in Transition* (1982); and Raymond Bonner, *Weakness and Deceit: U.S. Policy and El Salvador* (1984).

Additional Bibliography

Lungo, Mario, and Arthur Schmidt. *El Salvador in the Eighties: Counterinsurgency and Revolution.* Philadelphia: Temple University Press, 1996.

Ross, Tara W. "Roberto D'Aubuisson, Spokesman for the Right in El Salvador," M.A. thesis, Ohio University, 1997.

STEPHEN WEBRE

DAVIDOVSKY, MARIO (1934–). Mario Davidovsky (*b.* 4 March 1934), Argentine composer who became a naturalized U.S. citizen. Born in Médanos, province of Buenos Aires, he was a composition student of Guillermo Graetzer in Buenos Aires, where he developed an atonal, abstract lyricism in his compositions, such as String Quartet no. 1 (1954), *Noneto* (1957), and *Pequeño concierto* (1957).

He then moved to the United States under a Guggenheim Fellowship and studied with Varèse, Babbitt, Ussachevsky, Luening, and Sessions. He was associated with the Columbia-Princeton Electronic Music Center in New York from its inception and was an assistant director from 1965 to 1980. He became director in 1981. Davidovsky has been particularly interested in the combination of acoustic instruments and electronically produced sounds on tape. He is celebrated for his series of Synchronisms, including no. 1 for flute and tape (1963), no. 2 for flute, clarinet, violin, cello, and tape (1964), which was commissioned by the Fromm Foundation for the Tanglewood Festival, and no. 3 for cello and tape (1965). If some of his earlier pieces were somewhat exploratory, Davidovsky's style and personality emerged strongly in his Synchronisms no. 5 for percussion and tape (1969) and no. 6 for piano and tape (1971), which in 1971 was awarded the Pulitzer Prize. The series was continued in 1974 with Synchronisms no. 7 for orchestra and tape and no. 8 for violin and tape; in 1988 with Synchronisms no. 9 for violin and tape; and in 1992 with Synchronisms no. 10 for guitar and electronic sounds. Synchronisms no. 11 for contrabass and tape (2005) and no. 12 for clarinet and tape (2006) premiered at the 2007 National Conference of the Society for Electro-Acoustic Music in the United States (SEAMUS).

Davidovsky has produced a remarkable series for solo tape called Electronic Studies. The first dates from 1960, and the third (1965) was written as an homage to Varèse. Other important works include Transients for Orchestra (1972), String Quartet no. 3 (1976), Festino (1994), and Sefarad: Four Spanish-Ladino Folkscenes (2004). Davidovsky is the Fanny P. Mason Professor of Music, Emeritus, at Harvard University.

See also **Music: Art Music.**

BIBLIOGRAPHY

Rodolfo Arizaga, *Enciclopedia de la música argentina* (1971), p. 110.

David Ernst, *The Evolution of Electronic Music* (1977), pp. 128–129, 142.

Gérard Béhague, *Music in Latin America: An Introduction* (1979), pp. 329, 338–339; *New Grove Dictionary of Music and Musicians* (1980).

Additional Bibliography

Kimura, Mari. "Peformance Practice in Computer Music." *Computer Music Journal* 19: 1 (Spring 1995), 64–75.

Perea, Andrew Rafael. "Electro-Acoustic Music: An Historical Overview, with an In-Depth Study of Preparatory Techniques for Mario Davidovsky's Synchronisms No. 9 for Violin and Tape." D.M.A. Thesis, University of Texas at Austin, 1998.

ALCIDES LANZA

DÁVILA, MIGUEL R. (?–1927).

Miguel R. Dávila (d. 1927), provisional president of Honduras (1907–1908), then elected president (1908–1911). Dávila, a member of the Liberal Party, headed a regime that exemplified the political instability prevailing in Central America at the beginning of the twentieth century. The legendary rivalry between the Nicaraguan dictator José Santos Zelaya and Guatemala's Manuel Estrada Cabrera brought Dávila to power in 1907 when Zelaya engineered a coup against Estrada Cabrera's ally General Manuel Bonilla. During Dávila's term in office, Honduras participated in the 1907 Washington Conference sponsored by Mexico and the United States to restore stability to Central America. He had to deal with numerous rebellions organized by Honduran exiles. Dávila's regime ended in 1911 when Bonilla, financed by banana interests, took advantage of the tensions created by the renegotiation of Honduras's debt with the United States (part of Secretary of State Philander Knox's Dollar Diplomacy) to regain power.

See also **Honduras.**

BIBLIOGRAPHY

There are no monographs on Dávila's presidency. For the Honduran context a standard source is Rómulo Ernesto Durón y Gamero, *Bosquejo histórico de Honduras,* 2d ed. (1956). A more analytical approach is in Mario Posas and Rafael Del Cid, *La construcción del sector público y del estado nacional en Honduras, 1876–1979,* 2d ed. (1983). The international rivalries of the period are detailed in Dana G. Munro, *Intervention and Dollar Diplomacy in the Caribbean, 1900–1921* (1964).

HÉCTOR LINDO-FUENTES

DÁVILA ESPINOZA, CARLOS GUILLERMO (1887–1955).

Carlos Guillermo Dávila Espinoza (b. 15 September 1887; d. 19 October 1955), Chilean political figure and newspaper publisher. After serving as ambassador to Washington, Dávila continued his education in the United States. Dávila was one of three men who led the Socialist Republic of 100 Days. More conservative than his colleagues, he eventually replaced them until he too was deposed, this time by a military coup under the leadership of General Bartolomé Blanche Espejo. Following the socialist republic's fall, Dávila resumed his newspaper career, working in the United States and eventually acting as editor of the government-owned journal *La Nación.* Having served as Chile's representative to various international organizations, he subsequently became secretary-general of the Organization of American States, a position he held at the time of his death.

See also **Chile, Socialist Republic of 100 Days.**

BIBLIOGRAPHY

Frederick B. Pike, *Chile and the United States, 1880–1962* (1963), pp. 210–211.

Frederick M. Nunn, *Chilean Politics: The Honorable Mission of the Armed Forces 1920–1931* (1970), pp. 171–173.

Additional Bibliography

Simonetti de Groote, Susana. "El gobierno de Carlos Dávila, 16 de junio–13 de septiembre de 1932." *Boletín de la Academia Chilena de la Historia* 62 (1995): 293–360.

WILLIAM F. SATER

DAWSON AGREEMENT.

The vehicle through which the United States granted Nicaragua a critical loan and recognition of its government in exchange for certain concessions. After the ouster of Nicaraguan dictator José Santos Zelaya in 1909, the U.S. wanted to control Nicaragua's finances. The new Nicaraguan president, Juan Estrada, needed a loan, but the U.S. first wanted assurances that any Zelayista influences would be purged from the government—Zelaya had been vehemently antiforeign, and presumably any of his supporters would oppose foreign interests. In October 1910 the U.S. dispatched Thomas Dawson to Managua, to assist in the re-establishment of a constitutional government by ensuring that no Zelayistas maintained power and by preparing Nicaragua for new elections. The Estrada government signed the Dawson Agreement on

October 27. Dawson intimated that if the Nicaraguans did not accept the agreement, there could be outside interference if disorder were to reoccur.

The Dawson Agreement called for the destruction of Zelaya's monopolies, the establishment of a claims commission to compensate foreigners for losses incurred during the civil war, U.S. supervision of a customs receivership based on the Dominican Republic model, and the creation of a new constitution by the Constituent Assembly. The U.S. agreed to recognize the Estrada government and to reorganize Nicaragua's finances through a loan secured by customs revenues.

See also **United States-Latin American Relations.**

BIBLIOGRAPHY

William Kamman, *A Search for Stability: United States Diplomacy Toward Nicaragua, 1925–1933* (1968), esp. pp. 12–13.

Langley, Lester D. *The Banana Wars: United States Intervention in the Caribbean, 1898–1934.* Wilmington, DE: SR Books, 2002.

Woodward, Ralph Lee, Jr. *Central America: A Nation Divided.* New York: Oxford University Press, 1999.

Additional Bibliography

Langley, Lester D., and Thomas David Schoonover. *The Banana Men: American Mercenaries and Entrepreneurs in Central America, 1880–1930.* Lexington: University of Kentucky Press, 1995.

SHANNON BELLAMY

DAWSON ISLAND.

Dawson Island, Chilean land mass of about 8 square miles located in the central section of the Strait of Magellan, where it takes a northwestern turn and travels away from the Seno del Almirantazgo. On the continental shore, and facing the northern tip of the island, lies Puerto del Hambre (Port Famine), the site where Pedro Sarmiento De Gamboa tried unsuccessfully in 1584 to establish a permanent settlement. Windswept Dawson Island houses a detachment of the Chilean Marines, whose barracks held political prisoners during the first dictatorship of Carlos Ibáñez Del Campo (1927–1931) and during the early years (1974–1978) of General Augusto Pinochet's rule.

According to an International Red Cross report in 1974, Dawson Island was home to ninety-nine political detainees who were sentenced to forced labor and live in squalor. When the camp was shut down in October 1974, the prisoners were transferred to the Punta Arenas prison, and some were released.

See also **Chile, Geography; Ibáñez del Campo, Carlos; Pinochet Ugarte, Augusto; Sarmiento de Gamboa, Pedro.**

BIBLIOGRAPHY

Additional Bibliography

Collier, Simon. *A History of Chile, 1808–1994.* New York: Cambridge University Press, 1996.

Spooner, Mary Helen. *Soldiers in a Narrow Land: The Pinochet Regime in Chile.* Los Angeles: University of California Press, 1994.

CÉSAR N. CAVIEDES

DAZA, HILARIÓN

(1840–1894). Hilarión Daza (*b.* 14 January 1840; *d.* 27 February 1894), president of Bolivia (1876–1879). Born in Sucre, Daza was trained as a soldier and rose to the rank of colonel under Mariano Melgarejo (1864–1871). In 1870 he defected to revolutionaries, who deposed Melgarejo on 15 January 1871. Gen. Agustín Morales, the leader of the revolution, died in 1872, and his civilian successors showed little ability to consolidate power. Daza, head of the elite Colorado battalion, seized power in 1876. In constant need of funds for his army, Daza imposed a new tax on the Chilean mining concessions along the Pacific Coast (1878). This tax, which immediately provoked a Chilean attack against Bolivia's coastal territory, resulted in the War of the Pacific (1879–1884). Repeated Chilean victories led not only to Daza's downfall at the end of December 1879, but also to Bolivia's loss of the guano and nitrate-rich coastal area. Daza's major political accomplishment was the calling of the Constitutional Convention of 1878, whose work led to the adoption of the Constitution of 1880, the longest lasting in Bolivian history (1938). Daza was assassinated in 1894 in Uyuni by persons who claimed he was trying to regain the presidency.

See also **War of the Pacific.**

BIBLIOGRAPHY

Herbert S. Klein, *Parties and Political Change in Bolivia, 1880–1952* (1969), pp. 14–19.

Enrique Vidaurre Retamozo, *El presidente Daza* (1975).

Additional Bibliography

Antezana Ergueta, Luis. *Daza no ocultó la noticia de la invasión chilena: (definitiva dilucidación histórica).* La Paz, 1982.

ERWIN P. GRIESHABER

DEATH SQUADS.

Death squads appeared in Latin America in the late 1960s as a clandestine way to confront increasing revolutionary activity. The aim of death squads is to destroy an opponent's infrastructure through terrorism. Although death squads exist on the left and on the right of the political spectrum, they are most often associated with extreme rightists. Members of right-wing death squads are often recruited from police and military forces, or from paramilitary organizations. Rightist death squads are usually financed by wealthy conservatives and work closely with repressive national governments and their security forces in an alliance that has allowed them to operate with impunity.

Death squads were originally associated mainly with political instability in Central America, but they have been active in South America too. In the late 1960s, the military government in Brazil gave covert approval for the use of death squads against real or suspected opponents of the regime. In the 1970s and early 1980s, death squads of both the Right and the Left operated in Argentina, but the military regime's use of death squads in its dirty war against suspected leftists was especially brutal. Victims of Brazilian and Argentine death squads included intellectuals, students, journalists, workers, priests and nuns, and common criminals. A late twentieth-century trend in Brazil was the use of death squads by businessmen to murder orphaned street children.

The Andean countries of Colombia and Peru were plagued by death squads in the 1980s. In 1987 there were 137 active paramilitary death squads in Colombia. The most notorious in Colombia is the right-wing death squad MAS, or Death to Kidnappers. Formed in 1981, MAS has links to the drug cartels and the armed forces, and is believed to have committed some 500 murders by decapitation of peasants and left-wing leaders, including the country's only Indian priest. In 1987 priests advocating liberation theology were killed at the rate of one each month. The most famous case of right-wing death squad brutality was the October 1987 murder of presidential candidate Jaime Pardo Leal, who had identified retired and active military officers as ringleaders of Colombian death squads.

Peru's state-sponsored police antiterrorist unit Sinchis also has gained notoriety. Founded in 1984 to combat leftists, especially the Marxist group Sendero Luminoso (Shining Path), Sinchis conducted summary executions of suspects with little fear of official condemnation. Sendero death squads were active during the 1980s and early 1990s, as were a variety of peasant groups who have committed retribution killings. Equally well known among government-funded death squad activities were the massacres at La Cantuta University and Barrios Altos during the early 1990s. Both of these were clandestinely committed by the infamous Colina Group, perhaps with the complicity of the highest levels of Alberto Fujimori's government. All told, some twenty-five people, including a small child and a professor, "disappeared" at La Cantuta University and Barrios Altos.

The most notorious death squads operated in Honduras, Guatemala, and El Salvador. The Honduran Anticommunist Movement, known by its Spanish acronym MACHO, appeared in 1982 and targeted liberal politicians, students, labor leaders, and Indians suspected of leftist tendencies. Emerging in the 1960s, the Guatemalan Organized National Anticommunist Movement murdered leftists and peasants suspected of being guerrilla sympathizers. Another Guatemalan group that appeared in the late 1970s, the Secret Anticommunist Army, specialized in the assassination of union leaders, students, politicians, and professionals who questioned the status quo. Until their exposure in the 1980s, urban death squads in Guatemala were controlled directly from the National Palace.

El Salvadorian death squads of the Left and Right have achieved special notoriety due to their violent acts. The Farabundo Martí Front for National Liberation (FMLN), a leftist organization, engaged in the murder of military and political leaders and their U.S.

advisers, while rightist death squads retaliated by killing intellectuals, clerics, and anyone else suspected of supporting the FMLN. In 1966 police and army officers joined with the National Liberation Movement, an extreme-right political party, to create the Mano Blanca (White Hand) death squads. When Mano Blanca's close association with the government and the police became public and embarrassed the regime, it was replaced by Ojo por Ojo (Eye for Eye). In 1977 the White Warriors Union became known for terrorism against Jesuits, and in 1980 the Maximiliano Hernández Martínez Brigade organized to assassinate Christian Democrat and Marxist leaders. Many of the recruits for El Salvador's death squads came from ORDEN, a paramilitary organization founded by ex-army major Roberto D'Aubuisson. It is believed that D'Aubuisson and the death squads associated with ORDEN were responsible for the murders of Archbishop Oscar Arnulfo Romero, four American Maryknoll nuns, and a group of Jesuit priests in 1980. Though the precise number of deaths in Latin America attributed to leftist and rightist death squads is unknown, some place the death toll at more than 100,000.

See also **Guatemala, Terrorist Organizations: Mano Blanca; Guatemala, Terrorist Organizations: Ojo por Ojo; Terrorism; Truth Commissions.**

BIBLIOGRAPHY

Peter Flynn, *Brazil: A Political Analysis* (1971).

Gary E. McCuen, *Political Murder in Central America: Death Squads and U.S. Policies* (1984).

Report of the Archdiocese of São Paulo, *Torture in Brazil* (1986).

David Rock, *Argentina, 1567–1987: From Spanish Colonization to Alfonsin* (1987).

Amnesty International, *El Salvador Death Squads, a Government Strategy* (1988).

Javier Torres, *The Armed Forces of Colombia and the National Front* (1990).

Martha K. Huggins, ed., *Vigilantism and the State in Modern Latin America: Essays on Extra-Legal Violence* (1991).

Debrah Poole and Gerjerdo Renikue, *Peru: Time of Fear* (1992).

Additional Bibliography

Burt, Jo-Marie. "Quien habla es terrorista": The Political Use of Fear in Fujimori's Peru." *Latin American Research Review* 41: 3 (2006), 32–62.

Godoy, Angela Snodgrass. "La Muchacha Respondona: Reflections on the Razor's Edge Between Crime and Human Rights." *Human Rights Quarterly* 27: 2 (May 2005), 597–624.

Grandin, Greg. *The Last Colonial Massacre: Latin America in the Cold War.* Chicago: University of Chicago Press, 2004.

Interamerican Commission on Human Rights. *Report No. 42/99: Case 11.045.* Washington, DC: Organization of American States, March 11, 1999. Online at: http://www.cidh.oas.org/annualrep/98eng/Admissibility/Peru%2011045.htm.

Menjívar, Cecilia, and Néstor Rodriguez, eds. *When States Kill: Latin America, the U.S., and Technologies of Terror.* Austin: University of Texas Press, 2005.

Saavedra, Alfredo. *El color de la sangre: 40 años de represión y de resistencia en Guatemala.* Guatemala: Grupo de Apoyo Mutuo, 2001.

Taussig, Michael T. *Law in a Lawless Land: Diary of a "Limpieza" in Colombia.* New York: New Press, 2003.

SONNY B. DAVIS

DEBRAY, [JULES] RÉGIS (1940–).

[Jules] Régis Debray (*b.* 2 September 1940), French intellectual and Marxist philosopher. Debray was Ché Guevara's most articulate interpreter, but after Guevara's death in the disastrous 1967 Bolivian revolution, he synthesized the Leninist traditional view of revolution and Guevarist *focoismo* (revolution from a rural guerrilla center, or *foco*).

Debray became a student of the French Communist ideologue Louis Althusser in the early 1960s. While traveling in revolutionary Latin America, he became convinced that only insurrection, conducted according to local conditions, could bring successful revolution. One of Debray's most influential books, *Revolution in the Revolution?* (1967), popularized the *foco* philosophy of Guevara.

Three years in a Bolivian prison (1967–1970) and Marxist successes achieved without *focoismo* caused Debray to admit strategic mistakes. Nonetheless, he never criticized Guevara, but did criticize Chilean president Salvador Allende and Uruguay's urban guerrilla Tupamaros for not adhering to the Cuban position. Many insist that his novel of revolutionary alienation, *The Undesirable* (1975), is autobiographical.

Since the 1980s, Debray has published numerous essays and books on philosophy and French politics. In the 1990s he founded the discipline of *médiologie*, which aims to "elucidate the mysteries and paradoxes of cultural transmission." Debray also founded the journal *Cahiers de Médiologie* (1996–2004). Recent works include *Introduction à la médiologie* (2000) and *Transmettre* (1997; *Transmitting Culture*, 2000).

See also **Allende Gossens, Salvador; Communism; Guevara, Ernesto "Che"; Philosophy: Overview.**

BIBLIOGRAPHY

Leo Huberman and Paul M. Sweezy, eds., *Régis Debray and the Latin American Revolution* (1968).

Richard Gott, *Guerrilla Movements in Latin America* (1970).

Hartmut Ramm, *The Marxism of Régis Debray* (1978).

Additional Bibliography

Harris, Richard L. *Death of a Revolutionary: Che Guevara's Last Mission.* Revised ed. New York: Norton, 2000.

Spoiden, Stéphanie. *Régis Debray et la médiologie.* Amsterdam and New York: Rodopi, 2007.

PAT KONRAD

DEBRET, JEAN-BAPTISTE (1768–1848).

Jean-Baptiste Debret (*b.* 1768; *d.* 1848), French painter. Under the leadership of Joachim Lebreton (1760–1819), secretary of the fine arts class in the Institute of France, Debret left his country in 1816 and went to Rio de Janeiro with the French group known as the French Artistic Mission, which had been invited by the Portuguese government. The group was composed of Nicolas Antoine Taunay (1755–1830), a landscape painter; his brother, Auguste Marie Taunay (1768–1824), a sculptor; Auguste Henri Victor Grandjean De Montigny (1776–1850), an architect; Charles S. Pradier (1768–1848), an engraver; Sigismund Neukomm (1778–1858), a composer; and François Ovide, a specialist in mechanics. Although Debret was classified as a history painter, his first works in Brazil were portraits of the royal family, decorative paintings for public festivities, and stage settings for the Royal Theatre São João in Rio de Janeiro. It took ten years to establish the Brazilian Academy of Fine Arts, where the members of the French group were supposed to teach. Meanwhile, Debret taught his students in a private house.

Debret's best-known work is a series of drawings depicting Brazilian life and culture, which was published in three volumes in 1834 and 1839 under the title *Voyage pittoresque et historique au Brésil.* The drawings and the explanatory texts that accompany them may be considered the most striking documents on Brazilian daily life in the first decades of the nineteenth century. Following what he calls a "logical order," Debret began his book with descriptions of Indians belonging to several tribes. Although he had not traveled outside Rio de Janeiro, various travelers gave him the information he needed to represent the Indian way of life in the interior. No one better than Debret depicted slave life in Rio de Janeiro, and his drawings shocked the members of the Brazilian Historical and Geographical Institute because of their realism.

As a history painter, Debret also depicted historical events of the late colonial period: Her Royal Highness Princess Leopoldina disembarking in Rio de Janeiro, the coronation of King João VI, the baptism of Princess María da Glória, the oath to the Constitution, and the coronation of Pedro I as emperor of Brazil.

See also **French Artistic Mission.**

BIBLIOGRAPHY

Afonso Arinos De Melo Franco, *Jean-Baptiste Debret: Estudos inéditos* (1974).

Affonso De Escragnolle Taunay, *A missão artística de 1816* (1956).

Additional Bibliography

Araujo, Ana Lucia. "Les représentations de l'esclavage dans les gravures des relations (Voyage pittoresque et historique au Brésil) de Jean-Baptiste Debret et (Deux années au Brésil) de François-Auguste Biard." *Canadian Journal of Latin American and Caribbean Studies* 30 (2005): 161–183.

Lima, Heloisa Pires. "Negros debretianos representações culturais presentes na obra voyage pittoresque et historique au Brésil (1816 a 1839)." Ph.D. diss., University of São Paulo, 2006.

Lima, Valéria. *Uma viagem com Debret.* Rio de Janeiro: Jorge Zahar Editor, 2004.

MARIA BEATRIZ NIZZA DA SILVA

DEBT PEONAGE. Labeled "debt slavery" by those critical of it, debt peonage is a general term for several categories of coerced or controlled labor resulting from the advancement of money or goods to individuals or groups who find themselves unable or unwilling to repay their debt quickly. As a consequence they are obliged to continue working for the creditor or his assignees until the debt is repaid, and are often further coerced to borrow more or to agree to other obligations or entanglements. According to the traditional view, these individuals, once indebted, whether because of inadequate wages or employer fraud, were reduced to servitude and, in theory, to an inability to leave the workplace to which they have contracted.

Such peonages are usually found in societies with deep class or caste divisions in which elites, in spite of labor shortages, are able to restrict movement, sometimes by so-called vagrancy laws, and to control custom or law so that migration or flight, reneging on debts, and formal protest against conditions, are limited or prohibited. Some observers have associated debt peonage with paternalistic societies in which wage labor has not yet emerged as a dominant form.

In the aftermath of the Conquest and faced with the obvious and precipitous decline of indigenous populations, the European rulers of the new colonies abandoned the haphazard measures of the early years and sought more formal organization of the labor they required for commercial agriculture and mining. Where Indians survived, they usually retained at least initial access to the resources needed for their subsistence. Therefore, they resisted working for the intruders under the conditions offered, prompting the state and wouldbe employers to adopt coercive measures. These included Indian slavery (abolished by about 1550 in the core areas of the empires) and African slavery, coerced wage labor (*repartimientos* or *mitas*), and debt peonage or servitude. Prohibitions against *adelantos* (advances) to Indians appear in the third quarter of the sixteenth century. Favorite spots to catch Indians were at the entrances to market towns or at church doors on days of obligatory attendance. Peonage of various kinds grew in the late seventeenth century and after as encomienda and draft-labor systems declined, as the labor shortage caused by Indian population decline worsened, and as new haciendas and textile *obrajes* searched for a resident workforce. Slavery and forced labor continued on the empire's fringes, in the mining industry in Upper Peru that relied on *mitas* until independence, and on lowland plantations where black slavery predominated. As the population recovered and the economy and society stabilized, however, the general tendency favored labor mobilization and control to shift over time from more to less coercive forms, including debt peonage.

As it developed, colonial debt peonage embraced several systems of labor recruitment. In its seasonal form, recruiters advanced money or goods (*enganche*) to induce Indians and peasants, usually from the highlands, to go to the lowlands to work the harvest season on monocultural plantations. Advances of money or the goods to be worked on were also behind many of the "putting out" *derramas* or *repartos de efectos* of the eighteenth century.

In the highlands of Mesoamerica and the Andes, subsistence villages and nearby plantations often lived in symbiosis. It was to the large landowners' advantage to have a reliable workforce for which they were not responsible outside the planting, weeding, and harvesting seasons. The villagers found the large estate useful for providing cash for tribute and other obligations as well as for money purchases. Often the bond was many small debts from landowners to peasants. Debt peonage, *mitas, derramas,* etc., continued from the colonial period into the twentieth century, although scholars now believe that colonial peonage, in most areas, was far from being as pervasive and dominant as once thought.

In the nineteenth and twentieth centuries debt peonage took new forms. In isolated or peripheral areas of the new nations, especially in semideserts or jungles, local landowners and political bosses became very powerful, and their mines or haciendas were able to recruit and control labor through the *tienda de raya,* a system characterized by the "company store" and the "running tab." In some places private police forces prevented escape; in others the national army or police cooperated by pursuing and punishing those who fled. Rubber plantations were especially notorious, and those of the Putumayo region in Colombia and Peru, and in Chiapas, Tabasco, and Campeche in Mexico were the scenes of scandalous brutalities, backed up by the indifference or cooperation of the government. While debt

An identity check at a plantation employing forced labor in Para, Brazil, 2004. In search of work, peasants from poor regions in Brazil sometimes find themselves tricked or coerced into near endless cycles of forced work and debt in Amazonia. © JOAO LUIZ BULCAO/CORBIS

may have been the official excuse for detention of workers in these cases, conditions were more like chattel slavery backed up by brute force.

The abolition of slavery in the nineteenth century created the problem of finding a substitute labor force, and debt was among the devices used. Sugar plantations in Cuba and the Dominican Republic used debt to finance Colonos through the dead season and to provide them with funds to buy seed, equipment, and daily necessities while they awaited the *zafra* (harvest) on their rented parcels, some of which were large and prosperous. Variations of debt peonage still surfaced from time to time in the late twentieth century, especially in poorer nations.

Academic debate has led to the abandonment of the old view that debt labor was monolithically exploitive and harsh. In the colonial period villagers sometimes preferred it to the difficulties of life in the village or *encomienda*. In the national

period, loans from employers were one of the few opportunities for the poor to obtain money for improvements.

Where elites lost their cohesion and competed for scarce labor, and when rural police were few and ineffective, peons could shop around for bargains, flee from creditors with impunity, and thus had some bargaining power. One must conclude, then, that in its numerous forms and degrees of exploitation and servitude, debt peonage varied widely over time and space.

More recent research, for example, on north-central Mexico (the Bajío) and coastal Peru, has suggested a different picture, particularly for the nineteenth century. The need for wage income among the rural poor and their willingness to work in the cash sector increased dramatically as population growth and land loss in the late colonial and early national periods made subsistence more difficult and survival less certain. With pressures mounting and more and more families seeking employment, those able to obtain steady work and food at advantageous prices on the haciendas and who were allowed to run up debts at the hacienda store, far from seeing their condition as "slavery," felt themselves a labor aristocracy, and their peers envied them as such. If the worker was dissatisfied with his or her situation or the hacienda with the worker, there were always large numbers of land-short, desperate peasants and "free" laborers ready to take their place. A feared punishment was expulsion from the property, and the haciendas made little effort to seek to bring back those who fled, even if they owed money.

Also, before the last quarter of the nineteenth century, employers and the state had such limited political control over the countryside that enforcing peonage on individuals or a population that actively resisted was almost impossible. Where—for example, in southern Mexico and Chiapas—planters depended on a seasonal labor force drawn from intact indigenous villages rather than on workers resident on the property, the Indians' attachment to their home communities made mobilization and control easier, but peonage remained largely voluntary.

The limit case for the severity of debt servitude, and one in which extraeconomic coercion did predominate, was the involuntary peonage enforced in late-nineteenth-century Guatemala. Under laws intended to provide workers for export coffee production, Guatemala's Indians faced the choice of "voluntary" contracts requiring several months' labor a year for very low wages on the export plantations or repeated stints of forced wage labor (*mandamientos*) demanded by the planters and mobilized by the state. The threat of direct coercion pushed individuals into the debt contracts that provided the only, and that imperfect, protection from such drafts.

Debt peonage, however, whether voluntary or involuntary, tended to be an expensive and unwieldy form of labor mobilization, requiring that employers carry on their books large amounts of "dead" capital committed as advances and in some cases to employ a number of recruiters and policing agents, all of which added to labor costs. By the early twentieth century, population growth in most areas of Latin America, together with declining resources available to rural populations and new

"needs" that could be satisfied only with cash, were at once pushing and drawing more and more individuals into free labor, without need of large advances or debt coercion.

See also **Encomienda; Mita; Obraje; Repartimiento; Sugar Industry.**

BIBLIOGRAPHY

Silvio Zavala, "Orígenes coloniales del peonaje en México," in *El trimestre económico* 10, no. 4 (1943–1944): 711–748.

Friedrich Katz, "Labor Conditions on Haciendas in Porfirian Mexico: Some Trends and Tendencies," in *Hispanic American Historical Review* 54, no. 1 (1974): 1–47.

Kenneth Duncan and Ian Rutledge, eds., *Land and Labour in Latin America* (1977).

Arnold J. Bauer, "Rural Workers in Spanish America: Problems of Peonage and Oppression," in *Hispanic American Historical Review* 59, no. 1 (1979): 34–63 (see also "Forum," a discussion of this essay, in 59, no. 2 [1979]: 478–489).

Peter Blanchard, "The Recruitment of Workers in the Peruvian Sierra at the Turn of the Century: The Enganche System, in *Inter-American Economic Affairs* 33, no. 3 (1979): 63–83.

Harry Cross, "Debt Peonage Reconsidered: A Case Study in Nineteenth-Century Zacatecas, Mexico," in *Business History Review* 53, no. 4 (1979): 473–495.

David McCreery, "Debt Servitude in Rural Guatemala, 1876–1936," in *Hispanic American Historical Review* 63, no. 4 (1983): 735–759.

Roger Plant, *Sugar and Modern Slavery: A Tale of Two Countries* (1987).

Additional Bibliography

Dore, Elizabeth. *Myths of Modernity: Peonage and Patriarchy in Nicaragua.* Durham: Duke University Press, 2006.

Figueira, Ricardo Rezende. *Pisando fora da própria sombra: A escravidão por dívida no Brasil contemporâneo.* Rio de Janeiro: Civilização Brasileira, 2004.

Lal, Brij V., Doug Munro, and Edward D. Beechert. *Plantation Workers: Resistance and Accommodation.* Honolulu: University of Hawaii Press, 1993.

Mora-Torres, Juan. *The Making of the Mexican Border.* Austin: University of Texas Press, 2001.

Nickel, Herbert J. *El peonaje en las haciendas mexicanas: Interpretaciones, fuentes, hallazgos.* Freiburg: Arnold Bergstraesser Institut, 1997.

Rey de Castro, Carlos. *La defensa de los caucheros.* Iquitos: CETA; Copenhague, Dinamarca: IWGIA, 2005.

Yarrington. Doug. *A Coffee Frontier: Land, Society, and Politics in Duaca, Venezuela, 1830-1936.* Pittsburgh: University of Pittsburgh Press, 1997.

DAVID MCCREERY
MURDO J. MACLEOD

DE CASTRO, AMILCAR (1920–2002).

A product of the modernist movement in the arts in Minas Gerais, Brazil, in the 1940s, the sculptor and designer Amilcar de Castro was one of several artists to sign the manifesto of *Neoconcretismo* (the Neoconcrete Movement) in 1959. He was part of a group of prominent young artists and writers, such as Lygia Clark, Lygia Pape, and Sergio de Camargo, who advocated for a freer, nondogmatic, less rational vision of art and language. During the 1950s De Castro began to reform the field of graphic design through his work for the popular photojournal *Manchete* and the magazine *A Cigarra.* During the 1960s he was a designer for several newspapers.

As a sculptor, De Castro earned national and international recognition for his innovative and eclectic use of nonconventional materials, including iron, in his colossal works. From the 1970s on, he was a professor at the Escola Guinard in Belo Horizonte and the School of Art in the Universidade Federal de Minas Gerais. His works were shown at many international exhibitions in Brazil as well as at the Museum of Modern Art in São Paulo and the Museum of Modern Art in Rio de Janeiro.

See also **Art: The Twentieth Century; Camargo, Sergio de; Clark, Lygia; Modernism, Brazil; Pape, Lygia.**

BIBLIOGRAPHY

Amaral, Aracy, ed. *Arte construtiva no Brasil.* São Paulo: DBA, 1998.

Mirzoeff, Nicholas, ed. *The Visual Culture Reader.* London and New York: Routledge, 1998.

PAULA HALPERIN

DECENA TRÁGICA.

Decena Trágica, "the tragic ten days" of violence that erupted in Mexico City as a result of a revolt against the government of Francisco I. Madero that began on 9 February 1913. The rebels, led by generals Félix Díaz, Manuel Mandragón, and Bernardo Reyes, failed to take the National Palace but seized a strong position at La Ciudadela, the army's ammunition depot. General Victoriano Huerta was appointed commander of the government forces.

For ten days artillery fire raked the capital, causing extensive damage and fueling cries for a settlement that weakened support for the already tottering Madero government. On 18 February troops loyal to Huerta, under the command of General Aureliano Blanquet, seized Francisco Madero, while Huerta arrested his brother Gustavo. With Madero effectively deposed, U.S. ambassador Henry Lane Wilson mediated talks between Huerta and Díaz, which led to the Pact of the Embassy recognizing Huerta as provisional president. Madero was assassinated four days later.

See also **Huerta, Victoriano; Madero, Francisco Indalecio; Pact of the Embassy; Wilson, Henry Lane.**

BIBLIOGRAPHY

Stanley R. Ross, *Francisco I. Madero: Apostle of Mexican Democracy* (1955).

Kenneth J. Grieb, *The United States and Huerta* (1969).

Michael C. Meyer, *Huerta: A Political Portrait* (1972).

Additional Bibliography

Guzmán, Martín Luis. *Febrero de 1913.* México: Empresas Editoriales, 1963.

Guzmán, Martín Luis. *Muertes históricas: Febrero de 1913.* México, DF: Editorial Planeta Mexicana, 2001.

Katz, Friedrich. *De Díaz a Madero.* México, DF: Ediciones Era, 2004.

Tablada, José Juan. *La Ciudadela del fuego: O ochenta años de la Decena Trágica.* Mexico: Consejo Nacional para la Cultura y las Artes, 1993.

KENNETH J. GRIEB

DECOUD, HECTOR FRANCISCO

(1855–1930). Hector Francisco Decoud (*b.* 1855; *d.* 1930), Paraguayan historian and journalist. Born in Asunción, Decoud was a mere youth when the disastrous War of the Triple Alliance began in 1864. Entering the army as a noncommissioned officer, he fought in several battles before being arrested, together with his mother, by the dictator Francisco Solano López. Though his imprisonment was brief, he was poorly treated, and this left him with a lifelong hatred of López, a hatred that was reflected in his historical writings.

After the war, Decoud dedicated himself to journalism, working for *La Regeneración* and other Asunción newspapers. In 1882, he was appointed district attorney, but he resigned that post the following year after having been elected a national deputy, a position he held until 1887.

Decoud found the time during subsequent years to produce many highly partisan historical works. He focused on the War of the Triple Alliance and on the figure of López, whom he regarded as the worst sort of tyrant. His many studies included *Sobre los escombros de la guerra: Una década de vida nacional, 1869–1880* (1925), *Guerra del Paraguay: La masacre de Concepción ordenada por el mariscal López* (1926), *La revolución del comandante Molas* (1930), and *Elisa Lynch de Quatrefages* (published posthumously in 1939). Decoud died in Asunción.

See also **War of the Triple Alliance.**

BIBLIOGRAPHY

William Belmont Parker, *Paraguayans of To-Day* (repr. 1967), pp. 305–306.

Jack Ray Thomas, *Biographical Dictionary of Latin American Historians and Historiography* (1984).

THOMAS L. WHIGHAM

DECOUD, JOSÉ SEGUNDO (1848–1909).

José Segundo Decoud (*b.* 1848; *d.* 4 March 1909), Paraguayan statesman. Born into a prominent Asunción family, Decoud began his studies in the Paraguayan capital before moving on to the Colegio Nacional of Concepción del Uruguay, in Argentina. At the beginning of the 1860s, he transferred to the University of Buenos Aires, where he studied law. At the beginning of the War of the Triple Alliance in 1864, Decoud joined with his brother Juan Francisco and other Paraguayan exiles to found the *Legión Paraguaya*, a military unit that fought with the Argentines

against Paraguayan president Francisco Solano López. An ardent Liberal, Decoud was anxious to see a constitutional regime established in Paraguay. When the secret clauses of the Triple Alliance treaty were published, however, he denounced the territorial claims they made against Paraguay and resigned his position in the *legión*.

After the war, Decoud returned to Asunción, where he became editor of *La Regeneración* and a key member of the 1870 Constitutional Convention. Annoyed by in-fighting among the Liberals, he supported the rise of Conservative Cándido Bareiro and, later, of generals Bernardino Caballero and Patricio Escobar. From 1879 until the end of the century, he was a member of every cabinet except one and was generally regarded as the most influential politician in the country throughout this time. He provided the ideological argument behind Paraguayan conservatism, formulating the original party platform when the Caballeristas organized the Asociación Nacional Republicana (or Colorado Party) in 1887.

Decoud was also active in diplomatic and educational affairs. He attempted at one point to create new *colegios nacionales* in several communities of the interior, but his plans were vetoed at the last moment. His fluency in many languages and his superb private library made him the focus of much intellectual interest, not only for Paraguayans but also for foreign visitors to the Platine countries.

See also **Paraguay, Political Parties: Colorado Party.**

BIBLIOGRAPHY

Harris G. Warren, *Rebirth of the Paraguayan Republic: The First Colorado Era, 1878–1904* (1985), *passim;* Carlos Zubizarreta, *Cien vidas paraguayas,* 2d ed. (1985), pp. 195–197.

Additional Bibliography

Lewis, Paul H. *Political Parties and Generations in Paraguay's Liberal Era, 1869-1940.* Chapel Hill: University of North Carolina Press, 1993.

Martínez, Ofelia, and Mary Monte. *Dios proteja destino patria: las concepcioneras de 1901.* Asunción: Centro de Documentación y Estudios, 1999.

Pesoa, Manuel. *José Segundo Decoud, estadista del Partido Colorado.* Asunción, 1979.

THOMAS L. WHIGHAM

DEGOLLADO, SANTOS

DEFENSORÍA DEL PUEBLO (HUMAN RIGHTS OMBUDSMAN OFFICE).

The Defensoría del Pueblo, created to receive and handle citizen claims of any rights violation, is one of Latin America's most popular agencies. National, regional, and local *Defensorías* carry out investigations on their own or on behalf of an aggrieved party and present cases to the courts for prosecution. In many countries *Defensorías* also formulate legislation, develop administrative reforms, mediate conflicts, push for social service improvements, educate the public, and advocate for oppressed groups. But although their independence is guaranteed by law, *Defensorías* throughout the region are limited by budget cuts, political pressures, judicial ineffectiveness, and socioeconomic problems beyond their reach.

See also **Democracy; Human Rights.**

BIBLIOGRAPHY

Briceño Vivas, Gustavo, ed. *El defensor del pueblo en Venezuela: La figura del Ombudsman.* Caracas: Editorial Kinesis, 1993.

Comisión Andina de Juristas (CAJ). *El defensor del pueblo: De la teoría a la práctica.* Lima: CAJ, 1999.

Comisión Andina de Juristas (CAJ), ed. *Acceso a la justicia y defensoría del Pueblo.* Lima: CAJ, 2001.

Quinzio Figueiredo, Jorge Mario. *El ombudsman: El defensor del Pueblo.* Santiago, Chile: Editorial Jurídica de Chile, 1992.

Uggla, Fredrik. "The Ombudsman in Latin America." *Journal of Latin American Studies* 36, no. 3 (August 2004): 423–450.

MARK UNGAR

DE FUENTES, FERNANDO (1894–1958).

The Mexican director Fernando de Fuentes is one of the most famous figures of Mexican cinema. Born in Veracruz on December 13, 1894, he studied engineering for a time but then transferred to the humanities department at Tulane University, New Orleans. Once back in Mexico, de Fuentes worked for the government in different capacities; eventually he took charge of a chain of theaters and became an ardent supporter of sound cinema.

Some critics have claimed that de Fuentes abandoned his artistic intentions by becoming a highly efficient commercial producer. However, he truly was a gifted director who not only understood the nature of sound cinema but also took advantage of its potential. De Fuentes's Revolution Trilogy—*El prisionero trece* (Prisoner Number Thirteen, 1933), *El compadre Mendoza* (Godfather Mendoza, 1933), and *Vámonos con Pancho Villa* (Let's Go with Pancho Villa, 1935)—is a remarkable analysis of the then recent civil war that had changed Mexican society. De Fuentes's portrayal of the Mexican Revolution is both pessimistic and honest, in a manner reminiscent of Mariano Azuela's novel *Los de abajo*.

But the film for which de Fuentes is best known—which broke all box-office records and established Mexican cinema in the Latin American market—is *Allá en el rancho grande* (Out on the Big Ranch, 1936). Beyond being a mere imitation of Hollywood's singing cowboy movies, this film featured the *canción ranchera* and helped to incorporate this song style into the broader popular culture. The achievements of early Mexican cinema with directors such as de Fuentes, Emilio "El Indio" Fernández, and the Brazilian Humberto Mauro helped establish the structural basis of the Latin American film industry.

See also **Azuela, Mariano; Cinema: From the Silent Film to 1990; Fernández, Emilio "El Indio"; Mauro, Humberto.**

BIBLIOGRAPHY

Ciuk, Perla. *Diccionario de directores del cine mexicano.* Mexico: Consejo Nacional para la Cultura y las Artes (CONACULTA) and Cineteca Nacional, 2000.

King, John. *Magical Reels: A History of Cinema in Latin America.* London and New York: Verso, 2000.

JUAN CARLOS GRIJALVA

DEGOLLADO, SANTOS (1811–1861).

Santos Degollado (*b.* 1811; *d.* 1861), Mexican liberal general and cabinet minister. Degollado was born in the city of Guanajuato during the wars for Mexico's independence from Spain. Since his father was a supporter of the insurgency, the Spanish government confiscated his property. On the death of his father, an uncle took Degollado to Mexico City. In October 1828, Degollado moved to Morelia, where he took a job as a notary's clerk and studied in his spare time. Recognizing Degollado's organizational skills, the governor of Michoacán, Melchor Ocampo, named him secretary of the Colegio de San Nicolás, and in 1846 Degollado served briefly as a substitute for Ocampo.

As a foot soldier, Degollado dedicated himself to the struggle against Santa Anna and rose through the ranks to general. After the triumph of the Revolution of Ayutla (1854), he was elected to the Constitutional Convention of 1856–1857 as a representative of the state of Michoacán. In 1857, he was elected governor of that state but served only a few months before resigning to join the forces of Benito Juárez in the War of the Reform. On 27 March 1858, Juárez named Degollado his minister of war and general of the federal army. Degollado also served briefly as minister of foreign relations during the first months of 1860. A talented and tireless organizer of armies, Degollado was notably less successful as their leader in battle. After his subordinate, Manuel Doblado, confiscated silver from British mine owners, Degollado took responsibility and promised repayment. Then, without authorization, he sought a negotiated settlement to the war, with a British official, George W. Mathew, as mediator. Juárez reacted to this step by removing Degollado from his command and replacing him with Jesús González Ortega, who led the army Degollado had organized to victory over the conservatives in late 1860. González Ortega paid homage to Degollado when the liberal army marched into Mexico City. Degollado received another command in Michoacán to pursue the guerrillas who had killed Melchor Ocampo, but he was ambushed, captured, and executed by the conservatives.

See also Santa Anna, Antonio López de.

BIBLIOGRAPHY

Walter V. Scholes, Mexican Politics During the Juárez Regime, 1855–1872 (1957).

Richard N. Sinkin, The Mexican Reform, 1855–1876: A Study in Liberal Nation-Building (1979); Diccionario Porrúa de historia, biografía y geografía de México, 5th ed. (1986).

D. F. STEVENS

DEGREDADO.

Degredado, a "degraded" person, one who was convicted of crimes by royal and Inquisition courts and sent to the colonies or the galleys to serve the sentence. The Portuguese crown used this punishment to rid Portugal of petty criminals and social deviants. As they explored Africa and Brazil, Portuguese sea captains left degredados ashore to learn local languages and customs. Later, degredados figured prominently in the early colonization of Angola and Brazil. Although officials protested receiving degredados in Brazil, they themselves adopted the practice and sentenced Brazilian criminals and deviants to Africa, the galleys, or frontier outposts.

See also Inquisition: Brazil.

BIBLIOGRAPHY

Sônia A. Siqueira, A Inquisição Portuguesa e a sociedade colonial (1978).

A. J. R. Russell-Wood, A World on the Move: The Portuguese in Africa, Asia, and America (1992).

Additional Bibliography

Bueno, Eduardo. Náufragos, traficantes e degredados: As primeiras expedições ao Brasil, 1500–1531. Rio de Janeiro: Objetiva, 1998.

Coates, Timothy J. Convicts and Orphans: Forced and State-sponsored Colonizers in the Portuguese Empire, 1550–1755. Stanford: Stanford University Press, 2001.

Pieroni, Geraldo. Vadios e ciganos, heréticos e bruxas: As degredados no Brasil-colônia. Rio de Janeiro: Ministério da Cultura, Fundação Biblioteca Nacional, Departamento Nacional do Livro: Bertrand Brasil, 2001.

ALIDA C. METCALF

DEIRA, ERNESTO (1928–1986).

Ernesto Deira (b. July 1928; d. 1986), Argentine artist. Born in Buenos Aires, Deira turned to pop art, expressionism, and informalism to define a style halfway between abstract and figurative painting. He studied with Leopoldo Torres Agüero and Leopoldo Presas in the 1950s. Early works were reminiscent of Goya's grotesque creatures. A member of the Argentine New Figuration group, in 1961 he received a fellowship from the Argentine National Fund for the Arts to study in Paris. In 1964 he won the Guggenheim International Award and two years later a Fulbright fellowship to study in New York City, where he was a visiting professor at Cornell University.

Deira's work is characterized by gestural brush-strokes and harsh contrasts of color. He allowed paint to drip freely over the canvas to generate informalist structures which he accentuated with graphic signs and dribbles to define distorted figures. Some of his segmented figures, with exposed entrails, are erotic. His images became more serene after 1966, although they still tended toward ironic, nightmarish themes. In his later years he settled in Paris, where he died.

See also **Art: The Twentieth Century.**

BIBLIOGRAPHY

Gilbert Chase, *Contemporary Art in Latin America* (1970), pp. 152, 155.

Félix Angel, "The Latin American Presence," in Luis R. Cancel et al., *The Latin American Spirit: Art and Artists in the United States, 1920–1970* (1988), p. 259.

Miguel Briante et al., *Nueva Figuración: 1961–1991* (1991).

MARTA GARSD

DE JESUS, CLEMENTINA (1902–1987).

Clementina de Jesus (*b.* 1902; *d.* 1987), Brazilian samba singer who achieved national acclaim late in life. Born to a musical family in Valença, Rio de Janeiro State, Clementina, as she is called, was singing by age twelve with the Carnaval singing group Moreninha das Campinas. At fifteen, she frequented *samba de roda* sessions in the Oswaldo Cruz neighborhood, and later paraded with the Portela and Mangueira *samba* schools. For most of her life, Clementina had to work as a maid to support herself, even though she was a superb samba vocalist and a living archive of old musical forms such as *lundu, jongo,* and *partido alto* (a type of samba). Finally, at the age of sixty she was "discovered" by critic-impresario Hermínio Bello de Carvalho, who arranged numerous concert appearances for Clementina. She performed on stage with the likes of classical guitarist Turíbio Santos and in 1963 starred with Paulinho da Viola, Araci Cortes, and several others in the musical *Rosa de ouro*. In 1970, when she was sixty-eight, Clementina recorded her first album, "Clementina, cade você?" (Clementina, Where Are You?), and was celebrated as a national musical treasure. Many leading Brazilian artists, such as Milton Nascimento, invited her to perform duets on their albums.

See also **Samba.**

BIBLIOGRAPHY

Rita Caúrio, *Brasil Musical* (1988).

CHRIS MCGOWAN

DE LA FUENTE, JUAN RAMÓN (1951–).

Mexican physician and educator Juan Ramón de la Fuente Ramírez is the son of Dr. Ramon del la Fuente Muñiz, a leading psychiatrist, and Dr. Beatriz Ramírez, an authority on pre-Hispanic art. He graduated from the National Autonomous University of Mexico (UNAM) and completed a master's degree in psychiatry at the Mayo Clinic in Rochester, Minnesota. He worked as a researcher at the National Institute of Nutrition and the Mexico Institute of Psychiatry before becoming the director of the health research program and the science program at UNAM. After teaching many years at the university, he was appointed dean of the UNAM School of Medicine from 1991 to 1994. In 1994 president Ernesto Zedillo (1994–2000) appointed him as his first secretary of health, a position he held until he was selected as the president of UNAM in November 1999. He served a full four-year term, and was selected for a second term from 2003 through 2007.

See also **National Autonomous University of Mexico (UNAM).**

BIBLIOGRAPHY

Diccionario Biográfico del Gobierno Federal, 3rd edition. Mexico City: Presidencia, 1992, p. 124.

RODERIC AI CAMP

DE LA HUERTA, ADOLFO (1881–1955).

Adolfo de la Huerta (*b.* 26 May 1881; *d.* 9 July 1955), interim president of Mexico in 1920 and an important figure among the Constitutionalists during the Mexican Revolution. De la Huerta was born to an important family of Guaymas, in the state of Sonora. His family supported his studies in Hermosillo, where he obtained a teaching certificate in music. In 1900 he abandoned a career in that field to maintain his family by working in a variety of book-keeping posts. In 1908 he joined the Anti-Reelectionist Club, becoming secretary in 1910. In that year, however, his antigovernment activities cost him his managerial job. In 1911 he entered local politics, defeating Plutarco Elías Calles to become the local deputy to the state legislature.

Having joined the Constitutionalists under Venustiano Carranza on 20 February 1913, de la Huerta served as Carranza's *oficial mayor* (chief clerk) of government from 1915 to 1916. His other positions included interim governor of Sonora (1916–1917), consul general in New York City (1918), senator (1918), and governor of Sonora (1919–1920).

De la Huerta supported the opposition to Carranza that resulted in the Plan of Agua Prieta and, after Carranza's death, served as provisional president of the republic, from 1 June to 30 November 1920. On the election of Alvaro Obregón he joined the cabinet as secretary of the treasury (1920–1923), but when Obregón supported Calles for the presidency, de la Huerta led the first major, and most important, rebellion against the post-Revolutionary government (7 December 1923). Despite the support of a large part of the army and the civilian political community, the rebellion failed, and de la Huerta went into exile in Los Angeles, where he survived by giving piano lessons until 1935.

President Lázaro Cardenas appointed him inspector general of Mexican consulates in the United States, a post he held until 1946, when he retired. His son, Adolfo, also became a senator from his home state, and his brother Alfonso was a revolutionary general.

See also **Calles, Plutarco Elías.**

BIBLIOGRAPHY

Adolfo De La Huerta, *Memorias* (1957).

John W. F. Dulles, *Yesterday in Mexico: A Chronicle of the Revolution, 1919–1936* (1961).

Alvaro Matute, *La carrera del caudillo: Historia de la Revolución, período 1917–1924* (1980).

Additional Bibliography

Castro Martínez, Pedro Fernando. *Adolfo de la Huerta: la integridad como arma de la revolución.* Mexico City: Universidad Autónoma Metropolitana Iztapalapa; Siglo Veintiuno Editores, 1998.

Castro Martínez, Pedro Fernando. *Adolfo de la Huerta y la Revolución Mexicana.* Mexico City: Instituto Nacional de Estudios Históricos de la Revolución Mexicana; Secretaría de Gobernación; Universidad Autónoma Metropolitana, Unidad Iztapalapa, 1992.

Tamayo, Jaime. *En el interinato de Adolfo de la Huerta y el gobierno de Alvaro Obregón (1920–1924).* Mexico City: Siglo Ventiuno, 1987.

RODERIC AI CAMP

DELEGATIVE DEMOCRACY. Delegative democracy is a term coined by the Argentine political scientist Guillermo O'Donnell to describe democratic regimes in which presidents do their utmost to ensure that their powers remain unchecked by legislatures, courts, or other mechanisms of horizontal accountability (in which state agencies oversee and, if necessary, sanction public officials). The diverse set of Latin American democracies that emerged in the 1980s, following transitions from authoritarian rule, were polyarchies (to use the scholar Robert Dahl's term); a polyarchy is a democracy in which officials are chosen in free, fair, and frequent elections based on inclusive suffrage, the right to run for office, freedom of expression, alternative sources of information, and associational autonomy (pp. 10–11). These polyarchies lacked features typically associated with established liberal democracies, such as a lawful state (*estado de derecho*) able to enforce inclusive democratic citizenship. O'Donnell criticized the literature on democratic consolidation for treating some Latin American democracies as incomplete versions of established liberal democracies and argued, instead, that they constituted a distinct type of regime.

In a delegative democracy, O'Donnell explains in a 1999 essay, "whoever wins election to the presidency is thereby entitled to govern as he or she sees fit, constrained only by the hard facts of existing power relations and by a constitutionally limited term of office" (p. 164). In this majoritarian conception of rule, the president is seen as the "embodiment of the nation" (1999, p. 164), and courts and legislatures are treated as nuisances to be, at best, tolerated. Examples include presidents Carlos Menem (Argentina, 1989–1999) and Alan García Pérez (Peru, 1985–1990). In some cases delegative democracies evolved into regimes in which elements of polyarchy were severely eroded, as in the cases of presidents Alberto Fujimori (Peru, 1990–2000) and Hugo Chávez (Venezuela, 1998–).

See also **Democracy; O'Donnell, Guillermo.**

BIBLIOGRAPHY

Collier, David, and Steven Levitsky. "Democracy with Adjectives: Conceptual Innovation in Comparative Research." *World Politics* 49, no. 3 (1997): 430–451.

Dahl, Robert A. *Dilemmas of Pluralist Democracy: Autonomy* vs. *Control.* New Haven, CT: Yale University Press, 1982.

O'Donnell, Guillermo A. "Delegative Democracy." In *Counterpoints: Selected Essays on Authoritarianism and Democratization.* Notre Dame, IN: University of Notre Dame Press, 1999.

O'Donnell, Guillermo A. "Horizontal Accountability in New Democracies." *Journal of Democracy* 9, no. 3 (1998): 112–126.

MAXWELL A. CAMERON

DE LEÓN, MARTÍN (1765–1833).

Martín de León (*b.* 1765; *d.* 1833), successful Mexican rancher, colonizer, and founder of Victoria, Texas. De León was born in Burgos, Tamaulipas, in Mexico, to Spanish parents. He became a muleteer and merchant, and in 1790 joined the Fieles de Burgos Regiment in Nuevo Santander, reaching the rank of captain. He married Patricia de la Garza in 1795 and had ten children who became community leaders in Texas and northern Mexico. In 1824, de León founded the colony of Victoria on the Guadalupe River with forty-one Mexican families from Tamaulipas. De León's cattle raising made Victoria one of the most prosperous of the Texas colonies. He died in the cholera epidemic of 1833.

See also **Texas.**

BIBLIOGRAPHY

Victor M. Rose, *Some Historical Facts in Regard to the Settlement of Victoria, Texas* (1883), repr. as *A Republication of . . . Victor Rose's History of Victoria,* edited by J. W. Petty, Jr. (1961).

Roy Grimes, ed., *300 Years in Victoria County* (1968).

Arthur B. J. Hammett, *The Empresario Don Martín de León* (1973).

Additional Bibliography

Crimm, A. Carolina Castillo. *De León, a Tejano Family History.* Austin: University of Texas Press, 2003.

A. CAROLINA CASTILLO CRIMM

DELFIM NETO, ANTÔNIO (1928–).

Antônio Delfim Neto (*b.* 1 May 1928), Brazilian minister of finance (1967–1974) and planning (1979–1985). Economist, professor, and legislator, Delfim Neto oversaw Brazil's substantial economic policy apparatus for two extended periods during the military regime of 1964–1985. Known as a pragmatist, he was professor of economics at the University of São Paulo (1952–1965), secretary of finance of the state of São Paulo (1966–1967), ambassador to France (1975–1978), minister of agriculture (1979), and federal deputy (1987–). From 1967 to 1974, Delfim Neto presided over the Economic Miracle, a period when Brazil experienced an average annual growth rate in excess of 10 percent. Building on economic stabilization and institutional reform (1964–1967) and with the backing of a strong military government, his policies stimulated the economy, in the presence of wage and price controls, through lower interest rates, loosening of credit, export promotion, expansion of public investment in transportation and energy, and strengthening of public administration. The period witnessed rapid expansion of production, while provoking criticism over the increasingly unequal distribution of income and controversy over manipulation of the price indexes in 1973 to mask rising rates of inflation.

Delfim Neto began his second period in power promising to avoid a recession while combating inflation. In spite of active management, inflation surged in 1980, and output fell markedly in 1981. After a slight improvement in 1982, a key election year in the redemocratization process, chronic problems in Brazil's balance of payments worsened into a debt crisis. The years 1983–1984 witnessed harsh stabilization and export-promotion programs that caused a major internal recession while generating a sizable trade surplus that mitigated the debt crisis and created the external preconditions for the Cruzado Plan of 1986. The plan was an attempt to fight inertial inflation by freezing prices; ending wage indexation; and generally deindexing the economy, including long-term contracts. Although it was unsuccessful, experience with the plan contributed to subsequent plans. Delfim Neto was elected to the nation's constituent assembly in 1986 and retained his seat for five four-year terms, until losing it in the 2006 elections. He continues to write articles regularly for the national press, including the column "Sextante" in the journal *Carta Capital.*

See also **Brazil: Since 1889; Brazil, Economic Miracle (1968-1974); Campos, Roberto (de Oliveira); Economic Development; Simonsen, Mário Henrique.**

BIBLIOGRAPHY

Israel Beloch and Alzira Alves De Abreu, eds., *Dicionário histórico-biográfico brasileiro, 1930–1983,* vol. 2 (1984).

Leôncio Martins Rodrigues, *Quem é quem na constituinte: Uma análise sócio-política dos partidos e deputados* (1987).

Werner Baer, *The Brazilian Economy: Growth and Development,* 3d ed. (1989).

Additional Bibliography

Setti, Ricardo A. *A história secreta do plano cruzado.* São Paulo: Editora Canarinho, 2001.

Winograd, Carlos D. *Learning from Failed Stabilisation: High Inflation and the Cruzado Plan in Brazil.* London: Institute of Latin American Studies, 1995.

RUSSELL E. SMITH

DELGADO, JOSÉ MATÍAS (1767–1832).

José Matías Delgado (*b.* 24 February 1767; *d.* 12 November 1832), Salvadoran cleric and leader of the independence movement. Born in the provincial capital of San Salvador, Father Delgado became a champion of the Kingdom of Guatemala's independence from Spain and his province's separation from the overbearing influence of neighboring Guatemala. Trained in canon law and jurisprudence at the University of San Carlos in Guatemala, Delgado was part of a generation of discontented creoles who passed through the university in these years. The Enlightenment ideas he learned at San Carlos and his provincial resentments of both Spanish and Guatemalan control over his native Salvador quickly bore fruit. Delgado, Manuel José Arce, and other Salvadorans organized the uprising of 1811, in which they planned to seize the Spanish magistrate, the armory, and the treasury and gain independence. The conspiracy failed, as did a similar revolt in Nicaragua, in the face of strong royalist military action. The repression following these conspiracies helped to postpone independence for another decade but could not quell the unrest that was their root cause.

Delgado soon went to Guatemala to contact other independence activists and begin agitating for the establishment of a separate bishopric for El Salvador. By 1821 he was again in the thick of political intrigue. With many of the leading Liberals of the day, such as José Cecilio del Valle, Pedro Molina, and José Francisco Barrundia, Delgado played an instrumental role in convincing Captain-General Gabino Gáinza to declare Central America's independence from Spain on 15 September 1821.

After the collapse of the Mexican Empire, Central America gained its independence in its own right, and Father Delgado presided over the assembly that promulgated the first constitution of the independent United Provinces of Central America in July of 1823. With union came the reward for Salvador's help in the cause of independence, the formation of a new bishopric of El Salvador in 1825, with Delgado as the first bishop. Seven years later he died while witnessing the bloodshed of the internecine fighting that would plague the former Kingdom of Guatemala for generations to come.

See also **Central America, Independence of.**

BIBLIOGRAPHY

Ramón López Jiménez, *José Matías Delgado y De León, su personalidad, su obra y su destino: Un ensayo histórico* (1962).

José Salvador Guandique, *Presbítero y doctor José Matías Delgado: Ensayo histórico* (1962).

Rudolfo Barón Castro, *José Matías Delgado y el movimiento insurgente de 1811* (1962).

Ralph Lee Woodward, Jr., *Central America: A Nation Divided,* 2d ed. (1985), esp. pp. 92–95.

Additional Bibliography

Meléndez Chaverri, Carlos. *José Matías Delgado, prócer centroamericano.* San Salvador: Dirección de Publicaciones e Impresos, Consejo Nacional para la Cultura y el Arte, 2000.

TODD LITTLE-SIEBOLD

DELGADO CHALBAUD, CARLOS

(1909–1950). Carlos Delgado Chalbaud (*b.* 20 January 1909; *d.* 13 November 1950), president of Venezuela's military junta (1948–1950). Son of a famous Venezuelan general, Delgado received a degree in military engineering in France. Upon his return to Venezuela, he entered the army and rose rapidly in the officer ranks. From 1945 to 1948 he served as a member of the revolutionary junta and as war minister. After the 1948 military coup, Delgado, now a lieutenant colonel, served as president of the military junta until his assassination in 1950. One of the best-educated Venezuelan military men of his generation, he was regarded as a voice of political moderation among his army colleagues.

BIBLIOGRAPHY

Ana Mercedes Pérez, *La verdad inédita: Historia de la Revolución de Octubre revelada por sus dirigentes militares,* 2d ed. (Buenos Aires, 1953).

Winfield J. Burggraaff, *The Venezuelan Armed Forces in Politics, 1935–1959* (1972).

Additional Bibliography

Altuve Carrillo, Leonardo. *Los idus de noviembre: asesinato del presidente de la Junta Militar.* Caracas: Ediciones Roca Interamericana, 1992.

WINFIELD J. BURGGRAAFF

DELLEPIANE, LUIS J. (1865–1941). Luis

J. Dellepiane (*b.* 26 February 1865; *d.* 2 August 1941), career army officer, engineer, minister of war (1928–1930). Dellepiane was born in Buenos Aires and attended the military college in his home city, graduating in 1884. A general by 1910, he established his reputation as the officer who did the most to foster the development of the engineering branch of the Argentine army. He was also closely involved in Argentine politics. Following the assassination of the Buenos Aires police chief, Dellepiane was named interim chief in 1909. During the quasi-revolutionary *Semana Trágica* (Tragic Week) in Buenos Aires in 1919, President Hipólito Irigoyen (1916–1922) placed him in command of all military and civilian forces to restore order. Dellepiane's loyal service to Irigoyen was later rewarded when Dellepiane was appointed minister of war during Irigoyen's second term (1928–1930). Concerned about rumors of a coup, Dellepiane advised Irigoyen to arrest officers believed to be involved in the conspiracy. When he refused, Dellepiane resigned on 2 September 1930, just four days before elements of the army drove Irigoyen from power. Dellepiane remained in retirement until his death.

See also **Buenos Aires.**

BIBLIOGRAPHY

Robert A. Potash, *The Army and Politics in Argentina, 1928–1945: Yrigoyen to Perón* (1969).

Marvin Goldwert, *Democracy, Militarism, and Nationalism in Argentina, 1930–1966: An Interpretation* (1972).

Additional Bibliography

Díaz Araujo, Enrique. *La semana trágica de 1919: precedida por un estudio de los antecedentes de la inmigración y rebelión social.* Mendoza: Facultad de Filosofía y Letras, Universidad Nacional de Cuyo, 1988.

Seibel, Beatriz. *Crónicas de la semana trágica: enero de 1919.* Buenos Aires: Corregidor, 1999.

PAUL GOODWIN

DEL PRADO, JORGE (1910–1999).

Jorge del Prado (*b.* 15 August 1910; *d.* 1999), leader of the Peruvian Communist Party for much of the twentieth century. Del Prado was born in Arequipa, where in 1928 he helped form the "Revolution Group" that united radical writers, artists, and union leaders. The group maintained close ties to the "Amauta Group" in Lima led by José Carlos Mariátegui. In 1929 he traveled to Lima, where he collaborated closely with Mariátegui during the rupture with Víctor Haya De La Torre and the APRA party and the creation of the Socialist Party that would soon become the Peruvian Communist Party (PCP). In the early 1930s, he worked in the mines of Morococha as a union organizer. In the following decades, he held many positions in the Communist Party. He was repeatedly imprisoned and exiled.

From 1961 to 1991, Del Prado was the secretary-general of the Communist Party (referred to as the PCP-Unidad since the withdrawal of pro-China factions in 1964). In 1978 he was elected to the Constituent Assembly. In 1980 he was a candidate for vice president for the United Left (IU). He served three terms in the Peruvian Senate (1980–1985, 1985–1990, and 1990–1992). He wrote almost a dozen books on the Peruvian left and on Mariátegui.

See also **Amauta; Mariátegui, José Carlos; Peru: Peru Since Independence.**

BIBLIOGRAPHY

Jorge Del Prado, *40 años de lucha: Partido comunista del Perú, 1928–1968* (1968).

Carlos Milla Batres, *Diccionario histórico y biográfico del Peru, siglos XV–XX* (1986), pp. 186–187.

Alberto Tauro, *Enciclopedia ilustrada del Perú* (1987), vol 5, pp. 1678–1679.

Additional Bibliography

Drinot De Echave, Paulo. "Workers, the State, and Radical Politics in Peru in the Early 1930s." Ph.D. diss., University of Oxford, 2000.

Herrera Montesinos, Guillermo. *Izquierda Unida y el Partido Comunista*. Lima: s.n., 2002.

Villanueva del Campo, Armando et al. *Jorge del Prado: Una figura de leyenda: Homenaje del Congreso de la República*. Lima: Fondo Editorial del Congreso del Perú, 2002.

CHARLES F. WALKER

DEL RIO, DOLORES (1905–1983). Dolores Del Rio (Dolores Asunsolo; *b.* 1905; *d.* 11 April 1983), Mexican stage and motion picture star. Born in Durango, Del Rio was discovered by the American director Edwin Carewe, who cast her in the silent film *Joanne* (1925) in Hollywood. She subsequently starred in various other silent and early sound Hollywood films, such as *Journey into Fear*, directed by Orson Welles. In 1942, director Emilio "El Indio" Fernández convinced her to return to Mexico and become a central part of his film team. Del Rio thus had major roles in the most acclaimed of Fernández's films: *Flor silvestre* (1943), *María Candelaria* (1943), *Bugambilia* (1944), and *Las*

abandonadas (1944). In later years, she continued her career in both Hollywood and Mexico, receiving numerous acting awards in Mexico and elsewhere.

See also **Cinema: From the Silent Film to 1990.**

BIBLIOGRAPHY

Luis Reyes De La Maza, *El cine sonoro en México* (1973).

E. Bradford Burns, *Latin American Cinema: Film and History* (1975).

Carl J. Mora, *Mexican Cinema: Reflections of a Society: 1896–1980* (1982).

John King, *Magical Reels: A History of Cinema in Latin America* (1990).

Additional Bibliography

Hershfield, Joanne. *The Invention of Dolores del Río*. Minneapolis: University of Minnesota Press, 2000.

Taibo, Paco Ignacio. *Dolores del Río, mujer en el volcán: biografía*. Mexico City: Planeta, 1999.

DAVID MACIEL

DEMOCRACY. On September 24, 1809, the canon of the Catholic Church in Santa Fé de Bogotá gave an oration in the city's cathedral at the request of the Spanish viceroy. As he prayed for "public peace," his attention became centered on questions of "legitimacy." He noted the spread of the "idol of liberty" in "pestilent writings" by "monsters [who] inspire rebellion among all the peoples." Against these ideas, Canon José Domingo Duquesne de Madrid reminded his audience that they owed "obedience and submission" to the "legitimate powers"; those who resisted these powers were resisting the will of God. Five months later, on February 22, 1810, the archbishop of Buenos Aires issued a pastoral letter with a similar message: The authority to command the peoples did not originate in the human will; contrary to what the "libertines" imagined, it "emanated from the supreme authority of God" (Duquesne de Madrid 1809; Carta Pastoral 1810).

The oration in Bogotá and the pastoral letter in Buenos Aires were reaffirmations of Spanish monarchical rule and its final source: the divine rights of the king. Yet, paradoxically, both texts were clear expressions of a deep concern among civilian and religious authorities regarding the emergence of alternative sources of legitimacy. Whom, and why, do people obey?

Of course, these questions already had been at the center of political theoretical discussion for a long time, but they suddenly permeated the political reality of the Hispanic world following the Napoleonic invasion of Spain in 1808. The vacuum of power left by the forced abdication of King Ferdinand VII (1784–1833) set in motion a process that finally led to the independence of Spanish America under a new legitimizing principle: the sovereignty of the people. At the core of this process was the crucial issue of "representation," which was addressed from the start by resorting to elections, first in 1809 and soon followed by a series of electoral contests, which, given their unprecedented nature and dimensions, were—according to François-Xavier Guerra and Danielle Demelas-Bohy— "the revolution itself" (Demélas-Bohy and Guerra 1996, p. 34).

Talk of "new democracies" in Latin America is part of the contemporary vocabulary when referring in particular to the processes of regime transition from the military dictatorships of the period 1960 to 1970. These are, however, old creatures, whose origins date back to the early decades of the nineteenth century. Indeed, inasmuch as there was a visible "first 'long' wave of democratization" in the world since the 1820s (to use Samuel Huntington's phrase), most Latin American countries were from their beginnings part of this "wave." Since then, however, each country has taken a singular, individual path, and none of them has seen democratic developments take place in a linear, progressive way (Huntington 1991).

It is nowadays common to state that democracy is one of those "essentially contested concepts," concepts whose use "inevitably involves endless disputes about their proper use on the part of their users" (Gallie 1955–1956, p. 169; see also Whitehead 2002 and Crick 2002). But what came to be known as "modern democracy" in the early twenty-first century is identified with the merge of two different and often contradictory traditions—liberalism (understood as limited power) and democracy proper (the rule of the majority)—especially after World War II. Thus, modern democracies are also known as "liberal democracies" or "representative democracies," terms

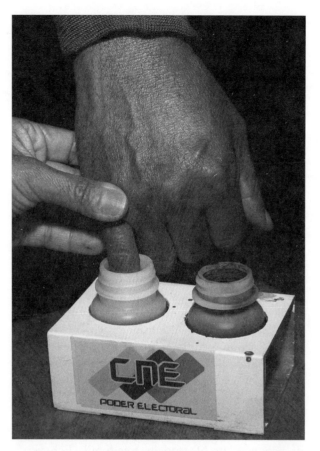

A Venezuelan voter's finger is inked at a polling station, December 2006. © SARAI SUAREZ/EPA/CORBIS

that will be used indistinctively in this essay (Bobbio 1990; Dunn 1995; Maier 1995; Urbinati 2006).

THE TERM *DEMOCRACY*

It seems that there is no history of the word *democracy* in Latin America like the account Pierre Rosanvallon has written for France (Rosanvallon 1995). Since the early nineteenth century the expression was certainly used by contemporaries in the region, albeit with the ambivalent connotations the term had elsewhere: The word was linked to Jacobin extremism following the French Revolution; it regained favor in the United States only with the founding of Jackson's Democratic Party in the late 1820s; and it became truly dominant in the political discourse of the West after the 1848 European revolutions (Maier 1995; Rosanvallon 1995).

During the first decades of Latin American independence, other words were probably favored over *democracy*—particularly *republic*, *representative government*, and *popular government*. Yet, contemporaries, even those who became suspicious of democracy, acknowledged the diffusion of "democratic ideas," as the Argentine Bernardo Monteagudo did, reflecting on his experiences in Peru in 1823 (Monteagudo 1916). Intellectuals and nation-builders often were aware of the tensions between liberalism and democracy (which, indeed, have persevered to the present). Some of them were also aware of the need to conciliate their principles. In 1833 Andrés Bello praised the newly reformed Chilean constitution for combining "a vigorous government with the complete enjoyment of well-ordered freedom": It gave "the government strength to defend itself against the attacks of insubordination produced by the excesses of democracy," and gave both the nation and individuals "resources to preserve them from despotism" (Bello 1997 [1833], pp. 254–255). In his *Dogma socialista* (1838) the Argentine Esteban Echeverría defined the two components of democracy: equality and freedom. Democracy was "the essence of all republican governments," the "government of the majorities," based on the "sovereignty of the people." But, Echeverría noted, people's sovereignty had limits, posed by "the individual, its conscience, its property, its life and its freedom" (Echeverría 1988 [1837], pp. 154–155). The extent to which the ideas and practices of democracy were originally understood in the region, and how they developed from the independence period, still remained understudied, in spite of some significant historiographical advances. In 1845 Domingo Faustino Sarmiento observed that there was a need for an Alexis de Tocqueville in South America—for someone who, knowledgeable in the social theories, could explain "the democracy brought about by the Revolution of 1810, the equality, whose dogma has penetrated even the lower levels of society" (Sarmiento 1976 [1845], p. 15; my own translation).

Although the evolution of the term *democracy* in Latin America had much in common with its history elsewhere in the Western world, here the focus is on those institutions and practices linked to the development of modern democracy in Latin America, particularly, though not exclusively, on those key aspects of democratization identified by Robert Dahl: inclusiveness and public contestation (Dahl 1971, p. 4). Hence the emphasis on the evolution of the suffrage and political parties, with the aim of

exploring the complex, long saga for free and fair competitive elections in Latin America. Democracies are not just about elections; but as Richard S. Katz observes, "elections are the defining institutions of modern democracies" (Katz 1997, p. 3). According to Pierre Rosanvallon, "elections amount to the most condensed and potent form of civic engagement." For this reason, he adds, "the history of democracy ... has for a long time simply been identified as a process of concentrating the political field of which the long struggle for universal suffrage has been both the means and the symbol" (Rosanvallon 2006, p. 236).

The following discussion adopts and adapts Huntington's idea of the three democratic "waves." This is done mostly to give some chronological order to a narrative of very disparate movements and to place the Latin American experience in a world context, rather than to suggest that democracy has come, reversed, and returned at the same pace throughout the region in the last two centuries.

THE FIRST "LONG DEMOCRATIC WAVE" IN LATIN AMERICA

The first world democratic "wave" in the 1820s was prefigured by what happened in Spanish America a decade or so earlier.

Between 1809 and 1814 there were at least five significant electoral processes in the American territories under Spanish control: for representatives to the Spanish Junta Central (1809); for deputies to the extraordinary Cortes (1810–1812); and for deputies to the ordinary Cortes, and members of municipal councils and provincial deputations (1812–1814). In addition, elections also took place in several provinces that declared their independence from Spain. Striking features of these movements were their abruptness and their inclusiveness: They showed the sudden evolution from absolutist rule to representative government based on almost universal male suffrage, particularly after the 1812 Cádiz constitution—some of the provinces adopted an even wider suffrage, like Cartagena in 1810 (Helg 2004, p. 129; Lasso 2007, p. 69; Rodríguez, 2000, p. 114. These were precocious exercises amidst extraordinarily circumstances.

On January 22, 1809, the Junta Central—which had been set up the previous September by deputies from the insurrectionary juntas throughout Spain to govern on behalf of the deposed king—called for the election of American representatives to that body. Widely publicized, the decree sparked an intense controversy about the nature of the Spanish territories in the Americas and their rights of representation, while opening up a process of mobilization that had few antecedents in the region: "from the Spring of 1809 to the Winter of 1810, from Sonora (Mexico) to Chile, all Spanish America lived according to the rhythm of this first experience of general elections" (Démelas-Bohy and Guerra 1996, p. 40; see also Guerra 1992; Haddick 1958; Benson 2004; Breña 2006). The elections were confined to the cities, though they were held in about a hundred locations. In some places—for example, Valladolid in New Spain (Mexico) and Cordoba in the River Plate—they evolved into seriously contested events, where anonymous leaflets contributed to the emergence of a public sphere with modern undertones.

The Cádiz Constitution (1812). The elections for deputies to the Junta Central were held under a restrictive system whose modalities of representation belonged to the *ancien régime*, but the Cádiz constitution in 1812 adopted a much wider and inclusive definition of the electorate.

As the *instrucción* to "facilitate" the elections in Guatemala explained, the notion of citizenship defined by the Cádiz constitution incorporated "the white, American or European: the Indian: the mestiso [person of mixed Indian and Spanish descent]." Although those "originating from Africa" were excluded in principle, they could qualify as citizens if they fulfilled certain conditions, such as servicing the "patria," or "distinguishing themselves by their talents, application and conduct." The "exercise of the rights of citizenship" was "suspended" in the cases of those under "judicial interdiction," of those in bankruptcy, and of domestic servants and vagrants (*Instrucción* 1812, pp. 5–9). Yet, there were no immediate literacy requirements for voting (they were to be applied only after 1830), nor were there income requirements. With the exceptions noted above, any male more than twenty-five years old and born in the Spanish dominions was a citizen, and thus entitled to vote in the first tier of a complex system of indirect elections.

It would be anachronistic to expect full universal suffrage in the region at that time; what is significant is how close the Cádiz constitution came to providing to universal male suffrage (Rodríguez 2005b and 2006). As José Antonio Aguilar has shown, the fact that elections were indirect should not detract from their modern nature either (Aguilar 1998, pp. 423–457; Aguilar 2000).

The Cádiz constitution did not remain a dead letter, in spite of its short life. Its text was received with festivities in América—in Lima, for example, people swore allegiance to the constitution with "splendor and pomp" during the celebrations that lasted from the first to the sixth of October 1812. It encouraged the publication of newspapers such as the *Verdadero Peruano*—a weekly journal specially founded to accompany the electoral process that followed, with pages devoted to related material, including an "Oda con motivo de la elección popular" written by the *pardo* (person of mixed African and Spanish ancestry) citizen José Manuel Valdes (*Verdadero Peruano* 1812, 1813). And of course it called for elections at various levels for the local *ayuntamientos*, provincial deputies and representative to the Cortes. Elections under the 1812 constitution did not take place everywhere, given the civil war conditions in much of the Hispanic world, but wherever they were held—in New Spain, Peru, Guatemala and Ecuador—they often proved to be significant events, for the intensity of the competition, the participation of voters from a wide range of social actors, and, often, their uncertainties (Rodríguez 2005a and 2006; Benson 1946; Chiaramonti 2005; Guedea 1991; Peralta Ruiz 1996 and 2005; Chust 2006; Chust and Serrano 2006; Morelli 2005; Dym 2006).

These initial processes of electoral mobilization were temporarily interrupted by Ferdinand's return to power in 1814, but their consequences were long-lasting. Above all, they severely undermined the legitimacy of colonial rule, thus paving the way for representative forms of government. The Cádiz constitution was reinstalled in 1820 after a liberal rebellion in Spain. By then, a few countries already had gained independence, but in those that still were under Spanish rule—such as Mexico, Guatemala, and Cuba—the return of the constitution motivated further electioneering. A liberal revolution also broke out in Portugal in 1820, provoking "the first colony-wide election in Brazil"—to select deputies to the Portuguese Cortes, under a "strictly limited suffrage"—which took place the following year (Bethell 1994, p. 3).

It is difficult to identify common patterns of political development from those early years of democracy. The representative governments of some of the new nations were rooted in the Cádiz constitution, but all the emerging countries had quite different experiences of fighting against Spanish forces or dealing with their own internal conflicts. And once they became independent, they all followed different paths.

Evolution of Voting Rights. A wide suffrage—a visible legacy of the Cádiz charter—prevailed in some countries and regions during the 1820s—in the province of Buenos Aires, or in Mexico after the 1824 constitution (Ternavasio 2002; Guardino 1996; Warren 2001). Restrictions to the vote that were introduced generally during the following decade varied and seemed to have kept a spirit of inclusiveness. Literacy requirements, for example, were set in New Granada, Peru, and Chile, but their applications were postponed for a few years, under the assumption that the lack of literacy was a colonial deficit to be remedied by the republics (Posada-Carbó 2003, p. 322). Income restrictions also were introduced, but sometimes the sum required was not that large; in other instances the wording of the restriction was vague, thus allowing for a flexible implementation. Domestic servants and dependent rural laborers were still explicitly excluded from suffrage in the 1832 constitution of New Granada, as in many other constitutions of the period.

A renewed drive to expand the suffrage took place in the mid-nineteenth century: In 1853 Colombia and Argentina fully adopted universal male suffrage, a measure also taken by Mexico and Venezuela in 1857 (Bushnell 1968 and 1972; Negretto and Aguilar 2000) Following in the footsteps of Cádiz, these also were precocious developments by world standards. However, none of the institutional advances became landmarks of democratic consolidation. In Mexico and Venezuela they soon were overshadowed by war and dictatorship. In Colombia universal male suffrage was partly reversed in 1863, when the electoral regime was decentralized—although some states kept it, others reintroduced voting restrictions. Voting restrictions became the norm for national elections after 1886, but universal male suffrage was

adopted for the elections of all city councils and departmental assemblies. The measure was never reversed in Argentina, but a later set of reforms, known as the Saenz Peña Law (1912)—which introduced a permanent register of electors, minority representation, and compulsory and secret voting—marked the effective expansion of male suffrage there.

Other countries also expanded the vote, though without fully embracing universal male suffrage. Peru came close to it after 1861, but returned to a restrictive regime in 1896. Ecuador relaxed its income requirements in 1861 but kept literacy restrictions, and in 1869, restricted voting to Catholics. Catholicism was a condition to vote in Brazil under the 1824 constitution, which also excluded slaves and imposed income requirements that were relatively modest, allowing for an extensive suffrage for some decades. In 1881 the Saraiva Law removed the income qualifications and allowed non-Catholics to vote, but introduced literacy requirements, drastically curtailing the suffrage: 80 percent of the adult male population lost the right to vote.

Such changes in the suffrage—expansion followed by restrictions time and again—are not specific to Latin American countries. Similar movements can be detected clearly in the history of European countries such as France, or in the ways the United States excluded blacks from the franchise at the end of the nineteenth century (Warren 2001, pp. 158,159; see also Keyssar 2000). Linear democratic developments towards universal suffrage, as in Great Britain, were more the exception than the norm. The closest to such an exception in Latin America was in Chile, where the expansion of the suffrage followed a gradualist path after adoption of the constitution of 1833, which set income and literacy restrictions. But the income restrictions were modest, and the literacy requirement was enforced with some flexibility. As J. Samuel Valenzuela has observed, income levels were never raised in later years, and they were "swept aside" by a 1874 reform that stated that it was presumed by law that all literates had the required income to vote (Valenzuela 1985 and 1996).

Unlike the precocious though interrupted enfranchisement of men, Latin America was relatively slow in giving the vote to women. The only country to embrace women's suffrage nationwide during the "first long wave of democratization" was Ecuador, and this was not until 1929 (Markoff 2003; Maza Valenzuela 1998). There had been a few earlier instances when women were formally given voting rights, but they were confined to particular regions and there is no evidence regarding their implementation. The earliest case seems to have been in the Colombian province of Vélez in 1853, when the provincial constitution provided the right of suffrage to all citizens "without distinction of sex." Similarly, women were entitled to vote in San Juan (Argentina) in 1862. These look like isolated and unsuccessful experiences; so were the attempts by women to register to vote in Chile in 1875, following vague legislation passed in 1874 (Maza Valenzuela 1995, p. 141). There were other provinces that also gave voting rights to women, but much later, in the 1920s: Yucatán, San Luis Potosí, and Chiapas, in Mexico, and Rio Grande do Norte in Brazil. The main organization to fight for women's suffrage in Brazil, the Federacao Brasileira pelo Progesso Femenino, was established in 1922 (Hahner 1979).

The final acceptance of universal male suffrage was generally a post-1930 conquest, except in Argentina and Mexico, where the constitutional provisions of the 1850s were never reversed, and in Uruguay, where it was adopted in 1916. In Costa Rica the vagueness of the restrictions introduced in the 1871 constitution "meant that, by the early twentieth century, all men at least twenty years old were registered to vote" (Lehoucq and Molina 2002, p. 41).

In spite of the "accidental" evolution of the suffrage, the institutional developments described above were not democratically insignificant: They not only reflected the early acceptance of popular sovereignty as an undisputed legitimacy principle, but also encouraged extraordinary levels of electoral popular politics (which, until recently, have been neglected by historians) (Annino 1995; Posada-Carbó 1997b; Sábato 1999). With the available information it is not possible to trace the movement of the electorates in a systematic fashion. Yet, some indicators show that electoral participation was often intense, with important variations in time and place, and according to the type of electoral contest and degree of competition.

There was a massive irruption of the electorate in most Spanish American countries from the early years of their independence through the 1830s. Some of the accounts of the elections under the Cádiz constitution reveal a picture of community involvement. Electoral participation continued to be high in Mexico City after independence: According to Richard Warren, "voter turnout for municipal elections of the late 1820s and early 1830s fluctuated in the range of 25 to 70 percent" (Warren 2001, p. 164). He also estimates that in 1829 to 1831, turnout "hovered around 27 percent" of the city's male population. Mexico City was perhaps not representative of all of Mexico, but as the capital of the country its importance should not be undervalued. The figures also suggest that in some areas there were extraordinarily high rates of participation by the world standards of the time. Electoral mobilization seems to have slowed down during the following decades in some countries as a result of new voting restrictions. In other countries—as in Argentina under the dictatorship of Juan Manuel de Rosas—elections simply lost significance except for their symbolic function.

Participation after Mid-Century. There was a second surge of extensive mass participation in the mid-nineteenth century, after some countries adopted universal male suffrage, or lowered voting requirements. In Colombia 210,000 people—40 percent of the electorate—voted in the presidential election of 1856. This was an extraordinarily high rate by world standards, as David Bushnell has shown, and even more when transport and communication difficulties are considered (Bushnell 1971). The electorate in Chile was around 30,000 people by the 1850s, but this figure more than tripled following the 1874 electoral reform. During that decade the largest electorate was in Brazil: One million people voted in the 1872 elections (11% of the total population), a rate higher than Italy (2%), Holland (2.5%), Portugal (9%), and Great Britain (7%). (Murilo de Carvalho 1995, p. 25; see also Graham 1990)

Although the voting populations of some countries shrank during the last quarter of the nineteenth century, there was a renewed general expansion of the electorate in the first three decades of the twentieth century. This was perhaps most dramatic in Argentina after 1912, and in Uruguay, where the electorate grew almost seven-fold between 1906 and 1930. In Colombia—as a result of the 1910 reforms that lowered the income requirements for voting at national elections—the electorate grew at a faster pace than the general population did in those same years. More than 800,000 voted in the presidential election of 1930, or about 48 percent of the adult male population (Posada-Carbó 1997a; Barrán 1996).

These successive "waves" of expansion and contraction must have produced substantial variation in the social composition of the electorate. But almost from the start, elections were not confined to the elites, as many historians long assumed.

Charles R. Berry might have exaggerated when he wrote that during the Mexican elections of 1810 to 1822, "the enfranchised populace participated enthusiastically, taking their obligations as citizens seriously" (Berry 1976, p. 41), but people from all classes and ethnic backgrounds voted in those early contests. The involvement of the popular sectors in electioneering persevered throughout the century, and was more intense of course during periods of suffrage expansion. Following the Peruvian electoral reforms of 1847 to 1849, "political participation increased among a wide cross section of Peruvians: tradesmen, teachers, journalists, professionals, small shopkeepers and villagers" (Peloso 1996, pp. 194–195). Artisans figured prominently in electoral campaigns in Peru, Chile, and Colombia (Sowell 1992).

There has been very little systematic research on the social composition of voters over time, but the available studies confirm the general picture of a socially diverse electorate where the popular element was often dominant, as in Buenos Aires, and in São Paulo, where low-income and illiterate voters—including those from rural districts—formed a large proportion of the electorate (Alonso 1996; Kline 1995). Closer examinations may reveal substantial variations in the electorate's social composition over time, as for example in Chile between 1863 and 1878: As the proportion of "property owners and capitalists," "professional, merchants, and other middle class sectors," and "public and private employees" declined, that of "artisans," "farmers," "miners," and "labourers" increased during those years (Valenzuela 1985, p. 118). During the first decades of the twentieth century, following urbanization and industrial development, the participation of the popular sectors in electoral politics became even more prominent. Even when suffrage restrictions remained, as in the Bolivian elections of 1904, parties had to court the artisan vote (Irurozqui 2000). The founder of the Chilean

Communist Party claimed that more than 60 percent of the Chilean electorate in the 1920s was made up of people who either were members of the Workers Federation or were somewhat linked it (Valenzuela 1998, p. 285). Undoubtedly this is an exaggeration of an interested party, but nonetheless it shows awareness of a new social landscape.

The development of labor unions often went hand in hand with the organization of socialist parties, sometimes with the explicit aim of gaining representation in congresses, state assemblies, and city councils. There were significant inroads for social democrats in Chilean representative politics. In other countries, however, they faced the resistance of fellow socialists who favored revolution over electioneering, or even more challenging, the competition of well-established parties with traditional links with the laboring classes. A good illustration of this was offered by the union leader Ignacio Torres Giraldo (1892–1968) in his account of the politics of the Colombian labor movement during the 1910s and 1920s (Torres Giraldo, n.d). The Liberal return to power in the presidential elections of 1930 owed a great deal to the support the party received from urban labor.

Many historians and social scientists have dismissed as insignificant the early experiences with a wide suffrage—even universal male suffrage—and the evidence of popular participation in electoral politics. In this view, Latin American elections before 1930 (especially in the nineteenth century) generally have been perceived as mere theatrical events, where voters were controlled by governments and elites through fraud, clientelism, bribery, and coercion. The regimes resulting from those elections have thus been labeled regimes of "democratic fiction" (Guerra 1994; see also Graham 1990 and Escalante Gonzalbo 1993).

Electoral Competition and the Formation of Political Parties. There were dictatorial regimes—such as Porfirio Díaz's in Mexico—where voters were regularly paraded at the polls in elections that were democratically meaningless. The politics of influence—be it by governments, the clergy, landowners, or politicians—were part and parcel of electioneering. Fraud and violence also were constant reminders of the shortcomings of democracy in the region. But these were far from typical of Latin America. As Alan Knight has observed regarding Francisco Madero's reform movement in revolutionary Mexico: "In no country were the constitutional practices admired by Madero and his fellow reformers rapidly implanted: they grew up gradually, often developing out of earlier 'corrupt' practices, associated with 'artificial' or 'limited' democracy and characterized by boss-rule, networks of patronage and machine politics" (Knight 1986, p. 412).

What needs to be acknowledged more fully is that the politics of influence or the existence of fraud and violence did not preclude democratic developments, which—it should be stressed once again—occurred with important variations over time and place, and often following what Hilda Sabato has referred to as a "zigzag path" (Sabato 2001; see also Deas 1973; Posada-Carbó 1994 and 2000b). Above all, scholars need to reconsider some of the stereotypes that tend to undermine the significance of elections during this period, and the extent to which elections reflected competitive politics—the realm of democratic aspirations and, indeed, achievements.

Electoral corruption coexisted with the development of competitive politics, and fraud did not always determine the results at the ballot box, as Lehoucq and Molina have demonstrated for Costa Rica. Moreover, an exclusive focus on corrupt methods draws attention from the constant efforts in some countries to develop a fairer competitive field. As early as the 1830s there was a body of experts on voting regulations in Colombia to challenge the results at the polls and foster a culture of electoral litigation. The adoption of the secret ballot was a late development, as it was also in Europe and in the United States. Chile established voting booths in 1890, more than two decades before France, where it was mandated in 1913 (Valenzuela 1998 and Markoff 1999).

Electoral competition went hand in glove with the formation of political parties. As in the earlier phases of other Western democracies, in Latin America the terms *party* and *opposition* had a pejorative sense well into the nineteenth century. Yet, as early as 1844 some figures such as Domingo Faustino Sarmiento defended their legitimacy, and the legitimacy of opposition parties contesting elections (Sarmiento 2001, pp. 63–85). Electoral clubs, much in evidence during the 1820s, again sprang up in Argentina after the fall of Rosas in 1852. Indeed, political organizations to fight elections emerged almost in

tandem with the adoption of suffrage throughout the continent. *Pipiolos* ("novices") and *pelucones* ("big wigs") were the nicknames in Chile for the Liberal and Conservative Parties, two of the four parties (together with the National and Radical) that formed Chile's first party system, during the administration of President Manuel Montt Torres (1851–1861) (Collier pp. 49–50; Valenzuela 1995). The Colombian Conservative and Liberal Parties, which also originated from earlier factions organized around the struggle for power, were established in 1849 to 1850. They, too, struggled for power in Mexico, but the Conservatives disappeared after 1863, whereas the Liberal Party was somewhat transformed under the Porfirio Díaz regime (Hale 1989).

Of course, party developments varied from country to country, and not all parties evolved into durable machines. There were no consolidated national parties in Brazil; instead, parties tended to be state-based, such as the Paulista Republican Party, organized in 1873, or the Democratic Party of São Paulo, established in 1926. The first national civilian party in Peru was founded in 1871 (McEvoy 1997; Muecke 2004). Argentine parties were also latecomers, and often had short lives. The Partido Autonomista Nacional was set up in 1880 but barely outlived his major leader, General Julio Argentino Roca. In contrast, the Unión Cívica Radical—established in 1891—became one of the two most important Argentine parties of the twentieth century (Alonso 2000). A significant number of parties founded during this period either ceased to exist or survived with diminished roles after 1930. The Blanco and Colorado in Uruguay, and the Liberals and Conservatives in Colombia, were exceptional for their influence in shaping their nations' party systems in the twentieth century. Nonetheless, there were other long-lasting parties that originated during this period, including the Cuban and Chilean and Communist Parties and the Alianza Popular Revolucionaria Americana (APRA), established in 1922.

The development of durable and competitive party systems was a slow, complex, and frustrating process. Party systems were more likely to evolve in countries that managed to hold regular elections because they helped to anchor social roots within the electorate. In the absence of strong electoral authorities, however, party competition unsurprisingly turned into violent conflict. Yet, civil war was no impediment to the evolution of competitive electoral politics between Blancos and Colorados in Uruguay, particularly after 1919, when elections were held almost annually (Barrán 1996, p. 52).

These reconsiderations by no means ignore the extent to which suffrage practices and political competition were still distant from the democratic ideal. Where in the world was that "ideal" in the nineteenth century? Indeed, a proper understanding of how democracy evolved in Latin America ought to reexamine the subject from a wider, comparative perspective. Furthermore, a detailed historical revision reveals a complex picture that cannot be framed by *caudillismo*—the common view of Latin American politics identified with personal, tyrannical rule that was popularized in the English-speaking world by Mary Mann's translation of Sarmiento's *Facundo* in 1868 (Jaksic 2007, pp. 306–308). Neither can it be framed within the usual history of permanent stagnation and failure.

Attempts at building constitutional regimes did meet with enormous difficulties from the start, and all countries subsequently suffered periods of instability and repression. Such setbacks should not be surprising. At the time of independence, republican liberal constitutionalism was a rarity in the world. As José Antonio Aguilar has noted, the emerging Latin American nations were "voluntary guinea pigs" in adopting a set of novel institutions considered to be appropriate for representative government—popular elections, separation of powers, individual rights, freedom of the press—but whose effectiveness was largely unknown: "Latin America represents the great post-revolutionary constitutional experiment" (Aguilar 2000, p. 24; see especially pp. 15–56). The menu of institutions chosen, the timing and circumstances of their adoption—without a proper state apparatus in place for their implementation—coupled with the lack of experience, help to explain why early attempts at democratization were frustrated (Valenzuela 2006).

The long-term consequences of those early experiences have not been assessed completely. An evident legacy, amply recognized in recent historiography, was the incorporation of popular sectors into electoral politics. Less studied has been the roles played by congresses and other representative assemblies since these nations' independence. Congresses might have been just rubber-stamping bodies under

conspicuous dictators, but their main function is "often overlooked" (Kinsbruner 1994, p. 119). They were most visible in imperial Brazil, in Chile during the crisis leading to the 1891 civil war and the subsequent parliamentary period, and under the federal regimes adopted in various nations. They also figured prominently in the politics of countries usually identified with *caudillo* rule, such as nineteenth-century Peru. Congresses represented provincial interests and served as constraints on the power of executives, even under centralist constitutions, as in Chile after 1833 or in Colombia under the Conservative hegemony (1886–1930).

Role of the Press and Civil Society.

In addition to congresses, another key actor in the early phases of Latin American democratization was the press, whose role also has been neglected by historians. The press flourished unprecedentedly during the first decades of independence. Repeated instances of repression, political instability, and undeveloped markets made for a bumpy ride for the consolidation of newspapers. "The history of the Mexican press is a narrative of failure," noted Walter McCaleb in 1920, following the destructive effects of the revolution (McCaleb 1920, p. 443). More often than not, newspapers had a short life, but some lasted for a number of significant years, even decades, and a few of those established during this period have survived to the present—notably *El Mercurio* (1827) in Chile, *El Comercio* (1839) in Peru, *La Nación* (1862) in Argentina, *O Estado de Sao Paulo* (1875) and *Jornal do Brasil* (1891) in Brazil, and *El Espectador* (1885) and *El Tiempo* (1911) in Colombia (Posada-Carbó 2007b; see also Soto 2004 and Alonso 2003). Regardless of their life spans, the history of newspapers is inextricably linked to the processes of democratization because their very existence is determined by a basic liberal principle: freedom of the press. Overall, newspapers were instrumental to most electoral campaigns: They publicized the candidates' profiles and platforms; they discussed the issues at stake; they informed about electoral regulations and procedures; and they helped to shape a fundamental aspect of modern democracies—*public opinion*, a term that was already in common usage in the press by the 1830s.

"Newspapers . . . were embedded in and constitutive of democratic life," Carlos Forment acknowledged in a stimulating attempt to revalue the "democratic tradition" of Latin America during the nineteenth century (Forment 2003, p. xviii). Newspapers were part of that terrain of associative practices through which Latin Americans became "democratic citizens," also exemplified by the more than seven thousand voluntary groups that formed in Mexico, Peru, Cuba, and Argentina throughout the century. But Forment presents a disjunctive picture of public life: Although "civil society" was the domain of "democratic-minded" Latin Americans, "political society" was the realm of authoritarians. Such generalized disjuncture is difficult to accept because it not only idealizes the former and demonizes the latter, but also assumes that there were no links between the two. Early artisan societies were set up with the encouragement and support of political leaders, and often with the purpose of contesting elections—consider those established by the *pelucones* in Chile in 1829, and by the *progresistas* in New Granada in 1836. Mutual societies such as the Argentinian Sociedad Tipográfica Bonaerense, founded in 1865, included politicians from its beginning, and "cultivated a special relation" with the political world: Its first president was a newspaper editor, the founder of *La Tribuna*, and later a government minister and senator (Sabato 1998, pp. 55–57). Rather than contradicting it, Forment's revisionist work serves to complement the narrative presented here, thus adding more elements—those from civil society—to underline that "the democratic tradition in Latin America is far more robust than most scholars have claimed" (Forment 2003, p. xi).

Moments of Democratization. As already suggested, this "democratic tradition" originating from independence did not develop in a linear, gradual way. Although all countries followed different paths, it is possible to identify two major "moments" of democratization during the first half of the nineteenth century: the early decades of independence, and the mid-nineteenth century, when developments were influenced to some extent by the 1848 European revolutions. The European revolutions had significant repercussions in Latin America, most visibly in Chile, Colombia, Peru, and Pernambuco (Brazil), but also indirectly and later in Argentina and Mexico. As Guy Thomson notes, "the revolutions of 1848 renewed and extended Latin America's democratic vocabulary and republican symbolism" (Thomson 2002, p. 7). Such "moments" of democratization also had deep practical consequences besides the massive enfranchisement of popular sectors. The abolition of slavery, which began during

the independence period—with Chile abolishing it altogether in 1823—was finally accomplished in the 1850s, except in Cuba, Puerto Rico, and Brazil. These "moments" of democratization also brought important reforms, some of them fostering social mobility and elite rotation, as exemplified by the career of Benito Juárez in Mexico. The drastic liberal reforms in Colombia during the 1840s and 1860s might not have produced all their desired effects, but there were a few democratic advancements (Posada-Carbó 2002). As José María Samper lamented in 1861, "the European world has made more efforts to study our volcanoes than our society…it has much more learning about how quinine bark is cut, or how hides are salted in Buenos Aires, than about the vitality of our infant democracy" (quoted in Deas 1985, pp. 537–538).

A third "moment" of democratization—this time more gradual and prolonged—took place from the 1880s to 1930, when liberal constitutional rule made significant inroads. This occurred, for example, in Brazil since the 1891 constitution, in Chile under the so-called "República parlamentaria" (1891–1925), and in Colombia after 1910. Electoral reforms made it possible for some political parties to achieve power via the ballot box, as did the Argentine Radicals, who won the presidency in 1916. During this period, under the influence of José Batlle y Ordóñez, Uruguayan democracy first embraced the welfare state. Some attempts at opening the political system ended in disaster, the most extreme example of which was Francisco Madero's anti-reelection campaign in 1910, which sparked the Mexican Revolution. With a few exceptions, however, this third moment came to an end with a succession of breakdowns after 1929—a democratic reversal similar to that which was already taking place in Europe.

THE SECOND WAVE: DEMOCRACY IN AN ILLIBERAL AGE

As the above narrative suggests, there was no easily identifiable "first democratic wave" in Latin America, but rather a mixed set of developments in different directions varying from country to country, though there were various "moments" of democratization that acquired a regional dimension. References to the "second wave" are at least as problematic. In Huntington's classification, this second global democratizing movement took place in 1943 to 1962; some Latin American scholars date it to 1956 to 1962 (Huntington 1991, p. 16; Hagopian and Mainwaring 2005, pp. 18–19).

A glance at some individual cases reveals the difficulties in fitting their experiences into such patterns. It is true that from 1929 to 1933 democracy in the region was in retreat following a succession of coups d'état. However, Costa Rica and Colombia avoided the trend—in the latter, power changed hands via democratic election in 1930, a landmark in the country's history (Posada-Carbó 2000a, pp. 35–47). In 1932 constitutional rule returned in Chile, where a military coup (as in Uruguay), "rather than leading to sharp breaks [with their] political evolution, represented serious but passing setbacks" (Hartlyn and Valenzuela 1995, p. 138). Indeed, as totalitarian and dictatorial regimes expanded in Europe in the 1930s and 1940s, the democratic perspectives in some Latin American countries did not look so dark. This was not the case, however, in Brazil under the authoritarian Estado Novo ("new state") inaugurated by Getúlio Dornelles Vargas in 1937, or in Argentina under Juan Domingo Perón's rule. But confronted with the horrors of Europe, the leading Colombian liberal statesman Alberto Lleras Camargo (1906–1990) optimistically claimed in the early 1940s that the future of world democracy was in the Americas.

After World War II, democracy did expand in the region. From 1945 to 1964, according to José Murilo de Carvalho, Brazil historically enjoyed its first "democratic experience" (Murilho de Carvalho 1995, pp. 95, 97). Venezuela, having emerged from the long dictatorial regime of Juan Vicente Gómez (1909–1935), underwent a period of political opening in the 1940s. Later significant developments encouraged Milton Eisenhower to report in 1959 to the president of the United States, Dwight D. Eisenhower (1953–1961), that dictatorships in Latin America had been "steadily" declining since 1933. J. Fred Rippy, critically commenting on Eisenhower's statement, skeptically observed that "with few exceptions, newsmen of every media of information (in the United States) have conveyed the idea that the general trend south of our border is toward democracy and more democracy" (Rippy 1960, p. 99). Rippy questioned the assumption that the recent downfall of tyrants signaled an "advance toward democracy" in the region. Four years later, the 1964 military coup in Brazil proved him right. Though the democratic regimes in Chile and Uruguay survived more than a decade beyond the end year of Huntington's second "wave," they did break down in 1973. "Those were the darkest of days," Fernando Enrique Cardoso recalled in his memoirs, "not just for us [Brazilians], but for all of Latin America. Like dominoes, democracies were collapsing everywhere: Uruguay, Chile, Argentina" (Cardoso 2006, p. 115).

Not everywhere. Costa Rica had been on the path towards a consolidated modern democracy since 1948. Democracy had flourished in Venezuela since 1958, and Colombia had returned to constitutional rule after the brief dictatorship of General Gustavo Rojas Pinilla (1953–1957). There was no regime breakdown in Mexico, though the long dominant rule by the PRI (Partido Revolucionario Institucional) brought into question the country's democratic credentials. Yet, in 1957 Russell Fitzgibbon argued that in spite of being "vitiated by the absence of genuine party competition, Mexico should be classed as a 'democratic country' [because] the democracy which is lacking in interparty competition may in part be supplied by the intraparty operation of the PRI" (Fitzgibbon 1957, pp. 18–19).

Suffrage Reform. Too much emphasis on the so-called "second wave" leaves out significant democratic developments that took place before and after the short "second wave." By and large, however, these developments occurred amidst a hostile ideological atmosphere. Arguably, there were conflicting views of democracy at play, but with a few exceptions, the guiding principles of political liberalism at best took second stage, and subsequently some of the major values of modern democracy lost currency (see Posada Carbo 2007a and 2008).

Nonetheless, beginning in the 1930s there was a significant expansion of the suffrage and, unlike those of earlier periods, few of these renewed constitutional achievements have been removed from the legal texts.

Universal male suffrage returned to Colombia (1936) and Venezuela (1947), and was officially adopted by Costa Rica in 1949. Literary restrictions were kept in some countries including Ecuador, Bolivia, Peru, Brazil, and Chile, though in Chile the 1874 electoral reform and the high literacy rates had made such restrictions redundant by the time they were finally abolished in 1970. This was also the period of incorporation of women into

Mexicans protest a lack of electoral ballots in polling stations, July 2000. Vicente Fox's victory in the 2000 presidential election unseated the Institutional Revolutionary Party (PRI), which had been in power since 1929, ending one-party rule in Mexico. © REUTERS/CORBIS

the political body. Country after country adopted female suffrage: Brazil and Uruguay in 1932, Cuba in 1934, El Salvador in 1939, Dominican Republic in 1942, Guatemala in 1945, Argentina and Venezuela in 1947, Costa Rica and Chile in 1949 (in Chile women had been granted the right to vote in municipal elections in 1935), Bolivia in 1952, Colombia and Honduras in 1955, and Haiti in 1958 (Brandenburg 1958, p. 212).

The electorate subsequently grew, even in countries that kept suffrage restrictions. Compulsory voting—adopted in Argentina, Uruguay, Costa Rica, Chile, Brazil, and Venezuela—might in some cases explain higher rates of electoral participation, but not in every case, as enforcement was not always strong. At any rate, the electorates grew more quickly than the general populations did in Argentina, Peru, Venezuela, Chile, and Brazil. By 1964 more than

fourteen million people voted in Brazil, a massive expansion from the 1.8 million who went to the polls back in 1930. The numbers seemed modest in Bolivia, yet its electorate doubled between 1940 and 1951, when about 200,000 people voted (Murilo de Carvalho 1995, p. 108; Whitehead 2002, p. 316). Although members of the laboring classes in some countries had been mobilized during the earlier period, the overall Latin American electorate acquired a new profile following this expansion.

The Growth of Parties. Wherever parties had developed strong social roots in the past, they often were successful in incorporating the respective expanding electorates, though in most cases they faced the challenges of new parties and populist figures. Some of the new parties were the results of merges, such as the Chilean Partido Socialista (founded in 1933), or of internal splits—the

Chilean Partido Demócrata Cristiano, set up in 1957, grew out of factions from the Conservatives. Christian democratic parties were established during this period and became leading actors in the politics of Costa Rica and Venezuela. Catholics in Mexico sponsored the foundation of the Partido de Acción Nacional (PAN). The Mexican Partido Revolucionario Institucional (PRI), originally known as Partido Nacional Revolucionario in 1929, consolidated as a party that was "almost unbelievably well organized": "No other political group in Latin America … can equal it in the completeness and effectiveness of its organization" (Fitzgibbon 1957, p. 19). Brazil saw the emergence of national political parties for the first time under the republic, such as the Uniao Democrática Nacional (UDN) and the Partido Social Democrático (PSD) (Bethell 1994, p. 9). Innovations in party politics were perhaps more significant in countries that had had dictatorships and thus required new organizations almost from scratch. This was the case in Venezuela, where Acción Democrática was established in 1946 and soon was followed by the Christian democratic party Comité de Organización Electoral Independiente (COPEI). These developments were interpreted positively by contemporary political scientists such as Fitzgibbon: "Party progress is erratic but there is ample evidence in many directions that parties are becoming more mature and sophisticated, more responsive and responsible, and a more significant part of the broad political landscape" (Fitzgibbon 1957, p. 21).

The extent to which party developments led to free and fair electoral contests during the 1940s to the 1960s varied from country to country. There were significant electoral reforms including the establishment of new electoral courts, and electoral rules to allow for minority representation and encourage party competition, as in Uruguay, Costa Rica, and Chile (McDonald 1967, p. 702; Brandenburg 1958, p. 217). Costa Rica's electoral code of 1946, adopted in a revised version by the 1949 National Constituent Assembly, is considered a landmark because it "contributed to the development of one of the most stable democratic regimes in the world" (Lehoucq 1995, pp. 24, 42). Contemporary foreign observers acknowledged important electoral developments, because some electoral contests were perceived as being relatively free and fair, including the presidential elections in Peru in

1956; in Uruguay in 1946 and 1950; in Venezuela in 1947; in Costa Rica in 1953; in Chile in 1946 and 1952; and in Ecuador's Galo Plaza in 1948, where the victor four years later became "the first popularly elected president in more than twenty-five years to complete his full term in office." But electoral irregularities persevered in most countries. Control of voters was made easier by preregistration arrangements and the general practice of parties and candidates printing their own ballots, though the state-printed ballot was introduced in Chile in 1958 (Brandenburg 1958, pp. 214–215; 218–220).

According to the surveys conducted by Fitzgibbon (and others) between 1945 and 1955, the nature of elections seriously hampered the quality of Latin America democracy, as did other factors that "were thought to be in a bad way": civilian supremacy over the military, freedom of party organization, and the state of local government. What impressed the "specialists" about the democratic progress during those years—and indeed encouraged their optimism about the future of democracy—were the improvements in education, the standard of living, and the status of social legislation (Fitzgibbon 1956, pp. 71–72). Whether or not the level of socioeconomic development should be a precondition for democratization is still a matter of scholarly debate today, but the frustrating experiences of the mid-twentieth century illustrate the difficulties of establishing any simple correlation. "The clearest … threat to civil liberty [in Latin America]," Germán Arciniegas wrote, "is that which has developed in the country with the lowest rate of illiteracy—Argentina" (1953, p. 10).

Military and Populist Regimes. Arciniegas, a Colombian liberal intellectual who lived in exile in the United States from 1942 to 1960, left a testimony of what he referred to as a "vast conspiracy against democracy, liberty, and respect for human rights"—an increasing movement away from representative government that was placing Latin America outside the "democratic orbit" (Arciniegas 1953; 1996 [1956], p. 18). His rallying cry was not just against military dictatorship but also against the rising populist regimes, which he labeled "neo-caudillism"; Perón and his party were the object of his harshest criticism. Arciniegas reflected on the

Armed guard observing voters in the congressional elections, Buenos Aires, Argentina, 1965. A year later a coup led by General Juan Carlos Ongania dissolved the congress and established military rule, spelling the end of democracy in Argentina for many years. © BETTMANN/CORBIS

dilemmas those regimes posed to democracy: "the caudillos … have started out with the backing of groups of people, sometimes with a real majority of popular support. Invariably their programmes have carried a glimmer of the democratic ideal." Demagoguery was an effective weapon, but "once the spellbinders have won power, their promises have gone up in smoke, leaving only the bitter bread of dictatorship" (Arciniegas 1953, pp. xv, 7, 384; 1996 [1956], p. 21). What was to Ariciniegas an "arbitrary use of words" was to populists a problem of definitions. Indeed, some foreign contemporary scholars were of the view that, in contrast to (U.S.) Americans, the average Latin American was "thinking more in terms of social and economic than of political democracy" (Fitzgibbon 1967, p. 130). However, Arciniegas supported the alternative notion of "representative, democratic government," a system that "would become a stimulus and challenge" for the alleviation of social problems, as they could be

"trashed out in the press, in the legislative chambers, in the streets and the homes" (Arciniegas 1953, p. 7).

As noted above, representative democracy seemed to flourish at the end of the 1950s. According to Mainwaring and Pérez Liñán, there were twelve democracies and "semi-democracies" in the region by 1961—a significant expansion since 1955. This was a "short wave." The impact of the Cuban Revolution (1959) was devastating. Added to the antidemocratic attitudes in traditional circles was now a devaluation of the suffrage by those who embraced guerrilla violence, further polarizing the struggle for power. After the military coups in Brazil and Bolivia in 1964, the breaking down of democracies seemed to be the rule for the next decade, in Argentina in 1966, Peru in 1968, Ecuador in 1970, Chile and Uruguay in 1973, and Argentina again in 1976—this was the "zenith of authoritarianism in Latin America" (Mainwaring 2000, p. 146).

The fact that democratic regimes survived in the 1970s in Costa Rica, Colombia, and Venezuela has often been obscured—firstly, by the dominant ideological climate of the time, which tended to despise liberal democracy as just "formal" or "bourgeois"; secondly, by the restrictive nature of the consociational pacts upon which those regimes were based, particularly in Colombia and Venezuela; thirdly, by the lack of recognition of their significance in relation to the rest of the continent; and finally, by their classification as "anomalies" in a region associated with an authoritarian tradition, where liberal democracy could find only an "inhospitable soil" (Peeler 1985, p. 134).

After the Pacto de Punto Fijo in 1958, Venezuela demonstrated that an authoritarian past was no impediment to democratic developments. The setbacks experienced since 1989 should not detract from the accomplishments of Venezuelan democracy during the second half of the twentieth century. For a start, a democratic system was established where there were limited democratic antecedents. Although Rómulo Betancourt became known as the "father of democracy," and other personalities played prominent roles, political parties were the major actors in the regime (Caballero 2004, p. 149). Party competition, though effectively confined to Acción Democrática (AD) and Comité de Organización Electoral Independiente (COPEI), became the rule for the peaceful transfer of power through regular electoral contests. The 1968 election was a "decisive turning point" as COPEI, hitherto in opposition, reached the presidency through the ballot box. Similar power turnovers took place in 1973, 1978, and 1983 (Levine 1989, p. 260). Parties were "broadly representative of society," and each had a large body of members (Coppedge 2003, p. 172). Freedom of the press flourished, together with other rights associated with free elections. Economic and social indicators also improved during the 1960s and 1970s. There were serious shortcomings, mostly related to corruption and clientelism, and the economy was severely hit in the 1980s when oil revenues declined. Yet, at the end of the decade, in spite of the unfolding crisis, Daniel Levine acknowledged that Venezuelan democracy had been remarkably successful: In less than three decades, the country had "built strong institutions, tamed the military, and combined high popular participation with social and political stability" (Levine 1989, p. 265; also Coppedge 2003, p. 172).

These democratic achievements are better appreciated in a comparative context, during a period when authoritarian rule was widespread not only in Latin America but also elsewhere, including in southern Europe. By 1974 only about forty countries in the world could be classified as "more or less democratic," and Venezuela, together with Colombia, and Costa Rica was among them (Huntington 1991, pp. 14–21; Diamond 1996, p. 20). A similar comparative perspective serves to highlight the significance of democratic survival in Colombia during the National Front (1958–1974). There are no doubts about Costa Rica's democratic credentials after 1949: Competitive elections were guaranteed by the establishment of the Supreme Election Tribunal, "a virtual fourth branch of the state." Its role became crucial in the evolution of a political system where free and fair elections prevailed, giving way to "an entrenched pattern of power alternation" every four years between 1958 and 1970 (Casas-Zamora 2005, pp. 63, 66).

Aside from these three countries, Latin American democracy was barely surviving by the late 1970s, but the electoral legacies of many nations may have contributed to the demise of some authoritarian regimes (Drake and Silva 1986, pp. 1–7). Elections were crucial in undermining military regimes and thus encouraging democratization; examples of this include the referendums of 1980 in Uruguay and 1988 in Chile, which inflicted serious defeats on their respective military rulers. The military junta in Brazil, which had been in power since 1964, allowed for an electoral opening. In the 1974 elections the "official opposition party" won a substantial number of seats in the Senate, and afterwards elections were the major vehicle through which Brazilians made the transition to democracy (Mainwaring 1999, pp. 83–87; Lamounier 1989, pp. 112–117). "Participating within the system, and using it to our own advantage, was the surest path to democratic change," recalled Fernando Henrique Cardoso (2006, p. 131). Cardoso himself, a member of the opposition, agreed to be a candidate for the Senate in 1978, and became a senator in 1983. "How can you participate in this fraud?" demanded his friends, who still believed that "Congress was just a farcical theater that the military tolerated in order to pretend Brazil was still a democracy" (Cardoso 2006, p. 147). Yet, the opposition persevered, and two years later its candidate,

Bolivian workers and students demonstrate in support of democracy, 1979. The 1960s and 1970s represented the height of authoritarianism in Latin America, with democracies surviving in Costa Rica, Colombia, and Venezuela alone. © JP LAFFONT/SYGMA/CORBIS

Tancredo Neves, was elected president by the Electoral College. On January 15, 1985, a billboard in Brasilia announced the new regime: "Good morning democracy."

CONTEMPORARY DEMOCRACIES OF THE THIRD WAVE: PERSPECTIVES AND CHALLENGES

By 1989 the "third wave" of democracy had reached most Latin American countries (with the exception of Cuba and Haiti). This wave started in 1978 when the opposition Dominican Revolutionary Party won power through the ballot box. As in the past, the third wave of democratization has not been a uniform process across all nations of the region.

Peru's successful general strike in 1977 has been singled out as the "most important event in triggering the...democratic transition of 1980" (Collier 1999, p. 118). In Argentina the "triggering event"

was the military's defeat in the 1982 Falklands/Malvinas War, which led to the collapse of the regime. Collier argues that any evaluation of Argentine democratization also should take account of the labor movement for its roles in undermining the authority of the military and in negotiating during the interim government that preceded the election of President Raúl Alfonsín in 1983 (Collier 1999, pp. 119–126; Foweraker 2004). Indeed, the extent to which these processes were affected by labor mobilization or by "elite settlements" (such as Uruguay's Naval Club Pact [1984] between the military and the leaders of the major parties) is a subject of academic debate. None of these processes were just "elite affairs." The leaders of the parties in conflict, along with key foreign powers, organizations, and individuals, were instrumental in negotiating a settlement that brought to an end the civil war in El Salvador in 1992, but such "pacted democratization" involved a wider social universe.

Whether the result of regime collapse, elite pacts, or any other modality, democratization in Latin America generally has expanded since the 1970s, and in this "third wave," it "has been far more extensive, involving far more countries, and has lasted for longer than any previous waves of democracy in Latin America" (Mainwaring and Pérez-Liñán 2005, p. 15). As the process unfolded, very few predicted that it would be long-lasting. "The dice are probably loaded in favour of repeated iterations and shaky and relatively short-lived democracy and ever-uglier authoritarian rule," Guillermo O'Donnell wrote in 1986. Although he tried to convey a message of moderate optimism, O'Donnell also considered that the "prospects for political democracy in Latin America" were "not very favorable" (O'Donnell 1993, p. 14). Three years later, in 1989, Larry Diamond and Juan Linz were also of the view that "the prospect of new democratic breakdowns in Latin America during the 1990s cannot be dismissed" (Diamond and Linz 1989, p. 52).

There were many reasons for pessimism, including fresh memories of the recent authoritarian experiences, the generally poor economic performance in the 1980s, and the continuing social problems of the region. Serious setbacks in the 1990s provided clear warnings against complacency. Threats to democratic stability were already visible in Venezuela during the Caracazo in 1989, and were made explicit during the failed military insurrections of 1992. In that year, in his infamous *autogolpe* (self-coup), President Alberto Fujimori closed down Peru's Congress. A year later, in 1993, the Guatemalan president Jorge Serrano Elías attempted a similar antidemocratic putsch, but failed and was forced to resign. These and other presidential crises (there were fourteen "interrupted presidents" in ten different countries between 1985 and 2004) added to a discouraging picture. According to Arturo Valenzuela, presidential failure was "among the reasons why democracy's future now hangs in the balance across a huge swath of the Western Hemisphere" (Valenzuela 2004, p. 18).

Current shortcomings are many and, once again, differ from place to place. The debate about the state of democracy in Latin America to some extent echoes earlier discussions in that often it focuses more on its socioeconomic performance than on political conditions. Poor social indicators (e.g., levels of poverty and inequality) are singled out as the major barriers to democratic development. From a liberal democratic perspective, however, the problems faced by representative institutions are of special concern. As the 2004 United Nations Development Programme (UNDP) report observed, "the crisis surrounding political parties in Latin America is one of the greatest threats to democracy in the region" (p. 37). The belief that some countries did not seem to be "on the path toward becoming representative democracies" led O'Donnell to coin the expression "delegative democracies" to refer to regimes where presidents, backed by the majority of voters, govern with few constitutional constraints (O'Donnell 1994). The "crisis of representation" has been particularly acute in the Andes (Mainwaring, Bejarano, and Pizarro Leongómez 2006).

Nonetheless, in spite of severe problems, what should be underlined is the perseverance of democracy in the last decades. As Marta Lagos pointed out in 2003, "public support for democracy has shown surprising resilience. Overall, the reaction of Latin American citizens to failures of economic and political performance has been one of dissatisfaction with the way in which democracy is working . . . , but not an abandonment of faith in democracy itself" (Lagos 2003, p. 163). Perhaps no other country exemplifies this better than Argentina since 1983, which has survived crisis after crisis (Levitsky 2005). Throughout the region, the ballot box is the means for transfer of power. Elections are regularly conducted and generally represent fairly genuine electoral competition. There were seventy national elections in Latin America between 1990 and 2002, and "in most instances where irregularities were observed they did not appear to have had a determining impact on the outcome of the polls" (United Nations Development Programme 2004, p. 35).

Mainwaring and Pérez-Liñán have noted that since 1978 Latin American democracies have been "more able to withstand polarized party systems" and "more likely to survive despite a vastly worst economic record after 1978" (2005, p. 38). In their view, this durability is due more to political than to socioeconomic factors. In what seems the most comprehensive survey of key variables, they conclude that "it is implausible that higher levels of development, changes in class structure, or better economic performance could account for the vastly

Chilean Socialist presidental candidate Michelle Bachelet at a campaign rally in Colina, Chile, 2005. Once a political prisoner of Augusto Pinochet's repressive military dictatorship, Bachelet was elected Chile's first female president in 2006. AP IMAGES

greater durability of democracy" in the last three decades (2005, p. 32). Instead, they attribute this success to a more favorable regional environment conducive to democracy, conditioned by a process of diffusion (i.e., "what happens in one country affects another"; idem, p. 58) and by the role played by international actors, including in particular the United States and the Organization of American States, which in 2001 adopted a Democratic Charter to respond to unconstitutional alterations of constitutional regimes. They also pay special attention to changes in attitudes towards democracy.

These changes, though difficult to accurately assess, are particularly significant. Hostility towards liberal democracy had not just been confined to right-wing quarters; it also dominated left-wing intellectual and political circles, where revolutionary violence was favored over electioneering. Jorge Castañeda pointed out that "much of the left

wrongly dismissed representative democracy for many years as a sham: a bureaucratic, corrupt device invented by local elites and foreign agents to trick the Latin masses into tolerating forms of government and domination contrary to their interests" (1993, p. 327). The end of the cold war eased ideological tensions, and the collapse of the Soviet Union and the Berlin Wall encouraged reconsideration of long-held beliefs. In his *Utopia Unarmed*, Castañeda described this reconciliation of the Left with liberal democracy as paradoxically motivated by the harsh experiences of living under dictatorship (Castañeda 1993; Mainwaring 2000, pp. 178–182; O'Donnell 1993, pp. 15–16; see also Posada-Carbó 2008). There were exceptions, notably in Cuba, and Marxist-inspired guerrilla warfare survived in Colombia.

Accepting some of its most basic tenets did not mean fully embracing representative democracy. By the early 1990s it seemed that it was becoming "more difficult to elaborate an alternative ideology to democracy [that raised] enthusiasm among the population," but conflicting views of democracy soon resurfaced (Nohlen 1995, p. 23). The common expression "competitive elections are not a sufficient condition for democracy" is often repeated to signal dissatisfaction with what liberal democracy can offer, undermining the pivotal significance of democratic procedures. Demand grew for "participatory democracy" instead, and this phrase was incorporated into many Latin American constitutions. ("Participatory democracy" calls for "direct participation of citizens in the regulation of key institutions of society; and making party official accountable to membership" [Held 1996, p. 271]). This provided a new conceptual framework, as well as a rhetorical device, for a revived populism. When signing the "democratic clause" in Canada in 2001, Venezuelan president Hugo Chávez said, after raising his hand: "We sign this but we have to reserve our vote from representative democracy, we believe in participatory democracy" (Chávez and Harnecker 2005, p. 107; see also Kornblit 2005, p. 136).

The challenges of a populist revival and the threats it poses to the prospects of liberal democracy should not be underestimated. Its revival has so far been limited, but instances of populist revivals capture international attention, feeding old Latin American stereotypes while obscuring the reformist democratic experiences of countries such as Brazil, Mexico, Uruguay, and especially Chile under the Concertación governments since 1990 (Angell 2007).

In a period of thirteen months during 2005 to 2006, Latin Americans voted "with an intensity never seen since the transition to democracy in the region": Eleven countries went to the polls to elect their respective presidents (Malamud 2007). The results painted a heterogeneous picture, both in terms of the politics of the various governments and the quality of their democratic institutions.

As the last "wave" of democratization in Latin America enters its third decade, questions of democratic performance have attracted increased attention from scholars. How have the democratically elected governments dealt with the acute socioeconomic problems of the region?: "Quite badly," with some exceptions, was Guillermo O'Donnell's assessment

(2001, p. 601). Nonetheless, O'Donnell warned against condemning the existing democratic regimes for their deficits in social and civil rights: These "political democracies," as he called them, "are not a fake." Their significance should not be dismissed as "purely formal"—the establishment of "political democracies" had been a "huge achievement," opening the avenue for further democratization (2001, pp. 599–609).

Such prolonged "waves" of democracy in the region, and above all the revaluation of "political democracy," should motivate historical reconsiderations of democracy in Latin America. The military regimes and dictatorships after the 1960s often prompted modern scholars to propagate the idea that Latin American societies had a "secular disposition" towards "authoritarian regimes" (Véliz 1980, p. 3). Some even suggested that the "use of the 'democratic' label" for Latin America, "implies not just political and economic imperialism but cultural imperialism as well" (Wiarda 1980, p. 18).

References to "new democracies" in Latin America ignore a rich history that dates back to the early nineteenth century. "Democracy," Margaret Lavinia Anderson points out, "is never a destination, a resting place" (2000, p. 437); "Democratic successes are never irreversible," notes Sean Wilentz (2005, p. xix). There is a long story of representative democracy in the region worthy of further study. If changing attitudes towards democracy partly explain its more recent fate, a fuller appreciation of that story may provide a better prospect for this "unfinished journey" (Dunn 1995).

See also **Batlle y Ordóñez, José; Caudillismo, Caudillo; Chávez, Hugo; Corruption; Cortes of Cádiz; Delegative Democracy; Echeverría, Esteban; Estado Novo; Falklands/Malvinas War; Ferdinand VII of Spain; Fujimori, Alberto Keinya; Gómez, Juan Vicente; Juárez, Benito; Junta: Spanish America; Liberalism; Lleras Camargo, Alberto; Madero, Francisco Indalecio; Mercurio, El; Mexico, Wars and Revolutions: Mexican Revolution; Nación, La (Buenos Aires); Organization of American States (OAS); Pardo; Perón, Juan Domingo; Rojas Pinilla, Gustavo; Sáenz Peña Law; Sarmiento, Domingo Faustino; Serrano Elías, Jorge Antonio; Slavery: Abolition; Vargas, Getúlio Dornelles; Women.**

BIBLIOGRAPHY

Aguilar, José Antonio. "La nación en ausencia: Primeras formas de representación em Mexico." *Política y gobierno* 5, no. 2 (Segundo Semestre 1998): 423–457.

Aguilar, José Antonio. *En pos de la quimera. Reflexiones sobre el experimento Atlántico*. México: Fondo de Cultura Económica, 2000.

Alonso, Paula. "Voting in Buenos Aires, Argentina, 1912." In *Elections before Democracy. The History Of Elections In Europe And Latin America*, ed. Eduardo Posada-Carbó Londons and Basingstoke: Macmillan and Institute of Latin American Studies, 1996.

Alonso, Paula. *Between Revolution and the Ballot Box: The Origins of the Argentina Radical Party in the 1890s*. Cambridge, U.K.: Cambridge University Press, 2000.

Alonso, Paula, ed. *Construcciones impresas: Panfletos, diarios y revistas en la formación de los estados nacionales en América Latina, 1820–1920*. Buenos Aires: Fondo ee Cultura Económica, 2003.

Anderson, Margaret Lavinia. *Practicing Democracy: Elections and Political Culture in Imperial Germany*. Princeton, NJ: Princeton University Press, 2000.

Annino, Antonio, ed. *Historia de las elecciones en Iberoamérica, siglo XIX*. Buenos Aires: Fondo de Cultura Económica, 1995.

Angell, Alan. *Democracy after Pinochet: Politics, Parties, and Elections in Chile*. London: Institute for the Study of the Americas, 2007.

Arciniegas, Germán. *The State of Latin America*. London: Cassell, 1953.

Arciniegas, Germán. *Entre la libertad y el miedo*. (1956). Bogotá: Planeta, 1996.

Barrán, José Pedro. "La democracia política y el Uruguay battlista: Un diálogo difícil, 1903–1933." In *Los caminos de la democracia. Alternativas y prácticas políticas, 1900–1943*, ed. Julio Melón Pirro and Elisa Tastoriza. Buenos Aires: Biblios, 1996.

Bello, Andrés. "Reforms to the Constitution." (1833). In *Selected Writings of Andrés Bello*, ed. Iván Jaksic. Oxford, U.K.: Oxford University Press, 1997.

Benson, Nettie Lee. "The Contested Mexican Election of 1812." *Hispanic American Historical Review* 26 (1946): 336–350.

Benson, Nettie Lee. "The Elections of 1809: Transforming Political Culture in New Spain." *Mexican Studies/Estudios Mexicanos* 20, no. 1 (Winter 2004): 1–20.

Berry, Charles R. "The Election of the Mexican Deputies to the Spanish Cortes, 1810–1822." In *Mexico and the Spanish Cortes, 1810–1822*, ed. Natalie Lee Benson. Austin and London: University of Texas Press, 1976.

Bethell, Leslie. "On Democracy in Brazil: Past and Present." Occasional paper no. 7. London: Institute of Latin American Studies, 1994.

Bobbio, Norberto. *Liberalism and Democracy*. London and New York: Verso, 1990.

Brandenburg, Frank R. "Political Parties and Elections." In *Government and Politics in Latin America*, ed. Harold E. Davis. New York: Ronald Press, 1958.

Breña, Roberto. *El primer liberalismo español y los procesos de emancipación de América, 1808–1824. Una revisión historiográfica del liberalismo hispánico*. México: El Colegio de México, 2006.

Bushnell, David. "El sufragio en la Argentina y en Colombia hasta 1853." *Revista del Instituto de Historia del Derecho* 19 (1968): 11–29.

Bushnell, David. "Voter Participation in the Colombian Election of 1856." *Hispanic American Historical Review* 51 (May 1971).

Bushnell, David. "La evolución del derecho del sufragio en Venezuela." *Boletín Histórico* 29 (May 1972): 189–206.

Caballero, Manuel. *Las crisis de la Venezuela contemporánea, 1903–1992*. Caracas: Alfadil Ediciones, 2004.

Cardoso, Fernando Henrique. *The Accidental President of Brazil: A Memoir*. New York: Public Affairs, 2006.

Carta Pastoral del Ilmo. *Sr Arzobispo de la Plata sobre obediencia y sumisión que se debe a las potestades legítimas*. Buenos Aires: Real Imprenta de los Niños Espósitos, 1810.

Casas-Zamora, Kevin. *Paying for Democracy: Political Finance and State Funding for Parties*. Colchester, U.K.: European Consortium for Political Research Press, 2005.

Castañeda, Jorge. *Utopia Unarmed: The Latin American Left After the Cold War*. New York: Alfred Knopf, 1993.

Chávez, Hugo, and Marta Harnecker. *Understanding the Venezuelan Revolution: Hugo Chávez Talks to Marta Harnecker*. New York: Monthly Review Press, 2005.

Chiaramonti, Gabriella. *Ciudadanía y representación en el Perú, 1808–1860. Los itinerarios de la soberanía*. Lima: Universidad Nacional de San Marcos, 2005.

Chust, Manuel, ed. *Doceañismos, constituciones e independencias. La constitución de 1812 y América*. Madrid: Mapfre, 2006.

Chust, Manuel, and José A. Serrano. "Guerra, revolución y liberalismo en México, 1808–1835." In *Bastillas, cetros y blasones. La independencia en Iberoamérica*, edited by Ivana Frasquet. Madrid: Mapfre, 2006.

Collier, Simon, and William F. Sater. *A History of Chile, 1808–1994*. Cambridge, U.K., and New York: Cambridge University Press, 1996.

Collier, Ruth Berins. *Paths toward Democracy: The Working Class and Elites in Western Europe and South America*. Cambridge, U.K.: Cambridge University Press, 1999.

Coppedge, Michael. "Venezuela: Popular Sovereignty Versus Liberal Democracy." In *Constructing Democratic Governance in Latin America*, ed. Jorge Domínguez and

Michael Shifter. Baltimore and London: John Hopkins University Press, 2003.

Crick, Bernard. *Democracy: A Very Short Introduction.* Oxford, U.K.: Oxford University Press, 2002.

Dahl, Robert. *Polyarchy: Participation and Opposition.* New Haven, CT, and London: Yale University Press, 1971.

Deas, Malcolm, "Algunas notas sobre el caciquismo en Colombia." *Revista de Occidente* 127 (1973).

Deas, Malcolm. "Venezuela, Colombia, and Ecuador." In *The Cambridge History of Latin America*, vol. 3, ed. Leslie Bethell. Cambridge, U.K.: Cambridge University Press, 1985.

Demélas-Bohy, Marie-Danielle, and François-Xavier Guerra. "The Hispanic Revolutions: The Adoption of Modern Forms of Representation in Spain and America, 1808–1810." In *Elections before Democracy: The History of Elections in Europe and Latin America*, ed. Eduardo Posada-Carbó. London: Macmillan, 1996.

Diamond, Larry. "Is the Third Wave Over?" *Journal of Democracy* 7, no. 3 (1996): 20–37.

Diamond, Larry, and Juan J. Linz. "Introduction: Politics, Society, and Democracy in Latin America." In *Democracy in Developing Countries: Latin America*, ed. Larry Diamond, Juan J. Linz, and Seymour Martin Lipset. Boulder, CO: Lynne Rienner, 1989).

Drake, Paul, and Eduardo Silva, eds. *Elections and Democratization in Latin America, 1980–1985.* San Diego: University of California Press, 1986.

Dunn, John, ed. *Democracy: The Unfinished Journey, 508 BC to AD 1993.* Oxford, U.K.: Oxford University Press, 1995.

Duquesne de Madrid, José Domingo. *Oración por la tranquilidad pública, pronunciada en la Santa Iglesia Catedral Metropolitana de esta muy noble y leal ciudad de Santa Fe de Bogotá.* Bogotá: Imprenta Real, 1809.

Duquesne de Madrid, José Domingo. *Carta Pastoral del Ilmo. Sr Arzobispo de la Plata sobre obediencia y sumisión que se debe a las potestades legítimas.* Buenos Aires: Real Imprenta de los Niños Espósitos, 1810.

Dym, Jordana. "'Our Pueblos, Fractions with No Central Unity': Municipal Sovereignty in Central America, 1808–1821." *Hispanic American Historical Review* 86, no. 3 (2006): 431–466.

Echeverría, Esteban. *Dogma socialista.* (1837). Buenos Aires: Hyspamerica, 1988.

Escalante Gonzalbo, Fernando. *Ciudadanos imaginarios.* Mexico City: El Colegio de Mexico, 1993.

Fitzgibbon, Russell H. "How Democratic Is Latin America?" *Inter-American Economic Affairs* 9, no. 4 (1956): 65–77.

Fitzgibbon, Russell H. "The Party Potpourri in Latin America." *Western Political Journal* 10, no. 1 (1957): 3–22.

Fitzgibbon, Russell H. "Measuring Democratic Change in Latin America." *Journal of Politics* 29, no. 1 (February 1967): 129–166.

Foweraker, Joe. "Transformation, Transition, Consolidation: Democratization in Latin America." In *The Blackwell Companion To Political Sociology*, ed. Kate Nash and Alan Scott. Malden, MA, and Oxford, U.K.: Blackwell, 2004.

Forment, Carlos. *Democracy in Latin America, 1760–1900*, Vol. I: *Civic Selfhood and Public Life in Mexico and Peru.* Chicago: University of Chicago Press, 2003.

Gallie, W. B. "Essentially Contested Concepts." *Proceedings of the Aristotelian Society* 56 (1955–1956): 167–198.

Graham, Richard. *Patronage and Politics in Nineteenth-Century Brazil.* Stanford, CA: Stanford University Press, 1990.

Guardino, Peter. *Peasants, Politics, and the Formation of Mexico's National State. Guerrero, 1800-1877.* Stanford, CA: Stanford University Press, 1996.

Guedea, Virginia. "Las primeras elecciones populares en la ciudad de México, 1812–1813." *Mexican Studies/Estudios Mexicanos* 7, no. 1 (Winter 1991): 1–28.

Guerra, François-Xavier. *Modernidad e independencias.* Madrid: Editorial Mapfre, 1992.

Guerra, François-Xavier. "The Spanish American Tradition of Representation and Its European Roots." *Journal of Latin American Studies* 26, no. 1 (February 1994): 1–35.

Haddick, Jack. "The Deliberative Juntas of 1808: A Crisis in the Development of Mexican Democracy." In *Essays on Mexican History*, ed. Thomas Cotner and Carlos Castañeda. Austin: Texas University Press, 1958.

Hagopian, Frances, and Scott Mainwaring, eds. *The Third Wave of Democratization: Advances and Setbacks.* Cambridge, U.K.: Cambridge University Press, 2005.

Hahner, June E. "The Beginnings of the Women's Suffrage Movement in Brazil." *Signs: Journal of Women on Culture and Society* 5, no. 1 (1979): 200–204.

Hale, Charles. *The Transformation of Liberalism in Late Nineteenth-Century Mexico.* Princeton, NJ: Princeton University Press, 1989.

Hartlyn, Jonathan, and Arturo Valenzuela. "Democracy in Latin America since 1930." In *The Cambridge History of Latin America*, vol. 6, ed. Leslie Bethell. Cambridge, U.K.: Cambridge University Press, 1995.

Held, David. *Models of Democracy.* Cambridge, U.K.: Polity Press, 1996.

Helg, Aline. *Liberty and Equality in Caribbean Colombia, 1770–1835.* Chapel Hill and London: University of North Carolina Press, 2004.

Huntington, Samuel P. *The Third Wave: Democratization in the Twentieth Century.* Norman and London: University of Oklahoma Press, 1991.

Instrucción formada de orden de la Junta Preparatoria para facilitar las elecciones de diputados y oficios consejiles. Guatemala, 1812. John Carter Brown Library, Providence, RI. B812J95i.

Irurozqui, Marta. "A bala, piedra y palo." *La construcción de la ciudadanía política en Bolivia, 1826–1952.* Sevilla: Diputación de Sevilla, 2000.

Jaksic, Iván. *Ven conmigo a la España lejana: Los intelectuales norteamericanos ante el mundo hispano, 1820–1880.* Santiago: Fondo de Cultura Económica, 2007.

Katz, Richard S. *Democracy and Elections.* New York and Oxford, U.K.: Oxford University Press, 1997.

Kinsbruner, Jay. *Independence in Spanish America.* Albuquerque: University of New Mexico Press, 1994.

Keyssar, Alexander. *The Right to Vote. The Contested History of Democracy in the United States.* New York: Basic Books, 2000.

Kline, Herbert. "Participación política en Brasil en el siglo XIX: Los votantes de San Pablo en 1880." In *Historia de las elecciones en Iberoamérica, siglo XIX*, ed. Antonio Annino Buenos Aires: Fonde de Cultura Económica, 1995.

Knight, Alan. *The Mexican Revolution: Porfirians, Liberals, and Peasants*, vol. 1. Lincoln and London: University of Nebraska Press, 1986.

Kornblit, Myriam. "Elections before Democracy." *Journal of Democracy* 16, no. 1 (January 2005): 124–137.

Lagos, Marta. "A Road with No Return?: Latin America's Lost Illusions." *Journal of Democracy* 24, no. 2 (April 2003): 163–173.

Lasso, Marixa. *Myths of Harmony: Race and Republicanism during the Age of Revolution: Colombia, 1795–1831.* Pittsburgh: University of Pittsburgh Press, 2007.

Lamounier, Bolívar. "Brazil: Inequality against Democracy." In *Democracy in Developing Countries Latin America*, ed. Larry Diamond, Juan J. Linz, and Seymour Martin Lipset. Boulder, CO: Lynne Rienner, 1989.

Lehoucq, Fabrice E. "Institutional Change and Political Conflict: Evaluating Alternative Explanations of Electoral Reform in Costa Rica." *Electoral Studies* 14, no. 1 (1995): 23–45.

Lehoucq, Fabrice E., and Iván Molina. "Political Competition and Electoral Fraud." *Journal of Interdisciplinary History* 30, no. 2 (Autumn 1999): 199–234.

Lehoucq, Fabrice E., and Iván Molina. *Stuffing the Ballot Box: Fraud, Electoral Reform, and Democratization in Costa Rica.* Cambridge, U.K.: Cambridge University Press, 2002.

Levine, Daniel. "Venezuela: The Nature, Sources, and Prospects of Democracy." In *Democracy in Developing Countries: Latin America*, ed. Larry Diamond, Juan J. Linz, and Seymour Martin Lipset. Boulder, CO: Lynne Rienner, 1989.

Levitsky, Steven, "Argentina: Democratic Survival amidst Economic Failure." In *The Third Wave of Democratization in Latin America: Advances and Setbacks*, ed. Frances Hagopian and Scott Mainwaring Cambridge, U.K., and New York: Cambridge University Press, 2005.

Maier, Charles S. "Democracy since the French Revolution." In *Democracy: The Unfinished Journey, 508 BC to AD 1993*, ed. John Dunn. Oxford, U.K.: Oxford University Press, 1995.

Mainwaring, Scott. *Rethinking Party Systems in the Third Wave of Democratization: The Case of Brasil.* Stanford, CA: Stanford University Press, 1999.

Mainwaring, Scott. "La capacidad de sobrevivencia democrática en América Latina." In *Democracia: Discusiones y nuevas aproximaciones*, ed. Ernesto López and Scott Mainwaring. Buenos Aires: Universidad Nacional de Quilmes, 2000.

Mainwaring, Scott, Ana María Bejarano, and Eduardo Pizarro Leongómez, eds. *The Crisis of Democratic Representation in the Andes.* Stanford, CA: Stanford University Press, 2006.

Mainwaring, Scott, and Aníbal Pérez-Liñán. "Latin American Democratization Since 1978: Democratic Transitions, Breakdowns, and Erosions." In *The Third Wave of Democratization: Advances and Setbacks*, ed. Frances Hagopian and Scott Mainwaring. Cambridge, U.K., and New York: Cambridge University Press, 2005.

Malamud, Carlos. "El Anuario Iberoamericano 2007 del Instituto Real Elcano y la Agencia EFE." Available from http:// www.ojosdepapel.com.

Markoff, John. "Where and When Was Democracy Invented?" *Comparative Studies in Society and History* 41, no. 4 (October 1999): 660–690.

Markoff, John. "Margins, Centers, and Democracy: The Paradigmatic History of Women's Suffrage." *Signs: Journal of Women in Culture and Society* 29, no. 1 (2003): 85–116.

Maza Valenzuela, Erika. "Catolicismo, anticlericalismo y extensión del sufragio a la mujer en Chile." *Estudios Públicos* 58 (Autumn 1995): 137–197.

Maza Valenzuela, Erika. "Liberales, radicales y la ciudadnía de la mujer en Chile, 1872–1930." *Estudios Públicos* 69 (1998): xx.

McCaleb, Walter. "The Press of Mexico." *Hispanic American Historical Review* 3, no. 3 (1920).

McDonald, Ronald H. "Electoral Systems, Party Representation, and Political Change in Latin America." *Western Political Quarterly* 20 (1967): 694–708.

McEvoy, Carmen. *La utopía republicana: Ideales y realidades en la formación política peruana, 1871–1919.* Lima: Pontificia Universidad Católica del Perú 1997.

Monteagudo, Bernardo. *Escritos políticos.* Buenos Aires: La cultura Argentina, 1916.

Morelli, Federica. *Territorio o nación. Reforma y disolución del espacio imperial en Ecuador, 1765–1830.* Madrid: Centro de Estudios Constitucionales, 2005.

Muecke, Ulrich. *Political Culture in Nineteenth-Century Peru: The Rise of the Partido Civil.* Pittsburgh, PA: University of Pittsburgh Press, 2004.

Murilo de Carvalho, José. *Desenvolvimiento de la ciudadanía en Brasil.* México: El Colegio de México, 1995.

Negretto, Gabriel, L., and José Antonio Aguilar-Rivera. "Rethinking the Legacy of the Liberal State in Latin America: The Cases of Argentina (1853–1916) and Mexico (1857–1910)." *Journal of Latin American Studies,* 32, no. 2 (2000): 361–397.

Nohlen, Dieter, ed. *Democracia y neocrítica en América Latina. En defensa de la transición.* Frankfurt am Main: Iberamoaericana, 1995.

O'Donnell, Guillermo. "Introduction to the Latin American Cases." In *Transitions from Authoritarian Rule: Latin America,* ed. Guillermo O'Donnell, Philippe C. Schmitter, and Laurence Whitehead. Baltimore and London: John Hopkins University Press, 1993.

O'Donnell, Guillermo. "Delegative Democracy." *Journal of Democracy* 5, no. 1 (1994): 55–69.

O'Donnell, Guillermo. "Reflections on Contemporary South American Democracies." *Journal of Latin American Studies* 33, no. 3 (August 2001): 599–609.

Peeler, John. *Latin American Democracies: Colombia, Costa Rica, Venezuela.* Chapel Hill: University of North Carolina Press, 1985.

Peloso, Vincent. "Liberals, Electoral Reform, and the Popular Vote in Mid-Nineteenth-Century Peru." In *Liberals, Politics, and Power: State Formation in Nineteenth-Century Latin America,* ed. Vincent Peloso and Barbara Tenenbaum. Athens: University of Georgia Press, 1996.

Peralta Ruiz, Victor. "Elecciones, constitucionalismo y revolución en el Cusco, 1809–1815." *Revista de Indias* 56, no. 206 (1996): 99–131.

Peralta Ruiz, Victor. "Los inicios del sistema representativo en Perú: Ayuntamientos constitucionales y diputaciones provinciales, 1812–1815." In *La mirada esquiva. Reflexiones históricas sobre la interacción del estado y la ciudadanía en los Andes (Bolivia, Ecuador y Perú). Siglo XIX,* ed. by Marta Irurozqui. Madrid: Consejo Superior de Investigaciones Científicas, 2005.

Posada-Carbó, Eduardo. "Elections and Civil Wars in Nineteenth-Century Colombia: The Presidential Campaign of 1875." *Journal of Latin American Studies* 26, no. 3 (1994): 621–649.

Posada-Carbó, Eduardo. "Limits of Power: Elections under the Conservative Hegemony in Colombia, 1886–1930." *Hispanic American Historical Review,* 77, no. 2 (1997a): 245–279.

Posada-Carbó, Eduardo, ed. *Elections before Democracy. The History of Elections in Europe and Latin America.* London and Basingstoke: Macmillan/Institute of Latin American Studies, 1997b.

Posada-Carbó, Eduardo. "Las elecciones presidenciales de Colombia en 1930." *Revista de Estudios Sociales* 7 (September 2000a): 35–47.

Posada-Carbó, Eduardo. "Electoral Juggling: A Comparative History of the Corruption of the Suffrage in Latin America, 1830–1930." *Journal of Latin American Studies* 32: (2000b): 611–644.

Posada-Carbó, Eduardo. "New Granada and the European Revolutions of 1848." In *The European Revolutions of 1848 and the Americas,* ed. Guy Thomson. London: Institute of Latin American Studies, 2002.

Posada-Carbó, Eduardo. "El estado Republicano y el proceso ee incorporación: Las elecciones en el mundo andino, 1830–1880. In *Historia de América Andina, vol. 5: Creación de las repúblicas y formación de las naciones,* ed. Juan Maiguashca. Quito: Universidad Andina Simón Bolívar, 2003.

Posada-Carbó, Eduardo. "Democracia, liberalismo y procesos electorales en América Latina since 1930." In *Historia General de América Latina,* vol. 8, ed. Marco Palacios. Madrid: Trota/UNESCO, 2007a.

Posada-Carbó, Eduardo. "Prensa y opinión pública en Latinoamérica, 1870–1930." In *Historia General de América Latina,* vol. 7, ed, Enrique Ayala and Eduardo Posada-Carbó. Madrid: Trota/UNESCO, 2007b.

Posada-Carbó, Eduardo. *Democracy, Parties and Political Finances in Latin America.* Working Paper, Helen Kellogg Institute. Notre Dame, IN: University of Notre Dame, 2008.

Rippy, J. Fred. "Dictatorship and Democracy in Latin America." *Inter-American Economic Affairs* 14, no. 1 (1960).

Rodríguez O, Jaime. E. "The Emancipation of America." *American Historical Review,* 105, no. 1 (2000): 131–152.

Rodríguez O, Jaime E. "Ciudadanos de la nación española: Los indígenas y las elecciones constitucionales en el régimen de Quito." In *La mirada esquiva, La mirada esquiva. Reflexiones históricas sobre la interacción del estado y la ciudadanía en los Andes (Bolivia, Ecuador y Perú). Siglo XIX,* ed. Marta Irurozqui. Madrid: Consejo Superior de Investigaciones Científicas, 2005a.

Rodríguez O, Jaime E. *La ciudadanía y la constitución de Cádiz.* Zacatecas, Mexico: Universidad Autónoma de Zacatecas, 2005b.

Rodríguez O, Jaime E. "La ciudadanía y la constitución de Cádiz." In *Bastillas, cetros y blasones. La independencia en Iberoamérica*, ed. Ivana Frasquet. Madrid: Mapfre, 2006.

Rosanvallon, Pierre. "The History of the Word 'Democracy' in France." *Journal of Democracy* 6, no. 4 (1995): 140–154.

Rosanvallon, Pierre. *Democracy Past and Future*. New York: Columbia University Press, 2006.

Sábato, Hilda. ed. *Ciudadanía política y formación de las naciones: Perspectivas históricas de América Latina*. México: Fondo de Cultura Económica, 1999.

Sabato, Hilda. *La política en las calles. Entre el voto y la movilización. Buenos Aires, 1862–1880*. Buenos Aires: Sidamericana, 1998.

Sabato, Hilda. "On Political Citizenship in Nineteenth-Century Latin America." *American Historical Review* 106, no. 4 (October 2001): 1290–1315.

Sarmiento, Domingo Faustino. *Facundo*. (1845). Buenos Aires: Losada, 1976.

Sarmiento, Domingo Faustino. *Obras completas*. Buenos Aires: Universidad Nacional de la Matanza, 2001.

Soto, Angel, ed. *Entre tintas y plumas: Historia de la prensa Chilena del Siglo XIX*. Santiago: Universidad de Los Andes, 2004.

Sowell, David. *The Early Colombian Labor Movement*. Philadelphia: Temple University Press, 1992.

Ternavasio, Marcela. *La revolución del voto. Política y elecciones en Buenos Aires, 1810–1852*. Buenos Aires, Siglo Veintinuo, 2002.

Thomson, Guy, ed. *The European Revolutions of 1848 in the Americas*. London: Institute of Latin American Studies, 2002.

Torres Giraldo, Ignacio. *Los inconformes: Historia de la rebeldía de las masas en Colombia*. Bogotá: Editorial Latina, vols. 3 and 4, n.d.

United Nations Development Programme, ed. *Democracy in Latin America: Towards a Citizens' Democracy*. New York: Author, 2004.

Urbinati, Nadia. *Representative Democracy. Principles and Genealogy*. Chicago and London: Chicago University Press, 2006.

Valenzuela, Arturo. "Latin American Presidencies Interrupted." *Journal of Democracy* 15, no. 4 (October 2004): 5–19.

Valenzuela, J. Samuel. *Democratización vía reforma. La expansión del sufragio en Chile*. Buenos Aires: Ides, 1985.

Valenzuela, J. Samuel. "Orígenes y transformaciones del sistema de partidos en Chile." *Estudios Públicos* 58 (Autumn 1995): 5–78.

Valenzuela, J. Samuel. "Building Aspects of Democracy before Democracy: Electoral Practices in Nineteenth-Century Chile." In *Elections before Democracy: The History of Elections in Europe and Latin America*, ed. Eduardo Posada-Carbó. London: Macmillan and Institute of Latin American Studies, 1996.

Valenzuela, J. Samuel. "La ley electoral de 1890 y la democratización del régimen político chileno." *Estudios Públicos* 71 (Winter 1998): 265–296.

Valenzuela, J. Samuel. "Caudillismo, democracia, y la excepcionalidad chilena en América Hispana." *Revista de Occidente* 305 (October 2006): 11–28.

Véliz, Claudio. *The Centralist Tradition of Latin America*. Princeton, NJ: Princeton University Press, 1980.

Verdadero Peruano. Lima, October 8, 1812; February 25, 1813. John Carter Brown Library, Providence, RI. BC812V383p.

Warren, Richard. *Vagrants and Citizens: Politics and the Masses in Mexico City From Colony to Republic*. Wilmington, DE: Scholarly Resources, 2001.

Whitehead, Laurence. *Democratization: Theory and Experience*. Oxford, U.K.: Oxford University Press, 2002.

Wiarda, Howard J., ed. *The Continuing Struggle for Democracy in Latin America*. Boulder, CO: Westview Press, 1980.

Wilentz, Sean. *The Rise of American Democracy*. New York: W.W. Norton, 2005.

EDUARDO POSADA-CARBÓ

DEMOGRAPHY. *See* **Population: Brazil; Population: Spanish America.**

DENEVI, MARCO (1922–1998). Marco Denevi (*b.* 12 May 1922, *d.* 12 December 1998), Argentine writer. Born in Sáenz Peña, in the last years of his life Denevi was considered perhaps more a gadfly presence in Argentine literary circles than a major voice. His works are best known for the absurdist humor with which he narrates the seemingly trivial comedy of quotidian existence. This is the salient feature of *Rosaura a las diez* (1955), cast as detective fiction but with several features atypical of the classic genre that has had so much influence in Argentina. As a consequence, the novel deals more with *porteño* idiosyncrasies within a register of gritty neorealism than with the dynamics of the thriller. *Ceremonia secreta* (1955; *Secret Ceremony*, 1961), an expressionistic tale of fatalistic human rituals reminiscent of Roberto Arlt, won a prize from *Life en*

Español magazine and was made into a movie (*Secret Ceremony*, 1967) with Elizabeth Taylor and Robert Mitchum, in which the shift from a Buenos Aires to a London locale deprives the story of any of its Argentine significance. *Falsificaciones* (1966) is a series of microtexts that are parables of human foibles, the dehumanization of modern social life, and the unknown lurking beneath the surface of routine existence. Denevi has written on Argentine national characteristics in *La república de Trapalanda* (1989). Other works include the novellas *Nuestra Señora de la Noche* (1993) and *Una familia argentina* (1998).

See also **Literature: Spanish America.**

BIBLIOGRAPHY

José María Carranza, "La crítica social en las fábulas de Marco Denevi," in *Revista Iberoamericana*, no. 80 (1972): 477–494.

Donald A. Yates, "Un acercamiento a Marco Denevi," in *El cuento hispanoamericano ante la crítica,* edited by Enrique Pupo-Walker (1973), pp. 223–234.

Ivonne Revel Grove, *La realidad calidoscópica de la obra de Marco Denevi* (1974).

Christina Pina, "Marco Denevi: La soledad y sus disfraces," in *Ensayos de crítica literaria año 1983* (1983), pp. 311–417.

Myron I. Lichtblau, "Narrative Perspective and Reader Response in Marco Denevi's *Rosaura a las diez,*" in *Symposium* 40, no. 1 (1986): 59–70.

Guillermo Gotschilich Reyes, "*Ceremonia secreta* de Marco Denevi: Enigma y ritualización," in *Revista Chilena de Literatura*, no. 33 (1989): 87–101.

Additional Bibliography

Delaney, Juan José. *Marco Denevi y la sacra ceremonia de la escritura: Una biografía literaria.* Buenos Aires: Corregidor, 2006.

Denevi, Marco, and Juan Carlos Pellanda. *Conversaciones con Marco Denevi, ese desconocido.* Buenos Aires: Corregidor, 1995.

DAVID WILLIAM FOSTER

DEPENDENCY THEORY. Dependency theory, a concept that emerged from Latin American intellectual centers in the early 1960s as a critique of the development programs then advocated by policymakers in national and international institutions. While popularly accepted as a new development theory or paradigm, many scholars, such as Fernando Henrique Cardoso, Peter Evans, Theotonio Dos Santos, and Andre Gunder Frank, maintain that dependency theory offers an approach to the study of political development that is related to the Marxian tradition of dialectical analyses of historical structures and social processes within a dynamic global economy.

The central premise of the dependency conception of Latin American economic history is that underdevelopment was created by the expansion of European capitalism. The same process by which the developed world, the "core" countries of western Europe and North America, became developed and wealthy, is the same one by which Latin American countries on the "periphery" became dependent and impoverished. Since the conquest and colonization of the Americas, the Latin American economic system has provided imperial powers with the raw materials required for an expanding industrial base and with captive markets for their surplus products. Colonial policies fashioned a monocultural export orientation on Latin America that political independence in the early nineteenth century did not change. With the assistance of a domestic elite, commercial capital, followed by financial and manufacturing capital, penetrated the area, perpetuating the dependency of Latin American economies on the export of one or two primary commodities and the import of manufactured goods.

The inequitable terms of trade stifled industrial growth, for capital accumulation in a dependent country requires the continued acceptance of its primary materials in the developed world. A dependent country can grow and expand only as a reflection of the growth and development of the developed countries to which it is subordinated. While the developed countries can achieve self-sustaining growth, the economy of the dependent country, being oriented toward external markets that it cannot control, is exceptionally vulnerable to the periodic fluctuations in the international market.

Dependency analysts concluded that the solution to Latin American underdevelopment, contrary to the opinions of policymakers in Europe and North America, did not lie in increased penetration of Latin America by foreign capital. Whereas economic policymakers from the core countries advocated increased levels of foreign investment in

Latin American industry as one of the solutions to underdevelopment and poverty, the dependency theorists argued that multinational industries would only strengthen the structure of international dependency, enrich the core, and impoverish the periphery. The immediate political implication of the dependency critique is that Latin America can only develop by severing its ties to the core and promoting self-sustaining economic growth through an industrialization program based on the expansion of the domestic market by agrarian reform and income redistribution.

Dependency theory provoked heated theoretical debates and inspired a wide range of empirical investigations. Charging that it was simply old Marxian wine in new Latin American bottles, critics (and some theorists) reduced it to simplistic hypotheses of external determination and domination by malicious foreign capitalists. Under continuous attack, dependency theory fell into disfavor to a substantial degree in the 1980s, even though it had established itself as one of the primary lenses through which scholars view Latin American political economy. It compelled scholars to analyze the dynamic international forces that condition Latin American development and distinguish it from the processes by which western Europe and North America have developed. While dependency theory undermined the assumptions on which previous development studies were based, its implicit political agenda has frequently been superseded by other models and approaches, such as post-imperialism, post-colonialism, imperial industrialization, and to some extent, post-modernism.

See also **Economic Development; Foreign Trade; Industrialization.**

BIBLIOGRAPHY

Andre Gunder Frank, *Latin America: Underdevelopment or Revolution* (1969).

Theotonio Dos Santos, "The Structure of Dependency," in *American Economic Review* 60, no. 2 (May 1970): 231–236.

Ronald Chilcote and Joel Edelstein, *Latin America: The Struggle with Dependency and Beyond* (1974).

Fernando Henrique Cardoso, "The Consumption of Dependency Theory in the United States," in *Latin American Research Review* 12, no. 3 (1977): 7–24.

Fernando Henrique Cardoso and Enzo Faletto, *Dependency and Development in Latin America* (1979).

Tulio Halperin-Donghi, " 'Dependency Theory' and Latin American Historiography," in *Latin American Research Review* 17, no. 1 (1982): 115–130.

Peter Evans, "After Dependency: Recent Studies of Class, State, and Industrialization," *Latin American Research Review* 20, no. 2 (1985): 149–160.

Additional Bibliography

Chilcote, Ronald H., ed. *Development in Theory and Practice: Latin American Perspectives.* Lanham: Rowman & Littlefield, 2003.

Roberts, J. Timmons, and Amy Hite, eds. *The Globalization and Development Reader: Perspectives on Development and Global Change.* Malden: Blackwell Pub., 2007.

Santiago, Silviano. *The Space in Between: Essays on Latin American Culture.* Ed. Ana Lúcia Gazzola. Trans. Tom Burns, Ana Lúcia Gazzola and Gareth Williams. Durham, NC: Duke University Press, 2001.

Seligson, Mitchell A., and John T Passé-Smith, eds. *Development and Underdevelopment: The Political Economy of Global Inequality.* 3rd ed. Boulder: Lynne Rienner Publishers, 2003.

PAUL J. DOSAL

DEPESTRE, RENÉ (1926–). René Depestre (b. August 29, 1926) is a Haitian poet, essayist, and novelist. After his self-published first volume of poetry, *Étincelles* (*Sparks*, 1945), Depestre participated in the movement to overthrow the Haitian president, Élie Lescot, in 1946. As a student in Paris (1946–1950), he collaborated with the Caribbean and African intellectuals Aimé Césaire, Léopold Senghor, and Léon Damas to found the Négritude movement. Expelled from France in 1950 for political activism, Depestre found asylum in Czechoslovakia as secretary to the Brazilian novelist Jorge Amado. Years of wandering through South America finally brought Depestre to a long stay in Cuba (1959–1978). He now lives in Lézignan-Corbières, France.

Depestre's poetry includes humanist, Marxist, and erotic elements. Since the 1980s he has written increasingly in prose, and in his early fictional works (for example, *Alléluia pour une femme-jardin*, 1981; Alleluia for a garden woman), he created a unique blend of humor and eroticism, a Haitian marvelous realism. His first novel, *Le mât de cocagne* (1979; translated by Carrol F. Coates as *The Festival of the Greasy Pole*, 1990), deftly applied similar narrative elements to political satire directed at the François Duvalier dictatorship (1957–1971). With his second novel, *Hadriana dans tous mes rêves* (1988; Hadriana in All My Dreams), Depestre continued to exploit his Haitian heritage by focusing on the tale of a young woman turned into a zombie on her wedding night in the lush tropical setting of Jacmel, where Depestre grew up. He returned to the erotic vein in the stories of *Éros dans un train chinois* (1990; Eros on a Chinese Train). Depestre's essays have also been influential in shaping Caribbean thought, especially his *Bonjour et adieu à la négritude* (1980; Hello and Farewell to Negritude). His collected poetry, titled *Rage de Vivre* (Lust for Life), was published in 2007.

See also **Césaire, Aimé; Damas, Léon-Gontran; Duvalier, François; Literature: Spanish America.**

BIBLIOGRAPHY

Couffon, Claude. *René Depestre*. Paris: Seghers, 1986.

Munro, Martin. *Shaping and Reshaping the Caribbean: The Work of Aimé Césaire and René Depestre*. Leeds, U.K.: MHRA, 2000.

Munro, Martin. *Exile and Post–1946 Haitian Literature: Alexis, Depestre, Ollivier, Laferrière, Danticat*. Liverpool, U.K.: Liverpool University Press, 2007.

CARROL F. COATES
MARTIN MUNRO

DERQUI, SANTIAGO (1809–1867).

Santiago Derqui (*b.* 19 June 1809; *d.* 5 September 1867), Argentine president. Trained as a lawyer, Derqui took an active role in the politics of his home province of Córdoba until, in the mid-1830s, it came firmly under the control of the dictatorship of Juan Manuel de Rosas. He then joined the Unitarist general José María Paz in the struggle against Rosas. After Rosas fell, Derqui served in the Constituent Convention of 1853 and collaborated with Justo José de Urquiza in the government of the Argentine Confederation. He succeeded Urquiza as president in 1860, just as rivalry between the Confederation and the secessionist province of Buenos Aires came to a head in

armed conflict. Defeated, he resigned the presidency in November 1861.

See also **Urquiza, Justo José de.**

BIBLIOGRAPHY

William H. Jeffrey, *Mitre and Argentina* (1952), pp. 141–158.

James R. Scobie, *La lucha por la consolidación de la nacionalidad argentina, 1852–1862* (1964).

Ana Rosa Ferías De Foulkes, *Después de la derrota—Derqui, desde el Pacto de San José de Flores hasta la batalla de Pavón (1859–1861)* (1970).

DAVID BUSHNELL

DESAGÜE. Desagüe, a drainage channel that was the greatest engineering project of colonial Spanish America. Designed to prevent the periodic flooding of Mexico City, the *desagüe* (with both open and tunneled sections) stretched from Lake Zumpango to the Tula River. Floods had plagued the capital since pre-Columbian times; colonial officials worked to maintain the Aztec system of dikes and causeways, but by the early seventeenth century it had become apparent that this was an inadequate solution. In 1607 the German-born engineer Enrico Martínez received approval for the construction of a drainage canal that would reduce water levels in the Valley of Mexico. Within a year, some 40,000 workers using hand tools had excavated 14 miles of channels, including a 4-mile tunnel that reached a depth of 175 feet.

Inaugurated on 17 November 1608, the *desagüe* soon proved to have numerous flaws, notably its inability to drain low-lying Lake Texcoco, the valley's largest body of water. The tunnel itself was too narrow and had poorly shored walls, and the entire system suffered from inattentive maintenance. As a result, the *desagüe* failed to prevent the great flood of 1629, which left parts of Mexico City inundated for five years. After this disaster, the authorities concentrated on converting the tunnel to open cut, removing obstructions from the channel, and increasing the *desagüe*'s capacity. But work proceeded sporadically, generally only in response to threats of severe flooding. In the end, the project outlasted the colonial government; construction was completed in the last two decades of the nineteenth century, at the cost of nearly 16 million pesos.

See also **Engineering; Mexico City.**

BIBLIOGRAPHY

For a detailed study of the *desagüe* see J. Ignacio Rubio Mañe, *El virreinato*, 2d ed., vol. 4 (1983). Much useful information can be found in Charles Gibson, *The Aztecs Under Spanish Rule: A History of the Indians of the Valley of Mexico, 1519–1810* (1964). Richard Everett Boyer, *La gran inundación: Vida y sociedad en México, 1629–1638* (1975); and Louisa Hoberman, "Bureaucracy and Disaster: Mexico City and the Flood of 1629," in *Journal of Latin American Studies* 6 (1974): 211–230, focus on the 1629 crisis. For the completion of the *desagüe*, see Moisés González Navarro, "México en una laguna," in *Historia mexicana* 4, no. 4 (April–June 1955): 506–522.

Additional Bibliography

Pascoe, Juan. *La obra de Enrico Martínez: Cosmógrafo del Rey, intérprete del Santo Oficio de la Inquisición, cortador y fundidor de caracteres, tallador de grabados, impresor de libros, autor, arquitecto y maestro mayor de la obra del desagüe del Valle de México.* Santa Rosa, Michoacán: Taller Martín Pescador, 1996.

Pérez-Rocha, Emma. *Ciudad en Peligro: Pobreza sobre el desagüe general de la ciudad de México, 1556.* México, D.F.: Instituto Nacional de Antropología e Historia, 1996.

Perló Cohen, Manuel. *El paradigma porfiriano: Historia del desagüe del valle de México.* México: Programa Universitario de Estudios Sobre la Ciudad, Instituto de Investigaciones Sociales: M.A. Porrúa Grupo Editorial, 1999.

R. DOUGLAS COPE

DESCAMISADOS. Descamisados, a term translated literally as the "shirtless ones," first used in a pejorative manner by Argentina's mainstream press on 17 October 1945 to describe the lower-class supporters of Juan Domingo Perón. Workers had gathered by the hundreds of thousands in the Plaza de Mayo to protest, successfully, the arrest of Perón, a symbol of working-class aspirations. They embraced the label and transformed it into a badge of honor that signified both their poverty and hard work. Perón himself first used the word publicly at a rally of the Labor Party early in 1946. At the end of his speech, he tossed his jacket aside and rolled up his sleeves. He, too, would be a *descamisado*,

and Eva, his wife, would become a symbol of both their dignity and their close identification with the regime. The attention given the *descamisados*, however, obscured the multiclass character of the Peronist movement.

See also **Argentina, Political Parties: Justicialist Party; Avellaneda, Nicolás; Mitre, Bartolomé; Perón, Juan Domingo; Perón, María Eva Duarte de.**

BIBLIOGRAPHY

Samuel L. Baily, *Labor, Nationalism, and Politics in Argentina* (1967), p. 90.

Julie M. Taylor, *Eva Perón: The Myths of a Woman* (1979), chaps. 4 and 6.

Joseph Page, *Perón: A Biography* (1983), pp. 136–137.

PAUL GOODWIN

D'ESCOTO BROCKMANN, MIGUEL

(1933–). Miguel D'Escoto Brockmann (*b.* 5 February 1933), Nicaraguan priest active in the Sandinista revolution; foreign minister of Nicaragua (1979–1989). Born in California to Nicaraguan parents, D'Escoto was educated in Managua, California, and New York. He studied theology, education, and political economy and became a Catholic priest in the Maryknoll Order. During the 1960s, he worked first for Maryknoll in New York, then in the slums of Brazil and Mexico. Returning to his own country, he established the Nicaraguan Foundation for Integral Community Development in 1973. In 1975 he became an active supporter of the Sandinista movement. He was a leader of the Group of Twelve (*Los Doce*), which organized resistance to the Somoza government. When the Sandinistas came to power in 1979 he was named foreign minister, a post he held for ten years. In 1980 he became a member of the party's political group, the Sandinista Assembly.

The Vatican made known in 1980 its desire that priests not be involved in politics. This policy was relayed to D'Escoto; Ernesto Cardenal, the minister of culture; and two other priests who were participating in the Nicaraguan government at the time. D'Escoto and the others proposed that they take a leave of absence from the church and continue with their work in the government. The Nicaraguan bishops accepted this compromise. Cardenal was subsequently expelled from the Jesuit order, but the Maryknollers did not expel D'Escoto. Throughout the 1980s, D'Escoto was a forceful spokesman for the Sandinista cause. Because of his fluency in English and his understanding of the political system of the United States he was particularly successful in communicating Sandinista positions to audiences in that nation. In 2006 the Sandinista presidential candidate Daniel Ortega was elected for a second time (his first term was 1985 to 1990). D'Escoto serves as a presidential advisor and continues to be a critic of neoliberalism and United States foreign policy towards Latin America.

See also **Cardenal, Ernesto; Maryknoll Order; Nicaragua, Sandinista National Liberation Front (FSLN).**

BIBLIOGRAPHY

Teofilo Cabestrero, *Un grito a Dios y al mundo* (1986).

Thomas P. Anderson, *Politics in Central America*, rev. ed. (1988).

Additional Bibliography

Canin, Eric. "'Work, a Roof, and Bread for the Poor': Managua's Christian Base Communities and the 'Revolution from Below.'" *Latin American Perspectives* 24: 2 (March 1997), 80–101.

Murphy, John W., and Manuel J. Caro. *Uriel Molina and the Sandinista Popular Movement in Nicaragua*. Jefferson, NC: McFarland, 2006.

DAVID L. JICKLING

advisory board and council on all matters of justice and legal administration. It became a central organ in the bureaucratic structure of the Portuguese Empire. The Desembargo do Paço appointed royal magistrates, promoted them, and evaluated their performance through the *residência* (investigation) at the end of their tours of duty. It settled conflicts of jurisdiction between subordinate tribunals or magistrates and, on occasion, conducted special examinations (*devassas*). By custom, the Desembargo do Paço consisted of six magistrates, including one ecclesiastic trained in church law. Into the twenty-first century, the title of *desembargador* remains in use throughout Brazil for certain members of federal tribunals.

See also **Judicial Systems: Brazil; Portuguese Empire; Residencia.**

BIBLIOGRAPHY

Stuart B. Schwartz, *Sovereignty and Society of Colonial Brazil* (1973).

Additional Bibliography

Bonelli, Maria da Glória. *Profissionalismo e política no mundo do direito: As relações dos advogados, desembargadores, procuradores de justiça e delegados de polícia com o Estado.* São Carlos: EdUFSCar; São Paulo: IDESP, Editora Sumaré: FAPESP, 2002.

Subtil, José Manuel Louzada Lopes. *O Desembargo do Paço (1750–1833).* Lisboa: Universidade Autónoma de Lisboa, Departamento de Ciências Humanas, 1996.

ROSS WILKINSON

DESEMBARGADORES.

Desembargadores, Brazilian high-court magistrates who were divided into *extravagantes,* unassigned judges who were appointed to cases on an as-needed basis, and *dos agravos,* or appellate judges. As a kind of traveling circuit judge in the colonies, the *desembargador* enforced royal policy and was regularly used as a judicial investigator in outlying areas.

Occupying the pinnacle of the Portuguese justice system was the Desembargo do Paço, which developed from an advisory committee to Dom João (1481–1495) into a fully institutionalized government board, established by the Ordenações Manuelinas of 1514. Although it could hear cases of special merit, its primary function was as an

DESNOES, EDMUNDO PÉREZ (1930–).

Edmundo Pérez Desnoes (*b.* 2 October 1930), Cuban novelist, essayist, and poet. Desnoes was born and raised in Havana and lived in New York, where he attended college from 1956 to 1959. He then returned to Cuba, where he held several posts in national cultural institutions, such as editorial board member of the Casa de las Américas. In 1967 he and film director Tomás Gutiérrez Alea adapted his 1965 novel *Memorias del subdesarrollo* (*Memories of Underdevelopment*) into a highly successful film that brought him immediate recognition. Largely because of this adaptation, Desnoes became a prominent figure in the Cuban cultural world of the 1960s, but in subsequent years his importance diminished as his literary output failed to live up to its earlier promise. Other works by Desnoes include the novel *El cataclismo,* an essay "Lam: Azul y negro," and a controversial anthology of Cuban literature, *Los dispositivos en la flor* (1981). In 2007, the film version of *Memorias de desarrollo* (*Memories of Overdevelopment*), a sequel to his most famous novel, was in its final stages of production.

See also **Cinema: From the Silent Film to 1990; Gutiérrez Alea, Tomás; Literature: Spanish America.**

BIBLIOGRAPHY

Paolo Gasparini, *Para verte mejor, América Latina* (1972).

Additional Bibliography

Davies, Catherine. "Surviving (on) Soup of Signs: Postmodernism, Politics, and Culture in Cuba." *Latin American Perspectives* 27: 4 (July 2000), 103–121.

Desnoes, Edmundo. "Para terminar (Excerpt from the unpublished novel entitled *Memorias de Desarrollo*)." *Casa de las Américas* 234 (Jan–Mar 2004), 69–72.

ROBERTO VALERO

DE SOTO, HERNANDO. *See* Soto, Hernando de.

DESSALINES, JEAN JACQUES (1758–1806).

Jean Jacques Dessalines (*b.* 1758; *d.* 17 October 1806), emperor of Haiti (1804–1806). In the early hours of an October morning in 1806, a fierce-looking black commander was trying to force his mount through a crowd of mutinous but stunned soldiers. Finally a shot rang out, the commander's horse rolled over, breaking and pinning the rider's leg, and with cries of anguish and curses rolling from the commander's lips, the stunned soldiers knew that their hated victim was mortal after all. They shot him to pieces and dragged his mutilated body from Pont Rouge to Port-au-Prince for public display. There but one person mourned his death—she was Défilée, an insane black woman. The object of her tears and flowers was the emperor, Jean Jacques Dessalines. No man in Haitian history has been more hated by

his contemporaries or loved and respected by future generations of his countrymen than Dessalines.

Born on the Cormiers Plantation in northern Saint-Domingue, young Jean Jacques Duclos (later Dessalines) experienced many of slavery's horrors. Master Duclos sold both his parents and a favorite aunt to neighboring plantation masters, a clear violation of the Code Noir (1685), which mandated that slave families be kept intact. In the late 1780s a free black master named Dessalines acquired the now mature Jean Jacques Duclos. His new master often whipped him, leaving him only pain and a new last name. Small wonder that Dessalines despised whites, mulattoes, and authority by the time of the Haitian Revolution.

When the revolution began, Dessalines may have been a maroon (slave fugitive), but runaway or not, he soon joined the black rebels. When Dessalines joined Toussaint Louverture is unclear, but he became indispensable to the "Black Spartacus" once he did. With a viciousness rare in Toussaint's generals, he figured heavily in crushing the rebellion of Theodore Hedouville at Le Cap (1798), in defeating and punishing the mulattoes of South Province, led by André Rigaud, during the War of the Knives (1799), in suppressing the rebellion of General Moyse (1801), and in opposing the expedition of French General Charles Leclerc (1802–1804). Clearly Dessalines was a gifted field commander, who earned the title of "Tiger."

But Dessalines's brutal manner and greed often tainted these achievements. At one time Dessalines had thirty plantations and an income so large that he refused to join the Moyse rebellion on the grounds that plantation division, one of its demands, threatened his economic interests. When Toussaint sent him to South Province as an occupation governor following the War of the Knives, the Tiger murdered hundreds of mulattoes. He also slaughtered practically the entire white population of Haiti in 1804. And he enforced *fermage* (system of forced labor and government management on plantations), introduced by Toussaint, with a severity seldom seen in any of the old colonial masters.

C. L. R. James is among those historians who emphasize that Dessalines acted largely on his own. But others, among them Hubert Cole, believe that

Dessalines usually acted with Toussaint's knowledge and approval, the War of the Knives providing their best argument. The brutal Dessalines served as a sort of alter ego for the gentle Toussaint. While Toussaint might have found Dessalines useful on the battlefield, he absolutely believed him unfit to rule the emerging black state. Toussaint was right.

Dessalines carried Haiti to independence on 1 January 1804 and himself to the emperorship at his coronation on 8 October 1804. That France might once again attack Haiti was his abiding fear and, as Hubert Cole indicated, may have triggered his mass slaughter of all whites in mid 1804. But his furious behavior extended to the mulattoes also. He once quipped that he murdered any mulatto who looked white during the massacres of 1804. Later he mellowed with regard to the mulattoes and remarked that blacks and mulattoes should intermarry and obliterate race lines. But rationality soon gave way to another volcanic eruption of rage in Dessalines. When the mulatto Alexandre Pétion refused to marry his daughter, Dessalines once again turned on them, and by the end of 1806 had planned their destruction. The Haitian national historian Thomas Madiou has treated Dessalines's social policies as those of a liberal. But other historians outside Haiti disagree. James Leyburn believes Dessalines brought social disaster on Haiti and fixed the caste system on the new state.

A reckless economic policy finally brought Dessalines down. He challenged mulatto land titles, put most of Haiti's able-bodied men under arms, enforced a harsh labor system, and neglected education. On 17 October 1806 most of Haiti rejoiced over his assassination.

See also **Louverture, Toussaint.**

BIBLIOGRAPHY

W. W. Harvey, *Sketches of Haiti* (1827).

Thomas Madiou, *Histoire d'Haiti*, 4 vols. (1847–1904).

C. L. R. James, *The Black Jacobins* (1938).

James Leyburn, *The Haitian People* (1944).

Hubert Cole, *Christophe: King of Haiti* (1967).

Thomas O. Ott, *The Haitian Revolution, 1789–1804* (1973).

David Nicholls, *From Duvalier to Dessalines: Race, Colour, and National Independence in Haiti* (1979).

Additional Bibliography

Dayan, Joan. *Haiti, History, and the Gods.* Berkeley: University of California Press, 1998.

Dubois, Laurent. *Avengers of the New World: The Story of the Haitian Revolution.* Cambridge, MA: Belknap Press of Harvard University Press, 2004.

THOMAS O. OTT

DESTERRO, NOSSA SENHORA DO.
See **Florianópolis.**

DEUSTUA, ALEJANDRO O. (1849–1945).

Alejandro O. Deustua (*b.* 1849; *d.* 1945), Peruvian philosopher, educator, politician, and lawyer. Born in Huancayo, Deustua initially was an exponent of the positivist school of thought prevalent in Latin America in the late nineteenth and early twentieth centuries. Subsequently he espoused idealist concepts developed by the European philosophers Karl Krause and his followers and Henri Bergson. This transition was not uncommon among Latin American intellectuals after the Mexican Revolution. In his later works, *Ante el conflicto nacional* (1931) and *La cultura nacional* (1937), Deustua expressed the need for a renewed sense of humanist nationalism among the elites. Deustua was a founding member of the historical Civilista Party (1872), minister of justice (1895) and government (1902), senator for Lima (1901–1904), a diplomat, and president of San Marcos University (1928–1930). He died in Lima.

See also **Peru, Political Parties: Civilista Party.**

BIBLIOGRAPHY

Frederick Pike, *The Modern History of Peru* (1967).

Additional Bibliography

Arpini, Adriana. "La concepción de la historia y la utopía en tres pensadores latinoamericanos: Alejandro Korn, Alejandro Deustua y José Vasconcelos." *Anuario de Historia del Pensamiento Argentino* 7 (1990): 123–152.

Frondizi, Risieri, and Jorge J. E. Gracia. *El hombre y los valores en la filosofía latinoamericana del siglo.* Mexico City: Fondo de Cultura Económica, 1975.

Himelblau, Jack J. *Alejandro O. Deústua: Philosophy in Defense of Man.* Gainesville: University Presses of Florida, 1979.

ALFONSO W. QUIROZ

DEVIL'S ISLAND. *See* **French Guiana.**

DÍA, EL. *El Día,* an Uruguayan newspaper founded by the great Colorado Party political leader and two-time president, José Batlle y Ordóñez, on 16 June 1886. The newspaper was the vehicle through which Batlle formulated and publicized his political ideology of the welfare state and support for the working class, which propelled him to the presidency (1903–1907 and 1911–1915). In the 1940s and 1950s the newspaper was controlled by Batlle's sons, César and Lorenzo. Although they were more conservative than their father, the sons used the newspaper to promote Batlle's long-sought dream of a purely collegial executive system, which was finally adopted under the 1952 Constitution but abandoned in 1966. In 1966, Jorge Pacheco Areco, editor of *El Día,* was elected vice president. When President Oscar Gestido died one year later, Pacheco became president.

El Día was the most influential newspaper in Uruguay for the first six decades of the twentieth century. During the military dictatorship (1973–1984), *El Día* remained a subdued but subtle voice of opposition to the regime by daily publishing a picture of Batlle with one of his pithy quotes about democracy or against dictatorship. The newspaper fell on hard times in the 1980s, with no major Colorado politician reflecting its legacy, and it ceased publication on 31 January 1991. Briefly resurrected, it again closed down.

See also **Batlle y Ordóñez, José; Journalism; Pacheco Areco, Jorge; Uruguay: The Twentieth Century; Uruguay, Political Parties: Colorado Party.**

BIBLIOGRAPHY

Roberto B. Giudici and Efraín González Conzi, *Batlle y el batllismo,* 2d ed. (1959).

Milton Vanger, *José Batlle y Ordóñez of Uruguay: The Creator of His Times, 1902–1907* (1963).

MARTIN WEINSTEIN

DÍA DE MUERTOS, CALAVERAS. Día de muertos, or Day of the Dead, is a festive occasion observed in Mexico on November 1 and 2. During the colonial era, a mixture of Spanish Catholic religious rites and pre-Hispanic traditions that commemorated people's deaths through the wearing of costumes gave rise to this celebration. On the Day of the Dead, people visit cemeteries and place flowers and candles on gravestones; they also make offerings of food and drinks to the spirits of the departed. In the early twenty-first century, celebrations occur across the entire country, with some regional and ethnic differences. A central element in every region is setting up an *ofrenda* ("offering"), both in cemeteries and homes; on and around these little altars, families arrange trinkets, food, drinks, *pan de muerto* ("bread of the dead"), and *calaveritas* or *calaveras,* small, skull-shaped candies with the names of family members on the forehead. The purpose of *ofrendas* is to offer the souls that visit their living relatives some of the food or drinks they used to taste in life. In some areas, people remain in graveyards all night. The towns Mixquic and Pátzcuaro are known for their traditional Day of the Dead celebrations.

See also **Posada, José Guadalupe.**

BIBLIOGRAPHY

Brandes, Stanley. *Skulls to the Living, Bread to the Dead: The Day of the Dead in Mexico and Beyond.* Malden, MA: Blackwell, 2006.

PERLA ORQUÍDEA FRAGOSO LUGO

DIAGUITAS. The Diaguitas were sedentary agriculturalists dispersed in the transversal valleys of the Andean cordillera (northwest Argentina and north-central Chile) from the mid-first millennium to the sixteenth century. Archaeological studies indicate that Diaguita culture in the region emerged in the transition from transhumant hunting and gathering to complete sedentary agriculture in the second half of the first millennium. Archaeologists detect three distinct periods in the material culture left by the Diaguitas in the following centuries until the mid-fifteenth century, when they were first conquered by the Inca, and then by the Spanish in the sixteenth century.

When the Spanish first contacted the Diaguitas, they found evidence of Inca domination in clothing, beliefs, and technology. Archaeological findings suggest also that the Diaguita culture was at its apogee when Inca expansion to the south incorporated the Diaguitas in the mid-fifteenth century. At that time, the Diaguitas occupied the transversal valleys on both sides of the cordillera from present-day Aconcagua to Copiapó, where they grew corn, beans, potatoes, quinoa, squash, and, according to the climate, cotton, in irrigated valleys fertilized with sardine heads or llama and alpaca manure. They herded llama and alpaca for wool and for transport; hunted Guanaco, chinchillas, and fowl; and also fished to supplement their diet.

In each settlement consanguineous relations linked all members; communal lands were assigned by the chief to each nuclear family. Within each valley settlements were further organized according to moieties with one half near the coast and the other half near the cordillera. The relative isolation of each of the valleys allowed the development of notable political autonomy, and even different dialects.

The incorporation of the Diaguitas under Spanish colonial rule was achieved without major resistance, and Diaguita tribute was important in providing the foundation of the colonial settlements in the region established to supply the Potosí mines with mules, textiles, and food.

Although many had previously believed that the Diaguitas were an extinct ethnic group, the 2001 Truth Commission (*Comisión de verdad y política del nuevo trato entre el estado, sociedad y mundo indígena en Chile*) launched by then-President Ricardo Lagos confirmed that many citizens still self-identify as Diaguita. Although contemporary Diaguita culture has been mostly overlooked by scholars, some anthropological studies conclude that Diaguita social and cultural patterns have indeed survived colonization and assimilation.

On September 8, 2006, the government passed Chilean Law 20.117, recognizing the "existence and cultural attributes of the Diaguita ethnicity and the indigenous nature of the Diaguita people." Whereas official state recognition should facilitate the recovery of ancestral lands, transnational corporations such as Nevada Ltd., a subsidiary of Canadian Barrack Gold Corporation, control a large portion of Diaguita territory. How the Chilean government will respond to this difficult situation is yet to be determined.

See also **Agriculture; Archaeology; Incas, The; Indigenous Peoples; Lagos, Ricardo; Truth Commissions.**

BIBLIOGRAPHY

Julian H. Steward, ed., *Handbook of South American Indians,* vol. 2 (1946), pp. 587–597.

Jorge Hidalgo L. et al., eds., *Prehistoria: Culturas de Chile desde sus orígenes hasta los albores de la conquista* (1989).

Grete Mostny, *Prehistoria de Chile* (1991), p. 117.

Additional Bibliography

Yáñez, Nancy, and Sarah Rea. "The Valley of Gold." *Cultural Survival Quarterly* 30, no. 4 (2006).

KRISTINE L. JONES

DIÁLOGOS DAS GRANDEZAS DO BRASIL.

Diálogos das Grandezas do Brasil, manuscript written in 1618 and attributed to Ambrósio Fernandes Brandão. The Dialogues were well known in manuscript form to the nineteenth-century scholars Francisco Adolfo de Varnhagen and João Capistrano de Abreu. Varnhagen made a copy of the manuscript in Leiden Library in 1874, and the Dialogues were printed in the *Revista do Instituto Arqueológico Histórico e Geográfico Pernambucano* between 1877 and 1887. Abreu tried to have them published in a volume in 1900, but the first edition did not appear until 1930 under the patronage of the Brazilian Academy of Letters.

There are six Dialogues. In the first one, the two characters, Alviano and Brandônio, talk about natural products and their possible use for colonists, distinguishing between those that were the result of human efforts through agriculture and those that were a kind offering from nature. In the same Dialogue, Portuguese settlement is discussed and the northern captaincies are described. The second Dialogue is a scholarly dissertation on the torrid zone and on the human races, with special emphasis on the original inhabitants of Brazil. It ends with some considerations of diseases and of Indian and white medical practices. Social groups, sugar mills, agriculture, fishing and hunting, and Indian culture occupy the remaining Dialogues. In historiographical debates concerning the Portuguese "discovery" of Brazil, scholarship in the early twenty-first century has revisited the

Dialogues and placed them within the framework of the "construction" of Brazilian national identity.

See also **Brazil: The Colonial Era, 1500-1808; Capistrano de Abreu, João; Literature: Brazil; Varnhagen, Francisco Adolfo de.**

BIBLIOGRAPHY

Francisco Adolfo De Varnhagen, *História geral do Brasil,* 9th ed. (1975).

João Capistrano De Abreu, *Ensaios e estudos: Crítica e história* (1st ser., 1975).

Ambrósio Fernandes Bran-Dão, *Dialogues of the Great Things of Brazil,* translated and annotated by Frederick Holden Hall et al. (1987).

Additional Bibliography

Cristóvão, Fernando. "Brasil: do 'descobrimento' à 'construção.'" *Camões: Revista de Letras e Culturas Lusofonas* 8 (January–March 2000).

MARIA BEATRIZ NIZZA DA SILVA

DIAMONDS. *See* **Gems and Gemstones.**

DIANDA, HILDA (1925–). Hilda Dianda (*b.* 13 April 1925), Argentine composer. Born in Córdoba, she studied under Honorio Siccardi and did postgraduate work in Europe (1958–1962) under Gian Francesco Malipiero and Hermann Scherchen. Dianda wrote some electroacoustic works at the Studío di Fonologia Musicale in Milan, Italy, and attended the new music summer courses in Darmstadt, Germany. Her early works have traces of moderated modernism—dissonant chords and jagged melodies—and a lyrical style. This is true of *Concertante* for cello and orchestra (1952) and *Poemas de amor desesperado* for voice and six instruments (1942). Later her style became more experimental, and she was one of the leading figures of the musical avant-garde in Argentina. Dianda participated in numerous international festivals, including Florence, Caracas, Rio de Janeiro, Madrid, Washington, D.C., Mexico, Zagreb, and Donaueschingen. Dianda has also written articles published in several publications around the world and one book, *Música en la Argentina de hoy* (1966). For several years Dianda

collaborated as a composer-member and concert organizer with the Agrupación Música Viva in Buenos Aires. This organization, which also included composers Gerardo Gandini, Armando Krieger, Antonio Tauriello, and Alcides Lanza, presented concerts in Buenos Aires consisting of their own compositions and contemporary music from other countries.

Other important compositions by Hilda Dianda are *Núcleos* for two pianos, vibraphone, xylorimba, eight percussionists, and string orchestra (1963); *Estructuras* nos. 1, 2, and 3 for cello and piano (1960); String Quartet no. 3 (1963–1964); *Percusión 11,* for eleven percussionists (1963); *Ludus* no. 1 for orchestra (1968); *Ludus* no. 2 for eleven performers (1969); *Idá-ndá's* for three percussionists (1969); *a7* for cello and five tapes (1966); *Resonancias* no. 3 for cello and orchestra (1965); *Resonancias* no. 5 for two choirs (1967–1968); *Ludus* no. 3 for organ (1969); *Impromptu* for string orchestra (1970); and *Cadencias* no. 2 for violin and piano (1986).

See also **Music: Art Music.**

BIBLIOGRAPHY

Fourth Inter-American Music Festival (1968), pp. 41, 67.

Rodolfo Arizaga, *Enciclopedia de la música argentina* (1971), p. 117.

John Vinton, ed., *Dictionary of Contemporary Music* (1974), pp. 184–185.

Gérard Béhague, *Music in Latin America: An Introduction* (1979), p. 336; *New Grove Dictionary of Music and Musicians* (1980).

Additional Bibliography

Dal Farra, Ricardo. "Something Lost, Something Hidden, Something Found: Electroacoustic Music by Latin American Composers." *Organised Sound* 11 (2006): 131–142.

ALCIDES LANZA

DIAS, ANTÔNIO GONÇALVES (1823–1864). Antônio Gonçalves Dias (*b.* 10 August 1823; *d.* 3 November 1864), Brazilian poet. An outstanding romantic poet, Dias was the founder of truly national Brazilian literature. Romanticism represented perfectly the ideals of freedom, patriotism, and nativism so fervent in Brazil in the time of Independence. These sentiments were well expressed by

Dias, whose work dealt mainly with Brazil's landscape and Indians (Indianism). He wrote exultant hymns to the beauty of tropical nature. With great imagination he treated Indian themes. Besides being a lyric poet, he was a prose writer, historian, ethnologist, and dramatist.

Born in Caxias, Maranhão, Dias was the illegitimate son of a Portuguese shopkeeper and a Brazilian *cafuza* (of mixed Indian and African blood). When his father married another woman, the child was separated from his mother and taken to live with the new couple. After his father's death, Dias went to Portugal to study at the University of Coimbra, where he received a bachelor's degree in 1845. His years in Portugal were very valuable. In addition to university work, he studied languages and literature, wrote intensively, made contact with great writers, and was loved and admired. Because of economic difficulties, however, he returned to Maranhão. In 1846 he went to Rio, where he published *Primeiros cantos* (First Songs, 1847), which was favorably reviewed by Alexandre Herculano. Other publications followed, including *Leonor de Mendonça* (1847); *Segundos cantos* (Second Songs, 1848), which contains "Sextilhas de Frei Antão" (Friar Antão's Sextets), a poem in the Portuguese troubadour style; and *Últimos cantos* (Last Songs, 1851).

Besides teaching positions, Dias held important government posts in Brazil and Europe. He published in Leipzig the second edition of his poems, titled *Cantos* (Songs, 1857), as well as *Os timbiras* (The Timbiras, 1857), and *Dicionário da língua tupi* (Dictionary of the Tupi Language, 1858). Additional works by Dias include *Obras póstumas* (6 vols., 1868–1869) and *Poesia completa e prosa escolhida* (1959).

In 1858 Dias traveled to Brazil, but in 1862 he returned to Europe seeking a cure for his poor health. Feeling worse, he sailed again for Brazil; although his wrecked ship was rescued from sinking, because he was ill, he was the only passenger who perished.

See also **Literature: Brazil.**

BIBLIOGRAPHY

Raymond Sayers, *The Negro in Brazilian Literature* (1956).

Fritz Ackermann, *A obra poética de Antônio Gonçalves Dias,* translated by Egon Schaden (1964).

David T. Haberly, "The Songs of an Exile: Antônio Gonçalves Dias," in *Three Sad Races: Racial Identity and National Consciousness in Brazilian Literature* (1983), pp. 18–31.

Almir C. Bruneti, "Antônio Gonçalves Dias," in *Latin American Writers,* edited by C. Solé and M. I. Abreu, vol. 1 (1989), pp. 185–193.

Additional Bibliography

Patriota, Margarida de Aguiar. *Eu sou marabá: vida e obra do poeta Gonçalves Dias.* Brasilia: Editora Universidade de Brasília, 2004.

Peres, Marcos Flamínio. *A fonte envenenada: Transcendência e história em três hinos de Gonçalves Dias.* São Paulo: Nova Alexandría, 2003.

MARIA ISABEL ABREU

DIAS, HENRIQUE (?–1662).

Henrique Dias (*d.* 8 June 1662), black military leader during the seventeenth-century Portuguese campaign against the Dutch occupation of northeastern Brazil. Although it is unknown whether or not he had ever been a slave, Henrique Dias was a free and literate man when he volunteered for service in 1633. At that time the Dutch were expanding their occupation of Pernambuco beyond the coastal towns of Recife and Olinda and would eventually overtake large portions of the northeastern captaincies.

Initially the captain of a small force, Dias later commanded over three hundred men of color, some of whom were slaves. By 1636 he was a master of the guerrilla tactics that were then the basis of the Luso-Brazilian strategy against the Dutch. His skills as a military tactician were evident in all of his engagements, which ranged from his participation in the defense of Salvador (the capital of Bahia) in 1638 to his role in the campaign to recover territory in Alagoas in 1639. Returning to Pernambuco in 1645, Dias resumed his part in the fight against the enemy, eventually traveling to Rio Grande do Norte, where he and his men took a Dutch fort in 1647. By 1648 he was in Olinda, where his fighting prowess contributed to the defeat of the enemy. Finally, he fought in the front lines in the recapture of Recife in January 1654.

Though subject to racist treatment during his long career, Dias received many honors for his service. In 1638, for example, King Philip IV awarded him a knighthood, a highly unusual status for a man of African descent. In Brazil, Portuguese commander the Count of Torre granted him a patent in 1639 that carried the title "Governor of All Creoles, Blacks, and Mulattoes." Finally, in March 1656, he traveled to Portugal, where, in an audience with the court, Dias requested and received the freedom of all slaves who had served in his *têrço* (unit) and the continued existence of his force, which was to have the rights and privileges of white units. Though he later died much as he had been born, in relative obscurity, his memory was preserved in the name given to all subsequent black militia companies. They were called the "Henriques."

See also **Militias: Colonial Brazil.**

BIBLIOGRAPHY

The most extensive sources about the life of Henrique Dias are in Portuguese. See especially José Antônio Gonsalves De Mello, *Henrique Dias: Governador dos pretos, crioulos, e mulatos do estado do Brasil* (1954). Many shorter sketches are available in English, but the older of these contain inaccuracies. The best is found in A. J. R. Russell-Wood, *The Black Man in Slavery and Freedom in Colonial Brazil* (1982), pp. 84–87 and 102–103. On the Dutch presence in Brazil, see Charles R. Boxer, *The Dutch in Brazil, 1624–1654* (1957).

                                          JUDITH L. ALLEN

DIAS GOMES, ALFREDO (1922–1999).

Alfredo Dias Gomes (*b.* 19 October 1922, *d.* 18 May 1999), Brazilian playwright. Born in Bahia, Dias Gomes tried and mastered all forms of drama, whether on the stage, radio, or television, and his theater continually evolved. Always he was both artist and social commentator. With his play *O pagador de promessas* (1960), Dias Gomes gained national prominence as a playwright. The central theme of the play is the tragic uphill struggle of the strong individual for true personal freedom in a capitalist society. This theme, a recurring one in Dias Gomes's theater, is closely related to two others: the problems of communication and intolerance, particularly religious intolerance, in modern society. The willful priest, every bit as intransigent as Zé, the title character, stands as the play's principal antagonist, and although Dias Gomes describes him as the symbol of

universal rather than merely religious intolerance, the priest's attitude and actions constitute a rather caustic commentary on religious dogmatism. Yet another strength of the play is the adroitness with which the dramatist parallels the "Afro-Catholic syncretism" that characterizes the religious views of Zé and several other characters with a similar syncretism in setting and symbol. *O pagador*, then, with a compelling plot, a carefully elaborated classical structure, and a protagonist who is perhaps the most memorable character of all Brazilian drama, deservedly ranks as one of the best plays of that country's theatrical tradition.

It is in *O berço do herói* (1965) that the satiric humor and the expressionistic techniques introduced in *A revolução dos beatos* (1962) and *Odorico, o bem amado* (1962) find their fruition. The work concerns itself chiefly with the problem of true individual liberty in a capitalist society, much as does *O pagador*. Various critics, in fact, have stated that *O berço* is a very pessimistic answer to the questions concerning individual freedom and liberty that are raised in *O pagador*. Both heroes experience one phase of Calvary—Zé the journey with the cross and Jorge the trial. The similarity between the plays is such, in fact, that they seem to comprise a dramatic experiment in which the same set of basic ingredients is poured into two distinct molds—one tragic and the other burlesque. The play, although long banned, is perhaps the best satire to be found in the contemporary Brazilian theater.

Dias Gomes's sixth major play, *O santo inquérito*, was first presented in Rio in September 1966. Based on the life of Branca Dias, it is the only one of his works whose setting is in the rather distant past: the year 1750, in the state of Paraíba. The major concerns or themes, just as in *O pagador*, are individual freedom within a tightly structured societal boundary (i.e., the church), existential communication, and religious fanaticism. The Inquisition is employed primarily as a metaphor to describe military and political repression in Brazil in the 1960s. Following *O santo inquérito* and representing yet another experiment in structure and technique is *Dr. Getúlio, sua vida e sua glória*, a piece in two acts in which verse and prose are mixed. It dramatizes the period of ultimate crisis in the life of the president-dictator Getúlio Vargas—the crisis that precipitated his suicide in 1954.

In *Os campeões do mundo,* Dias Gomes tells the story of two lovers who are involved in terrorism during the World Soccer Cup in Rio in the 1970s. It is a story of political oppression and torture whose outcome is known to the public; the dialectic of how and why things happened takes precedence over plot. With little of the usual interest in the denouement, spectators can be more objective and better able to exercise critical judgment, which was the goal of the author.

See also **Literature: Brazil; Theater.**

BIBLIOGRAPHY

Leon F. Lyday and George Woodyard, *Dramatists in Revolt: The New Latin American Theater* (1976), pp. 221–242.

Additional Bibliography

Albuquerque, Severino João Medeiros. "Alfredo Dias Gomes (1922–1999)." *Latin American Theatre Review* 33:1 (Fall 1999): 169.

RICHARD A. MAZZARA

DIAS LOPES, ISIDORO (1865–1949). Known as the "Rebel General," Isidoro Dias Lopes was one of the most dynamic military leaders in the Brazilian army. Born in Dom Pedrito, Rio Grande do Sul, in 1865, he joined the army in 1883, enlisting in the Thirteenth Infantry Battalion of Porto Alegre. Even though he supported the Republic, he left the army to join the Federalist revolution. Defeated, he went into exile in Paris in 1895. He was granted amnesty and returned to the army to continue his military career.

In 1924, even as a retired general (he had retired in 1923), he played a prominent role in the *tenentista* movement. Chosen as one of its leaders, he was among those largely responsible for the uprising of July 5th. After a few weeks Isidoro ordered the rebels to withdraw to Paraná, where they would later join Luís Carlos Prestes's group. Even without participating directly in the Prestes Column march, Isidoro still enjoyed great prestige among its leaders. In October 1930 he took command of the Second RM (Military Region). In 1931 he disagreed with the course taken by the Getúlio Vargas administration and began defending a return of the country to constitutional rule. He

participated in the controversial Constitutionalist revolution of 1932 and was deported to Portugal after its defeat. He returned to Brazil in 1934, after being pardoned once again. In 1937 he criticized the Vargas coup. He died in Rio de Janeiro in 1949.

See also **Brazil, Revolutions: Federalist Revolt of 1893; Prestes, Luís Carlos; Prestes Column; Tenentismo; Vargas, Getúlio Dornelles.**

BIBLIOGRAPHY

Capelato, Maria Helena. *O movimento de 1932: A causa paulista.* São Paulo: Editora Brasiliense, 1981.

Carvalho, José Murilo de. *Forças armadas e política no Brasil.* Rio de Janeiro: Jorge Zahar Editor, 2005.

Castro, Celso, Vitor Izecksohn, and Hendrik Kraay. *Nova história militar brasileira.* Rio de Janeiro: FGV/Bom Texto, 2004.

Prestes, Anita Leocádia. *A Coluna Prestes.* São Paulo: Editora Brasiliense, 1990.

FERNANDO VALE CASTRO

DÍAZ, ADOLFO (1874–1964). Adolfo Díaz (*b.* 1874; *d.* 27 January 1964), president of Nicaragua (1911–1916, 1926–1928). Previously a secretary for La Luz and Los Angeles Mining Company, a U.S. firm based in Bluefields, the Costa Rican–born Díaz entered Nicaraguan politics during the Conservative overthrow of Liberal dictator José Santos Zelaya in 1909. He served as a source of funds for the rebel leader Juan Estrada. After Zelaya's ouster, Estrada became president and Díaz, his vice president. On 8 May 1911, Estrada resigned in the face of a revolt led by Minister of War Luis Mena. Díaz succeeded to the presidency and quickly cultivated U.S. goodwill. One month into his presidency he signed a treaty with the U.S. that permitted the Nicaraguan government to negotiate a loan with U.S. private banks.

Díaz desired financial and political security, but his forging of closer ties between Nicaragua and the United States caused him to lose support at home. Mena declared that Díaz had sold out, and sought supporters in the National Assembly. In July 1912 Mena led a revolt against Díaz. Although Conservative Party leader Emiliano Chamorro defeated Mena, Díaz failed to control this tumultuous situation and finally turned to the United States for assistance. President William Howard Taft dispatched the marines on 4 August 1912.

Díaz was reelected president in 1926 after Chamorro's unsuccessful coup d'état. A reinstated national assembly acknowledged him as president, and the United States promptly recognized his government. The former Liberal vice president, Juan Bautista Sacasa, however, claimed the presidency for himself, and with the support of José María Moncada, rose against the Conservative administration. With the help of the United States, Díaz was able to end the resulting civil war, and gain control of the government until 1928. During this period he cooperated with the United States in the development and training of the National Guard.

See also **Zelaya, José Santos.**

BIBLIOGRAPHY

William Kamman, *A Search for Stability: United States Diplomacy Toward Nicaragua, 1925–1933* (1968).

Lester D. Langley, *The Banana Wars: United States Intervention in the Caribbean, 1898–1934* (1985).

James Dunkerley, *Power in the Isthmus: A Political History of Modern Central America* (1988).

Additional Bibliography

Bolaños, Pío. *Génesis de la intervención norteamericana en Nicaragua.* Managua: Editorial Nueva Nicaragua, 1984.

SHANNON BELLAMY

DÍAZ, FÉLIX JR. (1868–1945). Félix Díaz, Jr. (*b.* 17 February 1868; *d.* 9 July 1945), Mexican general, diplomat, and politician. He was the son of Félix Díaz (1833–1872), a general and governor of Oaxaca (1867–1871), and a nephew of Porfirio Díaz, the dictatorial president. Díaz is best known for his role in the overthrow of President Francisco I. Madero in February 1913 during the so-called *Decena Trágica* (tragic ten days).

Born in the city of Oaxaca, Díaz graduated from the National Military College with a degree in engineering in 1888. By 1909 he had become a brigadier general. He served as alternate federal deputy from Oaxaca (1894–1896) and Veracruz (1896–1900)

and federal deputy from Veracruz (1900–1912). In 1902 he was a candidate for governor of Oaxaca, and in 1910 he served as that state's interim chief executive. He was a member of the Exploratory Geographic Commission (1901); consul general in Chile (1902–1904); inspector of police, Mexico City (1904); chief of the presidential staff (1909); and ambassador to Japan (1913).

Díaz was separated from the army and jailed by President Madero, who overthrew Díaz's uncle, Porfirio. Díaz initiated, along with generals Manuel Mondragón (1859–1922) and Bernardo Reyes (1850–1913), the February 1913 rebellion against Madero that, when joined by federal army commander General Victoriano Huerta, successfully ousted the president. Díaz subsequently lost the power struggle he waged with Huerta, briefly served as ambassador to Japan, and then went into self-imposed exile in Havana and New York. In 1916 he returned to Mexico to head the National Reorganizing Army against revolutionary chief Venustiano Carranza. He remained active against the Carranza regime until 1920, when he was again exiled until 1937. He died in Veracruz.

See also **Carranza, Venustiano; Díaz, Porfirio; Huerta, Victoriano; Madero, Francisco Indalecio.**

BIBLIOGRAPHY

Luis Licéaga, *Félix Díaz* (1958).

Peter V. N. Henderson, *Félix Díaz, the Porfirians, and the Mexican Revolution* (1981).

Alan Knight, *The Mexican Revolution*, 2 vols. (1986), esp. pp. 1: 473–490, 2: 375–392.

Additional Bibliography

Plana, Manuel. *Pancho Villa and the Mexican Revolution.* New York: Interlink Books, 2002.

Guzmán, Martín Luis. *Muertes históricas: Febrero de 1913.* México, D.F.: Editorial Joaquín Mortiz, 2001.

DAVID LAFRANCE

DÍAZ, GONZALO (1947–). Gonzalo Díaz (*b.* 1947), Chilean artist. Throughout his career Díaz has addressed what he has termed the conceptualization of Chile as "cultural landscape" and the troubled status of painting in contemporary Chilean art. Born in Santiago, he studied art at the Escuela de Bellas Artes, Universidad de Chile, Santiago, from

1965 to 1969. Like the conceptually minded artists associated with the Avanzada, he was strongly affected by the institution of General Augusto Pinochet's military dictatorship in 1973. However, while most of the Avanzada artists abandoned painting, Díaz remained captivated by its theory, practice, and history in the era of photography. In the late 1970s he began producing labyrinthine installations that incorporate paintings as well as objects. His painting *Historia sentimental de la pintura chilena* (1982) exemplifies his central thematic concerns: the troubled status of painting in contemporary Chilean art, which in the late 1970s and early 1980s was largely dominated by conceptual and photographic practices, and the relationship between painting and the construction of national identity. Díaz has taught at the Universidad de Chile (1969), the Universidad Católica (1974), and the Instituto de Arte Contemporáneo (1977–1986), all in Santiago. He continues to teach at the Universidad de Chile and won the Premio Nacional de Artes in 2003.

See also **Art: The Twentieth Century.**

BIBLIOGRAPHY

Adriana Valdés, "Gonzalo Díaz," in *Contemporary Art from Chile,* edited by Fatima Bercht (1991), pp. 10–21.

Mari Carmen Ramírez, "Blueprint Circuits: Conceptual Art and Politics in Latin America," in *Latin American Artists of the Twentieth Century* (1993), pp. 156–167.

Additional Bibliography

Mellado, Justo Pastor. *Gonzalo Díaz: El padre de la patria.* Santiago: Eds. de la Cortina de Humo, 1999.

Oyarzún R., Pablo. "Estética de la sed: 'Lonquén 10 años,' diez años después." *Revista Iberoamericana* 69: 202 (Jan.–Mar. 2003), 85–94.

JOHN ALAN FARMER

DÍAZ, JORGE (1930–2007). Jorge Díaz (*b.* 1930, *d.* 13 March 2007) was born to Spanish parents in Rosario, Argentina, but raised in Chile. He graduated in architecture and first entered the theater as a scenographer. The Latin American playwright most closely associated with theater of the absurd, he achieved early success with *El cepillo de dientes* (1961), a two-character play that in language and structure epitomizes the clichés of contemporary life. Although his linguistic dexterity creates an illusion of vacuous and sterile relationships and the difficulties of authentic communication, his plays are underscored by a strong social and political reality. His early pieces played with language, time, music, humor, and the stultifying effects of bourgeois society.

In 1965 Díaz immigrated to Spain to escape the administrative responsibilities of ICTUS, a vanguard theater in Santiago. In Spain his plays became more aggressive, using mixed-media techniques to denounce greed and insensitivity, such as a massacre in a Brazilian *favela* and the ITT intervention in Chilean politics. After Franco's death in 1975 brought a new sense of freedom to the Spanish theater, Díaz began to experiment with two distinctly different styles, one focusing on the sociopolitical, the other more personal and intimate. He wrote about the archetypal qualities of sex and death, which he claimed was to write about life. Some plays were intended for a Madrid audience, others for Santiago. On two occasions Díaz has dramatized his compatriot, the Nobel laureate Pablo Neruda, most recently in *Pablo Neruda viene volando* (1991). In 2003 he published a collection of eight previously unpublished works, *Antología de la perplejidad.* Among the many awards he won were the Premio Nacional de las Artes y la Comunicación y Audiovisuales (1993) and the Premio Antonio Buero Vallejo de Guadalajara (1992).

Díaz returned to Chile in 1994, where he continued to write and paint for the remainder of his life. Díaz's trenchant style and playful language earned him the epithet of "absurdist" writer, but he sought only to express his view of contemporary human existence. Díaz was also a prolific writer of theater for children.

See also **Favela; Neruda, Pablo; Theater.**

BIBLIOGRAPHY

Teodosio Fernández, "Jorge Díaz," in *El teatro chileno contemporáneo (1941–1973)* (1982), pp. 153–67.

Tamara Holzapfel, "Jorge Díaz y la dinámica del absurdo teatral," in *Estreno* 9, no. 2 (1983): 32–35.

George Woodyard, "Jorge Díaz and the Liturgy of Violence," in *Dramatists in Revolt: The New Latin American Theater,* edited by Leon F. Lyday and George W. Woodyard (1976), pp. 59–76.

Additional Bibliography

Bauer, Oksana M. "Jorge Diaz: Evolución de un teatro ecléctico." Ph.D. diss., City University of New York, 1999.

Díaz, Jorge, and Eduardo Guerrero del Río. *Jorge Díaz: Un pez entre dos aguas.* Santiago: Universidad Finis Terrae, RiL Editores, 2000.

GEORGE WOODYARD

DÍAZ, JOSÉ EDUVIGIS (1833–1867).

José Eduvigis Díaz (*b.* 1833; *d.* 7 February 1867), Paraguayan soldier. Born in Pirayú, Díaz entered the military at age nineteen and showed sufficient promise as a soldier to receive several important appointments by the early 1860s. He was police chief of Asunción when the War of the Triple Alliance broke out in 1864. One year later, Díaz participated in the Corrientes campaign, during which he caught the eye of President Francisco Solano López for having ferried 100,000 head of cattle to the Paraguayan lines with the Allied armies in close pursuit. Díaz rose quickly to the rank of general and fought in engagements at Corrales, Tuyutí, and Boquerón. His greatest achievement, however, came in September 1866, when his troops, defending reinforced trenchworks at Curupayty, repulsed a massive Allied attack, killing 9,000 of the enemy and suffering almost no losses themselves.

For a short time, Díaz was feted as López's favorite, but in January 1867, while on a reconnaissance patrol along the Paraguay River, his canoe was hit by a Brazilian cannonball, which shattered his leg. Despite the ministrations of several army doctors, septicemia soon set in, and Díaz died at López's encampment at Paso Pucú.

See also **Paraguay: The Nineteenth Century.**

BIBLIOGRAPHY

Charles J. Kolinski, *Independence or Death! The Story of the Paraguayan War* (1965).

Carlos Zubizarreta, *Cien vidas paraguayas,* 2d ed. (1985), pp. 164–170.

Additional Bibliography

Chaves, Julio César. *El general Díaz; biografía del vencedor de Curupaity.* Buenos Aires: Ediciones Nizza, 1957.

Leuchars, Chris. *To the Bitter End: Paraguay and the War of the Triple Alliance.* Westport: Greenwood Press, 2002.

Marco, Miguel Angel de. *La Guerra del Paraguay.* Buenos Aires: Planeta, 1995.

Montezuma Hurtado, Alberto. "Un héroe griego." *Correo de los Andes* 40 (September–October 1986): 88–93.

THOMAS L. WHIGHAM

DÍAZ, JOSÉ PEDRO (1921–2006).

José Pedro Díaz (*b.* 1921, *d.* 3 July 2006), Uruguayan writer, literary critic, and educator. Formerly Uruguay's foremost critic of French literature, Díaz wrote about French as well as Uruguayan literature in the weekly *Correo de los viernes.* He was also one of Uruguay's most important novelists. His *Los fuegos de San Telmo* (1964), one of the best novels produced by the Uruguayan Generation of 1945, investigates the Italian origins of Uruguay's majority population. *Partes de naufragios* (1969) focuses on the complacent life in Montevideo of the 1930s and 1940s, a view that assumes ironic dimensions, given the productive and moral crisis affecting the country at the time of its publication. Also important are Díaz's conceptual essays treating the Spanish poet Gustavo Adolfo Bécquer (1953), the Uruguayan fantasy writer Felisberto Hernández, and the poet Delmira Agustini.

See also **Literature: Spanish America.**

BIBLIOGRAPHY

Fernando Ainsa Amigues, *Tiempo reconquistado: Siete ensayos sobre literatura uruguaya* (1977).

Marie Johnston Peck, *Mythologizing Uruguayan Reality* (1985).

Additional Bibliography

Sosnowski, Saúl, and Louise B. Popkin. *Repression, Exile, and Democracy: Uruguayan Culture.* Durham, NC: Duke University Press, 1993.

Peck, Marie J. "José Pedro Díaz y Hemingway: una mitología comparada." *Texto Crítico* 12: 34–35 (Jan.–Dec. 1986): 189–203.

WILLIAM H. KATRA

DÍAZ, PORFIRIO (1830–1915).

Porfirio Díaz (*b.* 15 September 1830; *d.* 2 July 1915), president of Mexico (1876–1880 and 1884–1911). In recognition of his prominence in Mexican politics and government, the period from 1876 to 1911 is called the Porfiriato. Much of the literature written about Díaz during his presidency reflects the sycophantic adulation of his biographers, while that dating from the Revolution of 1910 has tended to castigate him as a repressive dictator. His life, of course, was more complicated.

Porfirio Díaz was born in the city of Oaxaca, the sixth child of a modest innkeeper and his wife. His father, José de la Cruz Díaz, died before Porfirio reached the age of three. His mother, Petrona Mori, was unable to keep the business going. As soon as he was old enough, Porfirio was sent to work for a carpenter, but he found time for his primary studies. At the age of fifteen, he began attending the seminary, apparently with the aid of his godfather, the canon and later bishop of Oaxaca, José Agustín Domínguez. Porfirio interrupted his studies to enlist in the national guard during the war of 1846–1847 with the United States but saw no fighting. After graduating in 1849, Díaz refused to be ordained and insisted on studying law at the Institute of Sciences and Arts, passing his first examination in civil and canon law in 1853.

With the triumph of the Plan of Ayutla (1854), Díaz was named subprefect of Ixtlán, the beginning of his political career. He joined the Oaxaca national guard in 1856 and fought for the liberals during the War of the Reform. He was promoted to the rank of brigadier general in August 1861. Elected to Congress that same year, he served only briefly.

Porfirio Díaz first achieved fame as a result of his crucial role in the victory against the invading French troops at Puebla on 5 May 1862. The following year he was twice captured but managed to escape and return to the struggle, sustaining guerrilla warfare against the occupying French army throughout 1866 and taking the city of Oaxaca on 31 October of that year. The following year he led his Army of the East to victory at Puebla on 2 April and drove the imperial army from the national capital on 21 June.

Díaz opposed President Benito Juárez's *convocatoria* of 1867, which attempted to increase presidential power and alter the constitution by referendum. Díaz regarded the *convocatoria* as both unconstitutional and a personal affront. The legislature of Oaxaca lauded him in recognition of his efforts against the French, gave him the hacienda of La Noria, and supported him for the presidency of the republic. After Juárez's reelection (1867), Díaz resigned from the army and turned his attention to agriculture, his investment in the telegraph connecting Mexico and Oaxaca, and the presidential election in 1871. With another reelection of Juárez, Díaz rebelled. His Plan of la Noria claimed the election had been fraudulent and demanded that the presidency be limited to a single term. Díaz failed to dislodge Juárez, who died in mid-1872. Sebastián Lerdo De Tejada, head of the supreme court, ascended to the presidency and was soon elected to a four-year term. Díaz retired to his hacienda, made furniture, and prepared for another campaign.

Díaz rebelled against Lerdo in January 1876, charging that the elections scheduled for July of that year would be fraudulent. His Plan of Tuxtepec retained the principle of no reelection and insisted on municipal autonomy. An expert in guerrilla warfare from his days fighting the French, Díaz designed a military strategy for the revolt that called for the use of hit-and-run tactics to force the government to diffuse its forces. Contrary to traditional histories, the "battle" of Icamole on 20 May did not indicate that Díaz's effort was crumbling. Although portrayed by Lerdo's government as a great victory over forces commanded personally by Díaz, the rebel leader was not present and his subordinate in charge of the encounter was under orders only to reconnoiter and skirmish with the enemy, not to engage in a decisive battle.

In any case, Lerdo's reelection prompted José María Iglesias to charge fraud and refuse to recognize the results. As head of the Supreme Court and next in line for the presidency, Iglesias tried to assume that office himself. Faced with the opposition of both Iglesias and Díaz, Lerdo resigned and went into exile. Díaz offered to acknowledge Iglesias as president if new elections could be held soon. Iglesias refused, but soon resigned when his forces were unable to stop Díaz's advance. After holding elections, Díaz took formal possession of the presidency on 5 May 1877 for a term to end on 30 November 1881.

Although the image of a repressive Díaz has been pervasive in the post-Revolutionary literature, his first term was notable for his efforts to conciliate his rivals and opponents as well as foreign governments. Díaz sent the proposal for no reelection to Congress and supported efforts to increase political competition for state and municipal posts as well. He attempted to divide and rule the economic elite by creating rivals for political power and expanding economic opportunities.

When the Grant administration in the United States attached conditions to its recognition of his government, Díaz arranged for payments on Mexico's debt. Rutherford B. Hayes soon succeeded Grant and raised the stakes, ordering U.S. troops to cross into Mexico in pursuit of raiders, bandits, and rustlers. Díaz ordered Mexican troops to resist any invasion, and only forbearance on both sides prevented a major escalation. Díaz defused the crisis by wooing U.S. investors (among them former president Grant) with concessions, thereby ending the clamor for intervention and achieving formal recognition of his government in 1878. To balance the tremendous weight of the United States, Díaz sought to renew ties to France and other European powers, using similar efforts to attract investment and diplomatic recognition.

At the end of his first term, Díaz made good on his promise and did not run for reelection; he accepted the post of secretary of development under President Manuel González and served as governor of the state of Oaxaca. In 1884, Díaz was again elected president, losing his antipathy to reelection in 1888, 1892, 1904, and 1910. He provided stable government, balanced the budget, and assured economic growth but increased Mexico's reliance on foreign capital and the subservience of Mexican capital and labor to foreign control. His power became dictatorial; he prevented the election of his opponents and muzzled the press. But if his skills had been limited to repression, he would never have lasted as long as he did. Díaz blocked formation of political parties but encouraged rivalries between elite factions. The two major contenders for favor were the *científicos*, led by his father-in-law, Manuel Romero Rubio (and after his death by Díaz's finance minister, José Yves Limantour), and a cohort of military officers, led by Manuel González and later by Bernardo Reyes. Research suggests Díaz was able to exercise a relative degree of autonomy from economic interests. He acted to limit the expropriation of Indian lands by surveying companies and was

flexible in dealing with peasant and labor grievances until the turn of the century.

After 1900, the system began to fall apart as the result of economic depression, political organization, increasing nationalism, blatant repression, and the fundamental uncertainty generated by the president's age. Díaz was either unwilling or unable to maintain the complex system of rivalries and balancing of contending interests that had provided stability for decades. In 1908, in an interview with the U.S. newspaper reporter James Creelman, he appeared to announce that Mexico was ready for competitive elections and that he would not run for reelection in 1910. Later Díaz changed his mind, but not until after the published remarks had created a sensation.

As he neared the age of eighty, it was obvious to everyone else that Díaz could not remain president much longer. Every level of Mexican society clamored for more nationalistic policies, from the *científicos*, who resented the interventionism of the U.S. government and the increasing size and power of U.S. corporations, to the railroad workers and miners, who were paid half as much as foreigners for the same work. Díaz rejected economic nationalism, but U.S. interests saw him as increasingly anti-American while his domestic opponents accused him of selling out to the United States. Finally, Díaz lost power the way he first gained it, as a result of guerrilla warfare. On 21 May 1911, his representative signed the Treaty of Ciudad Juárez with Francisco Madero. Díaz resigned the presidency on 25 May, and by the end of the month was on his way to exile in Paris, where he died.

See also **Mexico: 1810–1910; Porfiriato; Oaxaca (City).**

BIBLIOGRAPHY

The literature on Porfirian Mexico is voluminous, but there is no good, recent biography of Díaz. See the classic indictments by John Kenneth Turner, *Barbarous Mexico* (1910; repr. 1969); Carleton Beals, *Porfirio Díaz, Dictator of Mexico,* (1932; repr. 1971). In Díaz's defense, see Jorge Fernando Iturribarría, *Porfirio Díaz ante la historia* (1967). As a guide, consult Thomas Benjamin and Marcial Ocasio-meléndez, "Organizing the Memory of Modern Mexico: Porfirian Historiography in Perspective, 1880s–1980s," in *Hispanic American Historical Review* 64 (May 1984): 323–364. For an excellent historical summary, see Friedrich Katz, "Mexico: Restored Republic and Porfiriato, 1867–1910," in Leslie Bethell, ed., *The Cambridge*

History of Latin America, vol. 5 (1986), pp. 3–78. On the restored republic and the Revolution of Tuxtepec, see Laurens Ballard Perry, *Juárez and Díaz: Machine Politics in Mexico* (1978). On Porfirian history, see Daniel Cosío Villegas, *Historia moderna de México,* 9 vols. (1955–1972); Daniel Cosío Villegas, *The United States Versus Porfirio Díaz* (1963); François-xavier Guerra, *México, del antiguo régimen a la Revolución,* 2 vols., translated by Sergio Fernández Bravo (1988). Recent works on Díaz's role in land-tenure questions include Donald F. Stevens, "Agrarian Policy and Instability in Porfirian Mexico," *The Americas* 39, no. 2 (1982): 153–166; and Robert H. Holden, "Priorities of the State in the Survey of the Public Land in Mexico, 1876–1911," *Hispanic American Historical Review* 70, no. 4 (1990): 579–608.

Additional Bibliography

Garner, Paul H., and Luis Pérez Villanueva. *Porfirio Díaz: del héroe al dictador, una biografía política.* Mexico City: Planeta, 2003.

González Navarro, Moisés. *Sociedad y cultura en el porfiriato.* Mexico City: Consejo Nacional para la Cultura y las Artes, Dirección General de Publicaciones, 1994.

Hale, Charles. *The Transformation of Liberalism in Late Nineteenth-century Mexico.* Princeton, NJ: Princeton University Press, 1989.

Johns, Michael. *The City of Mexico in the Age of Díaz.* Austin: University of Texas Press, 1997.

Katz, Friedrich. *De Díaz a Madero.* Mexico Ciy: Ediciones Era, 2004.

Krauze, Enrique. *Porfirio Díaz: místico de la autoridad.* Mexico City: Fondo de Cultura Económica, 1995.

Krause, Enrique, and Fausto Zerón-Medina. *Porfirio.* Mexico City: Clío, 1993.

Weiner, Richard. "Battle for Survival: Porfirian Views of the International Marketplace." *Journal of Latin American Studies* 32 (October 2000): 645–670.

D. F. STEVENS

DÍAZ AROSEMENA, DOMINGO

(1875–1949). Domingo Díaz Arosemena (*b.* 25 June 1875; *d.* 23 August 1949), Panamanian politician and president (1948–1949) and a member of one of the most prominent political families in the country. He spent many years in public service as a member of the Panama City Council and deputy to the National Assembly. After the revolution of 1931 Díaz Arosemena founded the Doctrinary Liberal Party, one of the many offshoots of the Liberal Party after the revolution. He was a candidate for president in the 1936 elections, one of the most hotly contested elections in the history of the country, but lost to the official candidate, Juan Demóstenes Arosemena. In 1948, Díaz Arosemena won the presidency with the backing of the country's major political forces. He died the following year.

See also **Panama.**

BIBLIOGRAPHY

Ernesto De Jesús Castillero Reyes, *Historia de Panamá,* 7th ed. (1962).

Joaquín A. Ortega C., *Gobernantes de la República de Panamá, 1903–1968,* 3d ed. (1965).

Additional Bibliography

Mendoza, Carlos Alberto, and Vicente Stamato. *Domingo Díaz: "El Bayardo panameño" en la guerra y en la independencia.* Panama: Comisión del Centenario de la Alcaldía de Panamá, 2003.

JUAN MANUEL PÉREZ

DÍAZ CASTRO, EUGENIO

(1804–1865). Eugenio Díaz Castro (*b.* 1804; *d.* 11 April 1865), Colombian author noted for his novels and local-color sketches (*cuadros de costumbre*). Born in Soacha, Díaz studied in Bogotá's Colegio de San Bartolomé but spent most of his life in agricultural endeavors. When he was over fifty, he became acquainted with José María Vergara y Vergara, who published his sketches of rural life in Vergara y Vergara's literary magazine *El Mosaico.* Díaz also wrote three novels: *Manuela* (1858), *Los aguinaldos en Chapinero* (1873), and *El rejo de enlazar* (1873), only the first of which is well regarded. Set in 1856 in a small town near Bogotá, it is partly a romantic love story centered on the simple but sharp-witted Manuela. The novel also effectively portrays the ideological disputes of the era and points up the gulf between recently enacted reform legislation and the realities of rural Colombia.

BIBLIOGRAPHY

Eugenio Díaz Castro, *Novelas y cuadros de costumbre,* 2 vols. (1985).

Raymond L. Williams, *The Colombian Novel, 1844–1987* (1991), esp. pp. 56–68.

Additional Bibliography

Botía Niño, Julio. *Análisis de Manuela, Eugenio Díaz Castro*. Bogota: Panamericana Editorial, 2003.

HELEN DELPAR

DÍAZ DE GUZMÁN, RUY (c. 1558–1629).

Ruy Díaz de Guzmán (*b.* ca. 1558; *d.* June 1629), known primarily for being the first creole historian of the Río de la Plata. Díaz de Guzmán was born in or near Asunción (modern Paraguay) and spent most of his early adult years fighting Indian wars and settling towns in the Río de la Plata, Paraguay, and Tucumán. Between the founding of Santa Fe in 1573, the recolonization of Buenos Aires in 1580, and the division of La Plata into two major jurisdictions in 1617, most littoral and interior towns had been permanently established. Díaz de Guzmán's history of the first half-century of Spanish rule is composed mainly of the accounts of town foundings and stories surrounding the early post-Conquest years. Known as the *Argentina Manuscrita*, it was first printed in 1835 and has had subsequent editions. Díaz de Guzmán died in Asunción. Ricardo Rojas (1882–1957), the Argentine writer and scholar whose pioneering *Historia de la literatura argentina* (4 vols., 1917) is a milestone in Argentine scholarship, traces influences of Díaz de Guzmán's history from the sixteenth to the twentieth century.

See also **Creole; Spanish Empire.**

BIBLIOGRAPHY

Marcos, Juan Manuel. "Ruy Díaz de Guzmán in the Context of Paraguayan Colonial Literature." *MLN* 102 (March 1987): 387–392.

Pistilli S., Vicente. *La primera fundación de Asunción: la gesta de Don Juan de Ayolas*. Asunción, Paraguay: Editorial El Foro, 1987.

Spagnuolo, Marta. *Tres visiones del encuentro de dos mundos*. Buenos Aires: Federación Argentina de la Industria Gráfica y Afines, 1992.

NICHOLAS P. CUSHNER

DÍAZ DEL CASTILLO, BERNAL (c. 1495–1584).

Bernal Díaz del Castillo (*b.* ca. 1495; *d.* 3 February 1584), Spanish conquistador and author. In a passage from his *Historia verdadera de la conquista de la Nueva España* (True History of the Conquest of New Spain), Díaz establishes his birthplace as Medina del Campo and recalls his first journey to America in Pedro Arias de Avila's expedition to the Darien in 1514. He subsequently participated in the explorations of the Yucatán by Francisco Hernández De Córdoba (1517) and of the Gulf of Mexico by Juan de Grijalva (1518), both of which preceded Cortés's conquest in 1519. After the Conquest, Díaz was awarded several *encomiendas* in Guatemala.

Like the other *encomenderos,* Díaz was adversely affected by a series of decrees in the mid-sixteenth century that eliminated *encomiendas* in perpetuity and personal services. However, his description of his poverty in the *Historia verdadera* should be taken as a rhetorical device. There are numerous documents that disprove his complaints about not having been sufficiently rewarded for his participation in the Conquest. Recently critics have insisted that his claims of "lacking letters" and his criticism of Francisco López de Gómara's elevated style in the *Historia de las Indias y la conquista de México* (1552) are a subterfuge to mask the fact that Bartolomé de Las Casas is the true target of his attacks. Díaz's and Gómara's styles are not as different as Díaz would lead us to believe; both cultivate a simple and clear language. Las Casas's condemnations of the colonial order, however, influenced the decrees against the *encomienda* system, and it was during the early 1550s that Díaz decided to write his *Historia verdadera.* He constantly revised the work until he finally finished it in 1568. The *Historia verdadera,* however, was not published until 1632. Although Díaz's expressed intent in writing the *Historia* was to better the lot of his children and grandchildren, his story is nevertheless a riveting account of the Conquest that ultimately constitutes a defense of the conquistadores. He died in Guatemala.

See also **Conquistadores; Las Casas, Bartolomé de.**

BIBLIOGRAPHY

Herbert Cerwin, *Bernal Díaz, Historian of the Conquest* (1963).

Bernal Díaz Del Castillo, *The Discovery and Conquest of Mexico, 1517–1521,* translated and edited by A. P. Maudslay (1970).

Rolena Adorno, "Discourses on Colonialism: Bernal Díaz, Las Casas, and the Twentieth-Century Reader," in *Modern Language Notes* 103 (March 1988): 239–258.

Bernal Díaz Del Castillo, *Historia verdadera de la conquista de la Nueva España,* edited by Carmelo Saenz de Santa María (1989).

Additional Bibliography

Campos Fernández-Fígares, María del Mar. *El caballo y el jaguar: Sobre la Historia verdadera de la conquista de la Nueva España.* Granada: Editorial Comares, 2002.

Cortínez, Verónica. *Memoria original de Bernal Díaz del Castillo.* Huixquilucan: Oak Editorial, 2000.

Mendiola Mejía, Alfonso. *Bernal Díaz del Castillo: Verdad romanesca y verdad historiográfica.* Mexico: Universidad Iberoamericana, Departamento de Historia, 1995.

Orquera, Yolanda Fabiola. *Los castillos decrépitos: O la "Historia verdadera" de Bernal Díaz del Castillo: una indagación de las relaciones entre cultura popular y cultura letrada.* Tucumán: Facultad de Filosofía y Letras, Universidad Nacional de Tucumán, 1996.

JOSÉ RABASA

DÍAZ DE SOLÍS, JUAN. *See* Solís, Juan Díaz de.

DÍAZ LOZANO, ARGENTINA (1909–1999).

Argentina Díaz Lozano (*b.* 15 December 1909, *d.* 1999), Honduran novelist. Born in Santa Rosa de Copán, Honduras, Díaz Lozano moved to Guatemala, the setting for many of her novels, in 1912 and returned to live in Tegucigalpa shortly before her death in 1999. She studied at the University of San Carlos and became the school's first woman to graduate in journalism. A prolific writer (whose work has been translated into French and English), she published her first novel at age seventeen and has received many awards for both her fiction and her journalism, among them the National Prize for literature in Honduras (1968) and awards from Guatemala, Brazil, and Italy. In 1957 ex-president Juan José Arévalo nominated her for the Nobel Prize in literature.

Her fiction belongs to the regionalist school predating the "Boom" of the 1960s in Latin American letters. Her novels focus on local themes, often exposing the plight of the poor, especially the tragic circumstances of Guatemalan Indians. Nevertheless, she shows little willingness to explore underlying issues of race, gender, and politics which might threaten the status quo. Her portrayal of women and Indians, while compassionate, essentially reflects the romantic and patronizing perspectives of the Ladino.

See also **Ladino; Literature: Spanish America.**

BIBLIOGRAPHY

The best-known novels include *Mayapán: Novela histórica* (1950), translated by Lydia Wright (1955); *Y tenemos que vivir* (1961), translated by Lillian Sears as *And We Have to Live* (1978); and *Ha llegado una mujer* (1991), based on Eugene O'Neill's *Desire Under the Elms.* She is mentioned briefly in Seymour Menton, *Historia crítica de la novela guatemalteca,* 2d. ed. (1985), and is exceedingly praised in José Francisco Martínez, *Literatura hondureña y su proceso generacional* (1987).

Additional Bibliography

Araya S., Seidy. *Historia y ficción educativa en la narrativa de las mujeres: Estudio de un caso centroamericano, la novelística de Argentina Díaz Lozano.* Heredia, Costa Rica: EUNA, 2004.

Díaz de Ortega, Rubenia. *Los años del ayer.* Tegucigalpa: s.n. (Alin Editora), 1996.

Umaña, Helena. *Narradoras Hondureñas.* Tegucigalpa: Editorial Guaymuras, 1990.

ANN GONZÁLEZ

DÍAZ ORDAZ, GUSTAVO (1911–1979).

Díaz Ordaz was the president of Mexico from 1964 to 1970. He was the last president to preside over a period of consistent, stable economic growth, but his administration is largely remembered and widely condemned for his handling of student unrest on the occasion of the 1968 Mexico City Olympics, resulting in the deaths of numerous citizens.

Díaz Ordaz was born March 12, 1911, in Chalchícomula, Ciudad Serdán, in the state of Puebla. His father was a government accountant and his mother a school teacher, his great grandfather was General José

María Díaz Ordaz, and one of his direct ancestors was the conquistador and chronicler Bernal Díaz del Castillo. After studying at elementary and preparatory schools in Oaxaca, Díaz Ordaz received his law degree from the University of Puebla in February 1937. While still a student he had begun his public career, starting as a modest court clerk in 1932. Upon graduation he became a prosecuting attorney, then a federal agent, and later the director of the labor arbitration board in Puebla.

After serving briefly as vice rector of the University of Puebla in 1940–1941, Díaz Ordaz became secretary general of government in Puebla and then a member of Congress from his home state in 1943–1946. He moved from the lower to the upper chamber, serving as senator from 1946 to1952, and then joined the government secretariat, first as director general of legal affairs in 1952–1956, then as *oficial mayor* in 1956–1958; and finally as secretary of government, the most influential political post in the cabinet, in the administration of President Adolfo López Mateos from 1958 to 1964.

López Mateos, who had become a close associate of his when both served in the senate, appointed him as the Institutional Revolutionary Party (PRI) candidate for president in 1964. Díaz Ordaz was serving as president when the Olympic Games took place in Mexico City in the fall of 1968. At the same time, his government became entangled in a conflict with a student movement that, as with such movements in many other countries, involved a number of issues. When students staged a demonstration in the Plaza of the Three Cultures in Mexico City's Tlatelolco district, the government called out army troops who fired on the demonstrators, leaving hundreds of students and bystanders dead. Archival research has revealed that the president used his personal presidential guard, dressed in civilian clothes, to fire first on the army troops, thus purposely perpetrating the army's violent response to what it believed was a student-initiated event. In short, neither the students nor the troops were responsible for what ensued.

The repercussions of this event shaped the generation of Mexican political and intellectual leaders of the 1990s, including former president Carlos Salinas, and altered the relationship between intellectuals and the government. Even more, this event raised serious questions about the legitimacy of the Mexican political and economic model and introduced pressures for political liberalization, the effects of which were to be seen in the 1970s and 1980s, culminating in the 1988 presidential election. Many analysts trace the ultimate demise of Mexico's one-party system, along with the introduction of political pluralism, to the divisions that emerged from the violent suppression of student demonstrators. Finally, Díaz Ordaz's policies led to a serious decline in the legitimacy of the Mexican presidency, which also affected his successors.

Even before the debacle of 1968, Díaz Ordaz had discouraged the early efforts of PRI president Carlos A. Madrazo to democratize the party in 1965. After his presidency, his successor appointed him its first ambassador to Spain after a reestablishment of relations in 1977, but he was so unpopular, and the public outcry against him was so intense, that he resigned the appointment before serving and remained out of the public eye until his death on July 15, 1979.

See also **Mexico, Political Parties: Institutional Revolutionary Party (PRI).**

BIBLIOGRAPHY

Cabrera Parra, José. *Díaz Ordaz y el '68.* 2nd ed. Mexico City: Grijalbo, 1982.

Hellman, Judith Adler. *Mexico in Crisis.* 2nd ed. New York: Holmes & Meier, 1983.

Krauze, Enrique. *El sexenios de Díaz Ordaz.* Mexico City: Clío, 1999.

Novo, Salvador. *La vida en el periodo presidencial de Gustavo Díaz Ordaz.* 2 vols. Mexico City: Conaculta, 1998.

RODERIC AI CAMP

DÍAZ SOTO Y GAMA, ANTONIO

(1880–1967). Antonio Díaz Soto y Gama was a distinguished Mexican political figure whose influence began with the founding of the Ponciano Arriaga Liberal Club in 1901 and culminated in the defeat of Ezequiel Padilla in the 1946 elections. He was born on January 23, 1880, in San Luis Potosí, the son of Conrado Díaz Soto and Concepción Gama Cruz. An attorney by profession, he fought as a member of the Liberal Party against the Porfirio Díaz dictatorship, together with Camilo Arriaga, the Flores Magón brothers, Juan Sarabia, and Antonio I. Villarreal, with whom he spent a brief period in exile. He was one of the founders of the Casa del Obrero Mundial (House of the International Worker) and worked closely with Emiliano Zapata, in whose name he gave a speech at the Aguascalientes Convention.

In 1920 Díaz Soto y Gama founded the Partido Nacional Agrarista (National Agrarian Party) and pursued an illustrious parliamentary career until 1929. He was involved in the agrarian program of his ally, President Álvaro Obregón, and worked for his reelection. Upon Obregon's death, he broke with General Plutarco Elías Calles. He collaborated with presidential candidates Antonio I. Villarreal (1934), Juan Andreu Almazán (1939), and Ezequiel Padilla (1946). An anticommunist Catholic, he was a critic of the agrarian program of President Lázaro Cárdenas. In 1948 a student movement designated him "rector by popular acclaim," a position he held for a short time. Until his death on March 14, 1967, he was a professor at the Law School of the National University of Mexico, a writer, and an editorial contributor to the national newspaper *El Universal.*

See also **Aguascalientes, Convention of; Almazán, Juan Andréu; Calles, Plutarco Elías; Cárdenas del Río, Lázaro; Casa del Obrero Mundial; Flores Magón, Ricardo; Mexico, Political Parties: Partido Liberal Mexicano; Mexico, Wars and Revolutions: Mexican Revolution; National Autonomous University of Mexico (UNAM); Obregón Salido, Álvaro; Zapata, Emiliano.**

BIBLIOGRAPHY

Cockroft, James D. *Precursores intelectuales de la Revolución Mexicana.* Mexico: Siglo XXI Editores, 1979.

Díaz Soto y Gama, Antonio. *La Revolución Agraria del Sur y Emiliano Zapata, su Caudillo.* Mexico: Centro de Estudios Históricos del Agrarismo en México, 1983.

Díaz Soto y Gama, Antonio. *Historia del Agrarismo en México.* Mexico: Ediciones Era-UAMI-FONCA, 2002.

RODERIC AI CAMP
PEDRO CASTRO

DÍAZ VÉLEZ, EUSTAQUIO ANTONIO (1782–1856).

A military officer and rural entrepreneur, Eustaquio Díaz Vélez was born in Buenos Aires on November 2, 1782. When British forces invaded the Viceroyalty of Río de la Plata in 1806,

Díaz Vélez enrolled in the regiment commanded by Viceroy Santiago Liniers that drove out the British in 1807. After the May Revolution of 1810, he was commissioned by the junta to bring Upper Peru into the revolutionary movement headed by Buenos Aires. Juan José Castelli sent Díaz Vélez to execute royalist leaders in Potosí. He also served in General Manuel Belgrano's Northern Army.

In 1814 the Directorio government designated Díaz Vélez as lieutenant governor of Santa Fe province. Constantly besieged by forces loyal to José Gervasio Artigas, fighting for province's autonomy against Buenos Aires government control, Díaz Vélez was eventually ousted by caudillo leader Estanislao López in 1816. In 1818 Díaz Vélez was designated as interim governor of Buenos Aires, a position he held until 1820.

Díaz Vélez retired to his *estancia* in Chascomús, south of Buenos Aires, where in 1839 he was imprisoned for participating in a conspiracy against Governor Juan Manuel de Rosas. When the latter was ousted from power in 1852, Díaz Vélez returned to Buenos Aires, where he died on April 1, 1856.

See also **Argentina: The Nineteenth Century; Artigas, José Gervasio; Belgrano, Manuel; Castelli, Juan José; López, Estanislao.**

BIBLIOGRAPHY

Rodríguez Bosch, Raúl. Eustoquio *Díaz Vélez: Soldado de la independencia y la organización Nacional.* Buenos Aires: Editora Selene, 1986.

KLAUS GALLO

DÍAZ VÉLEZ, JOSÉ MIGUEL (1770–1833).

José Miguel Díaz Vélez (*b.* 1770; *d.* 1833), Argentine patriot. Born in Tucumán and trained as a lawyer, Díaz Vélez was military commandant of Entre Ríos province from 1810 to 1814. He later held various positions in Buenos Aires. In 1825 he was a member of a mission to Upper Peru that sought a treaty with Simón Bolívar concerning the future status of that region and collaboration in a possible war against Brazil. The mission was a failure, as Upper Peru was by then committed to becoming a separate nation-state and Bolívar proved ambivalent regarding an anti-Brazilian alliance. Díaz Vélez served in the Unitarist regime set up in Buenos Aires by Juan Lavalle in 1828; when it collapsed, he emigrated to Uruguay, where he died at Paysandú.

See also **Argentina, Movements: Unitarists.**

BIBLIOGRAPHY

Jacinto R. Yaben, *Biografías argentinas y sudamericanas,* vol. 2 (1938), pp. 294–295.

Thomas B. Davies, Jr., *Carlos de Alvear: Man of Revolution* (1955, repr. 1968), pp. 63–83.

DAVID BUSHNELL

DI CAVALCANTI, EMILIANO (1897–1976).

Emiliano Di Cavalcanti (*b.* 1897; *d.* 1976), Brazilian painter. In 1914 Di Cavalcanti initiated his artistic career with the publication of one of his drawings in a magazine entitled *Fon-Fon*. In 1916 he moved from Rio de Janeiro to São Paulo, where he studied law and worked as an illustrator and journalist. In 1918, one year after exhibiting a series of "antiacademic" Beardsley-inspired caricatures in São Paulo, he began studying painting with the German painter Elpons. His first exhibition of paintings took place in 1921. During this period, Di Cavalcanti, in collaboration with modernist Paulistas Anita Malfatti and Vítor Brecheret, became one of the leaders of the Brazilian modernist movement. These three artists conceptualized and ultimately organized the 1922 Semana de Arte Moderna (Modern Art Week), a week-long series of poetry, dance, and fine arts exhibitions. It coincided with the centenary celebration of Brazilian independence and is regarded as a watershed for Brazilian cultural expression.

Di Cavalcanti's first trip to Europe in 1923 introduced him to the European avant-garde in art and literature. While the cubism and surrealism of Picasso, Braque, Léger, and Matisse influenced his own painting greatly, he remained devoted to national themes such as the bohemian life in Rio de Janeiro, mulatto women, and Carnival. In his memoirs he affirmed that "the mulata for me is a Brazilian symbol. She is not black or white, neither rich nor poor. Like our people, she likes to dance, she likes music and soccer . . . the mulata is feminine and Brazil is one of the most feminine countries in the world."

Upon his return to Brazil, he settled in Rio. Between 1927 and his return to Paris in 1935, Di Cavalcanti received a commission to prepare two wall panels for the João Caetano Theater. During this same period he exhibited in Rio de Janeiro and São Paulo. By the 1950s he had attained international recognition as one of the greatest modernist painters. In the second São Paulo Biennial in 1954, he won the highest honor, Best National Painter, and in the seventh São Paulo Biennial there was a special room devoted exclusively to an exhibition of his paintings.

See also **Modernism, Brazil.**

BIBLIOGRAPHY

Luis Martins, *Emiliano Di Cavalcanti* (1953).

Emiliano Di Cavalcanti, *Reminiscências líricas de um perfeito carioca* (1964).

Aracy Amaral, *Artes plásticas na Semana de 22: Subsídios para una história da renovação das artes no Brasil* (1992), esp. pp. 99–128, 246–248.

Additional Bibliography

Simioni, Ana Paula Cavalcanti. *Di Cavalcanti, ilustrador: Trajetória de um jovem artista gráfico na imprensa (1914–1922)*. São Paulo: Editora Sumaré; FAPESP, 2002.

Zílio, Carlos. *A querela do Brasil: A questão da identidade da arte brasileira: A obra de Tarsila, Di Cavalcanti e Portinari, 1922–1945*, 2nd edition. Rio de Janeiro: Relume Dumará, 1997.

CAREN A. MEGHREBLIAN

DICKMANN, ADOLFO (1882–1938).

Adolfo Dickmann, Argentine Socialist councilman and congressman, was born on September 1, 1882, in Finland. Dickmann immigrated as a youth with his family to Entre Ríos Province, Argentina, in the late nineteenth century. After joining the Socialist Party in 1900, he received his degree in dentistry from the University of Buenos Aires in 1905. He served first on the city council of Morón, province of Buenos Aires, and then in 1914 was elected to the provincial legislature, where he introduced legislation to create a provincial department of labor, to modify the tax on inheritances, and to regulate child and female labor.

In 1919 Dickmann was elected to the city council of the federal capital and then served two terms as a Socialist representative to the national Chamber of Deputies (1922–1930). After the military coup of 1930 that ousted democratic president Hipólito Irigoyen from office, Dickmann returned to Congress for the third time as a national deputy (1932–1936). A prominent member of the Socialist delegation in the national Congress, he was associated with legislation intended to improve the management of municipal administration and to better the living and working conditions of employees, workers, and rural laborers. However, the popular strength of the Unión Cívica Radical between 1916 and 1930 and the electoral fraud perpetrated by the conservatives after the coup of 1930 kept the Socialist Party as a minor political force. Himself a naturalized citizen, Dickmann wrote several works on immigration and nationalism (*Nacionalismo y socialismo*, 1933) as well as on tax policy, collective bargaining, and state control of the petroleum industry (*En defensa del petróleo nacional*, 1932).

See also **Argentina, Political Parties: Radical Party (UCR); Argentina, Political Parties: Socialist Party; Irigoyen, Hipólito.**

BIBLIOGRAPHY

Primary Work

Dickmann, Adolfo. *En defensa del petróleo nacional y por la dignidad de la función pública.* Buenos Aires: Durry y Kaplan, 1932.

Secondary Works

Suriano, Juan, comp. *La cuestión social en Argentina, 1870–1943.* Buenos Aires: La Colmena, 2000.

Sanguinetti, Horacio. *Los socialistas independientes.* Buenos Aires: Editorial de Belgrano, 1981.

RICHARD J. WALTER
VICENTE PALERMO

DICKMANN, ENRIQUE (1874–1955).
Enrique Dickmann (*b.* 20 December 1874; *d.* 30 December 1955), Argentine Socialist congressman and party leader. Born in present-day Latvia, Dickmann settled in Argentina in 1890. He became a naturalized citizen in 1897 and graduated from the medical school of the University of Buenos Aires with a medal of honor in 1904. In 1905 he was appointed chief of the clinic in a local hospital. As with several other Socialists, however, he became better known as a politician than as a physician. He joined the Socialist Party in 1896 and soon became an important figure in that organization, serving as editor of the party newspaper, *La Vanguardia,* first in 1898 and then for several periods thereafter.

Dickmann was elected for the first time to the national Chamber of Deputies from the federal capital in 1914 and served in that body for more than three decades (1914–1916, 1916–1920, 1920–1924, 1924–1928, 1932–1936, 1936–1940, and 1942–1946). An energetic and outspoken legislator, Dickmann was a prominent figure in the Socialist bloc of deputies. He had a hand in most of the Socialists' initiatives of these years, ranging from measures to promote and protect the rights of workers, including women and children, to opposition to what the Socialists viewed as overly favorable concessions to foreign investors. In 1931–1932, Dickmann played an important role in helping to form a joint presidential ticket with the Progressive Democratic Party, one of the few instances when the Socialists agreed to participate in a political coalition. In the late 1930s and early 1940s, Dickmann was a vocal opponent of the rise of fascism in Europe and warned of its possible extension to and growing influence in Argentina. He was close to party founder Juan B. Justo and remained steadfast in his loyalty to the central party until the 1940s, when, contrary to the stance of most Socialists, he expressed sympathy with the goals and achievements of President Juan Perón (1946–1955). The author of numerous books, his best-known work is his autobiography, *Recuerdos de un militante socialista* (1949).

See also **Argentina, Political Parties: Socialist Party.**

BIBLIOGRAPHY

Adelman, Jeremy. "Socialism and Democracy in Argentina in the Age of the Second International." *Hispanic American Historical Review* 72 (May 1992): 211–238.

Petra, Adriana. *Los socialistas argentinos a través de su correspondencia: Catálogo de los fondos de archivo de N. Repetto, J. A. Solari y E. Dickmann (1894–1980).* Buenos Aires: CeDInCI, 2004.

Walter, Richard J. *The Socialist Party of Argentina: 1890–1930.* Austin: University of Texas, Institute of Latin American Studies, 1977.

RICHARD J. WALTER

DICTATORS LEAGUE.

Dictators League, a myth concerning four Central American dictators that was popularized during 1936 and 1937 by the growing hysteria over the rise of fascism in Europe. Rumors spread by exile movements and the press in Mexico, Costa Rica, and the United States presumed an alliance among the regimes of generals Jorge Ubico in Guatemala (1931–1944), Maximiliano Hernández Martínez in El Salvador (1931–1944), Tiburcio Carías Andino in Honduras (1933–1949), and Anastasio Somoza García in Nicaragua (1937–1956). The similarities of the methods used by these personalistic caudillos and their prompt recognition of the Spanish regime of Generalíssimo Francisco Franco alarmed U.S. opinion-makers and journalists. In fact, the dominance and actions of the Central American dictators reflected each country's domestic political situation, all the results of the global depression.

The dictators were rivals who contested supremacy in the isthmus for many years. The only cooperation among them was a mutual tolerance stemming from belated recognition that none was capable of overthrowing the others—a standoff that resulted in a tacit accord to stop aiding exiles from neighboring nations.

BIBLIOGRAPHY

Kenneth J. Grieb, "The Myth of a Central American Dictators' League," in *Journal of Latin American Studies* 10, no. 2 (1978): 329–345; and *Guatemalan Caudillo: The Regime of Jorge Ubico, Guatemala, 1931–1944* (1979).

Additional Bibliography

Holden, Robert H. *Armies Without Nations: Public Violence and State Formation in Central America, 1821–1960.* Oxford: Oxford University Press, 2004.

Little-Siebold, Todd R. *Guatemala and the Dream of a Nation: National Policy and Regional Practice in the Liberal Era, 1871–1945.* Ph.D. diss., Tulane University, 1995.

Schmitz, David F. *Thank God They're on Our Side: The United States and Right-wing Dictatorships, 1921–1965.* Chapel Hill: University of North Carolina Press, 1999.

KENNETH J. GRIEB

DIEGO, ELISEO (1920–1994).

Eliseo Diego (*b.* 2 July 1920; *d.* 2 March 1994), Cuban poet and essayist. Diego was born in Havana, where he studied law for two years at the University of Havana. He was part of the editorial board of the literary publication *Clavileño* and was one of the founders of the influential magazine *Orígenes*, where his first poems and short stories appeared between 1944 and 1956. He taught English and served as inspector of English instruction for the Ministry of Education. In 1959 he earned a degree in education from the University of Havana. In 1962 Diego was put in charge of the Department of Children's Literature at the José Martí National Library in Havana, a post he occupied until 1970. He was secretary of public relations for the Cuban Union of Writers and Artists (UNEAC), and served on juries for several important literary contests in Cuba, including those of the UNEAC and the Casa de las Américas. He traveled widely to represent Cuba officially at international cultural events.

In 1993 Diego was awarded Mexico's Juan Rulfo literary prize, among the most important in Latin America. One of the foremost Cuban poets of the century, Diego exerted great influence on the younger generation of Cuban poets, especially after the publication of his first book, *En la calzada de Jesús del Monte* (1949). There is one compendium of his poems in prose, essays, and short stories (*Prosas escogidas*, 1983) and another of his poetry up to 1983 (*Poesía*). Both were published in Havana in beautiful editions. Other works by Diego include *Entre la dicha y la tiniebla: Antología poetica, 1949–1985* (1986), and *Veintiséis poemas recientes* (1986). His poetry has been translated widely. Diego died in Mexico City.

See also **Cuba: Cuba Since 1959.**

BIBLIOGRAPHY

Arcos, Jorge Luis. *Los poetas de "Orígenes".* Mexico City: Fondo de Cultura Económica, 2002.

López Lemus, Virgilio. *Oro, crítica y Ulises, o, Creer en la poesía: Figuras claves de la poesía cubana del siglo XX.* Santiago de Cuba: Editorial Oriente, 2004.

Padrón Barquín, Juan Nicolás. *La violenta música de la libertad: Antología poética de la Revolución.* Havana: Editorial José Martí, 1999.

Redonet, Salvador. *Entre dos origenistas y un eterno disidente: La cuentística de José Lezama Lima, Eliseo Diego y Virgilio Piñera.* Cienfuegos: Ediciones Mecenas y Reina del Mar Editores, 2001.

ROBERTO VALERO

DIEGO, JOSÉ DE (1866–1918).

José de Diego (*b*. 16 April 1866; *d*. 16 July 1918), Puerto Rican poet. Born in Aguadilla, Puerto Rico, de Diego studied law at the University of Barcelona in Spain, where he began writing poetry and prose. After completing his degree in Havana in 1892, he returned to Puerto Rico and became a prosecutor, later serving as undersecretary of justice and government, congressional representative, and Supreme Court justice. A staunch autonomist, he advocated the primacy of the Spanish language and Puerto Rico's independence from the United States. He was Speaker of the House of Representatives from 1907 until his death, president of the Union Party from 1914 to 1916, and president of the Puerto Rico Athenaeum from 1916 to 1918. De Diego was famous as an orator and for his books of poetry, among them *Pomarrosas* (Rose apples, 1904), *Cantos de rebeldía* (Songs of rebellion, 1916), and *Cantos de Pitirre* (Songs of Pitirre, published posthumously in 1949). Patriotism, Puerto Rico's country life, Americanism, the Antilles, and romantic love are his major themes. He also published a volume of selected prose, *Nuevas campañas* (New campaigns) in 1916.

See also **Puerto Rico, Political Parties: Overview.**

BIBLIOGRAPHY

Margot Arce De Vázquez, *La obra literaria de José de Diego* (1967).

Concha Meléndez, *José de Diego en mi memoria* (1966).

Delma S. Arrigoitia, *José de Diego: A Legislator in Times of Political Transition (1903–1918)* (1985).

Additional Bibliography

Arce de Vázquez, Margot. *Obras completas* vol. 2, "La obra literaria y el pensamiento poético de José de Diego." San Juan: Editorial de la Universidad de Puerto Rico, 1998.

Arrigoitía, Delma S. *José de Diego, el legislador: su visión de Puerto Rico en la historia (1903–1918)*. San Juan: Instituto de Cultura Puertorriqueña, 1991.

Rodríguez Escudero, Néstor A. *José de Diego: el caballero de la patria*. Puerto Rico[?], 1992.

ESTELLE IRIZARRY

DIEGUES, CARLOS (1940–).

A significant figure in Brazilian political and cultural life from the late 1950s, Carlos (Cacá) Diegues was central to the Cinema Novo movement.

EARLY YEARS

In 1959 Diegues began legal studies at the Ponificia Universidade Católica (Catholic University) in Rio de Janeiro, an institution increasingly engaged in politics. Diegues became active in politics through the Juventude Universitária Católica (Catholic Youth Movement) and the Centros Populares de Cultura (Popular Cultural Centers), or CPCs, both originating in leftist student politics. In the CPCs Diegues started his career as a filmmaker. The Centers stimulated political discussion and artistic innovation related to the creation of a genuine popular culture and the problematic linkage between intellectuals and artists, on the one hand, and the popular sectors on the other. Other independent and communist intellectuals joined the discussions, among them filmmakers Glauber Rocha (1938–1981), Nelson Pereira dos Santos (b. 1928), Arnaldo Jabor (b. 1940), Leon Hirszman (1937–1987), and Joaquim Pedro de Andrade (1932–1988).

In 1962, Diegues participated in the collective film *Cinco vezes favela* (Five times favela), making the episode *Escola de samba: Alegría de viver* (Samba school: Joy of living), in which he criticized the popular classes' involvement in Carnival and urged them to unionize as workers. The film's five episodes depicted landlords and bosses as exploitative, cruel, and decadent and the popular classes as alienated but with elements of solidarity and hopes for social change. This movie marked the distinctive engagement of the Cinema Novo group with social issues that flourished during the 1960s. Diegues radicalized his ideas and social vision, presenting a portrayal of the brutality of seventeenth-century slavery and Afro-Brazilian resistance in *Ganga Zumba* (1963) that was in tune with the leftist ideas of the CPCs and a political atmosphere permeated by the anti-colonial ideas of Frantz Fanon. From the mid-1960s, divergences of opinion about engaged art led Diegues and other Cinema Novo members to distance themselves from the CPC and leftist groups, creating a more sophisticated aesthetic language and demonstrating a more commercial sensibility.

LATER WORK

Amidst the growing repression of the dictatorship in Brazil after 1968, the experiment of the CPC disappeared, and Diegues and the cinemanovistas transformed their project in content and aesthetics.

Diegues made *Joana Francesa* (Joanne the Frenchwoman) in 1975, at a moment of extreme repression. In this film, the author depicted the decadence of a family belonging to the Northeastern aristocracy of Alagoas that disappeared as a consequence of modernization. *Xica da Silva*, made at a moment of opening in Brazilian cultural and intellectual life in 1976, told the story of an eighteenth-century black slave woman who gained power through a liaison with a rich Portuguese official of the Crown. The film gave rise to a significant debate in the public sphere about the depiction of black characters, the relationship between art and politics, and the public role of the intellectuals. Leftist critics judged the film banal and less complex than his previous films dealing with racial themes.

Intellectuals such as Roberto da Matta and Gilberto Freire, the critic Paulo Emílio Salles Gomes (1916–1977), and the filmmaker Glauber Rocha (1938–1981) participated in the discussion. The controversy persisted and increased with the release of his movie *Chuvas de verão* (Summer Rains) in 1978, when some of the former Cinema Novo filmmakers were accused by leftist intellectuals of being co-opted by the cultural industry and abandoning their old ideas about art and politics. In 1984 he made *Quilombo*, continuing his representation of Brazil's endemic racial issues. The film sustained the process opened with *Ganga Zumba*. Where in the first film the slaves escaped from the plantation to Palmares (a community of runaway slaves), in *Quilombo* the black women and men built a new community. As in *Xica da Silva*, Diegues depicted Afro-Brazilian culture imbued with carnivalesque images, creating at certain moments a romantic idea of slavery and the Afro-Brazilian condition. An idealistic vision of poverty and blackness in the favelas (slums) pervades his later works, especially *Orfeu* (1999).

Creative, passionate, and controversial, Diegues has been a major figure in modern Brazilian cinema. He has built a personal representation of the popular in his movies that eclectically combines elements of mass culture, folklore, popular culture, and high culture far from his former ideas about the popular classes' culture.

See also **Cinema: From the Silent Film to 1990; Cinema: Since 1990; Cinema Novo; Rocha, Glauber; Santos, Nelson Pereira dos.**

BIBLIOGRAPHY

Diegues, Carlos. *Cacá Diegues: Os filmes que não filmei.* Interviewed by Silvia Oroz. Rio de Janeiro: Rocco, 1984.

Johnson, Randal. *Cinema Novo x 5: Masters of Contemporary Brazilian Film.* Austin: University of Texas Press, 1984.

Stam, Robert. *Tropical Multiculturalism: A Comparative History of Race in Brazilian Cinema and Culture.* Durham, NC: Duke University Press, 1997.

PAULA HALPERIN

DIESELDORFF, ERWIN PAUL (1868–1940). Erwin Paul Dieseldorff (*b.* 10 June 1868; *d.* 3 November 1940), German-born coffee planter and merchant in the Alta Verapaz, Guatemala. A member of a wealthy Hamburg family active in trade with Central America, Dieseldorff worked for three years in his uncle's export firm in London before going to Guatemala in 1888 to search for investment opportunities. On the advice of relatives who had preceded him, he engaged in the production and export of coffee. He acquired properties from the Polochic River to the Petén and became the largest private landowner in Guatemala. His coffee business was vertically integrated with plantations that served different complementary functions. Dieseldorff had a lifelong interest in and wrote extensively about the Maya and the medicinal plants of the Alta Verapaz.

See also **Coffee Industry.**

BIBLIOGRAPHY

Erwin P. Dieseldorff, *Der Kaffeebaum* (1908), *Kunst und Religion der Mayavölker,* 3 vols. (1926–1933), and *Las plantas medicinales del Departamento de Alta Verapaz* (1940).

Guillermo Náñez Falcón, "Erwin Paul Dieseldorff, German Entrepreneur in the Alta Verapaz of Guatemala, 1889–1937" (Ph.D. diss., Tulane University, 1970).

Additional Bibliography

Kit, Wade A. "Costumbre Conflict and Consensus Kekchi-finquero Discourse in the Alta Verapaz, Guatemala, 1880–1930." Ph.D. diss., Tulane University, 1998.

GUILLERMO NÁÑEZ FALCÓN

DIET. *See* **Cuisines; Food and Cookery; Nutrition.**

DIEZMO.

Diezmo (tithe; in Portuguese, *dízimo*), an ecclesiastical tax of 10 percent levied on agricultural production. The tithe has biblical roots but came to be the standard level of support of the Catholic Church by the faithful. As the tithe was implemented in the Hispanic Americas it was levied only on agricultural and pastoral production: of a harvest of ten bushels of wheat, for instance, one bushel would be paid to the church; of ten lambs born in a given year, one would go to the church. Usually the tithe was paid on the raw material produced. Bulk wool was subject to the tithe, not woven cloth. Nevertheless, sugar was taxed, not cane. Generally all Christians were subject to the tithe. In Mexico, however, the practice evolved to require that natives pay only on three things (*tres cosas*): silk, wheat, and cattle. In other regions natives had to pay on all European products, but not on native goods, whereas in other regions they were fully liable.

The tithe could be collected directly by the ecclesiastical authorities, yet often the right to collect the tithe was rented to local contractors. By renting out the collection, the church received slightly less income, but with little or no delay. When the church collected the tithe directly, it often took quite a long time to complete collections for a given year, but it also gave the church more income and an opportunity to speculate in local commodity markets.

The tithe was used for the support of the ecclesiastical hierarchy under the local bishop or archbishop. According to the scheme under which the tithe was divided, one quarter went to the bishop and one quarter to the cathedral chapter. The remaining half was divided into nine parts, with two parts going to the king as patron, four to the local curates, and the remaining three divided equally between the local hospital and the cathedral for its upkeep.

The tithe in Brazil was controlled by the Portuguese crown. The right to collect and administer the tithe in Portuguese overseas possessions had been granted to the military-religious Order of Christ (Ordem de Cristo). Consequently, the tithe collected in Brazil was then sent to Portugal, where crown officials divided it, returning part to Brazil to support the local church.

See also **Catholic Church: The Colonial Period.**

BIBLIOGRAPHY

John F. Schwaller, *Origins of Church Wealth in Mexico: Ecclesiastical Revenues and Church Finances, 1523–1600* (1985).

Additional Bibliography

Brading, D. A. *Church and State in Bourbon Mexico: The Diocese of Michoacán, 1749-1810.* New York: Cambridge University Press, 1994.

Ferreira, Tito Lívio. *A Ordem de Cristo e o Brasil.* São Paulo: Instituição Brasileira de Difusão Cultural, 1980.

Jaramillo Magaña, Juvenal. *Hacia una iglesia beligerante: La gestión espiscopal de Fray Antonio de San Miguel en Michoacán, 1784-1804.* Zamora: El Colegio de Michoacán, 1996.

JOHN F. SCHWALLER

DIHIGO, MARTÍN (1906–1971).

One of the most famous Latin American baseball players of all time, Martín Dihigo of Cuba is the only player to have been elected to all three Baseball Halls of Fame in Cuba, Mexico, and the United States. Throughout his career, Dihigo was known for his great strength and speed and his ability to play almost any position on the field.

Born on May 25, 1906, in the town of Cidra in Cuba's Matanzas Province, Dihigo began playing professional baseball as a substitute infielder for the Havana team of the Cuban League when he was only sixteen years old. In 1923 he went to the United States for summer baseball, where he played first base for the Cuban Stars in the Negro Leagues. (Because he played before Jackie Robinson broke the baseball color barriers in 1947, he was eligible only for segregated black teams.) Dihigo continued to play with the Negro Leagues through 1936, moving through all nine positions on the field.

Dihigo later played throughout Latin America, most often as a pitcher with an infamous fastball. He threw the first no-hitter in the history of the Mexican baseball league as well as no-hitters in Venezuela and Puerto Rico. In Mexico he was given the nickname "El Maestro" (the master); in Cuba he was called "El Inmortal" (the immortal one.) After retiring from the baseball field, Dihigo served as Cuba's minister of sport. He died on May 20, 1971, in Cienfuegos, Cuba.

See also **Sports.**

BIBLIOGRAPHY

Bjarkman, Peter C. *A History of Cuban Baseball, 1864–2006.* Jefferson, NC: McFarland, 2007.

Santana Alonso, Alfredo. *El inmortal del béisbol: Martín Dihigo.* Ciudad de la Habana: Editorial Científico-Técnica, 1997.

Wilson, Nick. *Early Latino Ballplayers in the United States: Major, Minor, and Negro Leagues, 1901–1949.* Jefferson, NC: McFarland, 2005.

EMILY BERQUIST

DIOMEDE, MIGUEL (1902–1974).

Miguel Diomede (*b.* 20 July 1902; *d.* 15 October 1974), Argentine painter. Diomede was born in La Boca, an Italian bohemian neighborhood on the outskirts of Buenos Aires, where he lived and worked all his life, except for a short trip to Italy in 1954. A self-taught artist, he earned a living in humble jobs (street photographer, stevedore, hospital orderly, ship painter). He received several awards, including the first prize at the Salón de La Plata in Buenos Aires Province, 1957, and the bronze medal at the International Exhibition of Brussels, 1958. In 1959 he had a show at the Organization of American States in Washington, D.C. He became a member of the National Academy of Fine Arts in Buenos Aires in 1973. In 1974, two months before his death, he had a retrospective exhibition at the Galería LAASa in Buenos Aires.

The Argentine critic Damián Bayón called Diomede "one of the great melancholics," comparing his style to that of Eugenio Daneri. Diomede's work is marked by soft tones and large-scale composition. The elegance of his still lifes is immediately suggestive of the Italian Giorgio Morandi. He had a refined perception of reality and a soft sense of rhythm.

BIBLIOGRAPHY

Museum of Modern Art of Latin America (1985).

Vincente Gesualdo, Aldo Biglione, and Rodolfo Santos, *Diccionario de artistas plásticos en la Argentina* (1988).

AMALIA CORTINA ARAVENA

DIRETÓRIO DOS ÍNDIOS.

Diretório dos Índios (Indian directorate), a legislative code (1757–1798) that secularized the administration of Indian mission villages in Portuguese America. As part of the Pombaline Reforms, the Diretório initially sought to weaken Jesuit economic influence in the Amazon, but in 1758 the code was extended to all of Brazil. To replace the missionaries, local governors appointed lay directors who were to stimulate settled agriculture, encourage mixed marriages, and facilitate the adoption of the Portuguese language and customs. The code was strengthened by other decrees, such as the elevation of missions to the status of *vilas* (towns) in 1758 and the expulsion of the Jesuits in 1759. In practice, the directors frequently disregarded Diretório guidelines and, entitled to one-sixth of the villages' output, organized forced-labor drafts and abusive collecting expeditions for personal gain.

As a "civilizing" project, the Diretório failed miserably. It was, in effect, more interested in the exploitation of native labor than in the development of a social program. As a result, the Diretório period proved disastrous for the Indians, as village populations declined, communal lands were usurped, and ethnic identity became eroded. Repeated complaints of corruption and abuses led to the abolition of the Diretório in 1798.

BIBLIOGRAPHY

Colin Mac Lachlan, "The Indian Directorate. Forced Acculturation in Portuguese America," in *The Americas* 28 (1972): 357–387, provides a detailed treatment, with particular emphasis on the Amazon. A more general discussion may be found in John Hemming, *Amazon Frontier* (1987).

Additional Bibliography

Anderson, Robin L. *Colonization As Exploitation in the Amazon Rain Forest, 1758–1911.* Gainesville: University Press of Florida, 1999.

Queiroz, Jonas Marçal de, and Mauro Cezar Coelho. *Amazónia: modernização e conflito, séculos XVIII e XIX.* Belém: Universidade Federal do Pará, 2001.

JOHN M. MONTEIRO

DIRTY WAR.

Dirty war (guerra sucia) is the term used in Argentina by supporters of the last military dictatorship to characterize the clandestine terrorist repression carried out by the state between 1976 and 1983. They claim that an unconventional war was waged during those years between two

In Buenos Aires, citizens and mothers protest the disappearance of their relatives, late 1970s. Argentina's military carried out state-sponsored kidnapping, torture, and murder of citizens considered "dissidents" during the period known as the Dirty War between 1976 and 1983. Due to the absence of a body, victims were declared "disappeared." © BETTMANN/CORBIS

equally matched, armed organizations, and that the military government may have committed occasional "excesses" during that time.

In fact, what occurred was a campaign of clandestine, state-sponsored terrorism. Its nature and scope first came to light in 1982, when the military regime began to fall apart. In 1985 the National Commission for the Disappeared (Comisión Nacional para la Desaparición de las Personas, or CONADEP), created under the democratic government, carried out an in-depth investigation of what had taken place since 1976. The findings of this investigation served as the basis for the prosecution and conviction of those military officers who were chiefly responsible for the repression. It became clear that the "dirty war" was a deliberate and precisely planned program carried out by the armed forces. The modus operandi typically began with the kidnapping of a suspect, who was then tortured to obtain information that would help in the arrest of

others, confined in a concentration camp where torture continued, and usually finally killed—this had to be ordered by one of the highest-ranking military officers. Either the body was concealed in a clandestine grave or the prisoner was thrown out of an airplane over the Atlantic Ocean while still alive. In either case, the absence of a body gave victims the status of "disappeared." CONADEP managed to gather evidence in about 10,000 cases; human rights organizations claim that there were at least 30,000 victims. One particularly horrifying aspect of the repression was that babies born to victims in captivity were given new identities and turned over to families with ties to the repressors.

The CONADEP report led many to refer to those who had suffered state-sponsored terrorism as "innocent victims of repression." This label was connected with the demands of building a democracy from 1984. However, since 2000 many of the victims have been acknowledged as militant activists who fought against the dictatorship. Moreover, it became clear that clandestine state terrorism began in 1975, or even in 1974, as part of the conflict between Peronist factions. In any case, from the mid-1960s, Argentine society was engulfed in a growing wave of violence, and virtually all those who participated in any of these conflicts called for violence, justified it, or saw it as natural. The victims of repression included many individuals who had little or nothing to do with the social and political conflicts; some were targets of personal revenge. Trade union members and social activists of all types suffered, along with academics, journalists, students, and members of the clergy. But there were also many who had ties to armed organizations, particularly the People's Revolutionary Army (Ejército Revolucionario del Pueblo, or ERP) and the Montoneros, or were linked to their related front groups such as the Peronist Youth (Juventud Peronista).

The clandestine repression was deliberately arbitrary, and it combined the open spectacle of the kidnappings with the secret nature of the victims' final destinations. Not only did the repression seek to eliminate all types of dissidents, it also aimed to strike fear into the hearts of the remainder of the population and silence any opposition. It met with great success at the start: Many people parroted military slogans about "wiping out the unpatriotic subversives," and few voices were raised in opposition. The most notable dissident voices came from human rights organizations, particularly the Mothers of the Plaza de Mayo, an association of mothers of "disappeared" persons who began demonstrating in 1977 on the plaza in front of the presidential palace. These exceptionally courageous women managed to find and exploit tiny cracks in the dense discourse of the oppressors. Their demands for the return of their children touched a core of deeply rooted human values that kept them from being written off by the military dictatorship as "subversives."

See also **Argentina, Truth Commissions; Human Rights; Truth Commissions.**

BIBLIOGRAPHY

Nunca más. *Informe de la Comisión Nacional sobre la Desaparición de Personas.* Buenos Aires: Eudeba, 1984.

Quiroga, Hugo. *El tiempo del "Proceso": Conflictos y coincidencias entre políticos y militares, 1976–1983.* 2nd edition. Rosario, Argentina: Homo Sapiens, 2004.

Vezzetti, Hugo. *Pasado y presente: Guerra, dictadura y sociedad en la Argentina.* Buenos Aires: Siglo Veintiuno Editores Argentina, 2002.

LUIS ALBERTO ROMERO

DISCÉPOLO, ENRIQUE SANTOS

(1901–1951). Enrique Santos Discépolo (*b.* 27 March 1901; *d.* 23 December 1951), Argentine radio commentator, movie director, and composer of tangos. Born in Buenos Aires and the brother of the neogrotesque dramatist Armando Discépolo, Enrique Santos was known as "Discepolín" to distinguish him from Armando. Discépolo participated fully in the enormous expansion of commercial popular culture based in Buenos Aires in the golden years following World War I and the 1930 watershed marked by economic collapse and the country's first fascist-inspired military dictatorship. A radio personality of considerable note and a successful movie director, Discépolo also wrote some of the most famous tangos of the period, compositions that have become an integral part of the classical repertoire: "¿Qué vachaché?" "Esta noche me emborracho," "¿Qué sapa, señor?" "Chorra," and, perhaps one of the most famous tango lyrics of all time, "Cambalache." The latter was banned by the military dictatorship in the late 1970s because of its harshly pessimistic tone, which was interpreted as socially disruptive.

See also **Tango.**

BIBLIOGRAPHY

Horacio Arturo Ferrer and Luis Adolfo Sierra, *Discepolín* (1965).

Norberto Galasso, *Discépolo y su época* (1967).

Homero Manzi, *Discépolo* (1973).

Osvaldo Pellettieri, *Tango (II)* (1976).

Additional Bibliography

Ferrer, Horacio Arturo, and Luis Adolfo Sierra. *Discepolín: Poeta del hombre que está solo y espera.* Buenos Aires: Editorial Sudamericana, 2004.

Gálvez, Lucía, and Enrique Espina Rawson. *Romances de tango.* Buenos Aires: Grupo Editorial Norma, 2002.

Tahier, Julio, Pedro G. Orgambide, Juan Carlos Ghiano, et al. *Tango y teatro*. Buenos Aires: Fundación Autores Editorial La Abeja, 2004.

DAVID WILLIAM FOSTER

DISEASES. Prior to the voyages of Columbus, the Americas, by no means disease-free, had not encountered many of the devastating illnesses prevalent in Europe, Asia, and Africa. The Indians suffered from some forms of trypanosomiasis—pinta to be sure, and perhaps yaws—but according to recent bioanthropological research, probably not syphilis. They had tuberculosis, hepatitis, and encephalitis, and a variety of intestinal parasites afflicted them as well. In certain locations, the distinctly American illnesses of Carrion's disease (Andean region) and American trypanosomiasis, or Chagas's disease, as it is more commonly known (tropical South and Central America), were in evidence.

In the past it has been argued that malaria and yellow fever were resident in the Western Hemisphere prior to contact with the wider world. But today, combined immunological, epidemiological, and etymological as well as historical evidence reveal these to be imported illnesses, as were a host of other maladies, including smallpox, chicken pox, measles, whooping cough, diphtheria, mumps, typhus, typhoid fever, scarlet fever, influenza, and bubonic plague, to name but a few of the most prominent of the diseases to which the Amerindians proved extraordinarily susceptible.

The Amerindians avoided these diseases due to protracted isolation from the rest of the world. Beginning some 180 million years ago, long before humankind made its appearance on the globe, first South America and then North America broke free of Pangaea, the primordial supercontinent, gradually to work their way into their current locations. The animals that sailed with them presumably carried pathogens. But those were the days when reptiles—dinosaurs and the like—were dominant, and as they perished it is likely that most of their diseases perished with them.

Homo sapiens emerged some 40,000 years ago to spread out over the Old World as far as Siberia, and there is speculation based on genetic evidence that Polynesian voyagers in sea-going canoes may have reached the Americas. Certainly during the last ice age, when the oceans were low, other bold pioneers set out on the frozen tundra that formed a land bridge between Asia and Alaska. They probably crossed in small groups over millennia. About 10,000 years ago when the ice caps melted, the seas rose to seal off the Americas once again.

While some pathogens might have made it into the Americas, when the continents were connected, the pioneers who crossed the Bering Straits came as bands of hunter-gatherers whose restless lifestyle and small numbers were not supportive of most of the diseases that have more recently assaulted humans who became sedentary and crowded together. Moreover, the long trek through harsh weather presumably would have weeded out those who were ill. And finally, the new Americans arrived before humans had begun domesticating animals, a process that introduced literally hundreds of illnesses.

The Amerindians hence had little experience with disease, but, the Iberians who first reached the Americas had perhaps the most sophisticated immune systems of any people on earth. A series of invaders from the Romans to the Muslims had exposed the people of the peninsula to the diseases of vast empires extending throughout much of the Eurasian landmass. Also, their own exploration of the African coast as well as contact with the African slaves they brought back to Europe had exposed them to many of the diseases of that continent as well. The port cities of Iberia had long been the clearinghouse of diseases, and its towns and cities were open sewers abounding with disease-bearing rodents and insects, while the Iberians' lack of hygiene encouraged the presence of lice, fleas, and intestinal parasites.

We may never know with certainty what pathogens launched the first New World epidemic that was killing Arawaks in the Caribbean as early as 1493, but swine influenza has been put forth as a likely candidate. The *modorra* that assaulted Spaniards (and presumably Indians as well) on the Spanish Main a bit later on produced symptoms that suggest typhus. Smallpox had arrived in the Caribbean at least by 1518, swept through Mexico between the years 1520 and 1524, and then raced on to precede Pizarro into the land of the Incas. By 1554, it had penetrated southward as far as Chile to mount assaults on the disappeared until 1849, when it was omnipresent until the end of the century. Because survivors of yellow fever cannot host the disease a second time, the significant numbers reported as resistant to the illness in both the 1685 and the 1849 epidemics suggest that yellow fever was in the country prior to 1685 and had returned prior to 1849.

This combination of diseases brought extermination to the Indians in the islands of the Caribbean and adjacent low-lying mainlands, and depopulation to the Amazon valley. In the higher elevations of the mainland, by contrast, the colder temperatures were not condusive to the mosquito vectors of yellow fever and malaria. Indian populations reeled under the onslaught of illnesses but, without the added burden of the tropical plagues, ultimately recovered.

Yellow fever and malaria afflicted whites to the same extent as they did Indians, while sparing blacks, who possessed acquired protection against them. The immunities of blacks to disease thus created an accelerating demand for African workers, and the ships that carried them also brought schistosomiasis, onchocerciasis, leishmaniasis, filariasis, hookworm disease, dengue fever, yaws, and a host of other African ailments, which settled onto the American tropics.

Cholera, originating in India during the nineteenth century, swept the globe in five pandemics. The Americas were hit by four of these; the first, in the 1830s, was limited to Cuba (and North America), but the remaining three devastated much of the Caribbean and Latin America, leaving hundreds of thousands of dead in their wake. The great epidemic of 1855–1856 in Brazil may have killed up to 200,000 individuals in that country alone, while in the Caribbean the disease rolled over island after island during the 1850s.

The last few decades of the nineteenth century and the first decades of the twentieth century saw the discovery of beriberi as a significant health problem in Cuba and especially in Brazil, but the turn of the century also brought with it dramatic advances against many old scourges. Carlos Finlay and the Yellow Fever Commission of Walter Reed unraveled much of the riddle of yellow fever's epidemiology and etiology, and yellow fever was stopped in Cuba. Subsequently, William Gorgas applied mosquito-control measures in Panama, which greatly facilitated

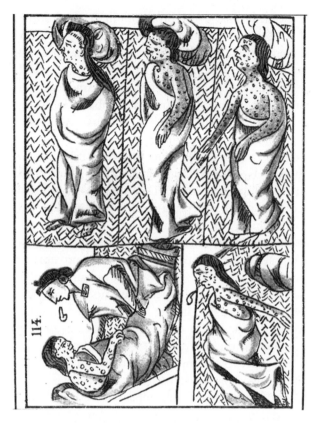

Smallpox victims in New Spain. Plate 114 from *Historia de las cosas de Nueva Espana* (also known as the Florentine Codex) by Bernardino de Sahagún, 16th century. Lacking previous exposure to European diseases, indigenous communities were ravaged by smallpox and other epidemics that swept through colonial Latin America. AKG LONDON. REPRODUCED BY PERMISSION

Araucanians. Measles hammered the Caribbean in 1529 and then spread to Mexico and Central America. A pandemic in 1545 that the Aztecs called *matlazáhuatl* was probably typhus or influenza. Diphtheria was another important killer of the Indians, and there is evidence that bubonic plague as well may have visited the New World in the sixteenth century.

Vivax malaria probably arrived in the blood of the first Europeans, whereas the far more deadly falciparum malaria, a tropical disease prevalent in Africa, reached the Americas through the slave trade. Yellow fever, another tropical disease, also rode the slave ships from Africa, but its debut was delayed until populations of its mosquito vector (which also required importation) and human hosts became sufficiently dense. The first recorded epidemic of yellow fever in the Caribbean is that which began in Barbados in 1647. Yellow fever is said to have occurred in Brazil between the years 1685 and 1694, to have the construction of the canal. In Rio de Janeiro, Oswaldo Cruz led successful campaigns against bubonic plague (which had broken out in 1899) and yellow fever, and soon mosquito-control programs had curbed yellow fever almost everywhere in the hemisphere. Effective control of the mosquito vectors of malaria, however, had to await DDT, which was widely used only after World War II.

Programs funded by the Rockefeller Foundation were launched early in the twentieth century to combat such diseases as hookworm infection and yellow fever. These attempts fell far short of the ambitious goal of eradication but represented important steps in controlling such diseases. In the case of yellow fever, Rockefeller researchers in Brazil discovered that the disease was alive in the monkey inhabitants of the great South American rain forest. With this knowledge came the realization that yellow fever was really a disease of monkeys that incidentally infected humans, and since the monkeys could not all be killed, the disease could not be eradicated but only controlled.

Over the course of the nineteenth century, tuberculosis became an ever-increasing threat to the health of Latin Americans, especially those of African descent. The disease generated mortality rates as high as 1,000 per 100,000 population in cities such as Bahia and Havana. After the turn of the century, however, tuberculosis began to fade slowly and by mid-century it was no longer an important threat, at least until very recently when strains of tuberculosis resistant to antibiotics have become menacing worldwide, and other strains are taking advantage of compromised immune systems.

Modern medicine can claim no credit for the decline of tuberculosis in the hemisphere, but medicine has made considerable headway against neonatal tetanus (once a massive killer of infants) and childhood diseases ranging from diphtheria to rubella. Yet far too many Latin Americans have little or no access to modern medicine, and thus in many places the circumstances of poverty with attendant malnutrition intertwine with pathogens in synergystic fashion to produce very high levels of morbidity and mortality. Protein-energy malnutrition, especially kwashiorkor, affects the young, while a variety of deficiency diseases can be found in those of all ages. Nor has the hemisphere been freed from the threat of epidemic diseases both ancient and modern.

Bubonic plague, which broke out in Ecuador during the first decade of the twentieth century, remained endemic there until well into the 1930s. In 1994, cholera once more returned to the Americas, spreading from Peru throughout the South American continent, in an epidemic that will probably kill thousands. In the late twentieth century, AIDS was widespread in Haiti and Brazil and threatened to become a serious problem throughout the hemisphere. As of 2006, an estimated 2 million people in the region have the AIDS virus. Brazil, Mexico, Colombia and Argentina make up more than half that number. In the Caribbean the infection rate stands at about two percent of the population. In Central American countries the rate is approximately one percent. While AIDS cases remain a public health concern, many experts have noted that AIDS has not been as devastating in Latin America as elsewhere. Public health researchers credit this positive outcome to the emergence of civil society, international agencies for providing education, and antiviral drugs. Together these mechanisms have helped limit the spread and the impact of AIDS, despite poverty, limited resources, and sometimes weak governments. However, many questions remain. Scientists, for instance, still do not know why Honduras has a much higher AIDS rate than neighboring Nicaragua or why Bolivia, a very poor country, has a low rate of infection. Consequently, scientists and health officials have begun to look at the interplay of social, cultural, and economic issues in the spread of diseases.

Indeed, scholars have examined how culture, race, and nation have influenced diagnosis, treatment, and public health policy. Some scientists have blamed the poor for contracting disease. Bubonic plague outbreaks in early twentieth-century Peru largely affected the poor, but often the state castigated the victims of the disease rather than seeking out a cure or better treatment. During the cholera outbreaks of the 1990s, many analysts suggested that public health administrators placed too much of an emphasis on individual responsibility, rather than addressing larger societal problems that created the conditions for cholera's spread. AIDS treatment in Latin America, as in the United States, involves differing values concerning sexuality.

Other academics have looked at how local traditions affect public health policy. In nineteenth century Costa Rica, government doctors relied on local popular healers to distribute medicine, because they often worked in remote areas of the country where few doctors would go and had greater credibility in small localities. Thus, public policy had to accommodate local customs to succeed.

The history of diseases challenges many of the stereotypes regarding Latin America. Commentators have assumed that ideas of modern medicine flowed from North America and Europe to developing countries. However, historical works have shown how Latin American scientists made important discoveries, insights, and innovations in the treatment of diseases. In nineteenth century Brazil, European and Brazilian doctors studying in the northeastern part of the country wrote papers countering ideas of Brazil's natural racial inferiority as a reason for disease. Thus, these physicians challenged much of the racist thinking which was popular in Europe at the time. Costa Rican doctors in the twentieth century identified hookworm induced anemia as one of the primary causes of sickness among rural labor and got the Rockefeller Foundation to follow its agenda. Locals identified the problem rather than being guided by international groups. While trying to provide better health care, Latin American scientists and physicians have made important, albeit sometimes unnoticed, advances in the treatment of diseases.

See also **Acquired Immune Deficiency Syndrome (AIDS); Medicinal Plants; Medicine: Colonial Spanish America; Medicine: The Modern Era.**

BIBLIOGRAPHY

Percy Moreau Ashburn, *The Ranks of Death: A Medical History of the Conquest of America* (1947).

Erwin H. Ackerknecht, *History and Geography of the Most Important Diseases* (1965).

Donald B. Cooper, *Epidemic Diseases in Mexico City, 1761–1813* (1965).

Lyeurgo De Castro Santos Filho, *História geral da medicina brasileira,* 2 vols. (1977).

Noble David Cook, *Demographic Collapse: Indian Peru, 1520–1620* (1981).

Kenneth F. Kiple, *The Caribbean Slave: A Biological History* (1984).

Alfred W. Crosby, *Ecological Imperialism: The Biological Expansion of Europe, 900–1900* (1986).

Guenter B. Risse, "Medicine in New Spain," in *Medicine in the New World: New Spain, New France, and New England,* edited by Ronald L. Numbers (1987).

Additional Bibliography

Armus, Diego. *Disease in the History of Modern Latin America from Malaria to AIDS.* Durham, NC: Duke University Press, 2003.

Armus, Diego. *Entre médicos y curanderos cultura, historia y enfermedad en la América Latina moderna.* Buenos Aires: Grupo Editorial Norma, 2002.

Guy, Donna J. *White Slavery and Mothers Alive and Dead: The Troubled Meeting of Sex, Gender, Public Health, and Progress in Latin America.* Lincoln: University of Nebraska Press, 2000.

Peard, Julyan G. *Race, Place, and Medicine: The Idea of the Tropics in Nineteenth Century Brazilian Medicine.* Durham, NC: Duke University Press, 1999.

KENNETH F. KIPLE
BYRON CRITES

DISTENSÃO. Distensão, the policy of decompression, or political liberalization, pursued by the Brazilian regime of General Ernesto Geisel during the late 1970s. Through a careful manipulation of the *distensão* process, the military government implemented democratic reforms.

In November 1974, President Geisel allowed an open election in which the opposition party, the Brazilian Democratic Movement (MDB), made substantial gains. The election results convinced Geisel that political liberalization would have to occur slowly in order to prevent the overthrow of his moderate military faction. To avoid future electoral surprises, President Geisel suspended Congress on 1 April 1977 for fifteen days and issued a decree providing for the indirect election of state governors and one-third of the federal senators. Ensured of keeping the government's party, the National Renovating Alliance (ARENA), in power, Geisel proceeded to dismantle components of the government's authoritarian structure.

Under the provisions of an executive-sponsored constitutional amendment in 1978, the regime stopped its censorship of the print media, reinstated habeas corpus for political detainees, and abolished the fifth Institutional Act, thereby ending the president's authority to suspend Congress, remove congressmen, and deny citizens their political rights.

Although the government retained significant arbitrary powers during Geisel's term, the *distensão* period prepared the way for the opening to democracy under General João Batista Figueiredo.

See also **Abertura; Brazil, Political Parties: Brazilian Democratic Movement (MDB); Brazil, Political Parties: National Renovating Alliance (ARENA).**

BIBLIOGRAPHY

Maria Helena Moreira Alves, *State and Opposition in Military Brazil* (1985).

Thomas Skidmore, *The Politics of Military Rule in Brazil, 1964–1985* (1988).

Alfred Stepan, *Rethinking Military Politics* (1988).

Additional Bibliography

Mathias, Suzeley Kalil. *A distensão no Brasil: O projeto militar, 1973–1979*. Campinas: Papirus Editora, 1995.

Salles, Severo. *Ditadura e luta pela democracia no Brasil: O início da distensão política (1974–1979)*. Salvador, Bahia: Quarteto, 2003.

MICHAEL POLL

DITELLA, GUIDO (1931–2001). Guido

DiTella, an Argentine politician and economist, was his country's minister of foreign affairs from 1991 to 1999. A son of the industrial magnate Torcuato DiTella (1892–1947), Guido graduated with an engineering degree from the National University of Buenos Aires and continued his studies in the United States at the Massachusetts Institute of Technology. During his university days he was an anti-Peronist activist, but after the 1955 coup d'état he became more closely allied to the movement headed by Juan Domingo Perón. With the Peronists back in power in 1973, DiTella was appointed director of the National Arts Foundation (Fondo Nacional de las Artes). During María Estela Martínez de Perón's brief term in office (1974–1976), he was deputy minister of the economy under Minister Antonio Cafiero. The military coup of 1976 led to death threats against DiTella, and he left for England.

DiTella returned to Argentina following the collapse of the de facto government in 1982. As a member of the so-called "Peronist renewal movement," he was elected a national deputy for the Justicialista Party, and in 1989 the newly elected president Carlos Saúl Menem named him ambassador to the United States. In February 1991 he was appointed minister of foreign affairs. DiTella's foreign policy, closely linked to economic policies of liberalization and open markets, was characterized by a strategic identification with the United States and the western powers that distanced it from the traditional nationalism of the Peronist movement. Argentina supported the United States in strategic areas, by participating in the 1991 Gulf War (even before DiTella joined the Ministry of Foreign Affairs) and openly supporting the White House in the Middle East. Argentina declared that it would refrain from using nuclear energy for military purposes, and deactivated the Condor II missile. Its "special relationship" with the United States enabled Argentina to attain the status of major non-NATO ally in 1998. During the prolonged conflict with Great Britain over the Falkland Islands (Islas Malvinas), DiTella put into practice an innovative policy of rapprochement with the islanders (inappropriately called a "policy of seduction") that sparked controversy at the Argentine local level.

See also **Argentina: The Twentieth Century; Argentina, Political Parties: Justicialist Party; Falkland Islands (Malvinas); Menem, Carlos Saúl; Perón, Juan Domingo; Perón, María Estela Martínez de.**

BIBLIOGRAPHY

Cisneros, Andrés, ed. *Política exterior argentina 1989–1999. Historia de un éxito*. Buenos Aires: Grupo Editor Latinoamericano/NuevoHacer, 1998.

Hirst, Mónica, ed. *Continuidad y cambio en las relaciones América Latina–Estados Unidos*. Buenos Aires: Grupo Editor Latinoamericano, 1987.

Palermo, Vicente, and Marcos Novaro. *Política y poder en el gobierno de Menem*. Buenos Aires: Norma, 1996.

VICENTE PALERMO

DITELLA, TORCUATO (1892–1948).

Torcuato DiTella (*b.* 15 May 1892; *d.* 22 July 1948), Argentine entrepreneur. Until age thirteen DiTella lived in Italy, at which time his family immigrated to Argentina. His entrepreneurial career was launched in 1910, when he linked his market study of the demand for dough-kneading machines to a mechanic who could build a machine capable of competing with imported technology. Operating from a converted garage, the fledgling business, which would eventually operate under the name S.I.A.M. (Sección Industria Amasadoras Mecánicas), expanded rapidly over the next five years.

DiTella's entrepreneurial career was interrupted by service with the Italian army in World War I. In 1919 he returned to Argentina, where he confronted a stagnant economy, sluggish market, and volatile labor force. The protectionist economic policies of the government and a labor policy that ranged from firing troublesome personnel to co-opting others through promotion allowed DiTella to overcome the difficulties. With an unmatched ability to take advantage of every opportunity and to anticipate markets, he expanded his operations. Gasoline pumps were added to bakery machinery, and by the end of the 1920s S.I.A.M.'s success was symbolic of the emergence of industry in Argentina. Management became the province of the extended DiTella family, which could be trusted to administer and operate the company. DiTella expanded his operations to Brazil, Chile, Uruguay, and, for a while, London. By the end of the 1930s, S.I.A.M. had diversified into household appliances. Operating in the style of a *patrón*, DiTella the man became "an integrating symbol for the company."

As a successful businessman, DiTella was sought out for a variety of national and international roles. He fought against the spread of fascism, both in Italy and Argentina, wrote several books, represented Argentina at important international meetings, and between 1944 and 1948 was a professor of economics and industrial organization at the University of Buenos Aires. He was a patron of the arts and owner of an experimental dairy farm.

See also **Argentina, Organizations: American Industrial Society for Machinery (SIAM).**

BIBLIOGRAPHY

Thomas C. Cochran and Ruben E. Reina, *Entrepreneurship in Argentine Culture: Torcuato Di Tella and S.I.A.M.* (1962).

Guido Di Tella, and Manuel Zymelman, *Las etapas del desarrollo económico argentino* (1967).

Additional Bibliography

Alcorta, Rodrigo. "'El Henry Ford argentino': Torquato di Tella; de los Apeninos a los Andes." *Todo Es Historia* 26 (May 1993): 64–67.

Di Tella, Torcuato S. *Torcuato Di Tella: industria y política.* Buenos Aires: Tesis, Grupo Editorial Norma, 1993.

PAUL GOODWIN

DITELLA FOUNDATION.

The Di-Tella Foundation was founded in Buenos Aires in 1958 by the economist Guido DiTella and his brother Torcuato DiTella, a sociologist, with the goal of further developing and reinforcing cultural and scientific creativity in Argentina. That same year the brothers established the DiTella Institute, a center promoting theatrical, musical, and other artistic endeavors, in honor of their father, also named Torcuato DiTella, who owned one of the largest machine manufacturing companies in Latin America, the Sección Industrial de Amasadoras Mecánicas (or SIAM). In 1991 Torcuato DiTella University, also associated with the foundation and the institute, opened in Buenos Aires. The foundation, institute, and the university cooperate in academic matters, including faculty research and conferences. The DiTella brothers personally endowed the foundation, although they conceived it as a corporate institution rather than a private body. At the time the practice of endowing a foundation was uncommon in Argentina. Following the downfall of Juan Domingo Perón in 1955, the DiTellas sought to invigorate an intellectual environment that, to a significant degree, had been suppressed by the Peronist government. The liberalizing policies of the Arturo Frondizi government (1958–1962) proved a fecund setting for the foundation's work, as the state also began dedicating funds to various forms of research and creativity in the humanities, social sciences, and sciences.

After the military coup of 1966, the intellectual openness and creative freedoms once enjoyed by the foundation and its benefactors were severely curtailed by the regime of General Juan Carlos Onganía. Given that the foundation drew on the profits of the DiTella-owned SIAM manufacturing company, the foundation and its related institutions also suffered as a result of the country's poor economic conditions in the late

1960s. During the 1970s the Argentine government seized control of the family's declining business. The foundation and institute managed to survive both financial hardship in the 1960s and the Argentine military dictators, or "Dirty Warriors," who ruled from 1976 to 1983. SIAM ultimately collapsed during the late-1980s. The foundation, however, continues its work in the early twenty-first century.

See also **DiTella, Guido; DiTella, Torcuato; Frondizi, Arturo; Onganía, Juan Carlos; Perón, Juan Domingo.**

BIBLIOGRAPHY

King, John. *El Di Tella y el desarrollo cultural argentino en la década del sesenta*, trans. Carlos Gardini. Buenos Aires: Ediciones de Arte Gaglianone, 1985.

King, John. "El Di Tella and Argentine Cultural Development in the 1960s." *Bulletin of Latin American Research* 1, no. 1 (1981): 105–112.

Plotkin, Mariano, and Federico Neiburg. "Elites intelectuales y ciencias sociales en la Argentina de los años 60: El Instituto Torcuato Di Tella y la Nueva Economía." *Estudios Interdisciplinarios de America Latina y el Caribe* 12, no. 1 (2003): 119–149.

PATRICK BARR-MELEJ

DITTBORN, EUGENIO (1943–). Eugenio Dittborn (*b.* 1943), Chilean artist. Born in Santiago, Dittborn studied painting and printmaking at universities in Chile and Europe from 1962 to 1969. Like many Chilean artists of his generation, he rejects traditional painting and the conservative values he believes it embodies. In the 1970s Dittborn became a leading member of the Avanzada, a group of Chilean artists and critics who developed an artistic language of metaphor and analogy related to conceptual art, in part to criticize General Augusto Pinochet's military dictatorship. In 1983 he produced his first Pinturas Aeropostales (Airmail Paintings), the works for which he has become best known. Consisting of appropriated photographic images, as well as drawings, texts, and objects, applied to wrapping paper and—after 1988—synthetic nonwoven fabric, they are folded in envelopes and airmailed to exhibitions throughout the world. Quintessential examples of the political-conceptual art Dittborn helped pioneer, they address, among other issues, the peripheral condition to which Latin Americans are often subject. Dittborn won the Premio Nacional de Artes Plásticas de Chile in 2005. He lives in Santiago.

See also **Art: The Twentieth Century; Pinochet Ugarte, Augusto.**

BIBLIOGRAPHY

Nelly Richard, "Margins and Institutions: Art in Chile Since 1973," in *Art and Text* 21 (May–June 1986).

Guy Brett, "Eugenio Dittborn," and Eugenio Dittborn, "Correcaminos—Roadrunner," both in Guy Brett, *Transcontinental: An Investigation of Reality. Nine Latin American Artists,* edited by Elizabeth A. Macgregor (1990).

Guy Brett and Sean Cubitt, *Camino Way: The Airmail Paintings of Eugenio Dittborn* (1991).

Mari Carmen Ramírez, "Blueprint Circuits: Conceptual Art and Politics in Latin America," in Museum of Modern Art, *Latin American Artists of the Twentieth Century* (1993).

Additional Bibliography

Goodwin, Alison. "Eugenio Dittborn and the Airmail Paintings: Remembrance in Chile After Pinochet." M.A. thesis, University of California, Santa Barbara, 2006.

Guernsey, Sarah E. "Memorial as a Tool of Dissent in the Work of Three Contemporary Latin American Artists: Doris Salcedo, Eugenio Dittborn, and Guillermo Kuitca." M.A. thesis, School of the Art Institute of Chicago, 2003.

Pastor Mellado, Justo. *Dos textos tácticos.* Santiago, Chile: Jeremy Button Ink, 1998.

JOHN ALAN FARMER

DJUKA. The Djuka are one of six tribes of Maroons (also known as Refugee Blacks or Bush Negroes), descendants of African slaves brought to Suriname as plantation laborers in the late seventeenth century. In the years before emancipation, large groups of slaves escaped from the plantations, and the Djuka settled in southeast Suriname, on the banks of the Ndjuka Creek, in the area between the Marowijne and Tapanahoni Rivers. The Djuka are distinct from other tribes of Maroons in language (they speak the Creole language Ndjuka), history, religion, and cultural traditions. A peace treaty was signed between the Dutch colonists and the Djuka in 1760: In return for autonomy, the Maroons were to abstain from acts of aggression against the plantation colony and not enter negotiations with other groups. After the treaty, the Djuka began to leave their first settlements, moving to new villages along the Tapanahoni River, which they named "River of the Ndjuk." This locale offered access to more resources and the ability to interact with other groups. By the beginning of the 1800s many of the Djuka found work in the colony. Males earned a living as lumberers, and through the timber trade they became a substantial part of the colonial economy.

The colonists felt ambivalent about their presence: Whereas the peace treaty was meant to keep the former slave groups away from the colony, the Djuka became valuable trading partners to the Dutch. The uneasy relationship between the Maroons and the colonial government continued over the years. In 1986 civil unrest between the Surinamese government and the Djuka escalated when a massacre of at least thirty-nine civilians at the Djuka village of Moiwana occurred. In 2005 the Inter-American Court of Human Rights found the Surinamese government guilty of human rights violations for the massacre and ordered reparations to survivors. In the early twenty-first century the Djuka and the Saramaka comprise the largest two Maroon tribes, with estimated populations of 15,000 to 20,000 each.

See also **Maroons (Cimarrones); Suriname and the Dutch in the Caribbean.**

BIBLIOGRAPHY

Huttar, George L., and Mary L. Huttar. *Ndyuka*. London; New York: Routledge, 1994.

Thoden van Velzen, H. U. E, and W. van Wetering. *The Great Father and the Danger: Religious Cults, Material Forces, and Collective Fantasies in the World of the Surinamese Maroons*. Dordrecht, Netherlands; Providence, RI: Foris Publications, 1988.

ALISON FIELDS

DOBLES SEGREDA, LUIS (1891–1956).

A Costa Rican educator, writer, and diplomat, Dobles Segreda was born on January 17, 1891, in Heredia. He attended the Liceo de Costa Rica, where he was mentored by the noted intellectual Joaquín García Monge. In 1910 he began writing articles for the *Havana Post* and founded, with others, the journal *Selenia*. In 1917 he became the director of the Normal School in Heredia, where he also received graduate degrees in geography, philology, and literature. In 1927 he taught in the United States at Marquette University and at the Louisiana State Normal College. He was Costa Rica's minister of education (1926–1928; 1930–1932, 1936) and later served as minister plenipotentiary in Chile, Argentina, Spain, France, Belgium, and the Vatican.

Dobles Segreda wrote fifteen books about Costa Rica, among them *Historia y tradiciones* (1920), *Caña brava* (1926) and his twelve-volume *Indice bibliográfico de Costa Rica* (1927–1935). The Library of Congress purchased his comprehensive collection of books about Costa Rica in 1943 and microfilmed it in 1995. Dobles Segreda served in Costa Rica's constitutional convention on 1948 and in 1950 again represented his country in Spain. A member of the Costa Rican Academy of Language, he was also awarded the Order of Isabel la Católica (Spain) and France's Legion of Honor. Dobles Segreda died in Heredia on October 27, 1956.

See also **Costa Rica.**

BIBLIOGRAPHY

Cordero, Abdenago. *Luis Dobles Segreda*. San José, Costa Rica: Instituto del Libro, Ministerio de Cultura, Juventud y Deportes, 1985.

GEORGETTE MAGASSY DORN

DOBRIZHOFFER, MARTÍN (1717–1791).

Martín Dobrizhoffer (*b.* 7 September 1717; *d.* 17 July 1791), Austrian missionary active in Paraguay. Born in the Bohemian town of Friedburg, Dobrizhoffer studied philosophy and physical sciences at the universities of Vienna and Graz. In 1748, after joining the Jesuits, he was sent to the Río de la Plata region in Argentina, where he finished his education at the University of Córdoba. He then went to work for four years among the Mocobí Indians of Santa Fe. From 1754 to 1762 Dobrizhoffer was stationed at the Jesuit settlements of Paraguay, at Santa María la Mayor on the Uruguay River, where he gained considerable fame as a learned man among his colleagues and among the Guaraní Indians.

In 1762, the royal governor at Asunción mandated the establishment of a new mission some fifty leagues to the west in the most inhospitable area of the Chaco. He ordered Dobrizhoffer to take charge of the mission, called Nuestra Señora del Rosario de Timbó. The Austrian's missionary goal there, the conversion of the "wild" Abipón Indians, eluded him. After many bitter experiences, he abandoned Rosario de Timbó in 1765 and was reassigned to San Joaquín, in northern Paraguay.

With the expulsion of the Jesuits two years later, Dobrizhoffer returned to Vienna. There he attracted the attention of the empress Maria Theresa, who begged him to write an account of his life in the New World. These memoirs, published in 1783–1784 as *Geschichte der Abiponer*, constitute a uniquely detailed examination of Indian-Caucasian relations in the eighteenth-century Chaco.

See also **Missions: Jesuit Missions (Reducciones).**

BIBLIOGRAPHY

Martin Dobrizhoffer, *An Account of the Abipones: An Equestrian People of Paraguay*, translated by Sara Coleridge, 3 vols. (1822).

Efraím Cardozo, *Historiografía paraguaya* (1959), pp. 344–351.

Additional Bibliography

Livi Bacci, Massimo. "The Missions of Paraguay: The Demography of an Experiment." *Journal of Interdisciplinary History* 35 (Autumn 2004): 185–224.

THOMAS L. WHIGHAM

DOCE, LOS. Los Doce, the twelve Franciscan friars who arrived in New Spain in 1524: Martín de Valencia (their superior), Luis de Fuensalida, Francisco de Soto, Andrés de Córdova, García de Cisneros, Martín de Coruña, Juan Suares, Toribio de Benavente (Motolinía), Juan de Palos, Antonio de Ciudad-Rodrigo, Juan de Ribas, and Francisco Jiménez. While they were not the first clergy or even the first Franciscans on the scene, their arrival represented the true beginning of the systematic Christianization program and the establishment of the Mexican church. Motolinía, the best-known member, wrote several important accounts of the indigenous society, and in general the prominence of these "Twelve Apostles" solidified the primacy of the Franciscan order in New Spain. From its privileged position, the order was able to obtain the best and most populous sites for its monasteries and to exert a great deal of influence on early colonial affairs, in part because a member of the order, Juan de Zumárraga, was Mexico's first bishop.

See also **Catholic Church: The Colonial Period; Missions: Spanish America.**

BIBLIOGRAPHY

Standard English-language accounts of the activities of the Franciscans (and other orders) in Mexico are John Leddy Phelan, *The Millennial Kingdom of the Franciscans in the New World: A Study of the Writings of Gerónimo de Mendieta (1525–1604)* (1956); Robert Ricard, *The Spiritual Conquest of Mexico* (1966); and John Frederick Schwaller, *The Church and Clergy in Sixteenth-Century Mexico* (1987). For a translation of Motolinía's work, see Toribio Motolinía, *History of the Indians of New Spain*, translated and edited by Elizabeth Andros Foster (1950). For an early history of the Franciscans in Mexico, consult Gerónimo De Mendieta, *Historia eclesiástica indiana* (1971). (Motolinía was Mendieta's mentor.)

Additional Bibliography

Díaz Balsera, Viviana. *The Pyramid under the Cross: Franciscan Discourses of Evangelization and the Nahua Christian Subject in Sixteenth-Century Mexico*. Tucson: University of Arizona Press, 2005.

Frost, Elsa Cecilia. *La historia de Dios en las indias: Visión franciscana del Nuevo Mundo*. México, D.F.: Tusquets Editores, 2002.

González y González, Luis. *Jerónimo de Mendieta: Vida, pasión y mensaje de un indigenista apocalíptico*. Zamora: Colegio de Michoacán, 1996.

Griffiths, Nicholas and Fernando Cervantes, eds. *Spiritual Encounters: Interactions Between Christianity and Native Religions in Colonial America*. Lincoln: University of Nebraska Press, 1999.

Mendieta, Gerónimo de., and Felix Jay. *Historia eclesiástica indiana: A Franciscan's View of the Spanish Conquest of Mexico*. Lewiston: Edwin Mellen Press, 1997.

Sandos, James A. *Converting California: Indians and Franciscans in the Missions*. New Haven, CT: Yale University Press, 2004.

ROBERT HASKETT

DOLLAR DIPLOMACY. Dollar Diplomacy, a stratagem closely associated with the foreign policy of U.S. President William Howard Taft (1909–1913) and his secretary of state, Philander Knox.

Dollar diplomacy was most clearly manifested in Latin America, especially Central America and the Caribbean, but the Taft-Knox team also labored hard to apply it to China. The proponents of dollar diplomacy intended to avoid direct military intervention to protect U.S. interests or to induce the stable political and social order necessary to establish a favorable environment for U.S. commercial and financial expansion. Their objective was to develop important U.S. political, economic, cultural, and strategic influence by substituting the power of U.S. capital and financial aid for more direct diplomatic or military pressure. These goals were pointedly expressed in 1911, when Knox declared: "It is rational to hold that a fatherland owes its children the duty of assuring them opportunity for self-advancement. The Department of State can help in this way by securing for our citizens equal and fair opportunity abroad commensurate with that which the National Government aims to secure for them at home." President Taft summarized his administration's foreign policy when he explained in his final message to Congress on 3 December 1912, that "the diplomacy of the present administration sought to respond to modern ideas of commercial intercourse. This policy has been characterized as substituting dollars for bullets. It is one that appeals alike to idealistic humanitarian sentiments, to the dictates of sound policy and strategy, and to legitimate commercial aims."

U.S. economic and security interests were most evident in the small Central American and Caribbean island states, which were the chief targets of dollar diplomacy, although historians have traced implementation of the policy to Ecuador and Mexico as well. The U.S. government induced the Caribbean and isthmian governments to accept U.S. customs collectors, financial advisers, tax administrators, and economic consultants appointed with the cooperation of the State Department. Dollar diplomacy resulted in numerous military interventions, despite claims to the contrary, because it insisted upon a U.S. role in the financial and economic life of the republics around the Caribbean. U.S. Marines occupied Nicaragua, Haiti, and Santo Domingo for long periods and landed frequently in Cuba and Panama and on at least two occasions in Honduras.

The core idea behind dollar diplomacy was an old one: managing another society's political economy without recourse to a costly and bloody conflict.

Early U.S. efforts to exert such influence in Mexico included the Corwin–Zamacona (1861) and the Corwin–Doblado (1862) loan treaties. These loans were to be used to pay the principal and interest on the outstanding Mexican debt to France, Great Britain, and Spain and thereby reduce the threat of European intervention in Mexico's La Reforma conflict. The U.S. Congress, however, rejected the loans, and the three European powers intervened.

U.S. officials and private parties had frequently compared the political and economic benefits and the costs of foreign and U.S. investment in Latin America, especially in the Caribbean–Central American regions, with alternative diplomatic-military activity. Emily Rosenberg has placed dollar diplomacy within a framework of liberal developmentalism that describes dollar diplomacy as merely one variation of numerous efforts to spread the American system abroad. For example, such considerations were common in the 1890s, when U.S. officials and private businessmen wished to replace British economic and financial involvement in Nicaragua's Mosquito region. Similar reasoning prompted President Theodore Roosevelt's decision to announce the policy that became known as the Roosevelt Corollary to the Monroe Doctrine. The Roosevelt administration assumed (as did the Taft administration) that financial and economic activity translated into political and strategic power. The U.S. government used the Roosevelt Corollary to claim a financial and economic supervisory authority over the economies of Latin American states. Under Taft and his successors, banks, financial institutions, humanitarian organizations, corporations, and other private agencies were selected as "chosen instruments" to advance U.S. objectives, but without formal involvement of U.S. institutions because that course would have been inconsistent with laissez-faire principles. However, by the 1920s, many of the original policymakers involved in dollar diplomacy criticized the program. For instance, several officials believed that the policy caused banks to make poor investment decisions based solely on the presence of U.S. advisors. Bad investments in turn created financial crises and economic instability. This reservation has stood the test of time. Simon G. Hanson has described the Alliance for Progress in the 1960s as a modern, unsuccessful, and formal U.S. governmental variation of that same policy outlook.

See also **Good Neighbor Policy; Monroe Doctrine; Roosevelt Corollary; United States-Latin American Relations.**

BIBLIOGRAPHY

Scott Nearing, *Dollar Diplomacy: A Study of American Imperialism* (1925).

Dana G. Munro, *Intervention and Dollar Diplomacy in the Caribbean, 1900–1921* (1964).

Robert Freeman Smith, "Cuba: Laboratory for Dollar Diplomacy, 1898–1917," *Historian* 28, no. 4 (1966): 586–609.

Eugene P. Trani, "Dollar Diplomacy," and Joan Hoff Wilson, "Economic Foreign Policy," in Alexander DeConde, ed., *Encyclopedia of American Foreign Policy,* vol. 1 (1978), pp. 265–274 and 281–291.

Emily Rosenberg, *Spreading the American Dream: American Economic and Cultural Expansion, 1890–1945* (1982).

Additional Bibliography

Drake, Paul W., ed. *Money Doctors, Foreign Debts, and Economic Reforms in Latin America from the 1890s to the Present.* Wilmington, DE: SR Books, 1994.

LaFeber, Walter. *Inevitable Revolutions: The United States in Central America.* 2nd ed. New York: W. W. Norton, 1993.

Rosenberg, Emily S. *Financial Missionaries to the World: The Politics and Culture of Dollar Diplomacy, 1900–1930.* Cambridge, MA: Harvard University Press, 1999.

Schell, William, Jr. *Integral Outsiders: The American Colony in Mexico City, 1876–1911.* Wilmington, DE: SR Books, 2001.

THOMAS SCHOONOVER

DOMADOR. In any ranching economy, certain skills are more highly esteemed because of their centrality to ranch work. Certainly, the broncobuster, or *domador,* held highest status. All gauchos could ride reasonably well. But the *domador* could tame, often with brutal efficiency, any wild horse to the saddle. Injury or death to the animal was not uncommon. Because of the demand for his skills, the *domador* earned higher wages than the average ranch worker. By the late nineteenth century wild horses were scarce and mounts became more costly. Harsh, traditional taming methods gave way to gentler ones. The Argentine writer Ricardo Güiraldes provides a memorable literary portrait of the *domador* in his novel *Don Segundo Sombra* (1926).

See also **Livestock.**

BIBLIOGRAPHY

Richard W. Slatta, *Gauchos and the Vanishing Frontier* (1983), p. 43; *Cowboys of the Americas* (1990), pp. 74–75.

Additional Bibliography

Assunção, Fernando O. *Historia del gaucho: El gaucho, ser y quehacer.* Buenos Aires: Editorial Claridad, 1999.

De la Fuente, Ariel. *Children of Facundo: Caudillo and Gaucho Insurgency During the Argentine State-Formation Process (La Rioja, 1853–1870).* Durham: Duke University Press, 2000.

RICHARD W. SLATTA

DOMESTIC SERVICE. Domestic servants have always been important to Latin American society and its economy. In the colonial period the patriarchal household was the primary basis of juridical identity and social control in Spanish and Portuguese America, with all persons being controlled through the male head of household. The Spanish *casa poblada* (the home of the *encomendero,* required by law to include room for at least forty guests and military retainers) was literally viewed as the basis for Spanish civilization in the New World. In sixteenth-century Latin America domestic servants were found not only in the houses of *encomenderos* and *senhores de engenho* (Brazilian sugar planters), with as many as forty, but also in the houses of merchants and artisans, with the former having as few as one. In addition, Spanish and Portuguese law mandated that women be maintained in a position of tutelage, which implied that most employment options for women prior to the end of the nineteenth century were domestic—in terms of where the work was executed, the type of labor demanded, and often the type of family relationship necessary to exercise a craft or trade.

The dominant race of domestic servants varied by location, depending upon the ethnic mix of the population, and also changed over time. However, Indians, slaves, freed slaves, persons of mixed races (*castas*), and white men and women were all part of the servant population in the sixteenth century. In Brazil, African and Indian slaves composed the servant population from the sixteenth through the eighteenth centuries. In Mexico, Indians were the dominant form of domestic labor in the sixteenth century, but blacks, slave and freed, became more important in the seventeenth century. By the eighteenth century, most Mexican domestic servants were *castas*. Spanish servants continued to be considered prestigious. Women seeking employment as wet nurses in Mexico City frequently claimed Spanish blood—probably because of the idea that a baby would imbibe qualities of character common to an ethnic group along with its milk. In Brazil, although most domestic servants were Indian or African slaves and freed persons until the middle of the nineteenth century, there was a definite preference for mixed-blood or "whiter" servants.

Domestics in the colonial period are difficult to trace. The only relevant regulations specified that domestic servants were under the authority and responsibility of the head of the household in which they worked. The significance of domestic servants in colonial Latin America becomes most apparent through studies on household composition. Studies of eighteenth-century Caracas, Buenos Aires, Mexico City, and various areas in Chile and Brazil indicate the high proportions of dependent members of the household who were not part of the nuclear family and were generally regarded as servants. These *allegados* or *agregados* frequently contributed from 20 to 40 percent of household members. Orphaned relatives, "adopted children," manumitted children and women in Brazil, Indians captured in frontier wars, illegitimate ("natural") offspring of the head of the household, and the adolescent children of neighbors or kinfolk were natural components of the servant category and contributed to the personalized, paternalistic master–servant relationship, which also was often strengthened through ritual kinship. This characteristic of domestic servitude declined in the nineteenth century. At the same time, the association of domestic service with the lower end of the class/caste/color system that dominated Latin American society caused a gradual alienation between employers and servants as well as a loss of status for the occupation of domestic service.

In the nineteenth century the effects of urbanization and structural economic changes increasing the size of the middle class led to renewed demand for domestic servants in the urban areas of Latin America. At the same time, domestic service acted to continue preindustrial social and productive relationships and to reinforce the patriarchal household. The private home was seen as a "protected place for a woman to work" and a "guardian of moral virtue." Most domestic servants were migrants from nearby villages. In nineteenth-century Mexico City and in Argentina about 60 percent of women workers were domestic servants.

Female labor participation during industrialization has followed a U-shaped path, according to studies on Brazil, Mexico, Peru, and the United States. In these countries the high proportions of women working in the mid-nineteenth century were followed by dramatic declines in the ranks of working women from the 1890s to the 1930s. In this period domestic service declined as well, though less than other forms of female employment. In the period from 1940 to 1970 female employment expanded throughout Latin America in response to generally improved economic conditions and to the expansion of the service sector. Middle-class and upper-class women entered the white-collar sector, which enlarged the demand for domestic service. This contrasts strongly with the experience of the United States and Europe, where domestic servants largely disappeared in this period. The difference in Latin America may be attributed to the much larger unskilled lower-class population, many of them rural migrants, desperately in need of jobs. Furthermore, with the continued use of domestics, upper-class and middle-class Latin American women were able to go to work without threatening the traditional patriarchal organization of the household.

Most domestic workers are recent migrants, frequently utilizing the "educational" and patronage advantages of a live-in domestic situation to provide them with a transition from the provinces. Nevertheless, the "mobility" experienced by domestic servants is not a move between types of employment, but rather a move as a domestic to a better neighborhood with a higher salary and more privileges. In the 1980s and 1990s the increased value of privacy, the growth of daycare and nursery schools, and improved technology in the middle-class home began to dampen the demand for full-time, live-in servants. More domestics were employed part-time for specific tasks—a change that has reduced the paternalistic privileges of the live-in situation as well as some of its oppressiveness in terms of hours and personal supervision. Although "casual" domestic labor was even less regulated and usually less secure than a live-in position, it did permit the domestic to acquire several employers.

Everywhere in Latin America domestic service has historically been the most important form of female employment. However, in part because of the colonial circumstances of conquest and caste/race relations, domestic service became an aspect of race and class subordination rather than the "stage-of-life" learning experience it usually was in pre-industrial Europe. In the sixteenth century many (perhaps half) domestic servants were male, and some were white. By the eighteenth century, most domestic servants were female and predominantly of mixed-blood or mixed-caste background, and those who were male were also of mixed blood or of slave status. Domestic service in the nineteenth twentieth, and twenty-first centuries has become an almost entirely female and lower-class occupation. Through women's organizations, federal labor laws throughout the Americas came to include domestic service, yet legal recourse in practice is often limited.

Globalization has brought changes to women's employment. While it has increased their participation in the export-manufacturing sector, globalization has also spurred women's migration across and within country borders. For instance, Bolivian, Paraguayan, and Ecuadorian, women often migrate to Chile and Argentina for domestic work. In the twenty-first century, domestic service continues to be important, particularly for new migrants and Afro-Brazilian women.

See also **Caste and Class Structure in Colonial Spanish America; Migration and Migrations; Women.**

BIBLIOGRAPHY

An excellent source on domestic service in Latin America, both historically and today, is Elsa M. Chaney and Mary Garcia Castro, eds., *Muchachas No More: Household Workers in Latin America and the Caribbean* (1989). On Brazil, see Sandra Lauderdale Graham, *House and Street: The Domestic World of Servants and Masters in Nineteenth-Century Rio de Janeiro* (1988), and Mary Karasch, "Suppliers, Sellers, Servants, and Slaves," in *Cities and Society in Colonial Latin America*, edited by Louisa Schell Hoberman and Susan Migden Socolow (1986). An accessible article relating larger economic changes, women's employment opportunities, and domestic service is Elizabeth Jelin, "Migration and Labor Force Participation of Latin American Women:

The Domestic Servants in the Cities," in *Signs* 3, no. 1 (1977): 129–141.

Additional Bibliography

Aymer, Paula L. *Uprooted Women: Migrant Domestics in the Caribbean*. Westport: Praeger, 1997.

Barbosa, Fernando Cordiro. *Trabalho e residência: Estudo das ocupações de empregada doméstica e empregado de edifício a partir de migrantes "nordestinos."* Niterói: Editora da Universidade Federal Fluminense, 2000.

Eckstein, Susan, and Timothy Wickham-Crowley. *Struggles for Social Rights in Latin America*. New York: Routledge, 2002.

Hondagneu-Sotelo, Pierrettte. *Doméstica: Immigrant Workers Cleaning and Caring in the Shadows of Affluence*. Berkeley: University of California Press, 2001.

Kofes, Suely. *Mulher, mulheres: Identidade, diferença e desigualdade na relação entre patroas e empregadas domésticas*. Campinas: Editora da Unicamp, 2001.

Momsen, Janet Henshall, ed. *Gender, Migration, and Domestic Service*. New York: Routledge, 1999.

Segura, Denise A., and Patricia Zavella, eds. *Women and Migration in the U.S.-Mexico Borderlands: A Reader*. Durham, NC: Duke University Press, 2007.

Vázquez Flores, Erika Julieta, and Horacio Hernández Casillas. *Migración, resistencia y recreación cultural: El trabajo invisible de la mujer indígena*. México, D.F.: Instituto Nacional de Antropología e Historia, 2004.

ELIZABETH ANNE KUZNESOF

DOMINGO, PLÁCIDO (1941–). Plácido Domingo is considered one of the great operatic tenors of his day. Born into a family of *zarzuela* performers in Madrid, Spain, on 21 January 1941, his family settled in Mexico shortly before his eighth birthday. He entered the Mexican National Conservatory at the age of fourteen as a nonmatriculating student. Marriage at sixteen years of age and fatherhood at seventeen cut short his conservatory studies, but he continued singing. He sang with the National Opera in supporting roles from 1959 to 1961. He also played piano with the Concierto de Mexico ballet troupe and acted in plays during those years. He and his second wife, singer Marta Ornelas, moved to Tel Aviv, Israel, to work with the Hebrew National Opera at the end of 1962 and stayed there until 1965, when he received his first invitations to perform in the

United States. He joined the New York City Opera in October of that year. In 1966 he began singing with the Hamburg State Opera. From that point on he sang in the major opera houses in the world, including Vienna, Milan, and London. He first performed at the Metropolitan Opera in September 1968. Domingo has been described as combining "a skillful and elegant power of expression with musical bridgings and melodic phrasings that border on the vocally miraculous" (Schnauber 1997, p. xv). Among the eighty different roles Domingo has performed in his career, he is most associated with the title roles in Offenbach's *Tales of Hoffman* and Verdi's *Otello*, as well as Cavaradossi in Puccini's *Tosca*. Domingo has had a varied career. He made his debut as a conductor with the New York City Opera in 1973. Among his more than 100 recordings are included performances of a wide variety of popular musical styles, many, but certainly not all, from the Hispanic world. (He had a hit song, "Perhaps Love," with John Denver in 1982.) Domingo has performed in more than twenty-four countries. In 1984 he co-founded the Los Angeles Music Center Opera. He became artistic director of the Washington Opera in 1996.

See also **Music: Popular Music and Dance.**

BIBLIOGRAPHY

Domingo, Plácido. *My First Forty Years.* New York: Knopf, 1983.

Schnauber, Cornelius. *Plácido Domingo.* Translated by Susan H. Ray. Boston: Northeastern University Press, 1997.

Snowman, Daniel. *The World of Plácido Domingo.* New York: McGraw-Hill, 1985.

ANDREW J. KIRKENDALL

DOMÍNGUEZ, MANUEL (1869–1935).

Manuel Domínguez (*b.* 1869; *d.* 1935), Paraguayan historian and essayist. Domínguez is widely regarded as the most important revisionist historian of Paraguay after Juan E. O'Leary. Born in the river port of Pilar toward the end of the War of the Triple Alliance, Domínguez grew up in an Asunción that had been terribly affected by the fighting. Despite these difficulties, he made major intellectual strides and ended up teaching subjects as varied as zoology, anatomy, and Roman history at the National College

and serving as rector of the university. He also held various political and diplomatic posts for brief periods.

Domínguez was instrumental in introducing Auguste Comte's positivism to Paraguayan historical studies, which meant applying more scientific methods to research. Domínguez himself put theory into practice in his *El Chaco Boreal,* a work that defended Paraguayan claims to the Gran Chaco region. He also wrote an influential series of essays entitled *El alma de la raza,* which argued for a portrayal of Paraguayan history in strongly nationalist terms; the book likewise championed the figure of Marshal Francisco Solano López, who had led Paraguay into the earlier war. In this respect, Domínguez broke with the virulently anti-López diatribes of earlier historians, particularly Cecilio Báez.

See also **Academia Literaria de Querétaro; Allende, Ignacio; Ortiz de Domínguez, Josefa.**

BIBLIOGRAPHY

William Belmont Parker, *Paraguayans of To-Day* (1921), pp. 299–302.

Jack Ray Thomas, *Biographical Dictionary of Latin American Historians and Historiography* (1984).

Carlos Zubizarreta, *Cien vidas paraguayas,* 2d ed. (1985), pp. 225–228.

THOMAS L. WHIGHAM

DOMÍNGUEZ, MIGUEL (1756–1830).

Miguel Domínguez (*b.* 20 January 1756; *d.* 22 April 1830), precursor of Mexican independence. A distinguished lawyer born in Mexico City, Domínguez was named *corregidor* of Querétaro in 1802. His opposition to the Law of Consolidation of *vales reales* (royal bonds) (1805) gained him the enmity of Viceroy José de Iturrigaray, who had him replaced, although he was eventually restored to his post. With his wife, Josefa Ortiz, he took part in the Querétaro conspiracy of 1810 against the colonial regime. When the plot was discovered, Domínguez, constrained by his office, locked his wife in their house and arrested some of the plotters. But she managed to notify others, causing Miguel Hidalgo to begin the revolution on 16 September. Domínguez was detained the same day; shortly thereafter he was released and restored to his post, although he was ousted again in 1820. He became a member of the Supreme Executive Power in 1823. At the end of 1824, he became president of the Supreme Court, a position he held for the rest of his life. He died in Mexico City.

See also **Academia Literaria de Querétaro; Allende, Ignacio; Ortiz de Domínguez, Josefa.**

BIBLIOGRAPHY

José María Miguel I. Vergés, *Diccionario de insurgentes* (1969), pp. 175–176.

Hugh M. Hamill, Jr., *The Hidalgo Revolt,* 2d ed. (1970); *Diccionario Porrúa de historia, geografía y biografía de México,* 5th ed. (1986), vol. 1, p. 922.

Additional Bibliography

Agraz García de Alba, Gabriel. *Los corregidores Don Miguel Domínguez y Doña María Josefa Ortiz y el inicio de la independencia.* Mexico City, 1992.

Archer, Christon I. *The Birth of Modern Mexico, 1780–1824.* Wilmington: Scholarly Resources Inc., 2003.

VIRGINIA GUEDEA

DOMINICA. Dominica, a small Caribbean island nation in the Lesser Antilles, located between Martinique and Guadeloupe in the chain of islands known as the Windwards. Dominica was sighted and named by Christopher Columbus on 3 November 1493, but the island remained a stronghold of the native Carib peoples until the flow of European settlers to the area increased in the late seventeenth century. The island was one of the many smaller islands that Spain could not or chose not to exclude other European powers from seizing, so in the era of imperial rivalries Dominica became the target of competing French and British claims. After driving the Caribs into the mountains, the French held most of the island until 1761. That year, however, the British seized the island as part of their effort to build an empire in North America, the Caribbean, and elsewhere during the Seven Years' War.

Under the British, Dominica became a classic slave society producing tropical agricultural products for export to Europe. The population of slaves and settlers skyrocketed. With the end of French efforts to claim the island in the first decade of the nineteenth century, coffee production was established as the first in a series of cash crops that would subject Dominica to cycles of economic boom and collapse. Around 1900 coffee and sugar gave way to cocoa, to be replaced by bananas in the middle of the twentieth century.

After the establishment of an elected assembly in 1763, Britain consistently dictated policy for the island, with minor changes in representation, until 3 November 1978, when Dominica gained its independence from Britain. The process toward autonomy had been a gradual one throughout most of the twentieth century, with increasing participation by Dominicans in self-rule and expanding suffrage.

See also **Banana Industry; Caribs; Coffee Industry; Slavery: Spanish America; Sugar Industry; Windward Islands.**

BIBLIOGRAPHY

Robert A. Meyers, *Dominica* (1987).

Michel-Rolph Trouillot, *Peasants and Capital: Dominica in the World Economy* (1988).

Additional Bibliography

Gimbernat González, Ester. *La poesía de mujeres dominicanas a fines del siglo XX.* Lewiston: E. Mellen Press, 2002.

Honychurch, Lennox. *The Dominicana Story: A History of the Island.* London: Macmillan, 1995.

TODD LITTLE-SIEBOLD

DOMINICAN REPUBLIC. In 1822, under President Jean-Pierre Boyer, the Haitians began a twenty-two-year occupation of the eastern two-thirds of Hispanolia. Dominican historians have traditionally described this period as the nadir of their country's history because of the imposition of high taxes, a military draft, the confiscation of church lands, the destruction of the prevailing educational system, and efforts of Haitianization. Recently, revisionist historians have stressed some of the positive aspects of the Haitian occupation, such as the freeing of the Dominican slaves. There is no doubt, however, that a substantial part of the Dominican people desired the end of Haitian rule.

The fight for Dominican liberation was led by Juan Pablo Duarte, who is regarded as "the father of

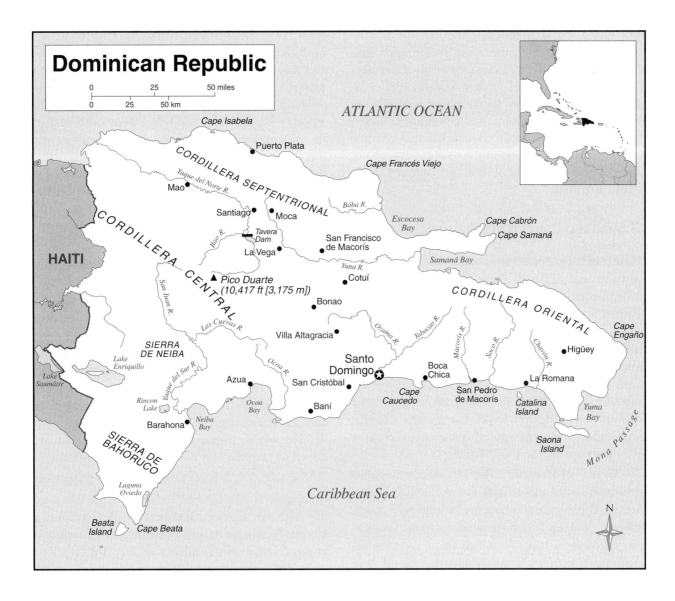

Dominican Republic

his country" and its greatest national hero. He was ably assisted by Ramón Matias Mella and Francisco del Rosario Sánchez, who are almost equally admired. On 27 February 1844, the Dominican Republic successfully proclaimed its independence from Haiti.

FROM SANTANA TO HEUREAUX (1845–1899)
Duarte's dream of establishing a liberal, democratic republic soon vanished with his permanent exile to Venezuela and his replacement by two caudillos (Pedro Santana and Buenaventura Báez) who for decades battled each other to control the country. The instability produced by this struggle was aggravated by the threat of frequent armed incursions by Haiti. Since neither Báez nor Santana believed in the viability of the Dominican Republic,

they searched for foreign protectors. Whereas Báez hoped for annexation by France or the United States, Santana looked for salvation to Spain, which reannexed its former colony of Santo Domingo in 1861. Most Dominicans objected to the reestablishment of Spanish control and commenced the War of Restoration (of Dominican independence) on 16 August 1863, a conflict that resulted in Spain's permanent withdrawal from Santo Domingo in 1865. Báez's U.S. annexation scheme was almost realized in the 1870s, when the administration of President Ulysses S. Grant strove to carry it out. The determined resistance of Senator Charles Sumner of Massachusetts narrowly defeated the annexation treaty's passage in the Senate.

The frequent turmoil that had plagued the nation ever since it attained independence was suspended temporarily during the last two decades of the nineteenth century, when General Ulises Heureaux (1882–1899) clamped an iron dictatorship on the country. His rule was marked by assassinations, bribery, and secret police surveillance. Nevertheless, the stability of the political situation led to a flurry of foreign investments that resulted in the building of telegraph lines, railways, roads, and the first large sugar mills in the southern Dominican Republic.

INCREASED UNITED STATES DOMINATION (1900–1926)

Heureaux's assassination in 1899 resulted in renewed political and financial destabilization, which was instrumental in persuading the government of the United States to take over the receivership of Dominican customs (1905) under the Roosevelt Corollary of the Monroe Doctrine. Under the beneficent presidency of Ramón Cáceres (1906–1911), the Dominican Republic experienced a brief spell of reform and modernization. Cáceres's assassination hurled the country into a new cycle of violence and financial indebtedness that persuaded President Woodrow Wilson to send in the U.S. Marines.

From 1916 to 1924 the Dominican Republic remained under the military control of the United States. The occupation resulted in improved roads, schools, and sanitation facilities as well as in the introduction of baseball, which became a national pastime. U.S. rule, however, also had its negative aspects, including the suppression of Dominican guerrilla activities, which was accompanied by incidents of torture. A pervasive attitude of racism on the part of the occupiers toward Dominicans created long-lasting resentments. Perhaps the worst legacy of the U.S. occupation was the creation of a Marine-trained National Guard under a commander in chief named Rafael Léonidas Trujillo Molina, who became the dictator of the Dominican Republic in 1930.

THE ERA OF TRUJILLO (1930–1961)

Trujillo followed in the footsteps of Báez, Santana, and Heureaux—he even patterned his uniforms after those worn by Heureaux. However, his regime was infinitely more encompassing than the governments of his three caudillo predecessors. Perhaps it would be more appropriate to compare him with his more famous contemporaries, Adolf Hitler and Joseph

Stalin. In terms of cruelty, *Gleichschaltung* (conformity laws), secret police terror, genocidal massacres, and megalomania, Trujillo certainly held his own in comparison with the German and Soviet rulers. He differed from them, however, in one important aspect: whereas Hitler and Stalin were indifferent to the accumulation of personal wealth, Trujillo, the son of a lower-middle-class postal officer, was determined to amass one of the world's great fortunes. He turned the Dominican Republic into his personal fiefdom by taking possession of most of the land, many industries, and many export-import monopolies. It is estimated that by the time of his death in 1961, his personal fortune amounted to more than U.S. $800 million. Members of Trujillo's extensive family were given important government positions that they used to make their own fortunes.

Trujillo added another bloody chapter to the long history of hostilities between Dominicans and Haitians by ordering the execution of all Haitians who could be found on Dominican soil. In October 1937, approximately 25,000 Haitian women, men, and children were massacred at the dictator's request. Trujillo, whose maternal grandmother was Haitian, hoped to "whiten" his country by this measure.

Owing his meteoric military career to the U.S. occupation forces, Trujillo sought to ingratiate himself with his former superiors. Besides creating a George Washington and Marine Corps Boulevard in Santo Domingo, Trujillo made sure that his country's debt to the United States was paid in full, within a decade. With the exception of the final phase of his reign, Trujillo elevated the maintenance of good relations with the United States to the cardinal principle of his foreign policy. These efforts resulted in the Trujillo–Hull Treaty (1940), by which the United States gave up its right to collect Dominican customs duties.

When the United States became involved in World War II, the Dominican Republic was one of the first Latin American countries to declare war on the Axis. The products of the Dominican Republic's agro-industries, which Trujillo had done so much to develop in the 1930s, found a ready market in the United States during the war. Dominican coffee, tobacco, and cocoa were in high demand, and the Dominican Republic became the second largest sugar exporter (after Cuba) to the United States. In 1944, when Franklin D. Roosevelt and Winston Churchill called for worldwide adherence to democratic principles, Trujillo even allowed the formation of opposition parties. He crushed them ruthlessly in 1947, at the beginning of the cold war, during which the Dominican dictator posed as Latin America's champion of anticommunism. His anticommunist stance, as well as the administering of favors and outright bribes, assured him support from a powerful group of U.S. senators and congressmen. Most North American journalists lavished praise on Trujillo for establishing a stable government in his country.

The Dominican ruler reached the apex of his reign in 1955, when he celebrated the twenty-fifth anniversary of his seizure of power by arranging for a Fair of Peace and Brotherhood of the Free World at Santo Domingo. After that event, Trujillo's fortunes began to decline rapidly. The toppling of dictators all over Latin America with the encouragement of the administrations of Dwight D. Eisenhower and John F. Kennedy left Trujillo an isolated relic. On 14 June 1959, Dominican exiles, with the encouragement of President Rómulo Betancourt of Venezuela and Fidel Castro of Cuba, launched an abortive invasion of the Dominican Republic. Trujillo ordered the captured rebels tortured and then killed. In retaliation for Betancourt's sponsorship of the invasion, Trujillo sent agents to Venezuela who dynamited Betancourt's car and injured the Venezuelan president. Other Dominican agents participated in the assassination of Guatemala's president, Carlos Castillo Armas, in 1957. These actions resulted in the imposition of economic sanctions against the Dominican Republic by the Organization of American States (OAS).

In his desperation, Trujillo began to abandon his principle of never antagonizing the United States. The 1956 kidnapping and subsequent murder of Columbia University instructor Jesús de Galíndez, who had infuriated the Dominican dictator by publishing a book dealing with Trujillo's many crimes, lessened Trujillo's support in the U.S. Congress. Many congressional members were outraged by Trujillo's murder of the North American pilot who had flown the kidnapped professor to his death in the Dominican Republic. The United States imposed an arms embargo on the Dominican Republic that was followed by a special excise tax on the importation of Dominican sugar. The latter measure dealt a crippling blow to the Dominican economy. Isolated abroad and increasingly opposed at home, the aging dictator was ambushed and murdered along Santo Domingo's waterfront (Malecón) on 30 May 1961.

THE AFTERMATH OF TRUJILLO (1961–1965)

The murdered dictator left behind a dislocated economy and a large power vacuum that his favorite son, Rafael Leónidas Trujillo Martínez (Ramfis), and Trujillo's last puppet president, Joaquín Balaguer, attempted to fill. While Ramfis was rounding up and torturing his father's assassins (they were all caught and killed, except for Luis Amiama Tío and General Antonio Imbert Barrera), Balaguer initiated some minor democratic reforms that failed to persuade the OAS to lift its economic sanctions. The reforms alarmed the late dictator's brothers, José Arismendi and Héctor Bienvenido, who tried to undo even these minor changes in order to preserve "Trujilloism with Trujillo." The protests of Santo Domingo's business community, backed by a show of force of U.S. naval units, persuaded the entire Trujillo clan to go into permanent exile on 20 November 1961. Before following suit, however, Balaguer formed and headed a seven-man Council of State. Consisting of members of the Dominican elite, this body was designed to preside over the country's transition to democracy until the national elections were held on 20 December 1962. These changes resulted in the lifting of sanctions by the OAS as well as a massive outpouring of economic and technical assistance by the United States.

The elections of 1962 proved to be a contest between two major parties: the conservative National Civic Union (UCN), which was backed by the elite, and the Dominican Revolutionary Party (PRD), which had been founded in 1939 by anti-Trujilloist exiles and consisted largely of members of the middle and lower classes. The PRD was led by the prominent Dominican novelist Juan Bosch, who won the presidential election. President John F. Kennedy, who was pleased by the outcome of the voting, invited the newly elected Dominican president to the White House and appointed his liberal speech writer, John Bartlow Martin, as ambassador to the Dominican Republic. The Kennedy administration's enthusiasm for Bosch soon vanished when the new president ignored the guidelines of the Alliance for Progress program and considered establishing

Dominican Republic

Population:	9,365,818 (2007 est.)
Area:	18,815 sq mi
Official language:	Spanish
National currency:	Dominican peso (DOP)
Principal religions:	Roman Catholicism, 95%
Ethnicity:	mixed 73%, white 16%, black 11%
Capital:	Santo Domingo
Other urban centers:	Concepción de la Vega, La Romana, San Francisco de Macorís, San Pedro de Macorís, and Santiago de los Caballerosii
Annual rainfall:	53 inches in the east, 17 inches in the west
Principal geographical features:	*Mountains:* Central and Northern Cordilleras; Duarte (10,417 ft) is the highest peak in the West Indies *Rivers:* Yanque del Norte, Yanque del Sur, Yuna *Lakes:* Enriquillo *Islands:* Alto Velo, Beata, Catalinita, Catalina, Saona
Economy:	*GDP per capita:* $8,400 (2006 est.)
Principal products and exports:	*Agricultural:* cocoa, coffee, sugar, tobacco *Manufacturing:* cement, cigars, food processing, sugar processing, textiles *Mining:* gypsum, salt Tourism is one of the most important components of the economy.
Government:	The Dominican Republic gained independence in 1865, and is governed as a democratic republic. The president is chief of state and head of government. The popularly elected legislature consists of a 32-seat Senate and a 178-seat House of Representatives.
Armed forces:	*Army:* 15,000 *Navy:* 4,000 *Air force:* 5,500 *Paramilitary:* 15,000 National Police
Transportation:	*Rail:* 321 mi *Ports:* Boca Chica, Puerto Plata, Rio Haina, Santo Domingo *Roads:* 3,867 mi paved; 3,962 mi unpaved *Airports:* 15 paved runway and 19 unpaved runway airports
Media:	Leading newspapers include *El Nacional, Hoy, La Información, Listín Diario,* and *Ultima Hora.* There are 120 AM and 56 FM radio stations, and 25 television stations, including the state-owned Radio-Televisión Dominicana.
Literacy and education:	*Total literacy rate:* 87% Nine years of education are required. There are 5 universities and 12 other institutes of higher education in the Dominican Republic.

diplomatic relations with Castro's Cuba. Elements of the Dominican armed forces, known as Loyalists and led by General Elías Wessín y Wessín, were well aware of the changed U.S. attitude toward Bosch, which enabled them to stage a successful military coup against Bosch in September 1963.

After Bosch's overthrow, the Dominican Republic was run by a triumvirate headed by business leader Donald Reid Cabral. The real power behind this civilian facade, however, was the military, which became so steeped in corruption and repression that the Dominican people revolted on 24 April 1965 in order to restore civilian rule under former president Bosch, who then was living in exile in Puerto Rico.

THE REVOLUTION OF 1965

The rebels of 24 April 1965 called themselves Constitutionalists because they advocated the reestablishment of a truly civilian, constitutionalist government headed by deposed president Juan Bosch. The Constitutionalists, who consisted of members of the PRD, some Christian Socialists, and part of the armed forces under Colonel Francisco Caamaño Deñó, stormed the National Palace and placed Reid Cabral under house arrest. When the people of Santo Domingo realized that the hated triumvirate had ended, they poured into the streets to support the Constitutionalists, who provided them with arms. General Wessín y Wessín, who headed those elements of the armed forces who called themselves Loyalists because they remained loyal to the triumvirate, unleashed the air force upon the defenseless population of the capital, which suffered thousands of casualties. He also sent heavily armed units backed by tanks across the Duarte Bridge, which spans the Ozama River. This river separated the Loyalist forces, headquartered at San Isidro Air Force base, from the Constitutionalists, who were concentrated in the old part of Santo Domingo (*zona colonial*). Armed with only light weapons and Molotov cocktails, the rebels were able to repel and defeat the Loyalists, capturing and disabling many armored vehicles.

With Caamaño's supporters on the verge of victory in the capital, the revolution threatened to spread to the rest of the country, a development that caused such panic at the U.S. embassy that Ambassador William Tapley Bennett informed President Lyndon Johnson that Communist-led hordes were committing atrocities and endangering the lives of U.S. citizens. On 28 April 1965, President Johnson sent tens of thousands of Marines (and, later, airborne units) into Santo Domingo, ostensibly to prevent a Communist takeover (a "second Cuba"), but in reality to obviate a Constitutionalist victory. On 29 April, the Constitutionalists formed a government with Caamaño as president. The Loyalists, too, formed a government, which was headed by General Antonio Imbert Barrera, one of the two surviving Trujillo assassins.

Johnson had been mistaken in his belief that U.S. intervention would put a quick end to the civil war. Instead, it lasted until 31 August 1965, when the Act of Dominican Reconciliation put an end to the conflict. This reconciliation pact called for the reintegration of the armed forces, the establishment of a temporary government, and the holding of national elections in June 1966.

THE ERA OF BALAGUER (1966–1978)

The ensuing electoral battle was fought between the PRD, once again led by Bosch, who had returned from exile, and the PR (Reformist Party), headed by Joaquín Balaguer, who had founded that party in 1963 during his exile in New York City. Balaguer, presenting himself as the candidate who could bring peace and reconciliation to his nation, won 57 percent of the vote. He was reelected in 1970 and 1974, thus creating the era of Balaguer, which coincided with a dramatic increase in the world price for sugar, the Dominican Republic's main export. Balaguer used the impressive revenues derived from the sugar export boom to construct schools, hospitals, roads, bridges, and dams. He concentrated particularly on the countryside, where he gained much political support from segments of the peasantry. The Dominican

president tried to reduce his country's dependence on sugar production by encouraging the tourist industry and by inviting foreign companies to explore the Dominican Republic's mineral resources (gold, silver, ferronickel, and bauxite).

The economic boom benefited the upper class and some strata of the bourgeoisie. It also produced much corruption, particularly among the top military leaders, many of whom became millionaires under Balaguer. Human rights violations constituted another negative aspect of the era. Especially in the 1970s, former leading Constitutionalists, Socialists, and Communists were murdered by a roving paramilitary gang known as La Banda (The Band), which was encouraged by the government. By 1978, as Balaguer was finishing his third consecutive term as president, his "economic miracle" was under assault by rising oil prices and the simultaneous decline in world demand for coffee, cocoa, and sugar. In June of that year, impoverished urban workers, illpaid professionals, and disillusioned Dominicans everywhere put an end to twelve years of Balaguerism by voting in the PRD's candidate for the presidency, Antonio Guzmán Fernández.

THE PRD INTERLUDE AND THE RETURN OF BALAGUER

During the electoral campaign, Guzmán had promised to bring about a change (*el cambio*) for all those Dominicans (the majority) who had been left out of the "economic miracle" of the Balaguer epoch. However, the continuing increase in the price of oil and the further decline in demand for the Dominican Republic's agricultural products prevented Guzmán from initiating the social reforms he had delineated during the campaign. The endemic political corruption continued under Guzmán. When the president learned that members of his immediate family were involved in a scandal, he committed suicide at the National Palace on 4 July 1982. His vice president, Jacobo Majluta Azar, served the remaining forty-three days of Guzmán's term. Although disappointed by Guzmán and Majluta, the Dominican voters showed that they still preferred the PRD to Balaguer's PR or Bosch's Party of Dominican Liberation (PLD, founded in 1973) when they elected the PRD's Salvador Jorge Blanco to the presidency in 1982.

Beset from the start by the Dominican Republic's enormous debt and the constantly falling world price for sugar, Jorge Blanco was as unable as his predecessors to improve the lot of the average Dominican. Under pressure from the International Monetary Fund (IMF), the Dominican president trebled the price of subsistence items such as cooking oil, rice, and beans in April 1984. The resulting outbursts of popular fury were bloodily suppressed by the police and armed forces. When Jorge Blanco was accused of personal corruption (for which he was jailed in 1988 and tried in 1991), the Dominican people's disillusionment with the PRD was complete. In the 1986 electoral battle of three ex-presidents (Balaguer, Bosch, and Majluta), Balaguer (and his party, the Reformist Social Christian Party [Partido Reformista Social Cristiano—PRSC]) emerged as the winner.

The government formed by the nearly blind, seventy-eight-year-old president seemed like an apparition from the past: former president of the triumvirate Reid Cabral as foreign minister, General Wessín y Wessín as minister of the interior (and later head of the armed forces), and Imbert Barrera as army chief. Balaguer, in his fifth term as president, faced nearly insurmountable problems. His country's agricultural exports were selling as poorly as ever and the U.S. Congress made the situation worse by cutting the Dominican sugar quota. The poor infrastructure of the Dominican Republic was crumbling everywhere. Electric power outages of up to twenty hours a day wrought havoc with industry, hotels, restaurants, and homes.

Balaguer's answer to these problems was a gigantic building program that included the construction of apartments, bridges, and highways as well as an immense lighthouse monument at Santo Domingo honoring Columbus. The building boom relieved unemployment but, at the same time, increased the country's already staggering debt. It also fueled a fierce inflation that threatened not only the survival of the poor but also the viability of the middle class. As far as the observance of human rights was concerned, the record of Balaguer's fifth term compared favorably with his previous tenures as head of state.

During the presidential elections of 1990, the PRD no longer proved to be a major factor because it had split into two hostile groupings: a left wing under the former mayor of Santo Domingo, José Francisco Peña Gómez, and a conservative faction, calling itself La Estructura, under former President Majluta. In the ensuing electoral battle, known as the "battle of the octogenarians," Balaguer was pitted against his old nemesis, Juan Bosch. The incumbent president defeated his opponent by a thin margin; Bosch claimed that he was cheated out of victory by electoral fraud.

Balaguer entered his sixth term as president in an atmosphere of rapid economic deterioration. He soon faced massive demonstrations against the prevailing inflation, unemployment, and dearth of medical and educational facilities, as well as the collapsing infrastructure. Only through the mediation of the Roman Catholic Church and his promise to step down as president in 1992 was Balaguer able to survive this crisis. (Although he remained in power through 1994 and was reelected.) After a temporary reprieve, a new crisis began building up during the summer of 1991, when severe power blackouts and continuing hyperinflation made life miserable for most Dominicans. Balaguer, at this point, apparently attempted to deflect attention from the domestic crisis by becoming embroiled in a bitter dispute with the Dominican Republic's old enemy, Haiti, over the expulsion of thousands of Haitians from Dominican soil. However, Balaguer lost the 1996 election to Leonel Fernández of the Dominican Liberation Party (PLD). The PRD regained the presidency in 2000 when Hipólito Mejía won the election. However, observers considered his administration ineffective and in 2004 the population reelected Leonel Fernández.

Future politicians will face long-standing challenges. The growth of tourism and remittances from Dominicans living in the United States have helped economic growth in the early twenty-first century. Also, the Dominican Republic, along with Central American countries, signed a free trade agreement with the United States in 2005. Nevertheless, of the 9 million Dominicans (2007), 2.25 million exist in poverty. Income inequality hampers development with the wealthiest 10 percent of the population owning 40 percent of the national income. Santo Domingo has already grown its population to 2.5 million and there will also be more pollution, more deforestation, more legal and illegal immigration, less agriculture, and less water. While the government has become democratic, future politicians still have to address these social and economic issues to ensure political stability.

See also Balaguer, Joaquín; Betancourt, Rómulo; Bosch Gaviño, Juan; Boyer, Jean-Pierre; Cáceres, Ramón; Castillo Armas, Carlos; Castro Ruz, Fidel; Duarte, Juan Pablo; Galíndez, Jesús de; Heureaux, Ulises; Mella, Ramón Matías; Monroe Doctrine; Organization of American States (OAS); Roosevelt Corollary; Trujillo Molina, Rafael Leónidas; Wilson, Woodrow.

BIBLIOGRAPHY

Sumner Welles, *Naboth's Vineyard: The Dominican Republic, 1844–1924*, 2 vols. (1928).

Selden Rodman, *Quisqueya: A History of the Dominican Republic* (1964).

Howard J. Wiarda, *The Dominican Republic: A Nation in Transition* (1969).

Frank Moya Pons, *Manual de historia dominicana* (1977).

Ian Bell, *The Dominican Republic* (1981).

H. Hoetink, *The Dominican People, 1850–1900* (1982).

Howard J. Wiarda and Michael J. Kryzanek, *The Dominican Republic: A Caribbean Crucible* (1982).

Jan Knippers Black, *The Dominican Republic: Politics and Development in an Unsovereign State* (1986).

Frank Moya Pons, *El pasado dominicano* (1986).

Michael J. Kryzanek and Howard J. Wiarda, *The Politics of External Influence upon the Dominican Republic* (1988).

Kai P. Schoenhals, *Dominican Republic* (1990).

Additional Bibliography

Domínguez, Jaime de Jesús. *Historia dominicana*. Santo Domingo, República Dominicana: ABC Editorial, 2001.

Gregory, Steven. *The Devil Behind the Mirror: Globalization and Politics in the Dominican Republic*. Berkeley: University of California Press, 2007.

Pérez, Odalís. *Nacionalismo y cultura en República Dominicana*. Santo Domingo, República Dominicana: Centro de Información Afroamericano, 2003.

Sagás, Ernesto. *Race and Politics in the Dominican Republic*. Gainesville: University Press of Florida, 2000.

KAI P. SCHOENHALS

DOMINICAN REPUBLIC, CONSTITUTIONS.

Since 1844, the Dominican Republic has had twenty-five constitutions. This number may appear to be extraordinary for a relatively young republic; however, it does not seem so large when taking into account the fact that the country followed the Spanish American model, in which virtually every new regime writes its own constitution—even though few substantive changes are made—to give it independence and validity in a very unstable system. To complicate matters further, the Dominican Republic was controlled by Haiti from 1822 to 1844, by Spain from 1861 to 1865, and by the United States from 1916 to 1924. Thus its status as an independent republic was a major constitutional issue that needed to be addressed. In general, all the constitutions have guaranteed basic human rights and have appeared to be democratic and progressive. In reality, however, they have been more symbolic than functioning documents. Adherence to the spirit of the many constitutions was more in the breach than in the observance.

The first constitution after the country's liberation from Haiti, promulgated in 1844, represented a compromise between conservative and liberal factions but was rhetorically quite liberal. It called for a popularly elected government and specified powers of the Congress and judiciary. It forbade the suspension of the constitution. Roman Catholicism was declared the state religion (although other sects were free to worship), and slavery was abolished. Ten years later (June 1854) a more liberal constitution briefly replaced the 1844 document. After political unrest, however, the caudillo Pedro Santana (1844–1848, 1853–1856, 1859–1861) returned to power and in December 1854 changed the constitution to fit his autocratic governing style. This authoritarian document was reflected in several later constitutions from the 1850s to the 1870s. An exception was the Moca Constitution of 1858, a more politically progressive document, which was reinstated after the Spanish occupation. It provided for universal male suffrage and direct voting by secret ballot for all elective offices. Its liberal provisions were extended by the Constitutions of 1865 and 1866.

Early-twentieth-century constitutions were influenced by the U.S. Constitution. The main features of the Constitution of 1924, promulgated after the U.S. military authorities withdrew, were retained in subsequent documents until the era of Generalíssimo Rafael Trujillo (1930–1961). Trujillo's constitutions enunciated principles of civilian democratic rule and representative government, called for three equal and independent branches of government, and included provisions for human rights. But constitutional theory and political reality were two very different things. Trujillo, while ruling as autocratically and ruthlessly as any Caribbean dictator, was scrupulous about upholding the narrow letter of the law—with no intention of abiding by the spirit of the constitution. Indeed, if examined closely, his 1955 Constitution, for example, granted almost absolute power to the president.

After Trujillo was assassinated in 1961, a provisional Council of State enacted a new Constitution of 1962, which remained in effect for less than a year. Its symbolic importance, however, was that it represented a continuation of *trujillismo*. Anti-Trujillo elements regarded it as a symbol of oppression and retention of privileges for the elites. It encountered bitter opposition from antidictatorial sectors and seemed strikingly unsuited to the needs of the impoverished country.

The reformist regime of Juan Bosch (1963) enacted a far different constitution. The 1963 Constitution not only retained the most politically and socially progressive features of the 1962 Constitution but also explicitly committed the government to an active role in fostering socioeconomic development and laid the bases for a modern welfare state. Unfortunately, several constitutional provisions alienated powerful traditional elements in society. The Catholic Church objected to the legalization of divorce and the new emphasis on secular education. The business community was alarmed over the emphasis on public rather than private economic interests. The landowners feared expropriation of their holdings, and the military feared a loss of power and subordination to civilian authority. These groups combined to overthrow Bosch in late 1963 and quickly restore the Constitution of 1962.

After the 1965 civil war, in which the United States intervened militarily, a compromise constitution was hammered out by a constituent assembly the following year. In essence the 1966 Constitution provides for modern progressive government and civil liberties but lacks the kind of social provisions that would alienate the traditional elites.

See also **Bosch Gaviño, Juan; Dominican Revolt (1965); Haiti; Santana, Pedro; Trujillo Molina, Rafael Leónidas.**

BIBLIOGRAPHY

Howard J. Wiarda, *The Dominican Republic: Nation in Transition* (1969).

Thomas E. Weil et al., *Area Handbook for the Dominican Republic* (1973).

Ian Bell, *The Dominican Republic* (1981).

Julio Brea Franco, *El sistema constitucional dominicano*, 2 vols. (1983).

Jan Knippers Black, *The Dominican Republic: Politics and Development in an Unsovereign State* (1986).

Additional Bibliography

Darío Espinal, Flavio. *Constitucionalismo y procesos políticos en la República Dominicana.* Santo Domingo: PUCMM, 2001.

Fiallo Billini, José Antinoe. *Democracia, participación popular y reforma constitucional.* Santo Domingo, República Dominicana: Instituto Tecnológico de Santo Domingo, 2001.

WINFIELD J. BURGGRAAFF

DOMINICAN REPUBLIC, DOMINICAN REVOLUTIONARY PARTY (PRD).

The PRD was founded in 1939 by Dominican anti-Trujilloist exiles for the purpose of toppling the Dominican dictator Rafael Trujillo. It established branches in Caracas, New York, and San Juan, Puerto Rico. Among its founders were Juan Bosch, Juan Isidro Jiménes Grullón, and Angel Miolán. Shortly after Trujillo's assassination in May 1961, a PRD delegation led by Angel Miolán, Nicolas Silfa, and Ramon Castillo returned to Santo Domingo to participate in the now reviving political life that had been stifled for over three decades. In the first national elections (December 1962) after Trujillo's death, PRD candidate Bosch defeated his National Civic Union (UCN) opponent. After only seven months in office, Bosch was toppled by a military coup. While the ensuing Triumvirate remained in power, the PRD spearheaded the opposition to a government that was dominated by UCN members and the military. During the revolution of 1965, the PRD led the struggle of the Constitutionalist cause.

In the first election (1966) after the end of the revolutionary and civil war of 1965, PRD candidate Juan Bosch was defeated by his Reformist Party (PR) opponent, Joaquín Balaguer, who also won the presidential elections of 1970 and 1974. After Bosch broke with the PRD in 1973 in order to form his own political party, the Dominican Liberation Party (PLD), PRD party affairs were taken over by José Francisco Peña Gómez, who went on to become vice president of the Socialist International after the

PRD, which considered itself a Social Democratic party, had become a member of that organization.

The PRD staged a political comeback in 1978, when its candidate, Antonio Guzmán Fernández, won the presidential election. That victory was followed in 1982 by Salvador Jorge Blanco's winning the presidency on behalf of the PRD. Thereafter, the PRD's fortunes declined as the party fragmented into diverse factions. However, the PRD won the presidential election in 2000. Although the party lost again in 2004, it still remains an important part of electoral politics.

See also **Balaguer, Joaquín; Bosch Gaviño, Juan; Dominican Republic; Peña Gómez, José Francisco; Trujillo Molina, Rafael Leónidas.**

BIBLIOGRAPHY

Michael J. Kryzanek, "Political Party Decline and the Failure of Liberal Democracy: The PRD in Dominican Politics," in *Journal of Latin American Studies* 9, pt. 1 (1977): 115–143.

Angel Miolán, *El Perredé desde mi ángulo* (1984).

Additional Bibliography

Agosto, Gabriela, and Francisco Cueto Villamán. *Los partidos por dentro estructura y funcionamiento del PRD, PRSC y PLD: 1978–2002*. Santo Domingo, República Dominicana: Centro de Estudios Sociales P. Juan Montalvo, S.J., 2002.

Gautreaux Piñeyro, Bonaparte. *El tiempo de la tormenta Bosch, Caamaño y el PRD*. Santo Domingo, República Dominicana: Editora de Colores, 1994.

KAI P. SCHOENHALS

DOMINICAN REVOLT (1965).

Dominican Revolt (1965), the civil conflict spurred by the military's overthrow of Juan Bosch and the installation of a repressive puppet regime. The September 1963 coup that removed the democratically elected Bosch after a mere seven months in office brought to power a military-backed civilian triumvirate, headed by businessman Donald Reid Cabral, that embarked on a course of corruption and repression that reminded Dominicans of the dictatorship of Rafael Trujillo. On 24 April 1965, members of the Dominican Revolutionary Party (PRD), some Christian Socialists, disgruntled professionals, and dissident elements of the armed forces led by

Colonel Francisco Caamaño Deñó, seized the government and arrested Reid Cabral. The Constitutionalists' appeal for the restoration of democracy and the return of the constitutionally elected President Juan Bosch from exile was met with enthusiasm from the Dominican populace but with consternation on the part of pro-Cabral elements among the armed forces and the U.S. embassy, represented by William Tupley Bennett.

The organizer of the coup against Bosch, General Elías Wessín y Wessín, ordered the bombing of Santo Domingo by his air force, which was followed by an attempted thrust into the old part of the capital. Not only were the Constitutionalists able to repulse Wessín's attack, but within a few days they were on the verge of victory. At this point U.S. President Lyndon B. Johnson ordered a massive armed intervention, ostensibly to rescue North American citizens and prevent a supposed Communist takeover, a "second Cuba," but in reality to obviate the return of Juan Bosch. There followed a bitter civil war between the Constitutionalists and Loyalists (loyal to Reid Cabral), with the supposedly neutral U.S. Marines and airborne units clearly siding with the forces of Wessín y Wessín. Contrary to Johnson's expectation of a brief skirmish, the conflict lasted the entire summer and resulted in thousands of Dominican casualties.

Johnson's intervention was criticized by Latin America's democracies (Mexico and Chile), which viewed his action as the end of Roosevelt's Good Neighbor Policy. The hemisphere's dictatorships, however, approved of the intervention and dispatched 500 Brazilian, Nicaraguan, Honduran, and Paraguayan soldiers to Santo Domingo to serve in an Inter-American Peace Force under U.S. General Bruce Palmer. A compromise settlement worked out by U.S. special envoy Ellsworth Bunker finally led to an end of the revolution and civil war on 31 August 1965. The Act of Dominican Reconciliation called for the creation of a provisional government, the reintegration of the country's armed forces, and the holding of national elections in June 1966.

See also **Bosch Gaviño, Juan; Caamaño Deñó, Francisco.**

BIBLIOGRAPHY

Dan Kurzman, *Santo Domingo: The Revolt of the Damned* (1965).

Tad Szulc, *Dominican Diary* (1965).

José Antonio Moreno, *Barrios in Arms* (1970).

Abraham F. Lowenthal, *The Dominican Intervention* (1972).

Piero Gleijeses, *The Dominican Crisis* (1978).

Hamlet Hermann, *Francis Caamaño* (1983).

Additional Bibliography

Bosch, Brian J. *Balaguer and the Dominican Military: Presidential Control of the Factional Officer Corps in the 1960s and 1970s.* Jefferson, NC: McFarland & Co., 2007.

Chester, Eric Thomas. *Red Tags, Scum, Riff-Raff, and Commies: the U.S. Intervention in the Dominican Republic, 1965–1966.* New York: Monthly Review Press, 2001.

Diedrich, Bernard. *Trujillo: Death of a Dictator.* Princeton: Markus Wiener, 2000.

Franco, Franklin J. *República Dominicana: Clases, crisis y comandos.* Santo Domingo: Ediciones Libería Trinitaria, 2000.

Peña Gómez, José Francisco. *Hitos de la revolución.* Santo Domingo: Editora el Nuevo Diario, 2005.

Kai P. Schoenhals

DOMINICANS.

DOMINICANS. Dominicans (Order of Preachers). The Dominican order was one of several religious orders important in colonial Latin America. Having been founded in medieval Europe as a means of combating heresy, it was particularly well suited to missionary activity in the Americas.

The Dominican order arrived in the New World in 1510 with a contingent of friars sent by the crown to Hispaniola. Although the Franciscans and others had begun the early missionary work on the island, the Dominicans would leave a lasting impression. The order was chosen for two reasons. The Spanish crown had received disquieting rumors of the outbreak of heresy in the new colony, and there was a generally conceded need for more priests. The first contingent was organized by Friar Alonso Loaisa. Although some fifteen friars were chosen, only nine, led by Friar Pedro de Córdoba, sailed for the New World, arriving in Santo Domingo in September 1510.

The impact of the Dominicans on Hispaniola was dramatic. Well trained in theology, as expounded by the famous Dominican, Saint Thomas Aquinas, the friars began to attempt to reform Spanish society.

They taught the doctrine of the equality of all human beings in the sight of God. In 1511, Friar Antonio de Montesinos began to rail in the pulpit against the system of forced Indian labor prevalent on the island. His sermons raised such ire in the colony that he was forced to return to Spain to defend his views. One settler, Bartolomé de Las Casas, deeply influenced by Montesinos, entered the Dominican order in 1523. Las Casas spent the remainder of his life continuing the struggle for social justice and for the protection of the American Indians.

The first contingent of Dominicans to arrive in Mexico after the Conquest came in 1526. The group of twelve friars, led by Friar Tomás Ortíz, suffered badly during the first year. Five of their number died, and four more were forced to return to Spain because of ill health, leaving only three friars: Domingo de Betanzos, Gonzalo Lucero, and Vicente de las Casas. Betanzos assumed leadership of the order in Mexico, overseeing its development until 1528, when seven more friars arrived.

In Mexico the Dominicans initiated their mission in the Valley of Mexico and surrounding regions. Their greatest efforts were made in the south, especially among the Mixteca and Oaxaca. In the south they had near complete autonomy. Some of the most impressive early churches were built by Dominicans, including Teposcolula, Yanhuitlán, and Cuilapán. Their devotion to Our Lady of the Rosary resulted in several magnificent works of ecclesiastical decoration, notably the Rosary chapel of the Church of Santo Domingo in Puebla.

The Dominicans were among the first orders to arrive in Peru. In 1529 a group of six Dominicans, led by Friar Reginaldo Pedraza, accompanied Pizarro on his return to the New World as participants in his expedition. Five of the six died or abandoned the enterprise, leaving only Friar Vicente de Valverde to participate with Pizarro in the conquest. He was counted among the men of Cajamarca and rewarded with the bishopric of Cuzco, in reality all of Peru, for his efforts.

The formal establishment of the order in Peru occurred in 1540, when Friar Francisco Toscano arrived with twelve other friars. The order quickly established monasteries in both Lima and Cuzco. Their church and convent in Cuzco was built upon the sacred temple of the Sun, the Coricancha. At the same time, the Dominicans under Friar Alonso de Montenegro established themselves in the other Inca capital of Quito.

Although the Dominicans were deeply involved in missionary activity among the Indians, they also had close ties to the Spanish population. In the capital cities, the Dominican conventual churches were often among the most ornate and best endowed. Many Dominicans also participated in the literary life of the colonies. In Lima, Friar Diego de Ojeda (Hojeda) won great repute for his poetry, especially the sacred epic *La cristiada.*

The Dominicans played an important role in the study of native languages. The order was responsible for the production of one of the most popular early catechisms in Mexico. In 1548 and 1550 their *Doctrina cristiana* was published. Later, in 1565, Friar Domingo de la Anunciación published his *Doctrina christiana breve,* another key early catechism, this one written in both Spanish and Nahuatl, the Aztec language. Among early students of the indigenous cultures, Friar Diego Durán ranks as very important. In his *Historia de las indias de la Nueva España* he compiled much information about the ancient rites and culture of the Aztecs, acquired during his childhood in Texcoco, near Mexico City. In Peru the efforts of the Dominicans to study the native languages was represented by Friar Domingo de Santo Tomás who published the first grammar and a dictionary of Quechua in 1560.

In Europe the Dominican order participated in the Holy Office of the Inquisition, but in the New World the Holy Office was organized under the monarch. The role played by the Dominicans was no greater than that of any other order. At the close of the sixteenth century one Dominican who had achieved some fame for his work in the Inquisition and for his skills as an historian was Friar Agustín Dávila y Padilla, author of the *Historia de la fundación y discurso de la provincia de Santiago,* a history of the Dominicans in Mexico.

As in other orders, by the end of the sixteenth century, nearly half of the membershp of local monasteries consisted of Creoles. Another important faction within the order were peninsular Spaniards who had entered the order in the New World, *hijos de provincia.* In order to cope with the competition for political power among these three groups, the Dominicans adopted the system known as the *alternativa* in their regular leadership elections. In this system, the leadership of local monasteries regularly rotated from peninsulars to creoles to *hijos de provincia.*

There were several Dominicans who became bishops during the colonial period. Some of the most famous of these include Friar Bartolomé de Las Casas, the first bishop of Chiapas, Friar Alonso de Montúfar, the second archbishop of Mexico and Friar Diego de Loaysa, first archbishop of Lima.

In Lima, during the seventeenth century a rich culture emerged out of the Dominican order. Saint Martín de Porres (1579–1639) was the mulatto son of a local gentleman. He sought entry into the Dominican order, but due to his illegitimate birth and mixed ancestry he was denied. Through quiet determination de Porres continued his quest, until in 1603 he was admitted as a lay brother. He was canonized in 1962. Juan Macias (1585–1645) arrived in Lima as a begging orphan. After living in the streets for several years, Macias entered the Dominican order and gained great fame for his piety and the austerity of his prayer life. He was beatified in 1837. Saint Rosa De Lima (1586–1617) was born into polite Lima society. Although baptized as Isabel, as a child she took the name Rose of Saint Mary. She did not formally enter the Dominican order, but dressed as a Dominican tertiary. She lived her life in extreme austerity, devoting long hours to prayer and mortification. She was canonized in 1671. Saint Mariana de Jesús Paredes (1618–1645) also was a member of the Dominican order. Born in Quito, she was orphaned at age five. Raised by her older sister, she soon demonstrated a vocation for the contemplative life. Although she studied with the Jesuits, she entered the Dominican convent of Santa Catalina in Quito. When an epidemic threatened to destroy everyone in the city, she offered herself to God as a sacrifice. The pestilence stopped, and within a day of her vow she died. Canonization proceedings began immediately and met with success in 1950.

See also **Catholic Church: The Colonial Period.**

BIBLIOGRAPHY

Daniel Ulloa, *Los predicadores divididos: Los dominicos en Nueva España, siglo XVI* (1977); *Los dominicos y el Nuevo Mundo* (1988).

Additional Bibliography

Brading, D.A. *First America: The Spanish Monarchy, Creole Patriots, and the Liberal State, 1492–1867.* New York: Cambridge University Press, 1991.

Casas, Bartolomé de las, and Stafford Poole. *In Defense of the Indians: The Defense of the Most Reverend Lord, Don Fray Bartolomé de las Casas, of the Order of Preachers, Late Bishop of Chiapas, Against the Persecutors and Slanderers of the Peoples of the New World Discovered Across the Seas.* DeKalb: Northern Illinois University Press, 1992.

Medina, Miguel Angel, O.P. *Los Dominicos en América: Presencia y actuación de los dominicos en la América colonial española de los siglos XVI–XIX.* Madrid: Editorial MAPFRE, 1992.

Mier Noriega y Guerra, José Servando Teresa de, Susana Rotker, and Helen R. Lane. *The Memoirs of Fray Servando Teresa de Mier.* New York: Oxford University Press, 1998.

Peréz Casado, Ángel. *En las fronteras de la fe: Dominicos en la Amazonía Peruana.* Salamanca: Editorial San Esteban, 1995.

                                        JOHN F. SCHWALLER

DONATÁRIOS. Donatários, lord proprietors. In 1534 King João III made donatary grants of fifteen strips of land in Brazil to a dozen noblemen to encourage permanent settlement and better defense from pirates. The lord proprietors who received these grants were required to defend and settle the land at their own expense, to found and charter townships, administer justice, collect tithes, and license sugar mills. The *donatários* were similar to the proprietors of large land grants in English North America, although in the case of Brazil, most were absentee landlords. As a recipient of a captaincy, the *donatário* had extensive administrative, fiscal, and judicial powers over colonists. They were empowered to make land grants (*sesmarias*) to prospective settlers who arrived to form permanent settlements and establish sugarcane plantations and cattle ranches to export crops.

None of the *donatários* came from the high nobility, but they were all members of the Order of Christ. Some of the *donatários* were soldiers of fortune, like Duarte Coelho Pereira and Francisco Pereira Coutinho. Others were well educated, like the historian João de Barros, or were government bureaucrats.

The original *donatários* of the captaincies around 1534 were:

João de Barros and Aires da Cunha (Pará)
Fernão Alvares de Andrade (Maranhão)
Antônio Cardoso de Barros (Piauí)
Pêro Lopes de Sousa (Itamaracá, Santo Amaro, Santa Ana)
Duarte Coelho Pereira (Pernambuco)
Francisco Pereira Coutinho (Bahia)
Jorge Figueiredo Correia (Ilhéus)
Pêro do Campo Tourinho (Pôrto Seguro)
Vasco Fernandes Coutinho (Espírito Santo)
Pêro de Góis (São Tomé)
Martim Afonso de Sousa (Rio de Janeiro, São Vicente)

See also **Captaincy System; João III of Portugal.**

BIBLIOGRAPHY

Carlos Malheiro Dias, ed., *História da colonização portuguesa do Brasil,* 3 vols. (1921–1926).

Alexander Marchant, *From Barter to Slavery: The Economic Relations of Portuguese and Indians in the Settlement of Brazil, 1500–1580* (1942).

Bailey W. Diffie, *Latin American Civilization: The Colonial Period* (1945), p. 642a, and *A History of Colonial Brazil, 1500–1792* (1987).

Additional Bibliography

Metcalf, Alida C. *Go-Betweens and the Colonization of Brazil, 1500–1600.* Austin: University of Texas Press, 2005.

Silva, Maria Beatriz Nizza da. *De Cabral a Pedro I: Aspectos da colonização portuguesa no Brasil.* Oporto, Portugal: Universidade Portucalense Infante D. Henrique, 2001.

                                        PATRICIA MULVEY

DONATARY CAPTAINCY SYSTEM. *See* **Captaincy System.**

DONOSO, JOSÉ (1924–1996). José Donoso (*b.* 5 October 1924, *d.* 7 December 1996), Chilean writer. Donoso was one of the most distinguished contemporary Latin American writers belonging to the generation of Gabriel García Márquez and Carlos Fuentes. Born in Santiago, Donoso began writing at the age of twenty-five. In 1951 he received a scholarship from the Doherty Foundation to study English literature at Princeton University. Upon returning to Chile he began a period of increased creative activity, writing short stories and publishing in 1955 his first book, *Veraneo y otros cuentos,* which won the Municipal Prize. His first novel, *Coronación* (1957) (*Coronation,* 1965) won the William Faulkner Foundation Prize for the Latin American Novel in 1962. He moved to Buenos Aires in 1958. Upon his return to Chile in 1960, he wrote for the weekly *Ercilla* and married María Pilar Serrano, a Bolivian painter. By the mid-1960s, Donoso was recognized as a major literary figure and was invited in 1965–1967 to the University of Iowa Writers' Workshop. He published his novels *Este domingo* (1966) (*This Sunday,* 1967) and *El lugar sin límites* (1966) (*Hell Has No Limits,* 1972) and a book of stories, *Los mejores cuentos de José Donoso* (1966).

In 1967 he left for Spain, eventually settling in Barcelona, where he published in 1970 what it had taken him eight years to write, *El obsceno pájaro de la noche* (*The Obscene Bird of Night,* 1973). This acclaimed novel placed Donoso among the top Latin American writers of his generation. There followed a series of outstanding novels: *Casa de campo* (1978) (*A House in the Country,* 1984), which won the Critics' Prize in Spain, *La misteriosa desaparición de la marquesita de Loria* (1980), *El jardín de al lado* (1981), and *La desesperanza* (1986) (*Curfew,* 1988), among others. In his 1972 *Historia personal del boom* (*The Boom in Spanish American Literature: A Personal History,* 1972) Donoso scrutinizes with humor and grace Emir Rodríguez Monegal's discussion of the publishing phenomenon of the 1960s. Donoso also created a series of masterful short story collections, among them *El charleston* (1960) (*Charleston and Other Stories,* 1977), *Tres novelitas burguesas* (1973) (*Sacred Families,* 1977), *Cuatro para Delfina* (1982), and *Taratuta* (1990). He also wrote a book of poetry, *Poemas de un novelista* (1981) and dramatic

versions of one of his short stories, *Sueños de mala muerte* (1985), and of his novel *Este domingo* (1990). The novellas *Nuevas novelas breves* and *El mocho* were published posthumously in 1997.

Donoso's fictional narratives stand out as the most important part of his production. His novels, *The Obscene Bird* and *House in the Country,* in particular, are the most valuable narratives of the contemporary period in Chile. They are also unique manifestations of the Spanish American novel, standing alongside García Márquez's *Cien años de soledad* (1967) and Carlos Fuentes's *Terra nostra* (1975). Donoso's literary expression represents the dark side of imagination, a grotesque recreation of myth, folklore, psychology, and the fantastic. The mixing of many voices constitutes the unmistakable stylistic feature of his narrative.

See also **Fuentes, Carlos; García Márquez, Gabriel; Literature: Spanish America.**

BIBLIOGRAPHY

Alfred J. MacAdam, *Modern Latin American Narratives: The Dreams of Reason* (1977).

George R. McMurray, *José Donoso* (1979).

Philip Swanson, *José Donoso: The Boom and Beyond* (1988).

Cedomil Goic, "José Donoso," in *Latin American Writers,* edited by Carlos A. Solé and María Isabel Abreu, vol. 3 (1989), pp. 1277–1288.

Additional Bibliography

Chesak, Laura A. *José Donoso, escritura y subversión del significado.* Madrid: Editorial Verbum, 1997.

Colvin, Michael. *Las últimas obras de José Donoso: Juegos, roles y rituales en la subversión del poder.* Madrid: Editorial Pliegos, 2001.

Magnarelli, Sharon. *Understanding José Donoso.* Columbia: University of South Carolina Press, 1993.

CEDOMIL GOIC

DONOVAN, JEAN (1953–1980). Jean Donovan (*b.* 10 April 1953, *d.* 2 December 1980), U.S. Catholic lay missionary murdered in El Salvador. Donovan was born in Westport, Connecticut. Influenced by an Irish priest who had served as a missionary in Peru, she applied to and was accepted for the Salvadoran mission program of the Cleveland diocese. Sent to La Libertad, El Salvador, in 1979, she taught religion, hygiene, and nutrition and worked with a Christian Base Community. Due to the escalation of the civil war, the Cleveland team soon joined Maryknoll nuns in transporting displaced peasants from war zones to Catholic refugee centers. On 2 December 1980, Donovan and her partner, Ursuline Sister Dorothy Kazel, picked up Maryknoll Sisters Ita Ford and Maura Clarke at the San Salvador airport. Their van was stopped by Salvadoran national guardsmen, who raped and murdered the four women. Their deaths and the cover-up of the crime by Salvadoran authorities shocked millions of North Americans and awakened them to the violent realities of El Salvador.

BIBLIOGRAPHY

Ana Carrigan, *Salvador Witness: The Life and Calling of Jean Donovan* (1984).

Donna Whitson Brett and Edward T. Brett, *Murdered in Central America: The Stories of Eleven U.S. Missionaries* (1988), pp. 189–252.

Additional Bibliography

Dear, John, and William Hart McNichols. *You Will Be My Witnesses: Saints, Prophets, and Martyrs.* Maryknoll, NY: Orbis Books, 2006.

Keogh, Dermot, ed. *Witness to the Truth: Church and Dictatorship in Latin America.* Cork: Cork University Press, 1989.

EDWARD T. BRETT

DORREGO, MANUEL (1787–1828).

Manuel Dorrego (*b.* 11 June 1787; *d.* 13 December 1828), Argentine military officer in the independence struggle and Federalist leader. Though born in Buenos Aires, Dorrego was studying law in Chile when the revolution against Spain began. He actively embraced the patriot cause, first in Chile and then in his own country, joining the 1811 campaign to liberate what later became Bolivia. Later still he fought in Uruguay with the forces of Buenos Aires against those of the Uruguayan leader José Artigas. He gained a reputation as quarrelsome and undisciplined, but he also took a principled stand against the centralism and monarchist intrigues of the

government of Juan Martín de Pueyrredón (1816–1819), which exiled him in 1817.

Dorrego spent three years in the United States, an experience that strengthened his Federalist convictions. After his return he held a number of military and other positions and became an active publicist in opposition to the Unitarist regime of Bernardino Rivadavia. At the collapse of Rivadavia's government in 1827, Dorrego became governor of Buenos Aires Province, in which capacity he brought to a close the war fought with Brazil over Uruguay, agreeing to accept Uruguayan independence. In December 1828 he was overthrown by Juan Lavalle, who by executing Dorrego made him a martyr in the eyes of Federalists and unleashed a round of bloody reprisals and counterreprisals between the two parties.

See also **Spain; Argentina, Movements: Federalists.**

BIBLIOGRAPHY

A biography is Marcos De Estrada, *Una semblanza de Manuel Dorrego* (1985). See also the treatment in the biography by John Lynch of his party ally and successor, *Argentine Dictator: Juan Manuel de Rosas, 1829–1852* (1981).

Additional Bibliography

Orsi, René. *Dorrego y la unidad rioplatense.* La Plata: Subsecretaría de Cultura, 1991.

Zuccherino, Ricardo Miguel. "Martín Miguel Juan de la Mata Güemes: el Señor Gaucho: Imagen de Manuel Dorrego: Ideólogo fundamental del federalismo." In *Caudillos e intelectuales de la Argentina tradicional,* Roberto Fernández Cistac, editor. Mar del Plata: EH, Fondo Editorial "Esto es Historia," 2001.

DAVID BUSHNELL

DORTICÓS TORRADO, OSVALDO

(1919–1983). Osvaldo Dorticós Torrado (*b.* 1919; *d.* 23 June 1983), president of Cuba from 1959 to 1976. Born in Cienfuegos, Dorticós Torrado graduated from the University of Havana Law School in 1941. He served as dean of the Cienfuegos Bar Association and subsequently as vice president of the Cuban Bar Association. After his release from a short imprisonment for anti-Batista activities, Dorticós joined Fidel Castro's Twenty-sixth of July Movement and soon became its Cienfuegos coordinator.

When President Manuel Urrutia resigned on 17 July 1959, Dorticós ascended to the presidency, becoming at forty the youngest president in the nation's history. Real power remained in Castro's hands, but Dorticós nevertheless remained loyal, receiving additional appointments, including minister of the economy in 1976. He held positions in the National Assembly of the People's Power and Council of State, was vice president of the Council of Ministers, and was a member of the Political Bureau of the Central Committee of the Cuban Communist Party. Dorticós committed suicide in 1983.

See also **Cuba: The Republic (1898–1959); Castro Ruz, Fidel.**

BIBLIOGRAPHY

Jaime Suchlicki, *Historical Dictionary of Cuba* (1988) and *Cuba: From Columbus to Castro,* 3d ed. (1990).

Additional Bibliography

Sweig, Julie. *Inside the Cuban Revolution: Fidel Castro and the Urban Underground.* Cambridge, MA: Harvard University Press, 2002.

JAIME SUCHLICKI

DOS PILAS. Dos Pilas, an important archaeological site of the Maya civilization located in the Petexbatún region of the Petén rain forest of Guatemala. Archaeological and epigraphic research has shown that Dos Pilas was the capital of a Classic Maya state remarkable for its late and rapid trajectory of florescence, expansion, and violent collapse.

The major occupation at the site began in the seventh century, when outcast members of the royal family of the great city of Tikal arrived at Dos Pilas and rapidly constructed the site center. From this new base, the first rulers concentrated their political and military efforts on defeating their relatives and rivals at Tikal. In the late seventh century, Dos Pilas defeated and sacrificed the king of Tikal, Shield Skull, enhancing the prestige of this newly created Maya polity. During the next century, the rulers of Dos Pilas successfully expanded their state across the Petexbatún region through royal marriages, alliance, and warfare. Even some large and ancient centers, such as Seibal, were subjugated. By 740 CE, the kingdom of Dos Pilas controlled much of the Pasión River valley, one of the major trade routes of the Maya world. During this period of expansionism, the Dos Pilas center acquired great wealth and prestige, as reflected in its tombs and cave deposits, and its many stone monuments. The site's numerous sculpted stelae and its four hieroglyphic stairways present military themes in both text and imagery.

The fall of Dos Pilas was as rapid and dramatic as its rise. In 761 CE, previously subordinate Petexbatún centers defeated the ruler of Dos Pilas. Archaeological remains corresponding to this date show that the site was besieged and destroyed. Evidence of the final years of the site includes concentric fortification walls around architectural complexes and impoverished occupation by small remnant populations. After the fall of Dos Pilas its Petexbatún kingdom fragmented into intensively warring smaller polities. This final violent period of Petexbatún history ended by 800 CE with the virtual abandonment of most of the region.

See also **Archaeology; Maya, The; Tikal.**

BIBLIOGRAPHY

Stephen Houston and Peter Mathews, "The Dynastic Sequence of Dos Pilas, Guatemala," in *Pre-Columbian Art Research Institute, Monograph 1* (1985).

Arthur Demarest et al., eds., *Petexbatún Regional Archaeological Project Preliminary Report 3* (1991) and *Petexbatún Regional Archaeological Project Preliminary Report 4* (1992).

Arthur A. Demarest, "The Violent Saga of a Maya Kingdom," in *National Geographic* 183, no. 2 (1993): 95–111.

Additional Bibliography

Brady, James E. "Settlement Configuration and Cosmology: The Role of Caves at Dos Pilas." *American Anthropologist* 99, no. 3 (Sept. 1997): 602–618.

Demarest, Arthur A. *The Petexbatun Regional Archaeological Project: A Multidisciplinary Study of the Maya Collapse.* Nashville: Vanderbilt University Press, 2006.

Houston, Stephen D. *Hieroglyphs and History at Dos Pilas: Dynastic Politics of the Classic Maya.* Austin: University of Texas Press, 1993.

Martin, Simon, and Nikolai Grube. *Chronicle of the Maya Kings and Queens: Deciphering the Dynasties of the Ancient Maya.* New York: Thames & Hudson, 2000.

ARTHUR A. DEMAREST

Habell-Pallán, Michelle, and Mary Romero, eds. *Latino/a Popular Culture.* New York: New York University Press, 2002.

ERIC ZOLOV

DOUBLE SIMULTANEOUS VOTE.
See **Uruguay, Electoral System.**

DOWNS, LILA

DOWNS, LILA (1968–). The leader of a six-member band whose members hail from across the Americas, Lila Downs has fashioned a unique musical fusion of sounds and aesthetic sensibilities rooted in her own Mixtec-Mexican-American identity and the diverse influences of her band members. Her band comprises both electric and acoustic instruments, including strings, saxophone, percussion, and both the electric and jarana guitar. Downs was born in Tlaxiaco, Oaxaca on September 19, 1968, to a Mixtec mother and an Anglo professor from Minneapolis, Minnesota. Her formative years were divided between Oaxaca, where she absorbed the indigenous and regional sounds of Mexico, and Minneapolis, where she studied music and social anthropology at the University of Minnesota. Downs's numerous albums reflect a wide exploration of musical genres, including ranchera, norteño, son jarocho, blues, and jazz. Her lyrics explore topics of Mexican immigration, indigenous spirituality, and feminist identity, blending English, Spanish, and the indigenous languages of southern Mexico to form a rich sonic experience. Her discography includes *La cantina* (2006); *Una sangre* (One Blood, 2004); *La sandunga* (2003); *Border* (*La linea*, 2001); and *Tree of Life* (2000).

See also **Music: Popular Music and Dance.**

BIBLIOGRAPHY

Aparicio, Frances R., and Cándida Jáquez, eds. *Musical Migrations: Transnationalism and Cultural Hybridity in Latin/o America.* New York: Palgrave Macmillan, 2003.

Habell-Pallán, Michelle. *Loca Motion: The Travels of Chicana and Latina Popular Culture.* New York: New York University Press, 2005.

DOWRY

DOWRY. Dowry, an important gift given to a woman contributing to her support in marriage or convent life. Until the end of the nineteenth century, parents had an explicit legal obligation to endow their daughters to the best of their abilities. Other relatives or, sometimes, charitable institutions also gave dowries or contributed toward them. In the sixteenth, seventeenth, and eighteenth centuries in Latin America most women who married and practically all nuns received a dowry.

The law and practice of dowry came from Iberia to Latin America with the first Spanish conquistadores and Portuguese settlers. In sixteenth-century Iberia it was customary for both spouses to bring property to marriage; the bride's contribution was her dowry and her inheritance (after one or both of her parents died). The practice of dowry, practically a requisite for marriage in Latin America in the sixteenth and seventeenth centuries, declined throughout the eighteenth and nineteenth centuries and disappeared by the early twentieth. The practice of a dowry to enter a convent persisted longer, although the relative size of the dowry had decreased considerably by the end of the nineteenth century.

When it was given by parents, the dowry was an advance on their daughter's inheritance. Daughters always inherited in Latin America, since Spanish and Portuguese law dictated equally partible inheritance and made all children forced heirs. (They could not be disinherited except for extremely serious causes.) When an endowed woman's parents died, the value of her dowry was usually added to the share of their estate that went by law to their children (usually four-fifths in Spanish America, and two-thirds in Brazil). The division was made equally among all heirs, and the daughter (whether a married woman or a nun) received the difference between her dowry and her inheritance.

Within marriage, dowry functioned differently in Spanish America from the way it did in Brazil because the marriage systems were different. In Spanish America there were three main kinds of property in a marriage: the property the husband brought to marriage; the property the wife brought to marriage, called her dowry, though it might not be restricted to the actual dowry given by her parents but could also include inherited property, or the property she had retained as a widow; and the property acquired in the course of the marriage through the husband's administration of all the couple's property (*bienes gananciales*). Because a wife's dowry was meant to revert to her when her husband died, her dowry could not be alienated or mortgaged and served as a kind of insurance for the wife. A widow received her dowry back and retained half the *bienes gananciales*. Brazil, in contrast, had full community property within the marriage (unless a prenuptial contract established otherwise), so that a woman's dowry disappeared into the pool of property. When she became a widow, she retained half the couple's property, no matter what proportion each spouse had contributed.

The system of equally partible inheritance with forced heirship combined with dowries for daughters meant that Latin American women of the propertied class made large economic contributions to their marriage or to the convents they entered. Furthermore, the marriage regimes by which widows retained considerable property gave Latin American widows of the propertied class importance as economic actors. Nuns likewise had significant economic roles.

The Latin American dowry system is now well understood, but its actual practice throughout the history of Latin America has been studied only in some regions and time periods, and more extensively in regard to marriage than in regard to convents. The main finding about dowry at marriage is that the practice varied somewhat from region to region and everywhere declined over the centuries. In the sixteenth and early seventeenth centuries, there was a tendency for brides to contribute greater amounts of property to marriage than did their husbands. By the late eighteenth or early nineteenth century, it was husbands who usually contributed more property to marriage than their wives. Simultaneously, fewer parents gave dowries and many marriages took place without a dowry. In São Paulo not only were dowries fewer and smaller in relation to the daughter's inheritance as the

centuries progressed, but the total divestment made by parents for their daughters' dowries in relation to the size of their estate dropped precipitously, and the contents of dowry changed from mainly means of production in the seventeenth century to mainly items for consumption in the nineteenth century.

The historical decline and disappearance of the practice of dowry was clearly related to changes in the roles of men and women and to alterations in marriage and the family which were a part of the general social changes experienced in the eighteenth and nineteenth centuries.

See also **Marriage and Divorce; Women.**

BIBLIOGRAPHY

For marriage dowry see Asunción Lavrin and Edith Couturier, "Dowries and Wills: A View of Women's Socioeconomic Role in Colonial Guadalajara and Puebla, 1640–1790," in *Hispanic American Historical Review* 59, no. 2 (1979): 280–304; Eugene H. Korth and Della M. Flusche, "Dowry and Inheritance in Colonial Spanish America: Peninsular Law and Chilean Practice," in *The Americas* 43, no. 4 (1987): 395–410; Muriel Nazzari, *Disappearance of the Dowry: Women, Families, and Social Change in São Paulo, Brazil (1600–1900)* (1991). For dowries in convents see Susan Soeiro, "The Social and Economic Role of the Convent: Women and Nuns in Colonial Bahia 1677–1800," in *Hispanic American Historical Review* 54, no. 2 (1974): 209–232; and Asunción Lavrin, "Women in Convents: Their Economic and Social Role in Colonial Mexico," in *Liberating Women's History: Theoretical and Critical Essays*, edited by Berenice Carroll (1976).

Additional Bibliography

Bazarte Martínez, Alicia. *Mujer y dotes en la Ciudad de Zacatecas durante la colonia.* Fresnilla: Museo de Minería, 2004.

Burns, Kathryn. *Colonial Habits: Convents and the Spiritual Economy of Cuzco, Peru.* Durham: Duke University Press, 1998.

Chowning, Margaret. *Wealth and Power in Provincial Mexico: Michoacán from the Late Colony to the Revolution.* Stanford: Stanford University Press, 1999.

Metcalf, Alida C. *Family and Frontier in Colonial Brazil: Santana de Parnaíba, 1580-1822.* Berkeley: University of California Press, 1992.

Seed, Patricia. *To Love, Honor, and Obey in Colonial Mexico: Conflicts over Marriage Choice, 1574-1821.* Stanford: Stanford University Press, 1988.

Silva, Maria Beatriz Nizza da. *Families in the Expansion of Europe, 1500-1800.* Brookfield: Ashgate, 1998.

MURIEL NAZZARI

DRAGO, LUIS MARÍA (1859–1921).
Luis María Drago (*b.* 6 May 1859; *d.* 9 June 1921), Argentine jurist. A native of Buenos Aires, Drago was elected three times to the Chamber of Deputies and became one of Argentina's most eminent international jurists. In 1909, at the request of Britain and the United States, he arbitrated two major disputes between them; he also was a judge on the Permanent Court of International Justice (1912–1916). His major contribution was in the context of American international law and another important doctrine, the Drago Doctrine, which was a narrowing of the Calvo Doctrine. This contribution, made while he was minister of foreign affairs, was in response to armed European intervention against Venezuela. In 1902, three European states (Britain, Germany, and Italy) imposed a naval blockade in order to force their financial claims resulting from default on bonds. On 29 December 1902 Drago sent an official note to the heads of the American governments stating that such use of force was contrary to international law: "The collection of loans by military means implies territorial occupation to make them effective [and it is] the suppression or subordination of the governments." His note received strong support in Latin America and at the Second Hague Conference (1907), where the United States had his doctrine modified.

See also **Drago Doctrine.**

BIBLIOGRAPHY

Luis María Drago, "State Loans in Their Relation to International Policy," in *American Journal of International Law* 1, no. 3 (1907): 692–726, and Harold Eugene Davis, John J. Finan, and F. Taylor Peck, *Latin American Diplomatic History: An Introduction* (1977).

Additional Bibliography

Bra, Gerardo. *La Doctrina Drago.* Buenos Aires: Centro Editor de América Latina, 1990.

Consalvi, Simón Alberto. "Luis M. Drago, 1902: una doctrina que hizo historia." *Boletín de la Academia Nacional de la Historia (Venezuela)* 85 (July–December 2002): 69–78.

LARMAN C. WILSON

DRAGO DOCTRINE.
Drago Doctrine, a principle of international law that rejects the right of a country to use military force against another country to collect debts. The doctrine was first enunciated on 29 December 1902 by Luis María Drago, Argentina's minister of foreign affairs, in a letter to the Argentine minister in Washington, D.C., in response to the naval blockade imposed on Venezuela by Germany, Great Britain, and Italy for the purpose of collecting debts incurred by the Venezuelan government with nationals of those countries.

Although based on the Calvo Doctrine, the Drago Doctrine goes further by rejecting the right of intervention and specifying that economic claims give no legal right to intervene militarily in another country. The Calvo Doctrine says, in essence, that investors have to accept the jurisdiction of the host country's laws and should not appeal to their own governments in case of any conflict in the enforcement of a contract. The Drago Doctrine stipulates that a nation, although it is legally bound to pay its debts, cannot be forced to do so.

The doctrine was innovative because it rejected categorically the right of military intervention or occupation of a country for the purpose of collecting debts. At the time, however, European powers were intervening and carving out empires everywhere and the United States had also joined the club of colonial powers after the Spanish-American War, and thus the doctrine was not readily accepted as a principle of international law. At the Second Hague Conference (1907) a toned-down form of the doctrine was adopted. The resolution declared illegal an intervention for the collection of debts, provided that the nation in question had accepted arbitration and the decisions adopted in that arbitration. Drago explained his doctrine extensively in two of his books: *La República Argentina y el caso de Venezuela* (1903) and *Cobro coercitivo de deudas públicas* (1906).

The general doctrine rejecting military force to collect debts seems to have become an accepted principle. After World War II, international institutions like the World Bank and the International Monetary Fund (IMF) arranged emergency loans when a country defaulted on its obligations. Even when Argentina defaulted on its foreign loans in 2001 and could not work out an agreement with international agencies, lenders had to resort to courts and arbitration to get any of their investments back.

See also **Calvo Doctrine; Drago, Luis María; International Monetary Fund (IMF); World Bank.**

BIBLIOGRAPHY

Alfredo N. Vivot, *La Doctrina Drago* (1911).

Victorino Jiménez y Núñez, *La Doctrina Drago y la política internacional* (1927).

Edwin M. Borchard, "Calvo and Drago Doctrines," in *Encyclopaedia of the Social Sciences,* vol. 3 (1930).

Isidro Fabela, *Las doctrinas Monroe y Drago* (1957).

Additional Bibliography

Drake, Paul W., ed. *Money Doctors, Foreign Debts, and Economic Reforms in Latin America from the 1890s to the Present.* Wilmington, DE: SR Books, 1994.

Lozada, Martín, and Lista, Guillermo. "Deuda externa y soberanía del estado deudor: Reflexiones en ocasión del centenario de la Doctrina Drago." *Realidad Económica* 192 (November–December 2002), 25–36.

Marichal, Carlos. *A Century of Debt Crises in Latin America: From Independence to the Great Depression, 1820–1930.* Princeton, NJ: Princeton University Press, 1989.

JUAN MANUEL PÉREZ

DRAGÚN, OSVALDO (1929–1999).

Osvaldo Dragún (*b.* 7 May 1929, *d.* 14 June 1999), Argentine playwright, achieved international status with his *Historias para ser contadas* (1957), a group of brief and dehumanizing vignettes that capture a pithy social reality with sparse language, minimal plot and scenery, and often grotesque elements. Dragún, a native of San Salvador, Entre Ríos, lacked formal training in the theater but learned quickly by acting, directing, and writing for community theater groups. His career was launched with the independent group Fray Mocho in 1956 and the production of two historical plays that underscored individual and political freedom, *La peste viene de Melos* (1956) and *Tupac Amaru* (1957). The writers of Dragún's generation (including Roberto Cossa, Carlos Gorostiza, and Ricardo Halac) sought to interpret an Argentine reality that was chaotic under Juan Perón but even more anarchic after his demise. This "new realism" found expression in the aesthetics of the grotesque, an honored tradition in

Argentina with its dehumanization of the individual. Dragún wrote many full-length plays, including Υ *nos dijeron que éramos inmortales* (1963), a study of the illusions of alienated generations, and *Milagro en el mercado viejo* (1964), a Brechtian play about crime and betrayal. Of his twenty or so theater pieces, the most successful are *El amasijo* (1968), an absurdist rendering of two lonely individuals who regularly miss the opportunities life hands them, and *Arriba corazón!* (1986), an expressionist piece with autobiographical overtones. Dragún spent many years outside Argentina, primarily in Cuba, where he was greatly involved with the International Theater School. In Argentina he was instrumental in creating the Teatro Abierto in 1981, a daring and ambitious presentation of twenty new plays, by various authors, structured to challenge Argentine political reality at its most vicious and repressive stage, the military dictatorship.

See also **Theater.**

BIBLIOGRAPHY

Donald L. Schmidt, "The Theater of Osvaldo Dragún," in *Dramatists in Revolt: The New Latin American Theater,* edited by Leon F. Lyday and George W. Woodyard (1976): 77–94.

Bonnie Hildebrand Reynolds, "Time and Responsibility in Dragún's *Tupac Amaru,*" in *Latin American Theatre Review* 13, no. 1 (Fall 1979): 47–53.

Jacqueline Eyring Bixler, "The Game of Reading and the Creation of Meaning in *El amasijo,*" in *Revista Canadiense de Estudios Hispánicos* 12, no. 1 (Fall 1987): 1–16.

Amalia Gladhart, "Narrative Foregrounding in the Plays of Osvaldo Dragún," in *Latin American Theatre Review* 26, no. 2 (Spring 1993): 93–109.

Additional Bibliography

Dragún, Osvaldo, and John F. Garganigo. *Osvaldo Dragún: Su teatro.* Medellín: Ediciones Otras Palabras, 1993.

Suppes, Patricia. "Audience and Message in Osvaldo Dragun's Historias Para Ser Contadas and Heroica De Buenos Aires." M.A. thesis, University of North Carolina at Chapel Hill, 1997.

GEORGE WOODYARD

DRAKE, FRANCIS (c. 1545–1596).

Francis Drake (*b.* ca. 1545; *d.* 28 January 1596), English privateer who became, from 1570 to 1595, the central figure in attacks by privateers on the Spanish Indies. A maritime genius and fervent Protestant, Drake was a glorious hero to the English and a frightening monster in the eyes of the Spanish. He developed a coherent West Indian strategy to replace the established pattern of small, uncoordinated raids on the Spanish. Although Drake achieved much success, acquiring great booty and inflicting considerable damage to Spanish holdings, he failed to break Spain's monopoly on territorial possession in the Caribbean.

Originally an illicit trader, Drake was with John Hawkins of Plymouth during the disastrous defeat at San Juan de Ulúa in late 1568. In 1571 he carried out reconnaissance activities and forged alliances with savage indigenous warriors, particularly on the Central American isthmus. A year later he led a voyage that attacked Nombre de Dios, Panama, and acquired a large booty of Peruvian treasure. After the English-Spanish peace of 1574, Drake remained active in the West Indies for eleven years, becoming the first captain to sail his own ship around the world (1577–1580).

In 1585, Drake resumed his naval efforts by carrying out a full-scale operation known as the Indies Voyage, with a fleet of over twenty sails, which aspired to attack Santo Domingo and Cartagena, Colombia, then Nombre de Dios and Panama (by land, in collaboration with runaway slaves), and, finally, Havana. In addition to establishing an English stronghold in the Indies, Drake hoped to disrupt the flow of Latin American resources, particularly Peruvian silver, to the Iberian Peninsula, thereby hindering Spain's military efforts in Europe. This plan proved to be too ambitious, however. After destroying much of Santo Domingo and Cartagena, Drake decided not to attack the isthmus, because of his depleted manpower, a result of shipboard health problems. When adverse weather also prevented him from attacking the Spanish treasure fleet, Drake sailed for home in June 1586. Despite its temporary successes and the great damage it caused Spain's possessions and prestige, Drake's Indies Voyage failed in its larger aims, for the Spanish maintained their territorial supremacy.

Spain's desire to destroy England's growing geopolitical power took the form of an enormous naval attack against England in 1588, in which Drake played a key role. Along with John Hawkins and others he contributed to one of the largest naval defeats in history, that of the Spanish Armada (1588). By 1595, however, the Spanish had clearly learned some lessons, particularly in regard to the activities of privateers. When another great fleet, under the direction of Hawkins and Drake, left England to attack Spain's possessions in the Indies, the Spanish were well prepared. They defeated the English at San Juan, Puerto Rico, and at Cartagena. Moreover, having established a more defensible harbor, Porto Bello, to replace Nombre de Dios, they emerged victorious on the isthmus as well. Sir Francis Drake died shortly thereafter, off the coast of Veragua, Panama.

See also **Piracy.**

BIBLIOGRAPHY

Sir Julian S. Corbett, *Drake and the Tudor Navy*, 2 vols. (1898, repr. 1988).

J. A. Williamson, *Sir John Hawkins: The Time and the Man* (1927, repr. 1970).

A. E. W. Mason, *The Life of Sir Francis Drake* (1941, repr. 1950).

J. A. Williamson, *Sir Francis Drake* (1951).

Garrett Mattingly, *The Armada* (1959).

George M. Thompson, *Sir Francis Drake* (1972).

J. H. Parry et al., *A Short History of the West Indies,* 4th ed. (1987).

John Sugden, *Sir Francis Drake* (1990).

Additional Bibliography

Kelsey, Harry. *Sir Francis Drake: The Queen's Pirate.* New Haven, CT: Yale University Press, 1998.

BLAKE D. PATTRIDGE

DROUGHT REGION (BRAZIL). Drought Region (Brazil), area encompassing most of eight states in Northeast Brazil; defined politically as the *polígono das sêcas* or drought polygon. Historically the designation has had more to do with social structure, politics, and psychology than with climate; generations of Brazilians have been conditioned through political debate, essays, novels, songs, and films to define the Northeast interior and its social problems in terms of drought. Meteorologically, the droughts are produced by Caribbean and South Atlantic weather systems, the instability of which can cause wide variations in seasonal rainfall. However, the human effects of these poorly understood natural phenomena derive historically from the social and political structure of the region.

The droughts entered the historical record in 1584, when Friar Fernão Cardim reported that over four thousand indigenes had fled from the interior to the Pernambucan coast because of a drought. The intermixture of meteorological, social, economic, and political factors in historical memory and contemporary perceptions has led to disagreement over the precise historical pattern of droughts, but most agree that severe droughts occurred in 1639, 1724–1725, 1736–1737, 1745–1746, 1777–1778, 1791–1793, 1825–1827, 1845–1847, 1877–1880, 1888–1889, 1906, 1915, 1936, 1953, 1958, and 1979–1983. The social and economic consequences of several of these earned them the label *grandes sêcas* (great droughts). The end of the great colonial northeastern cattle kingdoms, the "Leather Civilization," is traditionally marked by the *grande sêca* of 1793, and exceptionally severe droughts since that time tend to be associated with periods of economic and political stress or rapid change: the drought of 1825–1827 coincided with the political confusion of Brazilian independence and its aftermath; the drought of 1845–1847 accompanied the political and economic transformations of midcentury; the Empire of Brazil was ushered out by the drought of 1888–1889; the drought of 1958 accompanied the regional development crisis of the 1950s.

The worst drought in Brazilian history, which had a profound influence on the regional image and on the perception of and reaction to droughts in Brazil ever since, was the Great Drought of 1877–1880. This event followed two decades of population growth and incipient development spurred by an illusory cotton boom associated with the U.S. Civil War, then debt, retrenchment, and stress during the middle 1870s. Practical and psychological unpreparedness, combined with a lack of political and economic cohesion, led to at least a quarter of a million deaths, forced the permanent migration from the region of perhaps an equal number, and so profoundly dislocated the lives of survivors that its effects, on individuals, families, and the Northeast as a whole, were felt for generations thereafter. The crisis persuaded the imperial

government to treat the droughts as a national problem for the first time, and added an important new factor to the Brazilian political equation. Politicians from the drought states, divided over other issues, unified to force central governments to issue drought aid.

Imperial funds injected into the Northeast provinces during the great drought of 1877–1880 and the decade following moved "drought fighting" into a central position in regional politics. The drought "solutions" that emerged—relocation of refugees, public works for emergency employment and infrastructure improvement, and hydraulic works—have persisted to the present time. The drought-fighting discourse that then engaged intellectuals contained enduring subthemes that help to explain why the region and the nation have never solved the social problems that underlie the climatic phenomena, such as the contention that the climate of the Northeast could somehow be restored through the building of large reservoirs and reforestation, or that the common people of the Sertão had been shaped permanently by the climate into an inferior race, incapable of rational, modern action.

After the establishment of the republic in 1889, the ill-managed projects initiated by the imperial government were reincarnated as a series of federal agencies: the Federal Institute of Anti-Drought Works (IFOCS), established in 1909, developed through a series of droughts, sharp regional pressure, and the politics of the Vargas years into the National Department of Drought-Fighting Works (DNOCS) in 1949. The 1934 and 1946 Brazilian constitutions stipulated that fixed percentages of national, state, and municipal revenues be set aside for antidrought works and emergency relief for drought victims. While this financial obligation to the drought polygon is absent from the 1988 constitution, mounting a "permanent defense" against natural calamities is listed among the twenty-five enumerated responsibilities of the federal government.

In the 1950s, comprehensive regional planning began to replace the single-minded "hydraulic approach" that saw building reservoirs as the answer. The corruption and inefficiency revealed in DNOCS during the severe drought of 1958 discredited (but did not end) the drought-fighting approach and brought favor to the integrated regional-development approach embodied in the giant Superintendency for the Development of the Northeast (SUDENE). After 1958, the focus of DNOCS shifted from reservoir building to irrigation projects, which often forced peasants off their land in the fertile river bottoms. Since 1970 the favored solution to the problems of the drought region has been integration into the national economy, including improved transportation and renewed encouragement of outmigration to the more developed center-south and developing Amazon basin, while paying somewhat more, but still far inadequate, attention to basic social problems and sustainable development within the region. Near the end of the twentieth century, as overpopulation, economic and social exploitation, and an inadequate resource base continue to shape recurrent climatic episodes into social disasters, the social solution to the drought problem seems as remote as it was in 1877.

See also **Brazil, Organizations: Development Superintendency of the Northeast (SUDENE).**

BIBLIOGRAPHY

Anthony L. Hall, *Drought and Irrigation in North-East Brazil* (1978), and Kempton E. Webb, *The Changing Face of Northeast Brazil* (1974), are geographical surveys with good historical and political background information. Manuel Correia De Andrade, *The Land and People of Northeast Brazil,* translated by Dennis V. Johnson (1980), is indispensable for any study of the Northeast. Joaquim Alves, *História das Sécas (séculos XVII a XIX),* is a scholarly survey from within the region, but limited to Ceará. The most complete account of any Brazilian drought is Roger Cunniff, "The Great Drought: Northeast Brazil, 1877–1880" (Ph.D. diss., Univ. of Texas, Austin, 1970), complemented by Gerald Greenfield, "The Great Drought and Elite Discourse in Imperial Brazil," *Hispanic American Historical Review* 72 (1992): 375–400. Antonio Magalhães and Pennie Magee, "The Brazilian Nordeste (Northeast)," in *Drought Follows the Plow,* edited by Michael H. Glantz (1994), surveys developments in the drought area.

Additional Bibliography

Heinrichs, G., and Voerkelius, S. *Climate, Water, Mankind: Impacts of Long-term Climatic Changes in the Drought Polygon of Northeast–Brazil.* Río de Janeiro, Brazil: 31st International Geological Congress, 2000.

Ponce, Victor Miguel. "Management of Droughts and Floods in the Semiarid Brazilian Northeast: The Case for Conservation." *Journal of Soil and Water Conservation* 50, no. 1 (September–October 1995): 422–431.

Roger Cunniff

DRUGS AND DRUG TRADE. Latin America is home to several important native drugs. The coca shrub (*Erythroxylon coca*), the basis for cocaine, grows in the Andean region. A variety of cactus, including the peyote cactus (*Lophophora williamsii*) and the San Pedro cactus (*Trichocereus pachanoi*), grown primarily in Mexico and on the west coast of South America respectively, have mescaline as their active principle. Various mushrooms, members of the *Stropharia* and *Psilocybe* genera, are found in Mexico and Central America and have psilocybin as their base.

The female hemp plant (*Cannabis sativa*), whose dried leaves and flowers are known as cannabis or marijuana, was introduced to North and South America in the sixteenth century by the Spanish and Portuguese, and to the Caribbean in the early eighteenth century by immigrants from India. The opium poppy (*Papaver somniferum*), from which heroin is distilled, was first planted in Latin America in Mexico in the early twentieth century.

DRUGS AND DRUG USE

The use of drugs by traditional Latin American societies can be traced to 3000 BCE. They were used in diverse cultural and religious activities, such as divination, meditation, and curing, and for relief from hunger and discomfort. Archaeological evidence suggests that the coca shrub originated on the eastern slopes of the Andes and spread by 500 CE to Panama. Once the mild stimulant and medical properties of the leaves were known, they were collected, dried in the sun, and masticated and held in the mouth as a quid. An alkaline substance (usually ash from vegetables) was added to facilitate the release of their chemical properties. During the Tiwanaku Empire (600–1200 CE) coca was integrated into cultural and religious activities such as ritual nocturnal intoxication. Coca chewing was widespread during the Inca Empire from about 1400 to 1532 at all levels of society.

A Bolivian soldier destroys coca leaves, 1991. Eighty percent of all coca is grown in Bolivia and neighboring Peru. Most of it is processed into cocaine and shipped to Colombia for distribution elsewhere. © BILL GENTILE/CORBIS

During Spanish colonial rule (1532–1825) in the Andean region, coca production and use by Indians continued, and the coca leaf was also chewed by the Spanish, primarily for medical reasons, despite attempts by the colonial administration at eradication and prohibition. The prohibition of the growth and trade of coca in the Spanish American Empire for political and humanitarian reasons was not successful, although the use of coca in shamanic activities was seen as fostering resistance to Spanish rule and the miserable conditions and high death rate of the workers in coca fields were condemned by Bartolomé de Las Casas.

In the late sixteenth century the crown accepted the fact that coca was an integral part of the Indian workforce and Viceroy Toledo regulated all aspects of the production and trade of the coca leaf in the

ordenanzas de la coca. Production increased over time because of more widespread consumption in highlands farming communities and in mining areas. The cycles of boom and bust that afflicted the mining industry affected the coca industry as miners depended on coca because of their difficult and demanding working conditions. The symbiotic relationship between coca production and mineral exportation continued after independence from Spain primarily in large haciendas in the Yungas region of Bolivia, one of the main coca-growing areas in the Andes until the boom in the 1970s.

After the Conquest, the coca leaf continued to play an important role in the cultural identity of Aymara and Quechua Indians in the Andean highlands, or Altiplano. Coca is still essential in many religious and nonreligious ceremonies for 3 million Andean Indians who, for example, use coca leaves in ritual exchanges between families or groups as part of systems of reciprocal labor or favors. The traditional use of coca continues also in communities of Amazonian Indians in Peru and Ecuador.

In addition to coca, traditional societies in Peru before and after the Conquest used a variety of different drugs. Archaeological evidence allows us to reconstruct the use of the San Pedro cactus, various nightshade plants, and the willka shrub by the Mochica (100 BCE–700 CE) and by the Nazca (100–800 CE). In both cultures psychotropic plants played an important part in shamanic activities. Their use continued after the Spanish Conquest despite attempts at prohibition, and Roman Catholic beliefs were eventually syncretized with their traditional use. The San Pedro cactus is still used among traditional societies in northern Peru to treat illness believed to be caused by witchcraft. In Peruvian Amazonian cities today, men and women use the plant hallucinogen ayahuasca in the diagnosis and treatment of witchcraft-related illness. Folk healers assemble groups of patients several times a week and administer the plant potion to allow their clients to obtain visions of the men and women who bewitched them.

Psychoactive substances have been used in Meso-america from Preclassic times (1650 BCE) until the present. An examination of ancient Maya art from Mexico, Guatemala, and Belize reveals the use of mind-altering mushrooms, toad venom, and the

Plane spraying herbicide on suspected coca fields in Colombia, 1996. This practice destroys illegal drug crops but also ruins legitimate crops and contaminates the water and soil. JB RUSSEL/SYGMA/CORBIS

rhizomes of the common water lily. These substances, some of which are referred to in the Popol Vuh, influenced the ancient Maya religion, especially in divination and healing. The hallucinogenic mushrooms of pre-Columbian Mexico were called "god's flesh" by the Aztecs, who used at least four major hallucinogenic plants for ceremonies connected with human sacrifice, entertainment of guests at ceremonial feasts, and payment of tribute. The drugs were also used by the Aztecs for medical purposes and to give warriors courage to fight. The use of hallucinogens in Mexico and Central America continued despite their prohibition by the Inquisition, which declared in 1620 that the use of the peyote cactus was the work of the devil, and peyotism eventually became fused with Christianity.

Marijuana is a relatively unimportant drug in most traditional Latin American cultures. Only in Jamaica and other Caribbean nations does the drug, usually referred to as ganja, have a significant role with certain societal groups, such as the Rastafarians.

THE DRUG TRADE

The Latin American drug trade is dominated by cocaine and to a lesser extent by marijuana and heroin. Since the rapid increase in demand in the 1970s, the production, refining, and trafficking of these drugs in a growing number of nations in the region have affected the economy, politics, social fabric, and relations with the United States, which is the primary market for drugs produced in Latin America.

Cocaine, one of thirteen alkaloids distilled from the coca plant, is produced exclusively in Latin America. While about 80 percent of the coca grows in the Bolivian Chaparé and the upper Huallaga Valley in Peru, coca production has spread to all neighboring countries, where it had not been planted traditionally and where the cocaine content is often lower. A small percentage of the coca production is exported legally to the United States for use in manufacturing Coca Cola, which requires de-cocainized leaves, and for pharmaceutical companies. Colombia has a dominant role in the cocaine trade, primarily because it has many processing laboratories and because it is strategically located between the main coca-producing nations and the routes through the Caribbean and Central America that lead to the lucrative U.S. and European markets. Brazil has also become an increasingly significant route for cocaine transshipment.

Marijuana has been exported to the United States since the nineteenth century, most of it coming from Latin America. While Mexico decreased its supply of the drug in the 1970s, Colombia and nations in Central America and the Caribbean increased production. Today, marijuana is most likely the largest cash crop in Jamaica and Belize.

During the 1980s Latin America became a significant source of heroin, supplying 40 percent of the U.S. market. Mexico's share of the U.S. market has increased from 10 to 15 percent in the 1980s to 30 percent in the 1990s. Production is increasing in Mexico and has spread to Guatemala and to the Cauca Valley in Colombia.

Drug production and processing have affected the economies of Latin American nations. Especially in the crisis decade of the 1980s, dollars earned in the drug trade became an important source of foreign exchange in the region's economies. It is probable that the difficult position of the Mexican economy became a major impetus for the drug trade, and it is alleged that the marijuana trade in Jamaica kept that economy afloat in 1980 when the country was exceedingly short of foreign exchange. In the Andean region, coca dollars helped to weaken the impact of the decline in mineral prices. Estimates of annual profits made by cocaine traffickers range from $5 billion to $6 billion, and the reflow of coca money to producing countries ranges from approximately 10 to 20 percent. The drug industry is also an important source of employment in producing nations. In Bolivia, for example, it is estimated that cultivating coca, initial processing of coca paste, and refining and smuggling cocaine provide jobs for 10 percent of the economically active population.

The drug trade influences the politics of the region. In the absence of strong political support for the war on drugs weak central governments are only partially successful in implementing programs of drug eradication and interdiction. Some governments have demonstrated the political will to acknowledge and strike out against corruption, but strong criminal syndicates threaten national sovereignty and institutions. In Colombia, where the Medellín cartel was weakened by the death of its leader, Pablo Escobar, in 1993, the Cali cartel emerged as the largest in the world in refining, smuggling, and distributing cocaine—until it, too, was weakened by the arrest of its leaders in 1995. The huge profits involved in the drug trade contribute to the weakening of the juridical system in some countries and have corrupted segments of the police and the armed forces. In some instances, narco-traffickers have been linked to terrorist activities. They threaten governments with occasional acts of terrorism and have reached agreements with the Shining Path in Peru and Colombian guerrillas to provide arms and money in exchange for protection of drug production and trade. Powerful political constituencies, such as the coca farmers in Bolivia and Peru, are well-organized pressure groups opposed to government programs of coca eradication and cocaine interdiction. Most Latin American nations have become involved in the transit of illegal drugs and are vulnerable to money laundering because of strict bank secrecy regulations and weak banking and criminal laws.

The social costs of the expanding drug production and trade in the region are reflected, for example, in the addiction to coca paste by a rapidly increasing number of abandoned children in Peru, Bolivia, and Colombia. Domestic demand-reduction programs in most Latin American countries indicate a growing awareness of drug abuse.

National and international efforts to deal with the drug crisis have had mixed results. Latin American governments have faced a dilemma pitting the economic benefits of the drug trade against its political and social costs. Most governments have favored demand-side solutions, such as treatment of addicts, education, and prevention programs. But the National Drug Control Strategy of successive U.S. governments has emphasized supply-side measures, such as border interdiction and suppression programs in the source countries. These efforts have had only limited success. For example, crop-eradication and crop-substitution programs in Bolivia and Peru have failed to significantly slow coca production because the income from coca, which has a high and stable rate of return, is far greater than the income from substitute crops, such as citrus fruit or macadamia nuts, and the programs have been violently resisted by coca growers. As part of President George H. W. Bush's Andean Strategy, a multifaceted effort to reduce the flow of cocaine into the United States announced in 1989, Andean countries have promised to cooperate with the United States in enhancing their drug-fighting capabilities by training special police forces and getting the Latin American armed forces more involved in the drug war. However, because of the military's history of intervention into politics, Peruvian and Bolivian leaders have been reluctant to accept the militarization of the drug war and have called for a more economic approach to the problem. In the antidrug accord reached between the United States and six Latin American nations in San Antonio, Texas, in February 1992, the expanded role by South American militaries was shifted to the police. International organizations such as the Organization of American States and the United Nations favor a more equal distribution of supply and demand reduction. They provide a juridical framework for dealing with illegal drugs, but their authority is limited because international cooperation remains voluntary. In 1998, Colombia's President Andrés Pastrana Arango proposed legislation known as Plan Colombia to combat the drug trade. This plan, which received extensive input and funding from the Unites States during the presidency of Bill Clinton, focused on bolstering economic programs, strengthening the military, and aerial fumigation of drug crops. While the U.S. and Colombian governments have claimed that this effort has reduced cocaine production, these figures have been disputed. The plan continued to receive funding from the United States under President George W. Bush.

Ever since the beginning of large-scale drug trade in the 1970s, the Latin American traffickers have adjusted to antinarcotic efforts by spreading production and smuggling over the entire region, opening new markets, and recruiting new allies. Because of a wide range of political, social, and economic factors, the fight against drugs remains an extremely complex and difficult issue.

See also **Criminal Justice; Medicinal Plants; Rastafarians; United States-Latin American Relations.**

BIBLIOGRAPHY

A good analysis of the use of drugs by pre-Columbian cultures and traditional societies is in Marlene Dobkin De Rios, *Hallucinogens: Cross-Cultural Perspectives* (1989). *Coca and Cocaine: Effects on People and Policy in Latin America* (1966), edited by Deborah

Pacini and Christine Franquemont, deals with coca from an interdisciplinary perspective. On drug production and trade in Latin America and the relations between drugs and terrorism, see Scott B. MacDonald, *Dancing on a Volcano: The Latin American Drug Trade* (1988). A good survey of the dilemma of Latin American nations in their fight against drugs is Rensselaer W. Lee, *The White Labyrinth: Cocaine and Political Power* (1990). On the socioeconomic and political impact of illicit drugs, see James Painter, *Bolivia and Coca: A Study in Dependency* (1994), part of a new series from the U.N. Research Institute for Social Development. For a critical assessment of U.S. policies, see Raphael Perl, ed., *Drugs and Foreign Policy: A Critical Review* (1994). For U.S. government views, see U.S. Department Of State, Bureau Of International Narcotic Matters, *International Drug Control Strategy Report* (annual).

Additional Bibliography

Crandall, Russell. *Driven by Drugs: U.S. Policy toward Colombia.* Boulder, CO: Lynne Rienner Publishers, 2002.

Gootenberg, Paul. "Between Coca and Cocaine: A Century or More of U.S.-Peruvian Drug Paradoxes, 1860–1980." *The Hispanic American Historical Review* 83:1 (February 2003), 119–150.

Joyce, Elizabeth, and Carlos Malamud, eds. *Latin America and the Multinational Drug Trade.* Basingstoke, U.K.: Macmillan; New York: St. Martin's Press, 1998.

Recio, Gabriela. "Drugs and Alcohol: US Prohibition and the Origins of the Drug Trade in Mexico 1910–1930." *Journal of Latin American Studies* 34:1 (February 2002), 21–42.

Thoumi, Francisco E. *Illegal Drugs, Economy and Society in the Andes.* Washington, DC: Woodrow Wilson Center Press; Baltimore, MD: Johns Hopkins University Press, 2003.

MARIA LUISE WAGNER

DRUMMOND DE ANDRADE, CARLOS. *See* Andrade, Carlos Drummond de.

DUARTE, AUGUSTO RODRIGUES

(1848–1888). Augusto Rodrigues Duarte (*b.* 1848; *d.* 1888), Portuguese-born history painter. Augusto Rodrigues Duarte came to Brazil in 1866 and entered the Imperial Academy of Fine Arts, where he studied under the painter Vítor Meireles. Upon completion of his academic training in the early 1870s, Duarte left Brazil to study in Paris. In 1874 he entered the atelier of the French history painter Jean-Léon Gérôme and shortly thereafter won a second prize in the Paris Salon. He was one of the few nineteenth-century painters in Brazil to portray the Indian as the subject of a monumental history painting, a role traditionally reserved for members of the royal family and military heroes.

His most important artistic achievement was the Indianist painting entitled the *Funeral of Atala,* which was exhibited at the 1878 Universal Exhibition in Paris. The subject matter of the work borrowed from Chateaubriand's 1826 novel *Les Natchez.* Duarte's paintings exhibit the influences of the European aesthetic formulas of impressionism, symbolism, and even art nouveau. Beyond history painting, he is also known for his landscapes and genre paintings. He was awarded the title of Knight of the Imperial Order of Roses at the 1884 academic exhibition, where he entered fourteen paintings.

See also **Art: The Nineteenth Century.**

BIBLIOGRAPHY

Arte no Brasil, vol. 2 (1979), p. 516.

Caren Meghreblian, "Art, Politics and Historical Perception in Imperial Brazil, 1854–1884." Ph.D. diss., UCLA, 1990.

Additional Bibliography

Denis, Rafael Cardoso, and Colin Trodd. *Art and the Academy in the Nineteenth Century.* Lima: Editorial Milla Batres, 2000.

CAREN A. MEGHREBLIAN

DUARTE, JUAN PABLO (1813–1876).

Juan Pablo Duarte (*b.* 26 January 1813; *d.* 15 July 1876), leader of Dominican independence. While studying abroad in Europe, Duarte was influenced by the French romantic literary movement. With his homeland under Haitian occupation (1822–1844), the ideals of liberty and equality became of great importance to him. In 1838, Duarte and two others, Francisco de Rosario Sánchez and Ramón Mella, formed La Trinitaria, a secret society whose goal was independence. The society proved very successful but resulted in Duarte's exile. After the Haitian president Jean-Pierre Boyer was overthrown in 1844, Duarte returned to Santo Domingo to take part in the formation of a new and independent government. Imbued with the ideals of the French Revolution, his idealism soon alienated him from the more militaristic leaders, and strongman General Pedro Santana jailed and ultimately exiled him once more. After a brief stay in Germany, Duarte spent fifteen years as a recluse in the jungles of Venezuela.

When Santana agreed to the country's reassumption of colonial status in 1864, Duarte returned to the Dominican Republic to take up the cause of independence again. Once more, however, Duarte was unable to participate in the provisional government of the Dominican Republic. It has been said of Duarte that he could inspire but not lead. He was exiled for the third time in 1865 and he returned to Venezuela, where he lived the rest of his life in poverty and obscurity. Like the achievements of many great men, Duarte's significance and value were recognized only after his death. He is now considered the father of Dominican independence.

See also **Dominican Republic.**

BIBLIOGRAPHY

Selden Rodman, *Quisqueya: A History of the Dominican Republic* (1964).

Howard J. Wiarda, *The Dominican Republic: Nation in Transition* (1969).

Ian Bell, *The Dominican Republic* (1981).

Howard J. Wiarda, and M. J. Kryzanek, *The Dominican Republic: A Caribbean Crucible* (1982).

Additional Bibliography

Duarte, Juan Pablo, and Vetilio Alfau Durán. *Ideario de Duarte, y su Proyecto e constitución.* Santo Domingo: CPEP, Comisión Permanente de Efemérides Batrias, 2006.

Martínez-Fernández, Luis. *Torn between Empires: Economy, Society, and Patterns of Political Thought in the Hispanic Caribbean, 1840–1878.* Athens: University of Georgia Press, 1994.

Miniño, Manuel Marino. *El pensamiento de Duarte en su contexto histórico e ideológico.* Santo Domingo: Instituto Duartiano, 1998.

HEATHER K. THIESSEN

DUARTE, PEDRO (1829–1903).

Pedro Duarte (*b.* 1829; *d.* 1903), Paraguayan soldier and statesman. At the beginning of the War of the Triple Alliance, Duarte, a relatively obscure officer, was chosen as second in command of an expeditionary force sent south to attack Brazil. As the Paraguayans approached the Brazilian frontier in June 1865, their commander, Colonel Antonio de la Cruz Estigarribia, split his forces, sending one column of 2,500 men under Major Duarte down the right bank of the Uruguay River, while he himself led the bulk of the troops down the left bank, toward the Riograndense town of Uruguaiana. The Argentines and Brazilians were waiting for both columns. Unable to secure help from Estigarribia and unwilling to consider withdrawal, Duarte was effectively isolated, and, on 17 August, at a spot called Yatai, 10,000 Argentine troops struck his column, annihilating almost everyone. Gravely wounded, Duarte was taken to Buenos Aires, where he spent the rest of the war as a prisoner. After the Allied victory in 1870, he returned to Paraguay and subsequently served as minister of war and marine in the governments of Cándido Bareiro, Bernardino Caballero, and Patricio Escobar.

See also **Paraguay: The Twentieth Century; War of the Triple Alliance.**

BIBLIOGRAPHY

Charles J. Kolinski, *Independence or Death! The Story of the Paraguayan War* (1965).

Harris G. Warren, *Rebirth of the Paraguayan Republic: The First Colorado Era, 1878–1904* (1985), pp. 52, 65.

Additional Bibliography

Carrón, Juan María. *El régimen liberal, 1870–1930: Sociedad, economía.* Asunción: Arandurã Editorial, 2004.

Lewis, Paul H. *Political Parties and Generations in Paraguay's Liberal Era, 1869–1940.* Chapel Hill: University of North Carolina Press, 1993.

THOMAS L. WHIGHAM

DUARTE FUENTES, JOSÉ NAPOLEÓN (1925–1990).

José Napoleón Duarte Fuentes (November 23, 1925–February 23, 1990) was president of El Salvador from 1984 to 1989. Duarte received a degree in engineering from the University of Notre Dame in 1948 and worked as a civil engineer in El Salvador before entering politics. A founding member of the Partido Demócrata Cristiano (PDC; Christian Democratic Party), he was elected to the party's organizing committee in 1960 and became the party's first general secretary in 1961. The PDC expanded significantly under his stewardship and developed relationships with Christian Democratic parties abroad. Duarte served as mayor of San Salvador from 1964 to 1970, winning three consecutive elections. As mayor, Duarte emphasized community development and infrastructure projects. One of his most successful programs was the community self-help program, Acción Communitaria, which organized neighborhoods throughout the capital. This program not only responded to the needs of the population, but also mobilized popular support for the PDC.

In 1972 Duarte ran for president on the Unión Nacional Opositora (UNO; National Opposition Union) coalition ticket, which included the PDC and two other parties. Duarte's campaign focused on the promotion of social justice and democracy. Although Duarte was leading the vote when the government halted the broadcast of election results, the Partido de Conciliación Nacional (PCN; National Conciliation Party) candidate, Colonel Arturo Armando Molina, was pronounced the winner. Amid protests and Duarte's call for a new election, a surprise session of the legislature ratified Molina as president. Weeks later, fraud in municipal and legislative elections prompted a military rebellion. Duarte was arrested in March 1972 following a radio address in support of the rebellion. Although initially exiled to Guatemala City, Duarte ultimately settled in Caracas, Venezuela, where he remained even after being acquitted of charges in the coup attempt.

Duarte returned from Venezuela following the 15 October 1979 reformist coup by junior military officers. He joined the more conservative second provisional junta in March 1980 as foreign minister and was appointed to the junta's presidency in December after other civilian members resigned in protest of continued military repression. His controversial role as the junta's figurehead resulted in the defection of numerous party officials and supporters. Duarte was critical of those who, in his opinion, abandoned the democratic process to support the Frente Democrático Salvadoreño (FDR; Revolutionary Democratic Front) and the guerrillas of the Frente Farabundo

Martí para la Liberación Nacional (FMLN; Farabundo Martí National Liberation Front). He believed that working with the military was vital to ensuring the transition to democracy and implementing redistributive programs, such as agrarian reform, whereas his critics argued that gross human rights abuses made such an alliance unacceptable.

Duarte's presidential campaign in 1984 received considerable support from the United States, which sought to promote elections in El Salvador while fighting the FMLN guerrillas and curbing the military's human rights abuses. Duarte was elected president following a second round of voting, defeating the right-wing Alianza Republicana Nacionalista (ARENA; National Republican Alliance) of Roberto D'Aubuisson. Duarte thereby became the first civilian president since 1931. Although voting was marred by violence and irregularities, he viewed the victory as a triumph of the democratic process, whereas skeptics argued that he never truly held power, but that the military was the real power. Duarte's presidency was characterized by continued violence, a deteriorating economy, and widespread corruption within the PDC, including the misappropriation of aid following an October 1986 earthquake. Perhaps his greatest struggle, however, was his unfulfilled campaign promise to end the war. Early talks with the FDR-FMLN in October 1984 at La Palma and in November 1984 at Ayagualo were unsuccessful. He met again with the FDR-FMLN in October 1987, shortly after signing the Esquipulas II agreements with other Central American presidents. Again, the talks were without success. Duarte continued to oppose political reforms demanded by the FDR-FMLN, insisting that the guerrillas disarm and join the democratic process. His position was, in part, fueled by his strong anticommunist sentiments and conviction that sufficient conditions existed for the left to participate in politics. He was also constrained by his alliance with the military, opposition by elites, and U.S. foreign policy.

Embattled by war and corruption, the PDC experienced losses in both the 1988 legislative and municipal elections and the 1989 presidential balloting. Although diagnosed with terminal stomach cancer in 1988, Duarte was able to complete his term. He transferred power to ARENA's Alfredo Cristiani in June 1989,

representing the first transfer of power from one civilian president to another in El Salvador's history.

See also **Cristiani, Alfredo; d'Aubuisson, Roberto; El Salvador; El Salvador, Political Parties: Farabundo Martí National Liberation Front (FMLN); El Salvador, Political Parties: National Republican Alliance (ARENA).**

BIBLIOGRAPHY

Baloyra, Enrique A. *El Salvador in Transition.* Chapel Hill: University of North Carolina Press, 1982.

Byrne, Hugh. *El Salvador's Civil War: A Study of Revolution.* Boulder, CO: Lynne Rienner, 1996.

Duarte, José Napoleón, with Diana Page. *Duarte: My Story.* New York: Putnam, 1986.

Montgomery, Tommie Sue. *Revolution in El Salvador: From Civil Strife to Civil Peace,* 2nd edition. Boulder, CO: Westview Press, 1995.

Webre, Stephen. *José Napoleón Duarte and the Christian Democratic Party in Salvadoran Politics, 1960–1972.* Baton Rouge: Louisiana State University Press, 1979.

CHRISTINE J. WADE

DUEÑAS, FRANCISCO (1817–1884).
Francisco Dueñas (*b.* 1817; *d.* 31 March 1884), last Conservative president of El Salvador (1851–1854, 1863–1871). Francisco Dueñas studied law and was active in letters, education, and public service before seizing power in 1851 and again in 1863 with the assistance of Guatemala's Rafael Carrera. As president, Dueñas strengthened the Salvadoran armed forces and enacted a new constitution (1864), which consolidated military and political power in his hands. He persecuted his political rivals and had a number of them killed, including his Liberal predecessor, Gerardo Barrios. The Dueñas regime created a stable environment for the growth of the coffee industry, which it encouraged with incentives similar to those more commonly associated with Liberal governments. Dueñas also promoted physical improvements in the country's infrastructure and in the capital city, San Salvador. Congress reelected Dueñas in 1870, but he lost the following year to a Liberal revolt under Santiago González. Dueñas spent much of his later life in exile. A pioneer coffee grower himself, he founded one of El Salvador's wealthiest and most powerful families.

See also **Coffee Industry.**

BIBLIOGRAPHY

Juan J. Cañas, "Doctor Don Francisco Dueñas," in *San Salvador y sus hombres,* 2d ed. (1967).

Enrique Chacón, *El presidente Dr. Francisco Dueñas y su época* (n.d.).

Additional Bibliography

Ching, Erik Kristofer. "From Clientelism to Militarism: The State, Politics and Authoritarianism in El Salvador, 1840–1940." Ph.D. diss., University of California, Santa Barbara, 1997.

Melgar Brizuela, José. *Liberalismo y conservadurismo en El Salvador durante la segunda mitad del siglo XIX.* La Libertad: Editorial Delgado, 2004.

STEPHEN WEBRE

DUHALDE, EDUARDO (1945–). The Argentine politician Eduardo Duhalde served as president of Argentina from December 2001 to May 2003. As a youth he was a member of the Justicialist Party, was active in the municipal trade union movement in Lomas de Zamora, and studied law at the University of Buenos Aires. In 1971 he married Hilda Beatriz González (b. 1946), who became his unfailing political companion. When democracy was restored in Argentina in 1973, Duhalde was elected to the council of Lomas de Zamora, and in 1974 became the city's mayor. During the military dictatorship that began in 1976 Duhalde was removed from his post, and he worked as an attorney. When democracy was reestablished in 1983, he was once again elected mayor of Lomas de Zamora.

Although he had been active in the most conservative faction of the Justicialist movement (Peronism), Duhalde now joined its "renewal" faction, which tried to give the party a more democratic appearance. In 1987, when the renewal group won at the polls, he was elected a national deputy for the province of Buenos Aires, and soon came to be first vice president of the Chamber of Deputies. In 1988 he became Carlos Menem's vice presidential candidate in the preliminary rounds of the Justicialist Party's elections, and, having won this battle, the Menem-Duhalde ticket defeated the radical candidates in the national presidential elections. As vice president of the republic, Duhalde advocated the creation of the Office of Planning and Coordination to Prevent Drug Addiction and Fight Drug Trafficking. In 1991 he left that post to run for governor of the province of Buenos Aires. After winning that office, he expanded social services in the province with the support of the *manzaneras* (neighborhood block leaders), a group of Peronist women activists led by his wife, and stepped up his public works programs. During Duhalde's term in office he was accused of corruption by his opponents and the press, but in 1994 he held a referendum that saw him reelected as governor. This victory consolidated his power as the indisputable *caudillo* (leader) of the most important province of Argentina.

Duhalde soon began to work toward the 1999 presidential elections. This put him at loggerheads with President Menem, in terms of both Menem's political ambitions and Duhalde's traditionalist economic policies, which were opposed to the president's neoliberal bent. Duhalde managed to win the Justicialist Party's nomination for the presidency, but the Menem government discredited him in the eyes of the public, and he was defeated by the alliance formed by the Radical Civic Union (UCR) and Front for a Country in Solidarity (FrePaSo), led by Fernando de la Rúa and Carlos Álvarez. However, with the nation in the grip of the worst economic and social crisis in its history, de la Rúa stepped down as president in December 2001, and shortly thereafter, the National Congress elected Duhalde to finish out his term.

Some of the measures Duhalde implemented during his brief term as president included the forced conversion of foreign currency deposits to the national peso, a currency devaluation that culminated in the Convertibility Law, and the largest social assistance plan in the nation's history. Forced to hold the presidential elections six months early because of widespread popular protest, pressure from other Justicialist leaders, and a few acts of political violence, Duhalde supported the governor of Santa Cruz, Néstor Kirchner, as the Peronist movement's candidate, once again opposing Menem. After Kirchner's victory in the presidential elections, Duhalde promised to end his political career. In late 2003 he was named head of the Commission of Permanent Representatives to MERCOSUR, a post he held until 2005.

See also **Argentina, Political Parties: Justicialist Party; Argentina, Political Parties: Radical Party (UCR); Kirchner, Néstor; Menem, Carlos Saúl; Mercosur; Rúa, Fernando de la.**

BIBLIOGRAPHY

Petras, James. "Argentina: 18 Months of Popular Struggle." *Canadian Dimension* 37, No. 4 (July–August 2003): 28–34.

"Political Wife and Weapon: Argentina's President." *The Economist* (U.S. edition) 375, no. 8429 (June 4, 2005): 35.

                                        VICENTE PALERMO

DULLES, ALLEN (1893–1969).

Allen Welsh Dulles was director of the Central Intelligence Agency (CIA) from 1953 to 1961, during some of the principal covert operations of the Cold War. Born in Watertown, New York, Dulles earned his M.A. from Princeton University in 1916 and served in the State Department until 1926, when he joined the law firm of his older brother, John Foster Dulles, a future secretary of state. Allen Dulles spent World War II in the Office of Strategic Services (OSS). With other OSS veterans he helped establish the CIA in 1951, becoming its director in 1953. Under his leadership the agency overthrew the democratically elected leader of Iran, Mohammed Mosaddeq (1882–1967), in 1953, and the democratically elected president of Guatemala, Jácobo Árbenz Guzmán, in 1954. The United Fruit Company, angered by Guatemala's expropriation of some of its unused lands for agrarian reform, used its close links to the Dulles brothers to argue that the Árbenz government was subservient to Moscow. Dulles drew on the Guatemalan experience to shape the plan for the ill-fated 1961 invasion by U.S.-trained Cuban exiles at Playa Girón in Cuba, known as the Bay of Pigs, approved by President John F. Kennedy. Dulles took responsibility for the failure and resigned the same year.

See also **Bay of Pigs Invasion; Arbenz Guzmán, Jacobo; Central Intelligence Agency (CIA); Dulles, John Foster; United Fruit Company.**

BIBLIOGRAPHY

Dulles, Allen W. *The Craft of Intelligence.* [1973]. New York: Lyons Press, 2006.

Grose, Peter. *Gentleman Spy: The Life of Allen Dulles.* Amherst: University of Massachusetts Press, 1996.

Kornbluh, Peter, ed. *Bay of Pigs Declassified.* New York: New Press, 1998.

                                        MAX PAUL FRIEDMAN

DULLES, JOHN FOSTER (1888–1959).

As U.S. Secretary of State (1953–1959) under President Dwight D. Eisenhower, John Foster Dulles promoted hard-line policies in the Cold War. Grandson of one secretary of state and nephew of another, Dulles attended Princeton University, George Washington University, and the Sorbonne before joining the New York law firm Sullivan and Cromwell in 1911. He played a role in founding the League of Nations and the United Nations. As secretary of state, he was driven by a powerful hatred of Communism to view diverse issues through the lens of superpower conflict. He promised to meet any Soviet aggression in Europe with "massive retaliation" (nuclear attack), and favored a confrontational approach to diplomacy, comparing both Joseph Stalin and the Egyptian nationalist Gamal Abdel Nasser to Adolf Hitler. In Latin America, Dulles supported dictators such as Marcos Pérez Jiménez of Venezuela, who allegedly brought stability, whereas he portrayed the democratically elected government of Jácobo Árbenz Guzmán of Guatemala as a pawn of the Soviets. At a summit meeting in Caracas in March 1954, Dulles sought hemispheric backing for his opposition to Árbenz, but Latin American delegates insisted on reaffirming the principle of nonintervention. The Central Intelligence Agency nonetheless proceeded with a coup that overthrew Árbenz and brought widespread condemnation.

See also **Arbenz Guzmán, Jacobo; Central Intelligence Agency (CIA); Dulles, Allen; Pan-American Conferences: Caracas Conference (1954).**

BIBLIOGRAPHY

Hoopes, Townsend. *The Devil and John Foster Dulles.* New York: Little, Brown, 1973.

Immerman, Richard H. *John Foster Dulles: Piety, Pragmatism, and Power in U.S. Foreign Policy.* Wilmington, DE: SR Books, 1998.

Rabe, Stephen G. *Eisenhower and Latin America: The Foreign Policy of Anti-Communism.* Chapel Hill: University of North Carolina Press, 1988.

MAX PAUL FRIEDMAN

Veloso, Caetano, and Barbara Einzig. *Tropical Truth: A Story of Music and Revolution in Brazil.* New York: Knopf, 2002.

SUSANA SALGADO

DUPRAT, ROGÉRIO (1932–2006).

Rogério Duprat (*b.* 7 February 1932, *d.* 26 October 2006), Brazilian composer. Born in Guanabara, Rio de Janeiro, Duprat studied philosophy at São Paulo University. He also studied music theory, harmony, and composition with Olivier Toni and Cláudio Santoro and cello with Varoli at the Villalobos Conservatory in São Paulo (1952–1960). From 1953 to 1963 he was a cellist with the São Paulo Municipal Orchestra and took summer courses at Darmstadt, Germany. He also studied electronic music at studios in Cologne, Paris, and Karlsruhe under Stockhausen, Ligeti, Boulez, and Pousseur. Duprat returned to São Paulo, where he cofounded the Estadual Orchestra and the São Paulo Chamber Orchestra; for the latter he was the director of an experimental music group. His early style was nationalist but later he turned to twelve-tone, serial, and electronic music. In 1963 he formed the group Música Nova with Gilberto Mendes, Willy Correia de Oliveira, and Damiano Cozzella, manifesting strict devotion to contemporary and avant-garde trends. He composed music for television and collaborated with members of the musical movement Tropicália, arranging the music for many albums by the Tropicálistas including the classic *Tropicália ou Panis et Circenses,* and he also taught at the University of Brazil. Late in life he was forced to refrain from much musical activity due to hearing difficulties.

See also **Music: Art Music.**

BIBLIOGRAPHY

R. Duprat, "En torno al pronunciamiento" in *Revista musical chilena* xvii/86 (1963): 30, 33.

John Vinton, ed., *Dictionary of Contemporary Music* (1974); *New Grove Dictionary of Music and Musicians,* vol. 5 (1980).

Additional Bibliography

Gaúna, Regiane. *Rogério Duprat: Sonoridades múltiplas.* São Paulo: Editora UNESP, 2001.

Moehn, Frederick. "Colonial-Era Brazilian Music: A Review Essay of Recent Recordings." *Notes* 62: 2 (2005), 448–472.

DURÁN, DIEGO (1537–1588).

Diego Durán (*b.* 1537; *d.* 1588), one of the more important chronicler/ethnographers who lived in sixteenth-century New Spain. A Dominican friar born in Seville and raised in Texcoco and Mexico City, Durán wrote a three-part work, *Historia de las Indias de Nueva España islas de tierra firme,* on the pre-Hispanic history, religion, and calendar of the Aztecs, respectively. He based it on indigenous manuscripts—including the Crónica X, now lost—and hundreds of indigenous informants. He also had some assistants, probably monastery-trained Nahuas, who helped him gather, copy, and interpret information, and he interviewed Spanish eyewitnesses who had been on the scene of the Conquest. The three parts of the *Historia,* containing many descriptions not duplicated in any other chronicles, were written approximately during the period 1576–1581. Durán's goal, like that of many chroniclers of his time, was to improve the Christian instruction of the indigenous people by first gaining a better grasp of their beliefs.

See also **Christian Base Communities; Nahuas.**

BIBLIOGRAPHY

There is a more vivid and human biographical sketch of Durán in Fernando Horcasitas and Doris Heyden's English ed. of two parts of Durán's *Historia,* the *Book of the Gods and Rites* and *The Ancient Calendar* (1971). The third part, *The Aztecs: The History of the Indies of New Spain* (1964), was also translated by Horcasitas and Heyden. In the *Handbook of Middle American Indians,* vol. 13, pt. 2, edited by Howard F. Cline (1973), J. Benedict Warren explains the relationships between Durán's work and that of others who borrowed from him and/or consulted some of the same sources.

Additional Bibliography

Heyden, Doris. *El templo mayor de Tenochtitlán en la obra de Fray Diego Durán.* México, D.F.: Instituto Nacional de Antropología e Historia, 2000.

STEPHANIE WOOD

DURÁN, FRAY NARCISO (1776–1846).

Fray Narciso Durán (*b.* 16 December 1776; *d.* 1 June 1846), Franciscan missionary. Durán was born at Castellón de Ampurias in Catalonia, where he entered the Franciscan order at Gerona in 1792. Ordained in 1800, Durán left Spain in 1803 for Mexico, arriving in the Alta California missions three years later.

Durán remained in the Alta California missions for forty years and died at the Santa Barbara mission in 1846. During most of this period (1806–1833) he was stationed at the San José mission in the San Francisco Bay region and at the Santa Barbara mission. In 1832 Durán became the *vicar forane* (foreign vicar) and ecclesiastical judge for Alta California. He was president of the missions from 1833 to 1838 and commissary prefect after 1838.

Durán tried to defend the missions against reforms initiated by Mexican politicians and was vocal in his criticism of these changes. For example, he criticized the emancipation of mission Indians in the late 1820s and early 1830s. Moreover, in the 1820s and 1830s he refused to take oaths of loyalty to Mexico. Despite his views, Durán, like the other Spanish-born Franciscans in Alta California, was not expelled. However, in 1833 the Mexican government sent Mexican-born Franciscans from the apostolic college in Zacatecas to staff its missions in the northern part of the province, which was especially sensitive politically because of the presence of the Russians at Fort Ross north of San Francisco Bay.

See also **Franciscans.**

BIBLIOGRAPHY

Maynard J. Geiger, O.F.M., *Franciscan Missionaries in Hispanic California, 1769–1848: A Biographical Dictionary* (1969).

Additional Bibliography

Sandos, James A. *Converting California: Indians and Franciscans in the Missions.* New Haven, CT: Yale University Press, 2004.

ROBERT H. JACKSON

DURÁN-BALLÉN, SIXTO (1921–).

As president of Ecuador from 1992 to 1996, Sixto Durán applied a technocratic, neoliberal approach to economic policy in his administration. Born in Boston on July 14, 1921, and trained as an architect in the United States, he worked in Washington, D.C., for the Inter-American Development Bank (1960–1968). He also served as Ecuador's minister of public works (1956–1960) and was mayor of Quito from 1970 to 1978. After two unsuccessful runs as the candidate of the conservative Partido Social Cristiano (PSC; Social Christian Party), Durán-Ballén was elected president in 1992 as the standard bearer of the Partido Unión Republicana (PUR; Party of Republican Unity).

Durán-Ballén's administration inherited a large budget deficit, heavy external debt obligations, and an annual inflation rate of nearly 60 percent. He and his economic czar, Vice President Alberto Dahik Garzoni, were committed to neoliberal, probusiness policies. These included devaluating the currency, freezing public sector wages, and privatizing state enterprises. Initial successes of these reforms included declining inflation, improved relations with the International Monetary Fund (IMF), and a period of modest economic growth. At the same time, however, like many neoliberal reforms elsewhere, these policies contributed to increased unemployment and growing labor unrest. The administration's Agrarian Development Law of 1994, designed to convert peasant communal lands to commercial enterprises, provoked intense protests led by the Confederación de Nacionalidades Indígenas de Ecuador (CONAIE; Ecuadorian Confederation of Indigenous Nationalities).

A short border war with Peru in 1995 briefly raised Durán's record low approval ratings, but the president's acrimonious relationship with Congress and a series of administration corruption scandals quickly undermined his public support. Most damaging, in 1995 Vice President Dahik, the architect of Durán's economic policies, fled the country to avoid charges of corruption. Later that year, unable to get his key legislative proposals through Congress, Durán submitted a series of constitutional amendments—some designed to strengthen presidential powers—to a national plebiscite. Voters rejected all eleven proposed amendments, effectively crippling the president for the rest of his term.

Sixto Durán was the last of four elected Ecuadorian presidents to complete his full term. In the decade after he stepped down, none of Ecuador's elected presidents served a full term. Durán later served as a congressional deputy.

See also **Ecuador, Political Parties: Overview; Neoliberalism.**

BIBLIOGRAPHY

Work by Durán-Ballén

Durán-Ballén, Sixto. *A mi manera–: Los años de Carondelet.* Quito: Universidad Andína Simón Bolívar, 2005; Guayaquil, Ecuador: Abya Yala, 2005.

Other Works

Conaghan, Catherine M. "Políticos versus partidos: Discordía y desunión en el sistema de partidos ecuatoriano." In *La construcción de instituciones democráticas: Sistemas de partidos en América Latina,* edited by Scott Mainwaring and Thomas Scully. Santiago, Chile: Cieplan, 1996.

Lucio-Paredes, Pablo, et al., eds. *Paquetazo: Las medidas de Sixto y Dahik.* Quito: Editorial El Conejo, 1992.

HOWARD HANDELMAN

DURAND, OSWALD (1840–1906). Oswald Durand (*b.* 17 September 1840; *d.* 22 April 1906), Haitian writer, journalist, and politician. Durand began work as a tinsmith and studied at night. He became a lycée principal and went into politics in 1885. After being elected president of the Chambre des Députés in 1888, he traveled to France and was introduced to the "Société des Gens de Lettres" by François Coppée. Upon his death in 1906, he was given a state funeral and was praised as the greatest Haitian poet.

The poetry of Durand was often an erotic evocation of the women he loved (he was divorced for philandering by the poet Virginie Sampeur), but he also evoked simple people and the landscapes and traditions of Haiti. Some poems in Creole contributed to the recognition of the language's literary citizenship.

Other works include *Rires et pleurs* (1896); *Quatre nouveaux poèmes* (1900). *Mosaïques* and *Primes fleurs et ballades* are both unpublished.

See also **Creole; Haiti.**

BIBLIOGRAPHY

Naomi M. Garret, *The Renaissance of Haitian Poetry* (1963), pp. 30–33; See also F. Raphaël Berrou and Pradel Pompilus, *Histoire de la littérature haïtienne illustrée par les textes,* vol. 1 (1975), pp. 322–396.

Additional Bibliography

Charles, Christophe. *La vie sentimentale du poète Oswald Durand.* Port-au-Prince: Choucoune, 2005.

CARROL F. COATES

DURÃO, JOSÉ DE SANTA RITA (c. 1722–1784). José de Santa Rita Durão (*b.* c. 1722; *d.* 24 January 1784), Brazilian poet. Durão was born in Minas Gerais, Brazil, but left, never to return, at age nine. He grew up and was educated in Portugal, entering the Augustinian Order in 1738 and earning a doctorate in theology from the University of Coimbra in 1758. After serving as a papal librarian in Rome, he returned to Portugal and served as a professor of theology at Coimbra before becoming prior of the Gration convent.

In 1781 Durão published his major work, *Caramuru.* Modeling himself on Luís de Camões's *Os Lusíadas* with its celebration of Portuguese accomplishments in the Orient, Durão produced an epic poem in ten ottava rima cantos celebrating similar accomplishments in Brazil. As Camões had elaborated his narrative around Vasco da Gama's voyage to India, Durão used the discovery of Bahia by Diogo Álvares Correia (1510) and Correia's subsequent adventures. Caramurú, or Dragon of the Sea, is Correia's Indian name.

Again like Camões, and contrary to the rationalism of the age, Durão endorsed the ideal of a Christian empire served by Portuguese conquests, but he accepted eighteenth-century natural law and viewed the savage as innately noble. His accurate descriptions of Brazilian nature, moreover, together with those of native life and customs, make him an important precursor of both literary nationalism and Indianism.

See also **Gama, Vasco da.**

BIBLIOGRAPHY

David M. Driver, *The Indian in Brazilian Literature* (1942), pp. 34–40.

Antônio Cândido, *Formação da literatura brasileira: Momentos decisivos,* 2d ed., vol. 1 (1964), pp. 183–193.

Claude L. Hulet, "The Noble Savage in *Caramurú*," in *Homage to Irving A. Leonard*, edited by Raquel Chang-Rodríguez and Donald A. Yates (1977), pp. 123–130.

Additional Bibliography

Brandão, Roberto de Oliveira. *Poética e poesia no Brasil (Colônia)*. São Paulo: Editora UNESP, 2001.

NORWOOD ANDREWS JR.

DURAZNO. Durazno, department of central Uruguay with an area of 4,713 square miles and a population of 56,966 (1996). Most of the departmental territory extends between the rivers Negro and Yi, often called Uruguay's Mesopotamia. The capital is the city of Durazno (30,529 inhabitants in 2004), founded in 1821. The main activities of the department are farming, cattle raising, and shoe manufacturing. A large reservoir on the Río Negro provides irrigation for a good part of central Uruguay and electric energy for Greater Montevideo. Since 1989 the state has held a Carnaval which has drawn large crowds in addition to the multi-band concert series *Pilsen Rock* which was initiated in 2005.

See also **Uruguay, Geography.**

CÉSAR N. CAVIEDES

DUTARY, ALBERTO (1932–1998). Alberto Dutary (*b.* 3 July 1932, *d.* 23 March 1998), Panamanian painter. Dutary studied at the Escuela Nacional de Pintura in Panama (1950–1952) and in Madrid, at the San Fernando Academy (1953–1955) and the Escuela Nacional de Artes Gráficas (1956–1958). From 1962 until 1992, he was art professor in private schools and at the University of Panama, where he became the first director of the Fine Arts Career Program in 1987.

A notable draftsman and figurative painter, his works from the 1960s, including the "Santos" series, combined the surface textures of Spanish informalism with dramatic ghostlike figures. He later turned to more realistic, and at times surrealistic, still lifes. In the 1970s, he focused on mannequinlike female figures that play with the concept of reality in paintings such as *Figuras frente a la Bahía* (1979).

See also **Art: The Twentieth Century.**

BIBLIOGRAPHY

Stanton Loomis Catlin and Terence Grieder, *Art of Latin America Since Independence* (1966).

X. Zavala Cuadra et al., "Alberto Dutary: Pintor panameño," in *Revista del Pensamiento Centroamericano*, no. 155 (April–June 1977): 1–9.

Additional Bibliography

Toral, Demetrio C. "Alberto Dutary: In memoriam." *Revista Cultural Lotería* 425 (July–Aug. 1999): 5.

MONICA E. KUPFER

DUTCH IN COLONIAL BRAZIL. One of the great tragedies in the history of Brazil took place between 1624 and 1654 when the Dutch West India Company attempted to occupy Portuguese America, with enormous loss of life and property and massive dislocation of populations. At least 10,000 Dutchmen, Germans, Frenchmen, and other Europeans in the service of the company lost their lives, as did a similar number of opposing Portuguese, Spaniards, and Italians. Untold numbers were maimed. In addition, at least a thousand Amerindians and possibly an equal number of blacks also died fighting for one side or the other. More than a thousand ships were captured or sunk during the thirty years of conflict. Several hundred sugar mills were destroyed, countless cane fields burned, and numerous oxen killed. Tens of thousands of inhabitants of northeastern and northern Brazil were uprooted and forced to march southward to Bahia or Rio de Janeiro, flee into the interior, or return to the Iberian Peninsula. The economy of northeastern Brazil was seriously disrupted, and many decades elapsed before parts of that region were restored to normalcy.

Initially, Dutch contacts with Portuguese America were peaceful. By the latter decades of the sixteenth century, despite Spanish Hapsburg prohibitions against foreign trade with Brazil, an increasing number of Dutch ships and crews were helping carry cargoes, especially textiles, from Europe to Brazil, returning with sugar and brazilwood. By 1621 an estimated ten to fifteen ships were built annually by the Dutch solely for the Brazil trade. By that time, the Dutch controlled about one–half to two–thirds of the carrying trade between Portuguese America and Europe. The end of the twelve–year truce (1609–1621) between the Spanish Hapsburgs and the United Provinces of the Netherlands was marked by the founding of the Dutch West India Company (1621). With governmental support, the Dutch West India Company and explorers began colonization efforts in Portuguese America, Chile, the Caribbean, Suriname, and the Northeastern United States.

BAHIA AND THE DUTCH, 1624–1627
In late 1623 and early 1624, twenty–six ships and 3,300 men left the Netherlands in a successful effort to capture the Brazilian capital, Salvador, in the captaincy of Bahia. By the time the Dutch troops reached the city's limits, Salvador's defenders had fled. However, the Portuguese soon rallied and succeeded in confining the invaders to the capital. In the meantime, a joint Spanish–Portuguese force of fifty–two ships and 12,566 men under Don Fadrique de Toledo y Osorio sailed from the Iberian Peninsula and recaptured the capital of Brazil (May 1625). Although the Dutch had been ousted from Brazil, they were able to capture a considerable amount of Portuguese shipping both off the coast of Brazil and in the Atlantic. In 1627, Piet Heyn twice sailed into Bahia's harbor and captured or destroyed dozens of ships. The following year Heyn captured the richly laden Spanish silver fleet in Cuba's Matanzas Bay, providing the Dutch West India Company with the wealth to make another attempt at conquest in Brazil.

THE DUTCH OCCUPATION OF BRAZIL, 1630–1654
In February of 1630, a Dutch West India Company fleet of sixty–seven ships and more than 7,000 men, under the command of Hendrick Corneliszoon Loncq, captured Olinda, Recife, and the island of Antônio Vaz in the sugar–rich captaincy of Pernambuco. Although most of the Portuguese defenders initially fled, the inhabitants of the captaincy were rallied by Matias de Albuquerque, brother of Pernambuco's lord–proprietor. Albuquerque and his forces were able to restrict the Dutch to their coastal positions and for the next two years successfully mounted a campaign of guerrilla warfare from the fortress called Arraial do Bom Jesus while awaiting a rescue armada from the Iberian Peninsula.

It was not until May 1631 that substantial reinforcements left Portugal for Brazil under the command of Biscayan Don Antonio de Oquendo. He landed troops in Bahia, but on his way to disembark additional troops in Pernambuco and Paraíba, he encountered a Dutch fleet of sixteen ships commanded by Adriaen Janszoon Pater. They fought to a draw. Although Pater was killed in the struggle, only 700 of Oquendo's men (including 300 Neapolitans) reached the Arraial do Bom Jesus. The remainder of Oquendo's fleet returned home, leaving the coastal waters of Brazil in Dutch hands. However, the Portuguese resistance continued to keep the Dutch fighting force of about 7,000 men hemmed in at Recife and forced the abandonment of Olinda in November 1631. Even though the Dutch erected a fort (Oranje) in the neighboring captaincy of Itamaracá to the north, Albuquerque's troops were able to prevent the Dutch from capturing the northern captaincies of Paraíba and Rio Grande do Norte and from occupying the *várzea*, the rich sugar lands of Pernambuco.

By mid–1632, the tide of war began to turn with the desertion to the Dutch side of the Pernambucan–born Domingos Fernandes Calabar. He knew the terrain intimately and directed the Dutch forces to the Portuguese weaknesses. In addition, substantial Dutch reinforcements arrived in Pernambuco. By mid–1633, the standoff between Albuquerque's troops and the Dutch had ended, and the latter were making major advances. The Dutch expanded into the sugar lands of Pernambuco and into the captaincy of Itamaracá. They also captured the fort of Reis Magos in the captaincy of Rio Grande do Norte. The Portuguese forces fought valiantly, but they were no match for the continuing reinforcements sent by the Dutch West India Company. By the end of 1634, the Dutch had occupied the Brazilian coastline from Rio Grande do Norte to Pernambuco's Cabo de Santo Agostinho. In addition, they continued to control the seas, thus largely cutting off resupply and export. By 1635, increasing numbers of Portuguese settlers were accepting Dutch offers of freedom of worship and security of their property in Pernambuco and in the three captaincies to the north.

Both sides employed Amerindian allies in the fighting. The majority of the indigenous of northeastern Brazil allied themselves with the Dutch, though they made up only a relatively small percentage of the fighting forces of either side. The most famous of the these Portuguese allies was the Petiguar chieftain Dom Antônio Filipe Camarão, who was rewarded by the Hapsburg crown with a patent of nobility and a knighthood and commandery in the Order of Christ. The Portuguese and the Dutch also used African slaves in the war, at times promising freedom to those who took up arms. The most famous of the black leaders fighting for the Portuguese cause was Henrique Dias, who was given a patent of nobility by King Philip IV but who never received the knighthood in the Order of Christ he was promised and awarded.

In 1635 the Dutch captured three Pernambucan strongholds: the town of Porto Calvo, the Arraial do Bom Jesus, and Fort Nazaré on Cabo de Santo Agostinho. Control at these areas gave the Dutch access to major sugar–growing lands of the captaincy. Additional settlers accepted Dutch terms, but more than 7,000 inhabitants of the captaincy, including women, children, Amerindians, and black slaves and freedmen retreated southward under the leadership of Albuquerque. On their way south, they temporarily recaptured Porto Calvo, apprehending Calabar and executing him as a traitor. In September 1635, the first major Iberian reinforcements since 1631 left Portugal for Pernambuco. The 2,500 soldiers (Spaniards, Portuguese, and Neapolitans) were under the command of the Spaniard Don Luis de Rojas y Borgia, who led the war against the Dutch until he was killed in combat less than two months after his arrival. The Italian Giovanni Vincenzo de San Felice, count of Bagnuoli, who had arrived in Brazil with Oquendo's 1631 armada, succeeded Rojas. Bagnuoli accelerated the tactics of guerrilla warfare, as did the Dutch. The victims frequently were those who were trying to continue or revive sugar production under Dutch control and who were caught in the middle of a "scorched earth" policy adopted by both sides.

The Dutch West India Company, deeply in debt, in an attempt to bring peace to the region and restore sugar production, named Johan Maurits, count of Nassau–Siegen, as governor–general of Netherlands Brazil in 1636. He arrived in Recife on 23 January 1637, and his stay of just over seven years marked the height of Dutch power in Portuguese America. Soon after his arrival in Brazil, Maurits, commanding 3,000 European soldiers, 1,000 sailors, and 1,000 Amerindians, easily ousted Bagnuoli from Porto Calvo. He then pursued him southward to the Rio São Francisco. Hoping to make that river the boundary between Portuguese and Dutch Brazil, he laid waste to Alagoas, forcing Bagnuoli's troops to cross the São Francisco into the captaincy of Sergipe del Rey. The Dutch leader then returned to Recife, where he began rebuilding the city, connecting it to the island of Antônio Vaz, which became the new town of Mauritsstad.

Maurits also restored discipline and attempted to conciliate the Portuguese living under Dutch control and restore the economy of the region. He increased protection for the large number of Dutch Jews, the great majority speaking Spanish or Portuguese, who had made a home in Brazil. A much smaller number of New Christians already living in the Northeast abjured the Catholicism forced upon their ancestors and openly proclaimed their Judaic heritage. Jews living in Dutch Brazil had their own synagogues. It is estimated that in 1645 the Jewish population under the protection of the Dutch West India Company was at its peak and numbered 1,450, a little less than half of the total white civilian population.

In order to gain easier access to African slaves, Maurits sent an expedition in 1637 that captured the Portuguese fortress and trading center of São Jorge da Mina (Elmina) on Africa's Gold Coast. Later that year he dispatched a Dutch fleet southward along the coast of Portuguese America to raid São Jorge de Ilhéus in the captaincy south of Bahia. Another expedition devastated Sergipe, forcing Bagnuoli to retreat to within forty miles of the Brazilian capital. To the north, the captaincy of Ceará was taken before year's end. In May 1638, a force of 4,600 Europeans and indigenous confederates, led by Maurits, attacked Salvador but was driven off by the town's defenders.

Toward the end of 1638, a large armada of forty–six ships and 5,000 soldiers under the command of Dom Fernão de Mascarenhas, count of Torre, left Portugal to reconquer the Brazilian Northeast. The voyage was a slow one, and more than 3,000 of the fighting men and sailors died en route to Brazil. Torre made what proved to be a costly decision by landing at the Brazilian capital rather than attacking Recife immediately. In Salvador the count organized an expedition to attack Recife. He dispatched bands of guerrilla fighters led by André Vidal de Negreiros, Camarão, and Dias overland to encourage the Portuguese settlers to revolt and to hem in the Dutch while he and the majority of his troops, loaded into eighty–seven ships, attacked by sea in late 1639. But unfavorable winds and strong ocean currents drove the count of Torre's armada northward past Recife. The Dutch fleet, which gave battle in January 1640, was relatively small, and the naval results were not decisive. But Torre's mission was a failure, and he was forced to put Luis Barbalho Bezerra and some 1,200 troops ashore near Cape São Roque to make the 1,200–mile trek through Dutch territory back to Bahia. En route, they joined up with the guerrilla fighters sent out from Bahia. Most of the armada was scattered, some ships making their way to northern Brazil, others to the Azores, while the bulk ended up in the Spanish Caribbean before attempting the return trip to the Iberian Peninsula.

The majority of Barbalho Bezerra's troops, after skirmishes with the Dutch and their Amerindian allies, reached Bahia. Both sides accused each other of atrocities, and a bitter war of reprisal followed. When fresh troops arrived from the Netherlands, an expedition led by Jan Corneliszoon Lichthart destroyed twenty–seven sugar mills in the environs of Salvador before it was driven off by the Portuguese defenders augmented by Barbalho Bezerra's men. On 1 December 1640, the Portuguese overthrew Hapsburg rule, and the eighth duke of Bragança became King João IV of Portugal. Most of Spain's enemies became Portugal's allies. A ten–year truce between Portugal and the Netherlands was signed on 12 June 1641. Although it took effect immediately in Europe, its implementation was delayed in the colonies. Maurits took advantage of the delay by occupying the captaincy of Sergipe del Rey and capturing São Luis do Maranhão. In 1641 he sent a force of twenty–one ships and 3,000 men (including 240 Brazilian natives) to Africa to capture Angola, Benguela, the islands of São Tomé and Ano Bom, and the fortress of Axim on the coast of Guinea. The Dutch West India Company had reached its territorial apogee.

King João IV found himself in a difficult position regarding the Dutch interlopers in Brazil since he needed Dutch help in Europe against King Philip IV of Spain. A number of influential Portuguese, including Padre Antônio Vieira, initially recommended that João IV give up claims to Dutch Brazil in exchange for further Dutch aid against Spain in Europe. However, there were others, such as Antônio Teles da Silva, governor–general of Brazil from 1642 to 1647, who clandestinely plotted to oust the Dutch and sent men and supplies to achieve this aim, especially after the departure of Maurits in 1644. Teles da Silva's envoy, the Paraíban–born military man André Vidal de Negreiros and Madeiran–born João Fernandes Vieira, a Portuguese planter living in Pernambuco under Dutch rule, secretly planned a revolt for 1645. Teles da Silva also covertly dispatched to Pernambuco experienced soldiers and leaders like Antônio Dias Cardoso, Henrique Dias, and Dom Antônio Filipe Camarão to join the revolt. Betrayal of the conspiracy forced Fernandes Vieira to begin the revolt prematurely, on 13 June 1645.

The Portuguese governor in Bahia used the pretext of helping the Dutch to send two Portuguese regiments under Martim Soares Moreno and Vidal de Negreiros to Pernambuco. The troops landed in Tamandaré. Salvador Correia de Sá, returning to Portugal with the sugar fleet from Rio de Janeiro and Bahia, was encouraged to attack Recife by sea. On 3 August 1645, at Monte das Tabocas, 30 miles from Recife, Fernandes Vieira and Dias Cardoso with 1,000 supporters defeated a Dutch contingent of 400 whites and 300 autochthonous allies. Ten days later, they joined up with the troops of Dias and Camarão. In the meantime, Moreno and Negreiros occupied the district of Serinhaém and captured the fort of Nazaré. On 16 August 1645, they joined Fernandes Vieira. The following day, another Dutch force was defeated at Casa Forte. However, Salvador de Sá failed to attack Recife by sea, and the sixteen caravels that had disembarked Portuguese troops at Tamandaré were defeated and destroyed by a Dutch fleet under Lichthart.

News of the Portuguese victories on land encouraged many of the settlers living under Dutch rule to join the revolt. In September 1645, the Portuguese insurgents recaptured much of the captaincy of Paraíba, the town of Porto Calvo, Fort Maurits on the Rio São Francisco, and Sergipe del Rey. By the end of 1645, the Dutch were confined to Recife and its environs, the islands of Itamaracá and Fernão de Noronha, and the coastal forts of Cabedelo and Reis Magos (Ceulen). The Portuguese had recovered most of Netherlands Brazil, including the best sugar–producing areas.

When news of these losses was relayed to the Netherlands, efforts were made by the Dutch West India Company to aid their beleaguered colony, but for a variety of reasons only twenty ships and 2,000 men were sent to Brazil by May 1646. In the meantime, King João IV claimed no involvement in the rebellion and emphasized that he wanted nothing to interfere with Dutch support in the war against Spain. Gradually, however, he was won over to the cause of the Pernambucan rebels. In December 1646, he appointed Francisco Barreto de Meneses as commander in chief of all forces involved in the restoration of Pernambuco to Portuguese control. However, en route to Brazil near Bahia, Barreto was captured by the Dutch and imprisoned in Recife until he managed to escape early in 1648.

In the meantime, because of the arrival of Dutch reinforcements, the insurgents decided to regroup and abandoned Paraíba, Goiânia, and Itamaracá after destroying as much of the sugar–producing land as possible. The Dutch recaptured Fort Maurits—albeit temporarily—and in February 1647 a Dutch force of twenty–six ships and 2,400 men, led by the German Sigismund von Schoppe, occupied the island of Itaparica in Bahia's Bay of All Saints, holding it until 14 December. This action spurred King João IV to abandon all efforts at secrecy, and plans were made to send the Portuguese royal fleet to recapture the island. On 18 October 1647, an armada of fifteen ships and almost 4,000 men, commanded by Antônio Teles de Meneses, newly created count of Vila Pouca de Aguiar and governor–general of Brazil, sailed from Lisbon. The following month, a fleet of seven ships, commanded by Salvador de Sá, sailed for Rio de Janeiro to prepare an expedition for the recovery of Angola.

At the same time, the Dutch were preparing a fleet, under the command of Witte Corneliszoon de With, to capture Bahia and drive the Portuguese insurgents from Pernambuco. Internal rivalries in the Netherlands prevented de With from leaving until 26 December 1647. His fleet, slowed by bad weather and scattered by storms, began to arrive in Recife after mid–March of 1648, although the last

of the ships did not reach port until late August. Many of his troops were in poor condition. After much debate, the Dutch decided to attack the insurgents by land rather than attack Bahia by sea. On 19 April 1648, at the site called Guararapes, more than 5,000 Dutch and their indigenous allies under von Schoppe met a Portuguese force, estimated to be between 2,200 and 3,000, commanded by Francisco Barreto, which included regiments headed by Fernandes Vieira, Negreiros, Camarão, and Dias. The Portuguese emerged victorious and also forced the Dutch to abandon Olinda. In August the Portuguese were reinforced by another infantry regiment with recruits from Madeira and the Azores, under the leadership of Francisco de Figueiroa.

In the meantime, Salvador de Sá had left Rio de Janeiro with fifteen ships and some 1,500–2,000 men to regain Angola from the Dutch. On 24 August, Sá captured Luanda, and shortly thereafter Benguela and São Tomé were in Portuguese hands. However, the Dutch still controlled the seas off Brazil. In December 1648 a Dutch force sailed into the Bay of All Saints and remained there for a month attacking the Bahian Recôncavo, destroying 23 sugar mills and capturing 1,500 chests of sugar while meeting little Portuguese resistance. Emboldened by this success, a Dutch army force of 3,500 left Recife on 17 February 1649 in an effort to avenge their loss at Guararapes a year earlier. Two days later, at the second battle of Guararapes, the Portuguese, led by Barreto and taking advantage of their superior knowledge of the terrain, gained another victory.

But the Dutch still ruled the seas. In fact, between 1 January 1647 and 31 December 1648, approximately 220 Portuguese ships were captured by the Dutch, most of the vessels being seized by ships fitted out by the Zeeland Privateering Board. To counter this superiority in sea power, the Portuguese organized a convoy system. The brainchild of Padre Antônio Vieira, the convoys were supplied by the newly organized (1649) monopoly called the Companhia Geral para o Estado do Brasil (Brazil Company), funded in large part by Portuguese New Christian investors, who were granted special privileges for their participation. In exchange for providing warships to escort merchant vessels to and from Brazil, the company was given the monopoly over the wine, flour, codfish, and olive oil entering Portuguese America. It was also given the right to levy taxes on such products as sugar, tobacco, cotton, and hides returning to Portugal.

Rivalries and disagreements among the seven provinces of the Netherlands over tactics regarding Brazil and Portugal hampered efforts to reverse Dutch losses in Portuguese America and West Africa, although the Dutch did recapture Ceará in April 1649. In May of that year, Admiral de With began an ineffectual blockade of Rio de Janeiro. Dutch forces in Recife continued to be hemmed in by land by the Portuguese insurgents. Since Recife had to be provisioned by the Netherlands, the besieged occupants were frequently close to starvation. Because of the dissension among the United Provinces, few supplies were being sent from Europe to feed the 4,000 white civilians and 3,000–4,000 troops living in Dutch Brazil. Discontent among the naval forces was so great that most of the Dutch warships returned home by the end of 1649 without authorization, leaving Recife largely unprotected by sea. However, because the Portuguese insurgents were almost equally short of supplies, a five–year stalemate ensued.

On 4 November 1649, the Brazil Company's first armada, composed of eighty–four ships, including eighteen warships, left Lisbon under the command of João Rodrigues de Vasconcelos e Sousa, count of Castelo Melhor, who was to replace the governor–general of Brazil. This expedition was probably strong enough to recapture Recife by sea, but a cautious King João IV did not want to expand the conflict. Futhermore, after the execution of King Charles I of England (30 January 1649), King João IV continued to back the royalist cause. In turn, the Puritan fleet under Admiral Robert Blake blockaded the Tagus in 1650. Blake hampered the second Brazil Company armada from going to America and captured most of the homeward–bound sugar fleet, upon which much of the Portuguese war effort against Spain was dependent.

Portugal's defensive posture in Brazil and Castelo Melhor's instructions not to risk a naval battle with the Dutch returned the mastery of Brazilian waters to the Dutch. Although naval losses continued, the Brazil Company was able to outfit a third armada of sixty ships, which arrived in Brazil in early 1652. Despite harassment by a small Dutch fleet, most of this armada reached Bahia safely. Shortly thereafter, the weakened Dutch fleet fled to Europe, thus enabling the Portuguese to regain control of Brazilian waters.

In June 1651 the ten–year truce between Portugal and the Netherlands expired. The United Provinces again were at odds with Amsterdam, which had commercial ties to Portugal and preferred peace to war. Even though João IV feared a Dutch blockade of the Tagus if he sent a Portuguese fleet to attack Recife, the outbreak of the First Anglo–Dutch War (May 1652) began to alleviate his fears. On 20 December 1653, the Brazil Company's fleet of seventy–seven ships, under the command of Pedro Jacques de Magalhães and Francisco de Brito Freire, arrived to blockade Recife while the Portuguese insurgents pressured the Dutch on land. On 26 January 1654, the Dutch surrendered and signed the capitulation of Taborda, giving up not only Recife and neighboring Mauritsstad but also the islands of Itamaracá and Fernão de Noronha and the captaincies of Paraíba, Rio Grande do Norte, and Ceará, all of which had been in Dutch hands at the time Recife surrendered. The Dutch, including 600 Jews still living under their control, were given generous terms. They were allowed three months to liquidate their assets or take their possessions with them and were provided with shipping to leave Brazil. On 28 January 1654, the victorious Portuguese insurgents, led by Barreto, entered Recife.

AFTERMATH OF THE DUTCH OCCUPATION

This evacuation did not end Portugal's problems with the Netherlands. A treaty between the Portuguese and the Dutch needed to be hammered out. Although the Dutch West India Company was virtually bankrupt, there was still talk in the Netherlands of declaring war on Portugal and blockading the Tagus River to prevent Brazilian sugar from arriving to pay for Portugal's continuing war with Spain. Various ultimatums were issued to King João IV and later to his widow, Queen Luisa de Guzmán. In November 1657, a Dutch fleet under Admiral Michiel Adriaanszoon de Ruyter, which was blockading the Tagus, captured twenty–one of the thirty–four ships in the returning Brazilian fleet. However, England and France could not stand by and see a weakened Portugal lose its struggle with Spain. A treaty between the Dutch and the Portuguese was finally signed on 6 August 1661, providing that the

Portuguese would pay an indemnity of 4 million cruzados over sixteen years to compensate the Dutch for their loss of Brazil. A special tax was instituted to pay this indemnity, almost half of which was to be paid by the Brazilians themselves. This tax lasted throughout the colonial period and late into the reign of Emperor Dom Pedro I (1822–1831) in an independent Brazil. A supplementary treaty of 1669 ensured that Portugal's part of the indemnity would be paid from Setúbal's salt duties. That part of the indemnity was not paid off until the early eighteenth century.

In the immediate aftermath of the restoration of northeastern Brazil to Portuguese control, old scores were settled as reprisals were carried out against Amerindians who had sided with the Dutch. Other problems festered. Animosity marked relations between the Portuguese who had lived under Dutch control and those who had fled the region and who now returned to recover their properties. Litigation over the ownership of sugar mills, houses, cane fields, and other properties dragged on for decades, leaving wounds that were slow to heal.

The Dutch were likewise expelled from Chile and North America. While the Dutch did not successfully set up a large colonial empire, they maintained important and lucrative trading posts in the Caribbean. The Dutch islands of Curaçao and St. Eustatius continued to be important trading outposts. Curaçao, for instance, became an important stop for illegal trade between the Netherlands and Venezuela. An active slave trade between the Dutch and the Spanish colonies also occurred on these islands. Suriname remained under Dutch control until the twentieth century and during the colonial era became an agricultural exporter based on slave labor.

See also **Companies, Chartered; Slavery: Brazil; Trading Companies, Portuguese.**

BIBLIOGRAPHY

Francisco Adolfo De Varnhagen, *Historia das lutas com os Hollandeses no Brazil desde 1624 a 1654* (1871).

José Antônio Gonsalves De Mello, *Tempo dos flamengos: Influência da ocupação holandesa na vida e na cultura do norte do Brasil* (1947).

Charles R. Boxer, *Salvador de Sá and the Struggle for Brazil and Angola, 1602–1686* (1952).

Charles R. Boxer, *The Dutch in Brazil, 1624–1654* (1957).

Evaldo Cabral De Mello, *Olinda restaurada: Guerra e açúcar no Nordeste, 1630–1654* (1975).

Pedro Calmon, *Francisco Barreto: Restaurador de Pernambuco* (1940).

Gonsalves De Mello, *Francisco de Figueroa: Mestre de campo do têrço das ilhas em Pernambuco* (1954).

Gonsalves De Mello, *Antônio Dias Cardoso: Sargento–mor do têrço de infantaria de Pernambuco* (1954).

Gonsalves De Mello, *Henrique Dias: Governador dos pretos, crioulos e mulatos do estado do Brasil* (1954).

Gonsalves De Mello, *D. Antônio Filipe Camarão: Capitão–mor dos Indios da costa do nordeste do Brasil* (1954).

Gonsalves De Mello, *Filipe Bandeira de Melo: Tenente de mestre de campo general do estado do Brasil* (1954).

Gonsalves De Mello, *Frei Manuel Calado do Salvador: Religioso da ordem de São Paulo, pregador apostólico por sua santidade, cronista da restauração* (1954).

Gonsalves De Mello, *João Fernandes Vieira: Mestre–de–campo do têrço da infantaria de Pernambuco*, 2 vols. (1956).

Francis A. Dutra, *Matias de Albuquerque: Capitão–mor de Pernambuco e governador–geral do Brasil* (1976).

José Honório Rodrigues, *Historiografia e bibliografia do domínio Holandês no Brasil* (1949).

Bernardino José De Sousa, *Luiz Barbalho (1601–1644)* (1940).

Afranio Peixoto, *Martim Soares Moreno: Fundador do Seará, iniciador do maranhão e do pará, herói da restauração do Brasil, contra Franceses e Holandeses* (1940).

Adriaen Van Der Dussen, *Relatório sôbre as capitanias conquistadas no Brazil pelos Holandeses (1639): Suas condições econômicas e sociais*. Translated by Gonsalves de Mello (1947).

Herman Wätjen, *Das Holländische Kolonialreich in Brasilien: Ein Kapitel aus der Kolonialgeschichte des 17. Jahrhunderts* (1921), which has been translated into Portuguese (1938).

Pieter J. Bouman, *Johan Maurits van Nassau, de Braziliaan* (1947).

W. J. Van Hoboken, *Witte de With in Brazilië, 1648–1649* (1955).

Arnold Wiznitzer, *Jews in Colonial Brazil* (1960). The diplomacy of the Dutch episode in Brazil is best handled in Edgar Prestage, *The Diplomatic Relations of Portugal with France, England, and Holland from 1640 to 1668* (1925).

Additional Bibliography

Emmer, P. C. *The Dutch in the Atlantic Economy, 1580–1880: Trade, Slavery and Emancipation*. Aldershot: Ashgate, 1998.

Herkenhoff, Paulo, and Evaldo Cabral de Mello. *O Brasil e os holandeses, 1630–1654*. Rio de Janeiro: Sextante Artes, 1999.

Klooster, Wim. *Illicit Riches: Dutch Trade in the Caribbean, 1648–1795*. Rio de Janeiro: Sextante Artes, 1999.

Lopez, Adriana. *Guerra, açúcar e religião no Brasil dos holandeses*. São Paulo: Editora SENAC São Paulo, 2002.

Mello, Evaldo Cabral de. *O negócio do Brasil: Portugal, os Países Baixos e o Nordeste, 1641–1669*. Rio de Janeiro: Topbooks, 1998.

FRANCIS A. DUTRA

DUTCH IN THE CARIBBEAN. *See* Suriname and the Dutch in the Caribbean.

DUTCH-LATIN AMERICAN RELATIONS.
In the sixteenth century the Dutch carried sugar, salt, and East and West Indian spices from Portugal to the north of Europe. However, when Portugal was occupied by the forces of Philip II of Spain in 1581, trade relations with the Netherlands—which had declared independence from that same king in 1568—changed to a war footing. Philip II sent troops to reconquer the United Provinces (the Netherlands), but managed to take only Flanders. A large number of Flemish Calvinist traders fled to the north, particularly to Amsterdam. Prosperous Portuguese Jews also settled in Amsterdam following their expulsion from Spain and Portugal. Thus, Amsterdam assumed the commercial and financial leadership that previously had been centered in Antwerp and Brussels. The Dutch gradually began to seek out the territories that produced salt, sugar, and spices in the East and West Indies, which previously had been occupied by Spain and Portugal.

In Asia, the Dutch established colonies in what became the present-day countries of Indonesia and Sri Lanka. In Africa they trimmed back much of Portugal's strength, and built permanent settlements in South Africa. They moved next to the Caribbean and Brazil. In 1621 the West India Company was created in Amsterdam for the purposes of trade, pirating, and conquest. In May 1624 the Dutch occupied Salvador de Bahía, capital of the Portuguese colony in Brazil, and stayed for a year. In 1630 they attacked the captaincy of Pernambuco and occupied its capital, Olinda. Over the next several years they also occupied the captaincies of Pernambuco, Itamaracá, Paraíba, and Río Grande do Norte. Many of the new colonizers were Portuguese Jews from Amsterdam.

In Brazil the Dutch became interested in the slave trade. As early as 1630 they had encountered some 45,000 black slaves in Pernambuco, and soon realized that sugar production needed a steady supply of slaves from Africa. The West India Company conquered São George del Mina in 1637 and São Paulo de Luanda in 1641, both Portuguese ports used to transport slaves to Brazil. From 1636 to 1645 the Dutch imported some 23,000 slaves to Brazil.

In 1637 Count Johan Maurits was named governor of Dutch Brazil. His government, which lasted until 1644, was relatively liberal. He founded Mauritsstad (present-day Recife), created a parliament, regulated sugar production, and struck a treaty with the Portuguese landowners in 1641. Nonetheless, the Portuguese started a rebellion in 1645. Dutch Brazil gradually shrank in size from 1645 to 1654, when the Dutch finally left to resettle themselves and their slaves in the Guyanas and the Caribbean. There the Dutch owned several islands, including Curação, which began to serve as a port for the slave trade. From 1651 to 1675 they brought 63,000 slaves from Africa to the New World. Usually more than half the slaves brought to Curação were sold to the Spaniards.

The formerly Brazilian Dutch and their slaves moved mostly to Tobago, Barbados, and the French colonies of Guadalupe and Martinique, where they introduced sugarcane farming and taught the technique of sugar processing. A Dutch colony also was founded in Cayenne, the present-day capital of French Guiana, where many of the Portuguese Jews settled. When the French took Cayenne from the Dutch in 1664, the settlers emigrated to the neighboring British colony of Suriname.

The West India Company fell into bankruptcy at the end of the eighteenth century. In 1821 the recently created Kingdom of the Netherlands formally converted the company's former holdings into colonies.

See also **Recife; Curaçao; Dutch in Colonial Brazil; Dutch West India Company; Maurits, Johan; Paraíba; Pernambuco; Rio Grande do Norte; Slavery: Brazil.**

BIBLIOGRAPHY

Boxer, Charles. *The Dutch in Brazil, 1624–1654.* Oxford, U.K.: Clarendon Press, 1957.

Lier, Rudolf Asveer Jacob van. *Frontier Society: A Social Analysis of the History of Surinam.* Den Haag: Martinus Nijhoff, 1971.

Mello Neto, Jose Antonio Gonsalves de. *Fontes para a História do Brasil Holandês: A Economia Açucareira.* Recife: Parque Histórico Nacional dos Guararapes Mec/Sphan, 1981.

Mello Neto, Jose Antonio Gonsalves de. *Tempo dos flamengos: Influencia da ocupação holandesa na vida e cultura do norte do Brasil.* Recife: Fundação Joaquim Nabuco, 3a ediçaõ aumentada, 1a ediçaõ. Rio de Janeiro: José Olympio, 1987 [1947].

DIRK KRUIJT

DUTCH WEST INDIA COMPANY.

Dutch West India Company (also Nederlandische West-Indische Compagnie or WIC), a trading and colonizing company. The Dutch West India Company received its first charter from the States General of the United Provinces of the Netherlands on 3 June 1621 for trade and colonization in Africa and the Americas (along the Atlantic coast from Newfoundland to the Strait of Magellan as well as on the Pacific coast). Previously, commercial adventuring and the search for salt pans to supply the herring fisheries of the North Atlantic had led Dutch ships to Cape Verde and across the Atlantic to the Caribbean as interlopers in areas where Spain and Portugal claimed colonial hegemony. The WIC was founded in the year of the expiration of the Twelve Years' Truce (1621), an interruption in the eighty-year war of rebellion by the Spanish Netherlands against Hapsburg rule. Through its board of directors, the Heeren XIX, who represented bodies of investors in Amsterdam, Zeeland, the Maas, the Northern Quarter (West Frisian towns), and Friesland (including Groningen), the WIC adopted a more hostile policy toward Spain than had been desired by its veteran propagandist, William Usselinx

(1567–1647). Buccaneering expeditions attacked Spanish shipping, and plans were made for extensive land conquest, beginning with a territory regarded as rich and vulnerable: Portuguese Brazil.

A first attempt to take Brazil, at Bahia in 1624–1625, was short-lived, but windfall wealth from the capture of the Spanish silver fleet at Matanzas (Cuba) by Piet Heyn in 1628 allowed the company to strike again in 1630 at the northeastern sugar capital of Pernambuco. At its height, under WIC governor Johan Maurits (1637–1644), Dutch-occupied Brazil (New Holland) was an exemplary plantation colony: Dutch merchants financed the sugar industry, supplied slave labor from newly secured African entrepôts on the Guinea coast south to Loango, and shipped the product to their refinery operations in the Netherlands. After being dislodged by Luso-Brazilian rebels in a protracted struggle (1645–1654), during a period of disputes over the extent of its trade monopolies and renewal of its charter as well as conflict with England, the WIC concentrated on its profitable slaving operations and trade and agricultural settlement in the Caribbean.

In Guiana, the "Wild Coast" between the Amazon and Orinoco rivers, French, English, and Dutch colonists fought for a piece of the Spanish American mainland. Sugar, coffee, cotton, and cocoa plantations thrived in the districts of WIC-administered outposts at Demerara, Essequibo, Berbice, and Suriname. In the Leeward Antilles, Saint Eustatius, Saint Martin, and Saba became subject to WIC control. A strategically located slave mart at Willemstad, Curaçao (in an island group including Bonaire and Aruba), flourished, especially between the 1670s and 1720, for successive holders of the Spanish Asiento until the contract passed to the WIC's chief rival, the Royal African Company.

Bankruptcy followed losses incurred during the Third Anglo-Dutch War (1672–1674), but the company reorganized in 1674 as the Second or New WIC under a smaller board, the Heeren X. Thus restructured, it enjoyed decades of prosperity in the eighteenth century based on slaving and the provisions trade in the Caribbean. Forced to relinquish most of its monopoly privileges after 1730, the conditions of free trade drove the company into insolvent obsolescence by 1791.

See also **Buccaneers and Freebooters; Dutch in Colonial Brazil; Slave Trade.**

BIBLIOGRAPHY

Charles R. Boxer, *The Dutch in Brazil, 1624–1654* (1957; repr. 1973).

Cornelis Ch. Goslinga, *The Dutch in the Caribbean and on the Wild Coast, 1580–1680* (1971) and *The Dutch in the Caribbean and in the Guianas, 1680–1791* (1985).

José Antônio Gonsalves De Mello Neto, *Tempo dos flamengos: Influência da ocupação holandesa na vida e na cultura do norte do Brasil*, 3d ed. (1987).

Johannes Menne Postma, *The Dutch in the Atlantic Slave Trade, 1600–1815* (1990).

Additional Bibliography

Emmer, P. C. *The Dutch in the Atlantic Economy, 1580–1880: Trade, Slavery and Emancipation*. Aldershot: Ashgate, 1998.

Herkenhoff, Paulo and Evaldo Cabral de Mello. *O Brasil e os holandeses, 1630–1654*. Rio de Janeiro: Sextante Artes, 1999.

Klooster, Wim. *Illicit Riches: Dutch Trade in the Caribbean, 1648–1795*. Rio de Janeiro: Sextante Artes, 1999.

CATHERINE LUGAR

DUTRA, EURICO GASPAR (1883–1974).

Eurico Gaspar Dutra (*b.* 18 May 1883; *d.* 11 June 1974), president of Brazil (1945–1951). Son of merchant José Florêncio Dutra and Maria Justina Dutra, Dutra was born in Cuiabá, state of Mato Grosso. He married Carmela Leite, widow of Uchoa Cintra, on 19 February 1914; they had two children.

Dutra studied at the Escola Preparatória e Tática of Rio Pardo and completed his military studies at the Escola Militar do Brasil. After distinguishing himself during the Constitutionalist Revolution, Dutra became a general in 1932. In 1935 he was made commandant of Military Region I and put down the Communist rebellion of 27 November 1935 in Rio de Janeiro.

As minister of war (1936–1945) during the Getúlio Vargas dictatorship, Dutra organized the Brazilian Expeditionary Force (FEB), which saw combat in Europe during World War II. During this period, he actively participated in the Golpe Integralista (Integralist Coup) of 1937, for which he laid the groundwork. Dutra was also deeply involved in Vargas's nationalistic campaign to maintain Brazilian ownership of the nation's petroleum under the banner of "O petróleo é nosso" (the oil is ours).

In 1946 Dutra was elected president of Brazil and served until 31 January 1951. Not known as a charismatic figure, Dutra was respected for his honesty and ability to complete a full presidential term. Two Brazilian municipalities were named in his honor. Pursuing a close relationship with the United States, Dutra received President Harry S. Truman in Brazil, made an official visit to the United States, and broke relations with the Soviet Union. During his presidency, Dutra implemented a number of reforms in the federal government, including the establishment of the Tribunal Federal de Recursos, the Conselho Nacional de Economia, and the regional planning commissions.

See also **Brazilian Expeditionary Force (FEB); Vargas, Getúlio Dornelles.**

BIBLIOGRAPHY

Additional Bibliography

Aggio, Alberto, Agnaldo de Sousa Barbosa, and Hercídia Mara Facuri Coelho Lambert. *Política e sociedade no Brasil, 1930-1964*. São Paulo: Annablume, 2002.

Johnson, Ollie A. *Brazilian Party Politics and the Coup of 1964*. Gainesville: University Press of Florida, 2001.

Pomar, Pedro Estevam da Rocha. *A democracia intolerante: Dutra, Adhemar e a repressão ao Partido Comunista, 1946–1950*. São Paulo: Arquivo do Estado: Imprensa Oficial do Estado, 2002.

Skidmore, Thomas E. *Politics in Brazil, 1930–1964: An Experiment in Democracy*. New York: Oxford University Press, 1986.

IÊDA SIQUEIRA WIARDA

DUVALIER, FRANÇOIS (1907–1971).

François Duvalier (*b.* 14 April 1907; *d.* 21 April 1971), president of Haiti (1957–1971). A *noir* (black), Duvalier was born in Port-au-Prince; his father was an elementary schoolteacher and his mother a bakery worker. His formal education included elementary and secondary school at the Lycée Pétion and a medical degree from the École de Médecine the same year that the U.S. occupation (1915–1934) ended. After his internship, he worked in a clinic and in 1939 married Simone Ovide Faine, a mulatto (*mulâtresse*) nurse whose father was a merchant. They had four children, three daughters and a son—Jean-Claude.

In the 1940s, Duvalier became involved in the campaign against yaws (*pian*), a contagious tropical disease caused by a parasite, and then went on to direct training in the U.S. Army's malaria program. In the mid-1940s, he assisted Dr. James Dwinelle in the U.S. Army Medical Corps' yaws program. During this time he had a year's fellowship and studied public health at the University of Michigan.

Duvalier's ideas about race and politics and his literary and political activities were developed and took place both before and during his medical studies and work with yaws. In the 1920s, he became important in an ethnology movement as one of its three Ds, *les trois D,* later known as the *Griots,* and was a cofounder of its journal, *Les Griots.* This movement was based upon black nationalism (*noirisme*), *indigénisme,* and *négritude,* stressing African roots, including *voudon* (voodoo, *vodun*). It opposed the control and rule of the mulattoes. Certain events also affected Duvalier's attitudes and values: the U.S. occupation; President Rafael Trujillo's anti-Haitian views and actions, particularly the 1937 massacre of Haitians in the Dominican Republic; foreign intervention; control of economic and political life by the mulattoes; army intervention in national politics; and the campaigns of the church against *voudon.*

François Duvalier became politically active in 1946, when presidential candidate Daniel Fignolé formed a new party and made him its secretary-general. After the army assured the election of President Dumarsais Estimé, in his "Revolution of 1946," he designed reforms that downgraded the mulattoes in government. President Estimé made Duvalier a part of his government, first as director of the yaws program, then as under-secretary of labor in 1948, which was followed the next year by minister of labor and public health. The growing rift between blacks and mulattoes resulted in Estimé's overthrow in 1950, and the army brought in General Paul Magloire, who lasted until 1956. There ensued great instability and virtual civil war, with five provisional governments, and then rule by a military council. In his 1957 campaign for president against Louis Déjoie, Duvalier called for honesty in government, stressed his background as a country doctor, and organized a paramilitary group to deal with his opponents. The army also "managed" this

election, assuring the defeat of Fignolé (the U.S. embassy count showed a victory for Fignolé).

Once he was inaugurated as president at the age of fifty, Duvalier began the transformation of "cultural *négritude*" into "political *négritude*" by destroying his critics; neutralizing the army; Haitianizing the church; legitimizing *voudon* and making it an instrument of government; and establishing a black nationalist, xenophobic, and personalist regime. He became the state.

Duvalier first silenced the press and broadcasters, who were arrested, attacked, and killed; he then burned and bombed their offices and stations. The major instrument was the Tonton Macoutes (in *créole,* bogeymen), who were officially recognized by the creation in 1962 of the *Volontaires de la Securité Nationale* (VSN). Second, he neutralized the army by transfers and by politicizing it, and he created a separate palace guard, which was quartered there with their arsenal located in the basement. At the same time he invited a U.S. Marine Corps mission to train the army as a means of showing U.S. support; but the mission (1958–1962), commanded by Colonel Robert D. Heinl, withdrew when the VSN replaced the army. Third, he took on the church in 1959, expelling high officials, including the archbishop; arresting members of the clergy; closing the seminary; and expelling the Jesuits. The Vatican responded by excommunicating him and his entire cabinet. Then he "Haitianized" the church by increasing the number of Haitian clergy until they were in the majority. (He reconciled with the church in 1966, mainly on his own terms.) He openly favored and practiced *voudon,* used some of its priests (*houngans*) as advisers, and always dressed in black.

What was unique about his rule was that Duvalier controlled everything and almost everyone by making them responsible to him—loyalty was more important than competence. He and his family and closest advisers got a financial cut from all government enterprises, thus, it was "government by franchise."

In relations with the United States, Duvalier played the anticommunist game in order to get aid, but when the administration of John F. Kennedy cut off most aid in 1963, he turned inward and toward Africa, stressing *négritude.* He invited and welcomed Ethiopia's Haile Selassie I with great fanfare and at great expense in 1966. Although a *noirist,* he really did not care about the black masses. After paving the way for naming his son Jean-Claude as his successor as "president for life," he died of natural causes at the age of sixty-four.

See also **Duvalier, Jean-Claude; Haiti.**

BIBLIOGRAPHY

Bernard Diederich and Al Burt, *Papa Doc: The Truth About Haiti Today* (1969).

François Duvalier, *Mémoires d'un leader du Tiers Monde* (1969)—although a public relations document, it has a useful vita plus many interesting photographs, showing "Haitianization" of the church plus apparent support of the church and the U.S. of his regime.

Harold E. Davis and Larman C. Wilson, *Latin American Foreign Policies: An Analysis* (1975), chap. 10.

Leslie F. Manigat, *Ethnicité, nationalisme et politique: Le cas d'Haiti* (1975).

Robert D. Heinl, Jr., and Nancy G. Heinl, *Written in Blood: The Story of the Haitian People, 1492–1971* (1978), esp. chaps. 13–14.

Frances Chambers, *Haiti* (1983), an annotated bibliography (see esp. sections on History, Politics and Government, Law and Constitution, and Foreign Relations).

Brian Weinstein and Aaron Segal, *Haiti: Political Failures, Cultural Successes* (1984), chaps. 2, 3, 5, and 7.

James Ferguson, *Papa Doc, Baby Doc: Haiti and the Duvaliers* (1987), esp. chap. 2.

Patrick Bellegarde-Smith, *Haiti: The Breached Citadel* (1990), esp. chaps. 3 5.

Michel-Rolph Trouillot, *Haiti, State Against Nation: The Origins and Legacy of Duvalierism* (1990), chaps. 5–6.

Additional Bibliography

Jean Jacques, Fritz. *Le régime politique haïtien: Une analyse de l'État oligarchique, 1930-1986.* Montréal: Éditions Oracle, 2003.

                                    LARMAN C. WILSON

DUVALIER, JEAN-CLAUDE (1951–).

Jean-Claude Duvalier (*b.* 3 July 1951), president of Haiti (1971–1986). An unsuccessful law student and playboy, Duvalier became "president for life" upon the death of his father, François Duvalier, but was only the titular head for the first few years, since decisions were made by a council of state appointed by his father before he died. This arrangement assured the continuation of *Duvalierisme*. The council members included his mother and his father's main advisers; Luckner Cambronne was the power behind the throne and also headed the Leopards, a counterinsurgency force created with U.S. aid in 1971. When Jean-Claude dismissed and exiled Cambronne in 1972, it marked the president's emerging control and influence.

Duvalier stated that his goal was to effect an "economic revolution" (he had little interest in *négritude* or *noirisme*), which he pursued by making some cosmetic and some real changes in reducing political repression. These changes plus some genuine economic incentives ended Haiti's isolation, brought about the resumption of U.S. aid, and attracted foreign investment and companies.

Duvalier's marriage in 1980 to a mulatto divorcée, Michèle Bennett, daughter of a wealthy exporter-importer, provoked criticism from the antimulatto blacks. Her lifestyle served as a catalyst—along with the corrupt and incompetent bureaucracy—for his downfall. Her shopping sprees in Paris and lavish parties in Haiti caused national revulsion, prompting riots and demonstrations, which began in rural cities in 1984. Supported by the church, these acts of opposition convulsed the country and led the United States to urge Duvalier's resignation and departure. He and his family along with several close advisers were flown out of Haiti on a U.S. cargo plane in early February 1986. They relocated to France, where they originally lived a lavish lifestyle with a home outside of Cannes and two apartments in Paris. But when Duvalier and his wife divorced in 1993, he lost much of his wealth. He applied for political asylum in France, but his request was denied and he was placed under house arrest. In 1994, he said he would return to Haiti after the ousting of President Jean-Bertrand Aristide, but as of 2007, he was reportedly still living in Paris.

See also **Aristide, Jean-Bertrand; Duvalier, François; Haiti.**

BIBLIOGRAPHY

Brian Weinstein and Aaron Segal, *Haiti: Political Failures, Cultural Successes* (1984), esp. pp. 43–45, 57–61, 114–118.

James Ferguson, *Papa Doc, Baby Doc: Haiti and the Duvaliers* (1987), esp. chaps. 3 and 4.

Patrick Bellegarde-Smith, *Haiti: The Breached Citadel* (1990), pp. 97–98, 104–107, 123–126, 134–141, 186.

Michel-Rolph Trouillot, *Haiti, State Against Nation: The Origins and Legacy of Duvalierism* (1990), pp. 181–183, 200–219.

Additional Bibliography

Franjul, Miguel. *Somoza y Duvalier: La caída de dos dinastías.* Santo Domingo: Franjul, Analistsas & Asesores, 1998.

Orizio, Riccardo, and Avril Bardoni. *Talk of the Devil: Encounters with Seven Dictators.* New York: Walker, 2003.

Pierre, Hyppolite. *Haiti, Rising Flames from Burning Ashes: Haiti the Phoenix.* Lanham, MD: University Press of America, 2006.

LARMAN C. WILSON

DZIBILCHALTÚN. Dzibilchaltún, an important and long–occupied Maya archaeological zone and site located 10 miles north of Mérida, Yucatán. Dzibilchaltún and nearby sites such as Komchen were populated as early as 800 BCE The earliest occupants of northern Yucatán lived in small farming villages, and by around 500 BCE there is good evidence for formally arranged, public buildings located near town centers. During the Late Formative period (c. 300 BCE–250 CE) the people of the Dzibilchaltún region were increasingly engaged in long–distance trade, and the production of salt may have provided them with a valuable resource for that trade. Ceramic and architectural similarities with Late Formative sites on the east coast of Yucatán (e.g., Cuello and Cerros) suggest maritime contacts.

During the period between 250 and 700, Dzibilchaltún and the surrounding area were sparsely populated for reasons that remain poorly understood. By 700, however, the site of Dzibilchaltún experienced rapid growth, becoming one of the largest centers in the Yucatán peninsula. An area covering 7.6 square miles with over 8,000 structures was occupied between 700 and 1000; population may have reached 25,000 or more at this time. Early in this period there are architectural similarities with Early Classic sites in the southern lowland (e.g., Uaxactun) because Dzibilchaltún architects revived an earlier style. There are also similarities with contemporary western Maya sites like Palenque. By around 830, the Puuc architectural style came to dominate Dzibilchaltún, and structures had veneer facings with geometric mosaics and three–dimensional masks.

By around 1000, Dzibilchaltún had lost its dominant position in the area and there was strong influence from Chichén Itzá to the east. The resident population of Dzibilchaltún declined dramatically, and the site appears to have become a ceremonial center in the Late Postclassic period (c. 1200–1540).

Today, many ruins of Dzibilchaltún have been rebuilt or restored, and the site is visited regularly by tourists year–round due to its close proximity to the urban center of Mérida. Tourism is especially busy for the Spring and Fall equinox; visitors flock to witness the sun align and shine directly through the doorways of the Temple of the Seven Dolls for the equinox only. Also at Dzibilchaltún one can visit the highly regarded Museo de Pueblo Maya.

See also **Archaeology; Maya, The.**

BIBLIOGRAPHY

E. Wyllys Andrews IV and E. Wyllys Andrews V, *Excavations at Dzibilchaltún, Yucatán, México* (1980).

E. Wyllys Andrews V, "Dzibilchaltún," in *Handbook of Middle American Indians,* suppl. 1, *Archaeology* (1981), pp. 313–341.

Additional Bibliography

Jennifer T. Taschek, *The Artifacts of Dzibilchaltún, Yucatán, Mexico: Shell, Polished Stone, Bone, Wood, and Ceramics* (1994).

JANINE GASCO

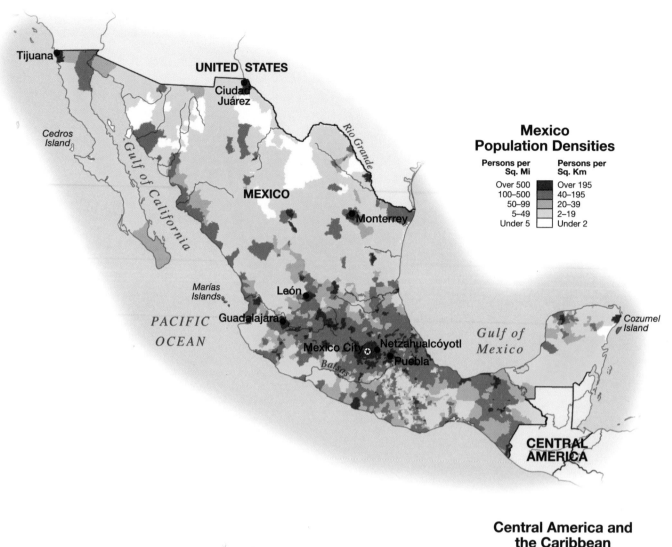

Mexico
Population Densities

Persons per Sq. Mi	Persons per Sq. Km
Over 500	Over 195
100–500	40–195
50–99	20–39
5–49	2–19
Under 5	Under 2

Tijuana

UNITED STATES

Ciudad Juárez

Cedros Island

Gulf of California

Rio Grande

MEXICO

Monterrey

Marías Islands

León

PACIFIC OCEAN

Guadalajara

Gulf of Mexico

Cozumel Island

Batsas

Mexico City Netzahualcóyotl

Puebla

CENTRAL AMERICA

Central America and the Caribbean
Population Densities

Persons per Sq. Mi	Persons per Sq. Km
Over 500	Over 195
100–500	40–195
50–99	20–39
5–49	2–19
Under 5	Under 2

Grand Bahama

Gulf of Mexico

UNITED STATES

BAHAMAS

ATLANTIC OCEAN

Nassau

Andros

Havana

CUBA

Isla de la Juventud

Turks and Caicos Islands (U.K.)

Cayman Islands (U.K.)

Virgin Islands (U.S.) *Virgin Islands (U.K.)*

HAITI DOMINICAN REPUBLIC

Puerto Rico (U.S.)

Anguilla (U.K.)

ANTIGUA AND BARBUDA

MEXICO

Port-au-Prince

Santo Domingo

San Juan

Basseterre St. John's

ST. KITTS AND NEVIS *Montserrat (U.K.)*

JAMAICA Kingston

Hispaniola

Belmopan

BELIZE

Guadeloupe (Fr.)

DOMINICA

Caribbean Sea

Roseau *Martinique (Fr.)*

GUATEMALA

Guatemala City

HONDURAS

San Salvador Tegucigalpa

EL SALVADOR

Grande

Castries ST. LUCIA

Kingstown Bridgetown

Netherlands Antilles (Neth.)

Aruba (Neth.)

ST. VINCENT AND THE GRENADINES BARBADOS

NICARAGUA

Managua

St. George's GRENADA

San José

TRINIDAD AND TOBAGO

COSTA RICA

PANAMA

Panama City

Port-of-Spain

Coiba Island

SOUTH AMERICA